THE QUOTABLE WOMAN
REVISED EDITION
THE FIRST 5,000 YEARS

ALSO BY ELAINE BERNSTEIN PARTNOW

Books
The Quotable Woman, 1800–1981
The Quotable Woman, Eve–1799
The New Quotable Woman
Breaking the Age Barrier
Photographic Artists and Innovators (coauthor, Turner Browne)
Everyday Speaking for All Occasions (coauthor, Susan Partnow)
The Female Dramatist (with Lesley Hyatt)
The Little Book of the Spirit
The Complete Idiot's Guide to Great Quotes for Any Occasion
The Complete Idiot's Guide to Your True Age (coauthor, Judith P. Hyman, Ph.D.)

Plays and Performance Pieces
Hear Us Roar, A Woman's Connection
Hispanic Women Speak
Sheroes: Living History Portraits of Notable Women
Funny Jewish Women
A Visit with Emily Dickinson
A Lovely Light: Edna St. Vincent Millay

THE QUOTABLE WOMAN
REVISED EDITION
THE FIRST 5,000 YEARS

Compiled and Edited by
Elaine Bernstein Partnow

✓ Facts On File
An imprint of Infobase Publishing

The Quotable Woman, Revised Edition: The First 5,000 Years

Copyright © 2011, 2001, 1992, 1986, 1985, 1983, 1977 by Elaine Partnow

Facts On File, Inc.
An imprint of Infobase Publishing
132 West 31st Street
New York NY 10001

Library of Congress Cataloging-in-Publication Data

The quotable woman, revised edition : the first 5,000 years / compiled and edited by Elaine Bernstein Partnow.
       p. cm.
  Includes index.
  ISBN 978-0-8160-7725-0 (hc : alk. paper) 1. Women—Quotations. 2. Quotations, English. I. Partnow, Elaine.
  PN6081.5.Q65 2010
  305.4—dc22   2009039139

Facts On File books are available at special discounts when purchased in bulk quantities for businesses, associations, institutions, or sales promotions. Please call our Special Sales Department in New York at (212) 967-8800 or (800) 322-8755.

You can find Facts On File on the World Wide Web at
http://www.factsonfile.com

"The Quotable Woman" is a trademark of Elaine Partnow.

Text design adapted by Kerry Casey
Composition by Hermitage Publishing Services
Cover printed by Sheridan Books, Ann Arbor, Mich.
Book printed and bound by Sheridan Books, Ann Arbor, Mich.
Date printed: August 2010
Printed in the United States of America

10 9 8 7 6 5 4 3 2 1

This book is printed on acid-free paper.

Stuffed © 2001 and *To My Dearest Friends* ©, Reprinted by permission of Patricia Volk and the Watkins/Loomis Agency

For Susan J. Herman
(1942–2009)
Mentor. Inspiration. Friend.

Contents

ACKNOWLEDGMENTS
ix
INTRODUCTION
xi
GUIDELINES FOR USE
xvii

QUOTATIONS
1

BIOGRAPHICAL INDEX
833
CAREER AND OCCUPATION INDEX
919
ETHNICITY AND NATIONALITY INDEX
958
SUBJECT INDEX
979

Acknowledgments

To Gina Hicks: Gina, dear, I cannot change more than a word or two of what I said last time. What could I have done without you? It would have been like the dinosaur days, when I did everything on 5×8 index cards and it took me four years and there were all kinds of inconsistencies that I couldn't even see until after the book was in galley stage, and even then there were some major mess-ups—until I got it all in the computer. Organized. Cross-referenced. Backed up. Integrated. Tabulated. Filterable. Reportable. Formidable. How do you do it, how do you do it, how do you do it? It's not just your wizardry with databases that dazzles me, though. It's your sense of equanimity, your reserve, your gentle humor, your infinite patience, your granite reliability. We've worked together, what, 13 years now? Despite the loose hours and lousy pay, you've never let us down. Even now, when we're thousands of miles apart. You created the right buttons for me to push. Thank you.

My lovely niece Jessica Partnow has been too busy doing her journalism with Common Language Project to actively help me on this edition, but the influence she exerted on the last one is still felt—the presence of contemporary songwriters such as Ani DiFranco, Liz Phair, and Lauryn Hill was a great contribution that helps the book be more current. And now, my dear goddess daughter, you and your journalism partner Sarah Stuteville are in the book! And most deservedly so.

My other wonderful, adored niece, Lesley Hyatt, with whom I've collaborated before, once again helped with the español, making it possible to include several Latinas; what fun it's been for us to build this additional level with which to connect hearts and minds. Dear sister Susan Partnow, you, too, helped, with the languages—Spanish, French, German—and the quotes you e-mailed me. And both your and sister Judy's constant moral support and enthusiasm kept me buoyed along the long way. My old friend Sue Witkovsky also helped with the Spanish, and my new friend Ellen Snortland sent a few fabulous women my way.

Jeff Soloway, my new editor, unfamiliar with the book when we set out on this long journey, has grown to appreciate the work and has generously let me know it, demonstrating patience and understanding with a few delays. Thank you so much.

Sheree Bykofsky and Janet Rosen, my agents, your attention and energy from the inception of this project will not be forgotten.

Photographer and translator Alice Forman was kind enough to help me with a Portuguese passage.

Thank you to all the wonderful literary critics who unwittingly did my work for me by culling superb bons mots in their book reviews.

My husband, Turner Browne, showed me every courtesy and indulgence in seeing to it I had the space and time to complete this enormous tome, making sure that I ate my meals and quit working at a decent hour and offering shoulder rubs.

I have corresponded via e-mail (about 2,500) with hundreds of the contributors, who have generously given of their time and information. They were, almost without exception, informative, supportive, and enthusiastic. This book would be nothing without them and without our foremothers.

I could not have done this work in the amount of time it was accomplished without the Internet—even though I struggled through the entire time on my pokey old dial-up (I live in a rural area—no cable; and, with all our thunderstorms, wi-fi is unreliable and very expensive)! The Internet provided me with superb informational and news sites such as WorldPulse.com, WomensMedia-Center.com, feminist.com, Wikipedia, the *New York Times* and *Washington Post* online: I'm grateful to each of them and other news teams for the work they do.

Looking over the acknowledgments in the last edition brought an ever sharper awareness to me of the solitude I have both enjoyed and mourned since moving to this small island off north Florida's coast. I've mainly done it alone this time, without the wonderful camaraderie of colleagues and friends. But I have had the rich companionship of a sisterhood of women, both living and dead, to provide me with warmth, encouragement, stimulation, and motivation. To all the women in this book, I say—thank you, from the depths of my soul.

Elaine Bernstein Partnow
Live Oak Island, Florida

Introduction

This thoroughly revised and expanded edition of *The Quotable Woman* features 1,350 new contributors and more than 4,000 new quotations. To make room for them, I had to weed thousands of quotes and even a few dozen contributors. Cutting was not easy. There were moments when my red pen would hover as I struggled to fully comprehend a quotation written in antiquated prose. But as the eminent sense of the passage emerged, I put my pen down and read on. Often, I could not bring myself to excise more than one or two quotes from a record, as with Jane Addams's *Newer Ideals of Peace:* each was so incisive and perceptive, together they could comprise a blueprint for how government should work today.

In order to perform this task, which felt to me like saying goodbye to old friends, I had to read the entire manuscript, cover to cover. I have always said *The Quotable Woman* is a serious reference book, but it is also a delight to thumb through. True, still. Yet reading it, which I have now done for the sixth time, so illuminated the depth and breadth of women's impact on world culture from history's first dawning, I recommend the experience to everyone. As Letty Cottin Pogrebin wrote, "The group entrusted with history-making remembers itself. Those who keep the books determine who is authorized to write in them and what is worth writing about. Authority means being the author of one's own reality as it is recorded for posterity. Remembering is not a neutral act." The experience in creating a work such as this may seem dry and tedious to the outsider, but I assure you, it is no such thing. In addition to being informative, it is inspiring and often quite moving. Sometimes I would burst into tears reading about someone like Wilma Rudolph, who was diagnosed with polio at the age of five and whose mother, after a long day of hard work, would sit on Wilma's bed, massaging her legs, telling her that one day she would walk without braces. She went on to win triple gold medals in track and field at the 1960 Olympics. Or someone like Helen Joseph, a white South African anti-apartheid activist who took in the children of her imprisoned comrades (she cared for Nelson and Winnie Mandela's children). Reading of Joseph's repeated arrests for standing up for her beliefs, right up until her 80th year, my breath caught, my eyes filled with tears, and I had to stop to center myself.

Nights would often find me lying awake, certain I would be criticized for having left out some terribly important woman. Why, for example, was it only at the 11th hour that I discovered Tzipi Malka Livni, acting prime minister of Israel? Or Sheikh Hasina Wajed, the prime minister of Bangladesh. Who else had I overlooked? Of course, hundreds of deserving historical women could not be included because, while we know of their lives, none of their works have survived. But many more—biographers, historians, scientists, athletes—who have made enormous contributions to society, simply were not quotable.

Happily, many contemporary giants of literature continue to produce wonderful works—Margaret Drabble, Margaret Atwood, Toni Morrison, Maya Angelou, Joan Didion, Joyce Carole Oates, to name but a few. So that I could bring them up to date, I had to snip away at some of their earlier works in order to keep their entries to a reasonable size. Even those who are no longer with us had to be whittled down to make room for the fabulous women making their first appearance in *The Quotable Woman*. But there are more new contributors in this edition than were in the entire first edition back in 1978! Cutting was a heartbreaking process. But it was the only way to keep this book down to a size that would not require a wagon to bring it home!

I pay homage to those who have died since I worked on the last edition. You are missed, you are missed, I repeat all too frequently, as I edit their works: Shirley Chisolm, Shana Alexander, Gwendolyn Brooks, Penelope Fitzgerald, Florynce Kennedy, Anne Morrow Lindbergh, Katharine Graham, Mary Kay Ash, Eudora Welty, Pauline Kael, June Jordan, Vinette Caroll, Joan Littlewood, Ann Landers, Indra Devi, Patsy Mink, Barbara Grizzuti Harrison, Eda Le Shan, Abigail Van Buren, Carolyn Heilbrun, Monique Wittig, Katherine Hepburn, Françoise Giroud, Jean Kerr, Françoise Lauder, June Singer, Elizabeth Kubler-Ross, Susan Sontag, Mary McGrory, Julia Child, Françoise Sagan, Bella Lewitzky, Andrea Dworkin, Judith Rossner, Anne Bancroft, Elizabeth Janeway, Molly Yard, Jean Baker Miller, Jane Jacobs, Oriana Fallaci, Shelley Winters, Betty Comden, Barbara Guest, Wendy Wasserstein, Coretta Scott King, Jeane Kirkpatrick, Molly Ivins, Benezir Bhutto, Eve Curie, Liz Claiborne, Peg Bracken, Beah Richards, Beverly Sills, Tillie Olsen, Madeleine L'Engle, Grace Paley, Eartha Kitt, Miriam Makeba, Uta Hagen, my old acting teacher, to name but a few. Lastly, my dear friend Susan Herman, who died only weeks after I told her this volume was being dedicated to her. I was only 32 when I started out on this life-long mission. The mortality of those near my own age has become more poignant as we have aged together.

CRITERIA & METHODOLOGY

Why is *The Quotable Woman* still necessary? Whenever I came across someone with a gender neutral first name (like Leigh, Dale, or Whitney) who was highly quoted, I always suspected, and was inevitably correct, that it was a man. In Random House's *The Quotationary,* published in 2001, of the thousands of contributors, only 386 are women, with about 500 quotations out of 20,000. There is no other collection that comes close to containing what is in this book.

An essay by Gertrude Himmelfarb in *The New York Times Book Review* entitled "Where Have All the Footnotes Gone?" put me in mind of the plethora of quotation sites on the Internet: but where have all the sources gone, I constantly ask? Putting a quotation next to a person's name with no citation whatsoever is, in my opinion, practically useless. On those few occasions in *The Quotable Woman* where I have had to claim "attributed," it was only after careful exploration that convinced me the words were, indeed, spoken by the person cited, but the original source is unknown. Otherwise, you will find thorough citations in the vast majority of quotations.

How do I choose quotations? What am I looking for? There is no easy answer. The woman being quoted must in some way be notable in her field—not famous, just notable—either as a public figure, a published person, or an expert. Generally, the quotation must grab me in some way. For years I have kept the following reminder above my computer screen:

NOT ONLY INFORM BUT
INSPIRE!
NOT ONLY EMOTE BUT
MOVE!
NOT ONLY AMUSE BUT
DELIGHT!
NOT ONLY INTIMATE BUT
REVEAL!

You will find thousands of bons mots of writers, poets, humorists and politicians. There are also thousands of quotations that may not be particularly catchy or memorable, but in terms of substance, are vital, stimulating, in some instances urgent; these are likely the voices of scientists, philosophers, and activists. They may not have a way with words, but they have breathtaking insights. *The Quotable Woman* is, after all, is not only a collection of quotations—it is a collection of women!

Sometimes I include three or four quotations from the same article or essay not so much because each by itself stands out but because together they tell a story, an important story, of who we are and where we are and where we are going. But at bottom, selection is subjective. During much of my research, two dear friends were battling cancer, so every quotation about fighting this scurrilous disease struck a particularly emotional chord within me. Had I edited the text last year, there might not be so many quotations reflecting the courage and insight of women who have gone head to head with this ogre.

Before I even began adding to my database, I checked each existing record for accuracy of biographical information, which resulted in hundreds of updates and corrections. I managed to track down e-mail addresses for more than 500 contributors, corresponding with each of them (my records show thousands of e-mails went back and forth between us). Even though the last contributor number is 4980, there are actually 5,005 contributors all told: that is because a couple of dozen were assigned contributor numbers like 1098.1, so you'll see contributor 1098 followed by 1098.1 followed by 1099.

I estimate that I deleted well over 1,000 quotes from the fifth edition to make space for new ones, so about a quarter of the 18,000 quotations in this volume are new to the collection.

I've glossed this tome heavily. Some of the notes may seem obvious to some of you—but this book is not just for this time; it is also for the future. How many readers can name all the presidents of the last 100 years, or all the wars, or all the Olympic champions or Pulitzer Prize winners? *The Quotable Woman* has now been in print for 35 years; I expect it will outlive me. Memory is short, and history is long.

I see *The Quotable Woman* as an educational tool as well as a collection. Ursula Le Guin has written, "Literature takes shape and life in the body, in the wombs of the mother tongue: always: and the Fathers of Culture get anxious about paternity. They start talking about legitimacy. They steal the baby. They ensure by every means that the artist, the writer, is male. This involves intellectual abortion by centuries of women artists, infanticide of works by women writers, and a whole medical corps of sterilizing critics working to purify the Canon, to reduce the subject matter and style of literature to something Ernest Hemingway could have understood." The same can be said for culture, for HIStory is simply the recording of culture. My prayer is that this book adds to the currency of the *whole* story of humankind.

THE INDEXES

The first of the four indexes is the Biographical Index, which offers the briefest of looks at a contributor's accomplishments: her full name, notable family relations, major achievements and awards. The Career and Occupation Index follows. Under six broad-based professions, a directory of which appears at its head, the 829 occupations of the women in this book are gathered—from slave to freedwoman, from householder to head of state. It is not always apparent how to categorize an occupation. There were some struggles. Under what category, for example, does one place a beggar or a laundress? For women such as these, who also were poets or diarists, as well as slaves and other day laborers, I created the category "Householders, Laborers, Slaves, and Miscellaneous," although I was tempted to place them under "Adventurers, Frontier Settlers, Heroes, and Pilots"; finally, I realized, acceptable or not, that these women were in the business of entertainment, and, in fact, were highly successful at it. So—"Arts and Entertainment" it was. Then there are the issues of gender-neutral language, vexing me in all the indexes. Do I use draftsman, draftsperson, drafter; fisherman, fisherwoman, or fisher? My most frequent choice was the most neutral—drafter, fisher, etc.

The Ethnicity and Nationality Index conveniently groups women for the ethnographic researcher. My protracted argument with myself as to whether or not to include an ethnicity index is antithetical to the argument I presented to my publishers in 1988, when I began work on the fourth edition. If I name one ethnicity, why not all? Why stop at African American, Asian American, white South African; why not name Italian English, Polish Mexican, Irish American? While it isn't disparaging to name one's nationality, might it be to name one's ethnicity? The various aspects of this argument remain, for me, unresolved. Ultimately, the ubiquitousness of ethnic studies programs influenced me to maintain this index for the present. I long for the day when these identifications are no more a matter of interest than, when looking through a family album, one notes the color of one's grandparents' eyes or whether their hair was straight, curly, or there.

The Subject Index attempts to break down popular subjects into subclassifications, thus enabling the reader to find what she is looking for more readily. "A word is dead when it is said, some say—/ I say it just begins to live that day" (Emily Dickinson). New words pop up, receive wide currency, then disappear: "empowerment" is less popular than it once was; "nurturing" lingers on; "conflict resolution" is very in; "ecofeminism" is practically newborn; so are "biodiversity" and "global thinking." "Blog" is brand new—as is the "Iraq War." This is the first edition in which the subclassification "by stoning" under "death" appears. And while "gender" has been around since the first edition, not until recently has it attained such lofty and abundant usage. It is certainly amusing and possibly instructive to look at the Subject Index in this way.

One of the challenges in categorizing quotations that are wide-ranging and whose contributors are rooted in so many different eras and ethnic and social backgrounds is using words that represent their thoughts with integrity, but without being offensive to today's sensibilities. *The Handbook of Non-Sexist Writing* by Kate Swift has been my Polaris through several editions now. I also consulted with professors of women's studies, African-American studies, and Hispanic studies to try and gauge the best usage today. Only in rare instances, when it very obligingly represents one and all, have I used the female form of a word. Thus, "comedian" and "writer" refer to professionals of both genders, except where otherwise noted in subclassifications ("women ~"); but "goddess" is in a class of its own, as is "heroine" (but in a telescoped mode: "hero/ine": see Notes to Subject Index). This is a word I personally shun. I much prefer Maya Angelou's clever "shero"; perhaps in the next edition I'll brave it. Other choices: "brotherhood" and "sisterhood" where literally applicable, but "esprit de corps" for expressing the larger sense of the word. "Actor," not "actress," since the latter's use in the 17th century when it was first applied was pejorative (just as the diminutive "authoress" and "poetess" have been all but done away with); but "princess" since, historically, it has always been in use with no derogation intended (with the exception of "Jewish-American princess"); "humankind" rather than "man" (as a race).

The struggle is ongoing and help is always welcome. As Gloria Steinem said, "Finding language that will allow people to act together while cherishing each other's individuality is probably the most feminist and therefore revolutionary function of writers."

Each section of the book is preceded by its own "Notes to . . .," which explains the nuts and bolts of abbreviations, format, etc.

CONCLUSION

While *The Quotable Woman* is, primarily, a collection of quotations, it is much more than that. By organizing the work chronologically, I've attempted to illustrate the arc of women's history and, along with that, the movement for human—and especially women's—rights. Therefore, in this edition, I've placed an emphasis on the new voices emerging from the developing world. We hear them more and more now, thanks to the Internet, and that has enabled me to include scores of women from the African, Middle Eastern and South Asian nations. The newest section of that arc is the environmental movement with dozens of ecofeminists leading the way. There are so many organizations in the world today filled with unselfish people who are working with all their might for the greater good. The source of women on an international level is enormous. I could have continued endlessly, adding to my burgeoning database, but the time came for me to stop, to get the book out there to you, the public. I have worked hard, but I've simply been a medium. In the words of painter and writer Emily Carr: "You yourself are nothing, only a channel for the pouring through of that which is something, which is all. Your job is to keep that channel clear and clean and pure so that which passes through may be unobstructed, unsullied, undiluted, and thus show forth its clear purity and intention."

The whole point of the work I'm doing is to share the rich fount of literature, art and thought gifted to the world by women. In the 35 years since I began this excavation of women's history my mission has been to raise the voices of women so that their contributions to world culture would be noted, spoken of, nay—shouted from the rooftops.

In sisterhood,
Elaine Bernstein Partnow
Live Oak Island, Florida

Guidelines for Use

The women quoted are presented in chronological order according to the year of their birth, then by year of death, then alphabetically. Each contributor has been assigned a number; guides to these contributor numbers appear in the running heads throughout the quotations section and are used in lieu of page numbers in all four indexes.

Where actual years of birth and/or death are not known, but could be estimated with reasonably accuracy, dates are followed by a question mark; dates that are less certain are preceded by "ca." (circa). Dates shown with a virgule (1734/37) indicate birth or death having taken place within that range of years. When the year of birth is not known but the year of death is, the latter has been used for placement in the chronology. When neither year is known, floruit (fl.) is used and the woman is placed alphabetically in the decade during which she was at her height (e.g. fl. ca. 1760–1770). It is often difficult to ascertain years of birth among emerging voices who have not yet been consigned to the dusty pages of history. Between the time the manuscript was submitted to the publisher and the proofreading of pages, new facts were found. Rather than omit this information in service to form, it has been included, putting some of the "fl. 1980s or 90s" contributors out of chronological order. This may cause annoyance at the end of the Quotations section, where some 50 or so contemporary women had to be listed as (fl. 1990s) or (Contemporary).

Quotations for each contributor are also laid out chronologically, in ascending order, based on year of publication. Parenthetical dates within a source indicate the time at which the quotation was originally spoken, written or published, if known, and, again, are laid out chronologically. When no date could be ascertained, the abbreviation n.d. (no date) appears; these quotations are placed at the end of entries with known dates.

Sic is used sparingly; for reasons of historical interest, whenever it would not muddle meaning, I have elected to maintain original spellings and references.

When possible, the location of a quotation within its source is given—chapter, stanza, act, page number, etc. Abbreviations used in source citations are: Vol.—volume; Pt.—part; Bk.—Book; Ch.—Chapter; St.—Stanza; Sec.—Section; No.—Number; Sc.—Scene, l.—line; l.l.—last line(s); Attr.—attributed; ca.—circa; ed.—editor; tr.—translator.

When a quotation is taken from a book, an article or any work by a writer other than the contributor, it is indicated by the words "Quoted in," followed by the source and its author. In the anthologies, "Quoted in" is not used; instead, editors are identified.

Quotation marks around a quotation indicate it was dialogue in the original source. Every effort has been made to maintain the integrity of form in all poetry.

For further information on the indexes, see the prefatory notes to each.

QUOTATIONS

1. Eve (pre-4000 B.C.E.)
1 The serpent beguiled me, and I did eat.

        Genesis 3:13 ca. ninth century B.C.E.

2. Spider Woman (3500?–? B.C.E.)
1 That is the Sun. You are meeting your Father the Creator for the first time. You must always remember and observe these three phases of your Creation. This time of the three lights, the dark purple, the yellow, and the red reveal in turn the mystery, the breath of life, and warmth of love. These comprise the Creator's plan of life for you as sung over you in the Song of Creation.

        "The Creation of Spider Woman," Quoted in *The Book of Hopi* by Frank Waters *1963*

3. Isis (3100?–? B.C.E.)
1 I am Nature, the universal Mother, mistress of all the elements, primordial child of time, sovereign of all things spiritual, queen of the dead, queen also of the immortals, the single manifestation of all gods and goddesses that are. My nod governs the shining heights of Heaven, the wholesome sea-breezes, the lamentable silences of the world below. Though I am worshiped in many aspects, known by countless names, and propitiated with all manner of different rites, yet the whole round earth venerates me.

        "The Goddess Isis Intervenes," *The Golden Ass by Apuleius,* Robert Graves, tr. *1978*

4. Enheduanna (ca. 2354–? B.C.E.)
1 You are in all our great rites.
  Who can understand you?

        "Inanna* and An," adapted by Aliki and Willis Barnstone, Quoted in *The Exaltation of Inanna* by William W. Hallo and J. J. A. van Dijk *1968*
    *Sumerian goddess of love.

2 cries of labor I gave birth to this hymn . . .

        "Inanna and An," adapted by Anne Draffkorn Kilmer, Ibid.

3 My honeyed tongue is tied with confusion

        Untitled, adapted by Anne Draffkorn Kilmer, Ibid.

5. Hagar (2300?–ca. 1850 B.C.E.)
1 Thou God seest me: . . . Have I also here looked after him that seeth me?

        Genesis 16:13 ca. ninth century B.C.E.

6. Inanna (fl. 2300 B.C.E.)
1 The shepherd! I will not marry the shepherd!
  His clothes are coarse; his wool is rough.
  I will marry the farmer.
  The farmer grows flax for my clothes.
  The farmer grows barley for my table.

        Quoted in *Inanna* by Diane Wolkstein and Samuel Noah Kramer *1983*

2 He put his hand in her hand.
  He put his hand to her heart.
  Sweet is the sleep of hand-to-hand.
  Sweeter still the sleep of heart-to-heart.

        Ibid.

7. Kubatum (fl. ca. 2030 B.C.E.)
1 my sweet and darling one with whom I would speak honey—
    youth, I am in love with you!

        "Love Song to King Shu-Suen," St. 6, Thorkild Jacobsen, tr., *Most Ancient Verse,* Thorkild Jacobsen and John A. Wilson, eds. *n.d.*

8. Sarah (1987?–1860 B.C.E.)
1 After I am waxed old shall I have pleasure, my lord being old also?

        Genesis 18:12 ca. ninth century B.C.E.

2 God hath made me to laugh, so that all that hear will laugh with me.

        21:6, Ibid.

9. Leah (fl. 18th century B.C.E.)
1 Is there yet an portion or inheritance for us [Leah and Rachel] in our father's house?
    Are we not counted of him strangers? For he hath sold us, and hath quite devoured also our money.

For all the riches which God hath taken from our father,
that is ours, and our children's . . .*

Genesis 31:14–16* *ca. ninth century* B.C.E.

*See 13.

10. Lot's daughter (the elder) (fl. 18th century B.C.E.)

1 Our father is old, and there is not a man in the earth to come in
unto us after the manner of all the earth;

Come let us make our father drink wine, and we will lie
with him, that we may preserve seed of our father.

Genesis 19:31, 32 *ca. ninth century* B.C.E.

11. Rebekah (fl. 18th century B.C.E.)

1 Drink my lord: . . .

I will draw water for thy camels also, until
they have done drinking.

Genesis 24:18, 19 *ca. ninth century* B.C.E.

2 Upon me be thy curse, my son: only obey my voice, and go
fetch me them.

27:13, 19, Ibid.

12. Eristi–Aya (1790?–1745 B.C.E.)

1 Even warriors seized as booty in war are treated humanely.
At least, treat me like them!

"A Letter to Her Mother," Willis Barnstone, tr., *A Book of
Women Poets,* Aliki and Willis Barnstone, eds. *1980*

13. Rachel (?–1732 B.C.E.?)

1 Give me children, or else I die.

Genesis 30:1 *ca. ninth century* B.C.E.

14. Hathshepsut (fl. 1500–d. 1482 B.C.E.)

1 My command stands firm like the mountains and the sun's disk
shines and spreads rays over the titulary of my August person,
and my falcon rises high above the kingly banner unto all eternity.

Quoted in *The Remarkable Women of Ancient Egypt*
by Barbara Lesko *1978*

15. Ankhesenpaton (fl. ca. 1390 B.C.E.)

1 My husband, Nib-khuruia,* has recently died, he and I have no
son. But thy sons, they say, are many. If thou wilt send me a son
of thine, he shall become my husband.

Letter to Shuppiluliuma, the Hittite king (62 B.C.E.), Quoted in
When Egypt Ruled the East by George Steindorff
and Keith C. Seele *1942*

*Official name of Tutankhamen, who ruled ca. 1379–1362 B.C.E.

16. Miriam (fl. 1250s–1230s B.C.E.)

1 Sing ye to the Lord, for he hath triumphed gloriously; the horse
and his rider hath he thrown into the sea.

Exodus 15:21 *ca. ninth century* B.C.E.

17. Pharaoh's daughter (fl. ca. 1250 B.C.E.)

1 Because I drew him [Moses] out of the water.

Exodus 2:10 *ca. ninth century* B.C.E.

18. Five Daughters of Zelophehad: Mahlah, Noah, Hoglah, Milcah and Tirzah (fl. 1240–1200 B.C.E.)

1 Our father died in the wilderness, and he was not in the company of them that hath gathered themselves together against
the Lord in the company of Kôr-ah; but died in his own sin,
and had no sons.

Why should the name of our father be done away from
among his family, because he hath no son? Give unto us therefore a possession among the brethren of our father.

Numbers 27:3, 4 *ca. ninth century* B.C.E.

19. Zipporah (fl. ca. 1230 B.C.E.)

1 Surely a bloody husband art thou to me . . .

A bloody husband thou art, because of the circumcision.

Exodus 4:25, 26 *ca. ninth century* B.C.E.

20. Penelope (1214?–? B.C.E.)

1 Careless to please, with insolence ye woo!

Quoted in *The Odyssey* by Homer *ca. 800* B.C.E.

2 When have I not been dreading dangers more grievous than the
reality? Love is a thing replete with anxious fears.

Quoted in *Epistulae Heroidum [Letters from Heroines]* by
Ovid *ca. 20* B.C.E.

21. Daughter of Jephthah the Gileadite (fl. ca. 1140 B.C.E.)

1 Let this thing be done for me: let me alone two months, that
I may go up and down upon the mountains, and bewail my
virginity.

Judges 11:37 *ca. 550* B.C.E.

22. Naomi (fl. ca. 1100 B.C.E.)

1 Go, return each to her mother's house . . .*

Ruth 1:8 *late fifth/fourth century* B.C.E.

*Spoken to her daughters-in-law, Ruth and Orpah. See 23.

23. Ruth (fl. ca. 1100 B.C.E.)

1 Intreat me not to leave thee,* or to return from following after
thee: for whither thou goest, I will go; and where thou lodgest,
I will lodge: thy people shall be my people, and thy God my
God:

Where thou diest, will I die, and there will I be buried: the
Lord do so to me, and more also, if ought but death part thee
and me.

Ruth 1:16, 17 *late fifth/fourth century* B.C.E.

*Her mother-in-law, Naomi: see 22.

24. Delilah (fl. ca. 1080 B.C.E.)

1 How canst thou say, I love thee, when thine heart is not with
me? Thou hast mocked me these three times, and hast not told
me wherein thy great strength lieth.

Judges 16:15 *ca. 550* B.C.E.

25. Wife of Manoah (fl. 1080 B.C.E.)

1 If the Lord were pleased to kill us, he would not have received a
burnt offering and a meat offering at our hands, neither would
he have shewed us all these things, nor would as at this time
have told us such things as these.

Judges 13:23 *ca. 550* B.C.E.

26. First wife of Samson (fl. ca. 1080 B.C.E.)

1 Thou dost but hate me, and lovest me not; thou hast put forth a riddle unto the children of my people, and hast not told it me.

Judges 14:16 *ca. 550 B.C.E.*

27. Deborah (fl. ca. 1070 B.C.E.)

1 Speak, ye that ride on white asses, ye that sit in judgment, and walk by the way.

Judges, with Barak,* 5:10 *ca. 550 B.C.E.*

*Leader who, with Deborah, delivered Israel from the Canaanites.

2 So let all think enemies perish, O Lord: but let them that love him be as the sun when he goeth forth in his might. And the land had rest forty years.

5:31, Ibid.

28. Jael (fl. ca. 1070 B.C.E.)

1 Turn in, my Lord, turn in to me; fear not.

Judges 4:18 *ca. 550 B.C.E.*

29. Woman of Abel of Beth-maacah (fl. 1040s–970s B.C.E.)

1 . . . why wilt thou swallow up the inheritance of the Lord?

2 Samuel 20:19 *ca. 550 B.C.E.*

30. Hannah (1040 B.C.E.?–?)

1 My heart rejoiceth in the Lord, mine horn is exalted in the Lord: my mouth is enlarged over mine enemies; because I rejoice in thy salvation.

There is none holy as the Lord: for there is none beside thee: neither is there any rock like our God.

Talk no more so exceeding proudly; let not arrogancy come out of your mouth: for the Lord is a God of knowledge, and by him actions are weighed.

The bows of the mighty men are broken, and they that stumbled are girded with strength.

They that were full have hired out themselves for bread; and they that were hungry ceased: so that the barren hath born seven; and she that hath many children is waxed feeble.

The Lord killeth, and maketh alive: he bringeth down to the grave, and bringeth up.

The Lord maketh poor, and maketh rich: he bringeth low, and lifteth up.

He raiseth up the poor out of the dust, and lifteth up the beggar from the dunghill, to set them among princes, and to make them inherit the throne of glory: for the pillars of the earth are the Lord's, and he hath set the world upon them.

He will keep the feet of his saints, and the wicked shall be silent in darkness; for by strength shall no man prevail.

The adversaries of the Lord shall be broken to pieces; out of heaven shall he thunder upon them: the Lord shall judge the ends of the earth; and he shall give strength unto his king, and exalt the horn of his anointed.

1 Samuel 2:1–10 *ca. 550 B.C.E.*

31. Wife of Phinehas (1040?–970 B.C.E.)

1 The glory is departed from Israel: for the ark of God is taken.

1 Samuel 4:22 *ca. 550 B.C.E.*

32. Michal (fl. 1010s–970s B.C.E.)

1 If thou save not thy life tonight, tomorrow thou shalt be slain.

1 Samuel 19:11 *ca. 550 B.C.E.*

33. Bathsheba (fl. 1000s–970s B.C.E.)

1 And thou, my lord, O king, the eyes of all Israel are upon thee, that thou shouldest tell them who shall sit on the throne of my lord the king after him.

1 Kings 1:20 *ca. 550 B.C.E.*

34. Abigail (fl. ca. 990 B.C.E.)

1 Behold, let thine handmaid be a servant to wash the feet of the servants of my lord.

1 Samuel 25:41 *ca. 550 B.C.E.*

35. Tamar (fl. ca. 990 B.C.E.)

1 Nay, my brother, do not force me; for no such thing ought to be done in Israel: do not thou this folly.

2 Samuel 13:12 *ca. 550 B.C.E.*

36. Prostitute of Jerusalem (mother of the dead child) (fl. ca. 950 B.C.E.)

1 Let it be neither mine nor thine, but divide it.

1 Kings 3:26 *ca. 550 B.C.E.*

37. Prostitute of Jerusalem (mother of the living child) (fl. ca. 950 B.C.E.)

1 O my lord, give her the living child, and in no wise slay it: she is the mother thereof.

1 Kings 3:26 *ca. 550 B.C.E.*

38. Queen of Sheba (fl. ca. 950 B.C.E.)

1 Howbeit I believed not the words, until I came, and mine eyes had seen it: and, behold, the half was not told me: thy wisdom and prosperity exceedeth the fame which I heard.

1 Kings, 10:7 *ca. 550 B.C.E.*

39. Woman of Tekoa (fl. ca. 940 B.C.E.)

1 For we must needs die, and are as water spilt on the ground, which cannot be gathered up again. . . .

2 Samuel 14:14 *ca. 550 B.C.E.*

40. Jezebel (fl. 870s–d. 853 B.C.E.)

1 . . . arise, and eat bread, and let thine heart be merry . . .

1 Kings 21:7 *ca. 550 B.C.E.*

41. Wife of Job (fl. eighth century B.C.E.)

1 Dost thou still retain thine integrity? Curse God, and die.

Job 2:9 *ca. early fifth century B.C.E.*

42. Semiramis (fl. eighth century B.C.E.)

1 Nature gave me the form of a woman; my actions have raised me to the level of the most valiant of men.

Quoted in *Women of Beauty and Heroism* by Frank B. Goodrich *1858*

43. Anna (fl. ca. 720 B.C.E.)
1 Alas! I let you leave me, my child, you, the light of my eyes.

Tobit 10:5 ca. 175–164 B.C.E.

44. Edna (fl. ca. 720 B.C.E.)
1 Courage, daughter! May the Lord of heaven turn your grief to joy! Courage, daughter!

Tobit 7:16 ca. 175–164 B.C.E.

45. Sarah (fl. ca. 720 B.C.E.)
1 I cannot cause my father a sorrow which would bring down his old age to the dwelling of the dead.

Tobit 3:10 ca. 175–164 B.C.E.

46. Sappho (ca. 630/610–ca. 570 B.C.E.)
1 When anger spreads through the breast, guard thy tongue from barking idly.

Untitled fragment, Quoted in Women in the Golden Ages by Amelia Gere Mason 1901

2 . . . death is an evil; the gods have so judged; had it been good, they would die.

Ibid.

3 Gentle ladies, you will remember till old age what we did together in our brilliant youth!

Untitled fragment, Quoted in Distinguished Women Writers by Virginia Moore 1934

4 Now Eros has shaken my thoughts, like a wind among highland oaks.

Ibid.

5 Love, fatal creature. . . .

Ibid.

6 all my flesh is wrinkled with age,
my black hair has faded to white,

my legs can no longer carry me,
once nimble like a fawn's,

but what can I do?
It cannot be undone,
no more than can pink-armed Dawn
not end in darkness on earth.

Untitled, Sts. 2–5, Greek Lyric Poetry, Willis Barnstone, ed. and tr. 1960

7   If I meet
you suddenly, I can't

speak—my tongue is broken;
a thick flame runs under
my skin; seeing nothing,
hearing only my own ears
drumming, I drip with sweat;
trembling shakes my body

and I turn paler than
dry grass. At such times
death isn't far from me.

Untitled, The Penguin Book of Women Poets, Carol Cosman, Joan Keefe, and Kathleen Weaver, eds. 1978

8 The angel of spring, the mellow-throated nightingale.

No. 39, Fragments n.d.

9 Art thou the topmost apple
The gatherers could not reach,
Reddening on the bough?
Shall I not take thee?

No. 53, Ibid.

47. Erinna (fl. 610s–d. 595 B.C.E.)
1 Little trails through my heart that are
Still warm—my remembrances of you.

"This Distaff," Marilyn Bentley Arthur, tr., Women Poets of the World, Joanna Bankier and Deirdre Lashgari, eds. 1983

48. Judith (fl. sixth century–d. 495 B.C.E.)
1 If you cannot sound the depths of the heart of man or unravel the arguments of his mind, how can you fathom the God who made all things, or sound his mind or unravel his purposes?

Judith 8:12–14 ca. 150 B.C.E.

2 But you have no right to demand guarantees where the designs of the Lord our God are concerned. For God is not to be coerced as man is, nor is he, like mere man, to be cajoled.

8:16, Ibid.

3 Her sandal ravished his eyes,
her beauty took his soul prisoner . . .
and the scimitar cut through his neck!

16:9, Ibid.

4 May your whole creation serve you!
For you spoke and things came into being,
you sent your breath and they were put together,
and no one can resist your voice.

16:14, Ibid.

5 A little thing indeed
is a sweetly smelling sacrifice. . . .

16:16, Ibid.

6 Woe to the nations
who rise against my race!

16:17, Ibid.

49. Mettika (fl. sixth century B.C.E.)
1 I sit here on this rock.
And over my spirit blows
The breath of liberty

"Though I am weak and tired now," Therigatha, Uma Chakravarti and Kumkum Roy, trs. 80 B.C.E.

50. Mutta (fl. sixth century B.C.E.)
1 So free am I, so gloriously free,
Free from three petty things—
From mortar, from pestle and from my twisted lord,

"So free am I, so gloriously free," Therigatha, Uma Chakravarti and Kumkum Roy, trs. 80 B.C.E.

51. Sumangalamata (fl. sixth century B.C.E.)
1 How wonderfully free, from kitchen drudgery.
Free from the harsh grip of hunger,
And from empty cooking pots

"A woman well set free! How free I am," Therigatha, Uma Chakravarti & Kumkum Roy, trs. 80 B.C.E.

52. Huldah (fl. ca. 580 B.C.E.)

1   Behold therefore, I will gather thee unto thy fathers, and thou shalt be gathered into thy grave in peace; and thine eyes shall not see all the evil which I will bring upon this place.

2 Kings 22:20 *ca. 550 B.C.E.*

53. Susanna (fl. 580s–d. 538 B.C.E.)

1   But I prefer to fall innocent into your power than to sin in the eyes of the Lord.

Daniel 13:23 *ca. 167–164 B.C.E.*

54. Ambapali (fl. 560s–d. 480 B.C.E.)

1   Such was my body once. Now it is weary and tottering, the home of many ills, an old house with flaking plaster. Not otherwise is the world of the truthful.

Untitled, St. 9, *The Wonder that was India,* A. L. Bashun, ed. and tr. *1959*

2   The truth of the Truth-speaker's words doesn't change.

"Therigatha XIII," St. 1 (refrain) *n.d.*

3   Swelling, round, firm, and high, both my breasts were once splendid. In the drought of old age, they dangle like empty old water bags.

St. 14 *n.d.,* Ibid.

55. Corinna (fl. ca. 520 B.C.E.)

1   When he sailed into the harbor his ship became a snorting horse.

Untitled, St. 1, *Greek Lyric Poetry,* Willis Barnstone, ed. and tr. *1962*

2   asleep forever? you were not like that, Corinna, in the old days.

Untitled, John Dillon, tr., *The Penguin Book of Women Poets,* Carol Cosman, Joan Keefe, and Kathleen Weaver, eds. *1978*

56. Esther (fl. 510s–d. 465 B.C.E.)

1   . . . if I perish, I perish.

Esther 4:16 *ca. 199–150 B.C.E.*

2   . . . you, lord, chose Israel out of all the nations and our ancestors out of all the people of old times to be your heritage for ever . . .

4:17, Ibid.

3   Never let men mock at our ruin.

Ibid.

57. Rebecca (fl. fifth century B.C.E.)

1   It is indeed better for us to live with wild beasts and perish of hunger than to be compelled by Greeks and idolaters to fall into the filth of marriage.

Acts of Xanthippe and Polyxena, XXXI, Ante-Nicene Fathers edition, Alexander Roberts and James Donaldson, eds. *1955* (repr).

58. Telesilla (fl. fifth century B.C.E.)

1   Run swiftly to escape the rape of the hunter Alpheus.

Untitled, *Greek Lyric Poetry,* Willis Barnstone, ed. and tr. *1978*

59. Xanthippe (fl. fifth century B.C.E.)

1   O beauty of the world! For that which we hitherto thought to come of itself, we know now that all things are beautifully fashioned by the beautiful One.

Acts of Xanthippe and Polyxena,* VI, Ante-Nicene Fathers edition, Alexander Roberts and James Donaldson, eds. *1955* (repr.)

*See 84.

2   Why is his* walk quiet and equable, as of one who expects to take in his arms one that is pursued? Why is his countenance kindly, as of one that tends the sick? Why does he look so lovingly hither and thither, as one who desires to assist those who are seeking to flee from the mouths of dragons?

VII, Ibid.

*St. Paul, the Apostle, biblical era.

60. Artemisia (fl. ca. 480 B.C.E.)

1   Spare your ships, and do not risk a battle; for these people [the Greeks] are as much superior to your people in seamanship, as men to women.

Remark to King Xerxes,* Bk. VIII, Quoted in *The Persian Wars* by Herodotus *ca. 450 B.C.E.*

*519?–465 B.C.E., King of Persia (486–465 B.C.E.)

61. Praxilla (fl. ca. 450 B.C.E.)

1   You gaze at me teasingly through the window: a virgin—and below—a woman's thighs.

Untitled, *Greek Lyric Poetry,* Willis Barnstone, ed. and tr. *1962*

2   Loveliest of what I leave is the sun himself Next to that the bright stars and the face of mother moon Oh yes, and cucumbers in season, and apples, and pears.

"Adonis Dying," John Dillon, tr., *The Penguin Book of Women Poets,* Carol Cosman, Joan Keefe, and Kathleen Weaver, eds. *1978*

3   Watch out, my dear, there's a scorpion under every stone.

Untitled fragment, Ibid.

62. Aspasia (fl. ca. 420 B.C.E.)

1   . . . if you don't endeavor that there be not a better husband and wife in the world than yourselves, you will always be wishing for that which you shall think best.

Quoted by Socrates in *Dialogue of Aeschines* by Plato *ca. 360–386 C.E.*

2   Your great glory is not to be inferior to what God has made you, and the greatest glory of a woman is to be least talked about by men, whether they are praising you or criticizing you.

Quoted in *History of the Peloponnesian War* by Thucydides *ca. 413 B.C.E.*

63. Theano (fl. ca. 420 B.C.E.)

1   Put off your shame with your clothes when you go in to your husband, and put it on again when you come out.

> Bk. VIII, Sec. 43, Quoted in *Lives, Teachings, and Sayings of Famous Philosophers* by Diogenes Laertius *ca. 300 B.C.E.*

2   The gods could not be honored by lies.

> Quoted in *Biography of Distinguished Women* by Sarah Josepha Hale* 1879

*See 807.

64. Phyrne (fl. fourth century B.C.E.)

1   He* is not a man but a statue.

> Quoted in *Lives, Teachings, and Sayings of Famous Philosophers* by Diogenes Laertius *ca. 300 B.C.E.*

*The Greek philosopher Xenocrates.

65. Lais (?–340 B.C.E.)

1   I do not understand what is meant by the austerity of philosophers, for with this fine name, they are as much in my power as the rest of the Athenians.

> Quoted in *Biography of Distinguished Women* by Sarah Josepha Hale* 1879

*See 807.

66. Anyte of Tegea (fl. ca. 300 B.C.E.)

1   This place is sacred to the goddess.
    Here her constant pleasure
    is to watch the sea as it shimmers from the shore

> Quoted in *Classical Women Poets*, Josephine Balmer, tr. 1966

67. Lady Ho (fl. 300 B.C.E.)

1   When a pair of magpies fly together
    They do not envy the pair of phoenixes.

> "A Song of Magpies," *The Orchid Boat, Women Poets of China*, Kenneth Rexroth and Ling Chung, eds. and trs. 1972

68. The Jewish Sibyl (fl. 190s–d. 165 B.C.E.?)

1   . . . here is a city, Chaldean Ur,
    Whence come a race of most upright men,
    Who are ever right-minded and their works good.
    They are neither concerned for the sun's course,
    Nor the moon's, nor for monstrosities on earth,
    Nor for satisfaction from ocean's depths,
    Nor for signs of sneezing and the augury from birds;
    Nor for soothsaying, nor sorcery, nor incantations;
    Nor for deceitful follies of ventriloquists.
    They do not, Chaldean fashion, astrologize,
    Nor watch the stars. . . .
    But they are concerned about rightness and virtue.

> *The Fourth Book of Sibylline Oracles ca. 100 B.C.E.*

69. Chuo Wên-chün (179?–117 B.C.E.)

1   Why should marriage bring only tears?
    All I wanted was a man
    With a single heart,
    And we would stay together
    As our hair turned white,
    Not somebody always after wriggling fish
    With his big bamboo rod.

> "A Song of White Hair," *The Orchid Boat, Women Poets of China*, Kenneth Rexroth and Ling Chung, eds. and trs. 1972

70. Mother of the Seven Brothers (164?–161 B.C.E.)

1   I do not know how you appeared in my womb; it was not I who endowed you with breath and life, I had not the shaping of your every part.
    It is the creator of the world, ordaining the process of man's birth and presiding over the origin of all things.

> 2 Maccabees 7:22–23 *ca. 41–44 C.E.*

2   I implore you, my child, observe heaven and earth, consider all that is in them, and acknowledge that God made them out of what did not exist, and that mankind comes into being the same way.

> Ibid., 7:28

71. Cornelia (fl. 160s–140s B.C.E.)

1   These are all the jewels of which I can boast.*

> Quoted in *Biography of Distinguished Women* by Sarah Josepha Hale** 1876

*Referring to her sons, Tiberius and Gaius Gracchi. **See 807.

72. Wife of Ch'in Chia (fl. first century B.C.E.)

1   I stood on tiptoe gazing into the distance
    Interminably gazing at the road that had taken you.

> "Ch'in Chia's Wife's Reply," *Translations from the Chinese*, Arthur Waley, tr. 1919

73. Hsi-chün (fl. ca. 100 B.C.E.)

1   Would I were a yellow stork
    And could fly to my old home!

> "Lament of Hsi-chün," *Translations from the Chinese*, Arthur Waley, tr. 1919

74. Hortensia (85 B.C.E.–?)

1   . . . you assume the glorious title of reformers of the state, a title which will turn to your eternal infamy, if, without the least regard to the laws of equity, you persist in your wicked resolution of plundering those [women] of their lives and fortunes, who have given you no just cause of offence.

> (ca. 45 B.C.E.), Vol. IV, Quoted in *Civil Wars* by Appian of Alexandria *32–34 C.E.*

2   Why should we pay taxes when we have no part in the honors, the commands, the state craft for which you contend?

> Speech before the Roman Triumvirate (42 B.C.E.), *Women in World History Curriculum*, http:womeninhistory.com, Lyn Reese, Director 1996–97

75. Cleopatra VII (69 B.C.E.–30 C.E.)

1   Leave the fishing-rod, Great General, to us sovereigns of Pharos and Canopus. Your game is cities and kings and continents.

> Remark to Marc Antony,* Quoted in Ch. 9, *Cleopatra of Egypt* by Philip W. Sergeant 1909

*83?–30 B.C.E. Roman general

2   As surely as one day I shall administer justice on the Capitol . . .*

> Ch. 13, Ibid.

*Her favorite oath, referring to the capital of the Roman Empire.

3   Fool! Don't you see now that I could have poisoned you a hundred times had I been able to live without you!

> Remark to Marc Antony, Quoted in Ch. 5, *Cleopatra's Daughter, the Queen of Mauretania* by Beatrice Chanler 1934

4 Nothing could part us while we lived, but death seems to threaten to divide us. You, a Roman born, have found a grave in Egypt. I, an Egyptian, am to seek that favour, and none but that, in your country.
   Spoken over Marc Antony's tombstone, Ch. 20, Quoted in *The Life and Times of Cleopatra* by Arthur Weigall *1968*

76. Sulpicia (fl. 60s B.C.E.–d. 14 C.E.)

1 Drat my hateful birthday
   to be spent in the boring old country.
   Untitled, John Dillon, tr., *The Penguin Book of Women Poets*, Carol Cosman, Joan Keefe, and Kathleen Weaver, eds. *1978*

2 At last love has come. I would be more ashamed
   to hide it in cloth than leave it naked
   Untitled, *A Book of Women Poets*, Aliki and Willis Barnstone, eds. and trs. *1980*

3 Friends worry about me and are upset that somehow
   I might tumble into bed with a nobody.
   Ibid.

4 Trips are often poorly timed.
   Ibid.

5 indiscretion has its charms
   Untitled (1), *Six Poems, from Corpus Tibullianum*, Lee T. Pearcy, tr. *1995*

6 What is sweeter than the city?
   Untitled (2), Ibid.

77. Porcia (?–42 B.C.E.)

1 Brutus,* I am Cato's** daughter, and I was brought into thy house, not, like a mere concubine, to share thy bed and board merely, but to be a partner in thy troubles. Thou, indeed, art faultless as a husband; but how can I show thee any grateful service if I am to share neither thy secret suffering nor the anxiety which craves a loyal confidant? I know that a woman's nature is thought too weak to endure a secret; but good rearing and excellent companionship go far towards strengthening the character, and it is my happy lot to be both the daughter of Cato and the wife of Brutus. Before this I put less confidence in these advantages, but now I know that I am superior even to pain.***
   From *Parallel Lives* by Plutarch (ca. 100 C.E.), Quoted in *Plutarch's Lives*, Vol. VI, B. Perrin, tr. *1914–26*
   *85?–42 B.C.E. Roman political and military leader. **95–46 B.C.E. Roman statesman. ***Spoken shortly before Caesar's murder, when she sensed Brutus' troubled mind; she wounded her thigh with a small knife just before making the above speech.

78. Saint Elisabeth (fl. 20s B.C.E.–? C.E.)

1 Blessed art thou [Mary*] among women, and blessed is the fruit of thy womb.
   And whence is this to me, that the mother of my Lord should come to me?
   For, lo, as soon as the voice of thy salutation sounded in mine ears, the babe [John the Baptist] leaped in my womb for joy.
   And blessed is she that believed: for there shall be a performance of those things which were told her from the Lord.
   Luke 1:42–45 *ca. 65–80 C.E.*
   *See 79.

79. Mary (fl. 7 B.C.E.–25 C.E.)

1 My soul doth magnify the Lord, And my spirit hath rejoiced in God my Savior.
   For he hath regarded the low estate of his handmaiden; for, behold, from henceforth all generations shall call me blessed.
   For he that is mighty hath done to me great things; and holy is his name.
   And his mercy is on them that fear him from generation to generation.
   He hath shewed strength with his arm; he hath scattered the proud in the imagination of their hearts.
   He hath put down the mighty from their seats, and exalted them of low degree.
   He hath filled the hungry with good things; and the rich he hath sent empty away.
   He hath helped his servant Israel, in remembrance of his mercy;
   As he spake to our fathers, to Abraham, and to his seed for ever.
   Luke 1:46–55 *ca. 65–80 C.E.*

80. Agrippina the Younger (14–59 C.E.)

1 No philosophy, my son [Nero*]; it is of no use to an emperor.
   Ch. 8, Quoted in *The Great Empress, A Portrait* by Maximilian Schele de Vere *1870*
   *(37–68 C.E.), Emperor of Rome (54–68 C.E.).

2 Strike the womb that bore a monster!
   Ch. 11, Ibid.

81. Mary Magdalene (fl. ca. 20 C.E.)

1 They have taken away the Lord out of the sepulchre, and we know not where they have laid him.
   John 20:2 *100 C.E.*

82. Salome (fl. ca. 20 C.E.)

1 I will that thou give me by and by in a charger the head of John the Baptist.
   Mark 6:25 *68*

83. Samaritan Woman (fl. ca. 20 C.E.)

1 How is it that thou [Christ], being a Jew, askest drink of me, which am a woman of Samaria? . . .
   John 4:9 *100*

84. Polyxena (fl. ca. 30 C.E.)

1 Would that I were as one of the wild beasts that I might not know what captivity is.
   Acts of Xanthippe and Polyxena, XXVI, Ante-Nicene Fathers edition, Alexander Roberts and James Donaldson, eds. *1955 (repr.)*
   *See 59.

2 No one sees or heeds or hears my groaning. Verily I shall beseech Him that sees the hidden things, for who is more pitiful and compassionate than He who always keeps watch over the oppressed?
   Ibid.

85. Poppæa Sabina (fl. 30–65 C.E.)

1 Rather die than see my beauty pass away!
   Ch. 9, Quoted in *The Great Empress, A Portrait* by Maximilian Schele de Vere *1870*

86. Boadicea (fl. 40s–65 C.E.)

1 It will not be the first time, Britons, that you have been victorious under the conduct of your queen. For my part, I come not here as one descended of royal blood, not to fight for empire or riches, but as one of the common people, to avenge the loss of their liberty, the wrongs of myself and children.

Speech, Quoted in *Biography of Distinguished Women* by Sarah Josepha Hale* *1876*

*See 807.

2 Roman lust has gone so far that not even our own persons remain unpolluted. If you weigh well the strengths of our armies, you will see that in this battle we must conquer or die. This is a woman's resolve. As for the men, they may live or be slaves.

Quoted in *The Dinner Party, A Symbol of our Heritage* by Judy Chicago* *1979*

*See 3133.

87. Arria the Elder (?–42 C.E.)

1 It does not hurt, my Paetus.*

Bk. III, epistle 16, Quoted in Epistles by Pliny the Younger *ca. 100–109*

*Remark to her husband, who had been ordered to commit suicide, after she had stabbed herself.

88–89. Pan Chao (Lady Pan) (fl.45 C.E.)

1 The virtues of women are not brilliant talent, nor distinction and elegance. The virtues of women are reserve, quiet, chastity, orderliness, governing herself to maintain a sense of shame, and conducting herself according to the rules of Confucian etiquette.

From *Nü Chieh* [Precepts for Women], Quoted in *Chinese Women: Yesterday and Today* by Florence Ayscough *1936*

2 Only needle-and-thread's delicate footsteps are truly broad-ranging yet without beginning!

"Needle and Thread," St. 3, Richard Mather and Rob Swigart, trs., *Women Poets of the World,* Joanna Bankier and Deirdre Lashgari, eds. *1983*

3 How can those who count pennies calculate their worth? They may carve monuments yet lack all understanding.

Ibid., St. 5

4 I took a piece of the rare cloth of Ch'i,
White silk glowing and pure as frost on snow,
and made you a fan of harmony and joy,
As flawlessly round as the full moon.

"A Present from the Emperor's New Concubine," *Love and the Turning Year: One Hundred More Poems from the Chinese,* Kenneth Rexroth, ed. and tr. *1970*

90. Lydia (fl. ca. 50 C.E.)

1 If ye have judged me to be faithful to the Lord, come into my house, and abide there.

Acts 16:15 *ca. 85–95 C.E.*

91. Imma Shalom (fl. 50 C.E.)

1 She once heard a sceptic mocking her brother, saying, "Your God is not strictly honest, or He would not have stolen a rib from sleeping Adam," and she asked him to fetch a police official whereupon he asked her why. "We were robbed last night of a silver cruet and the thief left in its place a golden one." He responded, "If that is all I wish that thief would visit me every day!" Imma retorted, "and yet you object to the removal of the rib from sleeping Adam! Did he not receive in exchange a woman to wait on him?"

The Status of Women in Formative Judaism by Leonard Swidler *2001*

92. Slave girl who was a soothsayer (fl. ca. 50 C.E.)

1 These men are the servants of the most high God, which shew unto us the way of salvation.

Acts 16:17 *ca. 85–95 C.E.*

93. Pompeia Plotina (80?–122)

1 May the gods send me forth from this august palace, whenever I may be destined to leave it, even as I now enter it; and may the high destiny to which fortune now raises me leave me in possession of the same qualities with which I this day assume it.

Speech (99), Quoted in *Biography of Distinguished Women* by Sarah Josepha Hale* *1876*

*See 807.

94. Sulpicia (80?–99 C.E.)

1 . . . Priscus Cato* held it of such deep import to determine whether the Roman stock would better be upheld by prosperity or adversity.—By adversity, doubtless; for when the love of country urges them to defend themselves by arms, and their wife held prisoner together with their household goods, they combine just like wasps, (a bristling band, with weapons all unsheathed along their yellow bodies,). . . .

Satire ca. 90

*Probably the same as Publius Valerius Cato, the first-century C.E. Roman poet and grammarian.

2 . . . when care-dispelling peace has returned, forgetful of labour, commons and fathers together lie buried in lethargic sleep.

Ibid.

95. Okkur Macatti (fl. ca. first–third centuries)

1 In Jasmine country, it is evening
for the hovering bees,
but look, he hasn't come back.

He left me and went in search
of wealth.

"What She Said," Speaking of Siva, A. K. Ramanujan, ed. and tr. *1973*

96. Myrta (fl. first century)

1 Paul the servant of the Lord will save many in Rome and will nourish many with the word . . . so that there will be great grace in Rome.

Quoted in "Word, Spirit and Power: Women in Early Christian Communities" by Elisabeth Schüssler Fiorenza,* *Women of Spirit,* Rosemary Ruether** and Eleanor McLaughlin, eds. *1979*

*See 3086. **See 3004.

97. Venmanipputi (fl. ca. first–third centuries)

1 my arms grow beautiful
in the coupling
and grow lean

as they come away
What shall I make of this?
> "What She Said to her Girlfriend," St. 2, *Interior: Landscape:
> Love Poems from a Classical Tamil Anthology,* A. K.
> Ramanujan, ed. and tr. *1967*

98. Ts'ai Yen (162?–239?)

1 Heaven was pitiless.
It sent down confusion and separation.
Earth was pitiless.
It brought me to birth in such a time.
War was everywhere.
Every road was dangerous.
Soldiers and civilians everywhere
Fleeing death and suffering.
> "Eighteen Verses Sung to a Tartar Reed Whistle," I:2, *The
> Orchid Boat, Women Poets of China,* Kenneth Rexroth and
> Ling Chung, eds. and trs. *1972*

2 Men here are as savage as giant vipers,
And strut about in armour, snapping their bows.
> II:1, Ibid.

99. Vivia Perpetua (180?–203)

1 "Father," said I, "do you see this vase here, for example, or water pot or whatever?"
"Yes, I do," said he.
And I told him: "Could it be called by any other name than what it is?"
And he said: "No."
"Well, so too I cannot be called anything other than what I am, a Christian."
> Ch. 3, Quoted in *Perpetua's Passion, The Death and Memory
> of a Young Roman Woman* by Joyce E. Salisbury* *1997*
*See 3537.

100. Zenobia of Palmyra (240–300)

1 By valor alone, by the force of arms only, can wars be brought to a close.
> Letter to Aurelian Augustus* (272), Quoted in *Women of
> Beauty and Heroism* by Frank B. Goodrich *1858*
*212?–75, Roman emperor (270–75).

101. Trieu Thi Trinh (fl. 270s)

1 My wish is to ride the tempest, tame the waves, kill the sharks. I will not resign myself to the usual lot of women who bow their heads and become concubines.
> Remark (270), Quoted in *Women in World History
> Curriculum* (womeninhistory.com), Lyn Reese, Director
> *1996–97*

102. Auvaiyar (fl. third century?)

1 This is the womb that carried him,
like a stone cave,
lived in by a tiger and now abandoned.
> Untitled, George Hart, tr., *Women Poets of the World,* Joanna
> Bankier and Deirdre Lashgari, eds. *1983*

103. Kaccipettu Nannakaiyar (fl. third century?)

1 . . . a dream
that lied like truth.
> "What She Said," St. 1, *Interior Landscape: Love Poems from
> a Classical Tamil Anthology,* A. K. Ramanujan, ed. and tr.
> *1967*

2 I grow lean
in loneliness,
like a water lily
gnawed by a beetle.
> St. 3, Ibid.

104. Tzu Tzu Yeh (fl. ca. third–fourth centuries)

1 I let down my silken hair
Over my shoulders
And open my thighs
Over my lover.
"Tell me, is there any part of me
That is not lovable?"
> "Song," II, *The Orchid Boat, Women Poets of China,* Kenneth
> Rexroth and Ling Chung, eds. and trs. *1972*

105. Monica (340–395)

1 Son, what I should here, and why I am here, I know not; the hope of this life is now quite spent.
> Quoted in *Biography of Distinguished Women* by Sarah
> Josepha Hale* *1876*
*See 807.

2 Nothing is far from God; and I do not fear that he will not know where to find me at the resurrection.
> Ibid.

106. Iwa no Hime (?–347)

1 In the autumn field,
Over the rice ears,
The morning mist trails,
Vanishing somewhere. . . .
Can my love fade too?
> "Longing for the Emperor," *The Penguin Book of Japanese
> Verse,* Goeffrey Bownas and Anthony Thwaite, eds. and trs.
> *1964*

107. Hypatia (355–415)

1 Life is an unfoldment, and the further we travel the more truth we can comprehend. To understand the things that are at our door is the best preparation for understanding those that lie beyond.
> "Hypatia," Quoted in *Little Journeys to the Homes of Great
> Teachers* by Elbert Hubbard *1908*

2 Men will fight for a superstition quite as quickly as for a living truth—often more so, since a superstition is so intangible you cannot get at it to refute it, but truth is a point of view, and so is changeable.
> Ibid.

3 He who influences the thought of his times, influences all the times that follow. He has made his impress on eternity.
> Ibid.

4 It does not make much difference what a person studies—all knowledge is related, and the man who studies anything, if he keeps at it, will become learned.
> Ibid.

5 To rule by fettering the mind through fear of punishment in another world, is just as base as to use force.
> Ibid.

6 All formal dogmatic religions are fallacious and must never be accepted by self-respecting persons as final.

> Quoted in *4000 Years of Women in Science,* astr. ua.edu4000WS *1 August 1997*

7 Reserve your right to think, for even to think wrongly is better than not to think at all.

> Ibid.

8 To teach superstitions as truth is a most terrible thing.

> Ibid.

108. Egeria (fl. 380s–d. 384)

1 I saw many holy monks from those parts when they came to Jerusalem on pilgrimage to the holy places, and all they told me about Uz* made me eager to take the trouble to make a further journey to visit it—if one can really speak of trouble when one sees one's wishes fulfilled.

> From *Travels,* Quoted in *Egeria: Diary of a Pilgrimage,* George E. Gingras, ed. and tr. *1970*
> *The Land of Uz was probably near Damascus, although there is little evidence of its actual location.

109. Aelia Pulcheria (399–454)

1 The more princes abstain from touching the wealth of their people, the greater will be their resources in the wants of the state.

> Quoted in *Biography of Distinguished Women* by Sarah Josepha Hale* *1876*
> *See 807.

110. Brigid of Kildare (453–523)

1 I should like a great lake of ale
   For the King of kings

> Prayer for the Heavenly Feast* *n.d.,* Attr.
> *Her feast day was February 1, the first day of spring according to the pagan calendar; she was worshipped as a goddess. Her canonization was an effort by the church to convert her followers.

2 I would like to be a tenant to the Lord, so if I should suffer distress, he would confer on me a blessing. Amen.

> Ibid.

111. Basine (fl. 460s)

1 Had I known a more valiant hero than yourself, I should have fled over the seas to his arms.

> Remark to Childeric [Merovingian king], Quoted in *Biography of Distinguished Women* by Sarah Josepha Hale* *1876*
> *See 807.

112. Maximilla (fl. 460s)

1 I am pursued like a wolf out of the sheep fold; I am no wolf: I am word and spirit and power.

> Quoted in "Word, Spirit and Power: Women in Early Christian Communities" by Elisabeth Schüssler Fiorenza,* *Women of Spirit,* Rosemary Ruether** and Eleanor McLaughlin, eds. *1979*
> *See 3086. **See 3004.

113. Theodora (508?–d. 547/8)

1 There was an anchorite who was able to banish the demons; and he asked them, "What makes you go away? Is it fasting?"

They replied, "We do not eat or drink." "Is it vigils?" They replied, "We do not sleep." "Is it separation from the world?" "We live in the deserts." "What power sends you away then?" They said, "Nothing can overcome us, but only humility."

> "Theta: Theodora," *The Sayings of the Desert Fathers: The Alphabetical Collection,* Benedicta Ward, tr. *1975*

2 For a King, death is better than dethronement and exile.

> Remark (ca. 532), Quoted in *Women in World History Curriculum* (womeninhistory.com) *1996–97*

114. Saint Radegunda (518?–587)

1 If you do not understand what is read, it is because you do not ask solicitously for a mirror of the soul.

> Quoted in *Vita Radegundis* [Life of Radegunda] by Fortunatus *ca. 580–600*

115. Bertegund (fl. 530s)

1 Go home and govern our children. I will not return to you [her husband], for the married will not see the kingdom of heaven.

> Ch. 6, Quoted in *Histoire Française* by Gregory of Tours* *ca. 538*
> *French bishop and writer (538/39–594/95).

116. Al-Khansa (600–670)

1 He is dead, who was the buckler of our tribe.

> "For Her Brother," St. 3, E. Powys Mathers, tr., *The Penguin Book of Women Poets,* Carol Cosman, Joan Keefe, and Kathleen Weaver, eds. *1978*

2 . . . every tribe is a journey to ruin
   and every treaty is erased by time.

> "In Death's Field," Sts. 12, 13, Willis Barnstone, tr., *A Book of Women Poets,* Aliki and Willis Barnstone, eds. *1980*

117. Baudonivia (fl. sixth century)

1 I am but the least among the least, small is my understanding and timid my heart.

> Letter to her abbess, Dedimia, Quoted in *Women and Their Letters in the Early Middle Ages* by Eleanor Shipley Duckett *1965*

118. Saint Caesaria (fl. sixth century)

1 . . . you cannot fight lust if you do not flee from the presence of men.

> Ch. 6, Quoted in *Women in Frankish Society, Marriage and the Cloister, 500–900* by Suzanne Fonay Wemple *1981*

2 . . . read and hear assiduously the divine lessons . . . to gather from them precious daisies for your ears and make from them rings and bracelets.

> Ch. 8, Ibid.

119. Herchenfreda (fl. 600s)

1 What shall I, an unfortunate mother, do now that I have lost your brothers? If you were also to die, I would have no children left! But you, my most pious son, my sweetest, you must constantly guard yourself against murder, for now that I have lost your brothers, I cannot lose you too!

> Ch. 3, Quoted in *Women in Frankish Society, Marriage and the Cloister, 500–900* by Suzanne Fonay Wemple *1981*

120. Hind bint Utba (fl. 600s–d. 635)
1 Rrrrrrrraaarghr
We have paid you back
Battle feeds battle
and war that follows war is always violent.
       "Fury Against the Moslems at Uhud," St. 1, Bridget Connelly
and Deirdre Lashgari, trs., *Women Poets of the World,* Joanna
Bankier and Deirdre Lashgari, eds. *1983*

121. Empress Wu Tse-t'ien (624–705)
1 My thoughts are many and tumultuous,
As troubled as the tossing branches,
All for thinking of you.
       "A Love Song of the Empress Wu," *The Orchid Boat, Women
Poets of China,* Kenneth Rexroth and Ling Chung, eds. and
trs. *1972*

122. Laila Akhyaliyya (fl. 660s–ca. 704)
1 He was honey—no, I see a beehive in his likeness
       "He reached the heights of things with ease," *Diwan Antara
ibn Shaddad ibn Qurad al Abs,* Arthur Wormhoudt, tr. *1974*

2 Our lungs are strong
when we wail with the first knives of dawn.
       "Laila Boasting," Willis Barnstone, tr., *A Book of Women
Poets,* Aliki and Willis Barnstone, eds. *1980*

3 No life is favored
nor corpse reborn
Every youth passes through destruction to Allah.
       "Lamenting Tauba," Ibid., St. 3

123. Nukada (fl. 660s–699)
1 When, loosened from the winter's bond, spring appears,
The birds that were silent
Come out and sing,
The flowers that were prisoned
Come out and bloom;
But the hills are so rank with trees
We cannot see the flowers,
And the flowers are so tangled with weeds
We cannot take them in our hands.
       Untitled, from *Manyō-Shū,* [Collection of Ten Thousand
Leaves], Harold P. Wright, tr. *ca. mid-eighth century*

124. Oku (661–701)
1 How will you cross
the autumn mountain
alone?
It was hard
for us,
even when we went
together.
       Untitled, Willis Barnstone, tr., *A Book of Women Poets,* Aliki
and Willis Barnstone, eds. *1980*

125. Maysun (fl. 670s)
1 I love the Bedouin's tent, caressed by the murmuring breeze,
and standing amid boundless horizons
More than the gilded halls of marble in all their splendor
I prefer a desert cavalier, generous and poor,
to a fat lout in purple living behind closed doors.
       Untitled poem, *Islamic Literature: an Introductory History,*
Najib Ullah, tr. *1963*

126. Safiya bint Musafir (fl. 670s)
1 Emptied with weeping
my eyes are
two buckets of the waterman
as he walks among the orchard trees
       "At the Badr Trench,"* St.1, Bridget Connelly and Deirdre
Lashgari, trs., *Women Poets of the World,* Joanna Bankier and
Deirdre Lashgari, eds. *1983*
*Burial place for 14 Muslim martyrs killed at Battle of Badr at
Medina (now in Saudi Arabia) in 674.

127. Yamatohime (fl. 670s)
1 Others may forget you, but not I.
I am haunted by your beautiful ghost.
       Untitled, *One Hundred Poems from the Japanese,* Kenneth
Rexroth and Ikuko Atsumi, eds. and trs. *1964*

128. Otomo no Sakano-e no Iratsume (700?–750)
1 Ah! I have handed over
    The jewel to its owner;
So from henceforth, my dear pillow,
    Let us two sleep together.
       "On the Marriage of a daughter," in toto, from *Manyō-Shū,*
Vol. IV, *An Anthology of Japanese Poems,* Miyamori Asatarō,
ed. and tr. *1938*

2 Do not smile to yourself
Like a green mountain
With a cloud drifting across it.
People will know we are in love.
       Untitled, *One Hundred Poems from the Japanese,* Kenneth
Rexroth and Ikuko Atsumi, eds. and trs. *1964*

3 My heart, thinking
"How beautiful he is"
Is like a swift river
Which though one dams it and dams it
Will still break through.
       Untitled, from *Manyō-Shū,* Quoted in *Japanese Poetry: The
Uta,* Arthur Waley, ed. and tr. *1976*

129. Liadan (fl. seventh century)
1 Not vain,
it seemed, our choice,
to seek Paradise through pain.
       "Liadan Laments Cuirithir,"* St. 3, *The Penguin Book of
Women Poets,* Carol Cosman, Joan Keefe, and Kathleen
Weaver, eds. *1978*
*Her lover who, after she became a nun, unknown to Liadan be-
came a monk.

2 Gain without gladness
Is in the bargain I have struck
       Untitled, St. 1, Frank O'Connor, tr., *The Penguin Book of Irish
Verse,* Brendan Kennelly, ed. *1981*

130. Mahodahi (fl. ca. seventh–11th centuries)
1 The sun's charioteer is lost. . . .
       Untitled, Willis Barnstone, tr., *A Book of Women Poets,* Aliki
and Willis Barnstone, eds. *1980*

131. Sila (fl. ca. seventh–11th centuries)
1 We knew long evenings wet with the moon.
       Untitled, Willis Barnstone, tr., *A Book of Women Poets,* Aliki
and Willis Barnstone, eds. *1980*

132. Silabhlattarika (fl. ca. seventh–11th centuries)
1 I too am still the same;
and yet with all my heart I yearn for the reedbeds by the
   stream
which knew our happy, graceful
unending bouts of love.
> "The Wanton" (*Treasury of Well-Turned Verse*, comp. by
> Vidya Kara, ca. 1100), Quoted in *Sanskrit Poetry*, Daniel H.
> H. Ingalls, ed. and tr. *1955*

133. Vidya (fl. ca. seventh–11th centuries)
1 I praise the disc of the rising sun
red as a parrot's beak, sharp-rayed,
friend of the lotus grove,
an earring for the goddess of the east.
> "The Sun" (*Treasury of Well-Turned Verse*, comp. by Vidya
> Kara, ca. 1100), Quoted in *Sanskrit Poetry*, Daniel H. H.
> Ingalls, ed. and tr. *1955*

2 Friends,
you are lucky you can talk
about what you did as lovers:
the tricks, the laughter, the words,
the ecstasy.
After my darling put his hand on the knot
of my dress,
I swear I remember nothing.
> Untitled, in toto, Willis Barnstone, tr., *A Book of Women
> Poets*, Aliki and Willis Barnstone, eds. *1980*

134. Young Woman of Harima (fl. 710s–719)
1 If you go away,
why should I adorn myself?
> Untitled, from the *Manyō-Shū*, Quoted in *Land of the Reed
> Plains*, Kenneth Yashuda, ed. and tr. *1972*

135. Chigami Sanu (fl. 710s–d. 784)
1 These are the garments
I, a helpless woman, sewed
with troubled longings
as a token of the day
when we two shall meet again.
> Untitled, from the *Manyō-Shū*, (ca. 800), Quoted in *Land of
> the Reed Plains*, Kenneth Yashuda, ed. and tr. *1972*

136. Rabi'a al-Adawiya (712/7–801)
1 My Lord
if I worship Thee from fear of Hell
burn me in Hell

and if I worship Thee from hope of Paradise
exclude me thence

but if I worship Thee
for Thine own sake alone
do not withhold from me Thine Eternal Beauty
> "A Prayer," Sts. 1–3, Quoted in *Rabi'a the Mystic and Her
> Fellow Saints in Islam* by Margaret Smith *1928*

2 O my Lord, the stars are shining and the eyes of men are
closed, and kings have shut their doors
and every lover is alone with his beloved,
and here am I alone with Thee.
> Prayer, Quoted in *Muslim Saints and Mystics* by Farid al-Din
> Attar; A. J. Arberry, tr. *1966*

3 My peace, O my brothers, is in solitude
> Untitled, Ibid.

137. Egburg (fl. 716–726)
1 No sailor tossed by the tempest hopes so keenly for the harbour, not thus does the thirsty field wait for the rain, not so
eagerly does the anxious mother look from the curving shore
for the coming of her son, as, My Father, I long for the sight of
you.
> Letter to St. Boniface (ca. 716–726), Quoted in *Women and
> Their Letters in the Early Middle Ages* by Eleanor Shipley
> Duckett *1965*

138. Khosrovidoukht Koghtnatsi (?–737)
1 More astonishing to me
than the lyrics made for you,
more amazing than the music composed
for your death,
is the sound of the sobbing mourning.
> "More Astonishing," St. 1 (737), *Anthology of Armenian
> Poetry*, Diana Der Hovanessian and Marzbed Margossian, eds.
> and trs. *1978*

139. Rabi'a bint Isma'il of Syria (?–755)
1 But if You consume me in fire, goal of my longing,
where then lies my hope of You, and where my fear?
> "Sufi Quatrain," St. 2, Deirdre Lashgari, tr., *Women Poets
> of the World*, Joanna Bankier and
> Deirdre Lashgari, eds. *1983*

140. Hsüeh T'ao (768–831)
1 Blossoms crowd the branches: too beautiful to endure.
Thinking of you, I break into bloom again.
> "Spring-Gazing Song," Carolyn Kizer, tr., *A Book of Women
> Poets*, Aliki and Willis Barnstone, eds. *1980*

2 He is gone, who knew the music of my soul.
> "Weaving Love Knots," St. 2, Ibid.

141. Xue Tao (768–831)
1 Then by chance she
took a nip
and bit a well-loved guest.

Now she no longer sleeps
upon his red silk rugs.
> "Dog parted from her master," Sts. 3–4, *Brocade River Poems:
> Selected works of the Tang Dynasty courtesan Xue Tao* Jeanne
> Larsen, tr. and intro. *1987*

2 Chirr after chirr,
as if in unison

But each perches
on its one branch
alone.
> "But each perches on its one branch, alone." [On cicidas], Sts.
> 3–4, Ibid.

3 He's done with reading holy texts.
He want to play a bit.
> "listening to a monk play the reed pipes," St. 3, Ibid.

142. Huneberc of Heidenheim (fl. 778–786)

1 I am but womanly, stained by the frailty and weakness of my sex, and supported neither by pretense to wisdom nor by exalted aspiration to great power, but freely prompted by my own willful impetuosity, like some ignorant child who at her heart's discretion plucks a few small things from trees rich in foliage and fruit. Nonetheless I would be pleased to pluck, collect, and display, with however small an art, a few tokens from the lowest branches for you to keep in your memory.

> Prologue (Thomas Head, tr.), *Hodoeporicon of St. Willibald*
> *pre-786*

2 These men come from the West where the sun sets; we know nothing of their country except that byond it lies nothing but water.

> Ibid., Text

143. Lady Ishikawa (fl. 780s–d. 800)

1 You were soaked, my lord,
  with the drops of mountain dew:
  how I wish that I were they!

> Untitled, from the *Manyō-Shū*, (ca. 800), Quoted in *Land of the Reed Plains*, Kenneth Yashuda, ed. and tr. 1972

144. Chao Luan-luan (fl. eighth century)

1 Small cherries sip delicately
  At the edge of the wine cup.

> "Red Sandalwood Mouth," *The Orchid Boat, Women Poets of China*, Kenneth Rexroth and Ling Chung, eds. and trs. 1972

2 Slender, delicate, soft jade,
  Fresh peeled spring onions—
  They are always hidden in emerald
  Sleeves of perfumed silk.

> "Slender Fingers," Ibid.

145. Kasa no Iratsume (fl. eighth century)

1 To love someone
  Who does not return that love
  Is like offering prayers
  Back behind a starving god
  Within a Buddhist temple.

> Untitled, from *Manyō-Shū*, (ca. 800; *Collection of Ten Thousand Leaves*), Harold P. Wright, tr. ca. mid-eighth century

146. Lady Kii (fl. eighth century)

1 . . . the idle ways
  of the beach.

> Untitled, *The Burning Heart: Women Poets of Japan*, Kenneth Rexroth and Ikuko Atsumi, eds. and trs. 1977

147. Li Yeh (fl. eighth century)

1 It is good to get drunk once in a while.
  What else is there to do?

> "A Greeting to Lu Hung-Chien," *The Orchid Boat, Women Poets of China*, Kenneth Rexroth and Ling Chung, eds. and trs. 1972

148. Sahakdoukht Siunetsi (fl. eighth century)

1 And spiritual orchard, bright flower,
  you conceived from God, as from rains
  flowing through the soul, the word,

and with the shield of your body
made it apparent to men.

> "Acrostic," St. 2, *Anthology of Armenian Poetry*, Diana Der Hovanessian and Marzbed Margossian, eds. and trs. 1978

149. Kassiane (804?–867?)

1 You meet your friend, your face
  brightens—you have struck gold.

> Untitled, Patrick Diehl, tr., *The Penguin Book of Women Poets*, Carol Cosman, Joan Keefe, and Kathleen Weaver, eds. 1978

2 Poverty? wealth? seek neither—
  One causes swollen heads,
  The other, swollen bellies.

> Ibid.

3 Better unborn than fool.
  If born, spare earth your tread.
  Don't wait. Go straight to hell.

> Ibid.

4 No remedy for fools,
  No helping them, but death.
  In office? puffed and strutting.
  Acclaimed? beyond endurance.
  Columns of stone will kneel
  Before you change a fool.

> Ibid.

5 A nun—a door unopened.

> Ibid.

6 Wealth covers sin—the poor
  are naked as a pin.

> "Epigrams" (ninth century), *Women Poets of the World*, Joanna Bankier and Deirdre Lashgari, eds. 1983

150. Ono no Komachi (834–880)

1 So lonely am I
  My body is a floating weed
  Severed at the roots.
  Were there water to entice me,
  I would follow it, I think.

> Untitled, in toto, from *Kokin Shū*, (905 C.E.), *Anthology of Japanese Literature*, Donald Keene, ed. and tr. 1955

2 A thing which fades
  With no outward sign—
  Is the flower
  Of the heart of man
  In this world!

> Untitled, *Japanese Poetry: The Uta*, Arthur Waley, ed. and tr. 1976

151. Empress Nijo (842–910)

1 Spring has already come round
  While on the ground lies snow;
  The frozen tears of uguisu*
  Soon in the soft warm breeze will thaw.

> "The Tears of Uguisu," in toto, from *Kokin Shū*, Vol. I, *An Anthology of Japanese Poems*, Miyamori Asatarō, ed. and tr. 1938

*A bird similar to a nightingale.

152. Yü Hsüan-chi (843?–868)

1 I lift my head and read their names
In powerless envy.
> "On a Visit to Ch'ung Chên Taoist Temple I See In the
> South Hall the List of Successful Candidates in the Imperial
> Examinations," *The Orchid Boat, Women Poets of China,*
> Kenneth Rexroth and Ling Chung, eds. and trs. *1972*

2 To find a rare jewel is easy.
To get a good man is harder.
> "For a Neighbor Girl," *A Book of Women Poets,* Aliki and
> Willis Barnstone, eds. *1980*

3 Evening, page by page, I hum beneath my quilt.
> "Rhyming a Friend's Poem," St. 3, Ibid.

4 Thinking hard, hunting rhymes, humming by my lamp,
Awake all night, I fear the cold quilt.
> "Sent to Wen T'ing on a Winter Night," St. 1, Ibid.

153. Han Ts'ui-p'in (fl. ca. 850)

1 Red leaf, I order you—
Go find someone
In the world of men.
> "A Poem Written on a Floating Red Leaf," *The Orchid Boat,*
> *Women Poets of China,* Kenneth Rexroth and Ling Chung,
> eds. and trs. *1972*

154. Lady Ukon (fl. ca. 860–d. 899)

1 It does not matter
That I am forgotten,
But I pity
His foresworn life.
> "I am forgotten now," *Poems from the Japanese,* Kenneth
> Rexroth, tr. *1964*

2 You gave me your solemn word, and I was
sure you would be constant.
I am moved to call down on you the penalty
of death for abandoning me!
> Untitled, from *Waga* (Mine), Quoted in *Women Poets of*
> *Japan,* Kenneth Rexroth and Ikuko Atsumi, ed. *1977*

155. Lady Ise (875?–938?)

1 Not even in dreams
Can I meet him anymore. . . .
> Untitled, *Japanese Literature: An Introduction for Western*
> *Readers,* Donald Keene, ed. and tr. *1955*

2 . . . my reputation
reaches to the skies
like a dust storm.
> Untitled, *The Burning Heart: Women Poets of Japan,* Kenneth
> Rexroth and Ikuko Atsumi, eds. and trs. *1977*

3 And like the maple leaves
of autumn, when members
of the household
have scattered
in their own ways,
uncertainty
fills the air.
> "Elegy: Ise Lamenting the Death of Empress Onshi," Etsuko
> Terasaki with Irma Brandeis, tr., *A Book of Women Poets,*
> Aliki and Willis Barnstone, eds. *1980*

156. Qernertoq (fl. ninth–14th centuries)

1 It seems as if
I'll never get beyond
the foot-prints that I made
> "The Widow's Song," St. 2, *Eskimo Poets of Canada and*
> *Greenland,* Tom Lowenstein, ed. and tr. *1973*

157. Vallana (fl. ninth–10th centuries)

1 who could save me from plunging into a sea
of shame
but the love god
who teaches us how to faint?
> Untitled, Willis Barnstone, tr., *A Book of Women Poets,* Aliki
> and Willis Barnstone, eds. *1980*

158. Hroswitha of Gandersheim (935?–1000)

1 I know that it is as wrong to deny a divine gift as to pretend
falsely that we have received it.
> "Epistle of the Same to Certain Learned Patrons of this Book,"
> *The Plays of Roswitha,* Christopher St. John, tr. *1923*

2 IRENA. Better far that my body should suffer outrage than my
soul.
> Sc. 12, *Dulcitius,* Ibid.

3 EPHREM. Out of the mouths of babes and sucklings!
> Sc. 1, *Abraham,* Ibid.

4 ABRAHAM. It is human to sin, but it is devilish to remain in
sin.
> Sc. 7, Ibid.

5 DISCIPLES. It is better to know nothing than to be bewildered.
> Sc. 1, *Paphnutius,* Ibid.

6 THAIS. Remorse has killed everything.
> Sc. 3, Ibid.

7 THAIS. Rumour never delays.
> Sc. 6, Ibid.

8 ANTONY. What pleasures God sends us, when we resign ourselves to have none!
> Sc. 10, Ibid.

9 PAPHNUTIUS. Grace is the free gift of God and does not depend on our merits. If it did, it could not be called grace.
> Sc. 12, Ibid.

159. Daughter of Ki no Tsurayuki (fl. ca. 940–d. 967)

1 But if the uguisu* inquire
For their home, oh! what shall I say?
> "The Uguisu's Home,"** from *Go-Shūi-Shū,* Vol. IX, *An*
> *Anthology of Japanese Poems,* Miyamori Asatarō, ed. and tr.
> *1938*

*A bird similar to a nightingale. **Poem in response to Emperor
Murakami's order to transplant a plum tree from the poet's garden
to his own.

160. Mother of Michitsuna (fl. ca. 950–d. 974)

1 Every day he promises that it shall be tomorrow. And when
tomorrow comes, it is to be the day after. Of course I do not

believe him; yet each time that this happens I begin imagining that he has repented,—that all has come right again. So day after day goes by.

Diary Entry (970), *Kagero Nikki* [Gossamer Diary] *954–74*

2 Have you any idea
How long a night can last, spent
Lying alone and sobbing?

Untitled, *One Hundred Poems from the Japanese*, Kenneth Rexroth and Ikuko Atsumi, eds. and trs. *1964*

161. 'Aisha bint Ahmad al-Qurtubiyya (fl. ca. 960–d. 999)

1 I am a lioness
and will never allow my body
to be anyone's resting place.

Untitled, Elene Margot Kolb, tr., *Women Poets of the World*, Joanna Bankier and Deirdre Lashgari, eds. *1983*

162. Nieh Shen-ch'iung (fl. ca. 960–1279)

1 I try to dream good dreams
But it is hard to do

"Farewell To Li," *The Orchid Boat, Women Poets of China*, Kenneth Rexroth and Ling Chung, eds. and trs. *1972*

163. Sei Shonagon (966?–1017)

1 One writes a letter, taking particular trouble to get it up as prettily as possible; then waits for the answer, making sure every moment that it cannot be much longer before something comes. At last, frightfully late, is brought in—one's own note, still folded or tied exactly as one sent it, but so fingermarked and smudged that even the address is barely legible. "The family is not in residence," the messenger says, giving one back the note.

Makura no Soshi [The Pillow-Book of Sei Shonagon], (ca. 991–1100), Arthur Waley, tr. *1928*

2 Among the five thousand arrogants, you too will surely find a place.

Ibid.

3 There is nothing in the whole world so painful as feeling that one is not liked. It always seems to me that people who hate me must be suffering from some strange form of lunacy.

Ibid.

4 Writing is an ordinary enough thing; yet how precious it is! When someone is in a far corner of the world and one is terribly anxious about him, suddenly there comes a letter, and one feels as though the person were actually in the room. It is really very amazing.

Ibid.

164. Lady Nakatsukasa (fl. 970s)

1 Before they bloomed I longed for them;
After they bloomed I mourned that they must fade;
The mountain cherry-flowers
Sorrow alone for my poor heart have made.

"Pining for a Dead Child," *in toto*, from *Go-Shūi-Shū*, Vol. I, *An Anthology of Japanese Poems*, Miyamori Asatarō, ed. and tr. *1938*

165. Izumi Shikibu (974?–1030?)

1 I am a drop of dew
Hanging from a leaf

Yet I am not unrestful
For on this branch I seem to have existed
From before the birth of the world.

III, *The Diary of Izumi Shikibu*, Annie Shepley Omori and Kochi Doi, trs. *1002–03*

2 Sleeves wet with tears are my bed-fellows.

Ibid.

3 Ah, when I count the years still left,
I find them quickly told;
In all the world is nought so sad
As growing old.

"At the Close of the Year," in toto, from Shin Kokin Shū, Vol. VI, *An Anthology of Japanese Poems*, Miyamori Asatarō, ed. and tr. *1938*

4 When you broke from me
I thought I let the thread
of my life break

Untitled, Willis Barnstone, tr., *A Book of Women Poets*, Aliki and Willis Barnstone, eds. *1980*

5 I wore out the darkness
until lazy dawn.

Ibid.

166. Murasaki Shikibu (974–1031?)

1 . . . so quick was I at picking up the language [Chinese] that I was soon able to prompt my brother whenever he got stuck. At this my father used to sigh and say to me: "If only you were a boy how proud and happy I should be." But it was not long before I repented of having thus distinguished myself; for person after person assured me that even boys generally become very unpopular if it is discovered that they are fond of their books. For a girl, of course, it would be even worse. . . .

Murasaki Shikibu Nikki [The Diary of Murasaki Shikibu], Hakubunkuwan text *ca. 994–1010*

2 There [at Princess Senshi's Court] I should be allowed to live buried in my own thoughts like a tree-stump in the earth . . .

Ibid.

3 Who has told you that the fruit belies the flower? For the fruit you have not tasted, and the flower you know but by report.*

Ibid.

*Addressing Michinaga, the prime minister, and implying that he has neither read her book, *The Tale of Genji*, nor won her love.

4 The truth is I now find that I have not the slightest pleasure in the society of any but a few indispensable friends. They must be people who really interest me, with whom I can talk seriously on serious subjects, and with whom I am brought into contact without effort on my side in the natural course of everyday existence.

Ibid.

5 "We are told," answered Genji, "that everything which happens to us in this life is the result of our conduct in some previous existence. If this is to be taken literally I suppose I must now accept the fact that in a previous incarnation I must have misbehaved myself in some way."

"The Sacred Tree," Ch. 3, *Genji Monogatari* [The Tale of Genji], (1001–15), Vol. II, Arthur Waley, tr. *1925–33*

6 "A night of endless dreams, inconsequent and wild, is this my life; none more worth telling than the rest."

Ch. 4, Ibid.

7 "You had best be quick, if you are ever going to forgive me at all; life does not last forever."

Ch. 5, Ibid.

8 Indeed, she had seen enough of the world to know that in few people is discretion stronger than the desire to tell a good story. . . .

Vol. III, "A Wreath of Cloud," Ch. 2, Ibid.

9 "Beauty without colour seems somehow to belong to another world."

Ibid.

10 "I have noticed that children of good families, assured of such titles and emoluments as they desire, and used to receive the homage of the world however little they do deserve it, see no advantage in fatiguing themselves by arduous and exacting studies."

Ch. 3, Ibid.

11 "You cannot simply disappear while people are talking to you."

Ch. 7, Ibid.

12 "But I have a theory of my own about what this art of the novel is, and how it came into being. . . . it happens because the storyteller's own experience of men and things, whether for good or ill . . . has moved him to an emotion so passionate that he can no longer keep it shut up in his heart."

Ibid.

13 "Some people have taken exception on moral grounds to an art [storytelling] in which the perfect and the imperfect are set side by side. But even in the discourses which Buddha in his bounty allowed to be recorded, certain passages contain what the learned call Up-aya or 'Adapted Truth'. . . ."

Ibid.

14 "I have never thought there was much to be said in favour of dragging on long after all one's friends were dead."

Vol. IV, "Blue Trousers," Ch. 1, Ibid.

15 "It would be fatal, for example, if this situation were suddenly sprung upon the world in all its details. But allowed to leak out piecemeal, it will do very little harm. What matters is that people should have plenty of time to get used to one part of a scandal before the next is allowed to leak out."

Ibid.

16 "Now faithlessness, that once was held a crime, rules all the world, and he a half-wit is accounted whose heart is steadfast for an hour."

Ch. 4, Ibid.

17 But unfortunately, Genji reflected, people who do not get into scrapes are a great deal less interesting than those who do.

Ch. 6, Ibid.

167. Andal (fl. 10th century)

1 Sing,
but not too loudly, so he will come.

Untitled, Willis Barnstone, tr., *A Book of Women Poets,* Aliki and Willis Barnstone, eds. *1980*

2 we will do good things,
use good words,
give away our possessions and live for him.

Ibid.

168. Akazome Emon (fl. 1000–1010)

1 I wish I could live
Long enough to see him soar
High above the clouds
When his cloak of crane feathers
Has grown out with the years.

"Composed after the birth of Masafusa,* on asking someone to sew baby clothes for him," Quoted in *Seeds in the Heart: Japanese Literature From Earliest Times to the Late Sixteenth Century* by Donald Keene *1993*

*Oe no Masafusa (1041–1111), her great-grandson, who became a brilliant and noted scholar.

169. Gormley (fl. 10th century)

1 though I have loved twenty men
this is not what women seek.

"Gormley's Laments," St. 1, Joan Keefe, tr., *The Penguin Book of Women Poets,* Carol Cosman, Joan Keefe, and Kathleen Weaver, eds. *1978*

170. Maryam bint Abi Ya'qub al-Ansari (fl. 1000s– d. 1035)

1 What can you expect
from a woman with seventy-seven years,
frail as the web of a spider?

Untitled, Elene Margot Kolb, tr., *Women Poets of the World,* Joanna Bankier and Deirdre Lashgari, eds. *1983*

171. Rabi'a of Balkh (fl. 10th century)

1 My wish for you
that God should make your love
fall on a heart as cold and stony as
your own

Untitled, Deirdre Lashgari, tr., *Women Poets of the World,* Joanna Bankier and Deirdre Lashgari, eds. *1983*

2 Love is as a sea with the shores you cannot see.
And a wise person can never swim in such a sea.

Untitled, *n.d.*

172. Wallada al-Mustakfi (fl. 1000s–d. 1035)

1 Expect my visit when the darkness comes.
The night I think is best for hiding all.
If the full moon felt like me she wouldn't rise;
if the star, it wouldn't move;
if the night, it wouldn't fall.

Untitled, Quoted in *The Troubadours and Their World of the Twelfth and Thirteenth Centuries* by Jack Lindsay *1976*

2 Time passes, yet I see no end to your long absence,
Nor does patience free me from the bondage of yearning!

"A Correspondence to Ibn Zaidun:* #4," A. R. Nykul, tr., *The Penguin Book of Women Poets,* Carol Cosman, Joan Keefe, and Kathleen Weaver, eds. *1978*

*Her lover, an Andalusian writer of classical Arabic poetry.

173. Lady Sarashina (1008–1060?)

1 They will come back next spring—those
cherry blooms
that scatter from the tree.
But how I yearn for her who left
And never will return!
*As I Crossed a Bridge of Dreams: Recollections of Woman in
Eleventh Century Japan*, Ivan Morris, tr. *1971*

2 There is no difference in their sounds—
This wind that blows across the Barrier now
And the one I heard so many years ago.
Ibid.

174. Lady Suo (fl. 1030–1065)

1 That spring night I spent
Pillowed on your arm
Never really happened
Except in a dream.
Unfortunately I am
Talked about anyway.
Untitled, *One Hundred Poems from the Japanese*, Kenneth
Rexroth and Ikuko Atsumi, eds. and trs. *1964*

175. Li Qingzhao (1081/84–1140/51)

1 Who can
Take a letter beyond the clouds?
Untitled, *Love and the Turning Year: One Hundred More
Poems from the Chinese*, Kenneth Rexroth, ed. and tr. *1970*

2 Search. Search. Seek. Seek.
Cold. Cold. Clear. Clear.
Sorrow. Sorrow. Pain. Pain.
Hot flashes. Sudden chills.
Stabbing pains. Slow agonies.
"A Weary Song to a Slow Sad Tune," Ibid.

3 But I am startled by the breaking cup of Spring.
to the tune "A Hilly Garden," *The Orchid Boat, Women Poets
of China*, Kenneth Rexroth and Ling Chung, eds. and trs.
1972

4 Nothing is left of Spring but fragrant dust.
"Spring Ends," Ibid.

5 Dense
sleep
doesn't
fade
a wine
hangover.
Untitled, St. 2, Willis Barnstone and Sun Chu-chin, trs., *A
Book of Women Poets*, Aliki and Willis Barnstone, eds. *1980*

176. Anna Comnena (1083–1153)

1 Indeed, so great a multitude of Gauls and Normans were cut
down by the Ishmaelite sword that when the dead bodies of the
killed, which were lying all about in the place, were brought
together, they made a very great mound, or hill, or lookout
place, lofty as a mountain, and occupying a space very conspicuous for its width and depth. So high did that mound of bones
tower, that some barbarians of the same race as the killed later
used the bones of the slain instead of stones in constructing a
wall, thus making that fortress a sort of sepulcher for them. It

stands to this day, an enclosure of walls built with mixed rocks
and bones.
"On the Crusades," *Alexiad*, Vol. 10 *1138–48*, M. Thiebaux,
tr. and ed. *1987*

2 Her expression, which revealed her true character, demanded
the worship of the angels but struck terror among demons . . .
from *Alexiad, The Writings of Medieval Women*, Vol. 14

3 For my grandmother* really had the gift of conducting the affairs of state. She knew so well how to organize and administer
that she was capable of governing not only the Roman Empire
but also every other kingdom under the sun. . . .
Ibid.

*Anna Dalassena, Byzantine empress.

177. Trotula of Salerno (?–1097)

1 Moreover, women, from the condition of their fragility, out of
shame and embarrassment do not dare reveal their anguish
over their diseases (which happen in such a private place) to a
physician. Therefore, their misfortune, which ought to be pitied, and especially the influence of a certain woman stirring my
heart, have impelled me to give a clear explanation regarding
their diseases in caring for their health.
Passionibus Mulierum Curandorum (1547), *The Diseases of
Women*, Elizabeth Mason-Hohl, tr. *1940*

2 When God the creator of the universe in the first establishment
of the world differentiated the individual natures of things
each according to its kind, He endowed human nature above
all other things with a singular dignity, giving to it above the
condition of all other animals freedom of reason and intellect.
Ibid.

178. Héloise (1098?–1164)

1 The blessings promised to us by Christ were not promised to
those alone who were priests; woe unto the world, indeed, if all
that deserved the name of virtue were shut up in a cloister.
Letter to Peter Abelard,* Quoted in *Women of Medieval
France* by Pierce Butler *1907*
*French theologian and philosopher (1079–1142)

2 Riches and power are but gifts of blind fate, whereas goodness
is the result of one's own merits.
Letter to Peter Abelard, #2, *The Letters of Abelard and
Héloise*, C. K. Scott Moncrieff, tr. *1925*

3 Prosperity seldom chooses the side of the virtuous . . .
First Letter to Abelard (ca. 1122), *The World's Great Letters*,
M. Lincoln Schuster, ed. *1940*

4 . . . I was more pleased with possessing your heart than with any
other happiness . . . the man was the thing I least valued in you.
Ibid.

5 We fluctuate long between love and hatred before we can arrive at tranquility.
Ibid.

6 To my lord/no/my father
my husband/no/my brother
his servant/no/his daughter
his wife/no/his sister
To my Abelard his Héloise.
Untitled, Quoted in *Women in the Middle Ages* by Sibylle
Harksen *1975*

7 When my self is not with you, it is nowhere.
Letter to Peter Abelard, Ibid.

179. Hildegarde von Bingen (1098–1179)

1 Greetings, greenest branch
Song 71, "About the Blessed Virgin Mary," St. 1, Symphony of
the Harmony of Heavenly Relations 1151–1158

2 I am that supreme and fiery force that sends forth all living sparks. Death hath no part in me, yet I bestow death, wherefore I am girt about with wisdom as with wings. I am that living and fiery essence of the divine substance that glows in the beauty of the fields, and in the shining water, and in the burning sun and the moon and the stars, and in the force of the invisible wind, the breath of all living things, I breathe in the green grass and in the flowers, and in the living waters. . . . All these live and do not die because I am in them . . . I am the source of the thundered word by which all creatures were made, I permeate all things that they may not die. I am Life.
Book of Divine Works ca. 1167

3 When a woman is making love with a man, a sense of heat in her brain, which brings with it sensual delight, communicates the taste of that delight during the act and summons forth the emission of the man's seed. And when the seed has fallen into its place, that vehement heat descending from her brain draws the seed to itself and holds it, and soon the woman's sexual organs contract, and all the parts that are ready to open up during the time of menstruation now close, in the same way as a strong man can hold something enclosed in his fist.
Ibid.

4 . . . man . . . rushes to woman like the stag to the spring, and the woman to him like the threshing floor of the barn, shaken and heated by the many blows of the flail when the grain is threshed.
Quoted in Women in the Middle Ages by Sibylle Harksen
1975

5 The prophetic spirit orders that God be praised with cymbals of jubilation and with the rest of the musical instruments which the wise and studious have created, since all of the arts (whose purpose is to fill uses and needs of man) are brought to life by that breath of life which God breathed into the body of man: and therefore it is just that God be praised in all things.
Letter to Prelates of Mainz, Quoted in Women in Music by
Carol Neuls-Bates 1982

6 The earth which sustains humanity must not be injured. It must not be destroyed!
Remark, Quoted in Hildegarde of Bingen: a visionary life by S.
Flanagan 1989

180. Matilda (1100?–1135)

1 Just as spiritual drink and food are necessary to the soul, so are physical drink and food necessary for the soul.
Letter to Saint Anselm ca. 1100

181. Sugawara no Takasue no musume (fl. 11th century)

1 Even into the mind always clouded with grief,
There is cast the reflection of the bright moon.
Quoted in "The Sarashina Diary," Diaries of Court Ladies of
Old Japan, Annie Shepley Omori and Kochi Doi, trs. 1920

182. Tao-hüsan Sun (fl. 1100–d. 1135)

1 The wind blows down from the emerald sky
A song like a string of pearls.
But the singer is invisible
Hidden behind her embroidered curtains.
"A Dream Song," The Orchid Boat, Women Poets of China,
Kenneth Rexroth and Ling Chung, eds. and trs. 1972

183. Eleanor of Aquitaine (1122?–1204)

1 Trees are not known by their leaves, nor even by their blossoms, but by their fruits. In this wise we have known your cardinals.
Letter to Pope Celestine III (1192), Quoted in Eleanor of
Aquitaine by Amy Kelly 1950

2 I have lost the staff of my age, the light of my eyes.
Comment on the death of her son, Richard I* (1199), Ibid.
*Known as "Coeur de Lion" or "the Lion-Hearted" (1157–1199)

184. Sun Bu-er (1124–?)

1 When you've cooked the marrow of the sun and moon,
The pearl is so bright you don't worry about poverty.
"Projecting the Spirit," Thomas Cleary, tr., Wise Women:
Over 2000 Years of Spiritual Writing by Women, Susan Cahill,
ed. 1996

185. Frau Ava (?–1127)

1 I am yours,
you are mine.
Of this we are certain.
You are lodged
in my heart,
the small key
is lost.
You must stay there
forever.
Attributed, attached to a letter to a cleric (ca. 1160), A Book
of Women Poets, Aliki and Willis Barnstone, eds. 1980

186. Lady Horikawa (fl. 1130–d. 1165)

1 Will he always love me?
I cannot read his heart.
This morning my thoughts
Are as disordered
As my black hair.
Untitled, One Hundred Poems from the Japanese, Kenneth
Rexroth and Ikuko Atsumi, eds. and trs. 1964

187. Tibors (1130?–1182)

1 nor did it ever come to pass, if you went off angry,
that I felt joy until you had come back
Untitled, from Die Provenzalischen Dicterinnen by Oscar
Schultz-Gora (1888), Quoted in The Women Troubadours by
Meg Bodin, tr. 1976

188. Almucs de Castelnau (1140–?)

1 Still, if you can get him to repent his perfidy you'll have no trouble in converting me.
Untitled, St. 2, with Iseut de Capio, Quoted in The Women
Troubadours by Meg Bodin, tr. 1976

189. Azalais de Porcairages (1140–?)

1 Now we are come to the cold time

Untitled, St. 1, Quoted in *The Women Troubadours* by Meg
Bodin, tr. *1976*

2 Handsome friend, I'll gladly stay
forever in your service—
such noble mien and such fine looks—
so long as you don't ask too much

Untitled, St. 5, Ibid.

190. Beatritz de Dia (1140?–post-1189?)

1 If all the pangs are mine, I say
unequal parts in love we play.

Untitled, Quoted in *The Troubadours and Their World of the
Twelfth and Thirteenth Centuries* by Jack Lindsay *1976*

2 Those bad-talking gossips
No one who counts
Pays any attention to them.
They are a fog that rises
Against the sunlight.

Untitled, St. 2, Doris Earnshaw, tr., *Women Poets of the World*,
Joanna Bankier and Deirdre Lashgari, eds. *1983*

191. Marula (fl. 1150s)

1 She was troubled with indescribable love.

"Meeting after Separation," *Indian Love Poems*, Tambimuttu
and R. Appalaswamy, eds. and trs. *n.d.*

192. Shikishi Naishinno (1151?–1201)

1 The blossoms have fallen.
I stare blankly at a world
Bereft of color.

Untitled, *Anthology of Japanese Literature*, Donald Keene, ed.
and tr. *1955*

193. Marie de France (1160?–1215?)

1 When a great good is widely heard of,
then, and only then, does it bloom,
and when that good is praised by man,
it has spread its blossoms.

Prologue, ll. 1–8, *The Lais of Marie de France*, Robert
Hannings and Joan Ferrante, trs. *1978*

2 You have to endure what you can't change.

"Guigemar," l. 410, Ibid.

3 But he who hides his sickness
can hardly be brought back to health;
love is a wound in the body,
and yet nothing appears on the outside.

ll. 481–484, Ibid.

4 But Fortune, who never forgets her duty, turns her wheel suddenly.

ll. 538–539, Ibid.

5 indeed, I condemned myself
when I slandered all womankind.

"Le Fresne [The Ash Tree]" ll. 79–80, Ibid.

6 whether it makes you weep or sing
justice must be carried out.

"Lanval," ll. 435–436, Ibid.

7 Whoever wants to tell a variety of stories
ought to have a variety of beginnings.

"Milun," ll. 1–2, Ibid.

8 With the two of them it was just
as it is with the honeysuckle
that attaches itself to the hazel tree:
when it has wound and attached
and worked itself around the trunk,
the two can survive together;
but if someone tries to separate them,
the hazel dies quickly
and the honeysuckle with it.
"Sweet love, so it is with us:
You cannot live without me, nor I without you."

"Chevrefoil [The Honeysuckle]," ll. 68–78, Ibid.

9 "Whoever believes in a man is very foolish."

"Eliduc," l. 1084, Ibid.

10 Desire can blind us to the hazards of our enterprises.

Medieval Fables of Marie de France, Jeanette Beer, tr. *1981*

194. Alamanda (fl. 1165–1199)

1 I'm so angry that my body's
all but bursting into flame.

Untitled, St. 1, Quoted in *The Women Troubadours* by Meg
Bodin, tr. *1976*

195. Marie de Ventadorn (1165?–?)

1 . . . the lady
ought to do exactly for her lover
as he does for her, without regard to rank;
for between two friends neither one should rule.

Untitled, St. 2, Quoted in *The Women Troubadours* by Meg
Bodin, tr. *1976*

2 . . . to me it's nothing short of treason
if a man says he's her equal *and* her servant.

Untitled, St. 5, Ibid.

196. Aldrude (fl. 1170s)

1 It is by those only who are truly great, that virtue is esteemed
more than riches or honours, or that virtuous actions can be
duly appreciated.

(1172), Quoted in *Biography of Distinguished Women* by
Sarah Josepha Hale* *1876*

*See 807.

2 Courage is relaxed by delay.

Ibid.

197. Chu Shu-chên (fl. 1180s–1200s)

1 I write poems, change and correct them,
And finally throw them away.

"Sorrow," *Love and the Turning Year: One Hundred More
Poems from the Chinese*, Kenneth Rexroth, ed. and tr. *1970*

2 Alone in the dark, I am
Going mad, counting my sorrow.

"Stormy Night in Autumn," *One Hundred Poems from the
Chinese*, Kenneth Rexroth, ed. and tr. *1971*

3   It is easier to see Heaven
    Than to see you.
                  "Spring Joy" (1182), *The Orchid Boat, Women Poets of
                  China,* Kenneth Rexroth and Ling Chung, eds. and trs. *1972*

198. Garsenda de Forcalquier (ca. 1180–ca. 1242)

1   . . . it's you who stands to lose
    if you're not brave enough to state your case
                  Untitled, St. 1, Quoted in *The Women Troubadours* by Meg
                  Bodin, tr. *1976*

199. Isabella (1180?–?)

1   . . . if I sang your praises
    it wasn't out of love
    but for the profit I might get from it
                  Untitled, St. 2, Quoted in *The Women Troubadours* by Meg
                  Bodin, tr. *1976*

200. Lombarda (1190?–?)

1   but then when I remember what my name records,
    all my thoughts unite in one accord.
                  Untitled, St. 3, Quoted in *The Women Troubadours* by Meg
                  Bodin, tr. *1976*

201. Clare of Assisi (1195–1253)

1   . . . sisters beware of all pride, vain ambition, envy, greed, and
    of taking part in the cares and busy ways of the world.
                  Rule and Testament 1253

202. Alais (fl. 12th century)

1   . . . shall I stay unwed? that would please me,
    for making babies doesn't seem so good,
    and it's too anguishing to be a wife.
                  Untitled, St. 1, with Iselda* and Carenza, Quoted in *The
                  Women Troubadours* by Meg Bodin *1976*
    *See 208.

203. Clara d' Anduza (1200–1235)

1   for the love that has me in its spell
    wants me to lock you up and guard you well;
    and I will . . .
                  Untitled, St. 3, Quoted in *The Women Troubadours* by Meg
                  Bodin, tr. *1976*

204. Beatrijs of Nazareth (ca. 1200–1268)

1   . . . the soul is like a maiden who serves her master only for her
    great love of him, not for any payment, sastisfied that she may
    serve him and that he suffers her to serve . . .
                  "Seven manieren van minne" (Seven Manners of Loving),
                  Mediaeval Netherlands religious literature, E. Colledge, tr. and
                  intro. *1965*

2   And you may see that now the soul is like a housewife who has
    put all her household in good order and prudently arranged it
    and well disposed it.
                  Ibid.

205. Bieiris de Romans (1200–1235)

1   Don't grant your love to a deceitful suitor.
                  Untitled, St. 3, Quoted in *The Women Troubadours* by Meg
                  Bodin, tr. *1976*

206. Castelloza (1200?–?)

1   . . . at any moment I might
    rediscover reason to rejoice.
                  Untitled, St. 4, Quoted in *The Women Troubadours* by Meg
                  Bodin, tr. *1976*

2   the more I sing
    the worse I fare in love.
                  Untitled, St. 1, Ibid.

3   And if you left me now,
    I wouldn't feel a thing,
    for since no joy sustains me
    a little pain won't drive me mad.
                  Untitled, St. 4, Ibid.

207. Domna H. (fl. 12th century)

1   for when a man is in love's grip
    it's wrong for him to knowingly
    ignore his lady's orders.
                  Untitled, St. 2, Quoted in *The Women Troubadours* by Meg
                  Bodin, tr. *1976*

208. Iselda (fl. 12th century)
Coauthor with Alais; see 202.

209. Kasmuneh (fl. 12th–13th centuries)

1   A vine I see, and though 'tis time to glean,
    No hand is yet stretched forth to cull the fruit.
                  "Overripe Fruit," *A Treasury of Jewish Poetry,* Nathan and
                  Maryann Ausubel, eds. *1957*

210. Stewardess of the Empress Koka (fl. 12th century)

1   For the sake of a night
    Short as the nodes
    Of the reeds of Naniwa
    Must I live on,
    My flesh wasted with longing?
                  Untitled, *One Hundred Poems from the Japanese,* Kenneth
                  Rexroth and Ikuko Atsumi, eds. and trs. *1964*

211. Mahadeviyakka (fl. 12th century)

1   husband, inside,
    lover outside.
    I can't manage them both.
                  Untitled, *Speaking of Siva,* A. K. Ramanujan, ed. and tr. *1973*

2   When all the world is the eye of the lord,
    onlooking everywhere, what can you
    cover and conceal?
                  Ibid.

212. Mahsati Ganjavi (fl. 12th century)

1   Better to live as a rogue and a bum,
        a lover all treat as a joke
    to hang out with a crowd of comfortable drunks,
        than crouch in a hypocrite's cloak.
                  Selected Quatrains, #1, Deirdre Lashgari, tr., *Women Poets
                  of the World,* Joanna Bankier and Deirdre Lashgari, eds.
                  1983

2 Gone are the games we played all night,
   gone the pearls my lashes strung.
   You were my comfort and my friend.
   You've left, with all the songs I'd sung.

                                    #4, Ibid.

213. T'ang Wan (fl. 12th century)

1 The world's love runs thin.
   to the tune "The Phoenix Hairpin," *The Orchid Boat, Women Poets of China,* Kenneth Rexroth and Ling Chung, eds. and trs. *1972*

2 My troubled mind sways
   Like the rope of a swing.

                                    Ibid.

214. Elizabeth of Thuringia (1206/07–1231)

1 We must not sadden God with sullen looks.
   Quoted in *Saint Elizabeth* by Elisabeth von Schmidt-Pauli; Olga Marx, tr. *1932*

2 We are made loveless by our possessions.

                                    Ibid.

3 We women were allowed to stand at the Cross. We saw His wounds bleed and His eyes grow dim. As He was dying Jesus put His faith in us, we were to carry His love through the whole world and here we sit and have forgotten Him.

                                    Ibid.

215. Mechtild von Magdeburg (1207?–1282/97)

1 I come to my Beloved
   Like dew upon the flowers.
   Introduction, *Das fliessende Licht der Gottheit* [The Flowering Light of God] *1344*

2 . . . a hungry man can do no deep study, and thus must God, through such default, lose the best prayers.

                                    Ibid.

3 Those who would know much, and love little, will ever remain at but the beginning of a godly life.

                                    Ibid.

4 Of the heavenly things God has shown me, I can speak but a little word, not more than a honey bee can carry away on its feet from an overflowing jar.

                                    Ibid.

216. Beruriah (fl. 1210s–d. 1280)

1 How do you make out [that such a prayer should be permitted]? Because it is written "Let *hattaim* [sins] cease"? Is it written *hottim* [sinners]? It is written *hattaim*! Further, look to the end of the verse "and let the wicked men be no more." Since the sins will cease, there will be no more wicked men! Rather pray for them that they should repent, and there will be no more wicked.
   Quoted in *The Jewish Woman: New Perspectives,* Elizabeth Koltun, ed. *1976*

217. Guillelma de Rosers (fl. 1230s–d. 1265)

1 a man who keeps his word is worth much more
   than one whose plans are constantly revised.
   Untitled, St. 2, Quoted in *The Women Troubadours* by Meg Bodin, tr. *1976*

2 . . . there's no such thing
   as chivalry that doesn't spring from love.

                                    Untitled, St. 3, Ibid.

218. Hadewijch of Brabant (fl. 1230s–1260/65)

1 All things
   Crowd me in!
   I am so wide!
   "All Things Confine," St. 1, Frans van Rosevelt, tr., *The Penguin Book of Women Poets,* Carol Cosman, Joan Keefe, and Kathleen Weaver, eds. *1978*

2 Things of great wonder come to those who give their all to love.
   Poem 12, *Strofische Gedichte* (Strophic Poems) *n.d.*

3 For this is love's truth: she joins two in one being, makes sweet sour, strangers neighbors, and the lowly noble.
   Poem 28, Ibid.

219–220. Angela of Foligno (1250–1309)

1 In that time, by the will of God, my mother, who was a severe obstacle to me, died. Then my husband and all my children died within a brief period. Since I had taken the path of the religious life, and had begged God to be released from every worldly tie, their death was a great consolation for me.
   The Book of Divine Consolation of the Blessed Angela of Foligno, Mary G. Steegmann, tr. *1908*

221. Gertrude the Great (1256–1302)

1 . . . growing in the knowledge of virtue like unto these trees, I flower in the greenness of good deeds . . .
   from *Legacy of Divine Piety,* Quoted in *Women in the Middle Ages: Religion, Marriage and Letters* by Angela M. Lucas *1983*

2 . . . looking down on things earthly in free flight like these doves, I approach heaven, and with my bodily senses removed from external turmoil, apprehend thee with my whole mind . . .

                                    Ibid.

222. Lady Nijo (1258–1306?)

1 "Even consolation brings pain."
   (1284), *The Confessions of Lady Nijo,* Karen Brazell, tr. *1973*

2 Its blossoms detaining travelers
   The cherry tree guards the pass
   On Osaka Mountain.

                                    (1289), Ibid.

223. Kuan Tao-shêng (1262–1319)

1 I am your clay.
   You are my clay.
   In life we share a single quilt.
   In death we will share one coffin.
   "Married Love," *The Orchid Boat, Women Poets of China,* Kenneth Rexroth and Ling Chung, eds. and trs. *1972*

224. Padeshah Khatun (fl. 1269–1273)

1 Two yards of veil won't make any woman a lady
   nor a hat make any head worthy of command
   "Sovereign Queen," Deirdre Lashgari, tr., *Women Poets of the World,* Joanna Bankier and Deirdre Lashgari, eds. *1983*

225. Empress Eifuku (1271–1342)

1 we
Were caught in bed by the dawn
Untitled, One Hundred More Poems from the Japanese,
Kenneth Rexroth and Ling Chung, eds. and trs. *1972*

226. Jeanne of Navarre (1271–1307/9?)

1 When you kill these Flemish boars, do not spare the sows; them
I would have spitted.
Attributed comment about revolt of Flanders (1302), Quoted
in *Women of Medieval France* by Pierce Butler *1907*

227. Abutsu (?–1283?)

1 Between the pines of the shore hills on the eastern road/
Even the waves rise in the image of flowers.
"The Diary of the Waning Loon," *The Penguin Book of
Women Poets,* Carol Cosman, Joan Keefe, and Kathleen
Weaver, eds. *1978*

228. Mahuat d' Artois (1285–1319)

1 . . . have pity upon me, a poor widow driven from her heritage,
and here without counsel! You see how your people besiege
me, one barking on my right, another at my left, till I know not
what to answer, in the great trouble of my mind.
Plea before the Duke de Noirs, Quoted in *Women of Medieval
France* by Pierce Butler *1907*

229. Mistress of Albrecht of Johannsdorf (fl. 13th century)

1 How can you combine two unlike things, to cross the sea and
bide with me? You leave the tenderness of my heart, then how
can you cherish it also?
Quoted in *Saint Elizabeth* by Elisabeth von Schmidt-Pauli;
Olga Marx, tr. *1932*

230. Mukta Bai (fl. 13th century)

1 What is beyond the mind,
has no boundary,
In it our senses end.
Untitled, Willis Barnstone, tr., *A Book of Women Poets,* Aliki
and Willis Barnstone, eds. *1980*

2 Mukta says: Words cannot contain him,
yet in him all words are.
Ibid.

231. La Compiuta Donzella (fl. 13th century)

1 To leave the world serve God
make my escape from all pretension . . .
That is my wish
For what I see flourish and ascend
the stalk is only
insanity, low acts and lies of men.
Untitled, Sts. 1–2, Laura Stortoni, tr., *Women Poets of the
World,* Joanna Bankier and Deirdre Lashgari, eds. *1983*

2 . . . all men find evil
a proper ornament.
Untitled, St. 3, Ibid.

232. Duchess of Lorraine (fl. early 13th century)

1 Churl death, who wars on all mankind,
you have taken from me what I most loved.

Now I am the Phoenix, alas! alone and bereft,
the single bird of which they tell.
"Elegy," St. 3, Quoted in *Medieval Lyrics of Europe,* Willard
R. Trask, tr. *1969*

233. Wang Ch'ing-hui (fl. 13th century)

1 Suddenly, one day, war drums on horseback
Came like thunder, tearing off the sky,
And all glorious flowery days were gone forever.
Untitled, *The Orchid Boat, Women Poets of China,* Kenneth
Rexroth and Ling Chung, eds. and trs. *1972*

234. Bridget of Sweden (1303–1373)

1 Pride alienates man from heaven; humility leads to heaven.
"Book of Questions," Vol. V, *Revelations,* Vol. III *1344–49*

2 The source of justice is not vengeance but charity.
Ibid.

3 JUDGE: If the nobleman is superior to the commoner, the
nobleman should fear that his ultimate Judgement will be the
more severe, because God has given him more.
Ibid.

4 To write well and speak well is mere vanity if one does not live
well.
Ibid.

5 Man, the author of evil, must bear it.
Ibid.

6 I beheld a Virgin of extreme beauty wrapped in a white mantle
and a delicate tunic . . . with her beautiful golden hair falling
loosely down her shoulders. . . . She stood with uplifted hands,
her eyes fixed on heaven, rapt, as it were, in an ecstasy of contemplation, in a rapture of divine sweetness. And while she
stood in prayer, I beheld her Child move in her womb and . . .
she brought forth her Son, from Whom such ineffable light and
splendor radiated that the sun could not be compared to it. . . .
And then I heard the wonderful singing of many angels. *
Vol. VII, Ibid.
*Her vision of the Nativity has become the standard, "influencing
Western art, music, literature, and even the decisions at the Council of Trent." (Anthony Butkovich, *Revelations,* 1972).

7 The world would have peace if the men of politics would only
follow the Gospel.
Prayer, "In Honor of our Lord Jesus Christ," Quoted in
Revelations by Anthony Butkovich *1972*

235. Lalleswari (1317?–1391?)

1 I set forth hopeful—cotton-blossom Lal.
Untitled, George Grierson, tr., adapted by Dierdre Lashgari,
Women Poets of the World, Joanna Bankier and Dierdre
Lashgari, eds. *1983*

2 Good repute is water carried in a sieve.
Untitled, George Grierson, tr., Ibid.

236. Juliana of Norwich (1342–1416?)

1 He shewed me a little thing, the quantity of a hazel nut, lying
in the palm of my hand. . . . I looked thereupon and thought:
"What may this be?" And I was answered . . . thus: "It is all

that is made. . . . It lasts and ever shall last because God loves it, and hath all-things its being through the love of God."

Ch. 4, *Revelations of Divine Love 1373*

2   And then our good Lord opened my ghostly eye, and shewed me my soul in the midst of my heart. I saw the soul so large as it were an endless world, and also as it were a blessed kingdom. And by the conditions that I saw therein, I understood that it is a worshipful city.

Ch. 68, Ibid.

3   He said not, "Thou shalt not be troubled, thou shalt not be travailed, thou shalt not be diseased;" but He said, "Thou shalt not be overcome."

Ibid.

237. Catherine of Siena (1347–1380)

1   Every evil, harm, and suffering in this life or in the next comes from the love of riches.

The Dialogue of the Seraphic Virgin Catherine of Siena, Algar Thorold, ed. and tr. *1896*

2   . . . the Devil invites men to the water of death . . . and blinding them with the pleasures and conditions of the world, he catches them with the hook of pleasure . . .

Ch. 44, Ibid.

3   Thy miseries are not hid from thee now, for the worm of conscience sleeps no longer . . .

Ch. 132, Ibid.

4   . . . if thou wish to reach the perfection of love, it befits thee to set thy life in order.

Letter to Monna Alessa dei Saracini, *Saint Catherine of Siena as Seen in her Letters,* Vida D. Scudder, ed. and tr. *1906*

5   . . . sometimes God works through rascally men, in order that they may execute justice on His enemy.

Letter to Giovanna, Ibid.

6   We are put here in this life like a battlefield and we must fight the good fight.

Dialogue with Divine Providence n.d.

238–239. Jefimija (1348?–1405?)

1   The sorrow for him is burning steadily in my heart
And I am overcome by my motherly ways.

"The Lament Over the Dead Son Overcome by Her Motherly Ways," St. 3, *An Anthology of Medieval Serbian Literature in English,* Mateja Matejic and Dragan Milivojevic, eds. *1978*

2   Who is this one?
Whisper into my ears!
Is this the one for whom I used to long. . . ?

"Who is This One?," St. 1, Ibid.

240. Chao Li-hua (fl. 1360s–d. 1644)

1   my boat goes west, yours east
heaven's a wind for both journeys

"Farewell," J. P. Seaton, tr., *A Book of Women Poets,* Aliki and Willis Barnstone, eds. *1980*

241. Margherita Datini (1360–1423)

1   You say, always sermonizing, that we will have a fine life, and every month and every week will be the one. You have told me

this for ten years, and today it seems more timely than ever to reply: it is your fault. . . .

If you delay so much, you will never seize this "fine life," and if you say, "Look at the hardships that I undergo every day, never can one live in the world without them:" that is no excuse for not living a fine life for the soul and the body.

Letter to [her husband] Francesco di Marco Datini (January 1386), Quoted in *Women in the Middle Ages* by Frances and Joseph Gies *1978*

242. Margaret of Nassau (fl. 1360s)

1   Know, my love, that I should like to call you a thief, because you have stolen my heart. . . .

Letter to Matilda of Cleves (1367), Quoted in *Women in the Middle Ages* by Sibylle Harsken *1975*

243. Leonor López de Córdoba (1361?–1420)

1   The rest of us were kept prisoner for nine years. . . . Our husbands had sixty pounds of iron each on their feet, and my brother Don Lope Lopez had a chain on top of the irons, in which there were seventy links. He was a child of thirteen years [when he died], the most beautiful creature there was in the world.

Memorias 1412

244. Christine de Pisan (1363/65–1430/31)

1   If justice were king,
neither female nor male would lose,
but mostly, I am certain
custom reigns, rather than justice.

La Livre de la Mutacion de Fortune, Vol. 1, (p. 21), Susan Groag Bell, tr. *1400*

2   If it were customary to send little girls to school and to teach them the same subjects as are taught to boys, they would learn just and fully and would understand the subtleties of all arts and sciences. Indeed, maybe they would understand them better . . . for just as women's bodies are softer than men's, so their understanding is sharper.

Prologue, *La Cité des Dames* [The City of Women] *1404*

3   She [Lady Reason] replied, "Rest assured, dear friend, that many noteworthy and great sciences and arts have been discovered through the understanding and subtlety of women, both in cognitive speculation, demonstrated in writing, and in the arts, manifested in manual works of labor."

Ibid.

4   . . . as says the Philosopher—he is not wise who knows not part of everything.

Pt. II, Ch. 9, "La Livre des Trois Vertus" *1405*

5   Knowledge has sweet savory, honeyed things which precede in value all other treasures as sovereign . . .

L'Avison-Christine, Sister Mary Louis Towner, ed.; Susan Groag Bell, tr. *1932*

6   Where true love is, it showeth; it will not feign.

"The Epistle of Othea to Hector," St. 27, *The Penguin Book of Women Poets,* Carol Cosman, Joan Keefe, and Kathleen Weaver, eds. *1978*

7   He is too unwise that, for default of one,
will therefore despise woman everyone.

"The Epistle of Othea to Hector," St. 45, Ibid.

8 I will not stay when you behave
   harshly, insult me like a cur,
   for things have changed. I won't concur
   and won't reveal my sorrow, save
   I'll always dress in black and rave.

   Untitled, St. 3, Willis Barnstone, tr., *A Book of Women Poets*,
   Aliki and Willis Barnstone, eds. *1980*

9 This wise lady ought to persuade her husband if she can by
   kind words and sensible admonitions to agree to discuss their
   finances together and try to keep to such a standard of living
   as their income can provide and not so far above it that at
   the end of the year they find themselves in debt to their own
   people or other creditors. There is absolutely no shame in living within your income, however small it may be, but there is
   shame if creditors are always coming to your door to repossess
   their goods or if they are obliged to make nuisances of themselves to your men or your tenants or if they have to try by
   hook or by crook to get their payment.

   "How ladies and young women who live on their
   manors ought to manage their households and estates," *The
   Treasure of the City of Ladies: or The Book of the Three
   Virtues* (pp. 130–133; 1404), Sarah Lawson, tr. *1985*

10 . . . help those who have need of it in humane compassion,
   remembering that you too will become powerless and weak
   if you live that long, and then you would surely wish to be
   comforted yourself. You should also do it for God as the greatest charity and almsgiving that there is, for there is no worse
   disease than old age.

   "How young women ought to conduct themselves towards
   their elders," Ibid.

11 . . . a woman with a mind is fit for any task . . .

   Quoted in *The Creation of Feminist Consciousness: From the
   Middle Ages to Eighteen-Seventy*, Gerda Lerner* *1993*
   *See 2380.

245. Margery Kempe (1373?–1438?)

1 She thought that she loved God more than He did her. She
   was smitten with the deadly wound of vainglory, and felt
   it not, for she many times desired that the crucifix should
   loosen His hands from the Cross, and embrace her in token
   of love.

   The Book of Margery Kempe ca. 1435

2 "I have oftentimes told thee, daughter, that thinking, weeping,
   and high contemplation is the best life on earth, and thou shalt
   have more merit in Heaven for one year of thinking in thy mind
   than for a hundred years of praying with thy mouth. . . ."

   Ibid.

3 And sometimes those that men think were revelations, are
   deceits and illusions, and therefore it is not expedient to give
   readily credence to every stirring, but soberly abide . . .

   Ch. 89, Ibid.

246. Chandidas (ca. 1375–1450)

1 I leave this black hair loosely knotted/
   so when my dark love comes to mind/
   I can let it down and brood.

   "Why Tell Me What To Do?," Tony Barnstone, tr., *World
   Poetry*, Katharine Washburn & John S. Major, eds., Clifton
   Fadiman, genl. ed. *1998*

247. Valentine Visconti (fl. 1390s–1405)

1 There is nothing more for me, nothing matters more. *[Rien ne
   m'est plus, plus ne m'est rien.]*

   Motto, adopted after her husband's death (ca. 1405), Quoted
   in *Women of Medieval France* by Pierce Butler *1907*

248. Lal Ded (fl. 14th century?)

1 Like water in goblets of unbaked clay
   I drip out slowly,
   and dry.

   Untitled, Willis Barnstone, tr., *A Book of Women Poets*, Aliki
   and Willis Barnstone, eds. *1980*

2 I came by the way
   but didn't go back by the way.

   Untitled, Ibid.

249. Jahan Khatun (fl. 14th century)

1 I do not know if it is wrong or right
   But if you could hold me tight
   That veil would no longer be in sight!

   Untitled, *n.d.*

250. Mehri (1404?–1447)

1 Each subtlety hard for the pedant to solve
   I found a drop of wine would dissolve.

   "Coming Across," Deirdre Lashgari, tr., *Women Poets of the
   World*, Joanna Bankier and Deirdre Lashgari, eds. *1983*

251. Alessandra de' Machingi Strozzi (1406–1471)

1 One has nothing to do now but to pay taxes. . . . It is miraculous how much money they extort from us, and yet we seem to
   gain no advantage.

   Letter to her son Lorenzo (1452), Quoted in *Famous Women
   of Florence* by Edgecumbe Staley, tr. *1909*

2 Those who have no money are bound to go down . . .

   Letter to her son Filippo (1464), Ibid.

3 If I had no other interruptions in my work than my grandson,
   that would be more than enough, but I get so much pleasure
   from it. He follows me everywhere, like a chicken following a
   hen.

   Letter to her son, Quoted in *Uppity Women of Medieval Times*
   by Vicki León *1997*

4 I pray to God that he frees you from your fears—if all men
   were as afraid of marriage as you are, the world would have
   long since died out!

   Letter to her son Filippo, Ibid.

252. Joan of Arc (1412?–1431)

1 Messire, I am but a poor village girl; I cannot ride on horseback nor lead men to battle.

   Attributed to vision of St. Michael (ca. 1425), Quoted in
   Women of Beauty and Heroism by Frank B. Goodrich *1858*

2 My brothers in Paradise tell me what to do.

   Remark, Ibid.

3 I know neither A nor B; but I come from God to deliver Orleans and consecrate the king.

   Ibid.

4   Children say that people are hung sometimes for speaking the
    truth.
                         Defense at her tribunal (23 February 1431), Ibid.

5   If I am not [in a state of grace], God bring me there; if I am,
    God keep me there!
                                                              Ibid.

253. Catherine of Bologna (1413–1463)

1   Let every lover who loves the Lord
    Come to the dance singing of love
    Let her come dancing all afire
    Desiring only him who created her
    And separated her from the dangerous
    worldly state.
            Preface, *The Seven Spiritual Weapons*, Hugh Feiss and Daniela
                                                    Re, trs., *1998*

2   My Lord, what should I do because I do not have my heart in
    the control of my free will and I cannot restrain the thoughts
    which come to me?
                                                     Text, Ibid.

254. Isotta Nogarola (1417–1461/68)

1   There are already so many women in the world! Why then . . .
    was I born a woman, to be scorned by men in words and deeds.
            Letter to Guarino Veronese, Quoted in "Book-Lined Cells,"
            Margaret King, tr., *Beyond Their Sex*, Patricia Labalme, ed.
                                                              1980

2   Hence the woman, but only because she had been first deceived
    by the serpent's evil persuasion, did indulge in the delights of
    paradise; but she would have harmed only herself and in no
    way endangered human posterity if the consent of the first-
    born man had not been offered. Therefore Eve was no danger
    to posterity but [only] to herself; but the man Adam spread the
    infection of sin to himself and to all future generations. Thus
    Adam, being the author of all humans yet to be born, was also
    the first cause of perdition.
            Letter to Ludovico Foscarini (1451), Quoted in *Her
            Immaculate Hand* by Margaret L. King and Albert Rabil, Jr.
                                                              1991

255. Lucrezia de' Medici (1425–1482)

1   Here is the mighty king
    He has conquered the evil
    Which has lasted many years,
    And makes the earth tremble
    removing sorrows from it
    Thus filling the seats of paradise
    To restore his court.
            "Here is the Mighty King," Claudia Alexander with Carlo
            Di Maio, trs., from *Laude*, Quoted in *Poesia italiana: Il
                            quatrocento*, Giulio Ferroni, ed. *1978*

256. Costanza Varano Sforza (1426–1447)

1   Even the wisest and most famous men would fear to attempt
    to praise you adequately. What then can I, an ignorant, unlet-
    tered, and inexperienced girl hope to do?
            "Oration to Bianca Maria Visconti,"* Quoted in "Book-Lined
            Cells," Margaret King, tr., *Beyond Their Sex*, Patricia Labalme,
                                                      ed. *1980*
    *Last surviving member of the Visconti family of Milan, who dom-
    inated the history of northern Italy in the 14th and 15th centuries.

257. Sister Bertken (1427?–1514?)

1   I must sow lilies by the light of the dawn,
    And start my work early as the new day is born.
            "A Ditty," St. 8, Jonathan Crewe, tr., *Women Poets of the
            World*, Joanna Bankier and Deirdre Lashgari, eds. *1983*

258. Margaret of Anjou (1430–1482)

1   The world is always disposed to consider what is done by a
    great and powerful monarch as of course right, and even when
    it would seem to them wrong they believe that its having that
    appearance is only because they are not in a position to form a
    just judgement on the question, not being full acquainted with
    the facts, or not seeing all the bearings of them.
            Ch. 9, Remark to Henry VI, her husband, Quoted in *The
            History of Marguerite d'Anjou* by Jacob Abbott *1861*

259. Macuilxochitl (1435–1499?)

1   Will my songs
    be borne to his house
    where he dwells in mystery?
    Or do thy flowers bloom
    here only?
    Let the dance begin!
            "Battle Song," St. 2, Miguel León-Portilla and Catherine
            Rodriguez-Nieto, trs., *Trece poetas del mundo azteca*
            [Thirteen Poets of the Aztec World], Miguel León-Portilla, ed.
                                                              1967

260. Elizabeth Woodville Grey (1437–1492)

1   . . . desire of kingdom knoweth no kindred . . .
            Speech to Archbishop of Canterbury (1483), Quoted in
                    Chronicles by Raphael Holinshed *1577*

2   . . . for as ye think I fear too much, be you well ware that you
    fear not as far too little.
                                                              Ibid.

261. Mihri Hatun (1440–1506)

1   At one glance
    I love you
    With a thousand hearts
            Untitled, St. 1, Tâlat S. Halman, tr., *The Penguin Book of
            Women Poets*, Carol Cosman, Joan Keefe, and Kathleen
                                                  Weaver, eds. *1978*

2   Let the zealots think
    Loving is sinful
    Never mind
    Let me burn in the hellfire
    Of that sin
                                                     St. 3, Ibid.

262. Margaret Mautby Paston (1441–1484)

1   I would that ye should not be too hasty to be married till ye
    were more sure of your livelode [livelihood], for ye must re-
    member what charge ye shall have; and if ye have not [the
    means] to maintain it it will be a great rebuke. And therefore
    labour that ye . . . be more in surety of your land ere than ye be
    married.
            Letter to her son, John Paston II (1469), *The Paston Letters
            and Papers of the Fifteenth Century*, Pt. II, Norman Davis, ed.
                                                              1976

263. Catherine of Genoa (1447–1510)

1   I am so washed in the tide of His measureless love that I seem
to be below the surface of a sea and cannot touch or see or feel
anything around me except its water.
La Vita della B. Caterina Fiesca Adorna Dama Genouese 1681

2   My Me is God, nor do I recognize any other
Me except my God himself.
Quoted in *The Perennial Philosophy* by Aldous Huxley* *1945*
*British writer (1894–1963).

264. Isabella I (1451–1504)

1   Whoever hath a good presence and a good fashion, carries continual letters of recommendation.
#99, Quoted in *Apophthegms New and Old*, Francis Bacon,
ed. *1625*

2   . . . kings who wish to reign have to labor . . .
Quoted in *Isabella of Spain* by William Thomas Walsh *1930*

3   Although I have never doubted it . . . the distance is great from
the firm belief to the realization from concrete experience.
Ibid.

265. Antonia Pulci (1452–1501)

1   SERVANT. All these husbands put their best forward:
When their lady is engaged to them
How humble, then, they wish to seem, and mild—
At least until they've led her to their home.
*The Plays of Saint Flavia Domitilla, Florentine Drama for
Convent and Festival*, James Wyatt Cook, tr. and annot. *1997*

2   SERVANT. So is virginity the glory true.
It wafts a sweet aroma up to God.
Ibid.

3   SERVANT. Lo, some keep mistresses or concubines,
and some their ladies batter painfully,
Torment them with harsh discipline so cruel;
Many scornful outbursts, too, they bear;
One needs to think through all things to their end—
Ibid.

266. Juliana Berners (1460?–?)

1   A faythfulle frende wold I fayne finde,
to fynde hym where he myghte be founde.
But now is the worlde wext so unkynde,
Yet frenship is fall to the grounde;
(Now a Frende I have Founde)
That I woll nother banne ne curse,
But of all frendes in felde or towne
Ever, gramercy, myn own purse.
"Song," St. 1, *Boke of Saint Albans 1486*

2   What are the means and the causes that lead a man into a merry
spirit! Truly, in my best judgment, it seems that they are good
sports and honest games in which a man takes pleasure without
any repentance afterward. Thence it follows that good recre-
ations and honorable pastimes are the cause of a man's fair old
age and long life. And therefore, I will now choose among four
good sports and honorable pastimes—to whit, among hunting,
hawking, fishing and fowling. The best, in my simple judgment,
is fishing, called angling, with a rod and a line and a hook.
The Treatise of Fishing With an Angle (A Treatyse of
Fysshynge Wyth an Angle) *1496*

3   Also you must not be too greedy in catching your said game,
as in taking too much at one time . . . That could easily be the
occasion of destroying your own sport and other men's also.
When you have a sufficient mess, you should covet no more at
that time. Also you should busy yourself to nourish the game
in everything that you can, and to destroy all such things as are
devourers of it.
Ibid.

267. Gwerfyl Mechain (1460?–1500)

1   Tiny snow of the stunningly cold black day
is white flour,
is flesh of the earth,
cold lamb fleece on the mountain.
"In the Snowfall," St. 1, Willis Barnstone, tr., *A Book of
Women Poets*, Aliki and Willis Barnstone, eds. *1980*

2   It's a sad state of affairs that a cock
completely deprives a woman of her senses.
"To Jealous Wives," St. 2, *Medieval Welsh Erotic Poetry*,
Dafydd Johnston, ed. and tr. *1991*

3   a girl's thick grove, circle of precious greeting,
lovely bush, God save it.
"The Female Genitals," *Ibid.*

4   I declare, the quim* is fair
circle of broad-edged lips
it is a valley longer than a spoon or a hand
a ditch to hold a penis two hands long
Ibid.

* Antiquated term for vagina.

268. Florencia del Pinar (fl. 1460s–d. 1499)

1   These birds were born
singing for joy;
such softness imprisoned
gives me much sorrow—
yet no one weeps for me.
"To Some Partridges, Sent to Her Alive" (ca. 1511), Julie
Allen, tr., *A Book of Women Poets*, Aliki and Willis Barnstone,
eds. *1980*

269. Caterina Sforza (1462–1509)

1   Could I write all, the world would turn to stone.
Letter to her Dominican confessor (ca. 1501–09),* Quoted in
The Medici by G. F. Young *1930*
*Written from her prison in the Castel Sant'Angelo, Rome.

2   War is not for ladies and children like mine.
Letter to her uncle, Ludovico Sforza il Moro (27 August
1498), Quoted in *Caterina Sforza* by Ernst Breisach *1967*

270. Clemence Isaure (1464–1515/16)

1   . . . I, alas, plaintive and solitary,
I who have known only that I love, and that I suffer,
I must—a stranger to the world, to happiness—
Weep . . . and die.
Untitled, St. 2, Michael Fanning, tr., *Dictats de Dona
Clamenza Isaure 1505*

271. Elizabeth of York (1465/66–1503)

1   Delivered from sorrow, annexed to pleasance,
Of all comfort having abundance.

This joy and I, I trust, shall never twin—
My heart is set upon a lusty pin.
"My Heart Is Set Upon a Lusty Pin," St. 1, The Women Poets
in English, Ann Stanford, ed. 1972

272. Cassandra Fedele (1465–1558)

1 Do that for which nature has suited you . . .
"Letter to Alessandra Scala," from Clarissimae feminae
Cassandra Fidelis benetae epistolae et orationes posthumae,
(1536), Quoted in "Book-Lined Cells," Margaret King, tr.,
Beyond Their Sex, Patricia Labalme, ed. 1980

2 . . . many of you no doubt will see it as audacious, that I, a maiden . . . have come forth to speak in this radiance of learned men . . .
"Oration delivered in Padua," Ibid.

273–274. Laura Cereta (1469–1499)

1 Burning with the fires of hatred, the more they gnaw others, spewing forth words, the more are they wordless, gnawed within.
from Epistolae, 1488

2 The free mind, not afraid to labor, presses on to attain the good.
Ibid.

3 For knowledge is not given as a gift but by study. For a mind free, keen, and unyielding in the face of hard work always rises to the good, and the desire for learning grows in the depth and breadth.
Letter to Bibolo Semproni, Laura Cereta, Collected Letters of
a Renaissance Feminist, Diana Robin, ed. and tr. 1997

4 Nature has granted to all enough of her bounty; she opens to all the gates of choice, and through these gates, reason sends legates to the will, for it is through reason that these legates transmit desires.
Ibid.

5 For some women worry about the styling of their hair, the elegance of their clothes, and the pearls and other jewelry they wear on their fingers. Others love to say cute little things, to hide their feelings behind a mask of tranquillity, to indulge in dancing, and to lead pet dogs around on a leash. For all I care, other women can long for parties. . . . But those women for whom the quest for the good represents a higher value restrain their young spirits and ponder better plans.
Letter to Bibolo Semproni (1488), Ibid.

6 Your mouth has grown foul because you keep it sealed so that no arguments can come out of it that might enable you to admit that nature imparts one freedom to all human beings equally—to learn.
Ibid.

275. Elisabetta Gonzaga (1471–1526)

1 Who is there among us whose conduct is so perfect as to close the mouth of slanderers? . . . trouble yourself no more on the subject, but . . . allow the wrong to recoil on the heads of those who invent these slanders, and who, in my judgement, are sufficiently punished by seeing how hateful they become in the eyes of all virtuous and honest persons.
Letter to Isabella d'Este* (1513), Quoted in Isabella d'Este,
Vol. II, by Julia Cartwright 1903
*See 276.

276. Isabella d' Este (1474–1530)

1 . . . the discontent of the people is more dangerous to a monarch than all the might of his enemies on the battlefield.
Letter to her husband (Milan, February 1495), Quoted in
Beatrice d'Este* by Julia Cartwright 1899
*See 278.

2 . . . resolve to think of nothing but . . . health in the first place and . . . honor and comfort in the second, because in this fickle world we can do nothing else, and those who do not know how to spend their time profitably allow their lives to slip away with much sorrow and little praise.
Letter to Elisabetta of Urbino (1492), Quoted in Lucrezia
Borgia* by Rachel Erlanger 1978
*See 281.

277. Guilia Farnese (1474–1524)

1 We look as if we had despoiled Florence [Italy] of brocade.
Letter to Pope Alexander VI, Quoted in Lucrezia Borgia * by
Rachel Erlanger 1978
*See 281.

278. Beatrice d' Este (1475–1497)

1 I cannot say much of the perils of the chase, since game is so plentiful here that hares are to be seen jumping out at every corner—so much so, that often we hardly know which way to turn to find the best sport.
Letter to Isabella d'Este* (1491), Quoted in Beatrice d'Este by
Julia Cartwright 1899
*See 276.

2 Wherever I turn, in the house or out-of-doors, I seem to see your face before my eyes, and when I find myself deceived, and realize that you are really gone, you will understand how sore my distress has been—nay, how great it still is.
Letter to Isabella d'Este, her sister (1495), Ibid.

279. Barbara Torelli (1475–1533)

1 Would that my fire might warm this frigid ice
And turn with tears, this dust to living flesh
Poem on the death of her husband* (1508), Quoted in
Lucrezia Borgia** by Rachel Erlanger 1978
*Her second husband was murdered by the Bentivoglio, the family of her first husband. **See 281.

280. Agnes Paston (?–1479)

1 This world is but a thoroughfare, and full of woe; and when we depart therefrom, right nought bear with us but our good deeds and ill.
Letter to her son John (ca. 1444), The Paston Letters and
Papers of the Fifteenth Century, Pt. II, Norman Davis, ed. 1976

2 There knoweth no man how soon God will call him; and therefore it is good for every creature to be ready. Whom God visiteth, he loveth.
Ibid.

281. Lucrezia Borgia (1480–1519)

1 . . . my husbands have been very unlucky.
Remark to her father after the murder of her second husband,
Quoted in Lucrezia Borgia by Rachel Erlanger 1978

2 The more I try to do God's will the more he visits me with misfortune.
Remark upon hearing of the death of her brother, Ibid.

282. Margaret of Austria (1480–1530)

1   The time is troubled, but time will clear;
     After the rain one awaits fair weather.
     Untitled roundelay, St. 1, Quoted in Margaret of Austria:
     Regent of the Netherlands *by Jane de Iongh, M. D.*
     Herternorton, tr. 1953

2   All goes awry and lawless in the land,
     Where power takes the place of justice.
     Ibid.

3   *Fortune. Infortune. Fort. Une.* (Fortune persecutes one
     harshly.)
     Motto (1506), Ibid.

283. Catherine of Aragon (1485–1536)

1   . . . I am in debt in London. . . . So that, my lord, I am in
     the greatest trouble and anguish in the world. . . . I have now
     sold some bracelets to get a dress of black velvet, for I was
     all but naked; . . . certainly I shall not be able to live in this
     manner.
     Letter to King Ferdinand of Spain (1505), Quoted in Letters
     of Royal and Illustrious Ladies of Great Britain, *Vol. I, Mary
     Anne Everett Wood Green,* ed. 1846*
     *See 948.

2   Our time is ever passed in continual feasts.
     Letter to King Ferdinand of Spain (1509), Ibid.

3   They tell me nothing but lies here, and they think they can
     break my spirit. But I believe what I choose and say nothing. I
     am not so simple as I seem.
     Letter to King Ferdinand of Spain (1508), Quoted in Catherine
     of Aragon *by Garrett Mattingly 1941*

4   I came not into this realm as merchandise, nor yet to be mar-
     ried to any merchant.
     *Letter replying to request she acquiesce to the marriage of
     Henry VIII and Anne Boleyn* (1533), Ibid.*
     *See 300.

284. Elisabeth of Brandenburg (1485–1545)

1   I believe in Him who made the sun and the moon and all the
     stars. . . . May he not tarry to fetch me. . . . I am so weary of
     life.
     Last words (1545), Quoted in Women of the Reformation,
     Vol. I, Germany and Italy by Roland H. Bainton 1971

285. Veronica Gambara (1485–1550)

1   It's Heaven's will we are without hope of
     renewal like everything else in nature,
     certain of nothing but that we must die,
     "How dream-like, fleeting earthly things," St. 5, Stanzas
     1532–33.

2   if without false emotion and sighs, we
     simply enjoyed what Heaven offers us,
     if we could live in modest, humble ways.
     St. 14, Ibid.

3   I'll stand here, glad to be rid of all else,
     loving virtue and the soul as long as I live.
     St. 27, last lines, Ibid.

4   . . . blissful in heaven you see dawn appear
     And under your feet you see the stars. . . .
     *Sonnet on the death of an unidentified poet, Claudia
     Alexander with Carlo DiMaio, trs., from* Rime (1759), Poesia
     italiana: il cinquecento, *Giulio Ferroni, ed. 1978*

286. Ursula Shipton (1488–1561)

1   Now shall the Mitered Peacock* first begin to plume, whose
     Train shall make a great show in the World for a time, but
     shall afterwards vanish away and his Honour come to nothing,
     which shall take its end at Kingston.
     *The Life, Prophecies and Death of the Famous Mother
     Shipton 1687*
     *Reference to Cardinal Wolsey (?–1530), whose pride and retinue
     of 800 followers inspired the metaphor, and whose death Shipton
     foretold.

287. Vittoria da Colonna (1490–1547)

1   Your virtue may raise you above the glory of being king. The
     sort of honour that goes down to our children with real lustre
     is derived from our deeds and qualities, not from power or
     titles.
     *Letter to Francesco, Marquis of Pescara, her husband, Quoted
     in* Biography of Distinguished Women *by Sarah Josepha Hale**
     1876
     *See 807.

2   Thou knowest, Love, I never sought to flee
     From thy sweet prison, nor impatient threw
     Thy dear yoke from my neck, nor e'er withdrew
     what, that first day, my soul bestowed on thee. . . .
     *Untitled sonnet (ca. 1525–29), in Letter to Francesco, Marquis
     of Pescara (1529), Quoted in* A Princess of the Italian
     Reformation: Giulia Gonzaga* *by Christopher Hare** 1912*
     *See 306. **Pseudonym of Marian Andrews.

3   . . . the swaggering knights prepare to ride.
     The war begins. They gloat and cannot wait.
     They think they are masters of their fate.
     Untitled sonnet (ca. 1529–49), Quoted in Women of the
     Reformation, Vol. I; Germany and Italy *by Roland H. Bainton
     1971*

4   A scissors cut the single noble thread
     which twisted our lives into one; he's gone
     and the life I lived through him is vanished.
     "By losing myself in a deepening," St. 3, Amaro Lagrimar, The
     Sonnets of Vittoria Colonna, *Ellen Moody, tr. 1999*

5   I would like to be deaf to the world's noise, . . .
     "I would like to be deaf to the world's noise," St. 1, Ibid.

6   See that lovely juniper, pressed so hard,
     angry winds swirl round her, but she'll not let
     her leaves fall or scatter; clenched, branches held
     high, she gathers strength; her refuge within.
     "See that lovely juniper, pressed so hard," Ibid.

288. Argula von Grumbach (1492–1564/68)

1   Where do you read in the Bible that Christ, the apostles, and the
     prophets imprisoned, banished, burned or murdered anyone?
     *Letter of protest to the faculty of the University of Ingolstadt
     (1523), Quoted in* Women of the Reformation, Vol. I;
     Germany and Italy *by Roland H. Bainton 1971*

2 To obey my man indeed is fitting,
But if he drives me from God's Word
In Matthew ten it is declared
Home and child we must forsake
When God's honor is at stake.

Untitled, Ibid.

3 I am distressed that our princes take the Word of God no more
seriously than a cow does a game of chess.

Letter to her cousin, Adam von Torring, Ibid.

4 I have even heard some say, "If my father and mother were in
hell, I wouldn't want to be in heaven." Not me, not if all my
friends were down there.

Ibid.

289. Marguerite of Navarre (1492–1549)

1 spite will make a woman do more than love. . . .

"Novel III, the First day," The Heptameron, or Novels of the Queen of Navarre 1558

2 I have heard much of these languishing lovers, but I never yet
saw one of them die for love.

Ibid.

3 . . . all the lovers I have had have invariably begun by talking
of my interests, and telling me that they loved my life, my
welfare, and my honor, and the upshot of it has no less invariably been their own interest, their own pleasure, and their
own vanity.

"Novel XIV, the Second Day," Ibid.

4 . . . no one ever perfectly loved God who did not perfectly love
some of His creatures in this world.

"Novel XIX, the Second Day," Ibid.

5 He who knows his own incapacity, knows something, after
all. . . .

"Novel XXIX, the Second Day," Ibid.

6 . . . God always helps madmen, lovers, and drunkards. . . .

"Novel XXXVIII, the Fourth Day," Ibid.

7 A prison is never narrow when the imagination can range in it
at will.

Ibid.

8 Blessed . . . is he who has it in his power to do evil, yet does it
not.

"Novel XLIII, the Fourth Day," Ibid.

9 I never knew a mocker who was not mocked . . . a deceiver who
was not deceived, or a proud man who was not humbled.

"Novel LI, the Sixth Day," Ibid.

10 I did not know that love could grow through death. But now I
know.

Dialogue on the death of her brother, King Francis I (ca. 1547/48), Quoted in Women of the Reformation, Vol. II: France and England by Roland H. Bainton 1973

290. Mary of France (1496–1533)

1 God's will sufficeth me. (La Volonté de Dieu me suffit.)

Personal motto (1514), Quoted in Mary Tudor: The White Queen by Walter C. Richardson 1970

2 Sir, your Grace knoweth well that I did marry for your pleasure
. . . and now I trust you will suffer me to marry as me liketh for
to do.

Letter to her brother, Henry VIII* (ca. 1514/15), Ibid.
*King of England (1509–47) who broke from the Catholic Church
in 1534 to form the Church of England.

291. Katherine Zell (1497/98–1562)

1 You remind me that the Apostle Paul told women to be silent
in church. I would remind you of the word of this same apostle
that in Christ there is no longer male nor female.

"Entschuldigung [Apology of] Katharina Schutzinn" (1524),
Quoted in Women of the Reformation, Vol. I; Germany and Italy by Roland H. Bainton 1971

2 Faith is not faith which is not tried.

"Den Leyenden Christgläubigen" [To Suffering Believers in Christ] (1524), Ibid.

3 Lead us not into the temptation of believing that we have truly
forgiven, while rancor lingers . . .

Ibid.

292. Huang O (1498–1569)

1 Once more I will shyly
Let you undress me and gently
Unlock my sealed jewel.

"A Farewell to a Southern Melody," The Orchid Boat, Women Poets of China, Kenneth Rexroth and Ling Chung, eds. and trs. 1972

2 I will allow only
My lord to possess my sacred
Lotus pond, and every night
You can make blossom in me
Flowers of fire.

to the tune "Soaring Clouds," Ibid.

3 Maybe you can fool some girls,
But you can't fool Heaven.

to the tune "Red Embroidered Shoes," Ibid.

4 Go and make somebody else
Unsatisfied.

Ibid.

293. Mirabai (1498–1547)

1 She drinks the honey of her vision.

Untitled, St. 4, Willis Barnstone and Usha Nilsson, trs., A Book of Women Poets, Aliki and Willis Barnstone, eds. 1980

2 The energy that holds up mountains is the one Mirabai bows
down to,
He lives century after century, and the test I set for him he has
passed.

"The Clouds," News of the Universe, Robert Bly,* ed. and adapter 1980
*American poet (1926–).

3 I have felt the swaying of the elephant's shoulders . . .
and now you want me to climb on a
jackass? Try to be serious!

"Why Mira Can't Go Back to her Old House," Ibid.

294. Diane de Poitiers (1499–1566)

1 Farewell sweet kisses, pigeon-wise,
    With lip and tongue, farewell again
    The secret sports betwixt us twain
        "To Henry II Upon His Leaving for a Trip" (ca. 1552), Quoted
            in *The Life and Times of Catherine de Medici** by Francis
                                                        Watson *1935*

    *See 310.

2 The years that a woman subtracts from her
    age are not lost. They are added to the
    ages of other women.
                                                    Attributed *n.d.*

295. Agnes the Martyr (1500–1535)

1 O Eternall Governour, vouchsafe to open the gates of heaven
    once shut up against all the inhabitants of the earth . . .
        "The praier of Agnes the Martyr at hir death," *The Monument
        of Matrones conteining seven severall Lamps of Virginitie, or
        distinct treatises . . .,* Vol. I, Thomas Bentley, ed. *1582*

296. Honor Lisle (1500?–1550)

1 Good my lord, whereas in my former letters I have written to
    you that you should write to me with your own hand, whereof
    two lines should be more comfort to me than a hundred of
    another man's hand.
            Letter to Arthur Plantagenet (1539), Quoted *in Letters of
            Royal and Illustrious Ladies of Great Britain,* Vol. III, Mary
                                        Anne Everett Wood Green,* ed. *1846*

    *See 948.

297. Caterina Cibo (1501–1557)

1 . . . all creatures are flames of love.
        Quoted in *Seven Dialogues* by Bernadino Orchino (n.d.), cited
            in *Women of the Reformation, Vol. I: Germany and Italy* by
                                            Roland H. Bainton *1971*

2 We have but a little knowledge of God. . . . We are like bats
    who cannot look upon the light of the sun. God is infinite,
    immense, uncircumscribed, but our intellect is finite, limited,
    imprisoned in this body of darkness, stained with primal sin.
                                                                Ibid.

298. Maria of Hungary and Bohemia (1505–1558)

1 Full well I know
    God is my sword,
    And of my Lord
    None is me relieving.
            Untitled, St. 1 (1529), Quoted in *Women of the Reformation,
            Vol. III: From Spain to Scandinavia* by Roland H. Bainton
                                                                1977

299. Hwang Chin-I (1506?–1544)

1 I cut in two
    A long November night
        Untitled, Peter H. Lee, tr., *The Penguin Book of Women Poets,*
            Carol Cosman, Joan Keefe, and Kathleen Weaver, eds. *1978*

2 Mountains are steadfast but the mountain streams
    Go by, go by
    And yesterdays are like the rushing streams,
    They fly, they fly,

And the great heroes, famous for a day,
They die, they die.
                                                                Ibid.

300. Anne Boleyn (1507–1536)

1 Commend me to the king, and tell him he is constant in his
    course of advancing me; from a private gentlewoman he made
    a marquise, and from a marquise a queen; and now, as he had
    left no higher degree of earthly honour, he hath made me a
    martyr.
            (19 May 1536), Quoted in *Apophthegms New and Old,* No.
                                        9, Francis Bacon, ed. *1625*

2 I will rather lose my life than my virtue, which will be the great-
    est and best part of the dowry I shall bring my husband.
        Letter to Henry VIII,* Quoted in *Women of Beauty and
            Heroism* by Frank B. Goodrich *1858*
        *King of England (1509–47) who broke from the Catholic Church
        in 1534 to form the Church of England.

3 I have heard say the executioner is very good, and I have a little
    neck.
                Remark shortly before execution (19 May 1536), Ibid.

4 Alas! poor head, in a very brief space thou wilt roll in the dust
    upon the scaffold; and as in life thou didst not merit to wear
    the crown of a queen, so in death thou deservest not better
    doom than this.*
                        Spoken at her execution (19 May 1536), Ibid.
        *The linen cap she placed over her head before submitting to the
        executioner.

5 What will be, will be, grumble who may. *(Ainsi sera, groigne
    qui groigne.)*
            Motto embroidered on servants' livery (ca. 1530/31), Quoted
                        in *Anne Boleyn* by Marie Louise Bruce *1972*

6 I am her death, as she is mine.
            Said of Catherine of Aragon's* death (January 1536), Ibid.
        *See 283.

7 The people will have no difficulty in finding a nickname for
    me, I shall be Queen Anne Lack-Head.
                        Spoken at her execution (19 May 1536), Ibid.

301. Tullia d'Aragona (1510–1556)

1 Yes, but I'll tell you something that's very true: when one is
    speaking of our mortal world, it's really not acceptable to in-
    troduce elements of the divine, because the latter is so perfect
    that we shall never be able to comprehend it, and each indi-
    vidual is entitled to pronounce his own opinion about it.
            (p. 63), *Dialogue on the Infinity of Love,* Rinaldina Russell
                        and Bruce Merry, eds. and trs. (repr. 1997) *1547*

2 VARCHI. So you want me to bow to authority!
    TULLIA. No, Sir. I want you to bow to experience, which I
    trust by itself far more than all the reasons produced by the
    whole class of philosophers.
                                                                Ibid.

302. Elisabeth of Braunschweig (1510–1558)

1 Obey God, the emperor, and your mother.
        Treatise on government written for her son, Erich II, Quoted
            in *Women of the Reformation, Vol. I; Germany and Italy* by
                                            Roland H. Bainton *1971*

2 Better be hurt than to hurt.

> Hymn, Ibid.

3 No one without the experience knows the anguish which children can cause and yet be loved.

> From *Book of Consolation for Widows*, Ibid.

303. Marina de Guevara (1510?–1559)

1 Better than the castigation of the flesh is the overcoming of pride and anger.

> Testimony before the Inquisition (1558/59), Quoted in *Women of the Reformation, Vol. III: From Spain to Scandinavia* by Roland H. Bainton *1977*

2 To bring the heart into tune with God is better than audible prayer.

> Ibid.

304. Renée de France (1510–1575)

1 . . . Satan is the father of lies and God of the truth . . .

> Letter to John Calvin* (1564), Quoted in *Queen of Navarre: Jeanne d'Albret** by Nancy Lyman Roelker *1968*
> *French religious reformer (1509–64). **See 327.

2 Had I had a beard I would have been the King of France. I have been defrauded by that confounded Salic law.*

> Quoted in *Women of the Reformation, Vol. I; Germany and Italy* by Roland H. Bainton *1971*
> *European law (derived from a fifth-century Frankish code) preventing women from succeeding to a throne.

305. Catherine Parr (1512/13–1548)

1 A goodly example and lesson for us to follow at all times and seasons, as well in prosperity as in adversity, to have no will but God's will. . . . But we be yet so carnal and fleshly, that we run headlong like unbridled colts, without snaffle or bit.

If we had the love of God printed in our hearts, it would keep us back from running astray. And until such time as it pleases God to send us this bit to hold us in, we shall never run the right way, although we speak and talk never so much of God and His word.

> "The Lamentation on or Complaint of a Sinner," *The Lamentation of a Sinner 1545*

2 We be so busy and glad to find and spy out other men's doings that we forget and can have no time to weigh and ponder our own.

> Ibid.

3 Set your affection on thynges that are above: and not on thinges, whiche are on the earthe.

> Epigraph, Ibid.

4 Let there be alwaye in me one wille, and one desire with thee, & that I have no desire to will, or not to will, but as thou wilte.

> Untitled prayer, Ibid.

306. Giulia Gonzaga (1513–1566)

1 What mad credulity is ours! How infinite is the cupidity of mortals!

> Letter to Livia Negra, Quoted in *A Princess of the Italian Reformation: Giulia Gonzaga* by Christopher Hare* *1912*
> *Pseudonym of Marian Andrews.

2 . . . what should we do if we had to remain in this world perpetually? We cannot inhabit a house for three days in this miserable world without being dissatisfied.

> Ibid.

3 The promises of the alchemist are like those of the astrologers, who boast that they can foretell future things, and do not even know the present or the past. . . . I do not know whether their fraud is more shameful, or our folly in believing, as we do . . .

> Ibid.

307. Chiara Cantarini Matraini (1514–post-1597)

1 Return soul of the sky, candid moon
To the first sphere, shining and beautiful,
And with your customary brilliance restore
The crown of silver to the darkened sky

> Untitled sonnet, Claudia Alexander with Carlo DiMaio, trs., from *Poemas* (1560), *Poesia Italiana: il cinquecento*, Giulio Ferroni, ed. *1978*

2 . . . that weak and tired vessel finding
Itself with broken mast and sail
Bereft of helmsman, tossed by monstrous waves,
Seems like my soul deprived of light, bereft of every hope.

> Ibid.

308. Teresa of Ávila (1515–1582)

1 The hour I have long wished for is now come.

> Last words (1582), Quoted in *Distinguished Women Writers* by Virginia Moore *1934*

2 How is it that there are not many who are led by sermons to forsake open sin? Do you know what I think? That is because preachers have too much worldly wisdom. They are not like the Apostles, flinging it all aside and catching fire with love of God; and so their flame gives little heat.

> "Life" (1562), *The Complete Works of Saint Teresa of Jesus*, Vol. I, E. Allison Peers, ed. and tr. *1946*

3 I only wish I could write with both hands, so as not to forget one thing while I am saying another.

> "Way of Perfection," Ch. 20 (1579), Vol. II, Ibid.

4 . . . I believe that honour and money nearly always go together . . . seldom or *never* is a poor man honoured by the world; however worthy of honour he may be, he is apt rather to be despised by it.

> Ch. 22, Ibid.

5 If we plant a flower or a shrub and water it daily it will grow so tall that in time we shall need a spade and hoe to uproot it. It is just so, I think, when we commit a fault, however small, each day, and do not cure ourselves of it.

> "Conception of Love of God" (1571), *Selected Writings of St. Theresa of Avila*, E. Allison Peers, tr.; William J. Doheny, ed. *1950*

6 Humility must always be doing its work like a bee making its honey in the hive: without humility all will be lost.

> "Interior Castle" (1577), Ibid.

7 Untilled soil, however fertile it may be, will bear thistles and thorns; and so it is with man's mind.

> "Maxim for Her Nuns," Ibid.

8 Accustom yourself continually to make many acts of love, for they enkindle and melt the soul.

> Ibid.

9 Be gentle to all and stern with yourself.

Ibid.

10 Remember that you have only one soul; that you have only one death to die; that you have only one life, which is short and has to be lived by you alone; and there is only one glory, which is eternal. If you do this, there will be many things about which you care nothing.

Ibid.

11 . . . about the injunction of the Apostle Paul that women should keep silent in church? Don't go by one text only.

Letter, Quoted in *Women of the Reformation, Vol. III: From Spain to Scandinavia* by Roland H. Bainton 1977

12 Let nothing disturb thee,
Nothing affright thee;
All things are passing;
God never changeth.
Patient endurance
Attaineth to all things;
Who Good possesseth
In nothing is wanting;
Alone God sufficeth.

"*Nada te turbe*" ("Nothing disturbs thee"; a.k.a. "Saint Theresa's Bookmark") in toto, Henry Wadsworth Longfellow,* tr., *An Anthology of Spanish Poetry,* John A. Crow, ed. 1979

*American poet (1807–1882).

13 God walks among the pots and pipkins.

Attributed *n.d.*

309. Mary I of England (1516–1558)

1 When I am dead and opened, you shall find "Calais" lying on my heart.

Quoted in *Chronicles,* Vol. III by Raphael Holinshed 1585

2 . . . there are two things only, soul and body. My soul I offer to God, and my body to your Majesty's service.

Letter to Edward VI (ca. 1552), Quoted in *Catherine of Aragon** by Garrett Mattingly 1942

*See 283.

3 May it please you to take away my life rather than the old religion.

Ibid.

310. Catherine de' Medici (1519–1589)

1 Ah, sentiments of mercy are in unison with a woman's heart.

Ch. 3, Quoted in *The Huguenots of France and America,* Vol. I by Hannah Farnham Lee* 1843

*See 782.

2 . . . suppress this violence of emotion. I have always found it best *to appear to yield.* Assume a seeming conformity to your husband's will, even attend mass, and you will more easily get the reins into your own hands.

Ch. 7, Remark to Queen of Navarre,* Ibid.

*Jeanne d'Albret; see 327.

3 *Lachrymae hinc, hinc dolor.* (Tears henceforth, henceforth sadness.)

Motto (1559), Quoted in *The Medici* by G. F. Young 1930

4 When I see these poor people burnt, beaten and tormented, not for thieving or marauding, but simply for upholding their reli-

gious opinions, when I see some of them suffer cheerfully, with a glad heart, I am forced to believe that there is something in this which transcendeth human understanding.

Letter regarding persecution of Protestants (1559/60), Ibid.

5 If things were even worse than they are after all this war they might have laid the blame upon the rule of a woman; but if such persons are honest they should blame only the rule of men who desire to play the part of kings. In future, if I am not any more hampered, I hope to show that women have a more sincere determination to preserve the country than those who have plunged it into the miserable condition to which it has been brought.

Letter to Ambassador of Spain (1570), Ibid.

6 . . . never did woman who loved her husband succeed in loving his whore. One must call a spade a spade, though the term is an ugly one on the lips.

Letter (1583), Quoted in *Women of Power* by Mark Strange 1976

311. Laura Terracina (1519?–1577?)

1 . . . alas, who has taken you from me?
Who has torn you from my breast so brazenly
And locked such beauty in a little grave?

Untitled sonnet, Claudia Alexander with Carlo DiMaio, trs., *Poesia italiana: il cinquecento,* Giulio Ferroni, ed. 1978

2 . . . I see virtue abandoned
and the muses enslaved by such baseness
that my brain is nearly overwhelmed.

"Sonnet to Marcantonio Passero," Claudia Alexander, tr., Ibid.

312. Catherine Willoughby (1519/20–1580)

1 Undoubtedly the greatest wisdom is not to be too wise. . . .

Letter to William Cecil (1559), Quoted in *Women of the Tudor Age* by Cecilie Gaff 1930

2 . . . though God wink. . . . He sleepeth not. . . .

Ibid.

3 Christ's plain coat without a seam is fairer to the older eyes than all the jaggs* of Germany.

Ibid.

*A slash made in a garment to show a different color beneath.

4 God is a marvellous man.

Quoted by Catherine Parr* in a letter to Thomas Seymour (ca. 1548), *Tudor Women* by Alison Plowdon 1979

*See 305.

313. Anne Askew (1520–1546)

1 . . . unadvised hasty judgement is a token apparent of a very slender wit.

Testimony at inquisition (1545), Quoted in *Actes and monuments of these latter and perillous dayes* (a.k.a *The Book of Martyrs*) by John Foxe 1563

2 God has given me the bread of adversity and the water of trouble.

Letter to King Henry VIII* (1546), Ibid.

*King of England (1509–47) who broke from the Catholic Church in 1534 to form the Church of England.

3   Like as the armed knight
Appointed to the field,
With this world will I fight,
And faith shall be my shield.
"The Ballad Which Anne Askew Made and Sang When She
Was in Newgate," St. 1 (1547), *The Women Poets in English,*
Ann Stanford, ed. *1972*

314. Madeleine Fradonnet (1520?–1587)
1   Distaff, my pride and care, I vow to thee
That I shall love thee ever nor exchange
Thy homely virtue for a pleasure strange
"To My Distaff," with Catherine Fradonnet,* *Anthology of
European Poetry, 13th to 17th century,* William Stirling, tr.;
Mervyn Savill, ed. *1947*
*Her sister; see 345.

315. Pernette du Guillet (1520?–1545)
1   True love, to whom my heart is prey,
How dost thou hold me in thy sway,
That in each day I find no fault
But daily wait for love's assault
"Song," St. 1, William Stirling, tr. (1947), *Rhymes de Gentille
et Vertueuse Dame de Pernette du Guillet* (Lyonaisse) *1545*

2   As the body denies the means to look
Into the spirit or know its force,
Likewise Error for me drew
Around my eyes the blindfold of ignorance.
"Epigram," Joan Keefe with Richard Terdiman, trs. (1978),
Ibid.

3   I no longer need be concerned
whether daylight goes or night comes,
. . . because my Day,* with tender brilliance,
enlightens me through and through.
"Epigram 8," Ann Rosalind Jones, tr. (1981), Ibid.
*Allusion to the poet Maurice Sceve, with whom she had a liaison.

316. Louise Labé (1520/22–1566)
1   A woman's heart always has a burned mark.
Sonnet II, *A Book of Women Poets,* Aliki and Willis
Barnstone, eds. *1980*

2   I live, I die, I burn myself and drown.
Sonnet VIII, Ibid.

3   Only outside my body can I live
or else in exile like a fugitive.
Sonnet XVII, Ibid.

4   Kiss me again, rekiss me, kiss me more,
give me your most consuming, tasty one,
give me your sensual kiss, a savory one,
I'll give you back four burning at the core.
Sonnet XVIII, Ibid.

5   Your brutal goal was to make *me* a slave
beneath the ruse of being served by you.
Pardon me, friend, and for once hear me through:
I am outraged with anger and I rave.
Sonnet XXIII, Ibid.

6   Don't blame me, ladies, if I've loved. No sneers
if I have felt a thousand torches burn
Sonnet XXIV, Ibid.

7   Since a time has come, Mademoiselle, when the severe laws of men no longer prevent women from applying themselves to the sciences and other disciplines, it seems to me that those of us who can, should use this long-craved freedom to study and to let men see how greatly they wronged us when depriving us of its honor and advantages. And if any woman becomes so proficient as to be able to write down her thoughts, let her do so and not despise the honor but rather flaunt it instead of fine clothes, necklaces, and rings. For these may be considered ours only by use, whereas the honor of being educated is ours entirely.
Letter to a friend, Quoted in *Uppity Women of Medieval
Times* by Vicki León *1997*

317. Isabella da Morra (1520–1546)
1   Once more, O arid valley
O wild river, O wretched, barbarous stones
You shall hear my eternal pain and weeping.
Untitled sonnet, Claudia Alexander with Carlo DiMaio, trs.,
Poesia italiana: il cinquecento, Giulio Ferroni, ed. *1978*

2   Turbid Siri,* now that my bitter end is here, proclaim my sorrow. . . .
Tumultuously incite your waves
And say, "Not merely tears, but the copious weeping
Of Isabella increased me while she lived."
Untitled poem, Ibid.
*A river that runs between Calabria and Basilicata in southern Italy.

318. Lucia dall'Orno Bertana (1521–1567)
1   . . . bless me Muse and I will go
Through thick woods and over pleasant hills
To bright fountains where I will find mercy.
Sonnet on her marriage, Claudia Alexander, tr., Quoted in *A
Women's Record* by Sarah Josepha Hale* *1855*
*See 807.

319. Ippolita Castiglione (?–1521)
1   My dear Lord,—I have got a little daughter, of which I think you will not be sorry. I have been much worse than I was last time, and have had three attacks of high fever, but to-day I feel better, and hope to have no more trouble. I will not try to write more, lest I overdo myself, but commend myself to you with all my heart—Your wife who is a little tired out with pain, your Ippolita.
Letter to Baldassare Castiglione, her husband (24 August
1521; four days before her death), Quoted in *Isabella d'Este*
by Julia Cartwright *1903*
*See 276.

320. Gulbadan Begam bint Babur Badshah (1522/23–1603)
1   "Brotherly custom has nothing to do with ruling and reigning. If you wish to act as a brother, abandon the throne. If you wish to be king, put aside brotherly sentiment. . . ."
Humayun-nama ca. *1552*

2   In short, after the death of my royal father and my lady [Mahan], his Majesty, in the fullness of his affection, showed this broken one such favour, and spoke with such boundless compassion to this helpless one, that she did not know she was orphaned and headless.
P. 111, Ibid.

3   They [the older begams*] had great friendship for one another, and they used to wear men's clothes and were adorned by various accomplishments, such as making of thumb-rings [for archery] and arrows, playing polo, and shooting with the bow and arrow. They also played many musical instruments.

Pp. 120–121, Ibid.

*(a.s.a. begum), a Muslim woman of rank; the women of the royal family.

321. Luisa Sigea (1522–1560)

1   You have written me a letter which . . . exudes the fragrance of a life unspotted, which I would inhale were I not so spoiled by the stench of the human as to be incapable of the divine. . . .

Letter to a friend (n.d.), Quoted in *Women of the Reformation, Vol. III: From Spain to Scandinavia* by Roland H. Bainton *1977*

2   Blaze with the fire that is never extinguished.

"Dialogue of Blesilla and Flaminia," Ibid.

322. Elizabeth Tyrwhit (1522–1578)

1   . . . from Sathan deliver me, with the bread of Angels feede me, from fleshlie lusts purge me, from sudden death and deadlie sinne, O Lord take me.

"Another praier at our uprising," Morning and evening praiers, with divers, Psalmes, Hymnes, and Meditations, made and set forth by the Ladie Elizabeth Tyrwhit *1582*

2   Sweets dews from heven to earth God grant,
of peace and quiet mind,
That we may serve the living God, as his statutes doo bind.

"The Hymne or praier to he sonne of God," Ibid.

323. Gaspara Stampa (1523–1554)

1   Love made me such that I live in fire
like a new salamander on earth
or like that other rare creature, the Phoenix,
who expires and rises at the same time.

Untitled sonnet, Lynne Lawner, tr., *The Penguin Book of Women Poets*, Carol Cosman, Joan Keefe, and Kathleen Weaver, eds. *1978*

2   I hate who loves me, love who scorns me.

Ibid.

3   O love, what strange and wonderful fits:
one sole thing, one beauty alone,
can give me life and deprive me of wits.

Untitled sonnet, J. Vitiello, tr., *A Book of Women Poets*, Aliki and Willis Barnstone, eds. *1980*

324. Cicely Ormes (1525–1557)

1   . . . this my death is and shall be a witness of my faith unto you all here present. Good People! As many of you as believe as I believe, pray for me.

Spoken at her execution (23 September 1557), Quoted in *Actes and monuments of these latter and perillous dayes* (a.k.a. *The Book of Martyrs*) by John Foxe *1563*

325. Olimpia Morata (1526–1555)

1   Never does the same desire enlist us all.
Tastes are not conferred by Zeus on all alike.

Untitled (ca. 1542), Jules Bonnet and Roland H. Bainton, trs., Quoted in *Women of the Reformation, Vol. I: Germany and Italy* by Roland H. Bainton *1971*

2   I, a woman, have dropped the symbols of my sex,
Yarn, shuttle, basket, thread

Ibid.

3   Remembering that the span of our life is but toil and trouble and we soon fly away, may I give myself to the contemplation of things eternal.

Letter to her sister, Vittoria (ca. 1553), Ibid.

4   Let us not be troubled by men, for what is man if not a fleeting shadow, a windblown leaf, a fading flower, and vanishing smoke!

Last letter, to Lavinia della Rovere (1555), Ibid.

326. Elizabeth Hoby Russell (1527–1609)

1   No one need honor me with tears, or lament my burial! This is why! I go through the stars to God! (*Nemo me lachrymis decoret, neque funera fletio! Faxit cur! Vado perastra deo!*)

Composed for and inscribed on her monument in Bisham Church near Great Marlow, England, John Williams, tr., Quoted in *Society Women of Shakespeare's Time* by Violet A. Wilson *1924*

2   I beseech your Majesty, let me have Justice, and I will then trust the law.

Spoken to King James I (1603), Quoted in *Diary of Lady Margaret Hoby,** Dorothy M. Meads, ed. *1930*

*See 375.

3   Though I be not so bad a bird as to defile mine own nest, yet I know my children. . . .

Letter to [William Cecil, Lord] Burghley (n.d.), Ibid.

327. Jeanne d'Albret (1528–1572)

1   . . . arms once taken up should never be laid down, but upon one of three conditions—a safe peace, a complete victory, or an honourable death.

Quoted in *Biography of Distinguished Women* by Sarah Josepha Hale* *1876*

*See 807.

2   . . . the task of women and men who do not bear arms . . . is to fight for peace . . . do your part, for God's sake. As for me I will spare nothing.

Letter to Cardinal de Bourbon (1568), Quoted in *Queen of Navarre: Jeanne d'Albret* by Nancy Lyman Roelker *1968*

3   . . . if religion separates us, does our common blood then separate? Do friendship and natural duty cease to exist? *Non, mon frère.*

Ibid.

4   Nothing is impossible to a valiant heart. (*À coeur valliant rien d'impossible*).

Motto (adopted by her son, Henry IV*) *n.d.*

*Known as "Henry of Navarre," King of France (1589–1610) who founded Bourbon royal line (1553–1610).

328. Anne Cooke Bacon (1528?–1610?)

1   Ignorance, especially of the heavenly things, is the greatest lack that can be seen in man.

15th sermon, *Sermons . . . concerning the predestination and election of God: very expedient to the setting forth of his glory among creatures* ca. *1570*

2 Simple ignorance hath not so much confused . . . wisdom, as Philosophie, which maketh men bold, unshamefaced, hot, lyers, proud, contentious, frenticke, foolysh, and wicked.
17th sermon, Ibid.

329. Margaret Bryan (fl. 1530s)

1 The minstrels played, and his grace [Edward VI] danced . . . so wantonly that he could not stand still, and was as full of pretty toys as ever I saw a child in my life.
Letter to [Thomas] Cromwell* (1539), *Letters of Royal and Industrious Ladies of Great Britain*, Vol. III, Mary Anne Everett Wood Green,** ed. *n.d.*
*Earl of Essex; English politician (1485?–1540). **See 948.

330. Maria Cazalla (fl. 1530s)

1 You do this to a woman? I dread more the affront than the pain.
Testimony before the Inquisition (ca. 1531–34), Quoted in *Women of the Reformation, Vol. III: From Spain to Scandinavia* by Roland H. Bainton *1977*

331. Catherine Killigrew (1530?–1583)

1 In thee my soul shall own combined
The sister and the friend.

If from my eyes by thee detained
The wanderer cross the seas,
No more thy love shall soothe, as friend,
No more as sister please.
Untitled, Sts. 2–3, Quoted in *Women of the Reformation, Vol. III: From Spain to Scandinavia* by Roland H. Bainton *1977*

332. Anne Locke (1530?–1590?)

1 My many sinnes in nomber are encreast,
With weight wherof in sea of depe despeire
My sinking soule is now so sore opprest,
That now in peril and in present fere,
I crye: susteine me, Lord, and Lord I pray,
With endlesse number of thy mercies take
The endlesse number of my sinnes away.
A Meditation of a Penitent Sinner: Written in Maner [sic] of A Paraphrase upon the 51. Psalme of David, Vol. 13 *1560*

2 So foule is sinne and lothesome in thy sighte,
So foule with sinne I see my selfe to be,
That till from sinne I may be washed white,
So foule I dare not, Lord, approche to thee.
Ibid.

333. Anne d' Este (1531–post-1563)

1 My sweet god, so much blood, surely some of it will fall upon our house.
Comment on the mass execution of conspirators (22 March 1560), Quoted in *Women of Power* by Mark Strange *1976*

334. Queen Elizabeth I of England (1533–1603)

1 Much suspected of me,
Nothing proved can be,
Quoth Elizabeth, prisoner.
Scratched with a Diamond on her Window at Woodstock Prison (ca. 1554–55), Quoted in *Actes and monuments of these later and perillous dayes* (a.k.a. *The Book of Martyrs*) by John Foxe *1563*

2 I am your anointed Queen. I will never be by violence constrained to do anything. I thank God I am endued with such qualities that if I were turned out of the Realm in my petticoat I were able to live in any place in Christendom.
Speech, Deputation of Lords and Commons *October 1566*

3 I know I have the body of a weak and feeble woman, but I have the heart and stomach of a king, and of a king of England too. . . .
Speech to the troops at Tilbury on the Approach of the Armada *8 August 1588*

4 All my possessions for a moment of time.
Last words, Attributed *1603*

5 For, what is a family without a steward, a ship without a pilot, a flock without a shepherd, a body without a head, the same, I think, is a kingdom without the health and safety of a good monarch.
Letter to King Edward VI (ca. 1551), *The Sayings of Queen Elizabeth*, Frederick Chamberlain, ed. *1923*

6 I am more afraid of making a fault in my Latin, than of the Kings of Spain, France, Scotland, the whole House of Guise, and all of their confederates.
To the Archbishop of St. Andrews (n.d.), Ibid.

7 . . . I cannot but muse for my part, and blush for theirs, to see the rebellious hearts and devilish intents of Christians in name, but Jews in deed. . . .
Letter to Mary, Queen of Scots* (22 August 1556), *The Letters of Queen Elizabeth the First*, G. B. Harrison, ed. *1935*
*See 341.

8 A strength to harm is perilous in the hand of an ambitious head.
Letter to Sir Henry Sidney (1565), Ibid.

9 Brass shines as fair to the ignorant as gold to the goldsmith.
Letter to "the Monk" (ca. 1581), Ibid.

10 I hope you will remember that who seeketh two strings to one bow, he may shoot strong but never straight.
Letter to James VI [of Scotland] (1585), Ibid.

11 No crooked leg, no bleared eye,
No part deformed out of kind,
Nor yet so ugly half can be
As in the inward suspicious mind.
Written in her French psalter, *The Poems of Queen Elizabeth I*, Leicester Bradner, ed. *1964*

12 *Semper eadem.* [Ever the same].
Motto *n.d.*

13 I am no lover of pompous title, but only desire that my name be recorded in a line or two, which shall briefly express my name, my virginity, the years of my reign, the reformation of religion under it, and my preservation of peace.
To her ladies, discussing her epitaph *n.d.*

335. Sofonisba Anguissola (1535/40?–1625)

1 It will be a great pleasure to me if I have gratified your Holiness's wish, but I must add that, if the brush could represent the beauties of the queen's [Isabel of Valois] soul to your eyes, they would be marvelous. However, I have used the utmost

diligence to present what art can show, to tell your Holiness the truth.

> Letter to Pope Pius IV (16 September 1561), Quoted in *The Lives of the Painters, Sculptors, and Architects*, Vol. III by Giorgio Vasari, A. B. Hinds, tr. *1927*

336. Jane Grey (1537–1554)

1 Think not, O mortal, vainly gay,
That thou from human woes art free;
The bitter cup I drink today,
Tomorrow may be drunk by thee.

> Lines written on a prison wall at the Tower of London (1554), Quoted in *Woman's Record* by Sarah Josepha Hale* *1855*

*See 807.

2 One of the greatest benefits that ever God gave me is, that he sent me so sharp and severe parents and so gentle a schoolmaster.

> "The Scholemaster" (1569), *The English Works of Roger Ascham*, William Aldis Wright, ed. *1904*

337. Anna Maria of Braunschweig (fl. 1540s)

1 I'd rather marry a wise old man than a young fool.

> Quoted in *Women of the Reformation, Vol. I; Germany and Italy* by Roland H. Bainton *1971*

338. Lettice Knollys (1540–1634)

1 . . . country life is fittest for disgraced persons.

> Letter to her son, the Earl of Essex (ca. 1595–98), Quoted in *Queen Elizabeth's* Maids of Honor* by Violet A. Wilson *n.d.*

*See 334.

339. Countess de Marcelle (fl. 1540s)

1 By compelling us to return to the world, it is not liberty the Calvinists offer us, but bondage.*

> Ch. 26, Quoted in *The Huguenots of France and America*, Vol. II by Hannah Farnham Lee** *1843*

*The Calvinists attempted to abolish monasteries and convents in France. **See 782.

340. Isabella Whitney (1540?–1573)

1 Some use the teares of Crocodiles,
contrary to their hart:
And yf they cannot alwayes weepe,
they wet their Cheekes by Art.

> "The admonition by the Auctor to all yong Gentilwomen: And to al other Maids being in Love," Sts. 4–5, *Letter 1567?*

2 Gold savours well, though it be got
with occupations vile:
If thou hast gold, thou welcome art,
though virtue thou exile.

> "The 103. Flower," *A Sweet Nosegay or Pleasant Posye Containing a Hundred and Ten Phylosophicall Flowers 1573*

3 Such poor folk as to law do go
are driven oft to curse:
But in mean while, the Lawyer thrives,
the money in his purse.

> "The 104. Flower," Ibid.

341. Mary Queen of Scots (1542–1587)

1 I am no subject to Elizabeth, but an independent queen as well as she; and I will consent to nothing unbecoming the majesty of a crowned head.

> Remark at her trial *October 1586*

2 If ever I have given consent by my words, or even by my thoughts, to any attempt against the life of the Queen of England, far from declining the judgment of men, I shall not even pray for the mercy of God.

> Ibid.

3 Time than fortune should be held more precious
For Fortune is as false as she is specious.

> "Book of Hours" *1579*

4 With sighing and crying bowed down as dying,
I adore thee, I implore thee, set me free!

> Quoted in *Book of Devotion* by Algernon Swinburne* *February 1587*

*British poet and critic (1837–1909).

5 Farewell, France! farewell beloved country, which I shall never more behold!

> (August 1559), Ibid.

6 No more tears now; I will think upon revenge.

> Remarking on the murder of her servant, David Riccio (1566), Quoted in *Memorials of Mary Stewart*, J. Stevenson, ed. *1883*

7 Look to your consciences and remember that the theater of the world is wider than the realm of England.

> Remark at her trial (1586), Quoted in *The Tragedy of Fotheringhay* by Mrs. Maxwell-Scot *1905*

8 As a sinner I am truly conscious of having often offended my Creator and I beg him to forgive me, but as a Queen and Sovereign, I am aware of no fault or offence for which I have to render account to anyone here below.

> To Sir Amyas Paulet (October 1586), Quoted in *Mary, Queen of Scots* by Antonia Fraser* *1969*

*See 2796.

9 In my end is my beginning. *(En ma fin est mon commencement.)*

> Motto, Ibid.

10 Constancy does become all folks well, but none better than princes, and such as have rule over realms.

> Quoted in *Women of the Reformation, Vol. III: From Spain to Scandinavia* by Roland H. Bainton *1977*

342. Isabella de' Medici Orsini (1542–1576)

1 Make yourself happy where you are adored, and on no account seek another abode.

> Letter to her sister-in-law, Bianca Capello (24 September 1572), Quoted in *Famous Women of Florence* by Edgecumbe Staley, tr. *1909*

343. Mary Grey (1543/44–1578)

1 . . . the princes favor is not so soon gotten agayn, and . . . to be without it is such a greff to any true subjectes harte, as no turment can be greater. . . .

> Letter to William Cecil, Lord Burghley (written from prison, 1566), *Original Letters Illustrative of English History*, Vol. II, Henry Ellis, ed. *1824–46*

344. Veronica Franco (1546–1591)

1   Now that my mind is bent on revenge,
    my disrespectful, my rebellious lover,
    step up and arm yourself with what you will.

    What battlefield do you prefer? this place?
    this secret hideaway where I have sampled—
    unwarily—so many bitter sweets?
        Untitled, Sts. 10, 11, Lynne Lawner, tr., *The Penguin Book
        of Women Poets*, Carol Cosman, Joan Keefe, and Kathleen
        Weaver, eds. *1978*

2   Alas! I say now and always will say
    That to live without you is cruel death to me
    And pleasures to me are cruel torments.
        "Lontana dall'Amante e da Venezia" ["Far from my Lover
        and from Venice"], Claudia Alexander with Carlo DiMaio,
        trs., *Poesia italiana: il cinquecento*, Giulio Ferroni, ed. *1978*

345. Catherine Fradonnet (1547–1589)

Coauthor with Madeleine Fradonnet; see 314.

346. Idelette de Bure Calvin (?–1549)

1   O glorious resurrection! God of Abraham and of all our fa-
    thers! The faithful have in so many ages hoped in Thee, and
    not one has been disappointed! I will also hope!
        Ch. 3, Dying words (1549), Quoted in *The Huguenots of
        France and America*, Vol. I by Hannah Farnham Lee* *1843*
        *See 782.

347. Mother Benet (fl. ca. 1550)

1   O man! be content, and let us be thankful; for God hath given
    us enough, if we can see it.
        Quoted in *Actes and monuments of these latter and perillous
        dayes* (a.k.a. *The Book of Martyrs*) by John Foxe *1563*

2   I cannot firkin [store] up my butter, and keep my cheese in the
    chamber and wait a great price, and let the poor want, and so
    displease God.
        Ibid.

348. Elizabeth Bowes (fl. ca. 1550)

1   Alas, wretched woman that I am, for the self-same sins that
    reigned in Sodom and Gomorrah reign in me!
        Letter to John Knox (ca. 1550), Quoted in *Women of the
        Reformation, Vol. III: From Spain to Scandinavia* by Roland
        H. Bainton *1977*

349. Anne Dowriche (1550?–1638?)

1   O noble France (quod he) that bor'st sometime the bell,
    And for thy pleasure and thy wealth all Nations didst excell!
    How art thou now of late with mischiefe so possest,
    That al the Realmes of Christendome thy falshoods do detest?
        The French Historie *1589*

2   As winde disperse the wavring chaffe, and toss it quite away,
    All worldly pompe shall so consume, and pass without delay.
        "Dedicatory poem to her brother," Ibid.

3   Who thinke they swim in wealth (blinded by guile):
    Yet wanting Truth; are wretched, poore and vile.
        Epilogue: "Veritie purtraied by the French pilgrim," St. 1, Ibid.

350. Zofia Olesnicka (fl. ca. 1550)

1   Better to safeguard Thy treasure,
    Which neither moth nor rust can corrupt
    Than enmeshed in the ways of the world
    To forfeit Thy favor forever.
        Hymn, St. 5 (1556), Quoted in *Women of the Reformation,
        Vol. III: From Spain to Scandinavia* by Roland H. Bainton
        1977

351. Renée de Chateauneuf Rieux (1550–1587)

1   Marriage is a lottery in which men stake their liberty and
    women their happiness.
        Attributed *n.d.*

352. Elizabeth Young (fl. 1550s)

1   . . . I had rather all the world should accuse me, than mine own
    conscience.
        Testimony at her first examination, Quoted in *Actes and
        monuments of these latter and perillous days* (a.k.a. *The
        Book of Martyrs*) by John Foxe *1563*

2   If ye take away my meat, I trust God will take away my hunger.
        Testimony at her second examination, Ibid.

3   Here is my carcase: do with it what you will . . . ye can have no
    more but my blood.
        Ibid.

4   No man can be the head of Christ's church; for Christ himself
    is the head, and his word is the governor of all.
        Testimony at her seventh examination, Ibid.

353. Grace Sherrington (1551/2–1620)

1   She [her governess] scoffed at all dalliance, idle talk, and wan-
    ton behaviour appertaining thereto. . . . She counseled us when
    we were alone so to behave ourselves as if all the worlde did
    looke upon us, and to doe nothing in secret whereof our con-
    science might accus us. . . .
        Quoted in *Diary of Lady Margaret Hoby*,* Dorothy M.
        Meads, ed. *1930*
        *See 375.

2   If all fathers and mothers were . . . provident and careful, and
    governors and governesses put in trust by them were diligent
    and faithful in performing their trust, so many parents should
    not be discomfited as they are in their age by the wickedness
    and misfortunes of their children.
        Ibid.

354. Gabrielle de Coignard (1552?–1594)

1   I'm dust and ashes, Lord; remember this.

    You are the wind and I am straw, or less,
    For you can sweep me into nothingness.
    Ah, do not let me fall in the abyss!
        "Prayer," Sts. 3–4, Raymond Oliver, tr., *Women Poets of the
        World*, Joanna Bankier and Deirdre Lashgari, eds. *1983*

355. Lucrezia Gonzaga (?–1552?)

1   . . . a poor man's life is like sailing near the coast, whereas that
    of a rich man resembles the condition of those who are in the
    main sea. The former can easily throw a cable on the shore,

and bring their ship safe into a harbour; whereas the latter cannot do it without much danger and difficulty.

Letter to Hortensio Lando, Quoted in *Woman's Record* by Sarah Josepha Hale* *1855*

*See 807.

2 . . . all things are good which are according to nature, and what is there more natural to all men than death?

Letter to Ippolita Gonzaga (ca. 1552), Quoted in *A Princess of the Italian Reformation: Giulia Gonzaga* by Christopher Hare** *1912*

*See 306. **Pseudonym of Marian Andrews.

3 . . . he alone acts wisely who, being mortal, expects nothing from this life of ours but mortal things.

Ibid.

356. Marguerite of Valois (1553–1615)

1 Joy takes far away from us the thoughts of our actions; sorrow it is that awakens the soul.

Memoirs (1594–1600) *1628*

2 . . . mistrust is the sure forerunner of hatred.

Letter IX, Ibid.

3 Adversity is solitary, while prosperity dwells in a crowd.

Letter XII, Ibid.

4 Science conducts us, step by step, through the whole range of creation, until we arrive, at length, at God.

Ibid.

5 In my sadness and solitude, I rediscovered the great gifts of study and devotion—gifts which, among the vanities and magnificence of my former good fortune, I had never truly tasted.

Ibid.

6 . . . let no one ever say that marriages are made in Heaven; the gods would not commit so great an injustice!

Letter to Jacques de Harlan (1582), Quoted in *Queen of Hearts* by Charlotte Haldane *1968*

357. Moderata Fonte (1555–1592)

1 And when it's said that women must be subject to men, the phrase should be understood in the same sense as when we say we are subject to natural disasters, diseases, and all the other accidents of this life: it's not a case of being subjected in the sense of obeying, but rather of suffering an imposition, not a case of serving them fearfully, but rather of tolerating them in a spirit of Christian charity, since they have been given to us by God as a spiritual trial.

The Worth of Women (p. 59; repr. 1996) *1600**

*Fonte's daughter, Cecelia, published her mother's manuscript eight years after her death from childbirth at age 37.

2 Men were created before women. But that doesn't prove their superiority—rather, it proves ours, for they were born out of the lifeless earth in order that we could be born out of living flesh. And what's so important about this priority in creation, anyway?

(p. 60) Ibid.

3 But we should not think that they behave like this only towards our sex, for even among themselves they deceive one another, rob one another, destroy one another, and try to do each other down. Just think of all the assassinations, usurpations, perjuries, the blasphemy, gaming, gluttony, and other such vicious deeds they commit all the time! Not to mention the murders, assaults, and thefts, and other dissolute acts, all proceeding from men! And if they have so few scruples about committing these kind of excesses, think of what they are like where minor vices are concerned: just give a thought to their ingratitude, faithlessness, falsity, cruelty, arrogance, lust, and dishonesty.

(p. 61) Ibid.

4 "Do you really believe," Cornelia replied, "that everything historians tell us about men—or about women—is actually true? You ought to consider the fact that these histories have been written by men, who never tell the truth except by accident."

(p. 77) Ibid.

5 "Homer used to say that men without wives were scarcely alive."

(p. 91) Ibid.

6 For it was with a good end in mind—that of acquiring the knowledge of good and evil—that Eve allowed herself to be carried away and eat the forbidden fruit. But Adam was not moved by this desire for knowledge, but simply by greed: he ate it because he heard Eve say it tasted good, which was a worse motive and caused more displeasure. And that is the reason why God did not chase them from Paradise as soon as Eve sinned, but rather after Adam had disobeyed him—in other words, he didn't respond to Eve's action, but Adam's prompted him to give both the punishment they deserved, which was and is common to all humankind.

(p. 94) Ibid.

7 Couldn't we live without them? Couldn't we earn our living and manage our affairs without help from them? Come on, let's wake up, and claim back our freedom, and the honor and dignity that they have usurped from us for so long.

(p. 237) Ibid.

358. Margaret Clitherow (1556?–1586)

1 They that think much and are not willing to do such base things [as housework], have little regard of well-doing or knowledge of themselves.

Quoted in *A True Report of the Life and Martyrdom of Mrs. Margaret Clitherow* by Fr. John Mush *1586*

2 God forbid that I should will any to do that in my house which I would not willingly do myself. . . .

Ibid.

359. Anne Dacre Howard (1557–1630)

1 In sad and ashy weeds I sigh. . . .

Elegy on the Death of Her Husband, St. 1 (1595), *The Women Poets in English*, Ann Stanford, ed. *1972*

2 I envy aire because it dare
Still breathe, and he not so;
Hate earthe, that doth entomb his youth,
And who can blame my Owe?

St. 3, Ibid.

360. Joyce Lewes (?–1557)

1 I thank my God that he will make me worthy to adventure my life in his quarrel.

At her execution (1557), Quoted in *Actes and monuments of these latter and perillous dayes* (a.k.a. *The Book of Martyrs*) by John Foxe *1563*

361. Wife of Prest (?–1558)

1   How save you souls, when you preach nothing but damnable lies. . . .

> Testimony to examining bishop, Quoted in *Actes and monuments of these latter and perillous dayes* (a.k.a. *The Book of Martyrs*) by John Foxe *1563*

2   God forbid that I should lose the life eternal, for this carnal and short life.

> At her execution (1558), Ibid.

362. Catherine de Bourbon (1559–1604)

1   . . . [King Henry of] Navarre can ill brook *words* when *deeds* are so much wanted.

> Ch. 15, Remark to Count de Soissons, Quoted in *The Huguenots of France and America*, Vol. I by Hannah Farnham Lee* *1843*
> *See 782.

2   Command me, my King, to make you a little page, for I fear that unless you command it yourself, he will not consent to lodge in my body.

> Letter to her brother, Henry IV of France (18 August 1599), Quoted in *Queen of Navarre: Jeanne d'Albret,** Nancy Lyman Roelker, tr. *1968*
> *See 327.

363. Blanche Parry (fl. ca. 1560)

1   . . . madam . . . if you ever marry without the Queen's [Elizabeth I*] writing, you and your husband will be undone, and your fate worse than that of my Lady Jane.**

> Letter to Lady Catherine Grey (ca. 1560), Quoted in *Queen Elizabeth's** Maids of Honor* by Violet A. Wilson *n.d.*
> *See 334. **Sister of Lady Catherine, see 336; subsequently, Catherine was imprisoned after her secret marriage to the earl of Hertford.

364. Rachel Susman Ashkenazi (fl. 1560s)

1   The saying, "Out of sight, out of mind" is not always correct. For a mother who has experienced pain does not do so. She does not forget the pain she suffered with her child.

> Letter to her son, Moses in Cairo (3 October 1567), *Four Centuries of Jewish Women's Spirituality*, Ellen M. Umansky* and Dianne Ashton, eds. *1992*
> *See 4011.

365. Mary Sidney Herbert (1561–1621)

1   My fellow, my companion, held most dear,
My soul, my other self, my inward friend

> Psalm LV, "Exaudi, Deus," St. 4, *The Psalmes of David* (ca. 1593), C. Whittingham, ed. *1823*

2   There is a God that carves to each his own.

> Psalm LVIII, *"Si Vere Utique,"* St. 4, Ibid.

3   O sun, whom light nor flight can match,
Suppose thy lightful flightful wings
Thou lend to me,
And I could flee
As far as thee the ev'ning brings

> Psalm CXXXIX, "Domine, Probasti," St. 5, Ibid.

4   If ever hapless woman had a cause
To breathe her plaints into the open air,

And never suffer inward grief to pause,
Or seek her sorrow-shaken soul's repair:
Then I, for I have lost my only brother,*
Whose like this age can scarcely yield another.

> "If Ever Hapless Woman Had a Cause," St. 1 (ca. 1599), Quoted in *The Woman Poets in English* by Ann Stanford *1972*
> *The poet Sir Philip Sidney (1554–1586), with whom she jointly translated the first 43 psalms.

366. Penelope Devereaux Rich (1562/63–post-1605)

1   . . . they will seem . . . such crafty workmen as will not only pull downe all the obstacles of theyr greatnes, but when they are in theyr full strengths (like gyants) make warr agaynst Heaven.

> Letter to Queen Elizabeth I* (1599), Quoted *in Society Women of Shakespeare's Time* by Violet A. Wilson *1924*
> *See 334.

2   Faction . . . careth not upon whose neck they buyld the walles of theyr owne fortunes . . .

> Ibid.

367. Elizabeth Grymeston (1563?–1603)

1   Crush the serpent in the head,
Break ill eggs ere they be hatched.
Kill bad chickens in the tread,
Fledged they hardly can be catched.
In the rising stifle ill,
Lest it grow against thy will.

> *Miscelanea: Prayer, Meditations, Memoratives 1604*

2   Our best life is to die well: for living her we enjoy nothing: things past are dead and gone: things present are always ending: things future always beginning: while we live we die; and we leave dying when we leave living.

> Ch. 4, Ibid.

3   If thou givest a benefit, keep it close; but if thou receivest one, publish it, for that invites another.

> Ch. 20, "Memoratives," Ibid.

4   Be not at any time idle. Alexander's* soldiers should scale molehills rather than rest unoccupied; it is the woman that sitteth still that imagineth mischief; it is the rolling stone that riseth clean, and the running water that remaineth clear.

> Ibid.
> *Alexander the Great or Alexander III (356–323 b.c.e.), king of Macedon; incontestably one of the greatest generals of all time.

5   There be four good mothers have four bad daughters: Truth hath Hatred; Prosperity hath Pride; Security hath Peril, and Familiarity hath Contempt.

> Ibid.

6   A fair woman is a paradise to the eye, a purgatory to the purse, and a hell to the soul.

> Ibid.

368. Ho Nansorhon (1563–1589)

1   Yesterday I fancied I was young;
But already, alas, I am aging.

> "A Woman's Sorrow," Peter H. Lee, tr., *The Penguin Book of Women Poets*, Carol Cosman, Joan Keefe, and Kathleen Weaver, eds. *1978*

2   Numberless are the sorrowful.

> Untitled, Ibid.

369. Marie le Jars de Gournay (1565–1645)

1   Suppose we believed that the Scriptures indeed order woman to submit to the authority of man because she cannot think as well as he can, see here the absurdity that would follow: women would be worthy of having been made in the likeness of the Creator, worthy of taking part in the holy Eurcharist, of sharing the mysteries of the Redemption, Paradise, worthy of the vision, even possession, of God, but not of the status and privileges of men. Wouldn't we be saying then that men are more precious and sacred than all these things, and wouldn't that be the most grievous blasphemy?

> *The Equality of Men and Women 1622*

2   . . . even if a woman has only the name of being educated she will be evilly spoken of.

> *Proumenoir* (1594), Quoted in *A Daughter of the Renaissance*
> by Marjorie Henry Ilsley *1963*

3   I am on the side of those who believe that vice comes from stupidity and consequently that the nearer one draws to wisdom the farther one gets from vice.

> Preface to *Essais* by Montaigne (1595), Ibid.

4   Knowledge not based on ethics cannot . . . bring real honor nor profit to its master. . . .

> "Advis" (1634), Ibid.

5   Since language and speech are the cement of human society whoever falsifies them should be punished for counterfeit or for poisoning the public water well.

> Ibid.

6   Society is a cage of idiots.

> "A Lenten" (1634), Ibid.

370. Elizabeth Raleigh (1565–1647)

1   I wish she would be as ambitious to do good as she is apt to the contrary.

> Letter to Sir Robert Cecil (ca. 1601), Quoted in *Society
> Women of Shakespeare's Time* by Violet A. Wilson *1924*

371. Elizabeth Joceline (1566–1622)

1   . . . all the delight a Parent may take in a child is honey mingled with gall.

> Introduction, *The Mothers Legacie to her Unborne Childe*
> *1624*

2   Drunkennesse . . . is the highway to hell. . . .

> Ch. 9, Ibid.

3   . . . there is nothing more contrary to our wicked nature than this loving our neighbour as our selves. Wee can with ease envie him if hee be rich, or scorne him if he be poore; but love him?

> Ch. 10, Ibid.

372. Aemilia Lanyer (1569–1645)

1   If Eve did err, it was for knowledge sake,
   No subtle Serpent's falsehood did betray him,
   If he would eat it, who had power to stay him?

> "Eve's Apology," *Salve Deus Rex Judeorum* (Hail, God, King
> of the Jews) *1611*

2   Then let us [women] have our liberty again,
   And challenge to your selves no sovereignty;
   You came not in the world without our pain,
   Make that a bar against your cruelty;
   Your fault being greater, why should you disdain
   Our being your equals, free from tyranny?

> Ibid.

3   As also in respect it pleased our Lord and Savior Jesus Christ, without the assistance of man, being free from original and all other sins, from the time of his conception, till the hour of his death, to be begotten of a woman, borne of a woman, nourished of a woman, obedient to a woman; and that he healed woman, pardoned women, comforted women: yea, even when he was in his greatest agony and bloody sweat, going to be crucified, and also in the last hour of his death, took care to dispose of a woman: after his resurrection, appeared first to a woman, sent a woman to declare his most glorious resurrection to the rest of his Disciples.

> Introduction, Ibid.

373. Frances Walsingham (1569–1631)

1   I will have more care of my self for your little one's sake.

> Letter to her husband, the Earl of Essex (ca. 1599), Quoted
> in *Society Women of Shakespeare's Time* by Violet A. Wilson
> *1924*

2   Simple thankes is a slender recompens. . . .

> Letter to Robert Cecil (December 1599), Ibid.

374. Antoinette de Pons Guercheville (1570–1632)

1   If I am not noble enough to be your wife, I am too much so to be your mistress.

> Remark to Henry IV,* Quoted in *Biography of Distinguished
> Women* by Sarah Josepha Hale** *1876*
> *Known as "Henry of Navarre," King of France (1589–1610) who
> founded the Bourbon royal line (1553–1610). **See 807.

2   A king, wherever he is, should always be master. As to myself, I also choose to be free.

> Message to Henry IV, Ibid.

375. Margaret Hoby (1570–1633)

1   . . . it is not sufficient only to have faith . . . but I must likewise pray especially for that virtue which is opposed to that vice whereunto I am then tempted.

> Diary Entry (10 December 1599), *Diary of Lady Margaret
> Hoby,* Dorothy M. Meads, ed. *1930*

2   They are unworthy of God's benefits and special favors that can find no time to make a thankful record of them.

> Diary Entry (1 April 1605), Ibid.

376. Lucrezia Marinella (1571–1653)

1   It is an amazing thing to see in our city [Venice] the wife of a shoemaker, or a butcher, or a porter dressed in silk with chains of gold at the throat, with pearls and a ring of good value . . . and then in contrast to see her husband cutting the meat, all smeared with cow's blood, poorly dressed, or burdened like an ass, clothed with the stuff from which sacks are made . . . but whoever considers this carefully will find it reasonable, because it is necessary that the lady, even if low-born and humble, be draped with such clothes for her natural excellence and

dignity, and that the man less adorned as if a slave, or a little ass, born to her service.

The Nobility and Excellence of Women together with the Defects and Deficiencies of Men 1600

377. Katherine Stubbes (1571–1591/92)

1 I would rather be a door keeper in the house of my God, than to dwell in the tents of the wicked.

Spoken during her final illness, Quoted in *Women of the Reformation, Vol. III: From Spain to Scandinavia* by Roland H. Bainton *1977*

378. Elizabeth Vernon (1572?–1648?)

1 . . . ever you like best I should be, that place shall be most pleasing to me. . . .

Letter to her husband, Henry Wriothesley, third earl of Southampton (8 July 1599), Quoted in *Society Women of Shakespeare's Time* by Violet A. Wilson *1924*

379. Elizabeth Clinton (1574–1630?)

1 Now who shall deny the own mother's suckling of their own children to be their duty, since every godly matron hath walked in these steps before them: Eve,* the mother of all the living; Sarah,** the mother of all the faithful; Hannah,*** so graciously heard of God; Mary,**** blessed among women, and called blessed of all ages.

The Countess of Lincoln's Nurserie 1622
*See 1. **See 45. ***See 30. ****See 79.

2 Whatsoever things are true, whatsoever things are honest . . . whatsoever things are just, whatsoever things are pure, whatsoever things are of good report . . . think on these things; these things do, and the God of peace shall be with you.

Ibid.

380. Feng Meng-lung (1574–1645)

1 When a crummy horse has no bridle, who enjoys the ride?

"My Old Man's Small," 1, Richard W. Bodman, tr. *World of Poetry*, Katharine Washburn and John S. Major, eds., Clifton Fadiman,* general ed. *1998*
*American writer and editor (1904–1999)

2 We share the same bedcurtains but not the same pillow.

2, Ibid.

3 But I rashly carried my lover into bed and out again
The two of us sharing a single pair of shoes.

"Smart," Richard W. Bodman, tr., Ibid.

381. Beatrice Cenci (1577–1599)

1 I am no Turk and no dog that I should wish to shed my own blood.

Testimony at her trial (1599), Quoted in *Beatrice Cenci* by Corrado Ricci, Morris Bishop, and Henry Longan Stuart, tr. *1925*

2 I no longer know what to do in order not to fall from one evil into another, and even though I slew myself, I would fall under the curse of the Holy Father.

Letter to her defense lawyer, Prospero Farinaccio (1599), Ibid.

3 Alas! Alas! O Madonna *santissima,* aid me! . . . Let me down! I will tell the truth.

Remark during torture on the rack (1599), Ibid.

382. Nur Jahan (1577–1645)

1 My eyes have one job: to cry.

Untitled, Willis Barnstone, tr., *A Book of Women Poets*, Aliki and Willis Barnstone, eds. *1980*

2 The key to my locked spirit is your laughing mouth.

Ibid.

383. Jane Anger (fl. ca. 1580)

1 Was there ever any so abused, so slandered, so railed upon, so wickedly handled undeservedly, as are we women.

Introduction, *For Protection for Women* 1589
*Written in response to *Boke His Surfeit in Love, with a farwel to the folies of his own phantasie* (1588) by Thomas Orwin.

2 Wild are men's lusts, false are their lips, besmeared with flattery

"A Protection for Women Etc.," Ibid.

3 The man that is of Cuckolds lot afraid,
From Lechery he ought for to refrain,
Else shall he have the plague he does forlorn:
and ought (perforce constrained) to wear the horn.

Ibid.

4 The lion rages when he is hungry, but man rails when he is glutted.

Ibid.

5 Deceit will give you fair words, & pick your pockets: nay he will pluck out your hearts, if you be not wary.

Ibid.

384. Anna of Saxony (fl. ca. 1580)

1 . . . many pregnant women in confinement and small children of noble as well as of common rank are often miserably neglected, injured, harmed and crippled at the time of the birth or in the following six weeks, all through the clumsiness, arrogance, and rashness of the midwives and assisting women; few sensible mid-wives are to be found in this country [Germany].

(ca. 1587), Quoted in *Women in the Middle Ages* by Sibylle Harksen *1975*

385. Mistress Bradford (fl. ca. 1580)

1 As Hanna* did applie, dedicate, and give her first child and sonne Samuel unto thee: even so doo I deere Father; beseeching thee, for Christ's sake, to accept this my gift.

"The praier that maister Bradford's mother said and offered unto God in his behalfe, a little before his martyrdom,"** *The Monument of Matrones conteining seven severall Lamps of Virginitie, or Distinct Treatises . . .*, Thomas Bentley, ed. *1582*
*See 30. **Her son, John Bradford, executed ca. 1582 for heresy.

386. Alice Harvey (fl. ca. 1580–d. 1600)

1 All the speed is in the morning.

Quoted in *Commonplace Book* by Gabriel Harvey *ca. 1580*

387. Margaret Lambrun (fl. ca. 1580)

1 I confess to you, that I suffered many struggles within my breast, and have made all possible efforts to divert my resolution from so pernicious a design, but all in vain; I found myself necessitated to prove by experience the certain truth of that

maxim, that neither reason nor force can hinder a woman from vengeance, when she is impelled thereto by love.

> Remark to Queen Elizabeth I* when caught attempting to assassinate her (1587), Quoted in *Biography of Distinguished Women* by Sarah Josepha Hale** *1876*
> *See 334. **See 807.

2   Your majesty ought to grant me a pardon [without assurances from me]. . . . A favour given under . . . restraint is no more a favour; and, in so doing, your majesty would act against me as a judge.

> Ibid.

388. Ann Wheathill (fl. ca. 1580)

1   . . . humilitie . . . the beautiful flowre of vertue that groweth in the garden of man's soule. . . .

> Prayer 9, *A Handfull of holesome (though homelie) Hearbs, gathered out of the Godlie Garden of Gods most Holie Word: for the common Benefit and comfortable Exercise of all such as are Devoutlie Disposed* *1584*

2   The young chickens, when the kite striketh at them, have no other refuge but to run dickering under the wings of the hen: no more hath mankind any other defense against his enemies, but onelie the covering of Thy grace, and the shaddowe of Thy most precious passion. . . .

> Prayer 28, Ibid.

389. Lucy Harington (1581–1627)

1   Death be not proud, thy hand gave not this blow. . . .

> "Elegy," l.1, Quoted in *The Woman Poets in English* by Ann Stanford *1972*

2   And teach this hymn of her with joy and sing,
The grave no conquest gets, Death hath no sting.

> "Elegy," last line, Ibid.

390. Elizabeth Melvill (1582?–1640)

1   The brain of man most surely did invent
That purging place, he answer'd me again:
For greediness together they consent
To say that souls in torment may remain,
Till gold and goods relieve them of their pain.

> *Ane Godlie Dreame Complit in Scottish Meter be M.M., Gentilwoman in Cul Ross, at the Request of her Friendes*, St. 1 *1606*

2   The fire was great, the heat did pierce me sore;
My faith was weak, my grip was wondrous small,
I trembled fast, my fear grew more and more. . . .

> St. 8, Ibid.

391. Elizabeth Carew (1585?–1639)

1   CHORUS. Tis not enough for one that is a wife
To keep her spotless from an act of ill:
But from suspicion she should free her life,
And bare herself of power as well as will.

> Act III, *The Tragedie of Mariam the Faire Queene of Jewry* *1613*

2   For in a wife it is no worse to find
A common body, than a common mind.

> Ibid.

3   CHORUS. The fairest action of our human life,
Is scorning to revenge an injury;
For who forgives without a further strife,
His adversary's heart to him doth tie:
And 't is a firmer conquest, truly said,
To win the heart, and overthrow the head.

> Act IV, Sc. 1, Ibid.

4   When she hath spacious ground to walk upon
Why on the ridge should she desire to go?

> Ibid.

392. Catalina de Erauso (1585–post-1624)

1   I went out of the convent; I found myself in the street, without knowing where to go; that was no matter; all I wanted was liberty.

> Quoted in *Biography of Distinguished Women* by Sarah Josepha Hale* *1876*
> *See 807.

2   In this attempt [to cross the deserts of the Andes] I *may* find death; by remaining here [in this sanctuary] I shall certainly find it.

> Ibid.

393. Mary Ward (1585–1645)

1   Fervour is not placed in feelings but in will to do well, which women may have as well as men. There is no such difference between men and women that women may not do great things as we have seen by example of many saints who have done great things.

> Quoted in *The Life of Mary Ward* by Mary Catherine Elizabeth Chambers *1884*

394. Francesca Caccini (1587–1640?)

1   I would rather lose my life before the desire to study and the affection I have always had for virtue, because this is worth more than all treasure and all grandeur.

> Letter to Michelangelo Buonarroti the Younger (Genoa, 26 May 1617), Quoted in *Women in Music* by Carol Neuls-Bates *1982*

395. Mary Sidney Wroth (1587–1651/53)

1   . . . wounds still cureless, must my rulers be.

> "Morea's Sonnet," St. 2, *The Countess of Montgomeries Urania* ca. *1615*

2   Had I not happy been, I had not known
So great a loss; a king deposed feels most
The torment of a throne-like-want when lost . . .

> "Pamphilia's Sonnet," St. 3, Ibid.

3   O Memory, could I but lose thee now . . .

> "Lindamira's Complaint," last line, Ibid.

396. Anne Clifford (1590–1676)

1   I am like an owl in the desert.

> Diary Entry (May 1616), *The Diary of the Lady Anne Clifford*, Vita Sackville-West,* ed. *1923*
> *See 1752.

2   I . . . strived to sit as merry a face as I could upon a discontented heart . . . knowing that God often brings things to pass by contrary means.

> Diary Entry (March 1617), Ibid.

397. Elizabeth Compton (fl. ca. 1590)

1 I would have two gentlewomen, lest one should be sick....
It is an indecent thing for a gentlewoman to stand mumping
alone when God hath blessed their Lord and Lady with a great
estate.

> Letter to her husband William, earl of Northampton, Quoted
> in *Court of King James* by Bishop Godfrey Goodman *1839*

398. Maria de Zayas y Sotomayor (1590–1661/69)

1 In conclusion, I have held her penned up, in the condition that
you have seen, for two years. She eats and drinks no more than
that ration which was allotted to her today. A heap of straw is
her only bed and the nook in which she stays is not any larger
than the space occupied by her reclining body. Her sole companion is the skull of her treacherous, beloved cousin.

> "Too Late for Disillusionment" *ca. 1637–47*

399. Anne Hutchinson (1591–1643)

1 An oath, sir, is an end of all strife, and it is God's ordinance.

> Spoken at her trial in Boston (1 November 1637), Quoted in
> *Antinomianism in the Colony of Massachusetts Bay, 1636–*
> *1638*, Charles Francis Adams, ed. *1894*

2 I thinke the soule to be nothing but Light.

> Ibid.

3 What from the Church at Boston? I know no such church, neither will I own it. Call it the whore and strumpet of Boston, no
Church of Christ!

> Remark (ca. 1638), Ibid.

400. Margaret Winthrop (1591?–1647)

1 I have many reasons to make me love thee, whereof I will name
two, first because thou lovest God, and secondly because that
thou lovest me.

> Letter to John Winthrop,* *The Winthrop Papers*, Samuel E.
> Morison et al., eds. *1929*
> *English colonial administrator (1588–1649); first governor of
> Massachusetts Bay Colony (1629–1649).

401. Nahabed Kouchak (?–1592)

1 My heart is turned into a wailing child,
In vain with sweets I seek to still its cries;
Sweet love, it calls for thee in sobbing wild
All day and night, with longing and with sighs.
What solace can I give it?

> "My Heart Is Turned into a Wailing Child," St. 1, *Armenian
> Legends and Poems*, Zabelle C. Boyajian, ed. *1916*

2 On the morning of thy birth
We were glad but thou wert wailing
See that when thou leav'st the earth
Thou art glad and we bewailing.

> "Birthday Song," St. 1, Ibid.

402. Sarah Copia Sullam (1592–1641)

1 The lying tongue's deceit with silence blight,
Protect me from its venom, you, my Rock,
And show the spiteful sland'rer by this sign
That you will shield me with your endless might.

> "My Inmost Hope," *A Treasury of Jewish Poetry,* Nathan and
> Maryann Ausubel, eds. *1957*

403. Artemisia Gentileschi (1593–1651/53)

1 As long as I live, I will have control over my being....

> Letter to Don Antonio Ruffo, a patron (March 1649), Quoted
> in *Women Artists: 1550–1950* by Ann Sutherland Harris and
> Linda Nochlin *1976*

2 You will find the spirit of Caesar in the soul of this woman.

> (November 1649), Ibid.

404. Pocahontas (1595?–1617)

1 You promised my father [Chief Powhatan] that whatever was
yours should be his, and that you and he would be all one.
Being a stranger in our country, you called Powhatan father;
and I for the same reason will now call you so.

> Remark to Captain John Smith* (ca. 1616), Quoted in
> *Women of Beauty and Heroism* by Frank B. Goodrich *1858*
> *English colonist, explorer and writer (1580–1631).

405. Rachel Speght (1597–1630?)

1 Some dogs barke more upon custome then curstnesse; and
some speake evill of others, not that the defamed deserve it,
but because through custome and corruption of their hearts
they cannot speak well of any.

> "Epistole Dedicatorie," *A Mouzell for Melastomus, the
> Cynicall Bayter of, and foule mouthed Barker against Evahs
> Sex. Or an apologeticall Answere to that Irreligius and
> Illiterate Pamphlet made by Jo[seph] Sw[etnam] and by him
> intituled, The Arraignment of Women 1617*

2 ... man was created of the dust of the earth, but woman was
made of a part of man, after that he was a living soule: yet was
shee not produced from Adam's foote, to be his too low infer-
iour; nor from his head to be his superiour, but from his side,
neare his heart, to be his equall....

> "Essay," Ibid.

3 For as Christ turned water into wine, a farre more excellent
liquor ... So the single man is by marriage changed from
Batchelour to a Husband, a farre more excellent title: from a
solitarie life unto a joyfull union....

> Ibid.

4 Marriage is a merri-age, and this world's Paradise, where there
is mutual love.

> Ibid.

5 Corne kept close in a garner feeds not the hungry; A candle put
under a bushell doth not illuminate an house ...

> Dedication, *Mortalitie's Memorandum, with a Dreame
> Prefixed, imaginarie in manner, reall in matter 1621*

6 Readers too common, and plentifull be;
For Readers they are that can read a, b, c.
And utter their verdict on what they doe view,
Though none of the Muses they yet euer knew.

> Prefatory Verse, in toto, Ibid.

7 And from the soul three faculities arise.
The mind, the will, the power; then wherefore shall
A woman have her intellect in vain
Or not endeavor Knowledge to attain.

> "A Dream," St. 14, Ibid.

406. Lucy Hay (1599–1660)

1 Spell well, if you can.

> *Thoughts n.d.*

407. Marie de L'Incarnation (1599–1672)

1 The air is excellent and in consequence this [Quebec] is an earthly paradise where crosses and thorns grow so lovingly that the more one is pricked by them, the more filled with tenderness is the heart.

> Letter to Mother Marie-Gillette Roland (1640), Quoted in
> *Word from New France* by Joyce Marshall *1967*

2 We see nothing, we walk gropingly, and . . . ordinary things do not come about as they have been foreseen and advised. One falls and, just when one thinks oneself at the bottom of an abyss, one finds oneself on one's feet.

> Letter to her son (1652), Ibid.

3 Everything is savage here [Quebec], the flowers as well as the men.

> Letter to her sister (1653), Ibid.

4 . . . if God strikes us with one hand, he consoles us with another.

> Letter to her son (1665), Ibid.

5 Writing teaches us our mysteries. . . .

> Letter to her son (1670), Ibid.

408. Madeleine de Souvré de Sablé (1599–1678)

1 Instead of taking care to acquaint ourselves with others, we only think of making ourselves known to them. It would be better to listen to other people in order to become enlightened rather than to speak so as to shine in front of them.

> *The Maxims of Madame de Sablé,* Arthur Chandler, tr. *1665*

2 Often the desire to appear competent impedes our ability to become competent, because we are more anxious to display our knowledge than to learn what we do not know.

> Ibid.

3 Mean-spirited mediocrities, especially those with a smattering of learning, are the most likely to be opinionated. Only strong minds know how to correct their opinions and abandon a bad position.

> Ibid.

4 It is such a great fault to talk too much that, in business and conversation, if what is good is also brief, it is doubly good, and one gains by brevity what one often loses by an excess of words.

> Ibid.

5 We judge matters so superficially that ordinary acts and words, done and spoken with some flair and some knowledge of worldly matters, often succeed better than the greatest cleverness.

> Ibid.

6 Man's greatest wisdom consists in knowing his own follies.

> Ibid.

7 To know how to unveil the inner workings of others, and how to hide one's own, is the great mark of the superior intellect.

> Ibid.

8 Sometimes we praise the way things used to be in order to blame the present, and we esteem what is no longer in order to scorn what is.

> Ibid.

9 Wealth does not teach us to transcend the desire for wealth. The possession of many goods does not bring the repose of not desiring them.

> Ibid.

409. Devorah Ascarelli (fl. ca. 1600)

1 Although a beautiful shock of golden hair swings across her forehead
And love finds nourishment in her eyes
The chaste Susannah never strays from the right path
And harbors not one thought without the Lord.

> Untitled poem, Quoted in *Written Out of History: Jewish*
> *Foremothers* by Sondra Henry and Emily Taitz *1990*

410. Virginie des Rieux (fl. 16th century)

1 "Gentlemen, in life, there is one thing that fascinates everybody, and that's rear ends. Talk about backsides and only backsides, and you will have friends everywhere always."

> Ch. 1, *La Satyre 1967 rev.*

2 Marriage is a lottery in which men stake their liberty and women their happiness.

> *Epigram n.d.*

411. Brilliana Harley (1600–1643)

1 . . . that is the evil in melancholy; it acts most, inwardly; full of thoughts they are, but not active in expressions. Many times they are so long in studying what is fit for them to do, that the opportunity is past.

> Letter to her son, Edward (4 January 1638), *Letters of the*
> *Lady Brilliana Harley,* Thomas Taylor Lewis, ed. *1854*

2 . . . man is so forgetful of his God, that all, and most of all great men, live in prosperity as if they were lords of what they had, forgetting that they are but tenants at will.

> Letter to her son (29 November 1639), Ibid.

3 . . . keep your heart above the world, and then you will not be troubled at the changes in it.

> Letter to her son (15 July 1642), Ibid.

412. Bathsua Makin (1600?–1675?)

1 . . . these men of Law and their confederates . . . the caterpillars of this Kingdom, who with their uncontrolled exactions and extortions, eat up the free-born people of this Nation. . . .

> *The Malady . . . and Remedy of Vexations and Unjust Arrests*
> *and Actions 1646*

2 A Learned woman is thought to be a comet, that bodes mischief whenever it appears.

> *An Essay to Revive the Ancient Education of the*
> *Gentlewomen 1673*

3 One generation passeth away and another cometh, but the earth, the theatre on which we act, abideth forever.

> Ibid.

4 Merely to teach gentlewomen to frisk and dance, to paint their faces, to curl their hair, to put on a whisk,* to wear gay clothes, is not truly to adorn, but to adulterate their bodies; yea (what is worse) to defile their souls.

> Ibid.

*A woman's scarf, worn around the neck.

5 Had God intended women only as a finer sort of cattle, He would not have made them reasonable. Brutes, a few degrees

higher than . . . monkeys . . . might have better fitted some men's lust, pride, and pleasure; especially those that desire to keep them ignorant to be tyrannized over.

Ibid.

6 . . . a little philosophy, carries a man from God, but a great deal brings him back again.

Ibid.

7 . . . a little knowledge, like windy bladders, puffs up, but a good measure of true knowledge, like ballast in a ship, settles down and makes a person move more even in his station; 'tis not knowing too much, but too little that causes irregularity.

Ibid.

413. Ann Sutcliffe (fl. ca. 1600–d. 1630)

1 . . . remember thy dayes of Darknes, for they are many.

Meditations of Man's Moralitie, Or, a Way to true Blessednesse, 2nd ed. *1634*

2 . . . the Glory of this World, is but the singing of Syrens, sweet but a deadly poison.

Ibid.

3 Pride, in it selfe doth beare a poyson'd breath. . . .

Ibid.

414. Anne of Austria (1601–1666)

1 God does not pay at the end of every week, but He pays.

Letter to Cardinal Mazarin, *Letters n.d.*

415. María de Agreda (1602–1664/65)

1 Earth has 2,502 leagues, and up to the half of it, which is the place or seat of Hell, there are 1,251 leagues of profundity. In this center or middle of the Earth are the Purgatory and the Limbo. Hell has many caverns and mansions of punishment, and everything in there forms a big infernal cavern with a mouth in it, and is a proven fact that there is a big stone, bigger than the mouth, to cover it, when Hell will be sealed with all the sinners inside of it, where they have to suffer for all the eternities to come.

Quoted in *Women in Myth and History* by Violeta Miqueli *1962*

416. Priscilla Alden (1602?–pre-1687)

1 John, why do you not speak for yourself?*

Quoted in *Collections of American Epitaphs and Inscriptions with Original Notes,* Vol. III, Rev. Timothy Alden, ed. *1814*
*Reply to John Alden, Pilgrim colonist (1559?–1687), who was intervening on behalf of Miles Standish, English colonial settler in America (1584?–1656).

417. Violante do Céu (1602?–1693)

1 . . . the end which ends with no way out.

"Voice of a Dissipated Woman Inside a Tomb, Talking to Another Woman Who Presumed to Enter a Church with the Purpose of Being Seen and Praised by Everyone, Who Sat Down Near a Sepulchar Containing This Epitaph, Which Curiously Reads," *Rimas Varias 1646*

418. Anna Maria Marchocka (1603–1652)

1 Humbly I beseech Thee, my Father. Cover me with Thy pinions, enlighten mine eyes that I wander not in a haze, knowing not what to write nor where.

Prayer found in her *Autobiography,* Quoted in *Women of the Reformation, Vol. III: From Spain to Scandinavia* by Roland H. Bainton *1977*

419. Arcangela Tarabotti (1604–1652)

1 When women are seen with pen in hand, they are met immediately with shrieks commanding a return to that life of pain which their writing had interrupted, a life devoted to the women's work of needle and distaff.

Remark (1654), Quoted in *Women in World History Curriculum* (womeninworldhistory.com) *1996–97*

420. Marcela de Carpio de San Feliz (1605–1688)

1 Love giving gifts
Is suspicious and cold;
I have all, my Belovèd,
When thee I hold.

"Amor Mysticus," St. 3, *The Catholic Anthology,* Thomas Walsh, ed. *1927*

2 But in Thy chastising
Is joy and peace.
O Master and Love,
Let Thy blows not cease.

St. 8, Ibid.

421. A. M. Bigot de Cornuel (1605/14?–1694)

1 Turenne's small change. *(La monnaie de M. Turenne.)**
Remark, Quoted in *Nouvelle Biographie Universelle 1853–1866*
*Reference to the eight generals appointed to take the place of the great French marshal Henri de La Tour d'Auvergne, vicomte de Turenne (1611–1675).

2 No man is a hero to his valet. *(Il n'y a point de héros pour son valet de chambre.)*
Letter (13 August 1628), *Lettres de Mlle. Aïssé,* * *n.d.*
*Charlotte Elizabeth Aïssé; see 540.

422. Anna Maria van Schurman (1607–1678)

1 Whoever longs greatly for a solid and enduring occupation is suited for the study of letters. And woman longs greatly for a solid and enduring occupation.

"Arguments: IV," *Whether the Study of Letters Is Fitting for a Christian Woman? 1645?*

2 Whatever fills the mind of man with distinguished and honest delight is fitting for a Christian woman.

"Arguments: XIII," Ibid.

3 To whomever ignorance is not fitting, the study of letters is fitting.

"Arguments: XIV," Ibid.

4 Woman has the same erect countenance* as man, the same ideals, the same love of beauty, honor, truth, the same wish for self-development, the same longing after righteousness, and yet she is to be imprisoned in an empty soul of which the very windows are shuttered.

Quoted in *The Dinner Party, A Symbol of our Heritage* by Judy Chicago** *1979*
*Probably a faulty translation; more likely, "stance" or "posture."
**See 3133.

423. Madeleine de Scudéry (1607–1701)

1 In order to represent the heroic spirit it is undoubtedly necessary to have the hero do something extraordinary, as in a moment of heroic rapture, but this should not continue too long or it will degenerate into something ridiculous and will not have any good effect on the reader.
> Preface, *Ibrahim or the Illustrious Bassa, an Excellent New Romance 1652*

2 Since the body and the mind are so closely linked that one cannot suffer without the other, I fell ill.
> Vol. I, Ibid.

3 Any road that can take us where we want to go is the right one. Don't trouble yourself in asking if what you do is just, but only if it is advantageous.
> Vol. II, Ibid.

4 When we know the truth in our own consciences it is unnecessary to be troubled about anything else.
> *Artamenes, or The Grand Cyrus, an Excellent New Romance*, Vol. I *1653–55*

5 I find nothing more extravagant than to see a husband still in love with his wife.
> Vol. VI, Ibid.

6 I don't think that she has ever been indisposed on a day when there was a party to attend.
> Vol. VII, Ibid.

7 I would, without a doubt, rather be a simple soldier than be a woman, because to be truthful, a soldier can become king, but a woman can never become free.
> *Celia, An Excellent New Romance*, Vol. I *1656–61*

8 In losing a husband one loses a master who is often an obstacle to the enjoyment of many things.
> Vol. IV, Ibid.

9 Victory follows me, and all things follow victory. *(La victoire me suit, et tout suit la victoire.)*
> "Tyrannic Love" *n.d.*

424. Queen Henrietta Maria (1609–1666)

1 Queens of England are never drowned.
> Written during a storm at sea (February 1642), *Letters of Queen Henrietta Maria*, Mary Anne Everett Wood Green,* ed. *1857*

*See 948.

425. Constantina Munda (fl. ca. 1610)

1 . . . printing that was invented to be the storehouse of famous wits, the treasure of Divine literature . . . is become . . . the nursery and hospitall of every spurious and pernicious brat, which proceeds from base phreneticall brainesicke bablers.
> *The Worming of a Mad Dogge 1617*

2 . . . you lay open your imperfections . . . by heaping together the . . . fragments . . . of diverse english phrases . . . by scraping together the glaunder and . . . the refuse of idle-headed Authors and making a mingle-mangle gallimauphrie of them . . . let every bird take his owne feathers, and you would be as naked as Aesop's jay.
> Answer to Joseph Swetnam's "The Arraignment of Lewd, Idle, Forward and Unconstant Women," Ibid.

426. Jane Owen (fl. ca. 1610–d. 1633?)

1 Among all the Passions of the mind, there is not any, which hath so great a sovereignty, and command over man, as the Passion of Feare.
> *An Antidote against Purgatory. Or Discourse, wherein is shewed that Good Workes, and Almes-Deeds, are a meanes for the preventing, or mitigating the Torments of Purgatory 1634*

427. Joane Sharp (fl. ca. 1610)

1 Any answere may serve an impudent lyar,
   Any mangie scab'd horse doth fit a scab'd Squire
> "Epilogue: A Defence of Women, against the Author of the Arraignment of Women," Quoted in *Ester Hath Hang'd Haman: or an Answere to a lewd Pamphlet, entituled, The Arraignment of Women** by Ester Sowernam*** 1617
> *Written by Joseph Swetnam in 1617. **See 428.

428. Ester Sowernam (fl. ca. 1610)

1 The world is a large field, and it is full of brambles, bryers, and weedes.
> "To the Reader," *Ester* Hath Hang'd Haman: or An Answere to a lewd Pamphlet, entituled, The Arraignment of Women*** 1617
> *See 56. **Written by Joseph Swetnam in 1617.

2 In all dangers, troubles, and extremities, which fell to our Saviour, when all men fled from Him, living or dead, women never forsook Him.
> Ch. 3, Ibid.

3 . . . forbeare to charge women with faults which come from the contagion of Masculine serpents.
> Ch. 7, Ibid.

429. Mary Dyer (1611–1660)

1 In obedience to the will of the Lord I came and in His will I abide faithful to the death.
> Last words on the gallows (Boston, 1 June 1660), Quoted in *Notable American Women*, Edward T. James, ed. *1971*

2 My life not availeth me in comparison of the liberty of the truth.
> Carved on monument to Mary Dyer at the Boston Statehouse *n.d.*

430. Anne Bradstreet (1612?–1672)

1 That there is a God my Reason would soon tell me by the wondrous workes that I see, the vast frame of the Heaven and the Earth, the order of all things, night and day, Summer and Winter, Spring and Autumn, the dayly providing for this great household upon the Earth, the preserving and directing of All to its proper end.
> Dedication, "To My Dear Children: Religious Experience and Occasional Pieces," *The Tenth Muse Lately Sprung Up in America 1650*

2 I am obnoxious to each carping tongue
   Who says my hand a needle better fits,
   A Poet's pen all scorn I should thus wrong,
   For such despite they cast on Female wits:
   If what I do prove well, it won't advance,
   They'll say it's stoln, or else it was by chance.
> Prologue, St. 5, *Several Poems Compiled with Great Variety of Wit and Learning 1678*

3 But thou art bound to me, above the rest
   Who am thy drink, thy blood, thy sap and best. . . .
                    "The Four Elements; Water," Ibid.

4 Let such as say our Sex is void of reason,
   Know 'tis Slander now, but once was Treason.
        "In Honour of that High and Mighty Princess, Queen
                                    Elizabeth," * Ibid.

   *See 334.

5 And he that knowes the most, doth still bemoan
   He knows not all that here is to be known.
                "The Vanity of All Worldly Things," Ibid.

6 If ever two were one, than surely we.
   If ever man were lov'd by wife, than thee.
                "To my Dear and Loving Husband," Ibid.

7 I had eight birds hatcht in one nest,
   Four Cocks there were, and Hens the rest,
   I nurst them up with pain and care,
   Nor cost nor labour did I spare.
            "In reference to her Children" (23 June 1656?), Ibid.

8 A prosperous state makes a secure Christian, but adversity
   makes him Consider.
                                            VIII, Ibid.

9 . . . those parents are wise that can fit their nurture according
   to their Nature.
                                            X, Ibid.

10 Authority without wisdom is like a heavy axe without an
   edg[e], fitter to bruise than polish.
                                            XII, Ibid.

11 Sweet words are like honey, a little may refresh, but too much
   gluts the stomach.
                                            Ibid.

431. Henriette de Coligny (1613?–1673)

1 His cleverness in the art of love is unequaled.

   He knows how to draw the soul out by the ear.
            Untitled sonnet (ca. 1725), Quoted in *Precious Women* by
                                    Dorothy Backer *1974*

432–433. Margaret Askew Fell Fox (1614–1702)

1 We who are the People of God called Quakers, who are hated
   and despised, and every where spoken against, as people not
   fit to live, as they were that went before us, who were of the
   same spirit, power, & Life and were as we are, in that they were
   accounted as the off-scouring of all things, by that Spirit and Nature that is of the world, and so the Scripture is fulfilled, he that
   is born of the flesh persecuteth him that is born of the Spirit . . .
                    A Declaration and an Information 1660

2 We are a People that follow after those things that make for
   Peace, Love and Unity, it is our desire that others feet may walk
   in the same, and do deny and beare our Testimony against all
   Strife, and Wars, and Contentions that come from the Lusts
   that warr in the members, that warr against the Soul, which
   we wait for and watch for in all People, and love and desire
   the good of all; for no other cause but love to the Souls of all
   People, have our sufferings been . . .
                                            Ibid.

3 And whereas it is said, I permit not a Woman to speak, as saith
   the Law: But where Women are led by the Spirit of God, they
   are not under the Law; for Christ in the Male and in the Female
   is one; and where he is made manifest in Male and Female, he
   may speak . . .
                                            Ibid.

434. Mary Oxlie of Morpet (fl. ca. 1616)

1 Perfection in a woman's work is rare;
   From an untroubled mind should verses flow;
   My discontent makes mine too muddy show;
   And hoarse encumbrances of household care,
   Where these remain, the Muses ne'er repair.
       "Til William Drummond, of Hawthornden," Quoted as Prefix
                    to *Poems* by William Drummond *1656*

435. Charlotte Bregy (1619?–1693)

1 I never oppose the opinions of any; but I must own that I never
   adopt them to the prejudice of my own.
            Letters (1688), Quoted in *Biography of Distinguished Women*
                            by Sarah Josepha Hale* *1876*

   *See 807.

2 I am indolent; I never seek pleasure and diversions, but when
   my friends take more pains than I do to procure them for me, I
   feel myself obliged to appear very gay at them, though I am not
   so in fact.
                                            Ibid.

436. Eleanor Audeley (fl. ca. 1620–d. 1651)

1 POPE. Kings I Depose, and all their Race, to Raigne.
   DIVELL. And Popes to Friers I can turne againe.
                    A Warning to the Dragon and all his Angels 1625

2 No man so well knowes his owne frailtie, as the Lord your God
   knowes how prone Devotion is to Superstition.
                                            Ibid.

437. Sarel Gutmans (fl. 1620s)

1 Nowadays nobody is ready to lend anything to other people,
   from one hand into the other. When I needed something for
   living, I was obliged to offer double pledges and to pay high
   interest. What shall I do? I wriggled about like a worm before
   I was prepared to borrow money on pawn in such a time. The
   saying goes: Need breaks iron, if you will or not. You must
   eat, domestics must eat, you may be as careful as you like, you
   must have money anyhow.
            Letter to her husband, Loeb Sarel G-, Prague (November
            1619), *A Treasury of Jewish Letters: Letters from the Famous
                    and the Humble* Franz Kobler, ed. *1953*

438. Lucy Hutchinson (1620–1671)

1 The greatest excellency she had was the power of apprehend-
   ing and the virtue of loving him; so, as his shadow, she waited
   on him everywhere, till he was taken into that region of light
   which admits of none, and then she vanished into nothing.
            Journal Entry, Quoted in *Leading Women of the Restoration*
                            by Grace Johnstone *1891*

2 'Twas not her face he loved, her honour and her virtue were his
   mistresses. . . .
                                            Ibid.

439. Ninon de L'Enclos (1620–1705)

1 Old age is woman's hell. (*La vieillesse est l'enfer des femmes.*)
La Coquette vengée 1659

2 We should take care to lay in a stock of provisions, but not of pleasures: these should be gathered day by day.
Correspondence authentique de Ninon de Lenclos, Émile Colombey, ed. *1886*

3 The joy of the mind is the measure of its strength. (*La joie de l'espirit est marque de sa force.*)
Ibid.

4 What you priests tell us is sheer nonsense. I don't believe a single word of it.
Quoted in *The Immortal Ninon* by Cecil Austin *1927*

5 I put your consolations by,
   And care not for the hopes you give:
Since I am old enough to die,
   Why should I longer wish to live?
Untitled, Ibid.

6 Love never dies of starvation, but often of indigestion.
Ch. 3, *L'Esprit des autres n.d.*

440. Margareta Ruarowna (fl. ca. 1620)

1 O King . . . The nations in Thy sight are as nothing and are esteemed as vain and empty. The world before Thee is as the quivering of the balance, as the drop of the morning dew when it lights upon the earth.
from *Prayer Book* (1621), Quoted in *Women of the Reformation, Vol. III: From Spain to Scandinavia*, by Roland H. Bainton *1977*

441. Jane Cavendish (1621–1669)

1 LUCENAY. My distruction is that when I marry Courtly I shall bee condemn'd to looke upon my Nose, whenever I walke and when I sitt at meate confin'd by his grave winke to looke upon the Salt, and if it bee but the paireing of his Nales to admire him.
The Concealed Fansyes, with Elizabeth Brackley *ca. 1644–46*

442. Leonora Christina (1621–1685)

1 . . . in the twinkling of an eye much may change; the hand of God, in whom are the hearts of kings, can change everything.
Preface, *Memoirs of Leonora Christina*, F. E. Bunnet, tr. *1929*

2 The past is rarely remembered without sorrow, for it has been either better or worse than the present.
Ibid.

3 Many a one has acquired great learning in captivity, and has gained a knowledge of things which he could not master before. Yes, imprisonment leads to heaven. I have often said to myself: "Comfort thyself, thou captive one, thou art happy."
Ibid.

4 Who can have any care for a child when one does not love its father?
"A Record of the Sufferings of the Imprisoned Countess Leonora Christina" (1674–1685), Ibid.

5 I am but dust and ashes,
   Yet one request I crave:
Let me not go unawares
   Into the silent grave.
"A Mourning Hymn," St. 6, Ibid.

443. Hannah Woolley (1621/23?–1675/76?)

1 . . . blows are fitter for beasts than for rational creatures.
The Gentlewoman's Companion 1675

2 . . . a woman in this age is considered learned enough if she can distinguish her husband's bed from that of another.
Ibid.

444. Anna Trapnel (1622?–?)

1 In another Vision she saw a great company of little children walking on the earth, and a light shining round about them, and a very glorious person in the midst of them, with a Crown on his head, speaking these words: These will I honour with my Reigning presence in the midst of them, and the Oppressor shall dye in the wilderness.
Strange and Wonderful Newes from White-Hall: or, The Mighty Visions Proceeding from Mistris Anna Trapnel . . . 1654

2 Thou art not only to receive pleasures at home, but to establish Righteousness abroad.
Ibid.

445. Elizabeth Brackley (1623?–1663)
Coauthor with Jane Cavendish; see 441.

446. Margaret Cavendish (1623–1673)

1 Mirth laughing came, and running to me, flung
Her fat white arms about my neck. . . .
"Mirth and Melancholy," *Mirth, Poems & Fancies 1653*

2 My music is the buzzing of a fly.
Ibid.

3 Since all heroic actions, public employments, powerful governments, and eloquent pleadings are denied our sex in this age, or at least would be condemned for want of a custom . . . I write.
"An Epistle to My Readers," *Nature's Pictures, Drawn by Fancies Pencil to the Life 1656*

4 LADY HAPPY. Let me tell you, that Riches ought to be bestowed on such as are poor, and want means to maintain themselves; and Youth, on those that are old; Beauty, on those that are ill-favoured; and Virtue, on those that are vicious: So that if I should place my gifts rightly, I must Marry one that's poor, old, ill-favoured, and debauch'd.
Act I, Sc. 2, *The Convent of Pleasure ca. 1662*

5 DICK. The truth is, Sir, that Women are always unhappy in their thoughts, both before and after Marriage; for, before Marriage they think themselves unhappy for want of a Husband; and after they are Married, they think themselves unhappy for having a Husband.
Act II, Sc. 1, Ibid.

6 COURT. They are not Civil Laws that punish Lovers.
ADVISER. But those are Civil Laws that punish Adulterers.

COURT. Those are Barbarous Laws that make Love Adultery.
ADVISER. No, Those are Barbarous that make Adultery Love.
Act II, Sc. 4, Ibid.

7 Women's minds are like shops of small-wares, wherein some have pretty toys, but nothing of any great value.
Sociable Letters 1664

8 But nature be thanked, she has been so bountiful to us as we oftener enslave men than men enslave us. They seem to govern the world, but we really govern the world in that we govern men. For what man is he that is not governed by a woman, more or less?
Letter XVI, Ibid.

9 I had rather die in the adventure of noble achievements, than live in obscure and sluggish security.
The Description of a New World Called the Blazing World 1666

10 Women make poems? burn them, burn them,
Let them make bone-lace, let them make bone-lace
(1662), Quoted in *Reconstructing Aphra** by Angeline Goreau 1980

*Aphra Behn; see 472.

11 . . . for all the Brothers were Valiant, and all the Sisters virtuous.
Epitaph, Westminster Abbey *n.d.*

447. Mary of Warwick (1624–1678)

1 I will begin my first rule of advice to your lordship, with desiring you not to turn the day into night . . . by sleeping so long in the morning. . . .
Letter to George, Earl of Berkeley, "Rules for a Holy Life,"
Quoted in *Leading Women of the Restoration* by Grace Johnstone 1891

2 This sweet river, which I looked upon with so much pleasure and delight, while it was smooth, serene, and calm, when a sudden tempest rose unexpectedly, and made it rough and troubled, proved rather frightful than delightful to me, and made me shut my window, and cease looking on it.
"Upon looking out of my window at Chelsea, upon the Thames" *n.d.*

448. Bessie Clarkstone (?–1625)

1 O for absolution! O for a drop to coole my tormented soule.
Quoted in *The Conflict in Conscience of a deare Christian, named Bessie Clarkstone, in the Parish of Lanark, which she lay under three yeare & an half* by John Wreittoun 1631

2 Alas, I have long to live, and a wretched life . . . sighs helpe not, sobs helpe not, groanes helpe not, and prayer is faint.
Ibid.

449. Ann Fanshawe (1625–1680)

1 Endeavour to be innocent as a dove, but as wise as a serpent.
Memoirs of Ann, Lady Fanshawe ca. 1670

2 . . . it was never seen that a vicious youth terminated in a contented, cheerful old age. . . .
Ibid.

3 . . . reserve some hours daily to examine yourself and fortune; for if you embark yourself in perpetual conversation or recreation, you will certainly shipwreck your mind and fortune.
Ibid.

4 My glory and my guide, all my comfort in this life, is taken from me.* See me staggering in my path, because I expected a temporal blessing as a reward for the great innocence and integrity of his whole life.
Ibid.

*Referring to the death of her husband, Sir Richard Fanshawe (1608–1666), diplomat and author.

450. Christina of Sweden (1626–1689)

1 There is a star above us which unites souls of the first order, though worlds and ages separate them.
Maxims (1660–1680), Included in *Pensées de Christine, reine de Suède* 1825

2 Life becomes useless and insipid when we have no longer either friends or enemies.
Ibid.

3 Fools are more to be feared than the wicked.
Ibid.

4 We grow old more through indolence, than through age.
Ibid.

5 Confessors of princes are like men engaged in taming tigers and lions: they can induce the beasts to perform hundreds of movements and thousands of actions, so that on seeing them one might believe they were completely tamed; but when the confessor least expects it, he is knocked over by one blow of the animal's paw, which shows that such beasts can never be completely tamed.
Ibid.

6 Nuns and married women are equally unhappy, if in different ways.
Ibid.

451. Marie de Sévigné (1626–1696)

1 . . . the most astonishing, the most surprising, the most marvelous, the most miraculous, the most magnificent, the most confounding, the most unheard of, the most singular, the most extraordinary, the most incredible, the most unforeseen, the greatest, the least, the rarest, the most common, the most public, the most private till today . . . I cannot bring myself to tell you: guess what it is.
Letter to M. de Coulanges, *Letters of Madame de Sévigné to Her Daughter and Friends* 1811

2 If I inflict wounds, I heal them.
from letters to her daughter, Ibid.

3 There is no real evil in life, except great pain; all the rest is imaginary, and depends on the light in which we view things.
Ibid.

4 There is no person who is not dangerous for someone. *(Il n'y a personne qui ne soit dangereux pour quelqu'un.)*
Ibid.

5 When I step into this library, I cannot understand why I ever step out of it.
Ibid.

6 Ah, how easy it really is to live with me! A little gentleness, a little social impulse, a little confidence, even superficial, will lead me such a long way.
                                                                    Ibid.

7 We like so much to hear people talk of us and our motives, that we are charmed even when they abuse us.
                                                                    Ibid.

8 The desire to be singular and to astonish by ways out of the common seems to me to be the source of many virtues.
                                                                    Ibid.

9 True friendship is never serene.
                                                    (10 September 1671) Ibid.

10 Luck is always on the side of the big battalions. *(La fortune est toujours pour les gros battaillons.)*
                                                    (22 December 1673) Ibid.

11 . . . it seldom happens, I think, that a man has the civility to die when all the world wishes it.
                                                    (1 March 1680) Ibid.

12 . . . a lucky marriage pays for all.
                                                    (11 September 1680) Ibid.

452. Ann-Marie-Louise d'Orléans (1627–1693)

1 . . . self-love is scarcely conducive to piety.
                    "Self-Portrait," *Mademoiselle's Portrait Gallery 1657*

2 Children who are the object of great respect . . . usually become horribly puffed up.
                    From *Memoirs* (1652–1688), Quoted in *The Grand Mademoiselle*, Francis Steegmuller, tr. *1956*

3 Nothing so disfigures a person, to my taste, as the inability to *talk.* . . .
                                                                    Ibid.

4 . . . there is no doubt that Cupid is French. . . .
                                                                    Ibid.

5 There is nothing so tiresome as other people's business.
                                                                    Ibid.

453. Dorothy Osborne (1627–1695)

1 . . . there are certain things that custom has made almost of absolute necessity, and reputation I take to be one of those . . .
                    Letter (ca. 1653), *Letters*, E. A. Perry, ed. *1914*

2 All letters, methinks, should be as free and easy as one's discourse, not studied as an oration, nor made up of hard words like a charm.
                    Letter to Sir William Temple (October 1653), Ibid.

454. Alice Thornton (1627–1707)

1 Therefore it highly concerned me to enter into this greatest change of my life [marriage] with abundance of fear and caution, not lightly, nor unadvisedly, nor, as I may take my God to witness that knows the secrets of hearts, I did it not to fulfill the lusts of the flesh, but in chastity and singleness of heart, as marrying in the Lord.
                    The Autobiography of Mrs. Alice Thornton, of East Newton, Co. York 1875

455. Anne Wentworth (1629/30?–1693?)

1 And there is no repentance in the Grave . . .
                    Revelation IX (9 April), *The Revelation of Jesus Christ*, Vickie Taft, ed. *1676*

2 Some are guilty of so much, that they cannot enter, except God give them repentance.
                                    Revelation I (6 September 1677), Ibid.

3 For my message is Truth, and in it there is no Lye,
  But Mercy and Judgment, that is still the Cry.
  You may take it or leave it, that is all one to me,
  For Judgments will come, good and bad, you will see:
                                    Revelation VI (8 March 1679), Ibid.

456. Dorothy Berry (fl. ca. 1630)

1 Whose Noble Praise
  Deserves a Quill pluckt from an Angels wing,
  And none to write it but a Crowned King.
                    Dedicatory Poem, Quoted in *A Chaine of Pearle. Or A Memoriall of the peerless Graces, and Heroick Vertues of Queene Elizabeth,* * *Glorious Memory* by Diana Primrose** *1630*
                    *Elizabeth I; see 334. **See 457.

2 Shee, Shee* it was, that gave us Golden Daies
                                                                    Ibid.
                    *Elizabeth I; see 334.

457–458. Diana Primrose (fl. ca. 1630)

1 . . . Great Eliza,* England's brightest Sun,
                    "The Induction," *A Chaine of Pearle. Or A Memoriall of the peerless Graces, and Heroick Vertues of Queene Elizabeth, of Glorious Memory 1630*
                    *Elizabeth I; see 334.

2 . . . that Vestall Fire
  Still flaming, never would Shee condescend
  To Hymen's* Rightes. . . .
                                    "The Second Pearle. Chastity," Ibid.
                    *Eponymous god of fruitfulness; also, in Attic legend, representative of married life.

3 O Golden Age! O blest and happy years!
  O music sweeter than that of the Spheres!
  When Prince and People mutually agree
  In sacred concord and sweet symphony!
                                    "The Fourth Pearle. Temperance," Ibid.

459. Katherine Fowler Philips (1631–1664)

1 Who to another does his heart submit,
  Makes his own idol, and then worships it
                    "Against Love," St. 2, Poems, *By the Incomparable Mrs. K. P. 1664*

2 How soon we curse what erst we did adore.
                    "A Sea-Voyage From Tenby to Bristol, Begun September 5, 1652. Sent From Bristol to Lucasia, September 8, 1652," Ibid.

3 He who commands himself is more a prince,
  Than he who nations keep in awe
                                                    Untitled, Ibid.

4   He only dies untimely who dies late.
    For if 'twere told to Children in the Womb,
    To what a Stage of Mischiefs they must come
    . . . .
    what we call their Birth would count their Death.
        "2 Cor. 5, 19. God was in Christ Reconciling the World to
        himself," "Upon the Double Murther of King Charles I in
        Answer to a Libellous Copy of Rimes by Vavasor Powell,"
        *Poems. By the most deservedly Admired Mrs. Katherine
        Philips, the Matchless Orinda* . . . 1678*
    *Philips's pseudonym.

5   I did but see him, and he disappear'd,
    I did but pluck the Rose-bud and it fell
        "Orinda upon little Hector Philips,"* St. 2, Ibid.
    *Her son.

6   But I can love, and love at such a pitch,
    As I dare boast it will ev'n you enrich
        "To my Lady M[argaret] Cavendish, chusing the Name of
        Polycrite," Ibid.
    *See 446.

7   For my sake talk of Graves no more
        "To my Atenor,* March 16, 1661/2," Ibid.
    *Her friend, Philip James.

8   And when our Fortune's most severe,
    The less we have, the less we fear.
                                                            Ibid.

9   Woes have their Ebb as well as Flood
                                                            Ibid.

10 Friendship's an abstract of this noble flame,
    'Tis love refin'd, and purged from all its dross,
    'Tis next to angel's love, if not the same,
    As strong in passion is, though not so gross.
                                                "Friendship," Ibid.

11 . . . we may generally conclude the Marriage of a Friend to be
    the Funeral of a Friendship. . . .
                                                            Ibid.

12 Waste not in vain the crystal Day,
    But gather your Rose-buds while you may.
                                                            Ibid.

460. Marie-Catherine Desjardins (1632–1683)

1   Beautiful lovers, hold your tongues, you err to the extreme;
    Taking turns a hundred times to say: I love you.
    In love, one must speak with elegance.
        "Madrigal," Elaine Bernstein Partnow,* tr.,
        Quoted in *Biography of Distinguished Women* by Sarah
                                        Josepha Hale** 1876
    *See 3291. **See 807.

2   A sweet languor takes me from my senses,
    I die away in the arms of my faithful lover,
    and in this death I rediscover life.
    (*Une douce langueur m'ôte le sentiment;
    Je Meurs entre les bras de mon fidèle amant,
    Et c'est dans cette mort que je trouve la vie.*)
        Untitled sonnet, Quoted in *Precious Women* by Dorothy
                                                    Backer 1974

461. Kawai Chigetsu-Ni (1632–1736)

1   Grasshoppers
    Chirping in the sleeves
    Of a scarecrow.
        Untitled haiku, *The Burning Heart: Women Poets of Japan*,
        Kenneth Rexroth and Ikuko Atsumi, eds. and trs. 1977

462. Anne Wharton (1632?–1685)

1   May yours* excel the matchless Sappho's** name;
    May you have all her wit, without her shame.
                                        "The Temple of Death" 1695
    *The English writer Aphra Behn; see 472. **See 46.

2   Sorrow may make a silent moan,
    But joy will be revealed.
        Untitled, St. 2, *Tooke's* Collection of Miscellaneous Poems*
                                                            n.d.
    *Probably John Horne Tooke (1736–1812), English politician and
    philologist.

463. Catharina Regina von Greiffenberg (1633–1694)

1   You empress of the stars, the heaven's worthy crown,
    The world's great eye, and soul of all spreading earth
        "Spring-Joy Praising God. Praise of the Sun," St. 1, George
        C. Schoolfield, tr., *Anthology of German Poetry through the
        Nineteenth Century*, Alexander Gode and Frederick Ungar,
                                                        eds. 1963

2   You mirror-spectrum-glance, you many-colored gleam!
    You glitter to and fro, are incomprehensibly clear
        "On the Ineffable Inspiration of the Holy Spirit," St. 3,
        Geistliche Sonnette (1662), Michael Hamburger, tr., *The
        Penguin Book of Women Poets*, Carol Cosman, Joan Keefe,
                                        and Kathleen Weaver, eds. 1978

464. Mary Evelyn (1634–1709)

1   Whoever has a mind to abundance of Trouble,
    Let him furnish himself with a Ship and a Woman,
    For no two things will find you more Employment,
    If once you begin to Rig them out with all their Streamers.
        A Voyage to Maryland; or, The Ladies Dressing-Room 1690

465. Marie Madeleine de La Fayette (1634–1693)

1   Most mothers think that to keep young people away from
    love-making it is enough never to speak of it in their presence.
        The Princess of Clèves, First Part 1678

2   Ambition and love-making were the soul of this Court,* and
    obsessed the minds of men and women alike.
                                                            Ibid.
    *The court of Henry II of France.

3   "If you judge by appearances in this place," replied Madame
    de Chartres, "you will often be deceived; what appears on the
    surface is almost never the truth."
                                                            Ibid.

4   The necessity of dying, which she saw close at hand, accus-
    tomed her to detaching herself from everything. . . .
                                                    Fourth Part, Ibid.

5 The shame and the unhappiness of libertinism presented itself to her spirit; she saw the abyss, where she was hurling herself and she resolved to avoid it.
> *La Comtesse de Tende,* Christy Sheffield Sanford, tr. (on-line 1996) *1718*

6 One cedes easily to that which is pleasing; . . .
> Ibid.

466. Françoise de Maintenon (1635–1719)

1 Nothing is more adroit than irreproachable conduct.
> Motto, *Maximes de Mme de Maintenon 1686*

2 Delicacy is to love what grace is to beauty.
> Ibid.

3 Frankness does not consist in saying a great deal, but in saying everything, and this everything is soon said when one is sincere, because there is no need of a great flourish and because one does not need many words to open the heart.
> Letter to Madame de Saint-Périer (21 October 1708), *Lettres sur l'education des filles 1854*

4 . . . thanks to the goodness of God, I have no passions, that is to say, I love no one to the point of being willing to do anything that God would not approve.
> Remark to Madame Glapion (October 1708), *Lettres historiques et édifantes,* Vol. II *1856*

5 [I wish] to remain an enigma to posterity.
> *Correspondance générale de Mme de Maintenon,* Vol. I, Théophile Lavallée, ed. *1865–66*

6 The longer I live, the more I grow in the opinion that it is useless to pile up wealth.
> Letter to Madame de Brinon (April 1683), Vol. II, Ibid.

7 There are few women who have sufficiently solid minds to carry great learning without a yet greater arrogance; furthermore, women never know but half-way, and the little they know generally renders them proud, disdainful, loquacious, and disgusted with essential matters.
> Quoted in *Souvenirs d'une Bleue élève à Saint-Cyr . . .* (p. 104) *1897*

8 You know that my mania is to make people hear reason.
> Letter to Madame de Ventadour (February 1692), *Lettres,* Vol. I, Marcel Langlois, ed. *1935–39*

9 I am determined to aid those who aid themselves, and to let the good-for-nothing suffer.
> Ibid.

10 [Marriage is] a state that causes the misery of three quarters of the human race.
> Letter to Gobelin (1 August 1674), Ibid.

467. Rachel Russell (1636–1723)

1 . . . the conversation of friends . . . is the nearest approach we can make to heaven while we live in these tabernacles of clay; so it is in a temporal sense also, the most pleasant and the most profitable improvement we can make of the time we are to spend on earth.
> Letter to Lady Sunderland, *Letters ca. 1793*

2 . . . who would live and not love?
> Ibid.

468. Mary Rowlandson (1637?–1711)

1 I had often before this said, that if the Indians should come, I should chuse rather to be killed by them than taken alive but when it came to the tryal my mind changed; their glittering weapons so daunted my spirit, that I chose rather to go along with those (as I may say) ravenous Bears, then that moment to end my dayes.
> *The Sovereignty & Goodness of God, Together, with the Faithfulness of His Promises Displayed; Being a Narrative of the Captivity and Restauration of Mrs. Mary Rowlandson 1682*

2 Now is the dreadful hour come, that I have often heard of (in time of war, as it was the case of others), but now mine eyes see it. Some in our house were fighting for their lives, others wallowing in their blood, the house on fire over our heads, and the bloody heathen ready to knock us on the head, if we stirred out.
> Ibid.

3 It is a solemn sight to see so many Christians lying in their blood, some here, and some there, like a company of sheep torn by wolves, all of them stripped naked by a company of hell-hounds, roaring, singing, ranting, and insulting, as if they would have torn our very hearts out; yet the Lord by His almighty power preserved a number of us from death, for there were twenty-four of us taken alive and carried captive.
> Ibid.

469. Antoinette Deshoulières (1638–1694)

1 It isn't easy for one who thinks
To be honest, and yet play the game;
The desire for gain, a day and night occupation,
    Is a dangerous spur
That goads one towards jeopardy.
> Untitled poem, Elaine Bernstein Partnow,* tr., Quoted in *Biography of Distinguished Women* by Sarah Josepha Hale** *1876*
>
> *See 3291. **See 807.

2 Alas! little sheep, you are blessed!
You pass through our fields without care, without alarm.
> "Idylle," Elaine Bernstein Partnow,* tr., from *Les Moutons* (1695), Ibid.
>
> *See 3291.

3 No one is satisfied with his fortune, nor dissatisfied with his intellect.
> *(Nul n'est content de sa fortune; Ni micontent de son esprit.)*
> "Epigram" *n.d.*

470. Makhfi (1639–1703)

1 I want to go to the desert
but modesty is chains on my feet.
> Untitled, Willis Barnstone, tr., *A Book of Women Poets,* Aliki and Willis Barnstone, eds. *1980*

2 My tears break forth, my will is overridden,
Reason retreats and resolutions wane;
The stormy bursts of weeping come unbidden,
Wayward and fitful as the April rain.
> Untitled, St. 2, Paul Whalley, tr., *Women Poets of the World,* Joanna Bankier and Deirdre Lashgari, eds. 1983

471. Mariana Alcoforado (1640–1723)

1 I gave myself out of love, my lord, as a free gift, neither buying myself a husband nor selling myself as though I were merchandise

p. 237, *The Portuguese Letters (a.k.a. Letters of a Portuguese Nun)** Donald E. Ericson, tr. *1975*

*Some scholars ascribe authorship to Gabriel-Joseph de la Vergne (1628–1685)

472. Aphra Behn (1640–1689)

1 AMINITA. While to inconstancy I bid adieu, I find variety enough in you.

Prologue, *The Forced Marriage 1670*

2 . . . I have heard the most of that which bears the name of learning, and which has abused such quantities of ink and paper, and continually employs so many ignorant, unhappy souls, for ten, twelve, twenty years in a university (who yet poor wretches think they are doing something all the while) as logic, etc. and several other things (that shall be nameless lest I misspell them) are much more absolutely nothing than the errantist play that e'er was writ.

"An Epistle to the Reader," *The Dutch Lover 1673*

3 OLINDA. . . . this marrying I do not like: 'tis like going on a long voyage to sea, where after a while even the calms are distasteful, and the storms dangerous: one seldom sees a new object, 'tis still a deal of sea, sea; husband, husband, every day,—till one's quite cloyed with it.

Act. IV, Sc. 1, *Ibid.*

4 SIR TIMOTHY. The Devil's in her tongue, and so 'tis in most women's of her age; for when it has quitted the tail, it repairs to the upper tier.

The Town Fop 1676

5 WILMORE. There is no sinner like a young saint.

Sc. 2., *The Rover 1677*

6 Variety is the soul of pleasure.

Act II, Sc. 1, last line *Ibid.*

7 Money speaks sense in a language all nations understand.

Act III, Sc. 1, *Ibid.*

8 She's a chick off the old cock.

Act IV, Sc. 4, *Sir Patient Fancy 1678*

9 Patience is a flatterer, sir—and an ass, sir.

Act III, Sc. 1, *The Feigned Curtezans 1679*

10 Love ceases to be a pleasure, when it ceases to be a secret.

"Four O'Clock," *The Lover's Watch 1686*

11 All I ask, is the privilege for my masculine part, the poet in me . . . if I must not, because of my sex, have this freedom, I lay down my quill and you shall hear no more of me. . . .

Preface, *The Lucky Chance 1686*

12 Too much curiosity lost Paradise.

Act. III, Sc. 3, *Ibid.*

13 Faith, Sir, we are here to-day, and gone tomorrow.

Act IV, *Ibid.*

14 Madam, 'twas a pious fraud, if it were one.

Act V, Sc. 7, *Ibid.*

15 Advantages are lawful in love and war.

Sc. 3, *Ibid.*

16 How many idiots has it [love] made wise! how many fools eloquent! how many homebred squires accomplished! how many cowards brave!

The Fair Jilt 1688

17 Love, like Reputation, once fled, never returns more.

History of the Nun 1689

18 . . . that perfect tranquility of life, which is nowhere to be found but in retreat, a faithful friend, a good library. . . .

The Lucky Mistake 1689

19 This money certainly is a most devilish thing!

The Court of the King Bantam 1696

473. Johanna Cartwright (fl. ca. 1640)

1 And that this Nation of England, with the Inhabitants of the Nether-lands, shall be the first and readiest to transport Izraells Sons & Daughters in their Ships to the Land promised to their fore-Fathers, Abraham, Isaac, and Jacob, for an everlasting Inheritance.

For the glorious manifestation whereof, and pyous meanes thereunto, your Petitioners humbly pray that the inhumane cruel Statute of banishment made against them, may be repealed, and they under the Christian banner of charity, and brotherly love, may again be received and permitted to trade and dwell amongst you in this Land, as now they do in the Nether-lands.

The Petition of the Jewes, For the Repealing of the Act of Parliament for their banishment out of England 1649

474. Ephelia (fl. ca. 1640–d. 1681?)

1 Beauty's but the smallest Grace,
Unless it be i'th' Mind as well as Face:

"Acrostic," *Female Poems On Several Occasions 1679*

2 Whole Months but hours seem, when you are here,
When absent, every Minute is a Year:

"First Farewell to J.G.," *Ibid.*

3 How strangely is my Life perplexed by fate!
I would not Love, and yet I cannot hate.

"To a Gentleman that durst not pass the door while I stood there," last lines, *Ibid.*

4 Why do I Love? go, ask the Glorious Sun
Why every day it round the world doth Run:
Ask *Thames* and *Tiber,* why they Ebb and Flow:
Ask Damask Roses, why in *June* they blow:

"To one that asked me why I loved J.G." last lines, *Ibid.*

5 How Happy was the World before men found
Those metals, Nature hid beneath the Ground!
All Necessary things She placed in View,
But this She wisely hid, because She knew
That it destructive to her work would be,
And jar the consort of her Harmony:

"Wealth's Power," *Ibid.*

475. Joane Hit-him-home (fl. ca. 1640)

Coauthor with Mary Tattlewell; see 477.

476. Anna Hume (fl. ca. 1640)

1   Reader, I have oft been told,
    Verses that speak not Love are cold.
        "To the Reader," *The Triumphs of Love, Chastity, Death:*
                        translated out of Petrarch* 1644
    *Italian poet (1304–74).

2   The fatal hour of her short life drew near,
    That doubtful passage which the world doth fear
                        "The Triumph of Death," Ch. 1, Ibid.

477. Mary Tattlewell (fl. ca. 1640)

1   . . . what have we women done,
    That any one who was a mother's sonne
    Should thus affront our sex? Hath he forgot
    From whence he came? or doth he seek to blot
    His own conception?
        "Epistle to the Reader: Long Megge of Westminster, hearing
        the abuse, offeres to women to riseth out of her grave and thus
                        speaketh," with Joane Hit-him-home* *1640*
    *See 475.

2   . . . the corrupt heart discovereth itself by the lewd tongue.
                                        Essay, Ibid.

3   Nature hath bestowed upon us two eares, and two eyes, yet
    but one tongue; which is an Embleme unto us that though we
    heare and see much, yet ought wee to speak but little. . . .
                                        Ibid.

4   . . . even fooles being silent have passed for wise men. . . .
                                        Ibid.

5   . . . hee never came to me empty mouth'd or handed; for he was
    never unprovided of stew'd Anagrams, bak'd Epigrams, sous'd
    Madrigalls, pickled Round delayes, broyld Sonnets, parboild
    Elegies, perfum'd poesies for Rings, and a thousand other such
    foolish flatteries, and knavish devices. . . .
                                        Ibid.

478. Mary Coffyn Starbuck (1644/45–1717)

1   . . . such who believed once in Christ, were always in Him,
    without possibility of falling away; and whom He had once
    loved, He loved to the End . . .
        Quoted in *An Account of the life of That Ancient Servant of*
                        Jesus Christ by John Richardson *1757*

479. Glückel of Hameln (1646–1724)

1   The kernel of the Torah is: "Thou shalt love thy neighbour as
    thyself." But in our days we seldom find it so, and few are they
    who love their fellow men with all their heart. On the contrary,
    if a man can contrive to ruin his neighbour nothing pleases
    him more . . .
                                        Memoirs (1692) *1896*

2   The best thing for you, my children, is to serve God from your
    heart without falsehood or deception, not giving out to people
    that you are one thing while, God forbid, in your heart you are
    another. Say your prayers with awe and devotion.
                                        Ibid.

3   If you have in hand money or goods belonging to other people,
    give more care to them than if they were your own, so that,
    please God, you do no one a wrong.
        (1692), *The Memoirs of Glückel of Hameln,* Marvin
                        Lowenthal, tr., *1977*

4   . . . honors and money are but for a space and not for eternity.
    A man may hoard his honors and his gold until the very last,
    and then comes bitter Death to make all forgotten; his honors
    and his gold are of no avail.
                                        Ibid.

5   A bird once set out to cross a windy sea with its three fledg-
    lings. The sea was so wide and the wind so strong, the father
    bird was forced to carry his young, one by one, in his strong
    claws. When he was half-way across with the first fledgling
    the wind turned to a gale, and he said, "My child, look how
    I am struggling and risking my life in your behalf. When you
    are grown up, will you do as much for me and provide for
    my old age?" The fledgling replied, "Only bring me to safety,
    and when you are old I shall do everything you ask of me."
    Whereat the father bird dropped his child into the sea, and
    it drowned, and he said, "So shall it be done to such a liar as
    you." Then the father bird returned to shore, set forth with
    his second fledgling, asked the same question, and receiving
    the same answer, drowned the second child with the cry, "You,
    too, are a liar!" Finally he set out with the third fledgling, and
    when he asked the same question, the third and last fledgling
    replied, "My dear father, it is true you are struggling mightily
    and risking your life in my behalf, and I shall be wrong not to
    repay you when you are old, but I cannot bind myself. This
    though I can promise: when I am grown up and have children
    of my own, I shall do as much for them as you have done for
    me." Whereupon the father bird said, "Well spoken, my child,
    and wisely; your life I will spare and I will carry you to shore
    in safety."
                                        Ibid.

480. Françoise de Grignan (1646–1705)

1   We [women] have not enough reason to use all our strength.
    (Nous n'avons pas assez de raison pour employer toute notre
    force.)
        Letter to her mother [Mme. de Sévigné],* Quoted in *Letters of*
            Madame de Sévigné to Her Daughter and Her Friends 1811
    *See 451.

481. Maria Sibylla Merian (1647–1717)

1   From my youth I have been interested in insects. First I started
    with the silkworms in my native Frankfurt am Main. After that
    . . . I started to collect all the caterpillars I could find in order
    to observe their changes . . . and I painted them very carefully
    on parchment.
        Quoted in "A Surinam Portfolio," *Natural History December*
                                        1962

482. Jeanne-Marie de la Motte Guyon (1648–1717)

1   But though my wing is closely bound,
    My heart's at liberty;
    My prison walls cannot control
    The flight, the freedom of the soul.
        "A Prisoner's Song," written while imprisoned at the Castle of
                                Vincennes *ca. 1695–1702*

2   I know but one path, but one way, but one road, which is that of
    continual renouncement, of death, of nothingness. Everybody
    flies this way and seeks with passion all that makes us live;
    nobody is willing to be nothing, yet how shall we find what we
    are all seeking by a road which leads precisely wrong?
        Lettres chrétiennes et spirituelles, Vol. III *1717–18*

3 My condition in marriage was rather that of a slave than that
of a free woman.
*La Vie de Mme J.-M. B. de La Mothe Guion, écrite par elle-
même* [Autobiography], Vol. I 1720

4 Let us love without reasoning about it, and we shall find ourselves filled with love before others have found out the reasons
that lead to loving.
Ibid.

5 Yet man, dim-sighted man, and rash as blind,
Deaf to the dictates of his better mind,
In frantic competition dares the skies,
And claims precedence of the Only wise.
"Glory to God Alone," St. 4, *The Works of William Cowper,**
Comprising His Poems, Correspondence and Translations,
William Cowper, tr. 1835
*Earl—(1664?–1773), English jurist.

6 'Tis love unites what sin divides;
The centre, where all bliss resides;
"The Testimony of Divine Adoption," St. 6, Ibid.

483. Anna Tompson Hayden (1648–1720)

1 For none Can tell who shall be next,
Yet all may it expect;
Then surely it Concerneth all,
Their time not to neglect.
"Upon the Death of the desireable young virgin, Elizabeth
Tompson, Daughter of Joseph & Mary Tompson of Bilerika,
who Deceased in Boston out of the house of Mr Legg, 24
August, 1712, aged 22 years," *Handkerchiefs from Paul:
Being Pious and Consolatory Verses of Puritan Massachusetts,*
Kenneth B. Murdock, ed. 1927

484. Maria Anna Mancini (1649–1714)

1 You weep, and you are the master! (*Vous pleurez, et vous êtes
le maître!*)
Remark to Louis XIV* (ca. 1658) in response to being sent
away from Paris, *Memoires n.d.*
*King of France (1638–1715; r. 1643–1715).

485. Anne Collins (fl. ca. 1650)

1 As in a cabinet or chest
One jewel may exceed the rest.
Untitled, St. 2, *Divine Songs and Meditacions* 1653

2 Cheerfulness
Doth express
A settled pious mind;
Which is not prone to grudging,
From murmuring refin'd.
"Song," St. 5, Ibid.

486. Nell Gwyn (1650–1687)

1 Shall the dog lie where the deer once crouched?*
Attributed 1685
*Her alleged rejection of a suitor after Charles II's death; she was
the king's mistress.

2 Here is a sad slaughter at Windsor, the young mens taking your
Leaves and going to France, and, although they are none of my
Lovers, yet I am loathe to part with the men.
Letter to Madam Jennings (14 April 1684), Quoted in *The
Story of Nell Gwynn* by Peter Cunningham 1892

487. Juana Inés de la Cruz (Sor Juana) (1651–1695)

1 The greater evil who is in—
When both in wayward paths are straying
The poor sinner for the pain,
Or he that pays for the sin?
"Redondillas," St. 9, Garrett Strange, tr., *The Catholic
Anthology,* Thomas Walsh, ed. 1927

2 I do not value wealth or riches,
Wherefore I shall be ever more content
To bring more richness to my mind
And not to keep my mind on riches.
"*En perseguirme, mundo, ¿qué interesas?*" ["Oh World,
Why do you thus pursue me?"], St. 2, Muriel Kittel, tr., *An
Anthology of Spanish Poetry, from Garcilaso to García Lorca,*
Angel Flores, ed. 1961

3 "*Diuturna enfermedad de la Esperanza . . .*" ("Perpetual Infir-
mity of Hope . . .")
Titular line of poem, Ibid.

4 What magical infusions, brewed
from herbals of the Indians
of my own country, spilled their old
enchantment over all my lines?
"*En reconocimiento a las inimitables plumas de la Europa*"
[In acknowledgment of the praises of European Writers"], St.
14, Constance Urdang, tr., Ibid.

5 I believed, when I entered this convent, I was escaping from
myself, but alas, poor me, I brought myself with me!
Quoted in *Women in Myth and History* by Violeta Miqueli
1962

6 Critics: in your sight
no woman can win:
keep you out, and she's too tight;
she's too loose if you get in.
Verses from "A Satirical Romance," St. 3, Samuel Beckett,**
tr., *The Penguin Book of Women Poets,* Carol Cosman, Joan
Keefe, and Kathleen Weaver, eds. 1978
*Irish born novelist and playwright (1906–1989).

7 . . . as love is union, it knows no extremes of distance.
"*Repuesta a Sor Filotea*" ["Reply to Sister Philotea:
1691], Quoted in *A Woman of Genius: The Intellectual
Autobiography of Sor Juana Inés de la Cruz* by Margaret
Sayers Peden 1982

8 One will abide, and will confess that another is nobler than
he, that another is richer, more handsome, and even that he is
more learned, but that another is richer in reason scarcely any
will confess: *Rare is he who will concede genius.*
Ibid.

9 But, lady, as women, what wisdom may be ours if not the
philosophies of the kitchen? Lupercio Leonardo spoke well
when he said: how well one may philosophize when preparing dinner. And I often say, when observing these trivial
details: had Aristotle* prepared victuals, he would have written more.
Ibid.
*Greek philosopher, logician and scientist (384 B.C.E.–322).

10 And I would add that a fool may reach perfection (if ignorance may tolerate perfection) by having studied his little
of philosophy and theology and by having some learning of

tongues, by which he may be a fool in many sciences and languages: a great fool cannot be contained solely by his mother tongue.

Ibid.

11 With you, no woman can hope to score;
whichever way, she's bound to lose;
spurning you, she's ungrateful—
succumbing, you call her lewd.
"You Men," St. 7, *Lesbian Poetry* (sappho.compoetry/index.
shtml) *21 January 1996*

12 In loss itself
I find assuagement:
having lost the treasure,
I've nothing to fear.
"Disillusionment," St. 5, Ibid.

13 No god is ever secure
against the lofty flight of human thought.
"My Divine Lysis," St. 1, Ibid.

14 Who has forbidden women to engage in private and individual studies? Have they not a rational soul as men do? . . . I have this inclination to study and if it is evil I am not the one who formed me thus—I was born with it and with it I shall die.
Letter to Father Nunez (1681), *Women in World History
Curriculum,* home.earthlink.net/~womenwhist/ *1996–97*

15 . . . given the total antipathy I felt towards marriage, I deemed convent life least unsuitable and the most honorable I could elect if I were to ensure my salvation. . . . wishing to live alone, and wishing to have no obligatory occupation to inhibit the freedom of my studies, nor the sounds of a community to intrude upon the peaceful silence of my books.
4000 Years of Women in Science, astr.ua.edu/4000WS *1
August 1997*

488. Anne Dacier (1651–1720)

1 Silence is the ornament of women.
Quoted in *Biography of Distinguished Women* by Sarah
Josepha Hale* *1876*
*See 807.

2 . . . let her [her granddaughter] conceal her learning with as much care as she might crookedness or lameness.
Letter to her daughter, Quoted in *The Life of Lady Mary
Wortley Montagu* by Robert Halsband *1956*
*See 533.

489. Margaret Godolphin (1652–1678)

1 If you speake anything they like, say 'tis borrowed. . . .
Quoted in *The Life of Mrs. Godolphin* by John Evelyn;* H.
Sampson, ed. *1939*

2 . . . may the Clock, the Candle, may everything I see, teach and instruct me some thing.
Ibid.

3 God knows a little pain makes one forget a long health, and the unkindes of one frind maks one forget the frindship of many for a time, for we by nateur are apter to grine than laugh, the first sound we make is crying, our childhood is scarce anything els but frowardnes, and so but in a little more reasonable

maner we proceed till we dye, so that unles we had hops of a beter world we wear of all things most miserable. . . .
Ch. 8, Letter to John Evelyn* (July 1675), Quoted in *John
Evelyn and Mrs. Godolphin* by W. G. Hiscock *1951*

4 . . . our wholl life is, in my opinion, a search after remedys, which doe often, if not always, exchange rather than cuer a deseas. . . .
Ch. 11, Last letter to John Evelyn,* Ibid.
*English author and diarist (1620–1706).

490. Francisca Gregoria (1653–1710)

1 Fair plaything of the breeze tonight.
"Envying a Little Bird," *The Catholic Anthology,* Thomas
Walsh, ed. *1927*

491. Elizabeth Bathurst (1655?–1685/91)

1 Oh! where was your patient Mind, that you could not hear what I had to say unto you, and have tried what Spirit I had been of, that so, if in Error, by sound Argument you might have convinced me.
"An Expostulatory Appeal to the Professors of Christianity"
1680

492. Mary Chudleigh Lee (1656–1710)

1 The restless atoms play. . . .
Of them, composed with wondrous art,
We are our selves a part,
And on us still they nutriment bestow;
To us they kindly come, from us they swiftly go,
And through our veins in purple torrents flow.
Vacuity is nowhere found,
Each place is full, with bodies we're encompassed round:
In sounds they're to our ears conveyed,
In fragrant odors they our smell delight,
And in ten thousand curious forms displayed
They entertain our sight.
"The Offering," Pt. One, *The Ladies' Defence: Or, the
Bride-Woman's Counsellor Answered: A Poem in a Dialogue
between Sir John Brute, Sir William Loveall, Melissa, and a
Parson 1701*

2 Wife and servant are the same
But only differ in the name,
For when that fatal knot is tied,
Which nothing, nothing can divide,
When she the word *obey* has said,
And man by law supreme has made,
Then all that's kind is laid aside,
And nothing left but state and pride.
"To the Ladies," Ibid.

493. Frances Boothby (fl. ca. 1660)

1 I'm hither come, but what d'ye think to say?
A Womans Pen present you with a Play:
Who smiling told me I'd be sure to see,
That once confirm'd, the House would empty be.
Not one yet gone!
Prologue, *Marcelia: or, The Treacherous Friend 1669*

2 You powerful Gods! if I must be
An injur'd offering to Love's deity,
Grant my revenge, this plague on men,
That woman ne'er may love again.
"Song," St. 1, Ibid.

494. Isobel Gowdie (fl. ca. 1660)

1 When we would ride, we take windle-straws, or beanstalks,
and put them betwixt our feet, and say thrice:
        Horse and Hattock, horse and go,
        Horse and pellattis, ho! Ho!
        And immediately we fly away wherever we would.
                Confession (1662), Quoted in "The Broomstick or Besom,"
                An ABC of Witchcraft, Past and Present by Doreen Valiente*
                                                        1973

        *See 2442.

495. Honnamma (fl. ca. 1660–d. 1699)

1 Wasn't your mother a woman?
                Untitled, Willis Barnstone, tr., *A Book of Woman Poets*, Aliki
                                and Willis Barnstone, eds. *1980*

2 Here and in the other world
        happiness
    comes to a person, not a gender.
                                                        Ibid.

496. Anne Killigrew (1660?–1685)

1 More rich, more noble I will ever hold
    The Muse's laurel, than a crown of gold.
                "Upon the Saying That My Verses Were Made by Another," St.
                                                2, *Poems 1686*

2 I willingly accept Cassandra's fate,
    To speak the truth, although believed too late.
                                                St. 6, Ibid.

3 But O, the laurel'd fool that doats on fame,
    Who's hope's applause, whose
        fear's to want a name:
    Who can accept for pay
    Of what he does, what others say
                                        "The Discontent," St. 2, Ibid.

4 Too loud, O Fame! thy trumpet is too shrill
                                                St. 3, Ibid.

5 Friendship, the Cement, that does faster twine
    Two Souls, than that which Soul and Body joyn:
                                "The Miseries of Man," St. 4, Ibid.

6 The bloody Wolf, the Wolf does not pursue;
    The Boar, though fierce, his Tusk will not embrue
    In his own Kind, Bares, not on Bares do prey:
    Then art thou, Man, more savage far than they.
                                                St. 7, Ibid.

7 How dares bold Vice unmasked walk,
    And like a Giant proudly stalk?
                                "To the Queen," St. 8, Ibid.

497. Anne Finch (1661–1720)

1 Alas! a woman that attempts the pen
    Such an intruder on the rights of men,
    Such a presumptuous Creature, is esteem'd
    The fault, can by no vertue be redeem'd.
                Introductory Verse, *Miscellany Poems on Several Occasions*
                                                        1713

2 . . . I have applied
    Sweet mirth, and music, and have tried

A thousand other arts beside,
To drive thee from my darkened breast,
Thou, who has banished all my rest.
                "To Melancholy," *Miscellany Poems, Written by a Lady 1713*
                                                        (repr. 1928)

3 Trail all your pikes, dispirit every drum,
    March in a slow procession from afar,
    Ye silent, ye dejected, men of war.
    Be still the hautboys, and the flute be dumb!
    Display no more, in vain, the lofty banner;
    For see where on the bier before ye lies
    The pale, the fall'n, the untimely sacrifice
    To your mistaken shrine, to your false idol
    Honour.
                        "Trail All Your Pikes," in toto, Ibid.

4 How gaily is at first begun
    Our life's uncertain race!
                                "Life's Progress," St. 1, Ibid.

5 He lamented for Behn,* o'er that
        place of her birth,
    And said amongst women there was none
        on earth
    Her superior in fancy, in language, or wit,
    Yet owned that a little too loosely she writ.
                        "Aristomenes," The Introduction, Ibid.
        *Aphra Behn; see 472.

6 How are we fal'n, fal'n, by mistaken rules?
                                                        Ibid.

498. Mary II of England (1662–1694)

1 There is but one command which I wish him* to obey; and
    that is, *"Husbands, love your wives."* For myself, I shall follow
    the injunction, *"Wives, be obedient to your husbands in all
    things."*
                Quoted in *Biography of Distinguished Women* by Sarah
                                        Josepha Hale** *1876*
        *Her husband, William III (1650–1702), king of England from
        1689 to 1702. **See 807.

499. Kata Szidónia Petröczi (1662–1708)

1 Hourly I howl the change in my fate.
                "Swift Floods," St. 1, Laura Schiff, tr, *Women Poets of the
                        World*, Joanna Bankier and Deirdre Lashgari, eds. *1983*

2 The winds of sadness lay siege
    To my forsaken mind, my wounded heart.
                                                St. 2, Ibid.

500. Elizabeth Bradford (1663–1731)

1 For 'tis no humane knowledge gain'd by art,
    But rather 'tis inspir'd into the heart
    By divine means; for true divinity
    Hath with this science great affinity
                Preface, "To the Reader, in Vindication of this Book," Quoted
                        in *War With the Devil* by Benjamin Keach

501. Delariviere Manley (1663/72–1724)

1 BELIRA. Poor cavillier, those who can jest with oaths can play
    with words.
                Act IV, Sc. ii, *The Lost Lover, or: The Jealous Husband 1696*

2   BELIRA. I would exchange thee for the last of men, and think the bargain cheap; would part with all that goodly form for honest ugliness, and think it fairer; thy youth for age, and doat upon his dotage, so in return I found but truth, mark well that word, that word has charms thou never knewest, and which out-weighs thine.

Ibid.

3   WILMORE. What woman's fair after we find her faulty? What lady innocent when no longer chaste? Or who so vain to hope for honour, or for pity from that soul who wants it for herself?

Ibid.

4   WILMORE. . . . vows that are made in love are writ in sand.

Act V, Sc. iii, Ibid.

5   ACMAT (a eunuch, speaking to the prince of Homais of his lady's behavior toward the prince's portrait).
How often have I seen this lovely Venus
Naked, extended, in the gaudy Bed,
Her snowy Breasts all panting with desire,
With gazing, melting Eyes, survey your Form,
And wish in vain, 't had Life to fill her Arms.

The Royal Mischief 1696

502. Elisabeth-Claude Jacquet de la Guerre (1664–1729)

1   He thinks he can escape the Lord by merely moving to a new place.

Recitatif, St. 2, *Jonas Cantata n.d.*

2   Such adversity! It seems that the world is returning to its primal, chaotic state.

Air, St. 1, Ibid.

503. Marie Jeanne L'Heritier (1664–1734)

1   You care for nothing but loving and joking.

"Rondeau, to a Young Girl," Elaine Bernstein Partnow,*
tr., Quoted in *Biography of Distinguished Women* by Sarah
Josepha Hale** 1876

*See 3291. **See 807.

504. Anne of England (1665–1714)

1   O, my dear brother, how I pity thee!

Remark to her brother, the future King William III,* on
her deathbed (20 July 1714), Quoted in *Biography of
Distinguished Women* by Sarah Josepha Hale** 1876

*(1650–1702; r. 1689–1702) **See 807.

505. Grisell Home (1665–1746)

1   When bonny young Johnnie cam' o'er the sea,
He said he saw naething sae lovely as me. . . .

"Warena My Heart Licht I Wad Dee," *Scottish Song,* Mary
Carlyle Aitken, ed. 1874

506. Henrietta Johnston (1665?–1728/29)

1   . . . reason and conscience startle not.

Letter to her husband (August 1713), Quoted in *Henrietta
Johnston, America's First Pastellist* by Margaret Simons
Middleton 1966

507. Mary Astell (1666/8–1731)

1   Women are from their very infancy debarr'd those advantages [of education] with the want of which they are afterwards reproached, nursed up in those vices with which will hereafter be upbraided them. So partial are Men as to expect Bricks when they afford no straw.

*A Serious Proposal to the Ladies for the Advancement of their
True and Greatest Interest* 1694

2   . . . Beauty with all the Helps of Art, is of no long Date; the more it is help'd the sooner it decays. . . .

Some Reflections Upon Marriage (repr. 1970) 1700

3   . . . he who only or chiefly chose for Beauty, will in a little Time find the same Reason for another Choice.

Ibid.

4   But how can a Woman scruple entire Subjection, how can she forbear to affirm the Worth and Excellency of the Superior Sex, if she at all considers it! Have not all the great Actions that have been performed in the World been done by Men? Have they not founded Empires and over-turned them? Do they not make Laws and continually repeal and amend them? Their vast Minds lay Kingdoms waste, no Bounds or Measures can be prescribed to their Desires. . . . What is it they cannot do? They make Worlds and ruin them . . .

Ibid.

5   There is not anything so excellent, but some will carp at it. . . .

Quoted in Preface (18 December 1724), *Letters of the Right
Honourable Lady Mary Wortley Montagu** 1767

*See 533.

508. Sarah Kemble Knight (1666–1727)

1   May all that dread the cruel fiend of night
Keep on, and not at this curs't mansion light.

Untitled (ca. 1704), *The Journal of Madame Knight,* Theodore
Dwight, Jr., ed. 1825

2   I ask thy Aid, O Potent Rum!
To charm these wrangling Topers Dum.
Thou hast their Giddy Brains possest—
The man confounded with the Beast—
And I, poor I, can get no rest.
Intoxicate them with thy fumes;
O still their Tongues till morning comes!

"Resentments Composed because of the Clamor of Town
Topers [drunkards] Outside My Apartment," in toto, Ibid.

509. Mary Griffith Pix (1666–1706/09?)

1   Deceiver Deceived, and Imposture cheated!. . . .
Our authoress, like true woman, showed her play
To some, who, like true wits, stole't half away.*

Prologue, *The Deceiver Deceived* 1698

*Reference to the plagiarism charges she and playwright William
Congreve brought against George Powell for his work, *The Imposture Defeated.*

2   The First Time she was grave, as well she might,
For Women will be damn'd sullen the first Night;
But faith, they'll quickly mend, so be n't uneasie:
To Night she's brisk, and trys New Tricks to please ye.

Prologue, *The Spanish Wives* 1696

3   MRS. RICH. . . . I quarrel daily with my destiny, that I was not at first a woman of quality . . . I had rather be the beggarliest

countess in the town, than the widow of the richest banker in Europe.

Act I, Sc. 1, *The Beau Defeated 1700*

4 LAURA. I find an Englishman true to one woman, nay even before he has had her is a miracle.

Act II, Sc. ii, *The Adventures in Madrid 1706*

5 GAYLOVE. Oh the affairs of love are quite different from those of war. We yield to all conditions before the engagement, but end alike, for when we have taken the town, we seldom keep them.

Act III, Sc. ii, Ibid.

510. Sophia Dorothea of Celle (1666–1726)

1 . . . my illness only comes from loving you, and I do not want to be cured of it.

Letter to George I (ca. 1689–1694), Quoted in *Lives of the Hanoverian Queens of England* by Alice Drayton Greenwood *1909*

511. Susanna Centlivre (1667–1723)

1 AMELIA. I have the best Proof in the World of it, ocular Demonstration.

Act III, Sc. 1, *The Beau's Duel 1702*

2 TOPER. Yesterday I carried to wait on a Relation of ours that has a Parrot, and whilst I was discoursing about some private Business, she converted the Bird, and now it talks of nothing but the Light of the Spirit, and the Inward man.

Ibid.

3 He surest strikes that smiling gives the blow.

Epilogue Ibid.

4 Friendship's a noble name, 'tis love refined.

Act II, Sc. 2, *The Stolen Heiress 1702*

5 Writing is a kind of Lottery in this fickle Age. . . .

Preface, *Love's Contrivance 1703*

6 OCTAVIO. . . . for I find by the beating of my Pulse, the Motion of my Brain, and the Heavings of my Heart, I am very far gone in that dangerous Distemper call'd Love, and you are the only Physician can save my life.

Act III, Sc. 1, Ibid.

7 LUCINDA. Once a week! I wou'd not for the World bed with you oftener; why 'tis not the Fashion, Sir Toby; and I assure you when I marry I hope to be my own Mistress, and follow my own Inclination, which will carry me to the utmost Pinnacle of the Fashion.

Act IV, Sc. 1, Ibid.

8 LADY LUCY. . . . nothing melts a Woman's Heart like gold.

Act IV, *The Basset-Table 1705*

9 VALERE. . . . there's nothing like ready Money to nick Fortune.

Act III, *The Gamester 1705*

10 HECTOR. Lying is a thriving Vocation.

Ibid.

11 HECTOR. What Business had you to get Children, without you had Cabbage enough to maintain 'em?

Ibid.

12 All policy's allowed in war and love.

Act I, *Love at a Venture 1706*

13 ISABINDA. The world cannot be more savage than our parents.

The Busie Body 1709

14 CHARLES. . . . Want, the Mistress of Invention, still tempts me on. . . .

Act I, Ibid.

15 MANAGE. . . . my present Profession is Physick—Now, when my Pockets are full, I cure a Patient in three Days; when they are empty, I keep him three months.

Act II, *The Man's Bewitched; or, The Devil to Do About Her 1709*

16 MARPLOT. I had rather fathom the Depth of Man's Thoughts, than his Pocket. . . .

Act III, Sc. 1, *Mar Plot, or, The Second Part of the Busy Body 1711*

17 FLORELLA. . . . nobody can boast of Honesty till they are try'd. . . .

Act III, Sc. 1, *The Perplex'd Lovers 1712*

18 DON LOPEZ. There is no Condition of Life without its Cares, and it is the Perfection of a Man to wear 'em as easy as he can. . . .

Act I, Sc. 1, *The Wonder: A Woman Keeps a Secret 1714*

512. Susanna Wesley (1668?–1742)

1 [To subdue the will of the child] is the only strong and rational foundation of a religious education, without which both precept and example will be ineffectual. But when this is thoroughly done, then a child is capable of being governed by the reason and piety of its parents till its own understanding comes to maturity, and the principles of religion have taken root in the mind.

Letter to her son, John Wesley,* *The Women of Methodism: Its Three Foundresses . . .* by Abel Stevens *1866*
*English preacher; founder of Methodism (1703–1791).

2 God's prescience is no more the effective cause of the loss of the wicked than our foreknowledge of the rising of tomorrow's sun is the cause of its rising.

Ibid.

513. Marie Thérèse Rodet Geoffrin (1669–1757)

1 Give and forgive.

Quoted in Biography of Distinguished Women by Sarah Josepha Hale* *1876*
*See 807.

2 We should not let the grass grow on the path of friendship.

Ibid.

3 Among those advantages which attract for us the most consideration are good manners, an erect bearing, a dignified demeanour, and to be able to enter a room gracefully; we dare not speak ill of a person who has all these advantages, for they presuppose thoughtfulness, order, and judgement.

Ibid.

514. Sarah Fyge Field Egerton (1670–1723)

1 When Heav'n survey'd the Works that it had done,
Saw Male and Female, but found Man

alone, A barren Sex, and insignificant,
then Heav'n made Woman to supply the want,
And to make perfect what before was
scant: Surely then she a Noble Creature is,
Whom Heav'n thus made to consummate all Bliss.

*The Female Advocate, or An Answer to a Late Satyr Against
the Pride, Lust, and Inconstancy, &c. of Woman* * 1683
*Her response to Robert Gould's misogynist tract *A Late Satyr
Against the Pride, Lust, and Inconstancy, etc. of Woman.*

2 For Adam most did of the guilt partake;
While he from God's own mouth had the Command,
But Woman had it at the second hand:

Ibid.

3 We find most Men have banish'd Truth for spight

Ibid.

515. Joan Philips (fl. ca. 1670–d. 1682)

1 Thou dull companion of our active years,
That chill'st our warm blood with thy frozen fears,
How is it likely thou shouldst long endure,
When thought itself thy ruin may procure?

"Maidenhead," *Female Poems on Several Occasions 1679*

2 Think me all man: my soul is masculine,
And capable of as great things as thine.

"To Phylocles, Inviting Him to Friendship," St. 3, Ibid.

516. Anne Baynard (1672–1697)

1 . . . it is a sin to be content with a little knowledge.

Quoted in *Biography of Distinguished Women* by Sarah
Josepha Hale* *1876*

*See 807.

2 I could wish that all young persons might be exhorted to . . .
read the great book of nature, wherein they may see the wisdom and power of the Creator, in the order of the universe,
and in the production and preservation of all things.

From her deathbed, Ibid.

517. Mary Davys (1674–1732)

1 As a Child born of a common Woman, has many Fathers, so
my poor Offspring has been laid at a great many Doors. . . . I
am proud they think it deserves a better Author.

Preface, *The Northern Heiress; or, The Humours of York 1716*

2 LADY GREASY. Love is like a bug, the longer it sticks in the
skin, the harder it is to pluck out.

Ibid.

3 The Pedant despises the most elaborate Undertaking, unless it
appears in the World with *Greek* and *Latin* Motto's; a Man
that would please him, must pore an Age over musty Authors,
till his Brains are as worm-eaten as the Books he reads, and his
Conversation fit for nobody else. . . .

The Reformed Coquet; or, the Memoirs of Amoranda 1724

4 How many brave Men, courageous Women, and innocent Children did I see butcher'd, to do God good Service? . . . I went
to the *Irish* Rebellion, where I saw more than three hundred
thousand Souls murder'd in cold Blood . . . crying, *Nits will
become Lice, destroy Root and Branch*: with a thousand other

Barbarities, too tedious as well as too dreadful to repeat, beside what has been transacted abroad.

"To Artander, November 10," *Familiar Letters, Betwixt a
Gentleman and a Lady 1725*

5 . . . we Women as naturally love Scandal, as you Men do Debauchery; and we can no more keep up Conversation without
one, than you can live an Age without t'other.

"To Artander, December 10," Ibid.

6 I cannot say I was ever so glutted with Pleasure in my Life,
as to be weary of it, nor properly speaking, can any body
say so; because, when once a Man is tir'd of a thing, it is no
longer a Pleasure, but retiring from it is; so that a Person
who has power to follow his own Inclinations, is always in
Pleasure. . . .

"To Berina, December 26," Ibid.

7 . . . Love, like Edg'd-Tools, shou'd never be play'd with.

"To Artander, January 12," Ibid.

8 MRS. FALLOW. So many Men and Women go together that, in
all probability, could never have met.

The Self-Rival; A Comedy 1725

518. Elizabeth Singer Rowe (1674–1737)

1 Thy numerous Works exalt Thee thus,
And shall I silent be?
No; rather let me cease to breathe,
Than cease from praising Thee!

"Hymn," St. 8, *Poems on Several Occasions by Philomela**
1696

* Her pseudonym.

2 . . . the studious follies of the great,
The tiresome farce of ceremonious state.

"Despair," Ibid.

3 By this thy glorious lineage thou dost prove
Thy high descent; for GOD himself is Love.

"Ode to Love," St. 11, *Miscellaneous Works in Prose and
Verse 1739*

519. Rosalba Carriera (1675–1757)

1 . . . I think that pleasures should be enjoyed with great sobriety
and moderation.

Ch. 6, Quoted in *Portraits and Backgrounds* by Evangeline
Wilbour Blashfield *1917*

2 You may be sure that I know that there is a world, men, and
bread beyond the lagoons [of Venice], but I submit to the will
of heaven which has decreed that my journeys shall be only
to my easel. I am contented with but little bread, while as to
men, believe me there is nothing in the world that I think less
of. . . .

Ibid.

3 . . . for three years I have been deprived of my sight. I wish you
to learn from my own hand that thanks to the Divine Goodness I have recovered it. I see but as one sees after an operation,
that is to say very dimly. Even this is a blessing for one who
has had the misfortune to become blind. When I was sightless I
cared for nothing, now I want to see everything. . . .

Ch. 7, Letter from Venice (23 August 1749), Ibid.

520. Elizabeth Thomas (1675/77?–1730/31)

1   Ah! strive no more to know what fate
       Is pre-ordain'd foe thee:
    'Tis vain in this my mortal state,
       For Heaven's inscrutable decree
    Will only be reveal'd in vast Eternity.
        "Predestination; or the Resolution," *Miscellany Poems on
        Several Subjects 1722*

521. Penelope Aubin (1679–1731)

1   Love and Honour had a sharp contest, but at last Love got the
    Victory, and the rose.
        Ch. 2, *The Life of the Lady Lucy 1726*

2   This is the vast difference betwixt doing well and ill; that in
    Vice the Pleasure is always momentary and of no duration, and
    the Remorse for having done it, sure and lasting; but in doing
    virtuous Deeds, tho' we may suffer Loss and Pain for some
    short time, yet we have always a secret Satisfaction within, that
    supports us under them, and the End brings us Honour and
    generally Reward, even in this world. . . .
        Ch. 10, Ibid.

522. Catherine Trotter (1679–1749)

1   . . . when a Woman appears in the World under any distin-
    guishing Character, she must expect to be the mark of ill
    nature.
        Dedication to Princess Anne, *Fatal Friendship 1698*

2   . . . We tax our Judgement, when we cease to love.
        Love at a Loss; or, Most Votes Carry It (a.k.a. *The
        Honourable Deceiver*) 1700

3   LESBIA. Hands, and Seals, and Oaths cannot secure
    A mind like Man's unfaithful and impure.
        Epilogue, Ibid.

4   But who the useful art can teach,
    When sliding down a steepy way,
    To stop, before the end we reach?
        "The Caution," St. 3, *The Female Wits*, Lucyle Hook, ed. *1704*

5   A heart whose safety but in flight does lie,
    Is too far lost to have the power to fly.
        "The Vain Advice," St. 2, *The Works of Mrs. Catharine
        Cockburn, Theological, Moral, Dramatic, and Poetical*,
        Thomas Birch, ed. *1751*

6   Women are as capable of penetrating into the grounds of things
    and reasoning justly as men are who certainly have no advan-
    tage of us but in their opportunities of knowledge . . .
        Vol. II, Ibid.

523. Jane Barker (fl. ca. 1680–d. 1715)

1   Happy life . . .
    Fearless of twenty-five and all its train,
    Of slights and scorns, or being called old maid. . . .
    Ah lovely state how strange it is to see,
    What mad conceptions some have made of thee,
    As though thy being was all wretchedness,
    Or foul deformity in the ugliest dress.
        "A Virgin Life," *Poetical Recreations 1688*

2   Poverty's the certain fate
    Which attends a poet's state.
        "Poetical Recreations," Ibid.

3   . . . thus we see that Human Projects are mere Vapours, carried
    about with every Blast of cross Accidents. . . .
        Love Intrigues 1713

524. Elizabeth Haddon Estaugh (1680–1762)

1   I'll venture to say, few, if any, in a married State, ever lived in
    sweeter Harmony than we did.
        Quoted in Introduction to *A Call to the Unfaithful Professors
        of Truth* by John Estaugh *1744*

2   I have received from the lord a charge to love thee, John Es-
    taugh.
        Attributed, Quoted in *Tales of a Wayside Inn* by Henry
        Wadsworth Longfellow* *1863*
    *American poet (1807–1882).

525. Eleonora von dem Knesebeck (fl. ca. 1680–d. 1713)

1   The [British] government must have done a deed of great injus-
    tice since they stop my mouth, for if they can answer to all the
    world for what they have done . . . why am I not [allowed to]
    speak? If their judgements are righteous, how should I dare to
    speak wrongfully?
        (ca. 1697), Quoted in *Lives of the Hanoverian Queens of
        England* by Alice Drayton Greenwood *1891*

526. Mrs. Taylor (fl. ca. 1680)

1   . . . tears,
    Those springs that water Love.
        "Song," St. 2, *Miscellany, Being a Collection of Poems by
        several Hands*, Aphra Behn,* ed. *1685*
    *See 472.

2   Alas! it does my soul perplex,
       When I his charms recall,
    To think he should despise the sex,
       Or what's worse, love them all.
        "Song," St. 3, Ibid.

527. Jane Wiseman (fl. ca. 1682–1717)

1   The Reception it [her play] met with in the World, was not
    kind enough to make me Vain, nor yet so ill, to discourage my
    Proceeding.
        Dedication, *Antiochus the Great; or, The Fatal Relapse 1701*

528. Elizabeth Elstob (1683–1756)

1   . . . I shou'd think it as Glorious an Employment to instruct
    Poor Children as to teach the Children of the Greatest Mon-
    arch.
        Letter to George Ballard (ca. 1740), Quoted in *A Galaxy of
        Governesses* by Bea Howe *1954*

2   . . . you can come into no company of Ladies and or Gentlemen,
    where you shall not hear an open and Vehement exclamation
    against Learned Women.
        Letter to George Ballard (ca. 1753), Ibid.

529. Jane Brereton (1685–1740)

1   Pope* is the emblem of true wit,

The sunshine of the mind.
"On Mr. Nash's** Picture at Full Length, Between the Busts of Sir Isaac Newton*** and Mr. Pope," St. 4, *Mrs. Jane Brereton's Poems 1744*
*British poet and satirist Alexander Pope (1688–1744). **British satirist and pamphleteer Thomas Nash (1567–1601). ***British physicist and mathematician (1643–1727).

2 I scorn this mean fallacious art
By which you'd steal, not win, my heart
"To Damon," St. 1, Ibid.

3 . . . Cupid's empire won't admit
Nor own, a Salic law.*
"To Philotinus," St. 2, Ibid.
*European law of succession (derived from a 5th-century Frankish code), prohibiting daughters from inheriting land and women from succeeding to a throne.

530. Claudine Alexandrine de Tencin (1685–1749)

1 Unless God visibly interferes, it is physically impossible that the state [France] should not fall to pieces.
Quoted in *Biography of Distinguished Women* by Sarah Josepha Hale* *1876*
*See 807.

531. Mary Chandler (1687–1745)

1 Fatal effects of luxury and ease!
We drink our poison and we eat disease.
"Temperance," *The Female Poets of Great Britain,* Frederic Rowton, ed. *1853*

532. Mary Collier (1689/90–ca. 1762)

1 In gleaning Corn, such is our frugal Care.
When Night comes on, unto our Home we go,
Our Corn we carry, and our Infant too;
Weary indeed! but 'tis not worth our while
Once to complain, or rest at ev'ry Stile;
We must make haste, for when we home are come,
We find again our Work has just begun;
So many Things for our Attendance call,
Had we ten hands, we could employ them all.
The Woman's Labour 1739

2 Our Toil and Labour's daily so extreme,
That we have hardly ever Time to Dream.
Ibid.

533. Mary Wortley Montagu (1689–1762)

1 But when the long hours of public are past,
And we meet with champagne and a chicken at last,
May every fond pleasure that moment endear;
Be banish'd afar both discretion and fear!
"The Lover: A Ballad (To Mr. Congreve),"* St. 4, *Six Town Ecologues 1747*
*English playwright (1670–1729).

2 In crowded courts I find myself alone,
And pay my worship to a nobler throne.
"In Answer to a Lady who advised Retirement," St. 1, *The London Magazine May 1750*

3 I enjoy vast delight in the folly of mankind; and, God be praised, that is an inexhaustible source of entertainment.
Letter to Countess of Mar (n.d.), *Letters of the Right Honourable Lady Mary Wortley Montagu 1767*

4 General notions are generally wrong.
Letter to Wortley Montagu, her husband (28 March 1710), Ibid.

5 A woman, till five-and-thirty, is only looked upon as a raw girl, and can possibly make no noise in the world till about forty.
Letter to Lady R[ich], (Vienna, 20 September 1716), Ibid.

6 . . . if it were the fashion to go naked, the face would be hardly observed.
(Sophia, Turkey, 1717), Ibid.

7 I am patriot enough to take pains to bring this useful invention [smallpox inoculation] into fashion in England; and I should not fail to write to some of our doctors very particularly about it, if I knew any one of them that I thought had virtue enough to destroy such a considerable branch of revenue for the good of mankind.
Letter to Lady Mar [her sister], (Belgrade, 1 April 1717), Ibid.

8 I give myself sometimes admirable advice, but I am incapable of taking it.
Letter to Lady Mar (1725), Ibid.

9 Nobody can deny but religion is a comfort to the distressed, a cordial to the sick, and sometimes a restraint on the wicked; therefore, whoever* would laugh or argue it out of the world, without giving some equivalent for it, ought to be treated as a common enemy.
Letter to Countess of Bute [her daughter] (1752), Ibid.
*Reference to Irish satirist Jonathan Swift (1667–1745).

10 . . . the knowledge of numbers is one of the chief distinctions between us and the brutes.
(28 January 1753), Ibid.

11 True knowledge consists in knowing things, not words.
Ibid.

12 People are never so near playing the fool as when they think themselves wise.
(1 March 1755), Ibid.

13 Civility costs nothing and buys everything.
(30 May 1756), Ibid.

14 . . . it is now eleven years since I have seen my figure in a glass, and the last reflection I saw there was so disagreeable, that I resolved to spare myself the mortification in the future.
Letter (Venice, ca. 1758–1761), Ibid.

15 It [her health] is so often impaired that I begin to be as weary of it as mending old lace; when it is patched in one place, it breaks out in another.
Ibid.

16 Be plain in dress, and sober in your diet;
In short, my dreary, kiss me! and be quiet.
"In Summary of Lord Lyttleton's Advice to a Lady," *Poetical Works 1768*

17 But the fruit that will fall without shaking,
   Indeed is too mellow for me.
   　　"To a Lady Making Love; or, Answered, for Lord Hamilton,"
   　　　　　　　　　　　　　　　　　　　　　　Ibid.

18 Consider, friend, but coolly, and you'll find
   Revenge the frailty of a feeble mind;
   　　"To the Same," St. 3, *The Letters and Works of Lady Mary
   　　　　　Wortley Montagu,* Lord Wharncliffe, ed. *1861*

19 A real marriage bears no resemblance to these marriages of
   interest or ambition. It is two lovers who live together. A
   priest may well say certain words, a notary may well sign certain papers—I regard these preparations in the same way that
   a lover regards the rope ladder that he ties to his mistress's
   window.
   　　　　　　　　　　　　　　　　　　　　　Essay *n.d.*

534. Mary Waite (?–1689)

1 All the
   sinners in Sion shall be
   afraid, fearfulnesse shall take hold on the
   Hypocrite. Dread and
   horror shall surprise them. O whither will
   you unfaithful fly!
   　　*A Warning to all Friends Who Professeth the Everlasting Truth
   　　of God, which he hath Revealed and made manifest in this his
   　　Blessed Day, (whether on this Side, or beyond the Seas.) 1679*

2 For the Devil is the King of pride . . .
   　　　　　　　　　　　　　　　　　　　　　　Ibid.

535. Ariadne (fl. ca. 1690)

1 [I] could not conquer the Inclination I had for Scribling from
   my Childhood. And when our Island enjoyed the Blessing of
   the incomparable Mrs. [Aphra] Behn,* even then I had much
   ado to keep my muse from shewing her Impertinence; but,
   since her death, has claim'd a kind of Privilege; and, in spite of
   me, broke from her Confinement.
   　　　　　　　　　　Preface, *She Ventures and He Wins 1695*
   *See 472.

2 (Enter CHARLOTTE and JULIANA in men's clothes.)
   JULIANA. Faith, Charlotte, the breeches become you so well
   'tis almost pity you should ever part with 'em.
   CHARLOTTE. Nor will I, till I can find one can make better
   use of them to bestow 'em on, and then I'll resign my title to
   'em for ever.
   JULIANA. 'Tis well if you find it so easy for a woman once
   vested in authority though 'tis by no other than her own making, does not willingly part with it.
   　　　　　　　　　　　　　　　　　Act I, Sc. 1, Ibid.

536. Mary Barber (1690?–1757)

1 A richer present I design,
   A finished form, of work divine,
   Surpassing all the power of art;
   A thinking head, a grateful heart.
   　　"On Sending my Son as a Present to Dr. [Jonathan] Swift,*
   　　Dean of St. Patrick's, on his Birthday," *Poems on Several
   　　　　　　　　　　　　　　　　　　　　　Occasions 1734*
   *Irish satirist (1667–1745)

537. Francisca Josefa del Castillo y Guevara (1691?–1743)

1 The land grew bright in a single flower—
   One great carnation rare. . . .
   　　"Christmas Carol," St. 1, *The Catholic Anthology,* Thomas
   　　　　　　　　　　　　　　　　　　　Walsh, ed. *1927*

2 "My sin has led me far
   As some wild thirsting bee
   Beneath Thy meadow star,
   Idly forgetting Thee;
   But Thou dost call me home; I hear
   Thy voice whose sweetness charms mine ear.
   　　　　　　　　　　　"The Holy Ecologue," St. 6, Ibid.

538. Martha Corey (?–1692)

1 Ye are all against me and I cannot help it.*
   　　　　Remark (1692), Quoted in *Notable American Women,*
   　　　　　　　　　　　　　　　Edward T. James, ed. *1971*
   *Remark at her trial for witchcraft in Salem, Massachusetts.

539. Eliza Haywood (1693?–1756)

1 Criticks! be dumb to-night—no Skill display;
   A dangerous Woman-Poet wrote the Play:
   One, who not fears your Fury, tho' prevailing,
   More than your match, in every thing, but Railing.
   Give her fair Quarter, and whene'er she tries ye,
   Safe in superior Spirit, she defies ye . . .
   　　　　　　　　　　　　　　　A Wife to Be Let 1723

2 Flattery is a Vice so much in Fashion, and, I am sorry to say,
   so much encouraged, that there is nothing more difficult than
   to find a Patron who not expects, nor would be pleased with
   it. . . .
   　　　　　　　　　　　Dedication, *The Rash Resolve 1724*

3 How little are the ill judging Multitude capable of chusing for
   themselves! How far are Wealth and Beauty, the two great
   Idols of the admiring world, from being real Blessings to the
   Possessors of them!
   　　　The Mercenary Lover; or, the Unfortunate Heiresses 1726

4 The base are always Cowards, the same Meaness of Spirit
   which makes them the one, inclines them to the other also;
   they are ever in Fear, and while there remains even the smallest
   Probability of Danger, peace is a Stranger to their Minds.
   　　　　　　　　　　　　　　　　　　　　　　Ibid.

5 The natural Propensity which all People have to listen to any Arguments which may serve to excuse the Errors they commit. . . .
   　　　　　　　　　　　　　　　　　　　　　　Ibid.

6 Philosophy is the toil which can never tire the persons engaged
   in it; all its ways are strewed with roses, and the farther you go,
   the more enchanting objects appear before you and invite you
   on.
   　　　"Study of Philosophy Recommended," *The Female Spectator
   　　　　　　　　　　　　　　　　　　　　　1744–46*

7 I desire no other Revenge for my abused Sincerity, than that you
   may, some time or other, find a Woman fair enough to create a
   real Passion in you; and as insensible of it, as you are of mine.
   　　　"The History of Graciana," *Memoirs of a Certain Island
   　　　　　　　　Adjacent to the Kingdom of Utopia 1775*

540. Charlotte Elizabeth Aissé (1694/95–1733)

1 We sup wretchedly, we have neither good fish nor good friends.
> Ch. 5, Letter, Quoted in *Portraits and Backgrounds* by
> Evangeline Wilbour Blashfield *1917*

2 . . . I could never love where I could not respect.
> Ch. 5, Letter, Ibid.

3 It seems to be a natural human impulse to profit by the weakness of others. I do not know how to use such arts; I know only one: to make life so sweet to him I love that he will find nothing preferable to it.
> Ch. 6, Letter, Ibid.

541. Elizabeth Tollet (1694–1754)

1 The conscious moon and stars above
   Shall guide me with my wandering love.
> "Winter Song," an Epistle to King Henry VIII, *Poems on
> Several Occasions*, with Anne Boleyn* *1755*
> *See 300.

2 'Tis vanished all! remains alone
   The eyeless scalp of naked bone;
   The vacant orbits sunk within;
   The jaw that offers at a grin.
   Is this the object, then, that claims
   The tribute of our youthful flames?
> "On a Death's Head," Ibid.

542. Cornelia Bradford (1695?–1755)

1 The Punsters are of Opinion, that though we could not Cope with the Rebellion at first, we shall make shift to Wade thro' it at last.*
> From article in *American Weekly Mercury*, Quoted in *Andrew
> Bradord, Colonial Journalist* by A. J. DeArmond *1949*
> *Neither Sir John *Cope* nor Field Marshal George *Wade* was successful in stemming the Jacobite invasion of 1745.

543. Anne Douglas Howard (1696–1764)

1 Nothing so like as male and female youth;
   Nothing so like as man and woman old
> "A defence to her sex in answer to [Alexander] Pope's*
> 'Characters of Women'," *The British Female Poets,* George W.
> Bethune, ed. *1848*
> *English poet and satirist (1688–1744).

2 In education all the difference lies . . .
> Ibid.

3 Culture improves all fruits, all sorts we find,
   Wit, judgement, sense, fruits of the human mind.
> Ibid.

544. Marie Anne du Deffand (1697–1780)

1 What more can you ask? He [Voltaire*] has invented history!
   (Que voulez-vous de plus? Il a inventé l'histoire!)
> Quoted in *L'Esprit dans histoire* by Fournier *1857*
> *Pen name of François Marie Arouet (1694–1798), French philosopher and writer.

2 The distance is nothing: it is only the first step that is difficult.*
> Letter to Jean Le Rond d'Alembert (7 July 1763),
> *Correspondence inédite 1859*
> *Refers to the legend that St. Denis, carrying his head in his hands, walked two leagues.

3 I do not know why Diogenes* went looking for a man: nothing could happen to him worse than finding one.
> Ibid.
> *Greek philosopher (412?–323 B.C.E.)

4 I hear nothings, I speak nothings, I take interest in nothing and from nothing to nothing I travel gently down the dull way which leads to becoming nothing.
> Ibid.

5 I remember thinking in my youth that no one was happy but madmen, drunkards and lovers.
> Ibid.

6 Faith is a devout belief in what one does not understand.
> Ibid.

7 Vanity ruins more women than love.
> Quoted in *Lettres à Voltaire,* Joseph Trabucco, ed. *1922*

545. Friederika Karoline Neuber (1697–1760)

1 Dear reader, here is something for you to read. To be sure, it is not written by a great, scholarly man. Oh, no! It is by a mere woman whose name you scarcely know and for whose station in life you have to look among the most humble of people, for she is nothing but a comedian. She cannot be responsible for anything but her own art, though she does know enough to understand another artist when he talks about his work. If you should ask her why she writes at all, her answer will be the customary feminine "Because." If any one asks you who helped her, you had better answer, "I don't know"—for it may very well be that she did it all herself.
> Preface to the play *Vorspiel,* Quoted in *Enter the Actress* by
> Rosamond Gilder *1931*

546. Susanna Wright (1697–1784)

1 Flowers on thy breast, and round thy head,
   With thee their sweets resign,
   Nipp'd from their tender stalks, and dead,
   Their fate resembles thine
> "On the Death of a Young Girl," St. 11 (1737), *Women Poets
> in Pre-Revolutionary America,* Patti Cowell, ed. *1981*

2 And what are they—a vision all the past,
   A bubble on the water's shining face,
   What yet remain, till the first transient blast,
   Shall leave no more remembrance of their place.
> "My Own Birth-Day," St. 2 (1 August 1761), Ibid.

547. Henrietta Luxborough (1699–1756)

1 Yon bullfinch, with unvaried tone,
   Of cadence harsh, and accent shrill,
   Has brighter plumage to atone
   For want of harmony and skill.
> "The Bullfinch in Town," St. 2, *A Collection of Poems. By
> Several Hands,* Robert Dodsley, ed. *1748*

548. Anne Bonny (1700–1782)

1 I am sorry to see you here Jack,* but if you had fought like a man, you need not be hanged like a dog.
> Quoted in, *A General History of the Robberies and Murders
> of the most notorious Pyrates* by Captain Charles Johnson
> (pseud.) *1724*
> *John Rackham, a.k.a. Calico Jack (1682–1720), English pirate with whom Bonny had an affair; upon his being sentenced to death; her husband threatened to sell her in divorce upon discovering her affair with pirate "Calico Jack."

2 I will not be bought and sold like cattle.

Ibid.

549. Mary Delany (1700–1788)

1 Hail to the happy times when fancy led
My pensive mind the flow'ry path to tread,
And gave me emulation to presume,
With timid art, to race fair nature's bloom

Preface, *Flora, or, Herbal n.d.*

550. Sarah Updike Goddard (1700?–1770)

1 . . . [the] mystick art of printing. . . .

Untitled poem, from *Providence Gazette* (16 March 1765),
Ch. 4, Quoted in *William Goddard, Newspaperman* by Ward
L. Miner *1962*

2 Ye learned physicians, whose excellent skill,
Can save, or demolish, can cure, or can kill;
To a poor forlorn damsel contribute your aid,
Who is sick, very sick of remaining a maid.

"The Distressed Maid" (30 August 1766), Ibid.

3 . . . every one who takes delight in publicly or privately taking
away any person's *good name*, or striving to render him ridiculous, are in the gall of bitterness, and in the bonds of iniquity,
whatever their pretences may be for it.

Letter to her son, William Goddard, Ch. 5, Ibid.

551. Kshetrayya (fl. 17th century)

1 He* set my heart floating on the honey stream of his words,
With his amorous kiss he burnt my lips,
And left me utterly alone, and unfulfilled.

"Dancing-Girl's Song," St. 2, *Indian Love Poems,* Tambimuttu
and R. Appalaswamy, eds. and trs. *n.d.*
*The god Krishna.

552. Marchioness de Tibergeau (fl. 17th century)

1 No, it isn't the point of poetry to write of the tenderness of
love:
To pick away at it, finding just the right words,
Arranging all in perfect measure and rhyme,
Stripping the heart to feed the mind.

Untitled, Elaine Bernstein Partnow,* tr., Quoted in *Biography
of Distinguished Women* by Sarah Josepha Hale** *1876*
*Author; see 3291. **See 807.

553. Wang Wei (fl. 17th century)

1 A traveler's thoughts in the night
Wander in a thousand miles of dreams.

"Seeking a Mooring," *The Orchid Boat, Women Poets of
China,* Kenneth Rexroth and Ling Chung, eds. and trs. *1972*

554. Fukuzoyo Chiyo (1701/03?–1775)

1 The dew of the rouge-flower
When it is spilled
Is simply water.

Untitled haiku, R. H. Blyth, tr., *The Penguin Book of Women
Poets,* Carol Cosman, Joan Keefe, and Kathleen Weaver, eds.
1978

2 After a long winter
giving

each other nothing, we collide
with blossoms in our hands.

Untitled, in toto, David Ray, tr., *A Book of Women Poets,* Aliki
and Willis Barnstone, eds. *1980*

555. Sidqi (?–1703)

1 From the hand of Power Unbounded draineth he the Wine of
Life,
Aye inebriate with Knowledge, learning's light, desireth not.

Untitled ghazel, *Wise Women: Over 2000 Years of Spiritual
Writing by Women,* Susan Cahill, ed. *1996*

556. Judith Boulbie (?–1706)

1 And (you). . . . scoffers (who say) those silly Quakers . . . setting up men and women's meeting their prescribing laws and
statutes . . . and decrees to what purpose is women's meetings
the men can do the business the women must be subject to
their husbands, but . . . there is a little remnant which is one
with our brethren and is entered into the work and service and
feels that heavenly reward in their bosoms which all that world
. . . can (not) . . . take it from us. Therefore my dear sisters let
nothing discompose your minds . . .

(p. 333), Quoted in *Visionary Women: Ecstatic Prophecy in
Seventeenth-Century England* by Phyllis Mack *1992*

557–558. Émilie du Châtelet (Gabrielle-Émilie le Tonnelier de Breteuil Du Châtelet) (1706–1749)

1 I am convinced that many women are either unaware of their
talents by reason of the fault in their education or that they
bury them on account of prejudice for want of intellectual
courage.

Preface, *The fable of the bees (1714),* Bernard Mandeville; tr.
ca. 1737

2 I feel the full weight of the prejudice which so universally ex-
cludes us from the sciences; it is one of the contradictions in
life that has always amazed me, seeing that the law allows us
to determine the fate of great nations, but that there is no place
where we are trained to think . . .

Ibid.

3 If I were king, I would establish *collèges* for women.

La Dame d'Esprit, A Biography of the Marquise Du Châtelet
Judith P. Zinsser *2006*

4 [I hope to win] the applause of posterity . . . from which one
expects more justice than from one's contemporaries.

Ibid.

559. Constantia Grierson (1706?–1733)

1 And if to wit, our courtship they pretend,
'Tis the same way that they a cause defend;
In which they give of lungs a vast expence,
But little passion, thought, or eloquence.

"To Miss Laetitia Van Lewen (Afterwards Mrs. Pilkington),*
at a Country Assize," *Poems on Several Occasions,* Mary
Barber, ed.** *1734*
*See 563. **See 536.

560. Mercy Wheeler (1706–1733?)

1 Poor, wretched and vile sinners all
Rank'd with the heathen nation,

Who unto God ne'er pray nor call,
For pardon and salvation.
> Untitled, St. 1 (1732), *Women Poets in Pre-Revolutionary America*, Patti Cowell, ed. *1981*

561. Anna Williams (1706–1783)

1 When Delia strikes the trembling string,
   She charms our list'ning ears;
   But when she joins her voice to sing,
   She emulates the spheres.
> "On a Lady Singing," St. 1, *Biography of Distinguished Women* by Sarah Josepha Hale* *1876*

*See 807.

562. Selina Hastings (1707–1791)

1 I am well; all is well—well for ever. I see, wherever I turn my eyes, whether I live or die, nothing but victory.*
> Quoted in *The Women of Methodism: Its Three Foundresses . . .* by Abel Stevens *1866*

*Remark after a stroke that presaged her death.

2 My work is done; I have nothing left to do but to go to my Father.*
>   Ibid.

*Some of her last words.

563. Laetitia Pilkington (1708–1750)

1 Lying is an occupation
     Used by all who mean to rise;
   Politicians owe their station
     But to well-concerted lies.

   These to lovers give assistance
     To ensnare the fair one's heart;
   And the virgin's best resistance
     Yields to this commanding art.

   Study this superior science,
     Would you rise in church or state;
   Bid to truth a bold defiance,
     'Tis the practice of the great.
> "Song," in toto, *Memoirs of Mrs. Laetitia Pilkington, written by herself, Wherein are occasionally interspersed all her Poems, with Anecdotes of several eminent persons living and dead* *1748*

564. Jane Colman Turell (1708–1735)

1 My good fat Bacon, and our homely Bread,
   With which my healthful Family is fed.
   Milk from the Cow, and Butter newly churn'd,
   And new fresh Cheese, with Curds and
   Cream just turn'd.
> "An Invitation Into the Country, In Imitation of Horace," St. 4, *Reliquiae Turellae et Lachrymae Paternae* [Relics of Turell and Paternal Tears] *1735*

*Roman poet (65–8 B.C.E.).

2 Dauntless you undertake th' unequal strife,
   And raise dead virtue by your verse to life.
   A woman's pen strikes the curs'd serpent's head,
   And lays the monster gaping, if not dead.
> "On Reading the Warning by Mrs. Singer",* *Women Poets in Pre-Revolutionary America*, Patti Cowell, ed. *1981*

*Elizabeth Singer Rowe; see 518.

3 . . . no pain is like a bleeding heart.
> "Part of the Fifth Chapter of Canticles Paraphras'd From the 8th Verse," St. 1 (14 September 1725), Ibid.

4 Thrice in my womb I've found the
     pleasing strife,
   In the first struggles of my infant's life:
   But O how soon by Heaven I'm call'd to mourn,
   While from my womb a lifeless babe is torn?
   Born to the grave ere it has seen the light,
   Or with one smile had cheer'd my longing sight.
> "Lines on Childbirth," St. 2, Ibid.

565. Mary Washington (1708–1789)

1 I am not surprised at what George* has done, for he was always a very good boy.
> *Recollections and Private Memoirs of Washington by his adopted son, George Washington Parke Curtis, with a Memoir of the Author, by his daughter . . .* *1860*

* G- Washington, 1st President of the United States (1732–1799).

566. Lydia Fish Willis (1709–1767)

1 The gate is straight,—the way is narrow,—my heart is hard,—my sins are great,—my strength is weak,—my faith is so benighted with doubts, that I am ready to cast all offered good away. . . .

   Such languid, faint desires I feel,
   Within this wicked, stupid heart,
   I should, I would, but that, I will,
   I hardly dare (with truth) assert.
> "Lines from an Undated Letter to her Niece," *Rachel's Sepulchre; Or, a Memorial of Mrs. Lydia Willis, taken Chiefly, from her Letters to Friends . . .* *1767?*

567. Sarah Pierpont Edwards (1710–1758)

1 My soul remained in a kind of heavenly elysium.
> Ch. XIV, Quoted in *The Works of President Edwards* (1738)*, Vol. I, Sereno E. Dwight, ed. *1830*

*Jonathan Edwards, American theologian and philosopher (1703–1758).

2 I seemed to myself to perceive a glow of divine love come down from the heart of Christ in heaven, into my heart, in a constant stream, like a stream or pencil of sweet light. At the same time, my heart and soul all flowed out in love to Christ.
>   Ibid.

568. Sarah Fielding (1710–1768)

1 " . . . the height of my distress lies in not knowing my own mind; if I could once find that out, I should be easy enough. I am so divided by the desire of riches on the one hand, and by my honour and the man I like on the other, that there is such a struggle in my mind I am almost distracted."
> *David Simple, ca. 1750*

2 "I hope to be excused by those gentlemen who are quite sure they have found one woman who is a perfect angel, and that all the rest are perfect devils. . . ."
>   Ibid.

3 "I think there is nothing so pleasant as revenge; I would pursue a man who had injured me to the very brink of life. I know it would be impossible for me ever to forgive him; and I would have him live only that I might have the pleasure of seeing him miserable."

Ibid.

569. Mary Hearne (fl. ca. 1710–20)

1 Love . . . generally hurries us on without Consideration. . . .
"The Third Day," *The Lover's Week* 1718

2 . . . Love and Reason, like a Fever and Ague, took their alternate Turns in my Breast. . . .
"The Amours of Calista and Torismond," *The Female Deserters* 1719

3 . . . therefore You should not by the vulgar Notion of Marriage make yourself uneasy, since that Ceremony is nothing but a piece of Formality, introduced on purpose to bring Profit to the Church; and I think that Love is much more to be Esteem'd, which has no other Motive but mutual Affection.

Ibid.

570. Mary Singleton Copley Pelham (1710–1789)

1 Your fame, my dear son, is sounded by all who are lovers of the art you bid fair to excel in. May God prosper and cause you to succeed in all your undertakings, and enroll your name among the first in your profession.
Letter to John Singleton Copley,* her son (Boston, 6 February 1788), Quoted in *The Domestic and Artistic Life of John Singleton Copley, R.A.* by Martha Babcock Amory 1882
*American loyalist painter (1738–1815).

571. Marie de Beauveau (1711–1786)

1 Say what you will in two
Words and get through.
"Air: Sentir avec ardeur," St. 1, Ezra Pound,* tr., *Confucius to Cummings; An Anthology of Poetry*, Ezra Pound and Marcella Spann, eds. 1964
*American poet and critic (1885–1972).

2 An idiot
Will always
Talk a lot.

St. 2, Ibid.

572. Catherine Clive (1711–1785)

1 WILLING. But don't your heart ache when you think of the first night, hey?
The Rehearsal: or, Boys in Petticoats 1753

2 MRS. HAZARD. Oh fie, Miss! that will never do: you speak your words as plain as a parish girl: the audience will never endure you in this kind of singing; if they understand what you say. You must give your words the Italian accent.

Ibid.

3 Necessity or inclination brings every one to the stage.
Quoted in *The Life of Mrs. Catherine Clive* by Percy Fitzgerald 1888

4 I am at present in such health and such spirits, that when I recollect I am an old woman, I am astonished.
Letter to Mr. [David] Garrick* (London, 14 April 1769), Ibid.

5 I have seen your lamb turned into a lion: by this your great labour was entertained; they thought they all acted very fine—they did not see you pull the wires.
Letter to Mr. Garrick* (Twickenham, 23 June 1776), Ibid.

*English actor and theater manager (1717–1779).

573. Ho Shuang-ch'ing (1712–?)

1 The hardest thing in the world
Is to reveal a hidden love.
to the tune "A Watered Silk Dress," *The Orchid Boat, Women Poets of China*, Kenneth Rexroth and Ling Chung, eds. and trs. 1972

574. Alicia Cockburn (1713–1794)

1 I've seen the smiling of fortune beguiling,
I've felt all its favours and found its decay;
Sweet was its blessing and kind its caressing,
But now it is fled—it is fled far away.
"The Flowers of the Forest,"* *Scottish Song*, Mary Carlyle Aitken, ed. 1874
*This is a reworking of a much older, anonymous song. (Cf. Jean Elliot, 599:1.) The reference is to the thousands of men led by James IV who were slain at the Battle of Flodden Field (9 September 1513).

2 The flowers of the forest are withered away.

Refrain, Ibid.

575. Esther Hayden (1713?–1758)

1 I'm sore distress'd, and greatly 'press'd
With filthy Nature, Sin;
I cannot rise to view the Prize
Of happiness within.
Untitled, *A Short Account of the Life, Death and Character of Esther Hayden, the Wife of Samuel Hayden of Braintree (Mass.)* 1759

576. Abigail Colman Dennie (1715–1745)

1 Yet still my fate permits me this relief,
To write to lovely Delia* all my grief.
To you alone I venture to complain;
From others hourly strive to hide my pain.
Lines from a letter to her sister, Jane Colman* (23 March 1733), Quoted in *New England Historical and Genealogical Register*, No. 14 1860
*Her sister, the poet Jane Colmam Turell; see 564.

577. Mary Monk (?–1715)

1 A just applause and an immortal name
Is the true object of the Poet's aim
"Epistle to Marinda," *Marinda: Poems and Translations on Several Occasions* 1716

2 Say, shouldst thou grieve to see my sorrows end?
Thou know'st a painful pilgrimage I've past;
And shouldst thou grieve that rest is come at last?
Rather rejoice to see me shake off life,
And die as I have liv'd, thy faithful wife.
"Verses written on her deathbed at Bath, to her husband in London," Ibid.

578. Elizabeth Carter (1717–1806)

1 For Wealth, the smiles of glad content,
For Power, its amplest, best extent,
An empire o'er the mind.
> "Ode to Wisdom," St. 7, *Poems Upon Particular Occasions*
> *1738*

2 I have nothing to assist me but industry; genius I have none, and I want mightily to know whether one can make any progress without it.
> Quoted in *A Woman of Wit and Wisdom* by Alice C. C.
> Gaussen *1906*

3 I am sick of people of sense because they can act like fools, and of fools because they cannot talk like people of sense, and of myself for being so absurd as to trouble my head about them.
> Letter to a friend (1745), Ibid.

4 Do you want employment? Choose it well before you begin, and then pursue it. Do you want amusement? Take the first you meet with that is harmless, and never be attached to any. Are you in a moderate station? Be content, though not affectedly so; be philosophical, but for the most part keep your thoughts to yourself. Are you sleepy? Go to bed.
> Ibid.

579. Maria Theresa (1717–1780)

1 My son,* as you are the heir to all my worldly possessions, I cannot dispose of them; but my children are still, as they have ever been, my *own*. I bequeath them to you; be to them a father.
> Last words (29 November 1780), Quoted in *Biography of
> Distinguished Women* by Sarah Josepha Hale** *1876*
> *Joseph II (1741–1790), Holy Roman Emperor, 1765–1790. **See
> 807.

2 I want to meet my God awake.
> Remark on her deathbed, refusing drugs; attributed by
> Thomas Carlyle* *November 1780*
> *Scottish-born author (1795–1881).

580. Anne Steele (1717–1778/79)

1 Little monitor, by thee
Let me learn what I should be;
Learn the round of life to fill,
Useful and progressive still.
> "To My Watch," *Poems on Subjects Chiefly Devotional 1760*

581. Maria Gaëtana Agnesi (1718–1799)

1 . . . proper clarity and simplicity . . . , that natural order which provides, perhaps, the best instruction and the greatest light.
> Preface, *Instituzioni analitiche ad uso della gioventù italiana*,
> Vol. 1 *1748*

2 With all the study, sustained by the strongest inclination towards mathematics, that I forced myself to devote to it on my own, I should have become altogether tangled in the great labyrinth of insuperable difficulty, had not [Rampinelli's*] secure guidance and wise direction led me forth from it . . . ; to him I owe deeply all advances (whatever they might be) that my small talent has sufficed to make.
> Ibid.
> *Ramiro Rampinelli, monk and mathematician.

582. Mary Draper (1718?–1810)

1 He [her son] is wanted and must go. You [her daughter] and I, Kate, have also service to do. Food must be prepared for the hungry; for before to-morrow night, hundreds, I hope thousands, will be on their way to join the continental forces.
> Response to a call to arms (1776), Quoted in *The Women of
> the American Revolution* by Elizabeth F. Ellet *1848*

583. Frances Fulke Greville (1720–1789)

1 No peace nor ease the heart can know,
Which, like the needle true,
Turns at the touch of joy or woe,
But, turning, trembles too.
> "Prayers for Indifference,"* St. 6 (1753), *Maxims and
> Characters 1756*
> *See Isabella Howard, 589:1, for reply poem.

2 And what of life remains for me
I'll pass in sober ease;
Half pleased, contented I will be,
Content but half to please.
> last stanza, Ibid.

584. Charlotte Lennox (1720–1804)

1 I am not cruel enough to wish his Death; say that I command him to live, if he can live without Hope.
> *Arabella; or, The Female Quixote*, Vol. I *1752*

2 "Oh! Sir," cried Sir George, "I have Stock enough by me, to set up an Author Tomorrow, if I please: I have no less than Five Tragedies, some quite, others almost finished; Three or Four Essays on Virtue, Happiness, etc., Three thousand Lines of an Epic Poem; half a Dozen Epitaphs; a few Acrostics; and a long String of Puns, that would serve to embellish a Daily Paper, if I was disposed to write one."
> Vol. II, Ibid.

3 The only excellence of Falsehood . . . is its Resemblance to Truth. . . .
> Ibid.

4 It is the Fault of the best Fictions, that they teach young Minds to expect strange Adventures and sudden Vicissitudes, and therefore encourage them often to Chance. A long Life may be passed without a single Occurrence that can cause much Surprize, or produce any unexpected Consequence of great Importance.
> Ibid.

5 " . . . I believe there is an intelligent cause which governs the world by physical rules. As for moral attributes, there is no such thing; it is impious and absurd to suppose it."
> *Henrietta*, Vol. II *1758*

6 "Whatever is, is best. The law of nature is sufficiently clear; and there is no need of supernatural revelation."
> Ibid.

7 The life of a good man is a continual prayer.
> *Euphemia*, Vol. IV *1790*

585. Elizabeth Montagu (1720–1800)

1 Will an intelligent spectator not admire the prodigious structures of Stone-Henge because he does not know by what law of mechanics they were raised?
> *An Essay on the Writing and Genius of Shakespeare*
> *Compared with Greek and French Dramatic Poets* . . . *1769*
> *William S— (1564–1616), English playwright, poet.

2 To judge therefore of Shakespeare by Aristotle's* rule is like trying a man by the Laws of one Country who acted under those of another.

> Ibid.

*Greek philosopher (384–322 B.C.E.).

3 Shakespeare seemed to have had the art of the Dervish in the Arabian tales who could throw his soul into the body of another man and be at once possessed of his sentiments, adopt his passions and rise to all the functions and feelings of his situation.

> Ibid.

4 Gold is the chief ingredient in the composition of worldly happiness. Living in a cottage on love is certainly the worst diet and the worst habitation one can find out.

> *The Letters of Mrs. Elizabeth Montagu 1810–13*

5 If she [Catherine the Great*] is not a good woman, she is a great Prince.

> Letter to Lord Lyttleton, Ibid.

*See 604.

6 Minds ripen at very different ages.

> Letter to Mrs. William Robinson, her sister-in-law, Ibid.

7 I endeavor . . . to be wise when I cannot be merry, easy when I cannot be glad, content with what cannot be mended and patient when there is no redress.

> Letter (ca. 1739), Ibid.

8 It is surprizing what money I have spent out of a principle of economy; because they are cheap I have bought more shoes than a millipede could wear in VII years. By my caps you would think I had more heads than Hydra.

> Letter to her brother (1776), Ibid.

9 Wit in women is apt to have bad consequences; like a sword without a scabbard, it wounds the wearer and provokes and assailants. I am sorry to say the generality of women who have excelled in wit have failed in chastity. . . .

> (1750), Quoted in *Reconstructing Aphra* by Angeline Goreau *1980*

586. Peg Woffington (1720–1760)

1 I count time by your absence; I have not seen you all morning, and is it not an age since then?

> Ch. 6, Remark to David Garrick* (1776), Quoted in *Days of the Dandies* by J. Fitzgerald Molloy *n.d.*

*English actor and theater manager (1717–1779).

587. Anna Dorothea Lisiewska-Therbusch (1721–1782)

1 I would not have dared suggest it to you, but you have done well, and I thank you.*

> (1767), Quoted by Denis Diderot in *Diderot Salons*, Vol. III, Jean Adhémar and Jean Seznec, eds. *1963*

*In response to Diderot's voluntary disrobing for his portrait bust by her; Diderot (1713–1784) was a French philosopher and writer.

588. Jeanne-Antoinette Poisson de Pompadour (1721–1764)

1 The King and I have such implicit confidence in you* that we look upon you as a cat, or a dog, and go on talking as if you were not there.

> Quoted in *The Memoirs of Louis XV and of Madame de Pompadour* by Mme du Hausset *1802*

*Mme. du Hausset, her bed-chamber attendant and author; see 661.

2 It is a wolf who makes the sheep reflect.

> Ibid.

3 After us the deluge! (*Après nous le déluge!*)

> Her motto, Ibid.

4 Wait a moment, monsieur, and we will set forth together. (*Attendez-moi, monsieur le curé, nous partirons ensemble.*)

> Last words, spoken to the priest, Ibid.

589. Isabella Howard (1722?–1793/95?)

1 "I dare not change a first decree:
She's doomed to please, nor can be free:
Such is the lot of beauty!"

> "Reply by the Countess of C—,"* St. 11 (ca. 1753), *The Female Poets of Great Britain*, Frederic Rowton, ed. *1853*

*Reply poem to Frances Greville's "Prayers for Indifference"; see 583:1–2.

590. Mary Leapor (1722–1746)

1 EMILIA. Our servile Tongues are taught to cry for Pardon
Ere the weak Senses know the Use of Words:
Our little Souls are tortur'd by Advice;
And moral Lectures stun our Infant Years:
Thro' check'd Desires, Threatnings, and Restraint
The Virgin runs; but ne'er outgrows her Shackles
They still will fit her, even to hoary Age.

> *The Unhappy Father 1751*

2 And all the arts that ruin while they please.

> "The Temple of Love—a Dream," St. 3, *Poems Upon Several Occasions*, Vol. II *1751*

591. Eliza Pinckney (1722?–1793)

1 Be particularly watchful against heat of temper; it makes constant work for repentance and chagrin.

> Letter to Charles Pinckney* (1761), *Journal and Letters of Eliza Lucas Pinckney*, Harriet R. Holbrook, ed. *1850*

*Her husband, a politician and judge.

592. Janet Graham (1723/24–1805)

1 Alas! my son, you little know
The sorrows that from wedlock flow,
Farewell to every day of ease,
When you have got a wife to please.

> "The Wayward Wife," *Scottish Song*, Mary Carlyle Aitken, ed. *1874*

2 Great Hercules* and Samson** too,
Were stronger men than I or you,
Yet they were baffled by their dears,
And felt the distaff and the shears.

> Ibid.

*Greek hero. **Israelite judge of Old Testament.

593. Frances Brooke (1724–1789)

1 To be happy in this world, it is necessary not to raise one's ideas too high. . . .

> Letter XV, *The History of Emily Montague*, Vol. I *1769*

2 I have said married women are, by my principles, forbidden fruit: I should have explained myself; I mean in England, for my ideas on this head change as soon as I land at Calais.

> Letter XXXVI, Ibid.

3 We have been saying, Lucy, that 'tis the strangest thing in the world people should quarrel about religion, since we undoubtedly all mean the same thing; all good minds in every religion aim at pleasing the Supreme Being; the means we take differ according to where we are born, and the prejudices we imbibe from education; a consideration which ought to inspire us with kindness and indulgence to each other.

Letter L, Ibid.

4 Parents should chuse our company, but never even pretend to direct our choice. . . .

Letter LXV, Ibid.

5 A marriage where not only esteem, but passion is kept awake, is, I am convinced, the most perfect state of sublunary happiness: but it requires great care to keep this tender plant alive. . . .

Letter LXVIII, Ibid.

6 . . . this love is the finest cosmetik in the world.

Letter XCIII, Ibid.

7 In my opinion, the man who conveys, and causes to grow, in any country, a grain, a fruit, or even a flower, it never possessed before, deserves more praise than a thousand heroes: he is a benefactor, he is in some degree a creator.

Letter CXXI, Ibid.

8 If the Supreme Creator had meant us to be gloomy, he would, it seems to me, have clothed the earth in black, not in that lively green, which is the livery of cheerfulness and joy.

Letter CXCIV, Vol. IV, Ibid.

9 RUSTIC. . . . I hate money when it is not my own.

Act II, Sc. 1, Rosina: A Comic Opera 1783

594. Sarah Ryan (1724?–1768)

1 My merciful God did not leave me to follow my own imaginations, but often checked me by that thought, "Must all men die? Must all have an end? And must I die?"

Quoted in The Women of Methodism: Its Three Foundresses . . . by Abel Stevens 1866

595. Frances Sheridan (1724–1766)

1 I must take her down a peg or so.

Act IV, Sc. 4, The Dupe 1760

2 What taught me silently to bear,
To curb the sigh, to check the tear,
When sorrow weigh'd me down?

'T was Patience!

"Ode to Patience," Sts. 3, 4, The Female Poets of Great Britain, Frederic Rowton, ed. 1853

596. Eva Maria Garrick (1725–1822)

1 Groans and complaints are very well for those who are to mourn but a little while; but a sorrow that is to last for life will not be violent or romantic.

Quoted by Hannah More* in Biography of Distinguished Women by Sarah Josepha Hale** 1876

*See 649. **See 807.

597. Bridget Fletcher (1726–1770)

1 God's only son by woman came,
To take away our shame;
And so thereby, to dignify,
Also to raise our fame.

Hymn XXXVI: St. 1, "The Greatest Dignity of a Woman, Christ Being Born of One," Hymns and Spiritual Songs 1773

598. Hester Chapone (1727–1801)

1 Affectation is so universally acknowledged to be disgusting, that it is among the faults which the most intimate friends cannot venture gravely to reprove in each other; for to tell your friends that they are habitually affected, is to tell them that they are habitually disagreeable; which nobody can bear to hear.

"Affectation," Miscellanies in Prose and Verse 1775

2 Thrice welcome, friendly Solitude,
O let no busy foot intrude,
Nor listening ear be nigh!

"Ode to Solitude," St. 1, A Volume of Miscellanies 1775

3 I make no scruple to call romances the worst of all species of writing; unnatural representation of the passions, false sentiment, false precepts, false wit, false honour, and false modesty, with a strange heap of improbable, unnatural incidents mixed up with true history. . . .

Letter to Elizabeth Carter (31 July 1750), The Works of Mrs. Chapone, Vol. I 1818

599. Jean Elliot (1727–1805)

1 I've heard them lilting, at the ewes milking.
Lasses a' lilting, before dawn of day;
But now they are moaning, on ilka green loaning;
The Flowers of the Forest* are a' wede away.

"The Flowers of the Forest," Scottish Song, Mary Carlyle Aitken, ed. 1874

*The forces of James IV who were slain at Flodden Field (9 September 1513). See note on Alicia Cockburn, 574:1.

2 The prime of our land, lie cauld in the clay.

Ibid.

600. Hannah Griffitts (1727–1817)

1 Then for the sake of Freedom's name,
(Since British wisdom scorns repealing)
Come sacrifice to Patriot fame,
And give up tea by way of healing.

"'Beware of the Ides of March,' Said the Roman Augur To Julius Caesar," St. 3 (1775), Women Poets in Pre-Revolutionary America, Patti Cowell, ed. 1981

2 Like a Newton,* sublimely he soar'd,
To a summit before unattain'd,
New regions of science explor'd,
And the palm of philosophy gain'd.

"Inscription On A Curious Chamberstove In the Form of an Urn, Contriv'd in Such A Manner as to Make the Flame Descend Instead of Rising, Invented By The Celebrated B.F.,"** St. 1 (1776), Ibid.

*British physicist and mathematician (1642–1727). **Benjamin Franklin, American printer and publisher, author, inventor and scientist, and diplomat (1706–1790); poem also attributed to Jonathan Odell.

601. Sarah Prince Gill (1728–1771)

1 —Thou, thou art all!
My soul flies up and down in thoughts of thee,
And finds herself but at the center still!
I AM, thy name! Existence, all thine own!
Creation's nothing to Thee, the great Original!

Untitled, St. 1, *Dying Exercises of Mrs. Deborah Prince and Devout Meditations of Mrs. Sarah Gill . . . 1784*

602. Margaret Klopstock (1728–1758)

1 I could not speak, I could not play; I thought I saw nothing but Klopstock.*

Letter to Samuel Richardson** (Hamburg, 14 March 1758), *Letters from the Dead to the Living post-1758*
*Her husband, the poet Friedrich Gottlieb Klopstock (1724–1803).
**English novelist (1689–1761).

2 It is long since I made the remark that the children of geniuses are not geniuses.

Letter to Samuel Richardson (26 August 1758), Ibid.

603. Mercy Otis Warren (1728–1758)

1 E------R. [sic.] Honors, places, pensions—
'Tis all a cheat, a damn'd, a cruel cheat.

Act V, Sc. 2, *The Adulateur 1773*

2 VALENTINIAN. I fear no storms but from an injur'd wife.

Act II, Sc. 1, *The Sack of Rome 1790*

3 GAUDENTIUS. Ambition, in a noble, virtuous mind,
Is the first passion that the gods implant,
And soars to glory till it meets the skies

Sc. 2, Ibid.

4 EDOXIA. Enough of life and all life's idle pomp—
Nor by a tyrant's fiat will I live—
I leave the busy, vain, ambitious world
To cheat itself anew, and o'er and o'er
Tread the same ground their ancestors have trod,
In chace of thrones, of sceptres, or of crowns,
'Till all these bubbles break in empty air,
Nor leave a trace of happiness behind.

Act V, Sc. 3, Ibid.

5 DON JUAN DE PADILLA. Let freedom be the mistress of thy heart.

Act I, Sc. 1, *The Ladies of Castile 1790*

6 DON JUAN. Most men are brave till courage has been try'd,
And boast of virtue till their price is known. . . .

Act II, Sc. 5, Ibid.

7 DON PEDRO. . . . the bubble freedom—empty name!—
'Tis all a puff—a visionary dream—
That kindles up this patriotic flame;
'Tis rank self love, conceal'd beneath a mask
Of public good. The hero's brain inflates—
He cheats himself by the false medium,
Held in virtue's guise, till he believes it just

Ibid.

8 DE HARO. Great souls—form's in the same etherial mould,
Are ne'er at war—they, different paths
Of glory may pursue, with equal zeal;

Yet not a cruel, or malignant thought,
Or rancorous design, deform the mind.

Act III, Sc. 1, Ibid.

9 DON JUAN. To learn to die is an heroic work

Act IV, Sc. 2, Ibid.

604. Catherine II of Russia (1729–1796)

1 For to tempt and to be tempted are things very nearly allied, and in spite of the finest maxims of morality impressed upon the mind, whenever feeling has anything to do in the matter, no sooner is it excited than we have already gone vastly farther than we are aware of.

Memoirs, A. Herzen, ed. and tr. *1857*

2 I may be kindly, I am ordinarily gentle, but in my line of business I am obliged to will terribly what I will at all.

Letter (30 August 1774), *Correspondance avec le Baron F. M. Grimm (1774–1796) 1878*

3 A great wind is blowing, and that gives you either imagination or a headache.

Letter (29 April 1775), Ibid.

4 I am one of the people who love the why of things.

Letter (20 January 1776), Ibid.

5 In my position you have to read when you want to write and to talk when you would like to read; you have to laugh when you feel like crying; twenty things interfere with twenty others, you have not time for a moment's thought, and nevertheless you have to be constantly ready to act with out allowing yourself to feel lassitude, either of body or spirit; ill or well, it makes no difference, everything at once demands that you should attend to it on the spot.

Letter (23 August 1794), Ibid.

6 Your wit makes others witty. (*Votre esprit en donne aux autres.*)

Letter to Voltaire,* *The Complete Works of Catherine II*, Evdokimov, ed. *1893*
*François-Marie Arouet, French philosopher and writer (1694–1778).

7 I praise loudly, I blame softly.

Letter, Ibid.

8 If Fate had given me in youth a husband whom I could have loved, I should have remained always true to him. The trouble is that my heart would not willingly remain one hour without love.

Letter to Prince Potemkin (1774), Quoted in *Memoirs*, Katharine Anthony, ed. and tr. *1925*

9 At the age of fourteen she made the three-fold resolution, to please her Consort, [Empress] Elizabeth, and the Nation.

Epitaph, written by herself (1789), Ibid.

10 To govern you have to have eyes and hands, and a woman has only ears.

Quoted in *Daughters of Eve* by Gamaliel Bradford *1928*

11 The most sure, but at the same time the most difficult expedient to mend the morals of the people, is a perfect system of education.

Remark (1767), Quoted in *Women in World History Curriculum* (womeninworldhistory.com) *1996–97*

605. Sarah Crosby (1729–1804)

1 The day after, at church, the Lord showed me that many things which I had thought were sins were only temptations, and also what a little thing it was for him to take the root of sin out of my heart.

> Quoted in *Women of Methodism: Its Three Foundresses . . .* by Abel Stevens *1866*

606. Marguerite Brunet (1730–1820)

1 Will I then really have no company here, and does the King absolutely insist that I sleep alone?

> Remark upon entering her prison cell, Quoted in *Enter the Actress* by Rosamond Gilder *1931*

2 . . . these special gala performances are always good for trade.

> Remark, Ibid.

607. Elizabeth Cooper (fl. 1730s)

1 BELLAIR. . . . Money is of no Value till 'tis used.

> *The Rival Widows; or, Fair Libertine 1735*

2 BELLAIR. We can talk of Murder, Theft, and Treason, without blushing: and surely there's nothing a-kin to Love that's half so wicked.

> Ibid.

608. Caterina Gabrielli (1730–1796)

1 In this case, your majesty has only to engage one of your field-marshals to sing.

> Reply to Catherine the Great's* response ("None of my field-marshals receive so enormous a sum!") to Gabrielli's fee of 5,000 ducats to sing, Quoted in *Biography of Distinguished Women* by Sarah Josepha Hale** *1876*
> *See 604. **See 807.

609. Sophie de la Briche Houdetot (1730–1813)

1 Youth, I loved you; those loveliest years,
Brief as they were, when love was my only occupation.

> "Imitation de Marot," Elaine Bernstein Partnow,* tr., Quoted in *Biography of Distinguished Women* by Sarah Josepha Hale** *1876*
>
> *See 3291. **See 807.

610. Mary Masters (fl. 1730–d. 1755)

1 What if the charms in him I see
Only exist in thought

> "To Lucinda," St. 2, *Poems on Several Occasions 1733*

2 Love is a mighty god, you know,
  That rules with potent sway;
And when he draws his awful bow,
  We mortals must obey.

> "To Lucinda," St. 6, Ibid.

611. Lucy Terry (1730?–1821)

1 Eunice Allen see the Indians comeing
And hoped to save herself by running
And had not her petticoats stopt her
The awful creatures had not cotched her

And tommyhawked her on the head
And left her on the ground for dead.

> "Bars Fight,"* *The Poetry of the Negro, 1746–1870*, Langston Hughes** and Arna Bontemps, eds. *1949*
> *Refers to an Indian raid on Deerfield, Massachusetts (25 August 1746). **American poet, writer (1902–1967).

612. Mrs. Weddell (fl. ca. 1730–1740)

1 . . . [they are] a wise People, and fond of Liberty, who consider all Men as Denizens of the Earth's plenteous Blessings, nor think the casual Tincture of the Skin, differing from the European Hue alienates any from the indubitable Right they are naturally entitled to, as Fellow Creatures.

> Preface, *Incle and Yarico 1742*

2 [Africa] . . .
Where the Remembrance of the Multitudes
Borne hence, to Slav'ry, by our Countrymen
Must make each Man we meet an Enemy.

> Ibid.

613. Martha Washington (1731–1802)

1 . . . the greater part of our happiness or misery depends on our dispositions, and not on our circumstances. We carry the seeds of the one or the other about with us in our minds wherever we go.

> Letter to Mrs. Warren* (26 December 1789), Quoted in *Lives of Celebrated Women* by Samuel Griswold Goodrich *1844*
> *Probably Mercy Otis Warren; see 603.

2 It is all over now. I shall soon follow him. I have no more trials to pass through.*

> Remark (1799), Ibid.
> *Referring to the death of her husband, George Washington (1732–99), 1st president of the United States (1789–97).

3 I live a very dull life here . . . indeed I think I am more like a state prisoner than anything else. . . .

> Letter to a relative, Quoted in *Martha Washington* by Anne Hollingsworth Wharton *1897*

4 . . . steady as a clock, busy as a bee, and cheerful as a cricket. . . .

> Letter to a friend, Ibid.

614. Julie-Jeanne-Eléonore de Lespinasse (1732–1776)

1 There is a certain hour in the day when I wind up my moral machine as I wind my watch. And then, the movement once given, it goes more or less well. . . . What is curious is that no one suspects the effort required to appear what I am thought really to be.

> Letter to Condorcet* (4 May 1771), *Lettres inédites 1887*
> *Marquis de Condorcet, French philosopher and politician (1743–1794).

2 . . . people observe very little, and it is fortunate, for there is not much to be gained by seeing more than others do.

> Ibid.

3 I do nothing but love, I know nothing but love.

> Letter to Guibert* (30 May 1773), *Lettres 1906*
> *François-Apollini Guibert, French military reformer (1744–1790).

4 The logic of the heart is absurd.
> Letter (27 August 1774), Ibid.

5 You know that when I hate you, it is because I love you to a point of passion that unhinges my soul.
> Letter (1774), Ibid.

615. Mary Knowles (1733–1807)

1 He [Dr. Johnson] gets at the substance of a book directly; he tears out the heart of it.
> Letter (15 April 1778), Quoted in *The Life of Samuel Johnson,** *LL.D.* by James Boswell *1791*
> *English author and lexicographer (1709–84).

616. Louise Honorine de Choiseul (1734–1801)

1 It is well to love even a dog when you have the opportunity, for fear you should find nothing else worth loving.
> Quoted in *Portraits of Women* by Gamaliel Bradford *1916*

2 If I have learned anything, I owe it neither to precepts nor to books, but to a few opportune misfortunes. Perhaps the school of misfortunes is the very best.
> Ibid.

3 He [Jean-Jacques Rousseau*] has always seemed to me to be a charlatan of virtue.
> Ibid.
> *French philosopher and writer (1712–1778).

4 He [Voltaire*] tells us he is faithful to his enthusiasms; he should have said, to his weaknesses. He has always been so cowardly where there was no danger, insolent where there was no motive, and mean where there was no object in being so. All which does not prevent his being the most brilliant mind of the century. We should admire his talent, study his works, profit by his philosophy, and be broadened by his teaching. We should adore him and despise him, as is indeed the case with a good many objects of worship.
> Ibid.
> *François Marie Arouet, French philosopher and writer (1694–1778).

5 My skepticism has grown so great that it falls over backward and from doubting everything I have become ready to believe anything.
> Ibid.

6 We grow old as soon as we cease to love and trust.
> Ibid.

7 Good-by, dear child, I wish you good sleep and a good digestion. I don't know anything better to desire for those I love.
> Ibid.

617. Mrs. Pennington (1734–1759)

1 On glories greater glories rise.
> "Ode to Morning," St. 1, *The Female Poets of Great Britain,* Frederic Rowton, ed. *1853*

618. Nancy Hart (1735?–1830)

1 Surrender your damned Tory carcasses to a Whig woman.
> On her capture of five Loyalists, Quoted in *The Women of the American Revolution,* Vol. II by Elizabeth F. Ellet *1848*

619. Caroline Keppel (1735–?)

1 What's this dull town to me?
>   Robin's not near—
> He whom I wished to see,
>   Wished for to hear;
> Where's all the joy and mirth
>   Made life a heaven on earth?
> O! they're all fled with thee,
>   Robin Adair
>
> "Robin Adair" *n.d.*

620. Theodosia De Visme Burr (1736–1794)

1 Piety teaches resignation.... The better I am acquainted with it, the more claims I find.
> Letter to her husband, Aaron Burr* (6 March 1781), *Memoirs of Aaron Burr,* Vol. I, Matthew L. Davis, ed. *1836–37*
> *American vice president (1801–1805) and politician (1756–1836); tried for treason.

2 I am impatient for the evening; for the receipt of your dear letter; for those delightful sensations which your expression of tenderness alone can excite. Dejected, distracted without them, elated, giddy even to folly with them, my mind, never at medium, claims everything from your partiality.
> Letter to Aaron Burr (August 1786), Ibid.

621. Mary Katherine Goddard (1736/38?–1816)

1 ... [it is] their duty to inquire into everything that has a tendency to restrain the liberty of the Press....
> Letter to the Baltimore Committee of Safety (May/June 1776), Quoted in Ch. 8, *William Goddard, Newspaperman* by Ward L. Miner *1962*

2 The stoppage of the *Paper-Mill,* near this Town, for the Want of a Supply of Rags, and the enormous Prices demanded at the Stores here for PAPER, constrains us to print the *Maryland Journal* on this dark and poor Sort, which our Readers will, we are persuaded to excuse, for one Week at least, when they are assured, that rather than deprive them of *the important Intelligence of the Times,* by the Discontinuance of our *Journal,* we have given from *Forty* to *Fifty Pounds* a Week for the Article of Paper *alone,* an equal Quantity of which, might, formerly, have been purchased for *Eight Dollars!*
> Notice in *Maryland Journal* (26 May 1778), Ibid.

622. Ann Lee (1736–1784)

1 By the Son, the *true* being and *true character* of the Father, was first revealed: and, the existence of the Son while it proved the existence of the Eternal *Father,* proved also the existence of the Eternal *Mother.*
  Neither argument, nor illustration, would seem necessary to prove this. For, without both a *father* and a *mother,* there can be neither son nor daughter; either natural or spiritual, visible or invisible!
> "The Order of Deity, Male and Female, in whose Image Man was Created," *Shaker Bible,* a.k.a. *Mother Ann's Bible ca. 1774*

2 It is not I that speak, it is Christ who dwells in me.
> Quoted in *The Testimony of Christ's Second Appearing* by Benjamin S. Youngs *1808*

3   You can never enter into the Kingdom of God with hardness against anyone, for God is love, and if you love God you will love one another.

> Remark, upon her release from prison (ca. 1776), Quoted in *Wise Women: Over 2000 Years of Spiritual Writing by Women*, Susan Cahill, ed. 1996

4   'Tis the gift to be simple,
'Tis the gift to be free,
'Tis the gift to come down where we ought to be,
And when we find ourselves in the place that's right
'Twill be in the valley of love and delight.

> "Simple Gifts" (Shaker Hymn), Ibid.

623. Annis Stockton (1736–1801)

1   . . . future ages shall enroll thy name
In sacred annals of immortal fame.

> "Addressed to General Washington* in the Year 1777 After the Battles of Trenton and Princeton," *Columbian Magazine January 1787*
> *George Washington (1732–1799), first president of the United States (1789–1797).

2   For, oh! I find on earth no charms for me
But what's connected with the thought of thee!

> "Epistle to Mr. S[tockton]," *Women Poets in Pre-Revolutionary America*, Patti Cowell, ed. 1981

3   Thousands of heroes from this dust shall rise.

> "On Hearing That General [Dr. Joseph] Warren Was Killed on Bunker Hill, the 17th of June, 1775," Ibid.

624. Elizabeth Graeme Ferguson (1737–1801)

1   A transient, rich, and balmy sweet
Is in thy fragrance found;
But soon the flow'r and scent retreat—
Thorns left alone to wound.

> "On a Beautiful Damask Rose, Emblematical of Love and Wedlock," St. 3, *Columbian Magazine May 1789*

2   Thus over all, self-love presides supreme

> "On the Mind's Being Engrossed By One Subject," Ibid.

3   Birth day odes to lords and kings,
Oft are strain'd and stupid things!
Poet laureate's golden lays,
Fulsome hireling's hackney'd praise!

> "An Ode Written on the Birthday of Mr. Henry Ferguson By His Wife When They Had Been Married Two Years, He Aged 26 Years," St. 1 (12 March 1774), *Women Poets in Pre-Revolutionary America*, Patti Cowell, ed. 1981

4   . . . angel-like he spake, and God-like died.

> "On the Death of Leopold, Hereditary Prince of Brunswick, Who was Drowned in the Oder, April 17, 1785, in Attempting to Save Some Children Whose Mother had Left Them on the Banks of that River," (Montgomery County, 5 July 1785), Ibid.

625. Margaret Morris (1737–1816)

1   A loud knocking at my door brought me to it. . . . I opened it, and a half a dozen men, all armed, demanded the key of the empty house. . . . I put on a very simple look and exclaimed— "Bless me! I hope you are not Hessians!"*
"Do we look like Hessians?" asked one rudely.

"Indeed, I don't know."
"Did you ever see a Hessian?"
"No—never in my life; but they are *men;* and you are men; and may be Hessians for aught I know!"

> from her Journal (16 December 1776), Quoted in *The Women of the American Revolution*, Vol. II by Elizabeth F. Ellet 1848
> *German mercenaries hired by the British.

2   . . . there is a god of battle as well as a God of peace. . . .

> (27 December 1776), Ibid.

626. Suzanne Chardon Necker (1737–1794)

1   . . . I cannot help thinking that the vows most women are made to take are very foolhardy. I doubt whether they would willingly go to the altar to swear that they will allow themselves to be broken on the wheel every nine months.

> Quoted in *Mistress to an Age: A Life of Madame de Staël** by J. Christopher Herold 1958
> *See 733.

2   Governesses have always one great disadvantage; if they are qualified for their calling, they intercept the child's affection for its mother.

> Ibid.

627. Mary Fletcher (1739–1815)

1   I was deeply conscious it [religion] is one of the most delicate subjects in the world, and requires both much wisdom and much love, to extinguish false fire, and yet keep up the true.

> Quoted in *The Women of Methodism: Its Three Foundresses* . . . by Abel Stevens 1866

2   I feel at this moment a more tender affection toward him* than I did at that time [of her marriage], and by faith I now join my hand afresh with his.

> Journal entry (12 November 1809), Ibid.
> *Her husband, Jean Guillaume de la Flechère; written during her widowhood, on the anniversary of her marriage.

628. Sophie Arnould (1740/4–1802)

1   We shall be rich as princes. A good fairy has given me a talisman to transform every thing into gold and diamonds at the sound of my voice.

> Quoted in *Queens of Song* by Ellen Creathorne Clayton 1865

2   Oh! that was the good time; I was very unhappy. (*Oh! c'était le bon temps; j'était bien malheureuse.*)

> Remark to Claude-Carlomande Rulhière,* Quoted in *Sophie Arnould; d'après sa correspondance et ses mémoirs inédits,* Edmond and Jules de Goncourt, eds. 1884
> *French writer and historian (1734–1791).

3   They give themselves to God when the Devil will no longer have them.

> Ch. 4, Quoted in *Sophie Arnould: Actress and Wit* by Robert B. Douglas 1898

629. Martha Brewster (fl. ca. 1740s–1757)

1   Oh!———he———is———gone.

> "To the Memory of that worthy Man Liet. NATHANIEL BURT of *Springfield* . . . [who died] in the Battle of Lake-George in the Retreat, September 8th, 1753," *Poems on Divers Subjects 1757*

2 There is a wheel within a wheel.
> "A Farewell to Some of My Christian Friends at Goshen, in
> Lebanon," St. 4 (5 April 1745), Ibid.

3 Dear friends, the life is more than meat,
The soul excels the clay;
O labor then for gospel food,
Which never shall decay.
> St. 14, Ibid.

4 O absence! absence! sharper than a thorn
> "A Letter to My Daughter Ruby Bliss," Ibid.

630. Madame de Charrière (1740–?)

1 I would prefer being my lover's laundress and living in a garret
to the arid freedom and the good manners of our great families.
> Quoted in *Mistress to an Age: A Life of Madame de Staël** by
> J. Christopher Herold *1958*
> *See 733.

631. Mrs. Hoper (fl. ca. 1740)

1 The Stage shall flourish, Tragedy shall thrive,
And Shakespear's Scenes ne'er die whilst They* survive
> Prologue, *Queen Tragedy Restores 1749*
> **Othello, Hamlet, Henry IV,* and *Richard II.*

632. Martha Milcah Moore (1740–1829)

1 Let the Daughters of Liberty nobly arise.
> "The Female Patriots, Addressed to the Daughters of Liberty
> in America," *William and Mary Quarterly April 1977*

633. Sarah Parsons Moorhead (fl. ca. 1740)

1 Despise the blest instructions of their tongue,
Conversion is become the drunkard's song;
God's glorious work, which sweetly did arise,
By this unguarded sad imprudence dies;
Contention spreads her harpy claws around,
In every church her hateful stings are found.
> "To the Reverend Mr. James Davenport on His Departure
> from Boston, By Way of a Dream," St. 1 *1742*

634. Clementina Rind (1740?–1774)

1 Open to ALL PARTIES, but Influenced by NONE
> Motto, Quoted in *Virginia Gazette* (first issue) *16 May 1766*

635. Hester Lynch Piozzi (1741–1821)

1 It is a maxim here [at Venice], handed down from generation to
generation, that change breeds more mischief from its novelty
than advantage from its utility.
> "Observations on a Journey Through Italy," *Autobiography,
> Letters and Literary Remains,* Abraham Hayward, ed. *1861*

2 The tree of deepest root is found
Least willing still to quit the ground:
'Twas therefore said by ancient sages,
That love of life increased with years
So much, that in our later stages,
When pain grows sharp and sickness rages,
The greatest love of life appears.
> "Three Warnings," Ibid.

3 Ah! he was a wise man who said Hope is a good breakfast but
a bad dinner. It shall be my supper, however, when all's said
and done.
> Vol. II, Ibid.

4 A physician can sometimes parry the scythe of death, but has
no power over the sand in the hourglass.
> Letter to Fanny Burney* (12 November 1781), Ibid.
> *See 671.

5 Johnson's conversation was by far much too strong for a person accustomed to obsequiousness and flattery; it was mustard
in a young child's mouth.
> (May 1781), Quoted in *Life of Samuel Johnson** by James
> Boswell *1791*
> *British writer and lexicographer (1709–1794).

636. Dorcas Richardson (1741?–1834)

1 I do not doubt that men who can outrage the feelings of a
woman by such threats, are capable of perpetrating any act
of treachery and inhumanity towards a brave but unfortunate
enemy. But conquer or capture my husband [Captain Richard
Richardson], if you can do so, before you boast the cruelty
you mean to mark your savage triumph! And let me tell you,
meanwhile, that some of you, it is likely, will be in a condition
to implore *his* mercy, before he will have need to supplicate, or
deign to accept yours.
> Remark to the British, Quoted by Dr. Joseph Johnson in *The
> Women of the American Revolution* by Elizabeth F. Ellet *1848*

637. Sarah Kirby Trimmer (1741–1810)

1 Happy would it be for the animal creation, if every human
being . . . consulted the welfare of inferior creatures, and neither spoiled them by indulgence, nor injured them by tyranny!
Happy would mankind be . . . by cultivating in their own
minds and those of their own children, the divine principle of
general benevolence.
> *Fabulous Histories: or, The History of the Robins. Designed
> for the Instruction of Children, Respecting Their Treatment of
> Animals,* 13th ed. *1821*

2 Every living creature that comes into the world has something
allotted to him to perform, therefore he should not stand an
idle spectator of what others are doing.
> Ibid.

638. Isabella Graham (1742–1814)

1 Hail! thou state of widowhood,
State of those that mourn to God;
Who from earthly comforts torn,
Only live to pray and mourn.
> "Widowhood" (1774), *Life and Writings n.d.*

639. Anne Home (1742–1821)

1 'Tis hard to smile when one would weep,
To speak when one would silent be;
To wake when one would wish to sleep,
And wake to agony.
> "The Lot of Thousands," *Poems by Mrs. John Hunter 1802*

2 My mother bids me bind my hair
With bands of rosy hue,
Tie up my sleeve with ribbons rare,
And lace my bodice blue.

"For why," she cries, "sit still and weep,
   While others dance and play?"
Alas! I scarce can go or creep
   While Lubin is away.
                    "My Mother Bids Me Bind My Hair," Ibid.

640. Darcy Maxwell (1742?–1810)

1   It is seldom that we go beyond our teachers.
                    Quoted in *The Women of Methodism: Its Three Foundresses*
                    . . . by Abel Stevens 1866

2   Suffice it to say, I was chosen in the furnace of affliction. The
    Lord gave me all I desired in this world, then took all from
    me;* but immediately afterward sweetly drew me to Himself.
                    Letter to a friend (ca. 1776), Quoted in *Biography of*
                    *Distinguished Women by Sarah Josepha Hale** 1876*
    *She was widowed at nineteen; six weeks later her only child died.
    **See 807.

641. Anna Seward (1742–1809)

1   O hours! more worth than gold
                    Untitled (December 1782), *Sonnets 1789*

2   This last and long enduring passion for Mrs. Thrale* was,
    however, composed of cupboard love, Platonic love, and vanity
    tickled and gratified.
                    Letter, *Letters,* Vol. II *n.d.*
    *Allusion to Dr. Samuel Johnson's relationship with Hester Lynch
    Piozzi, a.k.a. Mrs. Thrale; see 635.

642. Anna Letitia Barbauld (1743–1825)

1   While Genius was thus wasting his strength in eccentric flights,
    I saw a person of very different appearance, named Applica-
    tion.
                    "The Hill of Science," *Miscellaneous Pieces in Prose 1773*

2   Education, in its largest sense, is a thing of great scope and
    extent. It includes the whole process by which a human being
    is formed to be what he is, in habits, principles, and cultivation
    of every kind. . . . You speak of *beginning* the education of our
    son. The moment he was able to form an idea his education
    was already begun. . . .
                    "On Education," Ibid.

3   Who can resist those dumb beseeching eyes,
    Where genuine eloquence pervasive lies?
    Those eyes, where language fails, display thy heart
    Beyond the pomp of phrase and pride of art.
                    "To A Dog," *Poems 1773*

4   . . . still Afric bleeds,
    Unchecked, the human traffic still proceeds
                    "Epistle to William Wilberforce, Esq."* (1791), *The Works of*
                    Anna Letitia Barbauld, Vol. I *1826*
    *English politician and abolitionist (1759–1833); the reference is
    to slavery.

5   . . . separate rights are lost in mutual love.
                    "The Right of Woman," Ibid.

6   When trembling limbs refuse their weight,
    And films, slow gathering, dim the sight,
    And clouds obscure the mental light,—
    'Tis nature's precious boon to die.
                    "A Thought on Death" (November 1814), Ibid.

7   To *repair* a ruin carries a better sound with it than to *build* a
    ruin, as we do in England.
                    Letter to Dr. Aiken (Thoulouse [sic], 27 February 1786), Ibid.

8   Nobody ought to be too old to improve; I should be sorry if I
    was; and I flatter myself I have already improved considerably
    by my travels. First, I can swallow gruel soup, egg soup, and all
    manner of soups, without making faces much. Secondly, I can
    pretty well live without tea. . . .
                    Letter to Miss Belshan (Geneva, 21 October 1785), Ibid.

9   Finding out riddles is the same kind of exercise to the mind
    which running and leaping are to the body.
                    "On Riddles," *A Legacy for Young Ladies n.d*

10 . . . Taste has one great enemy to contend with . . . Fashion—an
    arbitrary and capricious tyrant, who reigns with the most des-
    potic sway over that department which Taste alone ought to
    regulate.
                    "On Female Studies, Letter Two," Ibid.

11 . . . a forest was never planted.
                    "On Plants," Ibid.

12 I often murmur, yet I never weep;
    I always lie in bed, yet never sleep;
    My mouth is large, and larger than my head,
    And much disgorges though it ne'er is fed;
    I have no legs or feet, yet swiftly run,
    And the more falls I get, move faster on.
                    "On Riddles," Ibid.

13 How patiently does she support the various burdens laid upon
    her! We tear her plows and harrows, we crush her with castles
    and palaces; nay we penetrate her very bowels, and bring to
    light the veined marble, the pointed crystal, the ponderous ores
    and sparkling gems, deep hid in darkness the more to excite
    the industry of man. Yet, torn and harassed as she might seem
    to be, our mother Earth is still fresh and young, as if she but
    now came out of the hands of her Creator.
                    "Earth," Ibid.

643. Hannah Cowley (1743–1809)

1   DOILEY. No, no; you must mind your P's and Q's* with him, I
    can tell you.
                    Act I, Sc. 2, *Who's the Dupe?* 1779
    *Originally abbreviation for "pints and quarts," used in taverns.

2   DOILEY. Well, good fortune never comes in a hurry. . . .
                    Ibid.

3   CHARLOTTE. You know very well, the use of language is to
    express one's likes and dislikes—and a pig will do this as effec-
    tually by its squeak, or a hen with her cackle, as you with your
    Latin and Greek.
                    Sc. 3, Ibid.

4   SAVILLE. Five minutes! Zounds! I have been five minutes too
    late all my life-time!
                    Act I, Sc. 1, *The Belle's Strategem* ca. 1780s

5   VILLERS. A lady at her toilette is as difficult to be moved as a
    quaker.
                    Sc. 3, Ibid.

6   COURTALL. But 'tis always so; your reserved ladies are like
    ice, 'egad!—no sooner begin to soften than they melt!
                    Act II, Sc. 2, Ibid.

7 LADY FRANCIS TOUCHWOOD. Every body about me seem'd happy—but every body seem'd in a hurry to be happy somewhere else.

Act III, Sc. 4, Ibid.

8 FLUTTER. "Live to love," was my father's motto: "Live to laugh," is mine.

Act IV, Sc. 1, Ibid.

9 VILLERS. The charms that helped to catch the husband are generally laid by, one after another, till the lady grows a down-right wife, and then runs crying to her mother, because she has transformed her lover into a downright husband.

Act V, Sc. 1, Ibid.

10 MRS. RACKET. It requires genius to make a good pun—some men of bright parts can't reach it.

Sc. 5, Ibid.

11 OLIVIA. But no gentle Katherine* will he find me, believe it. Katherine!—Why, she had not the spirit of a roasted chestnut. A few big words, an empty oath, and a scanty dinner, made her as submissive as a spaniel. My fire will not be so soon extin-guished: it shall resist big words, oaths, and starving!

A Bold Stroke for a Husband 1784
*Reference to Katharine in Shakespeare's *Taming of the Shrew.*

12 OLIVIA. He has a very pretty kind of conversation; 'tis like a parenthesis.
DON CAESAR. Like a parenthesis!
OLIVIA. Yes, it might be all left out, and never missed.

Ibid.

644. Ekaterina Vorontsova Dashkova (1743–1810)

1 As there were no other two women at the time, apart from the Grand Duchess* and myself, who did any serious reading, we were mutually drawn to each other; and the charm which she knew how to exert whenever she wanted to win over anyone, was too powerful for an artless little girl like myself, to refuse her the gift of my heart forevermore.

The Memoirs of Princess Dashkova, Kyril Fitzlyon, tr. and ed. *1995*
*Reference to Catherine the Great; see 604.

2 My life had been spent in constant sacrifice of my own wishes and pleasures for the sake of my children.

Ibid.

3 God himself, by creating me a woman, had exempted me from accepting the employment of a Director of an Academy of Sciences.*

Ibid.

*She later founded and became director of the Russian Academy of Sciences.

645. Eibhlín Dhubh Ní Chonaill (1743–1790)

1 Till Art O'Leary returns
There will be no end to the grief
That presses down on my heart,
Closed up tight and firm
Like a trunk that is locked
And the key mislaid.

"The Lament for Arthur O'Leary," St. 35, Ellis Dillon, tr., *The Penguin Book of Women Poets,* Carol Cosman, Joan Keefe, and Kathleen Weaver, eds. *1978*

646. Abigail Adams (1744–1818)

1 Do not put such unlimited power into the hands of the Hus-bands. Remember all Men would be tyrants if they could.

Letter to her husband, John Adams* *1776*

2 I am more and more convinced that man is a dangerous crea-ture . . . ; and that power, whether vested in many or a few, is ever grasping, and, like the grave, cries "Give, give."

Letter to John Adams* (27 November 1775), *Letters of Mrs. Adams 1840*
*(1735–1826) second president of the United States (1797–1801).

3 We are no ways dispirited here, we possess a Spirit that will not be conquered. If our Men are all drawn off and we should be attacked, you would find a Race of Amazons in America.

(1776) Ibid.

4 If particular care and attention is not paid to the Ladies we are determined to foment a Rebellion, and will not hold ourselves bound by any Laws in which we have no voice, or Representa-tion.

(31 March 1776) Ibid.

5 . . . had nature formed me of the other Sex, I should certainly have been a rover.

Letter to Isaac Smith, Jr. (20 April 1771), *The Adams Papers,* L. H. Butterfield, ed. *1963*

6 The Natural tenderness and Delicacy of our Constitution, added to the many Dangers we are subject to from your Sex, renders it almost impossible for a Single Lady to travel without injury to her character.

Ibid.

7 I can not say that I think you very generous to the Ladies, for whilst you are proclaiming peace and good will to Men, Eman-cipating all Nations, you insist upon retaining an absolute power over Wives.

Letter to John Adams (7 May 1776), Ibid.

647. Sarah Bache (1744–1808)

1 The subject now is Stamp Act, and nothing else is talked of. The Dutch talk of the "Stamp tack," the negroes of the "tamp"—in short, every body has something to say.

Letter to Benjamin Franklin,* her father (ca. November 1764), Quoted in *The Women of the American Revolution* by Elizabeth F. Ellet *1848*
*American statesman, author, and scientist (1706–1790).

2 In this country there is no rank but rank mutton.

Note to an Englishwoman who ran a school for girls that Bache's daughters attended, Ibid.

648. Elizabeth Martin (1745?–post-1776)

1 Go, boys; fight for your country! fight till death, if you must, but never let your country be dishonored. Were I a man I would go with you.

Remark to her seven sons at the call to arms, Quoted in *The Women of the American Revolution* by Elizabeth F. Ellet *1848*

2 I wish I had fifty.

Reply to a British officer's query regarding her sons in arms, Ibid.

649. Hannah More (1745–1833)

1   . . . dost thou know
      The cruel tyranny of tenderness?

Percy 1778

2   The keen spirit
      Ceases* the prompt occasion,—makes the thought
      Start into instant action, and at once
      Plans and performs, resolves and executes!

Daniel 1782

      *Seizes.

3   No adulation; 'tis the death of virtue;
      Who flatters, is of all mankind the lowest
      Save he who courts the flattery.

Pt. VI, Ibid.

4   Books, the Mind's food, not exercise!
      "Conversation," St. 1, *The Bas Bleu* [The Blue Stocking] *1784*

5   But sparks electric only strike
      On souls electrical alike

"Conversation," St. 2, Ibid.

6   He liked those literary cooks
      Who skim the cream of others' books;
      And ruin half the author's graces
      By plucking *bon-mots* from their places.

Florio 1786

7   And Pleasure was so coy a prude,
      She fled the more, the more pursued. . . .

Ibid.

8   Fell luxury! more perilous to youth
      Then storms or quicksands, poverty or chains.
      "Belshazzar," *The Complete Works of Hannah More 1856*

9   That silence is one of the great arts of conversation is allowed
      by Cicero* himself, who says, there is not only an art, but even
      an eloquence in it.
      "Thoughts on Conversation," *Essays on Various Subjects 1856*
      *Roman statesman, orator and philosopher (106–43 B.C.E.)

10 Subduing and subdued, the petty strife,
      Which clouds the colour of domestic life;
      The sober comfort, all the peace which springs
      From the large aggregate of little things;
      On these small cares of daughter, wife or friend,
      The almost sacred joys of home depend.

"Sensibility," *Poems 1856*

11 Going to the opera, like getting drunk, is a sin that carries its
      own punishment with it.
      Letter to her sister (1775), *The Letters of Hannah More 1925*

650. Stephanie Félicité Genlis (1746–1830)

1   For which reason, you may observe that the man whose
      probity consists in merely obeying the laws, cannot be truly
      virtuous or estimable; for he will find many opportunities of
      doing contemptible and even dishonest acts, which the laws
      cannot punish.

"Laws," *Tales of the Castle ca. 1793*

2   Hence it is that men act ill, and judge well. Feeble and corrupted,
      they give way to their passions; but when they are cool—that

is to say, when they are uninterested—they instantly condemn
what they have often been guilty of; they revolt against every
thing that is contemptible; they admire every thing generous,
and they are moved at every thing affecting.

"Virtue," Ibid.

3   Can any one be a connoisseur in music, without knowledge of
      the science?
      No; it is absolutely impossible.

"Music," Ibid.

4   "A philosopher, desirous of praising a princess, who had been
      dead these fifty years, could not accomplish his purpose but at
      the expense of all the princesses, and all the women, who have
      ever existed or do exist; and that in a single phrase."
      "He has been very laconic indeed."
      "You shall hear—*Though a woman and a princess,* said he,
      she loved learning!"
      "The orator ought to have been answered, that *though a
      philosopher,* and an academician, he did not, on this occasion,
      show either much politeness or equity."

"The Two Reputations," Ibid.

651. Esther De Berdt Reed (1746–1780)

1   . . . if these great affairs must be brought to a crisis and de-
      cided, it had better be in our time than our children's.
      Letter to Dennis De Berdt, her brother (1775), Quoted in *The
      Life of Esther De Berdt, Afterwards Esther Reed* by William
      H. Reed *1853*

652. Frederica de Riedesel (1746–1808)

1   Britons never retrograde.
      Quoted in *The Women of the American Revolution,* Vol. II by
      Elizabeth F. Ellet *1848*

2   Seizing some maize, I begged our hostess to give me some of
      it to make a little bread. She replied that she needed it for her
      black people. "They work for us," she added, "and you come
      to kill us."

Ibid.

3   It is astonishing how much the frail human creature can en-
      dure. . . . *

Ibid.

      *Referring to the breakout of a malignant fever in New York in
      1780.

653. Susanna Blamire (1747–1794)

1   Till soft remembrance threw a veil
      Across these een o' mine,
      I closed the door, and sobbed aloud,
      To think on aul langsyne!
      "The Nabob," St. 4 *The Poetical Works of Miss Susanna
      Blamire, the Muse of Cumberland 1842*

2   I come, I come, my Jamie dear;
      And O! wi' what good will
      I follow wheresoe'er ye lead!
      Ye canna lead to ill.

"The Weafu' Heart," St. 5, Ibid.

3   Of aw things that is I think thout* is meast queer,
      It brings that that's by-past and sets it down here.
      "Auld Robin Forbes," St. 1, Ibid.
      *Thought.

654. Anna Gordon Brown (1747–1810)

1   O first he sang a merry song,
    An then he sang a grave,
    And then he peckd his feathers gray,
    To her the letter gave.
    "The Gay Goshawk," St. 10, *The English and Scottish Popular
    Ballads*, Francis James Child, ed. *1898*

655. Marie Letitia Bonaparte (1748–1836)

1   Napoleon has never given me a moment's pain, not even at
    the time which is almost universally woman's hour of suffer-
    ing.*
    Quoted in *Biography of Distinguished Women* by Sarah
    Josepha Hale** *1876*
    *Reference to the birth of her son, Napoléon Bonaparte, French
    general and emperor (1769–1821). **See 807.

656. Olympe de Gouges (1748–1793)

1   Observe the Creator in his wisdom; survey in all her grandeur
    that nature with whom you seem to want to be in harmony,
    and give me, if you dare, an example of this tyrannical empire.
    Go back to animals, consult the elements, study plants, finally
    glance at all the modifications of organic matter, and surren-
    der to the evidence when I offer you the means; search, probe,
    and distinguish, if you can, the sexes in the administration of
    nature. Everywhere you will find them mingled; everywhere
    they cooperate in harmonious togetherness in this immortal
    masterpiece.
    *Declaration of the Rights of Woman and the Female Citizen**
    1791*
    *Retort to Emmanuel Sieyès's *Declaration of the Rights of Man
    and the Citizen* (1789), preamble to the French Constitution
    (1791).

2   Postcript: Woman, wake up; the tocsin of reason is being heard
    throughout the whole universe; discover your rights.
    Ibid

3   Postcript: Marriage is the tomb of trust and love. The married
    woman can with impunity give bastards to her husband, and
    also give them the wealth which does not belong to them. The
    woman who is unmarried has only one feeble right; ancient
    and inhuman laws refuse to her for her children the right to the
    name and the wealth of their father; no new laws have been
    made in this matter.
    Ibid.

4   Article 6: The laws must be the expression of the general will;
    all female and male citizens must contribute either personally
    or through their representatives to its formation; it must be
    the same for all: male and female citizens, being equal in the
    eyes of the law, must be equally admitted to all honors, posi-
    tions, and public employment according to their capacity and
    without other distinctions besides those of their virtues and
    talents.
    Ibid.

5   We,_____and_____, moved by our own will, unite our-
    selves for the duration of our lives, and for the duration of
    our mutual inclinations, under the following conditions: We
    intend and wish to make our wealth communal, meanwhile
    reserving to ourselves the right to divide it in favor of our chil-
    dren and of those toward whom we might have a particular
    inclination, mutually recognizing that our property belongs
    directly to our children, from whatever bed they come, and

that all of them without distinction have the right to bear
the name of the fathers and mothers who have acknowledged
them . . .
    Form for a Social Contract Between Man and Woman, Ibid.

657. Gertrude Elizabeth Mara (1749–1833)

1   When I give a lesson in singing, I sing with my scholars; by so
    doing they learn in half the time they can if taught in the usual
    way—by the master merely playing the tune of the song on the
    piano. People cannot teach what they don't know—my schol-
    ars have my singing to imitate—those of other masters seldom
    any thing but the tinkling of a piano.
    Quoted in *Queens of Song* by Ellen Creathorne Clayton *1865*

658. Charlotte Smith (1749–1806)

1   Sweet poet of the woods.
    "The Departure of the Nightingale," *Elegiac Sonnets and
    Other Essays 1782*

2   Another May new buds and flowers shall bring;
    Ah! why has happiness—no second Spring?
    "The Close of Spring," Ibid.

3   But Reason comes at—Thirty-eight.
    "Thirty-Eight," St. 4, Ibid.

4   Stripp'd of their gaudy hues by Truth,
    We view the glitt'ring toys of youth.
    St. 7, Ibid.

5   "'Tis an uneasy thing," said he, "a very uneasy thing, for a man
    of probity and principles to look in these days into a newspa-
    per."
    Ch. 6, *Desmond*, Vol. I *1792*

6   When the imagination soars into those regions, where the
    planets pursue each its destined course, in the immensity of
    space—every planet, probably, containing creatures adapted
    by the Almighty, to the residence he has placed them in; and
    when we reflect, that the smallest of these is of as much con-
    sequence in the universe, as this world of our's; how puerile
    and ridiculous do those pursuits appear in which we are so
    anxiously busied; and how insignificant the trifles we toil to
    obtain, or fear to lose.
    Ch. 12, Ibid.

7   Having never heard anything but her own praises, she
    really believed herself a miracle of knowledge and accomplish-
    ments. . . .
    The Old Manor House 1793

8   "And let me tell you, Mrs. Winslow," said the Doctor, "that you
    are too apt to fall into these fits of admiration."
    Ch. 7, *The Young Philosopher*, Vol. I *1798*

9   "Youth, even when deprived of all viable support—makes a
    long and often a successful stand against calamity."
    Ch. 6, Vol. II, Ibid.

659. Anne Barnard (1750–1825)

1   The waes o' my heart fa' in showers frae my e'e,
    While my gudeman lies sound by me.
    "Auld Robin Gray" *1771*

2 My father couldna work, and my mother couldna spin;
   I toiled day and night, but their bread I couldna win.
                                                    Ibid.

3 They gied him my hand, tho' my heart was at sea.
                                                    Ibid.

660. Sophia Burrell (1750?–1764)

1 Blindfold I should to Myra run,
   And swear to love her ever;
   Yet when the bandage was undone,
   Should only think her clever.

   With the full usage of my eyes,
   I Chloe should decide for;
   But when she talks, I *her* despise,
   Whom, dumb, I could have died for!
                        "Chloe and Myra," Sts. 4–5, *Poems 1793*

2 Cupid and you, it is said, are cousins,
   (*Au faith** in stealing hearts by dozens,)
                                        "To Emma," Ibid.
   *Proficient.

3 And you should be arraign'd in court
   For practising this cruel sport,
   In spite of all the plaintiff's fury
   Your smile would bribe both judge and jury.
                                                    Ibid.

661. Madame du Hausset (fl. ca. 1750–1764)

1 Great people have had the bad habit of talking very indiscreetly
   before their servants.
                Quoted in *The Memoirs of Louis XV, and of Madame de
                Pompadour** 1910 ed.

2 See what the Court is; all is corruption there, from the highest
   to the lowest.
                            Remark to Mme de Pompadour,* Ibid.

   *Jeanne-Antoinette Poisson de Pompadour; see 588.

662. Caroline Herschel (1750–1848)

1 Many a half or whole holiday he* was allowed to spend with
   me was dedicated to making experiments in chemistry, where
   generally all boxes, tops of tea-canisters, pepper-boxes, teacups,
   etc, served for the necessary vessels and the sand-tub furnished
   the matter to be analyzed. I only had to take care to exclude
   water, which would have produced havoc on my carpet.
                Memoir and Correspondence of Caroline Herschel, Mrs. John
                                            Herschel, ed. *1876*
   *Her nephew, the astronomer Sir John Frederick Herschel (1792–
   1871).

2 I am now so enured to receiving honours in my old age, that I
   take them all upon me without blushing.
                                                    Ibid.

663. Mary Jones (fl. ca. 1750–d. 1778)

1 How much of paper's spoil'd! what floods of ink!
   And yet how few, how very few can think!
                I. "Extract from an Epistle to Lady Bowyer," St. 1, *Miscellanies
                                        in Prose and Verse 1750*

2 For what is beauty but a sign?
   A face hung out, through which is seen
   The nature of the goods within.
                    II. "To Stella, after the Small-Pox," St. 1, Ibid.

664. Sophia Lee (1750–1824)

1 Society, that first of blessings, brings with it evils death only
   can cure.
                                            The Recess 1785

665. Judith Madan (fl. ca. 1750)

1 Doubt not to reap, if thou canst bear to plough.
                "Verses. Written in her brother's Coke upon Littleton",* *The
                Female Poets of Great Britain,* Frederic Rowton, ed. *1853*
   *I. e., a copy of the commentary by the English jurist Sir Edward
   Coke on the *Tenures of Sir Thomas Littleton.*

666. Elizabeth Peabody (1750–1815)

1 Lost to virtue, lost to humanity must that person be, who can
   view without emotion the complicated distress of this injured
   land. Evil tidings molest our habitations, and wound our peace.
   Oh, my brother! oppression is enough to make a wise people
   mad.
                Letter to John Adams,* her brother-in-law, Quoted in *The
                Women of the American Revolution,* Vol. II, by Elizabeth F.
                                                        Ellet *1848*
   *(1735–1826), second U.S. president (1797–1801).

667. Caroline Matilda (1751–1775)

1 O God, keep me innocent; make others great!
                    Scratched with a diamond on a window of the castle of
                                        Frederiksborg, Denmark *n.d.*

668. Jeanne Isabelle Montolieu (1751–1832)

1 Here lies the child [Voltaire] spoiled by the world which he
   spoiled. (*Ci git l'enfant gâté du monde qu'il gâta.*)
                                "Epitaph on Voltaire"* *n.d.*
   *François-Marie Arouet, French philosopher and writer (1694–
   1778).

669. Judith Sargent Murray (1751–1820)

1 To the absorbing grave I must resign,
   All of my first born child that e'er was mine!
                "Lines, Occasioned by the Death of an Infant," St. 4, *The
                            Massachusetts Magazine January 1790*

2 Will it be said that the judgement of a male two years old, is
   more sage than that of a female's of the same age? I believe the
   reverse is greatly observed to be true. But from that period what
   partiality! how is the one exalted and the other depressed, by
   the contrary modes of education which are adopted! the one is
   taught to aspire, and the other is early confined and limited.
                                "On the Equality of the Sexes," Ibid.

3 I know there are those who assert, that as the animal powers
   of the one sex are superiour, of course their mental faculties
   also must be stronger; thus attributing strength of mind to the
   transient organization of this earth born tenement. But if this
   reasoning is just, man must be content to yield the palm to
   many of the brute creation. . . .
                                                    Ibid.

4 I would be Cesar, or I would be nothing.
The Gleaner, Vol. I *1798*

5 Religion is 'twixt God and my own soul,
Nor saint, nor sage, can boundless thought control.
"Lines Prefacing Essay No. XIX. A Sketch of the Gleaner's
Religious Sentiment," Ibid.

6 I may be accused of enthusiasm, but such is my confidence in
the sex, that I expect to see our young women forming a new
era in female history.
Vol. III, Ibid.

670. Ann Eliza Bleecker (1752–1783)

1 New worlds to find, new systems to explore:
When these appear'd, again I'd urge my flight
Till all creation open'd to my sight.
"On the Immensity of Creation," St. 1 (Tomhanick, 1773),
*The Posthumous Works of Ann Eliza Bleecker, in Prose and
Verse*, Margaretta Faugeres, ed. *1793*

2 But think not I dislike my situation here; on the contrary, I am
charmed with the lovely scene the spring opens around me.
Alas! the wilderness is within: I muse so long on the dead until
I am unfit for the company of the living.
Letter (8 April 1780), Ibid.

3 . . . Oh leave the city's noxious air.
"To the Same," St. 1, Ibid.

4 You've broke th' agreement, Sir, I find;
(Excuse me, I must speak my mind)
It seems in your poetic fit
You mind not jingling, where there's wit
"To Mr. L***,*" Ibid.

671. Fanny Burney (1752–1840)

1 "What a jabbering they make!" cried Mr. Braughton; "there's
no knowing a word they say. Pray what's the reason they can't
as well sing [opera] in English?—but I suppose the fine folks
would not like it, if they could understand it."
Letter XXI, *Evelina 1778*

2 Concealment, my dear Maris, is the foe of tranquility. . . .
Letter LX, Ibid.

3 . . . *Imagination* took the reins, and *Reason,* slow-paced,
though sure-footed, was unequal to a race with so eccentric
and flighty a companion.
Letter XVII, Ibid.

4 I'd do it as soon as say "Jack Robinson."
Letter LXXXII, Ibid.

5 CECILIA. Oh, how unequally are we affected by the progress
of time! Winged with the gay plumage of hope, how rapid
seems its flight,—oppressed with the burden of misery, how
tedious its motion!—yet it varies not,—insensible to smiles
and callous to tears, its acceleration and its tardiness are mere
phantasms of our disordered imaginations.
Act V, Sc. 1, *The Witlings 1779?*

6 "How true is it, yet how consistent . . . that while we all desire
to live long, we have all a horror of being old!"
Bk. II, Ch. 3, *Cecilia 1782*

7 "Report is mightily given to magnify."
Ch. 4, Ibid.

8 " . . . childhood is never troubled with foresight. . . ."
Bk. III, Ch. 2, Ibid.

9 Travelling is the ruin of all happiness! There's no looking at a
building here after seeing Italy.
Bk. IV, Ch. 2, Ibid.

10 "But if the young are never tired of erring in conduct, neither
are the older in erring of judgement. . . ."
Ch. 11, Ibid.

11 The shill I, shall I, of Congreve* becomes shilly shally.
Bk. V, Ibid.
*William Congreve, Restoration dramatist (1670–1729).

12 " . . . he looked around him for any pursuit, and seeing distinction was more easily attained in the road to ruin, he galloped
along it, thoughtless of being thrown when he came to the bottom, and sufficiently gratified in showing his horsemanship by
the way."
Ch. 7, Ibid.

13 "Far from having taken any positive step, I have not yet even
formed any resolution."
Bk. II, Ch. 13, Ibid.

14 Whatever there is new and splendid, is sure of a run for at least
a season.
Bk. X, Ch. 3, Ibid.

15 'Tis best to build no castles in the air.
Diary entry, Vol. II, *Diary and Letters of Madame D'Arblay,
1778–1840*, Vol. I, Charlotte Barrett, ed. *1904*

16 All the delusive seduction of martial music. . . .
Diary Entry (1802), Vol. VIII, Ibid.

672. Jeanne Louise Campan (1752–1822)

1 I have put together all that concerned the domestic life of an
unfortunate princess [Marie Antoinette*], whose reputation is
not yet cleared of the stains it received from the attacks of calumny, and who justly merited a different lot in life, a different
place in the opinion of mankind after her fall.
Memorandum, Quoted in *The Memoirs of Marie Antoinette*,
editor reissue *1910*
*See 682.

2 His [Louis XVI's*] heart, in truth, disposed him towards reforms; but his prejudices and fears, and the clamours of pious
and privileged persons, intimidated him, and made him abandon plans which his love for the people had suggested.
Ch. 6, Ibid.
*King of France (1754–1793), r. 1779–1792.

3 Tremble at the moment when your child has to choose between
the rugged road of industry and integrity, leading straight
to honour and happiness; and the smooth and flowery path
which descends, through indolence and pleasure, to the gulf of
vice and misery. It is then that the voice of a parent, or of some
faithful friend, must direct the right course.
"To Her Only Son," *Familiar Letters to her Friends n.d.*

4   Learn to know the value of money. This is a most essential point. The want of economy leads to the decay of powerful empires, as well as private families. Louis XVI perished on the scaffold for a deficit of fifty millions. There would have been no debt, no assemblies of the people, no revolution, no loss of the sovereign authority, no tragical death, but for this fatal deficit.

Ibid.

673. Hannah Mather Crocker (1752–1829)

1   . . . the wise Author of nature has endowed the female mind with equal powers and faculties, and given them the same right of judging and acting for themselves, as he gave to the male sex.

Observations on the Real Rights of Women 1818

674. Jemima Wilkinson (1752–1819)

1   Live peaceably with all men as much as possible; in an especial manner do not strive against one another for mastery, but all of you keep your ranks in righteousness, and let not one thrust another [aside].

The Universal Friend's Advice, to Those of the Same Religious Society 1784

2   It is a Sifting time; Try to be on the Lord's side. . . .

Letter to John and Orpha Rose (1789), Quoted in *Pioneer Prophetess* by Herbert A. Wisbey, Jr. *1964*

3   . . . that way the tree inclineth while it groweth that way it pitcheth when it falleth and there it Lieth. . . . So we Lie down to Eternity whether it Be towards heaven or towards hell Being Once fallen there is no removing for as in war an Error is death So in death an Error is damnation therefore Live as you intend to die and die as you intend to Live

"As We Live So we Die," Ibid.

4   . . . I am weary of them that hate peace.

Letter to James Parker (1788), Ibid.

675. Catharine Greene (1753–1815?)

1   If you expect to be an inhabitant of this country [Georgia], you must not think to sit down with your netting pins; but on the contrary, employ half your time at the toilet, one quarter to paying and receiving visits; the other quarter to scolding servants, with a hard thump every now and then over the head; or singing, dancing, reading, writing, or saying your prayers. The latter is here quite a phenomenon; but you need not tell how you employ your time.

Letter to Miss Flagg (ca. 1783), Quoted in *The Women of the American Revolution*, Vol. II by Elizabeth F. Ellet *1848*

676. Elizabeth Inchbald (1753–1821)

1   LADY EUSTON. There is as severe a punishment to men of gallantry (as they call themselves) as sword or pistol; laugh at them—that is a ball which cannot miss; and yet kills only their vanity.

Act III, Sc. 1, *I'll Tell You What 1786*

2   LADY EUSTON. "You are the most beautiful woman I ever saw," said Lord *Bandy*; "and your Ladyship is positively the most lovely of mankind"—"What eyes," cried he; "what hair," cried I; "what lips," continued he; "what teeth," added I; "What a hand and arm," said he; "and what a *leg* and *foot*," said I—

"Your Ladyship is jesting," was his Lordship's last reply; and he has never since paid me one compliment.

Ibid.

3   MARQUIS. . . . love is a general leveller—it makes the king a slave; and inspires the slave with every joy a prince can taste.

Act I, Sc. 1, *The Midnight Hour 1787*

4   MR. TWINEALL. Why, Madam, for instance, when a gentleman is asked a question which is either troublesome or improper to answer, you don't say you *won't* answer it, even though you speak to an inferior—but you say—"really it appears to me e-e-e-e-e—[mutters and shrugs]—that is—mo-mo-mo-mo-mo— [mutters]—if you see the thing—for my part—te-te-te-te—and that's all I can tell about it at *present*."

Act I, Sc. 1, *Such Things Are 1788*

5   DOCTOR. They have refused to grant me a *diploma;* forbid me to practice as a physician, and all because I do not know a parcel of insignificant words; but exercise my profession according to the rules of *reason* and *nature.*—Is it not natural to die? Then, if a dozen or two of my patients *have* died under my hands, is not that natural?

Act I, Sc. 1, *Animal Magnetism 1789*

6   SIR ROBERT RAMBLE. We none of us endeavour to *be* happy, Sir, but merely to be *thought* so; and for my part, I had rather be in a state of misery, and envied for my supposed happiness, than in a state of happiness, and pitied for my supposed misery.

Act I, Sc. 1, *Every One Has his Fault 1793*

7   LORD PRIORY. I know several women of fashion, who will visit six places of different amusement on the same night, have company at home besides, and yet, for want of something more, they'll be out of spirits. . . .

Act I, Sc. 1, *Wives as they Were, and Maids as they Are 1797*

8   COTTAGER. Wife, Wife, never speak ill of the dead. Say what you please against the living, but not a word against the dead. COTTAGER'S WIFE. And yet, husband, I believe the dead care the last what is said about them—

Act II, Sc. 1, *Lover's Vows 1798*

9   GIRONE. . . . women's power seldom lasts longer than their complexion.

Act I, Sc. 1, *A Case of Conscience 1833*

10   GIRONE. My Lord, I *do* know, but I am sworn to secrecy; and 'tis so unmanly to tell! But I will lead you to my wife, who knows also; and being a woman, she would unsex herself as much by keeping the secret, as I should by revealing it.

Act II, Sc. 1, Ibid.

11   My present apartment is so small, that I am all over black and blue with thumping my body and limbs against my furniture on every side; but then I have not far to *walk* to reach anything I want, for I can kindle my fire as I lie in bed, and put on my cap as I dine. . . .

from her Journal, Quoted in *English Women of Letters*, Vol. II by Julia Kavanagh* *1863*

*See 993.

677. Phillis Wheatley (1753?–1784)

1   Suppress the deadly serpent in its egg.
Ye blooming plants of human race divine,

An Ethiop tells you 'tis your greatest foe;
Its transient sweetness turns to endless pain,
And in immense perdition sinks the soul.
> "To the University of Cambridge, in New-England," St. 3
> (1767), *Poems on Various Subjects, Religious and Moral 1773*

2 Some view our sable race with scornful eye,
"Their colour is a diabolic dye."
Remember, *Christians*, *Negroes* black as Cain,
May be refin'd and join th' angelic train.
> "On Being Brought From Africa to America" (ca. 1768), Ibid.

3 I, young in life, by seeming cruel fate
Was snatch'd from Afric's fancy'd happy seat:
What pangs excruciating must molest,
What sorrows labor in my parent's breast?
Steel'd was that soul and by no misery mov'd
That from a father seiz'd his babe belov'd:
Such, such my case. And I can then but pray
Others may never feel tyrannic sway?
> "To the Right Honourable William, Earl of Dartmouth, His
> Majesty's Principal Secretary of State for North America, &
> C.," St. 3, Ibid.

4 The land of freedom's heaven-defended race!
> "To His Excellency General Washington,"* St. 3, Ibid.
> *George Washington (1732–1799), first U.S. president (1789–
> 1797).

5 . . . civil and religious liberty . . . are so inseparably united, that
there is little or no enjoyment of one without the other: . . . in
every human breast, God has implanted a principle, which we
call love of freedom; it is impatient of oppression and pants for
deliverance. . . .
> Letter to Rev. Samson Occom (11 February 1774), *Boston
> Post-Boy 21 March 1774*

678. Jeanne-Marie Roland (1754–1793)

1 O liberty! what crimes are committed in thy name!* *(O liberté!
que de crimes on commêt dans ton nom!)*
> Ch. LI, Last words before being guillotined (8 November
> 1793), Quoted in *Histoire des Girondins* by Alphonse
> Lamartine *1847*
> *Words inscribed on front of Statue of Liberty in New York City;
> also recorded as: "O Liberty, how you have been trifled with!" *(O
> Liberté, comme on t'a jouée!)*

2 I shall soon be there [at the guillotine]; but those who send me
there will follow themselves ere long. I go there innocent, but
they will go as criminals; and you, who now applaud, will also
applaud them.
> Remark en route to execution (8 November 1793),
> Quoted in *Biography of Distinguished Women*
> by Sarah Josepha Hale* *1876*
> *See 807.

3 The more I see of men, the more I admire dogs. *(Plus je vois les
hommes, plus j'admire les chiens.)*
> Attributed* *n.d.*
> *Also attributed to Ouida (see 1089) and to Mme de Sévigné (see
> 451).

679. Frances Thrynne (?–1754)

1 To thee, all glorious, ever-blessed power,
I consecrate this silent midnight hour.
> "A Midnight Hour," *Miscellanies,* Dr. Watt, ed. *n.d.*

680. Anne Grant (1755–1838)

1 Gem of the heath! whose modest bloom
Sheds beauty o'er the lonely moor
> "On A Sprig of Heath," St. 3, *The Highlanders and Other
> Poems 1808*

2 O where, tell me where, is your Highland laddie gone?
He's gone with streaming banners, where noble deeds are
done,
And my sad heart will tremble till he comes safely home.
> "O Where, Tell Me Where,"* *Scottish Song,* Mary Carlyle
> Aitken, ed. *1874*
> *Both this and "The Blue Bells of Scotland" by Dorothea Jordan
> (see 712:1) are variants on an older popular song.

681. Anna Maria Lenngren (1755–1817)

1 'Tis plain to see what pride within her glance reposes,
And mark how nobly curved her nose is!
> "The Portraits," St. 2, *Anthology of Swedish Lyrics from
> 1750–1915,* C. W. Stork, ed. and tr. *1917*

2 The fairer sex possessed a mind
Of sturdy fabric, like her cloak.
Now all is different in our lives—
Other fabrics, other mores!
Taffetas, indecent stories
> "Other Fabrics, Other Mores!" Nadia Christensen and
> Mariann Tiblin, trs., *The Penguin Book of Women Poets,*
> Carol Cosman, Joan Keefe, and Kathleen Weaver, eds. *1978*

682. Marie Antoinette (1755–1793)

1 Let them eat cake.* *(Qu'ils mangent de la brioche.)*
> Quoted in *Confessions* by Jean-Jacques Rousseau** *1740*
> *Brioche, or "cake," was, in that day, equivalent to a round, hard-
> crusted bread. **French philosopher and writer (1712–1778).

2 Courage! I have shown it for years; think you I shall lose it at
the moment when my sufferings are to end?
> Remark (16 October 1793; on way to guillotine), Quoted in
> *Women of Beauty and Heroism* by Frank B. Goodrich *1858*

3 Adieu, once again, my children, I go to join your father.
> Last words (16 October 1793), Ibid.

4 I have seen all, I have heard all, I have forgotten all.
> Reply to inquisitors (October 1789), Quoted in *Biography of
> Distinguished Women* by Sarah Josepha Hale* *1876*
> *See 807.

5 I was a queen, and you took away my crown; a wife, and you
killed my husband; a mother, and you deprived me of my children. My blood alone remains: take it, but do not make me
suffer long.
> Remark at the revolutionary tribunal (14 October 1793),
> Quoted in *Biography of Distinguished* Women by Sarah
> Josepha Hale* *1876*
> *See 807.

6 There is nothing new except what has been forgotten.
> Remark, Quoted in *Women in World History Curriculum*
> (womeninworldhistory.com) *1996–97*

7 I allow the public to believe that I have more credit [with the
King] than I do in reality.
> Quoted in *Queen of Fashion* by Caroline Weber, *2006*

683. Renier Giustina Michiel (1755–1832)

1 For me ennui is among the worst evils—I can bear pain better.
Quoted in *Biography of Distinguished Women* by Sarah
Josepha Hale* *1876*
*See 807.

2 The world improves people according to the dispositions they
bring into it.
Ibid.

3 Time is a better comforter than reflection.
Ibid.

684. Sarah Siddons (1755–1831)

1 I pant for retirement and leisure, but am doomed to inexpress-
ible and almost unsupportable hurry.
Letter to Rev. Sedgwick Whalley (Dublin, 21 June 1784),
Quoted in *Journals and Correspondence of Thomas Sedgwick
Whalley*, Vol. I, Rev. Hill Wickham, ed. *1863*

2 This woman* is one of those monsters (I think them) of perfection, who is an angel before her time, and is so entirely resigned
to the will of heaven, that (to a very mortal like myself) she appears to be the most provoking piece of still life one had ever
had the misfortune to meet.
(ca. 1787) Ibid.
*The lead character in a new play by Bertie Greatheed.

3 I have paid severely for eminence.
Letter to the Rev. and Mrs. Whalley (15 March 1785), Quoted
in *The Kembles*, Vol. I, by Percy Fitzgerald *1871*

4 Alas! How wretched is the being who depends on the stability
of public favour!
(1824), *The Reminiscences of Sarah Kemble Siddons*, William
Van Lennep, ed. *1942* (repr.)

5 The awful consciousness that one is the sole object of attention
to that immense space, lined as it were with human intellect
from top to bottom, and on all sides round, may perhaps be
imagined but can not be described, and never never to be forgotten. . . .
Ibid.

6 Alas, why had I enemies, but because to be prosperous is sufficient cause for enmity.
Ibid.

7 . . . . I believe one half of the world is born for the convenience
of the other half. . . .
Ch. 5, Letter to Hester Lynch Piozzi* (27 August 1794),
Quoted in *Sarah Siddons, Portrait of an Actress* by Roger
Manvell *1970*
*See 635.

685. Elisabeth Vigée-Lebrun (1755–1842)

1 I was so fortunate as to be on very pleasant terms with the
Queen [Marie-Antoinette].* When she heard that I had something of a voice we rarely had a sitting without singing some
duets . . . together, for she was exceedingly fond of music. . . .
(1835), *Memoirs of Madame Vigée-Lebrun*,
Lionel Strachey, tr. *1907*
*See 682.

2 The women reigned then; the Revolution dethroned them.
Ibid.

686. Eliza Wilkinson (1755?–?)

1 . . . they [soldiers] really merit every thing, who will fight from
principle alone; for from what I could learn, these poor creatures had nothing to protect them, and seldom got their pay;
yet with what alacrity will they encounter danger and hardships of every kind!
Quoted in *The Women of the American Revolution*, Vol. II by
Elizabeth F. Ellet *1848*

687. Hester Ann Rogers (1756–1794)

1 What I suffered is known only to God.
Quoted in *The Women of Methodism: Its Three Foundresses
. . . by Abel Stevens *1866*

688. Anna Young Smith (1756–1780?)

1 But should we know as much as they,
They fear their empire would decay;
For they know women heretofore
Gained victories, and envied laurel's war.
And now they fear we'll once again
Ambitious be to reign,
And so invade the territories of the brain.
Sylvia's Complaint of her Sex's Unhappiness 1788

2 But now, so oft filth chokes thy sprightly fire,
We loathe one instant, and the next admire—
Even while we laugh, we mourn thy wit's abuse,
And while we praise thy talents, scorn their use.
"On Reading Swift's* Works" (Philadelphia, 1774), *Universal
Asylum & Columbian Magazine* September 1790
*Jonathan Swift, English satirist (1667–1745).

3 Teach my unskilled mind to sing
The feelings of my heart.
"An Ode to Gratitude," Pt. 1 (Philadelphia, 1770), *Women
Poets in Pre-Revolutionary America*, Patti Cowell, ed. *1981*

689. Augusta (1757–1831)

1 How can his [Napoleon's*] conscience be quite in abeyance,
with so many thousands of lives sacrificed to his insane ambition? What would I not give to read his inner thoughts. If
he will ever awake from his mad dream of power, God only
knows, Who has permitted him to become the scourge of the
nations of the earth.
Diary Entry (26 January 1813), *In Napoleonic Days,
Extracts from the private diary of Augusta, Duchess of Saxe-
Coburg-Saalfeld, Queen Victoria's** maternal grandmother,
1806–1821*, H. R. H., the Princess Beatrice, ed. and tr. *1941*
*Emperor of the French (1769–1821; r. 1804–1814) **See 960.

2 When one gets old one is so thankful to be quiet.
Diary entry (19 December 1817), Ibid.

690. Georgiana Cavendish (1757–1806)

1 Their Liberty requir'd no rites uncouth,
No blood demanded, and no slaves enchain'd;
Her rule was gentle, and her voice was truth,
By social order form'd, by law restrain'd.
Passage of the Mountain of Saint Gothard, St. 26 *1802*

691. Elizabeth Hamilton (1758?–1816)

1 "Those who wait till evening for sunrise," said Mrs. Mason,
"will find that they have lost the day."
Ch. 8, *The Cottagers of Glenburnie: A Tale for the Farmer's
Ingle-nook* 1808

2   Of a' roads to happiness were ever tried,
    There's nane half so sure as ane's ain fireside.
    My ain fireside, my ain fireside,
    O there's naught to compare wi' ane's ain fireside.
                "My Ain Fireside," *Scottish Song*, Mary Carlyle Aitken, ed.
                                                                    1874

3   With expectation beating high,
    Myself I now desire to spy;
    And straight I in a glass surveyed
    An antique lady, much decayed
            Untitled, Quoted in *Biography of Distinguished Women* by
                                        Sarah Josepha Hale* 1876
    *See 807.

4   It is only by the love of reading that the evil resulting from the
    association with *little* minds can be counteracted.
                    "The Benefits of Society," *Private Letters n.d.*

5   I perfectly agree with you in considering castles in the air as
    more useful edifices than they are generally allowed to be. It is
    only plodding matter-of-fact dullness that cannot comprehend
    their use.
                                            "Imagination," Ibid.

692. Henrietta O'Neill (1758–1793)

1   Hail, lovely blossom! thou canst ease
    The wretched victims of Disease
    Canst close those weary eyes in gentle sleep,
    Which never open but to weep;
    For oh! thy potent charm
    Can agonizing Pain disarm;
    Expel imperious Memory from her seat,
    And bid the throbbing heart forget to beat.
            "Ode to Poppy," St. 5, Quoted in *Elegaic Sonnets and Other
                            Essays*, Charlotte Smith, ed. *1782*

693. Mary Robinson (1758–1800)

1   Yet when love and hope are vanished,
    Restless memory never dies.
        "Stanzas, written between Dover & Calais," St. 4, *Poems 1775*

2   I have wept to see thee weep.
                                            St. 13, Ibid.

3   The proudest of the purring band:—
    So dignified in all her paces,
    She seem'd a pupil of the Graces!
    There never was a finer creature
    In all the varying whims of Nature!
                "Mistress Gurton's Cat. A Domestic Tale," St. 1, Ibid.

4   For friends, whom trifling faults can sever,
    Are valued most—when lost for ever!
                                            St. 12, Ibid.

5   The proud inheritor of Heaven's best gifts—
    The mind unshackled, and the guiltless soul!
                    "The Widow's Home," St. 5, last lines, Ibid.

6   Insatiate TIME shall steal those tints away,
    Warp thy fine form, and bend thy beauties low:

    But the rare wonders of thy polish'd MIND
    Shall mock the empty menace of decay;
            "To Her Grace the Duchess of Devonshire," Sts. 2–3, Ibid.

694. Jane West (1758–1852)

1   Great and sudden reverses of fortune are not frequent; yet little
    disappointments hourly occur, which fall with the greatest se-
    verity on those, whose amiable, though dangerous enthusiasm,
    induces them to expect too much, and to feel too severely.
                Preface, *The Advantage of Education; or, The History of
                Maria Williams, a tale for Misses and their Mammas*, Vol. I
                                                                    1793

2   " . . . your newly acquired taste for reading, prevents even
    the hazard of your ever perceiving time to be an intolerable
    burden."
                                            Ch. 7, Ibid.

3   There are some secrets which scarcely admit of being disclosed
    even to ourselves.
                            Ch. 8, *A Gossip's Story*, Vol. I 1797

4   As wise people often defeat their aims by too great caution,
    cunning also frequently overshoots the mark by too much
    craft.
                                            Ch. 11, Ibid.

5   Man. Lord of all, beneath the reign of time,
    Awaits perfection in a nobler clime.
                        Ch. 24, "To a Rose Bush," Vol. II, Ibid.

6   "How disgraceful are these baby quarrels! how ridiculous these
    high theatrical passions, which subject them to the laugh of the
    neighbourhood! nay, worse, which point out to artful villany,
    means whereby it may *effectually* undermine domestick happi-
    ness."
                                            Ch. 31, Ibid.

695. Martha Wilson (1758–post-1848)

1   . . . let it never be forgotten by you that the reputation estab-
    lished by a boy at school and college, whether it be of merit or
    demerit, will follow him through life.
                Letter to C. S. Stewart, her nephew and adopted son (16
                February 1811), Quoted in *The Women of the American
                Revolution*, Vol. II by Elizabeth F. Ellet *1848*

2   Industry is the handmaid of good fortune. . . .
                        Letter to C. S. Stewart (31 May 1814), Ibid.

3   Man can do much for himself as respects his own improve-
    ment, unless self-love so blinds him that he cannot see his own
    imperfections and weaknesses.
                                            Ibid.

4   The exercise of a little self-denial for the time being will be
    followed by the pleasure of having achieved the greatest of tri-
    umphs—a triumph over one's self.
                                            Ibid.

696. Agnes Craig (1759–1841)

1   Talk not of love, it gives me pain,
    For love has been my foe;
    He bound me with an iron chain,
    And plunged me deep in woe.
    But friendship's pure and lasting joys,
    My heart was formed to prove.
            "Talk Not of Love," *Scottish Song*, Mary Carlyle Aitken, ed.
                                                                    1874

697. Hannah Webster Foster (1759–1840)

1 An unusual sensation possesses my breast—a sensation which I once thought could never pervade it on any occasion whatever. It is *pleasure*, pleasure, my dear Lucy, on leaving my paternal roof.

Letter I, *The Coquette; or, The History of Eliza Wharton* 1797

2 In whatever situation we are placed, our greater or less degree of happiness must be derived from ourselves. Happiness is in a great measure the result of our own dispositions and actions.

Letter XXI, Ibid.

3 Our greatest mistakes may teach lessons which will be useful through life.

Letter XLIII, Ibid.

698. Sarah Wentworth Morton (1759–1846)

1 When life hung quiv'ring on a single hair

"To Constantia," St. 1, *Massachusetts Magazine* May 1790

2 To the mere superficial observer, it would seem that man was sent into this breathing world for the purpose of enjoyment— woman for that of trial and suffering.

"The Sexes," *My Mind and Its Thoughts* 1823

3 Expression in its finest utterance lives,
And a new language to creation gives.

"To Mr. [Gilbert] Stuart.* Upon Seeing Those Portraits Which were Painted by Him at Philadelphia, in the Beginning of the Present Century," St. 1, Ibid.
*Famed American portrait painter (1755–1828).

4 Did all the Gods of Afric sleep,
Forgetful of their guardian love,
When the white tyrants of the deep
Betrayed him in the palmy grove?

"The African Chief," St. 2, Ibid.

699. Martha Laurens Ramsay (1759–1811)

1 . . . the bucks, the fops, the idlers of college. . . .

Letters to her son at college *n.d.*

2 . . . of all the mean objects in creation, a lazy, poor, proud gentleman, especially if he is a dressy fellow, is the meanest. . . .

Ibid.

700. Anna Green Winslow (1759–1780)

1 Those golden arts* the vulgar never knew.

"To her Parents" (17 March 1772), *Diary of Anna Green Winslow: A Boston School Girl of 1771*, Alice Morse Earle, ed. *1895*

*Virtues.

701. Mary Wollstonecraft (1759–1797)

1 If the abstract rights of man will bear discussion and explanation, those of woman, by a parity of reasoning, will not shrink from the same test: though a different opinion prevails in the country.

Dedication, *A Vindication of the Rights of Women* 1792

2 Independence I have long considered as the grand blessing of life, the basis of every virtue; and independence I will ever secure by contracting my wants, though I were to live on a barren heath.

Ibid.

3 Perhaps the seeds of false-refinement, immorality, and vanity, have ever been shed by the great. Weak, artificial beings, raised above the common wants and defections of their race, in a premature and unnatural manner, undermine the very foundation of virtue, and spread corruption through the whole mass of society!

Introduction to 1st ed., Ibid.

4 . . . elegance is inferior to virtue. . . .

Ibid.

5 Virtue can only flourish among equals.

Ibid.

6 Standing armies can never consist of resolute robust men; they may be well-disciplined machines, but they will seldom contain men under the influence of strong passions, or with very vigorous faculties.

Ch. 2, Ibid.

7 Taught from infancy that beauty is woman's sceptre, the mind shapes itself to the body, and roaming round its gilt cage, only seeks to adorn its prison.

Ch. 3, Ibid.

8 Would man but generously snap our chains, and be content with rational fellowship instead of slavish obedience, they would find us more observant daughters, more affectionate sisters, more faithful wives, more reasonable mothers—in a word, better citizens. We should then love them with true affection, because we should learn to respect ourselves. . . .

"Of the Pernicious Effects which Arise from the Unnatural Distinctions Established in Society," Ibid.

9 But a child, though a pledge of affection, will not enliven it, if both father and mother be content to transfer the charge to hirelings; for they who do their duty by proxy should not murmur if they miss the reward of duty—parental affection produces filial duty.

"Parental Affection," Ibid.

10 From the respect paid to property flow, as from a poisoned fountain, most of the evils and vices which render this world such a dreary scene to the contemplative mind.

Ibid.

11 . . . only that education deserves emphatically to be termed cultivation of mind which teaches young people how to begin to think.

"On National Education," Ibid.

12 . . . as blind obedience is ever sought for by power, tyrants and sensualists are in the right when they endeavour to keep women in the dark, because the former only want slaves, and the latter a play-thing.

"The Prevailing Opinion of a Sexual Character Discussed," Ibid.

13 I begin to love this little creature, and to anticipate his birth as a fresh twist to a knot, which I do not wish to untie.

Letter to William Godwin, her husband (March 1797), Quoted in *Godwin and Mary* by Ralph M. Wardle 1966

14 Society fatigues me inexpressibly. So much so, that finding fault with everyone, I have only reason enough to discover that the fault is in myself.

Letter XXXVII (19 February 1795), *Letters to Imlay** n.d
*Captain Gilbert Imlay, her lover.

15 I never wanted but your heart—That gone, you have nothing more to give.

> Letter LXX (London, November 1795), Ibid.

702. Sally Sayward Wood (1759–1855)

1 Amelia was not a disciple of Mary Woolstonecraft* [sic], she was not a woman of fashion, nor a woman of spirit. She was an old-fashioned wife, and she meant to obey her husband: she meant to do her duty in the strictest sense of the word.

> *Amelia; or, the Influence of Virtue* 1802

*See 701.

703. Elizabeth "Betty" Zane (1759–1823)

1 You have not one man to spare.*

> Quoted in *Chronicles of Border Warfare* by Alexander S. Withers 1831

*Attributed remark as she volunteered to run a dangerous mission.

704. Margaret Shippen Arnold (1760–1804)

1 . . . my ambition has sunk with my fortune.

> Letter to E. Burd (15 August 1801), Quoted in "Life of Margaret Shippen" by Lewis Burd Walker, *Pennsylvania Magazine of History and Biography,* Vol. XXV 1901

2 At one period, when I viewed everything through a false medium, I fancied that nothing but the sacrifice of my life would benefit my children, for that my wretchedness embittered every moment of their lives; and dreadful to say, I was many times on the point of making the sacrifice.

> Letter to her father (1801), Ibid.

705. Charlotte Charke (?–1760)

1 MRS. TRAGIC. 'Tis every Parent's Duty to breed their Children with every Advantage their Fortunes will admit of . . .

> *The Art Management, or Tragedy Expelled* 1735

2 Your two friends, PRUDENCE and REFLECTION, I am inform'd, have lately ventur'd to pay you a visit; for which I heartily congratulate you, as nothing can possibly be more joyous to the Heart than the Return of absent Friends, after a long and painful Peregrination.

> Dedication, *A Narrative of the Life of Mrs. Charlotte Charke* 1755

3 . . . forced again to . . . find fresh means of Subsistence . . . 'till even the last thread of Invention was worn out.

> Ibid.

4 Misfortunes are too apt to wear out Friendship. . . .

> Ibid.

706. Susannah Farnum Copley (fl. ca. 1760–d. 1836)

1 It was his* own inclination and persevering industry that brought him forward in the art of painting, for he had no instructor.

> Ch. 1, Letter, Quoted in *The Domestic and Artistic Life of John Singleton Copley, R.A.,* by Martha Babcock Amory** 1882

*Her husband, the artist John Singleton Copley (1738–1815).
**Copley's granddaughter.

2 I tell [your father] I don't know what might be the effect if our comfort, as well as our delight, was not so interwoven with the arts, which it is mortifying to know do not find a place among the other refinements of our native country [the United States]. . . .

> Ch. 11, Letter to her daughter (1 June 1801), Ibid.

3 . . . but we find the law, as well as many other pursuits, requires much perseverance and patience to obtain the object; it is well for us that we do not always foresee the degree that it is necessary . . .

> (15 March 1805), Ibid.

4 A happy calm prevails after great apprehension of the reverse.

> Ch. 16, Letter to her daughter (22 March 1821), Ibid.

707. Rebecca Franks (1760–1823)

1 I have gloried in my rebel countrymen! Would to God I, too, had been a patriot!

> Remark to General Winfield Scott (ca. 1816), Quoted in *Rebecca Franks: An American Jewish Belle of the Last Century* by Max J. Kohler 1894

708. Hô Xuân Hu?o?ng (fl. ca. 1760–d. 1799)

1 I am like a jackfruit on the tree.
To taste you must pluck me quick, while fresh:
the skin rough, the pulp thick, yes,
but oh, I warn you against touching—
the rich juice will gush and stain your hands.

> "The Jackfruit," in toto, *A Thousand Years of Vietnamese Poetry,* Nguyen Ngoc Bich, ed. and tr. 1975

2 Pray hard: you too can be a Superior
And squat, proud, on a lotus.

> "A Buddhist Priest," Nguyen Ngoc Bich and Burton Raffel, trs., Ibid.

709. Mary Slocumb (1760–1836)

1 Allow me to observe and prophesy, the only land in these United States which will ever remain in possession of a British officer, will measure but six feet by two.

> Remark to a British colonel, Quoted in *The Women of the American Revolution,* Vol. II by Elizabeth F. Ellet 1848

2 My husband is not a man who would allow a duke, or even a king, to have a quiet [titled] seat upon his ground.

> Ibid.

710. Anne Yearsley (1760–1806)

1 Earth by the grizzly tyrant desert made
The feathered warblers quit the leafless shade;
Quit those dear scenes where life and love began,
And, cheerless seek the savage haunts of man.

> "Clifton Hill," St. 1 (January 1785), *The British Female Poets,* George W. Bethune, ed. 1848

2 The portals of the swelling soul ne'er ope'd
By liberal converse, rude ideas strove
Awhile for vent, but found it not, and died.
Thus rust the mind's best powers.

> "A Poem on Mrs. Montague",* *The Female Poets of Great Britain,* Frederic Rowton, ed. 1853

*Mary Wortley Montagu; see 533.

711. Margaret Wrench Holford (1761?–1834)

1 They are solemn and low, and none can hear
The whispers which come to Memory's ear!
"On Memory; Written at Aix-la-Chapelle," St. 3, *Poems* 1811

2 "Bright success
May only for a while sustain Man's feeble spirit!"
4th canto, "Margaret of Anjou:* A Poem in Ten Cantos" 1816
*See 258.

3 "Let me Fate's awful page explore!
Leaf after leaf would I unfold,
E'en to the final word!—till *all* the tale be told!"
7th canto, Ibid.

4 And, hark! the signal!—Now begin,
Of those who lose and those who win,
The strife, the shout, the mortal din!
Behold!—they meet!—they clash!—they close!—
They mix!—Sworn friends and deadly foes,
In one dire mass, one struggling host,
All order and distinction lost,
Roll headlong, guideless, blind, like waves together toss'd!
Ibid.

712. Dorothea Jordan (1761–1816)

1 'Oh, where, and Oh! where is your Highland laddie gone?'
'He's gone to fight the French, for King George upon the throne,
And it's Oh! in my heart, how I wish him safe at home!'
"The Blue Bells of Scotland"* *n.d.*
*Both this and "Oh Where, Tell Me Where" by Anne Green are
variants on an older popular song.

713. Joanna Baillie (1762–1851)

1 O! who shall lightly say that fame
Is nothing but an empty name?
"The Legend of Christopher Columbus,"* St. 1, ix,
Fugitive Verses 1790
*Italian explorer (1451–1506).

2 "Ah! happy is the man whose early lot
Hath made him master of a furnish'd cot;
Who trains the vine that round his window grows,
And after setting sun his garden hoes;
Whose wattled pails his own enclosure shield,
Who toils not daily in another's field."
"A Reverie," St. iii, Ibid.

3 "What hollow sound is that?" approaching near,
The roar of many wheels breaks on his ear.
It is the flood of human life in motion!
"London," St. iii, Ibid.

4 Sweet bud of promise, fresh and fair,
Just moving in the morning air.
The morn of life but just begun,
The sands of time just set to run!
Sweet babe with cheek of pinky hue,
With eyes of soft ethereal blue,
With raven hair like finest down
Of unfledged bird, and scant'ly shown
Beneath the cap of cumbrous lace,
That circles round thy placid face!

Ah, baby! little dost thou know
How many yearning blossoms glow,
How many lips in blessings move,
How many eyes beam looks of love
At sight of thee!
"To Sophia J. Baillie, an Infant," in toto, Ibid.

5 Busy work brings after ease;
Ease brings sport and sport brings rest;
For young and old, of all degrees,
The mingled lot is best.
"Rhymes," St. I, Ibid.

6 COUNTESS OF ALBINI. For she who only finds her self-esteem
In other's admiration, begs in alms;
Depends on others for her daily food,
And is the very servant of her slaves. . . .
Act II, Sc. 4, *Basil* 1798

7 COUNT ROSINBERG. The brave man is not he who feels no fear,
For that were stupid and irrational;
But he, whose noble soul its fear subdues,
And barely dares the danger nature shrinks from.
Act III, Sc. 1, Ibid.

8 SONG. Child, with many a childish wile,
Timid look, and blushing smile,
Downy wings to steal thy way,
Gilded bow, and quiver gay,
Who in thy simple mien would trace
The tyrant of the human race?
Sc. 3, Ibid.

9 A willing heart adds feather to the heel.
Act III, Sc. 2, *De Monfort* 1798

10 The bliss e'en of a moment still is bliss.
Act I, Sc. 2, *The Beacon* 1802

11 WORSHIPTON. Curse your snug comfortable ways of living!
my soul abhors the idea of it. I'll pack up all I have in a knapsack first, and join the wild Indians in America.
Act V, Sc. 2, *The Country Inn* 1804

12 Still on it creeps,
Each little moment at another's heels,
Till hours, days, years and ages are made up
Of such small parts as these, and men look back
Worn and bewilder'd, wondering how it is.
Rayner 1804

13 Pampered vanity is a better thing perhaps than starved pride.
Act II, Sc. 2, *The Election* 1811

14 ORRA. He was not all a father's heart could wish;
but oh, he was my son!—my only son.
Act III, Sc. 2, *Orra* 1812

15 SANCHO. Me care for te laws when te laws care for me.
Act V, Sc. 2, *The Alienated Manor* 1836

16 Words of affection, howso'er express'd,
The latest spoken still are deem'd the best.
"Address to Miss Agnes Baillie on Her Birthday," ll.125–126
n.d.

714. Mrs. Lyon (1762–1840)

1 Yet the doctors they do a' agree,
That whiskey's no the drink for me.
Saul! quoth Neil, 'twill spoil my glee,
Should they part me and whiskey, O
"Neil Gow's Farewell to Whiskey," *Scottish Song*, Mary
Carlyle Aitken, ed. *1874*

715. Susanna Haswell Rowson (1762–1824)

1 To raise the fall'n—to pity and forgive,
This is our noblest, best prerogative.
By these, pursuing nature's gentle plan,
We hold—in silken chains—the lordly tyrant man.
Epilogue, *Slaves in Algiers, or a Struggle for Freedom* 1794

2 Nay, start not, gentle sirs; indeed, 'tis true,
Poor woman has her rights as well as you;
And if she's wise, she will assert them too.
"Rights of Women," *Miscellaneous Poems* 1804

716. Helen Maria Williams (1762–1827)

1 No riches from his scanty store
My lover could impart;
He gave a boon I valued more,
He gave me all his heart.
"Song," St. 1, *An Ode to Peace and Other Poems* 1782–88

2 The night is dark, the waters deep,
Yet soft the billows roll;
Alas! at every breeze I weep,
The storm is in my soul.
St. 5, Ibid.

3 Come, gentle Hope! with one gay smile remove
The lasting sadness of an aching heart.
"Sonnet to Hope," *Poems, moral, elegant and pathetic: viz.
Essay on Man, by Pope* . . . And Original Sonnets* by Helen
Maria Williams *1796*
*English poet and satirist (1688–1744).

717. Empress Josephine (1763–1814)

1 Trust to me, ladies, and do not envy a splendor which does not
constitute happiness.
Quoted in *Lives of Celebrated Women* by Samuel Griswold
Goodrich *1844*

2 . . . patience and goodness will ever in the end conciliate the
goodwill of others.
Letter to her children (1794), Ibid.

718. Elizabeth Trefusis (1763–1808)

1 Thus the vain man, with subtle feigning,
Pursues, o'ertakes poor woman's heart;
But soon his hapless prize disdaining,
She dies!—the victim of his art.
"The Boy and Butterfly," *Poems and Tales* 1808

719. Anne Willing Bingham (1764–1801)

1 The women of France interfere in the politics of the Country,
and often give a decided Turn to the Fate of Empires.
Letter to Thomas Jefferson* (ca. 1783–1786), Quoted in *The
Papers of Thomas Jefferson*, Vol. XI, Julian P. Boyd, ed. *1955*
*(1743–1826), third president of United States (1801–1809).

720. Helene Marie Phillipine Elizabeth (1764–1794)

1 I am Elizabeth of France, the aunt of your king [Louis XVII].
In answer to request for her identity at her tribunal
(May 10, 1794), Quoted in *Biography of Distinguished
Women* by Sarah Josepha Hale* 1876
*See 807.

721. Juliana Krudener (1764–1824)

1 Stay quiet; refuse nothing; flowers grow only because they tran-
quilly allow the sun's rays to reach them. You must do the same.
Remark to Germaine de Staël,* Quoted in *Mistress to an Age:
A Life of Madame de Staël* by J. Christopher Herold *1958*
*See 733.

722. Mary Ann Lamb (1764–1847)

1 Who, that e'er could understand
The rare structure of a hand,
With its branching fingers fine,
Work itself of hands divine,
Strong, yet delicately knit,
For ten thousand uses fit
"Cleanliness," *Poetry for Children* 1809

2 His conscience slept a day or two,
As it is very apt to do
"The Boy and the Skylark," I, St. 5, Ibid.

3 An infant is a selfish sprite.
"The Broken Doll," St. 1, Ibid.

4 A child is fed with milk and praise.
"The First Tooth," Ibid.

5 Know ye not, each thing we prize
Does from small beginnings rise?
"The Brother's Reply," I, Ibid.

6 A child's a plaything for an hour.
"Parental Recollections," Ibid.

7 Thou straggler into loving arms,
Young climber up of knees,
When I forget thy thousand ways,
Then life and all shall cease.
"A Child," St. 3, Ibid.

8 . . . I have lost all self confidence in my own actions & one
cause of my low spirits is that I never feel satisfied with anything I do—a perception of not being in a sane state perpetually
haunts me.
Letter to Sarah Stoddart (9–14 November 1805), *The Letters
of Charles and Mary Lamb*, Vol. II, 1801–1809, Edwin W.
Marrs, Jr., ed. *1976*

9 If you fancy a very young man, and he likes an elderly gentlewoman, if he likes a learned & accomplished lady, and you
like a not very learned youth who may need a little polishing
which probably he will never acquire; it is all very well &
God bless you both together & may you both be very long in
the same mind.
(23 October 1806), Ibid.

10 . . . you must begin the world with ready money. . . .
>(21? December 1807), Ibid.

723. Ann Radcliffe (1764–1823)

1 At first a small line of inconceivable splendour emerged on the horizon, which, quickly expanding, the sun appeared in all of his glory, unveiling the whole face of nature, vivifying every colour of the landscape, and sprinkling the dewy earth with glittering light. The low and gentle responses of the birds, awakened by the morning ray, now broke the silence of the hour, their soft warbling rising by degrees till they swelled the chorus of universal gladness.
>*The Romance of the Forest 1791*

2 "We in Italy are not so apt to despair. . . ."
>*The Italian 1797*

3 Then let me stand amidst thy glooms profound
On some wild woody steep, and hear the breeze
>"Night," St. 8, *Poems 1834*

724. Catherine Rilliet-Huber (1764–post-1810)

1 All I can say is that she [Germaine de Staël*] is as lively and brilliant as ever—which proves the advantage of organizing one's heart in a system of multiple hiding places.
>Letter to Henri Meister (13 November 1810), Quoted in *Mistress to an Age: A Life of Madame de Staël* by J. Christopher Herold *1958*

*See 733.

725. Sun Yün-fêng (1764–1814)

1 Under the waning moon
In the dawn—
A frosty bell.
>"Starting at Dawn," *The Orchid Boat, Women Poets of China,* Kenneth Rexroth and Ling Chung, eds. and trs. *1972*

2 Along the shore the willows
Wait for their Spring green.
>"On the Road Through Chang-te," Ibid.

726. Catherine Marie Fanshawe (1765–1834)

1 'Twas whisper'd in heaven, 'twas mutter'd in hell,
And echo caught faintly the sound as it fell;
On the confines of earth 'twas permitted to rest,
And the depths of the ocean its presence confess'd.
>"Enigma: The Letter H," *Memorials 1865*

2 At their speed behold advancing
Modern men and women dancing;
Step and dress alike express
Above, below from heel to toe,
Male and female awkwardness.
>"The Abrogation of the Birth-Night Ball," Ibid.

727. Emma Hamilton (1765–1815)

1 When she [her daughter] comes and looks in my face and calls me "mother," indead [sic] I then truly am a mother. . . .
>Letter to Charles Greenville (June 1774), Quoted in *Memoirs of Emma, Lady Hamilton 1815*

728. Nancy Storace (1765–1815)

1 I have as good a right to show the power of my *bomba** as anyone else.
>Quoted in *Queens of Song* by Ellen Creathorne Clayton *1865*

*Tremolo or vibrato.

729. Barbara Frietschie (1766–1862)

1 "Shoot, if you must, this old gray head
But spare your country's flag"
>Attributed, Quoted by John Greenleaf Whittier* in "Barbara Fritchie," *Atlantic Monthly* (Boston) *October 1863*
*American poet (1807–1892).

730. Laodicea "Dicey" Langston (1766–1837)

1 Shoot me if you dare! I will not tell you.*
>Quoted by the Hon. B. F. Perry in *The Women of the American Revolution,* Vol. II, by Elizabeth F. Ellet *1848*
*Response to Loyalist's demand for intelligence concerning the Whigs; Langston was 16 years old at the time.

731. Carolina Nairne (1766–1845)

1 The Laird o' Cockpen, he's proud an' he's great,
His mind is ta'en up wi' things o' the State. . . .
>"The Laird o' Cockpen," St. 1, *Lays from Strathearn 1846*

2 A penniless lass wi' a lang pedigree.
>St. 2, Ibid.

3 Oh, ye may ca' them vulgar farin',
Wives and mithers maist despairin',
Ca' them lives o' men.
>"Caller* Herrin'," Ibid.
*Fresh.

4 Wi' a hundred pipers an' a', an' a',
Wi' a hundred pipers an' a', an' a',
We'll up an' gie them a blaw, a blaw,
Wi' a hundred pipers an' a', an' a'.
>"The Hundred Pipers," Ibid.

5 O, Charlie is my darling,
My darling, my darling;
Charlie is my darling,
The young Chevalier.
>"Charlie* Is My Darling," *Scottish Song,* Mary Carlyle Aitken, ed. *1874*
*The reference is to Charles Stuart, a.k.a. "Bonnie Prince Charlie," or The Young Pretender (1720–1788).

732. Nancy Dennis Sproat (1766–1826)

1 How pleasant is Saturday night,
When I've tried all the week to be good,
Not spoken a word that is bad,
And obliged every one that I could.
>"How Pleasant is Saturday Night," *n.d.*

733. Germaine de Staël (1766–1817)

1 . . . inventiveness is childish, practice sublime.
>*Réflexions sur la paix intérieure* (Reflections on internal peace) *1795*

2 Love is the whole history of a woman's life, it is but an episode in a man's.
Preface (1 July 1796), *De l'influence des passions sur le bonheur des individus et des nations* (A Treatise on the Influence of the Passions upon the Happiness of Individuals and of Nations) 1796

3 Intellect does not attain its full force unless it attacks power.
De la littirature considérée dans ses rapports avec les institutions sociales (The Influence of Literature upon Society) 1800

4 Every time a new nation, America or Russia for instance, advances toward civilization, the human race perfects itself; every time an inferior class emerges from enslavement and degradation, the human race again perfects itself.
Ibid.

5 Happy the land where writers are sad, the merchants satisfied, the rich melancholic, and the populace content.
Ibid.

6 Scientific progress makes moral progress a necessity; for if man's power is increased, the checks that restrain him from abusing it must be strengthened.
Ibid.

7 Why should it not be possible some day to compile tables that would contain the answer to all questions of a political nature based on statistical knowledge, on positive facts gathered from every country?
Ibid.

8 The entire social order . . . is arrayed against a woman who wants to rise to a man's reputation.
Ibid.

9 Between God and love, I recognize no mediator but my conscience.
Delphine 1802

10 "Follow me, let this instant decide our lives! There are decisions that must be made in the heat of passion, without giving bitter reflections the time to revive!"
Ibid.

11 Magnificence is the characteristic of everything one sees in Russia.
Dix années d'exil (Ten Years of Exile) 1813

12 Life resembles Gobelin tapestry; you do not see the canvas on the right side but when you turn it, the threads are visible.
Quoted in *Lives of Celebrated Women* by Samuel Griswold Goodrich 1844

13 The greatest happiness is to transform one's feelings into actions. . . .
Letter to de Pange (Coppet, ca. May 1796), *Madame de Staël et François de Pange: lettres et documents inédits,* Jean de Pange, ed. 1925

14 What I love about noise is that it camouflages life.
Letter to Eric Staël von Holstein, *Revue des Deux Mondes* June/July 1932

15 Money alone determines your entire life, political as well as private.
Letter to Benjamin Constant* (Coppet, April 1815), *Lettres à un ami,* Jean Mistler, ed. 1949
*Baron d'Estourelles, French politician, diplomat and Nobel laureate (1832–1924)

16 The pursuit of politics is religion, morality, and poetry all in one.
Quoted in *Mistress to an Age: A Life of Madame de Staël* by J. Christopher Herold 1958

17 Those gentlemen [Lafayette* and Sylvain Bailly, mayor of Paris] are like the rainbow; they always appear after the storm is over.
Ibid.
*French soldier and politician (1757–1834).

18 Genius has no sex!
Ibid.

19 If one hour's work is enough to govern France, four minutes is all that is needed for Italy. There is no nation more easily frightened; even its poetic imagination predisposes it to fear, and they look upon power as on an image that fills them with terror.
(1804), Letter to her cousin Juliette, Ibid.

20 I shall have to conquer myself once more, despite everything.
(near Blois, 27 September 1810), Ibid.

21 I must keep on rowing, not until I reach port but until I reach my grave.
Letter to Albertine Necker de Saussure, her daughter (Coppet, July 1814), Ibid.

22 You [America] are the vanguard of the human race. You are the world's future.
Spoken to George Ticknow* (ca. Spring 1817), Ibid.
*American author and teacher of languages (1791–1871).

734. Maria Edgeworth (1767–1849)

1 Man is to be held only by the *slightest* chains; with the idea that he can break them at pleasure, he submits to them in sport. . . .
Letter I (1787), *Letters of Julia and Caroline* 1795

2 "Pleasing for a moment," said Helen, smiling, "is of some consequence; for, if we take care of the moments, the years will take care of themselves, you know."
Mademoiselle Panache 1795

3 I've a great fancy to see my own funeral afore I die.
Ch. 1, *Castle Rackrent* 1800

4 "It is quite fitting that charity should *begin* at home," said Wright; "but then it should not *end* at home; for those that help nobody shall find none to help them in time of need."
Ch. 2, *The Will* 1800

5 How success changes the opinion of men!
Ch. 4, Ibid.

6 Business was his aversion; pleasure was his business.
Ch. 2, *The Contrast* 1801

7 All work and no play makes Jack a dull boy,
All play and no work makes Jack a mere toy.
Harry and Lucy 1801

8 Bishop Wilkins prophesied that the time would come when gentlemen, when they were to go on a journey, would call for their wings as regularly as they call for their boots.
Ch. 2, *Essay on Irish Bulls* 1802

9 Those who are animated by hope can perform what would seem impossibilities to those who are under the depressing influence of fear.

The Grateful Negro 1802

10 "The law, in our case, seems to make the right; and the very reverse ought to be done—the right should make the law."

Ibid.

11 Children were pretty things at three years old; but began to be great plagues at six, and were quite intolerable at ten.

Ch. 1, *The Manufacturers 1803*

12 I was ever searching for some *short cut* to the temple of Fame, instead of following the beaten road.

Ch. 3, *To-Morrow 1803*

13 I now attempted too much: I expected to repair by bustle the effects of procrastination.

Ch. 4, Ibid.

14 " . . . sometimes the very faults of parents produce a tendency to opposite virtues in their children . . ."

Ch. 1, *Manoeuvring 1809*

15 Well! some people talk of morality, and some of religion, but give me a little snug property.

Ch. 2, *The Absentee 1812*

16 "My mother took too much, a great deal too much, care of me; she over-educated, over-instructed, over-dosed me with premature lessons of prudence: she was so afraid that I would ever do a foolish thing, or not say a wise one, that she prompted my every word, and guided my every action. So I grew up, seeing with her eyes, hearing with her ears, and judging with her understanding, till, at length, it was found out that I had no eyes, or understanding of my own."

Ch. 1, *Vivian 1812*

17 "Fortune's wheel never stands still—the highest point is therefore the most perilous."

Ch. 2, *Patronage 1814*

18 "Of all men, I think a dissipated clergyman is the most contemptible."

Ch. 19, Ibid.

19 We must be content to begin at the beginning, if we would learn the history of our own mind; we must condescend to be even as little children, if we would discover or recollect those small causes which early influenced the imagination, and afterward become strong habits, prejudices, and passions.

Ch. 1, *Harrington 1817*

20 An orator is the worst person to tell a plain fact. . . .

Ch. 10, Ibid.

21 After a certain age, if one lives in the world, one can't be astonished—that's a lost pleasure.

Ch. 15, *Ormond 1817*

22 The everlasting quotation-lover dotes on the husks of learning. He is the infant-reciting bore in second childishness.

Thoughts On Bores 1826

735. Rachel Robards Jackson (1767–1828)

1 Believe me, this country [Florida] has been greatly overrated. One acre of our fine Tennessee land is worth a thousand here.

Letter to friends, Quoted in *Dames and Daughters of the Young Republic* by Gamaliel Bradford *1901*

2 To tell you of this city [Washington, D.C.], I would not do justice to the subject. The extravagance is in dressing and running to parties; but I must say they regard the Sabbath and attend preaching, for there are churches of every denomination and able ministers of the gospel.

Letter to a friend, Ibid.

736. Charlotte Corday (1768/69–1793)

1 I have done my task, let others do theirs.

Reply during interrogation at Abbaye Prison, Paris (13 July 1793), Quoted in *Biography of Distinguished Women* by Sarah Josepha Hale* *1876*
*See 807.

2 I considered that so many brave men need not come to Paris for the head of one man [Jean Paul Marat*]. He deserved not so much honour: the hand of a woman was enough. . . .

Letter to Barbaroux (from Abbaye prison), Ibid.
*Swiss-born French revolutionary (1743–93); assassinated by Corday.

3 . . . we do not execute well that which we have not ourselves conceived.

Remark at her trial (17 July 1793), Ibid.

737. Caroline Amelia Elizabeth (1768–1821)

1 I find him* very fat and not half as handsome as his portrait.

Ch. 1, Recorded by Lord Malmesbury, Quoted in *Caroline the Unhappy Queen* by Lord Russell of Liverpool *1967*
*Her future husband, King George IV.

2 . . . my dear, Punch's wife is nobody when Punch is present.*

Ch. 3, Recorded by Lady Charlotte Bury, Ibid.
*Punch and Judy, traditional English puppets, derived from *commedia dell' arte* characters.

3 The wasp leaves his sting in the wound and so do I.

Ch. 4, Recorded by a friend, Ibid.

738. Dolley Madison (1768–1849)

1 I would rather fight with my hands than my tongue.

Memoirs and Letters of Dolley Madison 1886

2 You may imagine me the very shadow of my husband.*

Letter to Mr. and Mrs. Barlow (1811), Ibid.
*James Madison (1751–1836), fourth president of the United States (1809–1817).

3 How the crowd jostles!

Quoted in *Dames and Daughters of the Young Republic* by Gamaliel Bradford *1901*

4 The profusion of my table is the result of the prosperity of my country, and I shall continue to prefer Virginia liberality to European elegance.

Retort to the wife of a foreign minister, Ibid.

739. Sarah Catherine Martin (1768–1826)

1 Old Mother Hubbard
Went to the cupboard,
To get her poor dog a bone;
But when she came there
The cupboard was bare,
And so the poor dog had none.
"The Comic Adventures of Old Mother Hubbard" 1805

740. Madame Necker de Saussure (1768?–1847)

1 . . . there are so many causes of excitement in early life, personal affections and the desire to win the love and esteem of others occupy the mind so fully, that the young rarely press steadily onward to the most elevated mark.
Quoted in Biography of Distinguished Women by Sarah Josepha Hale* n.d.

*See 807.

741. Maria-Louise-Rose Pitigny de Saint-Romain (1768–1800)

1 How enviable, thy destiny
Blessed, nimble butterfly!
To live constant life,
Then—so change yourself!
"Le Papillon," St. 1, Elaine Bernstein Partnow, tr.,* Idylles n.d.

*See 3291.

742. Melesina Trench (1768–1827)

1 A fat, fair, and fifty card-playing resident of the Crescent.
(18 February 1816), Letters ca. 1820

743. Anne Brunton Merry (1769–1808)

1 The business of the Theatre has been and is very, very bad indeed.
Letter to Mrs. Thackerson, Quoted in The Career of Mrs. Anne Brunton Merry in the American Theatre by Gresdna Ann Doty 1971

744. Amelia Opie (1769–1853)

1 Thy love, thy fate, dear youth, to share,
Must ever be thy happy lot;
But thou may'st grant this humble prayer,
Forget me not! forget me not!
"Go, Youth Beloved," St. 1 (1802), The Warrior's Return & Other Poems 1808

2 Yet still enchant and still deceive me,
Do all things, fatal fair, but leave me.
"Song," St. 1, Ibid.

3 Had I been an artful woman, and could I have condescended to make him doubtful of the extent of my love, by a few woman's subterfuges; could I have feigned a desire to return to the world, instead of owning, as I did, that all my enjoyment was comprised in home and him, I do think that I might have been, for a much longer period, the happiest of wives; but then I should have been, in my own eyes, despicable as a woman; and I was always tenacious of my own esteem.
"Two Years of Wedded Life," A Wife's Duty n.d

745. Anne Newport Royall (1769–1854)

1 . . . the evangelical-tractical-biblical-Sabbath School-prayer meeting—good, honest, pious, sound Presbyterians of Capitol Hill.
Remarking on witness at her trial (28 November 1817), Mrs. Royall's Pennsylvania; or, Travels Continued in the United States, Vol. II 1829

2 Hitherto I have only learned mankind in theory—but I am now studying him in practice. One learns more in a day, by mixing with mankind, than he can in an age shut up in a closet.
Letter XIII (22 December 1817), Letters from Alabama 1830

3 . . . true to their nature, the people, or rabble, rather always think the greatest fool the wisest man. They have proved it in this instance, by their selecting him [a local politician] to make laws for them. Alas, for my country! all your citizens want is a rope.
Letter XLIV (2 June 1821), Ibid.

4 The United States Bank [is] not a political machine! It is a despot. It is the rack. It is the inquisition. It is a monster of corruption.
Quoted in "Anne Royall, Tireless Traveler and Common Nuisance," Anne Royall's Letters from Alabama, Lucille Griffith, ed. 1969

746. Martha Bratton (fl. ca. 1770–d. 1816)

1 It was I who did it.* Let the consequence be what it will, I glory in having prevented the mischief contemplated by the cruel enemies of my country.
Quoted in The Women of the American Revolution, Vol. II by Elizabeth F. Ellet 1848

*She set fire to a cache of ammunition to prevent its falling into the hands of the British.

747. Anna Elliott (fl. ca. 1770)

1 [It is called] the rebel flower . . . because it always flourishes most when trampled upon.
Remark to a British soldier, Quoted in The Women of the American Revolution, Vol. II by Elizabeth F. Ellet 1848

2 Let not oppression shake your fortitude, nor the hope of a gentler treatment cause you for a moment to swerve from strict duty.
Remark to her father, Thomas Ferguson, on his removal as a prisoner of war, Ibid.

748. Mrs. Daniel Hall (fl. ca. 1770–80)

1 What is it you wish to look for? [Treason, came the reply.] Then you may be saved the trouble of search, for you may find enough of it at my tongue's end.
Upon handing over the key of her trunk to a British officer, Quoted in The Women of the American Revolution, Vol. II by Elizabeth F. Ellet 1848

749. Mary Lacy (fl. ca. 1770)

1 Perceiving her forwardness I thought it was no wonder the young men took such liberties with the other sex when they gave them such encouragement . . . I must confess that if I had been a young man I could not have withstood the temptations which this young person laid in my way.
The History of the Female Shipwright 1773

750. Ann Murry (fl. ca. 1770–d. 1799)

1 Mark but the hist'ry of a modern day,
Composed of nonsense, foppery, and play.

"A Familiar Epistle," *Poems on Various Subjects 1779*

751. Mary Scott (fl. ca. 1770)

1 Owl, that lov'st the cloudy sky,
Sure, thy notes are harmony!

St. 1, "The Owl," *The Female Poets of Great Britain*, Frederic
Rowton, ed. *1853*

752. Mrs. Richard Shubrick (fl. ca. 1770–d. 178-?)

1 To men of honor, the chamber of a lady should be sacred as a
sanctuary!

Remark to British soldiers hunting for an American hiding
in her bedroom, Quoted in *The Women of the American
Revolution,* Vol. II by Elizabeth F. Ellet *1848*

753. Elizabeth Wallbridge (1770–1801)

1 But when I consider what a high calling, what honor and dignity God has conferred upon me, to be called his child, to be
born of his Spirit, made an heir of glory, and joint heir with
Christ; how humble and circumspect should I be in all my
ways, as a dutiful and loving child to an affectionate and loving Father! When I seriously consider these things it fills me
with love and gratitude to God, and I do not wish for any
higher station, nor envy the rich. I rather pity them if they are
not good as well as great.

Quoted in *The Women of Methodism: Its Three Foundresses
. . .* by Abel Stevens *1866*

754. Mary Wordsworth (1770–1859)

1 O My William! it is not in my power to tell thee how I have
been affected by this dearest of all letters—it was so unexpected—so new a thing to see the breathing of thy inmost
heart upon paper that I was quite overpowered. . . .

Letter to William Wordsworth,* her husband (Grasmere,
1 August 1810), *The Love Letters of William and Mary
Wordsworth,* Beth Darlington, ed. *1982*
*English poet (1770–1850).

2 Bad as this is, it is some satisfaction to think this act* could
only be done by a Lunatic—We were fearful that it was some
dreadful Plot which might now be raging, the first act only
being gone through—Alas for this Country [England], Who
have we now—I fear a shadow pated Creature** to take his
Place. . . .

(13–14 May 1812), Ibid.
*The assassination of British Prime Minister Spencer Perceval
(1762–1812) in the House of Commons. **Robert Banks Jenkinson (1770–1828), second earl of Liverpool; Tory statesman and
prime minister (1812–1827).

755. Margaretta Van Wyck Faugères (1771–1801)

1 *There,* wrapt in musings deep, and steadfast gaze,
In solemn rapture hath she past the night.

"Winter," *Essays in Prose and Verse 1795*

2 "When I am gone—ah! who will care for thee?"

"Elegy to Miss Anna Dundass," Ibid.

756. Elizabeth Holland (1771–1845)

1 Your poetry is bad enough, so pray be sparing of your prose.

Remark to Samuel Rogers,* Quoted in *Portraits of Women* by
Gamaliel Bradford *1916*
*English poet (1763–1855) known for his wit.

2 I am sorry to hear you are going to publish a poem. Can't you
suppress it?

Remark to Lord Porchester, Ibid.

3 There is a sensation in a mother's breast at the loss of an infant
that partakes of the feeling of instinct. It is a species of savage
despair.

Letter to her husband, Lord Holland, Ibid.

4 . . . as nobody can do more mischief to a woman than a woman,
so perhaps might one reverse the maxim and say nobody can
do more good.

Ibid.

757. Rachel Levin Varnhagen (1771–1833)

1 Poor woman [Germaine de Staël*], she has seen nothing, heard
nothing, understood nothing.

Quoted in *Mistress to an Age: A Life of Madame de Staël* by J.
Christopher Herold, *1958*
*See 733.

2 My whole day is a feast of doing good!

Letters n.d.

758. Dorothy Wordsworth (1771–1855)

1 The half dead sound of the near sheep-bell in the hollow of the
sloping coombe, exquisitely soothing.

The Alfoxden Journal 1897

2 I found a strawberry blossom in a rock. I uprooted it rashly
and felt as if I had been committing an outrage, so I planted it
again.

Ibid.

3 One only leaf upon the top of a tree—the sole remaining leaf—
danced round and round like a rag blown by the wind.

(7 March 1798), Ibid.

759. Maria Falconar (1772–?)

1 Once Superstition, in a fatal hour,
O'er Europe rais'd the sceptre of her power;
She reign'd triumphant minister of death,
And Peace and Pleasure faded in her breath;
Deep in monastic solitude entomb'd,
The bud of beauty wither'd ere it bloom'd

Untitled, *Poems,* by Maria and Harriet Falconar* *1788*
*See 768.

2 Ye foes of heav'n, and Britain's dire disgrace,
Unjust oppressors of an injur'd race,
Tell us, who form'd the slave you thus deride,
The sport of insult, indolence, and pride?

"Slavery"*, Ibid.
*Written at age 17.

760. Mary Tighe (1772–1810)

1 Oh! how impatience gains upon the soul,
When the long promised hour of joy draws near!
How slow the tardy moments seem to roll!

What specters rise of inconsistent fear!
To the fond doubting heart its hopes appear
Too brightly fair, too sweet to realize;
all seem but day-dreams of delight too dear!
Psyche, or the Legend of Love 1795–1805

2 Change is the lot of all.
Ibid.

3 Oh! have you never known the silent charm
That undisturb'd retirement yields the soul
Ibid.

4 Who can speak a mother's anguish
"Hagar* in the Desert," St. 2, *The British Female Poets*,
George W. Bethune, ed. *1848*
*See 5.

5 The careless eye can find no grace,
Nor beauty in the scaly folds,
Nor see within the dark embrace
What latent loveliness it hold.
Yet in that bulb, those sapless scales,
The lily wraps her silver vest.
"The Lily," Sts. 2–3, *The Female Poets of Great Britain*,
Frederic Rowton, ed. *1853*

761. Harriet Auber (1773–1862)

1 And His that gentle voice we hear,
Soft as the breath of even,
That checks each fault, that calms each
fear,
And speaks of heaven.
"Our Blest Redeemer, ere He breathed," *Spirit of the Psalms*
1829

762. Sophie Cottin (1773–1807)

1 We have resisted a little while, and we think we have done
wonders; because we estimate the merit of our resistance, not
by its duration, but by the difficulty it has cost us.
Quoted in *Biography of Distinguished Women* by Sarah
Josepha Hale* *1876*
*See 807.

2 It is in affliction that the imagination elevates itself to the great
thoughts of eternity and supreme justice, and that it takes us of
ourselves, to seek a remedy for our pains.
Ibid.

3 But still, amidst the horror and gloom of an eternal winter, na-
ture displays some of her grandest spectacles. . . .
"The Exiles and their Home," *Elizabeth, or the Exile of
Siberia n.d.*

763. Mary Moody Emerson (1774–1863)

1 Rose before light every morn; . . . commented on the Scriptures; . . . touched Shakespeare,—washed, carded, cleaned
house, baked.
Diary Entry (1805), *Notable American Women*, Edward T.
James, ed. *1971*

2 Scorn trifles, lift your aims; do what you are afraid to do.
Remark to Ralph Waldo Emerson,* Quoted in *Notable
American Women*, Edward T. James, ed. *1971*
*American essayist and poet (1803–1882).

764. Cecile Renard (1774?–1794)

1 I wanted to see how a tyrant looks.
Reply at inquiry on her attempted assassination of
Robespierre* (1794), Quoted in *Biography of Distinguished
Women* by Sarah Josepha Hale** *1876*
*French revolutionary leader (1758–1794); guillotined. **See
807.

2 We have five hundred tyrants, [but] I prefer one king.
Ibid.

765. Elizabeth Seton (1774–1821)

1 Afflictions are the steps to heaven.
Notable American Women, Edward T. James, ed. *1971*

766. Louisa Catherine Adams (1775–1852)

1 Go flatter'd image tell the tale
Of years long past away;
Of faded youth, of sorrow wail,
Of times too sure decay. . . .
Ch. 3, "To my Sons with my Portrait by Stuart"* (18
December 1825), Quoted in *Portraits of John Quincy
Adams** and His Wife* by Andrew Oliver *1970*
*Gilbert Stuart, famed American portrait painter (1755–1828).
**Sixth president of the United States (1825–1829).

767. Jane Austen (1775–1817)

1 "Beware of the insipid Vanities and idle Dissipations of the
Metropolis of England; Beware of the unmeaning Luxuries of
Bath and of the stinking fish of South Hampton."
Letter Fourth, *Love and Friendship 1790*

2 She is probably by this time as tired of me, as I am of her; but
as she is too polite and I am too civil to say so, our letters are
still as frequent and affectionate as ever, and our Attachment
as firm and sincere as when it first commenced.
Letter the Fourth, *Lesley Castle 1792*

3 "It is not time or opportunity that is to determine intimacy; it
is disposition alone. Seven years would be insufficient to make
some people acquainted with each other, and seven days are
more than enough for others."
Ch. 12, *Sense and Sensibility, 1811*

4 Lady Middleton . . . exerted herself to ask Mr. Palmer if there
was any news in the paper.
"No, none at all," he replied, and read on.
Ch. 19, Ibid.

5 It is a truth universally acknowledged, that a single man in possession of a good fortune, must be in want of a wife.
Ch. 1, *Pride and Prejudice 1813*

6 A lady's imagination is very rapid; it jumps from admiration to
love, from love to matrimony in a moment.
Ch. 6, Ibid.

7 "You have delighted us long enough."
Ch. 18, Ibid.

8 "You ought certainly to forgive them as a Christian, but never
admit them in your sight, or allow their names to be mentioned
in your hearing."
Ch. 57, Ibid.

9 I have been a selfish being all my life, in practice, though not in principle.

> Ch. 58, Ibid.

10 "Those who see quickly, will resolve quickly, and act quickly. . . ."

> Ch. 6, *Mansfield Park 18*

11 "Selfishness must always be forgiven, you know, because there is no hope of a cure."

> Ch. 7, Ibid.

12 "Oh! do not attack me with your watch. A watch is always too fast or too slow. I cannot be dictated by a watch."

> Ch. 9, Ibid.

13 "If I lay it down as a general rule, Harriet, that if a woman *doubts* as to whether she should accept a man or not, she certainly ought to refuse him. If she can hesitate as to 'Yes,' she ought to say 'No,' directly."

> Ch. 7, *Emma 1815*

14 "Vanity working on a weak head produces every sort of mischief."

> Ch. 8, Ibid.

15 The truth is, that in London it is always a sickly season. Nobody is healthy in London, nobody can be.

> Ch. 12, Ibid.

16 It was a delightful visit—perfect, in being much too short.

> Ch. 13, Ibid.

17 Nobody who has not been in the interior of a family can say what the difficulties of any individual of that family may be.

> Ch. 18, Ibid.

18 Business, you know, may bring money, but friendship hardly ever does.

> Ch. 34, Ibid.

19 "It is very difficult for the prosperous to be humble."

> Ch. 50, Ibid.

20 "To look *almost* pretty is an acquisition of higher delight to a girl who has been looking plain the first fifteen years of her life than a beauty from the cradle can ever receive."

> Ch. 1, *Northanger Abbey 1818*

21 "And what are you reading, Miss—?" "Oh! it is only a novel!" replies the young lady; while she lays down her book with affected indifference, or momentary shame. "It is only *Cecilia*, or *Camilla*, or *Belinda*"; or, in short, only some work in which the greatest powers of the mind are displayed, in which the most thorough knowledge of human nature, the happiest delineation of its varieties, the liveliest effusions of wit and humour, are conveyed to the world in the best chosen language.

> Ch. 5, Ibid.

22 " . . . I am sure of *this,* that if everybody was to drink their bottle a day, there would be not half the disorders in the world there are now. It would be a famous good thing for us all."

> Ch. 9, Ibid.

23 History, real solemn history, I cannot be interested in. . . . I read it a little as a duty; but it tells me nothing that does not either vex or weary me. The quarrels of popes and kings, with wars and pestilences in every page; the men all so good for nothing, and hardly any women at all.

> Ch. 14, Ibid.

24 Personal size and mental sorrow have certainly no necessary proportions. A large bulky figure has as good a right to be in deep affliction as the most graceful set of limbs in the world. But, fair or not fair, there are unbecoming conjunctions, which . . . taste cannot tolerate —which ridicule will seize.

> *Persuasion 1818*

25 How quick come the reasons for approving what we like!

> Ch. 2, Ibid.

26 "My idea of good company, Mr. Elliot, is a company of clever, well-informed people, who have a great deal of conversation; that is what I call good company."

"You are mistaken," said he, gently, "that is not good company; that is the best."

> Ch. 16, Ibid.

27 One does not love a place the less for having suffered in it, unless it has been all suffering, nothing but suffering.

> Ch. 20, Ibid.

768. Harriet Falconar (1775–?)

1 Shall Britain view, unmov'd, sad Afric's shore
Delug'd so oft in streams of purple gore!

> Untitled, St. 2, *Poems,* by Maria* and Harriet Falconar *1788*
> *See 759.

2 Britain, where science, peace, and plenty smile,
Virtue's bright seat, and freedom's favour'd isle!

> "Slavery,"* Ibid.
> *Written at age 13.

769. Mary Martha Sherwood (1775–1851)

1 "The book of Nature, my dear Henry, is full of holy lessons, ever new and ever varied; and to learn to discover these lessons should be the work of good education; for there are many persons who are exceedingly wise and clever in worldly matters, and yet with respect to spiritual things are wholly blind and dark, and are as unable to look on divine light as the bats and moles to contemplate the glory of the sun's rays at midday."

> *The History of Henry Milner,* Pt. First, Ch. 16, from *The Works of Mrs. Sherwood,* Vol. I *1856*

2 "Where the habits are simple, and the mind truly elevated, then is society in the best state. . . . "

> Pt. Third, Ch. 2, Ibid.

3 "And why not?" returned the *fakeer,* "I can read books and men, too, and I tell you that the latter is a much more profitable branch of study than the former."

> *Arzoomund,* Ch. 5, Ibid.

4 "To speak the plain truth, all religions seem alike to me, one mass of absurdities and lies— . . . I know that there is a God, but I know no more of him; and I believe that all those who are liars who pretend to know more than I do."

> Ibid.

5 . . . what is the zest of argument when the antagonist is not allowed to answer?

> *The Monk of Climiés,* Ch. 5, Vol. XIV, Ibid.

6 "...my father has lived abroad till he has lost his judgement...."

The History of John Marten, Ch. 1, Vol. XVI, Ibid.

7 ...a dirty exterior is a great enemy to beauty of all descriptions.

Ch. 13, Ibid.

770. Sydney Owenson Morgan (1776?–1859)

1 Literary fiction, whether directed to the purpose of transient amusement, or adopted as an indirect medium of instruction, has always in its most genuine form exhibited a mirror of the times in which it is composed; reflecting morals, customs, manners, peculiarity of character, and prevalence of opinion. Thus, perhaps, after all, it forms the best history of nations....

Preface, *O'Donnell: A National Tale,* Vol. I 1813

2 "That you are an Irishman, *genuine* and thorough bred, there can be no doubt; with your porcupine spirit, rising before it is assailed, and throwing its quill before it receives a wound...."

Ch. 3, Vol. III, Ibid.

3 "...as is usual among the semi-barbarous, improvement is resisted as innovation; ...the old muddling system must go on for ever in the same old muddling way."

Ibid.

4 "...if foreigners won't understand one another, who do they expect will, I wonder."

Ch. 1, *Florence Macarthy: An Irish Tale,* Vol. I 1819

5 "What is wisdom *to-day* in the conduct of a government may be madness *to-morrow.*"

Ch. 3, Vol. III, Ibid.

6 "You are right, madam; the soul is of no sect, no party: it is, as you say, our passions and our prejudices, which give rise to our religious and political distinctions."

Ch. 12, *The Novice of St. Dominick,* Vol. II 1823

7 It is under the pressure of great and sudden exigencies that the faculties of a strong and comprehensive mind awaken to a full sense of their own power.

Ch. 35, Vol. IV, Ibid.

771. Adelaide O'Keeffe (1776–1855?)

1 Little Ann and her mother were walking one day
Through London's wide city so fair,
And business obliged them to go by the way
That led them through Cavendish Square.

"A True Story," St. 1, *Little Ann and other poems* 1883

2 'Twere better to starve than to steal;
For the great God, who even through darkness can look,
Writes down every crime we commit, in His book;
Nor forgets what we try to conceal.

Ibid., "The Apple-Tree," St. 6

3 The butterfly, an idle thing,
Nor honey makes, nor yet can sing.

"The Butterfly" *n.d.*

772. Jane Porter (1776–1850)

1 Such, thought she, O Sun, art thou!—The resplendent image of the Giver of All Good. Thy cheering beams, like His All-

cheering Spirit, pervades the very soul, and drives thence the despondency of cold and darkness.

Life of Sir William Wallace; * or, *The Scottish Chiefs* [a novel]
1810

*Scottish hero (ca. 1270–1305).

2 "The cruel are generally false."

Ch. 3, Ibid.

3 "No country is wretched, sweet lady," returned the knight, "till by a dastardly acquiescence it consents to its own slavery."

Ch. 9, Ibid.

4 "You would teach confidence to Despair herself...."

Ibid.

5 "For shame, Murray!" was the reply of Wallace; "they are dead, and our enemies no more. They are men like ourselves; and shall we deny them a place in that earth whence we all sprung?"

Ch. 13, Ibid.

6 "Earthly crowns are dross to him who looks for a heavenly one."

Ch. 33, Ibid.

7 "You are like a bad mirror that, from radical defect, always gives false reflections."

Ch. 17, *Thaddeus of Warsaw,* Vol. II 1835

773. Hester Lucy Stanhope (1776–1839)

1 If you were to take every feature in my face, and lay them one by one on the table, there is not a single one that would bear examination. The only thing is that, put together and lighted up, they look well enough. It is homogeneous ugliness, and nothing more.

Quoted in *Little Memoirs of the Nineteenth Century,* Pt. I by George Paston 1902

2 ...I shall go on making sublime and philosophical discoveries, and employing myself in deep, abstract studies.

Letter to Dr. Meryon (1827), Pt. II, Ibid.

3 Nobody is such a fool as to moider [waste] away his time in the slipslop conversation of a pack of women.

Remark, Ibid.

4 My roses are my jewels, the sun and moon my clocks, fruit and water my food and drink. I see in your face that you are a thorough epicure; how will you endure to spend a week with me?

Ibid.

774. Anna Chamber (?–1777)

1 But modern quacks have lost the art,
And reach of life the sacred seat;
They know not how its pulses beat,
Yet take their fee and write their bill,
In barb'rous prose resolved to kill.

"To the Duchess of Leeds, who, being ill, desired a copy of my verses to cure her," *Poems, printed at Strawberry Hill 1764*

775. Mary Brunton (1778–1818)

1 ...little acquainted with other minds, deeply studious of her own, she concluded that all mankind were like herself engaged in a constant endeavour after excellence....

"Sketch of the Heroine," *Self-Control 1811*

2 The passion which we do not conquer will, in time, reconcile us to any means that can aid its gratification.

"The Lover and his Declaration," Ibid.

776. Margaret Holford (1778–1852)

1 'T is man's pride,
His highest, worthiest, noblest boast,
The privilege he prizes most,
To stand by helpless woman's side.

"Margaret of Anjou,"* *Fanny and Selina, Gresford Vale and Other Poems 1798*

*See 258.

777. Margaret Bayard Smith (1778–1844)

1 Ladies and gentlemen only had been expected at this Levee, not the people en masse. Of all tyrants, they are the most ferocious, cruel and despotic.

Quoted in *First Ladies* by Betty Boyd Caroli *1987*

778. Angelica Catalani (1779–1848)

1 For when God has given to a mortal so extraordinary a talent as I possess, people ought to applaud and honour it as a miracle: it is profane to depreciate the gifts of Heaven!

Quoted in *Queens of Song* by Ellen Creathorne Clayton *1865*

779. Tabitha Moffatt Brown (1780–1858)

1 Worse than alone, in a savage wilderness, without food, without fire, cold and shivering, wolves fighting and howling all around me.

Letter (ca. 1846), Quoted in *Women Pioneers* by Rebecca Stefoff *1995*

2 Father Time is no respecter of persons, he is busily engaged in drawing furrows and disfiguring our faces to convince me that we are but mortal. Our next change will be from mortality to immortality. Oh, that we may all be prepared for this great and lasting change!

Letter (25 January 1858), Ibid.

780. Elizabeth Fry (1780–1845)

1 Does Capital punishment tend to the security of the people?

By no means. It hardens the hearts of men, and makes the loss of life appear light to them; and it renders life insecure, inasmuch as the law holds out that property is of greater value than life.

From her Journal, Quoted in *Biography of Distinguished Women* by Sarah Josepha Hale* *1876*

*See 807.

2 Punishment is not for revenge, but to lessen crime and reform the criminal.

Ibid.

781. Ann Holbrook (1780–1837)

1 An actress can never make her children comfortable . . . The mother returning with harassed frame and agitated mind, from the varying passions she has been pourtraying [sic], instead of imparting healthful nourishment to her child, fills it with bile and fever, to say nothing of draging them long journies, at all seasons of the year.

The Dramatist, or Memoires of the Stage 1809

782. Hannah Farnham Lee (1780–1865)

1 Astronomers tell us of countless worlds;—if we look within our own precincts we shall find an equal multiplication; every class of society talks of *the world,* and every class means something different.

Ch. 1, *Elinor Fulton 1837*

2 No one can have any high degree of virtue, without self-respect; it is the twin-sister of virtue.

Ch. 8, Ibid.

3 Liberty has set her foot on our shore, and she is not to be restricted in her walks.

Ibid.

4 We have arrived at that period when there is no putting a padlock on the human mind; every one is contending for his rights, every one ready to strike for them.

Ibid.

5 "Blessings on the Savings Bank! It is truly, to those who resolutely deposit their earnings there, the purse of Fortunatus. . . ."

Ch. 11, Ibid.

6 . . . is there no exterminating the shoots of vanity where it has once taken root?

Ibid.

7 He [John Calvin*], who had so loudly declaimed against the tyranny of Rome, was doomed to prove how dangerous an instrument is power in the hands of a human being.

Ch. 3, *The Huguenots in France and America,* Vol. I *1843*
*French-born Swiss Protestant theologian and religious reformer (1509–1564).

8 It is amusing to observe in every age the ingenuity of dress in changing the human figure.

Ch. 13, Ibid.

9 It is those in whom the power of virtue is formed and matured, that are truly great. It matters not how many millions a man may command, the next day may strip him of all; but the *undying principle* of duty is his own, and can only be surrendered by his will.

Ch. 29, Vol. II, Ibid.

10 There is nothing old tolerated in this new world [America].

Part Second, *The Log-Cabin; or, the World Before You 1844*

11 "The school may do much; but alas for the child where the instructor is not assisted by the influences of home!"

Ibid.

12 Surely we ought to prize those friends on whose principles and opinions we may constantly rely—of whom we may say in all emergencies, "I know what they would think."

Ibid.

13 . . . a good nurse is of more importance than a physician.

Pt. Third, Ibid.

783. Mary Somerville (1780–1872)

1 And who shall declare the time allotted to the human race, when the generation of the most insignificant insect existed for unnumbered ages? Yet man is also to vanish in the ever-changing course of events. The earth is to be burnt up, and the elements to melt with fervent heat—to be again reduced to

chaos—possibly to be renovated and adorned for other races of beings. These stupendous changes may be but cycles in those great laws of the universe, where all is variable but the laws themselves and He who ordained them.

"God and His Works," *Physical Geography 1848*

2 . . . no circumstance in the natural world is more inexplicable than the diversity of form and colour in the human race.

"Varieties of the Human Race," Ibid.

3 . . . one of the greatest improvements in education is that teachers are now fitted for their duties by being taught the art of teaching.

"Benevolence," Ibid.

4 The moral disposition of the age appears in the refinement of conversation.

"Influence of Christianity," Ibid.

784. Frances Milton Trollope (1780–1863)

1 "Is not amusement the very soul of life?"

Ch. 6, *The Life and Adventures of Michael Armstrong, the Factory Boy 1839*

2 "That's nonsense, Michael," said Fanny. "They can't keep us here for ever. When we die, we are sure to get away from them."

Ch. 17, Ibid.

3 "Times are altered with me now, nurse Tremlett," replied Mary; "I have left off living for myself, and I feel my temper improving already by it."

Ch. 22, Ibid.

785. Lucy Aiken (1781–1864)

1 No! instead of aspiring to be inferior men, let us content ourselves with becoming noble women:. . . . but let not sex be carried into every thing. Let the impartial voice of History testify for us, that, when permitted, we have been the worthy associates of the best efforts of the best of men; let the daily observation of mankind bear witness, that no talent, no virtue, is masculine alone; no fault or folly exclusively feminine; . . . that there is not an endowment, or propensity, or mental quality of any kind, which may not be derived from her father to the daughter, to the son from his mother.

Introduction, *Epistles on Women, Exemplifying Their Character and Condition in Various Ages and Nations. With Miscellaneous Poems 1810*

2 Stretch wide and wider yet thy liberal mind,
And grasp the sisterhood of womankind:

Epistle II, St. 3, Ibid.

3 Shepherd people on the plain
Pitch their tents and wander free;
Wealthy cities they disdain,
Poor,—yet blest with liberty.

"Arabia," St. 3, *The Female Poets of Great Britain*, Frederic Rowton, ed. *1853*

4 That life may not be prolonged beyond the power of usefulness, is one of the most natural, and apparently of the most reasonable wishes man can form for the future. . . .

"Memoirs" (of her father, Dr. Aiken), Quoted in *Biography of Distinguished Women* by Sarah Josepha Hale* *1876*
*See 807.

786. Janet Colquhoun (1781–1846)

1 This day I am thirty years old. Let me now bid a cheerful adieu to my youth. My young days are now surely over, and why should I regret them? Were I never to grow old I might be always here, and might never bid farewell to sin and sorrow.

Ch. 2, Diary entry (17 April 1811), Quoted in *A Memoir of Lady Colquhoun* by James Hamilton, D. D. *1851*

2 The world? it is nothing to me; its pomps, its pleasures, its vanities—all nothing, nothing.

(19 July 1816), Ibid.

3 I feel something within me that lives for God, that delights in God, that cannot exist without God, that must be derived from God.

Ch. 6, Diary entry (8 September 1844), Ibid.

787. Maria de Fleury (fl. 1781–1791)

1 Thou soft-flowing Keedron,* by thy silver stream
Our Saviour at midnight, when Cynthia's pale beam
Shone bright on the waters, would often times stray,
And lose in thy murmurs the toils of the day.

"Thou Soft-Flowing Keedron" *1804*
*Stream on the east side of Jerusalem near Mount of Olives; a.k.a. Kidron, Kedron.

788. Rebecca Gratz (1781–1869)

1 No event in this troubled life brings us nearer to our God than the taking away from us of those so loved & cherished . . .

Letter to Miriam Moses Cohen (Philadelphia to Charleston, 12 September 1853), *Four Centuries of Jewish Women's Spirituality*, Ellen M. Umansky* and Dianne Ashton, eds. *1992*
*See 4011.

2 As descendants of the great nation to whom God entrusted his Holy Law, which was to enlighten all the people of the earth, and the living witnesses of His sacred Legacy, the Jews ought to be among the purest and wisest of the sons of men, and the most faithful adherents to their religious duties; therefore it is incumbent on them to "teach their children diligently."

"Hebrew Sunday School Report" (25 April 1858, Philadelphia), *Occident and American Jewish Advocate 16 1858*
*Presented at the Sunday School on 25 April 1858; published in *Occident*, May 1858.

789. Anna Jane Vardill (1781–1852)

1 Behold this ruin! 'Twas a skull
One of the ethereal spirit full!
This narrow cell was Life's retreat;
This place was Thought's mysterious seat!
What beauteous pictures fill'd that spot,
What dreams of pleasure, long forgot!
Nor Love, nor Joy, nor Hope, nor Fear,
Has left one trace, one record here.

"Lines to a Skull," *European Magazine November 1816*

790. Susan Edmonstone Ferrier (1782–1854)

1 . . . petty ills; like a troup of locusts, making up by their number and their stings what they want in magnitude.

Ch. 6, *Marriage 1818*

2 . . . as . . . the surface was covered with flowers . . . who would
have thought of analysing the soil?

> Ch. 28, Ibid.

3 There are plenty of fools in the world; but if they had not been
sent for some wise purpose, they wouldn't have been here; and
since they are here they have as good a right to have elbow-
room in the world as the wisest.

> Ch. 68, Ibid.

4 Oh, how easy it must be to be good when one has the power of
doing good!

> Ch. 4, *The Inheritance 1824*

5 ". . . the synagogin', the tabernaclin', the psalmin', that goes on
in this hoose, that's enough to break the spirits o' ony young
creature."

> Ch. 46, Ibid.

6 " . . . there is no doctor like meat and drink. . . . "

> Ch. 98, Ibid.

7 "Which of all the gifts a liberal Creator has endowed you with
would you exchange for those empty distinctions which one
creature bestows upon another? Would you exchange your
beauty for rank, your talents for wealth, your greatness of
mind for extended power; for all of them would you exchange
your immortal soul?'

> Ch. 101, Ibid.

8 . . . the sickness of hope deferred crept like poison through her
veins.

> Ch. 102, Ibid.

9 But who can count the beatings of the lonely heart?

> Ibid.

10 "It was the saying, sir, of one of the wisest judges who ever
sat upon the Scottish bench, that a *poor* clergy made a *pure*
clergy—a maxim which deserves to be engraven in letters of
gold on every manse in Scotland."

> "A Bustling Wife," *Destiny, or the Chief's Daughter 1831*

11 " . . . I do assure you, it is a very tiresome thing to be trained up
to be a person of consequence. . . . "

> Ch. 47, Ibid.

12 " . . . the stomach requires to be amused as well as the mind."

> Ch. 55, Ibid.

13 " . . . there's no face like the face that loves us."

> Ch. 78, Ibid.

791. Sophie-Jeanne Soymonof Swetchine (1782–1857)

1 My Faith is to me what Benjamin was to Rachel, the child of
my sorrow.

> Letter, *Mme. Swetchine, sa vie, ses oeuvres* (2 vols.), De
> Falloux, ed. *1860*

2 The fact that God has prohibited despair gives misfortune
the right to hope all things, and leaves hope free to dare all
things.

> Ibid.

3 In order to have an enemy, one must be somebody. One must
be a force before he can be resisted by another force. A malicious enemy is better than a clumsy friend.

> Ibid.

4 Resignation is putting God between ourselves and our troubles.

> Ibid.

792. Ann Taylor (1782–1866)

1 Who ran to help me when I fell,
And would some pretty story tell,
Or kiss the place to make it well?
My Mother.

> "My Mother," St. 6, *Original Poems for Infant Minds,* with
> Jane Taylor* *1804*

2 Twinkle, twinkle, little star
How I wonder what you are,
Up above the world so high,
Like a diamond in the sky!

> "The Star," St. 1, *Rhymes for the Nursery,* with Jane Taylor*
> *1806*

3 And willful waste, depend upon 't,
Brings, almost always, woeful want!

> "The Pin," St. 6, *Hymns for Infant Minds,* with Jane Taylor*
> *1810*

4 So, while their bodies moulder here
Their souls with God himself shall dwell, —
But always recollect, my dear,
That wicked people go to hell.

> "About Dying," with Jane Taylor* *n.d.*

*See 795.

793. Theodosia Burr Alston (1783–1813)

1 What a charming thing a bustle is! Oh, dear, delightful confusion! It gives a circulation to the blood, an activity to the mind,
and a spring to the spirits.

> Letter to her father (December 1803), Quoted in *Memoirs of
> Aaron Burr,** Vol. II, Matthew L. Davis, ed. *1836–37*

*(1756–1836), third vice president of the United States (1801–
1805), tried for treason.

2 You know, I love to convict you of an error, as some philosophers seek for spots in the sun.

> Letter to her father (1 February 1809), Quoted in *The Private
> Journal of Aaron Burr,* Vol. I, Matthew L. Davis, ed. *1838*

3 Alas! my dear father, I do live, but how does it happen? Of what
am I formed that Live, and why? . . . You talk of consolation.
Ah! you know not what you have lost. I think Omnipotence
could give me no equivalent for my boy; no, none—none.

> Letter to her father on the death of her son (12 August 1812),
> Vol. II, Ibid.

794. Amelia (1783–1810)

1 Unthinking, idle, wild, and young,
I laugh'd and danc'd and talk'd and sung.

> "Youth" *n.d.*

795. Jane Taylor (1783–1824)

1 Though man a thinking being is defined,
Few use the grand prerogative of mind.

How few think justly of the thinking few!
How many never think, who think they do!
> "Prejudice, or, Essay on Morals and Manners," St. 45,
> *Original Poems for Infant Minds,* with Ann Taylor* *1804*

2 How pleasant it is, at the end of the day,
No follies to have to repent;
But reflect on the past, and be able to say,
That my time has been properly spent.
> "The Way to be Happy," *Rhymes for the Nursery,* with Ann
> Taylor* *1806*

3 I like little Pussy, her coat is so warm;
And if I don't hurt her she'll do me no harm.
> "I Like Little Pussy," St. 1, Ibid.

*See 792.

796. Mary Austin Holley (1784–1846)

1 How hard it is to be poor.
> *Texas: Observations Historical, Geographical and Descriptive*
> *1833*

2 Taste does not spring up in the wilderness, nor in prairies, nor in log cabins!
> Quoted in *Letters of an Early American Traveller: Mary*
> *Austin Holley* by Mattie Austin Hatcher *1933*

797. Judith Montefiore (1784–1862)

1 Humans have not the power to dive into futurity, therefore cannot say what will be, but trusting in God Almighty and ever keeping reason in view, I have as good a prospect for future happiness as I at present enjoy.
> Diary (10 June 1812), *Essays in Jewish History,* Cecil Roth,
> ed. *1934*

2 The gentlemen here tell me, it is not considered essential for ladies to observe that strict piety which is required of themselves; but surely at a place of devotion the mind ought to testify due respect and gratitude toward the Omnipotent.
> Diary (Alexandria; Sunday, 30 September 1836), Ibid.

3 There is no city in the world which can bear comparison in point of interest with Jerusalem,—fallen, desolate, and abject even as it appears—changed as it has been since the days of its glory.
> Diary (Jerusalem; Thursday, 18 October 1836), Ibid.

798. Bettina von Arnim (1785–1859)

1 Without trust, the mind's lot is a hard one; it grows slowly and needily, like a hot plant betwixt rocks: thus am I—thus was I till today....
> Various letters to Goethe,* Quoted in *Correspondence*
> *Between Goethe and a Young Girl 1835*
> *Johann Wolfgang von Goethe, German poet, dramatist, novelist
> (1749–1832).

2 O yes! the ascending from out of unconscious life into revelation,—that is music!
> Ibid.

3 Whoever is come to something in art, did forget his craftiness, his load of experience, became shipwreck, and despair led him to land on the right shore.
> Ibid.

4 To inhale the divine spirit is to engenerate, to produce; to exhale the divine breath is to breed and nourish the mind....
> Ibid.

5 Body is art, art is the sensual nature engenerated into the life of the spirit.
> Ibid.

799. Caroline Lamb (1785–1828)

1 Then, for the first time, Camioli beheld, in one comprehensive view, the universal plan of nature—unnumbered systems performing their various but distinct courses, unclouded by mists, and unbounded by horizon—endless variety in infinite space!
> Ch. 1, *Glenarvon,* Vol. I *1816*

2 It is the common failing of an ambitious mind to over-rate itself....
> Ch. 2, Ibid.

3 "...she is in love with ruin: it stalks about in every possible shape, she hails it:—woe is it; victim of prosperity, luxury and self indulgence."
> Ch. 28, Ibid.

4 "I had rather be the cause of her laughter, than of her tears."
> Ch. 24, Vol. II, Ibid.

5 Women, like toys, are sought after, and trifled with, and then thrown by with every varying caprice.
> Ch. 81, Vol. II, Ibid.

6 "...my mind is a world in itself, which I have peopled with my own creatures."
> Ch. 94, Ibid.

7 Mad, bad, and dangerous to know.*
> *Journal n.d.*
> *Her description of her lover, Lord Byron, English poet (1788–1824).

800. María Augustín (1786–1857)

1 Death or victory!*
> Speech at siege of Zaragoza (2 June 1808), Quoted in *Women*
> *of Beauty and Heroism* by Frank B. Goodrich *1858*
> *Cry that led the Spanish resistance to Napoleon's assault.

801. Marceline Desbordes-Valmore (1786–1859)

1 Shall I never play again in my mother's garden-close?
> "Tristesse," (Sadness), St. 1 *Elegies and Romances 1842*

2 Why are our joys remembered more bitter than our woes?
> St. 21, Ibid.

3 "I wonder who will take the oar
When my poor bark is at last found"
> "To Alphonse de Lamartine,"* St. 6, Ibid.
> *French poet and statesman (1790–1869).

4 We must make our lives as we sew,—stitch by stitch.
> Remark, Quoted in *Memoirs of Madame Desbordes-*
> *Valmore* by C. A. Sainte-Beuve; Harriet W. Preston, tr. *1872*

5 God will gather like bruised flowers
The souls of babes and women who to him

Are fled,—the air with outraged souls is dim,
On earth men wade in blood,—Merciful Powers!
>> Ch. 3, "Lyons," St. 2 (1834), Ibid.

6 Are we* not like the two volumes of one book?
>> Ch. 4, Letter, Ibid.
>> *Referring to her friend, Pauline Duchambge, composer, with whom Valmore frequently collaborated on songs.

7 I am climbing, as best I may, to the goal of an existence in which I speak very much oftener to God than to the world.
>> Letter to M. Antoince de Latour (7 February 1837), Ibid.

8 All the miseries of Lyons are added to my own,—twenty or thirty thousand workmen begging daily for a little bread, a little fire, a garment, lest they die. Can you realize, monsieur, this universal and insurmountable despair which appeals to one in God's name, and makes one ashamed of daring to have food and fire and two garments, when these poor creatures have none? I see it all, and it paralyzes me.
>> Ibid.

9 . . . the more I read, the farther I penetrate into the shadows which have hidden our great lights from me, the less I dare to write: I am smitten with terror,—I am like a glowworm in the sun.
>> Letter to her son, Hippolyte (26 October 1840), Ibid.

10 . . . if I were not poor, you would not be so.
>> Letter to her brother, Felix Desbordes (14 January 1843), Ibid.

11 In these days the rich will come and tell you their troubles with such utter candor, such bitter bewailings, that you are compelled to pity them more than you do yourself.
>> Letter to Pauline Duchambge (10 February 1843), Ibid.

12 An attack of hope is the same for us as an attack of fever.
>> Ibid.

13 The last result of misfortune is to sow seeds of discord in families in which happiness would have united. When it becomes necessary for each member to work hard in order to escape absolute indigence, the wings of the soul are folded, and soaring is postponed to a future day.
>> Letter to her niece (6 September 1854), Ibid.

14 . . . the sum and substance of volumes that I feel . . . will remain unwritten, like seeds put away in closets, which dry up and are never sown.
>> Letter to Mme. Derains (ca. September 1854), Ibid.

15 You say, my dear and true friend, that poetry is my consolation. On the contrary, it torments me, as with a bitter irony. I am like the Indian who sings at the stake.
>> Letter to Pauline Duchambge (15 January 1856), Ibid.

16 Are we not always young?
>> (5 January 1857), Ibid.

17 Ah, how many stabs are concealed by the smiles and sweet "goodmornings" of the world.
>> (April 1857), Ibid.

18 The are times when one cannot lift a blade of grass without finding a serpent under it.
>> (11 May 1857), Ibid.

802. Caroline Anne Southey (1786–1854)

1 Sleep, little baby! sleep!
Not in thy cradle bed,
Not on thy mother's breast
>> "To A Dying Infant," St. 1, *Solitary Hours, and Other Poems* 1826

2 You must love—*not my faults*—but in *spite* of them, me,
For the very caprices that vex ye;
Nay, the more should you chance (as it's likely) to see
'T is my special delight to perplex ye.
>> "The Threat," St. 6, Ibid.

3 But I have drunk enough of life
(The cup assign'd to me
Dash'd with a little sweet at best,
So scantily, so scantily)
>> "To Death," St. 4, Ibid.

4 This weak, weak head! this foolish heart! they'll cheat me to the last:
I've been a dreamer all my life, and now that life is past!
>> "The Dying Mother to her Infant," St. 11, *Autumn Flowers, and Other Poems* 1844

5 How happily, how happily, the flowers die away!
Oh, could we but return to earth as easily as they!
>> "The Death of the Flowers," St. 1, Ibid.

803. Eliza Lee Follen (1787–1860)

1 The night comes on,
And sleep upon this little world of ours,
Spreads out her sheltering, healing wings; and man—
The heaven-inspired soul of this fair earth,
The bold interpreter of nature's voice,
Giving a language even to the stars—
Unconscious of the throbbings of his heart,—
Is still
>> "Winter Scenes in the Country," St. 1, *Poems 1839*

804. Eliza Leslie (1787–1858)

1 "The truth is," pursued Mr. Culpepper, "I am travelling for my health, and therefore I am taking cross-roads, and stopping at out of the way places. For there is no health to be got by staying in cities, and putting up at crowded hotels, and accepting invitations to dinner-parties and tea-parties, or in doing any thing else that is called fashionable."
>> "The Red Box, or, Scenes at the General Wayne," *Pencil Sketches; or Outlines of Character and Manners 1837*

2 Servility and integrity rarely go together.
>> Ibid.

3 "There is no better cure for folly, and particularly for romantic folly, than a good burlesque. . . . "
>> "The Serenades," Ibid.

4 "Why, Pharaoh—my old fellow!" exclaimed Lindsay, "Is this really yourself?"
"Can't say, masser," replied Pharaoh. "All people's much the same—Best not be too personal—But I b'lieve I'm he."
>> "The Old Farm House," Ibid.

5 "And the Newman girls mix up their talk with all sorts of French words that sound very ugly to me. Instead of 'good

night' they say *bone swear,** and a 'trifle' they call a *bag-tail,**
and they are always talking about having a *Gennessee Squaw,**
though what they mean by that I cannot imagine; for I am sure
I never saw any such thing in this part of the country."

Ibid.

**bon soir; bagatelle; je ne sais quoi.*

6   " . . . there's a considerable difference between doing without a
thing of your own accord, and being made to do without it."
"Chase Loring. A Story of the Revolution," Ibid.

7   "Love at first sight is certainly a most amusing thing," remarked Mrs. Seabright, "at least to the by-standers."
"Love at First Sight," *Kitty's Relations, and other pencil
sketches 1847*

8   "Some goes by coffee-grounds, which is low and vulgar; and
some goes by the lines on the parms of your hands, which is
nothing but plexity and puzzledom; and some goes by the stars
and planipos [planets], which is too far off to be certain. But
cards is the only true things, as all the best judges can scratify
[certify]."
"The Fortune-Teller," *Leonilla Lynmore, and Mr. and Mrs.
Woodbridge or A Lesson for young wives 1847*

805. Mary Russell Mitford (1787–1855)

1   Of all living objects, children, out of doors, seem to me the most
interesting to a lover of nature . . . Within doors . . . I am one of
the many persons who like children in their places,—that is to
say, anyplace where I am not. But out of doors there is no such
limitation: from the gypsy urchins under a hedge, to the little
lords and ladies in a ducal demesne, they are charming to look
at, to watch, and to listen to. Dogs are less amusing, flowers
are less beautiful, trees themselves are less picturesque.
"The Carpenter's Daughter," *Belford Regis; or, Sketches of a
Country Town,* Vol. I *1835*

2   COLONNA. The fool's grown wise—
A grievous change.
Act II, Sc. 1, *Rienzi 1857*

3   COLONNA. Joined! by what tie?
RIENZI. By hatred—
By danger—the two hands that tightest grasp
Each other—the two cords that soonest knit
A fast and stubborn tie: your true love knot
Is nothing to it.
Ibid.

4   I have discovered that out great favourite, Miss [Jane] Austen,* is my countrywoman . . . with whom mamma before her
marriage was acquainted. Mamma says that she was then the
prettiest, silliest, most affected, husband-hunting butterfly she
ever remembers.
Letter to Sir William Elford (3 April 1815), Quoted in
Life of Mary Russell Mitford, Vol. I by Rev. A. G. L'Estrange,
ed. *1870*

*See 767.

806. Emma Hart Willard (1787–1870)

1   'T is best to make the Law our friend.
Harry Guy 1848

2   In searching for the fundamental principles of the science of
teaching, I find few axioms as indisputable as is the first principles of mathematics. One of these is this, HE IS THE BEST

TEACHER WHO MAKES THE BEST USE OF HIS OWN
TIME AND THAT OF HIS PUPILS. For TIME is all that is
given by God in which to do the work of Improvement.
"How to Teach," Address to the Columbian Association *n.d.*

3   He is not necessarily the best teacher who performs the most
labour; makes his pupils work the hardest, and bustle the most.
A hundred cents of copper, though they make more clatter and
fill more space, have only a tenth of the value of one eagle of
gold.
Ibid.

4   Reason and religion teach us that we too are primary exis-
tences, that it is for us to move in the orbit of our duty around
the holy center of perfection, the companions not the satellites
of men.
Inscribed beneath her bust in the Hall of Fame of Great
Americans, Bronx, New York *n.d.*

807. Sarah Josepha Hale (1788–1879)

1   O wondrous power! how little understood,
—Entrusted to the mother's mind alone
To fashion genius, form the soul for good,
Inspire a West,* or train a Washington!**
The Genius of Oblivion and Other Poems 1823
*Benjamin West, American painter (1738–1820). **George W—
(1732–99) first president of the United States (1789–1797).

2   . . . . there is a period when nations as well as individuals quit
their minority. . . .
Northwood, A Tale of New England 1828

3   You may easily tell a rich Yankee farmer—he is always pleading poverty.
Ibid.

4   In this age of innovation perhaps no experiment will have an
influence more important on the character and happiness of
our society than the granting to females the advantages of a
systematic and thorough education.
Editorial, *The Ladies' Magazine and Literary Gazette January
1828**
*First issue of first woman's magazine in the United States.

5   There is no influence so powerful as that of the mother, but
next in rank in efficacy is that of schoolmaster.
Ibid.

6   Victoria's reign will be one of the longest in English annals. . . .
She may so stamp her influence on the period in which she
flourishes that history shall speak of it as her own. . . .
It will be the Victorian, as a former one now is the Elizabe-
than age . . . *
Ibid.
*Predicted two years before Victoria (see 960) ascended the
throne.

7   Mary had a little lamb,
Its fleece was white as snow,
And everywhere that Mary went
The lamb was sure to go.
"Mary's Little Lamb," St. 1, *Poems for Our Children 1830*

8   O, beautiful rainbow, all woven of light!
There's not in thy tissue one shadow of night;
"Beautiful Rainbow," Ibid.

9 I consider every attempt to induce women to think they have a just right to participate in the public duties of government as injurious to their best interests and derogatory to their character. Our empire is purer, more excellent and spiritual. . . .

Editorial, *The Ladies' Magazine and Literary Gazette*
February 1832

10 Americans have two ardent passions; the love of liberty and the love of distinction.

Traits of American Life 1835

11 There is small danger of being starved in our land of plenty; but the danger of being stuffed is imminent.

Ibid.

12 The barbarous custom of wresting from women whatever she possesses, whether by inheritance, donation or her own industry, and conferring it all upon the man she marries, to be used at his discretion and will, perhaps waste it on his wicked indulgences, without allowing her any control or redress, is such a monstrous perversion of justice *by law,* that we might well marvel how it could obtain in a Christian community.

"The Rights of Married Women," *Godey's Lady's Book May 1837*

13 " . . . it's might hard for a man like me, that could be as good as any body, if his skin were a shade or two lighter, to be kept down so all the time, and not get drunk or wicked."

Ch. 3, *Liberia 1853*

14 " . . . what's de good of strong arms when de heart is a coward's?"

Ch. 5, Ibid.

15 "Africa . . . is the home . . . of the mysterious Negro races yet lying dormant in the germ, destined, perhaps, to rule this earth when our proud Anglo-Saxon blood is as corrupt as that of the descendents of Homer* or Perricles** [sic]."

Ch. 7, Ibid.
*Greek epic poet (fl. 850 B.C.E.). **Athenian leader (d. 429 B.C.E.)

16 If men cannot cope with women in the medical profession let them take an humble occupation in which they can.

Editorial, *Godey's Lady's Book January 1853*

17 Lambs skip and bound, kittens and puppies seem wild with the joy of life; and little children naturally run, leap, dance and shout in the exuberance of that capacity for happiness which the young human heart feels as instinctively as the flower buds open to the sun. To repress their natural joyousness, not to direct and train it for good, seems to be the object of most parents.

Ibid.

18 Growing old! growing old! Do they say it of me?
Do they hint my fine fancies are faded and fled?
That my garden of life, like the winterswept tree,
Is frozen and dying, or fallen and dead?

"Growing Old" [written on her 70th birthday], Ibid.

19 . . . the whole process of home-making, housekeeping and cooking, which ever has been woman's special province, should be looked on as an art and a profession. . . .

Editorial, Ibid.

20 The most welcome guest in society will ever be the one to whose mind everything is a suggestion, and whose words suggest something to everybody.

"Manners," Ibid.

21 What has made this nation great? Not its heroes but its households.

Editorial Ibid.

808. Marguerite Blessington (1789–1849)

1 "Och! Jim, and this is the way you keep the Bible oath you took over to Father Cahill last Easther Sunday, that you would not dhrink a dhrop in any sheban-house for a year and a day? . . ."
"I did not dhrink a dhrop in the sheban-house, for I put my head clean out the window while I was dhrinking, so my oath is safe. . . ."

Ch. 1, *The Repealers 1833*

2 "How is it, Jim dear, that I, who love you betther than ever I loved myself, and you, who say you love me—that we, who have but one heart, can have two minds?"

Ibid.

3 "Sure there's different roads from this to Dungarvan*—some thinks one road pleasanter, and some think another; wouldn't it be mighty foolish to quarrel for this?—and sure isn't it twice worse to thry to interfere with people for choosing the road they like best to heaven?"

Ch. 2, Ibid.
*Seaport and seat of Waterford County, Ireland; dating back to seventh century.

4 "Imagination, which is the eldorado of the poet and of the novel-writer, often proves the most pernicious gift to the individuals who compose the talkers instead of the writers in society."

Ch. 40, Ibid.

5 Politeness, that cementer of friendship and soother of enmities, is nowhere so much required, and so frequently outraged, as in family circles. . . .

Ch. 57, Ibid.

6 "My spaniel Dido is not more submissive," said Scamper; "for though I try Lady Janet by contradicting flatly to-day, what I maintained yesterday, it is all the same to her; she never has any opinion but mine: this is what I call the only solid foundation to build matrimonial happiness upon; and so I have made up my mind to marry."

Ch. 28, *The Two Friends 1835*

7 Love is, I think, like fever; one severe attack leaves the patient subject to relapses through youth; and each succeeding one renders him more weakened, and consequently, more exposed to future assaults.

"My Fourth Love," *The Confessions of an Elderly Gentleman 1836*

8 Injurious as are the examples of bad conduct, the impunity which too frequently attends the perpetration is still more fatally pernicious.

"Lord Delaward to Lady Delaward," *The Victims of Society 1837*

9 . . . with a good fortune, a brilliant position, and a weak, indulgent husband, what more could she desire?

"La Marquise Le Villeroi to Miss Montressor," Ibid.

10 How soothing is affection! and how do those who, like me, know little of this sweetener of life, turn, with awakened tenderness, to him who administers the cordial!
"The Countess of Anandale to La Marquise Le Villeroi," Ibid.

11 A mother's love! O holy, boundless thing!
Fountain whose waters never cease to spring!
"Affection," *Gems of Beauty 1837–38*

12 People seem to lose all respect for the past; events succeed each other with such velocity that the most remarkable one of a few years gone by, is no more remembered than if centuries had closed over it.
The Confessions of an Elderly Lady 1838

13 . . . if those only wrote, who were sure of being read, we should have fewer authors; and the shelves of libraries would not groan beneath the weight of dusty tomes more voluminous than luminous.
Ibid.

14 There is no magician like Love. . . .
Ibid.

15 Novels and comedies end generally in a marriage, because, after that event, it is supposed that nothing remains to be told.
"The Honey-Moon," *The Works of Lady Blessington 1838*

16 Reason dissipates the illusions of life, but does not console us for their departure.
Desultory Thoughts and Reflections 1839

17 Love-matches are made by people who are content, for a month of honey, to condemn themselves to a life of vinegar.
Commonplace Book n.d.

18 When the sun shines on you, you see your friends. Friends are the thermometers by which one may judge the temperature of our fortunes.
Ibid.

19 Religion converts despair, which destroys, into resignation, which submits.
Ibid.

809. Charlotte Elliott (1789–1871)

1 Just as I am, without one plea
But that Thy blood was shed for me,
And that Thou bidd'st me to come to Thee,
O Lamb of God, I come!
"Just As I Am," *Invalid's Hymn Book 1834*

2 "Christian! seek not yet repose,"
Hear thy guardian angel say;
Thou art in the midst of foes—
"Watch and pray."
"Christian! Seek Not Yet Repose," *Morning and Evening Hymns ca. 1840*

810. Hannah Flagg Gould (1789–1865)

1 He went to the windows of those who slept,
And over each pane, like a fairy, crept;
Wherever he breathed, wherever he *stepped*
By the light of the morn, were seen
Most beautiful things. . . .
"The Frost," *Poems 1832*

2 O Thou, who in thy hand dost hold
The winds and waves that wake or sleep,
Thy tender arms of mercy fold
Around the seamen on the deep.
"Changes on the Deep," Ibid.

811. Ann Hasseltine Judson (1789–1826)

1 Either I have been made, through the mercy of God, a partaker of divine grace, or I have been fatally deceiving myself, and building upon a sandy foundation. Either I have, in sincerity and truth, renounced the vanities of this world, and entered the narrow path which leads to life, or I have been refraining from them for a time only, to turn again and relish them more than ever. God grant that the latter may never be my unhappy case!
Journal Entry (22 December 1806), Quoted in *Memoir of Mrs. Ann H. Judson, Late Missionary to Burma* by James D. Knowles *1829*

812. Catherine Maria Sedgwick (1789–1867)

1 "There is some pure gold mixed with all this glitter; some here that seem to have as pure hearts and just minds as if they had never stood in the dazzling sunshine of fortune."
"The Opinions of a Yankee Spinster," *Redwood 1824*

2 " . . . contentment is a modest, prudent spirit; and . . . for the most part she avoids the high places of the earth, where the sun burns and the tempests beat, and leads her favourites along quiet vales to sequestered fountains."
Ibid.

3 The fountains are with the rich, but they are no better than a stagnant pool till they flow in streams to the labouring people.
"His Advice to his Children," *The Poor Rich Man and the Rich Poor Man 1836*

4 "If parents are civil and kind to one another, if children never hear from them profane or coarse language, they will as naturally grow up well-behaved, as that candle took the form of the mould it was run in.
"His Remarks on Manners," Ibid.

813. Eliza Townsend (1789–1854)

1 . . . let that come now,
Which soon or late must come. For light
like this
Who would not dare to die?
"The Incomprehensibility of God," St. 1, *The Female Poets of America,* Rufus Griswold, ed. *1849*

814. Harriette Wilson (1789–1846)

1 I shall not say why and how I became, at the age of fifteen, the mistress of the Earl of Craven.
Memoirs (first sentence) *n.d.*

815. Ann Eliza Bray (1790–1883)

1 Never fear spoiling children by making them too happy. Happiness is the atmosphere in which all good affections grow . . . unhappiness—the chilling pressure which produces . . . "the mind's green and yellow sickness"—ill temper.
Attributed *n.d.*

816. Mary Cole (fl. ca. 1790)

1 If all writers upon Cookery had acknowledged from whence they took their receipts, as I do, they would have acted with more candour by the public. Their vanity to pass for Authors, instead of Compilers, has not added to their reputation.

The Lady's Complete Guide 1791

817. Louisa Macartney Crawford (1790–1858)

1 Kathleen Mavourneen; what, slumbering still?
Oh, hast thou forgotten how soon we must sever?
O hast thou forgotten this day we must part?
It may be for years, and it may be for ever!
Oh, why art thou silent, thou voice of my heart?

"Kathleen Mavourneen" (Attributed) *n.d.*

818. Catharine Crowe (1790–1872)

1 The great proportion of us live for this world alone, and think very little of the next . . . whilst . . . what is generally called the religious world, is so engrossed by its struggles for power or money, or by its sectarian disputes and enmities, and so narrowed and circumscribed by dogmatic orthodoxies, that is has neither inclination nor liberty to turn back or look around, and endeavour to gather up, from past records and present observation, such hints as are now and again dropt in our path, to give us an intimation of what the truth may be.

The Night-Side of Nature 1848

2 A great many things have been pronounced untrue and absurd, and even impossible, by the highest authorities in the age in which they lived, which have afterwards, and indeed, within a very short period, been found to be both possible and true.

Ibid.

819. Hannah Godwin (fl. ca. 1790)

1 Good sense without vanity, a penetrating judgment without a disposition to satire, with about as much religion as my William likes, struck me with a wish that she [Miss Gay] was my William's wife.

Letter to William Godwin,* her brother, Quoted in *William Godwin: His Friends and Contemporaries* by C. K. Paul *1876*
*English political philosopher (1756–1836); married to Mary Wollstonecraft; see 701.

820. Rahel Morpurgo (1790–1871)

1 Wherever you go, you will hear all around:
The wisdom of woman to the distaff is bound.

Untitled, St. 4, *Ugab Rachel* (The Harp of Rachel), I. Castiglione, ed. *1890*

2 I will tell thee an idea that has come into mind that "oil from the flinty rock"* is *petroleum,* and there is nothing new under the sun.

Letter to Isaac Luzzatto (1869), Ibid.
*From Deuteronomy 32:13.

3 Woe! my knowledge is weak,
My wound is desperate.

Last poem (1871), Ibid.

4 I take me eagles' wings, with vision flying
And brow upraised to look upon the sun.

Untitled poem (1867), Nina Davis Salaman, tr., *Four Centuries of Jewish Women's Spirituality,* Ellen M. Umansky* and Dianne Ashton, eds. *1992*
*See 4011.

821. Charlotte Elizabeth Tonna (1790–1846)

1 When we name the infliction of a wrong, we imply the existence of a right. Therefore, if we undertake to discuss the wrongs of women, we may be expected to set out by plainly defining what are the rights of women.

Ch. 1, "Milliners and Dress-makers," *The Wrongs of Women,* Pt. I *1833–34*

2 There can be no doubt that the hand which first encloses the waist of a girl in these cruel contrivances [stays], supplying her with a fictitious support, where the hand of God has placed bones and muscles that ought to be brought into vigorous action, that hand lays the foundation of bitter suffering. . . .

Letter II, *Personal Recollections 1841*

3 How very much do they err who consider the absence of order and method as implying greater liberty or removing a sense of restraint!

Letter IV, Ibid.

4 "And how do you feel when you have got absolution?" "I feel all right; and I go out and begin again." "And how do you know that God has really pardoned you?" "He doesn't pardon me directly; only the priest does. He [the priest] confesses my sins to the bishop, and the bishop confesses them to the pope, and the pope sees the Virgin Mary every Saturday night, and tells her to speak to God about it."

Letter VII, Ibid.

5 Nothing rights a boy of ten or twelve years like putting him on his manhood. . . .

Letter XIV, Ibid.

6 "The weight seemed to be not only on my head, but all over me; and then the sickening smell and the whirring noise—I'll tell you what, the first few days in a factory would make me ill, and when I got over that, I should become stupid."

Helen Fleetwood, Ch. 19, from *The Works of Charlotte Elizabeth,* Vol. I *1844*

7 A self-sold, suicidal world.

"The Watchman," St. 4, *Posthumous and Other Poems,* Ibid.

8 Haste to set thy people free;
Come; creation groans for thee!

"The Millennium," St. 4, *The Female Poets of Great Britain,* Frederic Rowton, ed. *1853*

822. Eliza Ware Farrar (1791–1870)

1 The queen* and princesses were all such common-looking people that they upset my childish notions of royalty.

Ch. 2, *Recollections of Seventy Years 1865*
*Queen Charlotte (1744–1818), consort of George III of England.

2 . . . Sir William Ellis . . . was at the head of the great lunatic asylum for paupers at Handwell near London. . . . No straitwaistcoats, no strapping patients into beds or chairs, no punishments of any kind were used,—nothing but the personal influence of Sir William and Lady Ellis; and their power over all under their care was extraordinary. Even persons in the height of an attack of mania yielded to it. Part of their system was to keep the patients as fully and as happily employed as was possible, and the whole establishment was like a great school of industry.

Ch. 38, Ibid.

823. Anne Marsh (1791–1874)

1 To say nothing of that brief but despotic sway which every woman possesses over the man in love with her—a power immense, unaccountable, invaluable; but in general so evanescent as but to make a brilliant episode in the tale of life—how almost immeasurable is the influence exercised by wives, sisters, friends, and, most of all, by mothers!

"Woman's Influence," *Angela 1848*

2 He [without education] enters life an ill-trained steed; and the best that can be hoped for him is, that the severe lash of disappointment, contradiction, and suffering, will during the course of his career, supply the omissions of his youth, and train him at last, through much enduring, to that point from which a good education would have started him.

Ibid.

3 Oh, vice is a hideous thing.
A hideous, dark mystery—the mystery of iniquity! Its secret springs are hidden from our view. . . .

"Sin and its Consequences," *Mordaunt Hall; or, A September Night 1849*

824. Sarah Martin (1791–1843)

1 I knew also that it sometimes seemed good in His sight to try the faith and patience of His servants, by bestowing upon them very limited means of support; as in the case of Naomi* and Ruth;** of the widow of Zarephath and Elijah; and my mind, in the contemplation of such trials, seemed exalted by more than human energy; for I had counted the cost; and my mind was made up.

Article in *Edinburgh Review 1847*

*See 22. **See 23.

825. Margaret Mercer (1791–1846)

1 *Conversation is to works what the flower is to the fruit.*

Ethics n.d.

2 . . . I confess that the 'unidea-ed chatter of females' is past my endurance; they are very capable of better things, but what of that? Is it not yet more annoying that they will do nothing better?

Quoted in *Memoirs* by Caspar Morris, M.D. *n.d.*

3 . . . steady laborious efforts to do good will doubtless be blessed, although we may in mercy be denied the luxury of seeing our work under the sun prosper.

Ibid.

826. Policarpa Salavarrieta (1791?–1817)

1 Although I am a woman and young, I have more than enough courage to suffer this death and a thousand more.

Statement before execution in wars of independence (1817), *Women in World History Curriculum* (womeninworldhistory. com) *1996–97*

827. Lydia Howard Sigourney (1791–1865)

1 "I was a worm till I won my wings."

"Butterfly on a Child's Grave," St. 2, *Poems 1834*

2 Not on the outer world
For inward joy depend;
Enjoy the luxury of thought,
Make thine own self friend

"Know Thyself," Ibid.

3 Bid the long-prisoned mind attain
A sphere of dazzling day,
Bid her unpinion'd foot
The cliffs of knowledge climb,
And search for Wisdom's sacred root
That mocks the blight of time.

"Female Education," St. 3, *Zinzendorff, and Other Poems 1836*

4 They, perchance,
Did look on woman as a worthless thing,
A cloistered gem, a briefly-fading flower,
Remembering not that she had kingly power
O'er the young soul.

"Establishment of a Female College in New-Grenada, South America," St. 1, Ibid.

5 Hope spreads her wing of plumage fair,
Rebuilds the castle bas'd on air

"The Soap Bubble," Ibid.

6 —I fear thee. Thou'rt a subtle husbandman,
Sowing thy little seed, of good or ill,
In the moist, unsunn'd surface of the heart.

"Thought," St. 2, *Select Poems 1841*

7 And yield the torn world to the angel of peace.

"The War Spirit," St. 5, Ibid.

8 This is the parting place; this narrow house

"The Tomb," St. 1, Ibid.

9 Thou who has toiled to earn
The fickle praise of far posterity,
Come, weigh it at the grave's brink, here with me,
If thou canst weigh a dream.

"The Dying Philosopher," St. 4, Ibid.

10 But their name is on your waters,
Ye may not wash it out.

"Indian Names," St. 1, Ibid.

11 Man's warfare on the tree is terrible.

"Fallen Forests," St. 1 *Poems 1854.*

12 For every quarrel cuts a thread
That healthful love has spun.

"The Thriving Family," St. 3, Ibid.

13 Admitting that it is the profession of our sex to teach, we perceive the mother to be first in point of precedence, in degree of power, in the faculty of teaching, and in the department allotted. In point of precedence she is next to the Creator; in power over her pupil, limitless and without competitor; in faculty of teaching, endowed with the prerogative of a transforming love; while the glorious department allotted is a newly quickened soul and its immortal destiny.

"Power of a Mother," *Letters to Mothers n.d.*

14 This, then, is the patriotism of woman; not to thunder in senates, or to usurp dominion, or to seek the clarion-blast of fame, but faithfully to teach by precept and example that wisdom, integrity, and peace which are the glory of a nation.

"Woman's Patriotism," Ibid.

828. Eliza Vestris (179197–1856)

1 Before you hear a 'venturous woman bends—
A warrior woman, who in strife embarks,

The first of all dramatic Joan-of-Arcs!*
Cheer on the enterprize thus dared by me,
The first that ever led a company;
What though until this very hour and age,
A Lessee lady never owned a stage,
I'm that *Belle Sauvage*—only rather quieter—
Like Mrs. Nelson, turn'd a stage proprietor.

> Composed for her Olympic Theatre (London) debut (3 January 1831), Quoted in *Enter the Actress* by Rosamond Gilder *1931*

*See 252.

829. Virginie Ancelot (1792–1875)

1 *"There are no longer any women! no, my dear, Count, there are no longer any women,"* mournfully exclaimed the Marchioness de Fontenay-Mareuil . . .

> Ch. 1, *Gabrielle 1840*

2 "Saloons* [sic] exist no longer; conversation has ceased; good taste has disappeared with it, and the mind has lost all its influences."

> Ibid.

*Reference to the French term 'salons,' social gatherings of distinguished guests.

830. James Stuart Miranda Barry (1792/95?–1865)

1 If I had had my sword on when Mr. Fiscal proposed sending me to the tronk (gaol), I would certainly have cut off both his ears to make him look smart.

> Quoted in "The Mysterious Doctor James Barry," vanhunks. com *2002*

831. Dorothea Primrose Campbell (1792–1863)

1 The winds of heaven are hushed and mild
As the breath of a slumbering child

> "Moonlight," *Poems 1816*

2 I dreamed not that a fairer spot
On earth's broad bosom lay;
Nor ever wished my wand'ring feet
Beyond its bounds to stray.

> "Address to Zetland [the Shetlands]," St. 4, Ibid.

832. Sarah Moore Grimké (1792–1873)

1 . . . the false translation of some passages [of the New Testament] by the MEN who did that work, and against the perverted interpretation by the MEN who undertook to write commentaries thereon. I am inclined to think, when we [women] are admitted to the honor of studying Greek and Hebrew, we shall produce some various readings of the Bible a little different from those we now have.

> Letter (Haverhill, 17 July 1837), *Letters on the Equality of the Sexes, and the Condition of Woman 1838*

2 Ah! how many of my sex feel . . . that what they have leaned upon has proved a broken reed at best, and oft a spear.

> Ibid.

3 In most families, it is considered a matter of far more consequence to call a girl off from making a pie, or a pudding, than to interrupt her whilst engaged in her studies.

> Letter (Brookline, 1837), Ibid.

4 Woman, instead of being elevated by her union with man, which might be expected from an alliance with a superior being, is in reality lowered. She generally loses her individuality, her independent character, her moral being. She becomes absorbed into him, and henceforth is looked at, and acts through the medium of her husband.

> Letter (Brookline, September 1837), Ibid.

5 Brute force, the law of violence, rules to a great extent in the poor man's domicile; and woman is little more than his drudge.

> Ibid.

833. Harriet Grote (1792–1878)

1 Politics and theology are the only two really great subjects.

> Bk. VIII, Ch. 1, Letter to Lord Rosebery* (16 September 1880), Quoted in *Life of Gladstone* by John Morley Morly *1903*

*Archibald Philip Primrose, fifth earl of Rosebery, English statesman (1847–1929).

834. Anne Isabella Milbanke (1792–1860)

1 Yes! Farewell—farewell forever!
Thou thyself has fixed our doom,
Bade hope's fairest blossoms wither,
Ne'er again for me to bloom.

> "Fare Thee Well" (to Lord Byron*) *ca. January 1816*

*English poet (1788–1824).

835. Caroline Symonds (1792–1803)

1 She planted, she lov'd it, she water'd its head,
And its bloom every rival defied;
But alas! what was beauty or virtue, soon fled,
In Spring they both blossom'd and died.

> "The Faded Rose, which grew on the tomb of Zelida," St. 4, *The Female Poets of Great Britain*, Frederic Rowton, ed. *1853*

2 Scarce had thy velvet lips imbib'd the dew,
And nature hail'd thee, infant queen of May;
Scarce saw thy opening bloom the sun's broad ray,
And on the air its tender fragrance threw;
When the north wind enamour'd of thee grew,
And from his chilling kiss, thy charms decay.

> "The Blighted Rosebud",* Ibid.

*Inscribed on the tomb of the writer, who died at the age of eleven.

836. Sarah Taylor Austin (1793–1867)

1 It is the peculiar and invaluable privilege of a translator, as such, to have no opinions, and this is precisely what renders the somewhat toilsome business of translating attractive to one who has a profound sense of the difficulty of forming mature and coherent opinions, and of the presumption of putting forth crude and incongruous ones. . . .

> Translator's Preface, Quoted in *England in 1835: being a series of Letters written to friends in Germany . . .* by Frederick von Raumer *1836*

837. Rebecca Burton Burlend (1793–1872)

1 I observed several groups of slaves linked together in chains, and driven about the streets like oxen under the yoke.

> On arriving in New Orleans (1 November 1831), *A True Picture of Emigration 1848*

2 I was now going to be an alien among strangers.

Ibid.

3 The nights in winter are at once inexpressibly cold, and poetically fine. The sky is almost invariably clear, and the stars shine with a brilliancy entirely unknown in the humid atmosphere of England.

On Homesteading in Illinois, Ibid.

4 Every thing here bears the mark of ancient undisturbed repose. The golden age still appears, and when the woodsman with his axe enters these territories for the first time, he cannot resist the impression that he is about to commit a trespass on the virgin loveliness of nature, that he is going to bring into captivity what has been free for centuries.

Ibid.

838. Felicia Dorothea Hemans (1793–1835)

1 We will give the names of our fearless race
To each bright river whose course we trace.

"Song of Emigration," Works 1839

2 The stately homes of England!
How beautiful they stand,
Amidst their tall ancestral trees,
O'er all the pleasant land!

"The Homes of England," St. 1, Ibid.

3 The boy stood on the burning deck,
Whence all but he had fled.

"Casabianca," St. 1, Ibid.

4 Life's best balm—forgetfulness.

"The Caravan in the Desert," Ibid.

5 Oh! what a crowded world one moment may contain.

"The Last Constantine," Ibid.

6 Talk not of grief till thou has seen the tears of warlike men!

"Bernardo del Carpio," l. 26, Ibid.

7 Oh! call my brother back to me!
I cannot play alone;
The summer comes with flower and bee—
Where is my brother gone?

"The Child's First Grief," St. 1, Ibid.

8 Is *all* that we see or seem
But a dream within a dream?

"A Dream Within a Dream," ll., Ibid.

839. Lucretia Mott (1793–1880)

1 Then, in the marriage union, the independence of the husband and wife will be equal, their dependence mutual, and their obligations reciprocal.

Discourse on Women 1850

2 Look at the heads of those [Quaker] women; they can mingle with men; they are not triflers; they have intelligent subjects of conversation.

Women's Rights Convention, Proceedings 1853

3 Learning, while at school, that the charge for the education of girls was the same as that for boys, and that, when they became teachers, women received only half as much as men for

their services, the injustice of this distinction was so apparent, that I resolved to claim for my sex all that an impartial Creator had bestowed, which, by custom and a perverted application of the Scriptures, had been wrested from woman.

Letter, Quoted in Biography of Distinguished Women by Sarah Josepha Hale* 1876

*See 807.

4 The cause of Peace has had a share of my efforts, taking the ultra non-resistance ground—that a Christian cannot consistently uphold, and actively support, a government based on the sword, or whose ultimate resort is to the destroying weapon.

Ibid.

5 . . . systems by which the rich are made richer, and the poor poorer, should find no favour among people professing to "fear God and hate covetousness."

Ibid.

6 Truth for authority, not authority for truth.

Motto, Quoted in The Peerless Leader by Paxton Hibben n.d.

840. Almira Lincoln Phelps (1793–1884)

1 What a pledge for virtuous conduct is the character of a mother!

"The Mother's Hopes," The Mother's Journal 1838

2 The universe, how vast! exceeding far
The bounds of human thought; millions of suns,
With their attendant world moving around
Some common centre, gravitation strange!
Beyond the power of finite minds to scan!

"The Wonders of Nature," St. 1, Poems n.d.

3 Each opening bud, and care-perfected seed,
Is as a page, where we may read of God.

St. 3, Ibid.

841. Sarah Alden Ripley (1793–1867)

1 What a vista! A whole new language!*

Notable American Women, Edward T. James, ed. 1971

*Reaction to satirical novel Don Quixote by Miguel de Cervantes, Spanish writer (1547–1616).

2 The sun looks brighter . . . as the evening of life draws near.

Letter to her sister-in-law, Ibid.

842. Catherine Spalding (1793–1858)

1 My heart still clings to the orphans.

Notable American Women, Edward T. James, ed. 1971

843. Caroline Gilman (1794–1888)

1 I know how the mind rushes back, in such moments, to infancy, when those stiffened hands were wrapped around us in twining love; when that bosom was the pillow of our first sorrows; when those ears, now insensible and soundless, heard our whispered confidence; when those eyes, now curtained by uplifted lids, watched our every motion. I know the pang that runs through the heart, and I can fancy the shrieking voice which says, "Thou mightst have done more for thy mother's happiness, for her who loved thee so!"

Ch. 3, Recollections of a Southern Matron 1837

2   I must ask indulgence of general readers for mingling so much
of the peculiarities of negroes with my details. Surrounded
with them from infancy, they form a part of the landscape
of a southern woman's life; take them away, and the picture
would lose half its reality. They watch our cradles; they are the
companions of our sports; it is they who aid our bridal decora-
tions, and they wrap us in our shroud.
Ch. 14, Ibid.

3   . . . convert schools into places for *teaching* instead of *recita-
tion*. . . . If the system continue as it its, the name of *teacher*
should be changed to *lesson-hearer*.
Ch. 28, Ibid.

4   . . . sitting down to *one* plate, that loneliest of all positions. . . .
Ch. 35, Ibid.

5   To repress a harsh answer, to confess a fault, and to stop (right
or wrong) in the midst of self-defence, in gentle submission,
sometimes requires a struggle like life and death; but these
three efforts are the golden threads with which domestic happiness is woven; once begin the fabric with this woof, and trials
shall not break or sorrow tarnish it.
Ibid.

844. Anna Brownwell Jameson (1794–1860)

1   To think of the situations of these women! . . . steeped in excitement from childhood, their nerves for ever in a state of
terror between severe application and maddening flattery; cast
on the world without chart or compass—with energies mis-
directed, passions uncontrolled, and all the inflammable and
imaginative part of their being cultivated to excess as part of
their profession—of their material!
"Women Artists—Singers—Actresses, & C.," *Visits and
Sketches at Home and Abroad; With Tales and Miscellanies
1834*

2   Conversation may be compared to a lyre with seven chords—
philosophy, art, poetry, politics, love, scandal, and the weather.
"Conversation," Ibid.

3   Truth is the golden chain which links the terrestrial with the celestial, which sets the seal of heaven on the things of this earth,
and stamps them with immortality.
The Loves of the Poets ca. 1835

4   The only competition worthy a wise man is with himself.
"Washington Allston,"* *Memoirs and Essays Illustrative of
Art, Literature, and Social Mores 1846*
*American painter (1779–1843).

5   As the rolling stone gathers no moss, so the roving heart gathers no affections.
"Sternberg's Novels," *Studies n.d.*

845. Maria Brooks (1795–1845)

1   Looks are its food, its nectar sighs,
Its couch the lips, its throne the eyes,
The soul its breath: and so possest,
Heaven's raptures reign in mortal breast,
Fratello del mio cor. [Brother of my heart.]
"Friendship," St. 2, *Judith,** *Esther,*** *and Other Poems 1820*
*See 48. **See 56.

2   Where passion is not found, no virtue ever dwelt.
X, St. 1, *Zóphiël; or the Bride of Seven 1825*

3   "The bird that sweetest sings can least endure the storm."
XIV, St. 1, Ibid.

4   . . . Reverie,
Sweet mother of the muses, heart and soul are thine!
XXII, St. 1, Ibid.

5   Soul, I would rein thee in.
Canto Third, "Palace of Gnomes," XXXII, St. 1, Ibid.

6   . . . cold ambition mimicks love so well,
That half the sons of heaven looked on deceived.
Canto Fourth, "The Storm," XLVIII, St. 2, Ibid.

7   How thrills the kiss, when feeling's voice is mute!
Canto Fifth, "Zameïa," III, St. 1, Ibid.

8   "If evil things can give
Dreams such as mine, let me turn foe to good,
And make a God of *Evil* while I live!"
XXIV, St. 1, Ibid.

9   "'The frailest hope is better than despair."
CII, St. 1, Ibid.

846. Frances Manwaring Caulkins (1795–1869)

1   The tendency of man among savages, without the watch of
his equals and the check of society, is to degenerate; to decline
from the standard of morals, and gradually to relinquish all
Christian observances.
Ch. 6, *History of New London, Connecticut 1852*

847. Eleanor Anne Franklin (ca. 1795–1825)

1   "Thine icy heart I well can bear,
But not the love that others share."
"Coeur de Lion,* an Epic Poem in Sixteen Cantos" *1822*
*Richard I (the Lion-Hearted; 1157–1199).

2   "The widow'd dove can never rest,
The felon kite has robb'd her nest;
With wing untir'd she seeks her mate,
To share or change his dreadful fate.
Ibid.

848. Rebecca Cox Jackson (1795–1871)

1   I always believed that if the Lord had a work for His children
to do, He was able to make it as plain as the light.
From her *Autobiography* (1833–1836), *Gift of Powers, The
Writings of Rebecca Jackson, Black Visionary, Shaker Eldress,*
Jean McMahon Humez, ed. *1981*

2   Jesus, the seed of the woman, is the manhood in which the seed
of God dwells. Which seed is called the Godhead dwelling in
manhood.
Ibid.

849. Mary Pyper (1795–1870)

1   When you had looked your last, and passed
With noiseless step into the vast,
Would I have hastened to forget,
Or loved you.—as I do, dear, yet?
"Ma Belle," St. 3, *Making of America Journals Articles,* vol.
XIX–10 *n.d.*

2   I sat me down; 'twas autumn eve,
And I with sadness wept;

I laid me down at night, and then
'Twas winter, and I slept.

"Epitaph: A Life" *n.d.*

850. Frances Wright (1795–1852)

1 The prejudices still to be found in Europe . . . which would confine . . . female conversation to the last new publication, new bonnet, and *pas seul* [nothing else] are entirely unknown here. The women are assuming their place as thinking beings. . . .

Views of Society & Manners in America 1821

2 No man can see his own prejudices.

A Few Days in Athens 1822

3 It is not as of yore. Eve puts not forth her hand to gather the fair fruit of knowledge. The wily serpent now hath better learned his lesson; and, to secure his reign in the garden, beguileth her *not* to eat.

Course of Popular Lectures 1829

4 . . . whenever we establish our own pretensions upon the sacrificed rights of others, we do in fact impeach our own liberties, and lower ourselves in the scale of being!

Ibid.

5 Let us enquire—not if a mother be a wife, or a father a husband, but if parents can supply, to the creatures they have brought into being, all things requisite to make existence a blessing.

(1828), Quoted in *Frances Wright, Free Enquirer* by A. J. G. Perkins and Theresa Wolfson *1939*

851. Sophia Smith (1796–1870)

1 It is my opinion that by the higher and more thoroughly Christian education of women, what are called their "wrongs" will be redressed, their wages will be adjusted, their weight of influence in reforming the evils of society will be greatly increased; as teachers, as writers, as mothers, as members of society, their power for good will be incalculably enlarged.

Last Will and Testament of Sophia Smith, Late of Hatfield, Massachusetts *1871*

852. Anette Elizabeth von Droste-Hülshoff (1797–1848)

1 At night, when heavenly peace is flying
Above the world that sorrow mars,
Ah, think not of my grave with sighing!
For then I greet you from the stars.

"Last words," St. 3, *The Catholic Anthology*, Thomas Walsh, ed. *1927*

2 So still the pond in morning's gray,
A quiet conscience is not clearer.

"*Der Weiher*" (The Pond), Herman Salinger, tr., *An Anthology of German Poetry from Hölderlin to Rilke*, Angel Flores, ed. *1960*

3 O spirit free, entrancing youth,
Here at the very railing, I
Would wrestle, hip to hip, against
Your hold; become alive—or die.

"*Am Turme*" (On the Tower), St. 1, James Edward Tobin, tr., *Ibid.*

4 If heaven listened to my plea,
Made me a man, even though small!
Instead, I sit here—delicate,
Polite, precise, well-mannered child.
Dreams shake my loosened hair—the wind
Lone listener to my spirit wild.

Ibid.

5 . . . dreams release the soul's love urge

"*Durchwachte Nacht*" (Sleepless Night), St. 6, Herman Salinger, tr., *Ibid.*

6 . . . all the ghosts within your breast
(Dead love, dead pleasure, and dead time)

"*Im Grase*" (In the Grass), St. 2, James Edward Tobin, tr., *Ibid.*

853. Emily Eden (1797–1869)

1 "You will soon see how naturally one acquires a distaste for any ill-judging individual who presumes not to like one's husband."

Pt. 1, Ch. 3, *The Semi-Attached Couple 1830*

2 What could be more absurd than to assemble a crowd to witness a man and a woman promising to love each other for the rest of their lives, when we know what human creatures are,—men so thoroughly selfish and unprincipled, women so vain and frivolous?

Ch. 7, *Ibid.*

3 "I said to myself the other day, that one never hears anything new till it is old. . . ."

Ch. 17, *Ibid.*

4 There is nothing so catching as refinement. . . .

Ch. 48, *Ibid.*

5 "Now is that so like the Post Office?" she said. "Letters that are of no consequence are always delivered directly, but when Arthur writes to me, they send his letters all over England."

Ch. 5, *The Semi-Detached House ca. 1860*

6 At last, there came the joyful whisper, "a fine boy," perhaps the only moment of a fine boy's existence in which his presence is more agreeable than his absence.

Ch. 18, *Ibid.*

854. Kamamalu (1797?–1824)

1 O! heaven; O! earth; O! mountains; O! sea; O! my counsellors and my subjects, farewell! O! thou land for which my father suffered, the object of toil which my father sought. We now leave thy soil; I follow thy command; I will never disregard thy voice; I will walk by the command which thou hast given me.

Farewell address to her people upon her departure to England* (27 November 1823), Quoted in *Biography of Distinguished Women* by Sarah Josepha Hale** *1876*
*She died in England, never returning to her native land. **See 807.

855. Mary Lyon (1797–1849)

1 There is nothing in the universe that I fear but that I shall not know all my duty, or shall fail to do it.*

Quoted in *Eminent Missionary Women* by Mrs. J. T. Gracey *1898*

*Inscribed on her monument at Mt. Holyoke College, which she founded (1837) in Hadley, Massachusetts.

2   When you choose your fields of labor go where nobody else is willing to go.

> Ibid.

3   Oh, how immensely important is this work of preparing the daughters of the land to be good mothers!

> Letter to her mother (Ipswich, 12 May 1834), Quoted in *Mary Lyon through Her Letters*, Marion Lansing, ed. *1937*

856. Penina Moïse (1797–1880)

1   I weep not now as once I wept
   At Fortune's stroke severe;
   Since faith hath to my bosom crept,
   And placed her buckler there.

> "Hymn," St. 1, *Hymnal of Penina Moise*, 1856

2   Lay no flowers on my grave. They are for those who live in the sun, and I have always lived in the shadow.

> Last words, *Notable American Women*, Edward T. James, ed. *1971*

857. Ida Laura Pfeiffer (1797–1858)

1   When I was but a little child, I had already a strong desire to see the world. Whenever I met a travelling-carriage, I would stop involuntarily, and gaze after it until it had disappeared; I used even to envy the postilion, for I thought he also must have accomplished the whole long journey.

> *Visit to Iceland 1953*

2   A small affair would it have been for me to sail around the world, as many have done; it is my land journeys that render my tour a great undertaking, and invest it with interest.

> Quoted in *Biography of Distinguished Women* by Sarah Josepha Hale* *1876*
> *See 807.

3   Never betray fear.

> Motto, Ibid.

858. Therese Albertine Louise Robinson (1797–1870)

1   Not the untamed passion of the human heart, which, bursting out into a flame, spreading ruinously, destroys all barriers; not the unbridled force, which, in wild outbreaks of savage roughness, crushes under foot tender blossoms, lovely flowers,—not these constitute the greatest, the truest evil of the world; it is cold, creeping *egotism*, heartless *selfishness;* which with its attendants, treachery, deceit, and hypocrisy, easily bears away the palm, because it knows what it is doing, while passion, in blind fury, shatters its own weapons.

> "Selfishness," *Life's Discipline; a Tale of the Annals of Hungary 1851*

2   Losing her faith in the moral worth of the man she loves, a woman loses all the *happiness* of love.

> "Loving Unworthily," Ibid.

3   Love is dead. We are cured,—but are we happy?

> Ibid.

859. Mary Wollstonecraft Shelley (1797–1851)

1   . . . my dreams were all my own; I accounted for them to nobody; they were my refuge when annoyed—my dearest pleasure when free.

> Introduction (1831 edition), *Frankenstein (or, the Modern Prometheus) 1818*

2   Learn from me, if not by my precepts, at least by my example, how dangerous is the acquirement of knowledge, and how much happier that man is who believes his native town to be the world, than he who aspires to become greater than his nature will allow.

> Ch. 4, Ibid.

3   I felt that blank incapability of invention which is the greatest misery of authorship, when dull Nothing replies to our anxious invocations.

> Ibid.

4   I beheld the wretch—the miserable monster whom I had created.

> Ch. 5, Ibid.

5   "Of what a strange nature is knowledge! It clings to the mind, when it has once seized on it, like a lichen on the rock."

> Ch. 13, Ibid.

6   His conversation was marked by its happy abundance.

> Preface, *Collected Edition of Shelley 1839*

7   Mrs. Shelley was choosing a school for her son,* and asked the advice of this lady, who gave for advice—to use her own words to me—"Just the sort of banality, you know, one does come out with: 'Oh, send him somewhere where they will teach him to think for himself!'" . . . Mrs. Shelley answered: "Teach him to think for himself? Oh, my God, teach him rather to think like other people!"

> Quoted in *Essays in Criticism, Second Series; Shelley* by Matthew Arnold *1888*
> *Percy Bysshe Shelley, English poet and husband of Mary (1792–1822).

860. Sojourner Truth (1797?–1883)

1   Ef women want any rights more'n dey got, why don't dey jes' *take 'em,* and not be talkin' about it.

> Comment *ca. 1863*

2   I . . . can't read a book but I can read de people.

> Address, Tremont Temple, Boston, Massachusetts *January 1871*

3   Religion without humanity is a poor human stuff.

> Interview, Battle Creek, Michigan *ca. 1877*

4   Wall, childern, whar dar is so much racket dar must be somethin' out o' kilter.

> Speech, The Akron, Ohio, Convention (1851), *History of Woman Suffrage*, Vol. I, Elizabeth Cady Stanton,* Susan B. Anthony,** and Mathilda Gage*** *1881*
> *See 931. **See 963. ***See 1007.

5   Dat man ober dar say dat womin needs to be helped into carriages, and lifted ober ditches, and to hab de best place everywhar. Nobody eber helps me into carriages, or ober mud-puddles, or gibs me any best place! An a'n't I a woman? Look at me! Look at my arm! I have ploughed, and planted, and gathered into barns, and no man could head me! And a'n't I a woman? I could work as much and eat as much as a man—when I could get it—and bear de lash as well! And a'n't I a woman? I have borne thirteen chilern, and seen 'em mos' all sold off to slavery, and when I cried out with my mother's grief, none but Jesus heard me! And a'n't I a woman?

> Ibid.

6 Den dat little man in black dar,* he say women can't have as much rights as men, 'cause Christ wasn't a woman! . . . Whar did your Christ come from? From God and a woman. Man had notin' to do wid Him.

Ibid.

*A clergyman in the audience.

7 If de fust woman God ever made was strong enough to turn the world upside down all alone, dese women togedder ought to be able to turn it back, and get it right side up again!

Ibid.

8 There is a great stir about colored men getting their rights, but not a word about the colored women; and if colored men get their rights, and not colored women theirs, you see the colored men will be masters over the women, and it will be just as bad as it was before. So I am for keeping the thing going while things are stirring; because if we wait till it is still, it will take a great while to get it going again.

Speech, Annual Meeting of Equal Rights Convention (New York City, 9 May 1867), Vol. II, Ibid.

9 I know that it is hard for one who has held the reins for so long to give up; it cuts like a knife. It will feel all the better when it closes up again.

Ibid.*

*Quotations have been printed as they appear in *History of Woman Suffrage.* One assumes that the difference in the use of the vernacular and standard English has to do with the choice of the scribe at the event.

10 Truth burns up error.

Comment *ca. 1882*

11 I will show my breast to the entire congregation. It is not my shame, but yours.*

Quoted in *Women Suffragists* by Diana Star Helmer *1998*
*Her response when challenged by a heckler to show her breast to some of the ladies present to prove that, despite her deep voice, she was indeed a woman.

12 [In New York City] . . . the rich rob the poor and the poor rob one another.

Ibid.

13 I left everything behind. I wa'n't goin' to keep nothin' of Egypt on me. So I went to the Lord and asked him to give me a new name. And the Lord gave me Sojourner, because I was to travel up and down the land showin' the people their sins and bein' a sign unto them. Afterward, I told the Lord I wanted another name, 'cause everybody else had two names. And the Lord gave me Truth, because I was to declare the truth to the people.

Remark to Lucretia Mott,* Ibid.

*See 839.

14 I sell the shadow to support the substance.*

Ibid.

*Inscription of photographs of herself she sold to make money for food; she always spoke for free.

15 I *am* a woman's rights. I am a woman's rights.

Speech, American Equal Rights Association Convention (1867), Ibid.

861. Katharine Augusta Ware (1797–1843)

1 I've looked on thee as thou wert calmly sleeping,
And wished—Oh, couldst thou ever be as blest

As now, when haply all thy cause of weeping
Is for a truant bird, or faded rose!

"A New-Year Wish, to a child aged five years," St. 1, *The Power of the Passions, and Other Poems 1842*

862. Louisa Caroline Tuthill (1798/99–1879)

1 Never ring for a servant unless it is absolutely necessary; consider whether you have a right to make even your own waiting-maid take forty steps to save yourself one.

"Behaviour to Servants," *The Young Lady's Home n.d.*

2 A cumbrous set of rules and maxims hung about one, like the charms which the gree-gree man* sells to the poor African, will not ward off the evils, nor furnish an antidote to the trials of life.

"Home Habits," Ibid.

*Voodoo witch.

863. Catherine Gore (1799–1861)

1 Waterton,* the naturalist . . . asserts that whenever he countered an alligator *tête-à-tête,* in the wilderness, he used to leap on his back, and ride the beast to death. This feat, so much discredited by the stay-at-home critics, was an act of neither bravery nor braggartry—but of necessity. Either the man or the alligator must have had the upper hand. *Il a fallu opter.***

Just so are we situated with regard to the world. Either we must leap upon its back, strike our spur into its panting sides, and, in spite of its scaly defenses, compel it to obey our glowing will, or the animal will mangle us with its ferocious jaws, leaving us expiring in the dust.

"How to Manage the World," *Modern Chivalry n.d.*
*Charles W- , Eng. naturalist and explorer (1782–1865). **He had to choose.

2 For the egöist has so far the advantage over every other species of devotee, that his idol is ever present.

"Society," Ibid.

3 Thanks to the march of civilization, privacy has been exploded among us, and individuality effaced. People feel in thousands, and think in tens of thousands. No quiet nook of earth remaining for the modern Cincinnatus* to cultivate his own carrots and opinions, where humours may expand into excrescence, or originality let grow its beard!

Self n.d.
*Legendary Roman hero, political leader and farmer (fl. 460 B.C.E.).

864. Mary Howitt (1799–1888)

1 "Will you walk into my parlor?" said a Spider to a Fly;
"'Tis the prettiest little parlor that ever you did spy."

"The Spider and the Fly," *Poems ca. 1822–31*

2 Old England is our home and Englishmen are we,
Our tongue is known in every clime, our flag on every sea.

"Old England is Our Home," Ibid.

3 Make beauty a familiar guest.

Untitled, *Ballads and Other Poems 1847*

4 Hunger, and cold, and weariness, these are a frightful three,
But another curse there is beside, that darkens poverty;
It may not have one thing *to love,* how small soe'er it be!

"The Sale of the Pet Lamb," St. 6, Ibid.

5 Oh, hapless heirs of want and woe!
>   "Pauper Orphans," St. 5, *The Female Poets of Great Britain*,
>   Frederic Rowton, ed. *1853*

6 I love the fields, the woods, the streams,
    The wild flowers fresh and sweet,
    And Yet I love, no less than these,
    The crowded city street
>   "A City Street," St. 1, *Ibid.*

7 For visions come not to polluted eyes!
>   "English Churches," St. 3, *Ibid.*

8 Let us take our proper station;
    We the rising generation,
    Let us stamp the age as ours!
>   "The Children," St. 5, *Birds and Flowers; or, Lays and Lyrics*
>   *of Rural Life 1873*

865. Catharine Esther Beecher (1800–1878)

1 Woman's great mission is to train immature, weak, and ignorant creatures to obey the laws of God; the physical, the
   intellectual, the social, and the moral—first in the family, than
   in the school, then in the neighborhood, then in the nation,
   then in the world. . . .
>   "An Address to the Christian Women of America," *Woman*
>   *Suffrage and Women's Professions 1871*

2 To open avenues to political place and power for all classes
   of women would cause [the] humble labors of the family and
   school to be still more undervalued and shunned.
>   *Ibid.*

3 The delicate and infirm go for sympathy, not to the well and
   buoyant, but to those who have suffered like themselves.
>   "Statistics of Female Health," *Ibid.*

4 How many young hearts have revealed the fact that what they
   had been trained to imagine the highest earthly felicity was but
   the beginning of care, disappointment, and sorrow, and often
   led to the extremity of mental and physical suffering
>   *Ibid.*

866. Julia Crawford (1800–1885)

1 Kathleen Mavourneen! The grey dawn is breaking
   The horn of the hunter is heard on the hill.
>   "Kathleen Mavourneen," St. 1 (Attributed) *1835*

2 Oh! Hast thou forgotten how soon we must sever?
   Oh! Hast thou forgotten this day we must part?
   It may be for years, and it may be forever;
   Then why art thou silent, thou voice of my heart?
>   *Ibid.*

867. Maria Jane Jewsbury (1800–1833)

1 But let not thy little heart think, Genie,
   Childhood the prophet of life:
>   "Birth-Day Ballad," St. 4, *Lays for Leisure Hours:*
>   *Phantasmagoria 1824*

2 When the tossed mind surveys its hidden world,
   And feels in every faculty a foe,
   United but in strife; waves urged and hurled
   By passion and by conscience, winds of woe,

Till the whole being is a storm-swept sea—
There's none like thee, O Lord! there's none like thee!
>   "There Is None Like Unto Thee (Jeremiah X.6)," St. 3, *Ibid.*

3 Unfortunately, I was twenty-one before I became a reader, and
   I became a writer almost as soon; it is the ruin of all young talent of the day, that reading and writing are simultaneous. We
   do not educate ourselves for literary enterprise. I would gladly
   burn almost everything I ever wrote, if so be I might start now
   with a mind that has seen, read, thought, and suffered somewhat, at least, approaching to a preparation.
>   Letter to Felicia Hemans,* *Three Histories 1830*
>   *See 838.

868. Frederika Bremer (1801–1865)

1 Thou mayest own the world, with health
   And unslumbering powers;
   Industry alone is wealth,
   What we do is ours.
>   "Home" *1885*

869. Jane Welsh Carlyle (1801–1866)

1 It's [society] like seasickness: one thinks at the time one will
   never risk it again, and then the impression wears off and one
   thinks perhaps one's constitution has changed and that this
   time it will be more bearable
>   Letter, *Letters and Memorials 1883*

2 If they had said the sun and the moon was gone out of the
   heavens, it could not have struck me with the idea of a more
   awful and dreary blank in the creation than the words: Byron*
   is dead.
>   Letter to Thomas Carlyle** (1824), *Ibid.*
>   **English poet (1788–1824). *English essayist, historian (1795–
>   1881).

3 . . . the only thing that makes one place more attractive to me
   than another is the quantity of *heart* I find in it. . . .
>   Letter (1829), *Ibid.*

4 Some new neighbors, that came a month or two ago, brought
   with them an accumulation of all the things to be guarded
   against in a London neighborhood, viz., a pianofort, a lap-dog,
   and a parrot.
>   Letter to Thomas Carlyle's mother (6 May 1839), *Ibid.*

5 It is sad and wrong to be so dependent for the life of my life on
   any human being as I am on you; that I cannot by any force of
   logic cure myself at this date, when it has become second nature. If I have to lead another life in any of the planets, I shall
   take precious good care not to hang myself round any man's
   neck, either as a locket or a millstone.
>   Letter to Thomas Carlyle (1850), *Ibid.*

6 Never does one feel oneself so utterly helpless as in trying to
   speak comfort for great bereavement. I will not try it. Time is
   the only comforter for the loss of a mother.
>   (27 December 1853), *Ibid.*

7 When one has been threatened with a great injustice, one accepts a smaller as a favour.
>   (21 November 1855), *Ibid.*

8 Blessed be the inventor of photography! I set him above even
   the inventor of chloroform! It has given more positive pleasure

to poor suffering humanity than anything else that has "cast up" in my time or is like to—this art by which even the "poor" can possess themselves of tolerable likenesses of their absent dear ones. And mustn't it be acting favourably on the morality of the country?

Letter (21 October 1859), *The Collected Letters of Thomas and Jane Welsh Carlyle 1970*

9 Of all god's creatures, Man alone is poor.
"To a Swallow Building Under Our Eaves," *n.d*

10 *On the death of her father:* I had no counselor that could direct me, no friend that understood me—the pole-star of my life was lost, and the world looked a dreary blank.
"The Carlyles' Courtship," *Parallel Lives: Five Victorian Marriages,* by Phyllis Rose 1983

870. Lydia Maria Child (1802–1880)

1 The old men gazed on them in their loveliness, and turned away with that deep and painful sigh, which the gladness of childhood, and the transient beauty of youth, are so apt to awaken in the bosom of the aged.
Ch. 8, *Hobomok 1824*

2 I sometimes think the gods have united human beings by some mysterious principle, like the according notes of music. Or is it as Plato* has supposed, that souls originally one have been divided, and each seeks the half it lost?
Ch. 1, *Philothea: A Romance 1836*
*Greek philosopher (427–399 B.C.E.).

3 Blessed indeed is the man who hears many gentle voices call him father!
Ch. 19, Ibid.

4 Now twilight lets her curtain down
And pins it with a star.
Quoted in obituary for MacDonald Clark *1842*

5 Reverence is the highest quality of man's nature; and that individual, or nation, which has it slightly developed, is so far unfortunate. It is a strong spiritual instinct, and seeks to form channels for itself where none exists; thus Americans, in the dearth of other objects to worship, fall to worshiping themselves.
Letter 18 (26 May 1842), *Letters from New York,* Vol. I *1843*

6 Flowers have spoken to me more than I can tell in written words. They are the hieroglyphics of angels, loved by all men for the beauty of the character, though few can decypher even fragments of their meaning.
Letter 26 (1 September 1842), Ibid.

7 Not in vain is Ireland pouring itself all over the earth. . . . The Irish, with their glowing hearts and reverent credulity, are needed in this cold age of intellect and skepticism.
No. 33 (8 December 1842), Ibid.

8 None speaks of the bravery, the might, or the intellect of Jesus; but the devil is always imagined as being of acute intellect, political cunning, and the fiercest courage.
Ibid.

9 Childhood itself is scarcely more lovely than a cheerful, kind, sunshiny old age.
Letter 37 (March 1843), Vol. II *1852*

10 Every man deems that he has precisely the trials and temptations which are the hardest of all others for him to bear; but they are so, simply because they are the very ones he most needs.
Letter 39 (27 April 1843), Ibid.

11 There are not many people who are conscientious about being kind in their relations with human beings; and therefore it is not surprising that still fewer should be considerate about humanity to animals. . . . The fact is, reasonable and kind treatment will generally produce a great and beneficial change in vicious animals as well as in vicious men.
"Kindness to Animals," *The Freedman's Book 1865*

12 Genius hath electric power
Which earth can never tame.
"Marius Amid the Ruins of Carthage" *n.d.*

13 Over the river and through the wood,
To grandfather's house we'll go.
"Thanksgiving Day," St. 1 *n.d.*

871. Sara Coleridge (1802–1852)

1 No musing mind hath ever yet foreshaped
The face to-morrow's sun shall first reveal,
No heart hath e'er conceived
What love that face will bring.
"O sleep, my babe," St. 6, *n.d*

2 Chill December brings the sleet,
Blazing fire, and Christmas treat.
"The Months," St. 12, *n.d.*

3 To a little lump of malignity, on being medically assured that it was not a fresh growth, but an old growth splitting.
Split away, split away,
split away, split!
Plague of my life, delay pretermit!
"Doggrel Charm," *n.d.*

872. Dorothea Dix (1802–1887)

1 I have myself seen more than nine thousand idiots, epileptics and insane in the United States . . . bound with galling chains, bowed beneath fetters, lacerated with ropes, scourged with rods.
First Petition to Congress *ca. 1848*

2 In a world where there is so much to be done, I felt strongly impressed that there must be something for me to do.
Letter (31 December 1944), *Letters from New York,* Vol. II, Lydia Maria Child,* ed. *1852*
*See 870.

3 I think even lying in my bed, I can still do something.
Quoted in *Twelve American Women* by E. Anticaglia *1975*

873. Letitia Landon (1802–1838)

1 As beautiful as woman's blush—
As evanescent too.
"Apple Blossoms," *The Poetical Works of Miss Landon 1842*

2 Ah tell me not that memory
Sheds gladness o'er the past;
What is recalled by faded flowers
Save that they did not last?
"Despondency," Ibid.

3 I loved him too as woman loves—
Reckless of sorrow, sin or scorn.
"The Indian Bride," Ibid.

4 Few, save the poor, feel for the poor.
"The Poor," Ibid.

5 We might have been—These are but common words,
And yet they make the sum of life's bewailing.
"Three Extracts from the Diary of a Week," Ibid.

874. Harriet Martineau (1802–1876)

1 . . . there is no country in the world where there is so much boasting of the "chivalrous" treatment she enjoys. . . . In short, indulgence is given her as a substitute for justice.
"Women," *Society in America 1837*

2 Religion is a temper, not a pursuit.
Ibid.

3 . . . the sum and substance of female education in America, as in England, is training women to consider marriage as the sole object in life, and to pretend that they do not think so.
Ibid.

4 Persecution for opinion, punishment for all manifestations of intellectual and moral strength, are still as common as women who have opinions and who manifest strength. . . .
Ibid.

5 If there is any country on earth where the course of true love may be expected to run smooth, it is America.
"Marriage," Ibid.

6 Retribution is known to impend over violations of conjugal duty.
Ibid.

7 . . . the early marriages of silly children . . . where . . . every woman is married before she well knows how serious a matter human life is.
Ibid.

8 It is clear that the sole business which legislation has with marriage is with the arrangements of property; to guard the reciprocal rights of the children of the marriage and the community. There is no further pretence for the interference of the law, in any way.
Ibid.

9 Anyone must see at a glance that if men and women marry those whom they do not love, they must love those whom they do not marry.
Ibid.

10 I have no sympathy for those who, under any pressure of circumstances, sacrifice their heart's-love for legal prostitution.
Ibid.

11 For my own part, I had rather suffer any inconvenience from having to work occasionally in chambers and kitchen . . . than witness the subservience in which the menial class is held in Europe.
"Occupation," Ibid.

12 Readers are plentiful: thinkers are rare.
Ibid.

13 What office is there which involves more responsibility, which requires more qualifications, and which ought, therefore, to be more honourable, than that of teaching?
Ibid.

14 . . . I declare that if we are to look for a hell upon earth, it is where polygamy exists: and that, as polygamy runs riot in Egypt, Egypt is the lowest depth of this hell.
"The Harem," *Eastern Life: Present and Past 1848*

875. Clara Brown (1803–1885)

1 All churches do the Lord's work.
Quoted in *Women Pioneers* by Rebecca Stefoff *1995*

876. Marjory Fleming (1803–1811)

1 the most Devilish thing is 8 times 8 and 7 times 7 it is what nature itselfe cant endure. . . .
Diary of Marjory Fleming (repr. 1934) *1811*

2 love is a very
papithatick thing as well as
troublesom and tiresome. . . .
Ibid.

3 Sentiment is what I am not acquainted with.
Ibid.

4 I confess that I have been
more like a little young
Devil than a creature. . . .
Ibid.

877. Sarah B. Judson (1803–1845)

1 Then gird thine armour on, love,
Nor faint thou by the way—
Till the Boodh* shall fall, and Burmah's sons
Shall own Messiah's sway.
Poem to her husband, departing on a long voyage, St. 3 (ca. 1845), Quoted in *Biography of Distinguished Women* by Sarah Josepha Hale** *1876*
*Buddha: Judson was a missionary in Burma. **See 807.

878. Marie Lovell (1803–1877)

1 PARTHENIA. Clear be mine eyes, and thou, my soul, be steel!
Act I, *Ingomar, the Barbarian 1896*

2 INGOMAR. Freedom is hunting, feeding, danger;
that, that is freedom—that it is which makes
the veins to swell, the breast to heave and glow.
Aye, that is freedom,—that is pleasure—life!
Act II, Ibid.

3 INGOMAR.—This slavery
that gives thee freedom, brings along with it
so rich a treasure of consoling joy,
liberty shall be poor and worthless by its side.
Act V, Ibid.

879. Maria McIntosh (1803–1878)

1 Beneficent Nature, how often does the heart of man, crushed beneath the weight of his sins or his sorrows, rise in reproach against thine unchanged serenity!
Ch. 1, *Two Lives 1846*

2 "Now, Jessie, there is some beauty and some goodness in every thing God has made, and he who has a pure conscience is like one looking into a clear stream; he sees it all; while him who has a bad conscience, all things look as you say they did in the muddy stream—black and ugly."

"Jessie Graham," *Aunt Kitty's Tales 1847*

3 To the inhabitants of the Southern States, not only the New Englander, but everyone who dwelt north of the Potomac was a Yankee—a name which was with him a synonym of meanness, avarice and low cunning—while the native of the Northern States regarded his southern fellow-citizens as an indolent and prodigal race, in comparison with himself but half civilized, and far better acquainted with the sword and the pistol than with any more useful instrument.

Ch. 1, *The Lofty and the Lowly 1852*

4 "... it is only death which is hopeless..."

Ch. 19, Ibid.

880. Susanna Moodie (1803–1885)

1 I had heard and read much of savages, and have since seen, during my long residence in the bush, somewhat of uncivilized life, but the Indian is one of Nature's gentlemen—he never says or does a rude or vulgar thing. The vicious, uneducated barbarians, who form the surplus of overpopulace European countries, are far behind the wild man in delicacy of feeling or natural courtesy.

Ch. 1, *Roughing It in the Bush 1852*

2 But hunger's good sauce.

Ch. 12, Ibid.

3 "I have no wish for a second husband. I had enough of the first. I like to have my own way—to lie down mistress, and get up master."

Ibid.

4 The pure beauty of the Canadian water, the somber but August grandeur of the vast forest that hemmed us in on every side and shut us out from the rest of the world, soon cast a magic spell upon our spirits, and we began to feel charmed with the freedom and solitude around us.

Ch. 13, Ibid.

5 Ah, Hope! what would life be, stripped of thy encouraging smiles, that teach us to look behind the dark clouds of to-day, for the golden beams that are to gild the morrow.

Ch. 1, *Life in the Clearing 1853*

6 The want of education and moral training is the only real barrier that exists between the different classes of men. Nature, reason, and Christianity recognize no other. Pride may say Nay; but Pride was always a liar, and a great hater of the truth.

Ch. 3, Ibid.

7 Large parties given to very young children, which are so common in this country [Canada], are very pernicious in the way in which they generally operate upon youthful minds. They foster the passions of vanity and envy, and produce a love of dress and display which is very repulsive in the character of a child.

Ch. 19, Ibid.

8 We left one by one
the cities rotting with cholera,

one by one our civilized
distinctions
and entered a large darkness.
It was our own
ignorance we entered

Quoted in *The Journals of Susanna Moodie* by Margaret Atwood* *1970*

*See 3119.

881. Sarah Childress Polk (1803–1891)

1 It is only the hope that you can live through the campaign that gives me a prospect of enjoyment.

Letter to her husband, James Polk* (1843), Quoted in *First Ladies* by Betty Boyd Caroli *1987*

*J—Knox P—(1795–1849), 11th president of the United States (1845–1849).

882. Maria W. Stewart (1803–1879)

1 What if I am a woman? Is not the god of ancient times the god of these modern days? Did he not raise up Deborah,* to be a mother, and a judge in Israel? Did not queen Esther** save the lives of the Jews?

Introduction, Essay (1835), *Spiritual Narratives*, Sue E. Houchins, ed. *1988*

*See 27. **See 56.

2 O, ye daughters of Africa, awake! awake! arise! no longer sleep nor slumber, but distinguish yourselves. Show forth to the world that ye are endowed with noble and exalted faculties ... How long shall the fair daughters of Africa be compelled to bury their minds and talents beneath a load of iron pots and kettles?

"Religion and the Pure Principles of Morality" (1831), Ibid.

883. Flora Tristan (1803–1844)

1 *Ne me demandez pas d'où je viens.* (Do not ask from where I come.)

Pt. I, *Méphis 1838*

2 In the future, when woman is conscious of her power, she will free herself from the need for social approval, and those little tricks which today aid her to deceive men, will become useless; when that time comes, woman will say:—"I choose this man for my lover, because my love will be a powerful force on his intelligence, and our happiness will be reflected on others."

Pt. II, Ibid.

3 To love one's fellow-man is rational self-love.

Ibid.

4 What a revolting contrast exists in England between the slavery of women and the intellectual superiority of women writers.

Ch. 17, *Promenades Dans Londres* (London Walks) *1840*

884. Sarah Power Whitman (1803–1878)

1 And evening trails her robes of gold
Through the dim halls of the night.

"Summer's Call" *n.d.*

2 Star of resplendent front! Thy glorious eye
Shines on me still from out yon clouded sky.

"Arcturus (To Edgar Allan Poe*)" *n.d.*

*American poet, author (1809–1849).

3 Raven from the dim dominions
On the Night's Plutonian shore,
Oft I hear thy dusky pinions
Wave and flutter round my door.

"The Raven" *n.d.*

885. Delphine de Girardin (1804–1855)

1 Business is other people's money.

Marguerite, Vol. II *1852*

886. Elizabeth Palmer Peabody (1804–1894)

1 The advantage to the community in utilizing the age from 4
to 6 in training the hand and eye; in developing the habits of
cleanliness, politeness, self-control, urbanity, industry; in training the mind to understand numbers and geometric forms, to
invent combinations of figures and shapes, and to represent
them with the pencil—these and other valuable lessons . . .
will, I think, ultimately prevail in securing to us the establishment of this beneficent institution in all the city school systems
of our country.

Statement to Congress, *12 February 1897*

887. George Sand (1804–1876)

1 "I know that I am a slave, and you are my lord. The law of
this country has made you my master. You can bind my body,
tie my hands, govern my actions: you are the strongest, and
society adds to your power; but with my will, sir, you can do
nothing. God alone can restrain it and curb it. Seek then a law,
a dungeon, an instrument of torture, by which you can hold it,
it is as if you wished to grasp the air, and seize vacancy."

Indiana, (1900 ed.; George Burnham Ives, tr.) *1832*

2 The wit of small towns is, as you doubtless know, the most ill-
natured in the world. Good people are always misunderstood
there, superior minds are sworn foes of the public.

Pt. III, Ch. XIX, Ibid.

3 Love is woman's virtue; it is for love that she glories in her
sins, it is from love that she acquires the heroism to defy her
remorse. The more dearly it costs her to commit the crime, the
more she will have deserved at the hands of the man she loves.
It is like the fanaticism that places the dagger in the hand of the
religious enthusiast.

Ch. XXVII, Ibid.

4 I had forgotten how to be young, and Nature had forgotten to
awaken me. My dreams had moved too much in the world of
sublimity, and I could no longer descend to the grosser level of
fleshly appetites. A complete divorce had come about, though I
did not realize it, between body and spirit.

Lelia, Vol. II *1833*.

5 As things are, they [women] are ill-used. They are forced to
live a life of imbecility, and are blamed for doing so. If they
are ignorant, they are despised, and if learned, mocked. In love
they are reduced to the status of courtesans. As wives they are
treated more as servants than as companions. Men do not love
them: they make use of them, they exploit them, and expect, in
that way, to make them subject to the law of fidelity.

"La Fauvette du Docteur" (November 1844), *Almanach du
Mois November 1844*

6 "And yet," plied my friend, "nature has not changed. The night
is still unsullied, the stars still twinkle, and the wild thyme
smells as sweetly now as it did then. . . . We may be afflicted

and unhappy, but no one can take from us the sweet delight
which is nature's gift to those who love her and her poetry."

Preface, *La Petite Fadette 1848*

7 No one makes a revolution by himself; and there are some revolutions, especially in the arts, which humanity, accomplishes
without quite knowing how, because it is everybody who takes
them in hand.

Preface, *The Haunted Pool 1851*

8 Art is not a study of positive reality, it is the seeking for ideal
truth. . . .

Ch. 1, Ibid.

9 He who draws noble delights from the sentiments of poetry is
a true poet, though he has never written a line in all his life.

Ch. 2, Ibid.

10 "One never knows how much a family may grow; and when a
hive is too full, and it is necessary to form a new swarm, each
one thinks of carrying away his own honey."

Ch. 4, Ibid.

11 "Parents . . . sacrifice all the time of youth, which is the best, to
foreseeing what will happen to one at the age when one is no
longer good for anything, and when it makes little difference
whether one ends in one way or another."

Ch. 13, Ibid.

12 For everything, alas! is disappearing. During even my own lifetime there has been more progress in the ideas and customs
of my village than had been seen during centuries before the
Revolution.

Appendix, Ibid.

13 Once my heart was captured [by religion], reason was shown
the door, deliberately and with a sort of frantic joy. I accepted
everything, I believed everything, without struggle, without
suffering, without regret, without false shame. How can one
blush for what one adores?*

Pt. 3, Ch. 14, Vol. III *The Story of My Life*, Vol. I *1856*
*Reference to her newfound religious faith.

14 "I hated the pride of men of rank, and thought that I should
be sufficiently avenged for their disdain if my genius raised me
above them. Dreams and illusions all! My strength has not
equalled my mad ambition. I have remained obscure; I have
done worse—I have touched success, and allowed it to escape
me. I thought myself great, and I was cast down to the dust; I
imagined that I was almost sublime, and I was condemned to
be ridiculous. Fate took me—me and my audacious dreams—
and crushed me as if I had been a reed. I am a most wretched
man!"

"The Marquise" *1869*

15 Classification is Ariadne's* clue through the labyrinth of nature.

Nouvelles Lettres d'un Voyageur 1869
*In Greek mythology, Ariadne, *the* daughter of Minos and Pa-
siphaë, gave Theseus the thread with which he found his way out
of the Minotaur's labyrinth.

16 Universal suffrage, that is to say the expression of the will of
all, whether for good or ill, is a necessary safety-valve. Without
it, you will get merely successive outbreaks of civil violence.
This wonderful guarantee of security is there to our hands. It is
the best social counterweight so far discovered.

Ch. 3, *Handsome Lawrence 1872*

17 I have had my belly full of great men (forgive the expression). I quite like to read about them in the pages of Plutarch,* where they don't outrage my humanity. Let us see them carved in marble or cast in bronze, and hear no more about them. In real life they are nasty creatures, persecuters, temperamental, despotic, bitter and suspicious.
Correspondence, Vol. II 1883
*Greek biographer and philosopher (46–120).

18 There is only one happiness in life, to love and be loved. . . .
Letter to Lina Calamatta (31 March 1862), Vol. IV, Ibid.

19 One is happy as a result of one's own efforts, once one knows the necessary ingredients of happiness—simple tastes, a certain degree of courage, self denial to a point, love of work, and, above all, a clear conscience. Happiness is no vague dream, of that I now feel certain.
Letter, Vol. V, Ibid.

20 One wastes so much time, one is so prodigal of life, at twenty! Our days of winter count for double. That is the compensation of the old.
Letter to Joseph Dessauer (5 July 1868), Ibid.

21 Liszt* said to me today that God alone deserves to be loved. It may be true, but when one has loved a man, it is very different to love God.
(1834), *The Intimate Journal of George Sand 1926*
*Franz L—, Hungarian composer (1811–1886).

22 But if these people of the future are better than we are, they will, perhaps, look back at us with feelings of pity and tenderness for struggling souls who once divined a little of what the future would bring.
Ibid.

23 I have the feeling now that one changes from day to day, and that after a few years have passed one has completely altered. Examine myself as I may, I can no longer find the slightest trace of the anxious, agitated individual of those years, so discontented with herself, so out of patience with others.
Ibid.

24 He is unaware that any man who is adored as a god is deceived, mocked and flattered.
(3 June 1837), Ibid.

25 Immodest creature, you do not want a woman who will accept your faults, you want one who pretends that you are faultless—one who will caress the hand that strikes her and kiss the lips that lie to her.
Ibid.

26 One approaches the journey's end. But the end is a goal, not a catastrophe.
"Final Comment by George Sand" (September 1868), Ibid.

27 It is quite wrong to think of old age as a downward slope. On the contrary, one climbs higher and higher with the advancing years, and that, too with surprising strides. Brain-work comes as easily to the old as physical exertion to the child. One is moving, it is true, towards the end of life, but that end is now a goal, and not a reef in which the vessel may be dashed.
(1865), Ibid.

28 Stupid men—you who believe in laws which punish murder by murder and who express vengeance in calumny and defamation!
Ibid.

29 She prided herself on being educated, erudite and eccentric. She had read a little of everything, even of politics and philosophy, and it was curious to hear her bringing out as her own, for the delectation of the ignorant, things that she had read that same morning in a book, or had heard the night before from the lips of some serious-minded man of her acquaintance.
"Horace" *n.d.*

30 The old woman I shall become will be quite different from the woman I am now. Another *I* is beginning, and so far I have not had to complain of her.
Isadora, Vol. II *n.d.*

888. Sarah Flower Adams (1805–1848)

1 And joys and tears alike are sent
To give the soul fit nourishment.
As comes to me or cloud or sun,
Father! thy will, not mine, be done.
"He Sendeth Sun, He Sendeth Shower" *n.d.*

2 Though like the wanderer,
the sun gone down,
Darkness be over me,
my rest a stone;
Yet in my dreams I'd be
Nearer, my God, to Thee,
Nearer to Thee.
"Nearer, My God, to Thee," St. 2 *n.d.*

3 Once have a priest for enemy, goodbye
To peace.
Act III, Sc. 2, *Vivia Perpetua** n.d.*
*See 99.

889. Jeanne-Françoise Deroine (1805–1894)

1 Because the revolutionary tempest, in overturning at the same time the throne and the scaffold, in breaking the chain of the black slave, forgot to break the chain of the most oppressed of all—of Woman, the pariah of humanity. . . .
Letter from Prison of St. Lazare (Paris, 15 June 1851), written with Pauline Roland,* *History of Woman Suffrage,* Vol. I, by Elizabeth Cady Stanton,** Susan B. Anthony,*** and Mathilda Gage**** *1881*
*See 891. **See 931. ***See 963. ****See 1007.

2 We have, moreover, the profound conviction that only by the power of association based on solidarity—by the union of the working classes of both sexes to organize labor—can be acquired, completely and pacifically, the civil and political equality of women, and the social right for all.
Ibid.

890. Angelina Grimké (1805–1879)

1 . . . When the books and papers of the Anti-Slavery Society were thrown out of the windows of the office, one individual laid hold of the Bible and was about tossing it out to the ground, when another reminded him that it was the Bible he had in his hand. "O! 'Tis all one," he replied, and out went the sacred volume, along with the rest. We thank him for the acknowledgment.
"Appeal to the Christian Women of the South," *The Anti-Slavery Examiner September 1836*

2 It is through the tongue, the pen, and the press that truth is principally propagated.

> Ibid.

3 What was the conduct of Shadrach, Meshach, and Abednego?* . . . Did these men *do right in disobeying the law* of their sovereign? Let their miraculous deliverance from the burning fiery furnace answer. . . .

> Ibid.

*In the Book of Daniel in the Old Testament, these young men defy King Nebuchadnezzar's order that they bow down and worship a golden idol. Nebuchadnezzar orders the boys thrown into a furnace, but they emerge unharmed.

4 I have not placed reading before praying because I regard it more important, but because, in order to pray aright, we must understand what we are praying for. . . .

> Ibid.

5 If a law commands me to *sin I will break it;* if it calls me to *suffer,* I will let it take its course *unresistingly.* The doctrine of blind obedience and unqualified submission to any human power, whether civil or ecclesiastical, is the doctrine of despotism, and ought to have no place 'mong Republicans and Christians.

> Ibid.

6 Slavery always has, and always will, produce insurrections wherever it exists, because it is a violation of the natural order of things, and no human power can much longer perpetrate it. . . .

> Ibid.

7 I am not afraid to trust my sisters—not I.

> Letter No. 11, *Letters to Catherine Beecher,** Isaac Knapp, ed. *1836*

*See 865.

8 I recognize no rights but *human* rights—I know nothing of men's rights and women's rights; for in Christ Jesus there is neither male nor female. It is my solemn conviction that, until this principle of equality is recognized and embodied in practice, the church can do nothing effectual for the permanent reformation of the world.

> Letter No. 12, Ibid.

891. Pauline Roland (1805–1852)

Coauthor with Jeanne-Françoise Deroine; see also 889: 1–2.

1 I protest against marriage because, in the way it is organized, it asserts the inferiority of women to men.

> Statement at trial *January 1851*

892. Elizabeth Barrett Browning (1806–1861)

1 And lips say "God be pitiful,"
Who ne'er said "God be praised."

> "The Cry of the Human," St. 1, *Graham's American Magazine 1842*

2 Then we talked—oh, how we talked! her voice so cadenced in the talking,
Made another singing—of the soul! a music without bars . . .

> "Lady Geraldine's Courtship," St. 45, *Poems of 1844 1844*

3 Thou large-brained woman and large-hearted man. . . .

> "To George Sand,* A Desire," Ibid.

*See 887.

4 Our Euripides,* the human,
With his dropping of warm tears,
And his touches of things common
Till they rose to touch the spheres!

> "Wine of Cyprus," St. 12, Ibid.

*Greek dramatist (480–406 B.C.E.).

5 "Yes," I answered you last night;
"No," this morning, sir, I say:
Colors seen by candle-light
Will not look the same by day.

> "The Lady's 'Yes'," St. 1, Ibid.

6 What I do
And what I dream includes thee, as the wine
Must taste of its own grapes.

> *Sonnets from the Portuguese,* I *1850*

7 Say thou dost love me, love me, love me—toll
The silver iterance!—only minding, Dear,
To love me also in silence, with thy soul.

> XXI, Ibid.

8 How do I love thee? Let me count the ways.
I love thee to the depth and breadth and height
My soul can reach. . . .

> XLIII, Ibid.

9 I love thee with a love I seemed to lose
With my lost saints,—I love thee with the breath,
Smiles, tears, of all my life!—and, if God choose,
I shall but love thee better after death.

> Ibid.

10 If we tried
To sink the past beneath our feet, be sure
The future would not stand.

> Pt. I, l. 416, *Casa Guidi Windows 1851*

11 Long live the people! How they lived! and boiled
And bubbled in the cauldron of the street. . . .

> Pt. II, l. 115, Ibid.

12 How many desolate creatures on the earth
Have learnt the simple dues of fellowship
And social comfort, in a hospital. . . .

> Bk. III, l. 1122, Ibid.

13 A little sunburnt by the glare of life. . . .

> Bk. IV, l. 1140, Ibid.

14 Measure not the work
Until the day's out and the labor done. . . .

> Bk. V, l. 76, Ibid.

15 Men get opinions as boys learn to spell,
By reiteration chiefly. . . .

> Bk. VI, l. 6, Ibid.

16 Since when was genius found respectable?

> l. 275, Ibid.

17 Earth's crammed with heaven,
And every common bush afire with God;

> Bk. VII, l. 820, Ibid.

18 The thinkers stood aside
To let the nation act.

> "Napoleon III in Italy," St. 3, *Poems Before Congress 1860*

19 "What a monster have we here?
  A great Deed at this hour of day?
  A great just Deed—and not for pay?
  Absurd,—or insincere."
  "A Tale of Villafrance," St. 4, *Athenoeum 24 September 1859*

893. Maria Weston Chapman (1806–1885)

1 If this is the last bulwark of freedom, we may as well die here as anywhere.*
  Remark to mayor, Boston Female Anti-Slavery Society *1835*
  *The meeting of 45 women was mobbed by 5,000 pro-slavery men.

2 As *wives* and *mothers,* as *sisters* and *daughters,* we are deeply responsible for the influence we have on the human race. We are bound to exert it; we are bound to urge man to cease to do evil, and learn to do well. We are bound to urge them to regain, defend and preserve inviolate the rights of all, especially those whom they have most deeply wronged.
  Address, Boston Female Anti-Slavery Society, Quoted in *Liberator 13 August 1836*

3 Confusion has seized us, and all things go wrong,
  The women have leaped from 'their spheres,'
  And instead of fixed stars, shoot as comets along,
  And are setting the world by the ears! . . .
  So freely they move in their chosen elipse,
  The 'Lords of Creation'
  do fear an eclipse
  "The Times that Try Men's Souls" *1837*

4 Custom is never, by her nature, the handmaid of freedom.
  Right and Wrong in Massachusetts 1839

5 Don't drag the engine, like an ignoramous, but bring wood and water and flame, like an engineer.
  Address, "How Can I Help to Abolish Slavery," New York *1855*

6 We may draw good out of evil; we must not do evil, that good may come.
  Address, "How Can I Help to Abolish Slavery," New York *1855*

894. Juliette Drouet (1806–1883)

1 I love you *because* I love you, because it would be impossible for me not to love you. I love you without question, without calculation, without reason good or bad, faithfully, with all my heart and soul, and every faculty.
  (1833), *Letters to Victor Hugo* 1915*
  *French poet, novelist (1802–1885).

2 If I were a clever woman, my gorgeous bird, I could describe to you how you unite in yourself the beauties of form, plumage, and song!
  (1835), Ibid.

3 There are no wrinkles in the heart, and you will see my face only in the reflection of your attachment, eh, Victor, my beloved?
  (19 November 1841), Ibid.

4 In my opinion, infidelity does not consist in action only; I consider it already accomplished by the sole fact of desire.
  (4 April 1847), Ibid.

5 I come to fetch my heart where I left it, that is to say in yours.
  (14 December 1881), Ibid.

895. Mary Ann Dwight (1806–1858)

1 Janus was invoked at the commencement of most actions; even in the worship of the other gods the voterie began by offering wine and incense to Janus. The first month in the year was named from him; and under the title of Matutinus he was regarded as the opener of the day.
  "Janus," *Grecian and Roman Mythology 1864*

896. Flora Hastings (1806–1839)

1 Grieve not that I die young. Is it not well
  To pass away ere life hath lost its brightness?
  "Swan Song" *n.d.*

897. Nomura Motoni (1806–1867)

1 The whistle of the samurai's arrow is changing today to the thunder of the cannon.
  Untitled Poem *1855*

2 The song of the warbler, joyful at his release, has drawn forth the cry of many other birds.
  Ibid.

898. Julia Pardoe (1806–1862)

1 Raising his truncheon above his head, he broke it in the centre, and throwing the pieces among the crowd, exclaimed in a loud voice, "Le roi est moi!" Then seizing another staff, he flourished it in the air as he shouted, "Vive le Roi!"
  Life of Louis XIV, Vol. III 1947*
  *Known as "Louis the Great" and "the Sun King," (1643–1715); his was the longest reign in French history; lived 1638–1715.

2 The heart is a free and fetterless thing—
  A wave of the ocean, a bird on the wing.
  "The Captive Greek Girl" *n.d.*

899. Elizabeth Oakes Smith (1806–1893)

1 Faith is the subtle chain
  which binds us to the infinite.
  "Faith" *n.d.*

2 Yes, this is life, and everywhere we meet,
  Not victor crowns, but wailings of defeat.
  "The Unattained" *n.d.*

3 My friends, do we realize for what purpose we are convened? Do we fully understand that we aim at nothing less than an entire subversion of the present order of society, a dissolution of the whole existing social compact?
  Speech *n.d.*

900. Helen Dufferin (1807–1867)

1 The poor make no new friends.
  "Lament of the Irish Immigrant" *1894*

2 They say there's bread and work for all,
  And the sun shines always there:
  But I'll not forget old Ireland,
  were it fifty times as fair.
  Ibid.

901. Mary Elizabeth Hewitt (1807–1894)

1 A sumptuous dwelling the rich man hath.
  And dainty is his repast;
  But remember that luxury's prodigal hand
  Keeps the furnace of toil in blast.
  "A Plea for the Rich Man," St. 3, *Poems 1853*

2 Then hail! thou noble conqueror!
  That, when tyranny oppressed,
  Hewed for our fathers from the wild
  A land wherein to rest.
  "The Axe of the Settler," St. 5, Ibid.

3 And I shall hear thy sound resound,
  Till from his shackles man shall bound
  And shout exultant, "LIBERTY!"
  "The Songs of Our Land," St. 12, Ibid.

902. Harriet Taylor Mill (1807–1858)

1 We deny the right of any portion of the species to decide for another portion what is and what is not their 'proper sphere.' The proper sphere for all human beings is the largest and highest which they are able to attain to.
  Remark (1850), Quoted in *The Complete Works of Harriet Taylor Mill* by Jo Ellen Jacobs *1998*

903. Lucretia Maria Davidson (1808–1825)

1 O, say, amid this wilderness of life,
  What bosom would have throbbed like thine for me?
  Who would have smiled responsive? Who, in grief,
  Would e'er have felt, and, feeling, grieved like thee?
  "To My Mother" (November 1824), Quoted in *Lives of Celebrated Women* by Samuel Griswold Goodrich *1844*

2 That thought comes o'er me in the hour
  Of grief, of sickness, or of sadness;
  'Tis not the dread of death; 'tis more,—
  It is the dread of madness.
  Untitled (1825), Ibid.

904. Frances Dana Gage (1808–1884)

1 The home we first knew on this beautiful earth,
  The friends of our childhood, the place of our birth,
  In the heart's inner chamber sung always will be,
  As the shell ever sings of its home in the sea.
  "Home" *n.d.*

905. Caroline Sheridan Norton (1808–1877)

1 God made all pleasures innocent.
  Pt. I, *The Lady of LaGaraye 1862*

2 They serve God well, who serve his creatures.
  Conclusion, Ibid.

3 O Friend, I fear the lightest heart makes sometimes heaviest mourning.
  "Bingen on the Rhine," St. 1 *1883*

4 A soldier of the legion lay dying in Algiers—
  there was a lack of woman's nursing,
  There was a dearth of woman's tears.
  Ibid.

5 Love not! Love not! Ye hapless sons of clay;
  Hope's gayest wreaths are made of earthly flowers—
  Things that are made to fade and fall away,
  Ere they have blossomed for a few short years.
  "Love Not" *n.d.*

6 The stranger hath thy bridle-rein, thy master hath his gold;—
  Fleet limbed and beautiful, farewell; thou'rt sold, my steed, thou'rt sold.
  "The Arab's Farewell to His Steed" *n.d.*

906. Sophia Amelia Peabody Hawthorne (1809–1871)

1 Men's accidents are God's purposes.
  Inscribed on the window glass of her husband's study (1843), *The American Notebooks*, Claude M. Simpson, ed. *1932*

2 How pleasant it is to see a human countenance which cannot be insincere!*
  13 October 1851, Ibid.

  *Re the face of her baby.

907. Jenny P. d'Hericourt (1809–1875)

1 To emancipate woman is not to acknowledge her right to use and abuse love; such an emancipation is only the slavery of the passions; the use of the beauty and youth of woman by man; the use of man by woman for his fortune or credit.

  To emancipate woman is to acknowledge and declare her free, the equal of man in the social and the moral law, and in labor.
  Preface, *A Woman's Philosophy of Woman; or Woman Affranchised 1864*

2 In marriage, woman is a serf.
  In public instructions, she is sacrificed.
  In labor, she is made inferior.
  Civilly, she is a minor.
  Politically, she has no existence.
  She is the equal of man only when punishment and the payment of taxes are in question.
  I claim the rights of woman, because it is time to make the nineteenth century ashamed of its culpable denial of justice to half the human species . . .
  Ibid.

3 You tell the child that lies, "it is wrong to deceive; you would not wish others to deceive you."
  You tell the child that pilfers, "it is wrong to steal; you would not wish others to steal from you."
  You tell the child that takes advantage of his strength and knowledge to torment his younger companion, "you would not wish others to do these things to you; you are wicked and cowardly."
  These are good lessons. Why then, when the child has become a young man, do you say: *Young men must sow their wild oats?*
  To sow their wild oats is to deceive young girls, to destroy their future, to practice adultery, to keep mistresses, to visit brothels.
  Yet mothers, women thus consent to the profanation of their sex!
  Ch. 6, "Love; Its Functions in Humanity," I, Ibid.

4 MOTHER. You know, my children, that humanity advances only by forming itself an ideal and endeavoring to realize it. Every passion has its ideal, which, is modified by that of the whole.
  III, Ibid.

908. Fanny Kemble (1809–1893)

1 . . . children are made of eyes and ears, and nothing, however minute, escapes their microscopic observation.

Journal of a Residence on a Georgian Plantation in 1838–1839, John Scott, ed. *1961*

2 Just in proportion as I have found the slaves on this plantation intellectual and advanced beyond the general brutish level of the majority, I have observed this pathetic expression of countenance in them, a mixture of sadness and fear, the involuntary exhibition of the two feelings, which I suppose must be the predominant experience of their whole loves, regret and apprehension. . . .

Ibid.

3 This is no place for me, since I was not born among slaves, and cannot bear to live among them.

Ibid.

4 Nature lay frozen dead,—and still and slow,
A winding sheet fell o'er her body fair,
Flakey and soft, from his wide wings of snow.

"Winter" *n.d.*

5 Better trust all and be deceived,
And weep that trust, and that deceiving,
Than doubt one heart that, if believed,
Had blessed one's life with true believing.

"Faith" *n.d.*

909. Mrs. R. Addison (fl. ca. 1810)

1 Why is the Ass so stubborn grown!
How many mount and then are thrown!
Oh say! that men forget, alas!
Their Saviour rode upon an Ass.

"Written for a School-piece," St. 1, *Poetry on Different Subjects n.d.*

910. Margaret Fuller (1810–1850)

1 And knowing that there exists, in the world of men, a tone of feeling towards women as towards slaves, such as is expressed in the common phrase, "Tell that to women and children." . . .

"The Great Lawsuit. Man Versus Men. Woman Versus Women," *The Dial July 1843*

2 The well-instructed moon flies not from her orbit to seize on the glories of her partner.

Ibid.

3 The especial genius of women I believe to be electrical in movement, intuitive in function, spiritual in tendency.

Ibid.

4 Male and female represent the two sides of the great radical dualism. But, in fact, they are perpetually passing into one another. Fluid hardens to solid, solid rushes to fluid. There is no wholly masculine man, no purely feminine woman.

Ibid.

5 George Sand* smokes, wears male attire, wishes to be addressed as Mon frère; perhaps, if she found those who were as brothers indeed, she would not care whether she were a brother or sister.

Ibid.

*See 887.

6 "You are not the head of your wife. God has given her a mind of her own."
"I am the head and she is the heart."
"God grant you play true to one another then."

Ibid.

7 It is a vulgar error that love, *a* love, to woman is her whole existence; she is also born for Truth and Love in their universal energy.

Ibid.

8 What woman needs is not as a woman to act or rule, but as a nature to grow, as an intellect to discern, as a soul to live freely and unimpeded, to unfold such powers as were given her when we left our common home.

Woman in the 19th Century 1845

9 It does not follow because many books are written by persons born in America that there exists an American literature. . . . Before such can exist, an original idea must animate this nation and fresh currents of life must call into life fresh thoughts along its shores.

Quoted in the *New York Tribune 1846*

10 Truth is the nursing mother of genius.

Ibid.

11 . . . the public must learn how to cherish the nobler and rarer plants, and to plant the aloe, able to wait a hundred years for its bloom, or its garden will contain, presently, nothing but potatoes and pot-herbs.

Ibid.

12 The soul of the great musician can only be expressed in music. . . . We must read them in their works; this, true of artists in every department, is especially so of the high priestesses of sound.

"Lives of the Great Composers," *Art, Literature and the Drama 1858*

13 This was one of the rye-bread days, all dull and damp without.

Ch. 7, Diary Entry, Quoted in *Life of Margaret Fuller-Ossoli* by Thomas Wentworth Higginson,* ed. *1884*
*American author and editor (1823–1922).

14 Genius will live and thrive without training, but it does not the less reward the watering-pot and pruning-knife.

Diary entry, Ibid.

15 It is so true that a woman may be in love with a woman, and a man with a man. It is pleasant to be sure of it, because it is undoubtedly the same love that we shall feel when we are angels, when we ascend to the only fit place for the Mignons, where *sie fragen nicht nach Mann und Weib* [they ask not about men and women].

Quoted in *Margaret Fuller, Whetstone of Genius* by Mason Wade *1940*

16 I myself am more divine than any I see.

Letter to Emerson* (1 March 1838, Quoted in *The Feminist Papers* by Alice Rossi** *1973*
* Ralph Waldo E-, American writer, poet, philosopher, and central figure of American transcendentalism (1803–1882). **See 2439.

17 What a difference it makes to come home to a child!

Letter to friends (1849), Ibid.

911. Elizabeth Gaskell (1810–1865)

1   What's the use of watching? A watched pot never boils.

>Ch. 31, *Mary Barton 1848*

2   A man. . . is *so* in the way in the house!

>Ch. 1, *Cranford 1851–53*

3   There, economy was always "elegant," and money-spending always "vulgar," and ostentatious—a sort of sour grapeism, which made us very peaceful and satisfied.

>Ibid.

4   One gives people in grief their own way.

>Ch. 6, Ibid.

5   I'll not listen to reason. . . . Reason always means what someone else has got to say.

>Ch. 14, Ibid.

6   A wise parent humours the desire for independent action, so as to become the friend and advisor when his absolute rule shall cease.

>Ch. 15, *North and South 1855*

7   To be sure a stepmother to a girl is a different thing to a second wife to a man!

>Ch. 6, *Wives and Daughters 1866*

8   People may flatter themselves just as much by thinking that their faults are always present to other people's minds, as if they believe that the world is always contemplating their individual charms and virtues.

>Ch. 50, Ibid.

9   Sometimes one likes foolish people for their folly, better than wise people for their wisdom.

>Ch. 54, Ibid.

912. Mrs. Henry Rolls (fl. ca. 1810–d. 1825)

1   Whence is that sad, that transient smile
That dawns upon the lip of owe;
That checks the deep-drawn sigh awhile,
And stays the tear that starts to flow?
'Tis but a veil cast o'er the heart,
When youth's gay dreams have pass'd away
When joy's faint lingering rays depart,
And the last gleams of hope decay!

>"Smiles," Sts. 7–8, *The Female Poets of Great Britain*, Frederic Rowton, ed. *1853*

913. Ernestine Rose (1810–1892)

1   Oh, she [Frances Wright]* had her reward!—that reward of which no enemies could deprive her, which no slanders could make less precious—the eternal reward of knowing that she had done her duty; the reward of springing from the consciousness of right, of endeavoring to benefit unborn generations.

>Convention Speech, "Petitions Were Circulated" (1860), *History of Woman Suffrage*, Vol. I by Elizabeth Cady Stanton,** Susan B. Anthony,*** and Mathilda Gage****
>*1881*

*See 850; **see 931; ***see 963; ****see 1007.

2   I was a rebel at the age of five.

>American Jewish Historical Society (ajhs.org) 2003

3   Emancipation from every kind of bondage is my principle.

>Ibid.

914. Fanny Fern (1811–1872)

1   The way to a man's heart is through his stomach.

>"Willis Parton" *n.d.*

915. Frances Sargent Osgood (1811–1850)

1   And now with flashing eyes she springs,—
Her whole bright figure raised in air,
As if her soul had spread its wings
And poised her one wild instant there!

>"A Dancing Girl," St. 5, *An American Anthology, 1787–1900,* Edmund Clarence Stedman, ed., *1900*

2   The hand that swept the sounding lyre
With more than mortal skill,
The lightning eye, the heart of fire,
The fervent lip are still!

>Ibid., "On a Dead Poet," St. 1

3   Work—for some good, be it ever so slowly;
Cherish some flower, be it ever so lowly;
Labor!—all labor is noble and holy!
Let thy great deeds be thy prayer to thy god!

>*"Laborare Est Orare,"* St. 6 *n.d.*

916. Harriet Beecher Stowe (1811–1896)

1   "Well, I've got just as much conscience as any man in business can afford to keep—just a little, you know, to swear by as 't were. . . . "

>Ch. 1, *Uncle Tom's Cabin 1852*

2   "I b'lieve in religion, and one of these days, when I've got matters tight and snug, I calculate to 'tend to my soul, and them are matters: . . ."

>Ch. 8, Ibid.

3   "Treat 'em like dogs, and you'll have dogs' works and dogs' actions. Treat 'em like men, and you'll have men's works."

>Ch. 11, Ibid.

4   "Cause I's wicked—I is. I's mighty wicked, any how. I can't help it."

>Ch. 20, Ibid.

5   "Who was your mother?"
"Never had none!" said the child, with another grin.
"Never had any mother? What do you mean? Where were you born?"
"Never was born!" persisted Topsy. . . .
"Do you know who made you?"
"Nobody, as I knows on," said the child with a short laugh . . . "I 'spect I grow'd. Don't think nobody never made me."

>Ibid.

6   Whipping and abuse are like laudanum: You have to double the dose as the sensibilities decline.

>Ibid.

7   Who can speak the blessedness of that first day of freedom? Is not the sense of liberty a higher and finer one than any of the five? To move, speak, and breathe, go out and come in, unwatched and free from danger! Who can speak the blessings of that rest which comes down on the free man's pillow, under laws which ensure to him the rights that God has given to man?

>Ch. 37, Ibid.

8 No one is so thoroughly superstitious as the godless man.

Ch. 39, Ibid.

9 He declared that the gold made in it [slavery] was distilled from human blood, from mother's tears, from the agonies and dying groans of gasping, suffocating men and women, and that it would sear and blister the soul of him that touched it; in short, he talked as whole-souled, impractical fellows are apt to talk about what respectable people sometimes do. Nobody had ever instructed him that a slave-ship, with a procession of expectant sharks in its wake, is a missionary institution, by which closely-packed heathen are brought over to enjoy the light of the Gospel.

Ch. 1, *The Minister's Wooing 1859*

10 So we go, so little knowing what we touch and what touches us as we talk! We drop out a common piece of news, "Mr. So-and-so is dead, Miss Such-a-one is married, such a ship has sailed," and lo, on our right hand or on our left, some heart has sunk under the news silently—gone down in the great ocean of Fate, without even a bubble rising to tell its drowning pang. And this—God help us!—is what we call living!

Ch. 4, Ibid.

11 . . . women are the real architects of society.

"Dress, or Who Makes the Fashions?," *Atlantic Monthly* (Boston) *1864*

12 The pain of discipline is short, but the glory of the fruition is eternal.

"The Cathedral," Ibid.

13 Everyone confesses in the abstract that exertion which brings out all the powers of body and mind is the best thing for us all; but practically most people do all they can to get rid of it, and as a general rule nobody does much more than circumstances drive them to do.

"The Lady Who Does Her Own Work," Ibid.

14 "Take us the foxes, the little foxes, that spoil the vines: for our vines have tender grapes." . . . "Little Foxes," by which I mean those unsuspected, unwatched, insignificant *little* causes that nibble away domestic happiness, and make home less than so noble an institution should be. . . . The reason for this in general is that home is a place not only of strong affections, but of entire unreserve; it is life's undress rehearsal, its backroom, its dressing room, from which we go forth to more careful and guarded intercourse, leaving behind us much *debris* of cast-off and everyday clothing.

Ch. 1, *Little Foxes 1865*

15 Irritability is, more than most unlovely states, a sin of the flesh. . . . It is a state of nervous torture; and the attacks which the wretched victim makes on others are as much a result of disease as the snapping and biting of a patient convulsed with hydrophobia.

Ch. 2, Ibid.

16 The bitterest tears shed over graves are for words left unsaid and deeds left undone.

Ibid.

17 Every human being has some handle by which he may be lifted, some groove in which he was meant to run; and the great work of life, as far as our relations with each other are concerned, is to lift each one by his own proper handle, and run each one in his own proper groove.

Ch. 5, Ibid.

18 "For my part," said my wife, "I think one of the greatest destroyers of domestic peace is Discourtesy. People neglect, with their nearest friends, those refinements and civilities which they practice with strangers."

Ch. 6, Ibid.

19 One must be very much of a woman for whom a man can sacrifice the deepest purpose of his life without awakening to regret it.

Ch. 2, *Old Town Folks 1869*

20 The burning of rebellious thoughts in the little breast, of internal hatred and opposition, could not long go on without slight whiffs of external smoke, such as mark the course of subterranean fire.

Ch. 11, Ibid.

917. Sarah Boyle (1812–1869)

1 Here I come creeping, creeping everywhere. . . .

"The Voice of Grass" *n.d.*

918. Sarah Ellis (1812–1872)

1 To act the part of a true friend requires more conscientious feeling than to fill with credit and complacency any other station or capacity in social life.

Ch. 4, *Pictures of Private Life 1834*

919. Geraldine Jewsbury (1812–1880)

1 People who are called to suffer much have always great elasticity of heart, for without that it must give way and break.

Ch. I, *The Half Sisters,* 1848

2 He kept up a true Englishman's silence, and endeavoured to turn his share of the room into his castle, by surrounding himself with an impassable moat of stiffness and reserve.

Ibid., Ch. II

3 I wish that I had a good husband and a dozen children! Only the difficulty is that "women of genius" require very special husbands—men of noble character, not intellect, but of a character and nature large enough, and strong enough, and wise enough to take them and their genius too, without cutting them down to suit their own crochets, or reprobating half their qualities because they don't know what to do with them, or what they are intended for.

*Selections from the Letters of Geraldine E. Jewsbury to Jane Welsh Carlyle,** Mrs. Alexander Ireland, ed. *1892*
*See 869.

920. Emily Nonnen (1812–1905)

1 The art of sculpture is way above the art of painting!

Quoted by Barbro Hedstrom,* *n.d.*
*See 3420.

921. Ann Preston (1813–1872)

1 Wherever it is proper to introduce women as patients, there also it is in accordance with the instinct of truest womanhood for women to appear as physicians and students.

Quoted in *The Liberated Woman's Appointment Calendar,* Lynn Sherr and Jurate Kazickas, eds. *1975*

922. Ellen Wood (1813–1887)

1 Petty ills try the temper worse than great ones.

Ch. 1, *East Lynne* (novel) *1861*

2 Years ago, by dint of looking things steady in the face, and by economizing, he might have retrieved his position; but he had done what most people do in such cases—put off the evil day *sine die*, and gone on increasing his enormous list of debts. The hour of exposure and ruin was now advancing fast.

Ibid.

3 When folks act childishly, they must be treated as children.

Ch. 37, Ibid.

4 LEVISON. But there are moments when our hearts' dearest feelings break through the conventionalities of life, and betray themselves in spite of our sober judgement.

Act II, Sc. 1, *East Lynne* (play) *1862*

5 Things often seem to go by the rule of contrary.

Ch. 8, *The Channings*, Vol. I *1862*

6 Life has become to the most of us one swift, headlong race—a continuous fight in which there is so much to do that the half of it has to be left undone. It is not so much what we have done amiss, as what we have left undone, that will trouble us, looking back.

Our Children 1876

7 We are truly indefatigable in providing for the needs of the body, but we starve the soul.

Ch. 1, *About Ourselves 1883*

923. Esther Hobart Morris (1814–1902)

1 Justice first, then after that the law.

Quoted in *The 50 Most Influential Women in American Law* by Dawn Bradley Berry* *1996*

*See 4399.

2 I have assisted in drawing a grand and petit jury, deposited a ballot, and helped canvass the voters after the electing, and in performing all those duties I do not know as I have neglected my family any more than in ordinary shopping.

Quoted in the *Laramie Sentinel* (1871), Ibid.

924–925. Fátimih Baraghání Táhirih (1814/17–1852)

1 With you who condemn both love and wine
for the hermit's cell and the zealot's shrine,
What can I do?

"Tahirih the Pure," Martha Root, tr. *n.d.*

2 You can kill me as soon as you like, but you cannot stop the emancipation of women.

Last words before execution, Quoted in *Religion and Women* Susan Maneck *1994*

926. Anne Botta (1815–1891)

1 The honey-bee that wanders all day long . . .
Seeks not alone the rose's glowing breast,
The lily's dainty cup, the violet's lips,
But from all rank and noxious weed he sips
The single drop of sweetness closely pressed
Within the poison chalice.

"The Lesson of the Bee" *n.d.*

927. Julia Margaret Cameron (1815–1879)

1 I longed to arrest all beauty that came before me, and at length the longing has been satisfied.

Annals of My Glass House 1874

928. Eliza Farnham (1815–1864)

1 Our own theological Church, as we know, has scorned and vilified the body till it has seemed almost a reproach and a shame to have one, yet at the same time has credited it with power to drag the soul to perdition.

Pt. I, Ch. 1, *Woman and Her Era 1864*

2 The ultimate aim of the human mind, in all its efforts, is to become acquainted with Truth.

Ibid.

3 Each of the Arts whose office it is to refine, purify, adorn, embellish, and grace life is under the patronage of a Muse, no god being found worthy to preside over them.

Pt. II, Ch. 1, Ibid.

929. Ada Byron King, Countess of Lovelace (1815–1852)

1 [The Analytical Engine is suited for] developing [sic] and tabulating any function whatever . . . the engine [is] the material expression of any indefinite function of any degree of generality and complexity.

The Calculating Passion of Ada Byron by Joan Baum *1986*

2 The Analytical Engine has no pretensions whatever to originate anything. It can do whatever we know how to order it to perform. It can follow analysis; but it has no power of anticipating any analytical relations or truths.

Ibid.

3 If you can't give me poetry, can't you give me "poetical science?"

Letter to her mother, Lady Byron (ca. 1845), Quoted in *Ada, The Enchantress of Numbers* by Betty Alexandra Toole *1998*

930. Elizabeth Phelps (1815–1852)

1 She found out there was no doctor for her like Dr. "Have-To."

"What Sent One Husband to California," *The Tell-Tale 1853*

2 "You gentleman," said she, "have such odd ideas of *housecleaning*! You imagine you can do it up just as you buy and sell—so much labor for so much money. Now, the fact is, the simple labor is the easiest part of it. It is the getting ready for labor—contriving, planning, arranging—that is so wearisome."

"The Old Leather Portfolio," Ibid.

3 Put in *your* oar, and share the sweat of the brow with which you must both start up the stream. You will richly enjoy the rest when you reach the harbor.

"First Trials of a Young Physician," Ibid.

931. Elizabeth Cady Stanton (1815–1902)

1 We ask no better laws than those you have made for yourselves. We need no other protection than that which your present laws secure to you.

Speech, NY State Legislature *1854*

2 In a republic where all are declared equal an ostracised class of half of the people, on the ground of a distinction founded in nature, is an anomalous position, as harassing to its victims as it is unjust, and as contradictory as it is unsafe to the fundamental principles of a free government.

History of Woman Suffrage, Vol. 1, Susan B. Anthony* and
Mathilda Gage,** coauthors *1881*

*See 963. **See 1007.

3 The mind always in contact with children and servants, whose aspirations and ambitions rise no higher than the roof that shelters it, is necessarily dwarfed in its proportions.

Ibid.

4 . . . the woman is uniformly sacrificed to the wife and mother.

Ibid.

5 The more complete the despotism, the more smoothly all things move on the surface.

Ibid.

6 *Declaration of Sentiments.* Now, in view of this entire disfranchisement of half the people of this country, through social and religious degradation—in view of the unjust laws above mentioned, and because women do feel themselves aggrieved, oppressed, and fraudulently deprived of their most sacred rights, we insist that they have immediate admission to all the rights and privileges which belong to them as citizens of the United States.

Ibid.

7 *Declaration of Sentiments: Resolved,* That the same amount of virtue, delicacy, and refinement of behavior that is required of woman in the social station, should also be required of man, and the same transgressions should be visited with equal severity on both man and woman.

Ibid.

8 *Declaration of Sentiments:* . . . We hold these truths to be self-evident: that all men and women are created equal. . . .

Ibid.

9 Two pure souls fused into one by an impassioned love—friends, counselors—a mutual support and inspiration to each other amid life's struggles, must know the highest human happiness;—this is marriage; and this is the only corner-stone of an enduring home.

Ibid.

10 They who give the world a true philosophy, a grand poem, a beautiful painting or statue, or can tell the story of every wandering star . . . have lived to a holier purpose than they whose children are of the flesh alone, into whose minds they have breathed no clear perceptions of great principles, no moral aspiration, no spiritual life.

Ibid.

11 Modern inventions have banished the spinning-wheel, and the same law of progress makes the woman of to-day a different woman from her grandmother.

Ibid.

12 But standing alone we learned our power; we repudiated man's counsels forevermore; and solemnly vowed that there should never be another season of silence until we had the same rights everywhere on this green earth, as man.

Ibid.

13 The prolonged slavery of women is the darkest page in human history.

Ibid.

14 The queens in history compare favorably with the kings.

Ibid.

15 . . . there is no force in the plea, that "if women vote they must fight." Moreover, war is not the normal state of the human family in its higher development, but merely a feature of barbarism lasting on through the transition of the race, from the savage to the scholar.

Ibid.

16 Reformers can be as bigoted and sectarian and as ready to malign each other, as the Church in its darkest periods has been to persecute its dissenters.

"The Kansas Campaign of 1867," Ibid.

17 So long as tens of thousands of Bibles are printed every year, and circulated over the whole habitable globe, and the masses in all English-speaking nations revere it as the word of God, it is vain to belittle its influence.

Pt. I, Ibid.

18 Why is it more ridiculous to arraign ecclesiastics for their false teaching and acts of injustice to women, than members of Congress and the House of Commons?

Ibid.

19 For so far-reaching and momentous a reform as her complete independence, an entire revolution in all existing institutions is inevitable.

Ibid.

20 The Bible and Church have been the greatest stumbling blocks in the way of woman's emancipation.

Quoted in *Free Thought Magazine September 1896*

21 Though motherhood is the most important of all the professions—requiring more knowledge than any other department in human affairs—there was no attention given to preparation for this office.

Eighty Years and More, rev. ed. *1902*

22 I am at a boiling point! If I do not find someday the use of my tongue on this question I shall die of an intellectual repression, a woman's rights convulsion.

Elizabeth Cady Stanton, Vol. II, Theodore Stanton and Harriot
Stanton Blatch, eds. *1922*

23 The custom of calling women Mrs. John This and Mrs. Tom That, and colored men Sambo and Zip Coon, is founded on the principle that white men are lords of all. I cannot acknowledge this principle as just; therefore, I cannot bear the name of another.

Letter to Rebecca R. Eyster (1 May 1847), Ibid.

24 I have no sympathy with the old idea that children owe such immense gratitude to their parents that they can never fulfill their obligations to them. I think the obligation is all on the other side. Parents can never do too much for their children to repay them for the injustice of having brought them into the world, unless they have insured them high moral and intellectual gifts, fine physical health, and enough money and education to render life something more than one ceaseless struggle for necessities.

Diary entry (1880), Ibid.

25 I asked them why . . . one read in the synagogue service every week the 'I thank thee, O lord, that I was not born a woman.' " . . . It is not meant in an unfriendly spirit, and it is not intended to degrade or humiliate women." "But it does, nevertheless. Suppose the service read, 'I thank thee, O Lord, that I was not born into a jackass.' Could that be twisted in any way into a compliment to the jackass?"

Diary entry (1895), Ibid.

26 Men as a general rule have very little reverence for trees.

Diary entry (1900), Ibid.

27 We who like the children of Israel have been wandering in the wilderness of prejudice and ridicule for forty years feel a particular tenderness for the young women on whose shoulders we are about to leave our burdens.

Speech, International Council of Women (1888), *Feminism: The Essential Historical Writings*, Miriam Schneir,*ed. *1972*
*See 2864.

28 In writing, we did better work together than either could alone. . . . She* supplied the facts and statistics, I the philosophy and rhetoric . . .

Quoted in *Women Suffragists* by Diana Star Helmer *1998*
*Reference to Susan B. Anthony; see 963.

29 . . . one of the best gifts of the gods . . . a good, faithful housekeeper . . . But for this noble, self-sacrificing woman,* much of my public work would have been quite impossible.

Ibid.

*Amelia Willard, who worked for the Stantons for 31 years.

30 I get more radical as I grow older, while [Susan*] seems to get more conservative.

Ibid.

*S—B. Anthony; see 963.

31 *Response to clergyman's accusation that "The Woman's Bible" is "the work of women and the devil":* This is a grave mistake. His satanic majesty was not to join the Revising Committee which consists of women alone. Moreover, he has been so busy of late years attending Synods, General Assemblies and Conferences, to prevent the recognition of women delegates, that he has no time to study the languages and "higher criticism."

Remark to reporter, Quoted in *In Memory of Her* by Elisabeth Schüssler Fiorenza* *1994*
*See 3086.

932. Grace Aguilar (1816–1847)

1 We must not remain Hebrews only because our fathers were.

Ch. 1, *The Spirit of Judaism 1842*

2 "Hear, O Israel! The Lord our God, the Lord is One!" Such is the literal translation of the Hebrew, *sh'ma yisrael adonai elohaynu, adonai ekad,* but it is impossible to give the full force of the Hebrew by English words. . . . It is the avowal of belief, belief in the unparalleled, unchanging, incomprehensible unity of God, the repetition and acknowledgment of which marks us as His chosen people,—His redeemed, His beloved, His firstborn,—that separates us from every other nation, every other religion of the world.

Ibid.

3 For prayer is the language of the heart,—needing no measured voice, no spoken tone . . .

Ibid.

933. Mary Dow Brine (1816–1913)

1 She's somebody's mother, boys, you know,
For all she's aged, and poor, and slow.

"Somebody's Mother," St. 15, *Harper's Weekly* 2 March 1878

934. Charlotte Brontë (1816–1855)

1 Vain favour! coming, like most other favours long deferred and often wished for, too late!

Ch. 3, *Jane Eyre 1847*

2 It is in vain to say human beings ought to be satisfied with tranquility: they must have action; and they will make it if they cannot find it.

Ch. 12, Ibid.

3 "Dread remorse when you are tempted to err, Miss Eyre: remorse is the poison of life."

Ch. 14, Ibid.

4 "I grant an ugly *woman* is a blot on the fair face of creation; but as to the *gentlemen,* let them be solicitous to possess only strength and valour: let their motto be:—Hunt, shoot, and fight: the rest is not worth a fillip."

Ch. 17, Ibid.

5 "Reason sits firm and holds the reins, and she will not let the feelings burst away and hurry her to wild chasms. The passions may rage furiously, like true heathens, as they are; and the desires may imagine all sorts of vain things, but judgment shall still have the last word in every argument, and the casting vote in every decision."

Ch. 19, Ibid.

6 Feeling without judgment is a washy draught indeed; but judgment untempered by feeling is too bitter and husky a morsel for human deglutition *[sic]*.

Ch. 21, Ibid.

7 "Laws and principles are not for the times when there is no temptation: they are for such moments as this, when body and soul rise in mutiny against their rigour; stringent are they; inviolate they shall be. If at my individual convenience I might break them, what would be their worth?"

Ch. 28, Ibid.

8 One does not jump, and spring, and shout hurrah! at hearing one has got a fortune, one begins to consider responsibilities, and to ponder business; on a base of steady satisfaction rise certain grave cares, and we contain ourselves, and brood over our bliss with a solemn brow.

Ch. 33, Ibid.

9 Reader, I married him.

Ch. 38, Ibid.

10 Prejudices, it is well known, are most difficult to eradicate from the heart whose soil has never been loosened or fertilized by education; they grow there, firm as weeds among stones.

Ibid.

11 Give him rope enough and he will hang himself.

Ch. 3, *Shirley 1849*

12 Look twice before you leap.

Ch. 9, Ibid.

13 Yes—there is no Emily in Time or on Earth now—yesterday—we put her poor, wasted mortal frame quietly under the Church pavement. . . . —we feel she is at peace—no need now to tremble for the hard frost and keen wind—Emily does not feel them. She has died in a time of promise—we saw her taken from life in its prime—but it is God's will and the place where she is gone is better than that she has left.*

> Letter to her friend, Ellen Nussey (23 December 1848),
> Quoted in *The Brontës: A Life in Letters* by Juliet Barker *1998*
> *Her sister Emily Brontë; see 945.

935. Frances Brown (1816–1879)

1 It was the richest city in all the land; merchants from every quarter came there to buy and sell, and there was a saying that people had only to live seven years in it to make their fortunes. Rich as they were, however, Snowflower thought she had never seen so many discontented, covetous faces as looked out from the great shops, grand houses, and fine coaches . . .

> Ch. 1, *Granny's Wonderful Chair 1857*

2 Oh! those blessed times of old! with their chivalry and state;
I love to read their chronicles, which such brave deeds relate. . . .

> "Oh! The Pleasant Days of Old," St. 7 *n.d.*

936. Charlotte Saunders Cushman (1816–1876)

1 To me it seems as if when God conceived the world, that was Poetry; He formed it, and that was Sculpture; He colored it, and that was Painting, He peopled it with living beings, and that was the grand, divine, eternal Drama.

> Quoted in *Charlotte Cushman* by Emma Stebbins *1879*

2 Art is an absolute mistress; she will not be coquetted with or slighted; she requires the most entire self-devotion, and she repays with grand triumphs.

> Ch. 10, Ibid.

3 There is a God! The sky his presence snares,
His hand upheaves the billows in their mirth,
Destroys the mighty, yet the humble spares
And with contentment crowns the thought of worth.

> "There Is a God" *n.d.*

937. Ellen Sturgis Hooper (1816–1841)

1 I slept, and dreamed that life was Beauty;
I woke, and found that life was Duty.

> "Beauty and Duty" *n.d.*

2 The straightest path perhaps which may be sought,
Lies through the great highway men call "I ought."

> "The Straight Road" *n.d.*

938. Eliza "Mother" Stewart (1816–1908)

1 No power on earth or above the bottomless pit has such influence to terrorize and make cowards of men as the liquor power. Satan could not have fallen on a more potent instrument with which to thrall the world. Alcohol is king!

> Ch. 1, *Memories of the Crusade 1888*

2 But you must know the class of sweet women—who are always so happy to declare "they have all the rights they want"; "they are perfectly willing to let their husbands vote for them"—are and always have been numerous, though it is an occasion for thankfulness that they are becoming less so.

> Ch. 7, Ibid.

939. Priscilla Cooper Tyler (1816–1889)

1 I am considered "charmante" by the Frenchmen, "lovely" by the Americans and "really quite nice, you know" by the English.

> Letter, Quoted in *First Ladies* by Betty Boyd Caroli *1987*

940. Malwida von Meysenbug (1816–1903)

1 'I know that the example of a single person is almost lost amidst the masses . . .

> (1850), p. 21, *A Journey to Ostend*, Beth Muellner, tr. *1905*

2 I travel third-class on principle, firstly because I feel better and more secure being closer to 'the people', those I want to belong to entirely, because my heart belongs to them, rather than in often very dubious proximity to people in the first class; but then it also angers me that the strict hierarchy of the old order has been transferred on to the democratic institution of the railway . . . that here too the propertied classes have such enormous privilege and enjoy every luxury, while the poor and needy are deprived of such.

> (1850), p. 21–22, Ibid.

3 I don't know if many of my sisters share my taste, but with regard to the present safety of travel, even for single women, there is a rare delight in this independence, for one has a sense of strong, compelling inner dignity. And no way of travelling increases this delight as much as the railway . . .

> (1850), p. 291, Ibid.

941. Jane Montgomery Campbell (1817–1879)

1 We plough the fields and scatter
The good seed on the land,
But it is fed and watered
By God's Almighty hand.

> "We Plough the Fields," *Garland of Songs n.d.*

942. Tahereh Ghoratolain (1817–1853)

1 I am a proud woman, a follower of logic and wisdom

> Untitled, *n.d.*

943. Mrs. Cecil Frances Alexander (1818–1895)

1 All things bright and beautiful,
All creatures great and small,
All things wise and wonderful,
The Lord God made them all.

> "All Things Bright" *n.d.*

2 The rich man at his castle,
The poor man at his gate,
God made them, high and lowly,
And ordered their estate.

> Ibid.

944. Amelia Jenks Bloomer (1818–1894)

1 Another cannot make fit to eat without wine or brandy. A third must have brandy on her apple dumplings, and a fourth comes out boldly and says she likes to drink once in a while too well. What flimsy excuses these! brandy and apple dumplings forsooth! That lady must be a wretched cook indeed who cannot make apple dumplings, mince pie, or cake palatable without the addition of poisonous substances.

> *Water Bucket 1842*

2 Ah, how steadily do they who are guilty shrink from reproof!
The Lily 1 January 1849

3 The costume of women should be suited to her wants and necessities. It should conduce at once to her health, comfort, and usefulness; and, while it should not fail also to conduce to her personal adornment, it should make that end of secondary importance.
Letter to Charlotte A. Joy 3 June 1857

4 Every woman who is tied to a confirmed drunkard should sunder the ties, and if she do it not otherwise, the law should compel it, especially if she has children.
Speech, Woman's State Temperance Society Convention (Rochester, New York, Spring 1852), Quoted in *Women Suffragists* by Diana Star Helmer *1998*

5 Adam first, then Eve, they say. To this we reply: Animals first—then Adam.
Speech, Ibid.

6 Stitch! Stitch! Stitch!
in poverty, hunger and dirt—
sewing at once with a double thread
a shroud as well as a shirt.
Song, sung during speech, Ibid.

7 Alas! Poor Adam! While it required all the persuasive powers and eloquence of the subtle tempter, all the promises of wisdom and knowledge and power to seduce the so-called "weaker" vessel from the right path, all that was necessary to secure *his* downfall was simply to offer him the apple.
Speech, Ibid.

945. Emily Brontë (1818–1848)

1 Vain are the thousand creeds
That move men's hearts: unutterably vain. . . .
"Last Lines," *Poems by Currer, Ellis, and Acton Bell** *1846*
*Pseudonyms of Charlotte B— (see 934), Emily B—, and Anne B— (see 965).

2 There is not room for Death.
Ibid.

3 Oh! dreadful is the check—intense the agony—
When the ear begins to hear, and the eye begins to see;
When the pulse begins to throb, the brain to think again;
The soul to feel the flesh, and the flesh to feel the chain.
"The Prisoner" *1846*

4 I'll walk where my own nature would be leading—
It vexes me to choose another guide. . . .
"Often Rebuked" *1846*

5 Love is like the wild-rose briar;
Friendship like the holly-tree.
The holly is dark when the rose-briar blooms,
But which will bloom most constantly?
"Love and Friendship" *1846*

6 I've dreamt in my life dreams that have stayed with me ever after, and changed my ideas . . . and altered the color of my mind.
Wuthering Heights 1847

7 "I am now quite cured of seeking pleasure in society, be it country or town. A sensible man ought to find sufficient company in himself."
Ch. 3, Ibid.

8 "A person who has not done one half his day's work by ten o'clock, runs a chance of leaving the other half undone."
Ch. 7, Ibid.

9 "My love for Linton is like the foliage in the woods: time will change it, I'm well aware, as winter changes the trees. My love for Heathcliff resembles the eternal rocks beneath: a source of little visible delight, but necessary. Nelly, I *am* Heathcliff!"
Ch. 9, Ibid.

10 Having levelled my palace, don't erect a hovel and complacently admire your own charity in giving me that for a home.
Ch. 11, Ibid.

11 The tyrant grinds down his slaves and they don't turn against him, they crush those beneath them.
Ibid.

12 Any relic of the dead is precious, if they were valued living.
Ch. 13, Ibid.

13 I lingered round them [tombstones], under that benign sky: watched the moths fluttering among the heath and harebells; listened to the soft wind breathing through the grass; and wondered how anyone could ever imagine unquiet slumbers for the sleepers in that quiet earth.
Conclusion, Ibid.

946. Emily Collins (1818?–1879?)

1 It is ever thus; where Theology enchains the soul, the Tyrant enslaves the body.
Quoted in "Reminiscences of Emily Collins," *History of Woman Suffrage*, Vol. I, by Elizabeth Cady Stanton,* Susan B. Anthony,** and Mathilda Gage*** *1881*
*See 931. **See 963. ***See 1007.

2 Every argument for the emancipation of the colored man was equally one for that of women; and I was surprised that all Abolitionists did not see the similarity in the condition of the two classes.
Ibid.

3 From press, and pulpit, and platform, she was taught that "to be unknown was her highest praise," that "dependence was her best protection," and "her weakness her sweetest charm."
Ibid.

4 . . . from the earliest dawn of reason I pined for that freedom of thought and action that was then denied to all womankind. I revolted in spirit against the customs of society and the laws of the State that crushed my aspirations and debarred me from the pursuit of almost every object worthy of an intelligent, rational mind.
Ibid.

5 Moral Reform and Temperance Societies may be multiplied *ad infinitum,* but they have about the same effect upon the evils they seek to cure as clipping the top of a hedge would have toward extirpating it.
Letter to Sarah C. Owen (23 October 1848), Ibid.

947. Eliza Cook (1818–1889)

1 Better build schoolrooms for "the boy,"
Than cells and gibbets for "the man."
"A Song for the Ragged Schools," St. 12 *n.d.*

2 Oh! much may be done by defying
The ghosts of Despair and Dismay;
And much may be gained by relying
On "Where there's a will there's a way."
"Where There's a Will There's a Way," St. 4 *n.d.*

3 'Tis well to give honour and glory to Age,
With its lessons of wisdom and truth;
Yet who would not go back to the fanciful page,
And the fairytale read but in youth?
"Stanzas" *n.d.*

4 Whom do we dub as Gentleman? The
Knave, the fool, the brute—
If they but own full tithe of gold, and
Wear a courtly suit.
"Nature's Gentleman," St. 1 *n.d.*

5 Who would not rather trust and be deceived?
"Love On," St. 16 *n.d.*

6 On what strange stuff Ambition feeds!
"Thomas Hood"* *n.d.*

*British poet and editor (1799–1845).

7 Oh! Better, then, to die and give
The grave its kindred dust,
Than live to see Time's bitter change
In those we love and trust.
"Time's Changes" *n.d.*

948. Mary A. E. Green (1818?–1895)

1 Of all the royal daughters of England who, by the weight of personal character, or the influence of advantageous circumstances, had exercised a permanent bearing on its destiny, few have occupied so prominent a place as Elizabeth, queen of Bohemia, the high-minded but ill-fated daughter of James I.
Ch. I, *Elizabeth, Queen of Bohemia* 1855

949. Harriet Brent Jacobs (1818–1896)

1 It seems less degrading to give one's self, than to submit to compulsion. There is something akin to freedom in having a lover who has no control over you, except that which he gains by kindness and attachment.
Incidents in the Life of a Slave Girl, Lydia Maria Child,* ed. *1861 (repr. 1973)*

*See 870.

2 You never knew what it is to be a slave; to be entirely unprotected by law or custom; to have the laws reduce you to the condition of a chattel, entirely subject to the will of another. You never exhausted your ingenuity in avoiding the snares, and eluding the power of a hated tyrant; you never shuddered at the sound of his footsteps, and trembled within hearing of his voice.
Ibid.

950. Mary Todd Lincoln (1818–1882)

1 The change from this gloomy earth, to be forever reunited to my idolized husband & my darling Willie, would be happiness indeed!
Letter to Mrs. Slataper (29 September 1868), *The Mary Lincoln Letters*, Justin G. Turner, ed. *1956*

2 I am convinced, the longer I live, that life & its blessings are not so entirely unjustly distributed [as] when we are suffering greatly, we are inclined to suppose. My home for so many years was so rich in love and happiness; now I am so lonely and isolated—whilst others live on in a careless lukewarm state—not appearing to fill Longfellow's* measure: "Into each life, some rain must fall."
Ibid.

*Henry Wadsworth L—American poet (1807–1882).

3 My evil genius Procrastination has whispered me to tarry 'til a more convenient season.
Letter (June 1841), *Mary Todd Lincoln: Her Life and Letters*, Justin G. Turner, ed. *1972*

4 My feelings & hopes are all so sanguine that in this dull world of reality 'tis best to dispell our delusive daydreams as soon as possible.
Letter to Mercy Levering (23 July 1840), Ibid.

5 Clouds and darkness surround us, yet Heaven is just & the day of triumph will *surely* come, when justice & truth will be vindicated. Our wrongs will be made right, & we will once more, taste the blessings of freedom, of which the degraded rebels, would deprive us.
Letter to James Gordon Bennet (October 25, 1861), Ibid.

951. Maria Mitchell (1818–1889)

1 Why can not a man act himself, be himself, and think for himself? It seems to me that naturalness alone is power; that a borrowed word is weaker than our own weakness, however small we may be.
Diary entry (1867), *Maria Mitchell, Life, Letters, and Journals*, Phoebe Mitchell Kendall, ed. *1896*

2 We travel to learn; and I have never been in any country where they did not do something better than we do it, think some thoughts better than we think, catch some inspiration from heights above our own.
Diary entry (July 1873), Ibid.

3 This ignorance of the masses leads to a misconception in two ways; the little that a scientist can do, they do not understand—they suppose him to be god-like in his capacity, and they do not see results; they overrate him and they underrate him—they underrate his work.
Diary entry (1874), Ibid.

4 . . . to-day I am ready to say, "Give no scholarships at all." I find a helping-hand lifts the girl as crutches do; she learns to like the help which is not self-help. If a girl has the public school, and wants enough to learn, she will learn. It is hard, but she was born to hardness—she cannot dodge it. Labor is her inheritance.
Diary entry (10 February 1887), Ibid.

5 . . . I do think, as a general rule, that teachers talk too much! A book is a very good institution! To read a book, to think it over, and to write our notes is a useful exercise; a book which will not repay some hard thought is not worth publishing.
Diary entry (July 1887), Ibid.

6 Every formula which expresses a law of nature is a hymn of praise to God.
Inscription on bust in the Hall of Fame, Bronx, N.Y. *1905*

7 The eye that directs the needle in the delicate meshes of embroidery will equally well bisect a star with the spider web of the micrometer . . .

Quoted in *4000 Years of Women in Science*, astr.ua.edu/ 4000WS *27 September 1997*

952. Elizabeth Prentiss (1818–1878)

1 How dreadfully old I am getting! Sixteen! Well, I don't see as I can help it. There it is in the big Bible in father's own hand: "Katherine, born Jan. 15, 1815."

Ch. 1, *Stepping Heavenward 1852*

2 One child and two green graves are mine,
This is God's gift to me;
A bleeding, fainting, broken heart—
This is my gift to Thee.

Untitled, on the death of her children *1852*

3 Sleep, baby, sleep!
Thy father's watching the sheep,
Thy mother's shaking the dreamland tree,
And down drops a little dream for the.
Sleep, baby, sleep.

"Cradle Song" *n.d.*

953. Lucy Stone (1818–1893)

1 The right to vote will yet be swallowed up in the real question, viz: has woman a right to herself? It is very little to me to have the right to vote, to own property, etc., if I may not keep my body, and its uses, in my absolute right.

Letter to Antoinette Brown* *1855*
*Antoinette Brown Blackwell; see 998.

2 We want rights. The flour-merchant, the house-builder, and the postman charge us no less on account of our sex; but when we endeavor to earn money to pay all of these, then, indeed, we find the difference.

Speech, "Disappointment Is the Lot of Women," (17–18 October, 1855), *History of Woman Suffrage,* Vol. 1, by Elizabeth Cady Stanton,* Susan B. Anthony,** and Mathilda Gage*** *1881*
*See 931. **See 963. ***See 1007.

3 "We, the people of the United States." Which "We, the people?" The women were not included.

Speech (*New York Tribune,* April 1853), Quoted in Ch. 6, *Morning Star,* Pt. II by Elinor Rice Hayes* *1961*
*See 1933.

4 My heart aches to love somebody that shall be all its own . . . [but] I shall not be married ever. I have not yet seen the person whom I have the slightest wish to marry, and if I had, it would take longer than my lifetime for the obstacles to be removed which are in the way of a married woman having any being of her own.

Letter to Nettie Brown (1853), Ch. 9, Ibid.

5 There was only one will in our home, and that was my father's.

Quoted in *Women Suffragists* by Diana Star Helmer *1998*

6 The great majority of women are more intelligent, better educated, and far more moral than multitudes of men whose right to vote no man questions.

Ibid.

7 Make the world better.

Last words, spoken to her daughter Alice Stone Blackwell (18 October 1893), Ibid.

954. Louise Amelia Clappe (1819–1906)

1 . . . there is a certain fascination about the place (San Francisco), which our friends in the States find it difficult to comprehend. For what with its many-costumed, many-tongued, many-visaged populations; its flashy looking squares, built one day and burnt the next; its wickedly beautiful gambling houses; its gay stores where the richest productions of every nation can be found, and its wild, free, unconventional style of living, it possesses for the young adventurer especially a strange charm.

Letter to sister Molly (Rich Bar mining camp, 1849), "Dame Shirley" letters, *The Pioneer* (1854–55), *The Shirley Letters 1933*

2 . . . no newspapers, no shopping, calling, nor gossiping, little tea-drinkings; no parties, no balls, no picnics, no tableaux, no charades, no latest fashions, no daily mail (we have an express once a month), no promenades, no rides or drives; no vegetables but potatoes and onions, no milk, no eggs, no *nothing.*

(1851), Ibid.

3 My heart is heavy at the thought of departing forever from this place. I like this wild and barbarous life; I leave it with regret. The solemn fir trees . . . the watching hills, and the calmly beautiful river, seem to gaze sorrowfully at me, as I stand in the moon-lighted midnight, to bid them farewell . . .

(1852), Ibid.

4 I would gladly write something which the world would not willingly let die.

(n.d), Ibid.

5 Though ye've not shaved your savage lips, nor cut your barbarous hair—
Ye are welcome, merry miners! All bearded as ye are.

Fourth of July Poem for Rich Bar miners (1852), Ibid.

955. George Eliot (1819–1880)

1 Hate is like fire—it makes even light rubbish deadly.

Scenes of Clerical Life 1857

2 Any coward can fight a battle when he's sure of winning; but give me the man who has pluck to fight when he's sure of losing. That's my way, sir; and there are many victories worse than a defeat.

"Janet's Repentance," Ch. 6, Ibid.

3 Opposition may become sweet to a man when he has christened it persecution.

Ch. 8, Ibid.

4 Animals are such agreeable friends—they ask no questions, they pass no criticisms.

"Mr. Gilfil's Love Story," Ibid.

5 Our deeds determine us, as much as we determine our deeds.

Adam Bede 1859

6 It's them as take advantage that get advantage i' this world.

Bk. 4, Ch. 32, Ibid.

7 That's what a man wants in a wife, mostly; he wants to make sure o' one fool as 'ull tell him he's wise.

Bk. 6, Ch. 53, Ibid.

8 It's but a little good you'll do a-watering the last year's crop.

Ch. 18, Ibid.

9 It was a pity he couldna be hatched o'er again, an' hatched different.

Ibid.

10 I'm not denyin' the women are foolish: God almighty made 'em to match the men.

Ch. 43, Ibid.

11 The law's made to take care o' raskills.

Bk. III, Ch. 4, The Mill on the Floss 1860

12 Nothing is so good as it seems beforehand.

Ch. 18, Silas Marner 1861

13 Justice is like the Kingdom of God—it is not without us as a fact, it is within us as a great yearning.

Romola 1862–63

14 There is a mercy which is weakness, and even treason against the common good.

Ibid.

15 In the vain laughter of folly wisdom hears half its applause.

Bk.1, Ch. 12, Ibid.

16 An ass may bray a good while before he shakes the stars down.

Ch. 50, Ibid.

17 There are glances of hatred that stab, and raise no cry of murder.

Introduction, Felix Holt, The Radical 1866

18 One way of getting an idea of our fellow-countrymen's miseries is to go and look at their pleasures.

Ch. 28, Ibid.

19 Best friend, my well-spring in the wilderness!

Bk. 3, The Spanish Gypsy 1868

20 Quarrel? Nonsense; we have not quarrelled. If one is not to get into a rage sometimes, what is the good of being friends?

Bk. 2, Ch. 12, Middlemarch 1871–72

21 Might, could, would—they are contemptible auxiliaries.

Bk. 2, Ch. 14, Ibid.

22 One must be poor to know the luxury of giving!

Ch. 17, Ibid.

23 Failure after long perseverance is much grander than never to have a striving good enough to be called a failure.

Ch. 22, Ibid.

24 To be a poet is to have a soul so quick to discern, that no shade of quality escapes it, and so quick to feel, that discernment is but a hand playing with finely-ordered variety on the chords of emotion—a soul in which knowledge passes instantaneously into feeling, and feeling flashes back as a new organ of knowledge. One may have that condition by fits only.

Ibid.

25 She was no longer wrestling with the grief, but could sit down with it as a lasting companion and make it a sharer in her thoughts.

Bk. 8, Ch. 80, Ibid.

26 If we had keen vision of all that is ordinary in human life, it would be like hearing the grass grow or the squirrel's heart beat, and we should die of the roar which is the other side of silence.

Ch. 22, Ibid.

27 What loneliness is more lonely than distrust?

Ch. 44, Ibid.

28 Gossip is a sort of smoke that comes from the dirty tobacco-pipes of those who diffuse it; it proves nothing but the bad taste of the smoker.

Daniel Deronda 1876

29 The Jews are among the aristocracy of every land; if a literature is called rich in the possession of a few classic tragedies, what shall we say to a national tragedy lasting for fifteen hundred years, in which the poets and actors were also the heroes.

Ibid.

30 A difference of taste in jokes is a great strain on the affections.

Bk. 2, Ch. 15, Ibid.

31 Genius at first is little more than a great capacity for receiving discipline.

Bk. 3, Ch. 23, Ibid.

32 You may try—but you can never imagine what it is to have a man's force of genius in you, and yet to suffer the slavery of being a girl.

Bk. 7, Ch. 51, Ibid.

33 Blessed is the man who, having nothing to say, abstains from giving wordy evidence of the fact.

Ch. 4, The Impressions of Theophrastus Such 1879

34 What a wretched lot of old shrivelled creatures we shall be by-and-by. Never mind—the uglier we get in the eyes of others, the lovelier we shall be to each other; that has always been my firm faith about friendship.

Letter (27 May 1852), George Eliot's Life as Related in Her Letters and Journals 1885–86

35 The years seem to rush by now, and I think of death as a fast approaching end of a journey—double and treble reason for loving as well as working while it is day.

Letter to Miss Sara Hennell (22 November 1861), Ibid.

36 Oh may I join the choir invisible
Of those immortal dead who live again
In minds made better by their presence.

"Oh May I Join the Choir Invisible," Poems n.d.

37 'Tis God gives skill,
But not without men's hands: He could not make
Antonio Stradivari's violins
Without Antonio.

"Stradivarius," l. 140, Ibid.

38 It is never too late to be what you might have been.

Quoted by Anna Quindlen* in her commencement speech, Mount Holyoke College (South Hadley, Mass.) 23 May 1999
*See 4136.

956. Julia Ward Howe (1819–1910)

1 Mine eyes have seen the glory
  Of the coming of the Lord
  He is trampling out the vintage
  Where the grapes of wrath are stored.
  He hath loosed the fateful lightning
  Of His terrible, swift sword;
  His truth is marching on!
  > "The Battle Hymn of the Republic" *1862*

2 They are the mothers of the boys who are killed in war. They have the right to ask that the sons they love have a happy life.
  > Cited in "Ahead of her time" by Rev. Dale Turner, *Seattle Times*, A8 *4 July 1992*

3 The peace crusade is going to take a long time. I will devote the rest of my life to world peace, but that will not be long enough. I will encourage others to carry on the work when I am done.
  > Ibid.

4 All the sugar was in the bottom of the cup.
  > Last words, Ibid.

957. Anna Cora Mowatt (1819–1870)

1 TRUEMAN. Fashion is an agreement between certain persons to live without using their souls! To substitute etiquette for virtue—decorum for purity—manners for morals!
  > *Fashion 1845*

958. Louise Otto (1819–1895)

1 For no sacred mission can be crowned,
  And there can be no peace or amity,
  Unless material prosperity, like the sun,
  Would shine its healing rays on everyone.
  > "For All," St. 1, S.L. Cocalis and G.M. Geiger, trs., *The Defiant Muse: German Feminist Poems From The Middle Ages To The Present—A Bilingual Anthology*, Susan L. Cocalis, ed. *1986*

2 In the proud procession of the truth the call
  Will ring out again: "Emancipation came for all!"
  > Ibid.

3 The history of all times, and of today especially, teaches that women will be forgotten if they forget to think about themselves.
  > *Women in World History Curriculum* (womeninworldhistory. com) *1996–97*

959. Harriet Sewall (1819–1889)

1 Why thus longing, thus forever sighing
  For the far-off, unattain'd and dim,
  While the beautiful all round thee lying
  Offers up its low, perpetual hymn?
  > "Why Thus Longing" *n.d.*

960. Queen Victoria (1819–1901)

1 We are not interested in the possibilities of defeat.
  > Letter to A. J. Balfour *1899*

2 We are not amused.
  > *Notebooks of a Spinster Lady 1900*

3 I sat between the King and Queen. We left supper soon. My health was drunk. I then danced one more quadrille with Lord Paget. . . . I was *very* much amused.
  > Journal entry (16 June 1833), *The Girlhood of Queen Victoria*, Vol. I, Viscount Esher, ed. *1912*

4 The Queen is most anxious to see the Government strengthened and supported, and she *does* think that want of firmness in the leader of the House of Commons is most detrimental to it.
  > (27 June 1890), Ibid.

5 . . . Now let me entreat you seriously not to do this, not to let your feelings (very natural and usual ones) of momentary irritation and discomfort be seen by others; don't (as you so often did and do) let every little feeling be read in your face and seen in your manner, pray don't give way to irritability before your ladies. All this I say with the love and affection I bear you—as I know what you have to contend with and struggle against.
  > Letter to Princess Royal (27 September 1858), *Dearest Child*, Roger Fulford, ed. *1964*

961. Susan Warner (1819–1885)

1 Many a bit we passed in our ignorance, in the days when we could see no metal but what glittered on the surface; and many a good time we went back again, long afterward, and broke our rejected lump with great exultation to find it fat with the riches of the mind.
  > Foreword, *The Law and the Testimony 1853*

2 "There is a world there, Winthrop—another sort of world— where people know something; where other things are to be done than running plow furrows; where men may distinguish themselves!—where men may read and write; and do something great; and grow to be something besides what nature made them!—I want to be in that world."
  > Ch. 1, *The Hills of the Shatemuc 1856*

3 "The back is fitted to the burden, they say; and I always *did* pray that if I had work to do, I might be able to do it; and I always was, somehow."
  > Ch. 3, *What She Could 1870*

4 "And I, Maria—am I not somebody?" her aunt asked.
  "Well, we're all *somebody*, of course, in one sense. Of course we're not *nobody*."
  "I am not sure what you think about it," said Mrs. Candy. "I think that in your language, who isn't somebody, is nobody."
  > Ch. 7, Ibid.

5 "He who serves God with what costs him nothing, will do very little service, you may depend on it."
  > Ch. 11, Ibid.

962. Amelia C. Welby (1819–1852)

1 As the dew to the blossom, the bud to the bee,
  As the scent to the rose, are those memories to me.
  > "Pulpit Eloquence" *n.d.*

2 Ten thousand stars were in the sky,
  Ten thousand on the sea.
  > "Twilight at Sea," St. 4 *n.d.*

963. Susan B. Anthony (1820–1906)

1 Men their rights and nothing more; women their rights and nothing less.

Motto, *The Revolution 1868*

2 ... gentlemen ... Do you not see that so long as society says a woman is incompetent to be a lawyer, minister, or doctor, but has ample ability to be a teacher, that every man of you who chooses this profession tacitly acknowledges that he has no more brains than a woman?

Speech, State Convention of Schoolteachers, *History of Woman Suffrage,* Vol. 1, Elizabeth Cady Stanton* and Mathilda Gage,** co-authors *1881*
*See 931. **See 1007.

3 Of all the old prejudices that cling to the hem of the woman's garments and persistently impede her progress, none holds faster than this. This idea that she owes service to a man instead of to herself, and that it is her highest duty to aid his development rather than her own, will be the last to die.

"The Status of Women, Past, Present and Future," *The Arena May 1897*

4 ... The day will come when men will recognize woman as his peer, not only at the fireside, but in the councils of the nation. Then, and not until then, will there be the perfect comradeship, the ideal union between the sexes that shall result to the highest development of the race.

Ibid.

5 ... who can measure the advantages that would result if the magnificent abilities of [women] ... could be devoted to the needs of government, society, home, instead of being consumed in the struggle to obtain their birthright of individual freedom?

Ibid.

6 ... and I shall earnestly and persistently continue to urge all women to the practical recognition of the old Revolutionary maxim, "Resistance to tyranny is obedience to God."

Quoted in Courtroom Speech (18 June 1873), *Jailed for Freedom* by Doris Stevens *1920*

7 So, for the love of me and for the saving of the reputation of womanhood, I beg you, with one baby on your knee and another at your feet, and four boys whistling, buzzing, halooing, "Ma, Ma," set yourself about the work.

Letter to Stanton, *Elizabeth Cady Stanton,** Vol. II, Theodore Stanton and Harriot Stanton Blatch, eds. *1922*
*See 931.

8 The preamble of the Federal Constitution says: We, the people of the United States ... It was we, the people, not we, the white male citizens, nor we, the male citizens; but we, the whole people, who formed this Union.

Ibid.

9 Whoever controls work and wages, controls morals.

Ibid.

10 Independence is happiness.

Ibid.

11 Oh, the voice is stilled which I have loved to hear for fifty years. Always I have felt that I must have Mrs. Stanton's* opinion of things before I knew where I stood myself.

Letter to Ida Husted Harper (1902), Ibid.
*See 931; Stanton died 26 October 1902.

12 With such women as these consecrating their lives, failure is impossible.*

Remark to celebrants at her 86th birthday gala, Ibid.
*These were the last words Anthony spoke in public and became the watchwords of the suffrage movement.

964. Urania Locke Bailey (1820–1882)

1 I want to be an angel,
And with the angels stand
A crown upon my forehead,
A harp within my hand.

"I Want to Be an Angel," St. 1 *n.d.*

965. Anne Brontë (1820–1849)

1 All true histories contain instruction; though, in some, the treasure may be hard to find, and when found, so trivial in quantity, that the dry, shrivelled kernel scarcely compensates for the trouble of cracking the nut.

Ch. II, *Agnes Gray 1847*

2 I would not send a poor girl into the world, ... ignorant of the snares that beset her path; nor would I watch and guard her, till, deprived of self-respect and self-reliance, she lost the power or the will to watch and guard herself. ...

Ch. III, *The Tenant of Wildfell Hall 1848*

3 "If you would have your son to walk honourable through the world, you must not attempt to clear the stones from his path, but teach him to walk firmly over them—not insist upon leading him by the hand, but let him learn to go alone."

Ibid.

4 They say such tears as children weep
Will soon be dried away;
That childhood's grief, however strong,
Is only for a day;
And parted friends, how dear so e'er,
Will soon forgotten be:
It may be so with other hearts;
It is not so with me.

"An Orphan's Lament" (1 January 1841), *The Complete Poems of Anne Brontë,* Clement Shorter, ed. *1920*

5 Domestic peace! best joy of earth,
When shall we all thy value learn?

"Domestic Peace," St. 7 (11 May 1846), Ibid.

6 Nothing is lost that thou didst give,
Nothing destroyed that thou hast done.

"Severed and Gone," St. 15 (April 1847), Ibid.

7 But he that dares not grasp the thorn
Should never crave the rose.

"The Narrow Way," St. 4 (27 April 1848), Ibid.

966. Alice Cary (1820–1871)

1 Three little bugs in a basket,
And hardly room for two.

"Three Bugs" *n.d.*

2 True worth is in *being,* not *seeming*—
In doing, each day that goes by,
Some little good—not in dreaming
Of great things to do by and by.

"Nobility," St. 1 *n.d.*

3 We cannot bake bargains for blisses,
   Nor catch them like fishes in nets;
   And sometimes the thing our life misses,
   Helps more than the thing which it gets.

   St. 4, Ibid.

4 Work, and your house shall be duly fed:
   Work, and the rest shall be won;
   I hold that a man had better be dead
   Than alive when his work is done.

   "Work" n.d.

5 Ah, don't be sorrowful darling,
   And don't be sorrowful, pray:
   Taking the year together, my dear,
   There isn't more night than day.

   "Don't be sorrowful, darling" n.d.

967. Lucretia Peabody Hale (1820–1900)

1 But behind the east wind is hidden the summer, and in these early spring days we feel a little of its breath, its warmth, and its languor.

   Ch. 4, The Struggle for Life 1867

2 All the years before, she had lived in a roving, aimless way, and the old love of change came up often to assert its power. Often came back the old longings to live where she would not be bound to anybody—where she might be free, even if she were only free to starve.

   Ch. 18, Ibid.

3 It is so hard to melt away the influences of an early life, to counteract all the lessons of the first ten years, to tear up the weeds that are early planted. There are evil inheritances to be struggled with, childish prejudices, and fancies banished.

   Ch. 33, Ibid.

968. Jean Ingelow (1820–1897)

1 Oh Land where all the men are stones,
   Or all the stones are men.

   "A Land that Living Warmth Disowns" n.d.

2 There's no dew left on the daisies and clover,
   There's no rain left in heaven:
   I've said my "seven times" over and over,
   Seven times one are seven.

   "Seven Times One," St. 1, Songs of Seven n.d.

3 I wait for my story—the birds cannot sing it,
   Not one as he sits on the tree;
   The bells cannot ring it, but long years, O bring it!
   Such as I wish it to be.

   Untitled, Quoted in *The Slaveholder's Daughter* by Belle Kearney* *1900*

   *See 1297.

969. Mme. de Launey (fl. 1820s)

1 I forgive the *nonchalance* which you assume about receiving a pension. . . . It flatters both the vanity and the purse.

   Letter to Desbordes-Valmore* (1 November 1826), Quoted in *Memoirs of Madame Desbordes-Valmore* by C. A. Sainte-Beuve; Harriet W. Preston, tr. *1872*

   *See 801.

970. Jenny Lind (1820–1887)

1 I have a brightness in my soul, which strains toward Heaven. I am like a bird!

   Quoted in *Jenny Lind: The Swedish Nightingale* by Gladys Denny Shultz *1962*

2 I have often wished for the blessing of motherhood, for it would have given me a much-needed focal point for my affections. With it, and through the varied experiences that accompany it, I could perhaps have achieved something better than that which I have attained up to now.

   Letter (11 July 1849), *The Lost Letters of Jenny Lind*, W. Porter Ware and Thaddeus C. Lockard, Jr., eds. *1966*

3 My voice is still the same, and this makes me beside myself with joy! Oh, *mon Dieu*, when I think what I might be able to do with it!

   Letter (10 January 1855), Ibid.

971. Mary Livermore (1820–1905)

1 For humanity has moved forward to an era when wrong and slavery are being displaced, and reason and justice are being recognized as the rule of life. . . . The age looks steadily to the redressing of wrong, to the righting of every form of error and injustice; and a tireless and prying philanthropy, which is almost omniscient, is one of the most hopeful characteristics of the time.

   Ch. 1, What Shall We Do with Our Daughters? 1883

2 Almost every one of the great religions of the world has made special provisions for them, and the woman who has preferred a celibate to a domestic life has been able to occupy a position of honor and usefulness.

   Ch. 7, Ibid.

3 Above the titles of wife and mother, which, although dear, are transitory and accidental, there is the title human being, which precedes and out-ranks every other.

   Ibid.

972. Mathilde (1820–1904)

1 But I think him lost forever for any kind of locomotion. Nowadays it is only his mind that travels; his body stays behind on the bank.

   Quoted in *Revue Bleu 6 August 1863*

2 He knew that his conversation had the power to fascinate, and he used it like a prodigal man who knew he had an everlasting fortune. . . .

   Quoted in *Le Moniteur Universelle 15 October 1869*

3 I was born in exile—civically dead. . . .

   "Souvenirs de Années d'Exile," *La Revue des Deux Mondes 15 December 1927*

973. Mary Ann Muller (1820–1901)

1 How long are women to remain a wholly unrepresented body of the people? This is a question that has of late been agitated in England, and women in this colony read, watch, and reflect . . . Why should not New Zealand also lead? . . . Why has a woman no power to vote, no right to vote, when she happens to possess all the requisites which legally qualify a man for that right?"

   (1869), *Women in World History Curriculum* (womeninworldhistory.com) *1996–97*

974. Florence Nightingale (1820–1910)

1 No *man,* not even a doctor, ever gives any other definition of what a nurse should be than this—"devoted and obedient." This definition would do just as well for a porter. It might even do for a horse. It would not do for a policeman.

Notes on Nursing 1859

2 Merely looking at the sick is not observing.

Ibid.

3 But when you have done away with all that pain and suffering, which in patients are the symptoms, not of their disease, but of the absence of one or all of the essentials to the success of Nature's reparative processes, we shall then know what are the symptoms of, and the sufferings inseparable from, the disease.

Ibid.

4 Just as the end of food is to enable us to live and work, and not to live and eat, so the end of most reading perhaps, but certainly of mystical reading, is not to read but to work.

Preface, *Mysticism 1873*

5 For what is Mysticism? Is it not the attempt to draw near to God, not by rites or ceremonies, but by inward disposition? Is it not merely a hard word for "The Kingdom of Heaven is within?" Heaven is neither a place nor a time.

Ibid.

6 So I never lose an opportunity of urging a practical beginning, however small, for it is wonderful how often in such matters the mustard-seed germinates and roots itself.

"Health Missionaries for Rural India," *India December 1896*

7 Nothing ever laughs and plays [in Egypt]. Everything is grown up and grown old.

Quoted in *The Life of Florence Nightingale* by Sir Edward Cook *1913*

8 I stand at the altar of murdered men, and, while I live, I fight their cause.

Private note (1856), *Ibid.*

9 I can stand out the war with any man.

Quoted in *The World Book Encyclopedia 1972*

10 What the horrors of war are, no one can imagine. They are not wounds and blood and fever, spotted and low, or dysentery, chronic and acute, cold and heat and famine. They are intoxication, drunken brutality, demoralisation and disorder on the part of the inferior . . . jealousies, meanness, indifference, selfish brutality on the part of the superior.

Letter to her family (5 May 1855), *Forever Yours, Florence Nightingale: Selected Letters 1989*

11 Instead of wishing to see more doctors made by women joining what there are, I wish to see as few doctors, either male or female, as possible. For, mark you, the women have made no improvement—they have only tried to be "men" and they have only succeeded in being third-rate men.

Letter to John Stuart Mill* (12 September 1860), *Ibid.*
*British philosopher and economist (1806–1873).

975. Ann Plato (1820?–post-1841)

1 . . . a good education is another name for happiness.

Essays 1841

976. Margaret J. Preston (1820–1897)

1 Pain is no longer pain when it is past.

"Nature's Lesson" ca. *1875*

2 'Tis the motive exalts the action;
'Tis the doing, not the deed.

"The First Proclamation of Miles Standish"* ca. *1875*
*English colonial settler in America (1584?–1656).

3 Who so lives the holiest life
Is fittest far to die.

"Ready" ca. *1875*

977. Anna Sewell (1820–1878)

1 . . . if we see cruelty or wrong that have the power to stop, and do nothing, we make ourselves sharers in the guilt.

Black Beauty 1877

2 . . . he said that cruelty was the Devil's own trademark, and if we saw anyone who took pleasure in cruelty we might know who he belonged to, for the Devil was a murderer from the beginning, and a tormentor to the end.

Pt. I, Ch. 13, *Ibid.*

3 I am never afraid of what I know.

Pt. II, Ch. 29, *Ibid.*

4 I said, "I have heard people talk about war as if it was a very fine thing."
  "Ah!" said he, "I should think they never saw it. No doubt it is very fine when there is no enemy, when it is just exercise and parade, and sham fight. Yes, it is very fine then; but when thousands of good, brave men and horses are killed or crippled for life, it has a very different look."

Pt. III, Ch. 34, *Ibid.*

978. Harriet Tubman (1820?–1913)

1 I had crossed the line. I was *free;* but there was no one to welcome me to the land of freedom. I was a stranger in a strange land; and my home, after all, was down in Maryland; because my father, my mother, my brothers, and sisters, and friends were there. But I was free, and *they* should be free. I would make a home in the North and bring them there, God helping me.

Quoted in *Scenes in the Life of Harriet Tubman* by Sarah H. Bradford *1869*

2 When I found I had crossed dat *line,* I looked at my hands to see if I was de same pusson. There was such a glory ober ebery ting; de sun came like gold through the trees, and ober the fields, and I felt like I was in Heaben.

*Ibid.**

3 Don't you think we colored people are entitled to some credit for that exploit, under the lead of the brave Colonel Montgomery? We weakened the rebels somewhat on the Combahee River, by taking and bringing away *seven hundred and fifty-six* head of their most valuable live stock, known up in your region as "contrabands," and this, too, without the loss of a single life on our part, though we had good reason to believe that a number of rebels bit the dust. Of these seven hundred and fifty-six contrabands, nearly or quite all the able-bodied men have joined the colored regiments here. . . .

Article in the *Boston Commonwealth* (30 June 1863), *Ibid.*

4 I tink dar's many a slaveholder'll git to Heaven. Dey don't know no better. Dey acts up to de light dey hab. You take dat sweet little child—'pears more like an angel dan anything else—take her down dere, let her nebber know nothing 'bout niggers but they was made to be whipped, an' she'll grow up to use the whip on 'em jus' like de rest. No, Missus, it's because dey don't know no better.

Ibid.*

*Quotations have been printed as they appear in *Scenes from the Life of Harriet Tubman.* One assumes that the difference in the use of the vernacular and standard English has to do with the various scribes who recorded the events.

5 I had reasoned this out in my mind, there was two things I had a right to, liberty and death. If I could not have one, I would have the other, for no man should take me alive.

Quoted in "Lost Women: Harriet Tubman—The Moses of her People" by Marcy Galen, *Ms.* (New York) *August 1973*

6 I never ran my train off the track, and I never lost a passenger.

ThinkQuest, library.advanced.org *1995*

979. Anna Bartlett Warner (1820–1912)

1 Daffy-down-dilly came up in the cold. . . .

"Daffy-Down-Dilly" *n.d.*

2 Jesus loves me, this I know
For the Bible tells me so.

"Jesus Loves Me" *n.d.*

980. Clara Barton (1821–1912)

1 It is wise statesmanship which suggests that in times of peace we must prepare for war, and it is no less wise benevolence that makes preparation in the hour of peace for assuaging the ills that are sure to accompany war.

Ch. 1, *The Red Cross 1898*

2 An institution or reform movement that is not selfish, must originate in the recognition of some evil that is adding to the sum of human suffering, or diminishing the sum of happiness. I suppose it is a philanthropic movement to try to reverse the process.

Ibid.

3 I have an almost complete disregard of precedent and a faith in the possibility of something better. It irritates me to be told how things always have been done . . . I defy the tyranny of precedent. I cannot afford the luxury of a closed mind. I go for anything new that might improve the past.

Quoted in *A Chosen Faith* by Robin Lane Fox *n.d.*

981. Elizabeth Blackwell (1821–1910)

1 . . . Every advance in social progress removes us more and more from the guidance of instinct, obliging us to depend upon reason for the assurance that our habits are really agreeable to the laws of health, and compelling us to guard against the sacrifice of our physical or moral nature while pursuing the ends of civilization.

Medicine as a Profession for Women, coauthor Emily Blackwell* *1860*

*Her sister; see 1005.

2 . . . health has its science as well as disease. . . .

Ibid.

3 Our school education ignores, in a thousand ways, the rules of healthy development . . .

Ibid.

4 For what is done or learned by one class of women becomes, by virtue of their common womanhood, the property of all women.

Ibid.

5 How often homes, which should be the source of moral and physical health and truth, are centers of selfishness and frivolity!

Ibid.

6 As teachers, then, to diffuse among women the physiological and sanitary knowledge which they need, we found the first work for women physicians.

Ibid.

7 This failure to recognize the equivalent value of internal with external structure has led to such a crude fallacy as a comparison of the penis with such a vestige as the clitoris, whilst failing to recognize that the vast amount of erectile tissue, mostly internal, in the female, which is the direct seat of sexual spasm.

The Human Element in Sex 1894

8 . . . the total deprivation of it [sex] produces irritability.

Ibid.

982. Mary Baker Eddy (1821–1910)

1 Whatever materializes worship hinders man's spiritual growth and keeps him from demonstrating his power over error.

Ch. 1, *Science and Health, with Key to the Scriptures 1875*

2 Chastity is the cement of civilization and progress. Without it there is no stability in society, and without it one cannot attain the Science of Life.

Ch. 3, Ibid.

3 Give up the belief that mind is, even temporarily, compressed within the skull, and you will quickly become more manly or womanly. You will understand yourself and your Maker better than before.

Ch. 12, Ibid.

4 God is Mind, and God is infinite; hence all is Mind.

Ch. 14, Ibid.

5 The highest prayer is not one of faith merely; it is demonstration.

Ibid.

6 Then comes the question, how do drugs, hygiene, and animal magnetism heal? It may be affirmed that they do not heal, but only relieve suffering temporarily, exchanging one disease for another.

Ibid., *1910 ed.*

7 Disease is an experience of so-called mortal mind. It is fear made manifest in the body.

Ibid.

8 Jesus of Nazareth was the most scientific man that ever trod the globe. He plunged beneath the material surface of things, and found the spiritual cause.

Ibid.

9 Sin brought death, and death will disappear with the disappearance of sin.

Ibid.

10 Truth is immortal; error is mortal.

Ibid.

11 I would no more quarrel with a man because of his religion than I would because of his art.

Miscellaneous Writings (rev. as *The First Church of Scientist, and Miscellany* 1913) 1883–1896

12 To live and let live, without clamor for distinction of recognition; to wait on divine Love; to write truth first on the tablet of one's own heart—this is the sanity and perfection of living, and my human ideal.

Message to the Mother Church 1902

983. Frances Cobbe (1822–1904)

1 The time comes to every dog when it ceases to care for people merely for biscuits or bones, of even for caresses, and walks out of doors. When a dog *really* loves, it prefers the person who gives it nothing, and perhaps is too ill ever to take it out for exercise, to all the liberal cooks and active dog-boys in the world.

The Confessions of a Lost Dog 1867

2 I could discern clearly, even at that early age, the essential difference between people who are *kind* to dogs and people who really *love* them.

Ibid.

3 Then the Sorcerer Science entered, and where e'er he waved
    his wand
Fresh wonders and fresh mysteries rose on every hand.

"The Pageant of Time," St. 1 (December, 1859), *Rest in the Lord* 1887

4 . . . I must avow that the halo which has gathered round Jesus Christ obscures Him to my eyes.

Ch. 15, *Life of Frances Power Cobbe,* Vol. II 1894

984. Caroline Dall (1822–1912)

1 The solution of an old mystery must bring justification and proof to every assertion.

Preface, *The Romance of the Association* 1875

2 I have seen no Hindu who seemed to me prepared intellectually and morally for the freedom he would find in American society; nor are Americans prepared for the air of innocence and exaltation worn by very undeserving Orientals.

*The Life of Doctor Anandabai Joshee** 1888
*See 1316.

3 It was the glorious function of [John Greenleaf] Whittier* to lift us nearer to the Infinite Spirit, to keep us intent upon our immortal destiny, and to fill us with that love of Beauty which is the love of God.

"L'Envoi," Pt. 1, *Barbara Fritchie*** 1892
*(1807–1892) American poet and abolitionist. **See 729.

985. Lilly Martin Spencer (1822–1902)

1 . . . fame is as hollow and brilliant as a soap bubble, it is all colors outside and nothing worth kicking at inside.

Letter to parents, *Women in the Arts,* Vol. X, No. 2 *Summer 1992*

986. Julia Carney (1823–1908)

1 Little drops of water, Little grains of sand,
    Make the mighty ocean, And the pleasant land.
So the little minutes, Humble tho' they be,
    Make the mighty ages Of Eternity!

"Little Things," St. 1 1845

987. Mary Bokin Chesnut (1823–1886)

1 "You know how women sell themselves and are sold in marriage, from queens downwards, eh? You know what the Bible says about slaves, and marriage. Poor women, poor slaves."

(4 March 1861), *Diary from Dixie* 1949

2 You see, Mrs. Stowe did not hit the sorest spot. She makes Legree* a bachelor.

(27 August 1861), *Ibid.*
*A cruel slave dealer in the novel *Uncle Tom's Cabin* by Harriet Beecher Stowe (see 916).

3 Conscription has waked the Rip Van Winkles. To fight and to be made to fight are different things.

(19 March 1862), *Ibid.*

4 Grief and constant anxiety kill nearly as many women as men die on the battlefield.

(9 June 1862), *Ibid.*

5 Is the sea drying up? It is going up into mist and coming down on us in this water spout, the rain. It raineth every day, and the weather represents our tearful despair on a large scale.

(5 March 1865), *Ibid.*

6 We are scattered, stunned, the remnant of heart left alive in us filled with brotherly hate. We sit and wait until the drunken tailor [President Andrew Johnson*] who rules the United States issues a proclamation and defines our anomalous position.

(16 May 1865), *Ibid.*
*1808–75, 17th president of the U.S. (1865–69).

988. Margaret Davidson (1823–1838)

1 When left alone, when thou art gone,
Yet still I will not feel alone;
Thy spirit still will hover near,
And guard thy orphan daughter here.

Untitled poem (ca. 1831), Quotes in *Lives of Celebrated Women* by Samuel Griswold Goodrich 1844

2 My sister! With that thrilling word
Let thoughts unnumbered wildly spring!
What echoes in my heart are stirred,
While thus I touch the trembling string.

Untitled poem (1836), *Ibid.*

989. Caroline Mason (1823–1890)

1 Do they miss me at home—do they miss me?
'Twould be an assurance most dear,
To know that this moment some loved one
Were saying, "I wish he were here."

"Do They Miss Me at Home," St.1 1850

2 . . . like a story well-nigh told,
Will seem my life—when I am old.

"When I Am Old," St. 1 *n.d.*

3   His grave a nation's heart shall be,
    His monument a people free!
                    "President Lincoln's* Grave" *n.d.*
    *1809–1865; the 16th President of the United States (1861–1865);
    assassinated.

990. Elizabeth Stoddard (1823–1902)

1   When I hear music, whether waltz or psalm,
    Among a crowd, I find myself alone;
    It does not touch me with a soothing balm,
    But brings an echo like a moan
                    "Music In A Crowd," St. 1, *Poems* 1860

2   So, I must believe that I loved you once!
    These letters say so;
    And here is your picture—how you have changed!
    It was long ago.
                    Ibid., "A Few Idle Words," St. 1

3   A woman despises a man for loving her, unless she returns his
    love.
                    Ch. 32, *Two Men* 1888

991. Charlotte Yonge (1823–1901)

1   As the most striking lines of poetry are the most hackneyed, be-
    cause they have grown to be the common inheritance of all the
    world, so many of the most noble deeds that earth can show
    have become the best known, and enjoyed their full meed of
    fame.
                    A Book of Golden Deeds 1864

992. Phoebe Cary (1824–1871)

1   Charley Church, was a preacher who praught,
    Though his enemies called him a screecher who scraught.
                    "The Lovers" *n.d.*

2   I think true love is never blind
    But rather brings an added light,
    An inner vision quick to find
    The beauties hid from common sight.
                    Ibid.

3   For all the hard things to bear and grin,
    The hardest is being taken in.
                    "Kate Ketchem" *n.d.*

4   Give plenty of what is given to you,
    And listen to pity's call;
    Don't think the little you give is great
    And the much you get is small.
                    "A Legend of the Northlands," I, St. 8 *n.d.*

5   There's many a battle fought daily
    The world knows nothing about.
                    "Our Heroes," St. 2 *n.d.*

6   Be steadfast, my boy, when you're tempted,
    To do what you know to be right.
    Stand firm by the colors of manhood,
    And you will o'ercome in the fight.
                    St. 3, Ibid.

7   And isn't it, my boy or girl,
    The wisest, bravest plan,

Whatever comes, or doesn't come,
To do the best you can?
                    "Suupose," St. 5, Ibid.

993. Julia Kavanagh (1824–1877)

1   Most children are aristocratic. . . .
                    Daisy Burns, Vol. I 1853

2   Alas! why has the plain truth the power of offending so many
    people. . . .
                    Ch. 4, Ibid.

3   A beauty must regret the past; a noble-born and impoverished
    lady cannot look with favour on a new order of things.
                    Ch. 2, *Adele* 1872

994. Sarah Anna Lewis (1824–1880)

1   The oblivious world of sleep—
    That rayless realm where Fancy never beams,
    That nothingness beyond the land of dreams.
                    "Child of the Sea" *n.d.*

995. Rachel Simon (1824–1900?)

1   In our days of prosperity it is more difficult to sustain a re-
    ligious spirit than in times of adversity, because we are apt
    to forget that God who has bountifully given may also take
    away.
                    "Aspiration" (3 April 1840), *Records and Reflections* 1894

2   I believe that it is possible for all of us to attain a far greater ex-
    pansion of soul than we imagine, but we do not give ourselves
    the time necessary for the cultivation of this higher growth.
                    "A Reflection" (8 December 1854), Ibid.

3   Turn every trial to account; however trifling in its character,
    make use of it as the polishing instrument that will change the
    roughest stone into the jeweler's prize.
                    "Small Trials (A few words of Comfort)" (1859), Ibid.

996. Adeline Dutton Whitney (1824–1906)

1   I bow me to the thwarting gale:
    I know when that is overpast,
    Among the peaceful harvest days
    An Indian Summer comes at last.
                    "Equinoctal," St. 6 *n.d.*

997. Mrs. Alexander (1825–1902)

1   ". . . it is impossible to rely on the prudence or common sense
    of any man. . . ."
                    Ch. 1, *Ralph Wilton's Weird* 1875

2   "There's nothing more mischievous than moping along and
    getting into the blue devils!—nothing more likely to drive a
    man to suicide or matrimony, or some infernal entanglement
    even worse!"
                    Ch. 6, Ibid.

998. Antoinette Brown Blackwell (1825–1921)

1   . . . the sexes in each species of beings . . . are always true equiv-
    alents—equals but not identicals. . . .
                    The Sexes Throughout Nature 1875

2 Any positive thinker is compelled to see everything in the light of his own convictions.

Ibid.

3 The poor man's motto, "Women's work is never done," leads inevitably to its antithesis—ladies work is never begun.

Ibid.

4 The brain is not, and cannot be, the sole or complete organ of thought and feeling.

Ibid.

5 The law of grab is the primal law of infancy.

Ibid.

6 If Evolution, as applied to sex, teaches any one lesson plainer than another, it is the lesson that the monogamic marriage is the basis of all progress.

Ibid.

7 Woman's share of duties must involve direct nutrition, man's indirect nutrition. She should be able to bear and nourish their young children, at a cost of energy equal to the amount expended by him as household provider. Beyond this, if human justice is to supplement Nature's provisions, all family duties must be shared equitably, in person or by proxy.

Ibid.

8 Women's thoughts are impelled by their feelings. Hence the sharp-sightedness, the direct instinct, the quick perceptions; hence also their warmer prejudices and more unbalanced judgements. . . . In this the child is more like the woman.

Ibid.

9 Every nursing mother, in the midst of her little dependent brood, has far more right to whine, sulk, or scold, as temperament dictates, because beefsteak and coffee are not prepared for her and exactly to her taste, than any man ever had or ever can have during the present stage of human evolution.

Ibid.

10 Work, alternated with needful rest, is the salvation of man or woman.

Ibid.

11 It has seemed to both Lucy Stone* and myself in our student days that marriage would be a hindrance to our public work.

Quoted in *Antoinette Brown Blackwell: Biographical Sketch* by Sarah Gibson *1909*

*See 953.

12 . . . you asked me one day if it [marriage] seemed like giving up much for your sake. Only leave me free, as free as you are and everyone ought to be, and it is giving up nothing.

Letter to future husband, *Ibid.*

999. Julia Dorr (1825–1913)

1 A new beatitude I write for thee,
"Blessed are they who are not sure of things."

"A New Beatitude," *Poems 1897*

2 Oh golden Silence, bid our souls be still,
And on the foolish fretting of our care
Lay thy soft touch of healing unaware!

"Silence" *n.d.*

3 The year grows rich as it groweth old,
And life's latest sands are its sands of gold!

"To the 'Bouquet Club'" *n.d.*

4 Come, blessed Darkness, come and bring thy balm
For eyes grown weary of the garish day!
Come with thy soft, slow steps, thy garments grey,
Thy veiling shadows, bearing in thy palm
The poppy-seeds of slumber, deep and calm.

"Darkness" *n.d.*

5 Grass grows at last above all graves.

"Grass-Grown" *n.d.*

1000. Frances Ellen Watkins Harper (1825–1911)

1 And, your sin-cursed, guilty Union,
Shall be shaken to its base,
Till ye learn that simple justice,
Is the right of every race.

"To the Union Savers of Cleveland," St. 11 *ca. 1850*

2 "Now, father, I do think it is a shame for this child to be a slave, when he is just as white as anybody; . . . He is so beautiful, I would like him for my brother; and he looks like us anyhow."

Minnie's Sacrifice 1869

1001. Henrietta Heathorn (1825–1915)

1 Be not afraid, ye waiting hearts that weep,
For God still giveth His beloved sleep,
And if an endless sleep He wills—so best.*

"Browning's Funeral"** *1889*
*Epitaph on T. H. Huxley's tombstone; English scientist and humanist (1825–1895). **Robert Browning, English poet (1812–1889).

2 To all the gossip that I hear
I'll give no faith; to what I see
But only half, for it is clear
All that led up is dark to me.
Learn we the larger life to live,
To comprehend is to forgive.

"*Tout Comprendre, C'est Tout Pardonner*" *n.d.*

1002. Adelaide Proctor (1825–1864)

1 Dreams grow holy put in action.

"Phillip and Mildred," *The Poems of Adelaide Proctor 1869*

2 One dark cloud can hide the sunlight;
Loose one string, the pearls are scattered;
Think one thought, a soul may perish;
Say one word, a heart may break

Ibid.

3 One by one the sands are flowing,
One by one the moments fall;
Some are coming, some are going;
Do not strive to grasp them all.

"One by One," St. 1, *Ibid.*

4 Tell her that the lesson taught her
Far outweighs the pain.

"Friend Sorrow," *Ibid.*

5 The Past and the Future are nothing
In the face of the stern To-day.

"Now," St. 1, *Ibid.*

1003. Harriet Robinson (1825–1911)

1   What if she did hunger and thirst after knowledge? She could do nothing with it even if she could get it. So she made a *fetish* of some male relative, and gave him the mental food for which she herself was starving; and devoted all her energies towards helping him to become what she felt, under better conditions, she herself might have been. It was enough in those early days to be the *mother* or *sister* of somebody.

"Early Factory Labor in New England," *Massachusetts in the Woman Suffrage Movement 1883*

2   Skilled labor teaches something not to be found in books or in colleges.

Ibid.

3   In those days there was no need of advocating the doctrine of the proper relation between employer and employed. *Help was too valuable to be ill-treated* . . .

Ibid.

1004. Laura Towne (1825–1901)

1   I want to agitate, even if I am agitated.

Journal Entry (1877), Quoted in *Woman's True Profession* by Nancy Hoffman *1981*

1005. Emily Blackwell (1826–1911)

Coauthor with Elizabeth Blackwell; see 981:1–6.

1006. Dinah Mulock Craik (1826–1887)

1   "I wonder," he said at last, "if, when I was born, my father was as young as I am; whether he felt as I do now. You cannot think what an awful joy it is to be looking forward to a child; a little soul of God's giving, to be made fit for His eternity. How shall we do it! we that are both so ignorant, so young—she will be only just nineteen when, please God, her baby is born. Sometimes, of an evening, we sit for hours on this bench, she and I, talking of what we ought to do, and how we ought to rear the little thing, until we fall into silence, awed at the blessing that is coming to us."

Ch. XXI, *John Halifax, Gentleman 1856*

2   Yet, I think either parent would have looked amazed, had any one pitied them for having a blind child. The loss—a loss only to them, and not to her, the darling!—became familiar, and ceased to wound; the blessedness was ever new.

Ch. XXII, Ibid.

3   "There is no such word as 'too late,' in the wide world—nay, not in the universe."

Ibid., Ch. XXXVI

4   Gossip, public, private, social — to fight against it either by word or pen seems, after all, like fighting with shadows. Everybody laughs at it, protests against it, blames and despises it; yet everybody does it . . .

Ch. 8, *A Woman's Thoughts About Women 1858*

5   What comfort there is in a cheerful spirit! how the heart leaps up to meet a sunshiny face, a merry tongue, an even temper, and a heart which either naturally, or, what is better, from conscientious principle, has learned to take all things on their bright side, believing that the Giver of life being all-perfect Love, the best offering we can make to Him is to enjoy to the full what He sends of good, and bear what He allows of evil!

Ibid., Ch. 10

6   I fear, the inevitable conclusion we must all come to is, that in the world happiness is quite indefinable. We can no more grasp it than we can grasp the sun in the sky or the moon in the water. We can feel it interpenetrating our whole being with warmth and strength; we can see it in a pale reflection shining elsewhere; or in its total absence, we, walking in darkness, learn to appreciate what it is by what it is not.

Ibid.

7   Forgotten? No, we never do forget:
We let the years go; wash them clean with tears,
Leave them to bleach out in the open day,
Or lock them careful by, like dead friends' clothes,
Till we shall dare unfold them without pain, —
But we forget not, never can forget.

"A Flower of a Day," *Poems 1866*

8   Lo! All life this truth declares,
Laborare est orare;
And the whole earth rings with prayers.

Ibid., "Labour is Prayer," St. 4

9   Now, I have nothing to say against uncles in general. They are usually very excellent people, and very convenient to little boys and girls.

Ch. 2, *The Little Lame Prince 1875*

10   "One cannot make oneself, but one can sometimes help a little in the making of somebody else."

Ch. 10, Ibid.

11   Oh, if I could live four weeks longer! but no matter, no matter!

Last words* 12 October 1887

*Spoken after suffering a heart attack, while in a period of preparation for her adopted daughter Dorothy's wedding.

12   And when I lie in the green kirkyard,
With mould upon my breast,
Say not that she did well—or ill,
Only "she did her best."

"Obituary" *1887*

13   Oh my son's my son till he gets a wife,
But my daughter's my daughter all her life.

"Young and Old," *Mulock's Poems, New and Old 1888*

14   God rest ye, little children; let nothing you afright,
For Jesus Christ, your Saviour, was born this happy night;
Along the hills of Galilee the white flocks sleeping lay,
When Christ, the child of Nazareth, was born on Christmas day.

"Christmas Carol," St. 2 *n.d.*

15   Keep what is worth keeping—
And with the breath of kindness
Blow the rest away.

"Friendship" *n.d.*

16   Faith needs her daily bread.

Ch. 10, *Fortune's Marriage n.d.*

1007. Mathilda J. Gage (1826–1898)

1 . . . the most grievous wrong ever inflicted upon woman has been in the Christian teaching that she was not created equal with man, and the consequent denial of her rightful place in Church and State.

> Ch. I, "The Matriarchate" (p. 12), *Woman, Church and State: A Historical Account of the Status of Woman Through the Christian Ages with Reminiscences of the Matriarchate* (repr. 1972) *1893*

2 The whole ancient world recognized a female priesthood . . .

> Ibid.

3 One of the most revered ancient Scriptures, The Gospel according to the Hebrews, which was in use as late as the second century of the Christian era, taught the equality of the feminine in the Godhead; also that daughters should inherit with sons. . . . The fact remains undeniable that at the advent of Christ, a recognition of the feminine element in the divinity had not entirely died out from general belief . . .

> Ch. II, "Celibacy" (pp. 50–51), Ibid.

4 To the theory of "God the Father," shorn of the divine attribute of motherhood, is the world beholden for its most degrading beliefs, its most infamous practices.

> (p. 69), Ibid.

5 In the fourteenth century the church decreed that any woman who healed others without having duly studied, was a witch and should suffer death; yet in that same century, 1527, at Basle, Paracelsus* threw all his medical works, including those of Hippocrates and Galen into the fire, saying that he knew nothing except what he had learned from witches.

> Ch. V, "Witchcraft" (pp. 240–241), Ibid.

*German-Swiss alchemist and physician (1493–1541)

6 The superior learning of witches was recognized in the widely extended belief of their ability to work miracles. . . . As knowledge has ever been power, the church feared its use in woman's hands, and leveled its deadliest blows at her.

> (pp. 243–244), Ibid.

7 Woman is not regarded as a person but as a field, cultivable or not, as the possessor desires. As a field can neither have faith, nor intellect, nor a will of its own, it would be absurd for a man to occupy himself about what a woman believes, thinks, or wishes. She is absolutely nothing but her husband's domain. He cultivates it and reaps the harvest, for the harvest belongs to the proprietor.

> (p. 321), Ibid.

8 Man in thrusting the enforcement of his "curse" upon woman in Christian lands has made her the greatest unpaid laborer of the world.

> Ch. VIII, "Women and Work" (p. 441), Ibid.

9 The individual and not the family is the social unit; the rights of individuals are foremost.

> Ch. IX, "The Church of Today" (p. 498), Ibid.

10 The church and civilization are antipodal; one means authority, the other freedom; one means conservatism, the other progress; one means the rights of god as interpreted by the priesthood, the other the rights of humanity as interpreted by humanity. Civilization advances by free-thought, free speech, free men.

> Ch. X, "Past, Present, and Future" (p. 540), Ibid.

1008. Lucy Larcom (1826–1893)

1 He who plants a tree
Plants a hope.

> "Plant a Tree," St. 1, *Poetical Works of Lucy Larcom 1885*

2 Canst thou prophesy, thou little tree,
What the glory of thy boughs shall be?

> Ibid.

3 I do not own an inch of land,
But all I see is mine.

> "A Strip of Blue," Ibid.

4 If the world seems cold to you,
Kindle fires to warm it!

> "Three Old Saws," Ibid.

5 If the world's a wilderness,
Go, build houses in it!

> Ibid.

6 Oh, her heart's adrift, with one
On an endless voyage gone!
Night and morning
Hannah's at the window binding shoes.

> "Hannah Binding Shoes," St. 2, Ibid.

7 The land is dearer for the sea,
The ocean for the shore.

> "On the Beach," St. 11, Ibid.

1009. Dorothy Nevill (1826–1913)

1 It seems to be that, had the educational authorities attempted to keep alive these local industries by encouraging the children under their charge not to abandon them, they would have been doing much more good than by teaching smatterings of many totally useless subjects, which, imperfectly understood and soon forgotted, have but served to convert the English rustic into a somewhat dissatisfied imitation of the Londoner, whilst thoroughly stamping out that local character and individuality which was such an admirable feature of old-time country life.

> Ch. 3, *The Reminiscences of Lady Dorothy Nevill 1907*

2 The commercial class has always mistrusted verbal brilliancy and wit, deeming such qualities, perhaps with some justice, frivolous and unprofitable.

> Ch. 8, Ibid.

3 Society to-day and Society as I formerly knew it are two entirely different things; indeed, it may be questioned whether Society, as the word used to be understood, now exists at all. . . . Now all is changed, and wealth has usurped the place formerly held by wit and learning. The question is not now asked, "Is So-and-so clever?" but, instead, "Is So-and-so rich?"

> Ibid.

1010. Jane Francesca Wilde (1826–1896)

1 We have now traced the history of women from Paradise to the nineteenth century and have heard nothing through the long roll of the ages but the clank of their fetters.

> "The Bondage of Women," *Social Studies 1893*

2 Weary men, what reap ye?—"Golden corn for the stranger."
What sow ye?—"Human corpses that await for the Avenger."

Fainting forms, all hunger-stricken, what see you in the offing?
   "Stately ships to bear our food away amid the stranger's scoffing."
   There's a proud array of soldiers—what do they round your door?
   "They guard our master's granaries from the thin hands of the poor."

"Ballad of the Irish Famine" n.d.

1011. Ethel Lynn Beers (1827–1879)

1   All quiet along the Potomac to-night,
No sound save the rush of the river,
While soft falls the dew on the face of the dead,
The picket's off duty forever.

"The Picket Guard," St. 6 (1861), *All Quiet Along the Potomac and Other Poems 1879*

2   Art thou a pen, whose task shall be
To drown in ink
What writers think?
Oh, wisely write,
That pages white
Be not the worse for ink and thee.

"The Gold Nugget" n.d.

3   Only a mother's heart can be
Patient enough for such as he.

"Which Shall It Be" n.d.

1012. Rose Terry Cooke (1827–1892)

1   Yet courage, soul! nor hold thy strength in vain,
In hope o'er come the steeps God set for thee,
For past the Alpine summits of great pain
Lieth thine Italy.

"Beyond," St. 4 n.d.

2   Darlings of the forest!
Blossoming alone
When Earth's grief is sorest
For her jewels gone. . . .

"Trailing Arbutus" n.d.

1013. Elizabeth Doten (1827–1913)

1   God of the granite and the rose,
Soul of the sparrow and the bee,
The mighty tide of being flows
Through countless channels, Lord, from Thee.

"Reconciliation" ca. 1870

1014. Ellen Howarth (1827–1899)

1   Who hath not saved some trifling thing
More prized than jewels rare,
A faded flower, a broken ring,
A tress of golden hair.

"'Tis But a Little Faded Flower" n.d.

2   Where is the heart that doth not keep,
Within its inmost core,
Some fond remembrance hidden deep,
Of days that are no more?

Ibid.

1015. Johanna Spyri (1827–1901)

1   "You mischievous child!" she cried, in great excitement. "What are you thinking of? Why have you taken everything off? What does it mean?"
   "I do not need them," replied the child, and did not look sorry for what she had done.

Ch. 1, *Heidi 1885*

2   "Oh, I wish that God had not given me what I prayed for! It was not so good as I thought."

Ch. 11, Ibid.

3   "If your ABC is not learned to-day,
Go to be punished to-morrow, I say."

Ch. 19, Ibid.

4   ". . . anger makes us all stupid."

Ch. 23, Ibid.

1016. Lakshmi Bai (1828–1858)

1   God has created you for the destruction of the destroyers of your creed. . . . but it is evident to all men that these English are perverters of all men's religion. From time immemorial have they endeavoured to contaminate the Hindoo and Mahomedan religions by the production and circulation of religious books through the medium of missionaries, and by extirpating such books as afford arguments against them. . . .

Proclamation, 14 February 1858, Quoted in *Bhargava's Freedom Struggle in Uttar Pradesh* by M.L. Bhargava *1957–61*

2   Victory of Religion: To God only belongs the World, and the command of it rests with Him . . .

Ibid.

1017. Elizabeth Charles (1828–1896)

1   To know how to say what others only know how to think is what makes men poets or sages; and to dare to say what others only dare to think makes men martyrs or reformers—or both.

Chronicle of the Schönberg-Cotta Family 1863

1018. Mary Jane Holmes (1828–1907)

1   ". . . but needn't tell me that prayers made up is as good as them as isn't. . . ."

Ch. 1, *The Cameron Pride 1867*

2   "Keep yourself unspotted from the world," Morris had said, and she repeated it to herself asking, "how shall I do that? how can one be good and fashionable too?"

Ch. 19, Ibid.

3   "If the body you bring back has my George's heart within it, I shall love you just the same as I do now. . . ."

Ch. 3, *Rose Mather 1868*

1019. Margaret Oliphant (1828–1897)

1   "There ain't a worm but will turn when he's trod upon. . . ."

Ch. 20, *The Perpetual Curate*, Vol. II *1864*

2   For everybody knows that it requires very little to satisfy the gentlemen, if a woman will only give her mind to it.

"The Rector," Ch. 4, *Chronicles of Carlingford*, No. 1 *1866*

3 As for pictures and museums, that don't trouble me. The worst of going abroad is that you've always got to look at things of that sort. To have to do it at home would be beyond a joke.
"Phoebe, Junior," Ch. 26, No. 5, Ibid.

4 Oh, never mind the fashion. When one has a style of one's own, it is always twenty times better.
Ch. 31, No. 4, Ibid.

5 Temptations come, as a general rule, when they are sought.
Ch. 47, Ibid.

6 She was not clever; you might have said she had no mind at all; but so wise and right and tender a heart, that it was as good as genius.
Ch. 1, *A Little Pilgrim 1882*

7 "One does not want to hear one's thoughts; most of them are not worth hearing."
Ch. 3, Ibid.

8 In the history of men and of commonwealth there is a slow progression, which, however faint, however deferred, yet gradually goes on, leaving one generation always a trifle better than that which preceded it, with some scrap of new possession, some right assured, some small inheritance gained.
Introduction, *The Literary History of England 1889*

9 It has been my fate in a long life of production to be credited chiefly with the equivocal virtue of industry, a quality so excellent in morals, so little satisfactory in art.
Preface, *The Heir Presumptive and the Heir Apparent 1892*

10 There is something very solemn in the thought of a great spirit like hers* entering the spiritual world which she did not believe in. If we are right in our faith, what a blessed surprise for her!
Letter (26 December 1880), *Autobiography and Letters of Mrs. Margaret Oliphant 1899*
*Reference to George Eliot (see 955), who had recently died.

11 Imagination is the first faculty wanting in those that do harm to their kind.
"Innocent" *n.d.*

1020. Martha Johnson Patterson (1828–1901)

1 We are plain folks from Tennessee, called here by a national calamity. I hope not too much will be expected of us.
Comment after President Lincoln's* assassination, when her father, Andrew Johnson,** took office, Quoted in *First Ladies* by Betty Boyd Caroli 1987
*(1809–1865), 16th president of the United States (1861–1865).
**(1808–1875), 17th president of the United States (1865–1869).

1021. Edna Dean Proctor (1829–1923)

1 Now God avenges the life he gladly gave,
Freedom reigns to-day!
"John Brown"* *n.d.*
*American militant abolitionist (1800–1859).

2 O there are tears for him,*
O there are cheers for him—
Liberty's champion, Cid of the West.
"Cid of the West" *n.d.*
*Referring to Theodore Roosevelt (1858–1919), 26th president of the United States (1901–1909).

3 The fasts are done; the Aves said;
The moon has filled her horn,
And in the solemn night I watch
Before the Easter morn.
"Easter Morning" *n.d.*

1022. Charlotte Barnard (1830–1869)

1 I cannot sing the old songs,
Or dream those dreams again.
"I Cannot Sing the Old Songs" *ca. 1860*

2 Take back the freedom thou cravest,
Leaving the fetters to me.
"Take Back the Heart" *ca. 1860*

1023. Helen Olcott Bell (1830–1918)

1 To a woman, the consciousness of being well-dressed gives a sense of tranquility which religion fails to bestow.
Letters and Social Aims by R. W. Emerson* 1876
*Ralph Waldo E—, American poet and essayist (1803–1882).

1024. Emily Dickinson (1830–1886)

1 Will you tell me my fault, frankly as to yourself, for I had rather wince, than die. Men do not call the surgeon to commend the bone, but to set it, Sir.
Letter (July 1862) to Thomas Wentworth Higginson,*
The Letters of Emily Dickinson, Vol. 2,
Thomas H. Johnson, ed. *1958*
*American clergyman, author and editor (1823–1911).

2 Success is counted sweetest
By those who ne'er succeed.
No. 67, St. 1 (ca. 1859), *The Complete Works of Emily Dickinson,* Thomas H. Johnson, ed. *1955*

3 Surgeons must be very careful
When they take the knife!
Underneath their fine incisions
Stirs the Culprit—Life!
No. 108, (ca. 1859), Ibid.

4 "Faith" is a fine invention
When Gentlemen can *see*—
But *Microscopes* are prudent
In an Emergency.
No. 185 (ca. 1860), Ibid.

5 "Hope" is the thing with feathers—
That perches in the soul—
And sings the tune without the words—
And never stops—at all—
No. 254, St. 1 (ca. 1861), Ibid.

6 There's a certain Slant of light,
Winter Afternoons—
That oppresses like the Heft
Of Cathedral Tunes—
No. 258, St. 1 (ca. 1861), Ibid.

7 A single Screw of Flesh
Is all that pins the Soul
No. 262 (ca. 1861), Ibid.

8 I'm nobody, Who are you?
Are you—Nobody—too?
No. 288, St. 1 (1861), Ibid.

9 I tasted—careless—then—
I did not know the Wine
Came once a World—Did you?

No. 296, St. 3 (ca. 1861), Ibid.

10 I reason, Earth is short—
And Anguish—absolute—
And many hurt,
But, what of that?

No. 301, St. 1 (ca. 1862), Ibid.

11 The Soul selects her own Society—
Then—shuts the Door—

No. 303, St. 1 (ca. 1862), Ibid.

12 I'll tell you how the Sun rose—
A Ribbon at a time—

No. 318 (ca. 1862), Ibid.

13 Some keep the Sabbath going to Church—
I keep it, staying at Home—
With a Bobolink for a chorister—
And an Orchard, for a Dome—

No. 324, St. 1 (ca. 1860), Ibid.

14 After great pain, a formal feeling comes—

No. 341, St. 1 (ca. 1862), Ibid.

15 Much Madness is divinest Sense—
To a discerning Eye—
Much Sense—the starkest Madness—

No. 435, St. 1 (ca. 1862), Ibid.

16 This is my letter to the World
That never wrote to Me—

No. 441, St. 1 (ca. 1862), Ibid.

17 I heard a Fly buzz—when I died—

No. 465, St. 1 (ca. 1862), Ibid.

18 I reckon—when I count at all—
First—Poets—Then the Sun—
Then Summer—Then the Heaven of God—
And then—the List is done—

No. 569, St. 1 (ca. 1862), Ibid.

19 The Brain—is wider than the Sky—
For—put them side by side—
The one the other will contain
With ease—and You—beside—

No. 632, St. 1 (ca. 1862), Ibid.

20 I dwell in Possibility—
A fairer House than Prose—
More numerous of Windows—
Superior—for doors—

No. 657, St. 1 (ca. 1862), Ibid.

21 Because I could not stop for Death—
He kindly stopped for me—

No. 712, St. 1 (ca. 1863), Ibid.

22 My Life had stood—a Loaded Gun—
In Corners . . .

No. 754, St. 1 (ca. 1863), Ibid.

23 If I can stop one Heart from breaking
I shall not live in vain

No. 919, St. 1 (ca. 1864), Ibid.

24 A great hope fell
You heard no noise
The Ruin was within

No. 1123, St. 1 (ca. 1868), Ibid.

25 Tell all the Truth but tell it slant—
Success in Circuit lies

No. 1129, St. 1 (ca. 1868), Ibid.

26 A word is dead
When it is said,
Some say.
I say it just
Begins to live
That day.

No. 1212 in toto (1872?), Ibid.

27 A Deed knocks first at Thought
And then—it knocks at Will—
That is the manufacturing spot

No. 1216, St. 1 (ca. 1872), Ibid.

28 There is no Frigate like a Book
To take us Lands away
Nor any Coursers like a Page
Of prancing Poetry.

No. 1263, Ibid.

29 A little Madness in the Spring
Is wholesome even for the King,
But God be with the Clown—

No. 1333, St. 1 (ca. 1875), Ibid.

30 Forbidden Fruit a flavor has
That lawful Orchards mocks—
How luscious lies within the Pod
The Pea that Duty locks—

No. 1377 (ca. 1876), Ibid.

31 To see the Summer Sky
Is Poetry, though never in a Book it lie—
True Poems flee—

No. 1472, Ibid.

32 The Pedigree of Honey
Does not concern the Bee—
A Clover, any time, to him,
Is Aristocracy—

No. 1627, version II (ca. 1884), Ibid.

1025. Maria von Ebner Eschenbach (1830–1916)

1 "Good heavens!" said he, "if it be our clothes alone which fit us for society, how highly we should esteem those who make them."

The Two Countesses 1893

2 He says a learned woman is the greatest of all calamities.

Ibid.

3 If there is faith that can move mountains, it is faith in your own power.

Ibid.

4 Many think they have a kind heart who only have weak nerves.

Ibid.

5 As far as your self-control goes, as far goes your freedom.

Ibid.

6 Even a stopped clock is right twice a day.

Ibid.

7 Conquer, but don't triumph.

Ibid.

8 No one is so eager to gain new experience as he who doesn't know how to make use of the old ones.

Ibid.

9 Only the thinking man lives his life, the thoughtless man's life passes him by.

Ibid.

10 You can stay young as long as you can learn, acquire new habits and suffer contradiction.

Ibid.

11 In youth we learn; in age we understand.

Ibid.

12 Fear not those who argue but those who dodge.

Ibid.

13 To be content with little is hard, to be content with much, impossible.

Ibid.

14 Imaginary evils are incurable.

Ibid.

15 We don't believe in rheumatism and true love until the first attack.

Ibid.

16 We are so vain that we even care for the opinion of those we don't care for.

Ibid.

1026. Harriet Hosmer (1830–1908)

1 Apropos of a Temple, I have long entertained the hope of seeing before I die a monument erected which shall record the great deeds of women wherever found and it is high time that such a memorial should assume form.

Quoted by Carole Simmons Oles, (p. 24) The Women's Review of Books, XVI, No. 2 November 1998

1027. Helen Fiske Hunt Jackson (1830–1885)

1 There is nothing so skillful in its own defense as imperious pride.

Ch. 13, Ramona 1884

2 There cannot be found in the animal kingdom a bat, or any other creature, so blind in its own range of circumstance and connection, as the greater majority of human beings in the bosom of their families.

Ibid.

3 Wounded vanity knows when it is mortally hurt; and limps off the field, piteous, all disguises thrown away. But pride carries its banner to the last.

Ibid.

4 My body, eh. Friend Death, how now?
Why all this tedious pomp of writ?
Thou hast reclaimed it sure and slow
For half a century, bit by bit.

"Habeas Corpus," St. 1 1885

5 Great loves, to the last, have pulses red;
All great loves that have ever died dropped dead.

"Dropped Dead" n.d.

6 Bee to the blossom, moth to the flame;
Each to his passion; what's in a name?

"Vanity of Vanities" n.d.

7 Love has a tide!

"Tides" n.d.

8 Oh, write of me, not "Died in bitter pains,"
But "Emigrated to another star!"

"Emigravit" n.d.

1028. Mother Jones (1830–1930)

1 Sometimes I'm in Washington, then in Pennsylvania, Arizona, Texas, Alabama, Colorado, Minnesota. My address is like my shoes. It travels with me. I abide where there is a fight against wrong.

Congressional Hearing, Quoted in The Rebel Girl, Pt. II by Elizabeth Gurley Flynn* 1955
*See 1706.

2 Sit down and read. Educate yourself for the coming conflicts.

Quoted in Ms. (New York) November 1981

3 Pray for the dead and fight like hell for the living.

Motto n.d.

4 Get it right, I ain't a humanitarian.... I'm a hell-raiser!

Comment n.d.

1029. Belva Lockwood (1830–1917)

1 I do not believe in sex discrimination in literature, law, politics, or trade—or that modesty and virtue are more becoming to women than to men, but wish we had more of it everywhere.

Quoted in Pt. II, Ch. 8, Lady for the Defense by Mary Virginia Fox 1975

2 I know we can't abolish prejudice through laws, but we can set up guidelines for our actions by legislation. If women are given equal pay for Civil Service jobs, maybe other employers will do the same.

Ch. 11, Ibid.

3 If nations could only depend on fair and impartial judgments in a world court of law, they would abandon the senseless, savage practice of war.

Ch. 15, Ibid.

4 No one can claim to be called Christian who gives money for the building of warships and arsenals.

Address at Westminster Hall, London (ca. 1886), Ibid.

5 I have been told that there is no precedent for admitting a woman to practice in the Supreme Court of the United States. The glory of each generation is to make its own precedents. As there was none for Eve in the Garden of Eden, so there need be none for her daughters on entering the colleges, the church, or the courts.*

Pt. III, Ch. 13, Ibid.

*Lockwood argued in favor of admitting women to practice in the U.S. Supreme Court, for which there was no precedent. In 1879 she became the first woman to do so.

1030. Louise Michel (1830–1905)

1 In rebellion alone, woman is at ease, stamping out both prejudices and sufferings; all intellectual women will sooner or later rise in rebellion.

Memoirs 1890

2 It is the people who will deliver us from the men who have been corrupting us, and the people themselves will win their liberty.

Speech (Paris) *21 November 1880*

3 It is not a question of breadcrumbs. What is at stake is the harvest of an entire world, a harvest necessary to the whole future human race, one without exploiters and without exploited.

The Memoirs of Louise Michel, the Red V, Bullitt Lowry and Elizabeth Ellington Gunter, eds. *1981*

4 . . . since it seems that any heart which beats for freedom has the right only to a lump of lead, I too claim my share. If you let me live, I shall never stop crying for revenge and I shall avenge my brothers. I have finished. If you are not cowards, kill me!

Versaille Government Tribunal *16 December 1871*

5 We revolutionaries aren't just chasing a scarlet flag. What we pursue is an awakening of liberty, old or new. It is the ancient Communes of France, it is 1703; it is June 1848; it is 1871. Most especially it is the next revolution which is advancing under this dawn.

Quoted by Jayacintha Danaswamy, *Workers Solidarity* No. 55 *October 1998*

6 I have seen criminals and whores
And spoken with them. Now I inquire
If you believe them made as now they are
To drag their rags in blood and mire
Preordained, an evil race?
You to whom all men are prey
Have made them what they are today.

Untitled *n.d.*

1031. Sarah Agnes Pryor (1830–1912)

1 The public does not tolerate the intrusion of a man's personal joys and griefs into his official life.

Comment on Franklin Pierce's* inaugural speech (4 March 1853), Quoted in *First Ladies* by Betty Boyd Caroli *1987*
*(1804–1869), 14th President of the United States (1853–1857).

1032. Christina Rossetti (1830–1894)

1 When I am dead, my dearest,
Sing no sad songs for me;
Plant thou no roses at my head,
Nor shady cypress tree.
Be the green grass above me
With showers and dew drops wet:

And if thou wilt, remember,
And if thou wilt, forget

"Song," St. 1 *12 December 1848*

2 To-day is still the same as yesterday,
To-morrow also even as one of them;
And there is nothing new under the sun. . . .

"One Certainty" *2 June 1849*

3 My friends have failed one by one,
Middle-aged, young, and old,
Till the ghosts were warmer to me
Than my friends that had grown cold.

"A Chilly Night," St. 2 *11 February 1856*

4 "Does the road wind up-hill all the way?"
"Yes, to the very end."
"Will the day's journey take the whole long day?"
"From morn to night, my friend."

"Up-Hill," St. 1 *1861*

5 My heart is like a singing bird.

"A Birthday," St. 1 *1861*

6 Too late for love, too late for joy,
Too late, too late!
You loitered on the road too long,
You trifled at the gate. . . .

"The Prince's Progress," St. 1 *11 November 1861*

7 For there is no friend like a sister
In calm or stormy weather;
To cheer one on the tedious way,
To fetch one if one goes astray,
To lift one if one totters down,
To strengthen whilst one stands.

"Goblin Market," *Goblin Market 1862*

8 One day in the country
Is worth a month in town.

"Summer," Ibid.

9 Better by far that you should forget and smile
Than that you should remember and be sad.

"Remember" (25 July 1849), Ibid.

10 If thou canst dive, bring up pearls. If thou canst not dive, collect amber.

Prefatory Note, *The Face of the Deep 1892*

11 Well spake the soldier who being asked what he would do if he became too weak to cling to Christ, answered, "Then I will pray Him to cling to me."

Ch. 16, Ibid.

12 Who has seen the wind!
Neither you nor I:
But when the trees bow down their heads,
The wind is passing by.

"Who Has Seen the Wind?", St. 2 *n.d.*

13 He bids me sing: O death, where is thy sting?
And sing: O grave, where is thy victory?

"The Thread of Life," St. 3, *n.d.*

1033. Amelia Barr (1831–1919)

1 "'Is she not handsome, virtuous, rich, amiable?' they asked, 'What hath she done to thee?' The Roman husband pointed

to his sandal. 'Is it not new, is it not handsome and well made? But none of you can tell where it pinches me.' That old Roman and I are brothers. Everyone praises 'my good wife, my rich wife, my handsome wife,' but for all that, the matrimonial shoe pinches me."

Ch. 9, *Jan Vedder's Wife* 1885

2 That is the greatest mistake about the affections. It is not the rise and fall of empires, the birth and death of kings or the marching of armies that move them most. When they answer from their depths, it is to the domestic joys and tragedies of life.

Ch. 14, Ibid.

3 It is only in sorrow bad weather masters us; in joy we face the storm and defy it.

Ibid.

4 "When men make themselves into brutes it is just to treat them as brutes."

Ch. 8, *The Belle of Bolling Green* 1904

5 I entered this incarnation on March-the-twenty-ninth, A.D. 1831, at the ancient town of Ulverston, Lancashire, England. My soul came with me. This is not always the case. Every observing mother of a large family knows that the period of spiritual possession varies. . . . I brought my soul with me—an eager soul, impatient for the loves and joys, the struggles and triumphs of the dear, unforgotten world.

Ch. 1, *All the Days of My Life* 1913

6 The great difference between voyages rests not with the ships, but with the people you meet on them.

Ch. 11, Ibid.

7 What we call death was to him only emigration, and I care not where he now tarries. He is doing God's will, and more alive than ever he was on earth.

Ch. 23, Ibid.

8 Whatever the scientists may say, if we take the supernatural out of life, we leave only the unnatural.

Ch. 26, Ibid.

1034. Elena Petrovna Blavatsky (1831–1891)

1 We live in an age of prejudice, dissimulation, and paradox, wherein, like dry leaves caught in a whirlpool, some of us are tossed helpless, hither and thither, ever struggling between our honest convictions and fear of that cruelest of tyrants—PUBLIC OPINION.

"A Paradoxical World," *Lucifer* February 1889

2 We must prepare and study truth under every aspect, endeavoring to ignore nothing, if we do not wish to fall into the abyss of the unknown when the hour shall strike.

Quoted in *La Revue Theosophique* 21 March 1889

3 It is the worst of crimes and dire in its results. . . . Voluntary death would be an abandonment of our present post and of the duties incumbent on us, as well as an attempt to shirk karmic responsibilities, and thus involve the creation of new Karma.

Sec. 12, *The Key to Theosophy* 1893

4 Just back from under the far-reaching shadow of the Eighth Wonder of the World—the gigantic iron carrot that goes by the name of the Eiffel Tower. Child of its country, wondrous

in its size, useless in its object, as shaky and vacillating as the republican soil upon which it is built, it has not one single moral feature of its seven ancestors, not one trait of atavism to boast of.

"The Eighth Wonder," *Lucifer* October 1891

5 If there were such a thing as a void, a vacuum in Nature, one ought to find it produced, according to a physical law, in the minds of helpless admirers of the "lights" of Science, who pass their time in mutually destroying their teachings.

Sec. 17, *The Secret Doctrine* (1893) 1918

1035. Myra R. Bradwell (1831–1894)

1 [Mary Lincoln*] is no more insane than I am.

Comment, Quoted in *First Ladies* by Betty Boyd Caroli 1987
*See 950.

1036. Isabel Burton (1831–1896)

1 Blessed be they who invented pens, ink, and paper!

Bk. I, Ch. II, *The Romance of Isabel, Lady Burton*, Vol. I, W. H. Wilkins, ed. 1897

2 Happy is she who meets at her first start the man who is to guide her for life, whom she is always to love. Some women grow fastidious in solitude, and find it harder to be mated than married. Those who fear and respect the men they love, those whose judgment and sense confirm their affection, are lucky.

Ch. IV, Ibid.

3 It was not only his eyes* which showed the gypsy peculiarity; he had the restlessness which could stay nowhere long, nor own any spot on earth, the same horror of a corpse, deathbed scenes, and graveyards, or anything which was in the slightest degree ghoulish, though caring little for his own life, the same aptitude for reading the hand at a glance. With many he would drop their hands at once and turn away, nor would anything induce him to speak a word about them.

Ibid.

*Her husband, Sir Richard Burton, British explorer and orientalist (1821–90).

4 They say it is time I married (perhaps it is); but it is never time to marry any man one does not love, because such a deed can never be undone.

Ch. V, Ibid.

5 I do not want to think it over [Burton's* proposal]. I have been thinking it over for six years, ever since I first saw you at Boulogne. I have prayed for you every morning and night, I have followed all your career minutely, I have read every word you ever wrote, and I would rather have a crust and a tent with you than be queen of all the world; and so I say now, 'Yes, yes, YES!'

Ch. VI, Ibid.

*Her husband, Sir Richard Burton (1821–90), British explorer & orientalist.

1037. Rebecca Harding Davis (1831–1910)

1 The idiosyncracy of this town is smoke. It rolls solemnly in slow folds from the great chimneys of the iron foundries, and settles down in black, slimy pools on the muddy streets. Smoke on the wharves, smoke on the dinghy boats, on the yellow river—clinging in a coating of greasy soot to the house-front, the two faded poplars, the faces of the passers-by.

"Life in the Iron Mills," *Atlantic Monthly* (Boston) April 1861

2 "I tell you, there's something wrong that no talk of 'Liberté' or 'Egalité' will do away. If I had the making of men, these men who do the lowest part of the world's work should be machines—nothing more—hands. It would be kindness. God help them! What are taste, reason, to creatures who must live such lives as that?"

Ibid.

3 Reform is born of need, not pity.

Ibid.

4 There are moments when a passing cloud, the sun glinting on the purple thistles, a kindly smile, a child's face, will rouse him to a passion of pain—when his nature starts up with a mad cry of rage against God, man, whoever it is that has forced this vile, slimy life upon him.

Ibid.

5 Nowhere in this country, from sea to sea, does nature comfort us with such assurance of plenty, such rich and tranquil beauty as in those unsung, unpainted hills of Pennsylvania.

Ch. 4, *Bits of Gossip 1904*

6 North and South were equally confident that God was on their side, and appealed incessantly to Him.

Ch. 5, Ibid.

7 But while the light burning within may have been divine, the outer case of the lamp was assuredly cheap enough. [Walt] Whitman* was, from first to last, a boorish, awkward *poseur*.

Ch. 8, Ibid.

*American poet (1819–1892).

1038. Henrietta Dobree (1831–1894)

1 Safely, safely, gather'd in,
Far from sorrow, far from sin.

"Child's Hymn Book" *n.d.*

1039. Mary Mapes Dodge (1831–1905)

1 . . . in Holland ice is generally an all-winter affair.

Preface, *Hans Brinker or the Silver Skates 1865*

2 What a dreadful thing it must be to have a dull father. . . .

"Boys and Girls," Ibid.

3 "It is an ugly business, boy, this surgery," said the doctor, still frowning at Hans, "it requires great patience, self-denial and perseverance."

"Broad Sunshine," Ibid.

4 How faithfully those glancing eyes shall yet seek for the jewels that live hidden in rocky schoolbooks!

Ibid.

5 Life is a mystery as deep as every death can be;
Yet oh, how dear it is to us, this life we live and see!

"The Two Mysteries," St. 3 *n.d.*

6 But I believe that God is overhead;
And as life is to the living, so death is to the dead.

St. 5, Ibid.

1040. Amelia Edwards (1831–1889)

1 The Queen has lands and gold, Mother
The Queen has lands and gold,

While you are forced to your empty breast
A skeleton Babe to hold. . . .

"Give Me Three Grains of Corn, Mother," St. 4 *n.d.*

2 What has poor Ireland done, Mother,
What has poor Ireland done,
That the world looks on, and sees us starve,
Perishing one by one?

St. 5, Ibid.

1041. Lucy Webb Hayes (1831–1889)

1 Women's mind is as strong as man's—equal in all things and his superior in some.

Quoted in *First Ladies* by Betty Boyd Caroli *1987*

1042. Nora Perry (1831–1896)

1 Some day, some day of days, threading the street
With idle, heedless pace,
Unlooking for such grace,
I shall behold your face!

"Some Day of Days" *n.d.*

2 What silences we keep, year after year,
With those who are most near to us,
And dear!

"Too Late," St. 1 *n.d.*

3 Who knows the thoughts of a child?

"Who Knows," St. 1 *n.d.*

1043. Elizabeth Chase Akers (1832–1911)

1 Backward, turn backward, O Time, in your flight,
Make me a child again, just for to-night!

"Rock Me to Sleep, Mother" *1860*

2 I have grown weary of dust and decay—
Weary of flinging my soul-wealth away;—
Weary of sowing for others to reap;
Rock me to sleep, Mother—rock me to sleep!

St. 2, Ibid.

3 Unremembered and afar
I watched you as I watched a star,
Through darkness struggling into view,
I loved you better than you knew.

"Left Behind," St. 5 *n.d.*

4 Carve not upon a stone when I am dead
The praises which remorseful mourners give
To women's graves—a tardy recompense—
But speak them while I live.

"Till Death," St. 6 *n.d.*

5 Though we be sick and tired and faint and worn,—
Lo, all things can be borne!

"Endurance," St. 5 *n.d.*

1044. Louisa May Alcott (1832–1888)

1 A little kingdom I possess,
Where thoughts and feelings dwell;
And very hard the task I find
Of governing it well.

"My Kingdom," St. 1 *ca. 1845*

2 "She would make a man of me. She puts strength and courage into me as no one else can. She is unlike any girl I ever saw; there's no sentimentality about her; she is wise, and kind, and sweet. She says what she means, looks you straight in the eye, and is as true as steel."
Ch. III, *Behind a Mask: or, A Woman's Power* 1866

3 "... rivalry adds so much to the charms of one's conquests."
Ch. VII, Ibid.

4 "I can't get over my disappointment in not being a boy."
Little Women 1868

5 "Christmas won't be Christmas without any presents."
Pt. I, Ibid.

6 "Housekeeping ain't no joke."
Ch. 11, Ibid.

7 ... public opinion is a giant which has frightened stouter-hearted Jacks on bigger beanstalks than hers.
Pt. II, Ibid.

8 ... she was one of those happily created beings who please without effort, make friends everywhere, and take life so gracefully and easily that less fortunate souls are tempted to believe that such are born under a lucky star.
Ibid.

9 It takes people a long time to learn the difference between talent and genius, especially ambitious young men and women.
Ibid.

10 ... she had a womanly instinct that clothes possess an influence more powerful over many than the worth of character or the magic of manners
Ibid.

11 ... when women are the advisers, the lords of creation don't take the advice until they have persuaded themselves that it is just what they intended to do; then they act upon it, and if it succeeds, they give the weaker vessel half the credit of it; if it fails, they generously give her the whole.
Ibid.

12 "... I'm not afraid of storms, for I'm learning how to sail my ship."
Ibid.

13 "... What *do* girls do who haven't any mothers to help them through their troubles?"
Ibid.

14 "... It's a great comfort to have an artistic sister."
Ibid.

15 "[I'm] very glad and grateful that my profession will make me a useful happy and independent spinster."
Jo's Boys 1886

16 My definition [of a philosopher] is of a man up in a balloon, with his family and friends holding the ropes which confine him to the earth and trying to haul him down.
Louisa May Alcott: Her Life, Letters, and Journals, Edna D. Cheney, ed. 1889

17 Resolved to take Fate by the throat and shake a living out of her.
Ch. 3, Ibid.

18 Father asked us what was God's noblest work. Anna said *men*, but I said *babies*. Men are often bad; babies never are.
Early diary kept at Fruitlands (1843), Ibid.

1045. Lucretia Rudolph Garfield (1832–1918)

1 My heart almost broke with the cruel thought that our marriage was based upon the cold, stern word duty.
Letter to James Garfield* (1858), Quoted in *First Ladies* by Betty Boyd Caroli 1987
*(1831–81), 20th president of the United States.

1046. Elizabeth Sarah Mazuchelli (1832–1914)

1 O scarlet poppies in the rich ripe corn! O sunny uplands striped with golden sheaves! O darkling heather on the distant hills, stretching away, away to the far-off sea, where little boats with white sails, vague and indistinct in the misty horizon, lie floating dreamily!
Ch. I, *The Indian Alps and How We Crossed Them* 1876

2 ... I recall the events of the day, and think with a shudder of the precipices we have passed, and the unknown dangers we have escaped, and how near we may have been to that mysterious life beyond, which awaits us all sooner or later, when the slender thread which binds us here will be loosed to let us free; a time that almost comes to us in the vicissitude of each day's travel, and would surely do so but for some restraining hand to hold us up.
Ch. XXIII, Ibid.

3 The sky is intensely blue, and the air so intoxicating in its freshness, that the very tea we had for breakfast on the way seems to have got into our heads, and so exhilarating is the atmosphere that one's very heart seems to throb as with new life.
Ch. XXV, Ibid.

1047. Mary Edwards Walker (1832–1919)

1 If men were really what they profess to be they would not compell women to dress so that the facilities for vice would always be so easy.
Quoted in *Saturday Review* 1935

2 Let the generations know that women in uniform also guaranteed their freedom.
"Mary Edwards Walker," *Women in History* 25 January 2008

1048. Mary Woolsey (1832–1864)

1 I lay me down to sleep with little thought or care
Whether my waking finds me here, or there.
"Rest" n.d

1049. Lillie Devereux Blake (1833–1913)

1 Among all these strong, pushing, busy men, there seemed no place, and no hope for a woman to expect justice and mercy. These resolute-browed, swift-going, strong-limbed animals, who represented the great brute force of nature, its resistless power, its relentless will could crush out so easily the gentler, more spiritual being, who represented the beauty, the grace, the harmony of creation!
Fettered for Life 1874; rev. 1997

2 Mr. Livingston regarded his daughter in astonishment, as much surprised as one would be, who should see a hummingbird, that was sporting in apparent contentment among the flowers,

on a sudden ask to be transformed into an eagle, and aspire to reach the sun.

Ibid.

1050. Hedwig Dohm (1833–1919)

1 For me the beginning of all true progress in the woman question lies in women's right to vote . . . The stronger the emphasis on the difference between the sexes, the clearer the need for the specific representation of women.

Remark (1873), Quoted in *Women in World History Curriculum* (womeninworldhistory.com) *1996–97*

1051. Gail Hamilton (1833–1896)

1 Every person is responsible for all the good within the scope of his abilities, and for no more, and none can tell whose sphere is the largest.

"Men and Women," *Country Living and Country Thinking 1862*

2 Whatever an author puts between two covers of his book is public property; whatever of himself he does not put there is his private property, as much as if he had never written a word.

Preface, Ibid.

3 What's virtue in man can't be virtue in a cat.

"Both Sides" *n.d.*

1052. Julia Harris May (1833–1912)

1 If we could know
Which of us, darling, would be the first to go,
Who would be first to breast the swelling tide
And step alone upon the other side—
If we could know!

"If We Could Know" *n.d.*

1053. Emily Miller (1833–1913)

1 They sing, young hearts that are full of cheer,
With never a thought of sorrow;
The old goes out, but the glad young year
Comes merrily in tomorrow.

"New Year Song," *The Little Corporal 1865*

2 I love to hear the story
Which angel voices tell.

"I Love to Hear," Ibid.

1054. Julia Woodruff (1833–1909)

1 Out of the strain of the Doing,
Into the race of the Done.

"Harvest Home," *Sunday at Home May 1910*

1055. Annie Adams Fields (1834–1915)

1 Once men could walk these roads
And hear no sound
Save the sad ocean beating on the shore . . .

"Unchanged," *The Singing Shepherd 1895*

1056. Katherine Hankey (1834–1911)

1 Tell me the old, old story
Of unseen things above,

Of Jesus and His glory
Of Jesus and His love.

Hymn *n.d.*

1057. Harriet Kimball (1834–1917)

1 All my room was dark and damp:
"Sorrow," said I, "trim the lamp,
Light the fire, and cheer thy face,
Set the guest-chair in its place."

"The Guest," St. 2, *An American Anthology, 1787–1900,* Edmund Clarence Stedman, ed. *1900*

2 A very rapturing of white;
A wedlock of silence and light:
White, white as the wonder undefiled
Of Eve just wakened in Paradise.

"White Azaleas" *n.d.*

1058. Virginia Backentoe Murphy (1834–1921)

1 O Mary I have not rote you half of the truble we have had but I have rote you anuf to let you now that you dont now what truble is but thank god we have all got throw. [sic]

Letter to her cousin (April 1847),* *Illinois Journal December 1847*

*First detailed account of the disastrous Donner Party trek westward.

2 It was a dreary, desolate, alkali waste; not a living thing was to be seen; it seemed as though the hand of death had been laid upon the country.

Article on the Donner Party (on reaching the shore of the Great Salt Lake, Utah), Quoted in *Century Magazine 1891*

1059. Josephine Pollard (1834–1892)

1 On a velocipede*
Harry would ride:
Quickly the splendid steed
Set him astride.

"On a High Horse," St. 1, *The Nursery,* vol. XVII, no. 101 *May 1875*

2 Beyond the sunset's radiant glow,
There is a brighter world, I know;
Beyond the sunset I may spend
Delightful days that never end.

"Beyond the Sunset" *n.d.*

3 Though he had Eden to live in,
Man cannot be happy alone.

"We Cannot Be Happy Alone," St. 5 *n.d*

1060. Ellen Palmer Allerton (1835–1893)

1 If you have a cherished secret,
Don't you tell:—
Not your friend, for his tympanum
Is a bell

"Don't You Tell," St. 1, *Walls of Corn, and Other Poems 1894*

2 Beautiful faces are those that wear
Whole-souled honesty printed there

"Beautiful Things," Ibid.

1061. Mary Bradley (1835–1898)

1 Of all the flowers that come and go
  The whole twelve months together,
  This little purple pansy brings
  Thoughts of the sweetest, saddest things.

  "Heartsease" *n.d.*

1062. Olympia Brown (1835–1900)

1 I comforted her [Mother Cobb] by telling her that while it was disagreeable and unreasonable to have our wearing apparel described in the papers, it was inevitable at this stage of woman's progress, editors and reporters being much more able to judge of our clothes than they were of our arguments.

  Ch. 10, *Acquaintances, Old and New Among Reformers 1912*

2 When I read of the vain discussions of the present day about the Virgin Birth and other old dogmas which belong to the past, I feel how great the need is still of a real interest in the religion which builds up character, teaches brotherly love, and opens up to the seeker such a world of usefulness and the beauty of holiness. . . .

  "Olympia Brown, An Autobiography," Gwendolen B. Willis,*
  ed. (1960), Quoted in Ch. 5, *The Annual Journal of the
  Universalist Historical Society,* Vol. 4 *1963*
  *Daughter of Olympia Brown; see 1486.

3 Our women's colleges are filled with young women, many of whom, with proper encouragement, would make good ministers. We must present the needs of the church and the fitness of the profession for women to these students. The difficulties and discouragements in their way must be overcome by the indefatigable efforts of individual women, so that prejudices will be conquered and church rules, where necessary, amended.

  Ibid.

4 I used to say that Susan B. Anthony* was my pole star until I learned to make no one my guide but to follow truth wherever it might lead and to do the duty of the hour at whatever cost.

  Ibid.

  *See 963.

5 The more we learn of science, the more we see that its wonderful mysteries are all explained by a few simple laws so connected together and so dependent upon each other, that we all see the same mind animating them all.

  Sermon (Mukwonago, Wisconsin, 13 January 1895?), Ibid.

6 The Old Testament teems with prophecies of the Messiah, but nowhere is it intimated that that Messiah is to stand as a God to be worshiped. He is to bring peace on earth, to build up the waste places—to comfort the broken-hearted, but nowhere is he spoken of as a deity.

  Ibid.

7 He who never sacrificed a present to a future good or a personal to a general one can speak of happiness only as the blind do of colors.

  Ibid.

1063. Augusta Evans (1835–1909)

1 Money is everything in this world to some people, and more than the next to other poor souls.

  Ch. 2, *Beulah 1859*

2 Oh! Duty is an icy shadow. It will freeze you. It cannot fill the heart's sanctuary.

  Ch. 13, Ibid.

3 Human genius has accomplished a vast deal for man's temporal existence. . . . But . . . what has it affected for philosophy, that great burden which constantly recalls the fabled labors of Sisyphus and the Danaides?* Since the rising of Bethlehem's star, in the cloudy sky of polytheism, what has human genius discovered of God, eternity, destiny?

  Ch. 41, Ibid.

  *In Greek mythology, Sisyphus was condemned forever to roll a huge stone up a hill in Hades only to have it roll down again on nearing the top; the Danaides were the daughters of Danaus, who at their father's command murdered their bridegrooms on their wedding night and were condemned in Hades to pour water eternally into a leaky vessel.

1064. Rebecca Latimer Felton (1835–1930)

1 When there is not enough religion in the pulpit to organize a crusade against sin; nor justice in the court house to promptly punish crime; nor manhood enough in the nation to put a sheltering arm about innocence and virtue—if it needs lynching to protect woman's dearest possession from the ravening human beasts—then I say lynch, a thousand times a week if necessary.

  Speech, *11 August 1897*

2 It was a time of madness, the sort of mad-hysteria that always presages war. There seems to be nothing left but war—when any population in any sort of a nation gets violently angry, civilization falls down and religion forsakes its hold on the consciences of human kind in such times of public madness.

  Ch. 1, *Country Life in Georgia in the Days of My Youth 1919*

3 When the women of the country come in and sit with you, though there may be but very few in the next few years, I pledge you that you will get ability, you will get integrity of purpose, you will get exalted patriotism, and you will get unstinted usefulness.

  Address to Senate *21 November 1922*

1065. Ellen Gates (1835–1920)

1 Sleep sweet within this quiet room,
  O thou! who'er thou art;
  And let no mournful yesterday,
  Disturb thy peaceful heart.

  "Sleep Sweet" *n.d.*

1066. Amanda Theodosia Jones (1835–1914)

1 Books were more necessary than daily bread to our parents.

  A Psychic Autobiography 1910

2 I see how fruit can be canned without cooking it. The air must be exhausted from the cells and fluid made to take its place. The fluid must be airless also—a light syrup of sugar and water—that, or the juice of fruit.*

  Ibid.

  *Jones maintained that she awoke from a nap with these exact words in her mind.

1067. Louise Moulton (1835–1908)

1 Bend low, O dusky night,
  And give my spirit rest,
  Hold me deep to your breast,
  And put old cares to flight.

  "Tonight" *n.d.*

2   The month it was the month of May,
    And all along the pleasant way,
    The morning birds were mad with glee,
    And all the flowers sprang up to see. . . .
                          "The Secret of Arcady" *n.d.*

3   This life is a fleeting breath. . . .
                  "When I Wander Away with Death" *n.d.*

1068. Harriet Spofford (1835–1921)

1   Beauty vanishes like a vapor,
    Preach the men of musty morals.
                          "Evanescence" *n.d.*

2   Something to live for came to the place,
    Something to die for maybe,
    Something to give even sorrow a grace,
    And yet it was only a baby!
                          "Only" *n.d.*

3   The awful phantom of the hungry poor.
                          "A Winter's Night" *n.d.*

1069. Celia Thaxter (1835–1894)

1   Across the narrow beach we flit,
    One little sandpiper and I.
                          "The Sandpiper," St. 1 *n.d.*

2   Sad soul, take comfort, nor forget
    That sunrise never failed us yet!
                  "The Sunrise Never Failed Us Yet," St. 4 *n.d.*

1070. Anna C. Brackett (1836–1911)

1   Is it not evident that for natures so entirely different, entirely
    different methods [of education] must be used?
                  "Indian and Negro," *Harper's September 1880*

2   Here, again, is another wide difference between the two races,
    for, while in no race more than in the negro is woman recog-
    nized to be on a full equality with man, in none more than the
    Indian is she looked upon with contempt.
                          Ibid.

3   They [blacks] come to Hampton [School], and go to their class
    recitations just as they go to their washing or ironing, sewing,
    planting, or reaping, between class hours, with a never-failing
    courage in spite of all difficulties, a cheerful, sunny humor,
    and yet with a sense of responsibility delightful to see and
    feel.
        Such is the Negro race in its essential characteristics.
                          Ibid.

4   Do not seek for information of which you cannot make use.
                          p. 2, *The Technique of Rest 1892*

5   We go on multiplying our conveniences only to multiply our
    cares. We increase our possessions only to the enlargement of
    our anxieties.
                          Ibid.

1071. Mary Frances Butts (1836–1902)

1   Build a little fence of trust
    Around today;

Fill the space with loving work,
And therein stay.
                          "Trust" *n.d.*

1072. Frances Ridley Havergal (1836–1879)

1   Doubt indulged soon becomes doubt realized.
          "The Imagination of the Thoughts of the Heart," *Royal
                                      Bounty n.d.*

2   Love understands love; it needs no talk.
          "Loving Allegiance," *Royal Commandments n.d.*

3   Silence is not certain token
    That no secret grief is there;
    Sorrow which is never spoken
    Is the heaviest load to bear.
                  "Misunderstood," St. 15 *n.d.*

1073. Marietta Holley (1836?–1926)

1   We are blind creeters, the fur-seein'-est of us; weak creeters, when
    we think we are the strong-mindedest. Now, when we hear of a
    crime, it is easy to say that the one who committed that wrong
    stepped flat off from goodness into sin, and should be hung. It is
    so awful easy and sort of satisfactory to condemn other folks'es
    faults that we don't stop to think that it may be that evil was fell
    into through the weakness and blindness of a mistake.
          "Kitty Smith and Caleb Cobb," *My Wayward Pardner; or My
          Trials with Josiah, America, the Widow Bump, and Etcetery
                                      1880*

2   And then when we read of some noble, splendid act of gener-
    osity, our souls burn within us, and it is easy to say, the one
    who did that glorious deed should be throned and crowned
    with honor—not thinkin' how, mebby, unbeknown to us, that
    act was the costly and glitterin' varnish coverin' up a whited
    sepulchre. That deed was restin' on self-seekin', ambitious lit-
    tleness.
                          Ibid.

3   Yes, this world is a curious place, very, and holler, holler as a
    drum. Lots of times the ground seems to lay smooth and se-
    rene under your rockin' chair, when all the time a earthquake
    may be on the very p'int of bustin' it open and swollerin' you
    up—chair and all.
                  "Josiah Allen Gits a Stray," Ibid.

4   But I am a-eppisodin' and a-eppisodin' to a length and depth al-
    most onprecedented and onheard of—and to resoom and go on.
                  Ch. 4, *Samantha at the World's Fair 1893*

5   And I sez, "Children and trees have to be tackled young, Josiah,
    to bend their wills to the way you want 'em to go."
          Ch. 18, *Around the World with Josiah Allen's Wife 1899*

1074. Isabella Mary Mayson Beeton (1837–1865)

1   We hear of those to whom a lawsuit is an agreeable relaxation,
    a gentle excitement. One of this class, when remonstrated with,
    retorted, that while one friend kept dogs, and another horses,
    he, as he had a right to do, kept a lawyer; and no one had a
    right to dispute his taste.
                  The Book of Household Management 1861

2   There should be a place for everything, and everything in its
    place.
                          Ibid.

1075. Anne Blunt (1837–1917)

1 His gallop, as I have said, is long and low, and faster in proportion to his height than that of any other breed. If one could conceive an Arabian seventeen hands high, he could not fail to leave the best horse in England behind him. As it is, he is too small to keep stride with our race-horses.

Pt. I, *Bedouin Tribes of the Eurphrates 1879*

2 In disposition the Arabians are gentle and affectionate, familiar indeed almost to the extent of being troublesome.

Ibid.

1076. Mary Elizabeth Braddon (1837–1915)

1 ". . . it is easy to starve, but it is difficult to stoop."

Ch. 23, *Lady Audley's Secret 1862*

2 There can be no reconciliation when there is no open warfare. There must be a battle, a brave boisterous battle, with pennants waving and cannon roaring, before there can be peace treaties and enthusiastic shaking of hands.

Ch. 32, Ibid.

3 ". . . exceptional talent does not always win its reward unless favoured by exceptional circumstances."

Ch. 4, *Dead-Sea Fruit,* Vol. II *1868*

4 "Are there not, indeed, brief pauses of mental intoxication, in which the spirit releases itself from its dull mortal bondage, and floats starward on the wings of inspiration?"

Ch. 9, Ibid.

5 "A priest can achieve great victories with an army of women at his command."

Ch. 1, *Hostages to Fortune,* Vol. I *1875*

6 It may be that Miranda had enjoyed too much of the roses and lilies of life, and that a girlhood of such absolute indulgence was hardly the best preparation for the battle which has to come in the lives of women—whatever their temporal advantage—the battle of the heart, or of the brain, the fight with fate, or the fight with man.

Bk. I, Ch. 2, *Miranda 1913*

7 When once estrangement has arisen between those who truly love each other, everything seems to widen the breach.

Ch. 8, *Run to Earth 1915?*

1077. Rosalia de Castro (1837–1885)

1 Give back the flower its fragrant scent
When it is dry;
From the waves that kiss the seashore
And one by one caress it as they die,
Go gather all the murmurs that are spent
And on bronze plates their harmonies inscribe.

"*El tiempo pasa*" (Life Passes By), John A. Crow, tr. *n.d.*

1078. Jean Detourbey (1837–1908)

1 Is it necessary to have read Spinoza* in order to make out a laundry list?

Quoted in *Forty Years of Partisan Society* by Arthur Meyer *1912*
*Baruch or Benedict Spinoza, Dutch philosopher and theologian (1632–1677).

2 Of course, fortune has its part in human affairs, but conduct is really much more important.

Ibid.

3 So I cannot bear to be told that So-and-so is lucky. Too often the phrase is a covert attack upon the man; for what does it amount to in plain speech but that he is an idiot with nothing but his luck to recommend him?

Ibid.

1079. Jane Ellice Hopkins (1837–1915)

1 Gift, like genius, I often think only means an infinite capacity for taking pains.

Work Amongst Working Men 1870

1080. Martha Gay Masterson (1837–1916)

1 He [the schoolteacher] marched around occasionally, and if he discovered any fun or idleness going on, down would come that switch causing the juveniles to draw themselves into small parcels to evade the rod.

One Woman's West (autobio., 2nd ed.), Lois Barton, ed. *1990*

2 . . . we had no news or word from home. So we originated our own news and mirth.

Ibid.

3 Usually an Indian woman told the whites when the men were preparing for war. I think they preferred peace to war.

Ibid.

4 A man is soon ready for a journey. Packs his grip, gets his ticket and is off before a woman can decide on the color of her traveling dress.

Ibid.

1081. Mary E. Bryan (1838/46–1913)

1 Men, after much demur and hesitation, have given women liberty to write; but they cannot yet consent to allow them full freedom. They may flutter out of the cage, but it must be with clipped wings; they may hop about the smooth-shaven lawns, but must, on no account, fly.

"How Should Women Write?" (1860), *Hidden Hands: An Anthology of American Women Writers, 1790–1870,* Lucy M. Freibert and Barbara A. White, eds. *1985*

2 Women are. . . . learning that genius has no sex. . . . How should a woman write? I answer, as men, as all should write to whom the power of expression has been given—honestly and without fear.

Ibid.

1082. Kate Field (1838–1896)

1 They talk about a woman's sphere,
As though it had a limit.
There's not a place in earth or heaven,
There's not a task to mankind given. . . .
Without a woman in it.

"Woman's Spirit" *n.d.*

1083. Lydia Kamekeha Liliuokalani (1838–1917)

1 The Hawaiian people have been from time immemorial lovers of poetry and music, and have been apt in improvising historic poems, songs of love, and chants of worship, so that praises of the living or wails over the dead were with them but the natural expression of their feelings.

Ch. 5, *Hawaii's Story 1898*

2   Oh, honest Americans, as Christians hear me for my down-trodden people! Their form of government is as dear to them as yours is precious to you. Quite as warmly as you love your country, so they love theirs. . . . do not covet the little vineyards of Naboth's, so far from your shores, lest the punishment of Ahab* fall upon you, if not in your day, in that of your children, for "be not deceived, God is not mocked."

Ch. 57, Ibid.

*Pagan king of Israel and husband of Jezebel who, according to the Old Testament, was overthrown by Jehu.

3   Farewell to thee, farewell to thee,
Thou charming one who dwells among the bowers,
One fond embrace before I now depart
Until we meet again.

"Aloha Oe" *n.d.*

1084. Lucy Rockefeller (1838–1878)

1   When it's raining porridge, you'll find John's* dish right side up.

Quoted in Ch. 2, *Ambition: The Secret Passion* Joseph Epstein
1980

*John D. R—, her brother, American industrialist

1085. Margaret E. Sangster (1838–1912)

1   And it isn't the thing you do, dear,
It's the thing you leave undone
Which gives you a bit of a headache
At the setting of the sun.

"The Sin of Omission" *n.d.*

2   Never yet was a springtime
When the buds forgot to blow.

"Awakening" *n.d.*

3   Not always the fanciest cake that's there
Is the best to eat!

"French Pastry," St. 3 *n.d.*

4   Out of the chill and the shadow,
Into the thrill and the shine;
Out of the dearth and the famine,
Into the fullness divine.

"Going Home" *n.d.*

5   We have careful thought from the stranger,
And smiles from the sometimes guest;
But oft from "our own" the bitter tone,
Though we love our own the best.

"Our Own," St. 3, Ibid.

1086. Victoria Claflin Woodhull (1838–1927)

1   While others of my sex devoted themselves to a crusade against the laws that shackle the women of the country, I asserted my individual independence; while others prayed for the good time coming, I worked for it; while others argued the equality of woman with man, I proved it by successfully engaging in business; while others sought to show that there was no valid reason why women should be treated, socially and politically, as being inferior to man, I boldly entered the arena of politics and business and exercised the rights I already possessed.

I now announce myself candidate for the Presidency.

Letter to the Editor, *New York Herald 2 April 1870*

2   I submit that I have established first, that by the mere fact of being citizens, women are possessed of the elective franchise; and second, that the elective franchise is one of the privileges of the 14th Amendment which the states shall not abridge.

Address to Judiciary Committee, House of Representatives *11 January 1871*

3   I have an inalienable constitutional and natural right to love whom I may, to love as long or as short a period as I can, to change that love every day if I please!

Article, *Woodhull and Claflin's Weekly 20 November 1871*

4   A Vanderbilt may sit in his office and manipulate stocks or declare dividends by which in a few years he amasses fifty million dollars from the industries of the country, and he is one of the remarkable men of the age. But if a poor, half-starved child should take a loaf of bread from his cupboard to appease his hunger, he would be sent to the tombs.

Campaign Speech *1872*

5   Woman's ability to earn money is a better protection against the tyranny and brutality of man than her ability to vote.

Quoted in *Women Suffragists* by Diana Star Helmer *1998*

6   All this talk of women's rights is moonshine. Women have every right. They have only to exercise them.

Ibid.

7   Those who are called prostitutes . . . are free women, sexually, when compared to the slavery of the poor wife. They are at liberty, at least to refuse; but she knows no such escape . . . Yet marriage is held to be synonymous with morality! I say, eternal damnation sink such morality!

Ibid.

8   If the very next Congress refuses women all the legitimate results of citizenship, we mean treason! We mean secession. We are plotting revolution! We will overthrow this bogus Republic and plant a government of righteousness in its stead!

Speech, "Great Secession," Ibid.

9   Suffrage is only one phase of the larger question of woman's emancipation. More important is the question of her social and economic position.

Editorial, *The Humanitarian** (1896), Ibid.

*A weekly publication founded and operated by Woodhull.

10   If I want sexual intercourse with one hundred men, I shall have it.

Quoted in *Other Powers: The Age of Suffrage, Spiritualism, and the Scandalous Victoria Woodhull* by Barbara Goldsmith
1998

1087. Mary Clemmer (1839–1884)

1   I lie amid the Goldenrod,
I love to see it lean and nod.

"Goldenrod" *n.d.*

2   The Indian Summer, the dead Summer's soul.

"Presence" *n.d.*

3   Only a newspaper! Quick read, quick lost,
Who sums the treasure that it carries hence?
Torn, trampled under feet, who counts thy cost,
Star-eyed intelligence?

"The Journalist" *n.d.*

4 A shining isle in a stormy sea,
We seek it ever with smiles and sighs;
To-day is sad. In the bland To-be,
Serene and lovely To-morrow lies.

"To-morrow" *n.d.*

1088. Mary Louisa Molesworth (1839–1921)

1 Time indeed seemed to stand still in and all about the old
house, as if it and the people who inhabited it had got so old
that they could not get any older, and had outlived the possibility of change.

Ch. I, *The Cuckoo Clock* 1877

2 "What a *very* funny house it is, Aunt Grizzel," she said, as she
followed her aunt down the steps. "Every room has so many
doors, and you come back to where you were just when you
think you are ever so far off. I shall never be able to find my
way about."

Ibid.

3 "Why not?" said Griselda. "Lots of children have been there."
"I doubt it," said the cuckoo. "Some may have thought
they had been there who hadn't really been there at all. And as
to those who have been there, you may be sure of one thing—
they were not taken, they found their own way. No one ever
was taken to fairyland—to the real fairyland. They may have
been taken to the neighbouring countries, but not to fairyland
itself."

Ch. IV, Ibid.

1089. Ouida (1839–1908)

1 . . . with peaches and women, it's only the side next the sun
that's tempting.

Strathmore 1865

2 What is it that love does to a woman? Without it she only
sleeps; with it alone, she lives.

Wisdom, Wit and Pathos 1884

3 A cruel story runs on wheels, and every hand oils the wheels as
they run.

"Moths" (1880), Ibid.

4 To vice, innocence must only seem a superior kind of chicanery.
"Two Little Wooden Shoes" (1874), Ibid.

5 Fame has only the span of a day, they say. But to live in the
hearts of the people—that is worth something.

"Signa" (1875), Ibid.

6 Petty laws breed great crimes.
"Pipistrello" (1880), Ibid.

7 Take hope from the heart of man, and you make him a beast of
prey.

"A Village Commune" (1881), Ibid.

8 Christianity has made of death a terror which was unknown to
the gay calmness of the Pagan.

"The Failure of Christianity" *n.d.*

1090. Frances Willard (1839–1908)

1 Here's a recipe for the abolishment of the Blues which is
worth a dozen medical nostrums:

Take one spoonful of Pleasant memories.
Take two spoonfuls of Endeavours for the Happiness of others.
Take two spoonfuls of Forgetfulness of Sorrow.
Mix well with half a pint of Cheerfulness.
Take a portion every hour of the day.

Journal entry (ca. 1860), Quoted in Ch. 2, *Frances Willard: Her Life and Works* by Ray Strachey 1912

2 Geology teaches that death was in the world before sin, which
is contrary to the Bible. But it is nowhere stated in the Bible
that sin was the cause of the death of any save man: he only
has sinned. Any other idea is a superstition and without foundation.

Ibid.

3 The world is wide, and I will not waste my life in friction when
it could be turned into momentum.

Journal entry (ca. 1860), Ch. 6, Ibid.

4 Everything is not in the temperance movement, but the temperance movement should be in everything.

Ch. 11, Ibid.

1091. Mary Branch (1840–1922)

1 So, I think, God hides some souls away,
Sweetly to surprise us, the last day.

"The Petrified Fern" *n.d.*

1092. Elizabeth York Case (1840?–1911)

1 There is no unbelief;
Whoever plants a seed beneath the sod
And waits to see it push away the clod,
He trusts in God.

"There Is No Unbelief" *n.d.*

1093. Emilia Dilke (1840–1904)

1 [Artistic] work which is not done for its own sake, in which
the chief place is claimed by the historical or the moral, in
which attention is seized by the subject rather than the rendering of the subject . . . loses its aesthetic character, and cannot
possess those poetic elements which fire the fancy and rouse
the emotions.

Quoted in *The Saturday Review* 23 August 1868

2 It was put before me that if I wished to command respect I
must make myself *the* authority on some one subject which
interested me. I was told, and it was good counsel, not to take
hack-work, and to reject even well-paid things that would lead
me off the track.

Quoted in "Memoir" by Sir Charles Dilke, *The Book of Spiritual Life* 1905

1094. Harriet King (1840–1920)

1 Measure thy life by loss instead of gain,
Not by the wine drunk, but by the wine poured forth.

"The Disciples" *n.d.*

1095. Helena Modjeska (1840–1920)

1 Alas! it was not my fate to die for my country, as was my cherished dream, but instead of becoming the heroine I had to be
satisfied with acting heroines, exchanging the armor for tinsel,
and the weapon for words.

Pt. I, Ch. 1, *Memories and Impressions* 1910

2 It is never right to be more Catholic than the Pope.

Ch. 25, Ibid.

3 . . . the word "great" is not sufficient anymore, if you do not add to it, "Genius!" In Europe the word "genius" is only applied to the greatest of the world, but here [in America] it has become an everyday occurrence.

Pt. III, Ch. 51, Ibid.

4 We foreigners, born outside of the magic pale of the Anglo-Saxon race, place Shakespeare upon a much higher pedestal. We claim that, before being English, he was human, and that his creations are not bound either by local or ethnological limits, but belong to humanity in general.

Ibid.

5 It seems to me that there are only two schools, one of good acting, the other of bad acting.

Ibid.

1096. Marilla Ricker (1840–1920)

1 The only thing that ever came back from the grave that we know of was a lie.

The Philistine, Vol. XXV ca. 1901

2 He [Thomas Paine]* was as democratic as nature, as impartial as sun and rain.

Ibid.

*British-born American writer and Revolutionary leader (1737–1809).

1097. Katharine Walker (1840–1916)

1 The elusiveness of soap, the knottiness of strings, the transitory nature of buttons, the inclination of suspenders to twist and of hooks to forsake their lawful eyes, and cleave only to the hairs of their hapless owner's head.

"The Total Depravity of Inanimate Things," Atlantic Monthly (Boston) September 1864

2 However divinity schools may refuse to "skip" in unison, and may butt and butter each other about the doctrine and origin of human depravity, all will join devoutly in the credo, I believe in the total depravity of inanimate things.

Ibid.

1098. Elizabeth Wordsworth (1840–1932)

1 If all the good people were clever,
And all the clever people were good,
The world would be nicer than ever
We thought that it possibly could.

But somehow, 'tis seldom or never
The two hit it off as they should;
The good are so harsh to the clever,
The clever so rude to the good.

"The Good and the Clever," St. Christopher and Other Poems 1890

1099. Mary Wood Allen (1841–1908)

1 Woman embroiders man's life—Embroidery is to beautify—
The embroidery of cleanliness—Of a smile—Of gentle words.

Summary, What a Young Girl Ought to Know 1897

1100. Mathilde Blind (1841–1896)

1 Blossoms of humanity!

"The St.-Children's Dance" n.d.

2 The moon returns, and the spring; birds warble, trees burst into leaf,
But love once gone, goes forever, and all that endures is the grief.

No. 3, "Love Trilogy" n.d.

3 The dead abide with us. Though stark and cold,
Earth seems to grip them, they are with us still:
They have forged our chains of being of good or ill,
And their invisible hands these hands yet hold.

"The Dead" n.d.

1101. Sarah Knowles Bolton (1841–1916)

1 He alone is great
Who by a life heroic conquers fate.

"The Inevitable" n.d.

1102. Ina Coolbrith (1841–1928)

1 Very patient, I can wait,
Knowing that, or soon or late,
There will dawn a clearer morrow:
When your heart will moan "Alas!
Now I know how true she was;
Now I know how dear she was"—
When the grass grows over me!

"When the Grass Shall Cover Me," St. 3, An American Anthology, 1787–1900, Edmund Clarence Stedman, ed. 1900

2 Living and blooming thy brief summer-day:—
So, wiser far than I,
That only dream and sigh,
And, sighing, dream my listless life away.

"Fruitionless," St. 1, Ibid.

3 It must be sweet to slumber and forget;
To have the poor tired heart so still at last:
Done with all yearning, done with all regret

"Beside the Dead," The Book of Sorrow, David M. MacPhail, ed. I

1103. Eliza Burt Gamble (1841–1920)

1 . . . with the dawn of scientific investigation it might have been hoped that the prejudices resulting from lower conditions of human society would disappear, and that in their stead would be set forth not only facts, but deductions from facts, better suited to the dawn of an intellectual age. . . .

The ability, however, to collect facts, and the power to generalize and draw conclusions from them, avail little, when brought into direct opposition to deeply rooted prejudices.

The Evolution of Woman 1894

1104. Mary Lathbury (1841–1913)

1 Day is dying in the west;
Heaven is touching earth with rest.

"Day Is Dying in the West," St. 1 1877

2 Children of yesterday,
Heirs of tomorrow,
What are you weaving?
Labor and sorrow?

"Song of Hope," St. 1 n.d.

1105. Minnie D. Louis (1841–1922)

1 . . . Woman is the ozone of the metaphysical atmosphere.
"The Influence of Women in Bringing Religious Conviction to
Bear upon Daily Life," *American Hebrew 28 June 1895*

2 A compulsory universal University education, which means the thorough education of the head, hand and heart of *every individual* human being, can be the only developer of the real divinity in man, of the altruism which can make earth beautiful with its glow.

Ibid.

1106. Kate Brownlee Sherwood (1841–1914)

1 One heart, one hope, one destiny, one flag, from sea to sea.
"Albert Sidney Johnstone," *Dreams of the Ages 1893*

2 The flaring of the furnaces and the fretting of the forge,
The clamor of the fast express a-down the smoky gorge,
The growth of great endeavor pressing on from main to main.
Around the world and back again, a continental chain
"The Home Heart," St. 1 *n.d.*

3 O vanished majesty of days! Rise, type and mould to-day,
And teach our sons to follow on where duty leads the way;
That whatsoever trial comes, defying doubt and fear,
They in the thickest fight shall stand and proudly answer,
"Here!"
"Thomas at Chickamauga," St. 17 *n.d.*

4 Molly Pitcher* sprang to his side,
Fired as she saw her husband do.
Telling the king in his stubborn pride
Women like men to their homes are true.
"Molly Pitcher," St. 4 *n.d.*
*Mary Ludwig Hays McCauley, a.k.a. Molly Pitcher (1754–1832), American Revolutionary heroine who carried water to the soldiers during the Battle of Monmouth (June 28, 1778) and took over the gun of her husband after he was overcome with heat.

1107. Sarah Sadie Williams (1841–1868)

1 Is it so, O Christ in heaven, that the highest suffer most,
That the strongest wander farthest, and more hopelessly are lost,
That the mark of rank in nature is capacity for pain,
That the anguish of the singer makes the sweetness of the strain?
"Is It So, O Christ in Heaven?" *n.d.*

1108. Mary Elizabeth Brown (1842–1917)

1 I'll go where you want me to go, dear Lord,
O'er mountain, or plain, or sea;
I'll say what you want me to say, dear Lord,
I'll be what you want me to be.
"I'll Go Where You Want Me to Go" *n.d.*

1109. Marie le Baron (1842–1894)

1 Love's kisses are common things,
And the stain of too common usage,
To their dainty essence clings.
"Kiss No One But Me" (song) 1879

2 It is only a summer, my darling,
A dream, a delight, a surprise;

A mem'ry to hide as the frost does,
In regret . . . the flow'r where it lies;
But a summer to cling to for ever;
To bloom again, darling, ah! Never.
"Only A Summer" 1882

3 Where deep and misty shadows float
In forest's depths is heard thy note.
Like a lost spirit, earthbound still,
Art thou, mysterious whip-poor-will.
"The Whip—Poor-Will" *n.d.*

4 They truly mourn, that mourn without a witness.
Untitled *n.d.*

1110. May Riley Smith (1842–1927)

1 Let us gather up the sunbeams
Lying all around our path;
Let us keep the wheat and roses,
Casting out the thorns and chaff.
"If We Knew," St. 6 1867

2 Strange we never prize the music
Till the sweet-voiced bird is flown. . . .
St. 14, Ibid.

3 God's plan, like lilies pure and white, unfold.
We must not tear the close-shut leaves apart.
Time will reveal the calyxes of gold.
"Sometime," *Sometime and Other Poems 1892*

1111. Anna Spafford (1842–1923)

1 Saved alone. What shall I do . . .
Cable to her husband* after November 1873 shipwreck,
The American Colony in Jerusalem, A Library of Congress
Exhibition *4 March 2005*
*Horatio S- (1828–1888), lawyer, psalmist, missionary

2 God gave me four daughters. Now they have been taken from me. Someday I will understand why. *
Quoted by Pastor Weiss, fellow survivor of November 1873
shipwreck, *The American Colony in Jerusalem*, A Library of
Congress Exhibition *4 March 2005*
*Her four daughters were drowned.

3 I left my country to be of service, and this is my supreme moment.*
Quoted in *American Priestess: the Extraordinary Story of
Anna Spafford and the American Colony in Jerusalem* by Jane
Geniesse** 2008
*Response to U.S. Consul, who urged her to flee as British Field
Marshall Edmund Allenby's army was approaching Jerusalem during World War I. **See 2977.

1112. Ellen Swallow (1842–1911)

1 The power of knowledge is appreciated by manufacturers. They take advantage of every new step in science. The woman must know something of chemistry in self-defense. . . . The housekeeper should know when to be frightened. . . . It is for women to institute reform.
Speech (1879), Quoted in *Ellen Swallow, The Woman Who
Founded Ecology* by Robert Clarke 1973

2 For this knowledge of right living, we have sought a new name. . . . As theology is the science of religious life, and bi-

ology the science of [physical] life . . . so let *Oekology* be henceforth the science of [our] normal lives . . . the worthiest of all the applied science which *teaches the principles on which to found . . . a healthy . . . and happy life.*

Speech (1892), Ibid.

3   Heretofore, civilized man has proclaimed, as his God-like privilege, and as a proof of his superiority to animals, the right to eat what he liked, whether it was suitable or not, and as a result, he has been compelled to employ a band of skilled magicians to exorcise the devils . . . invited to enter his body. But man is . . . only an upright animal, amenable to the same laws of growth and decay as others. . . . The science of human nutrition is to play a larger part in therapeutics than heretofore and it will be of great advantage to the physician [who] . . . at present has less confidence in the cook than in the druggist.

Ch. 13, *The New England Kitchen Magazine* (1893), Ibid.

4   The essential principles of health are not understood by the people . . . and, alas! not by all our physicians, who as a rule have been educated to cure disease, not to prevent it. Too many have been taught to fight Nature's Laws, not stand by . . . as her adjutant.

Ch. 15, Ibid.

5   Woman was originally the inventor, the manufacturer, the provider. She has allowed one office after another gradually to slip from her hand until she retains, with loose grasp, only the so called housekeeping. . . . she rightly feels that what is left is mere deadening drudgery, and that escape from this condition is essential to her well being as an individual.

The Outlook (magazine; 1897), Ibid.

6   It is hard to find anyplace in the world where the water does not show the effect of human agencies.

Ch. 17, Ibid.

1113. Sarah Doudney (1843–1926)

1   Oh, the wasted hours of life
That have drifted by!
Oh, the good that might have been,
Lost without a sigh.

"The Lesson of the Water-Mill" *1864*

2   "No," said Faith sternly, "we don't want this girl to be hanged; we wish her to spend a useful life, full of repentance and good deeds."

Ch. 4, *Faith Harrowby; or, The Smuggler's Cave 1871*

3   "There are no such thing as mermaids," exclaimed Frank, her schoolboy brother; "and if there are, their company wouldn't suit you, Ada. How do you suppose you would get on under the sea, with no circulating library, no dress-makers and milliners, and knick knacks and fallals?"

Ch. 19, Ibid.

4   But the waiting time, my brothers,
Is the hardest time of all.

"The Hardest Time of All," *Psalms of Life n.d.*

1114. Violet Fane (1843–1905)

1   Ah, "All things come to those who wait,"
(I say these words to make me glad),
But something answers soft and sad,
"They come, but often come too late."

"Tout Vient à Qui Sait Attendre" n.d.

2   Let me arise and open the gate,
To breath the wild warm air of the heath,
And to let in Love, and to let out Hate,
And anger at living and scorn of Fate,
To let in Life, and to let out Death.

"Reverie" *n.d.*

3   Nothing is right and nothing is just;
We sow in ashes and reap in dust.

Ibid.

1115. Anna Hamilton (1843–1875)

1   This learned I from the shadow of a tree,
That to and fro did sway against a wall,
Our shadow selves, our influence, may fall
Where we ourselves can never be.

"Influence" *n.d.*

1116. Gertrude Jekyll (1843–1932)

1   The love of gardening is a seed that once sown never dies, but grows to the enduring happiness that the love of gardening gives.

Remark *n.d.*

1117. Caroline Bigelow Le Row (1843–?)

1   The health of the child should be the first thing considered in the school. In reality it is the last thing considered. If weak eyes, sunken chests, crooked spines, and diseased lungs were the exception rather than the rule among our school children, it is owing more to good luck than to good looking to.

Speech, The New York Assoc. of Collegiate Alumnae *30 March 1889*

2   A one-sided, purely literary education is not sufficient for many-sided human nature.

Ibid.

3   People are just discovering that a sound mind is to some extent dependent upon a sound body.

Ibid.

4   But I will right of him who fights
And vanquishes his sins,
Who struggles on through weary years
Against himself and wins.

"True Heroism" *n.d.*

1118. Isabella S. Stephenson (1843–1890)

1   Holy Father, in Thy mercy,
Hear our anxious prayer,
Keep our loved ones, now far absent,
'Neath thy care.

"Holy Father, in Thy Mercy" *n.d.*

1119. Bertha von Suttner (1843–1914)

1   After the verb, "To Love," "To Help" is the most beautiful verb in the world!

"Epigram," *Ground Arms 1892*

1120. Carmen Sylva (1843–1916)

1   "'Tis the ignorant who boast. . . ."

"The Nixies' Cleft," *Legends from River and Mountain 1896*

2 Surely he could never have borne such a life, and must have died of misery, save for one only consolation. Every man must have some such, be it only a dog, a flower, or a spider. Ovid had a snake, a tiny, bewitching snake. . . .

"The Serpent Isle," Ibid.

3 Complaints were heard no longer, for dull despair had reduced all men to silence; and when the starving people tore one another to pieces, no one even told of it.

"Rîul Doamnei," Ibid.

4 "One cannot help those who will not help themselves, so we felt it would be quite useless for us to come again."

"The Little People," *Real Queen's Fairy Tales* 1901

5 There was another thing that did not exist in these islands; that was money. The swans would never have permitted anything so low and degrading to enter their domain. Gold they tolerated, but merely for ornamentation, where it could light up some dull surface. But to traffic with money, and to bargain, and barter—that was unheard of.

"The Swan Lake," Ibid.

6 "Ill could I resign myself to dwell forever shut in between four walls. I must be free, free to roam where I please, like the birds in the woodlands."

"Carma, the Harp-Girl," Ibid.

7 Our life is seldom open,
For love and fear have shut it.

"Out of the Deep," St. 2, *Sweet Hours* 1904

8 Great Solitude
Hath one thousand voices and a flood of light,
Be not afraid, enter the Sanctuary,
Thou wilt be taken by the hand and led
To Life's own fountain, never-ending Thought!

"Solitude," Ibid.

1121. Saint Bernadette (1844–1923)

1 I fear only bad Catholics.

Quoted in *Lourdes* by Edith Sanders 1940

1122. Sarah Bernhardt (1844–1923)

1 Cloister existence is one of unbroken sameness for all. . . . The rumor of the outside world dies away at the heavy cloister gate.

Ch. 3, *Memories of My Life* 1907

2 For the theatre one needs long arms; it is better to have them too long than too short. An artiste with short arms can never, never make a fine gesture.

Ch. 6, Ibid.

3 Those who know the joys and miseries of celebrity . . . know . . . It is a sort of octopus with innumerable tentacles. It throws out its clammy arms on the right and on the left, in front and behind, and gathers into its thousand little inhaling organs all the gossip and slander and praise afloat to spit out again at the public when it is vomiting its black gall.

Ch. 22, Ibid.

4 We must live for the few who know and appreciate us, who judge and absolve us, and for whom we have the same affection and indulgence. The rest I look upon as a mere crowd,

lively or sad, loyal or corrupt, from whom there is nothing to be expected but fleeting emotions, either pleasant or unpleasant, which leave no trace behind them.

Ch. 9, *The Memoirs of Sarah Bernhardt* 1977

1123. Madeline Bridges (1844–1920)

1 When Psyche's friend becomes her lover,
How sweetly these conditions blend!
But, oh, what anguish to discover
Her lover has become—her friend!

"Friend and Lover" *n.d.*

2 Then give to the world the best you have,
And the best will come back to you.

"Life's Mirror," St. 1 *n.d.*

3 And a smile that is sweet will surely find
A smile that is just as sweet.

St. 3, Ibid.

1124. Bertha Buxton (1844–1881)

1 After all, the eleventh commandment (thou shalt not be found out) is the only one that is virtually impossible to keep in these days.

Ch. 3, *Jenny of the Princes* 1879

1125. Minna Canth (1844–1897)

1 HOMSANTUU. Your law and justice . . . These are what I ought to have shot.

The Working Man's Wife 1885

1126. Mary Cassatt (1844–1926)

1 I am independent! I can live alone and I love to work.

Quoted in *Sixteen to Sixty, Memoirs of a Collector* by Louise W. Havemeyer 1930

2 A woman artist must be . . . capable of making the primary sacrifices.

Quoted in "Mary Cassatt" by Forbes Watson, *Arts Weekly* 1932

3 Yet in spite of the total disregard of the dictionary of manners, he [Paul Cézanne*] shows a politeness toward us which no other man here would have shown. . . . Cézanne is one of the most liberal artists I have ever seen. He prefaces every remark with *Pour moi* it is so and so, but he grants that everyone may be as honest, and as true to nature from their convictions; he doesn't believe that everyone should see alike.

Letter to Mrs. Stillman (1894), Quoted in *Mary Cassatt: A Biography of the Great American Painter* by Nancy Hale** 1975

*French impressionist painter (1839–1906). **See 2089.

4 Why do people so love to wander? I think the civilized parts of the World will suffice for me in the future.

Letter to Louise Havemeyer (11 February 1911), Ibid.

1127. Elizabeth Stuart Phelps (1844–1911)

1 Who originated the most exquisite of inquisitions, the condolence system?

Ch. 2, *The Gates Ajar* 1869

2 "There are several disadvantages in being a girl, my dear, as you will find out, occasionally," said Tom, with a lordly air.

Ch. 4, *Gypsy Breynton* 1876

3 I must say distinctly that, though after the act of dying I departed from the surface of the earth, and reached the confines of a different locality, I cannot yet instruct another *where* this place may be.

Ch. 3, *Beyond the Gates* 1883

4 The great law of denial belongs to the powerful forces of life, whether the case be one of coolish baked beans, or an unrequited affection.

Ch. 1, *A Singular Life* 1896

5 She had accomplished nothing, that she could see, but keep her house in order. . . . Unsatisfied longings for something which she had not attained, often clouded what, otherwise, would have been a bright day to her; and yet the causes of these feelings seemed to lie in a dim and misty region, which her eye could not penetrate.

The Angel Over the Right Shoulder n.d.

1128. Sarah Ann Sewell (1844?–1920?)

1 It is a man's place to rule, and a woman's to yield. He must be held up as the head of the house, and it is her duty to bend so unmurmuringly to his wishes, that the rest of the household will follow her example, and treat him with the due respect his sex demands.

Woman and the Times We Live In 1869

1129. Margaret Sidney (1844–1924)

1 The little old kitchen had quieted down from the bustle and confusion of mid-day; and now, with its afternoon manners on, presented a holiday aspect, that as the principal room in the brown house, it was eminently proper it should have.

"A Home View," *Five Little Peppers and How They Grew* 1881

2 "It's better'n a Christmas," they told their mother, "to get ready for it!"

"Getting a Christmas for the Little Ones," Ibid.

3 "You're just the splendidest, *goodest* mamsie in all the world. And I'm a hateful cross old bear, so I am!"

"Polly's Dismal Morning," Ibid.

4 ". . . it can't be Christmas all the time."

"Christmas Bells," Ibid.

5 "Corners are for little folks; but when people who know better, do wrong, there aren't any corners they *can* creep into, or they'd get into them pretty quick!"

"Which Treats of a Good Many Matters," Ibid.

1130. Arabella Smith (1844–1916)

1 Oh, friends! I pray to-night,
Keep not your roses for my dead, cold brow
The way is lonely, let me feel them now.

"If I Should Die To-Night" *n.d.*

1131. Harriet Williams Russell Strong (1844–1926)

1 . . . it takes brains, not brawn, to make farms pay . . . We need more women farmers!

p. 96, Quoted in *Women Pioneers* by Rebecca Stefoff 1995

2 The pink and white, helpless prettiness; the delicate, fainting, clinging doll is fast becoming a thing of the past.

Speech, Ebell Club (Los Angeles, 1895), Quoted by Jane Apostol in *California History 1 March 2008*

1132. Sophie Tolstoy (1844–1919)

1 One can't live on love alone; and I am so stupid that I can do nothing but think of him.*

(13 November 1862), *A Diary of Tolstoy's Wife, 1860–1891* 1928

*Count Leo Tolstoy, Russian philosopher and novelist (1820–1910).

2 Of course I am idle, but I am not idle by nature; I simply haven't yet discovered what I can do here. . . .

Ibid.

3 I want nothing but his love and sympathy, and he won't give it me; and all my pride is trampled in the mud; I am nothing but a miserable crushed worm, whom no one wants, whom no one loves, a useless creature with morning sickness, and a big belly, two rotten teeth, and a bad temper, a battered sense of dignity, and a love which nobody wants and which nearly drives me insane.

(12 September 1867), Ibid.

4 It makes me laugh to read over this diary. It's so full of contradictions, and one would think I was such an unhappy woman. Yet is there a happier woman than I?

(31 July 1868), Ibid.

5 He would like to destroy his old diaries and to appear before his children and the public only in his patriarchal robes. His vanity is immense!

(17 December 1890), Ibid.

6 I am a source of satisfaction to him, a nurse, a piece of furniture, a *woman*—nothing more.

(13 November 1893), Ibid.

1133. Sarah Winnemucca (1844–1891)

1 I would be the first Indian woman who ever spoke before white people, and they don't know what the Indians have got to stand sometimes.

Newspaper interview (1879), Quoted in *Sarah Winnemucca of the Northern Paiutes* by Gae Whitney Canfield 1983

2 I assure you that there is an Indian ring; that it is a corrupt ring, and that it has its head and shoulders in the treasury at Washington.

Lecture, Ibid.

3 Everyone knows what a woman must suffer who undertakes to act against bad men. My reputation has been assailed, and it is done so cunningly that I cannot prove it to be unjust.

Ibid.

4 If I possessed the wealth of several rich ladies whom you all know, I would place all the Indians of Nevada on ships in our harbor, take them to New York and land them there as immigrants, that they might be received with open arms, blessed with the blessings of universal suffrage, and thus placed beyond the necessity of reservation help and out of the reach of Indian agents.

Lecture (1885), Ibid.

1134. Marie Chona (1845?–1937?)

1 You see, we have power. Men have to dream to get power from the spirits and they think of everything they can—song and speeches and marching around, hoping that the spirits will notice them and give them some power. But we have power . . . Children. Can any warrior make a child, no matter how brave and wonderful he is?

Papago Woman, Ruth M. Underhill, ed. *1936 (rev. ed. 1979)*

2 It is not good to be old, not beautiful.

Ibid.

1135. Tennessee Claflin (1845–1923)

1 At the ballot-box is not where the shoe pinches. . . . It is at home where the husband . . . is the supreme ruler, that the little difficulty arises; he will not surrender this absolute power unless he is compelled.

"Constitutional Equality, a Right of Women" *1871*

2 A *free* man is a noble being; a *free* woman is a contemptible being. . . . In other terms, the use of this one word, in its twofold application to men and to women, reveals the unconscious but ever present conviction in the public mind that men tend, of course, heavenward in their natures and development, and that women tend just as naturally hellward.

Article, *Woodhull* and Claflin's Weekly 1871*
*Victoria W-, her sister; see 1086.

3 The revolt against any oppression usually goes to an opposite extreme for a time; and that is right and necessary.

Ibid.

4 When people had slaves, they expected that their pigs, chickens, corn, and everything lying loose about the plantation would be stolen. But the planters began by stealing the liberty of their slaves, by stealing their labor, by stealing, in fact, all they had; and the natural result was that the slaves stole back all they could.

"Which Is to Blame?", Ibid.

5 The world enslaves our sex by the mere fear of an epithet; and as long as it can throw any vile term at us, before which we cower, it can maintain our enslavement.

Article, Ibid.

1136. Susan Coolidge (1845–1905)

1 "A commonplace life," we say and we sigh;
But why would we sigh as we say?
The commonplace sun in the commonplace sky
Makes up the commonplace day.

"Commonplace" *n.d.*

2 Men die, but sorrow never dies;
The crowding years divide in vain,
And the wide world is knit with ties
Of common brotherhood in pain.

"The Cradle Tomb in Westminster Abbey" *n.d.*

3 Yesterday's errors let yesterday cover.

"Every New Morning" *n.d.*

4 New morn has come
And with the morn the punctual tide again.

"Floodtide" *n.d.*

5 Slow buds the pink dawn like a rose
From out night's gray and cloudy sheath;
Softly and still it grows and grows,
Petal by petal, leaf by leaf.

"The Morning Comes Before the Sun" *n.d.*

1137. Emily Hickey (1845–1913)

1 Beloved, it is morn!
A redder berry on the thorn,
A deeper yellow on the corn,
For this good day new-born!

"Beloved, It Is Morn" *n.d.*

1138. Margaret Janvier (1845–1913)

1 You needn't try to comfort me—
I tell you my dolly is dead!
There's no use in saying she isn't, with
A crack like that in her head.

"The Dead Doll," St. 1 *n.d.*

1139. Marie de La Coste (1845–1936)

1 Into a ward of the whitewashed walls
Where the dead and dying lay—
Wounded by bayonets, shells, and balls—
Somebody's darling was borne one day.

"Somebody's Darling," St. 1 *n.d.*

2 Tenderly bury the fair young dead,
Pausing to drop on his grave a tear;
Carve on the wooden slab at his head,
"Somebody's darling lies buried here!"

St. 5, Ibid.

1140. Meta Orred (1845/46–1925)

1 A little wild will-o'-the-wisp did sit
Alone in a marsh, with his lantern dark;
And he watched the pied swallows fly over it,
And he watched the pied swallows so softly flit,

And he thought to himself: I am only a spark;
But what would the marsh-buds think of it,
If my little lantern were gone? thought he.

"The Little Wild Will-o'-the-Wisp," St. 1, *Berthold and Other Poems 1878*

2 In the gloaming, O, my darling!
When the lights are dim and low,
And the quiet shadows falling
Softly come and softly go.

"In the Gloaming" *1890*

1141. Katharine Bradley (1846–1914)

1 Come, mete out my loneliness, O wind,
For I would know
How far the living who must stay behind
Are from the dead who go.

"Mete Out My Loneliness," with Edith Cooper* *n.d*
*See 1285.

2 Sweet and of their nature vacant are the days I spend—
Quiet as the plough laid by at the furrow's end.

"Old Age," with E— C—* *n.d.*

3 The enchanting miracles of change.
> "Renewal," with E— C—* *n.d.*

1142. Anna Dostoevsky (1846–1918)

1 From a shy, timid girl I had become a woman of resolute character, who could not longer be frightened by the struggle with troubles.
> (ca. 1871), *Dostoevsky* * *Portrayed by His Wife* 1926
> *Feodor M. D—, Russian novelist (1821–1881).

2 It seems to me that he has never loved, that he has only imagined that he has loved, that there has been no real love on his part. I even think that he is incapable of love; he is too much occupied with other thoughts and ideas to become strongly attached to anyone earthly.
> (1887), *Ibid.*

1143. Anna Green (1846–1935)

1 Hath the spirit of all beauty
Kissed you in the path of duty?
> "On the Threshold" *n.d.*

1144. Kazu-no-Michi (1846–1877)

1 Please understand the heart of one who leaves as the water in the streams; never to return again.
> Untitled Poem *1861*

2 I wear the magnificent dress of brocade and damask in vain, now that you are not here to admire it.
> *Ibid.*

1145. Josephine Lazarus (1846–1910)

1 Come down from your watch-towers, come out of your Ghettos, and bear witness to that unity in the world to-day, not as an abstract, metaphysical truth, but in spirit and in deed.
> "Judaism, Old and New" (1894), *The Spirit of Judaism* 1895

2 Let us take our Judaism fearlessly out into the world, to be put to any test, but, above all, freely to be used, not in its own service, but in the service of the God in whom it believes, the universal Father of all, and, therefore, in the world's highest service. And in order to do this, first and foremost we must be rid of self, of this intense preoccupation to survive in any form, as race or creed or nation, this desperate struggle to exist in name, if nothing else.
> *Ibid.*

1146. Carry Nation (1846–1911)

1 God is a politician; so is the devil.
> *The Use and Need of the Life of Carry A. Nation* 1904

2 It's not possible to make a bad law. If it is bad, it is not a law.
> *Ibid.*

3 The women and children of Barber County are calling to you men for bread, for clothes, and education. . . . [Instead] men in Medicine Lodge and other towns of Barber County are selling whiskey. . . . No wonder the women want the ballot.
> Quoted in *Cyclone Carry* by Carleton Beals *1962*

4 Who hath sorrow? Who hath woe?
They who do not answer no;

They whose feet to sin incline,
While they tarry at the wine.
> Ch. 12, *Ibid.*

5 You have put me in here [jail] a cub, but I will come out roaring like a lion, and I will make all hell howl!
> Ch. 14 (ca. 1901), *Ibid.*

1147. Amalie Skram (1846–1905)

1 The battle between what she wanted to paint and what she actually painted left her in a confused state of misery that gnawed at her brain, colored everything she heard and experienced, paralyzed her spirit and destroyed her will.
> Ch. 1, *Professor Heironimus* Katherine Hanson and Judith Messick, trs. *1895*

2 It was immoral to go on living when you couldn't manage to accomplish a thing, when you knew you were a burden and a plague to the people you wanted most to please, and knew, also, that it would never be otherwise.
> *Ibid.*

3 Still it was strange how long a human being, no matter how miserable and racked with pain, could hesitate when it came to casting off the burden and removing oneself from the ranks of the living. The dread of slipping into the ternal darkness of oblivion must be deeply rooted, since she still kept dragging herself on, day after night, day after night.
> *Ibid.*

1148. Annie Wood Besant (1847–1933)

1 For I believe that the colour bar and all it implies are largely due to thoughtlessness, to silly pride, to the pride of race, which has grown mad in a country where there is no public opinion to check it.
> *Wake Up, India: A Plea for Social Reform* 1913

2 . . . when there shall be no differences save by merit of character, by merit of ability, by merit of service to the country. Those are the true tests of the value of any man or woman, white or coloured; those who can serve best, those who help most, those who sacrifice most, those are the people who will be loved in life and honoured in death, when all questions of colour are swept away and when in a free country free citizens shall meet on equal grounds.
> *Ibid.*

3 Spirituality does not depend upon the environment; it depends upon one's attitude towards life.
> *Spiritual Life* (rev. ed. *The Spiritual Life in the World*) 1991

4 To call one day the Lord's Day is to deny that same lordship to every other day in the week and to make six parts of life outside the spiritual, while only one remains recognized as dedicated to the Spirit.
> *Ibid.*

5 The wheels of the world are turned by God, and we are only his hands, which touch the rim of the wheel.
> *Ibid.*

6 The clerk behind his counter and the doctor in the hospital are quite as much engaged in a divine activity as any preacher in his church. Until that is realized the world is vulgarized, and until we can see one life everywhere and all things rooted in

that life, it is we who are hopelessly profane in attitude, we who are blind to the beatific vision which is the sight of the one life in everything, and all things as expressions of that life.

Ibid.

7 You grow, not by what you gain of outer fruit, by the inner unfolding necessary for your success in the struggle.

"Worldly Attractions," Ibid.

1149. Mary Catherwood (1847–1901)

1 They [the Chippewa] were a people ruled only by persuasive eloquence moving on the surface of their passion....

Pt. I, *The White Islander* 1893

2 She might struggle like a fly in a web. He wrapped her around and around with beautiful sentences.

"The King of Beaver," *Mackinac and Lake Stories* 1899

3 Two may talk together under the same roof for many years, yet never really meet; and two others at first speech are old friends.

"Marianson," Ibid.

4 Though in those days of the young century a man might become anything; for the West was before him, an empire, and woodcraft was better than learning.

"The Black Feather," Ibid.

5 The world of city-maddened people who swarmed to this lake for their annual immersion in nature....

"The Cursed Patois," Ibid.

1150. Millicent Garrett Fawcett (1847–1929)

1 The Income-Tax presses more heavily on the possessors of small incomes than on the possessors of large incomes.

Political Economy for Beginners 1870

2 There are many excuses for the person who made the mistake of confounding money and wealth. Like many others they mistook the sign for the thing signified.

Ibid.

1151. Eliška Krásnohorská (1847–1926)

1 Remember the protests which broke out all over the country when the female teachers wanted to be paid the same as the male teachers. It was said, "It may seem unjust, but in spite of the fact that the same education and job responsibilities are required for female teachers as for male teachers, the male teacher needs more money to live on. But," she continued, "when the shopkeeper replaces a male shop assistant with a female shop assistant to do the same work but at a lower wage, will the displaced male worker then claim that the man has greater needs? Lower wages for women are just not just."

(pp. 16–17) *Women Question* 1871

2 Poor women had to work: they, quite literally, could not live any other way. On the other hand, rich women will never have to work for their daily bread even if there is much progress in the women's movement. It is in the middle-class, between the iron need of poverty and the comforts of wealth, where the women's movement finds its reason for existence and will be taken seriously.

(pp. 18–19) Ibid.

3 It is impossible for a small artisan, a shopkeeper, or a clerk in normal times to feed not only his family, but all destitute kinswomen, and to secure an income sufficient for his wife and daughters to refrain from paid labor in the event of his death.... Not only does every father know this, but all men know it. Nonetheless, men are against the women's movement, calling it nonsense. They must have been born mad to be able to honor their prejudices by naming them "principles."

(p. 22) Ibid.

1152. Alice Christiana Meynell (1847–1922)

1 It is easy to replace man, and it will take no great time, when Nature has lapsed, to replace Nature.

"The True Colour of Life," *Essays 1914*

2 It is principally for the sake of the leg that a change in the dress of man is so much to be desired.... The leg is the best part of the figure ... and the best leg is the man's.... Man should no longer disguise the long lines, the strong forms, in those lengths of piping or tubing that are of all garments the most stupid.

"Unstable Equilibrium," Ibid.

3 With the first dream that comes with the first sleep
I run, I run, I am gathered to thy heart.

"Renouncement" *n.d.*

4 My heart shall be thy garden.

"The Garden" *n.d.*

5 And when you go
There's loneliness in loneliness.

"Song" *n.d.*

6 Dear Laws, be wings to me!
The feather merely floats, O be it heard
Through weight of life—the skylark's gravity—
That I am not a feather, but a bird!

"The Laws of Verse" *n.d.*

7 I come from nothing: but from where
Come the undying thoughts I bear?

"The Modern Poet, or a Song of Derivations" *n.d.*

8 She walks—the lady of my delight—
A shepherdess of sheep
Her flocks are thoughts.

"The Shepherdess," St. 1 *n.d.*

1153. Julia A. Moore (1847–1920)

1 The character of "Lord Byron"*
    Was of a low degree,
Caused by his reckless conduct,
    And bad company.

"Lord Byron," *The Sentimental Song Book* 1876
*George Gordon, Sixth Baron Byron of Rochdale, British poet (1788–1824).

2 You have come here and paid twenty-five cents to see a fool; I receive seventy-five dollars, and see a whole houseful of fools.

Speech, Grand Rapid opera house (Michigan) 1878

3 And now, kind friends, what I have wrote
I hope you will pass over,
And not criticize as some have done
Hitherto herebefore.

"To My Friends and Critics" *n.d.*

4 Leave off the agony, leave off style,
   Unless you've got money by us all the while.
                              "Leave off the Agony in Style" *n.d.*

1154. Anna Howard Shaw (1847–1919)

1 Her work will not be finished, nor will her last word be spoken, while there remains a wrong to be righted or a fettered life
   to be free in all the earth.
              Elegy at funeral of Susan B. Anthony* (13 March 1906),
              Quoted in *Women Suffragists* by Diana Star Helmer *1998*
   *See 963.

1155. Kate Sheppard (1847/48–1934)

1 Is it right that your mother, your sister . . . should be classed
   with criminals and lunatics. . . ? Is it right that while the loafer,
   the gambler, the drunkard, and even the wife-beater has a vote,
   earnest, educated and refined women are denied it? . . . Is it
   right . . . that a mother . . . should be thought unworthy of a
   vote that is freely given to the blasphemer, the liar, the seducer,
   and the profligate?
                                                   Is it right? 1892

2 The news is being flashed far and wide, and before our earth
   has revolved on her axis every civilized community within the
   reach of the electric wires will have received the tidings that civic
   freedom has been granted to the women of New Zealand. . . . It
   does not seem a great thing to be thankful for, that the gentlemen
   who confirm the laws which render women liable to taxation
   and penal servitude have declared us to be "persons". . .
              Statement after the New Zealand legislature gave women the
              right to vote, *September 1893*

3 All that separates, whether of race, class, creed, or sex, is inhuman, and must be overcome.
              p. 47, Quoted in *Women, Politics, And Power: A Global
              Perspective* by Melanie M. Hughes *2007*

1156. Rosa Sonneschein (1847–1932)

1 Not what has happened, but what is recorded makes history.
                                      The American Jewess, Vol. 1 *1895*

1157. Annie Rankin Annan (1848–1925)

1 A dandelion in his verse,
   Like the first gold in childhood's purse.
                                             "Dandelions" *n.d.*

1158. Hubertine Auclert (1848–1914)

1 Ladies, we must remind ourselves that the weapon of the vote
   will be for us, just as it is for man, the only means of obtaining
   the reforms we desire. As long as we remain excluded from civic
   life, men will attend to their own interests rather than to ours.
              1879, *Women in World History Curriculum*
              (womeninworldhistory.com) *1996–97*

1159. Alice Williams Brotherton (1848–1930)

1 Books we must have though we lack bread.
                                      "Ballade of Poor Bookworms" *n.d.*

2 Heap high the board with plenteous cheer, and gather to the
   feast,
   And toast the sturdy Pilgrim band whose courage never ceased.
                                      "The First Thanksgiving Day" *n.d.*

1160. Alice James (1848–1892)

1 It is so comic to hear oneself called old, even at ninety I suppose!
              Letter to William James* (14 June 1889), *The Diary of Alice
              James,* Leon Edel, ed. *1964*
   *American philosopher and psychologist (1842–1910), her
   brother.

2 . . . The immutable law that however great we may seem to our
   own consciousness no human being would exchange his for
   ours. . . .
                                           (7 July 1889), Ibid.

3 How sick one gets of being "good," how much I should respect
   myself if I could burst out and make everyone wretched for
   twenty-four hours; embody selfishness.
                                           (11 December 1889), Ibid.

4 It is an immense loss to have all robust and sustaining expletives
   refined away from one! At . . . moments of trial refinement is a
   feeble reed to lean on.
                                           (12 December 1889), Ibid.

5 . . . who would ever give up the reality of dreams for relative
   knowledge?
                                                         Ibid.

6 Every hour I live I become an intenser devotee to common-
   sense!
                                           (16 June 1890), Ibid.

7 I suppose one has a greater sense of intellectual degradation
   after an interview with a doctor than from any human experience.
                                           (27 September 1890), Ibid.

8 Having to look forward to something for a while seems to
   double the value of the event. . . .
                                           (1 June 1891), Ibid.

9 . . . physical pain however great ends in itself and falls away
   like dry husks from the mind, whilst moral discords and nervous horrors sear the soul.
                                           (4 March 1892), Ibid.

1161. Catherine Liddell (1848–1927)

1 "O God! but to be Thy laborer there,
      On the gentle hill's green side,
   To leave the struggle of want and wealth,
      And the battle of lust and pride!"
              "The Poet in the City," St. 3, *A Victorian Anthology, 1837–
              1895,* Edmund Clarence Stedman, ed. *1895*

2 "Isn't this Joseph's son?" —ah, it is He;
   Joseph the carpenter—same trade as me.
                                      "Jesus the Carpenter" *n.d.*

1162. Ellen Terry (1848–1928)

1 Imagination, industry, and intelligence—"the three I's"—are all
   indispensable to the actress, but of these three the greatest is,
   without any doubt, imagination.
                                      Ch. 2, *The Story of My Life 1908*

2 Some people are "tone-deaf," and they find it physically impossible to observe the law of contrasts. But even a physical

deficiency can be overcome by that faculty for taking infinite pains which may not be genius but is certainly a good substitute for it.

Ch. 4, Ibid.

3   What is a diary as a rule? A document useful to the person who keeps it, dull to the contemporary who reads it, invaluable to the student, centuries afterwards, who treasures it!

Ch. 14, Ibid.

4   Wonderful women! Have you ever thought how much we all, and women especially, owe to Shakespeare, for his vindication of women in these fearless, high-spirited, resolute and intelligent heroines?

"The Triumphant Women," Lecture (1911), *Four Lectures on Shakespeare* 1932

1163. Harriet Hubbard Ayer (1849–1903)

1   I know that good women are happier and better if they keep their good looks, their youthful grace and elasticity, their girlish figures throughout life, than when through ignorance or carelessness, or both, they lose their personal charms and become old and bent, wrinkled and fat, or emaciated before they have reached the golden prime of life.

Preface, *Harriet Hubbard Ayer's Beauty Book: A Complete and Authentic Treatise on the Laws of Health and Beauty* 1899

2   There are women who are constitutionally exempt from dowdiness, but the average woman of moderate means and, above all, the woman who has to count every penny and make it the equivalent of a five-cent piece is in great danger of drifting into that most unattractive condition called dowdiness.

"The Sin of Dowdiness", Ibid.

3   There is a chance for every one of us to be attractive in appearance, and there is no such thing as a hopelessly ugly girl or woman.

Ibid.

4   I am always a bit amused when anathemas are hurled at the present use of cosmetics, particularly when a hopelessly-soured and pitilessly-unattractive female or a blatant, tobacco-smoking, spirituously-odorous male addresses me on the subject.

Quoted in Ch. 1, *Hope in a Jar* by Kathy Peiss* 1998
*See 4283.

5   When a wife sees a haggard-looking ghost of herself reflected from her mirror, when perhaps she is painfully conscious that the eyes she loves best are turning from her faded beauty to a less worthy object, then I think she is not only justified in delicately simulating, by every aid known to cosmetic art, the charms she has lost, but she is stupid not to do so.

Ibid.

1164. Frances Burnett (1849–1924)

1   "Are you a 'publican, Mary?" "Sorra a bit," sez I; "I'm the bist o' dimmycrats!" An' he looks up at me wid a look that ud go to yer heart, an' sez he: "Mary," sez he, "the country will go to ruin." An' nivver a day since thin has he let go by widout argyin' wid me to change me polytics.

Ch. 1, *Little Lord Fauntleroy* 1888

2   It is astonishing how short a time it takes for very wonderful things to happen.

Ch. 14, Ibid.

1165. Clara Shortridge Foltz (1849–1934)

1   A woman would be better off almost anywhere than home raising men like you.

Quoted by Sandra Day O'Connor* in Foreword, "First Women: Contribution of American Women to the Law," 28, *Valparaiso Law Review,* xiii 1994
*See 2733.

2   They called me the lady lawyer—a dainty sobriquet—which enabled me to maintain a dainty manner as I browbeat my way through the marshes of ignorance and prejudice.

Quoted in *The 50 Most Influential Women in American Law* by Dawn Bradley Berry* 1996
*See 4399.

3   Narrow-gauge statesmen grew red as turkey gobblers mouthing their ignorance against the [women lawyers'] bill, and staid old grangers who had never seen the inside of a courthouse seemed to have been given the gift of tongues and delivered themselves of maiden speeches pregnant with eloquent nonsense.

Debate on California senate floor (ca. 1876), Ibid.

1166. Sarah Orne Jewett (1849–1909)

1   A harbor, even if it is a little harbor, is a good thing. . . . It takes something from the world and has something to give in return.

"River Driftwood," *Country By-Ways* 1886

2   This was one of those perfect New England days in late summer where the spirit of autumn takes a first stealthy flight, like a spy, through the ripening country-side, and, with feigned sympathy for those who droop with August heat, puts her cool cloak of bracing air about leaf and flower and human shoulders.

"The Courting of Sister Wisby," *Atlantic Monthly* (Boston) 1887

3   "Now I'm a believer, and I try to live a Christian life, but I'd as soon hear a surveyor's book read out, figgers an' all, as try to get any simple truth out o' most sermons."

Ibid.

4   The thing that teases the mind over and over for years, and at last gets itself put down rightly on paper—whether little or great, it belongs to Literature.

Preface, Letter to author Willa Cather,* *The Country of the Pointed Firs and Other Stories* 1896
*See 1408.

5   You must find your own quiet center of life, and write from that to the world.

Ibid.

6   Wrecked on the lee shore of age.

Ch. 7, Ibid.

7   Tact is after all a kind of mind reading.

Ch. 10, Ibid.

8   "Yes'm, old friends is always best, 'less you can catch a new one that's fit to make an old one out of."

Ch. 12, Ibid.

9   "T'ain't worthwhile to wear a day all out before it comes."

Ch. 16, Ibid.

10 The road was new to me, as roads always are, going back.

Ch. 19, Ibid.

1167. Ellen Key (1849–1926)

1 Poverty hinders suitable marriages.

Ch. 1, *The Century of the Child 1909*

2 The emancipation of women is practically the greatest egoistic movement of the nineteenth century, and the most intense affirmation of the right of the self that history has yet seen.

Ch. 2, Ibid.

3 According to my method of thinking, and that of many others, not woman but the mother is the most precious possession of the nation, so precious that society advances its highest well-being when it protects the functions of the mother.

Ibid.

4 At every step the child should be allowed to meet the real experiences of life; the thorns should never be plucked from his roses.

Ch. 3, Ibid.

5 Nothing would more effectively further the development of education than for all flogging pedagogues to learn to educate with the head instead of with the hand.

Ibid.

6 Anyone who would attempt the task of felling a virgin forest with a penknife would probably feel the same paralysis of despair that the reformer feels when confronted with existing school systems.

Ch. 5, Ibid.

7 I wrote in the sand [at age ten], "God is dead." In doing so I thought, If there is a God, He will kill me now with a thunderbolt. But since the sun continued to shine, the question was answered for the time being; but it soon turned up again.

Ch. 7, Ibid.

8 A destroyed home life, an idiotic school system, premature work in the factory, stupefying life in the streets, these are what the great city gives to the children of the under classes. It is more astonishing that the better instincts of human nature generally are victorious than the fact that this result is occasionally reversed.

Ch. 8, Ibid.

9 Love is moral without legal marriage, but marriage is immoral without love.

"The Morality of Woman," *The Morality of Woman and Other Essays 1911*

10 Conventionality is the tacit agreement to set appearance before reality, form before content, subordination before principle.

"The Conventional Woman," Ibid.

11 The educator must above all understand how to wait; to reckon all efforts in the light of the future, not the present.

Ibid.

12 Woman, however, as the bearer and guardian of the new lives, has everywhere greater respect for life than man, who for centuries, as hunter and warrior, learned that the taking of lives may be not only allowed, but honourable.

Pt. I, Ch. 2, *The Renaissance of Motherhood 1914*

13 No emancipation must make women indifferent to sexual self-control and motherly devotion, from which some of the highest life values we possess on this earth have sprung.

Ch. 4, Ibid.

14 Art, that great undogmatized church.

Pt. 2, Ch. 1, Ibid.

15 The socially pernicious, racially wasteful, and soul-withering consequences of the working of mothers outside the home must cease. And this can only come to pass, either through the programme of institutional upbringing, *or* through the intimate renaissance of the home.

Pt. 3, Ch. 2, Ibid.

16 The belief that we shall some day be able to prevent war is to me one with the belief in the possibility of making humanity *really* human.

Preface, *War, Peace, and the Future 1916*

17 Formerly, a nation that broke the peace did not trouble to try and prove to the world that it was done solely from higher motives.... *Now war has a bad conscience.* Now every nation assures us that it is bleeding for a human cause, the fate of which hangs in the balance of its victory. All now declare themselves to be fighting for right, against might, the very thing that the pacifists urged. No nation will admit that it was solely to insure its own safety and to increase its power that it declared war. No nation dares to admit the guilt of blood before the world.

Ch. 1, Ibid.

18 Everything, everything in war is barbaric.... But the worst barbarity of war is that is forces men collectively to commit acts against which individually they would revolt with their whole being.

Ch. 6, Ibid.

19 ... feelings of sympathy and admiration are the indispensable mortar that holds the stones of international justice together.

Ch. 16, Ibid.

1168. Emma Lazarus (1849–1887)

1 Although our stock is naturally so vigorous that in Europe the Jews remain after incalculable suffering and privation the healthiest of races, yet close confinement and sedentary occupations have undeniably stunted and debilitated us in comparison with our normal physical status. For nearly nineteen hundred years we have been living on an idea; our spirit has been abundantly fed, but our body has been starved, and has become emaciated past recognition, bearing no likeness to its former self.

Let our first care to-day be the re-establishment of our physical strength, the reconstruction of our national organism, so that in future, where the respect due to us cannot be won by entreaty, it may be commanded, and where it cannot be commanded, it may be enforced.

"An Epistle to the Hebrews," *American Hebrew 3 November 1882–23 February 1883*

2 Until we are all free, we are none of us free.

Ibid.

3 The word "Jew" is in constant use, even among so-called refined Christians, as a term of opprobrium, and is employed as a verb, to denote the meanest tricks.

"The Jewish Problem," *Century February 1883*

4 Give me your tired, your poor,
Your huddled masses yearning to breathe free,
The wretched refuse of your teeming shore,
Send these, the homeless, tempest-tossed to me,
I lift my lamp beside the golden door!*
"The New Colossus" ca. 1886
*Carved at the base of the Statue of Liberty in New York City.

5 Here at our sea-washed, sunset gates shall stand
A mighty woman with a torch, whose flame
Is the imprisoned lightning, and her name
Mother of exiles.
Ibid.

6 What prayers were in this temple offered up,
Wrung from sad hearts that knew no joy on earth,
By these lone exiles of a thousand years,
From the fair sunrise land that gave them birth!
"In the Jewish Synagogue at Newport," St. 3 (27 July 1867),
Emma Lazarus: Selections from Her Poetry and Prose, Morris
U. Schappes, ed. 1982

7 Each separate soul contains the nation's force,
And both embrace the world.
"Rosh-Hashanah, 5643" (1882), Ibid.

8 Blow, Israel, the sacred cornet! Call
Back to thy courts whatever faint heart throb
With thine ancestral blood, thy need craves all.
"The New Year, Rosh-Hashanah, 5643 (1882)" St. 3, Ibid.

9 Still ours the dance, the feast, the glorious Psalm,
The mystic lights of emblem, and the Word.
"The Feast of Lights," St. 6, Emma Lazarus: Selected Poems
2005

10 Still on Israel's head forlorn,
Every nation heaps its scorn.
"The World's Justice" n.d.

1169. Geneviève Straus (1849–1926)
1 The feminine chest was not made for hanging orders on.
Quoted in Pomp and Circumstance by E. de Gramont 1929

1170. Abby Langdon Alger (1850–?)
1 In the beginning, God made Adam out of the earth, but he did not make Gl-us-k-abé (the Indian God). Gl-us-k-abé made himself out of the dirt that was kicked up in the creation of Adam. He rose and walked about, but he could not speak until the Lord opened his lips.
God made the earth and the sea, and then he took counsel with Gl-us-k-abé concerning them. He asked him if it would be better to have the rivers run up on one side of the earth and down on the other, but Gl-us-k-abé said, "No, they must all run down one way."
Then the Lord asked him about the ocean, whether it would do to have it always lie still. Gl-us-k-abé told him, "No!" It must always rise and fall, or else it would grow thick and stagnant.
In Indian Tents: Stories Told by Penobscot, Passamaquoddy
and Mimac Indians to Abby L. Alger 1897

1171. Frances Xavier Cabrini (1850–1917)
1 But I don't think that my Institute can be confined to one city or one diocese. The whole world is not wide enough for me.
Quoted by Bishop Gelmini in Pt. I, Ch. 3, Too Small a World
by Theodore Maynard 1945

2 To become perfect, all you have to do is to obey perfectly. When you renounce your personal inclinations you accept a mortification countersigned with the cross of Christ.
Ibid.

3 Love is not loved, my daughters! Love is not loved! And how can we remain cold, indifferent and almost without heart at this thought? . . . If we do not burn with love, we do not deserve the title which ennobles us, elevates us, makes us great, and even a portent to the angels in heaven.
Diary (1891), Ibid.

1172. Emma Carleton (1850–1927)
1 Reputation is a bubble which a man bursts when he tries to blow it for himself.
The Philistine, Vol. IX, No. 82 n.d.

1173. Florence Earle Coates (1850–1927)
1 Age, out of heart, impatient, sighed;—
"I ask what will the Future be?"
Youth laughed contentedly, and cried:—
"The future leave to me!"
"Youth and Age" n.d.

2 Fear is the fire that melts Icarian wings.
"The Unconquered Air" n.d.

3 He turned with such a smile to face disaster
That he sublimed defeat.
"The Hero" n.d.

4 Though his beginnings be but poor and low,
Thank God a man can grow!
"Per Aspera" n.d.

5 Death—Life's servitor and friend—the guide
That safely ferries us from shore to shore!
"Sleep" n.d.

6 Ah me! the Prison House of Pain!—what lessons there are bought!—
Lessons of a sublimer strain than any elsewhere taught.
"The House of Pain" n.d.

1174. Margaret Collier Graham (1850–1910)
1 "Harvest's a poor time fer wishin'; it's more prof'table 'long about seedin'-time. . . ."
"Idy," Stories of the Foot-hills 1875

2 . . . it's no more 'n fair to be civil to a man when you're gettin' the best of 'im; but I hain't.
"The Withrow Water Right," Ibid.

3 The mind of the most logical thinker goes so easily from one point to another that it is not hard to mistake motion for progress.
Gifts and Givers 1906

4 People need joy quite as much as clothing. Some of them need it far more.
Ibid.

5 We are all held in place by the pressure of the crowd around us. We must all lean upon others. Let us see that we lean gracefully and freely and acknowledge their support.
Ibid.

6 Conscience, as I understand it, is the impulse to do right because it is right, regardless of personal ends, and has nothing whatever to do with the ability to distinguish between right and wrong.

"A Matter of Conscience," *Do They Really Respect Us? And Other Essays* 1911

1175. Leylâ Hanim (1850–1936)

1 Leylâ, indulge in pleasure
With your lovely friend:
Enjoy yourself in this world,
Never mind what they say.

Untitled, St. 4, Tâlat S. Halman, tr., *The Penguin Book of Women Poets,* Carol Cosman, Joan Keefe, and Kathleen Weaver, eds. *1978*

1176. Jane Harrison (1850–1928)

1 Youth and Crabbed Age stand broadly for the two opposite poles of human living, poles equally essential to any real vitality, but always contrasted. . . . The whole art of living is a delicate balance between the two tendencies.

"Crabbed Age and Youth," *Alpha and Omega* 1915

2 Your thoughts are—for what they are worth—self-begotten by some process of parthenogenesis. But there comes often to me, almost always, a moment when alone I cannot bring them to birth, when, if companionship is denied, they die unborn.

"*Scientlae Sacra Fames,*" Ibid.

3 A child's mind is, indeed, throughout the best clue to understanding of savage magic . . . Like the artist, he goes forth to the work of creation, gloriously alone.

"Darwinism and Religion," Ibid.

4 To be womanly is one thing, and one only; it is to be sensitive to man, to be highly endowed with the sex instinct; to be manly is to be sensitive to woman.

"Homo Sum," Ibid.

5 Whenever at an accusation blind rage burns up within us, the reason is that some arrow has pierced the joints of our harness. Behind our shining armour of righteous indignation lurks a convicted and only half-repentant sinner . . . [and] we may be almost sure some sharp and bitter grain of truth lurks within it, and the wound is best probed.

"Epilogue on the War," Ibid.

6 Old age, believe me, is a good and pleasant thing. It is true you are gently shouldered off the stage, but then you are given such a comfortable front stall as spectator. . . .

"Conclusion," *Reminiscences of a Student's Life* 1925

7 If I think of Death at all it is merely as a negation of life, a close, a last and necessary chord. What I dread is disease, that is, bad disordered life, not Death, and disease, so far, I have escaped. I have no hope whatever of personal immortality, no desire even for a future life. My consciousness began in a very humble fashion with my body; with my body, very quietly, I hope it will end.

Ibid.

8 Here was a big constructive imagination; here was a mere doctor laying bare the origins of Greek drama as no classical scholar had ever done, . . . for generations almost every branch of human knowledge will be enriched and illumined by the imagination of Freud.*

Ibid.

*Sigmund F- , Austrian physician and founder of psychoanalysis (1856–1939).

1177. Sofia Vasilyevna Kovalevskaya (1850–1891)

1 The meaning of these concepts I naturally could not yet grasp, but they acted on my imagination, instilling in me a reverence for mathematics as an exalted and mysterious science which opens up to its initiates a new world of wonders, inaccessible to ordinary mortals.

A Russian Childhood 1987

2 I began to feel an attraction for my mathematics so intense that I started to neglect my other studies.

Ibid.

3 Say what you know, do what you must, come what may.

Motto on her paper "On the Problem of the Rotation of a Solid Body about a Fixed Point," Cited in *4000 Years of Women in Science* astr.ua.edu/4000WS *1 August 1997*

1178 Mary Lease (1850/1853–1933)

1 What you Kansas farmers ought to do is to raise less corn and raise more hell.

Political Speech *1890*

2 Wall street owns the country. It is no longer a government of the people, by the people, and for the people, but a government of Wall Street, by Wall Street, and for Wall Street. The great common people of this country are slaves, and monopoly is the master.

Speech (1890s), *History of Kansas, State and People,* Vol. 1, W. E. Connelley, ed. *1928*

3 No more millionaires, and no more paupers; no more gold kings, silver kings and oil kings, and no more little waifs of humanity starving for a crust of bread. No more gaunt faced, hollow-eyed girls in the factories, and no more little boys reared in poverty and crime for the penitentiaries and the gallows

Speech, Women's Christian Temperance Union (1890), Quoted in *With These Hands: Women Working on the Land* by Joan M. Jensen 1981

4 Yet, after all our years of toil and privation, dangers and hardships upon the Western frontier, monopoly is taking our homes from us by an infamous system of mortgage foreclosure, the most infamous that has ever disgraced the statutes of a civilized nation. It, takes from us at the rate of five hundred a month the homes that represent the best years of our life, our toil, our hopes, our happiness. How did it happen?

Ibid.

5 For we are living in a grand and wonderful time—a time when old ideas, traditions and customs have broken loose from their moorings and are hopelessly adrift on the great shoreless, boundless sea of human thought—a time when the gray old world begins to dimly comprehend that there is no difference between the brain of an intelligent woman and the brain of an intelligent man; no difference between the soul-power or brainpower that nerved the arm of Charlotte Corday* to deeds of heroic patriotism and the soul-power or brain-power that

swayed old John Brown** behind his death dealing barricade at Ossawattomie.

Ibid.

*See 736. **(1800–1859) American abolitionist who led a rebellion at Harper's Ferry in 1859; tried and hung.

1179. Mary A. Owen (1850–1935)

1 "She's French quick an' Injun stubborn; it don't pay to rile her . . ."

The Taming of Tarias 1889

2 The astute Dave was a fisher of men, if not of catfish, and listened at supper with a proper admixture of astonishment and enthusiasm to an eager narration of piscatorial adventure more remarkable than anything he remembered since the day, some twenty-odd years before, when his mother explained how the whale caught Jonah instead of Jonah's catching the whale.

Ibid.

3 "To be strong in de haid"—that is, of great strength of will—is the most important characteristic of a "conjurer" or "voodoo". Never mind what you mix—blood, bones, feathers, grave-dust, herbs, saliva, or hair—it will be powerful or feeble in proportion to the dauntless spirit infused by you, the priest or priestess, at the time you represent the god or "Old Master".

Among the Voodoos 1891

1180. Laura Howe Richards (1850–1943)

1 "And the storm went on. It roared, it bellowed, and it screeched: it thumped and it kerwhalloped. The great seas would come bunt agin the rocks, as if they were bound to go right though to Jersey City, which they used to say was the end of the world."

Ch. 2, *Captain January* 1890

2 "There's times when a man has strength given to him, seemin'ly, over and above human strength. 'Twas like as if the Lord ketched holt and helped me: maybe he did, seein' what 'twas I was doing. Maybe he did!"

Ibid.

3 Be you clown or be you King, Still your singing is the thing.

"Dedication," *Tirra Lirra* 1890

4 Every little wave has its nightcap on.

"Song for Hal," Refrain, Ibid.

5 Once there was an elephant Who tried to use the telephant— No! No! I mean an elephone Who tried to use the telephone.

"Eletelephony," St. 1, Ibid.

1181. Rose Hartwick Thorpe (1850–1939)

1 And her face so sweet and pleading, yet with sorrow pale and worn,
Touched his heart with sudden pity—lit his eye with misty light;
"Go, your lover lives!" said Cromwell;* "Curfew shall not ring tonight!"

"Curfew Shall Not Ring Tonight" 1866
*Oliver C- , English military, political, and religious figure (1599–1658).

2 At death's door faint hearts grow fearless,
Miracles are sometimes wrought,
Springing from the heart's devotion
In the forming of a thought.

"Down the Track," St. 3, *Ringing Ballads* 1887

1182. Florence Bell (1851–1930)

1 Ursula had what the French call "genre" . . . The nearest English equivalent to the expression is "style," but that . . . suggests being dashing and assertive; "genre" is a grace inherent in the wearer, and does not depend upon clothes, but upon the way they are put on. And the reason there is no word for it in English, is that the thing is so rarely found that it is unnecessary to have a term on purpose.

Ch. 1, *The Story of Ursula* 1895

2 The girl was ill at ease with the downright Yorkshire women who surrounded her . . . In that class of life when people have nothing to say they say nothing; their rough blunt manner, when they did speak, alarmed her still more.

Ibid.

3 What a huge difference it makes in the whole aspect of life to be married—that there is some one who cares as much for the thing that happens to one as one does oneself!

Letter to daughter Molly Trevelyan (ca. 1878), Quoted in Ch. 1, *Gertrude Bell, Queen of the Desert, Shaper of Nations* by Georgina Howell* 2006
*See 3346.

1183. Nellie Cashman (1851–1904)

1 When I saw something that needed doing, I did it.

Interview, *Daily British Colonist* 1898

1184. Kate Chopin (1851–1904)

1 The voice of the sea speaks to the soul. The touch of the sea is sensuous, enfolding the body in its soft, close embrace.

Ch. 6, *The Awakening* 1889

2 A certain light was beginning to dawn dimly within her—the light which, showing the way, forbids it. . . . But the beginning of things, of a world especially, is necessarily vague, tangled, chaotic, and exceedingly disturbing. How few of us ever emerge from such beginning! How many souls perish in its tumult!

Ibid.

3 "Pirate gold isn't a thing to be hoarded or utilized. It is something to squander and throw to the four winds, for the fun of seeing the golden specks fly."

Ch. 12, Ibid.

4 The past was nothing to her; offered no lesson which she was willing to heed. The future was a mystery which she never attempted to penetrate. The present alone was significant. . . .

Ch. 15, Ibid.

5 "The way to become rich is to make money, my dear Edna, not to save it. . . ."

Ch. 18, Ibid.

6 It sometimes entered Mr. Pontellier's mind to wonder if his wife were not growing a little unbalanced mentally. He could see plainly that she was not herself. That is, he could not see that

she was becoming herself and daily casting aside that fictitious self which we appear before the world.

> Ch. 19, Ibid.

7 ... "a wedding is one of the most lamentable spectacles on earth."

> Ch. 22, Ibid.

8 Alcée Arobin's manner was so genuine that it often deceived even himself.

> Ch. 25, Ibid.

9 "There are some people who leave impressions not so lasting as the imprint of an oar upon the water."

> Ch. 34, Ibid.

10 "The years that are gone seem like dreams—if one might go on sleeping and dreaming—but to wake up and find—oh! well! perhaps it is better to wake up after all, even to suffer, rather than to remain a dupe to illusions all one's life."

> Ch. 38, Ibid.

11 Only the birds had seen, and she could count on their discretion.

> "A Shameful Affair" 1891

12 There would be no one to live for her during these coming years; she would live for herself. There would be no powerful will bending hers in that blind persistence with which men and women believe they have a right to impose a private will upon a fellow-creature.

> "The Story of an Hour" 1894.

13 "I don't hate him," Athenaise answered.... "It's jus' being married that I detes' an' despise."

> "Athenaise" 1895

1185. Anna Garlin Spencer (1851–1931)

1 And when her biographer says of an Italian woman poet, "during some years her Muse was intermitted," we do not wonder at the fact when he casually mentions her ten children.

> Woman's Share in Social Culture 1912

2 It is not alone the fact that women have generally had to spend most of their strength in caring for others that has handicapped them in individual effort; but also that they have almost universally had to care wholly for themselves.

> Ibid.

3 A successful woman preacher was once asked "what special obstacles have you met as a woman in the ministry?" "Not one," she answered, "except the lack of a minister's wife."

> Ibid.

1186. Mariana Griswold Van Rensselaer (1851–1934)

1 Let us shun self-analyzation, self-consciousness, morbidness, affectation, attitudinizing. Let us look ahead as little as possible, keeping our eyes on our brushes and on the world of beauty around us.

> "Some Aspects of Contemporary Art," Lippincott's
> [Philadelphia] December 1878

2 ... we also, and not our artists only, have a duty to perform if we wish the stream of progress to grow wider, deeper, swifter.

We must give ourselves more earnestly and intelligently and generously than we have to the happy duty of appreciation.

> The Book of American Figure Painters 1886

1187. Mary Augusta Ward (1851–1920)

1 "Every man is bound to leave a story better than he found it."

> Bk. I, Ch. 3, Robert Elsmer 1888

2 In my youth people talked about Ruskin;* now they talk about drains.

> Bk. II, Ch. 12, Ibid.
> *John R—, British writer and art critic (1819–1900).

3 "Put down enthusiasm." ... The Church of England in a nutshell.

> Ch. 16, Ibid.

4 Conviction is the Conscience of the Mind.

> Bk. IV, Ch. 26, Ibid.

5 All things change, creeds and philosophies and outward system—but God remains!

> Ch. 27, Ibid.

6 Truth has never been, can never be, contained in any one creed.

> Bk. VI, Ch. 38, Ibid.

7 For that final clash—that Armageddon that all think must come, our sailors wait, not despising their enemy, knowing very well that they—the Fleet—are the pivot of the situation, that without the British Navy, not all the valour of the Allies in France or Russia could win the war, and that with it, Germany's hope of victory is vain. While the Navy lives, England lives, and Germany's vision of a world governed by the ruthless will of the scientific soldier is doomed.

> Ch. IV, England's Effort, Vol. II 1918

1188. Mary A. Barr (1852–?)

1 I sing the Poppy! The frail snowy weed!
The flower of Mercy! That within its heart
Doth keep "a drop serene" of human need,
A drowsy balm of every bitter smart.
For happy hours the rose will idly blow
The Poppy hath a charm of pain and woe.

> "White Poppies" n.d.

1189. Emilia Pardo Bazan (1852–1921)

1 Nature, they call you a mother; they ought to call you a cruel stepmother.

> La madre naturaleza (Mother Nature) 1887

2 I don't know how men are different from hogs.... They chase after the same things: food, drink, women. In short, we're all made of the same stuff.

> Ibid.

3 Men can hardly form an idea of how difficult it is for a woman to acquire culture and to fill in her education by teaching herself. Boys, from the age they can walk and talk, attend elementary schools, then secondary institutes, the academies, the university.... For them, all advantages; for women, all obstacles.

> "Apuntes autobiograficos," Quoted in Emilia Pardo Bazan by
> R. E. Osborne 1964

4   . . . those of us who came into the world a third of a century
     after Concepción Arenal* found public opinion just as hos-
     tile (perhaps more so) to women who were called poetesses or
     bluestockings, and we read every day furious articles intended
     to demonstrate that the object of woman's life is to darn
     socks.

                                    "La Lectura" (1907), Ibid.
     *Spanish feminist writer and activist (1820–1893).

1190. Martha Jane Burke (1852–1903)

1   During the month of June I acted as a pony express rider car-
     rying the U.S. mail between Deadwood and Custer, a distance
     of fifty miles. . . . It was considered the most dangerous route
     in the hills, but as my reputation as a rider and quick shot was
     well known, I was molested very little, for the toll gatherers
     looked on me as being a good fellow, and they knew that I
     never missed my mark.

                          Life and Adventures of Calamity Jane 1896

2   I Jane Hickok Burke better known as Calamity Jane of my own
     free will and being of sound mind do this day June 3, 1903
     make this confession. I have lied about my past life. . . . People
     got snoopy so I told them lies to hear their tongues wag. The
     women are all snakes and none of them I can call friends.

                       Document to James O'Neill (2 June 1903), Quoted in
                  Calamity Was the Name for Jane by Glenn Clairmonte *1959*

1191. Vera Figner (1852–1942)

1   Generally speaking, there was in her* nature both feminine
     gentleness and masculine severity. Tender, tender as a mother
     with the working people, she was exacting and severe toward
     her comrades and fellow-workers, while toward her political
     enemies, the government, she could be merciless. . . .

                                      Memoirs of a Revolutionist 1927
     *Reference to Sofia Perovskaya; see 1198.

1192. Mary Wilkins Freeman (1852–1930)

1   . . . it took her a long time to prepare her tea; but when ready it
     was set forth with as much grace as if she had been a veritable
     guest to her own self.

                                        A New England Nun 1891

2   Louisa's feet had turned into a path . . . so straight and un-
     swerving that it could only meet a check at her grave, and so
     narrow that there was no room for anyone at her side.

                                                              Ibid.

3   She gazed ahead through a long reach of future days strung
     together like pearls in a rosary, every one like the others, and
     all smooth and flawless and innocent, and her heart went up in
     thankfulness.

                                                              Ibid.

1193. Augusta Gregory (1852–1932)

1   CHRISTIE. It's a grand thing to be able to take your money in
     your hand and to think no more of it when it slips away from
     you than you would of a trout that would slip back into the
     stream.

                                                   Twenty Five 1903

2   MRS. TARPEY. Business, is it? What business would the people
     here have but to be minding one another's business?

                                               Spreading the News 1905

3   MRS. DONOHOE. There is many a thing in the sea is not de-
     cent, but cockles is fit to put before the Lord!

                                            The Workhouse Ward 1908

4   HAZEL. To have no power of revenge after death! My strength
     to go nourish weeds and grass!

                                                       Coats 1910

5   DARBY. I am maybe getting your meaning wrong, your tongue
     being a little hard and sharp because you are Englified, but I
     am without new learnments and so I speak flat.

                                                The Bogiemen 1912

6   O'MALLEY. Well, there's no one at all, they do be saying, but
     is deserving of some punishment from the very minute of his
     birth.

                                              Act II, *Shanwalla 1915*

7   GIANT. One person to know it, and you to know him to know
     it, is the same as if it was known to all the world.

                                      Act II, Sc. 2, *The Golden Apple 1916*

8   MOTHER. Them that have too much of it [learning] are seven
     times crosser than them that never saw a book.

                                         Act I, *Aristotle Bellows 1921*

9   CELIA. It is better to be tied to any thorny bush than to be
     with a cross man.

                                                              Ibid.

10   JESTER. There's more learning than is taught in books.

                                                Act I, *The Jester 1923*

11   OGRE. I'll take no charity! What I get I'll earn by taking it. I
     would feel no pleasure it being given to me, any more than a
     huntsman would take pleasure in being made a present of a
     dead fox, in place of getting a run across country after it.

                                               Act II, Sc. 1, Ibid.

1194. Gertrude Kasebier (1852–1934)

1   . . . from the first days of dawning individuality, I have longed
     unceasingly to make pictures of people . . . to make likenesses
     that are biographies, to bring out in each photograph the es-
     sential personality that is variously called temperament, soul,
     humanity.

                          Quoted in *The Woman's Eye* by Anne Tucker* *1973*
     *See 3620.

1195. Qurrat al-'Ayn (?–1852)

1   The tangled curls of thy darling's hair, and thy saddle
     and steed are thine only care;
     In thy heart the Infinite hath no share, nor the thought
     of the poor man's poverty.

                           Untitled ghazal, *Wise Women: Over 2000 Years of Spiritual
                                      Writing by Women,* Susan Cahill, ed. *1996*

2   The country of "I" and "We" forsake; thy home in
     Annihilation make,
     Since fearing not this step to take, thou shalt gain the
     highest felicity.*

                                                              Ibid.
     *This is the core philosophy of Babism, a "systemized Sufism," of
     which Qurrat was a leader and martyred saint.

1196. Octavia Victoria Rogers Albert (1853–1889/90)

1 None but those who resided in the South during the time of slavery can realize the terrible punishments that were visited upon the slaves. Virtue and self-respect were denied them.

Ch. I, *The house of bondage, or, Charlotte Brooks and other slaves* 1890

2 "The white people thought in slave-time we poor darkies had no soul, and they separated us like dogs. So many poor colored people are dead from grieving at the separation of their children that was sold away from them."

Ch. IV, Ibid.

3 "I tell you, I have seen black people, in slave-time, drove along—may be one hundred in a drove—just like hogs to be sold. Sometimes men were sold from their wives and mothers from their children. I saw a white man in Virginia sell his own child he had by a colored woman there. They say a 'Merican man never would take care of his children he would have in slave-time by the black women, as a Frenchman would here in Louisiana."

Ch. VIII, Ibid.

1197. Lillie Langtry (1853–1929)

1 The sentimentalist ages far more quickly than the person who loves his work and enjoys new challenges.

Quoted in the *New York Sun* 1906

2 Anyone who limits his vision to his memories of yesterday is already dead.

Quoted in *Because I Love Him* by Noel B. Gerson 1971

1198. Sofia Perovskaya (1853–1881)

1 . . . my lot is not at all such a dark one. I have lived as my convictions have prompted me; I could not do otherwise; therefore I await what is in store for me with a clear conscience.

Letter to her Mother, *Woman as Revolutionary*, Fred C. Giffin, ed. 1973

1199. Emilie Poulsson (1853–1939)

1   Upon each hand
A little band
For work or play is ready.
The first to come
Is Master Thumb;
Then Pointer, strong and steady;

Then Tall Man high;
And just close by
The Feeble Man doth linger;
And last of all,
So fair and small,
The baby—Little Finger.

"The Little Men", *Finger-Plays* 1893

2   O, clap, clap the hands,
And sing out with glee!
For Christmas is coming
And merry are we!

"Santa Claus," Ibid.

3 Books are keys to wisdom's treasure;
Books are gates to lands of pleasure;

Books are paths that upward lead;
Books are friends. Come, let us read.

Inscription in Children's Reading Room, Hopkington, Massachusetts *n.d.*

1200. Susan Hamilton Ardagh (1854–1935)

1 What are necessaries? What are luxuries? For I need hardly point out to any one who has felt the grip of an English winter, that what constitutes riches in Capri would mean poverty and privation in a climate like ours. So much depends on the class we happen to associate with, and the sky under which we live.

The Modern Marriage Market 1897

2 The exhilarating and stimulating effect of certain minds upon our own is within the experience of most of us, while another perhaps superior intellect may leave us cold and dull.

Ibid.

1201. Jennie Jerome Churchill (1854–1921)

1 Of all nationalities, Americans are the best in adapting themselves. With them, to see is to know—and to know is to conquer.

Quoted in the *New York World-Telegram* 13 October 1908

2 You may be a princess or the richest woman in the world, but you cannot be more than a lady.

Ibid.

3 ALMA. I rather suspect her of being in love with him.
MARTIN. Her own husband? Monstrous! What a selfish woman!

His Borrowed Plumes 1909

4 Italians love—sun, sin, and spaghetti.

Ibid.

5 It is so tempting to try the most difficult thing possible.

Quoted in the *Daily Chronicle* (London) 8 *July* 1909

6 . . . we owe something to extravagance, for thrift and adventure seldom go hand in hand. . . .

"Extravagance" *October* 1915

7 Treat your friends as you do your pictures, and place them in their best light.

"Friendship," *Small Talk on Big Subjects* 1916

8 There is no such thing as a moral dress. . . . It's people who are moral or immoral.

Quoted in *Daily Chronicle* (London) 16 *February* 1921

9 But I suppose experience of life will in time teach you that tact is a very essential ingredient in all things.

Letter to Winston Churchill* (4 October 1895), Quoted in *Jennie*, Vol. II by Ralph G. Martin 1971

10 Life is not always what one wants it to be, but to make the best of it as it is, is the only way of being happy. . . .

Letter to Lord Kitchener* (27 November 1896), Ibid.
*Horatio Herbert, First Earl Kitchener of Khartoum and of Broome, British soldier and colonial administrator (1850–1916).

11 You seem to have no real purpose in life and won't realize at the age of twenty-two that for a man life means work, and hard work if you mean to succeed.

Letter to Winston Churchill* (26 February 1897), Ibid.
*(1874–1965) British statesman, prime minister (1940–1945 and 1951–1955), her son.

1202. Mary M. Cohen (1854–1911)

1 Those who have spoken of Judaism as a "kitchen religion" lose sight of the fact that spirit and body are equally in need of nourishment, and that to closely associate the material and the religious is to dignify the one without injuring the other.

> Address, "The Influence of the Jewish Religion in the Home",
> *Papers of the Jewish Women's Congress (Chicago) 1894*

2 The observances of the faith are so entwined with the everyday atmosphere of the home as to make the Jewish religion and the family life one, a bond in sanctity. In this sense the synagogue is the home, and the home the synagogue. I mean that the intelligent and devout Hebrew parent is the priest or priestess of the family alter. There is no need, if there is a desire to worship the God of Israel, to visit the sanctuary . . .

> Ibid.

1203. Eva March Tappan (1854–1930)

1 We drove the Indians out of the land,
But a dire revenge those Redmen planned,
For they fastened a name to every nook,
And every boy with a spelling book
Will have to toil till his hair turns gray
Before he can spell them the proper way.

> "On the Cape," St. 1 *n.d.*

1204. Edith Thomas (1854–1925)

1 How on the moment all changes!

> "*Optimi Consiliarii Mortui,* XXXIV," Sts. 1–2, *The Inverted Torch 1890*

2 When the wind through the trees makes a path for the moon!
Praise June!

> "Praise June," *In Sunshine Land 1894*

3 And Heaven gave me strivings blind
By Justice to be schooled,
And purpose branded in the mind,
To rule not, nor be ruled. . . .

> "Of the Middle World," St. 2, *The Guest at the Gate 1909*

4 The God of Music dwelleth out of doors.

> "The God of Music" *n.d.*

1205. Margaret Wolfe Hungerford (1855?–1897)

1 Beauty is in the eye of the beholder.

> *Molly Bawn 1878*

2 ". . . what the deuce did Wynter mean by leaving me his daughter? A real live girl of seventeen! It'll be the death of me," says the professor, mopping his brow.

> Ch. 1, *A Little Rebel 1891*

3 "I am a poor man, and poor men cannot afford such luxuries as hearts."

> Ibid.

1206. Alice Freeman Palmer (1855–1902)

1 A good society of scholars and of libraries and laboratories has no place and no attraction for her who finds no message in Plato, no beauty in mathematical order, and who never longs to know the meaning of the stars over her head or the flowers under her feet.

> Speech, Why Go to College? 1897

2 Pre-eminently the college is a place of education. That is the ground of its being. We go to college to know, assured that knowledge is sweet and powerful, that a good education emancipates the mind and makes us citizens of the world.

> Ibid.

3 Imagination and knowledge should be the hourly companions of her who would make a fine art of each detail in kitchen and nursery.

> Ibid.

4 Only a moment! Ah, how short the day!
Yet all the winters cannot blow its sweetness quite away.

> "A Spring Journey" *n.d.*

5 Exquisite child of the air.

> "The Butterfly" *n.d.*

1207. Julia Richman (1855–1912)

1 God needs hearts more than heads in His service.

> Report of National Committee on Religious School Work,
> Proceedings of First Convention of the National Council of
> Jewish Women 1896

2 Take your children to the Religious School at a very early age. Select for them a teacher who loves little ones and who loves God. What do these babies care about Adam and Eve, or the order of creation? Introduce them to the wonders of plant and animal life. *Show them God* in the bursting seed, in the budding flower, in the bird-producing egg, the glorious sunshine. Let them see God and learn to love Him for His blessings in which they share. Let them be made to feel that God means protection, that to Him they owe love and respect and gratitude and loyalty. Make God the starting point and the goal. Love of God, confidence in God, fear, not of God, but of His disapproval, these are the steps by which to develop the feeling of moral obligation, first to the world, then to Judaism.

> Ibid.

3 We are not Jews first and Americans afterward, we are American Jews.

> *Julia Richman: A Notable Woman* by Selma C. Berrol 1993
> "Life's Scars," St. 3 *n.d.*

1208. Olive Schreiner (1855–1920)

1 The troubles of the young are soon over; they leave no external mark. If you wound the tree in its youth the bark will quickly cover the gash; but when the tree is very old, peeling the bark off, and looking carefully, you will see the scar there still. All that is buried is not dead.

> Pt. 1, Ch. 13, *The Story of an African Farm 1883*

2 A little weeping, a little wheedling, a little self-degradation, a little careful use of our advantages, and then some man will say—"Come, be my wife!" With good looks and youth marriage is easy to attain. There are men enough; but a woman who has sold herself, even for a ring and a new name, need hold her skirt aside for no creature in the street. They both earn their bread in one way. Marriage for love is the beautifullest external symbol of the union of souls; marriage without it is the uncleanliest traffic that defiles the world.

> Pt. 2, Ch. 4, "Lyndall," Ibid.

3 Power! You may dam up the fountain of water, and make it a stagnant marsh, or you may let it run free and do its work; but

you cannot say whether it shall be there; it is there. And it will act, if not openly for good, then covertly for evil; but it will act.

Ibid.

4 They are called finishing-schools and the name tells accurately what they are. They finish everything. . . .

Ibid.

5 "*We* bear the world, and we make it. . . . There was never a great man who had not a great mother—it is hardly an exaggeration."

Ibid.

6 "Men are like the earth and we are the moon; we turn always one side to them, and they think there is no other, because they don't see it—but there is."

Ibid.

7 I have seen some souls so compressed that they would have fitted into a small thimble, and found room to move there—wide room.

Ibid.

8 "Wisdom never kicks at the iron walls it can't bring down."

Ibid.

9 "Look at this little chin of mine, Waldo, with the dimple in it. It is but a small part of my person; but though I had a knowledge of all things under the sun, and the wisdom to use it, and the deep loving heart of an angel, it would not stead me through life like this little chin. I can win money with it, I can win love; I can win power with it, I can win fame."

Ibid.

10 "If the bird *does* like its cage, and *does* like its sugar, and will not leave it, why keep the door so very carefully shut?"

Pt. 2, Ch. 4, Ibid.

11 I said to God, "What are they doing?"
God said, "Making pitfalls into which their fellows may sink."
I said to God, "Why do they do it?"
God said, "Because each thinks that when his brother falls he will rise."

"Across My Bed," *Dreams* 1890

12 "I suppose the most absolutely delicious thing in life is to feel a thing needs you, and to give at the moment it needs. Things that don't need you, you must love from a distance."

"The Buddhist Priest's Wife," *Stories, Dreams, and Allegories* 1892

13 "There is nothing ridiculous in love."

Ibid.

14 If Nature here wishes to make a mountain, she runs a range for five hundred miles; if a plain, she levels eighty; if a rock, she tilts five thousand feet of strata on end; our skies are higher and more intensely blue; our waves larger than others; our rivers fiercer. There is nothing measured, small nor petty in South Africa.

Ch. 1, *Thoughts on South Africa* 1892

15 I know there will be spring; as surely as the birds know it when they see above the snow two tiny, quivering green leaves. Spring cannot fail us.

"The Woman's Rose" 1893

16 I suppose there is no man who to-day loves his country who has not perceived that in the life of the nation, as in the life of the individual, the hour of external success may be the hour of irrevocable failure, and that the hour of death, whether to nations or individuals, is often the hour of immortality.

The English South African's View of the Situation ca. 1899

17 We have in us the blood of a womanhood that was never bought and never sold; that wore no veil and had no foot bound; whose realized ideal of marriage was sexual companionship and an equality in duty and labor.

Woman and Labor 1911

18 We have always borne part of the weight of war, and the major part. . . . Men have made boomerangs, bows, swords, or guns with which to destroy one another; we have made the men who destroyed and were destroyed! . . . *We pay the first cost on all human life.*

Ch. 4, Ibid.

1209. Ella Wheeler Wilcox (1855–1919)

1 Laugh and the world laughs with you;
Weep, and you weep alone;
For the sad old earth must borrow its mirth,
But has trouble enough of its own.

"Solitude" St. 1, *New York Sun 25 February 1883*

2 'Tis easy enough to be pleasant,
When life flows along like a song;
But the man worth while is the one who will smile
When everything goes dead wrong.

"Worth While" *n.d.*

3 Give us that grand word "woman" once again,
And let's have done with "lady"; one's a term
Full of fine force, strong, beautiful, and firm,
Fit for the noblest use of tongue or pen;
And one's a word for lackeys.

"Woman" *n.d.*

4 I love your lips when they're wet with wine
And red with wicked desire.

"I Love You," St. 1, *n.d.*

5 It ever has been since time began,
And ever will be, till time lose breath,
That love is a mood—no more—to man,
And love to a woman is life or death.

"Blind," St. 1 *n.d.*

6 Sweep up the debris from decaying faiths;
Sweep down the cobwebs of worn-out beliefs,
And throw your soul open to the light
Of Reason and Knowledge.

"Progress," St. 2 *n.d.*

7 Love lights more fires than hate extinguishes,
And men grow better as the world grows old.

"Optimism" *n.d.*

8 All love that has not friendship for its base,
Is like a mansion built upon the sand.

"Upon the Sand" *n.d.*

9 Keep on with your weary battle against triumphant might;
No question is ever settled until it is settled right.

"Settle the Question Right" *n.d.*

10 The splendid discontent of God
   With chaos, made the world.
   And from the discontent of man
   The world's best progress springs.

   "Discontent" *n.d.*

11 We flatter those we scarcely know,
   We please the fleeting guest,
   And deal full many a thoughtless blow
   To those who love us best.

   "Life's Scars," St. 3 *n.d.*

1210. Fannie Barrier Williams (1855–1944)

1 Few of the happy, prosperous, and eager living Americans can appreciate what it all means to be suddenly changed from irresponsible bondage to the responsibility of freedom and citizenship!

   Speech, "The Intellectual Progress of Colored Women of the United States Since the Emancipation Proclamation," *World's Congress of Representative Women (Chicago) 1893*

2 What can religion further do to advance the condition of the colored people? More religion and less church. . . . Less theology and more of human brotherhood, less declamation and more common sense and love for truth. . . .

   Speech, "Religious Duty to the Negro," World's Parliament of Religions (Chicago) *1893*

3 What men and women do, rather than what they say or profess, shall be the standard of religion.

   Speech, "Opportunities and Responsibilities of Colored Women" (Memphis, TN) *1895*

4 I never quite recovered from the shock and pain of my first bitter realization that to be a colored woman is to be discredited, mistrusted and often meanly hated.

   A Northern Negro's Autobiography 1904

5 In nothing was slavery so savage and relentless as in its attempted destruction of the family instincts of the Negro race in America.

   Quoted in Ch. 3, *Black Women in Nineteenth-Century American Life* by James Loewenberg and Ruth Bogin *1976*

1211. Elisabeth Marbury (1856–1933)

1 I began to realize that the world was divided into three groups: wasters, mollusks, and builders.

   Ch. 1, *My Crystal Ball 1923*

2 "Ah, daughter," said Mother, "where there is room in the heart, there is always room on the hearth."

   Ibid.

3 Throughout my life, I have always found that events which seemed at the time disastrous ultimately developed into positive blessings. In fact, I have never known one instance when this has not proved to be the case.

   Ch. 5, Ibid.

4 The richer your friends, the more they will cost you.

   "Careers for Women" *n.d.*

5 A caress is better than a career.

   Ibid.

6 No influence so quickly converts a radical into a reactionary as does his election to power.

   Ibid.

1212. Mrs. N. F. Mossell (1856–1946)

1 . . . keeping a clean house will not keep a man at home.

   The Work of the Afro-American Women 1894

2 . . . women must not be blamed because they are not equal to the self-sacrifice of always meeting husbands with a smile.

   Ibid.

1213. Lizette Reese (1856–1935)

1 A book may be a flower that blows;
   A road to a far town;
   A roof, a well, a tower;
   A book
   May be a staff, a crook.

   "Books" *n.d.*

2 Creeds grow so thick along the way,
   Their boughs hide God.

   "Doubt" *n.d.*

3 The old faiths light their candles all about,
   But burly Truth comes by and puts them out.

   "Truth" *n.d.*

4 When I consider life and its few years—
   A wisp of fog betwixt us and the sun;
   A call to battle, and the battle done
   Ere the last echo dies within our ears,
   I wonder at the idleness of tears.

   "Tears" *n.d.*

5 Fame is a bugle call
   Blown past a crumbling wall.

   "Taps" *n.d.*

1214. Kate Douglas Wiggin (1856–1923)

1 Women never hit what they aim at: but if they just shut their eyes and shoot in the air they generally find themselves in the bull's eye.

   New Chronicles of Rebecca 1907

2 My heart is open wide tonight
   For stranger, kith or kin.
   I would not bar a single door
   When love might enter in.

   "The Romance of a Christmas Card" *n.d.*

1215. Ada Alden (1857–1936)

1 Can this be Italy, or but a dream
   Emerging from the broken waves of sleep? . . .
   This world of beauty, color, and perfume,
   Hoary with age, yet of unaging bloom.

   "Above Salerno" *n.d.*

2 The years shall right the balance tilted wrong,
   The years shall set upon his* brows a star.

   "Ave" *n.d.*

   *Reference to Woodrow Wilson, (1856–1924), 28th president of the United States (1913–1921).

1216. Gertrude Atherton (1857–1948)

1 We love the lie that saves their pride, but never the unflattering truth.

   Bk. III, Ch. 6, *The Conqueror 1902*

2   No matter how hard a man may labor, some woman is always in the background of his mind. She is the one reward of virtue.

Bk. IV, Ch. 3, Ibid.

3   Better extirpate the whole breed, root and branch. And this, unless the German people come to their senses, is what we propose to do.

The New York Times 18 August 1918

1217. Myrta Lockett Avary (1857–1946)

1   Memoirs and journals written not because of their historical or political significance, but because they are to the writer the natural expression of what life has meant to him in the moment of living, have a value entirely apart from literary quality. They bring us close to the human soul—the human soul in undress.

Introduction, *A Virginia Girl in the Civil War, 1861–1865,* ed. *1903*

1218. Alice Brown (1857–1948)

1   Praise not the critic, lest he think
You crave the shelter of his ink.

"The Critic" *n.d.*

2   Yet thou, O banqueter on worms,
Who wilt not let corruption pass!—
Dost search out mildew, mound and stain,
Beneath a magnifying-glass.

"The Slanderer" *n.d.*

1219. Mary Lee Demarest (1857–1888)

1   Like a bairn to his mither, a wee birdie to its nest,
I wud fain be ganging nod unto my Saviour's breast;
For he gathers in his bosom witless, worthless lambs like me
An' he carries them himsel' to his ain countree

"My Ain Countree" *n.d.*

1220. Lina Eckenstein (1857–1931)

1   The contributions of nuns to literature, as well as incidental remarks, show that the curriculum of study in the nunnery was as liberal as that accepted by the monks, and embraced all available writing whether by Christian or profane authors.

Women Under Monasticism 1896

1221. Fannie Farmer (1857–1915)

1   Progress in civilization has been accompanied by progress in cookery.

Ch. 2, *The Boston Cooking-School Cookbook 1896*

2   I certainly feel that the time is not far distant when a knowledge of the principles of diet will be an essential part of one's education. Then mankind will eat to live, be able to do better mental and physical work, and disease will be less frequent.

Preface to the First Edition, Ibid.

3   . . . France, that land to which we ever look for gastronomic delights. . . .

Ch. 1, *Chafing Dish Possibilities 1898*

1222. Alexandra Gripenberg (1857–1913)

1   The miracle has happened! On May the 29th the Finnish Diet agreed to an Imperial proposal from the Czar concerning changes in the constitution of Finland, which changes also include political suffrage and eligibility to the Diet for Women, married and unmarried, on the same conditions as for men.

Statement (1906), *Women in World History Curriculum* (womeninworldhistory.com) *1996–97*

1223. Martha Matilda Harper (1857–1950)

1   The great achievement of the Harper empire is the women it has made.

Martha Matilda Harper and the American Dream by Jane R. Plitt *2001*

2   Base everything on service.

Ibid.

3   When a [person] is healthy, [she] is beautiful.

Ibid.

1224. Minna Irving (1857–1940)

1   He's cheerful in weather so bitterly cold
It freezes your bones to the marrow;
I'll admit he's a beggar, a gangster, a bum,
But I take off my hat to the sparrow.

"The Sparrow" *n.d.*

2   The flowery frocks and the ancient trunk,
And Grandmother Granger, too, are dust,
But something precious and sweet and rare
Survives the havoc of moth and rust.

"The Wedding Gift," St. 6 *n.d.*

3   A nation thrills, a nation bleeds,
A nation follows where it leads,
And every man is proud to yield
His life upon a crimson field
For Betsy's battle flag.

"Betsy's Battle Flag" *n.d.*

1225. Edna Lyall (1857–1903)

1   Two is company, three is trumpery, as the proverb says.

Ch. 24, *Wayfaring Men 1897*

1226. A. Mary F. Robinson (1857–1944)

1   You hail from dream-land, Dragon-fly?
A stranger hither? So am I.

"To a Dragonfly" *n.d.*

2   When I was young the twilight seemed too long.

"Twilight" *n.d.*

1227. Ida Tarbell (1857–1944)

1   The first and most imperative necessity in war is money, for money means everything else—men, guns, ammunition.

Ch. 1, *The Tariff in Our Times 1906*

2   Sacredness of human life! The world has never believed it! It has been with life that we settled our quarrels, won wives, gold and land, defended ideas, imposed religions. We have held that a death toll was a necessary part of every human achievement, whether sport, war, or industry. A moment's rage over the horror of it, and we have sunk into indifference.

Ch. 3, *New Ideals in Business 1914*

3 Those who talk of the mine, the mill, the factory as if they were inherently inhuman and horrible are those who never have known the miner, the weaver, or the steel or iron worker.

Ch. 7, Ibid.

4 A mind truly cultivated never feels that the intellectual process is complete until it can reproduce in some media the thing which it has absorbed.

Ch. 5, *The Ways of Woman* 1914

5 They did not understand it [culture] to be ripeness and sureness of mind, it was not taste, discrimination, judgement; it was an acquisition—something which came with diplomas and degrees and only with them.

Ibid.

6 "Yes, sir; he was what I call a *godly* man. Fact is, I never knew anybody I felt so sure would walk straight into Heaven, everybody welcomin' him, nobody fussin' or fumin' about his bein' let in, as Abraham Lincoln."

In Lincoln's Chair 1920

7 The Eighties dripped with blood.

p. 89, *All in the Day's Work: An Autobiography* 1939

1228. Martha "Minnie" Thomas (1857–1935)

1 Women are one-half of the world but until a century ago . . . it was a man's world. The laws were man's laws, the government a man's government, the country a man's country. . . . The man's world must become a man's and a woman's world. Why are we afraid? It is the next step forward on the path to the sunrise, and the sun is rising over a new heaven and a new earth.

Address, North American Woman Suffrage Association, (Buffalo, New York) *October* 1908

1229. Klara Zetkin (1857–1933)

1 In agreement with the class-conscious, political and trade union organizations of the proletariat of their respective countries, the Socialist women of all countries will hold each year a Women's Day, whose foremost purpose it must be to aid the attainment of women's suffrage. This demand must be handled in conjunction with the entire women's question according to Socialist precepts. The Women's Day must have an international character and is to be prepared carefully.*

Proposal to the Second International Women's Conference (Copenhagen, 27 August 1910), *Die Gleicheit* (Stuttgart), with Käthe Duncker and Comrades *29 August 1910*
*International Women's Day was first honored by several nations on 19 March 1911; it is now celebrated on 8 March.

2 The automatic machine . . . works with the powers of a giant, possesses unbelievable skill, speed and exactness and renders muscle power and acquired skills superfluous. The capitalist entrepreneur can employ only female labor at those places where he previously had to use male employees. And he just loves to hire women because female labor is cheap, much cheaper than male labor.

"Women's Work and the Trade Unions" *(Die Gleicheit),* (Stuttgart, 1 November 1893), *The Organization of Trade Unions n.d.*

3 . . . women are house as well as factory slaves and are forced to bear a double workload.

Ibid.

4 The larger the number of organized female workers who fight shoulder to shoulder with their comrades from the factory or workshop for better working conditions, the sooner and the greater will women's wages rise so that soon there may be the realization of the principle: Equal pay for equal work regardless of the difference in sex.

Ibid.

5 If during the Age of the Family, a man had the right . . . to tame his wife occasionally with a whip, capitalism is now taming her with scorpions. In former times, the rule of a man over his wife was ameliorated by their personal relationship. Between an employer and his worker, however, exists only a cash nexus.

Speech, "Only in Conjunction with the Proletarian Woman Will Socialism Be Victorious," presented to Party Congress of the Social Democratic Party of Germany (Gotha, 16 October 1896), Ibid.

6 Once the family as an economic unit will vanish and its place will be taken by the family as a moral unit, the woman will become an equally entitled, equally creative, equally goal-oriented, forward-stepping companion of her husband; her individuality will flourish while at the same time, she will fulfill her task as wife and mother to the highest degree possible.

Ibid.

1230. Marie Bashkirtseff (1858–1884)

1 Ah, when one thinks what a miserable creature man is! Every other animal can, at his will, wear on his face the expression he pleases. He is not obligated to smile if he has a mind to weep. When he does not wish to see his fellows he does not see them. While man is the slave of everything and everybody!

(6 May 1873) *The Journal of a Young Artist* 1884

2 Let us love dogs; let us love only dogs! Men and cats are unworthy creatures. . . .

(16 July 1874) Ibid.

3 In the studio all distinctions disappear. One has neither name nor family; one is no longer the daughter of one's mother, one is one's self—an individual—and one has before one art, and nothing else. One feels so happy, so free, so proud.

(5 October 1877) Ibid.

4 . . . I write down everything, everything, everything. Otherwise why should I write?

(1 May 1884) Ibid.

5 If I had been born a man, I would have conquered Europe. As I was born a woman, I exhausted my energy in tirades against fate, and in eccentricities.

(25 June 1884) Ibid.

6 For my own part I think love—impossible—to one who looks at human nature through a microscope, as I do. They who see only what they wish to see in those around them are very fortunate.

(1 August 1884) Ibid.

7 I was born to be a remarkable woman; it matters little in what way or how . . . I shall be famous or I will die.

I Am the Most Interesting Book of All: The Diary of Marie Bashkirtseff, Vol. 1, Phyllis Howard Kernberger with Katherine Kernberger, tr. 1997

1231. Anna Julia Cooper (1858–1964)

1 Only when the BLACK WOMAN can say "when and where I enter, in the quiet, undisputed dignity of my womanhood, without violence and without suing or special patronage, then and there the whole Negro race enters with me."

Introduction, A Voice from the South; By a Black Woman of the South 1892

2 The cause of freedom is not the cause of a race or a sect, a party or a class—it is the cause of humankind, the very birthright of humanity.

"Woman vs. The Indian," Ibid.

3 We take our stand on the solidarity of humanity, the oneness of life, and the unnaturalness and injustice of all special favoritisms, whether of sex, race, country, or condition. . . . The colored woman feels that woman's cause is one and universal; and that . . . not till race, color, sex, and condition are seen as accidents and the pursuit of happiness is conceded to be inalienable to all; not till then is woman's . . . cause won—not the white woman's nor the black woman's, not the red woman's but the cause of every man and of every woman who has writhed silently under a mighty wrong.

Speech (1893), Quoted in The Woman That I Am, The Literature and Culture of Contemporary Women of Color, D. Soyini Madison, ed. 1976

*See 3912.

1232. Dorothy Gurney (1858–1932)

1 The kiss of sun for pardon,
The song of the birds for mirth—
One is nearer God's Heart in a garden
Than anywhere else on earth.

"The Lord God Planted a Garden," St. 3 n.d.

1233. Selma Lagerlöf (1858–1940)

1 Just fancy what an effect his violin could have! It made people quite forget themselves. It was a great power to have at his disposal. Any moment he liked he could take possession of his kingdom.

"The Story of a Country House," Ch. 1, From a Swedish Homestead 1901

2 Anyone who has ever sat in a train as it rushes through a dark night will know that sometimes there are long minutes when the coaches slide smoothly along without so much as a shudder. All rustle and bustle cease and the sound of the wheels becomes a soothing, peaceful melody. The coaches no longer seem to run on rails and sleepers but glide into space.

Acceptance Speech, Nobel Prize (Stockholm) 1909

3 "Father, how shall I ever repay them for teaching me to love fairy tales and sagas of heroes, the land we live in and all of our human life, in all its wretchedness and glory?"

Ibid.

4 There is nothing so terrible as perjury. There is something uncanny and awful about that sin. There is no mercy or condonation for it.

"The Girl from the Marsh Croft," The Girl from the Marsh Croft 1911

5 "When I see a stream like this in the wilderness," he thought, "I am reminded of my own life. As persistent as this stream have I been in forcing my way past all that has obstructed my path. Father has been my rock ahead, and Mother tried to hold me back and bury me between moss-tufts, but I stole past both of them and got out in the World. Hey—ho, hi, hi!"

"The Musician," Ibid.

6 Thinking is never so easy as when one follows a plow up a furrow and down a furrow.

Bk. I, Ch. 1, Jerusalem 1915

7 There isn't much that tastes better than praise from those who are wise and capable . . .

Ch. 5, The Wonderful Adventures of Nils, Velma Swanston Howard, tr. 1922

8 Could I ever be happy again now that I knew there was so much evil in the world?

(24 March 1872) The Diary of Selma Lagerlöf 1936

9 To be sure, I believe in the power of the dead, but I also know that Selma Otilla Lovisa Lagerlöf is inclined to imagine things that are utterly impossible.

(26 March 1872), Ibid.

1234. Edith Nesbit (1858–1924)

1 Little brown brother, oh! little brown brother,
Are you awake in the dark?

"Baby Seed Song" n.d.

2 The chestnut's proud, and the lilac's pretty,
The poplar's gentle and tall,
But the plane tree's kind to the poor dull city—
I love him best of all!

"Child's Song in Spring" n.d.

1235. Emmeline Pankhurst (1858–1928)

1 We are here, not because we are law-breakers; we are here in our efforts to become law-makers.

Speech, at her trial in London 21 October 1908

2 Those men and women are fortunate who are born at a time when a great struggle for human freedom is in progress.

My Own Story 1914

3 It was rapidly becoming clear to my mind that men regarded women as a servant class in the community, and that women were going to remain in the servant class until they lifted themselves out of it.

Ibid.

4 "I have never felt a prouder woman than I did one night when a police constable said to me, after one of these demonstrations, 'Had this been a man's demonstration, there would have been bloodshed long ago.' Well, my lord, there has not been any bloodshed except on the part of the women themselves—these so-called militant women. Violence has been done to us, and I who stand before you in this dock have lost a dear sister in the course of this agitation."

Ibid.

5 Why is it that men's blood-shedding militancy is applauded and women's symbolic militancy punished with a prison-cell and the forcible feeding horror?

Ibid.

6 There is something that governments care far more for than human life, and that is the security of property, and so it is through property that we shall strike the enemy.

Speech, "I Incite This Meeting to Rebellion" (17 October 1912), Ibid.

7 You have to make more noise than anybody else, you have to make yourself more obtrusive than anybody else, you have to fill all the papers more than anybody else, in fact you have to be there all the time and see that they do not snow you under, if you are really going to get your reform realized.

Ibid.

8 I am what you call a hooligan!

Speech (1909), Quoted in *The Fighting Pankhursts* by David Mitchell *1967*

*See Christabel P—, 1553; Adela P—, 1636; Sylvia P—, 1583.

9 I have no sense of guilt. I look upon myself as a prisoner of war. I am under no moral obligation to conform to, or in any way accept, the sentence imposed upon me.

Speech to the Court (April 1913), *Ibid.*

10 Over one thousand women have gone to prison in the course of this agitation, have suffered their imprisonment, have come out of prison injured in health, weakened in body, but not in spirit. . . . I ask you . . . if you are prepared to go on doing that kind of thing indefinitely, because that is what is going to happen. There is absolutely no doubt about it. . . . We are women, rightly or wrongly convinced that this is the only way in which we can win power to alter what for us are intolerable conditions, absolutely intolerable conditions. From the moment I leave this court I shall deliberately refuse to eat food—I shall join the women who are already in Holloway [Women's Prison] on the hunger strike. I shall come out of prison, dead or alive, at the earliest possible moment; and once again, as soon as I am physically fit I shall enter into this fight again. Life is very dear to all of us. I am not seeking, as was said by the Home Secretary, to commit suicide. I do not want to commit suicide. I want to see the women of this country enfranchised, and I want to live until that is done.

Speech to the Court (2 April 1913), *Shoulder to Shoulder,* Midge Mackenzie, ed. *1975*

1236. Agnes Repplier (1858–1950)

1 . . . the children of to-day are favored beyond their knowledge and certainly beyond their deserts.

"Children, Past and Present," *Books and Men 1888*

2 But self-satisfaction, if as buoyant as gas, has an ugly trick of collapsing when full blown, and facts are stony things that refuse to melt away in the sunshine of a smile.

"Some Aspects of Pessimism," *Ibid.*

3 Memory cheats us no less than hope by hazing over those things that we would fain forget; but who that has plodded on to middle age would take back upon his shoulders ten of the vanished years, with their mingled pleasures and pains? Who would return to the youth he is forever pretending to regret?

Ibid.

4 Amusement is merely one side of pleasure, but a very excellent side, against which, in truth, I have no evil word to urge. The gods forbid such base and savorless ingratitude!

"Pleasure: A Heresy," *Points of View 1891*

5 A villain must be a thing of power, handled with delicacy and grace. He must be wicked enough to excite our aversion, strong enough to arouse our fear, human enough to awaken some transient gleam of sympathy. We must triumph in his downfall, yet not barbarously nor with contempt, and the close of his career must be in harmony with all of its previous development.

"A Short Defense of Villains," *Essays in Miniature 1892*

6 It is hard for us who live in an age of careless and cheerful tolerance to understand the precise inconveniences attending religious persecution.

Ch. 1, *Philadelphia: The Place and the People 1898*

7 Necessity knows no Sunday. . . .

Ch. 18, *Ibid.*

8 It is not what we learn in conversation that enriches us. It is the elation that comes of swift contact with tingling currents of thought.

"The Luxury of Conversation," *Compromises 1904*

9 People who cannot recognize a palpable absurdity are very much in the way of civilization.

Ch. 9, *In Pursuit of Laughter 1936*

10 It is not depravity that afflicts the human race so much as a general lack of intelligence.

Ibid.

11 Humour brings insight and tolerance. Irony brings a deeper and less friendly understanding.

Ibid.

12 Science may carry us to Mars, but it will leave the earth peopled as ever by the inept.

Ibid.

1237. Ethel Mary Smyth (1858–1944)

1 The habit some writers indulge in of perpetual quotation is one it behooves lovers of good literature to protest against, for it is an insidious habit which in the end must cloud the stream of thought, or at least check spontaneity. If it be true that *le style c'est l'homme,* what is likely to happen if *l'homme* is for ever eking out his own personality with that of some other individual?

"The Quotation-Fiend," *Streaks of Life 1924*

2 Because I have conducted my own operas and love sheep-dogs; because I generally dress in tweeds, and sometimes, at winter afternoon concerts, have even conducted in them; because I was a militant suffragette and seized a chance of beating time to "The March of the Women" from the window of my cell in Holloway Prison with a tooth-brush; because I have written books, spoken speeches, broadcast, and don't always make sure that my hat is on straight; for these and other equally pertinent reasons, in a certain sense I am well known.

Epilogue, *As Time Went On 1936*

1238. Hannah Greenebaum Solomon (1858–1942)

1 Even Paradise was not complete without a woman, and no paradise on earth can be perfectly complete unless we have men and women.

Presidential Address (New York), Proceedings of the First Convention of the National Council of Jewish Women *1896*

2 The only part of the program they [the men] wished us to fill was the chairs.*

from her Memoirs, quoted in *The Journey Home* by Joyce Antler* *2007*

*Response to being told she "could be hostess" at the Parliament of Religions held at the 1893 World's Columbian Exposition in Chicago. **See 3320.

3 Who is this new woman? . . . She is the woman who dares to go into the world and do what her convictions demand. She is

the woman who stays at home in the smallest, narrowest circle, foregoing all the world may offer to her, if there her duty lies ..."

Jewish Women's Archive (jwa.org) *n.d.*

4 We must add our voices to those who cry out that there is a standard below which we will not allow human beings to live, and that that standard is not at the freezing nor starving point. . . . In a democracy all are responsible.

Ibid.

1239. Beatrice Potter Webb (1858–1943)

1 The underlying principle of the industrial revolution—the creed of universal competition—the firm faith that every man free to follow his own self-interest would contribute most effectively to the common weal, with the converse proposition that each man should suffer the full consequences of his own actions—this simple and powerful idea was enabling a rising middle class to break up and destroy those restraints on personal freedom, those monopolies for private gain, with which a Parliament of landowners had shackled the enterprise and weighted the energies of the nation.

Ch. 1, *The Cooperative Movement in Great Britain 1891*

2 For the committee-man or the officer who accepts a bribe or neglects his duty must be fully aware that he is not simply an indifferently honest man, like many of his fellows in private trade, but the deliberate betrayer of the means of salvation to thousands of his fellow-countrymen of this and all future generations.

Ch. 7, Ibid.

3 All along the line, physically, mentally, morally, alcohol is a weakening and deadening force, and it is worth a great deal to save women and girls from its influence.

Ch. 10, *Health of Working Girls 1917*

4 Religion is love; in no case is it logic.

Ch. 2, *My Apprenticeship 1926*

5 For any detailed description of the complexity of human nature, of the variety and mixture in human motive, of the insurgence of instinct in the garb of reason, of the multifarious play of the social environment of the individual ego and of the individual ego on the social environment, I had to turn to novelists and poets. . . .

Ch. 3, Ibid.

6 . . . if I had been a man, self-respect, family pressure and the public opinion of my class would have pushed me into a money-making profession; as a mere woman I could carve out a career of disinterested research.

Ch. 8, Ibid.

1240. Eva Rose York (1858–1935?)

1 I shall not pass this way again;
Then let me now relieve some pain,
Remove some barrier from the road,
Or brighten some one's heavy load.

"I Shall Not Pass This Way Again," St. 2, *n.d.*

2 . . . I have drunk the cup of bliss
Remembering not that those there be
Who drink the dregs of misery.

St. 3, Ibid.

1241. Katherine Lee Bates (1859–1929)

1 O beautiful for spacious skies,
For amber waves of grain,
For purple mountains majesties
Above the fruited plain!
America! America!
God shed his grace on thee
And crown thy good with brotherhood
From sea to shining sea!

"America the Beautiful." St. 1 *1893*

2 Nay, brother of the sod,
What part hast thou in God?
What spirit art thou of?
It answers, "Love."

"Laddie" *n.d.*

3 Dawn love is silver,
Wait for the west:
Old love is gold love—
Old love is best.

"For a Golden Wedding" *n.d.*

1242. Louise de Koven Bowen (1859–1947)

1 By the time I made my entry into society I was ignorant of everything and accomplished in nothing.

Ch. 1, *Growing Up with a City 1926*

2 I hated myself because I smelt of onions and meat, and I seriously considered suicide in the cistern which supplied the house.

Ibid.

1243. Lettie Burlingame (1859–1890)

1 I have determined to make a specialty of equity. It is very interesting to me, and a very nice subject for a lady to pursue.

Diary Entry, Quoted in *The 50 Most Influential Women in American Law* by Dawn Bradley Berry* 1996

*See 4399.

1244. Carrie Chapman Catt (1859–1947)

1 There are two kinds of restrictions upon human liberty—the restraint of law and that of custom. No written law has ever been more binding than unwritten custom supported by popular opinion.

Speech, "For the Sake of Liberty" (8–14 February 1900), Quoted in *History of Woman Suffrage*, Vol. IV, by Susan B. Anthony* and Ida Husted *1902*

*See 963.

2 The sacrifice of suffering, of doubt, of obloquy, which has been endured by the pioneers in the woman movement will never be fully known or understood. . . .

Ibid.

3 There they swell that horrid, unspeakably unclean peril of civilisation, prostitution—augmented by the White Slave Traffic and by the machinations of the male parasites who live upon the earnings of women of vice. . . . We must be merciful, for they are the natural and inevitably consequence of centuries of false reasoning concerning woman's place in the world. . . . Upon these women we have no right to turn our backs. Their existence is part of our problem. They have been created by the very injustice against which we protest.

Speech, "Is Woman Suffrage Progressing?" Stockholm *1911*

4 When a just cause reaches its flood-tide, as ours has done in that country, whatever stands in the way must fall before its overwhelming power.

Ibid.

5 Parliaments have stopped laughing at woman suffrage, and politicians have begun to dodge! It is the inevitable premonition of coming victory.

Speech, International Woman Suffrage Association (1913),
Women in World History Curriculum (womeninworldhistory.
com) *1996–97*

6 Women are not in rebellion against men. They are in rebellion against worn-out traditions.

Quoted in *Women Suffragists* by Diana Star Helmer *1998*

7 My husband used to say that he was as much a reformer as I, but that he couldn't work at reforming and earn a living at the same time . . . what he could do was to earn a living enough for two and free me from all economic burden, and thus I could reform for two. That was our bargain, and we happily understood each other.

Ibid.

8 You must think internationally. You are members of the human race . . . Let us be a nation with sympathy enough to put war out of the world.

Speech, Iowa State College graduation (1921), Ibid.

9 We [Caucasians] stole land, whole continents.

(ca. 1940s), Ibid.

1245. Helen Gray Cone (1859–1934)

1 A song of hate is a song of Hell;
Some there be who sing it well.

"Chant of Love for England" *1945*

2 Bind higher, grind higher, burn higher with fire,
Cast her ashes into the sea,—
She shall escape, she shall aspire,
She shall arise to make men free.

Ibid.

3 Peerless, fearless, an army's flower!
Sterner soldiers the world never saw,
Marching lightly, that summer hour,
To death and failure and fame forever.

"Greencastle Jenny," St. 4 *n.d.*

4 Upon a showery night and still,
Without a second of warning,
A trooper band surprised the hill,
And held it in the morning.
We were not waked by bugle notes,
No cheer our dreams invaded,
And yet at dawn their yellow coats
On the green slopes paraded.

"The Dandelions" *n.d.*

1246. Eleanora Duse (1859–1924)

1 Before passing my lips each word seemed to have coursed through the ardor of my blood. There wasn't a fiber in me that did not add its notes to the harmony. Ah, grace—the state of grace!

Quoted in *Il Fuoco* by Gabriele D'Annunzio* *1900*
*Italian writer, poet and Fascist activist (1863–1938).

2 To save the theatre, the theatre must be destroyed, the actors and actresses must all die of the plague. They poison the air, they make art impossible. It is not drama that they play, but pieces for the theatre. We should return to the Greeks, play in the open air; the drama dies of stalls and boxes and evening dress, and people who come to digest their dinner.

"Eleanora Duse," Quoted in *Studies in Seven Arts* by Arthur Symons *1906*

3 I did not use paint, I made myself up morally.

Quoted in *Le Gaulois* by Louis Schneider 27 *July 1922*

4 Do you think one can speak about art? It would be like trying to explain love. There are many ways of loving and there are as many kinds of art. There is the love that elevates and leads to good—there is the love that absorbs all one's will, all one's strength and intelligence. In my opinion this is the truest love—but it is certainly fatal. . . . So it is with art. . . .

Quoted in *Eleanora Duse* by C. Antonia-Traversi *1926*

5 The strongest is the loneliest and the loneliest is the strongest.

Quoted in *Vita de Arrigo Boito* by Piero Nardi *1942*

6 Work means so many things! So many! Among other things Work also means Freedom. . . . Without it even the miracle of love is only a cruel deception.

Ibid.

1247. Alice Eastwood (1859–1953)

1 My own destroyed work I do not lament, for it was a joy to me while I did it, and I can still have the same joy in starting it again . . . *

(p 96), Quoted in *Alice Eastwood's Wonderland: The Adventures of a Botanist* by Carol Wilson *1955*
*Reference to the destruction, by the San Francisco earthquake of 1906, of her meticulously gathered botanical collections at the California Academy of Sciences where she was curator of botany.

2 . . . there is a part of me that will not die . . .

(p. 222), Ibid.

3 Never in all my experience have I had the slightest discourtesy and I have never had any fear. I believe that fear brings danger.*

Quoted in "Alice Eastwood" by Marcia Bonta (pp. 10–15), *American Horticulturist* October *1983*
*Reference to her travels to the Western frontier in the 1880s.

1248. Florence Kelley (1859–1932)

1 Tonight while we sleep, several thousand little girls will be working in textile mills, all the night through, in the deafening noise of the spindles and the looms spinning and weaving cotton and wool, silks and ribbons for us to buy.

Speech (Philadelphia) 22 *July 1905*

2 . . . the utter unimportance of children compared with products in the minds of the people. . . .

"My Philadelphia," *The Survey Graphic* 1 October *1926*

3 Keeping the light on is probably the best contribution that we can make where there is now Stygian darkness.

Quoted in "Second-Place Citizens" by Robin Morgan,* *The New York Times* 25 August *2008*
*See 3284.

1249. Bertha Pappenheim (1859–1936)

1 There is only one domain which the Jewish woman shares equally with the man, and that is in the fulfillment of that command, which was said by one of our sages to contain the whole of the Jewish religion, "Love thy neighbor as thyself."

Address, "The Jewish Woman in Religious Life" (Woman's Congress, Munich: 1912), *Jewish Review January 1913*

2 The Jewish religion is purest Monotheism. It knows no dogmas, no church, no sects, no proselytes, no mission, no worldly or political ambitions. It is in the best sense a matter of private conscience; it has and needs no outward forms and authorities to bind its members together.

Ibid.

3 The considerate exemption of woman from duties outside the home is not the only reason for her having become a sort of domestic recluse; the important precept of early marriage, and a certain fear of sexual passion in man, have cut the woman off from free intercourse with the male world, and thereby from all intellectual life.

Ibid.

4 Time, thou all kindly, confer upon me, at the ripeness of old age, mildness.

Prayers, I, Stephanie Forchheimer, tr. (a former student) *1946*

5 Oh that the sound of the Shofar might rouse the congregation, . . . That a generation would arise, born of strength and love and reverence for the holy *Schechina** [sic], who blesses those who live and govern with a pure heart. Amen.

Prayers, II, A Prayer for Women, Ibid.
*A visible manifestation of the divine presence as described in Jewish theology, usually associated with the feminine aspects of God; a.s.a. Shekinah.

6 *Malach homowes* [Angel of Death], . . . What signal did you follow when, although conscious of your eternal and universal triumph, you yielded for awhile?

Is there still a mission for me to perform, which accomplished, shall complete the significance of my life? If so I shall rally and seek strength for it and pull myself together to accomplish whatever is commanded.

Prayers, III, Ibid.

1250. Nora Archibald Smith (1859–1934)

1 "Good counsel and skill may do as much as a giant's will."

"The Ram and the Pig Who Went into the Woods to Live by Themselves," *Fairy Stories Every Child Should Know*, Kate Douglas Wiggin,* coauthor *1910*
*See 1214.

2 They'd knock on a tree and would timidly say
To the spirit that might be within there that day:
"Fairy fair, Fairy fair, wish thou me well;
'Gainst evil witcheries weave me a spell!"

"Knocking on Wood," St. 3 *n.d.*

1251. Jane Addams (1860–1935)

1 The word "non-resistance" is misleading, because it is much too feeble and inadequate. It suggests passivity, the goody-goody attitude of ineffectiveness. The words "overcoming," "substituting," "re-creating," "readjusting moral values," "forming new centres of spiritual energy" carry much more of the meaning implied. For it is not merely the desire for a conscience at rest, for a sense of justice no longer outraged, that would pull us into new paths where there would be no more war nor preparations for war. There are still more strenuous forces at work reaching down to impulses and experiences as primitive and profound as are those of struggle itself.

Ch. I, *Newer Ideals of Peace 1907*

2 A little examination will easily show that in spite of the fine phrases of the founders, the [U.S.] Government became an entity by itself away from the daily life of the people. There was no intention to ignore them nor to oppress them. But simply because its machinery was so largely copied from the traditional European Governments which did distrust the people, the founders failed to provide the vehicle for a vital and genuinely organized expression of the popular will.

Ch. II, Ibid.

3 It has been discovered that the city which is too careless to provide playgrounds, gymnasiums, and athletic fields where the boys legitimately belong and which the policeman is bound to respect, simply puts a premium on lawlessness.

Ibid.

4 A city is in many respects a great business corporation, but in other respects it is enlarged housekeeping. . . . May we not say that city housekeeping has failed partly because women, the traditional housekeepers, have not been consulted as to its multiform activities?

Ch. VII, Ibid.

5 Unless our conception of patriotism is progressive, it cannot hope to embody the real affection and the real interest of the nation.

"Utilization of Women in City Government," Ibid.

6 You do not know what life means when all the difficulties are removed! I am simply smothered and sickened with advantages. It is like eating a sweet dessert the first thing in the morning.

Twenty Years at Hull House 1910

7 Private beneficence is totally inadequate to deal with the vast numbers of the city's disinherited.

Ibid.

8 Perhaps I may record here my protest against the efforts, so often made, to shield children and young people from all that has to do with death and sorrow, to give them a good time at all hazards on the assumption that the ills of life will come soon enough. Young people themselves often resent this attitude on the part of their elders; they feel set aside and belittled as if they were denied the common human experiences.

Ibid.

1252. Mary Gardiner Brainard (fl. 1860s)

1 I would rather walk with God in the dark than go alone in the light.

"Not Knowing," St. 1 *n.d.*

2 And what looks dark in the distance may brighten as I draw near.

St. 2, Ibid.

1253. Ellen Thorneycroft Fowler (1860–1929)

1 Though outwardly a gloomy shroud,
The inner half of every cloud
Is bright and shining:

I therefore turn my clouds about
And always wear them inside out
To show the lining.

"Wisdom of Folly" *n.d.*

1254. Charlotte Perkins Gilman (1860–1935)

1 I do not want to be a fly,
I want to be a worm!

"A Conservative," *In This Our World* 1893

2 The labor of women in the house, certainly, enables men to produce more wealth than they otherwise could; and in this way women are economic factors in society. But so are horses.

Ch. 1, *Women and Economics* 1898

3 The women who do the most work get the least money, and the women who have the most money do the least work.

Ibid.

4 To be surrounded by beautiful things has much influence upon the human creature: to make beautiful things has more.

Ch. 4, Ibid.

5 When we see great men and women, we give credit to their mothers. When we see inferior men and women—and that is a common circumstance—no one presumes to the question of the motherhood which has produced them.

Ch. 9, Ibid.

6 A family unity which is only bound together with a table-cloth is of questionable value.

Ch. 11, Ibid.

7 The child learns more of the virtues needed in modern life—of fairness, of justice, of comradeship, of collective interest and action—in a common school that can be taught in the most perfect family circle.

Ch. 13, Ibid.

8 Work the object of which is merely to serve one's self is the lowest. Work the object of which is merely to serve one's family is the next lowest. Work the object of which is to serve more and more people, in widening range . . . is social service in the fullest sense, and the highest form of service we can reach.

Ibid.

9 Eternity is not something that begins after you are dead. It is going on all the time. We are in it now.

Quoted in *The Forerunner Magazine* 1909–16

10 I am the squaw—the slave—the harem beauty—
I serve and serve, the handmaid of the world.

Introduction, Pt. I, "Two Callings," *The Home* 1910

11 So when the great word "Mother!" rang once more,
I saw at last its meaning and its place;
Not the blind passion of the brooding past,
But Mother—the World's Mother—come at last,
To love as she had never loved before—
To feed and guard and teach the human race.

Pt. II, Ibid.

12 The original necessity for the ceaseless presence of the woman to maintain the altar fire—and it was an altar fire in very truth at one period—has passed with the means of prompt ignition; the matchbox has freed the housewife from that incessant service, but the *feeling* that women should stay at home is with us yet.

Ch. 3, Ibid.

13 It will be a great thing for the human soul when it finally stops worshipping backwards.

Ibid.

14 You may observe mother instinct at its height in a fond hen sitting on china eggs—instinct, but no brains.

Ibid.

15 Human life consists in mutual service. No grief, pain, misfortune, or "broken heart," is excuse for cutting off one's life while any power of service remains. But when all usefulness is over, when one is assured of an unavoidable and imminent death, it is the simplest of human rights to choose a quick and easy death in place of a slow and horrible one.

Suicide Note *17 August 1935*

16 Death? Why all this fuss about death. Use your imagination, try to visualize a world *without* death! . . . Death is the essential condition of life, not an evil.

The Living of Charlotte Perkins Gilman 1935

17 We are told to hitch our wagons to a star, but why pick on Betelgeuse?*

Ibid.

*Largest star in the galaxy.

18 . . . New York . . . that unnatural city where everyone is an exile, none more so than the American.

Ibid.

19 There is no female mind. The brain is not an organ of sex. As well speak of a female liver.

Quoted in *The Liberated Woman's Appointment Calendar,* Lynn Sherr and Jurate Kazickas, eds. *1975*

20 The people people have for friends
Your common sense appall,
But the people people marry
Are the queerest folks of all.

"Queer People" *n.d.*

1255. Florence Kling Harding (1860–1924)

1 If the career is the husband's, the wife can merge her own with it, if it is to be the wife's as it undoubtedly will be in an increasing proportion of cases, then the husband may, with no sacrifice of self respect or of recognition by the community, permit himself to be the less prominent and distinguished member of the combination.

Remark (1922), Quoted in *First Ladies* by Betty Boyd Caroli *1987*

2 They can't hurt you now.

Posthumous remark to her husband, Warren Harding,* Ibid.
*(1865–1923), 29th president of the United States (1921–1923).

1256. Amy Leslie (1860–1939)

1 No animal is so inexhaustible as an excited infant.

Amy Leslie at the Fair 1893

2 Those who make the most memorable racket are of two classes—wary diplomats looking for the best of a business

proposition and irresponsible parrots who croak and yell and chatter simply because exclamation points and interrogatories swim through the misty Chicago air.

Ibid.

3 As a singer you're a great dancer.

Quoted by George Primrose in They All Sang by E. W. Marks
1934

1257. Juliette Low (1860–1927)

1 To put yourself in another's place requires real imagination, but by doing so each Girl Scout will be able to live among others happily.

Letter to Girl Scouts of America (31 October 1923*), Juliette Low and the Girl Scouts, Anne Hyde Choate and Helen Ferris, eds. 1928

*Low's 63rd birthday.

2 I hope that during the coming year we shall all remember the rules of this Girl Scouting game of ours. To play for your side and not for yourself. And as for the score, the best thing in a game is the fun and not the result. . . .

(31 October 1924*), Ibid.

*Low's 64th birthday.

1258. Harriet Monroe (1860–1936)

1 Great ages of art come only when a widespread creative impulse meets an equally widespread impulse of sympathy. . . . The people must grant a hearing to the best poets they have else they will never have better.

Quoted in "Harriet Monroe," Famous American Women by Hope Stoddard 1970

2 . . . poetry, "The Cinderella of the Arts."

Ibid.

1259. Grandma Moses (1860–1961)

1 I don't advise any one to take it [painting] up as a business proposition, unless they really have talent, and are crippled so as to deprive them of physical labor. Then with help they might make a living, But with taxes and income tax there is little money in that kind of art for the ordinary artis [sic]. But I will say that I have did remarkable for one of my years, and experience. As for publicity, that Im [sic] too old to care for now. . . .

"How Do I Paint?" The New York Times 11 May 1947

2 What a strange thing is memory, and hope; one looks backward, the other looks forward. The one is of today, the other is the Tomorrow. Memory is history recorded in our brain, memory is a painter, it paints pictures of the past and of the day.

Ch. 1, Grandma Moses, My Life's History, Aotto Kallir, ed. 1947

3 If I didn't start painting, I would have raised chickens.

Ch. 3, Ibid.

1260. Annie Oakley (1860–1926)

1 I can shoot as well as you [her husband].

Quoted in Ch. 4, Annie Oakley: Woman at Arms by Courtney Ryley Cooper 1927

2 The contents of his [Sitting Bull's*] pockets were often emptied into the hands of small, ragged little boys, nor could he understand how so much wealth should go brushing by, unmindful of the poor.

Quoted in Ch. 7, Ibid.

*Dakota Indian leader (1834?–1890).

1261. Henrietta Szold (1860–1945)

1 To the women who have been the creators I commend the task of becoming preachers and prophets.

Address, Women's Day (Tel Aviv) 31 May 1934

2 My misfortune is my ability to see both sides even of the fundamental religious question.

p. 303, Summoned to Jerusalem: The Life of Henrietta Szold by Joan Dash 1979

3 If we are Zionists, as we say we are, what is the good of meeting and talking and drinking tea? Let us do something real and practical—let us organize the Jewish women of America and send nurses and doctors to Palestine.

Quoted in Pride of Our People by David C. Gross 1979

4 We hope for friendship with our Arab neighbors, we want to develop the country for the good of both the Jews and the Arabs. . . . We do not know what the future will bring but we pray and work for healing and peace.

Letter to her sister, Bertha (prior to 1948), Ibid.

5 . . . I had begun to preach to myself that my feelings were absurd in a woman of my age, and in relation to him, so many years my junior. I examined my face in the mirror, and went away saying, never again shall this foolish, hopeless feeling master me—only to succumb the next time I saw him.

Journal, "Meditation on Lost Love," Lost Love, The Untold Story of Henrietta Szold by Baila Round Shargel 1997

6 So one chamber after the other is locked up in our hearts as we go through life, and sometimes the very key is lost. And what a world goes with a beloved father, what a big chamber is locked after he leaves us!

Letter to Dr. Ginzberg, New York (28 July 1907), Ibid.

7 Why isn't there one Techninnah* in all the books to fit my modern case—not one to raise up the spirit of a so-called emancipated woman, Heaven save the mark!

(23 August 1907), Ibid.

*The feminine principal in God.

8 [Zionism is] Jewish messianism in a practical form. It is Jewish hope, aspiration, dream, prayer made practical.

Cited in "The Speaking Heart" by Jessie Sampter,* The Journey Home, How Jewish Women Shaped Modern America by Joyce Antler** 1997

*See 1600. **See 3320.

9 In the life of the spirit there is no ending that is not a beginning.

Comment n.d.

10 We [Hadassah] are an organization of Jewish women who believe in the "healing of the daughter of the people," in the healing of the soul of the Jewish people as well as its body.

Speech to Hadassah (Hotel Astor, New York City) n.d.

1262. Minna Antrim (1861?–1950?)

1 A homely face and no figure have aided many women heaven-ward.

Naked Truth and Veiled Allusions 1902

2 Man forgives woman anything save the wit to outwit him.

Ibid.

3 Experience has no text books nor proxies. She demands that her pupils answer her roll-call personally.

Ibid.

4 To know one's self is wisdom, but to know one's neighbor is genius.

Ibid.

5 Smiles are the soul's kisses. . . .

Ibid.

6 To control a man a woman must first control herself.

Ibid.

7 Golden fetters hurt as cruelly as iron ones.

Ibid.

8 To be loved is to be fortunate, but to be hated is to achieve distinction.

Ibid.

9 The "Green-Eyed Monster" causes much woe, but the absence of this ugly serpent argues the presence of a corpse whose name is Eros.

Ibid.

10 Experience is a good teacher, but she sends in terrific bills.

Ibid.

1263. Mary C. G. Byron (1861–1936)

1 Out of the uttermost ridge of dusk, where the dark and the day are mingled,
The voice of the Night rose cold and calm—it called through the shadow—swept air;
Through all the valleys and lone hillsides, it pierced, it thrilled, it tingled—
It summoned me forth to the wild sea-shore, to meet with its mystery there.

"The Tryst of Night," St. 1, *A Little Book of Lyrics ca.* 1892

2 On gossamer nights when the moon is low,
And stars in the mist are hiding,
Over the hill where the foxgloves grow
You may see the fairies riding.

"The Fairy Thrall" *A Victorian Anthology, 1837–1895,*
Edmund Clarence Stedman, ed. 1895

1264. Mary Coleridge (1861–1907)

1 The fruits of the tree of knowledge are various; he must be strong indeed who can digest all of them.

Gathered Leaves from the Prose of Mary E. Coleridge 1910

2 Solitude effects some people like wine; they must not take too much of it, for it flies to the head.

Ibid.

3 Mother of God! No lady thou:
Common woman of common earth!

"Our Lady" *n.d.*

4 We were young, we were merry, we were very, very wise,
And the door stood open at our feast,
When there passed us a woman with the West in her eyes,
And a man with his back to the East.

"Unwelcome" *n.d.*

5 Where is delight? and what are pleasures now?—
Moths that a garment fret.

"Mandragora" *n.d.*

1265. Dorothy Dix (1861–1951)

1 I have learned in the great University of Hard Knocks a philosophy that no woman who has had an easy life ever acquires. I have learned to live each day as it comes, and not to borrow trouble by dreading tomorrow. It is the dark menace of the future that makes cowards of us.

Introduction, *Dorothy Dix, Her Book* 1926

2 So many persons think divorce a panacea for every ill, who find out, when they try it, that the remedy is worse than the disease.

Ch. 13, Ibid.

3 Confession is always weakness. The grave soul keeps its own secrets, and takes its own punishment in silence.

Ch. 20, Ibid.

4 In reality, the mother who rears her children up to be monsters of selfishness has no right to expect appreciation and gratitude from them because she has done them as ill a turn as one human being can do another. She has warped their characters.

Ch. 44, Ibid.

5 For in all the world there are no people so piteous and forlorn as those who are forced to eat the bitter bread of dependency in their old age, and find how steep are the stairs of another man's house.

Ch. 69, Ibid.

6 Nobody wants to kiss when they are hungry.

News Item *n.d.*

7 The reason that husbands and wives do not understand each other is because they belong to different sexes.

Ibid.

1266. Josephine "Josie" Sarah "Sadie" Earp (1861?–1944)

1 Doc [Holliday]* was good company to his friends and bad news for his enemies.

Quoted in *I Married Wyatt Earp: The Recollections of
Josephine Sarah Marcus Earp* by Earp and Glenn G. Boyer
1982

*John Henry "Doc" H— (1852–1887), American dentist, gambler and gunfighter.

2 The years rolled back on my shoulders, and my friends departed. I was alone—alone in the dark hotel room, looking out to the drug store where Wyatt Earp* had once been an owner of the luxurious Oriental gambling palace.

"Lady Sadie" by Carol Mitchell, *True West February/
March 2001*

*(1848–1929) American frontier law officer involved in the famous gunfight at the O.K. Corral in Tombstone, Arizona (1881).

1267. Frances Greville (1861–1938)

1 Love and Misery proverbially go together. There is a popular notion . . . that a lover could not get along without a little misery. . . .

Quoted in Anglo-Saxon Review *June 1900*

1268. Louise Imogen Guiney (1861–1920)

1 To be Anonymous is better than to be Alexander. Cowley said it engagingly, in his little essay on *Obscurity:* "*Bene qui latuit, bene vixit;* he lives well that has lain well hidden." The pleasantest condition of life is in Incognito.

"The Delights of an Incognito," Patrins *1897*

2 Quotations (such as have point and lack triteness) from the great old authors are an act of filial reverence on the part of the quote, and a blessing to a public grown superficial and external.

Quoted in Scribner's Magazine *January 1911*

3 The fears of what may come to pass,
I cast them all away,
Among the clover scented grass,
Among the new-mown hay.

"A Song from Sylvan," St. 2 *n.d.*

4 A short life in the saddle, Lord!
Not long life by the fire.

"The Knight Errant," St. 2 *n.d.*

5 High above hate I dwell,
O storms! Farewell.

"The Sanctuary" *n.d.*

1269. Gracy Hebard (1861–1936)

1 These Indians [Shoshones] believe also that God pulled out the upper teeth of the elk because the elk were meant to be eaten by the Indians, and not the Indians by the elk.

Washakie *1930*

2 The buffaloes were the original engineers, as they followed the lay of the land and the run of the water. These buffalo paths became Indian trails, which always pointed out the easiest way across the mountain barriers. The white man followed in these footpaths. The iron trail finished the road.

Ch. 9, The Pathbreakers from River to Ocean *1932*

3 While we are enjoying the luxuries of this new era of the great west let us not forget to honor those who endured hardships and privations, encountered dangers and peril; yes, even gave up their lives to make these things possible. . . . It is all a story that has never had its equal in the world's history. The great American desert is no more.

Ibid.

1270. Katharine Tynan Hinkson (1861–1931)

1 O you poor folk in cities,
A thousand, thousand pities!

"June Song" *n.d.*

2 To me the wonderful charge was given,
I, even a little ass, did go
Bearing the very weight of heaven;
So I crept cat-foot, sure and slow.

"The Ass Speaks" *n.d.*

1271. Alice Hubbard (1861–1915)

1 [Thomas] Paine* was a Quaker by birth and friend by nature. The world was his home, mankind were his friends, to do good was his religion.

Introduction, An American Bible *1911*

*English-born American revolutionary leader (1737–1809).

1272. Emily Pauline Johnson (1861–1913)

1 Captive! But never conquered; Mohawk brave
Stoops not to be to anyman a slave;

"As Red Men Die," St. 1, Flint and Feather: collected verse *1913*

2 O! soft responsive voices of the night
I join your minstrelsy,
And call across the fading silver light
As something calls to me

"Moonset," St. 3, *Ibid.*

3 And we swing, swing,
While your branches sing,
And we drowse to your dreamy whispering.

"The Bird's Lullaby," III, *Ibid.*

1273. Amy Levy (1861–1889)

1 When first the world grew dark to me
I call'd on God, yet came not he.
Whereon, as wearier wax'd my lot,
On Love I call'd, but Love came not.
When a worse evil did befall,
Death, on thee only did I call.

"A Cross-Road Epitaph," in toto, Xantrippe *1880*

2 The lion remembers the forest,
The lion in chains;/
To the bird that is captive a vision
Of woodland remains.

"Captivity," *Ibid.*

1274. Nellie Melba (1861–1931)

1 The first rule in opera is the first rule in life: see to everything yourself.

Melodies and Memories *1925*

2 One of the drawbacks of Fame is that one can never escape from it.

Ibid.

3 Music is not written in red, white and blue. It is written in the heart's blood of the composer.

Ibid.

1275. Jessie Brown Pounds (1861–1921)

1 Somewhere, Somewhere, Beautiful Isle of Somewhere,
Land of the true, where we live anew,
Beautiful Isle of Somewhere.

"Beautiful Isle of Somewhere" *1901*

2 Modern life is getting to be more and more a vulgar display. Expenses are so rapidly exceeding incomes that there is no longer any home life. All the adults of families are forced to go out and work to meet the heavy expenses that modern conditions impose. We would much better keep our daughters at home, and let them make a home, than to send them out to work in

order to increase the family income. Let us lead simpler lives and develop more home-makers.

> Speech, Christian Women's Board of Missions Convention (Detroit) *17 October 1903*

1276. Corinne Roosevelt Robinson (1861–1933)

1 Though Love be deeper, Friendship is more wide. . . .

> "Friendship," *The Call of Brotherhood and Other Poems 1912*

2 Is life worth living?
Aye, with the best of us,
Heights of us, depths of us,—
Life is the test of us!

> "Life, A Question," *One Woman to Another 1914*

3 Nothing is as difficult as to achieve results in this world if one is filled full of great tolerance and the milk of human kindness. The person who achieves must generally be a one-ideaed individual, concentrated entirely on that one idea, and ruthless in his aspect toward other men and other ideas.

> Ch. 1, *My Brother Theodore Roosevelt* 1921*
> *(1858–1919) 26th president of the United States (1901–1909).

4 Thy love was like a royal accolade. . . .

> "Afterward," *Out of Nymph 1930*

5 Spirit of the air,
And of the seas, and of the fragrant earth,
I thank thee that thou didst attend my birth
To dower me with wonder. . . .

> "The Gift of Wonder," Ibid.

1277. Edith Carow Roosevelt (1861–1948)

1 Women who marry pass their best and happiest years in giving life and fostering it.

> *American Backlogs,* Quoted in *First Ladies* by Betty Boyd Caroli *1987*

1278. Ernestine Schumann-Heink (1861–1936)

1 One can never either hear or see himself, and there is a need—if one would make real progress in art—for constant criticism.

> Quoted in *Schumann-Heink, The Last of the Titans* by Mary Lawton *1935*

2 This shall be my parting word—know what you want to do—then do it. Make straight for your goal and go undefeated in spirit to the end.

> Ibid.

1279. Nettie Maria Stevens (1861–1912)

1 How could you think your questions would bother me? They never will, so long as I keep my enthusiasm for biology; and that, I hope, will be as long as I live.

> Letter to a student, Quoted in "Nettie Maria Stevens" by Marilyn Bailey Oglivie and Clifford J. Choquette (p. 373), *Proceedings of the American Philosophical Society*, Vol. 125, No. 4 *August 1981*

1280. Helen Herron Taft (1861–1943)

1 I have thought that a woman should be independent and not regard matrimony as the only thing to be desired in life.

> Diary entry (at 22), Quoted in *First Ladies* by Betty Boyd Caroli *1987*

2 I do not dislike teaching when the boys behave themselves.

> Ibid.

1281. Sadie American (1862–1944)

1 Because her work has been done largely in the home, because the man has been the medium of communication, the Jewish woman has been a little slower to feel the heart-beats of her time than other women. . . . [A]s a body Jewish women are behind the times, they have done nothing.

> *Writing Their Nations: The Tradition of Nineteenth-Century American Jewish Women Writers* by Diane Lichtenstein *1992*

1282. Helen Bannerman (1862–1946)

1 But the Tiger said, "What would your shoes be to me? I've got four feet, and you've got only two; you haven't got enough shoes for me."

> But Little Black Sambo said, "You could wear them on your ears."

> "So I could," said the Tiger: "that's a very good idea. Give them to me, and I won't eat you this time."

> *The Story of Little Black Sambo 1899*

2 And there he saw all the Tigers fighting, and disputing which of them was the grandest. And at last they got so angry that they jumped up and took off all the fine clothes, and began to tear each other with their claws, and bite each other with their great big white teeth.

> Ibid.

1283. Carrie Jacobs Bond (1862–1946)

1 When God made up this world of ours,
He made it long and wide,
And meant that it should shelter all,
And none should be denied.

> "Friends," St. 1, *Little Stories in Verse 1905*

2 Kind words smooth all the "Paths o' Life"
And smiles make burdens light,
And uncomplainin' friends can make
A daytime out o' night.

> "The Path o' Life," St. 11, Ibid.

3 And we find at the end of a perfect day,
The soul of a friend we've made.

> "A Perfect Day," St. 2 *1926*

1283.1. Ts'ai-t'ien Chang (1862–1945)

1 . . . I wanted to study and not to marry. My brother and Mao Tse-tung* also hated marriage and declared they would never marry. . . .

> Quoted in *Women in Modern China* by Helen Foster Snow** *1967*
> *Founder of the People's Republic of China (1893–1976). **See 2073.

1284. Susan Cocroft (1862–?)

1 Don't be ashamed of your desire for beauty.

> (p. 14), *A New Method of Physical Culture for the Face 1912*

2 The women of today, yesterday, and tomorrow are the same, but our horizons are broadening. And this will not make us mannish. We can be as sweet and dear and lovable in the street as in the home.

> "Miss Cocroft Tells How to Build a Neck," *The New York Times 21 April 1915*

1285. Edith Cooper (1862–1913)
Coauthor with Katharine Bradley; see 1141:1–3.

1286. Loie Fuller (1862–1928)
1 "Light" and "Color" thrown on great masses of silk, was my real representation and not dancing at all . . . called dance for want of a more appropriate title.

Fifteen Years of My Life 1913

2 Education is wonderful but nobody wants it rubbed in . . . when you don't even know what they are talking about & you don't want to know.

Ibid.

1287. Ella Higginson (1862–1940)
1 Forgive you?—Oh, of course, dear,
A dozen times a week!

"Wearing Out Love," St. 1 *n.d.*

2 It's what you do, unthinking,
That makes the quick tear start;
The tear may be forgotten—
But the hurt stays in the heart.

St. 2 *n.d.,* Ibid.

3 One leaf is for hope, and one is for faith,
And one is for love, you know,
And God put another in for luck.

"Four-Leaf Clover," St. 2 *n.d.*

1288. Ada Leverson (1862–1933)
1 Absurdly improbable things happen in real life as well as in weak literature.

The Twelfth Hour 1907

2 Before he left, Aunt William pressed a sovereign into his hand guiltily, as if it were conscience money. He, on his side, took it as though it were a doctor's fee, and both ignored the transaction.

"Aunt William" *1907*

1289–1290. Maud Nathan (1862–1946)
1 We must make our business ethics . . . correspond with Bible ethics.

"Bible Ethics versus Business Ethics," *The Review* 11, No. 4 *March 1907*

2 . . . Men and women think differently. Men think in terms of dollars and cents while women think along the lines of conservation of human life. Just as a party of men is called a stag party so is a nation with men serving alone stag-nation.

"Jews Besiege Theater to Hear Suffrage Plea", *Philadelphia Record 1 November 1915*

3 . . . No one ought to be more sympathetic to the ideal of enfranchisement than Jews.

Letter to rabbis (New York) *23 April 1917*

4 I so often found myself in the minority. It seemed cowardly to me not to protest whenever I considered an act of injustice was being done to me or to others. Many a time when I was considered fearless, my actions were due rather to a sense of fear—fear lest I be weak and cowardly; fear lest I be weighed and found wanting.

Once Upon a Time and Today 1974

1291. Ida B. Wells (1862–1931)
1 Let the Afro-American depend on no party, but on himself for his salvation. Let him continue to develop his education, character, and above all, put money in his purse.

"Iola's Southern Field," *The New York Age 11 November 1892*

2 The first excuse given to the civilized world for the murder of unoffending Negroes was the necessity of the white man to repress and stamp out "race riots." . . . It was always a remarkable feature in these insurrections and riots that only Negroes were killed during the rioting, and that all the white men escaped unharmed.

The Red Record 1895

3 True chivalry respects all womanhood. . . . Virtue knows no color lines, and the chivalry which depends upon complexion of skin and texture of hair can command no honest respect.

Ibid.

4 I felt that one had better die fighting against injustice than to die like a dog or a rat in a trap. I had already determined to sell my life as dearly as possible if attacked. I felt if I could take one lyncher with me, this would even up the score a little bit.

Crusade for Justice: The Autobiography of Ida B. Wells, Alfreda M. Duster, ed. *1970*

5 Not all or nearly all of the murders done by white men, during the past thirty years in the South, have come to light, but the statistics as gathered and preserved by white men, and which have not been questioned, show that during these years more than ten thousand Negroes have been killed in cold blood without the formality of judicial trial and legal execution.

Black Women in White America, Gerda Lerner,* ed. *1972*
*See 2380.

1292. Edith Wharton (1862–1937)
1 A New York divorce is in itself a diploma of virtue. . . .

Ch. 1, "The Other Two," *The Descent of Man 1904*

2 "It feels uncommonly queer to have enough cash to pay one's bills. I'd have sold my soul for it a few years ago!"

Ch. 3, Ibid.

3 If he paid for each day's comfort with the small change of his illusions, he grew daily to value the comfort more and set less store upon the coin.

Ch. 4, Ibid.

4 When she spoke it was only to complain, and to complain of things not in his power to remedy; and to check a tendency of impatient retort he had first formed the habit of not answering her, and finally of thinking of other things while she talked.

Ch. 4, *Ethan Frome 1911*

5 . . . they seemed to come suddenly upon happiness as if they had surprised a butterfly in the winter woods. . . .

Ch. 9, Ibid.

6 Mrs. Ballinger is one of the ladies who pursue Culture in bands, as though it were dangerous to meet it alone.

"Xingu," *Xingu and Other Stories 1916*

7 There's no such thing as old age, there is only sorrow.

"A First Word," *A Backward Glance 1934*

8 I think sometimes that it is almost a pity to enjoy Italy as much as I do, because the acuteness of my sensations makes them rather exhausting; but when I see the stupid Italians I have met here, completely insensitive to their surroundings, and ignorant of the treasures of art and history among which they have grown up, I begin to think it is better to be an American, and bring to it all a mind and eye unblunted by custom.

> Letter (8 March 1903), *The Letters of Edith Wharton* 1988

9 I despair of the Republic!* Such dreariness, such whining sallow women, such utter absence of the amenities, such crass food, crass manners, crass landscape!!

...What a horror it is for a whole nation to be developing without the sense of beauty, & eating bananas for breakfast.

> Letter to Sara Norton (19 August 1904), Ibid.
> *The republic of the United States.

10 How much longer are we going to think it necessary to be "American" before (or in contradistinction to) being cultivated, being enlightened, being humane, & having the same intellectual discipline as other civilized countries? It is really too easy a disguise for our shortcomings to dress them up as a form of patriotism!

> Letter (19 July 1919), Ibid.

11 It's a turgid welter of pornography (the rudest schoolboy kind) & unformed & unimportant drivel; & until the raw ingredients of a pudding make a pudding, I shall never believe that the raw material of sensation & thought can make a work of art without the cook's intervening.*

> Letter to Bernard Berenson** (6 January 1923), Ibid.
> *Reference to James Joyce's (1882–1941) novel *Ulysses* (1922).
> **Lithuanian art critic and historian (1865–1959).

12 My little dog:
A heartbeat at my feet.

> "A Lyrical Epigram" *n.d.*

13 There are two ways of spreading light: to be
The candle or the mirror that receives it.

> "Vesalius in Zante" *n.d.*

1293. Annie Jump Cannon (1863–1941)

1 ...a life spent in the routine of science need not destroy the attractive human element of a woman's nature.

> Quoted in *Science* 30 June 1911

2 They [streaks of light in spectrograms] aren't just streaks to me. Each new spectrum is the gateway to a wonderful new world.

> (p. 17), Quoted in *Science: Contributions of Women* by Diane Emberlin 1977

3 In these days of great trouble and unrest, it is good to have something outside our own planet, something fine and distant and comforting to troubled minds. Let people look to the stars for comfort.

> Interview (ca. 1941; p. 27), Ibid.

4 Classifying the stars has helped materially in all studies of the structure of the universe. No greater problem is presented to the human mind. Teaching man his relatively small sphere in the creation, it also encourages him by its lessons of the unity of Nature and shows him that his power of comprehension allies him with the great intelligence overreaching all.

> *4000 Years of Women in Science*, astr.ua.edu/ 4000WS *11 July 1997*

1294. Binodini Dasi (1863–1941)

1 In many regions water turns rock-hard! That is how it is with us! Falling helpless victims of oppression again and again, our hearts grow hardened one day.

> Essay (1924), Quoted in, *Women Writing in India*, Susie Tharu and K. Lalita, eds. 1991

1295. Elaine Goodale (1863–1953)

1 We feel our savage kind,—
And thus alone with conscious meaning wear
The Indian's moccasin.

> "Moccasin Flower," *In Berkshire with the Wild Flowers* 1879

2 Bronzed and molded by wind and sun,
Maddening, gladdening everyone
With a gypsy beauty full and fine,—
A health to the crimson columbine!

> "Columbine" *n.d.*

1296. Annie Fellows Johnston (1863–1931)

1 Her ideas of grandfathers, gained from stories and observation, led her to class them with fairy godmothers. She had always wished for one.

> Ch. III, *The Little Colonel* 1895

1297. Belle Kearney (1863–1939)

1 The popular delusion is that the ante-bellum Southern woman, like Christ's lilies, "toiled not." Though surrounded by the conditions for idleness she was indolent after she became the head of her own household. Every woman sewed, often making her own dresses; the clothing of all the slaves on a plantation was cut and made by negro seamstresses under her direct supervision, even the heavy coats of the men; she ministered personally to them in cases of sickness, frequently maintaining a well managed hospital under her sole care. She was a most skillful housekeeper, though she did none of the work with her own hands, and her children grew up around her knees; however, the black "mammy" relieved her of the actual drudgery of child-worry.

> Ch. 1, *The Slaveholders' Daughter* 1900

2 There was born in me a sense of the injustice that had always been heaped upon my sex, and this consciousness created and sustained in me a constant and ever increasing rebellion. The definite idea of the political emancipation of woman, as a happy and logical solution of the vexed question, did not present itself to me in a positive guise until some time after my entrance upon the list of wage-earners.

> Ch. 11, Ibid.

3 There are moments when one cannot weep, nor speak, nor pray,—only be quiet before God.

> Ch. 22, Ibid.

1298. Margaret Alice Murray (1863–1963)

1 Among the believers in witchcraft everything which could not be explained by the knowledge at their disposal was laid to the credit of supernatural powers; and as everything incomprehensible is usually supposed to emanate from evil, the witches were believed to be possessed of devilish arts.

> Introduction, *The Witch-Cult in Western Europe* 1921

2 ...I make a sharp distinction between Operative Witchcraft and Ritual Witchcraft. Under Operative Witchcraft I class all

charms and spells, whether used by a professed witch or by a professed Christian, whether intended for good or for evil, for killing or for curing. Such charms and spells are common to every nation and country, and are practised by the priests and people of every religion. They are part of the common heritage of the human race and are therefore of no practical value in the study of any one particular cult.

Ibid.

1299. Mary Church Terrell (1863–1954)

1 Lynching is the aftermath of slavery.

"Lynching from a Negro's Point of View," *North American Review June 1904*

2 The whole country seems tired of hearing about the black man's woes. The wrongs of the Irish, of the Armenians, of the Roumanian and Russian Jews, of the exiles of Russia and of every other oppressed people upon the face of the globe, can arouse sympathy and fire the indignation of the American public, while they seem to be all but indifferent to the murderous assaults upon the negroes in the South.

Ibid.

3 I cannot help wondering sometimes what I might have become and might have done if I had lived in a country which had not circumscribed and handicapped me on account of my race, but had allowed me to reach any height I was able to attain.

A Colored Woman in a White World 1940

4 It is impossible for any white person in the United States, no matter how sympathetic and broad, to realize what life would mean to him if his incentive to effort were suddenly snatched away. To the lack of incentive for effort, which is the awful shadow under which we live, may be traced the wreck and ruin of scores of colored youth.

"What It Means to Be Colored in the Capital of the United States" (1907), Ibid.

5 Please stop using the word "Negro" . . . We are the only human beings in the world with fifty-seven variety of complexions who are classed together as a single racial unit. Therefore, we are really truly colored people, and that is the only name in the English language which accurately describes us.

Letter to the Editor, *The Washington Post* (14 May 1949), Ibid.

6 Hanging, shooting, and burning black men, women and children in the United States have become so common that such occurrences create but little sensation and evoke but slight comment now.

Quoted in *Black Women in White America*, Gerda Lerner,* ed. 1972

*See 2380.

7 Colored women are the only group in this country who have two heavy handicaps to overcome, that of race as well as that of sex.

Quoted in *Women Suffragists* by Diana Star Helmer 1998

8 If we do not use the franchise, we shall give our enemies a stick with which to break our heads, and we shall not be able to live down the reproach of our indifference for 100 years. Hold meetings! Every time you meet a woman, talk to her about going to the polls to vote.

Speech to Women's Republican League, Ibid.

1300. Kishida Toshiko (1863–1901)

1 If it is true that men are better than women because they are stronger, why aren't our sumo wrestlers in the government?

Remark *n.d.*

1301. Margot Asquith (1864–1945)

1 Rich men's houses are seldom beautiful, rarely comfortable, and never original. It is a constant source of surprise to people of moderate means to observe how little a big fortune contributes to Beauty.

Ch. 17, *The Autobiography of Margot Asquith,* Vols. I and II 1920–22

2 The first element of greatness is fundamental humbleness (this should not be confused with servility); the second is freedom from self; the third is intrepid courage, which, taken in its widest interpretation, generally goes with truth; and the fourth—the power to love—although I have put it last, is the rarest.

Ch. 8, Vol. 1, Ibid.

3 Journalism over here [in America] is not only an obsession but a drawback that cannot be overrated. Politicians are frightened of the press, and in the same way as bull-fighting has a brutalising effect upon Spain (of which she is unconscious), headlines of murder, rape, and rubbish, excite and demoralise the American public.

Ch. 10, *My Impressions of America 1922*

4 It is always dangerous to generalise, but the American people, while infinitely generous, are a hard and strong race and, but for the few cemeteries I have seen, I am inclined to think they never die.

Ch. 14, Ibid.

5 The ingrained idea that, because there is no king and they despise titles, the Americans are a free people is pathetically untrue. . . . There is a perpetual interference with personal liberty over there that would not be tolerated in England for a week.

Ch. 17, Ibid.

6 . . . her one idea was to exercise a moderating influence; and without knowing it she would in a subtle and disparaging manner check the enthusiasm, dim the glow, and cramp the extravagance of everyone around her.

Ch. 1, *Octavia 1928*

7 She was not an individual when she was with him, she was an audience—

Ch. 12, Ibid.

8 Life was cruel, demanding wisdom from the young before they had the chance of acquiring it! Innocence was admired, ignorance despised: yet, in their effects, they had a dangerous resemblance.

Ch. 22, Ibid.

1302. Mary Berenson (1864–1945)

1 Love in whatever form it comes is a god, and even if it destroys all one's so-called "moral nature," it remolds the world nearer to the heart's desire. Why should we put faithfulness above it?

Diary Entry (1895), *Mary Berenson: A Self-Portrait from Her Letters and Diaries,* Barbara Strachey and Jayne Samuels, eds. *1984*

1303. Elinor Glyn (1864–1943)

1 Marriage is the aim and end of all sensible girls, because it is the meaning of life.

"Letters to Caroline," *Harper's Bazaar September 1913*

1304. Rebekah Bettelheim Kohut (1864–1951)

1 No foreign tongue, no jargon! We are Israelites, but we are Americans as well.

"Mission Work Among the Unenlightened Jews," Papers of the Jewish Women's Congress *1893*

2 Instilling habits of cleanliness promotes ideas of economy and exactness in the recipient, awakens dormant ambitions, and instills a feeling of self-respect. With a pure soul must be a clean body.

Ibid.

3 Every true Jewess is a priestess, and by the very strength of her unobtrusive belief is a witness for religion; and when faith in God is the source of her virtues, truth and integrity, gentleness and purity the foundation stones of her life, then truly is she a blessing in Israel.

"Welcoming Address" (Philadelphia), Proceedings of the First Convention of the National Council of Jewish Women *1896.*

4 The denial of woman's ability to serve the synagogue in every part of its work is cruel and dangerous.

"Women and the Synagogue: A Symposium," *American Hebrew 31 December 1897*

5 Social Service . . . can not be a substitute for religion.

Ibid.

6 Deborah* became to me not a prophetess but a great political emancipator. Mother Sarah** stood for the single standard of wife and mother in the home.

My Portion: An Autobiography 1927

*See 27; **see 8.

7 My sisters and I had always felt that while a woman's interests ought to begin at home and ought to end there, they need not necessarily confine themselves to it alone.

Ibid.

1305. Moira O'Neill (1864–1955)

1 Youth's for an hour,
Beauty's a flower,
But love is the jewel that wins the world.

"Beauty's a Flower," *Songs of the Glens of Antrim 1901*

2 The first time me foot got the feel o' the ground
I was strollin' along in an Irish city,
That hasn't its aquil the world around
For the air that is sweet an' the girls that are pretty.

"The Sailor Man," St. 1, Ibid.

3 For the love of her,
The love of her
That would not be my wife;
An' the loss of her,
The loss of her
Has left me lone for life.

"Denny's Daughter," St. 2, Ibid.

4 Now we're past the darklin' caves,
Where the breakin' summer waves
Wander in wi' their trouble from the sea.

"At Sea," St. 2, Ibid.

1306. Margaret P. Sherwood (1864–1955)

1 Whisper some kindly word, to bless
A wistful soul who understands
That life is but one long caress
Of gentle words and gentle hands.

"In Memoriam—Leo: A Yellow Cat" *n.d.*

1307. Wenonah Stevens Abbott (1865–1950)

1 To-day the journey is ended,
I have worked out the mandates of fate;
Naked, alone, undefended,
I knock at the Uttermost Gate.

"A Soul's Soliloquy" *n.d.*

1308. Evangeline Booth (1865–1950)

1 Drink has drained more blood,
Hung more crepe,
Sold more houses,
Plunged more people into bankruptcy,
Armed more villains,
Slain more children,
Snapped more wedding rings,
Defiled more innocence,
Blinded more eyes,
Twisted more limbs,
Dethroned more reason,
Wrecked more manhood,
Dishonored more womanhood,
Broken more hearts,
Blasted more lives,
Driven more to suicide, and
Dug more graves than any other poisoned
Scourge that ever swept its death—
Dealing waves across the world.

"Good Housekeeping" *n.d.*

1309. Mrs. Patrick Campbell (1865–1940)

1 I believe I was impatient with unintelligent people from the moment I was born: a tragedy—for I am myself three-parts a fool.

Ch. 2, *My Life and Some Letters 1922*

2 To be made to hold his [George Bernard Shaw's*] tongue is the greatest insult you can offer him—though he might be ready with a poker to make you hold yours.

Ch. 16, Ibid.

*Irish-born English author (1856–1950).

3 Wedlock—the deep, deep peace of the double bed after the hurly-burly of the chaise-longue.

(1914), Quoted in *Jennie*, Vol. II by Ralph G. Martin *1971*

4 It doesn't matter what you do in the bedroom as long as you don't do it in the street and frighten the horses.

Attributed *n.d.*

1310. Edith Louisa Cavell (1865–1915)

1 I realize that patriotism is not enough. I must have no hatred or bitterness towards anyone.

Last Words, Quoted in *The Times* (London) *23 October 1915*

1311. Elsie De Wolfe (1865–1950)

1 It is the personality of the mistress that the home expresses. Men are forever guests in our home, no matter how much happiness they may find there.

Ch. 1, *The House in Good Taste* 1920

2 What a joyous thing is color! How influenced we all are by it, even if we are unconscious of how our sense of restfulness has been brought about.

Ch. 6, Ibid.

3 It does not matter whether one paints a picture, writes a poem, or carves a statue, simplicity is the mark of a master-hand. Don't run away with the idea that it is easy to cook simply. It requires a long apprenticeship.

"Why I Wrote This Book," *Recipes for Successful Dining* 1934

1312. Minnie Fiske (1865–1932)

1 "Bosh! Do not talk to me about the repertory idea. It is an outworn, needless, impossible, *harmful* scheme. . . . This, my friend, is an age of specialization, and in such an age the repertory theatre is an anachronism, a ludicrous anachronism."

Quoted in Ch. 1, *Mrs. Fiske* by Alexander Woollcott* 1917

2 The essence of acting is the conveyance of truth through the medium of the actor's mind and person. The science of acting deals with the perfecting of that medium. The great actors are the luminous ones. They are the great conductors of the stage.

Ch. 5, Ibid.

3 You must make your own blunders, must cheerfully accept your own mistakes as part of the scheme of things. You must not allow yourself to be advised, cautioned, influenced, persuaded, this way and that.

Letter to Alexander Woollcott* (1908), Ibid.

*American columnist, critic (1887–1943).

1313. Ray Frank (1865–1948)

1 The grandest temples we have ever had or the world has even known were those which had the blue sky for a roof, and the grandest psalms ever sung were those rendered under the blue vaults of heaven . . .

Speech, Yom Kippur sermon (Spokane Falls, Washington, 1890), Quoted in *Ray Frank Litman: A Memoir* by Simon Litman 1957

2 There may be repentance at the eleventh hour, but who can say which hour may not be the eleventh one?

Ibid.

3 . . . think of it, ye Israelites, the chosen of the earth, so divided as to how you will worship Jehovah that you forget to worship at all!

Ibid.

4 From the beginning, she sought knowledge; perceive, it does not say wisdom, but knowledge; and this was at the expense of an Eden. She lost Eden, but she gained that wisdom which has made sure of man's immortality.

Address, "Woman in the Synagogue" (5 September 1893, Chicago), Papers of the Jewish Women's Congress 1984

5 But when the Lord said unto Moses, "And ye shall be unto Me a nation of priests and a holy nation," the message was not to one sex; and that the Israelites did not so consider it,

is proved by the number of women who were acknowledged prophets, and who exercised great influence on their time and on posterity.

Ibid.

6 Learning is not wisdom. Innovation is not progress, and to be identical with man is not the ideal of womanhood. Some things and privileges belong to him by nature; to these, true woman does not aspire; but every woman should aspire to make of her home a temple, of herself a high priestess, of her children disciples, then will she best occupy the pulpit, and her work run parallel with man's. She may be ordained rabbi or be the president of a congregation—she is entirely able to fill both offices—but her noblest work will be at home, her highest ideal, a home.

Ibid.

1314. Yvette Guilbert (1865–1944)

1 Try to make a woman who does badly on the stage understand that she might do better in trade, or in any other occupation. She will never believe you. It seems impossible to her to make linen garments or millinery, but very simple to enact the dandy on the stage.

La Vedette 1902

2 One cannot remain the same. Art is a mirror which should show many reflections, and the artist should not always show the same face, or the face becomes a mask.

Ibid.

3 Caper without cease, and caper again. . . . You are gaiety, which passes away.

Ibid.

1315. Laurence Hope (1865–1904)

1 For this is wisdom: to love, to live,
To take what Fate, or the Gods, may give.

"The Teak Forest," *India's Love Lyrics* 1922

2 Speed passion's ebb as you greet its flow—
To have, to hold, and in time let go!

Ibid.

3 Less than the dust beneath thy chariot wheel,
Less than the weed that grows beside thy door,
Less than the rust that never stained thy sword,
Less than the need thou hast in life of me,
Even less am I.

"Less Than the Dust," St. 1, Ibid.

4 Pale hands I loved beside the Shalimar,
Where are you now? Who lies beneath your spell?

"Kashmiri Song," St.1, Ibid.

5 Your work was waste? Maybe your share
Lay in the hour you laughed and kissed;
Who knows but that your son shall wear
The laurels that his father missed?

"The Masters" n.d.

6 Men should be judged, not by their tint of skin,
The Gods they serve, the Vintage that they drink,
Nor by the way they fight, or love, or sin,
But by the quality of thought they think.

"Men Should Be Judged" n.d.

1316. Anandabai Joshee (1865–1887)

1 Holes are bored through the lower part of the left nostril for the nose-ring, and all around the edge of the ear for jewels. This may appear barbarous to the foreign eye; to us it is a beauty! Everything changes with the clime.
Letter to Mrs. Carpenter (1880), Quoted in *The Life of Anandabai Joshee* by Caroline H. Dall *1888*

2 When I think over the sufferings of women in India in all ages, I am impatient to see the Western light dawn as the harbinger of emancipation.
Ibid.

3 Your American widows may have difficulties and inconveniences to struggle with, but weighed in the scale against ours, all of them put together are but as a particle against a mountain.*
Ibid.

*Reference to the now illegal act or practice of suttee (or sati), wherein a Hindu widow cremates herself on her husband's funeral pyre in order to fulfill a marital duty.

4 Had there been no difficulties and thorns in the way, then man would have been in his primitive state and no progress made in civilization and mental culture.
Letter to her aunt (27 August 1881), Ibid.

5 . . . I regard irreligious people as pioneers. If there had been no priesthood the world would have advanced ten thousand times better than it has now.
Ibid.

1317. Baroness Orczy (1865–1947)

1 Marguerite St. Just was from principle and by conviction a republican—equality of birth was her motto—inequality of fortune was in her eyes a mere untoward accident, but only inequality she admitted was of talent. "Money and titles may be hereditary," she would say, "but brains are not. . . ."
Ch. 6, *The Scarlet Pimpernel 1905*

2 "We seek him here, we seek him there,
Those Frenchies seek him everywhere
Is he in heaven?— Is he in hell?
That damned elusive Pimpernel?"
Ch. 12, Ibid.

3 It is only when we are very happy that we can bear to gaze merrily upon the vast and limitless expanse of water, rolling on and on with such persistent, irritating monotony, to the accompaniment of our thoughts, whether grave or gay. When they are gay, the waves echo their gaiety; but when they are sad, then every breaker, as it rolls, seems to bring additional sadness, and to speak to us of hopelessness and of the pettiness of all our joys.
Ch. 21, Ibid.

4 An apology? Bah! Disgusting! cowardly! beneath the dignity of any gentleman, however wrong he might be.
Prologue, *I Will Repay 1906*

5 "But a wife! . . . What matters what she thinks and feels? if she be cold or loving, gentle or shrewish, sensitive to a kind word or callous to cruelty? A wife! . . . Well! so long as no other man hath ever kissed her lips—for that would hurt masculine vanity and wound the pride of possession!"
Bk. I, Ch. 3, *Leatherface 1918*

6 "My dear, since the beginning of all times, men have perpetrated horrors against one another. It is the devil in them, but the devil would have no power over men if God did not allow it. Could He not, if He so willed, quell this revolution with His Word? Must we not rather bow to His will and try to realize that something great, something good, something, at any rate, that is in accordance with the great scheme of the universe must in the end come out of all this sorrow?"
Bk. III, Ch. 31, *A Child of the Revolution 1932*

1318. Emily James Putnam (1865–1944)

1 Until changing economic conditions made the thing actually happen, struggling early society would hardly have guessed that woman's road to gentility would lie through doing nothing at all.
Introduction, *The Lady 1910*

2 Maternity is on the face of it an unsocial experience. The selfishness that a woman has learned to stifle or to dissemble where she alone is concerned, blooms freely and unashamed on behalf of her offspring.
Ibid.

1319. Kathe Schirmacher (1865–1930)

1 In the greater part of the world woman is a slave and a beast of burden. . . . In most cases she is overworked, exploited, and (even when living in luxury) the oppressed sex. . . . These conditions are opposed by the woman's right movement. . . . Most men do not understand this ideal; they oppose it with unconscious egotism.
The Modern Rights Movement 1905

1320. Louisa Thomas (1865–?)

1 Charm is the measure of attraction's power
To chain the fleeting fancy of the hour.
"What Is Charm?" St. 1 *n.d.*

1321. Lady Troubridge (1865–1946)

1 A bad woman always has something she regards as a curse—a real bit of goodness hidden away somewhere.
The Millionaire 1907

2 If I had had a pistol I would have shot him—either that or fallen at his feet. There is no middle way when one loves.
Ibid.

3 It is far easier to love a woman in picturesque rags than in the common place garments of respectability.
Ibid.

4 A girl can't analyze marriage, and a woman—daren't.
Ibid.

1322. Mary Elizabeth Arnim (1866–1941)

1 Who can begin conventional amiability the first thing in the morning? It is the hour of savage instincts and natural tendencies; it is the triumph of the Disagreeable and the Cross. I am convinced that the Muses and the Graces never thought of having breakfast anywhere but in bed.
"September 15th," *Elizabeth and Her German Garden 1898*

2 Life was certainly a queer business—so brief, yet such a lot of it; so substantial, yet in a few years, which behaved like minutes, all scattered and anyhow.

Ch. 1, *Mr. Skeffington* 1940

3 She had been dragged in the most humiliating of all dusts, the dust reserved for older women who let themselves be approached, on amorous lines, by boys. . . . It had all been pure vanity, all just a wish, in these waning days of hers, still to feel power, still to have the assurance of her beauty and its effects.

Ch. 3, Ibid.

4 . . . without it [love], without, anyhow, the capacity for it, people didn't seem to be much good. Dry as bones, cold as stones, they seemed to become, when love was done; inhuman, indifferent, self-absorbed, numb.

Ch. 5, Ibid.

5 Strange that the vanity which accompanies beauty—excusable, perhaps, when there is such great beauty, or at any rate understandable—should persist after the beauty is gone.

Ch. 6, Ibid.

1323. Martha Dickinson Bianchi (1866–1943)

1 Deeper than chords that search the soul and die,
Mocking to ashes color's hot array,—
Closer than touch,—within out hearts they lie—
The words we do not say.

"The Words We Do Not Say" *n.d.*

1324. Sophonisba Preston Breckinridge (1866–1948)

1 You must remember, Lyman, that the work of the world is not done by going to bed when you get sleepy.

Three Against Time: Edith and Grace Abbott and Sophonisba P. Breckinridge by Helen R. Wright 1954

2 The preference of the social worker would probably be for public rather than private service . . . For the social worker can be satisfied with nothing less than a universal provision for continuous service. And only the state can be both universal and continuous.

"Organized Mother Love, and the Obligations of the State in the Later Nineteenth Century" by Elizabeth B. Clark, *Women in the Welfare State Conference* 11 1989

3 I don't want to cook any at all unless I have to, and I like the idea of bread factories or cake factories where people are paid honest wages for a professional product.

"A Profession for Women: Education, Social Service Administration, and Feminism in the Life of Sophonisba Preston Breckinridge," Stanford Law School Ph.D. dissertation Nancy Ellen Barr 1993

1325. Voltairine de Cleyre (1866–1912)

1 [Anarchism is] . . . not only the denial of authority, not only a new economy, but a revision of the principles of morality. It means . . . self-responsibility, not leader-worship.

"The Burial of My Past Self" (1885), *The Selected Works of Voltairine de Cleyre*, Alexander Berkman, ed. 1914

2 Consider the soul reflected on the advertising page. . . . Commercial man has set his image therein; let him regard himself when he gets time.

Ibid.

3 [Language] . . . this great instrument which men have jointly built . . . Every word the mystic embodiment of a thousand years of vanished passion, hope, desire, thought.

Ibid.

4 Do I repent? Yes, I do; but wait till I tell you of what I repent and why. I repent that I ever believed a man could be anything but a living lie!

"Betrayed," Ibid.

5 I had never seen a book or heard a word to help me in my loneliness.

"The Making of an Anarchist," Ibid.

6 I die, as I have lived, a free spirit, an Anarchist, owing no allegiance to rulers, heavenly or earthly. . . . If my comrades wish to do aught for my memory, let them print my poems.

Journal (1912), Ibid.

1326. Annie Johnson Flint (1866–1932)

1 Have you come to the Red Sea place in your life
Where, in spite of all you can do,
There is no way out, there is no way back,
There is no other way but through?

"At the Place of the Sea," St. 1 *n.d.*

1327. Dora Read Goodale (1866–1915)

1 The modest, lowly violet
In leaves of tender green inset,
So rich she cannot hide from view,
But covers all the bank with blue.

"Spring Scatters Far and Wide" *n.d.*

1328. Eleanor Prescott Hammond (1866–1933)

1 Prone on my back I greet arriving day,
A day no different than the one just o'er;
When I will be, to practically say,
Considerably like I have been before.
Why then get up? Why wash, why eat, why pray?
—Oh, leave me lay!

"Oh, Leave Me Lay," *Atlantic Monthly* (Boston) *August 1922*

1329. Florence Prag Kahn (1868–1948)

1 On being asked if she would favor birth control laws, she replied: "I will if you make it retroactive."

San Francisco Chronicle August 1926

2 Preparedness never caused a war and unpreparedness never prevented one.

Quoted in American Political Women by Esther Stineman 1980

1330. Beatrix Potter (1866–1943)

1 Once upon a time there were four little Rabbits, and their names were—Flopsy, Mopsy, Cottontail, and Peter.

The Tale of Peter Rabbit 1904

2 The water was all slippy-sloppy in the larder and the back passage. But Mr. Jeremy liked getting his feet wet; nobody ever scolded him, and he never caught a cold.

The Tale of Mr. Jeremy Fisher 1906

1331. Katherine Routledge (1866–1935)

1 In dealing with any scientific problem, the first step naturally is to find out all that can be discovered ... while the second is to co-ordinate that material with similar examples elsewhere, so that knowledge which may fail from one source, can be supplied from another.

(1920), *Among Stone Giants* by Jo Anne Van Tilburg, Ph.D. *2003*

1332. Annie Sullivan (1866–1936)

1 I have thought about it a great deal, and the more I think the more certain I am that obedience is the gateway through which knowledge, yes, and love, too, enter the mind of the child.

Letter (11 March 1887), Quoted in *The Story of My Life* by Helen Keller* *1903*

*See 1548.

2 My heart is singing for joy this morning. A miracle has happened! The light of understanding has shown upon my little pupil's mind, and behold, all things are changed!

Letter (20 March 1887), Ibid.

3 It is a rare privilege to watch the birth, growth, and first feeble struggles of a living mind. ...

Letter (22 May 1887), Ibid.

4 It's queer how ready people always are with advice in any real or imaginary emergency, and no matter how many times experience has shown them to be wrong, they continue to set forth their opinions, as if they had received them from the Almighty!

Letter (12 June 1887), Ibid.

5 It's a great mistake, I think, to put children off with falsehoods and nonsense, when their growing powers of observation and discrimination excite in them a desire to know about things.

Letter (28 August 1887), Ibid.

6 ... people seldom see the halting and painful steps by which the most insignificant success is achieved.

Letter (30 October 1887), Ibid.

7 Why, it is as easy to teach the name of an idea, if it is clearly formulated in the child's mind, as to teach the name of any object.

Letter (15 May 1888), Ibid.

1333. Emily Greene Balch (1867–1961)

1 ... I am hoping that 1946 will mark a turning point in the age-old effort to rid the world of war, to national disarmament, to renunciation of power politics, and to development of international trusteeship ...

Acceptance Speech, Nobel Awards (Oslo) *10 December 1946*

2 Thought and will and emotion, as we know about them, are bound up with the brains and nerves. They are as physical as a beefsteak.

"An Exploration of the Infinite," *The Christian Register* (American Unitarian Association) *1952*

3 Science suffers whenever there is a refusal to face evidence or accept results, however revolutionary.

Ibid.

4 If all the good people were clever
And all clever people were good,

The world would be nicer than ever
We thought it possibly could.

Quoted in "Emily Greene Blach: Nobel Peace Laureate" by Heather Miller (1955), *Notable American Unitarians: 1936–1961*, Herbert F. Vetter, ed. *2007*

5 It was not an apple but a book that did the mischief.

Ibid.

6 [I look to] an age in which the unlikeness of other races will be conceived as much of an asset as the unlikeness of wind and string instruments in a symphony.

Ibid.

7 Those of us who are not Jews are oppressed by a sense of our own responsibility for we too are guilty. We are all answerable in part for the development of a state of things where the moral insanity of Hitler Germany was possible. And for a state of things where the civilized world can find no better way out than competition in reciprocal slaughter and destruction. We were not ready in time with any other method than this slow and cruel one.

Ibid.

1334. Pearl Craigie (1867–1906)

1 To love is to know the sacrifices which eternity exacts from life.

Ch. 25, *Schools of Saints 1897*

2 Women may be whole oceans deeper than we are, but they are also a whole paradise better. She may have got us out of Eden, but as a compensation she makes the earth very pleasant.

Act III, *The Ambassador 1898*

1335. Marie Curie (1867–1934)

1 All my life through, the new sights of Nature made me rejoice like a child.

Pierre Curie *1923*
*French chemist, her partner and husband (1859–1906).

2 You cannot hope to build a better world without improving the individuals. To that end each of us must work for his own improvement, and at the same time share a general responsibility for all humanity, our particular duty being to aid those to whom we think we can be most useful.

Ibid.

3 One never notices what has been done; one can only see what remains to be done. ...

Letter to her brother (18 March 1894), Ibid.

4 After all, science is essentially international, and it is only through lack of the historical sense that national qualities have been attributed to it.

"Intellectual Co-operation," *Memorandum* (magazine) *16 June 1926*

5 Indeed, if the mentality of the scholars of the various countries, as revealed by the recent war, often appears to be on a lower level than that of the less cultured masses, it is because there is a danger inherent in all power that is not disciplined and directed toward the higher aims which alone are worthy of it.

Ibid.

6 I have no dress except the one I wear every day. If you are going to be kind enough to give me one, please let it be

practical and dark so that I can put it on afterwards to go to the laboratory.

Letter to a Friend (1849?), Quoted in "She Did Not Know How to Be Famous," *Party of One* by Clifton Fadiman* *1955*
*American writer, editor and radio host (1904–1999).

7 The shattering of our voluntary isolation was a cause of real suffering for us and had all the effects of disaster.*

Quoted in Lecture by Nanny Fröman, Royal Academy of Sciences (Stockholm) *27 September 1997*
*In response to the enormous interest from the public and the media after she and her husband won the Nobel Prize in 1903.

8 I am 38 and able to support myself.*

Remark (1906), Ibid.
*Reference to her refusal of a pension after Pierre was killed by a horse-drawn wagon; at the time her daughters Irène and Eve (see 1990) were nine and two years old.

9 Nothing in life is to be feared. It is only to be understood.

Ibid.

10 Life is not easy for any of us. But what of that? We must have perseverance and above all confidence in ourselves. We must believe that we are gifted for something, and that this thing, at whatever cost, must be attained.

Ibid.

1336. Edith Hamilton (1867–1963)

1 The Greeks were the first intellectualists. In a world where the irrational had played the chief role, they came forward as the protagonists of the mind.

Ch. 1, *The Greek Way 1930*

2 The anthropologists are busy, indeed, and ready to transport us back into the savage forest where all human things . . . have their beginnings; but the seed never explains the flower.

Ibid.

3 Mind and spirit together make up that which separates us from the rest of the animal world, that which enables a man to know the truth and that which enables him to die for the truth.

Ibid.

4 The English method [of poetry] is to fill the mind with beauty; the Greek method was to set the mind to work.

Ch. 4, Ibid.

5 A people's literature is the great textbook for real knowledge of them. The writings of the day show the quality of the people as no historical reconstruction can.

Preface, *The Roman Way 1932*

6 There are few efforts more conducive to humility than that of the translator trying to communicate an incommunicable beauty. Yet, unless we do try, something unique and never surpassed will cease to exist except in the libraries of a few inquisitive book lovers.

Introduction, *Three Greek Plays 1937*

7 No facts however indubitably detected, no effort or reason however magnificently maintained, can prove that Bach's* music is beautiful.

Witness to the Truth 1948
*Johann Sebastian B— (1685–1970), German composer and organist.

8 "Bless me," he [Socrates*] said, looking around the market where all an Athenian wanted lay piled in glowing profusion, "what a lot of things there are a man can do without."

Ch. 1, Ibid.
*Greek philosopher (470?–399 B.C.E.).

9 A life can be more lasting than systems of thought.

Ch. 2, Ibid.

10 Ages of faith and of unbelief are always said to mark the course of history.

Ch. 9, Ibid.

11 But it is not hard work which is dreary; it is superficial work. That is always boring in the long run, and it has always seemed strange to me that in our endless discussions about education so little stress is ever laid on the pleasure of becoming an educated person, the enormous interest it adds to life. To be able to be caught up in the world of thought—that is to be educated.

Quoted in the Bryn Mawr School Bulletin *1959*

1337. Käthe Kollwitz (1867–1945)

1 No longer diverted by other emotions, I work the way a cow grazes.

(April 1910), *Diaries and Letters,* Hans Kollwitz, ed. *1955*

2 Sensuality is burgeoning. . . . I feel at once grave, ill at ease and happy as I watch our children—our *children*—growing to meet the greatest of instincts. May it have mercy on them!

(5 May 1910), Ibid.

3 Where do all the women who have watched so carefully over the lives of their beloved ones get the heroism to send them to face the cannon?

(27 August 1914), Ibid.

4 Men without joy seem like corpses.

(19 September 1918), Ibid.

5 Age remains age, that is, it pains, torments and subdues. When others see my scant achievements, they speak of a happy old age. I doubt that there is such a thing as a happy old age.

(1 January 1932), Ibid.

6 I am afraid of dying—but being dead, oh yes, that to me is often an appealing prospect.

(December 1941), Ibid.

7 Although my leaning toward the male sex was dominant, I also felt frequently drawn toward my own sex—an inclination which I could not correctly interpret until much later on. As a matter of fact I believe that bisexuality is almost a necessary factor in artistic production; at any rate, the tinge of masculinity within me helped me in my work.

(1942), Ibid.

1338. Mary, Queen Consort of Great Britain (1867–1963)

1 God grant we may not have a European war thrust upon us, and for such a stupid reason too, no I don't mean stupid, but to have to go to war on account of tiresome Serbia beggars belief.

Letter to her aunt, Princess Augusta, Grand-Duchess of Mecklenburg-Strelitz (Germany) *28 July 1914*

1339. Annie Nathan Meyer (1867–1951)

1 . . . We women should be mastered, we want to be mastered—we adore our masters.

The Dominant Sex (play) 1911

2 [Women ought to] put more thought in their husbands soup and less into their careers!

"Spreadhenism" *n.d.*

3 Why have we permitted it that their God seems one of Love and ours one of Vengeance?

Ibid.

4 We endeavor to raise wages instead of spreading knowledge. We clean streets instead of our hearts, we build better houses, instead of better homes.

Ibid.

1340. Ellen O'Grady (1867–1938)

1 Crime takes but a moment but justice an eternity.

Quoted in "Woman Police Deputy Is Writer of Poetry" by Djuna Barnes,* *New York Sun Magazine* 1918

*See 1739.

1341. Emmeline Pethick-Lawrence (1867–?)

1 Under the flagstones of the pavements in London lie the dormant seeds of life—ready to spring into blossom if the opportunity should ever occur. And under our cruel and repressive financial and economic system lie dormant human energy and joy that are ready to burst into flower. So far as a drop may be compared to the ocean, we witnessed in many individual cases that releasing of the spirit that is possible when the conditions of life afford some modicum of dignity and of leisure.

Ch. 7, *My Part in a Changing World* 1938

2 I find in many writers of the present day a persistent inclination to refer to the suffrage movement as inspired by enmity towards men. So far as my own experience goes, during the six years with which I was connected with the campaign no effort was spared to instruct the public that we had no enemy except a Government that was false to its professions. We refused to have any quarrel even with the police who, acting under their orders, did us violence, or the prison officials and doctors who became the agents of torture in prison because their livelihood depended upon their obedience.

Ch. 19, Ibid.

3 A change of heart is the essence of all other change and it is brought about by a re-education of the mind.

Ch. 23, Ibid.

1342. Lillian D. Wald (1867–1940)

1 Over five million women are at work in the United States according to the 1900 census. Despite such figures, as a nation we superstitiously hug the belief that our women are at home and our children at school. As a whole the community is reluctant to face the situation frankly and seriously, that women no longer spin and weave and card, no longer make the butter and the cheese, scarcely sew and put the preserves at home, but accomplish these same industries in the factories, in open competition with men, and except in the relatively few instances of trade organization, in competition with each other.

"Organization Amongst Working Women," *Annals of the American Academy of Political Science*, Vol. 27 May 1906

2 Over broken asphalt, over dirty mattresses and heaps of refuse we went . . . There were two rooms and a family of seven not only lived here but shared their quarters with boarders . . . [I felt] ashamed of being a part of society that permitted such conditions to exist . . . What I had seen had shown me where my path lay. That morning's experience was a baptism of fire. Deserted were the laboratory and academic work of college. I never returned to them . . . I rejoiced that I had a training in the care of the sick that in itself would give me an organic relationship to the neighborhood in which this awakening had come.

The House on Henry Street 1915

3 Out they pour, the little hyphenated Americans, more conscious of their patriotism than perhaps any other large group of children, unaware that to some of us they carry on their shoulders our hopes of a finer, more democratic America, when their old-world traditions shall be mingled with the best that lies in our new-world ideals. They bring a hope that a better relationship—even the great brotherhood—is not impossible, and that through living love and understanding we shall come to know the shame of prejudice.

Ibid.

4 His most precious gift, if foreign born, is the absence of class distinction in the public school—the stronghold of democracy.

Ibid.

5 No one class of people can be independent of each other.

Quoted in *The 'Mutuality' of Society: The Life and Work of Lillian D. Wald* by Marjorie N. Feld 1995

1343. Madam C. J. Walker (Sarah Breedlove Walker) (1867–1919)

1 We must not let our love of our country, our patriotic loyalty, cause us to abate one whit in our protest against wrong and injustice.

Speech, "Women's Duty to Women," Walker Convention* 1917

*More than 200 agents of Walker's beauty business attended.

2 I am not ashamed of my past; I am not ashamed of my humble beginning. Don't think because you have to go down in the wash-tub that you are any less a lady!

Quoted in Ch. 3, *Hope in a Jar, The Making of America's Beauty Culture* by Kathy Peiss* 1998

*See 4203.

3 I am a woman who came from the cotton fields of the South. I was promoted from there to the washtub. Then I was promoted to the cook kitchen, and from there I promoted *myself* into the business of manufacturing hair goods and preparations. I have built my own factory on my own ground.

Quoted in *Women Inventors* by Linda Jacobs Altman 1997

4 There is no royal flower-strewn path to success. And if there is, I have not found it—for if I have accomplished anything in life it is because I have been willing to work hard.

The New York Times Magazine 14 November 1917

5 I got myself a start by giving myself a start.

Ibid.

1345. Laura Ingalls Wilder (1867–1957)

1 It was so hard to be good all the time, every day, for a whole year.

Ch. 4, *Little House in the Big Woods* 1932

2 "Did little girls have to be as good as that?" Laura asked, and Ma said: "It was harder for little girls. Because they had to behave like little ladies all the time, not only on Sundays. Little girls could never slide downhill, like boys. Little girls had to sit in the house and stitch on samplers."

Ch. 5, Ibid.

3 "That machine's a great invention!" he said. "Other folks can stick to old-fashioned ways if they want to, but I'm all for progress. It's a great age we're living in."

Ch. 12, Ibid.

1346. Mary Hunter Austin (1868–1934)

1 When a woman ceases to alter the fashion of her hair, you guess that she has passed the crisis of her experience.

The Land of Little Rain 1903

2 Choose a hill country for storms. There all the business of the weather is carried on above your horizon and loses its terror in familiarity. When you come to think about it, the disastrous storms are on the levels, sea or sand or plains. There you get only a hint of what is about to happen, the fume of the gods rising from their meeting place under the rim of the world; and when it breaks upon you there is no stay nor shelter. The terrible mewings and mouthings of a Kansas wind have the added terror of viewlessness. You are lapped in them like uprooted grass; suspect them of a personal grudge. But the storms of hill countries have other business.

"Nurslings of the Sky," Ibid.

3 Life set itself to new processions of seed-time and harvest, the skin newly turned to seasonal variations, the very blood humming to new altitudes. The rhythm of walking, always a recognizable background for our thoughts, altered from the militaristic stride to the jog of the wide unrutted earth.

The American Rhythm 1923

4 What need has he of clocks who knows
When highest peaks are gilt and rose
Day has begun?

"Clocks and Calendars," St. 1 *n.d.*

5 Never was it printed on a page,
Never was it spoken, never heard.

"Whisper of the Wind" *n.d.*

1347. Gertrude Bell (1868–1926)

1 The Arab is never safe and yet he behaves as though security were his daily bread.

The Desert and the Sown 1907

2 Life seized us and inspired us with a made sense of revelry. The humming wind and the teeming earth shouted "Life! Life!" as we rode. Life! Life! The bountiful, the magnificent! Age was far from us—death far; we had left him enthroned in his barren mountains, with ghostly cities and outworn faiths to bear him company. For us the wide plain and the limitless world, for us the beauty and the freshness of the morning!

Persian Pictures 1928

3 We people of the west can always conquer, but we can never hold Asia—that seemed to me to be the legend written across the landscape.

Quoted in "Gertrude Bell 1868–1916" by Lesley Gordon, British Council/University of Newcastle exhibition booklet *1994*

4 . . . there comes a moment in very evil days when they are too evil for anything but silence . . .

Quoted in Ch. 3, p. 43, *Gertrude Bell, Queen of the Desert, Shaper of Nations* by Georgina Howell* 2006
*See 3346.

5 Here we sit, and lives run out like water with nothing done.

Letter home, Ch. 10, p. 233, Ibid.

6 Political union is a conception unfamiliar to a society which is still highly coloured by its tribal origins and maintains in its midst so many strongly disruptive elements of tribal organization.

Undated white paper, Ch. 11, p. 248, Ibid.

7 How can we, who have managed our own affairs so badly, claim to teach others to manage their better?

Letter to Florence* (February 1920), Ch. 13, p. 325, Ibid.
*F— Bell, her stepmother; see 1182.

1348. Alexandra David-Néel (1868–1969)

1 I wish to live philosophy on the spot and undergo physical and spiritual training, not just read about them.

Quoted in "Walker in the Sky" by Jane Dedman, *Quest May/June 1978*

2 Whatever those unacquainted with it may think, solitude and utter loneliness are far from being devoid of charm. Words cannot convey the almost voluptuous sweetness of the feelings experience . . . Mind and senses develop their sensibility in this contemplative life made up of continual observations and reflections. Does one become a visionary or, rather, is it not that one has been blind until them?

Ibid.

3 To the one who knows how to look and feel, every moment of this free wandering life is an enchantment.

Ibid.

1349. Guida Diehl (1868–?)

1 Never did Hitler* promise to the masses in his rousing speeches any material advantage whatever. On the contrary he pleaded with them to turn aside from every form of advantage-seeking and serve the great thought: Honor, Freedom, Fatherland!

The German Woman and National Socialism 1933
*Adolf H—, Austrian-born Nazi dictator (1889–1945).

2 We long to see Men and Heroes who scorn fate. . . . Call us to every service, even to weapons!

Ibid.

1350. Mary Parker Follett (1868–1933)

1 Majority rule rests on numbers; democracy rests on the well-grounded assumption that society is neither a collection of units nor an organism but a network of human relations.

The New State—Group Organisation, the Solution for Popular Government (p. 7) *1918*

2 Conflict is resolved not through compromise, but through invention.

Ibid.

3 We cannot put the individual on one side and society on the other, we must understand the complete interrelation of the

two. Each has no value, no existence without the other. The individual is created by that process. There is no such thing as a self-made Man.

Ibid.

4 The enthusiasm and unanimity of a mass-meeting may warm an inexperienced heart, but the experienced know that this unanimity is largely superficial and is based on the spread of similar ideas, not the unifying of differences.

Ibid.

5 The unifying of opposites is the eternal process.

Ch. II, Ibid.

6 The object of a conference is not to get at a lot of different ideas, as is often thought, but just the opposite—to get at one idea. There is nothing rigid or fixed about thoughts, they are entirely plastic, and ready to yield themselves completely to their master—the group spirit.

Ibid.

7 But compromise is still on the same plane as fighting. War will continue—between capital and labor, between nation and nation—until we relinquish the ideas of compromise and concession.

Ibid.

8 Imitation is for the shirkers, like-mindedness for the comfort lovers, unifying for the creators.

Ch. III, Ibid.

9 The higher the degree of social organization the more it is based on a very wide diversity among its members.

Ibid.

10 I think it better when practicable to keep to verbs; the value of nouns is chiefly for post mortems.

(p. 88), *Creative Experience* 1924

11 All majority control is getting power over. Genuine control is activity between, not influence over.

(p. 186) Ibid.

1351. Maude Glasgow (1868–1955)

1 When new-born humanity was learning to stand upright, it depended much on its mother and stood close to her protecting side. Then women were goddesses, they conducted divine worship, woman's voice was heard in council, she was loved and revered and genealogies were reckoned through her. . . .

As the race grew older, rationality flourished at the expense of moral sense.

The Subjection of Women and the Traditions of Men 1940

1352. Agnes Lee (1868–1939)

1 Bed is the boon for me!
It's well to bake and sweep,
But hear the word of old Lizette:
It's better than all to sleep.

"Old Lizette on Sleep," St. 1 *n.d.*

2 But I'll not venture in the drift
Out of this bright security,
Till enough footsteps come and go
To make a path for me.

"Convention" *n.d.*

1353. Caroline Otero (1868–1965)

1 . . . Paco took care of me; protected me; taught me to dance and sing, and was my lover. It was the first time in over two years that I knew where I was going to sleep every night, and the first time in my life that I knew there would be something for me to eat when I woke up. Then Paco fell in love with me; wanted me to marry him, and spoiled everything.

Quoted in *The Pittsburgh Leader* 11 April 1904

2 There are two things in Spain which are not found elsewhere—flowers, lovely flowers in such abundance, and bull fights. I love both.

Quoted in *New York World* 10 May 1908 Ibid.

1354. Eleanor H. Porter (1868–1920)

1 "Oh, yes, the game was to just find something about everything to be glad about—not matter what 'twas," rejoined Pollyanna earnestly. "And we began right then—on the crutches."

"Well, goodness me! I can't see anythin' ter be glad about—getting' a pair of crutches when you wanted a doll!"

"Goosey! Why, just be glad because you *don't—need—'em*!"

Ch. 5, *Pollyanna* 1912

2 "Oh, but Aunt Polly, Aunt Polly, you haven't left me any time at all just to—to live."

"To live, child! What do you mean? As if you weren't living all the time!"

"Oh, of course I'd be *breathing* all the time I was doing those things, Aunt Polly, but I wouldn't be living. You breathe all the time you're sleep, but you aren't living. I mean *living*—doing the things you want to do. . . . That's what I call living, Aunt Polly. Just breathing isn't living!"

Ch. 7, Ibid.

3 "What men and women need is encouragement. . . . Instead of always harping on a man's faults, tell him of his virtues. Try to pull him out of his rut of bad habits. Hold up to him his better self, his *real* self that can dare and do and win out . . . People radiate what is in their minds and in their hearts."

Ch. 5, Ibid.

4 ". . . he said, too, that he wouldn't *stay* a minister a minute if 'twasn't for the rejoicing texts. . . . Of course the Bible didn't name 'em that. But it's all those that begin 'Be glad in the Lord,' or 'Rejoice greatly,' or 'Shout for joy,' and all that, you know—such a lot of 'em. Once, when father felt specially bad, he counted 'em. There were eight hundred of 'em."

Ch. 22, Ibid.

1355. Margaret Fairless Barber (1869–1901)

1 . . . Earth, my Mother, whom I love.

Dedication, *The Roadmender*, Vol. I 1900

2 The people who make no roads are ruled out from intellectual participation in the world's brotherhood.

Ch. 5, Ibid.

3 Necessity can set me helpless on my back, but she cannot keep me there; nor can four walls limit my vision.

Ch. 6, Vol. II, Ibid.

4 Revelation is always measured by capacity.

Ch. 3, Vol. III, Ibid.

5 To look backward for a while is to refresh the eye, to restore it, and to render it the more fit for its prime function of looking forward.

Ibid.

6 This place is peace and would be silent peace were it not for an Eisteddfod of small birds outvying each other with an eagerness which cannot wait until the last candidate has finished.

Letter (19 May 1900), *The Complete Works of Michael Fairless 1932*

1356. Elsa Barker (1869–1954)

1 They never fail who light
Their lamp of faith at the unwavering flame
Burnt for the altar service of the Race
Since the beginning.

"The Frozen Grail" *1910*

1357. Nancy Ford Cones (1869–1962)

1 Lonely? Dull? At Road's End [her home]? Not as long as I can see the catkins from my door and our maple trees in early spring, or tramp through the misty April wood in search of wildflowers to photograph and color, or watch the birds nesting about our house. Not as long as I can have our friends gather around our fireplace or about our stone tables for a picnic under the maples in the summer.

Quoted in "Rediscovering the Lady from Loveland" by Owen Findsen, *The Cincinnati Enquirer 9 November 1980*

1358. Olive Dargan (1869–1968)

1 Be a God, your spirit cried;
Tread with feet that burn the dew;
Dress with clouds your locks of pride;
Be a child, God said to you.

"To William Blake"* *n.d.*

*English artist and poet (1757–1827).

2 The mountains lie in curves so tender
I want to lay my arm about them
As God does.

"Twilight" *n.d.*

1359. Anna Bunston De Bary (1869–?)

1 A bird do sing, a bee do hum,
The flowers in the border blow,
And all my heart's so glad and clear
As pools when mists do disappear:

"Under a Wiltshire Apple Tree," St. 4, *The Oxford Book of English Mystical Verse*, Nicholson and Lee, eds. 1917

2 Close to the sod there can be seen
A thought of God in white and green.

"The Snowdrop" *n.d.*

1360. Emma Goldman (1869–1940)

1 In taking out an insurance policy one pays for it in dollars and cents, always at liberty to discontinue payments. If, however, woman's premium is a husband, she pays for it with her name, her privacy, her self-respect, her very life, "until death doth part."

"Marriage and Love," *Anarchism and Other Essays 1910*

2 The State is the altar of political freedom and, like the religious altar, it is maintained for the purpose of human sacrifice.

"Anarchism: What It Really Stands For," *Ibid.*

3 The political arena leaves one no alternative, one must either be a dunce or a rogue.

Ibid.

4 There is no hope even that woman, with her right to vote, will ever purify politics.

Ibid.

5 If love does not know how to give and take without restrictions, it is not love, but a transaction that never fails to lay stress on a plus and a minus

Ibid.

6 . . . true emancipation begins neither at the polls nor in courts. It begins in woman's soul.

Ibid.

7 Man has bought brains, but all the millions in the world have failed to buy love. Man has subdued bodies, but all the power on earth has been unable to subdue love. Man has conquered whole nations but all his armies could not conquer love. Man has chained and fettered the spirit, but he has been utterly helpless before love. High on a throne, with all the splendor and pomp his gold can command, man is yet poor and desolate, if love passes him by. And if it stays, the poorest hovel is radiant with warmth, with light and color. Thus love has the magic power to make of a beggar a king. Yes, love is free; it can dwell in no other atmosphere. In freedom it gives itself unreservedly, abundantly, completely.

"Marriage and Love," *Ibid.*

8 Capitalism . . . has . . . grown into a huge insatiable monster.

"The Social Aspect of Birth Control," *Mother Earth April 1916*

9 . . . the soldier's business is to take life. For that he is paid by the State, eulogized by political charlatans and upheld by public hysteria. But woman's function is to give life, yet neither the State nor politicians nor public opinion have ever made the slightest provision in return for the life woman has given.

Ibid.

10 After all, that is what laws are for, to be made and unmade.

Ibid.

11 Anarchy stands for the liberation of the human mind from the dominion of religion; the liberation of the human body from the dominion of property; liberation from the shackles and restraints of government.

Anarchism 1917

12 . . . no great idea in its beginning can ever be within the law. How can it be within the law? The law is stationary. The law is fixed. The law is a chariot wheel which binds us all regardless of conditions or place or time.

"Address to the Jury," *Mother Earth July 1917*

13 . . . democracy must first be safe for America before it can be safe for the world.

Ibid.

14 The ultimate end of all revolutionary social change is to establish the sanctity of human life, the dignity of man, the right of every human being to liberty and well-being.

My Further Disillusionment in Russia 1924

15 Every daring attempt to make a great change in existing conditions, every lofty vision of new possibilities for the human race, has been labeled Utopian.
Lecture, "Socialism: Caught in the Political Trap" (ca. 1912), Ibid.

16 Revolution is but thought carried into action.
Quoted in *The Feminist Papers* by Alice Rossi* 1973
*See 2439.

17 There's never been a good government.
Quoted by Katherine Anne Porter* in *The Los Angeles Times* 7 July 1974
*See 1715.

18 Two years imprisonment for having made an uncompromising stand for one's Ideal. Why that is a small price.
Quoted in *Emma Goldman in America* by Alice Wexler 1984

19 If there's no dancing, it is not my revolution.
Popularly attributed *n.d*

1361. Alice Hamilton (1869–1970)

1 In those days [her childhood] children invented their own games; grownups looked after health, studies, manners, and morals, but amusement was not their responsibility.
(p. 25), *Exploring the Dangerous Trades* (autobiography) 1943

2 I had to accept the thinly veiled contempt of many of my teachers and fellow students because I was at once a woman and an American, therefore uneducated and incapable of real study.*
(p. 47), Ibid.
*Reference to the time when she and her sister, Edith, studied in Germany in 1894.

1362. Corra May Harris (1869–1935)

1 The deadly monotony of Christian country life . . .
Ch. 3, *A Circuit Rider's Wife* 1910

2 No one has yet had the courage to memorialize his wealth on his tombstone. A dollar mark would not look well there.
Ch. 11, Ibid.

3 Adam was a man who could believe any statement he could evolve out of his ambitious imagination easier than he could believe the literal facts of his life.
Ch. 7, *Eve's Second Husband* 1910

4 "The world smacks most of us out of shape so soon."
Ch. 14, Ibid.

5 A woman would rather visit her own grave than the place where she has been young and beautiful after she is aged and ugly.
Ibid.

1363. Nadezhda Konstanitovna Krupskaia (1869–1939)

1 Solidarity among the male and female workers, a general cause, general goals, a general path to that goal—that is the solution to the "woman" question in the working-class environment.
Editorial, *Rabotnitsa* (Woman Worker) 1913

1364. Else Lasker-Schüler (1869–1945)

1 MEPHISTO. Let me ask you, Doctor Faust, with all due respect, why He created me, the Devil, from slime and scorn to live forever?
Act I, *IandI*, Beate Hein Bennett, tr. 1940

2 We shall rest from love like two rare beasts
In the high reeds behind this world.
"A Love Song" (ca. 1902), *The Other Voices*, Carol Cosman, ed. 1975

3 Theater is theater! Theater isn't a lecture hall for medicine or any other scientific discipline. . . . We do not want to go home from a performance saddened or refined but rather shaken by the joy of sorrow or even pleasure.
"Das Konzert" (1920–32) in *Gesammelte Werke*, Vol. 2, Nos. 635–38 (1962), cited in *The Divided Home/Land: Contemporary German Women's Plays*, Sue-Ellen Case,* ed. 1988
*See 3328.

1365. Constance Lytton (1869–1923)

1 After a hunger strike of nearly four days eighty-nine hours I was fed by force without my heart being tested or my pulse felt. I was fed twice a day through the mouth by means of a stomach tube . . . In spite of the first-hand accounts that I had heard of this process the reality surpassed all I had anticipated. It was a living nightmare of pain, horror, and revolting degradation.
"Titled Suffragette Tells of Being Fed," *The New York Times* 30 January 1910

2 The monster of industrialism, which followed in the wake of the discovery of steam and the dethroning of handicraft by artificially-propelled machinery, may one day be bridled and controlled so as to be a servant of humanity, a fellow worker in the day-to-day glory of creation; but for the present it is still a wild beast, a dragon at large, dealing pestilence and death with its fiery breath, combated in panic, its evils evaded rather than faced, its power a nightmare breeding fear and subjection. Instead of harnessing this new force to every branch of our existence, ordering it to serve us at our command, we have cringed before it, left our normal lives and drained our energies to congregate in its grimy temples and worship at its shrine.
Introduction, *Prisons & Prisoners: Some Personal Experiences* 1914

3 Votes and riot are the only form of appeal to which this Government will respond. They refuse us votes, we fall back on riot. The wrongs they inflict on women are intolerable, and we will no longer tolerate them.
Ch. XVI, Ibid.

1366. Charlotte Mew (1869–1928)

1 When us was wed she turned afraid
Of love and me and all things human;
Like the shut of a winter's day.
"The Farmer's Bride", *Collected Poems* 1916

2 . . . Oh! my God! the down,
The soft young down of her, the brown,
The brown of her. . . .
St. 5, Ibid.

1367. Jessie Rittenhouse (1869–1948)

1 I worked for a menial's hire,
Only to learn, dismayed,
That any wage I had asked of life,
Life would have paid.

"My Wage" n.d.

2 My debt to you, Beloved,
Is one I cannot pay
In any coin of any realm
On any reckoning day.

"Debt" n.d.

1368. Carolyn Wells (1869–1942)

1 A Tutor who tooted the flute
Tried to teach two young tutors to toot;
Said the two to the Tutor,
"Is it harder to toot, or
To tutor two tutors to toot?"

"Limericks," No. 6, The Book of Humorous Verse 1920

2 I love the Christmas-tide, and yet;
I notice this, each year I live;
I always like the gifts I get,
But how I love the gifts I give!

"A Thought" n.d.

3 When Venus said "Spell no for me,"
"N-O" Dan Cupid wrote with glee,
And smiled at his success:
"Ah, child," said Venus, laughing low,
"We women do not spell it so,
We spell it Y-E-S."

"The Spelling Lesson" n.d.

4 A canner can can
Anything that he can,
But a canner can't can a can, can he?

"The Canner" n.d.

5 The books we think we ought to read are poky, dull, and dry;
The books that we would like to read we are ashamed to buy;
The books that people talk about we never can recall;
And the books that people give us, oh, they're the worst of all.

"On Books" n.d.

1369. Rida Johnson Young (1869–1926)

1 I'm sure I could love someone madly,
If someone would only love me.

"I'm Falling in Love with Someone," Naughty Marietta (musical) 1910

2 For 'tis love, and love alone, the world is seeking;
And it's love, and love alone, I've waited for;

"Ah, Sweet Mystery of Life," Ibid.

3 Sure I love the dear silver that shines in your hair,
And the brow that's all furrowed, and wrinkled with care.
I kiss the dear fingers, so toil-worn for me.
Oh, God bless you and keep you, Mother Machree.

"Mother Machree", Barry of Ballymore 1911

1370. Jessie Tarbox Beals (1870–1942)

1 Too many photographers try too hard. They try to lift photography into the realm of Art, because they have an inferiority complex about their Craft. You and I would see more interesting photography if they would stop worrying, and instead, apply horse-sense to the problem of recording the look and feel of their own era.

Quoted in PM Magazine April 1941

2 I have learned that to get a job done and have fun in it is all you can get out of life.

Quoted in Jessie Tarbox Beals: First Woman News Photographer by Alexander Alland 1978

3 Mere feminine, delicate, Dresden china type of women get nowhere in business or professional life. They marry millionaires, if they are lucky. But if a woman is to make headway with men, she must be truly masculine.

Ibid.

4 I miss New York with its fairy-like towers
With Liberty's torch high in the air
I'd give all of California's damn flowers
For the sight of Washington Square.

Poem in diary (1936), Ibid.

1371. Elizabeth Botume (fl. 1870s)

1 It was not an unusual thing to meet a woman coming from the fields, where she had been hoeing cotton, with a small bucket or cup on her head, and a hoe over her shoulder, contentedly smoking a pipe and briskly knitting as she strode along. I have seen, added to all these, a baby strapped to her back.

First Days Amongst the Contrabands 1893

1372. Laura Lee Davidson (1870–1949)

1 If I have learned nothing else in all these months in the woods, I have thoroughly learned to keep hands off the processes of nature.

A Winter of Content 1922

1373. Lena Guilbert Ford (1870–1918)

1 Keep the home fires burning,
While your hearts are yearning,
Though your lands are far away
They dream of home.
There's silver lining
Through the dark cloud shining:
Turn the dark cloud inside out,
Till the boys come home.

"Keep the Home Fires Burning" 1915

1374. Sharlot Mabridth Hall (1870–1943)

1 I stayed not, I could not linger; patient, resistless, alone,
I hewed the trail of my destiny deep in the hindering stone.

"Song of the Colorado," Cactus Pine 1910

1375. Florence Hurst Harriman (1870–1967)

1 Next to entertaining or impressive talk, a thoroughgoing silence manages to intrigue most people.

Ch. 4, From Pinafore to Politics 1924

1376. Grace Hibbard (1870?–1911)

1 Is his life threaded with day-time dreams?
Or is it really just what it seems—

"Sacks and umbrellas, paper and bags,
Bits of old iron, bottles, and rags."
"The Ragman," St. 4, *Wild Roses of California 1902*

2 The moaning cypress trees lift somber arms
Up to skies of cloudless blue.
"Golden Gate Park in Midwinter," Ibid.

3 O close-clasped towns across the bay,
Whose lights like gleaming jewels stray
"Oakland—Berkeley—Alameda," *Forget-me-nots from California 1907*

4 "An Honest Lawyer"—book just out—
What can the author have to say?
Reprint perhaps of ancient tome—
A work of fiction anyway.
"Books Received" *n.d.*

1377. Mary Johnston (1870–1936)

1 "I am weary of swords and courts and kings. Let us go into the garden and watch the minister's bees."
Ch. 9, *To Have and To Hold 1899*

1378. Marie Lloyd (1870–1922)

1 They don't pay their sixpences and shillings at a music hall to hear the Salvation Army. If I was to try to sing highly moral songs, they would fire ginger beer bottles and beer mugs at me. I can't help it if people want to turn and twist my meanings.
Interview, *New York Telegraph ca. 1897*

2 She'd never had her ticket punched before.
Music Hall patter *n.d.*

3 A little of what you fancy does you good.
Song *n.d.*

4 I'm one of the ruins that Cromwell* knocked about a bit.
Ibid.

*English military, political and religious leader (1599–1658).

1379. Rosa Luxemburg (1870–1919)

1 . . . profits are springing, like weeds, from the fields of the dead.
The Crisis in the German Social Democracy 1919

2 Shamed, dishonored, wading in blood and dripping with filth, thus capitalist society stands.
Ibid.

3 The high state of world-industrial development in capitalistic production finds expression in the extraordinary technical development and destructiveness of the instruments of war. . . .
Ibid.

4 Passive fatalism can never be the role of a revolutionary party. . . .
Ibid.

5 Freedom for supporters of the government only, for the members of one party only—no matter how big its membership may be—is not freedom at all. Freedom is always freedom for the man who thinks differently.
Prison notes (1918), Quoted in *Die Russische Revolution* by Paul Froelich *1940*

6 Without general elections, without freedom of the press, freedom of speech, freedom of assembly, without the free battle of opinions, life in every public institution withers away, becomes a caricature of itself, and bureaucracy rises as the only deciding factor.
Ibid.

7 I hope to die at my post; on the street, or in prison.
Letter to Sonia Liebnicht* *n.d.*
*Wife of Karl L—(1871–1919), German journalist and politician.

1380. Lucia Clark Markham (1870–1967)

1 To-night from deeps of loneliness I wake in wistful wonder
To a sudden sense of brightness, an immanence of blue.
"Bluebells" *n.d.*

1381. Maria Montessori (1870–1952)

1 The teacher must derive not only the capacity, but the desire, to observe natural phenomena. In our system, she must become a passive, much more than an active, influence, and her passivity shall be composed of anxious scientific curiosity and of absolute *respect* for the phenomenon which she wishes to observe. The teacher must understand and *feel* her position of observer: the activity *must lie in the phenomenon.*
The Montessori Method, Anne Everett George, tr. *1912*

2 The prize and the punishment are incentives toward unnatural or forced effort, and, therefore we certainly cannot speak of the natural development of the child in connection with them. The jockey offers a piece of sugar to his horse before jumping into the saddle, the coachman beats his horse that he may respond to the signs given by the reins; and, yet, neither of these runs so superbly as the free horse of the plains.
Ch. I, Ibid.

3 Our servants are not our dependents, rather it is we who are dependent upon them.
Ch. V, Ibid.

4 Discipline must come through liberty. . . . If discipline is founded upon liberty, the discipline itself must necessarily be active. We do not consider an individual disciplined only when he has been rendered as artificially silent as a mute and as immovable as a paralytic. He is an individual annihilated, not disciplined.
Ibid.

5 But if for the physical life it is necessary to have the child exposed to the vivifying forces of nature, it is also necessary for his psychical life to place the soul of the child in contact with creation, in order that he may lay up for himself treasure from the directly educating forces of living nature. The method for arriving at this end is to set the child at agricultural labour, guiding him to the cultivation of plants and animals, and so to the intelligent contemplation of nature.
Ch. X, Ibid.

6 If one considers the charm of human speech one is bound to acknowledge the inferiority of one who does not possess a correct spoken language; and an aesthetic conception in education cannot be imagined unless special care be devoted to perfecting articulate language.
Ch. XVIII, Ibid.

7 If help and salvation are to come, they can only come from the children, for the children are the makers of men.
Ch. 1, *The Absorbent Mind 1949*

8 We teachers can only help the work going on, as servants wait upon a master.

Ibid.

9 The babies . . . sought to render themselves independent of adults in all the actions which they could manage on their own, manifesting clearly the desire not to be helped, except in cases of absolute necessity. And they were seen to be tranquil, absorbed and concentrating on their work, acquiring a surprising calm and serenity.

The Child in the Family 1956

10 Love and the hope of it are not things one can learn; they are a part of life's heritage.

The Absorbent Mind 1967 ed.

11 The greatness of the human personality begins at the hour of birth. From this almost mystic affirmation there comes what may seem a strange conclusion: that education must start from birth.

Ibid.

12 And so we discovered that education is not something which the teacher does, but that it is a natural process which develops spontaneously in the human being.

Ibid.

13 . . . humanity is still far from that stage of maturity needed for the realizations of its aspiration, for the construction, that is, of a harmonious and peaceful society and the elimination of wars. Men are not yet ready to shape their own destinies, to control and direct world events, of which—instead—they become the victims.

Ibid.

14 And if education is always to be conceived along the same antiquated lines of a mere transmission of knowledge, there is little to be hoped from it in the bettering of man's future. For what is the use of transmitting knowledge if the individual's total development lags behind?

Ibid.

1382. Alice Caldwell Rice (1870–1942)

1 Life is made up of desires that seem big and vital one minute, and little and absurd the next. I guess we get what's best for us in the end.

Ch. 2, *A Romance of Billy-Goat Hill 1912*

2 To him work appeared a wholly artificial and abnormal action, self-imposed and unnecessary. The stage of life presented so many opportunities for him to exercise his histrionic ability, that the idea of settling down to a routine of labor seemed a waste of talent.

Ch. 6, Ibid.

3 The arbitrary division of one's life into days and weeks and hours seemed, on the whole, useless. There was but one day for the men, and that was pay day, and one for the women, and that was rent day. As for the children, every day was theirs, just as it should be in every corner of the world.

Ch. 15, Ibid.

4 "Fer my part I can't see it's to any woman's credit to look nice when she's got the right kind of a switch and a good set of false teeth. It's the woman that keeps her good looks without none of them luxuries that orter be praised."

Ch. 2, *Calvary Alley 1918*

5 When one has a famishing thirst for happiness, one is apt to gulp down diversions wherever they are offered. The necessity of draining the dregs of life before the wine is savored does not cultivate a discriminating taste.

Ch. 14, Ibid.

1383. Helena Rubinstein (1870–1965)

1 The cosmetic business is interesting among modern industries in its opportunities for women. Here they have found a field that is their own province—working for women with women, and giving that which only women can give—an intimate understanding of feminine needs and feminine desires.

"Manufacturing—Cosmetics," *An Outline of Careers for Women*, Doris Fleischman Bernays, ed. *1928*

2 I have always felt that a woman had the right to treat the subject of her age with ambiguity until, perhaps, she passed into the realm of over ninety. Then it is better she be candid with herself and with the world.

Pt. I, Ch. 1, *My Life for Beauty 1965*

3 There are no ugly women, just lazy ones.

Pt. II, Ch. 1, Ibid.

4 But what parent can tell when some such fragmentary gift of knowledge or wisdom will enrich her children's lives? Or how a small seed of information passed from one generation to another may generate a new science, a new industry—a seed which neither the giver nor the receiver can truly evaluate at the time.

Ch. 10, Ibid.

5 Production on a small scale is now practically prohibitive.

(ca. 1920), Quoted in *Hope in a Jar, The Making of America's Beauty Culture* by Kathy Peiss* *1998*

*See 4203.

1384. Maud Younger (1870–1936)

1 "See here. How am I ever going to get experience if everyone tells me that I must have it before I begin?"

"New York, May 6, 1907," *McClure's Magazine 1907*

2 It is not pleasant to have a stranger doubt your respectability.

Ibid.

3 I did not know the working classes were so united. There is more affection and loyalty toward one another than among other people. Perhaps this is because the working people feel that there is a class struggle, and the leisure class does not know it yet.

"New York, May 15, 1907," Ibid.

4 "Then why don't all girls belong to unions?" I asked, feeling very much an outsider; but she of the gents' neckwear replied: "Well, there's some that thinks it ain't fashionable; there's some that thinks it ain't no use; and there's some that never thinks at all."

"New York, June 8," Ibid.

5 A trade unionist—of course I am. First, last, and all the time. How else to strike at the roots of the evils undermining the moral and physical health of women? How else grapple with the complex problems of employment, overemployment, and underemployment alike, resulting in discouraged, undernourished bodies, too tired to resist the onslaughts of disease and crime?

Speech, Quoted in *Ms.* (New York) *January 1973*

1385. B. M. Bower (1871–1940)

1 Do you like children? In other words, are you human?

Ch. I, *The Ranch at the Wolverine 1914*

2 Marthy was clumsy with words, and she was always coming to the barrier between her powers of expression and the thoughts that were prisoned and dumb.

Ibid.

3 "I didn't know there was a woman in the world like you," Ward said irrelevantly and looked into the fire. "I thought women were just soft things a man had to take care of and carry along through life, a dead weight when they weren't worse. I never knew a woman could be a friend—the kind of friend a man can be."

Ch. IV, Ibid.

4 "You know you belong to me, don't you? And I belong to you—body and soul. You know that, don't you? I've known it ever since the world was made. I knew it when God said, 'Let there be light,' and there was light. You were it."

Ch. IX, Ibid.

1386. Mary E. Buell (1871–1972)

1 Something made of nothing, tasting very sweet,
A most delicious compound, with ingredients complete;
But if, as on occasion, the heart and mind are sour,
It has no great significance and loses half its power.

"The Kiss" *n.d.*

1387. Emily Carr (1871–1945)

1 You yourself are nothing, only a channel for the pouring through of that which is something, which is all. Your job is to keep that channel clear and clean and pure so that which passes through may be unobstructed, unsullied, undiluted, and thus show forth its clear purity and intention.

Hundreds and Thousands 1966

2 Life's an awfully lonesome affair. . . . You come into the world alone and you go out of the world alone yet it seems to me you are more alone while living than even going and coming.

"The Elephant" (16 July 1933), Ibid.

3 Oh, the glory of growth, silent, mighty, persistent, inevitable! To awaken, to open up like a flower to the light of a fuller consciousness!

(17 October 1933), Ibid.

4 It is not all bad, this getting old, ripening. After the fruit has got its growth it should juice up and mellow. God forbid I should live long enough to ferment and rot and fall to the ground in a squash.

(12 December 1933*), Ibid.

*The eve of her 62nd birthday.

5 It is wonderful to feel the grandness of Canada in the raw, not because she is Canada but because she is something sublime that you were born into, some great rugged power that you are a part of.

(16 April 1937), Ibid.

6 I am not half as patient with old women now that I am one.

(6 March 1940), Ibid.

7 Everything holds its breath except spring. She bursts through as strong as ever.

(7 March 1941), Ibid.

8 Work and more work! . . . loving everything terrifically. . . . The outstanding event to me is the doing—which I am still at. Don't pickle me away as a done.

Interview (1945), Author's Afterword, *The Forest Lover* by Susan Vreeland* 2004

*See 3704.

1388. Maxine Elliott (1871–1940)

1 Beauty, what is that? There are phalanxes of beauty in every comic show. Beauty neither buys food nor keeps up a home.

News Item *1908*

1389. Margaret Witter Fuller (1871–1954)

1 I am immortal! I know it! I feel it!
Hope floods my heart with delight!
Running on air, mad with life, dizzy, reeling,
Upward I mount—faith is sight, life is feeling,
Hope is the day-star of might!

"Dryad Song" *n.d.*

2 It was thy kiss, Love, that made me immortal.

Ibid.

1390. Pamela Glenconnor (1871–1928)

1 Giving presents is a talent; to know what a person wants, to know when and how to get it, to give it lovingly and well. Unless a character possesses this talent there is no moment more annihilating to ease than that in which a present is received and given.

Ch. 5, *Edward Wyndhan Tennant: A Memoir 1919*

2 Bitter are the tears of a child:
Sweeten them.
Deep are the thoughts of a child:
Quiet them.
Sharp is the grief of a child:
Take it from him.
Soft is the heart of a child:
Do not harden it.

"A Child" *n.d.*

1390.1. Lugenia Burns Hope (1871–1947)

1 The joys and sorrows [of my clients] were poured into my ears and heart. They came for advice . . . We thought these problems through and they were helped.

Quoted in *Lugenia Burns Hope: Black Southern Reformer* by Jacqueline A. Rouse, *1989*

2 It is difficult for me to understand why my white sisters so strenuously object to this honest expression of colored women . . . After all, when we yield to public opinion and make ourselves say only what we think the public can stand, is there not a danger that we may find ourselves, with our larger view, conceding what those with the narrow view demand?

Ibid.

*Responding to leadership resistance from The Association of Southern Women for The Prevention of Lynching in creating a national bill prohibiting the practice.

1391. Georgiana Goddard King (1871–1939)

1 English spelling is an affair of memory, not of reason.

The Bryn Mawr Spelling Book 1909

2 Like other things that came out of the East, it [architecture] is always a little intoxicating.

"Castles in Spain," *The Journal of the American Institute of Architects*, Vol. 9 1921

1392. Agnes C. Laut (1871–1936)

1 They had reached the fine point where it is better for the weak to die trying to overthrow strength, than to live under the iron heel of brute oppression.

Ch. 4, *Vikings of the Pacific 1905*

2 Countless hopes and fears must have animated at the breasts of the Frenchmen.* It is so with every venture that is based on the unknown. The very fact that possibilities *are* unknown gives scope to unbridled fancy and the wildest hopes; gives scope, too, when the pendulum swings the other way to deepest distrust.

Ch. 7, *The Conquest of the Great Northwest 1908*
*Radisson and Groseiller's voyage in 1668 to Hudson Bay.

3 The ultimate umpire of all things in life is—Fact.

Ch. 20, Ibid.

4 Canada's prosperity is literally overflowing from a cornucopia of superabundant plenty. Will her Constitution, wrested from political and civil strife; will her moral stamina, bred from the heroism of an heroic past, stand the strain, the tremendous strain of the new conditions? . . . Above all, will she stand the strain, the tremendous strain, of prosperity, and the corruption that is attendant on prosperity? *Quien sabe?*

Ch. 16, *Canada, the Empire of the North 1909*

5 Yet when you come to trace when and where national consciousness awakened, it is like following a river from the ocean to its mountain springs. . . . You can guess the eternal striving, the forward rush and the throwback that have carved a way through the solid rock; but until you have followed the river to its source and tried to stem its current you can not know.

Ch. 1, *The Canadian Commonwealth 1915*

1393. Florence Sabin (1871–1953)

1 The prohibition law, written for weaklings and derelicts, has divided the nation, like Gaul, into three parts—wets, drys and hypocrites.

Speech *9 February 1931*

1394. Ella Jane S. Stewart (1871–?)

1 The real goddesses of Liberty in this country do not spend a large amount of time standing on pedestals in public places; they use their torches to startle the bats in political cellars.

Quoted in *New Directions for Women November/December 1980*

1395. Margaret Floy Washburn (1871–1939)

1 One of the difficulties in writing these recollections has been that the present is so much more interesting than the past. It is hard to keep one's attention on reminiscence.

4000 Years of Women in Science, astr.ua.edu/4000WS 27 *September 1997*

1396. Maude Adams (1872–1953)

1 If I smashed the traditions it was because I knew no traditions.

Quoted in *Maude Adams: A Biography* by Ada Patterson 1907

2 Genius is the talent for seeing things straight. It is seeing things in a straight line without any bend or break or aberration of sight, seeing them as they are, without any warping of vision. Flawless mental sight! That is genius.

Ibid.

1397. Mary Reynolds Aldis (1872–1949)

1 They flush joyously like a cheek under a lover's kiss;
They bleed cruelly like a dagger—wound in the breast;
They flame up madly of their little hour,
Knowing they must die.

"Barberries" *n.d.*

1398. Eva Gore-Booth (1872–1949)

1 The little waves of Breffney go stumbling through my soul.

"The Little Waves of Breffney," *Poems n.d.*

1399. Mildred Howells (1872–1966)

1 And so it criticized each flower,
This supercilious seed;
Until it woke one summer hour,
And found itself a weed.

"A Different Seed." St. 5 *n.d.*

1400. Emily "Pat" [Martha] Kelly (1872/3–1922)

1 Perhaps we got tired of being taken in hand by men climbers. . . . As in other walks of life, women wanted to find their own feet: it was very splended for some women to be always able to borrow crutches in the form of a man's help, and a man's rope, but it is even better to find that we have feet of our own.

Quoted in Introduction, *Mountaineering Women: Stories by Early Climbers* by David Mazel 1994

1401. Winifred Kirkland (1872–1943)

1 We are each launched in life with an elfin shipmate—set jogging upon earth beside a fairy comrade. When our ears are clear, he pipes magic music; when our feet are free he pleads with us to follow him on witching paths. We cannot often hear, we cannot often follow, but when we do, we know him for what he is; when we sail or run or fly with him, we know him for the gladdest fellow with whom life ever paired us, a companion rarely glimpsed, but glorious, for he is our own true Self.

Foreword, "The Ego in the Essay," *The Joys of Being a Woman and Other Papers 1918 (repr. 1968)*

2 Of all literary forms the personal essay appears the most artless, a little boat that sails us into pleasant havens, without any sound of machinery and without any chart or compass.

Ibid.

3 It is a feminist argument accepted as axiomatic that every woman would be a man if she could be, while no man would be a woman if he could help it. Every woman knows this is not fact but falsehood, yet knows also that it is one of those falsehoods on which depends the stability of the universe. The idea that every woman is desirous of becoming a man is as comforting to every male as its larger corollary is alarming, namely, that women as a mass have resolved to become men. The former notion expresses man's view of femininity, and is flattering; the latter expresses his view of feminism, and is fearsome. Man's panic, indeed, before the hosts he thinks he sees

advancing, has lately become so acute that there is danger of his paralysis.

"The Joys of Being a Woman," *The Joys of Being a Woman and Other Papers 1918 (repr. 1968)*

1402. Aleksandra Kollontai (1872–1952)

1 In place of the indissoluble marriage based on the servitude of women, we shall see rise the free union, fortified by the love and the mutual respect of the two members of the workers' state, equal in their rights and in their obligations.

Communism and the Family 1918

2 The practice of [political] appointments rejects completely the principle of collective work; it breeds irresponsibility.

The Workers' Opposition in Russia ca. 1921

3 The "upper" elements may divert the masses from the straight road of history which leads toward communism only when the masses are mute, obedient, and when they passively and credulously follow their leaders.

Ibid.

4 Bureaucracy, as it is, is a direct negation of mass self-activity. . . .

Ibid.

5 Fear of criticism and freedom of thought by combining together with bureaucracy quite often produce ridiculous forms.

Ibid.

1403. Julia Morgan (1872–1957)

1 I don't think you understand just what my work has been here. The decorative part was all done by a New York firm. My work was structural [on the rebuilding of the Fairmont Hotel following the 1906 earthquake].

Quoted in San Francisco Call 1907

2 The building should speak for itself.

Quoted in "Some Examples of the Work of Julia Morgan" by Walter T. Steilberg, Architect and Engineer November 1918

3 Never turn down a job because you think it's too small, you don't know where it can lead.

Ibid.

1404. Eleanor Rathbone (1872–1946)

1 Pluck from under the family all the props which religion and morality have given it, strip it of the glamour, true or false, cast round it by romance, it will still remain a prosaic, indisputable fact, that the whole business of begetting, bearing and rearing children, is the most essential of all the nation's business.

The Disinherited Family 1924

1405. Grace Seton-Thompson (1872–1959)

1 . . . the outfit I got together for my first [hunting] trip appalled that good man, my husband, while the number of things I had to learn appalled me.

Ch. 1, A Woman Tenderfoot 1900

2 I know what it means to be a miner and a cowboy, and have risked my life when need be, *but,* best of all, I have felt the charm of the glorious freedom, the quick rushing blood, the bounding motion, of the wild life, the joy of the living and of

the doing, of the mountain and the plain; I have learned to know and feel some, at least, of the secrets of the Wild Ones.

Ch. 19, Ibid.

3 Many times I have looked into the eyes of wild animals
And we have parted friends.
What did they see, and recognize,
Shining through the windows of a human soul?

"Windows of the Soul," St. 9, Ibid.

4 Butterflies and birds fly over me unconcerned . . .
The forest accepts me.

"Forest," St. 4, Ibid.

5 My Mother is everywhere . . .
In the perfume of a rose,
The eyes of a tiger,
The pages of a book,
The food that we partake,
The whistling wind of the desert,
The blazing gems of sunset,
The crystal light of the moon,
The opal veils of sunrise.

"Hindu Chant," St. 4, Ibid.

6 Courage! Speed the day of world perfection.
Straining from the Wheel of Things,
Let us break the bonds of lost direction!
Godward! Borne on Freedom's wings!

"The Wheel of Life," St. 6, Ibid.

1406. Leonora Speyer (1872–1956)

1 You gave me wings to fly;
Then took away the sky.

Introduction, Pt. V, *Fiddler's Farewell 1926*

2 Let me declare
That music never dies;
That music never dies.

"Fiddler's Farewell," St. 13, Ibid.

3 I'll sing, "Here lies, here lies, here lies—"
Ah, rust in peace below!
Passers will wonder at my words,
But your dark dust will know.

"I'll Be Your Epitaph," Ibid.

4 Poor patch-work of the heart,
This healing love with love;
Binding the wound to wound,
The smart to smart!

"Therapy," St. 3, Ibid.

5 Houses are like the hearts of men,
I think;
They must have life within,
(This is their meat and drink),
They must have fires and friends and kin,
Love for the day and night,
Children in strong young laps:
Then they live—then!

"Abrigada," St. 10, Ibid.

6 . . . I quote a great deal in my talks. . . . I do like to call upon my radiant cloud of witnesses to back me up, saying the thing I would say, and saying it so much more eloquently.

"On the Teaching of Poetry," *The Saturday Review of Literature 1946.*

7 There is not much stitching and unstitching in some of the hasty and cocksure writing of today.

Ibid.

1407. Sara Josephine Baker (1873–1945)

1 The way to keep people from dying from disease, it stuck me suddenly, was to keep them from falling ill. Healthy people didn't die. That sounds like a completely absurd and witless remark, but at that time it really was a startling idea.

Fighting for Life 1939

2 A baby has the right to be born whole.

Ibid.

3 I literally sat on [Mary Mallon]* all the way [to the hospital laboratory]. It was like being in a cage with an angry lion.

Ibid.

*A.k.a. Typhoid Mary; it was Baker who tracked her down as a typhoid carrier, and apprehended her.

4 We need more information. All we have is this one quote: It is true that the laboratory and the X-ray have added much that is valuable to our knowledge of diagnosis, but in this change of tactics the average doctor has lost much of his basic skill. Thirty years ago, we had to depend upon our sense of touch, sight, and hearing to make a diagnosis, and experience developed alertness that is not completely replaced by routine laboratory reports . . .

Quoted in *4000 Years of Women in Science* (astr.ua.edu/ 4000WS) *27 September 1997*

1408. Willa Cather (1873–1947)

1 There are only two or three human stories, and they go on repeating themselves as fiercely as if they had never happened before.

Pt. II, Ch. 4, *O Pioneers! 1913*

2 Artistic growth is, more than it is anything else, a refining of the sense of truthfulness. The stupid believe that to be truthful is easy; only the artist, the great artist, knows how difficult it is.

Pt. IV, Ch. 11, *The Song of the Lark 1915*

3 That is happiness; to be dissolved into something completely great.

Bk. I, Ch. 2, Epitaph, *My Ántonia 1918*

4 It was a highly respectable street, where all the houses were exactly alike, and where business men of moderate means begot and reared large families of children, all of whom went to sabbath-school and learned the shorter catechism, and were interested in arithmetic; all of whom were as exactly alike as their homes, and of a piece with the monotony in which they lived.

"Paul's Case," *Youth and the Bright Medusa 1920*

5 He . . . knew now, more than ever, that money was everything, the wall that stood between all he loathed and all he wanted.

Ibid.

6 Art, it seems to me, should simplify. That, indeed, is very nearly the whole of the higher artistic process; finding what conven-

tions of form and what details one can do without and yet preserve the spirit of the whole. . . .

On the Art of Fiction 1920

7 The dead might as well try to speak to the living as the old to the young.

Bk. II, Ch. 6, *One of Ours 1922*

8 Yes, inside of people who walked and worked in the broad sun, there were captives dwelling in darkness,—never seen from birth to death.

Bk. III, Ch. 6, Ibid.

9 When kindness has left people, even for a few moments, we become afraid of them as if their reason had left them. When it has left a place where we have always found it, it is like shipwreck; we drop from security into something malevolent and bottomless.

My Mortal Enemy 1926

10 That irregular and intimate quality of things made entirely by the human hand.

Bk.1, Ch. 3, *Death Comes for the Archbishop 1927*

11 CECILE. Do you think it wrong for a girl to know Latin?
PIERRE. Not if she can cook a hare or partridge as well as Mademoiselle Auclaire! She may read all the Latin she pleases.

Shadows on the Rock 1931

12 Only solitary men know the full joys of friendship. Others have their family; but to a solitary and an exile his friends are everything.

Bk. III, Ch. 5, Ibid.

13 "Nothing really matters but living—accomplishments are the ornaments of life; they come second."

Lucy Gayheart 1935

14 Religion and art spring from the same route and are close kin. Economics and art are strangers.

On Writing 1949

15 Give the people a new word and they think they have a new fact.

"Four Letters: Escapism" (1936), Ibid.

16 Writing ought either to be the manufacture of stories for which there is a market demand—a business as safe and commendable as making soap or breakfast foods—or it should be an art, which is always a search for something for which there is no market demand, something new and untried, where the values are intrinsic and have nothing to do with standardized values.

"On the Art of Fiction" (1920), Ibid.

17 The fact that I was a girl never damaged my ambitions to be a pope or an emperor.

Quoted by Joan Acocella in "Cather and the Academy," *The New Yorker 27 November 1995*

18 So blind is life, so long at last is sleep,
And none but love to bid us laugh or weep.

"Evening Song" *n.d.*

19 Where are the loves that we have loved before
When once we are alone, and shut the door?

"L'Envoi" *n.d.*

20 Oh, this is the joy of the rose:
   That it blows,
   And goes.

   "In Rose-Time" n.d.

21 Whatever is felt upon the page without being specifically named there—that, one might say, is created. It is the inexplicable presence of the thing not named, of the overtone divined by the ear but not heard by it, the verbal mood, the emotional aura of the fact or the thing or the deed, that gives high quality to the novel or the drama, as well as to poetry itself.

   Essay, "The Novel Démeublé" n.d.

1409. Colette (1873–1954)

1 Privation prevents all thought, substitutes for any other mental image that of a hot, sweet-smelling dish, and reduces hope to the shape of a rounded loaf set in rays of glory.

   Music Hall Sidelights 1913

2 I look like a discouraged beetle battered by the rains of a spring night. I look like a moulting bird. I look like a governess in distress. I look—Good Lord, I look like an actress on tour, and that speaks for itself.

   "On Tour," Ibid.

3 Nothing ages a woman like living in the country.

   Ibid.

4 . . . her smile was like a rainbow after a sudden storm.

   Ibid.

5 Give me a dozen such heart-breaks, if that would help me to lose a couple of pounds.

   Ibid.

6 . . . The sudden desire to look beautiful made her straighten her back. "Beautiful? For whom? Why for myself, of course."

   Ibid.

7 It's pretty hard to retain the characteristics of one's sex after a certain age.

   "My Mother and Illness," My Mother's House 1922

8 You'll understand later that one keeps on forgetting old age up to the very brink of the grave.

   Ibid.

9 "What are you thinking about, Bel-Gazou?" "Nothing, Mother."
   An excellent answer. The same that I invariably gave when I was her age.

   "The Priest on the Wall," Ibid.

10 It is not a bad thing that children should occasionally, and politely, put parents in their place.

   Ibid.

11 Whenever I feel myself inferior to everything about me, threatened by my own mediocrity, frightened by the discovery that a muscle is losing its strength, a desire its power, or a pin the keen edge of its bite, I can still hold up my head and say to myself: . . . "Let me not forget that I am the daughter of a woman who bent her head, trembling, over a cactus, her wrinkled face full of ecstasy over the promise of a flower, a woman who herself never ceased to flower, untiringly, during three quarters of a century."

   Break of Day 1928

12 My true friends have always given me that supreme proof of devotion, a spontaneous aversion for the man I loved.

   Ibid.

13 He was such an inoffensive little boy, she could find no fault with him, except his tendency to disappear.

   "The Savages," Sido 1929

14 It is wise to apply the oil of refined politeness to the mechanism of friendship.

   Ch. 9, The Pure and the Impure 1933

15 She [the cat] hasn't had her full ration of kisses-on-the-lips today. She had the quarter-to-twelve one in the Bois, she had the two o'clock one after coffee, she had the half-past-six one in the garden, but she's missed tonight's.

   The Cat 1933

16 "She never misses an opportunity to shrink away from anything that can be tasted or touched or smelled."

   "Armande" 1944

17 . . . one word escaped, crisp and lively, and made a beeline for Jean, the word "crisis." Sometimes it entered ceremoniously, like a lady dressed up to give away prizes, with an <i>h</i> behind its ear and a <i>y</i> tucked into its bodice: Chrysis, Chrysis Salutari.

   "The Sick Child" 1944

18 "Don't be too nice to me. When anyone's too nice to me, I don't know what I'm doing—I boil over like soup."

   "The Photographer's Missus" 1944

19 "But once I had set out, I was already far on my way."

   Ibid.

20 "Madame, people very seldom die because they lost someone. I believe they die more often because they haven't had someone."

   Ibid.

21 "Explain yourself without gestures. The moment you gesticulate you look common."

   Gigi 1944

22 "If only her brain worked as well as her jaws!"

   Ibid.

23 "Call your mother, Gigi! Liane d'Exelmans has committed suicide."
   The child replied with a long drawn-out "Oooh!" and asked, "Is she dead?"
   "Of course not. She knows how to do these things."

   Ibid.

24 "All that's in the past. All that's over and done with."
   "Of course, Tonton, until it begins again."

   Ibid.

25 A line of verse need not necessarily be beautiful for it to remain in the depths of our memory and occupy maliciously the place overrun by certain condemnable but unerasable melodies.

   "The Blue Lantern" 1949

26 You must not pity me because my sixtieth year finds me still astonished. To be astonished is one of the surest ways of not growing old too quickly.

   Speech, Belgian Academy,* Pt. 4, "Lady of Letters," Earthly Paradise, Robert Phelps, ed. 1966

   *On the occasion of her election to the Academy.

27 The writer who loses his self-doubt, who gives way as he grows old to a sudden euphoria, to prolixity, should stop writing immediately: the time has come for him to lay aside his pen.
> "Lady of Letters," Pt. 4, Ibid.

28 January, month of empty pockets! . . . Let us endure this evil month, anxious as a theatrical producer's forehead.
> "Empty Pockets," *Journey for Myself 1971*

1410. Mary Elizabeth Crouse (1873–?)

1 How often do the clinging hands, though weak,
  Clasp round strong hearts that otherwise would break.
> "Strength of Weakness" *n.d.*

1411. Daisy, Princess of Pless (1873–?)

1 Either of my parents would have done anything in the world for me—except tell me the truth.
> Ch. 1, *Daisy, Princess of Pless 1923*

2 How seldom people find their happiness on a darkened stage; they must turn up all the limelights to find it.
> Entry (16 August 1903), *From My Private Diary 1926*

3 No theater is prosperous, or a play complete, unless there is a bedroom scene in the second act. . . .
> Entry (28 April 1904), Ibid.

4 For each of us, after middle-age, the world is always emptying.
> Ch. 3, *Better Left Unsaid 1931*

5 The Irish sit by a peat fire; the English by a coal one. That is the unbridgeable difference between the two peoples: We prefer the glamorous, the quick, the pungent; they the lasting and substantial.
> Ch. 1, *What I Left Unsaid 1936*

1412. Marie Dressler (1873–1934)

1 Fate cast me to play the role of an ugly duckling with no promise of swanning. Therefore, I sat down as a mere child—fully realizing how *utterly* "mere" I was—and figured out my life early. Most people do it, but they do it too late. At any rate, from the beginning I have played my life as a comedy rather than the tragedy many would have made of it.
> Ch. 1, *The Life Story of an Ugly Duckling 1924*

2 . . . poor had no terror for me! It was pie for me! My whole life had been a fight!
> Ch. 5, Ibid.

3 I was born serious and I have earned my bread making other people laugh.
> Ch. 1, *My Own Story 1934*

4 In order to represent life on the stage, we must rub elbows with life, live ourselves.
> Ch. 3, Ibid.

5 Love is not getting, but giving. It is sacrifice. And sacrifice is glorious! I have no patience with women who measure and weigh their love like a country doctor dispensing capsules. If a man is worth loving at all, he is worth loving generously, even recklessly.
> Ch. 7, Ibid.

6 By the time we hit fifty, we have learned our hardest lessons. We have found out that only a few things are really important. We have learned to take life seriously, but never ourselves.
> Ch. 17, Ibid.

7 There is a vast difference between success at twenty-five and success at sixty. At sixty, nobody envies you. Instead, everybody rejoices generously, sincerely, in your good fortune.
> Ibid.

1413. Frances Alice Kellor (1873–1952)

1 From the moment [the immigrant] arrives in America he needs the creative aggressive attention of American institutions.
> *Straight America - A Call to National Service 1916*

2 The English language is a highway of loyalty. It is the open door to opportunity; it is a means of common defense.
> *Immigration and the Future 1920*

1414. Nellie McClung (1873–1951)

1 When they felt tired, they called it laziness and felt disgraced and thus they had spent their days, working, working from the grey dawn, until the darkness came again, and all for what? When in after years these girls, broken in health and in spirits, slipped away to premature graves, or, worse still, settled into chronic invalidism, of what avail was the memory of the cows they milked, the mats they hooked, the number of pounds of butter they made.
> *Sowing Seeds in Danny 1908*

2 "While we are side by side" the violins sang, glad, triumphant, that old story that runs like a thread of gold through all life's patterns; that old song, old yet ever new, deathless, unchangeable, which maketh the poor man rich and without which the richest becomes poor!
> Ibid.

1415. Virginia Taylor McCormick (1873–1957)

1 Not any leaf from any book
  Can give what Pan, in going took.
> "Regret from Pan" *n.d.*

2 Now she is dead she greets Christ with a nod,—
  (He was a carpenter)—*but she knows God.*
> "The Snob" *n.d.*

1416. Lily Montagu (1873–1963)

1 We believe in one moving force through which we and all the universe are created. God is manifested in us and in all our doings.
> Sermon to the Reform Synagogue, Berlin (August 1928), *Lily Montagu: Sermons, Addresses, Letters and Prayers*, Ellen M. Umansky,* ed. *1985*
> *See 4011.

2 There would be no value in worship services and symbols did they not, preserved in their Purity and Beauty, serve as aids to right living.
> Ibid.

3 Organized religion has a part in the evolution of personal religion. It is the material upon which personal religion is grafted, but the process of grafting must be individual. Every human

soul must, through thought, prayer, and study, cultivate his [sic] own religion to suit himself.

Ibid.

1417. Elizabeth Cutter Morrow (1873–1955)

1 My friend and I have built a wall
   Between us thick and wide:
   The stones of it are laid in scorn
   And plastered high with pride.

"Wall," St. 1 n.d.

2 There is no lover like an island shore
   For lingering embrace;
   No tryst so faithful as the turning tide
   At its accustomed place.

"Islands," St. 1 n.d.

1418. Emily Post (1873–1960)

1 Considering manners even in their superficial aspect, no one—unless he be a recluse who comes in contact with no other human being—can fail to reap the advantage of a proper, courteous and likeable approach, or fail to be handicapped by an improper, offensive and resented one.

Ch. 1, Etiquette 1922

2 Ideal conversation must be an exchange of thought, and not, as many of those who worry most about their shortcomings believe, an eloquent exhibition of wit or oratory.

Ch. 6, Ibid.

3 To do exactly as your neighbors do is the only sensible rule.

Ch. 33, Ibid.

4 To the old saying that man built the house but woman made it a "home" might be added the modern supplement that woman accepted cooking as a chore but man has made of it a recreation.

Ch. 34, Ibid.

5 The honor of a gentleman demands the inviolability of his word, and the incorruptibility of his principles. He is the descendant of the knight, the crusader; he is the defender of the defenseless and the champion of justice—or he is not a gentleman.

Ch. 48, Ibid.

1419. Dorothy Miller Richardson (1873–1957)

1 "There; how d'ye like that, eh? A liberal education in twelve volumes, with an index."

Ch. 24, Pilgrimage, Vol. II 1938

2 If there was a trick, there must be a trickster.

Ibid.

3 No future life could heal the degradation of having been a woman. Religion in the world had nothing but insults for women.

Ibid.

4 They invent a legend to put the blame for the existence of humanity on women and, if she wants to stop it, they talk about the wonders of civilizations and the sacred responsibilities of motherhood. They can't have it both ways.

Ibid.

5 <i>Coercion.</i> The unpardonable crime.

Ch. 9, Vol. IV, Ibid.

6 "Women carry all the domesticity they need about with them. That is why they can get along alone so much better than men."

Ibid.

7 In and out of every year of his ascent her life had been woven. She had been a witness, and was now a kind of compendium for him of it all, one of his supports, one of those who through having known the beginnings, through representing them every time she appeared, brought to him a realization of his achievements.

Ibid.

1420. Margaret Baillie Saunders (1873–1949?)

1 I've often known people more shocked because you are not bankrupt than because you are.

A Shepherd of Kensington 1907

2 One's old acquaintances sometimes come upon one like ghosts—and most people hate ghosts.

Ibid.

1421. Janet Scudder (1873–1940)

1 I don't believe artists should be subjected to experiences that harden the sensibilities; without sensibility no fine work can ever be done.

Ch. 2, Modeling My Life 1925

2 Someone has said that even criticism is better than silence. I don't agree to this. Criticism can be very harmful unless it comes from a master; and in spite of the fact that we have hundreds of critics these days, it is one of the most difficult of professions.

Ibid.

1422. Thérèse de Lisieux (1873–1897)

1 Love proves itself by deeds, so how am I to show my love? Great deeds are forbidden me. The only way I can prove my love is by scattering flowers and these flowers are every little sacrifice, every glance and word, and the doing of the least actions for love.

"Little Way," L'histoire d'une âme (Story of a Soul) 1897

2 For me, prayer is a surge of the heart; it is a simple look turned toward Heaven, it is a cry of recognition and of love, embracing both trial and joy; in a word, something noble, supernatural, which enlarges my soul and unites it to God.

Ibid.

1423. Edith Franklin Wyatt (1873–1958)

1 Every true poem is a lone fount, of whose refreshment the traveler himself must drink, if he is to quench his thirst for poetry.

"Modern Poetry," Art and the Worth-While, Baker Brownell, ed. 1929

2 Our criticism is always devoting itself to . . . watching the sticks and straws on the surface of the current, without interest, apparently, in the natural force of the stream, the style and turn of the whole composition, its communicative social imagination.

Ibid.

1424. Harriet Emma Burton (1874–?)

1 Say; can no healing art restore
The pulse of health and life;
Or still, within this feeble frame,
The long, unequal strife?
"The White-Rose Wreath," St. 6, *The White-Rose Wreath* 1835.

2 Love, indestructible as pure,
Till memory leaves her, will endure:
And each attempt to quench the flame,
But strengthens it within her frame:
With one calm, gradual, sacred light,
It burns ethereal, firm and bright.
"Woman's Love," St. 2, Ibid.

1425. Ch'iu Chin (1874–1907)

1 We'll follow Joan of Arc—*
With our own hands our land we shall regain!
"Ch'iu Chin—A Woman Revolutionary" (1905), Quoted in
Women of China by Fan Wen-Lan 1956
*See 252.

2 We want to unite our two hundred million sisters into a solid whole, so that they can call to each other. Our journal will act as the mouthpiece for our women. It is meant to help our sisters by giving their life a deeper meaning and hope and to advance rapidly toward a bright, new society. We Chinese women should become the vanguard in rousing the people to welcome enlightenment.
Ibid.

1426. Isabel La Howe Conant (1874–?)

1 He who loves an old house
Never loves in vain.
"Old House," St. 1 *n.d.*

1427. Mrs. Edmund Craster (?–1874)

1 The Centipede was happy quite,
Until the Toad in fun
Said, "Pray which leg goes after which?"
And worked her mind to such a pitch,
She lay distracted in a ditch
Considering how to run.
"Pinafore Poems," *Cassell's Weekly* 1871

1428. Olive Custance (1874–1944)

1 Spirit of Twilight, through your folded wings
I catch a glimpse of your averted face,
And rapturous on a sudden, my soul sings
"Is not this common earth a holy place?"
"Twilight" *n.d.*

1429. Clara Dolliver (fl. 1874–1891)

1 No merry frolics after tea,
No baby in the house.
"No Baby in the House," *No Baby in the House and Other Stories for Children* 1868

1430. Anne Crawford Flexner (1874–1955)

1 MRS. WIGGS. The worse Mr. Wiggs would act, the harder I would pat him on the back. And as for the children, I always did use compliments on 'em instead of switches.
Act I, *Mrs. Wiggs of the Cabbage Patch* 1903

2 MRS. FROST. If there were no women in the world, what would become of you men? FROST. We would be scarce, Emily, but we might be happier.
Act I, *The Marriage Game* 1913

3 KEATS. One must have health! You may banish money—banish sofas—banish wine! but right Jack Health, true Jack Health, honest Jack Health—banish health, and you banish all the world!
Act II, Sc. 3, *Aged Twenty-six* 1937

1431. Zona Gale (1874–1938)

1 Loving, like prayer, is a power as well as a process. It's curative. It is creative.
Ch. 3, *Birth* 1918

2 DWIGHT. Energy—it's the driving power of the nation.
Act I, Sc. 1, *Miss Lulu Bett* 1920

3 NINIAN. Education: I ain't never had it and I ain't never missed it.
Sc. 2, Ibid.

4 He faced the blind wall of human loneliness. He was as one who, expecting to be born, is still-born, and becomes aware not of the cradle, but of eternity.
"The Biography of Blade," *Century Magazine* 1924

5 He was integrated into life,
He was a member of life,
He was harmonized, orchestrated, identified with the program of being.
"Walt Whitman"* *n.d.*
*American poet (1819–1892).

1432. Mary Garden (1874–1967)

1 I have never been nervous in all my life and I have no patience with people who are. If you know what you're going to do, you have no reason to be nervous. And I knew what I was going to do.
Ch. 3, *Mary Garden's Story,* with Louis Biancolli 1951

2 If I ever had complete charge of an opera house, the chances are I wouldn't get anybody to sing for me. I would be very emphatic about some things. I would never have a curtain call. I would never allow an encore. I would never permit a claque. There would be only art in my theatre.
Ch. 11, Ibid.

3 I used my voice to color my roles. Salomé was blood red. Melissande was ice, melting ice. . . .
Ch. 21, Ibid.

1433. Theodosia Garrison (1874–1944)

1 The hardest habit of all to break
Is the terrible habit of happiness.
"The Lake" *n.d.*

2 I have known laughter—therefore I
May sorrow with you far more tenderly
Than those who never guess how sad a thing
Seems merriment to one's heart's suffering.
"Knowledge" *n.d.*

3 The kindliest thing God ever made,
   His hand of very healing laid
   Upon a fevered world, is shade.
                              "The Shade," St. 1 *n.d.*

1434. Lulu Glaser (1874–1958)

1 Anyone with any real blood in his or her . . . veins cannot help
   being a fan. . . . Being a true American and being a fan are synonymous.
          Baseball Magazine (1909), Quoted in *Women in Baseball: The
                       Forgotten History* by Gai Ingham Berlage *1994*

1435. Ellen Glasgow (1874–1945)

1 It was not the matter of the work, but the mind that went into
   it, that counted—and the man who was not content to do
   small things well would leave great things undone.
                         Bk. II, Ch. 4, *The Voice of the People* 1900

2 "A farmer's got to be born, same as a fool. You can't make a
   corn pone out of flour dough by the twistin' of it."
                                                       Ibid.

3 "What a man marries for's hard to tell," she returned; "an'
   what a woman marries for's past findin' out."
                                          Bk. III, Ch 1, Ibid.

4 "I ain't never seen a head so level that it could bear the lettin' in
   of politics. It makes a fool of a man and a worse fool of a fool.
   The government's like a mule, it's slow and it's sure; it's slow to
   turn, and it's sure to turn the way you don't want it."
                                                 Ch. 2, Ibid.

5 "Maria has been so long at her high-and-mighty boarding-
   school," he said, "that I reckon her head's full of fancies as a
   cheese is of maggots."
                           Bk. I, Ch. 3, *The Deliverance* 1904

6 "Oh, but it feels so nice to be hard! If I had known how nice it
   felt, I should have been hard all my life."
                          Pt. I, Ch. 12, *They Stooped to Folly* 1929

7 Women like to sit down with trouble as if it were knitting.
                          Pt. 3, Sct. 3, *The Sheltered Life* 1932

8 No idea is so antiquated that it was not once modern. No idea
   is so modern that it will not someday be antiquated.
                         Address, Modern Language Association *1936*

9 To seize the flying thought before it escapes us is our only touch
   with reality.
                                                       Ibid.

10 "Grandpa says we've got everything to make us happy but
   happiness."
                              Pt. I, Ch. 1, *In This Our Life 1941*

11 "I don't like human nature, but I do like human beings."
                                          Pt. II, Ch. 1, Ibid.

12 "We didn't talk so much about happiness in my day. When it
   came, we were grateful for it, and, I suppose, a little went farther than it does nowadays. We may have been all wrong in
   our ideas, but we were brought up to think other things more
   important than happiness."
                                                 Ch. 10, Ibid.

13 No matter how vital experience might be while you lived it, no
   sooner was it ended and dead than it became as lifeless as the
   piles of dry dust in a school history book.
                                          Pt. III, Ch. 9, Ibid.

1436. Beatrice Hinkle (1874–1953)

1 Fundamentally the male artist approximates more to the psychology of woman, who, biologically speaking, is a purely
   creative being and whose personality has been as mysterious
   and unfathomable to the man as the artist has been to the average person.
           "The Psychology of the Artist," *Recreating the Individual
                                                            1923*

2 . . . woman is a being dominated by the creative urge and . . .
   no understanding of her as an individual can be gained unless
   the significance and effects of that great fact can be grasped.
                                                       Ibid.

3 When one looks back over human existence, however, it is
   very evident that all culture has developed through an *initial
   resistance against adaptation to the reality in which man finds
   himself.*
                                                       Ibid.

4 The amount which cannot be harnessed and domesticated, but
   insists on its own form of activity rather than one which is offered ready made, is the energy used for the creation of art.
                                                       Ibid.

5 . . . the artist has always been and still is a being somewhat
   apart from the rest of humanity.
                                                       Ibid.

6 The mystics are the only ones who have gained a glimpse into
   what is possible. . . .
                                                       Ibid.

1437. Louise "Lou" Henry Hoover (1874–1944)

1 My chief hobbies are my husband* and my children.
                Comment, Quoted in *First Ladies* by Betty Boyd Caroli *1987*

   *Herbert Clark H— (1874–1964), 31st President of the United
   States (1929–1933).

2 Boys, remember you are just as great factors in the home making of the family as are the girls.
                           Radio speech to 4-H Club (June 1929), Ibid.

1438. Bettina von Hutten (1874–1957)

1 A good many women are good tempered simply because it
   saves the wrinkles coming too soon.
                                              The Halo 1907

2 Everybody in the world ought to be sorry for everybody else.
   We all have our little private hell.
                                                       Ibid.

1439. Yamamuro Kieko (1874–1915)

1 . . . I realize that were I a man, I would be at the battlefront
   fighting amidst bullets and explosives, instead of sitting se-
   renely at my desk.
                                          Untitled Essay *1895*

1440. Amy Lowell (1874–1925)

1 Brave idolatry
Which can conceive a hero! No deceit,
No knowledge taught by unrelenting years,
Can quench this fierce, untamable desire.
"Hero-Worship," *A Dome of Many-Coloured Glass 1912*

2 My words are little jars
For you to take and put upon a shelf.
"A Tulip Garden," *Sword Blades and Poppy Seeds 1914*

3 Happiness, to some, elation;
Is, to others, mere stagnation.
"Happiness," Ibid.

4 All books are either dreams or swords,
You can cut, or you can drug, with words.
"Sword Blades and Poppy Seeds," St. 3, Ibid.

5 A pattern called a war.
Christ! What are patterns for?
St. 7, "Patterns," *Men, Women, and Ghosts 1916*

6 Youth condemns; maturity condones.
Tendencies in Modern American Poetry 1917

7 Let the key-guns be mounted, make a brave
show of waging war, and pry off the lid of
Pandora's box once more.
"Gun's as Keys: And the Great Gate Swings," Pt. I, *Can Grande's Castle 1918*

8 A wise man,
Watching the stars pass across the sky,
Remarked:
In the upper air the fireflies move more slowly.
"Meditation," *Picture of the Floating World 1919*

9 There are few things so futile, and few so amusing,
As a peaceful and purposeless sort of perusing
Of old random jottings set down in a blank-book
You've unearthed from a drawer as you looked for your bank-book....
"A Critical Fable," St. 1, *A Critical Fable 1922*

10 I went a-riding, a-riding,
Over a great long plain.
And the plain went a-sliding, a-sliding
Away from my bridle-rein.
"Texas," St. 1, *What's O'Clock 1925*

11 And what are we?
We, the people without a race,
Without a language;
Of all races, and of none;
Of all tongues, and one imposed;
Of all traditions and all pasts,
With no tradition and no past.
A patchwork and an altar-piece....
"The Congressional Liberty," St. 1, Ibid.

12 Love is a game—yes?
I think it is a drowning....
"Twenty-four Hokku on a Modern Theme," XIX, Ibid.

13 Sappho* would speak, I think, quite openly,
And Mrs. Browning** guard a careful silence,

But Emily*** would set doors ajar and slam them
And love you for your speed of observation.
"The Sisters," St. 2, Ibid.
*See 46; **Elizabeth Barrett B—, see 892; ***E— Dickinson, see 1024.

14 Finally, most of us believe that concentration is the very essence of poetry.
"Imagist Poetry" *n.d.*

15 Time! Joyless emblem of the greed
Of millions, robber of the best
Which earth can give ...
"New York at Night" n.d.

1441. María Martínez Sierra (1874–1974)

1 SISTER JOANNA OF THE CROSS. They say canaries are born in cages and, see, how he doesn't care to fly away.
SISTER MARÍA. Then you're a great fool, birdie. God made the air for wings and He made wings to fly with. While he might be soaring away above the clouds, he is satisfied to stay here all day shut up in his cage, hopping between two sticks and a leaf of lettuce! What sense is there in a bird?
Act I, *The Cradle Song*, with Gregorio Martínez Sierra* *1911*

2 ANTONIO. . . . there is no longer in the world either far or near.
Act II, Ibid.

3 DON GUILLERMO. When we have once peeped into the Garden of Knowledge, even at the tiniest gate, it is astounding what marvelous voyages we are able to make, and what sights we can see, without taking the trouble of leaving our chairs.
Act II, *Madame Pepita*, with Gregorio Martínez Sierra* *1912*

4 RAMÓN. Just as sure as you name a street after a man, he goes and disgraces hiD3mself afterwards ...
Act I, *Wife to a Famous Man*, with Gregorio Martínez Sierra* *1914*

5 SISTER GRACIA. It is by no will of his that some are poor and neglected while some are set up in pride. For God is Love and he loves us all and to each one he gives a share in heaven and in this earth.
FELIPE. Don't listen to her . . . she's just preaching lies to you. Nuns have all sold themselves to the rich. Do they ever go hungry? And as long as they can get us to keep up the sham they're left to stuff themselves with food in peace.
Act III, *The Kingdom of God*, with Gregorio Martínez Sierra* *1915*

6 SISTER DIONISIA. But where are you going ... what are you going to do?
FELIPE. What men do ... take by force what we can't get by asking nicely.
Ibid.

7 IRENE. He's the untidiest man in the world, and the one thing he won't stand is untidiness. That's where his secretary comes in. He'll go out leaving his writing strewn all over the place, pages unnumbered, books on the floor, torn up paper in the drawers and his notes in the waste paper basket. But when he comes back, he likes to find everything just so.
Act II, *Romantic Young Lady*, with Gregorio Martínez Sierra* *1918*
*Her husband, famed Spanish novelist, poet, essayist, theatrician (1881–1947); shortly before his death it was revealed that María

had been his constant collaborator and had, in many instances, been the principal author of their dramatic works.

1442. Dorothy Reed Mendenhall (1874–1964)

1 My early life had been fed with dreams and a deep feeling that if I waited, did my part and was patient, love would come to me and with it such a family life as fiction depicted and romance built up. It seems to me that I have always been waiting for something better—sometimes to see the best I had snatched from me.

> Quoted in "Dorothy Mendenhall: 'Childbirth is Not a Disease'" by Gena Corea, *Ms.* (New York) *April 1974*

2 When hurry in the attendant meets fear in the mother, the combination . . . militates against safe and sane obstetrics.

> Ibid.

1443. Alice Duer Miller (1874–1942)

1 And now too late, we see these things are one:
The art is sacrifice and self-control,
And who loves beauty must be stern of soul.

> "An American to France," *Welcome Home 1928*

2 Frenchmen, when
The ultimate menace comes, will die for France
Logically as they lived.

> "Forsaking All Others," XXI, *Forsaking All Others 1931*

3 When a woman like that who I've seen so much
All of a sudden drops out of touch,
Is always busy and never can
Spare you a moment, it means a Man.

> Ibid.

4 They make other nations seem pale and flighty,
But they do think England is God almighty,
And you must remind them now and then
That other countries breed other men.

> "The White Cliffs," *The White Cliffs 1940*

5 The white cliffs of Dover, I saw rising steeply
Out of the sea that once made her [England] secure.

> St. 1, Ibid.

1444. Lucy Maud Montgomery (1874–1942)

1 "There's such a lot of different Annes in me. I sometimes think that is why I'm such a troublesome person. If I was just one Anne it would be ever so much more comfortable, but then it wouldn't be half so interesting."

> Ch. 20, *Anne of Green Gables 1908*

2 "As for Horace Baxter, he was in financial difficulties a year ago last summer, and he prayed to the Lord for help; and when his wife died and he got her life insurance he said he believed it was the answer to his prayer. Wasn't that like a man?"

> Ch. 15, *Anne's House of Dreams 1917*

3 "When a man is alone he's mighty apt to be with the devil—if he ain't with God. He has to choose which company he'll keep, I reckon."

> Ibid.

4 What had seemed easy in imagination was rather hard in reality.

> Ch. XII, *Rainbow Valley 1919*

5 "Mrs. Leander Crawford is always crying in church," said Susan contemptuously. "She cries over every affecting thing the minister says. But you do not often see her name on a subscription list, Mrs. Dr. dear. Tears come cheaper."

> Ibid.

6 "The only thing I envy a cat is its purr," remarked Dr. Blythe once, listening to Doc's resonant melody. "It is the most contented sound in the world."

> Ch. I, *Rilla of Ingleside 1921*

7 Certainly, Monday's looks were not his strong point. Black spots were scattered at random over his yellow carcass, one of them blotting out an eye. His ears were in tatters, for Monday was never successful in affairs of honour. But he possessed one talisman. He knew that not all dogs could be handsome or eloquent or victorious, but that every dog could love. Inside his homely hide beat the most affectionate, loyal, faithful heart of any dog since dogs were; and something looked out of his brown eyes that was nearer akin to a soul than any theologian would allow.

> Ch. II, Ibid.

8 "We know the real charm of night here as town-dwellers never do. Every night is beautiful in the country—even the stormy ones. I love a wild night storm on this old gulf shore. As for a night like this, it is almost too beautiful—it belongs to youth and dreamland and I'm half afraid of it."

> Ch. III, Ibid.

1445. Roselle Mercier Montgomery (1874–1933)

1 I would always be with the thick of life,
Threading its mazes, sharing its strife;
Yet—somehow, singing!

> "Somehow, Singing," *Ulysses Returns 1925*

2 Never a ship sail out of the bay
But carries my heart as a stowaway.

> "The Stowaway," Ibid.

3 The fates are not quite obdurate.
They have a grim sardonic way
Of granting men who supplicate
The things they wanted—yesterday!

> "The Fates," *Many Devices 1929*

4 Companioned years have made them comprehend
The comradeship that lies beyond a kiss.

> "For a Wedding Anniversary" *n.d.*

1446. Angela Morgan (1874?–1957)

1 I'd rather have the want of you,
The rich, elusive taunt of you
Forever and forever and forever unconfessed
Than claim the alien comfort
Of any other's breast.

> "Choice," St. 2, *The Second Book of Modern Verse,* Jessie B. Rittenhouse, ed. *1919*

2 Though guns may roar and cannon boom,
Roses are born and gardens bloom

> "In Spite of War," St. 2, Ibid.

3 The signals of the century
Proclaims the things that are to be—

The rise of woman to her place,
The coming of a nobler race.

"Today," St. 3, Ibid.

4 I will hew new windows for my soul.

"Room" *n.d.*

5 Praised be the gods that made my spirit mad;
Kept me aflame and raw to beauty's touch.

"June Rapture" *n.d.*

6 Work!
Thank God for the swing of it,
For the clamoring, hammering ring of it,
Passion of labor daily hurled
On the mighty anvils of the world.

"Work: A Song of Triumph" *n.d.*

7 God, when you thought of a pine tree,
How did you think of a star?

"God, the Artist," St. 1 *n.d.*

8 Past war and reeking sod,
In the book unbound their names are found
They are known in the courts of God!

"The Unknown Solder" l.l. *n.d.*

9 Nature's plan is wondrous kind
Could we understand her mind . . .
Fools are they who call her blind.

"When Nature Wants a Man," St. 9 *n.d.*

1447. Rose O'Neill (1874–1944)

1 Remember, men of guns and rhymes,
And kings who kill so fast,
That men you kill too many times
May be too dead at last.

"When the Dead Men Die," *The Master's Mistress 1922*

2 They lose least who have least to lose.

Ch. 11 *Garda 1929*

3 Her mind was as spry as a hummingbird, but its beak was not so long for the inward flower of things. Still, she had always been looked upon as a wit; and when a creature is witty enough, he will occasionally say something that smacks of the profound.

Ibid.

4 It was not her way to invent obstacles, that blood-thinning process of the sickly imaginative.

Ch. 15, Ibid.

1448. Josephine Preston Peabody (1874–1922)

1 That you should follow our poor humanhood,
Only because you would!

"To a Dog," *Collected Poems of Josephine Preston Peabody 1927*

2 . . . The elements rehearse
Man's urgent utterance, and his words traverse
The spacious heav'ns like homing birds.

"Wireless," Ibid.

3 The little Road says, Go;
The little House says, Stay;

And oh, it's bonny here at home,
But I must go away.

"The House and the Road," Ibid.

1449. Mabel Louise Robinson (1874–1962)

1 "Can't you have sense?"
Thankful, [the girl] hurried him on. "Not if I can have anything else."

Pt. I, *Bright Island 1937*

2 What if the truth does make them sad, what if it haunts them? Better be saddened than dead.

"Writing for the Younger Generation," *The Writer's Book,* Helen Hull, ed. *1950*

3 If this generation, like those before it, repeats the blunders of the past, we might possibly be to some degree at fault.

Ibid.

4 From the dog's point of view his master is an elongated and abnormally cunning dog.

Quoted in *The New York Times* Magazine *14 May 1967*

1450. Gertrude Stein (1874–1946)

1 "You are so afraid of losing your moral sense that you are not willing to take it through anything more dangerous than a mud puddle."

"Adele," *Q. E. D.,* Bk. I *1903*

2 "I could undertake to be an efficient pupil if it were possible to find an efficient teacher."

Ibid.

3 I am writing for myself and strangers. This is the only way that I can do it.

The Making of Americans 1906–08

4 "Rose is a rose is a rose is a rose."

"Sacred Emily" *1913*

5 I suppose I pose I expose, I repose, I close the door when the sun shines so, I close the door when the wind is so strong and the dust is not there. . . .

"Mildred's Thoughts" *1922*

6 Pigeons on the grass alas.

Four Saints in Three Acts (opera) *1927*

7 "Before the flowers of friendship faded friendship faded."

Story title *1931*

8 Remarks are not literature.

*The Autobiography of Alice B. Toklas** *1933*
*See 1502.

9 She always says she dislikes the abnormal, it is so obvious. She says the normal is so much more simply complicated and interesting.

Ibid.

10 In the United States there is more space where nobody is than where anybody is. That is what makes America what it is.

The Geographical History of America 1936

11 Everybody knows if you are too careful you are so occupied in being careful that you are sure to stumble over something.

Ch. 1, *Everybody's Autobiography 1937*

12 ... native always means people who belong somewhere else, because they had once belonged somewhere. That shows that the white race does not really think they belong anywhere because they think of everybody else as a native.

Ibid.

13 ... one never discusses anything with anybody who can understand, one discusses things with people who cannot understand. . . .

Ibid.

14 ... if anything is a surprise then there is not much difference between older or younger because the only thing that does make anybody older is that they cannot be surprised.

Ch. 2, Ibid.

15 ... money ... is really the difference between men and animals, most of the things men feel animals feel and vice versa, but animals do not know about money, money is a purely human conception and that is very important to know very very important.

Ibid.

16 ... considering how dangerous everything is nothing is really very frightening.

Ibid.

17 ... what is the use of thinking if after all there is to be organization.

Ibid.

18 It takes a lot of time to be a genius, you have to sit around so much doing nothing, really doing nothing.

Ibid.

19 America is not old enough yet to get young again.

Ch. 3, Ibid.

20 Counting is the religion of this generation it is its hope and its salvation.

Ibid.

21 I understand you undertake to overthrow my undertaking.

Ibid.

22 ... I do want to get rich but I never want to do what there is to do to get rich.

Ibid.

23 ... what is the use of being a little boy if you are going to grow up to be a man.

Ch. 4, Ibid.

24 ... it is a peaceful thing to be one succeeding.

Ibid.

25 A saint a real saint never does anything, a martyr does something but a really good saint does nothing and so I wanted to have Four Saints that did nothing and I wrote the *Four Saints in Three Acts* and they did nothing and that was everything. Realistically speaking anybody is more interesting doing nothing than doing anything.

Quoted in Introduction, *Last Operas and Plays* by Carl Van Vechten* 1949

*American music critic and novelist (1880–1964).

26 Nothing has happened today except kindness. . . .

"A Diary," *Alphabets and Birthdays* 1957

27 What is the answer? (I was silent.) In that case, what is the question?

Quoted in *What Is Remembered* by Alice B. Toklas* 1963
*See 1502.

28 All of you young people who served in the war. You are a lost generation. . . .

Remark to Ernest Hemingway,* Quoted in Ch. 3, *A Moveable Feast* 1964

*American writer (1899–1961).

29 And how do you look backward. By looking forward. And what do they see. As they look forward. They see what they had to do before they could look backward. And there we have it all.

"Thoughts on an American Contemporary Feeling" (1932), *Reflection on the Atomic Bomb*, Vol. I 1973

30 Everybody gets so much information all day long that they lose their common sense.

Untitled essay (1946), Ibid.

1451. Etsu Inagaki Sugimoto (1874?–1950)

1 A careless or perturbed state of mind always betrays itself in the intricate shadings of ideographs, for each one requires absolute steadiness and accuracy of touch. Thus, in careful guidance of the hand were we children taught to hold the mind in leash.

Ch. 2, *A Daughter of the Samurai* 1925

2 "Look in the mirror every day," she said, "for if scars of selfishness or pride are in the heart, they will grow into the lines of the face. Watch closely."

Ch. 6, Ibid.

1452. Margaret Eliza Ashmun (1875–1940)

1 We are the whirlwinds that winnow the West—
We scatter the wicked like straw!
We are the Nemeses, never at rest—
We are Justice, and Right, and the Law!

"The Vigilantes," *Pacific Monthly* 1907

1453. Mary McLeod Bethune (1875–1955)

1 If our people are to fight their way up out of bondage we must arm them with the sword and the shield and the buckler of pride. . . .

"Clarifying Our Vision with the Facts," *Journal of Negro History January* 1938

2 Mr. Lincoln* had told our race we were free, but mentally we were still enslaved.

"Faith That Moved a Dump Heap," *Who, The Magazine About People June* 1941
*Abraham Lincoln (1809–1865), 16th president of the United States (1861–65); assassinated.

3 I never stop to plan. I take things step by step.

Ibid.

4 For I am my mother's daughter, and the drums of Africa still beat in my heart. They will not let me rest while there is a single Negro boy or girl without a chance to prove his worth.

Ibid.

5 "For God so loved the world, that He gave His only begotten Son, that whosoever believeth in Him should not perish, but have everlasting life." With these words the scales fell from my eyes and the light came flooding in. My sense of inferiority, my fear of handicaps, dropped away. "Whosoever," it said. No Jew nor Gentile, no Catholic nor Protestant, no black nor white; just "whosoever." It meant that I, a humble Negro girl, had just as much chance as anybody in the sight and love of God. These words stored up a battery of faith and confidence and determination in my heart, which has not failed me to this day. . . .

Ibid.

6 The true worth of a race must be measured by the character of its womanhood. . . .

Address, "A Century of Progress of Negro Women" (Chicago Women's Federation, 3 June 1933), *Black Women in White America*, Gerda Lerner,* ed. *1972*

*See 2380.

7 I leave you love . . . hope . . . the challenge of developing confidence in one another . . . a thirst for education . . . a respect for the uses of power . . . faith . . . racial dignity . . . a desire to live harmoniously with your fellow men . . . a responsibility to our young people.

Last will and testament, Quoted in "Chronicles of Black Courage" by L. Bennett, *Ebony December 1982*

1454. Anna Hempstead Branch (1875–1937)

1 His screaming stallions maned with whistling wind.

"Nimrod Wars with the Angels" *1910*

2 Oh, grieve not, ladies, if at night
Ye wake to feel your beauty going.
It was a web of frail delight,
Inconstant as an April snowing.

"Grieve Not, Ladies," St. 1 *n.d.*

3 Order is a lovely thing;
On disarray it lays its wing,
Teaching simplicity to sing.

"The Monk in the Kitchen" *n.d.*

4 God wove a web of loveliness,
Of clouds and stars and birds,
But made not anything at all
So beautiful as words.

"Songs for My Mother: Her Words," St. 5 *n.d.*

5 If there is no God for thee
Then there is no God for me.

"To a Dog" *n.d.*

1455. Abbie Farwell Brown (1875–1927)

1 No matter what my birth may be,
No matter where my lot is cast,
I am the heir in equity
Of all the precious past.

"The Heritage," St. 1 *n.d.*

2 They named their rocky farmlands,
Their hamlets by the sea,
For the mother-towns that bred them
In racial loyalty.

"Names," St. 7 *n.d.*

1456. Louise Driscoll (1875–1957)

1 Power and gold and fame denied,
Love laughs glad in the paths aside.

"The Highway" *n.d.*

2 There you will find what
Every man needs,
Wild religion
Without any creeds.

"Spring Market," St. 5 *n.d.*

3 Some men die early and are spared much care,
Some suddenly, escaping worse than death;
But he is fortunate who happens where
He can exult and die in the same breath.

"The Good Hour" *n.d.*

1457. Alice Ruth Dunbar-Nelson (1875–1935)

1 In its dark bosom many secrets lie buried. It is like some beautiful serpent, languorous, sinister. It ripples in the sunshine, sparkles in the moonlight, glooms in the dusk and broods in the dark. But it thinks unceasingly, and below its brightest sparkle you feel its unknown soul.

Sketch about a Louisiana bayou, *The Schomburg Library of Nineteenth-Century Black Women Writers*, Henry Louis Gates, Jr., ed. *1988*

1458. Elie Faure (1875–1937)

1 The stamping out of the artist is one of the blind goals of every civilization. When a civilization becomes so standardized that the individual can no longer make an imprint on it, then that civilization is dying. The "mass mind" has taken over and another set of national glories is heading for history's scrap heap.

Quoted in *Forbes* magazine *n.d.*

1459. Minnie Haskins (1875–1957)

1 And I said to the man who stood at the gate of the year:
"Give me a light that I may tread safely into the Unknown."
And he replied: "Go out into the darkness and put your hand
Into the hand of God. That shall be to you better than light
And safer than a known way."

"The Desert" *1908*

1460. Helen Huntington (1875?–1950)

1 With the bitter past I will deck to-morrow.

"The Wayfarer" *n.d.*

1461. Marie Lenéru (1875–1940)

1 One *sees* intelligence far more than one hears it. People do not always say transcendental things, but if they are *capable* of saying them, it is always visible.

Journal 1945

2 If I were honest, I would admit that money is one half of happiness; it makes it so much more attractive!

(1898), Ibid.

3 Isolation has led me to reflection, reflection to doubt, doubt to a more sincere and intelligent love of God.

Ibid.

4 I have discovered that in an intellectual society individual intelligence is no more frequent than anywhere else, and its absence is more tedious, for not to speak in a superior manner of superior subjects is both boring and ridiculous.

Ibid.

5 To succeed is nothing, it's an accident. But to feel no doubts about oneself is something very different: it is character.

Ibid.

1462. Belle Livingstone (1875–1957)

1 That winter two things happened which made me see that the world, the flesh, and the devil were going to be more powerful influences in my life after all than the chapel bell. First, I tasted champagne; second, the theater.

Belle Out of Order 1959

2 Like Moses, I wasn't born. I was found.

Pt. I, Ch. 1, *Ibid.*

3 Odd how the erotic appeal has swung away from legs; today a smart girl takes her legs for granted and gets herself a good sweater.

Ch. 2, *Ibid.*

4 The courtesan, alas, is gone, extinct as the American buffalo . . . . Anyone can become a mistress; one has to be born a courtesan.

Ibid.

5 Much has been written about the beauty, the stillness, the terror of the desert but little about its flies.

Ch. 5, *Ibid.*

6 Oddly enough, a gambler never entertains the thought of loss. He can't afford to. No one who has never gambled can possibly understand the projects, plans, dreams a gambler can create on the turn of a card or the chance of a horse going to the post.

Ch. 9, *Ibid.*

1463. Anne Henrietta Martin (1875–1951)

1 The movement to enfranchise Nevada's women and give them full electoral and constitutional rights with men is not exclusively local, nor is it sporadic or ephemeral. It is part of the great world movement for democracy and freedom which is one of the dominant characteristics of the history of the nineteenth century, the realization of which will be the crowning achievement of the twentieth century.

"Woman Suffrage", *The History of Nevada,* Vol. II, Sam P. Davis, ed. *1912*

2 When a democracy based on human instead of sex-rights is established, there will be less waste and destruction of human material by blind government Juggernauts which cannot see their goal, there will be more and more conservation of human and social forces, and greater usefulness and happiness for a far greater number. We are living in great and stirring times.

Ibid.

1464. Vilda Sauvage Owens (1875–1950)

1 If ever I have time for things that matter,
If ever I have the smallest chance,
I'm going to live in
Little Broom Gardens,

Moat-by-the-Castle,
Nettlecomb, Hants.

"If Ever I Have Time for Things That Matter," St. 1 *n.d.*

1465. Qui Jin (1875–1907)

1 A country's salvation relies on exceptional genius.
I pledge the spilled blood from a hundred thousand skulls
To restore the universe with all our strength.

Untitled poem, 1904

2 Autumn rain, autumn wind; my heart dies of sorrow.

Death poem 1907

3 Today the two hundred million men in our country are entering into a civilized new world . . . but we, the two hundred million women, are still kept down in the dungeon.

Remark (1907), Quoted in *Women in World History Curriculum* (womeninworldhistory.com) *1996–97*

1466. Christopher Marie St. John (1875?–1960)

1 WINIFRED. The majority of men in this country shouldn't for years have kept alive the foolish superstition that all women are supported by men. For years we have told them it was a delusion, but they could not take our arguments seriously.

How the Vote Was Won 1909

1467. Anne Goodwin Winslow (1875–1959)

1 And how can curses make him yours
When kisses could not make him so?

"The Beaten Path" *n.d.*

1468. Josephine Dodge Bacon (1876–1961)

1 "Girls, it isn't likely that we'll win, *but we can give 'em something to beat!*"

"The Emotions of a Sub-Guard," *Smith College Stories 1900*

2 You musn't say anything that won't be perfectly true when he's grown up, you see. It's learning two sets of things that makes a child distrust you.

Ch. 6, *The Memoirs of a Baby 1904*

3 You mark my words, Toots, if you ever hear a darn-fool thing to-day, you can make up your mind some woman said it that writes books. . . . It ought to be a crime for any woman to have children that writes books.

Ch. 2, *The Biography of a Boy 1910*

4 I do not see how there can be any real respect,
Or any real privacy such as women love,
When you marry a man.
A man makes trouble.

Ch. 20, *Truth o' Women 1923*

5 To you in reality dead,
Dragging your bodies after you,
Persistently vital,
I say this:
Death will come. Be patient.

Ch. 42, *Ibid.*

1469. Elizabeth Baker (1876–1962)

1 MAGGIE. Office work is awf'lly monotonous.
MRS. MASSEY. Of course it is. So is all work. Do you expect work to be pleasant? Does anybody ever like work? The idea

is absurd. Anyone would think work was to be pleasant. You don't come into the world to have pleasure. We've got to do our duty, and the more cheerfully we can do it, the better for ourselves and everybody else.

Act III, *Chains 1909*

1470. Natalie Clifford Barney (1876–1972)

1 Renouncement: the heroism of mediocrity.

"Gods," *Adam*, No. 299 1962

2 Would that well-thinking people should be replaced by thinking ones.

Ibid.

3 Eternity—waste of time.

Ibid.

4 It is time for dead languages to be quiet.

"On Writing and Writers," Ezra Pound,* tr. (from French), Ibid.
*American poet, critic (1885–1972).

5 Why grab possessions like thieves, or divide them like socialists when you can ignore them like wise men?

"My Country 'tis of Thee," Ibid.

6 The advantage of love at first sight is that it delays a second sight.

"Samples from Almost Illegible Notebooks," Ibid.

7 Youth is not a question of years: one is young or old from birth.

Ibid.

8 If we keep an open mind, too much is likely to fall into it.

Ibid.

9 Fatalism is the lazy man's way of accepting the evitable.

Ch. 10, Quoted in *The Amazon of Letters* by George Wickes *1976*

10 Lovers should also have their days off.

Ibid.

1471. Mary Ritter Beard (1876–1958)

1 The prosecution of modern wars rests completely upon the operation of labor in mines, mills and factories, so that labor fights there just as truly as the soldiers do in the trenches.

Ch. 1, *A Short History of the American Labor Movement 1920*

2 The trade agreement has become a rather distinct feature of the American labor movement. It does not represent any revolutionary tendency in industry. It is based on the idea that labor shall accept the capitalist system of production and makes terms of peace with it.

Ch. 9, Ibid.

3 Viewed narrowly, all life is universal hunger and an expression of energy associated with it.

Ch. 1, *Understanding Women 1931*

4 In matters pertaining to the care of life there has been no marked gain over Greek and Roman antiquity.

Ch. 5, Ibid.

5 In other words, those who sit at the feast will continue to enjoy themselves even though the veil that separates them from the world of toiling reality below has been lifted by mass revolts and critics.

Ch. 6, Ibid.

6 The dogma of women's complete historical subjection to men must be rated as one of the most fantastic myths ever created by the human mind.

Woman as a Force in History 1946

7 Beneath the surface of civilian interests and capitalistic enterprises smoldered embers of the world's war spirit—humanity's traditional flare—now to be inflamed by new instruments for fighting and the associated aspiration for world trade and world power.

Ch. 9, *The Force of Women in Japanese History 1963*

1472. Anne Bronaugh (1876–1961)

1 Life is a patchwork—here and there,
Scraps of pleasure and despair
Join together, hit or miss.

"Patchwork" *n.d.*

1473. Sarah Norcliffe Cleghorn (1876–1959)

1 The golf links lie so near the mill
That almost every day
The laboring children can look out
And watch the men at play.

"The Conning Tower," *New York Herald Tribune 1 January 1915*

2 Since more than half my hopes came true
And more than half my fears
Are but the pleasant laughing-stock
Of these my middle years . . .
Shall I not bless the middle years?
Not I for youth repine
While warmly round me cluster lives
More dear to me than mine.

"Contented at Forty" *1916*

3 Come, Captain Age,
With your great sea-chest full of treasure!
Under the yellow and wrinkled tarpaulin
Disclose the carved ivory
And the sandalwood inlaid with pearl:
Riches of wisdom and years.

"Come, Captain Age," *Three Score 1936*

4 "The unfit die—the fit both live and thrive."
Alas, who say so? They who do survive.

"Survival of the Fittest" *n.d.*

1474. Susan Glaspell (1876/82–1948)

1 STEPHEN. If you're going to separate from psychoanalysis, there's no reason why I should separate from you!
MABEL. What am I supposed to do with my suppressed desires?
STEPHEN. Mabel, you just keep right on suppressing them!

Suppressed Desires 1914

2 HENRIETTA. It is through suppression that hells are formed in us.

Sc. 1, Ibid.

3   MABEL. Why, if it wasn't for psychoanalysis you'd never find
    out how wonderful your own mind is!

    Sc. 2, Ibid.

4   "We all go through the same things—it's all just a different
    kind of the same thing!"

    "A Jury of Her Peers," *Every Week* 1917

5   GRANDMOTHER. That's the worst of a war—you have to go
    on hearing about it so long.

    Act I, *Inheritors* 1921

6   GRANDMOTHER. Seems nothing draws men together like
    killing other men.

    Ibid.

7   HOLDEN. And I think a society which permits things to go on
    which I can prove go on in our federal prisons had better stop
    and take a fresh look at itself. To stand for that and then talk
    of democracy and idealism—oh, it shows no mentality, for one
    thing.

    Act. II, Sc. 2, Ibid.

8   A new town was only the same town in a different place. . . .

    "His Smile," *The Pictorial Review* 1921

1475. Mata Hari (1876–1917)

1   The dance is a poem of which each movement is a word.

    Scrapbook 1905

2   The [military] officer is a being apart, a kind of artist breathing
    the grand air in the brilliant profession of arms, in a uniform
    that is always seductive. . . . To me the officer is a separate
    race.

    Life 1906

3   I firmly believe that the only means of living in beauty consists
    in avoiding the thousand and one daily annoyances which in-
    terfere with an existence in the full ideal.

    Quoted in *Mata Hari* by Major Thomas Coulson, O.B.E.
    (1917) 1930 *(reissue)*

1476. Norah M. Holland (1876–1925)

1   Life has given me of its best—
    Laughter and weeping, labour and rest,
    Little of gold, but lots of fun;
    Shall I then sigh that all is done?

    "Life" *n.d.*

1477. Sally Kinsolving (1876–1962)

1   Ships, young ships,
    I do not wonder men see you as women—
    You in the white length of your loveliness
    Reclining on the sea!

    "Ships," *Many Waters* 1942

1478. Mary Sinton Leitch (1876–1954)

1   And deaf, he sings of nightingales
    Or, blind, he sings of stars.

    "The Poet" *n.d.*

2   He who loves the ocean
    And the ways of ships

May taste beside a mountain pool
Brine on his lips.

    "He Who Loves the Ocean" *n.d.*

3   While far below men crawl in clay and cold,
    Sublimely I shall stand alone with God.

    "The Summit, Mt. Everest" *n.d.*

1479. Grace Fallow Norton (1876–1926)

1   I have loved many, the more and the few—
    I have loved many that I might love you.

    "Song of the Sum of All" *n.d.*

2   Take me upon thy breast,
    O River of Rest.
    Draw me down to thy side,
    Slow-moving tide.

    "O Sleep" *n.d.*

3   "O would I were free as the wind on wing;
        Love is a terrible thing!"

    "Love Is a Terrible Thing" *n.d.*

1480. Mary Roberts Rinehart (1876–1958)

1   Conscription may form a great and admirable machine, but it
    differs from the trained army of volunteers as a body differs
    from a soul. But it costs a country heavy in griefs, does a vol-
    unteer army; for the flower of the country goes.

    Introduction, *Kings, Queens, and Pawns* 1915

2   It is easier to die than to send a son to death.

    Ch. 37, Ibid.

3   "You're a perfect child, a stubborn child! Your mind's in pig-
    tails, like your hair."

    "The Family Friend," *Affinities and Other Stories* 1920

4   LIZZIE. I've stood by you through thick and thin—I stood by
    you when you were a Vegetarian—I stood by you when you
    were a Theosophist—and I seen you through Socialism, Fletch-
    erism and Rheumatism—but when it comes to carrying on
    with ghosts—

    Sc. 1, *The Bat* (play based on her novel, *The Circular
    Staircase*, 1908), with James Avery Hopwood 1920

5   The great God endows His children variously. To some He
    gives intellect—and they move the earth. To some he allots
    heart—and the beating pulse of humanity is theirs. But to
    some He gives only a soul, without intelligence—and these,
    who never grow up, but remain always His children, are God's
    fools, kindly, elemental, simple, as if from His palette the Artist
    of all had taken one colour instead of many.

    "God's Fool," *Love Stories* 1920

6   But it is interesting to see how the Socialist becomes the con-
    servative when given power; Mussolini, Briand, Masaryk,* all
    considered radicals at one time. Or is it that our own ideas
    change, and that we are after all moving slowly toward a
    greater justice?

    Ch. 40, *My Story* 1931
    *Benito M - , a.k.a. "Il Duce," Italian Fascist dictator and prime
    minister from 1922–1943 (1883–1945); Aristide B— , French poli-
    tician who became prime minister for the first of 11 times in 1909
    (1862–1932); Tomáš Garrigue M—, Czech politician who served
    as the first president of independent Czechoslovakia from 1918–
    1935 (1850–1937).

1481. Helen Rowland (1876–1950)

1 Woman: the peg on which the wit hangs his jest, the preacher his text, the cynic his grouch, and the sinner his justification.

Reflections of a Bachelor Girl 1903

2 When you see what some girls marry, you realize they must hate to work for a living

Ibid.

3 Love, the quest; marriage, the conquest; divorce, the inquest.

Ibid.

4 It takes a woman twenty years to make a man of her son, and another woman twenty minutes to make a fool of him.

Ibid.

5 A husband is what is left of a lover, after the nerve has been extracted.

"Prelude," *A Guide to Men 1922*

6 A fool and her money are soon courted.

"First Interlude," Ibid.

7 Falling in love consists merely in uncorking the imagination and bottling the common-sense.

"Variations," Ibid.

8 At twenty, a man feels awfully aged and blasé; at thirty, almost senile; at forty, "not so old"; and at fifty, positively skittish.

"Personally Speaking," *The Book of Diversion,* F. P. Adams, D. Taylor, and J. Bechdolt, eds. *1925*

9 Alas, why will a man spend months trying to hand over his liberty to a woman—and the rest of his life trying to get it back again?

Ibid.

10 Marriage is the only thing that affords a woman the pleasure of company and the perfect sensation of solitude at the same time.

Ibid.

11 The woman who appeals to a man's vanity may stimulate him; the woman who appeals to his heart may attract him; but it's the woman who appeals to his imagination who *gets* him.

Ibid.

1482. Githa Sowerby (1876–1970)

1 RUTHERFORD. When men steal, Martin, they do it to gain something.

Rutherford & Son 1912

2 JANET. Me a lady? What do ladies think about, sitting the day long with their hands before them? What have they in their idle hearts? . . . The women down there [in the village] know what I wanted . . . I've envied them their pain, their poorness—the very times they hadn't bread. Theirs isn't the empty house, the blank o' the moors; they got something to fight, something to be feared of. They got life, those women we send cans o' soup to out o' pity when their bairns are born.

Ibid.

3 RUTHERFORD. Life! I've had nigh on sixty years of it, and I'll tell you. Life's work—keeping your head up and your heels

down. Sleep, begetting children, rearing them up to work when you're gone—that's life. And when you know better than the God that made you, you can begin to ask what you're going to get by it. And you'll get more work and six foot of earth at the end of it.

Ibid.

1483. Elinore Pruitt Stewart (1876–1933)

1 I am very enthusiastic about women homesteading. . . . Any woman who can stand her own company, can see the beauty of the sunset, loves growing things, and is willing to put in as much time at careful labor as she does over the washtub, will certainly succeed; will have independence, plenty to eat all the time, and a home of her own in the end.

Article, *Atlantic Monthly* (Boston) *1913*

2 I had not thought I should ever marry again. Jerrine was always such a dear little pal, and I wanted to just knock about footloose and free to see life as a gypsy sees it. I had planned to see the Cliff-Dwellers' home; to live right there until I caught the spirit of the surrounding enough to live over their lives in imagination anyway. I had planned to see the old missions and to go to Alaska; to hunt in Canada. I even dreamed of Honolulu. Life stretched out before me one long, happy jaunt. I aimed to see all the world I could, but to travel unknown by-paths to do it.

Letters of a Woman Homesteader 1914

3 I have had more than half a century of such happiness. A great deal of worry and sorrow, too, but never a worry or sorrow that was not offset by a purple iris, a lark, a bluebird, or a dewy morning glory.

Letter to a friend, Quoted in *Women Pioneers* by Rebecca Stefoff *1995*

1484. Helen L. Sumner (1876–1933)

1 . . . the history of women's work in this country shows that legislation has been the only force which has improved the working conditions of any large number of women wage-earners.

Senate Report, *History of Women in Industry in the United States,* Vol. IX *1911*

2 The story of women's work in gainful employment is a story of constant changes or shifting of work and workshop, accompanied by long hours, low wages, insanitary conditions, overwork, and the want on the part of the woman of training, skill, and vital interest in her work.

Ibid.

1485. Bertye Young Williams (1876–1951)

1 He who follows Beauty
Breaks his foolish heart.

"*Song Against Beauty*" *n.d.*

1486. Gwendolen Willis (1876–1969)

1 When we write the history of our feminists we must begin not with them but with their mothers.

Quoted by Nancy S. Prichard in a letter to Elaine Bernstein Partnow* from Unitarian Universalist Women's Federation *17 December 1981*

*See 3291.

1487. Katharine Anthony (1877–1965)

1   Personal ambitions and disappointments, personal desire and weaknesses, personal shrewdness or slackness play their part in these narrow homes as they do in more spacious ones.
Ch. 8, *Mothers Who Must Earn* 1914

2   The cult of "arms and the man" must reckon with a newer cult, that of "schools and the woman." Schools, which exalt brains above brawn, and women, who exalt life-giving above life-taking, are the natural allies of the present era.
Ch. 2, *Feminism in Germany and Scandinavia* 1915

3   There can be no doubt as to who began the literary war between the sexes. Also there is no comparison between the severity and harshness of the tone of criticism in the opposing camps. If we search the polemic writings of the most militant feminists, we can nowhere find expressions which compare in venom and ruthlessness with the woman-hating sentiments of certain medieval "saints" and modern "philosophers."
Ch. 9, Ibid.

4   The generosity of childless people toward the children of near relatives and favorite friends strikes one as mere justice and propriety, after all, and such voluntary acts of evening-up between one generation and the next are not at all uncommon among the families and classes who can afford to be kind.
Preface, *The Endowment of Motherhood* 1920

5   Principles are a dangerous form of social dynamite. . . .
Introduction, Ibid.

6   Foremost among the barriers to equality is the system which ignores the mother's service to Society in making a home and rearing children. The mother is still the unchartered servant of the future, who receives from her husband, at *his* discretion, a share in *his* wages.
Ibid.

7   To the biographer all lives bar none are dramatic constructions.
"Writing Biography," *The Writer's Book*, Helen Hull, ed. 1950

1488. Teresa Billington-Greig (1877–1964)

1   No passing of legal enactments can set free a woman with a slave mind.
The Militant Suffrage Movement: Emancipation in a Hurry 1911

2   The only time that power changes hands, there is a struggle.
Ibid.

3   It will be the fact that women are in revolt, rather than the revolt itself, which will win the day.
Ibid.

1489. Katherine Dunlap Cather (1877–1926)

1   Wherever there is no written language, wherever the people are too unlettered to read what is written, they still believe the legends. They love to hear them told and retold. . . . As it is with unlettered peasants today, as it was with tribesmen in primitive times and the great in medieval castle halls, it still is with the child.
(pp. 5–6), *Educating by Story-telling* 1918

2   When the time of rising came, I climbed joyfully into my mother's warm bed, and never did I listen to more beautiful fairy tales than at those hours. They became instinct with life to me and have always remained so. . . . It is a singular thing that actual events which happened in those early days have largely vanished from my memory, but the fairy tales I heard and secretly experienced became firmly impressed on my mind.
(p. 22), Ibid.

1490. Grace Noll Crowell (1877–1969)

1   I am one ever journeying toward the "light that never was on land or sea," and yet ever beckons one onward and upward to the glory ahead.
Foreword, "Focus," St. 7, *Grace Noll Crowell* 1938

2   The woman who can move about a house,
Whether it be a mansion or a camp,
And deftly lay a fire, and spread a cloth,
And light a lamp,
And by the magic of a quick touch give
The look of home wherever she may be—
Such a woman always will seem great
And beautiful to me.
"The Home Makers," St. 1 *n.d.*

3   God wrote His loveliest poem on the day
He made the first tall silver poplar tree.
"Silver Poplars," St. 1 *n.d.*

1491. Isabelle Eberhardt (1877–1904)

1   For those who know the value and the exquisite taste of solitary freedom (for one is only free when alone), the act of leaving is the bravest and most beautiful of all.
Journal entry, Quoted in *The Destiny of Isabelle Eberhardt* by Cecily Mackworth 1975

2   I love to dive into the bath of street life, the waves of the crowds flowing over me, to impregnate myself with the fluids of the people.
Ibid.

3   Death does not frighten me, but dying obscurely and above all uselessly does.
Ibid.

1492. Rose Fyleman (1877–1957)

1   The queen—now can you guess who that could be
(She's a little girl by day, but at night she steals away)?
Well—it's me!
"The Fairies," St. 3 *n.d.*

2   The Fairies have never a penny to spend,
They haven't a thing put by,
But theirs is the dower of bird and of flower,
And theirs are the earth and the sky.
"The Fairies Have Never a Penny to Spend," St. 1 *n.d*

3   I wish I liked rice pudding,
I wish I were a twin,
I wish some day a real live fairy
Would just come walking in.
Ibid.

1493. Virginia Gildersleeve (1877–1965)

1   Medicine is a profession which naturally appeals deeply to women, as they are instinctively concerned with conserving life.
"The Advancement of Women," *Many a Good Crusade* 1954

2 Now our witch-hunters are trying to drive students and teachers into conformity with a rigid concept of Americanism defined by ignorant and irresponsible politicians. If we do not check this movement, we shall become a totalitarian state like the Fascist and Communist models and our colleges and universities will produce frightened rabbits instead of scholars with free minds.

"The Inescapable Desert," Ibid.

3 The delicate first moment of dawn, before its mystery is invaded by the clatter of daily living, the bright hour of sunset before it is quenched in darkness, the last days of health unbroken, the last year of man's assurance that his civilization moves "ever upward and onward"—these are the moments, hours, days, years that have for us a poignant significance.

"The Turning of the Tide," Ibid.

1494. Mary Barnett Gilson (1877–1959)

1 Men's minds must be free, and that means the minds of all, not the minds of a select few.

What's Past Is Prologue: Reflections on My Industrial Experience 1940

2 The matter of consulting experienced workers, of keeping all the workers informed of changes . . . and how the changes are arrived at, seems to me the most important duty in the whole field of management.

Ibid.

3 To find ways of practicing democracy, not ways of orating about it, is our great problem.

Ibid.

4 The higher one climbs the lonelier one is.

Ibid.

5 How much time, approximately, can a worker in a hectic, speeded-up world give to his work and be a sane, all-round, informed, and recreated citizen? Unless he lives near his work, due allowance must be made for going and coming. Eight hours for sleep and eight hours for family and social life, education, recreation, and other activities which include, in the case of many women workers, keeping house and clothes in order and taking care of a family, and in the case of all workers, occasional visits to dentists and doctors, paying gas bills and the thousand and one other things an increasingly complicated life thrusts upon even the humblest, seem minimal for the "mechanics of living."

Ch. 17, Ibid.

1495. Mathilda von Kemnitz (1877–?)

1 Since the fundamental principle of eroticism imperiously governs every human life, since the manner of the first erotic happiness determines in a far-reaching manner the laws of the individual's eroticism throughout his entire life, the majority of men have become entirely incapable of concentrating their erotic will consistently on one human being; therefore, they have become incapable of monogamy.

The Triumph of the Immortal Will 1932

2 The man experiences the highest unfolding of his creative powers not through asceticism but through sexual happiness.

Ibid.

1496. Marian Le Sueur (1877–1954)

1 The American destiny is what our fathers dreamed, a land of the free, and the home of the brave; but only the brave can be free. Science has made the dream of today's reality for all the earth if we have the courage and vision to build it. American Democracy must furnish the engineers of world plenty—the builders of world peace and freedom.

Quoted in *Crusaders* by Meridel Le Sueur* 1955
*Her daughter; see 1911.

1497. Anne Shannon Monroe (1877–1942)

1 I have never been much cheered by the "stenciled smile," the false front, the pretending that there was no trouble when trouble stalked, that there was no death when Death laid his cold hand upon one dearer to us than life: but I have been tremendously cheered by the *brave* front; the imagination that could travel past the trouble and see that there were still joys in the world. . . .

Ch. 1, *Singing in the Rain,* with Adolph Green 1926

2 For loneliness is but cutting adrift from our moorings and floating out to the open sea; an opportunity for finding ourselves, our *real* selves, what we are about, where we are heading during our little time on this beautiful earth.

Ch. 6, Ibid.

3 "Don't get hung up on a snag in the stream, my dear. Snags alone are not so dangerous—it's the debris that clings to them that makes the trouble. Pull yourself loose and go on."

Ch. 13, Ibid.

1498. Maude Royden (1877–1956)

1 The belief that the personality of men and women are of equal dignity in the sight of God is necessary to a right moral standard.

The Church and Woman ca. 1920

1499. Rosika Schwimmer (1877–1948)

1 I am no uncompromising pacifist. . . . I have no sense of nationalism, only a cosmic consciousness of belonging to the human family.

Court testimony, Citizenship Hearing 1928

2 Women's rights, men's rights—human rights—all are threatened by the ever-present spectre of war so destructive now of human material and moral values as to render victory indistinguishable from defeat.

Speech, Centennial Celebration of Seneca Falls Convention of Women's Rights *July 1948*

3 Women's function of homemaker, we once dreamed, would extend into politics and economics our highest creative and conserving instincts. Let us go back to the task of building that safe, decent and wholesome home for the entire human family to which we once pledged ourselves.

Ibid.

4 We who successfully freed half of the human race without violence must now undertake with equal devotion, perseverance and intelligence the supreme act of human statesmanship involved in the creation of institutions of government on a world scale.

Ibid.

1500. Elizabeth Shane (1877–1951)

1 He's gone to school, wee Hughie,
An' him not four,

Sure I saw the fright was in him
When he left the door.

"Wee Hughie" 1947

2 But every road is tough to me
That has no friend to cheer it.

"Sheskinbeg" *n.d.*

1501. Laura Simmons (1877–1949)
1 The face within that passport book
Will rise to haunt you yet.

"Your Passport Picture" *n.d.*

1502. Alice B. Toklas (1877–1967)
1 What is sauce for the goose may be sauce for the gander, but it is not necessarily sauce for the chicken, the duck, the turkey, or the guinea hen.

The Alice B. Toklas Cook Book 1954

2 Re "Haschich Fudge": This is the food of Paradise. . . . it might provide an entertaining refreshment for a Ladies' Bridge Club or a chapter meeting of the DAR. . . . Euphoria and brilliant storms of laughter; ecstatic reveries and extensions of one's personality on several simultaneous planes are to be complacently expected.

Ibid.

3 Take 1 teaspoon black peppercorns, 1 whole nutmeg, 4 average sticks of cinnamon, 1 teaspoon coriander. These should all be pulverized in a mortar. About a handful each of stone dates, dried figs, shelled almonds and peanuts: chop these and mix them together. A bunch of canibus sativa can be pulverized. This along with the spices should be dusted over the mixed fruit and nuts, kneaded together. About a cup of sugar dissolved in a big pat of butter. Rolled into a cake and cut into pieces or made into balls about the size of a walnut, it should be eaten with care. Two pieces are quite sufficient. Obtaining the canibus may present certain difficulties. . . . It should be picked and dried as soon as it has gone to seed and while the plant is still green.

Recipe for Haschich Fudge, Ibid.

4 I am staying on here alone now.*
Letter to Julian Beck (8 September 1946), *Staying On Alone,*
Ed Burns, ed. Ibid.
*Her partner Gertrude Stein (see 1450) had recently died.

5 Well, I've gotten to the end of the subject—of the page—of your patience and my time.
Letter to Elizabeth Hansen (19 July 1949), 1973.

6 Haven't you learned yet that it isn't age but lack of experience that makes us fall off ladders or have radiators fall on us.
Letter to Princess Dilkusha de Rohan (5 March 1955), Ibid.

7 . . . the past is not gone—nor is Gertrude.*
Letter to Samuel Steward (7 August 1958), Ibid.
*Gertrude Stein; see 1450.

8 Dawn comes slowly but dusk is rapid.
Letter to Virginia Knapik (9 August 1958), Ibid.

1503. Elizabeth Arden (1878–1966)
1 The great days of the salons are over.
"I Am a Famous Woman in This Industry," *Fortune* October 1938

2 Nothing that costs only a dollar is worth having.
Quoted in "In Cosmetics the Old Mystique is No Longer Enough" by Eleanore Carruth, Ibid.

1504. Florence Ayscough (1878–1942)
1 Ideals determine government, and government determines social life, and social life, with all that the term connotes, is the essence of every literature.
Introduction, *Fir-Flower Tablets 1921*

1505. Eleanor Robson Belmont (1878–1979)
1 I was trained by my husband. He said, "If you want a thing done—go. If not—send." I belong to that group of people who move the piano themselves.
Quoted in *The New York Times* 18 December 1960

2 A private railroad car is not an acquired taste. One takes to it immediately.
The Fabric of Memory 1957

3 An actor must communicate his author's given message—comedy, tragedy, serio-comedy; then comes his unique moment, as he is confronted by the looked-for, yet at times unexpected, reaction of the audience. This split second is his; he is in command of his medium; the effect vanishes into thin air; but that moment has a power all its own and, like power in any form, is stimulating and alluring.

Ibid.

4 Never be afraid to meet to the hilt the demand of either work or friendship—two of life's major assets.
Pt. I, Ch. 4, Ibid.

5 In retrospect, the past seems not one existence with a continuous flow of years and events that follow each other in logical sequence, but a life periodically dividing into entirely separate compartments. Change of surroundings, interests, pursuits, has made it seem actually more like different incarnations.
Quoted in her obituary 24 October 1979

1506. Mary Grant Bruce (1878–1958)
1 "An' town ladies can't never compre'end country children, any'ow. Our little maid's jus' grown up like a bush flower, an' all the better she is for it."
Ch. I, *Mates at Billabong 1911*

2 "It's the most extraordinary place I was ever at," he told himself later, dressing for dinner, in the seclusion of his own room. . . . "Absolutely no class limits whatever, and no restrictions—why, she kept me waiting for my second cup while she looked after that fat old black in the dirty white turban!"
Ch. XI, Ibid.

1507. Amelia Burr (1878–1940?)
1 Because I have loved life, I shall have no sorrow to die.
"A Song of Living," St. 3, *Life and Living 1916*

2 Spring comes laughing down the valley
All in white, from the snow
Where the winter's armies rally
Loath to go.

"New Life," Ibid.

3 Swift and sure go the lonely feet,
And the single eye seems cold and true,

And the road that has room and to spare for one
May be sorely narrow for two.

"The Lovers" *n.d.*

1508. Hattie Wyatt Caraway (1878–1950)

1 I haven't the heart to take a minute away from the men. The poor dears love it so.*

Remark (1932), *Silent Hattie Speaks, The Personal Journal of Senator Hattie Caraway 1979*

*Re her never having made a speech in the Senate.

2 The time has passed when a woman should be placed in a position and kept there only while someone else is being groomed for the job.

Ibid.

1509. Grace H. Conkling (1878–1958)

1 I have an understanding with the hills.

"After Sunset" *n.d.*

2 The forest looks the way
Nightingales sound.

"Frost on a Window" *n.d.*

3 To build the trout a crystal stair.

"The Whole Duty of Berkshire Brooks" *n.d.*

4 Invisible beauty has a world so brief
A flower can say it or a shaken leaf,
But few may ever snare it in a song.

"After Sunset" *n.d.*

1510. Adelaide Crapsey (1878–1914)

1 These be
Three silent things:
The falling snow . . . the hour
Before the dawn . . . the mouth of one
Just dead.

"Cinquain: Triad" *n.d.*

2 Wouldst thou find my ashes? Look
In the pages of my book;
And, as this thy hands doth turn,
Know here is my funeral urn.

"The Immortal Residue" *n.d.*

3 Is it as plainly in our living shown,
By slant and twist, which way the wind hath blown?

"On Seeing Weather-Beaten Trees" *n.d.*

1511. Rachel Crothers (1878–1958)

1 WELLS (reading a book review). Her first work attracted wide attention when we thought Frank Ware was a man, but now that we know she is a woman we are more than ever impressed by the strength and scope of her work.

Act I, *A Man's World 1910*

1512. Isadora Duncan (1878–1927)

1 You were once wild here. Don't let them tame you!

Curtain speech, Symphony Hall (Boston) *1922*

2 . . . [I] would rather live in Russia on black bread and vodka than in the United States at the best hotels. America knows nothing of food, love, or art.

Interview aboard ship *1922*

3 . . . when I listened to music the rays and vibrations of the music streamed to this one fount of light within me—there they reflected themselves in Spiritual Vision, not the brain's mirror, but the soul's, and from the vision I could express them in Dance. . . .

My Life 1927

4 I have discovered the dance. I have discovered the art which has been lost for two thousand years.

Ibid.

5 Any intelligent woman who reads the marriage contract, and then goes into it, deserves all the consequences.

Ibid.

6 No composer has yet caught this rhythm of America—it is too mighty for the ears of most.

Ibid.

7 It seems to me monstrous that anyone should believe that the jazz rhythm expresses America. Jazz rhythm expresses the primitive savage.

Ch. 30, Ibid.

8 The whole world is absolutely brought up on lies. We are fed nothing but lies. It begins with lies and half our lives we live with lies.

"Memoirs" (1924), *This Quarter* (Paris) *Autumn 1929*

9 So long as little children are allowed to suffer, there is no true love in this world.

Ibid.

10 Art is not necessary at all. All that is necessary to make this world a better place to live in is to love—to love as Christ loved, as Buddha loved.

Ibid.

1513. Lillian Moller Gilbreth (1878–1962)

1 . . . the base of his* favorite concept which was "the quest of the one best way."

"Pioneers in Improvement and our Modern Standard of Living", *IW/SI News #18* (also see gilbrethnetwork.tripod. com) *September 1968*

*Ref. Her husband Frank G— (1868–1924), Am. engineer.

2 The things which concerned him more than anything else were the what and the why—the what because he felt it was necessary to know absolutely what you were questioning and what you were doing or what concerned you, and then the why, the depth type of thinking which showed you the reason for doing the thing and would perhaps indicate clearly whether you should maintain what was being done or should change what was being done.

Ibid.

3 I have had more in twenty years than any other woman I have known has had in a lifetime.*

Ibid.

*Ref. The death of her husband in 1924.

1514. Lise Meitner (1878–1968)

1 Women have a great responsibility . . . to try . . . to prevent another war. I hope . . . that we will be able to use this great [atomic] energy . . . for peaceful work.

Frontspiece, Quoted in *Twentieth-Century Women Scientists* by Lisa Yount *1996*

2 It is an unfortunate accident that this discovery [fission] came about in time of war. . . . You must not blame us scientists for the use to which war technicians have put our discoveries.*
Interview, Ibid.

*Her oft-said response about the atomic bomb.

3 It's tempting to speculate . . . about uranium-charged trains and flivvers [cars], and—why not?—about a trip to the moon . . . in rockets propelled by atomic energy. But . . . neither our generation nor the next one will sample the possibilities of atomic energy.
Interview (1946), Ibid.

4 I got so frightened, my heart almost stopped beating. I knew that the Nazis had just declared open season on Jews, that the hunt was on. For ten minutes I sat there and waited, minutes that seemed like so many hours.*
Ibid.

*Reference to the occasion when a military patrol took her passport as she was fleeing Germany.

1515. Edith Ronald Mirrielees (1878–1962)

1 In the thinking out of most stories, the thing the story is about, as apart from merely what happens in it, is of the utmost importance. For a story is not the sum of its happenings.
"The Substance of the Story," *Story Writing* 1947

2 Incident piled on incident no more makes life than brick piled on brick makes a house.
Ibid.

3 Experience shows that exceptions are as true as rules.
Ibid.

4 . . . belief that persistence is all and is bound to be rewarded has no . . . foundation.
Ibid.

1516. Ethel Watts Mumford (1878–1940)

1 God gives us our relatives—thank God we can choose our friends.
Pt. 1, *The Cynic's Calendar,* with Addison Mizner and Oliver Herford 1903

2 There was a young lady from Skye,
With a shape like a capital I;
She said, "It's too bad!
But then I can pad,"
Which shows you that figures can lie.
"Appearances Deceitful," *The Limerick Up to Date Book* 1903

3 There was a young lady named Julie,
Who was terribly fond of patchouli;
"Lavishness," Ibid.

4 There was a young person of Tottenham,
Whose manners, good Lord! she'd forgotten 'em.
"Good Manners," Ibid.

5 In the midst of life we are in debt.*
The Altogether New Cynic's Calendar, with Addison Mizner and Oliver Herford 1907
*A parody of *The Book of Common Prayer* anthem: "In the midst of life we are in death" (1662).

1517. Bertha Runkle (1878–1958)

1 We own the right of roaming, and the world is wide.
"Songs of the Sons of Essau" *n.d.*

1518. Bertha Spafford (1878–1968)

1 *Re soup kitchen:* We make no distinction in nationality or creed, the only requirement being if they absolutely need the help. We have Syrians and Arabs . . . Latins and Greeks, and Armenians, Russians, Jews, and Protestants.
Letter to Edward Loud (December 1915), Quoted in "The American Colony in Jerusalem," A Library of Congress Exhibition 4 March 2005

2 We have got to do something to give confidence and bring back the friendship of the Arabs for America—which we have lost. It is urgently necessary that the Arabs become convinced of the often expressed American policy of neutrality between Israel and the Arab states . . . In the present strained situation, such aid cannot come too quickly, for the cleavage between East and West is dangerously sharp in this vital region.
1954 fund-raising letter, Quoted in *American Priestess: the Extraordinary Story of Anna Spafford and the American Colony in Jerusalem* by Jane Geniesse* 2008
*See 2977.

1519. Nancy Astor (1879–1964)

1 I can conceive of nothing worse than a man-governed world—except a woman-governed world.
"America," Ch. 1, *My Two Countries* 1923

2 It is no use blaming the men—we made them what they are—and now it is up to try and make ourselves—the makers of men—a little more responsible.
Ibid.

3 I believe that the safest and surest way to get out of war is to join some sort of league of nations. That misrepresented and much despised League has already prevented three small wars, it has registered over one hundred treaties, has repatriated nearly four hundred thousand prisoners—not a bad record for only half a league.
"America," Ch. 2, Ibid.

4 Real education should educate us out of self into something far finer—into a selflessness which links us with all humanity. Political education should do the same.
Ch. 7, Ibid.

5 My vigor, vitality and cheek repel me. I am the kind of woman I would run from.
News Item 1955

6 I married beneath me. All women do.
Womanlist by Marjorie P. Weiser and Jean S. Arbeiter 1981

1520. Ethel Barrymore (1879–1959)

1 That's all there is, there isn't any more.
Curtain speech after a performance of *Sunday* 1904

2 For an actress to be a success she must have the face of Venus, the brains of Minerva, the grace of Terpsichore, the

memory of Macaulay, the figure of Juno, and the hide of a rhinoceros.

> Quoted in *The Theatre in the Fifties*
> by George Jean Nathan* *1953*

*American art critic (1882–1958).

3 I never let them cough. They wouldn't dare.

> *New York Post* 7 June *1956*

4 You grow up the day you have your first real laugh at yourself.

> Comment *n.d.*

1521. Margarete Bieber (1879–1978)

1 Hope for the best, and expect the worst.

> Quoted in "Margarete Bieber: An Archaeologist in Two
> Worlds" by Larissa Bonfante, *Women as Interpreters of the
> Visual Arts,* Claire Richter Sherman, ed. *1981*

2 Sweets are good for the nerves.

> Ibid.

1522. Catherine Carswell (1879–1946)

1 . . . it wasn't a woman who betrayed Jesus with a kiss.

> *The Savage Pilgrimage 1932*

1523. Grace Goodhue Coolidge (1879–1957)

1 This was I and yet not I—this was the wife of the President of the United States and she took precedence over me; my personal likes and dislikes must be subordinated to the consideration of those things which were required of her.

> Quoted in *First Ladies* by Betty Boyd Caroli *1987*

1524. Mabel Dodge (1879–1962)

1 . . . I knew instinctively that the strongest, surest way to the soul is through the flesh.

> *Lorenzo in Taos 1932*

2 The womb behind the womb—the significant, extended and transformed power that succeeds in primary sex, that he [D. H. Lawrence]* was ready, long since, to receive from woman.

> Ibid.

*British novelist (1885–1930).

3 A mania of love held me enthralled. . . . Nothing counted for me but Reed* . . . to lie close to him and to empty myself over and over, flesh against flesh. And I was proud I had saved so much to spill lavishly, without reckoning, passion unending.

> *Movers and Shakers 1936*

*John "Jack" Reed, American poet, adventurer, revolutionary writer (1887–1920).

4 Something in us wants men to be strong, mature, and superior to us so that we may admire them, thus consoled in a measure for our enslavement to them. But something else in us wants them to be inferior, and less powerful than ourselves, so that obtaining the ascendancy over them we gain possession, not only of them, but of our own souls, once more.

> Quoted in "The Passions of Mabel Dodge" by Rusty Brown,
> *Ms.* (New York) March *1984*

5 Nature is so strong here [Taos, New Mexico] that one has to be on one's guard not to be absorbed by it.

> Ibid.

1525. Dorothy Canfield Fisher (1879–1958)

1 "He divides us all into two kinds: the ones that get what they want by taking it away from other people—those are the dolichocephalic* blonds—though I believe it doesn't refer to the color of their hair. The other kind are the white folks, the unpredatory ones who have scruples, and get pushed to the wall for their pains."

> Bk. I, Ch. 5, *The Bent Twig 1915*

*Literally, long heads; metaphorically, top dogs.

2 A mother is not a person to lean on but a person to make leaning unnecessary.

> *Her Son's Wife 1926*

3 This was a nightmare memory, one of those that never comes to you at all in daylight, but when you get about so far asleep, start to unroll themselves in the dark.

> Pt. I, Ch. 2, *The Deepening Stream 1930*

4 "Father sticks to it that anything that promises to pay too much can't help being risky."

> Pt. II, Ch. 1, Ibid.

5 The skull of life suddenly showed through its smile.

> *Bonfire 1933*

6 Freedom is not worth fighting for if it means no more than license for everyone to get as much as he can for himself. And freedom *is* worth fighting for. Because it does mean more than unrestricted grabbing.

> *Seasoned Timber 1939*

1526. Katherine Gerould (1879–1944)

1 There are only three things worth while—fighting, drinking, and making love.

> "The Tortoise," *Vain Oblations 1914*

2 The commonest field may be chosen by opposing generals to be decisive; and in a day history is born where before only the quiet wheat has sprung.

> "The Case of Paramore," Ibid.

3 . . . I have always, privately and humbly, thought it a pity that so good a word [as culture] should go out of the best vocabularies; for when you lose an abstract term, you are very apt to lose the thing it stands for.

> "The Extirpation of Culture," *Modes and Morals 1920*

4 Politics, which, the planet over, are the fly in the amber, the worm in the bud, the rift in the loot, had, with great suddenness, deprived Wharton Cameron of a job.

> Ch. 1, *Conquistador 1923*

5 Codes cohabit easily until it comes to women. Then jungle and steppe, delta and forest, proceed to argue their differences.

> Ch. 5, Ibid.

1527. Bella da Costa Greene (1879–1950)

1 . . . every woman who comes within a mile of J.P.* immediately loses her head. . . . They flock to him all day long in rapid and sickening succession. Each one pluming her feathers and thinking she is the hen pheasant, when in reality she is forgotten before her successor appears.

> Quoted in *Morgan, American Financier* by Jean Strouse**
> *1999*

*John Pierpont Morgan (1837–1913), American financier and philanthropist. **See 3617.

2 Just because I am a librarian doesn't mean I have to dress like one!

Quoted in *An Illuminated Life, Belle da Costa Greene's Journey From Prejudice to Privilege* by Heidi Ardizzone 2007

1528. Annie Kenney (1879–1953)

1 . . . Paradise would be there once the vote* was won! I honestly believed every word I said. I had yet to learn that Nature's works are very slow but very sure. Experience is indeed the best though the sternest teacher.

Memoirs of a Militant 1924

*Woman's suffrage was granted in 1918 in Great Britain, subject to limitations; full enfranchisement came in 1928.

2 Prison. It was not a prison for me. Hunger-strikes. They had no fears for me. Cat and Mouse Act. I could have laughed. A prison cell was quiet—no telephone, no paper, no speeches, no sea sickness, no sleepless nights. I could lie on my plank bed all day and all night and return once more to my day dreams.

Ibid.

3 I was once told that the lesson I had to learn in life was patience. If that is true, I can only say I began life very badly indeed!

Ibid.

1529. Wanda Landowska (1879–1959)

1 Obviously the good lady [melody] has a tough constitution. The more attempts made against her, the more she blooms with health and rotundity. It is interesting to note that all those accused of being her murderers are becoming, in turn, her benefactors and saviors.

"Why Does Modern Music Lack Melody?" (9 February 1913), *Landowska on Music*, Denise Resout, ed. 1964

2 To embrace an epoch in all its splendor and truth, to understand the fluctuations of taste, one needs perspective.

Letter (8 September 1948), Ibid.

3 But I cannot help it if, having never stopped working, I have learned a great deal, especially about this divine freedom that is to music the air without which it would die. What would you say of a scientist or of a painter who, like stagnant water, would stop his experimentation and remain still?

Letter to a former pupil (1950), Ibid.

4 The most beautiful thing in the world is, precisely the conjunction of learning and inspiration. Oh, the passion for research and the joy of discovery!

Ibid.

1530. Frieda Lawrence (1879–1956)

1 Everything he* met had the newness of a creation, just that moment come into being.

Not I, But the Wind 1934

*D. H. Lawrence, English author (1885–1930).

2 In spite of his age and strong passions he [D.H. Lawrence] had never let himself go. Sex was suppressed in him with ferocity. He had suppressed it so much, put it away so entirely, that now, married, it overwhelmed him.

Frieda Lawrence: The Memoirs and Correspondence, E. W. Tedlock, ed. 1961

3 . . . he hated me for being miserable, not a moment of misery did he put up with; he denied all the suffering and suffered all the more. . . .

Letter to Edward Garnett (ca. 1914), Ibid.

4 Of course in war all madnesses come out in a man, that is the fault of war not of a man or a nation.

Letter (ca. 13 September 1914), *The Letters of D. H. Lawrence*, Vol. 2, George J. Zytaruk and James T. Boulton, eds. 1979

1531. Lillian Leveridge (1879–1953)

1 Over the hills of home, laddie, over the hills of home.

"A Cry from the Canadian Hills," St. 9, *Over the Hills of Home* 1918

2 Laddie! Laddie! Laddie! "Somewhere in France" you sleep,
Somewhere 'neath alien flowers and alien winds that weep,
Bravely you marched to battle, nobly your life laid down,
You unto death were faithful, laddie; yours is the victor's crown.

Ibid.

1532. Alma Mahler–Werfel (1879–1964)

1 He soured my enjoyment of life and made it an abomination. That is, he tried to. Money—rubbish! Clothes—rubbish! Beauty—rubbish! Traveling—rubbish! Only the spirit was to count. I know today that he was afraid of my youth and beauty. He wanted to make them safe for himself by simply taking from me any atom of life in which he himself played no part. I was a young thing he had desired and whose education he now took in hand.

"Marriage and Life Together," *Gustav Mahler** 1946

*Her first husband, Austrian composer (1860–1911).

2 I can never forget his dying hours and the greatness of his face as death drew nearer. His battle for the eternal values, his elevation about trivial things and his unflinching devotion to truth are an example of the saintly life.

"The End," Ibid.

3 . . . we exchanged a voluptuous glance—for a long, wonderful moment—regardless of on-lookers. Such a glance can be stunningly sensual—and he's the very picture of a man. . . . There's good stock for you. Mahler* can't compete with that.

Diaries 1898–1902, Selected and tr., Antony Beaumont 1999

4 No one will ever succeed in completely describing me; not even I myself succeeded. I am full of enigmas that can't be solved. In distant days, they'll say of me: She was a sphinx.

Quoted by Berndt Wessling, her chief biographer, Ibid.

1533. Frances Maule (1879–1966)

1 It is just as impossible to pick out a single feminine type and call it "woman," as it is to pick out a single masculine type and call it "man."

"The 'Woman' Appeal'," *J. Walter Thompson News Bulletin*, No. 105 *January 1924*

1534. Sarojini Naidu (1879–1949)

1 And spirits of Truth were the birds that sang,
And spirits of Love were the stars that glowed,

And spirits of Peace were the streams that flowed
In that magical wood in the land of sleep.
> "Song of a Dream," St. 1, *The Golden Threshold 1890*

2   Shall hope prevail where clamorous hate is rife,
Shall sweet love prosper or high dreams find place
Amid the tumult of reverberant strife.
> "At Twilight," St. 2, *The Bird of Time 1912*

3   What do you know in your blithe, brief season
Of dreams deferred and a heart grown old?
> "A Song in Spring," St. 2, Ibid.

4   The Indian woman of to-day is once more awake and pro-foundly alive to her splendid destiny as the guardian and interpreter of the Triune Vision of national life—the Vision of Love, the Vision of Faith, the Vision of Patriotism.
> Foreword, *The Broken Wing 1916*

5   Can ye measure the grief of the tears I weep
Or compass the woe of the watch I keep?
> "The Gift of India," St. 3, Ibid.

6   What, O my heart, though tomorrow be tragic,
Today is inwoven of rapture and magic.
> "Spring in Kashmir," St. 9, *The Feather of the Dawn 1927*

1535. Margaret Sanger (1879–1966)

1   Women of the working class, especially wage workers, should not have more than two children at most. The average working man can support no more and the average working woman can take care of not more in decent fashion.
> *Family Limitations 1914*

2   A mutual and satisfied sexual act is of great benefit to the aver-age woman, the magnetism of it is health giving. When it is not desired on the part of the woman and she gives no response, it should not take place. The submission of her body without love or desire is degrading to the woman's finer sensibility, all the marriage certificates on earth to the contrary notwithstanding.
> "Coitus Interruptus," Ibid.

3   The basic freedom of the world is woman's freedom.
> *Women and the New Race ca. 1920*

4   When we voice, then, the necessity of setting the feminine spirit utterly and absolutely free, thought turns naturally not to rights of the woman, nor indeed of the mother, but to the rights of the child—of all children in the world.
> Ibid.

5   Women are too much inclined to follow in the footsteps of men, to try to think as men think, to try to solve the general prob-lems of life as men solve them. . . . The woman is not needed to do man's work. She is not needed to think man's thoughts. . . . Her mission is not to enhance the masculine spirit, but to ex-press the feminine; hers is not to preserve a man-made world, but to create a human world by the infusion of the feminine element into all of its activities.
> Ibid.

6   Diplomats make it their business to conceal the facts. . . .
> Ibid.

7   Upon women the burden and the horrors of war are heavi-est. . . . When she sees what lies behind the glory and the horror, the boasting and the burden, and gets the vision, the human perspective, she will end war. She will kill war by the simple process of starving it to death. For she will refuse longer to produce the human food upon which the monster feeds.
> Ibid.

8   When motherhood becomes the fruit of a deep yearning, not the result of ignorance or accident, its children will become the foundation of a new race.
> Ibid.

9   Like begets like. We gather perfect fruit from perfect trees. . . . Abused soil brings forth stunted growths.
> Ibid.

10   Eugenics aims to arouse the enthusiasm or the interest of the people in the welfare of the world fifteen or twenty genera-tions in the future. On its negative side it shows us that we are paying for and even submitting to the dictates of an ever increasing, unceasingly spawning class of human beings who never should have been born at all—that the wealth of indi-viduals and of states is being diverted from the development and the progress of human expression and civilization.
> Ch. 8, *The Pivot of Civilization 1922*

11   . . . There was not a darkened tenement, hovel, or flat but was brightened by the knowledge that motherhood could be volun-tary; that children need not be born into the world unless they are wanted and have a place provided for them.
> "A Public Nuisance," *My Fight for Birth Control 1931*

12   The menace of another pregnancy hung like a sword over the head of every poor woman. . . .
> "Awakening and Revolt," Ibid.

13   . . . we explained simply what contraception was; that abortion was the wrong way—no matter how early it was performed it was taking a life; that contraception was the better way, the safer way—it took a little time, a little trouble, but was well while in the long run, because life had not yet begun.
> Ch. 30, *Margaret Sanger: An Autobiography 1938*

14   No woman can call herself free who does not own and control her body. No woman can call herself free until she can choose consciously whether she will or will not be a mother.
> Quoted in *Parade* (New York) *1 December 1963*

1536. Huda Shaarawi (1879–1947)

1   Men have singled out women of outstanding merit and put them on a pedestal to avoid recognizing the capabilities of all women.
> Remark (1924), Quoted in *Women in World History Curriculum* (womeninworldhistory.com) *1996–97*

1537. Rose Pastor Stokes (1879–1933)

1   If you put the grease from sewerage in butter and sell it, that's called good business. But if you put kerosene oil in a custard pie, that's sabotage.
> Speech to striking hotel workers, *Cincinnati Times Star 1912*

2   To go to prison for big principles will be truly a privilege.
> Quoted in *Fire and Grace: the life of Rose Pastor Stokes* by Arthur and Pearl Zipser *1989*

3 I am merely honoring the law by breaking it.
                                          Remark to reporters, Ibid.

4 No government which is for the profiteers can be also for the people, and I am for the people, while the government is for the profiteers.*
                                          Kansas City Star (1917), Ibid.
*Arrested for this statement, found guilty, and sentenced to 10 years in prison.

5 Whether you believe in a creed, or what you call religion, or not, there is something in Socialism that must move you. How can you love God, whom you have not seen, if you do not love your fellow man, whom you have seen?
                                          American Israelite (newspaper), "Daughters of the Book: A Study of Gender and Ethics in the Lives of Three American Women" (Ph.D. diss., Univ. of Mass.) Harriet Marla Sigerman *1992*

6 I slipped into the world while my mother was on her knees, scrubbing the floor.
                                          I Belong to the Working Class, Herbert Shapiro and David L. Sterling, eds. *1992*

1538. Beth Slater Whitson (1879–1930)

1 Meet me in Dreamland, sweet dreamy Dreamland,
   There let my dreams come true.
                                          "Meet Me To-Night in Dreamland" *1909*

1539. Mary F. Armstrong (fl. 1880s–d. 1903)

1 The introduction of negroes into the country as slaves was made at a time when only a few minds, here and there, had any true conception of the rights of individuals, or could put a fair interpretation upon that higher law which makes us our brothers' keepers; and the virgin soil and relaxing climate of the South made slavery so temptingly easy and profitable as to insure its continuance until a Power stronger than humanity interfered to bring it to an end.
                                          "The School and Its Story," *Hampton and its students*, coauthor, Helen W. Ludlow *1874*

2 Paint and powder, however skillfully their true names may be concealed under the mask of "Liquid Bloom," or "Lily Enamel," can never change their real character, but remain always unclean, false, unwholesome.
                                          (p. 31), *On Habits and Manners 1888*

1540. Nora Bayes (1880–1928)

1 I ain't had no lovin' since January, February, June or July . . .
                                          "Shine on Harvest Moon" *1907*

2 [My parents believed] the theater and all its works represented the lowest damnation and mortal sin.
                                          "1860–1919," *Women in Comedy* by Linda Martin and Kerry Segrave *1986*

3 Marriage is the only state to be in. I believe a woman should have as many love affairs as she likes, but only one at a time.
                                          Ibid.

1541. Ophelia Guyon Brown (fl. 1880s)

1 She knows Omnipotence has heard her prayer
   And cries, "It shall be done—sometime, somewhere."
                                          "Pray Without Ceasing," *Singing with Grace 1882*

1542. E. T. Corbett (fl. 1880s)

1 Ef you want to be sick of your life,
   Jest come and change places with me a spell—for I'm an inventor's wife.
                                          The Inventor's Wife 1883

1543. Ellen Eglui (fl. 1880s)

1 You know I am black and if it was known that a Negro woman patented the invention white ladies would not buy the wringer,* I was afraid to be known because of my color, in having it introduced into the market, that is the only reason.
                                          "The Innovative Woman" (p. 10), *New Scientist 24 May 1984*
*Hand-cranked roller device used to squeeze water out of fabric.

1544. Miles Franklin (1880–1956)

1 Bravely you jog along with the rope of class distinction drawing closer, close, tighter, tighter, around you. . . . I see it and know it, but I cannot help you. . . . I am only an unnecessary, little, bush commoner, I am only a—woman.
                                          My Brilliant Career 1901

1545. Radclyffe Hall (1880–1943)

1 Acknowledge us, o God, before the whole world. Give us also the right to our existence.
                                          The Well of Loneliness 1928

2 "You're neither unnatural, nor abominable, nor mad; you're as much a part of what people call nature as anyone else; only you're unexplained as yet—you've not got your niche in creation."
                                          Ibid.

3 But the intuition of those who stand midway between the two sexes is so ruthless, so poignant, so accurate, so deadly as to be in the nature of an added scourge.
                                          Ibid.

4 But when told that to appear naked in a drawing-room might be considered somewhat odd, since it was no longer the custom, she had argued that our bodies were very unimportant, only there so that people might perceive us. "We couldn't see each other without them, you know," she had said, smiling up at her mother.
                                          Ch. 1, *A Saturday Life 1930*

5 Cry out until the world shook with her cries: "You shall not take him, I care nothing for honour. I care only for the child that my womb has held, that my pain has brought forth, that my breasts have nourished. I care nothing for your wars. He was born of love; shall the blossom of love be destroyed by your hatreds? I care nothing. . . ."
                                          Ch. 41, *The Master of the House 1932*

1546. Ellen M. Hutchinson (fl. 1880s–d. 1933)

1 They are all in the lily-bed, cuddled close together—
   Purple, yellow-cap, and baby-blue;
   How they ever got there you must ask the April weather,
   The morning and the evening winds, the sunshine and the dew.
                                          "Vagrant Pansies" *n.d.*

1547. Maria Jotuni (1880–1943)

1 Life is laughable indeed, if one takes it seriously.
                                          Tohvelisankarin rouva (The Wife of the Henpecked Man) *1924*

1548. Helen Keller (1880–1968)

1 Knowledge is happiness, because to have knowledge—broad, deep knowledge—is to know true ends from false, and lofty things from low. To know the thoughts and deeds that have marked man's progress is to feel the great heart-throbs of humanity through the centuries; and if one does not feel in these pulsations a heavenward striving, one must indeed be deaf to the harmonies of life.

Pt. 1, Ch. 5, The Story of My Life 1903

2 There is much in the Bible against which every instinct of my being rebels, so much that I regret the necessity which has compelled me to read it through from beginning to end. I do not think that the knowledge which I have gained of its history and sources compensates me for the unpleasant details it has forced upon my attention.

Ch. 21, Ibid.

3 Literature is my Utopia. Here I am not disenfranchised. No barrier of the senses shuts me out from the sweet, gracious discourse of my book friends. They talk to me without embarrassment or awkwardness.

Ibid.

4 Everything has its wonders, even darkness and silence, and I learn, whatever state I may be in, therein to be content.*

Ch. 22, Ibid.

*Keller was blind and deaf since infancy.

5 . . . militarism . . . is one of the chief bulwarks of capitalism, and the day that militarism is undermined, capitalism will fail.

Ibid.

6 The hands of those I meet are dumbly eloquent to me. The touch of some hands is an impertinence. I have met people so empty of joy, that when I clasped their frosty fingertips, it seemed as if I were shaking hands with a northeast storm. Others there are whose hands have sunbeams in them, so that their grasp warms my heart.

Ch. 23, Ibid.

7 . . . as the eagle was killed by the arrow winged with his own feather, so the hand of the world is wounded by its own skill.

"The Hand of the World," American Magazine December 1912

8 I look upon the whole world as my fatherland, and every war has to me a horror of a family-feud. I look upon true patriotism as the brotherhood of man and the service of all to all.

"Menace of the Militarist Program," New York Call 20 December 1915

9 The only moral virtue of war is that it compels the capitalist system to look itself in the face and admit it is a fraud. It compels the present society to admit that it has no morals it will not sacrifice for gain.

Ibid.

10 We may have found a cure for most evils; but it has found no remedy for the worst of them all—the apathy of human beings.

Pt. I, Ch. 6, My Religion 1927

11 Security is mostly a superstition. It does not exist in nature, nor do the children of men as a whole experience it. Avoiding danger is no safer in the long run than outright exposure. Life is either a daring adventure, or nothing.

The Open Door 1957

1549. Elizabeth Kenny (1880–1952)

1 . . . panic plays no part in the training of a nurse.

And They Shall Walk, with Martha Ostenso 1943*

*See 1916.

2 O sleep, O gentle sleep, I thought gratefully, Nature's gentle nurse!

Ch. 2, Ibid.

3 Fortunately, perhaps, I was completely ignorant of the orthodox theory of the disease [polio-myelitis].

Ibid.

4 He looked at the book, took my name, and consulted his records. Then he informed me that I had been lost at sea and was dead. Under the circumstances, he could not possibly give me any money. . . . Even the fact that he was dealing with someone who had been dead for several days failed to awaken the slightest interest in his official heart.

Ch. 3, Ibid.

5 I was wholly unprepared for the extraordinary attitude of the medical world in its readiness to condemn anything that smacked of reform or that ran contrary to approved methods of practice.

Ch. 6, Ibid.

6 Some minds remain open long enough for the truth not only to enter but to pass on through by way of a ready exit without pausing anywhere along the route.

Ibid.

7 His response was remarkable for its irrelevance, if for nothing else.

Ch. 7, Ibid.

8 A measure of victory has been won, and honors have been bestowed in token thereof. But honors fade or are forgotten, and monuments crumble into dust. It is the battle itself that matters—and the battle must go on.

Ch. 14, Ibid.

1550. Sophie Kerr (1880–1965)

1 Freud and his three slaves, Inhibition, Complex and Libido.

"The Age of Innocence," Saturday Evening Post 9 April 1932

2 The longing to produce great inspirations didn't produce anything but more longing.

Ch. 1, The Man Who Knew the Date 1951

3 If peace, he thought (as he had often thought before), only had the music and pageantry of war, there'd be no more wars.

Ch. 8, Ibid.

1551. Edith Lewis (1880?–1955?)

1 . . . it is not in any form of biographical writing, but in art alone, that the deepest truth about human beings is to be found.

Willa Cather Living 1953*

*See 1408.

1552. Kathleen Thompson Norris (1880–1966)

1 "If you have children, you never have anything else!"

Ch. 2, Mother 1911

2 We cooked, cleaned, labored, worried, planned, we wept and laughed, we groaned and sang—but we never despaired. All this was but a passing phase; "we will certainly laugh at this someday," we all said buoyantly, laughing even then.

Ch. 1, Noon 1924

3 And so came middle-age, for I have discovered that middle-age is not a question of years. It is that moment in life when one realizes that one has exchanged, by a series of subtle shifts and substitutes, the vague and vaporous dreams of youth for the definite and tangible realization.

Ch. 3, Ibid.

4 Never in the history of the big round world has anything like us occurred. A country without caste, without serfs, peons or slaves, without banishment or exile or whipping post, without starvation and oppression!

Home 1928

5 Home ought to be our clearinghouse, the place from which we go forth lessoned and disciplined, and ready for life.

Ibid.

6 When they were going to be flagrantly, brutally selfish, how men did love to talk of being fair!

Ch. 2, Bread into Roses 1936

7 "There seems to be so much more winter than we need this year."

Ch. 14, Ibid.

1553. Christabel Pankhurst (1880–1958)

1 We are not ashamed of what we have done, because, when you have a great cause to fight for, the moment of greatest humiliation is the moment when the spirit is proudest. The women we do pity, the women we think unwomanly, the women for whom we have almost contempt, if our hearts could let us have that feeling, are the women who can stand aside, who take no part in the battle—and perhaps even more, the women who know what the right path is and will not tread it, who are selling the liberty of other women in order to win the smiles and favour of the dominant sex.

Speech, Albert Hall (London) 19 March 1908

2 Some people are tempted to say that all war is wrong, and that both sides in every war must be in the wrong. I challenge that statement and deny it utterly, absolutely, and with all the power I have at my disposal. All wars are not wrong. Was your war against a British Government wrong? As an Englishwoman, I say that when you fought us for the principle of freedom, for the right of self-government, you did right. I am glad you fought us and I am glad you beat us.

Speech, "America and the War," Carnegie Hall (New York) 25 October 1915

3 What we suffragettes aspire to be when we are enfranchised is ambassadors of freedom to women in other parts of the world, who are not so free as we are.

Ibid.

4 Never lose your temper with the Press or the public is a major rule of political life.

Unshackled 1959

5 The spirit of the movement was wonderful. It was joyous and grave at the same time. Self seemed to be laid down as the women joined us. Loyalty, the greatest of the virtues, was the keynote of the movement—first to the cause, then to those who were leading, and member to member. Courage came next, not simply physical courage, though so much of that was present, but still more the moral courage to endure ridicule and misunderstandings and harsh criticism and ostracism. There was a touch of the "impersonal" in the movement that made for its strength and dignity. Humour characterized it, too, in that our militant women were like the British soldier who knows how to joke and smile amid his fighting and trials.

Ibid.

6 Remember the dignity of your womanhood. Do not appeal, do not beg, do not grovel. Take courage, join hands, stand beside us, fight with us.

Remark, Quoted in Women in World History Curriculum (womeninworldhistory.com) 1996–97

1554. Julia Peterkin (1880–1961)

1 The black people who live in the Quarters at Blue Brook Plantation believe they are far the best black people living on the whole "Neck," as they call that long, narrow, rich strip of land lying between the sea on one side and the river with its swamps and deserted rice-fields on the other. . . .
   Since the first days of slavery they have been the best of field workers. They make fine mechanics and body servants for their masters. Their preachers and conjure doctors have always known many things besides how to save men's lives and souls.

Ch. 1, Scarlet Sister Mary 1928

2 "Times is changed. Women ain' like dey used to be. When I was young, a married man was a married man an' nobody didn' bother em. But dese days, it don' matter if a man is married or single, de womens don' let em rest. No. Gawd knows what de world is a-comin to."

Ch. 11, Ibid.

3 Everything gets out of order sometimes; men and women and pots and pans and axes; everything needs to be ruled.

Ibid.

4 Spoken words are safer. If Keepsie would keep his ears open he could hear plenty of good wise talk. Spoken words can cut and sting and beat down almost any enemy. They can bring tears or make people split their sides with laughter. Instead of reading all the time out of books and papers covered with printed words, he would do better to learn how to read other things: sunrises, moons, sunsets, clouds and stars, faces and eyes.

Ch. 18, Ibid.

5 Everything has its way of speaking and telling things worth knowing. Even the little grass-blades have their way of saying things as plain as words when human lips let them fall. Book-learning takes people's minds off more important things.

Ibid.

1555. Jeannette Rankin (1880–1973)

1 If the hogs of the nation are ten times more important than the children, it is high time that women should make their influence felt.

Campaign Speech* 1916
*Reference to the government's appropriation of $300,000 to study fodder for hogs and only $30,000 to study children's needs.

2 We're half the people, we should be half the congress.
> Remark (1966), Quoted in *Jeannette Rankin: First Lady in Congress* by Hannah Josephson *1974*

3 As a woman I can't go to war, and I refuse to send anyone else.
> Congressional remark (December 1941), Ibid.

4 You can no more win a war than you can win an earthquake.
> Ch. 8, Ibid.

5 Men and women are like right and left hands: it doesn't make sense not to use both.
> Quoted in *American Political Women* by Esther Stineman *1980*

6 If they are going to have a war, they ought to take the old men and leave the young men to carry on the race.
> Campaign speech (1916), Quoted in *Women Suffragists* by Diana Star Helmer *1998*

7 Today as never before, the nation needs its women, needs the work of their hands and their hearts and their minds. Are we now going to refuse these women the opportunity to serve, in the face of their plea, in the face of the nation's great need? . . . The boys at the front know something of the democracy for which they are fighting. These courageous lads who are paying with their lives testified to their sincerity when they sent home their ballots in the New York election and voted two to one in favor of woman suffrage and democracy at home. Can we afford to permit a doubt as to the sincerity of our protestations of democracy?
> Speech to Congress presenting the Anthony Amendment* (10 January 1918), Ibid.
> *After Susan B. A— (see 963), the 19th Amendment was commonly referred to as such.

8 We could have peace in one year if women were organized.
> Acceptance speech, NOW* Hall of Fame (12 February 1972), Ibid.
> *She was the first member of the National Organization for Women's Susan B. Anthony Hall of Fame.

9 It was women's work which was destroyed by war. Their work was raising human beings, and war destroyed human beings to protect profits and property.
> Interview, *The New York Times* (1972), Ibid.

1556. Ruth Sawyer (1880—1970)

1 Perhaps you have discovered this for yourself; you may have in mind this minute some of the stories that you wished had begun long before they did—and others that ended before you thought they had any business doing so. These have a very unpleasant way of leaving your expectations and your interest all agog; and I have not a doubt that you have always blamed the author. This is not fair. In a matter of this kind an author is just as helpless as a reader, and there is no use in trying to coax or scold a story into telling itself her way. As sure as she tries the story gets sulky or hurt, picks up its beginning and ending, and trails away, never to come back; and that story is lost for all time.
> Ch. I, *This Way to Christmas 1916*

1557. Ruth St. Denis (1880–1968)

1 I used to say that if a person wanted to keep alive, in distinction to merely existing, he should change his occupation every ten years.
> Ch. 3, *Ruth St. Denis: An Unfinished Life 1939*

2 I want to dance always, to be good and not evil, and when it is all over not to have the feeling that I might have done better.
> Ch. 6, Ibid.

3 I am a child of nature. Too much civilization and a touch of luxury have only depressed me. I must find a way to live more simply.
> Ibid.

4 We were a Poet* and a Dancer; and we became lovers. And let it be said of us that Beauty was our god whom we worshipped in rites of such pure loveliness that he became my Emperor and I became Moon to his Imperial Sun. Poems, like shy white birds, rose from our union: records of the strange drama of our love.
> Ch. 15, Ibid.
> *Reference to her husband, Ted Shawn.

1558. Marie Carmichael Stopes (1880–1958)

1 Each heart knows instinctively that it is only a mate who can give full comprehension of all the potential greatness in the soul, and have tender laughter for all the childlike wonder that lingers so enchantingly even in the white-haired.
> Ch. 1, *Married Love 1918*

2 An impersonal and scientific knowledge of the structure of our bodies is the surest safeguard against prurient curiosity and lascivious gloating.
> Ch. 5, Ibid.

3 . . . each coming together of man and wife, even if they have been mated for many years, should be a fresh adventure; each winning should necessitate a fresh wooing.
> Ch. 10, Ibid.

4 London, scarred mistress of proud Freedom's heart,
The love we bear you has no counterpart.
> "London," *Joy and Verity 1952*

5 We are not much in sympathy with the typical hustling American business man, and we have often felt compunction for him, seeing him nervous and harassed, sleeplessly, anxiously hunting dollars, and all but overshadowed by his over-dressed, extravagant and idle wife, who sometimes insists that her spiritual development necessitates that she shall have no children. Such husbands and wives are also found in this country; they are a growing produce of the upper reaches of the capitalist system. Yet such wives imagine that they are upholding women's emancipation.
> Article in *Dreadnought* (ca. 1919), Quoted in *The Fighting Pankhursts* by David Mitchell *1967*
> *See Adela P—, 1553; Christabel P—, 1636; Emmeline P—, 1235; Sylvia P—, 1583.

1559. Mabel Elsworth Todd (1880–1956)

1 In the expiratory phase lies renewal of vigor through some hidden form of muscular release. . . .
> *The Balancing of Forces in the Human Body 1929*

2 Emotion constantly finds expression in bodily position. . . .
> Ibid.

1560. Nancy Byrd Turner (1880–1971)

1 Burn, wood, burn—
Wood that once was a tree, and knew

Blossom and sheaf, and the Spring's return,
Nest, and singing, and rain, and dew—
Burn, wood, burn!

"Flame Song" *n.d.*

2 Death is only an old door
Set in a garden wall.

"Death Is a Door" *n.d.*

1561. Margaret Widdemer (1880–1978)

1 I have shut my little sister in from light and life
(For a rose, for a ribbon, for a wreath across my hair),
I have made her restless feet still until the night,
Locked from sweets of summer and from wild spring air.

"The Factories," St. 1 ca. *1916*

2 To grown people a girl of fifteen and a half is a child still; to
herself she is very old and very real; more real, perhaps, than
ever before or ever after. . . .

"The Changeling," *The Boardwalk* 1920

3 But the young are improvident—not having yet learned how hard
to come by money is and of how little account are other things.

"The Congregation," Ibid.

4 No one had told them that Age was a place
Where you sat with a curious mask on your face.

"Old Ladies," St. 6, *Hill Garden* 1936

5 And all that you are sorry for is what you haven't done.

"De Senectute" *n.d.*

1562. Anzia Yezierska (1880/1–1970)

1 "If you have no luck in this world, then it's better not to live."

"The Fat of the Land," *Hungry Hearts and Other Stories* 1920

2 "Woe to America where women are let free like men."

The Bread Givers 1925.

3 "A woman alone, not a wife and not a mother, has no existence.
No joy on earth, no hope of heaven. . . . You're not human!"

Red Ribbon on a White Horse (autobio) 1950

4 "Poverty becomes a Jew like a red ribbon on a white horse"

Ibid.

5 When you deny your parents, you deny the ground under
your feet, the sky over your head. You become an outlaw, a
pariah. . . .

Ibid.

6 Give a beggar a dime and he'll bless you. Give him a dollar
and he'll curse you for withholding the rest of your fortune.
Poverty is a bag with a hole at the bottom.

Ch. 9, Ibid.

7 A person who cuts himself off from his people cuts himself off
at the roots of his being; he becomes a shell, a cipher, a spiritual suicide.

"We Can Change Our Moses but Not Our Noses", *Anzia
Yezierska: A Writer's Life* by Louise Levitas Henriksen 1988

1563. Mary Antin (1881–1949)

1 So at last I was going to America! Really, really going, at last!
The boundaries burst. The arch of heaven soared. A million
suns shone out of every star. The winds rushed out into outer
space, roaring in my ears, "America! America!"

The Promised Land 1912

2 . . . The past was only my cradle, and now it cannot hold me,
because I am grown too big.

Ibid.

3 I have so little mastered the art of tranquil living that wherever
I go I trail storm clouds of drama around me.

Letter to Caroline Goodyear, Mary Antin Papers (Gould Farm,
Monterey, MA) *18 March 1930*

4 I can no more return to the Jewish fold that I can return to my
mother's womb.

"House of One Father", *Common Ground Spring 1941*

5 I have found my wider world of the spirit, and nothing can dislodge me. . . . In all those places where race lines are drawn, I
shall claim the Jewish badge; but in my Father's house of many
mansions I shall continue a free spirit.

Ibid.

6 "What are my daughters worth? They're only good to sit in
the house, a burden on their parents' neck, until they're married off. A son, at least, prays for the souls of his parents when
they're dead; it's a deed of piety to raise sons."

"Malinke's Atonement," *America and I: Short Stories by
American Jewish Women Writers,* Joyce Antler,* ed. 1990
*See 3320.

7 . . . If you have never been poor, you don't know what life is
worth.

The Speaking Heart (unpublished autobiography) *n.d.*

1564. Marie L. Bonaparte (1881–1962)

1 On the one hand, then, in the reproduction functions proper—
menstruation, defloration, pregnancy, and parturition—woman
is biologically doomed to suffer. Nature seems to have no hesitation in administering her strong doses of pain, and she can
do nothing to submit passively to the regimen prescribed. On
the other hand, as regards sexual attraction, which is necessary
for the act of impregnation, and as regards the erotic pleasure
experienced during the act itself, the woman may be on equal
footing with the man.

"Passivity, Masochism, and Femininity" (1934), *International
Journal of Psycho-Analysis*, Vol. 16 1935

1565. Mary Breckinridge (1881–1965)

1 To meet the needs of the frontiersman's child, you must begin
before he is born and carry him through the hazards of childbirth. His care not only means the care of the mother before,
during and after his birth, but the care of his whole family as
well. . . . Health teaching must also be on a family basis—in
the homes.

Quoted in "Birth Control Gains in the Mountains of
Kentucky" by Kenneth Reich, *Los Angeles Times 9 May 1975*

1566. Grace Stone Coatés (1881–1976)

1 And a woman can leave a man, without quitting his dwelling,
To loneliness deeper than night with no star-spawn;
The dearth he has of her is beyond his telling.
In the crook of his arm she is gone from him, she is gone.

"The Hardness of Women," St. 2, *Mead and Mangel-Wurzel
1931*

2 Do not be kind to me;
It is too late to be tender.
It is too late to rant
And accuse. Can you restore
The trampled grape to the vender,
Or water a dead plant?

"Conclusion," St. 1, Ibid.

3 "Where were you, last night?"
"I was in bed . . . Sleeping
Beside you . . . of course!"
"And I was leaping
Broomsticks, and burying Jesus,
And patting Godiva's horse."

"At Breakfast," in toto, Ibid.

4 Why should a dusty desk
Command my life,
When God is offering hills
Washed clean with the rain?

"Hills," St. 2, *Portulacas in the Wheat 1932*

5 Her occupation is housewifery: her delight, writing; her passion, music. All she has learned in 20 years of housekeeping
drops from her in one half-hour's intense writing, so that she
has to learn her business of housewifery each morning anew;
and all she knows of anything is drowned in one half-hour of
music.
Fortunately, her husband is sane.

*"Food of Gods and Starvelings": Selected Poems of Grace
Stone Coates,* Lee Rostad & Rick Newby, eds. *2007*

1567. Alice Corbin (1881–1949)

1 I know we grow more lovely
Growing wise.

"Two Voices" *n.d.*

2 Then welcome Age, and fear not sorrow;
Today's no better than tomorrow.

Ibid.

1568. Crystal Eastman (1881–1928)

1 A good deal of tyranny goes by the name of protection.

Equal Rights 1924

2 . . . with the feminist ideal of education accepted in every home
and school, and with all special barriers removed in every field
of human activity, there is no reason why women should not
become almost a human thing.

Quoted in *The 50 Most Influential Women in American Law*
by Dawn Bradley Berry* *1996*

*See 4399.

3 . . . establish new values, to create an overpowering sense of the
sacredness of life, so that war would be unthinkable.

Remark (ca. 1914–17), Ibid.

1569. Esther Lape (1881–1949)

1 We have no illusions about the flexibility of the Nobel Committee. Its statements reflect a rigidity *extraordinaire.*

Letter to A. David Gurewitsch (30 December 1964), Quoted
in *Eleanor:* *The Years Alone* by Joseph P. Lash *1972*

*E— Roosevelt; see 1618.

1570. Rose Macaulay (1881–1958)

1 Decades have a delusive edge to them. They are not, of course,
really periods at all, except as any other ten years would be.
But we, looking at them, are caught by the different name
each bears, and give them different attributes, and tie labels on
them, as if they were flowers, in a border.

Pt. II, Ch. 1, *Told by an Idiot 1923*

2 Sleeping in a bed—it is, apparently, of immense importance.
Against those who sleep, from choice or necessity, elsewhere
society feels righteously hostile. It is not done. It is disorderly,
anarchical.

"Beds and 'Omes," *A Casual Commentary 1925*

3 Does conduct rank with food, wine, and weather as a department of life in which goodness is almost universally admired?

"A Platonic Affection," Ibid.

4 . . . he desired to exaggerate. And here we have what may
be called a primary human need, which should be placed by
psychologists with the desire for nourishment, for safety, for
sense—gratifications, and for appreciation, as one of the elemental lusts of man.

Catchwords and Claptrap 1926

5 . . . the desire not to work; indeed, I share it to the full. As to
one's country, why should one feel any more interest in its welfare than in that of any other countries? And as to the family,
I have never understood how that fits in with any of the other
ideals at all. A group of closely related persons living under
one roof; it is a convenience, often a necessity, sometimes a
pleasure, sometimes the reverse; but who first exalted it as admirable, an almost religious ideal?

Ch. 20, *The World My Wilderness 1950*

6 "Take my camel, dear," said my aunt Dot, as she climbed down
from this animal on her return from High Mass.

Ch. 1, *The Town of Trebizond 1956*

1571. Mountain Wolf Woman (1881–1960)

1 I cried as loud as I could and cried as much as I wanted to. That
is the way I cried. Then when I got enough crying, I stopped
crying. When I stopped crying my anxiety seemed to be relieved. Then, after I cried it out, this pain in my heart, I felt
better.

Mountain Wolf Woman, Sister of Thunder, Nancy Oestreich
Lurie, ed. *1961*

2 I do not know why, but whatever the white people say, that is
the way it has to be. I guess it must be that way.

Ibid.

1572. Eleanor Patterson (1881–1948)

1 Perhaps a woman editor is resented because an editor is supposed to possess wisdom, and something in the masculine
mind objects to the suggestion that a woman can know anything except what she has already been told by a man.

Quoted in *Cissy* by Ralph G. Martin *1979*

1573. Anna Pavlova (1881–1931)

1 . . . although one may fail to find happiness in theatrical life,
one never wishes to give it up after having once tasted its fruits.
To enter the School of the Imperial Ballet is to enter a con-

vent whence frivolity is banned, and where merciless discipline reigns.

"Pages of My Life," *Pavlova: A Biography*, A. H. Franks, ed.
1956

2 To tend, unfailingly, unflinchingly, toward a goal, is the secret of success. But success? What exactly is success? For me it is to be found not in applause, but in the satisfaction of feeling that one is realising one's ideal. When a small child ... I thought that success spelled happiness. I was wrong. Happiness is like a butterfly which appears and delights us for one brief moment, but soon flits away.

Ibid.

3 As is the case in all branches of art, success depends in a very large measure upon individual initiative and exertion, and cannot be achieved except by dint of hard work. Even after having reached perfection, a ballerina may never indulge in idleness.

Ibid.

1574. Margaret Sackville (1881–1963)

1 When all is said and done, monotony may after all be the best condition for creation.

Introduction, *The Works of Susan Ferrier*,* Vol. I *1929*
*See 790.

2 Great imaginations are apt to work from hints and suggestions and a single moment of emotion is sometimes sufficient to create a masterpiece.

Ibid.

3 ... extreme modernity is apt very quickly to become old-fashioned.

Ibid.

4 Laughter is ever young, whereas tragedy, except the very highest of all, quickly becomes haggard.

Ibid.

1575. Mary Heaton Vorse (1881–1966)

1 "Some folks is born in the world feeling it and knowing it in their hearts that creation don't stop where the sight of the eyes stop, and the thinner the veil is the better, and something in them sickens when the veil gets too thick."

"The Other Room," *McCall's 1919*

2 He had seized the one loophole that life had given her and had infused her relentless courage into another's veins.

"The Wallow of the Sea," *Harper's* (New York) *1921*

1576. Mary Webb (1881–1927)

1 The past is only the present become invisible and mute; and because it is invisible and mute, its memoried glances and its murmurs are infinitely precious. We are tomorrow's past.

Foreword, *Precious Bane 1924*

2 Saddle your dreams afore you ride 'em.

Bk. I, Ch. 6, Ibid.

3 If you stop to be kind, you must swerve often from your path.

Bk. II, Ch. 3, Ibid.

4 It's the folks that depend on us for this and for the other that we most do miss.

Bk. IV, Ch. 4, Ibid.

1577. Charlotte Brown (1882–1961)

1 As a part of my argument for education for Negroes I used the incident as illustration that most white people looked upon every Negro, regardless of his appearance, modulated tones that reflected some culture and training, as a servant....

Autobiographical Sketch, *Black Women in White America*,
Gerda Lerner,* ed. *1972*
*See 2380.

2 ... I propose the raising of dollars to $500,000 as an endowment.... This seems tremendous, I know, for me to undertake but folks don't seem to pay much attention nowadays to anything that's small and a fund like this places a sort of permanence to the thing.

Letter to Mr. and Mrs. Galen Stone (19 June 1920), Ibid.

3 A few of us must be sacrificed perhaps in order to get a step further.

Letter to F. P. Hobgood, Jr. (19 October 1921), Ibid.

1578. Emma Jung (1882–1955)

1 Neither arrogance nor presumption drives us to the audacity of wanting to be like God—that is, like man; we are not like Eve of old, lured by the beauty of the fruit of the tree of knowledge, nor does the snake encourage us to enjoy it. No, there has come to us something like a command; we are confronted with the necessity of biting into the apple, whether we think it good to eat or not, confronted with the fact that the paradise of naturalness and unconsciousness, in which many of us would only too gladly tarry, is gone forever.

"On the Nature of Animus" (1931), *Animus and Anima 1957*

2 And now we come to the magic of words. A word, also, just like an idea, a thought, has the effect of reality upon undifferentiated minds. Our Biblical myth of creation, for instance, where the world grows out of the spoken word of the Creator, is an expression of this.

Ibid.

3 Learning to cherish and emphasize feminine values is the primary condition of our holding our own against the masculine principle....

Ibid.

4 For by her unconsciousness, woman exerts a magical influence on man, a charm that lends her power over him. Because she feels this power instinctively and does not wish to lose it, she often resists to the utmost the process of becoming conscious.... Many men take pleasure in woman's unconsciousness. They are bent on opposing her development of greater consciousness in every possible way, because it seems to them uncomfortable and unnecessary.

Ibid.

5 Very frequently, feminine activity also expresses itself in what is largely a retrospectively oriented pondering over what we ought to have done differently in life, and how we ought to have done it; or, as if under compulsion, we make up strings of causal connections. We like to call this thinking; though, on the contrary, it is a form of mental activity that is strangely pointless and unproductive, a form that really leads only to self-torture.

Ibid.

1579. Melanie Klein (1882–1960)

1 The sexual development of the child is inextricably bound up with his object relations and with all the emotions

which from the beginning mould his attitude to mother and father.

"The Oedipus Complex in the Light of Early Anxieties", *Int. Journal of Psycho-Analysis, 26: 11–33 1945*

2 Fears have to do with parts of the personality (possibly intro-jected) that cannot be accepted.

"Infantile Anxiety Situations," *The Selected Melanie Klein*, Juliet Mitchell, ed. *1987*

3 I hold that anxiety arises from the operation of the death in-stinct within the organism, is felt as fear of annihilation (death) and takes the form of fear of persecution.

Ibid.

4 "There is an empty space in my being which I can never fill."

Ibid.

1580. Winifred Letts (1882–1972)

1 Age after age the children give
Their lives that Herod still may live.

"The Children's Ghosts," *Hallow-e'en, and Poems of War 1916*

2 God rest you, happy gentlemen,
Who laid your good lives down,
Who took the khaki and the gun
Instead of cap and gown.

"The Spires of Oxford," St. 4, *The Spires of Oxford and Other Poems 1917*

3 I do be thinking God must laugh
The time he makes a boy,
All element the creatures are,
And divilment and joy.

"Boys," Ibid.

4 That God once loved a garden
We learn in Holy writ.
And seeing gardens in the spring
I well can credit it.

"Stephen's Green," St. 1 *n.d.*

1581. Mina Loy (1882–1966)

1 Pig Cupid his rosy snout
Rooting erotic garbage
"Once upon a time"

"Songs to Johannes," *The Lost Lunar Baedeker: The Poems of Mina Loy*, Roger L. Conover, ed. *1996*

2 Curie*
of the laboratory
of vocabulary
she crushed
the tonnage
of consciousness
congealed to phrases
to extract
a radium of the word

"Homage to Gertrude Stein,"** Ibid.
*Reference to Marie C—; see 1335; **see 1450.

3 Silver, circular corpse
your decease
infects us with unendurable ease

"Moreover, the Moon——," St. 3, Ibid.

4 I am the centre
Of a circle of pain
Exceeding its boundaries in every direction

"Parturition" (1914), Ibid.

5 the eye-white sky-light
white-light district
of lunar lusts

"Lunar Baedeker," St. 6, Ibid.

1582. Anne O'Hare McCormick (1882–1954)

1 Whoever goes to Russia discovers Russia.

Ch. 1, *The Hammer and the Scythe 1927*

2 There is no place where you can see more human nature in a few hours than in a season of the Parliament of Italy.

"A Papal Consistory and a Political Debut" (24 July 1921), *Vatican Journal, 1921–1954*, Marion Turner Sheehan, ed. *1957*

3 One little angry, brooding man [Hitler] has put the whole world on wartime. A man who could never keep step with any-body has forced millions of free and intelligent human beings to keep the time he sets.

"Reflections in Time of War" (4 April 1942), Ibid.

1583. Sylvia Pankhurst (1882–1960)

1 Hourly the War drew nearer; threat followed threat; ultimatum, ultimatum. My mind shrank from the menace sweeping down on us, as children's do from belief in death and misfortune, vainly clinging to the fancy that great disasters only happen to other people.

Ch. 1, *The Home Front 1932*

2 I could not give my name to aid the slaughter in this war, fought on both sides for grossly material ends, which did not justify the sacrifice of a single mother's son.

Ch. 25, Ibid.

3 My belief in the growth and permanence of democracy is undimmed. I know that the people will cast off the new dicta-torship as they did the old. I believe as firmly as in my youth that humanity will surmount the era of poverty and war. Life will be happier and more beautiful for all. I believe in the GOLDEN AGE.

Essay in *Myself When Young*, Margot Asquith,* ed. *1938*
*See 1301.

4 I have gone to war too. . . . I am going to fight capitalism even if it kills me. It is wrong that people like you should be com-fortable and well fed while all around you people are starving.

Courtroom Speech (January 1921), Quoted in *The Fighting Pankhursts* by David Mitchell *1967*
*See Adela P—, 1636, Christabel P—, 1553; Emmeline P—, 1235.

5 Love and freedom are vital to the creation and upbringing of a child. I do not advise anyone to rush into either legal or free marriage without love, sympathy, understanding, friendship and frankness. These are essential, and having these, no legal forms are necessary.

Article in *News of the World* (April 1928), Ibid.

6 Socialism is the greatest thing in life for me. You will never crush it out of me or kill it. I am only one of thousands or mil-lions. Socialists make it possible to practice what you say in

church, that we should love our neighbors as ourselves. If you work against socialism, you are standing with reaction against life, standing with the dead past against the coming civilization.

Pt. II, Ch. 4, Ibid.

1584. Frances Perkins (1882–1965)

1 In America, public opinion is the leader.

Sec. I, *People at Work* 1934

2 But with the slow menace of a glacier, [the] depression came on. No one had any measure of its progress; no one had any plan for stopping it. Everyone tried to get out of the way.

Sec. IV, Ibid.

3 The quality of his [F. D. Roosevelt*] being one with his people, of having no artificial or natural barriers between him and them, made it possible for him to be a leader without ever being or thinking of being a dictator.

Ch. 7, *The Roosevelt I Knew* 1946

4 He [F. D. Roosevelt*] didn't like concentrated responsibility. Agreement with other people who he thought were good, right-minded, and trying to do the right thing by the world was almost as necessary to him as air to breathe.

Ch. 12, Ibid.

*(1882–1945), 32nd president of the United States (1933–1945).

1585. Gisela Richter (1882–1972)

1 . . . a series of failures may culminate in the best possible result.

My Memoirs: Recollection of an Archaeologist's Life 1972

1586. Mabel Ulrich (1882?–?)

1 It can't be so easy being the husband of a "modern" woman. She is everything his mother wasn't—and nothing she was.

"A Doctor's Diary, 1904–1932," *Scribner's June* 1933

2 But, oh, what a woman I should be if an able young man would consecrate his life to me as secretaries and technicians do to their men employers.

Ibid.

3 Verily what bishops are to the English, bankers are to Americans.

Ibid.

4 A man, it seems, may be intellectually in complete sympathy with a woman's aims. But only about ten percent of him is his intellect—the other ninety his emotions.

Ibid.

1587. Sigrid Undset (1882–1949)

1 Mrs. Nielsen's school was co-educational and heavily committed to progressive educational ideas. It played an important role in shaping my character, inspiring me with an indelible distrust of enthusiasm for such beliefs! It was not that I disliked Mrs. Nielsen or suspected her of not being so noble-minded or attached to her principles as she appeared to be. No, it was those very principles which filled me with boundless skepticism; I knew not why either then or for a long time afterwards. Many years later I was to find some kind of an answer in the words uttered by St. Augustine concerning the leader of

the Donatists: "*securus judicat orbis terrarum*".* At the time, however, my only reaction was to roll myself up into a tight ball of resistance and it was thus, hedgehog-wise, that I went through my school years.

Autobiographical Essay, Nobel Lectures *1928*

*Tr.: The whole world judges in safety, or, its judgement is unswayed by fear.

1588. Virginia Verona (1882–?)

1 I blame the unions, first, last and all the time. The nation has gotten to the place where unskilled labor is getting paid more than skilled. The unions have gone too far. They rule this country, and they have no compassion, no mercy for people, not even other union members.

Quoted in "Fighting for Her—and Our—Rights" by Ursula Vils, *Los Angeles Times 5 January* 1975

2 People are too easygoing. The American people will not stand up for their rights. They'll be violent, of course, but they will not stand up for their rights.

Ibid.

1589. Margaret Wilson (1882–1973)

1 The prairie lay that afternoon as it had lain for centuries of September afternoons, vast as an ocean; motionless as an ocean coaxed into very little ripples by languid breezes; silent as an ocean where only very little waves slip back into their element.

Ch. 1, *The Able McLaughlins* 1923

2 The tidings of Lincoln's death sickened him desperately. He got to thinking he was never again to be a strong man. And he could see no reason for wanting to be.

Ch. 4, Ibid.

3 Now that he had been in Chicago he had a growing contempt, which never failed to amuse Wully, for the speech of his own people. What was it they spoke, he demanded scornfully, swinging a violent hoe among the weeds. It was Scotch no longer. It wasn't English. It wasn't American, certainly. It was just a kind of—he tried all summer to describe it satisfactorily in a word. Once he called it "the gruntings of the inarticulate forthright."

Ch. 14, Ibid.

4 They had acres of sod corn that summer, and wheat to make a miser chuckle. Both men, and whatever neighborly passer-by they might be able to hire, worked day after day till they staggered. To have stopped while yet there was sufficient daylight to distinguish another hill of corn would have been shirking; to go to supper while yet one could straighten up without a sharp pain in his back would have been laziness.

Ibid.

1590. Virginia Woolf (1882–1941)

1 But when the self speaks to the self, who is speaking?—the entombed soul, the spirit driven in, in, in to the central catacomb; the self that took the veil and left the world—a coward perhaps, yet somehow beautiful, as it flits with its lantern restlessly up and down the dark corridors.

"An Unwritten Novel," *Monday or Tuesday* 1921

2 The older one grows the more one likes indecency.

"The String Quartet," Ibid.

3   Rigid, the skeleton of habit alone upholds the human frame.

Mrs. Dalloway 1925

4   We all indulge in the strange, pleasant process called thinking, but when it comes to saying, even to someone opposite, what we think, then how little we are able to convey! The phantom is through the mind and out of the window before we can lay salt on its tail, or slowly sinking and returning to the profound darkness which it has lit up momentarily with a wandering light.

"Montaigne,"* *The Common Reader* (First Series) *1925*
*Michel Eyquem de M— , French essayist (1533–1592).

5   Humour is the first of the gifts to perish in a foreign tongue.

"On Not Knowing Greek," Ibid.

6   A good essay must have this permanent quality about it; it must draw its curtain round us, but it must be a curtain that shuts us in not out.

"The Modern Essay," Ibid.

7   Those comfortably padded lunatic asylums which are known, euphemistically, as the stately homes of England.

"Lady Dorothy Nevill," Ibid.

8   Different though the sexes are, they inter-mix. In every human being a vacillation from one sex to the other takes place, and often it is only the clothes that keep the male or female like-ness, while underneath the sex is very opposite of what it is above.

Ch. 6, *Orlando 1928*

9   Suppose . . . that men were only represented in literature as the lovers of women, and were never the friends of men, soldiers, thinkers, dreamers; how few parts in the plays of Shakespeare could be allotted to them; how literature would suffer! We might perhaps have most of Othello; and a good deal of Antony; but no Caesar, no Brutus, no Hamlet, no Lear, no Jacques—literature would be incredibly impoverished, as indeed literature is impoverished beyond our counting by the doors that have been shut upon women.

A Room of One's Own 1929

10   One cannot think well, love well, sleep well, if one has not dined well.

Ch. 1, Ibid.

11   A woman must have money and a room of her own if she is to write fiction.

Ibid.

12   Women have served all these centuries as looking-glasses pos-sessing the magic and delicious power of reflecting the figure of a man at twice its natural size.

Ch. 2, Ibid.

13   If truth is not to be found on the shelves of the British Museum, where, I asked myself, picking up a notebook and a pencil, is truth?

Ibid.

14   Why are women . . . so much more interesting to men than men are to women?

Ibid.

15   Who shall measure the heat and violence of the poet's heart when caught and tangled in a woman's body?

Ch. 3, Ibid.

16   . . . for fiction, imaginative work that it is, is not dropped like a pebble upon the ground, as science may be; fiction is liked a spider's web, attached ever so lightly perhaps, but still attached to life at all four corners. . . . But when the web is pulled askew, hooked up at the edge, torn in the middle, one remembers that these webs are not spun in midair by incorporeal creatures, but are the work of human beings and are attached to grossly mate-rial things, like health and money and the houses we live in.

Ibid.

17   When, however, one reads of a witch being ducked, of a woman possessed by devils, of a wise woman selling herbs, or even a very remarkable man who had a mother, then I think we are on the track of a lost novelist, a suppressed poet . . . indeed, I would venture to guess that Anon, who wrote so many poems without signing them, was often a woman.

Ibid.

18   There is the old brute, too, the savage, the hairy man who dab-bles his fingers in ropes of entrails; and gobbles and belches; whose speech is guttural, visceral—well, he is here. He squats in me.

(p. 205), *The Waves 1931*

19   On the outskirts of every agony sits some observant fellow who points.

Ibid.

20   Against you I will fling myself, unvanquished and unyielding, O Death!

Final words,* Ibid.
*Her husband, Leonard Woolf, chose these words as her epitaph at her burial-place and former home, Monk's House, Rodmell, Sus-sex, England. Woolf committed suicide by drowning on 28 March 1941.

21   To depend upon a profession is a less odious form of slavery than to depend upon a father.

(p. 20), *Three Guineas 1938*

22   "I will not cease from mental fight," Blake* wrote. Mental fight means thinking against the current, not with it. The current flows fast and furious. It issues a spate of words from the loud-speakers and the politicians. Everyday they tell us that we are a free people fighting to defend freedom. That is the current that has whirled the young airman up into the sky and keeps him circulating there among the clouds. Down here, with a roof to cover us and a gas mask handy, it is our business to puncture gas bags and discover the seeds of truth.

Article in *The New Republic* 21 October 1940
*William Blake, English poet and engraver (1757–1827).

23   There can be no two opinions as to what a highbrow is. He is the man or woman of thoroughbred intelligence who rides his mind at a gallop across country in pursuit of an idea.

"Middlebrow," *The Death of the Moth 1942*

24   He's like an express train running through a tunnel—one shriek, sparks, smoke and gone.

Letter to poet Stephen Spender (25 June 1935), *The Sickle Side of the Moon: Letters of Virginia Woolf,* Vol. V, Nigel Nicolson, ed. *1979*

25   My own brain is to me the most unaccountable of machin-ery—always buzzing, humming, soaring, roaring, diving, and then buried in mud.

(8 March 1941), Ibid.

26 This is not "writing" at all. Indeed, I could say that Shakespeare surpasses literature altogether, if I knew what I meant.
　　(13 April 1930), *Leave the Letters Till We're Dead: Letters of Virginia Woolf*, Vol. 3, Nigel Nicolson, ed. *1980*

27 These are the soul's changes. I don't believe in ageing. I believe in forever altering one's aspect to the sun. Hence my optimism.
　　(2 October 1932), Vol. 4, Ibid.

28 Now, aged 50, I'm just poised to shoot forth quite free straight & undeflected my bolts whatever they are.
　　Ibid.

1591. Dorothy Brett (1883–1977)

1 She [Mabel Dodge*] had an insatiable appetite for tasting life in all its aspects. She tasted and spat it out.
　　"My Long and Beautiful Journey," *South Dakota Review* Summer *1967*

　*See 1524.

1592. Nannie Helen Burroughs (1883–1961)

1 What every woman who bleaches and straightens out needs, is not her appearance changed, but her mind. She has a false notion as to the value of color and hair in solving the problem of her life. Why does she wish to improve her appearance? Why not improve her real self?
　　"Not Color but Character," *Voice of the Negro* July *1904*

2 Many Negroes have colorphobia as badly as the white folk have Negrophobia.
　　Ibid.

3 In fact, America will destroy herself and revert to barbarism if she continues to cultivate the things of the flesh and neglect the higher virtues.
　　"With All They Getting," *The Southern Workman* July *1927*

4 When the Negro learns what manner of man he is spiritually, he will wake up all over. He will stop playing white even on the stage. He will rise in the majesty of his own soul. He will glorify the beauty of his own brown skin. He will stop thinking white and go to thinking straight and living right. He will realize that wrong-reaching, wrong-bleaching and wrong-mixing have "most nigh ruin't him" and he will redeem his body and rescue his soul from the bondage of that death. . . .
　　Ibid.

5 Don't wait for deliverers. . . . I like that quotation, "Moses, my servant, is dead. Therefore arise and go over Jordan." There are no deliverers. They're all dead. We must arise and go over Jordan. We can take the promised land.
　　Article, *Louisiana Weekly* 23 December *1933*

6 The framers of the Declaration of Independence prophesied that uprisings would occur "in the course of human events," if people are denied those inalienable rights to which the "laws of nature and of nature's God entitle them." Reread their prophecy. . . . If that's Red, then the writers of the Declaration of Independence were very Red. They told Americans not to stand injustice after "patient sufferance."
　　"Declaration of 1776 Is Cause of Harlem Riot," *The Afro-American* 13 April *1935*

7 We specialize in the wholly impossible
　　Motto, National Training School for Girls (Washington D.C., ca. 1909), *Black Women in White America*, Gerda Lerner,* ed. *1972*

　*See 2380.

1593. Coco Chanel (1883–1971)

1 Fashion is made to become unfashionable.
　　Life (New York) *19 August 1957*

2 A fashion for the young? That is a pleonasm: there is no fashion for the old.
　　Quoted in *Coco Chanel, Her Life, Her Secrets* by Marcel Haedrich *1971*

3 My friends, there are no friends.
　　Ibid.

4 Since everything is in our heads, we had better not lose them.
　　Ibid.

5 "Where should one use perfume?" a young woman asked. "Wherever one wants to be kissed," I said.
　　Ibid.

6 Fashion is architecture; it is a matter of proportions.
　　Ibid.

7 There goes a woman who knows all the things that can be taught and none of the things that cannot be taught.
　　Ch. 21, Ibid.

8 Nothing is ugly as long as it is alive.
　　Ibid.

9 I am doing an optimistic collection because things are going badly.
　　Ibid.

10 You see, that's what fame is: solitude.
　　Ibid.

1594. Edith Clarke (1883–1959)

1 There is no demand for women engineers, as such, as there are for women doctors; but there's always a demand for anyone who can do a good piece of work.
　　Interview, *Daily Texan* 14 March *1948*

1595. Imogen Cunningham (1883–1976)

1 People who are living aren't famous—they're just infamous.
　　Quoted in *Never Give Up* (film) by Ann Hershey *1975*

2 One thing about being born without beauty—you don't look for it.
　　Ibid

1596. Elsa Maxwell (1883–1963)

1 First I want a woman guest to be beautiful. Second, I want her to be beautifully dressed. Third, I demand animation and vivacity. Fourth, not too many brains. Brains are always awkward at a gay and festive party.
　　Interview, *New York Mirror 1938*

2   I married the world—the world is my husband. That is why I'm so young. No sex. Sex is the most tiring thing in the world.
"I Married the World," *This Fabulous Century: 1930–1940*
1940

3   Most rich people are the poorest people I know.
Ch. 1, *R.S.V.P. 1954*

4   I have lived by my wits all my life and I thank the Lord they are still in one, whole piece. I don't need glasses, Benzedrine or a psychiatrist.
Ch. 16, Ibid.

5   Intolerance of mediocrity has been the main prop of my independence. . . .
Ibid.

6   Anatomize the character of a successful hostess and the knife will lay bare the fact that she owes her position to one of the three things: either she is liked, or she is feared, or she is important.
Ch. 3, *How to Do It 1957*

1597. Sara Murphy (1883–1975)

1   It was like a great fair, and everybody was so young.*
Quoted in *Everybody Was So Young: Gerald and Sara Murphy—A Lost Generation Love Story*
by Amanda Vaill *1998*
*Paris in the 1920s.

2   I don't think the world is a very nice place. And all there seems to be left to do is to make the best of it while we are here, & be VERY grateful for one's friends because they are the best there is, & make up for many another thing that is lacking.
Ibid.

1598. Frances Newman (1883–1928)

1   . . . she did not understand how her father could have reached such age and such eminence without learning that all mothers are as infallible as any pope and more righteous than any saint.
The Hard-Boiled Virgin 1926

2   For the first time, she realised that conversation might have been entirely satisfactory if women had been allowed to admit they understood the limited number of subjects men were interested in, and she was so excited by her idea that she almost committed the social crime of allowing a conversation to pause.
Ibid.

3   And while she wondered at all the things civilization can teach a woman to endure, she was able to take Mrs. Abbott's departing hand, and to watch Mrs. Abbott walk out of a door into the temporary silence civilization would require of her until she found another acquaintance on whom her conversation could pour as if she were emerging from a year and a day of solitary confinement.
Dead Lovers Are Faithful Lovers 1928

1599. "Sister" Evelyn Pollard (1883?–1960?)

1   Yes, my feets is tired, but my soul is rested.
(1955), Quoted by Martin Luther King, Jr. in a sermon at the New Covenant Baptist Church, (Chicago, IL) *9 April 1967*

2   Now come close to me and let me tell you something one more time, and I want you to hear it this time. Now I done told you we is with you. Now, even if we ain't with you, the Lord is with you. The Lord's going to take care of you
Ibid.

1600. Jessie Ethel Sampter (1883–1938)

1   A new light is coming into the world, as it has always come in moments of darkness and must come as inevitably as the sun rises. . . . A new synthesis of our hate of war and love of our land, . . . of our social reconstruction and our individual deepening, of radios and music, machines and art, time and eternity, man and God. . . . This is the burning bush.
"Anti-Semitism Is War," *Opinion: A Journal of Jewish Life and Letters May 1937*

2   I have never had the home-feeling anywhere since I was twelve years old; perhaps I never shall. I seem always to be standing on tiptoe at the edge of another, a different world. Perhaps Palestine, like the world of my childhood, will be nearer that world.
Remark to Elvie Wachenheim (16 July 1919), Quoted in *The Journey Home, How Jewish Women Shaped Modern America* by Joyce Antler* *1997*
*See 3320.

3   "And why shouldn't a girl be the Messiah?"
In the Beginning (unpub.novel) *n.d.*

4   I am reading James* Psychology [and] a history of Germany. The history I cannot abide; it deals only with wars and dates and kings; those are matters that do not interest me and that I cannot remember. History does not tell the real things.
The Speaking Heart (unpub. autiobio.) *n.d*
*William J- (1842–1920), American psychologist, philosopher.

5   My heart went out, seeking the God of my people. In thousands of homes those white candles burned tonight. I joined an invisible congregation.
Ibid.

1601. Florida Scott-Maxwell (1883–1979)

1   Age puzzles me. I thought it was a quiet time. My seventies were interesting and fairly serene, but my eighties are passionate. I grow more intense as I age.
The Measure of My Days 1972

2   No matter how old a mother is she watches her middle-aged children for signs of improvement.
Ibid.

3   I wonder why love is so often equated with joy when it is everything else as well. Devastation, balm, obsession, granting and receiving excessive value, and losing it again. It is recognition, often of what you are not but might be. It sears and it heals. It is beyond pity and above law. It can seem like truth.
Ibid.

4   When a new disability arrives I look about me to see if death has come, and I call quietly, "Death, is that you? Are you there?" So far the disability has answered, "Don't be silly, it's me."
Ibid.

5   If a grandmother wants to put her foot down, the only safe place to do it these days is in a note book.
Ibid.

6 Is there any stab as deep as wondering where and how much you failed those you loved?

Ibid.

7 Order, cleanliness, seemliness make a structure that is half support, half ritual, and—if it does not create it—maintains decency.

Ibid.

8 You need only claim the events of your life to make yourself yours. When you truly possess all you have been and done, which may take some time, you are fierce with reality.

Ibid.

1602. Marguerite Wilkinson (1883–1928)

1 God bless pawnbrokers!
They are quiet men.

"Pawnbrokers" n.d.

2 My father got me strong and straight and slim
And I give thanks to him.
My mother bore me glad and sound and sweet,
I kiss her feet!

"The End" n.d.

1603. Florence Ellinwood Allen (1884–1966)

1 Liberty cannot be caged into a charter and handed on ready made to the next generation. Each generation must re-create liberty for its own times. Whether or not we establish freedom rests with ourselves.

This Constitution of Ours 1940

2 The attainment of justice is the highest human endeavor.

Quoted in The 50 Most Influential Women in American Law by Dawn Bradley Berry* 1996

*See 4399.

1604. Ethel Percy Andrus (1884–1967)

1 To Serve, Not To Be Served.

Motto for American Association of Retired Persons (AARP) 1958

2 Aging is not a problem; it represents a real and thrilling challenge. It is one thing to recognize that older people represent the nation's greatest single human resource available, and it is quite another to do something about it.

Modern Maturity July 1958

3 To bring to each [student] a sense of his own worth by treating him with dignity and respect, by honoring his racial background not as a picturesque oddity, but as a valued contribution in the tapestry of American life.

Quoted in Modern Maturity January 1968

4 The human contribution is the essential ingredient. It is only in the giving of oneself to others that we truly live.

Quoted in The Wisdom of Ethel Percy Andrus by Ruth Lana and Jean Libma 1968

1605. Laura Benét (1884–1979)

1 Lost in the spiral of his conscience, he
Detachedly takes rest.

"The Snail" n.d.

2 No voice awoke. Dwelling sedate, apart
Only the thrush, the thrush that never spoke,
Sang from her bursting heart.

"The Thrush" n.d.

1606. Phyllis Bottome (1884–1963)

1 In my early life, and probably even today, it is not sufficiently understood that a child's education should include at least a rudimentary grasp of religion, sex, and money. Without a basic knowledge of these three primary facts in a normal human being's life—subjects which stir the emotions, create events and opportunities, and if they do not wholly decide must greatly influence an individual's personality—no human being's education can have a safe foundation.

Ch. 9, Search for a Soul 1947

1607. Mary "Molly" Colum (1884–1957)

1 Joyce* had devoted friends: he was a reliable friend himself, and would help one with any old thing—with finding an apartment or a maid or a doctor, with planning a journey or picking out a hotel. If one of his friends was ill, he would shower him with attentions—principally bottles of wine.

Pt. II, no. 10, Our Friend James Joyce 1958

*James Joyce (1882–1941), Irish novelist.

2 The only difference between the rich and other people is that the rich have more money.

Comment to Ernest Hemingway,* Quoted in Some Sort of Epic Grandeur: The Life of F. Scott Fitzgerald by Matthew J. Bruccoli 1981

*Ernest Miller H- (1899–1961), American writer.

1608. Helene Deutsch (1884–1982)

1 They have an extraordinary need of support when engaged in any *activity directed outward*, but are absolutely independent in such feeling and thinking as related to their inner life, that is to say, in their *activity directed inward*. Their capacity for identification is not an expression of inner poverty but of inner wealth.

The Psychology of Women, Vol. I 1944–45

2 After all, the ultimate goal of all research is not objectivity, but truth.

Ibid.

3 . . . adolescence is the period of the decisive last battle fought before maturity. The ego must achieve independence, the old emotional ties must be cast off, and new ones created.

Ch. 2, Ibid.

4 It is no exaggeration to say that among all living creatures, only man, because of his prehensile appendages, is capable of rape in the full meaning of this term—that is, sexual possession of the female against her will.

Ch. 6, Ibid.

5 All observations point to the fact that the intellectual woman is masculinized; in her, warm, intuitive knowledge has yielded to cold unproductive thinking.

Ch. 8, Ibid.

6 Psychoanalysis was my last and most deeply experienced revolution; and Freud,* who was rightly considered a conservative

on social and political issues, became for me the greatest revolutionary of the century.

> Ch. 10, Ibid.

*Sigmund F— (1856–1939), Austrian physician and founder of psychoanalysis.

7 The embattled gates to equal rights indeed opened up for modern women, but I sometimes think to myself: "That is not what I meant by freedom—it is only 'social progress.'"

> Ch. 1, *Confrontations with Myself* 1973

1609. Aalamtaaj Ghaaem-Maghami (1884–1947)
1 I never lived in Freedom but I know it now and forever
That Freedom is the only medicine for my pain and injure.

> Untitled poem *n.d.*

1610. Caroline Giltinan (1884–?)
1 To be alone, when Spring is being born,
One should be dead—or suddenly grown old.

> "Alone in Spring," *Anthology of Magazine Verse for 1920,*
> William Stanley Braíthwaite, ed. *1920*

2 Betrayer of the Master,
He sways against the sky,
A black and broken body,
Iscariot—or I?

> "Identity" *n.d.*

3 Let me keep my eyes on yours;
I dare not look away
Fearing again to see your feet
Cloven and of clay.

> "Disillusioned" *n.d.*

1611. Texas Guinan (1884–1933)
1 Fifty million Frenchmen can be wrong.

> Quoted in the *New York World-Telegram* 21 March 1931

2 I've been married once on the level, and twice in America.

> Nightclub Act *n.d.*

3 Success has killed more men than bullets.

> Ibid.

4 I would rather have a square inch of New York than all the rest of the world.

> Ibid.

5 It's having the same man around the house all the time that ruins matrimony.

> Ibid.

1612. Rose Henniker Heaton (1884–?)
1 She left no little things behind
Except loving thoughts and kind.

> "The Perfect Guest" *n.d.*

1613. Sara Murray Jordan (1884–1959)
1 In medicine, as in statecraft and propaganda, words are sometimes the most powerful drugs we can use.

> Quoted in *Reader's Digest* (New York) October 1958

2 A much more effective and lasting method of facelifting than surgical technique is happy thinking, new interests and outdoor exercise.

> Ibid.

3 Every businessman over 50 should have a daily nap and nip—a short nap after lunch and a relaxing highball before dinner.

> Ibid.

1614. Edith Summers Kelley (1884–1956)
1 ... the barnyard was an expression of something that was real, vital, and fluid, that ... was of natural and spontaneous growth, that ... turned with its surroundings, that ... was a part of the life that offered itself to her.

> *Weeds* 1923

2 The only break in what would seem to an outsider an intolerable stretch of tedium was the dinner. This usually consisted of salt hog meat, fried or boiled potatoes and some other vegetable, followed by a heavy-crusted apple pie or a soggy boiled pudding.

> Ibid.

1615. Fanny Heaslip Lea (1884–1955)
1 Children should be the result of love, not love the result of children.

> *Lolly* 1929

2 I have a little painted doll
Which wears the face of me;
I dress her up and send her out
With proper folk to tea.

> "I Have a Little Painted Doll," St. 1

3 It's odd to think we might have been
Sun, moon and stars unto each other—
Only, I turned down one little street
As you went up another.

> "Fate," St. 5 *n.d.*

1616. Alice Roosevelt Longworth (1884–1980)
1 He [Coolidge*] looks as if he had been weaned on a pickle.

> *Crowded Hours* 1934

*Calvin C— (1872–1933), 30th president of the United States (1923–29).

2 Were it not for Czolgosz [the assassin of President McKinley*], we'd all be back in our brownstone-front houses. That's where we'd be. And I would have married for money and been divorced for good cause.

> Quoted by Jean Vanden Heuvel in the *Saturday Evening Post*
> *4 December 1965*

*William M— (1843–1901), 25th president of the United States (1897–1901).

3 I have a simple philosophy. Fill what's empty. Empty what's full. And scratch where it itches.

> Quoted in *The Best* by Peter Russell and Leonard Ross 1974

1617. Ruth Mason Rice (1884–1927)
1 An oval, placid woman who assuaged men's lives;
Her comely hands wrought forth a century

Of oval, placid women who engaged, as wives,
In broideries and tea.

"Queen Victoria," *Afterward 1927*

2 Where are you going, multitude of feet?

"New York," *Ibid.*

3 But now—a loaf's an easy thing;
Made quickly by a blind machine;
And still—I find me hungering
For fare—unseen.

"Daily Bread," *Ibid.*

1618. Eleanor Roosevelt (1884–1962)

1 No one can make you feel inferior without your consent.

This Is My Story 1937

2 It is very difficult to have a free, fair and honest press anywhere in the world. In the first place, as a rule, papers are largely supported by advertising, and that immediately gives the advertisers a certain hold over the medium which they use.

If You Ask Me 1946

3 I used to tell my husband that, if he could make *me* understand something, it would be clear to all the other people in the country.

"My Day," syndicated newspaper column *12 February 1947*

4 Justice cannot be for one side only, but must be for both....

Ibid. *15 October 1947*

5 ... certain rights can never be granted to the government, but must be kept in the hands of the people.

Quoted in *The New York Times 3 May 1948*

6 A society in which everyone works is not necessarily a free society and may indeed be a slave society; on the other hand, a society in which there is widespread economic insecurity can turn freedom into a barren and vapid right for millions of people.

Speech, "The Struggle for Human Rights," (Paris) 27 *September 1948*

7 My own feeling is that the Near East, India and many of the Asiatic people have a profound distrust of white people. This is understandable since the white people they have known intimately in the past have been the colonial nations and in the case of the United States, our businessmen....

Report to President Truman* 1950
*Harry S. T— (1884–1972), 33rd president of the United States (1945–53).

8 We must preserve our right to think and differ.... The day I'm afraid to sit down with people I do not know because five years from now someone will say five of those people were Communists and therefore you are a Communist—that will be a bad day.

Speech, Americans for Democratic Action *2 April 1950*

9 There is a small articulate minority in this country which advocates changing our national symbol which is the eagle to that of the ostrich and withdrawing from the United Nations.

Speech, Democratic National Convention *23 July 1952*

10 Too often the great decisions are originated and given form in bodies made up wholly of men, or so completely dominated by them that whatever of special value women have to offer is shunted aside without expression.

Speech, United Nations *December 1952*

11 A mature person is one who does not think only in absolutes, who is able to be objective even when deeply stirred emotionally, who has learned that there is both good and bad in all people and in all things, and who walks humbly and deals charitably with the circumstances of life, knowing that in this world no one is all-knowing and therefore all of us need both love and charity.

It Seems to Me 1954

12 Could we have the vision of doing away in this great country with poverty? ... what can make us not only the nation that has some of the richest people in the world, but the nation where there are no people that have to live at a substandard level. That would be one of the very best arguments against Communism that we could possibly have.

Speech, Democratic National Convention *13 August 1956*

13 I have always felt that anyone who wanted an election so much that they would use those* methods did not have the character that I really admired in public life.

"Meet the Press," NBC TV *16 September 1956*
*Reference to Richard Nixon's smear campaign against Helen Gahagan Douglas; see 1897.

14 Where, after all, do universal human rights begin? In small places, close to home—so close and so small that they cannot be seen on any maps of the world. Yet they *are* the world of the individual persons; the neighborhood he lives in; the school or college he attends; the factory, farm or office where he works. Such are the places where every man, woman and child seeks equal justice, equal employment, equal dignity without discrimination. Unless these rights have meaning there, they have little meaning anywhere. Without concerned citizen action to uphold them close to home, we shall look in vain for progress in the larger world.

Speech, "The Great Question," United Nations *1958*

15 We cannot exist as a little island of well-being in a world where two-thirds of the people go to bed hungry every night.

Speech, Democratic Fund-Raising Dinner *8 December 1959*

16 You gain strength, courage, and confidence by every experience in which you really stop to look fear in the face.

"You Learn by Living" *1960*

17 You must do the thing you think you cannot do.

Ibid.

18 We have to face the fact that either all of us are going to die together or we are going to learn to live together and if we are to live together we have to talk.

Quoted by A. David Gurewitsch in *The New York Times 15 October 1960*

19 Perhaps the most important thing that has come out of my life is the discovery that if you prepare yourself at every point as well as you can, with whatever means you may have, however meager they may seem, you will be able to grasp opportunity for broader experience when it appears. Without preparation you cannot do it. The fatal thing is the rejection. Life was meant to be lived, and curiosity must be kept alive. One must never, for whatever reason, turn his back on life.

The Autobiography of Eleanor Roosevelt 1961

20 Both the President and his wife can never give way to appre-hension even though they are probably more aware than most citizens of the dangers which may surround us. If the country is to be confident, they must be confident.

"My Day," Syndicated newspaper column *29 May 1962*

21 They [Israelis] are still dreamers, but they make their dreams come true. . . .

Quoted by Ruth G. Michaels in *Hadassah December 1962*

22 This I know. This I believe with all my heart. If we want a free and peaceful world, if we want to make the deserts bloom and man grow to greater dignity as a human being—*we can do it!*

Tomorrow Is Now 1963

23 I think, at a child's birth, if a mother could ask a fairy god-mother to endow it with the most useful gift, that gift would be curiosity.

Today's Health (Chicago) *2 October 1966*

24 I'm glad I never *feel* important, it does complicate life.

Ch. 2, Quoted in *Eleanor: The Years Alone* by Joseph P. Lash *1972*

25 I cannot believe that war is the best solution. No one won the last war, and no one will win the next war.

Letter to Harry S. Truman* (22 March 1948), Ibid.
*(1884–1972), Am. politician; 33rd president of the United States (1945–1953).

26 Spiritual leadership should remain spiritual leadership and the temporal power should not become too important in any Church.

Letter to Cardinal Francis Spellman* (23 July 1949), Ibid.
*Francis Joseph S - (1889–1967), American prelate who was ap-pointed archbishop of New York in 1939 and cardinal in 1946.

27 The Jews in their own country are doing marvels and should, once the refugee problem is settled, help all the Arab countries.

Letter to Maude Gray (5 March 1952), Ibid.

28 Television has completely revolutionized what should go on at a convention.

Letter to Frank E. McKinney (13 July 1952), Ibid.

29 . . . I have spent many years of my life in opposition and I rather like the role.

Letter to Bernard Baruch* (18 November 1952), Ibid.
*B— Mannes B— (1870–1965), American financier and political adviser.

30 I believe that it is essential to our leadership in the world and to the development of true democracy in our country to have no discrimination in our country whatsoever. This is most impor-tant in the schools of our country.

Letter to Richard Bolling (20 January 1956), Ibid.

31 I doubt if Eisenhower can stand a second term and I doubt if the country can stand Nixon as President.

Letter to Lord Elibank (20 January 1956), Ibid.

32 When you cease to make a contribution you begin to die.

Letter to Mr. Horne (19 February 1960), Ibid.

33 To say he [John F. Kennedy]* would not make mistakes would be silly. Anyone would make mistakes with the problems that lie ahead of us.

Letter to Peter Kamitchis (21 October 1960), Ibid.
*(1917–63), 35th U.S. President of the United States (1961–1963); assassinated.

34 . . . on the whole, life is rather difficult for both the children and their parents in the "fish bowl" that lies before you.

Letter to Jacqueline Kennedy* (1 December 1960), Ibid.
*Later, Jacqueline Kennedy Onassis; see 2676.

35 You seem to think that everyone can save money if they have the character to do it. As a matter of fact, there are innumer-able people who have a wide choice between saving and giving their children the best possible opportunities. The decision is usually in favor of the children.

Letter to Franklin Roosevelt III (15 January 1962), Ibid.

1619. Sara Teasdale (1884–1933)

1 When I am dead and over me bright April
Shakes out her rain-drenched hair,
Though you should lean above me broken-hearted,
I shall not care.

"I Shall Not Care," St. 1, *Rivers to the Sea 1915*

2 One by one, like leaves from a tree,
All my faiths have forsaken me.

"Leaves," Ibid.

3 Joy was a flame in me
Too steady to destroy.

"The Answer," Ibid.

4 O beauty, are you not enough?
Why am I crying after love?

"Spring Night," *Love Songs 1918*

5 Spend all you have for loveliness.

"Barter," Ibid.

6 When I can look Life in the eyes,
Grown calm and very coldly wise,
Life will have given me the Truth,
And taken in exchange—my youth.

"Wisdom," Ibid.

7 I shall not let a sorrow die
Until I find the heart of it,
Nor let a wordless joy go by
Until it talks to me a bit.

"Servitors" *n.d.*

8 No one worth possessing
Can be quite possessed.

"Advice to a Girl" *n.d.*

9 Then, like an old-time orator
Impressively he rose;
"I make the most of all that comes
And the least of all that goes."

"The Philosopher," St. 4 *n.d.*

1620. Sophie Tucker (1884–1966)

1 Once you start carrying your own suitcases, paying your own bills, running your own show, you've done something to yourself that makes you one of those women men may like and call "pal" and a "good sport," the kind of woman they tell their troubles to. But you've cut yourself off from the orchids and the diamond bracelets, except those you buy yourself.

Some of These Days, with Dorothy Giles *1945*

2   Success in show business depends on your ability to make and
keep friends.

Ch. 4, Ibid.

3   From birth to age eighteen, a girl needs good parents. From
eighteen to thirty-five, she needs good looks. From thirty-five
to fifty-five, she needs a good personality. From fifty-five on,
she needs good cash.

Attributed 1953

4   Keep breathing.

Anniversary Speech 13 January 1964

5   Re radio: You can't do this, you can't do that. I couldn't even
say "hell or damn," and nothing, honey, is more expressive
than the way I say "hell or damn."

Quoted in "1860 to 1919," Women in Comedy by Linda
Martin & Kerry Segrave 1986

6   Gentlemen don't love love. They just like to kick it around.

Quoted in "Vaudeville Legends," Funny Women: American
Comediennes, 1860–1985 by Mary Unterbrink 1987

7   To me the mention of Israel is like the clang of a fire bell to a
fireman.

Address to trustees of Israel (7 February 1965), Quoted in The
Journey Home, How Jewish Women Shaped Modern America
by Joyce Antler* 1997

*See 3320.

8   Nothing mattered [to my mother] but the kinder*.... They
were her whole life just as children are the whole life of Judaism itself.

Speech (Hartford), Ibid.

*Yiddish for children.

9   I've been rich and I've been poor. Rich is better.

Performance patter n.d.

1621. Sophie Tunnell (1884–?)

1   Fear is a slinking cat I find
Beneath the lilacs of my mind.

"Fear" n.d.

1622. Anna Wickham (1884–1947)

1   It is well within the order of things
That man should listen when his mate sings;
But the true male never yet walked
Who liked to listen when his mate talked.

"The Affinity," The Contemplative Quarry 1915

2   I desire Virtue, though I love her not—
I have no faith in her when she is got:
I fear that she will bind and make me slave
And send me songless to the sullen grave.

"Self-Analysis," St. 3, Ibid.

3   I smother in the house in the valley below,
Let me out to the night, let me go!

"Divorce," The World Split Open, Louise Bernikow,* ed. 1974
*See 3174.

4   Because of the body's hunger we are born,
And by contriving hunger we are fed;
Because of hunger is our work well done,
And so our songs well sung, and things well said.

"Sehnsucht" n.d.

5   Desire and longing are the whips of God.

Ibid.

6   I have been so misused by chaste men with one wife
That I would live with satyrs all my life.

"Ship Near Shoals" n.d.

7   Alas! For all the pretty women who marry dull men,
Go into the suburbs and never come out again.

"Meditation at Kew" n.d.

1623. Theda Bara (1885–1955)

1   During the rest of my screen career, I am going to continue
doing vampires as long as people sin. For I believe that humanity needs the moral lesson and it needs it in repeatedly large
doses.

Tripod.com n.d.

2   I have the face of a vampire, but the heart of a feminist.

IMDb.com n.d

1624. Billie Burke (1885–1970)

1   To survive there, you need the ambition of a Latin-American
revolutionary, the ego of a grand opera tenor, and the physical
stamina of a cow pony.

Quoted in Filmgoer's Companion by Leslie Halliwell 1984

1625. Helen M. Cam (1885–1968)

1   We must not read either law or history backwards.

Introduction, Selected Essays of F. W. Maitland, H. D.
Hazeltine, G. Gapsley, and P. H. Winfield, eds. 1936

2   The authority of a statute made in Parliament is universally
recognized as superior to that of any other legislative act.

Ch. 12, England Before Elizabeth 1950

3   If civilisation is the art of living together with people not entirely like oneself, the first step in civilisation is not so much
the invention of material tools as the regularisation of social
habits. As soon as you begin to say "We always do things this
way" the foundations are laid. "Custom is before all law." As
soon as you begin to say "We have always done things this
way—perhaps that might be a better way," conscious law-mak-
ing is beginning. As soon as you begin to say "We do things
this way—they do things that way—what is to be done about
it?" men are beginning to feel towards justice, that resides between the endless jar of right and wrong.

Lecture, "Law as It Looks to a Historian," Girton College 18
February 1956

4   Historical fiction is not only a respectable literary form: it is a
standing reminder of the fact that history is about human beings.

Historical Novel 1961

5   . . . every historian knows that belief itself is a historical fact,
and that legend and myth cannot be left out of account in tracing the sequence of cause and effect.

Lecture, "Magna Carta—Event or Document?" Old Hall of
Lincoln's Inn 7 July 1967

1626. Gladys Cromwell (1885–1919)

1   Sorrow can wait,
For there is magic in the calm estate

Of grief; lo, where the dust complies
Wisdom lies.

"Folded Power" *n.d.*

1627. Isak Dinesen (1885–1962)

1   "What is man, when you come to think upon him, but a minutely set, ingenious machine for turning, with infinite artfulness, the red wine of Shiraz* into urine?"

Seven Gothic Tales 1934

*City in Iran famous for its wine.

2   I do not know if you remember the tale of the girl who saves the ship under mutiny by sitting on the powder barrel with her lighted torch . . . and all the time knowing that it is empty? This has seemed to me a charming image of the women of my time. There they were, keeping the world in order . . . by sitting on the mystery of life, and knowing themselves that there was no mystery.

"The Old Chevalier," Ibid.

3   "If only I could so live and so serve the world that after me there should never again be birds in cages. . . ."

"The Deluge at Norderney," Ibid.

4   I have seen a herd of elephants travelling through dense native forest . . . pacing along as if they had an appointment at the end of the world.

Pt. I, Ch. 1, *Out of Africa* 1938

5   The giraffe, in their queer, inimitable, vegetating gracefulness, as if it were not a herd of animals but a family of rare, long-stemmed, speckled gigantic flowers slowly advancing.

Ibid.

6   "All Natives are masters in the art of the pause, and thereby give perspective to a discussion."

Pt. V, Ch. 1, Ibid.

7   I don't believe in evil, I believe only in horror. In nature there is no evil, only an abundance of horror: the plagues and the blights and the ants and the maggots.

"Phantoms," *Prokosch, Voices: A Memoir* 1983

1628. Florence Kiper Frank (1885–1976)

1   The canny among the publishers know that an enormous popular appetite for the insulting of the famous must be gratified, and the modern biographer emerges from the editorial conference a sadist and a wiser man.

Morrow's Almanac 1929

2   Pooh-men!
We are done with them now,
Who had need of them then,-
I and you!

"Baby" *n.d.*

1629. Alice Gerstenberg (1885–1972)

1   HARRIET. I am what you wish the world to believe you are.
HETTY. You are the part of me that has been trained.
HARRIET. I am your educated self.
HETTY. I am the rushing river; you are the ice over the current.

*Overtones** 1915

*Harriet/Hetty are the conscious/unconscious of the same character; this was the first depiction of the subconscious on stage and made a tremendous impact on expressionism and psychological realism in theater.

1630. Malvina Hoffman (1885–1966)

1   My true center of work was not commissions. It was an enormous capacity for falling in love with everything around me. . . .

Quoted in "Malvina Hoffman," *Famous American Women* by Hope Stoddard 1970

2   . . . at heart we are really working for the angels. . . . What counts is the lasting integrity of the artist and the enduring quality of his work.

Ibid.

1631. Karen Horney (1885–1952)

1   Is not the tremendous strength in men of the impulse to creative work in every field precisely due to their feeling of playing a relatively small part in the creation of living beings, which constantly impels them to an overcompensation in achievement?

"The Flight from Womanhood," *Feminine Psychology* 1926

2   Like all sciences and all valuations, the psychology of women has hitherto been considered only from the point of view of men.

Ibid.

3   . . . it is necessary not to be too easily satisfied with ready-at-hand explanations for a disturbance.

Self-Analysis 1942

4   . . . concern should drive us into action and not into a depression.

Ibid.

5   But miracles occur in psychoanalysis as seldom as anywhere else.

Ibid.

6   Fortunately [psycho]analysis is not the only way to resolve inner conflicts. Life itself still remains a very effective therapist.

Our Inner Conflicts 1945

1632. Frances Parkinson Keyes (1885–1970)

1   Women were cats, all of them, unless they were fools, and there was no way of getting even with them, even, except by walking off with the men they wanted. . . .

Pt. I, Ch. 3, *The Great Tradition* 1939

2   "Well, it's a good thing to trust in Providence. But I believe the Almighty likes a little cooperation now and again."

Pt. III, Ch. 10, Ibid.

3   "I can't see that the Nazis are any different from the Communists, except that they're cleaner and better looking and better drilled. They're both stirring up trouble, they're both bent on destruction and despotism, they're both ready to go to any lengths to gain their ends!"

Pt. V, Ch. 15, Ibid.

4   Folks with their wits about them knew that advertisements were just a pack of lies—you had only to look at the claims of patent medicines!

Pt. I, Ch. 3, *Blue Camellia* 1957

5   ". . . young folks, them, don' never think 'bout nothin' only spend, spend, spend money, instead of save, save, save money, like us used to do, us. It's education, or either it's clothes, or

either it's something else, as long as somebody got to spend, spend, spend. Boys is plenny bad, I got to admit, yes, but girls is even worser."

Pt. V, Ch. 22, *Ibid.*

1633. Marie Laurencin (1885–1956)

1 Why should I paint dead fish, onions and beer glasses? Girls are so much prettier.

Quoted in *Time* (New York) *18 June 1956*

1634. Ettie Lee (1885–1974)

1 Every child has a right to a good home.

Quoted in *The Los Angeles Times 27 April 1974*

1635. Aline Triplett Michaelis (1885–1958)

1 Alone, yet never lonely,
Serene, beyond mischance,
The world was his, his only,
When Lindbergh flew to France.

"Lindbergh"* *n.d.*

*Charles A. L—, American aviator (1902–1974) who made the first nonstop solo trans-Atlantic flight.

1636. Adela Pankhurst (1885–1961)

1 We have no religious doctrine to preach, only a morality that is big enough to include all religions and that should give offence to none.

Quoted in *The Fighting Pankhursts** by David Mitchell *1967*

2 Profits and prostitution—upon these empires are built and kingdoms stand. . . .

"Communism and Social Purity," *Dreadnought* (London; February 1921), *Ibid.*

3 Their [politicians'] most outstanding characteristic, I should say, would be their inability to manage anything properly. What industry have they ever promoted but the gambling industry? What have they ever produced but strife and deficits? What resolve have they shown but a determination to grab for themselves, their friends and supporters whatever is available to grab?

Speech (ca. 1929), *Ibid.*

4 Capital and labour in alliance will require neither government control nor political interference, and the vast network of government which is impoverishing us today will become useless and will shrivel up and die away.

Ibid.

*See Christabel P—, 1553; Emmeline P—, 1235; Sylvia P—, 1583.

1637. Alice Paul (1885–1977)

1 Equality of rights under the law shall not be denied or abridged by the United States or by any State on account of sex.

Equal Rights Amendment* *1923*

*The wording of the proposed amendment was likely contributed to by several members of the National Woman's Party, of which Paul was founder and president.

2 It is better, as far as getting the vote is concerned I believe, to have a small, united group than an immense debating society.

Letter to Eunice R. Oberly (6 March 1914), Quoted in *Alice Paul and the National Woman's Party, 1912–1920* by Loretta Ellen Zimmerman *1964*

3 I have never doubted that equal rights was the right direction. Most reforms, most problems are complicated. But to me there is nothing complicated about ordinary equality. Which is a nice thing about our campaign. It really is true, at least to my mind, that only good will come to everybody with equality. . . . It seems to me it is not our problem how women use their equality or how men use their equality.

Quoted in *Women Suffragists* by Diana Star Helmer *1998*

4 You can't have peace in a world in which some women or some men or some nations are at different stages of development.

Ibid.

5 There had never [before] been a procession of women for any cause under the sun.*

Ibid.

*Reference to 3 March 1913, the day before Woodrow Wilson's inauguration as 28th United States president; 8,000 marchers, 10 bands, five squadrons of cavalry with chariots, 26 floats, and more, gathered together to demand women's suffrage.

6 Until women vote, every piece of legislation undertaken by the administration is an act of injustice to them. All laws affect the interests of women.

Motto, The *Suffragist,** *Ibid.*

*Official publication of the Congressional Committee of NAWSA, debut edition (November 1913)

7 It is not a war of women against men, for the men are helping loyally, but a war of women and men together against the politicians.

Ibid.

1638. Elizabeth Madox Roberts (1885–1941)

1 The wind found out my coat was thin.
It tried to tear my clothes away.
And the cold came in.

"Cold Fear," St. 3, *Under the Tree 1922*

1639. Constance Rourke (1885–1941)

1 An emotional man may possess no humor, but a humorous man usually has deep pockets of emotion, sometimes tucked away or forgotten.

Ch. 1, *American Humor 1931*

2 Comic resilience swept through them in waves, transcending the past, transcending terror, with a sense of comedy, itself a wild emotion.

Ch. 2, *Ibid.*

3 It is a mistake to look for the social critic—even Manqué—in Mark Twain.* In a sense the whole American comic tradition had been of social criticism: but this had been instinctive and incomplete, and so it proved to be in Mark Twain. . . . He was primarily a *raconteur*. . . . He was never the conscious artist, always the improviser.

Ch. 7, *Ibid.*

*Pen name of Samuel Langhorne Clemens (1835–1910), American author and humorist.

4 Humor has been a fashioning instrument in America, cleaving its way through the national life, holding tenaciously to the spread elements of that life. Its mode has often been swift and coarse and ruthless, beyond art and beyond established civilization. It has engaged in warfare against the established heritage, against the bonds of pioneer existence. Its objective—

the unconscious objective of a disunited people—has seemed to be that of creating fresh bonds, a new unity, the semblance of a society and the rounded completion of an American type.

> Ch. 9, Ibid.

1640. Marjorie Allen Seiffert (1885–1968)

1 Sorrow stands in a wide place,
Blind—blind—
Beauty and joy are petals blown
Across her granite face,
They cannot find sight or sentience in stone.

> "Sorrow," *A Woman of Thirty* 1919

2 Spring raged outside, but ghostly in my bed
A dead self lay and knew itself for dead.

> "A Full Storm," *The King with Three Faces and Other Poems* 1929

3 And love is worth what it cost you, nothing more.

> "The Horse-Leech's Daughter," Ibid.

4 Lust is the oldest lion of them all.

> "An Italian Chest" *n.d.*

1641. Clare Sheridan (1885–1970)

1 At the end of her days, she became superbly squaw-like, and would sit impassively for hours, staring into the fire, her head shrouded in a shawl. A figure of great moral fortitude and self-oblation was gradually fading out.

> *To the Four Winds* 1955

1642. Anna Louise Strong (1885–1970)

1 Some day I shall go by the world's highest mountains and most secret waters, traveling with the nomads in the heart of Asia!

> *The Road to the Gray Pamir* 1931

2 I'm reporter enough to know there is no absolute truth. Truth is for each of us - our picture of the world. When I say I want to tell the truth, I mean I want to paint my picture.

> Quoted in *Witness to Revolution: The Story of Anna Louise Strong* (documentary film), Maria Garigulo, author; Lucy Ostrander, producer/director 1986

1643. Sophie Treadwell (1885–1970)

1 PRISON BARBER (to Woman). You'll submit my lady, right to the end, you'll submit.

> Episode 9, *Machinal* 1928

1644. Bess Truman (1885–1982)

1 A woman's place in public is to sit beside her husband, be silent, and be sure her hat is on straight.

> Quoted in *Bess W. Truman* by Margaret Truman* 1986
> *Her daughter; see 2500.

2 I'm not used to this awful public life.

> Comment to Frances Perkins,* Quoted in *First Ladies* by Betty Boyd Caroli 1987
>
> *See 1584.

1645. Elinor Wylie (1885–1928)

1 I was, being human, born alone;
I am, being woman, hard beset;

I live by squeezing from a stone
The little nourishment I get.

In masks outrageous and austere
The years go by in single file;
And none has merited my fear,
And none has quite escaped my smile.

> "Let No Charitable Hope," Sts. 2–3 (1923),
> *Collected Poems* 1932

2 Honeyed words like bees,
Gilded and sticky, with a little sting.

> "Pretty Words," Ibid.

3 I love smooth words, like gold-enameled fish
Which circle slowly with a silken swish. . . .

> Ibid.

4 The worst and best are both inclined
To snap like vixens at the truth;
But, O, beware the middle mind
That purrs and never shows a tooth!

> "Nonsense Rhyme," St. 2, Ibid.

5 If you would keep your soul
From spotted sight and sound,
Live like the velvet mole,
Go burrow underground.

> "The Eagle and the Mole," St. 5(1921), Ibid.

1646. Zoë Akins (1886–1958)

1 LADY HELEN. To accuse is so easy that it is infamous to do so where proof is impossible!

> Act I, *Déclassé* 1919

2 OSCAR. But you've got a wife. It's all right to tell a wife the brutal truth, but you've got to go sort of easy with your lady-love.

> Act II, *Daddy's Gone A-Hunting* 1921

3 MRS. DAHLGREN. Shutting one's eyes is an art, my dear. I suppose there's no use trying to make you see that—but that's the only way one *can* stay married.

> Ibid.

4 CANAVA. The success-haters. . . . That's what I call them—the people who have never got what they want and turned sour on everybody who has. The world's full of them. . . . As soon as you've made good they begin to watch for you to fail. . . .

> Act I, *Greatness* 1922

5 CLEOFANTE. Work alone qualifies us for life, Sentoni.

> *The Portrait of Tiero* 1924

6 Mine was a love so exquisite that I
Rather than watch it wither chose to die:
So dress my grave, O friend, with no poor flower
Which in your quiet garden blooms an hour!

> "Epitaph," *The Hills Grow Smaller* 1937

7 In all my locked-up songs
No one but you belongs.

> "To H. R.," St. 1, Ibid.

1647. Margaret Anderson (1886–1973)

1 My unreality is chiefly this: I have never felt much like a human being. It's a splendid feeling.

> *My Thirty Years' War* 1930

2 I didn't know what to do about life—so I did a nervous breakdown that lasted many months.

Ibid.

3 In real love you want the other person's good. In romantic love
you want the other person.

The Fiery Fountains 1969

1648. Margaret Ayer Barnes (1886–1967)

1 There they were. Opinions. Jane bumped into them, tangible
obstacles in her path, things to be recognized, and accepted or
evaded, as the exigencies of the situation demanded.

Pt. 1, Ch. 1, *Years of Grace 1930*

2 "Curious, isn't it," he went on airily, "that 'talking with the
right people' means something so very different from 'talking
with the right person'?"

Pt. 3, Ch. 1, Ibid.

3 Childless women, Olivia reflected, slipped gracefully into middle age. There was no one particular awkward moment when
they climbed up on the shelf.

Ch. 1, *Westward Passage 1931*

4 "There's nothing half so real in life as the things you've done,"
she whispered. "Inexorably, unalterably *done*."

Ch. 4, Ibid.

5 "Character comes before scholarship. . . ."

Pt. I, Ch. 1, *Within This Present 1933*

1649. Frances Darwin Cornford (1886–1960)

1 A young Apollo, golden-haired,
Stands dreaming on the verge of strife,
Magnificently unprepared
For the long littleness of life.

"On Rupert Brooke,"* in toto, *Poems 1910*
*English poet (1837–1915).

2 O fat white woman whom nobody loves,
Why do you walk through the fields in gloves?

"To a Fat Lady Seen from the Train" *n.d.*

3 With what attentive courtesy he bent
Over his instrument;
Not as a lordly conquerer who could
Command both wire and wood,
But as a man with a loved woman might,
Inquiring with delight
What slight essential things she had to say
Before they started, he and she, to play.

"The Guitarist Tunes Up," in toto *n.d.*

1650. Hilda Doolittle (1886–1961)

1 "Why couldn't I have a dog? Cats are girls' animals."

"Old Tommy," *The Comrade 30 April 1911*

2 "Well, young man, if I'm not much mistaken, you'll have to
begin at the beginning, if ever you want to get to the end. That's
a platitude, if you know what that means. That means that it's
seven times seven times true, if you know how true that is. And
I'll tell you this, you'd better hurry and begin at the beginning,
or you can be quite sure you'll be pretty well forgotten at the
end."

Ibid.

3 "There never is anything a boy can do when he's not allowed
to go out because it rains. There never is anything a boy can
do!"

Ibid.

4 "I wonder how girls get such fun out of nothing!"

Ibid.

5 Why not let the pears cling
to the empty branch?
All your coaxing will only make
a bitter fruit—
let them cling, ripen of themselves,
test their own worth,
nipped, shrivelled by the frost,
to fall at last but fair
with a russet coat.

"Sheltered Garden," St. 6, *Sea Garden 1916*

1651. Hazel Hall (1886–1924)

1 *I am the dream of youth, and life is fair!*
Footfall, footfall;
I am a dream, divinely unaware!
Footfall, footfall;
I am the burden of an old despair!
Footfall.

"Footsteps" *n.d.*

1652. Clementine Hunter (1886/1887–1988)

1 My papa taught me how to pick cotton when I was 8 years old.
I didn't mind it. I'd rather pick cotton than to paint.

Quoted in "Clementine Hunter" by Mimi Read, *Dixie
Magazine 14 April 1985*

2 Work don't kill nobody. It make you tired though.

Ibid.

1653. Georgia Douglas Johnson (1886–1966)

1 I'm folding up my little dreams
Within my heart tonight,
And praying I may soon forget
The torture of their sight.

"My Little Dreams," St. 1, *The Book of American Negro
Poetry*, James Weldon Johnson, ed *1931 rev.*

2 The heart of a woman falls back with the night,
And enters some alien cage in its plight,
And tries to forget it has dreamed of the stars,
While it breaks, breaks, breaks on the sheltering bars.

"The Heart of a Woman," l. 5–8, *The Poetry of the Negro*,
Langston Hughes and Arna Bontemps, eds. *1970 rev.*

3 I want to die while you love me,
And never, never see
The glory of this perfect day
Grow dim, or cease to be!

"I Want to Die While You Love Me," l. 13–16, *American
Negro Poetry*, Arna Bontemps, ed. *1974 rev.*

1654. Rose Wilder Lane (1886–1965)

1 Even the street, the sunshine, the very air had a special Sunday quality. We walked differently on Sundays, with greater
propriety and stateliness. Greetings were more formal, more
subdued, voices more meticulously polite. Everything was so

smooth, bland, polished. And genuinely so, because this was Sunday. In church the rustling and the stillness were alike pervaded with the knowledge that all was for the best. Propriety ruled the universe. God was in His Heaven, and we were in our Sunday clothes.

Ch. 1, *Old Hometown 1935*

2   It was not seen that woman's place was in the home until she began to go out of it; the statement was a reply to an unspoken challenge, it was attempted resistance to irresistible change.

Ibid.

3   Two deep human desires were at war . . . the longing for stability, for form, for permanence, which in its essence is the desire for death, and the opposing hunger for movement, change, instability and risk, which are life. Men came from the east and built these American towns because they wished to go no farther, and the towns they built were shaped by the urge to go onward.

Ibid.

4   The prairies were dust. Day after day, summer after summer, the scorching winds blew the dust and the sun was brassy in a yellow sky. Crop after crop failed. Again and again the barren land must be mortgaged for taxes and food and next year's seed. The agony of hope ended when there was not harvest and no more credit, no money to pay interest and taxes; the banker took the land. Then the bank failed.

Ibid.

5   Making the best of things is . . . a damn poor way of dealing with them. . . .

Letter to Guy Moyston (25 August 1924), Quoted in *The Ghost in the Little House* by William V. Holtz *1993*

6   We joined long wagon trains moving south; we met hundreds of wagons going north; the roads east and west were crawling lines of families traveling under canvas, looking for work, for another foothold somewhere on the land. . . .   The country was ruined, the whole world was ruined; nothing like this had ever happened before. There was no hope, but everyone felt the courage of despair.

(1935), Ch. 1, Ibid.

7   I somehow always have this idea that as soon as I can get through this work that's piled up ahead of me, I'll really write a beautiful thing. But I never do. I always have the idea that someday, somehow, I'll be living a beautiful life.

(1923 journal entry), Ch. 7, Ibid.

8   Life is a thin narrowness of taken-for-granted, a plank over a canyon in a fog. There is something under our feet, the taken-for-granted. A table is a table, food is food, we are we—because we don't question these things. And science is the enemy because it is the questioner. Faith saves our souls alive by giving us a universe of the taken-for-granted.

(1920s), Quoted in Ch. 8, Ibid.

1655. Frances Marion (1886–1973)

1   The thought had taken root in his imagination and grown as a tree grows from a tiny seed until it crowded out all other thoughts in his mind.

Pt. I, Ch. 1, *Westward the Dream 1948*

2   The land around San Juan Capistrano is the pocket where the Creator keeps all his treasures. Anything will grow there, from wheat and beans to citrus fruit.

Ch. 3, Ibid.

3   "Do we really know anybody? Who does not wear one face to hide another?"

Ch. 10, Ibid.

4   What a strange pattern the shuttle of life can weave. . . .

Pt. II, Ch. 14, Ibid.

5   This is not dead land, it is only thirsty land.

Pt. II, Ch. 22, Ibid.

6   "A coin, Mr. Fox, can only fall heads or tails, and I'll gamble on heads, they last longer."

Off with Their Heads 1972

7   I shall refrain from mentioning to our southern neighbors that San Franciscans look upon the City of the Queen of the Angels as California's floating kidney transplanted from the Middle West.

"1914 Through 1924," Ibid.

8   Promises that you make to yourself are often like the Japanese plum tree—they bear no fruit.

Ibid.

9   We have a little catch phrase in our family which somehow fits almost everyone in the movie colony: "Spare no expense to make everything as economical as possible."

Ibid.

10   One thing you learned when you wrote for the movies: all nationalities were sensitive except Americans. The Arabs were always to be pictured as sweet, friendly people. So were the Greeks, the Dutch, Turks, Laps, Eskimos, and so on down the line. Everyone was honest and virtuous, except Americans. You could make them the most sinister villains and never hear a word of protest from Washington, Chicago, Kalamazoo, or all points south. But should you describe a villain belonging to any country but America, you found yourself spread-eagled between the Board of Censors and the diplomatic service of some foreign power.

"1925 Through 1928," Ibid.

1656. Cecilia Razovsky (1886/1891–1968)

1   We owe it to ourselves and to our families to take an active part in the civic and communal affairs of the city in which we live.

"Paying Our Rent" (n.d.), p. 223, *The Journey Home, How Jewish Women Shaped Modern America* by Joyce Antler* *1997*

*See 3320.

2   As intelligent voters we must try to understand state and national issues. Above all, we must help create an intelligent public opinion as how best to promote international understanding.

Ibid.

1657. Ida Rosenthal (1886–1973)

1   Nature made woman a bosom, so nature thought it was important. Why argue with nature? . . . A sister shouldn't look like a brother.*

Quoted in *Women Inventors* by Linda Jacobs Altman *1997*

*Discoursing her reasons for rejecting the flattening bandeau of the 1920s and devising the modern-day bra.

1658. Mary Wigman (1886–1973)

1   Art is communication spoken by man for humanity in a language raised above the everyday happening.
"The New German Dance," *Modern Dance*,
Virginia Stewart, ed. *1935*

2   During the process of artistic creation, man descends into the primordial elements of life. He reverts to himself to become lost in something greater than himself, in the immediate, indivisible essence of life.
Ibid.

3   Strong and convincing art has never arisen from theories.
Ibid.

1659. Ruth Benedict (1887–1948)

1   No man ever looks at the world with pristine eyes. He sees it edited by a definite set of customs and institutions and ways of thinking.
Ch. 1, *Patterns of Culture 1934*

2   War is, we have been forced to admit, even in the face of its huge place in our own civilization, an asocial trait.
Ibid.

3   "Hybrid vigor" has been shown in studies of American Indian-White mixture, stature in the half-breeds being greater than that of either race contributing to the cross. Mixed bloods also show over and over again evidence of increased fertility. . . . Nature apparently does not condemn the half-caste to physiological inferiority. The rule for the breeding of good human stock is that both parents be of good physique and good mental ability.
Ch. 4, Ibid.

4   Racism in its nationalistic phase, therefore, has been a politician's plaything. . . . It is a dangerous plaything, a sword which can be turned in any direction to condemn the enemy of the moment.
Ch. 7, *Race: Science and Politics 1940*

5   But the Thai have an indestructible conviction that existence is good, and they have characteristically placed the promised rewards of Buddhism in this life rather [than] in the life to come.
Pt. II, Ch. 5, *Thai Culture and Behavior 1943*

6   The Japanese are, to the highest degree, both aggressive and unaggressive, both militaristic and aesthetic, both insolent and polite, rigid and adaptable, submissive and resentful of being pushed around, loyal and treacherous, brave and timid, conservative and hospitable to new ways.
Ch. 1, *The Chrysanthemum and the Sword 1946*

7   A man's indebtedness . . . is not virtue; his repayment is. Virtue begins when he dedicates himself actively to the job of gratitude.
Ch. 6, Ibid.

8   . . . the passionate belief in the superior worth-whileness of our children. It is stored up in us as a great battery charged by the accumulated instincts of uncounted generations.
Quoted in *An Anthropologist at Work* by Margaret Mead*
1951
*See 1935.

9   I long to speak out the intense inspiration that comes to me from the lives of strong women.
(January 1917), Ibid.

10   . . . work even when I'm satisfied with it is never my child I love nor my servant I've brought to heel. It's always busy work I do with my left hand, and part of me watches grudging the wastes of a lifetime.
(9 June 1934), Ibid.

1660. Violet Bonham-Carter (1887–1969)

1   Hold on, hold out; we are coming.
Journal of Liberal Democrat History 1937

2   [He] has a brilliant mind until it is made up.*
Quoted in Ch. 12, *The Fine Art of Political Wit* by Leon Harris *1964*
*Reference to British Labour politician Sir Stafford Cripps.

3   I have never before . . . met anyone so completely un-house-trained.
Daring to Hope: the diaries and letters of Violet Bonham Carter 1946–1969, Mark Pottle, ed. *2000*
"Heart and Mind" *n.d.*

1661. Jessie Chambers (1887–1965)

1   So instead of a release and deliverance from bondage, the bondage was glorified and made absolute. His [D. H. Lawrence's] mother conquered indeed, but the vanquished one was her son.
D. H. Lawrence: A Personal Record * 1935*
*D. H. Lawrence, English author (1885–1930).

1662. Elizabeth Drew (1887–1965)

1   Just as it is still in her close personal relationships that woman most naturally uses her human genius and her artistry in life, so it is still in the portrayal of those relationships that she perfects her most characteristic genius in writing.
"Is There a 'Feminine' Fiction?," *The Modern Novel 1926*

2   The test of literature is, I suppose, whether we ourselves live more intensely for the reading of it. . . .
Ibid.

3   The world is not run by thought, nor by imagination, but by opinion. . . .
"Sex Simplexes and Complexes," Ibid.

4   Sown in space like one among a handful of seeds in a suburban garden, the earth exists; a revolving, tepid sphere, whose every rotation brings it relentlessly nearer to the moon's dim, white, rotten desolation. Dwelling in this spinning island of terror, under immutable sentence of death, is Man, who, whether we regard him with the Psalmist as a little lower than the angels, or as "an ape, reft of his tail and grown rusty at climbing"; whether we see him shouting exultantly that he is the captain of his soul, or meeting his fate with all the lumbering discomfort of a cow being hustled into a railway truck, remains yet the ultimate mystery.
"The New Psychology," Ibid.

5   But though personality is a skin that no writer can slip, whatever he may write about: though it is a shadow which walks inexorably by his side, so also is the age he lives in.
"The Novel and the Age," Ibid.

6 The pain of loss, moreover, however agonizing, however haunting in memory, quiets imperceptibly into acceptance as the currents of active living and of fresh emotions flow over it.

Pt. II, Ch. 9, Poetry: A Modern Guide to Its Understanding and Enjoyment 1959

7 Propaganda has a bad name, but its root meaning is simply to disseminate through a medium, and all writing therefore is propaganda for *something*. It's a seeding of the self in the consciousness of others.

Ch. 10, Ibid.

8 How frail and ephemeral . . . is the material substance of letters, which makes their very survival so hazardous. Print has a permanence of its own, though it may not be much worth preserving, but a letter! Conveyed by uncertain transportation, over which the sender has no control; committed to a single individual who may be careless or inappreciative; left to the mercy of future generations, of families maybe anxious to suppress the past, of the accidents of removals and housecleanings, or of mere ignorance. How often it has been by the veriest chance that they have survived at all.

"The Literature of Gossip," The Literature of Gossip 1964

1663. Edna Ferber (1887–1968)

1 From supper to bedtime is twice as long as from breakfast to supper.

Ch. 1, Foreword, Roast Beef, Medium 1911

2 "There are only two kinds of people in the world that really count. One kind's wheat and the other kind's emeralds."

Ch. 1, So Big 1924

3 "Woman's work! Housework's the hardest work in the world. That's why men won't do it."

Ch. 8, Ibid.

4 "But 'most any place is Baghdad if you don't know what will happen in it."

Ch. 10, Ibid.

5 "Any piece of furniture, I don't care how beautiful it is, has got to be lived with, kicked about, and rubbed down, and mistreated by servants, and repolished, and knocked around and dusted and sat on or slept in or eaten off of before it develops its real character," Salina said. "A good deal like human beings."

Ch. 15, Ibid.

6 But his gifts were many, and not the least of them was the trick of appearing sartorially and tonsorially flawless when dishevelment and a stubble were inevitable in any other male.

Ch. 1, Show Boat 1926

7 "Don't you believe 'em when they say that what you don't know won't hurt you. Biggest lie ever was. See it all and go your own way and nothing'll hurt you. If what you see ain't pretty, what's the odds! See it anyway. Then next time you don't have to look."

Ch. 13, Ibid.

8 Wasn't marriage, like life, unstimulating and unprofitable and somewhat empty when too well ordered and protected and guarded. Wasn't it finer, more splendid, more nourishing, when it was, like life itself, a mixture of the sordid and the magnificent; of mud and stars; of earth and flowers; of love and hate and laughter and tears and ugliness and beauty and hurt?

Ch. 19, Ibid.

9 "The gaudiest star-spangled cosmic joke that ever was played on a double-dealing government burst into fireworks today when, with a roar that could be heard for miles around, thousands of barrels of oil shot into the air on the miserable desert land known as the Osage Indian reservation and occupied by those duped and wretched—!"

Ch. 20, Cimarron 1929

10 "If American politics are too dirty for women to take part in, there's something wrong with American politics."

Ch. 23, Ibid.

11 "I am not belittling the brave pioneer men, but the sunbonnet as well as the sombrero has helped to settle this glorious land of ours."

Ibid.

12 KITTY (a social climber). I was reading a book the other day . . . It's all about civilization or something. A nutty kind of a book. Do you know that the guy said that machinery is going to take the place of every profession?
CARLOTTA (a former stage star). Oh my dear. That's something you need never worry about.

Dinner at Eight, with George S. Kaufman 1932

13 The calla lilies are in bloom again.

Stage Door, with George S. Kaufman 1936

14 America—rather, the United States—seems to me to be the Jew among the nations. It is resourceful, adaptable, maligned, envied, feared, imposed upon. It is warm-hearted, overfriendly; quick-witted, lavish, colorful; given to extravagant speech and gestures; its people are travelers and wanderers by nature, moving, shifting, restless; swarming in Fords, in ocean liners; craving entertainment; volatile. The schnuckle* among the nations of the world.

Ch. 1, A Peculiar Treasure 1939
*German or Yiddish for sheep; an expression of endearment approximating "darling pet."

15 The goat's business is none of the sheep's concern.

Ch. 2, Saratoga Trunk 1941

16 "You lose in the end unless you know how the wheel is fixed or can fix it yourself."

Ch. 14, Ibid.

17 It was part of the Texas ritual. We're rich as son-of-a-bitch stew but look how homely we are, just as plain-folksy as Grandpappy back in 1836. We know about champagne and caviar but we talk hog and hominy.

Ch. 2, Giant 1952

18 A woman can look both moral and exciting—if she also looks as if it was quite a struggle.

Quoted in The Reader's Digest December 1954

19 If men ever discovered how tough women actually are, they would be scared to death.

A Kind of Magic 1963

1664. Helen Hoyt (1887–1972)

1 At present most of what we know, or think we know, of women has been found out by men, we have yet to hear what woman will tell of herself, and where can she tell more intimately than in poetry?

Quoted in Others: A Magazine of the New Verse 1916

2 My heart led me past and took me away;
  And yet it was my heart that wanted to stay.
  "In the Park" n.d.

1665. Violet Jessop (1887–1971)

1 One awful moment of empty, misty blackness enveloped us in its loneliness, then an unforgettable, agonizing cry went up from 1500 despairing throats, a long wail and then silence and our tiny craft tossing about at the mercy of the ice field.
  Titanic Survivor, John Maxtone-Graham, ed. and annot. *1997*

1666. Florence Luscomb (1887–1985)

1 . . . there is no end to what you can accomplish if you don't care who gets the credit.
  Quoted in *Moving the Mountain* by Ellen Cantarow *1980*

2 The tragedy in the lives of most of us is that we go through life walking down a high-walled land with people of our own kind, the same economic situation, the same national background and education and religious outlook. And beyond those walls, all humanity lies, unknown and unseen, and untouched by our restricted and impoverished lives.
  Oral History Project, University of Rhode Island (1972/73), Ibid.

3 And when women are working side by side with them on all the great public issues, and carrying on the life of humanity, I think that men are going to get comradeship that only the really advanced men have now. And when we have amended the Declaration of Independence so that it reads, "All men and women are created equal," this new force of men and women will be able to go forward and create a society of peace and of social justice and of beauty we haven't ever known in this world.
  Ibid.

4 I have come face-to-face with the question, "Is America still a democracy? Is it ruled by the people, by their votes?" and I have been forced to answer, "No." Behind the screen of the ballot, the real holders of power who decide national policies and laws, and control public opinion by their ownership of all the mass media of information are the great industrial and monetary monopolies who own our national economic life. They, together with the armed forces—the military industrial complex—are the real rulers of our country today.
  Ibid.

5 Capitalism, by definition, sets money as the sole model of power which keeps us running. Every man for himself. From my lifetime experiences, I have reached the firm conviction that the only possible basis for a successful, just, and peaceful world society is a cooperative economy of production for human needs, not for individual profits. That is the basic principle of communism.
  Ibid.

6 It is subversive to set up inquisitions like this, state or national, into the thoughts and consciences of Americans. . . . It is subversive for commissions like this to spread hysteria and intimidation throughout the land that Americans are afraid to sign petitions, afraid to read progressive magazines, afraid to make out checks for liberal causes, afraid to join organizations, afraid to speak their mind on public issues. Americans dare not be free citizens! This is the destruction of democracy.
  Statement to Commission to Investigate Communism in Massachusetts (7 January 1955), Ibid.

1667. Mother Maribel (1887–1970)

1 Silence is not a thing we make; it is something into which we enter. It is always there. We talk about keeping silence. We keep only that which is precious. Silence is precious, for it is of God. In silence all God's acts are done; in silence alone can his voice be heard and his word spoken.
  Quoted by Sister Janet CSMV, *Mother Maribel of Wantage [England] 1973*

2 Our real work is prayer. What good is the cold iron of our frantic little efforts unless first we heat it in the furnace of our prayer? Only heat will diffuse heat.
  Ibid.

3 So often we try to alter circumstances to suit ourselves, instead of letting them alter us, which is what they are meant to do.
  Ibid.

1668. Agnes Meyer (1887–1970?)

1 What the Nation must realize is that the home, when both parents work, is non-existent. Once we have honestly faced the fact, we must act accordingly.
  "Living Conditions of the Woolworker," *Washington Post 10 April 1943*

2 An orderly existence creates primarily an unconscious relation to the silent progression of the days, seasons, and the music of the spheres.
  Out of These Roots 1953

3 In the pursuit of an educational program to suit the bright and the not-so-bright we have watered down a rigid training for the elite until we now have an educational diet in many of our public high schools that nourishes neither the classes nor the masses.
  Ch. 2, Ibid.

4 Let us hope that in the process of integration in our society, which fortunately is now well underway, the Negro will not allow the American steam roller of conformity to destroy his creative gifts.
  Ch. 8, Ibid.

5 The children are always the chief victim of social chaos.
  Ch. 13, Ibid.

6 Christianity must now rise above the limits of orthodoxy just as the free world must rise above the limitations of nationalism if we are not to pull the civilized world down around our ears.
  Lecture, "Democracy and Clericalism" *21 May 1954*

7 We Americans must now throw off our childishness and parochialism and create a new idea of man acceptable to thinking people the world over.
  Ch. 1, *Education for a New Morality 1957*

8 There is a need for heroism in American life today.
  Ibid.

9 From the nineteenth-century view of science as a god, the twentieth century has begun to see it as a devil. It behooves us now to understand that science is neither one nor the other.
  Ch. 3, Ibid.

1669. Marianne Moore (1887–1972)

1 There is a great amount of poetry in unconscious fastidiousness.
  "Critics and Connoisseurs," *Collected Poems 1935*

2 The deepest feeling always shows itself in silence;
   not in silence, but restraint. . . .
                                    "Silence," Ibid.

3   we
   do not admire what
   we cannot understand.
                                    "Poetry," St. 1, Ibid.

4 I wonder what Adam and Eve
   think of it by this time.
                                    "Marriage," Ibid.

5 My father used to say,
   "Superior people never make long visits,
   Have to be shown Longfellow's* grave
   or the glass flowers at Harvard."
                                    "Silence," Ibid.
   *Henry Wadsworth Longfellow, American poet (1807–82).

6 I'm troubled, I'm dissatisfied, I'm Irish.
                              "Spenser's* Ireland," St. 1, Ibid.
   *Edmund Spenser, English poet (1552?–99).

7 Among animals, one has a sense of humor.
   Humor saves a few steps, it saves years.
                              "The Pangolin," St. 1, Ibid.

8 . . . The world's an orphan's home. . . .
                              "In Distrust of Merits," St. 7, Ibid.

9 Beauty is everlasting
   And dust is for a time.
                                    Ibid.

10 Three foremost aids to persuasion which occur to me are humility, concentration, and gusto.
        Speech, "Humility, Concentration, and Gusto," Grolier Club
                                    21 December 1948

11 [The] whirlwind fife-and-drum of the storm
   bends the salt
   marsh grass, disturbs stars in the sky and
   the star on the steeple; it is a privilege to
   see so much confusion.
                              "The Steeple-Jack," Collected Poems 1951

12 To wear the arctic fox
   you have to kill it.
                        "The Arctic Fox (or Goat)," O to Be a Dragon 1959

13 O to be a dragon
   a symbol of the power of Heaven—of silkworm
   size or immense; at times invisible.
   Felicitous phenomenon!
                                    "O to Be a Dragon," Ibid.

14 Fanaticism? No. Writing is exciting
   and baseball is like writing.
      You can never tell with either
      how it will go
      or what you will do;
              "Baseball and Writing," St. 1, The Complete Poems of
                                    Marianne Moore 1961

15 The power of the visible is the invisible
                        "He 'Digesteth Harde Yron'," St. 8, Ibid.

16 He fights and he writes.

   Is there something I have missed?
   He is a smiling pugilist.
              Liner notes, "On Muhammad Ali",* I Am the Greatest
                              (album), Cassius Clay 1963
   *American boxer (né Cassius Clay; 1942–).

17 A writer is unfair to himself when he is unable to be hard on
   himself.
              Interview in Writers at Work (Second Series), George
                              Plimpton,* ed. 1963
   *American writer and editor (1917–2003).

18 Egotism is usually subversive of sagacity.
              No. 82 (New York, March 1927), Complete Prose 1987

19 Those who are deaf to the sublime, have to be without it; that
   is their honorarium.
              Letter to e. e. cummings* (5 March 1938), The Selected
                    Letters of Marianne Moore, Bonnie Costello, ed. 1997
   *American poet (1894–1962).

20 With its baby rivers and little towns, each with its
      abbey or its cathedral,
   with voices—one voice perhaps, echoing through
      the transept—The
   criterion of suitability and convenience.
                                    "England" n.d.

1670. Georgia O'Keeffe (1887–1986)

1 . . . nobody sees a flower—really—it is so small—we haven't
   time—and to see takes time like to have a friend takes time. If I
   could paint the flower exactly as I see it no one would see what
   I see because I would paint it small like the flower is small. So I
   said to myself—I'll paint what I see—what the flower is to me
   but I'll paint it big and they will be surprised into taking time
   to look at it—I will make even busy New Yorkers take time
   to see what I see of flowers. . . . Well, I made you take time to
   look at what I saw and when you took time to really notice
   my flower you hung all your own associations with flowers on
   my flower and you write about my flower as if I think and see
   what you think and see of the flower—and I don't.
              (ca. 1939), Quoted in Georgia O'Keeffe by Lloyd Goodrich
                                    and Doris Bry 1970

2 I grew up pretty much as everybody else grows up, and one
   day . . . [in 1916] found myself saying to myself—I can't live
   where I want to—I can't go where I want to—I can't do what
   I want to—I can't even say what I want to—School and things
   that painters have taught me even keep me from painting as I
   want to. I decided I was a very stupid fool not to at least paint
   as I wanted to and say what I wanted to when I painted as
   that seemed to be the only thing I could do that didn't concern anybody but myself—that was nobody's business but my
   own. . . .
                                    Ibid.

3 . . . that Blue [of the sky] . . . will always be there as it is now
   after all man's destruction is finished.
              Quoted in "Flowers, Bones, and the Blue" by Alfred
              Frankenstein (ca. 1919), San Francisco Chronicle 14 March
                                    1971

4 The desert is the last place you can see all around you. The
   light out here makes everything close, and it is never, never the

same. Sometimes the light hits the mountains from behind and front at the same time, and it gives them the look of Japanese prints, you know, distances in layers.

> Quoted in "A Visit with Georgia O'Keeffe" by Beth Coffelt, *San Francisco Examiner & Chronicle* 11 April 1971

5 Where I was born, and where and how I lived is unimportant. It is what I have done and where I have been that should be of interest.

> *Georgia O'Keeffe 1985*

6 My first memory is of the brightness of light, light all around.

> Ibid.

7 One can not be an American by going about saying that one is an American. It is necessary to feel America, like America, love America and then work.

> *Chicago Evening Post* (2 March 1926), Ibid.

8 Singing has always seemed to me the most perfect means of expression. It is so spontaneous. And after singing, I think the violin. Since I cannot sing, I paint.

> *New York Sun* (5 December 1922), Ibid.

9 I hate flowers—I paint them because they're cheaper than models and they don't move.

> *New York Herald Tribune* (18 April 1954), Ibid.

1671. Ruth Law Oliver (1887–1970)

1 I had a great desire to take off and go somewhere in flight, never having done it.

> Ch. 4, *The American Heritage History of Flight 1962*

1672. Rebecca Shelley (1887–1984)

1 Humanity above all nations!

> "Bicentennial Prayer for Peace" 1976

1673. Edith Sitwell (1887–1964)

1 Every one hundred years or so it becomes necessary for a change to take place in the body of poetry. . . . A fresh movement appears and produces a few great men, and once more the force and vigour die from the results of age; the movement is carried on by weak and worthless imitators, and a change becomes necessary again.

> *Poetry and Criticism 1926*

2 Daisy and Lily
Lazy and silly. . . .

> "Façade" (1922), *Façade and Other Poems 1920–1935 1950*

3 I have often wished I had time to cultivate modesty. . . . But I am too busy thinking about myself.

> Quoted in *Observer* (London) *30 April 1950*

4 I'm not the man to baulk at a low smell,
I'm not the man to insist on asphodel.
This sounds like a He-fellow, don't you think?
It sounds like that. I belch, I brawl, I drink.

> "One-Way Song," *Collected Poems 1954*

5 Jane, Jane
Tall as a crane,
The morning light creaks down again.

> "Aubade," Ibid.

6 Alas, that he who caught and sang the sun in flight, yet was the sun's brother, and never grieved it on its way, should have left us with no good-bye, good night.

> "Dylan Thomas,"* *Atlantic Monthly* (Boston) February *1954*
> *Welsh poet (1914–1953).

7 A lady asked me why, on most occasions, I wore black. "Are you in mourning?"
"Yes."
"For whom are you in mourning?"
"For the world."

> Ch. 1, *Taken Care Of 1965*

8 . . . I have never, in all my life, been so odious as to regard myself as "superior" to any living being, human or animal. I just walked alone—as I have always walked alone.

> Ch. 2, Ibid.

9 MR. MUGGLEBY LION. I hate to disturb you, but I have just finished a *Little Sonnet*, that I *must* read to you.
HIERATIC WOMAN (coldly). It can't be a *Little* Sonnet, Mr. Muggleby Lion. Sonnets are all of the same size.

> Ch. 13, Ibid.

10 Rhythm is one of the principal translators between dreams and reality. Rhythm might be described, as to the world of sound, what light is to the world of sight. It shares and gives new meaning. Rhythm was described by Schopenhauer* as melody deprived of its pitch.

> Ch. 14, Ibid.

> *(1788–1860), German philosopher.

11 A pompous woman of his acquaintance, complaining that the head-waiter of a restaurant had not shown her and her husband immediately to a table, said, "We had to tell him who we were." Gerald [Lord Berners], interested, enquired, "And who were you?"

> Ch. 15, Ibid.

12 . . . the heartless stupidity of those who have never known a great and terrifying poverty.

> Ch. 22, Ibid.

1674. Vicki Baum (1888–1960)

1 GRUSINSKAYA. I want to be alone.

> *Grand Hotel* (play) *1930*

2 Fame always brings loneliness. Success is as ice cold and lonely as the north pole.

> *Grand Hotel* (novel) *1931*

3 A woman who is loved always has success.

> Ibid.

4 Pity is the deadliest feeling that can be offered to a woman.

> *And Life Goes On 1932*

5 Marriage always demands the greatest understanding of the art of insincerity possible between two human beings.

> Ibid.

6 To be a Jew is a destiny.

> Ibid.

1675–1676. Marjorie Bowen (1888–1952)

1 "If you live in the world you must live on the world's terms."

> Ch. 10, *General Crack 1928*

2 "If you can't command your own soul, how can I give you enlightenment how to do so?"

Ibid.

3 Useless for one who did not believe in Heaven to renounce the World: that would be to fall into a void.

Ibid.

4 "It is more difficult, my lord, to rule the King's favourites that for the favourites to rule the King."

Ch. 1, *My Tattered Loving 1937*

5 Meanwhile, he continued to search for a brisk and subtle poison, for it seemed to him that one who could make the discovery of such a weapon as this would be more powerful than the greatest of kings.

Ch. 2, Ibid.

6 Flattery is so necessary to all of us that we flatter one another just to be flattered in return. . . .

"The Art of Flattery," *World's Wonder 1937*

7 As civilisation advanced, people began to discover that more was to be gained by flattery than by force—and that flattery had a larger purchasing power than coin of the realm.

Ibid.

8 "Leave well alone, my dear Miss Lawne."
   "But perhaps we are leaving evil alone," replied the lady, smiling.
   "In that case, also, have nothing to do with it."

Ch. 1, *Mignonette 1948*

9 Custom reclaimed her. . . . So, insidiously, her middle-class respectability hemmed in Barbara Lawne. . . . Only in her dreams did she explore wild and darkling landscapes. . . .

Ch. 2, Ibid.

10 Even a fool can deceive a man—if he be a bigger fool than himself.

"The Glen o' Weeping" *n.d.*

1677. Clemence Dane (1888–1965)

1 SYDNEY. It's extraordinary to me—whenever you middle-aged people want to excuse yourselves for anything you've done that you know you oughtn't have done, you say it was the war.

Act I, *A Bill of Divorcement 1921*

2 It's the things I might have said that fester.

Act II, Ibid.

3 DR. ALLIOT. That young, young generation found out, out of their own unhappiness, the war taught them, what peace couldn't teach us—that when conditions are evil it is not your duty to submit—that when conditions are evil, your duty, in spite of protests, in spite of sentiment, your duty, though you trample on the bodies of your nearest and dearest to do it, though you bleed your own heart white, your duty is to see that those conditions are changed. If your laws forbid you, you must change your laws. If your church forbids you, you must change your church. And if your God forbids you, why then, you must change your God.

Ibid.

4 HILARY. I was a dead man. You know what the dead do in heaven? They sit on their golden chairs and sicken for home.

Ibid.

5 ZEDEKIAH. How else should I treat an idol but tread on it?

Act I, Sc. 1, *Naboth's Vineyard 1925*

6 JEZEBEL. How often must I stoop to hold you up?

Sc. 2, Ibid.

7 JEZEBEL. Toss back the ball! Shall I flinch because a heavy hand flings it? At least it is a friend's hand.

Ibid.

8 JEZEBEL. What is it to sit on a throne? Weariness! But to shift the dolls that sit there, that's a game. Jehu, for a man or a woman! Let me teach you my game!

Ibid., Act II, Sc. 1

9 I think of our century as a sixty-year-old housewife in love with modern ideas.

Speech, "Approach to Drama," London *1961*

10 I suppose there is not one of us here who has not, at some time or other, evoked the good in which we believe to take our part, to speak for us, to put our case to the invisible evil (if it is evil) that thwarts and destroys our efforts toward happiness.

Ibid.

1678. Sophie Hutchinson Drinker (1888–1968)

1 Music gives access to regions in the subconscious that can be reached in no other way.

Music and Women 1948

2 Great music has always been rooted in religion—when religion is understood as an *attitude* toward superhuman power and the mysteries of the universe.

Ibid.

1679. Edith Evans (1888–1976)

1 When a woman behaves like a man, why doesn't she behave like a nice man?

Quoted in "Sayings of the Week," *Observer* (London) *30 September 1956*

1680. M. Esther Harding (1888–1971)

1 The chief characteristic of the goddess in her crescent phase is that she is a virgin. Her instinct is not used to capture or possess the man whom she attracts. . . . Her divine power does not depend on her relation to a husband-god, and thus her actions are not dependent on the need to conciliate such a one or to accord with his qualities and attitudes. For she bears her divinity in her own right.
   In the same way, the woman who is virgin, one-in-herself, does what she does—not because of any desire to please, not to be liked, or to be approved, even by herself; not because of any desire to gain power over another, to catch his interest or love, but because what she does is true.

Woman's Mysteries 1935

1681. Rose Gell Jacobs (1888–1975)

1 I never regretted that I assumed the burden nor that I laid it down when I did. *

Rose Jacobs Papers (Brandeis University), p. 214, *The Journey Home, How Jewish Women Shaped Modern America* by Joyce Antler** 1997

*Referring to her resignation as chairman of the Committee on the Study of Arab-Jewish Relations, with which she'd been associated for three decades. **See 3320.

I have independence, and am able to carry myself by my own guides to action. What has happened is that I am a pioneer ploughing the way and seeking the path for those who will come after me. There is always resistance to women in political affairs in general, and especially so in Jewish political life.

Ibid.

3 [Louis Brandeis]* expressed confidence in women. [H]e saw no reason why the contribution made by women on the voluntary base in welfare work should make any difference in evaluation.

"On Louis D. Brandeis," Midwinter conference of Hadassah (15 January 1957), *Ibid.*

*Louis Dembitz Brandeis (1856–1941), American jurist who served as an associate justice of the U.S. Supreme Court.

1682. Aline Murray Kilmer (1888–1941/44)

1 I'm sorry you are wiser,
I'm sorry you are taller;
I liked you better foolish,
And I liked you better smaller.

"For the Birth of a Middle-Aged Child," St. 1 *n.d.*

2 I cannot see myself as I once was;
I would not see myself as I am now.

"To Aphrodite: With a Mirror" *n.d.*

3 I sing of little loves that glow
Like tapers shining in the rain,
Of little loves that break themselves
Like moths against the window-pane.

"Prelude" *n.d.*

4 For there is only sorrow in my heart;
There is no room for fear.
But how I wish I were afraid again,
My dear, my dear.

"I Shall Not Be Afraid" *n.d.*

5 Things have a terrible permanence
When people die.

"Things," St. 6 *n.d.*

1683. Olga Knopf (1888–?)

1 ... the sexes are living, we might say, in a vast communal neurosis; a highly contagious neurosis which parents pass on to their children and men and women pass on to each other.

The Art of Being a Woman 1932

2 The outer limitations to woman's progress are caused by the fact we are living in a man's culture.

Women on Their Own 1935

3 No choice is ever all for love or all for convenience. . . . Even in love we understand that there is a valuation of the part-

ner and beneath the blindness of love there is often much calculation.

The Essential Elements in Marriage 1936

1684. Clare Kummer (1888–1948)

1 ETHEL. Did you sell your verses to Binder?
JENNINGS. No—he seemed to think they were indecent and when I explained to him that they weren't he lost interest in them—so that's all.

Act I, *Good Gracious, Annabelle* 1916

2 STEIN. It's the public. You can't count on it. Give 'em something good and they'll go to see something bad. Give 'em something bad and they don't like that either.

Act I, Sc. 1, *Rollo's Wild Oat* 1922

3 STEIN. Pictures are a great business. You take a picture and you got something.
MRS. PARK-GALES. Yes, but what?
STEIN. You get all through with the actors and there they are playing for you every night. If they are sick or dead, it don't make any difference. They are working just the same.
LUCAS. Anything to make us work for nothing!

Sc. 2, *Ibid.*

4 AUNT MIN. He should have started worrying before he had things to worry about.

Act I, *Her Master's Voice* 1933

5 Oh, there was a woman-hater hated women all he could,
And he built himself a bungle in a dingle in the wood;
Here he lived and said of ladies things I do not think he should,
"If they're good they're not good-looking; if good-looking, they're not good."

"In the Dingle-Dongle Bell" *n.d.*

1685. Lotte Lehman (1888–1976)

1 But to me the actual sound of the words is all important; I feel always that the words complete the music and must never be swallowed up in it. The music is the shining path over which the poet travels to bring his song to the world.

"The Singing Actor," *Players at Work*, Morton Eustis, ed. 1937

2 I have never understood the star who enjoys playing with a mediocre cast in order to shine out the more brilliantly himself, for the essence of any fine dramatic or operatic production is harmonious integration of all performances.

Ibid.

3 For what mission can be greater than that of giving the world hours of exaltation in which it may forget the misery of the present, the cares of everyday life and lose itself in the eternally pure world of harmony. . . .

Introduction, *More Than Singing* 1945

4 That fine God-given instrument—the voice—must be capable of responding with the greatest subtlety to every shade of each emotion. But it must be subordinate, it must only be the foundation, the soil from which flowers true art.

Ibid.

5 Imitation is, and can only be, the enemy of artistry. Everything which breathes the breath of life is changeable. . . . Only from life itself may life be born.

Ibid.

1686. Anita Loos (1888–1981)

1 "I really think that American gentlemen are the best after all, because . . . kissing your hand may make you feel very, very good, but a diamond and sapphire bracelet lasts forever."
Ch. 4, *Gentlemen Prefer Blondes 1925*

2 So this gentlemen said, "A girl with brains ought to do something else with them besides think."
Ibid.

3 JUDGE. Always go to a solitary drinker for the truth!
Act I, *Happy Birthday 1947*

4 ADDIE. I was making love to a man, a man I hardly even know. He was kissing the face off me and I was kissing the face off him. And I found it highly satisfactory.
Act II, Ibid.

5 Of course, everybody knows that the greatest thing about Motherhood is the "Sacrifices," but it is quite a shock to find out that they begin so far ahead of time.
Ch. 1, *A Mouse is Born 1951*

6 So after a Star has received five or six million of those Fan letters, you begin to realize you must be wonderful without having to read all those monitinous *[sic]* letters.
Ibid.

7 So I am beginning to wonder if maybe girls wouldn't be happier if we stopped demanding so much respeckt for ourselves and developped *[sic]* a little more respeckt for husbands.
Ch. 19, Ibid.

8 The people I'm furious with are the Women's Liberationists. They keep getting up on soapboxes and proclaiming women are brighter than men. That's true, but it should be kept quiet or it ruins the whole racket.
Observer (London) *30 December 1973*

9 . . . memory is more indelible than ink.
Ch. 1, *Kiss Hollywood Goodbye 1974*

10 Pleasure that isn't paid for is as insipid as everything else that's free.
Ch. 2, Ibid.

11 Show business is the best possible therapy for remorse.
Ch. 13, Ibid.

12 That our popular art forms become so obsessed with sex has turned the U.S.A. into a nation of hobbledehoys; as if grown people don't have more vital concerns, such as taxes, inflation, dirty politics, earning a living, getting an education, or keeping out of jail. It's true that the French have a certain obsession with sex, but it's a particularly adult obsession. France is the thriftiest of all nations; to a Frenchman sex provides the most economical way to have fun. The French are a logical race.
Ch. 21, Ibid.

13 If we have to tell Hollywood good-by, it may be with one of those tender, old-fashioned, seven-second kisses exchanged between two people of the opposite sex, with all their clothes on.
Ibid.

1687. Katherine Mansfield (1888–1923)

1 How idiotic civilization is! Why be given a body if you have to keep it shut up in a case like a rare, rare fiddle?
"Bliss," *Bliss and Other Stories*

2 ". . . Why! Why! Why is the middle-class so stodgy—so utterly without a sense of humour!"
Ibid.

3 It is as though God opened his hand and let you dance on it a little, and then shut it . . . so tight that you could not even cry.
(February 1914), *The Journal of Katherine Mansfield 1927*

4 Oh, the times when she had walked upside down on the ceiling . . . Floated on a lake of light . . . !
(31 December 1918), Ibid.

5 There is no limit to human suffering. When one thinks "Now I have touched the bottom of the sea—now I can go no deeper," one goes deeper. . . . Suffering is boundless, is eternity. One pang is eternal torment. Physical suffering is—child's play.
(19 December 1920), Ibid.

6 Whenever I prepare for a journey I prepare as though for death. Should I never return, all is in order. This is what life has taught me.
(1922), Ibid.

7 *Important.* When we can begin to take our failures nonseriously, it means we are ceasing to be afraid of them. It is of immense importance to learn to laugh at ourselves.
(October 1922), Ibid.

8 By health I mean the power to live a full, adult, living, breathing life in close contact with . . . the earth and the wonders thereof—the sea—the sun.
(14 October 1922), Ibid.

9 Risk! Risk anything! Care no more for the opinions of others, for those voices. Do the hardest thing on earth for you. Act for yourself. Face the truth.
Ibid.

10 Now perhaps you understand what "indifference" means. It is to learn not to mind, and not to show your mind.
(17 October 1922), Ibid.

11 Would you not like to try *all* sorts of lives—one is so very small—but that is the satisfaction of writing—one can impersonate so many people.
Letter (24 April 1907), *Collected Letters*, Vol. 1, Vincent O'Sullivan and Margaret Scott, eds. *1984*

12 To work—to work! It is such infinite delight to know that we still have the best things to do.
Letter to Bertrand Russell* (December 1916), Ibid.
*English mathematician and philosopher (1872–1970).

13 I'm a writer first and a woman after.
Letter to her husband John Middleton Murry (3 December 1920), Ibid.

1688. Carlotta Monterey O'Neill (1888–1970)

1 To understand his [Eugene O'Neill's*] work you must understand the man, for the work and the man are one.
Quoted in *O'Neill* by Arthur and Barbara Gelb *1960*
*American playwright (1888–1953), her husband.

2 I had to work like a dog. I was Gene's secretary, I was his nurse. His health was always bad. I did everything. He wrote the plays, but I did everything else. I loved it. It was a privilege to

work with him, because he was mentally stimulating. My God, how many women have husbands who are very stimulating?

Ch. 4, Ibid.

3 He got a racing car, a Bugatti, and when he was very nervous and tired he would go out in it and drive ninety-five miles an hour and come back looking nineteen years old and perfectly relaxed.

Ibid.

4 O'Neill was a tough mick and never loved a woman who walked. He loved only his work. But he had respect for me. I had an independent income, and I told him I'd marry him if he would let me pay half of all the household expenses. . . . He said he needed a home. "I want a home properly run," he told me. And that is what I did for him, I saw to it that he was able to work.

Ibid.

1689. Agnes Sligh Turnbull (1888–1982)

1 "Now ain't that funny! I thought it was you, an' you thought is was me; an' begob, it's nayther of us!"

Bk. I, Ch. 6, The Rolling Years 1936

2 "The older I get, Jeannie, the more I wonder whether a life shouldn't perhaps be like a river—flowing along in the channel God gave it. Not too many radical deflections."

Bk. II, Ch. 1, Ibid.

3 "There is still vitality under the winter snow, even though to the casual eye it seems to be dead."

Ch. 4, Ibid.

4 "The trouble with the average human being is that he never goes on mountain journeys. He stops at the first way station and refuses to believe there is country beyond."

Ch. 5, Ibid.

5 "You must learn to drink the cup of life as it comes, Connie, without stirring it up from the bottom. That's where the bitter dregs are!"

Ibid.

6 "Wasn't it [religion] invented by man for a kind of solace? It's as though he said, 'I'll make me a nice comfortable garment to shut out the heat and the cold; and then it ends by becoming a straitjacket."

Ch. 6, Ibid.

7 "I don't know that I care so much about going far," he said at last; "but I should like to go deep where I go."

Epilogue, Ibid.

8 "You can put city polish on a man, but by golly, it seems you can't ever rub it off him."

Ch. 2, The Golden Journey 1955

9 There would seem to be a law operating in human experience by which the mind once suddenly aware of a verity for the first time immediately invents it again.

Ch. 10, Ibid.

10 Oh, the utter unpredictability of a quarrel! How inflammable words were to ignite each other until the blaze of them scorched and seared.

Ibid.

11 "Do you know that the tendrils of graft and corruption have become mighty interlacing roots so that even men who would like to be honest are tripped and trapped by them?"

Ch. 11, Ibid.

12 Defeat in itself was part and parcel of the great gambling game of politics. A man who could not accept it and try again was not of the stuff of which leaders are made.

Ch. 12, Ibid.

13 . . . she was a widow, that strange feminine entity who had once been endowed with a dual personality and was now only half of what she had been.

Ch. 1, The Flowering 1972

14 "Dogs' lives are too short. Their only fault, really."

Ch. 2, Ibid.

1690. Miriam Ulinover (1888/94–1944)

1 Throw yourselves at happiness, sisters,
Burst into silvery laughter!

"With the Taytsh-Khumesh", Der bobes oytser (The grandmother's treasure) Kathryn Hellerstein, tr. 1922

2 A girl's voice yowling can carry high as heaven.

"The Old Prayer Book," Ibid.

1691. Mary Day Winn (1888–1965)

1 Sex is the tabasco sauce which an adolescent national palate sprinkles on every course in the menu.

Adam's Rib 1931

2 In the argot of the sub-deb, "U.S.A." has long ago lost its patriotic meaning. It now stands for "Universal Sex Appeal."

Ibid.

1692. Anna Akhmatova (1889–1966)

1 There is a sacred, secret line in loving which attraction and even passion cannot cross,—

Untitled, St. 4 (1915), White Flock, Jane Kenyon, tr. 1917

2 I remember how the gods turned people into things, not killing their consciousness.
And now, to keep those glorious sorrows alive,
you have turned into my memory of you.

Untitled, St. 3 (1916), Ibid.

3 How quiet is it after the volley!
Death sends patrols into every courtyard.

Untitled (1917), Ibid.

4 O great language we love:
It is you, Russian tongue, we must save, and we swear
We will give you unstained to the sons of our sons.

"Courage" 1942

5 And the sun goes down in waves of ether in such a way that I can't tell
if the day is ending, or the world,
or if the secret of secrets is within me again.

"On the Road," St. 3 (1964), Twenty Poems of Anna Akhmatova, Jane Kenyon, tr. 1985

6 One less hope becomes
One more song.

"Song about Song" n.d.

1693. Enid Bagnold (1889–1981)

1 "She keeps 'er brains in 'er 'eart. An' that's where they ought ter be. An' a man or woman who does that's one in a million an' 'as got my backing."

National Velvet 1935

2 "Love don't seem dainty on a fat woman."

Ibid.

3 MADRIGAL. Truth doesn't ring true in a court of law.

The Chalk Garden 1953

4 JUDGE. A judge does not always get to the bottom of a case.
MADRIGAL. No. It takes the pity of God to get to the bottom of things.

Ibid.

5 I shall continue to explore—the astonishment of living.

Ibid.

6 MADRIGAL. One can lie, but truth is more interesting.

Ibid.

7 MRS. ST. MAUGHAM. Privilege and power make selfish people—but gay ones.

Act I, Ibid.

8 MAITLAND. Praise is the only thing that brings to life again a man that's been destroyed.

Ibid.

9 ALICE. What is this ghastly difference between men and women? What is this closeness that works—and doesn't work! That boils, that burns and blisters, and is so near love!

The Chinese Prime Minister 1964

10 BENT. You were meant to be a single woman. Women of individuality are damned uncomfortable for men.

Ibid.

11 SIR GREGORY. Marriage. The beginning and the end are wonderful. But the middle part is hell.

Act II, Ibid.

12 SHE. We were so different that when two rooms separated us for half an hour—we met again as strangers.

Act III, Ibid.

13 To note, to pin down, to build up, to create, to be astonished at nothing, to cherish the oddities, to let nothing go down the drain, to make something, to make a great flower out of life, even if it's a cactus.

Ch. 3, *Autobiography 1969*

14 The theatre is a gross art, built in sweeps and over-emphasis. Compromise is its second name.

Ibid.

15 A father is always making his baby into a little woman. And when she is a woman he turns her back again.

Ch. 4, Ibid.

16 In marriage there are no manners to keep up, and beneath the wildest accusations no real criticism. Each is familiar with that ancient child in the other who may erupt again. . . . We are not ridiculous to ourselves. We are ageless. That is the luxury of the wedding ring.

Ch. 6, Ibid.

17 If a dog doesn't put you first where are you both? In what relation? A dog needs God. It lives by your glances, your wishes. It even shares your humour. This happens about the fifth year. If it doesn't happen you are only keeping an animal.

Ch. 10, Ibid.

1694. Agnes E. Benedict (1889–1950)

1 The only thing better than education is more education.

Progress to Freedom 1942

2 A democratic home is the foundation of a democratic state.

The Happy Home 1948

1695. Mildred Cram (1889–1965)

1 Publicity tripped upon the heels of publicity.

"Billy," *Harper's Bazaar 1924*

2 He was capitalized, consolidated, incorporated, copyrighted, limited, protected, insured, and all rights reserved, including the Scandinavian.

Ibid.

3 "I am vulgar, my friend! I mix tears with idiocy. I put the grotesque into love. I tickle sluggish minds. My recipe is a mixture of legend and pep, pantomime and beauty, artifice and art."

Ibid.

1696. Sarah "Sadie" Delany (1889–1999)

1 We were good citizens, good Americans! We loved our country, even though it didn't love us back.

Having Our Say, The Delany Sisters' First 100 Years with Elizabeth Delany* and Amy Hill Hearth *1993*
*Her sister; see 1725.

2 Back in slavery days, things were bad, but in some ways getting your freedom could be worse! To a small boy,* it meant leaving the only home you ever knew.

Ibid.
*Ref. their father, who was seven years old at the end of the Civil War.

3 Well, we didn't order any credit cards! We don't spend what we don't have. . . . Imagine a bank sending credit cards to two ladies over a hundred years old! What are those folks thinking!

Ibid.

4 Your job is to help somebody.

Family motto, Ibid.

1697. Fannie Hurst (1889–1968)

1 It's hard for a young girl to have patience for old age sitting and chewing all day over the past.

"Get Ready the Wreaths," *Cosmopolitan* (New York) *1917*

2 "I always say he wore himself out with conscientiousness."

"She Walks in Beauty," *Cosmopolitan* (New York) *1921*

3 It is doubtful if in all its hothouse garden of women the Hotel Bon Ton boasted a broken finger-nail or that little brash place along the forefinger that tattles so of potato peeling or asparagus scraping.

Ibid.

4 To housekeep, one had to plan ahead and carry items of motley nature around in the mind and at the same time preside, as mother had, at table, just as if everything, from the liver and bacon, to the succotash, to the French toast and strawberry jam, had not been matters of forethought and speculation.

Ch. 2, Imitation of Life 1932

5 He had always said of himself that people first tasted the command in his voice and then came nibbling at his products.

Ch. 14, Ibid.

6 "I know it, and when I know a thing wid my knowin', I knows it."

Ch. 33, Ibid.

7 "Honey-chile, it will shore seem a funny world up dar widout washin'. If de Lawd's robes only needed launderin', I'd do his tucks de way He's never seen 'em done."

Ch. 36, Ibid.

8 Papa lived so separately within himself that I retreated to Mama, who wore herself on the outside. Everything about her hung in view like peasant adobe houses with green peppers and little shrines, drying diapers and cooking utensils on the façade.

Bk. I, Anatomy of me; a wonderer in search of herself 1958

9 From the hour that I gave mama my first stare from her bed of my birth, I must have braced my new spine against being overpowered by the rush of her personality.

p. 3, Ibid.

10 Mama, Mama, my regrets for all the pain I caused you crowd in on me in these after-years. Your virtues transcended your faults. Papa knew that and bent his neck to your storms. I had neither his sweet humility nor fortitude . . . If only—I could live it over again.

p. 170, Ibid.

11 A chance acquaintance in an English railway carriage, a member of the peerage, once said to me in four unadorned words: I hate my mother. It was the first time I had heard such blasphemy uttered. Surely God would strike him dead. But God did not take action, and the lovely countryside through which we were riding kept smiling.

p. 235, Ibid.

1698. Elsie Janis (1889–1956)

1 When I think of the hundreds of things I might be,
I get down on my knees and thank God that I'm me.

"Compensation," Poems Now and Then ca. 1927

2 Why do we do it?
Oh, Hell! What's the use?
Why battle with the universe?
Why not declare a truce?

"Why," Ibid.

3 Up and down the burning sidewalks
Praying ever for a job,
In my heart a curse for mankind,
In my pocket not a bob.

"The Actor's Lament," Ibid.

4 It was Mother who fought. Fought! To keep me up to par! To make me study and improve. Fought! To keep my name in the

large type she believed I merited. Fought for heat in trains to protect my health. Fought to make ends meet, when each week she had finished sending money to the many dependents that automatically arrived on the high heels of success. Invincible! best describes her.

Pt. I, So Far, So Good! 1931

1699. Dorothy McCall (1889–?)

1 One cannot have wisdom without living life.

Quoted in The Los Angeles Times 14 March 1974

2 Technology dominates us all, diminishing our freedom.

Ibid.

3 Lawmakers and employers should not be allowed to continue their shameful practice of punishing still-producing and competent people merely because of age.

Ibid.

1700. Gabriela Mistral (1889–1957)

1 Let me be more maternal than a mother; able to love and defend with all of a mother's fervor the child that is not flesh of my flesh. Grant that I may be successful in molding one of my pupils into a perfect poem, and let me leave within her deepest-felt melody that she may sing for you when my lips shall sing no more.

"La Oracion de la Maestra" (The Teacher's Prayer), Desolacion 1922

2 Let me make my brick schoolhouse into a spiritual temple. Let the radiance of my enthusiasms envelop the poor courtyard and the bare classroom. Let my heart be a stronger column and my goodwill purer gold than the columns and gold of rich schools.

Ibid.

3 A son, a son, a son! I wanted a son of yours and mine, in those distant days of burning bliss when my bones would tremble at your least murmur and my brow would glow with a radiant mist.

"Poem of the Son," St. 1, Ibid.

4 he kissed me and now I am someone else

"He Kissed Me," St. 1, Ibid.

5 My grief and my smile begin in your face, my son.

"Eternal Grief," St. 2, Ibid.

6 The crimson rose
plucked yesterday,
the fire and cinnamon
of the carnation,

the bread I baked
with anise seed and honey,
and the goldfish
flaming in its bowl.

All these are yours, baby born of woman,
if you'll only go to sleep.

"If You'll Only Go to Sleep," Sts. 1–3, Tenura (Tenderness) 1924

7 And I wished I were born with them.
Could it not be so another time?

To leap from a clump of banana plants
one morning of wonders—
a dog, a coyote, a deer;
to gaze with wild pupils, to run, to stop, to run, to fall,
to whimper and whine and jump with joy,
riddled with sun and with barking,
a hallowed child of God, his secret, divine servant.

> *Ocho Perritos"* (Eight Puppies), Ibid.

8 I have all that I lost
and I go carrying my childhood
like a favorite flower
that perfumes my hand

> *"Todas Ibamos a Ser Reinas"* (We Were All to Be Queens),
> Ibid.

9 I love the things I never had
along with those I have no more.

> "Things," St. 1, Ibid.

10 At this moment, by an undeserved stroke of fortune, I am the
direct voice of the poets of my race and the indirect voice for
the noble Spanish and Portuguese tongues. Both rejoice to have
been invited to this festival of Nordic life with its tradition of
centuries of folklore and poetry.

> Acceptance speech, Nobel Prize Awards (Stockholm) *1945*

11 I will leave behind me the dark ravine, and climb up gentler
slopes toward that spiritual mesa where at last a wide light will
fall upon my days. From there I will sing words of hope, without looking into my heart. As one who was full of compassion
wished: I will sing to console men.

> Quoted in Introduction to *Tala, Selected Poems of Gabriela
> Mistral*, Doris Dana, tr. and ed. rev. ed. *1971*

1701. Julia Seton (1889–1975)

1 Dancing is a universal instinct—zoölogic, a biologic impulse,
found in animals as well as in man.

> "Why Dance?" *The Rhythm of the Redman 1930*

2 In its natural, primitive form, dancing is vigorous muscular
action to vent emotion. Originally, it was the natural expression of the basic impulses of a simple form of life. Triumph,
defeat, war, love, hate, desire, propitiation of the gods—all
were danced by the hero or the tribe to the rhythm of beaten
drums.

> "Dance in the Animal World," Ibid.

3 I have listened by a thousand fires as the Buffalo Wind blew
through our lives. . . . And so would come a flood of revelation, an unceasing flow of inspiration such as could not be
courted. Many a time have I sat by the embers, in motionless
silence for hours, while the words came in unhesitating rhythm
of passionate life—for we did not measure our life together
with a shallow cup. Each time we dipped, we brought up the
chalice brimming full and running over.

> Prologue, *By a Thousand Fires 1967*

4 But life has taught me that it knows better plans than we can
imagine, so that I try to submerge my own desires, apt to be
too insistent, into a calm willingness to accept what comes,
and to make the most of it, then wait again. I have discovered
that there is a Pattern, larger and more beautiful than our short
vision can weave. . . .

> Epilogue, Ibid.

1702. Margaret Turnbull (1889?–1942)

1 No man is responsible for his father. That is entirely his mother's affair.

> *Alabaster Lamps 1925*

2 When a man confronts catastrophe on the road, he looks in his
purse—but a woman looks in her mirror.

> *The Left Lady 1926*

1703. Mabel Walker Willebrandt (1889–1963)

1 When we sum up the columns that make "success" for the boy
on the one hand and the girl on the other, you find the girl has
the much longer column to add.

> "Give Women a Fighting Chance," *The Smart Set 1930*

2 Why the devil they have to put on that "girly-girly" tea party
description every time they tell anything about a professional
woman is more than I can see.

> Quoted in *The 50 Most Influential Women in American Law*
> by Dawn Bradley Berry* 1996

*See 4399.

1704. Daisy Ashford (1890?–1972)

1 I am parshial [sic] to ladies if they are nice. I suppose it is my
nature. I am not quite a gentleman but you would hardly notice it.

> Ch. 1, *The Young Visitors* * 1919

*Written when the author was nine years old.

2 My life will be sour grapes and ashes without you.

> Ch. 8, Ibid.

1705. Hallie Flanagan (1890–1969)

1 We were a violent lot,* a thorn in the body bureaucratic. Possibly that is one function of art in society. In the midst of learning
the necessary lingo of procedures, allotments, authorizations,
we found time for exchange of ideas, ideas for salvaging the
quickly receding past of our country, capturing it in plays, pictures, books; ideas for penetrating and illuminating our own
age, finding quicksilver ways in which to express the mercurial
present.

> "Danger: Men Not Working," *Arena, The Story of the Federal
> Theatre 1940*

*The Federal Theatre of the New Deal's WPA (Work Projects Ad-
ministration).

2 We live in a changing world: man is whispering through space,
soaring to the stars in ships, flinging miles of steel and glass
into the air. Shall the theatre continue to huddle in the confines of a painted box set? The movies, in their kaleidoscopic
speed and juxtaposition of external objects and internal emotions are seeking to find visible and audible expression for the
tempo and psychology of our time. The stage too must experiment—with ideas, with psychological relationships of men and
women, with speech and rhythm forms, with dance and movement, with color and light—or it must and should become a
museum product.

> Comment at meeting (8/9 October 1935), Ibid.

3 The greatest achievement of these public theatres was in their
creation of an audience of many millions, a waiting audience. . . . Neither should the theatre in our country be regarded
as a luxury. It is a necessity because in order to make democracy work the people must increasingly participate; they can't

participate unless they understand; and the theatre is one of the greatest mediums of understanding.

> "Blasting: Work Suspended," Ibid.

1706. Elizabeth Gurley Flynn (1890–1964)

1 He was *an agitator,* born of the first national awakening of American labor. The shame of servitude and the glory of struggle were emblazoned in the mind of every worker who heard Debs.*

> "Eugene V. Debs," *Debs, Haywood, Ruthenberg 1939*
> *American socialist leader and pacifist (1855–1926).

2 Time was, when the ACLU was young, they were Anarchists, Socialists, Christian pacifists, trade unionists, I.W.W., Quaker, Irish, Republican and Communist! Today, they are no longer heretics, non-conformists, radicals,—they are respectable.

> "I Am Expelled from Civil Liberties!," *Sunday Worker 17 March 1940*

3 History has a long-range perspective. It ultimately passes stern judgement on tyrants and vindicates those who fought, suffered, were imprisoned, and died for human freedom, against political oppression and economic slavery. Pioneers who were reviled, persecuted, ridiculed, and abused when they fought for free public schools, woman's suffrage against chattel slavery, for labor unions, are honored and revered today.

> *Labor's Own: William Z. Foster* 1949
> *American labor leader and Communist Party leader (1881–1961).

4 We hated the rich, the trusts they owned, the violence they caused, the oppression they represented.

> Pt. I, *The Rebel Girl 1955*

5 "What freedom?" we asked again. To be wage-slaves, hired and fired at the will of a soulless corporation, paid low wages for long hours, driven by the speed of a machine? What freedom? To be clubbed, jailed, shot down—and while we spoke, the hoofs of the troopers' horses clattered by on the street.

> Pt. III, Ibid.

6 So confident was he [Nicola Sacco*] of his innocence that sunny afternoon that he had no fear. He was sure when he told his story in court he would go free. He did not know that he was approaching the valley of the shadow of death. He feared no evil because the truth was with him. But greed, corruption, prejudice, fear and hatred of radical foreign-born workingmen were weaving a net around him.

> Pt. VII, Ibid.
> *Italian-born American anarchist (1891–1927); executed.

7 I was a convict, a prisoner without rights, writing a censored letter. But my head was unbowed. Come what may, *I was a political prisoner* and proud of it, at one with some of the noblest of humanity who had suffered for conscience's sake. I felt no shame, no humiliation, no consciousness of guilt. To me my number 11710 was a badge of honor.

> Ch. 3, *The Alderson Story* 1963
> *The Federal Reformatory for Women at Alderson, West Virginia.

8 One of my correspondents asked me: "What do you think are the main differences between a women's prison and a men's prison?" I replied: "You would never see diapers hung on a line at a men's prison or hear babies crying in the hospital on a quiet Sunday afternoon." The physiological differences—

menstruation, menopause, and pregnancy—create intense emotional problems among many women in prison.

> Ch. 13, Ibid.

9 A popular saying at Alderson went as follows: "They work us like a horse, feed us like a bird, treat us like a child, dress us like a man—and then expect us to act like a lady."

> Ch. 25, Ibid.

1707. Frances Noyes Hart (1890–1943)

1 "I cried at first . . . and then, it was such a beautiful day, that I forgot to be unhappy."

> "Green Garden," *Scribner's 1921*

2 Death cannot alter facts, only feelings.

> *The Crooked Lane 1933*

1708. Anne Hocking (1890–1966)

1 Other sins only speak,
  Murder cries out.

> *Death Leaves a Shining Mark 1943*

1709. Hedda Hopper (1890–1966)

1 His footprints* were never asked for, yet no one has ever filled his shoes.

> *From Under My Hat 1952*
> *Reference to D. W. Griffith, American filmmaker (1875–1948), and Grauman's Theatre in Hollywood.

2 In Hollywood gratitude is Public Enemy Number One.

> Ibid.

3 I decided that [Arthur] Brisbane* was a member of the 7-H club—Holy howling hell, how he hates himself.

> Ibid.
> *American newspaper editor infamous for yellow journalism (1864–1936).

1710. Rose Fitzgerald Kennedy (1890–1995)

1 The secret of the Kennedy successes in politics was not money but meticulous planning and organization, tremendous effort and the enthusiasm and devotion of family and friends.

> *Times to Remember 1974*

2 Sedentary people are apt to have sluggish minds. A sluggish mind is apt to be reflected in flabbiness of body and in a dullness of expression that invites no interest and gets none.

> Ibid.

3 Birds sing after a storm; why shouldn't people feel as free to delight in whatever remains to them?

> Ibid.

4 We cannot always understand the ways of Almighty God—the crosses which He sends us, the sacrifices which He demands of us. . . . But we accept with faith and resignation His holy will with no looking back to what might have been, and we are at peace.

> "After Robert Kennedy's Death" (Television Broadcast; 1968), Ibid.

1711. Beatrice Llewellyn-Thomas (1890–?)

1 O We have a desperate need of laughter!
  Give us laughter, Puck!*

> "To Puck" *n.d.*
> *Character from Shakespeare's *A Midsummer Night's Dream.*

1712. Maria, Grand Duchess of Russia (1890–1958)

1 Girls' games never had any interest for me; I hated dolls; the congealed expression on their porcelain faces provoked me. It was with lead soldiers that we played, without ever growing tired.

Ch. 3, Education of a Princess 1930

2 The mouthpieces of the so-called public opinion; those men, who by high-sounding formulas had so impressed the densely ignorant masses. . . . They had neither sufficient moral force nor experience necessary to build up a new system. Their mental store was limited to theories, often excellent but inapplicable to reality.

Ch. 8, Ibid.

3 Russia still writhed and stumbled. The wave of revolts and uprisings, the constant agitations, the incessant inflammatory orations of men possessed of little political competence. . . .

Ibid.

1713. Aimee Semple McPherson (1890–1944)

1 O Hope! dazzling, radiant Hope!—What a change thou bringest to the hopeless; brightening the darkened paths, and cheering the lonely way.

Pt. I, Ch. 1, This Is That 1923

2 We are all making a crown for Jesus out of these daily lives of ours, either a crown of golden, divine love, studded with gems of sacrifice and adoration, or a thorny crown, filled with the cruel briars of unbelief, or selfishness, and sin, and placing it upon His brow.

Pt. II, "What Shall I Do with Jesus," Ibid.

3 "Pit-a-pat! Pit-a-pat!"—say the hundreds and thousands of feet, surging by the church doors of our land. "Pat! Pat! Pit-a-pat!"—hurrying multitudes, on business and pleasure bent.

"Is Jesus Christ the Great 'I Am' or Is He the Great 'I Was'?"
Ibid.

4 Right here let us make it plain, that each individual is either a sinner or a saint. It is impossible to be both; it is impossible to be neutral; there is no half-way business with God. Either you are the child of the Lord or you are serving the devil—there is no middle territory.

"The Two Houses," Ibid.

1714. Anita Owen (fl. 1890s–1920s)

1 And in these eyes the love-light lies
And lies—and lies and lies!

"Dreamy Eyes" ca. 1894

2 . . . Daisies won't tell.

"Sweet Bunch of Daisies" 1894

1715. Katherine Anne Porter (1890–1980)

1 She laid the purse on the table and sat down with the cup of chilled coffee, and thought: I was right not to be afraid of any thief but myself, who will end by leaving me nothing.

"Theft," Flowering Judas and Other Stories 1930

2 "*What* could you buy with a hundred dollars?" she asked fretfully.

"Nothing, nothing at all," said their father, "a hundred dollars is just something you put in the bank."

Pt. II, "Old Morality" 1936

3 "It don't *look* right," was his final reason for not doing anything he did not wish to do.

Noon Wine 1937

4 After working for three years on a morning newspaper she had an illusion of maturity and experience; but it was fatigue merely. . . .

Pale Horse, Pale Rider 1939

5 "The mind and the heart sometimes get another chance, but if anything happens to the poor old human frame, why, it's just out of luck, that's all."

Ibid.

6 All believed they were bound for a place for some reason more desirable than the place they were leaving, but it was necessary to make the change with the least possible delay and expense. Delay and expense had been their common portion at the hands of an army of professional tip-seekers, fee-collectors, half-asleep consular clerks and bored migration officials who were not in the least concerned whether the travelers gained their ship or dropped dead in their tracks.

Pt. I, Ship of Fools 1962

7 "People on a boat, Mary, can't seem to find any middle ground between stiffness, distrust, total rejection, or a kind of evasive, gnawing curiosity. Sometimes it's a friendly enough curiosity, sometimes sly and malicious, but you feel as if you were being eaten alive by fishes."

Pt. II, Ibid.

8 Miracles are instantaneous, they cannot be summoned, but come of themselves, usually at unlikely moments and to those who least expect them.

Pt. III, Ibid.

9 "The real sin against life is to abuse and destroy beauty, even one's own—even more, one's own, for that had been put in our care and we are responsible for its well-being. . . ."

Ibid.

10 A cultivated style [of writing] would be like a mask. Everybody knows it's a mask, and sooner or later you must show yourself—or at least, you show yourself as someone who could not afford to show himself, and so created something to hide behind. . . . You do not create a style. You work, and develop yourself; your style is an emanation from your own being.

Writers at Work, Second Series, George Plimpton,* ed. 1963
*American writer and editor (1927–2003).

11 Our being is subject to all the chances of life. There are so many things we are capable of, that we could be or do. The potentialities are so great that we never, any of us, are more than one-fourth fulfilled.

Ibid.

12 No man can be explained by his personal history, least of all a poet.

Quoted in "A Lioness of Literature Looks Back" by Henry Allen, Los Angeles Times 7 July 1974

13 Such ignorance. All the boys were in military schools and all the girls were in the convent, and that's all you need to say about it.

Ibid.

14 I do not understand the world, but I watch its progress.

Ibid.

1716. Rachel (1890–1931)

1 Like a bird in the butcher's palm you flutter in my hand, insolent pride.

"Revolt," *Poems from the Hebrew*, Robert Mezey, ed. *1973*

2 This is a bond nothing can ever loosen.
What I have lost: what I possess forever.

"My Dead," Ibid.

1717. Jean Rhys (1890–1979)

1 She respected Americans: they were not like the English, who, under a surface of annoying moroseness of manner, were notoriously timid and easy to turn round your finger.

"Mannequin," *The Left Bank 1927*

2 The feeling of Sunday is the same everywhere, heavy, melancholy, standing still. Like when they say, "As it was in the beginning, is now, and ever shall be, world without end."

Act IV, *Voyage in the Dark 1934*

3 We can't all be happy, we can't all be rich, we can't all be lucky—and it would be so much less fun if we were. Isn't it so, Mr. Blank? There must be the dark background to show off the bright colours. Some must cry so that others may be able to laugh the more heartily. Sacrifices are necessary. . . .

Pt. I, *Good Morning, Midnight 1939*

4 Next week, or next month, or next year I'll kill myself. But I might as well last out my month's rent, which has been paid up, and my credit for breakfast in the morning.

Pt. II, Ibid.

5 She could give herself up to the written word as naturally as a good dancer to music or a fine swimmer to water. The only difficulty was that after finishing the last sentence she was left with a feeling at once hollow and uncomfortably full. Exactly like indigestion.

"The Insect World," *Sleep It Off, Lady 1976*

1718. Fradel Schtok (1890–193-?)

1 She sensed the truth of what was said when the wedding trumpet sounds, "This too will be your fate, this too will be your fate . . ." and the fiddle laments, "Oh, how you will be blighted!" while the bass angrily booms, "Just like this, just like this."

"The Veil," *Found Treasures: Stories by Yiddish Women Writers*, Frieda Forman, Ethel Raicus, Sarah Silberstein Swartz, and Margie Wolf, eds. *1994*

1719. Hattie Starr (fl. 1890s)

1 Nobody loves me, well do I know,
Don't all the cold world tell me so?

"Nobody Loves Me" *1893*

2 Somebody loves me; How do I know?
Somebody's eyes have told me so!

"Somebody Loves Me" *1893*

3 I wish I was a little black coon once mo'
Yes I does, 'deed I does,
A gettin' into mischief an' rollin' on de flo'
Yes I does, 'deed I does,

"Climb de Golden Fence" *1895*

4 Go to sleep, my little pickaninny,—
Brer' Fox 'll catch you if yo' don't;
Slumber on de bosom of yo' ole Mammy Jinny,—
Mammy's gwine to swat yo' if you won't.

"Little Alabama Coon" (1893), *An American Anthology, 1787–1900*, Edmund Clarence Stedman, ed. *1900*

1720. Dixie Willson (1890–1974)

1 I had to be where the world was moving. I had to be where the world was moving.

"Famous Iowans: Dixie Willson" by Tom Longden, *The Des Moines Register n.d.*

2 He may look just the same to you,
And he may be just as fine,
But the next-door dog is the next-door dog,
And mine—is—mine!

"Next-Door Dog" *n.d.*

1721. Margaret Culkin Banning (1891–1982)

1 It isn't easy to be the person who sometimes has to try to preserve your happiness at the expense of your fun.

Letters to Susan 1936

2 You wouldn't be caught wearing cheap perfume, would you? Then why do you want to wear cheap perfume on your conduct?

Ibid.

3 Did it ever occur to you that there's something almost crooked in the way decent girls nowadays use the shelter of their established respectability to make things awkward for men?

Ibid.

1722. Fanny Brice (1891–1951)

1 . . . everything about me has stopped growing except my nose.

Quoted on p. 148, *The Fabulous Fanny* by Norman Katkov *1952*

2 Your audience gives you everything you need. They tell you. There is no director who can direct you like an audience.

Ch. 6, Ibid.

3 Being a funny person does an awful lot of things to you. You feel that you mustn't get serious with people. They don't expect it from you, and they don't want to see it. You're not entitled to be serious, you're a clown, and they only want you to make them laugh.

Ch. 9, Ibid.

4 When love is out of your life, you're through in a way. Because while it's there it's like a motor that's going, you have such vitality to do things, big things, because love is goosing you all the time.

Ch. 19, Ibid.

5 Let the world know you as you are, not as you think you should be, because sooner or later, if you are posing, you will forget the pose, and then where are you?

Ch. 24, Ibid.

6 In the theater I was always at ease, but in pictures there was the camera following me around like a cop.

p. 184, Ibid.

7   A verbal agreement is not worth the paper it's written on.
  "Vaudeville Legends," *Funny Women, American Comediennes,*
  1860–1985 by Mary Unterbrink *1987*

8   I've done everything in the theater except marry the property man.
  Ibid.

9   Any woman who can't say a four-letter word sometimes is deceitful.
  New York Herald Tribune (22 March 1964), "Conclusion,"
  Funny Woman, The Life and Times of Fanny Brice by Barbara
  W. Grossman *1991*

1723. Harriet L. Childe-Pemberton (fl. 1891–1912)

1   MRS. CATERMOLE MacFADIE. No one will deny that things that are wrong frequently have their roots in things that are right; therefore, things that are right are things that are wrong. We are nothing if not logical; and when you have once become a member of the Sour Grape Club, of the Ishmaelites Club, and of the Clean-Sweepers League, you will understand these matters with a more enlightened apprehension.
  "The Deuce of Clubs," *Dead Letters and Other Narrative and*
  Dramatic Pieces 1896

2   O beautiful Earth! alive, aglow,
  With your million things that grow,
  I would lay my head on your ample knee. . . .
  "Songs of Earth," St. 1, *Nenuphar 1911*

3   "There is no fear for those who truly see
  What is, or will be, springs from all that was,—
  How all that happens fitly has to be,
  And what ye name 'effect' and 'cause'
  Make up but one degree."
  "Songs of Fire," IX, St. 7, Ibid.

4   For passion has come to the verge and leaps
  Headlong to the blind abyss,
  Yet gathers thereby the strength of deeps,
  And eddies a moment and swirls and sweeps
  Till peril is one with bliss!
  "Songs of Water," IV, St. 4, Ibid.

1724. Agatha Christie (1891–1975)

1   Every murderer is probably somebody's old friend.
  The Mysterious Affair at Styles 1920

2   It is completely unimportant. That is why it is so interesting.
  The Murder of Roger Ackroyd 1926

3   Crime is terribly revealing. Try and vary your methods as you will, your tastes, your habits, your attitude of mind, and your soul is revealed by your actions.
  Ch. 17, *The ABC Murders 1936*

4   There is nothing so dangerous for anyone who has something to hide as conversation! . . . A human being, Hastings, cannot resist the opportunity to reveal himself and express his personality which conversation gives him. Every time he will give himself away.
  Ch. 31, Ibid.

5   She lied with fluency, ease and artistic fervor.
  They Came to Baghdad 1951

6   LADY ANGKATELL. People are quite right when they say nature in the mild is seldom raw.
  Act I, *The Hollow 1952*

7   An archaeologist is the best husband any woman can have: the older she gets, the more interested he is in her.
  Quoted by Sir Max Mallowan, her husband, news item *9*
  March 1954

8   CLARISSA. Oh dear, I never realized what a terrible lot of explaining one has to do in a murder!
  Spider's Web 1956

9   SIR ROWLAND. You must know better than I do, Inspector, how very rarely two people's account of the same thing agrees. In fact, if three people were to agree exactly, I should regard it as suspicious. Very suspicious, indeed.
  Act II, Sc. 2, Ibid.

10 TREVES. If one sticks too rigidly to one's principles one would hardly see anybody.
  Act I, *Towards Zero 1957*

11 Is there ever any particular spot where one can put one's finger and say, "It all began that day, at such a time and such a place, with such an incident."
  Ch. 1, *Endless Night 1967*

12 . . . money isn't so hot, after all. What with incipient heart attacks, lots of bottles of little pills you have to take all the time, and losing your temper over the food or the service in hotels. Most of the rich people I've known have been fairly miserable.
  Bk I, Ch. 3, Ibid.

13 "Look here," I said, "people like to collect disasters."
  Ch. 5, Ibid.

14 To put it quite crudely . . . The poor don't really know how the rich live, and the rich don't know how the poor live, and to find out is really enchanting to both of them.
  Bk. II, Ch. 9, Ibid.

15 "Doctors can do almost anything nowadays, can't they, unless they kill you first while they're trying to cure you."
  Ch. 11, Ibid.

1725. Elizabeth "Bessie" Delany (1891–1995)

1   We've outlived those old rebby boys!* They're turning in their graves while Sadie** and me are getting the last word, in this book.
  Having Our Say, The Delany Sisters' First 100 Years, with
  Sarah Delaney** and Amy Hill Hearth *1993*
  *Term they used to call racist white men [probably stemming from Civil War]. **Sarah Delany, her sister; see 1696.

2   When Negroes are average, they fail, unless they are very, very lucky. Now, if you're average and *white,* honey, you can go far. Just look at Dan Quayle.* If that boy was colored he'd be washing dishes somewhere.
  Ibid.
  *James Danforth Quayle, 41st vice president of United States (1947–   ).

3   Oppressed people have a good sense of humor. Think of the Jews. They know how to laugh, and to laugh at themselves!

Well, we colored folks are the same way. We colored folks are survivors.

Ibid.

4   The first thing I would do if I was President would be to say that people over 100 years of age no longer have to pay taxes! Ha ha! Lord knows I've paid my share.

Ibid.

5   As a child, every time I encountered prejudice—which was rubbed in your face, once segregation started under Jim Crow*—I would feel it down to my core. I would go home and sit on my bed and weep and weep and weep, the tears streaming down my face.

Ibid.

*The practice of discriminating against and segregating black people.

1726. Laura Gilpin (1891–1979)

1   A river seems a magic thing. A magic, moving, living part of the very earth itself—for it is from the soil, both from its depth and from its surface, that a river has its beginning

Introduction, *The Rio Grande* 1949

2   . . . much earnest philosophical thought is born of the life which springs from close association with nature.

"The Source," *Ibid.*

3   Since the earliest-known existence of human life in the Western World, all manner of men have trod the river's banks. With his progressing knowledge and experience, man has turned these life-giving waters upon the soil, magically evoking an increasing bounty from the arid land. But through misuse of its vast drainage areas—the denuding of forest lands and the destruction of soil-binding grasses—the volume of the river has been diminished, as once generous tributaries have become parched *arroyos*. Will present and future generations have the vision and wisdom to correct these abuses, protect this heritage, and permit a mighty river to fulfill its highest destiny?

"The Delta," *Ibid.*

1727. Zora Neale Hurston (1891–1960)

1   Sometimes, I feel discriminated against, but it does not make me angry. It merely astonishes me. How can any deny themselves the pleasure of my company? It is beyond me.

"How It Feels to Be Colored Me," *The World Tomorrow* May 1928

2   Ah done been in sorrow's kitchen and Ah done licked out all de pots. Ah done died in grief and been buried in de bitter waters, and Ah done rose agin from de dead lak Lazarus.

Jonah's Gourd Vine 1934

3   Now, women forget all those things they don't want to remember and remember everything they don't want to forget. The dream is the truth. Then they act and do things accordingly.

Their Eyes Were Watching God 1937

4   Ships at a distance have every man's wish on board. For some they come in with the tide. For others they sail forever on the horizon, never out of sight, never landing, until the Watcher turns his eyes away in resignation, his dreams mocked to death by Time. That is the life of men.

Ch. 1, *Ibid.*

5   Gods always behave like the people who make them.

Ch. 15, *Tell My Horse* 1938

6   There is no agony like bearing an untold story inside you.

Dust Tracks on a Dirt Road (autobiography) 1942

7   Mama exhorted her children at every opportunity to "jump at de sun." We might not land on the sun, but at least we would get off the ground.

Ch. 2, *Ibid.*

8   Research is formalized curiosity. It is poking and prying with a purpose. It is a seeking that he who wishes may know the cosmic secrets of the world and they that dwell therein.

Ch. 10, *Ibid.*

9   Love, I find is like singing. Everybody can do enough to satisfy themselves, though it may not impress the neighbors as being very much.

Ch. 14, *Ibid*

10 "You love like a coward. Don't take no steps at all. Just stand around and hope for things to happen outright. Unthankful and unknowing like a hog under an acorn tree. Eating and grunting with your ears hanging over your eyes, and never even looking up to see where the acorns are coming from."

Seraph on the Suwanee 1948

11 "Don't you realize that the sea is the home of water? All water is off on a journey unlessen it's in the sea, and it's homesick, and bound to make its way home someday."

Ch. 27, *Ibid.*

1728–1729. Irene Rutherford McLeod (1891–1964?)

1   I'm a lean dog, a keen dog, a wild dog, and lone;
I'm a rough dog, a tough dog, hunting on my own;
I'm a bad dog, a mad dog, teasing silly sheep;
I love to sit and bay the moon, to keep fat souls from sleep.

"Lone Dog," *Songs to Save a Soul* 1916

2   Only because of you
Labor is sweet,
And all the song of you
Sings in my feet.

"Song," *Ibid.*

3   Though tongues of all the ages shout
That only death may not deceive—
I'll not believe! I'll not believe!

Untitled, *Ibid.*

4   Since I was a little child
My spirit has been swift and wild.

Untitled, *Ibid.*

5   Is love, then, so simple my dear?
The opening of a door,
And seeing all things clear?
I did not know before.

"Is love, then, so simple," St. 1, *Modern British Poetry,* Louis Untermeyer, ed. *1920*

1730. Anne Nichols (1891–1966)

1   MRS. COHEN. How early it is of late!

Act I, *Abie's Irish Rose* 1922

2   FATHER WHALEN. Shure, we're all trying to get to the same place when we pass on. We're just going by different routes. We can't all go on the same train.
RABBI. And just because you are not riding on my train, why should I say your train won't get there?

Act II, Ibid.

1731. Victoria Ocampo (1891–1979)

1   He [T. E. Lawrence] was of the same stuff as the saints, and like them he had to find perfection in himself, and not like a great artist in the work he had conceived and executed.

"Childhood," 33817TE (Lawrence of Arabia)* 1947
*T. E. Lawrence, British soldier and writer (1888–1935).

2   Morality, like physical cleanliness, is not acquired once and for all: it can only be kept and renewed by a habit of constant watchfulness and discipline.

"Scruples and Ambitions," Ibid.

3   Some regions of the earth, which are not rich or picturesque, attract us because of a mysterious relationship we have with them.

"A Man of the Desert," Ibid.

4   Sadism, masochism, neuroses, suppressed desires, complexes, all those things which psychoanalysis invents in order to debunk the scruples and ardent aspirations of mankind and their rebirth in secular disguises, are not sufficient to explain them.

"The Flesh," Ibid.

5   The eagerness to seek hidden but necessary connections, connections that revealed a close relationship between the world where I was born in the flesh and the other worlds where I was reborn, has been the enterprise of my whole life.

Speech, American Academy of Arts and Letters, New York 1973

1732. Edith Quimby (1891–1982)

1   The start of my professional life placed me in a field that was then full of fascinating problems, and which time has made only more interesting. I have always had good health and the ability to work at a fairly high pace and to keep several balls in the air at once. But any success which I have achieved I owe largely to the help and encouragement of others. . . . I can indeed count myself among the fortunate people.

Speech, Nuclear Pioneer Lecture, n.d.

1733. Marie Rambert (1891–1982)

1   We want to create an atmosphere in which creation is possible.

Quoted in "Ballet Rambert: The Company That Changed Its Mind" by John Percival, Dancemagazine February 1973

2   I don't do cartwheels any more, but I still do a barre to keep supple.

Quoted in "Old School Tights" by Beryl Hilary Ostlere, Ibid.

1734. Nelly Sachs (1891–1970)

1   Butterflies fluttering
soon feel at home in the sea—
This stone
inscribed with the 'fly
has placed itself in my hand—

In place of a homeland
I hold out for the world to transform—

Acceptance speech poem, Nobel Prize Awards (Stockholm),
Janice Price with Elaine Bernstein Partnow,* trs. 1966
*Author; see 3291.

2   When sleep leaves the body like smoke
and man, sated with secrets,
drives the overworked nag of quarrel
out of its stall,
then the fire-breathing union begins anew. . . .

"When Sleep Enters the Body Like Smoke," St. 3, Ibid.

3   You, the inexperienced, who learn nothing in the nights.
Many angels are given you
But you do not see them.

"Chorus of Clouds," The Seeker and Other Poems 1970

4   Are graves breath-space for longing?

"Are Graves Breath-Space for Longing?," Ibid.

1735. Edith Stein (1891–1942)

1   Every time I feel my powerlessness and inability to influence people directly, I become more keenly aware of the necessity of my own holocaust.

Vatican News 1930

2   In the synagogues and Protestant churches I had visited people simply went to the services. Here, however, I saw someone coming straight from the busy marketplace into this empty church, as if she was going to have an intimate conversation. It was something I never forgot.

"The Problem of Empathy" (dissertation; 1917), Ibid. n.d.

3   Things were in God's plan which I had not planned at all. I am coming to the living faith and conviction that—from God's point of view—there is no chance and that the whole of my life, down to every detail, has been mapped out in God's divine providence and makes complete and perfect sense in God's all-seeing eyes.

Ibid.

4   [It is possible to] pursue scholarship as a service to God . . . It was not until I had understood this that I seriously began to approach academic work again.

Ibid.

5   During the time immediately before and quite some time after my conversion I . . . thought that leading a religious life meant giving up all earthly things and having one's mind fixed on divine things only. Gradually, however, I learnt that other things are expected of us in this world . . . I even believe that the deeper someone is drawn to God, the more he has to 'get beyond himself' in this sense, that is, go into the world and carry divine life into it.

Ibid.

6   We who grew up in Judaism have a duty to bear witness . . . to the young generation who are brought up in racial hatred from early childhood.

"The Life of a Jewish Family," Ibid.

1736. Katherine Stinson (1891–1977)

1   When I began to talk about flying, she already had confidence in me. My mother never warned me not to do this or that for fear of being hurt. Of course I got hurt, but I was never afraid.

Quoted in Women Aviators by Lisa Yount 1995

2   It's all right if your automobile goes wrong while you are driving it. You can get out in the road and tinker with it. But if your airplane breaks down, you can't sit on a convenient cloud and tinker with that!

Article, American Magazine (1917), Ibid.

1737. Mary Ambrose (1892–?)

1   The true vocation [of a nun is] settled on the day a girl looks around her and sees a young woman her own age in pretty clothes wheeling a baby carriage by the convent. Then her heart takes an awful flop and she knows what it is God really is asking of her.

Quoted in *Life* (New York) *15 March 1963*

1738. Mary Baker (1892–197-?)

1   Women must organize and think strategically about creating ongoing pressure for change. Access is easy. Getting in law schools and getting a job is easy. To actually change the structure at law schools and law firms is really difficult.

"Back to the Future," *Perspectives Fall 1997*

1739. Djuna Barnes (1892–1982)

1   She wanted to be the reason for everything and so was the cause of nothing.

Nightwood 1936

2   Dreams have only the pigmentation of fact.

Ch. 5, Ibid.

3   Sleep demands of us a guilty immunity. There is not one of us who, given an eternal incognito, a thumbprint nowhere set against our souls, would not commit rape, murder and all abominations.

Ibid.

4   I'm a fart in a gale of wind, a humble violet, under a cow pat.

Ibid.

5   We are beginning to wonder whether a servant girl hasn't the best of it after all. She knows how the salad tastes without the dressing, and she knows how life's lived before it gets to the parlor door.

"The Home Club: For Servants Only," (*Brooklyn Daily Eagle*, 12 October 1913), *Djuna Barnes's New York 1989*

6   New York is the meeting place of the peoples, the only city where you can hardly find a typical American.

"Greenwich Village As It Is" (*Pearson's Magazine*, October 1916), Ibid.

1740. Stella Benson (1892–1933)

1   Call no man foe, but never love a stranger.
    Build up no plan, nor any star pursue.
    Go forth in crowds, in loneliness is danger.
    Thus nothing fate can send,
    And nothing fate can do
    Shall pierce your peace, my friend.

"To the Unborn," St. 3, *This Is the End 1917*

2   Family jokes, though rightly cursed by strangers, are the bond that keeps most families alive.

Ch. 9, *Pipers and a Dancer 1924*

1741. Pearl S. Buck (1892–1973)

1   It is better to be first with an ugly woman than the hundredth with a beauty.

Ch. 1, *The Good Earth 1931*

2   "Hunger makes a thief of any man."

Ch. 15, Ibid.

3   "Men do not take good iron to make nails nor good men to make soldiers."

Ch. 8, *The Young Revolutionist 1932*

4   "There was an old abbot in one temple and he said something of which I think often and it was this, that when men destroy their old gods they will find new ones to take their place."

Ch. 15, Ibid.

5   "But that land—it is one thing that will still be there when I come back—land is always there.

Ch. 1, *A House Divided 1935*

6   Freedom—it is today more than ever the most precious human possession.

Acceptance speech, Nobel Prize Awards (Stockholm) *1938*

7   I feel no need for any other faith than my faith in human beings.

I Believe 1939

8   "We shall fight until all anti-Japanese feeling is stamped out and the Chinese are ready to cooperate with us."
    I-wan stared at him, not believing what he heard.
    "You mean," he repeated, "you will kill us and bomb our cities—and—and—rape our women—until we learn to love you?"

Pt. II, *The Patriot 1939*

9   None who have always been free can understand the terrible fascinating power of the hope of freedom to those who are not free.

What America Means to Me 1942

10   Every great mistake has a halfway moment, a split second when it can be recalled and perhaps remedied.

Ch. 10, Ibid.

11   For our democracy has been marred by imperialism, and it has been enlightened only by individual and sporadic efforts at freedom.

Speech, "Freedom for All" (New York) *14 March 1942*

12   I remember as a child hearing my impatient missionary father . . . [as] he explained to an elderly Chinese gentlemen, "Does it mean nothing to you that if you reject Christ you will burn in hell?"
    The Chinese gentleman smiled as he replied, "If, as you say, my ancestors are all in hell at this moment, it would be unfilial of me not to be willing to suffer with them."

Speech, "The Chinese Mind and India" (Boston) *28 April 1942*

13   "Believing in gods always causes confusion."

Ch. 1, *Peony 1948*

14   "Obey—obey—and do what you like. The two go together—if you are clever."

Ch. 3, Ibid.

15   "War is costly, love is cheap."

Ch. 4, Ibid.

16   She had been so pretty when she was young that it had taken Kung Chen some years to discover that she was stupid.

Ch. 5, Ibid.

17   "We do not yet serve man as we should; how then can we know how to serve God?"

Ibid.

18 He longed to be free of them all, and yet he knew that no man is ever free of the women who have made him what he is.

> Ch. 12, Ibid.

19 Endurance can be a harsh and bitter root in one's life, bearing poisonous and gloomy fruit, destroying other lives. Endurance is only the beginning. There must be acceptance and the knowledge that sorrow fully accepted brings its own gifts. For there is an alchemy in sorrow. It can be transmuted into wisdom. . . .

> Ch. 1, *The Child Who Never Grew* 1950

20 Americans are all too soft. I am not soft. It is better to be hard, so that you can know what to do.

> Ibid.

21 Euthanasia is a long, smooth-sounding word, and it conceals its danger as long, smooth words do, but the danger is there, nevertheless.

> Ch. 2, Ibid.

22 Children who never grow are human beings, and suffer as human beings, inarticulately but deeply nevertheless. The human creature is always more than an animal.

> Ch. 3, Ibid.

23 The average person, fool that he often is, interests and amuses me more than the rare and extraordinary individual. The ways of common people are enchanting and funny and profound.

> "In Search of Readers," *The Writer's Book,* Helen Hull, ed. 1950

24 We had no police and needed none, because the family was responsible for all its members. . . . The child in Asia is loved not only for its own sake but as a symbol of hope for the future of both family and nation.

> Ch. 1, *Children for Adoption* 1964

25 What is a neglected child? He is a child not planned for, not wanted. Neglect begins, therefore, before he is born.

> Ch. 3, Ibid.

26 If our American way of life fails the child, it fails us all.

> Ch. 9, Ibid.

27 Nothing and no one can destroy the Chinese people. They are relentless survivors. They are the oldest civilized people on earth. Their civilization passes through phases but its basic characteristics remain the same. They yield, they bend to the wind, but they never break.

> Ch. 1, *China, Past and Present* 1972

28 Ah well, perhaps one has to be very old before one learns how to be amused rather than shocked.

> Ch. 6, Ibid.

29 "A hand is not only an implement, it's a sense organ. It's the eye of a blind man, it's the tone of those who cannot speak."

> Pt. II, *The Goddess Abides* 1972

30 Go out and be born among gypsies or thieves or among happy workaday people who live with the sun and do not think about their souls.

> "Advice to Unborn Novelists" *n.d.*

1742. Bessie Coleman (1892–1926)

1 I decided blacks should not have to experience the difficulties I had faced, so I decided to open a flying school and teach other black women to fly.

> Memoir, Quoted in *Ladybirds* by Henry M. Holden 1991

2 I wasn't going to let them humiliate *my* people, who were coming to see me. I told them I would not fly until they let the blacks through the same gate as the whites.

> Remark to Waxahachie, Texas stadium managers (1925),
> Quoted in *Women Aviators* by Lisa Yount 1995

1743. Ivy Compton-Burnett (1892–1969)

1 "We do not discuss the members of our family to their faces. . . ."

> Ch. 11, *A House and Its Head* 1935

2 "It is a lonely business, waiting to be translated to another sphere."

> Ch. 7, *Elders and Betters* 1944

3 "I do like approving of things. It is disapproving of them that is disturbing."

> Ch. 4, *Two Worlds and Their Ways* 1949

4 "Parents have too little respect for their children, just as the children have too much for the parents. . . ."

> Ch. 5, Ibid.

5 "We can build upon foundations anywhere, if they are well and truly laid."

> Ch. 7, Ibid.

6 "She should be thinking of higher things."
> "Nothing could be higher than food," said Leah.

> Ch. 1, *The Mighty and Their Fall* 1961

7 "They must release each other in time for their lives to grow."

> Ch. 3, Ibid.

8 When an age is ended you see it as it is.

> Quoted in *The Life of Ivy Compton-Burnett* by Elizabeth Sprigge 1973

1744. Diana Cooper (1892–1986)

1 Naturally good until now, I had never lied, for nothing tempted me to lie except fear of wounding and I had nothing to fear. But now with the advent of the young men—benign serpents—came the apple . . . Childhood was over.

> Ch. 5, *The Rainbow Comes and Goes* 1958

2 In astrology there is room for precaution and obstruction; the disaster is not inevitable. One can dodge the stars in their courses.

> *Trumpets from the Steep* 1960

3 Childhood is stamped on the fair face of one's uncluttered memory as clearly as morning, and a heart beating with love, enterprise and procreancy seemed recordable, but when I come to armies clashing in the dark, to destruction, to the rulers and their strength, shortcomings or ambivalence . . . I am lost in a rabble of stampeding thought that can never be rounded up.

> Ch. 2, Ibid.

4   It helped me in the air to keep my small mind contained in earthly human limits, not lost in vertiginous space and elements unknown.

        Ch. 5, Ibid.

1745. Janet Flanner (1892–1978)

1   Paris is now the capital of limbo.

        "Paris, Germany," *The New Yorker 7 December 1940*

2   The German passion for bureaucracy—for written and signal forms, for files, statistics, and lists, and for printed permissions to do this or that, to go here or there, to move about, to work, to exist—is like a steel pin pinning each French individual to a sheet of paper, the way an entomologist pins each specimen insect past struggling to his laboratory board.

        Ibid.

3   Never have nights been more beautiful than these nights of anxiety. In the sky have been shining in trinity the moon, Venus and Mars. Nature has been more splendid than man.

        "Letter from Paris," *Ibid.*

4   In place of certainty there is only a vast, tangled ball of rumor. In place of sensible, humane procedure, now destroyed by wars, revenge, suspicion and power politics, petty official strictures have been built up against which the individual is as helpless as a caged animal.

        "The Escape of Mrs. Jeffries," *Ibid.*

5   By jove, no wonder women don't love war nor understand it, nor can operate in it as a rule; it takes a man to suffer what other men have invented . . . Women have invented nothing in all that, except the men who were born as male babies and grew up to be men big enough to be killed fighting.

        Letter to Natalia Danesi Murray (1944), *Darlinghissima: Letters to a Friend 1985*

1746. Lady Willie Forbus (1892–1993)

1   But now that I'll be 100 years old, I think it's about time that I get out of the profession. I don't know any lawyers who are practicing at 100.

        Quoted in "Lawyer observes 100 years" by Robert L. Jamieson, Jr., *Seattle Post-Intelligencer,* B1 *24 August 1992*

2   I thought I'd go out West because it was more up-to-date. More open and receptive to women.*

        Ibid.

  *Reference to the difficulty for a woman lawyer to find a position ca. 1916.

3   When you become 100, life changes completely.

        Ibid.

1747. Clarissa Graves (1892–1985?)

1   What a man sows, that shall he and his relations reap.

        Letter (February 1928), Bk. 2, Ch. 9, *Robert Graves: The Years with Laura 1926–1940* * *1990*

  *Robert Ranke Graves (1895–1985), British writer, critic, poet.

1748. Eleanor Murdock Johnson (1892–1987)

1   Mission: to present selected, well-written news of interest and value to children with accuracy and fairness, colorful but uncolored.

        Motto

1749. Vivian Yeiser Laramore (1892?–1975)

1   Talk to me tenderly, tell me lies;
  I am a woman and time flies.

        "Talk to Me Tenderly" *n.d.*

2   I've shut the door on yesterday
  And thrown the key away-
  To-morrow holds no fears for me,
  Since I have found to-day.

        "To-day" *n.d.*

3   The tick of time is out of rhyme,
  Where wild things wait for death,
  Watching the stars through iron bars,
  And breathing each other's breath.
  But little man with his civic plan,
  To conquer and subdue,
  Acquires a thrill from broken will,
  Of beasts in the city zoo

        "City Zoo," in toto *n.d.*

1750. Maude Mayberg (fl. 1892)

1   Training and skills being equal, the woman who looks better will get the job, so why not make the most of your appearance?

        Quoted in Ch. 1, *Hope in a Jar, The Making of America's Beauty Culture by* Kathy Peiss* *1998*

  *See 4203.

2   Women may be divided into two classes, those who have good complexions and those who have not.

        Ch. 3, Ibid.

3   The day has passed forever for self-beautifying to be considered a confession of weakness.

        Ibid.

1751. Edna St. Vincent Millay (1892–1950)

1   I think our heart-strings were, like warp and woof
  In some firm fabric, woven in and out. . . .

        "Interim," St. 12, *Renascence and Other Poems 1917*

2   A grave is such a quiet place.

        "Renascence," St. 4, *Ibid.*

3   God, I can push the grass apart
  And lay my finger on Thy heart.

        St. 7, *Ibid.*

4   The soul can split the sky in two,
  And let the face of God shine through.

        St. 8, *Ibid.*

5   Life goes on forever like the gnawing of a mouse.

        "Ashes of Life," St. 3, *Ibid.*

6   COLUMBINE. I cannot *live*
  Without a macaroon!

        Aria Da Capo 1919

7   PIERROT. I am become a socialist. I love Humanity; but I hate people.

        Ibid.

8 CORYDON. *Your* sheep! You are mad, to call them
  Yours—mine—they are all one flock!

  Ibid.

9 Was it for this I uttered prayers,
  And sobbed and cursed and kicked the stairs,
  That now, domestic as a plate,
  I should retire at half-past eight?

  "Grown-Up," *A Few Figs from Thistles* 1920

10 Whether or not we find what we are seeking
   Is idle, biologically speaking.

   "I shall forget you presently," Ibid.

11 The fabric of my faithful love
   No power shall dim or ravel
   Whilst I stay here,—but oh, my dear,
   If I should ever travel!

   "To the Not Impossible Him," St. 3, Ibid.

12 My candle burns at both its ends;
   It will not last the night;
   But ah, my foes, and oh, my friends—
   It gives a lovely light.

   "First Fig," Ibid.

13 Spring will not ail nor summer falter;
   Nothing will know that you are gone. . . .

   "Elegy Before Death," St. 3, *Second April* 1921

14 *Down you mongrel, Death!*
   Back into your kennel!

   "The Poet and His Book," St. 1, Ibid.

15 I turn away reluctant from your light,
   And stand irresolute, a mind undone,
   A silly, dazzled thing deprived of sight
   From having looked too long upon the sun.

   "When I too long have looked upon your face," Ibid.

16 I make bean-stalks, I'm
   A builder, like yourself.

   "The Bean-Stalk," St. 4, Ibid.

17 Life is a quest and love a quarrel. . . .

   "Weeds," St. 1, Ibid.

18 Life must go on;
   I forgot just why.

   "Lament," Ibid.

19 Your body was a temple to Delight. . . .

   "As to some lovely temple tenantless," Ibid.

20 If I ever said, in grief or pride,
   I tired of honest things, I lied. . . .

   "The Goose-Girl," *The Harp-Weaver and Other Poems* 1923

21 I know I am but summer to your heart,
   And not the full four seasons of the year. . . .

   "I know I am but summer to your heart," Ibid.

22 I drank at every vine.
   The last was like the first.
   I came upon no wine
   So wonderful as thirst.

   "Feast," St. 1, Ibid.

23 Music my rampart, and my only one.

   "On Hearing a Symphony of Beethoven,"* St. 1, *The Buck in the Snow* 1928

   *Ludwig van B—, German composer (1770–1827).

24 The anguish of the world is on my tongue.
   My bowl is filled to the brim with it; there is more than I can
   eat.
   Happy are the toothless old and the toothless young,
   That cannot rend this meat.

   "The Anguish," St. 2, Ibid.

25 Breed, crowd, encroach, expand, expunge yourself, die out,
   Homo called *sapiens*.

   "Apostrophe to Man," *Wine from These Grapes* 1934

26 Childhood is the Kingdom Where Nobody Dies.

   "Childhood Is the Kingdom Where Nobody Dies," III, Ibid.

27 Soar, eat ether, see what has never been seen; depart, be lost,
   But climb.

   "On Thought in Harness," St. 3, Ibid.

28 I shall die, but that is all that I shall do for Death; I am not on
   his pay-roll.

   "Conscientious Objector," St. 3, Ibid.

29 Ease has demoralized us, nearly so; we know
   Nothing of the rigours of winter. . . .

   "Underground System," St. 2, *Huntsman, What Quarry?* 1939

30 Love does not help to understand
   The logic of the bursting shell.

   "Three Sonnets in Tetrameter," III, Ibid.

31 Any person who publishes a book willfully appears before the
   populace with his pants down. . . .

   Letters of Edna St. Vincent Millay, Allen R. Macdougall, ed. 1952

32 It's not true that life is one damn thing after another—it's one
   damn thing over and over.

   Ibid.

1752. Vita Sackville-West (1892–1962)

1 Travel is the most private of pleasures. There is no greater bore
  than the traveller to bore. We do not in the least want to hear
  what he has seen in Hong-Kong.

  Ch. 1, *Passenger to Teheran* 1926

2 . . . the fingers which had once grown accustomed to a pen
  soon itched to hold one again: it is necessary to write, if the
  days are not to slip emptily by. How else, indeed, to clap the
  net over the butterfly of the moment? for the moment passes,
  it is forgotten; the mood is gone; life itself is gone. That is
  where the writer scores over his fellows: he catches the
  changes of his mind on the hop. Growth is exciting; growth
  is dynamic and alarming. Growth of the soul, growth of the
  mind. . . .

  Ch. 1, *Twelve Days* 1928

3 For a young man to start his career with a love affair with an
  older woman was quite *de rigueur*. . . . Of course, it must not
  go on too long.

  Ch. 3, *The Edwardians* 1930

4 Click, clack, click, clack, went their conversation, like so many knitting-needles, purl, plain, purl, plain, achieving a complex pattern of references, cross-references, Christian names, nicknames, and fleeting allusions. . . .

Ch. 6, Ibid.

5 It is very necessary to have makers of beauty left in a world seemingly bent on making the most evil ugliness.

Country Notes 1940

6 I have grown wise, after many years of gardening, and no longer order recklessly from wildly alluring descriptions which make every annual sound easy to grow and as brilliant as a film star. I now know that gardening is not like that.

"January," In Your Garden Again 1953

7 I have come to the conclusion, after many years of sometimes sad experience, that you cannot come to any conclusion at all.

"May," Ibid.

8 Ambition, old as mankind, the immemorial weakness of the strong.

No Signposts in the Sea 1961

9 When, and how, and at what stage of our development did spirituality and our strange notions of religion arise? the need for worship which is nothing more than our frightened refuge into propitiation of a Creator we do not understand? A detective story, the supreme Who-done-it, written in indecipherable hieroglyphics, no Rosetta stone supplied, by the consummate mystifier to tease us poor fumbling unravellers of his plot.

Ibid.

10 Women, like men, ought to have their youth so glutted with freedom they hate the very idea of freedom.

Letter to her husband, diplomat and author Harold Nicolson (1 June 1919), Quoted in Portrait of a Marriage by Nigel Nicolson* 1973

*Her son.

11 You have met and understood me on every point. It is this which binds me to you through every storm, and makes you so unalterably the one person whom I trust and love.

(1 November 1919), Ibid.

12 . . . I hold the conviction that as centuries go on, and the sexes become more nearly merged on account of their increasing resemblances, I hold the conviction that such connections will to a very large extent cease to be regarded as merely unnatural, and will be understood far better, at least in their *intellectual* if not in their physical aspects.

"Autobiography" (27 September 1920), Ibid.

13 Things were not tragic for us then, because although we cared passionately we didn't care deeply.

(29 September 1920), Ibid.

1753. Blanche Stuart Scott (1892–1970)

1 Something must have happened to the throttle block.*

Quoted in Introduction, Women Aviators by Lisa Yount 1995

*Excuse she made to her instructor, who had blocked the throttle, upon safely landing an unauthorized solo flight.

1754. Agnes Smedley (1892–1950)

1 I have always detested the belief that sex is the chief bond between man and woman. Friendship is far more human.

Bk. I, "The Pattern," Battle Hymn of China 1943

2 The belief in immortality has always seemed cowardly to me. When very young I learned that all things die, and all that we wish of good must be won on this earth or not at all.

Ibid.

3 There's something dreadfully decisive about a beheading.

Bk. IX, "Farewell!," Ibid.

4 . . . Commercialism seemed to have eaten into the very heart of American life and culture.

Bk. X, "Hong Kong," Ibid.

5 There was waste and softness on every hand.

Ibid.

1755. Alfonsina Storni (1892–1938)

1 Miles overhead there is a light in space:
He sees a star; aroused, inspired, he reaches up to hold it,
And then another hand cuts off the hand he raises.

"Man," John A. Crow, tr., El duce dano (The sweet injury) 1918

2 I gutted your belly as I would a doll's
Examining its artifice of cogs
And buried deep within its golden pulleys
I found a trap bearing this label: sex.

"To Eros," Mask and Trefoil ca. 1930

3 . . . Ah, one favor:
If he telephones again,
Tell him it's no use, that I've gone out. . . .

"I Shall Sleep",* La Nacion (Buenos Aires) 1938

*Sent to La Nacion the day before she drowned herself.

4 You want me to be white
(God forgive you)
You want me to be chaste
(God forgive you)
You want me to be immaculate!

"You Want Me White" n.d.

5 To tell you, my love, that I desired you
With no instinctive hypocritic blush,
I was incapable, as tightly bound as Prometheus,
Until one day I burst my bonds.

"Twenty Centuries" n.d.

1756. Ruth Suckow (1892–1960)

1 To have someone tell his boys to do this and that! To take away his help on the farm just when he needed it most! To have somebody just step in and tell him where they had to go! Was that what happened in this country? Why had his people left the old country, then if things were going to be just the same?

Pt. II, Ch. 4, Country People 1924

2 To most of the people it [World War I] had seemed far away, something that could never come close. Some resented it, others seized upon it now to help break up the long monotony of everyday living—more terribly thrilling than a fire in the business district, a drowning in the river, or the discovery that the cashier of the Farmers' Bank had been embezzling. Something had come, it seemed, to shake up that placid, solid, comfortable life of home, changing things around, shifting values that had seemed to be fixed.

Pt. IV, Ch. 3, The Odyssey of a Nice Girl 1925

3   That would be the most terrible thing of all, if she began to forget. Then her heart would have to close. Yes, but if she kept it open, to feel the happiness, then she would have to feel the rest, too. . . . She would have to feel again, like blows on her open heart, every cruel detail of Harold's suffering, and the awful blank fact of his death.

"Experience," *Children and Other People* 1931

4   Exercises, songs and recitations—pieces by children whose mothers would be offended if they were left off the program: good or bad, the audience clapped.

"Eminence," Ibid.

1757. Marina Tsvetaeva (1892–1941)

1   HENRIETTE. God created his marvelous world in a week.
    A woman is a hundred worlds. With one breath,
    How can I become a woman in just one day?
    Yesterday a hussar—in spurs and sword.
    Today, a lace and satin angel.
    And tomorrow, perhaps, who knows?

Priklyuchenie (An Adventure) 1923

2   HENRIETTE. I am a moonbeam, free to go wherever I choose.

Ibid.

3   Word-creation . . . is only a journeying in the track of the hearing ear of nation and nature. A journey by ear.

"Art in the Light of Conscience," *Russian Poets on Poetry* 1976

4   Art does not pay its victims. It does not even know them. The worker is paid by the master, not by the lathe. The lathe can only leave you without an arm. How many of them I have seen, poets without an arm. With an arm lost for any other work.

Marina Tsvetaeva, A Captive Spirit: Selected Prose, Janet Marin King, ed. and tr.; Susan Sontag,* intro. 1983
*See 2866.

5   I have been trying on death for a year. It's all ugly and terrifying. Poison is vile, drowning—repulsive. . . . I do not want to die, I [just] want not to be.*

Diary entry (September 1940), Ibid.
*She hanged herself on 31 August 1941.

6   I cannot tolerate the slightest turning of the head away from me. I HURT, do you understand? I am a person skinned alive, while all the rest of you have armor.

Letter to a lover, Quoted in *Passionate Minds* by Claudia Roth Pierpont* 2000
*See 4134.

1758. Brenda Ueland (1892–1985)

1   Everybody is talented, original and has something important to say.

Ch. 1, *If You Want To Write* 1938

2   You know how all children have this creative power. You have all seen things like this: the little girls in our family used to give play after play. . . . these small ten-year-olds were working with feverish energy and endurance. . . . If they had worked that hard for school it probably would have killed them. They were working for nothing but fun, for that glorious inner excitement. It was the creative power working in them. It was

hard, hard work but there was no pleasure or excitement like it and it was something never forgotten

Ibid.

3   For when you come to think of it, the only way to love a person is not, as the stereotyped Christian notion is, to coddle them and bring them soup when they are sick, but by listening to them and seeing and believing in the god, in the poet, in them. For by doing this, you keep the god and the poet alive and make it flourish.

Ibid.

4   . . . orthodox criticism . . . is a murderer of talent. And because the most modest and sensitive people are the most talented, having the most imagination and sympathy, these are the first ones to get killed off. It is the brutal egotists that survive.

Ibid.

5   Self-trust is so important. When you launch on a story, make your neck loose, feel free, good-natured. And be lazy. Feel that you are going to throw it away. Try writing utterly unplanned stories and see what comes out.

Ch. 16, Ibid.

6   When we are listened to, it creates us, makes us unfold and expand. Ideas actually begin to grow within us and come to life.

Strength to Your Sword Arm 1993

1759. Rebecca West (1892–1983)

1   I myself have never been able to find out precisely what feminism is: I only know that people call me a feminist whenever I express sentiments that differentiate me from a doormat.

The Clarion 1913

2   "The point is that nobody likes having salt rubbed into their wounds, even if it is the salt of the earth."

Ch. 2, *The Salt of the Earth* 1935

3   "Why must you always try to be omnipotent, and shove things about? Tragic things happen sometimes that we just have to submit to."

Ibid.

4   It is queer how it is always one's virtues and not one's vices that precipitate one into disaster.

Ch. 1, *There Is No Conversation* 1935

5   There is no such thing as conversation. It is an illusion. There are intersecting monologues, that is all.

"The Harsh Voice," Sct. 1, Ibid.

6   We all drew on the comfort which is given out by the major works of Mozart,* which is as real and material as the warmth given up by a glass of brandy.

"Serbia," *Black Lamb and Grey Falcon* 1941
*Wolfgang Amadeus M- (1756–1791), Austrian composer.

7   . . . any authentic work of art must start an argument between the artist and his audience.

Pt. I, Ch. 1, *The Court and the Castle* 1957

8   All men should have a drop of treason in their veins, if nations are not to go soft like so many sleepy pears.

Pt. 4, "Conclusion," *The Meaning of Treason* 1949 rev. 1982

9 He is every other inch a gentleman.*

> Pt. 3, Ch. 5, Quoted in *Rebecca West: A Life* by Victoria Glendinning *1987*

*Reference to Bulgarian-born English novelist Michael Arlen (1895–1956).

10 Motherhood is the strangest thing, it can be like being one's own Trojan horse.

> Pt. 5, Ch. 8, Letter (20 August 1959), Ibid.

11 Everyone realizes that one can believe little of what people say about each other. But it is not so widely realized that even less can one trust what people say about themselves.

> Quoted in *Sunday Telegraph* (London, 1975), Epigraph, Ibid.

1760. Madeline Talmage Astor (1893–1940)

1 [Being helped over the rail of the Titanic*] I rang for ice, but *this* is ridiculous!

> Attributed *15 April 1912*

*British luxury passenger liner that sank during its maiden voyage after it struck an iceberg near Newfoundland; 1,513 lives were lost.

1761. Faith Baldwin (1893–1978)

1 The kiss was so much a part of the routine that it embarrassed him to withhold it.

> Ch. 2, *Alimony 1928*

2 "Compromises aren't enough."
"But," he protested, stupidly, "they're life, aren't they?"
"If they are, then life isn't enough either!"

> Ch. 8, Ibid.

3 Sometimes entering the ward he felt himself a god, with the gifts of life, of hope, of alleviation, of promise in his hands.

> Pt. V, Ch. 28, *Medical Center 1938*

4 . . . it is hard to convince editors . . . that people of—or past—forty are not senile, and might even have problems, emotions and—*mirabile dictu*—romances, licit and illicit.

> "Writing for the Women's Magazines," *The Writer's Book,* Helen Hull, ed. *1950*

5 Oh well, one must adopt a New England attitude, saying not yea, nor nay, but perhaps, maybe, and sometimes.

> Ibid.

6 Men's private self-worlds are rather like our geographical world's seasons, storm, and sun, deserts, oases, mountains and abysses, the endless-seeming plateaus, darkness and light, and always the sowing and the reaping.

> "April," *Harvest of Hope 1962*

7 Character builds slowly, but it can be torn down with incredible swiftness.

> "July," Ibid.

8 Gratitude is a humble emotion. It expresses itself in a thousand ways, from a sincere thank you to friend or stranger, to the mute, upreaching acknowledgment to God—not for the gifts of this day only, but for the day itself; not for what we believe will be ours in the future, but for the bounty of the past.

> "December," Ibid.

9 I think that life has spared these mortals much—
And cheated them of more—who have not kept
A breathless vigil by the little bed
Of some beloved child.

> "Vigil" *n.d.*

1762. Monica Baldwin (1893–1975)

1 . . . all the magic of the countryside which is ordained from the healing of the soul.

> *I Leap Over the Wall 1950*

2 You might have been standing in the heart of an iceberg, so strange it was, so silent, so austere.

> Ibid.

1763. Bessie Breuer (1893–1975)

1 The habit of worry had settled so firmly into her mother's being that her worries were her aspects of love. . . .

> Ch. 1, *The Actress 1955*

2 Hollywood . . . scripts . . . a medium where both syntax and the language itself were subjected to horrid mutilation by young men who thought of themselves as writers and who proved it by the enormous salaries they received from those higher up who were even less knowledgeable of the mother tongue.

> Ch. 15, Ibid.

3 When they first brought the baby in to her . . . she stared, inert, and thought, This is the author of my pain.

> Ch. 21, Ibid.

4 Did I stay with him the very next night because I, way deep down, thought I would learn the secret of acting by sleeping with him; was that it—the way women are always snatching at poets and composers and writers to bedizen themselves with a rag, a knuckle, a toe, the sacred toe of art?

> Ch. 32, Ibid.

1764–1765. Vera Brittain (1893–1970)

1 I found in you a holy place apart,
Sublime endurance, God in man revealed,
Where mending broken bodies slowly healed
My broken heart.

> "Epitaph on My Days in Hospital" (1919), *Poems of the War and After 1934*

2 Meek wifehood is no part of my profession;
I am your friend, but never your possession.

> "Married Love" (1926), Ibid.

3 The idea that it is necessary to go to a university in order to become a successful writer, or even a man or woman of letters (which is by no means the same thing), is one of those phantasies that surround authorship.

> Ch. 2, *On Being an Author 1948*

4 His secret realisation of his physical cowardice led him to underrate his exceptional moral courage. . . .

> Pt. I, Ch. 1, *Born 1949*

5 "There is a spiritual fellowship in suffering which unites men and women as nothing else can. Perhaps it will be by the world-wide members of this fellowship, in which those whom we call

our enemies share, that the temple of civilisation will be rebuilt when peace returns."

Pt. II, Ch. 8, Ibid.

6 The history of men and women in the past fifty years suggests that the old conflict between male and female will ultimately reach reconciliation in a new synthesis which is already in sight. The organic type of human being which will emerge from that synthesis may well be the constructive achievement of the next half-century.

Ch. 1, *Lady into Woman* 1953

7 It is probably true to say that the largest scope for change still lies in men's attitudes to women, and in women's attitudes to themselves.

Ch. 15, Ibid.

8 Politics are usually the executive expression of human immaturity.

Ch. 1, *The Rebel Passion* 1964

9 The pacifists' task today is to find a method of helping and healing which provides a revolutionary constructive substitute for war.

Ch. 12, Ibid.

1766. Elizabeth Coatsworth (1893–1986)

1 Only of one thing I am sure:
when I dream
I am always ageless

Personal Geography 1976

2 To a life that seizes
Upon content,
Locality seems
But accident.

"To Daughters, Growing Up," St. 1 *n.d.*

1767. Elizabeth Cotton (1893–1987)

1 But I didn't know people could take songs from you.
Quoted by Stephen March in *Southern Voices August/ September 1974*

2 Freight train, freight train, goin' so fast. . . .
"Freight Train" *n.d.*

1768. Lillian Day (1893–1991)

1 A lady is one who never shows her underwear unintentionally.
Kiss and Tell 1931

1769. Emma Ehrlich (1893–?)

1 For her, beauty begins with order, and it is her aesthetic sense which makes her so systematic. Everything around her is perfectly arranged; she can put her hand on any of her belongings in the dark. The same system and order which are an integral part of her public work are also part of her personal program, each item having its assigned time and place. The careful ordering of her life in mechanical things, she thinks, saves her time, keeps her in good condition, and leaves her mind free for the important problems of the day.
Quoted in *The Journey Home, How Jewish Women Shaped Modern America* by Joyce Antler* 1997
*See 3320.

1770. Marie Gilchrist (1893–1989)

1 But the life of poetry lies in fresh relationships between words, in the spontaneous fusion of hitherto unrelated words.
Ch. 1, *Writing Poetry 1932*

2 All American Indian poems are songs, and an Indian was once asked which came first, the words or the music. "They come together," he replied.
Ch. 3, Ibid.

3 Nouns and verbs are almost pure metal; adjectives are cheaper ore.
Quoted in "On the Teaching of Poetry" by Leonora Speyer,*
The Saturday Review of Literature 1946
*See 1406.

1771. Lillian [Diana] Gish (1893–1993)

1 It had been drilled into us that when an audience pays to see a performance, it is entitled to the best performance you can give. Nothing in your personal life must interfere, neither fatigue, illness, nor anxiety—not even joy.
Ch. 3, *The Movies, Mr. Griffith and Me 1969*

2 The stage was our school, our home, our life.
Ch. 7, Ibid.

3 No sacrifice was too great to get the film right, to get it accurate, true, and perfect. We weren't important in our minds; only the picture was.
Ch. 17, Ibid.

4 Young man, if God had wanted you to see me that way, he would have put your eyes in your bellybutton.*
Quoted by Richard Thomas in "Salute to Lillian Gish," CBS-TV *17 April 1984*
*Re a low camera angle.

5 Movies nowadays are all alike, as if they were made on an assembly line. Hollywood has turned into an emotional Detroit.
An Actor's Life For Me with Selma G. Lanes *1987*

6 The love scenes I did years ago were sensitive and romantic, but in today's (films) lovemaking, couples are trying to swallow each other's tonsils.
Ibid.

7 I'm a believing person. I believe in God even though I can't see him. You can't see the air in this room, right? But take it away and you're dead.
Ibid.

8 You only get one body to live in so you better take care of it.
Ibid.

1772. Helen Hathaway (1893–1932)

1 More tears have been shed over men's lack of manners than their lack of morals.
Manners for Men n.d.

1773. Lorena A. Hickok (1893–1968)

1 [The giant redwoods* made me feel] almost prayerful, and, above all, I wanted to be quiet. However, we were surrounded, not only by tourists, but guides, who kept hurling statistics at us. . . . The final indignity, so far as I was concerned, was to

name one of those trees—which was probably a sapling when Christ walked this earth—after General Sherman. Or anyone else. To me, it seemed positively sacrilegious. And I said so, right out loud.

(p. 170), *Empty Without You: The Intimate Letters of Eleanor Roosevelt*** *and Lorena Hickok*, Roger Streitmatter, ed. *1998*
*In California. **See 1618.

2   What is it you offer to send me, a Bible or a Girdle? . . . Since you mention it right after something about your riding and spell it with a small "b"—it might be a bridle. On the other hand, I have no horse, so a Bible would make better sense. I'm very curious!

Letter (20 May 1937), Ibid.

1774. Margery Eldredge Howell (1893–1946)

1   There's dignity in suffering—
Nobility in pain—
But failure is a salted wound
That burns and burns again.

"Wormwood" *n.d.*

1775. Emily Beatrix Jones (1893–1966)

1   O, do we burn on our suburban hearth
Fragments of fabulous trees that roofed a younger earth
When men were still inferior apes, and swung
In a twilight of green boughs where no birds sung?

"Forest," *Songs For Sale: An Anthology of Recent Poetry*, ed. and contr. *1918*

2   The pools of art and memory keep
Reflections of our fallen towers,
And every princess there asleep,
Whom once we kissed, is always ours.

"Middle-Age" *n.d.*

1776. Suzanne LaFollette (1893–1983)

1   The revolutionists did not succeed in establishing human freedom; they poured the new wine of beliefs in equal rights for all men into the old bottle of privilege for some; and it soured.

"The Beginnings of Emancipation," *Concerning Women* 1926

2   . . . where divorce is allowed all . . . society demands a specific grievance of one party against the other. . . . The fact that marriage may be a failure spiritually is seldom taken into account.

Ibid.

3   If responsibility for the upbringing of children is to continue to be vested in the family, then the rights of children will be secured only when parents are able to make a living for their families with so little difficulty that they may give their best thought and energy to the child's development. . . .

Ibid.

4   . . . most people, no doubt, when they espouse human rights, make their own mental reservations about the proper application of the word "human."

Ibid.

5   . . . nothing could be more grotesquely unjust than a code of morals, reinforced by laws, which relieves men from responsibility for irregular sexual acts, and for the same acts drives women to abortion, infanticide, prostitution, and self-destruction.

"Women and Marriage," Ibid.

6   . . . when one hears the argument that marriage should be indissoluble for the sake of children, one cannot help wondering whether the protagonist is really such a firm friend of childhood. . . .

Ibid.

7   The claim for alimony . . . implies the assumption that a woman is economically helpless . . .

Ibid.

8   No system of government can hope to survive the cynical disregard of both law and principle which government in America regularly exhibits.

"What Is to Be Done," Ibid.

9   It is impossible for a sex or a class to have economic freedom until everybody has it, and until economic freedom is attained for everybody, there can be no real freedom for anybody.

Ibid.

10   People never move towards revolution; they are pushed towards it by intolerable injustices in the economic and social order under which they live.

"Institutional Marriage and its Economic Aspects," Ibid.

11   No one . . . who has not known that inestimable privilege can possibly realize what good fortune it is to grow up in a home where there are grandparents.

Letter to Alice Rossi* (July 1971), *The Feminist Papers*, Alice Rossi,* ed. *1973*
*See 2439.

12   I . . . watch with growing concern the disintegration of the Western World—above all our own country—and the steady growth of totalitarian influence and power. . . .

Ibid.

1777. Margaret Leech (1893–1974)

1   England was the friend whose policy stood like a bulwark against Continental animosity to the ambitions of the American republic.

Ch. 11, *In the Days of McKinley** 1959
*William McKinley, 25th president of the United States (1897–1901); assassinated.

2   Charity stood ready to atone for the heartlessness of the War Department.

Ch. 13, Ibid.

3   The colonial fever was mildly infectious in Washington. Some of the President's closest friends and counselors came down with it.

Ch. 17, Ibid.

4   Never in history had the Union of the States been joined in such universal sorrow. North and South, East and West, the people mourned [William McKinley] a father and a friend, and the fervent strains of "Nearer, My God, to Thee"* floated, like a prayer and a leave-taking, above the half-masted flags in every city and town.

Ch. 26, Ibid.
*McKinley's favorite hymn and last words.

5   Yet, for a space, Americans turned from the challenge and the strangeness of the future. Entranced and regretful, they remembered McKinley's firm, unquestioning faith; his kindly,

frock-coated dignity; his accessibility and dedication to the people: the federal simplicity that would not be seen in Washington.

Ibid.

1778. Hesper Le Gallienne (1893–?)

1 The loose foot of the wanderer
Is curst as well as blest!
It urges ever, ever on
And never gives him rest.

"The Wanderer" n.d.

1779. Tehilla Lichtenstein (1893–1973)

1 If you believe only what you see, your world will consist only of molecules and atoms, of inert matter, having little soul and meaning, you yourself will be but a moving mechanism, having neither significance nor permanency, nor connection with the central meaning of things.

"Believing Is Seeing," *Four Centuries of Jewish Women's Spirituality: A Sourcebook,* Ellen M. Umansky* and Dianne Ashton, eds. 1992

*See 4011.

2 But the Divine Mind, and the divine attributes of God, have residence within man, they are within yourself, and therefore, healing, too, is within yourself; the healing that you seek is within yourself . . .

Ibid.

3 God has given us the physical eye, a miraculous instrument, with which to behold reality, the world about us, but he has given us the still more miraculous instrument of the imagination, he has given us the power of visualization, with which to create new and greater realities . . .

p. 181, Ibid.

1780. Dorothy Parker (1893–1967)

1 By the time you swear you're his,
Shivering and sighing,
And he vows his passion is
Infinite, undying—
Lady, make a note of this:
One of you is lying.

"Unfortunate Coincidence," *Enough Rope* 1927

2 Four be the things I am wiser to know:
Idleness, sorrow, a friend, and a foe.

Four be the things I'd be better without:
Love, curiosity, freckles, and doubt.

"Inventory," Sts. 1–2, Ibid.

3 Men seldom make passes
At girls who wear glasses.

"News Item," Ibid.

4 Oh, life is a glorious cycle of song,
A medley of extemporanea;
And love is a thing that can never go wrong;
And I am Marie of Roumania.

"Comment," Ibid.

5 Razors pain you
Rivers are damp;
Acids stain you;

And drugs cause cramp.
Guns aren't lawful;
Nooses give;
Gas smells awful;
You might as well live.

"Resumé," Ibid.

6 Her mind lives tidily, apart
From cold and noise and pain,
And bolts the door against her heart,
Out wailing in the rain.

"Interior," St. 3, *Sunset Gun* 1928

7 They sicken of the calm, who knew the storm.

"Fair Weather," St. 1, Ibid.

8 She was always pleased to have him come and never sorry to see him go.

"Big Blonde," Pt. II, *Laments for the Living* 1929

9 She had spent the golden time in grudging its going.

"The Lovely Leave," Ibid.

10 He [Ernest Hemingway]* has a capacity for enjoyment so vast that he gives away great chunks to those about him, and never even misses them. . . . He can take you to a bicycle race and make it raise your hair.

Quoted in *The New Yorker* 30 November 1929

*American novelist (1899–1961).

11 There was nothing more fun than a man!

"The Little Old Lady in Lavender Silk," St. 3, *Death and Taxes* 1931

12 That woman speaks eighteen languages and can't say No in any of them.

"Our Mrs. Parker," Quoted in *While Rome Burns* by Alexander Woollcott* 1934

*American drama critic and journalist (1887–1943).

13 Brevity is the soul of lingerie.

Ibid.

14 There's a helluva distance between wisecracking and wit. Wit has truth in it; wisecracking is simply calisthenics with words.

Interview in *Writers at Work* (First Series), Malcolm Cowley, ed. 1958

15 She [Katherine Hepburn*] runs the gamut of emotions from A to B.

Quoted in *Publisher's Weekly* 19 June 1967

*See 2110.

16 This is not a novel to be tossed aside lightly. It should be thrown with great force.

Quoted in *Algonquin Wits,* Robert E. Drennan, ed. 1968

17 I love to drink Martinis,
Two at the very most
Three, I'm under the table;
Four, I'm under the host.

The New Yorker, Quoted in *Shaken Not Stirred,* by Anistatia R. Miller and Jared M. Brown 1997

18 Excuse my dust.

"Epitaph" n.d

1781. Mary Pickford (1893–1979)

1 I was forced to live far beyond my years when just a child, now I have reversed the order and I intend to remain young indefinitely.

> Quoted in "How Mary Pickford Stays Young" by Athene Farnsworth, *Everybody's Magazine May 1926*

2 I left the screen because I didn't want what happened to Chaplin* to happen to me. When he discarded the little tramp, the little tramp turned around and killed him.

> Quoted in "America's Sweetheart Lives" by Aljean Harmetz, *The New York Times 28 March 1971*

*Charlie (Sir Charles Spencer) Chaplin, English actor and director (1889–1977)

1782. Dorothy L. Sayers (1893–1957)

1 "A man goes and fights for his country, gets his insides gassed out, and loses his job, and all they give him is the privilege of marching past the Cenotaph once a year and paying four shillings in the pound income-tax."

> Ch. 1, *The Unpleasantness at the Bellona Club 1928*

2 "And a continued atmosphere of hectic passion is very trying if you haven't got any of your own."

> Ch. 10, Ibid.

3 "People who make some other person their job are dangerous."

> *Gaudy Night 1936*

4 ". . . love's a nervous, awkward, overmastering brute; if you can't rein him in it's best to have no truck with him."

> Ibid.

5 "The only sin passion can commit is to be joyless."

> *Busman's Honeymoon 1947*

6 "Except ye become as little children," except you can wake on your fiftieth birthday with the same forward-looking excitement and interest in life that you enjoyed when you were five, "ye cannot enter the kingdom of God." One must not only die daily, but every day we must be born again.

> "Strong Meat," *Creed or Chaos? and Other Essays in Popular Mythology 1947*

7 ". . . What? Sunday morning in an English family and no sausages? God bless my soul, what's the world coming to, eh . . .?"

> Ch. 2, *Clouds of Witness 1956*

8 "Lawyers enjoy a little mystery, you know. Why, if everybody came forward and told the truth, the whole truth, and nothing but the truth straight out, we should all retire to the workhouse."

> Ch. 3, Ibid.

9 "She always says, my lord, that facts are like cows. If you look them in the face hard enough they generally run away."

> Ch. 4, Ibid.

10 "Well-bred English people never have imagination. . . ."

> Ch. 11, Ibid.

11 "Time and trouble will tame an advanced young woman, but an advanced old woman is uncontrollable by any earthly force."

> Ch. 16, Ibid.

12 There is no waste with God. He cancels nothing but redeems all.

> Quoted in *Dorothy L. Sayers: Her Life and Soul* by Barbara Reynolds *1993*

13 . . . passionate flesh and passionate intellect fused together in . . . a furnace of the passionate spirit. . . . Dante* is sublime, intellectual, and on occasion, grim; but we must also be prepared to find him simple, homely, humorous, tender and bubbling over with ecstasy.

> Ibid.

*Alighieri D—, Italian poet (1265–1321).

14 What we make is more important than what we are, particularly if making is our profession.

> Letter to John Anthony, her son (ca. 1930s), Ibid.

15 People are always imagining that if they get hold of the writer himself and, so to speak, shake him long enough and hard enough, something exciting and illuminating will drop out of him. But it doesn't. What's due to come out has come out, in the only form in which it ever can come out.

> Ibid.

16 I have a foolish complex against allying myself publicly with anything labeled feminist. . . . The more clamor we make about "the women's point of view," the more we ram into people that the women's point of view is different, and frankly I do not think it is.

> Letter to her agent (1936), Ibid.

1783. Evelyn Scott (1893–1963)

1 If I could only *feel* the child! I imagine the moment of its quickening as a sudden awakening of my own being which has never before had life. I want to *live* with the child, and I am as heavy as a stone.

> *Escapade 1913*

2 I realized a long time ago that a belief which does not spring from a conviction of the emotions is no belief at all.

> Ibid.

3 It is impossible to control creation.

> Ibid.

4 Inwardly shrinking and cold with an obscure fear, I make it a point to look very directly at all the men who speak to me. I want to shame them by the straightforwardness of my gaze.

> Ibid.

5 To have one's individuality completely ignored is like being pushed quite out of life. Like being blown out as one blows out a light.

> Ibid.

1784. Laura Frost Smith (1893–1998)

1 No one at home has the faintest idea how they are getting killed [here]. . . . I'm sure no one realizes the suffering of the boys. It's their spirit that affects me. I can watch them amputate a leg and dress a wound that is open from the hip down, but when a boy tells you he is sorry he lost [his leg] because it puts him out and he can't go back, well I have to walk away.

> Letter, cited in "Witness to War" by Carol Smith,* *Seattle Post-Intelligencer,* E1–5 *24 September 1998*

*Carol Smith is the granddaughter of Laura Frost Smith.

2 At the end of my ward there were several wounded German prisoners, young towheaded, blue-eyed boys. A guard stood over them with a .45. Having American and German patients together brought home the fact of how stupid any war is.

Ibid.

3 Finally, one day, the 11th of November,* everything became quiet about 11 a.m. And you wondered what was different. There wasn't a sound, for there were no birds to sing, or no cows to moo. We still couldn't believe it possible, as we had so many patients. A group of French trumpeters came in the afternoon and played for us, so that was the only celebration we had.

Ibid.

*Armistice Day, 1918; the end of World War I.

4 [On hearing her home town was displaying a flag for the nurses:] I'm glad someone appreciates the nurses. The patients are the only ones here that do. . . . We just have to fight for our very existence here.

Ibid.

5 It really was a wonderful parade. . . . They didn't say much about the nurses in it. We thought we were the whole show. They just said 400 [women] marched and there were at least 1,400. It is funny, because a paper usually exaggerates so much.

Letter (6 July 1918), Ibid.

1785. Freya Madeline Stark (1893–1993)

1 The great and almost only comfort about being a woman is that one can always pretend to be more stupid than one is and no one is surprised.

Ch. 2, The Valleys of the Assassins 1934

2 The slightest living thing answers a deeper need than all the works of man because it is *transitory*. It has an evanescence of life, or growth, or change: it passes, as we do, from one stage to the other, from darkness to darkness, into a distance where we, too, vanish out of sight. A work of art is static; and its value and its weakness lie in being so: but the tuft of grass and the clouds above it belong to our own travelling brotherhood.

Ch. 14, Perseus in the Wind 1948

3 The true gardener then brushes over the ground with slow and gentle hand, to liberate a space for breath round some favourite; but he is not thinking about destruction except incidentally. It is only the amateur like myself who becomes obsessed and rejoices with a sadistic pleasure in weeds that are big and bad enough to pull, and at last, almost forgetting the flowers altogether, turns into a Reformer.

Ch. 17, Ibid.

4 Persia is not good for one's morals.

Quoted in Passionate Nomad: the Life of Freya Stark by Jane Geniesse* 1999

*See 2977.

5 I have been] feeling so old . . . as if my whole life were wasted and now it was too late to do anything with it. As if what I *do* do were not worth doing: no one seems to think it is, but just wonder at me and are sorry for me if they are nice, and disapprove if they are not. To be just middle-aged with no particular charm or beauty and no position is a dreary business.

Letter to her mother (1930), Ibid.

1786. Madame Sun Yat-sen (1893–1981)

1 In the last analysis, all revolutions must be social revolutions, based upon fundamental changes in society; otherwise it is not revolution, but merely a change of government. . . .

Article in The People's Tribune 14 July 1927

2 Let us exert every ounce of man's energy and everything produced by him to ensure that everywhere the common people of the world get their due from life. This is to say that our task does not end until every hovel has been rebuilt into a decent house, until the products of the earth are within easy reach of all, until the profits from the factories are returned in equal amount to the effort exerted, until the family can have complete medical care from the cradle to the grave.

Address, "The Chinese Women's Fight for Freedom" (21 September 1949), Asia July–August 1956

3 . . . I want especially to say to our young people . . . learn from Sun Yat-sen!* Imbibe his continuous zeal, study his demand for constant progress, emulate his lack of subjectiveness, his humbleness and his closeness to the people. Make these characteristics part of your own makeup. With these you can surely go forward to build a great socialist China.

Ibid.

*Her husband, Chinese politician and revolutionary leader (1866–1925), who served as provisional president of the Republic after the fall of the Manchu dynasty (1911–1912).

1787. Clara Thompson (1893–1958)

1 The question that is raised in any study of change, whether by evolution or revolution, takes the form: Can one say that people are more benefitted or harmed?

Ibid.

2 Sexual freedom [for women] can be an excellent instrument for the expression of neurotic drives arising outside the strictly sexual sphere, especially drives expressive of hostility to men, or of the desire to be a man. Thus promiscuity may mean the collecting of scalps with the hope of hurting men, frustrating them, or taking away their importance, or in another case it may mean to the woman that she is herself a man.

Ibid.

3 Although [the upper class] is a special group within the culture, it is an important group because, on the whole, it is a thinking group, nonconformist, and seeking to bring about changes in the cultural situation.

Ibid.

4 Industry has been taken out of the home.

Ibid.

5 People who have low self-esteem . . . have a tendency to cling to their own sex because it is less frightening.

"Changing Concepts of Homosexuality in Psychoanalysis," A Study of Interpersonal Relations, New Contributions to Psychiatry, Patrick Mullahy, ed. 1949

6 The fact that one is married by no means proves that one is a mature person.

Ibid.

1788. Malka Heifetz Tussman (1893–1987)

1 For leaves don't fall. They descend.
   Longing for earth, they come winging.

"Leaves," St. 1, With Teeth in the Earth: Selected Poems of Malka Heifetz Tussman, Marcia Falk, tr. 1992

2 I hang all my heavy needs
   on a bird's wing.
                                   "Mild, My Wild," St. 2, Ibid.

3 Keep me from saying right now in the ripeness of my years.
   Unharness the horses, Mitika, I dont want to go anywhere.
   Keep me from saying such things.
                                   "Keep Me," Ibid.

1789. Sylvia Townsend Warner (1893–1978)

1 . . . Audrey carried in *The Daily Telegraph*. Mother turned with
   avidity to the Deaths. When other helpers fail and comforts
   flee, when the senses decay and the mind moves in a narrower
   and narrower circle, when the grasshopper is a burden and the
   postman brings no letters, and even the Royal Family is no
   longer quite what it was, an obituary column stands fast.
                   "Their Quiet Lives," *Swans on an Autumn River* 1966

2 There are some women . . . in whom conscience is so strongly
   developed that it leaves little room for anything else. Love is
   scarcely felt before duty rushes to encase it, anger impossible
   because one must always be calm and see both sides, pity evap-
   orates in expedients, even grief is felt as a sort of bruised sense
   of injury, a resentment that one should have grief forced upon
   one when one has always acted for the best.
                                   "Total Loss," Ibid.

3 But no one would possibly listen to her. No one ever listened to
   one unless one said the wrong thing.
                                   "Fenella," Ibid.

4 . . . somewhere out to sea . . . was a bell buoy, rocking and
   ringing. It seemed as though a heart was beating—a serene,
   impersonal heart that rocked on a tide of salt water.
                       "Healthy Landscape with Dormouse," Ibid.

5 Efficient people are always sending needless telegrams.
                                   "The View of Rome," Ibid.

6 You are only young once. At the time it seems endless, and is
   gone in a flash; and then for a very long time you are old.
                       "Swans on an Autumn River," Ibid.

1790. Mae West (1893–1980)

1 Come up 'n' see me some time.
                                   Diamond Lil 1928

2 TIRA. She's the kind of girl who climbed the ladder of success,
   wrong by wrong.
                                   I'm No Angel 1933

3 It is better to be looked over than overlooked.
                       Belle of the Nineties (screenplay) 1934

4 FRISCO DOLL. Between two evils, I always pick the one I
   never tried before.
                                   Klondike Annie 1936

5 It wasn't what I did, but how I did it. It wasn't what I said, but
   how I said it and how I looked when I did it and said it. I had
   evolved into a symbol and didn't even know it.
                   Goodness Had Nothing to Do with It 1959

6 I've always had a weakness for foreign affairs.
                                   Quoted in *Time* (New York) 1959

7 I believe in the single standard for men and women.
                   The Wit and Wisdom of Mae West, Joseph Weintraub, ed.
                                   1967

8 He who hesitates is last.
                                   Ibid.

9 A man in the house is worth two in the street.
                                   Ibid.

10 When women go wrong, men go right after them.
                                   Ibid.

11 It's not the men in my life that counts—it's the life in my men.
                                   Ibid.

12 Too much of a good thing can be wonderful.
                                   Ibid.

13 I used to be Snow White . . . but I drifted.
                                   Ibid.

14 The best way to hold a man is in your arms.
                                   Ibid.

15 My advice to those who think they have to take off their clothes
   to be a star is, once you're boned, what's left to create the illusion? Let 'em wonder. I never believed in givin' them too much
   of me.
                       Ch. 4, *Mae West on Sex, Health and ESP* 1975

16 Is that a gun in your pocket, or are you just glad to see me?
                                   Sextette 1978

17 I've made it my business to make business my business.
                   Quoted in "My Side" by M. George Haddad, *Working Woman*
                                   February 1979

18 Men have structured society to make a woman feel guilty if she
   looks after herself. Well, I beat men at their own game. I don't
   look down on men but I certainly don't look up to them either.
   I never found a man I could love—or trust—the way I loved
   myself.
                                   Ibid.

1791. Katherine Bowditch (1894–1933)

1 And what am I but love of you made flesh,
   Quickened by every longing love may bring,
   A pilgrim fire, homeless and wandering.
                                   "Reincarnation" *n.d.*

1792. Crystal Bird Fauset (1894–1965)

1 . . . what I am to do this year is to lift the curtain that separates
   the white people and the colored people, to lift the curtain of
   misunderstanding that is so dividing us.
                   Summary of work with Interracial Section, American Friends
                   Service Committee (1925), *The Face of Our Past: Images of
                   Black Women from Colonial America to the Present 2000*

2 The types of questions asked [me] give clear evidence that white
   students, both high school and college, think of the American
   Negro as being not quite human, think of him as being more
   or less of an alien, associating him with an African rather than
   American background, and that whatever advantages and
   privileges he enjoys are due solely to the magnanimity of white
   people. They do not seem to realize that these advantages and

privileges are due him as a native-born American citizen and as a normal human being - at least as normal as the attitude of the white world permits him to be.

Ibid.

1793. Rachel Lyman Field (1894–1942)

1 You won't know why, and you can't say how
Such a change upon you came,
But—once you have slept on an island
You'll never be quite the same!

"If Once You Have Slept on an Island," *Taxis and Toadstools*
1926

2 Doorbells are like a magic game,
Or the grab-bag at a fair—
You never know when you hear one ring
Who may be waiting there.

"Doorbells" *n.d.*

1794. Esther Forbes (1894–1967)

1 Women have almost a genius for anticlimaxes.

O Genteel Lady! *1926*

2 Most American heroes of the Revolutionary period are by now two men, the actual man and the romantic image. Some are even three men—the actual man, the image, and the debunked remains.

Paul Revere* 1942

*American silversmith, engraver and Revolutionary War hero (1735–1818).

1795. Martha Graham (1894–1991)

1 Nothing is more revealing than movement.

"The American Dance," *Modern Dance,* Virginia Stewart, ed.
1935

2 America does not concern itself with Impressionism. We own no involved philosophy. The psyche of the land is to be found in its movement. It is to be felt as a dramatic force of energy and vitality. We move; we do not stand still. We have not yet arrived at the stock-taking stage.

Ibid.

3 We look at the dance to impart the sensation of living in an affirmation of life, to energize the spectator into keener awareness of the vigor, the mystery, the humor, the variety, and the wonder of life. This is the function of the American dance.

Ibid.

1796. Agnes Kendrick Gray (1894–?)

1 There's only one corner of the universe that you can be certain of improving, and that's your own self.

Time Must Have A Stop 1944

2 Sure, 'tis God's ways is very quare,
An' far beyont my ken,
How o' the selfsame clay he makes
Poets an' useful men.

"The Shepherd to the Poet," St. 4 *n.d.*

1797. Osa Johnson (1894–1953)

1 When I was most tired, particularly after a hot safari in the dry, dusty plains, I always found relaxation and refresh-

ment in my garden. It was my shop window of loveliness, and Nature changed it regularly that I might feast my hungry eyes upon it. Lone female that I was, this was my special world of beauty: these were my changing styles and my fashion parade.

Ch. 9, *I Married Adventure 1940*

2 "A woman that's too soft and sweet is like tapioca pudding—fine for them as likes it."

Ch. 10, Ibid.

3 Theirs, it might be said, was a Utopian existence, for they [pygmies] showed neither hate, greed, vanity, not any other of the dominatingly unpleasant emotions of our so-called civilized world. Each dusky hop-o'-my-thumb plays his pleasant game of life with no desire to interfere with, and caring little about, the conduct of his fellows.

Ch. 27, Ibid.

4 "Animals and primitive people are alike in one thing," he said. "They know when you are friendly, they can sense it.... They can even smell fear."

Ch. 18, *Bride in the Solomons 1944*

1798. Blanche Wolf Knopf (1894–1966)

1 There is not a German writer left in Germany who is worth thinking about. The gifted writers and enterprising publishers who had any independence had left Germany. Only the Nazi writers and publishers remain so as to please the Nazi government.

Interview, *The New York Times 14 July 1936*

1799. Gertrud Kolmar (1894–1943)

1 If only I could raise my voice to be a blazing torch
Amidst the darkened desert of the world, and thunder:
JUSTICE! JUSTICE! JUSTICE!

"We Jews," St. 7, Henry A. Smith, tr., *Dark Soliloquy: The
Selected Poems of Gertrude Kolmar,* Henry A. Smith, tr. and
intro. *1975*

2 A woman always tries,
Her very life is but a single "You . . ."

"The Woman Poet," St. 5 Ibid.

1800. Jackie "Moms" Mabley (1894–1975)

1 You know who hipped me? My grandmother. This is the truth! She lived to be 118 years old. And you wonder why Moms is hip today? Granny hipped me. She said, "They lied to the rest of them, but I'm not gonna let you be dumb." One day she's sitting out on the porch and I said, "Granny, how old does a woman get before she don't want no more boyfriends?" She was around 106 then. She said, "I don't know honey, you'll have to ask somebody older than me."

Interview, *Black Stars May 1973*

2 A woman's a woman until the day she dies, but a man's only a man as long as he can.

Stand-up Routine, Quoted in *An Uncommon Scold* by Abby
Adams *1989*

3 There ain't nothin' an ol' man can do but bring me a message from a young one.

Stand-up Routine, Quoted in *And I Quote* by Ashton
Applewhite *1992*

4 They say you shouldn't say nothin' about the dead unless it's good. He's dead. Good!

Stand-up routine n.d.

1801. Kadya Molodowsky (1894–1975)

1 Sow in me your living breath,
As you sow a seed in the earth.

"Prayers," I, *Paper bridges: selected poems of Kadya Molodowsky*, Kathryn Hellerstein, ed. and tr. 1999

2 [I] . . . stretch my hands
With an entreaty . . .
To show me the light
And give light to my eyes,
To each worm that glows in the darkness at night,
That it shall bring its wonder before my heart
And redeem the darkness that is enclosed in me.

"Prayers," III, Ibid.

3 At any hour God may open the sealed womb.

"Songs of Women," Ibid.

1802. Madre Pascalina (1894–1983)

1 The Pope* should stop all overt political activity by the clergy.

Ch. 5, Quoted in *La Popessa* by Paul I. Murphy with R. Rene Arlington 1983
*Pius XII (1876–1958), pope of Roman Catholic Church (1939–1958).

2 Pius spurned ecumenism and feared the increasing democratization of ecclesiastical decision-making. The vernacular Mass, the growing role of the laity in Church policies, and the rising debate over the Holy See's sexual ethics [are] signs of decadence and profanation of Catholic heritage.

Epilogue, Ibid.

1803. Dora Russell (1894–1986)

1 Marriage, laws, the police, armies and navies are the mark of human incompetence.

The Right to Be Happy 1927

2 We have never yet had a Labour Government that knew what taking power really means; they always act like second-class citizens.

Quoted in *Observer* (London) 30 January 1983

3 We do not want our world to perish. But in our quest for knowledge, century by century, we have placed all our trust in a cold, impartial intellect which only brings us nearer to destruction. We have heeded no wisdom offering guidance. Only by learning to love one another can our world be saved. Only love can conquer all.*

Ch. 14, *Challenge to the Cold War*, Vol. 3 1985
*Final words of final volume of her autobiography.

1804. Adela Rogers St. Johns (1894–1988)

1 People don't think the only American saint is a woman [Mother Cabrini].* I knew her and didn't know she was a saint. She didn't know, either. She built the first school and first hospital in every town.

Some Are Born Great 1974
*Saint Frances Xavier Cabrini (1850–1917); see 1171.

2 Mrs. [Margaret] Sanger* said the best birth control is to make your husband sleep on the roof.

Ibid.
*See 1535; Sanger *reported* this advice—she did not give it.

3 I've often thought with Nixon* that if he'd made the football team, his life would have been different.

Quoted in "She's Had the Last Word for Sixty Years" by Joyce Haber, *Los Angeles Times* 13 October 1974
*Richard Milhous N— (1913–1994), 37th president of the United States (1969–1974); resigned.

4 The modern woman is the curse of the universe. A disaster, that's what. She thinks that before her arrival on the scene no woman ever did anything worthwhile before, no woman was ever liberated until her time, no woman really ever amounted to anything. . . .

Quoted in "Some Are Born Great" by Mert Guswiler, *Los Angeles Herald-Examiner* 13 October 1974

5 About twenty-five years ago . . . I made three resolutions of what I would never do again. They were: to put on a girdle, to wear high heels, and to go out to dinner.

Ibid.

6 I think every woman's entitled to a middle husband she can forget.

Ibid.

1805. Genevieve Taggard (1894–1948)

1 Try tropic for your balm,
Try storm,
And after storm, calm.
Try snow of heaven, heavy, soft and slow,
Brilliant and warm.
Nothing will help, and nothing do much harm.

"Of the Properties of Nature for Healing an Illness," St. 1 n.d.

1806–1807. Fabiola Cabeza de Baca (1895–?)

See Tey Diana Rebolledo, 3052.

1808. Babette Deutsch (1895–1974)

1 But the poet's job is, after all, to translate God's poem (or is it the Fiend's?) into words.

"Poetry at the Mid-Century," *The Writer's Book*, Helen Hull, ed. 1950

2 . . . the poet . . . like the lover . . . is a person unable to reconcile what he knows with what he feels. His peculiarity is that he is under a certain compulsion to do so.

Ibid.

3 The poets were among the first to realize the hollowness of a world in which love is made to seem as standardized as plumbing, and death is actually a mechanized industry. . . .

Ibid.

4 Their memories: a heap of tumbling stones,
Once builded stronger than a city wall.

"Old Women" n.d.

5 You, also laughing one,
Tosser of balls in the sun,
Will pillow your bright head
By the incurious dead.

"A Girl" n.d.

1809. Rose Franken (1895–1988)

1   CLAUDIA. Nothing, and no one really belongs to anyone.
DAVID. If you've learned that, you've learned a lot, my dearest.
Act III, Claudia 1941

1810. Anna Freud (1895–1982)

1   The war acquires comparatively little significance for children so long as it only threatens their lives, disturbs their material comfort or cuts their food ration. It becomes enormously significant the moment it breaks up family life and uproots the first emotional attachments of the child within the family group.
War and Children, with Dorothy Burlingham 1943

2   . . . it is normal for an adolescent to behave for a considerable length of time in an inconsistent and unpredictable manner; to fight his impulses and to accept them; to ward them off successfully and to be overrun by them; to love his parents and to hate them; to revolt against them and to be dependent on them; to be deeply ashamed to acknowledge his mother before others and, unexpectedly, to desire heart-to-heart talks with her; to thrive on imitation of and identification with others while searching unceasingly for his own identity; to be more idealistic, artistic, generous, and unselfish than he will ever be again, but also the opposite: self-centered, egoistic, calculating. Such fluctuation between extreme opposites would be deemed highly abnormal at any other time of life. At this time they may signify no more than that an adult structure of personality takes a long time to emerge . . .
"Adolescence," *The Psychoanalytic Study of the Child,* Vol. 13 *1958*

1811. Alberta Hunter (1895–1984)

1   I didn't care what time my time was up [at work]. If my patient was restless, I'd stay there and try to soothe my patient to sleep, no matter how long it took. Then when they'd go to sleep, I'd go on home.
Quoted in *Alberta Hunter: A Celebration in Blues* by Frank C. Taylor with Gerald Cook 1987

2   It upset me so to think that they have rules that make you leave something that you love.*
Ibid.

*Reference to her forced retirement as a nurse when, according to hospital records, she'd reached the age of seventy (actually she was eighty-two].

3   I gotta man, he's kinda old and thin.
But there are plenty of good tunes left
in an old violin'
"Workin' Man" (song) *n.d.*

1812. Juana de Ibarbourou (1895–1989)

1   I give you my naked soul
Like a statue unveiled.
"The Hour," *Diamond Tongues* 1919

2   For if I am so rich, if I have so much,
If they see me surrounded by every luxury,
It is because of my noble lineage
That builds castles on my pillow.
"Small Woman," Ibid.

1813. Dolores Ibarruri (1895–1989)

1   It is better to die on your feet than to live on your knees!
Radio Speech 18 July 1936

2   It is better to be the widow of a hero than the wife of a coward.
Speech (Valencia, Spain) 1936

3   Wherever they pass they [the fascists] sow death and desolation.
Speeches and Articles, 1936–1938 1938

4   We dip our colors in honor of you, dear women comrades, who march into battle together with the men.
Ibid.

5   !No pasaran!
Quoted in Ch. 4, *Passionate War, the Narrative History of the Spanish Civil War (1936–39)* by Peter Wyden 1983

6   I am a simple woman; granddaughter, daughter and sister of miners. A woman who has fought much and hard to bring socialism to Spain.
Quoted in "Entrevista" by Antonio del Corral, *Carta de España,* Hélène Lopez, tr. 15 December 1985

1814. Bessie Rowland James (1895–1974)

1   No matter how lofty you are in your department, the responsibility for what your lowliest assistant is doing is yours.
Quoted in Adlai's Almanac by Adlai Ewing Stevenson* 1952
*American politician, governor of Illinois (1900–1965).

1815. Eva Jessye (1895–1992)

1   I traveled and made money and I wouldn't let anybody get between me and my music. If I belong to anything, I belong to my music. . . . What you were born to do, you don't stop to think, should I? could I? would I? I only think, will I? And, I shall!
I Dream a World by Brian Lanker 1989

1816. Dorothea Lange (1895–1965)

1   These [country women] are women of the American soil. They are a hardy stock. They are the roots of our country. . . . They are not our well-advertised women of beauty and fashion. . . . These women represent a different mode of life. They are of *themselves* a very great American style. They live with courage and purpose, a part of our tradition.
Quoted in *The Women's Eye* by Anne Tucker* 1973
*See 3620.

2   The camera is an instrument that teaches people how to see without a camera.
Quoted in "The Photographer Who Showed Americans How to See Themselves" by Robert Kirsch, *The Los Angeles Times 13 August 1978*

3   . . . being disabled* gave me an immense advantage. People are kinder to you. It puts you on a different level than if you go into a situation whole and secure.
Ibid.

*A bout of polio at age seven left Lange with a wizened right leg and a limp.

4   The megalopolis is not just an American phenomenon, it's international and we are creating this environment, teeming with unfamiliar ways of living, almost without scrutiny.
Ibid.

1817. Susanne K. Langer (1895–1985)

1　Feeling, in the broad sense of whatever is felt in any way, as sensory stimulus or inward tension, pain, emotion or intent, is the mark of mentality.

> Pt. I, Ch. 1, *Mind, An Essay on Human Feeling,* Vol. I *1967*

2　Art is the objectification of feeling.

> Pt. II, Ch. 4, Ibid.

3　The secret of the "fusion" is the fact that the artist's eye sees in nature . . . an inexhaustible wealth of tension, rhythms, continuities and contrasts which can be rendered in line and color; and those are the "internal forms" which the "external forms"—painting, musical or poetic compositions or any other works of art—expresses for us.

> Ibid.

4　"Consciousness" is not an entity at all, let alone a special cybernetic mechanism. It is a condition built up out of mental acts of a particular life episode. . . .

> Ch. 11, Ibid.

1818. Marguerite Rawalt (1895–1989)

1　The ERA will rise again.*

> "A Century of Achievement," The Centennial of the National Association of Women Lawyers by Selma Moidel Smith, *Experience Fall 1998*
> *Commenting on 1982 failure of passage of the Equal Rights Amendment.

1819. Lillian Symes (1895–?)

1　. . . evidently fair wages and fair conditions cannot be left to the altruism of the individual employer where the worker is unable to enforce her own demands. . . .[O]n the whole, the young unorganized worker must look to the public for some protection until she is able to protect herself.

> "Behind the Scenes in Candy Factories," The Consumers' League of New York *March 1928*

2　[The new] gentleman who expects you to assume half the financial obligations and all the domestic ones.

> "Still a Man's Game: Reflections of a Slightly Tired Feminist," *Harper's Monthly Magazine 158 May 1929*

3　. . . man has acquired the habits of superiority and because that superiority is now being challenged, he is suffering more than woman from the ravages of this conflict. If it is ever resolved, the new masculinism will go the way of the old feminism.

> "The New Masculinism," pp. 105–107, *Harper's Monthly Magazine 161 June 1930*

4　The feminist movement is dying of partial victory and inanition.

> (ca. 1920s), Quoted by Susan Faludi in "Second-Place Citizens", *The New York Times 26 August 2008*

1820. Lenore J. Coffee (1896–1984)

1　They pick your brains, break your heart, ruin your digestion— and what do you get for it? Nothing but a lousy fortune.

> *The Grove Book of Hollywood,* Christopher Silvester, ed. *2000*

1821. Gerty Cori (1896–1957)

1　For a research worker the unforgotten moments of life are those rare ones, which come after years of plodding work, when the veil over nature's secret seems suddenly to lift and when what was dark and chaotic appears in a clear and beautiful light pattern.

> Radio interview,* Quoted in "Gerty Cori" by John Parascandola, *Notable American Women 1980*
> *This interview was played at her memorial service.

2　I believe that in art and science are the glories of the human mind. I see no conflict between them.

> Ibid.

1822. Nancy Cunard (1896–1965)

1　[Africa is] in the iron grip of its several imperialist oppressions . . . The white man is killing Africa.

> Introduction, *Negro: An Anthology 1934*

2　I've always had the feeling that everyone alive can [do] something that is worthwhile.

> Quoted in *Nancy Cunard: Heiress, Muse, Political Idealist* by Lois Gordon 2007

3　All that remains is a furious sense of indignation.

> "Parallex" (1925), Ibid.

4　But if I were free
I would go on, see all the northern continents
Stretch out before me under winter sunsets;
Look into the psychology
Of Iceland, and plumb the imaginations
of strange people in faraway lands.

> Ibid.

5　Sleep? Warmth? Food? No! Somewhere someone was suffering. . . . I should own absolutely NOTHING.

> Ibid.

1823. Gordon Daviot (1896–1952)

1　JOHN OF GAUNT.* He holds England in his two hands and laughs like a wicked child and men pause and hold their breath.

> *Richard Bordeaux** (play) 1932*
> *Duke of Lancaster (1340–1399), English soldier. The fourth son of Edward III who ruled England for a time. **Richard II (1367–1400), King of England (1377–1399).

1824. Mamie Eisenhower (1896–1979)

1　I stayed busy all the time and loved being in the White House, but I was never expected to do all the things you have to do.

> Comment to Rosalyn Carter* (1977), Quoted in *First Ladies* by Betty Boyd Caroli *1987*
> *See 2589.

1825. Ruth Gordon (1896–1985)

1　MAX. Say, is it too early for a drink?
POLLY. What's early about it? It's tomorrow in Europe and yesterday in China.

> Act III, *Over Twenty-One 1943*

2　POLLY. Do you realize you've come damn close to breaking a man's spirit?
GOW. Well, it was his spirit or my bank account.

> Ibid.

3　FATHER. . . . there's always plenty of room at the bottom.

> *Years Ago 1946*

4 CLYDE. I'm sure the way to be happy is to live well beyond your means!

Act I, *The Leading Lady 1948*

5 CLYDE. The best impromptu speeches are the ones written well in advance.

Ibid.

6 MRS. GILSON. Up and the world is your oyster! This time you can't miss! Whack comes down the old shillay and you're down again bitin' the dust! Can't face it! Screeching into your pillow nights! Put back your smile in the morning, trampin' to managers' offices! Home again in the evenin' ready to give up the ghost. Somebody come by, to tell you: "Go see Frohman nine-thirty sharp!" Luck's turned, you're on the trolley again! Curl up your ostrich feathers! Sponge off the train of your skirt! Because it's all aboard tomorrow....

Act III, Ibid.

7 To get it right, be born with luck or else make it. *Never* give up. Get the knack of getting people to help you and also pitch in yourself. A little money helps, but what *really* gets it right is to *never*—I repeat—*never* under any condition face the facts.

"Myself Among Others," *Myself Among Others 1970*

8 The good that men do lives after them. That's a quote from myself. I know the correct one, but I don't think so. I think the *good* lives after. The evil gets accepted or forgotten. Or becomes hearsay. The *good* lives on and does us all some good.

"The Good That Men Do," Ibid.

1826. Vivien Kellems (1896–1975)

1 Our tax law is a 1,598-page hydra-headed monster and I'm going to attack and attack and attack until I have ironed out every fault in it.

Quoted in *Los Angeles Times 26 January 1975*

2 ... the IRS has stolen from me over the past 20 years because I am single. It is unconstitutional to impose a penalty tax of 40 percent on me because I have no husband.

Quoted in "Unforgettable Vivien Kellems" by Gloria Swanson, *Reader's Digest October 1975*

3 Of course I'm a publicity hound. Aren't all crusaders? How can you accomplish anything unless people know what you're trying to do?

Ibid.

4 Men always try to keep women out of business so they won't find out how much fun it really is.

Ibid.

1827. Martha Martin (1896–1959)

1 I killed a sea otter today. I actually did kill a sea otter. I killed him with the ax, dragged him home, and skinned him.

O Rugged Land of Gold 1952

2 I told her the deer are our helpers and our friends, our subjects and our comfort, and they will give us food and clothing according to our needs. I told her of the birds.... Told her of the fishes.... Told her of the mink and the otter, and the great brown bear with his funny, furry cub. Told her of the forest and of the things it will give us ... of the majestic mountain uprising behind us with a vein of goldbearing ore coming

straight from its heart. Told her that all these things were ours to have and to rule over and to care for.

Ibid.

3 The Indians have come, good, good Indians. Shy, fat, smelly, friendly, kindhearted Indians.

Ibid.

4 My darling little girl-child, after such a long and troublesome waiting I now have you in my arms. I am alone no more, I have my baby.

Ibid.

1828. Tina Modotti (1896–1942)

1 ... I never realized before that a letter—a mere sheet of paper—could be such a spiritual thing—could emanate so much feeling—you gave a soul to it!

Letter to Edward Weston* (25 April 1921), Quoted in Ch. 1, *Tina Modotti, A Fragile Life* by Mildred Constantine *1975*
*American photographer (1850–1936) with whom she collaborated and who was her companion.

2 The love of revolutionaries is not separate from their other activities; it is related to their political ideals.

Courtroom Interrogation* (16 January 1929), Ibid.
*After the shooting death of Julio Antonio Mella, Cuban revolutionary, in Mexico, who was her companion.

3 I consider myself a photographer, nothing more ... Photography, precisely because it can only be produced in the present and because it is based on what exists objectively before the camera, takes its place as the most satisfactory medium of registering life in all its aspects, and from this comes its documental value. If to this is added sensibility and understanding and, above all, a clear orientation as to the place it should have in the field of historical development, I believe that the result is something worthy of a place in social production, to which we should all contribute.

Comment at exhibition, Mexico City (December 1929), Ibid.

1829. Rose Pesotta (1896–1965)

1 Wasn't it a little superficial to maintain that all the good qualities rest with the wage earners, and everything evil is part of the employing class?

Remark to Emma Goldman, Rose Pesotta Papers (N.Y. Public Library Rare Books & Ms. Div.) *15 April 1935*

1830. Dawn Powell (1896–1965)

1 She knew exactly what she wanted from life, which was, in a word, everything.

A Time to Be Born 1942

2 She had a genuine distaste for sexual intimacy ... but there were so many things to be gained by trading on sex and she thought so little of the process that she itched to use it as currency once again.

Ibid.

3 I reflected that he [her husband] was the only person in the world I found it always a kick to run into on the street.

Diary entry, Quoted in *Dawn Powell* by Tim Page *1998*

4 Satire is people as they are; romanticism, people as they would like to be; realism, people as they seem with their insides left out.

Attributed *n.d.*

1831. Beata Rank (1896–1967)

1 Because she is so barren of spontaneous manifestations of maternal feelings, she studies vigilantly all the new methods of upbringing and reads treatises about physical and mental hygiene.

"Adaptation of the Psychoanalytic Technique . . .," *American Journal of Orthopsychiatry January 1949*

2 . . . examine the personality of the mother, who is the medium through which the primitive infant transforms himself into a socialized human being.

Ibid.

1832. Marjorie Kinnan Rawlings (1896–1953)

1 You can't change a man, no-ways. By the time his mammy turns him loose and he takes up with some innocent woman and marries her, he is what he is.

"Benny and the Bird-Dogs," *When the Whippoorwill 1931*

2 When she settled down for a life-time's quarreling at him, it was for the same reason syrup sours—the heat had just been put to her too long.

Ibid.

3 There was something about the most fertile field that was beyond control. A man could work himself to skin and bones, so that there was no flesh left on him to make sweat in the sun, and a crop would get away from him. There was something about all living that was uncertain.

Ch. 3, *South Moon Under 1933*

4 Sorrow was like the wind. It came in gusts, shaking the woman. She braced herself.

Ch. 9, Ibid.

5 It seemed a strange thing to him, when earth was earth and rain was rain, that scrawny pines should grow in the scrub, while by every branch and lake and river there grew magnolias. Dogs were the same everywhere, and oxen and mules and horses. But trees were different in different places.

Ch. 1, *The Yearling 1938*

6 The game seemed to him to be two different animals. On the chase, it was the quarry. He wanted only to see it fall. . . . When it lay dead and bleeding, he was sickened and sorry. . . . Then when it was cut into portions . . . his mouth watered at its goodness. He wondered by what alchemy it was changed, so that what sickened him one hour, maddened him with hunger the next. It seemed as though there were either two different animals or two different boys.

Ch. 8, Ibid.

7 "A woman has got to love a bad man once or twice in her life, to be thankful for a good one."

Ch. 12, Ibid.

8 "You figgered I went back on you. Now there's a thing ever' man has got to know. Mebbe you know it a'ready. 'Twa'n't only me. 'Twa'n't only your yearlin' deer havin' to be destroyed. Boy, life goes back on you."

Ch. 33, Ibid.

9 Living was no longer the grief behind him, but the anxiety ahead.

Ibid.

1833. Ida P. Rolf (1896–1979)

1 Word's going around Esalen* that Ida Rolf thinks the body is all there is. Well, I want it known that I think there's more than the body, but the body is all you can get your hands on.

Quoted in *The Protean Body* by Don Johnson 1977
*Esalen Institute, founded in 1962 and located in Big Sur, California; known for its blend of East/West philosophies, experiential/didactic workshops, and a steady influx of philosophers, psychologists, artists, and religious thinkers.

2 Form and function are a unity, two sides of one coin. In order to enhance function, appropriate form must exist or be created.

Preface, *Rolfing: The Integration of Human Structures 1977*

3 Twentieth-century medicine, which has worked so many miracles, has been chemically not structurally oriented. Hence, the lay mind thinks of chemistry as the only outstanding healing medium—a drug for this, a shot for that. But any mirror photograph would reveal that a great many problems are matters of structure, of physics . . .

Ibid.

1834. Elsa Schiaparelli (1896–1973)

1 So fashion is born by small facts, trends, or even politics, never by trying to make little pleats and furbelows, by trinkets, by clothes easy to copy, or by the shortening or lengthening of a skirt.

Ch. 9, *Shocking Life 1954*

2 A good cook is like a sorceress who dispenses happiness.

Ch. 21, Ibid.

3 Eating is not merely a material pleasure. Eating well gives a spectacular joy to life and contributes immensely to goodwill and happy companionship. It is of great importance to the morale.

Ibid.

4 The moment that people stop copying you, it means that you are no longer any good, and that you have ceased to be news.

Ibid.

1835. Betty Smith (1896–1972)

1 There's a tree that grows in Brooklyn. Some people call it the Tree of Heaven. No matter where its seed falls, it makes a tree which struggles to reach the sky. It grows in boarded-up plots and out of neglected rubbish heaps. It grows up out of cellar gratings. It is the only tree that grows out of cement. It grows lushly . . . survives without sun, water, and seemingly without earth. It would be considered beautiful except that there are too many of it.

A Tree Grows in Brooklyn 1943

2 Miss Gardner had nothing in all the world excepting a sureness about how right she was.

Ch. 42, Ibid.

3 "The difference between rich and poor," said Francie, "is that the poor do everything with their own hands and the rich hire hands to do things."

Ch. 45, Ibid.

4 She felt, vaguely, that she had given away her childhood that night. She had given it to him or he had taken it from her, and made it into something wonderful. In a way, her life was his now.

Ch. 23, *Maggie—Now 1958*

5 "... I can never give a 'yes' or a 'no.' I don't believe everything in life can be settled by a monosyllable."

Ch. 39, Ibid.

1836. Dodie Smith (1896–1990)

1 ROGER. You know, you women with this skinny complex are laying up a wretched old age for yourselves. String, that's what you'll be. Stringy and desiccated.
DOROTHY. Well, that's better than having two double chins and three double stomachs.
ROGER. I have no stomach whatsoever.
DOROTHY. How inconvenient.

Call It a Day 1935

2 Noble deeds and hot baths are the best cure for depression.

Ch. 3, *I Capture the Castle 1948*

3 "... she happens to belong to a type [of American woman] I frequently met—it goes to lectures. And entertains afterwards. ... Amazing, their energy," he went on. "They're perfectly capable of having three or four children, running a house, keeping abreast of art, literature and music—superficially of course, but good lord, that's something—and holding down a job into the bargain. Some of them get through two or three husbands as well, just to avoid stagnation."

Ch. 7, Ibid.

4 What a difference there is between wearing even the skimpiest bathing-suit and wearing nothing! After a few minutes I seemed to live in every inch of my body as fully as I usually do in my head and my hands and my heart. I had the fascinating feeling that I could think as easily with my limbs as with my brain. ...

Ch. 12, Ibid.

5 Perhaps the effect wears off in time, or perhaps you don't notice it if you are born to it, but it does seem to me that the climate of richness must always be a little dulling to the senses. Perhaps it takes the edge off joy as well as off sorrow.

Ch. 14, Ibid.

6 "... I don't like the sound of all those lists he's making—it's like taking too many notes at school; you feel you've achieved something when you haven't."

Ch. 15, Ibid.

1837. Mildred Witte Struven (1896?–post-1983)

1 A clay pot sitting in the sun will always be a clay pot. It has to go through the white heat of the furnace to become porcelain.

Quoted by her daughter Jean Harris, *Stranger in Two Worlds 1986*

1838. Ethel Waters (1896–1977)

1 I sang "Stormy Weather" from the depths of the private hell in which I was being crushed and suffocated.

His Eye is on the Sparrow: An Autobiography with Charles Samuels 1951

2 The roustabouts and the concessionaires were the kind of people I'd grown up with, rough, tough, full of larceny towards strangers, but sentimental, and loyal to their friends and co-workers.

Ibid.

3 I never was a child. I never was coddled, or liked, or understood by my family.

To Me, It's Wonderful (autobiography) 1972

4 I wanted love and to get love back. I didn't want a man. Don't misunderstand me, I'm a normal woman. But I'd been so hurt.

Ibid.

1839. Charlotte Whitton (1896–1975)

1 Whatever women do they must do twice as well as men to be thought half as good. Luckily, this is not difficult.

Quoted in *Canada Month June 1963*

1840. Wallis Simpson Windsor (1896–1986)

1 I don't remember any love affairs. One must keep love affairs quiet.

Quoted in *Los Angeles Times 11 April 1974*

2 One can never be too thin or too rich.

Comment *n.d.*

1841. Judith Anderson (1897–1992)

1 There is nothing enduring in the life of a woman except what she builds in a man's heart.

News item *8 March 1931*

1842. Elizabeth Asquith Bibesco (1897–1945)

1 Being in a hurry is one of the tributes he pays to life.

"Balloons" 1922

2 I have made a great discovery.
What I love belongs to me. Not the chairs and tables in my house, but the masterpieces of the world.
It is only a question of loving them enough.

Ibid.

3 It is sometimes the man who opens the door who is the last to enter the room.

Ch. 13, *The Fir and the Palm 1924*

4 It is never any good dwelling on good-byes. It is not the being together that it prolongs, it is the parting.

Ch. 15, Ibid.

1843. Louise Bogan (1897–1970)

1 Eat it, and you will taste more than the fruit:
The blossom, too,
The sun, the air, the darkness at the root,
The rain, the dew,

"The Crossed Apple," St. 7, *Dark Summer 1929*

2 Yeats's faith in the development of his own powers has never failed.

"William Butler Yeats,"* *Atlantic Monthly* (Boston) *May 1938*
*Irish writer, world renowned poet, and cofounder of Irish National Theatre (1865–1939).

3 Women have no wilderness in them,
They are provident instead,
Content in the tight hot cell of their hearts
To eat dusty bread.

"Women," St. 1, *Body of this Death 1943*

4   True revolutions in art restore more than they destroy.
      "Reading Contemporary Poetry," *College English February 1953*

5   It is a dangerous lot, that of the charming, romantic public poet, especially if it falls to a woman. . . . it is almost impossible for the poetess, once laurelled, to take off the crown for good or to reject the values and taste of those who tender it.*
      "Unofficial Feminine Laureate" (1939), *Selected Criticism: Poetry and Prose 1955*
      *Reference to Edna St. Vincent Millay; see 1751.

6   But childhood prolonged, cannot remain a fairyland. It becomes a hell.*
      "Childhood's False Eden" (1940), Ibid.
      *Reference to Katherine Mansfield; see 1687.

7   I burned my life, that I might find
    A passion wholly of the mind
      "The Alchemist," St. 1, *The Blue Estuaries: Poems 1923–1968 1968*

8   Once form has been smashed, it has been smashed for good, and once a forbidden subject has been released it has been released for good.
      "Experimentalists of a New Generation" (1957), *A Poet's Alphabet 1970*

9   How fortunate the rich and/or married, who have servants and *wives* to expedite matters.
      What the Woman Lived: Selected Letters 1920–1970, Ruth Limmer, ed. *1974*

10 A second blooming and the bough can scarcely bear it.
      Ibid.

11 I cannot believe that the inscrutable universe turns on an axis of suffering; surely the strange beauty of the world must somewhere rest on pure joy!
      Letter to John Hall Wheelock, Ibid.

1844. Catherine Drinker Bowen (1897–1973)

1   I know what these people want; I have seen them pick up my violin and turn it over in their hands. They may not know it themselves, but they want music, not by the ticketful, the purseful, but music as it should be had, music at home, a part of daily life, a thing as necessary, as satisfying, as the midday meal. They want to *play*. And they are kept back by the absurd, the mistaken, the wicked notion that in order to play an instrument one must be possessed by that bogey called Talent. . . .
      Ch. 2, *Friends and Fiddlers 1934*

2   "We don't want her to take music too seriously." Real concern came into her voice. "We don't want her to become intense over something, and warped and queer. Such women are unhappy in later life. They don't" she rang the bell for more tea, "they don't make good wives."
      Ch. 4, Ibid.

3   Many a man who has known himself at ten forgets himself utterly between ten and thirty.
      Ch. 9, Ibid.

4   Holmes divided lawyers into kitchen knives, razors, and stings. Brandeis, he said, was a sting.
      Yankee from Olympus 1944

5   The professors laugh at themselves, they laugh at life; they long ago abjured the bitch-goddess Success, and the best of them will fight for his scholastic ideals with a courage and persistence that would shame a soldier. The professor is not afraid of words like *truth;* in fact he is not afraid of words at all.
      Ch. 5, *Adventures of a Biographer 1946*

6   For your born writer, nothing is so healing as the realization that he has come upon the right word.
      Ch. 11, Ibid.

7   In writing biography, fact and fiction shouldn't be mixed. And if they are, the fictional points should be printed in red ink, the facts printed in black ink.
      Quoted in *Publishers Weekly 24 March 1958*

8   People who carry a musical soul about them are, I think, more receptive than others. They smile more readily. One feels in them a pleasant propensity toward the lesser sins, a pleasing readiness also to admit the possibility that on occasion they may be in the wrong—they may be mistaken.
      Speech, "The Nature of the Artist" Scripps College *27 April 1961*

9   Great artists treasure their time with a bitter and snarling miserliness.
      Ibid.

10 The things we believe in and want done will not be done until women are in elective office.
      Quoted in *National Business Week September 1974*

1845. Catherine Cate Coblentz (1897–1951)

1   "Sing your own song," said the River, "sing well."
      The Blue Cat of Castle Town 1949

2   Life is an archer, fashioning an arrow
    With anxious care, for in it life must trust;
    A single flash across the earthly spaces
    Straight to the throat of death—one conquering thrust!
      "Life" *n.d.*

1846. Dorothy Day (1897–1980)

1   Tradition! We scarcely know the word anymore. We are afraid to be either proud of our ancestors or ashamed of them. We scorn nobility in name and in fact. We cling to a bourgeois mediocrity which would make it appear we are all Americans, made in the image and likeness of George Washington.
      Pt. 1, *The Long Loneliness 1952*

2   . . . who were the mad and who were the sane? . . . People sold themselves for jobs, for the pay check, and if they only received a high enough price, they were honored. If their cheating, their theft, their lies, were of colossal proportions, if it were successful, they met with praise, not blame.
      Pt. I, Ibid.

3   In our disobedience we were trying to obey God rather than men, trying to follow a higher obedience. We did not wish to act in a spirit of defiance and rebellion.
      Ch. 16, *Loaves and Fishes 1963*

4   The greatest challenge of the day is: how to bring about a revolution of the heart, a revolution which has to start with each one of us? When we begin to take the lowest place, to wash the feet of others, to love our brothers with that burning love, that

passion, which led to the Cross, then we can truly say, "Now I have begun."

Ch. 19, Ibid.

5 The best thing to do with the best things in life is to give them up.

Quoted in "Saints Among Us," *Time* (New York) *29 December 1975*

6 If you feed the poor, you're a saint. If you ask why they're poor, you're a Communist.

Entertaining Angels [bio pic] *1996*

1847. Amelia Earhart (1897–1937)

1 There is so much that must be done in a civilized barbarism like war.

Ch. 1, *20 Hours: 40 Minutes—Our Flight in the Friendship 1928*

2 In soloing—as in other activities—it is far easier to start something than it is to finish it.

Ch. 2, Ibid.

3 Of course I realized there was a measure of danger. Obviously I faced the possibility of not returning when first I considered going. Once faced and settled there really wasn't any good reason to refer to it again.

Ch. 5, Ibid.

4 Courage is the price that Life exacts for granting peace,
The soul that knows it not, knows no release
From little things.

"Courage" (1927), Quoted in Ch. 1, *The Sound of Wings* by Mary S. Lovell *1989*

5 The woman who can create her own job is the woman who will win fame and fortune.

The New York Times (29 July 1928), Ch.12, Ibid.

6 You must know again my reluctance to marry, my feeling that I shatter thereby chances in work which means most to me . . . Please let us not interfere with the other's work or play. . . . I may have to keep some place where I can go to be by myself now and then, for I cannot guarantee to endure at all times the confinement of even an attractive cage.

Letter to her future husband, George P. Putnam,* Ibid.
*(1887–1950), Am. Publisher, author, explorer.

7 I cruised inland until I found a suitable pasture. I landed there after frightening all the cows in the neighborhood and rolled up to the farmer's front door.*

Quoted on "100 Years of Great Women," *ABC News Special with Barbara Walters*** 30 April 1999*
*Comment on landing after piloting the first trans-Atlantic flight by a woman. **See 2687.

1848. Hermione Gingold (1897–1987)

1 My father dealt in stocks and shares and my mother also had a lot of time on her hands.

Pt. I, *The World is Square 1945*

2 To call him a dog hardly seems to do him justice, though inasmuch as he had four legs, a tail, and barked, I admit he was, to all outward appearances. But to those of us who knew him well, he was a perfect gentleman.

Pt. II, Ibid.

3 This isn't a recipe for soup, although it can land you right in the *potage* if you aren't careful.

"I Make Summer Stock," *Sirens Should Be Seen and Not Heard 1963*

4 "Have you anything to back up your theory?"
"I cannot truthfully say I have," Mr. Smith replied. "I just believe implicitly."
"Well," I said, "I suppose it's like believing in the creation. There is much less to back up that theory these scientific days, and yet in spite of everything people still believe."

"The Bomb That Had Mr. Smith's Name on It," Ibid.

1849. Constance McLaughlin Green (1897–1975)

1 Geographical influences have indicated the sites. Immigration and natural increase of the native population; a revolution in means of communication and transportation; the mechanization of life until the farm itself has been brought within the realm of the machine world; these are general answers to the question, why cities have arisen.

Preface, *Holyoke, Massachusetts: A Case History of the Industrial Revolution in America 1939*

2 The slowly developing New England farming community was to be subjected to sudden violent changes. No longer evolution but revolution by exploitation of the water power was to be the new order and Ireland [County, MA] was to be swept along by forces the extent of which few could guess, least of all the farmers of the parish.

Ch. 2, Ibid.

3 What had government, particularly municipal government, to do with business? For a time the political scene is the obverse of the economic, the foreign-born citizen or his sons dominating the political arena, the native American the industrial.

Ch. 9, Ibid.

4 . . . until the late [eighteen-]eighties there was no source of help for the needy other than the churches. Catholic charities far outdid anything the Protestant churches attempted and eventually stirred the more well-to-do Protestant groups to emulating collaboration. So in the second generation the city saw the growth of a series of non-sectarian philanthropies.

Ch. 12, Ibid.

1850. Edith Head (1897–1981)

1 The subjective actress thinks of clothes only as they apply to her; the objective actress thinks of them only as they affect others, as a tool for the job.

The Dress Doctor, with Jane Kesner Ardmore *1959*

2 Your dresses should be tight enough to show you're a woman and loose enough to show you're a lady.

Ibid.

3 I have yet to see one completely unspoiled star, except for the animals-like Lassie.

Ibid.

1851. Irène Joliot-Curie (1897–1956)

1 That one must do some work seriously and must be independent and not merely amuse oneself in life—this our mother

[Marie Curie]* has told us always, but never that science was the only career worth following.

> Quoted in Ch. 10, *A Long Way from Missouri* by Mary Margaret McBride** *1959*

*See 1335. **See 1888.

1852. Caroline Lejeune (1897–1973)

1   Nothing is said that can be regretted. Nothing is said that can even be remembered.

> "Dietrich* as an Angel," *The Observer* (London) *1936*

*Marlene D— ; see 1930.

2   For a good book has this quality, that it is not merely a petrification of its author, but that once it has been tossed behind, like Deucalion's* little stone, it acquires a separate and vivid life of its own.

> Introduction, *Chestnuts in Her Lap, 1936–1946 1947*

*In Greek mythology, a son of Prometheus who with his wife, Pyrrha, built an ark and floated in it to survive the deluge sent by Zeus. The couple became the ancestors of the renewed human race.

3   It's odd how large a part food plays in memories of childhood. There are grown men and women who still shudder at the sight of spinach, or turn away with loathing from stewed prunes and tapioca. . . . Luckily, however, it's the good tastes one remembers best.

> Ch. 1, *Thank You for Having Me 1964*

4   Sometimes it seems to me as if the only quality admired in modern writing, or play-making, or film-making, is truth-and-ugliness. This, for some reason, is described as realism; as if nothing could be real that is not sordid, disagreeable or violent.

> Ch. 21, Ibid.

1853. Margaret Mahler (1897–1985)

1   . . . the emotional growth of the mother in her parenthood, her emotional willingness to let go of the toddler—to give him, as the mother bird does, a gentle push, as encouragement toward independence—is enormously helpful. It may even be a *sine qua non* of normal (healthy) individuation.

> *The Psychological Birth of the Human Infant 1975*

1854. Isabel Briggs Myers (1897–1980)

1   We cannot safely assume that other people's minds work on the same principles as our own. All too often, others with whom we come in contact do not reason as we reason, or do not value the things we value, or are not interested in what interests us.

> Pt. I, Ch. 1, *Gifts Differing*, with Peter B. Myers *1980*

2   Whatever the circumstances of your life, whatever your personal ties, work, and responsibilities, the understanding of type can make your perceptions clearer, your judgements sounder, and your life closer to your heart's desire.

> Pt. IV, Ch. 19, Ibid.

1855–1856. Ruth Pitter (1897–?)

1   The place is hidden apart
Like the nest of a bird:
And I will not show you my heart
By a look, by a word.

> "If You Came," St. 4, *Collected Poems 1996*

2   I go about, but cannot find
The blood-relations of the mind.

> "The Lost Tribe," St. 1 *n.d.*

3   And high and high and high in the diamond light,
They soar and they shriek in the sunlight when heaven is bare.

> "The Swifts," St. 2 *n.d.*

1857. Margaret Chase Smith (1897–1995)

1   I believe that in our constant search for security we can never gain any peace of mind until we secure our own soul.

> Essay, *This I Believe,* Raymond Swing, ed. *1952*

2   My creed is that public service must be more than doing a job efficiently and honestly. It must be a complete dedication to the people and to the nation with full recognition that every human being is entitled to courtesy and consideration, that constructive criticism is not only to be expected but sought, that smears are not only to be expected but fought, that honor is to be earned but not bought.

> "My Creed," *Quick 11 November 1953*

3   In today's growing, but tragic, emphasis on materialism, we find a perversion of the values of things in life as we once knew them. For example, the creed once taught children as they grew up was that the most important thing was not in whether you won or lost the game but rather in "how you played the game." That high level attitude that stresses the moral side no longer predominates in this age of pragmatic materialism that increasingly worships the opposite creed that "the end justifies the means" or the attitude of get what you can in any way, manner, or means that you can.

> RCA Victor Recording *1964*

4   We are sick to death of war, defense spending and all things military. We are disgusted with and weary of the vilification that has been heaped upon us, at home as well as abroad, for our attempts to block communist enslavement in Southeast Asia. We yearn to turn away from foreign entanglements and to begin making our own house a better place to live in

> "It's Time to Speak Up for National Defense," *Reader's Digest March 1972*

5   The key to security is public information.

> Ibid.

6   I ignored any discrimination [in the Senate]. I never, never acknowledged it. Never.*

> Interview with author (1995), *No Place For A Woman, A Life of Senator Margaret Chase Smith* by Janann Sherman *2000*

*Ref. being forced to stand in line at public toilets since there were no facilities for women off the Senate floor.

7   I never was a woman. I never was a woman politician. I never was a woman senator.

> Ibid.

1858. Opal Whiteley (1897–1992)

1   The mamma where I love
says I am a new sance.
I think it is something grown-ups
don't like to have around.

> *The Story of Opal* 1920

*Written between the ages of five and twelve.

2 Potatoes are very interesting folks
I think they must see a lot
of what is going on in the earth
They have so many eyes.

Ibid.

3 And this I have learned
grown-ups do not know the language of shadows.

Ibid.

4 Some days are long.
Some days are short.
The days that I have to stay in the house
are the most long days of all.

Ibid.

1859. Berenice Abbott (1898–1991)

1 Photography can never grow up if it imitates some other medium. It has to walk alone; it has to be itself.

"It Has to Walk Alone," *Infinity* (magazine) *1951*

2 If a medium is represented by nature of the realistic image formed by a lens, I see no reason why we should stand on our heads to distort that function. On the contrary, we should take hold of that very quality, make use of it, and explore it to the fullest.

Ibid.

3 I took to photography like a duck to water. I never wanted to do anything else. Excitement about the subject is the voltage which pushes me over the mountain of drudgery necessary to produce the final photograph.

Preface, *The Berenice Abbott Portfolio 1976*

4 Photography helps people to see.

Quoted in "Berenice Abbott: An American Master," *ASMP Bulletin October 1989*

5 I am so fascinated with this century it will help keep me alive. I'll be there until the last minute, fighting.

Ibid.

1860. Katharine "Katie" Burr Blodgett (1898–1979)

1 A woman who wants to do something in science must have three things besides formal training—patience, persistence and a knack at solving problems, or at least the desire to try to solve them. A girl who is not interested in the little problems of everyday life will not find it easy to learn to solve the problems of work in a laboratory.

Quoted in *Women Inventors* by Linda Jacobs Altman *1997*

2 That formaldehyde polyvinyl—
If you eat it, you're certain to dine ill.
    One night at a party,
    When the guests all ate hearty,
By actual count it made nine ill.

Ibid.

1861. Rachel Fuller Brown (1898–1980)

1 Recently I had a severe shock. A high school girl who wanted to [study] biology was advised by her counselor not to do so because "the opportunities are few for women." It is hard to understand why the many life sciences should not offer just

the right chances for women to express themselves. Consider Rachel Carson's* *Silent Spring* . . .

Comment (15 April 1977), Quoted in *Women Inventors* by Linda Jacobs Altman *1997*

*See 2061.

1862. Lillian Carter (1898–1983)

1 I know folks all have a tizzy about it, but I like a little bourbon of an evening. It helps me sleep. I don't much care what they say about it.

The New York Times 20 December 1976

2 Every time I think that I am getting old, and gradually going to the grave, something else happens.

Quoted in *The Decade of Women* Suzanne Levine and Harriet Lyons, eds. *1980*

3 Sometimes when I look at all my children, I say to myself, "Lillian, you should have stayed a virgin."

Comment to 1980 Democratic Convention, Quoted in *Newsweek 29 December 1980*

1863. Madame Chiang Kai-shek (1898?–2003)

1 Of all the inventions that have helped to unify China perhaps the airplane is the most outstanding. Its ability to annihilate distance has been in direct proportion to its achievements in assisting to annihilate suspicion and misunderstanding among provincial officials far removed from one another or from the officials at the seat of government.

"Wings Over China," *Shanghai Evening Post 12 March 1937*

2 This changing world is rolling towards the abyss of self-destruction with a breath-taking rapidity.

Speech, International Women's Conference (Sydney, Australia, February 1938), Quoted in *War Messages and Other Selections 1938*

3 No nation that descends to murder, rape and rapine can expect to prosper or be respected.

Article in the *Birmingham Post* (England; May 1938), Ibid.

4 Out of the ashes which the Japanese are spreading over our country will arise a phoenix of great national worth.

"People's Spiritual Mobilization" (18 March 1939), Ibid.

5 Hammered out on the anvil of experience are four cardinal principles of life, as we Chinese understand life: 1. The way in which human beings behave one toward another. 2. Justice for all classes within our social framework. 3. Honesty in public administration and in business. 4. Self-respect, and a profound sense of the value of personality.

Sec. I, Ch. 1, *This Is Our China 1940*

6 I am convinced that we must train not only the head, but the heart and hand as well.

Sec. II, Ibid.

7 Every clique is a refuge for incompetence. It fosters corruption and disloyalty, it begets cowardice, and consequently is a burden upon and a drawback to the progress of the country. Its instincts and actions are those of the pack.

Pt. I, Ch. 8, *China Shall Rise Again 1941*

8 The universal tendency of the world as represented by the United Nations is as patent and inexorable as the enormous

sheets of ice which float down the Hudson in winter. The swift and mighty tide is universal justice and freedom.

Speech, Madison Square Garden (New York) *3 March 1943*

9 Truth requires that each people live according to its own traditions in a climate of human liberty and dignity. That has been the soul of Chinese civilization.

Radio Address (New York), *9 January 1950*

10 China's struggle now is the initial phase of a gigantic conflict between good and evil, between liberty and communism.

Ibid.

1864–1865. Ariel Durant (1898–1981)

1 You* love me because you know I love you to distraction.

Quoted in "The Philosopher and the Schoolgirl" by Jim Bishop, *Reader's Digest October 1969*

*Since the lion's share of Ms. Durant's monumental work was in collaboration with her husband, historian Will Durant, (1885?–1981), little can be found that is purely her own.

1866. Gracie Fields (1898–1979)

1 You can get good fish and chips at the Savoy; and you can put up with fancy people once you understand that you don't have to be like them.

Ch. 4, *Sing as We Go 1960*

2 Now sometimes it can be a very dangerous thing to go in search of a dream for the reality does not always match it. . . .

Ibid.

1866.1. Cecily R. Hallack (1898–1938)

1 Make me a saint by getting meals; and washing up the plates!

"The Divine Office of the Kitchen," St. 1 *ca. 1928*

1867. Winifred Holtby (1898–1935)

1 I don't see how I can write an autobiography. I never feel I've really had a life of my own. My existence seems to me like a clear stream which has simply reflected other people's stories and problems.

Quoted in *Testament of Friendship: The Story of Winifred Holtby* by Vera Brittain* *1940*

*See 1764.

2 God give me work, till my life shall end/And life, till my work is done.

Ibid.

3 Sixteen when the war started. The first thing it made me do was to fall in love. Brevity of life makes passion more insistent. The youngest and fittest in uniform. The erotic attraction of death.

Ibid.

4 I often forget what a strange distance there is between ill people and well ones.

Ibid.

5 The New Feminist emphasizes the importance of the "women's point of view," the Old Feminism believes in the primary importance of the human being.

(1926), Quoted in *Who Stole Feminism? How Women Have Betrayed Women* by Christina Hoff Sommers* *1994*

*See 4007.

6 . . . all curiosity an' asking questions about other folks' business—archeology they call it. Danged impertinence, *we* say! Now in the old days, a bit of talk about angels and devils was good enough for any one. These days they must have dates and Romans and civilisations and all that . . .

"The Legend of Rudson" (1935), *Remember! Remember!: Selected Stories of Winifred Holtby 1999*

1868. Lotte Lenya (1898–1981)

1 [I have] a heavenly vase full of autumn leaves today. They looks so beautiful. How much closer to God can one get? And a beautiful blue heron flew over the brook. Nature can make me cry faster than anything.

Letter to Mary Daniel (April 1957), Quoted in *Lenya, a Life* by Donald Spoto *1989*

2 I don't like holidays, not here [the United States]—it's a giant supermarket, and I'm thinking with nostalgia of my childhood with a tiny Christmas tree . . .

Christmas card to Hilde Halpern (1980), *Ibid.*

1869. Beatrice Lillie (1898–1989)

1 I'll simply say here that I was born Beatrice Gladys Lillie at an extremely tender age because my mother needed a fourth at meals.

Ch. 1, *Every Other Inch a Lady 1927*

2 I took up knitting from time to time as a relaxation, but I always put it down again before going out to buy a rocking chair.

Ch. 15, *Ibid.*

3 The vows one makes privately are more binding than any ceremony or even a Shubert contract.

Ibid.

4 In my experience, anyone can paint if he doesn't have to. . . . During my apprentice days, I felt encouraged by the advice of Winston Churchill,* who used to say, "Don't be afraid of the canvas." I have now reached the point where the canvas is afraid of me.

Ibid.

*Sir Winston Leonard Spenser C— (1874–1965), British politician, writer, and prime minister (1940–1945 and 1951–1955).

1870. Golda Meir (1898–1978)

1 I want to say to you, friends, that the Jewish community in Palestine is going to fight to the very end. If we have arms to fight with, we will fight with those, and if not, we will fight with stones in our hands.

"In the Midst of Battle: 1948," Speech, Council of Jewish Federations (Chicago) *21 January 1948*

2 We desire nothing more than peace, but we cannot equate peace merely with an apathetic readiness to be destroyed. If hostile forces gather for our proposed destruction, they must not demand that we provide them with ideal conditions for the realization of their plans. . . . The concept of annihilating Israel is a legacy of Hitler's war against the Jewish people, and it is no mere coincidence that the soldiers of Nasser* had an Arabic translation of *Mein Kampf* in their knapsacks.

"The Israeli Action in Sinai: 1956," Statement, General Assembly of United Nations *5 December 1956*

*Gamal Abdel N— (1918–1970), Egyptian prime minister (1954–1956) and president (1956–1958); president of United Arab Republic (1958–1970).

3 We have not the slightest doubt that eventually there will be peace and cooperation between us. This is a historic necessity for both peoples. We are prepared; we are anxious to bring it about now.

"A Solemn Appeal to the Arabs," Statement, General Assembly of United Nations 7 October 1957

4 . . . The deserts of the Middle East are in need of water, not bombers.

Ibid.

5 Those that perished in Hitler's gas chambers were the last Jews to die without standing up to defend themselves.

"In the Hour of Deliverance: 1967," Speech, United Jewish Appeal rally at Madison Square Garden (New York) 11 June 1967

6 But the individual was not a tool for something. He was the maker of tools. He was the one who must build. Even for the best purpose it is criminal to turn an individual into simply a means for some ultimate end. A society in which the dignity of the individual is destroyed cannot hope to be a decent society.

"The Zionist Purpose," Speech at Dropise College 26 November 1967

7 When peace comes we will perhaps in time be able to forgive the Arabs for killing our sons, but it will be harder for us to forgive them for having forced us to kill their sons.

Press conference (London) 1969

8 A leader who doesn't hesitate before he sends his nation into battle is not fit to be a leader.

(1967), As Good as Golda, Israel and Mary Shenker, eds. 1970.

9 We intend to remain alive. Our neighbors want to see us dead. This is not a question that leaves much room for compromise.

Quoted in "The Indestructible Golda Meir" by David Reed, Reader's Digest July 1971

10 Women's Liberation is just a lot of foolishness. It's the men who are discriminated against. They can't bear children. And no one's likely to do anything about that.

Quoted in Newsweek (New York) 23 October 1972

11 At work, you think of the children you've left at home. At home, you think of the work you've left unfinished. Such a struggle is unleashed within yourself: your heart is rent.

Quoted by Oriana Fallaci* in L'Europeo 1973
*See 2656.

12 Those who do not know how to weep with their whole heart don't know how to laugh either.

Ibid.

13 . . . there's no difference between one's killing and making decisions that will send others to kill. It's exactly the same thing, or even worse.

Ibid.

14 I took a great deal with me from America to Palestine, more perhaps than I can express. . . . An understanding of the meaning of freedom, an awareness of the opportunities offered to the individual in a true democracy and a permanent nostalgia for the great beauty of the American countryside.

My Life 1975

15 I didn't leave [America] because of anti-Semitism. I left to help build a nation of our own. In any country where Jews are a small minority, you cannot live fully as a Jew. Your language, history, holidays, are those of the minority culture. You don't need a pogrom to feel unwanted. As one of my friends said, "Jews have believed for two thousand years in what they did not have." Now we have it. Our past and our present are in one place.

Ch. 10, Meeting in Tel Aviv, 24 December 1976, Quoted in Deborah, Golda, and Me by Letty Cottin Pogrebin 1991

16 The only alternative to war is peace and the only road to peace is negotiations.

Quoted in Twentieth-Century Women Political Leaders by Claire Price-Groff 1998

17 I think women often get not so much an unfair deal as an illogical one. Once in the Cabinet we had to deal with the fact that there had been an outbreak of assaults on women at night. One minister (a member of an extreme religious party) suggested a curfew. Women should stay home after dark. I said: "But it's the men who are attacking the women. If there's to be a curfew, let the men stay at home, not the women."

Speech n.d.

1871. Clementine Paddleford (1898–1967)

1 We all have hometown appetites. Every other person is a bundle of longing for the simplicities of good taste once enjoyed on the farm or in the hometown [he or she] left behind.

Quoted by Jose Iraels II in Saturday Evening Post 1949

2 The maples are budding, snow is on the cherry boughs; peepers are shouting, Spring! Spring! Spring! Shad on the platter, fresh ducklings in the market.

"Food Flashes" column, Gourmet magazine April 1950

3 "Never grow a wishbone, daughter, where your backbone ought to be."

A Flower for My Mother 1958

4 Stirred-in joy. . . . Every last dish seasoned well with love,. She knew that eating was more than just filling hollow legs, just as environment is more than a place. This is one of the things she tried to teach her daughter. Cooking should never be made a chore.

Ibid.

5 How does America eat? She eats on the fat of the land. She eats in every language. For the most part, however, even with the increasingly popular trend toward foreign foods, the dishes come to the table with an American accent.

How America Eats 1960

6 Tell me where your grandmother came from and I can tell you how many kinds of pie you serve for Thanksgiving.

Ibid.

7 His Majesty the Oyster is indigenous to this city, and New Yorkers insist there are no oysters better than the fat firm Long Island kind, no dish to beat oyster stew as it's made at Grand Central Oyster Bar.

"New York," Ibid.

8 Beer is the Danish national drink, and the Danish national weakness is another beer.

Quoted in New York Herald Tribune 20 June 1964

1872. Molly Picon (1898–1992)

1 Mama's philosophy and approach to life were succinct: If it's good it's not forever, and if it's bad it's not forever.

Ch. 1, *Molly! An Autobiography* with Jean Bergantini Grillo *1980*

2 Everyone wanted to take me out to dinner. . . . Many of them were those moneyed men looking for romance and full of bicarbonate.

Ch. 5, Ibid.

3 It's never too late to begin a life or a book.

Ch. 20, Ibid.

4 An old lady was asked to come to the funeral of her next-door neighbor and she answered, "Why should I go to her funeral? She won't come to mine."

Ibid.

5 An old couple came to a rabbi for a divorce. They had been married for sixty-five years. The rabbi, astounded, asked the wife, "Why, after sixty-five years, would you want a divorce?" And the old lady answered, "Because enough is enough!"

Ibid.

1873. Lily Pincus (1898–1981)

1 Why not acknowledge and satisfy without shame the baby needs stirred up by bereavement?

Death and the Family 1974

2 Regression in grief must be seen and supported as a means toward adaptation and health.

Ibid.

1874. Edith Spurlock Sampson (1898?–1979)

1 I knew that I could never make my law practice the primary business of my life; I would have to devote myself to the cause of world brotherhood and world peace.

"I Like America," *Negro Digest December 1950*

2 To me, the U.N. is the most ambitious experiment in adult education at the highest level ever attempted in history.

Speech, "Show the East How the Freedom Revolution Works," *Vital Speeches of the Day 272 15 February 1951*

3 I would rather be a Negro in America than a citizen in any other land.

Round-the World Town Meeting, India (1949), Quoted in "The Programs of Negro Civil Rights Organizations" by Oliver C. Cox, *The Journal of Negro Education* 20 (3) *Summer 1951*

4 The question is, quite bluntly, 'Do Negroes have equal rights in America?' My answer is no, we do not have equal rights in all parts of the United States. But let's remember that 85 years ago Negroes in America were slaves and were 100 per cent illiterate. And the record shows that the Negro has advanced further in this period than any similar group in the entire world. You here get considerable misinformation about American Negroes and hear little or nothing that is constructive.

Ibid.

5 I talk from my heart and let the law take care of itself.

Quoted in "Justice—Edith Sampson Style" by J. D. Ratlcliff, *Reader's Digest* (New York) *November 1968*

6 The president did not ask me to represent six million Negroes, but 150 million Americans.

"Edith Sampson," *Black Women in America: An Historical Encyclopedia* by Gloria Marrow *1993*

7 I've been colored a long time, and if I stopped eating every time something like this happened to me, I'd be thin as a rail. And you can see I have no problems in that direction.*

Ibid.

*Re refusal by a hotel to serve dinner to a delegation with blacks. Delegation moved to another hotel.

8 The millions of uncommitted people in the East, whom we need as partners for peace, are watching every move we make in America. You may not realize that these peoples represent two-thirds of the population of the world, and they are dark people. We need their help and co-operation. They are questioning our sincerity. They are of the opinion that the same discriminatory practices affecting Negroes in this country would affect them because of their color if they joined with America.

Lecture, "World Security Begins at Home," *Journal of Home Economics 516, 517 1993*

9 Don't tear down the old homestead until you have a clear idea of what you'll build in its place.

Quoted in *The James Logan Courier n.d.*

1875. Esther Savitsky (1898?–197-?)

1 I can't understand it. Bella's been against the war in Vietnam so long and it's still going on.

"Bella* on Bella", *Moment 1, No. 7 February 1976*
*Bella Abzug; see 2360.

2 I knew Bella would be a success because she always did her homework and practiced her violin.

Quoted on p. 17, *Bella Abzug* by Doris Faber *1976*

3 In response to her daughter's rejection by Harvard: Why do you want to go to Harvard, anyway? It's far away and you can't afford the carfare. Go to Columbia University. They'll probably give you a scholarship, and it's only five cents to get there on the subway.

Bella Abzug Exhibit, Jewish Women's Archive (jwa.org) *September 2003*

1876. Helen Sekaquaptewa (1898–1990)

1 We were as stubborn about going back to the old ways as they were about changing their way.

Me and Mine 1969

2 I was stuck here, so I might as well learn everything.

Interview (3 June 1981), Quoted in *American Indian Women, Telling Their Lives*, Gretchen M. Bataille and Kathleen Mullen Sands, eds. *1984*

1877. Anna Moore Shaw (1898–1975)

1 We were not allowed to speak the Pima tongue at school. Some students would report on those who spoke in Indian and as a punishment our mouths would be taped. We did not mind, for the matron, teachers, and other employees were good to us, despite our naughty ways.

A Pima Past 1974

2   The educations they had strived so hard to give us had prepared us to bring in money from the white man's work; it would be wrong to waste all those years of schooling on a life of primitive farming.

Ibid.

1878. Bessie Smith (1898–1937)

1   No time to marry, no time to settle down;
I'm a young woman, and I ain't done runnin' aroun'.
"Young Woman's Blues" *1927*

2   While you're living in your mansion, you don't know what hard times mean.
Poor working man's wife is starving; your wife is living like a queen.
"Poor Man's Blues" *1930*

3   It's a long old road, but I know I'm gonna find the end.
"Long Old Road" *1931*

1879. Dorothy Speare (1898–1951)

1   The intoxication of rouge is an insidious vintage known to more girls than mere man can ever believe.
Dancers in the Dark 1922

1880. Léonie Adams (1899–1988)

1   You wander late alone,
The flesh frets on the bone,
Your love fails in your breast,
Here is the pillow.
Rest.
"Lullaby," *Poems: A Selection 1954*

2   The last majority attained,
And shut from its small house of dust,
Into the heritage of air
The spirit goes because it must
"Many Mansions," Ibid.

3   O heart more frightened than a wild bird's wings
Beating at green, now is no fiery mark
Left on the quiet nothingness of things.
"Thought's End," Ibid.

1881. Anni Albers (1899–1994)

1   We often look for an underlying meaning of things while the thing itself is the meaning.
pp. 30, 45, *Anni Albers: On Designing 1945*

2   When the painter or the weaver or someone has to prepare the material, you learn what the material tells you and what the technique tells you.
Oral History Interview with Sevim Fesci (New Haven, CT), Archives of American Art, Smithsonian *5 July 1968*

3   Sometimes one talks more easily than one thinks.
Ibid.

4   And I find today that, if the New York scene people would stick to or turn to a craft, it would save their soul. Because they are, I think, in this really hopeless situation of constantly searching their inners and not finding a way to something that is really satisfactory. They splatter and they spit and they do

heavens knows what and try to be awfully original. And the results to my mind are very awful things that you have one look at and wouldn't look again or turn away sometimes even in disgust. And I have this very what you call today "square" idea that art is something that makes you breathe with a different kind of happiness.

Ibid.

5   I think [weaving] is closest to architecture because it is a building up out of a single element, to building a whole out of single elements.

Ibid.

6   The one great worrying question in a student's mind is this: where do I go from here? And my answer has always been, you can go anywhere from anywhere. For any new beginning is puzzling and where it may lead is hidden in the folds of the future.
p. 13, *The Woven and Graphic Art of Anni Albers 1985*

7   The reality of art is concluded in itself. It sets up its own laws as completion of vision.
p. 11, *Anni Albers 1999*

1882. Gertrude Berg (1899–1966)

1   MOLLY GOLDBERG. So who's to know?
Me and Molly 1948

2   Jake wants the children to have everything money can buy, and I want them to have everything money can't buy.
Quoted in "'The Goldbergs' Jewish Humor" by Charles Angoff, *Congress Weekly 18 5 March 1951*

3   It's late, Jake, and time to expire.
Quoted in "The 1920's and 1930's," *Women in Comedy* by Linda Martin and Kerry Segrave 1986

4   Better a crust of bread and enjoy it than a cake that gives you indigestion.

Ibid.

5   Yoo Hoo, Mrs. Bloom!
Quoted in "Funny Women of Radio," *Funny Women, American Comediennes, 1860–1985* by Mary Unterbrink *1987*

6   It is impossible to improve on reality. The good radio story should never escape reality and the problems of real people.
Quoted in *Who's Who in Comedy* by Ronald L. Smith 1992

1883. Elizabeth Bowen (1899–1973)

1   "The best type of man is no companion."
The Hotel 1928

2   Intimacies between women go backwards, beginning with revelations and ending up in small talk without loss of esteem.
Pt. 2, Ch. 1, *The Death of the Heart 1938*

3   Only in a house where one has learnt to be lonely does one have this solicitude for things. One's relation to them, the daily seeing or touching, begins to become love, and to lay one open to pain.

Ch. 2, Ibid.

4   Nobody can be kinder than the narcissist while you react to life in his own terms.

Pt. 3, Ch. 3, Ibid.

5 The charm, one might say the genius of memory, is that it is choosy, chancy, and temperamental: it rejects the edifying cathedral and indelibly photographs the small boy outside, chewing a hunk of melon in the dust.

Article, *Vogue* (New York) *15 September 1955*

6 "There being nothing was what you were frightened of all the time, eh? Yes."

The Little Girls 1963

1884. Indra Devi (1899–2002)

1 Like an ugly bird of prey, tension hovers over the heads of millions of people, ready to swoop down on all its victims at any time and in any place. More and more men, women, and even children are caught up in its cold grip and held for years, sometimes for the whole of their lives. Tension, in fact, is probably one of the greatest menaces the civilized world must face these days.

Ch. 1, *Renewing Your Life Through Yoga 1963*

2 Tranquilizers . . . dull the keen edge of the angers, fears, or anxiety with which we might otherwise react to the problems of living. Once the response has been dulled, the irritating surface noise of living muted or eliminated, the spark and brilliance are also gone.

Ibid.

3 Like water which can clearly mirror the sky and the trees only so long as its surface is undisturbed, the mind can only reflect the true image of the Self when it is tranquil and wholly relaxed.

Ibid.

4 Our body is a magnificently devised, living, breathing mechanism, yet we do almost nothing to insure its optimal development and use. . . . The human organism needs an ample supply of good building material to repair the effects of daily wear and tear.

Ch. 2, Ibid.

5 Yoga is not a religion, nor is it a magic formula or some form of calisthenics. In the country of its origin it is called a science—the science of living a healthy, meaningful, and purposeful life—a method of realizing the true self when the body, mind, and spirit blend into one harmonious whole. . . . Yoga is a philosophy, a way of life, and organized religion forms no part of it.

Ch. 10, Ibid.

1885. Hildegarde Flanner (1899–1987)

1 I saw a hawk devour a screaming bird,
Devour the little ounce sugared with song.

"Hawk Is a Woman," *If There is Time 1942*

2 May she, the very she, may that hawk hear
The ugly female laughter of a hawk.

Ibid.

1886. Marguerite Harris (1899–1978)

1 In tidy terminal homes,
agape at the stalking Rorschach
shapes that menace our cosmos,
pawns, now, we itch and surmise.

"The Chosen," St. 1, *The East Side Scene*, Allen de Loach, ed.
1968

1887. Eva Le Gallienne (1899–1991)

1 . . . no mechanical device can ever, it seems to me, quite take the place of that mysterious communication between players and public, that sense of an experience directly shared, which gives to the living theater its unique appeal.

Ch. 1, *The Mystic in the Theater: Eleanora Duse* 1965*
*See 1246.

2 Innovators are inevitably controversial.

Ibid.

3 People who are born even-tempered, placid and untroubled—secure from violent passions or temptations to evil—those who have never needed to struggle all night with the Angel to emerge lame but victorious at dawn, never become great saints.

Ch. 2, Ibid.

4 But the breathtaking part of it all was not so much the planning as the fantastic skill with which the planning was concealed.

Ch. 5, Ibid.

5 There can be no generalizations as far as the art of acting is concerned. There can be no over-all "method"—above all no short cuts. Each actor must find his own way for himself.

Ch. 6, Ibid.

1888. Mary Margaret McBride (1899–1976)

1 Yes, we have a good many poor tired people here already, but we have plenty of mountains, rivers, woods, lots of sunshine and air, for tired people to rest in. We have Kansas wheat and Iowa corn and Wisconsin cheese for them to eat, Texas cotton for them to wear. So give us as many as come—we can take it, and take care of them.

Ch. 1, *America for Me 1941*

2 This country began with people moving, and we've been moving ever since. . . . As long as we keep at that I guess we'll be all right.

Ch. 2, Ibid.

3 "Terrible things happen to young girls in New York City. . . ."

Ch. 1, *A Long Way from Missouri 1959*

1889. Helen Hill Miller (1899–1995)

1 France prides itself on being very old, on being not only the first-born among the modern nations but the heir of the ancient world, the transmitter to the West of Mediterranean civilization.

Pamphlet, "The Spirit of Modern France" *1934*

2 Logical clarity is the genius of the French language.

Ibid.

3 Women scientists at colleges and universities have a double opportunity: that of pursuing their own research, and that of capturing the imagination of the next generation and attracting it into their specialty.

"Science: Careers for Women," *The Atlantic Monthly* [Boston]
October 1957

4 Much of the time and energy of women who entered the scientific professions in the nineteenth century was spent in either contriving to take barriers gracefully or crashing into them

with results demolishing sometimes the woman, sometimes the barrier.

Ibid.

5 Then, the word tyrant did not carry the pejorative meaning it conveys today. Tyrants seized and held their power by force, exercised it subject to no restraint, and perpetuated notorious cruelties. But many of them were great generals who fought wide-sweeping wars, lavish patrons of the arts, public figures who brought their cities riches and renown. The times combined civilization and savagery.

Sicily and Western Colonies of Greece 1965

6 It isn't very often that a person who has been at the very center of one period in the life of a political party has the forward-lookingness and the resilience to note the transition to a new time, much less to bring it forcefully to the attention to the current members of the party.

Letter to Eleanor Roosevelt* (1956), Quoted in Eleanor: The Years Alone by Joseph P. Lash 1972

*See 1618.

1890. Louise Nevelson (1899–1988)

1 The freer that women become, the freer will men be. Because when you enslave someone—you *are* enslaved.

Quoted in AFTRA Magazine Summer 1974

1891. Bella Spewack (1899–1990)

1 BENSON. You were saying that this is one of the greatest picture scripts ever written.

C.F. Now, just a minute—

LAW. And do you know why? Because it's the same story Larry Toms has been doing for years.

BENSON. We *know* it's good.

LAW. Griffith used it. Lubitsch used it. And Eisenstein's coming around to it.

BENSON. Boy meets girl. Boy loses girl. Boy gets girl.

LAW. The great American fairy-tale. Sends the audience back to the relief rolls in a happy frame of mind.

BENSON. And why not?

LAW. The greatest escape formula ever worked out in the history of civilization . . .

C.F. Of course, if you put it that way . . . but, boys, it's hackneyed.

LAW. You mean classic.

C.F. *Hamlet* is a classic—but it isn't hackneyed!

LAW. *Hamlet* isn't hackneyed? Why, I'd be ashamed to use that poison gag. He lifted that right out of the Italians.

Sc. 4, Boy Meets Girl 1935

1892. Gloria Swanson (1899–1983)

1 When I die, my epitaph should read: *She Paid the Bills.* That's the story of my private life.

Quoted in "Gloria Swanson Comes Back" by S. Frank, Saturday Evening Post 22 July 1950

1893. Grace Adams (1900–?)

1 Whenever serious intellectuals, psychologists, sociologists, practicing physicians, Nobel prize novelists take time off from their normal pursuits to scrutinize and appraise the Modern American Woman, they turn in unanimously dreary reports.

"American Women Are Coming Along," Harper's (New York) 1939

1894. Polly Adler (1900–1962)

1 Too many cooks spoil the brothel.

A House is Not a Home 1953

2 . . . I am one of those people who can't help getting a kick out of life—even when it's a kick in the teeth.

Ch. 1, Ibid.

3 The degree to which a pimp, if he's clever, can confuse and delude a prostitute is very nearly unlimited.

Ch. 4, Ibid.

4 What it comes down to is this: the grocer, the butcher, the baker, the merchant, the landlord, the druggist, the liquor dealer, the policeman, the doctor, the city father and the politician—these are the people who make money out of prostitution, these are the real reapers of the wages of sin.

Ch. 9, Ibid.

5 The women who take husbands not out of love but out of greed, to get their bills paid, to get a fine house and clothes and jewels; the women who marry to get out of a tiresome job, or to get away from disagreeable relatives, or to avoid being called an old maid—these are whores in everything but name. The only difference between them and my girls is that my girls gave a man his money's worth.

Ch. 10, Ibid.

1895. Dorothy Arzner (1900–1980)

1 It is my theory that if you have authority, know your business and know you have authority, you have the authority.

Quoted in The New York Times 15 June 1972

2 I was led by the grace of God to the movies. I would like the industry to be more aware of what they're doing to influence people. . . .

Quoted in Popcorn Venus by Marjorie Rosen* 1973

*See 3372.

1896. Taylor Caldwell (1900–1985)

1 ". . . I knew you would not betray us. Not because of—honor. But profit. And profits are not bedfellows of honor."

Bk. I, Ch. 12, Dynasty of Death 1938

2 "Honest men live on charity in their age; the almshouses are full of men who never stole a copper penny. Honest men are the fools and the saints, and you and I are neither."

Ibid.

3 A civilization based purely on agriculture was a civilization which never went hungry. But a raucous and ruthless civilization, dependent on the churning of the "devil machines" within brick walls, was vulnerable to every sensitive wind that blew from Wall Street.

Pt. III, Ch. 43, This Side of Innocence 1946

4 "Learning," he would say, "should be a joy and full of excitement. It is life's greatest adventure; it is an illustrated excursion into the mind's noble and learned men, not a conducted tour through a jail. So its surroundings should be as gracious as possible, to complement it."

Pt. I, Ch. 9, The Sound of Thunder 1957

5 One, if one is sensible, blames government, not the servers of the government, not those entangled in their governments.

Pt. I, Ch. 10, Great Lion of God 1970

6 "... it is not always wise to appear singular."
Pt. III, Ch. 35, Ibid.

7 Is it not deplorable that a few heedless zealots can bring calamity to their law-abiding fellows?
Ch. 43, Ibid.

8 The old [Roman] gods understood that life was reasonable and favors were exchanged for favors, and that is how it should be.
Ch. 53, Ibid.

9 At the end—and as usual—God had betrayed the innocent and had left them comfortless.
Pt. I, Ch. 1, *Captains and the Kings* 1972

10 It was business, and none of them had allegiances or attachments or involvements with any nation, not even their own ... Joseph immediately called them "the gray and deadly men," and did not know why he detested them, or why he found them the most dangerous of all among the human species.
Ch. 21, Ibid.

11 "Mankind is the most selfish species this world has ever spewed up from hell, and it demands, constantly, that neighbors and politicians be 'unselfish,' and allow themselves to be plundered—for its benefit."
Pt. II, Ch. 13, Ibid.

1897. Helen Gahagan Douglas (1900–1980)

1 Such pip-squeaks as Nixon and McCarthy* are trying to get us so frightened of Communism that we'll be afraid to turn out the lights at night.
Speech *1950*
*Richard Milhous N—(1913–94), 37th president of the United States (1969–74); Joseph Raymond M— (1908–57), U.S. senator from Wisconsin (1947–57) who presided over the House Committee on Un-American Activities.

2 The Eleanor Roosevelt* I shall always remember was a woman of tenderness and deep sympathy, a woman with the most exquisite manners of anyone I have known—one who did what she was called upon to do with complete devotion and rare charm.
The Eleanor Roosevelt We Remember 1963
*See 1618.

3 I know the force women can exert in directing the course of events.
Ibid.

4 ... the first step toward liberation of *any* group is to use the power in hand. ... And the power in hand is the vote.
Quoted in "Helen Gahagan Douglas" by Lee Israel, *Ms.* (New York) *October 1973*

5 If the national security is involved, anything goes. There are no rules. There are people so lacking in roots about what is proper and what is improper that they don't know there's anything wrong in breaking into the headquarters of the opposition party.
Ibid.

1898. Elizabeth, Queen Mother (1900–2002)

1 The children will not leave unless I do. I shall not leave unless their father does, and the King will not leave the country in any circumstances whatever.
Attributed *1940*

2 I'm glad we've been bombed. It makes me feel I can look the East End in the face.
Pt. 3, Ch. 6, Remark (September 1940),* Quoted in *King George VI* by John Wheeler-Bennett *1958*
*Reference to the bombing of Buckingham Palace. The East End (London) bore the brunt of the bombing during the blitz in World War II.

1899. Joanna Field (1900–1998)

1 ... the growth of understanding follows an ascending spiral rather than a straight line.
A Life of One's Own 1934

2 I used to trouble about what life was for—now being alive seems sufficient reason.
(8 June), Ibid.

3 I came to the conclusion then that "continual mindfulness" ... must mean, not a sergeant-major-like drilling of thoughts, but a continual readiness to accept whatever came.
(10 October), Ibid.

4 I began to suggest that thought, which I had always before looked on as a cart-horse to be driven, whipped and plodding between shafts, might be really a Pegasus, so suddenly did it alight beside me from places I had no knowledge of.
Ibid.

1900. Margaret Fishback (1900–1985)

1 Fashion makes the fur fly.
"Sisters Under the Skin...," *Time for a Quick One* 1940

2 At six weeks Baby grinned a grin
That spread from mouth to eyes to chin,
And Doc, the smartie, had the brass
To tell me it was only gas!
"Infant Prodigy," *Look Who's a Mother* 1945

3 The same old charitable lie
Repeated as the years scoot by
Perpetually makes a hit—
"You really haven't changed a bit!"
"The Lie of the Land" *n.d.*

1901. Zelda Fitzgerald (1900–1948)

1 Most people hew the battlements of life from compromise, erecting their impregnable keeps from judicious submissions, fabricating their philosophical drawbridges from emotional retractions and scalding marauders in the boiling oil of sour grapes.
Ch. 1, *Save Me the Waltz* 1932

2 Wasn't any art the expression of the inexpressible? And isn't the inexpressible always the same, though variable—like the *Time* in physics?
Ch. 3, Ibid.

3 "By the time a person has achieved years adequate for choosing a direction, the die is cast and the moment has long since passed which determined the future."
Ch. 4, Ibid.

4 "... We grew up founding our dreams on the infinite promise of American advertising. I *still* believe that one can learn to

play the piano by mail and that mud will give you a perfect complexion."

Ibid.

5 Mr. Fitzgerald*—I believe that is how he spells his name— seems to believe that plagiarism begins at home. . . . On one page, I recognized a portion of an old diary of mine which mysteriously disappeared shortly after my marriage.

Tribune review of F. Scott Fitzgerald's The Beautiful and Damned (New York, 2 April 1922), Pt. 2, Ch. 7, Quoted in Zelda by Nancy Mitford** 1970

*Her husband (1896–1940), American writer. **See 2000.

6 Don't you think I was made for you? I feel like you had me ordered—and I was delivered to you—to be worn—I want you to wear me, like a watch-charm or a button-hole boquet [sic]—to the world.

Letter to F. Scott Fitzgerald (1919), Pt. 3, Ch. 17, Ibid.

7 . . . I have often told you that I am that little fish who swims about under a shark and, I believe, lives indelicately on its offal. Anyway, that is the way I am. Life moves over me in a vast black shadow and I swallow whatever it drops with relish . . .

Letter to F. Scott Fitzgerald (1932), Ibid.

1902. Lisa Gardiner (1900–1956)

1 And remember, expect nothing and life will be velvet.

Quoted in Don't Fall Off the Mountain by Shirley MacLaine* 1970

*See 2903.

1903. Elizabeth Goudge (1900–1984)

1 Her birthdays were always important to her; for being a born lover of life, she would always keep the day of her entrance into it as a very great festival indeed. . . .

Bk. I, Pt. II, Ch. 1, Green Dolphin Street 1944

2 His hatred of his wife horrified him. It was the first hatred of his life, it was growing in bitterness and intensity day by day, and he had no idea what to do about it.

Pt. III, Ch. 1, Ibid.

3 She had a deep sense of justice and sometimes this made her feel as uncomfortable in her spirit if she deserved a whipping and did not get it as she felt it on her body if she did get it, and of the two she preferred to suffer in body.

Bk. I, Ch. 1, The Child from the Sea 1970

4 Peace, she supposed, was contingent upon a certain disposition of the soul, a disposition to receive the gift that only detachment from self made possible.

Ch. 7, Ibid.

5 ". . . The travail of creation of course exaggerates the importance of our work while we engage in it; we know better when the opus is finished and the lion is perceived to be only a broken-backed mouse. . . ."

Pt. III, Ch. 2, Ibid.

6 "All we are asked to bear we can bear. That is a law of the spiritual life. The only hindrance to the working of this law, as of all benign laws, is fear."

Ch. 17, Ibid.

1904. Helen Hayes (1900–1992)

1 An actress's life is so transitory—suddenly you're a building.*

News item November 1955

*Reference to a New York theater named for her.

2 We rely upon the poets, the philosophers, and the playwrights to articulate what most of us can only feel, in joy or sorrow. They illuminate the thoughts for which we only grope; they give us the strength and balm we cannot find in ourselves. Whenever I feel my courage wavering I rush to them. They give me the wisdom of acceptance, the will and resilience to push on.

Introduction, A Gift of Joy, with Lewis Funke 1965

3 One has to grow up with good talk in order to form the habit of it.

Ibid.

4 The hardest years in life are those between ten and seventy.

Remark on turning 73 1973

5 Actors cannot choose the manner in which they are born. Consequently, it is the one gesture in their lives completely devoid of self-consciousness.

Ch. 1, Ibid.

6 When I get panicky at rehearsals, I reassure myself, "They wouldn't dare fire me. It would be like spitting on the American flag."

Remark (1966), Cited in "'First Lady of Theater' . . ." by Rayer Pike, Seattle Post-Intelligencer 18 March 1993

1905. Laura Z. Hobson (1900–1986)

1 It was the rhythm of all living, apparently, and for most people. Happiness, and then pain. Perhaps then happiness again, but now, with it, the awareness of its own mortality.

Ch. 1, Gentlemen's Agreement 1946

2 Did it never occur to one of them to write about a fine guy who was Jewish? Did each one feel some savage necessity to pick a Jew who was a swine in the wholesale business, a Jew who was a swine in the movies, a Jew who was a swine in bed?

Ch. 3, Ibid.

3 The anti-Semite offered the effrontery—and then the world was ready with harsh yardsticks to measure the self-control and dignity with which you met it. You were insensitive or too sensitive; you were too timid or too bellicose; they gave you at once the wound and the burden of proper behavior toward it.

Ch. 8, Ibid.

4 What trouble it was to be young! At sixty you grieved for the world; in youth you grieved for one unique creature.

Ch. 13, Ibid.

5 What was it, this being "a good father"? To love one's sons and daughters was not enough; to carry in one's bone and blood a pride in them, a longing for their growth and development—this was not enough. One had to be a ready companion to games and jokes and outings, to earn from the world this accolade. The devil with it.

Pt. I, Ch. 2, The First Papers 1964

6 She forced herself to stop thinking. . . . She was disciplined enough to do this nonthinking for short stretches, during the daytime at least. She had done it in other crises of her life; at times it was the only way to manage.

Consenting Adults 1975

7 "Dear Mama. . . . I have something to tell you that I guess I better not put off any longer . . . you see, I am a homosexual. I have fought it off for months and maybe years, but it just grows truer. . . ."

Ibid.

8 Why didn't children ever see that they could damage and harm their parents as much as parents could damage and harm children?

Ibid.

1906. Kathryn Hulme (1900–1981)

1 I saw more of them [concentration-camp brands] on that first day. I saw so many that I was sure my memory was branded forever and that never again would I be able to think of mankind with that certain friendly ease which characterizes Americans like a birthright.

Ch. 2, The Wild Place 1953

2 Interior silence, she repeated silently. That would be her Waterloo. How without brain surgery could you quell the rabble of memories? Even as she asked herself the question, she heard her psychology professor saying quite clearly across a space of years, "No one, not even a saint, can say an Ave straight through without some association creeping in; this is a known thing."

Ch. 1, The Nun's Story 1956

3 "You must never lose the awareness that in yourself you are nothing, you are only an instrument. An instrument is nothing until it is lifted."

Ch. 8, Ibid.

4 "I believe, Father," she said, "that even the smallest gesture of charity made in the world, with joy, would be ten times more pleasing to God than all the work I do here under the Holy Rule I only pretend to obey."

Ch. 18, Ibid.

5 Then there had been the inspection of their child from head to toe as he watched Annie undress the baby before bedtime. The tiny perfect fingernails and toenails astonished him the most. They were like the small pink shells you scuffed up in the sands of tropical beaches, he whispered, counting them.

Ch. 9, Annie's Captain 1961

6 Their fright seemed to turn them into children.

Ch. 18, Ibid.

1907. Loran Hurnscot (1900?–1970)

1 It came over me, blindingly, for the first time in my life, that suicide was a wrong act, was indeed "mortal sin." In that moment, God stopped me. I did not want my life, but I knew I was suddenly forbidden by something outside myself to let it go.

(9 July 1939), A Prison, a Paradise, Vol. II 1959

2 It had always been pride that had held me off from Him. Now it was broken the obstacle was gone. One is never simple enough, while things go well.

Ibid.

1908. Guion Griffis Johnson (1900–1989)

1 Government existed for the best people—the intelligent, educated, and wealthy. In a society where all are equally free and share alike in political privileges, there are some more fit for the exercise of good government than others.

"Southern Paternalism Toward Negroes After Emancipation,"
The Journal of Southern History November 1957

2 The argument against mixing in the schools stresses again the concept of superior and inferior races and the obligation of the superior to give the inferior equal but separate facilities so that the Negro may have the opportunity to rise within his own social system.

Ibid.

1909. Wilhelmina Kemp Johnstone (1900–1970)

1 But how glad I am, how very glad and grateful for that window looking out upon the sea!

"My Window," Bahamian Jottings 1973

2 The dawn artist was already out, tipping the clouds with glory, and transforming the sky into a glow of wonder.

"Our Trip to Green Cay," Ibid.

3 Pride, we are told, my children, "goeth before a fall," and oh, the pride was there and so the fall was not far away!

"The Old Ship's Story," Ibid.

1910. Eva Lathbury (fl. early 1900s)

1 The fall, like the serpent, was mythical: the apple was sound and Eve hysterical.

My Meyer's Pupil 1907

2 I can't help it . . . that's what we all say when we don't want to exert ourselves.

Ibid.

1911. Meridel Le Sueur (1900–1996)

1 Every generation must go further than the last or what's the use of it?

"The Dead in Steel," Salute to Spring 1940

2 Hard times ain't quit and we ain't quit.

"Salute to Spring," Ibid.

3 . . . the history of an oppressed people is hidden in the lies and the agreed-upon myth of its conquerors.

Ch. 3, Crusaders 1955

4 For none shall die who have the future in them.

Ch. 6, Ibid.

5 Memory in America suffers amnesia.

Ibid.

6 Money is only money, beans tonight and steak tomorrow. So long as you can look yourself in the eye.

Ch. 7, Ibid.

7 Perhaps women like me of another generation are a bridge. Pass over, use the energy of the root in our witness and our singing. So we will never be gone. You have more tools now. The fog is lifting over the illusions. You have begun to tell it. You will bear sharper witness. Be bold. Tell it all. Don't spare the horses. The earth is waiting to hear you. All the children and the ancients are waiting. We shall come home together.

Afterword, Ripening: Selected Work (2nd ed.) 1990

1912. Paula Ludwig (1900–1974)

1 Because I betrayed myself there in the dim
no leaf moved
no drop fell
But in the stillness could be heard
my hands growing toward you.

"To the Dark God," St. 3, Candice L. McRee, tr. *n.d.*

1913. Viviane Carter Mason (1900–1982)

1 Poverty was no barrier to what we wanted to do. It was just a condition of life that you were in and you had to work yourself out of it. We never felt that the "world owes me a living and it better give it to me!" We never had that feeling that we couldn't rise. We knew there were obstacles, very vivid obstacles; but, they weren't strong enough to destroy in us the feelings that we had to get there and we were going to get there and that nothing was going to stop us!

Interview by Zelda Silverman, Old Dominion University (Norfolk, VA) *29 March 1978*

2 Men are still savages under certain kinds of pressures. Thus, we must never forget the atrocities of the past, in order that we may not repeat it in the future.

Ibid.

3 But, to read was tantamount to eating. You have to read. That is part of living. My father was a voracious reader. My mother was a voracious reader. And I was a voracious reader. All of us were. This was the one thing that we had put into us with great force and consistency, that to get anywhere in this world, you had to be able to read and understand what you are reading.

Ibid.

1914. Margaret Mitchell (1900–1949)

1 Land is the only thing in the world that amounts to anything, for 'tis the only thing in this world that lasts, ... 'Tis the only thing worth working for, worth fighting for—worth dying for.

Pt. I, Ch. 2, *Gone With the Wind 1936*

2 "I'm tired of everlastingly being unnatural and never doing anything I want to do. I'm tired of acting like I don't eat more than a bird, and walking when I want to run and saying I feel faint after a waltz, when I could dance for two days and never get tired. I'm tired of saying 'How wonderful you are!' to fool men who haven't got one-half the sense I've got and I'm tired of pretending I don't know anything, so men can tell me things and feel important while they're doing it. . . ."

Ch. 5, Ibid.

3 "Until you've lost your reputation, you never realize what a burden it was or what freedom really is."

Pt. II, Ch. 9, Ibid.

4 "What most people don't seem to realize is that there is just as much money to be made out of the wreckage of a civilization as from the upbuilding of one."

Ibid.

5 Fighting is like champagne. It goes to the heads of cowards as quickly as of heroes. Any fool can be brave on a battlefield when it's be brave or else be killed.

Pt. IV, Ch. 31, Ibid.

6 Southerners can never resist a losing cause.

Ch. 35, Ibid.

7 Now he disliked talking business with her as much as he had enjoyed it before they were married. Now he saw that she understood entirely too well and he felt the usual masculine indignation at the duplicity of women. Added to it was the usual masculine disillusionment in discovering that a woman has a brain.

Ch. 36, Ibid.

8 If! If! If! There were so many ifs in life, never any certainty of anything, never any sense of security, always the dread of losing everything and being cold and hungry again.

Ch. 38, Ibid.

9 "Death and taxes and childbirth! There's never any convenient time for any of them!"

Ibid.

10 "You kin polish a mule's feets an' shine his hide an' put brass all over his harness an' hitch him ter a fine cah'ige. But he a mule jes' de same. He doan fool nobody."

Ch. 48, Ibid.

11 "My pet, the world can forgive practically anything except people who mind their own business."

Ibid.

12 "Life's under no obligation to give us what we expect. We take what we get and are thankful it's no worse than it is."

Pt. V, Ch. 53, Ibid.

13 "I won't think of it now. I can't stand it if I do. I'll think of it tomorrow at Tara. Tomorrow's another day."

Ch. 57, Ibid.

14 "What's broken is broken—and I'd rather remember it as it was at its best than mend it and see the broken places as long as I lived."

Ch. 63, Ibid.

15 "You're so brutal to those who love you, Scarlett. You take their love and hold it over their heads like a whip."

Ibid.

16 I wish I could care what you do or where you go, but I can't. My dear, I don't give a damn.

Ibid.

1915. Barbara Morgan (1900–1992)

1 The Navajo and Pueblo Indian tribes who danced the rituals . . . as partners in the cosmic process, attuned me to the universally primal—rather than to either the "primitive" or the "civilized."

Quoted in *The Woman's Eye* by Anne Tucker* *1973*
*See 3620.

2 . . . as the life style of the Space Age grows more inter-disciplinary, it will be harder for the "one-track" mind to survive. . . . I see simultaneous intake, multiple awareness, and synthesized comprehension as inevitable, long before the year 2000 A.D.

Ibid.

1916. Martha Ostenso (1900–1963)

1 The garden cost Amelia no end of work and worry; she tended the delicate tomato vines as though they were new born infants, and suffered momentary sinking of the heart whenever she detected signs of weakness in any of the hardier vegetables.

She was grateful for the toil in which she could dwell as a sort of refuge from deeper thought.

Ch. 7, *Wild Geese 1925*

2 Wherever the wind was bound, Elsa thought, there the whole world seemed to be going.

Ch. 4, *The Mad Carews 1927*

3 She was especially happy in the violence, the stride of the great, obstreperous city [Chicago], the fierce roar of the wind that was its voice, the white-green tumult of the waves breaking on the shore of Lake Michigan, its soul.

Ch. 21, Ibid.

4 "You have stirred the soil with our plow, my friend. It will never be the same again."

Ch. 4, *O River, Remember 1943*

5 It came to him sharply then that his mother had gradually discarded every vestige of her immigrant past, while his father was still—well, what *was* his father? Surely an American now, but with the best, the most vigorous and honest and spiritually simple qualities of the old land giving something to the new.

Ch. 8, Ibid.

6 Pity the Unicorn,
Pity the Hippogriff,
Souls that were never born
Out of the land of If!

"The Unicorn and the Hippogriff," St. 1 *n.d.*

1917. Vijaya Lakshmi Pandit (1900–1990)

1 It [political imprisonment] is a slow daily sacrifice which can be so much more deadly than some big heroic gesture made in a moment of emotional upheaval....

(3 May 1943), *Prison Days 1946*

2 When my public activities are reported it is very annoying to read how I looked, if I smiled, if a particular reporter liked my hair style.

Quoted in *The Statesman* (Glasgow) *29 August 1955*

3 You know, what happens to anybody who has been in these two places [Moscow and Washington D.C.] and looked at them objectively, is the horrifying thought—if I may use that word in quotes—that they are so similar.... Take that passion for science—they're both absolutely dedicated to the machine, they are both extroverts, they both function in much the same way....

Ibid.

4 The Indian temperament exceeds in emotionally worded epistles, which keep one in suspense as to what the aim of the writer is, until one has waded through a sea of beautiful metaphors to the final paragraphs.

(ca. 1963), Quoted in *The Envoy Extraordinary* by Vera Brittain* *1965*

*See 1764.

5 Freedom is not for the timid.

(ca. 1964), Ibid.

1918. Frances Partridge (1900–2004)

1 [Friendship] fertilises the soil of one's life, sends up fresh shoots, encourages cross-pollination and the creation of new species. Here and now I declare my infinite gratitude to my friends.

Last words, *Love in Bloomsbury: Memories 1981*

2 It is a purely relative matter where one draws the plimsoll-line of condemnation, and ... if you find the whole of humanity falls below it you have simply made a mistake and drawn it too high. And are probably below it yourself.

Ch. 17, Entry (3 September 1959), *Julia 1983*

1919. Cecilia Helena Payne-Gaposchkin (1900–1979)

1 The reward of the young scientist is the emotional thrill of being the first person in the history of the world to see something or to understand something. Nothing can compare with that experience; it engenders what Thomas Huxley* called the Divine Dipsomania. The reward of the old scientist is the sense of having seen a vague sketch grow into a masterly landscape. Not a finished picture, of course; a picture that is still growing in scope and detail with the application of new techniques and new skills. The old scientist cannot claim that the masterpiece is his own work. He may have roughed out part of the design, laid on a few strokes, but he has learned to accept the discoveries of others with the same delight that he experienced his own when he was young.

Acceptance speech, Henry Norris Russell Prize, American Astronomical Society *1977*

*English biologist (1825–95).

1920. Malvina Reynolds (1900–1978)

1 Where are you going, my little one, little one,
Where are you going, my baby, my own?
Turn around and you're two,
Turn around and you're four,
Turn around and you're a young girl going out of my door.

"Turn Around" *1958*

2 Everybody thinks my head's full of nothing,
Wants to put his special stuff in,
Fill the space with candy wrappers,
Keep out sex and revolution,
But there's no hole in my head,
Too bad.

"No Hole in My Head" *1965*

3 While that baby is a child it will suffer from neglect,
Be picked up and pecked, run over and wrecked,
And its head will be crowned with the thorn,
But while it's inside her it must remain intact,
And it cannot be murdered till it's born.

"Rosie Jane" *1973*

4 They've got the world in their pocket,
But the pocket's got a hole.

"World in Their Pocket," Verse 1 *1975*

5 Celebrate my death for the good times I've had,
For the work that I've done and the friends that I've made.
Celebrate my death, of whom it could be said,
"She was a working class woman, and a red."

Last song, untitled *1978*

1921. Nathalie Sarraute (1900–1999)

1 Neither reproaches nor encouragements are able to revive a faith that is waning.

"The Age of Suspicion" (February 1950), *The Age of Suspicion*, Maria Jolas, tr. (1963) *1956*

2   . . . what is hidden beneath the exterior monologue: an immense profusion of sensations, images, sentiments, memories, impulses, little larval actions that no inner language can convey, that jostle one another on the threshold of consciousness, gather together in compact groups, and loom up all of a sudden, then immediately fall apart, combine otherwise and reappear in new forms; while unwinding inside us, like the ribbon that come clattering from a telescriptor slot, in an uninterrupted flow of words.

   "Conversation and Sub-conversation" (January–February 1956), Ibid.

3   "We're swallowed up only when we are willing for it to happen."

   The Planetarium, Maria Jolas, tr. 1959

4   "But there are no more holy of holies, no more sacred places, no more magic, no more mirages for the thirsty, no more unsatisfied desires . . ."

   Ibid.

5   "There are people we should not allow to come near us, not for anything. Parasites who devour our very substance . . . Microbes that settle on us . . ."

   The Golden Fruits, Maria Jolas, tr. 1963

1922. Violet Alleyn Storey (1900–?)

1   I think God feels Himself the Owner here,
   Not just rich Host to some self-seeking throng,
   But Friend of village folk who want Him near
   And offer Him simplicity and song.

   "A Country Church," St. 2 1936

2   Of course, I thought I'd never let him stay,
   But, anyhow, I'd save him from the street
   And dreadful woes that might befall a cat
   So very small and wobbly on his feet.

   "Silhouette," St. 1 n.d.

3   Milton, the blind, who looked on paradise!
   Beethoven, the deaf, who heard vast harmonies.
   Byron, the lame, who climbed toward Alpine skies.
   Who pleads a handicap remembering these?*

   Untitled 1 n.d.
   *John M— (1608–1675), Eng. Poet and scholar; Ludwig van B— (1770–1827), Ger. Composer; Lord George Gordon B— (1788–1824), British poet.

1923. Frances Winwar (1900–1985)

1   In her [Eleanora Duse]* intellectual acquisitiveness she selected people as a bee chooses its flowers, for what they had to offer. Her lack of formal education made her the eternal disciple.

   Ch. 14, Wingless Victory 1956
   *See 1246.

1924. Nicola Abbagnano (1901–1990)

1   Reason itself is fallible, and this fallibility must find a place in our logic.

   The Daily Telegraph (London) 14 September 1990

1925. Yocheved Bat-Miriam (1901–1980)

1   Singing like a hope, shining like a tear,
   Silent the echo of what will befall.

   "Parting," St. 1, Poems from the Hebrew, Robert Mezey, ed. 1973

2   I shall put on my dead face with a silence free
   Of joy and of pain forevermore,
   And dawn will trail like a child after me
   To play with shells on the shore.

   St. 5, Ibid.

3   Not to be, to be gone—I pray for this.
   At the gates of infinity, like a fey child.

   "Distance Spills Itself," St. 5, Ibid.

1926. Miriam Beard (1901–1983)

1   "Haven't you some small item I could send her, very attractive—typically American?"
   The sales expert looked depressed. . . .
   "American, you say? . . . Why, my dee-ur, we don't carry those Colonial goods. All our things are imported."

   Ch. 1, Realism in Romantic Japan 1930

2   A country honeycombed with agitation and a life made vivid by unending clash and controversy—that is what the traveler finds in Japan to-day.

   Ch. 5, Ibid.

1927. Nina Berberova (1901–1993)

1   I had learnt to seek intensity rather than happiness, not joys and prosperity but more of life, a concentrated sense of life, a strengthened feeling of existence, fullness and concentration of pulse, energy, growth, flowering, beyond the image of happiness or unhappiness.

   The Italics Are Mine 1969

2   If the payment has sometimes been excessive, it was after all the payment for life, and there cannot be and is no excessive payment for life.

   Ibid.

3   Not losing time has been my permanent concern since I was three years old, when it dawned on me that time is the warp of life, its very fabric, something that you cannot buy, trade, steal, falsify, or obtain by begging.

   Ibid.

1928. Barbara Cartland (1901–2000)

1   What did we in our teens realize of war? Only that we were unsatisfied after our meals, bored, in the selfishness of youth, with mourning and weeping, sick of being told plaintively that the world would "never be the same again."

   Ch. 1, The Isthmus Years 1942

2   I always say what I think and feel—it's got me into a lot of trouble but only with women. I've never had a cross word with a man for speaking frankly but women don't like it—. I can't think why, unless it's natural love of subterfuge and intrigue.

   Ch. 8, Ibid.

3   Only through freedom will man find salvation, only through freedom can civilization survive and progress. We shall win, I am as sure of that as I am that England with all her faults, her mistakes, her snobbery and her social injustices is worth any individual sacrifice—this England which means far more in the sum total of human existence than a small green island surrounded by blue seas.

   Epilogue, Ibid.

4 To sleep around is absolutely wrong for a woman; it's degrading and it completely ruins her personality. Sooner or later it will destroy all that is feminine and beautiful and idealistic in her.

Interview, Quoted in *Speaking Frankly* by Wendy Leigh *1978*

5 France is the only place where you can make love in the afternoon without people hammering on your door.

The Guardian (London) *24 December 1984*

6 Only the English and the Americans are improper. East of Suez everyone wants a virgin.

Attributed *n.d.*

1929. Margaret Craven (1901–1980)

1 The tide-book open by the compass because you came with the tide, you went with the tide, you waited for the tide, and sometimes you prayed for the tide.

Pt. I, Ch. 1, *I Heard the Owl Call My Name 1973*

2 "Where there is no written language, anything which must be remembered must be said."

Ch. 2, Ibid.

3 "Here in the village my people are at home as the fish in the sea, as the eagle in the sky. When the young leave, the world takes them, and damages them. They no longer listen when the elders speak. They go, and soon the village will go also."

Pt. II, Ch. 8, Ibid.

4 "The church belongs in the gutter. It is where it does some of its best work."

Pt. III, Ch. 12, Ibid.

5 Here every bird and fish knew its course. Every tree had its own place upon this earth. Only man had lost his way.

Ch. 16, Ibid.

6 Past the village flowed the river, like time, like life itself, waiting for the swimmer [salmon] to come again on his way to the climax of his adventurous life, and to the end for which he had been made.

"*Wa Laum* (That is all)," Pt. IV, Ch. 23, Ibid.

1930. Marlene Dietrich (1901–1992)

1 The average man is more interested in a woman who is interested in him than he is in a woman—any woman—with beautiful legs.

News item *13 December 1954*

2 Latins are tenderly enthusiastic. In Brazil they throw flowers at you. In Argentina they throw themselves.

Quoted in *Newsweek* (New York) *24 August 1959*

3 Sex. In America an obsession. In other parts of the world a fact.

"Sex," *Marlene Dietrich's ABC 1962*

4 Once a woman has forgiven her man, she must not reheat his sins for breakfast.

"Forgiveness," Ibid.

5 The weak are more likely to make the strong weak than the strong are likely to make the weak strong.

"Weakness," Ibid.

6 He is gentle, as all real men are gentle; without tenderness, a man is uninteresting.

Ch. 1, *Papa Hemingway,** A. E. Hotchner *1966*
*Ernest H—, American writer and journalist (1899–1961).

1931. Doris Fleeson (1901–1970)

1 At this stage, it appears that for women, the New Frontiers are the old frontiers.

Column, *New York Post 1961*

2 It is occasionally possible to charge Hell with a bucket of water but against stupidity the gods themselves struggle in vain.

Newspaper column *17 February 1964*

1932. Marie-Luise Fleisser (1901–1974)

1 OLGA. Oh, that we fall every day into a world of viciousness, just as we fell into our bodies, and now we're stuck with them.

Sc. 5, *Purgatory in Ingolstadt,* Annie Castledine, tr. (1991) *1924*

1933. Elinor Hayes (1901–1994)

1 It was not childbearing that wore away women's lives. There were slower erosions.

Pt. I, Ch. 1, *Morning Star 1961*

2 Those most dedicated to the future are not always the best prophets.

Pt. IV, Ch. 29, Ibid.

1934. Gertrude Lawrence (1901–1952)

1 In London I had been by turns poor and rich, hopeful and despondent, successful and down-and-out, utterly miserable and ecstatically dizzily happy. I belonged to London as each of us can belong to only one place on this earth. And, in the same way, London belonged to me.

Ch. 1, *A Star Danced 1945*

2 "So this is America!" I exclaimed. "Look at that bath, will you? Feel that delicious warmth. Central heating, my girl. No wonder they call this the most luxurious country on earth."

Ch. 11, Ibid.

3 Perhaps you have to be born an Englishwoman to realize how much attention American men shower on women and how tremendously considerate all the nice ones among them are of a woman's wishes.

Ch. 12, Ibid.

1935. Margaret Mead (1901–1977)

1 The negative cautions of science are never popular.

Ch. 1, *Coming of Age in Samoa 1928*

2 To insist that there are no sex-differences in a society that has always believed in them and depended upon them may be as subtle a form of standardizing personality as to insist that there are many sex-differences.

Sex and Temperament in Three Primitive Societies 1935

3 An occupation that has no basis in sex-determined gifts can now recruit its ranks from twice as many potential artists.

Ibid.

4 The removal of all legal and economic barriers against women's participating in the world on an equal footing with men may be in itself a standardizing move towards the wholesale stamping-out of the diversity of attitudes that is such a dearly bought product of civilization.

Ibid.

5 If little boys have to meet and assimilate the early shock of knowing that they can never create a baby with the sureness and incontrovertibility that is a woman's birthright, how does that make them more creatively ambitious, as well as more dependent upon achievement?

Male and Female 1948

6 Man's role is uncertain, undefined, and perhaps unnecessary. By a great effort, man has hit upon a method of compensating himself for his basic inferiority.

Ibid.

7 Women, it is true, make human beings, but only men can make men.

Ibid.

8 Each home has been reduced to the bare essentials—to barer essentials than most primitive people would consider possible. Only one woman's hands to feed the baby, answer the telephone, turn off the gas under the pot that is boiling over, soothe the older child who has broken a toy, and open both doors at once. She is a nutritionist, a child psychologist, an engineer, a production manager, an expert buyer, all in one. Her husband sees her as free to plan her own time, and envies her; she sees him as having regular hours and envies him.

Ch. 16, Ibid.

9 Women want mediocre men, and men are working to be as mediocre as possible.

Quoted in *Quote Magazine 15 May 1958*

10 Early domesticity has always been characteristic of most savages, of most peasants and of the urban poor.

Quoted in "New Look at Early Marriages," *U.S. News & World Report 6 June 1960*

11 The first step in the direction of a world rule of law is the recognition that peace no longer is an unobtainable ideal but a necessary condition of continued human existence.

The New York Times Magazine 26 November 1961

12 It is an open question whether any behavior based on fear of eternal punishment can be regarded as ethical or should be regarded as merely cowardly.

Quoted in *Redbook* (New York) *February 1971*

13 . . . I had no reason to doubt that brains were suitable for a woman. And as I had my father's kind of mind—which was also his mother's—I learned that the mind is not sex-typed.

Blackberry Winter 1972

14 We are living beyond our means. As a people we have developed a life-style that is draining the earth of its priceless and irreplaceable resources without regard for the future of our children and people all around the world.

"The Energy Crises—Why Our World Will Never Again Be the Same," *Redbook* (New York) *April 1974*

15 The contempt for law and the contempt for the human consequences of lawbreaking go from the bottom to the top of American society.

Quoted in "Impeachment?" by Claire Safran, *Ibid.*

16 Our treatment of both older people and children reflects the value we place on independence and autonomy. We do our best to make our children independent from birth. We leave them all alone in rooms with the lights out and tell them, "Go to sleep by yourselves." And the old people we respect most are the ones who will fight for their independence, who would sooner starve to death than ask for help.

Quoted in "Growing Old in America" by Grace Hechinger, *Family Circle 26 July 1977*

17 In this country, some people start being miserable about growing old while they are still young.

Ibid.

18 If I were to be taken hostage, I would not plead for release nor would I want my government to be blackmailed. I think certain government officials, industrialists and celebrated persons should make it clear they are prepared to be sacrificed if taken hostage. If that were done, what gain would there be for terrorists in taking hostages?

Quoted in "Comment," *Parade Magazine 20 May 1979*

19 The first thing we have to get rid of is this horrible independent little misery called the suburban home. It is using up an unprecedented amount of hardware, creating an unprecedented amount of pollution, and producing unhappy people.

Quoted by Joni Seager* in "Blueprints for inequality," *The Women's Review of Books,* Vol. X, No. 4 *January 1993*
*See 4273.

20 . . . [to] nest in the gale [means] being able to be at home anywhere in the world, in any house, in any time band, eating any different kind of food, learning new languages as needed, never afraid of the new, sad to leave anywhere where one has been at home for a few days, but glad to go forward.

Letter, Library of Congress *n.d*

1936. Grace Moore (1901–1947)

1 There, in repressed defiance, lies the natural instinct to tell the world where to get off: an instinct, alas, that too often takes itself out in the tardy report framed *sotto voce,* or the year-in, year-out threat mumbled to oneself, "Just wait till I write that book!"

Ch. 1, You're Only Human Once 1944

2 I think that to get under the surface and really appreciate the beauty of any country, one has to go there poor.

Ch. 4, Ibid.

1937. Ruth Rowland Nichols (1901–1961)

1 Many newspaper articles . . . discussed the supposed rivalry between Amelia Earheart* and me. I have no hesitation in stating that they were exaggerated or slanted or untrue. . . . We were united by common bond of interest. We spoke each other's language—and that was the language of pioneer women of the air.

Wings for Life 1957
*See 1847.

2 It was a great source of concern, to put it mildly, when I finally had reached my altitude peak and discovered that I was down to my last five gallons of gasoline.

Quoted in Ch. 7, *The American Heritage History of Flight 1960*

1938. Laura Riding (1901–1991)

1   I met God.
    "What." he said, "you already?"
    "What," I said, "you still?"
                    "Then Follows," *Collected Poems 1938*

2   You have pretended to be seeing.
    I have pretended that you saw.
                                "Benedictory," Ibid.

3   The mercy of truth—it is to be truth.
                        "The Last Covenant," Ibid.

4   In our unwilling ignorance we hurry to listen to stories of old
    human life, new human life, fancied human life, avid of some-
    thing to while away the time of unanswered curiosity.
                        "The Telling," *The Telling 1967*

5   May our Mayness become All-embracing. May we see in one
    another the All that was once All-one rebecome One.
                                            Ibid.

6   To a poet the mere making of a poem can seem to solve the prob-
    lem of truth. . . . but only a problem of art is solved in poetry.
                Preface, *Selected Poems: In Five Sets 1975*

7   Art, whose honesty must work through artifice, cannot avoid
    cheating truth.
                                            Ibid.

8   Father, I have begun to think.
    Come and listen at my head.
    It is frightful, like being dead
    and having to hide.
            "Addresses," *First Awakenings, The Early Poems. . . ,* Elizabeth
                Friedmann, Alan J. Clark, and Robert Nye, eds. *1993*

1939. Ruth Crawford Seeger (1901–1953)

1   I often feel quite pessimistic about the future of "our" mod-
    ern music, though it is impossible for me to lose my feeling
    that surely such a dead thing as Neo-Classicism cannot perma-
    nently grip either the people or the composers.
                (1930), Quoted in "Ruth Crawford Seeger: A Virtual
                Autobiography" by Judith Tick, *ISAM Newsletter,* vol. XXXI,
                                            No. 1 *Fall 2001*

2   It is the belief of this composer that, just as the child becomes
    acquainted with his own home environment before experi-
    encing the more varied contacts of school and community, so
    should the music student be given the rich musical heritage of
    his own country as a basis upon which to build his experience
    of the folk and art music of other countries.
                                    (1936–1938), Ibid.

3   [Folk music] knows and tells what people have thought about
    the ways of living. It bears many fingermarks. It has been
    handled roughly and gently. It has been used. . . . It is not "fin-
    ished" or crystalized—it invites improvisation and creative
    aliveness. . . . It invites participation
                                        (1948), Ibid.

1940. Cornelia Otis Skinner (1901–1979)

1   I can enjoy flowers quite happily without translating them into
    Latin. I can even pick them with success and pleasure. What,
    frankly, I can't do is arrange them.
                    "Floral Piece," *Dithers and Jitters 1937*

2   It's not that I don't want to be a beauty, that I don't yearn to be
    dripping with glamour. It's just that I can't see how any woman
    can find time to do to herself all the things that must appar-
    ently be done to make herself beautiful and, having once done
    them, how anyone without the strength of mind of a foreign
    missionary can keep up such a regime.
                            "The Skin-Game," Ibid.

3   It is disturbing to discover in oneself these curious revelations
    of the validity of the Darwinian theory. If it is true that we
    have sprung from the ape, there are occasions when my own
    spring appears not to have been very far.
                        "The Ape in Me," *The Ape in Me 1959*

4   Courtesy is fine and heaven knows we need more and more of it
    in a rude and frenetic world, but mechanized courtesy is as pal-
    lid as Pablum . . . in fact, it isn't even courtesy. One can put up
    with "Service with a Smile" if the smile is genuine and not mere
    compulsory tooth baring. And while I am hardly advocating
    "Service with a Snarl," I find myself occasionally wishing for
    "Service with a Deadpan," or just plain Service, executed with
    efficiency and minus all the Charm School garnish.
                        "Production-Line Courtesy," Ibid.

5   . . . that amenity which the French have developed into a great
    art . . . conversation.
                Ch. 4, *Elegant Wits and Great Horizontals 1962*

6   Woman's virtue is man's greatest invention.
                        Quoted in *Paris '90 n.d.*

1941. Edith Mendel Stern (1901–1975)

1   The role of the housewife is, therefore, analogous to that of
    the president of a corporation who would not only determine
    policies and make over-all plans but also spend the majority of
    his time and energy in such activities as sweeping the plant and
    oiling the machines.
            "Women Are Household Slaves," *American Mercury January
                                                1949*

2   For a woman to get a rewarding sense of total creation by way
    of the multiple monotonous chores that are her daily lot would
    be as irrational as for an assembly line worker to rejoice that
    he had created an automobile because he tightened a bolt.
                                            Ibid.

1942. Jan Struther (1901–1953)

1   It took me forty years on earth
    To reach this sure conclusion:
    There is no Heaven but clarity,
    No Hell except confusion.
            "All Clear," *The Glass Blower and Other Poems 1940*

2   She saw every personal religion as a pair of intersecting cir-
    cles. . . . Probably perfection is reached when the area of the two
    outer crescents, added together, is exactly equal to that of the
    leaf-shaped piece in the middle. On paper there must be some
    neat mathematical formula for arriving at this; in life, none.
                                    Mrs. Miniver 1940

1943. Edith Summerskill (1901–1980)

1   Nagging is the repetition of unpalatable truths.
            Speech, Married Women's Association, House of Commons,
                                    London *14 July 1960*

2 I learned that economics was not an exact science and that the most erudite men would analyze the economic ills of the world and derive a totally different conclusion. . . . [Yet] governments still pin their faith to some new economic nostrum which is produced periodically by some bright young man. Only time proves that his alleged magic touch is illusory.

Ch. 5 A Woman's World 1967

3 Prize-fighting is still accepted as a display worthy of a civilized people despite the fact that all those connected with it are fully aware it caters to the latent sadistic instincts.

Ch. 12, Ibid.

4 The practice of abortion is as old as pregnancy itself. . . . Today, literate people of the space age, in well-populated countries, are not prepared to accept taboos without question; and in the matter of abortion the human rights of the mother with her family must take precedence over the survival of a few weeks' old foetus without sense or sensibility.

Ch. 19, Ibid.

5 There are those who believe that a divorce is better than subjecting a child to frequent scenes and quarrels but I am not among them. According to the report of some Judges sitting in custody, it is at the moment of the break-up of the home that the child shows signs of serious deterioration in bad behaviour and speech defects.

Ch. 20, Ibid.

1944. Anda Amir (1902–1980?)

1 You will be a blessing to me, magic spell that is in the heart,
for bringing me to the fruit,
through it I will be redeemed,
Though I will no longer know flighty pleasure.

"Eve," St. 12, Land of Israel, Sue Ann Wasserman, tr. 1987

2 I am drunk on yesterday.
Its murmuring is preserved with every pounding of my blood

"Lot's Wife," St. 5, Ibid.

3 . . . women more than men, weave their lives out of the people, places, and everyday events that they experience.

Quoted in "Women's Voices through the Past and Present" by Sue Ann Wasserman, Rabbinic thesis, Hebrew Union College-Jewish Institute of Religion (New York) *1987*

1945. Marian Anderson (1902–1993)

1 Where there is money, there is fighting.

Quoted in *Marian Anderson, a Portrait* by Kosti Vehanen *1941*

2 I could see that my significance as an individual was small. . . . I had become, whether I liked it or not, a symbol, representing my people. I had to appear. . . . I could not run away from this situation.

Quoted in "Marian Anderson," *Famous American Women* by Hope Stoddard *1970*

3 As long as you keep a person down, some part of you has to be down there to hold him down, so it means you cannot soar as you otherwise might.

Interview on CBS-TV 30 December 1957

4 Sometimes it's [prejudice] like a hair across your cheek. You can't see it. You can't find it with your fingers, but you keep brushing at it because the feel of it is irritating.

Interview (1960), Cited in "Death stills voice . . ." (AP), *Seattle Post-Intelligencer*, A9 *9 April 1993*

1946. Brooke Astor (1902–2007)

1 I am beginning to think 1929 is going to be a great year for us. There is nothing that makes me feel more alive than making money.

The Last Blossom on the Plum Tree 1986

1947. Kay Boyle (1902–1992)

1 It had been these mountains here and the others like them that all his life had wooed him from the streets and the houses as the thought of women wooed him. He knew their sloping icy shoulders and he knew their paths as one knows the roads to home.

Ch. 1, Death of a Man 1936

2 Logic, reason, disease, and the menace of death, these things meant nothing at all to us. We were committed to other values by which the poet has always lived in defiance of all that society demanded of him.

"Kay Boyle: 1926–1928," Being Geniuses Together 1968

3 What a gold mine it was to come into the stable on an early morning that sparkled with rain and to start the horses tossing their manes on their shoulders, stamping and lashing with fury because she passed by them.

"Episode in the Life of an Ancestor," Fifty Stories 1992

4 So much had she heard about Jews that the joints of his tall, elegant frame seemed oiled with some special, suave lubricant that was evil, as a thing come out of the Orient, to their clean, Nordic hearts.

"The Austrian Group," Ibid.

1948. Stella Gibbons (1902–1995)

1 Graceless, Pointless, Feckless and Aimless waited their turn to be milked.

Ch. 3, Conference at Cold Comfort Farm 1932

2 Something nasty in the woodshed.

Ch. 8, Ibid.

1949. Madeline Gray (1902–)

1 Sex, as I said, can be summed up in three P's: procreation, pleasure, and pride. From the long-range point of view, which we must always consider, procreation is by far the most important, since without procreation there could be no continuation of the race. . . . So female orgasm is simply a nervous climax to sex relations . . . and as such it is a comparative luxury from nature's point of view. It may be thought of as a sort of pleasure-prize like a prize that comes with a box of cereal. It is all to the good if the prize is there, but the cereal is valuable and nourishing if it is not.

The Normal Woman 1967

1950. Elsa Lanchester (1902–1986)

1 Comedians on the stage are invariably suicidal when they get home.

Charles Laughton* and I 1938
*Her husband, British-born American actor (1899–1962).

2 Every artist should be allowed a few failures.

          Ibid.

3 Perhaps the beginning of our interest in each other was first shown by the fact that although we are both the kind of people who can usually express ourselves and our ideas with great ease in conversation, we were practically dumb when we were alone together . . .

          Ch. 3, Ibid.

4 To complain too bitterly of the load of mischief that notoriety brings with it would mean that you are unsuited to the position you have made for yourself.

          Ch. 20, Ibid.

1951. Beryl Markham (1902–1986)

1 I have a trunk containing continents.

          "World without Walls: Beryl Markham's African Memoir,"
          KQED-TV 8 October 1986

1952. Barbara McClintock (1902–1992)

1 They* thought I was crazy, absolutely mad.

          Quoted in "Honoring a Modern Mendel" by Claudia Wallis,
          Time (New York) 24 October 1983
          *The National Academy of Sciences (1944), in response to her theory that genes could "jump" around in a chromosome; she later won the Nobel Prize for medicine (1983).

2 When you know you're right, you don't care what others think. You know sooner or later it will come out in the wash.

          Ibid.

3 Well, you know, when I look at a cell I get down in that cell and look around.

          (p. 69), Quoted in *A Feeling for the Organism: The Life and
          Work of Barbara McClintock* by Evelyn Fox Keller* 1983
          *See 2988.

4 You let the material tell you where to go.

          Quoted in *Twentieth-Century Women Scientists* by Lisa Yount
          1996

5 It seems a little unfair to reward a person for having so much pleasure over the years.*

          Ibid.

          *Her response to having received the Nobel Prize.

6 I start with the [corn] seedling, and I don't want to leave it. I don't feel I really know the story if I don't watch the plant all the way along. So I know every plant in the field. I know them intimately, and I find it a great pleasure to know them.

          Ibid.

1953–1954. Alva Reimer Myrdal (1902–1986)

1 An established tendency to drive values underground, to make the analysis appear scientific by omitting certain basic assumptions from the discussion, has too often emasculated the social sciences as agencies for rationality in social and political life. To be truly rational, it is necessary to accept the obvious principles that a social program, like a practical judgement, is a conclusion based upon premises of values as well as upon facts

          Pt. I, Ch. 1, Nation and Family 1941

2 The family of old could rightly be called the mutually supported family. All family members, without calculation as to exact shares, took part in both production and consumption. The nature and the degree of dependency were relatively similar for all. Only in the transition stage, when the male heads of households had surrendered to industrialism but that process had not yet markedly changed the functions of women, did the special dilemma of wives [as wage earner] appear.

          Pt. II, Ch. 22, Ibid.

3 The plight of the hitherto less privileged nations is beginning to weigh heavily on our conscience. Today, when all the modern means of communication keep us supplied with an incessant, vivid flow of information, we can no longer ignore that plight, as our forefathers did. Such is the dilemma of our time . . .

          "A Scientific Approach to International Welfare," *America's
          Role in International Welfare 1955*

4 It's not worthy of human beings to give up.

          Quoted in "Sissela Bok,"* *A World of Ideas* by Bill Moyers
          1989

          *See 2881.

1955. Leni Riefenstahl (1902–2003)

1 I state precisely: it is *film-verité*. It reflects the truth that was then, in 1934, history. It is therefore a documentary. Not a propaganda film. Oh! I know very well what propaganda is. That consists of recreating certain events in order to illustrate a thesis or, in the face of certain events, to let one thing go in order to accentuate another.

          Quoted by Michael Delahaye in *Cahiers du Cinema,* No. 5
          1966

2 My life became a tissue of rumors and accusations through which I had to beat a path. . . .

          Ibid.

3 I only know how happy it makes me when I meet good men, simple men. But it repulses me so much to find myself faced with false men that it is a thing to which I have never been able to give artistic form.

          Ibid.

4 Whatever is purely realistic, slice-of-life, what is average, quotidian, doesn't interest me. Only the unusual, the specific, excites me.

          Ibid.

1956. Stevie Smith (1902–1971)

1 Solitary Solitary
She would go and watch the pictures
In the National Gallery

          "Deeply Morbid," St. 2 *n.d.*

2 Fourteen-year-old, why must you giggle and dote,
Fourteen-year-old, why are you such a goat?
I'm fourteen years old, that is the reason,
I giggle and dote in season.

          "The Conventionalist" *n.d.*

3 This Englishwoman is so refined
She has no bosom and no behind.

          "This Englishwoman" *n.d.*

4 O lovers true
   And others too.
   Whose best is only better
   Take my advice
   Shun compromise
   Forget him and forget her.
   > To the tune of "The Coventry Carol," St. 4 *n.d.*

1957. Christina Stead (1902–1983)

1 . . . the waste, the insane freaks of these money men, the cynicism and egotism of their life . . . I'll show that they are not brilliant, not romantic, not delightful, not intelligent.
   > *The House of All Nations 1938*

2 "I know your breed; all your fine officials debauch the young girls who are afraid to lose their jobs: that's as old as Washington."
   > Ch. 4, *The Man Who Loved Children 1940*

3 "I do not want to go to heaven; I want my children, forever children, and other children, stalwart adults, and a good, happy wife, that is all I ask, but not paradise; earth is enough for me: it is because I believe earth is heaven, Naden, that I can overcome all my troubles and face down my enemies.'
   > Ch. 7, Ibid.

4 She was able to feel active creation going on around her in the rocks and hills, where the mystery of lust took place; and in herself, where all was yet only the night of the senses and wild dreams, the work of passion was going on.
   > *For Love Alone 1944*

5 "We are primitive men; we taboo what we desire and need. How did the denying of love come to be associated with the idea of morality?"
   > Ibid.

6 "When Europe's ruined after the war and the kids are starving and the old people dropping dead like flies, everybody sick, and without any hats or shoes, you'll see, we'll make a fortune."
   > *A Little Tea, A Little Chat 1948*

1958. Leonor Kretzer Sullivan (1902–1988)

1 Millions of American women would like to see the nation which can dress men in the garments necessary to withstand the hostile environment of the moon help women to get through a day without a bag, sag, wrinkle or tear in an expensive and frequently essential article of wearing apparel here on earth.
   > *The Congressional Record 1970*

2 A woman with a woman's viewpoint is of more value than when she forgets she's a woman and begins to act like a man.
   > Ibid.

1959. Jessamyn West (1902–1984)

1 "After a good heart," she said, "the least a woman can do is pick a face she fancies. Men's so much alike and many so sorry, that's the very least. If a man's face pleasures thee, that doesn't change. That is something to bank on."
   > "Lead Her Like a Pigeon," *The Friendly Persuasion 1945*

2 She intended to forgive. Not to do so would be un-Christian; but she did not intend to do so soon, nor forget how much she had to forgive.
   > "The Buried Leaf," Ibid.

3 "Men ain't got any heart for courting a girl they can't pass—let alone catch up with."
   > "A Likely Exchange," Ibid.

4 "It's better to learn to say good-by early than late. . . ."
   > "Learn to Say Good-by," *Love, Death, and the Ladies' Drill Team 1955*

5 Being consistent meant not departing from convictions already formulated; being a leader meant making other persons accept these convictions. It was a narrow track, and a one-way, but a person might travel a considerable distance on it. A number of dictators have.
   > Ch. 7, *To See the Dream 1956*

6 We want the facts to fit the preconceptions. When they don't, it is easier to ignore the facts than to change the preconceptions.
   > Introduction, *The Quaker Reader 1962*

7 Friends [Quakers] refused to take legal oaths, since by doing so they acquiesced in the assumption that, unless under oath, one was not obliged to tell the truth.
   > Ibid.

8 A religious awakening which does not awaken the sleeper to love has roused him in vain.
   > Ibid.

9 Fiction reveals truths that reality obscures.
   > Quoted in *Reader's Digest April 1973*

10 "He should have put his wife to work. That's the way doctors and lawyers pay for their education nowadays."
   > Ch. 1, *Hide and Seek 1973*

11 Visitors to Los Angeles, then and now, were put out because the residents of Los Angeles had the inhospitable idea of building a city comfortable to live in, rather than a monument to astonish the eye of jaded travelers.
   > Ch. 22, Ibid.

1960. Edna Gardner Whyte (1902–1993)

1 I must have been competitive from the day I was born.
   > *Rising Above It 1991*

2 A shrinking violet would not last a day in a career in aviation. If the men didn't browbeat her to death the other women would.
   > Ibid.

3 I hope that I have helped hold open the door to [the] sky so that every woman can "rise above it."
   > Ibid.

4 Just watch, all of you men. I'll show you what a woman can do. . . . I'll go across the country, I'll race to the moon. . . . I'll never look back.
   > Reflections after her first solo flight, New Year's Day, 1931, Ibid.

1961. Marya Zaturenska (1902–1982)

1 The cold dream melts, the frost
   Dissolves—the dream has sown
   A harvest never lost.
   > "Song," St. 5 *1960*

2 It's hard to breathe in a tenement hall,
So I ran to the little park,
As a lover runs from a crowded ball
To the moonlit dark.
"Song of a Factory Girl," St. 2 *n.d.*

3 Once they were flowers, and flame, and living bread;
Now they are old and brown and all but dead.
"Spinners at Willowsleigh" *n.d.*

1962. Ella J. Baker (1903–1986)

1 I don't think it ever occurred to our immediate family to in-doctrinate children against sharing. Because they had had the privilege of growing up where they'd raised a lot of food. They were never hungry. They could share their food with people. And so, you share your *lives* with people.
Quoted in *Moving the Mountain* by Ellen Cantarow *1980*

2 The best country in the world, you hear them say. I guess it may be. I haven't lived anywhere else. But it's not good enough as far as I'm concerned.
Ibid.

1963. Bettina Ballard (1903–1961)

1 Steichen* had a talent for making people drop their affecta-tions and pretensions so that what came through on his film were true portraits, whether that was what the sitter wanted or not. Steichen himself was incapable of pretense.
Ch. 1, *In My Fashion 1960*
*Edward S— , American photographer and pioneer in fine art photography (1879–1973).

2 None of the people I wrote about were as exciting in reality as I imagined them to be.
Ch. 3, Ibid.

3 The feeling about time and what to do with it has changed. What has become of those long hours when we brushed our hair, fooled with our nails, tried for the most effective place of a beauty spot? Fashion is just one of the great sacrifices of the jet age—there just isn't time to play at it.
Ch. 21, Ibid.

1964. Tallulah Bankhead (1903–1968)

1 I have three phobias which, could I mute them, would make my life as slick as a sonnet, but as dull as ditch water: I hate to go to bed, I hate to get up, and I hate to be alone.
Ch. 1, *Tallulah 1952*

2 Cocaine habit-forming? Of course not. I ought to know. I've been using it for years.
Ch. 4, Ibid.

3 I've been called many things, but never an intellectual.
Ch. 15, Ibid.

4 If you really want to help the American theater, don't be an actress, dahling, be an audience!
Quoted by Liz Smith, newsday.com *29 April 1999*

5 I am as pure as the driven slush.
Comment *n.d.*

1965. Jessie Barnard (1903–1986)

1 Your father thinks parents ought to get down on their knees and beg forgiveness of children for bringing them into such

a world. And there is much truth in that. But I hope you will never feel like that. I hope you will never regret the life we have created for you out of our seed. To me the only answers a woman can make to the destructive forces of the world is creation. And the most ecstatic form of creation is the creation of new life.
Letter to her unborn child (4 May 1941), Quoted in *Mother's Nature: Timeless Wisdom for the Journey into Motherhood* by Andrea Alban Gosline, Lisa Burnett Bossi, and Ame Mahler Beanland *1999*

2 To be happy in a relationship which imposes so many impedi-ments on her, as traditional marriage does, women must be slightly mentally ill.
Quoted in *Women Who Make the World Worse* by Kate O'Beirne *2006*

1966. Sula Benet (1903–1982)

1 The astonishing resemblance between the Semitic 'kanbos' and the Scythian 'cannabis' leads me to suppose that the Scythian word was of Semitic origin. . . . The Semites could also have spread the word during their migrations through Asia Minor.
"Tracing One Word Through Different Languages" (1936), *The Book of Grass 1967*

2 Taking into account the matriarchal element of Semitic culture, one is led to believe that Asia Minor was the original point of expansion for both the society based on the matriarchal circle and the mass use of hashish.
Ibid.

3 . . . in the original Hebrew text of the Old Testament there are references to hemp, both as incense, which was an integral part of religious celebration, and as an intoxicant.
"Early Diffusions and Folk Uses of Hemp," *Cannabis and Culture,* Vera Rubin, ed. *1975*

1967. Jessie Shirley Bernard (1903–1996)

1 Women may think like men, act like men, live the rules of the male world, and think they live in the male world until some-thing happens that shows how wide the chasm really is.
The Female World 1981

2 Many women find female solidarity hard to reconcile with almost any other of the many competing pulls on them; ethnic, racial, religious—and male. Perhaps especially male. Men seem better able to "gang up" against women than vice versa.
Ibid.

3 There are two marriages, then, in every marital union, his and hers.
The Future of Marriage 1982

1968. Dorothy Dow (1903–1979)

1 Shall I tremble at a gray hair. . . .
"Unbeliever," *Time and Love 1942*

2 Things that are lovely
Can tear my heart in two—
Moonlight on still pools,
You.
"Things," Ibid.

1969. Elizabeth "Babe" Hawes (1903–1971)

1 Dress to please yourself. . . . Forget you are what you wear. . . . Wear what you are.

Fashion Is Spinach 1938

2 There is no word in English for chic. Why should there be? Everything chic is by legend French. Perhaps everything chic is in reality French. The French invented chic and they keep it alive by what has come to be a very complicated machinery.

Ch. 1, Ibid.

3 I don't know when the word fashion came into being, but it was an evil day. For thousands of years people got along with something called style and maybe, in another thousand, we'll go back to it.

Ibid.

4 Style is the thing which, being looked back upon after a century, gives you the fundamental mental feeling for a certain period in history. . . . Style doesn't change every month or every year. It only changes as often as there is a real change in the point of view and lives of the people for whom it is produced. . . .

Ibid.

5 It took a war to get women out of corsets, and it will take a more drastic upheaval to get men into sensible clothes.

Ibid.

6 As for the bright hues in clothes, men always snort . . ." Only pansies wear colored clothes!" So I say to myself, heaven help the American male with his complex of having to be masculine.

Article in *Reader's Digest* (1938), Cited in "Early Feminist Fashion" by Bettina Berch, *Ms.* (New York) March 1987

1970. Barbara Hepworth (1903–1975)

1 . . . I rarely draw what I see. I draw what I feel in my body.

Quoted by A. M. Hammersmith in *The World of Art Series* 1968

1971. Fanny Ellen Holtzman (1903–1980)

1 Gentlemen, women have the vote. Further progress is inevitable. Our common concern should be to attract the best types of women to the law, to set honorable standards. Why admit a woman to the practice of law if you're going to ban her from the Bar Building? A tolerant approach will reflect greater dignity on all of us.

p. 57, Quoted in *The lady and the law: the remarkable life of Fanny Holtzmann* by Ted Berkman 1976

2 I don't follow precedent, I establish it.

Quoted in *The 50 Most Influential Women in American Law* by Dawn Bradley Berry* 1996
*See 4399.

1972. Kathleen Yardley Lonsdale (1903–1971)

1 Any country that wants to make full use of all its potential scientists and technologists could do so, but it must not expect to get the women quite so simply as it gets the men. It seems to me that marriage and motherhood are at least as socially important as military service. Government regulations are framed to ensure (in the United Kingdom) that a man returning to work from military service is not penalized by his absence. Is it Utopian, then, to suggest that any country that really wants married women to return to a scientific career when her children no longer need her physical presence should make special arrangements to encourage her to do so?

Quoted in "Women in Science: Reminiscences and Reflections" by Kathleen Lonsdale, *Impact of Science on Society,* Vol. 20 1970

1973. Clare Boothe Luce (1903–1987)

1 CHRYSTAL. There's a name for you ladies, but it isn't used in high society . . . outside of a kennel.

The Women 1936

2 MARY. Reno's full of women who all have their pride.

Act II, Ibid.

3 EDITH. Always remember, Peggy, it's matrimonial suicide to be jealous when you have a really good reason.

Act III, Ibid.

4 Much of what Mr. [Vice-President Henry] Wallace calls his global thinking is, no matter how you slice it, still Globaloney.

Speech, U.S. House of Representatives *9 February 1943*

5 To put a woman on the ticket would challenge the loyalty of women everywhere to their sex, because it would be made to seem that the defeat of the ticket meant the defeat for a hundred years of women's chance to be truly equal with men in politics.

Quoted in *Vanity Fair 28 June 1948*

6 I am for lifting everyone off the social bottom. In fact, I am for doing away with the social bottom altogether.

Quoted in *Time* (New York) *14 February 1964*

7 NORA. Know what Freud wrote in his diary when he was 77? "What do women want? My God, what do they want?" Fifty years this giant brain spends analyzing women. And he still can't find out want they want. So this makes him the world's greatest expert on female psychology?

Slam the Door Softly 1970

8 BLACK WOMAN'S VOICE. There's no human being a man can buy anymore—except a woman.

Ibid.

9 NORA. But if God had wanted us to think with our wombs, why did He give us a brain?

Ibid.

10 The American Republic is now almost 200 years old, and in the eyes of the law women are still not equal with men. The special legislation which will remedy that situation is the Equal Rights Amendment. Its language is short and simple: *Equality of rights under the law shall not be abridged in the United States or by any state on account of sex.*

Quoted in the *Bulletin of the Baldwin School* (Pennsylvania) *September 1974*

*See Alice Paul, 1637.

11 A man's home may seem to be his castle on the outside; inside, it is more often his nursery.

Ibid.

12 Male supremacy has kept women down. It has not knocked her out.

Quoted in *Saturday Review/World 15 September 1974*

13 I'll marry for money. Lots of it . . . Damned if I'll ever love any
   mere man. Money! I need it and the power it brings, and someday you shall hear my name spoken of as famous.
   Diary entry, Quoted in *Rage for Fame: The Ascent of Clare
   Boothe Luce* by Sylvia Jukes Morris *1997*

14 I do not like to go to bed without you. But somehow, lately,
   even when I'm with you, I seem to go to bed without you.
   Letter to her husband, Henry Luce,* Ibid.
   *American editor and publisher; founder of *Time, Life, Fortune*
   and *Sports Illustrated* (1898–1967).

15 Most everyone that knew me casually preferred to think of me
   as a cold, remote, shrewd and ambitious woman: I have always
   contrived to behave so in their company.
   Note to her husband, Henry Luce, Ibid.

16 What rage for fame attends both great and small.
   School yearbook entry, Ibid.

1974. Caroline Miller (1903–1992)

1 Cean's eyes followed the rows of young corn, all of a size, all
  of a green. She was thinking how she had dropped the grains
  of seed corn: and they had lain in the dark through cool nights
  and hot days; they had burst the soil, new and different, unrecognizable in poison green, disowning the seed that sought
  sustenance downward with white roots in black earth, sustenance for bright-green blades growing toward the sun, toward
  far-off tassels high in the air, and heavy ears of corn that would
  be other new seeds of grain.
  Lamb in His Bosom 1933

2 Lonzo had brought her a century plant from the Coast, and Cean
  set it in a far corner of her yard and watered it. She wondered
  how anybody would ever know if it counted a hundred years
  right till it was time for it to bloom. She would not be here, nor
  Lonzo, nor the last youngest child that she might bear. . . . In a
  hundred years . . . she would be dead and rotten long ago. There
  would be nothing alive that she had known-not a child, nor a
  cow, nor a bird. . . . She and hers would be gone, like prince's
  feathers and old-maid flowers and bachelor-buttons that die
  with killing frost, leaving only dried seeds for a careful hand to
  garner if it will; blazing-star and mulberry geraniums will leave
  roots to sleep in the earth like a wild thing; Cean would leave no
  roots to wake again to the sun of another year. Her children, she
  judged, were her seeds and roots and new life.
  Ibid.

3 One day it occurred to me that I was not half so weighted
  down with duties as the pioneer women used to be. Even my
  mother and grandmother, who had such large families, seemed
  to get through with much less effort and energy than I was ex-
  pending. I couldn't help wondering why. They had something,
  something very real, very tangible, yet almost indefinable, that
  anchored them and gave them faith and courage, and I needed
  that something so much. From that day I turned to the examples set by the pioneer women of Georgia.
  "An Ethnographic Study of the 1934 Pulitzer Prize Novel
  Lamb in His Bosom" by Joanne Bishop, Caroline Pafford
  Miller Collection, Emory University n.d.

1975. Virginia Moore (1903–1993)

1 Fortunately there is excess in greatness: it can lose more than
  mediocrity possesses, and still be great.
  "Sappho,"* *Distinguished Women Writers 1934*
  *See 46.

2 A poet is a state of mind.
  "Saint Teresa,"* Ibid.
  *See 308.

3 Suspicion is the badge of base-born minds,
  And calculation never understands.
  "Tragic Conclusions" *n.d.*

1976. Kuni Nagako (1903–2000)

1 We have always been trained in the past to a life of service and
  I am afraid that as these new changes come about there may be
  a loss of real values.
  Meeting with Eleanor Roosevelt* (1953), Quoted in *Eleanor:
  The Years Alone* by Joseph P. Lash *1972*
  *See 1618.

1977. Irène Némirovsky (1903–1942)

1 There are laws that regulate the fate of beehives and of people,
  that's all there is to it. The spirit of the people is undoubtedly
  also ruled by laws that elude us, or by whim we know nothing
  about. How sad the world is, so beautiful yet so absurd . . .
  "Dolce," Ch. 12, *Suite Française*, Sandra Smith, tr. *2004*

2 The people around him believed that fate was tracking them
  down, them and their pitiable generation; but not Maurice: he
  knew there had been exoduses throughout history. How many
  people had died on this land (on land everywhere in the world),
  dripping with blood, fleeing the enemy, leaving cities in flames,
  clutching their children to their hearts: no one gave a thought
  to these countless dead, or pitied them. To their descendants
  they were no more important than chickens who'd had their
  throats slit.
  "Storm in June," Ch. 11, Ibid.

3 "Ah! Madame, this is the principal problem of our times: what
  is more important, the individual or society? War is the collaborative act par excellence, *is it not?* We Germans believe in the
  communal spirit—the spirit one finds among bees, the spirit of
  the hive. It comes before everything: nectar, fragrance, love . . .
  "Dolce," Ch. 12, Ibid.

4 What separates or unites people is not their language, their
  laws, their customs, their principles, but the way they hold
  their knife and fork.
  Ch. 16, Ibid.

5 "In the heart of every man and every woman a kind of Garden
  of Eden endures, where there is no war, no death, where wild
  animals and deer live together in peace. All we have to do is to
  reclaim that paradise, just close our eyes to everything else."
  Ch. 20, Ibid.

6 People get used to everything, everything that happens in the
  occupied zone: massacres, persecution, organised pillaging, are
  like arrows shot into mire! . . . the mire of our hearts.
  Appendix I, Ibid.

7 They're trying to make us believe we live in the age of the
  "community," when the individual must perish so that society
  may live, and we don't want to see that it is society that is
  dying so that tyrants can live.
  Ibid.

8 Sacrifice (everyone agrees about the necessity of sacrifice just
  as long as it's your neighbour's) . . .
  Ibid.

9   How is this fire lit within us? It devours everything and then, in a few years, a few months, a few hours even, it burns itself out. Then you see how much damage has been done.

> Ch. 1, *Fire in the Blood,* Sandra Smith, tr. 2007

10   For I sometimes feel I've been rejected by life, as if washed ashore by the tide. I've ended up on a lonely beach, an old boat, still solid and seaworthy, but whose paint has faded in the water, eaten away by salt.

> Ibid.

11   Everyone lives in his own house, on his own land, distrusts his neighbors, harvests his wheat, counts his money and doesn't give a thought to the rest of the world. No châteaux, no visitors.

> Ibid.

1978. Lorine Niedecker (1903–1970)

1   My friend tree
I sawed you down
but I must attend
an older friend
the sun

> "My friend tree," in toto, *The Granite Pail: The Selected Poems of Lorine Niedecker 1985*

2   Grandfather
   advised me:
      Learn a trade

I learned
   to sit at desk
     and condense

> "Poet's Work," Sts. 1 & 2, *Lorine Niedecker: Collected Works 2002*

3   Know amazedly how
often one takes his madness
into his own hands
and keeps it.

> "When Ecstasy is Inconvenient," St. 3, Ibid.

1979. Anaïs Nin (1903–1977)

1   He wove a veritable spider web about himself. No man was ever more completely installed in the realm of possessions. . . . He had prepared a fortress against need, war and change.

> *Winter of Artifice 1945*

2   . . . all elegant women have acquired a technique of weeping which has no . . . fatal effect on the make-up.

> Ibid.

3   This enthusiasm which must be held in check was a great burden for a child's soul. . . . to restrain meant to kill, to bury.

> Ibid.

4   He had a mania for washing and disinfecting himself. . . . For him the only danger came from the microbes that attacked the body. He had not studied the microbe of conscience which eats into the soul.

> Ibid.

5   There is blood in my eyes. A tunnel. I push into this tunnel, I bite my lips and push. There is a fire and flesh ripping and no air. Out of the tunnel! All my blood is spilling out. Push! Push! Push! It is coming! It is coming! I feel the slipperiness, the sudden deliverance, the weight is gone.

> "Birth," *Under a Glass Bell 1948*

6   Too much awareness, without accompanying experience, is a skeleton without the flesh of life.

> (February 1937), *The Diary of Anaïs Nin,* Vol. II 1967

7   I can remember what I did but not the reflection of what I did.

> (March 1937), Ibid.

8   Woman does not forget she needs the fecundator, she does not forget that everything that is born of her is planted in her.

> (August 1937), Ibid.

9   Electric flesh-arrows . . . traversing the body. A rainbow of color strikes the eyelids. A foam of music falls over the ears. It is the gong of the orgasm.

> (October 1937), Ibid.

10   The crowd is a malleable thing, it can be dominated, dazzled, it's a public, it is faceless. This is the opposite of relationship.

> Ibid.

11   What I consider my weaknesses are feminine traits: incapacity to destroy, ineffectualness in battle.

> (January 1943), *The Diary of Anaïs Nin,* Vol. III 1969

12   How wrong it is for women to expect the man to build the world she wants, rather than set out to create it herself.

> *The Diary of Anaïs Nin,* Vol. V 1974

13   The role of the writer is not to say what we can all say but what we are unable to say.

> Ibid.

14   Memory is a great betrayer.

> Letter to Geismar, Ibid.

15   If we are unable to make passion a relationship of duration, surviving the destruction and erosions of daily life, it still does not divest passion of its power to transform, transfigure, transmute a human being from a rather limited, petty, fearful creature to a magnificent figure reaching at moments the status of a myth.

> "San Francisco," Ibid.

16   Anxiety is love's greatest killer, because it is like the strangle hold of the drowning.

> Ibid.

17   The drugs, instead of bringing fertile images which in turn can be shared with the world . . . have instead become a solitary vice, a passive dreaming which alienates the dreamer from the whole world, isolates him, ultimately destroys him.

> "Sierra Madre,"Ibid.

1980. Eileen O'Casey (1903–1995)

1   I was liberated but not too liberated. I was Catholic, you see, and my conscience always bothered me.

> Quoted in "Eileen O'Casey Remembers" by Lee Grant, *The Los Angeles Times 13 November 1974*

2   Unless it's right next door, people don't notice killing and bloodshed. We take it in like the sun shines and the rain falls.

> Ibid.

1981. Justine Wise Polier (1903–1987)

1 *Explaining why she never wore her heavy judicial robes in Family Court:* There is nothing about a black robe that encourages a child to talk to me like a human being.
> Quoted in *Jewish Heroes and Heroines of America* by Seymour "Sy" Brody 1996

2 Passionate concern may lead to errors of judgment, but the lack of passion in the face of human wrong leads to spiritual bankruptcy.
> Address, "Basic Elements of Friendly Frontiers" (Christ Church, 14 October 1952), *The Journey Home, How Jewish Women Shaped Modern America* by Joyce Antler* 1997
> *See 3320.

3 As case after case came up, I saw the vast chasms between our rhetoric of freedom, equality and charity, and what we were doing to, or not doing for poor people, especially children.
> Interview (n.d.), Ibid.

4 If I were a good judge it was because I felt I might have committed every crime or offense charged against the children brought before me. That I had not was largely a matter of luck, privilege, and always feeling loved.
> Oral Histories of Justine Wise Polier (4), Ibid.

5 We have lost a sense of personal responsibility and sensitivity to people, and our faith that we can do more for people who need help if we care. In other words, I don't believe we can have justice without caring, or caring without justice. These are inseparable aspects of life and work for children as they are for adults.
> Jewish Women's Archive (jwa.org) *n.d.*

1982. Nelly Ptaschkina (1903–1920)

1 Youth does not know how to concentrate, and, on the other hand, does not want to confide in others. Hence the diary. The old work out everything in themselves.
> (23 January 1918), *The Diary of Nelly Ptaschkina 1923*

2 Whatever I neglect now I shall have to pay for later.
> (26 January 1918), Ibid.

3 It seems to me that man at birth does not represent a lump of clay, which can be shaped at will: for instance, either he is born intelligent or he is born stupid. Goodness can, on the other hand, be acquired.
> Ibid.

4 Give women scope and opportunity, and they will be no worse than men.
> (1 October 1918), Ibid.

5 Yes, one must renounce that which is too emotional. There is no need for these moods, this longing, these *attendrissements.* . . . Work is waiting for us.
> (27 May 1919), Ibid.

1983. Teng Ying-ch'ao (1903–?)

1 . . . in order to fight the Japanese we must study Japanese!
> Quoted in *Women in Modern China* by Helen Foster Snow* 1967
> *See 2073.

1984. Diana Vreeland (1903–1989)

1 Elegance is innate . . . it has nothing to do with being well dressed.
> Quoted in *Time* (New York) 4 September 1989

1985. Thyra Samter Winslow (1903–1961)

1 Platonic love is love from the neck up.
> Quoted by James Simpson in *Interview* 19 August 1952

1986. Marguerite Yourcenar (1903–1987)

1 One reaches all great events of life a virgin.
> *Fires 1935*

2 One doesn't know what to do with delirium while experimenting with the mingling and mixing of bodies.
> Ibid.

3 And you are going? You are going? . . . No, you are not going: I am keeping you . . . You leave your soul, like a coat, in my hands.
> Ibid.

4 We say: mad with joy. We should say: wise with grief.
> Ibid.

5 To possess is the same thing as to know: the Bible is always right.
> Ibid.

6 Thieves are only after our rings, lovers our bodies, preachers our souls, murderers our lives.
> Ibid.

7 The successive phases of love follow a monotonous course; what they still seem to me to resemble the most are the endless but sublime repetitions and returns in Beethoven's* Quartets.
> *Coup de Grâce 1939*
> *Ludvig van B— (1770–1827), German composer.

8 This morning it occurred to me for the first time that my body, my faithful companion and friend, truly better known to me than my own soul, may be after all only a sly beast who will end by devouring his master.
> "*Animula Vagula Blandula,*" Ibid.

9 I have done much rebuilding. To reconstruct is to collaborate with time gone by, penetrating or modifying its spirit, and carrying it toward a longer future. Thus beneath the stones we find the secret of the springs.
> "*Tellus Stabilita,*" Ibid.

1987. Margery Allingham (1904–1966)

1 Lying, they say, is a new modern art of the enemy's, but telling the truth is not easy.
> Preface, *The Oaken Heart 1941*

2 It is always difficult to escape from youth; its hopefulness, its optimistic belief in the privileges of desire, its despair, and its sense of outrage and injustice at disappointment, all these spring on a man inflicting indelicate agony when he is no longer prepared.
> Ch. 21, Ibid.

3 Normally he was the happiest of men. He asked so little of life that its frugal bounty amazed and delighted him. . . . He believed in miracles and frequently observed them, and nothing astonished him. His imagination was as wild as a small boy's and his faith ultimate. In ordinary life he was, quite frankly, hardly safe out.

Ch. 2, *The Tiger in the Smoke* 1952

4 Chemists employed by the police can do remarkable things with blood. They can find it in shreds of cloth, in the interstices of floor boards, on the iron of a heel, and can measure it and swear to it and weave it into a rope to hang a man.

Ch. 9, Ibid.

1988. Elaine Frances Burton (1904–1991)

1 A woman in authority is often unpopular, only because she is efficient.

What of the Women? 1941

2 If you get a good woman, you get the finest thing on earth.

Ibid.

1989. Mary Steichen Calderone (1904–1998)

1 Interference with self-pleasure is a very bad thing for children.

60 Minutes, CBS-TV 25 October 1981

2 I don't want to control anybody's mind or anybody's heart—I just want to help free people from the concept of sex as evil instead of a gift from God.

Ibid.

3 The significance of revolutions never lies in what they are *against*, but in what they are *for*.

Friends and Womankind (pamphlet, Friends General Conference) 1984

4 Being a Quaker lays on one the responsibility for engaging in a continuing internal process of finding out what one really believes in, and relentlessly tracking down one's own bigotries, prejudices, inconsistencies, blindnesses, and refusals to recognize truth and accept it as such.

Ibid.

1990. Ève Curie (1904–2007)

1 We discovered that peace at any price is no peace at all. . . . We discovered that life at any price has no value whatever; that life is nothing without the privileges, the prides, the rights, the joys which make it worth living, and also worth giving. And we also discovered that there is something more hideous, more atrocious than war or than death; and that is to live in fear.

Address, American Booksellers Association, New York 9 *April 1940*

2 Let's face it: however old-fashioned and out of date and devaluated the word is, we like the way of living provided by democracy.

Ibid.

3 Public opinion waged the war. Statesmen, diplomats, government officials waged the war. To beat the Axis, it was not enough to win battles in the field, to kill millions of men. We also had to kill ideas that knew no frontiers and spread like diseases.

Pt. V, Ch. 26, *Journey Among Warriors* 1943

1991. Lilly Daché (1904–1989)

1 When I was six I made my mother a little hat—out of her new blouse.

Newspaper interview *3 December 1954*

2 Today, there is no excuse for a woman to grow old, unless she is ill . . . If you want to keep up with this modern, wonderful world, you must be young in thought, feeling, and appearance.

Glamour Book 1956

1992. Adelle Davis (1904–1974)

1 Nutrition is a young subject; it has been kicked around like a puppy that cannot take care of itself. Food faddists and crackpots have kicked it pretty cruelly. . . . They seem to believe that unless food tastes like Socratic hemlock, it cannot build health. Frankly, I often wonder what such persons plan to do with good health in case they acquire it.

Ch. 1, *Let's Eat Right to Keep Fit 1954*

2 When the blood sugar is extremely low, the resulting irritability, nervous tension, and mental depression are such that a person can easily go berserk. . . . Add a few guns, gas jets, or razor blades, and you have the stuff murders and suicides are made of. The American diet has become dangerous in many more ways than one.

Ch. 2, Ibid.

3 Thousands upon thousands of persons have studied disease. Almost no one has studied health.

Ch. 29, Ibid.

4 If this country is to survive, the best-fed-nation myth had better be recognized for what it is: propaganda designed to produce wealth but not health.

Ch. 30, Ibid.

5 You can't eat well and keep fit if you don't shop well.

Quoted in "The Great Adelle Davis Controversy" by Daniel Yergin, *The New York Times Magazine 20 May 1973*

1993. Fumiko Hayashi (1904–1951)

1 Kin refused to forget her femininity.
Death itself was preferable to the
blowsiness of the average old woman.
There was a poem—composed, they said, by
some famous woman of the past—
Never could human form
Aspire, I know,
To beauty ripe as that now bends
This rose. Yet, somewhere here,
I see myself.

"Late Chrysanthemum," John Bester, tr. *1948*

2 Love in itself, she felt should be like the creation of a succession of works of art.

Ibid.

1994. Eugenia Ginzburg (1904–1967)

1 . . . how thin the line is between high principles and blinkered intolerance.

Eugenia Ginzburg: Within the Whirlwind (1979), Ian Boland, tr. *1981*

2 Maternal feelings are a splendid rationale for misbehavior.

Pt. I, Ch. 1, Ibid.

3 When you have lived for years on end without any sense of the future or any real feeling for the reality of the morrow, the whole idea of putting something aside, of saving, goes clean out of your head. There had been periods when we had been earning quite a lot of money. We could have saved up for a rainy day. But when every day is rainy, you somehow don't think about it. And now we were ourselves astonished at where all the money had gone; all at once we were without means.

Pt. II, Ch. 14, Ibid.

1995. Sheilah Graham (1904–1988)

1 . . . you have to really drink a lot to enjoy parties.

Quoted in "Sheilah Graham: Still Upwardly, Verbally Mobile" by Kathleen Hendrix, *The Los Angeles Times* 13 October 1974

2 You just never know when you're going into eternity.

Ibid.

3 I think people still want to marry rich. Girls especially. . . . [It's] simple. Don't date poor boys. Go where the rich are. . . . You don't have to be rich to go where they go.

Ibid.

1996. Helen Lawrenson (1904–1982)

1 They are a curious mixture of Spanish tradition, American imitation, and insular limitation. This explains why they never catch on to themselves.

"Latins Are Lousy Lovers," *Esquire* (New York) October 1939

2 A skirt is no obstacle to extemporaneous sex, but it is physically impossible to make love to a girl while she is wearing trousers.

"Androgyne, You're a Funny Valentine," *Latins Are Still Lousy Lovers* 1968

3 Most of today's film actresses are typical of a mass-production age: living dolls who look as if they came off an assembly line and whose uniformity of appearance is frequently a triumph of modern science, thanks to which they can be equipped with identical noses, breasts, teeth, and hair.

"Where Did It Go?," Ibid.

1997. Victoria Lincoln (1904–1981)

1 This is the art of courage: to see things as they are and still believe that the victory lies not with those who avoid the bad, but those who taste, in living awareness, every drop of the good.

"The Art of Courage", *Vogue* 1 October 1952

1998. Marya Mannes (1904–1990)

1 Promiscuous. . . . That was a word I had never applied to myself. Possibly no one ever does, for it is a sordid word, reducing many valuable moments to nothing more than dog-like copulation.

"The Second Month," *Message from a Stranger* 1948

2 They had no serenity, for true serenity comes after knowledge of pain. They had only the stillness of spiritual inertia. They were half alive.

"The Seventh Month," Ibid.

3 The real demon is success—the anxieties engendered by this quest are relentless, degrading, corroding. What is worse, there is no end to this escalation of desire. . . .

"The Roots of Anxiety in Modern Women," *Journal of Neuropsychiatry* May 1964

4 What I call the destructive anxieties are not the growth of women's minds and powers, but quite the contrary: the pressures of society and the mass media to make woman conform to the classic and traditional images in men's eyes.

Ibid.

5 Affluent as it was for the majority, the society we had produced was not admirable. It might be better than others, but it was nowhere near what it should have been. It was, in fact, going rotten. The private gain had for so long triumphed over the public need that the cities had become unlivable, the country desecrated, the arteries choked, and pollution—of air, of water, yes, of spirit too—a daily, oppressive fact. And who else but our generation (if not ourselves) had made it so?

Them 1968

6 Timing and arrogance are decisive factors in the successful use of talent. The first is a matter of instinct, the second part carapace and part self-hypnosis; the shell that protects, the ego that assumes, without question, that the talent possessed is not only unique but important, the particular vision demanding to be shared.

Preface, *Out of My Time* 1971

7 While the young fight the official barbarism of unsentient power—the insanities of war and the ruinous priorities imposed by leaders and organizations in the *name* of reason, perhaps our last duty is to fight for the civilization *of* reason.

Ch. 9, Ibid.

1999. Dorothy Eugenia Miner (1904–1973)

1 The book with pages was the stimulus to everything that we think of when we discuss book design.

The History of Bookbinding, 525–1950 A.D. 1957

2 . . . labels—a favorite device by which insignificant things can *reflect* significance.

Letter to Eleanor P. Spencer (3 November 1970), Quoted in "The Varied Career of a Medievalist" by Claire Richter Sherman, *Women As Interpreters of the Visual Arts,* Claire Richter Sherman, ed. 1981

2000. Nancy Mitford (1904–1973)

1 "I simply don't see the point of getting up at six all the time you are young and working eighteen hours a day in order to be a millionaire, and then when you are a millionaire still getting up at six and working eighteen hours a day. . . . What does it all mean?"

Ch. 1, *Pigeon Pie* 1940

2 An aristocracy in a republic is like a chicken whose head has been cut off: it may run about in a lively way, but in fact it is dead.

Noblesse Oblige 1956

3 Americans relate all effort, all work, and all of life itself to the dollar. Their talk is of nothing but dollars. The English seldom sit happily chatting for hours on end about pounds. In England, public business is its own reward, nobody would go into Parliament in order to become rich, neither do riches bring public appointment.

Ibid.

4 The reason for my resignation is that I'm no use to you. When things go badly you don't need me, when they go well you

turn to other, prettier, ladies. So I seem to have no function—*le portefeuille est vide.**

> Letter to Gaston Palewski** (1858), *Love From Nancy, The Letters of Nancy Mitford*, Charlotte Mosely, ed. *1993*
> *An empty pocketbook. **A French diplomat of Polish descent; both married to others, he was the love of her life.

2001. Helen Nearing (1904–1995)

1   Do the best that you can in the place where you are, and be kind.

> *The Good Life*, with Scott Nearing* *1990*
> *Her husband: (1883–1983) American radical economist, educator, writer, political activist, and advocate of simple living.

2   A month or two before he [her husband Scott] died he was sitting at table with us at a meal. Watching us eat he said, "I think I won't eat anymore." "Alright," said I. "I understand. I think I would do that too. Animals know when to stop. They go off in a corner and leave off food."

> "At The End Of A Good Life," *What is Enough?* (Context Institute #26) *Summer 1990*

3   In a soft voice, with no quiver or pain or disturbance he said "All . . . right," and breathed slower and slower and slower till there was no movement anymore and he was gone out of his body as easily as a leaf drops from the tree in autumn, slowly twisting and falling to the ground.

> So he returned to his Maker after a long life, well-lived and devoted to the general welfare.

> Ibid.

4   Satisfaction in life seems to come from living in tune with your beliefs, in tune with other humans and animals you encounter, and in tune with your environment.

> "Going It Alone", Ibid.

5   A communal life is richer than a single one. Mankind was doubtless meant to live in company, not isolation.

> Ibid.

2002–2003. Virgilia Peterson (1904–1966)

1   In Reno, there is always a bull market, never a bear market for the stocks and bonds of happiness.

> *A Matter of Life and Death 1961*

2   A lady, that is an enlightened, cultivated, liberal lady—the only kind to be in a time of increasing classlessness—could espouse any cause: wayward girls, social diseases, unmarried mothers, and/or birth control with impunity. But never by so much as the shadow of a look should she acknowledge her own experience with the Facts of Life.

> Ibid.

3   European society . . . automatically assumes its superiority to Americans whether they have money or not, but money tends to blur the sharpness of the distinction.

> Ibid.

2004. Anne Roe (1904–1991)

1   Nothing in science has any value to society if it is not communicated. . . .

> Ch. 1, *The Making of a Scientist 1952*

2   Freedom breeds freedom. Nothing else does.

> Ch. 16, Ibid.

2005. Bobbie Rosenfeld (1904–1969)

1   *Responding to patron's offer of "anything she wanted":* Well, sir, if it's all the same to you, I'll take a nice ham.

> "She Made Track Record and Joshed the Umpire", *Heritage Toronto 20 September 1924*

2   We gals were babes in the wood then and clung to that old cliche about sports for sports sake.

> "Lamp Shades and Ribbon" (1950), Jewish Women's Archive (jwa.org) *n.d.*

3   Athletic maids to arms! . . . We are taking up the sword, and high time it is, in defense of our so-called athletic bodies to give the lie to those pen flourishers who depict us not as paragons of feminine physique, beauty and health, but rather as Amazons and ugly ducklings all because we have become sports-minded . . .

> "Crashing the Sacred Sanctum," Ibid.

2006. Anya Seton (1904–1990)

1   People in England seemed to think nothing of false teeth, even when they got them from the National Health.

> Pt. I, Ch. 1, *Green Darkness 1972*

2   "As I grew up I got cynical. I'd see Mother enthusiastic and involved with charlatans. Numerologists and astrologers who charged five hundred dollars for a 'reading' which was so vague you could twist the meaning any way you wanted. And faith healers who couldn't seem to heal themselves, and a Yogi in California who preached purity, sublimity, and continence, and then tried to seduce me one day while Mother was out."

> Ch. 2, Ibid.

3   "Truth is naturally universal," said Akananda, "and shines into many different windows, though some of them are clouded."

> Pt. III, Ch. 19, Ibid.

2007. Sally Stanford (1904–1982)

1   No, no one sets out to be a madam; but madams answer the call of a well-recognized and very basic human need. Their responsibilities are thrust upon them by the fundamental nitwittedness and economic shortsightedness of most hustling broads. And they become tempered and sharpened and polished to the highest degree of professional awareness by constant intercourse with men devoutly dedicated to the policy of getting something for nothing.

> Prologue, *The Lady of the House 1966*

2   Well, there's a Book that says we're all sinners and I at least chose a sin that's made quite a few people happier than they were before they met me, a sin that's left me with very little time to consider other extremely popular moral misdemeanors, like usury, intolerance, bearing false tales, extortion, racial bigotry, and the casting of the first stone. And, I might add, a hell of a lot worse.

> Ch. 4, Ibid.

3   No man can be held throughout the day by what happens throughout the night.

> Ch. 13, Ibid.

4   Romance without finance is a nuisance. Few men value free merchandise. Let the chippies fall where they may.

> Ibid.

2008. Charlotte Wolff (1904–1986)

1 I have no doubt that lesbianism makes a woman virile and open to *any* sexual stimulation, and that she is more often than not a more adequate and lively partner in bed than a "normal" woman.

Love Between Women 1971

2 A niggling feeling of discomfort and unease follows masturbation, even in those who do not feel guilty about it.

Ibid.

2009. Jane Ace (1905–1974)

1 Home wasn't built in a day.
Comment, "Easy Aces" radio show (ca. 1928–1945), Quoted in *The Fine Art of Hypochondria* by Goodman Ace* 1966
*American humorist and radio personality; her husband (1899–1982).

2 Familiarity breeds attempt

Ibid.

3 He's a ragged individualist.

Ibid.

4 Time wounds all heels.

Ibid.

2010. Loma Chandler (1905–1988)

1 Sometimes asylums are just what they should be—a resting place for people who get lost in life.
"They're Expecting Us," *Reader's Digest October 1973*

2 A smile appeared upon her face as if she'd taken it directly from her handbag and pinned it there.

Ibid.

2011. Ilka Chase (1905–1978)

1 She thought of all foreign lands as lands of promise, and with the same yearning that so many Europeans had for America.
Ch. 1, *I Love Miss Tilli Bean 1946*

2 She knew that no human being is immune to sorrow and she wanted me to be tough, the way a green branch is tough, and to be independent, so that if anything happened to her I would be able to take hold of my own life and make a go of it.
Ch. 6, Ibid.

3 The very fact that we make such a to-do over golden weddings indicates our amazement at human endurance. The celebration is more in the nature of a reward for stamina. . . .
Ch. 15, *Free Admission 1948*

4 When he said we were trying to make a fool of him, I could only murmur that the Creator had beat us to it.
"Mrs. Crankhurst," *Violets and Vinegar*, Jilly Cooper and Tom Hartman, eds. *1980*

2012. Agnes de Mille (1905–1993)

1 I learned three important things in college—to use a library, to memorize quickly and visually, to drop asleep at any time given a horizontal surface and fifteen minutes. What I could not learn was to think creatively on schedule.
Dance to the Piper 1952

2 No trumpets sound when the important decisions of our life are made. Destiny is made known silently.

Ibid.

3 Dancing is not taught as an art in any university. There it is still in the gymnasium.

Ibid.

4 A good education is usually harmful to a dancer. A good calf is better than a good head.
News item *1 February 1954*

5 The truest expression of a people is in its dances and its music. Bodies never lie.
"Do I Hear a Waltz?," *The New York Times Magazine 11 May 1975*

2013. Viña Delmar (1905–1990)

1 "We have strict orders on how to teach. There are certain methods that must be employed. Your way is easier to learn, but it hasn't been approved by the school board for use in the classroom."
The Becker Scandal 1968

2 . . . her plumpness was so neat and firm that she was rather like one of the better apples that are purchased for fruit-bowl display.

Ibid.

2014. Dorothy Fields (1905–1974)

1 Gee, I'd like to give you something swell, baby,
Diamond bracelets Woolworth's doesn't sell, baby.
Till that lucky day, you know darn well, baby,
That I can't give you anything but love.
"I Can't Give You Anything But Love," with Jimmy McHugh *ca. 1920*

2 Now I know why mother
Taught me to be true
She knew I'd meet someone
Exactly like you.
"Exactly Like You," *The International Revue*, with Jimmy McHugh *1930*

3 Grab your hat and grab your coat,
Leave your worries on the doorstep.
Just direct your feet
To the sunny side of the street.
"The Sunny Side of the Street," Ibid.

4 I'm in the mood for love
simply because you're near me;
Funny, but when you're near me
I'm in the mood for love.
"I'm in the Mood for Love" with Jimmy McHugh *1935*

5 Lovely, never never change
Keep that breathless charm
Won't you please arrange it
'Cause I love you, just the way you look tonight.
"The Way You Look Tonight," Swing Time (film) *1936*

6 To think the highest-brow,
Which I must say is he,

Should pick the lowest-brow,
Which there's no doubt is me . . .

"If My Friends Could See Me Now," Act I, Sc. 6, *Sweet Charity* 1966

7   No matter where I run,
I meet myself there.

"Where Am I Going?" Act II, Sc. 6, Ibid.

2015. Frances Frost (1905–1959)

1   I am the keeper of wall and sill,
I kneel on the hearth to a tempered fire:
(Flesh that was wild can learn to be still,
But what of a heart that was born to briar?)

"Capture," St. 4, Hemlock Wall 1929

2   But the trees that lost their apples
In the early windy year-
Hard-cheeked little apples,
Round and green and clear,-
They have nothing more to lose
And nothing more to fear.

"Loss," St. 2, Ibid.

3   Grow, white boy! Drink deep of living,
Deeper yet of mirth,
For there is nothing better than laughter
Anywhere on earth!

"White Boy," St. 3, Ibid.

2016. Enchi Fumiko (1905–?)

1   Chigako had no interest in pornographic pictures and books; even in the first days of their marriage, when Keisaku had shown her his private store of pictures she had, far from enjoying them, ended by shutting the book unread, thus affording her husband simultaneously both disappointment and a sense of relief at his wife's lack of the lecherous instinct.

"Enchantress," John Bestor, tr. *n.d.*

2   . . . their daughter was gone, Kiriko had been invaluable—a solid, flesh-and-blood barrier between them. Now she had vanished, and the gap she had left must, whatever happened, be filled with something else.

Ibid.

3   Spectacles, false teeth eventually, false locks made of other people's hair—all kinds of things foreign to her own flesh which she donned like armor in her hungry craving to appear young, to be beautiful. What kind of creature was she?

Ibid.

2017. Greta Garbo (1905–1990)

1   There are many things in your heart you can never tell to another person. They are you, your private joys and sorrows, and you can never tell them. You cheapen yourself, the inside of yourself, when you tell them.

Quoted in *The Story of Greta Garbo* by Bruce Biery 1928

2   I never said, "I want to be alone." I only said, "I want to be *left* alone." There is all the difference

Quoted in *Garbo* by John Bainbridge 1955

3   Why can't we avoid being followed and examined? It is cruel to bother people who want to be left in peace. This kills beauty for me.

Newspaper Interview (Naples, 1938), Ibid.

2018. Peggy Gilbert (1905–2007)

1   Women are never hired because of their ability as musicians, but as an attraction for the very reason that they are women, and men like to look at attractive women. Consequently, the manager is continually reminding the girls not to take the music so seriously, but to relax, to smile. How can you smile with a horn in your mouth? How can you relax when a girdle is throttling you and the left brassiere strap holds your arm in a vise? If we quaver a little on the high notes, it's because we are asked to do a Houdini . . . On the other hand, men's orchestras are usually hired because of their ability as musicians. Their good looks, their presentability other than neatness, will rarely enter the question.

"Peggy Gilbert," *1930s Jazz Excerpts April 1938*

2   The first time I picked up a sax, I said, 'This is it!.' I loved the feel of it—free and loose.

Quoted in *The Los Angeles Times 2006*

2019. Emily "Mickey" Hahn (1905–1997)

1   And never have a love affair with a man whose friendship you value. Because there's nothing like sex to make people hate and misunderstand one another.

Ch. 9, New York Sunday World (17 April 1930), *Nobody Said Not to Go, The Life, Loves, and Adventures of Emily Hahn* by Ken Cuthbertson 1998

2   Arthur Mann is going with me to a notary public to swear out an affidavit that I have morals. The [Belgian] consul demands this. Arthur says he's used to lying; he's a newspaper man and won't go to Heaven anyway.

Ch. 9, Letter to Hannah H— (mother; 23 December 1930), Ibid.

3   The mind of a traveler has only one spotlight, and it is always trained on the present scene.

Ch. 14, Times and Places (p. 212), 1970, Ibid.

4   I have deliberately chosen the uncertain path whenever I had a chance.

Ch. 16, Interview, *Saturday Review of Literature* (26 March 1955), p. 13, Ibid.

5   [The Japanese] know that it is the quickest, surest way to humiliate a community. I think that they rape almost as a religious duty, a sacrifice to the God of Victory, a symbol of their triumphant power.

Ch. 23, China to Me (pp. 287–288), 1944, Ibid.

6   Woman after woman comes into this house [in England] . . . and tells me women oughtn't to have equal pay because their place is in the home, and a man has commitments and women aren't really any good at their jobs in any case, and if you give equal pay it will only do a lot of them out of jobs because people will only hire men. Every . . . female says the same things in the same order. Every now and then a man says it as well, but it is usually some flat-faced English nag.

Ch. 31, Letter to Muriel Hanson (29 March 1954), Ibid.

2020. Clara Mcbride Hale (1905–1992)

1   I'm not an American hero. I'm a person that loves children.*

I Dream a World by Brian Lanker 1989

*Response when President Ronald Reagan cited her as "an American hero."

2021. Lillian Hellman (1905–1984)

1 MRS. MORTAR. But the cinema is a shallow art. It has no—no—no fourth dimension.

Act I, *The Children's Hour 1934*

2 EASTER. When you got nothin' to do, we can't do it for you.

Act. II, Sc. 1, *Days to Come 1936*

3 WILKIE. You're a noble lady and I am frightened of noble ladies. They usually land the men they know in cemeteries.

Sc. 3, Ibid.

4 ANDREW. Polite and blind, we lived.

Act III, Ibid.

5 Cynicism is an unpleasant way of saying the truth.

Act I, *The Little Foxes 1939*

6 God forgives those who invent what they need.

Ibid.

7 Fashions in sin change.

Watch on the Rhine 1941

8 MARCUS. Carry in your own valise, son. It is not seemly for a man to load his goods on other men, black or white.

Act I, *Another Part of the Forest 1946*

9 LAVINIA. I'm not going to have any Bibles in my school. That surprise you all. It's the only book in the world but it's just for grown people, after you know it don't mean what it says.

Act III, Ibid.

10 I am not willing, now or in the future, to bring bad trouble to people who, in my past association with them, were completely innocent of any talk or any action that was disloyal or subversive. . . . I cannot and will not cut my conscience to fit this year's fashions, even though I long ago came to the conclusion that I was not a political person and could have no comfortable place in any political group.

Letter to the House Committee on Un-American Activities, *The Nation 31 May 1952*

11 ALBERTINE. You do too much. Go and do nothing for a while. Nothing.

Act II, *Toys in the Attic 1959*

12 CARRIE. I read in a French book that there was nothing so abandoned as a respectable young girl.

Ibid.

13 CARRIE. There are lives that are shut and should stay shut. . . .

Act III, Ibid.

14 ANNA. Well, people change and forget to tell each other. Too bad—causes so many mistakes.

Ibid.

15 I didn't know what she was saying when she moved her lips in a Baptist church or a Catholic cathedral or, less often, in a synagogue, but it was obvious that God could be found anywhere. . . .

An Unfinished Woman 1969

16 Mamma seemed to do only what my father wanted, and yet we lived the way my mother wanted us to live.

Ibid.

17 It is a mark of many famous people that they cannot part with their brightest hour.

"Theatre," *Pentimento 1973*

2022. Ethel Jacobson (1905?–)

1 Behind every man who achieves success
Stands a mother, a wife, and the IRS.

Quoted in *Reader's Digest April 1973*

2 Insects are creatures with three pairs of legs,
Some swim, some fly; they lay millions of eggs. . . .

When five billion trillion keep munching each day,
It's a wonder the world isn't nibbled away!

"The Insects' World" *n.d.*

3 At first just a trickle,
Two drops splash and tickle.
And then there's a spurt,
A sudden big squirt,
Right smack in my eye:
The fountain must think
That I need a face-wash
More than a drink!

"Drinking Fountain" *n.d.*

2023. Adelaide Johnson (1905–1960)

1 The neurotic needs of the parent . . . are vicariously gratified by the behavior of the child.

"The Genesis of Antisocial Acting Out in Children and Adults," *Psychoanalytic Quarterly*, Vol. 21 *1952*

2 Firmness bespeaks a parent who has learned . . . how all of his major goals may be reached in some creative course of action. . . .

Ibid.

2024. Helen Joseph (1905–1992)

1 I . . . don't doubt for a moment that the revolution will result in a nonracial society. I have just come from being a patient in Groote Schuur Hospital where they now have integrated wards. For the first time in my life, I have seen it working. The patients were mixed, the staff was mixed, and the medical officers were mixed; it was totally integrated. It was beautiful. White and black together. And it works. To me that is terribly exciting.

Ch. 15, *Lives of Courage* by Diana E. H. Russell *1989*

2025. Maggie Kuhn (1905–1995)

1 Arbitrary retirement at a fixed age ought to be negotiated and decided according to the wishes of the people involved. Mandatory retirement ought to be illegal.

Quoted in "Profile of a Gray Panther" by Carol Offen, *Retirement Living December 1972*

2 Ageism is any discrimination against people on the basis of chronological age—whether old or young. It's responsible for an enormous neglect of social resources.

Ibid.

3 Men and women approaching retirement age should be recycled for public service work, and their companies should foot the bill. We can no longer afford to scrap-pile people.

"Gray Panthers Versus Ageism," *Ms.* (New York) *July 1973*

4 Power should not be concentrated in the hands of so few, and powerlessness in the hands of so many.

Quoted in "How to Forget Age Bias," Ibid.

5 I think of age as a great universalizing force. It's the only thing we all have in common. It doesn't begin when you collect your social security benefits. Aging begins with the moment of birth, and it ends only when life itself has ended. Life is a continuum; only, we—in our stupidity and blindness—have chopped it up into little pieces and kept all those little pieces separate.

Quoted in "Liberating Aging" by Ken Dychtwald, *New Age February 1979*

6 Old age is not a disease—it is strength and survivorship, triumph over all kinds of vicissitudes and disappointments, trials and illnesses.

Ibid.

7 I'm having a glorious old age. One of my greatest delights is that I have outlived most of my opposition.

Speech, Vermont state legislature *1991*

8 Learning and sex until *rigor mortis*.

Motto *n.d.*

2026. Erika Mann (1905–1969)

1 "I want the child to become a human being, a good and decent man who knows the difference between lies and truth, aware of liberty and dignity and true reason, not the opportunistic reason 'dictated by policy' which turns black white if it's useful at the moment. I want the boy to become a decent human being—a man and not a Nazi!"

Prologue, *School for Barbarians 1938*

2 But the Hitler Youth organization, that third circle around the child, is the most expansive, most important, and by far the most comprehensive of his influences.

"The State Youth," Ibid.

3 "There's absolutely no discipline in the democracies. The other day our propaganda minister said that the democracies strike him as being a collection of comical old fogies. But I've got to say it myself; they're rotten and corrupt to the marrow."

"The City," *The Lights Go Down 1940*

4 Music, theater, the beauty of men and things, a fine day, a child, an attractive animal—from all these he [Thomas Mann]* drew much pleasure, provided he was getting on with his work. Without work—that is, without active hope—he would not have known how to live.

Quoted in *The Last Year of Thomas Mann,* a Revealing Memoir by His Daughter 1958
*German writer (1875–1955) who won the Nobel Prize (1929).

2027. Phyllis McGinley (1905–1978)

1 Oh, shun, lad, the life of an author.
It's nothing but worry and waste.
Avoid that utensil,
The laboring pencil,
And pick up the scissors and paste.

"A Ballad of Anthologies," *A Ballad of Anthologies 1941*

2 Gossip isn't scandal and it's not merely malicious. It's chatter about the human race by lovers of the same. Gossip is the tool of the poet, the shop-talk of the scientist, and the consolation

of the housewife, wit, tycoon and intellectual. It begins in the nursery and ends when speech is past.

"A New Year and No Resolutions," *Woman's Home Companion January 1957*

3 Sometimes I have a notion that what might improve the situation is to have women take over the occupations of government and trade and to give men their freedom. Let them do what they are best at. While we scrawl interoffice memos and direct national or extranational affairs, men could spend all their time inventing wheels, peering at stars, composing poems, carving statues, exploring continents—discovering, reforming, or crying out in a sacramental wilderness. Efficiency would probably increase, and no one would have to worry so much about the Gaza Strip or an election.

The Province of the Heart 1959

4 It's this no-nonsense side of women that is pleasant to deal with. They are the real sportsmen. They don't have to be constantly building up frail egos by large public performances like over-tipping the hat-check girl, speaking fluent French to the Hungarian waiter, and sending back the wine to be recooled.

Ibid.

5 Sin . . . has been made not only ugly but passé. People are no longer sinful, they are only immature or under privileged or frightened or, more particularly, sick.

"In Defense of Sin," Ibid.

6 The thing to remember about fathers is, they're men.
A girl has to keep it in mind.

"Girl's-Eye View of Relatives: First Lesson," *Times Three: 1932–1960 1960*

7 Oh, high is the price of parenthood,
And daughters may cost you double.
You dare not forget, as you thought you could,
That youth is a plague and a trouble.

"Homework for Anabelle," Ibid.

8 The knowingness of little girls
Is hidden underneath their curls.

"What Every Woman Knows," Ibid.

9 Time is the thief you cannot banish.

"Ballade of Lost Objects," St. 4, Ibid.

10 Oh! *do* you remember Paper Books
When paper books were thrilling,
When something to read
Was seldom Gide
Or Proust or Peacock
Or Margaret Mead
And seldom Lionel Trilling?

"Dirge for an Era," St. 4, Ibid.

11 I'm a middle-bracket person with a middle-bracket spouse
And we live together gaily in a middle-bracket house.
We've a fair-to-middlin' family; we take the middle view;
So we're manna sent from heaven to internal revenue.

"The Chosen People," St. 1, Ibid.

12 . . . "I am he
Who champions total liberty—
Intolerance being, ma'am, a state
No tolerant man can tolerate."

"The Angry Man," St. 2, Ibid.

13 We might as well give up the fiction
That we can argue any view.
For what in me is pure Conviction
Is simple Prejudice to you.
"Note to My Neighbor," Ibid.

14 History must always be taken with a grain of salt. It is, after all, not a science but an art. . . .
"Aspects of Sanctity," Saint-Watching 1969

15 We live in the century of the Appeal. . . . One applauds the industry of professional philanthropy. But it has its dangers. After a while the private heart begins to harden. We fling letters into the wastebasket, are abrupt to telephone solicitations. Charity withers in the incessant gale.
Ibid.

16 Benevolent, stormy, patient, or out of sorts.
God knows which God is the God God recognizes.
"The Day After Sunday" n.d.

2028. Dorothy Norman (1905–1997)

1 To adopt the posture of the hero is the most unheroic of all acts.
Ch. 16, The Hero: Myth/Image/Symbol 1969

2 Is it not the artist who—like our dreams—dissolves the pretenses that hide us from ourselves, disclosing both our self-serving fantasies and our unsuspected potentialities?
Ch. 18, Ibid.

3 Desire for gain and fear of loss burn like fire.
Ch. 20, Ibid.

4 Without Satan, no Christ.
Ch. 24, Ibid.

2029. Gretta Brooker Palmer (1905–1935)

1 Happiness is a by-product of an effort to make someone else happy.
Permanent Marriage n.d.

2030. Vera Fedorovna Panova (1905–1973)

1 SHEMETOVA. Sometimes, when the accustomed pattern of things is suddenly broken . . . like today's emergency landing . . . as if you were going along and suddenly: Stop! and you look up . . . and it's terrifying—why has this happened to me? But it's only for a moment; no more. You, too, know how it is: you fall asleep, see something terrible, and you make yourself wake up.
Act III, It's Been Ages! (Skolko let, skolko zhit!) 1966

2031. Ivy Baker Priest (1905–1975)

1 We women ought to put first things first. Why should we mind if men have their faces on the money, as long as we get our hands on it?
Ch. 1, Green Grows Ivy 1958

2 We seldom stop to think how many peoples' lives are entwined with our own. It is a form of selfishness to imagine that every individual can operate on his own or can pull out of the general stream and not be missed.
Ch. 18, Ibid.

3 My father had always said that there are four things a child needs—plenty of love, nourishing food, regular sleep, and lots of soap and water—and after those, what he needs most is some intelligent neglect.
Ch. 11, Ibid.

2032. Ayn Rand (1905–1982)

1 "Civilization is the progress toward a society of privacy. The savage's whole existence is public, ruled by the laws of his tribe. Civilization is the process of setting man free from men."
The Fountainhead 1943

2 Great men can't be ruled.
Ibid.

3 If you learn how to rule one single man's soul, you can get the rest of mankind.
Ibid.

4 Kill reverence and you've killed the hero in man.
Ibid.

5 "Throughout the centuries there were men who took first steps down new roads armed with nothing but their own vision. Their goals differed, but they all had this in common: that the step was first, the road new, the vision unborrowed, and the response they received—hatred. The great creators—the thinkers, the artists, the scientists, the inventors—stood alone against the men of their time."
Ibid.

6 "We are one in all and all in one.
There are no men but only the great WE.
One, indivisible and forever."
Ch. 1, Anthem 1946

7 My happiness is not the means to any end. It is the end. It is its own goal. It is its own purpose. Neither am I the means to any end others may wish to accomplish. I am not a tool for their use. I am not a servant of their needs. I am not a bandage for their wounds. I am not a sacrifice on their altars.
Ch. 9, Ibid.

8 If I were to speak your kind of language, I would say that man's only moral commandment is: Thou shalt think. But a 'moral commandment' is a contradiction in terms. The moral is the chosen, not the forced; the understood, not the obeyed. The moral is the rational, and reason accepts no commandments.
Atlas Shrugged 1957

9 "Disunity, that's the trouble. It's my absolute opinion that in our complex industrial society, no business enterprise can succeed without sharing the burden of the problems of other enterprises."
Pt. I, Ch. 3, Ibid.

10 "The entire history of science is a progression of exploded fallacies, not of achievements."
Pt. II, Ch. 1, Ibid.

11 "To demand 'sense' is the hallmark of nonsense. Nature does not make sense. Nothing makes sense."
Ibid.

12 "People don't look for *kinds* of work anymore, ma'am," he answered impassively. "They just look for work."
Ch. 10, Ibid.

13 The modern mystics of muscle who offer you the fraudulent alternative of "human rights" versus "property rights," as if one could exist without the other, are making a last, grotesque attempt to revive the doctrine of soul versus body. Only a ghost can exist without material property; only a slave can work with no right to the product of his effort.

Pt. III, Ch. 7, Ibid.

14 Man's unique reward, however, is that while animals survive by adjusting themselves to their background, man survives by adjusting his background to himself.

For the New Intellectual 1961

15 Professional intellectuals are the voice of a culture and are, therefore, its leaders, its integrators and its bodyguards.

Ibid.

2033. Mary Renault (1905–1983)

1 Miss Searle had always considered boredom an intellectual defeat.

Ch. 1, *North Face* 1948

2 Which of youth's pleasures can compare with the making ready for one's first big war?

Bk. II, Ch. 3, *The King Must Die* 1958

3 I thought of my life, the good and evil days; of the gods, and fate; how much of a man's life and of his soul they make for him, how much he makes for himself. . . . Fate and will, will and fate, like earth and sky bringing forth the grain together; and which the bread tastes of, no man knows.

"Skyros," *The Bull from the Sea* 1962

4 Men have more fun.

Letter (p. 176), Quoted in *Mary Renault: A Biography* by David Sweetman 1993

5 . . .Shakespeare and Beethoven & Co do seem to have, as men, some extra reserve of neural strength, some capacity for sustained intensity and inner drive, which women do not possess. I will believe otherwise when given evidence.

Ibid.

2034. Anna F. Trevisan (1905–?)

1 ELZA. Some things are very important and some are very unimportant. To know the difference is what we are given life to find out. . . .

Easter Eve 1946

2 ELZA. The mother! She is what keeps the family intact. . . . It is proved. A fact. Time and time again. The father, no matter how good . . . a father cannot keep the family intact.

Ibid.

3 MRS. BRENTA. When they're grown up, you might just as well not have them. They come home and they go out. This is like a railroad station and a restaurant.

Ibid.

4 ANNIE. How was they to know the ould war would take them so soon and last so long?

In the Valley of the Shadow 1946

5 MRS. GRISWOLD. The world is exhausted.

Ibid.

2035. Margaret Webster (1905–1972)

1 When an actor says a line, he makes his point and his thought moves on to the next; but a singer has to repeat the same words over a dozen times, the emotional shading varying with the music, the thought progressing only in terms of sound.

Don't Put Your Daughter On the Stage 1972

2036. Hannah Arendt (1906–1975)

1 Totalitarianism is never content to rule by external means, namely, through the state and a machinery of violence; thanks to its peculiar ideology and the role assigned to it in this apparatus of coercion, totalitarianism has discovered a means of dominating and terrorizing human beings from within.

Ch. 10, Sct. 1, *The Origins of Totalitarianism* 1951

2 The concentration camps, by making death itself anonymous (making it impossible to find out whether a prisoner is dead or alive), robbed death of its meaning as the end of a fulfilled life. In a sense they took away the individual's own death, proving that henceforth nothing belonged to him and he belonged to no one. His death merely set a seal on the fact that he had never existed.

Pt. 3, Ch. 12, Sct. 3, Ibid.

3 Thought . . . is still possible, and no doubt actual, wherever men live under the conditions of political freedom. Unfortunately . . . no other human capacity is so vulnerable, and it is in fact far easier to act under conditions of tyranny than it is to think.

The Human Condition 1958

4 Wherever the relevance of speech is at stake, matters become political by definition, for speech is what makes man a political being.

Prologue, Ibid.

5 The new always happens against the overwhelming odds of statistical laws and their probability, which for all practical, everyday purposes amounts to certainty; the new therefore always appears in the guise of a miracle.

Pt. 5, Ch. 24, Ibid.

6 Poets . . . are the only people to whom love is not only a crucial, but an indispensable experience, which entitles them to mistake it for a universal one.

Ch. 33, (footnote), Ibid.

7 Love, by its very nature, is unworldly, and it is for this reason rather than its rarity that it is not only apolitical but antipolitical, perhaps the most powerful of all antipolitical human forces.

Pt. 5, Ch. 33, Ibid.

8 Have we now come to the point where it is the children who are being asked to change or improve the world?

"Reflections on Little Rock" 1959

9 The banality of evil.

Eichmann in Jerusalem 1963

10 The trouble with Eichmann* was precisely that so many were like him, and that the many were neither perverted nor sadistic, that they were, and still are, terribly and terrifyingly normal. . . . This new type of criminal, who is in actual fact *homo generis humani,* commits his crimes under circumstances

that make it well-nigh impossible for him to know or to feel that he is doing wrong.

Epilogue, Ibid.

*Adolf E——, German Nazi official who as head of the Gestapo's Jewish section from 1939 to 1945 was responsible for the slaughter of millions of Jews during World War II, (1906–1962).

11 Wars and revolutions . . . have outlived all their ideological justifications. . . . No cause is left but the most ancient of all, the one, in fact, that from the beginning of our history has determined the very existence of politics, the cause of freedom versus tyranny.

Introduction, *On Revolution* 1963

12 . . . What makes it so plausible to assume that hypocrisy is the vice of vices is that integrity can indeed exist under the cover of all other vices except this one. Only crime and the criminal, it is true, confront us with the perplexity of radical evil; but only the hypocrite is really rotten to the core.

Ch. 2, Ibid.

13 Economic growth may one day turn out to be a curse rather than a good, and under no conditions can it either lead into freedom or constitute a proof for its existence.

Ch. 6, Ibid.

14 The chief reason warfare is still with us is neither a secret death-wish of the human species, nor an irrepressible instinct of aggression, nor, finally and more plausibly, the serious economic and social dangers inherent in disarmament, but the simple fact that no substitute for this final arbiter in international affairs has yet appeared on the political scene.

"On Violence," *Crises of the Republic* (rev. ed.) 1972

15 The most radical revolutionary will become a conservative the day after the revolution.

"Civil Disobedience," Ibid.

16 There is all the difference in the world between the criminal's avoiding the public eye and the civil disobedient's taking the law into his own hands in open defiance. This distinction between an open violation of the law, performed in public, and a clandestine one is so glaringly obvious that it can be neglected only by prejudice or ill will.

Ibid.

17 The defiance of established authority, religious and secular, social and political, as a world-wide phenomenon may well one day be accounted the outstanding event of the last decade.

Ibid.

18 What really distinguishes this generation in all countries from earlier generations . . . is its determination to act, its joy in action, the assurance of being able to change things by one's own efforts.

"Thoughts on Politics and Revolution," Ibid.

19 There are no dangerous thoughts; thinking itself is dangerous.

The Life of the Mind, Vol. 1 1978

20 When we were young enough to have children, we had no money. And when we had money, we were too old.

Quoted in *Hannah Arendt: For Love of the World* by Elisabeth Young-Burial 1981

2037. Mary Astor (1906–1987)

1 Eventually, every actor on the Metro lot called me Mom. I was in my late thirties, and it played havoc with my image of myself.

A Life on Film 1969

2 One day in the makeup room Perc Westmore* and I played around with mixing the Stein's Pink with a just a touch of the brown eyeshadow. We melted it together, and stirred it up and put it on, and there was an ivory cast to the color that had never been used. On the screen it was miraculous. Bones began to show, skin looked natural and the tiny muscles of facial expression that had blanked out before were more evident. It was the beginning of panchromatic makeup. I wish I had held a patent on it!

Ibid.

*Famed Eng./Am. make-up artist (1904–1970).

2038. Dorothy Gillam Baker (1906–1990)

1 In the past no dominant political, economic, religious or military power has voluntarily relinquished its position.

Transformation or Catastrophe? 1978

2 I am convinced that the promise of harmonious resolution as a united people of the world, capable of living on a higher level of consciousness . . . is not a utopian vision, but the new revolutionary form that lies within our grasp.

Ibid.

2039. Josephine Baker (1906–1975)

1 Surely the day will come when color means nothing more than skin tone, when religion is seen uniquely as a way to speak one's soul; when birth places have the weight of a throw of the dice and all men are born free, when understanding breeds love and brotherhood.

Ch. 16, *Josephine* 1977

2 I like Frenchmen very much, because even when they insult you they do it so nicely.

Remark *n.d.*

2040. Rita Boumi Pappa (1906–1984)

1 I did not let them nail my soul as they do butterflies.

"Roxane M." *1975*

2 My fine days? Oh, a few fleeting birds,
I had no other treasure than my tears.
That is why none of those who tortured me
have seen me weep.

Ibid.

2041. Margaret Bourke-White (1906–1971)

1 Usually I object when someone makes overmuch of men's work and women's work, for I think it is the excellence of the results which counts.

Portrait of Myself 1963

2 What makes Soviet Russia the new land of the machine are the new social relationships of the men and women around the machine. The new man . . . and with him, on equal footing, the new woman—operating drill presses, studying medicine and engineering—are integral parts of a people working collectively toward a common goal.

Quoted in *The Woman's Eye* by Anne Tucker* 1973

*See 3620.

2042. Louise Brooks (1906–1985)

1 I have a gift for enraging people, but if I ever bore you it will be with a knife.

Lulu in Hollywood 1982

2 Anyone who has achieved excellence in any form knows that it comes as a result of ceaseless concentration.

"The Other Face of W. C. Fields,"* Ibid.

*(1880–1946) American entertainer.

3 For me, nice, soft, easy men were never enough—there had to be an element of domination.

Quoted in "The Girl in the Black Helmet" by Kenneth Tynan,* *The New Yorker* 1979

*(1927–1980) British theater critic, writer.

2043. Jacqueline Cochran (1906–1980)

1 I have found adventure in flying, in world travel, in business, and even close at hand . . . Adventure is a state of mind—and spirit. It comes with faith, for with complete faith there is no fear of what faces you in life or death.

Article, *Guideposts* magazine 1954

2 The objective in every one of my flights was to go faster or farther through the atmosphere or higher into it than anyone else and to bring back some new information about plane, engine, fuel, instruments, air, or pilot that would be helpful in the conquest of the atmosphere.

Quoted in *Women Aviators* by Lisa Yount 1995

3 I'd have given my right eye to be an astronaut.

Ibid.

4 To live without risk for me would be tantamount to death.

Ibid.

2044. Catherine Cookson (1906–1998)

1 "Catholic, be damned! They tell 'em to have bairns, but do they bloody well keep them?"

Ch. 1, *The Fifteen Streets* 1952

2 God knew there was no happiness came out of a mixed marriage. With a Church of England one it would be bad enough, but with a Spiritualist! . . . And yet . . . what was the obstacle of religion compared with the obstacle of class?

Ch. 7, Ibid.

3 "It's no good saying one thing and thinking another."

Ch. 8, Ibid.

2045. Gertrude Ederle (1906–2003)

1 To me, the sea is like a person—like a child that I've known a long time. It sounds crazy, I know, but when I swim in the sea I talk to it. I never feel alone when I'm out there.

New York Post 5 September 1956

2 People said women couldn't swim the Channel but I proved they could.

Interview (2001), *CBS News* 1 December 2003

2046. Anna Roosevelt Halsted (1906–1975)

1 There are so many indignities to being sick and helpless. . . .

Letter to David Gray (1 November 1962), Quoted in *Eleanor:* *The Years Alone* by Joseph P. Lash 1972

*Eleanor Roosevelt; see 1618.

2047. Mrs. Robert Henrey (1906–2004)

1 One must leave one's parents early, especially one's mother. Mothers are never any good for their daughters. They forget they were just as ugly and silly and scraggy when they were little girls.

Ch. 3, *Paloma* 1951

2048. Grace Murray Hopper (1906–1992)

1 A ship in a harbor is safe, but that is not what a ship is built for.

"Grace Hopper: The Youthful Teacher of Us All" by Henry S. Tropp, *Abacus* 2 (1), p. 18 *Fall 1984*

2 We're just getting started. We're just beginning to meet what will be the future—we've got the model T.

60 Minutes, CBS-TV 24 August 1986

3 It's just as well to be told you're too old at 40. Then you're over it.*

Quoted by Sara C. Medina in *Time* (New York) 25 August 1986

*Reference to regular Navy's rejection of her in 1946.

2049–2050. Hsieh Ping-ying (1906–2000)

1 Ah! Mother really loved me, but why did she beat me so hard? Is not a child a person too? Can she never have her own way? Must she obey every word a grown-up says? These questions went round and round in my head.

Girl Rebel, Adet and Anor Lin, trs. 1940

2 The spring came, warm and intoxicating, and planted the seeds of love in the hearts of many young boys and girls. But it also sprayed the dew of blood on the young bodies of boy and girl soldiers. The call to "fight on" had waked young people from their dreams. They came out of the pink palace of romance, going to the social front which was covered in corpses and reeked with the smell of blood. They gave up their ideas of love, and substituted for it the love of the masses suffering under suppression, the love of the poor, the love of their comrades.

Ibid.

2051. Dilys Laing (1906–1960)

1 Vague, submarine, my giant twin
swims under me, a girl of shade
who mimics me.

"Ego," *Collected Poems* 1967

2 The end will be, perhaps, the end of me,
which will, I humbly guess, be his beginning.

"Private Entry in the Diary of a Female Parent," Ibid.

3 The women took a train
away away from herself.

"The Double Goer," St. 1, Ibid.

4 . . . memory is a storm I can't repel.

"Venus Petrified," St. 3, Ibid.

5 Women receive
the insults of men
with tolerance,
having been bitten
in the nipple
by their toothless gums.

"Veterans," Ibid.

6 To be a woman and a writer
is double mischief, for
the world will slight her
who slights "the servile house," and who would rather
make odes than beds.
"Sonnet to a Sister in Error," St. 2, Ibid.

2052. Estée Lauder (1906–2004)

1 I would give the woman a sample of whatever she did not buy as a gift. It might be a few teaspoonfuls of powder in a wax envelope. I just knew, even though I had not yet named the technique, that a gift with a purchase was very appealing.
Estée: A Success Story 1985

2 You may have great inner resources, but they don't show up as confidence when you don't feel pretty. People are more apt to believe you and like you when you know you look fine. And when the world approves, self-respect is just a little easier . . .
Ibid.

2053. Anne Morrow Lindbergh (1906–2001)

1 One can never pay in gratitude; one can only pay "in kind" somewhere else in life.
Ch. 19, North to the Orient 1935

2 . . . the fundamental magic of flying, a miracle that has nothing to do with any of its practical purposes—purposes of speed, accessibility, and convenience—and will not change as they change.
Ch. 23, Ibid.

3 Lost time was like a run in a stocking. It always got worse.
Ch. 3, The Steep Ascent 1944

4 Perhaps middle-age is, or should be, a period of shedding shells; the shell of ambition, the shell of material accumulations and possessions, the shell of the ego.
Gift from the Sea 1955

5 One cannot collect all the beautiful shells on the beach.
Ibid.

6 It isn't for the moment you are struck that you need courage, but for the long uphill climb back to sanity and faith and security.
Hours of Gold, Hours of Lead 1973

7 Love is a force. . . . It is not a result; it is a cause. It is not a product; it produces. It is a power, like money, or steam or electricity. It is valueless unless you can give something else by means of it.
Locked Rooms and Open Doors 1974

8 People talk about love as though it were something you could give, like an armful of flowers.
Ibid.

2054. Maria Goeppert Mayer (1906–1972)

1 No one has ever seen, nor probably ever will see, an atom, but that does not deter the physicist from trying to draw a plan of it, with the aid of such clues to its structure as he has.
"The Structure of the Nucleus," Scientific American March 1951

2 Of course my father always said I should have been a boy. He said, Don't grow up to be a woman, and what he meant by that was, a housewife . . . without any interests.
Quoted in "Maria Goeppert-Mayer," *A Life of One's Own* by Joan Dash *1973*

3 Mathematics began to seem too much like puzzle solving. Physics is puzzle solving, too, but of puzzles created by nature, not by the mind of man.
Ibid.

2055. Kathryn Murray (1906–1999)

1 Don't try to teach a whole course in one lesson.
Training Manual, The Arthur Murray Dance Studios *1950–60*

2 Put a little fun into your life. Try dancing.
Motto, *The Arthur Murray Party* (radio and TV syndicated show) *1950–60*

2056. Viola Spolin (1906–1994)

1 Through spontaneity we are re-formed into ourselves. It creates an explosion that for the moment frees us from handed-down frames of reference, memory choked with old facts and information and undigested theories and techniques of other people's findings. Spontaneity is the moment of personal freedom when we are faced with reality, and see it, explore it and act accordingly. In this reality the bits and pieces of ourselves function as an organic whole. It is the time of discovery, of experiencing, of creative expression.
Ch. 1, Improvisation for the Theater 1963

2 We learn through experience and experiencing, and no one teaches anyone anything.
Ibid.

3 In a culture where approval/disapproval has become the predominant regulator of effort and position, and often the substitute for love, our personal freedoms are dissipated.
Ibid.

4 The audience is the most revered member of the theater. Without an audience there is no theater. . . . They are our guests, our evaluators, and the last spoke in the wheel which can then begin to roll. They make the performance meaningful.
Ibid.

5 It is the avant-garde teachers who . . . have come to realize that body release, not body control, is what is needed for natural grace to emerge, as opposed to artificial movement.
Ch. 5, Ibid.

6 One must be chary of words because they turn into cages.
Quoted in "Spolin Game Plan for Improvisational Theater" by Barry Hyams, *The Los Angeles Times 26 May 1974*

7 First teach a person to develop to the point of his limitations and then—pfft!—break the limitation.
Ibid.

2057. Alice Stewart (1906–2002)

1 We have already doubled the level of background radiation today. What is the effect on human genes? That is the really important question: it won't show up for two or three more generations.
Acceptance Speech, Right Livelihood Award (Stockholm), *8 December 1986*

2058. Ting Ling (1906–1985/6)

1 In the Chinese family system, there is superficial quiet and calmness and quarreling is frowned upon, but in reality all is in conflict.

Quoted in *Women in Modern China* by Helen Foster Snow*
1967

*See 2073.

2 I wanted to escape from love but didn't know how.

Ibid.

2059. Dominique Aury (1907–1998)

1 Thus he would possess her as a god possesses his creatures, whom he lays hold of in the guise of a monster or bird, of an invisible spirit or a state of ecstasy. He did not wish to leave her. The more he surrendered her, the more he would hold her dear. The fact that he gave her was to him a proof, and ought to be for her as well, that she belonged to him: one can only give what belongs to you. He gave her only to reclaim her immediately, to reclaim her enriched in his eyes, like some common object which had been used for some divine purpose and has thus been consecrated.

The Story of O (1954), Richard Seaver, tr. *1965*

2 . . . no pleasure, no joy, no figment of her imagination could ever compete with the happiness she felt at the way he used her with such utter freedom, at the notion that he could do anything with her, that there was no limit, no restriction in the manner with which, on her body, he might search for pleasure.

Ibid.

3 As long as I am beaten and ravished on your behalf, I am naught but the thought of you, the desire of you, the obsession of you. That, I believe, is what you wanted. Well, I love you, and that is what I want too.

Ibid.

4 [She was] lying on her side with her feet tucked up under her, a soft black pencil in her right hand . . . the girl was writing the way you speak in the dark when you've held back the words of love too long and they flow out at last. For the first time in her life, she was writing without hesitation, without stopping, rewriting or discarding; she was writing the way one breathes, or dreams . . . she was still writing when the street cleaners came by at the first touch of dawn.

A Girl in Love 1974

5 [Mother] didn't like men. She didn't like women, either. She hated flesh.

Quoted in "I wrote the story of O" by Geraldine Bedell, *The Observer* (London) *25 July 2004*

6 Existence filled him* with wonder. Both the admirable and the horrible aspects of experience, equally so. The atrocious fascinated him. The enchanting enchanted him.

Ibid.

*Her lover, Jean Paulhan (1884–1968), Fr. writer, literary critic, publisher.

2060. Dorothy Baker (1907–1968)

1 In the first place maybe he shouldn't have got himself mixed up with Negroes. It gave him a funny slant on things and he never got over it. It gave him a feeling for undisciplined expression, a hot, direct approach, a full-throated ease that never did

him any good in his later dealings with those of his race, those whom civilization has whipped into shape, those who can contain themselves and play what's written.

Bk. I, Ch. 1, *Young Man with a Horn 1938*

2 Fortune, in its workings, has something in common with the slot-machine. There are those who can bait it forever and never get more than an odd assortment of lemons for their pains; but once in a while there will come a man for whom all the grooves will line up, and when that happens there's no end to the showering down.

Bk. IV, Ch. 2, Ibid.

3 "She wastes herself, she drifts, all she wants to do with her life is lose it somewhere."

Cassandra at the Wedding 1962

4 "Same thing everywhere I'd looked. Large amounts of safety, very few risks. Let nothing endanger the proper marriage, the fashionable career, the nonirritating thesis that says nothing new and nothing true."

Ibid.

2061. Rachel Carson (1907–1964)

1 To stand at the edge of the sea, to sense the ebb and the flow of the tides, to feel the breath of a mist moving over a great salt marsh, to watch the flight of shore birds that have swept up and down the surf lines of the continents for untold thousands of years, . . . is to have knowledge of things that are as nearly eternal as any earthly life can be.

Under the Sea Wind 1941

2 Beginnings are apt to be shadowy and so it is the beginnings of that great mother of life, the sea.

Pt. I, Ch. 1, *The Sea Around Us 1951*

3 For the sea lies all about us. . . . In its mysterious past it encompasses all the dim origins of life and receives in the end, after its many, many transmutations, the dead husks of that same life. For all at last return to the sea—to Oceanus, the ocean river, like the everflowing stream of time, the beginning and the end.

Pt. III, Ch. 14, Ibid.

4 Always the edge of the sea remains an elusive and indefinable boundary. The shore has a dual nature, changing with the swing of the tides, belonging now to the land, now to the sea.

"The Marginal World," *The Edge of the Sea 1955*

5 The discipline of the writer is to learn to be still and listen to what his subject has to tell him.

Speech, American Association of University Women *22 June 1956*

6 In every outthrust headland, in every curving beach, in every grain of sand there is a story of the earth.

"Our Ever-Changing Shore," *Holiday July 1958*

7 As cruel a weapon as the cave man's club, the chemical barrage has been hurled against the fabric of life.

Silent Spring 1962

8 For the first time in the history of the world, every human being is now subjected to contact with dangerous chemicals, from the moment of conception until death.

Ch. 3, Ibid.

9 If we are going to live so intimately with these chemicals—eating and drinking them, taking them into the very marrow of our bones—we had better know something about their nature and their power.

Ibid.

10 Under the philosophy that now seems to guide our destinies, nothing must get in the way of the man with the spray gun.

Ch. 7, Ibid.

11 Over increasingly large areas of the United States, spring now comes unheralded by the return of the birds, and the early mornings are strangely silent where once they were filled with the beauty of bird song.

Ch. 8, Ibid.

12 The "control of nature" is a phrase conceived in arrogance, born of the Neanderthal age of biology and convenience of man.

Ch. 17, Ibid.

13 This is an era of specialists, each of whom sees his own problems and is unaware or intolerant of the larger frame into which it fits. It is also an era dominated by industry, in which the right to make a dollar at whatever cost is seldom challenged.

(p. 228), Quoted in *The House of Life: Rachel Carson at Work* by Paul Brooks 1972

2062. Mary Chase (1907–1981)

1 VETA. It's our dreams that keep us going. That separate us from the beasts. I wouldn't even want to live if I thought it was all just eating and sleeping and taking off my clothes.

Harvey 1943

2 It's quite possible to leave your home for a walk in the early morning air and return a different person—beguiled, enchanted.

Introduction, *Bernardine* 1952

2063. Daphne du Maurier (1907–1989)

1 . . . like most sleepers I knew that I dreamed.

Ch. 1, *Rebecca* (novel) 1938

2 MRS. DANVERS. Why don't you go? Why don't you leave Manderley? He doesn't need you. He's got his memories. He doesn't love you. He wants to be alone again, with her. You've nothing to stay for. You've nothing to live for, really, have you? *(Pointing to the sea, several stories below.)* Look down there. It's easy, isn't it? Why don't you, why don't you. Go on, go on, don't be afraid . . .

Rebecca (screenplay) 1940

3 She could not separate success from peace of mind. The two must go together; her observation pointed to this truth. Failure meant poverty, poverty meant squalor, squalor led, in the final stages, to the smells and stagnation of Bowling Inn Alley.

Pt. I, Ch. 10, *Mary Anne* 1954

4 One second's hesitation. Tears, or laughter? Tears would be an admission of guilt, so laughter was best.

Pt. II, Ch. 7, Ibid.

5 The pair were playing a game that defied intervention, they were matched like reel and rod and there was no unwinding. They

juggled in jargon, dabbled in *double-entendres*, wallowed in each other's witticisms, and all at the expense of the Defendant.

Pt. IV, Ch. 2, Ibid.

6 . . . The little festive atmosphere of strangeness, of excitement, that only a holiday bedroom brings. This is ours for the moment, but no more. While we are in it we bring it life. When we have gone it no longer exists, it fades into anonymity.

Don't Look Now 1970

7 "The trouble is," said Laura, "walking in Venice becomes compulsive once you start. Just over the next bridge, you say, and then the next one beckons."

Ibid.

2064. Parvin Etessami (1907–1940)

1 Beneath this soil which verdure refuse,
Lies Parvin, literary star and muse.
She who, while suffering the bitterness of times,
Composed charming, sugar-laden rhymes.

Untitled, Iraj Bashiri, tr. 1940

2065. Laura Capon Fermi (1907–1977)

1 They were the first men to see matter yield its inner energy, steadily, at their will. My husband was their leader.

Atoms in the Family: My Life with Enrico Fermi 1954

2066. Frida Kahlo (1907–1954)

1 I'd rather sit on the floor in the market of Toluca and sell tortillas, than to have anything to do with these "artistic" bitches of Paris. They sit for hours on the "cafes" warming their precious behinds, and talk without stopping about "culture" "art" "revolution" and so forth thinking themselves the gods of the world. . . . Gee whiz! It was worthwhile to come here only to see why Europe is rottening.

Letter to Nikolas Muray (1939), Quoted in *Frida: A Biography of Frida Kahlo* by Hayden Herrera 1983

2 Why do you study so much? What secret are you looking for? Life will reveal it to you soon. I already know it all, without reading or writing. A little while ago, not much more than a few days ago, I was a child who went about in a world of colors, of hard and tangible forms. Everything was mysterious and something was hidden, guessing what it was was a game for me. If you knew how terrible it is to know suddenly, as if a bolt of lightning elucidated the earth. Now I live in a painful planet, transparent as ice; but it is as if I had learned everything at once in seconds. My friends, my companions became women slowly, I became old in instants and everything today is bland and lucid. I know that nothing lies behind, if there were something I would see it. . . .

Ch. 5, Letter to Alejandro Gómez Arias (1927), Ibid.

3 He [Diego] is irritated by only two things, loss of time from work—and stupidity. He has said many times that he would rather have many intelligent enemies than one stupid friend.

Ch. 7, Ibid.

4 I suffered two grave accidents in my life. One in which a streetcar knocked me down. . . . The other accident is Diego.

Ch. 8, Ibid.

5 Mexico is as always, disorganized and gone to the devil, the only thing that it retains is the immense beauty of the land and

of the Indians. Each day the United States' ugliness steals away a piece of it, it is a sad thing but people must eat and it can't be helped that the big fish eats the little one.
> Ch. 9, Letter to Dr. Eloesser (14 June 1931), Ibid.

6 High society here [in New York City] turns me off and I feel a bit of rage against all these rich guys here, since I have seen thousands of people in the most terrible misery without anything to eat and with no place to sleep, that is what has most impressed me here, it is terrifying to see the rich having parties day and night while thousands and thousands of people are dying of hunger....
> (26 November 1931), Ibid.

7 They thought I was a Surrealist, but I wasn't. I never painted dreams. I painted my own reality.
> Ch. 10, Ibid.

8 I drank, because I wanted to drown my sorrows, but now the damned things have learned to swim, and now decency and good behavior weary me!
> Ch. 13, Letter to Ella Wolfe (1938), Ibid.

9 I want you to know, dear children, that there does not exist in the whole world a single teacher who is capable of teaching art. To do that is truly impossible.
> Quoted by Guillermo Monroy, describing his maestra's first day teaching at La Esmeralda, Ch. 19, Ibid.

10 If a masterpiece can be made only by a master and a master is defined as "a man having control or authority,": you can see what we're up against. Considering the history of slavery, we suggest changing the word to "massa" and "massa's piece."
> Quoted in *Confessions of the Guerilla Girls* by Guerilla Girls 1995

2067. Kathryn Kuhlman (1907–1976)

1 I didn't have any looks, I didn't have any talent, and it was easy for me to say to the Lord, "I don't have anything." If you only knew where I came from . . . this leetle-bitty town with no more than twelve hundred people in it. So . . . anything I am today, He is the one who has done it . . .
> Quoted in *Ms.* (New York) *January 1975*

2 The Bible is the Word of God, its author is the Holy spirit, and in its entirely it is the revelation of Jesus Christ.
> Ch. 1, *The Greatest Power in the World 1997* rev.

2068. Violette Leduc (1907–1972)

1 "She is killing me and there's nothing I can accuse her of."
> *La Bâtarde 1965*

2 I was and I always shall be hampered by what I think other people will say.
> Ibid.

3 To give oneself, one must annihilate oneself.
> *Therese and Isabelle 1968*

4 The pearl wanted what I wanted. I was discovering the little male organ we all of us have. A eunuch taking heart again.
> Ibid.

5 "I desire, am only able to desire, myself."
> *Mad in Pursuit 1971*

2069. Astrid Lindgren (1907–2002)

1 She was nine years old, and she lived there all alone. She had no mother or father, which was actually quite nice, because it meant that no one could tell her that she had to go to bed just when she was having most fun.
> *Pippi Longstocking 1945*

2 Why should some people have the good luck to be born in London's slums or Chicago's underworld, where murder and gunplay were the order of the day!
> *Bill Bergson, Master Detective 1946*

3 She was so willing to be good and obedient, that it was a pity she didn't always succeed.
> *Mardie 1960*

4 "How can things be so terrible," I asked. "How can things be so terrible that some people have to die, when they're not even ten years old?"
> *The Brothers Lionheart 1973*

2070. Helen M. Mallicoat (1907–1984)

1 I was regretting the past and fearing the future.
Suddenly my Lord was speaking.
"My name is I Am"
He paused. I waited. He continued.
"When you live in the past with its mistakes and regrets, it is hard. I am not there.
My name is not I WAS.
"When you live in the future with its problems and fears, it is hard.
My name is not I WILL BE.
"When you live in this moment it is not hard. I am here.
My name is I AM."
> *Listen for the Lord 1977*

2071. Helen Dick Megaw (1907–2002)

1 Much has been said about the difficulties of women in science, but I would like to say explicitly that I at least was never or rarely aware of discrimination. Perhaps I was particularly lucky, in that everyone who advised me on my education and guided my career assumed that women should be given the same opportunities as men. First and foremost I am thankful to my parents for this, and then to those far-sighted women of earlier generations who founded Girton College as a college for women, within Cambridge University and an integral part of it
> Acceptance Speech, Roebling Medal of the Mineralogical Society of America (1989), *American Mineralogist*, Vol. 75 *1990*

2072. Lee Miller (1907–1977)

1 I'm not Cinderella. I can't force my foot into the glass slipper.
> Quoted in *The Lives of Lee Miller* by Anthony Penrose* 1985
> *Her son.

2 In all the great sieges, the defenders eat rats, and if I have to eat rats, they are going to be well spiced!*
> Ibid.
> *Remark to store manager on purchasing a basketful of spices at start of the Blitz in London, 1940.

2073. Helen Foster Snow (1907–1997)

1 The war between the artist and writer and government or orthodoxy is one of the tragedies of humankind. One chief enemy is stupidity and failure to understand anything about the cre-

ative mind. For a bureaucratic politician to presume to tell any artist or writer how to get his mind functioning is the ultimate in asininity. The artist is no more able to control his mind than is any outsider. Freedom to think requires not only freedom of expression but also freedom from the threat of orthodoxy and being outcast and ostracized.

"Women and Kuomintang," *Women in Modern China 1967*

2 . . . one can judge a civilization by the way it treats its women.
"Bound Feet and Straw Sandals," Ibid.

2074. Barbara Stanwyck (1907–1990)

1 Sponsors obviously care more about a ninety-second commercial and *want* to pay you more than any guest star gets for a ninety-minute *acting* performance.
Quoted in *McCall's March 1965*

2 There is a point in portraying surface vulgarity where tragedy and comedy are very close.
Quoted in *Starring Miss Barbara Stanwyck* by Ella Smith *1974*

3 My only problem is finding a way to play my fortieth fallen female in a different way from my thirty-ninth.
Interview with Hedda Hopper,* Ibid.
*See 1709.

2075. Fay Wray (1907–2004)

1 Only in your imagination can you revise.
Quoted in *International Herald Tribune* (Paris) *22 February 1989*

2076. Anne Anastasi (1908–2001)

1 . . . it is apparent that we cannot speak of inferiority and superiority, but only of specific differences in aptitudes and personality between the sexes. These differences are largely the result of cultural and other experiential factors. . . .
Differential Psychology 1937

2 Tests can serve a predictive function only insofar as they indicate to what extent the individual has acquired the prerequisite skills and knowledge for a designated criterion performance. What persons can accomplish in the future depends not only on their present intellectual status, as assessed by the test, but on their subsequent experience.
Differential Psychology (4th ed.) *1981*

3 Intelligence is not a single, unitary ability, but rather a composite of several functions. The term denotes that combination of abilities required for survival and advancement within a particular culture.
"What counselors should know about the use and interpretation of psychological tests" (p. 613), *Journal of Counseling and Development,* 70 (5) *1992*

2077. Rita Angus (1908–1970)

1 You have been trying to make me into a legend. I am a painter and paintings are paintings—line, tone, form and colour, mass, light. You cannot make a legend out of a painting.
Remark, Quoted at exhibition, Security Pacific Art Gallery, Seattle *1992*

2078. Harriette Arnow (1908–1986)

1 "If a religion is unpatriotic, it ain't right."
Ch. 4, *The Dollmaker 1954*

2 "I've been readen th Bible an a hunten God fer a long while—off an on—but it ain't so easy as picken up a nickel off th floor."
Ch. 15, Ibid.

3 "You never did see them ads an signs an letters beggen all th people back home to come up here an save democracy far you all. They done it in a last war, too. Now you can git along without us, so's you cain't git shet a us quick enough. Want us to go back an raise another crop a youngens at no cost to you an Detroit, so's they'll be all ready to save you when you start another war—huh?"
Ch. 33, Ibid.

4 There was something frantic in their blooming, as if they knew that frost was near and then the bitter cold. They'd live through all the heat and noise and stench of summertime, and now each widely opened flower was like a triumphant cry, "We will, we will make seed before we die."
Ch. 34, Ibid.

5 Christ had had no money, just his life. Life and money: could a body separate the two? What had Judas done for his money? Whispered a little, kept still as she did now.
Ch. 37, Ibid.

2079. Sylvia Ashton-Warner (1908–1984)

1 When love turns away, now, I don't follow it. I sit and suffer, unprotesting, until I feel the tread of another step.
Teacher 1963

2 I've got to relearn what I was supposed to have learned.
(February 1941), *Myself 1967*

3 I flung my tongue round like a cat-o'-nine-tails so that my pleasant peaceful infant room became little less than a German concentration camp as I took out on the children what life should have got.
(August 1941), Ibid.

4 I am my own Universe. I my own Professor.
Ibid.

5 Your work means more to me than my own does to me because your work involves your contentment and that comes before my work with me.
(22 March 1942), Ibid.

6 "Quite nice women suddenly have to wear this title with the stigma on it and a crown of thorns. We're so frightened of it that we change our nature to avoid it and in so doing we end up the classical mother-in-law we feared in the first place; so gravely have we twisted ourselves."
Three 1970

7 In mind I lay a hand on his arm but only in mind. That would be revealing a feeling, an offense against London.
Ibid.

8 "God, the illogic! The impossibility of communicating in this house. The sheer operation alone of getting something through to somebody."
Ibid.

2080. Simone de Beauvoir (1908–1986)

1 . . . the time that one gains cannot be accumulated in a storehouse; it is contradictory to want to save up existence, which,

the fact is, exists only by being spent, and there is a good case for showing that airplanes, machines, the telephone, and the radio do not make men of today happier than those of former times.

Ch. 3, The Ethics of Ambiguity 1948

2 A man would never get the notion of writing a book on the peculiar situation of the human male.

The Second Sex 1953

3 For him she is sex—absolute sex, no less. She is defined and differentiated with reference to man and not he in reference to her; she is the incidental, the inessential as opposed to the essential. He is the Subject, he is the Absolute—she is the Other.

Ibid.

4 ... the only public good is that which assures the private good of the citizens. ...

Ibid.

5 Between women love is contemplative. ... There is no struggle, no victory, no defeat; in exact reciprocity each is at once subject and object, sovereign and slave; duality becomes mutuality.

Ibid.

6 Society, being codified by man, decrees that woman is inferior; she can do away with this inferiority only by destroying the male's superiority.

Ibid.

7 ... when we abolish the slavery of half of humanity, together with the whole system of hypocrisy that it implies, then the "division" of humanity will reveal its genuine significance and the human couple will find its true form.

Ibid.

8 Whatever the country, capitalist or socialist, man was everywhere crushed by technology, made a stranger to his own work, imprisoned, forced into stupidity. The evil all arose from the fact that he had increased his needs rather than limited them; ... As long as fresh needs continued to be created, so new frustrations would come into being. When had the decline begun? The day knowledge was preferred to wisdom and mere usefulness to beauty. ... Only a moral revolution—not a social or political revolution—only a moral revolution would lead man back to his lost truth.

Ch. 3, Les Belles Images 1966

9 It's frightening to think that you mark your children merely by being yourself. ... It seems unfair. You can't assume the responsibility for everything you do—or don't do.

Ibid.

10 I had grown very fond of this dying woman [her mother]. As we talked in the half-darkness I assuaged an old unhappiness; I was renewing the dialogue that had been broken off during my adolescence and that our differences and our likenesses had never allowed us to take up again. And the early tenderness that I had thought dead forever came to life again. ...

A Very Easy Death 1966

11 I find it absurd to assume that all coitus is rape. By saying that, one agrees to the masculine myth that a man's sex is a sword, a weapon.

Quoted in "The Radicalization of Simone de Beauvoir" by Alice Schwarzer, *The First Ms. Reader,* Francine Klagsbrun, ed. *1972*

12 ... it is old age, rather than death, that is to be contrasted with life. Old age is life's parody, whereas death transforms life into a destiny: in a way it preserves it by giving it the absolute dimension—"And into himself eternity changes him at last." Death does away with time.

Conclusion, The Coming of Age 1972

13 One is not born a genius, one becomes a genius.

Quoted in *The Woman's Eye* by Anne Tucker* 1973
*See 3620.

14 I tore myself away from the safe comfort of certainties through my love for truth; and truth rewarded me.

All Said and Done 1974

15 Patience [is one of those] "feminine" qualities which have their origin in our oppression but should be preserved after our liberation.

Interview by Alice Schwarzer, *Marie-Claire* October *1976*

2081. Elizabeth L. Chittick (1908–2008)

1 If the economic perspective is to be the dominant perspective for the next few years, then we must change the name "women's issues" and broaden our base and call such issues "economic issues affecting everyone." Fresh strategies for the E.R.A. will be on the top of the National Woman's Party agenda for 1985. We will not give up on the E.R.A. until it becomes law of the land.

"Required Reading; Whither the E.R.A.?," *The New York Times 18 January 1985*

2082. Bette Davis (1908–1989)

1 I have always been driven by some distant music—a battle hymn no doubt—for I have been at war from the beginning. I've never looked back before. I've never had the time and it has always seemed so dangerous. To look back is to relax one's vigil.

Ch. 1, The Lonely Life 1962

2 The weak are the most treacherous of us all. They come to the strong and drain them. They are bottomless. They are insatiable. They are always parched and always bitter. They are everyone's concern and like vampires they suck our life's blood.

Ch. 20, Ibid.

3 This became a credo of mine ... attempt the impossible in order to improve your work.

Ch. 10, Mother Goddamn 1974

4 If you don't work, what the hell do you do? Sit around and rot! The retirement age of 65 has killed *millions.* Luckily, I'm in an industry with no retirement. They only retire you if you don't make money for them.

Quoted in "The Story of a Winner" by Dotson Rader, *Parade Magazine 6 March 1983*

5 You know what I'm going to have on my gravestone? "She did it the hard way."

Interview, CBS-TV *5 May 1985*

2083. Hildegarde Dolson (1908–1981)

1 Perhaps the surest way to tell when a female goes over the boundary from childhood into meaningful adolescence is to watch how long it takes her to get to bed at night.

"How Beautiful with Mud," *We Shook the Family Tree 1946*

2 I too would be beautiful. I would also be Flower-Fresh, Fastidious and Dainty—a triple-threat virtue obviously prized above pears by the entire male sex, as depicted in the *Ladies' Home Journal.*

Ibid.

2084. Helen Dudar (1908–2002)

1 Contrary to the folklore of abortion as lifelong trauma, it is not necessarily a profoundly scarring one either.

"Abortion for the Asking," *Saturday Review of the Society April 1973*

2 In this era of radicalized and politicized clergy, it is no longer even surprising when a woman shows up at [an abortion] clinic with the blessing of her priest.

Ibid.

2085. M. F. K. Fisher (1908–1992)

1 One of the stupidest things in an earnest but stupid school of culinary thought is that each of the three daily meals should be 'balanced.' Of course, where countless humans are herded together, as in military camps or schools or prisons, it is necessary to strike what is ironically called the happy medium. In this case, what kills the least number with the most ease is the chosen way.

How to Cook a Wolf 1942

2 When I write of hunger, I am really writing about love and the hunger for it.

Foreword, *The Gastronomical Me 1943*

3 Sharing food with another human being is an intimate act that should not be indulged in lightly.

"A Is for Dining Alone," *An Alphabet for Gourmets 1949*

4 "In France we have lived with the law for so long that we know how and when to make use of it. We are not afraid of it. In your country you are still so inexperienced, that you are in awe of it. The law is your stern parent, like God, and you fear its punishment. Here we respect it, but only if we respect ourselves more. We use it when we need it."

Ch. 5, Ibid.

5 Tell me what you eat, and I shall tell you what you are.

Quoted by Michiko Kakutani in *The New York Times Book Review 14 June 1983*

6 "There is a communion of more than our bodies when bread is broken and wine is drunk. And that is my answer when people ask me: Why do you write about hunger, and not wars or love?"

Quoted in "With Bold Pen and Fork" by Mimi Sheraton, *Time (New York) 26 January 1987*

7 He loved what he wanted me to be.

Stay Me, Oh Comfort Me: Journals and Stories, 1933–1941 1993

2086. Joan Fleming (1908–1980)

1 "It's the money," Molly said clumsily, "if you've once had no money, and I mean no money at all, it means something always ever afterwards."

Ch. 7, *The Chill and the Kill 1964*

2 "Folks love being told things about themselves they already know."

Ibid.

2087. Martha Gellhorn (1908–1998)

1 I see mysteries and complications wherever I look, and I have never met a steadily logical person.

Introduction, *The Face of War 1959*

2 It took nine years, and a great depression, and two wars ending in defeat, and one surrender without war, to break my faith in the benign power of the press. Gradually I came to realize that people will more readily swallow lies than truth, as if the taste of lies was homey, appetizing: a habit.

Ibid.

3 People may correctly remember the events of twenty years ago (a remarkable feat), but who remembers his fears, his disgusts, his tone of voice? It is like trying to bring back the weather of that time.

"The War in Finland," Introduction, Ibid.

4 America has made no reparation to the Vietnamese, nothing. We are the richest people in the world and they are among the poorest. We savaged them, though they had never hurt us, and we cannot find it in our hearts, our honor, to give them help—because the government of Vietnam is Communist. And perhaps because they won.

"The War in Vietnam—Vietnam Again, 1986," Ibid.

2088. Lillian Gideon (1908–?)

1 Racial discrimination hasn't ended, it's just become more difficult to prove. It's subtle, unspoken, covert.

"Her dream: Give hope a chance" by Judi Hunt, *Seattle Post-Intelligencer, C1–2 18 January 1993*

2 You know, we're all going in the same direction, or at least trying to. So we need to live together, get along together and give each other enough space to be comfortable on that road.

Ibid.

3 It must be very tempting to join the drug culture when you're second or third generation on welfare, you have nothing, not even enough to eat.

It has to be difficult, if not impossible, to say "no" when he's suddenly offered $200 a week to deliver or deal drugs. I don't know if I were in the same situation if I could say "no."

Ibid.

2089. Nancy Hale (1908–1988)

1 After my mother's* death I began to see her as she had really been. . . . It was less like losing someone than discovering someone.

"A Good Light," *The Life in the Studio 1957*
*Reference to Lillian Westcolt H—, American artist (1881–1963).

2 Like all real artists', her objective had been to create riches with modest means; squandering seemed to her a kind of stupidity. Since she never had but one standard, perfection—which in the nature of things fits art better than life—she often gave a misleading impression of Yankee parsimony.

Ibid.

3 She could never get used to the idea that most people don't use their eyes except to keep from running into things.

"Eyes or No Eyes, or The Art of Seeing," Ibid.

4 ... the cynicism of the young about society is as nothing to the cynicism of young artists for the art establishment.

> Pt. I, Ch. 4, *Mary Cassatt:* * *A Biography of the Great American Painter 1975*
> *See 1126.

5 The best work of artists in any age is the work of innocence liberated by technical knowledge. The laboratory experiments that led to the theory of pure color equipped the impressionists to paint nature as if it had only just been created.

> Pt. II, Ch. 7, Ibid.

6 I had wanted to say then to the young man, "Painting one picture—even a mediocre picture—is more important than collecting a hundred." I'd wanted to say, "You couldn't have any collections at all unless you first had pictures."

> Epilogue, Ibid.

2090. Josephine Jacobsen (1908–2003)

1 Life is absolutely brimming with terror.

> Quoted in interview by Betty Parry, *Belles Lettres May/June 1986*

2 For me, it's like Jacob wrestling with the angel. In every encounter with a poem there is a possibility of an abysmal failure. It's like the difficulty of trying to climb a mountain: the chances that you are going to fall are very steep, and the sense of triumph if you get there is very strong.

> Ibid.

3 The essence of poetry is the unique view—the unguessed relationship, suddenly manifest. Poetry's eye is always aslant, oblique.

> Lecture, "One Poet's Poetry," Ibid.

4 Galaxies are simpler. There is an awful grace
in such mystery.

> "Presence I" *n.d.*

2091. Amy Johnson (1908?–1941)

1 Had I been a man I might have explored the Poles or climbed Mount Everest, but as it was my spirit found outlet in the air.

> Essay in *Myself When Young,* Margot Asquith,* ed. *1938*
> *See 1301.

2092. Eve Langley (1908–1974)

1 It is a thought as sweet as heaven to know that in the minds of each of us the may by the fence still blooms in an eternal springtime; that the snowdrop has in our hearts a triple birth, and blooms in three separate minds, faultlessly. . . . So that if all the flowers and grasses and hollows and hills of the old house were razed and mutilated—as they are now, I suppose—we keep them intact in three minds, each depending on the other to supply it with the delicate minutiae of remembrance.

> First Part, I, *Not Yet the Moon* 1946

2 The sun was a warrior whom I gladly contested and whom I overthrew. Dazzling and magnificent was the sun's army on my back and joyous were the blades of sweat that came from my pores and vanquished him.

> Second Part, X, Ibid.

2093. Betty MacDonald (1908–1958)

1 Men are quite humorless about their own businesses.

> "I Learn to Hate Even Baby Chickens," *The Egg and I* 1945

2 Gammy used to say, "Too much scrubbing takes the life right out of things" . . .

> Ibid.

3 Nobody know how old Mrs. Piggle-Wiggle is. She says she doesn't know herself. She says, "What difference does it make how old I am when I shall never grow any bigger?"

> Ch. 1, *Mrs. Piggle-Wiggle* 1947

2094–2095. Jean Sutherland MacLeod (1908–   )

1 Oh! why does the wind blow upon me so wild?
Is it because I'm nobody's child?

> "Nobody's Child" *1954*

2096. Beatrice M. Murphy (1908–1992)

1 Not until you live more years and
Acquire deeper wisdom will you know
They paved and pointed the way
You are now impatient to go.

> "To Any Negro Youth," St. 2, *The Rocks Cry Out*

2 All I know of the South
Is what I've been told
And the telling has filled
My veins with brackish hate
And made my blood run cold.

> "Disclaimer," St. 2, Ibid.

3 Please send me a miracle
By noon tomorrow.

> "Deadline for Miracles," St. 1, Ibid.

2097. Alice Neel (1908–1984)

1 You can't leave humanity out. If you didn't have humanity, you wouldn't have anything.

> Quoted in "Alice Neel: Portraits of Four Decades" by Cindy Nemser, *Ms.* (New York) October 1973

2 You may use your penis but I use a paint brush.*

> Cited by Ann Sutherland Harris in "Portrait of a lady," *New Directions for Women,* Vol. XIV, No. 4 *January 1997*
> *Her retort to the men who taunted her as a young woman artist by telling her she needed a penis to paint.

2098. Peace Pilgrim (1908–1981)

1 I wish that every child could have growing space because I think children are a little like plants. If they grow too close together they become thin and sickly and never obtain maximum growth. We need room to grow.

> Ch. 1, *Peace Pilgrim: Her Life and Work in Her Own Words 1982*

2 I don't eat junk food and I don't think junk thoughts.

> Ch. 2, Ibid.

3 Truth is the pearl without price. . . . Those who have the truth would not be packaging it and selling it, so anyone who is selling it, really does not possess it.

> Ch. 3, Ibid.

4 Prayer is a concentration of positive thought.

Ibid.

5 I would say to the military: yes, we need to be defended; yes, we need you. The Air Force can clean up the air, the Marines can take care of the despoiled forests, the Navy can clean the oceans, the Coast Guard can take care of the rivers, and the Army can be used to build adequate drainage projects to prevent disastrous floods, and other such benefits for mankind.

Ch. 8, Ibid.

6 We seem always ready to pay the price for war. Almost gladly we give our time and our treasures—our limbs and even our lives—for war. But we expect to get peace for nothing.

Ibid.

2099. Zenobia Powell Perry (1908–2004)

1 To not get discouraged by the things that happen that distract (you), and to remember where you're going and what you're doing and stick to it.

"Xenia to Honor Zenobia" by Meth Michaels,
Dayton Daily News 11 July 2002

2100. Ann Petry (1908–1997)

1 It took me quite a while to realize that there were fashions in literary criticism and that they shifted and changed much like the fashions in women's hats.

"The Novel as Social Criticism," *The Writer's Book,*
Helen Hull, ed. 1950

2 I told myself that if I were a maker of perfumes I would make one and call it "Spring," and it would smell like this cool, sweet, early-morning air and I would let only beautiful young brown girls use it, and if I could sing I would sing like the song sparrow and I would let only beautiful young brown boys hear me.

"The New Mirror," *Miss Muriel and Other Stories 1971*

2101. Kathleen Jessie Raine (1908–2003)

1 I couldn't claim that I have never felt the urge to explore evil, but when you descend into hell you have to be very careful.

Times (London) 18 April 1992

2 I set out in a dream
To go away—
Away is hard to go, but no one
Asked me to stay
And there is no destination for away.

Untitled, *Collected Poems 2001*

3 Stone into man must grow,
the human word carved by our whispers in the passing air is
the authentic utterance of cloud,
the speech of flowing water, blowing wind,
of silver moon and stunted juniper.

"Night in Martindale," Ibid.

4 Sleep at the tree's root,
where the night is spun Into the stuff of worlds,
listen to the winds,
the tides, and the night's harmonies,
and know All that you knew before you began to forget . . .

"Message from Home," Ibid.

2102. Ann Ronell (1908–1993)

1 Willow weep for me, willow weep for me,
Bend your branches green along the stream that runs to sea;
Listen to please, listen willow, weep—for me.

"Willow, Weep For Me" (song) 1932

2 Who's afraid of the big bad wolf?

"Who's afraid of the big bad wolf?," *Walt Disney's Three
Little Pigs 1933*

2103. Amy Vanderbilt (1908–1974)

1 Ceremony is really a protection, too, in times of emotional involvement, particularly at death. If we have a social formula to guide us and do not have to extemporize, we feel better able to handle life.

Introduction, Pt. I, *New Complete Book of Etiquette 1963*

2 Good manners have much to do with the emotions. To make them ring true, one must feel them, not merely exhibit them.

Introduction, Pt. II, Ibid.

3 One face to the world, another at home makes for misery.

Introduction, Pt. VI, Ibid.

2104. Gale Wilhelm (1908–1991)

1 "I'm going to turn on the light and we'll be two people in a room looking at each other and wondering why on earth they were afraid of the dark."

We Too Are Drifting 1953

2105. Yang Ping (1908–?)

1 That I should think, even now, of wanting to continue to exist only as the vessel of a chemical experimentation heartlessly, inexorably formulating itself within me! And against my will . . . And yet I love this little life! With all the pain of it, I long for the wonderful thing to happen, for a tiny human creature to spring from between my limbs bravely out into the world. I need it, just as a true poet *needs* to create a great undying work.

"Fragment from a Lost Diary," *Fragment from a Lost Diary
and Other Stories,* Naomi Katz and Nancy Milton, eds.
1973

2 Women and revolution! What tragic, unsung epics of courage lie silent in the world's history!

Ibid.

3 Only when the beat of life is lifted to this pitch, this fury, and this danger, only when destiny . . . poses the choice between irreconcilable desires at a given moment, only when a human being feels the necessity of ignoring personal feeling in the decision taken—only then can one talk of a revolutionary awakening!

Ibid.

2106. Hedda Bolgar (1909–   )

1 I was put on this Earth to accomplish certain things. I'm so far behind, I can never die.

"At 99, she's living life for others" by Steve Lopez, *Los Angeles
Times 14 September 2008*

2 I don't see why people are so afraid of being old. It seems to me that what people see is only the loss or the deteriora-

tion or the "minus." They don't see that there are tremendous gains.

> The Beauty of Aging (film) (beautyofaging.com) *2010*

3 I have a very strong feeling of connection with everything that's alive and the importance of now.

> Ibid.

2107. Agnes "Sis" Cunningham (1909–2004)

1 We . . . were young radicals who felt that by singing ideas straightforwardly we could get more said in five minutes than in hours, or days, of talking.

> "Songs of Hard Years" with Madeline B. Rose, *Ms.* (New York) *March 1974*

2 Oh, it's good to be living and working
when we know the land's our own
To know that we have got a right to
all the crops we've grown.

> "When We Know the Land's Our Own" *n.d.*

2108. Anne Fremantle (1909–2002)

1 Among the most truly responsible of all people are artists and revolutionaries, for they most of all are prepared to pay with their lives.

> Introduction, *Woman as Revolutionary,* Fred C. Giffin, ed. *1973*

2 The revolutionary attempts a secular denial of mortality, the artist a spiritual one.

> Ibid.

2109. Eleanor Hamilton (1909–?)

1 Good lovers have known for centuries that the hand is probably the primary sex organ.

> Quoted in "Hue & Cry," *San Francisco Chronicle 29 October 1978*

2 Intimacy of soul is often dependent on intimacy of body.

> "Body Image & Aging," grandtimes.com *n.d.*

2110. Katharine Hepburn (1909–2003)

1 The average Hollywood film star's ambition is to be admired by an American, courted by an Italian, married to an Englishman and have a French boyfriend.

> *New York Journal-American 22 February 1954*

2 Television, which sank the picture industry, has turned the Academy Awards into a big television show. I think it should be an intimate honor.

> Quoted in "Hepburn: She Is the Best," *The Los Angeles Times 24 November 1974*

3 Without discipline, there's no life at all.

> *Dick Cavett Show,* ABC-TV *4 April 1975*

4 You never feel that you have fame. It's always in back of you.

> Ibid.

5 . . . plain women know more about men than beautiful ones do.

> Quoted in *Kate* by Charles Higham *1975*

6 As for me, prizes mean nothing. My prize is my work.

> Ibid.

2111. Queen Juliana (1909–2004)

1 You people of the United States of America have the wonderfully farseeing conception of being Democracy's material and spiritual arsenal, to save the world's highest values from annihilation.

> Radio address, NBC *13 April 1941*

2 I want to emphasize that for a queen the task of being a mother is just as important as it is for every other Netherlands woman.

> Inauguration address, Amsterdam *6 September 1948*

3 Though previous generations were also inspired by the fervent will to improve the world, they failed because they did not call a final halt to the forces of destruction. To do this is precisely the task of the present generation. . . .

> Address, University of Paris *25 May 1950*

2112. Rita Levi-Montalcini (1909–)

1 At twenty, I realized that I could not possibly adjust to a feminine role as conceived by my father, and asked him permission to engage in a professional career. In eight months I filled my gaps in Latin, Greek and mathematics, graduated from high school, and entered medical school in Turin.

> Ibid.

2 Wrapped in a black mantle, he bowed before the king and, for a moment, lowered the veil covering his face. We recognized each other in a matter of seconds when I saw him looking for me among the applauding crowd. He then replaced his veil and disappeared as suddenly as he had appeared.*

> *In Praise of Imperfection* (autobiography) *1988*
> *Her description of receiving the Nobel Prize from the King of Sweden; the "he" in the passage refers to NGF (nerve growth factor), the discovery for which she received the prize.

3 The answer* lies in the desperate . . . desire of human beings to ignore what is happening in situations where full awareness might lead one to self-destruction.

> Quoted in *Twentieth-Century Women Scientists* by Lisa Yount *1996*
>
> *Explaining how she, a Jew in hiding, could concentrate on research when Mussolini and the Germans took over Italy.

4 For a long time [in the late 1960s and early 1970s] people didn't mention how NGF* was discovered. . . . People repeated my experiment and didn't mention my name! I am not a person to be bitter, but it was astonishing to find it completely canceled.

> Ibid.
>
> *Nerve growth factor, which she discovered in 1950.

2113. Margaret [Ursula] Mee (1909–1988)

1 I know my death will not be the end of my work. Wherever I go I will try to influence those who are destroying our planet, so the Earth will have a chance to survive.

> *Margaret Mee's Amazon: The Diaries of an Artist Explorer 2004*

2114. Ethel Merman (1909–1984)

1 Broadway has been very good to me—but then, I've been very good to Broadway.

> Quoted in "She Had Rhythm and Was the Top" by William A. Henry III, *Time* (New York) *27 February 1984*

2 I take a breath when I have to.

> Ibid.

2115. Gabrielle Roy (1909–1983)

1 The city was made for couples, not for four or five silly girls with their arms interlaced, strolling up St. Catherine Street, stopping at every shop-window to admire things they would never own.

Ch. 1, The Tin Flute 1947

2 When there was enough money for their needs, the ties between them had been strong, but once the money was lacking, what a strain was put on their love!

Ch. 32, Ibid.

3 The Christian Scientists held that it was not God who wanted sicknesses, but man who puts himself in the way of suffering. If this were the case, though, wouldn't we all die in perfect health?

Ch. 3, The Cashier 1955

4 How clearly he realized that men did not like what they called love. That most embarassing of subjects between men they approached with half-utterances, with false carelessness, or else with a vulgar leer, never easily and comfortably.

Ch. 8, Ibid.

2116. Simone Weil (1909–1943)

1 I would suggest that barbarism be considered as a permanent and universal human characteristic which becomes more or less pronounced according to the play of circumstances.

"Hitler and Roman Foreign Policy," Nouveaux Cahiers 1 January 1940

2 There is something else which has the power to awaken us to the truth. It is the works of writers of genius. . . . They give us, in the guise of fiction, something equivalent to the actual density of the real, that density which life offers us every day but which we are unable to grasp because we are amusing ourselves with lies.

"Morality and Literature," Cahiers du Sud January 1944

3 The capacity to give one's attention to a sufferer is a very rare and difficult thing; it is almost a miracle; it is a miracle. Nearly all those who think they have this capacity do not possess it. Warmth of heart, impulsiveness, pity are not enough.

"Reflections on the Right Use of School Studies," Waiting on God 1950

4 Obvious and inexorable oppression that cannot be overcome does not give rise to revolt but to submission.

Factory journal, "The Mystery of the Factory" (1934–35), La Condition Ouvrière 1951

5 Nothing is less instructive than a machine.

Ibid.

6 Two prisoners whose cells adjoin communicate with each other by knocking on the wall. The wall is the thing which separates them but is also their means of communication. It is the same with us and God. Every separation is a link.

"Metaxu" (1947), Gravity and Grace 1952

7 Money destroys human roots wherever it is able to penetrate, by turning desire for gain into the sole motive. It easily manages to outweigh all other motives, because the effort it demands of the mind is so very much less. Nothing is *so* clear and *so* simple as a row of figures.

"L'Enracinement," Pt. II (1949), The Need for Roots 1952

8 Propaganda is not directed towards creating an inspiration; it closes, seals up all the openings through which an inspiration might pass; it fills the whole spirit with fanaticism.

Pt. III, Ibid.

9 Evil becomes an operative motive far more easily than good; but once pure good has become an operative motive in the mind, it forms there a fount of a uniform and inexhaustible impulsion, which is never so in the case of evil.

Ibid.

10 War, which perpetuates itself under the form of preparation for war, has once and for all given the State an important role in production.

"Revolution Proletarienne" (25 August 1933), Oppression and Liberty 1958

11 What a country calls its vital economic interests are not the things which enable its citizens to live, but the things which enable it to make war. Petrol is more likely than wheat to be a cause of international conflict.

"The Power of Words" (Nouveaux Cahiers, 1 & 15 April 1937), Selected Essays (1934–1953), Richard Rees, ed. 1962

12 Who were the fools who spread the story that brute force cannot kill ideas? Nothing is easier. And once they are dead they are no more than corpses.

"Three Letters on History: Théophile de Viau" (ca. 1938/39), Ibid.

13 Real genius is nothing else but the supernatural virtue of humility in the domain of thought.

"Human Personality" (1943; La Table Ronde, December 1950), Ibid.

14 There is one, and only one, thing in modern society more hideous than crime—namely, repressive justice.

Ibid.

15 Equality is the public recognition, effectively expressed in institutions and manners, of the principle that an equal degree of attention is due to the needs of all human beings.

"Draft for a Statement of Human Obligation" (1943), Ibid.

16 . . . when a man's life is destroyed or damaged by some wound or privation of soul or body, which is due to other men's actions or negligence, it is not only his sensibility that suffers but also his aspirations toward the good. Therefore there has been a sacrilege towards that which is sacred in him.

Ibid.

17 Art is the symbol of the two noblest human efforts: to construct . . . and to refrain from destruction.

The Pre-War Notebook (1933–39), First and Last Notebooks, Richard Rees, ed. 1970

18 To get power over is to defile. To possess is to defile.

"The New York Notebook" (1942), Ibid.

19 Charity. To love human beings in so far as they are nothing. That is to love them as God does.

Ibid.

20 In relation to God, we are like a thief who has burgled the house of a kindly householder and been allowed to keep some of the gold. From the point of view of the lawful owner this gold is a gift; From the point of view of the burglar it is a theft.

He must go and give it back. It is the same with our existence. We have stolen a little of God's being to make it ours. God has made us a gift of it. But we have stolen it. We must return it.

"New York Notebook" (1950), Ibid.

21 Human beings are so made that the ones who do the crushing feel nothing; it is the person crushed who feels what is happening. Unless one has placed oneself on the side of the oppressed, to feel with them, one cannot understand.

Pt. 3, Ch. 2, *Lectures on Philosophy* 1978

22 In the Church, considered as a social organism, the mysteries inevitably degenerate into beliefs.

Ch. 9, Quoted in *Simone Weil: Utopian Pessimist* by David McLellan 1989

2117. Eudora Welty (1909–2001)

1 I have been sick and I found out, only then, how lonely I am. Is it too late?

"Death of a Travelling Salesman," *A Curtain of Green and Other Stories* 1936

2 This time, when his heart leapt, something—his soul—seemed to leap too, like a little colt invited out of a pen.

Ibid.

3 "We're walking along in the changing-time," said Doc. "Any day now the change will come. It's going to turn from hot to cold. . . . Old Jack Frost will be pinching things up. Old Mr. Winter will be standing in the door. Hickory tree there will be yellow. Sweet-gum red, hickory yellow, dogwood red, sycamore yellow. . . . Persimmons will all git fit to eat, and the nut will be dropping like rain all through the woods here. And run, little quail, run, for we'll be after you too."

"The Wide Net," *The Wide Net and Other Stories* 1943

4 In a shadowy place something white flew up. It was a heron, and it went away over the dark treetops. William Wallace followed it with his eyes and Brucie clapped his hands, but Virgil gave a sigh, as if he knew that when you go looking for what is lost, everything is a sign.

Ibid.

5 His memory could work like the slinging of a noose to catch a wild pony.

"First Love," Ibid.

6 Haven't you noticed it prevail, in the world in general? Beware of a man with manners.

Ch. 1, *The Golden Apples* 1949

7 She was dead as a doornail. And she'd died laughing. I could have shaken her for it. She'd never laughed for Uncle Daniel before in her life. And even if she had, that's not the same thing as smiling; you may think it is, but I don't.

The Ponder Heart 1954

8 He loved being happy! He loved happiness like I love tea.

Ibid.

9 Ah, I'm a woman that's been clear around the world in my rocking chair.

"Circe," *The Bride of Innisfallen and Other Stories* 1955

10 "Never think you've seen the last of anything. . . ."

Pt. I, Ch. 1, *The Optimist's Daughter* 1969

11 All they could see was sky, water, birds, light and confluence. It was the whole morning world. And they themselves were a part of the confluence. Their own joint act of faith had brought them here at the very moment and matched its occurrence, and proceeded as it proceeded. Direction itself was made beautiful, momentous. They were riding as one with it, right up front.

Pt. IV, Ibid.

12 What I do in the writing of any character is to try to enter into the mind, heart and skin of a human being who is not myself. Whether this happens to be a man or a woman, old or young, with skin black or white, the primary challenge lies in making the jump itself. It is the act of a writer's imagination that I set most high.

Preface, *The Collected Stories of Eudora Welty* 1980

13 . . . listening to the magical percussion, the world beating in their ears. They heard through falling rain the running of the horse and bear, the stroke of the leopard, the dragon's crusty slither, and the glimmer and the trumpet of the swan.

"June Recital," Ibid.

14 She has spent her life trying to escape from the parlor-like jaws of self-consciousness.

"Old Mr. Marblehall," Ibid.

15 They were not really old—they were only 50; still, their lives were filled with tiredness, with a great lack of necessity to speak, with poverty which may have bound them like a disaster too great for any discussion but left them still separate and undesirous of sympathy. Perhaps, years ago, the long habit of silence may have been started in anger and passion. Who could tell now?

"The Whistle," Ibid.

16 The story and its analyses are not mirror-opposites of each other. They are not reflections, either one. Criticism indeed is an art, as a story is, but only the story is to some degree a vision; there is no explanation outside fiction for what the writer is learning to do.

On Writing 2002

2118. Dora Alonso (1910–?)

1 The shadow, the color of the man, and the kind of living, all are the same; black in one hundred tones, either so light as to be cinnamon flesh or as dark as black coffee, it carries the sign of subjection.

"Times Gone By," *Fragment from a Lost Diary and Other Stories*, Naomi Katz and Nancy Milton, eds. 1973

2 Life goes on, buried in pain for those who wait; swollen with haughtiness and arrogance for those who fear.

Ibid.

3 Her body broke down like the collapse of forked poles which could no longer bear the weight of an entire life dedicated to obedience, without a single pillar of rebellion to hold up the structure.

Ibid.

4 There's no higher right than might, and I am mighty.

"Time Gone By," Ibid.

2119. Bertha Adams Backus (fl. 1910s)

1 Build for yourself a strong-box,
Fashion each part with care;

When it's strong as your hand can make it,
Put all your troubles there.

"Then Laugh," St. 1 *1911*

2120. Janet Begbie (fl. 1910s–1970?)

1   Carry on, carry on, for the men and boys are gone,
But the furrow shan't lie fallow while the women carry on.

"Carry On" *n.d.*

2121. Mary Ingraham Bunting (1910–1998)

1   When her last child is off to school, we don't want the talented woman wasting her time in work far below her capacity. We want her to come out running.

Quoted in *Life* (New York) *13 January 1961*

2122. Barbara Anne Castle (1910–2002)

1   We want jam today, not jam tomorrow.

Speech, Labour Party conference *1943*

2   In politics, guts is all.

The Castle Diaries 1974–1976 1980

2123. Hilda Conkling (1910–1986)

1   The hills are going somewhere;
They have been going on the way a long time.
They are like camels in a line
But they move more slowly.

"Hills" *n.d.*

2   The world turns softly
Not to spill its lakes and rivers.

"Water" *n.d.*

3   Poems come like boats
With sails for wings;
Crossing the sky swiftly
They slip under tall bridges
Of cloud.

"Poems" *n.d.*

2124. Elizabeth Gould Davis (1910–1974)

1   The deeper the archaeologists dig, the further back go the origins of man and society—and the less sure we are that civilization has followed the steady upward course so thoroughly believed in by the Victorians. It is more likely that the greatest civilizations of the past have yet to be discovered.

Prologue, *The First Sex 1971*

2   Maleness remains a recessive genetic trait like color-blindness and hemophilia, with which it is linked. The suspicion that maleness is abnormal and that the Y chromosome is an accidental mutation boding no good for the race is strongly supported by the recent discoveries by the geneticists that congenital killers and criminals are possessed of not one but *two* Y chromosomes, bearing a double dose, as it were, of genetically undesired maleness.

Pt. I, Ch. 1, Ibid.

3   When man substituted God for the Great Goddess he at the same time substituted authoritarian for humanistic values.

Ch. 7, Ibid.

4   It is men, not women, who have promoted the cult of brute masculinity; and because men admire muscle and physical force, they assume that women do too.

Pt. IV, Ch. 21, Ibid.

5   If the human race is unhappy today, as all modern philosophers agree that it is, it is only because it is uncomfortable in the mirror image society man has made—the topsy-turvy world in which nature's supporting pillar is forced to serve as the cornice of the architrave, while the cornice struggles to support the building.

Ch. 22, Ibid.

2125. Esther Lillian Duff (fl. 1910s)

1   Some of the roofs are plum-color
Some of the roofs are gray,
Some of the roofs are silverstone,
And some are made of clay;
But under every gabled close
There's a secret hid away.

"Not Three, But One," *Bohemian Glass 1916*

2126. Raya Dunayevskaya (1910–1987)

1   Ever since the myth of Eve giving Adam the apple was created, women have been presented as devils or as angels, but definitely not as human beings.

"We Speak in Many Voices," *Notes on Women's Liberation 1970*

2   The first act of liberation is to demand back our own heads.

Ibid.

3   Only live human beings can recreate the revolutionary dialectic forever anew. And these live human beings must do so in theory as well as in practice.

Rosa Luxemburg, Women's Liberation, and Marx's Philosophy of Revolution 1991 rev.

4   All of history is the history of the struggle for freedom.

Marxism and Freedom, from 1776 until Today 2000

2127. Millicent Fenwick (1910–1992)

1   The curious fascination in this job* is the illusion that either you are being useful or you could be—and that's so tempting.

60 Minutes, CBS-TV *1 February 1981*

*U.S. Representative.

2   When you're old, everything you do is sort of a miracle.

Ibid.

3   Party organization matters. When the door of a smoke-filled room is closed, there's hardly ever a woman inside.

Ibid.

4   It has been said that one man's loophole is another man's livelihood. Even if this is true, it certainly is not fair, because the loophole-livelihood of those who are reaping undeserved benefits can be the economic noose of those who are paying more than they should.

Speaking Up 1982

5   We cannot continue to deny American women the full rights and responsibilities of citizenship.

Quoted by the National Women's Political Caucus *n.d.*

2128. Edith Starrett Green (1910–1987)

1   I have never believed that race, sex, religion, or national origin are valid criteria for either "favorable" or "unfavorable" treat-

ment. This is one reason why I have been opposed to programs which give an advantage in job consideration and promotion to members of those groups who have suffered historic discrimination.

Speech, Brigham Young University *1977*

2 I've always argued that it is just as desirable, just as possible, to have philosopher plumbers as philosopher kings.

Quoted in *American Political Women* by Esther Stineman *1980*

2129. Joyce Phipps Grenfell (1910–1979)

1 They look quite promising in the shop; and not entirely without hope when I get them back into my wardrobe. But then, when I put them on they tend to deteriorate with a very strange rapidity and one feels so sorry for them.

"Stately as a Galleon," *English Lit.* *1978*

2 Progress everywhere today does seem to come so very heavily disguised as Chaos.

Ibid.

2130. Margaret Halsey (1910–1997)

1 The attitude of the English . . . toward English history reminds one a good deal of the attitude of a Hollywood director toward love.

With Malice Toward Some 1938

2 All of Stratford, in fact, suggests powdered history—add hot water and stir and you have a delicious, nourishing Shakespeare.

Ibid.

3 . . . in England, having had money . . . is just as acceptable as having it, since the upper-class mannerisms persist, even after the bankroll has disappeared. But never having had money is unforgivable, and can only be atoned for by never trying to get any.

Ibid.

4 What I know about money, I learned the hard way—by having had it.

The Folks at Home 1952

2131. Jessie Hawkes (1910–1996)

1 We live in a world made seemingly secure by the four walls of our houses, the artificiality of our cities, and by the four walls of habit. Volcanoes speak of insecurity, of our participation in progress. They are openings not any longer into a properly appointed hell, but into an equally alarming abysm of thought.

A Land 1952

2 . . . the universe is substantially homogeneous, and shooting stars are chips from globes very much like our own. They are, as the label in the Geological Museum soberly states, "fragments of former worlds."

Ibid.

3 The only inequalities that matter begin in the mind. It is not income levels but differences in mental equipment that keep people apart, breed feelings of inferiority.

Quoted in *New Statesman* (London) *January 1957*

4 This dedication to a Goddess involved also a glorification of the meaning of sex. Fertility and abundance were the purpose

and the desire, sex was the instrument, and for this reason its symbols were everywhere.

Dawn of the Gods 1968

2132. Dorothy Crowfoot Hodgkin (1910–1994)

1 There are certain letters which I dread to open, and when I saw one from Buckingham Palace I left it sealed, fearing that they wanted to make me Dame Dorothy.

Remark to Max Perutz, Quoted in his obituary of her, *The Independent* (London) *1994*

2133. Marjorie Holmes (1910–2002)

1 The man who treasures his friends is usually solid gold himself.

Love and Laughter 1967

2 Descartes said, "Because I think, I am."
Because I am, I pray.
Prayer, to the thinking person, is almost inescapable.

Introduction, *I've Got to Talk to Somebody, God 1968*

3 A child's hand in yours—what tenderness it arouses, what power it conjures. You are instantly the very touchstone of wisdom and strength.

Calendar of Love and Inspiration 1981

4 I made the Holy Family as real as the folks next door.*

Quoted in obituary, *Los Angeles Times 2 April 2002*
*Re her trilogy: "Two From Galilee," "Three From Galilee: The Young Man From Nazareth," and "The Messiah."

5 If nobody else in this world gives a darn or believes in me, let me believe in myself.

"Faith In Myself" *n.d.*

2134. Hsiang Chin-yu (fl. 1910s–d. 1927)

1 . . . the emancipation of women can only come with a change in the social structure which frees men and women alike.

Quoted in *Women in Modern China* by Helen Foster Snow* *1967*

*See 2073.

2135. Josephine Winslow Johnson (1910–1990)

1 I can look back now and see the days as one looking down on things past, and they have more shape and meaning than before. But nothing is really finished or left behind forever.

Ch. 1, *Now in November 1934*

2 I used to wonder how men who had murdered or done crude and slimy things could go on living with the self which had made them do it still inside like a worm or ulcer; but now I could see how simple it was to make excuses.

Ch. 9 Ibid.

3 "It's late, and we got some work to do." It was always late with Father, even at four in the mornings; I think that his sleep was a race between dark and light, and he lay with his boots a hand away on the chair beside him.

Ch. 11, Ibid.

4 "I've got a fool hopeless belief," he said, "that the more we know the more we'll be able to understand."
"Maybe for you," I told him, "but for me only more confusion.

Ch. 14, Ibid.

5 A vast throng of people are working night and day, destroying all they still call their native land. Who are these people. . . . Who pollutes the air? Who cuts down the trees, builds houses on the stripped hillsides? Who poisons the sheep, shoots the deer, oils the beaches, dams and rivers, dries up the swamps, concretes the countrysides?

The New York Times 1969

6 If I were mad, I'd sit and talk to this stone. There's much to be said of mutual interest. I would tell him of Stonehenge, by which the seasons were marked, the time of day, the coming of eclipses known.

The Inland Island 1969

7 I am obsessed with the thought of starting over. Starting again with everything gone. A March thought. Fifty-seven years of accumulation. But man is not earth. He does not change to marble under pressure. Just assumes a curious shape. Living conglomerate.

Ibid.

8 Integrity. Conscience. That which separates me from all these fortunate small animals, insects, birds and stone.

Ibid.

9 We hear they [the scarlet tanagers] died by the thousand in New England. The sadness of that red-feathered rain, dropping from the cold skies. They could not stay in this warmer region. They were programmed to go on. Driven by that which can never be revised, never unlearned, never suited to the circumstances, never tempered to the wind. We humans have certain advantages we do not use.

Ibid.

2136. Mary Keyserling (1910–1997)

1 Occupationally women are relatively more disadvantaged today than they were twenty-five years ago. . . . This deterioration has occurred despite the increase in women's share of total employment over the same period and the rising number of women who enroll in and graduate from institutions of higher education.

Windows on Day Care 1972

2 There shouldn't be a single little child in America left alone to fend for himself.

Ch. 2, Ibid.

3 Our ultimate goal as a nation should be to make available comprehensive, developmental childcare services to all families that wish to use them.

Ch. 9, Ibid.

2137. Elizabeth Layton (1910–1993)

1 I never did dislike the world. I just dislike myself.

Quoted in "A Hidden Talent" by Michael Ryan, Parade Magazine 28 May 1989

2 There's a wonderful story. There was a little sparrow, lying out on the ground with his feet up in the air. Somebody asked him what he was doing, and he said, "The sky is going to fall." And this person said, "What do you think you can do about it?" And the little sparrow said, "One must do what one can."

Ibid.

2138. Alicia Markova (1910–2004)

1 . . . glorious bouquets and storms of applause. . . . These are the trimmings which every artist naturally enjoys. But to *move* an audience in such a role, to hear in the applause that unmistakable note which breaks through good theatre manners and comes from the heart, is to feel that you have won through to life itself. Such pleasure does not vanish with the fall of the curtain, but becomes part of one's own life.

Ch. 18, Giselle and I 1960

2139. Pauli Murray (1910–1985)

1 The wake had the solemnity of a high religious observance with an undertone of family reunion. There was subdued merriment among the more distant relatives while the chief mourners stayed in a special room surrounded by only the closest of friends. The atmosphere was hushed most of the time except for the occasional irreverent laughter of children.

Proud Shoes: The Story of an American Family 1956

2 Not Eden's gate, but freedom
Lures us down a trail of skulls
Where men forever crush the dreamers—
Never the dream.

"Dark Testament," 1, Dark Testament and Other Poems 1970

3 Hope is a crushed stalk
Between clenched fingers.

8, Ibid.

4 Seeing the relationship between my personal cause and the universal cause of freedom released me from a sense of isolation, helped me rid myself of vestiges of shame over my racial history, and gave me an unequivocal understanding that equality of treatment was my birthright and not something to be earned.

Song in a Weary Throat: An American Pilgrimage 1987

5 An African man may house his family in a mud hut, sleep on the ground, barely make a living scrabbling in parched earth, and have only one ceremonial cloth of cheap fabric. Yet when he drapes his toga about his shoulder and comes to greet a stranger, he walks with such self-assurance that I cannot help thinking how his proud bearing contrasts with the bearing of his sharecropper counterparts I have seen in rural America.

Ibid.

6 One person plus one typewriter constitutes a movement.

Letter to Dr. Ware of Harvard Law School, Ibid.

7 Somewhere along the way I adopted the slogan "Don't get mad, get smart."

Letter to Mrs. [Eleanor] Roosevelt, Ibid.
*See 1618.

2140. Mary Orr (1910–2006)

1 A young girl is on her way to Hollywood with a contract for one thousand dollars a week from a major film company in her pocketbook. In a year or two I am sure Miss Harrington will be as much of a household word to you as Ingrid Bergman or Joan Fontaine.

"The Wisdom of Eve," Cosmopolitan May 1946
*Story was the basis for the film classic *All About Eve* as well as the Broadway musical *Applause*.

2141. Anna Sokolow (1910–2000)

1   I certainly didn't expect to be affected so deeply, but the minute the plane landed [in Israel] I was overwhelmed with an indescribable feeling about being there. I didn't have any kind of strong Zionist background, but going there changed my point of view. [Israel] is now one of the deepest things in my life.

> Jewish Women's Archive (jwa.org) 20 August 2003

2   I prefer to work with people who can dance and act rather than dancers who act or actors who dance.

> Ibid.

3   . . . art should be a reflection and a comment on contemporary life.

> Ibid.

4   The artist should belong to his society, yet without feeling that he has to conform to it. . . Then, although he belongs to his society, he can change it, presenting it with fresh feelings, fresh ideas.

> Ibid.

5   I don't end [my dances], because I don't feel there's any ending. *Rooms** ends where it began. *Dreams*** no ending. That's the Jew in me. Ask the world a question, and there's no answer. All I do is present what I feel, and you, you answer. You answer.

> Ibid.

*1955 dance dealing with urban alienation. **1961 dance dealing with the Holocaust.

2142. Mother Teresa (1910–1997)

1   Loneliness and the feeling of being unwanted is the most terrible poverty.

> Quoted in "Saints Among Us," *Time* 29 December 1975

2   Our intellect and other gifts have been given to be used for God's greater glory, but sometimes they become the very god for us. That is the saddest part: we are losing our balance when this happens. We must free ourselves to be filled by God. Even God cannot fill what is full.

> Ibid.

3   To keep a lamp burning we have to keep putting oil in it.

> Ibid.

4   The spiritual poverty of the western world is much greater than the physical poverty of our people.

> "Who Are the Poor?," *Life in the Spirit*, Kathryn Spink, ed. *1986*

5   I don't claim anything of the work. It is his work. I am like a little pencil in his hand. That is all. He does the thinking. He does the writing. The pencil has nothing to do with it. The pencil has only to be allowed to be used.

> Speech, Awakening Conference, Colorado *15 June 1986*

6   The hunger for love is much more difficult to remove than the hunger for bread.

> Ibid.

2143. Aline Thomas (1910–?)

1   I must laugh and dance and sing
    Youth is such a lovely thing.

> "A Song of Youth" *n.d.*

2144. Adeline Wanatee (1910–1996)

1   Men have visions, women have children.

> Oral Interview (28 February 1980), Quoted in Ch. 2, *American Indian Women, Telling Their Lives* by Gretchen M. Bataille and Kathleen Mullen Sands *1984*

2   When two different patterns join together to form a third, we call that "art."

> Quoted in *Native North American Art* by Janet Catherine Berlo and Ruth B. Phillips *1998*

2145. Annie Dodge Wauneka (1910–1997)

1   I ask them [Navajo youth], "What is your biggest problem?" They tell me alcohol, drugs.
    I ask them, "What is the most beautiful machine?" They tell me they don't know how to answer.
    I tell them it's their heads, and they must not let alcohol and drugs ruin that machine.

> Quoted in "'Our Mother' Shepherds a Nation of Navajos" by Rusty Brown, *The Albuquerque Tribune 1 May 1984*

2146. Margaret R. Wilcox (1910?–?)

1   Children ask the world from us.

> Women's Action of Nuclear Disarmament (WAND), Boston *n.d.*

2147. Mary Lou Williams (1910–1981)

1   I am praying through my fingers when I play. I get that good 'soul sound,' and I try to touch people's spirits.

> Quoted in "The Prayerful One," *Time 21 February 1964*

2   You've got to play, that's all. They don't think of you as a woman if you can really play. I think some girls have an inferiority complex about it and this may hold them back. If they have talent, the men will be glad to help them along. [And] working with men, you get to think like a man when you play. You automatically become strong, though this doesn't mean you're not feminine.

> Quoted on p. 67, *Stormy Weather: The Music and Lives of a Century of Jazzwomen* by Linda Dahl 1984

3   The term jazz is perhaps corny and can have derogatory meanings, but I keep it because our music comes under the heading of jazz. We Americans have supported European music for centuries, but we are too stupid to support what was created here in America.

> Quoted in "Mary Lou Williams: First Lady of the Jazz Keyboard" by D. Antoinette Handy, The Kennedy Center: Women in Jazz Festival *n.d.*

4   Real jazz has love, and it has the spirit of God coming out of the suffering of black people. There are two things I express, the religious ideas and the musical ideas—both, otherwise it would be cold and have no feeling. When I'm playing, it seems as though someone else takes over. What I play comes from God, and I write it for the benefit of other people.

> Ibid.

5   I don't need to test the piano. During my sixty-plus years of playing, doing all those one-nighters, I've had to play on all kinds of pianos. If a few keys aren't working, you merely make the necessary changes. It makes you a better musician, having to transpose to different keys. [Art] Tatum* played his best when keys were missing.

> Ibid.

*(1909–1956) American jazz pianist and virtuoso.

2148. Leontine Young (1910–1988)

1 We do the same thing to parents that we do to children. We insist that they are some kind of categorical abstraction because they produced a child. They were people before that, and they're still people in all other areas of their lives. But when it comes to the state of parenthood they are abruptly heir to a whole collection of virtues and feelings that are assigned to them with a fine arbitrary disregard for individuality.

Introduction, *Life Among the Giants* 1965

2 The confusion of emotions with behavior causes no end of unnecessary trouble to both adults and children. Behavior can be commanded; emotions can't. An adult can put controls on a child's behavior—at least part of the time—but how do you put controls on what a child feels? An adult can impose controls on his own behavior—if he's grown up—but how does he order what he feels?

Ch. 1, Ibid.

3 [How] the young . . . can grow from the primitive to the civilized, from emotional anarchy to the disciplined freedom of maturity without losing the joy of spontaneity and the peace of self-honesty is a problem of education that no school and no culture have ever solved.

Ibid.

4 This is no argument against teaching manners to the young. On the contrary, it is a fine old tradition that ought to be resurrected from its current mothballs and put to work . . . In fact, children are much more comfortable when they know the guide rules for handling the social amenities. It's no more fun for a child to be introduced to a strange adult and have no idea what to say or do than it is for a grownup to go to a formal dinner and have no idea what fork to use.

Ibid.

5 Unfortunately the laughter of adults too often carries to the ears of the young the ring of ridicule, that annihilating enemy of human dignity. Like grownups, children enjoy participating in a joke and appreciate admiration of their wit and cleverness, but do not enjoy being the butt of the jokes.

Ch. 12, Ibid

2149. Virginia Mae Axline (1911–1988)

1 Out again into the night where the dulled light obscures the decisive lines of reality and casts over the immediate world a kindly vagueness. . . . The darkened sky gives growing room for softened judgments, for suspended indictments, for emotional hospitality. What *is,* seen in such light, seems to have so many possibilities that definitiveness becomes ambiguous.

Ch. 2, *Dibs: In Search of Self* 1965

2 "So much to say. And so much not to say! Some things are better left unsaid. But so many unsaid things can become a burden."

Ch. 8, Ibid.

3 Asking questions in therapy would be so helpful if anyone ever answered them accurately. But no one ever does.

Ch. 12, Ibid.

2150. Lucille Ball (1911–1989)

1 Luck? I don't know anything about luck. I've never banked on it, and I'm afraid of people who do. Luck to me is something else: Hard work—and realizing what is an opportunity and what isn't.

Quoted in Ch. 1, *The Real Story of Lucille Ball* by Eleanor Harris *1954*

2 I think knowing what you can *not* do is more important than knowing what you can do. In fact, that's good taste.

Ch. 7, Ibid.

3 I expected to only do the show for a year and then have some, like, home movies to show the baby that I had just had.*

"100 Years of Great Women," *ABC News Special with Barbara Walters* 30 April 1999

*Reference to *I Love Lucy,* a television comedy that ran from 1951 to 1956.

2151. Belle Barth (1911–1971)

1 I had my disappointments in the service; I discovered that a 21-inch Admiral was only a television set.

Quoted in "The 1920's and 1930's," *Women in Comedy* by Linda Martin and Kerry Segrave 1986

2 There's only two Yiddish words you need to know. *Gelt* and *schmuck.* If a man has no *gelt,* he is.

Quoted in "Is There Any Group I Haven't Offended?," *The Haunted Smile, The Story of Jewish Comedians in America* by Lawrence J. Epstein *2001*

3 If I embarrass you, tell your friends.

Stand-up routine *n.d.*

4 I don't mean to be vulgar, but it's profitable!

Ibid.

2152. Sybille von Schoenbeck Bedford (1911–)

1 A part, a large part, of travelling is an engagement of the ego v. the world. . . . The world is hydra headed, as old as the rocks and as changing as the sea, enmeshed inextricably in its ways. The ego wants to arrive at places safely and on time.

"The Quality of Travel," *Esquire* (repr. in *As It Was,* 1990) *November 1961*

2153. Elizabeth Bishop (1911–1979)

1 The Seven Wonders of the World are tired
and a touch familiar, but the other scenes,
innumerable, though equally sad and still, are foreign.

"Over 2000 Illustrations and a Complete Concordance," *A Cold Spring 1955*

2 We stand as still as stones to watch the leaves and ripples
while light and nervous water hold their interview.

"Quai d'Orleans," Ibid.

3 Brazilians are very quick, both emotionally and physically. Like the heroes of Homer, men can show their emotions without disgrace.

Ch. 1, *Brazil 1962*

4 The masses of poor people in the big cities, and the poor and not-so-poor of the "backlands," love their children and kill them with kindness by the thousands. The wrong foods, spoiled foods, warm medicines, sleeping syrups—all exact a terrible toll. . . .

Ibid.

5 You left North Haven, anchored in its rock,
afloat in mystic blue . . . And now, you've left
for good. You can't derange, or rearrange,
your poems again. (But the sparrows can their song.)
The words won't change again. Sad friend, you cannot change.

"North Haven (in memoriam—Robert Lowell*)," St. 6, *Questions of Travel 1965*

*Robert L— (1917–1977), Pulitzer Prize-winning American poet.

6 There is a magic made by melody
                              Sonnet, Ibid.

7 The waves are running in verses this fine morning.
      "Invitation to Miss Marianne Moore,"* St. 2, *The Complete
                              Poems 1927–1979 1983*
      *See 1669.

8 The art of losing isn't hard to master
   so many things seem filled with the intent
   to be lost that their loss is no disaster.
                      "One Art," St. 1, Ibid.

9 The whole shadow of Man is only as big as his hat,
                      "The Man Moth," St. 1, Ibid.

10 the sweet peas cling
   to their wet white string
   on the whitewashed fences;
   bumblebees creep
   inside the foxgloves,
   and evening commences.
                      "The Moose," St. 9, Ibid.

11 I sometimes wish that I had nothing, or little more, to do but
   write letters to the people who are not here.
              Letter (ca. 1930), *One Art*, Robert Giroux, ed. *1994*

2154. Hortense Calisher (1911–2009)

1 A happy childhood can't be cured. Mine'll hang around my
   neck like a rainbow, that's all, instead of a noose.
                              Pt. I, *Queenie 1971*

2 Every sixteen-year-old is a pornographer, Miss Piranesi. We
   had to know what was open to us.
                              Ibid.

3 . . . the circulation of money is different from the circulation
   of the blood. Some eras obscure that; not that it was nakedly
   appearing. I began to understand why the banker had jumped.
   A circulatory failure.
                              Pt. I, *Herself 1972*

4 Every art is a church without communicants, presided over by a
   parish of the respectable. An artist is born kneeling; he fights to
   stand. A critic, by nature of the judgement seat, is born sitting.
                              Pt. IV, Ibid.

5 When anything gets freed, a zest goes round the world.
                              Ibid.

6 When you come to the end of the past—no more peroration.
   Tolerate life—a poem which annoys when it falls into grandeur. The past will come round again.
                              Pt. V, Ibid.

2155. Jean Carroll (1911–   )

1 I've always been proud of the Jews, but never so proud as tonight because tonight I wish I had my old nose back.
          Quoted in "Early Stand-Up Comics," United Jewish Appeal
          appearance (Madison Square Garden, May 1948), *Funny
          Women, American Comediennes, 1860–1985* by Mary
                              Unterbrink *1987*

2 I don't feel differently inside, like there's an old woman living
   in there. Who determines when you should stop enjoying life,

that you should stop enjoying a raunchy joke or mixed company?
          Quoted in "Milton Berle, With Charm and a Mink" by Jane
          Wollman Rusoff, *The New York Times 5 November 2006*

3 He's a wonderful man, a regular do-it-yourselfer. I say, 'Honey,
   help me.' He says, 'Do it yourself!
                              Stand-up routine *n.d.*

2156. Lea Goldberg (1911–1970)

1 There is a law of life in her hands milking,
   For quiet seamen hold a rope like her.
      "Of Bloom," Pt. II, St. 2, *Poems from the Hebrew*, Robert
                              Mezey, ed. *1973*

2 Land of low clouds, I belong to you.
   I carry in my heart your every drop of rain.
      "Song of the Strange Woman," Pt. III, St. 1, Ibid.

2157. Ruth Gruber (1911–)

1 I realized that even if we were born Jews, there was a moment
   in our lives when we became *Jews*.
          p. 133, *Haven: The Unknown Story of 1,000 World War II
                              Refugees* *1983*
      *Referring to a refugee camp in Oswego, New York, at former
      army camp Fort Ontario.

2 To write with my heart. To think and speak with my heart. To be
   adventurous, to be an activist, to be a rebel, to be compassionate, and most of all, to be a *mensch*—a decent human being.
                              p. 197, Ibid.

3 That every Jew in the world was alive through a miracle. That
   since Egypt's Pharaoh, persecutors had tried to do to Jews
   what Hitler was now trying to do in Europe. Before Hitler,
   I was an innocent, convinced that some day there would be
   no more nationalism, no more racism, no more anti-Semitism.
   Hitler had taught me I was wrong. I became a "Hitler Jew"
   with three thousand years of history.
                              p. 267, Ibid.

2158. Hsiao Hung (1911–1941)

1 "I've never abused her all the time she's been in my home.
   Where else will you find another family that has not abused
   its child-bride by giving her beatings and tongue lashings all
   day long? Now I may have beaten her a little, just to get her
   started off on the right foot, and I only did that for a little
   over a month. Maybe I beat her pretty severely sometimes, but
   how was I expected to make a well-mannered girl out of her
   without being severe once in a while? Believe me, I didn't enjoy
   beating her so hard, what with all her screaming and carrying
   on. But I was doing it for her own good, because if I didn't beat
   her hard, she'd never be good for anything."
      "The Child Bride," *Tales of the Hulan River*, Howard
                              Goldblatt, tr. *1940*

2 "Each of the 360 trades in this world of ours has its share of
   miseries."
                              Ibid.

2159. Mahalia Jackson (1911–1972)

1 It's easy to be independent when you've got money. But to be independent when you haven't got a thing—that's the Lord's test.
              Ch. 1, *Movin' On Up*, with Evan McLoud Wylie *1966*

2 Gospel music in those days of the early 1930s was really taking wing. It was the kind of music colored people had left behind them down south and they liked it because it was just like a letter from home.

Ch. 5, Ibid.

3 Blues are the songs of despair, but gospel songs are the songs of hope.

Ch. 6, Ibid.

4 The grass is still green. The lawns are as neat as ever. The same birds are still in the trees. I guess it didn't occur to them to leave just because we moved in.

Quoted in "Unforgettable Mahalia Jackson" by Mildred Falls, *Reader's Digest March 1973*.

2160. Bel Kaufman (1911–)

1 "What is the meaning of this noise?"
"It's the sound of thinking, Mr. McCabe," I said.

Up the Down Staircase 1994

2 Good teachers, like Tolstoy's happy families, are alike everywhere.

Ibid.

*(1828–1910) Russian writer and philosopher.

3 "Hi, teach!"

Ibid.

4 Children are the true connoisseurs. What's precious to them has no price—only value.

Ibid.

5 Education is not a product: mark, diploma, job, money—in that order; it is a process, a never-ending one.

Ibid.

2161. Ruth McKenney (1911–1972)

1 If modern civilization had any meaning it was displayed in the fight against Fascism.

Letter to George Seldes, *The Great Quotations*, George Seldes, ed. *1960*

2 Man has no nobler function than to defend the truth.

Ibid.

2162. Josephine Miles (1911–1985)

1 All our footsteps, set to make
Metric advance,
Lapse into arcs in deference
To circumstance.

"On Inhabiting an Orange," St. 2, *Poems (1930–1960) 1960*

2 This weight of knowledge dark on the brain is never
To be burnt out like fever.

"*Physiologus*," St. 2, Ibid.

3 Where is the world? not about.
The world is in the heart
And the heart is closed in the sea lanes out of port.

"Merchant Marine," St. 1, Ibid.

4 How conduct in its pride
Maintains a place and sits

At the head of the table at the head of the hall
At the head of the hosts and guests.

"Conduct," St. 1, Ibid.

5 Accustomed as we are to change, or unaccustomed, we think of a change of heart, of clothes, of life, with some uncertainty. We put off the old, put on the new, yet say that the more it changes the more it remains the same. Every age is an age of transition.

Introduction, *Poetry and Change 1974*

6 True, translation may use the value terms of its own tongue in its own time; but it cannot force these on a truly alien text.

Ch. 12, Ibid.

2163. Ethel L. Payne (1911–1991)

1 Progressive legislation either directly or indirectly pertaining to civil rights is really getting the run around in Congress these days. Unless some drastic action is taken to goad the lawmakers into action, they are slated for the graveyard.

"Need Prodding to Get Congress to Act on Civil Rights Program," *Chicago Defender 1954*

2 I was put into deep freeze and given the silent treatment by the White House.

Quoted in "Loneliness in the Capital: The Black National Correspondent" (1974), *Reporting Civil Rights, Part Two: American Journalism* by Clayborne Carson, et al. *2003*

3 Things came to a head when I asked Ike what he intended to do about ending segregation in interstate travel. The Interstate Commerce Commission has handed down an opinion saying that the time had come when the practice should cease.

But Ike* took this as a personal affront. Drawing himself up to his five-star general authority, he proceeded to chew me out as he would one of his top sergeants.

Ibid.

*Dwight D. Eisenhower (1890–1969), American general, Republican politician, 34th U.S. president.

2164. Anne Porter (1911–)

1 Good-bye sweet whistling quail
Milkweed and Queen Anne's lace
Good-bye shy cottontail
Quit your secret room . . ."

"House Lots," *An Altogether Different Language 1994*

2 Lovers lie sleeping
Side by side
A wilderness between them

"Here On Earth," St. 3, Ibid.

3 Now the smallest creatures, who do not know they have names,
In fields of pure sunshine open themselves and sing.

"The First of May," St. 1

4 Give praise with children chanting their skip-rope rhymes,
A poetry not in books, a vagrant mischievous poetry
living wild on the Streets through generations of children.

"A List of Praises," St. 1, *Living Things 2006*

2165. Matilda White Riley (1911–2004)

1   People are aging better than they used to. Already about one-third of the average American's adult life is spent in retirement.

   A structural revolution is needed.

   "Matilda Riley's revolution," *AARP Bulletin,* Vol. 33, No. 11
   December 1992

2   There shouldn't be a certain age for learning, a certain age for working and a certain age for retiring.

   Ibid.

3   I see a society where the structural revolution has provided more choices and more varied roles for older people. A society where lifelong learning replaces the lockstep of traditional education, a society where the burdens of the middle generation are spread over the life course.

   Ibid.

2166. Ginger Rogers (1911–1995)

1   When two people love each other, they don't look at each other, they look in the same direction.

   "I Don't Want to Live without Love" by Dotson Rader, *Parade*
   (New York) *8 March 1987*

2167. Anna Russell (1911–2006)

1   The reason that there are so few women comics is that so few women can bear being laughed at.

   Quoted in *The Sunday Times* (London) *25 August 1957*

2168. Rosalind Russell (1911–1976)

1   . . . taste. You cannot buy such a rare and wonderful thing. You can't send away for it in a catalogue. And I'm afraid it's becoming obsolete.

   Quoted in "Rosalind Russell: Screen's Career Career Girl,"
   The Los Angeles Times 31 March 1974

2   Sex for sex's sake on the screen seems childish to me, but it's violence that really bothers me. I think it's degrading. It breeds something cancerous in our young people. We have a great responsibility to the future in what we're communicating.

   Ibid.

3   The sex symbol always remains, but the sophisticated woman has become old hat.

   Ibid.

2169. Kay Thompson (1911–1999)

1   The Plaza is the only hotel in New York that will allow you to have a turtle.

   Eloise; a book for precocious grown-ups 1955

2   There is absolutely nothing but rooms in the Plaza.

   Ibid.

3   Getting bored is not allowed.

   Ibid.

2170. Audrey Wurdeman (1911–1960)

1   I walk in ambush bright
   With terror and delight,

The savage lovely beast
Pacing within my breast
   "Bright Ambush," St. 1, *Bright Ambush: Poems 1934*

2   It was as though, thus caught and mine,
   A flying fish, a silver line
   With wings of gauze grown softer still,
   Lay in my hands and at my will,
   And of my will it was set free,
   And plunged like moonlight in the sea.
   "Love's Instant," St. 2, *Ibid.*

3   Behold, my dear, the dream we saw,
   The thing we built without a flaw,
   The amber and the agate rime,
   The interstitial beat of time,
   The microcosmos of our wit,
   The sweetness that we sucked from it
   "Text," St. 2, *Ibid.*

4   Being born is only knowing
   Less of growth and more of growing.
   "Being Born," *Ibid.*

2171. Yang Jiang (1911–   )

1   SHEN. In the spring the flower blooms in the sun, the spring breeze blows it away where it will—ideals, love: they're nothing more than spring sunlight and spring breeze. Tomorrow that blossom will fall to earth, sprout, grow roots, nothing more than seed—if the environment lets it live. . . . There are botanical types that don't know their place. Here they fly, there they fly, thinking they have so much strength, that they're in charge! The law-abiding ones, like rice and wheat, have already quietly let themselves rot in the soil and turn into fertilizer for the next generation.

   Act I, *Fen hsü* (Windswept Blossoms) 1946

2172. Madeline Bingham (1912–1988)

1   In every country the organization of society is like a section of a rock face, with new layers and old layers built one upon the other. The decay of old ways of behaving and old laws does not take place within a few years; it is a gradual process of erosion.

   Ch. 2, *Scotland Under Mary Stuart** 1971
   *See 341.

2   Once the fervour has gone out of it, a revolution can turn out to be dull work for the ordinary people.

   Ch. 7, *Ibid.*

3   A country which is engaged in constant war, both internal and external, does not provide good ground in which the arts may flourish.

   Ch. 12, *Ibid.*

4   Too many cooks may spoil the broth, but it only takes one to burn it.

   The Bad Cook's Guide n.d.

5   There may be as many good fish in the sea as ever came out of it, but cooking them is even more difficult than catching them.

   Ibid.

2173. Chien Shiung Wu (1912–1997)

1   . . . even the most sophisticated and seemingly remote basic nuclear physics research has implications beneficial to human welfare.

   4000 Years of Women in Science, astr.ua.edu/4000WS *16*
   October 1998

2 There is only one thing worse than coming home from the lab to a sink full of dirty dishes, and that is not going to the lab at all.

Contributions of 20th Century Women to Physics, UCLA, physics.ucla.edu/~cwp *16 March 1999*

2174. Julia Child (1912–2004)

1 This is a book for the servantless American cook who can be unconcerned on occasion with budgets, waistlines, time schedules, children's meals, the parent-chauffeur-den mother syndrome or anything else which might interfere with the enjoyment of producing something wonderful to eat.

Introduction, *Mastering the Art of French Cooking*, with Simone Beck and Louisette Bertholle *1961*

2 Sometimes . . . It takes me an entire day to write a recipe, to communicate it correctly. It's really like writing a little short story.

Quoted in "The Making of a Masterpiece" by Patricia Simon, *McCall's October 1970*

3 Learn how to cook! That's the way to save money. You don't save it buying hamburger helpers, and prepared food; you save it buying fresh foods in season or in large supply, when they are cheapest and usually best, and you prepare them from scratch at home. Why pay for someone else's work, when if you know how to do it, you can save all that money for yourself?

Introduction, *Julia Child's Kitchen 1975*

4 I still feel that French cooking is the most important in the world, one of the few that has rules. If you follow the rules, you can do pretty well.

Quoted in Obituary by Regina Schrambling, *The New York Times Book Review 13 August 2004*

5 I don't think it's a real cuisine [Italian] because you don't do much.

Ibid.

6 Remember, you are alone in the kitchen, and no one can see you.

The French Chef (PBS TV show) *n.d.*

2775. Amalia Fleming (1912–1986)

1 I am working on a problem which fascinates me but I keep failing to do what I try. Still there is an end even to failures.

(December 1954), Quoted in *The Life of Sir Alexander Fleming** by André Maurois *1959*
*English bacteriologist (1881–1955).

2 He, too, I thought, possesses, like Pasteur,* and in the highest degree, the art of choosing the crucial experiment and of grasping the capital importance of a chance observation. . . . But . . . for Fleming there was a wide world lying beyond the confines of his lab. The appearance of a new flower in his garden was as interesting to him as the work he might be engaged on. . . . [He] felt himself to be an infinitesimal part of nature, and from that feeling was born his refusal to indulge in self-importance and his dislike of big words. It was almost possible to say that he was a genius in spite of himself, and reluctantly.

Ch. 16, Ibid.
*Louis P— (1822–1895), French chemist who founded modern microbiology.

3 I respect every idealogy, including communism, provided they are not trying to impose their will through force. I am against any totalitarian regime.

Quoted in *Newsweek* (New York) *11 October 1971*

4 The innocent people who have nothing to say are tortured the most because when a prisoner admits something, the torture stops.

Quoted in "Greece: Survival of the Shrewdest" by Susan Margolis, *Ms.* (New York) *October 1973*

2176. Lucille Fletcher (1912–1973)

1 Such amazing things happen to the female sex on an ocean cruise. The sea air acted like an aphrodisiac. Or maybe it was the motion. Or the carnival atmosphere. Whatever it was, and he had never seen it otherwise, the ladies, married or single, young or old, simply went to pieces aboard the S.S. *Columbia*. They toppled like tenpins—into bed.

Ch. 2, *The Girl in Cabin B54 1968*

2 "The brain, of course, is still an unknown country in many respects—like outer space. And as a psychologist, I myself can believe that certain people, extraordinarily sensitive people, may possess special mental equipment which can tune in, as it were, certain waves, vibrations, even imagery, which other people cannot sense at all."

Ch. 8, Ibid.

2177. Virginia Graham (1912–1998)

1 It will be the firm intention of your hosts to take you, as soon as possible, away from their homes. Remember, they do not know what on earth to do with you and have been arguing about it for weeks, so do not be difficult and announce that all you want to do is sit still and look at the view. They are irrevocably determined you should be entertained, and it is a matter of little importance whether you wish to be or whether you don't.

Ch. 1, *Say Please 1949*

2 Good shot, bad luck, and hell are the five basic words to be used in a game of tennis, though these, of course, can be slightly amplified.

Ch. 8, Ibid.

3 In society it is etiquette for ladies to have the best chairs and get handed things. In the home the reverse is the case. That is why ladies are more sociable than gentlemen.

Ch. 14, Ibid.

4 Be blind. Be stupid. Be British. Be careful.

Ch. 25, Ibid.

2178. Martha Wright Griffiths (1912–2003)

1 This amendment [the Equal Rights Amendment*], if passed, would be like a beacon which should awaken nine sleeping Rip Van Winkles to the fact that the twentieth century is passing into history. It is a different world and they [the Supreme Court] should speak for justice, not prejudice. . . . I seek justice, not in some distant tomorrow, not in some study commission, but now while I live.

Quoted in *American Political Women* by Esther Stineman *1980*
*See Alice Paul, 1637.

2 My grandmother wanted to live long enough to vote for a woman president. I'll be satisfied if I live to see a woman go before the Supreme Court and hear the justices acknowledge, "Gentlemen, she's human. She deserves the protection of our laws."

Ibid.

3 The error of most women [in Congress] was they were trying to make the men who sat in Congress not disapprove of them. I think they wanted to be liked, they didn't want to make enemies. So they didn't try to do things they thought the men would disapprove of. I didn't give a damn whether the men approved or not.

> "A Woman's Place; The 1950s Were Not Easy for Females in Congress" by Elizabeth Kastorm, *Washington Post* 17 *November 1996*

4 I am tired of paying into a pension fund to support your widow but not my widower.

> Comment, House Ways and Means Committee, Quoted in "Martha Griffiths, Fighter for Women's Rights, Dies at 91" by Wolfgang Saxon, *The New York Times* 25 April 2003

2179. Louise Levitas Henriksen (1912–1997)

1 There was no way back to the ghetto.
> *Anzia Yezierska: A Writer's Life* 1988

2180. Lady Bird Johnson (1912–2007)

1 It all began so beautifully. After a drizzle in the morning, the sun came out bright and clear. We were driving into Dallas. In the lead car were President and Mrs. Kennedy....

> (22 November 1963),* *A White House Diary* 1970
> *The day John F. Kennedy, 35th president of the United States, was assassinated.

2 It's odd that you can get so anesthetized by your own pain or your own problem that you don't quite fully share the hell of someone close to you.

> (8 February 1964), Ibid.

3 As I record this several days later, I must say that being with President Truman* those days has been one of the biggest pluses of this period of my life. It has been an insight into history for me, a joy to see a man who has lived through so much public rancor and condemnation and has emerged philosophic, salty, completely unembittered, a happy man—and vindicated by history on most of his major decisions.

> (12 March 1964), Ibid.
> *Harry S. T—, politician (1884–1972); 33rd president of the United States (1945–1953).

4 The first lady is, and always has been, an unpaid public servant elected by one person, her husband.

> (14 March 1968), Ibid.

5 I've had a long love affair with the environment. It is my sustenance, my pleasure, my joy. Flowers in a city are like lipstick on a woman—it just makes you look better to have a little color.

> Quoted in *Time* (New York) 5 September 1989

6 Where flowers bloom, so does hope.
> Motto for Society for a More Beautiful National Capital *n.d*

2181–2182. Pamela Hansford Johnson (1912–1981)

1 There are few things more disturbing than to find, in somebody we detest, a moral quality which seems to us demonstrably superior to anything we ourselves possess. It augurs not merely an unfairness on the part of creation, but a lack of artistic judgement.... Sainthood is acceptable only in saints.

> Ch. 23, *Night and Silence, Who is Here?— An American Comedy* 1963

2 You slam a politician, you make out he's the devil, with horns and hoofs. But his wife loves him, and so did all his mistresses.

> Ibid.

2183. Dena Justin (1912–)

1 Mythologically speaking, the ancients scooped our modern-day biologists by unknown thousands of years in their recognition of the female principle as the primal creative force. And they too buried the truth, restructuring the myths to accommodate male ideology.

> "From Mother Goddess to Dishwasher," *Natural History February 1973*

2 Although the witch, incarnate or in surrogate mother disguise, remains a universal bogey, pejorative aspects of the wizard, her masculine counterpart, have vanished over the patriarchal centuries. The term *wizard* has acquired reverential status—wizard of finance, wizard of diplomacy, wizard of science.

> Ibid.

3 It is remarkable how many legends survive among preliterate cultures of an earlier matriarchal period and a violent uprising by men in which they usurped female authority.

> Ibid.

4 The earth Mother, the womb from which all living things are born and to which all return at death, was perhaps the earliest representation of the divine in protohistoric religions.

> Ibid.

2184. Mary Lavin (1912–1996)

1 "Take my own father! You know what he said in his last moments? On his deathbed, he defied me to name a man who had enjoyed a better life. In spite of the dreadful pain, his face *radiated* happiness!" said Mother, nodding her head comfortably. "Happiness drives out pain, as fire burns out fire."

> "Happiness," *The New Yorker* 14 December 1968

2 Our father, while he lived, had cast a magic over everything, for us as well as for her. He held his love up over us like an umbrella and kept off the troubles that afterward came down on us, pouring cats and dogs!

> Ibid.

3 "Life is a vale of tears," they said. "You are privileged to find it out so young!" Ugh! After I staggered onto my feet and began to take hold of life once more, they fell back defeated. And the first day I gave a laugh—pouf, they were blown out like candles. They weren't living in a real world at all; they belonged to a ghostly world where life was easy: all one had to do was sit and weep. It takes effort to push back the stone from the mouth of the tomb.

> Ibid.

4 ... a new noise started in her head; the noise of a nameless panic that did not always roar, but never altogether died down.

> "Via Violetta," *A Memory and Other Stories* 1972

2185. Mary McCarthy (1912–1989)

1 I felt caught in a dilemma that was new to me then but which since has become horribly familiar: the trap of adult life, in which you are held, wriggling, powerless to act because you can see both sides. On that occasion, as generally in the future, I compromised.

Memories of a Catholic Girlhood 1946

2 The happy ending is our national belief.

"America the Beautiful," *Commentary* (New York) *September 1947*

3 . . . Elinor was always firmly convinced of other people's hypocrisy since she could not believe that they noticed less than she did.

Ch. 1, *The Group 1954*

4 "You mustn't force sex to do the work of love or love to do the work of sex."

Ch. 2, Ibid.

5 She had tried to bind him with possessions, but he slipped away like Houdini.

Ch. 13, Ibid.

6 Sometimes she felt that he was postponing being a success till he could wear out her patience; as soon as she gave up and left him, his name would mock her in lights.

Ibid.

7 Bureaucracy, the rule of no one, has become the modern form of despotism.

"The *Vita Activa*," *The New Yorker 18 October 1958*

8 The labor of keeping house is labor in its most naked state, for labor is toil that never finishes, toil that has to be begun again the moment it is completed, toil that is destroyed and consumed by the life process.

Ibid.

9 When an American heiress wants to buy a man, she at once crosses the Atlantic.

On The Contrary 1961

10 An unrectified case of injustice has a terrible way of lingering restlessly, in the social atmosphere like an unfinished question.

Pt. 3, "My Confession," Ibid.

11 Every age has a keyhole to which its eye is pasted.

Ibid.

12 The horror of Gandhi's* murder lies not in the political motives behind it or in its consequences for Indian policy or for the future of non-violence; the horror lies simply in the fact that any man could look into the face of this extraordinary person and deliberately pull a trigger.

Pt. 1, "Gandhi" (1949), Ibid.
*Mohandas G—, Indian nationalist leader and father of nonviolent resistance; assassinated (1869–1948).

13 He had never outgrown the feeling that a quest for information was a series of maneuvers in a game of espionage.

"Winter Visitors," *Birds of America 1965*

14 In politics, it seems, retreat is honorable if dictated by military considerations and shameful if even *suggested* for ethical reasons.

"Solutions," *Vietnam 1967*

15 In the Stalinist* days, we used to detest a vocabulary that had to be read in terms of antonyms—"volunteers," denoting conscripts, "democracy," tyranny, and so on. Insensibly, in Vietnam, starting with the little word "advisors," we have adopted this slippery Aesopian language ourselves . . .

"Language," *Hanoi 1968*
*Josef Stalin, Soviet leader (1879–1953), premier of U.S.S.R. (1941–1953).

16 It has to be acknowledged that in capitalist society, with its herds of hippies, originality has become a sort of fringe benefit, a mere convention, accepted obsolescence, the Beatnik model being turned in for the Hippie model, as though strangely obedient to capitalist laws of marketing.

Ibid.

17 My grandmother had statutory ages for everything, sixteen for boys, fourteen for real, non-ribbed silk stockings, fifteen perhaps for lipstick.

How I Grew 1987

2186. Pat Nixon (1912–1993)

1 I have sacrificed everything in my life that I consider precious in order to advance the political career of my husband.*

Quoted in *Women at Work* by Betty Medsger *1975*
*Richard Milhous N—(1913–1994), 37th President of the United States (1969–1974); Vice President (1953–1961).

2187. Tillie Olsen (1912–2007)

1 And when is there time to remember, to sift, to weigh, to estimate, to total?

"I Stand Here Ironing," (1954) *Tell Me a Riddle 1960*

2 My wisdom came too late.

Ibid.

3 . . . the Law and the Wall: only so far shall you go and no further, uptown forbidden, not your language, not your people, not your country.

"Hey Sailor, What Ship?" (1955), Ibid.

4 In the beginning there had been youth and the joy of raising hell . . . And later there were memories to forget, dreams to be stifled, hopes to be murdered.

Ibid.

5 "Not everybody feel religion the same way. Some it's in their mouth, but some it's like a hope in their blood, their bones."

"O Yes" (1956), Ibid.

6 It is a long baptism into the seas of humankind, my daughter. Better immersion than to live untouched. . . .

Ibid.

7 For forty-seven years they had been married. How deep back the stubborn, gnarled roots of the quarrel reached, no one could say—but only now, when tending to the needs of others no longer shackled them together, the roots swelled up visible, split the earth between them, and the tearing shook even the children, long since grown.

Ch. 1, "Tell Me a Riddle" (1960), Ibid.

8 He could not, could not turn away from this desire: to have the troubling of responsibility, the fretting with money, over

and done with; to be free, to be *care*free where success was not measured by accumulation. . . .

Ibid.

9   The television is shadows, Mrs. Enlightened! Mrs. Cultured! A world comes into your house—and it is shadows. People you would never meet in a million lifetimes. Wonders.

Ibid.

10   Like the hide of a drum shall you be, beaten in life, beaten in death.

Ibid.

11   "Vinegar he poured on me all his life; I am well marinated; how can I be honey now?"

Ibid.

12   Heritage. How have we come from the savages, now no longer to be savages—this to teach. To look back and learn what humanizes man—this to teach. To smash all ghettos that divide us—not to go back, not to go back—this to teach.

Ch. 2, Ibid.

13   "Remember your advice, easy to keep your head above water, empty things float. Float."

Ch.3, Ibid.

14   ". . . life may be hated or wearied of, but never despised."

Ch.4, Ibid.

15   . . . the circumstances for sustained creation are almost impossible.

Silences: When Writers Don't Write 1965

16   More than in any other human relationship, overwhelmingly more, motherhood means being instantly interruptible, responsive, responsible. . . .

Ibid.

17   Time granted does not necessarily coincide with time that can be most fully used.

Ibid.

18   The mute inglorious Millions: those whose waking hours are all struggle for existence; the barely educated; the illiterate; women—their silence the silence of centuries as to how life was, is, for most of humanity.

Ibid.

19   "The joy, the reason to believe," my mother said, "the hope for the world, the baby, holy with possibility, that is all of us at birth." And she began to cry, out of the dream and its telling now.

"Dream-Vision," *Mother to Daughter, Daughter to Mother 1984*

2188.   Anne Barbara Ridler (1912–2001)

1   CRANMER. A scholar, you know, is a wingless creature
More tortoise than bird.
MARGARET. But with a bird's domain . . .

Sc. 1, *The Trial of Thomas Cranmer 1956*

2   . . . live each now in the illumination
Of what's to come

"A Waving Hand," *A Matter of Life and Death 1959*

3   It is not that the dead return—
They are about us always, although unguessed

"Nothing Is Lost," Ibid.

4   And when our baby stirs and struggles to be born
It compels humility: what we began
Is now its own.

"For a Child Expected" *n.d.*

2189.   May Sarton (1912–1995)

1   Learning is such a very painful business. It requires humility from people at an age where the natural habit is arrogance.

The Small Room 1961

2   Excellence costs a great deal.

Ibid.

3   The Lord is not my shepherd. I shall want.

Mrs. Stevens Hears the Mermaids Singing 1965

4   We are all monsters, if it comes to that, we women who have chosen to be something more and something less than women.

Ibid.

5   "There was such a thing as women's work and it consisted chiefly, Hilary sometimes thought, in being able to stand constant interruption and keep your temper. . . ."

Ibid.

6   The poet must be free to love or hate as the spirit moves him, free to change, free to be a chameleon, free to be an enfant terrible. He must above all never worry about his effect on other people. Power requires that one do just that all the time. Power requires that the inner person never be unmasked. No, we poets have to go naked. And since this is so, it is better that we stay private people; a naked public person would be rather ridiculous, what?

Pt. 2, Ibid.

7   A man with a talent does what is expected of him, makes his way, constructs, is an engineer, a composer, a builder of bridges. It's the natural order of things that he construct objects outside himself and his family. The woman who does so is aberrant. . . . We have to *expiate* for this cursed talent someone handed out to us, by mistake, in the black mystery of genetics.

Ibid.

8   I would predicate that in all great works of genius masculine and feminine elements in the personality find expression, whether this androgynous nature is played out sexually or not.

Journal of a Solitude 1973

9   My faults too have been those of excess; I too have made emotional demands, without being aware of what I was asking; I too have imagined that I was giving when I was battering at someone for attention.

Ibid.

10   I think men do not want women poets to talk about their feelings. It's the *feminine* poet men don't like.

Quoted in *May Sarton: A Biography* by Margot Peters 1997

11   I know my biographer will be my enemy.

Cited in "Licking her wounds" by Brenda Wineapple, *The Women's Review of Books*, Vol. XIV, No. 8 *May 1997*

2290. Kate Simon (1912–1990)

1 Girls' prayers counted for nothing; like animals, they had no souls and no voices to God's ear.
Bronx Primitive: Portraits in A Childhood 1982

2 One assumes that foreign ladies, English and Americans particularly, because they are tremulous, neurotic bags of bones reduced by sexual malnutrition, find all Italians irresistible.
Italy: The Places In Between n.d.

3 I had no time for step-by-step projects; the urgent need was for swift voyages, with short stops at many ports of call.
A Wider World: Portraits in Adolescence 1986

4 The susurrus of silks dragging through pools of blood, chivalric elegance living with bestiality in high places, the silver rose boxed with the dagger, fidelity bedded with perfidy, remain a collage whose fascination has never quite faded.
A Renaissance Tapestry: The Gonzaga of Mantua 1988

5 Her impressive knowledge of Virgil, every line, didn't matter, nor did her command of Greek, and so what if she could explain the propositions of Euclid? Her vocation was marriage.
Ibid.

2191. Claire Trevor (1912–2000)

1 What a holler would ensue if people had to pay the minister as much to marry them as they have to pay a lawyer to get them a divorce.
Quoted in *New York Journal-American 12 October 1960*

2192. Barbara Tuchman (1912–1989)

1 War is the unfolding of miscalculations.
The Guns of August 1962

2 Dead battles, like dead generals, hold the military mind in their dead grip.
Ch. 2, Ibid.

3 Honor wears different coats to different eyes. . . .
Ch. 7, Ibid.

4 No more distressing moment can ever face a British government than that which requires it to come to a hard, fast and specific decision.
Ch. 9, Ibid.

5 For one August in its history Paris was French—and silent.
Ch. 20, Ibid.

6 In April 1917 the illusion of isolation was destroyed, America came to the end of innocence, and of the exuberant freedom of bachelor independence. That the responsibilities of world power have not made us happier is no surprise. To help ourselves manage them, we have replaced the illusion of isolation with a new illusion of omnipotence.
"How We Entered World War I," *The New York Times Magazine 5 May 1967*

7 We're being made to look like Lolitas and lion tamers.
Quoted in *The Beautiful People* by Marilyn Bender* 1968
*See 2511.

8 Reasonable orders are easy enough to obey; it is capricious, bureaucratic or plain idiotic demands that form the habit of discipline.
Pt. I, Ch. 1, *Stilwell* and the American Experience in China: 1911–1945 1970*
*Joseph W. S—, American army general (1883–1946).

9 In a country where misery and want were the foundation of the social structure, famine was periodic, death from starvation common, disease pervasive, thievery normal, and graft and corruption taken for granted, the elimination of these conditions in Communist China is so striking that negative aspects of the new rule fade in relative importance.
Ch. 1, *Notes from China 1972*

10 The farmer is the eternal China.
Ch. 3, Ibid.

11 The open frontier, the hardships of homesteading from scratch, the wealth of natural resources, the whole vast challenge of a continent waiting to be exploited, combined to produce a prevailing materialism and an American drive bent as much, if not more, on money, property, and power than was true of the Old World from which we had fled.
"On Our Birthday—America As Idea," *Newsweek* (New York) *12 July 1976*

12 In the United States we have a society pervaded from top to bottom by contempt for the law.
Ibid.

13 Our government . . . learns no lessons, employs no wisdom and corrupts all who succumb to the Potomac fever.
Ibid.

14 Our sins in the twentieth century—greed, violence, inhumanity—have been profound, with the result that the pride and self-confidence of the nineteenth century have turned to dismay and self-disgust.
Ibid.

15 Every French town has an Avenue Victor Hugo.* We never have a Mark Twain** Street.
Quoted in "Nothing Wicked About Being Elite . . ." by Nan Robertson, *The New York Times 28 February 1979*
*French novelist (1801–1885). **Pen name of American author and humorist Samuel Langhorne Clemens (1835–1910).

16 I ask myself, have nations ever declined from a loss of moral sense rather than from physical reasons or the pressure of barbarians? I think that they have.
"Barbara Tuchman," Quoted in *A World of Ideas* by Bill Moyers *1989*

17 We're a public that is brought up on deception, through advertising. . . . We're accustomed to being deceived. We allow ourselves to be deceived. Advertising is really responsible for a lot in the deterioration of American public perceptions.
Ibid.

2193. Charleszetta Waddles (1912–2001)

1 Hungry people can be dangerous people—it's the best excuse to do the lowest thing.
Quoted by James K. Davis in *Life* (New York) *21 March 1969*

2 We're trying to show what the church could mean to the world if it lived by what it preached. I read the Bible. It didn't say just go to church. It said, "Do something."
Quoted in *Newsweek 1 May 1972*

3 You can't give people pride, but you can provide the kind of understanding that makes people look to their inner strengths and find their own sense of pride.
> Quoted in "Mother Waddles: Black Angel of the Poor" by Lee Edson, *Reader's Digest October 1972*

4 God knows no distance.
> Ibid.

2194. Roberta Wohlstetter (1912–2007)

1 If the study of Pearl Harbor has anything to offer for the future, it is this: We have to accept the fact of uncertainty and learn to live with it. No magic, in code or otherwise, will provide certainty. Our plans must work without it.
> *Pearl Harbor: Warning and Decision 1962*

2 After the event, of course, a signal is always clear; we can now see what disaster it was signaling since the disaster has occurred. But before the event it is obscure and pregnant with conflicting meanings.
> Ibid.

3 We cannot *count* on strategic warning. We *might* get it, and we might be able to take useful preparatory actions that would be impossible without it . . . [But] if we accept the fact that the signal picture for impending attacks is almost sure to be ambiguous, we shall pre arrange actions that are right and feasible in response to ambiguous signals, including signs of attack that might be false.
> Ibid.

2195. Eleanor Clark (1913–1996)

1 "He was the kind of man, if a mule kicked somebody down the street, he'd work till he gut it on his conscience."
> Pt. III, Ch. 2, *Baldur's Gate 1955*

2 "We Occidentals have a congenital, it may even be fatal, need for good manners, or you might say ceremony, in our approach to meaning, I suppose to make up for our crudeness in living."
> Ch. 3, Ibid.

3 The little *and,* the tiny *if,*
   The ardent *ahs* and *ohs,*
   They haunt the lane of poesy,
   The boulevards of prose.
> "Alliances" *n.d.*

2196. Nathalia Crane (1913–1998)

1 But my heart is all aflutter like the washing on the line.
> "The Flathouse Roof," St. 1 *n.d.*

2 In the darkness, who would answer for the color of a rose,
   Or the vestments of the May moth and the pilgrimage it goes?
> "The Blind Girl," *n.d.*

3 The sign work of the Orient it runneth up and down;
   The Talmud stalks from right to left, a rabbi in a gown;
   The Roman rolls from left to right from Maytime unto May;
   But the gods shake up their symbols in an absent-minded way.
> "The Symbols," *n.d.*

4 You cannot choose your battlefield,
   The gods do that for you,

But you can plant a standard
Where a standard never flew.*
> "The Colors," *n.d.*

*Sometimes misattributed to author Stephen Crane.

5 There is a glory
   In a great mistake.
> "Imperfection," *Swear By the Night and Other Poems 1936*

2197. Sylvia Fine (1913–1991)

1 And why do I sew each new chapeau
   With a style they most look positively grim in?
   Strictly between us, entre-nous
   I hate women.
> "Anatole of Paris," *The Secret Life of Walter Mitty* (musical) 1947

2 An unemployed court jester is nobody's fool.
> "The Court Jester," *The Court Jester* (musical) 1956

3 So rock-a-bye my baby
   Don't you cry my baby
   Sleepy time is nigh
   Won't you rock me to a ragtime lullabye
> "Lullaby in Ragtime," *The Five Pennies 1959*

4 He is full of pith and vinegar.
> Quoted by Marie Shear* *n.d.*

*See 3228.

2198. Grace Hansen (1913–1985)

1 For some time I've had my eye on Tom McCall's* seat—which is a great deal more than he's had on it.
> Quoted in her obituary, *Register-Guard* (Eugene, Oreg.) *14 January 1985*

*On her 1970 race against incumbent Tom McCall (1913–1983), governor of OR, 1967–75.

2 Don't be afraid your life will end; be afraid that it will never begin.
> Ibid.

3 A wedding is just like a funeral except that you get to smell your own flowers.
> Ibid.

2199. Ruth Beebe Hill (1913–   )

1 I live in a world of reason and choice as opposed to faith and force.
> Quoted in "'Hanta Yo': The Book of the Indian" by Kathleen Hendrix, *The Los Angeles Times 4 February 1979*

2 Bear with me. I'll get back on the track. Actually I'm not off the track. I'm off the train, but not off the track.
> Ibid.

3 I own my life. And only mine. And so I shall appreciate my person. And so I shall make proper use of myself.
> *Hanta Yo 1979*

4 I am Ahbleza. I own the earth.
> Ibid.

2200. Attia Hosain (1913–1998)

1 "Listen to me child. You will be a woman soon and must behave well and modestly. The Kazi will ask you three times whether you will marry Kalloo Mian. Now don't you be shameless, like these modern educated girls, and shout gleefully "Yes." Be modest and cry softly and say 'Hoon.'"

Phoenix Fled, introduction by Anita Desai *1953 (repr. 1988)*

2 My life changed. It had been restricted by invisible barriers almost as effectively as the physically restrictive lives of my aunts in the *zenana.* A window had opened here, a door there, a curtain had been drawn aside; but outside lay a world narrowed by one's field of vision.

Sunlight on a Broken Column, introduction by Anita Desai *1961 (repr. 1988)*

2201. Elizabeth Janeway (1913–2005)

1 ... it is through the ghost [writer] that the great gift of knowledge which the inarticulate have for the world can be made available.

Ch. 29, *The Writer's Book,* Helen Hull, ed. *1950*

2 Poets are the leaven in the lump of civilization.

Ch. 30, Ibid.

3 As long as mixed grills and combination salads are popular, anthologies will undoubtedly continue in favor.

Ch. 32, Ibid.

4 ... it is almost shockingly delightful to read a book which could have been written by absolutely no one else in the world than the great and important figure whose name is signed to it ...

"This I Remember," *Accident on Route 37 1964*

5 I admire people who are suited to the contemplative life.... They can sit inside themselves like honey in a jar and just be. It's wonderful to have someone like that around, you always feel you can count on them. You can go away and come back, you can change your mind and your hairdo and your politics, and when you get through doing all these upsetting things, you look around and there they are, just the way they were, just being.

"Elizabeth Jowett," Ibid.

6 After the city, where we had always lived, those country years were startling.... The surprise of animals ... in and out, cats and dogs and a milk goat and chickens and guinea hens, all taken for granted, as if man was intended to live on terms of friendly intercourse with the rest of creation instead of huddling in isolation on the fourteenth floor of an apartment house in a city where animals occurred behind bars in the zoo.

"Steven Benedict," Ibid.

7 American women are not the only people in the world who manage to lose track of themselves, but we do seem to mislay the past in a singularly absent-minded fashion.

"Reflections on the History of Women," *Women: Their Changing Roles 1973*

8 Sex cannot be contained within a definition of physical pleasure, it cannot be understood as merely itself for it has stood for too long as a symbol of profound connection between human beings.

Between Myth and Morning 1974

9 Love between women is seen as a paradigm of love between equals, and that is perhaps its greatest attraction.

Ibid.

10 We have to see, I think, that questioning the values of old rules is different from simply breaking them.

Ibid.

11 I am not sure how many "sins" I would recognize in the world. Some would surely be defused by changed circumstances. But I can imagine none that is more irredeemably sinful than the betrayal, the exploitation, of the young by those who should care for them.

"Incest: A Rational Look at the Oldest Taboo," *Ms.* (New York) *November 1981*

12 To prepare for the future we need to interpret the past. I wish people would read more history. So many people believe that if something happened more than five years ago, it doesn't matter anymore.

"Trendspotters" (p. 59), *Working Woman Magazine July 1987*

13 Women must do their part to invent the future. We must start thinking of ourselves as the people responsible for making public policy.

Ibid.

2202. Margo Jones (1913–1955)

1 Neither the building, nor the organization, not the finest plays and actors in the whole world will help you create a fine theatre if you have no consistent approach of your own, a true philosophy of the theater.

Theatre in the Round 1951

2 Everything in life is theatre.

Quoted in *The New York Times 26 July 1955*

3 The theatre has given me a chance not only to live my own life but a million others. In every play there is a chance for one great moment, experience or understanding.

Ibid.

4 There are two kinds of theatre, good and bad. Much as I should like to see theatre in America, I would rather have no theatre than bad theatre. What we must strive for is perfection and come as close to it as is humanly possible.

"Theatre '50: A Dream Come True," *Ten Talents in the American Theatre,* David H. Stevens, ed. *1957*

2203. Dorothy Kilgallen (1913–1965)

1 The world is grand, awfully big and astonishingly beautiful, frequently thrilling. But I love New York.

Girl Around the World 1936

2 Doorman—a genius who can open the door of your car with one hand, help you in with the other, and still have one left for the tip.

"Come Away, Poverty's Catching," *Violets and Vinegar,* Jilly Cooper and Tom Hartman, eds. *1980*

2204. Vivien Leigh (1913–1967)

1 In Britain, an attractive woman is somehow suspect. If there is talent as well it is overshadowed. Beauty and brains just can't be entertained; someone has been too extravagant.

Quoted by Robert Ottaway in *Light of a Star* by Gwen Robyns *1968*

2205. Mary Morris (1913–1986)

1   "It's like dependency on foreign oil.... We should be able to live alone, even if we don't want to."

"Summer Share," *The Bus of Dreams* 1985

2   ... how easy it is for a heart to turn to stone.

"The Hall of Meteorites," Ibid.

2206. Rosa Parks (1913–2005)

1   My only concern was to get home after a hard day's work.*

Quoted in *Time* (New York) *15 December 1975*
*Reference to her refusal to give up her seat on a bus in Montgomery, Alabama, in 1955 to a white who was standing. From her act of defiance grew the Montgomery bus boycott and the leadership of Martin Luther King, Jr.

2   In these times, none of us seem safe from this type of treatment and violation by a sick-minded person.*

"Nation," A3, *Seattle Post-Intelligencer 1 September 1994*
*Remark after having been robbed and beaten in Detroit.

3   I had been pushed as far as I could stand.

Quoted in "Women Who Could Be President" by Jane Ciabattari, *Parade Magazine 7 February 1999*

4   By the time I was 6, I was old enough to realize that we were not actually free.

Quoted in *Rosa Parks* by Doughlas Brinkley 2000

5   I just wanted to be free like everybody else. I did not want to be continually humiliated over something I had no control over: the color of my skin.

Ibid.

2207. Sylvia Porter (1913–1991)

1   The average family exists only on paper and its average budget is a fiction, invented by statisticians for the convenience of statisticians.

Ch. 1, *Sylvia Porter's Money Book* 1975

2   Money never remains just coins and pieces of paper. It is constantly changing into the comforts of daily life. Money can be translated into the beauty of living, a support in misfortune, an education, or future security. It also can be translated into a source of bitterness.

Ibid.

3   We are into an "era of aspirations" in our economy. In this era, most of us will spend a shrinking share of our income on the traditional necessities of food, clothing, shelter, and transportation while we spend a steadily increasing share of our income for goods and services which reflect our hopes and wants.

Ibid.

4   For millions, the retirement dream is in reality an economic nightmare. For millions, growing old today means growing poor, being sick, living in substandard housing, and having to scrimp merely to subsist. And this is the prospect not for the one out of every ten Americans now over sixty-five ... but also for the sixty-five million who will reach retirement age within the next thirty-three years.

Ch. 19, Ibid.

5   One of the soundest rules I try to remember when making forecasts in the field of economics—a profession which is still far

more an art than a science—is that whatever is to happen is happening already.

Speech, Economic Club (Detroit), Quoted in "Sylvia & You",
Time 28 November 1960

2208. Barbara Pym (1913–1980)

1   My thoughts went round and round and it occurred to me that if I ever wrote a novel it would be of the 'stream of consciousness' type and deal with an hour in the life of a woman at the sink.

Excellent Women 1952

2   I began piling cups and saucers on to a tray. I suppose it was cowardly of me, but I felt that I wanted to be alone, and what better place to choose than the sink, where neither of the men would follow me?

Ibid.

3   I should have liked the kind of life where one ate food flavoured with garlic, but it was not to be.

Jane and Prudence 1953

4   I'm not one of those excellent women, who can just go home and eat a boiled egg and make a cup of tea and be very splendid, she thought, but how useful it would be if I were!

Less Than Angels 1955

5   "Research with a good-looking man. That's an enviable lot."

No Fond Return of Love 1961

6   "You were lucky to find [a poet] so obscure that not even the Americans had done him. It's quite serious, this shortage of obscure poets."

Ibid.

2209. Nancy Reeves (1913–   )

1   Today the hemisphere of the public has been assigned to the male and the hemisphere of the private to the female. Each sex has become a symbol for its territory. The conflict between them can then be seen as a reflection of the longing of each to be part of the other's sphere, to link the public with the private in our schizoid world, to embrace the whole of life.

Womankind Beyond the Stereotypes 1971

2210. Muriel Rukeyser (1913–1980)

1   Women and poets see the truth arrive,
Then it is acted out,
then lives are lost, and all the newsboys shout.

"Letter to the Front," *Beast in View* 1944

2   The universe of poetry is the universe of emotional truth. Our material is in the way we feel and the way we remember.

The Life of Poetry 1949

3   ... on second cry I woke
fully and gave to feed and fed on feeding.

"Night Feeding," *Selected Poems* 1951

4   You will enter the world which eats itself
Naming faith, reason, naming love, truth, fact.

"Nine Poems for the Unborn Child," VII, St. I, *Waterlily Fire*
(1935–1962) 1962

5   The strength, the grossness, spirit and gall of choice.

VI, Ibid.

6   Escape the birthplace; walk into the world
Refusing to be either slave or slaveholder.
"Secrets of American Civilization," St. 3, *The Speed of Darkness* 1968

7   No more masks! No more mythologies!
"The Poem as Mask," St.3, Ibid.

8   The universe is made of stories,
not of atoms.
"The Speed of Darkness," IX, St. 2, Ibid.

9   the revolutionary look
that says   I am in the world
to change the world.
"Women as Market," St. 2, Ibid.

10 What would happen if one woman told the truth about her life?
The world would split open.
"Käthe Kollwitz,"* III, St. 4, Ibid.
*See 1337.

11 Whatever we stand against
We will stand feeding and seeding.
"Wherever," St. 3, *Breaking Open* 1973

12 The wars say it to us—all of Europe, all of Vietnam—and Nuremberg: never wait to speak against these horrors.
To act against these horrors
Do not let them be abstract and distant.
They look at you with human eyes. . . .
"Searching Not Searching," Quoted in *The Poetic Vision of Muriel Rukeyser*, p. 387, by Louise Kertesz 1980

13 . . . if we look long enough and hard enough . . . we will begin to see the connections that bind us together, and when we recognize those connections, we will begin to change the world.
Quoted in "The Critique of Consciousness and Myth in Levertov, Rich and Rukeyser," *Writing Beyond the Ending: Narrative Strategies of 20th Century Women Writers*, p. 129, by Rachel B. du Plessis 1985

2211. Elizabeth Smart (1913–1986)

1   I am over-run, jungled in my bed, I am infested with a menagerie of desires: my heart is eaten by a dove, a cat scrambles in the cave of my sex, hounds in my bed obey a whipmaster who cries nothing but havoc as the hours test my endurance with an accumulation of tortures. Who, if I cried, would hear me among the angelic orders?
Pt. 1, *By Grand Central Station I Sat Down and Wept* 1945

2   Vanity is a vital aid to nature: completely and absolutely necessary to life. It is one of nature's ways to bind you to the earth.
Journal entry (25 June 1933), Pt. 1, Ch. 2, *Necessary Secrets*, Alice Van Wart, ed. 1991

3   O I know they make war because they want peace; they hate so that they may live; and they destroy the present to make the world safe for the future. When have they not done and said they did it for that?
(18 February 1941), Ibid.

2212. May Swenson (1913/19–1989)

1   The summer that I was ten—
Can it be there was only one summer that I was ten? It must have been a long one then—
"The Centaur," Sts. 1 & 2, *To Mix with Time* 1963

2   I was the horse and the rider . . .
St. 13, Ibid.

3   We play in the den of the Gods and snort at death
"To Confirm a Thing," St. 2, *New and Selected Things Taking Place* 1978

4   You're back,
barefoot, brought
some fruit. Split me
an apple. We'll
get red, white
halves each, our
juice on the
Indian spread.
"In the Yard," *The Love Poems of May Swenson* 1991

5   . . . Elemental form simplified as an egg,
you held perfectly still on your artificial perch. You, too,
might be a crafty fake, stuffed or carved. Except your eyes.
   Alive,
enormous, yellow circles containing black circles, clear, slick,
heartstopping double barrels of concentrated rage pointed
   at me.
"The Snowy," *Nature: Poems Old and New* 1994

6   Intermittent moon
that we say climbs
or sets, circles only.
"Sleeping Overnight on the Shore," Ibid.

2213. Honor Tracy (1913–1989)

1   He was a member of the eccentric race of fiscophobes, Englishmen who would do anything and live anywhere, no matter how bored and miserable they might be, rather than stay at home and pay English taxes.
Ch. 1, *The Butterflies of the Province* 1970

2   "Early upbringing," David moaned. "One struggles against it in vain."
Ch. 5, Ibid.

2214. Julia de Burgos (1914–1953)

1   You are the bloodless doll of social lies
And I the virile spark of human truth . . .
"To Julia de Burgos," *The Nation* (New York) 1972

2   You curl your hair and paint your face.
Not I:
I am curled by the wind, painted by the sun.
Ibid.

2215. Aurora Castillo (1914–1998)

1   We used to say we can't fight the government. But we are the government.
Quoted in "Earth Day Greening From the Roots Up" by Priscilla Painton, *Time* (New York) 23 April 1990

2 The Mothers of East Los Angeles will fight like lionesses for the safety, welfare and security of their children.

Speech, GoldmanPrize.org 1995

2216. Stella Chess (1914–2007)

1 A child is nothing like a racing car … Souping up babies doesn't work that way. The child is what she is. There is a certain irreducible if elusive core. Pushing, pulling, stretching, and shrinking will not really change it. There may be spectacular interim results. The baby may say the alphabet before she walks, master two-times or even ten-times table at three. In the long run, however, this forced precocity tends to be irrelevant …

Ch. 2, Daughters, coauthor, Jane Whitbread* 1978

*See 2231.

2 An actress reading a part for the first time tries many ways to say the same line before she settles into the one she believes suits the character and situation best. There's an aspect of the rehearsing actress about the girl on the verge of her teens. Playfully, she is starting to try out ways to be a grown-up person.

Ch. 6, Ibid.

3 Preventive care concentrated on changing the mother's or father's behavior, and cultural influences were often ignored. But it became clear that some children with serious problems had adequate or excellent parents.

Harvard Mental Health Letter 1997

2217. "Babe" Didrikson Zaharias (1914–1956)

1 Boy, don't you men wish you could hit a ball like that!

Quoted in "'Babe' Didrikson Zaharias," Famous American Women by Hope Stoddard 1970

2 All my life I've been competing—and competing to win. I came to realize that in this way, this cancer was the toughest competition I'd faced yet. I made up my mind that I was going to lick it all the way. I not only wasn't going to let it kill me, I wasn't even going to let it put me on the shelf.

Ibid.

3 It's not enough to just swing at the ball. You've got to loosen your girdle and really let fly.

"100 Years of Great Women," ABC News Special with Barbara Walters 30 April 1999

2218. Marguerite Duras (1914–1996)

1 One must talk. That's how it is. One must.

The Vice-Consul, Eileen Ellenbogen, tr. 1966

2 Thousands on the causeways, carrying their loads, laying them down, returning empty-handed. People surrounding the bare, watery spaces of the rice-field, fields of upright stalks. People everywhere, ten thousand, a hundred thousand, crowded like grains of millet, walking along the causeways, an endless procession, continually on the move, each one with his tools of naked flesh hanging down on either side.

Ibid.

3 CLAIRE. I am not intelligent enough for the intelligence within me.

The Lovers of Viorne 1971

4 Clarity is a disease of the French. They believe in it, it is everywhere!

Quoted in Current Biography Yearbook, Charles Moritz, ed. 1980–85

5 Journalism without a moral position is impossible. Every journalist is a moralist. It's absolutely unavoidable. A journalist is someone who looks at the world and the way it works, someone who takes a close look at things every day and reports what she sees, someone who represents the world, the event, for others. She cannot do her work without judging what she sees.

Foreword, Outside: Selected Writings 1984

6 Nowhere is one more alone than in Paris … and yet surrounded by crowds. Nowhere is one more likely to incur greater ridicule. And no visit is more essential.

"Tourists in Paris," France-Observateur (Paris, 1957), Ibid.

7 Alcohol doesn't console, it doesn't fill up anyone's psychological gaps, all it replaces is the lack of God. It doesn't comfort man. On the contrary, it encourages him in his folly, it transports him to the supreme regions where he is master of his own destiny.

"Alcohol," Practicalities 1987

8 The woman is the home. That's where she used to be, and that's where she still is. You might ask me, What if a man tries to be part of the home—will the woman let him? I answer yes. Because then he becomes one of the children.

"House and Home," Ibid.

9 I believe that always, or almost always, in all childhoods and in all the lives that follow them, the mother represents madness. Our mothers always remain the strangest, craziest people we've ever met.

Ibid.

10 In heterosexual love there's no solution. Man and woman are irreconcilable, and it's the doomed attempt to do the impossible, repeated in each new affair, that lends heterosexual love its grandeur.

"Men," Ibid.

11 You have to be very fond of men. Very, very fond. You have to be very fond of them to love them. Otherwise they're simply unbearable.

Ibid.

12 A writer is a foreign country.

"The M.D. Uniform," Ibid.

13 The best way to fill time is to waste it.

"Wasting Time," Ibid.

2219. Etty Hillesum (1914–1943)

1 Mysticism must rest on crystal-clear honesty, and can only come after things have been stripped down to their naked reality.

Entry (1942), An Interrupted Life: The Diaries of Etty Hillesum 1941–1943, Arno Pomerans, tr. 1983

2 It is good to have such moments of despair and of temporary extinction; continuous calm would be superhuman.

Ibid.

3 When I pray, I never pray for myself, always for others, or else I hold a silly, naive or deadly serious dialogue with what is deepest inside me, which for the sake of convenience I call God. Praying to God for something for yourself strikes me as being

too childish for words. . . . To pray for another's well-being is something I find childish as well; one should only pray that another should have enough strength to shoulder his burden. If you do that, you lend him some of your own strength.

Ibid.

4 The soul has a different age from that recorded in the register of births and deaths. At your birth, the soul already has an age that never changes. One can be born with a 12-year-old soul. One can also be born with a thousand-year-old soul. . . . I believe the soul is that part of man that he is least aware of . . .

Entry (12.10.42), Ibid.

5 But let me impress just one thing upon you, sister . . . Your imagination and your emotions are like a vast ocean from which you wrest small pieces of land that may well be flooded again. That ocean is wide and elemental, but what matter are the small pieces of land you reclaim from it. The subject right before you is more important than those prodigious thoughts on Tolstoy and Napoleon that occurred to you in the middle of last night . . .

Entry, Ibid.

6 We are always in search of the redeeming formula, the crystallising thought . . .

Ibid.

2220. Carolina Maria de Jesus (1914–1977)

1 I classify Sao Paulo this way: The Governor's Palace is the living room. The mayor's office is the dining room and the city is the garden. And the *favela** is the back yard where they throw the garbage.

Diary entry (15 May 1958), Child of the Dark: The Diary of
Carolina Maria de Jesus 1962

*Barrio or ghetto.

2 She neglects children and collects men.

Diary entry (1 June 1958), Ibid.

3 A child is the root of the heart.

Ibid.

2221. Jiang Qing (1914–1991)

1 There cannot be peaceful coexistence in the ideological realm. Peaceful coexistence corrupts.

Remark (April 1967), Quoted in Ch. 15, Mao and China:
From Revolution to Revolution by Stanley Karnow 1972

2222. Gypsy Rose Lee (1914–1970)

1 Mother, in a feminine way, was ruthless. She was, in her own words, a jungle mother, and she knew too well that in a jungle it doesn't pay to be nice. "God will protect us," she often said to June and me. "but to make sure," she would add, "carry a heavy club."

Ch. 1, Gypsy 1957

2 [He] often said I was the greatest no-talent star in the business.

Ibid.

2223. Joan Littlewood (1914–2002)

1 I do not believe in the supremacy of the director, designer, actor, or even of the writer. It is through collaboration that this knockabout art of theatre survives and kicks.

"A Goodbye Note from Joan," Encore (Natl. Assoc. of
Dramatic and Speech Arts) October 1961

2 War is for clowns.*

Remark (1963), Quoted in Obituary, BBC News
21 September 2002

*Commenting on her most celebrated creation, *Oh What a Lovely War.*

2224. Catherine Marshall (1914–1983)

1 Often God has to shut a door in our face, so that He can subsequently open the door through which He wants us to go.

Ch. 2, A Man Called Peter 1951

2 . . . truth could never be wholly contained in words. All of us know it: At the same moment the mouth is speaking one thing, the heart is saying another . . .

Prologue, Christy 1967

3 So once I shut down my privilege of disliking anyone I chose and holding myself aloof if I could manage it, greater understanding, growing compassion came to me. . . .

Ch. 12, Ibid.

4 . . . in rejecting secrecy I had also rejected the road to cynicism.

Ch. 33, Ibid.

5 . . . I learned that true forgiveness includes total acceptance. And out of acceptance wounds are healed and happiness is possible again.

Ibid.

6 Usually passion wants to grab and to yank.

Ibid.

2225. Noor Inayat Khan (1914–1944)

1 I wish some Indians would win high military distinction in this war.
It would help to build a bridge between English and the Indians.

Quoted in Indian Heroes and Heroines of World War II by
Vidya Anand 1995

2226. Anna Maria Ortese (1914–1998)

1 It was the easiest and at the same time the most sinister thing possible that was happening to me: when one thing recalls another, and so on, till your present vanishes, and everything before you is purely past, the echo of a life that was more real than this one.

"The Lights of Genoa," Italian Writing Today, Raleigh
Trevelyna, ed. 1967

2 People were alone, and at the same time never alone, at least not in the terrible way you are in Milan and in Rome, where, if you aren't socially eminent or rich or important, others simply don't notice you, and if you're ill you could be thrown out with the rubbish . . .

Ibid.

3 Make a place for aesthetics—and its laws—within this prison, this dullness, of human life. You will have made a place for freedom—the suspension of pain—for elegance, for tenderness.

"Where Time Is Another" (Henry Martin, tr., 1997),
Micromega May 1990

4 And yet if democracy is ever to prove its worth as the tool most suited for creating a certain happiness, I believe that the problem of self-expression—the problem of achieving a true individuality—may well have to occupy the very first place, and I mean within the lives of people in general.

Ibid.

2227. Dixy Lee Ray (1914–1994)

1 My answer to why did I choose the Democratic Party is that I spent three years in Washington under a Republican administration.

Quoted in *The Wall Street Journal* 15 March 1976

2 Everybody's in favor of resolving the energy crisis and everybody is in favor of preserving the environment. But the people in the Northwest, where the big coal deposits are, don't want their terrain upset; and the people in the Northeast, who need heating fuel the most, don't want an oil port and refineries on their coast, and some of the Nader people don't want any nuclear plants at all generating electric power because of some theoretical dangers. I understand these conflicts, but this isn't a perfect world. Somebody—and I mean every one of us—has to make some sacrifices.

Interview (1974), Quoted in *American Political Women* by Esther Stineman 1980

3 The reality is that zero defects in products plus zero pollution plus zero risk on the job is equivalent to maximum growth of government plus zero economic growth plus runaway inflation.

Speech, Scientist and Engineers for Secure Energy (1980), Ibid.

2228. Hazel Brannon Smith (1914–1994)

1 I ain't no lady. I'm a newspaperwoman.

Quoted in "The 11-Year Siege of Mississippi's Lady Editor" by T. George Harris, *Look* (New York) 16 November 1965

2 I can't think of but one thing that's worse than being called a nigger-lover. And that's a nigger-hater!

Ibid.

3 A crusading editor is one who goes out and looks for the wrongs of the world. I just try to take care of things as they come up. I try to make them a little better.

Ibid.

2229. Billy Tipton (1914–1989)

1 Some people might think I'm a freak or a hermaphrodite. I'm not. I'm a normal person. This has been my choice.*

Quoted in *Suits Me: The Double Life of Billy Tipton* by Diane Wood Middlebrook 1998

*Tipton lived most of her life as a man.

2230. Barbara Ward (1914–1981)

1 It is very much easier for a rich man to invest and grow richer than for the poor man to begin investing at all. And this is also true of nations.

Ch. 1, *The Rich Nations and the Poor Nations* 1962

2 There is no human failure greater than to launch a profoundly important endeavor and then leave it half done. This is what the West has done with its colonial system. It shook all the societies in the world loose from their old moorings. But it seems indifferent whether or not they reach safe harbour in the end.

Ch. 2, Ibid.

3 ... mankind must go beyond the limits of purely national government and begin to find out what the "post-national community" is like ... [But] it cannot, must not, mean a suppression of all variety and a civilization so standardized that we all end up hideously the same.

"Only One Earth," *Who Speaks for Earth?*, Maurice F. Strong, ed. 1973

4 We ... live in an epoch in which the solid ground of our preconceived ideas shakes daily under our uncertain feet.

Ibid.

2231. Jane Whitbread (1914–?)

1 Actually, every laborsaving device of the past century has added to women's work ... A man invents a vacuum cleaner and ... a co-conspirator popularizes Venetian blinds, so there will be something else for the vacuum cleaner to do in a jiffy. A man turns out a simple little mechanism to make melon balls, and it's no longer comme il faut to toss a plain hunk of melon into a fruit salad ... In the period when beer came in kegs, the man of the house hauled it himself. Now that it comes in handy little cans, even a woman can lug a dozen from the delicatessen. The man who speeds by a woman, stopped by a flat tire, can't be accused of lack of chivalry. He knows that the way they make jacks these days, even a woman can change a tire.

The Intelligent Man's Guide to Women, coauthor Vivian Cadden-Schuman* 1951

*See 2264.

2 The American man has high standards for everything but marriage. As long as his wife doesn't run off with another man, commit suicide, develop acute dementia praecox, or stab him with the carving knife, he considers his marriage reasonably successful ... [The American woman] is frustrated, unfulfilled, humiliated, and bored by the routine existence that passes for family life in her native land. If Groggle doesn't change, she can only hope to get worse.

Ibid.

Also see Chess, Stella, 2216:1–2

2232. Pearl Williams (1914–1991)

1 Women come in here and sit at the tables up front, and I can hear them whispering, "Oh, she's so dirty! She's so dirty!" Well, if they're so pure, how the hell do they know what I'm talking about? People want to know where I learn all these words. I went to a grammar school one day and went up to the bathroom. There they were, right on the wall.

Stand-up routine *n.d.*

2 What's the difference between the Italian wife, the French wife, and the Jewish wife? When the Italian wife is having an affair, she says, "Mamma mia." When the French wife is having an affair, she says, "Ooh-la-la." When the Jewish wife is having an affair, she says, "Jake, the ceiling needs painting."

Ibid.

2233. Molly Yard (1914–2005)

1 Don't buy the garbage that you're over the hill at 50. This country makes such a big thing about age, particularly if you're a woman. What I think is relevant is your experience, what you have to offer. I hope people will recognize that and keep going.

(p. 71), *Time* (New York) 3 August 1987

2 I thought it would be different in this country [than it is in China], but I learned quickly that females weren't valued in this society, either. It is indeed a worldwide problem.

Quoted in "NOW Head Assails President's Policies" by Alex Tizon, *Seattle Times February 1989*

2234. Hortensia Bussi de Allende (1915–   )

1 We want a Chile where the rights of man will be fully respected. Our message is not fear but hope, not hate but joy. It is not the past, but the future, that we will build together.

Speech, Santiago, Chile *24 September 1988*

2235. Phyllis Shand Allfrey (1915–1986)

1 She went out on the portico and looked down on the land, sighing as if her heart had broken and the wind was whistling through it. "Beauty grows like a weed here," she said, "and so does disease."

The Orchid House 1953

2236. Ingrid Bergman (1915–1982)

1 You know, one looks at herself in the mirror every morning, and she doesn't see the difference, she doesn't realize that she is aging. But then she finds a friend who was young with her, and the friend isn't young anymore, and all of a sudden, like a slap on her eyes, she remembers that she, too, isn't young anymore.

Quoted in "Ingrid Bergman," *The Egotists* by Oriana Fallaci* *1963*

*See 2656.

2 I've never sought success in order to get fame and money; it's the talent and the passion that count in success.

Ibid.

3 Things came to me asking to be done, and I did them—spontaneously, without asking whether it was wise or not. And the day after, I could say, "Maybe I shouldn't have done it." But years later, I always realized I was right in doing them.

Ibid.

2237. Caroline Bird (1915–   )

1 Secretaries may be specially prized, and the top secretaries exceptionally well paid, because they give men who can afford to pay well the subservient, watchful and admiring attention that Victorian wives used to give their husbands.

Ch. 4, *Born Female 1968*

2 Equity speaks softly and wins in the end. But it is expedience, with its loud voice, that sets the time of victory.

Ch. 10, Ibid.

3 Femininity appears to be one of those pivotal qualities that is so important no one can define it.

Ch. 11, Ibid.

4 The big advantage of getting your college money in cash now is that you can invest it in something that has a higher return than a diploma.

The Case Against College 1975

5 A liberal-arts education is supposed to provide you with a value system, a standard, a set of ideas, not a job. The fact is, of course, that the liberal arts are a religion in every sense of that term. [And if] the liberal arts are a religious faith, the professors are its priests.

Ibid.

6 In fact there is no real evidence that the higher income of college graduates is due to college. College may simply attract people who are slated to earn more money anyway: those with higher IQs, better family backgrounds, a more enterprising temperament.

Ibid.

7 College, then, may be a good place for those few young people who are really drawn to academic work, who would rather read than eat, but it has become too expensive, in money, time and intellectual effort, to serve as a holding pen for large numbers of our young. We ought to make it possible for those reluctant, unhappy students to find alternative ways of growing up, and more realistic preparation for the years ahead.

Ibid.

2238. Fawn M. Brodie (1915–1981)

1 There is, of course, a gold mine or a buried treasure on every mortgaged homestead. Whether the farmer ever digs for it or not, it is there, haunting his daydreams when the burden of debt is most unbearable.

Ch. 2, *No Man Knows My History 1945*

2 Mormon theology was never burdened with otherworldliness. There was a fine robustness about it that smelled of the frontier and that rejected an asceticism that was never endemic to America.

Ch. 13, Ibid.

3 A man's memory is bound to be a distortion of his past in accordance with his present interests, and the most faithful autobiography is likely to mirror less what a man was than what he had become.

Ch. 19, Ibid.

4 Show me a character whose life arouses my curiosity, and my flesh begins crawling with suspense.

Quoted in "Home Q&A" by Marshall Berger in *The Los Angeles Times Home Magazine 20 February 1977*

5 Housework is a breeze. Cooking is a pleasant diversion. Putting up a retaining wall is a lark. But teaching is like climbing a mountain.

Ibid.

2239. Nien Cheng (1915–?)

1 I would rather die than tell a lie.

Life and Death in Shanghai 1987

2 The past is forever with me and I remember it all.

Pt. I, Ch. 1, Ibid.

3 The [Chinese] leaders who ordered this killing of innocent people* will never ever recover the good reputation they'd worked so hard for and gained in the eyes of the world and the Chinese people.

Quoted in "China Hears a Voice of Experience" by Judi Hunt, *Seattle Post-Intelligencer 10 June 1989*
*Referring to the gunning down by the military of Chinese students and workers demonstrating for democracy in Tiananmen Square, Beijing, 15 April 1989.

4   I think the democratic movement will be repressed for now, only to erupt again somewhere down the line.

And more blood will be shed, just like it was when Americans fought and died to bring independence, democracy, and freedom to the United States. It's not something you can sit back and wait for someone to give to you voluntarily.

Ibid.

5   The transformation of China from feudal autocracy into a modern democratic state is a long and agonizing process. It is not just a matter of changing the political and economic system. Much of China's traditional culture will have to be jettisoned. The urban idealists must involve the 70 per cent of China's population that lives in the countryside. When the wish for change blossoms in every heart, democracy will come to China. The massacre in Peking will bring that day nearer.

"China Devours Its Children," *National Review 4 August 1989*

6   The pattern of China's history has been one of alternating periods of unity and disintegration. China is now a nuclear power. If control of those weapons should fall into irresponsible hands, world peace will be threatened.

Ibid.

7   Half of China's villages now can elect their own boss, so to speak, their own official. Eventually, this will be carried to the county level and gradually, gradually to the central government. So China has already taken the first step towards democracy. It's a long road, but step by step China will get there.

"An American's Perspective", The News Hour with Jim Lehrer *3 July 1998*

2240. Marie-Louise von Franz (1915–1998)

1   Unfortunately the conscious representation we make of the Godhead undergoes the same fate as all other contents of our consciousness: it suffers from the tendency to wear out, and becomes mere words which lose their emotional and feeling substructure.

Ch. 4, *Individuation in Fairytales 1977*

2   The inner experience consolidates, and instead of being a kind of emotional spiritual experience, it becomes a realization in the most literal sense of the word. We use the word "realization" rather too lightly; but if we "realize" something in its basic meaning, it becomes a real thing forever.

Ch. 5, *Ibid.*

3   The only way the Self can manifest is through conflict. To meet one's insoluble and eternal conflict is to meet God, which would be the end of the ego with all its blather.

Alchemy: An Introduction to the Symbolism and the Psychology 1980

2241. Ketti Frings (1915–1981)

1   EUGENE. If he hates it so much here, why does he stay?
BEN. You stupid little fool, it's like being caught in a photograph. Your face is there, and no matter how hard you try, how are you going to step out of a photograph?

Act I, Sc. 1, *Look Homeward, Angel* 1957*
*Stage adaptation of Thomas Wolfe's 1929 novel. In 1978, Frings collaborated on a musical version of her adaptation by the same name.

2242. Carolyn Goodman (1915–2007)

1   I still feel that I would let Andy* go to Mississippi again . . . [E]ven after this terrible thing happened to Andy, I couldn't make a turnabout of everything I believe in.

The New York Times 1965
*Re permitting her son Andrew to go to Mississippi to help register blacks to vote in 1964; he, along with two others, was murdered by Ku Klux Klan members. He was 20 years old.

2   I'm totally against capital punishment. Who's it going to help?

Monitor (American Psychological Association) *2005*

3   It was somewhat frightening to realize that the Klan is not just a matter of history but is still very much around.

Interview with Henry Foner, *Jewish Currents September 2005*

2243. Janet Harris (1915–   )

1   I'm the ultimate in the throwaway society, the disposable woman.

The Prime of Ms. America: The American Woman at Forty 1975

2   . . . one searches the magazines in vain for women past their first youth. The middle-aged face apparently sells neither perfume nor floor wax. The role of the mature woman in the media is almost entirely negative.

Ibid.

3   Quite a few women told me, one way or another, that they thought it was sex, not youth, that's wasted on the young. . . .

Ibid.

4   At its most basic root, the death or disintegration of one's parents is a harsh reminder of one's own mortality.

Ibid.

5   Reared as we were in a youth—and beauty-oriented society, we measured ourselves by our ornamental value.

Ibid.

6   We were brought up with the value that as we sow, so shall we reap. We discarded the idea that anything we did was its own reward.

Ibid.

7   The first crisis of middle age is within the psyche itself, as the values and aspirations of youth come up for examination in the light of the experience and knowledge which we have gained through living.

Ibid.

2244. Billie Holiday (1915–1959)

1   Southern trees bear a strange fruit,
Blood on the leaves and blood at the root,
Black bodies swinging in the Southern breeze,
Strange fruit hanging from the poplar trees.

"Strange Fruit" *1939*

2   Mama may have
Papa may have
But God bless the child that's got his own

"God Bless the Child" *1941*

3   And when you're poor, you grow up fast.

Ch. 1, *Lady Sings the Blues,* with William Dufty *1956*

4   I can't stand to sing the same song the same way two nights in succession, let alone two years or ten years. If you can, then it ain't music, it's close-order drill or exercise or yodeling or something, not music.

Ch. 4, Ibid.

5   You can be up to your boobies in white satin, with gardenias in your hair and no sugar cane for miles, but you can still be working on a plantation.

Ch. 11, Ibid.

6   Sometimes it's worse to win a fight than to lose.

Ch. 13, Ibid.

7   If you think dope is for kicks and for thrills, you're out of your mind. There are more kicks to be had in a good case of paralytic polio or by living in an iron lung. If you think you need stuff to play music or sing, you're crazy. It can fix you so you can't play nothing or sing nothing.

Ch. 23, Ibid.

2245. Lena May Jeger (1915–2007)

1   . . . no legislation can compel anybody to give an unmarried mother what she usually most needs—friendship, understanding and companionship in what is almost inevitably a lonely and deeply traumatic experience.

Foreword, *Illegitimate Children and Their Parents* 1951

2   The child is different, not because he is illegitimate, but because he is fatherless and he is going to miss a father in the same way that any child who loses his father early, through death or separation, misses him.

Ibid.

3   . . . we feel that there is often too little concern with the unmarried father. In our social records he is an elusive figure, often anonymous, alternately reviled, beloved or blackmailed. . . . Often he needs as much help as the mother to regain a mental and emotional equilibrium and so to make subsequently a good husband to somebody, if not to the mother of his first child.

Ibid.

2246. Moya Olson Lear (1915–2001)

1   No. Mr. President, I never tell him what to do. I sometimes tell him where to go, but . . .*

"If Bill** Could See Me Now: The Story of Moya Lear" by Phyllis R. Moses, wingsandstars.com
*Response to President Truman's query as to whether she helped him in the business. **William L— (1902–1978), Am. businessman and inventor who created the Lear jet.

2   I didn't run the company. What I did was motivate the workforce. I listened to what was going on. I helped solve their problems so they could do their jobs. I helped expedite some critical policy decisions, and made sure they had the machinery they needed. I validated everybody's place in the organization; I let them know they were all important to the project.

Ibid.

2247. Isobel Lennart (1915–1971)

1   FANNY. Look, suppose all you ever had for breakfast was onion rolls. All of a sudden one morning, in walks a bagel. You'd say, "Ugh! What's that?" Until you tried it. *That's* my trouble. I'm a bagel on a plate full of onion rolls!

Act I, Sc. 3, *Funny Girl* 1964

2   NICK. Fanny, would you say you were a woman of—wide experience? . . .
FANNY . . . I've been too busy. What about you? *Hundreds* of girls, huh?
NICK. The count is in mere dozens. Of very minor entanglements. I like to feel free.
FANNY. You can get lonesome—being that free.
NICK. You can get lonesome—being that busy.

Sc. 11, Ibid.

2248. Abigail McCarthy (1915–2001)

1   Despite the fact that the campaign* brought almost unbearable emotional strain and disaster to our family, I cannot wish that the campaign did not happen. Through it I crossed the barrier into the world of my children and of all the young people to whom this world really belongs. I see the world now as they see it. I feel a sense of surprise that it is so easy to lay aside what once were rocklike basic assumptions as I look at injustice in the fierce light of their outrage. But I do not wish to have crossed this barrier having brought nothing from the other side, as have so many older people in a kind of headlong rush to join the young. What I would like to bring with me is a sense of the past, its continuity in the present, and a sense of identity stemming from the past which enables each one of us to withstand the assault of change.

Private Faces/Public Places 1972
*Senator Eugene McCarthy, her husband, made a bid for the presidency in 1968.

2   I began to live out the role for which I had been preparing the last month. This was what I had been trained to do, not only by the demands of political life but by my heritage—from those daughters of the pioneers, my grandmother, my aunts, my mother—to face disaster with as much dignity as possible, to affirm whatever was positive.

Ibid.

3   For those of us whose lives have been defined by others—by wifehood and motherhood—there is no individual achievement to measure, only the experience of life itself.

Ibid.

2249–2250. Margaret Ellis Millar (1915–1994)

1   As soon as she opened her eyes Priscilla could feel in her bones that it was Saturday. The air smelled different, and it seemed to quiver with anticipation.

"A Problem in Economics," *It's All in the Family* 1948

2   "And when I was eleven and wanted ten cents I went out and got me a ten-cent task to do."
"I can't think of any ten-cent tasks except just being good."
"In this world, you don't get paid for being good."

Ibid.

2251. Barbara "Babe" Paley (1915–1978)

1   You can never be too skinny or too rich.*

Attributed *n.d.*
*Also see Windsor, Wallis Simpson: 1840:2; also attributed to Gloria Vanderbilt, 2502.

2252. Eleanor Perry (1915–1981)

1   "We've all known each other so long there's not even anyone to flirt with."

The Swimmer (screenplay) 1967

2 "That's your hang-up, Neddy-boy. You're afraid the sky will fall down if everybody doesn't love you. You'll lose the popularity contest, you won't be elected Head Boy—as if the whole world's a prep school!"

Ibid.

3 . . . so long as a woman is dependent on a man for her self-image or her self-esteem she will remain without any sense of her own worth—can never be a fully realized human being.

Quoted in "Rebirth" by Kay Loveland and Estelle Changas, *The Hollywood Screenwriters*, Richard Corliss, ed. *1972*

4 Given a skillful cinematographer and technical staff almost any creative person can direct a film.

Ibid.

2253. Aurelia Potor (1915–1999)

1 Middle-aged rabbits don't have a paunch, do have their own teeth and haven't lost their romantic appeal.

Quoted in *The New York Times 22 September 1956*

2254. Janet Mary Riley (1915–2008)

1 We [women law students] bore the burden of representing womankind, whether we liked it or not.

If you goofed, if you failed, if you cried in public or received bad grades, they'd say, "What do you expect: She's only a woman."

So we didn't cry in public. We didn't get bad grades. The result was that the woman students did remarkably well. For years, the women were the tops in their class. There was a lot of self-inflicted pressure not to cry. But I did my share of crying in the women's lounge.

Quoted in "Women Win Their Case as Legal Eagles" by Jean Blake, *The Times/Picayune* (New Orleans) *2 November 1986*

2 The role of mother is probably the most important career a woman can have.

Ibid.

2255. Ethel Rosenberg (1915–1953)

1 Together we hunted down the answers to all the seemingly insoluble riddles which a complex and callous society presented. . . . And yet for the sake of these answers, for the sake of American democracy, justice and brotherhood, for the sake of peace and bread and roses, and children's laughter, we shall continue to sit here [in prison] in dignity and in pride—in the deep abiding knowledge of our innocence before God and man, until the truth becomes a clarion call to all decent humanity.

Letter to Julius Rosenberg, Sing Sing (27 May 1951), *Death House Letters of Ethel and Julius Rosenberg 1953*

2 Work and build, my sons, and build
a monument to love and joy,
to human worth, to faith we kept
for you, my sons, for you.

"If We Die" (24 January 1953), Ibid.

2256. Natalie Shainess (1915–   )

1 As we have become a thing-oriented, impulse-ridden, narcissistically self-preoccupied people, we are increasingly dedicated to the acquisition of things, and cultivate little else.

"A Psychiatrist's View: Images of Woman—Past and Present, Overt and Obscured," *American Journal of Psychotherapy January 1969*

2 Our society has tended since medieval times, when the odor of the great unwashed was everywhere, to work at eliminating unpleasant aspects of smell. The sense of smell is tied up with paranoia—one of the classic paranoid symptoms is the feeling, "I smell bad. That's why no one likes me." The sense of being malodorous is connected with more serious disturbances.

Quoted in *Crazy Salad: Some Things About Women* by Nora Ephron* *1975*

*See 3258.

3 An overprotective mother binds her child to her by refusing to allow the child to move away from her. Unable to recognize the separateness of her daughter, unable to acknowledge the boundaries between them, such a mother refuses to let the child develop her own thoughts and perceptions. This symbiotic relationship breeds passivity and a sense of inadequacy in the child.

Sweet Suffering: Woman as Victim 1984

4 Once a wife has been hit, it is likely to recur; some standard has been lowered, some barrier broken down.

Ibid.

2257. Alice Bradley Sheldon (1915–1987)

1 She didn't provide a model for me, she provided an impossibility.

Quoted in Ch. 1, *James Tiptree, Jr.: The Double Life of Alice B. Sheldon* by Julie Phillips* *2006*

*See 4710.

2 "Alice," it was made clear to me early, belonged to my mother, who chose it because it had no nickname. How cruel can you get, unintentionally—I hope? But one's nicknames-they are one's own.

Ibid.

2258. Jean Stafford (1915–1979)

1 There were two objects of conversation; one was the food they were eating and the other was the food they had eaten at other times . . .

"Maggie Meriwether's Rich Experience," *The Innocents Abroad*, from *The Collected Stories of Jean Stafford 1969*

2 Abby's preconception of gambling derived from scenes in movies, and as she moved from table to table, endeavoring to understand the games, she realized that either her memory was at fault or Hollywood had carelessly added an apocryphal glitter and subtracted an essential gloom.

"The Children's Game," Ibid.

3 . . . "From time to time, I need a rest from the exercitation of my intellect."

"The Echo and the Nemesis," Ibid.

2259. Margaret Walker (1915–1998)

1 For my people thronging 47th Street in Chicago and Lenox Avenue in New York and Rampart Street in New Orleans, lost disinherited dispossessed and happy people filling the cabarets and taverns and other people's pocket. . . .

"For My People," St. 6, *For My People 1942*

2 Let a new earth rise. Let another world be
born. Let a bloody
peace be written in the sky. Let a second
generation

full of courage issue forth;
let a people loving free—
dom come to growth.

St. 10, Ibid.

3 Now this here gal warn't always tough
Nobody dreamed she'd turn out rough.

"Kissie Lee," St. 2, Ibid.

4 Old women working by an age-old plan to make
their bread in ways as best they can.

"Whores," St. 1, Ibid.

5 ...the filthy
privies marked "For Colored Only"
and the drinking-soda-fountains
tasting dismal and disgusting
with a dry and dusty flavor
of the deep humiliation....

"Now," *Prophets for a New Day* 1970

6 Hurry up, Lucille, Hurry up
We're Going to Miss Our Chance to go to Jail.

"Street Demonstration," Ibid.

2260. Judith Wright (1915–2000)

1 South of my days' circle,
I know it dark against the stars, the high lean country
Full of old stories that still go walking in my sleep.

"South of My Days' Circle," *The Moving Image* 1946

2 My days burn with the sun
my nights with moon and star,
since into myself I took
all the living things that are.

"The Maker," *Woman to Man* 1949

3 Look—I'll spell it out for you. War is no good! (When will you
people ever learn?)

"Christmas Ballad," *Shadow* 1970

4 They did not breed nor love,
each in his cell alone
cried as the wind now cries
through this flute of stone.

"The Old Prison," St. 4, *Collected Poems* 1971

5 Autobiography is not what I want to write. It forces the writer
into far too much introversion or into arrogance.

Half a Lifetime 1999

6 They [her family] were those who chose to adapt themselves
to the new environment rather than superimpose their class
values of Englishness upon it. They were ... set against the
squattocracy ... and underwent a convulsive change in social
values and patterns and from them came not only an authentic
patriotic fervour, but a tradition of warmth, hospitality and
egalitarianism.

Ibid.

2261. Helen Yglesias (1915–2008)

1 They never ask the patient. The patient is anesthetized on the
operating table, cut open. They call in the husband. "We think
it best to remove this precancerous breast. Since this is your
hunk of meat, do we have your permission, husband?"

Ch. 1, *How She Died* 1972

2 "Life is too short to understand God altogether, especially
nowadays."

Ibid.

3 I wanted to pull him toward me and comfort him with my
body as I had when he was a child, but that time was over. We
could only be to each other what any two human beings might
be, close or far, quick or dull, yielding or hard.

Ch. 11, Ibid.

4 Listening was a three times a day ritual with her, the news
made even more nightmarish in the repetition: the war, the
official statements, the enemy's denial, the traffic deaths,
conspiracy charges, abortion reform rights, kidnappings,
terrorism, peace talks, negotiations of all kinds, hijackings,
charges and countercharges of anti-Semitism, Panther trials,
civilian massacre trials, murder trials, riots, demonstrations,
flaring wars between nations in corners of the world that
didn't seem to really exist, the nonsense item they always
found to end each broadcast with—and then the weather,
reported as if every dip of the wind was a judgement day
warning.

Ch. 16, Ibid.

2262. Lindy Boggs (1916–)

1 In the past we in the United States had thought we could escape direct participation in world events, but there was no way
we could do so again.

Ch. 6, *Washington Through a Purple Veil, Memoirs of a
Southern Woman,* with Katherine Hatch 1994

2 Our presidents often depict themselves as trying to save the
people from Congress or the Supreme Court or both.

Ch. 14, Ibid.

3 My dear, I am the author of the law that forbids this type of
requirement for female persons and the elderly. You are not
complying with the federal regulation, you are in defiance of
it.*

p. 126, Quoted in *Why Women Should Rule the World: A
Memoir* by Dee Dee Myers** 2008
*Re a bank loan officer demanding detailed financial statements
and insurance policies of her, saying they were required by law.
**See 4590.

2263. Maeve Brennan (1916–1993)

1 She had found that the more the child demanded of her, the
more she had to give. Strength came up in waves that had their
source in a sea of calm and unconquered devotion. The child's
holy trust made her open her eyes, and she took stock of herself and found that everything was all right, and that she could
meet what challenges arose and meet them well, and that she
had nothing to apologize for—on the contrary, she had every
reason to rejoice.

"The Eldest Child," *The New Yorker* 23 June 1968

2 She ... enjoyed the illusion that life had nothing to teach her.

Ibid.

3 He wished they could go back to the beginning and start
all over again, but the place where they had stood together,
where they had been happy, was all trampled over and so
spoiled that it seemed impossible ever to make it smooth
again.

Ibid.

2264. Vivian Cadden (1916–1995)
See Whitbread, Jane, 2231:1–2.

2265. Dorothy Salisbury Davis (1916–)

1 There are seasons in Washington when it is even more difficult than usual to find out what is going on in the government. Possibly it is because nothing is going on, although a great many people seem to be working at it.

Ch. 1, Old Sinners Never Die 1959

2 We are all at the mercy of God as well as one another. And for that we can be grateful, He has so much more of it than we have.

Ch. 7, Black Sheep Among White Lambs 1963

3 She dressed more severely than was her fashion, needing herringbone for backbone . . .

"The Purple Is Everything," *Ellery Queen's Mystery Magazine 1964*

4 The law is above the law you know.

Ch. 8, The Little Brothers 1973

5 You know what truth is, gentlemen? Truth is self-justification. That is everybody's truth. . . .

Ibid.

2266. Penelope Fitzgerald (1916–2000)

1 [She] cared nothing for the future, and had, as a result, a great capacity for happiness.

Offshore 1978

2 "She wants an Arts Centre. How can the arts have a centre?"

The Bookshop 1979

3 Broadcasting House was in fact dedicated to the strangest project of the war, or of any war, that is, telling the truth.

Human Voices 1980

4 Without prompting, the BBC* had decided that truth was more important than consolation, and, in the long run, would be more effective.

Ibid.

*British Broadcasting Corporation.

5 Truth ensures trust, but not victory, or even happiness.

Ibid.

6 . . . how dangerous generosity is to the giver . . .

The Gate of the Angels 1990

7 If they don't depend on true evidence, scientists are no better than gossips.

Ch. 3, Ibid.

8 However, no two people see the external world in exactly the same way. To every separate person a thing is what he thinks it is—in other words, not a thing, but a think.

Ch. 6, Ibid.

9 It's very good for an idea to be commonplace. The important thing is that a new idea should develop out of what is already there so that it soon becomes an old acquaintance. Old acquaintances aren't by any means always welcome, but at least one can't be mistaken as to who or what they are.

Ch. 20, Ibid.

10 "The universe, after all, is within us. The way leads inwards, always inwards."

The Beginning of Spring 1997

11 The benign indifference of the universe . . .

Ibid.

12 Now that he saw everything was going well, his mind was turning to his next charitable enterprise. With the terrible aimlessness of the benevolent, he was casting round for a new misfortune.

Ibid.

2266.1 Betty Furness (1916–1994)

1 You fellows have got to get this [phosphate-pollution problem] straightened out, because the laundry's piling up.

Quoted in *Bella!** by Mel Ziegler, ed. *1972*

*B— Abzug; see 2360.

2267. Natalia Ginzburg (1916–1991)

1 . . . it hurts me not to love music, because I feel my spirit is hurt by not loving it. But there's nothing to be done about it; I shall never understand music, and never love it. If I occasionally hear music I like, I can't remember it; so how could I love a thing I can't remember.

"He and I" (1963), *Italian Writing Today*, Raleigh Trevelyan, ed. *1967*

2 My tidiness, and my untidiness, are full of regret and remorse and complex feelings.

Ibid.

3 As far as the education of children is concerned I think they should be taught not the little virtues but the great ones. Not thrift but generosity and an indifference to money; not caution but courage and a contempt for danger; not shrewdness but frankness and a love of truth; not tact but love for one's neighbour and self-denial; not a desire for success but a desire to be and to know.

"The Little Virtues" (1962), *The Little Virtues*, Dick Davis, tr. *1985*

4 A vocation is man's one true wealth and salvation.

Ibid.

5 Not too soon and not too late; the secret of education lies in choosing the right time to do things.

Ibid.

6 The money we give our children should be given for no reason; it should be given indifferently so that they will learn to receive it indifferently; but it should be given not so that they learn to love it, but so that they learn not to love it, so that they realize its true nature and its inability to satisfy our truest desires, which are those of the spirit. When we elevate money into a prize, a goal, an object to be striven for, we give it a position, an importance, a nobility, which it should not have in our children's eyes. We implicitly affirm the principle—a false one—that money is the crowning reward for work, its ultimate objective.

Ibid.

7 School should be from the beginning the first battle which a child fights for himself, without us; from the beginning it should be clear that this is his battlefield and that we can give him only very slight and occasional help there. And if he suffers from injustice there or is misunderstood it is necessary to

let him see that there is nothing strange about this, because in life we have to expect to be constantly misunderstood and misinterpreted, and to be victims of injustice; and the only thing that matters is that we do not commit injustices ourselves.

Ibid.

2268. Françoise Giroud (1916–2003)

1 Are there still virgins? One is tempted to answer no. There are only girls who have not yet crossed the line, because they want to preserve their market value. . . . Call them virgins if you wish, these travelers in transit.

Quoted in *Coronet November 1960*

2 Nothing is more difficult than competing with a myth.

I Give You My Word 1974

3 . . . the present evolution of women . . . is to my mind the most profound revolution that highly developed societies will have to contend with. . . .

Ibid.

4 As though femininity is something you can lose the way you lose your pocketbook: hmm, where in the world did I put my femininity?

Ibid.

5 When mores are no longer founded on the law of civilization but on habit, then comes the revolt.

Ibid.

2269. Ruth Handler (1916–2002)

1 Domestic chores bored me silly. I missed the fast-paced business world and the adrenaline rush that came with closing a tough sale and delivering a gigantic order on time.

Quoted in *Women Inventors* by Linda Jacobs Altman *1997*

2 I was—I *am*—a fiercely independent woman, one who has always felt the need to prove myself, even when I was just a child.

Ibid.

3 . . . the most gratifying memories . . . from my sixteen years with Nearly Me* are the many times . . . I stood toe to toe in fitting rooms with women I was really helping. . . . some came in depressed, confused, self-pitying. I'd fit them, and sometimes they would cry when they saw how Nearly Me had restored their looks.

Ibid.

*A company she founded that produced prosthetic breasts she designed for mastectomy patients.

2270. Elizabeth Hardwick (1916–2007)

1 Letters are above all useful as a means of expressing the ideal self; and no other method of communication is quite so good for this purpose. . . . In letters we can reform without practice, beg without humiliation, snip and shape embarrassing experiences to the measure of our own desires. . . .

"Anderson, Millay, and Crane" in Their Letters" (1953), *A View of My Own 1962*

*Margaret A—, see 1647; Edna St. Vincent—, see 1751; Nathalia C—, see 2196.

2 Mothers born on relief have their babies on relief. Nothingness, truly, seems to be the condition of these New York people. . . . They are nomads going from one rooming house to another, looking for a toilet that functions.

"The Insulted and Injured: Books About Poverty," Ibid.

3 The fifties—they seem to have taken place on a sunny afternoon that asked nothing of you except a drifting belief in the moment and its power to satisfy.

"Domestic Manners," *Bartleby in Manhattan and Other Essays 1968*

4 Sex can no longer be the germ, the seed of fiction. Sex is an episode, most properly conveyed in an episodic manner, quickly, often ironically. It is a bursting forth of only one of the cells in the body of the omnipotent "I," the one who hopes by concentration of tone and voice to utter the sound of reality.

Address, "Seduction and Betrayal" (1972), *Seduction and Betrayal: Women in Literature 1974*

5 The "book"—a plaguing growth that does not itself grow, but attaches, hangs on, a tumorous companion made up of the deranged cells of learning, experience, thinking.

Sleepless Nights 1979

6 Biographers, the quick in pursuit of the dead, research, organize, fill in, contradict, and make in this way a sort of completed picture puzzle with all the scramble turned into a blue eye and the parts of the right leg fitted together.

"Katherine Anne Porter,"* *Sight-Readings: American Fictions 1998*

*See 1715.

7 How certain human beings are able to create works of art is a mystery, and why they should wish to do so, at a great cost to themselves usually, is another mystery. Works are not created by one's life; every life is rich in material.

Ibid.

8 Manhattan is not altogether felicitous for fiction. It is not a city of memory, not a family city, not the capital of America so much as the iconic capital of this century. It is grand and grandiose with its two rivers acting as a border to contain the restless. Its skyscrapers and bleak, rotting tenements are a gift for photographic consumption, but for the fictional imagination the city's inchoate density is a special challenge.

"Locations: An Introduction," *Ibid.*

9 There's a leveling homogeneity in America today created by television. Each day it passes over the vast land mass, over the states nudging each other like the sovereignties of the Balkans, creating a unifying cloud of aesthetic properties and experience. East and West, North and South are wrapped in a sort of over-soul of images, facts, happenings, celebrities.

Ibid.

10 It is often the task of the historian and the imaginative writer to discover the silences behind speech.

"Norman Mailer:* The Teller and the Tape," Ibid.

*American writer (1923–2007).

11 Like all writers I know of, the early days were dominated by love of reading, just reading, like eating, anything around.

Interview (1979), Quoted in Obituary, *The New York Times 5 December 2007*

2271. Jane Jacobs (1916–2006)

1 But look what we have built . . . Low-income projects that become worse centers of delinquency, vandalism, and general social hopelessness than the slums they were supposed to replace. . . . Cultural centers that are unable to support a good bookstore. Civic centers that are avoided by everyone but bums. . . . Promenades that go from no place to nowhere and

have no promenades. Expressways that eviscerated great cities. This is not the rebuilding of cities. This is the sacking of cities.
Introduction, *The Death and Life of Great American Cities 1961*

2 There is a quality even meaner than outright ugliness or disorder, and this meaner quality is the dishonest mask of pretended order, achieved by ignoring or suppressing the real order that is struggling to exist and to be served.
Ibid.

3 Streets and their sidewalks, the main public places of a city, are its most vital organs . . . If a city's streets are safe from barbarism and fear, the city is thereby tolerably safe from barbarism and fear . . . To keep the city safe is a fundamental task of a city's streets and its sidewalks.
Pt. I, Ch. 2, Ibid.

4 Conventionally, neighborhood parks or park-like open spaces are considered boons conferred on the deprived populations of cities. Let us turn this thought around, and consider city parks deprived places that need the boon of life and appreciation conferred on them.
Ch. 5, Ibid.

5 But because development subverts the status quo, the status quo soon subverts governments.
Ch. 8, *The Economy of Cities 1969*

6 The bureaucratized, simplified cities, so dear to present-day city planners and urban designers, and familiar also to readers of science fiction and utopian proposals, run counter to the processes of city growth and economic development. Conformity and monotony, even when they are embellished with a froth of novelty, are not attributes of developing and economically vigorous cities. They are attributes of stagnant settlements.
Ibid.

2272. Florynce R. Kennedy (1916–2000)

1 . . . There can be no real pervasive system of oppression, such as that in the United States, without the consent of the oppressed.
"Institutionalized Oppression vs. the Female," *Sisterhood Is Powerful*, Robin Morgan,* ed. *1970*
*See 3284.

2 Women are dirt searchers; their greatest worth is eradicating rings on collars and tables. Never mind real-estate boards' corruption and racism, here's your soapsuds. Everything she is doing is peripheral, expendable, crucial, and nonnegotiable. Cleanliness is next to godliness.
Ibid.

3 Every form of bigotry can be found in ample supply in the legal system of our country. It would seem that Justice (usually depicted as a woman) is indeed blind to racism, sexism, war and poverty.
Ibid.

4 Oppressed people are frequently very oppressive when liberated.
Ibid.

5 Being a mother is a noble status, right? Right. So why does it change when you put "unwed" and "welfare" in front of it?
Quoted in "The Verbal Karate of Florynce R. Kennedy, Esq." by Gloria Steinem,* *Ms.* (New York) *March 1973*
*See 2916.

6 The biggest sin is sitting on your ass.
Ibid.

7 Don't agonize. Organize.
Ibid.

8 If men could get pregnant, abortion would be a sacrament.
Ibid.

9 There are very few jobs that actually require a penis or vagina. All other jobs should be open to everybody.
Quoted in "Freelancer with No Time to Write" by John Brady, *Writer's Digest February 1974*

2273. Bella Lewitzky (1916–2005)

1 Making social comment is an artificial place for an artist to start from. If an artist is touched by some social condition, what the artist creates will reflect that, but you can't force it.
Quoted in "Modern Dance Group Plants Western Roots" by Didi Moore, *San Francisco Chronicle 4 March 1979*

2 When you dance, it's only for now. When you choreograph, it's with you day and night. But when you get through, the creation leaves you like a child.
Ibid.

3 To exist merely to exist is stupidity. To exist to make art is a pretty grand act.
Quoted in *The New York Times 1990*

2274. Eve Merriam (1916–1992)

1 MARY JONES. I asked a man in prison once how he happened to be there and he said that he had stolen a pair of shoes. I told him if he had stolen a railroad he would be a United States Senator.
Out of Our Fathers' House, with Paula Wagner and Jack Hofsiss *1975*

2 Poetry is the liveliest use of language, and nobody knows more instinctively how to take delight in that playfulness than children.
"Serious Play: Reading Poetry with Children," *The Academy of American Poets Web Site*, poets.org *April 1999*

2275. Sylvia Sleigh (1916–   )

1 I am a portrait painter in every way. Even if I paint a leaf, it should be a portrait. It is my belief that if we could all appreciate every living thing in detail, we would be kinder and better to one another.
"Sylvia Sleigh", *Exposures, Women & Their Art* by Ann Brown and Arlene Raven* *1989*

*See 3533.

2276. Mary Stewart (1916–   )

1 This turf, this sky, the heartsease in the grass; the old lines of ridge and furrow, and the still older ghosts of Roman road and Wall; the ordered, spare beauty of the northern fells; this, in front of me now, was England. *This other Eden, demi-paradise. This dear, dear land.*
Ch. 1, *The Ivy Tree 1961*

2 It is harder to kill a whisper than even a shouted calumny.
Bk.1, Ch. 1, *The Last Enchantment 1979*

3 There are few men more superstitious than soldiers. They are, after all, the men who live closest to death.

Bk. 2, Ch. 3, Ibid.

2277. Patricia Swerda (1916–)

1 Go to nature. Once you learn how plants grow, you will know how to arrange them.

Quoted in "Ikebana, a Zen way with flowers" by Karen Mathieson, *Pacific Magazine* 28 May 1989

2 The only difference between a rut and a grave are the dimensions.

Ibid.

2278. Dagmar Wilson (1916–)

1 You know how men are. They talk in abstractions and prestige and the technicalities of the bomb, almost as if this were all a game of chess. Well, it isn't. There are times, it seems to me, when the only thing to do is let out a loud scream. . . . Just women raising a hue and cry against nuclear weapons for all of them to cut it out

Remark (26 October 1961), Quoted in *Women Strike for Peace: Traditional Motherhood and Radical Politics in the 1960s* by Amy Swerdlow* 1993

*See 2470.

2 Since we came into being 35 years ago as a protest against atmospheric nuclear tests and the danger of radioactive pollution to children's health, WSP has remained a strong voice in the struggle for our unfinished goal—the Comprehensive Test Ban Treaty and for total nuclear disarmament. . . . As we celebrate our 35th anniversary, we call on women to recommit themselves to the total elimination of nuclear weapons and removing the nuclear threat from future generations.

News release, Women Strike for Peace 24 September 1996

3 As women we feel a peculiar moral passion of revolt against both the cruelty and the waste of war . . . we are especially the custodian[s] of life.

Quoted in ""Women Strike for Peace: Success or Failure?" by Joe Newlin, *Voices: Santa Monica Women's College Magazine*, vol. 1, no. 2 *Summer 2000*

2279. Hiltgunt Zassenhaus (1916–2004)

1 If they bomb my home in Hamburg, all I have left is what I can carry with me. . . . [But] there was something no suitcase could hold. It was intangible and the prisoners hungered for it. Only our minds and hearts could give truth and hope.

Walls: Resisting the Third Reich—One Woman's Story 1974

2280. Martha Bacon (1917–1981)

1 She* soothed and solaced and celebrated, destroying her gift by maiming it to suit her hearers.

Quoted in *Christian Science Monitor* 24 June 1965
*Re Phillis Wheatley; see 677.

2281. Gwendolyn Brooks (1917–2000)

1 What she wanted was to donate to the world a good Maude Martha. That was the offering, the bit of art, that could not come from any other. She would polish and hone that.

Ch. 6, *Maude Martha* 1943

2 She had a tremendous impatience with other people's ideas— unless those happened to be exactly like hers; even then, often

as not, she gave hurried, almost angry, affirmative, and flew onto emphatic illumination of her own.

Ch. 23, Ibid.

3 Abortions will not let you forget.
You remember the children you got that you did not get. . . .

"The Mother," St. 1, *A Street in Bronzeville* 1945

4 I hold my honey and I store my bread
In little jars and cabinets of my will.
I label clearly, and each latch and lid
I bid, Be firm till I return from hell.
I am very hungry. I am incomplete.
And none can tell when I may dine again.

"My dreams, my works, must wait till after hell," Ibid.

5 People like definite decisions,
Tidy answers, all the little ravellings
Snipped off, the lint removed, they
Hop happily among their roughs
Calling what they can't clutch insanity
Or saintliness.

"Memorial to Ed Blanc," St. 3, *Annie Allen* 1949

6 We real cool. We
Left school. We

Lurk late. We
Strike straight. We

Sing sin. We
Thin gin. We

Jazz June. We
Die soon.

"We Real Cool," *The Bean Eaters* 1960

7 I wonder if the elephant
Is lonely in his stall
When all the boys and girls are gone
And there's no shout at all,
And there's no one to stamp before,
No one to note his might.
Does he hunch up, as I do,
Against the dark of night?

"Pete at the Zoo," Ibid.

8 He opened us—
who was a key,

who was a man.

"Malcolm X,"* Sts. 4–5, *In the Mecca* 1968
*Assumed name of Malcolm Little, American Black activist and founder of the Organization of Afro-American Unity (1964); assassinated (1925–1965).

9 Does man love Art? Man visits Art, but squirms
Art hurts. Art urges voyages—
and it is easier to stay at home,
the nice beer ready.

"The Chicago Picasso," St. 1, Ibid.

10 Live not for battles won.
Live not for the-end-of-the-song.
Live in the along.

"Speech to the Young: Speech to the Progress-Toward," St. 2 *n.d.*

11 You did not know the Black continent
that had to be reached
was you.
"To the Diaspora," St. 2 *n.d.*

2282. Leonora Carrington (1917–)

1 Sentimentality is a form of fatigue.
"The Happy Corpse Story" (*Le Nouveau Commerce*, No. 31, 1975), *The Seventh Horse and Other Tales 1988*

2283. Janet Colins (1917–2003)

1 I said no. I sat on the steps and I cried and cried.*
Interview by Anna Kisselgoff, *The Times (London) 1974*
*Re the Ballet Russe telling her she would have to dance in white face.

2284. Anne Cumming (1917–)

1 Sex is a short cut to everything.
Ch. 1, *The Love Quest* (autobio.) *1991*

2285. Barbara Deming (1917–1984)

1 It is particularly hard on us as pacifists, of course, to face our own anger. It is particularly painful for us—hard on our pride, too—to have to discover in ourselves murderers.
"On Anger," *We Cannot Live Without Our Lives 1974*

2 If men put from them in fear all that is "womanish" in them, then long, of course, for that missing part of their natures, so seek to possess it by possessing us; and because they have feared it in their own souls seek, too, to dominate it in us— seek even to slay it—well, we're where we are now, aren't we?
"Two Perspectives on Women's Struggles," Ibid.

3 A liberation movement that is nonviolent sets the oppressor free as well as the oppressed.
p. 172, *Seeds of Peace*, Jeanne Larson and Made Micheels-Cyrus, comps. *1986*

2286. Phyllis Diller (1917–)

1 Cleaning your house while your kids are still growing
Is like shoveling the walk before it stops snowing.
Phyllis Diller's Housekeeping Hints 1966

2 Never go to bed mad. Stay up and fight.
Ibid.

3 You know you're getting old, when your back starts going out more than you do.
Quoted in Earl Wilson's syndicated "Broadway" column *8 September 1978*

4 Men have this silly, witchy . . . attitude that a woman who is a comic has lost her femininity.
Quoted in "The 1960's to the 1980's," *Women in Comedy* by Linda Martin and Kerry Segrave *1986*

5 Comedy is tragedy revisited or hostility. It is mock hostility, of course, or it would be ugly.
Ibid.

6 Next to gold and jewelry, health is the most important thing you can have.
Quoted in "Early Stand-Up Comics," *Funny Women, American Comediennes, 1860–1985* by Mary Unterbrink *1987*

7 *Re her promiscuous sister:* It took a driving instructor two days to teach her how to sit up in a car.
Ibid.

8 Life is a do-it-yourself kit, so do it yourself. Work. Practice.
Ibid.

2287. Zsa Zsa Gabor (1917–)

1 I never hated a man enough to give him his diamonds back.
Quoted in *Observer* (London) *28 August 1957*

2 Husbands are like fires. They go out when unattended.
Quoted in *Newsweek* (New York) *28 March 1960*

3 I'm a vunderful housekeeper. Effry time I get a divorce I keep the house.
Remark *n.d.*

4 I know nothing about sex, because I was always married.
"Sex," *Hammer and Tongues: The Best of Women's Wit and Humor,* Michele Brown and Ann O'Connor, comps. *1986*

2288. Indira Gandhi (1917–1984)

1 Peace we want because there is another war to fight against poverty, disease and ignorance. We have promises to keep to our people of work, food, clothing, and shelter, health and education.
Radio Broadcast (26 January 1966), Quoted in *Indira Gandhi* by Mithrapuram K. Alexander *1968*

2 The young people of India must recognize that they will get from their country tomorrow what they give her today.
Ibid.

3 You cannot shake hands with a clenched fist.
Press Conference, New Delhi (19 October 1971), Quoted in *Indira Speaks* by Dhiren Mullick *1972*

4 Is it possible, was it ever possible, to keep alive in India the beautiful dream of parliamentarian democracy the British imported along with five o'clock tea?
Quoted in "Indira's Coup" by Oriana Fallaci,* *New York Review of Books 18 September 1975*
*See 2656.

5 To bear many children is considered not only a religious blessing but also an investment. The greater their number, some Indians reason, the more alms they can beg.
Ibid.

6 There exists no politician in India daring enough to attempt to explain to the masses that cows can be eaten.
Ibid.

7 I think that the highly industrialized Western world has neglected to the utmost degree to leave room for man. The infernal production-consumption cycle has completely dehumanized life. The individual has become a tool. He hardly has any contact with nature anymore. That is, with himself. He has lost his soul and is not even trying to find it again.
Quoted in "Conversation with Indira Gandhi," by José-Luis de Villalonga, *Oui 1975*

8 Never forget that when we are silent, we are one. And when we speak, we are two.
Ibid.

9 Every democratic system evolves its own conventions. It is not only the water but the banks which make the river.
Remark (1967), Quoted in *Speeches and Writings 1975*

10 You must learn to be still in the midst of activity and to be vibrantly alive in repose.

Quoted in "The Embattled Woman" by James Shepherd, *People* 30 June 1975

11 Even if I died in the service of the nation, I would be proud of it. Every drop of my blood . . . will contribute to the growth of this nation and to make it strong and dynamic.

Speech, Delhi *30 October 1984**

*The eve of her assassination by Sikh militants.

12 People tend to forget their duties but remember their rights.

Last words *1984*

2289. Katharine Graham (1917–2001)

1 If one is rich and one's a woman, one can be quite misunderstood.

Quoted in "The Power That Didn't Corrupt" by Jane Howard,* *Ms.* (New York) *October 1974*

*See 2936.

2 To love what you do and feel that it matters—how could anything be more fun?

Ibid.

3 The power is to set the agenda. What we print and what we don't print matter a lot.

Quoted in "All the Publisher's Presidents" by Donald I. Bartlett, *The New York Times Book Review* 28 February 1993

2290. Fannie Lou Hamer (1917–1977)

1 Ain' no such thing as I can hate anybody and hope to see God's face.

Quoted in Introduction (p. xi), *Civil Wars* by June Jordan* *1981*

*See 2987.

2 Let's face it. What's hurtin' the Black folks that's without, is hurtin' the white folks that's without. If the white folk fight for theyself, and the Black folk for theyself, we gonna crumble apart. These are things that we gonna have to fight together. We got to fight in America for ALL the people . . . and I'm perfectly willing to make this country what it have to be.

Slogan, Women for Racial & Economic Equality *n.d.*

2291. Han Suyin (1917–)

1 "Your laws are ineffective," Wen declared. "Why? Because no system of control will work as long as most of those administering the law against an evil have more than a finger dipped into it themselves."

Ch. 13, *Destination Chungking* 1942

2 "I'd sell my love for food any day. The rice bowl is to me the most valid reason in the world for doing anything. A piece of one's soul to the multitudes in return for rice and wine does not seem to me a sacrilege."

Preface, *A Many-Splendored Thing* 1950

3 Afterwards, as happens when a man is safely dead, they sang his praise.

Pt. IV, Ibid.

4 . . . all humans are frightened of their own solitude. Yet only in solitude can man learn to know himself, learn to handle his own eternity of aloneness. And love from one being to another can only be that two solitudes come nearer, recognize and protect and comfort each other.

Pt. V, Ch. 1, *The Mountain Is Young* 1958

5 The world needs the artist who records, with dispassionate compassion, more than the missionary who proclaims with virulence unreal crusades against reality, especially those who want to put the clock back to an ideal past that never was.

Pt. I, Ch. 1, *The Crippled Tree* 1965

6 For exploitation and oppression is not a matter of *race*. It is the system, the apparatus of world-wide brigandage called imperialism, which made the Powers behave the way they did. I have no illusions on that score, nor do I believe that any Asian nation or African nation, in the same state of dominance, and with the same system of colonial profit-amassing and plunder, would have behaved otherwise.

Ch. 9, Ibid.

7 These ways to make people buy were strange and new to us, and many bought for the sheer pleasure at first of holding in the hand and talking of something new. And once this was done, it was like opium, we could no longer do without this new bauble, and thus, though we hated the foreigners and though we knew they were ruining us, we bought their goods. Thus I learned the art of the foreigners, the art of creating in the human heart restlessness, disquiet, hunger for new things, and these new desires became their best helpers.

Ch. 15, Ibid.

8 A country is not truly betrayed to the enemy outside its gates unless there are also traitors within. For money, for power, these can be found.

Ch. 17, Ibid.

9 "Goldfish are flowers," said Papa, "flowers that move."

Pt. II, Ch. 26, Ibid.

2292–2293. Ruth Herschberger (1917–)

1 I was driven off the playing field
By Ginsberg* & pals.
I went quietly.
Benched.

"The Playing Field", *Adam's Rib* 1948

*Re Allen G— (1926–1997), Am. poet of the Beat generation.

2 I cannot be a different thing although
For your sake, to win you, I would grow
  Wings and shed thorns,
  Be weed, or newly born,
Anything so to please you,
But I'm myself and cannot ease you.

"So If You Love Me," St. 1, *Nature & Love Poems* 1969

3 I would say for the expenditure of love,
And the atrophy of longing, there is no cure

"The Huron," Ibid.

2294. Lena Horne (1917–2010)

1 It's ill-becoming for an old broad to sing about how bad she wants it. But occasionally we do.

Quoted in *Time* (New York) *17 October 1988*

2 Always be smarter than the people who hire you.

Remark *n.d.*

2295. Fay Kanin (1917–)

1 JUDGE. Now, where were we? Oh, yes, plaintiff and defendant were in bed—talking.

His and Hers, with Michael Kanin *1948*

2 While other [film] crafts have to sit around chewing their fingernails waiting for a movie to be put together, writers have one great strength. They can sit down and generate their own employment and determine their own fate to a great extent by the degree of their disciplines, their guts, and their talents.

Quoted in "Fay Kanin," *The Screenwriter Looks at the Screenwriter* by William Froug *1972*

3 She* was an early activist for freedom of expression. She stood up for what she believed in and fought all the negative elements. What recommended her to me was that she made sex fun. She put humor into sex, and I found that absolutely delicious.

Quoted in "Mae West still figures prominently . . ." Associated Press *17 August 1993*

*Reference to Mae West; see 1790.

4 It's my feeling that the highest aspiration of the [screen] writer is to be a writer-executive in the sense that he goes on to control his material in one further aspect by producing or directing it. I believe every writer who can should try to accomplish that. Because it's the best way he can get his work done well.

Froug, Ibid.

2296. Sybil Leek (1917–1982)

1 You can't be sure who the Devil is these days. He might be a TV or movie producer in disguise.

Ch. 1, *Diary of a Witch 1968*

2 Perhaps telepathy will remain a mystery for many more years but it has always been within the power of a few people in every generation to transmit and receive thoughts. People in love often claim this power. Maybe we are being forced to realize that love is in itself a magical power and that awareness may be instrumental in preventing our own destruction.

Ch. 6, Ibid.

3 Reincarnation is nothing more than the law of evolution applied to the consciousness of the individual. . . . The spirit is our only link with the Godhead, the divine force of life, and it is the indestructible part of ourselves.

Ch. 12, Ibid.

4 We seem to be trapped by a civilization that has accelerated many physical aspects of evolution but has forgotten that other vital part of man—his mind and his psyche.

Ch. 13, *ESP—The Magic Within You 1971*

2297. Carson McCullers (1917–1967)

1 "Today we are not put up on the platforms and sold at the courthouse square. But we are forced to sell our strength, our time, our souls during almost every hour that we live. We have been freed from one kind of slavery only to be delivered into another."

Pt. II, Ch. 6, *The Heart is a Lonely Hunter 1940*

2 "Say a man died and left his mule to his four sons. The sons would not wish to cut up the mule into four parts and each take his share. They would own and work the mule together. That is the way Marx says all of the natural resources should

be owned—not by one group of rich people but by all the workers of the world as a whole."

Ibid.

3 Three words were in the captain's heart. He shaped them soundlessly with his trembling lips, as he had not breath to spare for a whisper: "I am lost." And having given up life, the Captain suddenly began to live.

Ch. 3, *Reflections in a Golden Eye 1941*

4 "We all of us somehow caught. We born this way or that way and we don't know why. But we caught anyhow. . . . And maybe we wants to widen and bust free. But no matter what we do we still caught. Me is me and you is you and he is he. We each one of us somehow caught all by ourself."

Pt. II, Ch. 2, *The Member of the Wedding* (novel) *1946*

5 F. Jasmine did not want to go upstairs, but she did not know how to refuse. It was like going into a fair booth, or fair ride, that once having entered you cannot leave until the exhibition or the ride is finished. Now it was the same with this soldier, this date. She could not leave until it ended.

Ch. 3, Ibid.

6 FRANKIE. The trouble with me is that for a long time I have been just an "I" person. . . . All people belong to a "we" except me . . . Not to belong to a "we" makes you too lonesome.

The Member of the Wedding (play) *1950*

7 His own life seemed so solitary, a fragile column supporting nothing amidst the wreckage of the years.

"The Sojourner," *The Ballad of the Sad Café 1951*

8 Ferris glimpsed the disorder of his life: the succession of cities, of transitory loves; and time, the sinister glissando of the years, time always.

Ibid.

9 Psychopathic people are very often charming.

Illumination and Night Glare, The Unfinished Autobiography of Carson McCullers, Carlos L. Dews, ed. *2000*

2298. Jessica Mitford (1917–1996)

1 Things on the whole are much faster in America; people don't *stand for election,* they *run for office.*

Ch. 11, *Sons and Rebels 1960*

2 [Undertakers have] successfully turned the tables in recent years to perpetrate a huge, macabre and expensive practical joke on the American public.

The American Way of Death 1963

3 No doubt prison administrators sense that to permit the media and the public access to their domain would result in stripping away a major justification for their existence: that they are confining depraved, brutal creatures.

Ch. 1, *Kind and Unusual Punishment 1971*

4 When is conduct a crime, and when is a crime not a crime? When Somebody Up There—a monarch, a dictator, a Pope, a legislator—so decrees.

Ch. 5, Ibid.

5 One of the nicest American scientists I know was heard to say, "Criminals in our penitentiary are fine experimental material—much cheaper than chimpanzees." I hope the chimpanzees don't come to hear of this.

Ch. 9, Ibid.

6 Radical and revolutionary ideologies are seeping into the prisons. Whereas formerly convicts tended to regard themselves as unfortunates whose accident of birth at the bottom of the heap was largely responsible for their plight, today many are questioning the validity of the heap.

> Ch. 13, Ibid.

2299. Violeta Parra (1917–1967)

1 I do not play the guitar for applause. I sing the difference that there is between what is true and is false; otherwise I do not sing.

> Remark *n.d.*

2 But the cry of the Indian
why will no-one hear it?
> "Sufferings of Arauco" (Arauco tiene una pena) *n.d.*

3 Gracias a la vida que me ha dado tanto
Me dio el corazón, que agita su marco.
Cuando miro el fruto del cerebro humano,
Cuando miro al bueno tan lejos del malo.
Cuando miro el fondo de tus ojos claros.

I'm grateful to, Life, that gives me so much.
My heart—that beats like a drum
When I see the fruits of the mind
When I see good distanced from evil
When I look in the depths of your beautiful eyes.
> "Gracias a La Vida" (In Gratitude to Life), St. 5 *n.d.*

2300. Estelle R. Ramey (1917–2006)

1 If it's testosterone the public wants in a president, as an endocrinologist I can't recommend a 70-year-old man in the White House. They should get a 16-year-old boy instead. It seems the only thing the public doesn't want to see in a president is estrogen.

> Letter to Editor, *Washington Evening Star* 1970

2 Women's chains have been forged by men, not by anatomy.

> Ibid.

3 It is said, for instance, that men are innately more aggressive than women. But conditioning, not sex hormones, makes them that way. Anyone seeing women at a bargain-basement sale—where aggression is viewed as appropriate, even endearing—sees aggression that would make Attila the Hun turn pale.

> Quoted in "Are Men and Women Different?" by Judith
> Viorst,* *Redbook* (New York) *November* 1978
> *See 2780.

4 Men were designed for short, nasty, brutal lives. Women are designed for long, miserable ones.

> Quoted in "Estelle R. Ramey: Used Wit in Women's Advocacy"
> by Patricia Sullivan, *The Washington Post* 10 September 2006

5 Asked if she wished to be called "chairperson": I'd rather be a chairman. They make more.

> Ibid.

2301. Muriel Resnik (1917–1995)

1 JOHN. . . . that's nothing but a tax dodge! . . . This is what the Internal Revenue Service expects. It's all part of the game. They play their part, we have to play ours. It's our duty as American citizens!

> Act I, Sc. 1, *Any Wednesday* 1963

2 HELEN . . . it's so horrible to be—oh God—*thirty* . . . Today is a turning point in my life, the beginning of the end. It's pushing forty—and menopause out there waiting to spring—and before you can even turn around you're a senior citizen.

> Ibid.

3 JOHN. But she doesn't *know* I'm hurting her, so I'm not. Is that a happy woman? Is she? You see? We're not hurting her, we're not taking anything away from her. In point of fact, having you in my life makes me happy, a happy husband for Dorothy! Far from hurting her, pet, we're *helping* her.
ELLEN. We are?
JOHN. Of course! If I didn't have you, Dorothy would be *miserable!*

> Act II, Sc. 1, Ibid.

2302. Christiane Rochefort (1917–1998)

1 JULIA. Never argue with them. You're always forgetting you're a woman. They never listen to what you're saying, they just want to listen to the music of your voice.

> *Les Stances à Sophie* 1970

2 You can go to the hospital. If you don't go to the hospital, you can go to marriage. And if you don't go to marriage you can go to the women's movement.

> Quoted in "Les Stances à Sophie" by Annette Levy, *Women
> and Film* (Vol. I, Nos. 3 and 4) 1973

2303. Helen Suzman (1917–)

1 Liberalism has a future in South Africa, but fundamental changes will take a lot longer than most people think.

> Quoted in World Notes, *Time* (New York) 29 May 1989

2 It is not my questions that embarrass South Africa, it is your answers.

> Quoted by The Helen Suzman Foundation 2003

3 I seem to have become the honorary ombudsman for all those people who have no vote and no MP . . . my desk here in Cape Town is a sad harvest of the seeds of apartheid.

> Ibid.

2304. Marie Vassiltchikov (1917–1978)

1 After dinner we had a long discussion with a famous zoologist about the best way to get rid of Adolf.* He said that in India natives use tigers' whiskers chopped very fine and mixed with food. The victim dies a few days later and nobody can detect the cause. But where do we find a tiger's whiskers?

> Diary entry, *Berlin Diaries, 1940–45* 1987
> *Reference to Adolf Hitler, Austrian-born German Nazi dictator
> (1889–1945).

2305. Rose Mary Woods (1917–2005)

1 I am most dreadfully sorry.

> Court testimony (November, 1973) Obituary, Quoted in
> *The New York Times* 23 January 2005

*Infamous apology regarding erasure of 18 minutes of subpoenaed tapes of President Richard M. Nixon.

2306. Mary Kay Ash (1918–2001)

1 Integrity is the ingredient that will enable you to forge rapidly ahead on the highway that leads to success. It advertises you as being an individual who will always come through. Whatever you say you will do, do it even if you have to move heaven and earth.

> Mary Kay Tribute, marykaytribute.com *n.d.*

2 The definition of successful people is simply ordinary people with extraordinary determination.

> Ibid.

3 When you reach an obstacle, turn it into an opportunity. You have the choice. You can overcome and be a winner, or you can allow it to overcome you and be a loser. The choice is yours and yours alone. Refuse to throw in the towel. Go that extra mile that failures refuse to travel. It is far better to be exhausted from success than to be rested from failure.

> Ibid.

4 I have learned to imagine an invisible sign around each person's neck that says, "Make me feel important!" I respond to it immediately, and I never cease to be amazed at how positively people react.

> Ibid.

5 A company is only as good as the people it keeps.

> Ibid.

2307. Pearl Bailey (1918–1986)

1 There are two kinds of talent, man-made talent and God-given talent. With man-made talent you have to work very hard. With God-given talent, you just touch it up once in a while.

> *Newsweek* (New York) *4 December 1967*

2 There's a period of life when we swallow a knowledge of ourselves and it becomes either good or sour inside.

> Ch. 13, *The Raw Pearl 1968*

3 The fact is that it takes more than ingredients and technique to cook a good meal. A good cook puts something of *himself* into the preparations—he cooks with enjoyment, anticipation, spontaneity, and he is willing to experiment.

> Preface, *Pearl's Kitchen 1973*

4 Hungry people cannot be good at learning or producing anything, except perhaps violence.

> Epilogue, Ibid.

2308. Marie Louise Berneri (1918–1949)

1 The authoritarian utopias of the nineteenth century are chiefly responsible for the anti-utopian attitude prevalent among intellectuals today. But utopias have not always described regimented societies, centralized states and nations of robots. Diderot's Tahiti or Morris's Nowhere gave us utopias where men were free from both physical and moral compulsion, where they worked not out of necessity or a sense of duty but because they found work a pleasurable activity, where love knew no laws and where every man was an artist.

Utopias have often been plans of societies functioning mechanically, dead structures conceived by economists, politicians and moralists; but they have also been the living dreams of poets.

> *Journey Through Utopia 1950*

2309. Peg Bracken (1918–2007)

1 . . . unnecessary dieting is because everything from television to fashion ads have made it seem wicked to cast a shadow. This wild, emaciated look appeals to some women, though not to many men, who are seldom seen pinning up a *Vogue* illustration in a machine shop.

> *The I Hate to Cook Book 1960*

2 Add the flour, salt, paprika and mushrooms, stir, and let it cook five minutes while you light a cigarette and stare sullenly at the sink.

> Skid Road Stroganoff, Ibid.

2310. Gertrude Louise Cheney (1918–)

1 All people are made alike.
They are made of bones, flesh and dinners.
Only the dinners are different.

> "People" *1927*

2311. Mildred McElroy Clingerman (1918–1997)

1 Nobody really looks at a bartender. . . . Even the bar philosophers (the dreariest customers of all) prefer to study their own faces in the back-bar mirror. And however they accept their reflected images, whether shudderingly or with secret love, it is to this aloof image that they impart their whiskey-wisdom, not to the bartender.

> *Stair Trick 1952*

2 She faced him as if he were Judgement and she standing up pleading for mankind.

> Ibid.

3 . . . people do not live by reason alone- . . . they only make up reasons to stop other people asking silly questions.

> "The Day of the Green Velvet Cloak," *A Cupful of Space 1961*

2312. Gertrude B. Elion (1918–1999)

1 I was a child with an insatiable thirst for knowledge and remember enjoying all of my courses almost equally. When it came time at the end of my high school career to choose a major in which to specialize I was in a quandary. One of the deciding factors may have been that my grandfather, whom I loved dearly, died of cancer when I was 15. I was highly motivated to do something that might eventually lead to a cure for this terrible disease.

> Autobiographical Essay, *Les Prix Nobel 1988*

2 When we began to see the results of our efforts in the form of new drugs which filled real medical needs and benefited patients in very visible ways, our feeling of reward was immeasurable.

> Ibid.

3 It's amazing how much you can accomplish when you don't care who gets the credit.

> Jewish Women's Archive (jwa.org) *n.d.*

2313. Betty Ford (1918–)

1 In our society, we get to know each other over drinks, we associate feast and celebrations with liquor. We think we have to drink, that it's a social necessity . . . It's romantic as long as you can handle it—for years I could and did—but it's misery when you become addicted.

> *The Times of My Life,* with Chris Chase *1978*

2 . . . a woman . . . told us she was forever getting herself into trouble. "But I just keep coming back," she said. "I just keep showing up for my life."

Showing up for life. Being blessed with the rebirth that recovery brings.

One day at a time.
Ch. 17, *Glad Awakening,* with Chris Chase *1987*

2314. Selma Fraiberg (1918–1981)

1 But the neurotic conscience behaves like a gestapo headquarters within the personality, mercilessly tracking down dangerous or potentially dangerous ideas and every remote relative of these ideas, accusing, threatening, tormenting in an interminable inquisition to establish guilt for trivial offenses or crimes committed in dreams. Such guilt feelings have the effect of putting the entire personality under arrest. . . .
The Magic Years 1959

2315. Marge Frantz (1918?–)

1 All memories are treacherous and made to order, and I have no doubt romanticized my own. But I would not trade the passion for social and racial justice that I inherited from my father for any other way of life.
Quoted in *Red Diapers: Growing Up in the Communist Left,* Judy Kaplan and Linn Shapiro, eds. *1998*

2 Our movement was a singing movement. We didn't listen to others sing; we all sang together.
Ibid.

3 We lived dangerously.
Ibid.

2316. Cecelia Helen Goetz (1918?–)

1 Once you put on a [judicial] robe, the male-female distinction disappears, at least as far as the people who appear before you are concerned. They don't see you as either male or female.
Quoted in *The 50 Most Influential Women in American Law* by Dawn Bradley Berry* *1996*
*See 4399.

2317. Doris Isaac Grumbach (1918–)

1 I am ready to begin the end.
Last lines, *Coming Into the End Zone 1991*

2 The end of life is too often like this, mean, without the grace in which a woman like this must have lived.*
Extra Innings 1993
*Reference to a former Harvard art professor who was moved to a nursing home.

3 [I have] abandoned the barricades for the veranda, the foxhole for the hammock.
Ibid.

4 . . . children are most apt to discover their inner selves in moments of misery.
The Book of Knowledge 1995

2318. Corita Kent (1918–1986)

1 There are so many hungry people that God cannot appear to them except in the form of bread.
"Enriched Bread" (silkscreen) *1965*

2 One of the things Jesus did was to step aside from the organized religion of his time because it had become corrupt and bogged down with rules. Rules became more important than feeding the hungry.
Quoted in "A Time of Transition for Corita Kent" by Lucie Kay Scheuer, *The Los Angeles Times 11 July 1974*

3 Women's liberation is the liberation of the feminine in the man and the masculine in the woman.
Ibid.

2319. Ann Landers (1918–2002)

1 Women complain about sex more often than men, Their gripes fall into two major categories: (1) Not enough. (2) Too much.
Ch. 2, *Ann Landers Says Truth Is Stranger . . . 1968*

2 What the vast majority of American children need is to stop being pampered, stop being indulged, stop being chauffeured, stop being catered to. In the final analysis it is not what you do for your children but what you have taught them to do for themselves that will make them successful human beings.
Ch. 3, Ibid.

3 All married couples should learn the art of battle as they should learn the art of making love. Good battle is objective and honest—never vicious or cruel. Good battle is healthy and constructive, and brings to a marriage the principle of equal partnership.
Ch. 11, Ibid.

4 At every party there are two kinds of people—those who want to go home and those who don't. The trouble is, they are usually married to each other.
International Herald Tribune (Paris) *19 June 1991*

5 Tact is the art of making people feel at home when that's where you wish they were.
Ann Landers Advice *22 December 1998*

6 The real test of class is how you treat people who cannot possibly do you any good.
Ann Landers Advice *22 January 1999*

7 Love is friendship that has caught fire.
Ann Landers Advice *23 April 2002*

2320. Madeleine L'Engle (1918–2007)

1 "It's my worst trouble, getting fond. If I didn't get fond I could be happy all the time."
Ch. 6, *A Wrinkle in Time 1962*

2 A self is not something static, tied up in a pretty parcel and handed to the child, finished and complete. A self is always becoming.
A Circle of Quiet 1972

3 I was in that area of despair where one is incapable of being ontological. In my definition, this is sin.
Ibid.

4 Her father said, "You know, my dears, the world has been abnormal for so long that we've forgotten what it's like to live in a peaceful and reasonable climate. If there is to be any peace or reason, we have to create it in our own hearts and homes."
Ch. 1, *A Swiftly Tilting Planet 1978*

5   "You know Where we are, then? I mean—When we are? Is it time gone, or time to be?"

"It is, I think, what you would call Once Upon a Time and Long Ago."

"So we're not in the present."

"Of course we are. Whenever we are is present."

"We're not in *my* present. We're not When we were when you came to me."

"When I was called to you," Guadior corrected. "And When is not what matters. It's what happens in the When that matters. Are you ready to go?"

Ch. 3, Ibid.

6   "Everything that happens within the created Order, no matter how small, has its effect. If you are angry, that anger is added to all the hate with which the Echthroi would distort the melody and destroy the ancient harmonies. When you are loving, that lovingness joins the music of the spheres."

Ibid.

7   "Hate hurts the hater more'n the hated."

Ch. 9, Ibid.

2321. Ida Lupino (1918–1995)

1   And believe me, *Bring it in on time* is such a major factor in television that I'd sometimes get absolutely sick to my stomach days beforehand. . . . So any ladies who want to take over men's jobs—if that's what they really want—had better have strong stomachs.

Quoted in *Popcorn Venus* by Marjorie Rosen* 1973

*See 3372.

2322. Anna Magnani (1918–1973)

1   Great passions, my dear, don't exist: they're liars' fantasies. What do exist are little loves that may last for a short or a longer while.

Quoted in "Anna Magnani," *The Egotists* by Oriana Fallaci* 1963

*See 2656.

2   Children are like puppies: you have to keep them near you and look after them if you want to have their affection.

Ibid.

2323. Mary McGrory (1918–2004)

1   But he [Richard M. Nixon]* was like a kamikaze pilot who keeps apologizing for the attack.

Syndicated newspaper column *8 November 1962*

*American politician (1913–1994); 37th president of the United States (1969–74); resigned.

2   He [John F. Kennedy]* came on, composed as a prince of the blood, chestnut thatch carefully brushed, facts straight, voice steady. "Look at him," breathed the proud Irishman next to me in the audience. "He's a thoroughbred."

Syndicated newspaper column *9 August 1974*

*American politician (1917–1963); 35th president of the United States (1961–63); assassinated.

3   The Holocaust* happened because a whole nation lined up behind a madman. Germany had a rich culture and vaunted family values. Germans prided themselves on their immaculate houses and their obedient children. Yet they tolerated the most horrendous mass murder of the 20th century.

"Holocaust Museum holds appalling relevance today," *Seattle Post-Intelligencer*, Op-Ed 27 April 1993

*The genocide of European Jews and others by the Nazis during World War II.

4   And the propensity of weak and empty people to follow a leader into the darkness from which there is no return is still flourishing, as ever.

Ibid.

2324. Marian McPartland (1918–)

1   When I started out, I had the wish, the need, to compete with men. But I don't feel that way anymore. I take pride in being a woman.

(1973), p. 75, Quoted in *Stormy Weather: The Music and Lives of a Century of Jazzwomen* by Linda Dahl 1984

2   I don't mind turning 90. It beats any alternative I can think of.

Quoted in "Pioneer Marian McPartland closing in on 90" by Howard Reich, *Chicago Tribune 16 March 2008*

3   There certainly was not a good feeling toward women musicians years ago. I remember [bassist] Milt Hinton* saying, "I don't mind working with a woman musician, so long as she can play." I think that was the prevailing thought at the time—that the woman couldn't play as well as the man. It wasn't until they found out we all could that things started to change.

Ibid.

*(1910–2000), African-American "dean of jazz bass players," photographer; a.k.a. "The Judge."

4   One day a professor heard me in the practice room, and he opened up the door while I was trying to play like [Art] Tatum,* and he said, "Stop playing that trash." And that really made me want to do jazz all the more.

Ibid.

*(1909–1956), African-American jazz pianist and virtuoso.

2325. Martha Mitchell (1918–1976)

1   I'm not certain that we should have Democrats in the Cabinet.

Interview, *Tonight Show* NBC-TV *11 February 1971*

2   I've never said I was against integration. It should have started right after the Civil War. But why single out the South? The South has been imposed on long enough. It's the orphan of the nation.

Quoted in *Martha: The Mouth That Roared* by Charles Ashman and Sheldon Engelmayer 1973

2326. Penelope Mortimer (1918–1999)

1   In all the years of her marriage, a long war in which attack, if not happening, was always imminent, she had learned an expert cunning. The way to avoid being hurt, to dodge unhappiness, was to run away.

Ch. 1, *Daddy's Gone A-Hunting 1958*

2   "There is an obsessive tenderness and passion, an eating out of one's heart, a sense of longing, an affliction, which remains buried and unchanged from childhood, this is what is called falling in love. The longing is for reciprocation, the affliction is in knowing that reciprocation is forbidden."

Ch. 5, Ibid.

3 "I thought I was supposed to lie on a couch and you wouldn't say a word. It's like the Inquisition or something. Are you trying to make me feel I'm wrong? Because I do that for myself."

Ch. 1, The Pumpkin Eater 1962

4 "What do your patients do while you're away? Commit suicide, murder their wives, or do they just sit and cry and take pills and think about what they told you last time? . . . If I'm sane enough to be left alone with my *thoughts* for two weeks then I'm too sane to need these futile, boring conversations—because my God, they bore me—at six guineas a time."

Ch. 11, Ibid.

5 Grief is a very antisocial state . . .

Long Distance 1974

2327. Raisa Davydovna Orlova (1918–1989)

1 Beliefs and convictions reach out from the past, and they cannot be altered by fervent desire alone. They possess their own logic and illogic, their own organic existence, their own rhythm of development.

Introduction, Memoirs, Samuel Cioran, tr. *1983*

2 The working morning. Now I love the morning more than the evening, the spring more than the fall. The promise more than the fulfillment.

Ch. 24, Ibid.

2328. Florence Rush (1918–2008)

1 The family itself is an instrument of sexual and other forms of child abuse. . . . [it] is permitted because it is an unspoken but prominent factor in socializing and preparing the female to accept a subordinate role. . . . In short the sexual abuse of female children is a process of education that prepares them to become the wives and mothers of America.

Speech, New York Radical Feminists 17 April 1971

2329. Cicely Saunders (1918–2005)

1 It appears to be that many patients feel deserted by their doctors at the end. Ideally the doctor should remain the centre of a team who work together to relieve where they cannot heal, to keep the patient's own struggle within his compass and to bring hope and consolation to the end.

Care of the Dying 1960

2 Deception is not as creative as truth. We do best in life if we look at it with clear eyes, and I think that applies to coming up to death as well.

Quoted in "Dying with Dignity" by David Brand, Time (New York) 5 September 1988

2330. June K. Singer (1918/20–2004)

1 Is it sufficient that you have learned to drive the car, or shall we look and see what is under the hood? Most people go through life without ever knowing.

Boundaries of the Soul, The Practice of June's Psychology 1972

2 And so Multi-Media Man, the contemporary successor to Renaissance Man . . .

Ch. 1, Ibid.

3 As a man's image of the world changes, so a man changes himself.

Ibid.

4 In learning to sail you do not change the current of the water nor do you have any effect on the wind, but you learn to hoist your sail and turn it this way and that to utilize the greater forces which surround you. By understanding them, you become one with them, and in doing so are able to find your own direction—so long as it is in harmony with, and does not try to oppose, the greater forces in being.

Ibid.

5 Despite the continuing expansion or even explosion of information, there will forever be limits beyond which the devices of science cannot lead a man.

Ch. 13, Ibid.

6 Despite the gradual nature of the impact it is making now, the Women's Movement is revolutionary in nature. Its aims are radical; its cutting edge is to enable woman to conceive of herself as possessing the inner potential to become economically and spiritually independent. The radical feminist of today recalls the mythic Amazon, a fearsome warrior who could defeat man at his own game. The rationale of the Movement, as the more liberal wing recognizes, is that if woman can get beyond a position of subservience to man, she can then begin to relate to him in a much more satisfying way for both, and that is as an equal.

Ch. 1, Androgyny: The Opposites Within 1976

7 The recent expansion of androgynous consciousness, brought about largely through the catalytic effect of the Women's Movement, has increased our awareness of the necessity for questioning the nearly impregnable fortress of male-oriented values.

Ibid.

2331. Muriel Spark (1918–2006)

1 Being over seventy is like being engaged in a war. All our friends are going or gone and survive amongst the dead and the dying as on a battlefield.

Ch. 4, Memento Mori 1959

2 There was altogether too much candour in married life; it was an indelicate modern idea, and frequently led to upsets in a household, if not divorce.

Ch. 12, Ibid.

3 "Give me a girl at an impressionable age, and she is mine for life."

Ch. 1, The Prime of Miss Jean Brodie 1961

4 "One's prime is elusive. You little girls, when you grow up, must be on the alert to recognize your prime at whatever time of your life it may occur. You must then live it to the full."

Ibid.

5 "Art and religion first; then philosophy; lastly science. That is the order of the great subjects of life, that's their order of importance."

Ch. 2, Ibid.

6 "To me education is a leading out of what is already there in the pupil's soul. To Miss Mackay it is a putting in of something that is not there, and that is not what I call education, I call it intrusion . . ."

Ibid.

7 "Nothing infuriates people more than their own lack of spiritual insight, Sandy, that is why the Moslems are so placid, they are full of spiritual insight."

Ch. 4, Ibid.

8 "It is impossible to persuade a man who does not disagree, but smiles."

Ibid.

9 She did not know then that the price of allowing false opinions was the gradual loss of one's capacity for forming true ones.

"Bang-Bang You're Dead," Collected Stories: I 1968

10 Kathleen, speaking from the Catholic point of view which takes some getting used to, said, "She was at Confession only the day before she died—wasn't she lucky?"

"The Portobello Road," Ibid.

11 I wouldn't take the Pope too seriously. He's a Pole first, a pope second, and maybe a Christian third.

International Herald Tribune (Paris) 29 May 1989

12 "I don't know how it struck you," said Hildegard (Dr Wolf) to her patient. "But to me, selling one's soul to the Devil involves murder. Anything less is not worthy of the designation. You can sell your soul to a number of agents, let's face it, but to the Devil there has to be a killing or so involved."

Ch. 1, Aiding and Abetting 2000

2332. Christine Stevens (1918–2002)

1 The basis of all animal rights should be the Golden Rule: we should treat *them* as we would wish them to treat us, were any other species in our dominant position.

Quoted in Returning to Eden by Michael Fox 1980

2 [There is a] widespread, ingrained problem of unnecessary suffering among the millions of laboratory animals used yearly in our country. . . . I was shocked by the attitude of Committee members who asserted that we have no moral obligation to animals and expressed hatred of the idea of having a report that puts emphasis on alternatives. . . . A balanced report should recognize the severity and extent of the problem.

Minority Statement to the Committee to National Research Council 1988

3 So long as I can, I feel it's a duty. Why would I stop?

Motto n.d.

2333. Abigail Van Buren (1918–2003)

1 People who fight fire with fire usually end up with ashes.

"Dear Abby" newspaper column 7 March 1974

2 Some people are more turned on by money than they are by love. . . . In one respect they're alike. They're both wonderful as long as they last.

"Dear Abby" newspaper column 26 April 1974

3 Religion, like water, may be free, but when they pipe it to you, you've got to help pay for the piping. And the piper!

"Dear Abby" newspaper column 28 April 1974

4 Psychotherapy, unlike castor oil, which will work no matter how you get it down, is useless when forced on an uncooperative patient.

"Dear Abby" newspaper column 11 July 1974

2334. June Wayne (1918–)

1 My art deals with information systems and astrophysical space because it is the new wilderness, the next frontier, a wilderness of an immensity we have yet to comprehend.

Quoted in "June Wayne," Exposures, Women & Their Art by Ann Brown and Arlene Raven* 1989

*See 3533.

2335. Faye Glenn Abdellah (1919–)

1 A nurse must maintain a close relationship with the patient. There is no machine that can take the place of a nurse holding a patient's hand and being there for moral support. I don't want to see the nurse become a machine, there has to be a balance. The focus has to be on the patient and the patient's welfare. A challenge for nurses today is to retain a personal connection with the patient. Nursing science without personal care does not work.

"Up Close and Personal: Interview with Rear Admiral Faye Glenn Abdellah" by Melvin Lessing, Military Medicine November 2004

2 I'll never forget my stopover in San Diego, where I observed the local nursing homes. Having some extra time, I toured the San Diego Zoo and realized that the zoo was better maintained than the nursing homes I had visited.

Ibid.

2336. Joy Adamson (1919–1980)

1 How could she [Elsa, the lion] know that it needed all the strength of my love for her to leave her now and give her back to nature—to let her learn to live alone until she might find her pride—her real pride?

"The Second Release," Born Free 1960

2 Since we humans have the better brain, isn't it our responsibility to protect our fellow creatures from, oddly enough, ourselves?

Born Free: A Lioness of Two Worlds 2000

2337. Isidora Aguirre (1919–)

1 CAROLINA. Besides when I say "nothing," what I mean is: everything.

Carolina (a.k.a. Express for Santiago) 1955

2 CARLOS. Remember: don't start conversations with strangers on a trip. No way of getting rid of them later!

Ibid.

3 CAROLINA. It's awful to be the wife of a lawyer.

Ibid.

2338. E. Margaret Burbidge (1919–)

1 Suddenly I saw my fascination with the stars . . . linked to my other delight, large numbers. I decided then and there that the occupation I most wanted to engage in "when I was grown up" was to determine the distances of the stars.

"Watcher of the Skies," Annual Review of Astronomy and Astrophysics 1994

*Upon receiving astronomy books from her grandfather when she was 12.

2 I often think about the joys of work in an open [observatory] dome, under the stars, next to the telescope, joys denied to most younger astronomers.*

Ibid.

*Today, like so many other sciences, much of the study of astronomy is via computers.

2339. Betty Comden (1919–2006)

1 I'm singing in the rain,
   Just singing in the rain.
   What a glorious feeling,
   I'm happy again.
   "Singin' in the Rain," *Singin' in the Rain* with Adolph Green
   1952

2 Moses supposes his toeses are roses
   But Moses supposes erroneously.
   "Elocution," Ibid.

3 The party's over—
   It's time to call it a day—
   No matter how you pretend
   You knew it would end this way.
   Act II, Sc. 4, "The Party's Over," *Bells Are Ringing,* with
   Adolph Green *1960*

2340. Frances Crowe (1919–)

1 . . . keep on keeping on . . .
   Quoted in "Karen Malpede,"* *Interviews with Contemporary
   Women Playwrights,* Kathleen Betsko** and Rachel Koenig,
   comps. *1987*

   *See 3590. **See 3125.

2 Anyone who is conscientiously opposed to participating in any
   war facing them, on moral, ethical, philosophical or religious
   grounds, with the same degree of intensity as you would hold a
   religious belief, has a right not to be drafted.
   Interview by Aaron Ford & Sunny Miller, grassrootspeace.org
   2008

2341. Jessie Lopez De la Cruz (1919–)

1 I'd hear them scolding their kids and fighting their husbands
   and I'd say, "Gosh! Why don't you go after the people that
   have you living like this? Why don't you go after the growers
   that have you tired from working out in the fields at low wages
   and keep us poor all the time? Let's go after them! *They're* the
   cause of our misery!"
   Quoted in *Moving the Mountain* by Ellen Cantarow *1980*

2 They tell us there's no money for food stamps for poor people.
   But if there is money enough to fight a war in Vietnam, and
   if there is money enough for Governor Reagan's wife* to buy
   a $3,000 dress for the Inaugural Ball, there should be money
   enough to feed these people.
   Ibid.
   *Nancy Reagan (see 2411), wife of Ronald Reagan, American
   politician, actor (1911–2003), governor of California (1967–75),
   40th president of the United States (1980–88).

3 America was built with small farms. They keep saying that the
   farmer is the country's backbone. I never heard anything about
   agribusiness being the backbone of the country, or corporations being the backbone.
   Ibid.

2342. Margot Fonteyn (1919–1991)

1 True art, in the end, is to do with character . . . what reaches us
   is the essence of a person.
   Quoted in *Margot Fonteyn* by Meredith Daneman *2004*

2 Genius is another word for magic, and the whole point of
   magic is that it is inexplicable.
   Attributed *n.d.*

3 The one important thing I have learned over the years is the
   difference between taking one's work seriously and taking
   one's self seriously. The first is imperative and the second is
   disastrous.
   Attributed *n.d.*

2343. Ella Grasso (1919–1981)

1 I'm opposed to abortion because I happen to believe life de-
   serves the protection of society.
   Quoted in "Ella Grasso of Connecticut" by Joseph B. Treaster,
   Ms. October 1974

2 I keep my campaign promises, but I never promised to wear
   stockings.
   Quoted in *Time 18 November 1974*

2344. Chaika Grossman (1919–1991?)

1 If you were a stranger, not known to some respectable person,
   you had no right to exist in an occupation regime. You became
   one of the suspected, maybe a Jew, or maybe a member of the
   underground.
   Step by step the difficulties and sacrifices piled up. Step by
   step our hearts forged the ability to hold firm.
   The Underground Army (1949) 1987

2 At age nineteen, I fought with the Partisans against the Nazis.
   In the Resistance, no one cared whether you were a man or a
   woman. Only your will and your work counted. Before 1948,
   it was the same in Israel, but since then women have suffered a
   deplorable setback. We are indeed the second sex. Even in the
   Knesset, we're expected to deal only with social and domestic
   problems.
   Quoted in Ch. 10, *Deborah, Golda, and Me* by Letty Cottin
   Pogrebin* *1991*
   *See 3145.

2345. Uta Hagen (1919–2004)

1 Talent is an amalgam of high sensitivity; easy vulnerability;
   high sensory equipment (seeing, hearing, touching, smelling
   tasting—*intensely*); a vivid imagination as well as a grip on
   reality; the desire to communicate one's own experience and
   sensations, to make one's self heard and seen.
   Pt. I, Ch. 1, *Respect for Acting 1973*

2 I would like to disagree with George Bernard Shaw's statement
   that "He who *can,* does. He who *cannot,* teaches" to express
   my personal belief that "Only he who *can* should teach!"
   Prologue, *A Challenge for the Actor 1991*

3 Since the time of the ancient Greeks a democracy has depended
   on its philosophers and creative artists. It can only flourish by
   continuous probing, prodding, and questioning of the social
   conditions under which man exists and tries to better himself.
   One of the first moves of a dictatorship is to stifle the artists
   and thinkers who have the ability to stir up dissent from any
   prescribed dogma which might enslave them. Because the artist
   can arouse the curiosity and conscience of his community, he
   becomes a threat to those who have taken power.
   Ch. 1, "The Actor's World," Ibid.

4 The desire to perform in order to attain fame or fortune *or* romantic dreams of starring in the classics are not real goals but
   notions that rattle in the void.
   Ch. 2, "The Actor's Goals," Ibid.

5   I truly believe there is *nothing* larger than life.

> Ch. 3, "The Actor's Techniques," Ibid.

6   Read out loud. Learn to relish the explosive ideas and phenomenal imagery contained in a body of contemporary and classic literature. Let language take shape on your tongue until it begins to spring from your soul.

> Ibid.

2346. Shirley Jackson (1919–1965)

1   "Listening to the young folks, nothing's good enough for *them*. Next thing you know, they'll be wanting to go back to living in caves, nobody work anymore, live *that* way for a while."

> *The Lottery, or, The Adventures of James Harris 1949*

2   "Cocoa," she said. "Cocoa. Damn miserable puny stuff, fit for kittens and unwashed boys. Did *Shakespeare* drink cocoa?"

> Pt. I, *The Bird's Nest 1954*

3   . . . I saw that Beth now, looking about her and drawing herself together, was endeavoring to *form* herself, as it were; let my reader who is puzzled by my awkward explanations close his eyes for no more than two minutes, and see if he does not find himself suddenly not a compact human being at all, but only a consciousness on a sea of sound and touch; it is only with the eyes open that a corporeal form returns, and assembles itself firmly around the hard core of sight.

> Pt. IV, Ibid.

4   . . . February, when the days of winter seem endless and no amount of wistful recollecting can bring back any air of summer . . .

> Pt. II, *Raising Demons 1956*

5   It has long been my belief that in times of great stress, such as a four-day vacation, the thin veneer of family unity wears off almost at once, and we are revealed in our true personalities. . . .

> Pt. IV, Ibid.

6   She looked out the window . . . savoring the extreme pleasure of being on a moving train with nothing to do for six hours but read and nap and go to the dining-car, going farther and farther every minute from the children, from the kitchen floor, with even the hills being incredibly left behind, changing into fields and trees too far away from home to be daily.

> "Pillar of Salt," *The Magic of Shirley Jackson*, Stanley Edgar Hyman, ed. *1966*

2347. Pauline Kael (1919–2001)

1   The first prerogative of an artist in any medium is to make a fool of himself.

> "Is There a Cure for Film Criticism?" *I Lost It at the Movies 1965*

2   Good movies make you care, make you believe in possibilities again.

> Pt. I, Ch. 1, *Going Steady 1968*

3   Art is still what teachers and ladies and foundations believe in, it's civilized and refined, cultivated and serious, cultural, beautiful, European, Oriental; it's what America isn't, and it's especially what American movies are not.

> Pt. II, Ch. 4, Ibid.

4   The words "Kiss Kiss Bang Bang," which I saw on an Italian movie poster, are perhaps the briefest statement imaginable of the basic appeal of movies.

> Title note, *Kiss Kiss Bang Bang 1968*

5   In the arts, the critic is the only independent source of information. The rest is advertising.

> *Newsweek December 1973*

6   Los Angeles, a mock paradise, is so perversely beautiful and so fundamentally unsatisfying that maybe just about everybody there secretly longs to see it come rattling down.

> "The Current Cinema," *The New Yorker 2 December 1974*

2348. Libby Koontz (1919–1989)

1   Curriculum has been a big hang-up between boards and teachers. It's like hiring a surgeon to perform delicate surgery, then expecting him to do it with a can opener, by candlelight, with everybody standing around telling him where to cut.

> "A Fighting Lady for N.E.A.," *Time* (New York) *12 July 1968*

2   We can be concerned about our kids—and well-paid at the same time. And we're not going to get able young people into teaching unless we improve conditions. All we're saying is that if the schools belong to the people, the people must act like it and support them.

> Ibid.

2349. Doris Lessing (1919–   )

1   "In university they don't tell you that the greater part of the law is learning to tolerate fools."

> Pt. III, Ch. 2, *Martha Quest 1952*

2   . . . he went on to remark gently that some women seemed to imagine birth control was a sort of magic; if they bought what was necessary and left it lying in a corner of a drawer, nothing more was needed. To this attitude of mind, he said, was due a number of births every year which would astound the public.

> Pt. I, Ch. 1, *A Proper Marriage 1952*

3   Love had brought her here, to lie beside this young man; love was the key to every good; love lay like a mirage through the golden gates of sex.

> Ibid.

4   The smell of manure, of sun on foliage, of evaporating water, rose to my head; two steps farther, and I could look down into the vegetable garden enclosed within its tall pale of reeds—rich chocolate earth studded emerald green, frothed with the white of cauliflowers, jeweled with the purple globes of eggplant and the scarlet wealth of tomatoes.

> Ch. 9, *The Habit of Loving 1957*

5   Effort, after days of laziness, seemed impossible.

> Ch. 15, Ibid.

6   A high price has to be paid for the happy marriage with the four healthy children in the large white gardened house.

> "To Room 19," *A Man and Two Women 1958*

7   "Small things amuse small minds. . . ."

> "A Woman on a Roof," Ibid.

8   "Don't you think there's something awful in two grown people stuck together all the time like Siamese twins?"

> "A Man and Two Women," Ibid.

9 After a certain age—and for some of us that can be very young—there are no new people, beasts, dreams, faces, events: it has all happened before . . . and everything is an echo and a repetition; and there is no grief even that it is not a recurrence of something long out of memory.

Ch. 2, Particularly Cats 1967

10 If a fish is the movement of water embodied, given shape, then cat is a diagram and pattern of subtle air.

Ibid.

11 What is charm then? The free giving of a grace, the spending of something given by nature in her role of spendthrift . . . Charm is something extra, superfluous, unnecessary, essentially a power thrown away—given.

Ch. 9, Ibid.

12 " . . . that is what learning is. You suddenly understand something you've understood all your life, but in a new way."

The Four-Gated City 1969

13 "The way to learn a language is to breathe it in. Soak it up! Live it!"

The Summer Before the Dark 1973

14 . . . older woman, younger man! Popular wisdom claims that this particular class of love affair is the most poignant, tender, poetic, exquisite one there is, altogether the choicest on the menu.

Ibid.

15 And what authority even the creases in a suit can convey . . .

Ibid.

16 There are certain types of people who are political out of a certain kind of religious reason. I think it's fairly common among socialists: they are, in fact, God-seekers, looking for the kingdom of God on earth. A lot of religious reformers have been like that, too. It's the same psychological set, trying to abolish the present in favor of some better future—always taking it for granted that there is a better future. If you don't believe in heaven, then you believe in socialism.

Quoted in "Doris Lessing on Feminism, Communism and 'Space Fiction'" by Lesley Hazleton, *The New York Times Magazine 25 July 1982*

17 The human community is evolving. . . . We can survive anything you care to mention. We are supremely equipped to survive, to adapt and even in the long run to start thinking.

Ibid.

18 Surely it is better to be poor here, in this sunlight, this beauty, than, let's say, Bradford or Leeds.

African Laughter: Four Visits to Zimbabwe 1992

19 I expected a period of incompetence. I expected every kind of mess and muddle. I knew nothing would work for a time. How could it when they didn't have trained people? But what I didn't expect was that these bastards would get into power and then not care about anything but feathering their own nests. There are dozens of them, noses in the trough, getting rich quick.

Ibid.

20 The great secret that all old people share is that you really haven't changed in seventy or eighty years. Your body changes, but you don't change at all. And that, of course, causes great confusion.

Sunday Times: Books (London) 10 May 1992

21 Political correctness is the natural continuum from the party line. What we are seeing once again is a self-appointed group of vigilantes imposing their views on others. It is a heritage of communism, but they don't seem to see this.

Ibid.

22 . . . we have not yet developed a system of education that is not a system of indoctrination.

Under My Skin: My Autobiography to 1949, Vol. 1 1994

23 . . . memory's little tricks . . . how it simplifies, tidies up, makes sharp contrasts of light and shade.

Walking in the Shade: Vol. Two of My Autobiography, 1949–1962 1997

24 Briefly and in passing: it is a sad thing that what is written has permanence, whereas what is said is often unnoticed. Something written is reprinted, becomes part of theses. Decades later it is quoted back at you. It is a millstone around your neck, and there is nothing you can do. "But you said, on page 123 . . ."

Ibid.

25 Projectiles that could carry diseases designed to kill all the people in a country or city? What were these ancient peoples, that they could do such things?

Mara and Dann: An Adventure 1998

26 There was a recklessness about the ways they used their soil and their water.

Ibid.

2350. Casey Geddes Miller (1919–1997)

1 Except for words that refer to females by definition (mother, actress, Congresswoman), and words for occupations traditionally held by females (nurse, secretary, prostitute), the English language defines everyone as male. The hypothetical person ("If a man can walk 10 miles in two hours . . ."), the average person ("the man in the street") and the active person ("the man on the move") are male. The assumption is that unless otherwise identified, people in general—including doctors and beggars—are men.

"One Small Step for Genkind," coauthor Kate Swift,* *The New York Times Magazine 16 April 1972*

*See 2471.

2 Language screens reality as a filter on a camera screens light waves.

Words and Women 1976

2351. Elizabeth Catlett Mora (1919–)

1 Don't work to make yourself important but to make your mind important.

Oral interview, National Visionary Leadership Project (visionaryproject.org) 2003

2352. Iris Murdoch (1919–1999)

1 "We can only learn to love by loving. . . ."

The Bell 1958

2 "You cannot have both civilization and truth. . . ."

A Severed Head 1961

3 There is no substitute for the comfort supplied by the utterly taken-for-granted relationship.

Ch. 28, Ibid.

4 "To be a complete victim may be another source of power."

The Unicorn 1963

5 Happiness is a matter of one's most ordinary everyday mode of consciousness being busy and lively and unconcerned with self. To be damned is for one's ordinary everyday mode of consciousness to be unremitting agonising preoccupation with self.

Ch. 22, *The Nice and the Good 1968*

6 Bereavement is a darkness impenetrable to the imagination of the unbereaved.

The Sacred and Profane Love Machine 1974

7 Human affairs are not serious, but they have to be taken seriously.

Pt. 2, "The Great Teacher," *Henry and Cato 1976*

8 He . . . had got into an intellectual muddle early on in life and never managed to get out.

"The Events in Our Town," *The Philosopher's Pupil 1983*

9 The sin of pride may be a small or a great thing in someone's life, and hurt vanity a passing pinprick, or a self-destroying or ever murderous obsession.

Ibid.

10 Moralistic is not moral. And as for truth—well, it's like brown—it's not in the spectrum. . . . Truth is *sui generis*.

Ibid.

11 PLATO. Art is the final cunning of the human soul which would rather do anything than face the gods.

"Art and Eros: A Dialogue about Art" (first performed on stage, February 1980), *The Nice and the Good* (play) *1986*

12 SOCRATES. In philosophy if you aren't moving at a snail's pace you aren't moving at all.

"Above the Gods: A Dialogue about Religion," Ibid.

13 Philosophy! Empty thinking by ignorant conceited men who think they can digest without eating!

Pt. 1, "Midsummer," *The Book and the Brotherhood 1987*

14 They [bars and pubs] are universal places, like churches, hallowed meeting places of all mankind.

Pt. 2, "Midwinter," Ibid.

15 But fantasy kills imagination, pornography is death to art.

Pt. 1, *The Message to the Planet 1989*

16 Every man needs two women, a quiet home-maker, and a thrilling nymph.

Ibid.

17 I daresay anything can be made holy by being sincerely worshipped.

Pt. 5, Ibid.

2353. Françoise Parturier (1919–1995)

1 In general all curvaceousness strikes men as incompatible with the life of the mind.

Lettre ouverte aux hommes (Open Letter to Men) 1968

2 And the more deodorants there are in the drugstores, the worse [woman] smells in literature.

Ibid.

3 That the most intelligent, discerning and learned men, men of talent and feeling, should finally put all their pride in their crotch, as awed as they are uneasy at the few inches sticking out in front of them, proves how normal it is for the world to be crazy. . . .

Ibid.

4 . . . we've never been in a democracy; we've always been in a phallocracy!

Ibid.

5 You say being a housewife is the noblest call in the world . . . You remind me of those company executives who . . . praise the "little guys" of their organization in their speeches . . .

Ibid.

6 Inaccessible women remain your loved ones: dead women, exiled women . . . women saints . . . angels. It is not women you love, sir, but Woman; that is an invention which "real presence" does not live up to. You have in you a secret preference for imaginary pleasures.

Ibid.

2354. Eva Duarte Perón (1919–1952)

1 Almsgiving tends to perpetuate poverty; aid does away with it once and for all. Almsgiving leaves a man just where he was before. Aid restores him to society as an individual worthy of all respect and not as a man with a grievance. Almsgiving is the generosity of the rich; social aid levels up social inequalities. Charity separates the rich from the poor; aid raises the needy and sets him on the same level with the rich.

Ibid.

2 When a woman goes into politics, the man eats cold *puchero* [stew].

Speech, Quoted in *Twentieth-Century Women Political Leaders* by Claire Price-Groff *1998*

3 Without fanaticism one cannot accomplish anything.

Ibid.

2355. Belva Plain (1919–)

1 How helpless we are, like netted birds, when we are caught by desire!

Evergreen 1978

2 I stand and listen to people speaking French in the stores and in the street. It's such a pert, crisp language, elegant as rustling taffeta.

Ibid.

3 All is pattern, all life, but we can t always see the pattern when we're part of it.

Crescent City 1984

4 If you don't see a child every day, if you have to wait for weeks or months, you'll be seeing a new child each time. You'll have missed everything.

Ch. 10, *From After the Fire 2000*

2356. Joy Rosenheim Simonson (1919–2007)

1 I love lobbying. It's my favorite Washington sport.

Quoted in *The Washington Post 1962*

2357. Nontsikelelo Albertina Sisulu (1919–   )

1   Women are the people who are going to relieve us from all this oppression and depression. The rent boycott that is happening in Soweto* now is alive because of the women. It is the women who are on the street committees educating the people to stand up and protect each other.

> Quoted in Ch. 10, *Lives of Courage* by Diana E. H. Russell**
> *1989*

*A group of black townships southwest of Johannesburg. **See 3104.

2358. Gladys Yang (1919–1999)

1   In China, literature is not viewed as a form of entertainment or simply as a source of aesthetic enjoyment, but as an effective means of education, of inspiring readers with high ideals and the belief that these can be attained.

> Preface, *Seven Contemporary Chinese Women Writers 1982*

2359. Louise Young (1919–   )

1   Sentimentality is a luxury that cannot be tolerated; it might get in the way of progress.

> Ch. 1, *Power Over People 1975*

2   In two weeks it is not possible to participate in the intricate interrelationship of living things or to sense the deep inner rhythms of nature. But the tune of our times is set to another rhythm—a noisy accelerating rhythm which searches out every quiet place.

> Ibid.

3   Will our grandchildren ever know the sudden glory of a dawn in an unpolluted sky or witness the slow fading of the violet light that floods a clear twilight heaven? Will they explore mountain meadow deep in columbine or walk the tranquil aisles of a virgin forest where the trees soar tall and proud to meet the sun? As these sights and sounds are replaced by cold stone and hard steel and plumes of acrid smoke, then these will become part of the child. A fabric woven of such coarse threads will make a harsher man.

> *Sowing the Wind: Reflections on the Earth's Atmosphere*
> *1990*

2360. Bella Abzug (1920–1998)

1   Woman's place is in the house—the House of Representatives.

> Motto *1970*

2   I've been described as a tough and noisy woman, a prize fighter, a man-hater, you name it. They call me Battling Bella, Mother Courage, and a Jewish mother with more complaints than Portnoy. There are those who say I'm impatient, impetuous, uppity, rude, profane, brash, and overbearing. Whether I'm any of those things, or all of them, you can decide for yourself. But whatever I am—and this ought to be made very clear at the outset—I am a very serious woman.

> Introduction, *Bella!*, Mel Ziegler, ed. *1972*

3   You can't have a Congress that responds to the needs of the workingman when there are practically no people here who represent him. And you're not going to have a society that understands its humanity if you don't have more women in government.

> Quoted in "Impeachment?" by Claire Safran, *Redbook* (New York) *April 1974*

4   We don't so much want to see a female Einstein become an assistant professor. We want a woman schlemiel to get promoted as quickly as a male schlemiel.*

> "Lois Gordon and Alan Gordon," *American Chronicle 1987*
> *Also attributed to Jeff Nyquist, journalist, radio show host.

5   I was running [for Congress] not because I happened to be a woman but *because* I was a woman.

> Induction Speech, National Women's Hall of Fame (Seneca Falls, New York) *24 September 1943*

6   I'll tell you what Zionism is. It is a liberation movement for a people who have been persecuted all their lives and throughout human history.

> Comment, U.N. Women's Conference (1980, Copenhagen), Quoted in *The Journey Home, How Jewish Women Shaped Modern America*, p. 275, by Joyce Antler *1997*

2361. Faith Bandler (1920–   )

1   [The constitutional amendment] will be of tremendous advantage to the indigenous Australian. It will mean that opportunities will be made available for better housing, for permanent employment and perhaps the most important of all is that of education.

> Comment (1967), quoted in profile by Victor Chang, *Australians* abc.net.au/btn/australians/f.bandler.htm *2000*

2362. Elise M. Boulding (1920–   )

1   The sense of play is so important. I mean, God plays! Creation plays! And who are we humans to get all tied up in knots and not get in there and play?!

> Quoted in "Concentrating On Essence" by Alan AtKisson In *Context Summer 1990*

2   We're never going to have respectful and reverential relationships with the planet—and sensible policies about what we put in the air, the soil, the water—if very young children don't begin learning about these things literally in their houses, backyards, streets and schools. We need to have human beings who are oriented that way from their earliest memories.

> Ibid.

3   All of the peace-making that we need on the planet begins with the infant and the infant's environment—the home.

> Ibid.

4   The word "development" has lost its human and spiritual meaning, and it is left with only an economistic kind of meaning.

> Ibid.

5   The tendency of planners and policymakers to prepare for worst-case scenarios leaves societies unprepared for the opportunities involved in best-case scenarios.

> "Peace Culture: An Overview," *Cultures of Peace: The Hidden Side of History 2000*

6   A static image of peace, as reflecting human inactivity, is dramatically opposed to the characterization of peace as process, of peacebuilding as adventure, exploration, and willingness to venture into the unknown. *Pacifism*, which literally refers to the *making* of peace (from *pace* and *facere*) is often mistakenly understood as passivism. One major attitudinal obstacle to the acceptance of peaceableness as a desireable norm is the connotation of inactivity associated with it.

> Ibid.

7 Peaceableness is an action concept, involving a constant shaping and reshaping of understandings, situations, and behaviors in a constantly changing lifeworld, to sustain well-being for all.

Ibid.

8 We must look towards societies that set a high value on non-aggression and noncompetitiveness, and therefore handle conflicts by nonviolent means. We can see how child rearing patterns produce nurturing adult behaviors.

Quoted in *Elise Boulding: A Life in the Cause of Peace* by Mary-Lee Morrison *2005*

2363. Liz Carpenter (1920–2010)

1 I thought that we would wake up this morning and have the same rights as our husbands, grandsons and garbagement—but we are still begging to be let into our country's Constitution.*

Speech, Thursday Caucus (New York City) *22 March 1979*
*After the defeat of the Equal Rights Amendment; see Alice Paul, 1637.

2 You can't complain if you don't participate.

Speech (University of Texas at Austin) *March 2004*

3 And here's to you, Mr. Wolfowitz*
Where did all those ugly weapons go?
Don't you know.

"The Wolfowitz Song" (sung to the tune of "Mrs. Robinson") *2004*

*Paul W— (1943–   ), Am. Deputy of Defense (2001–2005); pres. World Bank Group (2005–2007)

2364. Alice Childress (1920–1994)

1 OLDTIMER. Child, when hard luck fall it just keep fallin'.

Wine in the Wilderness 1969

2 TOMMY. I'm independent as a hog on ice and a hog on ice is dead, cold, well-preserved and don't need a mother'grabbin' thing.

Ibid.

3 TOMMY. I'm just sick-a hair, hair, hair. Do it this way, don't do it, leave it natural, straighten it, process, no process. I get sick-a hair and talkin' 'bout it and foolin' with it. That's why I wear the wig.

Ibid.

4 We think of poverty as a condition simply meaning a lack of funds, no money, but when one sees fifth, sixth, and seventh generation poor, it is clear that poverty is as complicated as high finance.

A Hero Ain't Nothin' But a Sandwich 1973

5 Today our youngsters can freely discuss sex. Soon they will even be able to openly discuss one of the results of sex—life.

"Alice Childress," *Interviews with Contemporary Women Playwrights*, Kathleen Betsko* and Rachel Koenig, comps. *1987*
*See 3125.

6 I think women need kindness more than love. When one human being is kind to another, it's a very deep matter.

Ibid.

2365. Amy Clampitt (1920–1994)

1 Think of it
undermining
the computer's
cheep, the time
clock's hiccup,
the tectonic
inchings of it
toward some
general crackup!
Think of it, think of
water running, running,
running till it
falls!

"Times Square Water Music," St. 7 *1987*

2 O drifting apotheosis of dust
exhumed, who will unseal
the crypt locked up within
the shimmer of the chromosomes

"Urn-Burial and the Bitterly Migration," St. 11 *1987*

2366. Kathryn Clarenbach (1920–1994)

1 The overemphasis on protecting girls from strain or injury and underemphasis on developing skills and experiencing teamwork fits neatly into the pattern of the second sex. . . . Girls are the spectators and the cheerleaders. . . . Perfect preparation for the adult role of woman—to stand decoratively on the sidelines of history and cheer on the men who make the decisions.

Sex Role Stereotyping in the Schools 1973

2 Women who have had the regular experience of performing before others, of learning to win and lose, of cooperating in team efforts, will be far less fearful of running for office, better able to take public positions on issues in the face of public opposition.

Quoted in "Old School System Curbed Sportswomen," *The Los Angeles Times 24 April 1974*

2367. Cecilia Colledge (1920–2008)

1 I can assure you it [practice] was not my idea of pleasure. Each time I had a lesson it would break all the little blood vessels in my eyes.

Quoted in Obituary, *The New York Times 24 April 2008*

2 My mother had this ghastly silver dress made for me. I was skating for a gold medal, and you don't wear silver. I wanted to wear my little green velvet dress. Whenever I wore my green dress, I thought I did well. I wouldn't dress anybody I knew in silver.

The Boston Globe (1998), Ibid.

2368. Selma Diamond (1920–1985)

1 Buying your own mink coat is real mass rejection.

Quoted in "Writers and Directors," *Funny Women, American Comediennes, 1860–1985* by Mary Unterbrink *1987*

2 [Working with all male writers is] like being Red China. I'm there, they just don't recognize me.

Ibid.

3 I have no patience with anyone born after World War II. You have to *explain* everything to these people.

Remark on *Johnny Carson Show*,* Ibid.
*(1925–2005) American comedian and mainstay of late-night television (1962–1992).

4 Judy Holliday:* I've worn strapless evening gowns since I was twelve years old.
Tallulah Bankhead:** Isn't twelve a little young for a strapless evening gown?
Judy Holliday: If it stays up, you're old enough.
> *The Big Show* (NBC Radio, ca. 1951–53), Ibid.
> *See 2401; **see 1964.

5 Tallulah Bankhead: I can't get used to this French money.
Fred Allen:* Yes, it's printed on the thinnest paper I've ever seen in public.
> Ibid.

> *(1894–1957), American radio comic.

2369. Mary J. Elmendorf (fl. 1920s)

1 Beauty's the thing that counts
In women; red lips
And black eyes are better than brains.
> "Beauty's the Thing" *n.d.*

2370. Rosalind Elsie Franklin (1920–1958)

1 This was my first continental holiday by car . . . and I confirmed my impression that cars are undesirable. . . . Travelling around in a little tin box isolates one from the people and the atmosphere of the place in a way that I have never experienced before. I found myself eyeing with envy all rucksacks and tents.
> Quoted in *Saint Elizabeth* by Anne Sayre *1975*

2370.1. Esther Gordy Edwards (ca. 1920–   )

1 I think that I was probably more strict than I needed to be. I just had a burning desire to protect the artist. These were young people who came from less fortunate families or one-parent families. Motown was a family itself. . . . I wound up learning a lot about young people.
> Quoted in *Detroit Free Press 2 November 1986*

2 Women didn't get credit for anything, [whether they were] black or white. They were taught to support their husbands, run carpools, and host charitable events.
> Quoted in "Ain't No Women (Like the Motown Women)" by Anna Clark, Women's Media Center (womensmediacenter. com) *12 May 2009*

2371. Barbara Guest (1920–2006)

1 I wonder if this new reality is going to destroy me.
> "The Hero Leaves His Ship," St. 1, *The Location of Things 1962*

2 I am talking to you
With what is left of me written off,
On the cuff, ancestral and vague,
As a monkey walks through the many fires
Of the jungle while the village breathes in its sleep.
> "Sunday Evening," St. 3, Ibid.

3 Then you took my hand. You told me that love was a sudden disturbance of the nerve ends that startled the fibers and made them new again.
> "Sadness," St. 3, Ibid.

4 Where goes this wandering blue,
This horizon that covers us without a murmur?

Let old lands speak their speech,
Let tarnished canopies protect us.
> "In the Alps" St. 1, Ibid.

2372. Mary Anne Guitar (1920?–   )

1 We have to stop being so teacher-centered, and become student-centered. It's not what you think they need but what they think they need. That's the functional approach.
> "College Marriage Courses—Fun or Fraud?" *Mademoiselle February 1961*

2373. Anna Halprin (1920–   )

1 As I continued teaching, it became apparent that the experience of movement connected to feelings generates long-buried and unknown emotions and images. When these emotions and images are expressed through movement, we dance. And when these dances are connected to our lives, they bring about dramatic release and change in our will to live.
> Prologue, Introduction, *Returning to Health: With Dance, Movement & Imagery 2000*

2 Dance as a healing art is traditional in many non-Western cultures, but this application of dance has been obscured and ignored in the Western world.
> Introduction, Ibid.

3 A way to create ritual is to invest the objects of our daily lives with new significance.
> p. 42, Ibid.

4 I believe if more of us could contact the natural world in a directly experiential way, this would alter the way we treat our environment, ourselves and one another.
> Artist's statement, annahalprin.org *2008*

2374. Leona Helmsley (1920–2007)

1 We don't pay taxes. Only the little people pay taxes.*
> Remark, Quoted in *The New York Times 12 July 1989*
> *She was jailed for tax evasion.

2375. Jane Screven Heyward (fl. 1920s–d. 1939)

1 More brightly must my spirit shine
Since grace of Beauty is not mine.
> "The Spirit's Grace" *n.d.*

2 The dear old ladies whose cheeks are pink
In spite of the years of winter's chill,
Are like the Autumn leaves, I think,
A little crumpled, but lovely still.
> "Autumn Leaves" *n.d.*

2376. Helen Hudson (1920–   )

1 A white casket with silver handles, she thought. Not a soft bed with a pink quilt but four sides and a lid that closes. To be shipped like a shoe in a box from this world to the next.
> "Sunday Morning," *American Scene: New Voices,* Don Wolfe, ed. *1963*

2 As he worked, putting the mask of sleep over the faces of death, he felt a vague excitement, as though he were, indeed, reviving her, as though the eyes he had closed so carefully might open again and see him, without reproach: a kindly man who knew his trade and did it well.
> Ibid.

2377. Ruth E. Iskin (1920–)

1 In the dealer-critic system, galleries exist primarily for sale purposes and it is the critic's role to promote the art product by establishing its value and providing a justification for its importance.

> "A Space of Our Own, Its Meaning and Implications,"
> *Womanspace February/March 1973*

2 The star system: the focus on the artist and his/her entire career, which was a by-product of the sale orientation developed in the dealer-critic system, replaced the older emphasis on individual paintings and schools of painters, which prevailed in the academy.

> Ibid.

2378. Janet Jagan (1920–)

1 There was much hatred and malice against me because I was a white person [married to a non-white], but also, they claimed that I was the brains behind Jagan* that wrote all his speeches. They were trying to say only white people had brains.

> Quoted in "Cheddi Jagan's widow . . ." by Bert Wilkinson,
> Associated Press *1 April 1997*
> *Reference to her husband, Cheddi Jagan (d. 1972), Guyanese prime minister (1971–1972).

2 I haven't even been an American citizen since 1947. I live here [Guyana] and I will die here.

> Ibid.

2379. P. D. James (1920–)

1 A politician is required to listen to humbug, talk humbug, condone humbug. The most we can hope is that we don't actually believe it.

> *A Taste for Death 1986*

2 A cup of tea. That English remedy for grief, shock and human mortality.

> Ch. 14, A Death in Chambers, *A Certain Justice 1997*

3 The almost superstitious tradition that the dead should be treated with reverence always failed at some point along the carefully documented final journey to the crematorium or the grave.

> Ch. 30, A Letter from the Dead, Ibid.

2380. Gerda Lerner (1920–)

1 . . . black women . . . are trained from childhood to become workers, and expect to be financially self-supporting for most of their lives. They know they will have to work, whether they are married or single; work to them, unlike to white women, is not a liberating goal, but rather an imposed lifelong necessity.

> Preface, *Black Women in White America 1972*

2 [I remember my passage to America] as six days of weeping, seasickness and fear. No matter what I tried to say and act, deep inside I was mourning. It was a tearing out, a violent uprooting, a voyage of death.*

> "A Personal Journey," p. 163, *A Death of One's Own 1978*
> *She never saw her mother again

3 I had to make the choice of how I was going to die. Once you've faced that, it's there for the rest of your life. It gives you a kind of basic courage.*

> p. 191, Ibid.
> *Referring to the six weeks she was held prisoner in a foul Nazi prison cell in Austria.

4 Long-term commitment to an intimate relationship with one person of whatever sex is an essential need that people have in order to breed the qualities out of which nurturant thought can rise.

> Quoted in "On the Future of Our Past" by Catharine R.
> Stimpson,* *Ms.* (New York) *September 1981*
> *See 3008.

5 . . . women's history is the primary tool for women's emancipation.

> Ibid.

6 Everything that explains the world has in fact explained a world that does not exist, a world in which men are at the center of the human enterprise and women are at the margin "helping" them. Such a world does not exist—never has.

> Ibid.

7 [There is a] depth and urgency of the search of Jewish and Christian women for connection to the Divine, which found expression in more than 1000 years of feminist Bible criticism and religious re-visioning.

> *The Creation of Feminist Consciousness: From the Middle Ages to Eighteen-Seventy 1993*

8 All of us, ultimately, will join one of the most despised, neglected and abused groups in [American] society—the old and the sick.

> *Why History Matters: Life and Thought 1997*

9 I learned first hand what it means to be defined as "the Other," the deviant. I was a respectable, bourgeois person, with class privileges . . . [a]nd then within weeks I was defined as a Jew, nothing else.

> Address, Awards ceremony (Vienna), Ibid.

2381. Clarice Lispector (1920–1977)

1 Around him, an emptiness blew, in which a man finds himself when he is going to create. Desolated, he provoked the great solitude. (. . .) And, like an old man who has not learned to read, he measured the distance that separated him from the word.

> *A maçã no escuro (The Apple in the Dark) 1959*

2 Oh! My love, don't be afraid of neediness: it is our greatest destiny.

> Ibid.

3 Do you know that hope sometimes consists only of a question without an answer?

> Ibid.

4 . . . how can I say it, if not timidly like this: life is it self my self. Life is it self my self, and I don't understand what I say. And then I adore.

> *A Paixão segundo G.H. (The Passion According to G.H.) 1967*

5 My love, you don't believe in the God, because we made a mistake when we humanized Him. We humanized Him because we did not understand Him, then it didn't work out. I'm certain that He is not human. But although He's not human, He sometimes makes us divine.

> *Uma aprendizagem ou O livro dos prazeres (An Apprenticeship or The Book of Pleasures) 1971*

6 Her curiosity instructed her more than the answers she was given.

> "Preciousness" (1960), *Family Ties*, Giovanni Pontiero, tr. *1972*

7 I am a concomitant being: in myself, I gather the time past, the present and the future, the time that pounds in the ticktack of the clocks.

"Água Viva" (Live Water) 1974

8 The word is my fourth dimension.

Interview by Rachel Gutierrez, Carla Sherman, tr. *n.d.*

2382. Carmen McRae (1920–1994)

1 Blues is to jazz what yeast is to bread—without it, it's flat.

Speech, "Blues is a Woman," Newport Jazz Festival, Avery Fisher Hall, New York City *2 July 1980*

2383. Elaine Morgan (1920–)

1 The trouble with specialists is that they tend to think in grooves.

Ch. 1, *The Descent of Woman 1972*

2 We had taken the first step along the tortuous road that led to the sex war, sado-masochism, and ultimately to the whole contemporary snarl-up, to prostitution, prudery, Casanova, John Knox, Marie Stopes, white slavery, women's liberation, *Playboy* magazine, *crimes passionels*, censorship, strip clubs, alimony, pornography, and a dozen different brands of mania. This was the Fall. It had nothing to do with apples.

Ch. 4, Ibid.

3 Evolution takes place in response to things which *have happened*, not things which are predestined to happen. Man is no more an evolutionary pinnacle than a tree is, or a termite or an octopus.

"The Emergence of Man," *The Scars of Evolution 1991*

2384. Ruth Morgan (1920–1978)

1 Pregnant women! They had that weird frisson, an aura of magic that combined awkwardly with an earthy sense of duty. Mundane, because they were nothing unique on the suburban streets; ethereal because their attention was ever somewhere else. Whatever you said was trivial. And they had that preciousness which they imposed wherever they went, compelling attention, constantly reminding you that they carried the future inside, its contours already drawn, but veiled, private, an inner secret.

Ch. 13, *Andrew's Revenge 1975*

2 What a let-down! I was ready for a tour round his Eiffel Tower, but all I got was a limp excuse and not-tonight-Josephine. Next time it had better be the real French stick, François, not a soggy brioche.

Ch. 9, *Jeu d'Esprit 1968*

2385. Portia Nelson (1920–2001)

1 I walk down the same street.
There is a deep hole in the sidewalk.
    I see it is there.
I still fall in . . . it's a habit.
    My eyes are open.
    I know where I am.
    It is my fault.
I get out immediately.

"Autobiography in Five Short Chapters," Ch. 3, *There's a Hole in My Sidewalk: The Romance of Self-Discovery 1977*

2386. Marjorie Newlin (1920–)

1 I see some people so terrified about getting older, but it's going to happen if you're still alive.

Quoted in "Sure, You'll Get Older. So What" by Jean-Noel Bassior, *Parade Magazine 22 November 1998*

2 People say, "When you get to this age, you can't do this and you can't do that," but that's not the way it is. I never considered my age when I went to the gym.

Ibid.

2387. Beah Richards (1920–2000)

1 Having grown up in a racist culture where two and two are not five, I have found life to be incredibly theatrical and theatre to be profoundly lifeless.

Preface, *A Black Woman Speaks and Other Poems 1974*

2 . . . nature is neither reasonable nor just. Nature is exact.

Ibid.

3 Heaven and earth!
How is it that bodies join
but never meet?

"It's Time for Love," St. 2, Ibid.

4 Lord,
there is no death,
no numb, no glacial sorrow
like the love of loveless love,
a tender grunting, sweating horror of obscenity.

"Love Is Cause It Has to Be," St. 6, Ibid.

5 If I cannot with my blind eyes see
that to betray or deny my brother
is but to diminish me
then you may pity me . . .

"The Liberal," St. 11, Ibid.

2388. Gabriela Roepke (1920–)

1 AMANDA. I just can't seem to go on—without a good morning in a big baritone voice.

A White Butterfly 1960

2 SMITH. . . . the reflection in my shaving mirror tells me things nobody else would.

Ibid.

3 OLD LADY. The best thing others can do for us is to tell us lies.

Ibid.

2389. Katsuko Saruhashi (1920–2007)

1 There are many women who have the ability to become great scientists. I would like to see the day when women can contribute to science and technology on an equal footing with men.

Quoted in *Twentieth-Century Women Scientists* by Lisa Yount *1996*

2 Each winner* has been not only a successful researcher but . . . a wonderful human being as well. They have become role models for those who will follow in their footsteps.

Ibid.

*Reference to the Saruhashi Prize, which she established in 1980 to be awarded to a Japanese woman 50 years old or younger who has made important contributions to the natural sciences.

2390. Hazel Scott (1920–1981)

1 There's only one free person in this society, and he is white and male.

Quoted in "Great (Hazel) Scott!" by Margo Jefferson, *Ms.* *November 1974*

2 Who ever walked behind anyone to freedom? If we can't go hand in hand, I don't want to go.

Ibid.

3 There's a time when you have to explain to your children why they're born, and it's a marvelous thing if you know the reason by then.

Ibid.

2391. Dinah Shore (1920–1994)

1 I earn and pay my own way as a great many women do today. Why should unmarried women be discriminated against—unmarried men are not.

Quoted in "Dinah," *The Los Angeles Times 16 April 1974*

2 I have never thought of participating in sports just for the sake of doing it for exercise or as a means to lose weight. And I've never taken up a sport just because it was a social fad. I really enjoy playing. It is a vital part of my life.

Ibid.

2392. Eileen Jackson Southern (1920–2002)

1 Who are our true rulers? The Negro poets, to be sure. Do they not set the fashion, and give laws to the public taste? Let one of them, in the swamps of Carolina, compose a new song, and it no sooner reaches the ear of a white amateur, than it is written down, amended (that is, almost spoilt), printed, and then put upon a course of rapid dissemination, to cease only with the utmost bounds of Anglo-Saxondom, perhaps with the world. Meanwhile, the poor author digs away with his hoe, utterly ignorant of his greatness.

Knickerbocker Magazine (1845), *The Music of Black Americans 1971*

2 Like him [W. E. B. DuBois*], I went to Harvard because it was a great opportunity for me as a black female scholar, and I accepted the reality of racial and sex discrimination. In its role as nurturer of scholars, Harvard never let me down!

"A Pioneer," *Blacks: an anthology* (Harvard) *1993*

2393. Helen Thomas (1920–)

1 You didn't tell a lie, you just left a big hole in the truth.

Vladimir Pozner* interview, *The Phil Donahue Show,** CNBC-TV July 1993*
*(1905–1992) Russian/American émigré who spied for Soviet intelligence while working for the U.S. War Department. **(1935–) American media personality and writer who hosted the talk show (1970–1996).

2 Anybody who runs for public office today has got to know his life or her life will be an open book. I've decided that if you want to run for public office you have to decide at the age of 5 and live accordingly.

"Uncovering the White House," *San Francisco Chronicle 29 January 1995*

3 You're only as good as your last story.

Acceptance Speech, Lifetime Achievement Award, White House Correspondents Dinner (Washington, D.C.) *25 April 1998*

4 The White House used to belong to the American people. At least that's what I learned from history books and from covering every president starting with John F. Kennedy.* But now the 201-year-old Executive Mansion belongs only to a select, elitist group of people, including top government officials, members of Congress and the press corps. They and some others, all of whom are screened in advance, are welcome. But most people are not—not anymore.

Syndicated column, Hearst Newspapers *15 October 2003*
*(1917–1963) 35th president of the United States; assassinated.

5 They don't understand that the presidential news conference is the only forum in our society where a president can be questioned. If he's not questioned, he can rule by edict; by government order. He can be a monarch. He can be a dictator, and who is to find out? No. He should be questioned and he should always be able to willingly reply and answer to all questions because these aren't our questions. They're the people's questions.

Interview, *The Majority Report 2 April 2004*

6 I'd like to ask you, Mr. President,* your decision to invade Iraq has caused the deaths of thousands of Americans and Iraqis, wounds of Americans and Iraqis for a lifetime. Every reason given, publicly at least, has turned out not to be true. My question is: Why did you really want to go to war? From the moment you stepped into the White House, from your Cabinet—your Cabinet officers, intelligence people, and so forth—what was your real reason? You have said it wasn't oil—quest for oil, it hasn't been Israel, or anything else. What was it?

White House press conference *21 March 2006*
*George W. Bush (1946–), 43rd president of the United States (2001–2009).

7 You don't spread democracy through the barrel of a gun.

Interview, *The Daily Show with Jon Stewart* 27 June 2006*
*(1962–) American political satirist, stand-up comedian, and host of "The Daily Show" (1996–) on Comedy Central.

8 It is sad to have to acknowledge that ethics—the simple difference between right and wrong—is the foremost internal problem facing journalism and other businesses today.

Ch. 1, *Watchdogs of Democracy?: The Waning Washington Press Corps and How It Has Failed the Public 2006*

9 The day Dick Cheney* is going to run for president, I'll kill myself. All we need is another liar . . . I think he'd like to run, but it would be a sad day for the country if he does.

Quoted in "Reporter: Cheney's Not Presidential Material" by Albert Eisele, *The Hill 28 August 2006*
*Richard C— (1941–) American political figure; 46th vice president of the United States (2001–2009).

2394. Harriet Van Horne (1920–1998)

1 Cooking is like love. It should be entered into with abandon or not at all.

Quoted in *Vogue October 1956*

2 We love newspapers the way a plain woman loves a charming, no-good husband.

Never Go Anywhere Without a Pencil 1972

3 Had I stayed in television, it would have killed me. Imagine reviewing "I Love Lucy" 20 times. Imagine reviewing "Gunsmoke" 20 times. It would rot anybody's brain.

Quoted in Obituary, *The New York Times 17 January 1998*

2395. Shelley Winters (1920–2006)

1 Every now and then, when you're on stage, you hear the best sound a player can hear. It's a sound you can't get in movies or in television. It is the sound of a wonderful, deep silence that means you've hit them where they live.

Theatre Arts June 1956

2 It was so cold I almost got married.

Quoted in *The New York Times 29 April 1956*

2396. Denise Bonal (1921–)

1 VINCENT. Yeah, being forty isn't so easy . . .
MOTHER. True, it was pretty hard for me, too, at forty. . . . Forty years old when Charles died! No man ever slept beside me since. Winter nights are the worst. Summer nights are violent. You keep cats. And you learn never to look at a couple kissing again.

A Picture Perfect Sky (Passions et Prairie), Timothy Johns, tr. *1987*

2397. Carol Emshwiller (1921–)

1 As a mother I have served longer than I expected.

"Autobiography," *Joy in Our Cause 1974*

2 For a long time I was powerless to resist: my father's opinions, marriage, and having three children, the lure of music.

Ibid.

2398. Betty Friedan (1921–2006)

1 The problem lay buried, unspoken for many years in the minds of American women. It was a strange stirring, a sense of dissatisfaction, a yearning that women suffered in the middle of the twentieth century in the United States. Each suburban housewife struggled with it alone. As she made the beds, shopped for groceries, matched slipcover material, ate peanut butter sandwiches with her children, chauffeured Cub Scouts and Brownies, lay beside her husband at night, she was afraid to ask even of herself the silent question: "Is this all?"

Ch. 1, *The Feminine Mystique 1963*

2 Over and over women heard in voices of tradition and Freudian sophistication that they could desire no greater destiny than to glory in their own femininity [and] to pity the neurotic, unfeminine, unhappy women who wanted to be poets or physicians or presidents.

Ibid.

3 How did Chinese women, after having their feet bound for many generations, finally discover they could run?

Ch. 4, Ibid.

4 How to put the libido back, restore the lost spontaneity, drive, love of life, the individuality, that sex in America seems to lack?

Ch. 9, Ibid.

5 Women, because they are not generally the principal breadwinners, can be perhaps most useful as the trail blazers, working along the bypaths, doing the unusual job that men cannot afford to gamble on.

Ch. 11, Ibid.

6 The feminine mystique has succeeded in burying millions of American women alive.

Ch. 13, Ibid.

7 It is easier to live through someone else than to become complete yourself.

Ch. 14, Ibid.

8 The problem that has no name—which is simply the fact that American women are kept from growing to their full human capacities—is taking a far greater toll on the physical and mental health of our countries than any known disease.

Ibid.

9 Sexual war against men is an irrelevant, self-defeating acting out of rage.

The Second Stage 1981

10 The most important effect of transcending those old sex roles may be an evolution of morality and religious thought. . . .

Ibid.

11 Today the problem that has no name,* is how to juggle work, love, home and children.

Ibid.

*See quotation 8.

12 I hereby affirm my own right as a Jewish American feminist to make chicken soup, even though I sometimes take it out of a can.

"Jewish Roots: An Interview with Betty Friedan," *Tikkun* 3, No. 1 *Jan./Feb. 1988*

13 In 1993 we've broken through the feminine mystique. Twenty-five years ago we doorbelled for politicians. Today, women are making policy. There are more women in Congress than ever before. Women have discovered the power to change their own lives.

Speech, Overlake Hospital (Bellevue, Washington) *28 January 1993*

14 Say "no" to the fountain of youth and turn on the fountain of age.

Ibid.

15 Down through the generations in history my ancestors prayed, "I thank thee, Lord, I was not created a woman," and from this day forward I trust that women all over the world will be able to say, "I thank Thee, Lord, I *was* created a woman."

Speech, Bryant Park, New York City (26 August 1970), "Marching in Front," *Hadassah Magazine November 1993*

2399. Mirija Gimbutas (1921–1994)

1 . . . the world of myth was not polarized into female and male as it was among the Indo-Europeans and many other nomadic and pastoral people of the steppes [in Neolithic Times]. Both principals were manifest side by side. The male divinity in the shape of a young man or male animal appears to affirm and strengthen the forces of the creative and active female. Neither is subordinate to the other: by complementing one another, their power is doubled.

(p. 237), *Gods and Goddesses of Old Europe 1981*

2 The difficulty with the term *matriarchy* in twentieth-century anthropological scholarship is that it is assumed to represent a complete mirror image of patriarchy or androcracy—that is to say, a hierarchical structure with women ruling by force in place of men. This is far from the reality of Old Europe. Indeed, we do not find in Old Europe, nor in all of the Old World, a system of autocratic rule by women with an equiva-

lent suppression of men. Rather, we find a structure in which the sexes are more or less on equal footing, a society that could be termed a gylany.*

(p. 324), *The Civilization of the Goddess* 1991

*Term coined by Riame Eisler; see 2756.

2400. Wilma Scott Heide (1921–1985)

1 The only jobs for which no man is qualified are human incubator and wet nurse. Likewise, the only job for which no woman is or can be qualified is sperm donor.

Quoted in NOW* Official Biography *1971*

2 . . . we whose hands have rocked the cradle, are now using our heads to rock the boat. . . .

Ibid.

3 . . . we will no longer be led only by that half of the population whose socialization, through toys, games, values and expectations, sanctions violence as the final assertion of manhood, synonymous with nationhood.

Ibid.

4 The pedestal is immobilizing and subtly insulting whether or not some women yet realize it. We must move up from the pedestal.

Ibid.

5 Now that we've organized [NOW]* . . . all over the United States and initiated an international movement and actions, it must be apparent that feminism is no passing fad but indeed a profound, universal behavior revolution.

Quoted in "About Women," *The Los Angeles Times* 12 May *1974*

*National Organization for Women.

2401. Judy Holliday (1921–1965)

1 All I have to do is remember to be dumb when I'm out, and smart when I'm home.

"The 1940s and 1950's," *Women in Comedy* by Linda Martin and Kerry Segrave *1986*

2 I started off as a moron in *Kiss Them for Me,** worked my way up to imbecile in *Adam's Rib*, and have carved my current niche [in *Born Yesterday*]** as a noble nitwit.

Ibid.

*Stage play, 1945. **Hollywood films, 1949, 1950.

2402. Ada Louise Huxtable (1921–   )

1 New York, thy name is irreverence and hyperbole. And grandeur.

"A Delightful Walk Downtown," *The New York Times* 20 July *1975*

2 Neatness counts.

The Unreal America: Architecture and Illusion 1997

3 Today form follows feeling . . . desire, not utility, dictates design.

Ibid.

4 What concerns me as much as the state of American building is the American state of mind, in which illusion is preferred over reality to the point where the replica is accepted as genuine and the simulacrum replaces the source. Surrogate experience and surrogate environments have become the American way of life.

Ibid.

5 Of course, we like our memories better all cleaned up. The gritty and sometimes unlovely accumulations that characterize cities are the best and worst of what we have produced; they exert a fascination that no neatly edited version can inspire. . . . To edit life, to sanitize the substance of history, is to risk losing the art, actuality, and meaning of the real past and its intrinsic artifacts.

Ibid.

6 At best, preservation is a necessary but ambiguous effort; there is nothing tidy about it.

Ibid.

7 Most disheartening of all in a place built on and dedicated to imagination is the lack of it . . . Let's face it, the Disney dream is terminally uptight!

Ibid.

8 It was not until our own day that this great art became irrelevant, that the tradition of building well ceased to matter. For those in positions of power, architecture has no redeeming value; it is a frill to be eliminated as a virtuous, cost-cutting, vote-getting measure; it can be abandoned without regret. It took today's mean mentality to see cathedrals and courthouses as "wasted space," to consider beauty as an extravagant and expendable add-on; only now has that impoverishment of the human spirit become politically and aesthetically correct. What no one appears to have noticed, while deploring the decline of public standards, is that trashy buildings trash the institutions and people they serve.

Ibid.

9 The poet Wallace Stevens reminded us that art helps us live our lives. Yet no one has had the courage, or conviction, to demand that the arts be restored to their proper place as one of the city's greatest strengths and a source of its spiritual continuity. We have lost what we hoped to gain—a creative rebirth downtown. At Ground Zero, what should be first is last. An affirmation of life is being reduced to a culture of death.

"Death of the Dream," *The Wall Street Journal* 20 April *2005*

2403. Juanita Kreps (1921–2010)

1 I'd like to get to the point where I can be just as mediocre as a man.

Quoted in *American Political Women* by Esther Stineman *1980*

2404. Carmen Laforet (1921–2004)

1 "Cities, my child, are hell. And in all of Spain no city resembles hell more than Barcelona,"

Nada (1923) Edith Grossman, tr. *2007*

2405. Rose MacMurray (1921–1997)

1 Now and then I would hear my mother's silk skirt whispering on the stairs, and the front door opening and shutting heavily as she left the house. Her presence was an absence, even when I knew she was at home.

Book I, *Afternoons with Emily* 2007

2 "My father is OBSESSED with keeping Lavinia and me on the proper moral path and reminding us of our inferiority as women. He would BREATHE for me if he could, since he thinks I don't breathe correctly without his supervision."

Book V, Ibid.

3 Affection was like bread, I mused. It was unnoticed until we starved, and then we dreamed of it, sang of it, hungered for it—and never knew anything else but the longing for it.
Ibid.

4 "I read the other day that it takes an entire TON of mimosa to make an ounce of a certain French perfume, Miranda. Then I thought, That's how I write my poetry!"
Book VI, *Ibid.*

5 "No one cares about whatever it is that makes each child unique. The children are taught just the way you fill muffin tins—each one right up to the brim, with exactly the same ingredients!"
Ibid.

6 "There are times in life when ceremony is the only balm."
Book VIII, *Ibid.*

7 Everything in New York was gray—the buildings, the streets, even the air. I always felt a dozen people had breathed it before it reached me!
Book IX, *Ibid.*

8 "War may be an armed angel with a mission, sir, but she has the personal habits of a slattern."
Book X, *Ibid.*

9 Forget her lies, forget her fantasies, her selfishness: genius lived by its own rules.
Book XII, *Ibid.*

2406. Eeva-Liisa Manner (1921–1995)
1 PAAVO. Modesty makes women insincere.
Act I, Sc. 1, *Snow in May 1966*

2 LASSI. Love makes *intelligent* beings depressed and flat. Only women, ostriches and monkeys are made happy by love. Oh yes, and parrots.
Act II, Sc. 1, *Ibid.*

3 PAAVO. Illusions! Illusions. Illusion of innocent love. Illusion of the heart's goodness, illusion of the sacredness of the pure life. But your virtuousness is only love of comfort, bourgeois self-satisfaction. Give up what you hold so dear: your illusions, and you can return to reality and become your real self.
Sc. 2, *Ibid.*

4 PAAVO. Great men are born in stable straw and they are put in a basket of reeds for the river to carry away. They are allowed to form their own souls—God looks after their bodies. They're not fed with warm milk, they must drink from the streams of the world, they do dirty work; the polisher of the mirror has dirty hands.
Sc. 3, *Ibid.*

5 LASSI. Women! There isn't anything so bad that they don't soon start to enjoy it. Even if they lived in a barrel of shit they'd start making a home out of it, with everything nice and cozy.
Act III, Sc. 1, *Ibid.*

2407. Del Martin (1921–)
1 To understand the lesbian as a sexual being, one must understand woman as a sexual being.
Lesbian/Woman, with Phyllis Lyon* 1972
*See 2489.

2 It is only when she can denounce the idiocy of religious scriptures and legal strictures that bind her and can affirm her Lesbian nature as but a single facet of her whole personality that she can become fully human.
Ibid.

3 There is nothing mysterious or magical about lesbian lovemaking . . . The mystery and the magic come from the person with whom you are making love.
Ibid.

4 Much polarity between men and women has centered around [sic] procreation. But the sex act itself is neither male nor female: it is a human being reaching out for the ultimate in communication with another human being.
Ibid.

5 We didn't give a damn about getting married [when we founded Daughters of Bilitis). We just wanted to get a law that said you can't fire us because we are gay.*
"Lesbian pioneers wed at San Francisco City Hall," CNN.com
17 June 2008
*Founded in 1955; after 55 years of co-habitation, Phyllis Lyon and Del Martin first lesbian couple to wed in California's 2004 challenge of same-sex marriage laws.

2408. Hazel McCallion (1921–)
1 We do things quickly here. We don't let any grass grow under our feet.
Quoted in "We do things quickly here" by Berry Hertz,
National Post (Toronto) 8 November 2007

2 If my councillors were saying we were wasting money, I'd be really concerned. I think we give value for tax dollars, we run our city like a business.
Ibid.

3 I do my own cleaning, grocery shopping, gardening . . . The assumption is that people in my position have others doing all these things for them but I like to be self sufficient. Housework and gardening are great forms of exercise and keep one humble.
Quoted in "Hazel: I don't believe in regrets" by Archie D'Cruz,
Confidence Bound June/July 2007

4 Having a life filled with purpose and meaning and living my life in a Christian-like manner helps to motivate me and keep me energized.
Ibid.

2409. Tami McIntyre (1921–)
1 *Thank goodness,* I said to myself, *footbinding* is now *outlawed!* That is not to say we, too, don't have our own weird and cruel customs and practices. Mama had worked with Aunt Raica in their dressmaking salon to make corsets for high-fashioned women to bind themselves in mercilessly. High heels tilted women forward so that they would be statuesque and shapely. Are these not barbaric customs and practices too?
Ch. 1, *Wait For Me 1995*

2 "I've asked innumerable questions in my lifetime, but I have found few real answers."
Ch. 14, *Ibid.*

3 "Don't judge people by what their government does," he told me quietly. "The wrongs of a few don't discredit the multitude . . ."
Ch. 15, *Ibid.*

4   "Love does not require a middleman."

Ch. 25, Ibid.

5   "Literature does not lead men astray."

Ch. 26, Ibid.

6   "Learning is a treasure that follows its owner everywhere."

Ibid.

2410. Marie Birmingham Ponsot (1921–)

1   In this stretch of the Atlantic
the whole Atlantic operates
"Separate in the Swim," *The Bird Catcher* 1998

2   What wd it be to be water, one body of water
(what water is is another mystery) (We are
water divided.) It wd be a self without walls
"Springing," *Springing* 2002

2411. Nancy Reagan (1921–)

1   I must say acting was good training for the political life which
lay ahead for us.

Nancy 1980

2   The Sixties, of course, was the worst time in the world to try
and bring up a child. They were exposed to all these crazy
things going on.

Quoted in "Reflections of a Woman in Love" by Dotson
Rader, *Parade Magazine* 8 November 1981

3   Where would we be without the movies?

Filmex Tribute to Elizabeth Taylor,* Quoted in "The Great Life"
by George Cristy, *The Hollywood Reporter November 1981*
*See 2826.

4   I had no idea I was walking into history.*

Quoted in *Ron's First Lady* by Peggy Noonan 2002

*Remarking on her marriage, when he was an actor, to Ronald
Reagan (1911–2003), 40th President of U.S., 1981–89).

2412. Donna Reed (1921–1986)

1   If nuclear power plants are safe, let the commercial insurance
industry insure them. Until these most expert judges of risk are
willing to gamble with their money, I'm not willing to gamble
with the health and safety of my family.

Quoted in *The Los Angeles Times* 12 March 1974

2413. Hannah Senesh (1921–1944)

1   Our two-thousand year history justifies us, the present compels
us, the future gives us confidence.

Diary Entry (12 November 1938), *Hannah Senesh: Her Life
and Diary* 1966

2   . . . woe to the individual who attempts to ingratiate himself
with the enemy instead of following his own route.

Diary Entry (11 December 1938), "Roots of Zionism or The
Fundamentals of Zionism," Ibid.

3   Even today, in its mutilated form, Palestine is big enough to be
an island in the sea of seemingly hopeless Jewish destiny, an island upon which we can peacefully build a lighthouse to beam
its light into the darkness, a light of everlasting human values,
the light of the one God.

Ibid.

4   I dream and plan as if there was nothing happening in the
world, as if there was no war, no destruction, as if thousands
upon thousands were not being killed daily. . . .

Diary entry (2 November 1940), Ibid.

5   There are events without which one's life becomes unimportant,
a worthless toy; and there are times when one is commanded
to do something, even at the price of one's life.

Diary entry (25 December 1943), Ibid.

2414. Simone Signoret (1921–1985)

1   Chains do not hold a marriage together. It is threads, hundreds of
tiny threads which sew people together through the years. That is
what makes a marriage last—more than passion or even sex!

Daily Mail (London) *4 July 1978*

2415. Mona Van Duyn (1921–2004)

1   For what is story if not relief from the pain
of the inconclusive, from dread of the meaningless?

"Endings," *Firefall* 1992

2   and not even the daffodils know if it's safe to come
up for air in this crazy, hot-and-cold weather.

"Notes from a Suburban Heart," St. 3, *If It Be Not I:
Collected Poems 1959–1982* 1994

3   There is no disorder but the heart's.

"The Gardener to His God," St. 2, *A Time of Bees n.d.*

2416. Rosalyn Yalow (1921–)

1   Through the years my mother has told me that it was fortunate
that I chose to do acceptable things, for if I had chosen otherwise no one could have deflected me from my path.

Autobiographical entry, *Les Prix Nobel Yearbook,* Tore
Frängsmyr, ed. *1977*

2   Whether we like it or not, women, even now, must exert greater
total effort than men for the same degree of success.

Quoted in *The Lady Laureates* (p. 229) by Olga S. Opfell
1978

3   I've always had time for my children. I went home every day
for lunch. When the children were small, if I worked on weekends, they came to the laboratory with me. When they were
older, I took them to museums, on trips . . .

Quoted in "Winner Woman!" by Letitia Kent (p. 174), *Vogue*
(New York) *January 1978*

4   We must believe in ourselves or no one else will believe in us.*

Acceptance speech, Nobel Prize, Quoted in *Mothers of
Invention* (p. 131) by Ethlie Ann Vare and Greg Ptacek *1988*
*Her challenge to young women in the sciences.

5   We still live in a world in which a significant fraction of people,
including women, believe that a woman belongs—and wants
to belong—exclusively in the home. . . . The world cannot afford the loss of the talents of half its people if we are to solve
the many problems which beset us.

Ibid.

2417. Phyllis Battelle (1922–)

1   A reporter discovers, in the course of many years of interview-
ing celebrities, that most actors are more attractive behind a
spotlight than over a spot of tea.

New York Journal-American 30 April 1961

2 If you haven't had at least a slight poetic crack in the heart, you have been cheated by nature.

Ibid. 1 June 1962

3 A broken heart is what makes life so wonderful five years later, when you see the guy in an elevator and he is fat and smoking a cigar and saying long-time-no-see.

Ibid.

2418. Liliane Schueller Bettencourt (1922–)

1 To the best ideas of our time, in realms as diverse as medicine, culture, and humanitarianism, the Foundation wants to offer the possibility to solidify. To exist, and . . . to last.

Mission Statement, *Bettencourt Schueller Foundation*, Jessica Partnow,* tr. *1987*

*See 4947.

2 Giving wings to talent supports it, so that the ideas come to life, solidify, exist and serve.

Ibid.

3 The capital structure of the group has remained unchanged for 26 years. This stability is surely one of the factors that has allowed the company to develop. Furthermore, the value of the shares is a good indicator of the confidence that investors have in the group's future in its current structure. Nothing in the short term seems to justify a change.

Quoted in "The Pyramid Behind The Perfume"* by R.C.M., *Forbes.com 27 November 2000*

*Re. L'Oréal, founded by her father, Eugène Schueller, in 1927.

2419. Alison Wyrley Birch (1922–)

1 There are sounds to seasons. There are sounds to places, and there are sounds to every time in one's life.

Quoted in *The Christian Science Monitor 23 January 1974*

2420. Ruth Brinker (1922–)

1 You have to go out and beg.*

Quoted in "Open Heart, Open Hand," *Time* (New York) *9 January 1989*

*Reference to fund-raising for her Project Open Hand, which feeds people with AIDS.

2421. Helen Gurley Brown (1922–)

1 You may marry or you may not. In today's world that is no longer the big question for women. Those who glom onto men so that they can collapse with relief, spend the rest of their days shining up their status symbol and figure they never have to reach, stretch, learn, grow, face dragons, or make a living again are the ones to be pitied. They, in my opinion, are the unfulfilled ones.

Sex and the Single Girl 1963

2422. Vinnette Carroll (1922–2002)

1 They told me that I had one-third less chance because I was a woman and a third less chance again because I was black, but I tell you, I'm going to do one hell of a lot with that remaining one third.

Newspaper article by S. Patterson, Billy Rose Collection, New York Public Library at Lincoln Center *n.d.*

2423. Eugenie Clark (1922–)

1 Not many appreciate the ultimate power and potential usefulness of basic knowledge accumulated by obscure, unseen investigators who, in a lifetime of intensive study, may never see any practical use for their findings but who go on seeking answers to their unknown without thought of financial or practical gain.

Ch. 1, *The Lady and the Sharks 1969*

2 In the beginning, I wanted to enter what was essentially a man's field. I wanted to prove I could do it. Then I found that when I did as well as the men in the field I got more credit for my work because I am a woman, which seems unfair.

Quoted in "Shark Tamer" by Madeleine Lundberg, *Ms.* (New York) *August 1979*

3 It seems as though women keep growing. Eventually they can have little or nothing in common with the men they chose long ago.

Ibid.

2424. Judith Crist (1922–)

1 The critics who love are the severe ones . . . we know our relationship must be based on honesty.

Introduction, *The Private Eye, the Cowboy, and the Very Naked Girl 1968*

2 In this era of affluence and of permissiveness, we have, in all but cultural areas, bred a nation of overprivileged youngsters, saturated with vitamins, television, and plastic toys. But they are nurtured from infancy on a Dick-and-Jane literary and artistic level; and the cultural drought, as far as entertainment is concerned, sets in when they are between six and eight.

"Forgotten Audience: American Children" (2 May 1965), Ibid.

3 . . . the outcry against the current spate of sadism and violence in films is . . . more than justified by the indecencies that we are being subjected to on the big screen (and more and more on the little one at home), by the puddles of blood and piles of guts pouring forth from the quivering flesh that is being lashed and smashed, by the bouncing of breast and the grinding of groin, by the brutalizing of men and the desecration of women being fed to us by the hour for no possible social, moral or intellectual purpose beyond our erotic edification and sensual delight and, above all, the almighty box-office return.

"Against the Groin" (December 1967), Ibid.

2425. Catherine De Vinck (1922–)

1 [My writing is] soaked in a theology of hope, that is, in the knowledge that death has no dominion, that light overcomes darkness, and that love is a divine power of transformation and renewal.

Quoted in *Wise Women: Over 2000 Years of Spiritual Writing by Women*, Susan Cahill* ed. *1996*

*See 3178.

2 I am a God of a thousand names:
   why cannot one of them be
Woman Singing?

"The Womanly Song of God," ll., Ibid.

3 Did you know the concordance
   that links not only heaven and earth

but the most antique fragment of baked clay
to the very blood that pumps your heart
full of desire and dream?
                          "Venus—Aghia Sophia," St. 1, Ibid.

2426. Mavis Gallant (1922–)

1   Success can only be measured in terms of distance traveled. . . .
                          Ch. 1, *Green Water, Green Sky 1959*

2   No people are ever as divided as those of the same blood. . . .
                          Its Image on the Mirror 1964

3   The Knights had been married nearly sixteen years. They considered themselves solidly united. Like many people no longer in love, they cemented their relationship with opinions, pet prejudices, secret meanings, a private vocabulary that enabled them to exchange amused glances over a dinner table and made them feel a shade superior to the world outside the house.
                          "Bernadette," *My Heart Is Broken 1964*

4   "What is the appeal about cats? he said kindly. "I've always wanted to know." . . .
       "They don't care if you like them. They haven't the slightest notion of gratitude, and they never pretend. They take what you have to offer, and away they go . . ."
                          "An Unmarried Man's Summer," Ibid.

5   Swedish films had given her the impression that conversation in an unknown tongue consisted of nothing except "Where is God?" and "Should one have children?" although, in reality, everyone in those foreign countries was probably saying "How much does it cost?" and "Pass the salt."
                          Ch. 5, *A Fairly Good Time 1970*

6   She had the loaded handbag of someone who camps out and seldom goes home, or who imagines life must be full of emergencies.
                          Ibid.

7   The worst punishment I can imagine must be solitary confinement with nothing for entertainment except news of the world.
                          Ch. 12, Ibid.

8   Now that he was rich he was not thought ignorant any more, but simply eccentric.
                          "The Pegnitz Junction," *The Pegnitz Junction 1973*

2427. Ava Gardner (1922–1990)

1   Deep down, I'm pretty superficial.
                          Ch. 8, Quoted in *Ava* by Roland Flamini *1983*

2428. Judy Garland (1922–1969)

1   I was born at the age of twelve on a Metro-Goldwyn-Mayer lot.
                          Quoted in *Observer* (London) *18 February 1951*

2   Before every free conscience in America is subpoenaed, please speak up!*
                          Quoted in Ch. 19 (ca. 1947), *Judy Garland* by Anne Edwards** *1975*
       *Re House Un-American Activities Committee "trials" that spiked fears of Communism—and ruined many careers. **See 2594.

3   How strange when an illusion dies
It's as though you've lost a child. . . .
                          "An Illusion," Ibid.

4   For 'twas not into my ear you whispered but into my heart.
'Twas not my lips you kissed, but my soul.
                          "My Love Is Lost," Ibid.

2429. Blanche H. Gelfant (1922–)

1   American literary mind, the city has made its impression not only as a physical place but more important as a characteristic and unique way of life.
                          The American City Novel 1954

2   Friendships, like geraniums, bloom in kitchens. Love runs up and down a flight of stairs and enters one flat and another in the housing projects.
                          Quoted in *Women Writing in America: Voices in Collage 1985*

2430. Grace Hartigan (1922–)

1   . . . the face the world puts on that sells itself to the world.
                          Quoted by Cindy Nemser in *Art Talk* (magazine) *1975*

2   There's a time when what you're creating and the environment you're creating it in come together.
                          Ibid.

3   . . . I don't mind being miserable as long as I'm painting well.
                          Ibid.

2431. Gladys Medalie Heldman (1922–2003)

1   Players are always in the foreground, and they should be . . . anything else would be like Sol Hurok* thinking that *he* was the star when it is really the ballet.
                          Quoted in "Queen of the Long-Way Babies" by Dan Rose, *Signature August 1974*
       *Russian-born American impresario (1888–1974).

2   It's a mental attitude you have about winning, about dying before you're willing to lose.
                          Ibid.

2432. Gertrude Himmelfarb (1922–)

1   The old feminism spoke the language of liberation. . . . The new feminism speaks the language of power.
                          Quoted in "Are Women Leaders Wielding Power Differently Than Men?" by Georgia Anne Geyer,* *Seattle Times 14 May 1989*
       *See 2930.

2   Virtues are very hard. Vices are easy to come by. Once young people had the leisure and money to indulge themselves, it was almost inevitable that they do it.
                          On Looking Into the Abyss: Untimely Thoughts on Culture and Society 1994

3   It is this reluctance to speak the language of morality, and to apply moral ideas to social policies, that separates us from the Victorians. In Victorian England every measure of poor relief had to justify itself by showing that it would promote the moral as well as the material well-being of the poor. In recent times we have so completely rejected any kind of moral principle that we have deliberately, systematically divorced poor relief

from moral sanctions and incentives. We are now confronting the consequences.

The Demoralization of Society: From Victorian Virtues to Modern Values 1995

4   No religion is as tradition-bound and history-centered as Judaism.

"Edmund Burke,"* *The Moral Imagination: From Edmund Burke to Lionel Trilling 2007*
*(1729–1797) Irish-born British politician and writer.

5   Of the 613 commandments prescribed for devout Jews, some are universal moral principles binding on all civilized human beings. But others are unique to Judaism; they are what distinguish it from all other faiths and peoples.

Ibid.

2433. Lucille Chernos Kallen (1922–1999)

1   A lawyer's relationship to justice and wisdom . . . is on a par with a piano tuner's relationship to a concert. He neither composes the music, nor interprets it—he merely keeps the machinery running.

Quoted in *Lawyer's Wit and Wisdom* and Bruce Nash and Allan Zullo, eds.; Kathryn Zullo, compiler *1995*

2434. Eda J. Le Shan (1922–2002)

1   . . . most of us carry into marriage not only our childlike illusions, but we bring to it as well the demand that it *has* to be wonderful, because it's *supposed* to be. Of course the biggest illusion of all is that we are going to do the job of parenthood so well: it will all be fun and always deeply satisfying.

Ch. 2, *How to Survive Parenthood 1965*

2   Psychotherapy can be one of the greatest and most rewarding adventures, it can bring with it the deepest feelings of personal worth, of purpose and richness in living. It doesn't mean that one's life situation will change dramatically or suddenly. . . . It does mean that one can develop new capacities and strengths with which to meet the natural vicissitudes of living; that one may gain a sense of inner peace through greater self-acceptance, through a more realistic perspective on one's relationships and experiences.

Ch. 11, Ibid.

3   . . . in all our efforts to provide "advantages" we have actually produced the busiest, most competitive, highly pressured and over-organized generation of youngsters in our history—and possibly the unhappiest. We seem hell-bent on eliminating much of childhood.

Ch. 1, *The Conspiracy Against Childhood 1967*

4   Babies are necessary to grown-ups. A new baby is like the beginning of all things—wonder, hope, a dream of possibilities. In a world that is cutting down its trees to build highways, losing its earth to concrete . . . babies are almost the only remaining link with nature, with the natural world of living things from which we spring.

Ch. 2, Ibid.

5   Excellence in life seems to me to be the way in which each human being makes the most of the adventure of living and becomes most truly and deeply himself, fulfilling his own nature in the context of a good life with other people . . . What he knows and what he feels have equal importance in his life . . .

Ch. 9, Ibid.

6   The highest compliment we can be paid today is to be told we don't look our age. Men and women spend millions of dollars every year on trying to remain youthful and glamorous—untouched by life and aging.

The Wonderful Crisis of Middle Age 1973

7   Someone once said that middle age is like rereading a book that you haven't read since you were a callow youth. The first time around you were dazzled by impressions, emotions, and tended to miss the finer points. In middle age you have the equipment to see the subtleties you missed before and you savor it more slowly.

Ibid.

2435. Rose Marie McCoy (1922–   )

1   I don't want my heart to be broken
Cause it's the only one I've got
"I Beg of You" (1957), *50,000,000 Elvis Fans Can't Be Wrong: Elvis' Gold Records Volume 2 1959*

2   Whole lotta women used to be my speed
Now pretty baby you're all I need
Oh darling, think it's gonna work out fine
"I Think It's Gonna Work Out Fine", co-lyricist, Sylvia McKinney *1961*

3   When I came to New York, I had six bucks. I got a job working in a Chinese hand laundry and I learned how to iron shirts. Then I worked weekends in nightclubs, singing.
"Lady Writes the Blues: The Life of Rose McCoy," *NPR Radio Diaries 27 February 2009*

4   [The kids] wanted to hear what you had. And if they liked it, they didn't care if you was black or white. We thought it was the blues and they called it rock 'n' roll; I still don't know the difference.

Ibid.

2436. Liz Moore (1922–   )

1   [My parents] both taught me, very early on, two things: one was that you respected anyone who was good at whatever he or she did, no matter what it was; and the second was that, if you were lucky, you gave something back.
Quoted in "Liz Moore: Giving HMOs a Checkup" by Vickie L. Bane, *Ms. (New York) November/December 1997*

2   You have these moments, I guess you call it epiphany . . . I thought, "This is the answer." I had been documenting how bad and how high the costs are of traditional energy, particularly coal, and here is the benign source [solar energy]. All we have to do is learn to harvest it in an economic way.

Ibid.

2437. Grace Paley (1922–2007)

1   He had had a habit throughout the twenty-seven years of making a narrow remark which, like a plumber's snake, could work its way though the ear down the throat, halfway to my heart. He would then disappear, leaving me choking with equipment.

Enormous Changes at the Last Minute 1960

2   Rosiness is not a worse windowpane than gloomy gray when viewing the world.

Ibid.

3 I was a fantastic student until ten, and then my mind began to wander.

> Quoted in "Grace Paley: 'Art Is on the Side of the Underdog'" by Harriet Shapiro, *Ms.* (New York) *March 1974*

4 There isn't a story written that isn't about blood or money. People and their relationship to each other is the blood, the family. And how they live, the money of it.

> *Ibid.*

5 "But the fun of talking, Ruthy. What about that? It's as good as fucking lots of times. Isn't it?"

   "Oh boy," Ruth said, "if it's that good, then it's got to be that bad."

> "The Expensive Moment," *Later the Same Day 1985*

6 You have an opinion. I have an opinion. Life don't have no opinion.

> "Zagrowsky Tells," *Ibid.*

7 I'm not a person who keeps things in. Tell! That opens up the congestion a little—the lungs are for breathing, not secrets. My wife never tells, she coughs, coughs. All night. Wakes up. Ai, Iz, open up the window, there's no air. You poor woman, if you want to breathe, you got to tell.

> *Ibid.*

8 Well, you have children so you know: little children little troubles, big children big troubles—it's a saying in Yiddish. Maybe the Chinese said it too.

> *Ibid.*

9 Thank God for the head. Inside the head is the only place you got to be young when the usual place gets used up.

> *Ibid.*

10 I often see through the appearance of things right to the apparition itself.

> *Just As I Thought 1998*

11 I had this idea that Jews *were* supposed to be better. I'm not saying they were, but they were *supposed* to be, and it seemed to me on my block that they often were. I don't see any reason in being in this world actually if you can't in some way be better, repair it somehow. . . . So to be like all the other nations seems to me a waste of nationhood, a waste of statehood, a waste of energy, and a waste of life.

> *Ibid.*

12 If there are prisons, they ought to be in the neighborhood, near a subway—not way out in distant suburbs, where families have to take cars, buses, ferries, trains, and the population that considers itself innocent forgets, denies, chooses to never know that there is a whole huge country of the bad and the unlucky and the self-hurters, a country with a population greater than that of many nations in our world.

> *Ibid.*

13 It's a terrible thing to die young. Still, it saves a lot of time.

> *Ibid.*

14 Let us go forth with fear and courage and rage to save the world.

> *Ibid.*

15 Though the world cannot be changed by talking to one child at a time, it may at least be known.

> *Ibid.*

16 It is the responsibility of the poet to say many times: there is no freedom without justice and this means economic justice and love justice.

> "Responsibility," *Begin Again: Collected Poems 2000*

2438. Vera Randal (1922–   )

1 Time, dough in a bowl, rose, doubling, trebling in bulk, and I was in the middle of the swelling, yeasty mass—lost.

> "Alice Blaine," *The Inner Room 1964*

2 "John is dead."

   "Yes."

   "I am also dead," I said numbly.

   "You're not dead. You're very far from dead."

   "I feel dead."

   "That's different."

   "Is it?" I said. "Is it really?"

   "It is. Really."

> *Ibid.*

3 "I believe in people, which I suppose is a way of believing in God."

> *Ibid.*

4 Fury gathered until I was swollen with it.

> *Ibid.*

2439. Alice Rossi (1922–   )

1 The emancipation or liberation of women involves more than political participation and the change of any number of laws. Liberation is equally important in areas other than politics; economics, reproduction, household, sexual and cultural emancipation are relevant.

> Preface, *The Feminist Papers 1973*

2 Scholars all too often move in a world as restricted as that in which their subjects lived or from which they escaped.

> Pt. I, "The Making of a Cosmopolitan Humanist," *Ibid.*

3 It is curious that it may be the help of a housekeeper and a friend that facilitates a woman's life's work, while the closest analogy . . . one would find from the pen of a man is typically a tribute to his wife.

> "A Feminist Friendship," *Ibid.*

4 Equal pay for equal work continues to be seen as applying to equal pay for men and women in the same occupation, while the larger point of continuing relevance in our day is that some occupations have depressed wages because women are the chief employees. The former is a pattern of sex discrimination, the latter of institutionalized sexism.

> *Ibid.*

5 The single most impressive fact about the attempt by American women to obtain the right to vote is how long it took.

> "Along the Suffrage Trail," *Ibid.*

6 Without the means to prevent, and to control the timing of conception, economic and political rights have limited meaning for women. If women cannot plan their pregnancies, they can plan little else in their lives. . . .

> "The Right to One's Body," *Ibid.*

7 For every war widow there may be several dozen wives who cope with the physical and emotional damage inflicted by war on their husbands and sons.

> Pt. IV, Introduction, *Ibid.*

8 *Eros* (infatuation and youthful passion) is a necessary stage in the development of sexual attraction to the point of mate choice and reproduction; *caritas* (loving kindness and attachment) is the more enduring and mature quality necessary to assure the care and protection of human young through the uniquely long human stage of youthful dependency.
Ch. 1, *Sexuality across the Life Course 1994*

9 To avoid intellectual sterility, it is wise to periodically reexamine our most deeply held presuppositions.
Ibid.

10 There have been numerous times in our history when contemporary critics claimed the social fabric was being frayed irrevocably, that people were losing trust in social institutions, that alienation was on the increase, crime rampant, behavior in public crude. In other words, any array of disturbing social indicators is not unique to the last few decades of the twentieth century, nor to the first few decades for that matter.
Introduction, *Caring and Doing for Others: Social Responsibility in the Domains of Family, Work, and Community 2001*

11 Indeed, one would be hard pressed to cite any indicator of social or psychological well-being that suggests life is good in America or that Americans are good people. If we were to take personally all the bad news and faults one hears and reads about, we should all be in a state of deep depression. Americans are berated in almost every aspect of their lives . . .
Ibid.

2440. Joyce Treiman (1922–1991)

1 You ask why I paint? Why do I breathe?
Quoted in "Joyce Treiman," *Exposures, Women & Their Art* by Ann Brown and Arlene Raven* 1989
*See 3533.

2 The major challenge is to be able to articulate and perform all of it—subject and concept and media. That's really tough. And that's the difference between painting and the performing arts. For instance, in theater, the authors, producers, directors and performers are separate. But in painting, you have to come up with the idea, and be the performer and producer—they're tied up together. It's wonderful to be able to do them all.
Ibid.

2441. Marjorie Tuite (1922–1986)

1 I think to work on one issue is a luxury in a global analogy. Because there is a basic problem: militarism out of a patriarchal structure, a world view of militarism that nurtures cultural violence.
Speech, National Assembly of Religious Women Annual Convention 1985

2442. Doreen Valiente (1922–1999)

1 In our present-day "permissive society," sex is blazoned forth everywhere, usually in some more or less commercialised form. . . . And yet, how . . . many, beneath their surface gaiety, are loveless, insecure, neurotic and miserable? Perhaps the old idea of the sacredness of sex was not so foolish after all? To degrade sex is to degrade life itself.
"Fertility, Worship of," *An ABC of Witchcraft 1973*

2 The heart of paganism is a philosophy based upon Nature, and veiled in symbol and myth.
"The Horned God," Ibid.

3 As the most conspicuous luminary of the night, and the nearest heavenly body to our earth, the moon has hung like a shining magic mirror, reflecting man's dreams. From the Stone Age to the age of space travel, she has bewitched and allured mankind.
"Moon Worship," Ibid.

4 An important point about witchcraft is that it *is* a craft, in the old sense of the word, the Anglo-Saxon *craeft*, implying art, skill, knowledge. The word "witch" means "wise one"; and a person cannot be *made* wise, they have to *become* wise.
"Witchcraft," Ibid.

5 Spaceship Earth is in deep trouble; when that happens, we need to get in touch with our base.
Our base is the Divine Life of the universe. Our means of keeping in touch with it cannot be through any man-made dogma, but through nature, which man did not make. Men's hands wrote all the holy books and sacred scriptures; only the book of nature was written by divinity.
"Witch Ethics," *Witchcraft for Tomorrow 1978*

2443. Renee Winegarten (1922–   )

1 We still tend to share the idea that civilization must be either growing and pressing ever upwards, or else disintegrating into nothingness, instead of going on, variously developing and changing in a multitude of different areas, in ways not always perceptible to the human eye.
"The Idea of Decadence," *Commentary* (New York) *September 1974*

2 . . . the quest for origin and end, zenith and nadir, growth and decline, rise and fall, florescence and decadence. Where would writers be without these essential props for their narratives?
Ibid.

3 Old age cannot be cured. An epoch or a civilization cannot be prevented from breathing its last. A natural process that happens to all flesh and all human manifestations cannot be arrested. You can only wring your hands and utter a beautiful swan song.
Ibid.

4 What lies behind the concept of decadence to render it so appealing to the imagination?
Ibid.

5 If epochs can grow old and die, what is to prevent them from becoming subject to disease?
Ibid.

2444. Diane Arbus (1923–1971)

1 I really believe there are things nobody would see if I didn't photograph them.
Diane Arbus 1972

2 Most people go through life dreading they'll have a traumatic experience. Freaks are born with their trauma. They've already passed it. They're aristocrats.
Ibid.

3   Something is ironic in the world and it has to do with the fact that what you intend never comes out like you intend it.

> Ibid.

4   . . . the camera is a kind of license.

> Ibid.

5   A photograph is a secret about a secret. The more it tells you the less you know.

> Preface, Quoted in *Diane Arbus: A Biography* by Patricia Bosworth *1985*

2445. Marie B. Assad (1923–   )

1   We managed to put FGM* on the agenda of Egypt.

> Quoted in "Critical Analysis of Interventions Against FGC in Egypt," p. 32, Population Council (New York), by Nahla Abdel-Tawab, M.D., Dr. P. H. and Sahar Hegazi, M.A. *June 2000*

*Female genital mutilation.

2   Tradition justifies everything. No woman ever establishes a cause and effect relationship with the pain that they feel for years, nor with certain problems that arise during childbirth (partem), nor, clearly, with sexuality. In the "ribanceiras" of the river Nile, almost all the women still suffer genital mutilation.

> Quoted in "Nas ribanceiras do rio Nilo . . ." by Hubert Prolongeau, *Le Monde,* tr. Alex Forman *23 December 2005*

2446. Ruth Tiffany Barnhouse (1923–1999)

1   To my mind the struggle for the ordination of women to the priesthood is not only, or even principally, another engagement in the continuing battle for women's rights. No doubt the temptation to pursue it at that level is very great, particularly for those women whose pursuit of their true vocation continues to be ignominiously frustrated. But to fall into that temptation is to secularize the issue, and it is a serious mistake to permit the vanguard of the development of human consciousness to be taken over by the secular arm of society. All secularization partakes to some extent of idolatry, because the secular perspective is never eternal. The Church, by including its women at last in full partnership, should be leading and shaping human development, because only in this way can she effect her role of mediating salvation, to and through all humankind.

> "An Examination of the Ordination of Women to the Priesthood in Terms of the Symbolism of the Eucharist," *Women and Orders,* Robert J. Heyer, ed. *1974*

2   I take issue with . . . contending that, even though involuntary, such incapability does have profound moral and theological significance. That the proper demands of true Christian charity have not been met in the past treatment of homosexuals will not be denied; but redressing this wrong in no way requires that homosexuality be accepted as a normal alternative life style.

> "Homosexuality," *Anglican Theological Review,* Supp. Series *6 June 1976*

3   I have often thought, if I "cure" no one else in my whole career, you are enough. I love you. Good luck,—Ruth B.

> Letter to Sylvia Plath, Quoted in "Sylvia* and Ruth" by Karen Maroda, *Salon.com 29 November 2004*
> *Re Sylvia Plath, 2817; Barnhouse was her therapist.

2447. Ylena Georgievna Bonner (1923–   )

1   Since I never at any time anywhere under any circumstances deliberately spread slanderous fabrications defaming the Soviet state or social system or other countries, or private persons, I will not participate in the investigation and will not answer the question.

> *Alone Together 1986*

2   Living under the surveillance of the KGB* is very strange and unpleasant. Wherever you go, you feel the KGB watching, sometimes making films, sometimes harassing.

> Ibid.

*Komitet Gosudarstvennoy Bezopasnosti (Committee of State Security), Soviet intelligence agency.

2448. Ursula Reilly Curtiss (1923–1984)

1   It was the old principle of getting back on the horse that had thrown you (although why, Kate had always wondered? Why not just take up some other sport?) but sometimes, like a number of laudable things, it was wearing.

> Ch. 1, *The Wasp 1963*

2   After a second's astonishment, Kate let the lie stand. Like most lies it was much easier than the truth, and to contradict it might turn out to be a very wearying affair.

> Ch. 3, Ibid.

3   This was not love; it was exactly what Georgia had said: ownership. If you owned a race horse, you got the winner's stakes. If you owned a play, you got the royalties. If you owned a son. . . .

> Ch. 17, Ibid.

2449. Marie-Thérèse Danielsson (1923–2003)

1   The sudden flooding of the beautiful and peaceful islands of French Polynesia by 20,000 foreign troops and merciless profiteers in the early 1960s, when General de Gaulle made his fateful decision to build nuclear testing bases there, is fully comparable, in both its swiftness and magnitude, to the destruction wrought by a tsunami.

> *Moruroa, Mon Amour,* with Bengt Danielsson *1974*

2450. Mary Dann (1923–2005)

1   *Re the Shoshone struggle for their lands:* We're the ones that know which is right and which is wrong.

> Interview, Associated Press *2003*

2451. Antoinette DeWit (1923–   )

1   Grab the Hope when it flies by, we* say.

> Letter to Elaine Bernstein Partnow** *16 June 1989*
> *Enabled Artists Guild, Portland, Oregon. **See 3291.

2   I really cannot, and never will, presume to "educate" the public . . . that being disabled never means "disabled en toto," but to recognize that "disabled" also means "enabled," and that I would like to see the public become more aware of.

> Quoted in "She's Got Art and Soul" by Kathy Brock, *Lake Oswego Review* (Oregon) *April 1989*

2452. Dorothy Dinnerstein (1923–1992)

1   So long as the first parent is a woman, then, woman will inevitably be pressed into the dual role of indispensable quasi-human

supporter and deadly quasi-human enemy of the human self. She will be seen as naturally fit to nurture other people's individuality; as the born audience in whose awareness other people's subjective existence can be mirrored; as the being so peculiarly needed to confirm other people's worth, power, significance that if she fails to render them this service she is a monster, anomalous and useless. And at the same time she will also be seen as the one who will not let other people be, the one who beckons her loved ones back from selfhood, who wants to engulf, dissolve, drown, suffocate them as autonomous persons.

The Mermaid and the Minotaur 1977

2453. Mari Evans (1923–   )

1 Who
can be born black
and not
sing the wonder of it
the joy
the
challenge

"Who Can Be Born Black?," St. 1, *Continuum: New and Selected Poems* 2007

2 Connoisseurs of gourmet garbage
Gluttons seldom filled and never
satisfied   decay and rot a sauce
for hardy souls who wage with death
a never-ending war   This
is America
to me

"Four Movements: I New York City," St. 2, Ibid.

3 Where have you gone
with your confident
walk your
crooked smile the
rent money
in one pocket and
my heart
in another . . .

"Where Have You Gone," St. 3, Ibid.

2454. Paula Fox (1923–   )

1 I was born and thrown away.

The Western Coast 1972

2 My heart had grown dull. Sorrow, and the changes in my life that were its cause, had worked its desolation upon me.

Borrowed Finery, A Memoir 2001

3 As I grew older, my attitude about money changed. I began to see how complex it was, how some people accumulate it for its own sake, driven by forces as mysterious to me as those that drive termites to build mounds that attain heights of as much as forty feet in certain parts of the world.

Ch. 1, Ibid.

2455. Clara Fraser (1923–1998)

1 People hear that word [socialism] and they think "rhetoric. Karl Marx."* People's eyes get that kind of glazed look. [Socialism] is when the whole family is sitting around the dinner table, sharing and everyone gets alike.

Quoted in "Still active" by Florangela Davila, *Seattle Times*, B2 *17 March 1996*

*German political philosopher and economist (1818–83).

2 Capitalism is constant change, but when you advocate change, people cry out, "That's revolutionary! Subversive!" And my favorite: "Un-American!" Of all the people who should be shocked—Americans. How the hell do they think they got here?

Ibid.

3 Capitalism is approaching a crisis. Everyone senses it. That's why they say "Throw out the immigrants. Put up tariff walls. Send women home. Get rid of affirmative action. Build more prisons."

Ibid.

2456. Nadine Gordimer (1923–   )

1 A line in a statute book has more authority than the claims of one man's love or another's. All claims of natural feeling are over-ridden alike by a line in a statute book that takes no account of humanness, that recognizes neither love nor respect nor jealousy nor rivalry nor compassion nor hate—nor any human attitude where there are black and white together. What Boaz felt towards Ann; what Gideon felt towards Ann, what Ann felt about Boaz, what she felt for Gideon—all this that was real and rooted in life was void before the clumsy words that reduced the delicacy and towering complexity of living to a race theory . . .

Occasion for Loving 1963

2 That was one of the things she held against the missionaries: how they stressed Christ's submission to humiliation, and so had conditioned the people of Africa to humiliation by the white man.

"Not for Publication," *Not for Publication and Other Stories* 1965

3 He was a Nyasa with a face so black that the blackness was an inverted dazzle—you couldn't see what he was thinking.

"The Pet," Ibid.

4 The two women gazed out of the slumped and sagging bodies that had accumulated around them.

"Vital Statistics," Ibid.

5 Time is change; we measure its passage by how much things alter.

The Late Bourgeois World 1966

6 Oh we bathed and perfumed and depilated white ladies, in whose wombs the sanctity of the white race is entombed! What concoction of musk and boiled petals can disguise the dirt done in the name of that sanctity?

Ibid.

7 "There's nothing moral about beauty."

Ibid.

8 She filled her house with blacks, and white parsons who went around preaching Jesus was a revolutionary, and then when the police walked in she was surprised.

The Conservationist 1975

9 In the beginning was the Word.
The Word was with God, signified God's Word, the word that was Creation. But over the centuries of human culture the word has taken on other meanings, secular as well as religious. To have the word has come to be synonymous with ultimate authority, with prestige, with awesome, sometimes dangerous

persuasion, to have Prime Time, a TV talk show, to have the gift of the gab as well as that of speaking in tongues. The word flies through space, it is bounced from satellites, now nearer than it has ever been to the heaven from which it was believed to have come. But its most significant transformation occurred for me and my kind long ago, when it was first scratched on a stone tablet or traced on papyrus, when it materialized from sound to spectacle, from being heard to being read as a series of signs, and then a script; and traveled through time from parchment to Gutenberg. For this is the genesis story of the writer. It is the story that wrote her or him into being.

> Nobel lecture, "Writing and Being" (Johannesburg, 7 December 1991), *The Electronic Nobel Museum*, nobel.se/ enm-index.html *1996*

10 Humans, the only self-regarding animals, blessed or cursed with this torturing higher faculty, have always wanted to know why.

> *Ibid.*

11 [Myth] has made a whirling comeback out of Space, an Icarus in the avatar of Batman and his kind, who never fall into the ocean of failure to deal with the gravity forces of life. These new myths, however, do not seek so much to enlighten and provide some sort of answers as to distract, to provide a fantasy escape route for people who no longer want to face even the hazard of answers to the terrors of their existence. (Perhaps it is the positive knowledge that humans now possess the means to destroy their whole planet, the fear that they have in this way themselves become the gods, dreadfully charged with their own continued existence, that has made comic-book and movie myth escapist.)

> *Ibid.*

12 Any writer of any worth at all hopes to play only a pocket-torch of light—and rarely, through genius, a sudden flambeau—into the bloody yet beautiful labyrinth of human experience, of being.

> *Ibid.*

13 . . . nothing from the past could be more remote than this present.

> *The House Gun 1997*

14 The beloved hasn't gone anywhere. He is dead. He is nowhere except in the possibility of recall, a calling-up of all the times, phases, places, emotions and actions of what he was, how he lived while he was.

> "Allesverloren," *Beethoven Was One-Sixteenth Black and Other Stories 2007*

2457. Aline Griffith (1923–   )

1 I wanted to tell him* I had three great-grandmothers who had braved crossing this country to lay down roots in the Midwest, despite Indian attacks, birth without doctors, sickness without medicine, helping to build homes with their own hands, but I was afraid he would laugh. Instead I said, "I love adventure."

> *The Spy Wore Red: My Adventures as an Undercover Agent in World War II 1987*
> *Office of Strategic services representative who recruited her to spy.

2458. Jean Harris (1923–   )

1 The problems of administering a prison or living in one as an inmate appear to me to be quite similar . . . mental illness, physical illness, ignorance, drugs and alcohol, racism, overcrowding,

inadequate vocational training, incompetent staff and homosexuality. Were I to be asked to choose, I would put mental illness at the top of the list. There are days on my floor when the shrieks and screams and banging on the metal doors and throwing of furniture against a wall make my blood run cold, leave me touching a blanket or a book or something that represents sanity and a degree of permanence in a world gone mad.

> *"They Always Call Us Ladies": Stories from Prison 1988*

2 My own observation is that many of the women here [in Bedford Hills Correctional Facility, New York] fall loosely into two groups. The first made up of those so damaged in childhood they have never learned to trust or love or even feel small pangs of compassion for others; the second made up of those in whom the need to love and be loved is the overriding drive in their lives.

> *Ibid.*

3 Don't ever be sanguine about justice, Shane. Who the hell can say what it is?

> *Marking Time* 1992
> *A book of letters to journalist Shana Alexander (see 2540).

2459. Dorothy Coade Hewett (1923–2002)

1 In the years of Stalin
I came to Russia
And saw flowers growing
out of the blinkers
of my eyes.

> Untitled, *ca. 1952*

2 They come spilling out of the schoolhouse on Christmas Eve men in shirtsleeves and serge trousers women in printed cotton with permed hair drunk stumbling wound round with streamers shouting kissing the air they essay a few dance steps throw a few punches and fall down laughing . . .

> "Christmas Eve in Queensland," *Hecate May 1999*

2460. Mildred Armstrong Kalish (1923–   )

1 "A body'd think you had no upbringing. They'd think that you'd been peed on a stump and hatched by the sun."

> *Little Heathens, Hard Times and High Spirits on an Iowa Farm During the Great Depression 2007*

2 . . . the privilege of inhaling "the sweet fragrance emanating from the clean body of a colt, calf, lamb, puppy or kitten that had been sleeping on the grass and warmed by the sun" is one of life's great "pagan pleasures."

> *Ibid.*

3 Childhood was generally considered to be a disease, or, at the very least, a disability, to be ignored for the most part, and remedied as quickly as possible.

> *Ibid.*

4 We were taught that if you bought something it should last forever—or as close to forever as we could contrive.

> *Ibid.*

5 Every family owned at least three guns: a .22 rifle, and ten- and twelve-gauge shotguns. From early childhood we were taught to respect and care for guns. "The most dangerous gun," we were cautioned, "is the one that isn't loaded."

> Ch. 1, *Ibid.*

6 I had never seen adults cry. I didn't know they could cry.

> *Ibid.*

2461. Shirley Kaufman (1923–)

1 Through every night we hate,
  preparing the next day's
  war. . . .

  "Mothers, Daughters," *The Floor Keeps Turning 1970*

2 Even now
  in this sweet flesh
  isn't there something starting to withdraw?

  "Milk" (1993) (p. 157) *Roots in the Air: New and Selected Poems 1996*

3 before
  I could be her daughter,
  she turned me into her mother.
  Taught me the names of love
  in her language: grief
  and sorrow, sorrow and grief.

  "Leftovers" (p. 160), Ibid.

2462. Virginia Cassidy Kelley (1923–1994)

1 He's a mighty good man, and it's not only due to my being perfect.*

  Leading with My Heart: My Life, with James Morgan *1994*
  *Reference to her son, William Jefferson Clinton (1946–), 42nd president of United States (1993–2001).

2 When I die, if I open my eyes and I'm standing in the middle of Marshall Field's makeup department, I'll know I made it to heaven.

  Ibid.

2463. Jean Kerr (1923–2003)

1 I feel about airplanes the way I feel about diets. It seems to me that they are wonderful things for other people to go on.

  "Mirror, Mirror, on the Wall," *The Snake Has All the Lines 1958*

2 TIFFANY. Practically everybody Daddy knows is divorced. It's not that they're worse than other people, they're just richer.

  Act I, *Mary, Mary 1960*

3 MARY. It was hard to communicate with you. You were always communicating with yourself. The line was busy.

  Act II, Ibid.

4 A lawyer is never entirely comfortable with a friendly divorce, any more than a good mortician wants to finish the job and then have the patient sit up on the table.

  Quoted in *Time* (New York) *14 April 1961*

5 SYDNEY. You don't seem to realize that a poor person who is unhappy is in a better position than a rich person who is unhappy. Because the poor person has hope. He thinks money would help.

  Act I, *Poor Richard 1963*

6 SYDNEY. Even though a number of people have tried, no one has yet found a way to drink for a living.

  Ibid.

7 FELICIA. Hope is the feeling you have that the feeling you have isn't permanent.

  Act III, *Finishing Touches 1973*

2464. Denise Levertov (1923–1997)

1 two by two in the ark of
  the ache of it.

  "The Ache of Marriage," *O Taste and See 1963*

2 Two girls discover
  the secret of life
  in a sudden line of
  poetry.

  I who don't know the
  secret wrote
  the line.

  "The Secret," Sts. 1–2, *Poems 1960–1967 1964*

3 No, God's in the wilderness next door
  —that huge tundra room, no walls and a sky roof—
  busy at the loom.

  "The Task," *Oblique Prayers 1984*

4 When shall we
  dare to fly?

  "Standoff," St. 8, *Breathing the Water 1987*

5 We must breathe time as fishes breathe water.

  "Variation and Reflection on a Theme by Rilke,"* Ibid.
  *Rainer Maria Rilke, German poet (1875–1926).

6 The day's blow
  rang out, metallic—or it was I, a bell awakened,
  and what I heard was my whole self
  saying and singing what it knew: I *can.*

  "Variation on a Theme by Rilke," Pt. I, Ibid.

7 I hear the books in all the rooms
  breathing calmly

  "August Daybreak," St. 1, Ibid.

8 Much happens when we're not there.

  "Window-Blind," Pt. II, Ibid.

9 Every day, every day I hear
  enough to fill
  a year of nights with wondering.

  "Every Day," Pt. III, St. 6, Ibid.

10 . . . I have just enough faith to believe it exists.

  "Work That Enfaiths," *New and Selected Essays 1992*

11 Every work of art is an "act of faith" in the vernacular sense of being a venture into the unknown. The artist must dive into waters whose depths are unplumbed, and trust that he or she will neither be swallowed up nor come crashing against a cement surface four foot down, but will rise and be buoyed upon them.

  Ibid.

12 Invisible wings are given to us too, by which, if we would dare to acknowledge and use them, we might transcend the dualities of time and matter—might be upheld to walk on water. Instead, we humans persistently say no, and persistently experience our wings only as a dragging weight on our backs.

  Ibid.

13 Thus for me the subject is really reversed: not "faith that works" but "work that enfaiths."

  Ibid.

14 Fully occupied with growing—that's
the amaryllis.
"The Métier of Blossoming," St. 1, *This Great Unknowing:
Last Poems 1998*

15 I'll dig in
into my days, having come here to live, not to visit.
Grey is the price
of neighboring with eagles, of knowing
a mountain's vast presence, seen or unseen.
"Settling" *n.d.*

2465. Naomi Long Madgett (1923–)

1 I will not feed your hunger with my blood
Nor crown your nakedness
With jewels of my elegant pain.
"The Race Question," lines 13–15, *1965*

2 Curse of the orchard,
Blemish on the land's fair countenance,
I have grown strong for strength denied, for struggle
In hostile woods. I keep alive by being the troublesome,
Indestructible
Stinkweed of truth.
"Tree of Heaven," lines 13–18 *1970*

2466. Alice Miller (1923–)

1 Experience has taught us that we have only one enduring
weapon in our struggle against mental illness: the emotional
discovery and emotional acceptance of the truth in the individual and unique history of our childhood.
Ch. 1, *The Drama of the Gifted Child: The Search for the True
Self,* 1st ed. *1979*

2 Society chooses to disregard the mistreatment of children,
judging it to be altogether normal because it is so commonplace.
"Childhood and Creativity," *Pictures of a Childhood,*
Hildegarde Hannum, tr. *1986*

3 We are often imprisoned in a cage of our own abilities and
routines, which provides us with a sense of security. We are
afraid to break free; yet we must gasp for air and keep seeking our way, probably over and over again, if we do not
want to be smothered in the womb of what is familiar and
well known to us, but rather to be born along with our new
work.
Ibid.

4 In my own therapy it was my experience that it was precisely
the opposite of forgiveness —namely, rebellion against mistreatment suffered, the recognition and condemnation of my
parents' destructive opinions and actions, and the articulation of my own needs— that ultimately freed me from the
past.
Breaking down the walls of silence 1990

5 Psychoanalysis does not distort the truth by accident. It does so
by necessity. It is an effective system for the suppression of the
truth about childhood, a truth feared by our entire society. Not
surprisingly, it enjoys great esteem among intellectuals . . . Fear
of the truth about child abuse is a leitmotif of nearly all forms
of therapy known to me.
Ibid.

6 We become free by transforming ourselves from unaware victims of the past into responsible individuals in the present,
who are aware of our past and are thus able to live with it.
Ch. 1, *The Drama of the Gifted Child: The Search for the True
Self,* 3rd ed., Andrew Jenkins, tr. *1996*

7 In order to become whole we must try, in a long process, to
discover our own personal truth, a truth that may cause pain
before giving us a new sphere of freedom. If we choose instead to content ourselves with intellectual "wisdom," we will
remain in the sphere of illusion and self-deception.
Ibid.

2467. Shri Mataji Nirmala Devi (1923–)

1 No Reality in those religions. These religions were money oriented or power-oriented. There was no Divine Force working,
actually it was all anti-divine. How to now turn human beings
away from these superficial religions, these perverted paths of
destruction? How to tell them about all these established organizations? For ages they have been ruling, making money,
making power.
Speech (Fregene, Italy), *8 May 1988*

2 Global unity of mankind can be achieved through this
awakening that can occur within each human being, so that
transformation takes place within us.
sahajayoga.org *2005*

3 Meditation is the only way you can grow . . . because when you
meditate, you are in silence. You are in thoughtless awareness.
Then the growth of awareness takes place.
Ibid.

2468. Miriam Schapiro (1923–)

1 A woman can make the choice to be an artist and decide to
go all the way, but there is still tremendous guilt. You feel as
though you're stealing power.
Quoted in "Miriam Schapiro", *Exposures, Women & Their
Art* by Ann Brown and Arlene Raven* *1989*
*See 3533.

2 Throughout history, many women who became artists trained
in their fathers' studios . . . [Mine] had a passion for art that
was very deep.
Ibid.

3 If you were to survey celebrated women, with every step toward real success there came a baby.
Ibid.

4 I felt that by making a large canvas magnificent in color, design
and proportion, filling it with fabrics and quilt blocks, I could
raise a housewife's lowered consciousness.*
Quoted in "Miriam in Wonderland" by Kate Mulligan,
Parade Magazine 1998
*At the center of this artwork is a small, white rectangle with the
embroidered words: "Welcome to our home"

5 The great thing about that quilt (the AIDS NAMES quilt)
is that everybody and their brother and sister made those
pieces without any thought of whether they had talent. You
have art giving you a healing process. You have art giving
you redemption.
Ibid.

2469. Liz Smith (1923–)

1 Gossip is news running ahead of itself in a red satin dress.
"American Way" (syndicated column) 3 September 1985

2 Black people were my secret passion. I wanted to sit separated with them at the movies. I was enthralled with how they
looked, their talk, their humor, their food, their music, their
laughter and the terrible way most them had to live without
seeming even to notice it.
"Frozen Justice in Texas," Natural Blonde 2000

2470. Amy Swerdlow (1923–)

1 In the eighth grade my stomach churned and I thought I would
faint as I had to stand up on the auditorium stage and refuse
a bronze medal for coming in third in a potato race with the
statement "I cannot accept a medal from William Randolph
Hearst."*
(p. 250), Red Diapers: Growing Up in the Communist Left,
Judy Kaplan and Linn Shapiro, eds. 1998
*American newspaper and magazine publisher (1863–1951).

2471. Kate Swift (1923–)

1 Webster's Ninth New Collegiate Dictionary (1986) defines a
man-about-town as "a worldly and socially active man." But
if man sometimes means "any human being," should not the
definition of man-about-town read "a worldly and socially active person of the male sex?"
Ch. 1, The Handbook of Nonsexist Writing, coauthor, Casey
Miller* 1988 rev.

*See 2350.

2472. Wislawa Szymborska (1923–)

1 Why does this written doe bound through these written
woods?
For a drink of written water from a spring
whose surface will xerox her soft muzzle?
"The Joy of Writing," St. 1, No End of Fun, Stanislaw
Baranczak and Clare Cavanagh, trs. 1967

2 For all its charms, the island is uninhabited,
and the faint footprints scattered on its beaches
turn without exception to the sea.

As if all you can do here is leave
and plunge, never to return, into the depths.

Into unfathomable life.
"Utopia," last lines, A large number, Stanislaw Baranczak and
Clare Cavanagh, trs. 1976

3 I think that dividing literature or poetry into women's and
men's poetry is starting to sound absurd. Perhaps there was a
time when a woman's world did exist, separated from certain
issues and problems, but at present there are no things that
would not concern women and men at the same time. We do
not live in the boudoir anymore.
Interview with Beata Chmiel, Ex Libris (Poland) 1984

4 All imperfection is easier to tolerate if served up in small doses.
Nobel lecture, "The Poet and the World," Stanislaw Baranczak
and Clare Cavanagh, trs., The Electronic Nobel Museum,
(nobel.se/enm-index.html) 7 December 1996

5 Bureaucrats and bus passengers respond with a touch of incre-
dulity and alarm when they find out that they're dealing with a
poet.
Ibid.

6 Films about painters can be spectacular, as they go about recreating every stage of a famous painting's evolution . . . Music
swells in films about composers . . . Of course this is all quite
naive and doesn't explain the strange mental state popularly
known as inspiration, but at least there's something to look at
and listen to.
But poets are the worst. Their work is hopelessly unpho-
togenic. Someone sits at a table or lies on a sofa while staring
motionless at a wall or ceiling. Once in a while this person
writes down seven lines only to cross out one of them fifteen
minutes later, and then another hour passes, during which nothing happens . . . Who could stand to watch this kind of thing?
Ibid.

7 And any knowledge that doesn't lead to new questions quickly
dies out: it fails to maintain the temperature required for sustaining life.
Ibid.

8 I prefer myself liking people
to myself loving mankind
"Possibilities," ll. 5, 6, Nothing Twice, Stanislaw Baranczak
and Clare Cavanagh, trs. 1997

9 trash does not pretend to be anything better than it is
"Kitschy" n.d.

2473. Katherine Tait (1923–)

1 Reason, progress, unselfishness, a wide historical perspective,
expansiveness, generosity, enlightened self-interest. I had heard
it all my life, and it filled me with despair.
Afterword, Quoted in Bertrand Russell* by Caroline
Moorehead 1992
*Her father, English mathematician and philosopher (1872–
1970).

2474. Inge Trachtenberg (1923?–)

1 . . . my tenth year is marked as the year in which Adolf Hitler came to power in Germany. . . . Yet, when that event took
place, Father wasn't sure that it was such a bad thing for Germany. Adolf Hitler had promised bread and order; Father was
in favor of bread and order . . . I, for one, had no premonition
of bad things to come.
Ch. 4, So Slow the Dawning 1973

2 Decent was more than moral, decent was also being a good
sport, a good friend, having a sense of humor, being tough.
Ch. 14, Ibid.

2475. May Yamada (1923–)

1 Not only the young, but those who feel powerless over their
own lives know what it is like not to make a difference on
anyone or anything. The poor know it only too well, and we
women have known it since we were little girls.
"Invisibility Is an Unnatural Disaster" (1981), This Bridge
Called My Back: Writings by Radical Women of Color,
Cherríe Moraga* and Gloria Anzaldúa,** eds. 1983
*See 4125. **See 3321.

2 The Japanese have an all-purpose expression in their language
for this attitude of resigned acceptance: "Shikataganai." "It
can't be helped." "There's nothing I can do about it." It is said
with the shrug of the shoulders and tone of finality, perhaps
not unlike the "those-were-my-orders" tone that was used at
the Nuremberg trials.
Ibid.

3 Asian American women still remain in the background and we are heard but not really listened to. Like Musak, they think we are piped into the airwaves by someone else.

Ibid.

4 Thank you people
of the village, if it had not been for your
kindness
in refusing me a bed
for the night
these humble eyes would never
have seen this
memorable sight.

Camp Notes and Other Poems 1992

2476. Lauren Bacall (1924–)

1 The purity of Jewish upbringing—the restrictions that one carries through life being a "nice Jewish girl"—what a burden.

Lauren Bacall By Myself 1978

2 A man's illness is his private territory and, no matter how much he loves you and how close you are, you stay an outsider. You are healthy.

Ibid.

3 I think your whole life shows in your face and you should be proud of that.

The Daily Telegraph (London) *2 March 1988*

2477. Dorothy Corkille Briggs (1924–)

1 The surest route to breeding jealousy is to compare. Since jealousy comes from feeling "less than" another, comparisons only fan the fires.

Ch. 7, *Your Child's Self-Esteem 1970*

2 The opposite of love is not hate, as many believe, but rather indifference.

Ibid.

3 Growth is not steady, forward, upward progression. It is instead a switchback trail; three steps forward, two back, one around the bushes, and a few simply standing, before another forward leap.

Ch. 13, Ibid.

4 The area [of toilet training] is one where a child really does possess the power to defy. Strong pressure leads to a powerful struggle. The issue then is not toilet training but who holds the reins—mother or child? And the child has most of the ammunition!

Ch. 15, Ibid.

2478. Sarah Caldwell (1924–)

1 If you approach an opera as though it were something that always went a certain way, that's what you get. I approach an opera as though I didn't know it.

Quoted in "Sarah Caldwell: The Flamboyant of the Opera" by Jane Scovell Appleton, *Ms.* (New York) *May 1975*

2 We must continually discipline ourselves to remember how it felt the first moment.

Ibid.

3 It [Tanglewood, summer home of the Boston Symphony Orchestra] was a place where gods strode the earth.

Quoted in "Music's Wonder Woman," *Time* (New York) *10 November 1975*

2479. Nina Cassian (1924–)

1 With a triumphant smile,
I confront time
as its edged diamond
sculpts my features.

"Poets," *Cheerleader for a Funeral 1992*

2 What's that tiny star on your left temple?
Maybe a bird scratched it with tender claws
to prod you into flying.

"Youthing," *Take My Word For It 1998*

2480. Shirley Chisholm (1924–2005)

1 It is not heroin or cocaine that makes one an addict, it is the need to escape from a harsh reality. There are more television addicts, more baseball and football addicts, more movie addicts, and certainly more alcohol addicts in this country than there are narcotics addicts.

Testimony, House Select Committee on Crime *17 September 1969*

2 Of my two "handicaps," being female put many more obstacles in my path than being black.

Unbought and Unbossed 1970

3 When morality comes up against profit, it is seldom that profit loses.

Ibid.

4 Tremendous amounts of talent are being lost to our society just because that talent wears a skirt.

Ibid.

5 The seniority system keeps a handful of old men, many of them southern whites hostile to every progressive trend, in control of the Congress. These old men stand implacably across the paths that could lead us toward a better future. But worse than they, I think, are the majority of members of both Houses who continue to submit to the senility system. Apparently, they hope they, too, will grow to be old.

Pt. II, Ch. 8, Ibid.

6 I ran because someone had to do it first. In this country everyone is supposed to be able to run for President, but that's never been really true. I ran *because* most people think the country isn't ready for a black candidate, not ready for a woman candidate. Some day . . .

Ch. 1, *The Good Fight 1973*

7 Richard M. Nixon* . . . has a deeper concern for his place in history than for the people he governs. And history will not fail to note that fact.

Ch. 11, Ibid.

*Richard M. Nixon, American politician (1913–1994), 37th president of the United States (1969–74); resigned.

8 We Americans have a chance to become someday a nation in which all racial stocks and classes can exist in their own selfhoods, but meet on a basis of respect and equality and live together, socially, economically, and politically. We can become

a dynamic equilibrium, a harmony of many different elements, in which the whole will be greater than all its parts and greater than any society the world has seen before. It can still happen.

Ch. 14, Ibid.

2481. Jane Cooper (1924–2007)

1   I don't want your rent, I want
a radiance of attention
like the candle's flame when we eat,

I mean a kind of awe
attending the spaces between us—
Not a roof but a field of stars.

"Rent," Sts. 3–4, *Scaffolding: Selected Poems 1993*

2   Must the anthropologist always dream animal dreams? Must we?

"Seventeen Questions About KING KONG," St. 12, *The Flashboat: Poems Collected and Reclaimed 1994*

3   The future weighs down on me
just like a wall of light!

"The Blue Anchor," St. 1, Ibid.

2482. Pamelia Dillin Fergus (1924–1987)

1   I know we like to count dollars and cents but what are they to a little enjoyment the short time we stay here on earth.

Letter (April 1961), Quoted in *Women Pioneers* by Rebecca Stefoff 1995

2483. Janet Frame (1924–2004)

1   Every morning I woke in dread, waiting for the day nurse to go on her rounds and announce from the list of names in her hand whether or not I was for shock treatment, the new and fashionable means of quieting people and of making them realize that orders are to be obeyed and floors are to be polished without anyone protesting and faces are made to be fixed into smiles and weeping is a crime.

Ch. 1, *Faces in the Water 1961*

2   Electricity, the peril the wind sings to in the wires on a gray day.

Ch. 2, Ibid.

3   For in spite of the snapdragons and the dusty millers and the cherry blossoms, it was always winter.

Ibid.

4   "For your own good" is a persuasive argument that will eventually make man agree to his own destruction.

Ch. 4, Ibid.

5   It would be nice to travel if you knew where you were going and where you would live at the end or do we ever know, do we ever live where we live, we're always in other places, lost, like sheep.

"The Day of the Sheep," *You Are Now Entering the Human Heart 1983*

2484. Bette Clair Graham (1924–1980)

1   As a young woman with a son to raise alone, I suffered greatly with extreme lack [of funds]. I was a Christian Scientist and had tried to work this problem out by turning to God, but I

never seemed to get anywhere until I was willing to humbly let go of my fear of, and dependency on, matter.

Quoted in *Women Inventors* by Linda Jacobs Altman 1997

2   In ten years we have come from production in a kitchen . . . to a corporation employing many people . . .

Excerpt from company speech (1968), Ibid.

2485. Patricia Roberts Harris (1924–1985)

1   I am one of them [the poor]. You do not seem to understand who I am. I am a Black woman, daughter of a dining-car worker. I am a Black woman who could not buy a house eight years ago in parts of the District of Columbia. I didn't start out as a member of a prestigious law firm, but as a woman who needed a scholarship to go to school. If you think that I have forgotten that, you are wrong.

Congressional Confirmation Hearings (addressing Senator William Proxmire*) 25–26 *July 1979*
*American politician (1915–2005).

2486. Marcella Hazan (1924–   )

1   You don't cook? What do you do? Starve?

Quoted in "Battling Spaghetti O Taste Buds" by Cathy Booth, *Time* (New York) 29 *May 1989*

2   Cooking is an art, but you can eat it too.

Ibid.

3   . . . the pallor of deep-freeze counters, those cemeteries of food, whose produce is sealed up in waxed boxes marked, like some tombstones, with photographs of the departed.

Marcella's Italian Kitchen 1995

2487. Ruth Hubbard (1924–   )

1   The mythology of science asserts that with many different scientists all asking their own questions and evaluating the answers independently, whatever personal bias creeps into their individual answers is cancelled out when the large picture is put together. This might conceivably be so if scientists were women and men from all sorts of different cultural and social backgrounds who came to science with very different ideologies and interests. But since, in fact, they have been predominantly university-trained white males from privileged social backgrounds, the bias has been narrow and the product often reveals more about the investigator than about the subject being researched.

"Have Only Men Evolved?," *Women Look at Biology Looking at Women*, Ruth Hubbard, Mary Sue Henifin, and Barbara Fried, eds. 1979

2   To overturn orthodoxy is no easier in science than in philosophy, religion, economics, or any of the other disciplines through which we try to comprehend the world and the society in which we live.

Ibid.

3   The decision to disbelieve all scientific explanations is not to be sneered at. The volume, contradictoriness, and limited comprehensibility of much scientific information leave most people bewildered.

Ch. 1, *The Politics of Women's Biology 1989*

4   There is no historical and political analysis of our hierarchically structured, exploitative society, in which scientists

work not so much because they believe that the knowledge they produce is relevant to human needs or values but often in order to generate publications, jobs, research funds, and prices.

Ibid.

2488. Alice Koller (1924–   )

1   If I could learn how to see with my own eyes, I'd be able to make a comparable leap, leaving behind everybody else's rules.... I don't know what I want, or want to do. I don't know how to use my own evidence ... I don't know what to look for inside me. I don't know how to identify that I'm feeling something, let alone give it a name. I think I've been anesthetized, deadened.

An Unknown Woman 1981

2   I've arrived at this outermost edge of my life by my own actions. Where I am is thoroughly unacceptable. Therefore, I must stop doing what I've been doing.

Ibid.

3   Being solitary is being alone well: being alone luxuriously immersed in doings of your own choice, aware of the fullness of your own presence rather than of the absence of others. Because solitude is an achievement.

The Stations of Solitude 1990

2489. Phyllis Lyon (1924–   )
Coauthor with Del Martin; see 2407.

2490. Lisel Mueller (1924–   )

1   Memory is the only
afterlife I can understand.
"Pillar of Salt," *Alive Together: New and Selected Poems 1996*

2   In any age, life has to be lived
Before we know what it is.
"Triumph of Life," Ibid.

3   I ...
placed my grief
in the mouth of language,
the only thing that would grieve with me.
"When I Am Asked," Ibid.

4   Because the story of our life
becomes our life
"Why We Tell Stories," Ibid.

5   Speaking of marvels, I am alive
together with you, when I might have been
alive with anyone under the sun ...
"Alive Together," Ibid.

6   The laughter of women sets fire
to the Halls of Injustice
and the false evidence burns
to a beautiful white lightness
"The Laughter of Women," St. 1, Ibid.

7   My country was struck by history more deadly than
earthquakes or hurricanes
"Curriculum Vitae," Ibid.

2491. Bess Myerson (1924–   )

1   ... the accomplice to the crime of corruption is frequently our own indifference.
Quoted in "Impeachment?" by Claire Safran, *Redbook April 1974*

2   It's always time for a change for the better, and for a good fight for the full human rights of every individual.
Quoted in *AFTRA Magazine Summer 1974*

2492. Geraldine Page (1924–1987)

1   That's the longest night I've ever seen.*
Quoted in Obituary by Elizabeth Kolbert,**
The New York Times 15 June 1987
*Her remark on being acclaimed an overnight success upon release of film versions of *Summer and Smoke* and *Sweet Bird of Youth;* she'd been acting on Broadway stage for 10 years. **See 4584.

2   A lot of people say I always play neurotic women. Well, who doesn't play neurotic women?

Ibid.

3   The main thing is the ability to control your instrument, which in the actor, is yourself. Look the way you want the character to look. Sound the way you want the character to sound. Once you've trained the instrument to do what you want, you're in control and you're free.
Profile in *The New Yorker*, Ibid.

2492.1. Maxine Powell (1924–   )

1   When I was young I came to realize how people were all born and conceived in the same manner; that since all children are helpless and innocent at birth, their differences are determined by their upbringing, not color.
Quoted *in Contemporary Black Biography: Profiles from the International Black Community*, Ashyia N. Henderson, ed. *2001*

2   I taught positive change through body language and word power. I told these young artists that they were not the best singers and dancers in the world, that our race has always had great performers. My job was to keep them from going on an ego trip—to remind them that each performance was a dress rehearsal.

Ibid.

3   Motown artists weren't disrespectful, but they were diamonds in the rough. I told them they trained for the number-one places around the world, for the Queen of England and president of the United States, and those youngsters laughed at me. They said all they wanted was a hit record. They didn't have the vision—yet.
Quoted in "Ain't No Women (Like the Motown Women)" by Anna Clark, Women's Media Center (womensmediacenter. com) *12 May 2009*

2493. Rosetta Reitz (1924–2008)

1   The blues women had a commanding presence and a refreshing robustness. They were nurturers, taking the yeast of experience, kneading it into dough, molding it and letting it grow in their minds to bring the listener bread for sustenance, shaped by their sensibilities.
Ch. 10, *The Political Palate* by Betsey Beaven et al. *1980*

2494. Harriet Rochlin (1924–)

1 "Laughter can be more satisfying than honor; more precious than money; more heart cleansing than prayer."

Ch. 1, *So Far Away* 1981

2 "Family life is a training ground," intoned Miss O'Hara, "for life in the world. Learn to get along at home, and you can get along everywhere."

Ch. 8, Ibid.

3 "A Jew is supposed to chase God, not gold."

Ch. 18, Ibid.

4 Had she made a mistake? If she had, it was too late to rectify. Now that they were married, he could carry her off like a valise, and no one would lift a finger to stop him.

Ch. 1, *The First Lady of Dos Cacahuates* 1998

2495. Alma Routsong (1924–1996)

1 [I] wonder if what makes men walk lordlike and speak so masterfully is having the love of women.

A Place for Us 1969

2496. Phyllis Schlafly (1924–)

1 The moral sickness of the Federal Government becomes more apparent every day. Public officials are caught in a giant web of payoffs, bribes, perversion, and conflicts of interest, so that few dare to speak out against the establishment.

Ch. 1, *Safe—Not Sorry* 1967

2 America is waiting for an Attorney General who will enforce the law—and a President with the courage to demand that he do so.

Ch. 8, Ibid.

3 The left wing forces—both obvious and hidden—which have been running our country for the last seven years understand and appreciate the importance of *political action*. Their long tentacles reach out in many fields: to "orchestrate" propaganda through the communications media, to indoctrinate youth in our schools and universities, to create a Socialist intellectual climate through tax-exempt foundations, and to bend business into line with Government contracts.

Ch. 12, Ibid.

4 The atomic bomb is a marvelous gift that was given to our country by a wise God.

"Topics; Invocations; The Godly Nuke," *The New York Times* 9 July 1982

5 It is long overdue for parents to realize they have the right and duty to protect our children against the intolerant evolutionists.

"Time to End the Censorship," Syndicated Column 29 December 2004

6 By getting married, the woman has consented to sex, and I don't think you can call it rape.

Quoted in "Schlafly cranks up agitation at Bates" by J. T. Leonard, *Sun Journal* 29 March 2007

7 A woman seeking help from a VAWA*-funded center is not offered any options except to leave her husband, divorce him, accuse him of being a criminal, and have her sons targeted as suspects in future crimes. VAWA ideology rejects joint counseling, reconciliation, and saving marriages.

"Time to Defund Feminist Pork—the Hate-Men Law," *The Phyllis Schlafly Report*, vol. 39, no. 3 October 2005
*Violence Against Women Act sponsored by Senator Joe Biden** and passed in 1994. **(1942–), Am. politician; 47th vice president of the United States (2009–).

8 The term domestic violence has morphed into domestic abuse, a far broader term. Domestic abuse doesn't have to be violent—it doesn't even have to be physical. The feminists' mantra is, "You don't have to be beaten to be abused."

Ibid.

2497. Irene Pierce Stiver (1924–2000)
See Miller, Jean Baker. 2607:06.

2498. Efua Theodora Sutherland (1924–1996)

1 AMPONA. I declare to earth and sky and water, and all things with which we shall soon be one, that I am slave to your flesh and happy so to be.*

Edufa 1962
*Ampona is volunteering to die in her husband's place.

2 LABARAN. I was impatient at the beginning; in haste. Seeing the raggedness of my people's homes, I was ashamed, even angry. I heard it, screamed: Progress! Development! I wanted it far and everywhere.

But now I have learned that I can roam all I please, and nothing will change. I can talk all I please—who cares? Friends, when you talk to people and see blankness in their faces, you have to give up. In these you can read the sum of their souls and whether or not they understand. From that derives the patience of which I speak.

Act I, *Foriwa* 1962

2499. Betty Shingler Talmadge (1924–)

1 If you love the law and you love good sausage, don't watch either of them being made.

Quoted in *The Reader* 25 November 1977

2 It's only a good town if you have a good seat, if you know what I mean, honey.

Quoted in *The Washington Post* 1988

2500–2501. Margaret Truman (1924–2008)

1 I know from experience that the barbs of the critics are more painful for a President's family to endure than they are for the President.

Women of Courage 1976

2 It's only when you grow up, and step back from him, or leave him for your own career and your own home—it's only then that you can measure his greatness and fully appreciate it. Pride reinforces love.

Address to Congress (on centenary of Harry S. Truman's* birth) 8 May 1984
*(1884–1972), Am. politician; 33rd president of the United States (1945–1953).

3 He loved politicians—even Republicans.

Ibid.

4 Mother* . . . considered a press conference on a par with a visit to a cage of cobras.

Bess W. Truman 1986
*See 1644.

2502. Gloria Vanderbilt (1924–   )

1 Rich people don't communicate. They rise above things.
"Living with Loss" by Kim Hubbard, *People* 6 *May* 1966

2 His death* shattered the glass bubble I've always felt I lived in. Tragedy happens and people say, "Why me?" I say, "Why should I be exempt?" Tragedy connects everyone in the world.

Ibid.

*Re her son Carter's suicide.

3 The creative risk-taking of passionate love not only gives you the chance to change the past, it gives the imagination one more chance at an exciting future.
"Romance", *It Seemed Important at the Time: A Romance Memoir* 2004

4 I find sex endlessly interesting. I suppose I always have. It's all in the head, of course; I realize that now. What we like, what we want, what we think we need is generated somewhere in that curious cortex of ours, created by the firing of synapses— the electricity of love.
"The Scarlet Sting of Scandal," Ibid.

2503. Sally Weinraub (1924–   )

1 Architects believe less and less in doors these days, so that houses were becoming like beehives, arches leading into chambers and more arches. It was lucky that Americans were still puritan in their habits. You could be alone in the bathroom.
"Knifed with a Black Shadow," *American Scene: New Voices*, Don Wolfe, ed. 1963

2504. Wakako Yamauchi (1924–   )

1 YO. What is there to fear? Life? Death? Just roll with the punches.
12–1-A 1982

2 YO. In a war, Obasan, one country wins; the other loses. . . . We all look the same to them. We lost both ways.
Act I, Sc. 1, Ibid.

3 [The internment camp] was a terrible place. You couldn't run away from it because you'd die in the desert*—*if you escaped the bullets from the sentries. . . . I felt very bitter there, and very closed in.
Between Worlds: Contemporary Asian-American Plays, Misha Berson, ed. 1990
*Yamauchi and her family were interred at a camp in 1941 in Poston, Arizona.

2505. Etel Adnan (1925–   )

1 The human race is going to the cemetery
in great upheavals
"The Beirut-Hell Express" (1991), *The Woman That I Am, The Literature and Culture of Contemporary Women of Color*, D. Soyini Madison,* ed. 1994
*See 3912.

2 City more unreal than the wind
although pregnant with the sins of
the world
it is in your belly that foreigners
exercise the alchemy of treason
Ibid.

2506. Dede Allen (1925–   )

1 Editing [film] is really a creative art. Any editor needs to know certain techniques, but the real decisions are made in her or his head.
Quoted in "The Power Behind the Screen" by Geraldine Febrikant, *Ms.* (New York) *February 1974*

2507. Svetlana Alliluyeva (1925–   )

1 Moscow, breathing fire like a human volcano with its smoldering lava of passion, ambition and politics, its hurly-burly of meetings and entertainment. . . . Moscow seethes and bubbles and gasps for air. It's always thirsting for something new, the newest events, the latest sensation. Everyone wants to be the first to know. It's the rhythm of life today.
Introduction (16 July 1963), *Twenty Letters to a Friend* 1967

2 He is gone, but his shadow still stands over all of us. It still dictates to us and we, very often, obey.*
Ch. 2, Ibid.
*Reference to her father, Josef Stalin, Soviet Communist revolutionary and political leader (1879–1953).

3 . . . as a result of half a century of Soviet rule people have been weaned from a belief in human kindness.
"The Journey's End," *Only One Year* 1969

2508. Helen Bamber (1925–   )

1 Above all else, there was the need to tell you everything, over and over and over again. And this was the most significant thing for me, realizing that you had to take it all.*
Quoted in *The Good Listener: Helen Bamber, a Life Against Cruelty* by Neil Belton 1999
*Reference to survivors of the Holocaust, the genocide of European Jews and others by the Nazis during World War II.

2 When you walk with a limp, when you can't sit comfortably, when you can't eat properly because your mouth has been damaged, or you can't hear because your ears are damaged, you are reminded daily of what happened to you, and you need a way to put that in some form to rest.
Returning to some kind of strength means that you are going to want your needs to be recognized, and that there has to be a journey from being a victim to being a survivor. I know that there's a lot of sentimentality about—and a lot of talk about—not using the word victim and only using the word survivor, and so on, but for me, there is often a journey to be made from being a victim to being a survivor.
Interview with history editor Sunny Delaney, Amazon.com 1999

3 Torture is not only about broken bodies and broken teeth and damaged limbs. It's about loss; it's about being helpless in the face of other people's torture. It's hearing the screams of others. It's the helplessness of torture that is so difficult to bear. To begin to live a normal life again is a monumental task!
Ibid.

4 The bystander, I think, is somebody who will find good reason not to take part, not to intervene, not to take an individual decision of their own to stand up and be counted.
Ibid.

2509. Helen Barolini (1925–   )

1 What they can't express verbally, they show. Show and Tell: that is the level of a people in a linguistic backwater, in a

backwater of old outdated attitudes; of a people uneducated in values beyond the blatant materialistic one that seduces so many newcomers to America: get rich and make good, defend your property values.

"Buried Alive by Language" (p. 52), *Chiaroscuro: Essays of Identity 1997*

2   It was not just the Convent School that taught me to efface myself before the male partner who was surely more important, worthier, better. It was also my Italian American education which upheld the eternal sacrificial position of the woman. We were the uprights of the home; we were there to give ourselves for our men and for our children. We were not there for ourselves.

"Shutting the Door on Someone" (p. 62), Ibid.

2510. Nina Bawden (1925–   )

1   Wars give ordinary people a chance to be more than just ordinary. . . . You can save your friend's life or betray him.

The Real Plato Jones 1993

2   . . . harder than belonging to a tribe . . . [is to be] A Citizen of the World.

Ibid.

3   All writers are liars.

In My Own Time: Almost An Autobiography 1995

4   . . . family stories . . . tell us who we are and help to shape our lives.

Ibid.

2511. Marilyn Bender (1925–   )

1   Female clothing has been disappearing literally and philosophically.

Ch. 1, *The Beautiful People 1967*

2   To whip up desire for something that people don't really need, at least not in endless quantity, glamorous idols are essential. If desire begets need, then envy begets desire. The stimulation of envy or a longing to imitate is the function of the idol. The fashion industry, through its press agents and an eagerly cooperative, self-serving press, had to manufacture new goddesses.

Ch. 3, Ibid.

3   Just as the court flunky tasted the king's food to screen it for poison, so today the corporate sovereign has his literary fare digested and presented in capsule form or laced into his speeches by his ghost writer.

"The Business of Reading About Business," *Saturday Review of the Society April 1973*

4   Any survey of what businessmen are reading runs smack into the open secret that most businessmen aren't. Reading books, that is.

Ibid.

2512. Carmel Budiardjo (1925–   )

1   For this regime [Suharto*], people in the middle are also extremists if they happen to be liberals or advocates of human rights.

Surviving Indonesia's Gulag 1997

2   [Indonesians] have a misplaced patriotism which says you must not attack your own government.

Quoted in "Britain's ex-tapol fights on" by Bob Hawkins, *New Internationalist, 116 October 1982*

3   Nationalism and militarism is a poisonous mix . . .

"West Papua: Land of Peace or Killing Field," *Tapol 30 April 2005*

4   Suharto* departed this world without facing justice for his multiple crimes against humanity or for the extremely brutal campaign carried out, by his troops in their attempt to crush the resistance movement in East Timor.

Obituary of Suharto, former president and dictator of Indonesia, *Tapol 27 January 2008*

*(1921–2008) Indonesian military leader and president of Indonesia (1969–1998).

2513. Sala Burton (1925–1987)

1   I saw and felt what happened in Western Europe when the Nazis were moving. You learn that politics is everybody's business.

Obituary, *The New York Times 2 February 1987*

2514. Barbara Bush (1925–   )

1   I got away with murder [as Second Lady]. I'm now slightly more careful about what I say. Slightly.

Quoted in "The Silver Fox" by Michael Duffy, *Time* (New York) *23 January 1989*

2   Why would he tell me any secrets when he says I begin every sentence with "Don't tell George* I told you this, but . . ."

Ibid.

3   What happens in your house is more important than what happens in the White House.

Attributed by George Bush,* Cited in "A troubled Bush . . ." by Marianne Means, *Seattle Post-Intelligencer,* A7 *3 August 1992*

*Her husband, G— H. W. Bush (1924–   ), 41st president of the United States (1989–1992).

4   To us, family means putting your arms around each other and being there.

Speech, Republic National Convention (Houston) *19 August 1992*

2515. Rosario Castellanos (1925–1974)

1   Indians are human beings no different from whites. They simply live in very different—and unfavorable—circumstances.

Introduction, Quoted in *Selected Works of Rosario Castellanos* by Myralyn F. Allgood *1990*

2   . . . dáme la muerte que me falta . . . (. . . give me the death I need)

Quoted in Ch. 5, *Women Who Run With the Wolves* by Clarissa Pinkola Estés* *1992*

*See 3567.

2516. Jacqui Michot Ceballos (1925–   )

1   Americans and Vietnamese were dying by the thousands in a long war. Antiwar activists were passionately involved and finding some pretty spectacular ways to protest. But we feminists remained steadfast, and rightly so. From time immemorial feminist activity had stopped when women devoted themselves to a war effort and we weren't about to let that happen now.

Veteran Feminists of America newsletter vfa.us March 2008

2517. Arvonne Fraser (1925–)

1 Politics is serious business. It's the art and science of govern-ing. In a democracy no major party should nominate for vice president a religious zealot who wants to ban books from pub-lic libraries and believes guns solve problems. The idea that she could be a heart beat away from having her finger on the nuclear button sends chills down my spine.
Speech, "Women, Politics and the World" (Baraboo, Wisconsin), *6 September 2008*

2 Rulers don't like the unruly—those who organize to change the rules.
Ibid.

3 We ought to be past the time when we think that some people are born to rule and others to be ruled. The idea that one's honor depends on whether your rule is respected and obeyed is just plain wrong. One's honor, we progressives know, is whether you are a decent citizen, a responsible citizen who cares about others and treats them as one would like to be treated.
Ibid.

4 We're worse than all the other industrialized countries. They all have paid maternity leave, they have a much better system of preschool and daycare. They call that social security.
Quoted in "Arvonne Fraser" by Elizabeth Noll, *Women's Press 12 November 2008*

5 I think when you put something in law you change culture.
Ibid.

2518. Pam Gems (1925–)

1 SUSANNAH. You've never been off the tit. Eleven-plus, schol-arships, research fellowship project grant. You're free—white and male. And you've caved in.
Loving Women 1984

2 All the stories have been told long ago. Your job is retelling. Relighting.
Quoted in "Pam Gems," *Interviews with Contemporary Women Playwrights* by Kathleen Betsko* and Rachel Koenig *1987*
*See 3125.

3 What you have to control, in the writing, is silence. You have to orchestrate that important member of the cast, the audience. Orchestrate, and conduct. One joke too many and they become flatulent, blowzy. One thought too many and they begin to move, restless, oppressed. The audience *must* be working, as hard as the actors. The audience must be alive, must create the play.
Ibid.

4 Art is of necessity. Which is why we need women playwrights just now very badly. We have our own history to create, and to write.
Introduction to *Queen Christina, Plays by Women,* Vol. 8, Mary Remnant, ed. *1990*

2519. Linda Goodman (1925–1970)

1 It seems to be quite a leap from the . . . lost continent of At-lantis to the jet-propelled twentieth century. But how far is it really? Perhaps only a dream or two.
Afterword, *Linda Goodman's Sun Signs 1968*

2 Alone among the sciences, astrology has spanned the centuries and made the journey intact. We shouldn't be surprised that it remains with us, unchanged by time—because astrology is truth—and truth is eternal.
Ibid.

2520. Julie Harris (1925–)

1 I learned faith from Ethel [Waters*]. . . . She was a great wheel to hold on to, an anchor. I always liken her to a phenomenon of nature, a Niagara Falls.
"Veteran actress personifies her characters . . . ," *Seattle Times,* L3 *16 August 1992*
*See 1838.

2 Courage. What is that? It's like faith. But you can't teach it to anybody. Only life teaches you courage.
Ibid.

2521. Eleanor Hoover (1925?–)
Coauthor with Marie Edwards; see 2548.

2522. Huang Zongying (1925–)

1 The woman growing wild herbs* aroused my interest for some unknown reason. Perhaps for her frankness, her composure, or perhaps because she looked as ordinary as any country midwife, who interrupts her pig-feeding and washes her hands before picking up her sterilized instruments.
"The Flight of the Wild Geese," Yu Fanqin and Wang Mingjie, trs., *Seven Contemporary Chinese Women Writers,* Gladys Yang,** ed. *1982*
*Quin Guanshu; see 2679.1. **See 2358.

2 God! In the world of plants, no two leaves have the same pat-tern of veins. But in the world of human beings, people have to be classified and tagged all over the country. But how can these tags express the complications of Chinese society? After all, class origin is not terribly important.
Ibid.

2523. Shirley M. Hufstedler (1925–)

1 I'm bilingual. I speak English and I speak educationese.
Quoted in *Newsweek 12 May 1980*

2524. Barbara "Penny" Kanner (1925–)

1 The institutional techniques of starvation, cold, flogging and fisticuffs were among the chief mechanisms for turning boys into brave, self-reliant, self-governing gentlemen committed to masculine ideals.
Introduction, *Women in English Social History 1800–1914 1990*

2525. Carol Kaye (1925–)
Coauthor with Elizabeth Douvan; see 2545.

2526. Lisa Kirk (1925–1990)

1 A gossip is one who talks to you about others; a bore is one who talks to you about himself; and a brilliant conversational-ist is one who talks to you about yourself.
Quoted in *New York Journal American 9 March 1954*

2527. Carolyn Kizer (1925–)

1 Our masks, always in peril of smearing or cracking,

In need of continuous check in the mirror or
    silverware,
Keep us in thrall to ourselves, concerned with our surfaces.
                                            "Pro Femina," Ibid.

2   Unfortunately we live in a society which cheers at naked self-
    exposure, and cares little if the stripper burns or freezes. But I
    care, as all people who love poetry for itself . . . care.
                                    Proses on Poems and Poets 1994

3   This dreadful century staggers to its close
    And the sky dies for us, its poisoned heirs.
            "On a Line from Valéry (The Gulf War)," St. 5, *Harping On*
                                                            1996

4   Water itself is not enough.
    Harness her turbulence to work
    For man: fill his reflecting pools.
    Drained for his cofferdams, or stored
    In reservoirs for his personal use:
    Turn switches! Let the fountains play!
        "A Muse of Water," St. 7, *Cool, Calm, and Collected: Poems
                                            1960–2000 2001*

5   We will be cows for a while, because babies howl for us,
    Be kittens or bitches, who want to eat grass now and then
    For the sake of our health. But the role of pastoral heroine
    Is not permanent, Jack. We want to get back to the meeting.
                            "Pro Femina," Two, St. 2, Ibid.

2528. Ida Kuklina (1925?–   )

1   There is a great necessity to continue the programmes of
    human rights education and training especially on the regional
    level. There are dangerous tendencies in the development of
    the military law system which demand the constant attention
    of the Committee. . . . These military monsters are continuing
    to kill the sons of Russia through hunger, illness, humiliation.
    The situation when the state takes the young men for compul-
    sory military service in order to defend itself and then makes a
    mess of its own responsibility for their health and lives could
    be called the tragic Russian absurdity.
        Acceptance Speech for Union of Soldiers Mothers Committees
            of Russia (UCSMR), Right Livelihood Awards, *9 December
                                                        1996*

2   Russian society still does not know the real and officially
    acknowledged scales of human losses in this war [with Chech-
    nya].
                                                        Ibid.

2529. Maxine Kumin (1925–   )

1   Now under the ice, under twelve knee-deep layers
    of mud in last summer's pond
    the packed hearts of peepers are beating
    barely, barely repeating
    themselves enough to hang on.
            "January 25th," St. 3, *The Atlantic Monthly,* Vol. 215, No. 1
                                                    January 1965

2   I plucked the memory splinter from your spine
    as we played at being normal, who
    had eased each other in the cold zoo
    of childhood.
        "The Man of Many L's," *Our Ground Time Here Will Be Brief
                                                            1982*

3   Cherish
    your wilderness.
        "You Are in Bear Country," *The Long Approach 1985*

4   Everything pays for growing tame
                            "Sunday in March," Ibid.

5   caring is small
    susceptible fits in a pocket
    not is it one thing to save animals
    and people another
    but seamless
                            "Caring: A Dream," Ibid.

6   Let me put my faith in the bean.
                "Shelling Jacob's Cattle Beans," Ibid.

7   I'm going home the old way with a light hand on the reins
    making the long approach.
                        "The Long Approach," Ibid.

8   three smacks for failing in long division,
    one more to instill the meaning of humble.
    As the twig is bent, said your harridan nuns.
        "The Nuns of Childhood: Two Views," 1., St. 2, *The Atlantic
                            Monthly,* Vol. 269, No. 2 *February 1992*

9   In the most direct, overt, and uncomplicated way, my writing
    depends on the well-being that develops from . . . chores un-
    dertaken and completed.
        "Menial Labor and the Muse," *Women, Animals, and
                                            Vegetables 1994*

10 . . . the vixen in the bottom meadow
    I ride across allows me under cover
    of horse scent to observe the education
    of her kits, how they dive for the burrow
    on command, how they re-emerge at another
    word she uses, a word I am searching for.
        "The Word," St. 5, *The Atlantic Monthly,* Vol. 273, No. 3
                                                    March 1994

11 The animals talk in reasonable tones that children
    can understand
            "In once a time," *Connecting the Dots: Poems 1996*

2530. Angela Lansbury (1925–   )

1   The greatest success stories are those who defied the tendency
    to just run with the crowd.
                Quoted in *Wise Women* by Joyce Tenneson* 2002
        *See 3619.

2531. Melina Mercouri (1925–1994)

1   When you are born and they tell you "what a pity that you are
    so clever, so intelligent, so beautiful but you are not a man,"
    you are ashamed of your condition as a woman. I wanted to
    act like a man because the man was the master.
            Quoted in "Greece: Survival of the Shrewdest" by Susan
                        Margolis, *Ms.* (New York) *October 1973*

2532. Geraldine "Jerrie" Mock (1925–   )

1   If I don't get out of this house, I'll go nuts.*
            "Shades of Amelia," *Newsweek* (New York) *30 March 1964*
        *The remark that purportedly launched her career as an aviator.

2 The tiny plane* raced down the runway and . . . leaped into the air, eager to explore the world.

Three-Eight Charlie 1970

*Her Cessna 180, officially dubbed the Spirit of Columbus.

3 [I] felt like a queen. . . . My subjects, the foamy clouds and glowing rainbows, put on a command performance just for me. It was worth all the hard work, worry, and sleepless nights. . . . After Christopher Columbus* discovered America, he became the Admiral of the Ocean Seas. In my red-and-white *Spirit of Columbus,* . . . . I became Queen of the Ocean Skies.

Ibid.

*Christopher Columbus (1451–1506), Italian navigator and explorer who, in 1492, opened the path from the Old World to the New.

2533. Tharon Musser (1925–   )

1 It's the lighting of moving sculpture. . . . Dance is heaven to light . . .

Quoted in "The Facts of Light" by Arnold Aronson, *American Theatre* (New York) *January 1986*

2 All design in theatre is a supportive art. It's there to help, to underline, to emphasize.

Ibid.

2534. Flannery O'Connor (1925–1964)

1 . . . the help was morally superior to all the guests.

Letter (of the Yaddo Artist Colony) *ca. 1948*

2 "I'm going to preach there was no Fall because there was nothing to fall from and no Redemption because there was no Fall and no Judgement because there wasn't the first two. Nothing matters but that Jesus was a liar."

Ch. 6, *Wise Blood* 1949

3 I preach there are all kinds of truth, your truth and somebody else's. But behind all of them there is only one truth and that is that there's no truth.

Ch. 10, Ibid.

4 Living had got to be such a habit with him that he couldn't conceive of any other condition.

"A Late Encounter with the Enemy," *A Good Man Is Hard to Find* 1955

5 "I call myself The Misfit," he said, "because I can't make what all I done wrong fit what all I gone through in punishment."

"A Good Man is Hard to Find," Ibid.

6 "Lady, a man is divided into two parts, body and spirit. . . . A body and a spirit," he repeated. "The body, lady, is like a house it don't go anywhere; but the spirit, lady, is like a automobile: always on the move, always. . . ."

"The Life You Save May Be Your Own," Ibid.

7 He had stuffed his own emptiness with good work like a glutton.

"The Lame Shall Enter First," *Everything That Rises Must Converge* 1965

8 Once or twice I have been asked what the peacock is "good for"—a question which gets no answer from me because it deserves none.

"Peacocks Are a Puzzle," *Mystery and Manners* 1969

9 While the South is hardly Christ-centered, it is most certainly Christ-haunted.

Address, "Some Aspects of the Grotesque in Southern Fiction," Wesleyan College for Women (Macon, Ga., Fall 1960), Ibid.

10 Being a Georgia author is a rather specious dignity, on the same order as, for the pig, being a Talmadge ham.

"The Regional Writer" (*Esprit*, Winter 1963), Ibid.

11 Faith is what you have in the absence of knowledge.

Letter to Alfred Corn (30 May 1962), *The Habit of Being* 1978

12 One of the effects of modern liberal Protestantism has been gradually to turn religion into poetry and therapy, to make truth vaguer and vaguer and more and more relative, to banish intellectual distinctions, to depend on feeling instead of thought, and gradually to come to believe that God has no power, that he cannot communicate with us, cannot reveal himself to us, indeed has not done so, and that religion is our own sweet invention.

Letter to Alfred Corn (16 June 1962), Ibid.

13 I find it reasonable to believe, even though these beliefs are beyond reason.

Ibid.

2535. Ru Zhijuan (1925–   )

1 The desolate grassland stretched out as if to the end of the world. On a piece of uncultivated land as vast as this, one could have made straight for anywhere . . .

"The Path Through the Grassland," Yu Fanqin, tr., *Seven Contemporary Chinese Women Writers*, Gladys Yang,* ed. 1982
*See 2358.

2 The hardest thing for a person to bear is not a dressing-down or a beating, but loneliness, ostracism.

Ibid.

3 Love needed a full stomach, but the two were quite different things.

Ibid.

2536. Naomi Streshinsky (1925–   )

1 The danger of a gift is an intriguing concept. Primitive man may have believed that the gift contained the spirit of the donor and therein lay its potential harm. The belief in the donor's spirit dissolved for modern man but the danger is still very much present.

Ch. 2, *Welfare Rights Organizations* 1970

2 Political acceptability of social welfare can be translated to mean what the general public will permit to be granted, out of its tax money to poor people, just because they are in need and with no strings attached. Attitudes of hostility toward and derogation of the assisted poor puts serious obstacles in the way of future programs and are precisely the ones which contribute to the present bind.

Ch. 6, Ibid.

2537. Margaret Thatcher (1925–   )

1 No woman in my time will be Prime Minister or Chancellor or Foreign Secretary—not the top jobs. Anyway I wouldn't want to be Prime Minister. You have to give yourself 100%.*

Interview in *Sunday Telegraph* (London) *26 October 1969*
*Ten years later she became England's first female prime minister; prior to that, she served in a cabinet post.

2 One of the things being in politics has taught me is that men are not a reasoned or reasonable sex.

> BBC interview *14 January 1972*

3 I owe nothing to Women's Lib.

> Remark (1982), Quoted in *Observer* (London) *1 December 1974*

4 In politics, if you want anything said, ask a man. If you want anything done, ask a woman.

> Quoted in *People 15 September 1975*

5 I am extraordinarily patient provided I get my own way in the end.

> Quoted in *Observer* (London) *2 January 1983*

6 It was then that the iron entered my soul.*

> Remark (1982), Quoted in *Observer* (London) *27 March 1983*
> *Reference to her nickname, "The Iron Lady," of her time in Edward Heath's cabinet (1970–74); Thatcher and Heath became political antagonists.

7 I always cheer up immensely if an attack is particularly wounding because I think, well, if they attack one personally, it means they have not a single political argument left.

> Quoted in *The Daily Telegraph* (London) *1986*

8 People think that at the top there isn't much room. They tend to think of it as an Everest. My message is that there is tons of room at the top.

> Interview in *The Daily Telegraph* (London) *30 September 1988*

9 You will only achieve higher growth, only release enterprise, only spur people to greater effort, only obtain their full-hearted commitment to reform, when people have the dignity and enjoyment of personal and political liberty, when they have the freedom of expression, freedom of association and the right to form free and independent trade unions.

> Remark to Gen. Wojciech Jaruzelski,* state banquet (Warsaw) *3 November 1988*
> *Polish military and political leader (1923–   ); premier (1982–1985), president (1985–1990).

10 To me, consensus seems to be the process of abandoning all beliefs, principles, values and policies. So it is something in which no one believes and to which no one objects.

> Pt. 4, Ch. 23, Quoted in *The Time of My Life* by Denis Healey *1989*

11 The cocks may crow, but it's the hen that lays the egg.

> Interview in *Sunday Times* (London) *9 April 1989*

12 Battles in life are never won. I mean, you don't have your household budget permanently balanced; you have to balance it every year. Life's a continuous business, and so is success, and requires continuous effort.

> Quoted in interview (London), *The New York Times 28 September 1989*

13 Unless we change our ways and our direction, our greatness as a nation will soon be a footnote in the history books, a distant memory of an offshore island, lost in the mists of time like Camelot, remembered kindly for its noble past.

> Campaign Speech, Quoted in *Twentieth-Century Women Political Leaders* by Claire Price-Groff *1998*

2538. Dottie Walters (1925–2007)

1 Speaking—speaking *well*—is like a great dance involving your audiences, your customers and the great minds of all the ages.

> Ch. 1, *Speak and Grow Rich*, and Lilly Walters* *1997*

2 Goals are dreams with deadlines.

> Ch. 12, Ibid.

> *See 4394.

2539. Mai Zetterling (1925–1994)

1 Women are on the whole more sensual than sexual, men are more sexual than sensual.

> *Times* (London) *17 May 1989*

2540. Shana Alexander (1926–2005)

1 Faithful horoscope-watching, practiced daily, provides just the sort of small but warm and infinitely reassuring fillip that gets matters off to a spirited start.

> "A Delicious Appeal to Unreason" (May 1966), in *The Feminine Eye* 1970

2 The sad truth is that excellence makes people nervous.

> "Neglected Kids—the Bright Ones" (June 1966), Ibid.

3 Roughly speaking, the President of the United States knows what his job is. Constitution and custom spell it out, for him as well as for us. His wife has no such luck. The First Lady has no rules; rather each new woman must make her own.

> "The Best First Lady" (December 1968), Ibid.

4 . . . when two people marry they become in the eyes of the law one person, and that one person is the husband!

> Introduction, *State-by-State Guide to Women's Legal Rights* 1975

5 The law changes and flows like water, and . . . the stream of women's rights law has become a sudden rushing torrent.

> Ibid.

2541. Ingeborg Bachmann (1926–1973)

1 For the facts that make up the world need the non-factual as a vantage point from which to be perceived.

> *Der Fall Franza* (The Franza Case), Jan van Heurck, tr. *n.d.*

2 He has taken my possessions from me. My laughter, my tenderness, my ability to feel joy, my compassion, my ability to help, my animality, my radiance; he has stamped out every sprout of all these things, until they stopped sprouting. But why does someone do that, I don't understand.

> Ibid.

3 your heart has business elsewhere
your mouth is annexing new languages.

> "Explain to Me, Love," St. 1, Jan van Heurck, tr. *n.d.*

2542. Gina Berriault (1926–   )

1 "I try to imagine them when they were girls, but I can't," she told the head nurse, Nancy and the nurse, already verging into that same anonymity of aging, turned her head for Angela to see her deliberately uncomprehending face. "Why would you ever think to do that anyway?"

> "Women in Their Beds" (p. 7), *Women in Their Beds 1996*

2 Just remember the beds where you wished you weren't and the bed where you wished you were, and then name any spot on this earth that's a bed for some woman at this very hour. A bed of stones and a bed of earth trampled by soldiers and a bed of ashes, and where you're lying now, where you never wanted to imagine yourselves. If I'd wished for a bed of roses and feathers, and *I did, I did,* now I don't want it so much anymore.

(p. 15), Ibid.

3 "Don't get scared, but in this box is all that remains of Clara Ruchenski. . . . she's in the palm of my hand," he said. "That's why I kept this. She's harmless. She's nothing. If I took the ashes between my fingers, it would powder off into air. But I'm alive, God damn it, and that means something."

"Around the Dear Ruin" (p. 221), Ibid.

2543. Antonia Brenner (1926–)

1 The Lord was a prisoner, just as you are a prisoner. You have something in common.

Comment to a prisoner, Quoted in "She Brings Hope to Prisoners" by Arnie Weissman, *Parade Magazine 19 January 1986*

2 I lived what most people call the good life. I was happy, but deep inside I always felt that, with the short amount of time we are given to live and love in this world, we spend too much time loving things instead of people.

Ibid.

3 To give help is easy. To ask for it is hard.

"'Prison angel' shuns luxury for jail" by Elliot Spagat, Associated Press *27 December 2005*

2544. Toni Carabillo (1926–1997)

1 But powerlessness is still each woman's most critical problem, whether or not she is a social activist. It is at the root of most of her psychological disorders.

Address, "Power Is the Name of the Game," California NOW* State Conference (San Diego) *28 October 1973*

2 . . . we have learned from the experience of the first feminist movement that to stop short of the basic reordering of society, as it is reflected in sex role stereotypes, is too small a victory.

Address, "Womanpower and the Media," National Association of Broadcasters *1974*

3 Rock music consistently degrades women and makes it clear her place in this man's world is limited to the kitchen and the bedroom. Rock music has been rightly characterized, in our view, as a "frenzied celebration of masculine supremacy."

Ibid.

4 We know that poverty in this country is primarily the problem of *all* women—that most women are only a husband away from welfare.

Address, "Sharing the Power, the Glory—And the Pain," NOW* Western Regional Conference (Long Beach, California) *24 November 1974*

5 Not only the CIA, but the FBI,** as well as many state and community police departments, have devoted vast resources to monitoring the activities of concerned citizens working in concert to make social changes within our system. The "flatfoot mentality" insists that any individual or organization that wants to change *anything* in our present system is somehow subversive of "the American way," and should be under con-

tinuous surveillance—a task that appears to absorb most of our resources for fighting genuine crime.

"The Flatfoot Mentality," Hollywood NOW* News *August 1975*

*National Organization for Women. **Central Intelligence Agency and the Federal Bureau of Investigation.

2545. Elizabeth Douvan (1926–2002)

1 The dream of college apparently serves as a substitute for more direct preoccupation with marriage: girls who do not plan to go to college are more explicit in their desire to marry, and have a more developed sense of their own sex role.

"Motivational Factors in College Entrance," *The American College,* with Carol Kaye* *1987*

*See 2525.

2546. Rosalyn Drexler (1926–)

1 [My characters] have all been invented only in order to rush madly around, armed to the teeth with language and also with the capacity to be quick-change artists, con men and false prophets, wolves in sheep's clothing and the reverse, so that they might do nothing else than establish an atmosphere of freedom . . . they make up new worlds of farce whose highly serious intention, as in all true examples of the genre, is to liberate us from the way things are said to be.

Quoted in *The Line of Least Existence and Other Plays,* Richard Gilman, ed. *1967*

2 WOMAN. You want it because it's mine. . . . And you think that I belong to you too, and that's why you want me. You want me and my art reproduction. you want my art reproduction and my entire reproduction system. You hate both my systems. The HOW TO LIE FOREVER System and the HOW TO LIVE HARMONIOUSLY AS A WOMAN system.

Skywriting 1968

3 "I'm just a dog. Look, no opposable thumb."

The Cosmopolitan Girl 1975

4 He visited the Museum of Modern Art, and was standing near the pool looking at his dark reflection when a curator of the museum noticed him. "My, my, what a fine work of art that is!" the curator said to himself. "I must have it installed immediately."

Ibid.

5 As Hemingway* once said, or was thought to have said, [to write well] one must have a built-in shit detector. But to have that, one must have smelled shit at least a few times.

Quoted in "Rosalyn Drexler," *Interviews with Contemporary Women Playwrights* by Kathleen Betsko** and Rachel Koenig *1987*

*Ernest H—, American writer (1899–1961). **See 3125.

6 Pornography is not a safety valve, it is a writ of permission. . . .

Ibid.

2547. Betty Edwards (1926–)

1 The key to learning to draw, therefore, is to set up conditions that cause you to make a mental shift to a different mode of information processing—the slightly altered state of consciousness—that enables you to see well. In this drawing mode you will be able to draw your perceptions even though you may never have studied drawing. Once the drawing mode is famil-

iar to you, you will be able to consciously control the mental shift.

Drawing on the Right Side of the Brain 1979

2   Training in perception has the same function as teaching people to read and write—that is, it reins those skills so they are honed up and useable at a conscious level, and useful for things other than just looking around, just as language skills are trained up through reading and writing, in ways that one doesn't achieve just talking.

Quoted in "Betty Edwards: Teaching the Tricks of Perception" by John Crutcher, *Common Ground of Puget Sound Fall 1989*

3   Computers can do all the left hemisphere processing better and faster than the human brain. So what's left for the human brain is global thinking, creative thinking, intuitive-problem solving, seeing the whole picture. All of that cannot be done by the computer. And yet the school system goes on, churning out reading, writing, and arithmetic, spelling, grammar.

Ibid.

2548. Marie Edwards (1926?–   )

1   Books, magazines, counselors, therapists sell one message to unmarrieds: "Shape up, go where other singles are, entertain more, raise your sex quotient, get involved, get closer, be more open, more honest, more intimate, above all, find Mr. Right or Miss Wonderful and *get married.*"

The Challenge of Being Single, with Eleanor Hoover* 1975
*See 2521.

2549. Queen Elizabeth II of Great Britain (1926–   )

1   My whole life, whether it be long or short, shall be devoted to your [the public's] service and the service of our great imperial family to which we all belong. But I shall not have the strength to carry out this resolution alone unless you join in it with me.

Radio Broadcast *21 April 1947*

2   Like all the best families, we have our share of eccentricities, of impetuous and wayward youngsters and of family disagreements.

Quoted in *Daily Mail* (London) *19 October 1989*

2550. Betty Skelton Erde (1926–   )

1   To me, there's hardly any feeling in the world that can equal the feeling of an airplane when the wheels leave the ground.

"What a ride: Woman, 82, inducted into Hall of Fame," *The New York Times 13 August 2008*

2   I wanted very much to fly in the Navy. But all they would do is laugh when I asked.

Ibid.

3   It's been quite a ride.

Ibid.

2551. Sissy Farenthold (1926–   )

1   I am working for the time when unqualified blacks, browns and women join the unqualified men in running our government.

Quoted in *The Los Angeles Times 18 September 1974*

2   There is no question that under the Equal Rights Amendment there will be debates at times, indecision at times, litigation at times. Has anyone proposed that we rescind the First Amendment on free speech because there is too much litigation over it? Has anyone suggested the same for the Fourteenth Amendment (I don't suppose there has ever been a constitutional amendment with so much litigation)?

Speech for International Women's Year, "Legal Rights," Vermont College *26 February 1977*

3   You change laws by changing lawmakers.

Quoted in "Interview with Sissy Farenthold" by Dave Anast, *The Bakersfield Californian 22 April 1978*

2552. Carolyn G. Heilbrun (1926–2003)

1   In former days, everyone found the assumption of innocence so easy; today we find fatally easy the assumption of guilt.

Quoted in *Poetic Justice* by Amanda Cross* 1970
*Her pseudonym.

2   Ideas move fast when their time comes.

Toward a Recognition of Androgyny 1973

3   What is important now is that we free ourselves from the prison of gender and, before it is too late, deliver the world from the almost exclusive control of the masculine impulse.

Introduction, Ibid.

4   Androgyny suggests a spirit of reconciliation between the sexes; it suggests, further, a full range of experience open to individuals who may as women be aggressive, as men, tender; it suggests a spectrum upon which human beings choose their places without regard to propriety or to custom.

Ibid.

5   Great periods of civilization, however much they may have owed their beginning to the aggressive dominance of the male principle, have always been marked by some sort of rise in the status of women. This in its turn is a manifestation of something more profound: the recognition of the importance of the "feminine" principle, not as other, but as necessary to wholeness.

Pt. I, Ibid.

6   Today's shocks are tomorrow's conventions.

Pt. II, Ibid.

7   From the critics of the past I have learned the futility of concerning oneself with the present.

Afterword, Ibid.

8   The genuine solitaries of life fear intimacy more than loneliness. The married are those who have taken the terrible risk of intimacy and, having taken it, know life without intimacy to be impossible.

"Marriage Is the Message," *Ms. August 1974*

9   Women must continue to invade the domains of power in order to change institutions as we know them, in order to offer places to other women . . . and to do justice to themselves.

Reinventing Womanhood 1979

10 In life, as in fiction, women who speak out usually end up punished or dead. I'm lucky to escape with my pension and a year of leave [from Columbia University].

Quoted in "Who Stole Feminism? How Women Have Betrayed Women," by Christina Hoff Sommers,* *The New York Times 1994*

*See 4007.

11 ... catch courage ...

The Last Gift of Time: Life Beyond Sixty 1997

12 To be alone if one has not been doomed to aloneness is a temptation so beguiling that it carries with it the guilt of adultery, and the promise of consummation.

"The Small House," Ibid.

13 If each day is a loan from eternity, one spends it with the joy known to gamblers betting everything on a last roll of the dice. The payoff is intensity.

Interview, *The Women's Review of Books* [Wellesley MA] *July 2003*

14 I have always believed that, over 70, one should be as free to choose one's death as one must, earlier, be free to choose whether or not to give birth.

Ibid.

2553. Aileen Clarke Hernandez (1926–)

1 My comments to the thousands of persons at the peace march [the 1971 Another Mother for Peace march in Los Angeles] were directed not just against the Vietnam War, but against *all* war, against the masculine mystique which glorifies violence as a solution to problems, and against the vast diverting of American energies and resources from socially needed programs into social destructive wars.

Letter to Eve Norman, Quoted in the NOW* Newsletter *29 April 1971*

2 There are no such things as women's issues! All issues are women's issues. The difference that we bring to existing issues of our society, the issues of war and peace; the issues of poverty; the issues of child care; the issues of political power—the difference that we bring is that we are going to bring the full, loud, clear determined voice of women into deciding how those issues are going to be addressed.

Address, National Conference of NOW* (Los Angeles) *3–6 September 1971*

3 This movement ... is the last stage of the drive for equality for women. We are determined that our daughters and granddaughters will live as free human beings, secure in their personhood, and dedicated to making this nation and the world a humane place in which to live.

Ibid.

*National Organization for Women.

2554. Elizabeth Jennings (1926–2001)

1 At last now you can be
What the old cannot recall
And the young long for in dreams,
Yet still include them all.

"Accepted," *Growing Pains* 1975

2 Do they know they're old,
These two who are my father and my mother
Whose fire from which I came, has now grown cold?

"One Flesh" *n.d.*

2555. Natasha Josefowitz (1926–)

1 Speaking is the most visible of the four uncommon skills. You may not be well read, you may not know how to count, you may write poorly, but as soon as you open your mouth people

get an impression of you based on both the content of your message and one the way you deliver it.

Ch. 4, *Paths to Power* 1980

2556. Sue Kaufman (1926–)

1 I was afraid that if I opened my mouth, like Gerald McBoing-Boing, terrible inhuman sounds would come out—brakes screeching, metal clashing, tires skidding, trains roaring past in the night.

"Saturday, October 7," *Diary of a Mad Housewife* 1967

2 "Make yourself a nice hot toddy, and while you sip it, read Proust.* Proust is the only thing when you're sick." ... I skipped the hot toddy, but by God it worked. Saved me. Was the antibiotic which wouldn't "touch" the Thing I had. Marvelous crazy poet. Marvelous Proust.

"Friday, November 17," Ibid.

*Marcel Proust, French writer (1871–1922)

3 Burt told her that he loved her, she told him that she loved him. She thought she didn't mean it. She thought she was being very advanced, very pre-liberated, shattering the damned double standard and lying while she did it, if that's what was required.

Falling Bodies 1974

4 Ever since she had gotten out of the hospital, her eyes kept seeking out and fastening on the cruel, the ugly, the sordid—trying to turn every nasty little incident or detail into some sort of concrete proof of just how rotten the world had become.

Ibid.

5 "In violent and chaotic times such as these, our only chance for survival lies in creating our own little islands of sanity and order, in making little havens of our homes."

Ibid.

2557. Gertrude Lemp Kerbis (1926–)

1 It was hell for women architects then. They didn't want us in school or in the profession. ... One thing I've never understood about this prejudice is that it's so strange in view of the fact that the drive to build has always been in women.

Quoted in *Women at Work* by Betty Medsger 1975

2558. Jeane Kirkpatrick (1926–2006)

1 Vietnam presumably taught us that the United States could not serve as the world's policeman; it should also have taught us the dangers of trying to be the world's midwife to democracy when the birth is scheduled to take place under conditions of guerrilla war.

"Dictatorship and Double Standards," *Commentary* (New York) *November 1979*

2 Tyranny and anarchy are alike incompatible with freedom, security, and the enjoyment of opportunity.

Speech, Third Committee of United Nations General Assembly *24 November 1981*

3 [Democrats] can't get elected unless things get worse—and things won't get worse unless they get elected.

Quoted in *Time* (New York) *17 June 1985*

4 It is a fact that successive presidents find so many different reasons not to appoint specific women to specific positions in

specific Cabinets. And it is a fact that men always get irritable if they get pressed about this.
> Cited by Solveig Torvik in "Clinton can't please everyone," *Seattle Post-Intelligencer,* Op-Ed, A7 *30 December 1992*

5   We have war when at least one of the parties to a conflict wants something more than it wants peace.
> Quoted in *Reader's Digest 1994*

2559. Mathilde Krim (1926–)

1   Now we [American Foundation for AIDS Research] can have theater benefits, cocktail parties, dinners, and people will come.* They're not as afraid anymore. It's as if, all of a sudden, it's chic to behave decently.
> Quoted in "When No One Dared" by Michael Ryan, *Parade Magazine 5 June 1988*
> *Since actor Elizabeth Taylor (see 2826) became honorary chair.

2   I've never known a virus that discriminates.
> Ibid.

3   There were some friends who didn't want to associate with me after I became identified with AIDS. But then, they weren't friends, were they?
> Ibid.

2560. Elizabeth Kübler–Ross (1926–2004)

1   . . . we have to ask ourselves whether medicine is to remain a humanitarian and respected profession or a new but depersonalized science in the service of prolonging life rather than diminishing human suffering. . . .
> Ch. 2, *On Death and Dying 1969*

2   Guilt is perhaps the most painful companion of death.
> Ch. 9, Ibid.

3   It is difficult to accept death in this society because it is unfamiliar. In spite of the fact that it happens all the time, we never see it.
> Ch. 2, *Death: The Final Stage of Growth 1975*

4   Dying is hard under any circumstances, but dying in the familiar surroundings of one's home, with those you love and who love you, can take away much of the fear.
> Ch. 3, Ibid.

5   Those who have been immersed in the tragedy of massive death during wartime, and who have faced it squarely, never allowing their senses and feelings to become numbed and indifferent, have emerged from their experiences with growth and humanness greater than that achieved through almost any other means.
> Ch. 5, Ibid.

6   It is not the end of the physical body that should worry us. Rather, our concern must be to *live* while we're alive—to release our inner selves from the spiritual death that comes with living behind a façade designed to conform to external definitions of who and what we are.
> "Omega," Ibid.

7   Death is the final stage of growth in this life. There is no total death. Only the body dies. The self or spirit, or whatever you may wish to label it, is eternal.
> Ibid.

8   Learn to get in touch with silence within yourself and know that everything in this life has a purpose. There are no mistakes, no coincidences; all events are blessings given to us to learn from. There is no need to go to India or anywhere else to find peace. You will find that deep place of silence right in your room, your garden or even your bathtub.
> Speech (1976), Quoted in "Elizabeth Kübler-Ross" by Lennie Kronisch, *Yoga Journal November/December 1976*

2561. Margaret Laurence (1926–1987)

1   Privacy is a privilege not granted to the aged or the young.
> Ch. 1, *The Stone Angel 1964*

2   Even if heaven were real, and measured as Revelation says, so many cubits this way and that, how gimcrack a place it would be, crammed with its pavements of gold, its gates of pearl and topaz, like a gigantic chunk of costume jewelry.
> Ch. 4, Ibid.

3   "The prime purpose of a funeral director is not all this beautician deal which some members of the profession go in for so much. No. It's this—to take over. Reassure people."
> Ch. 7, *A Jest of God* (a.k.a. *Rachel, Rachel*) 1966

4   "Death's unmentionable?"
> "Not exactly unmentionable, but let's face it, most of us could get along without it."
> "I don't see how."
> Ibid.

5   How strange to have to keep on retreating to the only existing privacy, the only place one is permitted to be unquestionably alone, the lavatory.
> Ch. 9, Ibid.

6   I was always afraid that I might become a fool. Yet I could almost smile with some grotesque light-headedness at that fool of a fear, that poor fear of fools, now that I really am one.
> Ch. 10, Ibid.

7   "You are out of danger," he said. I laughed, I guess, and said, "How can I be—I don't feel dead yet."
> Ch. 11, Ibid.

2562. Cloris Leachman (1926–)

1   Why can't we build orphanages next to homes for the elderly? If someone's sitting in a rocker, it won't be long before a kid will be in his lap.
> Quoted in "I Love My Career and I Love My Children . . ." by Jane Wilkie, *Good Housekeeping October 1973*

2563. Harper Lee (1926–)

1   The day was twenty-four hours long but seemed longer. There was no hurry, for there was nowhere to go, nothing to buy and no money to buy it with, nothing to see outside the boundaries of Maycomb County. But it was a time of vague optimism for some of the people: Maycomb County had recently been told that it had nothing to fear but fear itself.
> Ch. 1, *To Kill a Mockingbird 1960*

2   Until I feared I would lose it, I never loved to read. One does not love breathing.
> Ch. 2, Ibid.

3 "The one thing that doesn't abide by majority rule is a person's conscience."

> Ch. 11, Ibid.

4 "Folks don't like to have somebody around knowin' more than they do. It aggravates 'em. You're not gonna change any of them by talkin' right, they've got to want to learn themselves, and when they don't want to learn there's nothing you can do but keep your mouth shut or talk their language."

> Ch. 12, Ibid.

5 Never, never, never, on cross-examination ask a witness a question you don't already know the answer to, was a tenet I absorbed with my baby-food. Do it, and you'll often get an answer you don't want, an answer that might wreck your case.

> Ch. 17, Ibid.

6 "Our courts have their faults, as does any human institution, but in this country our courts are the great levelers, and in our courts all men are created equal. I'm no idealist to believe firmly in the integrity of our courts and in the jury system—that is no ideal to me, it is a living, working reality. Gentlemen, a court is no better than each man of you sitting before me on this jury. A court is only as sound as its jury, and a jury is only as sound as the men who make it up."

> Ch. 20, Ibid.

7 "As you grow older, you'll see white men cheat black men every day of your life, but let me tell you something and don't you forget it—whenever a white man does that to a black man, no matter who he is, how rich he is, or how fine a family he comes from, that white man is trash."

> Ch. 23, Ibid.

2564. Carolyn Leigh (1926–1983)

1 I've got your number,
I know you inside out,
You ain't no Eagle Scout,
You're all at sea.

> "I've Got Your Number," Little Me 1962

2 When you arouse the need in me
My heart says yes, indeed, to me
Proceed with what you're leading me to

> "Witchcraft" n.d.

3 Out of the tree of life
I done picked me a plum

> "The Best is Yet to Come" n.d.

4 It's hard, you will find
To be narrow of mind
If you're young at heart

> "Young at Heart" n.d.

2565. Pat Loud (1926–)

1 College for women was a refinement whose main purpose was to better prepare you for your ultimate destiny . . . to make you a more desirable product.

> Pat Loud: A Woman's Story, with Nora Johnson 1974

2 A miserable marriage can wobble along for years until something comes along and pushes one of the people over the brink. It's usually another man or woman. For me, it was a whole production staff and camera crew.

> Ibid.

2566. Alison Lurie (1926–)

1 "You see, actually, Roger, the very second a plant is cut from its roots, or pulled out of the ground, it starts to die and lose its nutritive values. That's why I've got started growing my own [vegetables], as much as I've got room for, and so's Elsie."

> Ch. 16, Imaginary Friends 1967

2 Then last year, when Jeffrey turned fourteen and Matilda twelve, they had begun to change; to grow rude, coarse, selfish, insolent, nasty, brutish, and tall. It was as if she were keeping a boarding house in a bad dream, and the children she had loved were turning into awful lodgers—lodgers who paid no rent, whose leases could not be terminated.

> Ch. 1, The War Between the Tates 1974

3 Without sex and death humans may become as angels.

> Don't Tell the Grown-Ups 1990

4 [The world is] going to hell in a nonbiodegradable plastic handbasket.

> The Last Resort 1998

5 "Nature can seem cruel, but she balances her books."

> Ibid.

6 "You don't have to be intellectually brilliant to be a famous American poet. It's a handicap, sometimes. Innocent egotism, good looks, romantic sensibility, a thrilling speaking voice, and a nice little lyric gift, that's what makes it with the reviewers and the public."

> Ibid.

2567. Joyce McDougall (1926–)

1 From the time she left the farm, Mater began to perform on the psychosomatic stage. For the rest of her long life, she suffered from angina pectoris and for some 30 years her death was considered imminent.

> Ch. 1, Theaters of the Body: A Psychoanalytic Approach to Psychosomatic Illness 1989

2 All of us use action instead of reflection when our usual defences against mental pain are overthrown. Instead of becoming aware that we are guilty, anxious, or angry, we might overeat, overdrink, have a car accident or a quarrel with our neighbor or our life-partner or, weather permitting, fall victim to the flu!

> Ibid.

3 Whether we will it or not, our inner characters are constantly seeking a stage on which to play out their tragedies and comedies. Although we rarely assume responsibility for our secret theater productions, the producer is seated in our own minds. Moreover, it is this inner world with its repeating repertory that determines most of what happens to us in the external world.

> Prologues, Theaters of the Mind: Illusion and Truth on the Psychoanalytic Stage 1991

2568. Marilyn Monroe (1926–1962)

1 I've been on a calender, but never on time.

> Quoted in Look (New York) 16 January 1962

2 A career is born in public—talent in privacy.

> Quoted in "Marilyn: The Woman Who Died Too Soon" by Gloria Steinem,*The First Ms. Reader, Francine Klagsbrun, ed. 1972

*See 2916.

3 I have too many fantasies to be a housewife.... I guess I *am* a fantasy.

Ibid.

4 I am always running into peoples' unconscious.

Quoted in *Marilyn* by Norman Mailer* 1973

*American writer (1923–).

5 Hollywood's a place where they'll pay you a thousand dollars for a kiss, and fifty cents for your soul. I know, because I turned down the first offer often enough and held out for the fifty cents.

"Acting," *Marilyn Monroe In Her Own Words 1990*

6 I want to grow old without face lifts. They take the life out of a face, the character. I want to have the courage to be loyal to the face I've made. Sometimes, I think it would be easier to avoid old age, to die young, but you'd never complete your life, would you? You'd never wholly know yourself.

Interview *n.d.*

2569. Jan Morris (1926–)

1 To me gender is not physical at all, but is altogether insubstantial. It is soul, perhaps, it is talent, it is taste, it is environment, it is how one feels, it is light and shade, it is inner music....

Ch. 3, *Conundrum 1974*

2 I had reached the conclusion myself that sex was not a division but a continuum, that almost nobody was altogether of one sex or another, and that the infinite subtlety of the shading from one extreme to the other was one of the most beautiful of nature's phenomena. Sex was like a biological pointer, but the gauge upon which it flickered was that very different device, gender.

Ch. 5, Ibid.

3 Englishmen . . . found the [sexual] ambiguity in itself beguiling . . . Frenchmen were curious, and tended to engage me in inquisitive conversation. . . . Italians, frankly unable to conceive the meaning of such a phenomenon, simply stared boorishly, or nudged each other in piazzas. Greeks were vastly entertained. Arabs asked me to go for walks with them. Scots looked shocked. Germans looked worried. Japanese did not notice.

Ch. 12, Ibid.

4 We are told that the social gap between the sexes is narrowing, but I can only report that having, in the second half of the twentieth century, experienced life in both roles, there seems to me no aspect of existence, no moment of the day, no contact, no arrangement, no response, which is not different for men and for women.

Ch. 17, Ibid.

5 Why, the garbage thrown away in this city every day—every *day*—would feed the whole of Europe for a week.

Manhattan '45 1987

6 ". . . a bum who ain't drunk by midnight ain't trying."

Ibid.

7 It takes guts to be a martyr, to have arrows stuck all over you or be pulled apart on racks: but it perhaps takes true holiness to be laughed at by louts for your convictions.

Fifty Years of Europe: An Album 1997

2570. Patricia Neal (1926–)

1 It's very important not to pamper or indulge them [brain-injured or handicapped children] or to treat them differently from the other children in the family. But this is very difficult . . .

Quoted in "Triumph Over Tragedy" by Patricia Baum, *Parents' Magazine November 1975*

2 Tennessee hillbillies don't conk out that easily.

Ibid.

3 In mid-life the man wants to see how irresistible he still is to younger women. How they turn their hearts to stone and more or less commit a murder of their marriage I just don't know, but they do.

Quoted in *The Daily Telegraph* (London) *22 June 1988*

2571. Mary Mamie O'Brien (1926–1998)

1 . . . we have a substantial intellectual movement, bearing the name if not always the perception of Marx, based on the necessity of subsistence. We have another body of thought, exemplified by the followers of Freud, resting upon the imperatives of human sexuality. We have a further body of thought, existentialism, resolutely anticipating the absurd necessity of death. We have no philosophy of birth.

The Politics of Reproduction 1981

2 Man Alone is a subject which has long preoccupied Western thought; woman alone is a welfare problem.

Cited in obituary, *New Directions for Women*, Vol. XVI, No. 4, p. 4 *January 1999*

2572. Charlotte Painter (1926–)

1 If a thing is absolutely true, how can it not also be a lie? An absolute must contain its opposite.

Confession from the Malaga Madhouse 1971

2 The passion for destruction, glorious destruction. Must we seek grace in violence, more than any other way?

Ibid.

3 . . . as awareness increases, the need for personal secrecy almost proportionately decreases.

Afterword, *Revelations: Diaries of Women*, with Mary Jane Moffat* 1974

*See 2859.

4 *Why, why, why?*—the question of adolescence. My experience in life had not brought me wisdom, but at least I know that *how* was a more appropriate question for maturity. How to live the rest of it in the right way, how to die.

Ch. 1, *Conjuring Tibet 1996*

5 The sanity of the Buddha's philosophy drew me, but my suspicion of the participation mystique has kept me away from the consolations of all religion.

Ibid.

2573. Teri Perl (1926–)

1 The general feeling is that girls are discouraged from pursuing tech careers and are treated differently. It's really an equity issue, offering girls the same opportunity to be a part of where society is going.

"Tech revolutionary pushes equality" by Cliff Edwards, *Associated Press 14 March 2000*

2574. R. Rajalakshmi (1926–)

1 . . . my capacity for insight and intuition . . . made [me] think of common-sense solutions to seemingly complex problems.
Quoted in Twentieth-Century Women Scientists by Lisa Yount 1996

2 It is time we realized that ultimately the future of this planet earth and the beings it houses depends on the promotion of the welfare of all.
Speech (1982), Ibid.

2575. Gerlind Reinshagen (1926–)

1 The discrepancy between imagination and reality, the persistent pursuit of the inner image, and the failure of the original concept—for all this I would like to find a form.
Interview by Anke Roeder, The Divided Home/Land: Contemporary German Women's Plays, Sue-Ellen Case,* ed. 1992

*See 3328.

3 Drama is only a revolt if it moves away from this [true to life] reality, if it forces people to think differently. I don't want to repeat the pragmatic way of life on stage.
Ibid.

2576. Rachel Rosenthal (1926–)

1 I look at performing as transcendental lovemaking. I put everything in it—I put who I am in it, all my passion, all my vulnerability, all my intelligence. When I come on stage and I feel the energy of the audience, all my fears disappear and the performance becomes a ritual of communion. In that way, it is extremely nourishing.
Quoted in "Rachel Rosenthal," Exposures, Women & Their Art by Ann Brown & Arlene Raven* 1989

*See 3533.

2577. Cynthia Propper Seton (1926–1982)

1 To Angela her grandmother was old but had not grown older and was never younger. This is a usual way with grandmothers.
Ch. 1, The Sea Change of Angela Lewes 1971

2 Well, banality is a terribly likely consequence of the underuse of a good mind. That is why in particular it is a female affliction.
Ch. 9, Ibid.

3 "Holding hands is a very intimate thing to do," she found herself whispering. "Even to hold a child's hand. It's very touch- ing."
Ch. 25, Ibid.

4 To pursue yourself is an interesting and absorbing thing to do. Once you have caught the scent of a hidden being, your own hidden being, you won't readily be deflected from the tracking down of it.
Ibid.

5 She had trouble defining herself independently of her husband, tried to talk to him about it, but he said nonsense, he had no trouble defining her at all.
The Half-Sisters 1974

2578. Alice Shalvi (1926–)

We are killing our youngsters physically, metaphorically, morally. We are killing our own future.
Ch. 16, Meeting, The Dialogue Project, Spring 1988 (New York), Quoted in Deborah, Golda, and Me by Letty Cottin Pogrebin* 1991

*See 3154.

2 We've got to talk to the Palestinians because they're there. We have to recognize their existence. They are our partners in dialogue . . .
Ibid.

3 Until we really manage to break away from all the traditional concepts of what functions belong to the respective sexes, there won't be equality in the true sense of the word.
"One on One with Alice Shalvi: A woman's work" by Ruthie Blum, The Jerusalem Post 19 April 2007

2579. Dorothy E. Smith (1926–)

1 The exclusion of women from the making of our culture is not the product of a biological deficiency or a biological configuration of some kind. As we learn more of our women's history we discover that a powerful intellectual and artistic current moves like an underground stream through the history of the last few centuries. It appears sometimes merely as a missing potentiality . . . We learn of the subordination of genius to the discipline of service in the home and in relation to children, and of the fragmentary realization of extraordinary powers of mind and dedication. . . .
Ch. 1, The Everyday Woman as Problematic 1987

2580. Nancy Spero (1926–)

1 The male standard has been universal. Images in art are images that men have made. The correction is simple—equally a female standard with images in art that women make.
Quoted in "Nancy Spero," Exposures, Women & Their Art by Ann Brown & Arlene Raven* 1989

*See 3533.

2 Only recently has women's history been uncovered. I'm recovering the past through all kinds of images by women, from goddesses to victims. An artist has power, if she has a voice that can enter the public discourse.
Ibid.

2581. Joan Sutherland (1926–)

1 If I weren't reasonably placid, I don't think I could cope with this sort of life. To be a diva, you've got to be absolutely like a horse.
Quoted in "Joan Sutherland," Divas: Impressions of Six Opera Superstars by Winthrop Sargeant 1959

2 I know I'm not exactly a bombshell, but one has to make the best of what one's got.
Ibid.

2582. Savina J. Teubal (1926–2005)

1 Wisdom is the process by which visions are realized.
Pt. IV, Introduction, Letter to Ellen M. Umansky (12 June 1989), Four Centuries of Jewish Women's Spirituality Ellen M. Umansky* & Dianne Ashton, eds. 1992

*See 4011.

2 Torah is the source of Jewish wisdom (hochmah), whose roots are our foundations and whose branches spread out to infinity.
"Simchat Hochmah: A Crone Ritual" (1986), Ibid.

3 The difference between our ancestors and ourselves is that they took visions and miracles as a matter of course, as proof of the

existence of the supernatural. Omens exist only if you believe in them. We have lost the capacity to recognize any omen or a vision.

Ibid.

4   In the early 1970s, when I was driving down Wilshire Boulevard in Santa Monica, I saw a bumper sticker on the car in front of me that read "Question Authority." Those two words did for me what the burning bush did for Moses: they changed my perception of reality. I began to ask myself: What authority asserted that I could not be bat mitzvah, could not attend college nor have a career simply because I was female?

Jewish Women's Archive jwa.org *n.d.*

2583. Johnnie Tillmon (1926–2001)

1   I'm a woman. I'm a black woman. I'm a poor woman. I'm a fat woman. I'm a middle-aged woman. And I'm on welfare. In this country, if you're any one of those things, you count less as a person. If you're *all* those things, you just don't count, except as a statistic.

"Welfare is a Woman's Issue," *The First Ms. Reader,* Francine
Klagsbrun, ed. *1972*

2   Wages are the measure of dignity that society puts on a job.

Ibid.

3   Welfare is like a traffic accident. It can happen to anybody, but especially it happens to women.

Ibid.

2584. Lois Wyse (1926–2007)

1   With a name like Smucker's,* it has to be good.

Tag line for client, Wyse Advertising *1960s*

*The J.M. Smucker Company, established in 1897.

2   All of a sudden, I'm older than my parents were when I thought *they* were old.

"Age-Old conversations," *Funny, You Don't Look Like a
Grandmother 1990*

3   So if you have a grandma
Thank the Good Lord up above,
And give Grandmama hugs and kisses,
For grandmothers are to love.

"Grandmothers Are to Love," last stanza, Ibid.

4   "What's that in your hand, honey?"
"A letter."
"To Katy or Danielle?"
"No, it's not for them, it's for my new best friend."
"And who is that, dear?"
"I don't know," Brooke answered forlornly. "I haven't met her yet."

"A New World," *Women Make the Best Friends:
A Celebration 1995*

2585. Itka Frajiman Zygmuntowicz (1926–)

1   My childhood world was gone, but not from my heart and mind. Nothing dies as long as it is remembered and transmitted from person to person, from generation to generation. Or, as my beloved grandmother used to say, "My child, you only have what you choose to give away!"

"Survival and Memory" (p. 290), *Four Centuries of Jewish
Women's Spirituality: A Sourcebook,* Ellen M. Umansky* and
Dianne Ashton, eds. *1992*

*See 4011.

2   There are those who claim that love is blind, but it seems to me that hatred is blind.

Ibid.

3   Death is only a physical separation, while love and remembrance are a spiritual union.

Ibid.

2586. Erma Bombeck (1927–1996)

1   If I had my life to live over again I would have waxed less and listened more.
      . . . There would have been more I love yous . . . more I'm sorrys . . . more I'm listenings . . . but mostly, given another shot at life, I would seize every minute of it . . . look at it and really see it . . . try it on . . . live it . . . exhaust it . . . and never give that minute back until there was nothing left of it . . .

"Experience life in its moments," Newsday Newspaper
Syndicate *1979*

2   Guilt: the gift that keeps on giving.

Quoted in *Time* (New York) *2 July 1984*

3   You hear a lot of dialogue on the death of the American family. Families aren't dying. They're merging into big conglomerates.

"Empty Fridge, Empty Nest," *San Francisco Examiner 1
October 1978*

4   I worry about scientist discovering that lettuce has been fattening all along. . . .

*If Life Is a Bowl of Cherries—What am I Doing in the Pits?
1978*

5   Insanity is hereditary. You can catch it from your kids.

"At Wit's End," Newspaper column, Newsday Newspaper
Syndicate *n.d*

6   The Rose Bowl is the only bowl I've ever seen that I didn't have to clean.

Ibid.

7   When humor goes, there goes civilization.

Ibid.

2587. Joyce Brothers (1927–)

1   Marriage is not just spiritual communion and passionate embraces; marriage is also three-meals-a-day and remembering to carry out the trash.

"When Your Husband's Affection Cools," *Good
Housekeeping May 1972*

2   Anger repressed can poison a relationship as surely as the cruelest words.

Ibid.

2588. Lynn Caine (1927–1987)

1   After my husband died, I felt like one of those spiraled shells washed up on the beach . . . Poke a straw through the twisting tunnel, around and around, and there is nothing there. No flesh. No life. Whatever lived there is dried up and gone.

Widow 1974

2   "Widow" is a harsh and hurtful word. It comes from the Sanskrit and it means "empty." I have been empty too long.

Ibid.

2589. Rosalyn Carter (1927–)

1 My greatest disappointment in all the projects I worked on during the White House years was the failure of the Equal Rights Amendment to be ratified . . . Why all the controversy and why such difficulty in giving women the protection of the Constitution that should have been theirs long ago?

First Lady From Plains 1984

2 Jimmy* and I were always partners.

Remark, Quoted in *First Ladies* by Betty Boyd Caroli *1987*
*James Carter, her husband (1924–), 39th president of the United States (1977–81).

3 If we have not achieved our early dreams, we must either find new ones or see what we can salvage from the old.

Something to Gain 1987

2590. Beatrice Conrad (1927–)

1 Their lives had intertwined into a comfortable dependency, like the gnarled wisteria on their front porch, still twisted around the frail support which long ago it had outgrown.

"The Night of the Falling Star," *American Scene: New Voices*, Don Wolfe, ed. *1963*

2 We are poor helpless creatures on an undistinguished planet in an obscure corner of a small and fading universe.

Ibid.

3 How can you no longer be?
Suppose that we could somehow meet again,
Might you have transmigrated
Into a mote? a molecule? a cloud?
And I an atom floating high
Above Grand Canyon or Antarctica,
Uniting with an atom that long ago was you?

"My Frank Sinatra Sweetheart" *2000*

2591. Nora Dauenhauer (1927–)

1 Trying to write
about you is like dragging
a fishing line through bushes.
I go a short distance
and my line hooks
on underbrush.

"Jessy," *in toto*, *That's What She Said*, Rayna Green, ed. *1984*
*See 3338.

2592. Midge Decter (1927–)

1 Shifts in prejudice can work both ways.

Pt. I, Ch. 3, *The Liberated Woman and Other Americans 1971*

2 . . . because I am a New Yorker, my experience is the more truly, the more typically, American one. It is my America that is moving in on them [Middle America]. God is about to bless them with an opportunity, and may He also save them from it, but there is no turning back now.

Pt. III, Ch. 6, Ibid.

3 The hatred of the youth culture for adult society is not a disinterested judgment but a terror-ridden refusal to be hooked into the, if you will, ecological chain of breathing, growing, and dying. It is the demand, in other words, to remain children.

Ch. 1, *The New Chastity and Other Arguments Against Women's Liberation 1972*

4 It might sound a paradoxical thing to say—for surely never has a generation of children occupied more sheer hours of parental time—but the truth is that we neglected you. We allowed you a charade of trivial freedoms in order to avoid making those impositions on you that are in the end both the training ground and proving ground for true independence. We pronounced you strong when you were still weak in order to avoid the struggles with you that would have fed your true strength. We proclaimed you sound when you were foolish in order to avoid taking part in the long, slow, slogging effort that is the only route to genuine maturity of mind and feeling. Thus, it was no small anomaly of your growing up that while you were the most indulged generation, you were also in many ways the most abandoned to your own meager devices by those into whose safe-keeping you had been given.

Ch. 1, *Liberal Parents/Radical Children 1975*

5 All they wished for her was that she should turn herself into a little replica of them.

Ch. 3, Ibid.

2593. Jean Edelstein (1927–)

1 I think that art is an internal investigation of who you are, what motivates you. It can't be something out there, it has to be something totally inside.

Quoted in "Jean Edelstein," *Exposures, Women & Their Art* by Ann Brown & Arlene Raven* *1989*
*See 3533.

2 My Marxist background certainly didn't prepare me for the Goddess! Then everything I had been doing finally came to fruition—my work became a temple for the Goddess.

Ibid.

2594. Anne Edwards (1927–)

1 What a difficult swallowing of ego and pride she [Judy Garland*] must have suffered with each pill—what a frightening loss of self.

Judy Garland 1975
*See 2428.

2 That was, of course, the problem—she *begged*, not demanded. She wanted a happy world and everyone in it happy, but she was at a loss as to how to accomplish this.

Ibid.

2595. Elizabeth Warnock Fernea (1927–2008)

1 We thought we knew what we were doing. We were going to spend a year Marrakech . . .

Ch. 1, *Street in Marrakech 1988*

2 . . . sadly, the people of the Middle East still remain as distant from the general American public as they were nearly half a century ago . . . Today, on television, on film, Arab peoples are seen running for cover in Beirut or Jerusalem, in Algiers or Basra; they turn away from the lens of the television journalist, shield themselves behind veils, robes, sunglasses, tears; or, masked, brandishing weapons at the screen. The very nearness of the television images, presented without explanation or background, accentuates the differences between "us" and "them"; they dress differently, look different, seem to worship a different god . . . These images of the Arab peoples regularly seen by millions of Americans are far removed from our own impressions, our own experiences of the Middle East.

The Arab World, Forty Years of Change, coauthor, Robert A. Fernea* *1997*
*Her husband, American anthropologist and educator.

3 [In America] the feminist emphasis on the individual woman has allowed the religious right to appropriate family values.

In Search of Islamic Feminism: One Woman's Global Journey
1998

4 Cover or hijab is an important new development in Muslim countries, where it is equated with piety and belief. Sometimes women are forced to cover, as in Iran and Afghanistan, and that is certainly a restriction. But in other countries, hijab appears to be a matter of the woman's choice, of her own decision based on her reading of religious texts. Sometimes this dress gives women extra authority as they struggle with male Muslims to achieve gender equality.

Ibid.

2595.1. Marianne Fredriksson (1927–2007)

1 . . . love is often a reflection of an inner longing, a state within the one who loves.

p. 278, *Hanna's Daughters: A Novel of Three Generations*
1994

2 But the body ages, and it doesn't lie. . . . I was old and I had to accept it.

Aging with dignity.

What does that mean? How idiotic. At eleven o'clock, I got up, phoned the hairdresser and made an appointment to have my hair cut and tinted. I bought an expensive "miracle" cream and the first ever lipstick in my life. . . .

pp. 283–4, Ibid.

3 "Didn't Anna tell you"? she went on. "My father's a count and has an estate, blue blood and all that, arrogant and generally somewhat limited."

I remember that moment so clearly, for it was the first time I understood that we see only according to our own prejudices. The peasant girl in front of me was transformed, the long curved nose and the heavy eyelids ecoming aristocratic.

How handsome she was!

p. 291, Ibid.

4 The years came and went, the children came and left. The worst of getting old is not tiredness and aches and pains, but that time rushes on so quickly that in the end it doesn't seem to exist. It's Christmas and then it's Easter. It's a clear winter's day and then a hot summer's day. In between is a vacuum.

p. 308, Ibid.

2596. Betty Harper Fussell (1927–)

1 When I traveled around the United States in the early 1980s looking for the genus and the genius of American food, I discovered that American cooking was rooted in corn.

Ch. 1, *Story of Corn 1992*

2 No matter what I touched, it turned to corn. Corn was everywhere.

Ibid.

3 Don't mind the mess. It's always this way, because a kitchen is in the middle of things, in the middle of life, as I'm living it now, this moment, the detritus of the past heaped like a midden everywhere you look.

"Assault and Battery," *My Kitchen Wars 1999*

4 The meat we cooked at home, including the rare holiday treat of Swiss steak in the pressure cooker, was designed to give way at the first touch of my grandparents' denture.

Ch. 1, *Raising Steaks: The Life and Times of American Beef*
2008

5 Presidents are mythmakers just as poets are, and the results of Jefferson's* attempt to mold the American West by England's agrarian mythology was but the first of many national policies driven by fictions mistaken for facts.

"The New Range Wars," Ibid.
*Thomas J- (1743–1826), 3rd president of the United States (1801–1809), political philosopher, educator, architect.

2597. Gao Yaojie (1927–)

1 Government officials, research foundations, NGOs, hospitals, pharmaceutical companies, unlicensed doctors—so many people have deceived the public in order to hide this disease* and profit.

Speech, Xingua University 5 April 2006
*AIDS.

2 I am a doctor, so I can't tell lies.

Quoted in "China's AIDS Heroine" by Wang Jingwen, *The Epoch Times 26 March 2007*

2598. Althea Gibson (1927–2003)

1 I always wanted to be somebody. I guess that's why I kept running away from home when I was a kid even though I took some terrible whippings for it.

Ch. 1, *I Always Wanted to Be Somebody 1958*

2 I don't want to be put on a pedestal. I just want to be reasonably successful and live a normal life with all the conveniences to make it so. I think I've already got the main thing I've always wanted, which is to be somebody, to have identity. I'm Althea Gibson, the tennis champion. I hope it makes me happy.

Ch. 9, Ibid.

2599. Lee Grant (1927–)

1 This is a period of great *angst*. The impermanence and flimsiness of houses built on faults, subject to landslides, add to a former apartment dweller's sense of insecurity. The stage-set quality of the streets, the green and blue spotlights illuminating every sallow palm in front of Hollywood court apartments, the 40-foot neon cross overlooking the freeway.

"Selling Out to Hollywood, or Home," *The New York Times 12 August 1973*

2 The more stringent the conditions are, the more the actor uses them—like hurdlers, or emotional stuntmen.

Ibid.

3 As more of us [actresses] are moving into producing and directing, the level of creativity among women has become very high, and therefore our relationships have changed—have themselves become more creative.

"Art Catches Up to Life," *Ms.* (New York) *November 1975*

4 . . . art always seems to be catching up to life.

Ibid.

2600. Ann Jellicoe (1927–)

1 TOLEN. Intuition is, to some degree, inborn, Colin. One is born with an intuition as to how to get women. But this feeling can be developed with experience and confidence, in certain people, Colin, to some degree. A man can develop the knack. First you must realize that women are not just individuals but types. No, not even types, just women. They want to surrender but they don't want the responsibility of surrendering.

The Knack 1961

2 The impulse to create is linked with the aggressive instinct.
Article by Carol Dix, quoted in *The Guardian* (London) *1972*

2601. Ruth Prawer Jhabvala (1927–)

1 "... what she wants is a live guru—someone to inspire her ... snatch her up and out of herself—simultaneously destroy and create her."
Travelers 1973

2 "India ... is not a place that one can pick up and put down again as if nothing had happened. In a way it's not so much a country as an experience, and whether it turns out to be a good or a bad one depends, I suppose, on oneself."
Ibid.

3 [India] was like being not in a different part of this world but in another world altogether, in another reality.
Heat and Dust 1983

4 I had come to India to be in India. I wanted to be changed. Henry didn't—he wanted a change, that's all, but not to be changed.
"An Experience of India," *Out of India 1986*

2602. Beverly Jones (1927–)

1 The married woman knows that love is, at its best, an inadequate reward for her unnecessary and bizarre heritage of oppression.
"The Dynamics of Marriage and Motherhood," *The Florida Paper on Women's Liberation* (a.k.a. The Florida Paper) *1968*

2 Now, as always, the most automated appliance in a household is the mother.
Ibid.

3 If enforced wakefulness is the handmaiden and necessary precursor to serious brainwashing, a mother—after her first child—is ready for her final demise.
Ibid.

4 Romance, like the rabbit at the dog track, is the illusive, fake, and never-attained reward which for the benefit and amusement of our masters keeps us running and thinking in safe circles.
Ibid.

5 Automation and unions have led to a continuously shortened day for men but the work day of housewives with children has remained constant.
Ibid.

2603. Coretta Scott King (1927–2006)

1 There is a spirit and a need and a man at the beginning of every great human advance. Each of these must be right for that particular moment of history, or nothing happens.
Ch. 6, *My Life with Martin Luther King, Jr.* 1969*

2 My husband* often told the children that if a man had nothing that was worth dying for, then he was not fit to live.
Press Conference (April 1968), Ibid.
*American clergyman and civil rights leader (1929–68); assassinated.

3 We are concerned not only about the Negro poor, but the poor all over America and all over the world. Every man deserves a right to a job or an income so that he can pursue liberty, life, and happiness. Our great nation, as he often said, has the resources, but his question was: Do we have the will?
Speech, Memphis City Hall, Ibid.

2604. Eartha Kitt (1927–2008)

1 You send the best of this country off to be shot and maimed. They rebel in the street. They don't want to go to school because they're going to be snatched off from their mothers to be shot in Vietnam.
Remark to Lady Bird Johnson, White House Luncheon, *1968*

2 In essence, I'm a sophisticated cotton picker.
Alone With Me (autobiography) 1976

3 The thing that hurts, that became anger, was when I realized that if you tell the truth—in a country that says you're entitled to tell the truth—you get your face slapped and you get put out of work.*
Interview, *Essence 1988*
*Re being blackballed after publicly criticizing the Vietnam War.

4 I'm a dirt person. I trust the dirt. I don't trust diamonds and gold.
Interview, *Ebony magazine 1993*

2605. Lolita Lebron (1927–)

1 I did not come here to kill, I came here to die.*
Quoted in *A Message from God in the Atomic Age* by Irene Vilar;** Gregory Rabassa, tr. *1996*
*Reference to 24 February 1954, when Lebron and three male companions opened fire on the U.S. House of Representatives in protest against U.S. colonial rule; she spent 27 years in prison.
**See 4805.

2606. Alice McGill (1927–)

1 The usual penalty for stealing was death, but the law said no one could be executed if they could read the Bible. Molly could read the Bible, so she was sentenced to indentured servitude in America for seven years.
Molly Bannaky 1999

2 That a lone woman should stake land was unheard of, but Molly's new neighbors saw the way she jutted out her chin.
Ibid.

3 [Miles] took to sleeping with his arm wrapped around his head to protect his knowledge.
Miles' Song 2000

4 The new Africans would have to learn hard work by the whip for the rest of their lives. If a hoe rested too long, the whip popped. If cottonseeds didn't hit the dirt fast enough, the whip popped. Nobody could tell from what direction the sound of the whip would pop.
Way Up and Over Everything 2008

2607. Jean Baker Miller (1927–2006)

1 Women are quite validly seeking something more complete than autonomy as it is defined by men, a fuller not lesser ability to encompass relationships to others, simultaneously with the fullest development of oneself.
(p. 115), *Toward a New Psychology of Women 1976*

2 Most so-called women's work is not recognized as real activity. One reason for this attitude may be that such work is usually associated with helping others' development, rather than with self-enhancement or self-employment. This is seen as *not doing anything*.

Ch. 5, Ibid.

3 The very essence of all life is growth, which means change. . . . Some societies, particularly ours, attempt to divert the need for change by entertainment, and a rapid succession of fads. All of these "circuses" may convey the illusion of change, but in fact they accomplish the opposite. They do not meet the need for growth and enlargement of the mind. Instead, they often confuse us so much that we overlook the terrible frustration of this true need. They thwart rather than fulfill it.

Ibid.

4 Practically everyone now bemoans the Western man's sense of alienation, lack of community, and inability to find ways of organizing society for human ends. We have reached the end of the road that built on the set of traits held out for male identity—advance at any cost, pay any price, drive out all competitors, and kill them if necessary.

Ch. 8, Ibid.

5 A backlash may be an indication that women really have had an effect, but backlashes occur when advances have been small, before changes are sufficient to help many people. . . . It is almost as if the leaders of backlashes use the fear of change as a threat before major change has occurred.

Quoted in Introduction, *Backlash: The Undeclared War Against American Women* by Susan Faludi* 1991

*See 4481.

6 We all know how extraordinarily hard it can sometimes be to connect with another person, and this is especially true when there are differences in power between individuals within a relationship.

Ch. 1, *The Healing Connection: How Women Form Connections in Both Therapy and in Life*, coauthor, Irene Pierce Stiver* 1998

*See 2497.

2608. Patsy Takemoto Mink (1927–2002)

1 We self-righteously expect all others to admire us for our democracy and our traditions. We are so smug about our superiority, we fail to see our own glaring faults, such as prejudice and poverty amidst affluence.

Speech, National Association of Student Affairs Conference (Atlanta) *May 1972*

2 It is easy enough to vote right and be consistently with the majority . . . but it is more important to be ahead of the majority and this means being able to cut the first furrow in the ground and stand alone for a while if necessary.

Remark posted on her Web site, News article *1973*

3 National security is not only building war machines to kill. National security is as much a policy of the living who prefer life over death, wellness over sickness, work over idleness, education over illiteracy, and food over hunger.

"Gazette News," *Ms.* (New York) *October 1981*

4 We have to build things that we want to see accomplished, in life and in our country, based on our own personal experiences

. . . to make sure that others . . . do not have to suffer the same discrimination. That is really the story of Title IX.

Speech, National NOW Conference (St. Paul, MN) *21–23 June 2002*

2609. Estela Portillo Trambley (1927/36–1998/99)

1 The hacienda is the fiber upon which existence hangs. The church, the fluid rose, assures the future promise of Elysian fields. No one dares ask for life.

The Day of the Swallows 1972

2 In earnest belief, they wash their hair in spring water to insure future marriages made in heaven. It is true, no one has seen a marriage made in heaven, but each girl hugs the private truth that hers will be the one.

Ibid.

3 The tierra of Lago de San Lorenzo is within memory of mountain sweet pine. The maguey thickens with the ferocity of chaotic existence. Here the desert yawns. Here it drinks the sun in madness.

Ibid.

4 No action yet. But who wanted action? Rico had transformed into a soldier, but he knew he was no soldier. He had been trained to kill the enemy in Vietnam. He watched the first curl of smoke coming out of the chimneys. They were the enemy down there. Rico didn't believe it. He would never believe it.

"Village" p. 436, *Literature Without Borders*, George R. Bozzini, ed. *2001*

5 It struck him again, the feeling—a bond—people all the same everywhere . . . The woman with the child on her shoulder mattered. Every human life in the village mattered. He knew this not only with the mind but with the heart.

p. 437, Ibid.

2610. Leontyne Price (1927–)

1 I think that recording is in a way much more personal than stage performance. In a theater the audience sees and hears you. So the costumes and the general *mise en scène* help you do the job, because they can see. In recording, you have to see and hear for them with the voice—which makes it much more personal.

Quoted in "Leontyne Price," *Divas: Impressions of Six Opera Superstars* by Winthrop Sargeant *1959*

2 All token blacks have the same experience. I have been pointed at as a solution to things that have not *begun* to be solved, because pointing at us token blacks eases the conscience of millions, and I think this is dreadfully wrong.

Ibid.

3 If I do have some success, I'd like to try to enjoy it, for heaven's sake! What is the point of having it otherwise? Everybody else gets excited, but *you're* the one who's always tired. That's not life. That's not living.

Ibid.

2611. Lillian Ross (1927–)

1 His name was not engraved on a brass plate on his door; it was typed on a white card placed in a slot, from which it could easily be removed.

Ch. 3, *Picture 1952*

2 All enduring love between two people, however startling or unconventional, feels unalterable, predestined, compelling, and intrinsically normal to the couple immersed in it.

Ch. 1, *Here But Not Here: My Life with William Shawn* and The New Yorker 1998*

*American editor of *The New Yorker,* 1952–1987 (1907–1992).

2612. Sonya Rudikoff (1927–1997)

1 Although there are countless alumni of the school of hard knocks, there has not yet been a move to accredit that institution.

"Women and Success," *Commentary* (New York) *October 1974*

2 The embattled gates to equal rights have indeed opened up for modern women, but I sometimes think to myself: "That is not what I meant by freedom—it is only 'social progress.'"

Ibid.

3 There are surely lives which display very few of the signs of success until very late, or after life is over. There are lives of great significance which go unrecognized by peers for a very long time, there are those who achieve nothing for themselves but leave a legacy for others who come after, there are lives sacrificed for causes.

Ibid.

4 History provides abundant examples of . . . women whose greatest gift was in redeeming, inspiring, liberating, and nurturing the gifts of others.

Ibid.

5 Should we, perhaps, see the development of the commune movement in another light, as a less expensive form of summer camp for a growing population—post-adolescent, post-industrial, post-Christian and unemployed?

Article, Quoted in *Commentary* (New York) *1974*

6 Euthanasia, from the Greek eu and thanatos, signifies a good or peaceful death. It conjures up images of dignity and repose, a calm, reconciled conclusion to a life whose meaning has been accorded its due. Euthanasia, often called "death with dignity," also implies the necessary medical efforts to reduce pain without needlessly prolonging the agony of one who is going to die. Few in the past have been fortunate enough to die such a death, and not so many in the present.

"The Problem of Euthanasia," *Commentary* (New York) *February 1974*

2613. Una Stannard (1927–2004)

1 Every day, in every way, the billion-dollar beauty business tells women they are monsters in disguise. . . . women are told they are the fair sex, but at the same time that their "beauty" needs lifting, shaping, dyeing, painting, curling, padding. Women are really being told that "the beauty" is a beast.

"The Mask of Beauty," *Woman in Sexist Society,* Vivian Gornick* and Barbara Moran, eds. *1971*

*See 2932.

2 Woman officially lost her head in Judeo-Christian cultures in Genesis 3, interestingly enough, for trying to acquire knowledge, for which sin God decided that a woman's head was good for nothing since it only got men into trouble.

Mrs. Man 1977

3 Freud,* living at a time when women were proving their heads were no different from men's, substituted the penis for the head as the organ of male superiority, an organ women could never prove they had.

Ibid.

*Sigmund F- (1856–1939), Austrian psychiatrist; founder of psychoanalysis.

4 To create more compassion in the world, we have to stop being like Fundamentalists and Sentimentalists, who treat the family as a holy icon. That icon has to be smashed if the world is to become a loving place. Truth is what smashes sacred beliefs, most of which turn out to be lies we were trained to think were true.

Ch. 1, *A Few Kind Words About Hate: The Dark Side of Family Life and the Bible 2006*

5 Hate should be a friend, for when we let it out of its shrouded cage, we see it's not a roaring beast but a hurt, frightened child who needs to be held and comforted, needs to be loved.

Ch. 2, Ibid.

6 I used to be a scholar, which is a kind of explorer. Exploring my mind was very different. No calm dredging facts out of books. I was the book that was laid open, forced to undergo surgery without anesthesia, I was like Prometheus, who was chained to a rock while an eagle tore at his liver, except the eagle of my awareness tore at my memory. . . .

Ibid.

2614. Arie P. Taylor (1927–2003)

1 When men restrict who can fight and die for America, they restrict who can run America.*

Letter to Sara Hammel, *Women Cross Generations to Talk About Family, Work, Sex, Love and the Future of Feminism,* Anna Bondoc and Meg Daly, eds. *1999*

*In response to being asked why women would choose to be in combat.

2615. C. DeLores Tucker (1927–2005)

1 People are frightened and fearful because of the culture of the gangstas*. . . . they're not afraid because of the enemy he had to fight, but because of their own brothers and sisters who are paid to glorify drugs and guns, to call black women obscene names.

Cited in "Black Activist crusades. . . ," *Seattle Times,* A12 *6 February 1994*

*A genre of music noted for driving beat and "talk-sing" modality, it is also a conduit for raunchy language and portrayals of violence.

2 We spent $500 billion on that war on Iraq, and Hussein* still lives. We could have spent $6,000 and sent the boys in the <0x201C8>hood over there, and they would have taken care of Hussein and taken care of him permanently.

TV interview, Cited in "Black activist crusades . . . ," Ibid.

*Iraqi military and political leader (1937–2006), president of Iraq (1979–2003).

2616. Lillian Vernon (1927–)

1 Mail order is truly an American business.

Ch. 1, *An Eye for Winners 1996*

2 Here is where some entrepreneurs fail. They are filled with creative juices and total commitment to their business, but too often they don't understand that they must also be managers, administrators, even gofers—at least for a while.

Afterword, Ibid.

2617. Doreen Gandy Wiley (1927–)

1 The feet of the enemy march like thunder. Swift as lightning, they deliver overwhelming change. The familiar is transformed into something strange, threatening. . . . This is not real. This is not real. As in a bad dream, the dreamer asks, "When will it end?" When will it end? A litany in the mass mind of a conquered people.

Fires of Survival 1994

2618. Maya Angelou (1928–)

1 She said that I must always be intolerant of ignorance but understanding of illiteracy. That some people, unable to go to school, were more educated and even more intelligent than college professors. She encouraged me to listen carefully to what country people called mother wit. That in those homely sayings was couched the collective wisdom of generations.

Ch. 15, *I Know Why the Caged Bird Sings 1969*

2 I find it interesting that the meanest life, the poorest existence, is attributed to God's will, but as human beings become more affluent, as their living standard and style begin to ascend the material scale, God descends the scale of responsibility at a commensurate speed.

Ch. 18, Ibid.

3 The fact that the adult American Negro female emerges a formidable character is often met with amazement, distaste and even belligerence. It is seldom accepted as an inevitable outcome of the struggle won by survivors, and deserves respect if not enthusiastic acceptance.

Ch. 34, Ibid.

4 Then the question began to live under my blankets: How did lesbianism begin? What were the symptoms? The public library gave information on the finished lesbian—and that woefully sketchy—but on the growth of a lesbian, there was nothing. I did discover that the difference between herma-phrodites and lesbians was that hermaphrodites were "born that way." It was impossible to determine whether lesbians budded gradually, or burst into being with a suddenness that dismayed them as much as it repelled society.

Ch. 35, Ibid.

5 My life has been one great big joke,
A dance that's walked
A song that's spoke,
I laugh so hard I almost choke
When I think about myself.

"When I Think About Myself," *Just Give Me a Cool Drink of Water 'fore I Diiie 1971*

6 "I probably couldn't learn to cook creole food, anyway. It's too complicated."

"Sheeit. Ain't nothing but onions, green peppers and garlic. Put that in everything and you got creole food."

Ch. 3, *Gather Together in My Name 1974*

7 The white American man makes the white American woman maybe not superfluous but just a little kind of decoration. Not really important to turning around the wheels of the state. Well the black American woman has never been able to feel that way. No black American man at any time in our history in the United States has been able to feel that he didn't need that black woman right against him, shoulder to shoulder—in that cotton field, on the auction block, in the ghetto, wherever.

Interview, "A Conversation with Maya Angelou" (21 November 1973), *Conversations with Maya Angelou 1989*

8 The sadness of the women's movement is that they don't allow the necessity of love. See, I don't personally trust any revolution where love is not allowed.

"Listening to Maya Angelou" (*California Living*, 14 May 1975), Ibid.

9 I love to see a young girl go out and grab the world by the lapels. Life's a bitch. You've got to go out and kick ass.

Interview, "Kicking Ass," *Girl About Town* (13 October 1986), Ibid.

10 There's a world of difference between truth and facts. Facts can obscure the truth.

Quoted in *I Dream a World* by Brian Lanker *1989*

11 History, despite its wrenching pain,
Cannot be unlived, and if faced
With courage, need not be lived again.

"A Rock, A River, A Tree,"* Sts. 9–10, *On The Pulse of Morning 1993*

*Commissioned for the inaugural of President William J. Clinton (20 January 1993).

12 When you learn, teach.
When you get, give.
As for me,

I shall not be moved.

"Our Grandmothers" (1990), *The Woman That I Am, The Literature and Culture of Contemporary Women of Color*, D. Soyini Madison,* ed. *1994*

*See 3912.

13 The word is Peace.
It is loud now. It is louder.
Louder than the explosion of bombs.

We tremble at the sound. We are thrilled by its presence.
It is what we have hungered for.
Not just the absence of war. But, true Peace.
A harmony of spirit, a comfort of courtesies.

"Amazing Peace: A Christmas Poem," sts. 7–8 *2005*

14 There is a world of difference between being a woman and being an old female. If you're born a girl, grow up, and live long enough, you can become an old female.

But to become a woman is a serious matter. A woman takes responsibility for the time she takes up and the space she occupies.

The Observer (London) *20 January 2008*

15 Loving someone liberates the lover as well as the beloved.

Interview, *Oprah Winfrey* Show 2008*

*See 4285.

16 Dressing in purples and pinks and greens
Exotic as rum and Cokes
Living our lives with flash and style
Ain't we colorful folks?

"Ain't That Bad?" *n.d.*

17 Televised news turns
a half-used day into
a waste of desolation.

"Televised," St. 1 *n.d.*

18 You may write me down in history
With your bitter, twisted lies,

You may trod me in the very dirt
But still, like dust, I'll rise.

"Still I Rise," St. 1 *n.d.*

2619. Shirley Temple Black (1928–)

1 Our whole way of life today is dedicated to the *removal of risk*. Cradle to grave we are supported, insulated, and isolated from the risks of life—and if we fall, our government stands ready with Band-Aids of every size.

Speech, Kiwanis International Convention, Texas (June 1967), Quoted in *The Sinking of the Lollipop* by Rodney G. Minott *1968*

2 No country has washed more dirty laundry in public than we have.

Quoted in *American Political Women* by Esther Stineman *1980*

3 I stopped believing in Santa Claus when I was six. Mother took me to see him in a department store and he asked for my autograph.

Quoted in *Halliwell's Filmgoer's Companion* by Leslie Halliwell *1984*

4 I was very sophisticated when I was 17. When I was 14, I was the oldest I ever was.

Quoted in "What Do You Do After You've Been Shirley Temple?" by Dotson Rader, *Parade Magazine* 7 December *1986*

2620. Anita Brookner (1928–)

1 She was a handsome woman of forty-five and would remain so for many years.

Ch. 4, *Hotel du Lac 1984*

2 You have no idea how promising the world begins to look once you have decided to have it all for yourself. And how much healthier your decisions are once they become entirely selfish.

Ibid.

3 There are moments when you feel free, moments when you have energy, moments when you have hope, but you can't rely on any of these things to see you through. Circumstances do that.

Novelists in Interview, John Haffenden, ed. *1985*

4 Great writers are the saints for the godless.

Ibid.

5 Time misspent in youth is sometimes all the freedom one ever has.

Ch. 10, *The Misalliance 1986*

6 Women don't sit at home any more, you know, dreaming of Prince Charming. They don't do it because they've found out that he doesn't exist. As you should have found out. I live in the real world, the world of deceptions. You live in the world of illusions.

A Friend from England 1987

7 A man of such obvious and exemplary charm must be a liar.

Ch. 3, Ibid.

8 No blame should attach to telling the truth. But it does, it does.

Ch. 10, Ibid.

9 Existentialism is about being a saint without God; being your own hero, without all the sanction and support of religion or society.

Interview, *Writers at Work* (Eighth Series), George Plimpton,* ed. *1988*

*American writer and editor (1927–2003).

10 Real love is a pilgrimage. It happens when there is no strategy, but it is very rare because most people are strategists.

Women Writers Talk, Olga Kenyon, ed. *1989*

11 Always let them think of you as singing and dancing.

Dolly 1993

2621. Barbara B. Brown (1928–1999)

1 The critical and quite new element that biofeedback brings to medical and psychologic therapeutics is the capacity to manipulate one's own body (and mind) by one's own mind. The implications of this newly discovered capacity are enormous. The uses are obvious, but the misuses are not obvious at all.

New Mind, New Body, Bio-Feedback: New Directions for the Mind 1974

2 Stress is a phenomenon generated almost exclusively by society's mad pace of the twentieth century. Diminished well being is the social Pac-Man that devours coping and psychic energy and inner strength. Before it wins the game of our lives, it needs some serious, sober attention.

Prologue, *Between Health and Illness 1974*

2622. Theo E. Colborn (1928–)

1 People should look to the scientific journals, but they should also look very carefully at where the scientists who research and write about this issue get their funding. . . . Follow the money. That's what the public is going to have to do.

Interview by Marilyn Berlin Snell, *Mother Jones March/April 1998*

2 Last night on television I saw a new advertisement on the wonders of plastic and how safe it makes the world for children. I know this is in direct response to our work. This is how they [corporations] are spending their money: to create the image of motherhood and apple pie where they know they are going to be blasted as the science comes forward.

Ibid.

3 We're never going to be able to prove a causal relationship of anything in a human being because we can't feed chemicals to human beings and wait for them to grow up. . . . Despite the fact that there are a lot of misdiagnosed kids, I still think ADHD is on the increase. And the evidence is almost overwhelming that these chemicals* are involved.

Ibid.

*Toxins such as lead, PCBs, and dioxins.

4 We are neutering the population—we are making females more masculine and we are making males more feminine.

Ibid.

5 The truth is that the protocols to test chemicals for their safety and the regulations to assure product safety failed to prevent the use of these chemicals with which we commingle continuously, moment to moment in our homes, schools, places of business, and outdoors.

Lifetime Achievement Acceptance Speech, Integrated Environment and Human Health Organization, The National Council for Science and the Environment *1 February 2007*

6   What a crazy world we live in when almost everyone knows what the acronym ED stands for. Millions have been poured into creating awareness of ED, erectile dysfunction, because it is profitable. This 21st century, sales-pitch strategy called "disease mongering", has proved good for the bottom line. The irony of all this is that there is another ED out there into which millions have also been poured—to keep it a secret. That ED is endocrine disruption, which, if the public was to learn about it, the bottom line could shrink.

Ibid.

2623. Mary Daly (1928–   )

1   It is the creative potential itself in human beings that is the image of God.

Ch. 1, *Beyond God the Father 1973*

2   ... "God's plan" is often a front for men's plans and a cover for inadequacy, ignorance and evil.

Ibid.

3   Courage to be is the key to the revelatory power of the feminist revolution.

Ibid.

4   Why indeed must "God" be a noun? Why not a verb—the most active and dynamic of all.

Ch. 2, *Ibid.*

5   The image of Mary as Virgin, moreover, has an (unintended) aspect of pointing to independence for women. This aspect of the symbol is of course generally unnoticed by theologians.

Ch. 3, *Ibid.*

6   I had explained that a woman's asking for equality in the church would be comparable to a black person's demanding equality in the Ku Klux Klan.

"New Autobiographical Preface" (1968), *The Church and the Second Sex 1975*

7   Elemental female Lust is intense longing/craving for the cosmic concrescence that is creation. It is charged, tense, in tension with the tenses of fabricated "father time." Incensed, it burns through the shallow impressions of insipid senses, sensing the Sources, Astral Forces, Angels and Graces that call from the Deep. This Lusting is divining: foreseeing, foretelling, forecasting. Unlike the dim divines and divinities, the deadheads of deadlands whose ill-illuminations blind us, Lusty women portend with luster, our radiance from within that radiates from and toward Original Powers of creation.

Introduction, *Pure Lust 1984*

8   If life is to survive on this planet, there must be a decontamination of the Earth. I think this will be accompanied by an evolutionary process that will result in a drastic reduction of the population of males. People are afraid to say that kind of stuff anymore.

Interview, *Quintessence ... Realizing the Archaic Future: A Radical Elemental Feminist Manifesto 1998*

2624. Carrie Dann (1928?–   )

1   To most indigenous thinking people, the United States is not a melting pot; it is a boiling mess. No longer do we have the clear blue skies, but acid rain, maybe soon cyanide and nuclear rain, destroying life on land and water. No longer clear cool waters, but outrageous pollution destroying all forms of water life—believe it or not folks, if we cannot drink our once clear blue waters, we are the next to go! The nuclear test site will be contaminated by the nuclear testing for thousands of years. To my way of thinking nuclear testing is not national security, but national death sentence for us, our children, the unborn and to all that we know as life.

Acceptance Speech, Right Livelihood Awards (Stockholm) *9 December 1993*

2   I strongly believe that the United States for many years has systematically and deliberately, through it acts and actions, made moves to destroy our ways and leave us with nothing.

If indeed the US took our land, extinguished treaty and our land rights—this is genocide.

Ibid.

3   I was indigenous and in one single evening they made me indigent. If you think the Indian wars are over, then think again.

Quoted in "For Mary Dann the Fight is Over" by Susan Bates, Snowwowl.com *31 October 2002*

4   It's disgraceful how the United States makes international statements about human rights and then commits this kind of assault in our own backyard.* It destroys their credibility and moral authority.

Ibid.

*In 2002 the 24 agents of the Bureau of Indian Affairs raided Dann's ranch, removing 2,400 head of cattle.

2625. Takako Doi (1928–   )

1   The people are aware of how politics affects their daily life. It's the politicians who are behind the times.

Quoted in "A Mountain Moves" by Jill Smolowe, *Time* (New York) *7 August 1989*

2   The underpinnings of our lives is hope. If we have the smallest margin of hope, we can continue to exist. I believe what is sought from politics is to expand that hope even by the smallest margin. When we think of it, however, it seems politics has cast a shadow over people's hopes.

Speech, Future of Hope International Conference (Hiroshima) *6 December 1995*

2626. Muriel Fox (1928–   )

1   Women and men have to fight together to change society—and both will benefit. We [her husband and herself] are strongly pro-marriage. I think it is a grave mistake for young girls to think that it has to be a career versus marriage, equality versus love. Partnership, not dependence, is the real romance in marriage.

Quoted in "Wait Late to Marry" by Barbara Jordan Moore, *New Woman October 1971*

2   Total commitment to family and total commitment to career is possible, but fatiguing.

Ibid.

3   While you don't need a formal written contract before you get married, I think it's important for both partners to spell out what they expect from each other. ... There are always plenty of surprises—and lots of give and take—once you're married.

Ibid.

2627. Sonia Pressman Fuentes (1928–   )

1   On watching a football game: "I don't understand," she said, "What do you get when they win?"

I didn't know the answer then and I haven't been able to come up with a satisfactory answer ever since. Whenever I'm tempted to go to a game of any sort, my mother's question comes to mind—and I stay home.

Eat First—You Don't Know What They'll Give You, The Adventures of an Immigrant Family and Their Feminist Daughter 1999

2 "Howja like dot?" asked my father.

"Not dot," corrected Mother, unperturbed by Father's twenty-year resistance to the niceties of English pronunciation. "Not dot. Dat. T-h-a-t. Dat." For some inexplicable reason, Mother's tutorial method with a man who had never mastered the alphabet was premised on spelling. I suspected this technique owed its application not so much to Mother's belief in its validity as a teaching tool but to her desire to demonstrate her own superior grasp of the language. "All right," said Father, in his I-stand-corrected tone. "Dat. Howja like dat?"

"If You Speak His Language," Ibid.

3 I don't feel I've done any service. I just did what needed to be done. If you see a baby in the middle of the road, you get it out of the way of oncoming cars. Your act may be considered heroic, but your motivation isn't service; it is simply to do what needs to be done. That's how I've responded with regard to women's issues.

"Making A Difference" by Frieda Craft Eakins, straightfromtheheart.org 1999

2628. Griselda Gambaro (1928–   )

1 FUNCTIONARY. Art is all that deserves to last—lofty sentiments, things and beings coming to life. You haven't smashed the doll so as to assure that there will be beauty in the world, order. In a word: so the trees can keep growing and putting forth new leaves, so the earth does not become a desolate wasteland.

The Walls (Las Paredes), Marguerite Feitlowitz, tr. 1964

2 LORENZO (a Siamese twin). What happens in operations like these, is that they can't save them both. One of them is ruined. In order to leave one of them in perfect condition, they have to ruin the other. They have to.

The Siamese Twins (Los siameses) 1965

3 ANTÍGONA. Let the laws, these vile laws! drag me to a grave that will be my tomb. No one will hear my weeping; no one will be aware of my suffering. They will live in the light as though nothing were happening. . . . I will be . . . uncounted among the living and among the dead. I will disappear from the world, alive.

Antígona Furiosa 1986

4 . . . What feminism means is to change our optic, our vision, which means we must also change our ethics.

"Griselda Gambaro," Albert Minero, tr., Interviews with Contemporary Women Playwrights, Kathleen Betsko* and Rachel Koenig 1987
*See 3125.

5 Theater is very much connected with the society, with the social situation. . . . A theater piece, of itself, demands a confrontation with an audience. It demands that you connect with other people; it demands a collective and social effort with the company and later with the audience.

Ibid.

6 This is a schizophrenic country, a country that lives two lives. The courteous and generous have their counterpart in the violent and the armed who move among the shadows . . . One never really knows what country one is living in, because the two co-exist . . .

Quoted in "Two Argentine Writers" by Marguerite Feitlowitz, Bomb, No. 32 Summer 1990

2629. Jane Gardam (1928–   )

1 The sex-act for Mrs Djinn was after the nature of a viral infection that might result in nasty flue, something not yet eradicated from the human species.

The Queen of the Tambourine 1991

2 Hetty was poor because her father, who had been four years in the trenches in the First World War, had returned miraculously unscathed in body but shattered to bits in mind. It had once been a remarkable mind but now it hid itself, looking out only now and then like sunlight between tree trunks.

Ch. 1, The Flight of the Maidens 2001

3 When she saw them in her house she forgot whether or not she disliked them. It was unconscious caution. The gods of hospitality were always on the watch.

Ch. 23, Faith Fox 2004

4 Filth had always said—of his Cases—"I am trained to forget." "Otherwise," he said, "how could I function?" Facts, memories, the pain of life—of lives in chaos—have to be forgotten.

Ch. 1, Old Filth 2006

5 All his working life he had been called Filth not only because of the olk joke (Failed In London Try Hong Kong) but because nobody had ever seen him other than immaculate: scrubbed, polished, barbered, manicured, brushed, combed, perfect. At any moment of his life Feathers could have been presented to the Queen.

Ch. 1, The People on Privilege Hill 2008

2630. Elizabeth G. Hainstock (1928?–   )

1 Never do for a child what he is capable of doing for himself.

Teaching Montessori in the Home 1968

2 Evidence clearly shows that the early years, from birth to six, are the most formative and are too often wasted by not realizing the child's true potential. . . . To the young child, learning is a natural function of childhood—effortless and challenging, and more meaningful than idle play.

p. 32, The Essential Montessori 1986

3 Each child is a unique individual and will develop at his own rate. You are simply giving him the tools and encouragement for learning when *he* is ready.

Ch. 1, Teaching Montessori in the Home: The Pre-School Years 1997

4 Today's fast-paced lifestyle—with so many more outside influences, the number of latch-key children at an all-time high, and single-parent homes prevalent—makes it more important than ever for you as a parent to find quality time to spend with your children.

Ibid.

2631. Shoshana Kalisch (1928?–   )

1   These songs became a witnessing message, a means to express sorrow and to give courage and hope. It's a personal matter to me. Somehow I could not free myself until I sang songs of the Holocaust.*

> Quoted in "Raising her Voice" by Janet Wallfisch (p. G-3), *Times-Picayune* (New Orleans) *1 May 1988*
> *The genocide of European Jews and others by the Nazis during World War II.

2   I realized that refusing to look [at those being marched to the gas chamber] would have been tantamount to abandoning these human beings during their last hours. And so, every evening at roll call in Auschwitz, we [her sister, Nany] shared with our eyes and hearts the fate of those about to die.

> Ibid.

2632. Joan Kelly-Gadol (1928–1982)

1   . . . there was no renaissance for women—at least not during the Renaissance.

> "Did Women Have a Renaissance?"
> *Becoming Visible: Women in European History*, Renate Bridenthal and Claudia Koonz, eds. *1976*

2   What emerges [in historic perspective] is a fairly regular pattern of relative loss of status for women precisely in those periods of so-called progressive change.

> "The Social Relation of the Sexes: Methodological Implications of Women's History," *Signs: A Journal of Women in Culture and Society*, vol. 1 *1976*

2633. Eva Clara Keuls (1928–   )

1   Like a slave, a woman [in classical Athenian society] had virtually no protection under the law except in so far as she was the property of a man. She was, in fact, not a person under the law. The dominance of male over female was as complete during the period in question as that of master over slave.

> *The Reign of the Phallus: Sexual Politics in Ancient Athens 1993*

2   The governing principle in a phallocracy is that the human race is essentially male, the female being a mere adjunct, unfortunately required for the purpose of reproduction. The natural consequence of this notion is the elimination of the female from all social processes.

> Ibid.

3   Rape is the ultimate translation of phallicism into action. Rape is committed not for pleasure or procreation, but in order to enact the principle of domination by means of sex.

> Ibid.

2634. Judith Krantz (1928–   )

1   "It's that or get fat again," she told herself, as she walked up Rodeo or down Camden, feeling a sexual buzz as she searched the windows for new merchandise. The thrill was in the trying on, in the buying. The moment after she had acquired something new it became meaningless to her. . . .

> Ch. 6, *Scruples 1978*

2   Billy thought privately that the rich are different only because people treat them as if they were. Sometimes she wondered why people bothered. It was not as if knowing someone rich rubbed off on them, put more money in their own bank ac-

counts. Yet, it was there, that slight self-consciousness, the faint over-consideration, that eagerness to charm, the instinctive putting-the-best-foot-forward that she heard all day.

> Ch. 8, Ibid.

2635. Rita Liljestrom (1928–   )

1   What good does it do to treat women and men alike if the whole system is permeated by a male culture? If all of society's prioritized values rest on a collective male consciousness, then what is equality but assimilation in the dominant culture?

> Quoted in *Sisterhood is Global*, Robin Morgan,* ed. *1984*
> *See 3284.

2636. Cynthia Macdonald (1928–   )

1   You genuflect?
Have you forgotten I was Jewish?
That made my heavenly Father Jewish,
Mary and Joseph, too.

> "Jesus Returns," *I Can't Remember 1997*

2   My working methods are to sit on my tail till inspiration,
that horsefly, bites. Then if I can, to throw the buzz away
and keep the path of flight.

> "Poet-Chicken Answers," Ibid.

3   Jingle words like coins, the change,
   or covering
for dead eyes. Fingers fiddle. Don't
   pick.
How many times have I told you not to?
Don't pick. But can choose.

> "The Weekend He Died," Ibid.

4   . . . stone yields
the language everyone
understands but no one speaks.

> "What No One Should Want to Have," Ibid.

2637. Jeanne Moreau (1928–   )

1   Success is like a liberation or the first phase of a love story. . . .

> Quoted in "Jeanne Moreau," *The Egotists* by Oriana Fallaci* *1963*
> *See 2656.

2   I don't think success is harmful, as so many people say. Rather, I believe it indispensable to talent, if for nothing else than to increase the talent.

> Ibid.

3   For me it's not possible to forget, and I don't understand people who, when the love is ended, can bury the other person in hatred or oblivion. For me, a man I have loved becomes a kind of brother.

> Ibid.

4   Acting deals with very delicate emotions. It is not putting up a mask. Each time an actor acts he does not hide; he exposes himself.

> *The New York Times 30 June 1976*

5   When people are alive, they have many deaths: not only cowards die a million deaths. What is incredible about existence is its toughness in extremity.

> Quoted in "Profiles: A Sense of Dream" by Penelope Gilliatt,* *The New Yorker 13 March 1978*
> *See 2799.

2637.1. Thea Musgrave (1928–)

1 Music is a human art, not a sexual one. Sex is no more important than eye color.

> Quoted in "A Matter of Art, Not Sex," *Time* (New York) *10 November 1975*

2 Yes, I am a composer, and I am a woman, but rarely at the same time.

> Frequent reply to questions about being a "woman composer" *n.d.*

2638. Cynthia Ozick (1928–)

1 He had once demonstrated that, since God had made the world, and since there was no God, the world in all logic could not exist.

> Pt. I, Ch. 1, *Trust 1966*

2 "He knows nothing about literature—most great writers don't; all they know is life."

> Pt. III, Ch. 1, Ibid.

3 If the fish had stuck to its gills there would have been no movement up to the land.

> "The Hole/Birth Catalog," *The First Ms. Reader,* Francine Klagsbrun, ed. *1972*

4 The engineering is secondary to the vision.

> Ibid.

5 Wondrous hole! Magical hole! Dazzlingly influential hole! Noble and effulgent hole! From this hole everything follows logically: first the baby, then the placenta, then, for years and years and years until death, a way of life. It is all logic, and she who lives by the hole will live also by its logic. It is, appropriately, logic with a hole in it.

> Ibid.

6 Judaism has no dying god, no embalming of dead bodies, above all no slightest version of death-instinct—"Choose life."

> Ibid.

7 I'm not afraid of facts, I welcome facts *but a congeries of facts is not equivalent to an idea*. This is the essential fallacy of the so-called "scientific" mind. People who mistake facts for ideas are incomplete thinkers; they are gossips.

> "We Are the Crazy Lady and Other Feisty Feminist Fables," Ibid.

8 After a certain number of years our faces become our biographies. We get to be responsible for our faces.

> *Writers at Work* (Eighth Series), George Plimpton,* ed. *1988*
> *American writer and editor (1927–2003).

9 . . . real apprenticeship is ultimately always to the self.

> "Old Hand as Novice," *Fame and Folley: Essays 1996*

10 Joyce's Molly rejoicing. Bellow fanning fire, Updike fingering apertures, Oates wildly sowing, Roth wroth. And so on.*

> "Puttermesser in Paradise," *The Puttermesser Papers 1997*
> *James Joyce, Irish writer (1882–1941); Saul Bellow, Canadian-born American writer (1915–); Joyce Carol Oates (see 2722); Philip Roth, American novelist (1933).

11 A genuine essay has no educational, polemical, or sociological use; it is the movement of a free mind at play. . . .

> "She: Portrait of the Essay as a Warm Body," *Quarrel & Quandary 2000*

12 [New York City] disappears and then . . . disappears again; or say that every 75 years or so another city bursts out, as if against nature—new shapes, new pursuits, new immigrants with their unfamiliar tongues and worried uneasy bustle.

> "The Synthetic Sublime," Ibid.

13 He had his seaman's good right hand, and the firm mast of his pen, and the blessed ocean of paper, as white as a sail and as relentless as the wind.

> "Dictation," *Dictation: A Quartet 2008*

14 Never mind, says Fiction; what fun, laughs Transgression; so what? mocks Dream.

> Ibid.

15 His mind was a secret cave, immaculately swept and spare.

> "At Fumicaro," Ibid.

2639. Franca Rame (1928–)

1 MOTHER. I went to see the corpse of one of those young policemen murdered by my son's comrades. Yes, I went to the funeral parlor. Because it's too easy to complain about things if you don't see them at first-hand.

> *La Madre 1983*

2 PROLOGUE. Beautiful, no? Man elevated his member to his image and likeness. It is him, his thing, his power . . . the power assoluto! If we think a little, the world does not revolve around the United States . . . or Russia: The world revolves around the Grand Phallsa! The real tiger, not the paper one, is what is it! Notwithstanding its modest proportions . . .

> Prologue, *Orgasmo Adulto Escapes from the Zoo* (a.k.a. *Female Parts,* Olwen Wymark, tr., 1981), Estelle Parsons,* tr. *1983*
> *American stage and screen actor (1927–).

3 WIFE (to audience). "Listen Luigi," I said, "You get mad about how nobody pays you for your traveling time but what about me? Do I get paid for all the working and slaving I do at home? No I do not. And believe you me everything I do here is for the multinational, oh yes! . . . We recondition you, regenerate you . . . reproduce you! And all for free!"

> "Waking Up," Ibid.

2640. Vera C. Rubin (1928–)

1 I returned to the subject of my Master's thesis, which had been believed by very few astronomers. But now I obtained my own data to look for large scale motions in the universe. This paper was also believed by very few, but the subject became a major branch of extragalactic astronomy a few years later.

> "Motion of the Galaxy and the Local Group Determined from the Velocity Anisotropy of Distant Sc I Galaxies," *Astrophysical Journal 289: 81: 687 and 719 1976*

2 I discovered from observations . . . that in the single disk of this galaxy, half the stars orbit clockwise, and half the stars orbit counterclockwise, both systems intermingled.

> "Cospatial Counterrotating Stellar Disks in the Virgo. . . ," with J. A. Graham and J. P. D. Kennedy, *Astrophysical Journal 394: L9-L12 1992*

2641. Bernice "Bunny" R. Sandler (1928–)

1 With the politics of change led by women and men of good will, campus, society and the world will never again be the same.

> Speech, "The Real Story Behind the Passage of Title IX 35 Years Ago" (Cleveland State University), Women in Higher Education (wihe.com) *March 2007*

2 Title IX* did more than encourage women. It acted like a shock wave. . . . It gave hope and courage to women to organize for change. Women became a new advocacy group and learned the politics of change.

Ibid.

Title IX of the Education Amendments of 1972 (a.k.a. the Patsy T. Mink Equal Opportunity in Education Act (*see 2608), states: "No person in the United States shall, on the basis of sex, be excluded from participation in, be denied the benefits of, or be subjected to discrimination under any education program or activity receiving Federal financial assistance."

3 I naively thought that since sex discrimination was wrong, there must be a law against it.

Ibid.

2642. Anne Sexton (1928–1974)

1 . . . I gather
guilt like a young intern
his symptoms, his certain evidence.
"The Double Image," *To Bedlam and Partway Back* 1960

2 You, Dr. Martin,* walk from breakfast to madness.
"You, Dr. Martin," St. 1, Ibid.
*Martin Luther King, Jr., American civil rights leader, (1929–68); assassinated.

3 Today life opened inside me like an egg. . . .
"Live," *Live or Die* 1966

4 The trouble with being a woman,
Skeezis,
is being a little girl
in the first place.
"Hurry Up Please It's Time," *The Death Notebooks* 1974

5 Even without wars, life is dangerous.
Ibid.

6 What is death, I ask: What is life, you ask.
Ibid.

7 Generally speaking, mental hospitals are lonely places, they are full of televisions and medications.
"A Small Journal" (November 8, 1971), *The Poet's Story,* Howard Moss, ed. *1974*

8 I took the radio, my vigil keeper, and played it for my waking, sleeping ever since. In memoriam. It goes everywhere with me like a dog on a leash.
Ibid.

9 The sea is mother-death and she is a mighty female, the one who wins, the one who sucks us all up.
(Entry for 19 November 1971), Ibid.

10 The eyes, opening and shutting like cameras and never forgetting, recording by thousands. . . .
"The Earth," St. 3, *The Awful Rowing Toward God* 1975

11 The tongue, the Chinese say,
is like a sharp knife:
it kills
without drawing blood.
"The Dead Heart," St. 3, Ibid.

12 I am tired of being brave.
"The Truth the Dead Know," St. 1, *The Complete Poems* 1981

13 I have gone out, a possessed witch,
haunting the black air, braver at night;
dreaming evil. . . .
"Her Kind," St. 1, Ibid.

14 Pride pumped in her like poison.
"Snow White and the Seven Dwarfs," St. 2, Ibid.

15 But suicides have a special language.
Like carpenters they want to know which tools.
They never ask why build.
"Wanting to Die," St. 3, Ibid.

16 Until I was twenty-eight, I had a kind of buried self who didn't know she could do anything but make white sauce and diaper babies. I didn't know I had any creative depths. I was a victim of the American Dream, the bourgeois, middle-class dream. All I wanted was a little piece of life, to be married, to have children. I thought the nightmares, the visions, the demons would go away if there was enough love to put them down. I was trying my damnedest to lead a conventional life, for that was how I was brought up, and it was what my husband wanted of me. But one can't build little white picket fences to keep nightmares out.
Quoted in Pt. I, Ch. 1, *The World Split Open: How the Modern Women's Movement Changed America* by Ruth Rosen* 2000

*See 3608.

17 Each night I am nailed into place and forget who I am.
"Sleeping Beauty" *n.d.*

18 but I grew, I grew
and God was there like an island I had not rowed to,
still ignorant of Him, my arms and my legs worked,
and I grew, I grew,
I wore rubies and bought tomatoes
and now, in my middle age,
about nineteen in the head I'd say,
I am rowing, I am rowing
"Rowing" *n.d.*

2643. Norma Merrick Sklarek (1928–   )

1 Do not give up on anything you find difficult.
Speech, Scripps College, *Scripps Magazine Fall 2001*

2 Until the end of World War II, I think there was strong discrimination against women in architecture. It was fairy obvious the schools had a quota against women and against blacks. Even after graduation from Barnard, with a professional architectural degree, it was tough to get a job. I applied at about twenty different offices before I was able to land an entry-level job. I don't know if the rejections were because I was a black person, because I was a young woman, or because of the economic recession at the time.
Ibid.

2644. Agnès Varda (1928–   )

1 You ask me, is it difficult to be a woman director? I'd say that it's difficult to be a director, period! It's difficult to be free; it's difficult not to be drowned in the system. It's difficult for women, and it's difficult for men, the same way.
Quoted in an "Interview with Agnès Varda" by Barbara Confino, *Saturday Review 12 August 1972*

2 The image of woman is crucial, and in the . . . movies that image is always switching between the nun and the whore, the

mama and the bitch. We have put up with that for years, and it has to be changed. It is the image that is important, not so much who is making the film.

Ibid.

2645. Frances Weaver (1928?–2004)

1 The sincere desire to lead a productive, interesting life at any age depends upon our own imagination and acceptance of new ideas.

Ch. 1, *Girls with Grandmother Faces: A Celebration of Life's Potential For Those Over 55 1987*

2 I don't want to sound mean, but the way a woman copes with the reality of the death of her husband tells the world a great deal about both of those people.

Ch. 1, *There's More to Me Than I've Used Yet 1994*

3 *I'm Not as Old as I Used to Be*

Book title *1997*

2646. Ruth Westheimer (1928–)

1 If you love to eat steak, you still wouldn't want to eat it every night for dinner, even if you didn't like the other foods as much. Why? Because if you ate steak every day, you'd become bored with it and there would come a time you'd never want to eat it again. The same effect can happen with sex, which is why it is good to throw in some variety, even if only once in a while.

Dr. Ruth (drruth.com) *1997*

2 Today we do know that from a scientific point of view that for many women masturbation is the best way for them to learn how to give themselves permission to have an orgasm.

Ibid.

3 Considering that I was to become famous as an advocate of contraception, it's somewhat ironic that my parents didn't use it at precisely the point when they should have.

Ibid.

2647. Katharine Whitehorn (1928–)

1 Cooking times do not include the time it takes you to find the salt in the suitcase under the bed.

Cooking in a Bedsitter * 1961
*The British equivalent to a studio apartment.

2 From a commercial point of view, if Christmas did not exist it would be necessary to invent it.

"The Office Party," *Roundabout 1962*

3 There are some circles in America where it seems to be more socially acceptable to carry a hand-gun than a packet of cigarettes.

The Observer (London) *30 October 1988*

4 Gavin* was only 70 when he died. "It is an amputation," said one of the letters I received—a good analogy. Nothing can put back what's gone, but sooner or later the person who has lost a leg learns to walk with a crutch, the woman with only one hand left somehow manages to cope, even if she feels phantom pains in the limb that's no longer there.

Selective Memory 2007
*Her husband, novelist Gavin Lyall, who died in 2003.

5 The main point of camping is to remind one why they invented the house.

Ibid.

6 Given how long we're all living, maybe people will start to have careers at the ends of their lives. Perhaps it won't be necessary to do everything at the beginning. We're living another 30 bloody years after retirement, and a 30-year sabbatical is not on the cards, so career patterns are going to have to change. I believe people are going to have to work longer, and that they will be a damn sight happier if they do, though I know it's easy for me, because I'm a journalist and that's fun; it's not the same if you're scrubbing floors.

Quoted in "The domestic goddess who couldn't cook" by Rachel Cook, *The Observer* (London) *17 August 2008*

2648. Marion Woodman (1928–)

1 It takes great courage to break with one's past history and stand alone

Ch. 2, *Addiction to Perfection, The Still Unravished Bride 1982*

2 The aim in analysis is to bring the magnificent energy of the wild horse under the control of the rider, without using a whip that will kill its spirit.

Ch. 5, Ibid.

3 The experience of the feminine is the psychological key to both the sickness of our time and its healing.

Ch. 7, Ibid.

4 Moreover, perfectionist standards do not allow for failure. They do not even allow for life, and certainly not for death.

Ibid.

5 Many people can listen to their cat more intelligently than they can listen to their own despised body. Because they attend to their pet in a cherishing way, it returns their love. Their body, however, may have to let out an earth-shattering scream in order to be heard at all.

Ch. 1, *The Pregnant Virgin, A Process of Psychological Transformation 1985*

6 Healing depends on listening with the inner ear—stopping the incessant blather, and *listening*. Fear keeps us chattering—fear that wells up from the past, fear of blurting out what we really fear, fear of future repercussions. It is our very fear of the future that distorts the *now* that could lead to a different future if we dared to be whole in the present.

Ch. 6, Ibid.

9 Dismissing poetry is dismissing the glory of the imagination. Teaching English to adolescents for twenty years gives me the authority to say, "Kill the imagination and you kill the soul. Kill the soul and you're left with a listless, apathetic creature who can become hopeless or brutal or both. Kill the metaphor and you kill desire; the image magnetizes the movement of the energy." I will make this clear as I speak. The tax money that is being withdrawn from arts programs in schools will be spent on prisons.

p. 165, *Bone: Dying into Life 2000*

2649. Zong Pu (1928–)

1 "But I can't play the cello all day long. I must read some books too. Since I can't find any good ones, I'm reading these, even though they're bad. It's like food. When there's nothing delicious, I eat anything. So there!"

Ch. 3, "Melody in Dreams," Song Shouquan, tr., *Seven Contemporary Chinese Women Writers*, Gladys Yang,* ed. *1982*
*See 2358.

2 Yuejun was outraged thinking how many families had been ruined by the gang*; how many young people had been deprived of their lives. They wouldn't even leave the premier** alone. Our great hero had left nothing of himself after his death. Even his ashes had been scattered over the mountains and rivers. Now they intended to blacken his reputation.

Ch. 4, Ibid.

*Reference to the "Gang of Four," the term of aspersion used by the Chinese authorities after the Cultural Revolution (1966–69) to identify those held responsible for its excesses. **Mao Tse Tung (a.k.a. Mao Zedong), Chinese communist leader (1893–1976).

2650. Shulamit Aloni (1929–   )

1 According to civil law, women are equal to men. But I have to go to a religious court as far as personal affairs are concerned. Only men are allowed to be judges there—men who pray every morning to thank God He did not make them women. You need prejudice before you open your mouth. And because they believe women belong in the home, you are doubly discriminated against if you work.

Quoted in "Women in Israel" (November 1973), *Crazy Salad* by Nora Ephron* 1975

*See 3258.

2 Even though Israel's "patriotic" media seek to ignore you, there is no doubt that your voice will be heard and that a great many others will join your cause. You will break through the silence because yours is a vision of freedom, justice, and peace.

Speech, March of Mourning, Coalition of Women for a Just Peace 2 January 2002

2651. Rosalie Bertell (1929–   )

1 With no biological testing of victims it is hard to prove causality. None of these problems are considered serious in the eyes of nuclear experts because they have not yet caused radiation-induced cancer death. We need a new word to describe this random damaging of life. I would suggest using nucleogenic or technogenic illness to describe these induced abnormalities.

In the face of such lack of sensitivity to human health considerations, concern for the future viability of the human race, placed under great stress by militarism and high tech, is rational, not irrational.

Acceptance Speech, Right Livelihood Award (Stockholm), 8 December 1986

2 If we truly want to assume stature as a mature global family of nations we need to extend responsibility to the people of the world through a representative assembly, rather than assign abnormal political power to countries with weapons of mass destruction. We need to invest power in international treaties, conflict resolution mechanisms and the World Court.

Ibid.

3 The people of the global village are longing to share in the benefits of human endeavor, not the garbage; to share in the wholesomeness of life and not to be handed death. It is my heart-felt wish that the good begun here will flow forth as a river of life justice, and hope for those people most broken and needy in our global village.

Ibid.

2652. Betty Boothroyd (1929–   )

1 Everyone thinks it [touring in a dance company] was all men drinking champagne from your shoes. But, like politics, it was damned hard and taught me about teamwork.

Article by Judith Newman and Ellin Stein, quoted in *People* 28 February 1994

2 You've got to ensure that the holders of an opinion, however unpopular, are allowed to put across their points of view.

Ibid.

2653. Meg Bowman (1929–   )

1 One of the worst sexists was the revered sage Confucius. This respected religious leader said, "One hundred women are not worth a single testicle."

Why We Burn: Sexism Exorcised 1988

2 Our foremothers, Susan B. Anthony, Elizabeth Cady Stanton, Matilda Joslyn Gage, Sojourner Truth and Alice Paul* knew that the major force against women's rights came from the male clergy.

Ibid.

*See 1487, 931, 1007, 860, 1637.

2654. Violeta Barrios de Chamorro (1929–   )

1 We [the newspaper staff] will die here.

Quoted in "Once-lively paper is dead under Sandinistas" by Rick Raber, *The Times/Picayune* (New Orleans) 22 February 1987

2 When you run a paper under a dictatorship, it's very difficult and dangerous.

Quoted in "I Had To Be Strong From the Beginning" by Larry Smith, *Parade Magazine* 17 February 1991

3 Before, it was one person who decided everything, who managed everybody, and a fly could not fly and a cat could not walk without asking permission from the dictator. Now that we are making democracy, it's completely different.... There's an explosion, we could say, a certain excess of liberty. After 50 years, *la gente*—the people—now want everything to be done quickly.

Ibid.

4 I think problems can be solved through dialogue, looking for solutions, but I want no intervention and no interference— from nobody!

Ibid.

5 There cannot be sovereignty without peace; no sovereignty without liberty. But to have liberty you must respect the rule of the law, other people's morals and opinions, and private property as well.

Quoted in *Twentieth-Century Women Political Leaders* by Claire Price-Groff 1998

6 Reconciliation is more beautiful than victory.

Ibid.

2655. Liz Claiborne (1929–2007)

1 I wanted to dress busy and active women like myself, women who dress in a rush and who weren't perfect. But loving clothes, I knew clothes could do a certain thing for you from

a flattering point of view. And I tried to bring good taste to a mass level.

> Interview, *Women's Wear Daily* 1989

2656. Oriana Fallaci (1929–2006)

1   Listening to someone talk isn't at all like listening to their words played over on a machine. What you hear when you have a face before you is never what you hear when you have before you a winding tape.

> Foreword, *The Egotists* 1963

2   Glory is a heavy burden, a murdering poison, and to bear it is an art. And to have that art is rare.

> "Federico Fellini,"* Ibid.

*Italian film director (1920–93).

3   We are all going to become Swedish, and we do not understand these Americans who, like adolescents, always speak of sex, and who, like adolescents, all of a sudden have discovered that sex is good not only for procreating children.

> "Hugh Hefner,"* Ibid.

*American magazine publisher (1926–   )

4   I'm going to show you the real New York—witty, smart, and international—like any metropolis. Tell me this—where in Europe can you find old Hungary, old Russia, old France, old Italy? In Europe you're trying to copy America, you're almost American. But here you'll find Europeans who immigrated a hundred years ago—and we haven't spoiled them. Oh, Gio! You must see why I love New York. Because the whole world's in New York.

> Ch. 8, *Penelope at War* 1966

5   Have you ever thought that war is a madhouse and that everyone in the war is a patient? Tell me, how can a normal man get up in the morning knowing that in an hour or a minute he may no longer be there? How can he walk through heaps of decomposing corpses and then sit down at the table and calmly eat a roll? How can he defy nightmare-like risks and then be ashamed of panicking for a moment?

> Ch. 6, *Nothing, and So Be It* 1972

6   Equality, Child, like freedom, exists only where you are now. Only as an egg in the womb are we all equal.

> *Letter to a Child Never Born* 1975

7   But what is this life by which you, who exist still incomplete, count for more than I, who exist completely already? What is this respect for you that removes respect for me? What is this right of yours to exist that takes no account of my right to exist?

> Ibid.

2657. Anne Frank (1929–1945)

1   I soothe my conscience now with the thought that it is better for hard words to be on paper than that Mummy should carry them in her heart.

> Entry (2 January 1944), *The Diary of a Young Girl* 1947 (tr. 1952)

2   I think what is happening to me is so wonderful, and not only what can be seen on my body, but all that is taking place inside. I never discuss myself or any of these things with anybody; that is why I have to talk to myself about them.

> Ibid.

3   The best remedy for those who are afraid, lonely or unhappy is to go outside, somewhere where they can be quiet, alone with the heavens, nature and God. Because only then does one feel that all is as it should be and that God wishes to see people happy, amidst the simple beauty of nature. As long as this exists, and it certainly always will, I know that then there will always be comfort for every sorrow, whatever the circumstances may be. And I firmly believe that nature brings solace in all troubles.

> Entry (23 February 1944), Ibid.

4   I don't believe that the big men, the politicians and the capitalists alone are guilty of the war. Oh, no, the little man is just as keen, otherwise the people of the world would have risen in revolt long ago! There is an urge and rage in people to destroy, to kill, to murder, and until all mankind, without exception, undergoes a great change, wars will be waged, everything that has been built up, cultivated and grown, will be destroyed and disfigured, after which mankind will have to begin all over again.

> Entry (3 May 1944), Ibid.

5   Parents can only give good advice or put them on the right paths, but the final forming of a person's character lies in their own hands. . . .

> Entry (15 July 1944), Ibid.

6   I'm awfully scared that everyone who knows me as I always am will discover that I have another side, a finer and better side. I'm afraid they'll laugh at me, think I'm ridiculous and sentimental, not take me seriously . . .*

> Ibid.

*Last words of last entry. Three days after writing this entry, Anne Frank was arrested and sent to a concentration camp in Germany

2658. Marilyn French (1929–2009)

1   One thing that makes art different from life is that in art things have a shape . . . it allows us to fix our emotions on events at the moment they occur, it permits a union of heart and mind and tongue and tear.

> Ch. 3, *The Women's Room* 1977

2   "Well, love is insanity. The ancient Greeks knew that. It is the taking over of a rational and lucid mind by delusion and self-destruction. You lose yourself, you have no power over yourself, you can't even think straight."

> Ch. 10, Ibid.

3   "When they kept you out it was because you were black; when they let you in, it is because you are black. That's progress?"

> Ch. 19, Ibid.

4   "I hate discussions of feminism that end up with who does the dishes," she said. So do I. But at the end, there are always the damned dishes.

> Ch. 21, Ibid.

5   In a patriarchal world, power is not just the highest but the only value.

> *Beyond Power; On Men, Women, and Morals* 1985

6   In personal and public life, in kitchen, bedroom and halls of parliament, men wage unremitting war against women.

> *The War Against Women* 1992

7   Men expect women to perform the most important of all human tasks [child-bearing] with no reward, without much help, and with almost no consideration.

> Ibid.

8 If you pay attention to history, and know what has happened in the past, you will realize that the rights we have so arduously won in the United States slowly but surely can be rescinded by a right-wing Supreme Court combined with a right-wing government. And are.

Introduction, "Origins," *From Eve to Dawn: A History of Women in the World*, vol. 1 2002

9 The feminist movement is the most important revolution that has ever occurred on earth.

Introduction, "Revolutions and the Struggles for Justice in the 20th Century," vol. 4, Ibid.

2659. Shirley Ann Grau (1929–)

1 And isn't it funny, she thought, that it takes two generations to kill off a man? . . . First him, and then his memory. . . .

"Margaret," *The Keepers of the House* 1964

2 Why does it take so much trouble to keep your stomach full and quiet?

Ibid.

3 Her Father was waiting. When she saw him, she felt the usual shift in her feelings. A lift, a jump, a tug. Pleasure, but not totally. Love, but not completely. Dependence. Fear, familiarity, identification. That's part of me there, walking along. Tree from which I sprang. His spasm produced me. Shake of his body and here I am. . . .

"Margaret," *The Condor Passes* 1971

4 "Haven't you ever noticed how highways always get beautiful near the state capital?"

"The Way Back," Ibid.

5 Trees come out of acorns, no matter how unlikely that seems. An acorn is just a tree's way back into the ground. For another try. Another trip through. One life or another. And what came out of sex now. Love maybe. But that wasn't as sure as a tree. Or maybe a tree was as unsure as Love. One capsule life or another.

Ibid.

6 Me? What am I? Nothing. The legs on which dinner comes to the table, the arms by which cocktails enter the living room, the hands that drive cars. I am the eyes that see nothing, the ears that don't hear. I'm invisible too. They look and don't see me. When they move, I have to guess their direction and get myself out of the way. If they were to walk into me—all six feet of black skin and white bone—they'd never again be able to pretend that I wasn't there. And I'd be looking for another job.

"Stanley," Ibid.

7 "You forget places you've been and you forget women you've had, but you don't forget fighting."

"Homecoming," *The Wind Shifting West* 1973

8 Women use children as excuses not to do anything.

Quoted in "Profile . . . Shirley Ann Grau" by Louis Gallo, *New Orleans February* 1974

2660. Elizabeth Dodson Gray (1929–)

1 It is not accidental that in the Genesis 2 account of creation Adam "named" all the animals. Naming is power, the power to shape reality into a form that serves the interest and goals of the one doing the naming.

Sunday School Manifesto 1988

2661. Jeanette Greene (1929–)

1 It's just the traditional thing for men to run the government here [in Alabama]. It's that Southern mentality, that let's let father do it. . . .

[But] I handled 10th-graders for years. I can handle those men in the Legislature.

Cited in "Olympian Women" by Dionne Searcey, *Seattle Times*, A18 31 January 1999

2662. Audrey Hepburn (1929–1993)

1 Keep trying. Take care of the small circle around you. When you have succeeded with them, then move outwards, one small step at a time.

Quoted by her son, Sean Hepburn Ferrer* in *Seattle Post-Intelligencer* 1994

*At the founding of the Audrey Hepburn Hollywood for Children Fund, Los Angeles, 1994.

2 For attractive lips, speak words of kindness.
For lovely eyes, seek out the good in people.
For a slim figure, share your food with the hungry.
For beautiful hair, let a child run his or her fingers through it once a day.
For poise, walk with the knowledge you'll never walk alone.

"Beauty Tips" *n.d.*

3 Remember, if you ever need a helping hand, you'll find one at the end of your arm. As you grow older, you will discover that you have two hands, one for helping yourself, the other for helping others.

Ibid.

2663. Florence Howe (1929–)

1 Thirty-five years later, and with Olsen* in early mid-stage Alzheimer's, I want to emphasize the contribution she has made not only to the Feminist Press as a nonprofit publishing house, but to the entire field of literature world-wide.

Statement, "Jewish Women and the Feminist Revolution", *Jewish Women's Archive* 2007

*Tillie O- ; see 2187.

2664. Barbara Marx Hubbard (1929–)

1 The vast effort of humanity to "be fruitful and multiply" would have to be curtailed in our generation. One more doubling of the world population will destroy our life support system. Our Mother will not support us if we continue to grow in numbers! We must stop.

The Revelation: A Message of Hope for the New Millennium 1995

2 It's the third great human drive: from self-preservation to self-reproduction to self-evolution.

"At the Crossroad: Living in Between," *The Fabric of the Future: Women Visionaries of Today Illuminate the Path to Tomorrow*, M. J. Ryan, ed. 1998

3 It has taken fifteen billion years of evolution, from the Big Bang to the present to develop a planetary species on Earth that is aware of itself as a whole and must become responsible for the future of the whole system. The entire story of creation has led to the birth of a species which must learn to cooperate and cocreate on a planetary scale.

Ibid.

4   *Conscious Evolution* carries us beyond the human potential movement toward the social potential movement and describes a new social architecture to enhance and connect social innovations now evolving our world.

> Ch. 1, *Conscious Evolution: Awakening our Social Potential* 1998

5   A "Universal Human" is one who is connected through the heart to the whole of life, attuned to the deeper intelligence of nature, and called forth irresistibly by spirit to creatively express his or her gifts in the evolution of self and the world.

> Introduction, *Emergence: The Shift from Ego to Essence* 2001

2665. Jill Johnston (1929–   )

1   It's necessary in order to attract attention, to dazzle at all costs, to be disapproved of by serious people and quoted by the foolish.

> *Lesbian Nation: The Feminist Solution* 1973

2   Bisexuality is not so much a copout as a fearful compromise.

> Ibid.

3   I never said I was a dyke even to a dyke because there wasn't a dyke in the land who thought she should be a dyke or even thought she was a dyke so how could we talk about it.

> Ibid.

4   . . . I want these women in office who're in touch with their feelings and who know perfectly well when they're bullshitting and who don't have to displace their concealed feelings by dropping bombs on people who live thousands of miles away. . . .

> *Gullible's Travels* 1974

2666. Louise J. Kaplan (1929–   )

1   Adolescence is the conjugator of childhood and adulthood.

> Ch. 3, *Adolescence: The Farewell to Childhood* 1984

2   When a child becomes an adult . . . the elders are fearful. And for good reason . . . not we but they are the germinators of future generations. Will they leave us behind as we did our parents? Consign us to neatly paved retirement villages? Trample us in the dust as they go flying out to their new galaxies? We had better tie them down, flagellate them, isolate them in the family cocoon, . . . indoctrinate them into the tribal laws and make sure they kneel before the power of the elders.

> Ch. 5, Ibid.

3   Children, even infants, are capable of sympathy. But only after adolescence are we capable of compassion.

> Ch. 12, Ibid.

4   The purpose of adolescence is to revise the past, not to obliterate it. . . . Adolescence entails the deployment of family passions to the passions and ideals that bind individuals to new family units, to their communities, to the species, to nature, to the cosmos. Therefore, given half a chance, the revolution at issue in adolescence becomes a revolution of transformation, not of annihilation.

> Ibid.

5   It didn't take elaborate experiments to deduce that an infant would die from want of food. But it took centuries to figure out that infants can and do perish from want of love.

> Ch. 1, *No Voice Is Every Wholly Lost* 1995

2667. Sheila Kitzinger (1929–   )

1   Health is not a medical artifact. Economics, politics, the social system in which we live, conditions in the work-place, poisons in the environment, and personal relationships are all elements in causing health and disease. Doctors treat illness; they do not make us healthy. For the vast majority of women physical health and a sense of well-being during pregnancy is nothing to do with how often they visit the doctor, but with the social conditions in which they live.

> *Birth over 35* 1994

2   I must have done something right.*

> Quoted in *Daily Telegraph* 16 January 1997
> *On three of her daughters being lesbians.

3   It is time to discuss the language of choice. "Choice" comes from the language of advertising It is used to promote products. Remember the advertisement, "You've come a long way baby! Smoke Virginia Slims." Statements about caesareans being a "woman's choice" grows the power differential between women and obstetricians. An emergency procedure has become routine practice. The language of choice has been appropriated by obstetricians.

> p. 284, *British Journal of Midwifery*, vol. 9 May 2001

4   Birth is the only sport I can do.

> *The New Experience of Childbirth* 2004

5   You don't need an MBA in baby management to be a good mother.

> *Understanding Your Crying Baby* 2005

6   To get women upright [in childbirth] is to do far more than help them find a comfortable posture. It is to turn them from passive patients to active birthgivers.

> *The Lancet*, vol. 369, no. 817 10 March 2007

2668. Ursula K. Le Guin (1929–   )

1   To hear, one must be silent.

> *A Wizard of Earthsea* 1968

2   When action grows unprofitable, gather information; when information grows unprofitable, sleep.

> Ch. 3, *The Left Hand of Darkness* 1969

3   . . . Primitiveness and civilization are degrees of the same thing. If civilization has an opposite, it is war. Of these two things, you have either one, or the other. Not both.

> Ch. 8, Ibid.

4   It is good to have an end to journey towards; but it is the journey that matters, not the end.

> Ch. 15, Ibid.

5   Nothing remains the same from one moment to the next, you can't step into the same river twice. Life—evolution—the whole universe of space/time, matter/energy—existence itself—is essentially change.

> *The Lathe of Heaven* 1971

6   He had grown up in a country run by politicians who sent the pilots to man the bombers to kill the babies to make the world safe for children to grow up in.

> Ch. 6, Ibid.

7   Love doesn't just sit there, like a stone, it has to be made, like bread; re-made all the time, made new.

> Ch. 10, Ibid.

8 "His soul is about the size of a toenail."
Ch. 7, *The Eye of the Heron* 1978

9 Art, like sex, cannot be carried on indefinitely solo; after all they have the same mutual enemy, sterility.
Pt. I, "A Citizen of Mondath," *The Language of the Night, Essays on Fantasy and Science Fiction,* Susan Wood, ed. and intro. *1979*

10 For the story—from *Rumplestilskin* to *War and Peace*—is one of the basic tools invented by the mind of man, for the purpose of gaining understanding. There have been great societies that did not use the wheel, but there have been no societies that did not tell stories.
Pt. II, "On Fantasy and Science Fiction," *Ibid.*

11 Now, I doubt that the imagination can be suppressed. If you truly eradicated it in a child, he would grow up to be an egg-plant. Like all our evil propensities, the imagination will out. But if it is rejected and despised, it will grow into wild and weedy shapes; it will be deformed.
Pt. V, "Why Are Americans Afraid of Dragons?" *Ibid.*

12 Fake realism is the escapist realism of our time. And probably the ultimate escapist reading is that masterpiece of total unre-ality, the daily stock market report.
Ibid.

13 Sure it's simple, writing for kids. Just as simple as bringing them up.
"Dreams Must Explain Themselves," *Ibid.*

14 Fantasy is nearer to poetry, to mysticism, and to insanity than naturalistic fiction is. It is a real wilderness, and those who go there should not feel too safe.
"From Elfland to Poughkeepsie," *Ibid.*

15 In art, "good enough" is not good enough.
Ibid.

16 The worst walls are never the ones you find in your way. The worst walls are the ones you put there—you build yourself. Those are the high ones, the thick ones, the ones with no doors in.
"The Stone Ax and the Muskoxen," *Ibid.*

17 Hating gets going, it goes round, it gets older and tighter and older and tighter until it holds a person inside it like a fist holds a stick.
Four Histories, "Old Woman Hating," *Always Coming Home* 1985

18 O brave new world that has no people in it!
"Time in the Valley," *Ibid.*

19 Almost everything is double like that for adolescents; their lies are true and their truths are lies, and their hearts are broken by the world. They gyre and fall; they see through everything, and are blind.
"Stone Telling," Pt. II, *Ibid.*

20 If we can get that realistic feminine morality working for us, if we can trust ourselves and so let women think and feel that an unwanted child or an oversize family is wrong—not ethically wrong, not against the rules, but morally wrong, all wrong, wrong like a thalidomide birth, wrong like taking a wrong step that will break your neck—if we can get feminine and human

morality out from under the yoke of a dead ethic, then maybe we'll begin to get somewhere on the road that leads to sur-vival.
Speech, "Moral and Ethical Implications of Family Planning," Planned Parenthood Symposium (March 1978, Portland, Maine), *Dancing at the Edge of the World* 1989

21 Translation is entirely mysterious. Increasingly I have felt that the art of writing is itself translating, or more like translating than it is like anything else. What is the other text, the original? I have no answer. I suppose it is the source, the deep sea where ideas swim, and one catches them in nets of words and swings them shining into the boat . . . where in this metaphor they die and get canned and eaten in sandwiches.
Address, "Reciprocity of Prose and Poetry," Poetry Series, Folger Shakespeare Library (Washington, D.C., 1983), *Ibid.*

22 Our roots are in the dark; the earth is our country. Why did we look up for blessing—instead of around, and down? What hope we have lies there. Not in the sky full of orbiting spy-eyes and weaponry, but in the earth we have looked down upon. Not from above, but from below. Not in the light that blinds, but in the dark that nourishes, where human beings grow human souls.
"A Left-Handed Commencement Address," Mills College (1983), *Ibid.*

23 Literature takes shape and life in the body, in the wombs of the mother tongue: always: and the Fathers of Culture get anxious about paternity. They start talking about legitimacy. They steal the baby. They ensure by every means that the art-ist, the writer, is male. This involves intellectual abortion by centuries of women artists, infanticide of works by women writers, and a whole medical corps of sterilizing critics work-ing to purify the Canon, to reduce the subject matter and style of literature to something Ernest Hemingway could have un-derstood.
Address, Bryn Mawr Commencement (1986), *Ibid.*

24 We are volcanoes. When we women offer our experience as our truth, as human truth, all the maps change. There are new mountains.
Ibid.

25 On Aka, *god* is a word without referent. No capital letters. No creator, only creation. No eternal father to reward and punish, justify injustice, ordain cruelty, offer salvation. Eternity not an endpoint but a continuity.
Ch. 4, *The Telling* 2000

26 "Don't hold on to things, they weigh you down. Keep in your head what's worth keeping."
Ibid.

27 To think that realistic fiction is by definition superior to imagi-native fiction is to think imitation is superior to invention.
"The Question I Get Asked Most Often," *The Wave in the Mind: Talks and Essays on the Writer, the Reader, and the Imagination* 2004

28 Whenever they tell me children want this sort of book and chil-dren need this sort of writing, I am going to smile politely and shut my earlids. I am a writer, not a caterer. There are plenty of caterers. But what children most want and need is what we and they don't know they want and don't think they need, and only writers can offer it to them.
"A Message About Messages," *CBC Magazine n.d.*

29 The book itself is a curious artifact, not showy in its technology but complex and extremely efficient: a really neat little device, compact, often very pleasant to look at and handle, that can last decades, even centuries. It doesn't have to be plugged in, activated, or performed by a machine; all it needs is light, a human eye, and a human mind. It is not one of a kind, and it is not ephemeral. It lasts. It is reliable. If a book told you something when you were fifteen, it will tell you again when you're fifty, though you may understand it so differently that it seems you're reading a whole new book.

"Staying Awake," *Harper's* February 2009

2669. Joanna Macy (1929–)

1 The Third Turning, I think, will be what Robinson Jeffers* called "falling in love outward." Our mission is not to escape from our world, or fix things by remote control, looking at charts and pushing buttons, and pulling levers, but to fall in love with our world. We are made for that, because we co-arise with her—in a dance where we discover ourselves and lose ourselves over and over.

World As Lover, World As Self 1990
*American poet (1887–1962).

2 Greed and fear are very isolating. They make us crazy. We have to see through them and refuse to be pitted against each other. Only through all beings and with all beings can we awaken to our peace and joy. Our daily adventure is to realize that.

Ibid.

3 In my mind I still hear the local Sarvodaya* workers, in their village meetings and district training centers. Development is not imitating the West. Development is not high-cost industrial complexes, chemical fertilizers and mammoth hydro-electric dams. It is not selling your soul for unnecessary consumer items or schemes to get rich quick. Development is waking up—waking up our true potential as persons and as a society.

(p. 132), Ibid.
*A Buddhist practice that means "everybody wakes up."

4 No magic bullet, not even the Internet, can save us from population explosion, deforestation, climate disruption, poison by pollution, and wholesale extinctions of plant and animal species. We are going to have to want different things, seek different pleasures, pursue different goals, than those that have been driving us and our global economy.

New values must arise *now*, while we still have room to maneuver—and that is precisely what is happening. They are emerging at this very moment, like green shoots through the rubble.

"The Great Turning," *The Fabric of the Future: Women Visionaries of Today Illuminate the Path to Tomorrow,* M. J. Ryan, ed. *1998*

5 We are opening our senses to the web of relationships, the deep ecology, in which we have our being. Like our primordial ancestors, we begin again to see the world as our body and (whether we say the word or not) as sacred.

Ibid.

2670. Imelda Marcos (1929–)

1 I was no Marie Antoinette,* I was not born to nobility, but I had a human right to nobility.

Quoted on *60 Minutes* with Diane Sawyer,** CBS-TV *21 September 1986*
*See 682. **See 3610.

2 If you know how much you've got, you probably haven't got much.

Ibid.

3 Life is not a matter of place, things or comfort; rather, it concerns the basic human rights of family, country, justice and human dignity.

Quoted in *Newsweek* (New York) *12 June 1989*

4 I get so tired listening to one million dollars here, one million dollars there, it's so petty.*

Quoted in *The Times* (London) *22 June 1990*
*Response to witnesses' testimony against her during her trial in New York on charges of embezzlement.

2671. Jane Roland Martin (1929–)

1 Just as no two individuals and no two circumstances are alike in every respect, no two are different in every respect.

"Methodological Essentialism, False Difference, and Other Dangerous Traps," *Signs, vol. 19, no. 31 1994*

2 Almost every schoolteacher has at one time or another been driven to the brink by the thought of how much there is to teach and how impossible it is to do it all. Just about every child has wondered at least once or twice why he or she was being told to learn this rather than that.

Ch. 1, *Cultural Miseducation: In Search of a Democratic Solution* 2002

3 How paradoxical that even as so many of the world's resources have been shrinking, the inheritance from which curriculum's content is drawn has been growing!

Ibid.

4 Just as the old economic wealth was eventually exposed as the loot of robber barons who exploited their workers, cheated their customers, bribed politicians, and waged war on their competitors, the creation of the scholarship of yore has been shown to depend on unacknowledged, unrewarded labor.

Ibid.

5 Culture in the broadest sense of the term includes not just artistic and scholarly products, whether masterpieces or works of lesser merit. It encompasses the institutions and practices, rites and rituals, beliefs and skills, attitudes and values, worldviews and localized modes of thinking and acting of *all* members of society over the *whole* range of contexts.

Ibid.

2672. Emma Mashinini (1929–)

1 That was the most horrible day of my detention. The whole day I could see my baby's face and wanted to call her name, "Dudu," "Dudu," but my mind was blank. I couldn't recollect it. "Can a mother forget her baby's name?" I wondered.*

Ch. 13, *Lives of Courage* Diana E. H. Russell** 1989
*Of her experience in police detention. **See 3104.

2673. Arna Mer-Khamis (1929–1995)

1 In this land were sown the seeds of racism and suffering, wars and death and pain. An entire nation stands before us bereft of human rights, where children grow up surrounded by the imagery of soldiers, stones and guns. They are scared, they are threatened, they are vulnerable. And their cries of suffering are

drowned by loudspeakers screaming about Law, Order, Security and Progress.
Acceptance Speech, Right Livelihood Award (Stockholm), 9 December 1993

2 We [Defence of the Children] have received the greatest prize of all—their smiles, their confidence, their friendship—all of which have served to breed a new human relationship between Jews and Arabs. The only basis for a real peace.
Ibid.

3 The child under military occupation is affected psychologically, emotionally and academically. So if one wants to support and strengthen these children, one has to consider them from all these aspects. The socialisation of the child is the most basic thing in its life; if you see children only as individuals, in fact you can be indirectly deepening their problems ... Our principle is to serve the child: to turn the pyramid [of education and authority] upside down.
Ibid.

4 Before 1948, Arabs and Jews were living together in harmony and fraternity. However, in a span of a few months the creation of the state of Israel caused racism and contempt towards the "Arab," an attitude that did not exist before. Arabs and Jews should live together. This is possible, as not only is there no other alternative, but it occurred in the past.
"The Work of Arna Mer-Khamis with Palestinian children under occupation" by Sanà A. Osseiran arna.info 10 June 2002

5 There is no freedom without knowledge. There is no peace without freedom. Peace and freedom are bound together.
Arna's Children (documentary film) 2003

2674. Ellen James Morphonios (1929–)

1 I have a saying—there's no justice in the law.
Lawyer's Wit and Wisdom, Bruce Nash, Allan Zullo, eds., Kathryn Zullo, compiler 1995

2675. Nel Noddings (1929–)

1 Many of the practices embedded in the masculine curriculum masquerade as essential to the maintenance of standards, ... [but in fact] they accomplish quite a different purpose: the systematic dehumanization of both female and male children through the loss of the feminine.
Caring 1984

2 It is time for the voice of the mother to be heard in education.
Ibid.

3 In direct opposition to the current emphasis on academic standards, a national curriculum, and national assessment, I have argued that our main educational aim should be to encourage the growth of competent, caring, loving, and lovable people.
"A Morally Defensible Mission for Schools in the 21st Century," Phi Delta Kappa January 1995

4 Programs for the noncollege-bound should be just as rich, desirable, and rigorous as those for the college-bound.
Ibid.

5 Teachers can be very special people in the lives of children, and it should be legitimate for them to spend time developing relations of trust, talking with students about problems that are

central to their lives, and guiding them toward greater sensitivity and competence across all the domains of care.
"Teaching Themes of Care," Ibid. May 1995

6 In an age when violence among school-children is at an unprecedented level, when children are bearing children with little knowledge of how to care for them, when the society and even the schools often concentrate on materialistic messages, it may be unnecessary to argue that we should care more genuinely for our children and teach them to care. However, many otherwise reasonable people seem to believe that our educational problems consist largely of low scores on achievement tests.
Ibid.

2676. Jacqueline Kennedy Onassis (1929–1994)

1 If you bungle raising your children, I don't think whatever else you do well matters very much.
Pt. 4, Ch. 15, Quoted in Kennedy by Theodore C. Sorenson 1965

2 Minimum information given with maximum politeness.*
Quoted in A Hero for Our Time by Ralph G. Martin 1983
*Her guidelines for dealing with the media.

3 The one thing I do not want to be called is First Lady. It sounds like a saddle horse.
Pt. 3, Ch. 2, Quoted in The Kennedys by Peter Collier and David Horowitz 1984

4 How can I explain these people [the Kennedys]? They were like carbonated water, and other families might be flat.
Letter to friend, reported in "A Woman Named Jackie," Pt. 1, by C. David Heymann, Seattle Post-Intelligencer 23 May 1994

5 The main thing for me was to do whatever my husband wanted. He couldn't—and wouldn't—be married to a woman who tried to share the spotlight with him.
Pt. 2, Ibid. 24 May 1994

6 Do you think seeing the coffin can upset me, doctor? I've seen my husband die, shot in my arms. His blood is all over me. How can I see anything worse than I've seen?
Quoted by physician at Parkland Memorial Hospital,* cited in "America's First Lady" by Peggy Noonan,** Time (New York) 30 May 1994
*The hospital in Dallas, Texas, where John F. Kennedy's body was taken after having been shot. **See 3996.

7 For a while I thought history was something that bitter old men wrote. But then I realized history made Jack* what he was. You must think of him as this little boy, sick so much of the time, reading in bed, reading history, reading the Knights of the Round Table, reading Marlborough. For Jack, history was full of heroes. And if it made him this way—if it made him see the heroes—maybe other little boys will see. Men are such a combination of good and bad. Jack had this hero idea of history, this idealistic view.
Interview with Theodore White** (1963), Ibid.
*Her husband, John F. Kennedy (1917–63), 35th U.S. president (1961–63); assassinated. **American political journalist (1915–1986).

8 I think my biggest achievement is that after going through a rather difficult time, I consider myself comparatively sane. I'm proud of that.
Remark (1979), "Portrait of a Friendship" by John Russell, Ibid.

2677. Vivian Gussin Paley (1929–   )

1   Turning sixty, I am more aware of the voices of exclusion in the classroom. "You can't play" suddenly seems too overbearing and harsh, resounding like a slap from wall to wall. How casually one child determines the fate of another.
You Can't Say You Can't Play 1992

2   In time we discovered that play was indeed work. First there was the business of deciding who to be and who the others must be and what the environment is to look like and when it is time to change the scene. Then there was the even bigger problem of getting others to listen to *you* and accept *your* point of view while keeping the integrity of the make-believe, the commitment of the other players, and perhaps the loyalty of a best friend.
"Young Children," *Ibid.*

3   Children do not pretend to be storytellers; they are storytellers. It is their intuitive approach to all occasions. It is the way they think.
The Girl With the Brown Crayon: How Children Use Stories to Shape Their Lives 1997

4   No longer am I tested each day as I was in the classroom. *There* it was quite impossible to cover my mistakes; here, upon this podium, the illusion of virtue comes easily.
The Kindness of Children 1999

2678. Peng Peiyun (1929–   )

1   China is one of the developing countries which invest substantively in reproductive health care. The service network extends to all cities and villages throughout the country and service facilities have been improved and service capacity upgraded.
Address, Conference on the Implementation of the ICPD* of Action (Ottawa, Canada), *21 November 2002*
*Internatl. Conference on Population and Development.

2   Women's health must be promoted, people's legitimate rights must be protected and family planning and other reproductive health performance should be upgraded. The adoption and enforcement of the "Population and Family Planning Law" will certainly exert a significant and profound impact on stabilizing low fertility, upgrading family planning performance, safeguarding the legal interests and rights of citizens, as well as on the coordinated development between population and economy, society, resource, environment, and sustainable development in China.
Ibid.

3   Global sustainable development requires the collective efforts of countries all over the world. For the sake of the common future of humankind, we . . . strongly urge the international community and the various national governments, the governments of the developed countries in particular, to further raise awareness for population and development, . . . fully understand the difficulties of developing countries in resource and technology, honor their pledges made at the ICPD, increase funding for population, family planning, and reproductive health programmes, so as to promote global sustainable development.
Ibid.

4   With great determination, defeat the drug devil, to create for yourself and your family a bright future.
Motto, Calligraphic work at Drug Treatment Center (China), *11 October 2006*

2679. Dory Previn (1930–   )

1   men wander
women weep
women worry
while men are asleep
"Men Wander" *1971*

2   I said
your words
till my throat
closed up
and I had
no choice
but to do your song
I was you baby
I was you too long
"I Was You" *1971*

3   Would you care to stay till sunrise
it's completely your decision
it's just the night cuts through me like a knife
would you care to stay awhile and save my life?
"The Lady With the Braid" *1971*

4   What most of us want is to be heard, to communicate—which are in the ballads of the wandering minstrel.
Quoted in "Sexism Seen But Not Heard" by Tracy Hotchner, *The Los Angeles Times 26 May 1974*

2679.1. Quin Guanshu (1929–   )

1   Wasting time is an unbearable punishment.
Quoted by Huang Zongying* in "The Flight of the Wild Geese," Yu Fanqin & Wang Mingjie, trs., *Seven Contemporary Chinese Women Writers*, Gladys Yang, ed. *1982*
*See 2358.

2680. Adrienne Rich (1929–   )

1   Weather abroad
And weather in the heart alike come on
Regardless of prediction.
"Storm Warnings," *A Change of World 1951*

2   A thinking woman sleeps with monsters.
"Snapshots of a Daughter-in-Law," Pt. III, St. 1 (1958–1960), *Snapshots of a Daughter-in-Law 1963*

3   Nothing changes. The bones of the mammoths are still in the earth.
"End of an Era," St. 1 (1961), *Ibid.*

4   I'd call it love if love
didn't take so many years
but lust too is a jewel
a sweet flower. . . .
"Two Songs," Pt. I (1964), *Necessities of Life 1966*

5   Only where there is language is there world.
"The Demon Lover," *Leaflets 1969*

6   Posterity trembles like a leaf
and we go on making heirs and heirlooms.
Ibid.

7   The victory carried like a corpse
from town to town
begins to crawl in the casket.
"Letters: March 1969: I," *The Will to Change 1971*

8 Rape is a part of war; but it may be more accurate to say that the capacity for dehumanizing another which so corrodes male sexuality is carried over from sex into war.

"Caryatid," *American Poetry Review* (repr. in *On Lies, Secrets, and Silence*, 1980) *May–June 1973*

9 A friend I can trust is the one who will let me have my death. The rest are actors who want me to stay and further the plot.

Untitled (1960s), *Poems: Selected and New (1950–1974) 1974*

10 . . . Love, our subject:
we've trained it like ivy to our walls
baked it like bread in our ovens
worn it like lead on our ankles

Untitled (1970s), *Ibid.*

11 Every journey into the past is complicated by delusions, false memories, false namings of real events.

Foreword, *Of Woman Born: Motherhood As Experience and Institution 1976*

12 My children cause me the most exquisite suffering of which I have any experience. It is the suffering of ambivalence: the murderous alternation between bitter resentment and raw-edged nerves, and blissful gratification and tenderness. Sometimes I seem to myself, in my feelings toward these tiny guiltless beings, a monster of selfishness and intolerance.

Ch. 1, *Ibid.*

13 The ocean, whose tides respond, like women's menses, to the pull of the moon, the ocean which corresponds to the amniotic fluid in which human life begins, the ocean on whose surface vessels (personified as female) can ride but in whose depths sailors meet their death and monsters conceal themselves . . . it is unstable and threatening as the earth is not; it spawns new life daily, yet swallows up lives; it is changeable like the moon, unregulated, yet indestructible and eternal.

Ch. 4, *Of Woman Born: Motherhood As Experience and Institution 1976*

14 The word "revolution" itself has become not only a dead relic of Leftism, but a key to the deadendedness of male politics: the "revolution" of a wheel which returns in the end to the same place; the "revolving door" of a politics which has "liberated" women only to use them, and only within the limits of male tolerance.

Introduction, "Power and Danger: Works of a Common Woman," *The Work of a Common Woman: The Collected Poetry of Judy Grahn,* 1964–1977 1977*
*See 3193.

15 how sister gazed at sister
reaching through mirrored pupils
back to the mother

"Sibling Mysteries," Pt. IV, St. 6, (1963), *The Dream of a Common Language, Poems (1974–1977) 1978*

16 Marriage is lonelier than solitude.

Pt. III, "Paula Becker to Clare Westhoff" (1975–1976), from *Twenty-One Love Poems, Ibid.*

17 But gentleness is active
gentleness swabs the crusted stump
invents more merciful instruments
to touch the wound beyond the wound

"Natural Resources," Pt. VIII, Sts. 3–4 (1979), *Ibid.*

18 I am a feminist because I feel endangered, psychically and physically, by this society and because I believe that the women's movement is saying that we have come to an edge of history when men—insofar as they are embodiments of the patriarchal idea—have become dangerous to children and other living things, themselves included.

On Lies, Secrets and Silence 1979

19 The connections between and among women are the most feared, the most problematic, and the most potentially transforming force on the planet.

"Disloyal to Civilization: Feminism, Racism, Gynophobia," *Chrysalis*, no. 7, *Ibid.*

20 False history gets made all day, any day,
the truth of the new is never on the news
False history gets written every day . . .

"Turning the Wheel," section 2 *1981*

21 Lesbian existence comprises both the breaking of a taboo and the rejection of a compulsory way of life. It is also a direct or indirect attack on the male right of access to women.

"Compulsory Heterosexuality and Lesbian Existence," *Blood, Bread, and Poetry: Selected Prose 1979–1985 1986*

22 Memory is a nutriment, and seeds stored for centuries can still germinate.

Lecture, Scripps College (Claremont, Calif., February 1983), *Ibid.*

23 . . . poetry can break open locked chambers of possibility, restore numbed zones to feeling, recharge desire . . .

What Is Found There: Notebooks on Poetry and Politics 1993

24 [Maya Lin's* Vietnam Memorial is] the only great public monument that allows the anesthetized holes in the heart to fill with a truly national grief.

Ibid.

*See 4492.

25 I am suspicious—first of all, in myself—of adopted mysticisms of glib spirituality, above all of white people's tendency to . . . vampirize American Indian, or African, or Asian, or other "exotic" ways of understanding.

Ibid.

26 The danger lies in forgetting what we had. The flow between generations becomes a trickle, grandchildren tape-recording grandparents' memories on special occasions perhaps—no casual storytelling jogged by daily life, there being no shared daily life what with migrations, exiles, diasporas, rendings, the search for work. Or there is a shared daily life riddled with holes of silence.

Ch. 11, *What Is Found There 1993*

27 MIRACLE's truck comes down the little avenue,
Scott Joplin ragtime strewn behind it like pearls,
and, yes, you can feel happy
with one piece of your heart.

"Miracle Ice Cream," *Dark Fields of the Republic 1995*

28 our country moving closer to its own truth and dread,
its own ways of making people disappear.

"What Kind of Times Are These," *Ibid.*

29 Art . . . means nothing if it simply decorates the dinner-table of power which holds it hostage. The radical disparities of wealth

and power in America are widening at a devastating rate. A president cannot meaningfully honor certain token artists while the people at large are so dishonored.

> Letter to Jane Alexander,* Quoted in "No thanks, NEA,**
> *Ms.* (New York) *November/December 1997*
> *See 3117. **National Endowment for the Arts. Rich's explanation for her refusal to accept the prestigious National Medal of Arts, awarded annually by the president of the United States.

30 I wanted to go somewhere
the brain had not yet gone

> "Letters to a Young Poet," *Midnight Salvage: Poems 1995–
> 1998 1999*

2681. Nafis Sadik (1929–)

1 More than one-half the world cannot be denied.

> Cited in "Population blueprint criticized" (AP), *Seattle Post-
> Intelligencer,* A14 *5 April 1994*

2 We should invest in people, especially in women, and let them make choices about family size.

> Ibid.

2682. Johanna Levelt Sengers (1929–)

1 As an immigrant to the United States I have found at the national Bureau of Standards [now NIST] a work environment where I felt welcome and accepted, where even in the 1960's women scientists had successful careers, where special arrangements were made for me while I was raising my family, and where I was given all support to succeed.

> *American Men and Women of Science 1990–1993*

2683. Louise Shivers (1929–)

1 He was holding me, and for the first time I had the feeling. The feeling of wanting to push, to push myself into another person. *So this is what it is,* I thought. *This is why people do the things they do.* The feeling made me sick, scared me, and I pulled away . . .

But he knew how to wait, and just how to work me, and unbutton me.

By harvest time in the fall I'd be there waiting for him. He'd walk up and put his hand behind my neck and slowly pull me to him.

I remember thinking, *I am a rider on an ancient horse.*

> *A Whistling Woman 1993*

2 I remember that old saying, "A whistling woman and a crowing hen never come to any good end." Well, I don't believe that just means that men want women to be quiet, or that if a woman whistles she's acting like a man. I've thought and thought on it. I believe that some women, most women, *know* so much that they never tell, know so many secret things that sometimes they're just making a little slow, low whistling sound of warning. Don't mess with a whistling woman.

> Ibid.

2684. Beverly Sills (1929–2007)

1 In a way, retarded children are satisfying. Everything is a triumph. Even getting Bucky to manage to get a spoon to his mouth was a triumph. God compensates.

> Quoted in "Beverly Sills," *Divas: Impressions of Six Opera
> Superstars* by Winthrop Sargeant *1959*

2 I would willingly give up my whole career if I could have just one normal child. . . .

> Ibid.

3 My singing is very therapeutic. For three hours I have no troubles—I know how it's all going to come out.

> Interview, *60 Minutes,* CBS-TV *1975*

4 A happy woman is one who has no cares at all; a cheerful woman is one who has cares but doesn't let them get her down.

> Ibid.

5 I've always tried to go a step past wherever people expected me to end up.

> Quoted in Obituary, *Time* (New York) *31 December 2007*

2685. Patricia Meyer Spacks (1929–)

1 Theories by women about women have only recently begun to appear in print. Theories by men about women are abundant.

> Ch. 1, *The Female Imagination 1975*

2 Dependency invites encroachment.

> Ch. 2, Ibid.

3 The cliché that women, more consistently that men, turn inward for sustenance seems to mean, in practice, that women have richly defined the ways in which imagination creates possibility; possibility that society denies.

> "Afterword," Ibid.

4 Gossip, like poetry and fiction, penetrates to the truth of things.

> "In Praise of Gossip," *Hudson Review,* 35 *1982*

5 Those understanding gossip as fellowship typically deny its malice; those stressing its destructiveness ignore its bonding.

> *Gossip 1985*

2686. Octavia Capuzzi Waldo (1929–)

1 "Living," he had said, "like studying, needs a little practice."

> "Roman Spring," *American Scene: New Voices,* Don Wolfe,
> ed. *1963*

2 The rain fell like a cascade of pine needles over Rome. Rain—thirty days of it. It marked the interlude between winter and spring, and spring was late in coming. There was nothing to do about it but wait. There is nothing to do about most things that are late in Rome, whether it be an appointment, or a bus, or a promise. Or even hope.

> Ch. 1, Ibid.

3 ". . . Adam Maxwell, age twenty-four, husband to Ruth. A boy who wants to go to the top. As if the world had a top!"

> Ibid.

4 "The war has carved the very heart out of modesty and has left her rather bare."

> Ch. 2, Ibid.

2687. Barbara Walters (1929–)

1 . . . I happen to disagree with the well-entrenched theory that the art of conversation is merely the art of being a good listener. Such advice invites people to be cynical with one another

and full of fake; when a conversation becomes a monologue, poked along with tiny cattle-prod questions, it isn't a conversation anymore.

How to Talk with Practically Anybody About Practically Anything 1970

2 Celebrities used to be found in clusters, like oysters—and with much the same defensive mechanisms.

Ch. 1, Ibid.

3 Most old people . . . are disheartened to be living in the ailing house of their bodies, to be limited physically and economically, to feel an encumbrance to others—guests who didn't have the good manners to leave when the party was over.

Ch. 4, Ibid.

4 Parents of young children should realize that few people, and maybe no one, will find their children as enchanting as they do.

Ibid.

5 A great many people think that polysyllables are a sign of intelligence. . . .

Ch. 8, Ibid.

6 Success can make you go one of two ways. It can make you a prima donna, or it can smooth the edges, take away the insecurities, let the nice things come out.

Quoted in "Barbara Walters—Star of the Morning,"
Newsweek (New York) 6 May 1974

2688. Alisa Wells-Witteman (1929–)
1 Now the real beginnings of the "freedom" which we have discussed for many years—and a heady freedom it is, coming after so many years of reaching outward for it—to finally discover all I had to do was reach inward, and it was there waiting all the time for me!

Quoted in *The Woman's Eye* by Anne Tucker* 1973
*See 3620.

2689. Christa Wolf (1929–)
1 Ten years of war. That was long enough to forget completely the question of how the wars started. In the middle of a war you think of nothing but how it will end. And put off living. When large numbers of people do that, it creates a vacuum within us, which the war flows in to fill.

Cassandra, Jan van Heurck, tr. 1983

2 "Try to understand, Mother," he said. "We want to spare you. The things we have to talk about in our council, now in wartime, are no longer the concern of women."
"Quite right," said Anchises. "Now they are the concern of children."

Ibid.

3 . . . We foreigners . . . incapable of deciphering even the signs outside the shops, must rely on pictures, smells.
But isn't the word the very thing that has taken over control of our inner life? The fact that I lack words here: doesn't this mean that I am losing myself? How quickly does lack of speech turn into lack of identity?

Ibid.

4 About reality. The insane fact that in all the "civilized" industrialized nations, literature, if it is realistic, speaks a completely different language from any and all public disclosures. As if every country existed twice over. As if every resident existed twice over: once as himself and as the potential perceiver of an artistic presentation; second, as an object of statistics, publicity, agitation, advertisement, political propaganda.

"3: A Work Diary, about the Stuff Life and Dreams Are Made Of," Ibid.

5 Awe is composed of reverence and dread. I often think that people today have nothing left but the dread.

"4: A Letter about Unequivocal and Ambiguous Meaning, Definiteness and Indefiniteness; about Ancient Conditions and New View-Scopes; about Objectivity," Ibid.

6 We lied and kowtowed and railed and slandered and we lusted for slavery and pleasure.

What Remains 1990

7 Whoever causes the people to lay hands on what they hold sacred makes himself their enemy.

Medea: A Modern Retelling 1998

2690. Patsy Abbott (fl. 1930s–50s)
1 "Have I Had You Before"

Album title *n.d.*

2 "They Don't Make Jews Like Jesus Anymore"

Song title *n.d*

2691. Nancy Banks-Smith (1930?–)
1 In my experience, if you have to keep the lavatory door shut by extending your left leg, it's modern architecture.

The Guardian (London) 20 February 1979

2 Anthropology is the science which tells us that people are the same the whole world over—except when they are different.

The Guardian (London) 21 July 1988

3 Agatha Christie* has given more pleasure in bed than any other woman.

Quoted in *The Guardian* (London) *n.d.*
*See 1724.

2692. Nguyen Thi Binh (1930–)
1 I was tortured [in the 1950s] by the Vietnamese, with the French directing, just as now it is with the Americans directing.

Quoted in "Madame Binh" by Beca Wilson, *New York Review of Books 25 June 1975*

2 We tell our children that the bombs cannot kill everyone, that they must not be afraid. . . . We know our sacrifice is necessary. If the bombs do not fall on you, they fall on friends. We accept fate. We are calm. It is useless to be a pessimist. Some day we will win a beautiful life, if not for ourselves, then for our children.

Ibid.

2693. Julie Anne Bovasso (1930–1991)
1 BEBE. I want to know you. And I want you to know me and understand me. What good is love without understanding? How can we love each other if we don't know each other and understand each other? And how can we know each other if we don't love each other?

Schubert's Last Serenade 1972

2 BEBE. I didn't take it all back: I simply adjusted my initial reaction.

> Ibid.

2694. Marion Zimmer Bradley (1930–1999)

1 And as men believe, so their world goes. And so the worlds which once were one are drifting apart.

> Bk. I, Ch. 1, *The Mists of Avalon* 1982

2 . . . one of the old priestesses had once said that the House of Maidens was for little girls whose whole duty in life was to spill things, break things, and forget things, the rules of their daily life among them, until they had spilled, broken, and forgotten everything they could, and thus made room in their lives for a little wisdom.

> Ch. 12, Ibid.

3 Some knowledge and some song and some beauty must be kept for those days before the world again plunges into darkness.

> Bk. IV, Ch. 7, Ibid.

4 Men had no divine power; they neither bred nor bore; yet somehow they felt they had some natural right in the fruit of their women's bodies, as if coupling with a woman gave them some power of ownership, as if children did not naturally belong to the woman whose body had sheltered and nourished them.

> Prologue, *The Firebrand* 1987

2695. E. M. Broner (1930–)

1 My friend healed. She began to push her troubles off her chest. They became smaller. Sometimes she could fit them in her pocket. Sometimes she could pluck them from her arm and keep them from burrowing into her skin, and squash them like ticks on her dog.

> "Body Memories" (1986), *Four Centuries of Jewish Women's Spirituality*, Ellen M. Umansky* & Dianne Ashton, eds. 1992
> *See 4011.

2 "Here's your last chance. Mary, the Virgin, is visited by the Angel. He has an announcement to make. Mary will give birth to a baby, a son, who will be the son of God."
  "Gee," says Mary, "I wanted a girl."
  "That's good, Mother," says my eldest, patting me.

> "Joking Around," *Ghost Stories* 1995

2696. Eileen Kampakuta Brown (1930?–)
See Eileen Wani Wingfield, 2747: 1–4.

2697. Rosemary Brown (1930–2003)

1 I'm not committed to welfare measures. I don't think they get at the root of the problem. I'm committed to the eradication of all poverty, to its being wiped out. I'm not hung up on guaranteed incomes and that sort of thing, because I don't think that's the solution. We've got to change the system and make it impossible to be poor.

> Quoted in "The Radical Tradition of Rosemary Brown" by Sharon Batt, *Branching Out July/August 1975*

2 We cannot swing our vote. We have to swing our party.

> Ibid.

2698. Mary Cantwell (1930–2000)

1 To earn one's death, I think of it as a kind of parlor game. How, I shall ask my friends, would you like to earn your deaths? And how would I like to earn mine? The question is strangely liberating, implying as it does action, energy, choice. In fact, it has an unexpectedly American ring: death as First Prize. I like it—it makes the nights less frightening.

> "Hers" column, *The New York Times* 1980

2 I have the resilience of a roach.

> *Speaking With Strangers* 1998

3 What I wanted from sex, when finally I did want something from it besides babies, was Communion.

> Ibid.

2699. Maria Castellani (fl. 1930s–1990s)

1 Fascism recognizes women as part of the life force of the country, laying down a division of duties between two sexes, without putting obstacles in the way of those women who by their intellectual gifts reach the highest positions.

> *Italian Women, Past and Present* 1937

2700. Blythe M. Clinchy (1930–)
See Mary Belenky, 2834: 1–3.

2701. Elisabeth Craigin (fl. 1930s)

1 A so-called Lesbian alliance can be of the most rarefied purity, and those who do not believe it are merely judging in ignorance of the facts.

> *Either Is Love* 1937

2702. Mildred Spiewak Dresselhaus (1930–)

1 All the hardships I encountered provided me with the determination, capacity for hard work, efficiency, and a positive outlook on life that have been so helpful to me in realizing my professional career.

> Quoted in *Contemporary Women Scientists of America* by Iris Noble 1979

2 Follow your interests, get the best available education and training, set your sights high, be persistent, be flexible, keep your options open, accept help when offered, and be prepared to help others.

> Letter to author, Quoted in *Women Scientists* by Nancy J. Veglahn 1991

3 There are some advocates out there who think that when women do science the science changes. I can't see that. I think that the facts are the facts and whoever discovers the facts, they will discover the same facts.

> Quoted in Ch. 6, *Rosalyn Yalow,* * *Nobel Laureat* by Eugene Straus, M.D. 1998
> *See 2416.

2703. Målfrid Grude Flekkøy (193-?–)

1 It's not a law that says parents will be punished for striking their child.* It's an attitude-creating piece of legislation. It says that society does not approve of physically punishing children.

> Quoted in "Who Speaks for Children?" by Michael Ryan, *Parade Magazine 8 July 1990*
> *Reference to a law passed by Norwegian Parliament at her urging.

2 Children are people of equal value—human beings with equal rights, including the right to state their own opinions and views on things. The important thing is to give them a channel through which they can be heard.

Ibid.

2704. Maria Irene Fornés (1930–)

1 "Let Me Be Wrong, but also Not Know It"

Song title, *The Successful Life of 3 1965*

2 DR. KHEAL. We can only do what is possible for us to do. But still it is good to know what the impossible is.

Dr. Kheal 1968

3 FEFU. Women are always eager for the men to arrive. When they do, they can put themselves at rest, tranquilized. . . . That's the closest they can be to feeling wholesome. The danger is gone, but the price is the mind and the spirit.

Fefu and Her Friends 1977

4 . . . the playwright is the "woman" of the theater . . . The playwright is the woman and the director is the husband.

Quoted in "Maria Irene Fornés," *Interviews with Contemporary Women Playwrights* by Kathleen Betsko* and Rachel Koenig *1987*

*See 3125.

5 I feel that the older I get, the more shameless I feel. And in a sense, more pure.

Ibid.

6 When I'm not doing something that comes deeply from me, I get bored. When I get bored I get distracted, and when I get distracted, I become depressed. It's a natural resistance, and it insures your integrity. You die when you are faking it, and you are alive when you are truthful.

Ibid.

2705. Priscilla Galloway (1930–)

1 The bicycle of my mood
Wavers,
Wobbles, as I
Uncertain rider, uneasy,
Seek surety in slowness

"The Bicycle of My Mood," St. 1 (1975), *Cross-Canada Writers' Quarterly* 7 (#1): *31 February 1985*

2 What are the special properties of sand? It shifts, moves out from under you. With sand there is no stability, no permanence. Things are not what they appear to be. Sand insinuates itself everywhere. It slips in, grain by gritty grain. In calm weather, you live with it under your fingernails, in your pubic har. When the dry wind rises, sand beats on your every door, into nostrils, under eyelids. The woman's dress of old Islam was created as a desperate defence against the invasion of sand, not the lascivious eyes of men.

In sandy places, the habit of silence develops early. Its alternative is a mouth forever full of grit. Those who cannot, will not learn to be silent, pay for their chatter with early loss of their worn-down teeth.

"A Bed of Peas," *Truly Grim Tales 1996*

3 It seemed to me that paradise ought to be more attractive than hell. The experience of paradise, if one may speak thus about a concept, must surely be preferable to the experience of hell. It is one of the paradoxes of literature, however, that hell is the best seller. There is a fascination about the anatomy of sin. Dante's *Inferno* satisfied my adolescent appetite for gothic images on a far more profound level than Frankenstein or Dracula.

Confessions of a Book Junkie n.d.

2706. Winefreda Estanero Geonzon (1930?–1990)

1 We find it futile to be criticizing without offering alternatives. We find it useless to curse the dark. It is always better to light a candle. We have proven countless times that man is by nature good. In our work we see the beauty of reconciliation rather than making direct confrontation.

Acceptance Speech, Right Livelihood Award (Stockholm), *9 December 1984*

2707. Elettra Marconi Giovanelli (1930–)

1 He [Marconi]* was so young, and all the big scientists, like Edison,** were saying it wasn't possible. He had the intuition. He knew he could succeed. And he succeeded.

Speech, Centennial Marconi Celebration (Wellfleet, Mass), *17 January 2003*

*(1875–1937) Noble Prize–winning (1909) Italian inventor of wireless transmission. **(1847–1931) American inventor of electricity et al.

2708. Lydia Gottschewski (fl. 1930s)

1 It is a curious fact that pacifism . . . is a mark of an age weak in faith, whereas the people of religious times have honored war as God's rod of chastisement . . . Only the age of enlightenment has wished to decide the great questions of world history at the table of diplomats.

Women in the New State 1934

2709. Francine Du Plessix Gray (1930–)

1 Woman—as tender of the hearth, custodian of most ethnic rituals and religious customs, safe-guarder of tribal memory—stands in contrast to man the explorer, innovator, technocrat, who in his nomadic obsession for power and control tends to neglects many time-honored traditions.

"Women's Rites," *Vogue* (New York) *September 1980*

2 If I were to describe the decline in quality of life enjoyed by women in the West, I'd say it decreased in proportion to the decrease of meaningful rituals in their lives.

Ibid.

3 This is indeed the nadir of women's history, the idle and lonely housewife, surrounded by kitchen appliances, who increasingly resorts, as medical figures show, to Valium and alcohol and the equally drugging effects of daytime television to relieve her sense of powerlessness and isolation.

Ibid.

4 The act of nutrition is not a purely physiological event. It remains, in its more civilized form, a way of communion. The family meal is a formality that cultivates in us from earliest age a curb of natural greed, a capacity for sharing, generosity, thoughtfulness, a talent for civilized conversation. It is a custom that can enrich our knowledge of our historic roots by carefully prepared food from our own ethnic tradition, that can enlarge our love of literature by readings of poetry easily adaptable to the beginning or the end of a meal.

Ibid.

5   In the terrifying orgies of his fictions he gave free rein to those
    darker inclinations, to the impulses that can compel us to re-
    gress if only in our fantasies to an archaic, animal-like stage,
    liberated from even the most fundamental taboos—incest, can-
    nibalism—imposed by civilization.

                              At Home with the Marquis de Sade 1998
    *Donatien Alphone Françoise de S—, French writer (1740–1814).
    The word "sadism" derives from the marquis.

2710. Meg Greenfield (1930–1999)

1   In Washington it is an honor to be disgraced. . . . you have to
    have *been* somebody to fall.

                              Quoted in *Newsweek 2 June 1986*

2   Now consider this settlement's profoundly high school nature.*
    It is psychologically fenced off from the larger community
    within which it makes its home, free—like irresponsible
    youth—of all but the minimal obligations of citizenship to that
    community, and absorbed to the exclusion of all else in its own
    eccentric aims and competitions. And the high-school-like feel
    political/governmental Washington takes on by virtue of all of
    this is intensified by certain givens of its existence . . . One is
    the only-passing-through nature of so much time spent here
    . . .

                                           Washington 2001

    *Re. Washington, D.C.

3   These are people who don't seem to live in the world so much
    as to inhabit some point on graph paper, whose coordinates
    are (sideways) the political spectrum, and (up and down) the
    latest overnight poll figures.

                                                    Ibid.

4   If the politicians and officials of Washington have an infinite
    number of chances to cheat every day (and an equal number of
    chances to decide not to), they have nothing on us in the press,
    who are their neighbors, just one precarious house down the
    slope.

                                                    Ibid.

2711. Lorraine Hansberry (1930–1965)

1   ASAGAI. Ah, I like the look of packing crates! A household in
    preparation for a journey! . . . Something full of the flow of
    life. . . . Movement, progress.

                              Act. III, *A Raisin in the Sun 1958*

2   BENEATHA. Don't you see there isn't any real progress, As-
    agai, there is only one large circle that we march in, around
    and around, each of us with our own little picture—in front of
    us—our own little mirage that we think is the future.

                                                    Ibid.

3   LENA. Child, when do you think is the time to love somebody
    the most; when they done good and made things easy for every-
    body? Well then you ain't through learning—because that ain't
    the time at all. It's when he's at his lowest and can't believe in
    hisself 'cause the world done whipped him so. When you starts
    measuring somebody, measure him right, child, measure him
    right. Make sure you done taken into account what hills and
    valleys he come through before he got to wherever he is.

                                                    Ibid.

4   GLORIA. Things as they are as they are and have been and will
    be that way because they got that way because things were as
    they were in the first place.

                              The Sign in Sidney Brustein's Window 1964

5   There is both joy and beauty and illumination and communion
    between people to be achieved through dissection of personal-
    ity. That's what I want to do. I want to reach a little closer to
    the world, which is to say people, and see if we can share some
    illuminations together about each other.

                              Quoted in *To Be Young, Gifted and Black* by Robert
                                                    Nemiroff* 1969
    *Hansberry's husband.

6   MARTA. I've lived without a confidante for years: it really isn't
    the strain it's painted to be.

                                           Act II, Sc. 1, *Les Blancs 1972*

7   TSHEMBE. Ntali, there are men in this world—I don't know
    how to say this so you will understand—who *see* too much to
    take sides.

                                                    Sc. 2, Ibid.

8   TSHEMBE. I said racism is a device that, of itself, explains
    nothing. It is simply a means. An invention to justify the rule of
    some men over others.

                                                    Ibid.

9   ABIOSEH. That is what you think, but God is raging in you,
    fighting for you!
    TSHEMBE. Why does He always tell you and not me what He
    is doing!

                                                    Sc. 4, Ibid.

10 DEKOVEN. We do not look down on the black because we
    really think he is lazy, we look down on him because he is wise
    enough to resent working for us. The problem, therefore, has
    been how *not* to educate him at all and—at the same time—
    teach him just enough to turn a dial and know which mining
    lever to raise. It has been as precise as that—and that much a
    failure. Because, of course, it is *impossible!* When a man knows
    that the abstraction *ten* exists—nothing on earth can stop him
    from looking for the fact of *eleven*.

                                                    Sc. 5, Ibid.

2712. Barbara Clementine Harris (1930–   )

1   A fresh wind is blowing across this church* of ours.
                  Sermon, Church of the Advocate (Philadelphia), Quoted in
                  "First Anglican Woman Bishop . . ." by Bruce Rule, Associated
                                                    Press *26 September 1988*
    *Anglican Communion.

2713. Rosanna Taylor Herndon (1930–   )

1   Family stories speak volumes about the communication pat-
    terns in the family unit. They remind us who we are and who
    we wish to become.
                  Introduction, *The Line from Here to There: A Storyteller's
                                                    Scottish West Texas 2008*

2714. Lorraine Hine (1930–   )

1   Women don't have halos built in.
                  Quoted in "Cleaning house in government . . ." by Carol M.
                              Ostrom, *Seattle Times, A1–9 2 August 1992*

2715. Maureen Howard (1930–   )

1   When I go home my mother and I play a cannibal game; we eat
    each other over the years, tender morsel by morsel, until there
    is nothing left but dry bone and wig.

                                           Bridgeport Bus 1966

2 I have a world now, about the size of a circle of light thrown by a desk lamp, that is mine and safe from my mother and the zipper company and my brother's children.

Ibid.

3 She was a survivor, frail, helpless, but a survivor: the past was one prop, the bottle another.

"Three Cheers for Mr. Spears," *Before My Time 1974*

4 "The process of losing my faith was so gradual," said Mr. Spears, "I didn't seem to notice it. I've thought since that it was a counterpart of attaining my physical growth, which I never noticed either. One day it was complete—my height and my loss of faith—and it was easy, painless. I wish that I had suffered."

Ibid.

5 Exhaustive events cover all possibilities. . . .

"A Lover's Almanac," *Big as Life: Three Tales for Spring 1998*

6 "It seems you must reinvent yourself to meet love's impossible demands."

Ibid.

2716. Dolores Huerta (1930–)

1 . . . if you haven't forgiven yourself something, how can you forgive others?

Quoted in "Stopping Traffic: One Woman's Cause" by Barbara L. Baer, *The Progressive September 1975*

2 Don't be a marshmallow. Walk the street with us into history. Get off the sidewalk. Stop being vegetables. Work for justice. *Viva* the boycott!

Ibid.

3 How do I stop eleven million people from buying the grape?

Ibid.

4 But we want to change people's lives. Farmworkers kill themselves working, living nowhere, traveling all the time, putting up with the pesticides because the growers want it that way. It's a feudal system which higher wages won't change. *We* know the work can be organized so people settle down in one place with their families, and control their lives through political power and their own union—which they run themselves.

Quoted in "Dolores Huerta: La Pasionaria* of the Farmworkers" by Judith Coburn, *Ms.* (New York) *November 1976*

*Dolores Ibarruri (see 1690) was known as *La Pasionaria* during the Spanish Civil War.

5 I consider myself a feminist, and the Women's Movement has done a lot toward helping me not feel guilty about my [two] divorces. But among poor people, there's not any question about women being strong—even stronger than men—they work in the fields right along with the men. When your survival is at stake, you don't have these questions about yourself like middle-class women do.

Ibid.

6 That's why Cesar* always reminds us of that *dicho: Hay mas tiempo que vida* (the saying: there is more time than life).

Ibid.

*Cesar Chavez, American migrant worker, labor leader, union organizer (1927–1993).

2717. Luce Irigaray (1930–)

1 Woman's desire most likely does not speak the same language as man's desire, and it probably has been covered over by the logic that has dominated the West since the Greeks.

"This sex which is not one," *New French Feminisms: An Anthology,* Elaine Marks and Isabelle de Courtivron, eds. *1981*

2 Contradictory words seem a little crazy to the logic of reason, and inaudible for him who listens with ready-made grids, a code prepared in advance.

Ibid.

3 [Before woman can] arrive at the point where she can enjoy her pleasure . . . a long detour by the analysis of the various systems of oppression which affect her is certainly necessary.

Ibid.

2718. Sandra Weinstein Jacobson (1930–)

1 Wasting limited assets by encouraging protracted litigation is a cause of, not a cure for, the feminization of poverty.

"Restricting Divorce Hurts Children and Women," *The New York Times 21 February 1996*

2719. Selma James (1930–)

1 In pre-capitalist patriarchal society *the home and the family* were central to agricultural and artisan production. With the advent of capitalism the socialization of production was organized with *the factory* as its center. Those who worked in the new productive center, the factory, received a wage. Those who were excluded did not.

Quoted in "Women and the Subversion of the Community," *The Power of Women & the Subversion of Community* by James and Mariarosa Dalla Costa* *1975*

*See 3081.

2 The role of the working class housewife, which we believe has indispensable to capitalist production, is *the* determinant for the position of all over women.

Ibid.

3 Revolutions are notorious for allowing even non-participants—even women!—new scope for telling the truth since they are themselves such massive moments of truth, moments of such massive participation.

Ch. 1, *The Ladies and the Mammies: Jane Austen* & Jean Rhys** 1983*

*See 767. **See 1717.

2720–2721. Foumiko Kometani (1930–)

1 In the West, ideologies and theologies traditionally proselytized; unable to leave foreign cultures alone; resulting inevitably in imperialism, evangelism, and even in Nazism

"Passover" (1986), *Passover 1989*

2722. Felicia Langer (1930–)

1 A second generation of heroes is sprouting from this land which is soaked with the blood of her children. And in the city streets there are soldiers patrolling, ready to shoot and kill instantly. The second generation of oppressors, the by-product of the occupation.

p. 32, *An Age of Stone 1987*

2 I am proud of those thousands of our sons and daughters who refuse to oppress, who prefer prison cells instead of serving in the army in the occupied territories, who demonstrate and solidarize with the oppressed. They are the conscience of Israel, faithful to the bright traditions of the Jewish people, not ready to betray our dead.

Acceptance Speech, Right Livelihood Awards (Stockholm), *9 December 1990*

3 Blood is spilled daily all over the occupied territories and in Israel too, sometimes of innocent Israelis, who are falling victims of Palestinians' revenge for the government's atrocities; a vicious circle of violence, turning us into a nation of killers and killed, a new Sparta of the Middle East, where the fathers are burying their sons.

Ibid.

4 Because we Jews know what it is to suffer, we must not oppress others.

Quoted on rightlivelihood.org/langer *9 December 1990*

5 I'm part of the other Israel. I'm for justice and against all those for whom the conclusion of the holocaust is hatred, cruelty and insensitivity.

Quoted by Christina Foerch in *The Daily Star 14 March 2002*

6 For the Palestinians in Israel, the years since the proclamation of the Israeli State have been years of discrimination and dispossession; years of the "Judaization of the Galilee." The democracy they enjoy is "half a democracy," a democracy for Jews only.

Address, "The Experience of Legal Representation of Palestinian Political Prisoners" conference (Nazareth) *13 May 2005*

2723. Abbey Lincoln (1930–)

1 The fact that white people readily and proudly call themselves "white," glorify all that is white, and whitewash all that is glorified, becomes unnatural and bigoted in its intent only when these same whites deny persons of African heritage who are Black the natural and inalienable right to readily— proudly—call themselves "black," glorify all that is black, and black- wash all that is glorified.

"Who Will Revere the Black Woman?," *Negro Digest September 1966*

2724. Gay Gaer Luce (1930–)

1 Swept along in the concepts of their business-oriented culture, many people berate themselves if they are not as consistent and productive as machines.

Preface, *Body Time 1971*

2 . . . people are beginning to resist the rhythm of the machine and suspect that the path of inner harmony and health demands an inward attention.

"Trust Your Body Rhythms," *Psychology Today* (New York) *April 1975*

3 Our harmony is maintained by nature, since we are not closed systems, but are part of the turning earth, the sun, moon and cosmos beyond. In contradiction with our inner clockwork, our urban culture bids us to forget our sources of health and harmony and live by artificial clocks.

Ibid.

4 In the past, respect for the wisdom of the elders was a central tenet of human societies—especially in indigenous populations, whose elders served as keepers of the cultures' knowledge. But today, in technological countries such as ours, respect has faded into bare tolerance, as we demand that older people act, look, and talk young.

"The Graying of America," *Utne Reader November/December 2000*

2725. Ann McGovern (1930–)

1 Dumb. Dumb. Tiny drum beats. Dumb. Dumb. Her sister's favorite word. She called her dumb more than she called her Jane.

"Wonder is Not Precisely Knowing," *American Scene: New Voices*, Don Wolfe, ed. *1963*

2 She shared much with her sister—the absence of a father, the presence of a shadowy unhappy mother. They had one bike and one sled between them and had learned long ago that these possessions were not worth the fights.

Ibid.

3 In those days, people did not think it was important for girls to read. Some people thought too much reading gave girls brain fever.

The Secret Soldier 1975

2726. Kinn Hamilton McIntosh (1930–)

1 As solemnly as a pair of cricket captains at a Test match, the two men advanced together the better to see how the coin lay on the ground.

Ch. 1, *Amendment of Life: A Mystery 2002*

2 "There's a girl downstairs, sir," reported Detective Constable Crosby, "who is saying that the hospital's killed her granny."
"They've been killing grannies over there for years," responded Detective Inspector C. D. Sloan dryly. "Par for the course, if you ask me."

"A Change of Heart" (1997), *Chapter and Hearse: And Other Mysteries 2004*

3 "That's the funny thing about golf—one day you can't hit a thing," mused Ursula, half to herself, "and suddenly the next day you can."

Ch. 1, *Hole in One 2005*

4 "Every man has his price," responded Jason. This was one thing that success and its consequent great wealth had already taught the young pop star.

Ch. 1, *Losing Ground 2007*

2727. Gracia Molina de Pick (1930–)

1 I began fighting for Chicano rights, even before Chicanos knew they were Chicanos.

Quoted by Geneva Gamez, *La Prensa San Diego 11 March 2005*

2 I don't have a lot of money—but I'm rich in so many other ways. Everything I have, I give to the causes. I hope others will also help in raising the consciousness of the people of our community.

Quoted by Judy Piercey, *UCSD News Center 20 March 2008*

3 Your individual life only has meaning if you unselfishly engage as sisters and brothers in the fight for equality, justice and peace.

Ibid.

2728. Faye S. Moskowitz (1930–)

1 If only she could remember what it was she had done to offend God so, perhaps she could make some sense of what He had done to her.

> "A Leak in the Heart" (1985), *Shaking Eve's Tree, Short Stories of Jewish Women* Sharon Niederman,* ed. 1990
> *See 3853.

2 The child had been like a strap that held them close. Now, unbuckled, they had to struggle to keep together.

> Ibid.

3 I close my eyes and think of Grandma tasting a bit of her childhood each Chanukah when she prepared the latkes as her mother had made them before her.

My mother, my aunts, my own grandmothers float back to me, young and vibrant once more, making days holy in the sanctuaries of their kitchens, feeding me, cradling me, connecting me to the intricately plaited braid of their past, and even at this moment, looking down the corridor of what's to come, I see myself join them as they open their arms wide to enfold my children and grandchildren in their embrace.

> *And the Bridge Is Love* 1991

4 As the Yiddish lessons continue, Jack's reading to me has become, along with dreams and old photographs, another key to memories squirreled away for over half a century. It is as if I have unlocked a trunk where the words had been stored like wedding linens, too precious for everyday use, or velvet draperies, no longer in fashion, but too good to give away.

> "Learning Yiddish," *Peace in the House* 2002

2729. Ora Namir (1930–)

1 It's a quiet period now, so women can insist that our issues be taken seriously. But something happens to this country when there's a war. You have to live here to understated the way priorities suddenly change. Just about every woman you meet has a husband or son in the army. Even feminist wives and mothers are wives and mothers first when the shooting starts. Then we worry more about their dying than about our civil rights.

> Ch. 10, *Deborah, Golda, and Me* Letty Cottin Pogrebin* 1991
> *See 3154.

2730. Naomi Newman (1930–)

1 And start digging. Dig in all directions. Up and down. Right and left. In and out. Not in a straight line. Nothing natural or interesting goes in a straight line! As a matter of fact, it is the quickest way to the wrong place. And don't try to pretend you know where you are going. Because if you know where you are going, you have already been there and are going to end up exactly where you came from.

> Rifke's monologue, *Snake Talk, Urgent Messages From the Mother* 1988

2 And do you know what you're supposed to do while you're waiting? You're supposed to do NOTHING. NOTHING. And if you can do that, if you can do nothing until the right thing comes along, then you have mastered the hardest part of all.

> Ibid.

3 Some people . . . they fall down and they lie there for the rest of their lives. But some people learn how to fall down—gaddup. That is one move. Fall down-gaddup.

> Ibid.

2731. Frances Newton (fl. 1930s–1940s)

1 There, in that manufactured park with its ghoulish artificiality, with its interminable monuments to bad taste, wealth and social position, we were planning to place the body of a beautiful and dignified old man who had lived generously and loved beauty.

> "Light, Like the Sun" (1937), *Reader's Digest (New York) January* 1948

2 I can stand what I know. It's what I don't know that frightens me.

> Ibid.

3 The soul is not anchored to a tombstone or a tiny plot of ground. Let us seek the ways to honor our dead not because they died, but because they lived.

> Ibid.

2732. Edna O'Brien (1930–)

1 He had what I call a very religious smile. An inner smile that came on and off, governed as it were by his private joy in what he heard or saw. . . .

> *The Love Object* 1963

2 It is impossible to insist that bad news delivered in a certain manner and at a certain time will have a less awful effect.

> Ibid.

3 When something has been perfect . . . there is a tendency to try hard to repeat it.

> Ibid.

4 I suppose you wonder why I torment myself like this, but I need it, I cannot let go of him now, because if I did, all our happiness and my subsequent pain . . . will have been for nothing, and nothing is a dreadful thing to hold on to.

> Ibid.

5 Later she came in the house and sat in front of the telephone, staring at it, waiting for it to come to life, hoping, beseeching, lifting it from time to time to make sure it was not out of order, then, relieved at its regular purr, she would drop it suddenly in case he should be dialing at that very moment, which he wasn't.

> Ch. 3, *August is a Wicked Month* 1965

6 Kindness. The most unkindest thing of all.

> Ch. 11, Ibid.

7 Do you know what I hate about myself, I have never done a brave thing, I have never risked death.

> "Over," *A Scandalous Woman* 1974

8 But it is not good to repudiate the dead because they do not leave you alone, they are like dogs that bark intermittently at night.

> "Love-Child," Ibid.

9 It hurt, with a raw hurt, to recall our gadfly days, and yet I did, our days, nights, beaded jackets, shawls, sometimes had our hands read . . . those days when every new love affair brought us, as we thought, to the brink of a sustained happiness. I thought of the day I too had gone a bit mad, slipped from behind this girl with all these hopes to the woman who would count in morsels from that moment onward the pleasures and excitements of her life.

> *The High Road* 1988

10 I would grow to forget him, the him that I believed had broken my heart, but in my saner moments I recognized as being probably the last to partake with me at that fount of sensuality, and vertigo and earthly love.

Ibid.

11 "Remember love is all bull, the only true love is that between mother and child."

The Light of Evening 2006

12 He would describe the forests and the different trees, pine and cedar and hemlock, trees two hundred feet high, tall and proud, like tall proud ships, and the fight that they put up against the hackings of the cross saw, the long battle, then the waver before the big crash, the long low hiss as it fell, a smell of wet sap, sap as alive as blood, as true as blood and the stumps sulky and lonely-looking, then the cut planks loaded onto the horse-drawn sleighs, down to the rapids to end up in the sawmills, for various items of furniture.

"Courtship" 2, Ibid.

2733. Sandra Day O'Connor (1930–   )

1 The more education a woman has, the wider the gap between men's and women's earnings for the same work.

Phoenix Magazine 1971

2 There is no question that the [Supreme] Court has now made clear that it will no longer view as benign archaic and stereotypic notions concerning the roles and abilities of males and females. Despite the encouraging and wonderful gains and the changes for women which have occurred in my lifetime, there is still room to advance and to promote correction of the remaining deficiencies and imbalances.

Conference Speech (Atlanta), Quoted in *The New York Times*
12 February 1989

3 The really expert riders of horses let the horse know immediately who is in control, but then they guide the horse with loose reins and very seldom use the spurs. So it was with our chief [William Rehnquist*]. He guided us with loose reins and used the spurs only rarely to get us up to speed with our work.

"Rehnquist mourners praise a life well lived," *Cox News
Service* 8 September 2005
*(1925–2005), Chief Justice of the U.S. Supreme Court (1986–
2005).

2734. Odetta (1930–2008)

1 School taught me how to count and taught me how to put a sentence together. But as far as the human spirit goes, I learned through folk music.

Interview, *NPR* 2005

2 They were liberation songs. You're walking down life's road, society's foot is on your throat, every which way you turn you can't get from under that foot. And you reach a fork in the road and you can either lie down and die or insist upon your life.

Interview (2007), Quoted in Obituary, *The New York Times* 3
December 2008

3 The folk songs were—the anger.

Ibid.

2735. Minako Ohba (1930–   )

1 We are the creatures who dream about things we cannot attain. Our dreams do not exist in reality.

"Candle Fish," *Unmapped Territories, New Women's Fiction
from Japan,* ed. & tr. 1991

2 "If you try to kill someone, you can't complain about being killed yourself, can you? By putting his hand around my neck, he slowly strangled himself."

Ibid.

3 It seems we discover the meaning of our unconscious behavior only when we are confronted with the unconscious behavior of others.

Ibid.

4 "But we don't learn from other people, I guess. If I were ten years younger, I'm sure I would do the same thing all over again. That's why I don't want to be younger. Why do people want to bring their youth back? For my part, I'm glad it's gone for good."

Ibid.

5 Then she would see that half her face was smiling like an affectionate mother, while the other half was seething with demonic rage. Blood would trickle down from half her mouth while it devoured and ripped the man's flesh apart. The other half of her lips was caressing the man who curled up his body in the shadow of one of her breasts, sucking it like a baby.

"The Smile of a Mountain Witch," *Japanese Women Writers:
Twentieth Century Short Fiction,* Noriko Mizuta Lippit and
Kyoko Iriye Selden, eds. & trs. 1991

2736. Carmen M. Pursufull (1930–   )

1 I traded in my almost disappearing wings
withdrawing to the borough of restraint.
It was a barren place.

"First Stop/City of Senses," St. 12 (1986), *The Woman That I
Am, The Literature and Culture of Contemporary Women of
Color,* D. Soyini Madison,* ed. 1994
*See 3912.

2 So where did this legend
Of Nobility come from
& the shade of Royal Blue?
What do Social Registers
contribute to the tincture
of blood?

"Blue Blood," *The Homestead Review* (Hartnell College), vol.
17, issue 2, *Spring/Summer* 2001

2737. Ruth Rendell (1930–   )

1 The worst has happened . . . it's rather liberating.

The Crocodile Bird 1993

2738. Elaine Roulet (1930–   )

1 When a man goes to prison the woman keeps the home together. But when the woman goes to prison, many times the home falls apart.

Quoted in "Sister Elaine" by Sherrye Henry, *Parade Magazine*
29 March 1987

2 Our lives may be the only Gospel some people ever read.

Ibid.

2739. Dorothy Rowe (1930–)

1 What is the difference between being depressed and being unhappy? There is a difference, and when you have experienced both you know what this difference is.

   When you are unhappy, even if you have suffered the most grievous blow, you are able to seek comfort and let that comfort come through to you to ease the pain. . . . But in depression neither the sympathy and concern of others nor the gentle love of oneself is available. . . . Depression is a prison where you are both the suffering prisoner and the cruel jailer.

   Ch. 1, *Depression: The Way Out of Your Prison 1983*

2 Real love cannot be used as a weapon to control others. It can only be freely given, and as a gift, it can be rejected. Loving is a very risky business.

   Ch. 3, Ibid.

3 Only the people who get depressed put between self and ideal self an unbridgeable chasm. And in the chasm is great despair—and pride.

   Ch. 6, Ibid

4 Most people grow up not understanding that all we can ever know are the meanings which we each create. Thus most people grow up believing that the world *is* the way they see it, and they *are* the way they see themselves. To them, they and their world are fixed and unchangeable. However, each of us is in a constant process of change because every new experience changes us. Similarly the world changes all the time whether we acknowledge the changes or not.

   Ch. 7, Ibid.

5 The key to the prison of depression is simply to become truly your own best friend.

   "The Wrong Sort of Depression," *Guardian Weekend (London) 25 March 1995*

2740. Dorothy Semenow (1930–)

1 I share with the client how I arrive at my responses. In doing so, I demonstrate that analytical methods are knowable and imply that the client too can master them. This demystifies my utterances and punctures the myth often held over from childhood by the client (and by many of the rest of us too) that *big people,* originally *her parents* and now *the analyst,* can read her mind and heart with their powerful X-ray vision and thus know her sins *and* her destiny.

   Address, "Principles of Feminist Psychoanalysis," Cedars-Sinai Hospital, Los Angeles *May 1975*

2 As early as possible in our analytic journey we try to sketch what kind of treasures the client wants to build into her life. True, she often comes to analysis caught up and spilling over with what is wrong. But buried in the suffering of those wrongs is some notion of stunted rights. We uncover those rights lost in the client's yesterdays and add to them her hopes for her tomorrow.

   Ibid.

2741. Alice M. Shepard (fl. 1930s)

1 They shall not pass, tho' battleline
   May bend, and foe with foe combine,
   Tho' death rain on them from the sky
   Till every fighting man shall die,
   France shall not yield to German Rhine.

   "They Shall Not Pass" *n.d.*

2742. Evelyn Elizabeth Smith (1930?–2002?)

1 Enemies whispered that he had bewitched the voting machines, but that wasn't true; he'd won fair and square through mass hypnosis.

   The Martian and the Magician 1952

2 That's always the way when you discover something new; everybody thinks you're crazy.

   Ibid.

3 It turned out that all the scientists had been doing the same thing, making a lot of hoopla about inventing stuff—atom bombs, jet planes, television—when actually they did it all with witchcraft. Seems all the magicians had gone underground since the Age of Enlightenment and had been passing off their feats as science—except for a few unreconstructed gypsies.

   Ibid.

2743. June L. Tapp (1930–)

1 The liberal view, it seems to me, encourages a diversity of views and open confrontation among them. . . . The due process of law as we use it, I believe, rests squarely on the liberal idea of conflict resolution.

   Quoted in "The Notion of Conspiracy Is Not Tasty to Americans" by Gordon Bermant, *Psychology Today* (New York) *May 1975*

2 Public participation—as in the jury trial—is the cornerstone in the administration of justice and vital to our system of law.

   Ibid.

3 . . . I cannot accept the idea of law as merely repressive or punitive. It can be expressive and conducive to the development of social values.

   Ibid.

2744. Barbara G. Walker (1930–)

1 Through making God in his own image, man has almost forgotten that woman once made the Goddess in hers. This is the deep secret of all mythologies . . .

   Introduction, *The Woman's Encyclopedia of Myths and Secrets 1983*

2 From a biological viewpoint, patriarchal religion denied women the natural rights of every other mammalian female: the right to choose her stud, to control the circumstances of her mating, to occupy and govern her own nest, or to refuse all males when preoccupied with the important business of raising her young.

   Ibid.

3 The church declared from the first that the Great Goddess "whom Asia and all the world worshippeth" must be despised "and her magnificence destroyed" (Acts 19:27). This is virtually the only Gospel tenet that churches followed through all their centuries with no deviation or contradiction. It seemed necessary to hide the fact that Christianity itself was an offshoot of Middle-Eastern Goddess worship. . . .

   Ibid.

2745. Maria Elena Walsh (1930–)

1 4. Because your mother is a saint, but all other women are witches. (4. Porque su mamá es una santa, por lo tanto las demás mujeres son unas brujas.)

   "Know Why You Are a Male Chauvinist," *1980*

9. Because the whole matter of gestation and birth scares and disgusts you, like sex ed at the Ministry of Education. (9. Porque todo ese asunto de la gestación y el parto le da miedo y asquete, como la educación sexual al Ministro de Educación.)

Ibid.

2746. Shirley Williams (1930–   )

1 No test tube can breed love and affection. No frozen packet of semen ever read a story to a sleepy child.

Daily Mirror (London) *2 March 1978*

2 The Catholic Church has never really come to terms with women. What I object to is being treated either as Madonnas or Mary Magdalenes.*

Observer (London) *22 March 1981*

*See 79 and 81.

2747. Eileen Wani Wingfield (1930?–   )

1 We are only the caretakers of the country. If we look after it, it will look after us.

Kungka Tjuta's Declaration of Opposition, coauthor
Eileen Kampakuta Brown* (1995), Quoted on
GoldmanPrize.org *2003*

*See 2696.

2 People said that you cannot win against the Government. Just a few women, us. We just kept talking and telling them to get their ears out of their pockets and listen.

Ibid.

3 Never mind our country is the desert. That's where we belong.

Ibid.

4 My grandfather and mother looked after the land; that was their manta, their duty. Now I am talking on behalf of them, so that the kids can have it when we leave it behind. My grandsons, daughters and sons.

Ibid.

5 It's from our grandmothers and our grandfathers that we've learned about the land. This learning isn't written on paper as the whitefellas knowledge is. We carry it in our heads and we're talking from our hearts, for the land.

Kungka Tjuta's Declaration of Opposition, *The Guardian*
(London) *8 March 2005*

2748. Hilma Wolitzer (1930–   )

1 I was drawn into the back seat of his father's green Pontiac and the pattern of those seat covers stays in my head forever.

"Waiting for Daddy," *Esquire* (New York) *July 1971*

2 It seemed strange that I could do all those things with him, discover all those sensations and odors and that new voice that came from the dark pit of my throat *Don't—oh yes, oh God* and that my mother and grandmother didn't know.

Ibid.

3 Their kitchen was full of piecework and vague hope.

Ibid.

4 The moment I awoke I knew that something was terribly wrong. I could feel it in that place behind my breastbone, where bad news always slides in like junk mail through a slot.

The Doctor's Daughter 2006

2749. Joanne Woodward (1930–   )

1 I'm tired of playing worn-out depressing ladies in frayed bathrobes. I'm going to get a new hairdo and look terrific and go back to school and even if nobody notices, I'm going to be the most self-fulfilled lady on the block.*

Quoted in *Ms.* (New York) *February 1975*
*She returned to school; she and her daughter received a B.A. from Sarah Lawrence College on the same day in 1990.

2 I remember the first Earth Day, my kids were small and Paul and I took them out and picked up garbage. I wanted them to know what it was about. Of course, doing such a small thing is not going to solve the world's complex environmental problems. But I do think it creates awareness among the next generations. It is upsetting that many people don't seem to observe what's happening to the environment, what's happening in terms of global warming, the loss of habitats and wild things.

Quoted on Web site of *The Nature Conservancy 2008*

2750. Joyce Aiken (1931–   )

1 Judy Chicago* influenced me . . . she gave permission for women to use their own life experiences and materials—those traditionally used by women but not by men—in mainstream art. Judy Chicago brought out that women hadn't been given a voice.

Artists Section, *Veteran Feminists of America* vfa.us *2007*
*See 3133.

2751. Simone Benmussa (1931–2001)

1 ALBERT NOBBS. I thought that regrets had passed away with the petticoats. But you've awakened the woman in me. You've brought it all up again.

"Albert Nobbs' Tale," *The Singular Life of Albert Nobbs 1977*

2752. Geraldyn Cobb (1931–   )

1 Even before [we] . . . had reached 300 feet, I recognized that the sky would be my home. I tumbled out of the airplane with stars in my eyes.*

Woman into Space 1963
*Her first flight, piloted by her father, taken when she was 12 years old.

2 . . . to marry . . . would be to cage an eagle.

Ibid.

3 I believe that . . . space exploration will reveal God's creations and purposes more clearly to us.

Ibid.

2753. Kathleen Collins (1931–1988)

1 MARIETTA. Dear Pop, always so full of fire, the need to be different . . . First colored to get a job with the Post Office, first colored to own property in Riverview . . . Kept us all in an uproar . . . He had such dreams, saw each of us living in angry defiance of all Negro rules, always standing tall and sturdy as the first of the first of the first of the coloreds . . . Dear Pop, he was so full of fire, none of us could breathe . . .

Act III, Sc. 2, *The Brothers 1982*

2754. Carmen de Lavallade (1931–   )

1 We're at an age now where we wonder how you can continue your art form without falling in a crack. I mean, you always

create, but it's just different now. People have become famous overnight just doing nothing. The poor darlings, I guess kids all want to be famous, but something's left out.

> Quoted in "Geoffrey Holder & Carmen de Lavallade" by Karen Kramer, *Thrive*, vol. 2, issue *5 February 2008*

2 I think there's far too much emphasis on counting [in dance today], and not, as I said, on what's underneath. You see these dancers with incredible technique and yet they don't seem to be enjoying themselves. You have to think about the texture and the poetry or there's no beauty. I also fear for them when the physicality becomes all. I think choreographers can be to blame there, too—asking dancers to do incredible things that in the long term will cripple them, [like] those extensions that mean nothing except that your leg is very high. It's kind of ugly.

> Quoted in "Carmen deLavallade" by Valerie Gladstone, *DanceTeacher magazine December 2008*

3 Once you master something that frightens you, it makes the next challenge much easier.

> Ibid.

2755. Olympia Dukakis (1931–)

1 The audience wants to be reminded of their own humanity.

> Graduation Address, American Conservatory Theater (San Francisco) *10 May 1997*

2 All of us as women feel there is a part of ourselves that is silenced.

> Quoted in "An Interview with Olympia Dukakis" by Jan Narqi, BroadwayWorld.com *10 January 2007*

2756. Riane Eisler (1931–)

1 The root of [society's] problem lies in a social system in which the power of the Blade is idealized—in which both men and women are taught to equate true masculinity with violence and dominance and to see men who do not conform to this ideal as "too soft" or "effeminate."

> Introduction, *The Chalice and the Blade 1987*

2 . . . all the modern, post-Enlightenment movements for social justice, be they religious or secular, as well as the more recent feminist, peace, and ecology movements, are part of an underlying thrust for the transformation of a dominator to a partnership system. Beyond this, in our time of unprecedentedly powerful technologies, these movements may be seen as part of our species' evolutionary thrust for survival.

> Ibid.

3 And if the central religious image [in Neolithic times] was a woman giving birth and not, as in our time, a man dying on a cross, it would not be unreasonable to infer that life and the love of life—rather than death and the fear of death—were dominant in society as well as art.

> Ch. 2, Ibid.

4 . . . something went terribly wrong with Christianity's original gospel of love. How otherwise could such a gospel be used to justify all the torture, conquest, and bloodletting carried out by devout Christians against others, and against one another, that makes up so much of our Western history?

> Ch. 9, Ibid.

5 History as taught in most schools is largely a matter of the struggle for power among men and nations. It is the dates of battles and the names of kings and generals noted for alter-

nately constructing and destroying fortresses, palaces, and religious monuments.

> Ch. 10, Ibid.

6 But ours is a time when "man's conquest of nature" threatens all life on our planet, when a dominator mind-set and advanced technology are a potentially lethal mix, when all around us institutions designed to maintain domination and exploitation are proving incapable of coping with the massive social, economic, and ecological problems they have created.

> Introduction, *Sacred Pleasure: Sex, Myth, and the Politics of the Body 1995*

7 Is it just accidental that *passion* is the word we use for both sexual and mystical experiences? Or is there some long-forgotten but still powerful connection?

> Ch. 1, Ibid.

8 For with consciousness and choice comes the possibility of change.

> Ch. 2, Ibid.

9 It is hard for us to imagine an art where scenes of men killing are virtually absent, where the act of giving birth is depicted as sacral in sculptures and paintings of the Goddess herself, and where . . . the act of coitus is a religious rite. It is also not easy for us to imagine menstrual blood as a divine gift, as we are not used to thinking of the human body, much less sex, as spiritual. And it is particularly hard for us to see woman's sexuality, her vagina, her pregnancy, her birth giving—as associated with a deity rather than as something shameful, unfit for polite discussion, much less religious art.

> Ch. 3, Ibid.

10 Laws are extremely useful indicators of the behaviors that are at a particular time and place considered acceptable or unacceptable. Of course, they do not tell us how people actually behave. But far more clearly than literary and historical accounts, laws do tell us what kinds of attitudes and behaviors the people who make the laws (and who have the power to enforce them) want to encourage or discourage.

> Ch. 6, Ibid.

11 To change our realities, we also have to change our myths. As history amply demonstrates, myths and realities go hand in hand.

> Ch. 7, Ibid.

12 Still another manifestation of the strong resistance to the mounting partnership thrust has been an intensive campaign for a return to "traditional family values"—the new code name for an authoritarian, male-dominated, patriarchal family designed to teach both boys and girls to obey orders from above, no matter how unjust or unloving they may be. This campaign has mainly come from fundamentalist and other religious groups who are still told by their leaders that the ranking of man over woman is divinely ordained.

> Ch. 10, Ibid.

13 For how can we speak of a free and democratic society with equality and justice for all at the same time that the domination of one half of humanity over the other half is accepted as only proper and right?

> Ch. 11, Ibid

14 Changes in consciousness are a very strange thing. Suddenly we see what was there all the time. And we wonder how it could for so long have been invisible to us.

> Ibid.

15 This notion that man can, and should, have absolute dominion over the "chaotic" powers of nature and woman . . . is what ultimately lies behind man's famous "conquest of nature"—a conquest that is today puncturing holes in the earth's ozone layer, destroying our forests, polluting our air and water, and increasingly threatening the welfare, and even survival, of thousands of living species, including our own.

Ch. 15, Ibid.

16 But, once again, the men who head the world's powerful religious hierarchies remain conspicuously silent about uncaring and violent sex—even when it is as extreme as genital mutilation and rape. Instead of pressuring world leaders to hold men fully accountable for rape, they expend their considerable resources on trying to stop women and men from the "sins" of contraception and abortion.

Ch. 16, Ibid.

17 . . . despite the fact that even though there are important official Catholic statements on the need for a more just redistribution of wealth, the Vatican has yet to redistribute its enormous wealth or, as attested by former priests who did join such grass-roots struggles, to actively support those who in many Catholic countries are fighting for just that.

Ibid.

18 But here too there is enormous opposition from the religious right, once again on the grounds that to educate young people about sex is immoral.

Actually, if we stop to think about it, what is immoral is *not* to educate young people about sex. Because for no other matter of importance in our lives—and sex is obviously of tremendous importance—would anyone think of advocating ignorance.

Ibid.

19 I now think of this courage to challenge unjust authority from a position of love rather than hate as spiritual courage. I think of it as the courage to question our most hallowed and sanctified norms—as the young Jew named Jesus did almost two thousand years ago when he defied the religion and secular authorities of his day. And I think of it as the kind of courage today being displayed by countless women and men in all walks of life who are through their lives and actions defying still firmly entrenched millennia-old dominator traditions.

Ch. 19, Ibid.

20 . . . to heal ourselves we also have to heal society.

Ibid.

21 This reclamation of divinity for Mary is particularly important, since we obviously need to leave behind the idealization of a family in which only the father and the son, and not the mother, are divine. In fact, we also need to add to the pantheon of a holy family a divine daughter. For only then will we have a model for families in which all members are equally valued and respected.

Ibid.

22 We all hunger for stories. Stories give form to our desires, feelings, and goals, molding how we view just about everything—from our own bodies to what is sacred or profane, good or bad, possible or impossible. Stories give us figures to emulate, imitate, admire, or abhor. And it is from the stories we are told that we in turn unconsciously fashion our own life scripts.

Ibid.

23 We must have the courage to open our eyes to the needs, suffering, and hopes of children worldwide, to question prescribed conventions, and to become the architects of a partnership future for generations to come through an enlightened, empathic global public education.

Tomorrow's Children: A Blueprint For Partnership Education in the 21st Century 1999

24 Partnership education helps students look beyond conventional social categories, such as capitalism versus communism, right versus left, religious versus secular, and even industrial versus preindustrial or postindustrial. They can instead begin to focus on relationships, and on the underlying question of what kinds of beliefs and social structures support or inhibit relations of violence or nonviolence, democracy or authoritarianism, justice or injustice, caring or cruelty, environmental sustainability or collapse.

Ibid.

25 I have chosen the phrase meaningful evolution to describe a view of evolution in which we can find a larger sense of purpose. . . . It is an approach that draws from an emerging body of scientific findings pointing to the evolutionary roots of caring for others and caring for what happens to future generations. It highlights that what we do in this lifetime is meaningful because it advances the evolution of our species and fulfills our responsibilities to this planet.

Ibid.

26 At the core of every child is an intact human.

"Reconstructing Education," Ibid.

27 Children are being given a false picture of what it means to be human. We tell them to be good and kind, nonviolent and giving. But on all sides they see media images and hear and read stories that portray us as bad, cruel, violent, and selfish.

"Refocusing and Reframing Education," Ibid.

2757. Totie Fields (1931–1978)

1 Obese, hefty, overweight, rotund. I never knew there were so many ways to say fatty.

Quoted in "The 1960's to the 1980's," *Women in Comedy* by Linda Martin & Kerry Segrave 1986

2 [Happiness is] getting a brown gravy stain on a brown dress.

Ibid.

3 I break all the rules and wear everything. Ruffles, ostrich feathers, fox coats. You look fat in fox anyway, so if you start fat, you only look a little fatter.

Quoted in "Early Stand-Up Comics," *Funny Women, American Comediennes, 1860–1985* by Mary Unterbrink 1987

4 I've been on a diet for two weeks and all I've lost is two weeks.

Stand-up routine *n.d*

2758. Sally Gearhart (1931–)

1 I look forward with great anticipation to the death of the church. The sooner it dies, the sooner we can be about the business of living the gospel.

"The Lesbian and God-the-Father or All the Church Needs Is a Good Lay—on Its Side" 1972

2 The proportion of men must be reduced to and maintained at approximately 10% of the human race.

The Future—If There Is One—Is Female 1982

3 Falling asleep, she thought. Sheer contentment, always, even with another Spooned body. But, she mused, there's a special balm to doing it in a wide bed all alone, with the margins of your body quite unbounded. . . .
"Flossie's Flashes," *Lesbian Love Stories,* Irene Zahava, ed. *1989*

2759. Bernice Gera (1931–1992)
1 When I work a game I am an umpire; the rest of the day I am a lady.
"Squeeze Play," *Time, 15 August 1969*

2 I could beat them in the courts, but I can't beat them on the field.
Quoted by her husband, Steve Gera, Obituary, *The New York Times 25 September 1992*

2760. Patricia Goedicke (1931–2006)
1 even the spiral notebooks I fill
with inky scratches to keep count.

From minute to minute disappear,

erase themselves from the mind's liquid,
dissolving pages.
"Uncharted," *Invisible Horses 1996*

2 . . . she lives in me like a crowd
of love songs and loud static . . .
"Because My Mother Was Deaf She Played the Piano," Ibid.

3 the flesh you live in is an anchor
of damp stones, you cannot move with or without it
"Recipe," Ibid.

4 The mind holds hands with itself in music
Untitled, Ibid.

2761. Martha Grimes (1931–)
1 "Just because you like birds doesn't mean you wouldn't take an ax to your mum, does it?"
"Wizards and Warlords," *The Anodyne Necklace 1983*

2 The sparrows—one attempting to escape, the other in hot pursuit—flew from hedge to tree to hedge. The pecking of one had bloodied the breast of the other. He was used to scenes of carnage; still he was shocked. But didn't it go on everywhere?
Ch. 1, *Jerusalem Inn 1983*

3 That really rankled. The man was clearly well off if that cashmere coat, that gold ring bore testimony: handsome—just the sort who made other men feel tatty: intelligent and well spoken. And besides all that he could blow proper smoke rings.
Ch. 1, *The Old Wine Shades 2006*

2762. Ossie Guffy (1931–)
1 I'm a woman, I'm black, I'm a little under forty, and I'm more of black America than Ralph Bunche* or Rap Brown** or Harry Belafonte,*** because I'm one of the millions who ain't bright, militant, or talented.
Ossie: The Autobiography of a Black Woman 1971
*American founder and key diplomat of the United Nations and recipient of the 1950 Nobel Peace Prize (1904–1971). **H. Rap Brown, American militant activist (1943–). ***Jamaican-born American actor, singer, director (1927–).

2 I got more children than I can rightly take care of, but I ain't got more than I can love.
Ibid.

2763. Shirley Hazzard (1931–)
1 "Sometimes, surely, truth is closer to imagination—or to intelligence, to love—than to fact? To be accurate is not to be right."
Ch. 11, *The Evening of the Holiday 1965*

2 "Perhaps if we lived with less physical beauty we would develop our true natures more."
Ch. 13, Ibid.

3 Algie was collecting contradictions in terms: to a nucleus of "military intelligence" and "competent authorities" he had added such discoveries as the soul of efficiency, easy virtue, enlightened self-interest, Bankers Trust, and Christian Scientist.
"Nothing in Excess," *People in Glass Houses 1967*

4 Pylos' first official act was to name his new department. The interim titles that had been used—"Economic Relief of Under Privileged Territories" and "Mission for Under-Developed Lands"—were well enough in their way, but they combined a note of condescension with initials which, when contracted, proved somewhat unfortunate.
"The Story of Miss Sadie Graine," Ibid.

5 Had I been accompanied, I might have laughed out loud . . . but solitude, which is held to be a cause of eccentricity, in fact imposes excessive normality, at least in public. . . .
Ch. 1, *The Bay of Noon 1970*

6 Like many men who are compulsively cruel to their womenfolk, he also shed tears at the cinema, and showed a disproportionate concern for insects.
Ch. 7, Ibid.

2764. Margaret O'Shaughnessy Heckler (1931–)
1 When you undermine faith in a system, your child may not necessarily see the difference between the politician who is no longer respected and the policeman, the teacher, the parent.
Quoted in "Impeachment?" by Claire Safran, *Redbook* (New York) *April 1974*

2 Once you start to separate public service from the enormous influence of the fat cats of society, you rob the vested interests of their most powerful weapons.
Ibid.

3 Women are the one minority group it is still considered fashionable to discriminate against.
Quoted on p. 134 *Women of Congress: A Twentieth-Century Odyssey* by Marcy Kaptur *1996*

2765. Kristin Hunter (1931–)
1 "A landlord is supposed to be brutal, stingy, insulting, and arrogant. Like the police, like the magistrates, like all the authority-figures of white society. That's what we're used to. That's what we understand. We're accustomed to our enemies, we know how to deal with them. A landlord who tries to be a friend only confuses us."
The Landlord 1966

2 "Love can't last around poverty. Neither can a woman's looks."
Ibid.

3 "But generally speaking I've always been too confused about who I was to decide who I was better than."

Ibid.

4 "First it is necessary to stand on your own two feet. But the minute a man finds himself in that position, the next thing he should do is reach out his arms."

Ibid.

5 Phosdicker was as honest as the day was long. He was an old-fashioned, dedicated civil servant; a fine, upright, honorable old man, Elgar thought. God help us all. A monster.

Ibid.

6 Just because I'm a big woman doesn't mean I can't be ravishing and gorgeously attired.

Ch. 1, *Kinfolks 2000*

7 She has a mouth full of razor blades disguised as pretty teeth, and she'll bare them and cut you up into person julienne in a minute.

Ibid.

8 She always politely accepted the diets he [her doctor] gave her, folded them, and put them in her bag, where they stayed until she changed pocketbooks. She was comfortable with the lush padding under her skin that made her resemble a sleek brown seal in the water . . . she had no plans to change.

Ch. 1, *Breaking Away 2003*

2766. Rona Jaffe (1931–2005)

1 A blonde in a red dress can do without introductions—but not without a bodyguard.

"Bottled in Blonde," *Roundabout 1962*

2767. Adrienne Kennedy (1931–)

1 SARAH. As for myself I long to become even a more pallid Negro than I am now; pallid like Negroes on the cover of American Negro magazines; soulless, educated and irrelevant. I want to possess no moral value, particularly value as to my being. I want not to be. I ask nothing except anonymity.

Funnyhouse of a Negro 1962

2 SARAH. For, like all educated Negroes—out of life and death essential—I find it necessary to maintain a stark fortress versus recognition of myself. My white friends like myself will be shrewd, intellectual and anxious for death. Anyone's death.

Ibid.

3 SARAH. . . . for relationships was one of my last religions.

Ibid.

4 I bleed.

A Lesson in Dead Language 1964

2768. Francine Klagsbrun (1931–)

1 The freedom of Shabbat comes from the potential it holds to control time, perhaps the most far-reaching form of freedom anyone can experience. Oppressed by unrelenting demands, many of us feel incapable of controlling our time. Shabbat offers such control. It offers a day when instead of fighting time we luxuriate in it. Instead of feeling chained to a routine, we may break loose and breathe freely.

The Fourth Commandment: Remember the Sabbath Day 2002

2 "Words" have a softness that "commandments" lack. "Words" suggest dialogue and connectedness. To use Martin Buber's terms, "words" presupposes an I-Thou relationship between humans and God, a degree of human nearness to the divine, the giver of those words.

Ch. 1, Ibid.

3 As the rabbis said, the commandments are all in the singular so that each person will feel that he or she, alone in the world, is responsible for studying, performing, and upholding them.

Ibid.

2769. Ella Leffland (1931–)

1 How could [the diplomats] keep from flinging themselves across the table and smashing each other's faces? Why had [innocent families] been killed if these leaders didn't even let go with a clenched fist? In such restraint, in such cordiality, there was something more horrifying than death itself.

Rumors of Peace 1979

2 Each century was the same; history was the same record played over and over. War was war, and peace was preparation for war; it was as if man were crazy, had always been, would always be. And the people on the street were man in his daily and abiding craziness.

Ibid.

2770. Jo Ann McNamara (1931–)

1 They [nuns] served their god and their church and in doing so they fulfilled themselves and laid a foundation for all women. Without the daring and sacrifice of these nuns, it is impossible to imagine the feminist movements of modern times finding any purchase in the public world. They created the image and reality of the autonomous woman. They formed the professions through which that autonomy was activated.

Sisters in Arms: Catholic Nuns Through Two Millennia 1996

2 For those of us formed by Western civilization, the Bible is the North Pole of our moral compass. We must know it to know ourselves.

"After the Fall," *The New York Times Book Review 6 September 1998*

2771. Toni Morrison (1931–)

1 "Which you want? A whipping and no turnips or turnips and no whipping?"

The Bluest Eye 1961

2 The difference between white and black females seemed to me an eminently satisfactory one. White females were *ladies,* said the sign maker, worthy of respect. And the quality that made ladyhood worthy? Softness, helplessness and modesty—which I interpreted as a willingness to let others do their labor and their thinking. Colored females, on the other hand, were *women*—unworthy of respect, independent and immodest.

"What the Black Woman Thinks About Women's Lib," *The New York Times Magazine 22 August 1971*

3 "I don't know everything, I just do everything."

Sula 1974

4 "I know what every colored woman in this country is doing."
"What's that?"
"Dying."

Ibid.

5 He meant that if you take a life, then you own it. You responsible for it. You can't get rid of nobody by killing them. They still there, and they yours now.

Song of Solomon 1977

6 "How come it [peacock] can't fly no better than a chicken?" Milkman asked.

"Too much tail. All that jewelry weighs it down. Like vanity. Can't nobody fly with all that shit. Wanna fly, you got to give up the shit that weighs you down."

Ch. 8, Ibid.

7 Bryn Mawr had done what a four-year dose of liberal education was designed to do: unfit her for eighty per cent of the useful work of the world.

Ch. 9, Ibid.

8 "Grab this land! Take it, hold it, my brothers, make it, my brothers, shake it, squeeze it, turn it, twist it, beat it, kick it, kiss it, whip it, stomp it, dig it, plow it, seed it, reap it, rent it, buy it, sell it, own it, build it, multiply it, and pass it on—can you hear me? Pass it on!"

Ch. 10, Ibid.

9 What they took for inattentiveness was a miracle of concentration.

Tar Baby 1981

10 But I think women dwell quite a bit on the duress under which they work, on how hard it is just to do it at all. We are traditionally rather proud of ourselves for having slipped creative work in there between the domestic chores and obligations. I'm not sure we deserve such big A-pluses for all that.

Quoted in "Toni Morrison's Black Magic" by Jean Strouse,*
Newsweek (New York) *30 March 1981*
*See 3617.

11 That's a pejorative term in critical circles now: if a work of art has any political influence in it, somehow it's tainted. My feeling is just the opposite: if it has none, it is tainted.

The problem comes when you find harangue passing off as art. It seems to me that the best art is political and you ought to be able to make it unquestionably political and irrevocably beautiful at the same time.

"Rootedness: The Ancestor as Foundation," *Black Women Writers (1950–1980)*, Mari Evans,* ed. *1983*
*See 2453.

12 Once upon a time she had known more and wanted to.

Pt. I, *Beloved 1987*

13 She couldn't read clock time very well, but she knew when the hands were closed in prayer at the top of the face she was through for the day.

Pt. II, Ibid.

14 "Tell me this one thing. How much is a nigger supposed to take? Tell me. How much?"

"All he can," said Stamp Paid. "All he can."

"Why? Why? Why? Why? Why?"

Ibid.

15 Two parents can't raise a child any more than one. You need a whole community—everybody—to raise a child. And the little nuclear family is a paradigm that just doesn't work. It doesn't work for white people or for black people. Why we

are hanging onto it, I don't know. It isolates people into little units—people need a larger unit.

Quoted in "The Pain of Being Black" by Bonnie Angelo, *Time* (New York) *22 May 1989*

16 How soon country people forget. When they fall in love with a city it is forever, and it is like forever. As though there never was a time when they didn't love it. The minute they arrive at the train station or get off the ferry and glimpse the wide streets and the wasteful lamps lighting them, they know they are born for it. There, in a city, they are not so much new as themselves: their stronger, riskier selves.

Ch. 2, *Jazz 1991*

17 In this country American means white. Everybody else has to hyphenate.

The Guardian (London) *29 January 1992*

18 Oppressive language does more than represent violence; it is violence; does more than represent the limits of knowledge; it limits knowledge.

Nobel Prize acceptance speech *7 December 1993*

19 In my country children have bitten their tongues and use bullets instead to iterate the voice of speechlessness.

Ibid.

20 We die. That may be the meaning of life. But we do language. That may be the measure of our lives.

Ibid.

21 Our inheritance is an affront. You want us to have your old, blank eyes and see only cruelty and mediocrity. Do you think we are stupid enough to perjure ourselves again and again with the fiction of nationhood? How dare you talk to us of duty when we stand waist deep in the toxin of your past?

Ibid.

22 What I think the political correctness debate is really about is the power to be able to define. The definers want the power to name. And the defined are now taking that power away from them.

Quoted in *The New York Times Magazine 11 September 1994*

23 "Parents idle, children sidle," his own mother used to say.

I, "Portrait," *Love 2003*

24 They seemed well suited to each other: vain, voluptuous, prouder of their pewter and porcelain than of their sons.

p. 19, *A Mercy 2008*

25 Jacob sneered at wealth dependent on a captured workforce that required more force to maintain. Thin as they were, the dregs of his kind of Protestantism recoiled at whips, chains and armed overseers. He was determined to prove that his own industry could amass the fortune, the station, D'Ortega claimed without trading his conscience for coin.

p. 28, Ibid.

26 Their drift away from others produced a selfish privacy and they had lost the refuge and the consolation of a clan.

p. 58, Ibid.

27 We never shape the world she says. The world shapes us.

p. 71, Ibid.

2772. Alice Munro (1931–)

1 But I never cleaned thoroughly enough, my reorganization proved to be haphazard, the disgraces came unfailingly to light, and it was clear how we failed, how disastrously we fell short of that ideal of order and cleanliness, household decency which I as much as anybody else believed in.

"Winter Wind," *Something I've Been Meaning to Tell You* 1974.

2 They were intimate. They had found out so much about each other that everything had got cancelled out by something else. That was why the sex between them could seem so shame-faced, merely and drearily lustful, like sex between siblings.

The Progress of Love 1986

3 Moments of kindness and reconciliation are worth having, even if the parting has to come sooner or later.

Ibid.

4 So you see against what odds, and with what unpromising-looking persons, love takes root and flourishes.

Selected Stories 1996

5 What if people really did that—sent their love through the mail to get rid of it? What would it be that they sent? A box of chocolates with centers like the yolks of turkey's eggs. A mud doll with hollow eye sockets. A heap of roses slightly more fragrant than rotten. A package wrapped in bloody newspaper that nobody would want to open.

"Before the Change," *The Love of a Good Woman* 1998

6 But once in a while came a moment when everything seemed to have something to say to you. The rocking bushes, the bleaching light. All in a flash, in a rush, when you couldn't concentrate. Just when you wanted summing up, you got a speedy, goofy view, as from a fun-ride.

"Jakarta," Ibid.

2773. Nisa (1931–)

1 When your child dies, you think . . . "This God . . . his ways are foul! Why did he give me a little one and then take her away?"

It is the same if it is your mother. You cry for her as you do for your child. You pull off your beads and ornaments so your neck and body are bare. You mourn for her, you miss her, and your heart is miserable.

Quoted in *The Life and Words of a !Kung Woman* by Marjorie Shostak

2 Babies, yes . . . the day your baby is about to be born, that day your heart is miserable. But once it is lying on the sand, a baby is a wonderful thing. Your heart is very happy because you love children. You and your child talk together, even if it is just tiny.

Ibid.

2474. Amanda Row (1931–)

1 Jocelyn's childhood stood on the bookcase: *Pollyanna, The Bobbsey Twins, Now We Are Six, Black Beauty,* and *The Little Minister* beside *Heidi.*

Where No Sea Runs 1963

2775. Jane Rule (1931–)

1 ". . . I think everything has value, absolute value, a child, a house, a day's work, the sky. But nothing will save us. We were never meant to be saved."

"What were we meant for then?"
"To love the whole damned world . . ."

Desert of the Heart 1964

2 Cleaving is an activity which should be left to snails for cleaning ponds and aquariums.

Introduction, *Lesbian Images* 1975

3 I didn't want to be a boy, ever, but I was outraged that his height and intelligence were graces for him and gaucheries for me.

Ibid.

4 I had never been as resigned to ready-made ideas as I was to ready-made clothes, perhaps because, although I couldn't sew, I could think.

Ibid.

5 What is is my domain. What ought to be is the business of politicians and preachers.

"Lesbian and Writer," *A Hot-Eyed Moderate* 1985

2776. Maxine Singer (1931–)

1 . . . Science is one of the grand human activities. It uses the same kind of talent and creativity as painting pictures and making sculptures. It's not really very different, except that you do it from a base of technical knowledge.

Quoted in *A World of Ideas* by Bill Moyers 1989

2 A society that turns its back on science has to face decay and deterioration.

Ibid.

3 The reasons we know that we will discover things that we can't describe now is that this has been the history of science. We do things to learn something we can define, and we wind up knowing things we never imagined even asking about.

Ibid.

4 Whether evil uses technology that's new or technology that's old, what motivates it are human problems that have nothing to do with the developments in technology.

Ibid.

2777. Kabita Sinha (1931–)

1 I was the first
rebel—
banished from paradise,
exiled.
I learned
that human life
was greater
than paradise.
I was first
to know.

"Ishwarke Eve" (Eve Speaks to God), *Poetry Is the Supreme Being,* Pritish Nandy, tr. 1976

2 can you pose naked then, chaste Savitri*—
not the flighted fairy frozen on temple walls
not Botticelli's distilled desire, Venus seductress
not the abashed arm covering breasts
not nudity as sanctimonious cloak then:
all masks come off, you hold your pose,
relaxed and nude, for all the rest of us.

"Alone like a Goddess," *Poetry Goddess* 1976
*Legendary Hindu princess who married for love.

2778. Merlin Stone (1931–)

1 It is difficult to grasp the immensity and significance of the extreme reverence paid to the Goddess over a period of (at least) seven thousand years and over miles of land cutting across national boundaries and vast expanses of sea. Yet it is vital to do just that to fully comprehend the longevity as well as the widespread power and influence this religion once held.

When God Was a Woman 1976

2 We may find ourselves wondering to what degree the suppression of women's rites has actually been the suppression of women's rights.

Ibid.

3 In each area in which the Goddess was known and revered, She was extolled not only as the prophetess of great wisdom, closely identified with the serpent, but as the original Creatress, and the patroness of sexual pleasures and reproduction as well. The Divine Ancestress was identified as She who brought life as well as She who decreed the destinies and directions of those lives, a not unnatural combination.

Ibid.

4 With blatant disregard for actual history, the Levite leaders announced that woman must be ruled by man, declaring that it was in agreement with the original decree of Yahweh, who, according to these new legends, had first created the world and people. The myth of Adam and Eve, in which male domination was explained and justified, informed women and men alike that male ownership and control of submissively obedient women was to be regarded as the divine and natural state of the human species.

Ibid.

5 They had so hoped that when the beings of Earth began to think about a very long past, it would help them to conceive of a very long future ahead.

"The Plasting Project," *Hear the Silence*, Irene Zahava, ed. *1986*

2779. Jolene Unsoeld (1931–)

1 I think fewer of the women [in politics] have deliberately set out to be on a leadership track the way many of our male colleagues have. We want to work on the issues that drove us to office.

Quoted in "Cleaning house in government . . ." by Carol M. Ostrom, *Seattle Times*, A1–9 2 August 1992

2 Reproductive health is at the very core of a woman's existence in its importance. If you want to be brutally frank what it compares [with] is if you had health care plans that did not cover any illness related to male testicles.

"Unsoeld 'brutally frank' on issue," *Seattle Post-Intelligencer* 13 May 1994

2780. Judith Viorst (1931–)

1 With four walk-in closets to walk in,
Three bushes, two shrubs, and one tree,
The suburbs are good for the children,
But no place for grown-ups to be.

"The Suburbs Are Good for the Children," *It's Hard to Be Hip Over Thirty and Other Tragedies of Married Life 1968*

2 But it's hard to be hip over thirty
When everyone else is nineteen . . .

"It's Hard to Be Hip Over Thirty," Ibid.

3 Love is much nicer to be in than an automobile accident, a tight girdle, a higher tax bracket or a holding pattern over Philadelphia.

"What Is This Thing Called Love?" *Redbook* (New York) *February 1975*

4 Brevity may be the soul of wit, but not when someone's saying, "I love you."

Ibid.

5 The world could maybe come to an end on next Tuesday.
The ceiling could maybe come crashing on my head.
I maybe could run out of things for me to worry about.
And then I'd have to do my homework instead.

"Fifteen, Maybe Sixteen Things to Worry About," St. 2, *If I Were in Charge of the World and Other Worries . . . 1981*

6 My mom says I'm her sugarplum.
My mom says I'm her lamb.
My mom says I'm completely perfect
Just the way I am.
My mom says I'm a super-special wonderful terrific little guy.
My mom just had another baby.
Why?

"Some Things Don't Make Any Sense at All," *in toto,* Ibid.

7 When we think of loss we think of the loss, through death, of people we love. But loss is a far more encompassing theme in our life. For we lose not only through death, but also by leaving and being left, by changing and letting go and moving on. And our losses include not only our separations and departures from those we love, but our conscious and unconscious losses of romantic dreams, impossible expectations, illusions of freedom and power, illusions of safety—and the loss of our own younger self, the self that thought it would always be unwrinkled and invulnerable and immortal.

Introduction, *Necessary Losses 1986*

8 Growing up means letting go of the dearest megalomaniacal dreams of our childhood. Growing up means knowing they can't be fulfilled. Growing up means gaining the wisdom and the skills to get what we want within the limitations imposed by reality—a reality which consists of diminished powers, restricted freedoms and, with the people we love, imperfect connections.

Ch. 11, Ibid.

2781. Frances West (1931–2007)

1 Human beings have a desire to worship because it scratches what itches in the human condition.

Quoted by Barbara Hamilton-Holway, *Spirit of Life Workshop* uua.org 2007

2782. Anouk Aimée (1932–)

1 You can only perceive real beauty in a person as they get older.

The Guardian (London) 24 August 1988

2783. Liliane Atlan (1932–)

1 We have all become little sharks.

The Carriage of Flames and Voices 1971

2 At first, men wrote on the walls of their caves, then on papyrus, then paper; why, in an age such as ours, should we not write with waves of sound and light?

"Liliane Atlan," Antoine Bootz and Catherine Ruello, trs., *Interviews with Contemporary Women Playwrights*, Kathleen Betsko* and Rachel Koenig *1987*

*See 3125.

3   Video is a great instrument—the cassette and television are small and intimate. I am convinced that the new mode of communication is not the theater play, the novel, or cinema, but videotexts.

Ibid.

2784. Natalie Babbitt (1932–)

1   The first week in August hangs at the very top of summer, the top of the live-long year, like the highest seat of a Ferris wheel when it pauses in its turning.

Prologue, *Tuck Everlasting 1985*

2   The ownership of land is an odd thing when you come to think of it. How deep, after all, can it go? If a person owns a piece of land, does he own it all the way down, in ever narrowing dimensions, till it meets all other pieces at the center of the earth? Or does ownership consist only of a thin crust under which the friendly worms have never heard of trespassing?

Ch. 1, *Ibid.*

3   . . . the cows, through some wisdom they were not wise enough to know that they possessed, were very wise indeed.

Ibid.

2785. Bai Fengxi (1932?–)

1   Women are not the moon. Emit your own light.

Return of an Old Friend on a Stormy Night 1983

2   If a woman is strong, there will be no peace in the house.

Ibid.

2786. Anne Bancroft (1932–2005)

1   [Live television] was the greatest school that one could go to. You learned to be concentrated and focused.

Remark, *1997*

2   Film critics said I gave a voice to the fear we all have: that we'll reach a certain point in our lives, look around and realize that all the things we said we'd do and become will never come to be—and that we're ordinary.

Ibid.

2787. Beverly Butcher Byron (1932–)

1   Legislation is not going to change discrimination. That is like trying to legislate morality. The quality of representation is neither hindered nor helped by gender; the quality is with the individual.

Speech, 96th Congress *January 1979*

2   I'm probably the only member of Congress who was elected having taken no campaign contributions and no stands on any issue. I came out of my kitchen into Congress.

Quoted in "The Widow's Run" by Frank Bruni, *The New York Times 29 March 1998*

2788. Yoko Nagae Ceschina (1932–)

1   I know nothing about politics, I don't care about the conflicts between North Korea, Japan, United States. I love music and music is a universal language. I am pleased I can make the concert possible, I hope it can contribute to peace.

"Note diplomatiche L'orchestra Usa in Corea del Nord" by Sandro Cappellletto, *La Stampa 2 May 2008*

2789. Olga Connolly (1932–)

1   Society feels that sport must be justified, and we have gotten away from the Greek concept of mind and body. That is the failure of the physical education process.

Quoted in "Women in Sports: The Movement Is Real," *The Los Angeles Times 23 April 1974*

2   Women must be accepted as human beings, and it can't be done until women are physically strong enough to stand on their own feet.

Ibid.

2790. Shirley Conran (1932–)

1   I make no secret of the fact that I would rather lie on a sofa than sweep beneath it. But you have to be efficient if you're going to be lazy.

"The Reason Why," *Superwoman 1975*

2   Life is too short to stuff a mushroom.

Epigraph, *Ibid.*

2791. Patricia Cumming (1932–)

1   We thought we could banish
the faceless
dark, the sticky
cobwebs in the hall:
we thought the
hollowness would go away.

"Further Notes for the Alumni Bulletin," Sts. 3–4, *Quartet*, vol. 6, nos. 15–16 *Winter/Spring 1974*

2792. Sheena Duncan (1932–)

1   The women made a plan to dig their own graves and they said, "We will stand beside our graves because we are not moving from here. You can shoot and we will lie in our land forever.

Quoted in Ch. 24, *Lives of Courage* by Diana E. H. Russell* *1989*

*See 3104.

2793. Alice Thomas Ellis (1932–)

1   Christmas [was a time when] . . . relations who throughout most of the year had the sense to stay apart confined themselves in small spaces to eat and drink too much.

The Birds of the Air 1980

2   Life is only, by definition, a use of time.

The Inn at the Edge of the World 1990

3   Death is the last enemy: once we've got past that I think everything will be alright.

"In the Psychiatrist's Chair," BBC Radio 4 *19 August 1992*

4   Humans were useful for breeding, when you could catch one, and every now and then . . . he ate one, but otherwise he avoided them on the whole. . . .

Fairy Tale 1998

5   The world was full of nutty housewives.

Pillars of Gold 1992

2794. Eva Figes (1932–)

1 When modern woman discovered the orgasm it was (combined with modern birth control) perhaps the biggest single nail in the coffin of male dominance.

> Quoted in *The Descent of Woman* by Elaine Morgan* 1972
> *See 2383.

2 The law of individualism and private enterprise is that God helps those who help themselves; what is more, He is actually on their side, since it is a sin not to make use of the talents God gave you. So poverty definitely implies not only laziness but a fall from grace: God disapproves of paupers.

> Ibid.

3 Providing for one's family as a good husband and father is a water-tight excuse for making money hand over fist. Greed may be a sin, exploitation of other people might, on the face of it, look rather nasty, but who can blame a man for "doing the best" for his children?

> "A View of My Own," *Nova January 1973*

4 . . . unless society recognises that its responsibility extends far beyond the provision of free schooling, the money spent on state education is largely wasted. School becomes just another way of institutionalising the poor.

> Ibid.

5 The much vaunted male logic isn't logical, because they display prejudices—against half the human race—that are considered prejudices according to any dictionary definition.

> *Women Writers Talk*, Olga Kenyon, ed. 1989

2795. Dian Fossey (1932–1985)

1 The more you learn about the dignity of the gorilla, the more you want to avoid people.

> Quoted in "Case of the Gorilla Lady Murder" by William E. Smith, *Time* (New York) 1 September 1986

2796. Antonia Fraser (1932–)

1 . . . As with all forms of liberation, of which the liberation of women is only one example, it is easy to suppose in a time of freedom that the darker days of repression can never come again.

> "Epilogue: How Strong?" *The Weaker Vessel 1984*

2 It is however an almost universal fact of history that women have done well in wartime when they have been able or compelled to act as substitutes for men, showing themselves resourceful, courageous and strong in every sense of the words; in short displaying without much difficulty all those qualities generally described as masculine. It is another fact that the postwar period has generally seen a masculine retreat from this view of the female sex when the vacuum no longer needs to be filled.

> Ibid.

2797. Sheila Fugard (1932–)

1 In a way it is much simpler to take upon oneself a discipline without the consolation of a visionary guide.

> I believe now that there is no need to find him, the Buddhist, that all I must do is progress in the knowledge of the void, the perennial nothingness of the moment.

> Pt. III, l.l., *The Castaways 1972*

2 I talk of the lives of others. I am fertilized, but not fulfilled, and my life insists on its own voice.

> Pt. I, *A Revolutionary Woman 1985*

3 The Karoo* is all space. The trees fail to fill the emptiness, and the fences are useless too. The Karoo swallows up everything; Brahmins and Untouchables, the flocks of sheep and goats, as well as the houses and possessions. There is much to contend with here.

> Ibid.

> *The harsh landscape of South Africa.

4 The butcher is mistaken. Justice is not weighed on a scale like a pound of steak. I'm aware of the cost of justice, and it's not measured in pounds. It's got to do with men's hearts.

> Pt. III, Ibid.

2798. Shirley Gee (1932–)

1 MOTHER. There's too much hate in the world. I'll not be part of it. Sometimes that's hard, but how I try to think of it is this. The boys on the streets, the soldiers. With them it's not so much the boredom, it's the tension of that boredom. And nobody wants them, and they feel it. That makes explosions in them, trapped inside them, not allowed to burst. So when they get the chance, there's a bit of trouble, then they let it out, they're full of spite, smash things, smash people.

> Act I, *Never in My Lifetime 1983*

2799. Penelope Gilliatt (1932–)

1 The reason why her face was unlined was perhaps that no expression ever passed through it, the owner having developed a reputation for herself as a sort of Delphic presence simply by a habit of nonparticipation that had begun as a defence against the efforts of a boisterous English nanny to boot her into vivacity.

> Pt. I, Ch. 3, *A State of Change 1967*

2 "Why is it that beautiful women never seem to have any curiosity?"

> "Is it because they know they're classical? With classical things the Lord finished the job. Ordinary ugly people know they're deficient and they go on looking for the pieces."

> Pt. II, Ch. 8, Ibid.

3 ALEX. I can't see why having an affair with someone on and off is any worse that being married for a course or two at mealtimes.

> "Monday," *Sunday Bloody Sunday 1971*

4 ALEX. I've had this business that anything is better than nothing. There are times when nothing has to be better than anything.

> "Saturday," Ibid.

5 The odd thing is, whatever you've been stingy about is something you never use anyway. It's like life itself . . . spend it—spend it because you have it.

> Quoted in "Rebirth?" by James Childs, *The Hollywood Screenwriters*, Richard Corliss, ed. 1972

2800. Raisa Maxima Gorbachev (1932–1999)

1 The calamity of war, wherever, whenever and upon whomever it descends, is a tragedy for the whole of humanity.

> *I Hope 1991*

2 No war, not even to punish an aggressor, is a good thing. Today people must learn to take into account each others' interests, if only for the sake of survival.

Ibid.

2801. Joanne Greenberg (1932–)

1 "On my surface . . . there must be no sign showing, no seam—a perfect surface."

Ch. 1, *I Never Promised You a Rose Garden* 1964

2 A child's independence is too big a risk for the shaky balance of some parents.

Ch. 5, Ibid.

3 She had opened her mind to the words the way an eye used to darkness, veiled with its lashes, opens cautiously to the light, and, finding it even a little blinding, closes itself too late. The light had come, and come invincibly, even after the eye had renounced it. It was too late to unsee.

Ch. 8, Ibid.

4 Later, they began to explore the secret idea that Deborah shared with all the ill—that she had infinitely more power than the ordinary person and was at the same time also his inferior.

Ch. 17, Ibid.

5 "And if I fight, then for *what?*"

"For nothing easy or sweet, and I told you that last year and the year before that. For your own challenge, for your own mistakes and the punishment for them, for your own definition of love and sanity—a good strong self with which to begin to live."

Ch. 21, Ibid.

6 "What cook can match herself against hunger and memory?"

"Children of Joy" (1966), *Shaking Eve's Tree, Short Stories of Jewish Women,* Sharon Niederman,* ed. 1990
*See 3853.

7 "Listen, when a woman can't have diamonds, she wears rhinestones; and when she can't have rhinestones, she wears glass and holds up her head."

Ibid.

8 There is no creativity in madness; madness is the opposite of creativity, although people may be creative in spite of being mentally ill.

Comment, National Association for Rights Protection and Advocacy 1998

2802. Jacquelyne Jackson (1932–)

1 Those black males who try to hold women down are expressing in sexist terms the same kinds of expression in racist terms which they would deny. . . .

Speech, First National Conference of Black Women *March 1974*

2803. Jenny Joseph (1932–)

1 When I am an old woman I shall wear purple
With a red hat which doesn't go, and doesn't suit me,
And I shall spend my pension on brandy and summer globes
And satin sandals, and say we've no money for butter.
I shall sit down on the pavement when I'm tired
And gobble up samples in shops and press alarm bells

And run my stick along the public railings
And make up for the sobriety of my youth.

"Warning," St. 1, *The Oxford Book of Twentieth Century English Verse,* Phillip Larkin, ed. 1973

2804. Nancy Kassebaum (1932–)

1 The professional politician, with his eye on the next election, quite naturally seeks to temporize or completely avoid potentially controversial issues. . . . The result is often the subjugation of the nation's common welfare.

Quoted in *American Political Women* by Esther Stineman 1980

2805. Lilian G. Katz (1932–)

1 Learning to deal with setbacks, and maintaining the persistence and optimism necessary for childhood's long road to mastery are the real foundations of lasting self-esteem.

"Reading, Writing, Narcissism," *The New York Times* 15 July 1993

2 As a way of learning, the project approach emphasizes children's active participation in the planning, development, and assessment of their own work; children are encouraged to take initiative and responsibility for the work undertaken.

Ch. 1, *Engaging Children's Minds: The Project Approach, Second Edition* co-author, Sylvia C. Chard* 2000, rev.
*See 3077.

3 All decision include errors. Life is a series of choices of which errors you prefer.

Intellectual Emergencies 2009

4 Every solution to every problem creates new problems. You have to decide whether you like the new problems more than the old ones.

Ibid.

5 Teach children to take pleasure in each others' gifts.

Ibid.

2806. Loretta Lynn (1932–)

1 A woman's two cents worth is worth two cents in the music business.

Quoted in "Sexism Seen But Not Heard" by Tracy Hotchner, *The Los Angeles Times* 26 May 1974

2 Yeah! I'm proud to be a coal miner's daughter
I remember the well where I drew water
The work we done was hard
At night we'd sleep 'cause we were tired
I never thought of ever leaving Butcher Holler

Title song, *Coal Miner's Daughter* (album) 1970

3 I'm about as old fashioned as I can be
And I hope you're lik'in what you see
'Cause if you're lookin' at me
You're lookin' at country

"You're Looking at Country," *The Definitive Collection* (album) 2004

2807. Miriam Makeba (1932– 2008)

1 I look at an ant and I see myself: a native South African, endowed by nature with a strength much greater than my size

so I might cope with the weight of a racism that crushes my spirit. I look at a bird and I see myself: a native South African, soaring above the injustices of apartheid on wings of pride, the pride of a beautiful people. I look at a stream and I see myself: a native South African, flowing irresistibly over hard obstacles until they become smooth and, one day, disappear—flowing from an origin that has been forgotten toward an end that will never be.

Prologue, *Makeba, My Story*, with James Hall *1987*

2 *"Age ain't nothin' but a number."* But age is other things, too. It is wisdom, if one has lived one's life properly. It is experience and knowledge. And it is getting to know all the ways the world turns, so that if you cannot turn the world the way you want, you can at least get out of the way so you won't get run over.

Ch. 16, Ibid.

3 Africa has her mysteries, and even a wise man cannot understand them. But a wise man respects them.

Ch. 20, Ibid.

4 I never understood why I couldn't come home. I never committed any crime.

Quoted by Associated Press *1990*

5 I kept my culture. I kept the music of my roots. Through my music I became this voice and image of Africa, and the people, without even realizing.

Quoted in Obituary by Celia Dugger, *The New York Times 10 November 2008*

2808. Vivienne Malone-Mayes (1932–1995)

1 . . . definitions, theorem, proof, then example; it was almost like a little song . . . once you began to understand it, the beauty of it began to shine through.

Quoted in *Women in Mathematics: The Addition of Difference* by Claudia Henrion* *1997*

*See 4454.

2809. Joan Manley (1932–)

1 The best direction is the least possible direction.

Quoted in "Hooked on Books" by Jurate Kazickas, *Working Woman February 1979*

2 Selling is the final step of the creative process—since I didn't have the ability to be in on the beginning of a book, the writing of it, then I wanted to be in on the end.

Quoted in "Wistful View From the Corporate Heights" by Lynn Darling, *The Washington Post 8 April 1979*

3 I would have made a terrible mother. For one thing, I hate to repeat myself.

Ibid.

4 Sometimes you wonder how you got on this mountain. But sometimes you wonder, "How will I get off?"

Ibid.

2810. Elaine May (1932–)

1 "Mama, let me tell you, I feel awful [for not writing you]."

"Oh, God, sonny, if I could only believe that, I'd be the happiest mother in the world.

Quoted in "Writers and Directors," *Funny Women, American Comediennes, 1860–1985* by Mary Unterbrink *1987*

2 I sat by that phone all day Friday, all day Saturday, and all day Sunday. Your father said to me, "Phyllis, eat something. You'll faint." I said, "No, Harry. No. I don't want my mouth to be full when my son calls me."

Quoted in "Is There Any Group I Haven't Offended?" *The Haunted Smile, The Story of Jewish Comedians in America* by Lawrence J. Epstein *2001*

3 Someday, someday, Arthur, you'll get married, and you'll have children of your own, and, honey, when you do, I only pray that they make you suffer. That's a mother's prayer.

Ibid.

4 It's so thrilling to be married to someone you don't really know.

Taller Than A Dwarf 2002

5 Let's face it, if women didn't sit by the phone waiting for the guys to call, why would you need a women's movement?

After the Night and the Music 2005

2811. Nobuko Mori (1932–)

1 Let the voice from the kitchen be heard in government.

Quoted in "A Mountain Moves" by Jill Smolowe, *Time* (New York) *7 August 1989*

2812. Maria Nemeth (1932–)

1 Energy requires a conduit, for without that, energy is nothing but pure potential.

"Becoming a Conduit of Money" by Diane M. Cooper, *The Spirit of M'aat, vol. 1, no. 12* (spiritofmaat.com) *2002?*

2 When we allow ourselves the energy of relationship, we find that we are not meant to go it alone. We are literally meant to allow ourselves to give other people support, and let them support us. True abundance occurs when you always allow that which is around you to nourish you.

Ibid.

3 I've learned that whatever I try to get away from only follows me, nipping at my heels.

Ch. 1, *Mastering Life's Energies 2007*

4 It takes daring to become focused on dreams instead of dilemmas.

Ibid.

5 Luminosity—it's worthy emphasizing—is clarity, focus, ease, and grace *in action*. It can't be invoked by psychological insight or analysis. It's fresh. Luminosity doesn't comb its hair but rather lets the winds of life blow freely through it.

Ibid.

2813. Pauline Oliveros (1932–)

1 Sonic awareness is a synthesis of the psychology of consciousness, the physiology of the martial arts, and the sociology of the feminist movement. . . .

Quoted in *The Music of Pauline Oliveros* by Heidi Von Gunden *1983*

2 Deep listening is listening in every possible way to every thing possible to hear no matter what you are doing. Such intense listening includes the sounds of daily life, of nature, of one's own thoughts as well as musical sounds. Deep listening is my life practice.

"Interactive Music," *The Roots of the Moment 1998*

2814. Suzy Parker (1932–2003)

1 I thank God for high cheekbones every time I look in the mirror in the morning.

Quoted in This Fabulous Century (1950–1960) 1970

2815. Linda Pastan (1932–)

1 Grief is a circular staircase

"The Five Stages of Grief," *The Five Stages of Grief 1978*

2 You have grown wings of pain
and flap around the bed like a wounded gull
calling for water, calling for tea, for grapes
whose skins you cannot penetrate.
Remember when you taught me
how to swim? Let go, you said,
the lake will hold you up.
I long to say, Father let go
and death will hold you up . . .

"Go Gentle," *PM/AM 1982*

3 I have banked the fires of my body

"Meditation by the Stove," *Carnival Evening: New and Selected Poems: 1968–1998*

2816. Sylvia Brinton Perera (1932–)

1 . . . so much of the power and passion of the feminine has been dormant in the underworld—in exile for five thousand years.

Introduction, *Descent of the Goddess, A Way of Initiation for Women 1981*

2 Our planet is passing through a phase—the rebirth of the goddess . . .

Ch. 1, Ibid.

3 "In ceremonies of riddance the evil is magically transferred to other persons, to animals, plants or inanimate objects. The evil is treated concretely, as if it were a contagion that could be drawn off into a material object which then becomes—on the concrete, literalistic level of magic consciousness—an incarnate pollution that can be disposed of.

Ch. 1, *Scapegoat Complex: Toward a Mythology of Shadow and Guilt 1985*

4 As the old ways trickled down through the millennia, they became secularized: rites became revels, gods became "little people," and sacred wine became intoxicating booze. A similar fate happens to the old gods in each of us.

Queen Maeve and Her Lovers: A Celtic Archetype of Ecstasy, Addiction, and Healing 1999

2817. Sylvia Plath (1932–1963)

1 His ardor snares me, lights the trees,
And I run flaring in my skin;

"Pursuit" (1956), *The Colossus 1960*

2 She judged petals in disarray,
The whole season, sloven.

"Spinster," St. 2 (1956), Ibid.

3 each day demands we create our whole world over,
disguising the constant horror in a coat
of many-colored fictions . . .

"Tale of a Tub," St. 5 (1956), Ibid.

4 Two virtues ride, by stallion, by nag,
To grind our knives and scissors:
Lantern-jawed Reason, squat Common Sense,
One courting doctors of all sorts,
One, housewives and shopkeepers.

"The death of myth-making," St. 1 (1957), Ibid.

5 . . . hearing the cut flowers
Sipping their liquids from assorted pots,
Pitchers and Coronation goblets
Like Monday drunkards.

"Leaving early," Ibid.

6 Now she's done for, the dewlapped lady
I watched settle, line by line, in my mirror . . .

"Face Lift," St. 4 *1961*

7 The woman is perfected
Her dead
Body wears the smile of accomplishment.

"Edge"* *1963*

*Her last poem, written a week before her suicide.

8 "What does a woman see in a woman that she can't see in a man?" Doctor Nolan paused. Then she said, "Tenderness."

The Bell Jar 1963

9 . . . I guess I feel about a hot bath the way those religious people feel about holy water. . . . The longer I lay there in the clear hot water the purer I felt, and when I stepped out at last and wrapped myself in one of the big, soft, white, hotel bath-towels I felt pure and sweet as a new baby.

Ch. 2, Ibid.

10 "Do you know what a poem is, Esther?"
"No, what?" I would say.
"A piece of dust."
Then just as he was smiling and starting to look proud, I would say, "So are the cadavers you cut up. So are the people you think you're curing. They're dust as dust as dust. I reckon a good poem lasts a whole lot longer than a hundred of those people put together."

Ch. 5, Ibid.

11 I never wanted to get married. The last thing I wanted was infinite security, and to be the place an arrow shoots off from. I wanted change and excitement and to shoot off in all directions myself, like the colored arrows from a Fourth of July rocket.

Ch. 7, Ibid.

12 If neurotic is wanting two mutually exclusive things at one and the same time, then I'm neurotic as hell. I'll be flying back and forth between one mutually exclusive thing and another for the rest of my days.

Ch. 8, Ibid.

13 . . . I had followed the green, luminous course of the second hand and the minute hand and the hour hand of the bedside clock through their circles, their circles and semi-circles, every night for seven nights, without missing a second, or a minute, or an hour.

Ch. 10, Ibid.

14 I stored the fact . . . in the corner of my mind the way a squirrel stores a nut.

Ch. 15, Ibid.

15 Sunday—the doctor's paradise! Doctors at country clubs, doctors at the seaside, doctors with mistresses, doctors with wives, doctors in church, doctors in yachts, doctors everywhere resolutely being people, not doctors.

Ch. 19, Ibid.

16 I took a deep breath and listened to the old brag of my heart. I am, I am, I am.

Ch. 20, Ibid.

17 A living doll, everywhere you look.
It can sew, it can cook,
It can talk, talk, talk.

It works, there is nothing wrong with it.
You have a hole, it's a poultice
You have an eye, it's an image.
My boy, it's your last resort.
Will you marry it, marry it, marry it.

"The Applicant," *Ariel* 1965

18 Out of the ash
I rise with my red hair
and I eat men like air.

"Lady Lazarus," Ibid.

19 Viciousness in the kitchen!

"Lesbos," Ibid.

20 How long can I be a wall around my green property?
How long can my hands
Be a bandage to his hurts, and my words
Bright birds in the sky, consoling? consoling?
It is a terrible thing
To be so open: it is as if my heart
Put on a face and walked into the world. . . .

"A Poem for Three Voices" 1968

21 Spiderlike, I spin mirrors,
Loyal to my own image,
Uttering nothing but blood.

"Childless Woman" 1968

22 Widow. The word consumes itself. . . .

"Widow," *Crossing the Water* 1971

23 I am no drudge
Though for years I have eaten dust
and dried plates with my dense hair.

"The Babysitters," *Collected Poems/ Sylvia Plath*, Ted Hughes,* ed. 1981
*Plath's British-born husband (1930–2000), Poet Laureate of England (1984).

24 Is there no way out of the mind?

"Apprehensions" *n.d.*

2818. Harriet Rosenstein (1932?–)

1 . . . violent outrage and equally violent despair seem inevitable responses to our era. All the horrors committed in the name of national honor or the sanctity of the family or individual integrity have caught up with us.

"Reconsidering Sylvia Plath,"* *The First Ms. Reader,* Francine Klagsbrun, ed. 1972
*See 2817.

2 Destiny is something men select; women achieve it only by default or stupendous suffering.

Quoted in *Ms. July 1974*

2819. Maggie Scarf (1932–)

1 There is no clearer, more commonly encountered example of a projective identification system than that seen in the relationship of the nonexpressive husband and his voluble, highly emotional wife. In this kind of marriage, each spouse has his or her own area of specialization. One partner carries all of the expressivity, warmth and feeling in the intimate system, while the other is in charge of cool rationality, attention to detail, and logic.

Ch. 12, *Intimate Partners: Patterns in Love and Marriage* 1991

2 . . . one cannot feel at ease and relaxed in an emotional minefield. In less competent, poorly functioning families, the emotional system shapes the individual's role, and the individual is that role and can be nothing otherwise. In better-functioning, healthier families, on the other hand, people tend to create their own roles, which are not unidimensional and which can change over time as both individual and family development proceed and continue.

Ch. 22, *Intimate Worlds: Life Inside the Family* 1995

3 Unbearable, unthinkable experiences have a way of demolishing the basic structure of the self, shattering those fundamental assumptions that have served to make life feel livable and safe.

Ch. 13, *Secrets, Lies, Betrayals: The Body/Mind Connection* 2004

4 Until the time of the affair's exposure, she's seen herself as someone unique and special in the eyes of another special person—the intimate partner who has bonded with her and promised to prize her above all others. Thus, when faced with the indisputable evidence of his horrifying dishonesty, her self-respect suffers a monumental reversal. In the wake of the revelation, she experiences herself as anything but special; she feels inconsequential and discardable, as if she'd been relegated to a kind of human waste dump.

Ibid.

5 For the biological bottom line is that when we humans are faced with threats of a potentially overwhelming nature, an inner siren is triggered and we switch into an altered state of high readiness to meet the challenge at hand.

Ibid.

2820. Rönnog Seaberg (1932–2007)

1 Old age like a tiger
ripping at your skin
to set your mind free.

"Old Age" 15 October 2007

2821. Joan Semmel (1932–)

1 I was an abstract painter in the abstract expressionist mode until 1970 . . . My whole life changed. Feminism brought me back to the figure.

Quoted in "Joan Semmel," *Exposures, Women & Their Art* by Ann Brown & Arlene Raven* 1989
*See 3533.

2 My erotic nudes of the early 1970s were my part of the sexual revolution and they were erotic from a woman's point of view.

Ibid.

2822. Alix Kates Shulman (1932–)

1 It was always the girl who was kept in the house after school if a boy molested her, never the boy. Ostensibly she was kept in for protection, but how was it different from punishment if she couldn't even play on the street?

Memoirs of an Ex-Prom Queen 1972

2 They say it's worse to be ugly. I think it must only be different. If you're pretty, you are subject to one set of assaults; if you're plain, you are subject to another.

Ibid.

3 "Come on, Sasha, you're torturing me," he would say. But it was really he who was torturing me, squeezing me between two guilts.

Ibid.

4 If, as the girls always said, it's never too early to think about whom to marry, then it could certainly not be too early to think about who to be. Being somebody had to come first, because, of course, somebody could get a much better husband than nobody.

Ch. 2, Ibid.

5 I don't think that there are individual ways of transforming the world. It's true that when enough individuals have changed the way they think and have decided that they want to see it in their lifetime, that's when you have a movement.

A Conversation with. . . , Womankind (womankindflp.org) *1995*

2823. Muriel "Mickie" Siebert (1932–)

1 You create opportunities by performing, not complaining.

Ch. 1, *Changing the Rules: Adventures of a Wall Street Maverick 2002*

2 Analyzing the market is both an art and a science. The financial data that indicate how a company fits into the economy make up the science part; seeing a pattern in those numbers and then looking ahead is an art.

Ibid.

3 Men at the top of industry and government should be more willing to risk sharing leadership with women and minority members who are not merely clones of their white male buddies. In these fast-changing times we need the different viewpoints and experiences, we need the enlarged talent bank. The real risk lies in continuing to do things the way they've always been done.

SiebertNet (siebertnet.com) *n.d.*

2824. Helen Somers (1932–)

1 The Legislature has changed in tone and tenor enormously since I came here because society has changed. There's no more locker-room kind of approach.

Cited in "Olympian Women" by Dionne Searcey, *Seattle Times, A18 31 January 1999*

2825. Polly Strand (1932–2003)

1 The road to health is paved with vegetables, fruits, beans, rice and grains.

Letter to editor, *San Francisco Chronicle 19 March 1993*

2 Let's see fewer Geezers paired with Babes as love interests in the movies.

Gray Guerillas slogan *n.d.*

3 Fur is Worn by Beautiful Animals and Ugly People.

T-shirt slogan *n.d.*

2826. Elizabeth Taylor (1932–)

1 When people say: she's got everything, I've only one answer: I haven't had tomorrow.

Elizabeth Taylor 1965

2 My God, I was on a merry-go-round for so long. Now I've stopped spinning. I'm not afraid of myself. I'm no longer afraid of what I will do. I have absolute faith in our future. Richard [Burton]* has given me all this.

Ibid.

*Welsh actor (1925–1984) to whom she was twice married.

3 I want to be known as an actress. I'm not royalty.

Interview in *The New York Times* (1964), Quoted in *Elizabeth* by Dick Sheppard *1974*

2827. Megan Terry (1932–)

1 CHESTER. My God, the human baby! A few weeks after birth, any other animal can fend for itself. But *you!* A basket case till you're twenty-one.

The Magic Realist 1968

2 CHESTER. Fourteen mewling brats and not a business brain in a bucketful.

Ibid.

3 Broadway is just a showcase for television now. Broadway is no longer the place I was taught about when I went to college, i.e., the place where The Theater was kept alive, the Theater of Ideas. A place where one could be in touch with human feelings, where you could see yourself, where society could see itself. Broadway is now a place for the tourists to go and be beguiled by stagecraft.

Quoted in "Megan Terry," *Interviews with Contemporary Women Playwrights* by Kathleen Betsko* and Rachel Koenig *1987*

*See 3125.

4 I think that people are too rarified in New York. They've been too long away from animals and plants and trees.

Ibid.

5 Isn't it strange that this American culture has valued everything but the people who create something out of thin air? What is left when a civilization dies? Only its art and a few tool fragments.

Ibid.

2828. Jill Tweedie (1932/36–1993)

1 Many of those who offer the longevity of their marriage as proof of enduring love are often only revealing their own endurance in the face of ravaging compromises and a resulting anesthesia that has left them half-way dead.

"On Love," *New Internationalist, #118 December 1982*

2 Contrary to the old wives' tales, the real joy of love lies in the knowledge that your lover could manage without you, that he

or she has no need of you but simply feels a great deal happier that you are there.

Ibid.

3   Equality does not guarantee happiness in love, but it is a gamble towards that happiness and not away from it.

Ibid

4   It is easy and dismally enervating to think of opposition as merely perverse or actually evil—far more invigorating to see it as essential for honing the mind, and as a positive good in itself. For the day that moral issues cease to be fought over is the day the word "human" disappears from the race.

Independent (London) *May 1989*

5   Assumptions about women are what has changed most radically. And a woman's whole psychic energy isn't wrapped up in men or nurturing the male ego. Young women don't appreciate that vast liberation.

Remark (1993), Quoted in "Introduction to Literature," *The Bedford* (bedfordstmartins.com) *2001*

2829. Robin Worthington (1932–   )

1   Mental health, like dandruff, crops up when you least expect it.

Thinking About Marriage 1971

2   The battle to keep up appearances unnecessarily, the mask—whatever name you give creeping perfectionism—robs us of our energies.

Ibid.

2830. Corazon Aquino (1933–2009)

1   The politicians think that I have not included enough of them; the nonpoliticians think that I have gone back to the old ways; and the mass public groups think I have forgotten them.

Interview with Sandra Burton,* Quoted in *Time* (New York) *10 March 1986*

*See 2883.

2   Marcos* underestimated me—and look where it got him!

Interview with Diane Sawyer,** *60 Minutes,* CBS-TV *14 September 1986*

*Ferdinand Marcos, Philippine politician (1917–1989); president of the Philippines (1966–1986); husband of Imelda (see 2387). **See 3066.

3   I think Ninoy's* joy is the knowledge that he pulled a fast one on me. Once more he has gone on his merry way and left me to pick up the mess.

Speech, St. Ignatius Roman Catholic Church (Newton, Massachusetts) *21 September 1986*

*Her husband, Benigno "Ninoy" A- (1932–1983), journalist and politician; assassinated.

4   Faith is not simply a patience which passively suffers until the storm is past. Rather, it is a spirit which bears things—with resignation, yes, but above all with blazing serene hope.

Quoted in *Twentieth-Century Women Political Leaders* by Claire Price-Groff *1998*

2831. Beryl Bainbridge (1933–   )

1   The carnage was horrid. Men died posed like the statues in Mr. Blundell's glass-house.

Master Georgie 1998

2   The authoritarian voice, the ring of confidence, is not for me. I'm not bothered with causes or hard facts; my preoccupation is not with the immediate how and why of the lives we lead, but rather with a raking over of the life we once knew.

Something Happened Yesterday 1998

2832. Judith M. Bardwick (1933–   )

1   Real confidence comes from knowing and accepting yourself—your strengths and your limitations—in contrast to depending on affirmation from others.

p. 8, *The Plateauing Trap 1988*

2   On the surface, unlimited growth would seem to be a good thing. Companies are strong and profitable and people have no trouble finding good jobs, so everyone is secure and happy. But . . . it is possible to have too much of a good thing, that those years of prosperity have now backfired. Gradually, insidiously, prosperity created the crippling condition called Entitlement, where workers have no real incentive to achieve and managers have stopped doing the work of requiring real work.

Ch. 1, *Danger in the Comfort Zone: From Boardroom to Mailroom—How to Break the Entitlement Habit That's Killing American Business 1991*

3   For increasing numbers of people, the traditional boundary between work time and place and personal time and space is gone. Although this flexibility can increase productivity and one's sense of control, it can also decrease any feelings of control and lead to burnout.

Ch. 1, *Seeking the Calm in the Storm: Managing Chaos in Your Business Life 2002*

4   A Psychological Recession is not just an idea; it is a real phenomenon with real consequences, all of them bad. When people are scared and depressed for a long time, despair and fear replace confidence and optimism. Try running a company with workers who feel like that.

One Foot Out the Door: How to Combat the Psychological Recession That's Alienating Employees and Hurting American Business 2007

2833. Evelyn Torton Beck (1933–   )

1   I was pained but not surprised to feel invisible as a lesbian among Jews. I was terribly disappointed and confused to feel invisible as a Jew among lesbians. . . .

Introduction, *Nice Jewish Girls: A Lesbian Anthology 1989*

2834. Mary Field Belenky (1933–   )

1   That they can strengthen themselves through the empowerment of others is essential wisdom often gathered by women.

Ch. 2, Pt. I, Ch. 1, *Women's Ways of Knowing, The Development of Self, Voice, and Mind,* with Blythe McVicker Clinchy,* Nancy Rule Goldberger,** and Jill Mattuck Tarule*** *1986*

*See 2700; **see 2891; ***see 3462.

2   Parents who enter into a dialogue with their children, who draw out and respect their opinions, are more likely to have children whose intellectual and ethical development proceeds rapidly and surely.

Pt. II, Ch. 8, Ibid.

3   Really listening and suspending one's own judgment is necessary in order to understand other people on their own terms.

As we have noted, this is a process that requires trust and builds trust.

Ibid.

4   When a tradition has no name people will not have a rich shared language for articulating and reflecting on their experiences with the tradition. Poorly articulated traditions are likely to be fragile.

A Tradition That Has No Name: Nurturing the Development of People, Families and Communities, with Lynne A. Bond and Jacqueline S. Weinstock *1997*

2835. Ela Bhatt (1933–   )

1   We face occupational hazards. We unshell peanuts with our teeth (the nation earns foreign exchange out of them), but our lips and mouth get sore so that we cannot eat food. When we unshell cottonpods our finger bleed. We break stones, we breathe stone dust, we sweep the streets and fill our lungs with dust, we roll cigarettes and breathe tobacco. We pull carts with 2000 kgs of load and lose our unborn babes. We are not ready to accept this life for our daughters. Our renowned researchers have made miracles like transplanting hearts or reaching the moon. Will our Research Institutes hurry up to design a proper mask, a glove, a footstool, a hammer, a fingercap?

Acceptance Speech, Right Livelihood Award (Stockholm), 9 December 1984

2   The Sewa women by organising themselves have faced many struggles, gulped bitterness, but in the process have attained self-dignity, a slice of power, increased their capability to think, act, react, manage and lead. Out of their miserable passive acceptance of all the injustices, they have attained courage to stand up and fight. Self-reliance is what they want ultimately. There is no development without self-reliance.

Ibid.

2836. Barbara Aronstein Black (1933–   )

1   Where I am today has *everything* to do with the years I spent hanging on to a career by my fingernails.

Quoted in The New York Times 2 January 1986

2   I refused to believe that studying history could be as boring and as onerous as it had always been for me. The fault had to lie with the teaching; it could not be the enterprise itself.

Faculty Profile, Columbia Law School 2008

3   History was always my worst subject.

Ibid.

2837. Bernice Braid (1933–   )

1   When explorers see themselves charting their own routes, they come to see themselves as natives in a new land. They come, in fact, to feel that they have developed new eyes.

Place as Text 2000

2   What we seek, all of us, are ways to reintegrate our thinking so that it does not divide us into "us and them" but instead connects us as participant observers in the same small world. We want an inventory of ways to create coherence. Out of the exclusionary cubbyholes that our disciplines appear to occupy because of how our institutions organize themselves administratively; out of the chaos that our world presents to us in embattled countries everywhere; out of the received knowledge that shifts and changes even as we acquire it for the first time, we must arrive at modes of thinking that help us make some sense out of conflicting view-

points and that embolden us with an organizing principle for all the disorganized information out there.

Address, "Honors in Practice," North Carolina Honors Assn. (Fayetteville State University) 28–29 September 2007

3   I know we all grow up with the admonition to "learn from experience," but we all know, probably by the time we are teenagers, that not many people do in fact learn from experience. Bigots are not bigoted because they have had a lot of experience with those they hate and want to exclude, but because no amount of experience or religious training has been able yet to dislodge from their closed minds the way they prefer to see the world. They are stuck, and cannot grow "new eyes." This behavior is extreme, though in today's world unfortunately not rare, but it exemplifies the worst effects of not being able to see old things in new ways, or maybe to see new things at all.

Ibid.

2838. Carol Burnett (1933–   )

1   When someone who is known for being comedic does something straight, it's always "a big breakthrough" or "a radical departure." Why is it no one ever says that if a straight actor does comedy? Are they presuming comedy is easier?

Quoted in "Death by 'Friendly Fire' and a Mother's Search" by Ellen Farley, San Francisco Chronicle 5 October 1978

2   I don't consider [the Equal Rights Amendment] a political issue. It is a moral issue as far as I am concerned. Where are women mentioned in the Constitution except in the Nineteenth Amendment, giving us the right to vote? When they said all *men* were created equal, they really meant it—otherwise, why did we have to fight for the Nineteenth Amendment?

Quoted in "Hue & Cry," San Francisco Chronicle 29 April 1979

2839. Jean Carnahan (1933–   )

1   When thoughts from the past come across my mind, there's always work that kind of pushes them out of the way and forces me to move on to the thing that's next. So in a sense, work is wonderful therapy.

"The Accidental Senator" by Matt Bai, The New York Times 27 October 2002

2   I had to be there and support my husband* and give him the things he needed to run for office. I had to give him a stable home and all that. So his dreams sort of became my dreams.

Ibid.

*Mel C- (1934–2000), Gov. of Missouri, 1993–2000.

3   I should have taken dancing lessons instead of playing baseball.

Ibid.

2840. Joan Collins (1933–   )

1   I've never yet met a man who could look after me. I don't need a husband. What I need is a wife.

Sunday Times (London) 27 December 1987

2841. Alice Denham (1933–   )

1   Sex was my great adventure

Sleeping with Bad Boys, a Juicy Tell-all of Literary New York in the Fifties and Sixties 2006

2   What these hotsy male writers knew about love was nada.

Ibid.

2842. Maureen Duffy (1933–)

1 We all have to rise in the end, not just one or two who were smart enough, had will enough for their own salvation, but all the halt, the maimed and the blind of us which is most of us.

The Microcosm 1966

2 All reduction of people to objects, all imposition of labels and patterns to which they must conform, all segregation can lead only to destruction.

Rites 1969

3 The pain of love is the pain of being alive. It's a perpetual wound.

Wounds 1969

4 Love is the only effective counter to death.

Ibid.

5 I think basically I just think I want everyone and don't really want anybody.

Love Child 1971

2843. Joycelyn "Minnie" Elders (1933–)

1 The most pervasive form of violence in America is interpersonal—domestic violence, partner abuse, abuse of children and adolescents, the elderly. If we ever expect to put an end to violence and victimization in America, we have to start where the violence starts—in our homes, in our families.

"Violence begins in the home...," *Seattle Post-Intelligencer*, B1 *12 February 1993*

2 When you are dancing with a bear, you do not sit down when you are tired; you sit down when the bear is tired.

Ibid.

3 We taught them what to do in the front seat of a car. Now it's time to teach them what to do in the back seat.

Quoted in "Blunt Style of Teen Sex and Health" by Philip J. Hilts, *The New York Times 14 September 1993*

4 I feel that denying young people health education, denying them the availability of contraceptives, and saying to them that you have to take this kind of risk, is almost child abuse.

Ibid.

5 I feel that God meant sex for more than procreation.

Quoted in *The Advocate March 1994*
Also see Judith Levine, 4118.

2844. Cynthia Fuchs Epstein (1933–)

1 Attacks on working mothers are an aspect of a cultural control system designed to keep women in "their place," which means, out of the centers of authority and decision making in the society. And the leftists who chastise women for employing household help unwittingly reinforce this system.

"Working Moms under Attack," *Dissent Magazine Fall 2004*

2 Fast food, twenty-four-hour supermarkets, and even synthetic fabrics were responses to what became the norm-dual-earner families. Within a decade the slow-baked casserole and the homemade layer cake disappeared along with the starched party dress, and no one seemed to miss them.

Ibid.

3 Our society's romance with child-care perfectionism, its absurd focus on producing "designer children," not only creates pressure on working mothers to reduce their hours in the paid labor force and downscale their hopes for achievement, but may also have poor effects on their children. We don't know yet, but the professionalization of mothering to include constant attention and involvement (from Mozart in the womb to attendance at every sports event and the review of every homework assignment) may not even produce the desired high-quality children. Indeed, it may produce cohorts of narcissistic young people who demand constant attention and never develop the skills of independence.

Ibid.

4 Wage-earning women are in a no-win situation. So are the women who work for them. Just as we have no meaningful collective policies for providing child care or elder care, so we have no effective policies for enforcing minimum wages, decent benefits, and limited work hours. We do not address care-work as a social priority.

Ibid.

2845. Pozzi Escot (1933–)

1 In our [Peruvian] schools we teach Bach, Beethoven and Brahms but nothing that has been composed in the past 70 years.

Quoted in "A Matter of Art, Not Sex," *Time* (New York) *10 November 1975*

2 Everything in life is very special to me. My life is simply alive with being at my desk, studying, reading, preparing the journal, lectures, cooking. I like to invent recipes. Bicycling is very special. I like to fix bicycles. Life is very special to me and music is just part of it.

Interview with Bruce Duffie, *Sonus* (journal) *Fall 1989*

3 ... music is one of those conditions of life that humans cannot live without. Music has always existed. It is a true function of human beings. Whatever is out there we are a reflection of it. Music is out there. Everything that moves makes some kind of music, some kind of sound. We copy that, we grasp that.

Ibid.

4 For superior art we must have challenge, future, grasp, originality and crystallization of technique. Art must not put you to sleep. Art must offer timeless semantics. It must grasp its world with wide and deep intelligence.

Ibid.

2846. Elizabeth Evatt (1933–)

1 I believe every woman should have the right to live in a home *free* of deadly weapons.

Interview with Robin Morgan,* *Ms.* (New York) *March/April 1993*

*See 3284.

2 You have to see human rights as an all-embracing concept. It could be something that would unite the world, if it could only be seen in that light.

Ibid.

2847. Myrlie Evers-Williams (1933–)

1 I recall this feeling of release that was very spiritual and it was as though all of the demons in my body exited through every

pore of my being. It was as though I could almost see it rushing out. For the first time in all those years, I became free, my children became free and I felt that Mississippi became freer, as did all of America. That was the point of closure.*

Quoted in "Saying 'The End' Doesn't Mean It's All Over" by Kevin Sack, *The New York Times 28 May 2000*
*Ref. the 1994 jury trial that found Byron de la Beckwith guilty of complicity in the assassination of civil rights activist Medgar Evers, her husband, in 1963.

2848. Dianne Feinstein (1933–   )

1   This city [San Francisco] typifies the American dream of a sense of tolerance and openness, with different people living closely together, carefully, with respect for the law, not impinging their will on others but living with a growing mutual respect.

Quoted in "Dianne Feinstein: Learning the Lessons of the Phoenix" by Mildred Hamilton, *San Francisco Examiner 4 March 1979*

2   Toughness doesn't have to come in a pinstripe suit.

Time 4 June 1984

3   It really comes down to a question of blood or guts—the blood of innocent people or the Senate of the United States having the guts to do what we should do when we take that oath to protect the welfare of our citizens.*

(p. 85), Quoted in *Politics in America* 1998 by Philip D. Duncan *1999*
*Reference to the legislative ban on assault weapons, which she championed, that was signed into law in 1994.

4   The position of America today really warrants someone in her* shoes, and the fact that her shoes may be have an inch or two of heels doesn't matter.

"She opened home to a close a door" by Noam N. Levey, *The Los Angeles Times 7 June 2008*
*Reference to Hillary Rodham Clinton; see 3731.

2849. Barbara C. Gelpi (1933–   )

1   . . . the masculine and feminine principles are not simply arbitrary manila folders for filing certain qualities; they are transcendent functions, spiritual realities which must be taken into account in the psychological makeup of every human being.

"The Androgyne," *Women and Analysis,* Jean Strouse,* ed. *1974*
*See 3617.

2   With myths, dreams, visions, poems, stories, conversations we must imagine a race in which both mind and soul are of equal importance and may be equally fulfilled for both sexes.

Ibid.

3   Consciousness, as we tend to conceive of it, brings humanity into being—and that is good—but has certain negative consequences as well. Though it is man's triumph, it is divisive, separating him from the natural rhythms of life by virtue of the fact that he can observe those rhythms, looking forward and backward. He becomes then subject to the peculiarly human fear of death and the human affliction of boredom. He becomes also aware of his separateness, his individuality—and that is an achievement—but at the same time becomes competitive, suffering all the endless human misery which competition involves.

Ibid.

2850. Ruth Bader Ginsburg (1933–   )

1   In commercial law, the person duped was too often a woman. In a section on land tenure, one 1968 textbook explains that "land, like women, was meant to be possessed."

Quoted in "Portia Faces Life—The Trials of Law School" by Susan Edmiston, *Ms. April 1974*

2   The emphasis must not be on the right to abortion but on the right to privacy and reproductive control.

Ibid.

3   Civil rights groups hold no monopoly position among those discontent with legislative or executive action who seek the aid of the courts.

15 Georgia Law Review 539 1981

4   A judge steps out of the proper judicial role most conspicuously and dangerously when he or she flinches from a decision that is legally right because the decision is not the one the home crowd wants.

Quoted in *The 50 Most Influential Women in American Law* by Dawn Bradley Berry* *1996*
*See 4399.

5   Motherly love ain't everything it has been cracked up to be. To some extent, it's a myth that men have created to make women think that they do this job to perfection.

Quoted in *Women Who Make the World Worse* by Kate O'Beirne *2006*

6   Certain attitudes about pregnancy and childbirth, throughout human history, have sustained pervasive, often law-sanctioned, restrictions on a woman's place among paid workers and active citizens.

U.S. Supreme Court, Dissent, *AT&T Corp. v. Hulteen et al. 21 December 2007*

2851. Faye Joan Girsh (1933–   )

1   [Dying] using to happen at home, children and pets would be on the dying person's bed, and it would be a natural, family-centered event. Now it occurs for most people alone, in a sterile hospital environment. Dying people should be able to have their loved ones present, say their good-bye's and I-love-you's, and die peacefully and gently with the help of a doctor.

"Kevorkian* serves public need," *USA Today 24 November 1998*
*Jack K- (1928–   ), Am. pathologist/activist who spearheaded a movement for physician assisted suicide; incarcerated 1999–2007.

2852. Niède Guidon (1933–   )

1   As you can see, this country doesn't have a government, this is not a democratic republic . . . there are political parties and these put a "king" in charge and they do whatever they want! They steal, devastate, leave the country without a penny, and then take off!

Quoted in Interview by Arara, *Maria-Brazil.com September 2005*

2   When men were in the guard stations everything got dirty, disorganized, the kitchen was filthy, the stove was filthy. They washed their underwear and hung it out in front, and the tourists saw all that, it was depressing for them, as well as for me! That's why I've hired only women now. They're more responsible. They put food on the table; the men spend all their money

on drink. The women seem really happy with having their own money and independence.

Ibid.

3　In about one hundred years Brazil will be like Africa, with a Sahara-like desert, extending from the Atlantic Ocean to the border with the Andean countries.

Ibid.

2853. Hazel Henderson (1933–　)

1　Seeking certainties can be comfortable but may not be the most realistic course. In a changing world, policymakers will need to scan broadly, make rapid course corrections, and sometimes resort to skillful improvisation.

Ch. 1, *Building a Win-Win World* 1997

2　Money isn't real. It's a tracking system, a scoring system, to keep track of people's transactions. The real resources are the human resources and the natural resources in these exchanges. We've gone from shells and barter to coins and paper money. Now we've gone to global electronic money. Suddenly people are realizing the possibilities in the "local information society."

Quoted in "To Stitch the World Back Together Again" by David Kupfer, *Whole Earth Review Fall* 1995

3　I like to call countries and corporations and other great institutions Non-Civil Organizations, NCOs. The global civil society and this proliferation of citizens' organizations are the social innovators.

Ibid.

4　If you think by now that GDP* is crazy—you are correct.

"New Scorecards for Real National Progress," InterPress Service *November* 2007

*Gross Domestic Product

2854. Joan Heron (1933–　)

1　Unable to sleep or even really relax, I saw the last few days in a blur of new people, airplane food, immunizations, paper forms, and Peace Corps passports. The buzzing of flies was constant as they flew unimpeded through the open window. As I lay there in my depleted state, flies began landing on my face and even my eyelids. I cringed and began to cry.

What have you gotten yourself into this time?
Can you stand two years of this?
Is this what retirement will be like?
Then a small voice within said:
What can you do to help yourself NOW?

"Turkmenistan" (September 1995), *Chai Budesh? Anyone for Tea? A Peace Corps Memoir of Turkmenistan* 2008

2　"Remember, we were a nomadic people for centuries, traveling the silk route and trading with other tribes. Only in the last century have these countries been formed and have we settled into one place. So we have practiced our religion in every setting we were in, however temporary."

As she spoke, I felt the long stream of history; camels loaded with beautiful silks and wool crossing the wide, hot desert, stopping by an oasis and sitting on the ground in a tent to eat churek and drink chai together off of a clean tablecloth, then ending their meal with the graceful prayer of gratitude I so admired.

"Chai Budesh," Ibid.

2855. Corinne Jacker (1933–　)

1　LOIS. I write down significant things about beginnings. See— I'm trying to get it all straight. All my life it turns out that I've come in at the middle. Korea, Viet Nam, the energy crisis. And when I try to talk about it, they say, "You don't understand. That wasn't when it really began." But when I ask when the start was, nobody knows.

Act I, Sc. 1, *Harry Outside* 1975

2　STEVE. I came back here to be safe, and it's not safe here either.

Domestic Issues 1980

3　It's true that women tend to think of domestic, encapsulated incidents as crucial. We look at the microcosm rather than the macrocosm. . . . Perhaps women find their metaphors in domestic experience because we are still new to the world of action.

"Corinne Jacker," *Interviews with Contemporary Women Playwrights*, Kathleen Betsko* and Rachel Koenig 1987
*See 3125.

2856. Devaki Jain (1933–　)

1　We were naïve and realized too late that this great goodness, development, into which our mandate had been to integrate women, and that this great public world, which men occupy and into which we were to bring women through employment and health strategies, was dangerous, even devastating.

Essay, Quoted in *The Politics of Women's Education: Perspectives from Asia, Africa, and Latin America* by Jill Ker Conway and Susan C. Bourque 1993

2　Democratic politics is a market place for different lobbies. It is those lobbies that influence political decisions.

"The needs of the poor come first" by Monte Leach, *Share International March* 1998

3　It is sound economics to put incomes in the hands of the masses of the poor, because these incomes generate the growth impulse. I call it the "bubbling up" theory of growth, as a different concept from the "trickle down" approach. The growth engine will bubble up from the production and consumption of the poor. Imagine the entire growth path coming that way. This whole issue of poverty would have been dealt with as a genuine priority.

We have to make the choice that the needs of the poor come first. Then we can transform the economy.

Ibid.

4　Women at the UN were able to have a significant impact on the founding principles of the world body in its early years because of their decades of experience as activists in freedom struggles, peace movements, political forums, and trade unions.

Ch. 1, *Women, Development, and the UN: A Sixty-year Quest for Equality and Justice* 2005

2857. Marjorie Karmel (1933?–　)

1　It is a great pity that a man should stand back, helpless and inadequate, *de trop*, while his wife alone knows the profound experience of the birth of the child they have created together.

Ch. 3, *Thank You, Dr. Lamaze** 1959
*French physician who developed a drugless, natural method of childbirth (1890–1957).

2　Who ever said that doctors are truthful or even intelligent? You're getting a lot if they know their profession. Don't ask any more from them. They're only human after all—which is to say, you can't expect much.

Ch. 7, Ibid.

3   "One-way first-name calling always means inequality—witness servants, children and dogs."

Ibid.

2858. Penelope Lively (1933–)

1   Chronology irritates me. There is no chronology inside my head. I am composed of a myriad of Claudias who spin and mix and part like sparks of sunlight on water.

Moon Tiger 1987

2   . . . the rainbow experience we all have lost but of which we occasionally retrieve a brilliant glimpse.

Oleander, Jacaranda: A Childhood Perceived: A Memoir 1994

3   There are realities which for most of us are beyond imagination.

The Five Thousand and One Nights 1996

4   In her trade [anthropology], you travelled most fruitfully if you travelled alone. And it helped if you were footloose and singularly unfettered by personal possessions.

Spiderweb 1999

5   A small ancient-looking chapel of perfect simplicity perched above a hedgebank that sparkled with flowers. Sometimes it was difficult to take this landscape seriously—to remember that it had evolved from centuries of agricultural endeavour and blithe environmental disregard.

Ibid.

2859. Mary Jane Moffat (1933–2004)

1   Why do women keep diaries? . . . The form has been an important outlet for women partly because it is an analogue to their lives: emotional, fragmentary, interrupted, modest, not to be taken seriously, private, restricted, daily, trivial, formless, concerned with self, as endless as their tasks.

Foreword, *Revelations: Diaries of Women,* with Charlotte Painter* *1974*

*See 2572.

2   The shock of first grief is an amazement that what was alive and of this world only a few moments ago is irrevocably gone.

"Shock," *In the Midst of Winter: Selections from the Literature of Mourning 1992*

2860. Yoko Ono (1933–)

1   Everybody's an artist. Everybody's God. It's just that they're inhibited. I believe in people so much that if the whole of civilization is burned so we don't have any memory of it, even then people will start to build their own art. It is a necessity—a function. We don't need history.

Interview with Abram Deswaan, Dutch TV *October 1968*

2   I wonder why men can get serious at all. They have this delicate long thing hanging outside their bodies, which goes up and down by its own will. . . . If I were a man I would always be laughing at myself.

"On Film No. 4" (1967), *Grapefruit 1970*

3   I have a woman inside my soul.

"I Have a Woman Inside My Soul" *n.d.*

4   On a windy day let's go flying
There may be no trees to rest on
There may be no clouds to ride
But we'll have our wings and the wind will be with us
That's enough for me, that's enough for me.

"Song for John"* *n.d.*

*Her husband, John Lennon, British singer-songwriter, member of the Beatles; murdered (1940–1980).

5   Don't be too clever or we'll scratch your goodies out . . . or we'll blow your sillies off.

"Catman" *n.d.*

2861. Ann Richards (1933–2006)

1   Poor George,* he can't help it. He was born with a silver foot in his mouth.

Quoted in *Independent* (London) *20 July 1988*

*George H. W. Bush, American politician (1924–); 41st U.S. president (1989–93).

2   Bill Clinton* isn't the first man I've had to forgive, and he isn't apt to be the last.

Cited by Susan Paynter in *Seattle Post-Intelligencer,* B1 *28 October 1996*

*William Jefferson Clinton, American politician and lawyer (1946–), 42nd president of the United States (1993–2001).

3   They* go up there and forget who brung 'em to the dance.

Ibid.

*Reference to congressional representatives in Washington, D.C.

4   When you think you've come so far and achieved so much, your impatience begins to take over. To give you a context, my grandmother, for a period of her life, couldn't vote. The law said [that] "imbeciles, idiots, the insane and women" could not vote in Texas. And, within that same single lifetime, I became the governor of Texas. What an incredible change that is.

Ibid.

5   A woman's place is in the dome.

Acceptance speech *1990*

2862. Joan Rivers (1933–)

1   I hate housework! You make the beds, you do the dishes—and six months later you have to start all over again.

"Work," *Woman Talk,* Michèle Brown and Ann O'Connor, eds. *1984*

2   My whole career has been one rejection after another . . . And then going back and back and pushing against everything and everybody. Getting ahead by small, ugly steps.

Quoted in "The 1960's to the 1980's," *Women in Comedy* by Linda Martin & Kerry Segrave *1986*

3   Would you have slept with Onassis for $26 million dollars?

Ibid.

4   She's do dumb that she studies for her Pap test.

Quoted in "Familiar Faces," *Funny Women, American Comediennes, 1860–1985* by Mary Unterbrink *1987*

5   Lemme get this straight. Bin Laden's top man has been released. The price of petrol is through the roof. There's inflation, depression. And people are hysterical because I said fuck [on television]?

"Rivers Revokes Swearing Apology," *Digital Spy 19 June 2008*

6 It's been so long since I made love I can't even remember who gets tied up.

Stand-up routine *n.d.*

7 Can we talk?

Catchphrase *n.d.*

2863. Masha Kabakow Rudman (1933–)

1 We need to give children successful experiences. Their pride in their accomplishment will help them overcome their fears if they're not punished for making mistakes.

"Parent & Child," *The New York Times* 17 December 1992

2 There's no such thing as a book that's too easy if the book has substance.

Ibid.

3 . . . we have to communicate that we only get at the truth if we are comprehensive and wide-ranging in our search for it.

"An Educator Speaks," *Journal of Youth Services in Libraries* Winter 1994

2864. Miriam Schneir (1933–)

1 The decline of feminism after the First World War is attributable at least in part to the eventual concentration of the women's movements on the single narrow issue of suffrage— which was won.

Introduction, *Feminism: The Essential Historical Writings* 1972

2 . . . centuries of slavery do not provide a fertile soil for intellectual development or expression.

Ibid.

2865. Mary Jane Sherfey (1933–)

1 The nature of female sexuality as here presented makes it clear that . . . woman's inordinate orgasmic capacity did not evolve for monogamous, sedentary cultures.

"A Theory on Female Sexuality," *Journal of the American Psychoanalytical Association* 1966

2 The strength of the drive determines the force required to suppress it.

Ibid.

3 There is no such thing as a vaginal orgasm distinct from a clitoral orgasm. The nature of the orgasm is the same regardless of the erotogenic zone stimulated to produce it.

Ibid.

2866. Susan Sontag (1933–2004)

1 The truth is always something that is told, not something that is known. If there were no speaking or writing, there would be no truth about anything. There would only be what is.

Ch. 1, *The Benefactor* 1963

2 Interpretation is the revenge of the intellect upon art.

"Against Interpretation" (*Evergreen Review*, December 1964), *Against Interpretation* 1966

3 Real art has the capacity to make us nervous. By reducing the work of art to its content and then interpreting that, one tames the work of art. Interpretation makes art manageable, conformable.

Ibid.

4 The whole point of Camp is to dethrone the serious. Camp is playful, anti-serious. More precisely, Camp involves a new, more complex relation to "the serious." One can be serious about the frivolous, frivolous about the serious.

"Notes on 'Camp'," Note 41 (1964), Ibid.

5 Science fiction films are not about science. They are about disaster, which is one of the oldest subjects of art.

"The Imagination of Disaster," Ibid.

6 American "energy" . . . is the energy of violence, of free-floating resentment and anxiety unleashed by chronic cultural dislocations which must be, for the most part, ferociously sublimated. This energy has mainly been sublimated into crude materialism and acquisitiveness. Into hectic philanthropy. Into benighted moral crusades, the most spectacular of which was Prohibition. Into an awesome talent for uglifying countryside and cities. Into the loquacity and torment of a minority of gadflies: artists, prophets, muckrakers, cranks, and nuts. And into self-punishing neuroses. But the naked violence keeps breaking through, throwing everything into question.

"What's Happening in America (1966)," (*Partisan Review*, Winter 1967), Ibid.

7 I do not think white America is committed to granting equality to the American Negro . . . this is a passionately racist country; it will continue to be so in the foreseeable future.

Ibid.

8 This is a doomed country, it seems to me; I only pray that, when America founders, it doesn't drag the rest of the planet down, too. But one should notice that, during its long elephantine agony, America is also producing its subtlest minority generation of the decent and sensitive, young people who are alienated as Americans.

Ibid.

9 What pornographic literature does is precisely to drive a wedge between one's existence as a full human being and one's existence as a sexual being—

"The Pornographic Imagination," Sct. 3, Ibid.

10 Bending the mind and shaking loose the body makes someone a less willing functionary of the bureaucratic machine. Rock, grass, better orgasms, freaky clothes, grooving on nature—really grooving on anything—unfits, maladapts a person for the American way of life.

Quoted in *Recreation* by Mark Estrin 1971

11 Industrial societies turn their citizens into image-junkies; it is the most irresistible form of mental pollution. Poignant longings for beauty, for an end to probing below the surface, for a redemption and celebration of the body of the world. Ultimately, having an experience becomes identical with taking a photograph of it.

"In Plato's Cave," *On Photography* 1977

12 Using a camera appeases the anxiety which the work-driven feel about not working when they are on vacation and supposed to be having fun. They have something to do that is like a friendly imitation of work: they can take pictures.

Ibid.

13 Though collecting quotations could be considered as merely an ironic mimetism—victimless collecting, as it were . . . in a world that is well on its way to becoming one vast quarry, the collector becomes someone engaged in a pious work of salvage. The course of modern history having already sapped the traditions and shattered the living wholes in which precious objects once found their place, the collector may now in good conscience go about excavating the choicer, more emblematic fragments.

"Melancholy Objects," Ibid.

14 Illness is the night-side of life, a more onerous citizenship. Everyone who is born holds dual citizenship, in the kingdom of the well and in the kingdom of the sick. Although we all prefer to use only the good passport, sooner or later each of us is obliged, at least for a spell, to identify ourselves as citizens of that other place.

Opening words, *Illness As Metaphor 1978*

15 A large part of the popularity and persuasiveness of psychology comes from its being a sublimated spiritualism: a secular, ostensibly scientific way of affirming the primacy of "spirit" over matter.

Ch. 7, Ibid.

16 Sisyphus, I. I cling to my rock, you don't have to chain me. Stand back! I roll it up—up, up. And . . . down we go. I knew that would happen. See, I'm on my feet again. See, I'm starting to roll it up again. Don't try to talk me out of it. Nothing, nothing could tear me away from this rock.

"Debriefing," I (*American Review, September 1973*), I, *Etcetera 1978*

17 Although none of the rules for becoming more alive is valid, it is healthy to keep on formulating them.

Ibid.

18 Like the effects of industrial pollution and the new system of global financial markets, the AIDS crisis is evidence of a world in which nothing important is regional, local, limited; in which everything that can circulate does and every problem is, or is destined to become, worldwide.

AIDS and Its Metaphors 1989

19 AIDS obliges people to think of sex as having, possibly, the direst consequences: suicide. Or murder.

Ch. 7, Ibid.

20 One set of messages of the society we live in is: Consume. Grow. Do what you want. Amuse yourselves. The very working of this economic system, which has bestowed these unprecedented liberties, most cherished in the form of physical mobility and material prosperity, depends on encouraging people to defy limits.

Ibid.

21 I envy paranoids; they actually feel people are paying attention to them.

Quoted in *Time Out* (London) *19 August 1992*

22 Not all violence is equally reprehensible; not all wars are equally unjust.

"Why Are We In Kosovo," *The New York Times Magazine 2 May 1999*

2867. Rosalie Sorrels (1933–)

1 Let her discover all the things that she can do.

Sooner or later, she's gonna discover
She can do without you.

"She Can Do Without You" 1974

2 What can I say, but that it's not easy?
I cannot lift the stones out of your way,
And I can't cry your bitter tears for you.
I would if I could, what can I say?

"Apple of My Eye" 1974

3 I like to sing for my friends; I don't want to sing in fucking stadiums. I like to be able to see who I'm singing too, look them right in the eye and talk to them. . . . I can't get into that thing where you keep swelling up bigger and bigger, publicity, super-hype, higher prices, more equipment. . . . If you come around with a seven-piece band, three roadies, a manager, and groupies . . . you lose your mobility and miss all the *good* times.

Quoted in "Rosalie Sorrels" by Amie Hill, *Rolling Stone* (New York) *28 January 1975*

4 It's not that I don't love the darlings
I'd do anything for my kids, but
If I had to go through all that one more time
I'd jump off the Golden Gate Bridge tra la la.

"Mother's Day Song" 1980

2868. Joanna T. Steichen (1933–)

1 To make the choice for independent survival, the great man's wife has to become convinced of her own intrinsic worth.

"Jacqueline Picasso* and Me" (p. 76), *Ms.* (New York) *March 1987*

*Wife of Spanish artist Pablo Picasso (1881–1973).

2 I was the only one of Steichen's wives who was not a natural photogenic beauty. Except for some vacation snapshots which are lost, he photographed me only once, and the inspiration to do so came from the accident of my being present when a reflection of the pond and hillside in a window offered an irresistibly puzzling composition.

Steichen's * *Legacy 2000*

*Edward S— (1879–1973) photographer.

2869. Renee Taylor (1933–)

1 Our marriage exists for a higher purpose, to write comedy. We see our marriage as comedy, and we're observers of that comedy.

Quoted in "Writers and Directors," *Funny Women, American Comediennes, 1860–1985* Mary Unterbrink 1987

2 We wrote together in a synagogue . . . In a public school cafeteria . . . Near a pool in Arizona . . . In our bedroom . . . In the double whirlpool. I wake him up in the middle of the night and say, "How about this?"*

Ibid.

**Her husband, Joe Bologna (1934–), writer-actor-director.

3 *Re secret of good marriage:* Fidelity and pasta.

Ibid.

4 *Re homes in New Jersey and Beverly Hills:* One keeps us real, the other keeps us phony.

Remark, *David Letterman* * *Show,* Ibid.

*American television host and comedian who has hosted *Late Night with David Letterman* since 1982.

2870. Minnie Thomas (1933?–)

1 Crack has taken away these women's pride.
   By the time they find their way here,* they'll beg, steal and trade their bodies to the dope man for more.

Quoted in "A Hand and a Home for Pregnant Addicts" by Dennis Wyss, *Time 27 February 1989*
*Mandela House, a halfway house for pregnant crack addicts in Oakland, California.

2 I tell the women constantly that I'm part of them. I tell them, "I was you."

Ibid.

2871. Dorothy Uhnak (1933–2006)

1 The only people left when the blacks and Puerto Ricans came spilling in were the old people who still paid nearly the same rents as they had for more than twenty-five years. Who had been fixed in income, fixed in a particular neighborhood, in a particular building, in a particular apartment. They stayed as though serving a life sentence; their next and only move would be in a box.

Pt. I, Ch. 7, *The Investigation 1977*

2 I like to deliver more than I promise instead of the other way around. Which is just one of my many trade secrets.

Ch. 13, Ibid.

3 He maintained that the case was lost or won by the time the final juror had been sworn in; his summation was set in his mind before the first witness was called. It was all in the orchestration, he claimed: in knowing how and when to pitch each and every particular argument; who to intimidate; who to trust, who to flatter and court; who to challenge; when to underplay and exactly when to let out all the stops.

Ch. 14, Ibid.

4 There weren't many unusual events to clutter up her memory, so she hung on to the ones she had.

Pt. II, Ch. 10, Ibid.

2872. Helen Vendler (1933–)

1 It is a crushing burden . . . to reinterpret in a personal, and personally acceptable, way every conventional liturgical and religious act; to make devotion always singular, never simply communal . . . to particularize, not to merge; to individuate, not to accede.

Introduction, *The Poetry of George Herbert* 1975
*English metaphysical poet (1593–1633).

2 Perhaps total immersion in the Sonnets—that is to say, in Shakespeare's mind—is a mildly deranging experience to anyone.

The Art of Shakespeare's Sonnets 1997
*William Shakespeare, English playwright and poet (1564–1616).

3 Seeing the Columbia [University] course use Dante and Conrad* as moral examples is rather like seeing someone use a piece of embroidery for a dishrag with no acknowledgment of the difference between hand-woven silk and a kitchen towel.**

Quoted in "The Closest Reader" by Rachel Donadio, *The New York Times Book Review 10 December 2006*
*Dante Alighieri (1265–1321), Italian poet; Joseph Conrad (1857–1924), Polish-born British novelist. **Ref. "Great Books" by David Denby (1996), which focuses on the Columbia University's course,

4 The monumental quality of "Kaddish"* makes it one of those poems that, as Wallace Stevens** said, take the place of a mountain.

Ibid.

*1961 poem by American beat poet Allen Ginsberg (1926–97). **American poet (1879–1955).

5 It [death] used to be easier to deal with when you had heaven to believe in, when there was another place to go at the end of your poem.

Ibid.

2873. Nina Voronel (1933–)

1 In Russia today, anything new is dangerous.

Quoted in "Russia: No Exit for These Four Women" by Ruth Gruber, *Ms. April 1974*

2 The echoes of pogroms sob in my verses
Making contacts with history.

"I Am a Jew," Ibid.

3 . . . I believe devoutly in the word. The Word can save all, destroy all, stop the inevitable, and express the inexpressible.

Ibid.

2874. Fay Weldon (1933–)

1 The New Women! I could barely recognise them as being of the same sex as myself, their buttocks arrogant in tight jeans, openly inviting, breasts falling free and shameless and feeling no apparent obligation to smile, look pleasant or keep their voices low. And how they live! Just look at them to know how! If a man doesn't bring them to orgasm, they look for another who does. If by mistake they fall pregnant, they abort by vacuum aspiration. If they don't like the food, they push the plate away. If the job doesn't suit them, they hand in their notice. They are satiated by everything, hungry for nothing. They are what I wanted to be; they are what I worked for them to be: and now I see them, I hate them.

Ch. 2, *Praxis 1978*

2 We shelter children for a time; we live side by side with men; and that is all. We owe them nothing, and are owed nothing. I think we owe our friends more, especially our female friends.

Ch. 19, Ibid.

3 You end up as you deserve. In old age, you must put up with the face, the friends, the health and the children you have earned.

Ch. 21, Ibid.

4 Women who live by the good will of men have no control over their lives, and that's the truth of it.

The Heart of the Country 1989

5 I am an ordinary person, but carried to extremes.

Leader of the Band 1989

6 Apart from the fact that it is mostly lies, [advertising] teaches you form.

Current Biography Yearbook 1990 1991

7 Life Force . . . leaping . . . like electricity, from this one to that one, burning us up, wearing us out, making us old, passing on, its only purpose its own survival . . . the best thing that ever happened to us.

Life Force 1991

8 The past may be another country, but there are frequent international flights from there to here.

Wicked Women 1997

2875. Shirley Abbott (1934–)

1 All fiction may be autobiographical, but all autobiography is of course fiction.

Quoted by Mickey Pearlman in *Listen to Their Voices*, #12
1993

2 *Love needs guidebooks and road signs, since it is forever terra incognita, the new world, the unmapped land of each heart.*

Prologue, *Love's Apprentice: The Romantic Education of a Modern Woman* 1998

3 "Civilization" was a word that came easily to us then, a thrilling word, not yet dismembered and exposed as a vile disguise of capitalism, an excuse for exploiting the poor of the earth.

p. 145, Ibid.

4 One could measure a civilization by how well it disposed of excrement.

Ch. 1, *The Future of Love* 2008

5 Sophie was beautiful with nothing on her face or body, and yet she creamed and combed and powdered and groomed, tweezed and depilated, exfoliated, moisturized, drew her eyebrows in with wispy lines.

Ch. 17, Ibid.

2876. Freda Adler (1934–)

1 Woman throughout the ages has been mistress to the law, as man has been its master. . . . the controversy between rule of law and rule of men was never relevant to women—because, along with juveniles, imbeciles, and other classes of legal nonpersons, they had no access to law except through men.

Sisters in Crime 1975

2 There is another side to chivalry. If it dispenses leniency, it may with equal justification invoke control.

Ch. 4, Ibid.

3 Of all the tyrannies which have usurped power over humanity, few have been able to enslave the mind and body as imperiously as drug addiction.

Ch. 5, Ibid.

4 Stripped of ethical rationalizations and philosophical pretensions, a crime is anything that a group in power chooses to prohibit.

Ch. 7, Ibid.

5 That man is a creature who needs order yet yearns for change is the creative contradiction at the heart of the laws which structure his conformity and define his deviancy.

Ch. 8, Ibid.

6 It is little wonder that rape is one of the least reported crimes. Perhaps it is the only crime in which the victim becomes the accused and, in reality, it is she who must prove her good reputation, her mental-soundness, and her impeccable propriety.

Ch. 9, Ibid.

2877. Rita Arditti (1934–)

1 The rules of the capitalist market, when applied to women's bodies and reproductive power, institutionalize women as breeders and devalue motherhood.

Essay, *The Politics of Motherhood: Activist Voices from Left to Right*, Alexis Jetter, Annelise Orlecks, and Diana Taylor, eds.
1996

2 The military, presenting itself as the defender of "tradition, family, and property," considered any criticism of its rule as a sign of anti-Argentine, subversive behavior that it needed to crush in order to protect the nation.

Ch. 1, *Searching for Life: The Grandmothers of the Plaza de May and the Disappeared Children in Argentina* 1999.

2878. Eileen Atkins (1934–)

1 It's a damn shame we have this immediate ticking off in the mind about how people sound. On the other hand, how many people really want to be operated upon by a surgeon who talks broad cockney?

The Daily Telegraph (London) 5 February 1992

2879. Brigitte Bardot (1934–)

1 I leave before being left. I decide.

Quoted in *Newsweek* (New York) 5 March 1973

2 I am leaving the town* to the invaders: increasingly numerous, mediocre, dirty, badly behaved, shameless tourists.

International Herald Tribune (Paris) 10 August 1989
*On leaving her home at Saint Tropez.

3 I gave my youth and beauty to men. Now I give the best of my wisdom and experience to animals.

Quoted in "Bardot Flies Again," *Parade Magazine* 3 May 1992

2880. Faith Barnebey (1934–)

1 Matriarchs are not born but rather formed, as though from the Earth's core—bits of iron, nuggets of gold, hammered into shape by the hand of God. Filled with grit and compassion in equal measure, things to be learned the hard way.
   That is the way of matriarchs.

"New challenges for next-generation matriarchs," *Tallahassee Democrat* 1 December 2002

2881. Sissela Ann Bok (1934–)

1 If you combine lying and secrecy, and if you also bring in violence so that secrecy covers up for schemes of lying and violence, then I think a republic can die. I don't think it's possible for citizens to have much of an effect if they literally don't know what's going on.

Quoted in *A World of Ideas* by Bill Moyers 1989

2 The predicament we're in now and that we have been in for some time is the threat of extinction from nuclear weapons, and the threat of extinction from environmental sources. It has simply never been the case before in human history that all of life—not just human life but really all of life—could be wiped out. That has made an enormous change for us. At the same time, this is also an extraordinary opportunity.

Ibid.

3 Our century has been unbelievably violent and brutal and filled with tyranny, but it has also brought forth countervail-

ing powers. We've had popular movements seeking to change nonviolently and, in fact, succeeding more and more often. . . . We have better history. We know much more how wars start and how they can get out of hand.

Ibid.

2882. Diana Chang (1934–)

1 The old are girlish now
Going to their grooms
They marry mysteries
"On Seeing My Great-Aunt in a Funeral Parlor," St. 5, *The American Scholar*, Vol. 28, No. 1 *Winter 1958/59*

2 I am the thin edge I sit on.
I begin to gray—white and black and in between.
My hair is America.
"Second Nature," St. 7, *The Woman That I Am, The Literature and Culture of Contemporary Women of Color*, D. Soyini Madison,* ed. *1994*
*See 3912.

2883. Eva M. Clayton (1934–)

1 We help men become what they think they are. Men are not without passion for children or equality, but those are peripheral issues for them.
Quoted by Mindy Cameron in "Win-win politics from a sisterhood of change," *Seattle Times, Op-Ed 3 April 1994*

2884. Inga Clendinnen (1934–)

1 . . . the theological struggle to comprehend the Holocaust* as an episode in an enigmatic deity's intentions regarding his chosen people continues to shadow putatively secular debate.
Reading the Holocaust 1999
*The genocide of European Jews and others by the Nazis during World War II.

2 Villains are rarely simple men.
Ibid.

3 Fractured identity is not confined to the innocent.
Ibid.

4 We will not understand an Eichmann* unless we grasp not only the individual character, but the exhilaration infused into that drab character by his context of revolutionary excitement and urgent high purpose, so that bullying brutal action was transformed into heroism.
Ibid.

*Adolf Eichmann, German Nazi official (1906–62).

2885. Sherry Suib Cohen (1934–)

1 What have been the costs of blind, cutthroat, unaffiliating competition? Lagging productivity, as the import figures reveal, a huge turnover of the best people, distrust and suspicion within the ranks, political infighting and sabotage, workers who expect to be ignored and who expect to fail (and who do exactly these two things). These are the costs the American corporation is paying.

Ch. 3, *Tender Power 1989*

2 Power is not a sorority for working women alone. A certain inner confidence is to be gained when, knowing one is following one's strongest instincts, one chooses, in defiance of current dogma, to stay home. For some, heeding that call is power. Moreover, those who decide they can afford to stay home, at least for a few years, are not alone in the wisdom of their decision.
Ch. 10, Ibid.

2886. Édith Cresson (1934–)

1 To get the country moving it is necessary to let off some bombs. I shall commence the bombardment.
"World: Europe: Cresson: The 'careless' commissioner," *BBC News 16 March 1999*

2 One of the most obvious characteristics of the bourgeoisie is the boredom it generates.
Ibid.

2887. Arlene Croce (1934–)

1 The gift of care can be both selfless and exploited.
The Price of Motherhood 2002

2 At least some of the men who write sex books admit they really don't understand female sexuality. Freud* was one. Masters** is another—that was why he got Johnson.***
Quoted in *Commentary n.d.*
*Sigmund Freud, Austrian physician and founder of psychoanalysis (1856–1939). **William H. Masters, gynecologist (1915–) and Virginia E. Johnson,*** psychologist (1925–), pioneering American research team in human sexuality.

2888. Margaretta D'Arcy (1934–)

1 SINGER (to the air "Long Lankin").
The cold rain of Ireland blows over the water
To furrow the face of fair England's proud daughter.

How long will it fall, O as sharp as a knife?
Till the dogteeth of England let go of our life.

Let go of our heart and the voice in our throat:
Till the day of that good-morning, no end to the fight . . .
Prologue, *Vandaleur's Folly*, with John Arden* *1978*
*British dramatist (1930–), her husband and collaborator.

2 I am not sure whether there is a connection between the loss of the concept of "play" and our present-day mechanistic bums-on-seats "task-profit" syndrome where the finished commodity of the cultural production-line is all that matters and to hell with the personal growth and vision of the workers.
Quoted by Elaine Turner in *Contemporary Dramatists*, 5th ed., K. A. Berney, ed. *1993*

2889. Judi Dench (1934–)

1 Lack of sense of humor—it's like not having a leg or an arm.
Quoted in "The Quiet Truth" by Laurie Winer, *Modern Maturity July/August 2002*

2 We have lost that feeling of a community all being together, and of course, irritatingly, wanting to know what everyone else's business is.
Quoted in "Judi Dench, Living Quietly in 'Cranford'" by John Ydstie, *National Public Radio* npr.org *16 June 2008*

2890. Diane Di Prima (1934–)

1 We buy the arms and the armed men, we have placed them on all the thrones of South America
we are burning the jungles, the beasts will rise up against us
"Goodbye Nkrumah," St. 1, *Intrepid #VI 1966*

2 Had you lived longer than your twenty-six years
You, too, would have come up against it like a wall—
That the Beauty you saw was bought
At too great a price
Even in those days. . . .
  "Ode to Keats,"* St. 1, *The East Side Scene,* Allen de Loach,
    ed. *1968*

*John Keats (1795–1821), British poet.

3 Don't forget, however great your visioning and your inspiration, you need the techniques of the craft and there's nowhere, really, to get them . . . they are passed on person to person and back then the male naturally passed them on to the male. I think maybe I was one of the first women to break through that in having deep conversations with Charles Olson* and Frank O'Hara.**
  Quoted in *Women of the Beat Generation* by Brenda Knight
    1996

*American avant garde poet and literary theorist (1910–70).
**American poet (1926–66).

2591. Nancy Rule Goldberger (1934–)
See Mary Field Belenky, 2834: 1–3.

2892. Jane Goodall (1934–)

1 You cannot get through a single day without having an impact on the world around you. What you do makes a difference, and you have to decide what kind of difference you want to make.
  My Life with the Chimpanzees 1996

2 You may not believe in evolution, and that is all right. How we humans came to be the way we are is far less important than how we should act now to get out of the mess we have made for ourselves.
  Ch. 1, *Reason for Hope: A Spiritual Journey 1999*

3 So here we are, the human ape, half sinner, half saint, with two opposing tendencies inherited from our ancient past pulling us now toward violence, now toward compassion and love. Are we, forever, to be torn in two different directions, cruel in one instance, kind the next? Or do we have the ability to control these tendencies, choosing the direction we wish go to?
  Ch. 10, Ibid.

4 Without hope, all we can do is eat and drink the last of our resources as we watch our planet slowly die. Let us have faith in ourselves, in our intellect, in our staunch spirit.
  Quoted in *Wise Women* by Joyce Tenneson* *2002*
  *See 3619.

5 We have a choice to use the gift of our lives to make the world a better place.
  janegoodall.org *2008*

2893. Barbara Grizzuti Harrison (1934–2002)

1 Profoundly ignorant, we are obliged to invent.
  "Talking Dirty," *Ms.* (New York) *October 1973*

2 Fantasies are more than substitutes for unpleasant reality; they are also dress rehearsals, plans. All acts performed in the world begin in the imagination.
  Ibid.

3 True revolutionaries are like God—they create the world in their own image. Our awesome responsibility to ourselves, to our children, and to the future is to create ourselves in the image of goodness, because the future depends on the nobility of our imaginings.
  Ch. 9, *Unlearning the Lie: Sexism in School 1973*

4 I refuse to believe that trading recipes is silly. Tuna-fish casserole is at least as real as corporate stock.
  "Secrets Women Tell Each Other," *McCall's August 1975*

5 Women's propensity to share confidences is universal. We confirm our reality by sharing.
  Ibid.

6 Kindness and intelligence don't always deliver us from the pitfalls and traps: there are always failures of love, of will, of imagination. There is no way to take the danger out of human relationships.
  Ibid.

7 I love my body when I'm having sex, nice body, so obedient, so capable. . . . I rise, like yeast . . . so beautifully able to give and to take . . .
  Introduction, *An Accidental Autobiography 1996*

2894. Nancy M. Henley (1934–)

1 Feminine atmosphere projects the image of immobility; these accoutrements are ones that one can only look beautiful in, not move, feel strong, or be active in. . . . It is no accident that coffins puff out with satin pads, lace, and frills. . . . and the funeral parlor is filled with flowers. These signs of femininity, common also to the beauty parlor, are symbolic of the powerlessness of the dead, as they are of the powerlessness of women.
  Ch. 4, *Body Politics: Power, Sex, and Non-Verbal*
    Communication 1977

2 "Polite" company, that is, the social elite and those who would imitate them, are so removed from their bodies—undoubtedly a sign of spirituality and near-divinity—that they are expected not to feel the need to itch, belch, or fart.
  Ch. 6, Ibid.

3 The history of power in fact shows us that victims of unfathomable oppression have arisen to claim their rights, that power is persistently being broken down and overturned. Every new insight into its workings may provide a new road to its overthrow.
  Ch. 11, Ibid.

2895. Anne Haw Holt (1934–)

1 You'd shame me in front of the world by joining the Yankee Army? You'll be fighting your mother's people and mine. Would you kill your own family?
  p. 36, *Blanco Sol 2005*

2 Don't you ever forget, big brother, you are not on the reservation here. This land is mine from my husband and it will belong to my sons.
  p. 122, *Blood Redemption 2008*

2896. Marilyn Horne (1934–)

1 Ninety percent of what's wrong with singers today is that they don't breathe right.
  Quoted in "Marilyn Horne," *Divas: Impressions of Six Opera*
  Superstars by Winthrop Sargeant *1959*

2 The thing to do [for insomnia] is to get an opera score and read *that*. That will bore you to death.

Ibid.

3 I've been a general for so long in many male roles, it's time I became emperor!

Highlights, *Modern Maturity December 1991/January 1992*

2897. Jeanne Wakatsuki Houston (1934–)

1 As the months at Manzanar* turned to years, it became a world unto itself, with its own logic and familiar ways. In time, staying there seemed far simpler than moving once again to another, unknown place. It was as if the war were forgotten, our reason for being there forgotten. The present, the little bit of busywork you had right in front of you, became the most urgent thing. In such a narrowed, world, in order to survive, you learn to contain your rage and your despair, and you try to re-create, as well you can, your normality, some sense of things, continuing. The fact that America had accused us, or excluded us, or imprisoned us, or whatever it might be called, did not change the kind of world we wanted. Most of us were born in this country; we had no other models.

Farewell to Manzanar, and James D. Houston 1973
*Owens Valley, California, the first permanent internment camp for Japanese, set up after the bombing of Pearl Harbor in 1941.

2898. Barbara Howar (1934–)

1 . . . the cocktail party remains a vital Washington institution, the official intelligence system.

Ch. 5, *Laughing All the Way 1973*

2 In our long history of shooting politicians . . . I have come to feel that Washington politicians look upon these events as little more than temporary setbacks in the continuing process of government.

Ch. 12, Ibid.

3 Eventually most television stations around the country achieved their minority quota by hiring "twofers," which is a trade expression meaning a "black, female, on-air personality," two television unthinkables, at one salary—a salary, I might add, that generally falls short of the "equal pay for equal work" cliché.

Ch. 15, Ibid.

4 Kissinger* likes intrigue rather than confrontation . . . [He] believes all power begins in the White House. It is his firm belief that he and the President know what is best; the rest of us are to be patient and they will announce our destiny.

Ch. 16, Ibid.
*Henry K—, German-born American diplomat (1923–) who shared the 1973 Nobel Peace Prize.

2899. Louise Kapp Howe (1934–)

1 Despite the focus in the media on the affluent and the poor, the average man is neither. Despite the concentration in TV commercials on the blond, blue-eyed WASP, the real American prototype is of Italian or Irish or Polish or Greek or Lithuanian or German or Hungarian or Russian or any of the still amazing number of national origins represented in this country—a "white ethnic," sociologists somberly call him.

Introduction, *The White Majority 1970*

2 . . . the assumption of a male-breadwinner society . . . ends up determining the lives of everyone within a family, whether a male breadwinner is present or not, whether one is living by the rules in suburbia or trying to break them on a commune.

Introduction, *The Future of the Family 1972*

3 While politicians carry on about the sanctity of the American family, we learn . . . that in the scale of national priorities our children and families really come last. After freeways. After pork subsidies. After the billions spent on munitions in the name of national defense. It is now time . . . to reverse the usual procedure. It is time to *change the economy* to meet the needs of American families.

Ibid.

2900. Diane Johnson (1934–)

1 A lesser life does not seem lesser to the person who leads one. His life is very real to him; he is not a minor figure in it.

"Lesser Lives," *The True History of the First Mrs. Meredity and Other Lesser Lives 1972*

2 We are surrounded by the enraged.

The Shadow Knows 1974

3 Waiting to be murdered has given me you might say something to live for.

Ibid.

4 Men are generally more law-abiding than women . . . Women have a feeling that since they didn't make the rules, the rules have nothing to do with them.

Lying Low 1978

5 Of course she had not really believed Iran would be a foreign land. She saw the deficiency in her imagination, that she had not been able to imagine with sufficient intensity the alien condition. A well-traveled American with no anxieties about hotels, headwaiters, planes—her imagination had provided her with no more than a benign region of camels, and mosques, and well-run hospitals of the American kind . . . She had assumed she could put things right . . . Now she saw that this presumption was naïve.

Persian Nights 1987

2901. Audre Lorde (1934–1992)

1 Since Naturally black is Naturally Beautiful
I must be proud
And, naturally,
Black and
Beautiful

Who always was a trifle
Yellow
And plain though proud
Before.

"Naturally," St. 1, *Cables to Rage 1970*

2 . . . Which me will survive all these liberations.

"From a Land Where Other People Live," *From a Land Where Other People Live 1975*

3 *It was in high school that I came to believe that I was different from my white classmates, not because I was Black, but because I was me.*

Zami: A New Spelling of My Name 1983

4 Militancy no longer means guns at high noon, if it ever did. It means actively working for change, sometimes in the absence of any surety that change is coming. It means doing the unromantic and tedious work necessary to forge meaningful coalitions, and it means recognizing which coalitions are possible and which coalitions are not. It means knowing that coalition, like unity, means the coming together of whole, self-actualized human beings, focused and believing, not fragmented automatons marching to a prescribed step. It means fighting despair.

> Speech, "Learning from the 60s," Harvard University (*February 1982*), *Sister/Outsider: Essays and Speeches 1984*

5 One of the most basic Black survival skills is the ability to change, to metabolize experience, good or ill, into something that is useful, lasting, effective. Four hundred years of survival as an endangered species has taught most of us that if we intend to live, we had better become fast learners.

> Ibid.

6 Decisions to cut aid for the terminally ill, for the elderly, for dependent children, for food stamps, even school lunches, are being made by men with full stomachs who live in comfortable houses with two cars and umpteen tax shelters.

> Ibid.

7 Revolution is not a one-time event.

> Ibid.

8 Black feminism is not white feminism in blackface.

> "Sexism: An American Disease in Blackface," Ibid.

9 Afrekete Afrekete my beloved
feel the sun of my Days surround you
binding our pathways

> "Today is Not the Day," *The Marvelous Arithmetics of Distance: Poems 1987–1992 1993*

10 The master's tools will never bring down the master's house.

> Quoted in "Harryette Mullen's* *Écriture féminine*" by Mike Jackman, Twentieth Century Literature Conference (Louisville, Kentucky) *26–28 February 1998*

*See 4197.

2902. Sophia Loren (1934–   )

1 Getting ahead in a difficult profession requires avid faith in yourself. You must be able to sustain yourself against staggering blows and unfair reversals. There is no code of conduct to help beginners. That is why some people with mediocre talent, but with great inner drive, go much further than people with vastly superior talent. I'm convinced that this inner drive is something you are born with, and no one can teach you how to acquire it.

> Quoted in *Sophia: Living and Loving* by A. E. Hotchner *1979*

2 Sex appeal is fifty percent what you've got and fifty percent what people think you've got.

> Quoted in *Halliwell's Filmgoer's Companion* by Leslie Halliwell *1984*

2903. Shirley MacLaine (1934–   )

1 In Japan, courtesy had an esthetic value far greater than good manners in the West. A negative truth is frequently subordinate to the virtue of courtesy. Courtesy, therefore, is more of a virtue than honesty.

> Ch. 5, *Don't Fall Off the Mountain 1970*

2 The more I traveled the more I realized that fear makes strangers of people who should be friends.

> Ch. 13, Ibid.

3 Africa seems the harmonious voice of creation. Everything alive was inextricably intertwined until death. And even death was part of the life harmony.

> Ibid.

4 India is a paradox, passionate, pulsating, even humorous in her poverty. And in her villages the subhuman drama plays itself out against a backdrop of such beauty that it seems grotesque mockery.

> Ch. 14, Ibid.

5 I realized that if what we call human nature can be changed, then absolutely *anything* is possible. And from that moment, my life changed.

> Epilogue, *You Can Get There from Here 1975*

6 Perhaps Western values, for the past five hundred years, had been a human distortion, perhaps competition was simply not compatible with harmony, not conducive to human happiness, perhaps the competitive urge came only from the exaggerated emphasis on the individual. Maybe the individual was simply not as important as the group.

> Ibid.

7 Within the family environment was every human conflict that could ultimately lead to a willingness, or a nonwillingness, to wage war. Most attitudes of, and toward, violence and hostility are spawned in the family. Just as attitudes of love and compassion are.

> Ch. 2, *Dancing in the Light 1985*

8 Experimentation in front of the big black giant* is enough to reduce an accomplished and seasoned performer to the rank of blithering idiot. . . . The audience never responds to artifice. They can detect sham immediately and just as swiftly respond positively to something you do that comes out of your gut. They want you to be real. That's what they're there for.

> Ch. 6, Ibid.

*Reference to song "The Big Black Giant" from Rodgers and Hammerstein's musical *Me and Juliet*.

9 Nothing should be permanent except struggle with the dark side within ourselves.

> Ch. 11, Ibid.

10 If I could know me, I could know the universe.

> Epilogue, Ibid.

2904. Janet Malcolm (1934–   )

1 Every journalist who is not too stupid or too full of himself to notice what is going on knows that what he does is morally indefensible. He is a kind of confidence man, preying on people's vanity, ignorance, or loneliness, gaining their trust and betraying them without remorse.

> *The Journalist and the Murderer 1990*

2 Fidelity to the subject's thought and to his characteristic way of expressing himself is the sine qua non of journalistic quotation.

> Ibid.

3 The dominant and most deep-dyed trait of the journalist is his timorousness. Where the novelist fearlessly plunges into the

water of self-exposure, the journalist stands trembling on the shore in his beach robe. . . . The journalist confines himself to the clean, gentlemanly work of exposing the griefs and shames of others.

Ibid.

2905. Winnie Madikizela-Mandela (1934–)

1 I am a living symbol of whatever is happening in the country. I am a living symbol of the white man's fear.

"My Little Siberia," *Part of My Soul Went With Him,* Anne Benjamin, ed. *1984*

2 The Afrikaner in the Free State—for him a black is something that sits on their tractor or plods behind their plough. What is more important to that farmer is his tractor and not that laborer. . . .

Ibid.

3 We never had him* physically to share that love he exudes so much of. I knew when I married him that I married the struggle, the liberation of my people.

"Life With Him Was Always a Life Without Him," Ibid. *Nelson Mandela, South African political and civil rights leader (1918–); incarcerated (1962–90); president (1994–99); Nobel Peace Prize, 1993.

4 Together, hand in hand, with that stick of matches, with our necklace*, we shall liberate this country.

Speech in black townships, quoted in *The Guardian* (London) *15 April 1986* *Slang for the practice of lighting a gasoline filled tire thrown around a victim's neck.

5 It dawned on me that you either had to survive apartheid or you had to perish with it. I decided to survive.

Quoted in *Twentieth-Century Women Political Leaders* by Claire Price-Groff *1998*

2906. Peggy McIntosh (1934–)

1 In my class and place, I did not see myself as a racist because I was taught to recognize racism only in individual acts of meanness by members of my group, never in invisible systems conferring unsought racial dominance on my group from birth.

"White Privilege and Male Privilege," *Peace and Freedom July/August 1989*

2 I have come to see white privilege as an invisible package of unearned assets that I can count on cashing in each day, but about which I was "meant" to remain oblivious. White privilege is like an invisible weightless knapsack of special provisions, maps, passports, codebooks, visas, clothes, tools, and blank checks.

Ibid.

2907. Marianne Means (1934–)

1 Conservatives are used to strong women; they just aren't used to strong women who don't give men all the credit.

"Conservatives make much of Clinton. . . ," Hearst Newspapers *12 February 1993*

2 In politics, the more things change, the more they remain the same.

Syndicated column, Hearst Newspapers *8 September 1997*

3 It is not surprising that young people feel their views will not be heard in distant, isolated Washington. Older adults feel that way, too. Such alienation is inevitable in an enormous nation of vast geographic contrasts, ethnic diversity and technical specialization.

"What's impeachment effect on younger set?," Hearst Newspapers *January 1999*

4 In politics, as in war, there is collateral damage, non-combatants who are injured because of their proximity to the real target. First lady Laura Bush* may be vulnerable to that problem.

"Laura Bush wastes unique opportunity," Hearst Newspapers *23 March 2006* *See 3641.

5 But in politics, memories are long. And often bitter. And this campaign was really about the two of them, not their policies. Even if he gets to the White House, he really can't win over the country without her.* She is the nation's pre-eminent heroine—her courage in the face of male sexism, ignorant youthful idealism and media hostility was incredible. Now that's a leader!

"Obama is making a big, surly mistake," Hearst Newspapers *12 June 2008* *Referencing Hillary Rodham Clinton; see 3731.

2908. Kate Millett (1934–)

1 The care of children, even from the period when their cognitive powers first emerge, is infinitely better left to the best-trained practitioners of both sexes who have chosen it as a vocation, rather than to harried and all too frequently unhappy persons with little time or taste for the work of educating minds however young or beloved . . . The family, as that term is presently understood, must go.

Sexual Politics 1969

2 . . . I see the function of true Erotica (writing which is pro—, not antisexual) as one not only permissible but worthy of encouragement and social approval, as its laudable and legitimate function is to increase sexual appetite just as culinary prose encourages other appetites.

Ibid.

3 Perhaps nothing is so depressing an index of the inhumanity of the male supremacist mentality as the fact that the more genial human traits are assigned to the underclass: affection, response to sympathy, kindness, cheerfulness.

Ibid.

4 Sexual congress in a Mailer* novel is always a matter of strenuous endeavor, rather like mountain climbing—a matter of straining after achievement.

Ibid. *Norman Mailer, American writer (1923–).

5 Whores are the political prisoners of the feminist movement . . . They are considered criminals for no other reason than the fact that they are women . . . men aren't jailed for solicitation . . . women are jailed. And they're jailed because they have cunts.

Quoted in *Radical Lifestyles* by Claudia Dreifus* *1971* *See 3495.

6 Standing by the car door he looks like a gent, taking out my bags. Says he went to university. Why does he drive a cab? Soft with the kindness of failure. Probably just got lost in life.

Part One, Vertigo, *Flying 1974*

7 Either I was never crazy or I have recovered and can be sane henceforth. To be whole, not a cracked egg, not an imperfect specimen, not a deformed intellect or a mental defective—but whole.

Part One, The Farm, 1, *The Loony-Bin Trip 1990*

2909. Sister Nirmala (1934–   )

1 I remember [when I was in college] the church bells ringing, it was the bells of Angelus, and my roommate suddenly knelt down right there and prayed. At that moment, something happened in my heart. Jesus came alive in me.

Quoted in "Life in the shadow of Mother Teresa"* by John Stackhouse, *Seattle Post-Intelligencer,* A12 *5 September 1998*

2 We have decided collectively to keep that title for Mother* only. For me it is definite. I like to be a sister. I like being sister to my sisters. When you are a sister, you can play with the sisters.

Ibid.

*See 2124.

2910. Mary Quant (1934–   )

1 I wanted to make clothes that you could move in, skirts you could run and dance in.

Quant by Quant 1966

2 The fashionable woman wears clothes. The clothes don't wear her.

Ibid.

3 A woman is as young as her knees.

Ibid.

4 Having money is rather like being a blond. It is more fun but not vital.

Quoted in *Observer* (London) *2 November 1986*

2911. Carol Lee Sanchez (1934–   )

1 For fifty years, children in this country have been raised to kill Indians mentally, subconsciously through the visual media, until it is an automatic reflex. That shocks you? Then I have made my point . . . The cheap western is still rolling out of Hollywood, the old shoot-'em-up westerns playing on afternoon kid shows, late night T.V. Would you allow your children to play Nazis and Jews? Blacks and KKKs?*

"Sex, Class and Race Intersections Visions of Women of Color," *A Gathering of Spirit,* Beth Brant,** ed. *1984*
*Ku Klux Klan, a secret, militant, white supremacist society, founded in 1915 in the U.S. state of Georgia. **See 3246.

2 We have been displaced, relocated, removed, terminated, educated, acculturated, and in our hearts and minds we will always "go back to the blanket" as long as we are still connected to our families, our Tribes and our land.

Ibid.

3 yo soy india
pero no soy
yo soy anglo
pero no soy
yo soy arabe
pero no soy
yo soy chicana
pero no soy

(I am indian/but I am not/I am anglo/but I am not/I am arabic/ but I am not/I am chicana/but I am not)

"Tribal Chant," St. 5, *That's What She Said,* Rayna Green,* ed. *1984*

*See 3338.

4 how come you kees me by
the reever, & on the strit
jou don told me hallo?

"The Way I Was. . . ." St. 2, Ibid.

5 somewhere on earth
on an ordinary day
a human hand understood
the magic of transcription

"symbols," St. 4, *From Spirit to Matter 1997*

6 i touch
eternal consciousness
with the tips of
my imagination

"meditation," st. 1, Ibid.

2912. Sonia Sanchez (1934–   )

1 Slow is not always dumb, and fast is not always smart.

The Adventures of Fathead, Smallhead, and Squarehead 1973

2 I want my body to carry my words like aqueducts.
I want to make the world my diary
and speak rivers.

"Past," 1. Woman, St. 1, *The Woman That I Am, The Literature and Culture of Contemporary Women of Color,* D. Soyini Madison,* ed. *1994*

*See 3912.

3 you held me so close
we were like the singing coming off drums.
you made me squeeze muscles
lean back on the sound
of corpuscles sliding in blood. I heard my thighs singing

Untitled, *Like the Singing Coming Off the Drums 1997*

2913. Carolyn See (1934–   )

1 Explosions wait in all of us, and we're just as surprised as everyone else when they go off.

Dreaming: Hard Luck and Good Times in America 1995

2 Scorn was my career.

Ibid.

3 Her boyfriend Tony bored her to tears. He was good and kind, but his idea was: go to work. Go to the movies. Take a class, hear a lecture, buy a few beers, smoke some dope, zone out in front of the TV, sleep, surf, be peaceful.

Ibid.

4 Don't do as we did. Do what it was we wanted to do when we started our lives. Adhere to *those* high ideals. . . . Learn from our mistakes.

Ibid.

2914. Patricia Simon (1934– 1993)

1 An old French farm built on levels up and down a hillside near Grasse—overlooking, in the middle distance, the quiet cluster

of the town and, in the further distance, hills, and beyond them other hills, and other hills, in a gentle, fertile, dreamlike landscape that continued forever—the Alpes-Maritimes.
"The Making of a Masterpiece," McCall's October 1970

2 Flowers and sunlight, air and silence—*"luxe, calme et volupté."*
Ibid.

2915. Jo Spence (1934–1992)

1 Passing through the hands of the medical profession can be terrifying when you have breast cancer.
"A Picture of Health?" Putting Myself in the Picture: A Political, Personal and Photographic Autobiography 1986

2 [Photographs] in newspapers, magazines and on high-street hoardings,* play an important part in our lives. With their messages—both explicit and hidden—they help to shape our concepts of what is real and what is normal. They give us information about the sort of sex roles we are expected to play in society, contribute to our image of ourselves, to our expectations and to our fantasies.
Television, cinema and all visual media echo the same ideology.
"The Politics of Photography" (1976), Cultural Sniping: The Art of Transgression 1995
*British term for billboards.

3 News and advertising have proved remarkably adept at listening to criticism and changing, whilst subtly remaining exactly the same.
"The Politics of Transformation" (1986), Ibid.

4 Two cameras standing side by side could take totally different pictures of the same moment.
Quoted in Ch. 1, Aged by Culture by Margaret Morganroth Gullette 2004*
*See 3268.

2916. Gloria Steinem (1934–   )

1 We [women] are not more moral, we are only less corrupted by power.
"A New Egalitarian Life Style," The New York Times Book Review 26 August 1971

2 ... no man can call himself liberal, or radical, or even a conservative advocate of fair play, if his work depends in any way on the unpaid or underpaid labor of women at home, or in the office.
Ibid.

3 The first problem for all of us, men and women, is not to learn, but to unlearn.
Ibid.

4 God knows (*she* knows) that women try.
"Sisterhood," The First Ms. Reader, Francine Klagsbrun, ed. 1972

5 The definition of women's work is shitwork.
Quoted in "Freelancer with No Time to Write" by John Brady, Writer's Digest February 1974

6 A government's responsibility to its young citizens does not magically begin at the age of six. It makes more sense to extend the free universal school system downward—with the neces-

sary reforms and community control that child care should have from the start.
"Victory with Honor," Ms. (New York) April 1974

7 Erotica is as different from pornography as love is from rape, as dignity is from humiliation, as partnership is from slavery, as pleasure is from pain.
"Erotic and Pornography, A Clear and Present Difference," Ms. (New York) November 1978

8 The real reasons for genital mutilation can only be understood in the context of the patriarchy: men must control women's bodies as the means of production, and thus repress the independent power of women's sexuality.
"The International Crime of Female Genital Mutilation," Ms. (New York) March 1979

9 We must understand the difference between what we mean by family and what the Right Wing means by family. . . . Women are the means of production, owned by the husband. Children are the labor, owned by the husband. And that's what they mean by family. Consequently, they oppose any direct guarantee of right between wife and the law or children and the law, because that is antithetical to their definition of the family.
Speech, National Women's Political Caucus Conference (Albuquerque, New Mexico) July 1981

10 Some of us are becoming the men we wanted to marry.
Speech, Yale University 23 September 1981

11 If the men in the room would only think how they would feel graduating with a "spinster of arts" degree they would see how important this [language reform] is.
Ibid.

12 . . . the authority of any governing institution must stop at its citizen's skin.
"Night Thoughts of a Media-Watcher," Ms. (New York) November 1981

13 Dying seems less sad than having lived too little.
Outrageous Acts and Everyday Rebellion 1983

14 Finding language that will allow people to act together while cherishing each other's individuality is probably the most feminist and therefore truly revolutionary function of writers.
Introduction, Ibid.

15 If the shoe doesn't fit, must we change the foot?
"If Men Could Menstruate" (1978), p. 206–210, Ibid.

16 If men started taking care of children, the job will become more valuable.
Quoted in "Onward, Women!" by Claudia Wallis, Time (New York) 4 December 1989

17 It's an incredible con job when you think about it, to believe something now in exchange for something after death. Even corporations with their reward systems don't try to make it posthumous.
Revolution From Within 1992

18 I thought seriously about whether the world still needs *Ms.* magazine. And I went out and picked up armloads of women's magazines and I looked at them and I thought: "Yes. The world does still need *Ms.* Magazine."
Quoted in "Ms. to balance today's 'women's magazines'" by Kimberly Mills, Seattle Post-Intelligencer 13 December 1998

19 Until we end the masculinization of wealth, we will not end the feminization of poverty.

Speech (Seattle), Women of Power Conference *6 April 2000*

20 Many of us are living out the unlived lives of our mothers, because they were not able to become the unique people they were born to be.

Quoted in *Wise Women* by Joyce Tenneson* 2002

*See 3619.

21 Gender is probably the most restricting force in American life, whether the question is who must be in the kitchen or who could be in the White House. This country is way down the list of countries electing women and, according to one study, it polarizes gender roles more than the average democracy.

"Women are Never the Front-runners," *The New York Times 8 January 2008*

22 Republicans may learn they can't appeal to right-wing patriarchs and most women at the same time. A loss in November could cause the centrist majority of Republicans to take back their party, which was the first to support the Equal Rights Amendment and should be the last to want to invite government into the wombs of women.

"Palin: wrong woman, wrong message," *The Los Angeles Times 4 September 2008*

23 Feminism has never been about getting a job for one woman. It's about making life more fair for women everywhere. It's not about a piece of the existing pie; there are too many of us for that. It's about baking a new pie.

Ibid.

24 I have yet to hear a man ask for advice on how to combine marriage and a career.

haruth.com/WomenToWomen.htm *n.d.*

2917. Jean Valentine (1934–   )

1 Together
   we are two stones like one stone rolling
   "Away from you," st. 3, *The Cradle of the Real Life 2000*

2 I had to die
   break the rope
   push through the stone fence

   of you, of myself, and fly
   "Mother," sts. 3–4, *Door in the Mountain: New and Collected Poems, 1965–2003 2004*

3 I needed a friend but
   I was in the other room
   "Hospital: strange lights," St. 1, *Little Boat 2007*

4 . . . I am poling
   my way into life. It seems
   like another life:
   "La Chalupa, the Boat," St. 1, Ibid.

2918. Shirley Hill Witt (1934–   )

1 I want to weep for La Vieja*
   Two booths away,
   But I can't: she is me.
   "Punto Final," St. 6, *That's What She Said*, Rayna Green,** ed. *1984*

*The old woman. **See 3338.

2 The campesinos* tend to smooth out the wrinkled places of legend for the better telling and also for their own better understanding. In this way, they discharge those questions left unanswered in their time as so much uselessness: the tale weaves better the more simply told, anyway.

"*La Mujer de Valor*" (The Brave Woman), Ibid.

*Farmers or farmworkers.

2919. Nellie Wong (1934–   )

1 when I was growing up, I felt
   dirty. I thought that god
   made white people clean
   and no matter how much I bathed,
   I could not change, I could not shed
   my skin in the gray water.
   "When I Was Growing Up," St. 11, *Dreams in Harrison Railroad Park 1977*

2 and now in my hours of awakening
   as my hair turns white
   my anger moves, a storm into the sunlight
   where women and men fight alongside each other
   "For an Asian Woman Who Says My Poetry Gives Her a Stomach-ache," St. 8 (1989), *The Woman That I Am, The Literature and Culture of Contemporary Women of Color,* D. Soyini Madison*, ed. *1994*

*See 3912.

3 Moving in concert with the forces of labor
   Solving problems with cooperation and care
   Workers' councils gather neighbor to neighbor
   With food and water and dwellings to share
   "Typewriter Keys Pantoum," st. 4 (2003), *An Anthology of Bay Area Women Writers,* Part 1, Katherine Hastings, ed. *n.d.*

2920. Angeles Arrien (1935–   )

1 Story opens us to discover where we really are in our journey rather than where we think we are.

"Transformation in the Millennium," *The Fabric of the Future: Women Visionaries of Today Illuminate the Path to Tomorrow,* M. J. Ryan, ed. *1998*

2 We need to bless those who challenge us to be fully loving; they mirror to us where we may withhold our love by being closed-hearted, half-hearted, and weak-hearted. They are great teachers for us, and remind us that the greatest remorse for human beings is love unexpressed.

Ibid.

3 Whenever we experience happiness and peace in our natures, we are at the gate where the medicines of joy, laughter, play, fun, and humor flourish.

Ibid.

4 The experiences of solitude are those in which we feel filled by silence, rather than empty or alone.

Ibid.

5 We know our behavior is authentic when we can consistently say what we mean, do what we say, and say what is so when it is so.

The Second Half of Life, Opening the Eight Gates of Wisdom 2006

2921. MaVynee Betsch (1935–2005)

1 I wear orange lipstick because, baby, during the days of segregation, they couldn't even leave the ocean alone. They put an orange rope in the water, and one side said "White," the other side said "Colored." A rope! Out! in! the! ocean! Can you believe it?

Quoted in "Madame Butterfly" by Michelle Nijhuis, *Sierra Magazine September/October 2005*

2 Understand that everything you do makes a statement, whether it's your jewelry, your clothes, or your house.

Ibid.

3 As long as we keep talking about it, American Beach* will stay alive. Younger people will create a new culture there. They'll start to etch in the sand what it means to have this leisure area for themselves.

Ibid.

*Historic African-American resort community; located on Amelia Island, just north of Jacksonville, Florida.

2922. Susan Brownmiller (1935–)

1 Man's discovery that his genitalia could serve as a weapon to generate fear must rank as one of the most important discoveries of prehistoric times, along with the use of fire and the first crude stone axe. From prehistoric times to the present, I believe, rape has played a critical function. It is nothing more or less than a conscious process of intimidation by which all men keep all women in a state of fear.

Against Our Will: Men, Women, and Rape 1975

2 It has been argued that, when killing is viewed as not only permissible but heroic behavior sanctioned by one's government or cause, the fine distinction between taking a human life and other forms of impermissible violence gets lost, and rape becomes an unfortunate but inevitable by-product of the necessary game called war.

Ibid.

3 Fighting back. On a multiplicity of levels, that is the activity we must engage in. . . .

Ibid.

4 Women are all female impersonators to some degree.

Femininity 1984

5 Femininity, in essence, is a romantic sentiment, a nostalgic tradition of imposed limitations. Even as it hurries forward in the 1980s, putting on lipstick and high heels to appear well dressed, it trips on the ruffled petticoats and hoopskirts of an era gone by.

Ibid.

6 Of the thousand or so white volunteers who joined the southern civil rights struggle during the mid-sixties, at least half, including myself, were women. Many of us went on to found—or to play a major role in—the Women's Liberation Movement a few years later. History seldom offers parallels this tidy, but as it happened, many of the female abolitionists of the nineteenth century had gone on to organize for women's suffrage. These two vivid epochs were separated by more than a century, yet nearly identical forces applied. After fighting alongside men in a radical movement to correct a grievous wrong, the women then woke up and wondered, "What about us?"

"The Founders," *In Our Time: Memoir of a Revolution 1999*

7 Political organizers understand that the important thing about action is reaction.

Ibid.

2923. Shirley Trusty Corey (1935–)

1 The arts must be considered an essential element of education, not an optional or lesser element in the consideration of time, materials, or appropriate teaching staff. They are the content and process by which we bring unity to isolated knowledge and feelings. They are tools for living life reflectively, joyfully, and with the ability to shape the future.

Letter to Elaine Bernstein Partnow* *19 December 1989*
*See 3291.

2 The arts personalize knowledge and visions, demanding an ever growing development of the mind and spirit. We do our children and our country ill service by not supporting them adequately in our schools.

Ibid.

2924. Gretchen Cryer (1935–)

1 Music is my one salvation
Singin' is my celebration
And playin' with a rock 'n roll band
Is a natural high

"Natural High," *I'm Getting My Act Together And Taking It On The Road 1977*

2 MOTHER. I prayed and prayed that my father would die before mother so that she could have a little time to herself, a little time to be happy. But he didn't, he held on, the old coot. Finally she died first and he died the next day. He just couldn't let her have anything.

Ibid.

3 HEATHER. You see, men would rather have a shitty thing than a good thing. It's less binding. As long as a relationship is shitty, they have a sense of freedom because they can say to themselves, "This is shitty and I really should get out of it." But if a relationship is good, that's very frightening, because then they don't have an excuse to get out. So the trick becomes to stay in a relationship and keep it shitty so the door is always open.

Ibid.

4 TRIO. If you smile in just the right way
You'll make a pretty wife
And someone will take care of you
For all your pretty life
If you smile, smile, smile.
If you smile

Ibid.

2925. Joan Didion (1935–)

1 New York is full of people on this kind of leave of absence, of people with a feeling for the tangential adventure, the risk adventure, the interlude that's not likely to end in any double-ring ceremony.

"New York: The Great Reprieve," *Mademoiselle February 1961*

2 Americans are uneasy with their possessions, guilty about power, all of which is difficult for Europeans to perceive because they are themselves so truly materialistic, so versed in the uses of power.

Run River 1963

3   Because when we start deceiving ourselves into thinking not that we want something or need something, not that it is a pragmatic necessity for us to have it, but that it is a *moral imperative* that we have it, then is when we join the fashionable madmen, and then is when the thin whine of hysteria is heard in the land, and then is when we are in bad trouble. And I suspect we are already there.
> "On Morality" (1965), Ibid.

4   Most of our platitudes notwithstanding, self-deception remains the most difficult deception. The tricks that work on others count for nothing in that very well-lit back alley where one keeps assignations with oneself: no winning smiles will do here, no prettily drawn lists of good intentions.
> "On Self-Respect" (1961), Ibid.

5   . . . California is a place in which a boom mentality and a sense of Chekovian loss meet in uneasy suspension; in which the mind is troubled by some buried but ineradicable suspicion that things had better work here, because here, beneath that immense bleached sky, is where we run out of continent.
> "Notes from a Native Daughter" (1965), Ibid.

6   She had to have a telephone. There was no one to whom she wanted to talk but she had to have a telephone.
> Ch. 35, *Play It As It Lays* 1970

7   . . . she had deliberately not counted the months but she must have been counting them unawares, must have been keeping a relentless count somewhere, because this was the day, the day the baby would have been born.
> Ch. 54, Ibid.

8   To hear someone's voice she looked in the telephone book and dialed a few prayers. . . .
> Ch. 60, Ibid.

9   Some nights he said that he was tired, and some nights she said that she wanted to read, and other nights no one said anything.
> Ch. 69, Ibid.

10   The apparent ease of California life is an illusion, and those who believe the illusion will live here in only the most temporary way.
> "Holy Water," *The White Album* 1979

11   A pool is, for many of us in the West, a symbol not of affluence but of order, of control over the uncontrollable. A pool is water, made available and useful, and is, as such, infinitely soothing to the western eye.
> Ibid.

12   Of course great hotels have always been social ideals, flawless mirrors to the particular societies they service.
> "In the Islands," Ibid.

13   . . . the freeway experience . . . is the only secular communion Los Angeles has. . . . Actual participation requires a total surrender, a concentration so intense as to seem a kind of narcosis, a rapture-of-the-freeway. The mind goes clean. The rhythm takes over. A distortion of time occurs. . . .
> "Bureaucrats" (1976), Ibid.

14   Many people I know in Los Angeles believe that the Sixties ended abruptly on August 9, 1969,* ended at the exact moment when word of the murders on Cielo Drive traveled like brushfire through the community, and in a sense this is true. The tension broke that day. The paranoia was fulfilled.
> "The White Album: A Chronicle of Survival in the Sixties,"
> *New West* 4 June 1979

*Day of the Tate-LaBianca murders, committed by Charles Manson (1937–   ) and his followers.

15   Because the reality of death has not yet penetrated awareness, survivors can appear to be quite accepting of the loss.
> *The Year of Magical Thinking* 2005

16   Nor can we know ahead of the fact (and here lies the heart of the difference between grief as we imagine it and grief as it is) the unending absence that follows, the void, the very opposite of meaning, the relentless succession of moments during which we will confront the experience of meaninglessness itself.
> Ibid.

17   These people who have lost someone look naked because they think themselves invisible. I myself felt invisible for a period of time, incorporeal. I seemed to have crossed one of those legendary rivers that divide the living from the dead, entered a place in which I could be seen only by those who were themselves recently bereaved. . . . I understood for the first time the meaning in the practice of suttee. Widows did not throw themselves in the burning raft out of grief. The burning raft was instead an accurate representation of the place to which their grief (not their families, not the community, not custom, their grief) had taken them.
> Ibid.

2926. Sylvia A. Earle (1935–   )

1   We have become frighteningly effective at altering nature.
> Quoted in "Call of the Sea" by Roger Rosenblatt, *Time* (New York) 5 October 1998

2   [The sea is] the place where the history of life actually can be found, not in fossils but in living creatures that represent life as it has been, perhaps, from the beginning of time.
> Ibid.

3   Look at the bark of a redwood, and you see moss. If you peer beneath the bits and pieces of the moss, you'll see toads, small insects, a whole host of life that prospers in that miniature environment. A lumberman will look at a forest and see so many board feet of lumber. I see a living city.
> Ibid.

4   [Marine exploration is] like having a chance to dive into your own circulatory system and swim around and see how it all fits together.
> Ibid.

5   I want to share the exhilaration of discovery and convey a sense of urgency about the need for all of us to use our talents and resources to continue to explore the nature of this extraordinary ocean planet.
> *Wild Ocean: America's Parks under the Sea,* with Wolcott Henry 1999

2927. Ann Faraday (1935–   )

1   I believe we have entered a new age of self-reliance and personal responsibility in which former reticence about the inner life is being abandoned and the demand for external conformity is being relaxed. The need in this new age is for more deliberate

inquiry into the hidden forces of the personality which shapes our waking behavior and for communication of our insights for public discussion.

Introduction, *Dream Power* 1972

2 Thus, learning to understand our dreams is a matter of learning to understand our heart's language.

The Dream Game 1974

2928. Forough Farrokhzad (1935–1967)
1 I speak out of the deep of night
Out of the deep of darkness

Untitled, Ahmad Karimi Hakkkak, tr. *n.d.*

2929. Geraldine A. Ferraro (1935–)
1 I don't think unnecessary suffering builds character at all. It doesn't make you a better person, it makes you a bitter person . . .

Ferraro: My Story, with Linda Bird Francke 1985

2 I'm a competitive person, but I have never understood people's competitiveness at the expense of their colleagues.

Ibid.

3 Any society that cannot respect its past by granting those who built it financial security faces moral bankruptcy in the future.

Ibid.

2930. Georgia Anne Geyer (1935–)
1 . . . Not only does the world scarcely know who the Latin American man is, the world has barely *cared*.

Introduction, *The New Latins* 1970

2 . . . the more revolutions occur, the less things change.

Ibid.

3 Because it was when "reporters" became "journalists" and when "objectivity" gave way to "searching for truth," that an aura of distrust and fear arose around the New Journalist.

"Whatever Happened to Lois Lane?," *The Los Angeles Times*
4 February 1979

4 Would women leaders wield power differently? Would they be more humane? Would they perhaps even usher in some gleaming, renascent era? And would men accept them?

Now that we have this veritable club of women leaders across the globe—ruling, scheming, changing the rules and the world—we can begin to answer those questions. But the answers are no simpler than the questions themselves.

"Are Women Leaders Wielding Power Differently Than
Men?," *Seattle Times 14 May 1989*

2931. Ellen Gilchrist (1935–)
1 "Well, for God's sake, find somebody with money," Sudie said. "Being married is bad enough without having to be poor at the same time. Whenever I get tired of Johnny's allergies I just go look at his Merrill Lynch portfolio. It turns me on. I swear it does."

Ch. 5, *The Annunciation* 1983

2 "Watch out for fame, Sissy. It ruined my life. I've spent my whole life watching men be jealous of me. It's dangerous to do

something everyone else wishes they could do, to be the thing they wish they could be."

Ch. 25, Ibid.

3 Don't ruin the present with the ruined past.

Ch. 27, Ibid.

4 Reality expands exponentially. It meets itself coming and going. It is a net, a web; touch one strand and the whole thing quivers. Get caught and you cannot get away. Sticky stuff, reality. Spiders understand this metaphor.

"Paris," *The Age of Miracles* 1995

5 We laughed again. It was incredibly, divinely, hilariously funny. No one ever gets that tickled when they are alone. Only two people can know something is that funny.

Ibid.

6 There is nothing on earth like friendship. It is God's love, God's ambrosia, the one thing we never have to pay for or regret.

Ibid.

7 Only sugar and whiskey made people feel better. Sugar and coffee and whiskey. Beignets and café au lait and taffy and Cokes and snowballs made with shaved ice and sugar and colored flavors. Gin and wine and vodka, whiskey and beer. It was too hot, too humid. The blood wouldn't move without sugar.

"The Stucco House," Ibid.

8 Teddy's vision of grown people was very astute. He envisioned them as large, very high-strung children who never sat still or finished what they started.

Ibid.

9 The language police had triumphed. Every opinion was hedged. Dialogue banished. Argument eschewed. Cant had displaced thought on American campuses.

"Death Comes to A Hero," Ibid.

2932. Vivian Gornick (1935/8–)
1 If the word for London is decency and the word for New York is violence, then, beyond doubt, the word for Cairo is tenderness. Tenderness is what pervades the air here.

Pt. I, *In Search of Ali-Mahmoud* 1973

2 The subjection of women, in my view, lies most deeply in the ingrained conviction—shared by both men and women—that for women marriage is the pivotal experience. It is this conviction, primarily, that reduces and ultimately destroys in women that flow of psychic energy that is fed in men from birth by the anxious knowledge given them that one is alone in this world; that one is never taken care of; that life is a naked battle between fear and desire, and that fear is kept in abeyance only through the recurrent urge of desire. . . .

"Toward a Definition of the Female Sensibility," *The Village
Voice 31 May 1973*

3 She takes daily walks on the land that was once the bottom of the sea, marking and classifying, sifting through her thoughts the meaning of the jagged edge of discontent that has begun to make inroads anew insider her.

"Stillness at the Center," *Ms.* (New York) *October 1973*

4 Being a housewife is an illegitimate profession . . . The choice to serve and be protected and plan towards being a family-maker

is a choice that shouldn't be. The heart of radical feminism is to change that.

> "The Daily Illini" *25 April 1981*

5 This is a population in a permanent state of intermittent attachment. Inevitably, the silent apartment waits.

> "On Living Alone," *Approaching Eye Level 1996*

6 Loneliness, when it came, came . . . like a surge of physical illness.

> Ibid.

7 These sentences are born of a concentration in the writer that runs so deep, is turned so far inward, it achieves the lucidity of the poet. . . . The material is at one with the voice speaking.

> On Grace Paley,* *The End of the Novel of Love 1997*
> *See 2437.

8 What was most striking about [Woody] Allen's* humor . . . Is that this Jewish anxiety at the center of his wit touched something alive in America at the moment and went out beyond us. . . . It made Jews of gentiles.

> *Village Voice* article, quoted in *The Haunted Smile, The Story of Jewish Comedians in America* by Lawrence J. Epstein *2001*
> *(1935–), Am. film director, writer, actor, comedian, musician, playwright.

2933. Shusha Guppy (1935–2008)

1 It is very important not to become hard. The artist must always have one skin too few in comparison to other people, so you feel the slightest wind.

> Interview, *The Guardian* (London) *6 April 1988*

2 Like a healthy body that can tolerate germs and impurities without succumbing to disease, the bazaar harboured a legion of parasites—layabouts, con-men, thieves, brokers, urchins and beggars.

> "Haji Mahmood," *The Blindfold Horse: Memories of a Persian Childhood 2004*

3 After a quarter of a century or more, life's colours fade, its contour blur, and even memory mellows.

> Ch. 1, *A Girl in Paris: A Persian Encounter with the West 2007*

2934. Sandra G. Harding (1935–)

1 Scientific and technological change are inherently political, since they redistribute costs and benefits of access to nature's resources in new ways. They tend to widen any pre-existing gaps between the haves and the have-nots unless issues of just distribution are directly addressed.

> *Is Science Multicultural? Postcolonialisms, Feminisms, and Epistemologies 1998*

2935. Barbara Harris (1935–)

1 The man with the navy-blue voice.*

> Quoted in *Observer* (London) *6 August 1976*
> *Re Sir Alfred Hitchcock (1899–1980), British filmmaker and producer.

2 Who wants to be up on the stage all the time? It isn't easy. You have to be awfully invested in the fame aspect, and I really never was. What I cared about was the discipline of acting, whether I did well or not.

> Quoted in *Arizona Republic News* (Phoenix) *2002.*

2936. Jane Howard (1935–1996)

1 The re-entry from encounter groups to reality, and the business of keeping alive the elusive benefits of sensitivity training, are problems that preoccupy every student of the human potential movement.

> "Back Home," *Please Touch 1970*

2 Parents, however old they and we may grow to be, serve among other things to shield us from our sense of doom. As long as they are around, we can avoid the fact of our mortality; we can still be innocent children.

> *A Different Woman 1973*

3 New links must be forged as old ones rust.

> Ch. 1, Ibid.

4 I wish women in the gay liberation movement God-speed, although I take issue with their premise that all men, without exception, are intruding vandals bent only on the oppression of womankind. I submit that some of them can be welcome guests.

> Ch. 9, Ibid.

5 The wider the age range, the stronger the tribe.

> "Families," *Today,* International Child and Youth Care Network (cyc-net.org) *22 November 2000*

2937. Jane Dee Hull (1935–)

1 This is like a freight train coming at us. . . . We've got to clean up these forests. Mother Nature is telling us to do so. We've got to get this under control.

> "Scorched Earth" by Michael Janofsky, *The New York Times 24 June 2002*

2 Congress passes laws, and bureaucracies make regulations. Most of the time, neither one of them makes a lot of sense.

> Ibid.

2938. Joy Kogawa (1935–)

1 The language of her grief is silence. She has learned it well, its idioms its nuances. Over the years the silence with her small body has grown large and powerful.

> p. 17, *Obasan 1981*

2 The memories were drowned in a whirlpool of protective silence. . . For the sake of the children, calmness was maintained.

> p. 26, Ibid.

3 "You have to remember. You are your history. If you cut any of it off you're an amputee. Don't deny the past. Remember everything. If you're bitter, be bitter. Cry it out! Scream! Denial is gangrene."

> p. 60, Ibid.

4 "It matters to get the facts straight . . . Reconciliation can't begin without mutual recognition of the facts."

> p. 219, Ibid.

2939. Myra MacPherson (1935?–)

1 Unless one pulls the plug, there is no escaping the psychic bludgeoning of cable talk shows.

> *Long Time Passing: Vietnam and the Haunted Generation 1984*

2   Above all, Vietnam was a war that asked everything of a few and nothing of most in America.

> Epilogue, Ibid.

3   All his adult life, Bush* has been an influence peddler—trading on his father's name. In quid pro quo fashion, Bush the younger found rich family friends or those seeking political access who were eager to find him a berth in that lily-white bastion for Vietnam draft avoiders, the National Guard, subsidize his baseball team, bail out his failing oil businesses, and drop fat checks into his political coffers.

> "Bush Lite, The record is slim," *The Washington Monthly*
> *April 2000*
> *George W. B- (1946), 43rd President of the United States (2001–09).

2940. Barbara Myerhoff (1935–1985)

1   All rituals are paradoxical and dangerous enterprises, the traditional and improvised, the sacred and the secular. Paradoxical because rituals are conspicuously artificial and theatrical, yet designed to suggest the inevitability and absolute truth of their messages. Dangerous because when we are not convinced by a ritual we may become aware of ourselves as having made them up, thence on the paralyzing realization that we have made up all our truths; our ceremonies, our most precious conceptions and convictions—all are mere inventions.

> *Number Our Days 1979*

2   . . . the Jewish world—and I mean the intensely Jewish world, not the usual secular circles that I move in—have more resources . . . [They] have rituals, they have ceremonies, they have knowledge, they have things to do that other people do not in the cases of illness or emergency of a crisis like this.

> *In Her Own Time* (documentary film) *1986*

3   I came to see the Center elderly as in possession of the philosophers' stone—that universally sought, ever-elusive treasure, harboring the secret that would teach us how to transmute base metals into pure gold. The stone, like the bluebird's feather of happiness, is said to be overlooked precisely because it is so close to us, hidden in the dust at our feet.

> Jewish Women's Archive (jwa.org) *n.d.*

4   Someday I'll be a little old Jewish lady myself.

> Ibid.

2941. Mary Oliver (1935–   )

1   Whoever you are, no matter how lonely,
the world offers itself to your imagination,
calls to you like the wild geese, harsh and exciting—
over and over announcing your place
in the family of things.

> "Wild Geese," *Dream Work 1986*

2   One day you finally knew
what you had to do, and began,
though the voices around you
kept shouting
their bad advice—

> "The Journey," Ibid.

3   Is the soul solid, like iron?
or is it tender and breakable, like
the wings of a moth in the beak of an owl?

> "Some Questions You Might Ask," *New and Selected Poems*
> *1992*

4   Tell me, what is it you plan to do
with your one wild and precious life?

> "The Summer Day," Ibid.

5   . . . creative work needs the whole sky to fly in, and no eye watching until it comes to that certainty which it aspires to . . .

> *Blue Pastures: New and Selected Poems 1995*

6   Only oddly, and not naturally . . . are we found, while awake, in the posture of deliberate or hapless inaction. But such is the posture of the poet, poor laborer.

> *Winter Hours 1999*

7   Everything is all right, say the meter and the rhyme; everything is not all right, say the words.

> Essay on Robert Frost,* Ibid.
> *American poet (1874–1963).

8   But I am devoted to Nature too, and to consider Nature without this appetite—this other-creature-consuming appetite—is to look with shut eyes upon the miraculous interchange that makes things work. . . .

> "Sister Turtle," Ibid.

2942. E. Annie Proulx (1935–   )

1   "Life cripples us in different ways but it gets to everybody . . . Gets you again and again and one day it wins."

> *Postcards 1992*

2   "How money does change a person. Glad I haven't got any to spoil me."

> Ch. 1, Ibid

3   His blood, urine, feces and semen, the tears, strands of hair, vomit, flakes of skin, his infant and childhood teeth, the clippings of finger and toenails, all the effluvia of his body were in that soil, part of that place. The work of his hands had changed the shape of the land, the weirs in the steep ditch beside the lane, the ditch itself, the smooth field were echoes of himself in the landscape, for the laborer's vision and strength persists after the labor is done.

> Ch. 12, Ibid.

4   When you lived alone you could shout at the ceiling.

> Ch. 34, Ibid.

5   The alchemist sea changed fishermen to wet bones, sent boats to drift among the cod, cast them on the landwash.

> Ch. 4, "Cast Away," *The Shipping News 1993*

6   What he knew was that women were shaped like leaves and men fell.

> Ch. 18, "Lobster Pie," Ibid.

7   No, they didn't have any money, the sea was dangerous and men were lost, but it was a satisfying life in a way people today do not understand. There was a joinery of lives all worked together, smooth in places, or lumpy, but joined. The work and the living you did was the same things, not separated out like today.

> Ch. 20, "Gaze Island," Ibid.

8   Archie was an expert at dividing the affairs of life into men's business and women's business. An empty cupboard and a full plate were the man's business, a full cupboard and an empty plate the concern of the woman.

> Ch. 38, "The Sled Dog Driver's Dream," Ibid.

9 The stale coffee is boiling up but he catches it before it goes over the side, pours it into a stained cup and blows on the black liquid, lets a panel of the dream slide forward. If he does not force his attention on it, it might stoke the day, rewarm that old, cold time on the mountain when they owned the world and nothing seemed wrong.

"Brokeback Mountain," *The New Yorker* 13 October 1997

10 There is no happiness like that of a young couple in a little house they have built themselves in a place of beauty and solitude.

"Them Old Cowboy Songs," *Fine Just the Way It Is: Wyoming Stories 3* 2008

2943. Anne Roiphe (1935–)

1 "What the world needs," he said, "is not a Joan of Arc,* the kind of woman who allows herself to be burned on the cross. That's just a bourgeois invention meant to frighten little girls into staying home. What we require is a real female military social leader."

"But that"—I smiled at him—"is just impossible. Women are tied to husband and children. Women are constructed to be penetrated; a sword or a gun in their hands is a joke or a mistake. They are open holes in which things are poured. Occasionally, it's true, a woman can become a volcano, but that's about it."

"Out of Week Two," *Up the Sandbox!* 1970
*See 252.

2 What I'm doing in this car flying down these screaming highways is getting my tail to Juarez so I can legally rid myself of the crummy son-of-a-bitch who promised me a tomorrow like a yummy fruitcake and delivered instead wilted lettuce, rotted cucumber, a garbage of a life.

Long Division 1972

3 She tried to be respectable because respectability kept away the chaos that sometimes overwhelmed her, causing her to call out in her sleep, screaming wild sounds, a warning to the future, a mourning for the past.

Ibid.

4 Reader, you forget that economics precedes religion; worship grew out of eating, not the other way around.

The Pursuit of Happiness 1991

5 "Be careful. . . . There's a reason he's still available."

If You Knew Me 1993

6 We were squeezed between that proverbial rock and hard place. Motherhood by definition requires tending of the other, a sacrifice of self-wishes for the needs of a helpless, hapless human being, and feminism by definition insists on attention being paid to the self, to the full humanity, wishes, desires, capacities of the self. This basic contradiction is not simply the nasty work of a sexist society. It is the lay of the land, the mother of all paradoxes, the irony we cannot bend with mere wishing or might of will. Here are the ingredients of our private and public human tragedy.

Nevertheless I still wanted more children.

Fruitful: A Real Mother in the Modern World 1996

7 He told me he would never do to his son what had been done to him. . . .

1185 Park Avenue: A Memoir 1999

8 If society is a pyramid in which the top comes to a point, they [the Episcopalians] were the point. They did not so much cast a shadow over the rest as provide a source of constant anxiety for the others. That is the place where you weren't wanted. That is the restricted hotel on this block. That is the hospital that doesn't allow Jewish doctors to admit patients. That is the school you won't bother to apply to. "Them" was the word spoken with a touch of awe and a spark of anger.

Ch. 1, Ibid.

9 This was a city that knew how to have a good time: tickertape parades down Wall Street, smoke from the Camel billboard on Times Square, ice skating at Rockefeller Center, bonnets at the Easter parade, tourists at the Empire State Building, bad guys, wannabes on the make at The Stork Club, 21, The Little Club, The El Morocco, drinking the night away watching the Copa girls lift their long legs, greeting the morning with cheesecake at Lindy's.

Ibid.

10 "Out of the void the beautiful world was once formed. These candles are not burning, and in their not burning they leave us in darkness, and this darkness tells us that light will surely return, spring will come, that men are brave and nations can defend themselves against evil-doers. We are not afraid of the dark."

Ch. 1, *Secrets of the City* 2003

2944. Judith Rossner (1935–2005)

1 "Being a witch is like royalty," I said calmly. "You have to inherit it from someone."

Pt. I, *Nine Months in the Life of an Old Maid* 1969

2 It is easier to betray than to remain loyal. It takes far less courage to kill yourself than it takes to make yourself wake up one more time. It's harder to stay where you are than to get out. (For everyone but you, that is.)

Pt. II, Ibid.

3 Love is the direct opposite of hate. By *definition* it's something you can't feel for more than a few minutes at a time, so what's all this bullshit about loving somebody for the rest of your life?

Ibid.

4 So often I heard people paying blind obeisance to change—as though it had some virtue of its own. Change or we will die. Change or we will stagnate. Evergreens don't stagnate.

Ibid.

5 He always said she was smart, but their conversations were a mine field in which at any moment she might make the wrong verbal move and find her ignorance exploding in her face.

Looking for Mr. Goodbar 1975

6 A lie was something that didn't happen but might just as well have.

Ibid.

7 Sometimes she thought that the TV wasn't so much an escape as a filter through which he saw and heard everything but was kept from being affected by it too much.

Ibid.

2945. Françoise Sagan (1935–2004)

1 A strange melancholy pervades me, to which I hesitate to give the grave and beautiful name of sorrow.

Bonjour Tristesse 1954

2 Jazz music is an intensified feeling of nonchalance.
Pt. 1, Ch. 7, *A Certain Smile 1956*

3 We had the same gait, the same habits and lived in the same rhythm; our bodies suited each other and all was well. I had no right to regret his failure to make the tremendous effort required of love, the effort to know and shatter the solitude of another.
Pt. II, Ch. 2, Ibid.

4 After Proust,* there are certain things that simply cannot be done again. He marks off for you the boundaries of your talent.
Interview, *Writers at Work* (First Series), Malcolm Cowley,** ed. *1958*
*Marcel P—, French writer (1871–1922). **American writer, editor, and literary critic (1898–1989).

5 Of course the illusion of art is to make one believe that great literature is very close to life, but exactly the opposite is true. Life is amorphous, literature is formal.
Ch. 9, *La Chamade 1965*

6 To jealousy, nothing is more frightful than laughter.
Ibid.

7 Whoever has not thrilled to speed has not thrilled to life. However madly and hopelessly in love you may be, at 120 miles an hour you are less so. Your blood no longer congeals around your heart; your blood throbs to the extremities of your body, to your fingertips, your toes and your eyelids, now the fateful and tireless guardians of your own life.
With Fondest Regards 1985

2946. Barbara Seaman (1935–2008)
1 In 1957, pregnant with my first child, I told my doctor that I planned to breast-feed. "You wouldn't make a good cow," he said. To his mind that settled the matter, for he gave me a laxative that went straight to the milk and almost finished off my son!
Doctors Against the Pill 1969

2 Probably the easiest thing would be to vasectimize males at the age of 13 after freezing some of their sperm. Then you could unfreeze it only after they have enough money to support a child up to the age of 18.
"The Contraception Conundrum: It's Not Just Birth Control Anymore" by Sarah Boxes, *The New York Times 22 June 1997*

3 I just started out to try and give women plain facts that would help them to make their own decisions and not have to rely on authority figures. I didn't start out to be a muckraker.
Quoted in interview, *Women's E-News* (womensenews.org) *17 October 2003*

4 The U.S. drug industry's responsibility is to employees and share holders. It's the doctors who have the duty to the patients. Too many of them let themselves be snookered, by the gifts and flattery of the drug [representatives] and the misplaced faith in certain eminent doctors and medical professors.
Ibid.

5 [Estrogens] have been used, in the main, for what doctors and scientists hope or believe they can do, not for what they know the products can do. Medical policy on estrogens has been to "shoot first and apologize later" . . . Over the years, hundreds of millions, possibly billions of women, have been lab animals in this unofficial trial. They were not volunteers. They were given no consent forms. And they were put at serious, often devastating risk.
The Greatest Experiment Ever Performed on Women 2007

2947. Merle Shain (1935–1989)
1 We tend to think of the rational as a higher order, but it is often the emotional that marks our lives. One often learns more from ten days of agony than from ten years of contentment. . . .
Pt. I, Ch. 1, *Some Men Are More Perfect Than Others 1973*

2 Most women would rather have someone whisper their name at optimum moments then rocket with contractions to the moon. . . .
Ch. 3, Ibid.

3 So mistresses tend to get a steady diet of whipped cream, but no meat and potatoes, and wives often get the reverse, when both would like a bit of each.
Pt. II, Ch. 4, Ibid.

2948. Shen Rong (1935–)
1 Never having imagined love could be so intoxicating, she almost regretted not finding it earlier.
"At Middle Age," Ch. 3 (1980) Yu Fanqin and Wang Mingjie, trs., *Seven Contemporary Chinese Women Writers*, Gladys Yang,* ed. *1982*
*See 2358.

2 "I don't want a medal or a citation. I just wish your hospital understood how hard it is to be a doctor's husband. As soon as the order comes to go off on medical tours or relief work, she's up and off, leaving the family. She comes back so exhausted from the operating theater, she can't raise a finger to cook a meal. That being the case, if I don't go into the kitchen, who will? I should really be grateful to the 'cultural revolution' for giving me all that time to learn to cook."
Ch. 9, Ibid.

3 "There's no pleasing you!" laughed Jiang. "When you're not used, you complain that your talents are wasted, you live at the wrong time. When you're fully used, you gripe that you're overworked and underpaid!"
Ibid.

4 She had performed such operations umpteen times, but every time she picked up her instruments, she felt like a raw recruit on the battlefield.
Ch. 13, Ibid.

5 So this was dying, no fear, no pain, just life withering away, the senses blurring, slowly sinking, like a leaf drifting on a river.
Ch. 17, Ibid.

2949. Carol Shields (1935–2003)
1 This business of being a guy, it never lets up.
The Republic of Love 1991

2 . . . men spend whole lifetimes preparing answers to certain questions that will never be asked of them.
Happenstance 1993

3 . . . the clean preserving gel of history.
Ibid.

4   Life is an endless recruiting of witnesses.
The Stone Diaries 1993

5   When we say a thing or an event is real, never mind how suspect it sounds, we honor it. But when a thing is made up—regardless of how true and just it seems—we turn up our noses. That's the age we live in. The documentary age.
Ibid.

2950. Fanchon Shur (1935–)

1   When we ignore human movement we ignore our innate ability to perceive and respond to the process of becoming. We are naturally expressive through our bodies, and our rituals either build spontaneity or inhibit that option.
"My Dance Work as a Reflection of a Jewish Woman's Spirituality" (1989), *Four Centuries of Jewish Women's Spirituality* Ellen M. Umansky* & Dianne Ashton, eds. *1992*
*See 4011.

2   Our tissues, our cells remember. . . .
Ibid.

4   . . . *I learned of Faith by touching earth, I learned of faith by listening to breath move through me . . . The faith I found was in my own body as spiritual truth, and my felt "thought" or symbol creation has me imaging my own body as goddess, as earth, as shechinah*. . . .*
Ibid.
*(a.k.a. shekinah) A visible manifestation of the divine presence as described in Jewish theology, usually associated with the feminine aspects of god.

4   Tradition implies process and change, the movement of the past into the future, the continual forging of links on an unending chain.
Introduction to New Blessings, *The Book of Blessings: A Feminist-Jewish Reconstruction of Prayer 1992*

5   *We will uproot violence by facing it in ourselves;*
by letting heal that which we have repressed;
by rejecting the religious, philosophical
and political beliefs that permit us to subordinate,
exclude,
isolate,
oppress,
and kill others.
Dedication, *Tallit: Prayer Shawl* (a dance) *n.d.*

2951. Joan Micklin Silver (1935–)

1   Standing erect, like overgrown bookends on either side of Mr. MacAfee's desk, were two Air Force officers.
Ch. 1, *Limbo,* with Linda Gottlieb* *1972*
*See 3265.

2   Just as war bound together the men under fire, Mary Kaye thought, it united the women left behind back home.
Ch. 5, Ibid.

3   The mother of an eighteen-year-old boy who had had to secure his mother's consent for enlisting in the Army, she now cried at the slightest provocation. "How could I tell him not to go?" she once asked Fay Clausen, the tears brimming in her eyes. "He always loved guns—from the time he was a little boy he would play with toy guns, BB guns—you know, pretended he was in the marines and things. I once got him that big il-lustrated history of the Second World War—it cost seventeen dollars—from American Heritage, and he read it over and over again."
Ch. 8, Ibid.

2952. Zulu Sofola (1935–1995)

1   ULOKO (to Ogoli, his mother). . . . Did you speak for me? Did you let Ibekwe know that an injustice was being done to you by his action? Did you let anyone know that, for money, the wife whom you had planned for your son was being forced from your hands and being given to someone else? Did you tell them that my life would become nothing if the one I love so much was given away to someone else? Did you?
Act II, Sc. 2, *Wedlock of the Gods 1971*

2   [There are] aspects in traditional society where customs and moral precepts set themselves at war against individual citizens.
Essay by Olu Obafemi in *Contemporary British Dramatists,*
K. A. Berney, ed. *1993*

2953. Audrey Grace Thomas (1935–)

1   How could I tell her that she was wrong about things when essentially she was right? Life was cruel, people hurt and betrayed one another, grew old and died alone.
Songs My Mother Taught Me 1973

2   . . . cats everywhere asleep on the shelves like motorized bookends.
Ibid.

2954. Sheila Tobias (1935–)

1   Not everyone learns everything. Many of us elect to stay within a fairly narrow comfort zone of knowledge.
Ch. 1, *Overcoming Math Anxiety 1978*

2   A slight discomfort with mathematics acquired in elementary or secondary school can develop into full-fledged syndrome of anxiety and avoidance by the time one has graduated from school and gone to work.
Ibid.

3   People who don't know what math is don't know what math isn't.
Ibid.

4   In feminist theory, gender, unlike sex, is defined as *socially constructed role,* which means that it is the result of political arrangements and is amenable to social and political analysis. To understand this idea, we have to think about roles the way social scientists do—not as God or nature determined, but as how and with what rationale a particular culture distributes certain tasks, certain privileges, and certain responsibilities.
Ch. 1, *Faces Of Feminism: An Activist's Reflections on the Women's Movement 1998*

5   In its narrowest definition, politics has to do with participation in government, party politics, and elective or appointed office. More broadly, however, politics has to do with power: getting people to do what you want them to do.
Ibid.

2955. Taeko Tomioka (1935–)

1   My favorite question was, "What would you do if we had a baby?" I always asked this question after I'd had sex with a

young man, and I always looked forward to hearing their responses.

"Straw Dogs," *Unmapped Territories, New Women's Fiction from Japan*, ed. and tr. *1991*

2 I've always wondered whether a relationship can be established simply by the entry of part of a stranger's body into mine.

Ibid.

3 I wanted to pull out the guts of his dark mood and devour them with my teeth.

Ibid.

4 Izumi hadn't seemed to be aware of the possibility that his penis was there to excite the woman and give her pleasure, that he could pierce the woman and her pleasure together like a skewer for barbecuing chicken and onions.

Ibid.

2956. Jane Wagner (1935–)

1 LILY.* One thing I have no worry about is whether
God exists.
But it has occurred to me that God has Alzheimer's and has forgotten
we exist.

Pt. 1, *The Search for Signs of Intelligent Life in the Universe 1986*

*Lily Tomlin; see 3009.

2 KATE. I am sick of being the victim of trends I reflect
but don't even understand.

Ibid.

3 TRUDY. See, it's not so much what we know,
but how we know, and what
it is about us that needs to know.
The intriguing part: Of all the things we've learned, we still haven't learned
where did this desire to want to know come from?

Pt. II, Ibid.

2957. Marina von Neumann Whitman (1935–)

1 I never took a lifetime view at 20 and decided where I wanted to be at 50. Since I was trailblazing, there weren't many rules about what you were and were not supposed to be. Young women today feel such a burden to prove themselves.

Quoted in "The Corporate Guru of Global Economics" by Beth McGoldrick, *Working Woman November 1988*

2 I've learned only that you never say never.

Ibid.

2958. Monique Wittig (1935–2003)

1 There was a time when you were not a slave, remember that . . . You say there are no words to describe this time. You say it does not exist. But remember. Make an effort to remember. Or, failing that, invent.

Les Guerillières 1969

*Female guerrilla warriors.

2 The women say that they perceive their bodies in their entirety. They say that they do not favor any of its parts on the grounds that it was formerly a forbidden object. They say that they do not want to become prisoners of their own ideology.

Ibid.

3 The language you speak poisons your glottis tongue palate lips. They say, the language you speak is made up of words that are killing you. They say, the language you speak is made up of signs that rightly speaking designate what men have appropriated.

Ibid.

2959. Madeleine Albright (1936–)

1 Force, and the credible possibility of its use, are essential to defend our vital interests and to keep America safe. But force alone can be a blunt instrument, and there are many problems it cannot solve.

Speech (7 February 1997), *Vital Speeches of the Day 15 April 1997*

2 Only in America could a refugee girl from Europe become Secretary of State.

"Albright retakes citizenship oath" (p. 19A), *USA Today 11 November 1998*

3 The United States will never apologize for speaking or publishing the truth.

"Albright chides China . . . ," *Seattle Post-Intelligencer 2 March 1999*

4 Societies are more, not less, likely to be stable when citizens have an outlet to express their political views.

Ibid.

5 We determined some time ago that it was not a good idea to link human rights and trade, and that we actually make better progress in both when they are not linked.

Ibid.

2960. Jean M. Auel (1936–)

1 "You cannot see the spirit of your totem because he is part of you, inside you. Yet, he will tell you. Only you must learn to understand. If you have a decision to make, he will help you. He will give you a sign if you make the right choice. . . . It may be a stone you have never seen before or a root with a special shape that has meaning to you. You must learn to understand with your heart and mind, not your eyes and ears, then you will know.

Ch. 9, *The Clan of the Cave Bear 1980*

2 Six men, pitifully weak by comparison, using skill and intelligence and cooperation and daring, had killed the gigantic creature no other predator could. No matter how fast or how strong or how cunning, no four-legged hunter could match their feat.

Ch. 14, Ibid.

3 Zoug's pride was the pride of a true teacher for a pupil who had exceeded; a student who paid attention, learned well, and then did the master one better.

Ch. 15, Ibid.

2961. Rona Barrett (1936–)

1 It's ironic, but until you can free those final monsters within the jungle of yourself, your life, your soul is up for grabs.

Prologue, *Miss Rona: An Autobiography 1974*

2 . . . the *healthy,* the *strong* individual, is the one who asks for help when he needs it. Whether he's got an abscess on his knee or in his soul.

Ch. 15, Ibid.

2962. Jeanine Basinger (1936–)

1 A small town is automatically a world of pretense. Since everyone knows everyone else's business, it becomes the job of the populace to act as if they don't know what is going on instead of its being their job to try to find out.

Ch. 1, *A Woman's View* 1993

2 In movies about women, all important historical and natural events are translated into the terms of a woman's daily life.... At the same time that big events are made small, personal, small events are made huge.... Thus, the woman's film is a genre that generously empowers a sex that society has relegated to secondary status.

Ch. 7, Ibid.

3 ...in the movies Paris is designed as a backdrop for only three things—love, fashion shows, and revolution.

Ibid.

4 The stars of silent film and of the great studio system were gods and goddesses.

The Star Machine 2007

2963. Rose Bird (1936–1999)

1 If our courts lose their authority and their rulings are no longer respected, there will be no one left to resolve the divisive issues that can rip the social fabric apart.... The courts are a safety valve without which no democratic society can survive.

The Los Angeles Times 11 September 1978

2 The role of the press and the protections which we afford it are today more important than ever before, because we dwell in a society where belief in our governments and in the strength of our institutions is declining.

Quoted in "Hue & Cry," *San Francisco Chronicle* 13 May 1979

3 We must use our courage to ensure a judiciary not governed by the daily polls but by the rules of law, serving not the special interest of the few but the best interest of all, devoted not to self-preservation, but to the preservation of those great constitutional principles which history has bequeathed to us.

The Los Angeles Times 20 July 1982

4 The courts are an easy scapegoat because at a time when everything has to be boiled down to easy slogans, we speak in subtleties.

Newsweek (New York) 9 August 1982

5 Courts are an aristocratic institution in a democracy. That's the dilemma for an institution that has the function of reviewing the will of the people. We're bound to be "anti-majoritarian."

Quoted in "Calm at the center of the storm," by Anthony Lewis, *The New York Times News Service* 23 October 1986

2964. Martha Gross Boesing (1936–)

1 ABIGAIL. I have this malady: I try to make sense out of everything that happens to me. I cling to the neurotic belief that if I could understand what events mean, then I could stop obsessing about them.

Act I, *The Web* 1981

2965. Jean Shinoda Bolen (1936–)

1 There is a potential heroine in every woman.

Ch. 14, *Goddesses in Every Woman: A New Psychology of Women* 1984

2 ...the necessity of choosing a "path with heart." I feel that one must deliberate and then act, must scan every life choice with rational thinking but then base the decision on whether one's heart will be in it. No other person can tell you if your heart is involved, and logic cannot provide an answer.

Ibid.

3 An estimated forty million baby-boomer generation women turn fifty in the few years preceding and following the year 2000, joining those women's movement-women who led the way a decade earlier. This could very well constitute a critical mass of women of wisdom, authority, and action who may determine the direction that humanity will take. What we do or fail to do at this liminal time will not only shape the course of our personal lives, but collectively will affect the third millennium and with that, the future of the planet.

"Wisewomen at the Crossroad," *The Fabric of the Future: Women Visionaries of Today Illuminate the Path to Tomorrow,* M. J. Ryan, ed. 1998

4 There is a stirring in the psyches of a generation of women's movement-influenced older women, one that calls on us to be an influence, to say what we know, to enter the phase of the wisewoman, whose concern is for other generations and the greater good.

Ibid.

2966. Sandy Boucher (1936–)

1 My father's voice says, Watch out for little men. They are more aggressive, meaner, nastier, trickier, more combative. A big man is secure in his strength, so he doesn't push it. A little man is always proving something. The same goes for little dogs versus big dogs.

"Mountain Radio," *Assaults and Rituals* 1975

2 Thus we were equally, though differently, sophisticated, and our game was the same: not to *care*—to arrive at each other without being there.

Ibid.

2967. Trisha Brown (1936–)

1 Yes, I am still dancing and still enraptured by it. In spite of the stereotype, I believe my dancing in some ways is better than ever. It got more amazing and deeper. Like everything.

Quoted in "Choreographer returns to NW ..." by R. M. Campbell, D1, *Seattle Post-Intelligencer, What's Happening* 9 April 1993

2 I've felt like an apprentice all my life, both as a dancer and choreographer. Now [that I'm older], it's different. I've discovered a new sense of freedom.

Wise Women Joyce Tenneson* 2002
*See 3619.

2968. A. S. Byatt (1936–)

1 Pain hardens, and great pain hardens greatly, whatever the comforters say, and suffering does not ennoble, though it may occasionally lend a certain rigid dignity of manner to the suffering frame.

Quoted in *The Daily Telegraph* (London) 21 July 1986

2969. Joan Chittister (1936–)

1 What is the depth of the American soul if we can allow destruction to be done in our name and the name of "liberation" and

never even demand an accounting of its costs, both personal and public, when it is over?

> "Is there anything left that matters?" *National Catholic Reporter 27 May 2003*

2 The spirit we have, not the work we do, is what makes us important to the people around us.

> Ibid.

3 . . . we may well be the ones Proverbs warns when it reminds us: "Kings take pleasure in honest lips; they value the one who speaks the truth." The point is clear: If the people speak and the king doesn't listen, there is something wrong with the king. If the king acts precipitously and the people say nothing, something is wrong with the people.

> Ibid.

2970. Lucille Clifton (1936–)

1 the question for you is
what have you ever traveled toward
more than your own safety?

> "further note to clark" from notes to clark kent,
> *The Book of Light 1993*

2 . . . come celebrate
with me that everyday
something has tried to kill me
and has failed.

> "Song at Midnight," Ibid.

3 maybe i should have wanted less.
maybe i should have ignored the bowl in me
burning to be filled.

> "climbing" *n.d.*

4 if the little girl lies
still enough
shut enough
hard enough
shapeshifter may not
walk tonight

> "shapeshifter poems," 3 *n.d.*

5 the time i dropped your almost body down
down to meet the waters under the city
and run one with the sewage to the sea
what did i know about waters rushing back
what did i know about drowning
or being drowned

> "the lost baby poem" *n.d.*

6 it is the great circulation
of the earth's body, like the blood
of the gods, this river in which the past
is always flowing. every water
is the same water coming round.

> "the mississippi river empties into the gulf" *n.d.*

2971. Johnnetta B. Cole (1936–)

1 The more we pull together toward a new day, the less it matters what pushed us apart in the past.

> Quoted by Mayor Shirley Franklin, State of the City Address
> (Atlanta), *5 January 2004*

2 But let our remembering and our learning and our transformation because of a day called September 11 never be the day after, but constantly present.

> Speech, "The Power of Diversity", 3rd Annual Women &
> Power Conference *September 2004*

3 Clearly when the good Lord, she made the world, she made us as an example of the wonderful Chinese saying; one flower never makes a spring. I don't care how gorgeous this bouquet of lilacs happens to be or how exquisite the rose is, how enticing this bunch of birds of paradise. It's only in the diversity of the blooming that we really embrace spring.

> Ibid.

4 In a time of great global change humanity is still relying on the old myth of survival and domination. We need a new myth, a new vision, a new definition of power and leadership.

We must go away from the old model and toward one of creative cooperation on our small and threatened planet. The world needs women to imagine, define, and lead us toward a sane and sustainable culture. A culture of soul. A culture that values life more than war. People more than profits. And hope more than despair.

> Ibid.

2972. Marva Nettles Collins (1936–)

1 I take the children no one else wants.

> Quoted in *Instructor January 1982*

2 [My father] never presumed that any task was too challenging for me to try nor any concept too difficult for me to grasp. He gave me assignments that helped build my confidence and gave me a sense of responsibility.

> Quoted in *Ebony February 1985*

3 I think what everybody calls a miracle is just common sense. . . . You can look at the attitudes when people come in.* That's why they call it a miracle. These are black kids and they're not supposed to know the things they know and achieve the way they are achieving.

> Quoted in *I Dream a World* by Brian Lanker *1989*
> *Re: Westside Preparatory School in Chicago, which she founded
> in 1975 for poor inner-city children.

2973. Meinrad Craighead (1936–)

1 I draw and paint from my own myth of personal origin. Each painting I make begins from some deep source where my mother and grandmother, and all my fore-mothers, still live; it is as if the line moving from pen or brush coils back to the original Matrix. Sometimes I feel like a cauldron of ripening images where memories turn into faces and emerge from my vessel. So my creative life is itself an image of God the Mother and her unbroken story of emergence in our lives.

> *The Mother's Songs, Images of God the Mother 1986*

2 When you wonder, you give thanks, and giving thanks is a ritual. Ritual is the need to do beautiful actions with beautiful things in order to say 'thank you' for this divine beauty we all share.

> Quoted in *Soul Sisters, The Five Sacred Qualities of a
> Woman's Soul* by Pythia Peay *2002*

2974. Marlene Dixon (1936–)

1 The institution of marriage is the chief vehicle for the perpetuation of the oppression of women; it is through the role of wife that the subjugation of women is maintained. In a very real way the role of wife has been the genesis of women's rebellion throughout history.

> *Why Women's Liberation? Racism and Male Supremacy 1969*

2 Whatever the faults and weaknesses of Women's Liberation in the United States and Canada, it was a historical event of worldwide importance.

The Rise and Demise of Women's Liberation: A Class Analysis 1977

2975. Elizabeth Hanford Dole (1936–)

1 The time is ripe for a woman President. Definitely in our lifetime. There are many women who are prepared.

Quoted in "Women Who Could Be President" by Jane Ciabattari, *Parade Magazine* 7 February 1999

2976. Nell Dunn (1936–)

1 JOSIE. He made me wild last night, we was having it and I was really getting into it and enjoying, when he's come. "Hold up!" I says. "What about me?" Well, after that I made him plate me for an hour till I come, every time he lifts his head I push it back down—I wouldn't even let him up to breathe . . . I can feel it from the bottom of my toes to the top of my skull. It's as if something pealed right through my body . . . I hadn't come like that for months. It did me the world of good.

Sc. 1, *Steaming* 1981

2977. Jane Fletcher Geniesse (1936–)

1 It was so important to be attractive. It was the crucial factor in a woman's life. A friend of her mother's had once remarked that sexiness in a woman brings power; for a man, power brings sexiness. Her mother had only partially inclined her head, as if she could not entirely concur with a view so baldly stated. But Sarah had agreed and now, more than ever as she grew older, she was aware of an insatiable need to be reassured by the nod of a bus driver, the smile of the doorman, a pleasantry from a sales clerk—those glances that not only confirmed that she was good-looking, even desirable, but were incontrovertible evidence that in this vast, anonymous city she did, in fact, exist.

The Riches of Life 1976

2 Together, from the white counterpane, they removed her folded laundry, pulled back the covers and joined in the hot familiar exercise of love that was no more exciting, yet not less so, than it had been since they first separately realized at some distinct but certain point that they were partners in a trust and no longer impassioned explorers of a mysterious frontier.

Yet, as he entered her, her eyes were tightly closed, and deep in a part of her that was beyond loyalty, she imagined no one in particular, merely another face and a different body from her husband's. As for him, when they were done, he asked softly in the darkness: "Will I have clean underwear for tomorrow in that pile over there?"

Ibid.

3 Freya could use the Koran to venture delicately into such intimate subjects as polygamy or concubinage and especially the lively topic of the veil, a custom dating back to Hammurabi's code and traditionally the mark of a virtuous woman. The farther she traveled, the more Freya would hear traditionalists among the ladies of the harems insist that the veil gave them freedom. Not only did it confer dignity but, concealed in the anonymous veil, they could go about their business in privacy.

Passionate Nomad: The Life of Freya Stark * 1999
*See 1785.

4 As she, Lucy and their guide, tied together with ropes, struggled up the Winkler Turm near Vajolet, Freya slipped. The others

were already out of sight. With the rope tight beneath her armpits, she swung in an excruciatingly slow circle over the Alpine meadow far below. As the arc brought her back to the cliff wall, she was just able to grasp a handhold and pull herself painfully up and over the rock, to where her friends were waiting. . . . The peace she'd felt in those minutes when she floated out of control remained a strangely comforting memory. If this was all there was to death, then death had lost its terror—and she could handle anything.

Ibid.

5 In times of confusion, suffering, or dread of the future, otherwise reasonable men and women have willingly handed over their freedom to another deemed stronger and endowed with greater certainty—usually a leader they believe to be in touch with a "higher" authority.

Ibid.

6 Listening, entranced, the pilgrims heard the city find its voice: shopkeepers chattering under them in the cobbled street, a donkey's bray, a semi-naked dervish ringing his bell and crying for alms, the pillowed feet of camels shuffling toward the souk,* their drivers shouting through the gathering crowds. As quickly as they could relish a breakfast of hot flatbread and strong coffee, the pilgrims sallied forth from their dirty caravanserai into the stream of varied humanity that was Jerusalem in 1881.

Ibid.

*An open-air market in an Arab city.

7 *Re the George W. Bush* administration:* Their lack of curiosity and their self-righteous conviction that they alone knew what was best for the country, that somehow they were entitled to flout its laws, has been a tragedy for millions and earned the world's opprobrium.

"Why Obama," ** largeheartedboy.com *8 August 2008*
*(1946–), 43rd President of the United States (2001–09).
**(1961–), 44th President of the United States (2009–).

8 Sarah Palin* is a throwback to this fundamentalist past and her autocratic inclinations (attempting to fire those who disagree), her reliance on an intimate circle of loyalists (her husband and her high school pals whom she has rewarded with high-paying jobs), her misuse of power (her per diem charges to the tax payer for days at home), her falsehoods and bombast (denying that she supported the "Bridge to Nowhere"), her invocations of God to determine her course (the Iraq war, she believes, was "God's plan"), and lastly her messianic world view (She has been quoted as saying that she believes "Jesus will return in my lifetime.")—all this disturbs me deeply.

Ibid. *1 October 2008*
*See 4684.

2978. Sandra Gilbert (1936–)

1 Examining the psychosocial implications of a "haunted" ancestral mansion, such a tale* explores the tension between parlor and attic, the psychic split between the lady who submits to male dicta and the lunatic who rebels. But in examining these matters the paradigmatic female story inevitably considers also the equally uncomfortable spatial options of expulsion into the cold outside or suffocation in the hot indoors, and in addition it often embodies an obsessive anxiety both about starvation to the point of disappearance and about monstrous inhabitation.

(p. 86), *The Madwoman in the Attic: The Woman Writer and The Nineteenth-Century Literary Imagination*, with Susan Gubar** 1979
**Jane Eyre* by Charlotte Brontë; see 934:2–14. **See 3507.

2 I wanted to fall, I was falling, I had fallen
into the hissing crevices, the lanes of ice

where I knew you wandered, shivering
even in your Irish sweater.
"October 6, 1991: Seattle, Looking for Mount Rainier," *Ghost Volcano* 1995

3 If you've lost a gorgeous orange, no number of delicious apples
can replace its glow and sweetness.
Wrongful Death: A Medical Tragedy 1995

2979. Carol Gilligan (1936–   )

1 Implicitly adopting the male life as the norm, they have tried
to fashion women out of a masculine cloth. It all goes back, of
course, to Adam and Eve—a story which shows, among other
things, that if you make a woman out of man, you are bound
to get into trouble. In the life cycle, as in the Garden of Eden,
the woman has been the deviant.
Ch. 1, *In a Different Voice* 1982

2 The blind willingness to sacrifice people to truth, however, has
always been the danger of an ethics abstracted from life. This
willingness links Gandhi to the biblical Abraham, who prepared to sacrifice the life of his son in order to demonstrate
the integrity and supremacy of his faith. Both men, in the limitations of their fatherhood, stand in implicit contrast to the
woman* who comes before Solomon and verifies her motherhood by relinquishing truth in order to save the life of her
child. . . .
Ch. 3, Ibid.
*Prostitute of Jerusalem, mother of the living child; see 37.

3 Thus changes in women's rights change women's moral judgements, seasoning mercy with justice by enabling women to
consider it moral to care not only for others but for themselves.
Ch. 5, Ibid.

4 While an ethic of justice proceeds from the premise of equality—that everyone should be treated the same—an ethic of
care rests on the premise of nonviolence—that no one should
be hurt.
Ch. 6, Ibid.

5 As the river of a girl's life flows into the sea of Western culture,
she is in danger of drowning or disappearing.
(1990), Quoted in Ch. 1, *The War Against Boys: How
Misguided Feminism Is Harming Our Young Men* by Christina
Hoff Sommers* 2000
*See 4007.

6 Maybe love is like rain, sometimes gentle, sometimes torrential,
flooding, eroding, quiet, steady, filling the earth, collecting in
hidden springs. When it rains, when we love, life grows.
Ch. 1, *The Birth of Pleasure* 2002

2980. Natalya Gorbanevskaya (1936–   )

1 Opening the window, I open myself.
Untitled poem, *Poems, the Trial, Prison* 1972

2 I am awaiting the birth of my child quite calmly, and neither
my pregnancy nor the birth will prevent me from doing what
I wish—which includes participating in every protest against
any act of tyranny.
Red Square at Noon 1972

2981. Blu Greenberg (1936–   )

1 The ink flows, the pen chases
Its shadow across the page
Seldom does the phone ring
Interrupting thought
"Resisting Yom Hashoah 1985," St. 4, *Four Centuries of
Jewish Women's Spirituality* Ellen M. Umansky* & Dianne
Ashton, eds. *1992*
*See 4011.

2 Why must I give them
Victory anew
The laughing tormentors
In their graves
Who rise to assault my calendar
"Resisting Yom Hashoah 1985," St. 7, Ibid.

3 Renewal of the cycle
Expectation and arousal
Women leaving clean and shiny
Young brides and premenopausals.
"The *Mikvah*," St. 1, Ibid.

4 Once I had tasted of the fruit of the tree of knowledge, there
was no going back.
Quoted in "Coming Out as Jewish Women," p. 292, *The
Journey Home, How Jewish Women Shaped Modern America*
Joyce Antler* 1997
*See 3619

2982. Judith Guest (1936–   )

1 The small seed of despair cracks open and sends experimental
tendrils upward to the fragile skin of calm holding him together.
Ch. 1, *Ordinary People* 1976

2 Riding the train gives him too much time to think, he has decided. Too much thinking can ruin you.
Ch. 4, Ibid.

3 He had left off being a perfectionist then, when he discovered
that not promptly kept appointments, not a house circum-
spectly clean, not membership in Onwentsia, or the Lake Forest
Golf and Country Club, or the Lawyer's Club, not power, or
knowledge, or goodness—not *anything*—cleared you through
the terrifying office of chance; that it is chance and not perfection that rules the world.
Ch. 11, Ibid.

4 How would you describe your marriage, in terms of knowing
each other? In terms of being friends? Of understanding that
hopelessly intricate network of clash and resolution that has
been woven over the last twenty years? Two separate, distinct
personalities, not separate at all, but inextricably bound, soul
and body and mind, to each other, how did we get so far apart
so fast?
Ch. 19, Ibid.

5 "Geez, if I could get through to you, kiddo, that depression is
not sobbing and crying and *giving vent*, it is plain and simple
reduction of feeling. Reduction, see? Of all feeling. People who
keep stiff upper lips find that it's damn hard to smile."
Ch. 27, Ibid.

2983. Sandra Hochman (1936–   )

1 What I wanted
Was to be myself again.
"The Inheritance," *Love Letters from Asia* 1967

2984. Glenda Jackson (1936–   )

1   Acting is not about dressing up. Acting is about stripping bare. The whole essence of learning lines is to forget them so you can make them sound like you thought of them that instant.
Sunday Telegraph (London) 26 July 1992

2985. Sonia Johnson (1936?–   )

1   I liked the *name* of the amendment. I couldn't help feeling uneasy that the church was opposing something with a name as beautiful as the *Equal Rights* Amendment.
From Housewife to Heretic 1981

2   In our patriarchal world, we are all taught—whether we like to think we are or not—that God, being male, values maleness much more than he values femaleness . . . that in order to propitiate God, women must propitiate men. After all, God won't like us if we don't please those nearest to his heart, if we don't treat his cronies well.
Ibid.

3   I am a warrior in the time of women warriors; the longing for justice is the sword I carry, the love of womankind is my shield.
Ibid.

4   Women cannot serve two masters at once who are urgently beaming antithetical orders. . . . Either we believe in patriarchy—the rule of men over women—or we believe in equality.
Ibid.

2986. Barbara Jordan (1936–1996)

1   I live a day at a time. Each day I look for a kernel of excitement. In the morning, I say: "What is my exciting thing for today?" Then, I do my day. Don't ask me about tomorrow.
Quoted in "Where is Barbara Jordan Today?" by Malcolm Boyd, *Parade Magazine* 16 February 1986

2   When the Constitution was completed on the Seventeenth of September in 1787, I was not included in that "We, the people . . ."
Speech, House Judiciary Committee hearings (1974),* Quoted in *Twentieth-Century Women Political Leaders* by Claire Price-Groff 1998
*Jordan was an African-American woman.

3   One hundred and forty-four years ago, members of the Democratic Party met for the first time in a convention to select their Presidential candidate. Since that time, Democrats have continued to convene once every four years to draft a party platform and nominate a Presidential candidate. Our meeting this week continues that tradition. There is something different and special about this opening night. I am a keynote speaker.*
Opening words, Keynote Address, Democratic National Convention (12 July 1976), Ibid.
*Reference to to her race and gender, both firsts at any major national party convention.

4   Are we to be one people bound together by common spirit . . . or will we become a divided nation?
Ibid.

5   We are a people in a quandary about the present and in search of the future . . . We are a people in search of a national community.
Closing words, Ibid.

6   This is the great danger America faces—that we will cease to be one nation and become instead a collection of interest groups: city against suburb, region against region, individual against individual; each seeking to satisfy private wants. If that happens, who then will speak for America? Who then will speak for the common good?"
Speech, Quoted in *Barbara Jordan: Speaking the Truth with Eloquent Thunder* by Max Sherman 2007

7   Don't call for black power or green power. Call for brain power.
Ibid.

2987. June Jordan (1936–2002)

1   "But what's more important. Building a bridge or taking care of a baby?"
New Life, New Room 1975

2   The purpose of polite behavior is never virtuous. Deceit, surrender, and concealment: these are not virtues. The goal of the mannerly is comfort, per se.
"Civil Wars" (1972), *Civil Wars* 1981

3   Self-determination has to mean that the leader is your individual gut, and heart, and mind or we're talking about power, again, and its rather well-known impurities.
Ibid.

4   We do not deride the fears of prospering white America. A nation of violence and private property has every reason to dread the violated and the deprived.
"Black Studies: Bringing Back the Person" (*Evergreen Review*, October 1969), *Moving Towards Home: Political Essays* 1989

5   In America, you can segregate the people, but the problems will travel.
"Problems of Language in a Democratic State" (1982), Ibid.

6   If any of us hopes to survive, s/he must meet the extremity of the American female condition with immediate and political response. The thoroughly destructive and indefensible subjugation of the majority of Americans cannot continue except at the peril of the entire body politic.
"The Case for the Real Majority" (1982), Ibid.

7   It sure did seem she wanted him to lose
his job because she could not find
the keys
he could not find
"War and Memory," I, St. 1 (1989), *The Woman That I Am, The Literature and Culture of Contemporary Women of Color*, D. Soyini Madison,* ed. 1994
*See 3912.

8   Crowd counts at the rallies.
Body counts on the news.
Ketchup on the steps of universities.
Blood on the bandages around the head of the Vietnamese woman shot between the eyes.
Big guys.
"War and Memory," V, St. 2 (1989), Ibid.

9   a make-
believe Black man
a mediocre mediocrity of apple polish
brown nose cut-throat
"Letter to Mrs. Virginia Thomas, Wife of Whatzhisname* Lamentably Appointed to the Supreme Courte, U.S.A.," St. 1, *Kissing God Goodbye: New Poems 1991–1996* 1997
*Reference to Clarence Thomas (1948–   ), appointed in 1991.

2988. Evelyn Fox Keller (1936–)

1 The complement of the scientific mind is, of course, Nature—viewed so ubiquitously as female.

"Gender and Science," *Psychoanalysis and Contemporary Thought: A Quarterly of Integrative Studies 1978*

2 [Barbara McClintock]* didn't adopt a masculine ideal, nor did she adopt a purely feminine ideal. She made use of the full range of human capacity . . . and all her intuitive strengths, in the service of science. . . . It doesn't matter that she was a woman. One could find men in that tradition as well.

Quoted in *A Feeling for the Organism: The Life and Work of Barbara McClintock 1983*

*See 1952.

3 The need to dominate nature is, in this view, a project of the need to dominate other human beings.

Reflections on Gender and Science 1985

4 In my vision of science, it is not the taming of nature that is sought, but the taming of hegemony.

Ibid.

5 Not only does our characterization of science thereby become colored by the biases of patriarchy and sexism, but simultaneously our evaluation of masculine and feminine becomes affected by the prestige of science.

Quoted in *Feminist Research Methods*, Joyce McCarl Nielsen, ed. *1990*

2989. Barbara B. Kennelly (1936–)

1 A vote to impeach on the basis of the facts and materials assembled by the Office of the Independent Counsel is a vote to lower dramatically and inalterably the bar to future impeachments.

Until now the House has very much held a high standard for impeachment, keeping with the Constitution dictum that impeachment be reserved exclusively for high crimes and misdemeanors.

House debate on impeachment against President Clinton,* *Federal News Service 19 December 1998*

*William Jefferson C- (1946–), 42nd President of the United States (1993–2001).

2 We should be using taxpayer dollars to promote quality in Medicare, instead of bestowing unwarranted subsidies on inefficient private plans that serve a fraction of Medicare beneficiaries.

Speech, Hearing on "Selling to Seniors: The Need for Accountability and Oversight of Marketing and Sales by Medicare Private Plans", *U.S. Senate Committee on Finance 7 February 2008*

2990. Florence King (1936–)

1 No matter which sex I went to bed with, I never smoked on the street.

Confessions of a Failed Southern Lady 1985

2 Chinks in America's egalitarian armor are not hard to find. Democracy is the fig leaf of elitism.

"Democracy," *Reflections in a Jaundiced Eye 1989*

3 Owning your own home is America's unique recipe for avoiding revolution and promoting pseudo-equality at the same time. To keep citizens puttering in their yards instead of sputtering on the barricades, the government has gladly deprived itself of billions in tax revenues by letting home "owners" deduct mortgage interest payments.

Ibid.

4 The proliferation of support groups suggests to me that too many Americans are growing up in homes that do not contain a grandmother. A home without a grandmother is like an egg without salt and Helpists know it. They have jumped into the void left by the disappearance of morbid old ladies from the bosom of the American family.

"Does Your Child Taste Salty?" Ibid.

5 Any hope that America would finally grow up vanished with the rise of fundamentalist Christianity.

"Good King Herod," Ibid.

6 He travels fastest who travels alone, and that goes double for she. Real feminism is spinsterhood.

"Spinsterhood Is Powerful," Ibid.

7 Humor inspires sympathetic good-natured laughter and is favored by the "healing-power" gang. Wit goes for the jugular, not the jocular, and it's the opposite of football; instead of building character, it tears it down.

"The State of the Funny Bone," Ibid.

2991. Dacia Maraini (1936–)

1 He talked and talked because he didn't know what to say.

Ch. 1, *The Holiday 1962*

2 "Our strength is like the sea," Pompei announced, lifting his chin up proudly. "Nothing can divert it."

Ch. 8, Ibid.

3 A woman who writes poetry and knows
she is woman, has no choice but to hang on
   tight
to contents because the sophistication
of forms is something that belongs to power
and the power that woman has is always an
un-power, a scorching inheritance never entirely
   hers.

"Woman's Poetry," *Donne Mie (My Dear Woman) 1974*

2992. Mary McIntosh (1936–)

See Michele Barrett, 3885: 1.

2993. Deena Metzger (1936–)

1 Stories are like a body. We can touch them and they touch the very heart of us.

"Writing for Your Life," *Ms.* (New York) *March/April 1993*

2 Following the creative is a path, but it is not a known path. It has to be carved out by each individual practitioner. . . . Each practitioner must discover her own prayers, sacrifices, offerings, rituals—everything has to be invented from the beginning. And so, as in the mystery religions, one travels with one's eyes closed, utterly alone, into the unknown.

Ibid.

3 Understanding and vision cannot be fully cultivated until the ego, the will, or the worldly self defers to other ways of being and knowing.

Ibid.

4　"What is your medicine?" I was asked.
　　"Story. Story is my medicine," I answered.
　　　　　　　　　　　　　Ch. 1, *Entering the Ghost River* 2002

5　If the spirits and the Divine are real then this world we humans
　have created has become a sacrilege.
　　　　　　　　　Ch. 1, *From Grief Into Vision: A Council* 2007

2994. Barbara Ann Mikulski (1936–)

1　America is not a melting pot. It is a sizzling cauldron for the
　ethnic American who feels that he has been politically courted
　and legally extorted by both government and private enter-
　prise.
　　　　　　　Speech, Catholic University of America (Washington, D.C.)
　　　　　　　　　　　　　　　　　　　　　　　1970

2　What is needed is an alliance of white and black, white collar,
　blue collar and no collar based on mutual need, interdepen-
　dence and respect, an alliance to develop the strategy for new
　kinds of community organization and political participation.
　　　　　　　　　　　　　　　　　　　　Ibid.

3　As we move from an economy of affluence to an economy of
　scarcity, we must be careful that the people who make $5,000
　a year are not pitted against those who make $25,000 a year
　by those who make $900,000. The two-martinis-for-lunch
　bunch would love for us to fight each other over the resources
　they have made scarce.
　　　　　　　Campaign Speech (1974), Quoted in *American Political
　　　　　　　　　　　　　　Women* by Esther Stineman 1980

2995. Jane O'Reilly (1936–)

1　. . . the click! of recognition, that parenthesis of truth around
　a little thing that completes the puzzle of reality in women's
　minds—the moment that brings a gleam to our eyes and means
　the revolution has begun.
　　　　　　　"The Housewife's Moment of Truth," *The First Ms. Reader,*
　　　　　　　　　　　　　　Francine Klagsbrun, ed. 1972

2　. . . housewives, the natural people to turn to when there is some-
　thing unpleasant, inconvenient or inconclusive to be done.
　　　　　　　　　　　　　　　　　　　　Ibid.

3　Men will always opt for things that get finished and stay that
　way—putting up screens, but not planning menus.
　　　　　　　　　　　　　　　　　　　　Ibid.

4　The one nice thing about sports is that they prove men do have
　emotions and are not afraid to show them.
　　　　　　　　　　　　　Ch. 5, *The Girl I Left Behind* 1980

5　Trying to be a perfect feminist . . . is not really a big improve-
　ment on trying to be a perfect wife, mother, and lady.
　　　　　　　　　　　　　　　　　Ch. 7, Ibid.

2996. Rochelle Owens (1936–)

1　CY. I wasn't near people. They came to me and looked under
　my trousers all the way up to their dirty hearts! They minded
　my *own* life.
　　　　　　　　　　　　　　　　　　Futz 1958

2　CY. I don't want no sow with two feet but with four! Them
　repeats true things with their grunts not like you human-
　daughter.
　　　　　　　　　　　　　　　　　Sc. 1, Ibid.

3　MARX. Labor! Sucking Capital! Capital! The exploiting class!
　The milking class—the ruling class!
　　　　　　　　　　　　　　　The Karl Marx* Play 1971
　*German political philosopher and economist (1818–83).

4　MARX. Economics is not only a cause. But the *only* cause for
　all human rancor. All human exploitation.
　　　　　　　　　　　　　　　　　　　　Ibid.

5　It's as if I was a chemist, an alchemist, mixing and playing
　around with fluids, living tissue, vapors, always testing the vi-
　ability of the matter—language.
　　　　　　　"Rochelle Owens," *Interviews with Contemporary Women
　　　　　　　　Playwrights,* Kathleen Betsko* and Rachel Koenig 1987
　*See 3125.

2997. Marge Piercy (1936–)

1　Reflecting the values of the larger capitalistic society, there is
　no prestige whatsoever attached to actual working. Workers
　are invisible.
　　　　　　　"The Grand Coolie Damn," *Sisterhood Is Powerful,* Robin
　　　　　　　　　　　　　　　　　Morgan,* ed. 1970
　*See 3284.

2　The ruling class isn't dissatisfied: they are healthy, well-fed, live
　in beauty, enjoy their own importance: fun-loving cannibals
　　　　　　　　　　　　　　　　　　　　Ibid.

3　The will to be totally rational
　is the will to be made out of glass and steel:
　and to use others as if they were glass and steel.
　　　　　　　　　"Song of the Fucked Duck" (1969), Ibid.

4　"You're not pretty, Miriam-mine, so you better be smart. But
　not too smart."
　　　　　　　　　　　　　　　Small Changes 1973

5　"All women hustle. Women watch faces, voices, gestures,
　moods. The person who has to survive through cunning."
　　　　　　　　　　　　　　　　　　　　Ibid.

6　She must learn again to speak
　starting with I
　starting with We
　starting as the infant does
　with her own true hunger
　and pleasure
　and rage.
　　　　　　　"Unlearning to Not Speak," *To Be of Use* 1973

7　As I kneel to put the seeds in
　careful as stitching, I am in love.
　You are the bed we all sleep on.
　You are the food we eat, the food
　we ate, the food we will become.
　We are walking trees rooted in you.
　　　　　　　"The Common Living Dirt," St. 3, *Stone, Paper, Knife* 1983

8　Heaven and earth observe how we cherish or spoil our world.
　　　　　　　"(Interpretation of the) She'ma,"* *The Art of
　　　　　　　　　　　　　　　Blessing the Day* 1999
　*A holy Jewish prayer.

9　Bless the teaching of how to open
　in love so all the doors and windows of the

body swing wide on their rusty hinges
and we give ourselves with both hands.
> "Amidah: On Our Feet, We Speak to You," 1, Ibid.

10 Holy is the hand that works for peace and for justice,
holy is the mouth that speaks for goodness
holy is the foot that walks toward mercy.
> 3, Ibid.

11 Blessed is the match that burned and kindled flames,
Blessed is the flame that set hearts on fire.
Blessed are the hearts that knew how to die with honor,
Blessed is the match that burned, and kindled flames
> "Blessed is the Match" *n.d.*

2998. Sharon Pollock (1936–)

1 SITTING BULL. In the beginning . . . was given . . . to everyone a cup . . . a cup of clay. And from this cup we drink our life. We all dip in the water, but the cups are different . . . My cup is broken. It has passed away.
> Act III, *Walsh 1973*

2 LIZZIE. You want me living life by the Farmer's Almanac; having everyone over for Christmas dinner; waiting up for my husband; and serving at socials..
> *Blood Relations 1981*

2999. Aishah Rahman (1936/37–)

1 GIRL. It's only in the head of a musician that I begin to understand. Only a musician can make sense for me. Only a musician knows how to connect shoes with cardboard to cover holes to P.S. 184 on 116th Street and Lenox Avenue to the red taste of watermelon and mocking white smiles to Anthony's smiles and smell of Florida Water to late night loneliness and . . . this . . . [her unborn baby].
> *Unfinished Woman Cry in No Man's Land While a Bird Die in a Gilded Cage 1984*

2 BIRD. My pain is not unbearable. In none of my secret places inside of me have I condemned myself.
> Ibid.

3 PREGNANT GIRL. One day we will not have to be afraid of our dreams.
> Ibid.

4 Such categories [as gender, culture, or sexual orientation] are only literary apartheid that marginalizes specific groups of writers. They are false commercial distinctions that have nothing to do with the quality of writing. There are only two kinds of writing. Good and bad.
> Quoted in *Moon Marked and Touched by Sun* by Sydné Mahone *1994*

3000. Margaret Randall (1936–)

1 In order to effectively reverse the centuries-old paradigm of male = ownership = control, versus female = dependence = powerlessness, we must begin to deal with the ways women have been made to *feel* about money.
> *The Price You Pay 1996*

2 . . . the management of memory—how it may be preserved, mishandled, abused, or offered as a touchstone to the understanding of history.
> "Eyes on the prizewinner," *The Women's Review of Books,* vol. XV, no. 12 *September 1998*

3 How could I live
without your temperature, deep river, perfect weight
of breast and reach of mind? How grow without your
silliness gene. . .
> "How Could I Live," St. 1, *Coming Up for Air 2001*

3001. Diane Rehm (1936–)

1 . . . I am reminded, as I have been so many times during my life, that when one door closes, others open. It may not be the door you expected to open, but if you keep moving in a direction in which you believe, things do happen.
> Pt. Two, p. 135, *My Voice 1999*

2 I understand very well the longing for the familiar, no matter how dangerous.
> p. 155, Ibid.

3 The whole question of marriage revolves around assumptions and expectations.
> "Dialogue on Assumptions and Expectations," *Toward Commitment: A Dialogue About Marriage*, John B. Rehm,* coauthor 2002

*Her husband.

4 I don't think most people regard food as part of the whole mix of the relationship, yet it's such an integral part.
> "Food," Ibid.

3002. Jill Robinson (1936–)

1 The fame fraud is so complete that all the Hollywood kids think everyone else has money. It is the suburban delusion. But then, suburbia was invented by Hollywood.
> Pt. I, *Bed/Time/Story 1974*

2 Somewhere there was a gentle man with a cock that wore a jaunty grin and stayed long enough for you to get to know him.
> Ibid.

3 The transcontinental jet flight is a condensed metaphor of the escapist's Geographical Change. One starts out with the gorgeous hope that the self one abhors can be left behind. Three thousand miles is a powerful distance; such speed, such height should get you away before that self can catch up.
> Pt. II, Ibid.

4 "Ambition is destruction, only competence matters. . . ."
> Ibid.

5 "Everyone's parent is only a fantasy finally, neither as magical as, forgive me, you are, nor as prosaic. It is the image one has created in the head that one is fighting. Not the real parent at all."
> Ibid.

3003. Betty Rollin (1936–)

1 How can birth-control programs really be effective as long as the concept of glorious motherhood remains unchanged? (Even poor old Planned Parenthood has to euphemize—why not Planned Unparenthood?)
> "Motherhood: Who Needs It," *Look 16 May 1971*

2 Publicity educates, and so does fear.
> Ch. 1, *First Your Cry 1976*

3   Two hours before my mother killed herself, I noticed she had put on makeup. This shocked me, but it shouldn't have. Whatever the occasion, my mother liked to look her best.

Ch. 1, Last Wish 1985

4   "My Leon died healthy," she said through her grief. The way he ate, she figured, how could he not be healthy? She couldn't get over how one organ, his heart, could have been impervious to all those green vegetables, all that sole broiled dry, all those skins of all those baked potatoes.

Ibid.

5   They don't make cards for cancer anniversaries. Not even for the twenty-fifth. That's okay. I don't need anyone else to tell me something nice has happened. As deeply as I've ever known anything, I know that I am one lucky woman. For no reason in particular, except luck, I'm still breathing. Breathing is my favorite thing. It's probably yours, too, if you've had cancer—or, for that matter, any disease that has made the possibility of not breathing real.

Introduction, First Your Cry 2000 edition.

3004. Rosemary Radford Ruether (1936–   )

1   It is through generating stories of our own crisis and hope and telling them to one another that we light the path.

Womanguides: Reading Toward a Feminist Theology 1985

2   The center of [my mother's] being was cultured leisure, in the sense of the cultivation of the mind, heart and soul through prayer, intellectual thought and service. This was more a state of being than of particular activities.

"A Wise Woman," The Christian Century 17 February 1993

3   I went to college to cultivate my mind, and it was the purest accident that this turned out also to be preparation for employment.

Ibid.

4   Prehistory—precisely because one can say so little about it or about the inner life of its people with certainty—easily becomes a tabula rasa on which to project our own theories about what humans necessarily are or should be and hence must have once been.

Ch. 1, Goddesses and the Divine Feminine: A Western Religious History 2005

3005. Sandra Marie Schneiders (1936–   )

1   The gender of god, god's presumed masculinity, has functioned as the ultimate religious legitimization of the unjust social structures which victimize women.

Women and the Word 1986

2   As feminist consciousness has gradually deepened, the feminist agenda has widened, from a concern to right a particular structural wrong, namely, the exclusion of women from the voting booth, to a demand for full participation of women in society and culture, to an ideal of recreating humanity itself according to a pattern of ecojustice, that is, of right relations at every level and in relation to all of reality.

Ch. 1, With Oil in Their Lamps: Faith, Feminism, and the Future 2000

3   Women belong to every class, including oppressor classes such as whites or the wealthy. What women have in common is not class but sex, and sex is not, like skin color, ethnic origin, language, age, or economic status, either irrelevant in the area of rights or remediable. Skin color is irrelevant and poverty is remediable. But sex is neither and most feminists do not want to argue otherwise.

Ch. 1, Beyond Patching: Faith and Feminism in the Catholic Church 2004

3006. Becky Simpson (1936–   )

1   What I wanted was justice for poor people. Then I realized that can also mean putting a good pair of shoes on somebody's feet, a meal on their table, clothes on their back—that's justice to me. I know it's ground level, but that's where I want to be.

Quoted in "You Just Have to Try" by Michael Ryan, Parade Magazine 28 May 1989

2   I guess I learned to look for the similarities in all of us. Even though their house doesn't have the nicest carpet, they're still human beings, and they still have the same wants and same needs that I have.

Quoted in "Mother Teresa of Appalachia" by Carol Davis, American Profile Magazine (Franklin, TN) 5 November 2000

3007. Carol Springer (1936–   )

1   We're going to do exactly the same thing we would do if there were no gender issue. You do your job.*

"Arizona's 'girl thing' . . ." (p. 6A), USA Today 11 November 1998

*Referring to 1998 election of five women to top state government offices.

3008. Catharine R. Stimpson (1936–   )

1   Identity politics is contemporary shorthand for a group's assertion that it is a meaningful group; that it differs significantly from other groups; that its members share a history of injustice and grievance; and that its psychological and political mission is to explore, act out, act on and act up its group identity. What makes a group a group may be race, ethnicity, religion, class, gender, sexual preference or any one of a number of conditions. . . . Identity politics offers stability in a shifting, swiftly changing world.

"Acting Up and Opting Out," The Nation (New York) 18 December 1995

2   The genius-dubbing business is never any better than its selection process.

"Dynamite Plan Bolsters Myth: The Nobel, Towering Genius," The New York Observer 12 November 2000

3   In general, the [Nobel] prizes have underwritten the misleading myth of the towering genius whose solitary work would eventually help many. This stress on the heroic individual may sooner or later conflict with the nature of contemporary science, in which major work is done by teams—scores or hundreds or even thousands of people.

Ibid.

4   Big fortunes left in unexpected ways excite bad feelings.

Ibid.

3009. Lily Tomlin (1936–   )

1   If you have a psychotic fixation and you go to the doctor and you want these two fingers amputated, he will not cut them off. But he *will* remove your genitals. I have more trouble getting

a prescription for Valium than I do having my uterus lowered and made into a penis.

> Quoted by David Felton in *Rolling Stone* (New York)
> *24 October 1974*

2 If you can't be direct, why be?

> "Mary Jean,"* Ibid.

3 Once poor, always wantin'. Rich is just a way of wantin' bigger.

> "Wanda V.,"* Ibid.

4 Lady . . . Lady, I do not make up things. That is lies. Lies is not true. But the truth could be made up if you know how. And that's the truth.

> "Edith Ann,"* Ibid.

*Characters created by Lily Tomlin.

5 If you win the rat race, you're still a rat.

> Quoted by Anna Quindlen* in her Commencement Speech,
> Mount Holyoke College *23 May 1999*

*See 4136.

6 The sensibility in this culture is so hard-edged, so brutal, so ridiculing, and so dismissive. I think the most radical thing you can do now is to be tender. That's really pushing the envelope.

> Quoted in "Who's Lily Now?" by Laurie Winer, *Modern Maturity March/April 2002*

3010. Esther Tusquets (1936–)

1 The passing of time . . . this time that has on some occasions paradoxically passed so slowly, has stretched, has given of itself to the point of improbability to be able to contain so many events, such intense sorrow, such fierce happiness, so that the months are remembered as years and the years expand into centuries, whereas on other occasions it has elapsed monotonously, senselessly, rapidly, in the large parentheses of boredom, large hollow parentheses that should seem interminable but are remembered later as the brevity of a few minutes. . . .

> p. 1, *Stranded 1992*

2 . . . skinny stray cats with sad eyes keep being so innocent, so foolish, so stubborn, and a little selfish, with their crazy, innocent, slightly selfish, so childish dreams, and they don't know or don't understand that the owners sometimes make mistakes or understand either or can't understand a certain kind of cat, stray skinny cats with sad eyes, cats of the street and of the night, who make a mess of things, and make mistakes and love badly, who love a lot and badly, and always always always lose their pretty owners. . . .

> p. 82, Ibid.

3011. Meredith "Marty" Walton (1936–)

1 It has only been recently that feminist consciousness has affected the Society of Friends just as it has affected the world at large. The old boys' network has been as much a factor in the Society of Friends as it has in the general society.

> Cited by Barbara Findlen, *Ms.* (New York) *March 1987*

2 There have been women models in Quaker history that have perhaps made it easier for women to assume leadership positions now.

> Ibid.

3012. Joan Myers Weimer (1936–)

1 She knows the Underworld like the palm of her hand.

> *Back Talk: Teaching Lost Selves to Speak 1994*

2 I think the biggest secret I've kept from myself is my hunger for a spiritual life.

> Ibid.

3 But every time we leave home and go where nothing is familiar, where everyone is a stranger, we discover each other with the same attention and wonder that we bring to a Gothic cathedral—craning our necks to admire the vaulted ceiling, descending into the crypt to stand on its ancient stones. When sun streams through the stained glass windows, we fall in love all over again.

> Ch. 1, *Awestruck, A Skeptic's Pilgrimage 2006*

4 Maybe this garden, not my desk, is the place for me to weed and water my memories of my mother.

> pp. 145–149, Ibid.

5 Maybe that's the way of the inner life—you dive into those dark waters where memory and magic live tangled together, and then you surface, gasping, amazed by snippets of blue sky between the branches of a willow tree.

> Ibid.

3013. Nancy Willard (1936–)

1 For me there is a very strong connection between listening to literature and telling stories and writing them. Finding your own voice grows out of hearing the spoken word.

> "Far from just kid stuff" by Berthe Amoss, *Times-Picayune* (New Orleans), E7 *27 March 1988*

2 . . . I found out it is not what happens, it is how you tell it and who does the telling.

> Ibid.

3 You know the work will not go well
If you should mispronounce a spell.
A single lapse in common sense
can have a fatal consequence.

> *The Sorcerer's Apprentice 1993*

3014. Elizabeth Wilson (1936–)

1 Postmodernism refuses to privilege any one perspective, and recognizes only difference, never inequality, only fragments, never conflict.

> Ch. 23, *Hallucinations: Life in the Postmodern City 1988*

3015. Sidney Abbot (1937–)

1 Lesbianism is far more than a sexual preference: it is a political stance.

> *Sappho* Was a Right-on Woman*, with Barbara J. Love** 1972
> *See 46. **See 3043.

2 . . . a woman who wants a woman usually wants a woman.

> Ibid.

3016. JoAnne Akalaitis (1937–)

1 JESSICA. One evening, I asked my evening school teacher to tell me the real difference between "I was writing" and "I have written" . . . "Well," he said grandly, "The imperfect tense refers to what WAS, while the present perfect tense refers to what HAS BEEN."

> Act I, "English," *Green Card 1986*

3017. Ann Arensberg (1937–)

1 Accepting a sexless marriage is a gradual process, subject to lapses. Every night brings a fresh opportunity for regression, reviving the hope that two bodies lying side by side will catch fire spontaneously. When proximity fails to work its remembered magic, every night is a new occasion for disappointment.

Incubus 1998

2 Ancient peoples bared themselves to the moon in adoration, but they knew, while we have forgotten, that the moon rules over death as well as fruitfulness.

Ibid.

3018. Cora Harvey Armstrong (1937?–)

1 Inside me lives a skinny woman crying to get out. But I can usually shut the bitch up with cookies.

Performance patter *n.d.*

2 Inside every older person is a younger person—wondering what the hell happened.

Ibid.

3019. Byllye Y. Avery (1937–)

1 I can't recall ever hearing a child say, "I want to be an activist when I grow up."

"Activism," *An Altar of Words: Wisdom to Comfort and Inspire African-American Women* 1999

2 Activists help make the world a better place. Many important changes have been made because something clicked and made people see the picture more clearly, focusing on the vision of what could be, and how changes can lead to a better society.

Ibid.

3 I know that birth and death are a part of my reality and I affirm the presence of the spirit.

"Death," Ibid.

4 The world is so full of stress that sometimes the only way we can deal with it is to hold our breath and plunge in.

"Breath," Ibid.

3020. Margaret Lowe Benston (1937–)

1 In sheer quantity, household labor, including child care, constitutes a huge amount of socially necessary production. Nevertheless, in a society based on commodity production, it is not usually considered as "real work" since it is outside of trade and the marketplace. . . . In a society in which money determines value, women are a group who work outside the money economy.

"The Political Economy of Women's Lib," *Monthly Review* September 1969

2 Once women are freed from private production in the home, it will probably be very difficult to maintain for any long period of time a rigid definition of jobs by sex.

Ibid.

3 Industrialization is, in itself, a great force for human good; exploitation and dehumanization go with capitalism and not necessarily with industrialization.

Ibid.

3021. Sallie Bingham (1937–)

1 . . . he wondered again, how much of her desire was passion and how much grasping: girls used sex to get a hold on you, he knew—it was so easy for them to pretend to be excited.

"Winter Term," *Mademoiselle* July 1958

2 The clock would never let him forget the amount of time he was wasting. . . .

Ibid.

3022. Elena Castedo-Ellerman (1937–)

1 "The best way to get where you want to be is to please those who own the road."

Paradise 1990

3023. Jane Chambers (1937–1983)

1 ELLIE. When I was your age, "lesbian" was a dictionary word used only to frighten teenage girls and parents. Mothers fainted, fathers became violent, landlords evicted you, and nobody would hire you. A Lesbian was like a vampire: she looked in the mirror and there was no reflection.

A Late Snow 1974

3024. E. Kitch Childs (1937–1993)

1 We need a whole new level of consciousness-raising groups and networks. We must learn how to speak our bitterness about each other *to* each other. It will liberate our energies to keep on working together.

Quoted in Introduction, *Women and Madness*, 25th anniversary ed. by Phyllis Chesler* 1997

*See 3184.

3025. Hélène Cixous (1937–)

1 Write your self. Your body must be heard.

"The Laugh of the Medusa," Keith Cohen and Paula Cohen, trs., *Signs: A Journal of Women in Culture and Society* 1976

2 I, too, overflow: my desires have invented new desires, my body knows unheard-of songs.

Ibid.

3 To Write [would be] an act which will not only "realize" the decensored relation of woman to her sexuality, . . . it will give her back her goods, her pleasures, her organs, her immense bodily territories which have been kept under seal. . . .

Ibid.

4 [Women] take pleasure in jumbling the order of space, in disorienting it, in changing around the furniture, dislocating things and values, breaking them all up, emptying structures, and turning propriety upside down.

Ibid.

5 You only have to look at the Medusa
straight on to see her,
And she's not deadly. She's beautiful
and she's laughing.

Ibid.

3026. Maryse Condé (1937–)

1 I can't understand why I placed all my hopes in this man whom I didn't know from Adam. Probably because he came from Elsewhere. From over there. From the other side of the water. He wasn't born on our island of malice that has been left to

the hurricanes and the ravages caused by the spitefulness in the hearts of black folks.

> *Traversé de la Mangrove* (Crossing the Mangrove, tr. 1995), Richard Philcox, tr. *1989*

2 . . . the wounds of childhood do not heal.

> Ibid.

3 "Maman, all that about slavery and shackles, that's ancient history. You've got to live with your times."

> Ibid.

3027. Ann Crittenden (1937–)

1 One learns, in theory and in practice, to try to resolve conflict in ways that do not involve the sheer imposition of will or brute force. One learns that violence just doesn't work.

> Article, *The Nation* (New York) 1991

2 For all of the ink spilled about the high-tech economy, the majority of American mothers are still primarily engaged in the oldest economy in the world: the household.

> Ch. 1, *The Price of Motherhood: Why the Most Important Job in the World is Still the Least Valued 2001*

3 . . . feminism only went so far. It got women in the game, but we have been expected to play by rules that we didn't write and that don't fit our lives. Now our challenge is to rewrite the rules and establish new norms that reflect our priorities. We need new societal norms that truly value conscientious parenting and that enable parents to integrate caring for children with a full and independent life.

> "Feminist Face-off," *The American Prospect 21 April 2004*

4 I am amazed that we still have to fight for that most basic personal freedom: the right to choose when, or whether, to become a mother, the biggest commitment one can make in life. That is the bedrock of the next stage of feminism.

> Ibid.

5 Multitasking is the only skill mothers are universally credited with possessing.

> Ch. 1, *If You've Raised Kids, You Can Manage Anything: Leadership Begins at Home 2004*

6 Psychologists have known for some time that the female brain is different from the male. Women tend to gather in more details of the world around them, and integrate that data into a more holistic picture of the world.

> Ibid.

3028. Helene Ferris (1937–)

1 I am not so naïve to believe that a change in liturgical language will have the slightest impact on the legal, economic, or social equality of women. After all, Sabbath "bride" and "queen" and the Hebrew prophets' references to Israel as "mother," "daughter," and "wife" have been of no help whatsoever to the status of women.

> Quoted in Ch. 4, *Deborah, Golda, and Me* by Letty Cottin Pogrebin* *1991*

*See 3154.

3029. Jane Fonda (1937–)

1 I don't care about the Oscar. I make movies to support the causes I believe in, not for any honors. I couldn't care less whether I win an Oscar or not.

> Quoted in Prologue, *Jane: An Intimate Biography of Jane Fonda* by Thomas Kiernan 1973

2 All I can say is that through the people I've met, the experiences I've had, the reading I've done, I realize the American system must be changed. I see an alternative to the usual way of living and relating to people. And this alternative is a total change of our structures and institutions—through Socialism. Of course I am a Socialist. But without a theory, without an ideology.

> Pt. IV, Ch. 26 (c. 1971), Ibid.

3 When a child enters the world through you, it alters everything on a psychic, psychological and purely practical level. You're just not free anymore to do what you want to do. And it's not the same again. Ever.

> Quoted in "At Home with Tom* and Jane" by Danae Brook, *Los Angeles Weekly 28 November–4 December 1980*
> *Reference to Tom Hayden, American politician and activist (1941–) who was one of the Chicago Seven in 1968 and later became a state legislator of California; once married to Fonda.

4 I am not a do-gooder. I am a revolutionary. A revolutionary woman.

> Comment (1971), Ibid.

5 [Coco Chanel]* freed us from the corset. You know, the foot in the back, Scarlett O'Hara,** whalebone corset. If you get a strong emotion, be it fear, sadness, anger, what happens? You pass out. Women don't pass out today. You know why? We can breathe. She stripped us of the corset. She put the A-frame dress on us, showed our legs, removed the focus from the waist, bobbed our hair, and we were off and running.

> "100 Years of Great Women," *ABC News Special with Barbara Walters*** 30 April 1999*
> *See 1593. **Reference to central character in Margaret Mitchell's *Gone with the Wind*; see 1914:1–16. ***See 2687.

3030. Kathleen Fraser (1937–)

1 He is all of him urge.

> Untitled poem, *What I Want 1974*

2 I think you have many shelves
but never put love there.

> Ibid.

3031. Nancy Friday (1937–)

1 Anger broke the pane of glass between us.

> Ch. 1, *My Mother, My Self 1977*

2 Spontaneous and honest love admits errors, hesitations, and human failings; it can be tested and repaired. Idealized love ties us because we already intuit that it is unreal and are afraid to face this truth.

> Ibid.

3 The older I get, the more of my mother I see in myself.

> Ibid.

4 We are the loving sex; people count on us for comfort, nurturing warmth. We hold the world together with the constant availability of our love when men would tear it apart with their needs for power.

> Ibid.

5 It was the promise of men, that around each corner there was yet another man, more wonderful than the last, that sustained me. You see, I had men confused with life. . . . You can't get what I wanted from a man, not in this life.

> Ch. 8, Ibid.

3032. Gail Godwin (1937–   )

1 "The only reason people forget is because they want to. If we were all clear, with no aberrations, we could remember everything, before we were born, even."

Ch. 1, The Perfectionists 1970

2 "Good teaching is one-fourth preparation and three-fourths theatre. . . ."

The Odd Woman 1974

3 I believe that dreams transport us through the undersides of our days, and that if we wish to become acquainted with the dark side of what we are, the signposts are there, waiting for us to translate them. Dreams say what they mean, but they don't say it in daytime language.

Ch. 1, The Finishing School 1984

4 Actors between plays are like ghosts looking for bodies to inhabit.

Ch. 7, Ibid.

5 Death is not the enemy; age is not the enemy. These things are inevitable, they happen to everybody. But what we ought to fear is the kind of death that happens in life. It can happen at any time. You're going along, and then, at some point, you congeal. You solidify at a certain point and from then on your life is doomed to be a repetition of what you have done before. That's the enemy.

Ibid.

6 "I was thinking how nice it would be to be a character in one of your novels . . . you take care of [your characters] so nicely. You let them suffer a little, just enough to improve their characters, but you always rescue them from the abyss at the last minute and reward them with love or money or the perfect job—or sometimes all three."

A Southern Family 1987

7 ". . . the Great Uncouth has taken up permanent residence inside me."

The Good Husband 1994

8 Mates are not always matches and matches are not always mates.

Ibid.

3033. Lois Gould (1937–2002)

1 Danny Mack got past the nurses at two-fifteen by impersonating a doctor. All he did was clip four ballpoint pens on his vest pocket and march in looking preoccupied.

Such Good Friends 1970

2 "Hogamous, Higamous, men are polygamous, Higamous, Hogamous, women monogamous."

Ibid.

3 Life is the only sentence which doesn't end with a period.

Ibid.

4 ". . . the city *requires* a funeral . . . All the ordinances are designed with your friendly funeral directors in mind—not to mention the cemeteries and coffin makers and gravestone cutters."

Ibid.

5 She hated the powdered oil smell they put on the baby. Rubbing away all his natural sourness and anointing him with foreign substances that were all ironically labeled *Baby*. So that he would never recognize his own body in the dark, the way she could recognize hers now. Small victory, discovering your acrid identity after eighteen years. Buried alive under thousands of layers of powdered oil.

Ibid.

6 "Women always run away," she said. "That's why women never get to run anything else. They can't stand the heat, so they get *back* in the kitchen."

Final Analysis 1974

7 Make up. Meaning invent. Make up something more acceptable, because that face you have on right there will not do.

Ibid.

8 The only reason I hated him was that I had needed him so much. That's when I found out about need. It goes much better with hate than with love.

Ibid.

3034. Louise Hart (1937–   )

1 *Raising healthy children is the most important work of the culture.*

Ch. 1, The Winning Family: Increasing Self-Esteem in Your Children and Yourself 1987

2 Our children give us the opportunity to become the parents we always wished we'd had.

Epigraph, Ibid.

3 Bringing a child into the world is the greatest act of hope there is.

"Postscript: On Nightmares," Ibid.

4 The purpose of the mature butterfly or moth is to bring more caterpillars into the world so the species will survive. Yet it also has a higher purpose within the web of life. It fills an ecological niche in the food chain and pollinates flowers, contributing to the well-being of all creatures on earth. For those who see it, the butterfly brings beauty to the world. It also shows us humans that transformation is a common and natural part of life's process.

Ch. 1, On the Wings of Self-Esteem: A Companion for Personal Transformation 1994

5 Childhood lasts only a few years, but the experience lasts a lifetime.

Motto n.d.

3035. Bessie Head (1937–1986)

1 But in a society like this, which man cared to be owned and possessed when there were so many women freely available? And even all the excessive love-making was purposeless, aimless, just like tipping everything into an awful cesspit where no one really cared to take a second look.

Ch. 8, When Rain Clouds Gather 1968

2 And if the white man thought that Asians were a low filthy nation, Asians could still smile with relief—at least, they were not Africans. And if the white man thought that Africans were a low, filthy nation, Africans in southern Africa could still smile—at least, they were not bushmen. They all have their monsters.

Pt. I, Maru 1971

3 Love is mutually feeding each other, not one living on another like a ghoul.

A Question of Power 1973

3036. Maria Teresa Horta (1937–)
Coauthor with Maria Isabel Barreno (see 3122) and Maria Fatima Velho da Costa (see 3080).

3037. Jean Houston (1937–)

1 Odysseus' voyage, with all its physical dangers and thrills, may also be perceived as a progressive journey into the far more chilling cartography of inner space.

Ch. 1, *The Hero and the Goddess: The Odyssey as Mystery and Initiation 1992*

2 Sacred psychology shows you that you are richer, deeper, stronger, and more a mystery than you know. The work of sacred psychology is to school you in your own depths. Your energies, power, stamina, and moral force seem limited only because your personal and cultural expectations set limits.

Ch. 1, *The Search For the Beloved 1997*

3 A myth is something that never was but is always happening . . . and that happening is upon us and within us, declaring its continued presence in whatever medium we choose to receive the news of the world.

"Living in One's and Future Myths" (1995), *The Fabric of the Future: Women Visionaries of Today Illuminate the Path to Tomorrow*, M. J. Ryan, ed. *1998*

4 As cultures come together and exchange their essence, they join in a cadence of awakening, a new idiom of consciousness that is exhilarating and revolutionary. This rhythm carries us from the ballads of local concerns to the concerto of a larger ecology of being.

Ch. 1, *Jump Time: Shaping Your Future in a World of Radical Change 2004*

5 Ultimately all is rhythm, all music. The world is sound. *Aum*, the beginning, heard now and forever.

Ibid.

3038. Tina Howe (1937–)

1 SANDY. When I looked in the mirror this morning, I saw an old lady. Not old old, just used up.

Birth and After Birth, coauthor, Honor Moore* *1974*
*See 3596.

2 Young mothers inhabit rather wild territory.

"Tina Howe," *Interviews with Contemporary Women Playwrights*, Kathleen Betsko* and Rachel Koenig *1987*
*See 3125.

3 The reason to pick up the pen or the paint brush is to fight back.

Ibid.

4 I've always thought women were much more dangerous than men.

Ibid.

3039. Bette Howland (1937–)

1 Reason is a passion; an instinct, a drive.

Ch. 3, *Blue in Chicago 1978*

2 My father is not a strictly observant Orthodox Jew. He does as others do. Sometimes he Observes. Sometimes he Looks the Other Way.

"The Life You Gave Me," *Things to Come and Go 1983*

3 Builders in South Florida are like God in the universe. Their handiwork is everywhere, but they are nowhere to be seen. They move on, leaving Gardens of Eden all over the place, and nothing quite finished.

Ibid.

4 In Florida, plants carry their roots with them; whole forests crawling on their bellies, recumbent trunks with roots that noose and lasso. They have claws, tusks, fangs, beaks. They can take anchor anywhere—the shallowest places; an inch or two of soil; on water; on other plants; on nothing at all—on air.

Ibid.

5 Beauty is here to stay. Beauty doesn't vanish. We do.

Ibid.

6 All their lives they believed in the Future; they struggled and slaved and sacrificed for the Future. Not that they had much choice; it was understood they had been born too soon. Things were going to get better. In the Future. The everlasting Future. And now all of a sudden they see the truth. The Future? What Future?

Ibid.

7 To the south, the mills gave off a thick, orange glow, mightier than the sinking clouds. Lights squiggled on the surface of the water.

Chicago rose from the horizon the way heat rises from the highway: staggering, shimmering. You could never be sure you were seeing it because it was there.

"Birds of a Feather," Ibid.

8 Snow was swirling, giddy in the headlamps, the light driving it all before them—threshing it like white grain.

"The Old Wheeze," Ibid.

9 For a long time it seemed to me
that real life was about to begin,
but there was always some obstacle in the way.

Something had to be got through first,
some unfinished business;
time still to be served,
a debt to be paid.

Then life would begin.

At last it dawned on me
that these obstacles were my life.

"Obstacles" *n.d*

3040. Ann Jones (1937–)

1 As we drove on toward Lovedu* land, we tried to imagine what it might mean to be a queen in Africa. All around us, all along the way, we saw women doing nothing but work. Debo,** who had been filming *Women at Work*, had footage of women hoeing, planting crops, weeding, harvesting, gathering wild edibles, shucking maize, pounding maize, grinding maize at the mill, carrying maize meal home, chopping wood, gathering firewood, carrying firewood home on their heads or on their backs, building fires, cooking, serving food, washing dishes, scouring pots, making clothes, buying

clothes, washing clothes (after first carrying the laundry to the river, or carrying the river water home), selling clothes and just about anything else in the marketplace or beside the road, building houses, painting houses, gathering thatch, preparing mud plaster, polishing floors with cattle dung (to keep out insects), scrubbing floors, weaving palm fibers, making mats, making baskets, making hats, dyeing fabrics, sewing, knitting, embroidering, making pots, minding children, doctoring children, teaching children, feeding children, washing children, dressing children, plaiting hair, milking cows, feeding chickens, butchering chickens, shopping, making brooms, sweeping houses, sweeping yards, cleaning churches, cleaning wells, planting trees and keeping accounts. So far she had no footage at all of women being queen. What would a queen *do*?

> "Finding the Lovedu," *The Women's Review of Books*, Vol. XV, No. 5 *February 1998*

*A Southern African people. **Debo Kinsland, Australian-born British-based filmmaker.

2 . . . the Lovedu believe that only a fool fails to find peaceable compromise, and only the truly stupid come to blows. Compromise, appeasement, reconciliation, tolerance, peace. The great ideals of Lovedu culture.

> Ibid.

3 And I remember how she'd laughed and what she'd said in response to Debo's last question: "Your majesty, is there something of importance that you and your people could teach the people of the West?"

"Yes," the Queen said. "We could teach you to dance."

> Ibid.

3041. Jan Karon (1937–)

1 God wastes nothing.

> Quoted in "Down-home Jan Karon..," Nanci Helmlmich, *USA Today 14 April 1999*

2 There were times when he didn't like being a priest, always on the front line for justice and mercy and forgiveness and redemption; trying to figure out the mind of God; giving the Lord his personal agenda, then standing around waiting for it to be fulfilled. He didn't have an agenda for Morris Love, anymore; he was giving up the entire self-seeking, willful notion.

> *A New Song 1999*

3042. Penelope Leach (1937–)

1 One day you will find that you have stopped regarding your baby as a totally unpredictable and therefore rather alarming novelty, and have begun instead to think of him as a person with tastes, preferences and characteristics of his own. When that happens you will know that he has moved on from being a "newborn" and has got himself settled into life.

> Ch. 3, *Your Baby and Child: From Birth to Age Five 1977*

2 For a small child there is no division between playing and learning; between the things he or she does "just for fun" and things that are "educational." The child learns while living and any part of living that is enjoyable is also play.

> Ch. 5, Ibid.

3 True spoiling is nothing to do with what a child owns or with amount of attention he gets. He can have the major part of your income, living space and attention and not be spoiled, or he can have very little and be spoiled. It is not what he gets that

is at issue. It is how and why he gets it. Spoiling is to do with the family balance of power.

> Ch. 6, Ibid.

4 When he was a crawler he left your feet to journey to the sofa and bring you a ball. When he was a toddler he left your side to journey across the grass and bring you a leaf. When he was a pre-school child he left your yard to journey next door and bring you back a neighbor's doll. Now he will journey into school and bring you back a piece of his new world. . . . His journeys are all outwards now, into that waiting world. But he feels the invisible and infinitely elastic threads that still guide him back to you. He returns to the base that is you, seeking rest and re-charging for each new leap into life.

> Ibid.

3043. Barbara J. Love (1937–)
Coauthor with Sidney Abbot; see 3015: 1–2.

3044. Lois Lowry (1937–)

1 . . . it was the sort of thing one didn't ask a friend about because it might have fallen into that uncomfortable category of "being different." Asher took a pill each morning; Jonas did not. Always better, less rude, to talk about things that were the same.

> *The Giver 1993*

2 "Why can't everyone see them? Why did colors disappear?"

The Giver shrugged. "Our people made that choice, the choice to go to Sameness. . . . We gained control of many things. But we had to let go of others."

> Ibid.

3 Once she read a book but found it distasteful because it contained adjectives.

> Ch. 1, *The Willoughbys 2008*

3045. Lydia Phindile Makhubu (1937–)

1 In my opinion, the major reason for the survival of the traditional system [of African medicine] in spite of the modern ways of life, is its approach. It is a holistic system utilizing treatment which focuses not only on symptoms but also on psychological and sociological factors.

> *The Traditional Healer 1978*

2 I'm very concerned about the appreciation of science, not only among those who had a formal education in science but the nation as a whole . . . because I think there is a very strong relationship between our everyday life and science.

> Ibid.

3046. A. G. Mojtabai (1937–)

1 What staggers me is not the persistence of illusion, but the persistence of the world in the face of illusion.

> *Mundome 1974*

2 Everything sags near the end: the earlobes flatten, lie close along the skull, the jaw goes slack, the head lolls, too heavy to lift; secretions pool and thicken in the throat, the fingers, before this so restlessly seeking, fold in and are still.

> *Soon: Tales from Hospice 1998*

3047. Marabel Morgan (1937–)

1 Be prepared mentally and physically for intercourse every night this week.

> *The Total Woman 1973*

3048. Marlo Morgan (1937–)

1 Little is gained in a lifetime if what you believe at age seven is still how you feel at age thirty-seven . . . New things cannot come where there is no room.

Mutant Mess Down Under 1994

3049. Liane Norman (1937–)

1 If conscience is regarded as imperative, then compliance with its dictates commends a society not to forgive, but to celebrate, its conscientious citizens.

"Selective Conscientious Objection," *The Center Magazine May/June 1972*

2 While the State may respectfully require obedience on many matters, it cannot violate the moral nature of a man, convert him into a serviceable criminal, and expect his loyalty and devotion.

Ibid.

3 Whenever government's interests become by definition more substantial than the humanity of its citizens, the drift toward government by divine right gathers momentum.

Ibid.

3050. Eleanor Holmes Norton (1937–)

1 Racial oppression of black people in America has done what neither class oppression nor sexual oppression, with all their perniciousness, has ever done: destroyed an entire people and their culture.

"For Sadie and Maude," *Sisterhood Is Powerful,* Robin Morgan,* ed. 1970
*See 3284.

2 There is no reason to repeat bad history.

Ibid.

3 With children no longer the universally accepted reason for marriage, marriages are going to have to exist on their own merits.

Ibid.

4 The only way to make sure people you agree with can speak is to support the rights of people you don't agree with.

Quoted in *New York Post 28 March 1970*

5 But feminist change is both irresistible and irreversible. American women are part of an international movement that affects virtually every country in the world.

Speech, National Women's Political Caucus Conference (Albuquerque, New Mexico) *July 1981*

6 I will not yield, sir! The District of Columbia has spent two hundred and six years yielding!

Speech, U.S. Congress,* *19 April 2007*
*Re: voting rights for residents of Washington, D.C.; her response to a fellow representative's request to take the floor.

3051. Alicia Suskin Ostriker (1937–)

1 Anyway, what is the soul
But a dream of itself?

"Message from the Sleeper at Hell's Mouth," *A Woman Under the Surface 1982*

2 Was I succulent? Was I juicy?

"Mastectomy," *The Crack in Everything 1996*

3 Like one of those trees with a major limb lopped,
I'm a shade more sublime today than yesterday

"Normal," *The Little Space: Poems Selected and New, 1968–1998 1998*

4 What woman doesn't die in childbirth
What child doesn't murder the mother.

"Surviving," *Ibid.*

5 As if there could be a world
Of absolute innocence
In which we forget ourselves

"The Dogs at Live Oak Beach, Santa Cruz," *Ibid.*

6 this wounded
World that we cannot heal, that is our bride.

"The Eighth and Thirteenth," *Ibid.*

7 Art destroys silence

Ibid.

3052. Tey Diana Rebolledo (1937–)

1 We have entered into the "Age of Criticism" which could be defined as a preoccupation with theoretical structures often not internalized: we feel that theory is power.

"The Politics of Poetics . . . ," *The Americas Review, 16 1988*

2 While contemporary writers may feel that they are seeing the world anew, those of us who are searching out our literary roots are finding women writers who were raising many of the same concerns women voice today—written in a different tone and style and conforming to a different mode; nevertheless, contemporary writers have not arisen from a complete void.

Ibid.

3 In the search for our own aesthetic, for our own analytical direction, we need to look to each other, to recognize that our literature and our cultural production does not need legitimization from the academy, that it already is legitimate in itself.

Ibid.

4 It is a lonely land because of its immensity, but it lacks nothing for those who enjoy Nature in her full grandeur. The colors of the skies, of the hills, the rocks, the birds and the flowers, are soothing to the most troubled heart. It is loneliness without despair. The whole world seems to be there, full of promise and gladness.

"The Llano,"* *We Fed Them Cactus,* coauthor Fabiola Cabeza De Baca** *1994*
*Referencing the Llano Estacado, an extensive, semiarid plateau region of the southern Great Plains. **See 1807.

3053. Caryl Rivers (1937–)

1 The laziness of pack journalism allows cultural stereotypes to multiply like bacteria on the locker-room floor. Your best bet, if you'd really like a glimpse of the press at work, is just to put the Friskies out on the porch.

Slick Spins and Fractured Facts: How Cultural Myths Distort the News 1996

2 The picture of the poor—welfare mothers in particular—that has emerged from the media as I write has been one that is so savage, so lacking in compassion, that it takes my breath away. . . .

Ibid.

3 Okay, let's build a superhighway; everybody bring one paving stone. That's how we approach family policy. We don't look at systems, just at individuals. And that's ridiculous.

Selling Anxiety: How the News Media Scare Women 2007

3054. Jill Ruckelshaus (1937–)

1 It occurred to me when I was thirteen and wearing white gloves and Mary Janes and going to dancing school, that no one should have to dance backward all their lives.

Speech 1973

2 The family is the building block for whatever solidarity there is in society.

Quoted in "Jill Ruckelshaus: Lady of Liberty" by Frederic A. Birmingham, *Saturday Evening Post 3 March 1973*

3 The best way to win an argument is to begin by being right. . . .

Ibid.

4 The Equal Rights Amendment* is designed to establish in our Constitution the clear moral value judgment that all Americans, women and men, stand equal under the law . . . It will give woman's role in the home new status, recognizing that the homemaker's role in a marriage has economic value. . . .

Quoted in "Forum," *Ladies' Home Journal August 1975*
*See Alice Paul, 1637.

5 We're not a fairy-tale couple. And there's no big strain on our relationship because of our careers. My family has to come first. We discuss work at home. I give him advice. He does the same to me. We commiserate.

"The Package Deal of Jill and Bill,"*
Time 11 July 1983
*Her husband, W. William R— (1932–), attorney and civil servant.

3055. Nancy Samalin (1937–)

1 We will never be able to avoid conflicts entirely because parents' needs and children's needs are so often opposed. When we need to hurry, they want to dawdle. When we crave ten minutes of solitude after a trying day, they issue eighteen demands for immediate attention. When we get a long-distance phone call, they interrupt us with a crisis.

Ch. 1, Loving Your Child Is Not Enough 1987

2 It is easy after a day full of hassles to experience a child as being just one more hassle, one more person who wants to sap our strength. We feel emotionally fragile and put upon. We long to have someone take care of us and soothe our emotions. Instead, we are required to take care of a child who might be exhausted and needy as well, and who is acting unreasonable.

Ch. 2, Love and Anger: The Parental Dilemma 1991

3 When we acknowledge our children's right to want things, as well as their right to be upset when they can't have what they want, it can go a long way toward defusing their anger and the tantrums that occur as a result.

Ibid.

3056. Dinae B. Schulder (1937–)

1 Legislation and case law still exist in some parts of the United States permitting the "passion shooting" by a husband of a wife; the reverse, of course, is known as homicide.

"Does the Law Oppress Women?," *Sisterhood Is Powerful,*
Robin Morgan,* ed. *1970*
*See 3284.

2 . . . prejudice (the mythology of class oppression) is enshrined in laws. Laws lead to enforcement of practices. Practices reinforce and lead to prejudice. The cycle continues. . . .

Ibid.

3057. Barbara Seuling (1937–)

1 I believe at the heart of writing for children is the author's own attachment, or emotional connection, to a certain period in her youth. . . .

Ch. 1, *How to Write a Children's Book and Get It Published 1984*

3058. Susan Sheehan (1937–)

1 It had never occurred to Crystal that little Dquan—let alone Crystal herself—might end up in New York City's foster-care system.

Ch. 1, *Life for Me Ain't Been No Crystal Stair: One Family's Passage Through the Child Welfare System 1993*

2 Sometimes Crystal was hit for what she considered just cause— her two younger brothers ate slowly, and if she was hungry she took food off their plates—but usually not.

Ibid.

3059. Gail Sheehy (1937–)

1 The prostitutes continue to take all the arrests, the police to suffer frustration, the lawyers to mine gold, the operators to laugh, the landowners to insist they have no responsibility, the mayor to issue press releases. The nature of the beast is, in a word, greed.

Ch. 5, Hustling 1971

2 The best way to attract money, she had discovered, was to give the appearance of having it.

Ch. 9, Ibid.

3 It is fitting that speed should be our chemical superstar. With the only certainty of our daily existence being change, and a rate of change growing always faster in a kind of technological leapfrog game, speed helps people to think they are keeping up.

Speed Is of the Essence 1971

4 It is a paradox that as we reach our prime, we also see there is a place where it finishes.

Pt. IV, Ch. 17, Passages 1976

5 Democratization is not democracy; it is a slogan for the temporary liberalization handed down from an autocrat. Glasnost is not free speech; only free speech, constitutionally guaranteed, is free speech.

"Looking for Mikhail Gorbachev," *Gorbachev 1991*

6 Transformation also means looking for ways to stop pushing yourself so hard professionally or inviting so much stress. . . . This momentous passage invites meditation and spiritual exploration. A wisewoman will make time to contemplate things eternal and appreciate the life she has.

"The Menopause Getaway," *The Silent Passage: Menopause 1991*

3060. Margo St. James (1937–)

1 A conservative estimate would be that 90 percent of politicians patronize public women. Imagine the wealth of information

available for bringing "undercover" pressure to bear regarding passage of certain legislation concerning minors, women, minorities, religious and political freedoms.

Quoted in The Realist, No. 94 October 1972

2 Punishing the prostitute promotes the rape of all women. When prostitution is a crime, the message conveyed is that women who are sexual are "bad," and therefore legitimate weapons of sexual assault.

Quoted in "Margo" by Mildred Hamilton, San Francisco Examiner 29 April 1979

3061. Rita Süssmuth (1937–)

1 . . . we can expect from women different approaches and solutions to a number of problems connected with people living together . . . [because] women tend to approach problems in a more pragmatic and action-oriented way which is more closely related to real life.

Quoted in the Kölner Staadt-Arzeiger, weekend edition, 4 2–3 October 1993

2 Given the accelerating pace of the worldwide exchange of information and knowledge, and against the background of increasing economic and social globalization, Lifelong Learning will be a key factor in the further peaceful development and social justice of this continent and indeed of the world community.

Speech, European Regional Conference (Sofia, Bulgaria) 6–9 November 2002

3 To the extent that Europe is becoming more varied as a result of the influx of new ethnic groups and cultures, the teaching of universal human values is increasingly important. While the inherited understanding of citizenship draws on national traditions, religion and culture, it also contains a hidden latent rejection of the Other.

Ibid.

3062. Marlo Thomas (1937–)

1 Women have gone through a real revolution in this country. They have started trusting one another.

Quoted in "Currents," U.S. News & World Report 12 October 1987

2 The message is a rather deep one, that you can choose your own role models, you can fight stereotypes. [Free to Be*] was a revolutionary book. Some people were even afraid of it.

Quoted in "Marlo Thomas: 'Free to Be' for you and me, 35 years later" by Craig Wilson, USA Today 6 October 2008
*A record album and songbook for children (1972) against gender stereotypes.

3063. Jennifer Tipton (1937–)

1 I often do feel that theatre might truly save the world. It is that expression on a stage in front of an audience—not the global communication that film and television can give—that tells us how we see ourselves, how we can better ourselves. It doesn't mean that all plays should be beautiful—we can better ourselves by picturing the worst, too. I'm deeply committed to theatre in all its forms.

Quoted in "The Facts of Light" by Arnold Aronson, American Theatre (New York) January 1986

2 You have to see the dancer to know what is going on, whereas in theatre that's not necessarily true; information can come from language.

Ibid.

3064. Diane Wakoski (1937–)

1 It happens all the time, I told her,
     some of us have bad vision, are crippled, have defects, and our reality is a different one, not the correct and ascertainable one, and sometimes it makes us dotty and lonely but also it makes us poets.

"The Birds of Paradise Being Very Plain Birds," St. 9, The East Side Scene, Allen de Loach, ed. 1968

2 My face
that my friends tell me is so full of character;
my face
I have hated for so many years;
my face
I have made an angry contract to live with
though no one could love it.

"I Have Had to Learn to Live with My Face," St. 2, The Motorcycle Betrayal Poems 1971

3 Mother-love: that is the only kind of love women are supposed to have; more importantly, there is no metaphor for women to be writers, singers, Orphic voices echoing the beauty of their longing and lost desire for the perfect mate or lost love.

"Lost and found," The Women's Review of Books, Vol. XII, Nos. 10–11 July 1995

3065. Jill Paton Walsh (1937–)

1 . . . no money has ever been minted which could pay for such conduct.

Grace 1994

2 Morning knowledge is different from evening knowledge. [Morning knowledge deals with] the nature of a straight line; evening knowledge is knowing that no line in the world is really straight.

A Knowledge of Angels 1995

3 "The world is more fun by far now it has you in it!"

When I Was Little Like You 1997

3066. Eleanor Wilner (1937–)

1 The woman, says the holy man, can never
   escape from *maya**; it grows in her like maggots
   in tainted meat, and drives her from his holy ground.

"maya" (p. 290), maya 1979
*The power of a god or demon to transform a concept into an element of the sensible world.

2 You can be chosen
or you can choose. Not both.

"Sarah's Choice" (p. 166), Sarah's Choice 1989

3 young men . . . filing into the black
belly of a huge cargo plane, each with a woman
in his wallet, her words on lilac paper,
her distant image as his aphrodisiac
in hell.

"Ume: Plum," (p. 100), Otherwise 1993

4 for there is no enlightenment
without immersion.

"Blessing," Reversing the Spell 1997

5 Shall we paste up the placards
of a revolution in which we no
longer believe?

"Up Against It" (p. 66), Ibid.

3067. Zhang Jie (1937–)

1 I am thirty, the same age as our People's Republic. For a republic thirty is still young. But a girl of thirty is virtually on the shelf.

"Love Must Not Be Forgotten" (1979) Gladys Yang,* tr.,
Seven Contemporary Chinese Women Writers, Gladys Yang,*
ed. *1982*

*See 2358.

2 Though not bound together by earthly laws or morality, though they never once clasped hands, each possessed the other completely. Nothing could part them. Centuries to come, if one white cloud trails another, two grasses grow side by side, one wave splashes another . . . believe me, that will be them.

Ibid.

3 I long to shout: "Mind your own business! Let us wait patiently for our counterparts. Even waiting in vain is better than willy-nilly marriage. To live single is not such a fearful disaster. I believe it may be a sign of a step forward in culture, education and the quality of life."

Ibid.

4 In China since the founding of the People's Republic, women have won equal rights in the social and economical spheres. But in social consciousness there is still a skepticism of women's abilities and there is still a degree of disrespect for women's dignity. But I don't think this problem can be solved by feminism alone. It depends on the progress of mankind as a whole, and that includes both material and spiritual progress.

Quoted in "The Art of the Chinese Writer" by Bruce Shenitz,
Newsweek (New York) *26 May 1986*

5 . . . there's no absolute freedom anywhere in the world. Freedom is always relative.

Ibid.

3068. Renata Adler (1938–)

1 If anything has characterized the [peace] movement, from its beginning and in all its parts, it has been a spirit of decentralization, local autonomy, personal choice, and freedom from dogma.

"Early Radicalism: The Price Of Peace Is Confusion" (11
December 1965), *Toward a Radical Middle 1969*

2 . . . nothing defines the quality of life in a community more clearly than people who regard themselves, or whom the consensus chooses to regard, as mentally unwell.

"The Thursday Group" (15 April 1967), Ibid.

3 I . . . doubt that film can ever argue effectively against its own material: that a genuine antiwar film, say, can be made on the basis of even the ugliest battle scenes. . . . the medium is somehow unsuited to moral lessons, cautionary tales or polemics of any kind. If you want to make a pacifist film, you must make an exemplary film about peaceful men.

"The Movies Make Heroes of Them All" (7 *January* 1968), *A
Year in the Dark: Journal of a Film Critic, 1968–69 1970*

4 At six one morning, Will went out in jeans and frayed sweater to buy a quart of milk. A tourist bus went by. The megaphone was directed at him. "There's one," it said. That was in the 1960s. Ever since, he's wondered. There's one what?

Speedboat 1976

5 In the strange heat all litigation brings to bear on things, the very process of litigation fosters the most profound misunderstandings in the world.

Lawyer's Wit and Wisdom, Bruce Nash, Allan Zullo, eds.;
Kathryn Zullo, compiler *1995*

3069. Antonia Arslan (1938–)

1 "No mercy for women, old men or children. If even one Armenian were to survive, he would later want revenge."

Skylark Farm, tr. Geoffrey Brock *2007*

2 "The pharmacist," he used to say, "ought to be equipped to send and receive telegrams. There could be an urgency."

Ch. 1, Ibid.

3 For Sempad, and all the others like him, it was literally inconceivable that a man could deceive—much less kill—someone with whom he drank tea *in his own home:* a guest!

Ibid.

3070. Ti-Grace Atkinson (1938–)

1 The continuance of the inheritance idea—the idea of living on through things, property, children—subverts any possibility of the communal society succeeding. For people to live communally instead of competitively, the bonds of inheritance must be completely broken.

Quoted in "The Second Feminist Wave" by Martha Weinman
Lear, *The New York Times Magazine 10 March 1968*

2 Love is the victim's response to the rapist.

Quoted in "Rebellion," *Sunday Times Magazine* (London) *14
September 1969*

3 The price of clinging to the enemy [a man] is your life. To enter into a relationship with a man who has divested himself as completely and publicly from the male role as much as possible would still be a risk. But to relate to a man who has done any less is suicide. . . . I, personally, have taken the position that I will not appear with any man publicly, where it could possibly be interpreted that we were friends.

Amazon Odyssey 1974

3071. Barbara Allen Babcock (1938–)

1 *Stock reply when asked what it felt like to have gotten her job because she was a woman:* It feels better than being rejected for the position because you're a woman.

Quoted in *Justice and gender: sex discrimination and the law*
by Deborah L. Rhode* *1989*

*See 4137.

2 Due process, both as aspiration and method, is at the heart of our study of procedure. Rules, statues, formal and informal decision making must all meet a due process standard. The United States Supreme Court has spoken on the subject in many settings. Sometimes, the process due is only what the legislature says must be done before the government takes property or liberty.

Even then, however, the government must notify the persons affected and afford them some chance to "tell the other side."

Ch. 1, *Civil Procedure: Cases and Problems* coauthors, Toni
Marie Massaro* & Norman Spaulding *2006*

*See 4316.

3072. Beatrix, Queen of the Netherlands (1938–)

1 I realize that much will be asked of me, yet I am resolved to accept it as a great and splendid task.*

Quoted in *The New York Times* 1 May 1980

*On succeeding to the throne.

2 Nature is under control but not disturbed.*

Quoted in *The New York Times* 5 October 1986

*On opening a new Dutch sea barrier.

3073. Mary Frances Berry (1938–)

1 If Rosa Parks* had taken a poll before she sat down in the bus in Montgomery, she'd still be standing.

Quoted in "Mary Frances Berry," *I Dream a World: Portraits of Black Women Who Changed America* by Brian Lanker 1989

*See 2206.

2 When it comes to justice, I take no prisoners and I don't believe in compromising.

Lawyer's Wit and Wisdom, Bruce Nash and Allan Zullo, eds.; Kathryn Zullo, compiler 1995

3074. Judy Blume (1938–)

1 "Are you there God? It's me, Margaret.
I just told my mother I want a bra.
Please help me grow God. You know where.
I want to be like everyone else."

Are You There God? It's Me, Margaret 1970

2 How come smart women like us keep falling in love with schmucks?

Smart Women 1983

3075. Helen Caldicott (1938–)

1 But the nuclear industry I've been debating for 35 years, and they lie. And it's hard to deal with people who lie. In medicine, if I lied about my patients or my treatment I would be deregistered. It's inappropriate to lie about science.

Quoted in interview by Monica Trauzzi, *E&E* TV talk show 5 October 2006

2 To go into Iraq and Afghanistan and kill people the way we are doing is enabling America's addiction to power, control and war. Rather, we should be trying to teach America how to live in peace with everyone in the world.

"NT takeover is nuke dump ploy," *The Age* 2 July 2007

3 We are the curators of life on earth. We hold it in the palm of our hand.

Remark *n.d.*

3076. Lois Capps (1938–)

1 First of all, Walter had me.* I don't have him.

Quoted in "Widows of Bono, Capps Are on Well-Worn Path to Office" by Jodi Wilgoren, *The Los Angeles Times* 26 January 1998

*Re: her late husband, Walter Holden Capps (1934–97), U.S. House of Representatives (D-CA); in office Jan.–Oct. 1997.

2 I have enormous respect for Sen. Clinton.* She is smart, dedicated and a champion of those often underserved and forgotten. She has a remarkable record of achievement that in-spires us all. And her election would fulfill a life long dream for so many of us who have been fighting for women's rights. She would make a great president.
But for me, Barack Obama is the best choice.

"Why I Am Supporting Barack Obama,"** *The Huffington Post* 30 April 2008

*See 3731. ** (1961–), 44th president of the United States (2001–).

3077. Sylvia C. Chard (1938–)

1 Children not only need to know *how* to use a skill but also *when* to use it.

"The Learner," *The Project Approach: Making Curriculum Come Alive* (Book 1) 1987

2 When a teacher is instructing a child in a new level of skill, the learning tasks have to be carefully matched to the child's abilities. When children are applying skills in which they have some fluency, they can work independently and with more confidence, make decisions, and solve problems as they arise.

Ibid.

3 When children are trusted to be competent and resourceful they will generally show those qualities.

Ch. 11, *Assessing Our Ways of Knowing*, Richard Sawa, ed. 2009

3078. Caryl Churchill (1938–)

1 CLEGG (speaking of his successful wife). It's very like having a talking dog, and it's on the front page at breakfast, the radio at dinner, the television at night—that's mine, look, that's my clever dog. But a time comes when you say, Heel. Home. Lie down.

Owners 1972

2 MARION. I can't be a failure just to help.

Ibid.

3 JOAN. Women, children, and lunatics can't be Pope.

Act I, Sc. 1, *Top Girls* 1982

4 NELL. Because that's what an employer is going to have doubts about with a lady as I needn't tell you, whether she's got the guts to push through to a closing situation. They think we're too nice. They think we listen to the buyer's doubts. They think we consider his needs and his feelings.

Act II, Sc. 1, Ibid.

5 Most theaters are still controlled by men and people do tend to be able to see promise in people who are like themselves.

"Caryl Churchill," *Interviews with Contemporary Women Playwrights*, Kathleen Betsko* and Rachel Koenig 1987

*See 3125.

6 [Margaret] Thatcher* had just become prime minister; there was talk about whether it was an advance to have a woman prime minister if it was someone with policies like hers: She may be a woman but she isn't a sister, she may be a sister but she isn't a comrade.

Ibid.

*See 2537.

3079. Alessandra Comini (1938?–)

1 One is born to it—to being an artist—by predisposition and talent; one achieves mastery of it by dint of study, hard

517

work, thought, experimentation, doubt, observation, striving, perseverance and above all, by following an inner imperative—sometimes buoyantly joyous, sometimes fatiguingly compulsive, always mysterious.

> Quoted in Foreword of *Exposures, Women & Their Art* by Ann Brown and Arlene Raven* 1989
> *See 3533.

2 To live in America in the 20th century means, for an increasing number of women, to have a chance at *multiple* creativity, artistic as well as biological.

> Ibid.

3080. Maria Fatima Velho da Costa (1938–)
Coauthor with Maria Isabel Barreno; see 3122, and Maria Teresa Horta; see 3036.

3081. Mariarosa Dalla Costa (1938?–)

1 In singling out the work of the housewife as that for which women are trained and by which women are defined; in identifying its product as labour power—the working class—this book broke with all those previous analyses of capitalist society which began and ended in the factory, which began and ended with men. Our isolation in the family while doing our work had hidden its social nature. The fact that it brought no wage had hidden that it was work.

> Foreword, *The Power of Women and the Subversion of the Community*, Selma James,* coauthor 1972
> *See 2719.

2 Behind the closed doors of the home, women provided a labour that had no retribution nor labour time nor holidays, whilst actually almost occupying the entire time of their lives.

> "The Door to the Garden: Feminism and Operaismo" (Rome) *June 2002*

3 Let's shed our coats and become less eurocentric, less anthropocentric and a little more animal, between rustic and ethical.

> "Rustic and Ethical" (Verona, Italy 9–10 April 2005), *Ephemera, Theory & Politics in Organization*, vol. 7 Giuseppina Mecchia, tr. *2007*

4 We need to preserve and respect the earth's vital cycles and biological balance if we want to maintain its ability to generate and regenerate harvests and crops every single year. . . . Most importantly, we have to remember that the earth can contain many human beings and create many working opportunities, if we do not upset it with big mechanical instruments, reducing it to a desolate landscape without trees, bushes or animals.

> Ibid.

5 This is the mother of all battles, where we see on one side the interests of multinationals and their scientists, and, on the other, the movement for another agriculture composed by peasants and citizens who refuse to be simple consumers and defend the seeds as common goods. In fact, the seeds are not only a gift of nature, but also of the work, the knowledge and the cooperation of entire generations of peasant men and women. Their being natural does not make them 'primitive'.

> Ibid.

6 Capitalist development is founded on the negation of women as persons and of the earth as living organism.

> Ibid.

3082. Paula B. Doress-Worters (1938–)

1 In the civil rights and feminist movements, we identified as universalists. We were afraid of seeing ourselves as too driven by our particularities; it wouldn't have been proper to call ourselves radical Jews. But that is exactly what we were.

> Interview with author (January 1996), p. 283, *The Journey Home, How Jewish Women Shaped Modern America*, Joyce Antler* 1997
> *See 3320.

2 [Ernestine Rose*] broke new ground for radical women's rights reform . . . through her activism, she helped shape progress toward the egalitarian society in which she wanted to live.

> Preface, *Mistress of Herself: Speeches and Letters of Ernestine L. Rose, Early Women's Rights Leader* 2008
> *See 913.

3 We must reclaim our right as a nation of voters to self-determination through fair and honest elections. As Ernestine Rose so cogently argued we must live up to the promise of the Declaration of Independence for universal rights, and in our time, resist the creation of new groups to be excluded. Finally, as Rose insisted, we must return to that core principle of our founding documents, the separation of church and state.

> Ibid.

3083. Colette Dowling (1938–)

1 I tell you, the great divide is still with us, the awful split, the Us and Them. Like a rubber band tautened to the snapping point, the polarization of the sexes continues, because we lack the courage to face our likenesses and admit to our real need.

> "A Woman Sounds Off on Those Sexy Magazines," *Redbook* (New York) *April 1974*

2 Here it was—the Cinderella Complex. It used to hit girls of sixteen or seventeen, preventing them, often, from going to college, hastening them into early marriages. Now it tends to hit women after college—after they've been out in the world a while. When the first thrill of freedom subsides and anxiety rises to take its place, they begin to be tugged by that old yearning for safety: the wish to be saved.

> *The Cinderella Complex 1982*

3 Once a man is on hand, a woman tends to stop believing in her own beliefs.

> Ch. 6, Ibid.

3084. Roxanne Dunbar-Ortiz (1938–)

1 "'What did the Wobblies* want?" I asked. No matter how many times he told me, I loved to hear his agenda of Wobbly dreams: abolition of interest and profits, public ownership of everything, no military draft, no military, no police, the equality of women and all races. "The O-B-U, One Big Union," he would say and smile to himself, lost in memory.

> Ch. 1, *Red Dirt: Growing Up Okie 1997*
> *The Industrial Workers of the World (IWW or the Wobblies), an international union currently headquartered in Cincinnati, Ohio, USA.

2 The political space that had been created by the 1960s movements began to contract even before Reagan'*s right-wing hardliners assumed power in 1981.

> Prologue, *Blood on the Border: A Memoir of the Contra War* 2005
> *Ronald R— (1911–2004), 40th president of the United States (1981–89).

3   I think we are becoming increasingly aware that History itself is an issue, often the issue: Who owns the history of the
United States? Do we accept the history of the Latino/Anglo
conquerors or the indigenous peoples in the Western Hemisphere? Whose version of history is valid in Palestine/Israel, in
Northern Ireland, in Cyprus, in Kashmir, in Afghanistan, in Sri
Lanka, and in hundreds of other situations?

Ibid.

3085. Marilyn Ferguson (1938–2008)

1   After a dark, violent age, the Piscean, we are entering a millennium of love and light—in the words of the popular song
"the Age of Aquarius," the time of "the mind's true liberation."

Ch. 1, *The Aquarian Conspiracy: Personal and Social
Transformation in the 1980s 1980*

2   Broader than reform, deeper than revolution, this benign
conspiracy for a new human agenda has triggered the most
rapid cultural realignment in history. The great shudder-
ing, irrevocable shift overtaking us is not a new political,
religious, or philosophical system. It is a new mind—the
ascendance of a startling worldview that gathers into its
framework breakthrough science and insights from earliest
recorded thought.

Ibid.

3   It is a dark, unspoken truth that the powerful—the "ruling
class"—make up the rules as they go along. Public policy is
designed by spin doctors who aim to keep our heads below the
water. The public good is not a consideration, and their self-
serving agendas prevail over common sense.

Introduction, *Aquarius Now: Radical Common Sense and
Reclaiming Our Personal Sovereignty 2005*

4   Most of us would prefer that others doubted our motives rather
than our intelligence.

Ch. 6, Ibid.

3086. Elisabeth Schüssler Fiorenza (1938–   )

1   To discuss the relationship between biblical-historical interpretation and feminist reconstruction of women's history in
biblical times is to enter an intellectual and emotional minefield.

Ch. 1, *In Memory of Her 1994*

2   No one who is even remotely aware of the history of feminist
biblical interpretation can deny that the scholarly discussion of
"Women in the Bible" can be abstracted from its apologetic-
political setting and function of legitimization. Whether the
bible is used in the trial of Anne Hutchinson* (1637) or in the
Vatican statement against the ordination of women (1977), its
function is the same, namely, the legitimization of societal and
ecclesiastical patriarchy and of women's "divinely ordained
place" in it.

Ibid.

*See 399.

3   In the past decade or so right-wing fundamentalist movements
around the world have insisted on portraying emancipated
women as signifiers of Western decadence or of modern atheist
secularism, but they have presented masculine power as the
expression of divine power.

Jesus: Miriam's Child, Sophia's Prophet (p.8) 1995

3087. Merrill Joan Gerber (1938–   )

1   Life was always life—this trip to death was just more of it.

Anna in the Afterlife 2002

2   Once her dying got underway, Anna could not really complain
about how the process moved along.

Ibid.

3   For her, indignation was a natural reaction. She found it a relief
to hold everything against everyone—it was almost her religion. For reasons she did not question, her life energy had been
powered by fury. She was actually surprised (now that she was
dead) that it hadn't kept her living forever.

Ibid.

4   Not suffer? What would be left if she didn't have suffering?

Ibid.

3088. Mary Ann Glendon (1938–   )

1   Laws are ways that society makes sense of things.

Quoted in *A World of Ideas* by Bill Moyers *1989*

2   Apparently we just don't feel that all American children of all
colors and social classes are our children, the way I think a
Swede quite easily feels that a child up in Lapland is very precious to a worker in Stockholm.

Ibid.

3   Pro-choice has some silent support among men who don't want
to take responsibility for fatherhood, among persons involved
in a profit-making abortion industry, and, maybe saddest of
all, among taxpayers who see abortion as a way of keeping
down the size of an underclass. So there's a lot of unspoken
support for the status-quo. On the other hand, pro-life has this
dark side of puntiveness toward women that I find absolutely
incomprehensible, but it seems to be there, as well as a certain
unwillingness to recognize that if you're going to be pro-life, it
shouldn't be with a view that life begins at conception and ends
at birth. You have to be pro-life all the way, and that means
supporting maternity, childbirth, and child raising, which has
become very difficult in our society, where both parents are
usually in the labor force.

Ibid.

4   There is always the danger that if you speak a language that
recognizes only individual rights, you will become a people
that can think only about individuals.

Ibid.

3089. Judith Partnow Hyman (1938–   )

1   The birth of a mother and a father is initiated by the Pro-
methean event of the birth of the first child.

"Shifting Patterns of Fathering in the First Year of Life,"
Becoming A Father, Jerrold Lee Shapiro, Michael J. Diamond,
and Martin Greenberg, eds. *1995*

2   The modern mother's dual interests in both briefcases and babies also has a significant influence on the way in which men
make the transition to fatherhood; among other things, there
is generally an increased vacuum in the care of the child, and
decreased pressure for him to be the sole provider. In this intermediate area a potential space is emerging that provides
an opportunity for men to be engaged in the procreation and
early care of children.

Ibid.

3   . . . the reawakened nurturance of the actively involved father whose infant is being breastfed is faced with a quandary: How does he cope with the fact that his partner is able to achieve a degree of intimacy with the infant of which he is totally denied? He has to deal with the paradox of being more involved, as he is expected to be, while simultaneously being excluded from the most intimate contact with his new baby.

Ibid.

4   Youth is as much a state of mind as it is a time and place in life. Just as in our later years we can be very young in some things, so during our so-called "youth" we may be very old in others.

Introduction, *The Complete Idiot's Guide to Your True Age,*
Elaine Bernstein Partnow,* coauthor 2009
*See 3291.

5   How many times have you heard an exchange like this: "Your daughter is darling, truly an amazing child. How old is she?" "Oh. She's 7 going on 35." Or what about this one: "Your husband is such a football enthusiast. I can't believe he still plays tackle with your boys." "Oh yes, my husband is 48 going on 16." Such dialogues may evoke laughter, a sagacious nodding of the head, or eyes rolling heavenward. Whatever your response, what such comments point out is that chronological age is just the tip of the iceberg. It doesn't begin to reveal what's underneath.

Ch. 1, Ibid.

6   Language is a boxing match in which you must spar daily, warding off negative suggestions that age is your worst enemy. Indeed, it is your best friend.

Ibid.

3090. Ellen Johnson-Sirleaf (1938–   )

1   We are a good people; we are a kind people. We are a forgiving people—and we are a God-fearing people.
So, let us begin anew, moving forward into a future that is filled with promise, filled with hope!

Inauguration Speech (Monrovia), *17 January 2006*

2   I would like to talk to the women—the women of Liberia, the women of Africa, and the women of the world. Until a few decades ago, Liberian women endured the injustice of being treated as second-class citizens. During the years of our civil war, they bore the brunt of inhumanity and terror. They were conscripted into war, gang raped at will, forced into domestic slavery. Yet, it is the women who labored and advocated for peace throughout our region.

Ibid.

3   We applaud the resilience of our people who, weighed down and dehumanized by poverty and rendered immobile by the shackles of fourteen years of civil war, went courageously to the polls, to vote. . . .

Ibid.

4   As a mother, I understand what is needed. As a grandmother, I'm thinking about our future.

Quoted in "Ma Ellen is Delivering Liberia" by Swanee Hunt,*
International Herald Tribune 14 March 2007
*See 3978.

5   The pace of development in any nation is contingent upon informed decision making, which is indispensably a function of

factual data collected, analyzed and propagated for the sustainability and viability of the nation.

Speech (Monrovia City Hall) *28 June 2007*

3091. Cheris Kramarae (1938–   )

1   For many feminists, pornography is the theory and rape is the practice.

A Feminist Dictionary, coauthor, Paula A. Treichler* 1987
*See 3643.

2   Perhaps a "talkative woman" is one who does talk as much as a man.

"Women's Speech: Separate but Unequal," *Quarterly Journal of Speech,* 60:1 1975

3   While some administrators and educators have predicted that bits and bytes will replace brick and mortar in the high-tech college of the 21st century, others are dubious that technology has or will change the fundamentals of education and university learning—for better or worse.

Pt. I: Introduction, *The Third Shift: Women Learning Online 2001*

3092. Jane Kramer (1938–   )

1   "It is a burden to have daughters," Dawia said, sighing. "My husband looks at Jmaa now and he says, 'What can I expect from her? More of the same problems I have suffered with the first two.'"
"He has a point," Musa remarked. "Having daughters is not profitable."

Pt. II, *Honor to the Bride 1973*

3093. Lilly Ledbetter (1938–   )

1   In my case, the money I should have been compensated hurt me, because my retirement was based on what I earned. So that was much lower. I'm like a second-class citizen for the rest of my life. I will never be compensated for my lower wages and my pension, and Social Security wages are much lower, because Goodyear* paid me less.

"TAP Talks with Lilly Ledbetter" by Ann Friedman, *The American Prospect 23 April 2008*
*Goodyear Tire & Rubber Co., established in 1898.

2   There's a lot of publicity about EEOC* and your rights, and I knew I was a lone female in a male-dominated factory. When I saw that note, it just floored me. I was so shocked at the amount of difference in our pay for doing the same exact job. When we got into the case, I was more shocked to see what all the other people were making, too. They all had much greater pay than I, and most had less seniority, less experience. And I worked there for 20 years. I was a good employee, and I worked hard; there was nothing I couldn't do.

Ibid.
*U.S. Equal Employment Opportunity Commission.

3   Women need to observe, pay attention, be alert. And if possible, have a mentor to help them along the way. If they get any written proof of discrimination, they need to hold onto it. But it's difficult if a corporation goes into it knowing they're going to discriminate.

Ibid.

4   Pay levels were a big secret [at Goodyear], but an anonymous person left a note in my mailbox at work one day, compar-

ing my pay to that of three male managers—and that's when I knew I'd been the victim of pay discrimination.*

"Senate approves landmark equal pay legislation" by David Lightman & Tony Pugh, McClatchy Newspapers
22 January 2009

*The Lilly Ledbetter Fair Pay Act of 2009 was signed into law by President Barack Obama on January 29, 2009; essentially, it eliminates the previous 180-day statute of limitations for filing an equal-pay lawsuit regarding pay; Ledbetter fought 10 years to win her case against Goodyear.

3094. Betty Bao Lord (1938–)

1 "If your heart did not break now and then, Spring Moon, how would you know it is there? Hearts break, then mend and break and mend again in a cycle without beginning, without end. As surely as dawn sows the evening, twilight sows the morn."

Prologue, *Spring Moon 1981*

2 "I fear, Lustrous Jade, that in broadening your mind, you have narrowed your heart."

Ch. 27, "Jade Phoenix," Ibid.

3 "If mortals wait until the gods remake the world to their liking to be happy, they are already in hell."

Ch. 38, "Sowing Dawn," Ibid.

4 "There is a season for sun, another for shadow. A season to sing, another to be silent. And, in all seasons, parting and re-union.

"In yielding we are like the water, by nature placid, conforming to the hollow of the smallest hand; in time, shaping even the mountains to its will.

"Thus we keep duty and honor. We cherish clan and civilization.

"We are Chinese."

Ibid.

3095. Beverly Lowry (1938–)

1 Gardening and scholarship were not so different; both took long hours and single-mindedness, resiliency in the face of major setbacks, a gift for tedium and a flair for the marriage of the unusual. Both strained the eyes and lower back and depended to some degree on fate, prejudice, perspective and the intuitive flash.

Breaking Gentle 1988

2 "Soup's on," she said in so low a voice not even the broccoli could have heard her.

Ibid.

3 I have always worked facing a blank white wall. With nothing to look at, no green view, no enticing piece of artwork to offer up distraction, the mind travels inside itself, into the imagination where—for writing fiction, making stuff up, or so I have always thought—the mind belongs.

"Snapshots," *Cross Over: A Murder, A Memoir 1992*

3096. Tatyana Mamonova (1938?–)

1 I, Tatyana Mamonova, the chief editor of *Woman and Russia*, the first free feminist publication in the Soviet Union, call the women of the whole world to solidarity with our struggle for our rights. I have been stripped of my Soviet citizenship and exiled from the Soviet Union, and now, as a

citizen of the world . . . I hope that all people of good will will support . . . women's moral resistance to the forces of evil and violence.

Quoted in *New Directions for Women November/December 1980*

3097. Judith Martin (1938–)

1 Dear Miss Manners: What should I say when I am introduced to a homosexual "couple?"

Gentle Reader: "How do you do?" "How do you do?"
Miss Manners' Guide to Excruciatingly Correct Behavior 1979

2 If you put together all the ingredients that naturally attract children—sex, violence, revenge, spectacle and vigorous noise—what you have is grand opera.

Ibid.

3 Etiquette doesn't have the great sanctions that the law has. But the main sanction we do have is in not dealing with these people and isolating them because their behavior is unbearable.

Quoted in *Netiquette* by Virginia Shea 1995

4 Civilized life begins with a boiled egg sitting upright in an egg cup.

Miss Manners column "Egg On Their Face," United Features Syndicate *19 June 2005*

5 In secular society, as in many religions, the willingness to share sustenance freely, even if one has little, is a test. Those who turn others away are in trouble, even if the visitor does not turn out to be a deity in disguise.

Ibid. *9 August 2008*

6 There are three possible parts to a date, of which at least two must be offered: entertainment, food, and affection. It is customary to begin a series of dates with a great deal of entertainment, a moderate amount of food, and the merest suggestion of affection. As the amount of affection increases, the entertainment can be reduced proportionately. When the affection is the entertainment, we no longer call it dating. Under no circumstances can the food be omitted.

Ibid. *n.d.*

7 It is far more impressive when others discover your good qualities without your help.

Ibid. *n.d.*

8 If written directions alone would suffice, libraries wouldn't need to have the rest of the universities attached.

Ibid. *n.d.*

9 "Dear Miss Manners: How is a hat correctly worn?
"Gentle Reader: Same as always; on the head."

Ibid. *n.d.*

3098. Glenna C. Matthews (1938–)

1 The notion of a "room of one's own" was unknown to colonial society, and privacy was an unheard-of luxury.

Ch. 1, *"Just a Housewife": The Rise and Fall of Domesticity in America 1989*

2 By 1850. . . . Women in their homes were the locus of moral authority in the society.

Ibid.

3 Would-be public women need more than just the removal of barriers to their access. They need imaginative new social arrangements so that they do not have to choose between the welfare of their loved ones and their public responsibilities. . . . Finally, we all need to recognize that women who stand up in public are still subject to scrutiny of their personal lives to an extent that often goes beyond what men experience. . . . Public woman will take her place alongside of public men only after the last residue of such unequal treatment has been obliterated.

The Rise of Public Woman: Woman's Power and Woman's Place in the United States 1630–1970 1993

3099. Joyce Carol Oates (1938–   )

1 She felt like a plant of some kind, like a flower on a stalk that only looked slender but was really tough, tough as steel, like the flowers in fields that could be blown down flat by the wind but yet rose again slowly coming back to life.

Pt. II, Ch. 6, *A Garden of Earthly Delights* 1967

2 She ransacked her mind, but there was nothing in it.

Pt. I, Ch. 15, *Them* 1969

3 ". . . women don't understand these things. They only understand money when they can see it. They're very crude essentially. They don't understand where money comes from or what it means or how a man can be worth money though he hasn't any at the moment. But a man understands all that."

Pt. II, Ch. 2, Ibid.

4 She would have a baby with her husband, to make up for the absence of love, to locate love, to fix herself in a certain place, but she would not really love him.

Pt. III, Ch. 1, Ibid.

5 The worst cynicism: a belief in luck.

Pt. II, Ch. 15, *Do With Me What You Will* 1970

6 . . . he believed in the justice of his using any legal methods he could improvise to force the other side into compromise or into dismissals of charges, or to lead a jury into the verdict he wanted. Why not? He was a defense lawyer, not a judge or a juror or a policeman or a legislator or a theoretician or an anarchist or a murderer.

Ibid.

7 . . . like all virtuous people he imagines he must speak the truth. . . .

Ibid.

8 Nothing is accidental in the universe—this is one of my Laws of Physics—except the entire universe itself, which is Pure Accident, pure divinity.

"The Summing Up: Meredith Dawe," Ibid.

9 "Loneliness is dangerous, it's bad for you to be alone, to be lonely, because if aloneness does not lead to God, it leads to the devil. It leads to the self."

"Shame" (1968), *The Wheel of Love and Other Stories* 1970

10 When a marriage ends, who is left to understand it?

"Unmailed, Unwritten Letters" (1969), Ibid.

11 Her mind churns so that she can't hear, she can't think.

"What Is the Connection Between Men and Women?" *Mademoiselle February 1970*

12 "Things move from invisibility to visibility," he said slowly. "There are tremendous forces, like hurricanes or floods, that people have inside them. Sometimes there is a break and the force rushes out. It can't be stopped. . . . But then there's calm again. It's as if there were terrible ghosts inside us that were always prodding and testing our skins, looking for weaknesses. Then one day they rush out into the world, outside us. And so a 'crime' is committed."

Do With Me What You Will 1973

13 I think of the improbable precision of the eye: the perfection of the iris, the pupil, the mirroring brain.

Son of the Morning 1977

14 It is not her body that he wants but it is only through her body that he can take possession of another human being, so he must labor upon her body, he must enter her body, to make his claim.

"In the Founders' Room," *Unholy Loves 1979*

15 The television screen, so unlike the movie screen, sharply reduced human beings, revealed them as small, trivial, flat, in two banal dimensions, drained of color. Wasn't there something reassuring about it!—that human beings were in fact merely images of a kind registered in one another's eyes and brains, phenomena composed of microscopic flickering dots like atoms. They were atoms—nothing more. A quick switch of the dial and they disappeared and who could lament the loss?

Pt. 1, Ch. 13, *You Must Remember This 1987*

16 She knows no more of how love ends than she knew as a child, she knows only of how love begins—in the belly, in the womb, where it is always present tense.

"Shopping," *Ms. (New York) March 1987*

17 Our house is made of glass . . . and our lives are made of glass; and there is nothing we can do to protect ourselves.

American Appetites 1988

18 Will is the conduit of fate.

Soul/Mate 1989

19 I used to think getting old was about vanity—but actually it's about losing people you love. Getting wrinkles is trivial.

"Master Race," Interview in *The Guardian* (London) *18 August 1989*

20 *Fear is good, fear is normal. Fear will save your life.*

First Love 1996

21 Past?—but the graveyard of Future.
   Future?—but the womb of Past.

My Heart Laid Bare 1998

22 There are places in the world where people vanish.

"Spider Boy," *High Lonesome, New & Selected Stories 1966–2006 2006*

23 . . . I am one of those individuals of a somewhat fantastical & nervous disposition, who entertains worries where there are none, as my late beloved V. observed of me, yet who does not sufficiently worry of what is.

"The Dying of the Light," *Wild Nights! Stories about the Last Days of Poe, Dickinson, Twain, James, and Hemingway 2008*

24 The truest life must always be hidden.

"Papa at Ketchum, 1961," Ibid.

25 In all of the Master's prose, not one bedpan.
  "The Master at St. Bartholomew's Hospital, 1914–1916," Ibid.

3100. Karen O'Connor (1938–)

1 [The] abortion issue may not be all that different from other policy issues, including civil rights and the environment. All such policy issues have gone off on tangents, incurred violence, and, ultimately, moved toward neutral ground. It appears that the abortion issue is now reaching that stage of equilibrium.
  No Neutral Ground? Abortion Politics in an Age of Absolutes
  1996

3101. Lyudmila Petrushevskaya (1938–)

1 YURA. . . . the family no longer exists. There is just the female tribe with their young ones, and lone males.
  The Stairwell 1983

2 All men are brothers.
  Not all—some are sisters!
  Three Girls in Blue (Tri devshki v golubom) 1983

3 She turned into a kind of commander, who knew the power of a retreat, of a withdrawal into the shadows, the power of silence.
  "Our Crowd," Helena Goscilo, tr., *Glasnost: An Anthology of Russian Literature under Gorbachev,* Helena Goscilo and Byron Lindsey, eds. *1990*

4 All people have remained animals internally and perceive everything that occurs without any words. . . .
  Ibid.

5 Russia is a land of female Homers . . . I'm just a listener among them.
  Told to Sally Laird, tr., Quoted by Oliver Ready, *The St. Petersburg Times* (Russia) *16 March 2001*

3102. Diane Ravitch (1938–)

1 The ladder was there, "from the gutter to the university," and for those stalwart enough to ascend it, the schools were a boon and a path out of poverty.
  The Great School Wars 1974

2 Everywhere the goals [of public schools] were few and simple: Children learned not only the basics of reading, 'riting, and 'rithmetic, but also the basics of good behavior. Principals and teachers considered character and intelligence to be of equal value, and neither was possible without "disciplining the will," which required prompt, unquestioning obedience to the teacher and the school rules.
  Ch. 1, *Left Back: A Century of Battles over School Reform*
  2001

3 Only by severing England's ties from the Catholic Church could Henry divorce his first wife, Catherine of Aragon,* and legitimize the male heir that he hoped Anne Boleyn** would produce. But instead of a son, Anne Boleyn gave birth to a mere daughter.***
  "Queen Elizabeth I," *The English Reader: What Every Literate Person Needs to Know 2006*
  *See 283; **see 300; ***see 334.

3103. Janet Reno (1938–)

1 Just as there should be a federal remedy for racial discrimination and for gender discrimination, I think in this instance somehow or another there has got to be a federal response to interference through physical conduct which restrains access to a woman's right to choose.
  Interview at swearing in ceremony (12 March), in "Reno takes an oath . . . ," *Seattle Post-Intelligencer*, A3 *13 March 1993*

2 There are too many people in this country who do not have competent counsel to represent them in capital cases.
  Quoted in "The Lawyers Live to Fight Again" by Jayson Blair, *The New York Times 25 June 2000*

3104. Diana E. H. Russell (1938–)

1 Wife rape has presumably been with us as long as the institution of marriage—at least in western culture.
  Ch. 1, *Rape In Marriage 1990*

2 But the viewing of wives as their husbands' property is not inevitable; it is part of our patriarchal heritage. The phenomenon of wife rape must be seen in the contest of the patriarchal family.
  Ibid.

3 Some people apparently find the information that a child has participated in a taboo sexual relationship exciting and provocative, regardless of the involuntary nature of the child's victimization. Incest victims, for example, appear to be particularly at risk of revictimization by male therapists and psychiatrists.
  p. 171, *Incest in The Life of Girls and Women* (rev) *1999*

3105. Nancy Simpson (1938–)

1 In hearing distance of a wave's yes, earth is a woman with plans.
  "Skin Underwater," *Night Student 1985*

3106. Queen Sofía of Spain (1938–)

1 The spirit of solidarity contained in that first loan of a few dollars which Professor Yunus* granted a young girl in the village of Jobra, to buy bamboo for making and selling her own chairs, has reached us today unchanged in its essence, while greatly multiplied in its successful results.
  Speech (Bangladesh) *2006*
  *Muhammad Y- (1940–), Bangladeshi banker and economist; fdr., Grameen Bank; Nobel Peace Prize, 2006.

2 . . . I believe that . . . we have managed to reinforce two concepts closely linked to the microcredit idea: the feeling of self-esteem experienced by its beneficiaries, and increased sense of responsibility towards their families and the society they live in.
  Ibid.

3 Children need an explanation of the origin of the world and life.
  Quoted in *The Queen Up Close* by Pilar Urbano *2008*

4 If those people want to live together, dress up like bride and groom and marry, they could have a right to do so, or not, depending on the law of their country, but they should not call this matrimony, because it isn't. There are many possible names: social contract, social union.
  Ibid.

3107. Susan Strasberg (1938–1999)

1 I'd rather not marry an actor because there isn't room in the house for two egos.
  Quoted in her obituary by Tom Vallance, *The Independent* (London) *25 January 1966*

3108. Liv Ullman (1938–   )

1   . . . we have to work to be good people . . . goodness always involves the choice to be good.

Quoted in Necessary Losses by Judith Viorst* 1986
*See 2780.

3109. Laurel Thatcher Ulrich (1938–   )

1   . . . it is in the very dailiness, the exhaustive repetitious dailiness, that the real power of Martha Ballard's book lies . . . For her, living was to be measured in doing. Nothing was trivial.

A Midwife's Tale: The Life of Martha Ballard, Based on Her Diary, 1785–1812 1991

2   *Well-Behaved Women Seldom Make History*

Book title 2007

3110. Luisa Valenzuela (1938–   )

1   In Victor's life, monotony and boredom had nothing to do with one another. He repeated his repertoire so often that even from miles away, Clara could follow his conversation with anyone who happened to be sitting next to him.

"The Body," Ch. 1, *Clara* (1967), Quoted in *Thirteen Short Stories and a Novel,* Hortense Carpenter and J. Jorge Castello, trs. *1976*

2   How good can freedom be if you're alone and broke, with just a few coins in the bottom of your purse, hidden in the lining, the forgotten coins nobody cares about.

Ch. 4, Ibid.

3   I am superior. I don't need any drugs, although at times I share those of others out of pure sociability, so as not to seem different. And to keep my business going: I produce drugs—no longer through my pores but in an industrial way, so others can attain, even if only in fleeting flashes, a little of the light that illuminates me.

For my personal use, I *am* the drug, the drug is I.

"The One," *The Lizard's Tale (El Brujo Hormiga Roja Señor Del Tacurú)*, Gregory Rabassa, tr. *1983*

4   The initial path can be repeated forever.

Ibid.

3111. Alena Vostrá (1938–   )

1   OFFSIDE. How should I put it? You have to ask yourself the question: are they governing you or are you governing them? This is the only defense. I tell myself: this is a sort of experiment as to what one can endure and what one can make another endure . . . It is all a game. . . . Finally we all shall get it. It is a sort of a merry-go-round.

Eeny Meeny Miney Mo 1966

3112. Gloria Jean Wade-Gayles (1938–   )

1   A metal comb placed on an open flame, heated, and then pulled through my hair suddenly seemed utterly ridiculous. . . . Straightened hair became a weight pulling my head down when I wanted to hold it up. High. . . . I decided to wear an Afro.

Pushed Back to Strength 1993

2   My students give me energy, pride, respect for the transforming power of literature and the learning experience. They are a magical mirror that reflects both the past and the future,

down this long, long stretch of years. I see myself, and I see my mother.

Quoted by Allison O. Adams in *Emory Magazine Spring 1994*

3   To scream, to know that you are heard, is the only right the violator has not taken from you.

"Fissures in the Moon: Sharing Pain in Order to Heal," *Rooted Against the Wind: Personal Essays 1996*

4   Perhaps I wore too heavy a scent of my fragrance in the grocery line or smiled too warmly when he cut in front of me at a traffic light. Perhaps I took the lighted darkness for granted and, as punishment, I lost the night. I whip myself.

Ibid.

3113. Davi Walders (1938?–   )

1   . . . we talk
of friends at fifty who buy answering machines,
wait for calls, keep money hidden in drawers, open
separate accounts, begin and end careers, take lovers,
let them go, reweave, unravel, gather and lose
tighten and loosen their hold on children, thighs,
lies and fears.

"Reflections in Green Glass," St. 4 *1992*

2   our eyes wear pouches
and hoods, as though expecting rain

"Anniversary," *A More Perfect Union: Poems and Stories About the Modern Wedding 1998*

3   People should be exposed to the art of poetry whether they are sick or well, rich or poor, or are college educated or not. The art of poetry speaks to the deepest parts of our hearts and I want to bring this to people who may have never experienced poetry.

"Poetry provides outlet for healing," *National Institutes of Health Newsletter April 2002*

4   We huddle
in coats, warming our hands
over freshly made vegetable soup, our eyes watching
the fragrant steam rise toward
glistening stars, listening to age-old prayers, comforted
by ritual, homes and heat to retreat to.

"Sukkot,"* *Poetica Magazine 9 October 2008*
*(a.k.a. Sukkos, Succoth) Feast of Booths or Feast of Tabernacles, it is a Jewish festival that occurs in autumn on the 15th day of the month of Tishreí (late September to late October) and lasts seven days; it celebrates the time when the Jewish populace traveled to the Temple in Jerusalem. The Hebrew word *Sukkot* means booths or huts.

3114. Maxine Waters (1938–   )

1   [President George W. Bush]* does not deserve to use the word "democracy" for he neither respects nor supports it, but simply promotes the rhetoric of democracy to his own advantage.

"Haiti: Maxine Waters denounces election fraud by coup government," haitiaction.net/News *15 February 2006*
*(1946–   ), Am. politician; 43rd president of the United States (2001–09).

2   The Haitian people have suffered greatly at the hands of the United States, France and Canada, powerful nations who preach democracy and yet orchestrated the removal of the democratically-elected president of Haiti and drove him from his own country.

Ibid.

3 I don't see white police officers slamming the heads of little white boys into police cars.

"FBI Probing Videotape Beating", CNN-TV 7 December 2006

4 Day after day, from Fallujah to Sadr City, our troops are placed in the midst of a civil war that cannot be contained by American forces.

While the president [George W. Bush] is determined to continue this war and has adopted the "cut and run" sound bite to intimidate those of us who disagree with him, the American people are demanding leadership, not safe political nuances by politicians who believe they can have it both ways.

"Bring the Troops Homes Now," feministpeacenetwork.org 15 March 2007

3115. Marie Winn (1938?–)

1 The television experience allows the participant to blot out the real world and enter into a pleasurable and passive mental state.

The Plug-In Drug 1977

2 Concern about the effects of television on children has centered almost exclusively upon the *content* of the programs children watch. . . . It is easy to overlook a deceptively simple fact: one is always *watching television* when one is watching television rather than having any other experience.

Ch. 1, The Plug-In Drug: Television, Computers, and Family Life 2002 rev.

3 Only through those self-propelled activities in which games are invented and dreams dreamed will children discover a self dependable enough to sustain them in place of those people and things they have been dependent on for so long.

p. 140, Ibid.

4 It's easy to see that there's time enough to begin teaching kids to be good drivers in high school. Yet the thought prevails that the children's future in a high-tech society requires them to start learning computer skills in kindergarten or earlier.

p. 170, Ibid.

5 The first time I walked through the Ramble at night I was terrified. I had been there in the daytime often enough; that thirty-seven-acre wilderness in the heart of Central Park is where I first became a birdwatcher. But the very features that enchanted me by day—the winding paths, the thicket of trees blocking out the city in all directions, the rock formations cropping up out of nowhere, the secret coves, the rustic bridges and sylvan streams—all looked grotesque and menacing in the darkness.

Ch. 1, Central Park in the Dark: More Mysteries of Urban Wildlife 2008

3116. Natalie Wood (1938–1981)

1 The only time a woman really succeeds in changing a man is when he is a baby.

Remark n.d.

3117. Jane Alexander (1939–)

1 The arts have tremendous economic power; they have the ability to communicate, to heal, to offer hope—to the troubled and disadvantaged, to the young child in the inner city, to the lonely and those looking for inspiration or solace or challenge.

Let that message ring out, and let us work toward getting more people into our theaters and introducing them to the arts.

Speech, Show Biz Expo-East (New York City, 6 January 1994), American Theatre (New York) March 1994

2 I knew what the endowment* did, because I had performed in regional theaters—it made those not-for-profit theaters possible in those communities. It made possible 13,000 art teachers in schools across the country. It provided seed money for the performing arts, for music, writing, painting, sculpture and folk crafts all across the nation, in every district, in villages and cities.

Quoted in "Let's Support Our Artists" by Dotson Rader, Parade Magazine 30 October 1994

*Reference to the National Endowment for the Arts.

3 There are two parts to the creative endeavor: making something, then disseminating it.

Ibid.

3118. Paula Gunn Allen (1939–)

1 Division
does not come easy to a woman,
it is against the tribe
laws which only women honor

III. Navajo, A Cannon between My Knees 1981

2 The best of the world slumps before me—minds
that eighteen years ago first turned earthward,
blinking.
oh yeah.
Wasted.
Turned off.
Tuned in to video narcosis,
stereophonic flight, transfixed.
naked angels burning their hopes, mine, on dust and
beer.

"Star Child Suit" II, St. 4, That's What She Said, Rayna Green, ed. 1984*

*See 3338.

3 We are the women of daylight; of clocks and steel
foundries, of drugstores and streetlights,
of superhighways that slice our days in two.
Our dreams are pale memories of themselves,
and nagging doubt is the false measure of our days.

"Kopis'taya," St. 3, Ibid.

4 The serene presence of the state, the faceless shadow of authority, of power, of those who controlled because they had seen fit to entomb themselves and their sacred honor in the vast caverns of city hall.

Untitled story, Ibid.

5 Human beings need to belong to a tradition and equally need to know about the world in which they find themselves.

"Something Sacred Going On out There" (1982), The Sacred Hoop 1986

6 [M]yth allows us to rediscover ourselves in our most human and ennobling dimensions. Through it we are allowed to see our own transcendent powers triumphant. . . .

Ibid.

3119. Margaret Atwood (1939–)

1 You fit into me
like a hook into an eye

a fish-hook
an open eye.

Epigraph, *Power Politics 1971*

2   I've never understood why people consider youth a time of
freedom and joy. It's probably because they have forgotten
their own.

"Hair Jewelry," *Ms.* (1976), *Dancing Girls and Other Stories
1982*

3   Who knows, your very flesh may be polluted, dirty as an oily
beach, sure death to shore birds and unborn babies. Maybe a
vulture would die of eating you. . . . Women took medicines,
pills, men sprayed trees, cows ate grass, all that souped-up piss
flowed into the rivers. Not to mention the exploding atomic
power plants.

The Handmaid's Tale 1986

4   Nobody dies from lack of sex. It's lack of love we die from.

Ibid.

5   "What's the point of continuing, in a society like this one,
where it's always two steps forward and two back?"

"Uglypuss," *Bluebeard's Egg and Other Stories 1986*

6   Time is not a line.

first line, *Cat's Eye 1989*

7   Nothing ever goes away

Ibid.

8   Popular art is the dream of society; it does not examine itself.

"A Question Of Metamorphosis," interview in *Malahat
Review,* No. 41 (1977), *Conversations,* Earl G. Ingersoll, ed.
1990

9   If a stranger taps you on the ass and says, "How's the little lady
today!" you will probably cringe. But if he's an American, he's
only being friendly.

Ibid.

10 The personal is not political, thinks Tony: the personal is military. War is what happens when language fails.

The Robber Bride 1993

11 There must be people like that around, because there are more
humans alive on the earth right now than have ever lived, altogether, since humans began, and if souls are recycled then there
must be some people alive today who didn't get one, sort of
like musical chairs.

Ibid.

12 Women don't want all the men eaten up by man-eaters; they
want a few left over so they can eat some themselves.

Ibid.

13 Men's bodies are the most dangerous things on earth.

"Making a Man," *Good Bones and Simple Murders 1994*

14 Men such as him do not have to clean up the messes they make,
but we have to clean up our own messes, and theirs into the
bargain. In that way, they are like children, they do not have to
think ahead, or worry about the consequences of what they do.

Alias Grace 1996

15 "Nothing is more difficult than to understand the dead, I've
found; but nothing is more dangerous than to ignore them."

The Blind Assassin 2000

16 We don't like bad news, but we need it. We need to know about
it in case it's coming our way.

"The Bad News," *Moral Disorder 2006*

3120. Nancy Azara (1939–   )

1   There is a similar kind of silence that is found in sculpture as
there is in a garden.

*Feminist Foremothers Women's Studies, Psychology, Mental
Health,* Phyllis Chesler,* Esther D. Rothblum, and Ellen Cole,
eds. *1995*

*See 3184.

2   Visual art, such as painting and sculpture, has its own kind of
language. It reaches us in a way that words cannot, for words
cannot be literally translated into visual form. Art is not only
the pictorial description of something beautiful. As defined in
this book, art is a visual description in a language of shape,
color and form, presenting the viewer with a dialogue different
from that found in words. It is a graphic manifestation of the
way we think and feel.

Introduction, *Spirit Taking Form: Art Making as a Spiritual
Practice 2002*

3   As a child, I would spend many silent hours in my grandfather's
garden lying on the earth and looking at the flowers and plants.
I would watch the shadows of the trees move and change on the
lawn, observe a baby bird learn to fly and sometimes I thought
I could see a flower open. In those moments I began to confirm my suspicion that there was something beyond that which
I could see, and although invisible and intangible, I could sense
that unseen presence, know somehow that it was connected to
the place of spirit and the divine in me.

"Painting, Sculpture, and the Spiritual Dimension: The
Kingston and Winchester Papers," *Pursuit of the Divine 2003*

4   Anyone can make art. Finding one's spiritual center can come
of making art. Making art can come of finding one's spiritual
center.

Artists Section, Veteran Feminists of America (vfa.us) *2007*

3121. Toni Cade Bambara (1939–1995)

1   The genocidal bloodbath of centuries and centuries of witch
hunts sheds some light on the hysterical attitude white men
have regarding their women.

Lecture, "The Scattered Sopranos," Livingston College Black
Women's Seminar, *The Black Woman 1970*

2   Revolution begins with the self, in the self.

Ibid.

3   Being American and being proud and they weren't the same
in her head. When Dada Bibi talked about Harriet Tubman*
and them, she felt proud. She felt it in her neck and in her
spine. When the brother who ran the program for the little kids
talked about powerful white Americans robbing Africa and
bombing Vietnam and doing ugly all over the world, causing
hard times for Black folks and other colored people, she was
glad not to be American.

"A Girl's Story," *The Sea Birds Are Still Alive 1974*
*See 978.

4   It was simpler to watch than to listen.

Ibid.

5   Bless the workers and beam on me if you please.

Dedication Page, *The Salt Eaters 1980*

6 "What is wrong, Old Wife? What is happening to the daughters of the yam? Seem like they just don't know how to draw up the powers from the deep like before."

Ibid.

3122. Maria Isabel Barreno (1939–)

1 . . . all friendship between women has a uterine air about it, the air of a slow, bloody, cruel incomplete exchange, of an original situation being repeated all over again.

New Portuguese Letters, coauthors, Maria Fatima Velho da Costa,* Maria Teresa Horta** *1972*
*See 3080. **See 3036.

2 The time of discipline began. Each of us the pupil of whichever one of us could best teach what each of us needed to learn.

Ibid.

3 . . . we are still the property of men, the spoils today of warriors who pretend to be our comrades in the struggle, but who merely seek to mount us. . . .

Ibid.

4 One lives and endures one's life with others, within matrices, but it is only alone, truly alone that one bursts apart, springs forth.

Ibid.

5 Let no one tell me that silence gives consent, because whoever is silent dissents.

Ibid.

3123. Kathleen Barry (1939?–)

1 Conning a girl or young woman by feigning friendship or love is undoubtedly the easiest and most frequently employed tactic of slave producers (and one that is also used for procuring young boys) and it is the most effective.

Ch. 1, *Female Sexual Slavery 1979*

2 Giving a false sense of earning money, and subsequent indebtedness, are traditional strategies for keeping enslaved prostitutes from rebelling.

Ibid.

3 Female sexual slavery is not an illusive condition; the word "slavery" is not merely rhetorical. Slavery is an objective social condition that requires escape in order for the victim to get out of it. Slavery is one aspect of the violation of women and children in prostitution, in marriage, and in families.

"Pimping: The World's Oldest Profession," *On The Issues* (ontheissuesmagazine.com) *Summer 1995*

3124. Mary Catherine Bateson (1939–)

1 The family is changing, not disappearing. We have to broaden our understanding of it, look for the new metaphors.

Quoted in *A World of Ideas* by Bill Moyers *1989*

2 There are few things as toxic as a bad metaphor. You can't think without metaphors.

Ibid.

3 Fear is not a good teacher. The lessons of fear are quickly forgotten.

Ibid.

4 Either we have to make the leap to a vision that includes all human beings, or we are locked up in tiny, local self-interest and prejudices—and at that point, why not just get rich and enjoy yourself? It's as if the time had come to recognize that we are one.

Ibid.

5 This is the century of the refugee.

Ibid.

3125. Kathleen Betsko (1939–)

1 Most war tales have been about male bravery. National history seen through men's militaristic eyes. I want to record the history of England's mothers at war . . . children at war.

"Kathleen Betsko," *Interviews with Contemporary Women Playwrights,* with Rachel Koenig *1987*

2 I think the theater should be a place to "get down and dirty" . . . passionate, visceral. Even unfair if necessary. Fairness is the opposite of passion.

Ibid.

3 In my own opinion, women think and write differently than men because they have different experiences, different myths, different needs and desires and dreams and memories. As feminist scholars have pointed out, we exist as a separate culture within the dominant culture. A culture distinct from men's, no matter how intimately we may live with or love them.

Ibid.

3126. Carol Brightman (1939–)

1 Naturally the most sophisticated person she [Mary McCarthy] would ever meet (at sixteen) would be a lesbian, for whom sex appeared to be a simple dalliance with one's own sex, and not the devil's bargain it often seemed to be with the *opposite* sex.

Prologue, *Writing Dangerously: Mary McCarthy and Her World 1992*

2 The character of any town is set by what takes place in it . . .

Ch. 2, Ibid.

3 "Never Trust Anyone under 80"

Article title, *The Nation* (New York) *17 January 1994*

4 True power, as Machiavelli* and Confucius** knew, asserts itself through countless channels, mostly pacific. On this score, Vietnam taught the U.S. a hard lesson, or tried to.

"The End of Deterrence," *Los Angeles Times 22 September 2002*
*Niccolò M- (1469–1527), Italian political theorist who developed means by amoral and calculating systems of maintaining power. ** (ca. 551–479 B.C.) Chinese philosopher who urged a system of morality and statecraft to bring about peace and stability.

3127. Maxine Brown (1939–)

1 In order to get them both (black teenagers and white teenagers] in the same building [to hear music], they would put a rope down the middle—the whites on one side and the blacks on this side of the rope. And they were enjoying the same music; everyone was having a ball. You just didn't cross over the rope.

"Lady Writes the Blues: The Life of Rose McCoy," *NPR Radio Diaries 27 February 2009*

3128. Rosellen Brown (1939–)

1 "Do you think there could be something like victims without crimes?"

"A Letter to Ismael in the Grave," *Street Games* 1974

2 "I wish you were alive. I wish, I wish, so I could hate you and get on with it."

Ibid.

3 I know how he dreams me. I know because I dream his dreams.

"How to Win," Ibid.

3129. Gro Harlem Brundtland (1939–)

1 We need a wider definition of national security . . . The destruction of the planet's environment is making the world a less stable place, politically, economically and militarily . . . Our environmental management practices have focused largely upon after-the-fact repair of damage . . . The ability to anticipate and prevent environmental damage will require that the ecological dimensions of policy be considered at the same time as the economic, trade, energy, agricultural and other dimensions.

From television broadcast, "Only One Earth," Quoted in *Ms.* (New York) *January 1989*

2 There is a very close connection between being a doctor and being a politician. The doctor first tries to prevent illness, then tries to treat it if it comes. It's exactly the same as what you try to do as a politician, but with regard to society.

Quoted in "Norway's Radical Daughter" by Nancy Gibbs,* *Time* (New York) *25 September 1989*

*See 3479.

3 I do not know of any environmental group in any country that does not view its government as an adversary.

Ibid.

4 Only by educating people and giving them a fair chance to break out of poverty can we help to find a sustainable relation between population and resources.

Technology Review 1993

5 Morality becomes hypocrisy if it means accepting mothers' suffering or dying in connection with unwanted pregnancies and illegal abortions and unwanted children.

Speech, U.N. Conference on Population and Development (Cairo) *5 September 1994*

6 The myth that men are the economic providers and women, mainly, are mothers and care givers in the family has now been thoroughly refuted. This family pattern has never been the norm, except in a narrow middle-class segment.

Remark (1995), Quoted in *Women in World History Curriculum* (home.earthlink.net/~womenwhist) *1996–97*

7 The environment is where we all live; and development is what we all do in attempting to improve our lot within that abode. The two are inseparable.

Quoted in *Twentieth-Century Women Political Leaders* by Claire Price-Groff *1998*

3130. Joan Busfield (1939?–)

1 It is only if we can manage to create a better society that we are likely to enhance the mental health of the population as a whole. The complete eradication of mental disorder in both women and men is a utopian dream; some reduction in disorder through making our social institutions and social arrangements less destructive and difficult is not.

Men, Women and Madness: Understanding Gender and Mental Disorder 1996

3131. Siv Cedering (1939–)

1 . . . when I finish my other work
I can spend all night sweeping
the heavens.

"Letter from Caroline Herschel* (1750–1848)," St. 4, *From Songs from Unsung Worlds (Science in Poetry)*, Bonnie B. Gordon, ed. *1985*

*See 662.

2 However long we live, life is short, so I
work. And however important man becomes,
he is nothing compared to the stars.
There are secrets, dear sister, and it is
for us to reveal them. Your name, like mine,
is a song.

St. 9, Ibid.

3132. Barbara Chase-Riboud (1939–)

1 Pride is never sinful when it is Justice.

Echo of Lions 1989

3133. Judy Chicago (1939–)

1 . . . I suddenly knew that I was alone forever, that I could lose the people I loved any time, any moment, and that the only thing I had in this life was myself.

Ch. 1, *Through the Flower: My Struggle as a Woman Artist 1975*

2 I did not understand that wanting doesn't always lead to action.

Ch. 4, Ibid.

3 The acceptance of women as authority figures or as role models is an important step in female education. . . . It is this process of identification, respect, and then self-respect that promotes growth.

Ch. 5, Ibid.

4 After some years in the art world trying to pretend I wasn't a woman, I decided for better or worse I had to be who I was.

Quoted in "Judy Chicago," *Exposures, Women & Their Art* by Ann Brown and Arlene Raven* *1989*

*See 3533.

5 When we look at the Empire State Building or the Washington Monument, nobody yells "Penis!" We are used to seeing the world through male images, not our own likenesses.

Ibid.

3134. Terry Cole-Whittaker (1939–)

1 Examine where money is an issue in your life—where the lack of it holds you back, where the abundance of it is a problem, or where the fear of having it or losing it is an obstacle. Are you a money victim or are you a money generator and curator? This doesn't have to be a have-not world.

How To Have More In A Have-Not World 1983

3135. Judy Collins (1939–)

1 In the future we will have pop song cycles like classical Lieder, but we will create our own words, music, and orchestrations, because we are a generation of whole people.

Quoted in Rock and Other Four Letter Words *by J. Marks*
1968

2 I look in the mirror through the eyes of the child that was me.
"Secret Gardens of the Heart" 1972

3 Secret gardens of the heart where the old stay young forever.
. . .
Ibid.

3136. Yaël Dayan (1939–)

1 Within me I would be the mistress; outside, if necessary, a slave. I would knit my world together, make contact with the outside world, write the right kinds of letters, and be as I thought appropriate to different people.

New Face in the Mirror 1959

2 He picked up some earth and poured it into the boy's palm. "Grasp it, feel it, taste it. There is your God. If you want to pray, boy, pray to the sky to bring rain to our land and not virtue to your souls."

Ch. 4, *Envy the Frightened 1960*

3 It wasn't a battle really, as it wasn't a war. Nor was it a game, not when you heard the poisonous shrieking of the bullets—confused, scattered, searching above your heads—there was no feeling of deep revenge or hatred. It was almost as quiet as a day's work, only moments seemed eternal and seconds endless . . . Not a war, or a battle, but a fight.

Ch. 18, Ibid.

4 She was friendless and yet a friend to others and the same intensity with which she ignored the future marked her passionate attitude to the past.

Ch. 8, *Death Had Two Sons 1967*

5 I'm not a feminist. I take my equality for granted. I'm not breaking away from the tradition. I cultivate it. I don't need sisters.

"Women in the Firing Line" by Betty Friedan,* *The New York*
Times 28 October 1984
*See 2398.

3137. Shelagh Delaney (1939–)

1 HELEN. The only consolation I can find in your immediate presence is your ultimate absence.

Act. I, Sc. 1, *A Taste of Honey 1959*

2 JO. In this country [England] there are only two seasons, winter and winter.

Sc. 2, Ibid.

3 HELEN. Why don't you learn from my mistakes? It takes half your life to learn from your own.

Ibid.

4 BOY. Women never have young minds. They are born three thousand years old.

Ibid.

5 NELL. Some women will have any sort of a man rather than no man at all.

The Lion in Love 1960

6 According to her, only a revolution will ever bring true democracy to this country and the sooner revolution comes (she said) the better and even though hundreds of innocents will be slaughtered they will die in a good cause and men must be willing to sacrifice themselves. But that depends I suppose on which men you're thinking of. . . .

"Sweetly Sings the Donkey," *Sweetly Sings the Donkey 1963*

7 He didn't play with his food anymore till it got cold; instead, down it went like fuel into a furnace keeping the ovens hot, and the energy at boiling point, as Tom hurtled through his life catching up with himself at last.

"Tom Riley," Ibid.

3138. Margaret Anne Doody (1939–)

1 One of the most successful literary lies is that the English claim to have invented the novel.

The True Story of the Novel 1996

2 We make a not unimportant spiritual and political as well as personal move when we open a novel and become initiates, entering upon the marshy margins of becoming.

Ibid.

3139. Margaret Drabble (1939–)

1 It appalled him, the complacency with which such friends would describe the advantages of living in a mixed area. As though they licensed seedy old ladies and black men to walk their streets, teaching their children of poverty and despair, as their pet hamsters and guinea pigs taught them of sex and death.

Pt. I, *The Needle's Eye 1972*

2 . . . she used to pray . . . and she still prayed, occasionally, not incessantly as she had done through childhood, but every now and then a natural or man-made calamity would push her imperiously to her knees, a massacre, an earthquake, a drowning, and she would implore justice, mercy, intercession, explanation, not praying any more for herself, as she had once so futilely done . . . wondering even as she knelt whether there were any use in such genuflections, and yet pushed down as certainly as if a hand had descended on her head to thrust her from above, crushing her hair and weighing on her skull.

Pt. II, Ibid.

3 How easy it was to underestimate what had been endured.

Ibid.

4 People like admiration more than anything. Whatever can one do about it?

"A Success Story," *Spare Rib Magazine 1972*

5 We seek a utopia in the past, a possible if not ideal society. We seek golden worlds from which we are banished, they recede infinitely, for there never was a golden world, there never was anything but toil and subsistence, cruelty and dullness.

The Realms of Gold 1975

6 . . . the human mind can bear plenty of reality but not too much intermittent gloom.

Ibid.

7 But his heart was another matter. It beat in his chest, soft and treacherous. It was invisible. Nobody had ever seen it. He had been unaware of it most of the time, until it had reminded him of its existence. And now he thought of it often, he nursed it

carefully, as though it were a baby or a bird, a delicate creature that must not be shocked or offended.

Pt. I, *The Ice Age* 1977

8   When nothing is sure, everything is possible.

The Middle Ground 1980

9   A male world, a world of suits and ties and speeches, of meetings and money. Charles had conquered it. First he had mocked it, then he had exposed it, then he had joined it, and now he represented it.

The Radiant Way 1987

10   I did not realize the dreadful facts of life. I did not know that a pattern forms before we are aware of it, and that what we think we make becomes a rigid prison making us. In ignorance and innocence I built my own confines, and by the time I was old enough to know what I had done, there was no longer time to undo it.

Ch. 1, *The Millstone* 1998

11   She enjoyed ill health. It was her earliest source of pleasure and indulgence.

Ch. 1, *The Peppered Moth* 2002

12   Mr. Beever preached docility, acceptance, littleness, the second-rate. But the Bible was different. It was grand, extreme and horrid. It spoke damnation and darkness, it sounded cymbals and trumpets, it flared its nostrils and it sniffed another air.

Ibid.

13   Nothing much happened to us, but we all wrote about it nonetheless.

Part One, Her Diary, *The Seven Sisters* 2003

14   I sometimes have fears that my Health Club may not be very healthy after all.

Ibid.

15   None of us has full access to even our own stories.

Ch. 1, *The Red Queen* 2005

3140. Roxanne Dunbar (1939–   )

1   Man, in conquering nature, conquered the female, who had worked with nature, not against it, to produce food and to reproduce the human race.

"Feminine Liberation as the Basis for Social Revolution,"
Sisterhood Is Powerful, Robin Morgan,* ed. 1970
*See 3284.

2   We live under an international caste system, at the top of which is the Western white male ruling class, and at the bottom of which is the female of the nonwhite colonized world.

Ibid.

3   In reality, the family has fallen apart. Nearly half of all marriages end in divorce, and the family unit is a decadent, energy-absorbing, destructive, wasteful institution for everyone except the ruling class for which the institution was created.

Ibid.

3141. Marian Wright Edelman (1939–   )

1   Just because a child's parents are poor or uneducated is no reason to deprive the child of basic human rights to health care, education, proper nutrition. Clearly we ignore the needs of black children, poor children, and handicapped children in the country.

Quoted in "Society's Pushed-Out Children" by Marge Casady,
Psychology Today (New York) *June 1975*

2   I've been struck by the upside-down priorities of the juvenile-justice system. We are willing to spend the least amount of money to keep a kid at home, more to put him in a foster home, and the most to institutionalize him.

Ibid.

3   Some school officials have forgotten the reason they are there. Expediency and efficiency in administration have somehow become more important than educating children.

Ibid.

4   Democracy is not a spectator sport.

Families in Peril 1987

5   It is a spiritually impoverished nation that permits infants and children to be the poorest Americans.

The Measure of Our Success 1992

6   Children must have at least one person who believes in them. It could be a counselor, a teacher, a preacher, a friend. It could be you. You never know when a little love, a little support, will plant a small seed of hope.

Ibid.

7   Service to others is the rent you pay for living on this planet.

Quoted in "Make Things Better For Somebody" by Wallace
Terry, *Parade Magazine 14 February 1993*

8   Our worst nightmares are coming true. After years of epidemic poverty, joblessness, racial intolerance, family disintegration, domestic violence and drug and alcohol abuse, the crisis of children having children has been eclipsed by the greater crisis of children killing children.

Annual Report, Children's Defense Fund *1993*

9   If we don't wake up and take care of our children, the country is going to go to hell. This is our moral and practical Achilles heel.

Quoted in Intelligence Report by Jane Ciabattari, *Parade
Magazine 3 May 1997*

3142. María Espinosa (1939–   )

1   Nuns weep tears of crystal
For the love of God.

Untitled, *Night Music, poems* 1969

2   Why was it difficult to get into the unions, he wondered? Wasn't this the land of opportunity? He didn't understand this country at all. The slang expression "oh boy"—how indicative it seemed. A country of boys and girls. They had not been hardened yet by suffering. They did not want to acknowledge their maturity but wished to remain adolescent forever. There was something wrong about those values.

Longing 1995

3   Invisible structures of steel-like strength constrict us or let us flow. These structures guide our movements and our thoughts, form our beliefs, form our sense of what is possible. These structures can be built on subtle as well as overt happenings—a glance, a smile, a tone of voice, what is spoken of or ignored. . . .

Dying Unfinished 2009

4 To pass afternoons in unfamiliar rooms with a stranger's hands on her body gave her pleasure and a sense of freedom. The stranger's touch was proof she existed; the stranger's fluids fertilized her with life . . . her body was her own, one thing she could salvage from the ruins.

Ibid.

3143. Terry Garthwaite (1939–)

1 from bessie to bebe to billie to boz
there's a lot more power than the wizard of oz

"Rock and Roller" 1975

3143.1. Galia Golan (1939?–)

1 Israel has changed enormously. I immigrated in 1966, exactly forty years ago. It was a socialist country. It had a mixed economy but it had a very strong welfare state, a good deal of social justice. We had the lowest gap between rich and poor in the world, and today we have the highest, or the second highest, only behind the U.S. It has changed enormously. The welfare state has been dismembered. We have privatization running wild, which by the way, began with the Labour Party in the eighties.

Quoted in "Conversation with Galia Golan: The Israeli Peace Movement and the 2006 Lebanon War" by Harry Kreisler, Institute of International Studies (UC Berkeley) *16 October 2006*

2 The truth is that today the United States is the only superpower, and while the Europeans are very helpful and they pour a good deal of money into the region and they have good will, they're not a force, they're not a power. It's the Americans, and the Americans could, if they wanted to, bring us together. They could. They could bring Israel and the Palestinians together, they could force us to talk to each other again. They could force us. And certainly, they could release us to talk with the Syrians.

Ibid.

3 I'm somebody who's always believed that the way to go with enemies is engagement and not confrontation. I believed that with the Soviet Union, I think it's the case with Hamas, for example, and I think it's the case with Iran. I think that engagement would be a lot smarter than confrontation but I don't see anybody taking that path. I certainly am hopeful that the United States doesn't decide to take a crazy position, that is, to attack Iran, which I think would be absurd. We would be the victims, because any response to the United States would be on us. I can only hope that the Americans will not go in that direction.

Ibid.

See also Zahira Kamal, 3586:1–2.

3144. Joan Goulianos (1939–)

1 . . . These . . . women [of history] . . . wrote in a world which was controlled by men, a world in which women's revelations, if they were anything but conventional, might not be welcomed, might not be recognized, and they wrote nevertheless.

Introduction, By a Woman Writt 1973

2 But, overall, it was men who were the critics, the publishers, the professors, the sources of support. It was men who had the power to praise women's work, to bring them to public attention, or to ridicule them, to doom them . . . to obscurity.

Ibid.

3145. Germaine Greer (1939–)

1 The consequences of militancy do not disappear when the need for militancy is over. Freedom is fragile and must be protected. To sacrifice it, even as a temporary measure, is to betray it.

Introduction, The Female Eunuch 1971

2 Every time a man unburdens his heart to a stranger he reaffirms the love that unites humanity.

"The Ideal," Ibid.

3 Every time a woman makes herself laugh at her husband's often-told jokes she betrays him. The man who looks at his woman and says "What would I do without you?" is already destroyed.

"Egotism," Ibid.

4 Revolution is the festival of the oppressed.

"Revolution," Ibid.

5 What is the arms race and the cold war but the continuation of male competitiveness and aggression into the inhuman sphere of computer-run institutions? If women are to cease producing cannon fodder for the final holocaust they must rescue men from the perversities of their own polarization.

"The Psychological Sell," Ibid.

6 There is no such thing as security. There never has been. . . .

"Security," Ibid.

7 Loneliness is never more cruel than when it is felt in close propinquity with someone who has ceased to communicate.

Ibid.

8 The most threatened group in human societies as in animal societies is the unmated male: the unmated male is more likely to wind up in prison or in an asylum or dead than his mated counterpart. He is less likely to be promoted at work and he is considered a poor credit risk.

Ch. 2, Sex and Destiny 1984

9 The management of fertility is one of the most important functions of adulthood.

Ibid.

10 All societies on the verge of death are masculine. A society can survive with only one man; no society will survive a shortage of women.

Ch. 3, Ibid.

11 The only perfect love to be found on earth is not sexual love, which is riddled with hostility and insecurity, but the wordless commitment of families, which takes as its model mother-love.

Introduction, The Madwoman's Underclothes 1986

12 Human beings have an inalienable right to invent themselves; when that right is pre-empted it is called brain-washing.

Times (London) 1 February 1986

13 English culture is basically homosexual in the sense that the men only really care about other men.

Daily Mail (London) 18 April 1988

14 Libraries are reservoirs of strength, grace and wit, reminders of order, calm and continuity, lakes of mental energy, neither warm nor cold, light nor dark. The pleasure they give is steady,

unorgiastic, reliable, deep and long-lasting. In any library in the world, I am at home, unself-conscious, still and absorbed.

"Still in Melbourne, *January 1987,*" *Daddy, We Hardly Knew You 1989*

15 To be unwanted is also to be free.

The Change: Women, Aging and the Menopause 1991

16 The older woman's love is not love of herself, nor of herself mirrored in a lover's eyes, nor is it corrupted by need. It is a feeling of tenderness so still and deep and warm that it gilds every grassblade and blesses every fly. It includes the ones who have a claim on it, and a great deal else besides. I wouldn't have missed it for the world.

Introduction, Ibid.

17 After centuries of conditioning of the female into the condition of perpetual girlishness called femininity, we cannot remember what femaleness is.

Ch. 2, Ibid.

18 Developing the muscles of the soul demands no competitive spirit, no killer instinct, although it may erect pain barriers that the spiritual athlete must crash through.

Ibid.

19 All that remains to the mother in modern consumer society is the role of scapegoat; psychoanalysis uses huge amounts of money and time to persuade analysands to foist their problems on to the absent mother, who has no opportunity to utter a word in her own defence. Hostility to the mother in our societies is an index of mental health.

Ch. 3, Ibid.

20 The Shakespeare wallahs have succeeded in creating a Bard in their own likeness, that is to say, incapable of relating to women.

Shakespeare's Wife 2008

3146. Gail E. Haley (1939–   )

1 Once, oh small children round my knee, there were no stories on earth to hear.

A Story, a story 1970

2 Children who are not spoken to by . . . responsive adults will not learn to speak properly. Children who are not answered will stop asking questions. They will become incurious. And children who are not told stories and who are not read to will have few reasons for wanting to learn to read.

Acceptance speech, Caldecott Medal *1971*

3 He's a young feller who'll risk just about everything to have an adventure. It's like a hunger he has, and his dreams will lead him into places where an older, wiser person might think twice about goin'. Course, if he didn't start out in a foolhardy sort of way, he might not have the adventure.

It's believing and taking chances that get him the beans. But it's losing everything and learning to cry that really set the beans a-growin'.

"Poppyseed's Invitation", *Mountain Jack Tales 2002*

3147. Molly Haskell (1940–   )

1 . . . the propaganda arm of the American Dream machine, Hollywood. . . .

From Reverence to Rape 1973

2 The mammary fixation is the most infantile—and most American—of the sex fetishes. . . .

Ibid.

3 There have been very few heroines in literature who defined their lives morally rather than romantically and likewise but a handful in film. . . .

Ibid.

4 There is a thin line between murderous anger and murder, and you have only to read the tabloids to know that more people are crossing it every day.

"Battle of the Sexes," *The New York Times 25 February 1982*

5 If the image of the lousy-woman-driver has been advanced with such relish, it is to disguise a truth that goes against the very definition of manhood in a country in which driving and virility are synonymous.

"He Drives Me Crazys," *The New York Times 24 October 1989*

6 The New York of "Law and Order" may be as much a myth as the skylines and dance floors and Park Avenue apartments that starred in an earlier, more rhapsodic vision of the city. But its myth is modern, multiethnic, capacious in its reach, and startlingly close, something you can reach out and touch.

"A 'Law and Order' Addict Tells All," *The New York Times 7 April 2002*

7 Not only have great theaters and their plush seats and majestic curtains disappeared, but so has the technical pride that went with them.

"It Used to Be So Easy. I Remember When. . . ," *The New York Times 14 March 2003*

3148–3149. Matina Horner (1939–   )

1 Unusual excellence in women was clearly associated for them with the loss of femininity, social rejection, personal or societal destruction or some combination of the above.

Women and Success: The Anatomy of Achievement 1964

3150. Barbara Kolb (1939–   )

1 . . . composing a piece of music is very feminine. It is sensitive, emotional, contemplative. By comparison, doing housework is positively masculine.

Quoted in "A Matter of Art, Not Sex," *Time 10 November 1975*

3151. Lynn Martin (1939–   )

1 In days when I grew up and before, job security meant one's union or one's company. For women it was often one's husband.

But in today's world of company closures and mergers, a union can't stop [a firm] from moving overseas or from shutting down.

Job security now has to be with each individual. This Department [of Labor], no matter how well meaning, has been tied to another past.

Quoted in "Lynn Martin's new message" by Robert Lewis, *AARP Bulletin, Vol. 33, No. 1 January 1992*

2 It seems a little odd to be talking about the older worker; maybe that's the 90-year-old.

Ibid.

3 It's never wise to keep the House [of Representatives] in after 11. It's like managing a nursery school without a nap.

p. 464, Quoted in *Politics in America* 1990 ed. by Philip D. Duncan, *1991*

3152. Erika Munk (1939–)

1 . . . even in a world with five billion inhabitants, people suffer history one by one.

"The world turned upside down," *The Women's Review of Books,* Vol. XIV, No 8 *May 1997*

2 We're back at the gates of Troy or the sack of Rome, but with better technology.

Ibid.

3 Hope is the commodity in shortest supply for all refugees.

Ibid.

4 The worldwide rise of fundamentalist nationalism, with its inevitable atrocity and misogyny, remains undeterred.

Ibid.

3153. Suzanne Pharr (1939–)

1 The eight Biblical references (and not a single one by Jesus) to alleged homosexuality are very small indeed when compared to the several hundred references (and many by Jesus) to money and the necessity for justly distributing wealth. Yet few people go on a rampage about the issue of a just economic system, using the Bible as a base.

Homophobia: A Weapon of Sexism 1988

2 The image I presented to the world was of a woman who was slightly odd and eccentric, mostly a loner, detached from close relationships, asexual, often mysterious, and always very, very serious about work. To keep my identity safe meant that I had to be constantly vigilant and lie, primarily through omission but sometimes through commission, virtually every minute of every day.

Introduction, Ibid.

3 Patriarchy—an enforced belief in male dominance and control—is the ideology and sexism is the system that holds it in place. The catechism goes like this: Who do gender roles serve? Men and the women who seek power from them. Who suffers from gender roles? Women most completely and men in part. How are gender roles maintained? By the weapons of sexism: economics, violence, homophobia.

Ibid. *1997* (expanded ed.)

4 I fear that we have achieved more integration than equality, more tolerance than justice, and more freedom for the middle-class than shared power and resources for those who live on the margins of society.

Letters of Intent: Women Cross the Generations to Talk about Family, Work, Sex, Love, and the Future of Feminism, Anna Bondoc and Meg Daly, eds. *1999*

3154. Letty Cottin Pogrebin (1939–)

1 . . . lifestyles and sex roles are passed from parents to children as inexorably as blue eyes or small feet.

"Down with Sexist Upbringing," *The First Ms. Reader,* Francine Klagsbrun, ed. *1972*

2 In school books, the Dick and Jane syndrome reinforced our emerging attitudes. The arithmetic books posed appropriate conundrums: "Ann has three pies . . . Dan has three rockets. . . ." We read the nuances between the lines: Ann keeps her eye on the oven; Dan sets his sights on the moon.

Ibid.

3 But in my experience, the most profound, life-changing insights always seem to arrive suddenly, like a rash, a fever, an epiphany straight from God.

Ch. 1, *Deborah, Golda, and Me; Being Female and Jewish in America 1991*

4 We can't forget that Judaism's worldview rests on a hierarchical paradigm (God over man, man over woman-child-animal-plant) that sanctifies male supremacy and diminishes the female in its theology, history, and daily ritual.

Ch. 4, Ibid.

5 The group entrusted with history-making remembers itself. Those who keep the books determine who is authorized to write in them and what is worth writing about. Authority means being the author of one's own reality as it is recorded for posterity. Remembering is not a neutral act.

Ch. 8, Ibid.

6 Having someone else peel your potatoes can be habit-forming.

Ch. 10, Ibid.

7 Racism is a bacterium, potentially curable but presently deadly; anti-Semitism is a virus, potentially deadly but presently contained.

Ch. 14, Ibid.

8 Cultural imperialism—no matter how admirable its intent—is doomed to fail.

Ch. 15, Ibid.

9 During centuries of dislocation and powerlessness, we kept our soul. Now, we have a homeland and an army but our soul is in mortal danger.

Ch. 16, Ibid.

3155. Helen Prejean (1939–)

1 The sheer weight of his loneliness, his abandonment, draws me. I abhor the evil he has done. But I sense something, some sheer and essential humanness, and that, perhaps, is what draws me most of all.

Dead Man Walking: An Eyewitness Account of the Death Penalty in the United States 1993

2 I realize that I cannot stand by silently as my government executes its citizens. If I do not speak out and resist, I am an accomplice.

Ibid.

3 Do you really believe that Jesus, who taught us not to return hate for hate and evil for evil and whose dying words were, "Father, forgive them," would participate in these executions? Would Jesus pull the switch?*

Ibid.

*Remark to the Louisiana prison warden.

4 The death penalty is an act of despair by society. It says that people can be sealed up and done away with—that there is absolutely nothing redeemable about them. And to those people and their families, it signals that they are nothing but human waste.

Speech, Seattle, quoted in "A personal journey into death row" by John Marshall, *Seattle Post-Intelligencer,* C1–4 *16 November 1993*

3156. Jane Bryant Quinn (1939–)

1 Lawyers are . . . operators of toll bridges across which anyone in search of justice must pass.
Remark, quoted in Newsweek *9 October 1978*

2 A poor man may still get into heaven, but after Reaganization, he may not be able to get into court.
Lawyer's Wit and Wisdom, Bruce Nash, Allan Zullo, eds.; Kathryn Zullo, compiler *1995*

3 The government had plenty of power to stop the frauds and financial pyramid schemes that brought home buyers down. It just didn't use it. You're looking at what amounts to a financial Katrina, brought to you by regulators who didn't do their jobs.
"No More Financial Katrinas," Newsweek *(New York) 14 April 2008*

4 Available wedding dates are few for brides of a certain age. You have to celebrate after your grandchildren get out of school and before your friends go away for the summer. So I'll be a June bride.
"Slicing Up Assets in Advance," Newsweek *9 June 2008*

3157. Willa Mae Reid (1939–)

1 What must be recognized is that the status of black women places us at the intersection of all the forms of subjugation in this society—racial oppression, sexual oppression, economic exploitation. We are a natural part of many different struggles—as Black people, as union members, as unemployed, as parents, as women.
"Changing Attitudes Among Black Women," International Socialist Review *March 1975*

2 The oppression of women, like the oppression of blacks, is one of the pillars of the capitalist system of exploitation. The fight to weaken any one of these pillars contributes to weakening the entire structure that victimizes all of us.
Ibid.

3158. Susan Sherman (1939–)

1 Analysis. Cross-reference analysis. The age of analysis. Psychological, philosophical, poetic analysis. Not the event, but the picture of the event.
"The Fourth Wall," St. 2, El Corno Emplumado *1966*

2 *In Soweto*
the people continue to rebel
in Soweto
the people continue to fight back
In Manhattan
my student looks at the 5 o'clock news

His head is filled with facts
He knows nothing
He learns nothing

He doesn't even know "Why?"
"Facts," A Poetics of Resistance: Women Writing in El Salvador, South Africa, and the United States, *Mary K. DeShazer, ed. 1994*

3159. Grace Slick (1939–)

1 Remember what the dormouse said:
"Feed your head.
Feed your head.
Feed your head."
"White Rabbit" 1965

2 All rock-and-rollers over the age of 50 look stupid and should retire.
Interview, Behind the Music *(documentary) 1988*

3 Man is the only animal that knows he's going to die, so we invent a heaven to keep from going crazy. Most people are hypnotized by organized religion from childhood.
Somebody to Love?: A Rock-and-Roll Memoir, with Andrea Cagan *1998*

3160. Eleanor Smeal (1939–)

1 We are a majority. We are determined to play majority politics. . . . We are not going to be reduced again to the ladies' auxiliary.
Quoted in "End of ERA Battle" by Sandra R. Gregg and Bill Peterson, The Washington Post *1 July 1982*

2 Just think—guns have a constitutional amendment protecting them and women don't.
Fundraising letter, Fund for the Feminist Majority 1989

3 Any system that produces 95% men members and 5% women members—like Congress—is sex discriminatory.
Ibid.

3161. Loretta Swit (1939–)

1 So much of life is luck. One day you make a right turn and get hit by a car. Turn left and you meet the love of your life. I think I made the correct turn.
Quoted in "M*A*S*H Supporting Players About Ready for Civilian Careers" by Bob Wisehart, The Times/Picayune *(New Orleans) 17 September 1981*

3162. Solveig Torvik (1939–)

1 And women surely won't be able to rest easy until it becomes just as routine for a woman to fail as a Cabinet officer as it has been for the legions of third-rate men who so ineptly have discharged those duties in recent decades.
"Clinton can't please everyone," Seattle Post-Intelligencer, *Op-Ed, A7 30 December 1992*

2 The world needs more mean women.
Ibid.

3163. Mierle Laderman Ukeles (1939–)

1 To me, the Sanitation Department was easily among the most essential services in the city, and yet it was perceived in this very repressed manner of being beneath, a displaced service. Even the facilities are always out of sight, out of mind.
Quoted in "Art Work Is (Yes, Really) Garbage" by James Barron, The New York Times *10 June 1993*

2 The design of garbage should become the great public design of our age. I am talking about the whole picture: recycling facilities, transfer stations, trucks, landfills, receptacles, water treatment plants, and rivers. They will be giant clocks and thermometers of our age that tell the time and health of the air, the earth, and the water. They will be utterly ambitious—our public cathedrals. For if we are to survive, they will be our symbols of survival.
Sculpting with the Environment, Baile Oakes, ed. *1995*

3 Sanitation is the beginning of culture. And the people who are serving [it] are inside the culture.

> Quoted in "Reinventing Maintenance with Artist Mierle Ukeles" by Regina Cornwell* The Women's Media Center (WomensMediaCenter.com) *14 December 2006*

3164. Penny Vincenzi (1939–)

1 Love was powerful, when it came to secrets. Huge, dangerous secrets. It saw them, it found them out.

> Ch. 25, *Sheer Abandon 2005*

2 The wheeling and dealing that goes on between politicians and the press, their mutual dependence, their ruthless pragmatism towards each other, is one of the most crucial ingredients in political life.

> Ch. 27, Ibid.

3 Sometimes they made her feel terribly hunted, her e-mails; they pursued her wherever she went.

> Ibid.

4 That was one of the worst things about being on your own, she had discovered: day to day was all right, even bad days could be coped with, but happiness, however small, needed to be shared.

> Ch. 31, Ibid.

5 It is virtually impossible for extremely—or even moderately—rich people not to expect to get what they want, whenever they want it. They may imagine themselves reasonable, patient, easy; the fact is that the various people who are dependent upon them work to make their lives so agreeable that they do not have to become unreasonable, or impatient, or difficult. This process is in direct proportion to how rich they are. . . .

> Ch. 38, Ibid.

3165. Naomi Weisstein (1939–)

1 Except for their genitals, I don't know what immutable differences exist between men and women. Perhaps there are some other unchangeable differences; probably there are a number of irrelevant differences. But it is clear that until social expectations for men and women are equal, until we provide equal respect for both sexes, answers to this question will simply reflect our prejudices.

> "Woman as Nigger," *Psychology Today* (New York) *October 1969*

2 Psychology has nothing to say about what women are really like, what they need and what they want, for the simple reason that psychology does not know. Yet psychologists will hold forth endlessly on the true nature of woman, with dismaying enthusiasm and disquieting certitude.

> Ibid.

3 Humor as a weapon in the social arsenal constructed to maintain caste, class, race, and sex inequalities is a very common thing.

> Introduction, *She Needs 1973*

4 Why have they been telling us women lately that we have no sense of humor—when we are always laughing? . . . And when we're not laughing, we're smiling.

> Ibid.

5 Evidence and reason: my heroes and my guides.

> "Adventures of a Woman in Science," *Women Look at Biology Looking at Women,* Ruth Hubbard,* Mary Sue Henifin and Barbara Fried, eds. *1979*

*See 2487.

3166. Ann Ruth Willner (1939?–)

1 . . . it is not what the leader is but what people see the leader as that counts in generating the charismatic relationship.

> Ch. 1, *The Spellbinders: Charismatic Political Leadership 1984* rev.

2 But political charisma alone has produced profound consequences in this century. Gandhi,* Roosevelt,** Hitler,*** and Castro**** were only four examples of political leaders whose charismatic hold over millions of followers gave them leverage to transform and transcend their times and countries.

> Ibid.

*Mohandas Karamchand Gandhi (1869–1948), a.k.a. "Mahatma"; Indian nationalist and spiritual leader. **Franklin Delano Roosevelt (1882–1945), 32nd president of the United States (1933–45). ***Adolf Hitler (1889–1945), a.k.a. "Der Führer"; Austrian-born founder of the German Nazi Party and chancellor of the Third Reich (1933–45). ****Fidel Castro (1926–), Cuban revolutionary leader; 23rd president of Cuba (1976–2008).

3 To a political scientist, a political leader* who had long been able to control a country without controlling a political party, a bureaucracy, or an army was a fascinating phenomenon.

> Ibid.

*Re Sukarno (1901–70), Indonesian politician who obtained his country's independence, then served as its first president, 1949–67.

3167. Judy Yung (1939?–)

1 Most prostitutes did not have the individual or collective means to resist their fate. Refusing to work only brought on beatings and other physical tortures. At best, a prostitute might hope to be redeemed by a wealthy client. For some, suicide, madness, or violent death proved to be the only way out of misery.

> *Chinese Women of America 1986*

2 Wives of merchants, who were at the top of the social hierarchy in Chinatown [in the second half of the 19th century], usually had bound feet and led bound lives.

> Ch. 1, *Unbound Feet: A Social History of Chinese Women in San Francisco 1995*

3168. Ellen Taaffe Zwilich (1939–)

1 I had gotten to the point where I was either going to play the violin much better or I was going to break it over my knee.

> "Encounters" by George Sturm, *MadAminA! (Music Assoc. of America) 2002–2005*

2 I've always bristled at the notion that people are "educated" at such-and-such a place. I think you learn habits of educating yourself, and when you stop doing that, the end is near.

> Ibid.

3 Art is not a trivial thing. It's at the center of life. It has to do with understanding ourselves as human beings.

> Ibid.

4 An artist's life can be very cruel. Artists with the loftiest ambitions, aspirations and intentions may not produce work that measures up to those qualities; on the other hand, a composer like Beethoven might write something just to pay the rent and it turns out to be a masterpiece.

> Ibid.

3169. Leila Ahmed (1940–)

1 Cut from its bed and fashioned into a pipe, the reed forever laments the living earth that it once knew, crying out, whenever life is breathed into it, its ache and its yearning and loss.

Ch. 1 *A Border Passage: From Cairo to America—A Woman's Journey* 2000

2 Though the atmosphere in Muslim countries is becoming more restrictive, no matter how conservative things get they can't put the genie back in the bottle.

Quoted in "Reform: Not Ignorant, Not Helpless . . ." by Lorraine Ali, *Newsweek* 12 December 2005

3 We're in the early stages of a major rethinking of Islam that will open Islam for women. [Muslim scholars] are rereading the core texts of Islam—from the Koran to legal texts—in every possible way.

Quoted in "US Latinas seek answers in Islam" by Christine Armario, *The Christian Science Monitor* 27 December 2004

4 Nobody has ever asked me to explain why there have been women heads of state in Turkey, Indonesia, Pakistan and Bangladesh. How many European and American women heads of state have there been? . . . The extraordinary achievements and freedoms of Muslim women are simply invisible.

Quoted in "Conversions unveiled; Appeal of Islam to women explored" by Mark Johnson, *Milwaukee Journal Sentinel* (Wisconsin) 15 March 2007

3170. Nobuko Albery (1940?–)

1 "Many may argue it's the lowest of the low among living creatures, to be performers. But don't forget, Buddha put us there, and we actors live in service to the gods. . . . We, the humblest leeches of the temples and shrines, though called untouchables, beggars and dung-worms, by singing, dancing, giving happiness to thousands of miserable souls should be the first amongst holy herons and peach blossoms to be allowed into Heaven of Blissful Peace."

Ch. 1, *The House of Kanze* 1986

2 "I'd rather forgo sleep today than sleeplessly lament my lost fortune tomorrow."

Ch. 9, Ibid.

3 "When you forget the beginner's awe, you start decaying."

Ch. 10, Ibid.

4 "Of course it is true that our art exists only when we are seen; we are slaves to our audiences. But at the same time, we must always be a step ahead of them. We must tantalize, not bore them. . . . To shock, Motomasa, is a Flower of our art, like a sting of a certain bee that is said to revive the dead."

Ch. 21, Ibid.

3171. Moira Bachman (fl. 1940s)

1 In my apron I carry nails, pliers, a heavy hammer, and pride.

Organization for Equal Education of the Sexes *n.d.*

3172. Elizabeth Bartholet (1940–)

1 A sane and humane society should encourage people to provide for these existing children rather than bring more children into the world.

Family Bonds: Adoption and the Politics of Parenting 1993

2 Despite . . . universal denigration, the available evidence shows that adoption works extremely well for all those immediately concerned. Why is the success story being suppressed? It may be too threatening. It means, among other things, that women can give away their children or lose their capacity for pregnancy and still function as full human beings. It means that children who are mistreated by their birth parents can be removed for parenting by others. It means that biology is *not* destiny. It raises questions about the goal of self-perpetuation and the value of promoting our own racial, cultural, and national groups. It forces us to think about the appropriate definition of family and community.

(p. 165), Ibid.

3 There may be some inborn need to procreate, but there are also inborn needs to nurture. Why does organized society seem to want to encourage its members to obsess over the former at the expense of the latter?

(p. 231), Ibid.

3173. Frances M. Beal (1940–)

1 The advertising media in this country continuously informs the American male of his need for indispensable signs of his virility. . . .

"Double Jeopardy: To Be Black and Female" (1969), *Sisterhood Is Powerful*, Robin Morgan,* ed. 1970

*See 3284.

2 Men may be cruelly exploited and subjected to all sorts of dehumanizing tactics on the part of the ruling class, but they have someone who is below them—at least they're not women.

Ibid.

3 To die for the revolution is a one-shot deal; to live for the revolution means taking on the more difficult commitment of changing our day-to-day life patterns.

Ibid.

3174. Louise Bernikow (1940–)

1 Every time I say "sure" when I mean "no," every time I smile brightly when I'm exploding with rage, every time I imagine my man's achievement is my own, I know the cheerleader never really died. I feel her shaking her ass inside me and I hear her breathless, girlish voice mutter "T-E-A-M, Yea, Team."

"Confessions of an Ex-Cheerleader," *Ms.* (New York) *October 1973*

2 The question arises as to whether it is possible *not* to live in the world of men and still to live in the world. The answer arises nearly as quickly that this can only happen if men are not thought of as "the world."

Introduction, *The World Split Open* 1974

3 A witch was a woman with enormous power, a woman who might change the natural world. She was "uncivilized" and in opposition to the world of the King, the court, polite society. She had to be controlled.

Ch. 1, *Among Women* 1980

4 I say you hurt me. You say I scorned you. We say we care. It begins. The conversation begins.

Ch. 6, Ibid.

3175. Carmel Bird (1940–)

1 Students always think I am joking when I say give up the housework. But you have the choice of a clean house or a finished story. The choice is yours; I am assuming you will make the right choice.

"Giving up Housework," *Dear Writer* 1996

2 Life is a crude inventor; fiction will only be convincing if it is more artful than life.

"Fact or Fiction," *Automatic Teller* 1997

3176. Barbara Boxer (1940–)

1 Before I lost my mother, she told me her greatest fear was being a burden to her children. Nothing, nothing I could say could ease her concern. Her dignity was at stake. So for the sakes of all our moms and dads who have reached the golden years, let's get them a benefit that means something, that's straightforward and not confusing, a benefit that they can trust—a true Medicare benefit.

Radio address, *21 June 2003*

2 We have made tremendous strides since 1920. Women have a stronger voice in our communities and in our workplaces. I am proud to serve as one of the 14 women, Republican and Democrat, in the United States Senate, and now we have 62 women in the House of Representatives. We have made progress, but much more needs to be done.

Letter re the Anniversary of the Ratification of the 19th Amendment *18 August 2003*

3177. Anita Bryant (1940–)

1 If homosexuality were the normal way, God would have made Adam and Bruce.

Remark, Quoted in *The New York Times* 1977

3178. Susan Cahill (1940–)

1 As many historians have pointed out, religious institutions, despite their petrified official hierarchies, have provided abundant opportunities for women's self-authorization and -actualization. In spite of themselves, these institutions have nurtured the love of freedom and goodness and justice within their own hidebound bodies.

Introduction, *Wise Women: Over 2000 Years of Spiritual Writing by Women*, ed. 1996

2 From Eros, the God/Goddess of Love, the timeless source of mystical longing, comes the sensory language of mysticism and its imagery of touching, dancing, arousal, penetration, ecstasy, suckling, satisfaction.

Ibid.

3179. Maria Campbell (1940–)

1 Cheechum [grandmother] would often say scornfully of this God that he took more money from us than the Hudson's Bay store.

Halfbreed 1973

2 She taught me to see beauty in all things around me; that inside each thing a spirit lived, that it was vital too, regardless of whether it was only a leaf or a blade of grass, and by recognizing its life and beauty I was accepting God. . . . that when my body became old my spirit would leave and I'd come back and live again. She said God lives in you and looks like you, and not to worry about him floating around in a beard and a white cloak; that the Devil lives in you and in all things, and that he looks like you and not like a cow. . . . Her explanation made much more sense than anything Christianity had ever taught me.

Ibid.

3 Dreams are so important in one's life, yet when followed blindly they can lead to the disintegration of one's soul.

Ibid.

4 I no longer need my blanket to survive.

Ibid.

3180. Isabel do Carmo (1940–)

1 The movement must be accompanied by force. . . . There must be an armed insurrection.

Quoted in *Time* (New York) *30 October 1975*

2 There can be no halfway solutions, no half measures. That won't work. We must have either pure socialism or we will go back to fascism.

Ibid.

3 In our party, being a woman is no problem. After all, it is a revolutionary party.

Ibid.

3181. Norma Carson (fl. 1940s–1950s)

1 I've never found it an advantage to be a girl. If a trumpet player is wanted for a job and somebody suggests me, they'll say 'What, a chick?' and put me down without even hearing me . . . I don't want to be a girl musician. I just want to be a musician.

Quoted on p. 85 (1951), *Stormy Weather: The Music and Lives of a Century of Jazzwomen* by Linda Dahl 1984

3182. Angela Carter (1940–1992)

1 Fine art, that exists for itself alone, is art in a final state of impotence. If nobody, including the artist, acknowledges art as a means of knowing the world, then art is relegated to a kind of rumpus room of the mind and the irresponsibility of the artist and the irrelevance of art to actual living becomes part and parcel of the practice of art.

"Polemical Preface," *The Sadeian Woman* 1979

2 Mother goddesses are just as silly a notion as father gods. If a revival of the myths of these cults gives woman emotional satisfaction, it does so at the price of obscuring the real conditions of life. This is why they were invented in the first place.

Ibid.

3 If Miss means respectably unmarried, and Mrs. respectably married, then Ms. means nudge, nudge, wink, wink.

"The Language of Sisterhood," *The State of the Language*, Christopher Ricks and Leonard Michaels, eds. 1980

4 I think it's one of the scars in our culture that we have too high an opinion of ourselves. We align ourselves with the angels instead of the higher primates.

Marxism Today (London) *January 1985*

5 Reading a book is like re-writing it for yourself. . . . You bring to a novel, anything you read, all your experience of the world. You bring your history and you read it in your own terms.

Ibid.

3183. Kim Chernin (1940–)

1 They could not see they were too thin because slenderness had become a statement of power. There could never be too much of it, since more implied that the will had grown even stronger in its relentless struggle to dominate matter.

The Obsession 1981

2 And so we leave home, we leave the apron and . . . put on . . . tailored executive suits. . . . And now we take ourselves in hand, tailoring ourselves to the specifications of this world we are so eager to enter. We strip our bodies of flesh, our hearts of the overflow of feeling, our language of exuberant and dramatic imprecisions. We cut back the flight of our fancy, make our thoughts rigorous and subject (this marvelous rushing intuitive leaping capacity of ours) to measure of demonstration and proof, trying not to talk with our hands, trying hard to subdue our voices, getting our bursts of laughter under control.

The Hungry Self 1985

3184. Phyllis Chesler (1940–)

1 [Within the feminist movement] non-Jewish men treated me the way white men treat black women—as more "sensual," earthy, sexually accessible; as Rebecca of *Ivanhoe*. I experienced the same treatment from feminists, when I was singled out by some comrades as somehow fleshier, earthier, sexier, pushier, more verbal: "Jewish."

Quoted in "An Exclusive Interview with Dr. Phyllis Chesler" by Aviva Cantor Zuckoff, *Lilith* 1, No. 2 *Winter 1976/1977*

2 The clinical distrust of mothers, simply because they are women, the eagerness to bend over backward to like fathers, simply because they are men, is mind-numbing. Mother-blaming and woman-hatred fairly sizzle on clinical pages.

Introduction, *Women and Madness*, 25th anniversary ed. *1997*

3 What does a feminist therapist do that's different? A feminist therapist tries to *believe* what women say. Given the history of psychiatry and psychoanalysis, this alone is a radical act.

Ibid.

4 We understand that rape is not about love or even lust, but about humiliating another human being through forced or coerced sex and sexual shame. The intended effect of rape is always the same: to utterly break the spirit of the rape victim, to drive the victim out of her (or his) body and to make her incapable of resistance and quite often out of her mind.

Ibid.

5 Freedom and justice do wonders for one's mental health. So, in response to my brother Sigmund Freud's* infamous query, what do women want? For starters, and in no particular order: freedom, food, nature, shelter, leisure, freedom from violence, justice, music, poetry, nonpatriarchal family, community, compassionate support during chronic or life-threatening illness and at the time of death, independence, books, physical/sexual pleasure, education, solitude, the ability to defend ourselves, love, ethical friendships, the arts, health, dignified employment, and political comrades.

Ibid.

*Austrian physician and founder of psychoanalysis (1856–1939).

6 Contrary to myth and propaganda, Israel is not an apartheid state. The largest practitioner of apartheid in the world is Islam which practices both gender and religious apartheid. In terms of gender apartheid, Palestinian women—and all women who live under Islam—are oppressed by "honor" killings, in which girls and women who are raped are then killed by family members for the sake of restoring the family "honor;" forced veiling, segregation, stonings to death for alleged adultery, seclusion/sequestration, female genital mutilation, polygamy, outright slavery, sexual slavery. Women have few civil, legal, or human rights under Islam.

"The Brownshirts of Our Time [the new Leftist anti-Semitism]," *FrontPageMagazine.com 19 November 2003*

3185. Claudette Colvin (1940–)

1 "Aren't you going to get up?" I said, "No, sir." He shouted "Get up" again. I started crying, but I felt even more defiant. I kept saying over and over, in my high-pitched voice, "It's my constitutional right to sit here as much as that lady. I paid my fare, it's my constitutional right!" I knew I was talking back to a white policeman, but I had had enough.

Quoted in *Claudette Colvin: Twice Toward Justice* by Phil Hoose *2009*

2 But worried or not, I felt proud. I had stood up for our rights. I had done something a lot of adults hadn't done. On the ride home from jail, coming over the viaduct, Reverend Johnson had said something to me I'll never forget. He was an adult who everyone respected and his opinion meant a lot to me. "Claudette," he said, "I'm so proud of you. Everyone prays for freedom. We've all been praying and praying. But you're different—you want your answer the next morning. And I think you just brought the revolution to Montgomery."

Ibid.

3 My head was just too full of black history, you know, the oppression that we went through. It felt like Sojourner Truth* was on one side pushing me down, and Harriet Tubman** was on the other side of me pushing me down. I couldn't get up.***

Ibid.

*See 860. **See 978. ***Re her refusal to give up her seat on 2 March 1955 in Montgomery, Alabama.

3186. Anne Commire (1940?–)

1 SHAY. I finally learned when I'm alone—I'm total. I'm not rude, boring, or stupid. In fact, I become a very nice person. I like me and I don't hurt anyone. I don't like what's in here when I'm with people: jealousy, anger, boredom . . . That's why I shouldn't be allowed to run around loose. I'm sealing myself off for society's sake.

Act I, *Shay 1978*

2 Funny, if I have any pride in my writing, it's not in what I wrote. It's because I dare to write, dare to face my demons and that enormously frightening machine daily. After fifteen years, I still face that machine with fear. Dreading there'll be nothing there. Dreading that today I'll find out I don't have an original thought left in my brain, that I squandered it on postcards to friends.

"Anne Commire," *Interviews with Contemporary Women Playwrights*, Kathleen Betsko* and Rachel Koenig *1987*
*See 3125.

3 Theater risks every night. It has the possibility of soaring in the air or landing on its ass. People come for the spectacle, for the danger. Some with holly in their hearts; some like spectators at the Colosseum, rooting for the lion.

Ibid.

4 LYNNE. I've always been a bit stiff; afraid to be seen having fun. Some ride roller coasters, some wait below, holding the coats. Now, there's a T-shirt if I ever heard one.

Starting Monday 1990

3187. Angela de Hoyos (1940–)

1 I must wait for the conquering barbarian
to learn the Spanish word for love:
HERMANO*

"Hermano," The Woman That I Am, *The Literature and Culture of Contemporary Women of Color*, D. Soyini Madison,** ed. *1994*

*Brother. **See 3912.

2 here's a guitar
for you
—a chicana guitar—
so you can spill out a song
for the open road
big enough for my people

"To Walt Whitman"* *n.d.*

*American poet (1819–92).

3188. Lydia Dunn (1940–   )

1 China will let Hong Kong survive not because it is just or right but because of our economic value.

Quoted in "Whither Hong Kong?" by Margaret Scott, *The New York Times Magazine October 1989*

2 We [Hong Kongers] have been told to stay out of politics and if we did we could make money. We did.

Ibid.

3189. Frances Fitzgerald (1940–   )

1 Americans see history as a straight line and themselves standing at the cutting edge of it as representatives for all mankind. They believe in the future as if it were a religion; they believe that there is nothing they cannot accomplish, that solutions wait somewhere for all problems, like brides.

Pt. I, Ch. 1, *Fire in the Lake 1972*

2 . . . the Americans were once again embarked upon a heroic and (for themselves) almost painless conquest of an inferior race. . . . [They] were white men in Asia, and they could not conceive that they might fail in their enterprise, could not conceive that they could be morally wrong.

Ch. 2, Ibid.

3 . . . the American government did not want to face the consequences of peace. It was, after all, one thing to wish for an end to the war and quite another to confront the issues upon which the war had begun. President Johnson* had wanted to end the war; so, too, had President Kennedy.** But to end the war and not to lose it: the distinction was crucial, and particularly crucial after all the American lives that had been spent and all the political rhetoric expended.

Ibid.

*American politician (1908–73), 36th president of the United States (1963–69). **John F. Kennedy, American politician (1917–63), 35th U.S. president (1961–63); assassinated.

4 Most Americans . . . did not seem to mind that the President who spoke of homespun virtues and old-fashioned family values was a divorcé who rarely saw his children or went to church and whose wife shopped on Rodeo Drive.*

Ch. 1, *Way Out There in the Blue, Reagan, Star Wars and the End of the Cold War 2000*

*Ronald Reagan (1911–2004), 40th President of the United States (1981–89), actor.

3190. Maria Mazziotto Gillan (1940–   )

1 Remember me, ladies,
the silent?
I have found my voice
and my rage will blow
your house down.

"Public School 18: Paterson, New Jersey," *The Dream Book: An Anthology of Writings by Italian American Women,* Helen Barolini,* ed. *1985*

*See 2509.

3191. Sue Grafton (1940–   )

1 He'd forgotten just how addictive crime can be. Repeat offenders are motivated more by withdrawal symptoms than necessity.

"H" is for Homicide 1991

2 "Take it from me, you can't trust a guy who's hell-bent on getting in your pants."
"Even if he loves you?"
"Especially if he loves you, and worse if you love him."

Ch. 1, *S is for Silence 2005*

3 She was a chameleon. Playing the loser was her disguise.

Ch. 1, *T Is for Trespass 2007*

3192. Laurie Graham (1940–   )

1 "Blue-collar people think that if you don't want to work you get a desk job."

Singing the City 1998

3193. Judy Grahn (1940–   )

1 . . . I looked into the mirror
and nobody was there to testify.

"A Woman is Talking to Death" *1974*

2 The shaman/priest/artist/teacher/leader does not operate for the sole benefit of herself and her kind but for the benefit of the people at large and of the universe and its patterns, as becomes what she perceives as fitting into place, into her sense of natural justice.

"Modern Lesbian Sex Domains: Flaming without Burning," *Another Mother Tongue 1984*

3 want of my want, I am your lust
wave of my wave, I am your crest
earth of my earth, I am your crust
may of my may, I am your must
kind of my kind, I am your best

"Funeral Poem: For Yvonne Mary Robinson" (October 10, 1939—November 22, 1974), Ibid.

3194. Joan Haggerty (1940–   )

1 It was the novelty of the attraction that captivated her as much as the woman herself.

Daughters of the Moon 1971

2 Afterwards, you know, afterwards, I often feel like being fucked by a man too. . . . You *tune* me, d'you see, and then I want a man to counter me, but we together, we just keep travelling to strung out space. We can't comfort each other.

Ibid.

3195. Ruth Mae Harris (1940–   )

1 He's [Obama]* of a different time and place, but he knows whose shoulders he's standing on.

Quoted in "A Time to Reap for Foot Soldiers of Civil Rights" by Kevin Sack, *The New York Times 4 November 2008*

*Barack Obama (1961–   ), 44th president of the United States (2009–   ).

2 They didn't give us our mule and our acre, but things are better. It's time to reap some of the harvest.

Ibid.

3196. Arlie Hochschild (1940–)

1 It has become a sad commonplace to associate being old with being alone. We call isolation a punishment for the prisoner, but perhaps a majority of American old people are in some degree isolated or soon will be.

> "Communal Living in Old Age," *The Future of the Family,*
> Louise Kapp Howe,* ed. 1972
> *See 2899.

2 In processing people, the product is a state of mind.

> Part One, *Exploring the Managed Heart 2003*

3 Is an emotion a resource like gold or ivory that can be extracted from one place and taken to another?

> "Love and Gold," *Global Woman: Nannies, Maids and Sex Workers in the New Economy,* Barbara Ehrenreich* and Hochschild, eds. 2003
> *See 3257.

3197. Fanny Howe (1940–)

1 —if on this unday—one
undoing would be undone

> "Unday," sts. 3–3, *Gone: Poems 2003*

2 Is it the case that technology also took us far far from warm bread while its nihilism showed that the past is all that is allowed to live. Face it. The minute the work is complete, it is obsolete.

> "The Sparkling Stone," *Glasstown: Where Something Got Broken 2005*

3 I learned that everything develops in exact proportion to something else that opposes it. I could measure my silence by the bumping noise around it.

> Ibid.

4 Lots of laughter
Before and after. Every meeting
Rhymed and fluttered into meter.
The beat was the message. . . .

> "Far and Away," St. 8, *The Lyrics: Poems 2007*

3198. Mary Hyde (fl. 1940s–d. 1982)

1 The art of managing men has to be learned from birth. . . . It depends to some extent on one's distribution of curves, a developed instinct, and a large degree of sheer feline cunning.

> *How to Manage Men 1955*

3199. Aisha Kahlil (1940?–)

1 Dance is more than just a discipline for me, it's a method of healing—a prayer. If I wasn't dancing I wouldn't be alive.

> Quoted in "Sweet Honey: A Cappella Activists" by Audreen Buffalo, *Ms.* (New York) *March/April 1993*

3200. Penelope Keith (1940–)

1 Shyness is just egotism out of its depth.

> Quoted in *Daily Mail* (London) *27 June 1988*

2 What sort of culture have we come to when two phrases are now pejorative? A "do-gooder" and "well-made". Isn't that dreadful? It's ghastly! If a few more people would do good, there wouldn't be so many people doing bad. People should aspire to being a do-gooder! It's the same as," oh, the well-made play. . . .

> Quoted in "Penelope Keith and the handbag landmine" by Dominic Maxwell, *The Times* (London) *29 January 2008*

3201. Linda Kaufman Kerber (1940–)

1 [Not until 1992] did the Supreme Court specifically announce that it would no longer recognize the power of husbands over the bodies of their wives. That is the moment when coverture, as a living legal principle, died.

> *No Constitutional Right To Be Ladies: Women and the Obligations of Citizenship 1998*

2 We cannot embrace the rights without acknowledging the obligations. Nor do we have the option of limiting ourselves to the voluntarily embraced duties; there waits a steel hand in a velvet glove to enforce obligation.

> Ibid.

3202. Wendy Kesselman (1940–)

1 MADAME DANZARD. You have no idea how lucky we are, Isabelle. The servants I've seen in my day. *(She watches her daughter stuff potatoes in her mouth.)* They eat like birds. Always looking so neat, so perfect. You wouldn't think they were maids at all.

> Sc. 4, *My Sister in This House 1981*

3203. Maxine Hong Kingston (1940–)

1 Night after night my mother would talk-story until we fell asleep. I couldn't tell where the stories left off and the dreams began, her voice the voice of the heroines in my sleep. . . . At last I saw that I too had been in the presence of great power, my mother talking-story.

> (p. 23), *The Woman Warrior 1976*

2 I learned to make my mind large, as the universe is large, so that there is room for paradoxes.

> (p. 35), Ibid.

3 Those of us in the first American generations have had to figure out how the invisible world the emigrants built around our childhood fits in solid America.

> Ibid.

4 "If that demon whips me, I'll catch the whip and yank him off his horse, crack his head like a coconut. In an emergency a human being can do miracles—fly, swim, lift mountains, throw them. Oh, a man is capable of great feats of speed and strength."

> *China Men 1980*

5 "You're going through the delusion of clarity. . . ."

> *Tripmaster Monkey: His Fake Book 1989*

6 Yesterday morning my car beeped at me, again—beep, beep, beep. It kept yelling at me until I did what it wanted me to do. The gas pump—the automatic bank teller—the telephone as I dialed—the phone answering machine—they all beeped loudly at me. They told me what to do or what not to do. They wore me down, so I obeyed their orders.

> "Sound Shy," *Veterans of War, Veterans of Peace 2006*

7 I appreciate having a warrior inside and available, but I do not want it to be always leading me.

> Ibid.

3204. Angela Lambert (1940–)

1 Pornography is literature designed to be read with one hand.
Independent on Sunday (London) *18 February 1990*

2 He [Adolf Hitler]* was the first politician to grasp the importance of projecting the right image, and he scrutinised every [photographic] print.
Ch. 1, *The Lost Life of Eva Braun*** 2007
*Known as "Der Führer" (1889–1945), Austrian-born founder of the German Nazi Party and chancellor of the Third Reich (1933–45). **(1912–45), mistress and later wife of Hitler.

3205. Prue Leith (1940–)

1 When you get to fifty-two food becomes more important than sex.
Quoted in *The Guardian* (London) *11 November 1992*

3206. Jane Litman (194-?–)

1 When, at the synagogue which I attended in my teens, the rabbi would say as he took the Torah from the Ark, "This is the covenant which declares the fatherhood of God and the brotherhood of man," I was never too excited, but every time I say to myself—the sisterhood of women—a chill runs down my spine.
"Judaism and Feminism," *The Jewish Radical February 1978*

2 We must always test the limits and be careful not to cross borders too hurriedly.
Interview with author (January 1996), p. 306, The Journey Home, *How Jewish Women Shaped Modern America* by Joyce Antler* 1997
*See 3320.

3207. Wangari Muta Maathai (1940–)

1 All of us have a God in us, and that God is the spirit that unites all life, everything that is on this planet.
"You Strike the Woman. . . ," *In Context,* #28 *Spring 1991*

2 I think what the Nobel* committee is doing is going beyond war and looking at what humanity can do to prevent war. Sustainable management of our natural resources will promote peace.
Interview, *Time* (New York) *10 October 2004*
*Re Nobel Peace Prize, established by Alfred B. N- in 1901.

3 Africa is not a poor continent. Africa is extremely rich, but it has been impoverished by injustice.
Speech, W8 Summit (Edinburgh, Scotland) *2005*

4 Until you dig a hole, you plant a tree, you water it and make it survive, you haven't done a thing. You are just talking.
Speech, Goldman Awards (San Francisco), *24 April 2006*

5 To create a more cohesive nation-state, ruling elites must devote time, energy and resources to ensuring universal freedom, security and an equitable distribution of resources. And far from trying to destroy the micro-nationalities, Africans should embrace their distinct cultures, languages and values. By bringing the best of their micro-nationality to the nation, they would enrich all.
"Creating a Path To Peace in Kenya," *Washington Post 8 February 2008*

3208. Margrethe II (1940–)

1 We are being challenged by Islam these years. Globally as well as locally. There is something impressive about people for whom religion imbues their existence, from dusk to dawn, from cradle to grave. There are also Christians who feel this way. There is something endearing about people who give themselves up completely to their faith. But there is likewise something frightening about such a totality, which also is a feature of Islam. A counterbalance has to be found, and one has to, at times, run the risk of having unflattering labels placed on you. For there are some things for which one should display no tolerance. And when we are tolerant, we must know whether it is because of convenience or conviction.
Quoted in *London Telegraph 2005*

3209. Bobbie Ann Mason (1940–)

1 "You can't get lost in the United States," Sam says. "I wish I could, though. I wish I'd wake up and not know where I was."
Part One, Ch. 1, *In Country 1984*

2 The pondweed is lovely. If it were up to me, I'd just admire it and let the fish have it. But then, I'm spoiled and lazy and have betrayed my heritage as a farmer's daughter by leaving the land and going off to see the world.
Ch. 1, *Clear Springs: A Family Story 1999*

3 Viewing the stars, he always felt privileged to witness ultimate mystery, to be in it. The universe tantalized and affronted him, ripping him out of his own petty corner.
An Atomic Romance 2005

3210. Stephanie Matthews-Simonton (1940–)

1 The most powerful tool we have for changing our environment is our ability to change ourselves.
Quoted in "The Good News About Cancer" by Peggy Elman Roggenbuck, *New Age May 1978*

2 Too often we associate healing only with medical treatment . . . [but] healing is more than just physiological . . . the patient can take part in his own recovery. The family can offer a vital supportive environment in this effort.
Introduction, *The Healing Family 1984*

3 Hope is essential; human beings can't live long without it. . . . When hope is taken away, people become so depressed that no matter what the outcome, their lives are miserable.
Ch. 3, Ibid.

3211. Fatima Mernissi (1940–)

1 The Christian concept of the individual as tragically torn between two poles—good and evil, flesh and spirit, instinct and reason—is very different from the Muslim concept. . . . It views the raw instincts as energy. The energy of instincts is pure in the sense that it has no connotation of good or bad. . . . It is the use made of the instincts, not the instincts themselves, that is beneficial or harmful to the social order.
Ch. 1, *Beyond the Veil: Male-Female Dynamics in a Modern Muslim Society 1987*

2 When Allah created the earth, said Father, he separated men from women, and put a sea between Muslims and Christians for a reason. Harmony exists when each group respects the prescribed limits of the other: trespassing leads only to sorrow and unhappiness.
Ch. 1, *Dreams Of Trespass: Tales of a Harem Girlhood 1994*

3   "To travel is the best way to learn and employ yourself," said Yasmina, my grandmother, who was illiterate and lived in a harem, a traditional household with locked gates that women were not supposed to open. "You must focus on the strangers you meet and try to understand them. The more you understand a stranger and the greater is your knowledge of yourself, the more power you will have."

Ch. 1, *Scheherazade Goes West: Different Cultures, Different Harems 2001*

4   Islam insists on the unbridgeable distance between the divine and the human, but Hallaj* believed that if you concentrate on loving God, without intermediaries, a blurring of the boundaries with the divine becomes possible.

Ibid.

*A famous 10th-century Sufi mystic.

3212. Juliet Mitchell (1940–)

1   Circumstantial accounts of the future are idealistic and, worse, static.

"Women-The Longest Revolution," *New Left Review November/December 1966*

2   Hysteria is the alternative or other side of the coin of what is regarded as normal behaviour. Women are thought to be, or assigned to be, its main practitioners.
Hysteria is also the mental condition which provides the relevant point of comparison for both witchcraft and spirit possession, for shamanism and even for cannibalism.

Ch. 1, *Mad Men and Medusas: Reclaiming Hysteria 2000*

3   All human emotions, psychic states, and indeed even organic illnesses, take place within specific social contexts. They cannot exist outside of them.

Ibid.

4   If we fail to overcome our desire for sibling incest or for sibling murder, will versions of these be more insistently played out with later lateral relationships, with peers and so-called equals—in love and in war?

Ch. 1, *Siblings: Sex and Violence 2004*

3213. Anne Moody (1940–)

1   I sat on the grass and listened to the speakers [28 August 1963, the March on Washington], to discover we had "dreamers" instead of leaders leading us. Just about every one of them stood up there dreaming. Martin Luther King* went on and on talking about his dream. I sat there thinking that in Canton [Mississippi] we never had time to sleep, much less dream.

Coming of Age in Mississippi 1968
*American civil rights leader (1929–68), assassinated.

2   ... the [Civil Rights] Movement was not in control of its destiny. We were like an angry dog on a leash who had turned on its master. It could bark and howl and snap, and sometimes even bite, but the master was always in control.

Quoted in *Contemporary Authors*, Vol. 65–68 *1977*

3   I realized that the universal fight for human rights, dignity, justice, equality and freedom is not and should not be just the fight of the American Negro or the Indians or the Chicanos. It's the fight of every ethnic and racial minority, every suppressed and exploited person, everyone of the millions who daily suffer one or another of the indignities of the powerless and voiceless masses.

Quoted by Katie Opartny and Jenny Noterman in "VG: Voices from the Gaps" (voices.cla.umn.edu) *1998*

3214. Luisa Morgantini (1940–)

1   The use of uranium weapons has devastating consequences on human health and the environment. That's why we call for an immediate end to the use of uranium weapons and for the disclosure of all locations where uranium weapons have been used.

Press Release (Brussels), International Day of Action against Depleted Uranium Weapons 6 *November 2007*

2   The time of empty words and of betrayed promises is ended: all the Palestinians and the Israelis who want the peace deserve our support and efforts to work concretely for guaranteeing the respect of the international humanitarian law. ...

"EP* re-calls for the end of the blockade in Gaza," Arabic Media Internet Network *21 February 2008*
*European Parliament.

3   If we call on Israel for the release of all political prisoners and for the end of systematic violations of international and humanitarian law we have to ask the same respect of law and human rights to the Palestinians: justice needs transparency and coherence.

Press Release (Brussels), "A call for transparent inquiry" 26 *February 2008*

3215. Cyntha Moss (1940?–)

1   Before we started our studies, people felt elephants were there to be used in the way man thought best. But the more we learn about them, the more arguments we have to protect them.

Quoted in "Kenya's Elephant Team" by Simon Robinson, *Time.com 28 February 2000*

2   [The elephants] turned out to have a very complex and multi-tiered society. One study indicates they have the largest social network of any land mammal save humans.

Ibid.

3216. Bharati Mukherjee (1940–)

1   Expensive girls' schools in Lausanne and Bombay have trained me to behave well. My manners are exquisite, my feelings are delicate, my gestures refined, my moods undetectable. They have seen me through riots, uprootings, separation, my son's death.

"A Wife's Story," *The Middleman and Other Stories 1988*

2   Taylor thought dull was the absence of action, but dull is its own kind of action. Dullness is a kind of luxury.

Ch. 2, *Jasmine 1989*

3   What novelists have the power to do is imagine the inner life of people who acted out the facts of history. And do it with sympathy for every side.

Interview by Joseph A. Cincotti (p. 7), *The New York Times Book Review October 1993*

4   Two servants walk ahead of the eight litter-bearers, holding naphtha lamps. No one has seen such brilliant European light, too strong to stare into, purer white than the moon. It is a town light, a rich man's light, a light that knows English invention.

Ch. 1, *Desireable Daughters 2002*

3217. Nuala O'Faolain (1940–2008)

1   When you're young, the endings of relationships are all swirling feeling, and the practical implications don't matter. But it's

different when you're a shade nearer sixty than fifty, and you had taken it for granted that what you had together would be your life to the end.

Ch. 1, *Almost There 2003*

2 I don't know of any other event that causes as much pain and destruction, and that is as little understood, as the end of love.

Ibid.

3 I had no idea of the abundance of pristine love a dog can release.

Ibid.

4 But there is a limit to the consolations of nature.

Ch. 4, Ibid.

5 I had enough self-belief to start off along any tightrope but not enough to get to the other side without beginning to falter.

Ibid.

6 The whole world is vibrant with the heroism of people who have had to start anew, and Manhattan is the greatest of all the cities created by such people.

Ibid.

3218. Gail Parent (1940–)

1 Don't we realize we're a business, we single girls are? There are magazines for us, special departments in stores for us. Every building that goes up in Manhattan has more than fifty percent efficiency apartments . . . for the one million girls who have very little use for them.

"On Jobs and Apartments," *Sheila Levine Is Dead and Living in New York 1972*

2 . . . volleyball is a Jewish sport. It's fun, and nobody can get hurt.

"Fire Island," Ibid.

3 *Fact:* Girls who are having a good sex thing stay in New York. The rest want to spend their summer vacations in Europe.

"Europe," Ibid.

4 Do you realize the planning that goes into a death? Probably even more than goes into a marriage. This, after all, really is for eternity.

"Enough Already," Ibid.

5 "Thank you, Agatha, for the lovely bracelet, but I still haven't changed my mind. I have no desire to touch you in places that I already own. Sincerely, Sheila Levine."

Ibid.

3219. Carole Pateman (1940–)

1 It is rather ironical that the idea of participation should have become so popular, particularly with students, for among political theorists and political sociologists the widely accepted theory of democracy (so widely accepted that one might call it the orthodox doctrine) is one in which the concept of participation has only the most minimal role. Indeed, not only has it a minimal role but a prominent feature of recent theories of democracy is the emphasis placed on the dangers inherent in wide popular participation in politics.

Ch. 1, *Participation and Democratic Theory 1970*

2 The dichotomy between the private and the public is central to almost two centuries of feminist writing and political struggle; it is, ultimately, what the feminist movement is about.

"Feminist Critiques of the Public/Private Dichotomy," *Public and Private in Social Life 281 1983*

3 . . . the private, womanly sphere (natural) and the public, masculine sphere (civil) are opposed but gain their meaning from each other.

The Sexual Contract 1988

4 . . . women have never been and still are not admitted as full and equal members and citizens in any country known as a 'democracy.'

"Feminism and Democracy," *Democratic Theory and Practice,* Graeme Duncan, ed. *1993*

5 No emergency or "war on terror" has ever been declared because of the scale of violence against women.

Ch. 5, *Contract and Domination,* Charles Mills, coauthor *1997*

3220. Nancy Pelosi (1940–)

1 Where we can find common ground on the economy, and on other domestic issues, we shall seek it. . . . Where we cannot find common ground, we must stand our ground.

Quoted in "Pelosi scores an easy victory" by David Espo, Associated Press *15 November 2002*

2 America must be a light to the world, not just a missile.

Response to State of the Union Address *2005*

3 A woman is like a teabag. You can't tell how strong she is until you put her in hot water.

Quoted by Hillary Rodham Clinton,* Interview on *ABC News 2006*

Also attributed to Nancy Reagan and Eleanor Roosevelt.*

4 Maybe it will take a woman to clean up the House.

Interview, *Barbara Walters* Specials 13 December 2006*

*See 2687.

3221. Janis-Rozena Peri (1940?–)

1 Mother* has accomplished extraordinary things under often difficult circumstances. With extremely limited financial and professional support, she has managed to maintain a life as a composer through circumstances that would have utterly defeated others. I often look at her as not only my mother but as a miracle worker.

Quoted in "Xenia to Honor Zenobia" by Meth Michaels, *Dayton Daily News 11 July 2002*

*Zenobia Perry; see 2099.

3222. Lois Phillips (1940–)

See Ferguson, Anita Perez: 4527:3–5, and Mankiller, Wilma: 3591:4.

3223. Navanethem "Navi" Pillay (1940–)

1 Rape had always been regarded as one of the spoils of war. Now it is a war crime, no longer a trophy.

Quoted in "Finally! The UN Gets One Right" by Robin Morgan,* Women's Media Center (womensmediacenter.com) *4 August 2008*

*See 3284.

3224. Jaune Quick-to-See Smith (1940–   )

1   The glaciers pushed
and the People moved.
> "The Ronan Robe Series," Pt. 1, *That's What She Said*, Rayna
> Green,* ed. *1984*

*See 3338.

2   The Jesuits enslaved the young Indians, forced them into
church and put them to work on cattle ranches or in the orchards. We were forbidden to drum, sing, dance, speak our
language, carry anything of our culture . . . but even with all
that people would gather in a cabin, cover the windows, and
drum and sing.
> Quoted in "Jaune Quick-to-See Smith," *Exposures, Women &*
> *Their Art* by Ann Brown & Arlene Raven* *1989*

*See 3533.

3   I'm going on a journey each time I begin a canvas.
> Ibid.

3225. Pattiann Rogers (1940–   )

1   the studious glory of a seeded dandelion scattering
its brilliant wind of stars before the sun.
> "Investigative Logic in a Study of Love," St. 6, *Eating Bread*
> *and Honey 1997*

2   Everything I assemble, all
the constructions I have rendered
are the metal and dust of my locked
and storied bones.
> "Nearing Autobiography," St. 4, Ibid.

3   It's no wonder then that leaves
can sing all summer long, even while
knowing for certain and remembering
the waiting winter ahead
> "Silva," St. 4, *The Cortland Review,* No. 7 *May 1999*

3226. Wilma "Skeeter" Rudolph (1940–1994)

1   When you come from a large, wonderful family, there's always
a way to achieve your goals.*
> Quoted in *Wilma Rudolph: Champion Athlete* by Tom
> Biracree *1988*

*She was the 20th of 22 siblings.

2   I don't know why I run so fast. I just run.
> Ibid.

3   Triumph can't be had without the struggle.
> Ibid.

3227. Patricia Schroeder (1940–   )

1   I have a brain and a uterus and I use them both.
> (1973), Quoted in *American Political Women* by Esther
> Stineman *1980*

2   There is an ancient Indian saying: "We do not inherit the earth
from ancestors; we borrow it from our children." If we use this
ethic as a moral compass, then our rendezvous with reality can
also become a rendezvous with opportunity.
> Quoted in *Ms. February 1989*

3   *24 Years of House Work . . . and the Place Is Still a Mess*
> Book title *1998*

4   [Ronald Reagan* is] the Teflon president.
> Cited in *Biographical Dictionary of Congressional Women* by
> Karen Foerstel *1999*

*American politician, actor (1911–2004), governor of California
(1967–75), 40th president of the United States (1980–88).

5   [Dan Quayle* thinks] *Roe versus Wade** are two ways to
cross the Potomac.***
> Ibid.

*J. Danforth Quayle (1947–   ), vice president of the United States
(1989–93). **U.S. Supreme Court decision re abortion rights
(1973); see Sarah Weddington, 3075. ***Potomac River, which
flows into Washington, D.C.

6   If you guys were women, you'd always be pregnant. You just
can't say no.
> Remark to Pentagon officials on the Armed Services
> Committee, Ibid.

7   The White House is still a great big tree house with a "No girls
allowed" sign on it.
> "Clinton broke ground, but what does it mean," *The Los*
> *Angeles Times 7 June 2008*

3228. Marie Shear (1940–   )

1   Millions of people have been using they, their and them as
third-person singulars all along. They are eminently sensible. As a reformed pedant, I don't say that casually. Until
a few years ago I scorned such people, considering them
fundamentally uncouth, like public smokers. But I've seen
the light.
> "Solving the Great Pronoun Problem: 12 Ways to Avoid
> the Sexist Singular," *Perspectives* (U.S. Commission on Civil
> Rights) *Spring 1981*

2   Philip Morris* is too modest about its concern for the environment. Its blurb in your special advertising section (September)
omitted P.M.'s finest biodegradable of all. Philip Morris makes
cigarettes, cigarettes make corpses, and worms eat corpses.
Human compost. Rah, rah, rah!
> Letter to the editor, *American Journalism Review November*
> *1991*

*Philip Morris USA is one of the world's largest tobacco
corporations.

3   I am entitled to assisted suicide, and so is anyone else who
chooses it, whether our miseries are terminal or interminable—real assistance, not help restricted to those who can
pass through the eye of a needle at the far end of an obstacle
course.
> Book review, "Unhappy Endings," *The Women's Review of*
> *Books* (Wellesley, MA) *June 1999*

4   If God had meant everyone to be thin, She'd have made us
taller.
> Letter to the editor, *The New York Times 11 June 2005*

3229. Karen Shepherd (1940–   )

1   I wonder if we would have to cough up all this money for prisons if we had fully funded Headstart* 20 years ago. We are
paying the price of benign neglect.
> Quoted by Mindy Cameron in "Win-win politics from a
> sisterhood of change," *Seattle Times,* Op-Ed *3 April 1994*

*A preschool program for underprivileged children, started in the
1960s.

3230. Valerie Solanis (1940–1988)

1 Life in this society being, at best, an utter bore and no aspect of society being at all relevant to women, there remains to civic-minded, responsible, thrill-seeking females only to overthrow the government, eliminate the money system, institute complete automation and destroy the male sex.

SCUM Manifesto* 1967–1968
*SCUM is an acronym for Society for Cutting Up Men.

2 Dropping out gives control to those few who don't drop out; dropping out is exactly what the establishment leaders want; it plays into the hands of the enemy; it strengthens the system instead of undermining it, since it is based entirely on non-participation, passivity, apathy and non-involvement....

Ibid.

3 Our society is not a community, but merely a collection of isolated family units.

Ibid.

3231. Marcia Tager (194?–2004)

1 Parents sighed, shrugged, lifted their eyes heavenward, asking God to witness the madness of their young, asking for the strength to bear the terrible burden of their children's lunacy.

"Cousins" (1982), *Shaking Eve's Tree, Short Stories of Jewish Women,* Sharon Niederman,* ed. 1990
*See 3855.

2 But Lilo never seemed to understand that you have to have things before you can throw them away. It's easy for Lilo to turn up her nose at the suburbs. To Lilo the word suburban is pejorative. But Lilo grew up in a suburb, in a white house guarded by a velvet lawn. I think you have to grow up on city streets to want lawns for your children.

Ibid.

3 ... if there's one kind of person in this world who makes other people feel miserable it's a saint.

Ibid.

3232. Yukiko Tanaka (1940–)

1 Both the [19]80s and the period from 1913–38 were periods of upheaval [in Japan], when women worked to free themselves of traditional social and psychological constraints. In both ... we see women compelled by the pressure of history to explore unfamiliar terrain, to reinvent themselves.

Introduction, *Unmapped Territories, New Women's Fiction from Japan,* ed. & tr. 1991

3233. Raymonda Tawil (1940?–)

1 Yesterday's terrorist is today's prime minister. And today's terrorist will be tomorrow's president of Palestine.

Quoted in Ch. 16, Meeting, Ms. Tour group, 7 March 1978, (King David Hotel, Jerusalem), *Deborah, Golda, and Me* by Letty Cottin Pogrebin* 1991
*See 3154.

2 We [Palestinians] are the Jews of the Arab world.

Ibid.

3 There is no place for the Jew in the Middle East!

Ibid.

4 Although Arab women suffer more gender discrimination than any other women in the world, it is impossible to ask us to care about the sexual revolution when the individual Palestinian is dehumanized, when there is a conspiracy against the realization of our human rights, when our being is threatened, when our identity is denied and when we have no home.

Ibid.

3234. Jane P. Tompkins (1940–)

1 The female subject par excellence, which is her self and her experiences, has once more been elided by literary criticism.

"Me and My Shadow" (1988), *The Intimate Critique: Autobiographical Literary Criticism,* Diane P. Freedman, Olivia Frey and Frances Murphy Zauhar, eds. 1993

3235. Theadora Van Runkle (1940–)

1 Death is very sophisticated. It's like a Noel Coward comedy. You light a cigarette and wait for it in the library.

Quoted in "People You Should Know" by Mary Reinholz, *Viva April 1974*

3236. Yuliya Voznesenskaya (1940–)

1 In the West they had invented disposable nappies and plastic pants long ago. Our people were supposed to be involved in industrial espionage, so why couldn't they steal some useful secrets instead of always going for electronics?

The Women's Decameron (Damskii Dekameron), W. B. Linton, tr. 1985

2 "I think, Larissa," she said, "that all your strength comes precisely from your insecurity. It happens to a lot of women these days. It's not so much that we're striving to be strong ourselves, but the weakness of the men forces us to be. It's frightening how unmanly they have become. A husband in the home is just another child, only greedier."

"The First Day, Story Two," Ibid.

3237. Michelene Wandor (1940–)

1 However it is true so far that on the whole women playwrights have tended to choose to write about their own sex—and actually, there is nothing at all unusual about that. Most male playwrights choose to write about their own sex—it is just that they rarely see that that is what they are doing.

Introduction, *Plays by Women,* Vol. 2 1984

2 Stupid word, that. Period. In America it means "full stop," like in punctuation. That's stupid as well. A period isn't a full stop. It's a new beginning. I don't mean all that creativity, life-giving force, earth-mother stuff, I mean it's a new beginning to the month, relief that you're not pregnant, when you don't have to have a child.

"Mother's Pride," *Guests in the Body 1986*

3 I have decided to give up heterosexuality. I have decided that, while the project of altering the balance of power within heterosexual relationships is still a valid one, it is no longer one I can espouse—so to speak. There is no revolutionary hope for the heterosexual, and I have therefore decided to love myself and become a lesbian.

"Meet My Mother," *Close Company: Stories of Mothers and Daughters,* Christine Park and Caroline Heaton, eds. 1987

4 If someone accuses me of ghettoizing women playwrights, I have two answers: one is unprintable, the other is that no one

ever accuses the editor of an all-male anthology of plays of ghettoizing playwrights.

> Quoted in "Michelene Wandor," *Interviews with Contemporary Women Playwrights* by Kathleen Betsko* and Rachel Koenig *1987*

*See 3125.

3238. Margot Adler (1941–   )

1   Although we know that on some level we are always connected, our most common experience is one of estrangement.

> *Drawing Down the Moon 1986*

2   Just as ecological theory explains how we are interrelated with all other forms of life, rituals allow us to re-create that unity in an explosive, non-abstract, gut-level way. Rituals have the power to reset the terms of our universe until we find ourselves suddenly and truly "at home."

> Ibid.

3239. Charlotte Vale Allen (1941–   )

1   There is a damned good reason why old people died: to spare youngsters the sight of them. Who the hell wanted to know at twenty that they'd one day look like a quirky assemblage of shapeless rubbery parts tacked any which way to a set of crumbling bones?

> *Painted Lives 1990* Ibid.

2   Men are just like little boys with money.

> Ibid.

3   "Do you dream in color or black and white?" . . .
    "Color, naturally. . . . Is this some kind of imbecilic psychological test?"
    "No, I'm serious. I've been dreaming lately in black and white. I think it must mean something."
    "Maybe it means you're too lazy to fill in the mental colors."

> *Dreaming In Color 1993*

3240. Gloria Allred (1941–   )

1   Lots of men, you see, simply aren't ready for assertive women. They expect us to tiptoe in, trembling and pleading for our rights and when those rights are denied, they expect us not to cause a furor but to tiptoe away quietly. But they underestimate how much we care.

> Quoted in "Home Q&A" by Marshall Berger in *The Los Angeles Times Home Magazine 7 January 1979*

2   . . . the media is still dominated by men, many of whom think of women in a very sexist way. They cover them in a sexist way, and they do *not* cover them because of sexism.

> Quoted in *Perspectives* Fall *1996*

3   They can't buy me, they can't rent me, they can't lease me, they can't silence me. All they can do is give me justice.

> "Victims' Rights Lawyer: TV Fixture," CBS-TV *The Early Show 25 May 2005*

3241. Joan Baez (1941–   )

1   Powerful Jesus gold and silver with young, hundred-year-old eyes.
    You look around and you know you must have failed somewhere.

> "Farewell Angelina" *1965*

2   If it's natural to kill why do men have to go into training to learn how?

> *Daybreak 1966*

3   By the middle of the twentieth century men had reached a peak of insanity. They grouped together in primitive nation-states, each nation-state condoning organized murder as the way to deal with international differences. . . .

> Ibid.

4   And if you're offering me diamonds and rust
    I've already paid.

> "Diamonds and Rust" *1975*

5   We are the warriors of the sun
    Fighting postwar battles
    That somehow never were won.

> "Warriors of the Sun," *Live Europe 83* (album) *1983*

6   We're the children of the eighties;
    Haven't we grown?
    We're softer than a lotus
    and tougher than stone*
    And the age of innocence
    Is somewhere in the garden.

> "(For the) Children of the Eighties," Ibid.

*Adapted from phrase by Mohandas Gandhi, Indian nationalist and spiritual leader (1869–1948), assassinated.

7   I've never had a humble opinion in my life. If you're going to have one, why bother to be humble about it?

> *International Herald Tribune* (Paris) *2 December 1992*

3242. Sandra Ables Benítez (1941–   )

1   In her hut, Remedios listens to someone's story, and the teller is revived.
    It is stories that save us, Remedios is certain.

> *A Place Where the Sea Remembers 1993*

3243. Sally Bingham (1941–   )

1   For me, the Holy Eucharist symbolizes not only Christ's presence, but also our dependence on nature; without bread, water, and land, we could not survive.
    It was that belief that led me to pursue my environmental commitments within the context of the Church. I didn't believe that we should be baptizing with polluted water.

> "The Regeneration Project," grist.org *25 March 2002*

2   If we say we love God, we are required to save God's creation. How can you listen to the second commandment—which is to love your neighbor as yourself—and then pollute your neighbor's air?

> "Meet Sally Bingham," PurposePrize.org *2007*

3   Why don't I ever hear about the destruction of creation from the pulpit?

> Ibid.

3244. Carol Bolt (1941–   )

1   EMMA. . . . freeing herself from the fear of public opinion and public condemnation will set a woman free, will make her a force hitherto unknown in the world.

> *Red Emma,* * Queen of the Anarchists 1974*

*Reference to Emma Goldman; see 1360.

3245. Erica Bouza (1941?–)

1 When you've written to your president, to your congressman, to your senator and nothing, nothing has come of it, you take to the streets.

> Quoted in "The Public Eye," *The Great Divide: Second Thoughts on the American Dream* by Studs Terkel* *1988*
> *(1912–2008) Pulitzer Prize-winning American author, historian, actor, broadcaster.

2 Don't you think we are heading for another McCarthy* period and shouldn't we remember Benjamin Franklin's** statement that "those who would sacrifice liberty for safety deserve neither liberty nor safety?"

> Letter to Senator Coleman,*** *Pulse of the Twin Cities* (pulsetc.com) *9 April 2003*
> *Re: the politically motivated practice of making accusations of disloyalty, subversion, or treason without proper regard for evidence; name for Senator Joseph McCarthy (1908–1957) of Wisconsin. **Benjamin Franklin (1706–90), U.S. statesman, writer. ***Norman Bertram C– (1949–), U.S. Senator (R-MN), 2003–09.

3 In WWII we all had gas masks. I read that you keep one by your desk. I assume all the senators have one, but should the rest of us get gassed, it means you will have only each other to govern.

> Ibid.

3246. Beth Brant (1941–)

1 Because in the unraveling, the threads become more apparent, each one with its distinct color and texture. And as I unravel, I also weave. I am the storyteller and the story.

> Introduction, *A Gathering of Spirit*, ed. *1984*

2 We have a spirit of rage. We are angry women. Angry at white men and their perversions. Their excessive greed and abuse of the earth, sky, and water. Their techno-christian approach to anything that lives, including our children, our people. We are angry at Indian men for their refusals of us. For their limited vision of what constitutes a strong Nation. We are angry at a so-called "women's movement" that always seems to forget we exist. Except in romantic fantasies of earth mother, or equally romantic and dangerous fantasies of Indian-woman-as-victim.

> Ibid.

3 Helen can't imagine that she is beautiful.
That her skin is warm
like redwood and fire.
That her thick black hair moves like a current.
That her large body speaks in languages stolen from her.
That her mouth is wide and full and when she smiles
people catch their breath.

> "Her Name Is Helen," St. 11, *Mohawk Trail 1985*

3247. Martha Gertrude Burk (1941–)

1 . . . the problem of unwanted pregnancy is largely one of uncontrolled sperm.

> "The Sperm Stops Here," *Ms.* (New York) *November/ December 1997*

3248. Lynne Ann Cheney (1941–)

1 We live in a land of shining cities and natural splendors, a beautiful land made more beautiful still by our commitment to freedom.

> Introduction, *America: A Patriotic Primer 2002*

2 In Abigail Adams's* time, women could not go to college, become professionals, own property once they were married, or vote. The transformation of women's lives from then to now is one of our great national narratives, an inspiring story that our children deserve to know.

> Introduction, *A is for Abigail: An Almanac of Amazing American Women 2003*
> *See 646.

3 I kind of like politicians that are more in the Dick Cheney* mold, who say what they mean and mean what they say.

> "A Cheney Speaks Out on 2008," *The Washington Post 23 October 2007*
> *Her husband, Richard Bruce "Dick" Cheney (1941–), 46th vice president of the United States (2001–09).

3249. Blanche Weisen Cook (1941–)

1 Revolution is a process and not an event. The power of women to come together, to support each other in community, in creative self-criticism and love, gives us the power to intensify the economic and political struggle. Wherever groups of women come together to define their own visions, economic and personal, and make connections with other groups of women working in our own interests, politically accountable to our own needs and wants, we are affirming a network of change. We are building the future.

> *Women and Support Networks 1979*

3250. Margarita Cota-Cárdenas (1941–)

1 yes yes I went yelling loud too why why and they said tie her up she's too forward too flighty she thinks she's a princess thinks she's her father's daughter thinks she's hot stuff that's it doesn't know her place a real threat to the tribe take her away haul her off she's a menace to our cause that's it only learned to say crazy things accuse with HER EYES and they didn't want them troublemakers in their country.

> *Puppet 1985*

3250.1 Dai Qing (1941–)

1 As a citizen of a country, I cannot leave her. And I have to criticise it in order to build a more perfect and stronger one.

> *Wo de Ruyu* (My Imprisonment) *1990*

2 The highest expression of dignity can be summed up in the single word "No!"—being able to say "No!" when you disagree.

> Quoted on goldmanprize.org *1993*

3 The new era is making new Chinese. The situation in China is different. Ordinary people are exercising their rights.

> "The Stars of Asia," *Business Week 14 June 1999*

4 My books are banned. But I can speak outside. I am a writer and a journalist. My voice is the most important. They only silence me on the inside [of China], not the outside.

> Ibid.

5 Hydropower is a clean form of energy that doesn't pollute the air. However, if a dam is built on the middle reaches of a river busy with ship traffic; if it's built in a densely populated agricultural region; on a river whose waters bear large volumes of sediment; in an area where the earth can split open and collapse at any time; in a place scattered with ancient tombs; in a place where rare animals and fish face extinction—then the contrast between the benefits brought by clean energy, and

disasters brought by environmental damage and social turmoil, is quite clear.

"Expert Roundtable," *The New York Times 21 November 2007*

6 The need to protect rivers—not just use them—has become a universal consensus at the end of 20th century

Ibid.

3251. Alma De Groen (1941–)

1 JOY. I can cope with being satirised. It's your sympathy I can't stand.

Vocations 1983

2 VICKI. I feel as if emotionally I might love you, but my head hasn't caught up yet. I don't know you.

Ibid.

3 WAYNE. I live in a room—and it isn't home. I live on earth—and it isn't home.

Rivers of China 1987

3252. Donna de Matteo (1941–)

1 A new play is like a child.

"Donna de Matteo," *Interviews with Contemporary Women Playwrights,* Kathleen Betsko* and Rachel Koenig *1987*
*See 3125.

2 Watching Miss [Uta] Hagen* during rehearsals is comparable to watching a superb musician playing a fine instrument. She is a master at her craft, very detailed, and patient in her approach to a character; but at the same time, she never loses sight of her instincts and emotions, and when you see her blend all of these elements together, it all looks so natural and effortless . . . It transcends life. It's art at its best.

Ibid.

*See 2345.

3 The wonderful thing about music is that it immediately evokes certain eras of one's life, brings you back to where you've been, even if you don't want to go there.

Ibid.

4 Women, generally, are apt to put things together rather than tear them apart.

Ibid.

3253. Margriet de Moor (1941–)

1 Religion is as beautiful and dangerous as poetry. It forges a direct connection with a sphere that the average sceptical West European is only prepared to enter with great reservation. The poetic dimension of religion, beautiful for its unrestrained and rapturous qualities, has always remained attractive: a world in which human reason has little to say, yet a world that touches us all the same.

"Alarm bells in Muslim hearts," signandsight.com
23 April 2007

2 The law of profit says rather matter-of-factly: avoid confrontation and do business.

Ibid.

3 How sex-obsessed is a culture that teaches a woman that she is basically a walking, sitting or reclining set of genitals? How over-aroused is a society in which men are expected to have no qualms about throwing themselves on any woman who

happens to walk by unless a powerful signal in the form of a divinely ordained dress code forbids them to do so?

Quoted by Suzanne Fields* in "The world is slouching toward '2084'," *Washington Times 5 May 2007*
*See 4572.

3254. Toi Derricotte (1941–)

1 When my legs gave out, my grandmother
dragged me up and held me like God
holds saints by the
roots of the hair.

"The Weakness," *Captivity 1989*

2 "She think she white" was said with a bitterness, irony, disgust, and even a humor that only one raised with generations of historical pain can understand. It was not only a judgment, it was a punishment as well, for it embodied the consequence of exile, of exclusion. Suddenly the accused had stepped outside of love, community, and entered that territory in another person's head that made her the thing hated. . . . "She think she white" seemed to guard a little sacred territory in the speaker's mind, a final defense against self-rejection, questioning the accused's sanity rather than one's own.

The Black Notebooks 1997

3 Some of us, in spite of our ambivalence, in spite of the roads back that vanish like the crumbs in Hansel and Gretel, are drawn by our ancestors' strength.

"The Bond of Living Things: Poems of Ancestry," poets.org
2008

4 Leaving the pain of the past behind necessitated terrible junctures in the self, repressions that often broke out in acts of inexplicable violence or self-mutilation.

Ibid.

3255. Bridget Rose Dugdale (1941–)

1 For how long you sentence me is of no relevance; I regard it with the contempt it deserves. I am guilty and proudly so if guilty has come to describe one who takes up arms to defend the people of Ireland against the English tyrant.

Quoted in "Englishwoman Trips on Revolutionary Road" by Tom Lambert, *The Los Angeles Times 26 June 1974*

3256. Jennifer Dunn (1941–2007)

1 I'm someone who has broken a lot of glass ceilings. I was the first woman president of our student body in the sixth grade and was the first woman Republican Party state chairman.

"Congresswoman: Leadership needs change of face" (p. 10A), *USA Today 11 November 1998*

2 I have the skills that can fill any gap. I can communicate. I can organize. I can feel what people want. I'm a woman.

Ibid.

3 I have always been a proponent of softening our [the Republican Party's] rhetoric. I believe we can pursue the same positions we have been, but we don't need to be as harsh and scary about it.

Quoted in *Biographical Dictionary of Congressional Women* by Karen Foerstel *1999*

3257. Barbara Ehrenreich (1941–)

1 The witch-craze was neither a lynching party nor a mass suicide by hysterical women. Rather, it followed well-ordered,

legalistic procedures. The witch-hunts were well organized campaigns, initiated, financed, and executed by Church and State.

Witches, Midwives, and Nurses: A History of Women Healers, coauthor, Deirdre English* 1973

*See 3825.

2   Exercise is the yuppie version of bulimia.
"Food Worship" (1985), *The Worst Years of Our Lives* 1991

3   Upscale young men seem to go for the kind of woman who plays with a full deck of credit cards, who won't cry when she's knocked to the ground while trying to board the six o'clock Eastern shuttle, and whose schedule doesn't allow for a sexual encounter lasting more than twelve minutes.
"The Cult of Busyness" (*The New York Times,* 1985), Ibid.

4   It seems to me that there must be an ecological limit to the number of paper pushers the earth can sustain, and that human civilization will collapse when the number of, say, tax lawyers exceeds the world's total population of farmers, weavers, fish-erpersons, and pediatric nurses.
"Premature Pragmatism" (*Ms.,* 1986), Ibid.

5   So why do people keep on watching? The answer, by now, should be perfectly obvious: we love television because television brings us a world in which television does not exist.
"Spudding Out" (1988), Ibid.

6   If men were equally at risk from this condition—if they knew their bellies might swell as if they were suffering from end-stage cirrhosis, that they would have to go nearly a year without a stiff drink, a cigarette, or even an aspirin, that they would be subject to fainting spells and unable to fight their way onto commuter trains—then I am sure that pregnancy would be classified as a sexually transmitted disease and abortions would be no more controversial than emergency appendectomies.
"Their Dilemma and Mine," Ibid.

7   No matter that patriotism is too often the refuge of scoundrels. Dissent, rebellion, and all-around hell-raising remain the true duty of patriots.
"Family Values," Ibid.

8   Unlike blue-collar people, the white-collar unemployed are likely to have some assets to invest in their job searches; they are, in addition, often lonely and depressed—a perfect market, in other words, for any service promising prosperity and re-newed self-esteem.
Ch. 1, *Bait and Switch: The (Futile) Pursuit of the American Dream* 2005

9   But if any other animals create music and move in synchrony to it, they have kept this talent well hidden from humans. We alone are gifted with the kind of love that Freud* was unable to imagine: a love, or at least affinity, holding people together in groups much larger than two.
Ch. 1, *Dancing in the Streets: A History of Collective Joy* 2007
*Sigmund F- (1856–1939), Austrian physician and founder of psychoanalysis.

10 Rock's contribution was to weigh in decisively on the side of hedonism and against the old puritanical theme of "deferred gratification."
"Rock Rebellion," Ibid.

3258. Nora Ephron (1941–   )

1   We have lived through the era when happiness was a warm puppy, and the era when happiness was a dry martini, and now we have come to the era when happiness is "knowing what your uterus looks like."
"Vaginal Politics" (December 1972), *Crazy Salad* 1975

2   No man can be friends with a woman he finds attractive. He always wants to have sex with her. Sex is always out there. Friendship is ultimately doomed and that is the end of the story.
When Harry Met Sally (screenplay) 1989

3   I am continually fascinated at the difficulty intelligent people have in distinguishing what is controversial from what is merely offensive.
"Barney Collier's Book," *Esquire January* 1976

4   The last four years of psychoanalysis are a waste of money.
Ch. 1, *I Feel Bad About My Neck* 2006

5   When your children are teenagers, it's important to have a dog so that someone in the house is happy to see you.
Ibid.

Also see Delia Ephron, 3498:3–4.

3259. Sheila Mary Fitzpatrick (1941–   )

1   *Homo Sovieticus* was a string-puller, an operator, a timeserver, a freeloader, a mouther of slogans and much more. But above all, he was a survivor.
Everyday Stalinism 1998

3260. Fannie Flagg (1941–   )

1   "It's funny, when you're a child you think time will never go by, but when you hit about twenty—time passes like you're on the fast train to Memphis."
"December 15, 1985," *Fried Green Tomatoes at the Whistle Stop Café* 1987

2   He was here—Slagtown on a Saturday night—and just one block away, white Birmingham was completely unaware that this exotic sepia spot even existed. Slagtown, where the High-land Avenue maid of that afternoon could be tonight's Queen of the Avenue, and red-caps and shoeshine boys were the lead-ers of Slagtown's after-dark fashion show.
"December 30, 1934," Ibid.

3   "A lot of people might have been sad to have a birth-injured child, but I think the good Lord made him like that so he wouldn't have to suffer. He never even knew there were mean people on this earth. He just loved everybody and ev-erybody loved him. I truly believe in my heart that he was an angel that God sent down to me, and sometimes I cain't wait to get to heaven to see him again. He was my pal, and I miss him . . ."
"March 15, 1986," Ibid.

4   She had stayed a virgin so she wouldn't be called a tramp or a slut; had married so she wouldn't be called an old maid; faked orgasms so she wouldn't be called frigid; had children so she wouldn't be called barren; had not been a feminist because she didn't want to be called queer and a man hater; never nagged or raised her voice so she wouldn't be called a bitch . . .
"August 8, 1986," Ibid.

5   . . . and is there anything worse than man who has a little pain? Guess that's why we have the babies . . .

"August 10, 1954," Ibid.

6   She had joined a health club, once, but was so exhausted by the time she'd pulled herself into those awful leotards, she went home to bed.

"October 14, 1986," Ibid.

3261. Elizabeth Fox-Genovese (1941–2007)

1   More than any other single issues, support for a woman's right to choose to have an abortion has become the litmus test of feminism. . . . Do feminists believe that feminism has no room for pro-life women even if they support equal pay for equal work and related women's issues? Apparently it does.

Ch. 1, *Feminism Is Not the Story of My Life 1995*

2   Having originated more as a relation between families, tribes, or clans than as a relation between individuals, marriage has gradually been transformed into an exclusively personal relation—a matter of an individual's "right" to specific benefits and privileges and, perhaps above all, community recognition and approval.

Ch. 1, *Marriage: The Dream That Refuses to Die 2008*

3   The gift has figured as a powerful symbol in virtually all cultures—the tangible embodiment and confirmation of intangible promises and intentions.

Ibid.

4   It is impossible to exaggerate our moral failures to children, but ultimately those failures are society's as much as individual parents'. We have indulged ourselves with a culture that puts the individual—"me, me, me"—first at the expense of all competing obligations. Under these conditions, binding ties dissolve into matters of personal choice that may change without warning or concern for the consequences to others.

Ch. 3, Ibid.

5   Symbolically, the reduction of privacy to the privacy of the solitary individual effectively sounds the death knell of the family as an organic unit with claims on its members.

Ch. 4, Ibid

3262. Marilyn Frye (1941–   )

1   We can be taken in by this equation of servitude with love because we make two mistakes at once: we think, of both servitude and love that they are selfless or unselfish.

(p. 73), *The Politics of Reality: Essays in Feminist Theory 1983*

2   The meanings one's life and experience might generate cannot come fully into operation if they are not woven into language; they are fleeting, or they hover, vague, not fully coalesced, not connected, and hence not useful for explaining or grounding interpretations, desires, complaints, theories.

"Lesbian 'Sex'," *Sinister Wisdom 35 Summer/Fall 1988*

3   Female heterosexuality is not a biological drive or an individual woman's erotic attraction or attachment to another human animal which happens to be male. Female heterosexuality is a set of social institutions and practices defined and regulated by [patriarchal mores, values, and law].

Willful Virgins: Essays In Feminism, 1976–1992 1992

3263. Diane Glancy (1941–   )

1   They couldn't remove us. Didn't the soldiers know we were the land? The cornstalks were our grandmothers. In our story of corn, a woman named Selu had been murdered by her sons. Where her blood fell, the corn grew. The cornstalks waved their arms trying to hold us. Their voices were the long tassels reaching the air. Our spirits clung to them. Our roots entwined.

Pushing the Bear: A Novel of the Trail of Tears 1996

2   I unbraided my hair and covered a small girl with it to keep her from shivering. "You are a small animal," I said. "Feel your fur." I took the child's hand and rubbed it over my hair. "You are warm under your fur, little rabbit."

Ibid.

3264. Ellen H. Goodman (1941–   )

1   I don't romanticize mental illness. But at the same time, I wonder what will happen if we are able to lighten the load of memory. Would we end up with a drug to make loss "lite," to speed up "closure," to make horrors "manageable"? At some point reducing human suffering is editing human experience. For better or for worse.

"Treating bad memories. . . ," *Boston Globe 15 November 2002*

2   . . . the White House and both houses of Congress are all securely in Republican hands, and all hands are ready to chip away at reproductive rights—one law, one rule, one regulation, one case at a time.

"Administration chips at abortion rights," *Boston Globe 21 January 2003*

3   I would like to say we're at a point where global warming is impossible to deny. Let's just say that global warming deniers are now on a par with Holocaust deniers, though one denies the past and the other denies the present and future.

Column, *Boston Globe 9 February 2007*

3265. Linda Gottleib (1941?–   )
Coauthor with Joan Silver; see 2951.

3266–3267. Toni Grant (1941–   )

1   There is a profound sense of alienation and loneliness here [in Southern California], and few traditional guidelines for behavior. I don't have any grand solutions, just my own idiosyncratic ones.

"Dial Dr. Toni for Therapy," *Time (New York) 26 May 1980*

2   . . . sometimes you have to give up an intense heat for a continuing warmth.

Quoted in "Sexy Guru for Kvetches" by Elaine Warren, *Los Angeles Herald-Examiner 20 July 1980*

3268. Margaret Morganroth Gullette (1941–   )

1   Midlife is a "contrast-gainer" (to borrow a phrase from Bellow* at his sixtyish wittiest). To feel good about the middle years it is helpful to have had a miserable young adulthood and, in particular, a trying time in the early years of marriage.

Safe at Last in the Middle Years 1988
*Saul B— (1915–2005), American novelist.

2   Is it too blissful to imagine, as our goal, being able to feel at home in the life course at every age?

Ch. 1, *Aged by Culture 2004*

3 On the calm surface, chronology is a bureaucratic convenience and a motive for annual potlatches of celebration. But the media increasingly exploit these automatic sequences for their associated story of decline.

> Ibid.

4 Decline is a metaphor as hard to contain as dye. Once it has tinged our expectations of the future (sensations, rewards, status, power, voice) with peril, it tends to stain our experiences, our views of others, our explanatory systems, and then our retrospective judgments.

> Ibid.

5 Women have less to fear from menopause than from menopause *discourse*.

> p. 6, *Our Bodies Ourselves: Menopause* 2006

3269. Lyn Hejinian (1941–)

1 I am among them thinking thought through the thinking thought to no conclusion.

> "Happily," *The Language of Inquiry* 2002

2 Nostalgia is another name for one's sense of loss at the thought that one has sadly gone along happily overlooking something, who knows what

> "Happily," St. 2, Ibid.

3 Language itself is never in a state of rest. And the experience of using it, which includes the experience of understanding it, either as speech or as writing, is inevitably active. I mean both intellectually and emotionally active.

> "The Rejection of Closure," Ibid.

4 Poetry takes as its premise that language (all language) is a medium for experiencing experience. It provides us with the consciousness of consciousness. To experience is to go through or over the limit (the word comes from the Greek peras (term, limit)); or, to experience is to go beyond where one is, which is to say to be beyond where one was. . . .

> "Some Notes toward a Poetics" 200-?

3270. Marie Herbert (1941–)

1 Unlike children in other countries, the Eskimos played no games of war. They played with imaginary rifles and harpoons, but these were never directed against people but against the formidable beasts that haunted the vast wastes of their land.

> Ch. 5, *The Snow Children* 1973

2 The Eskimos described everyone other than themselves as Kasdlunas. They called themselves the Inuit—which simply means "the people." For centuries, since they never saw anyone else, they believed they were the only human beings in the world.

> Ibid.

3271. Elizabeth Holtzman (1941–)

1 If the mood of the country is for fiscal responsibility, then let's get at that area of government which is the biggest waster of funds—the Defense Department.

> Quoted in *American Political Women* by Esther Stineman 1980

3272. Libby Houston (1941–)

1 The base emotions Plato banned
have left a radio-active and not radiant land.

> "Judging Lear," *At the Mercy* 1981

2 When your dreams tire, they go underground
and out of kindness that's where they stay.

> "Gold," *Necessity* 1988

3273. Shirbey Johnson (1941–)

1 . . . women are carrying a new attitude. They've cast aside the old stereotypes. They don't believe you have to be ugly or have big muscles to play sports.

> Quoted in "Women in Sports: The Movement is Real,"
> *The Los Angeles Times* 23 April 1974

2 As coaches and facilities are slowly upgraded, as girls get interested at earlier ages, they become integrated into the sports system more naturally.

> Ibid.

3274. Christine H. Kellett (1941–)

1 They were political animals before they got to the Supreme Court, and they don't change when they get there.

> *Lawyer's Wit and Wisdom* Bruce Nash, Allan Zullo, eds.;
> Kathryn Zullo, compiler 1995

3275. Joyce L. Kennard (1941–)

1 I can assure you I am not a token presence. . . . It's nice . . . to see so many women in their proper place—here at the State Bar . . . rubbing elbows with the "old boys."

> Speech, California Women Lawyers, Quoted in "Kennard
> Seeks Her Own Way on High Court" by Philip Hager,
> *The Los Angeles Times* 17 September 1989

2 Individuals in "loving" same-sex relationships have waited years, sometimes several decades, for a chance to wed, yearning to obtain the public validation that only marriage can give.

> Quoted in "Two Pro-Gay CA. Judges On Calif. Ballot" by
> James Hartline, *The Conservative Voice* 24 October 2006

3 In holding today that the right to marry guaranteed by the state constitution may not be withheld from anyone on the ground of sexual orientation, this court discharges its gravest and most important responsibility under our constitutional form of government. There is a reason why the words "Equal Justice Under Law" are inscribed above the entrance to the courthouse of the United States Supreme Court.

> Concurring opinion, Supreme Court of California 15 May 2008

3276. Irena Klepfisz (1941–)

1 at night the vestiges
of other ages influence
us.

> "dinosaurs and larger issues," vii, *periods of stress* 1975

2 My first conscious feeling about being Jewish was that it was dangerous, something to be hidden.

> "Resisting and Surviving America," *Dreams of an Insomniac:*
> *Jewish Feminist Essays, Speeches and Diatribes* 1990

3 You learned Russian in the street
spoke Yiddish at home wrote Polish
in the segregated schools. You were
a linguist at eight ready to master
even more tongues for the sake of survival.

> "'67 Remembered," St. 2, *A Few Words in the Mother Tongue:*
> *Poems Selected and New (1971–1990)* 1990

4 I see now the present dangers, the dangers of the void, of the American hollowness in which I walk calmly day and night as I continue my life. I begin to see the incessant grinding down of lines for stamps, for jobs, for a bed to sleep in, of a death stretched imperceptibly over a lifetime. I begin to understand the ingenuity of it. The invisibility. The Holocaust without smoke.

> "Bashert,"* Ibid.

*Yiddish for destiny; often used in the context of one's divinely foreordained spouse or soulmate.

5 By making literature in *mame-loshn** patrilineal rather than matrilineal, Sholem Aleichem** instantly created a male Yiddish literary dynasty ... Just when Yiddish was being championed as an authentic national *mame-loshn* [he] declared—and everyone agreed—its literature now belonged to the fathers.

> Introduction, *Found Treasures: Stories by Yiddish Women Writers*, Frieda Forman, Ethel Raicus, Sarah Silberstein Swartz & Margie Wolf, eds. *1994*

*Yiddish: mother tongue. **nee S- Yakov Rabinowitz (1859–1916), Russian writer who popularized Yiddish literature.

3277. Julia Kristeva (1941–)

1 FLASH—instant of time or of dream without time; inordinately swollen atoms of a bond, a vision, a shiver, a yet formless, unnamable embryo. Epiphanies. Photos of what is not yet visible and that language necessarily skims over from afar, allusively. Words that are always too distant, too abstract for this underground swarming of seconds, folding into unimaginable spaces. Writing them down is an ordeal of discourse, like love. What is loving, for a woman, the same thing as writing. Laugh. Impossible. Flash on the unnamable, weavings of abstraction to be torn. Let a body venture at last out of its shelter, take a chance with meaning under a veil of words. WORD FLESH. From one to the other, eternally, broken up visions, metaphors of the invisible.

> "Herethique de l'amour," *Tel Quel* 74 *Winter 1977*

2 Our philosophies of language, embodiments of the idea, are nothing more than the thoughts of archivists, archaeologists, and necrophiliacs. Fascinated by the remains of a process which is partly discursive, they substitute this fetish for what actually produced it. Egypt, Babylon, Mycenae: we see their pyramids, their carved tablets, and fragmented codes in the discourse of our contemporaries, and think that by codifying them we can possess them.

> "Prolegomenon," *Revolution in Poetic Language (La revolution du langage poetique*, 1974), Margaret Waller, tr. *1984*

3278. Eunice Lipton (1941–)

1 Selling is what is crucial and Now is the only moment that counts. So you can treat anyone as malevolently as you like today and tomorrow you can smile at them. And mean it. The disingenuousness and flattery one experiences if one is seen as powerful, and the rudeness if one isn't, takes the breath away.

> "Monkey business," *The Women's Review of Books*, Vol. XII, Nos. 10–11 *July 1995*

2 Is that why I'm here in France? Because it is such a locus of maddening extremes: seduction and betrayal, beauty and ugliness, love and hate? Because it's such a tease?

> *French Seduction, An American's Encounter With France, Her Father, and the Holocaust 2006*

3 I want to chew and lick and wallow, far from rules and regulations, where boys don't get more than girls, where I can live eternally anchored in pleasures that never go away.

> Ibid.

3279. Mary Lowry (1941?–)

1 One of the many root causes of youth violence is prenatal chemical dependency. Children born to women who use alcohol and other drugs often suffer brain damage, causing them great difficulty controlling their emotions. . . .

If we are indeed serious about solving the problem of youth violence, addressing the problem of chemical dependency during pregnancy is a great place to start.

> "Mother's chemical dependency . . . ," *Seattle Post-Intelligencer*, Op-Ed, A9 *25 January 1994*

3280. Suzanne Massie (1941?–)

1 Love is always a mystery. No one can define it exactly, but when it happens it is the most real and important thing in one's existence.

> Commencement address, Holy Trinity Orthodox Seminary (Jordanville, N.Y.) *7 June 1981*

2 I have been studying, working and going to Russia for 34 years. From the beginning I was lucky enough to meet and get to know a wide variety of Russians. During these many years whenever I went, it was always apparent that what I saw and heard was often diametrically different from both the official and the journalistic perception in the United States. I came to call it my worm's eye view. The more I studied Russian history and culture the more I saw that the picture was always far more nuanced and complex than the judgments often characteristic of the American approach to affairs Russian.

> Speech, "Why Are We Always Wrong about Russia?", World Affairs Council (Washington, D.C.) *16 May 2001*

3 In these days of acerbic language and mutual sabre rattling between the United States and the Soviet Union, it is difficult to recall that throughout our history, with the exception of recent times, Russia and the United States enjoyed the most amicable relations.

> Pt. 1, "The Grand Duke Alexis in the U.S.A.," *The Gilcrease Magazine of American History & Art* (Tulsa) *2003*

3281. Evelyn Mattern (1941–2003)

1 The mystic can see God with the eyes of love.

> *Why Not Become Fire? Encounters With Women Mystics 1999*

2 Despite the presence of evil in the world, the mystic believes that the universe is ultimately friendly.

> Ibid.

3 I don't think we're going to have a mass movement [to halt global warming] anytime soon, but I don't think it takes that many people to make a difference.

> Quoted in "Kyoto, U.S.A." by Katherine Ellison,* grist.org *31 July 2002*

*See 4405.

4 I think I'm really ready to die, But I know from the experience of other people you can't always have it when you want it. I would be happy if it would be over now.

Quoted in "Sr. Evelyn Mattern, mystic and activist . . ." by Patrick O'Neill, *National Catholic Report 23 January 2004*

5   I think people are much more serious about prayer, not as a ritual, but as an inner movement of the spirit.

Ibid.

3282. Donella "Dana" Meadows (1941–2001)

1   I've done the numbers. I believe it's possible for 7 billion or 8 billion people to live in a way that doesn't degrade the earth, in a way that meets basic human needs better than we do today—including the nonmaterial ones.

Quoted by Jay Walljasper, *Utne Reader May–June 2001*

2   Scientists go through an anti-religious, anti-spiritual brainwashing. If you can't measure it, it doesn't exist.

Ibid.

3   Speak the truth. Speak it loud and often, calmly but insistently, and speak it, as the Quakers say, to power. Material accumulation is not the purpose of human existence. All growth is not good. The environment is a necessity, not a luxury. There is such a thing as "enough."

Limits to Growth: The 30-Year Update, with Jorgen Randers and Dennis L. Meadows *2004*

3283. Janice Mirikitani (1941–   )

1   if you're too dark
they will kill you
if you're too swift
they will buy you
if you're too beautiful
they will rape you

watch with eyes open
speak darkly
turn your head like the owl
behind you

"Japs," *Awake in the River 1978*

2   Some imprisonments are permanent:
white walls encaged her
with a single syllable:
JAP.

"Generations of Women," II, St. 5 (1987), *The Woman That I Am, The Literature and Culture of Contemporary Women of Color* D. Soyini Madison,* ed. *1994*

*See 3912.

3   No, I do not answer to Geisha Girl, China Doll, Suzie Wong, mamasan, or gook, jap or chink.
No, to us life is not cheap.

"Yes, We Are Not Invisible," *We the Dangerous, New and Selected Poems 1995*

4   For me, the role of poet is as a voice to connect with the community. What's great about San Francisco is its diversity. It's the mecca for diversity and that's what turns me on about being the laureate.

Acceptance remarks as Poet Laureat (San Francisco), *San Francisco Chronicle 7 February 2000*

5   The woman
spins her thread
from the spool of her heart,

knotted to her daughter's
departing
wedding slippers.

"For a Daughter Who Leaves," *Love Works 2001*

3284. Robin Morgan (1941–   )

1   . . . although every organized patriarchal religion works overtime to contribute its own brand of misogyny to the myth of woman-hate, woman-fear, and woman-evil, the Roman Catholic Church also carries the immense power of very directly affecting women's lives everywhere by its stand against birth control and abortion, and by its use of skillful and wealthy lobbies to prevent legislative change. It is an obscenity—an all-male hierarchy, celibate or not, that presumes to rule on the lives and bodies of millions of women.

Introduction, *Sisterhood Is Powerful 1970*

2   There's something contagious about demanding freedom.

Ibid.

3   Don't accept rides from strange men,
and remember that all men are strange as hell.

"Letter to a Sister Underground," Ibid.

4   All the secretaries hunch at their IBM's, snickering at keys.
What they know could bring down the government.

"On the Watergate Women," St. 7, *Monster 1972*

5   Only she who attempts the absurd can achieve the impossible.

Sisterhood is Global 1984

6   The historical persons who were Gautama Buddha, Moses, Jesus Christ, Mohammed—among the other great philosopher-leaders—were remarkably progressive for their own times, a fact most of their followers have overlooked ever since. Religion may be the last resort of the patriarchal scoundrel, because the distortion of those original teachings is so drastic and pervasive.

Introduction: "Planetary Feminism: The Politics of the 21st Century," Ibid.

7   *We are formulating revolution in its most profound sense:* a complete social, political, economic, cultural, technological, sexual, and emotional transformation of human society. We are daring to redefine everything, from sexuality to power, from development to peace, from economics to psychology. We are even daring to try to free the human soul, to create a physical *and* metaphysical revolution.

Ibid.

8   Because virtually all existing countries are structured by patriarchal mentality, the standard for being human is being male—and female human beings *per se* become "other," and invisible. This permits governments and international bodies to discuss "the world's problems"—war, poverty, refugees, hunger, disease, illiteracy, overpopulations, ecological imbalance, the abuse or exploitation of children and the elderly, etc.—without noticing that those who suffer most from "the world's problems" are *women,* who, in addition, are not consulted about possible solutions.

Ibid.

9   The invisible woman continues her visible work.

Ibid.

10   When a sexist idiot screamed "Iron my shirt!" at HRC,* it was considered amusing; if a racist idiot shouted "Shine my shoes!"

at BO,** it would've inspired hours of airtime and pages of newsprint analyzing our national dishonor.

"Goodbye to All That," The Women's Media Center
(womensmediacenter.com) *2 February 2008*
*Hillary Rodham Clinton; see 3731. **Barack Obama (1961–),
44th president of the United States (2009–).

11 John McCain* answering "How do we beat the bitch?" with "Excellent question!" Would he have dared reply similarly to "How do we beat the black bastard?" For shame.

Ibid.

*(1936–), U.S. Senator (R-AZ), 1987– , and Republican Presidential candidate (2008); response to a constituent on the campaign trail in 2008.

3285. Claire Goldberg Moses (1941–)

1 Among the peasantry, to be sure, inequalities based on sex were less important: a blanket of poverty spread itself equally over both men and women, and a lack of property made the idea of protection of the patrimony meaningless.

Ch. 1, *French Feminism in the 19th Century 1984*

2 Women's studies, even at the graduate level, intends to change society, not simply to fit our students into the society we inherit.

"Passing on the torch," *The Women's Review of Books,* Vol.
XV, No. 5 *February 1998*

3286. Suzanne Mubarak (1941–)

1 We must never underestimate the power of the word. It is through words and images that people have shared their thoughts and feelings, their fears and aspirations—and their dreams to create a better future . . .

Speech, IBBY Jubilee, *6 May 2003*

2 Polygamy cannot be prevented by force, but through education.

Speech *March 2007*

3287. Suniti Namjoshi (1941–)

1 Circe,*
all animals adore you,
you are all things to each
in the tutelary garden, at the continuous feast.

"Homage to Circe," *The Jackass and the Lady 1980*
*In Greek mythology, enchantress; daughter of Helios.

2 I give her the rose with unfurled petals.
She smiles
and crosses her legs.

"I Give Her the Rose," Ibid.

3288. Judith Niemi (1941–)

1 On the main Amazon, sheer volume overwhelms the imagination, wipes out thought.

"Bitten by the jungle," *The Women's Review of Books,* Vol.
XII, Nos. 10–11 *July 1995*

2 Floating downstream silently in the dark, the air a perfect temperature, or no-temperature—could this be what it feels like in the womb?

Ibid.

3 Fay raises a plastic cup of *siepte raices,* powerful sugar-cane rum with seven roots that offer endless aphrodisiac and cura-

tive properties. It promises long life; it tastes like woody, acrid Mogen David. She surveys the tangled jungle and in her lady-like, 75-year-old voice offers a toast: "To chaos."

Ibid.

3289. Mary O'Malley (1941–2006)

1 MOTHER PETER. Of course nobody ever passed any exam of their own accord. Only prayer will get results. The best thing each one of you can do is to pick out a particular saint and pray to him or her to get you through. Your Confirmation Saint perhaps, or any saint you fancy. But not St. Peter the Apostle, if you wouldn't mind. He's my saint, so he is, and don't any of you go annoying him now.

Act I, Sc. 1, *Once a Catholic 1977*

3290. Pamela Painter (1941–)

1 For his father it had all been said, as if words had been stripped away like coal from the hollows and hills that had once been farms. And he too had nothing to say as he kept his father's silence.

"Winter Evenings: Spring Night," *Getting to Know the
Weather 1985*

2 "I'm going to be a wild woman," she told me. "I'm going to do wild things. . . . You won't recognize me," she said. "I'm tired of doing other people's tax returns. Adding numbers rich people have an uncanny way of multiplying. Sending my ex-husband whining notes with Astrid's college bills attached. She graduates in one more year. Then it's my turn."

"going wild," *The Long and Short of It 1998*

3291. Elaine Bernstein Partnow (1941–)

1 We are remarkable creatures, able to mold and shape ourselves just as we do the world we live in. Just as having opposable thumbs differentiates us primates from all other species, enabling us to grasp and wield tools and other objects in our hands, having "opposable minds," if you will, enables Homo sapiens, unlike our primate cousins, to develop logic, self-argument, inner opposition, so that we can grasp any situation and mold it into an agreeable and useful shape with our minds.

Pt. II, Ch. 15, *Breaking the Age Barrier 1981*

2 The serpent's name was Hollywood.

Act I, *Hear Us Roar: A Woman's Connection 1988*

3 I have seen how heart cells from different organisms, when placed together in the same petri dish, begin to pulsate in unison.

There is a connection between all living things, and more so between all like things.

Ibid.

4 It's all an experiment, isn't it? Aren't we just one great big petri dish in the cosmos?

Ibid.

5 Theater is a democratic art form—it speaks to the myriad complexities of mood, intellect, station, age, and social status that make up an audience. If it succeeds in moving that amorphous body, whether to laughter, tears, reflection, or anger, it is good theater. If it happens to speak particularly to the members of "the ruling class"—upper class, white, powerful—it may garner the reputation of great theater.

Preface, *The Female Dramatist,* with Lesley A. Hyatt* *1998*
*See 4700.1.

3292–3293. Jean Peelen (1941–)

1 Turning 50, for me, did not involve the fear of the loss of beauty. I did, however, fear losing youth.

"Comments About Age," *Invisible No More: The Secret Lives of Women over Fifty,* Renee Fisher* and Joyce Krame,** coauthors 2005

*See 3743. **See 3357.

2 Given that I wasn't going to get through life on a beauty pass, I didn't have to waste time playing with things like make up, fashion and hairstyles. I could play girls' basketball and run for class president.

Ibid.

3 The fear of failing this most basic of female "accomplishments," having and keeping a man, has led us to be insecure and inauthentic with our loves.

"Rational Women Repeating Irrational Patterns," Ibid.

4 The man I lived with said to me, much after the break up when it had become less painful to talk to each other, "I knew when you quite smoking that my days were numbered." He was right. Strength begets strength.

"Accepting Our Bodies," Ibid.

3294. Sally Quinn (1941–)

1 Washington is . . . a company town.

We're Going to Make You a Star 1975

2 There are a thousand reasons to have a party or to entertain, but as far as I'm concerned there is only one legitimate one. And that is to have a good time. If you don't care about having fun, then have a meeting.

Ch. 1, *The Party: A Guide to Adventurous Entertaining 1997*

3 No matter what anyone says about how Romney's* religion doesn't matter, being a Mormon is simply not acceptable to Bush's** base. Several right-wing evangelicals have told me they don't see Mormons as "true Christians."

"A GOP Plan to Oust Cheney," *The Washington Post 26 June 2007*

*Mitt R- (1947–), Am. businessman, politician; governor of Massachusetts (2003–07). **George W. B— (1946–), Am. politician; 43rd president of the United States (2001–09).

3295. Judith Rascoe (1941–)

1 "There are more important rights than the so-called right to know. That is not the right that is being violated nowadays. People have the right to know *something.* They have the right to know that something is being done. That is more important than the right to know. They have the right to know how long they will have to wait until something is done. That is more important than the right to know. I know you would rather know that I am doing something than know what I am doing."

"Evening's Down Under," *Yours and Mine 1973*

2 . . . the grandmother opens the envelope with the letter-opener that Helen's first husband gave her and finds a colored photograph of Helen's second husband and his new wife, Myrna, surrounded by Myrna's children from her first marriage: "Season's Greetings from the Hannibals!"

"Yours and Mine," Ibid.

3296. Maureen Reagan (1941–2001)

1 We're an ideal political family, as accessible as Disneyland.

Quoted in *The Guardian* (London) *24 December 1984*

3297. Helen Reddy (1941–)

1 At that point [the 2000 political coup in Florida] I could no longer trust the Supreme Court, and America had become a one-party state. I said, "I'm not going to live under totalitarianism, I'm out."

Quoted in "Reddy's miles away from her singing days" by Howard Cohen, *Miami Herald 15 April 2008*

2 Glamour to me is being spotlessly clean and courteous at all times.

Quoted in *The Los Angeles Times 23 April 1974*

3 If I have to, I can do anything
I am strong, I am invincible, I am Woman.

"I Am Woman" *1972*

4 The most exciting thing about women's liberation is that this century will be able to take advantage of talent and potential genius that have been wasted because of taboos.

Quoted in the *The Los Angeles Times 23 April 1974*

3298. Ann Rice (1941–)

1 People who cease to believe in God or goodness altogether still believe in the devil. I don't know why. No, I do indeed know why. Evil is always possible. And goodness is eternally difficult.

Interview with the Vampire 1976

2 "Evil is a point of view. God kills indiscriminately and so shall we. For no creatures under God are as we are, none so like him as ourselves."

Ibid.

3 Nothing in all the world is so nonsensical and contradictory, save mortals, that is, who live in the grip of the superstitions of the past.

The Vampire Lestat 1985

4 I moved slowly towards what was at last going to separate me from all around me . . . I had to see it beyond hamlet or town or camp, . . . I had to seek it where there was nothing but the burnt sand, and the searing wind, and the highest cliffs of the land. I had to seek it as if it was nowhere and as if it contained nothing—when in fact it was the palm of the hand that held me. . . . Well, now I knew just what it meant to be the man who knew he was God.

The Road to Cana 2008

5 I've entered history for the whole of it. And I won't be stopped.

Ibid.

3299. Barbara Paul Robinson (1941–)

1 It is irresponsible for public officials, especially those who are lawyers, to use our courts as a political football, when they must know that an independent judiciary is essential to our system of justice.

Editorial, *The New York Times n.d.*

3300. Lillian Robinson (1941–2006)

1 (Greer* suggests that much of the animosity against Thatcher** originated in societal contempt for aging women. I believe that if a stereotype was involved it was Thatcher's violation of the image of woman as nurturer. In fact, contemplating the former

Prime Minister, I think I really understand for the first time what the term Phallic Mother means.)

"Consciousness lowering," *The Women's Review of Books,*
Vol. X, No. 4, pp. 11–12 *January 1993*
*Germaine G- ; see 3145. **Margaret T- ; see 2537.

2 Nothing has prepared us for growing older, . . .

Ibid.

3 I am not terribly interested in whether feminism becomes a respectable part of academic criticism; I am very much concerned that feminist critics become a useful part of the women's movement.

Quoted in "Remembering Lillian Robinson" by Greg
Robinson, *The Minnesota Review,* no. 67 *Fall 2006*

3301. Buffy Sainte-Marie (1941–)

1 He's five feet two and he's six feet four.
He fights with missiles and with spears.
He's all of thirty-one and he's only seventeen.
He's been a soldier for a thousand years.

"The Universal Soldier" *1963*

2 We'll make a space in the lives that we planned
And here I'll stay until it's time for you to go.

"Until It's Time for You to Go" *1965*

3 And yet where in your history books is the tale
of the genocide basic to this country's birth?
of the preachers who lied?
how the Bill of Rights failed.

"My Country 'Tis of Thy People You're Dying" *1966*

4 You have to sniff out joy, keep your nose to the joy-trail.

Quoted by Susan Braudy in *Ms.* (New York) *March 1975*

5 The white man wants everyone who isn't white to think white.

Ibid.

3302. Susan Fromberg Schaeffer (1941–)

1 The sky is reduced,
A narrow blue ribbon banding the lake.
Someone is wrapping things up.

"Post Mortem," St. 1, *The Witch and the Weather Report*
1972

2 What can be wrong
That some days I hug this house
Around me like a shawl, and feel
Each window like a tatter in its skin,
Or worse, bright eyes I must not look through?

"Housewife," St. 1, Ibid.

3 In her drugged state, she felt only a euphoria, as if all the pain of her life had become a vast salty water, buoying up, where she floated on the great blue waves of a vast, melodramatic sea.

Ch. 1, *Falling 1973*

4 "Time is only a force; it is neither good nor evil, only necessary."

Ch. 6, Ibid.

5 "There are many ways people stop living. Some people live so long life forgets all about them, and so they stop living. But most people stop because they made a mistake."

Ch. 1, *Poison 2006*

3303. Vicki Sears (1941–)

1 Now
at 57 years
she sits crying for a
barren womb stolen by Nagasaki.
tears bumping down her rippled skin
bound in pain thirty years past its time
unable to answer why.

"Nagasaki Elder," St. 4, *Backbone,* Vol. I, No. 1 *Fall 1984*

2 Almost every recent day my mind tongue tasted the bitter heat of scotch. I salivated. It seemed real again. That getting drunk would make everything better. All the world issues and ordinary life problems would fade into oblivion. Nothing would hurt. I would have control of my environment again. Fool's talk on a fool's walk. Splurges of dirges, I mused.

"Sticktalk" (1984), *Hear the Silence,* Irene Zahava, ed. *1986*

3 My father had repeatedly proven, when I was a child, that all things have their own spirits and lessons to share. I am just as the sticks and rocks. I may not always know my purpose, but it will be clear to me when I need to know. I will behave just as I am supposed to at that moment.

Ibid.

4 "You can't possess anything but yourself. Let me loose."

Ibid.

3304. Donna Shalala (1941–)

1 Her [Joycelyn Elders's*] style is straightforward and very American. We like plain-spoken, outspoken people in this country, particularly on health issues.

Quoted in "Blunt Style of Teen Sex and Health" by Philip J.
Hilts, *The New York Times 14 September 1993*
*See 2843.

3305. Elaine Showalter (1941–)

1 In a society that not only perceived women as childlike, irrational, and sexually unstable but also rendered them legally powerless and economically marginal, it is not surprising that they should have formed the greater part of the residual categories of deviance from which doctors drew a lucrative practice and asylums much of their population.

The Female Malady: Women, Madness, and English Culture,
1830–1980 1985

2 Hysteria is part of everyday life. It not only survives in the 1990s, but it is more contagious than in the past. Newspapers, magazines, talk shows, self-help books, and of course the Internet ensure that ideas, once planted, manifest themselves internationally as symptoms.

Hystories: Hysterical Epidemics and Modern Media 1997

3 From Mary Wollstonecraft* to Naomi Wolf,** feminism has often taken a hard line on fashion, shopping, and the whole beauty Monty. . . . But for those of us sisters hiding *Welcome to Your Facelift* inside *The Second Sex,****** a passion for fashion can sometimes feel a shameful secret life. . . . I think it's time I came out of the closet.

Article, *Vogue 1997*
*See 701. **See 4635. ***By Simone de Beauvoir; see 2080:4–11.

3306. Madeleine St. John (1941–2006)

1 What was he saying? Nicola was paralysed by dread—a dread which in weaker doses had become almost familiar to her during the past few months: now, with this preposterous invitation, *Come in here* (for where else might she have gone?), this ominous announcement, *I want to talk to you,* she saw that something wholly dreadful had at last begun.

Ch. 1, *The Essence of Things 1997*

2 *Wrong* is one of those words which sound like what they signify, not by virtue of onomatopoeia, but by virtue of a more subtle correspondence: the same being true, to a lesser degree only, of *right.*

Ibid.

3 He was suddenly on much firmer ground: he was down to brass tacks, now. Brass tacks were his stock-in-trade, he being after all a lawyer.

Ch. 2, Ibid.

4 *On being nominated for the Booker Prize:* There are squillions of books out there. Who knows what the best six are? It's not about me being brilliant. It's about me being lucky. . . . We won't know for a hundred years the truth about whether it's any good. It's one of the things about literature; you just can't tell until you're dead.

Quoted in "Writer exposed British mores" by Tony Stephens, *The Sydney Morning Herald 29 June 2006*

3307. Martha Stewart (1941–)

1 What follows is the story of the restoration, the renovation, the decoration, and the initial landscaping of the new old house. Each project like this is really a work in progress, an ever-changing environment that is altered by time, by weather, by whim, and by necessity. One learns, one experiments, one is frustrated, and one enjoys the extraordinary variety of problems and solutions posed by such a commitment. The thrill of near completion keeps one going.

Introduction, *Martha Stewart's New Old House 1992*

2 [Home is] a sense of security, a sense of being able to relax within the confines of your own world. Have your own world. That's what I'm about. Having some place to think, to do, to make, to enjoy.

Interview, *Charlie Rose* (TV interview show) *15 September 1995*

3 We're all trying to do the same thing. Live well.

Ibid.

3308. Barbara Trapido (1941–)

1 Claire Crouchley's older sister was currently attending a finishing school where she was learning how to emerge gracefully from a Rolls-Royce in a hat.

p. 4, *Temples of Delight 1990*

2 "They're all stupid, that's why," Alice said. It didn't occur to her how dramatically, with the utterance, she was separating herself from the coziness of that dominant consenting world to which she had always, more or less, belonged.

p. 65, Ibid.

3309. Anne Tyler (1941–)

1 Sad people are the only real ones. They can tell you the truth about things; they have always known that there is no one you can depend upon forever and no change in your life, however great, that can keep you from being in the end what you were in the beginning: lost and lonely, sitting on an oilcloth watching the rest of the world do the butterfly stroke.

(p. 85), *Celestial Navigation 1974*

2 . . . she thought of the hall lamp she used to leave on so they wouldn't be scared in the dark. Then later she'd left just the bathroom light on, further down the hall of whatever house they'd been living in; and later still just the downstairs lights if one of them was out for the evening. Their growing up amounted, therefore, to a gradual dimming of the light at her bedroom door, as if they took some radiance with them as they moved away from her.

Ch. 1, *Dinner at the Homesick Restaurant 1982*

3 "You almost died," a nurse told her. But that was nonsense. Of course she wouldn't have died; she had children. When you have children, you're obliged to live.

Ibid.

4 He was back to his boyhood, it seemed, fearing that his mother could read his mind as unhesitatingly as she read the inner temperature of a roasting hen by giving its thigh a single, contemptuous pinch.

Ch. 10, Ibid.

5 I've always thought a hotel ought to offer optional small animals. . . . I mean a cat to sleep on your bed at night, or a dog of some kind to act pleased when you come in. You ever notice how a hotel room feels so lifeless?

The Accidental Tourist 1985

6 "It used to be 'Love Me Forever' and now it's 'Help Me Make It Through the Night.'"

Breathing Lessons 1988

7 I think we're each allowed one single life to live on this planet. We never get another chance in all eternity . . . And if you let that go to waste—now, that is sinning.

(p. 210), *Saint Maybe 1991*

8 . . . how life was not a straight line—either downward or upward, either one—but something more irregular, a zigzag or a corkscrew or sometimes a scribble. "And sometimes . . . you get to what you thought was the end and you find it's a whole new beginning."

(p. 219), *Ladder of Years 1995*

9 Just because we were related didn't mean we were any good at understanding each other.

A Patchwork Planet 1998

10 "You can start to believe that your life is defined by your foreignness. You think everything would be different if only you belonged. 'If only I were back home,' you say, and you forget that you wouldn't belong there either, after all these years."

Digging to America 2006

11 "Sometimes it seems to me that most of the adapting in this country is done by Americans."

Ibid.

3310. Vivienne Westwood (1941–)

1 Every time I hear that word, I cringe. Fun! I think it's disgusting; it's just running around. It's not my idea of pleasure.

Independent on Sunday (London) *18 February 1990*

2   It is not possible for a man to be elegant without a touch of femininity.

Independent (London) *12 July 1990*

3311. Margaret Wheatley (1941–   )

1   In a self-organizing world, one of the things that works on our behalf is not only that we have a natural tendency toward change, that we can constantly reorganize, or that we can structure ourselves without leaders (as long as we're well connected and informed and focused) but that, underneath it all, what we're doing is discovering our connections.

"The Unplanned" (pp. 17–23), *Noetic Sciences Review* Spring 1996

2   You can't change people, but people change all the time.

Ibid.

3   The image of the world as a machine that came into our consciousness in the seventeenth century was a wonderful metaphor that then went out of control. Ultimately, we came to believe not only that the world is a machine but that people can best be understood as machines.

Ibid.

4   Life is self-organizing. It seeks to create patterns, structures, organization, without pre-planned directive leadership.

Ibid.

5   Leadership is a series of behaviors rather than a role for heroes.

Ibid.

6   It is Gaia who reaches into the void that is Chaos and pulls forth life. It is Gaia who works with the creative impulse that is Eros and creates the world. She is the created universe, the mother of all life, the great partner of chaos and creativity. In modern science, she is planet Earth, a living being who creates for herself the conditions that nourish and sustain life. And in this millennial era, Gaia is us. She is the feminine energy that compels us to care about the future of Earth. She is the feminine sensibility that inspires us to dream of harmony among all beings. She is the feminine voice that yearns to speak through us of the law of love.

"Reclaiming Gaia, Reclaiming Life," *The Fabric of the Future: Women Visionaries of Today Illuminate the Path to Tomorrow,* M. J. Ryan, ed. 1998

3312. E. Faye Williams (1941–   )

1   We believe in the right to free speech, but we also believe in decent speech. . . . women, especially we black women and our children, have been bombarded with misogyny, violence and obscenity through public airways day after day.

Quoted in "From Imus* to Industry—What Price Dignity?" by Faye M. Anderson, The Women's Media Center (womensmediacenter.com) *9 October 2007*
*Don I- (1940–   ), American radio host, humorist.

2   America's media companies . . . need to display more responsibility, and refrain from disseminating degrading, misogynistic content in order to make a simple buck. Members are all too aware of the examples of media companies jumping at opportunities to produce movies, videos, music and other content that portray African Americans as debased caricatures. They hide behind the First Amendment, which is their right, but ignore the larger issue about assuming corporate responsibility to remove this poison from our airwaves.

Remarks, House Subcommittee on Telecommunications and the Internet *5 December 2007*

3313. Merle Woo (1941–   )

1   Abrasive teacher, incisive comedian,
Painted Lady, dark domestic—
Sweep minds' attics; burnish our senses;
keep house, make love, wreak vengeance.

"Yellow Woman Speaks," St. 5, *Breaking Silence: An Anthology of Contemporary Asian American Poets,* Joseph Bruchac, ed. 1982

2   We decided that gender expressions
Like racial expressions
Were like jelly beans—
One alone is pretty enough
But one among many
Multi-flavored, multi-colored
Jelly beans
Is
Ecstasy!

"Jelly Beans," *Yellow Woman Speaks: Poems of A Woman Warrior 2003*

3314. Anne Wortham (1941–   )

1   A civilized society is one whose members expect that each will address at all times, as far as possible, the rational in man; that even when I may want to bash you over the head, I will be checked by my awareness of you as a rational entity, and I will not resort to force as an expression of my disagreement with you or even my feeling that you have been unjust to me; that in my disagreements with you, I will rely on the power of persuasion.

Quoted in *A World of Ideas* by Bill Moyers 1989

2   Rationality has the capacity for betraying itself. Rational men have the capacity to be irrational and to institutionalize irrationality. We've seen that in Nazi Germany.

Ibid.

3   Respect means that you leave me alone, that you don't build up in your own mind scenarios for my salvation and that you respect me enough to trust me, even when I'm an idiot, even when I'm wrong.

Ibid.

4   Government is not a savior—the American federal government has not acted as a liberator. Civil rights for minorities was no great favor, for Christ's sake! This is what they should have done two hundred years ago.

Ibid.

3315. Susan Yankowitz (1941–   )

1   BILL. Is she going to be "all there"? I don't know. But during a solar eclipse, the sun is still there, isn't it? And when a star collapses in on itself, isn't that star still there?*

Sc. 3, *Night Sky 1991*
*Referring to a woman who suffers from aphasia, the loss of the ability to use words.

3316. Ama Ata Aidoo (1942–   )

1   People are worms, and even the God who created them is immensely bored with their antics.

No Sweetness Here & Other Stories 1970

2   "Our Auntie Araba is going to heaven."
If there is any heaven and God is not like man, my sister.

"Something to Talk About on the Way to the Funeral," Ibid.

3 ANOWA. I hear in other lands a woman is nothing. And they let her know this from the day of her birth. But here, O my spirit mother, they let a girl grow up as she pleases until she is married. And then she is like any woman anywhere: in order for her man to be a man, she must not think, she must not talk.

Anowa 1970

4 Eternal death has worked like a warrior rat, with a diabolical sense of duty, to gnaw at my bottom.

"The Message," *Fragment from a Lost Diary and Other Stories,* Naomi Katz and Nancy Milton, eds. 1973

5 It's a sad moment, really, when parents first become a bit frightened of their children.

Ibid.

3317. Isabel Allende (1942–)

1 "The Congress and the armed forces are above corruption. It would be better if we used the money to buy the mass media. That would give us a way to manipulate public opinion, which is the only thing that really counts."

Ch. 12, *The House of the Spirits,* Magda Bogin, tr. 1982

2 They were unable to bribe the members of Congress, and on the date stipulated by law the left calmly came to power. And on that date the right began to stockpile hatred.

Ibid.

3 The things we forget may as well never have happened, but she had many memories, both real and illusory, and that was like living twice.

Part One, Eliza, *Daughter of Fortune* 1999

4 What matters is what you do in this world, not how you come into it. . . .

Ibid.

5 "The only good thing about marriage is becoming a widow," she said.

The English, Ibid.

6 Doors opened to him because of his skill with cards and dice; he lost with such grace that very few realized how much he won.

Ibid.

7 "People with original ideas always end up being considered mad. . . ."

Part Two, The Farewell, Ibid.

8 He said that knowledge was of little use without wisdom, and that there was no wisdom without spirituality, and that true spirituality always included service to others.

The Fourth Son, Ibid.

9 "The wise man desires nothing; he does not judge, he makes no plans, he keeps his mind open and his heart at peace."

Ibid.

10 "Agriculture is the true gold of California."

Part Three, Joaquin, Ibid.

3318. Ghada al-Samman (1942–)

1 The liberated woman is not that modern doll who wears make-up and tasteless clothes. . . . The liberated woman is a person who believes that she is as human as a man. The liberated woman does not insist on her freedom so as to abuse it.

Remark (1961), Quoted in *Women in World History Curriculum* (womeninworldhistory.com) 1996–97

2 ink is sobriety's wine. . . .

"A Rebellious Owl," Noel Abdulahad, tr., *Dancing With the Owl* 2003

3 Every time you embrace me
I become a virgin again,
I feel it is my wedding night!

"A Revived Owl," in toto, Ibid

3318–3319. Alta (1942–)

1 [Of] course, if you think only terrible people go to prison, that solves that problem.

Untitled poem 1972

2 if you come in me
a child is likely to
come back out.
my name is alta.
i am a woman.

Untitled poem 1969–1973

3320. Joyce Antler (1942–)

1 Jewish women today constitute the most important resource for Jewish revival. Their complex and in many ways unique legacy deserves to be placed in the foreground of Jewish memory and identity so that it can help shape American Jewish life in the century to come.

p. 327, *The Journey Home, How Jewish Women Shaped Modern America* 1997

2 For more than half a century, the media have used Jewish mothers as convenient targets for a humor that, while sometimes affectionate, easily veers into misogyny and anti-Semitism.

"The Mother's Day Gift I Want," The Women's Media Center (womensmediacenter.com) 10 May 2007

3 Today's "helicopter" mother who hovers over her children and is on call 24/7—self-sacrificing, overprotective, deeply identified with her child's success and embedded in every aspect of her children's lives—resembles the fabled Jewish mother caricature more than ever before.

Quoted in "Mothering Heights" by Ellen K. Rothman, *Mass Humanities* (mfh.org) Fall 2007

4 From Biblical tales through the narratives of early modern Europe, the image of the Jewish mother in song and story has been that of a strong, determined, family-bound, and loyal matriarch, raising her children, helping to sustain the family economically, and keeping the domestic flame of Judaism alive.

Ch. 1, *You Never Call! You Never Write!: A History of the Jewish Mother* 2007

3321. Gloria Anzaldúa (1942–2004)

1 Indigenous like corn, like corn, the *mestiza* is a product of crossbreeding, designed for preservation under a variety of conditions. Like an ear of corn—a female seed-bearing organ—the *mestiza* is tenacious, tightly wrapped in the husks of her culture. Like kernels she clings to the cob; with thick

stalks and strong brace roots, she holds tight to the earth—she will survive the crossroads.
"La conciencia de la mestiza: Towards a New Consciousness," *Borderlands/La Frontera: The New Mestiza 1987*

2 The dominant white culture is killing us slowly with its ignorance.
Ibid.

3 "We can no longer camouflage our needs, can no longer let defenses and fences sprout around us. We can no longer withdraw. To rage and look upon you with contempt is to rage and be contemptuous of ourselves. We can no longer blame you, nor disown the white parts, the male parts, the pathological parts, the queer parts, the vulnerable parts. Here we are weaponless with open arms, with only our magic. Let's try it our way, the *mestiza* way, the Chicano way, the woman way."
Ibid.

4 my face shut like a door.
"Nightvoice," St. 5, *Chicana Lesbians: The Girls Our Mothers Warned Us About,* Carla Trujillo, ed. *1991*

3322. Sue Armstrong (1942–)
1 There is no doubt that the practice is a means of suppressing and controlling the sexual behaviour of women. Female circumcision is a physiological chastity belt.
New Scientist 2 February 1991

2 Many of the beautiful game reserves of Africa became and remain oases of plenty in deserts of rural poverty.
"The people who want their parks back," *New Scientist 6 July 1991*

3323. Rivka Weiss Bar-Yosef (1942?–)
1 The original humanistic ideals of the Jewish state, included the equality of women.
Quoted in "Women in the Firing Line" by Betty Friedan,* *The New York Times 28 October 1984*
*See 2398.

3324. Carol Bellamy (1942–)
1 In a global economy worth over $30 trillion, it is clear that the necessary resources and know-how to reach every child are well within our grasp.
Address (Stockholm) *2002*

2 For eight years the FLA [Fair Labor Association] has been strengthening its capacity to work with companies, factories, civil society organizations and others to end sweatshop labor and protect workers' rights. It is now moving beyond its rigorous monitoring program to focus greater attention on identifying the root causes of these problems and to develop sustainable compliance programs.
"FLA Elects Carol Bellamy Chair of Its Board of Directors", *The Earth Times 25 July 2007*

3325. Charlotte Bingham (1942–)
1 I was thinking in bed the other night I must have been out with nearly three hundred men, and I still haven't found a Superman. I don't know what a Superman is, but I know there must be one somewhere.
Ch. 1, *Coronet Among the Weeds 1963*

2 I think it must have been quite fun when women were rather mysterious and men didn't know all about them. Look at the end product of women being free. I mean, go on, look at it. It's a poor old career girl sitting in her digs, wondering whether she ought to ring up her boyfriend or not.
Ibid.

3 "And the only way to avoid playing the game is never to belong to the club, class, set, or trade union. As soon as you do, you're accepting someone else's rules, and as soon as you do that, you start looking down on the other chap with different rules."
Ch. 3, *Lucinda 1966*

4 "I'm glad you understand, Mr. Flint, I'm the last person in the world who would wish to ruin my life by inheriting a fortune. There are quite enough evils in it, without complicating the issues with money."
Ch. 8, Ibid.

3326. Mary Bricker-Jenkins (1942–)
1 Having been so long in ascendancy, patriarchal ideology has also determined the interpretation and recording of history. Therefore, we women must reclaim history, exposing the myths that distort our experiences and limit our vision of our capabilities.
"A Feminist World View," *Not For Women Only*, with Nancy R. Hooyman,* eds. *1986*
*See 3582.

2 The notion that the personal is political is a primary analytic tool in feminist practice—a precision instrument with which we examine the myths and structures of oppression that contain us. It also is another of the fundamental organizing principles of our practice: we change our world by changing our selves as we change our world. It is by this process that fundamental structural changes may occur.
Ibid.

3 We have a long and enduring history of struggle to implement such values as egalitarianism, consensus democracy, nonexploitation, cooperation, collectivism, diversity, and nonjudgmental spirituality even though these values are not ascendant in the American tradition. In the fabric of our society, these values can be reclaimed and rewoven into a transformed social order. That is the feminist agenda.
Ibid.

3327. Sila María Calderón (1942–)
1 The people from Puerto Rico already decided they want to be permanently linked to the United States. There's nothing else to be said about that matter.
Caribbean Business 3 December 1998

2 The people of Puerto Rico want an immediate halt to the naval exercises.* Sixty years of a menace to the health and security of our countrymen is unacceptable for any civilized and peaceful society.
Inaugural Address *2 January 2001*
*Re the 60 years of bombing on the island of Vieques.

3328. Sue-Ellen Case (1942–)
1 . . . the Church [by the late Middle Ages] had secured the notion that such immoral conduct was the province of women: that is, that prostitutes caused prostitution. Therefore the control

of prostitutes would control prostitution, or, more specifically, banning women from the stage would prevent the stage from becoming the site for immoral sexual conduct.

Feminism and Theatre 1988

3329. Amy Cohen (1942–)

1 Yet I cannot accept the politically dangerous doctrine that some sex-linked characteristic of females leads them to avoid rigorous thought.

"No safety in numbers?" *The Women's Review of Books,* Vol. XVI, No. 2 *November 1998*

2 A love for mathematics is a rare thing; it's a terrible thing to waste wherever it is found.

Ibid.

3 Doing mathematics requires a tolerance for frustration.

Ibid.

3330. Camilla T. Crespi (1942–)

1 "Women have never waited for authority, have we? We just go ahead and do whatever has to be done century after century. Even when we don't get recognition or a share of the authority, we still keep doing what needs to be done."

The Trouble With Thin Ice 1994

2 Depending on your mood, the fog was dreary, romantic or scary.

The Trouble With Hot Summer 1997

3 "Ozone layer's thinner than a Park Avenue wife."

Ibid.

4 Our lives are like anyone else's, I have to believe. A simple gathering of facts, of sad little coincidences, with no discernable pattern. Random twists of direction is all anyone can expect, twists that can turn into tragedy and overwhelm you, against which we have tried to defend ourselves by burying them in the basement of our souls, by building a wall of silence to lean on.

Prologue, *The Price of Silence 2008*

3331. Martha Craig Daughtrey (1942–)

1 In the early '70s, we had a real sense that women would humanize the legal profession . . . how law was practiced and how law firms were structured. Not only has the legal profession not gotten to be more humane and a better place, it has become worse and harder to maintain a law practice and have a full and well-rounded life.

"Back to the Future," *Perspectives* Fall *1997*

3332. Margie Eugene-Richard (1942–)

1 Communicating without hostility—communicating with truth, coming face to face with community people, government, and industrial people. The changes needed to come from within the government, the people, and the industry. We had the Clean Air Act, the Clean Water Act, the Civil Rights Act, and the Good Neighbor Policy that had been written by the industry. My plea was that we had all this written on paper—there had to be some accountability for following what was already written.

Quoted in "Shell Game" by Michelle Nijhuis, grist.org *20 April 2004*

2 Every time we as black Americans stand up for what is right, they say it's for greed of money. It's a fight for longevity. If we don't put a face to it, we can't make change. Truth and justice for the betterment of life, the environment and government is the stairway to upward mobility.

Quoted on GoldmanPrize.org *2004*

3333. Gloria Feldt (1942–)

1 It's absolutely incumbent on us to put our agenda forward [Planned Parenthood] and let our adversaries justify why they don't support it. Let them run the risk of looking like unreasonable Neanderthals.

Quoted by Evan Smith, *Mother Jones March/April 1997*

2 So on the 35th anniversary of a decision that should have guaranteed women's human rights to make their own childbearing decisions without a bazillion legislators and a bunch of fundamentalist preachers weighing in, I and all women are rapidly becoming nameless and faceless Roes,* the pseudonymous name used to represent a whole class of people in intrusive and volatile cases. In this case, clearly second class.

"I Am Roe and I Have Questions for the Candidates," *The Huffington Post 21 January 2008*
Roe v. Wade was a United States Supreme Court case that resulted in a landmark decision regarding a woman's right to choose abortion.

3 I am Roe and I have these questions for presidential candidates:
1. Do you agree that reproductive rights are human rights? (If your answer is "no", do not pass go, do not collect my paltry campaign contribution, and no two-stepping explanation will bail you out.)

Ibid.

3334. Maureen Fiedler (1942–)

1 Why organize? First, because it ends isolation. Many women feel treated as second-class citizens—in church, in society. In organizing we lose the sense of being alone. Second, in organizing the whole is greater than the sum of its parts, and our energy is increased when we come together. And third, we are building base communities which struggle for change and give us a place to talk.

Speech, Annual Conference, National Assembly of Religious Women *1985*

3335. Barbara Garson (1942–)

1 JOHN. The Pox Americana, a sweet haze
Shelt'ring all the world in its deep shade.

Act I, Sc. 2, *MacBird 1966*

2 JOHN. Consensus is the thing.

Sc. 3, *Ibid.*

3 4TH VOICE. Let's get the facts. Let's go and watch TV.

Sc. 7, *Ibid.*

4 EGG OF HEAD. Security makes cowards of us all.

Act II, Sc. 1, *Ibid.*

5 EGG OF HEAD. I know you think I'm acting like a toad
But I still choose the middle of the road.

Ibid.

3336. Carol Glassman (1942?–   )

1   For its recipients, the Welfare system carried with it most of the hazards of "housewife and mother," and a few of the rewards. Domination by a husband was replaced with control over every aspect of a woman's life by the welfare agency. Strangers could knock at any hour to pass judgment on her performance as mother, housekeeper, and cook—as well as her fidelity to the welfare board. The welfare board, like a jealous husband, doesn't want to see any men around who might threaten its place as provider and authority.

"Women and the Welfare System," *Sisterhood Is Powerful,*
Robin Morgan,* ed. *1970*

*See 3284.

2   Throughout the welfare department one finds the combined view that poverty is due to individual *fault,* and that *something is wrong with women who don't have men.*

Ibid.

3   It is the woman who is ultimately held responsible for pregnancy. While not being allowed to have control over her body, she is nevertheless held responsible for its products.

Ibid.

3337. J. B. Goodenough (1942–   )

1   Wisteria ties the roof
of the porch down; morning-
Glory anchors the mailbox;
Green peas keep the garden
Fence from taking off.

"Among Vines," St. 1, *Dower Land 1984*

2   No, they said,
You cannot be a tree.
You are a human child.

"Changes," Ibid.

3338. Rayna Green (1942–   )

1   But "identity" is never simply a matter of genetic make-up or natural birthright. Perhaps once, long ago, it was both. But not now. For people out on the edge, out on the road, identity is a matter of will, a matter of choice, a face to be shaped in a ceremonial act.

Introduction, *That's What She Said,* Rayna Green, ed. *1984*

2   women's hands are never empty
women's mouths are never empty
women's arms are never empty

"Spider Woman," Ibid.

3   Indian silence
leaves no room to hide
except in dreams
visions of light and spirit
to wipe terror away

"Old Indian Trick," St. 6, Ibid.

4   There's nothing like funerals for good eating.

"High Cotton," Ibid.

3339. Linda Gregg (1942–   )

1   Fish! Fish! White Sun! Tell me we are one
and that it's the others who scare me,
not you.

"The Girl I Call Alma" 1, *Too Bright to See 2002*

2   Certainly one can make good poems without feeling much or discovering anything new. You can produce fine poems without believing anything, but it corrodes the spirit and eventually rots the seed-corn of the heart. Writing becomes manufacturing instead of giving birth.

"The Art of Finding," *American Poet 2006*

3   Believed in the miracle because of the half heard
and the other half seen.

"Now I Understand," *In the Middle Distance 2006*

3340. Marilyn Hacker (1942–   )

1   The child of wonder, deep in his
gut, knows how long forever is,
and, like a haunted anarchist,
hears a repeated order hissed
not to exist.

"Chanson de L'Enfant Prodigue," *Presentation Piece 1974*

2   I am in exile in my own land.

"Exiles," St. 1, Ibid.

3   Between us on our wide bed we cuddle an incubus
whom we have filled with voyages. We wake
more apart than before, with open hands.

"The Navigators, I" St. 1, Ibid.

4   A dozen times, she looked at the long scar
studded with staples, where I'd suckled her.

"Cancer Winter," *Winter Numbers 1994*

5   O blight that ate my breast like worms in fruit,
be banished by the daily pesticide
that I ingest.

Untitled, Ibid.

3341. Joan Halifax (1942–   )

1   I visited my grandmother in a plain and cavernous room in the nursing home, a room filled with beds of people who had all been unwittingly abandoned by their kin—and I can never forget hearing her beg my father to let her die, to help her die. She needed us to be present for her, and we withdrew in the face of her suffering.

Part I, Ch. 1, *Being with Dying: Cultivating Compassion and Fearlessness in the Presence of Death 2008*

2   Planting seeds of kindness, love, compassion, and joy helps us ride the waves of change without drowning. Equanimity, grounded in letting go, is the capacity to be in touch with suffering and at the same time not be swept away by it.

Part I, Ch. 5, Ibid.

3   Out of our expectations, beliefs, and fears, most of us fabricate a version of how things are. We defend ourselves against the fear of pain with our story; we like to use it as a buffer against impermanence, trying to protect ourselves from the fact that death comes for everyone, often without warning.

Part II, Introduction, Ibid.

3342. Judith Lewis Herman (1942–   )

1   This idea of the child's right to her own body is a radical one. In the traditional patriarchal family, there is no such concept. The child is the legal property of the father. Only in the last century have reforms of law and custom recognized the *mother's* custodial rights to her child. The concept that the child,

too, might have some individual rights or interests not represented by either parent is even more recent.

Father-Daughter Incest 1981

2 As long as fathers rule but do not nurture, as long as mothers nurture but do not rule, the conditions favoring the development of father-daughter incest will prevail.

Ibid.

3 The ordinary response to atrocities is to banish them from consciousness. Certain violations of the social compact are too terrible to utter aloud: this is the meaning of the word unspeakable.

Trauma and Recovery 1992

4 . . . to some degree, everyone is a prisoner of the past. . . .

Ibid.

5 In the absence of strong political movements for human rights, the active process of bearing witness inevitably gives way to the active process of forgetting.

Ibid.

3343. Susan J. Herman (1942–2009)

1 Fairness is an abstract concept with no foundation in reality.

Remark to Elaine Bernstein Partnow,* Interlocken (Antrim, N. H.) *16 February 1984*

*See 3291.

2 You can have the best service, the best service delivery plan, the sexiest product, the most efficient production system, the wisest financial plan. But without the best people, your organization simply can't function at its optimum.

Ch. 1, *Hiring Right 1994*

3 We brought you up to know that people are more important than things.

Startup.com (documentary film) *2001*

4 I am also particularly motivated by a realization that our human capacity for cruelty hasn't changed; but the technology we have at our disposal to execute this cruelty becomes more potent every day.

Keynote speech, "Leadership, the Holocaust, Genocide, and Education," 2009 Hildebrandt Award Presentation, Cohen Center for Holocaust Studies at Keene State College (N.H.) *20 April 2009*

5 I define leadership as having three parts: first is seeing what needs to be done to make things better or seeing a problem that needs fixing; second is having the vision, the skill, and the wherewithal to change the system; and third is the most important task of mobilizing the energy of others to organize and act in ways to achieve that vision.

Ibid.

6 Anwar Sadat,* one of the most inspiring leaders for me, showed us how a political leader can transform international relationships with a vision of a solution to a seemingly intractable problem. When his plane touched down on Israeli soil, half the world thrilled to his courage while the other half, fearing his leadership, mobilized to kill him for damaging the status quo.

Ibid.

*Muhammad Anwar Al Sadat, or Anwar El Sadat (1918–81), the third president of Egypt (1970–81; assassinated; with Israeli prime minister Menachem Begin, won the 1979 Nobel Peace Prize for formulating an Egyptian-Israeli peace treaty.

3344. Shere Hite (1942–)

1 I renounced my US citizenship in 1995. After a decade of sustained attacks on myself and my work, particularly my "reports" into female sexuality, I no longer felt free to carry out my research to the best of my ability in the country of my birth. The attacks included death threats delivered in my mail and left on my telephone answering machine.

"Why I became a German," *New Statesman 17 November 2003*

2 The tragedy for the US is that it has lost its leadership as a beacon of idealistic democracy. It is not only the west that has functioning democratic government. But the idea of full, participatory democracy for all—even though there has never been a black or a female US president . . . is what the west, and in particular the US, should strive to represent, not only in words but also in deeds.

Ibid.

3 *[The Hite Report*]* became so popular because it was the only book to say there is nothing wrong with women—that women can have orgasms very easily, but the kind of stimulation women need isn't being included in sex.

Quoted in "Decades later, Hite reports back" by Sharon Jayson, *USA Today 15 May 2006*

*The Hite Report on Female Sexuality (1976, 2004), a controversial work on intercourse and orgasm.

4 I think it was trying to say that women need to be half of the equation, and, if we're going to have equality in sex, it has to be re-thought because female orgasm happens in a different way than during the act. This implies many things for redefining intimate activity. I'm arguing for sex to be two bodies trying to communicate. We should be trying to get each other as aroused as possible rather than racing each other for orgasm.

Ibid.

3345. Janette Turner Hospital (1942–)

1 We inherit [literary] plots. . . . There are only two or three in the world, five or six at most. We ride them like treadmills.

Independent (London) *7 April 1990*

2 Anything, it transpires, absolutely anything, can be the mysterious machinery of desire, can be eroticized, fetishized, tantalized, sandwiched between peanut butter and raspberry jam.

The Last Magician 1992

3 " . . . the world is crammed with messages. We'll never have time to read them all."

Ibid.

4 I didn't know what I was looking for before I saw it. . . .

Ibid.

5 From time to time, I find myself inside the skin of other people. I see out of their eyes. This affliction swoops down like seasickness. It changes things irrevocably.

Ibid.

3346. Georgina Howell (1942–)

1 By the mid-nineteenth century, the concept of Empire was evolving from one of commercial exploitation to one capable of taking a pride in honest and benevolent government.

Ch. 1, p. 15, *Gertrude Bell,* Queen of the Desert, Shaper of Nations 2006*

*See 1347.

2 Every day, in her head, she heard the bombardment that was the prelude to an infantry assault, saw the . . . dead, the wounded, the missing, all of them, all the mud and the blood, to be reduced to names on lists on a desk in Boulogne.

Ch. 10, p. 233, Ibid.

3 Arabs spoke a common language but were not a common people.

Ch. 12, p. 277, Ibid.

4 The single incentive for joining forces with the British remained the Arab prize of self-determination, so far the vaguest of concepts. To the shia *mujtahids*, the religious representatives of the biggest proportion of the population, it meant a theocratic state under Sharia law; to the Sunnis and free-thinkers of Baghdad it meant an independent Arab state under an amir; to the tribes in the deserts and mountains it meant no government at all.

p. 280, Ibid.

5 She had long outgrown the complacent English milieu in which she now swam like a rainbow fish among tadpoles.

Ch. 8, Ibid.

3347. Charlayne Hunter-Gault (1942–   )

1 Even if you drove slowly, it would have been easy to drive right through Due West without realizing a town was there.

Ch. 1, *In My Place* 1993

2 While America made (or was forced to make) the right choices in that battle (Brown v. Board of Education*), the country went on to make a series of wrong choices in several newly liberated nations of Africa, backing despots . . . who abused their people, denying them the promise of freedom held out by independence.

Ch. 1, *New News Out of Africa: Uncovering Africa's Renaissance* 2002
*The Supreme Court's 1954 decision re segregation in schools.

3 A little over a decade into its new democracy, South Africa is in some ways where America was in 1968, when the country's inner cities erupted in flames sparked by rage.

Ibid.

4 Generally, the media cover death, disease, disaster, and despair. What I call the four D's of the African apocalypse. And there is so much going on on the continent these days, in terms of the movement towards Democracy, in terms of Africans attempting to take control of their own destinies, solve their own problems.

Interview, *Tavis Smiley* Show* (NPR) 22 June 2006
*(1964–   ), African-American author, journalist, political commentator, and talk show host.

5 Afro-pessimism has been the prism through which many journalists and many policymakers and others have viewed the continent.

Ibid.

3348. Frances Itani (1942–   )

1 "If you can say your name, you can tell the world who you are."

Deafening 2003

2 She is brimming with questions, but there is no one to ask.

Ibid.

3 "The world . . . is divided into things that move and things that don't move . . . It keeps me alive. Movement and shadow."

Ibid.

4 . . . people die holding their secrets, their loves, their pains.

Remembering the Bones 2007

3349. Erica Jong (1942–   )

1 Everyone has talent. What is rare is the courage to follow the talent to the dark place where it leads.

"The Artist as Housewife: The Housewife as Artist," *The First Ms. Reader*, Francine Klagsbrun, ed. 1972

2 Solitude is un-American.

Ch. 1, *Fear of Flying* 1973

3 Throughout all history, books were written with sperm, not menstrual blood.

Ch. 2, Ibid.

4 There is nothing fiercer than a failed artist. The energy remains, but, having no outlet, it implodes in a great black fart of rage which smokes up all the inner windows of the soul.

Ch. 9, Ibid.

5 Coupling doesn't always have to do with sex. . . . Two people holding each other up like flying buttresses. Two people depending on each other and babying each other and defending each other against the world outside. Sometimes it was worth all the disadvantages of marriage just to have that: one friend in an indifferent world.

Ch. 10, Ibid.

6 The idea of the future is our greatest entertainment, amusement, and time-killer. Take it away and there is only the past—and a windshield spattered with dead bugs.

Ch. 11, Ibid.

7 It was easy enough to kill yourself in a fit of despair. It was easy enough to play the martyr. It was harder to do nothing. To endure your life. To wait.

Ch. 17, Ibid.

8 Each month
the blood sheets down
like good red rain.

I am the gardener.
Nothing grows without me.

"Gardener," *Half-Lives* 1973

9 I can live without it all—
love with its blood pump,
sex with its messy hungers.
men with their peacock strutting,
their silly sexual baggage,
their wet tongues in my ear
and their words like little sugar suckers
with sour centers.

"Becoming a Nun," *About Women*, Stephen Berg and S. J. Marks, eds. 1973

10 He had been in analysis for seven years and he regarded life as a long disease, alleviated by little fifty-minute bloodlettings of words from the couch.

How to Save Your Own Life 1977

11 "How do I save my own life?" the poet asked.
"By being a fool," God said.

Ibid.

12 "The trick is not how much pain you feel—but how much joy you feel. Any idiot can feel pain. Life is full of excuses to feel pain, excuses not to live, excuses, excuses, excuses."

Ibid.

13 Books go out into the world, travel mysteriously from hand to hand, and somehow find their way to the people who need them at the *times* when they need them. . . . Cosmic forces guide such passings-along.

Ibid.

14 Advice is what we ask for when we already know the answer but wish we didn't. . . .

Epigraph, Ibid.

15 Every country gets the circus it deserves. Spain gets bullfights. Italy gets the Catholic Church. America gets Hollywood.

"Take the Red-Eye. . . ," Epigraph, Ibid.

16 There is a rhythm to the ending of a marriage just like the rhythm of a courtship—only backward. You try to start again but get into blaming over and over. Finally you are both worn out, exhausted, hopeless. Then lawyers are called in to pick clean the corpses. The death has occurred much earlier.

"There Is a Rhythm to the Ending. . . ," Ibid.

17 The only difference between men and women is that women are able to create new little human beings in their bodies while simultaneously writing books, driving tractors, working in offices, planting crops—in general, doing everything men do.

Quoted in "Are Men and Women Different?" by Judith Viorst*, *Redbook* (New York) *November 1978*
*See 2780.

3350–3351. Temma E. Kaplan (1942–)

1 By placing human need above other social and political requirements and human life above property, profit, and even individual rights, female consciousness creates the vision of a society that has not yet appeared.

"Female Consciousness and Collective Action: the case of Barcelona, 1910–1918," *Signs: A Journal of Women in Culture and Society,* Vol. 7 *Spring 1982*

2 Americans like to believe in the good intentions of their government, and they frequently consider the absence of politics to constitute an ideal state of being.

"Suburban Blight and Situation Comedy," *Crazy for Democracy: Women in Grassroots Movements 1996*

3352. Byron Katie (1942–)

1 If you want reality to be different than it is, you might as well try to teach a cat to bark.

Ch. 1, *Loving What Is: Four Questions That Can Change Your Life 2003*

2 The only time we suffer is when we believe a thought that argues with what is. When the mind is perfectly clear, what is is what we want.

Ibid.

3 (For me, the word *God* means "reality." Reality is God, because it rules. Anything that's out of my control, your control, and everyone else's control—I call that God's business.)

Ibid.

3353. Kitty Kelley (1942–)

1 A hero is someone we can admire without apology.

"An 80-Year Hitting Streak," *The New York Times 25 February 1995*

2 . . . moving an icon out of the moonlight and into the sunlight . . .

Quoted in "Kitty Kelley, colonoscopist to the stars" by Michael Crowley, *Slate.com 15 September 2004*

3 I try and live by what Abraham Lincoln* said. Never explain. It tires your friends, and your enemies won't believe you.

Quoted in "For the Queen of Exposé, Four Walls That Won't Talk" by Frank Bruni, *The New York Times 16 September 2004*
*(1809–65), 16th United States president (1861–65); assassinated.

4 Oprah Winfrey* has fascinated me for many years. As a woman, she has wielded an unprecedented amount of influence over the American culture and psyche. There has been no other person in the 20th century whose convictions and values have impacted the American public in such a significant way.

Quoted in "Fact or fiction? The incredible world of Kitty Kelley" by David Usborne, *The Independent* (London) *15 December 2006*
*See 4285.

3354. Elaine Haikyung Kim (1942–)

1 British and American scholarship traditionally placed Asians between blacks and whites on a racial continuum: if whites were born to lead, blacks were best at hard labor, and Asians were suited to carry out orders. This notion has been sedimented into our interpretations of economic development in Asia today. . . .

"Defining Asian American Realities through Literature," *Spring 1987*

3355. Carole King (1942–)

1 When my soul was in the lost-and-found
You came along to claim it.

"A Natural Woman" *1967*

2 You've got to get up every morning with a smile on your face
And show the world all the love in your heart
Then people gonna treat you better
You're gonna find, yes you will
That you're beautiful as you feel.

"Beautiful" *1971*

3 Doesn't anybody stay in one place anymore?

"So Far Away" *1971*

4 Winter, spring, summer or fall
All you have to do is call
And I'll be there,
You've got a friend.

"You've Got a Friend" *1971*

5   My life has been a tapestry of rich and royal hue.
    An everlasting vision of the everchanging view.
                                        "Tapestry" 1971

3356. Gloria DeVidas Kirchheimer (1942?–)

1   In our house, the direct statement was seldom used as a vehicle
    for communication. Innuendo was the order of the day.
                            Preface, *Goodbye, Evil Eye* 2000

2   She found it difficult to make decisions but attributed this to
    being ambidextrous.
                                "A Story of Blood," Ibid.

3   To Salvo, the shortest distance between New York and Cal-
    ifornia was the number of relatives one could count on for
    accommodations.
                                                    Ibid.

4   "Psychiatry shmuckiatry," my father says. "A racket. They
    make money so families can split up. Look at the divorce
    rate."
                                "A Case of Dementia," Ibid.

5   "Only what is written in French is poetry, and only what is
    sung in Italian is music. The rest is holy—the Hebrew—or
    harsh—the German."
                                                    Ibid.

3357. Joyce Kramer (1942–)

1   Aging has never been about diminishing physical appearance,
    or whether I look my age. Aging, for me, is not about num-
    bers. . . . Aging is growing wiser, putting my past behind me,
    and being fully alive. Aging means healing and maturing on the
    inside, accepting myself and who I am.
            "Comments on Age," *Invisible No More: The Secret Lives of
            Women over Fifty,* coauthors Renee Fisher* and Jean Peelen**
                                                    2005
    *See 3743. **See 3292.

2   If I hadn't liked my body when I was younger, how was I sup-
    posed to like it now that it was coming apart at the seams? In
    my secret thoughts, I felt my body was a cruel joke.
                                "Accepting Our Bodies", Ibid.

3   I embrace the notion that my generation is changing the face
    of aging. At any age, at any stage in our lives we can create
    powerful possibilities for ourselves and others. In my experi-
    ence, it wasn't until I was in my mid-fifties that I began to
    stop taking my life for granted and began creating the life I
    truly wanted.
                            "The Realities of Breast Cancer," Ibid.

4   This [breast cancer] was an opportunity to grow emotionally
    and spiritually in ways I never imagined. It was a hint of what
    was to come for me in my personal transformation: I knew for
    the first time in my life that I wanted to live.
                                                    Ibid.

3358. Lili Lakich (1942–)

1   Neon is the great American art form. America's monuments
    are the neon signs. Places like Times Square and Las Vegas are
    meccas for the American dream.
                    Quoted in "Lili Lakich," *Exposures, Women & Their Art* by
                            Ann Brown and Arlene Raven* 1989
    *See 3533.

2   Neon is associated with the highest aspirations and fantasies of
    the American dream as well as the lowest expression of com-
    mercialism and banality. There is no other art form that is as
    symbolic of the American spirit.
                                                    Ibid.

3359. Carolyn Chappell Lougee (1942–)

1   Historical studies are the terrain on which sociologists, anthro-
    pologists, and psychologists can test the universality of their
    categories and the possibly limited applicability of their expla-
    nations of social continuity and change.
                "Modern European History," *Signs: A Journal of Women in
                        Culture and Society,* vol. 2, no. 3 *Spring 1977*

2   Restoring women to the historical record not only reclaims for
    women their own past but also provides for modern men and
    women the understanding of a comprehensive past needed by
    the creators of a human future.
                                                    Ibid.

3360. Sarah J. McCarthy (1942–)

1   On close scrutiny, the beast within us looks suspiciously like a
    sheep.
                    "Why Johnny Can't Disobey," *The Humanist September/
                                            October 1979*

2   Despite our rich literature of freedom, a pervasive value
    instilled in our society is obedience to authority. Unquestion-
    ing obedience is perceived to be in the best interests of the
    schools, churches, families, and political institutions. Nation-
    alism, patriotism, and religious ardor are its psychological
    vehicles.
                                                    Ibid.

3   The concept of religious tolerance has been stretched to its
    outer limits, implying freedom from criticism and the non-
    payment of taxes. Neither patriotism nor religion should be
    justification for the suspension of reason.
                                                    Ibid.

4   Squelching spontaneous behaviors like teasing, joking and
    chasing members of the opposite sex is an outrageous thing to
    do to an entire nation of school children because a few have
    gone out of bounds.
                    "Punitive Damages: The Only Cure in Town?" *The Women's
                    Freedom Network Newsletter,* vol. 6, no. 4 *July/August 1999*

3361. Kate Michelman (1942–)

1   [*Roe vs. Wade*]* is solely responsible for saving women's lives,
    saving women's health, and saving women from shame and
    degradation. It is an important milestone in the quest for
    equality and liberation.
                    Quoted in interview in *USA Today 22 January 1989*
    *The U.S. Supreme Court case legalizing abortions (1973); see
    Sarah Weddington, 3075.

2   Nobody likes abortion. It's a difficult choice. Women don't
    have abortions they want. They have abortions they need.
                    Quoted in "Whose Life Is It?" by Richard Lacayo, *Time
                                            1 May 1989*

3   It's more important to change history than to make history.
                    Quoted by Alexandra Silver in *Time
                                            5 November 2007*

3362. Hedda Nussbaum (1942–)

1 I worshipped him.*

Comment, Manhattan courtroom, Quoted in "Hedda's Hellish Tale" by David Ellis, *Time* (New York) *12 December 1988*
*Response to lawyer's enquiry as to why she never left Joel Steinberg, abuser and murderer.

2 I pray that my story will be an inspiration to women to see the truth before it's too late and to use their inner strength to save their own lives and those of their children.

Prologue, *Surviving Intimate Terrorism 2005*

3363. Christiane Nüsslein-Volhard (1942–)

1 To find out whether I could be attracted to studying medicine, I did a one month course as a nurse in a hospital. This experience greatly supported my conviction not to become a doctor.

Les Prix Nobel 1995

2 We believe that the combination of several approaches and systems in one laboratory provides a powerful basis for further understanding of the development of complexity in the life of an animal.

Ibid.

3364. Sharon Olds (1942–)

1 I want to live . . . I say
Do what you are going to do, and I will tell about it
"I Go Back to May 1937," *The Gold Cell 1987*

2 There are creatures whose children float away
at birth, and those who throat-feed their young
for weeks and never see them again. My daughter
is free and she is in me—no, my love
of her is in me, moving in my heart,
changing chambers, like something poured
from hand to hand, to be weighed and then reweighed.
"High School Senior," *The Wellspring 1996*

3 You are drinking gin
night-blue juniper berry
dissolving in your body, I am drinking Fumé,
chewing its fragrant dirt and smoke, we are
taking on earth, we are part soil already
"The Promise," *Blood, Tin, Straw: Poems 1999*

3365. Nell Painter (1942–)

1 Poll taxes were head taxes of $1 to $2 per year whose payment was mandatory for voting, but for nothing else. Prospective voters had to pay poll taxes well in advance of elections, preserve their receipts, and pay any missed taxes cumulatively in order to vote. Because paying poll taxes was optional unless one wanted to vote, this burdensome fee proved an effective disfranchiser of the poor, who in the South were disproportionately black.

Ch. 9, *Standing at Armageddon: The United States 1877–1919 1987*

2 Whenever she spoke in public, she also sang. No one ever forgot the power and pathos of Sojourner Truth's* singing, just as her wit and originality of phrasing were also of lasting remembrance.

Ch. 1, *Sojourner Truth: A Life, a Symbol 1996*
*See 860.

3 It sounds as if people who are throwing populism around are throwing it around as a dirty word. And if it is a dirty word, they don't know what they're talking about.

Interview, *Bill Moyers Journal*, PBS-TV *29 February 2008*

4 What I'm saying is that we need the engagement of citizens, of voters, of ordinary people to push; to push back against the tremendous amount of money that goes into electing our representatives. It's not an accident that there's so much money in politics. And that politics tend to serves the needs of those who can pay.

Ibid.

5 Because families are so short of wealth. . . . families come under tremendous pressure. And you see it in the breakdown of families, the brittleness of family relations. You see it in children left home by themselves, because their parents are working two or three jobs at a time. You see it in people not being able to keep their families together, because of the stresses, the psychological stresses of hard times. And you see the culture taking the place of parents. And our culture, as you know is full of guns, and violence and sex. And so, we have lots of guns, and violence and sex moving in where parents might be if they weren't under so much stress.

Ibid.

3366. Rosalind Petchesky (1942–)

1 [The decades before *Roe** were] years of terror, of silently fearing pregnancy, of sneaking off to possible sterility or death, and of sex ridden with shame.

Abortion and Woman's Choice: The State, Sexuality, and Reproductive Freedom 1990
*Re to *Roe vs. Wade*, U.S. Supreme Court decision affirming abortion rights (1973); see Sarah Weddington, 3622.

2 What if women's voices tell us things we would rather not hear, or simply cannot hear—because they express values and priorities that are different from those we espouse?

Negotiating Reproductive Rights: Women's Perspectives Across Countries and Cultures, with Karen Judd, eds. *1998*

3367. Bonnie Phillips (1942–)

1 There aren't enough women environmentalists. Women can fight without making it personal. Work with the opposition when we can . . . and sue them when we have to.

"The Great Northwest" by John Skow, *Time 21 December 1998*

3368. Flora Purim (1942–)

1 Clear days, feel so good and free
So light as a feather can be. . . .
"Light as a Feather" *1973*

2 I try to reinvent myself as often as I can.

Quoted in "Flora Purim-Queen of Brazilian Jazz" by Beatrice Richardson, *Jazz Review* (jazzreview.com) *n.d.*

3 So I asked him [Dizzy Gillespie*] what was his religion and he told me he had been a Bahá'í for thirty years. I asked him what was the philosophy of Bahá'í religion and he said among other things, is the oneness of mankind, universal peace upheld by a world government, equality between men and women, mandatory education for all children of the world and a spiritual solution to the economic power. I was impressed.

Ibid.

*(1917–93) African-American jazz musician, composer.

3369. Bernice Johnson Reagon (1942–)

1   Life's challenges are not supposed to paralyze you, they're supposed to help you discover who you are. They're the prod that moves you forward.

> Quoted in "Sweet Honey: A Cappella Activists" by Audreen
> Buffalo, *Ms.* (New York) *March/April 1993*

2   When I work with young people, I tell them, don't hand me anything with a missing step. A missing step is a hole that will break your leg and can pull your whole project down. I have no tolerance for people who skip steps; they're dangerous to themselves, their work, and everything else. If you want to be someplace else you have to start walking. Do the steps—I get that from my mother.

> Ibid.

3   You can't even tell what you created until you give it away.

> Ibid.

3370. Anita Roddick (1942–)

1   I am still looking for the modern-day equivalent of those Quakers who ran successful businesses, made money because they offered honest products and treated their people decently, worked hard, spent honestly, saved honestly, gave honest value for money, put back more than they took out and told no lies. This business creed, sadly, seems long forgotten.

> Frontispiece, *Body and Soul 1991*

2   I hate the beauty business. It is a monster industry selling unattainable dreams. It lies. It cheats. It exploits women. Its major product lines are packaging and garbage. It is no wonder that Elizabeth Arden* once said that the cosmetics business was the "nastiest in the world."

> Ch. 1, Ibid.

*See 1503.

3   Conventional retailers trained for a sale; we trained for knowledge. They trained with an eye on the balance sheet; we trained with eye on the soul.

> Ch. 7, Ibid.

4   When you take the high moral road it is difficult for anyone to object without sounding like a complete fool.

> Ibid.

5   Too often development aid is a process by which you collect money from poor people in rich countries and give it to rich people in poor countries.

> Ch. 8, Ibid.

6   Losing the collected wisdom of the rainforest tribes would be like burning every library in the world without bothering to look what was on the shelves.

> Ch. 9, Ibid.

3371. Phyllis Rose (1942–)

1   There comes a time in your life when you dead end on the search for your identity as something unique. At that point, you start looking around for what connects you to other people, not what distinguishes you alone.

> *Writing of Women, Essays in a Renaissance 1985*

2   . . . whether you choose to destroy or to redeem what you perceive as Other, the problem begins with perceiving it as Other.

> "Helen Bannerman,"* Ibid.

*Author of *Little Black Sambo* (1899); see 1282.

3   In starkly political terms, biography is a tool by which the dominant society reinforces its values. It has ignored women; it ignores the poor and working class; it ignores the unprivileged; it ignores noncelebrities. Such a formulation is useful only up to a point, because in fact biography ignores almost everyone.

> "Fact and Fiction in Biography," Ibid.

4   Almost all the love affairs in Proust* are variations on Groucho Marx's** insight that any club that wants you is not a club you want to join.

> "Reading Proust," *The Year of Reading Proust: A Memoir in
> Real Time 1997*

*Marcel P— (1871–1922), French writer. **(1895–1977), U.S. comic actor.

3372. Marjorie Rosen (1942–)

1   Which is strongest—the reality out of which the illusion is created, the celluloid illusion itself, or the need for illusion? Do we hold the mirror up and dive in? And if we do, what are the consequences? And what are the responsibilities of the illusion makers?

> Pt. I, Ch. 2, *Popcorn Venus 1973*

2   It's unfortunate that Hollywood could not visualize a woman of mental acumen unless she was fixing up a mess her man/boss had made, covering a scoop to prove herself to a man, or deftly forging a life of dishonesty.

> Pt. III, Ch. 8, Ibid.

3   If proof were needed of the power of woman's film image on women in life, the number of platinum heads tells the story.

> Ch. 9, Ibid.

4   Studios, purporting to ease the anguish of Depression reality, transformed movies into the politics of fantasy, the great black-and-white opiate of the masses.

> Ibid.

5   On December 7, 1941, the Japanese bombed the hell out of Pearl Harbor. Johnny got his gun. America mobilized. And social roles shifted with a speed that would have sent Wonder Woman into paroxysms of power pride.

> Pt. IV, Ch. 12, Ibid.

6   Women's films [in the fifties] became "how-to's" on catching and keeping a man. Veneer. Appearance. Sex Appeal. Hollywood descended into mammary madness.

> Pt. V, Ch. 17, Ibid.

3373. Susan C. Ross (1942–)

1   . . . alimony is one way of compensating women for those financial disabilities aggravated, or caused, by marriage: unequal educational opportunities; unequal employment opportunities; and an unequal division of family responsibilities, with no compensation for the spouse who works in the home. . . . Thus, women should not be cowed into believing that to ask for alimony is to be unliberated, or that their husbands provide alimony out of the largess of their noble hearts.

> Ch. 7, *The Rights of Women 1973*

2   Law then is not a preordained set of doctrines, applied rigidly and unswervingly in every situation. Rather, law is molded from the arguments and decisions of thousands of persons. It is very much a human process, a game of trying to convince others . . . that your view of what the law requires is correct.

> Ch. 10, Ibid.

3 The concept of *enforcing* a right gives meaning to the concept of the right itself.

> Ibid.

4 For many persons, law appears to be black magic—an obscure domain that can be fathomed only by the professional initiated into its mysteries.

> Ibid.

3374. Gillian Rubenstein (1942–)

1 I had never imagined men and women could actually be torn into eight pieces, their strong, honey-colored limbs wrenched from sockets and thrown to the waiting dogs. Raised among the Hidden, with all their gentleness, I did not know men did such things to each other.

> Ch. 1, *Across the Nightingale Floor* (as Lian Hearn) 2002

2 How irretrievable the dead are, how completely they go from us! Even when their spirits return, they do not speak of their own deaths.

> Ch. 1, *Brilliance of the Moon* (as Lian Hearn) 2004

3 He who had killed so many times would never kill anyone again, not even to save his own life. He had made that vow, and he knew he was not going to break it.

> Ch. 1, *Heaven's Net Is Wide* (as Lian Hearn) 2007

3375. Ghada Samman (1942–)

1 The liberated woman is not that modern doll who wears make-up and tasteless clothes. . . . The liberated woman is a person who believes that she is as human as a man. The liberated woman does not insist on her freedom so as to abuse it.

> Remark (1961), Quoted in *Women in World History Curriculum* (home.earthlink.net/~womenwhist/) 1996–97

2 ink is sobriety's wine. . . .

> "A Rebellious Owl," Noel Abdulahad, tr., *Dancing With the Owl* 2003

3 Every time you embrace me
I become a virgin again,
I feel it is my wedding night!

> "A Revived Owl," in toto, Ibid.

3376. Sally E. Shaywitz (1942–)

1 . . . just as breast milk cannot be duplicated, neither can a mother.

> "Catch 22 for Mothers," *The New York Times Magazine* 4 March 1973

2 To be somebody, a woman does not have to be more like a man, but has to be more of a woman.

> Ibid.

3 As virulent as any virus that courses through tissues and organs, dyslexia can infiltrate every aspect of a person's life.

> Ch. 1, *Overcoming Dyslexia* 2003

3377. Judith Sheindlin (1942–)

1 You're no less dead if your killer is fifteen or fifty.

> *Don't Pee on My Leg and Tell Me It's Raining*, with Josh Getlin 1996

2 Where I come from, grandparents and family members are supposed to take care of neglected children. It's an obligation, not something you do for a government paycheck.

> Ibid.

3 I think you will agree with me that there are two kinds of people in the world: ulcer givers and ulcer getters.

> Ch. 1, Ibid.

4 I have no time, no room, for excuses and tales of victimization, usually by victimizers. They are all designed to minimize responsibility, individual and bureaucratic.
The price we pay for this buck-passing is staggering.

> Ibid.

5 This is the dirty little secret that women share and rarely talk about. You can be the president of a corporation, an astronaut, a neurosurgeon, a judge—it doesn't matter. All of us started from the same ground zero with the lesson:
If you want to get along in life, you'd better defer to men.

> Ch. 1, *Beauty Fades, Dumb is Forever: The Making of a Happy Woman* 1999

6 I think what we really need to impress upon our daughters is that for a teenage girl, sex is *stupid*. . . . Teenage girls have to recognize that what they will get out of sex is probably not pleasure. It's definitely not love. What they get, in most cases, is social acceptance, a Saturday night date, the chance to be a member of the popular crowd.
Maybe they'll also get a sexually transmitted disease. Or they'll get pregnant.

> Ch. 2, Ibid.

3378. Johanna Sigurdardottir (1942–)

1 My time will come.

> Concession speech 1994

2 I'm always talking with the Left-Greens.

> Quoted in *Iceland Review* 27 January 2008

3 Now we need a strong government that works with the people.

> Press conference, upon appointment as prime minister 28 January 2009

3379. Barbra Streisand (1942–)

1 Until there is a critical mass of women, whether it be as senators, chief executive officers or film directors, we're not going to be able to make a difference—to effect any real change.

> "Women fast becoming most powerful . . ." *Seattle Post-Intelligencer*, Op-Ed, A9 10 February 1994

2 Somebody once said to me—asked me if I was happy, and I said, "Are you kidding? I'd be miserable if I was happy!" And I'd like to thank all the members of the Academy for making me really miserable. Thank you!

> Acceptance speech, Academy Awards, Ch. 17, Quoted in *Streisand: Her Life* by James Spada 1995

3 That's why I love being in movies—I'm performing all over the world—while I'm home taking a bath.

> Ch. 20, Ibid.

4 I don't feel like a legend. I feel like a work in progress.

> Ch. 38, Ibid.

5 We've come a long way. Not too long ago we were referred to as dolls, tomatoes, chicks, babes, broads. We've graduated to being called tough cookies, foxes, bitches, and witches. I guess that's progress. Language gives us an insight into the way women are viewed in male-dominated society. A man is commanding—a woman is demanding. A man is forceful—a woman is pushy. A man is uncompromising—a woman is a ball breaker. A man is a perfectionist—a woman's a pain in the ass.

(Article, 1994), Ibid.

6 I'm also very proud to be a liberal. Why is that so terrible these days? The liberals were liberating. They fought slavery, fought for women to have the right to vote . . . fought to end segregation, fought to end apartheid. Thanks to liberals, we have Social Security, public education, consumer and environmental protection, Medicare, Medicaid, the minimum-wage law, unemployment compensation. Liberals put an end to child labor. They even gave us the five-day work week. What's to be ashamed of?

Speech, "The Artist as Citizen" (Harvard, Boston, 3 February 1995), pp. 511–512, Ibid.

3380. Barrie Thorne (1942–)

1 In working to create political change, feminists seek to create organizations based on power understood as energy and initiative, while challenging institutions that embody power understood as domination. Although fraught with contradictions, the feminist process uses methods of organization as a strategy for redefining political power itself.

Review of Building Feminist Theory: Essays for Quest," *Signs: A Journal of Women in Culture and Society*, Vol. 7 1982

3381. Robin Tyler (1942–)

1 I think the Democratic emblem should be changed from a donkey to a prophylactic. It's perfect. It supports inflation, keeps production down, helps a bunch of pricks and gives a false sense of security when one is being screwed.

Quoted in "The 1960's to the 1980's," *Women in Comedy* by Linda Martin & Kerry Segrave 1986

2 I would like to become president of a major TV network, and then I would ban all commercials that make women look like imbeciles—that would mean 24 hours of uninterrupted programming.

Ibid.

3 If I've offended any of you, you needed it.

Last remark, *Always a Bridesmaid, Never a Groom* (comedy album) 1988

4 The suicide rate of gay youth is still three times higher than that of straight youth. Our communities alcoholism and drug addiction rates are among the highest of any group. You can't grow up being called faggot and dyke and sissy and freak and being rejected by your family and being condemned by society and being told you are sick by science and sinful by religion and still be healthy. Pride is about self-esteem, and self-esteem comes from honesty.

"So, You Aren't Marrying a Jewish Girl?," *Huffington Post 10 June 2008*

5 If homosexuality is a disease, let's all call in queer to work. "Hello, can't work today. Still queer."

Stand-up routine *n.d.*

3382. Karen Uhlenbeck (1942–)

1 I didn't mind being a woman doing math [at the University of Texas], not supposed to be doing it, working on the fringes, succeeding in a small way . . . I was really sort of doing it for myself.

Quoted in *Women in Mathematics: The Addition of Difference* by Claudia Henrion* 1997

*See 4454.

3383. Virginia Valian (1942–)

1 In white, Western middle-class society, the gender schema for men includes being capable of independent, autonomous action . . . [and being] assertive, instrumental, and task-oriented. Men act. The gender schema for women is different; it includes being nurturant, expressive, communal, and concerned about others.

Why So Slow? The Advancement of Women 1998

2 We don't accept biology as destiny. We vaccinate, we inoculate, we medicate. . . . I propose we adopt the same attitude toward biological sex differences.

Ibid.

3 Egalitarian parents can bring up their children so that both boys and girls play with dolls and trucks. . . . From the standpoint of equality, nothing is more important.

Ibid.

4 The notion of a flat earth is a notable example of a natural concept, a concept most people's experiences seem to verify. People need very special data or specific instruction to discover that the flat-world hypothesis is false. . . . Gender schemas, I suggest, are similar to a belief that the earth is flat.

p. 118, Ibid.

3384. Sally Roesch Wagner (1942–)

1 Iroquois women fired the revolutionary vision of early feminists by providing a model of freedom at a time when EuroAmerican women experienced few rights. Women of the Six Nations Iroquois Confederacy possessed freedom far beyond those of their white sisters: decisive political power, control of their bodies, control of their own property, custody of the children they bore, the power to initiate divorce, satisfying work, and a society generally free of rape and domestic violence.

Veteran Feminists of America Newsletter 10 November 2008

2 I think white women are not the natural leaders of this movement. I think it's the women who have been living in a place of authority, despite the best efforts of this government and the churches, Native American and African American women, and not just ones who have been recognized by the white world.

Interview by Stephanie Hiller, *Awakened Woman* (awakenedwoman.com) *n.d.*

3 The women of all red nations have said that the stealing of spirituality now is comparable to the stealing of land in the past.

Ibid.

4 My heritage [as a white person], my legacy, is to do damage. I know I'm going to be culturally inappropriate. This is what white people do. We carry with us the arrogance of believing that ours is the norm. We don't understand the cultural garbage we carry, and it makes us dangerous.

Ibid.

5 I sleep well each night knowing that native elders are meeting regularly and talking about the survival of the planet. People who have been caretakers of the planet for a long long time are talking.

Ibid.

3385. Ruth Weisberg (1942–)

1 I feel nourished by teaching. I have a great sense of vocation about teaching. . . .

Quoted in "Ruth Weisberg," *Exposures, Women & Their Art* by Ann Brown and Arlene Raven* 1989
*See 3533.

2 Time turns out to be far more precious than any other thing. I have a heightened awareness that I might not have all the time in the world. I don't want to waste it.

Ibid.

3386. Susan Witkovsky (1942–)

1 All children are musicians; all children are artists.

Quoted in "A New Era in Day Care" by Mildred Hamilton, *San Francisco Chronicle* 19 December 1971

2 I am opposed to the custodial idea of day care. That is a mistake. Enrichment is what we are after.

Ibid.

3 The merits of good child care for all who need it or want it are many. The health and well-being of our society depends on it. Those unconvinced are people who have no need of high quality public programs, and who choose not to see the children and parents who suffer from lack of them.

"The Impediments to Public Day Care Programs in San Francisco" 1974

4 The provision of child care on even a moderate scale requires the use of institutional money, public money. I have no trouble with using public money. Child care and other services [are] exactly what it should be used for.

Address, University of California Conference on Child Care (Berkeley) *April 1975*

3387. Rachel Adler (1943–)

1 Ultimately, law is maintained or remade, not by orthodoxies or visions but by commitments of communities either to obey the law as it stands or to resist and reject it in order to live out some alternative legal vision.

Engendering Judaism: A New Ethics and Theology 1997

2 . . . a theology requires a method that can connect what we believe with what we do.

Ibid.

3388. Hikari Agata (1943–)

1 "For my wife I'd rather have a good-looking woman who just sits there than an ugly one who works hard."

"A Family Part," *Unmapped Territories, New Women's Fiction from Japan*, ed. and tr. 1991

2 "It's strange, but now that I have my own money, I don't feel like spending it on myself."

Ibid.

3389. Glynn Marsh Alam (1943–)

1 We get along with the help of instinct, a bit of knowledge, and a large dose of fear.

Prologue, *Deep Water Death* 2001

2 I have learned to live with this river, to keep perfectly still when a spider stretches its legs across my chest, probably like moving over a continent to him.

Ch. 1, *River Whispers* 2002

3 The waters of the South are like its people, with dangerous undercurrents and a deep beauty.

Prologue, *Bilge Water Bones* 2005

4 The idea that I held one end of a weapon and touched the snake with the other was too much connection with primitive forces.

Ch. 3, Ibid.

5 . . . no one gets suspicious when a ninety-year-old drops dead.

Ch. 1, *High Water Hellion* 2006

3390. Lourdes Arizpe (1943/6–)

1 . . . people are becoming poorer in knowledge and, what is even worse, *poorer in the confidence that they can continue to create knowledge.* . . . Rural women, those formidable sources of resilience, practical knowledge, emotional strength, and otherworldly wisdom, find their capacities and skills are undermined.

Essay, Quoted in *The Politics of Women's Education: Perspectives from Asia, Africa, and Latin America* by Jill Ker Conway and Susan C. Bourque 1993

2 Of far greater utility [than increasing money spent on education] would be a reassessment of the kind of society we hope to construct and the type of education likely to promote it.

Ibid.

3391. Eve Babitz (1943–)

1 There are three basic personality factors in cats: The kind who run up when you say hello and rub against you in cheap romance; the kind who run away certain that you mean to ravish them; and the kind who just look back and don't move a muscle. I love all three kinds.

Eve's Hollywood 1974

2 It takes a certain kind of innocence to like L.A., anyway.

"Daughters of the Wasteland," Ibid.

3 Packaging is all heaven is.

"Rosewood Casket," Ibid.

4 But by the time I'd grown up, I naturally supposed that I'd grown up.

"The Academy," Ibid.

5 . . . fun was all the truth we needed.

"Black Swans," *Black Swans* 1993

6 I was raised on Tabasco and gumbo by my mother at a time in America when onions and garlic were considered a shock.

Two by Two 1999

3392. Patricia Barker (1943–)

1 A woman's flesh learns slow by fire and pestle,
Like succulent meats, it must be sucked and eaten.

"From Deep Within," St. 3, *Movement in Black* 1983

2 The war.... Nobody benefits. Nobody's in control. Nobody knows how to stop.

The Ghost Road 1996

3 He might even have missed the war altogether, perhaps spent the rest of his life goaded by the irrational shame of having escaped.

Ibid.

3393. Susan V. Berresford (1943?–)

1 But I don't think as a society we've thought enough about what institutions we really need to raise children well and to have workers who can do the kind of work they are *best* able to do, and not be stressed completely. We have an aging population. We don't have good care options for everybody. The cost of all these things is enormous. So there are *huge* barriers for us to keep talking about and keep working on.

"Work Life Legacy Award Interview" (New York), *Families and Work Institute 1 April 2005*

2 I think change comes in a society in a lasting way when the different sectors of society—government, business, the nonprofit, independent sector—all are engaged in a variety of ways and come to some consensus over time. So we have to look for champions in all of these areas.

Ibid.

3 Leading means doing something that isn't happening naturally. And, if it's not happening naturally, it means you have to step out from the way things are. And, if you do something different, not everybody welcomes that. Not everybody admires it—some people think it's even dangerous, sometimes irresponsible. And so, you are often characterized in negative ways. So, you have to have a pleasure from doing something different and a *confidence* in yourself.

Ibid.

3394. Elinor Burkett (1943?–)

1 While the coddling made many students feel good about themselves, it provided them with none of the academic benefit promised by proponents of self-esteem training. In fact, feeling good about themselves led kids to achieve less, not more, researchers report. Why work hard and strive to improve if you are praised no matter what you do?

p. 92, *Another Planet: A Year in the Life of a Suburban High School 2001*

2 There's a moment in any voyage, just after I clear customs, when I pause in the netherworld between the timeless, placeless, plastic surreality of the airplane and my chimera about what's to come. On the one side is the familiar, the routine; on the other, the door to the unknown. It's a delicious interlude, fantasy ruling for one final instant. Then the doors swing open....

Introduction, *So Many Enemies, So Little Time: An American Woman in All the Wrong Places 2004*

3 It was a strange phenomenon, the majority petrified of the minority. But in that odd corner of Eastern Europe called the Pale of Settlement, Christians had been tormenting Jews ever since Catherine the Great set her mind on protecting the masses from "evil influences" by banishing Russia's Jews to the farthest and least economically significant reaches of her empire ... There, the Jews coped by insulating themselves in their own world.

Ch. 1, *Golda 2008*

4 Can you imagine what it's like to live with editorials in Arab newspapers saying that only Israel's disappearance can bring peace? What it's like to be a citizen of a small country without a single alliance when Soviet dignitaries regularly visit Cairo, Damascus, and Beirut?

Ch. 11, Ibid.

3395. Jocelyn Bell Burnell (1943–)

1 Because [physics and astronomy] are predominately male, inevitably, the standards, the norms are the male's. The system doesn't always stop to think, "Has this person had a career break, perchance, or are there other constraints?" ... Do we use a quantity of achievement as a measure of ability?

Quoted in "The Woman Who Discovered Pulsars" by Arthur M. K. Marsh Weatherall *26 October 1995*

2 Although we are now much more conscious about equal opportunities I think there are still a number of inbuilt structural disadvantages for women. I am very conscious that having worked part-time, having had a rather disrupted career, my research record is a good deal patchier than any man's of a comparable age ... The life experience of a woman is rather different from that of the male....

"Interview with Jocelyn Bell Burnell" by Robert Lambourne, *Education and the Profession*, Vol. 31, No. 3 *May 1996*

3396. Susan Cheever (1943–)

1 Death is terrifying because it is so ordinary. It happens all the time.

Home before Dark 1984

2 Addiction is always a broken promise, whether it's a promise made to oneself or to another person.

Desire: Where Sex Meets Addiction 2008

3 We are a nation of puritanical love junkies.

Ibid.

3397. Barbara T. Christian (1943–2000)

1 For she [Alice Walker]* reminded us that Art, and the thought and sense of beauty on which it is based, is the province not only of those with a room of their own, or of those in libraries, universities and literary Renaissances—that *creating* is necessary to those who work in kitchens and factories, nurture children and adorn homes, sweep streets or harvest crops, type in offices or manage them.

"The Highs and the Lows of Black Feminist Criticism" (1990), *The Woman That I Am, The Literature and Culture of Contemporary Women of Color*, D. Soyini Madison,** ed. *1994* *See 3547. **See 3912.

2 I sometimes wonder if we critics read stories and poems, or, if as our language indicates, our reading fare is primarily that of other critics and philosophers?

Ibid.

3 If movements have any effect, it is to give us a context within which to imagine questions we might not have asked before.

New Black Feminist Criticism, 1985–2000 2007

3398. Linda Ann Cinciotta (1943–)

1 There is the continuing problem of client generation. Money talks. Without the power, we cannot make the calls and the plays.

"Back to the Future," *Perspectives Fall 1997*

3399. Margaret D. Clark (1943–)

1 "Start a diary," she said. "Write your dreams. It'll help you understand yourself." I did. Writing it down made me feel worse.

Back on Track 1995

2 If my sister Babeth won the Miss Daydream quest for looking beautiful she'd come home with a gold cup, new clothes and money. If I got dux* of my year in math I'd get a piece of paper.

No Fat Chicks 1998

*Top of the class.

3 In caveman days you would have been having hordes of babies from the age of twelve. Nature says "You're a woman." But our society says, "You're still a kid. You have to live with your family until you leave school." This could mean you're twenty five before you leave home.

Secret Girls' Stuff 1999

3400. Charlotte Bonny Cohen (1943–)

1 For the Chinese Communists, ideology is always ahead of practice.

"Chung-kuo Fu Nu (Women of China)," *Sisterhood Is Powerful*, Robin Morgan,* ed. *1970*

*See 3284.

2 China is not our model. . . . But Mao and the Chinese Communists do show us that society is changed by changing people's daily lives. Working side by side with men partially liberates women. Freedom—however you want it—comes from new ways of living together.

Ibid.

3401. Cecilia Danieli (1943–)

1 It's the company that's important, not me as an individual.

Quoted in "Italy's First Lady of Steel" by Gordon M. Henry, *Time* (New York) *19 May 1986*

3402. Catherine Deneuve (1943–)

1 It is very fashionable for good-looking ladies to say how hard it is to be beautiful, but that's not true. There are times when it depresses and bothers me to see just how easy things are made for a beautiful woman.

Quoted in *People* (New York) *2 September 1974*

2 No, I don't enjoy. I suffer from enjoying. It's very Christian.

Interview with Geoff Andrew, *The Guardian* (London) *21 September 2005*

3403. Judith Durham (1943–)

1 We must teach our children
That man didn't weave life's web
For he's just one strand in it
So don't destroy the thread*

"We Must Teach Our Children," St. 1, colyricist, Ted Perry, *The Chief Seattle Suite* (album) *1983*

*Adapted from a speech of Chief Seattle.

2 And nowhere, nowhere could I find
That sweet peace, oh peace of mind
Till I found where I should start . . .
Right in my heart

"Let Me Find Love," *Let Me Find Love* (album) *1994*

3 Your name means everything to me
My special name for you
No mother could be lovelier
Than you

"No Mother Could Be Lovelier (Than You)," Ibid.

4 Music in our heart brings love to the world and music in the world brings love to our heart.

Motto, judithdurham.com *n.d.*

3404. Darlene Fairley (1943–)

1 Guys look at this [breast feeding]], and say it's indecent exposure. Women look at this, and say this is an issue for the workplace.

Cited in "Olympian Women" by Dionne Searcey, *Seattle Times*, A18 *31 January 1999*

3405. Mary Flanagan (1943–)

1 Everyone turns, expectant smiles on their faces, hankies at the ready. Then they see it, seven yards of deep-purple silk chiffon falling in five five tiers over Nora's slender body. The tiers are cut on the bias, so that the bottom tier hangs longer on the right side, ending in a graceful point while the left side exposes Nora's black silk-stockinged leg as far as her knee. The sleeves are trimmed at the wrist in black fur, the same fur as the hat that adorns her head, tilted at a rakish angle and covering the top of her face with a black-net veil. . . .

"The Wedding Dress," *The Blue Woman and Other Stories 1994*

3406. Carol Lee Flinders (1943–)

1 The precious beginnings of a different kind of world are not impossibly hard to imagine, and each of us needs to be imagining them—strenuously. But we don't have to start from scratch. Important as it is to recall all those wrong turns, it may be even more crucial to identify the women and men who know, or knew, what a right turn looks like.

"Feminism Reimagined: A Civil Rights Movement Grounded in Spirituality," *The Fabric of the Future: Women Visionaries of Today Illuminate the Path to Tomorrow*, M. J. Ryan, ed. *1998*

2 The selflessness, the austerity, and the communality of resistance work kindles a kind of flame.

Ibid.

3 Feminism has no better friend or more ardent champion than Gandhi.*

Ibid.

*Mohandas Gandhi, Indian nationalist leader and father of non-violent resistance (1869–1948); assassinated.

4 . . . one of the real sticking points for would-be feminists all along—one of the reasons the movement has not attracted the large numbers of women it should have, or held all it *has* attracted—is the oppositional paradigm that we've inherited from patriarchy itself—the winner-take-all model that assumes a champion and a challenger, one who is victorious, and one who is vanquished.

Ibid.

3407. Anna Ford (1943–)

1 Let's face it, there are no plain women on television.

Quoted in *Observer* (London) *23 September 1979*

2 The world men inhabit . . . is rather bleak. It is a world full of doubt and confusion, where vulnerability must be hidden, not shared; where competition, not co-operation, is the order of the day; where men sacrifice the possibility of knowing their own children and sharing in their upbringing, for the sake of a job they may have chosen by chance, which may not suit them and which in many cases dominates their lives to the exclusion of much else.

Men 1985

3408. Ellen Galinsky (1943?–)

1 Awaiting the birth of a child is strangely similar to the time before entering a new junior high, before moving, before getting married. Something is about to happen that will change everything. A new person, a mystery person, will enter the lives of those parents-to-be, and nothing again will be quite the same . . . .

1. "The Image-Making Stage," *The Six Stages of Parenthood 1981*

2 Prospective and new parents often fear that they will, by some ironic twist of fate, turn out exactly like their own parents. It seems as if parenthood is automatically accompanied by an unwanted personality implantation.

2. "The Nurturing Stage," Ibid.

3409. Tess Gallagher (1943–)

1 I stop writing the poem
to fold the clothes. No matter who lives
or who dies, I'm still a woman.
I'll always have plenty to do.
I bring the arms of his shirt
together. Nothing can stop
our tenderness. I'll get back
to the poem. I'll get back to being
a woman. But for now
there's a shirt, a giant shirt
in my hands, and somewhere a small girl

standing next to her mother
watching to see how it's done.
"I stop writing the poem ," *in toto, Instructions to the Double 1976*

2 Like a swarm
the heart moves with its separate
wings under the eaves.
"The Calm," St. 2, Ibid.

3 Take care when you speak to me.
I might listen. . . .
"When You Speak to Me," St. 1, Ibid.

4 Raymond Carver* used to say "use it all up." I like that. Each time you're working on something, throw your whole self into the balance of what you're doing.
"A Conversation with Tess Gallagher" by Katie Bolick, *Atlantic Monthly* (Boston) 10 July 1997
*Her late husband, American writer, poet, and screenwriter (1938–88).

5 Writing fiction is more like sitting in a clearing and waiting to see if the deer will come. All that gray waiting and watching and slow magic. Poetry to me is lightning of the moment. It's second nature.
Ibid.

3410. China Galland (1943?–)

1 Going into the wilderness involves the wilderness within us all. This may be the deepest value of such an experience, the recognition of our kinship with the natural world.
Women in the Wilderness 1980

2 We take on the attributes of one sex or another by virtue of only a chromosome or two. Wholeness is a composite or union of what we know as male and female: it is not a contemporary psychological insight, but a biological fact.
Ch. 1, *Longing for Darkness 1991*

3411. Gloria Gervitz (1943–)

1 Silence is a job that lasts all your life. It occurs in the most deep, in the most dark places like a mortal illness.
From the Book of Yiskor 1981

3412. Nikki Giovanni (1943–)

1 His headstone said
FREE AT LAST, FREE AT LAST
But death is a slave's freedom
We seek the freedom of free men
"The Funeral of Martin Luther King, Jr.,"* Ibid.
*American civil rights leader (1929–68); assassinated.

2 But we can't be Black
And not be crazy
"A Short Essay on Affirmation Explaining Why," St. 7, Ibid.

3 Mistakes are a fact of life
It is the response to error that counts
"Of Liberation," St. 16, Ibid.

4 And you will understand all too soon
That you, my children of battle, are your heroes
You must invent your own games and teach us old ones
how to play
"Poem for Black Boys," St. 8, Ibid.

5 In the name of peace
They waged the wars
ain't they got no shame
"The Great Pax Whitie," St. 3, Ibid.

6 You could say we've lost our innocence. That's a little worse than losing the nickel to put in Sunday school, though not quite as bad as losing the dime for ice cream afterward.
Introduction, *Spin a Soft Black Song 1971*

7 You can have Jesus but give me the world. I'll take it even though it's losing twenty-five percent of its energy every one hundred years or something ridiculous.
James Baldwin—Nikki Giovanni: A Dialogue 1973*
*American writer (1924–87).

3413. Louise Elisabeth Glück (1943–)

1 Birth, not death, is the hard loss.
I know. I also left a skin there.
"Cottonmouth Country" *1987*

2 If there is justice in some other world, those like myself, whom nature forces into lives of abstinence, should get the lion's share of all things. . . .
"Vespers," St. 3, *The Wild Iris 1992*

3 I thought my life was over and my heart was broken. Then my heart was broken
Vita Nova 1999

4 It is true there is not enough beauty in the world.
It is also true that I am not competent to restore it.
Neither is there candor, and here I may be of some use.
"October," *Averno* 2006

5 A night in summer. Sounds of a summer storm.
The great plates invisibly shifting and changing —
And in the dark room, the lovers sleeping in each other's arms.
We are, each of us, the one who wakens first,
who stirs first and sees, there in the first dawn,
the stranger.
"Prism," Ibid.

3414. Sylvia Alicia Gonzales (1943–)

1 *todo seré ... y hasta bastarda seré, antes de dejar de ser mujer.**
"Chicana Evolution," last stanza, Quoted by Marcela Christine Lucero-Trujillo in "The Dilemma of the Modern Chicana Artist and Critic," *The Woman That I Am, The Literature and Culture of Contemporary Women of Color*, D. Soyini Madison,** ed. 1994
*Trans.: I will be everything ... I will even be illegitimate before forsaking my womanhood. **See 3912.

2 ... the artist must be true to her own soul and her own personal experiences, and in so doing, the message will be universal and eternal.
"Ars Poetica," *De Colores* (Albuquerque) *n.d.*

3 There are many Mexican cultural values that we can relate to, but are they reliable in our search for an identity within the Anglo American cultural tradition?
Article, Ibid.

3415. Doris Kearns Goodwin (1943–)

1 ... one fundamental principle of politics is to always be on the side of your country in a war. It kills any party to oppose a war.
*Team of Rivals: The Political Genius of Abraham Lincoln** 2005
*Abraham Lincoln (1809–1865), 16th president of the United States (1861–65); assassinated.

2 ... in the pioneer world of rural Kentucky and Indiana, where physical labor was essential for survival and mental exertion was rarely considered a legitimate form of work, Lincoln's book hunger was regarded as odd and indolent.
Ibid.

3 Just as a hologram is created through the interference of light from separate sources, so the lives and impressions of those who companioned Lincoln give us a clearer and more dimensional picture of the president himself.
Ibid.

4 Lincoln, after winning the presidency, made the unprecedented decision to incorporate his eminent rivals into his political family, the cabinet was evidence of a profound self-confidence and a first indication of what would prove to others a most unexpected greatness.
Ibid.

5 His political genius was not simply his ability to gather the best men of the country around him, but to impress upon them his own purpose, perception and resolution at every juncture.
Ibid.

6 The most important thing for a president when a war is going on is to sustain the morale and support of the American people to fight as long as necessary, and to give them the aims of the war which they believe in, so they're willing to continue to sacrifice until those aims are met.
Interview with Rebecca Myers, *Time* (New York) *18 April 2006*

3416. Gayle Greene (1943–)

1 ...—I felt abandoned in ways I can't even begin to describe. Where was the medical profession? Where were the doctors my mother had known for decades? They were there, of course, issuing the orders that determined what medication and services she was entitled to, but from the day my mother became bedridden through the long terrible slide to the end, they were nowhere near the scene. They had vanished behind desks in posh offices, surrounded by receptionists, secretaries, nurses.
"Unhappy endings," *The Women's Review of Books*, vol. 15, No. 7 *April 1998*

2 ... death, like birth, is women's work ... And poorly paid work at that: it seemed salaries went down in proportion to nearness to the messy, awful work of tending the dying. It was a radicalizing experience, to say the least.
Ibid.

3 Nothing prepared me for the horror of the months I spent caring for my mother, watching her lose her functions, her faculties, her mind. I would console myself that at least this ordeal might soften the blow of death itself, but I was wrong. I emerged from it stunned, dazed, having to learn baby steps back to life.
Ibid.

3417. Susan Griffin (1943–)

1 In no state of mind can a man be accused of raping his wife. How can any man steal what already belongs to him?
Quoted in *Ramparts September 1971*

2 sleep leads to dreaming
waking to imagination and to
imagine what we
could be, o,
what we could be.
"To Gather Ourselves," *Dear Sky* 1973

3 The legal answer
to the problem of feeding children
is ten free lunches every month,
being equal, in the child's real life,
to eating lunch every other day.
Monday but not Tuesday.
I like to think of the President
eating lunch Monday, but not
Tuesday.
And when I think of the President
and the law, and the problem of
feeding children, I like to
think of Harriet Tubman*
and her revolver.
"I Like to Think of Harriet Tubman," St. 2, *Like the Iris of an Eye* 1976
*See 978.

4 We rise from the wave. We are gazelle and doe, elephant and whale, lilies and roses and peace, we are air, we are flame, we are oyster and pearl, we are girls. We are woman and nature.
Women and Nature: The Roaring Inside Her 1980

5 How old is the habit of denial? We keep secrets from ourselves that all along we know.
"Denial," *A Chorus of Stones 1992*

6 For perhaps we are like stones; our own history and the history of the world embedded in us, we hold a sorrow deep within and cannot weep until that history is sung.
Ibid.

3418. Tarja Kaarina Halonen (1943–)

1 Expertise is not just the business of universities; it must be an objective in all aspects of working life. . . . Lifelong learning is an objective we have all heard of, but it needs to be urgently put into practice because of the shift in our business world and working life and because of the ageing of our population.
Inauguration speech (Helsinki), *29 January 2006*

2 A more just world is a safer world, and also a better place for us to live in.
Ibid.

3 Environmental care in the future will require more comprehensive national and international cooperation. Climate change affects everyone, and we must continue to work towards getting all countries on board in this effort. We have not only a shared responsibility but an individual responsibility for the state of our environment. I would like to be able to contribute to this effort. We do not inherit the earth from our ancestors, we borrow it from our children.
Ibid.

4 The welfare of citizens and the international competitiveness of our country are not mutually exclusive; they are mutually complementary and mutually supportive.
Ibid.

3419. Maureen Harris (1943–)

1 The children are in line at the edge of the world where we've placed them.
"The Herdsman's Children," St. 3, *A Possible Landscape 1993*

2 Today I would like to be only the woman in the poem
"Reading(s)," St. 1, *Vintage 95: League of Canadian Poets National Poetry Contest* Linda Rogers, ed. *1996*

3 Year after year I looked at you looking away.
"Looking at Pictures of My Daughters," St. 1, Ibid.

4 The life I made up is so solid.
How can I be evaporating in the midst of it?
"Cleaning Cupboards," St. 1, Ibid.

3420. Barbro Hedström (1943–)

1 Art should awaken the senses and compassion in people. We *shall* interfere, we *shall* protest, the rebellion must be kept alive! We must not disintegrate to silent agreement to deeds that are damaging and destructive for the earth and humanity.
Interview by Annika E. Ortmark, *Kvinna Nu,* No. 2 *1989*

2 I am one who carves away rather than builds up.
Ibid.

3 If Picasso* could then I can.
Interview by Nicole de Bouczan, *Karlstads Tidningen* 6–12 *July 1989*
*Pablo Picasso, renowned Spanish painter (1881–1973).

4 I had a "real" job for seven months. My soul fell asleep.
Ibid.

3421. Xaviera Hollander (1943–)

1 *Mundus vult decipi decipiatur ergo.* The world wants to be cheated, so cheat.
Ch. 1, *The Happy Hooker,* with Robin Moore and Yvonne Dunleavy *1972*

2 There is only one other profession that outranks bankers as dedicated clients, and that is the stockbroker. . . . When the stocks go up, the cocks go up!
Ch. 11, Ibid.

3 . . . if my business could be made legal . . . I and women like me could make a big contribution to what Mayor Lindsay* calls "Fun City," and the city and state could derive the money in taxes and licensing fees that I pay off to crooked cops and political figures.
Ch. 14, Ibid.
*John V. Lindsay, American politician (1921–2000), mayor of New York City (1966–74).

3422. Lauren Hutton (1943–)

1 Men are doing what they were meant to do—patrolling the borders, protecting the house. Men have vision. They build bridges. We'd still be sitting at the edge of the river without them. But two thousand years of second-class citizenship is enough! Enough!
"Walk on the Wild Side" by Martha Sherrill, *Modern Maturity November/December 2003*

2 The great thing about dangerous situations is that you are so alive. I can remember every day of all my hunter-gatherer trips—every single day—better than I can remember what happened on any day last week.
Ibid.

3 [At 44]. I hadn't looked at fashion magazines for years because they hurt my feelings. I felt like I had disappeared, along with an entire generation. And we had.
Ibid.

4 I feel a sense of urgency about the planet—not just about sharks, but about all living things. I've been diving for 40 years in the most remote spots and I can tell you with certainty that the sea is emptying out. There's less of everything. We don't have much time left to turn things around. . . .
Ibid.

3423. Susan Isaacs (1943–)

1 So she would meet Yussel in the dank shadows behind the stairs where sometimes people threw their garbage, and she prayed the rats wouldn't climb up her skirt. They didn't; Yussel did. He lifted her skirt and pulled down her drawers and stuck it into her every single night. Of course, she became pregnant.
Book One, *Almost Paradise 1984*

2 He wore white shirts so starched they could carry on a life of their own.

Shining Through 1988

3 I'm an historian. I have inordinate warmth for anyone who invokes the past in public.

Ch. 1, *Long Time No See 2002*

3424. Ada Maria Isasi-Diaz (1943–   )

1 . . . women's theologies simply reclaim that, as women, we are made in the image of God.

Quoted in "A new forum for voices decrying violence against women" by Pamela K. Brubaker,* *Seattle Post-Intelligencer,* Focus Section *10 January 1999*

*See 3640.

2 I believe that ethnicity is a social construct and that the construction and maintenance of ethnicity is a vital process of Hispanic Women's struggle to survive.

Ch. 1, *En La Lucha/In the Struggle: Elaborating a Mujerista Theology* (10th ed.) *2004*

3 . . . it is not important whether the USA is a Christian nation or not. What is important is for the USA to uphold and promote the value of all life.

"Fullness of Life for All Should Be US Aim," WashingtonPost. com *18 December 2006*

3425. Elaine Jackson (1943–   )

1 WOMAN. You see, the color *black* has within itself many colors. It is a very complex color and at the same time simple and delicate. It can be made to appear formidable and mysterious in a dark, unlit cave, or can appear as bright and inviting as the twinkling eyes of a child.

Paper Dolls (1979), *Nine Plays by Black Women,* Margaret B. Wilkerson, ed. *1986*

2 GUERRA (singing). Wont you make my belly cut
   Into something delicate?

Birth Rites 1987

3426. Judith Jamison (1943–   )

1 If you study dances from the world you realize that the older the dance, the more natural the stance—before it became totally erect or turned out. The most extraordinary thing to realize is that the basis of your movement, historically, is coming from a very "primitive" tradition.

Ch. 2, *Dancing Spirit: An Autobiography 1993*

2 Alvin* taught me how to be generous with movement, that there is no step that is not useful to your growth, that there is no *feeling* that is not useful to your growth.

Ch. 8, Ibid.
*Alvin Quin Ailey, African-American choreographer (1931–89).

3 Nobody can be you. Uniqueness needs to be celebrated. There's only one of you. You're totally and absolutely individual. . . . Self-definition is very important. You define who you are by actions, by what you do with your life.

Ch. 20, Ibid.

4 Dancers have to go "over the edge" onstage. It's no place to be safe. What's the point? What are you waiting for? The stage is the perfect arena for you to let out all the stops.

Ibid.

3427. Paulette Jiles (1943–   )

1 The reins were telegraph lines through which he spoke to his horses in a silent code. . . .

Ch. 1, *Stormy Weather 2007*

2 A young man named Conrad Hilton* borrowed money to buy a hotel in Cisco and packed in cots so tightly you could step from one to another. He said the place was a cross between a flophouse and a gold mine.

Ibid.
*(1887–1979) American hotelier who founded the Hilton Hotel chain.

3 "Americans are not comfortable with tragedy. Because of its insolubility."

The Color of Lightning 2009

4 The justice of the peace said it was a shame to manumit the man, look at what a likely buck he was, a great big strong nigger, and Moses Johnson said, You are going to meet your Maker before long, sir. You will meet him with tobacco on your breath and smelling of the Indian devil weed, and what will you say to Him who is the Author of your being? You will say Yes I did my utmost to keep a human being in the bonds of slavery and robbed of his liberty, and moreover I spent my precious breath a-smoking of filthy black cigars.

Ch. 1, Ibid.

3428. Janis Joplin (1943–1970)

1 Believe in your brother, have faith in man,
   Help each other, honey, if you can
   Because it looks like everybody in this whole round world
   Is down on me.

"Down on Me," *Big Brother & the Holding Company* (album) *1968*

2 They ain't never gonna love you any better, babe
   And they're nee-eeever gonna love you ri-ight
   So you better dig it right now, right now.

"Kozmic Blues" *I Got Dem Ol' Kozmic Blues Again Mama!* (album) *1969*

3 You say that it's over, baby, no,
   You say that it's over now,
   But still you hang around me, come on
   Won't you move over.

"Move Over," St. 6, *Pearl* (album) *1971*

4 Oh Lord won't you buy me a night on the town?

"Oh Lord Won't You Buy Me a Mercedez-Benz," Ibid.

5 Don't compromise yourself. You are all you've got.

Quoted in *Reader's Digest April 1973*

3429. Rosabeth Moss Kanter (1943–   )

1 People seem to matter in direct proportion to an awareness of corporate crisis.

Pt. One, Ch. 1, *Change Masters 1985*

2 Innovations, whether in products, market strategies, technological processes, or work practices, are designed not by machines but by people.

Ibid.

3 Managers who can embed change capabilities in everyday operations and who empower their people to serve as agents of

change are less likely to be blindsided by surprises or to face resistance from the work force.

Pt. One, Ch. 1, *Rosabeth Moss Kanter on the Frontiers of Management 1997*

4 Managers have the fundamental, enduring job of mobilizing and motivating individual human talent in pursuit of collective ends.

Ibid.

3430. Sally Kempton (1943–)

1 Men define intelligence, men define usefulness, men tell us what is beautiful, men even tell us what is womanly.

"Cutting Loose," *Esquire* (New York) *July 1970*

2 Women are natural guerrillas. Scheming, we nestle into the enemy's bed, avoiding open warfare, watching the options, playing the odds.

Ibid.

3 It is hard to fight an enemy who has outposts in your head.

Ibid.

4 When men imagine a female uprising they imagine a world in which women rule men as men have ruled women: their guilt, which is the guilt of every ruling class, will allow them to see no middle ground.

Ibid.

5 Meditation is the secret of effective inner work. We might struggle conscientiously to change our limiting qualities; we might saturate ourselves with instructions and help, both concrete and subtle. Yet in the end, it is the direct, naked encounter with our own inner awareness that shifts our understanding of who we are, and gives us the power to stand firmly in the center of our being. No one else can do this for us. Meditation can.

Quoted in "Meditation for the Love of It," *The Heart of Meditation: Pathways to a Deeper Experience* by Swami Durgananda *2002*

3431. Marilyn Moats Kennedy (1943–)

1 [Secretaries] are professionals with needs and ambitions of their own. Treat the relationships you build with them as trading relationships between equals.

Office Politics: Seizing Power, Wielding Clout 1980

2 Politics is the process of getting along with the querulous, the garrulous and the congenitally unlovable.

"Playing Office Politics," *Newsweek 16 September 1985*

3432. Karen Kijewski (1943–)

1 "I can shoot." They looked at me. I can not only shoot, I can use correct grammar; I let that slide, though.

Alley Cat Blues 1995

3433. Jean Kilbourne (1943–)

1 If you're like most people, you think that advertising has no influence on you. This is what advertisers want you to believe.

Ch. 1, *Can't Buy My Love: How Advertising Changes the Way We Think and Feel 2000*

2 Children are especially vulnerable on the Internet, where advertising manipulates them, invades their privacy, and transforms them into customers without their knowledge.

Ibid.

3 Advertising performs much the same function in industrial society as myth performed in ancient and primitive societies. It is both a creator and perpetuator of the dominant attitudes, values, and ideology of the culture, the social norms and myths by which most people govern their behavior.

Ch. 2, Ibid.

4 The crimes committed when alcohol is involved are often especially heinous. . . . it is often gasoline on the fire of racism, sexism, and homophobia, as well as a convenient excuse for the perpetrators of such violence (in their own minds, as well as to the world).

Ch. 7, Ibid.

Also see Diane E. Levin, 3764:1–4.

3434. Billie Jean King (1943–)

1 I think self-awareness is probably the most important thing towards being a champion.

Quoted by Marlene Jensen in *The Sportswoman November/ December 1973*

2 I just want equal rights for boys and girls—finished. That's what feminism is to me. Not just legislate it—feel it. Do it. Accept it. Want it.

Quoted in Grapevine, *Ms.* (New York) *May/June 1996*

3 I'd like to see women's achievements become part of the landscape, instead of an unusual occurrence. Anytime women do better, it also helps men.

People, P-I News Service (Seattle) *16 May 1998*

4 No one changes the world who isn't obsessed.

Quoted in "Billie Jean King, Is There Life After Tennis" by Jane Gross, *San Francisco Chronicle 8 August 1978*

5 I think most people think I am like the mother of modern sports. . . . I happened to come along at a time when the world was ready for some change.

"100 Years of Great Women," *ABC News Special with Barbara Walters* 30 April 1999*

*See 2687.

3435. Frances Kissling (1943–)

1 Those opposed to abortion have marketed pro-life very successfully as a pro-children, pro-family, pro-nice, pro-flowers way of looking at the world. In the absence of any threat, it's easy.

Quoted in "Administration chips at abortion rights" by Ellen Goodman,* *Boston Globe 21 January 2003*

*See 3264.

2 The sad fact is that Clinton has felt compelled to run as a stereotypical male. In her own mind it is only a certain kind of man who is qualified to be president and she will be that man: tough on everything from war, flag burning, kids' access to video games, illegal immigrants and Palestinians. She has missed the opportunity to talk about what it really means for women to be equal in this country.

"Why I'm still not for Hillary Clinton,"* *Salon.com 10 January 2008*

*See 3731.

3 We'd like to see a woman president, but more than anything we want to be able to say at the end of the first woman's tenure in the highest political office that it really mattered.

That the first woman president did things no man would have done, that feminist values were at the core of her decisions—and that the country was on the road to further transformation.

Ibid.

3436. Jane D. Lazarre (1943–)

1 . . . there is only one image in this culture of the "good mother." At her worst this mother image is a tyrannical goddess of stupefying love and murderous masochism which none of us can or should hope to emulate. But even at her best, she is . . . quietly receptive and intelligent in only a moderate, concrete way; she is of even temperament, almost always in control of her emotions. She loves her children completely and unambivalently. Most of us are not like her.

Preface, *The Mother Knot 1976*

2 The only thing that seems eternal and natural in motherhood is ambivalence.

Ch. 16, *The Last Word: A Treasury of Women's Quotes,* Carolyn Warner, ed. *1992*

3 But what do white students and other white people mean when they talk about being silenced? Is it wrong to feel silenced if being silenced is taken to mean feeling humbled by all one does not yet understand, including the scope of one's own prejudice?

Beyond the Whiteness of Whiteness: Memoir of a White Mother of Black Sons 1996

4 What is this whiteness that threatens to separate me from my own child? Why haven't I seen it lurking, hunkering down, encircling me in some irresistible fog? I want to say the thing that will be most helpful to him, offer some carefully designed, unspontaneous permission for him to discover his own road, even if that means leaving me behind. On the other hand, I want to cry out, don't leave me, as he cried to me when I walked out of day-care centers, away from baby-sitters, out of his first classroom in public school.

Ibid.

5 But there is a sense one gains irrevocably after a life-threatening illness, that the mind, or spirit, and body are indeed one, or at least in intimate communion.

Wet Earth and Dreams: A Narrative of Grief and Recovery 1998

3437. Vera Litricin (1943–)

1 We know that if we are to say aloud who we are and what we want, there will be no historically accepted political patterns for our experience or our language. And yet here we are.

"Serbian nation," with Lepa Mladjenovic* (p. 185), *Ana's Land: Sisterhood in Eastern Europe* Tanya Renne,** ed. *1996* *See 4264. **See 4830.

3438. Susan Lydon (1943–2005)

1 Our society treats sex as a sport, with its record-breakers, its judges, its rules and its spectators.

"The Politics of Orgasm," *Ramparts December 1968*

2 I felt as though I had been and would continue to be falling down those stairs forever, like Alice down the rabbit hole. "Everything will be different now," I thought to myself. Somewhere in the far reaches of my mind loomed a clear understanding of how, in a single second, one tiny misstep could suddenly change a person's life.

Ch. 1, *The Knitting Sutra: Craft as a Spiritual Practice 1997*

3439. Rosalie Maggio (1943–)

1 Although an impressive amount of business and social interaction takes place over the telephone and fax, by e-mail, or in person today, the well-written letter remains a staple of business success and one of the strongest connecting links between human beings.

Introduction, *How to Say It 1991*

2 At the heart of good education are those gifted, hardworking, and memorable teachers whose inspiration kindles fires that never quite go out, whose remembered encouragement is sometimes the only hard ground we stand upon, and whose very selves are the stuff of the best lessons they ever teach us. Most of us, no matter how long ago it's been, can name our kindergarten teacher. Our first music teacher. Our junior high algebra teacher. Good teachers never die.

Introduction, *Quotations on Education 1997*

3 Language doesn't belong to grammarians, linguists, wordsmiths, writers, or editors. It belongs to the people who use it.

Introduction, *Talking About People 1997*

4 And yet if there's one thing consistent about language it is that it is constantly changing. The only languages that do not change are those whose speakers are dead.

Ibid.

5 . . . cutting edges are always a little rough. . . .

Ibid.

3440. Nancy Mairs (1943–)

1 Now, I don't object to selling books, but neither have I found the prospect of selling them a motivation for writing them.

"The Way In," *Remembering Bone House 1989*

2 God is no White Knight who charges into the world to pluck us like distressed damsels from the jaws of dragons, or diseases. God chooses to become present to and through us. It is up to us to rescue one another.

"God's Will," *Ordinary Time: Cycles in Marriage, Faith and Renewal 1993*

3 Gradually, however, I began to see that "the Christ" referred not so much to an entity as to an accretion of ideas, formed across centuries, largely by men, many of whom appeared to suffer from considerable sexual anxiety, and imposed systematically, often by intimidation, upon various populations (among them my own gender), not all of whom benefited from their espousal. This setup sounded to me more descriptive of the Romans than the Christians.

"Left at the Altar," *A Dynamic God: Living an Unconventional Catholic Faith 2007*

3441. Sandra McPherson (1943–)

1 On the third afternoon one bud tore off its green glove
And burst out brazen as Baby New Year.

"Poppies," St. 4, *Elegies for the Hot Season 1970*

2 Math soothed you; music
Made you bold; and science, completely
Understanding.

"Helen Todd: My Birthname," St. 2, *Patron Happiness 1979*

3 Dominion—death has it, beauty has it,
water has it, drought
has it.
"Path Through a Few Things that Must Be Said for Putah
Creek, at the Foot of Monticello Dam," St. 27, *Edge Effect*
1996

3442. Sue Miller (1943–)

1 It was her intense loving that frightened us, her desperate quick
embraces, her sudden anger, her "internal combustion engine"
my father called it—a set of mysterious, primal emotions which
ruled her. You could never tell in what direction she'd suddenly
veer.

Pt. One, Ch. 1, *Family Pictures 1998*

2 But that's the way it is in a family, isn't it? The stories get passed
around, polished, embellished. Liddie's version or Mack's version changes as it becomes my version. And when I tell them,
it's not just that the events are different but that they all mean
something different too. Something I want them to mean. Or
need them to.

Ibid.

3 They'd spent a good part of this strange day, the day of their
mother's burial, laughing. Laughing nervously, perhaps with
even a touch of hysteria, mostly because they didn't know what
they ought to feel or think. Laughter was the easiest course.
It was their way to ward off all the dark feelings waiting for
them.

Pt. One, Ch. 1, *The World Below 2002*

4 The croissant, the seedless raspberry jam, the rich dark coffee
with steamed milk. . . . *The consolation of the daily.*

The Senator's Wife 2008

5 "Do you remember when everyone thought Bush had a mistress
too? But she was rumored to be someone wealthy and WASPy,
of course. . . . The problem here is the goddamn Democrats,
who sleep *down,* you see. They love that white trash. . . . And
white trash loves publicity, so the Democrats are the ones who
get into all the trouble. As opposed to the Republicans. They
sleep *up* . . . Up, where all is Episcopalian and quiet as death
itself, and no one ever has to hear a thing about it."

Ibid.

3443. Joni Mitchell (1943–)

1 Moons and Junes and Ferris wheels
The dizzy dancing way you feel
As every fairy tale comes real
I've looked at love that way

"Both Sides, Now" *1969*

2 Woke up, it was a Chelsea morning,
and the first thing that I knew
There was milk and toast and honey
and a bowl of oranges, too
And the sun poured in like butterscotch
and stuck to all my senses

"Chelsea Morning" *1969*

3 Sweet bird you are
Brighter than a falling star
All these vain promises on beauty jars
Somewhere in your wings of time
You might be laughing. . . .

"Sweet Bird" *1975*

4 We are stardust, we are golden.

"Woodstock" *1975*

5 If you avoid doing what's cool, you won't have bell-bottom
pants on your songs down the road.
Quoted in "Joni Mitchell shelves talk of retirement . . ." by
Carrie Bell, *Seattle Post-Intelligencer,* D1 *8 October 1998*

6 The introspective artist is like a canary in a coal mine in that
they are the first to feel things. If they are worth a salt, they
should turn a jaundiced eye toward society and look for a vac-
cine. That's the difference between artists and stars. Stars are
only concerned with twinkling.

Ibid.

3444. Maureen Ann Orth (1943–)

1 It is one of the grotesqueries of the tabloid culture we live in that
no matter what heinous crimes an individual commits, a temptation of the individual's family is to make money off the tragedy.
Ch. 1, *Vulgar Favors: Andrew Cunanan, Gianni Versace, and*
the Largest Failed Manhunt in U.S. History 1999

2 South Beach [Florida] is a riot of loose luxury and easy sleazy,
where dancing the night away amid hundreds of tanned, undu-
lating bodies is a standard prelude to hot, anonymous sex.

Ibid.

3 You don't have to be famous anymore to be famous.
Ch. 1, *The Importance of Being Famous: Behind the Scenes of*
the Celebrity-Industrial Complex 2004

4 Welcome to the world of the reality soap opera, where celebrity
sells everything, where complicated news stories are served up
in entertaining ways and then get made into movies—where
it's harder and harder to tell fact from fiction.

Ibid.

3445. Elaine Pagels (1943–)

1 The idea that each individual has intrinsic, God-given value and
is of infinite worth quite apart from any social contribution—
an idea most pagans would have rejected as absurd—persists
today as the ethical basis of western law and politics. Our secularized Western idea of democratic society owes much to that
early Christian vision of a new society—a society no longer
formed by the natural bonds of family, tribe, or nation but by
the voluntary choice of its members.

"The 'Paradise of Virginity' Regained," *Adam, Eve, and the*
Serpent 1988

2 As Augustine* grew older, he argued that even the most saintly
ascetic was not, in himself, capable of self-mastery; that all
humankind was fallen; and that the human will was incor-
rigibly corrupt. This cataclysmic transformation in Christian
thought from an ideology of moral freedom to one of universal
corruption coincided . . . with the evolution of the Christian
movement from a persecuted sect to the religion of the emperor himself.

Ibid.

*St. Augustine, philosopher (354–430); considered the founder
of theology.

3 For millennia, Jews and Christians have attempted to explain
the mystery of human suffering as moral judgment—the price
of Adam and Eve's sin. The creation story of Genesis, addressing the question Why do we suffer and why do we die?, makes
the empirically absurd claim that death does not constitute the

natural end of all lives but intruded upon our species solely because Adam and Eve made the wrong choice.

"The Nature of Nature," Ibid.

4 I would suggest [that] . . . guilt, however painful, offers reassurance that such [disastrous] events do not occur at random but follow specific laws of causation; and that their causes, or a significant part of them, lie in the moral sphere, and so within human control.

Ibid.

5 When you look at the history of Christianity, you see that what the Bible says has been interpreted so many ways that one has to acknowledge that one chooses an interpretation.

Quoted in *A World of Ideas* by Bill Moyers *1989*

6 I began to reflect on how our culture has taught us that suffering and death and disease are not natural, are not part of nature, but were brought in because of human guilt and sin. That belief can lead people to blame themselves in ways that are not constructive.

Ibid.

3446. Gail Thain Parker (1943–)

1 . . . Quaker meetings [were] the first enclaves in American society in which women were encouraged to speak out in public . . . [with] the faith . . . that each individual, regardless of sex, had to act according to his own inner lights. . . .

Introduction, Pt. I, *The Oven Birds 1972*

2 Literature was a great factor in the socialization of women, and without novels (and poems) which portrayed women on an heroic scale, whole generations of nascent feminists might be stunted in their development.

Ibid.

3 Sentimentalism restructured the Calvinist model of salvation, making the capacity to feel, and above all to weep, in itself evidence of redemption.

Ibid.

3447. Charlotte Pierce-Baker (1943–)

1 For black women, where rape is concerned, race has preceded issues of gender. We are taught that we are first black, then women. . . . Black women have survived by keeping quiet, not solely out of shame, but out of a need to preserve the race and its image. In our attempts to preserve racial pride, we black women have often sacrificed our souls.

Surviving the Silence: Black Women's Stories of Rape 1998

2 The way out is to tell: speak the acts perpetrated upon us, speak the atrocities, speak the injustices, speak the personal violations of the soul. Someone will listen, someone will believe our stories, someone will join us.

Ibid.

3447.1. Sally Jessy Raphaël

1 You learn more from ten days of agony than from ten years of content.

Sally on the Net (sallyjr.com) *2000*

2 The advice show made me realize how compelling real people's stories are. I never heard the same love story twice. I became interested in the human condition as opposed to hard news.

Biography, Ibid.

3448. June Machover Reinisch (1943–)

1 When people say women can't be trusted because they cycle every month, my response is that men cycle every day, so they should only be allowed to negotiate peace treaties in the evening.

Times (London) *20 January 1992*

3449. Margaret "Peggy" Milner Richardson (1943–)

1 Well, I think I'm now going into the biggest fund-raising job there is. And this time, I won't even have to use my Rolodex.

Quoted in "Washington at Work; A Tax Lawyer Now Atop the I.R.S." by Robert D. Hershey, Jr., *The New York Times 30 March 1994*

2 No matter how much talk we hear about the problems of the tax system or the Internal Revenue Service, we should not forget that our federal tax administration is the envy of the rest of the world.

Speech, Ohio Tax Conference (16 January 1997), *Vital Speeches of the Day 1 April 1997*

3450. Cokie Roberts (1943–)

1 The truth is, the notion that gay marriage is harmful to marriage, is sort of mind-boggling, because these are people trying to get married. But it seems to me, if you want to defend marriage against something, defend it against divorce.

Real Time with Bill Maher, * HBO-TV *6 August 2004*
*(1956–) American stand-up comedian, television host, social and political commentator, and author.

2 I know his grandmother lives in Hawaii and I know Hawaii is a state, but it has the look of him going off to some sort of foreign, exotic place. He should be in Myrtle Beach, and, you know, if he's going to take a vacation at this time.*

Comment, *This Week with George Stephanopoulos,** ABC-TV *10 August 2008*
*Re President Barack Obama's visit during the 2008 presidential campaign. **(1961–) American broadcaster and former political adviser.

3451. Marilynne Robinson (1943–)

1 All this is fact. Fact explains nothing. On the contrary, it is fact that requires explanation.

Housekeeping 1996

2 She was an old woman, but she managed to look like a young woman with a ravaging disease.

Ch. 1, Ibid.

3 To crave and to have are as like as a thing and its shadow.

Ch. 8, Ibid.

4 . . . the medicalization of sorrow . . .

The Death of Adam: Essays on Modern Thought 1998

5 I miss civilization, and I want it back.

Ibid.

6 It seems ridiculous to suppose the dead miss anything. If you're a grown man when you read this—it is my intention for this letter that you will read it then—I'll have been gone a long time. I'll know most of what there is to know about being dead, but I'll probably keep it to myself. That seems to be the way of things.

Gilead 2004

7 And there was the oak tree in front of the house, much older than the neighborhood or the town, which made rubble of the pavement at its foot and flung its imponderable branches out over the road and across the yard, branches whose girths were greater than the trunk of any ordinary tree. There was a torsion in its body that made it look like a giant dervish to them. Their father said if they could see as God can, in geological time, they would see it leap out of the ground and turn in the sun and spread its arms and bask in the joys of being an oak tree in Iowa.

Ch. 1, Home 2008

3452. Lesley Rogers (1943–)
See Gisela Kaplan, 3516.1:2.

3453. Lorna Sage (1943–2001)

1 In concentrating on women's writing . . . you stress the extent and pace of change, for the scale of women's access to literary life has reflected and accelerated democratic, diasporic pressures in the modern world.

Preface, The Cambridge Guide to Women's Writing in English 1999

2 As long as austerity lasted, the vicarage could maintain its shaky claims to gentility. There was virtue in shabbiness.

Bad Blood 2000

3 The sinner I was expecting was guilty of pride, lust and spiritual despair, not merely of sloth and ineptitude. This was the diary of a nobody. . . . But in truth this is what we should be exposed to—the awful knowledge that when they're not breaking the commandments, the antiheroes are mending their tobacco pipes and listening to the wireless.

Ibid.

3454. Susan Schnall (1943–)

1 The professed purpose of the United States military is to maintain the peace, but its methods towards this goal are destructive and have resulted in the promotion of suffering and death of foreign peoples, as well as of its own.

"Women in the Military," Sisterhood Is Powerful, Robin Morgan, ed. 1970

*See 3284.

2 Because I wore a peace symbol, I had to have an extra interview to determine my suitability as a member of the military.

Ibid.

3455. Sandra Scofield (1943–)

1 "If you aren't nurturing your *self,* what kind of mother can you be, anyway?"

More Than Allies 1993

2 The vastness, the emptiness, terrified me. I couldn't imagine we would ever come out on the other side.*

Ibid.

*Reference to to Texas.

3 She had a rampant dream life and a vivid sense of herself in another kind of world entirely. She had an imagination, she read novels and poetry. It was a short leap to religion.

Ch. 1, Occasions of Sin: A Memoir 2004

4 She was not much more than a girl trapped in a grown-up's life without the taste for it or the stamina, either; she was trembling with longing for something larger than her life.

Ibid.

3456. Silvia of Sweden (1943–)

1 Trafficking of human beings functions like any commercial business: with no demand there is no supply.

Address, Round Table of Business Community against the Trafficking of Human Beings (Athens), INTERPOL 23 January 2006

2 To see but not to see,
to see but to deny,
to see but not to act,
is a crime against a child!
You can make a difference!
You can stop this slavery!
You can save a child!

Ibid.

3 Be a responsible company, a clean company, by guaranteeing your employees and your clients that there is no access possible on your company computers to child pornography.

Do inform your employees to be alert, do cooperate with the police and never erase this illegal material if it ever is downloaded.

Every pimp and every perpetrator should know: also you are watching them!

Ibid.

4 The advantage of being queen is that it's possible to help turn things around for the better.

"Sweden's German-Born Queen Silvia Going Strong at 65," Deutsche Welle 23 December 2008

3457. Ann Snitow (1943–)

1 "Woman" is my slave name; feminism will give me freedom to seek some other identity altogether.

Quoted in "A Gender Diary," Conflicts in Feminism by Marianne Hirsch & Evelyn Fox Keller 1990

*See 2988.

2 Never has the baby been so delicious. A feminist theorist tells me she is more proud of her new baby than of all her books.

Essay, The Politics of Motherhood: Activist Voices from Left to Right, Alexis Jetter, Annelise Orlecks, and Diana Taylor, eds. 1997

3458. Dale Spender (1943–)

1 . . . for centuries there has been a long and honorable tradition of women who have resisted and protested against men and their power.

Feminist Theorists: Three Centuries of Key Women Thinkers 1983

2 It is partly the absence of recorded history which sends women now to the lives of women past for the detailed documentation of their daily lives.

Foreword, All Sides of the Subject, Women and Biography, Teresa Iles, ed. 1992

3 Sexual harassment is becoming the modus operandi of the new world [on-line]. . . . It is the means by which some males are conquering and claiming the new territory as their own.

Nattering on the Net: Women, Power and Cyberspace 1996

3459. Linda Stein (1943–)

1 (You know, we artists think we are in control when we make art. We sometimes feel like gods or masters of the universe, but

in reality, though we sit in the driver's seat, we are merely acting as chauffeur. We take orders from some internal power and follow it feverishly.)

"Notes on My Obsession," *Smith College Exhibition Catalog 2004*

2   To this day, when my eyes settle on a tall building, I cannot stop my mind from imagining it go poof, melting in a slow downward slump as I gaze, watching it evaporate in air.

Artists Section, Veteran Feminist of America (vfa.us) 2007

3460. Elaine Storkey (1943–   )

1   Disappointment within marriage has one very clear answer: acceptance. The issue of acceptance is the core spiritual issue which lies at the heart of every marriage. For we are all failures. We are all disappointments. No one person can be all that another dreamed of. And so often we have to let go of our ideal of what a husband or wife should be like, and give ourselves in love instead to the one we actually have.

The Search for Intimacy 1996

2   The clergy role is a combination of so many things that women are good at: nurturing, loving, organizing, managing people, preaching, networking with people, encouraging, counseling, setting examples. There's also a strong teaching ministry there which is challenging intellectually.

Ch. 8, *Conversations on Christian Feminism,* coauthor, Margaret Hebblethwaite* 1999

*See 4250.1.

3   So we have a healthy caution towards selling techniques. We know that claims can be suspect, promises hollow and that a sensible response to bargains in our inbox is 'delete'.

It's not surprising then, that we have a similar distrust to people selling religion.

"Thought for the Day," BBC.co.uk *27 November 2008*

3461. Roberta Sykes (1943–   )

1   A woman said to me
T'other day. . . .
I read one of your poems
About women,
I thought it very good
But
It didn't say that you
were BLACK

"racism/many faces," *Love Poems and Other Revolutionary Claims 1979*

3462. Jill Tarule (1943–   )
See Mary Belenky, 2834:1–3.

3463. Paula Antonia Treichler (1943–   )
See Cheris Kramarae, 3091:1.

3464. Rose Tremain (1943–   )

1   Life is not a dress rehearsal.

Sunday Correspondent (London) *24 December 1989*

2   Even in an age in which we wisely practise the excellent art of oblivion, certain things remain.

Restoration 1990

3   "What's up?"
"Nothing."
"When men cry, it is never for nothing."

The Road Home 2008

4   They both longed to return to a time before the people they loved most were lost.

Ibid.

3465. Joanna Trollope (1943–   )

1   . . . [she is] a true Oxford spinster, one of that dwindling band of elderly, dignified, clever women living out frugal lives in small flats and rooms, sustained by thinking.

The Men and the Girls 1993

2   She looked around the kitchen. Mrs. Cheng had left it as she usually did, with the floor and taps and surfaces gleaming, and all the room's intractable muddle of living piled in a reproachful heap on the table.

Ibid.

3466. Gina Valdés (1943–   )

1   *Hay tantisimas fronteras*
que dividen a la gente,
pero por cada frontera
existe también un puente.
     (There are so many borders/that divide people,/but for every border/there is also a bridge.)

Untitled, Lesley A. Hyatt,* tr., *Puentes y Fronteras: Coplas Chicanas 1982*

*See 4700.1.

3467. Viva (1943–   )

1   If Mother had let us go to bed whenever we wanted, not forced us to go to church, allowed us to masturbate, go to bars at night, see any movie we wanted, eat whenever we felt like it, sleep with her and Daddy, then I'm sure we'd now be exactly the way she had hoped us to be.

The Baby 1975

2   I think that he exercised a lot of restraint, limiting his kicks to the wall and a painting. I only wish that the heads of governments had the same instincts.

Ibid.

3   Like marriage, nursing was turning out to be one of those painful addictions; damned if you do, damned if you don't.

Ibid.

3468. Patricia Volk (1943–   )

1   "Are you sick?" my mother would ask if I left a scrap from a twelve-ounce Delmonico. You weren't considered fed unless you were in pain. The more somebody loved you, the more they wanted you to eat.

Ch. 1, *Stuffed 2001*

2   The beauty of a marriage is its ongoingness. The staying together, the sharing of history, the appreciation of wrinkles and sag in flesh once known in its taut prime. And the longest stretches of all, the plowing comfort of the quotidian, intimacy with all its lows and reprieves. Marriage is like liver. It regenerates.

Ch. 1, *To My Dearest Friends 2007*

3   Aging is merely a substitution of things that alarmed you then for things that alarm you now. All of life has equal alarm weight.

    Ch. 2, Ibid.

4   Do you have to know a man when he was a boy to still see the boy in him?

    p. 71, Ibid.

3469. Faye Wattleton (1943–   )

1   If we can't preserve the privacy of our right to procreate, I can't imagine what rights we will be able to protect.

    Quoted in "Nothing Less Than Perfect" by Richard Stengel, *Time* (New York) *11 December 1989*

2   Social change rarely comes about through the efforts of the disenfranchised. The middle class creates social revolutions. When a group of people are disproportionately concerned with daily survival, it's not likely that they have the resources to go to Washington and march.

    Ibid.

3   For Mama, all of life was inalterably directed toward the realm of God, and her mission was to persuade everyone who listened to join her in seeking a place in that realm. For me, life was a more earthly endeavor consisting of day-to-day struggles, and my commitment was—and is—toward making sure that all people have the freedom and the power to make the choices they need to make it through. There was no middle ground between our two perspectives.*

    Life on the Line 1996

    *Wattleton's mother was a fundamentalist preacher.

4   I was determined that these men* and their callow ideologies not run roughshod over women's lives.

    Ibid.

    *Re members of the Senate and House Hearing Committees for Title X, 1981.

5   We don't see the issue of parenting as a matter of convenience; we see the issue of parenting as a profoundly important decision, one that has lifelong implications. The whole debate over the rights of the unborn is ethically, morally, and religiously based. There is a wide range of views. The decision should be left to the individuals coping with the circumstances.

    Testimony, Senate Committee hearing re: Title X (31 March 1981), Ibid.

3470. Lotus Weinstock (1943–1997)

1   I Brake For Insights.

    Stand-up routine 1970s

2   Curb Your Dogma.

    Ibid.

3   It may be lonely at the top, but it's so fucking crowded at the bottom.

    Ibid.

4   Even if you don't believe a word of the Bible, you've got to respect the person who typed all that!

    Ibid.

5   Laughter is one of the strongest medicines on the planet . . . If it's strong enough to kill an orgasm, surely it's strong enough to kill cancer.

    Ibid.

6   With all the Jewish comics in the world, how come Israel doesn't have a Laughing Wall?

    Lotus Position 1982

7   Angels can fly because they take themselves lightly.

    Sign-off line, Ibid.

3471. Betty Williams (1943–   )
See Maireád Corrigan Maguire, 3491.

3472. Sandra Alcosser (1944–   )

1   If love were water
    not a drop would be left

    "Dancing the Tarantella at the County Farm," *Except By Nature 1998*

2   I know this world, said the farmer,
    I've listened to worms my whole life
    stirring in slime. I know where
    we come from, and despite all our slick
    designs, I know where we return.

    "Worms," St. 8, Ibid.

3   And when I went off to college I lied. I denied that I had won blue ribbons for butterscotch bars and tight little stitches in skirts, because that was female, and I denied I'd grown up in a body shop, because that was laughable, lower class, and not female. So began a dance, of learning then denying experience. Not exactly the way to build intelligence, though silence sharpens the senses, creates an oily, pungent memory.

    Untitled prose poem, St. 3, Ibid.

4   Surely this is not the place of women in our world, that when we are old and curled like crustaceans, young girls will laugh at us, point their fingers, run as fast as they can in the opposite direction.

    "Hats," Ibid.

3473. Lisa Alther (1944–   )

1   I happen to feel that the degree of a person's intelligence is directly reflected by the number of conflicting attitudes she can bring to bear on the same topic.

    Ch. 7, *Kinflicks 1976*

2   I have been well and happy, Mother. In between being sick and miserable.

    Ibid.

3   ". . . drop kick me, Jesus, through the goal posts of life. . . ."

    Original Sins 1981

4   I had to wonder . . . where modern Americans ever got the idea that physicians should somehow be more competent than the rest of us. . . . When we writers make mistakes, we erase them with our delete buttons. When doctors make mistakes, they get labeled "oafish." Yet I also remember all the trips cancelled because of my father's patients, all the family dinners presided over by his empty chair, all the sleep interrupted by desperate phone calls. I remember my father crying in his armchair over a patient who had died that day on the operating table. I remember, too, my siblings' exhaustion from long hours on duty at urban medical centers, their terror at having lives depend on their split-second decisions, their despair after sleepless nights spent mopping up after other people's brutality, addictions and misfortunes.

    "American tragedies," *The Women's Review of Books,* Vol. XII, Nos. 10–11 *July 1995*

3474. Karen Armstrong (1944–)

1   I say that religion isn't about believing things. It's about what you do. It's ethical alchemy. It's about behaving in a way that changes you, that gives you intimations of holiness and sacredness.
A History of God: The 4000-Year Quest of Judaism, Christianity and Islam 1993

2   One of the reasons why religion seems irrelevant today is that many of us no longer have the sense that we are surrounded by the unseen. Our scientific culture educates us to focus our attention on the physical and material world in front of us.
Ch. 1, Ibid.

3   Yet it seems that creating gods is something that human beings have always done.
Ibid.

4   I don't think, in our kind of society, we'll be able to develop a full-blown mystical religion or concept of God because we seek instant gratification, fast food, endless talk and noise. The silence in mysticism is alien. People want to do a few courses in mysticism, rather like the way you do French before going on holiday, and emerge a mystic. Mysticism isn't like that.
Quoted in "Ex-Nun Challenges Major Religions to Reinvent God" by Janet Silver Ghent, Jewish Bulletin of Northern California 28 October 1994

3475. Lynn Barber (1944–)

1   The best interviews—like the best biographies—should sing the strangeness and variety of the human race.
Independent (London) 24 February 1991

3476. Judith Barrington (1944–)

1   They want women to be like gardens
cultivated possessed
perfected by man.
"A Remarkably Vigorous Rose," Trying to be an Honest Woman 1985

2   Awful truths can mutter under the breastbone
hide their heads, grow fat on opulent time.
"Sonnet for a Stiff Upper Lip," Ibid.

3   They say memory resides in the head
but I say it lives in the tips of fingers
the insides of thighs and forearms
"For a Friend Whose Lover Has Left," St. 1, History and Geography 1989

4   That kind of longing
turns your whole torso into a cavern
where despair echoes wall to wall
and hope leaps like a fœtus.
"Body Language," St. 1, An Intimate Wilderness, Lesbian Writers on Sexuality, ed. 1991

3477. Evelyn S[ilten] Bassoff (1944–)

1   It is only after young women are confident of their individuality and secure that they are strong enough to resist being pulled back into childish ways that they can return to their mothers.
Ch. 1, Mothers and Daughters: Loving and Letting Go 1988

2   Most of life's meaning and beauty are derived from our intimate attachments, yet these attachments also promise frustration, confusion, and sorrow.
Ibid.

3   In our culture, mothers who remain always available to their children, always the "essential" ones, are deified as the "good mother," while the mothers who discourage their children's dependence may be labeled "cold" or "unmotherly."
Last chapter, Between Mothers and Sons: The Making of Vital and Loving Men 1994

4   Mother is the child's most trusted "interpreter," the one who defines the child's inner and outer worlds by telling her what to approach in the world, what to avoid, whom to like, whom to dislike; she gives words to name the things around her and feelings within her. . . .
Cherishing Our Daughters 1998

3478. Ingrid Bengis (1944–)

1   The real questions are the ones that obtrude upon your consciousness whether you like it or not, the ones that make your mind start vibrating like a jackhammer, the ones that you "come to terms with" only to discover that they are still there. The real questions refuse to be placated. They barge into your life at the times when it seems most important for them to stay away. They are the questions asked most frequently and answered most inadequately, the ones that reveal their true natures slowly, reluctantly, most often against your will.
"Man-Hating," Combat in the Erogenous Zone 1973

2   For me words still possess their primitive, mystical, incantatory healing powers. I am inclined to use them as part of an attempt to make my own reality more real for others, as part of an effort to transcend emotional damage. For me, words are a form of action, capable of influencing change. Their articulation represents a complete, lived experience.
Ibid.

3   Imagination has always had powers of resurrection that no science can match.
"Monroe According to Mailer,"** Ms. (New York) October 1973*

*Marilyn M- ; see 2568. **American writer (1923–2007).

4   The form that our bodies take, particularly with women, dictates more often than we wish it would the form that a portion of our lives will take.
Ibid.

3479. Sandra Lipsitz Bern (1944–)

1   When I entered the Stanford Universe, I entered a fast-track, high-stakes game, the likes of which I never knew existed. . . .
An Unconventional Family 1998

2   . . . how much better it would be for both women and men if society would stop stereotyping virtually all aspects of the human personality as either feminine or masculine . . . if everyone were free to be their own unique blending of temperament and behavior.
Ibid.

3480. Eavan Boland (1944–)

1   After the wolves and before the elms
the bardic order ended in Ireland.
Only a few remained to continue
a dead art in a dying land.
"My Country in Darkness" (p. 15), The Lost Land: Poems 1998

2 and memory itself
has become an emigrant. . . .
"Mother Ireland" (p. 40), Ibid.

3 How much longer
will I see girlhood in my daughter?
"The Blossom" (p. 45), Ibid.

4 *Beautiful land* the patriot said
and rinsed it with his blood.
"Whose?" (p. 67), Ibid.

3481. Rita Mae Brown (1944–)

1 I move in the shadow of the great guillotine
That rhythmically does its work
On heads remaining unbowed.
"The Self Affirms Herself" (1966), *The Hand That Rocks the
Cradle 1971*

2 An army of lovers shall not fail.
"Sappho's* Reply" (1970), Ibid.
*See 46.

3 Love is the wild card of existence.
In Her Day 1976

4 I am a comic writer, which means I get to slay the dragons, and
shoot the bull.
Speech (San Jose, Calif.) *18 November 1978*

5 This is a celebration of individual freedom, not of homosexuality. No government has the right to tell its citizens when or
whom to love. The only queer people are those who don't love
anybody.
Speech, Gay Games (San Francisco) *8 August 1982*

3482. Joan Jacobs Brumberg (1944–)

1 In the course of the twentieth century, a girl's body has come to
loom very large in her sense of personal identity.
*The Body Project: An Intimate History of American Girls
1997*

2 Can you imagine what would happen if girls took all the energy they spend worrying about their image and put it into
painting, writing, theorizing, science, or sports?
Ibid.

3483. Charlotte Bunch (1944–)

1 Feminism is an entire world view or gestalt, not just a laundry
list of "women's issues."
"Understanding Feminist Theory," *New Directions for Women
September/October 1981*

2 We know that priorities are amiss in the world when a man
gets a military medal of honor for killing another man and a
dishonorable discharge for loving one.
"Speaking Out, Reaching Out," *Passionate Politics 1987*

3 Violence against women is an issue that has come onto the global
agenda from the grassroots level of the women's movement, that
is, from women's lives and feminist organizing. No issue better
illustrates how the women's movement can and has moved a
concern from local women's spaces to the tables of power.
"Listen Up: UN Must Hear Women on Violence," *On the
Issues Spring 2009*

4 Violence against women highlights both the universality of
women's experiences around the world, as well as the particularities of the diversity of women's lives. The commonality is
that almost all women experience violence, or the threat of
violence, as a tool aimed at controlling us—our behavior and
our bodies. But the forms and ways in which women experience such threats and acts of violence are shaped by many
factors including race, class, culture, sexual orientation, age
and physical abilities, as they intersect with gender. One-size-
fits all solutions will not work. Remedies and efforts to end
violence against women must be intersectional, particular
and context-driven. This is especially important in relation to
women whose lives and experiences are often marginalized,
such as refugee and migrant women, sexual and racial minorities, disabled women.
Ibid.

3484. Andrea Carlisle (1944–)

1 If the world were made of language, what kind of world would
I create?
The Riverhouse Stories 1989?

3485. Ana Carrigan (1944?–)

1 . . . back to *campesino* country, to Indian country, where there
are no historical monuments or archives or television cameras
to worry about, and where the casualties are politically invisible.*
The Palace of Justice, A Colombian Tragedy 1993
*Re the November 6, 1985 guerilla attack on the Palace of Justice,
and the army's brutal response to it.

2 It is hard to care about a place we don't understand, particularly when our only images are the interminably familiar ones
of destruction and death.
"The Supply and Demand for Colombia's Misery," *In These
Times* (inthesetimes.com) *9 May 2003*

3 Even in Colombia, hope dies last.
Quoted in "War and Hope in Colombia," Ibid. *9 December
2004*

3486. Judi Chamberlin (1944–)

1 "Empowerment" is a term that has become very popular in
mental health services. . . . Still lacking a definition, the word
has become common political rhetoric, with a flexibility of
meaning so broad that it seems to be in danger of losing any
inherent meaning at all.
"A Working Definition of Empowerment," *Psychiatric
Rehabilitation Journal,* vol. 20, no. 4 *Spring 1977*

2 The desire to protect (and to be protected) is a strong one;
nonetheless, there are genuine benefits when clients begin to
control their own lives, and when practitioners become guides
and coaches in this process, rather than assuming the long-
term, paternalistic role of supervisors. Such a shift of roles and
practices would make rehabilitation services truly transformative in the lives of their clients.
Ibid.

3487. Nancy Chodorow (1944–)

1 To understand how men and women love requires that we
understand how any particular woman or man loves; to understand femininity and masculinity and the various forms
of sexuality requires that we understand how any particular

woman or man creates her or his own cultural and personal gender and sexuality.

Femininities, Masculinities, Sexualities: Freud and Beyond 1994

3488. Laurie Colwin (1944–1992)

1 "You believe in happy endings. I don't. You think everything is going to work out fine. I don't. You think everything is ducky. I don't. . . . I come from a family that fled the Czar's army, got their heads broken on picket lines, and has never slept peacefully anywhere."

Happy All the Time 1978

2 Misty felt that life was a battle. You had to fight and think. You had to hack your way through life with your intelligence as a machete cutting down what obstacles you could. You were born knowing nothing: you had to fight for what you knew.

Ibid.

3 It was just as she suspected: love turned you into perfect mush.

Ibid.

4 Oh, domesticity! The wonder of dinner plates and cream pitchers. You know your friends by their ornaments. You want everything. If Mrs. A. has her mama's old jelly mold, you want one too, and everything else that goes with it—the family, the tradition, the years of having jelly molded in it. We domestic sensualists live in a state of longing, no matter how comfortable our own places are.

The Lone Pilgrim 1981

5 She was tender on the subject of animals, but the cats reminded her of herself: so willing, so hungry for love.

Ibid.

6 She was married to Alfred Hendershot, the political adviser, and was an almost perfect person. She gave elaborate dinner parties and belonged to the Royal Guild of Needleworkers— she did fine embroidery in her two minutes of spare time.

"A Big Storm Knocked It Over" (1987), *Shaking Eve's Tree, Short Stories of Jewish Women,* Sharon Niederman,* ed. 1990
*See 3853.

3489. Mary Coombs (1944–)

1 The law has been written with men in mind. Feminist jurisprudence puts women at the center and asks, "To what extent is this doctrine or this area of law designed in a way that implicitly assumes people are men?"

Quoted in "Now for a Woman's Point of View" by Anastasia Touflexis, *Time* (New York) *17 April 1989*

3490. Stephanie Coontz (1944–)

1 The triumph of private family values discourages us from meeting our emotional needs through mutual aid associations, political and social action groups, or other forms of public life that used to be as important in people's identity as love or family.

The Way We Never Were 1992

2 . . . families have been most successful wherever they have built meaningful, solid networks and commitments *beyond* their own boundaries.

Ibid.

3 Many of the problems commonly blamed on breakdown of the traditional family exist not because we've changed too much but because we haven't changed enough.

The Way We Really Are: Coming to Terms with America's Changing Families 1997

3491. Mairéad Corrigan Maguire (1944–)

1 Love everybody and don't let flags and religions get in the way of looking somebody in the eye and seeing the beauty of the human person.

Interview conducted by Dawn Engle and Ivan Suvanjieff, (August 14, 1995), *PeaceJam.org 2000*

2 Official violence begets illegal violence as surely as night follows day.

Speech, I.P.J.E.T (International Platform of Jurists for East Timor) Conference (Dublin; 8 November 1996), Ibid.

3 Terrorism is invariably the response of powerless people to oppression of some sort. And terrorism can become endemic to a whole community, if solutions are not found to the sources of oppression.

Ibid.

4 At first, some people might imagine the silence of guns to be nonviolence; but such a silence is merely the dim early enlightenment of anti-violence. To commit oneself to live without arms, no matter what happens, requires a much deeper pilgrimage—and that pilgrimage is one that many conventional politicians who lecture terrorists have not themselves made.

Ibid.

5 I have come to know for certain that our first identity is not nationalist or unionist, but our humanity. I have come to know for certain that love and compassion are the greatest and strongest forces operating in our world today.

"A New Vision—An Open Letter to the IRA" Ibid.

3492. Nancy Cotton (1944?–)

. . . she [Margaret Cavendish]* fulfills the popular fantasy that a woman writer is necessarily slightly demented.

Women Playwrights in England, ca. 1363–1750 1980
*See 446.

3493. Angela Davis (1944–)

1 . . . the master needs the slave far more than the slave needs the master.

"Reflections on the Black Woman's Role in the Community of Slaves," *The Black Scholar December 1971*

2 We, the black women of today, must accept the full weight of a legacy wrought in blood by our mothers in chains. As heirs to a tradition of perseverance and heroic resistance, we must hasten to take our place wherever our people are forging toward freedom.

Ibid.

3 . . . the brother . . . had painted a night sky on the ceiling of his cell, because it had been years since he had seen the moon and stars.

An Autobiography 1974

4 Jails and prisons are designed to break human beings, to convert the population into specimens in a zoo—obedient to our keepers, but dangerous to each other.

Ibid.

5 Media mystifications should not obfuscate a simple, perceivable fact; Black teenage girls do not create poverty by having babies. Quite the contrary, they have babies at such a young age precisely because they are poor—because they do not have the opportunity to acquire an education, because meaningful, well-paying jobs and creative forms of recreation are not accessible to them . . . because safe, effective forms of contraception are not available to them.
Address, "Facing Our Common Foe" (15 November 1987),
Women, Culture and Politics 1989

6 Radical simply means "grasping things at the root."
Address, "Let Us All Rise Together," Spelman College" (5 June 1987), Ibid.

3494. Thadious M. Davis (1944–)

1 *Girls together* once in the city that care forgot
during hot evenings elongated summers
the two of us in the sweat of days
growing through ankle socks knee-highs
ribbons and headbands
"Reunion," Sts. 2–3 (1981), *The Woman That I Am, The Literature and Culture of Contemporary Women of Color*, D. Soyini Madison*, ed. 1994
*See 3912.

3495. Claudia Dreifus (1944–)

1 We spent a winter learning the feminist basics from the textbook of each other's lives. . . .
Introduction, *Woman's Fate* 1973

2 . . . girls enforce the cultural code that men invent.
"The Adolescent Experience," Ibid.

3496. Linda Ellerbee (1944–)

1 Only dead fish swim with the stream.
Move On 1991

2 Adventure is to take big bites of elsewhere. I believe in elsewhere. I believe in taking big bites.
Introduction, *Take Big Bites* 2005

3 After years spent shelling peas, stringing beans, cutting the corn off the cob, peeling this and slicing that and then cooking everything—in a big pot of water with a big a piece of pork—until Tuesday, my mother thought Mr. Birdseye was a saint.
Ibid.

3497. Buchi Emecheta (1944–)

1 That was life, she said to herself. Be as cunning as a serpent and as harmless as a dove.
Ch. 2, *Second-Class Citizen* 1974

2 But how was she to tell this beautiful creature that in her society she could only be sure of the love of her husband and the loyalty of her parents-in-law by having and keeping alive as many children as possible, and that though a girl may be counted as one child, to her people a boy was like four children put together? And if the family could give the boy a good university education, his mother would be given the status of a man in the tribe. How was she to explain all that?
Ch. 6, Ibid.

3 The whole world seemed so unequal, so unfair. Some people were created with all the good things ready-made for them, others were just created like mistakes. God's mistakes.
Ch. 9, Ibid.

4 . . . shame kills faster than disease.
The Rape of Shavi 1985

3498. Delia Ephron (1944?–)

1 If you are a girl, worry that your breasts are too round. Worry that your breasts are too pointed. Worry that your nipples are the wrong color. Worry that your breasts point in different directions.
If you are a boy, worry that you will get breasts.
. . . If you are a boy, worry that you'll never be able to grow a mustache.
If you are a girl, worry that you have a mustache.
Teenage Romance 1981

2 As complicated as joint custody is, it allows the delicious contradiction of having children and maintaining the intimacy of life-before-kids.
Funny Sauce 1986

3 JOE: The whole purpose of places like Starbucks is for people with no decision-making ability whatsoever to make six decisions just to buy one cup of coffee. Short, tall, light, dark, caf, decaf, low-fat, non-fat, etc. So people who don't know what the hell they're doing or who on earth they are can, for only $2.95, get not just a cup of coffee but an absolutely defining sense of self: Tall! Decaf! Cappuccino!
You've Got Mail, cowriter, Nora Ephron* 1998
*See 3258.

4 GEORGE: As far as I'm concerned, the Internet is just another way to be rejected by a woman.
Ibid.

5 Divorce is the destruction of childhood.
Big City Eyes 2000

6 . . . diehard Manhattanites. To leave the city, unless it was to go someplace thrilling like Paris, they would have to be towed.
Ibid.

3499. Anne Fausto-Sterling (1944–)

1 . . . in modern usage, a cuckold is the husband of an unfaithful wife—a far nastier and more humiliating state, apparently, than being the wife of a philanderer, for which in fact no word exists.
Myths of Gender 1985

2 . . . to take even very extensive animal research, define it according to uniquely human behavior, and then use it to analyze human behavior is both logically flawed and politically dangerous. . . .
Ibid.

3500. Fatima Gallaire-Bourega (1944–)

1 LELLA. When the mad speak of calamity, it's best to listen.
You Have Come Back (Ah! Vous êtes venus . . . là òu il y a quelques tombes), Jill MacDougall, tr. 1988

3501. Marjorie B. Garber (1944–)

1 ... [the] extraordinary power of the transvestite as an aesthetic and psychological agent of destabilization, desire, and fantasy.

Vested Interests: cross dressing & cultural anxiety 1992

2 Historians record dozens, probably hundreds, of ... stories of lifelong cross-dressers whose "true" gender identities were disclosed only after death.

Ibid.

3502. Jane F. Garvey (1944–)

1 We cannot regain our innocence we lost on Sept. 11, but we will—we must—regain confidence in the safety of air travel. ... Americans have long known that "eternal vigilance is the price of liberty." Now, we know, it is the price of mobility.

Speech, National Press Club, October 2001

3503. Inge Genefke (1944?–)

1 Today we know that the most essential purpose of torture is not to gather information and evidence, no, the most essential purpose is the most evil in the world: to break down a personality, to destroy an identity, you could call it: to kill a soul. And to use it is worse than murder.

Acceptance Speech, Right Livelihood Awards (Stockholm), 9 December 1988

2 Because torture is the worst, the most hideous thing on earth. Torture is not just ... a person is burnt with cigarettes or with iron bars, is hit and kicked all over, or is tormented until being unconscious.

No, torture is far worse, and it is something which is difficult for us to imagine. Torture is mainly of psychological character. This means that a person is forced to witness the torture of a child or a spouse ... to have to watch helplessly and to have to listen to their screams and crying, and their appeals to stop the torture—and you can do nothing.

This is the worst form of torture. It creates great suffering—and, of course, the torturers know it, and they use it.

Ibid.

3504. Margaret Gibson (1944–)

1 When I say
   love, I mean what we've had to lose
      to be what we are.
   I mean what continues without us,
      and somehow,
   because.

(p. 138), *Memories of the Future: the daybooks of Tina Modotti*: poems 1986

*See 1828.

2 Doing nothing, I
   no longer wait for whole
   other worlds to break open,
   more beautiful than this one
   whose wild darkness
   stains my fingers,
   my mouth, my tongue.

"Doing Nothing" (p. 87), *Out in the Open 1989*

3505. Marcia Gillespie (1944–)

1 We have been looking at it [feminism] warily. Black women need economic equality but it doesn't apply for me to call a black man a male chauvinist pig. Our anger is not at our men. I don't think they have been the enemy.

Quoted in "About Women," *The Los Angeles Times 12 May 1974*

2 One of the reasons I became active politically was from reading history, the movements, the oppression, the sacrifices. Unless we look at ourselves from that model, nothing is ever going to make sense. And nothing is ever going to change.

Speech, University of Massachusetts (Dartmouth) March 1998

3 You can't just talk about freedom for some people. You have to talk about freedom for all people.

Ibid.

4 I did not stand up for myself as a black person in America to be told to sit down because I'm a woman.

Quoted in "Kindred Spirits" by Rachel G. Thomas, *The Standard Times 18 March 1998*

3506. Rita M. Gross (1944?–)

1 If it is daring, degrading or alienating to speak of God using female pronouns and imagery, perhaps that indicates something about the way women and the feminine are valued. God language does not really tell us about God, but it does tell us a considerable amount about those who use the God language. I only wish the people who argue to retain solely male imagery were as aware that God is not really male as I am that God is not really female.

Quoted in Ch. 4, *Deborah, Golda, & Me* by Letty Cottin Pogrebin* 1991

*See 3154.

3507. Susan Gubar (1944–)
See Sandra Gilbert, 2978:1.

3508. Daphne Hampson (1944–)

1 If one is not fundamentalist ... then there are questions which need to be brought to the [biblical] text. What authority could, for example, the text of the creation story possibly have post-Darwin?

Ch. 1, *Theology and Feminism 1990*

2 It will be clear that human religion need not ... be historical. It could be believed that God, whatever was understood by God, was equally close to all times and places; that no particular period, and no particular events, were to be held to be more revelatory of God than others.

Ibid.

3 Since at least the Enlightenment we have been clear that there is a regularity to nature and to history. That is ... to say that one event follows from another. Caesar crossed the Rubicon because he put one foot in front of the other; he did not suddenly find himself transported to the other side. History forms a causal nexus.

Ch. 1, *After Christianity 1996*

3509. Bernadine Healy (1944–)

1 The race to discover new genes was visible and competitive, the promise of substantial economic returns for screening tests compelling, and the public hunger for a breakthrough in breast-cancer treatment intense.

1997, Quoted in *Future Perfect* by Lori B. Andrews 2001

2   Yet the school years are a critical time in the development of minds and brains. In fact, the brain does not fully mature until late adolescence and early adulthood, when the prefrontal cortex undergoes the final stages of building and organization. This area controls impulses, moral reasoning, judgment, and rational thinking and accounts for that magical time parents yearn for when their emotion-driven teens morph into people capable of nuanced thinking. This is also the time when two major brain illnesses emerge—schizophrenia, a disorder marked by irrational thought, and bipolar or manic-depressive illness, a disorder of mood.

"A Path to Mental Health," U.S. News and World Report 19 April 2007

3   The doctor-patient relationship rests on a moral foundation as well. A vulnerable patient turns over a measure of privacy and control to a doctor only because of need, creating an asymmetric partnership that demands physician integrity. This has always been so, explaining the oath, handed down from the time of Hippocrates, which says, simply: Tell the truth, do no harm, take no advantage, keep secrets.

"Medicine, the Art," U.S. News and World Report 15 July 2007

3510. Joan D. Hedrick (1944–   )

1   The outward acts of Jack London's* life received enormous publicity while he was living, and they continue to exercise a fascination that often eclipses his work. Like his hero, Burning Daylight, he "had the fatal facility for self-advertisement."

Introduction, Solitary Comrade, Jack London and His Work 1982

*Am. author (1876–1916).

2   London was engaged in a covert alliance with his readers, who preferred the illusions of Van Weyden to the brutal truths of Wolf Larsen.*

Ch. 9, Ibid.

*Central characters from The Sea-Wolf (1904).

3   Describing himself as "harnessed to the chariot of Christ," [Lyman Beecher*] spent his life winning souls in what turned out to be a futile attempt to outflank the enemy. He died in 1863, just before the onslaught of Material and secular excess called the Gilded Age.

Ch. 1, Harriet Beecher Stowe: A Life 1995

*American cleric, father of Harriet B— Stowe (see 916).

3511. Nancy Hopkins (1944–   )

1   There won't be many women scientists at the top until prejudice against them abates and until it becomes fashionable to admit that children take more of a woman's time than a man's. The system needs to change to make the playing field equal. We owe it to young women to make the institutional changes needed so that more can have it all—or even have it at all.

Letter to the Editor, The New York Times 12 June 1996

2   When he* started talking about innate differences in aptitude between men and women, I just couldn't breathe because this kind of bias makes me physically ill. Let's not forget that people used to say that women couldn't drive an automobile.

*Quoted by Jonah Goldberg**, Ibid. 19 January 2005*

*Re Larry Summers (1945–   ), Am. Economist. **(1969–   ), Am. Syndicated columnist, author.

3   It's hard to end your experiment in time to go home to make dinner. I was just going to be a scientist.

Quoted by Devan Sipher, Ibid. 29 July 2007

4   At 60, if you don't have time to take the weekend off, there's something wrong.

Ibid.

3512. Molly Ivins (1944–2007)

1   She is convinced there is no civilization without bialys, a bialy being a sort of a Brooklyn tortilla.

Column, The Texas Observor 30 December 1977

2   Government is a tool, like a hammer. You can use a hammer to build with or you can use a hammer to destroy.

Column, Fort Worth Star-Telegram 1992

3   It's all very well to run around saying regulation is bad, get the government off our backs, etc. Of course our lives are regulated. When you come to a stop sign, you stop; if you want to go fishing, you get a license; if you want to shoot ducks, you can shoot only three ducks. The alternative is dead bodies at intersections, no fish and no ducks.

Column, Fort Worth Star-Telegram 1994

4   He owes his political life to big corporate money: He's a CEO's wet dream. He carries their water . . . George W. Bush* is a wholly owned subsidiary of corporate America. . . .

Shrub: The Short But Happy Political Life of George W. Bush 2000

*(1946–   ), Amer. politician; 43rd president of the United States (2001–09).

5   The state of the union is that money talks and public policy is sold to the highest bidder.

"The actual state of the union," Creators Syndicate 29 January 2003

6   We suffer the worst attack on this country since Pearl Harbor, and the Bush administration sends the FBI after the American Civil Liberties Union. The ACLU exists to protect every citizen's rights as defined in the Bill of Rights in the Constitution of the United States.

Syndicated Column, Fort Worth Star-Telegram July 2005

7   Newt Gingrich,* the Boy Scout. Newt Gingrich, the man who sat there and watched Congress impeach and try Bill Clinton for lying about having an extramarital affair while he, Newt Gingrich, was lying about having an extramarital affair.

Ibid., 16 November 2006

*Newton "Newt" Leroy G— (1943–   ), Am. politician, author; served as the Speaker of the United States House of Representatives, 1995–99.

8   . . . if Republicans want to continue to rubber-stamp this administration's idiotic 'plans' and go against the will of the people, they should be thrown out as soon as possible, to join their recent colleagues. . . . We are the people who run this country. We are the deciders.

Ibid., 7 January 2007

3513. Sarah James (1944–   )

1   We believe everything is related. If everything is balanced, the earth will work for all of us, not just for our own little lot. We are talking about sharing the whole world together, because

there are some people with too much that are not sharing and too many without enough.

"Fun and James", grist.org *15 December 2006*

2 Conservation is long-range protection for our people and for our children. It's not only for us, it's for the whole world. We are one of the last people living off the land; it's still natural. We have to educate people because after this there is no more. It's the only place for birds and ducks, migratory animals, fish, and all kinds of life. Here in Alaska the ecosystem still works.

Ibid.

3 We are going to continue to educate the world about global warming. People will see that it makes no sense to open a new place to drilling for oil, which will ultimately release more greenhouse-gas emissions.

Ibid.

4 We are caribou people. It's our clothing, our story, our song, our dance and our food that's who we are. If you drill for oil here, you are drilling right into the heart of our existence.

goldmanprize.org *2002*

3514. J. A. Jance (1944–)

1 People die. Quarrels don't.

Dismissed with Prejudice 1989

2 Despite what the Constitution says, all men are not created equal—not in life and not in death either. Rank hath its privilege, even in the medical examiner's wagon.

Ch. 5, *Payment in Kind 1991*

3 I know from experience that homicide is no respecter of philosophy or religion. At the moment of crisis, those who pull the triggers of murder weapons are far beyond the pale of their own moral imperatives, to say nothing of society's as a whole.

Ch. 7, Ibid.

4 I was struck by the fact that even after all those years, the exact time of her child's death was still engraved in her heart and brain. Mothers are like that, I guess.

Ch. 15, Ibid.

3515. Lisa Jardine (1944–)

1 The practice of science has been one and the same throughout its history—a story of chance, creative misunderstanding, wrong turnings, sudden opportunities taken, succumbing to sponsorship and the inspired ingenuity of individual men and women.

Ingenious Pursuits, Building the Scientific Revolution 2000

3516. Carol Jenkins (1944–)

1 This is our true mission as we leave the scene of great celebration: to remember the homeless we saw sleeping in doorways as we made our way to the fancy inaugural balls last night. To determine acts to accompany the words that will counter the deepening economic distress we woke up to this morning—affecting, increasingly, not only the anonymous buried in the statistics, but people we know, perhaps even ourselves. To remember the women, still the poor and vulnerable of the world. And to remember that ever more importantly, we must tell their stories—tell them straight and strong so we move people to act, as well as think and feel.

"Remaking America," Women's Media Center (womensmediacenter.com) *21 January 2009*

2 As a result, in part, of the media's coverage of our candidates, the fracturing of our identities into gender, race, class, and age has been so thorough that the main task we have as a nation now is pulling ourselves together into a whole. If we're lucky, this new nation will be an improvement on what we had. If we don't exert every effort at reconciliation, these historic breakthroughs in political participation will be for naught. Media's involvement in our division—and its responsibility in the healing—cannot be underestimated.

Ibid.

3516.1. Gisela Kaplan (1944–)

1 . . . the political agenda of the day very often *a priori* determined the "findings." . . . These extreme examples of academic behavior in a specific political climate in very recent times may inculcate a good measure of mistrust toward academics.

"Irreducible 'Human Nature': Nazi Views on Jews and Women," *Challenging Racism and Sexism: Alternatives to Genetic Explanations,* Ethel Tobach and Betty Rosoff, eds. *1994*

2 For Haeckel the only morality lay in the process of natural selection. According to him, this "morality" of natural selection in human society now required positive intervention in order to correct the errors humans had already brought upon themselves. He advocated the extermination of anybody with any failings—racial, physical, social, or otherwise—because such an artificial process of selection would make "the struggle for life among the better portion of mankind . . . easier."

"Race and Gender Fallacies," coauthor Lesley Rogers,* Ibid.
*See 3452.

3517. Leslie King-Hammond (1944–)

1 That these women* would do this: to push forward against apparently insurmountable odds when there was absolutely no promise of their recognition, no access for them to be received. . . . They were women, and they were African American women. Society did not recognize them beyond being maids, or maybe teachers or nurses. But fine artists? American society did not recognize that as even a remote possibility.

Quoted in "Breaking the Mold" by Sharon Fitzgerald, *Ms.* (New York) *September/October 1996*
*Re traveling art exhibit, "Three Generations of African American Women Sculptors: A Study in Paradox," curated by King-Hammond and Tritobia Hayes Benjamin (1996–97).

2 For the better part of the nineteenth century and really until the break of the twentieth century, women were not allowed to be in classes with nudes. So how possibly could a woman become a sculptor if she was denied the basic education and experience that was necessary?

Ibid.

3518. Frances Moore Lappé (1944–)

1 . . . much agricultural land which might be growing food is being used instead to "grow" money (in the form of coffee, tea, etc.)

Foreword, *Diet for a Small Planet 1971*

2 The act of putting into your mouth what the earth has grown is perhaps your most direct interaction with the earth.

Pt. I, Ibid.

3   People often disparage their [charitable] efforts as mere "drops in the bucket." Yet drops fill up a bucket quite fast—as long as there is a bucket!

Acceptance Speech, Right Livelihood Awards (Stockholm) *9 December 1987*

4   How could we ever believe "the world" can change unless we experience ourselves changing?

Introduction, *Getting A Grip 2007*

5   As long as we conceive of power as the capacity to exert one's will over another, it is something to be wary of. Power can manipulate, coerce, and destroy. And as long as we are convinced we have none, power will always look negative.

Ch. 4, Ibid.

6   It is culture, not fixed aspects of human nature, which largely determines the prevalence of cooperation or brutality, honesty or deceit. And since we create culture through our daily choices, then we do, each of us, wield enormous power.

Ibid.

3519. Harriet Goldhor Lerner (1944–)

1   In our rapidly changing society we can count on only two things that will never change. What will never change is the will to change and the fear of change.

Ch. 2, *The Dance of Intimacy 1989*

2   Men chart the stars, create language and culture as we know it, record history as they see it, build and destroy the world around us, and continue to run every major institution that generates power, policy, and wealth. Men define the very "reality" that—until the current feminist movement—I, for one, accepted as a given, and although women throughout history have exercised a certain power as mothers, we have not created the conditions in which we mother, nor have we constructed the predominant myths and theories about "good mothering."

Epilogue, Ibid.

3   All the assertiveness training and communication skills in the world can't prevent a relationship from becoming fertile ground for silence and stonewalling, or for anger and frustration, or for just plain hard times.

Ch. 1, *The Dance of Connection 2002*

4   It is an interesting sidelight that our language—created and codified by men—does not have *one* unflattering term to describe men who vent their anger at women. Even such epithets as "bastard" and "son of a bitch" do not condemn the man but place the blame on a woman—his mother!

Ch. 1, *The Dance of Anger 2005*

5   Just as physical pain tells us to take our hand off the hot stove, the pain of our anger preserves the very integrity of our self.

Ibid.

3520. Sara Lawrence Lightfoot (1944–)

1   Good schools have a sense of mission that kids and adults can all articulate. They have an identity. They have a character, a quality that's their own, that feels quite sturdy. They have a set of values . . . Good schools are also disciplined places. I don't mean by that just behavioral discipline, but a place where people set goals and standards and hold each other accountable.

Quoted in *A World of Ideas* by Bill Moyers *1989*

2   Somehow the American public has to get back to the great richness and mystery of learning, the playfulness and seriousness of learning, and how that can be nurtured in schools by teachers in classrooms.

Ibid.

3   Schooling is what happens inside the walls of the school, some of which is educational. Education happens everywhere, and it happens from the moment a child is born—and some people say before—until a person dies.

Ibid.

4   Respect is not just carried through talk, it is also conveyed through silence. I do not mean an empty, distracted silence. I mean a fully engaged silence, that permits us to think, to feel, to breathe, and take notice, silence that gives the other person permission to let us know what he or she needs. In nourishing respectful relationships then, we must develop receptive antennae, take on the role of witness, and learn to live in stillness. . . . I believe that respect is the single most important ingredient in creating authentic relationships and building healthy communities.

Speech, "Will anybody know who I am: On witness, justice, and respect," Coalition of Essential Schools (Seattle) Fall Forum *2001*

3521. Shirley Geok-Lin Lim (1944–)

1   If the women's movement has discovered difference to be a liberating rather than an oppressive principle, through which new visions, new understanding and new orders of society can be generated, the experiences of being an Asian American woman is an exemplar of living in difference.

Introduction (p. 10), *The Forbidden Stitch: An Asian-American Women's Anthology,* Lim, Mayumi Tsutakawa, and Margarita Donnelly, eds. *1989*

2   Life's miseries dissipated into the sharp fertility of sense through my fixed idea that all I saw and felt would become words one day. The ambition for poetry, a belief in the vital connection between language and my specific local existence, was clearly irrational, even perhaps a symptom of small madness.

Among the White Moon Faces: An Asian-American Memoir of Homelands 1996

3522. Elizabeth Loftus (1944–)

1   What am I doing here? What business does a research psychologist have in a court of law, offering facts taken from countless scientific experiments, hoping to communicate that our memories are sometimes distortions of reality, inaccurate images of the past?

Part One, *Witness for the Defense: The Accused, the Eyewitness and the Expert Who Puts Memory on Trial,* coauthor, Katherine Ketcham* *1992*

*See 3904.

2   In a chaotic world, where so much is out of control, we need to believe that our minds, at least, are under our command. We need to believe that our memories, inherently trustworthy and reliable, can reach back into the past and make sense of our lives.

The Myth of Repressed Memory, coauthor, Kathrine Ketcham *1994*

3   Sometimes we might be better off with distorted memories. And sometimes it just plain old doesn't matter if our memory is perfectly accurate or not. It only matters when you start to use memories to accuse people, and you want to imprison them or take their money.

"Into the Past Imperfect" by Kit Boss, *Seattle Times,* Pacific Northwest section *25 September 1994*

3523. Annette Lu (1944–)

1 It took the People's Republic of China 22 years [to gain United Nations membership]. It took Korea 15 years. Taiwan has been forgotten, and the process itself will remind the world.

> Quoted in "Taiwan's Don Quixote," *Parade Magazine* 13 *February 1994*

2 The more trials I stand, the stronger I become. It is encouraging for me to say that I have never played political tricks. I have never resorted to violence. I always touch the hearts of others and lead people with my ideals and ideas through peaceful and democratic procedures, even if it needs to sacrifice myself.

> Acceptance Speech, World Peace Prize *4 December 2001*

3524. Shena MacKay (1944–)

1 ... carousing on a sandbank in time, music and laughter drowning the sound of tomorrow's tide.

> *An Advent Calendar 1997*

2 Every artist leaves behind a shadowy retrospective exhibition of the pictures that were never painted.

> *The Artist's Widow 1999*

3525. Alice Tepper Marlin (1944–)

1 As more and more shoppers make informed, socially sound choices, such as recycling, selecting goods with simple, biodegradable packaging, buying only what we need, and looking at the companies behind the products we buy, we are converting our shopping carts into vehicles for social change.

> Acceptance Speech, Right Livelihood Awards (Stockholm) 9 *December 1990*

2 But, imbued with a newly influential concept, consumers have begun to embrace the simple, quiet activism of casting their economic vote conscientiously at the checkout counter, an act which can empower us all.

> Ibid.

3 If the U.S. had spent as much from August through December on improving energy efficiency as we've spent mobilizing in the Gulf, the U.S. could have eliminated our oil imports from the Gulf.

> Ibid.

3526. Emily Martin (1944–)

1 It is remarkable how femininely the egg behaves and how masculinely the sperm. The egg is seen as large and passive. It does not move or journey, but passively "is transported," "is swept," or even "drifts" along the fallopian tube. In utter contrast, sperm are small, "streamlined," and invariably active. They "deliver" their genes to the egg, "activate the developmental program of the egg," and have a "velocity" that is often remarked upon. Their tails are "strong" and efficiently powered. Together with the forces of ejaculation, they can "propel the semen into the deepest recesses of the vagina."

> "The Egg and the Sperm: How Science Has Constructed a Romance Based on Stereotypical Male-Female Roles," *Signs: A Journal of Women in Culture and Society*, Vol. 16, Spring *1991*

3527. Doris Okada Matsui (1944–)

1 When you hear the word "incubator," an image is called to mind of a safe environment that allows growth to happen. Business incubators are entities that do just that: they provide

our innovators and entrepreneurs a stable environment in which to move their ideas from concept to reality.

> News Release, cleanstart.org 23 *April 2008*

2 Cultivating our workforce, which is largely comprised of small businesses, will help ensure that America remains competitive in the evolving global market. By providing resources to innovative new businesses, we are taking action now to grow the cutting-edge workforce of tomorrow.

> Ibid.

3528. Susan Miller (1944–)

1 PERRY. There is a moment, like the black holes in space, of complete and irrevocable loss. To allow that moment is to let go of the sides of times, to fall into another place where it is not likely any of your old friends will recognize you again.

> *Cross Country 1976*

2 I always wonder in the movies when the female star has to appear topless in a love scene and the male star is caressing her nipples, how the actress is supposed to remain professional. See, I don't think this would be expected of a man whose penis was being fondled.

> *My Left Breast 1994*

3529. Ann Oakley (1944–)

1 Being a "good" mother does not call for the same qualities as being a "good" housewife, and the pressure to be both at the same time may be an insupportable burden. Children may suffer, because the goal of housework may become the goals of child-care, and a dedication to keeping children clean and tidy may override an interest in their separate development as individuals.

> Ch. 5, *Woman's Work: The Housewife, Past and Present 1974*

2 The primary function of myth is to validate an existing social order. Myth enshrines conservative social values, raising tradition on a pedestal. It expresses and confirms, rather than explains or questions, the sources of cultural attitudes and values. . . . Because myth anchors the present in the past it is a sociological charter for a future society which is an exact replica of the present one.

> Ch. 7, Ibid.

3 Clearly, society has a tremendous stake in insisting on a woman's natural fitness for the career of mother: the alternatives are all too expensive.

> Ch. 8, Ibid.

4 Housework is work directly opposed to the possibility of human self-actualization.

> Ch. 9, Ibid.

5 Men are the enemies of women. Promising sublime intimacy, unequalled passion, amazing security and grace, they nevertheless exploit and injure in a myriad subtle ways. Without men the world would be a better place: softer, kinder, more loving; calmer, quieter, more humane.

> "A French Letter," *Taking It like a Woman 1984*

3530. Suzanne Osten (1944–)

1 Despair and humour are inseparable.

> "Creating Theatre with Lars Norén,"* *An Introduction to the Unga Klara Company 1993*

*(1944–) Swedish playwright, novelist, poet.

2 We at the theater always strive for clarity and always ask for clarification. . . . We keep fantasizing about the characters' lies and illusions. . . . We become like gluttons at a banquet from all the possibilities.

Ibid.

3531. Pat Parker (1944–1989)

1 If I close my eyes
  I can feel your tongue
  dart
  from my ear
  to my neck
  to the crevice
  a prospector
  pause to take samples
  inspect the ore
  then move on.

"aftermath," St. 2, Jonestown & Other Madness 1985

2 They will come in robes
  to rehabilitate
  and white coats
  to subjugate
  and where will you be
  when they come?

"Where Will You Be?" St. 5 (1978), The Woman That I Am,
The Literature and Culture of Contemporary Women of Color,
D. Soyini Madison, *ed. 1994

*See 3912.

3532. Julia Phillips (1944–2001)

1 Here's how I define the role of producer: the producer is there long before the shooting starts, and way after the shooting stops.

Quoted in American Film (New York) December 1975

2 It [filmmaking] has to be in your blood because three times a day you ask yourself why are you doing this. Especially when you've done it before and you know up front it's going to be pure torture. But if you love the screenplay, and the director and cast amplify it, then it's magic—and the rewards are fantastic.

Ibid.

3 Hollywood is a place that attracts people with massive holes in their souls.

Times (London) 3 April 1991

4 Her life was like running on a treadmill or riding on a stationary bike; it was aerobic, it was healthy, but she wasn't going anywhere.

You'll Never Eat Lunch in This Town Again 1991

3533. Arlene Raven (1944–2006)

1 In my view, the content of feminist art, and its deepest meaning, is consciousness: a woman's full awareness of herself as an entity, including her sensations, her emotions, and her thoughts—mind in its broadest sense.

"Woman's Art: The Development of a Theoretical
Perspective," Womanspace February/March 1973

2 An artist who shows us his/her world without this essential sense of optimism is without hope and without power: We can empathize with that art, but it cannot inspire in us the high level of human aspiration that we need to enrich ourselves, to grow, and to change.

Ibid.

3 Animals which are traditionally referred to as female include the cow, sow, bitch and cat—all derogatory words in our language when they are applied to human beings. English does not use gender extensively, but its linguistic sexism is intact because sexism is intact.

Ibid.

3534. Mandy Rice-Davies (1944–)

1 My life has been one long descent into respectability.*

Quoted by Lynn Barber Independent on Sunday (London) 31
March 1991

*In connection with 1963 reports that she was on social terms with Sir Denis Thatcher, husband of ex-prime minister Margaret Thatcher; see 2537.

3535. Janet Radcliffe Richards (1944–)

1 Slavery can be not only enforced unpaid labour, but also underpaid work into which people are coerced by the unfair power of other. This description can apply to a great number of women, especially housewives and even mothers: but it can also be extended to the situation of many others.

The Sceptical Feminist: A Philosophical Enquiry 1980

2 Some men are quite as capable of logical thinking and scientific investigation as women.

p. 41, Ibid.

3 But if you're so poor that you want to sell an eye, are we doing you a favour by refusing to let you so that you die of hunger instead? In fact, one of the things I've argued is that if people are so disgusted by it, then they'll realize how bad poverty is and do something about it. I mean, can you imagine how badly off you must be to want to sell an eye?
  But we don't think about such a thing as poverty because it doesn't disgust us in the same way taking an eye out does.

"Their pound of flesh" by Jacquie Charlton, The Front
(MontrealMirror.com) 23 July 1998

4 Technological progress is changing our existence at such a rate that every week seems to confront us with decisions about what to do in situations we have never encountered before. We try to apply our existing moral standards to them; and sometimes this works perfectly well. But increasingly, the advances are throwing up situations of such unfamiliarity that our normal standards seem of no help at all.

"The wrong moral autopilot," New Statesman (London) 20
November 2000

5 We hate this kind of thinking; but no state of any kind—religious or secular—can take the view that all life is beyond price; and in a secular state, trying to make the best of a morally unstructured universe, it is morally essential to address questions about the acceptable cost of saving any life.

Ibid.

3536. Michelle Zimbalist Rosaldo (1944–1981)

1 . . . women's status will be lowest in conditions of sharp segregation of domestic life from the public sphere of activity, and when women are isolated from each other in homes belonging to men.

Quoted in "Blueprints for inequality" by Joni Seager, The
Women's Review of Books, Vol. X, No. 4 January 1993

3537. Joyce Ellen Salisbury (1944–)

1 Things are never simple when paradigms shift and ideologies conflict. Martyrdom represents perhaps the most vivid moment in such a clash of cultures. During the early centuries of Christianity, individuals were willing to die, and die horribly, to bear witness to a new idea that was displacing an old one.
Introduction, *Perpetua's* Passion, The Death and Memory of a Young Roman Woman* 1997

*Vivia P—, see 99.

2 Even among modern dream analysts who allow for transcendent or even prophetic dreams, none whose works I have read share the ancient belief that dreams may originate from outside the dreaming psyche. Modern dreams originate within the dreamer.
Ch. 4, Ibid.

3538. Susan Polis Schutz (1944–)

1 We all hear the same sounds. We look up and see the same sky. We cry the same tears.
Introduction, *One World, One Heart* 2001

2 We need to give more
and take less
We need to share more
and own less
Untitled, St. 2, Ibid.

3 A mother tries to teach her daughter
to not be afraid to stick to her beliefs
to not follow the majority when the majority is wrong
to always realize that she is a woman equal to all men
Title poem, st. 4, *To My Daughter with Love on the Important Things in Life* 2007

3539. Judee Sill (1944–1979)

1 I heard the thunder come rumblin'
The light never looked so dim
I see the junction git nearer'
And danger is in the wind
And either road's lookin' grim
"Jesus Was a Cross Maker," St. 7, *Judee Sill* (album) 1971

2 While you sit and seek a crescent moon
Is layin' at your feet,
With hope that's made of sand,
You don't think you can
But you have held it all in your hand
Lady-O.
"Lady-O," Ibid.

3 Come on, the light is gone
Hope's slowly dyin'
Tell me how you come ridin' through
Gainin' steady till this round is won
On the long and lonely road to kingdom come
"There's A Rugged Road," St. 3, *Heart Food* (album) 1972

3540. Lee Smith (1944–)

1 I hate all this active-listening shit. Ever since they learned it last year in that class, you can't have a decent conversation with them. If you ever could. But now I mean you come home from school really pissed, and they say something like, "Gee, son, you're very angry!" and then if you say "Well, yes, I am pretty goddamn angry," they say "Yes! Yes, you are! I can tell you're angry!" and that's it.
Family Linen 1985

2 I am like the ruby-throated hummingbird that comes again again and again to Fannie's red rosebush but lights down never for good and all, always flying on. And it is true that often I feel so lonesome for all of them that are gone.
On Agate Hill 2006

3 The things that people really want are the most like to kill them, it seems to me, such as war and babys. [sic]
Ibid.

3541. Robyn Smith (1944–)

1 Don't ever call me a jockette.
Quoted in "Sportswomanlike Conduct," *Newsweek* 3 June 1974

3542. Natalie J. Sokoloff (1944–)

1 Prisons are a wasteland, places of punishment, degradation and disempowerment; warehouses for the poor, minorities, the disadvantaged, the disenfranchised. Above all, prisons don't stop crime.
"In the criminal injustice system," *The Women's Review of Books*, Vol. XIV, No. 1, p. 19 October 1996

2 The frequent use of the term "illegals" in our public dialogues today, in fact, summons up an image that conflates the civil infraction of entering the country without documents with a more serious infraction of criminal law.
"Locking up Hope: Immigration, Gender, and the Prison System" coauthored with Susan C. Pearce,* *The Scholar & Feminist Online*, Issue #6.3 (barnard.edu/sfonline) *Summer 2008*

*See 4387.

3 The roundup and jailing of immigrant mothers who are at work, and their removal to prisons far away from their children and their homes, is a situation of terrible trauma all the way around. We must be aware of both the immigrant and non-immigrant children whose mothers have been ripped from their lives—sometimes without any notice and with tragic consequences.
Ibid.

3543. Leonore Tiefer (1944–)

1 At the dawn of transgender studies, it behooves those of us in all of our categories to practice the respect for diversity we preach.
"Forced choices," *The Women's Review of Books,* vol. 16, no. 2 *November 1998*

2 Over just a few decades, linkages thought to be fixed for all time were severed and then crushed by the weight of literature, history and social science.
Pills separated sex from reproduction. Women's studies separated sex from gender. Technology eliminated any fixed notion of reproduction, while gay studies and gender studies exploded the meaning of gender. The natural desire of the sexes for each other evaporated under close inspection.
Ibid.

3544. Amaryllis Tigalo Torres (1944?–)

1 The decision of the American government to educate the Filipino masses was not an act of magnanimity. Education was correctly perceived to be the most effective way to pacify the nation.

> Essay, Quoted in *The Politics of Women's Education: Perspectives from Asia, Africa, and Latin America* by Jill Ker Conway and Susan C. Bourque *1993*

2 [Education should transmit] concepts, perspectives, and skills that respond to the needs of people for good-paying and self-fulfilling jobs, for democratic processes, and for peace and security in their daily lives.

> Ibid.

3545. Emily Toth (1944–)

1 A Ph.D., Ms. Mentor declares, should be pursued only by those who love what they are doing. They should burn with curiosity and wonder; they should delight in discovering new things. Otherwise the graduate school apprenticeship is too long, and the required studies often dreary.

> "Graduate School: The Rite of Passage," *Ms. Mentor's Impeccable Advice for Women in Academia 1997*

2 Ms. Mentor has always been intrigued by the idea that one needs "balls" in order to do anything other than the work for which they were intended—I.e., the propagation of our species and the recreational pleasures of the bearer thereof.

> Ibid.

3546. Alma Villanueva (1944–)

1 Who is this woman with
words dangling from
the ends of her
hair? leaping
out from her
eyes? dripping
from her
breasts? seeping
from her
hands?

> Untitled, *Bloodroot ca. 1977*

2 *Oh, the summer was beautiful in spite of the fog, death, lack of her own bed, a pillow to fit her head, food. There was still color everywhere, sprayed randomly by the feeble city sun. And she was still free to roam, like a boy, on her bike.*

> Ch. 1, *Naked Ladies 1994*

3 I figure if I don't pray to him he'll kinda leave me alone and not punish me for the stupid things I have to do some times like steal stuff to eat like the phoney ham with El Diablo on it kinda a joke of mine, like El Diablo doesn't scre me on the front of the pham, like hes kinda telling me You hungry kid? Well go to Hell with me and hes sort of dancing, kinda having a good time, well hes not hungry. Hes on the pham can right? (phony ham = PHAM, *my new word* cool!)

> Ch. 1, *Luna's California Poppies 2002*

3547. Alice Walker (1944–)

1 How to teach a barren world to dance? It is a contradiction that divides the world.

> "The Diary of an African Nun," *Freedomways Summer 1968*

2 Be nobody's darling;
Be an outcast

> "Be Nobody's Darling," *Revolutionary Petunias and Other Poems 1973*

3 But evil all over her today. She smile, like a razor opening.

> Letter 27, *The Color Purple 1982*

4 Anyhow, I say, the God I been praying and writing to is a man. And act just like all the other mens I know. Trifling, forgitful, and lowdown.

> Letter 73, Ibid.

5 She says, Celie, tell the truth, have you ever found God in church? I never did. I just found a bunch of folks hoping for him to show. Any God I ever felt in church I brought in with me. And I think all the other folks did too. They come to church to share God, not to find God.

> Ibid.

6 Yeah, It. God ain't a he or a she, but a It.
But what do it look like? I ast.
Don't look like nothing, she say. It ain't a picture show. It ain't something you can look at apart from anything else, including yourself. I believe God is everything, say Shug. Everything that is or ever was or ever will be. And when you can feel that, and be happy to feel that, you've found it.

> Ibid.

7 It [marijuana] just like whiskey, I say. You got to stay ahead of it. You know a little drink now and then never hurt nobody, but when you can't git started without asking the bottle, you in trouble.
You smoke it much, Miss Celie? Harpo ast.
Do I look like a fool? I ast. I smoke when I want to talk to God. I smoke when I want to make love. Lately I feel like me and God make love just fine anyhow. Whether I smoke reefer or not.

> Letter 78, Ibid.

8 I believe that the truth about any subject only comes when all sides of the story are put together, and all their different meanings make one new one. Each writer writes the missing parts to the other writer's story. And the whole story is what I'm after.

> *In Search of Our Mothers' Gardens: Womanist Prose 1983*

9 Black women are called, in the folklore that so aptly identifies one's status in society, "the *mule* of the world," because we have been handed the burdens that everyone else—*everyone else*—refused to carry.

> "In Search of Our Mothers' Gardens," Ibid.

10 Guided by my heritage of a love of beauty and a respect for strength—in search of my mother's garden, I found my own.

> Ibid.

11 Anybody can observe the Sabbath, but making it holy surely takes the rest of the week.

> Letter to the Editor, *Ms. August 1974*

12 As for those who think the Arab world promises freedom, the briefest study of its routine traditional treatment of blacks (slavery) and women (purdah) will provide relief from all illusion. If Malcolm X* had been a black woman his last message to the world would have been entirely different. The brotherhood of Moslem men—all colors—may exist there, but part of

the glue that holds them together is the thorough suppression of women.

Ibid.

*African-American leader; née Little, (1925–65); assassinated; founder, Organization for Afro-American Unity, 1964.

13 ... the reasons millions of Africans are exterminating themselves in wars is that the superpowers have enormous stores of outdated weapons to be got rid of.

The Temple of My Familiar 1989

14 She was soon meditating and masturbating and finding herself dissolved into the cosmic All. Delicious.

Ibid.

15 The Secret of Joy ... is Resistance.

Possessing the Secret of Joy 1992

16 No one could wish for a more advantageous heritage than that bequeathed to the black writer in the South: a compassion for the earth, a trust in humanity beyond our knowledge of evil, and abiding love of justice. We inherit a great responsibility ... for we must give voice to centuries not only of silent bitterness and hate but also of neighborly kindness and sustaining love.

(p. 104), Quoted in *Everyday Use* by Barbara T. Christian *1994*

17 A person's work is her only signature; we forget this at our peril. It is to the work and the life we must turn.

"How Long Shall They Torture Our Mothers? The Trials of Winnie Mandela,"* *Anything We Love Can Be Saved: A Writer's Activism 1997*

*See 2905.

3548. Alice Waters (1944–)

1 I wanted a café to hang out in, in the afternoon, and I wanted civilized meals, and I wanted to wear French clothes. The cultural experience, that aesthetic, that paying attention to every little detail—I wanted to live my life like that.

Quoted in *Alice Water, Chez Panisse* by Thomas McNamee *2007*

2 Remember when Kennedy* put physical fitness in schools? We had to exercise four times a week, and we all went for it. We need that kind of passion. Going into public schools and teaching [children] about the consequences of the food that they eat can have remarkable results.**

Quoted in "Heroes of the Environment: Alice Waters" by Joel Stein, *Time 2008*

*John F. Kennedy (1917–63), 35th president of the United States; assassinated. **Re: her Edible Schoolyard project.

3 We need a President to speak about the issues of food, nourishment and stewardship, and I have great hope that will happen.

Ibid.

3549. Brita Westergaard (1944?–)

1 We are not just changing Norway.* When people realize that this is possible in the Cabinet of one country, they must realize it is possible everywhere.

Quoted in "An Experiment in Woman Power" by Michael S. Serrill, *Time* (New York) 6 October 1986

*Re stunning increase in the number of women selected to serve on the Norwegian Cabinet by Gro Brundtland; see 3129.

3550. Joy Williams (1944–)

1 Compost was as munificent as God to them, just as interesting as God certainly. They said that the reason healthy plants repel pests is that they have such intense vibrations in the molecules of their cells. The higher the state of health, the higher the vibrations. Because pests' vibrations are on a much lower level, they receive a distinct shock when they come into contact with a healthy plant.

Ch. 1, *The Quick and the Dead 2000*

2 The desert knew no drought, really. Anything so habitual and prolonged was simply life—a life invisible and anticipatory.

Ibid.

3 You don't believe in Nature anymore. It's too isolated from you. You've abstracted it. It's so messy and damaged and sad. Your eyes glaze as you travel life's highway past all the crushed animals and the Big Gulp cups.

"Save the Whales, Screw the Shrimp" 1, *Ill Nature 2001*

4 This is the time of machines and models, hands-on managements and master plans. Don't you ever wonder as you pass that billboard advertising another MASTER PLANNED COMMUNITY just what master they are actually talking about?

Ibid.

5 Sharks move boneless from the sea light into the darkness of our worst imaginings. And as the impossible terminus, as the inconceivable hazard, they slip from our dreams into the sea.

"Sharks and Suicide" 93, Ibid.

3551–3552. Sherley Anne Williams (1944–1999)

1 "Oh, we have paid for our children's place in the world again, and again...."

Dessa Rose 1986

2 The buildings of the
Projects were arrayed
like barracks in
uniform rows we
called regulation
ugly, the World in
less than one square block.

"The Iconography of Childhood," v, St. 1 (1983), *The Woman That I Am, The Literature and Culture of Contemporary Women of Color*, D. Soyini Madison,* ed. *1994*

*See 3912.

3553. Ruth Ann Anderson (1945?–)

1 I have never really abandoned my childhood goal of missionary work. Only, my guidebook isn't the Bible anymore.

Quoted in "Ruth Ann Anderson," *Exposures, Women & Their Art* by Ann Brown and Arlene Raven* *1989*

*See 3020.

2 Being a social worker and being a Christian are not necessarily compatible. Social work has a wider view of the world, it draws from several different disciplines and sees society as the dominant factor in personality. Prior to that, I believed God was the all determining factor.

Ibid.

3 When I first started [in the Women's Spirituality Movement], I saw the word "goddess" as being a metaphor for nature. I think now it's more an understanding of a feminine energy that

I would qualify as nurturing and powerful and also terrifying in her destructive aspects—all the elements of the universe in a very powerful feminine entity who has a thousand ways of being manifested.

Ibid.

3554. Aung San Suu Kyi (1945–)

1 "We must make democracy the popular creed. . . . If we should fail to do this, our people are bound to suffer. . . ." That is what my father* said. It is the reason why I am participating in this struggle.

Speech (August 1988),** Quoted in *Twentieth-Century Women Political Leaders* by Claire Price-Groff *1998*
*General Aung San activist and hero (d. 1947; assassinated.)
**The Shwedagon Pagoda protests in August 1988 during which 3,000 protesters were killed.

2 Let the world know that under this administration the Burmese people are like prisoners in their own homes.

Letter to various political parties, Quoted in *Time 31 July 1989*

3 It must be very exhausting for them [the government] to go on lying.

Interview,* "Democracy leader vows never to leave Burma" by Phillip Shenon (14 February 1994), *Seattle Post-Intelligencer*, A2 *15 February 1994*
*This was her first opportunity to speak publicly since her house arrest in 1989.

4 I only ask one thing: that should my people need me, you would help me do my duty by them.

Letter to Michael Aris, her future husband, quoted in *Twentieth-Century Women Political Leaders* by Claire Price-Groff *1998*

5 You should not let your fears prevent you from doing what you know is right. Not that you shouldn't be afraid. Fear is normal. But to be inhibited from doing what you know is right, that is what is dangerous. You should be able to lead your life in the right way—despite your fears.

Speech (August 1988),* Ibid.
*The Shwedagon Pagoda protests in August 1988 during which 3,000 protesters were killed.

6 It is not enough to simply "live and let live." Genuine tolerance requires an active effort to try to understand the point of view of others.

Ibid.

3555. Doris Baizley (1945–)

1 DOT. This isn't a contest I'm in up here, it's every day of my life and I'm so damned good at it I can't stop.

Mrs. California 1986

2 MEG. Being me is no hobby.

Shiloh Rules 2001

3556. Jennifer M. Belcher (1945?–)

1 We continue to consume more than our natural systems can replace, and the result is a downward spiral in the health of our natural world and in our quality of life.

If current trends continue, our descendants will live in a state that will be unrecognizable to us.

"Changing Our Water Ways: Trends in Washington's Water Systems" *2001*

2 These trends (of ecodamage) can be reversed. To succeed, we must recognize that our [current] ways of managing our natural resources are all better suited to the last century than to the new one we've just begun.

Ibid.

3 I don't pick fights. I just try to enforce the law.

"DNR and Live-aboards Are Locked in Tug of War," *Seattle Post-Intelligencer 15 April 2000*

4 I'm never quite sure whether the public pushes or the public follows, but they certainly take their cues from the active organizations like the environmental groups. They take their cues from politicians who are leaders, they take their cues from the Governor.

Quoted in Interview by Rita R. Robison, secstate.wa.gov/oralhistory *11 August 2005*

5 If you don't have water, you can't build. And if you can't guarantee that you have water you shouldn't be able to build.

Ibid.

3557. Francine M. Benes (1945?–)

1 Understanding the chemistry of cells in diseased regions of the brain . . . can help scientists determine what went wrong, and develop diagnostic tests and treatments.

Quoted in "Brain banks: Crucial for research, clamouring for donors" by Gloria Troyer, *CBC News 22 September 2008*

2 Stem cell research will lead us to new forms of therapy that can be applied early in the course of the illness and prevent its progression. We can only dream about such therapies right now, but they will become a reality in the future.

Ibid.

3 All of the drugs that we use now in psychiatry have been discovered by accident. We have no theoretical basis for any of our pharmacologic treatments, whether they be antipsychotics, antidepressants, mood stabilizers, or anxiolytics. It's incredible that our patients have done as well as they have.

Ibid.

3558. Victoria Billings (1945–)

1 Whether he admits it or not, a man has been brought up to look at money as a sign of his virility, a symbol of his power, a bigger phallic symbol than a Porsche.

"Getting It Together," *The Womansbook 1974*

2 The best thing that could happen to motherhood already has. Fewer women are going into it.

"Meeting Your Personal Needs," Ibid.

3 Constant togetherness is fine—but only for Siamese twins.

"A Love to Believe In," Ibid.

4 Rape is a culturally fostered means of suppressing women. Legally we say we deplore it, but mythically we romanticize and perpetuate it, and privately we excuse and overlook it. . . .

"Sex: We Need Another Revolution," Ibid.

3559. Janis Lynn Birkeland (1945–   )

1 Because it is identified with the "feminine," nature is regarded as existing to serve Man's physical needs (and the reverse). This association of nature and women in Patriarchal societies underwrites instrumentalism, whereby things are valued only to the extent that they are useful to Man.

> Essay, *Ecofeminism: Women, Animals, Nature*, Greta Gaard, ed. *1993*

2 [Ecofeminism is] about changing from a morality based on "power over" to one based on reciprocity and responsibility ("power to").

> Ibid.

3560. Wendy Mary Cope (1945–   )

1 I'm aiming by the time I'm fifty to stop being an adolescent.

> Quoted in *Daily Telegraph* (London) *9 December 1992*

2 Bloody men are like bloody buses—
You wait for about a year
And as soon as one approaches your stop
Two or three others appear.

> "Bloody Men," *Serious Concerns 1992*

3561. Lucha Corpi (1945–   )

1 Steeped in tradition, mystic
and mute she was sold—
from hand to hand, night to night,
denied and desecrated, waiting for the dawn
and for the owl's song

> "Marina,"* I. Marina Mother, St. 2 (1976), *The Woman That I Am, The Literature and Culture of Contemporary Women of Color*, D. Soyini Madison,** ed. *1994*
> *Doña Marina, also known as La Malinche, was an Aztec noblewoman given to Spanish explorer Hernán Cortés upon his landing in Veracruz, Mexico. Her Indian name, Malinche, is synonymous in Mexico with treachery and betrayal. **See 3912.

2 a promise of milk in her breasts,
vanilla scent in her hair
cinnamon flavor in her eyes,
cocoa-flower between her legs

> "Dark Romance," St. 4 (1978), Ibid.

3562. Sharon Creech (1945–   )

1 Gramps says that I am a country girl at heart, and that is true. I have lived most of my thirteen years in Bybanks, Kentucky, which is not much more than a caboodle of houses roosting in a green spot alongside the Ohio River. Just over a year ago, my father plucked me up like a weed and took me and all our belongings (no, that is not true—he did not bring the chestnut tree, the willow, the maple, the hayloft, or the swimming hole, which all belonged to me) and we drove three hundred miles straight north and stopped in front of a house in Euclid, Ohio.

> *Walk Two Moons 1994*

2 Life is a bowl of spaghetti. Every now and then you get a meatball.

> *Chasing Redbird 1997*

3 Although . . . my uncle Bill
who is a teacher
in a college
said those words I wrote
about Sky

were NOT poems.
He said they were just
words
coming
out
of
my
head
and that a poem has to rhyme
and have regular meter
and SYMBOLS and METAPHORS
and onomoto-something and
alliter-something.

> *Hate That Cat 2008*

3563. Annie Dillard (1945–   )

1 We wake, if we ever wake at all, to mystery, rumors of death, beauty, violence.

> Ch. 1, *Pilgrim at Tinker Creek 1974*

2 Every live thing is a survivor on a kind of extended emergency bivouac.

> Ibid.

3 The world's spiritual geniuses seem to discover universally that the mind's muddy river, this ceaseless flow of trivia and trash, cannot be dammed, and that trying to dam it is a waste of effort that might lead to madness.

> Ch. 2, Ibid.

4 The secret of seeing is to sail on solar wind. Hone and spread your spirit till you yourself are a sail, whetted, translucent, broadside to the merest puff.

> Ibid.

5 Somewhere, and I can't find where, I read about an Eskimo hunter who asked the local missionary priest, "If I did not know about God and sin, would I go to hell?" "No," said the priest, "not if you did not know." "Then why," asked the Eskimo earnestly, "did you tell me?"

> Ch. 7, Ibid.

6 Every day is a god, each day is a god, and holiness holds forth in time.

> Pt. I, *Holy the Firm 1977*

7 Feeding our mother lines, we were training as straight men. The straight man's was an honorable calling, a bit like that of the rodeo clown: despised by the ignorant masses, perhaps, but revered among experts who understood the skills required and the risks run. We children mastered the deliberate misunderstanding, the planted pun, the Gracie Allen remark that can make of any interlocutor an instant hero.

> *An American Childhood 1987*

8 Write as if you were dying. At the same time, assume you write for an audience consisting solely of terminal patients. That is, after all, the case. What would you begin writing if you knew you would die soon? What could you say to a dying person that would not enrage by its triviality?

> "Write Till You Drop," *The New York Times 28 May 1989*

9 One of the few things I know about writing is this: spend it all, shoot it, play it, lose it, all, right away, every time. Do not hoard what seems good for a later place in the book, or for another book; give it, give it all, give it now.

> Ibid.

10 When I switched from poetry to prose, it was like switching from a single reed instrument to a full orchestra. I thought: 'My God, you can do everything with this stuff. You can do everything you do with poetry, and more besides.'

> Quoted in "A Pilgrim's Progress" by Mary Cantwell, *The New York Times 26 April 1992*

11 Why are we reading, if not in hope of beauty laid bare, life heightened and its deepest mystery probed? Can the writer isolate and vivify all in experience that most deeply engages our intellects and our hearts?

> *The Writing Life 1999*

12 Falling in love, like having a baby, rubs against the current of our lives: separation, loss and death. That is the joy of them.

> *The Maytrees 2007*

13 Only the lover sees what is real, he thought. . . . Far from being blind, love alone can see.

> Ibid.

3564. Jacqueline Du Pré (1945–1987)

1 Water overflows from the gutter down one's neck and the beautiful brilliant sunshine and the blue, blue sky which go with the intense cold have given way to the grayness of the undecided season. Everyone waits, longs for the first glimpse of fresh green and from then on there will be no looking back.

> Letter to her friend, Madeleine Dinkel, Quoted in *Jacqueline du Pré: Her Life, Her Music, Her Legend* by Elizabeth Wilson* *1999*
>
> *See 3014.

2 [Mstislav Rostropovich]* has spent most of his time digging away at the hysteria and extravagance which are so firmly rooted in my playing.

> Ibid.
>
> *Her teacher in Moscow.

3565. Katherine "Karen" Dunn (1945–)

1 "When your mama was the geek, my dreamlets," Papa would say, "she made the nipping off of noggins such a crystal mystery that the hens themselves yearned toward her, waltzing around her, hypnotized with longing. 'Spread your lips, sweet Lil,' they'd cluck, 'and show us your choppers!'"

This same Crystal Lil, our tar-haired mama, sitting snug on the built-in sofa that was Arty's bed at night, would chuckle at the sewing in her lap and shake her head. "Don't piffle to the children, Al. Those hens ran like whiteheads."

> Ch. 1, *Geek Love 1989*

2 Miss Lick's purpose is to liberate women who are liable to be exploited by male hungers. The exploitable women are, in Miss Lick's view, the pretty ones. She feels great pity for them. . . . If all these pretty women could shed the traits that made men want them (their prettiness) then they would no longer depend on their own exploitability but would use their talents and intelligence to become powerful.

> Ch. 12, Ibid.

3 ". . . Isolation is a standard cult technique but I don't use it. It's standard procedure to get the poor buggers in a low moment, hustle them off to the boonies, and surround them with a strong-arm/soft-spiel combo. . . .

"As it is, I don't need all that crap. For what I've got to say, the more exposure the folks have to the outside world, the better. Feed 'em newspapers, TV, world reports. Tell 'em about terrorist attacks, mass murders, disease, divorce, crooked politicians, pollution, war and rumors of war! Then go ahead and tell 'em that only fools and half-wits join my outfit. The first half of the news cancels out that particular message. Let the relatives and lovers loose on 'em. All they can stand. Because it's the world that drives them to me. You news guys are my allies."

> Ch. 19, Ibid.

3566. Alice Embree (1945?–)

1 Shortly after the turn of the century, America marshaled her resources, contracted painfully, and gave birth to the New Technology. The father was a Corporation, and the New Technology grew up in the Corporate image.

> "Media Images I: Madison Avenue Brainwashing—The Facts," *Sisterhood Is Powerful*, Robin Morgan,* ed. *1970*
>
> *See 3284.

2 Humans must breathe, but corporations must make money.

> Ibid.

3 The message of the media is the commercial.

> Ibid.

4 America's technology has turned in upon itself; its corporate form makes it the servant of profits, not the servant of human needs.

> Ibid.

3567. Clarissa Pinkola Estés (1945–)

1 Intuition is the treasure of a woman's psyche.

> Ch. 2, *Women Who Run With the Wolves 1992*

2 Many women are in recovery from their "Nice-Nice" complexes, wherein, no matter how they felt, no matter who assailed them, they responded so sweetly as to be practically fattening.

> Ibid.

3 . . . at bottom is where the living roots of psyche are. It is there that a woman's wild underpinnings are. At bottom is the best soil to sow and grow something new again. In that sense, hitting bottom, while extremely painful, is also the sowing ground.

> Ch. 8, Ibid.

4 If we could realize that the work is to keep doing the work, we would be much more fierce and much more peaceful.

> Ibid.

5 Creativity is not a solitary movement. That is its power. Whatever is touched by it, whoever hears it, sees it, senses it, knows it, is fed. That is why beholding someone else's creative word, image, idea, fills us up, inspires us to our own creative work. A single creative act has the potential to feed a continent. One creative act can cause a torrent to break through tone.

> Ch. 10, Ibid.

6 Remember, if logic were all there really was to the world, then surely all men would ride sidesaddle.

> Ibid.

7 Art is not meant to be created in stolen moments only.

> Ibid.

8 Women across the world—your mother, my mother, you and I, your sister, your friend, our daughters, all the tribes of women not yet met—we all dream what is lost, what next must rise from the unconscious. We all dream the same dreams world-wide. We are never without the map. We are never without each other. We unite through our dreams.

Ch. 15, Ibid.

9 The stories are medicine. The storyteller is the medicine maker, is the physician of the soul.
"Stories that heal the soul" by Bo Emerson (Cox), *Seattle Post-Intelligencer*, C2 *1992*

10 There are not two 'm's to governing, as many PolySci courses have taught: 'Money and Management.' There are three m's. The third one is Mercy. The third "M" constitutes the difference between a country and a corporation.
Testimony, Federal Ways and Means Committee on Social Programs (Washington, D.C.) *1996*

11 We are all *los immigrantes,* the Soul is The First Immigrant: The Soul cannot be held back by any imaginary boundary drawn against it; not by mountain ranges, not by rivers, nor by human scorn. The Soul, goes everywhere, like an old woman in her right mind, going anywhere she wishes, saying whatever she wants, bending to mend whatever is within her reach. Wherever she goes, the Soul brings new life.
The Dangerous Old Woman 2008

3568. Michèle Fabien (1945–1999)

1 JOCASTA. One does not gaze upon one's mother when she is a woman. One does not gaze upon a woman when she is one's mother.
Sc. 5, *Jocasta*, Richard Miller, tr. *1981*

3569. Abla Farhoud (1945–)

1 AMIRA. In the village, there was a woman who could take anything . . . poverty, misery, anything. She'd raised about ten kids. She took everything as it came, never complained. She didn't even mind being beaten. She just smiled. But one day, a day like any other when her husband was about to beat her, she snuck into the kitchen and grabbed a butcher knife. She looked her husband straight in the eye and said, "No, not one more time, not ever again."
The Girls from the Five and Ten, Jill MacDougall, tr. *1986*

3570. Shulamith Firestone (1945–)

1 A man is allowed to blaspheme the world because it belongs to him to damn.
The Dialectic of Sex 1970

2 I submit that women's history has been hushed up for the same reasons that black history has been hushed up . . . and that is that a feminist movement poses a direct threat to the establishment. From the beginning it exposes the hypocrisy of the male power structure.
Ch. 2, Ibid.

3 The bar is the male kingdom. For centuries it was the bastion of male privilege, the gathering place for men away from their women, a place where men could go to freely indulge in The Bull Session . . . a serious political function: the release of the guilty anxiety of the oppressor class.
"The Bar as Microcosm," *Voices for Women's Liberation*, Leslie B. Tanner, ed. *1970*

3571. Doris Ann Foster (1945/55–)

1 I've put life in one hand and death in the other and weighed the two. To me, death is my only route to freedom.
"I Want to Die," *Time* (New York) *24 January 1983*

2 I'm dying slowly. I need to feel the earth under my feet. This place resembles a tomb. I'm sealed away from the things that make living living. I need fresh air and space to move. I often ask the guards to bring me a cup of fresh air. . . .
Letter to Beth Brant* (6 January 1983), *A Gathering of Spirit*, Beth Brant, ed. *1984*
*See 3246.

3 Many Christians write [to me], but I do not believe the way they do. They are really weird sometimes. I usually ignore them. They only want to save my soul. I need to save my life.
(26 January 1983), Ibid.

4 Death row is a state of mind.
Quoted in *Times* (London) *31 August 1984*

3572. Jo Freeman (1945–)

1 Bitches are aggressive, assertive, domineering, overbearing, strong-minded, spiteful, hostile, direct, blunt, candid, obnoxious, thick-skinned, hard-headed, vicious, dogmatic, competent, competitive, pushy, loud-mouthed, independent, stubborn, demanding, manipulative, egoistic, driven, achieving, overwhelming, threatening, scary, ambitious, tough, brassy, masculine, boisterous and turbulent. . . . A Bitch takes shit from no one. You may not like her, but you cannot ignore her.
The Bitch Manifesto 1969?

2 The mythology that women are inferior and need to be protected by men went out with the mythology about the superiority of the Aryan race.
"The 51 Percent Minority Group," *The Voice of the Women's Liberation Movement* (newsletter) *1960s*

3 Trashing is a particularly vicious form of character assassination which amounts to psychological rape. It is manipulative, dishonest, and excessive. It is occasionally disguised by the rhetoric of honest conflict, or covered up by denying that any disapproval exists at all. But it is not done to expose disagreements or resolve differences. It is done to disparage and destroy.
"Trashing: The Dark Side of Sisterhood," *Ms.* (New York) *April 1976*

4 Sometimes myth becomes history.
Introduction, Ibid.

5 Long before women could vote they ran for public office, including the highest office—the Presidency of the United States. They ran for the same reasons that men run who don't have a chance: because a Presidential candidacy is a great platform from which to talk about issues and sometimes just to talk about yourself.
Ch. 6, *We Will Be Heard: Women's Struggles for Political Power in the United States 2008*

3573. Helen Fremont (1945?–)

1 I had been living my life with flawed vision, stumbling in the dark, bumping into things I hadn't realized were there. No one

acknowledged anything. Yet each time I walked into my parents' house, I fell over something, or dropped into something, a cavernous silence, an unspoken, invisible danger.

After Long Silence 1998

2 Perhaps the war had not changed them so much as selected their strengths, reinforced them and made them rigid. Their secret was their armor, but it was a mask of silence imposed on all of us.

Ibid.

3574. Laura Furman (1945–)

1 My own mother might have wished nothing more than for me to have a real second mother, but out of loyalty to her I didn't acknowledge even to myself for decades that I wanted a mother. *I had a mother,* I would say fiercely if anyone suggested that this or that might betoken a search for a mother.*

Ordinary Paradise 1998

*Her mother died at age 46 of cancer when Furman was 13.

2 It is true for every adult that we must learn to be our own best parent. Long after I was finished with my stay at the [psychiatric] hospital, I still waited for the adults around me—at home, in school, on the job—to be good parents at last. The waiting retarded my maturing and perpetuated that twilight of my childhood far too long.

Ibid.

3575. Jennifer Greene (1945–)

1 Water, in a very deep way, is a women's issue. It is vital to the role women play in caring for their families. Women bathe and nourish their young, often tend the crops, and are the keepers of the waters. When fetching potable water requires distance, there is less time for the family and abject poverty and disease result.

"Our Model for the Future," *World Pulse Magazine* (worldpulsemagazine.com) *21 March 2008*

2 . . . outward activism arises out of a charged stillness within. Here, in active listening into a situation or condition, we hear and see what to do.

Ibid.

3 Water that is allowed to move according to its own nature cleanses itself and sustains life. This is our model for the future. If water is not allowed to move and change and be open to organizing principles, if it becomes stagnant, then it becomes dead. . . . when water moves freely, it is answered by a system of organic forms, movements and rhythms—an integrated system of life processes and substances that allows water to mediate all life needs in order to exist on earth.

Ibid.

3576. Janet Hamill (1945–)

1 Soaring wings over choppy waters. Away from this world/
the genie of the alphabet rises out of the typewriter/
with his rosary of fire. Twenty-six beads of blood for twenty-six/
letters. To fly in the face of finitude.

"Lost Ceilings," *Lost Ceilings 1999*

2 Standing by a body of water. Moving or/
standing still. In the dark green depths my soul/
finds its own level

"Body of Water," St. 1, *Body of Water 2008*

3 Will she learn to dance with her head brushing the clouds/
and her feet patterning figure eights in clover?

"Nine Card Spread," Ibid.

3577. Goldie Hawn (1945–)

1 I do have this quality that is very childlike. But how long can it last? How long can you be cute?

Quoted in "The 1960's to the 1980's," *Women in Comedy* by Linda Martin & Kerry Segrave *1986*

2 I don't want to be a star! I just want to get married.

Ibid.

3 I never looked at myself as a nitwit. I never looked at anything I did as vacant or dumb or bubble-headed. There was always a sensibility about what I did. Because someone is hopeful, because someone likes to have fun, because someone is trusting and open, does not necessarily mean that someone is stupid.

Ibid.

3578. Lesley Hazleton (1945–)

1 Some say that a writer's life is a permanent vacation.

"Floating World," *The Women's Review of Books,* Vol. XII, Nos. 10–11 *July 1995*

2 Binoculars and a bird book sit on one corner of my desk, because what work could be more important than watching a pair of trumpeter swans swim up the channel out of the early morning mist?

Ibid.

3 There was a fine romance to this: the very American romance of taking to the road. For if the history of the United States is one of settlement, its romance is one of abandoning the settled life.

Driving to Detroit: An Automotive Odyssey 1998

4 Outside, my white horse was in fact red, and had wheels instead of legs.* But it was a magnificent steed, the kind that drew quiet nods of appreciation from exactly the kind of young men who might otherwise give me trouble, which was partly why I'd chosen it.

Ibid.

*Re her 1998 red Ford Expedition 4×4.

3579. Carter Heyward (1945–)

1 I'm a priest, not a priestess. . . . "Priestess" implies mumbo jumbo and all sorts of pagan goings-on. Those who oppose us would love to call us priestesses. They can call us all the names in the world—it's better than being invisible.

Quoted in "Who's Afraid of Women Priests?" by Malcolm Boyd, *Ms.* (New York) *December 1974*

2 It's obvious throughout secular and church history that significant legislation follows only after dramatic action.

Ibid.

3 As we come to experience the erotic as sacred, we begin to know ourselves as holy and to imagine ourselves sharing in the creation of one another and of our common well-being.

Touching Our Strength 1989

4 Openly lesbian women are dangerous to heterosexist patriarchy because, whether or not it is our intention, our visibility

signals an erotic energy that has gotten out of control—out of men's control.

> "The Erotic As Sacred Power," *Coming Out and Relational Empowerment: A Lesbian Feminist Theological Perspective* 1989

3580. Dianne Highbridge (1945–   )

1   . . . [to know] what it is to be irrevocably other, and to be able to call it, most of the time, peace.

> *In the Empire of Dreams* 1999

2   . . . fumbling for the right words in a language made for not explaining . . . still hopefully clapping hands before the shrines of gods who will never know them but whose indifference itself seems sweet.

> Ibid.

3581. Eva Hoffman (1945–   )

1   [History] tends to dissolve as you get closer, to fragment into a billion bits of ordinariness.

> *Exit Into History, A Journey Through the New Eastern Europe* 1993

2   We in the West . . . should be careful of judging whole societies that have survived an epoch when to act morally often involved not only the risk of death, but also the risk of torture.

> Ibid.

3   . . . [Jews] are the specter haunting Eastern Europe these days . . . an absence that is itself felt as a presence, a wrongness. . . . Perhaps, if we don't always have a conscious conscience, we have a subliminal one, from which the memory of past wrongs is not so easily erased.

> Ibid.

4   Every immigrant becomes a kind of amateur anthropologist.

> Quoted by Andrew Brown in *Guardian Unlimited* (London) 28 April 2001

3582. Nancy R. Hooyman (1945–   )

1   As we age, we pass through a sequence of defined stages, each with its own social norms and characteristics. In sum, age is a social construct with social meanings and social implications.

> Ch. 1, *Social Gerontology: A Multidisciplinary Perspective*, coauthor, H. Asuman Kiyak* 2007

*See 4054.

2   The attempts to discover a substance to rejuvenate the body and mind have driven explorers to far corners of the globe, and have inspired alchemists and scientists to search for a way to restore youth and extend life.

> Ibid.

Also see Mary Bricker-Jenkins, 3326: 1–3.

3583. Lynn Hunt (1945–   )

1   Revolutionary language did not simply reflect the realities of revolutionary changes and conflicts, but rather was itself transformed into an instrument of political and social change. . . . The language itself helped shape the perception of interests and hence the development of ideologies.

> *Politics, Culture, and Class in the French Revolution* 1984

2   Revolutionaries placed such emphasis on the ritual use of words because they were seeking a replacement for the charisma of kingship.

> Ibid.

3   Every great interpreter of the French Revolution—and there have been many such—has found the event ultimately mystifying.

> Presidential Address, 117th Annual Meeting of the American Historical Assoc. (Chicago) *3 January 2003*

4   Voluntarism—the idea that humans could shape their future—and determinism were two faces of the same coin. This coin—this new apprehension of time—was forged in the crucible of revolution.

> Ibid.

5   The rat-a-tat-tat of scholarly and political crossfire threatens to obliterate the real accomplishments made in historical understanding over the centuries.

> Ibid.

6   . . . human rights require three interlocking qualities: rights must be natural (inherent in human beings), equal (the same for everyone) and universal (applicable everywhere).

> *Inventing Human Rights, A History* 2007

7   . . . we should not forget the restrictions placed on rights by 18th-century men, but to stop there, patting ourselves on the back for our own comparative "advancement," is to miss the point. How did these men, living in societies built on slavery, subordination and seemingly natural subservience, ever come to imagine men not at all like them and, in some cases, women too, as equals?

> Ibid.

3584. Susan Jacoby (1945–   )

1   I have always regarded the development of the individual as the only legitimate goal of education. . . .

> *Inside Soviet Schools* 1974

2   Soviet schools are extraordinarily good at squeezing the fight out of the individuals they process.

> Ibid.

3   I was troubled at a young age by the idea that pouring water over someone's head could change . . . his relationship to God. . . .

> *Half Jew: A Daughter's Search for Her Family's Buried Past* 2000

4   Trying to discern the true religious opinions of the founders [of the U.S.A.] from their voluminous writings is rather like searching for the real Jesus in the conflicting passages of the Scriptures.

> Ch. 1, *Freethinkers: A History of American Secularism* 2004

5   Then as now, American scientific interest focused not on theory but on the immense practical benefits to be derived from discovering the secrets of the natural world. . . .

> Ibid.

6   In Europe the subject matter of science and history lessons taught to children in all publicly supported schools has always been determined by highly educated employees of central education ministries. In America the image of an educated elite

laying down national guidelines for schools was and is a bête noire for those who consider local control of education a right almost as sacred as any of the rights enumerated in the Constitution.

The Age of American Unreason 2008

3585. Kathy Kahn (1945–   )

1   There is still a natural tendency for the people of one class to look down on people who they think are lower class—as if they are less than human.

Quoted in "Kathy Kahn: Voice of Poor White Women" by Meridee Merzer, *Viva April 1974*

2   In places like the textile mills, where superhuman production rates are set, the people have to take speed (amphetamines) in order to keep up production. . . . Virtually every factory is this country is run on speed, grass, or some other kind of upper.

Ibid.

3   I do not believe in being paid for organizing . . . because a revolution is a revolution. And nobody—*nobody*—gets paid for making a revolution.

Ibid.

3586. Zahira Kamal (1945–   )

1   Perhaps the most striking difference is in the presence of emotion and personal accounts in the opening of women's dialogue . . . as distinct from the more confrontational and accusatory openings of men in mixed groups. The clear implication is that "the personal is political."

"Women's People-to-People Activities: Do We Do It Better?" *Palestine-Israel Journal*, vol. 12, no. 4 & vol. 13, no. 1, coauthor, Galia Golan *6 May 2008*

2   Women on both sides are consistently concerned about reaching the grass roots, not remaining elitist. Men, while speaking of broadening constituencies, rarely seem to express the need for grass-roots participation.

Ibid.

3   We like to stress that the women's movement is part of the national movement. We believe that both personal and national liberation go hand in hand.

"Profiles of Peace: Zahira Kamal," American Friends Service Committee (afsc.org) *n.d.*

3587. Linda Kintz (1945–   )

1   The corporation is defined in spiritual terms as a natural extension of God's natural law, with the belief in the corporation and the protection of corporate activity . . . saturated with moral passion [which] . . . justifies an admonition to Americans that it is their religious and moral duty to export unregulated free enterprise to the rest of the globe.

Between Jesus and the Market: The Emotions that Matter in Right-Wing America 1997

2   How can hate sound so *nice?*

Ibid.

3588. Chandrika Bandaranike Kumaratunga (1945–   )

1   Poverty and unemployment are very often the underlying causes of social conflict and violence, which undermines and erodes the social fabric upon which human prosperity and happiness rest.

Address, United Nations World Summit For Social Development (Copenhagen), *12 March 1995*

2   We believe in simultaneously strengthening the democratic and legal framework within which people participate in the formulation and implementation of policy. This involves the fullest respect for human rights and fundamental freedoms and the rule of law, access to justice, elimination of discrimination as well as transparent and accountable government.

Ibid.

3   Conflict resolution has become today, a high profile subject taught in universities and lectured on, at many a seminar and conference. Experts in this field are held in awe in some circles in many countries. Yet, conflict resolution is not new. It has only been packaged differently in our age.

Speech, Asia Society (New York City) *Fall 2004*

3589. Enriqueta Longauex y Vasquez (1945?–   )

1   A woman who has no way of expressing herself and of realizing herself as a full human has nothing else to turn to but the owning of material things.

"The Mexican-American Woman," *Sisterhood Is Powerful,* Robin Morgan,* ed. *1970*

*See 3284.

2   The Anglo woman is always there with her superiority complex.

Ibid.

3   When a family is involved in a human rights movement, as is the Mexican-American family, there is little room for a woman's liberation movement alone.

Ibid.

3590. Karen Malpede (1945–   )

1   The flowing of blood and of milk, the turning of blood into milk, renewable ecstasies—these are commonplaces of female sexuality.

Women in Theatre: Compassion and Hope (p.255) 1983

2   MICHEL. Nothing we do sullies us; why is that?

Us 1987

3   . . . in order for me to reveal the divine in "man" I had to come to feminism. There was no other way, I had to come to an understanding of the divine in women. Now I can truly be one within a long tradition of people who believe that theater is a way to reveal the spirit, the deep essence, the unrealized desires, the true holiness of humankind.

Quoted in "Karen Malpede," *Interviews with Contemporary Women Playwrights* by Kathleen Betsko* and Rachel Koenig *1987*

*See 3125.

4   The great artist speaks a truth so personal it becomes universal. There's no way you can do that with one eye on the marketplace.

Ibid.

5   Pregnancy can be a tremendously creative time in the life of a woman; the body itself is tied up in the act of creation so it's easy for the mind and heart to be similarly engaged.

Ibid.

3591. Wilma Mankiller (1945–2010)

1 Cherokees have stated that they are ready for female leadership. . . . We all knew this was coming. . . . The issues are our programs, the breaking of the circle of poverty, not me.

Inaugural Speech* 5 December 1985
*Elected chief of the Cherokee Nation of Oklahoma in 1987, she was the first woman to head a major Native American tribe.

2 We can look back over the 500 years since Columbus* stumbled onto this continent and see utter devastation among our people. But as we approach the 21st century, we are very hopeful. Despite everything, we survive in 1991 as a culturally distinct group. Our tribal institutions are strong. And I think we can be confident that, 500 years from now, someone like Wilma Mankiller will say that our languages and ceremonies from time immemorial still survive.

Quoted in "She Leads A Nation" by Hank Whittemore, Parade Magazine 18 August 1991
*Christopher Columbus (1451?–1506), Italian navigator and explorer who, in 1492, opened the path from the Old World to the New.

3 *Have a good mind.* No matter what situation you're in, find something good about it, rather than the negative things. And in dealing with other human beings, find the good in them as well.
We are all interdependent. Do things for others—tribe, family, community—rather than just for yourself.
Look forward. Turn what has been done into a better path. If you're a leader, think about the impact of your decisions on seven generations into the future.

Credo, Ibid.

4 This young man come out to the airport to pick me up . . . and he asked me, he said, "Well, since principal chief is a male term, how should I address you?" . . . I just looked out the window of the car. Then he said "Well, should we address you as chiefteness?" So I looked out the window for a little longer. Then he thought he would get real funny and cute, and he asked me if he should address me "chiefette," so I looked out the window for a real long time . . . and so I told him to call me "Ms. Chief," [as in] mischief.

p. 176, Women Seen and Heard: Lessons Learned from Successful Speakers, coauthor, and Lois Phillips* 2003
*See 3222.

3592. Bernadette Mayer (1945–)

1 Now it's your turn to fall down from the love of my look
Untitled, St. 2 (p. 1), Midwinter Day 1982

2 I've nothing at all to say but to exercise
my freedom to speak about everything
"Ode on Periods," St. 2, Another Smashed Pinecone 1998

3 It was hard to have no money today
"On Gifts for Grace," Scarlet Tanager 2005

3593. Patricia McLaughlin (1945–)

1 Discoveries have reverberations. A new idea about oneself or some aspect of one's relations to others unsettles all one's other ideas, even the superficially related ones. No matter how slightly, if shifts one's entire orientation. And somewhere along the line of consequences, it changes one's behavior.
Quoted in American Scholar Autumn 1972

2 Obviously, nothing that comes in a tube, bottle or jar can stop time in its tracks. And, in fact, most Americans probably hope they'll be lucky enough to keep aging (consider the alternative.) They just don't want to look like it. It's the visual appearance of aging these zillions of lotions and potions promise to delay or disguise or spackle over. It's as if looking old has become indecent, un-American—something that simply must not on any account be allowed to show.
"Whither the absconded glamour of the grown-up?," St. Louis Dispatch 24 June 2008

3 And notice the proliferation of so-called "senior moments." Once upon a time—until recently, in fact—people routinely forgot things without seeing it as a foretaste of imminent mental decline.
Ibid.

3594. Bette Midler (1945–)

1 For Tillie had been (in the Days of her Youth)
Adored as a Terpsichorine.
She danced with Abandon and not too much else,
Yet never approached the Obscene.
The Saga of Baby Divine, St. 16 1983

2 "Make sure that your Life is a Rare Entertainment!
It doesn't take anything drastic.
You needn't be gorgeous or wealthy or smart
Just Very Enthusiastic!"
St. 153, Ibid.

3 If Dick Nixon* would only do to Pat what he's done to the country.
Quoted in "The 1960's to the 1980's," Women in Comedy by Linda Martin and Kerry Segrave 1986
*Richard Milhouse N— (1913–94), 37th president of the United States (1969–74); resigned.

4 My boyfriend Ernie asked me, "Soph, how come you never tell me when you're having an orgasm?"
"Well, Ernie, you're never around."
Quoted in "Familiar Faces," Funny Women, American Comediennes, 1860–1985 by Mary Unterbrink 1987

5 In your young life, you rebel against values you think are square. After a while, you realize they are good values and there's a reason they've been around for thousands of years.
Ibid.

6 Marriage involves big compromises all the time. International-level compromises. You're the U.S.A., he's the USSR, and you're talking nuclear warheads.
Quoted in "I Can't Play the Victim" by Tom Seligson, Parade Magazine 5 February 1989

3595. Gertrude Ibengwe Mongella (1945–)

1 Women have always struggled with their men-folk for the abolition of slavery, the liberation of countries from colonialism, the dismantling of apartheid and the attainment of peace. It is now the turn of men to join women in their struggle for equality.
Speech, U.S. Fourth Conference on the World's Women 1995

2 It is not enough just to open the door to the rooms of power—we have to get inside and rearrange the furniture!
Speech, Parliamentary Meeting, UN Commission on the Status of Women (New York) 27 February 2008

3596. Honor Moore (1945–   )

1 MARGARET. Halfway down the
stairs I stop and put the dishes down,
sit there and remember
as hard as I can where I am, hard as
I can: I am myself, a woman,
nursing a woman who may be dying.
My mother can't feed me any more.

Mourning Pictures (verse play) 1974

2 A ring or two.
Her turquoise beads
The green-striped chair
What will she leave me
Except alone. . . .

"What Will She Leave Me?," Ibid.

3 M-A-D* is the filter through which we're pressed to see
ourselves—
If we don't, we won't get published, sold, or exhibited—
I blame none of us for not challenging it
Except not challenging it may drive us mad.

"Polemic #1" (poem) 1974

*Acronym for Male Approval Desire.

4 The all-male world he found "a sort of magical utopian
place." . . . [It] represented mental freedom, an entrance into
the world of thinking and imagining.

Ch. 1, *The Bishop's Daughter: A Memoir* 2008

3597. Susanna Moore (1945–   )

1 She used to say laughingly that she knew the ritual ceremony
for wrapping the bones of a chief, but she could not divide
fractions. She could steer an outrigger canoe through rough
seas, but she had never learned to iron.

Sleeping Beauties 1993

2 The whole class was having trouble with irony. They do much
better with realism. Realism, they think, is simply a matter of
imitating Ernest Hemingway.

Ch. 1, *In the Cut* 1995

3 Stream of consciousness, which to some of them at first was
stream of conscienceness, doesn't seem to give them much
trouble. They think it's like writing down your dreams except
without punctuation.

Ibid.

3598. Carol Muske-Dukes (1945–   )

1 I considered how we twisted into ourselves to live.

"An Octave Above Thunder," 1, St. 11, *An Octave Above
Thunder: New and Selected Poems* 1997

2 Look. Messages the dead send
take time to arrive.

"Like This," St. 2, Ibid.

3 Will is back in the diminished atmosphere of pre-Needs. Here,
the living hurry to purchase the pay-by-the-month La-Z-Boy
death lounger, the faux-Hellenic vault, the *Star Trek* sepulchre
(the lost one is beamed up on a video screen)—padding the
threshold to the afterlife.

Ch. 1, *Life After Death* 2001

4 *Haunted? Of course I'm haunted, I bury the dead. I sell eternal
resting compartments to the dead. The dead come to me to get
out of this world with a little dignity. I shake hands with the
dead every day.*

People offer their suffering to him and he orchestrates it.

Ibid.

3599. Paula Nelson (1945–   )

1 Society still traditionally assigns to woman the role of money-
handler rather than money-maker, and our assigned specialty
is far more likely to be home economics than financial economics.

Ch. 1, *The Joy of Money* 1975

2 The making of money simply is not a sex-linked skill. Women
can and are turning it all around. We are discovering for ourselves the challenge—and the joy—of money.

Ibid.

3 A credit card is a money tool, *not* a supplement to money. The
failure to make this distinction has "supplemented" many a
poor soul right into bankruptcy.

Ch. 4, Ibid.

4 . . . launching your own business is like writing your own personal declaration of independence from the corporate beehive,
where you sell bits of your life in forty-hour (or longer) chunks
in return for a paycheck. . . . Going into business for yourself,
becoming an entrepreneur, is the modern-day equivalent of
pioneering on the old frontier.

Ch. 6, Ibid.

3600. Mary D. Nichols (1945–   )

1 If buildings are built that draw nothing from the (electrical)
grid, but all of the materials in that building were built in
China using machines from factories that were all powered
by Chinese coal, I don't think we would have made the globe
a cleaner, safer place. So we've got to think about life-cycle
emissions in a whole different way then we've ever had to do
before. If we're not thinking at a truly global level, we're not
actually going to save our planet.

Panel Discussion, Stanford University 4 March 2008

2 Especially in times like these, we must be extraordinarily
mindful of the economic effects of our actions. We know
that the economic crisis we will face from unmitigated climate change could dwarf anything we have ever seen. That
alone is a compelling enough reason to take swift action. But
there's another reason also, which is that developing a new
clean energy economy that drives and rewards investment
and innovation, creates jobs and serves as the engine for sustainable economic growth is exactly what we need at a time
like this.

Speech, University of Rhode Island 12 November 2008

3601. Jessye Norman (1945–   )

1 Marian Anderson* was the personification of all that I admire—wonderful, simple, pure and majestic in the human
spirit. She wore the glorious crown of her voice with the grace
of an empress. I have loved her all my life.

Interview (1960), Cited in "Death stills voice . . ." (AP), *Seattle
Post-Intelligencer*, A9 9 April 1993

*See 1945.

3602. Alice Notley (1945–)

1 Everybody in
any room is a
smuggler.

"At Night the States," st. 7, *Grave of Light: New and Selected Poems, 1970–2005* 2006

2 No world is intact
and no one cares about you.

"No word is intact," St. 1, Ibid.

3 —who would not
be released from the
Book of Knowledge?

"World's Bliss," Ibid.

3603. Frances Olsen (1945–)

1 Transcending the male/female dichotomy . . . does not mean making women more like men, or men more like women. . . . Rather than shades of grey as an alternative to all black and all white, I envision reds and greens and blues.

"The Family and the Market: A Study of Ideology and Legal Reform," *Harvard Law Review,* vol. 96 1983

2 The differences between men and women are as natural as starvation, religion, and brutality. Inequality between men and women has existed throughout recorded history and has persisted across widely divergent cultures. So too have starvation, religion, and brutality. That each of these phenomena has been long lived does not mean that any of them is immutable.

Ibid.

3 Some adoptive parents say that they thank God that their adopted child was not aborted, but should they not also thank God that the natural father and mother failed to use effective birth control or that their child's natural mother was denied a meaningful opportunity to refuse intercourse? An adopted child conceived the result of a violent rape would have died as an egg and a sperm, never allowed to join or to be born, had the rape not taken place. Should the adoptive parents be glad that their child's natural father had not been sent to jail for an earlier rape or that the arrival of a police office had not prevented the rape that "saved" their adopted daughter?

"Unraveling Compromise," *Harvard Law Review,* vol. 103 1989

4 If women were not devalued, a pregnant woman's control over reproduction would seem natural and inevitable. Most people would not conceptualize an early fetus as a baby or as a person with interests separate from and potentially hostile to those of its mother.

Ibid.

3604. Younhee Paik (1945?–)

1 I like to think about the source or power of the universe. Both art and life are derived from the power which reigns in the universe. I believe that power is truth. All beauty comes from the truth that has always been. I don't create art or create beauty, I just discover what has always been there.

Quoted in "Younhee Paik," *Exposures, Women & Their Art* by Ann Brown and Arlene Raven* 1989

*See 3533.

3605. Jurgenne Primavera (1945?–)

1 We scientists in developing countries need to come down from the Ivory Tower and disseminate results not only in peer-re-viewed journals but also through advocacy and the popular media. We must not forget our hearts even as we apply our minds. We do science not in a vacuum but against the grinding poverty and environment-unfriendly character of modern times, and we can use our scientific knowledge to reduce suffering and make life more full for fellow humans and creatures.

"Mangroves, Fishponds, and the Quest for Sustainability," *Science 7 October 2005*

2 In the 1980s, I began to ring warning bells about the perils of runaway shrimp farming. At the time, aquaculture was perceived as the coming Blue Revolution that would help solve world hunger, provide jobs, and fight poverty. . . . And in recent years, momentum to develop sustainable aquaculture practices has been building.

Ibid.

3 Troubles . . . come with the mission of protecting the world's mangroves—the lushly forested environmental buffer zones by which the sea meets land in so many places around the world—even as these areas become ever more exploited for aquaculture and other uses. It is a mission that teeters on the always difficult negotiation by which ecological and environmental goals, on the one hand, and economic, social, and immediate human needs, on the other, are adjudicated.

Ibid.

4 People might think the mangroves are just wet trees, but they give us so much. All we have to do is use them.

Quoted in "Heroes of the Environment: Jurgenne Primavera" by Hannah Beech, *Time* 2008

3606. Rosa Hilda Ramos (1945?–)

1 We dream of forming a tropical wetland garden where the world can see how diverse nature is in our little corner of the world.

Acceptance Speech (San Francisco), Goldman Environmental Prize *14 April 2008*

2 We are now working hard to bring our wetlands to their past splendor, restoring our natural butterfly gardens, protecting our bird sanctuary, the Secret lagoon, and our dragonfly habitats. We are helping to build a glass house museum for our beloved Coqui frogs where people will fall under the spell of the Coqui song.

Ibid.

3 Moving on, holding hands together—that is the secret of success.

goldmanprize.org 2008

3607. Carolyn M. Rodgers (1945–)

1 not too smart not too bitchy not too sapphire
not too dumb not too not to not too
a little less a little more

add here detract there
lonely.

"Poem for Some Black Woman," St. 10 (1981), *The Woman That I Am, The Literature and Culture of Contemporary Women of Color,* D. Soyini Madison,* ed. 1994

*See 3912.

2 And my mouth has been open
Most of the time but

I ain't been saying nothin but
Thinking about ev'rything

"Breakthrough" *n.d.*

3608. Ruth Rosen (1945–)

1 Bursts of artillery fire, mass strikes, massacred protesters, bomb explosions—these are our images of revolution. But some revolutions are harder to recognize: no cataclysms mark their beginnings or ends, no casualties are left lying in pools of blood. Though people may suffer greatly, their pain is hidden from public view. Such was the case with the modern women's movement.

The World Split Open: How the Modern Women's Movement Changed America 2000

2 The great accomplishment of the modern women's movement was to name such private experiences—domestic violence, sexual harassment, economic discrimination, date rape—and turn them into public problems that could be debated, changed by new laws and policies or altered by social customs. That is how the personal became political.

"The Care Crisis," *The Nation 12 March 2007*

3 People suffer their private crises alone, without realizing that the care crisis is a problem of national significance. Many young women agonize about how to combine work and family but view the question of how to raise children as a personal dilemma, to which they need to find an individual solution. Most cannot imagine turning it into a political debate. More than a few young women have told me that the lack of affordable childcare has made them reconsider plans to become parents.

Ibid.

4 Although Americans famously root for the underdog, they have shown far less compassion for the poor, the vulnerable and the homeless in recent years.

Ibid.

5 The irrational belief that markets can, and should, solve all our problems has made us forget that the profit motive does not always produce better results and that, moreover, there is still such a thing as a common good that should be protected from markets.

"And You're Worried About Oil?," *San Francisco Chronicle 2007*

3609. Kay Ryan (1945–)

1 Doubt uses albumen
at twice the rate of work.

"Doubt," Elephant Rocks: Poems 1996

2 Lacunae aren't
what was going to be
empty anyway.

"Lacunae," Ibid.

3 Don't you wonder
how people think
the banks of space
and time don't matter?

"Nothing Ventured," *Say Uncle 2000*

4 Who would
have guessed

it possible
that waiting
is sustainable—

"Patience," Ibid.

3610. Diane Sawyer (1945–)

1 When someone's life is shattered, there is only humanity.*

Quoted in "Star Power" by Richard Zoglin, *Time 7 August 1989*

*Re: to Richard Nixon (1913–94), 37th president of the United States (1969–74), forced to resign after the Watergate scandal.

2 We're a Madison Avenue country. I'm not sure that we make a distinction between news people and celebrities. And I think there is a distinction. The distinction lies in what you do every day—what you do to get stories and how far you will go and how much you will dig for them. All of the rest of the attention that comes to you because you're on the air seems to me as irrelevance.

Ibid.

3611. Karen Anne Schmidt (1945–)

1 I've been accused of being aggressive. I wonder what they would call me if I was a man doing the same thing.
    If you work and fight hard for something you believe in, why is it different depending on what sex you are?

Cited in "Olympian Woman" by Dionne Searcey, *Seattle Times, A18 31 January 1999*

3611.1. Hanan al-Shaykh (1945–)

1 How can I answer your questions about the state of the country when my chief worry is the rat occupying our kitchen?

Beirut Blues, Catherine Cogham, tr. 1995

2 I carry my war wherever I go.

Ibid.

3 Despite the regularity of the routine, I can't concentrate. I keep reliving the shock of my kidnapping and I shall never be free of it even if I'm released. . . . I no longer think about life outside.

(p. 40), Ibid.

4 He turned to me and asked me my age. "The age of madness," I replied.

I Sweep the Sun Off Rooftops (Aknus al-Shams 'an al-Sutuh, 1994), Catherine Cobham, tr. 1998

5 "Marriage is like everything else in life—a matter of luck. Who says a worm-eaten apple can't look red and juicy from the outside?"

Ibid.

3612. Mary Sheepshanks (1945?–)

1 I go for weekly channelling
- Burnt Feathers is my guide.
In a previous incarnation
he says he was my bride.
He is very wise and holy
but it's well within his range
to give me helpful little hints
about the Stock Exchange.

"Shall We Go Alternative," St. 4, *Thinning Grapes 1992*

2 "Sonia's so gifted, you know. She was a promising artist before she married Archie." It was pleasant to hear people say that

and to rest on this half-earned reputation with no further effort.

Ch. 1, A Price for Everything 1996

3 [Cecily's driving was] a source of constant anxiety to her family . . . her use of the horn . . . which she regarded as a perfectly legitimate signal to other road users that she claimed priority under all circumstances.

Picking Up the Pieces 1999

4 "Well, hello there, Tilly," said the Bishop, who suffered little children to come unto him with all the enthusiasm of one determined to wear a hair shirt and look as if he liked it.

Ibid.

5 If they would only binge on chips
- while scribbling plots of love or gore -
they might get bigger round the hips
but oh—I'd like them so much more!
"Working Out," St. 5, *Dancing Blues to Skylarks 2004*

3613. Karin P. Sheldon (1945–)

1 Environment, in all its forms and relations, sustains us. We depend upon it. I truly believe that the fundamental principles of ecology govern our lives, wherever we live, and that we must wake up to this fact or be lost.

Quoted in "Found Women: Defusing the Atomic Establishment" by Anna Mayo, *Ms. October 1973*

2 My ideal West would be a region where there is still wild country, wild rivers, and wildlife in abundance, a region where human beings live in balance with their environment.

Quoted by Ashley McPhee for Western Resource Advocates, *Western Views, vol. 18 Fall 2007*

3614. Ruth Simmons (1945?–)

1 We can educate our youth using many, many modalities. They can go to magnet schools. They can go to Montessori schools. They can go to an incredible range of institutions. They need several things in those institutions. They need to feel that somebody there respects them and their ability; that somebody there encourages them to work up to and beyond their potential; and they need to have someone there who promotes the idea that they can succeed in life. The important thing is to give students the tools to be educated, but, more than that, to give them every encouragement to succeed.

"Celebrating Black History Month" by Harry Allen, *USA Weekend Magazine 11 February 2001*

2 . . . I don't want people to find a formula for success in education. Not at all. I want lots of successful models that are different. . . . What I don't want is to make education so homogenized it eliminates the possibility for us to choose what we need.

Ibid.

3 I ended up going to a historically black college [Dillard University in New Orleans] because I wanted to major in theater. And I didn't want to be relegated to playing black roles in a white university. I wanted to play Antigone. I wanted to play all roles. And my drama teacher said, "If you go to a black college, you'll be able to play any role." So I went to an African-American institution.

Ibid.

3615. Carly Simon (1945–)

1 You're so vain, I'll bet you think this song is about you. . . .
"You're So Vain" 1972

2 I have no need of half of anything
No half time, no half of a man's attention
Give me all the earth and sky
And at the same time add a new dimension
Half the truth is of no use
Give it all, give it all to me
"Give Me All Night," St. 1, *Coming Round Again* (album) 1987

3 Just because you don't see shooting stars
Doesn't mean it isn't perfect
Can't you see

It's the stuff that dreams are made of
It's the slow and steady fire
"The Stuff That Dreams Are Made Of," Sts. 2–3, Ibid.

4 Let it all go now
Like smoke from a candle
Like the trace of a song
That you hear in the wind
"Better Not Tell Her," St. 4, *Have You Seen Me Lately?* (album) 1990

5 Let the river run
Let all the dreamers
Wake the nation
Come, the New Jerusalem
"Let the River Run," *Working Girl* (film) 1990

3616. Jacqueline "Jackie" St. Joan (1945–)

1 I swallow the Sunday news
with my coffee: Yet another woman
killed by her husband-who-shot-himself-too.
But
this one,
this client might have been mine,
this one,
had I not been booked up
and had to say no,
this one,
had she had the money on Thursday
instead of on Monday,
this one.
"The Drama of the Long Distance Runners," *Ms.* (New York) *November/December 1997*

2 I stand here now, still at the kitchen sink
the belly of my dress wet and stinking
this running faucet of words
running out of my mouth,
the choking generations of daughters
spitting both privilege and bitterness
from their mothers' broken cups.
"Virginia, 1957–1977–1997," St. 5, Ibid.

3617. Jean Strouse (1945–)

1 His* authority—in his office, over railroads, in the world's capital markets—came not from what he said but from he did.
Morgan, American Financier 1999

2   . . . the country's economic welfare could no longer be left to private bankers. . . . Morgan's* extraordinary authority endangered the public welfare.

Ibid.

*John Pierpont Morgan, American financier and philanthropist (1837–1913).

3618. Deborah F. Tannen (1945–   )

1   We cannot lump all men or all women into fixed categories. But the seemingly senseless misunderstandings that haunt our relationships can in part be explained by the different conversational rules by which men and women play.

You Just Don't Understand: Men and Women in Conversation
1990

2   There is a sense in which every woman is seen as a receptionist—available to give information and help, perennially interruptible.

Talking from 9 to 5 1994

3   The Pavlovian view of women voters—plug the words in, and they will respond—sends a chill down my spine because it sounds like an adaptation of something I have written about communication between the sexes: When a woman tells a man about a problem, she doesn't want him to fix it; she just wants him to listen and let her know he understands. But there's a difference between a private conversation and a presidential election, between what we want from our lovers and what we want from our leaders.

"Bush's Sweet Talk," Op-Ed, *The New York Times 20 January*
2000

3619. Joyce Tenneson (1945–   )

1   In my work, I try to open myself and let the unconscious take over—and I am always surprised by the transformations that emerge in front of the lens. I don't give my subjects any specific directions. I just provide a safe space for them to be open, to let down their external shields, and to expose an essence or kernel of their being that is normally secret or hidden.

Introduction, *Light Warriors 2000*

2   I've always found it amusing that our society conceals the human body under clothing, yet we leave our faces—the part of the body that has the potential to reveal everything—naked.

Wise Women 2002

3   I want to allow others to reveal and celebrate aspects of themselves that are usually hidden. My camera is a witness. It holds a light up for my subjects to help them feel their own essence, and gives them the courage to collaborate in the recording of these revelations.

joycetenneson.com *n.d*

3620. Anne Tucker (1945–   )

1   All art requires courage.

Introduction, *The Woman's Eye 1973*

2   Exploration, whether of jungles or minds, is considered unfeminine.

Ibid.

3   For centuries men have defined themselves in terms of other men, but women have been defined by and in terms of men.
        . . . The ubiquitous nature of masculine images of Woman has contributed significantly to the struggles of women artists because that which is publicly acceptable art does not conform

with their own needs and experiences, and their own art does not conform with popular standards.

Ibid.

3621. Anne Waldman (1945–   )

1   Write down everything you mentally / linguistically / orally juxtapose with all five senses plus mind. Study steadily for a week and the rest of your life. It's the preternatural primordial assignment.

Prelude: "My Song and Only Afterlife," *Vow to Poetry 2001*

2   the manatee has no natural enemies but unnatural man
the manatee is constantly threatened by man unnaturally
man with his boats and plastic and attitude

"Manatee/Humanity," *The Brooklyn Rail* (brooklynrail.org)
February 2008

3622. Sarah Weddington (1945–   )

1   I can't say, "I'm tired of this fight, let's do something else." To say that is to lose everything that was won.

Quoted in "For Roe v. Wade attorney, the crusade goes on" by
Lily Eng, *Seattle Times*, B9 27 September 1992

2   For me and the countless women who put their lives at risk to control their own destinies, the world did change in 1973 when *Roe v. Wade** became the law of the land.

Ch. 1, *A Question of Choice 1992*

*The landmark 1973 Supreme Court ruling that allows medical abortion; Weddington was the attorney who fought for and won the case.

3623. Leslie Kanes Weisman (1945–   )

1   Malls are insular fantasy worlds where the relatively well-off pursue the study and acquisition of superfluous goods as a form of entertainment, in a society in which millions are in desperate need of something to eat and a safe, warm place to sleep.

Discrimination by Design: A Feminist Critique of the Man-
Made Environment 1992

3624. Khaleda Zia Rahman (1945–   )

1   There can be no talks with this corrupt and repressive Government.*

"Bangladesh frees dissident leaders," *The New York Times*
Book Review 11 December 1987

*Re Bangladesh Nationalist Party.

3625. Susan Au Allen (1946–   )

1   The quiet but steady revolution in affirmative action puts individual rights over group rights.

Speech, National Order of Women Legislators (11 November
1996), *Vital Speeches of the Day 1 April 1997*

3626. Lisa Appignanesi (1946–   )

1   Patients could well find themselves the victims of a doctor's prejudice about what kind of behavior constituted sanity: this could all too easily work against women who didn't conform to the time's norms of sexual behavior or living habits.

Mad, Bad and Sad: Women and the Mind Doctors 2008

2   [The diagnosis of hysteria] best expresses women's distress at the clashing demands and no longer tenable restrictions placed on women in the fin de siècle.

Ibid.

3627. Hanan Ashrawi (1946–   )

1 We should not make any further political concessions but we should persist in what we're doing, and keep repeating our message. Education is a long process. The public needs to hear it over and over again: we want two states for two peoples; there is no alternative to the PLO; and Jews and Palestinians don't have to love each other, we just have to understand each other.

> Quoted in Ch. 16, *Deborah, Golda, and Me* by Letty Cottin
> Pogrebin* *1991*

*See 3154.

2 In the moment that I give up hope, I will not be in the peace process. If we lose faith, there will be no peaceful solution to the conflict. Peace will be very difficult and very painful, but I think we have to do it.

> Quoted in "The Palestinians' tough negotiator is Israel's best
> hope for peace" by Israel Amrani, *Mother Jones March/April*
> *1993*

3 You will see that it is going to be very difficult to send these women* back to the kitchen or to relegate them to the status of second class citizens.

> *Palestinian Women of Gaza and the West Bank*, Suha
> Sabbagh, ed. *1998*

*Re to Palestinian women after the Intifada of 1987–92.

3628. Kit Bakke (1946–   )

1 Louisa* made her life, she didn't just live it. She wore her heart, as well as her brain, on her sleeve—always in the open, unprotected and brave.

> p. xi, *Miss Alcott's E-Mail, Yours for Reforms of All Kinds*
> *2006*

*L- May Alcott; see 1044.

2 Sometimes I just want to get through the next hour without doing anything stupid. With my switchback tracks, I must look like a bug wandering blindly around on the wrong side of the tapestry.

> p. 235, Ibid.

3 . . . ideas count. It matters what you think, what I think, what each of us thinks. . . . Following fads is lazy; assuming that the people in charge have the best ideas is folly.

> Ibid.

3629. Christina Baldwin (1946–   )

1 Ritual is the way you carry the presence of the sacred. Ritual is the spark that must not go out.

> *Life's Companion 1991*

2 Change is the constant, the signal for rebirth, the egg of the phoenix.

> Ibid.

3 Journal writing is a voyage to the interior.

> Ibid.

4 Every person is born into life as a blank page—and every person leaves life as a full book. Our lives are our story, and our story is our life. Story is the narrative thread of our experience—not what literally happens, but what we make out of what happens, what we tell each other and what we remember.

> First Lines, *Storycatcher 2005*

5 How we remember, what we remember and why we remember form the most personal map of our individuality.

> Ibid.

3630. Mary Jo Bang (1946–   )

1 the mind is made by eye.

> "Pear and O, an Opera" st. 8, *The Downstream Extremity of
> the Isle of Swans: Poems 2001*

2 Uneasy acceptance of rampant destruction.
In April's court, you talk—sure—but she don't listen.

> "When April Was Beginning, and End," St. 3, Ibid.

3 Wasn't the skeptic invented to nourish an interest in science?

> "Eclipsed," *Louise in Love 2001*

4 The day is dragged here and there but still can't be saved.

> "Three Trees," *Elegy: Poems 2007*

5 And how can it be
that this means nothing to anyone but me now.

> "Landscape with the Fall of Icarus," Ibid.

3631. Joan Barfoot (1946–   )

1 I remember now that in the old life, I watched clocks. They told me everything: when to do each thing, walking, cooking, laundering, watching television, reading the newspaper, even having a cigarette. And sleeping. Time was how I counted off my life. Now I see that it was time I was accomplishing. I was not timing my tasks, but making the tasks into time; and all that is gone.

> Ch. 3, *Gaining Ground* (a.k.a. *Abra*) *1978*

2 "I've often thought that if we just put all our energy into raising the next generation, and they do the same and so on and so on, it makes us no better than ants, really, or bees. Save something for yourself."

> Ch. 5, Ibid.

3 "I can't know anything about you if you're doing something that's a lie, and I can't be myself if I have to keep worrying about whether or not you're happy."

> Ch. 14, Ibid.

3632. Mary Barley (1946–   )

1 Everglades is one of our most important natural cathedrals.

> Quoted in "Everglades Forever" by Tim Padgett, *Time.com 12
> August 1999*

2 The money that Everglades damage costs us in areas like tourism could be 10 times more than what industries like sugar contribute to the economy.

> Ibid.

3633. Ysaye Barnwell (1946–   )

1 . . . it's impossible to perform and interpret* for someone else at the same time. In interpreting, you're listening to someone else and expressively transposing their statements and lyrics into another language.

> Quoted in "Sweet Honey: A Cappella Activists" by Audreen
> Buffalo, *Ms.* (New York) *March/April 1993*

*American Sign Language, for the deaf.

2 I believe very strongly that the way African and African American music is practiced, composed, and performed embodies a

set of values that ought to be applied in the broader society. Part of that is allowing yourself to be open, not controlling. Cooperation as opposed to competition.

Ibid.

3634. Georgette Bennett (1946–)

1   . . . take the profit out of drugs . . .

Crime-warps: The Future of Crime in America 1988

2   [The poor] are victimized by the most crimes, they have to live with the dealers and junkies, they suffer the most.

Ibid.

3635. Candice Bergen (1946–)

1   THE MAN. Man has always been under death's dictatorship, always questioned it, always challenged it.

The Freezer 1968

2   THE MAN. You've been renovated, my sweet, like an urban renewal project!

Ibid.

3   I may not be a great actress but I've become the greatest at screen orgasms. Ten seconds of heavy breathing, roll your head from side to side, simulate a slight asthma attack and die a little.

Quoted in *Halliwell's Filmgoer's Companion* by Leslie Halliwell *1984*

3636. Ellen Berman (1946–)

1   From the time [my daughter] was 18 months old, my life changed radically. Not only because it's different to live day-to-day with someone who's handicapped, but because it's changed my sensibilities in every way. It's changed my perceptions about how people get along in the world, how they look at each other, treat each other—especially how people view other people.

Quoted in "Ellen Berman" *Exposures, Women & Their Art* by Ann Brown and Arlene Raven* *1989*

*See 3533.

3637. Jacqueline Bisset (1946–)

1   Character contributes to beauty. It fortifies a woman as her youth fades. A mode of conduct, a standard of courage, discipline, fortitude and integrity can do a great deal to make a woman beautiful.

Quoted by Lydia Lane in *The Los Angeles Times 16 May 1974*

3638. Joan Borysenko (1946?–)

1   The work of healing is in peeling away the barriers of fear and past conditioning that keep us unaware of our true nature of wholeness and love.

Introduction, *Minding the Body, Mending the Mind 1987*

2   It's only through our relations with others that we develop the outlook of hardiness and come to believe in our own capabilities and inner goodness.

Ch. 1, *Ibid.*

3   As the hours dragged by, we were beckoned into the mysteries of Indian time. Things happen when they happen. There is no rush. Nothing to do, no place to go better than where you are. This is a great clinical exercise for type A personalities. You

either learn to go with the flow here or resign yourself to dropping dead from a heart attack.

A Woman's Journey to God 1999

4   I have always loved the Virgin Mary,* who I think of as a dark-haired Semitic Jewish sister who had some fast talking to do when she got pregnant out of wedlock. And I love the rebel Rabbi Jesus who, if you know anything about Judaism, preached its highest truths.

Ibid.

*See 79.

5   Emily Dickinson* wrote about faith as a fragile thing, a winged thing. Like a thin diaphanous membrane, it changes the color of the world. Under the spell of faith the ordinary shimmers. The mundane becomes miraculous. The daily sunrise and sunset are a call to celebration. The seasons in their majestic turning, a succession of holy days. Every face holds the possibility of love, and strangers are just friends whom we don't yet know.

Ibid.

*See 1024.

3639. Kathleen Brown (1946–)

1   East Coast journalists wrote us [Californians] off after the Gold Rush, again after the 1906 earthquake, after world War II, Korea, Vietnam.
     In each of those we had devastating economic times and social upheavals. But in each the spirit of California reasserted itself. I believe there is something special about California. It attracts risk-takers. It's still the West. It's not for the fainthearted.

"Kathleen Brown knows . . . ," *Seattle Post-Intelligencer,* Op-Ed, A9 *25 January 1994*

2   I love a good fight. I prefer fair fights, but I take them as they come and I like to win.

Ibid.

3640. Pamela K. Brubaker (1946–)

1   It is crucial that we speak out against violence perpetrated by differences on theological and ethical issues if justice is to prevail.

"A new forum for voices decrying violence against women", *Seattle Post-Intelligencer* Focus Section *10 January 1999*

2   We believe that equity and human rights are central to poverty eradication; poverty is not just lack of monetary resources. Our vision is of a world filled with just, sustainable communities which affirm the sacred nature of all creation.

"Wealth Creation, Poverty Reduction and Social Justice," A World Council of Churches Perspective.", International Conference on Religion and Globalization (Chiang Mai, Thailand) *27 July–2 August 2003*

3641. Laura Bush (1946–)

1   A lasting victory in the war against terror depends on educating the world's children because educated children are much more likely to embrace the values that defeat terror.

Speech (Paris), Organization for Economic Cooperation and Development *14 May 2002*

2   Every parent, every teacher, every leader has a responsibility to condemn the terrible tragedy of children blowing themselves up to kill others.

Ibid.

3 We talk about issues, but I'm not his adviser, I'm his wife . . . I find that it's really best not to give your spouse a lot of advice. I don't want a lot of advice from him.
Interview, CBS News 24 *June* 2004

4 In contrast to my husband,* I can pronounce the word *nuclear*.
Interview, *Metro* (Dutch-Belgian) 2 *May* 2005
*George W. B- (1946–), Am. politician; 43rd president of the United States (2001–09).

5 AIDS respects no national boundaries; spares no race or religion; devastates men and women, rich and poor. No country can ignore this crisis. Fighting AIDS is an urgent calling—because every life, in every land, has value and dignity.
Remarks, High Level Meeting on HIV/AIDS, United Nations General Assembly 2 *June* 2006

6 Education is spreading hope. Millions are now learning to live with HIV/AIDS—instead of waiting to die from it.
Ibid.

3642. Kim Campbell (1946–)

1 Charisma without substance is a dangerous thing.
Quoted in "Canada's intellectual defense chief . . . "by Joel Connelly, *Seattle Post-Intelligencer*, A8 24 *March* 1993

2 Does fashion matter? Only if you're out of it.
Quoted in "Does Fashion Matter?" by Eric P. Nash, *New York Time Magazine* 24 *October* 1993

3643. Cher (Cherilyn Sarkisian) (1946–)

1 I'd like to look really great for as long as I can. If some people think that makes me terminally vain, then yes, I am that. I don't think feminists should get upset if women want to change their looks. This is the real world and we're going to get older no matter what. It's just that I'd rather get older looking like Loretta Young* than get older looking like, say, Thelma Ritter,** even though she was one of my favorite actresses.
Forever Fit 1991
*(1913–2000), American award-winning film and television actor.
**(1902–69), American award-winning stage and film actor.

3644. Meg Christian (1946–)

1 Mama, oh, my Mama, well, do you understand
Why I've not bound myself to a man?
Is something buried in your old widow's mind
That blesses my choice of our own kind?
Oh, Mama, Mama.
"Song to My Mama," Verse 3, *I Know You Know* (album) 1974

2 She was a big tough woman, the first to come along
That showed me being female meant you still could be strong;
And though graduation meant that we had to part,
She'll always be a player on the ballfield of my heart.
"Ode to a Gym Teacher," Chorus, Ibid.
Also see Holly Near, 3921:4.

3645. Michelle Cliff (1946–)

1 When did we (the light-skinned middle-class Jamaicans) take over for them [the whites] as oppressors? I need to see when and how this happened. When what should have been reality

was overtaken by what was surely unreality. When the house nigger became master.
"If I Could Write This In Fire, I Would Write This In Fire," *The Land of Look Behind* 1985

2 It was a hot afternoon after a day of solid heavy rain. Rain which had drenched them and seemed not to have finished with them, but only to have taken itself off somewhere to return soon, replenished, with a new strength.
Ch. 1, *No Telephone to Heaven* 1987

3646. Sheila Cronan (1946?–2003)

1 Since marriage constitutes slavery for women, it is clear that the Women's Movement must concentrate on attacking this institution. Freedom for women cannot be won without the abolition of marriage.
"Marriage" (1970), *Radical Feminism*, Anne Koedt, Ellen Levine, and Anita Rapone, eds. 1973

2 The simple fact is that every woman must be willing to be identified as a lesbian to be fully feminist.
National NOW Times January 1988

3647. Alison Hawthorne Deming (1946–)

1 I haven't lived anywhere long enough to be anything other than an outsider.
Temporary Homelands 1994

2 Wise and frightened ancestors, tell me this: If faith blinds, makes us cold to another's suffering, must we be faithless to see?
"Exiled in America," Ibid.

3648. Sharon Doubiago (1946–)

1 "Ever since you were born, I've tried to understand why, since women birth and raise the boys, they grow up to be soldiers. Why isn't the world a more sensuous, loving place? and you know what Danny? There's almost nothing on this subject. Women and war, mothers and soldiers—the most fundamental, crucial issue."
"The Football Player and the Poet: Mother and Child Reunion," *Clinton Street Quarterly Fall* 1986

2 "The football player in America is like the artist in America! The same loner, the same heroic figure so outside the mainstream, but performing for it. Both are like the shaman, the one who heals oneself, who comes back transformed from the mutilating experience to show the world how.
"Still I have these funny moments. Is this what I birthed and raised my child for? Football? What would my son be, with his perfect giant body, in a perfect society? And there remains the other great mystery. What is the function of the game for the spectators? Why do Americans love football?"
Ibid.

3649. Patty Duke (1946–)

1 I don't mind being thought of as someone who was crazy, because I had no control over that situation. What I don't like is for people to think that I chose to do destructive things. I was someone who didn't have a choice about my actions, yet I fought like a son of a bitch to get to a place where I could have one.
Ch. 1, *Call Me Anna: The Autobiography of Patty Duke* 1987

2 One of the things I've discovered in general about raising kids is that they really don't give a damn if you walked five miles to school. They want to deal with what's happening now.
Quoted in *Woman to Woman* by Gilden and Mark Riedman
1994

3650. Marcia Falk (1946–)
1 Washing the hands, we call to mind
the holiness of body.
"Handwashing Before the Meal," *The Book of Blessings: New Jewish Prayers for Daily Life, the Sabbath, and the New Moon Festival 1996*

2 The recognition of difference is part of the very appreciation of life.
Ibid.

3 Let us distinguish parts within the whole
and bless their differences.
"Blessing of Distinctions," Ibid.

4 Hear O Israel—
The divine abounds everywhere
and dwells in everything;
the many are One.
Sh'ma*, Ibid.
*Her interpretation of the most famous prayer in the Jewish liturgy.

3651. Elizabeth Fee (1946–)
1 The voice of the scientific authority is like the male voice-over in commercials, a disembodied knowledge that cannot be questioned, whose author is inaccessible.
"Women's Nature and Scientific Objectivity," *Woman's Nature: Rationalizations of Inequality,* M. Loew and R. Hubbard, eds. *1983*

3652. Irene Fernandez (1946–)
1 *Tenaganita* means women's force. We are a force that does not use guns or goons to make our point or dominate others. We are a force that conscientizes, builds, and empowers the oppressed communities, in particular women and migrant workers, by creating spaces and opportunities for expression, for sharing and for taking actions to protect and claim their rights. Where they are invisible, we become a voice for them. Where they are discriminated, we make them our equals.
Acceptance Speech, Right Livelihood Awards (Stockholm), 9 *December 2005*

2 Governments are more interested in exporting their last resource, the human being, as labor in order to get their remittances. The remittance is a source of foreign exchange to pay the countries' debts to the rich countries via the international financial institutions. In short, the human person has become a commodity to be bought, sold, resold, used and discarded like a piece of tissue. It is the modern day slavery.
Ibid.

3 But we must change the rules of the global economy, for it is the logic of global capitalism that is the source of the disruption of society and of the environment. The challenge is that even as we deconstruct the old, we dare to imagine and win over people to our visions and programs for the new.
Ibid.

4 We belong to one race, the human race and we have only one earth. This solidarity of people must ensure that we put people and the planet before profits. The earth we are given is not just for us but also for those who come after us. They need a tomorrow and that rests on us today.
Ibid.

5 I read what Christ has gone through. It really motivates me—he never compromised on love and justice, nor the truth.
"The Longest Trial," *Christian Solidarity Worldwide,* #96 *December 1998*

3653. Sally Field (1946–)
1 If the mothers ruled the world, there would be no goddamn wars in the first place!
Acceptance Speech, Emmy Awards *1977*

2 I haven't had an orthodox career, and I've wanted more than anything to have your respect. The first time I didn't feel it, but this time I feel it, and I can't deny the fact that you like me, right now, you like me!
Acceptance Speech, Academy Awards *April 1985*

3654. Arden Fingerhut (1946–1994)
1 It's a cellular, biological reaction. We understand images because of who we are physically.
Quoted in "The Facts of Light" by Arnold Aronson, *American Theatre* (New York) *January 1986*

3655. Louise Fréchette (1946–)
1 Multilateralism is not a panacea, of course, but a world in which all, including the most powerful, agree to abide by the same rules is likely to be more stable and less conflicted than one where "might makes right."
"Canada's priorities: Trade, climate change," *The Des Moines Register 28 January 2009*

2 America is uniquely placed to induce a paradigm shift in our societies. Your position as a role model may have suffered of late, but for millions of people, American-style prosperity is still the standard to emulate.
Ibid.

3 The health of the American economy is the No. 1 preoccupation in Canada, just as it is in your country. Our economies are deeply intertwined, and we cannot hope to thrive if you do not. We fervently hope that America's commitment to open trade will be part of any strategy the new administration adopts to cope with the current crisis.
Ibid.

3656. Judith Freeman (1946–)
1 [Las Vegas, a] . . . meta-theme park arising amidst a surreal expanse of windblown nothingness . . .
A Desert of Pure Feeling 1996

2 I've lived in the world of women all my life and yet never understood there is another world of women, heretofore unseen by me, that intersects so baldly with the raw world of men. . . .
Ibid.

3657. Biruté M. F. Galdikas (1946–)
1 I remember thinking that if we understood our closest human relatives we'd understand our origins . . . maybe our own behavior.
Quoted in *Twentieth-Century Women Scientists* by Lisa Yount *1996*

2 Sometimes I felt as though I were surrounded by wild, unruly children in orange suits* who had not yet learned their manners. . . . It was a continual battle of wits and they won!

Ibid.

*Re orangutans.

3 My main contribution [to science] is staying in one place, following one population longer than anyone.

Ibid.

4 [Once people] pay attention to orangutans, they also have to pay attention to the tropical rain forest, which is their only home.

Ibid.

5 . . . it's a victory here, a loss there, a victory there and a loss here. But if we weren't doing what we're doing now, the forests and where we work would've been gone a long time ago—long time ago. I mean there's so many foresters arrayed against the forest.

Reflections of Eden: My Years with the Orangutans of Borneo
1996

3658. Sonia Gandhi (1946–)

1 I never felt they look at me as a foreigner. Because I'm not. I am Indian.

"Italy heralds 'first woman PM,'" BBC News 14 May 2004

2 Following the principles of probity and my inner conscience I am resigning my post in the parliament. I have done this because I think it is the right thing to do. Some people in the country have been trying to create an environment as if the government and the parliament are being used only to favour me. This has pained me greatly.

I did not enter public life for any personal gains. I have made a resolve to serve the country and Indian society and to protect secular values. That is why, in keeping with the ideals of public life and politics as well as my own beliefs, I am resigning as an MP.

"Sonia Gandhi quits as MP," The Independent (London) 24
March 2006

3 It is not the relevance of Mahatma Gandhi* that is in question today . . . it is whether we have the courage to emulate his preachings and what he lived and died for.

Address, International Day of Non-violence, United Nations
General Assembly 2 October 2007

*Mohandas Karamchand Gandhi (1869–1948), a.k.a. "Mahatma"; Indian nationalist and spiritual leader.

4 Yet even though all the world's religions preach non-violence, there is no affirmative, independent word for it. Thus, in our very thought processes, the concept of violence has been central, that of non-violence marginal.

Ibid.

5 [Mahatma Gandhi] held that means and ends are inseparable, and that in fact the means themselves shape the ends. He believed unworthy means can never produce worthy ends.

Ibid.

6 To practice [non-violence] in its true spirit demands strict discipline of mind: the courage to face aggression, the moral conviction to stay the course and the strength to do so without harbouring any malice towards the opponent.

Ibid.

3659. Marielle Goitschel (1946–)

1 I might have skied more recklessly if Christine* was not in first place. But I wanted to make sure that we would win two medals, so I made sure not to make any mistakes.

Quoted in "The Greater Part of Glory" by Bud Greenspan,
Parade Magazine 21 April 1991

*Her sister, with whom she shared the silver and gold, the first and only time that two sisters have done so.

3660. Kimi Gray (1946–)

1 Poor people are allowed the same dreams as everyone else.

Quoted in "Turning Public Housing Over to Resident
Owners" by Jerome Cramer, Time (New York) 12 December
1988

2 People don't throw trash on the ground when they know it soon will be their turn to pick it up.

Ibid.

3661. Patricia Hampl (1946–)

1 Poetry has always laid claim to the spirit. And it probably should be no surprise that a secular society like ours conceals plenty of religious ache. Yet the assumption of a secular consciousness in American cultural life is so strong that when contemporary American poets not only address God directly but make it clear that the search for God lies at the core of their enterprise, it can become a jolt.

Review of A Silence Opens by Amy Clampitt,* Virgin Time
1992

*See 2365.

. . . the world was not set up for sitting and staring. . . .

Blue Arabesque, A Search for the Sublime 2006

3 A painting must depict the act of seeing, not the object seen.

Ibid.

3662. Ewa Hauser (1946–)

1 These young women have not experienced any oppression themselves, have had free access to education, and have not yet gone through the drudgery of household chores and childbearing, and so they express a sincere regret that they grew up in a society where they were expected to be emancipated.

Ana's Land: Sisterhood in Eastern Europe, Tanya Renne,* ed.
1996

*See 4830.

3663. Ursula Hegi (1946–)

1 By then Trudi had come up against that moment when she knew that praying for something did not make it happen, that this was it: that there was no God-magic; that she was as tall as she would ever be; that she would die some day; and that anything that would happen to her until that day of her death would be up to her to resolve.

Ch. 1, Stones from the River 1994

2 Without men, the barriers between the married and unmarried women blurred: suddenly they were more alike than different. No longer did respect come to them because of their husbands' positions, but because of their own abilities.

Ibid.

3 "Getting what you want has to do with holding it in your mind so strongly that you keep returning to it . . . so that you are always linked to it."

The Vision of Emma Blau 2000

4 It made him uneasy, this vision of a time he hadn't lived . . . yet, it rooted itself in his mind as potent as memory, influencing his decisions, shaping his future.

Ibid.

3664. Sylvia Ann Hewlett (1946–)

1 Women can be playwrights, presidential candidates, and CEOs, but increasingly, they cannot be mothers.

Ch. 1, *Creating a Life: Professional Women and the Quest for Children* 2004

2 Most women become stalled or sidelined during the early or midpoint stretches of the career highway. Few make it into the fast lane or get to participate in the end game.

Ibid.

3665. Sarah Blaffer Hrdy (1946–)

1 Biology, it is sometimes thought, has worked against women.

Ch. 1, *The Woman That Never Evolved* 1982

2 A woman who is committed to being a mother will learn to love any baby, whether it's her own or not; a woman not committed to or prepared for being a mother may well not be prepared to love any baby, not even her own.

Mother Nature: A History of Mothers, Infants, and Natural Selection 1999

3 As I would learn, mothers have worked for as long as our species has existed, and they have depended on others to help them rear their children.

Introduction, Ibid.

4 Today, mothers in developed countries, and with them fathers and children, enter uncharted terrain. Without anyone raising their hands to volunteer, we have become guinea pigs in a vast social experiment that reveals what women who can control reproduction really want to do.

Ch. 1, Ibid.

5 Human mothers learn to recognize their own babies in the days right after birth, and gradually "fall in love." Since babies return the favor, the baby's attachment to the mother further reinforces her commitment. This is why when babies are adopted, the younger the better.

Ch. 5, Ibid.

3666. Sibyl James (1946–)

1 The Chinese government was offering me a free roundtrip, a modest salary, and housing . . . for the first time in my life I was being offered a one-year contract with medical benefits . . . And that is the heart of the tale. For these pages are the stories and meditations of a resident foreigner, not a tourist—and all the sickness and cures, the struggle and trust that such a status confers.

Preface, *In China With Harpo and Karl* 1990

2 First, be short. Or stand beneath an open skylight in the bus roof. Be thin. Be very thin. To get on or off be Kung Fu elbows and not worry. . . . Last week at Hong Kou Park I saw a bonsai exhibition—stalls and stalls of tiny trees bent into shapes the

Chinese find pleasing, a sort of stay against the chaos of the natural. Suddenly I understood the secret of buses. My bones leaned together, my chest concaved. I found a space that fit me when the doors shut.

"Busing," Ibid.

3667. Kathleen Hall Jamieson (1946–)

1 I'm a real purist, and I believe that when people move into the Senate or the House they ought to put everything they own in a blind trust. . . . Our elected officials are in a position to influence stock prices and get special access to information that is potentially useful to their personal interests. And you don't want them to make public policy decisions about something they have a self-interest in.

Quoted in "The Perils and Profits of Lawmakers in the Market" by Don Van Natta, Jr., *The New York Times,* Sct. 4, p. 1 *16 July 2000*

3668. Marcia Carolyn Kaptur (1946–)

1 The American people have the right to know who holds the mortgage on America.

Congressional Speech *October 1988*

2 This generation* was the most unselfish America has ever seen. They never asked anybody for anything in return.

"Veterans Gather to Dedicate World War II Memorial," *The New York Times 30 May 2004*

*Re "the greatest generation," World War II vets.

3669. Mary Jo Leddy (1946–)

1 The evil of the Holocaust was realized through the exercise of a certain kind of power—coercive power. It was a power that sought to dominate and control. It was a power legitimated through law, buttressed by propaganda, augmented by terror, and affected through all the institutions of society.

"A Different Power," *Different Voices: Women and the Holocaust,* Carol Rittner & John K. Roth, eds. *1993*

2 What we say with our words is so much less important than what we mean with our lives. Only our lives give weight to our words.

Ch. 1, *Radical Gratitude* 2002

3 Like Jacob we each have an angel to wrestle with, the messenger who reveals our true name which is both wound and blessing.

Ibid.

4 Ours is a culture constituted through craving. It works as long as people want more, want to go shopping, want to think that freedom has to do with a range of choices available to the shopper. Without consumption there would be no production—and no profit.

"The Captivity of Craving," Ibid.

5 We are held captive when our deep spiritual longings are transformed into cravings for more.

Ibid.

6 There are people, religiously committed people and men and women of good will, who hunger and thirst for justice. However, if this hunger for justice is more akin to a craving for a *more* just and perfect world, then even the finest efforts for

justice will replicate the patterns of craving that lie close to the heart of our culture.

"Partial Liberations," Ibid.

3670. Barbara Lee (1946–)

1 In the past, women have been judged on the Three H's—hair, husband and hemlines. If one woman runs, she's judged on the Three H's; if two women run, they're considered by the press as candidates in a cat fight. But when three run, the scrutiny of them as women diminishes, and they are viewed as capable people who are looked at through their accomplishments, their agenda and their vision of the future.

Quoted in "Women Who Could Be President" by Jane Ciabattari, *Parade Magazine* 7 February 1999

2 I do not dispute the president's* intent to rid the world of terrorism—but we have many means to reach that goal, and measures that spawn further acts of terror or that do not address the sources of hatred do not increase our security.

"Why I opposed the resolution to authorize force," *San Francisco Chronicle* 23 September 2001

*Re George W. Bush (1946–), 43rd president of USA (2001–09).

3671. Candy Lightner (1946–)

1 Death by drunken driving is a socially acceptable form of homicide.

Quoted in "Legislature Eyes Harsher Laws . . ." by Chuck Buxton, *San Jose Mercury* 20 April 1981

2 Victims of drunk drivers have no place to turn. Judges drink and drive, juries drink and drive, D.A.'s drink and drive. They're going to have sympathy for the drunk driver. They don't have sympathy for the rapist, the murderer, the mugger.

Quoted in "Mother's Crusade to Get Drunk Drivers Off the Streets" by Beverly Beyette, *The Los Angeles Times* 11 June 1981

3672. Genny Lim (1946–)

1 A woman is a ritual
A house that must accommodate
A house that must endure
Generation after generation
Of wind and torment, of fire and rain
A house with echoing rooms
Closets with hidden cries
Walls with stretchmarks
Windows with eyes.

"Wonder Woman," St. 6 (1981), *The Woman That I Am, The Literature and Culture of Contemporary Women of Color*, D. Soyini Madison,* ed. 1994

*See 3912.

3673. Kristin Carol Luker (1946–)

1 Early childbearing doesn't make young women poor; rather poverty makes women bear children at an early age. Society should worry not about some epidemic of "teenage pregnancy" but about the hopeless, discouraged and empty lives that early childbearing denotes.

Dubious Conceptions: The Politics of Teenage Pregnancy 1996

2 Early childbearing would decrease if poor teenagers had better schools and safe neighborhoods, if their mothers and fathers had decent jobs so that teens could afford the luxury of being children for a while longer.

Ibid.

3674. Catherine A. MacKinnon (1946–)

1 The law sees and treats women the way men see and treat women.

"Viewpoint: Feminism, Marxism, Method, and the State: Towards Feminist Jurisprudence," *Signs: A Journal of Women in Culture and Society* 1983

2 Lawyers considering whether anything can be done for a woman who is damaged in ways that make her less than the perfect case rarely conclude that they should confront or change the law. They look at cases the way surfers look at waves.

Introduction, *Feminism Unmodified* 1987

3 . . . anyone with an ounce of political analysis should know that freedom before equality, freedom before justice, will only further liberate the power of the powerful and will never free what is most in need of expression.

Ibid.

4 For purposes of sex discrimination law, to be a woman means either to be like a man, or to be like a lady. We have to meet either the male standards for males or the male standards for females.

"On Exceptionality: Women as Women in Law," Ibid.

5 . . . it is only the exceptional woman who escapes gender inequality enough to be able to claim that she is injured by it. It seems that we already have to be equal before we can complain of inequality.

Ibid.

6 This has been at the heart of every women's initiative for civil equality from suffrage to the Equal Rights Amendment: the simple notion that law—only words, words that set conditions as well as express them, words that are their own kind of art, words in power, words in authority, words in life—respond to women as well as men.

Afterword, Ibid.

3675. Helena Matheopoulos (1946?–)

1 As an interpreter, he has to form an opinion about the musical and spiritual meaning of each work and acquire a mental image of the sound contained in the score [. . .] the quality of his musicianship, his personality, his depth and quality as a human being (or lack of it) will greatly affect his perceptions of what lies behind those black dots. For musical notation is an inexact, mysterious language, and even instructions written in words—like allegro or pianissimo—are subject to different and highly individual interpretations.

Maestro 1982

2 [Pavarotti* was] the first to understand, manipulate and exploit, aided by an expert, well-oiled publicity machine, the American yen for "hype" . . .

Divo 1986

*Luciano P— (1835–2007), Italian operatic tenor; one of "The Three Tenors."

3 The past eight years have seen the steady rise of divas capable of drawing mass audiences as well as enthralling the cognoscenti, and who deliver performances to rival those of the great singers of the past.

The message of the decade is: forget nostalgia.

Introduction, Diva, The New Generation: The Sopranos and Mezzos of the Decade Discuss Their Roles 1998

3676. Jessica Tuchman Mathews (1946–)

1   The automobile reaches to the heart of the American self-image in the way the horse once did in the West. It's going to be hard to change.

>Quoted in *A World of Ideas* by Bill Moyers *1989*

2   Countries are starting to see that they can't have economic growth without protecting their resource base. The economic growth disappears as the fisheries disappear, as the forest disappears, as soil erosion progresses. They can't have real growth without environmental management.

>Ibid.

3   We're going to need a new sense of shared destiny, that we're in this together. We, the family of nations, are going to have to develop somehow some shared sense, almost like a joint business venture, that we work together, or we're all going to suffer.

>Ibid.

4   Diplomacy is kind of like a basketball game. An awful lot can happen in the last 30 seconds.

>Quoted by Jon Sawyer in "Diplomacy leaves U.S. isolated in end game," Knight Ridder Tribune *9 March 2003*

5   It is imperative for the United States to rescue and then rejuvenate the nonproliferation regime. It is critical to our security interests in the Middle East, a region in which a nuclear arms race could be fatally destabilizing, and throughout the world.

>"Reinvigorate Nuclear Nonproliferation," *Democracy: A Journal of Ideas,* #6 Fall *2007*

3677. Mary McCaslin (1946?–)

1   Bury me out on the lone prairie
Near the mountains I could never see

>The speakers, they all gasp to clear their lungs for their luncheon speeches
This year's new campaign is to save the canyons and the beaches

>"The Dealers" *1975*

2   There's a ghost in every machine. What else explains the disappearance of that all important piece of writing from the computer screen? Did it fly off into the ether when you weren't looking, or was it gobbled up and digested by the hard drive?

>"Confessions of a Near Luddite," *Santa Cruz Style 3 March 2007*

3678. Liza Minnelli (1946–)

1   In Hollywood now when people die they don't say, "Did he leave a will?" but "Did he leave a diary?"

>Quoted in *Observer* (London) *13 August 1989*

2   I have the best taste in friends and the worst taste in husbands.

>Quoted by Shannon Breen, *St. Petersburg Times 6 October 2007*

3679. Janet Horowitz Murray (1946–)

1   . . . for now we have to listen very, very carefully to hear, amid the cacophony of cyberspace, the first fumbling chords of the awakening bard.

>*Hamlet on the Holodeck: The Future of Narrative in Cyberspace 1997*

2   Mouse-clicking through the mind of the insomniac is like a walk through a labyrinth.

>Ibid.

3   In order for electronic narrative to reach a higher level of expressiveness, the medium as a whole must make that shift that Charlotte [Brontë]* made, that is, away from adolescent rehearsal fantasies and toward the expression of more realistic desires.

>Ibid.

*See 934.

3680. Marilyn Nelson (1946–)

1   slow lips recite the credo, smother yawns,
and ask forgiveness for being so bored.

>"Churchgoing," St. 1, *For the Body 1978*

2   I have no answer to the blank inequity
of a four-year-old dying of cancer.
I saw her on TV and wept
with my mouth full of meatloaf.

>"Mama's Promise," St. 1, *Mama's Promises 1985*

3   Big deal,
said Abba Jacob.
Miracles happen all the time.
We're here,
aren't we?

>"Abba Jacob and Miracles," St. 2, *Magnificat 1994*

4   *The true magic is the love contained in the universe.*
This is the original enchanter.

>"The Plotinus Suite," VIII. The True Magic, St. 4, Ibid.

5   Go into yourself, look around.

>And if what you see there isn't beautiful,
don't stop smoothing, polishing, cutting away until
you are *wholly yourself, nothing but pure light.*

>"The Plotinus Suite," X. Ennead I.vi., St. 3, Ibid.

3681. Linda Niemann (1946–)

1   On-the-road books are the Ur-narratives of our invading culture; they hearken back to voyages of discovery and to the building of the roads themselves. The road was created through the westward "manifest destiny" genocidal land rush, the stories it inspired having arrival as their ending. And the impulse to go on the road is a given: it was both the initiating act of our culture and its answer to any unsolvable problem.

>"Wheels of fortune," *New Directions for Women,* Vol. XVI, No. 4 *January 1999*

3682. Helena Norberg-Hodge (1946–)

1   In the traditional culture, villagers provided for their basic needs without money. They developed skills that enabled them to grow barley at 12,000 feet (3,600 metres) and to manage yaks and other animals at even higher elevations. People knew how to build houses with their own hands from the materials of the immediate surroundings. The only thing they actually needed from outside the region was salt, for which they traded.

>*Ancient Futures: Learning from Ladakh 1991*

2   Equal voice should be given to female perspectives and values.

>Quoted in "Survival Economics," *Earth Island Journal Spring 1992*

3   The [World Trade Organisation] demonstrations [in Seattle in December 1999] , came about as a result of a build-up of awareness by millions of people worldwide that the root cause

of escalating unemployment and environmental breakdown wasn't what they'd been led to believe. It wasn't dark-skinned immigrants taking their jobs away. It wasn't a question of right or left politics. It wasn't the result of some sort of evolutionary "progress," innate human greed or even propensity to over-populate. It was a result of institutional structures that had been imposed by governments.

Interview by David Leser, *Good Weekend* 27 May 2000

4 There is almost nothing more important than the localisation of food. Every human being has to eat three times a day, so to call a system efficient that separates people further and further from their source of food is nothing short of madness.

Ibid.

5 What happened under colonialism was that powers from Europe moved across the entire globe in search of resources, and they used force, and as we know, even killing, slaughtering, enslaving people, or carrying them to another part of the world, to work in monocultures for export. In the Western world, we came to identify countries according to what resource they provided for the center; so whole countries became tin countries, coffee countries and so on.

Interview by Nermeen Shaikh, *Asia Source* (asiasource.org) *15 July 2008*

6 Conditions are not ideal in most rural areas of the so-called "Third World" (terrible poverty following generations of colonialism, monocropping, an exploding population, to give only a few indicators), but they are vastly better than in most urban slums.

Ibid.

7 Children need to have real live role models because real live role models never have perfect eyes and perfect teeth and perfect bodies; they are just human beings.

Ibid.

3683. Virginia O'Brien (1946–)

1 You can succeed on your own terms, but you can't succeed alone.

Success on Our Own Trems: Tales of Extraordinary, Ordinary Business Women 1998

2 The intrinsic value of work, the ability to have an impact and operate in relationship with others, seem to motivate women more than anything else—more than climbing to the top, more than financial reward, more than power for power's sake.

Ibid.

3684. Susan Moller Okin (1946–2004)

1 What should be done when the claims of minority cultures or religions clash with the norm of gender equality that is at least formally endorsed by liberal states (however much they continue to violate it in their practice)?

"Is Multiculturalism Bad for Women?" *Is Multiculturalism Bad for Women?* Joshua Cohen and Matthew Howard, eds. *1999*

2 Discrimination against and control of the freedom of females is practiced, to a greater or lesser extent, by virtually all cultures, past and present, but especially religious ones and those that look to the past—to ancient texts or revered traditions—for guidelines or rules about how to live in the contemporary world.

Ibid.

3 Thus, many culturally-based customs aim to control women and render them, especially sexually and reproductively, servile to men's desires and interests. Sometimes, moreover, "culture" or "traditions" are so closely linked with the control of women that they are virtually equated.

Ibid.

4 Home is, after all, where much of culture is practiced, preserved, and transmitted to the young.

Ibid.

5 I think we—especially those of us who consider ourselves politically progressive and opposed to all forms of oppression—have been too quick to assume that feminism and multiculturalism are both good things which are easily reconciled.

Ibid.

3685. Susie Orbach (1946–)

1 Fat is a social disease, and fat is a feminist issue.

Introduction, *Fat is a Feminist Issue 1978*

2 An obsessive involvement with food flows out of a cultural insistence that what they eat, how much they eat, and how they cook for others, is their especial domain. Food is the medium through which women are addressed; in turn, food has become the language of women's response.

Ch. 1, *Hunger Strike: Starving Amidst Plenty 2000*

3 Anorexia nervosa is perhaps the most dramatic outcome of the culture's obsession with regulating body size.

Ibid.

3686. Dolly Parton (1946–)

1 Now that I have won my freedom, like an eagle,
I am eager for the sky.

"Light of a Clear Blue Morning" *1976*

2 Butterflies are colorful and bright and gentle and have no way to harm you. They go about their business and bring others pleasure while doing it, because just seeing one flying around makes people happy. I'd like to think of myself as bringing people happiness while I do my business, which is my music. I'm content with what I am, and butterflies seem to be content to be just what they are, too. They're gentle, but determined.

Quoted in "Introduction: Hello, Dolly," *Dolly* by Alanna Nash *1978*

3 Sure we had runnin' water. When we'd run and get it!

Ch. 1, Ibid.

4 Oh, sometimes I go walking through fields where we walked
Long ago in the sweet used to be
And the flowers still grow, but they don't smell as sweet
As they did when you picked them for me

"Do I Ever Cross Your Mind" (1973), *Trio II* (album) *1999*

3687. Candace B. Pert (1946–)

1 There's another form of energy that we have not yet understood. For example, there's a form of energy that appears to leave the body when the body dies. . . . Your mind is in every cell of your body. . . . There are many phenomena that we can't explain without going into energy.

from *Bill Moyer's Healing of the Mind*, Quoted in Ch. 1, *Anatomy of the Spirit: The Seven Stages of Power and Healing*, Caroline Myss* *1996*

*See 4126.

2 The molecules of emotion run every system in the body.
Molecules of Emotion: Why You Feel the Way You Feel 1997

3688. Adrian Piper (1946–)

1 I would never have believed it could be so agonizingly difficult to make verbal sense of my immediate creative impulses. I felt dull and completely helpless. I wanted to say what I was doing, and why, and I couldn't. Words careened into mental view, collided, and joined or separated randomly, as I flailed wildly among them, trying dimly to grasp their connections and pin them to my thoughts. It was a nightmare.
Essay (p. 11), *Out of Order, Out of Sight,* Vol. I *1996*

2 Performance art necessarily has human subjectivity as part of its content. To situate human subjectivity in the role of the art object is to invite the audience to engage with it, and with its own subjectivity, and to transcend them. But this requires a high degree of skill in interpersonal fine-tuning, and attention to the subtle psychologistics of social interaction. Most of us, who have been trained to pummel, slash, and besmirch objects in the isolation of our studios, have yet to achieve the requisite expertise.
Essay (1984; p. 104), Vol. II, Ibid.

3 Doing philosophy disciplines my urge to fly, improves my sense of direction, and enables me to soar, for a time, above the moral cretins. But it doesn't change their behavior . . . so they always bring me down again eventually. And there is no escape: . . . My art practice is a reflecting mirror of light and darkness, a high sunny window that holds out to me the promise of release into the night.
"Flying" (1987; p. 231–232), Ibid.

3689. Gail Pool (1946–)

1 Even with the best of maps and instruments, we can never fully chart our journeys.
"The war at home," *The Women's Review of Books,* Vol. XII, Nos. 10–11 *July 1995*

2 Editors are forced to rely upon secondhand information, much of it insufficient, biased, or inappropriate, about the nature and quality of the book they're selecting or rejecting for review.
Ch. 1, *Faint Praise: The Plight of Book Reviewing in America 2006*

3690. Minnie Bruce Pratt (1946–)

1 She has three sisters, Lethean, Evie, and Ora Gilder.
When they aggravate her she wants to pinch
their habits off like potato bugs off the leaf.
But she meets them each weekend for cards and jokes
while months go by without her speaking to her brother.
"My Mother Loves Women," *The Sound of One Fork 1981*

2 You had not acted like a man
and I never loved you better
"Love Poem to an Ex-Husband," St. 4, Ibid.

3 We don't say we're too old for this.
"#65 Parked Down by the Potomac," St. 1 (5 October 1987), *An Intimate Wilderness, Lesbian Writers on Sexuality,* Judith Barrington,* ed. *1991*
*See 3476.

4 "You are not only a lesbian, but very, very queer. You love a woman who is manly, and yet do not want her to be completely man. In fact, you desire her *because* she is both."
"You," *S/he 1995*

5 But now I have spoken, my self, I can ask
for you: that you'll know evil when you smell it;
that you'll know good and do it, and see how both
run loose through your lives; that then you'll remember
you come from dirt and history; that you'll choose
memory, not anesthesia. . . .
"Poem for My Sons," St. 5, *Walking Back up Depot Street 1999*

3691. Gilda Radner (1946–1989)

1 [Audiences] all applaud, but none of them will come home with you and look at your back someplace to see if you have a pimple.
Quoted in "The Many Faces of Gilda" by Roy Blount, Jr., *Rolling Stone* (New York) *2 November 1978*

2 I think of my illness [ovarian cancer] as a school, and finally I've graduated.
Quoted in *Life* (New York) *1988*

3 Television was earthbound, but the movies were up in the stars.
"The Baby and the Movie Star," *It's Always Something 1989*

4 You cannot live in Los Angeles for any period of time without eventually trying to write a screenplay. It's like a flu bug that you catch . . . Even the plumber has a screenplay in his truck.
Ibid.

5 Nothing in our personal lives was sacred. We used all of it for material on the show. The most important thing was those ninety minutes live on Saturday night. So what if your whole world was falling apart as long as you could find a joke in it and make up a scene. Millions of Americans saw what we did, and it was a charmed time. We thought we were immortal, at least for five years. But that doesn't exist anymore.
"Cancer," Ibid.

6 It is so hard for us little human beings to accept this deal that we get. It's really crazy, isn't it? We get to live, then we have to die. What we put into every moment is all we have. You can drug yourself to death or you can smoke yourself to death or eat yourself to death, or you can do everything right and be healthy and then get hit by a car. Life is so great, such a neat thing, and yet all during it we have to face death, which can make you nuts and depressed.
Ibid.

7 It just goes to show you, it's always something.
Coined by her character, Roseanne Rosanna-Danna on *Saturday Night Live passim*

3692. Nancy Venable Raine (1946–)

1 Before I sat down to write about the seventh anniversary of my rape, I had come to the conclusion that my continued silence was a wounding disguised as a healing. Denial had been ticking, and when the timer went off—seven years after the rape—and words finally came, I was discovering that truthtelling could be healing disguised as a wounding.
After Silence: Rape and My Journey Back 1998

2 The words "shut up" are the most terrible words I know. The man who raped me spat these words out over and over during the hours of my attack—when I screamed, when I tried to talk him out of what he was doing, when I protested.

Ibid.

3 I have noted what has come into my view as I go about my life, seeing the world through the eyes of a woman who remembers rape.

Ibid.

3693. Shulamit Reinharz (1946–)

1 I will never know the experience of others, but I can know my own, and I can approximate theirs by entering their world. This approximation marks the tragic, perpetually inadequate aspect of social research.

On Becoming a Social Scientist 1984

2 But there is another form [of anti-Semitism] that flourishes today—Jewish anti-Semitism. It seems like a contradiction in terms, but it is not. In fact, Jewish anti-Semitism is particularly troublesome because it seems to corroborate the views of anti-Semitic non-Jews.

"Fighting Jewish anti-Semitism," *The Jewish Advocate 23 July 2008*

3694. Linda Ronstadt (1946–)

1 The thing you have to be prepared for is that other people don't always dream your dream.

Quoted in "Ronstadt Backed into Her Notoriety" by Lawrence DeVine, Knight-Ridder Newspapers *3 October 1986*

2 The great temper tantrum of the 60's . . .

Ibid.

3 We were raised with the idea that we had limitless chances and we got very shocked to learn that wasn't the case.

Ibid.

3695. Susan Sarandon (1946–)

1 Peace is compassion. Peace is understanding and acceptance. Peace is the absence of hunger, thirst and illness . . . Let us stand up for our dream and try to prove that artists can make a difference.

Speech, Cinema for Peace (Berlin), *2005*

2 You can't tend to somebody's soul and ignore their body. You can't talk in abstract terms.

Quoted in "'The Power of One': Interview with Susan Sarandon" by Linda Sheahen, beliefnet.com *14 January 2008*

3 I want [my children] to respect the divine in everyone. And understand that with privilege comes responsibility. Everyone has a responsibility towards this larger family of man, but especially if you're privileged, that increases your responsibility. I want them to understand the joy of empowerment, of service. I want them to understand that doing the right thing is a joyful experience, that it isn't a grind.

Ibid.

4 I think I'm an actor because I have very strong imagination and empathy. I never studied acting, but those two qualities are exactly the qualities that make for an activist.

Ibid.

3696. Patti Smith (1946–)

1 Jesus died
For somebody's sins
But not mine.

"Gloria (In Excelsis Deo)," *Horses* (album) *1975*

2 Americans just don't know what being a movie star's all about.

Quoted in "Patti Smith: Can You Hear Me Ethiopia?" by Scott Cohen, *Circus Magazine 14 December 1976*

3 He spared the child and spoiled the rod
I have not sold myself to God

"Babelogue," *Easter* (album) *1978*

4 People have the power
To redeem the work of fools
Upon the meek the graces shower
It's decreed the people rule

"People Have the Power," *Dream of Life* (album) *1988*

5 I'm an American, I pay taxes in my name and they are giving millions and millions of dollars to a country such as Israel and cluster bombs and defense technology and those bombs were dropped on common citizens in Qana.* It's terrible. It's a human rights violation.

Quoted in "Patti Smith rails against Israel and US" by Louise Jury, *The Independent* (London) *9 September 2006*
*(a.k.a. Cana), a village in Lebanon shelled by Israeli forces on 18 April 1996.

3697. Barbara Smith (1946–)

1 Then there was the magazine called LIFE which promised more about the Deaths.

"Poem for My Sister (One) Birmingham Sunday" (1963), *Southern Voices August/September 1974*

2 Autonomy and separatism are fundamentally different. Whereas autonomy comes from a position of strength, separatism comes from a position of fear. When we're truly autonomous we can deal with other kinds of people, a multiplicity of issues, and with difference, because we have formed a solid base of strength.

Introduction (p. xl), *Home Girls, A Black Feminist Anthology 1983*

3698. Charlene Spretnak (1946–)

1 Many feminists feel there is good reason to use female metaphors for the divine. First, it overturns a cornerstone of gender politics in patriarchal cultures. Second, the symbolization matches physical reality; has anyone ever seen anything spring into existence because a male finger was pointed toward it? We are not amused by the mythic narratives that steal the generative power of the female; womb envy should find less aggressive outlets.

"Essay: Wholly Writ," *Ms.* (New York) *March/April 1993*

2 Democratic rule by the people, once considered a scared trust, has become so irrelevant to the majority of our countrymen that they do not even vote.

Ch. 1, *The Resurgence of the Real 1997*

3 We are told that the world is shrinking, that vast distance has been conquered by computer and fax, and that the Earth is now a "global village" in which all of us are connected as never

before. It feels, however, quite the opposite. It feels as if distancing and disconnection are shaping modern life.

If anything is shrinking, it is the fullness of being that is experienced by the modern self.

Ibid.

3699. Gila Svirsky (1946–   )

1   The women's peace movement in Palestine and in Israel believes that the time has come to end the bloodshed. We refuse to accept more warfare in our lives. We refuse to go along with the fear. We refuse to give in to the violence. We refuse to be enemies of each other.

Address, UN Security Council 22 October 2002

2   At the moment there are two entirely separate things going on in the minds of Israelis. On the one hand there is the patriotic fervour that accompanies military action. When the general announces that this is a matter of survival, everyone rallies behind him. But the other side of this is an underlying belief that ultimately there is no military solution to this. That belief is as well entrenched as the current belief that says right now we have no alternative but to use arms.

"Voices from the Conflict," *BBC News 2005?*

3   Women can plant subversive ideas of peace in the minds of the young before the agents of war have even noticed.

GilaSvirsky.com *n.d.*

4   Women are not just the mothers, teachers, nurses, and social workers of our societies. We are also secret agents serving up politics with dinner, teaching the lessons of nonviolence to every child in our classrooms, every patient in our care, every client we advise, every son and daughter that we love.

Ibid.

3700. Meredith Tax (1946?–   )

1   A woman comes to believe that personal truth, the truth of the nuances of individual behavior, is ultimate . . . But this concentration of the personal is another way society makes her unfit to run her mind. . . . Once people have gotten past the realization that they are neurotic as individuals, they are able to realize that their problem is not an individual one, but one they share with the rest of their community. At this point, the realm of psychology becomes the proper sphere of political analysis. . . .

"Anais Nin:* A Woman's Diary" (*The Old Mole*, No. 13),
Quoted in *The Journey Home, How Jewish Women Shaped
Modern America*, p. 281, by Joyce Antler 1997

*See 1979.

3701. Shirley M. Tilghman (1946–   )

1   I was very organized. It sounds ridiculous, but I think I jettisoned everything except family and work. I had this mindset: I was not going to feel guilty when I was at work, and I was not going to feel guilty when I was with the children.

Quoted in "A conversation with Shirley Tilghman" by Claudia
Dreifus, *The New York Times 8 July 2003*

2   We knew [in 1977] that this was a major moment in the history of molecular biology. The idea that we were looking at the chemical composition of the first few genes that had ever been studied in biology was just an amazing moment.

What made it truly thrilling was that the genes were organized in a way that was totally unexpected. So nature took us by surprise.

Ibid.

3   Stem cells, I see it as an ethical debate, which, in my view, devolves down to a single question: whether you invest in an embryonic stem cell sitting in a petri dish the same moral status as you do a living human being. If your answer is yes, then you have to be opposed to the use of human embryonic stem cells. If your answer is no, stem cells are a perfectly legitimate subject for study.

Ibid.

4   I'd like to see us teaching more than a canon, a collection of [scientific] facts, but why this is exciting, why is the exploration of nature one of the most wonderful ways to spend one's life.

Ibid.

3702. Sue Townsend (1946–   )

1   Friday, January 2nd. BANK HOLIDAY IN SCOTLAND, FULL MOON. I felt rotten today. It's my mother's fault for singing "My Way" at two o-clock in the morning at the top of the stairs. Just my luck to have a mother like her. There is a chance my parents could be alcoholics. Next year I could be in a children's home.

The Secret Diary of Adrian Mole, Aged 13 3/4 1982

2   Babies hardly take any space at all. They are only about 21 inches long.

Ibid.

3   I was racked with sexuality but it wore off when I helped my father put manure on our rose bed.

Ibid.

3703. Marilyn vos Savant (1946–   )

1   Moderation may be fine for parents and politicians, but science, literature and art need the bold.

"Ask Marilyn," *Parade Magazine 18 August 1991*

2   To me, the major difference between a broken heart and a broken spirit is that people break hearts and time mends them, but *time* breaks spirits and *people* mend them.

Ibid., *February 1993*

3   A fool is someone whose pencil wears out before its eraser does.

"Ask Marilyn," *Parade Magazine* n.d.

4   Being defeated is often a temporary condition. Giving up is what makes it permanent.

Ibid.

5   A good idea will keep you awake during the morning, but a great idea will keep you awake during the night.

Ibid.

3704. Susan Vreeland (1946–   )

1   In the end, it's only the moments that we have, the kiss on the palm, the joint wonder at the furrowed texture of a fir trunk or at the infinitude of grains of sand in a dune. Only the moments.

"Adagia," *Girl in Hyacinth Blue 1999*

2   I came to see that knowing what love isn't might be just as valuable, though infinitely less satisfying, as knowing what it is.

"Hyacinth Blues," Ibid.

3 "The line between defeat and immortality is sometimes as thin as thread."

Ch. 14, *The Passion of Artemisia* 2002

4 Regardless of Galileo's logic, the highest of arts, I realized, is to uplift the spirit, whatever means one uses.

Ch. 15, Ibid.

5 "It's Stanley Park.* The interior. It's so deep and quiet and still. It could heal a person, body and soul. I get a sense of some presence breathing there. God's too big to be squeezed into a stuffy church, but I feel Him there in the spaces between the trees.

Ch. 8, *The Forest Lover* 2004
*A 1,000-acre park that abuts Vancouver, British Columbia, Canada; established in 1888.

6 "We start this life and we've got, most of us, all that we need. Then circumstance or accident robs us—a finger or a toe or a friend or a dream—and we go on, and maybe we even learn something. Loss or no loss, we go on."

Ch. 10, Ibid.

7 "Scrape scales off a fish, feathers off a bird, skin off a man and you get the same thing underneath," William said.

Ch. 26, Ibid.

8 Why was such a forest called virgin, as if it were untouched? Nothing here was untouched.

Ch. 42, Ibid.

3705. Anna Lee Walters (1946–)

1 The ever swollen hills in Oklahoma have given birth many times. . . . It is a land that drinks a lot of water and never seems to swallow much.

"Autobiography" (1977), *American Indian Women, Telling Their Lives*, Gretchen M. Bataille and Kathleen Mullen Sands, eds. 1981

2 The old folks are all gone. They were tired, prepared and they went on. Life goes on. Nothing diminishes it. We have been taught also that life is a fragile thing. Grandma always said that it almost feels too good to be alive.

Ibid.

3706. Marina Warner (1946–)

1 For while Mary* provides a focus for the steeliest asceticism, she is also the ultimate of fertility symbols. The mountain blossoms spontaneously; so does the mother maid.

Alone of All Her Sex 1978

2 The Virgin Mary* has inspired some of the loftiest architecture, some of the most moving poetry, some of the most beautiful paintings in the world; she has filled men and women with deep joy and fervent trust; she has been an image of the ideal that has entranced and stirred men and women to the noblest emotions of love and pity and awe. But the reality her myth describes is over; the moral code she affirms has been exhausted. . . .

As an acknowledged creation of Christian mythology, the Virgin's legend will endure in its splendor and lyricism, but it will be emptied of moral significance, and thus lose its present real powers to heal and to harm.

Ibid.

*See 79.

3 The BBC* is a fine institution which I care very deeply about, yet the striking absence of women reproduces very clearly the prejudices of the country.

"Sex, symbols and the fallen virgin," The *Times* (London) 14 January 1994
*British Broadcasting Corporation.

4 If only life were more hospitable to children, there wouldn't be this tragic controlling tension that gives women their only power and authority. I'm all for women having authority, but it is easier to be fond of children in climates where children are welcome.

Ibid.

5 . . . I don't think behavior should disqualify people from being MPs,* not because I condone it but because MPs should be representative of us all, with all our difficulties. . . .

Ibid.

*Members of Parliament (Britain).

3707. Sheila Pelz Weinberg (1946–)

1 We work all week, and on the seventh day we remember creation and pause, so that we can look around and feel more, take in all the wonders around us that we often miss the other six days.

Address, "Campus Pilgrimage to Reverse the Nuclear Arms Race" (1983), *Four Centuries of Jewish Women's Spirituality*, Ellen M. Umansky* & Dianne Ashton, eds. 1992
*See 4011.

2 An awareness of statistics, figures—numbers—is crucial to any serious endeavor. Sometimes we would like to ignore this dimension of our struggle, but we do so only at a cost to ourselves.

Ibid.

3 The task of peace, the journey in the wilderness that you are on, is a gathering from the four corners and a bringing to wholeness, which means *shalom*, which means peace.

Ibid.

3708. Kutlu Aslihan Yener (1946–)

1 [Growing up] I almost lived at the Natural History Museum in New York.

Quoted in *Twentieth-Century Women Scientists* by Lisa Yount 1996

2 [I] was interested in the fundamental blocks that make up the world.

Ibid.

3709. Patricia Aburdene (1947?–)

1 The most important thing you can master for the next decade won't be Fiber Optics 101 but rather learning how to learn.

"Trendspotters" (p. 60), *Working Woman Magazine* July 1987

2 The Industrial Age relied on brute strength, but the Information Age will rely on mental stamina—women's strong suit.

Ibid.

3710. Kathy Acker (1947–1997)

1 New York City is a pit-hole: Since the United States government, having decided that New York City is no longer part of

the United States of America, is dumping . . . all the people they don't want (artists, poor minorities and the media in general) on the city and refusing the city federal funds; the American bourgeoisie has left. Only the poor: artists, Puerto Ricans who can't afford to move . . . and rich Europeans . . . inhabit this city.

Meanwhile the temperature is getting hotter and hotter so no one can think clearly. No one perceives. No one cares. Insane madness come out like life is a terrific party.

> "New York City in 1979", *Up Is Up but So Is Down, New York's Downtown Literary Scene, 1974–1992*, Brandon Stosuy, ed. 2006

3711. Ai (1947–)

1 Pretend you don't owe me a thing
and maybe we'll roll out of here,
leaving the past stacked up behind us:
old newspapers nobody's ever got to read again.

> "Twenty-Year Marriage," *Vice: New and Selected Poems 1999*

2 the poor have no children, just small people

> "Abortion," Ibid.

3 I traveled back through time
to the dark and heavy breathing part of my life
I thought was gone,
but it had only sunk from view
into the quicksand of my mind.

> "Grandfather Says," *Dread 2003*

3712. Paulette Bates Alden (1947–)

1 It would be funny—if it weren't so painful—how up until about the age of twenty-one the worst mistake a girl like me could make would be to have a baby before she got married, and then almost overnight the worst mistake became to get married and have a baby . . . both of which I had avoided. . . . But now I was beginning to wonder if maybe I wasn't about to make—if I hadn't already—the biggest mistake of all: I was about to miss out on having a child.

> *Crossing the Moon: A Journey Through Infertility 1996*

2 The maternal instinct waiting to be unleashed in me might turn out to be like the plant in *Little Shop of Horrors*.

> Ibid.

3713. Catherine Anderson (1947–)

1 All day she'll guide cloth along a line
of whirring needles, her arms & shoulders
rocking back & forth
with the machines—
200 porch size rugs behind her
before she can stop
to reach up, like her mother,
and pick the lint
out of her hair.

> "Womanhood," St. 2, *Working Classics: Poems on Industrial Life*, Peter Oresick and Nicholas Coles, eds. 1983

3714. Laurie Anderson (1947–)

1 All of nature talks to me. If I could just make out what it was trying to tell me. Listen!

> "Sharkey's Way," St. 3, *Spectral Display 1984*

2 If I were queen for a day
I'd give the ugly people all the money.
I'd rewrite the book of love
I'd make it funny.

> "Kerjillions of Stars," *Empty Places 1989*

3 What is history? It is an angel, being blown backwards into the future. It is a pile of debris.

> "The Dream Before," Ibid.

4 The willingness to be a fool, that's what I love most about this country. We don't have the same rules as Europeans.

> Quoted in "Hitching a Ride on the Great White Whale" by Roselee Goldeberg, *The New York Times*, Arts & Leisure 3 October 1999

5 Paradise
is exactly like
Where you are right now
Only much much
Better

> "Language Is a Virus," *Laurie Anderson n.d.*

3715. Louise Arbour (1947–)

1 China has declared its commitment to human rights and has raised expectations for the country to match its growing prosperity with a firm commitment to advancing human rights.

> Quoted in "U.N. Official Urges China to Deepen Commitment to Rights" by Chris Buckley, *The New York Times* 3 September 2005

2 There is an urgent need for the international community to monitor the unfolding human rights situation [in Sri Lanka], as these are not merely cease-fire violations, but grave breaches of international human rights and humanitarian law.

> Quoted in "U.N. Right Chief Urges Monitors for Sri Lanka" by Somini Sengupta, *The New York Times* 29 September 2006

3 Human rights protection begins in the national framework. There is no doubt about that. By the time you have to come to Geneva for redress, that means there's been a total collapse of the human rights protection system nationally and regionally. Asia, unfortunately, is not very well equipped with regional mechanisms, as compared to, say, Europe or Latin America, that has a human rights protective framework, or Africa, for that matter. So protection starts at home. And I think the embracing of human rights values has to be done very much by home communities.

> *Democracy Now! with Amy Goodman*,* Pacifica Radio 7 September 2007

*See 4408.1.

4 It seems to me that anything that is related to full gender equality is a fundamental human right. But the dictates of culture or religion or tradition are often put forward as clashing with that. It's the wrong debate.

> Quoted in "Departing Rights Official Raised Volume on Issues" by Marlise Simons, *The New York Times* 6 July 2008

5 It's a small miracle to see how far we have come since the 50 years of silence after Nuremberg.* All things considered, in human rights law we have achieved more in the past 15 years than in the previous 50 in taking personal criminal accountability to where it is now.

> Ibid.

*Re the trials of Nazi war criminals after World War II.

3716. Rae Armantrout (1947–)

1 We love our cat
   for her self
   regard is assiduous
   and bland

"Thing," *7 Poems Beard of Bees,* No. 15 *June 2004*

2 The present
   must be kept empty
   so that anything
   can happen

"Empty," Ibid.

3 The opposite
   of nothingness
   is direction

"Once," 3, Ibid.

4 Can dreamer
   outwit her dream?

   Not on a first date.

"My Advantage," *Up to Speed 2004*

3717. Gloria Macapagal Arroyo (1947–)

1 I'd rather be right than Popular.

State of the Nation Address *25 July 2005*

2 Join me as we begin to tear down the walls that divide. Let us build an edifice of peace, progress and economic stability.

Ibid.

3 The people want government that works for them at every level. They want good government that begins at their doorstep in the barangay,* and does not end before the closed door of a bureaucrat in Metro Manila.

Ibid.

*(a.k.a. Barrio), Native Filipino term for village.

3718. Barbara Lazear Ascher (1947?–)

1 [There] is a need to find and sing our own song, to stretch our limbs and shake them in a dance so wild that nothing can roost there, that stirs the yearning for solitary voyage.

Playing after Dark 1986

2 The hot, moist smell of babies fresh from naps.

Ibid.

3719. Maude Barlow (1947–)

1 A [United Nations] Covenant on the right to water would serve as a common, coherent body of rules for all nations and clarify that it is the role of the state to provide clean, affordable water to all of its citizens. Such a Covenant would also safeguard already accepted human rights and environmental principles.

"It's Time for the UN to Make Water a Human Right," *AlterNet.org 21 February 2008*

2 U.S. policies should not be dictating the world's fate. We need robust international standards and communities of action so that the world's diverse peoples may, together, identify key problems and enact viable solutions.

Ibid.

3 We are living in a period of history when the common heritage of both humanity and the earth appears to be under systemic siege. Under the current model of globalization, everything is for sale. Areas once considered our common heritage are being commodified, commercialized and privatized at an alarming rate. Today, more than ever before, the targets of this assault comprise the building blocks of life as we know it on this planet, including fresh water, the human genome, seeds and plant varieties, the air and atmosphere, the oceans and outer space. The assault on, and defence of, the commons is one of the great ideological and social struggles of our times.

Acceptance Speech, with Tony Clarke, Right Livelihood Awards (Stockholm), *9 December 2005*

4 Water is a sacred component of the commons; it belongs to our common humanity, the earth and all living species.

Ibid.

5 You can't really charge for a human right; you can't trade it or deny it to someone because they don't have money. And we need laws at every level of government, from the most local to international, on the current abuse of water. All of us are going to have to change our relationship with water.

Quoted in "Blue Gold: An Interview with Maude Barlow" by Jeff Fleischer, *Mother Jones 14 January 2005*

3720. Ellen Bass (1947–)

1 People say "time heals all wounds," and it's true to a certain extent. Time will dull some of the pain, but deep healing doesn't happen unless you consciously choose it.

Ch. 1, *The Courage to Heal,* coauthor Laura Davis,* 1988
*See 4361.

2 But they kissed lavish
   kisses like the ocean in the early morning,
   the way it gathers and swells, sucking
   each rock under, swallowing it
   again and again.

"Gate 22," St. 2, *The Human Line 2007*

3 god in trouble, god at the end of his rope—
   sleepless, helpless—
   desperate god, frantic god, whale heart
   lost in the shallows

"God's Grief", Ibid.

4 What would people look like
   if we could see them as they are,
   soaked in honey, stung and swollen,
   reckless, pinned against time?

"If You Knew," St. 4, Ibid.

5 Make your eating and drinking a supplication.
   Make your slicing of carrots a holy act,
   each translucent layer of the onion, a deeper prayer.

"Pray for Peace," St. 3, Ibid.

3721. Mei-mei Berssenbrugge (1947–)

1 I have an ideal that there could exist unity in a poem—the way a bird opens its mouth and sings. Even though I can't "sing," I imagine that's possible. But also with inside and outside, woman and not-woman—these don't necessarily need to be dichotomies. They can also be continuities.

Quoted in "In the Margin, Fertile Things Happen" by Laura Hinton (October 2003), *American Poet Winter 2006*

2   I don't think artists are happy with the world and they feel a
need to make another world.

Ibid.

3722. Flora Miller Biddle (1947?–)

1   Don't memoirs allow writers to keep from revealing all they
know?

The Whitney Women and the Museum They Made 2000

2   He [the artist Richard Tuttle*] transforms my perception. . . . I
see beauty, suddenly, where I've never seen it before.

Ibid.

*(1941–), American postminimalist artist.

3723. Madeleine Blais (1947/9–)

1   "Why can't you be more obedient?"
"Dogs are obedient!"

The Heart Is an Instrument: Portraits in Journalism 1992

2   I am most often drawn to people walking the edge, curiously
undefeated.

Ibid.

3724–3275. Shelley Bovey (1947–)

1   Every day the fat woman dies a series of small deaths.

Ch. 1, *Being Fat Is Not a Sin* 1989

3726. Karen Brodine (1947–)

1   "will you hold please? I'll see if he's in."
(are you in?)
"I'm sorry, sir, he's out."

the receptionist is by definition underpaid to lie.

"The Receptionist Is By Definition," St. 3, *Workweek: Poems*
1977

3727. Octavia Butler (1947–1970)

1   [Religion is] a dangerous prod, because it can always be misused and get out of hand, but it's useful for keeping people on
the straight and narrow.

Interview, Amazon.com *24 March* 1999

2   God
Gives shape to the universe
As the universe
Shapes God.

Ch. 1, *Parable of the Talents (Earthseed: The Books of Living)*
1999

3   Back when he vanished, dying by violence was even easier than
it is today. Living, on the other hand was almost impossible.

Ibid.

4   Hyperempathy syndrome is a delusional disorder, after all.
There's no telepathy, no magic, no deep spiritual awareness.
There's just the neurochemically-induced delusion that I feel
the pain and pleasure that I see others experiencing. Pleasure
is rare, pain is plentiful, and, delusional or not, it hurts like
hell.

Ibid.

3728. Beatrix Campbell (1947–)

1   Sexual abuse is like a corpse on a slab, saying nothing. You've
got nothing to go on. It's a police officer's nightmare. You just
want it to go away.

Quoting a police source, Introduction, *Unofficial Secrets* 1988

2   Sexual abuse of children now presents society with the ultimate
crisis of patriarchy, when children refuse to protect their fathers by keeping secrets.

Ch. 2, Ibid.

3   A society in which adults are estranged from the world of children, and often from their own childhood, tends to hear children's
speech only as a foreign language, or as a lie. . . . Children have
been treated . . . as congenital fibbers, fakers and fantasisers.

Ibid.

4   Children's bodies aren't like automobiles with assailant's fin-
gerprints lingering on the wheel. The world of sexual abuse is
quintessentially secret. It is the perfect crime.

Ibid.

3729. Andrea R. Canaan (1947?–)

1   The enemy is our urgent need to stereotype and close off people, places, and events into isolated categories. Hatred, distrust,
irresponsibility, unloving, classism, sexism, and racism, in their
myriad forms, cloud our vision and isolate us.

"Brownness," *This Bridge Called My Back: Writing by Radical
Women of Color*, Cherríe Moraga* and Gloria Anzaldúa,**
eds. 1982

*See 4125. **See 3321.

2   Since before I can remember, brownness was always compared to whiteness in terms that were ultimately degrading for
brownness. Lazy, shiftless, poor, non-human, dirty, abusive,
ignorant, uncultured, uneducated, were used to convey conscious and unconscious messages that brown was not a good
thing to be and the ultimate model of things right and good
was white.

Ibid.

3   It's as if we think liberation a fixed quantity, that there is only
so much to go around. That an individual or community is
liberated at the expense of another. *When we view liberation
as a scarce resource, something only a precious few of us can
have, we stifle our potential, our creativity, our genius for living, learning, and growing.*

Ibid.

4   I call up my names: Woman who has been born in the arms of
a woman and welcomed home.
I shout Truth-teller, Silence-breaker, Life-embracer,
Death-no-longer-fearing, woman reunited with her child self.
I sing woman who is daughter, sister, lover and mother to her-
self
I hum woman planter, gatherer, healer.
I drum woman warrior, siren, woman-who-stands-firmly-on-
her-feet, woman who reaches
   inward to her centre and outward to the stars.
I am woman who is child no longer, woman who is making
herself sane, whole

"My Names" 2006

3730. Carolyn Chute (1947–)

1   Gram plays the organ at church. Her fingers in her pocketbook move around in many directions at once, over the readin'

glasses, tappin' the comb, pressin' the change purse and plastic rain hat, as if from these objects one of my favorite hymns WE ABIDE will come.

"Lizzie, Annie, and Rosie's Rescue of Me with Blue Cake", *The Beans of Egypt, Maine 1985*

2 "There should be a law that after you've had nine kids and no husband, you get the knife," Lee mutters.

"Earlene's Yellow Hair", *Ibid.*

3 "Big Lucien has what you call a HEART OF GOLD! He'd take in a poison snake if it begged him."

Ch. 1, *Letourneau's Used Auto Parts 1988*

4 The militias grow. And the resisters, the raised fists, the pamphlets, the huddles, the blocking of streets. Cries for liberty, libertad, free will. The hydra coalesces. It is beautiful to its mother.

The School on Heart's Content Road 2008

5 Today, somewhere in America, more foreclosures. More auctions. Another farmer plots his own death. And another. There is an art to making your death by combine look like an accident.

"Out in the World," *Ibid.*

3731. Hillary Rodham Clinton (1947–   )

1 We are, all of us, exploring a world none of us understands. . . . searching for a more immediate, ecstatic, and penetrating mode of living. . . . [for the] integrity, the courage to be whole, living in relation to one another in the full poetry of existence. The struggle for an integrated life existing in an atmosphere of communal trust and respect is one with desperately important political and social consequences.

Student Commencement Speech, Wellesley College Government Association *31 May 1969*

2 We currently have a system for taking care of sickness. We do not have a system for enhancing and promoting health.

Speech *1993*

3 Service means you get as well as you give, your life is changed as you change the lives of others. . . . It is the way we find meaning in our lives, both individually and collectively.

Speech, Youth Service Day (The White House, Washington, D.C.) *24 April 1993*

4 In the Bible it says they asked Jesus how many times you should forgive, and he said 70 times 7. Well, I want you all to know that I'm keeping a chart.

Speech at the National Prayer Luncheon, quoted by Connie Bruck in *The New Yorker 30 May 1994*

5 If there is one message that echoes forth from this conference, let it be that human rights are women's rights, and women's rights are human rights, for once and for all.

Speech, Fourth World Conference on Women (Beijing) *5 September 1995*

6 It is a violation of human rights when babies are denied food, or drowned, or suffocated, or their spines broken, simply because they are born girls. It is a violation of human rights when woman and girls are sold into the slavery of prostitution. It is a violation of human rights when women are doused with gasoline, set on fire and burned to death because their marriage dowries are deemed too small. It is a viola-

tion of human rights when individual women are raped in their own communities and when thousands of women are subjected to rape as a tactic or prize of war. It is a violation of human rights when a leading cause of death worldwide among women ages 14 to 44 is the violence they are subjected to in their own homes. It is a violation of human rights when women are denied the right to plan their own families, and that includes being forced to have abortions or being sterilized against their will.

Ibid.

7 Let us use government as we have in the past, to further the common good.

It Takes a Village and Other Lessons Children Teach Us 1996

8 It is a national shame that many Americans are more thoughtful about planning their weekend entertainment than about planning their families.

Ibid.

9 If I am going to be criticized for doing what I believe in, I might as well just keep doing what I believe in.

Remark (1994), Quoted in *The 50 Most Influential Women in American Law* by Dawn Bradley Berry *1996*

10 We shouldn't leave the work of politics to people who run for public office.

Quoted in *The Unique Voice of Hillary Rodham Clinton* by Claire G. Osborne *1997*

11 The idea that I would check my brain at the White House door is something that just doesn't make any sense to me.

Ibid.

12 You know, we've been married for 22 years. And I've learned a long time ago that the only people who count in a marriage are the people who are in it.

Interview with Matt Lauer, *NBC's Today Show 27 January 1999*

13 Americans are ready to consider voting for a woman President within the next 10 years. This is good news for our country, for qualified women willing to enter the public arena at the highest level and for every young girl interested in public service who can be told with a straight face that she too could grow up to be President.

Quoted in "Women Who Could Be President" by Jane Ciabattari, *Parade Magazine 7 February 1999*

14 Every nation has to either be with us, or against us. Those who harbor terrorists, or who finance them, are going to pay a price.

Speech *13 September 2001*

15 And Israel is not only our ally; it is a beacon of what democracy can and should mean. . . . If the people of the Middle East are not sure what democracy means, let them look to Israel.

Speech, Hanukkah dinner, Yeshiva University *December 2005*

16 Democracy is far more than just holding elections. Democracy has to spring from an active and open citizenry dedicated to tolerance, to respect for differences, to the rule of law, to policies that lift us up not tear us down as fellow human beings, and to the value of human life.

Speech, American Israel Public Affairs Committee (AIPAC) *1 February 2007*

17 We are here today because the price that has been paid in blood and treasure; through the rush to war in Iraq and the incompetence of its execution and managing the aftermath; in the excesses of military contracting abuses and the inadequate supply of body armor and armored vehicles on the ground have led to a loss of confidence among our allies and the American people in this Administration.

Speech 14 February 2007

18 Lady Liberty's presence and the towers' absence are a constant reminder that here in America we are resilient, we are courageous, we embrace all of our people, and that, when we face our challenges together, there is no barrier we can't overcome, no dream we can't realize, nothing we can't do if we just start acting like Americans again.

Speech (New York City) 3 June 2008

19 As we gather here today, the 50th woman to leave this Earth is orbiting overhead.* If we can blast 50 women into space, we will someday launch a woman into the White House.

Democratic Nomination Concession Speech, National Building Museum (Washington, D.C.) 7 June 2008
*Dr. Karen L. Nyberg (1969–), Am. mechanical engineer.

20 Although we weren't able to shatter that highest, hardest glass ceiling this time, thanks to you, it's got about 18 million cracks in it. And the light is shining through like never before, filling us all with the hope and the sure knowledge that the path will be a little easier next time.

Concession Speech, National Building Museum (Washington, D.C.) 7 June 2008

21 From now on, it will be unremarkable for a woman to win primary state victories, unremarkable to have a woman in a close race to be our nominee, unremarkable to think that a woman can be the president of the United States. And that is truly remarkable.

Ibid.

22 I believe that American leadership has been wanting, but is still wanted.

Confirmation hearing, U.S. Senate Foreign Relations Committee 13 January 2009

23 When you are in politics, you have to have a high threshold for pain.

Quoted in "The Global Listening Tour" by Glenn Kessler, The Washington Post 20 February 2009

3732. Sara Davidson (1947–)

1 Overexposure to women's liberation leads, I found, to headaches, depression and a fierce case of the shakes.

Quoted in interview, Life (New York) 1969

2 In that time [the sixties], that decade which belonged to the young, we had thought life was free and would never run out. There were good people and bad people and we could tell them apart by a look or words spoken in code. We were certain we belonged to a generation that was special. We did not need or care about history because we had sprung from nowhere.

Loose Change: Three Women of the Sixties 1977

3 He had attacked hypocrisy everywhere but at home. He couldn't deal with pain. He was always telling stories, playing with the energy and ranting about capitalist society. But he couldn't face himself, Susie, their life or his problems.

Ch. 20, Ibid.

4 The sight of the Marlboro man on a billboard can give me a jolt of longing as I drive through traffic on my way to work. I imagine that the way some men respond to the sight of a woman in seamed stockings and garter belt is the way I feel when I see a man in chaps.

Cowboy 2000

5 The imperative was to shift from creating for a purpose to creating for the joy and challenge of the undertaking.

"The First Day of the Rest of My Life," Newsweek 22 January 2007

3733. Lydia Davis (1947–)

1 Wassily was so extremely self-conscious that at times even the soft eyes of his dog made him blush with embarrassment when he tried to attract her attention by some stupid action.

"Sketches for a Life of Wassily," 3, Break It Down 1986

2 I copied the address into my address book, erasing an earlier one that had not been good for very long. No address of his was good for very long and the paper in my address book where his address is written is thin and soft from being erased so often.

p. 1, The End of the Story 1995

3 The fact that he came back to me after leaving me, that time, may have made me think that no matter what I said, no matter what I did, and no matter how long he stayed away from me, he would always come back to me, and that I did not have to love him very deeply, or considerately, for him to go on loving me.

p. 117, Ibid.

4 How he is curious to the limits of his understanding; how he attempts to approach what arouses his curiosity, to the limits of his motion; how confident he is, to the limits of his knowledge; how masterful he is, to the limits of his competence; how he derives satisfaction from another face before him, to the limits of his attention; how he asserts his needs, to the limits of his force.

What You Learn About the Baby, Varieties of Disturbance 2007

3734. Paula Deen (1947–)

1 My best thoughts on life still seem to appear when I'm stirrin' my pots, and the freshest impressions and even the sweetest memories of family and friends come bubblin' up along with the intoxicatin' smells from the jambalaya on my stove.

"A Word from Paula," Paula Deen's Kitchen Wisdom and Recipe Journal, with Sherry Suib Cohen 2008*
*See 2885.

3735. Carla Del Ponte (1947–)

1 (So many decorative columns that feign to support so many decorative cornices and lintels. I had not seen such a failed struggle to exude vigor, stability, and permanence since my last stroll among the Bourbon palaces of central Paris.)*

Prologue, Madame Prosecutor: Confrontations with Humanity's Worst Criminals and the Culture of Impunity coauthor, Chuck Sudetic 2009
*Of the Old Executive Office Building, Washington, D.C.

2 I know something of Sicilian thugs. And Tenet, a jowly Greek by extraction, exuded a Mediterranean passion, an overbearing will, and other qualities of Sicilian toughs. I loved it, because any spymaster needs these qualities to perform effectively.

Ibid.

3   The Serbs are bastards . . . But the Croats are sneaky bastards.

Ch. 10, p.242, Ibid.

4   There is no way to . . . cushion the disappointment and sense of anticlimax because the simple fact of failure is the simple fact of failure.

Epilogue, Ibid

3736. Bernadette Devlin (1947–)

1   To gain that which is worth having, it may be necessary to lose everything else.

Preface, *The Price of My Soul 1969*

2   She* attended demonstrations against abuse of power, so that makes her guilty of disrespect for British institutions.

Quoted in "In the Name of the Mother" by Neil McCafferty, *Ms.* (New York) *November/December 1997*
*Reference to her daughter, Róisín McAliskey, political activist (1971–).

3737. Ellen Carol DuBois (1947–)

1   History never stops; it is stubborn that way. Besides, what could be more Jewish, more Talmudic, than continuing, endless debate? As a Jew, I think I prefer it that way. it seems wiser to remain in the diaspora, to keep the messiah just over the horizon, where I can aspire to but never quite attain her.

Quoted on *Women in World History Curriculum* (womeninworldhistory.com) *1996–97*

2   Extending over more than a century and including most nations of the globe, the cause of woman suffrage has been one of the great democratic forces in human history.

Remark (1989), Ibid.

3738. Andrea Dworkin (1947–2005)

1   The will to domination is a ravenous beast. There are never enough warm bodies to satiate its monstrous hunger. Once alive, this beast grows and grows, feeding on all the life around it, scouring the earth to find new sources of nourishment. This beast lives in each man who fattens on female servitude.

Ch. 8, Speech, "Our Blood: The Slavery of Women in Amerika," National Organization for Women (Washington, D.C., 23 August 1975), *Our Blood 1976*

2   We think that we live in a heterosexual society because most men are fixated on women as sexual objects; but, in fact, we live in a homosexual society because all credible transactions of power, authority, and authenticity take place among men; all transactions based on equity and individuality take place among men. Men are real; therefore, all real relationship is between men; all real communication is between men; all real reciprocity is between men; all real mutuality is between men.

Ch. 9, Speech, "The Root Cause," Massachusetts Institute of Technology (Cambridge, 26 September 1975), Ibid.

3   Undernourished, intelligence becomes like the bloated belly of a starving child: swollen, filled with nothing the body can use.

Ch. 2, *Right-Wing Women 1978*

4   She is the pinup, the centerfold, the poster, the postcard, the dirty picture, naked, half-dressed, laid out, legs spread, breast or ass protruding. She is the thing she is supposed to be: the thing that makes him erect.

Pornography: Men Possessing Women 1981

5   Erotica is simply high-class pornography; better produced, better conceived, better executed, better packaged, designed for a better class of consumer.

Preface, Ibid.

6   Male supremacy is fused into the language, so that every sentence both heralds and affirms it.

Ch. 1, Ibid.

7   One of the differences between marriage and prostitution is that in marriage you only have to make a deal with one man.

Letters From a War Zone 1988

8   In the world I'm working for, nation states will not exist. But in the world I live in, I want there to be an Israel.

Quoted in Ch. 11, *Deborah, Golda, and Me* by Letty Cottin Pogrebin,* *1991*
*See 3154.

3739. Shirin Ebadi (1947–)

1   In my view, there is no difference between Islam and human rights. Therefore, the religious ones should also welcome this award. The prize means you can be a Muslim and at the same time have human rights.

"Iranian activist wins peace Nobel," Associated Press *11 October 2003*

2   An interpretation of Islam that is in harmony with equality and democracy is an authentic expression of faith. It is not religion that binds women, but the selective dictates of those who wish them cloistered. That belief, along with the conviction that change in Iran must come peacefully and from within, has underpinned my work.

Iran Awakening: A Memoir of Revolution and Hope 2006

3   The fight for human rights is conducted in Iran by the Iranian people, and we are against any foreign intervention in Iran.

"Nobels with a Message," *The Washington Post 12 October 2007*

3740. Helen Epstein (1947–)

1   When it comes to fighting AIDS, our greatest mistake may have been to overlook the fact that, in spite of everything, African people often know best how to solve their own problems.

The Invisible Cure: Africa, the West, and the Fight Against AIDS 2007

3741. Linda A. Fairstein (1947–)

1   Each false accusation makes too many skeptics think that every accusation is a false one—which is a danger that cannot be overstated.

Quoted in "Rancorous Liaisons—The Morning After" by Cathy Young,* *Reason February 1994*
*See 4661.

3743. Renee Fisher (1947–)

1   We cannot change time. What we can do is change how we view our choices, and stop measuring and judging the success of our decisions solely by their permanency. It is not the permanency of what we have that creates the value; rather, it is our investment or experience that creates the value of our time in our lives.

Introduction, *Invisible No More: The Secret Lives of Women over Fifty,* coauthors Joyce Kramer* and Jean Peelen** *2005*
*See 3092. **See 3292.

2 "You don't look your age." From age five to just under age thirty, this comment borders on insult. From ages 30 to 50, the same comment morphs into a compliment. Past age 50, for many women it can be a veritable lifeboat, sent to save them from the shark-infested waters of decrepitude.

"Comments on Age," Ibid.

3 If I stop trying to look like someone else's age, I can make my age, whatever that is, fabulous. I can set new standards for whatever age I am. I can keep raising the bar as I raise the numbers. I can change the world as well as my hair color.

Ibid.

4 Coffee Haagen Dazs does for me what alcohol does for others. It provides a profound sense of well being and joy, followed the morning after by angst and guilt.

"Weighing In," Ibid.

5 Self dignity and self love do not necessarily depend on how well we are loved or protected in our lives.

"Realities of Breast Cancer," Ibid.

3744. Mary Gallagher (1947–)

1 MARINA. Well, you can't be afraid all the time, or you won't do anything!

Act II, Sc. 16, *Dog Eat Dog 1983*

2 Publication is the only thing that makes me stop rewriting.

Quoted in "Mary Gallagher," *Interviews with Contemporary Women Playwrights* by Kathleen Betsko* and Rachel Koenig 1987

*See 3125.

3 Good theater incorporates the personal, the social, the political, seamlessly.

Ibid.

4 The theater brigades are a major tool for unifying the Nicaraguan people. Music, dance, poetry are taught in every community because the Sandinistas believe that Nicaraguans can't explore their national identity till they are making art.

Ibid.

5 INS* OFFICER. You think we're so tough on them**—but they still keep coming! If we coddled 'em like you folks want, every goddamn country south of Texas'd be empty!

¿De Donde? 1991

*Immigration and Naturalization Service. **Immigrants, especially from Mexico and Central America.

3745. Farooka Gauhari (1947–)

1 Concealing your identity behind a veil and watching the world through a four-by-six inch rectangle of fine mesh had certain advantages. It was a sign of respect, of growing up and womanhood.

Searching for Saleem: An Afghan Woman's Odyssey 1996

2 Whenever I sat down to write, thousands of teardrops would fall and the paper would disappear behind the shadows of my mind.

Ibid.

3746. Kathleen Gerson (1947–)

1 A lengthy, leisurely childhood and prolonged adolescence are thus modern inventions that came into existence only after the rise of the mass system of education.

Ch. 1, *Hard Choices: How Women Decide About Work, Career and Motherhood 1986*

2 The child-centered housewife is actually a relatively recent historical development and is a social position that has generally been reserved for the more privileged members of the female population.

Ibid.

3 We need to worry less about the family values of a new generation and more about the institutional barriers that make them so difficult to achieve. Most young adults do not wish to turn back the clock, but they do hope to combine the more traditional value of making a lifelong commitment with the more modern value of having a flexible, egalitarian relationship. Rather than trying to change individual values, we need to provide the social supports that will allow young people to overcome work/family conflicts and realize their most cherished aspirations.

"What Do Women and Men Want?" *The American Prospect 19 February 2007*

4 Women and men both want to balance family and work in their own lives and balance commitment and autonomy in their relationships. Yet women and men also share a concern that—in the face of workplaces greedy for time and communities lacking adequate child care—insurmountable obstacles block the path to achieving these goals.

Ibid.

5 Grappling with their own family experiences has led most young women and men to affirm the intrinsic importance of family life, but also to search for ways to combine lasting commitment with a substantial measure of independence.

Ibid.

3747. Lorna Goodison (1947–)

1 I'm a poet, but I didn't choose poetry—it chose me [. . .] it's a dominating, intrusive tyrant. It's something I have to do—a wicked force.

I Am Becoming My Mother 1986

2 All that she needed
was salt.
And widows have that.

"From the Book of Local Miracles, Largely Unrecorded," *To Us, All Flowers are Roses 1995*

3 Speaking for small
dreamers of this earth, plagued with nightmares, yearning for healing dreams
we want the stone to move

"Mother, the Great Stones Got to Move," St. 4, Ibid.

4 It is that cooked-down
near-burned state which produces that taste
of redeemed and rescued richness.

"The Domestic Science of Sunday Dinner," *Turn Thanks 1999*

5 Every once in a while, when the culture of a people undergoes great stress, stitches drop out of existence, out of memory.

From Harvey River, A Memoir of My Mother and Her Island 2008

3748. Temple Grandin (1947–)

1 I think using animals for food is an ethical thing to do, but we've got to do it right. We've got to give those animals a de-

cent life and we've got to give them a painless death. We owe the animal respect.

> "Animals Are Not Things," *Animals in Translation: Using the Mysteries of Autism to Decode Animal Behavior,* coauthor, Catherine Johnson *2005*

2   I think in pictures. Words are like a second language to me. I translate both spoken and written words into full-color movies, complete with sound, which run like a VCR tape in my head.

> Ch. 1, *Thinking in Pictures, Expanded Edition: My Life with Autism 2006*

3   Many of the behaviors of people with autism seem strange, but they are reactions to distorted or overly intense sensory input. Observation of the behaviors can provide clues to the underlying sensory problems.

> Ch. 3, Ibid.

4   The best thing a parent of a newly diagnosed child can do is to watch their child, without preconceived notions and judgments, and learn how the child functions, acts, and reacts to his or her world.

> Ch. 1, *The Way I See It: A Personal Look at Autism and Asperger's 2008*

5   The prohibition against really bad things is universal in all civilized societies.

> Ch. 6, Ibid.

3749. Batya Gur (1947–   )

1   He tried to suppress the feeling that there was something stupefying about the tranquility here. . . .

> *Murder on a Kibbutz: A Communal Case 1995*

2   He reflected that it was a moot point whether a man called on music to wake sleeping worlds within him. Or whether he sought in it a great echo for his conscious feelings or listened to it in order to create a particular mood when he himself was steeped in fog and emptiness. . . .

> Ch. 1, *Murder Duet: A Musical Case 2000*

3   There comes a moment in a person's life when he fully realizes that if he does not throw himself into action, if he does not stop being afraid to gamble, and if he does not follow the urgings of his heart that have been silent for many a year—he will never do it.

> Ch. 1, *Bethlehem Road Murder: A Michael Ohayon Mystery 2004*

4   Every work of art must be the result of overcoming obstacles; the more meaningful its execution is, the harder the obstacles seem to be, as if the creator has been put to the test against the very right that was granted him—or that he took for himself—to fulfill his own dream.

> Ch. 1, *Murder in Jerusalem: A Michael Ohayon Mystery 2007*

3750. Cynthia Heimel (1947–   )

1   Nobody, but nobody, is as fat as she thinks she is.

> *Sex Tips for Girls 1983*

2   Dogs act exactly the way we would act if we had no shame.

> *Get Your Tongue Out of My Mouth, I'm Kissing You Good-Bye! 1993*

3   The only women who don't believe that sexual harassment is a real problem in this country are women who have never been in the workplace.

> Ibid.

4   If you leave me, can I come too?

> *If You Leave Me, Can I Come Too? 1995*

3751. Carolivia Herron (1947–   )

1   Once the old lady was young and leaned over Myrna for a kiss, the kiss that explained what they meant, what everybody meant really when they said love will take you, passion will come, this was that kiss to make true the love lies, to clear the confusion from all they said about how love feels. . . .

> She could have lived with Myrna but Myrna was breaking her own heart over being a pervert. . . .

> "The Old Lady," *Afrekete: An Anthology of Black Lesbian Writing,* Catherine E. McKinley and L. Joyce DeLaney, eds. *1995*

3752. Darlene Clark Hine (1947–   )

1   The encyclopedia [*Black Women in America,* 1994] is intended to place a stone in the shoe of every American historian. The encyclopedia will make it difficult, if not impossible, to exclude black women and their deeds, contributions, and experiences. . . .

> "Darlene Clark Hine," *Contemporary Authors,* vol. 143 *1994*

2   If I can . . . impress upon the historical profession how important it is to talk to those people who do not leave written records, but who have remembrances and have influenced generations and people all over the globe, then I feel that my career is worthwhile.

> Quoted in interview by Roger Adelson, *The Historian Winter 1995*

3   To me, the historical profession is still too caught up with the wealthy and the influential in political, social, and cultural arenas, who actually number only a very small minority of the human population. . . . Because so few of the new social historians have included black women, who remained at the very bottom of the ladder in the United States, we continue to lose much understanding and wisdom.

> Ibid.

4   Historians can write a history of anything or anyone, but the key is the historian must decide that thing, event, person or group is worthy of investigation. And apparently no one had ever thought black women were worth studying.

> *Shattering the Silences: Minority Professors Break into the Ivory Tower* (PBS documentary film) *1997*

5   In Modern American mythology, a family is a group composed of a father, mother, and their children. The more enlightened recognize aunts, uncles, grandparents, and cousins as an integral part of the family unit. For African Americans, however, family is a much more flexible concept, and Black women have had to stretch to meet is requirements. The terrible exigencies of the institution of slavery tore husbands from their wives, children from their parents, and sisters from their brothers, but those who were enslaved held to the idea of family with a fierce intensity. It provided practical and emotional support in a world where survival demanded both.

> Introduction, *The Face of Our Past: Images of Black Women from Colonial America to the Present,* Kathleen Thompson and Hilary MacAustin, eds. *2000*

3753. Linda Hogan (1947–)

1 On the bus two elderly women sat in front of her. They were both speaking and neither one listened to the other. They carried on two different conversations the way people did in the city, without silences, without listening. Trying to get it all said before it was too late, before they were interrupted by thoughts.

"New Shoes," *A Gathering of Spirit*, Beth Brant,* ed. *1984*

*See 3246.

2 The land is the house
we have always lived in.
The women,
their bones are holding up the earth.

"calling myself home," St. 4, *That's What She Said*, Rayna
Green,* ed. *1984*

*See 3338.

3 We're full of bread and gas, getting fat on the outside
while inside we grow thin.

"Oil," St. 5, Ibid.

4 Us Chickasaws have lost so much we hold on to everything. Even our muscles hold on to their aches. We love our lovers long after they are gone, better than when they were present.

"Making Do" 2 (1988), *Spider Woman's Granddaughters*,
Paula Gunn Allen,* ed. *1986*

*See 3118.

5 We have survived and in that survival is our life, our strength, our spirituality. And we are telling about it. . . .

Preface (p. xiv), *The Stories We Hold Secret: Tales of Women's
Spiritual Development,* Carol Bruchac and Judith McDaniel,
co-eds. *1986*

6 I don't remember when
the girl of myself turned her back
and walked away . . .

"The Lost Girls," St. 1 (1988), *The Woman That I Am, The
Literature and Culture of Contemporary Women of Color*, D.
Soyini Madison,* ed. *1994*

*See 3912.

3754. Amber Hollibaugh (1947?–)

1 The bottom line for any woman in the sex trades is economic. However a woman feels when she finally gets into the life, it always begins as survival—the rent, the kids, the drugs, pregnancy, financing an abortion, running away from home, being undocumented, having a "bad'" reputation, incest—it always starts as trying to get by.

"On the Street Where We Live," *Women's Review of Books
January 1988*

2 Imagine at a moment of extraordinary racism and injustice to live in a world without prejudice and oppression. It's an extraordinary thing to hope for when you can see no real example in front of you that suggests that that's any kind of possibility.

Speech, Cornell University (New York) *4 March 2008*

3 Liberation is the question of imagining what's possible, dreaming what's possible, engaging in a dialogue in your life that never ends, about hope. It says that there is never a time when it is impractical to imagine change. There is never a time when it is ridiculous and hopeless to want things to be different. It says you are your own agent of change.

Ibid.

3755. Keri Hulme (1947–)

1 They were nothing more than people, by themselves. Even paired, any pairing, they would have been nothing more than people by themselves. But all together, they have become the heart and muscles and mind of something perilous and new, something strange and growing and great.

Together, all together, they are the instruments of change.

Prologue, *The Bone People 1983*

2 "I have everything I need, but I have lost the main part."

Pt. I, Ch. 2, Ibid.

3 She thought of the tools she had gathered together, and painstakingly learned to use. Future probes, Tarot and I Ching and the wide wispfingers from the stars . . . all these to scry and ferret and vex the smokethick future. A broad general knowledge, encompassing bits of history, psychology, ethology, religious theory and practices of many kinds. Her charts of self knowledge. Her library. The inner thirst for information about everything that had lived or lives on Earth that she'd kept alive long after childhood had ended.

None of them helped make sense of living.

Ibid.

4 A man can find satisfaction with enough.

Pt. IV, Ch. 10, Ibid.

3756. Kathryn Jacobi (1947–)

1 On of the most important functions of the artist at this point in history is to create symbols of continuance. Religious messages have become unsatisfactory for most of us, leaving us with a void in our experience of life continuing . . .

Quoted in "Kathryn Jacobi," *Exposures, Women & Their Art*
by Ann Brown and Arlene Raven* *1989*

*See 3533.

2 My people's history has been blown to smithereens. I could not and cannot come to terms with that idea. I am appalled that holocaust is a possibility of human behavior.

Ibid.

3 I do have an awareness of the fragility of life, an awareness of the incredible sweetness of every moment of existing in good health and good condition. I take nothing for granted. I try to capture what comes alive while making a painting, so it will live for somebody else; live and tell the truth.

Ibid.

3757. Rayda Jacobs (1947?–)

1 The middle people* have had it better than the black people, yes, but the middle people have suffered too. . . . At least, if you have a black skin, you know you're black. The devil isn't at your elbow telling you to just get into the white section of the train 'cause there you'll have a seat, or leave out your race on the job ap because you're damn qualified and want the job. Whiteskins are tempted everyday into falseness and deceit . . . We've all been fucked by apartheid.

"For the Smell of the Sea" (p. 143), *The Middle Children 1994*
*Term used for multiracial, or "Coloured," people in South Africa.

2 They couldn't possibly be serious about a monkey for a president, and the vote for everyone.

"Give Them Too Much" (p. 149), Ibid.

3 I saw for the first time my black brothers and sisters. I didn't know them in 1968. They were not on my street, not in my

school, not in my thoughts. But I watched now, through the smoke and tear gas, and was ashamed that the middle children have had it better than them.

"Make the Chicken Run," Ibid.

4 The emotional damage of apartheid is large. It clogs the pores, deadens the heart.

Ibid.

3758. Karla Jay (1947–)

1 History is so precarious, it could hinge on one careless trip to the laundry without first checking the contents of the pants pockets.

Tales of the Lavender Menace 1999

3759. Margaret Jenkins (1947–)

1 I believe that things happen when they're supposed to if one is fully engaged in the process and doing it for the right reason.

Quoted by Rita Feliciano in "Dancing Through the Fragments of Memory," Arts & Leisure, *The New York Times 28 March 1999*

2 [There is a] necessary disorder that is crucial to making work.

Ibid.

3760. Shirley Childress Johnson (1947?–)

1 To interpret American Sign Language is one function. To sing is yet another function. To think about the song, the singing, and the production of the song, and to interpret that into a clear, flowing rhythmic rendition at the same time is a great, great challenge.

Quoted in "Sweet Honey:* A Cappella Activists" by Audreen Buffalo, *Ms.* (New York) *March/April 1993*
*Sweet Honey in the Rock is a vocal group; also see Bernice Johnson Reagon, 3369, and Ysaye Barnwell, 3633.

2 Interpreting music and the performing arts is very specialized. My first goal is to convey Sweet Honey's message in a way that reflects its tempo, passion, and melodious intent. My expertise in this area was earned at the School of Hard Knocks, acquired through on-the-job training and from the suggestions and input of deaf people.*

Ibid.

*Johnson is the child of deaf parents.

3761. Laila Iskandar Kamel (1947–)

1 Survival strategies of the poor are often good survival strategies for the Earth.

goldmanprize.org 1994

2 It is a common practice in a crowded classroom, I've seen this in many villages in Egypt, where they have girls sitting in the back of the classroom. Or when the teacher calls on kids to answer questions, he never calls on the girls. And when there are sports activities, they never involve the girls. . . . Parents felt that they were investing in a useless endeavor, and since it costs poor parents money to send kids to school, if you're investing in something that's useless, you pull them out.

"The Source of Illiteracy" by Waleed Khalil Rasromani, *Daily News Egypt 10 April 2006*

3 No child in a poor village has the luxury just to go to school. They have other things to do at home, or in the fields, or in the workshops in urban areas. Children are a source of income in this economy, so it's an opportunity cost. Parents that send their kids to school really sacrifice.

Ibid.

4 Child labor is a transitional phase. We're hoping that it will be phased out in the next generation. But while these kids are working, rather than deny the reality, let's work with it and do something constructive to improve the situation of these working children.

Ibid.

5 If you compare where the issue of literacy is versus economic development, you don't hear ministers and high political figures talk about literacy; it's not there. They're not yet linking the issue of literacy with economic development. It's as if our high-tech industries can zoom at a fast pace and leave the rest of the country behind. There's still not a full-blown recognition of how illiteracy drags a country down.

Ibid.

3762. Petra Kelly (1947–1992)

1 All too long we have been told that to gain equal chances and equal opportunities, we must accept the equal rights and equal duties of men. But it cannot be emancipation, to stand beside men in the various national armies and learn to shoot and learn to kill. It cannot be emancipation to learn how to operate a nuclear reactor or to be able to sit in a nuclear silo and control the control board.

Acceptance Speech (Stockholm), RightLivelihood.org *9 December 1982*

2 The Green Party has an underlying thought which states clearly that humankind must not consider the land and what it supports in terms of property or real estate. We are all temporary custodians of the land entrusted to us for passing on unimpaired to future generations.

Ibid.

3 The anti-war and anti-nuclear movement does not mean negative protest: it is necessarily pro-environment, pro-woods- and pro-fields, pro-rivers and oceans, pro-plants and animals, pro-solar energy, pro clean air and above all, pro-people. It is a planetary vision, planetary moral standard, for hungry people, poor people, women, youth, the handicapped, the old people, the Amazone tribes, the Aborgines, the inner-city slum dwellers, the oppressed minorities everywhere—we are all in this together. . . . We are in fact the realists, we are not only the dreamers of brother- and sisterhood, of nonviolence and of survival.

Ibid.

4 Without a bullet having been fired and without a bomb having been dropped, without a missile having been launched, it can be truthfully said, that the arms race is killing us. The military escalation and poverty are closely related to one another.

Ibid.

5 We, the generation that faces the next century, can add the . . . solemn injunction "If we don't do the impossible, we shall be faced with the unthinkable."

Quoted in *Vanity Fair* (New York) *January 1993*

3763. Jane Kenyon (1947–1995)

1 I am the maker, the lover, and the keeper . . .

"Briefly It Enters, and Briefly Speaks," st. 2, *The Boat of Quiet Hours 1986*

2   I divested myself of despair
and fear when I came here.
    "Notes from the Other Side," St. 2, *Constance 1993*

3   With psalters
in their breast pockets, and gloves
knitted by their sisters and sweethearts,
the men in gray hurled themselves
out of the trenches, and rushed against
blue. It was what both sides
agreed to do.
    "At the Public Market Museum: Charleston, South Carolina,"
    St. 3, *Otherwise: New and Selected Poems 1996*

4   There's just no accounting for happiness,
or the way it turns up like a prodigal
who comes back to the dust at your feet
having squandered a fortune far away.
    "Happiness," St. 1, *The Breath of Parted Lips: Voices From the
    Robert Frost Place,* David Graham et al., eds. *2000*

5   I took the last
dusty piece of china
out of the barrel.
It was your gravy boat,
with a hard, brown
drop of gravy still
on the porcelain lip.
I grieved for you then
as I never had before.
    "What Came to Me," in toto, *The Sorrow Psalms: A Book of
    Twentieth-Century Elegy,* Lynn Strongin, ed. *2006*

3764. Diane E. Levin (1947–   )

1   In today's cultural environment, products that channel children
into narrowly focused content and activities threaten to consume every aspect of their lives.
    Ch. 2, *So Sexy So Soon: The New Sexualized Childhood and
    What Parents Can Do to Protect Their Kids,* Jean Kilbourne,*
    coauthor *2008*

    *See 3433.

2   Marketers have put a great deal of money and talent into using
violence to market products to boys.
    Ibid.

3   Deregulation [by the FCC]* made it possible for marketers
to develop products for children directly linked to children's
television programs. And the program-length commercial, a
program made for the sole purpose of selling products, was
born.
    Ibid.

    *Federal Communications Commission.

4   Raising children in a society where you're constantly worried
about the physical and psychological dangers that can befall
them harms both your relationship with your children and
your ability to parent well.
    Ch. 4, Ibid.

3765. Alicia F. Lieberman (1947–   )

1   Toddlers have the gift of living in the moment and finding
wonder in the ordinary. They share those gifts by helping the
adults they love to reconnect with the simple pleasures of life.
    Ch. 1, *Emotional Life of the Toddler 1993*

2   Physical punishment, such as spanking, teaches a toddler that
might makes right and that it is fine to hit when one is stronger
and can get away with it.
    Ch. 7, Ibid.

3766. Mary Ann Lindley (1947–   )

1   I celebrate Christmas as a spiritual person if not a strongly
religious one and have no doubt that this is not the second-
best way to observe it. All those of non-Christian faiths, of
unformed faiths, of no faith are welcome at the table of human
happiness.
    "Dogmatic view of Christmas. . . ," *Tallahassee Democrat 22
    December 2002*

2   Every cutback has a trickle-down effect that, instead of making
things better or even just holding the fort, has the potential to
make things worse.
    "Universities need more than good ideas," *Tallahassee
    Democrat 15 June 2008*

3767. Deborah Lipstadt (1947–   )

1   It was the only time in recorded history that a state tried to
destroy an entire people, regardless of an individual's age, sex,
location, profession, or belief. And it is the only instance in
which the perpetrators conducted this genocide for no osten-
sible material, territorial, or political gain.
    *Beyond Belief: The American Press and the Coming of the
    Holocaust 1986*

2   When a former president* of the United States writes a book
on the Israeli-Palestinian crisis and writes a chronology at the
beginning of the book in order to help them understand the
emergence of the situation and in that chronology lists nothing
of importance between 1939 and 1947, that is soft-core denial.
    Quoted by Jonny Paul in "Holocaust Scholar Warns of New
    'soft-core' Denial," Jerusalem Center for Public Affairs *1
    August 2003*

    *James Earl "Jimmy" Carter (1924–   ), 39th president of the
    United States; re his book *Palestine Peace Not Apartheid.*

3   When groups of people refuse to commemorate Holocaust
Memorial Day unless equal time is given to anti-Muslim prejudice, this is soft-core denial.
    Ibid.

3768. Jane Lubchenco (1947–   )

1   We now live on a human dominated planet. The growth of
the human population and the growth in amount of resources
used are altering Earth in unprecedented ways.
    Quoted in *Science 23 January 1998*

2   The oceans have long been thought to be so vast and bountiful that they must be impervious to human depredation. The
evidence is now overwhelming that even the immense oceans
are depleted and disrupted. Turns out that oceans are more
vulnerable—and more valuable—than we thought.
    Quoted in "Sea Champion Picked for Ocean, Air Agency" by
    Andrew C. Revkin, *The New York Times 18 December 2008*

3   The appearance of large zones of low-oxygen or no-oxygen
along exposed outer coasts like Oregon and Washington came
as a complete surprise. If someone had told me this rich, diverse, productive ecosystem could rapidly become a 'dead
zone', I would have thought they were nuts.
    Ibid.

4 There is no way we can control marine ecosystems, we only control human activities that affect them.

Ibid

5 The Bush* administration has not been respectful of the science. But I think that's not true of Republicans in general. I know it's not.

Quoted in "Advocates for Action on Global Warming Chosen as Obama's Top Science Advisers" by Juliet Eilperin and Joel Achenbach, *The Washington Post 19 December 2008*
*George W. B- (1946–), Am. politician; 43rd president of the United States (2001–09).

3769. Norma McCorvey (1947–)

1 We're not like other lesbians, going to bars. We're lesbians by ourselves. We're homers.

Quoted in interview, *The New York Times ca. 1994*

2 I felt crushed under the truth of this realization. I had to face up to the awful reality. Abortion wasn't about "products of conception." It wasn't about "missed periods." It was about children being killed in their mother's wombs.

Won by Love 1998

3 We're getting our babies back. . . . I feel like the weight of the world has just been lifted off my shoulders.

Quoted in "'Jane Roe' Wants Case Overturned" by Lisa Falkenberg, Associated Press *17 June 2003*

3770. Martha McFerren (1947–)

1 Honey, if I can park in it,
I can back out of it.

"The Best Advice I Received as an Adolescent," *Contours for Ritual 1988*

2 . . . we bourgeoisie
can't afford to dawdle.
Yes, history needs me.

"The Saga Continues," Ibid.

3 It is better to be the magician
than the magicked

Untitled, *Women in Cars: Poems 1992*

4 There's simply nothing out there.
Some people say Texans
think more about wheels than sex,
but you have to understand
the distances involved.

"Women in Cars," St. 7, Ibid.

3771. Merikay McLeod (1947–)

1 There is no truth or integrity in this room full of church men.

McCloud v. Seventh-day Adventist trial *May 1975*

2 All the love, all the idealism, all the pride I've had in my church and its institutions bubbles to the surface, only to be snuffed by the reality I've experienced.

Betrayal 1985

3 The spirit of Christ and the spirit of the church are contradictory.

Ibid.

3772. Melanie (1947–)

1 We were so close, there was no room
We bled inside each others wounds
We all had caught the same disease
And we all sang the songs of peace
Some came to sing, some came to pray
Some came to keep the dark away

"Lay Down (Candles in the Rain)," *Candles in the Rain* (album) *1970*

2 Look what they done to my brain ma
Look what they done to my brain
Well they picked it like a chicken bone
And I think I'm half insane ma
Look what they done to my song

"Look what they done to my song," St. 2, Ibid.

3 Well, I got a brand new pair of roller skates
You got a brand new key
I think that we should get together and try them out you see

"Brand New Key," St. 1, *Gather Me* (album) *1971*

4 don't hold the sprout against the seed
don't hold this need against me. . . .

"Gather on a Hill of Wildflowers" *1975*

3773. Elizabeth Morgan (1947–)

1 For the average middle-class American, living in the D.C. jail* is a horror. It's dirty, it's noisy, it's crowded, and you have no privacy. But I chose this because the middle-class American existence is worthless to me if my daughter is being raped. The destruction of my child is not worth any possessions. Just having her safe makes me happy.

Quoted in "A Hard Case of Contempt" by Jon Elson, *Time 18 September 1989*
*Incarcerated in Washington, D.C., for refusing to disclose the whereabouts of her allegedly sexually abused five-year-old daughter.

3774. Carol Moseley Braun (1947–)

1 There are those who would keep us slipping back into the darkness of division, into the snake pit of racial hatred, of racial antagonism and of support for symbols of the struggle to keep African-Americans in bondage.

Speech to Senate, quoted in *Newsweek 16 December 1991*

2 He looked at Senator Hatch* and said, "I'm going to make her cry. I'm going to sing 'Dixie' until she cries." And I looked at him and said, "Senator Helms,** your singing would make me cry if you sang 'Rock of Ages'."

Quoted in *Newsweek 16 August 1993*
*Orrin Grant H— (1934–), United States Senator (R-UT; 1977–). **Jesse Alexander H— (1921–2008), U.S. Senator (R-NC; 1973–2003).

3 This crowd has turned record surpluses into record deficits. We have gone into a war, an unelected president sending us into a war that the Congress frankly had no right, I believe, to authorize. We have misspent money, giving tax cuts to those who need it the least, cutting programs for those who need it the most. We're failing our children with education, we're failing our environment. They're pandering to fear and to hate and it's just all wrong.

"Morning Edition with Bob Edwards," NPR *6 May 2003*

4 I want to rebuild America. If we can rebuild Iraq, we can rebuild Illinois and Indiana and if we can do Baghdad, we can do Baltimore.

Ibid.

5 If anything, our representative democracy should have the voices of women as much as of men, of working people as of gazillionaires.

Ibid.

6 My late mother used to say that it did not matter if you came to this country on the Mayflower or a slave ship, across the Rio Grande or through Ellis Island; we are all in the same boat now. I believe that the challenge for all of us is to work to make certain that Americans now come together. We must now transform this nation so that we can live up to the promise of our democracy, the promise of our Constitution and so that we can be America again.

Oft repeated remark during her bid for presidency *2004*

7 Biodynamic farming is the most sustainable farming model in the world, and we are the first company in America to market a line of biodynamic organic products.*

Quoted in interview by Amanda Griscom Little, grist.com *3 January 2008*

*Re her food line, Ambassador Dynamics.

8 I decided to run when my little 10-year-old niece said, "But Auntie Carol, all the presidents are boys." And I stood there and I said, "Sweetie, girls can be president, too"—knowing I was lying to her. And I just decided I was not going to let that lie stand. That was the reason I got out there to run.*

Ibid.

*Re her brief 2004 bid for the presidency.

9 Food trumps politics any day!

Ibid.

3775. Vicki Noble (1947–)

1 The garden within is the sacred sanctuary where we reconnect with the Goddess, the deep Feminine, the underground source of female empowerment and expression. We were once deeply rooted in that place, expressing power and sexuality from there without any splitting. That's the unambiguous wholeness we see in the ancient female figurines. We were snake and bird, earth and sky, body and spirit. We could invite the male into that place for an encounter, and he came.

Shakti Woman 1990

3776. Marsha Norman (1947–)

1 JESSIE. I'm just not having a very good time and I don't have any reason to think it'll get anything but worse.

'night, Mother 1983

2 There are things that music can do that language can never do, that painting can never do, or sculpture. Music is capable of going directly to the source of the mystery. It doesn't have to explain it. It can simply celebrate it.

Quoted in "Marsha Norman," *Interviews with Contemporary Women Playwrights* by Kathleen Betsko* and Rachel Koenig *1987*

*See 3125.

3 As women, our historical role has been to clean up the mess. Whether it's the mess left by war or death or children or sick-

ness. I think the violence you see in plays by women is a direct reflection of that historical role. We are not afraid to look under the bed, or to wash the sheets; we know that life is messy. We know that somebody has to clean it up, and that only if it is cleaned up can we hope to start over, and get better.

Ibid.

4 My attitude toward the computer has changed. In the first year I owned it, I was a true believer. I wrote articles and gave interviews saying it was our only hope as writers. Now I've gone back to the yellow pad. . . . I found I was having conversations with the screen, rather than with the audience, or with myself. The screen appreciates a very particular kind of talk. You might say I was talking head-to-head rather than heart-to-heart.

Ibid.

5 Success is always something that you have to recover from.

Ibid.

6 But a vibrant theater is possible only when the critics stop leaving the audience out of the review. I'm not saying the critics have to distort their opinions. I am saying that critics have to accept responsibility for what they write. They can do enormous good . . . And they can do great harm. . . . The theater community needs to feel that even if critics don't like a particular work, they at least like plays. We need critics to use their power for good. . . . Otherwise, what on earth is the point of having them?

"The Critic as Advocate," *The New York Times 2 March 2008*

3777. Kathleen Norris (1947–)

1 And it is precisely the skills of celibate friendship—fostering intimacy through letters, conversation, performing mundane tasks together (thus rendering them pleasurable), savoring the holy simplicity of a shared meal, or a walk together at dusk— that can help a marriage survive the rough spots.

The Cloister Walk 1996

2 I'd begun to realize that the apprenticeship as a writer that I'd embarked on in my early twenties was in essence a religious quest.

Ibid.

3 The monastic life has this in common with the artistic one: both are attempts to pay close attention to objects, events, and natural phenomena that otherwise would get chewed up in the daily grind.

Ibid.

4 Often it is by doing things all wrong the first time that I make them come out right in the end.

"Eschatology," *Amazing Grace: A Vocabulary of Faith 1998*

3778. Martha C. Nussbaum (1947–)

1 To be a good human being is to have a kind of openness to the world, an ability to trust uncertain things beyond your own control, that can lead you to be shattered in very extreme circumstances for which you were not to blame. . . . But the life that no longer trusts another human being and no longer forms ties to the political community is not a human life any longer.

Quoted in *A World of Ideas* by Bill Moyers *1989*

2 Often, when people are measuring the quality of life, what they're doing is measuring the opulence of the society.

Ibid.

3 Advertising simplifies us, when I think what we want to do is to become more aware of complexity, nuance, and the complicated messiness of human situations. Advertising gives us a simple, two-second message in language that has to be grasped right away whereas the great works of literature draw us into a complex, highly textured language that is much more adequate for a grasp of ethical reality.

> Ibid.

4 Philosophy heals human diseases, disease produced by false beliefs. Its arguments are to the soul as the doctor's remedies are to the body.

> Ch. 1, *The Therapy of Desire* 1994

5 Commending it in the public sphere is difficult, since many people who think of literature as illuminating about the workings of the personal life and the private imagination believe that it is idle and unhelpful when the larger concerns of classes and nations are at issue. Here, it is felt, we need something more reliably scientific, more detached, more sternly rational. But I shall argue that here, all the more, literary forms have a unique contribution to make.

> Ch. 1, *Poetic Justice: The Literary Imagination and Public Life* 1996

6 This is a country that has long understood that liberty of conscience is worth nothing if it is not equal liberty. Liberty of conscience is not equal, however, if government announces a religious orthodoxy, saying that this, and not that, is the religious view that defines us as a nation.

> Ch. 1, *Liberty of Conscience: In Defense of America's Tradition of Religious Equality* 2008

3779. Laura Nyro (1947–1997)

1 And when I die
and when I'm gone
there'll be one child born
and a world to carry on....

> "And When I Die" 1966

2 I was born from love
and my poor mother worked the mines
I was raised on the good book Jesus
till I read between the lines....

> "Stoney End" 1966

3 Nothing cures like time and love....

> "Time and Love" 1970

4 I've got a lot of patience, baby
And that's a lot of patience to lose.

> "When I Was a Freeport" 1971

5 money money money
do you feel like a pawn
in your own world?
you found the system
and you lost the pearl....

> "Money" 1975

6 ... you will find
your own way
hard and true
And I'll find mine
cause I'm growing with you

> "To a Child...." *n.d.*

3780. Camille Paglia (1947–   )

1 Capitalism is an art form, an Apollonian fabrication to rival nature. It is hypocritical for feminists and intellectuals to enjoy the pleasures and conveniences of capitalism while sneering at it.... Everyone born into capitalism has incurred a debt to it. Give Caesar his due.

> Ch. 1, *Sexual Personae* 1990

2 Pregnancy demonstrates the deterministic character of woman's sexuality. Every pregnant woman has body and self taken over by a chthonian* force beyond her control. In the welcome pregnancy, this is a happy sacrifice. But in the unwanted one, initated by rape or misadventure, it is a horror. Such unfortunate women look directly into nature's heart of darkness. For a fetus is a benign tumor, a vampire who steals in order to live. The so-called miracle of birth is nature getting her own way.

> Ibid.

*In Greek mythology, of or relating to the gods and spirits of the underworld.; Paglia explains "chthonian" as "my symbol for unregenerate nature."

3 There are no accidents, only nature throwing her weight around. Even the bomb merely releases energy that nature has put there. Nuclear war would be just a spark in the grandeur of space. Nor can radiation "alter" nature: she will absorb it all. After the bomb, nature will pick up the cards we have spilled, shuffle them, and begin her game again.

> Ibid.

4 How many modern transsexuals are unacknowledged shamans? Perhaps it is to poets they should go for counsel, rather than surgeons.

> Ch. 2, Ibid.

5 Popular culture is the new Babylon, into which so much art and intellect now flow. It is our imperial sex theater, supreme temple of the Western eye. We live in the age of idols. The pagan past, never dead, flames again in our mystic hierarchies of stardom.

> Ch. 4, Ibid.

6 Television is actually closer to reality than anything in books. The madness of TV is the madness of human life.

> *Harper's* (New York) *March 1991*

7 My thinking tends to be libertarian. That is, I oppose intrusions of the state into the private realm—as in abortion, sodomy, prostitution, pornography, drug use, or suicide, all of which I would strongly defend as matters of free choice in a representative democracy.

> Introduction, *Sex, Art, and American Culture 1992*

8 A woman simply is, but a man must become. Masculinity is risky and elusive. It is achieved by a revolt from woman, and it is confirmed only by other men.... Manhood coerced into sensitivity is no manhood at all.

> "Alice in Muscle Land," book review, *Boston Globe* (27 January 1991), Ibid.

9 You have to accept the fact that part of the sizzle of sex comes from the danger of sex. You can be overpowered.

> Interview in *San Francisco Examiner* (7 July 1991), Ibid.

10 Gay men are the guardians of the masculine impulse. To have anonymous sex in a dark alleyway is to pay homage to the dream of male freedom. The unknown stranger is a

wandering pagan god. The altar, as in prehistory, is anywhere you kneel.

> "Homosexuality at the Fin de Siècle," *Esquire* (New York, October 1991), Ibid.

11 Madonna* is the true feminist. She exposes the puritanism and suffocating ideology of American feminism, which is stuck in an adolescent whining mode. Madonna has taught young women to be fully female and sexual while still exercising control over their lives.

> "Madonna 1: Animality and Artifice," *The New York Times* (14 December 1991), Ibid.
> *See 4459.

12 The penis is shaping up to be the central metaphor of the gender crisis of the Nineties. In too much feminist thought of the last several decades, the penis has been defined as an instrument of intimidation, aggression, violation, and destruction.

> "The Penis Unsheathed," *Vamps & Tramps: New Essays 1994*

3781. Sara Paretsky (1947–)

1 I believe in the dull lie—make your story boring enough and no one will question it.

> *Blood Shot 1988*

2 The smell was sweet, not like the icky, fake-flavored corn syrup you got with your pancakes at the diner, but a clean, light sweetness, before anyone took the corn and started manufacturing things from it.

> Ch. 1, *Bleeding Kansas 2008*

3 "They'll make the corn dirty," Lara told it. "Here in the field, it's clean. But then they'll take it to their stupid factories and turn it into gasoline or plastic or some other nasty thing."

> Ibid.

3782. Susan Partnow (1947–)

1 It is within the families themselves where peace can begin. If families can learn to respect their members, and deal with conflict resolution, that would be the first step to keeping peace on a global level.

> "Families For Peace," *Puget Sound Consumers Coop Newsletter Spring 1986*

2 Children learn about the world through their play. When we choose toys and games that encourage creativity, problem solving and learning, and we resolve to keep violence and racial stereotypes out of our homes, we are taking important steps towards a world without hatemongers.

> Letter to the editor, *The Seattle Time 3 December 1988*

3 Every person has a piece of the truth. If we listen deeply enough we will find that. Through compassionate listening, we can connect without judgment.

> *Ballard-Tribune* (Seattle) *April 2008*

4 When it comes to education, we don't know how to count what really counts.

> Remark to Elaine Bernstein Partnow* *27 October 2000*
> *See 3291.

5 How do we, especially Americans, awaken to our inter-connectedness as global citizens and our mutual responsibility so that we will be fully engaged as active citizens of the world? How are we going to come to a world of peace? It doesn't

mean we are going to sit around and sing Kumbaya. It's messy and challenging. We have to embrace confusion and conflict. That's why we need compassionate listening skills.

> Quoted on PeacebyDesign.com *August 2008*

3783. Angela Marie Phillips (1947–)

1 . . . children . . . need the intoxicating pleasure of the passionate devotion of someone who thinks they are the bee's knees, the cat's pajamas, or the best thing since sliced bread.

> *The Trouble with Boys: A Wise and Sympathetic Guide to the Risky Business of Raising Sons 1994*

2 Most teenage boys are treated as a general nuisance to be swatted like flies. Men seeing a boy without a father do not think: here is a young man to talk to, to listen to, to make friends with. They think: here is a young man who lacks male discipline. They wade in with orders and instructions.

> Ibid.

3 The trouble with boys is that they must become men.

> Ibid.

3784. Mary Pipher (1947–)

1 Something dramatic happens to girls in early adolescence. Just as planes and ships disappear mysteriously into the Bermuda Triangle, so do the selves of girls go down in droves. They crash and burn.

> *Reviving Ophelia: Saving the Selves of Adolescent Girls 1994*

2 Adolescent girls are saplings in a hurricane. They are young and vulnerable trees that the winds blow with gale strength.

> Ch. 1, Ibid.

3 Women often know how everyone in their family thinks and feels except themselves. They are great at balancing the needs of their co-workers, husbands, children and friends, but they forget to put themselves into the equation.

> Ibid.

4 Remembering is more like taking a Rorschach test than calling up a computer file. It's highly selective and revealing of one's deep character.

> Ch. 12, Ibid.

5 Let's work toward a culture in which there is a place for every human gift, in which children are safe and protected, women are respected and men and women can love each other as whole human beings. Let's work for a culture in which the incisive intellect, the willing hands and the happy heart are beloved.

> Ch. 15, Ibid.

3785. Judith Plaskow (1947–)

1 Obviously Judaism is patriarchal. This hurts us deeply. Yet it's one thing when we articulate it in our terms and another when it is taken up by Christians as evidence that Jews are more patriarchal than any other people. Just as Jews have been called more communist, or more stiff-necked, or more whatever, this kind of projection of humanities ills onto one group has been used against women. It is what we as feminists are committed to destroy.

> Quoted in Ch. 11, *Deborah, Golda, and Me* by Letty Cottin Pogrebin* *1991*
> *See 3154.

2 If women are invisible from the first moment of Jewish history, can we hope to become visible now? How many of us will fight for years to change the institutions in which we find ourselves only to achieve token victories? Perhaps we should put our energy elsewhere, into the creation of new communities where we can be fully present and where our struggles will not come up against walls as old as our beginnings.

Standing Again at Sinai 1991

3786. Riv-Ellen Prell (1947–)

1 They were wage earners who supported families and sent money to the Old World to bring relatives to the New World. Many sought education; virtually all longed for marriage. They were cultural pioneers, exploring the terrain of a new urban American life with immigrant parents who could provide few tools for mapping this world.

Ch. 1, *Fighting to Become Americans: Assimilation and the Trouble Between Jewish Women and Jewish Men* 1999

2 In contrast to Europe, professions lacked a distinctive tradition in the United States. With the urbanization and industrialization of America at the turn of the century, entering the professions depended upon advanced training and specialization, and afforded a form of status that rewarded achievement and loyalty to a specific group.

Ch. 3, Ibid.

3787. Sally Priesand (1947–)

1 Clergy are father figures to many women, and sometimes they are threatened by another woman accomplishing what they see as strictly male goals. But I can see them replacing that feeling with a sense of pride that women can have that role.

Quoted in *Women at Work* by Betty Medsger 1975

2 When I was in rabbinical school I believed in an all-powerful God, but the older I get, the more I believe in a limited God, a God who loves and cares, who weeps with us, but who can't change things. I hope the message I give to my congregants is that we need strength to accept where we find ourselves.

Quoted in "Reflections of a 'Woman Who Dare'" by Sally Friedman, *The New York Times* 19 September 1993

3788. Francine Prose (1947–)

1 When he first started teaching, he'd settled for nothing less than the whole class falling in love with him. Now he's content to get through the hour without major psychic damage.

Ch. 1, *Blue Angel* 2000

2 "I want to help you guys save guys like me from becoming guys like me."

A Change Man 2005

3 You can assume that if a writer's work has survived for centuries, there are reasons why this is so, explanations that have nothing to do with a conspiracy of academics plotting to resuscitate a zombie army of dead white males.

Reading Like A Writer, A Guide for People Who Love Books and for Those Who Want to Write Them. 2006

4 If all the clocks and calendars vanished, children would still know when Sunday came.

Ch. 1, *Goldengrove* 2008

5 Margaret's death had shaken us, like three dice in a cup, and spilled us out with new faces in unrecognizable combinations.

We forgot how we used to live in our house, how we'd passed the time when we lived there. We could have been sea creatures stranded on the beach, puzzling over an empty shell that reminded us of the ocean.

Ch. 4, Ibid.

3789. Margo Sappington (1947–)

1 Choreography is more than just making up movements. It's what they express. It's how you pick up a glass, how you feel about something in that particular moment of time. It's . . . not just arbitrary jiggling around.

Quoted in "Choreographer returns to NW . . ." by R.M. Campbell, D1, *Seattle Post-Intelligencer* 12 January 1999

3790. Sandy Eisenberg Sasso (1947–)

1 Women's center of focus is on people rather than principles.

"How Women Are Changing the Rabbinate" by Janet Marder, *Reform Judaism* Summer 1991

2 The farmer whose skin was dark like the rich brown earth from which all things grew called God *Source of Life*.

In God's Name 1994

3 Sometimes I think the clouds are made
of white balls of cotton yarn,
God's way of painting pictures in the sky.

God's Paintbrush 2004

4 I think the wind is God breath moving through the world, making it come alive.

Ibid.

3791. Susan Scanlan (1947?–)

1 It's time to inform WFAN, CBS, and MSNBC—and their corporate sponsors—that a company is known by the man it keeps.*

Open letter to CBS and NBC, National Council of Women's Organizations 9 April 2007

*Re radio host Don Imus's sexist and racist diatribe on the Rutgers College women's basketball team.

2 You don't have to be an expert to realize there is a lot of inappropriate television programming all too easily accessible by kids. But there also is excellent programming and easy to use technology. Parents need to know about the good alternatives for their kids to watch. STA* will focus our energy on promoting the best of kid's TV, how to find it easily, and how to watch it on families' timetables, not the broadcast schedule.

Kids First! News release 16 October 2007

*Smart Television Alliance.

3792. Laura Catherine Schlessinger (1947–)

1 If women change their minds, men must take it. When men change their minds, they're brutes.

Ch. 1, *The Proper Care and Feeding of Husbands* 2005

2 If there is one basic assumption I believe that most married women make, it is that their husbands are to serve them, and that any demands husbands make are insensitive and selfish.

Ch. 2, Ibid.

2 I don't believe anyone does life well alone; I believe you lose your humanity by isolating yourself. It is up to you to reach out.

Introduction, *Bad Childhood—Good Life: How to Blossom and Thrive in Spite of an Unhappy Childhood* 2006

3793. Vera Schwarcz (1947–)

1 . . . Jews . . . had to nurture memory through prolonged exile from the land of Israel. Over time remembrance became its own homeland [and] memory has kept Jews Jewish.

Bridge Across Broken Time: Chinese and Jewish Cultural Memory 1998

2 Far from being liberating, memory seeks to arrest us in our flight toward the present moment. It would be such a relief to be done with the past, or better yet, be headed for the future with a confidence unburdened by the details of sorrows gone by. But memory won't leave us alone.

Ibid.

3794. Jill Severn (1947–)

1 Getting pregnant helps fill the void in a way that nothing else can. In spite of a lot of messages to the contrary, most teenage girls know that parents are the most important people in the world and that to become a mother is to become a VIP.

Being pregnant becomes the source of new status, new power and a new definition of self. It is a rite of passage not just from adolescence to adulthood but from alienation to connectedness. Giving birth is an opportunity to work your own personal miracle. It is a way to prove to yourself and everyone else that you are in league with the divine power of creation.

"Why teens feel pregnancy their only option," *Seattle Post-Intelligencer*, Op-Ed *27 January 1994*

3795. Charlotte Shelton (1947–)

1 Chaos is the progenitor of all progress. Without the chaos of change, life stagnates and entropy ensues.

"If you only have a hammer," *Perspective* (World Business Academy) *March 1999*

2 Everything in the universe is a part of a correlated, complex whole in which each part influences and is influenced by every other part.

Ibid.

3 Both quantum theory and contemporary research in human perception suggest that over eighty percent of what we see in the external world is a function of internal assumptions and beliefs. Yet we, for the most part, continue to live our lives and manage our organizations with little regard for the subjectiveness of external reality.

Ibid.

4 If we are to re-create our organizations for the twenty-first century, we must release our outdated beliefs about the way the world works and we must replace our time-worn hammers with a radically new tool kit. Such a kit would contain new skills—skills that are congruent with the new paradigm view of organizations as unpredictable, interactive, living systems, rather than stable, clock-like machines.

Ibid.

3796. Margaret Sloan-Hunter (1947–2004)

1 We feel that there can't be liberation for less than half a race. We want *all* black people in this country to be free.

Manifesto, National Black Feminist Organization *1975*

2 It has been hard for black women to emerge from the myriad of distorted images that have portrayed us as grinning Beulahs, castrating Sapphires, and pancake-box Jemimahs.

Ibid.

3797. Sarah Smith (1947–)

1 It takes a second to shoot a man. Thinking about it takes the rest of one's life.

Ch. 1, *The Knowledge of Water 1996*

2 Love made Milly nervous. Sex, that was easy; one says yes, one says no; but when the person was in love, who knows where it ended. Milly liked things clear and definite; love, like stories, should have a beginning, a middle, and especially an end.

Ch. 11, Ibid.

3 "They have been divorcing for years, they are always divorcing, they are almost always almost divorced, but they are not divorced yet."

Ch. 17, Ibid.

4 Differences in upbringing are never stronger than in the kitchen.

Ch. 30, Ibid.

5 It is an advantage to be raised in a diplomatic family; one learns to keep one's emotions in separate drawers.

Ch. 56, Ibid.

6 "I'm afraid of doing what I want instead of doing what I ought."

Ch. 66, Ibid.

7 "Art's to fail at," Mallais said. "Art's not a whore for hire. She insults you, strips you bare, loses you your dignity, shows you you know nothing about loving her. She makes impossible demands—you know, mademoiselle."

Ch. 93, Ibid.

8 If you're a kid, two plays can start you on Shakespeare, *Macbeth* or *Hamlet*. I goggle-eyed my way through witches and murders and ghosts, having as much fun as if it was Stephen King. And then I got to the end of the play. Lady Macbeth is dead, and Macbeth is so torn up he can't even realize it, all he can do is wish it were sometime else when he could sit down and work up to grieving her. And he realizes he's got forever because she'll be dead forever.

Introduction, *Chasing Shakespeares 2004*

3798. Olympia Snowe (1947–)

1 People are rightfully fed up. More than ever, we need centrist values in the U.S. Senate and the political system.

Quoted in "Snowe aims for GOP road less taken" by Tom Bell, *Portland Press Herald 14 April 2006*

2 Designating the SBA Administrator with Cabinet-level status— as was the case during the previous Administrations—will help to ensure that the voice of small business is heard loud and clear within our Federal government.

Quoted in "Senator Olympia Snowe on Change at the SBA" by Jeremy Quittner, *Business Week 2 December 2008*

3 I sense that President-elect Obama is truly genuine and forthright about getting to work across the aisle,. The White House and administration have not been bringing people into the process. . . . If you're not willing to take the risk of working across the political aisle, you lose the chance to do major things for the country.

Quoted in "Maine's GOP senators may control the moderate middle" by Sasha Issenberg, *The Boston Globe 21 December 2008*

4 It is true that being a Republican moderate sometimes feels like being a cast member of "Survivor"*—you are presented with multiple challenges, and you often get the distinct feeling that you're no longer welcome in the tribe. But it is truly a dangerous signal that a Republican senator** of nearly three decades no longer felt able to remain in the party.

"We Didn't Have to Lose Arlen Specter,"* *The New York Times 28 April 2009*

*Popular reality TV series wherein contestants compete for cash as they attempt to survive in wilderness areas; 1992– . **(1930–), U.S. Senator (PA), 1980– ; switched from Republican to Democrat, 28 April 2009.

5 I have said that, without question, we cannot prevail as a party without conservatives. But it is equally certain we cannot prevail in the future without moderates.

Ibid.

6 We can't continue to fold our philosophical tent into an umbrella under which only a select few are worthy to stand. Rather, we should view an expansion of diversity within the party as a triumph that will broaden our appeal. That is the political road map we must follow to victory.

Ibid.

3799. Danielle Steel (1947–)

1 If you see the magic in a fairy tale, you can face the future.

Family Album 1985

2 Nick* was like a burning cigarette tossed to the dry grass at the edge of a summer forest. He was a forest fire waiting to happen, and while the conflagration began to burn, and the flames began to devour him, none of us could yet see it.

His Bright Light: The Story of Nick Traina 1998

*N- Traina, her son, who committed suicide at age 19.

3 It was a time of terrifying frustration. I am a capable, reasonable, rational, intelligent, fairly strong-willed, competent person, with ample funds at my disposal, terrific resources, and an ability to get things on track quickly. If I couldn't make things happen for Nick, and get help for him, I shudder to think at what happens to people who are too shy or too frightened to speak up, people who don't know their way around.

Ibid.

4 . . . [his] kisses were as intoxicating as everything else about him.

Rogue 2008

5 Love is wonderful, but hope is more important. Without hope you can't live.

Quoted in "Danielle Steel puts heart into giving hope" by Mark Kennedy, Associated Press 27 July 2008

6 I still never finish a book without being terrified I can't write another one. I never start one without being terrified I can't finish it. It's sort of a torturous process.

Ibid.

3800. Megawati Sukarnoputri (1947–)

1 To my children across the nation, I ask you to sincerely return to your work and not to engage in emotional acts because, as you can see for yourself, your mother now stands on this podium.

Presidential concession speech, Quoted by David Lamb, *Los Angeles Times 23 October 1999*

3801. Lynn M. Thomas (1947–)

1 There are for starters, grandeur and silence, pure water and clean air. There is also the gift of distance . . . the chance to stand away from relationships and daily ritual . . . and the gift of energy. Wilderness infuses us with its own special brand of energy. I remember lying by the Snake River in Idaho once and becoming aware I could not sleep . . . nature's forces had me in hand. I was engulfed in a dance of ions and atoms. My body was responding to the pervasive pull of the moon.

The Backpacking Woman 1980

3802. Lynne Tillman (1947–)

1 We were a ragtag band of inhibited outsiders, each a secret and keeping secrets from the others. And ourselves, I suspect.

Cast in Doubt 1992

2 I am a ride, a roller coaster, the fun house. I'm what frightens you in the palace of horror. I'm pleasure . . . fire engine red inside your brain . . . Lie down, I'll speak for you.

The Madame Realism Complex 1992

3 People need to be protected from others, who may hurt them, as I need to be protected, but I don't listen to everyone, though I'm a good listener, and I'm curious, though curiosity killed the cat, my mother would say, but she had the cat killed.

American Genius, A Comedy 2006

4 She doesn't know me, I don't know her, and each time she asks why I'm leaving or where I'm going, I tell her, but then she forgets. I tell her again and again, and then she says she misses and loves me, which she never said when I was young and she wasn't incontinent.

Ibid.

3803. Yūko Tsushima (1947–)

1 Running away out of habit was more of a problem than the other kind, since there was no way to stop it. The family was sure she'd have learned her lesson after Yutaka was born, yet in the third year the habit came back and away she went. . . .

"A Sensitive Season," *The Shooting Gallery* Geraldine Harcourt, comp. & tr. 1988

2 Silence is essential. As long as we maintain silence, and thus avoid trespassing, we leave open the possibility of resuming negotiations at any time. I believe the system of bartering used by the mountain men and the villagers was called "silent trade." I am coming to understand that there was nothing extraordinary in striking such a silent bargain for survival.

"The Silent Traders," Ibid.

3 I thought that if he, who had a life with his wife and child elsewhere, was a normal human being then I, whose existence was unknown, unseen and unacceptable to his family, had to be a creature without human form, like an evil spirit that inhabits the mountains and rivers.

"The Marsh," *Unmapped Territories, New Women's Fiction from Japan,* ed. and tr. 1991

4 I felt like teasing them and so I spoke up without thinking. It's an important issue, and we ought to give them accurate information, I said. I should've stopped there. But they were nodding their heads, you know. So I went ahead and told them how I would open my legs to let my kid see what's between them. I let him see the hole and told him that he came out of it, I told them. It's the same hole where men stick their penises

and pour in this thing that makes babies. It's the hole that blood comes out of when babies are not made. I said I told my son all these things. They looked at me with shocked faces. Don't you think it's strange? I got a bit scared afterward and felt depressed. I felt I had said something silly again . . .

Ibid.

3804. Laura D'Andrea Tyson (1947–   )

1 [The economic expansion in the Bush* years] has been marked by the fact that employment growth has been extremely weak. It's marked by the fact that this is the first economic expansion on record—on record—where the family incomes of working families have declined in real terms.

"Your World with Neil Cavuto," *Fox News 2008*
*George W. B- (1946–   ), Am. politician; 43rd president of the United States (2001–09).

3805. Hasina Wazed (1947–   )

1 We shall brave the tortures in jail and are even prepared to die, but we will not talk to him.*

"Bangladesh frees dissident leaders," *The New York Times 11 December 1987*
*Re: President H. M. Ershad, who seized power in 1982.

2 Can we afford islands of prosperity in an ocean of suffering and darkness? Let us resolve that as part of a global village, we should work together so that all can benefit from the process of globalization and we can have a win-win at the end.

Speech, United Nations World Summit *6 September 2000*

3 Globalization and a borderless world are not a panacea for all social and economic ills. While they can reinforce the rich and the powerful, they can also impoverish the weak and the vulnerable.

Ibid.

3806–3807. Roberta Hill Whiteman (1947–   )

1 "I remember the moon shimmering
loss and discovery along a water edge, and skirting

a slice of carrot, I welcome eternity in that sad eye of autumn. Rare and real, I dance while vegetables sing in pairs . . ."

"Leap In The Dark," III, sts. 5–8, *Star Quilt 1984*

2 The wagon people
do not think relationship is wealth.

"In the Summer After 'Issue Year' Winter (1873)," St. 2 (1984), *The Woman That I Am, The Literature and Culture of Contemporary Women of Color*, D. Soyini Madison,* ed. *1994*
*See 3912.

3808. Diane Ackerman (1948–   )

1 The senses don't just *make sense* of life in bold or subtle acts of clarity, they tear reality apart into vibrant morsels and reassemble them into a meaningful pattern.

Introduction, *A Natural History of the Senses 1990*

2 Most of all, the twentieth century will be remembered as the time when we first began to understand what our address was. . . . The fragile euphoria of the complex ecosystem that is Earth, an Earth on which, from space, there are no visible fences, or military zones, or national borders. . . . The view from space is offering us the first chance we evolutionary tod-

dlers have had to cross the cosmic street and stand facing our own home, amazed to see it clearly for the first time.

"Vision," Ibid.

3 Perception is itself a form of grace.

"Postscript," Ibid.

4 The great affair, the love affair with life, is to live as variously as possible, to groom one's curiosity like a high-spirited thoroughbred, climb aboard, and gallop over the thick, sun-struck hills every day.

Ibid.

5 Why do the same images come to mind when people describe their romantic feelings? Custom, culture and tastes vary, but not love itself, not the essence of the emotion.

A Natural History of Love 1994

6 What would life be without play?

Deep Play 1999

7 Challenge, discovery, exploration, novelty, pushing one's limits, losing one's self in the activity—all elements of deep play . . .

Ibid.

8 Sometimes I try to sing the birds on the telephone wires (who look like notes on a musical staff). . . . I am mentally far far away from civilization. The world is breaking someone else's heart.

Ibid.

3809. Laurel Gordon Bellows (1948–   )

1 Like Sisyphus . . . women have long been pushing for equal integration into the [law] profession.

Quoted in *Perspectives Winter 1995*

3810. Sheila Bender (1948–   )

1 Your blank book, loose-leaf papers or computer are where you can make sure that by thinking in writing, you allow yourself to take leaps in the dark. In such places, you can write every day or week in a quest to keep describing your world from a state in which you are present in the moment but not knowing what is next. If you write from this state, you will find writing offers you epiphanies, meaningful evocations of places and people and things past and present, as well as knowledge essential to your well-being that you would not have been able to gain any other way.

Ch. 1, *A Year in the Life: Journaling for Self-Discovery 2000*

2 How sad that one of the best ways we have to communicate with ourselves—thinking through writing, making leaps of imagination and association to find our true thoughts and feelings—is contaminated with the imposed idea that how we do something is more important than what we are attempting to do.

Ch. 5, Ibid.

3811. Elizabeth Berg (1948–   )

1 I do not believe the army is a good idea for people with regular human hearts.

Durable Goods 1993

2 . . . he can only go so far in a good direction. Then something happens. He is all broken apart.

Ibid.

3 . . . he said, "Oh." And the bottom fell out. What I am seeing now is that it was never up to him. He could have been more generous. He could have been more sensitive. But how I felt was not up to him. I only let it be.

Pull of the Moon 1996

3812. Julia Blackburn (1948–)

1 Daisy Bates was a liar, of that I am sure, but the extent and the exact details of her lies remain a difficult territory for which no good maps have survived. . . . It would seem that for her the past had no fixed shape or pattern; it was a crystal ball into which she would gaze and she was free to interpret whatever images she saw emerging out of the glimmering refractions of light and colour.

Daisy Bates in the Desert: A Woman's Life Among the Aborigines 1994

2 It was like eternity, that place. Something about the transparency of the light and the way the land seemed to merge with the air and the water as if the elements were interchangeable and the one could become the other. But it was also the silence.

Ibid.

3 My father never hit me; except once when the three of us were sitting down to Sunday lunch at the big round table and he had lunged sideways at my mother with his fist, but got me instead by mistake. "So sorry darling," he said, genuinely apologetic. "No blood I hope?"

Ch. 1, *The Three of Us* 2008

3813. Mary Kay Blakely (1948–)

1 This is a perilous time for those living outside traditional family units.

American Mom: Motherhood, Politics and Humble Pie 1994

2 Motherhood is not a job I ever wanted to outgrow. But here I am, 20 years later: I have become unnecessary.

Ibid.

3 Even with all the shocking evidence of what's been going on behind closed doors, myths about the superiority of "the traditional family" continue to be stronger than our grip on reality.

Red, White, and Oh So Blue: A Memoir of Political Depression 1996

4 With our current politicians in a protracted state of arrested development, salvation depends on the bystanders asserting their power.

Ibid.

5 Bertha Pappenheim* chose not to detach from the pain of her childhood—she let it move her. Then she moved the world.

Ibid.

*The real name of Freud's famously pseudonymous patient, Anna O; Freud, the Austrian physician and founder of psychoanalysis (1856–1939), believed she was only fantasizing about incestuous abuse; see 1249.

3814. Catherine Breillat (1948–)

1 It happens under the eye of the camera that the actors are transfigured, like people in love. Because the camera is a way of loving people. The way you look at them transforms them totally. That's why directors sign their films, even though they're not the ones holding the camera, or saying the words. But their vision transforms things so totally that the film belongs to them.

Quoted by Leslie Camhi in "Baring the Intricacies of Desire and Shame," *The New York Times,* Arts & Leisure 14 March 1999

2 I make moral films. But mine is a rather ambiguous, Dostoyevskian morality. I believe that human beings are forever torn between their worst and best impulses. And nothing represents that better than sex—what is most trivial, most obscene, most debased and most beautiful in human beings.

Ibid.

3 I don't make films in order to present a realistic vision of society, but rather to track down the truths we are not supposed to see. It's not realism that interests me, but reality, truth, which is very incorporeal.

Ibid.

3815. Castell Bryant (1948–)

1 If the rate of change inside an institution is less than the rate of change outside, the end is in sight.

"Bryant to faculty . . ." by Bill Cotterell, *Tallahassee Democrat* 18 August 2005

2 We need [tomorrow's graduates]. This nation needs them. And for those who don't know how the Social Security system works, you need them.

Ibid.

3 I'm what you call a free black woman. Sometimes, we can be dangerous but one thing, we've always been consistent. You can't break us down.

Ibid.

3816. Denise Elia Chávez (1948–)

1 ISABEL. When people tell me it's an easy time to be a woman, *me río*! As far as I'm concerned, when you're a woman, no time is easy. And when you're an artist, it's worse. Those born rich suffer as much as those born poor. But I'm not complaining. I might worry, but then I either sing or pray or laugh. Ríanse,* as my *gramita* used to say. And love! One of the greatest powers we all possess is the ability to love.

"Novena Narrativas," *Chicana Creativity and Criticism . . . Americas Review* 15 (3–4) 1987

*Laugh.

2 JESUSITA. I'm too busy with God to be worrying about people.

Ibid.

3 MINDA. She tells me, "Don't be afraid of your body, Minda. All women are the same that way. It's beautiful! A gift from God the Mother. The female thing won't kill you, or your mother being dead. All things have to die. It's natural."

Ibid.

3817. Ann-ping Chin (1948–)

1 One cannot say that all China's cultural symbols and cultural assumptions were reduced to ruins. They seem to be endowed with a life of their own.

Children of China 1989

3818. Pearl Cleage (1948–   )

1   MISS LEAH. I needed to be someplace big enough for all my sons and all my ghost grandbabies to roam around. Big enough for me to think about all that sweetness they had stole from me and just holler about it as loud as I want to holler.

Flyin' West 1992

2   JENNY. No horror stories please! I can't stand it when people tell a pregnant woman horror stories, especially when I'm the pregnant woman!

Hospice (1989), *The Woman That I Am, The Literature and Culture of Contemporary Women of Color,* D. Soyini Madison,* ed. *1994*

    *See 3912.

3   ALICE. Nobody chooses to be alone. You might choose your sanity, or your freedom, or some other wild thing that results in your being alone, but that's the fallout. The unavoidable consequences. Not the choice.

Ibid.

4   ALICE. Ordinary people often mistake courage for insanity. It frightens them.

Ibid.

5   As a playwright I don't want to spend all my time fussing at white racism, but as a feminist, I don't want to spend all my time fussing at men . . . The responsibility is to tell the complete truth, and if you do that, the whole question of role models is really moot.

Quoted in "Making Our History" by Douglas Langworthy, *American Theatre* (New York) *July/August 1996*

3819. Marcelle Clements (1948–   )

1   If I had imagined the life I now lead, I doubt I would have wanted it, but it also wouldn't have occurred to me that I could handle it, . . . so I'm surprised and pleased to find that I do.

(p. 11), *The Improvised Woman: Single Women Reinventing Single Life 1998*

3820. Deborah S. Cohen (1948–   )

1   Measured in terms of violence and prejudice, college campuses often look to be altogether nastier places than they were thirty years ago. Even the presence of Women's Studies, Jewish Studies and African American Studies doesn't stop women from being raped, Holocaust revisionists from creeping up to the door of the Hillel, Ku Klux Klan banners from making surreptitious appearances on dormitory walls.

"Strangers in a strange land," *The Women's Review of Books,* Vol. XII, No. 4 *January 1995*

2   Must remember to incorporate gory or libidinous material in every lecture to ensure wakefulness.

"Chronicle of higher education," *The Women's Review of Books,* Vol. XV, No. 5 *February 1998*

3821. Patricia Hill Collins (1948–   )

1   Groups unequal in power are correspondingly unequal in their ability to make their standpoint known to themselves and others.

"Defining Black Feminist Thought," *Black Feminist Thought 1991*

2   Being black encompasses *both* experiencing white domination *and* individual and group valuation of an independent, long-standing Afrocentric consciousness.

Ibid.

3821.1. Candy Crowley (1948–   )

1   The interviewee has something to say, born of experiences I haven't had. I am so curious to know what they think that my opinions just don't pop into my head. No interview is about me or what I think.

"Candy Crowley Q & A," All Things CNN 7 June 2009

2   I tell people that balancing career and children is not a daily act. It's a minute-to-minute act. When the kids were young, they would inevitably call the bureau when I was crashing to get a story on air. These were known as "Crowley Kid Calls." At deadline time, I asked whoever answered the phone to give the kids the "three B" test: Is anything broken, burning or bleeding? And if not, I'll call right back. One day the oldest said "BLEEDING" and I was home in 15 minutes and at the hospital in 30.

Ibid.

3   Here is a secret: almost nothing ever goes the way you planned on live TV.

Ibid.

4   I have been a print reporter, a radio reporter and a TV reporter. The jobs were far more alike than different. Print, radio and TV are not journalism; they are venues through which you put your journalism. And journalism is journalism.

Ibid.

3822. Nance K. Dicciani (1948?–   )

1   More than any other profession, engineers will bear the responsibility of those challenges that humans [will face in the future].

Keynote address, Society of Women Engineers Region E Conference (Pennsylvania), *21 November 1992*

2   Let's not be self-limiting. Let's go instead where there is no path and leave a trail.

Ibid.

3823. Dianne Dugaw (1948–   )

1   We in the West may be living our way out of one of the most constrained and unimaginative epochs in the history of human sexual expression. (One can only hope.)

"Delusions of gender," *The Women's Review of Books,* Vol. XIV, No. 7 *April 1997*

2   People who have had themselves refashioned from "woman" to "man" or vice versa almost necessarily stand in a parodying relationship to the binary gender system, and may well be more aware of it as a superstructure than people whose gender has been achieved with less contrivance.

Ibid.

3824. Sue Levi Elwell (1948–   )

1   When will we learn that isolation is *not* the answer to our fear of difference, that separation is not how we must treat those who embody our own greatest fears of isolation and alienation? We, of all people, must remember the basic right of each human being to dignity and to justice.

Sermon, Rosh Hashanah (Los Angeles, 1987), *Four Centuries of Jewish Women's Spirituality* Ellen M. Umansky* & Dianne Ashton, eds. *1992*

    *See 4011.

2   How do we save our own lives? By taking risks, by pushing against the boundaries and limits that others have established,

by being fully present. By stretching. By paying attention to the small acts of kindness that make up our everyday lives.

Ibid.

3825. Deirdre English (1948–)

Coauthor with Barbara Ehrenreich; see 3257:1.

3826. Connie Field (1948–)

1 Many people think that the woman who responded to the call to "do the job he left behind," were suburban housewives who trotted back to their homes after the war. The newsreels would have you believe that too. But for a majority, the women were working before, and had to work after.

Quoted in "'Rosies' Were There When U.S. Needed Them" by Anita Alverio, *New Directions for Women July/August 1981*

2 . . . making a [documentary] film is not writing a textbook. Someone can have a terrifically wonderful story, but if they can't say it in a way that makes you want to listen, then it's not useful.

Ibid.

3827. Shakti Gawain (1948–)

1 Creative visualization is magic in the truest and highest meaning of the word. It involves understanding and aligning yourself with the natural principles that govern the workings of our universe, and learning to use these principles in the most conscious and creative way.

Creative Visualization 1978

2 Humanity is in an ongoing process of conscious evolution. At this time, we are taking a giant step in consciousness—a great leap in that evolutionary process.

"Facing the Future," *The Path of Transformation 1993*

3 The overall process of physical healing takes place in our lives as we learn to feel, listen to, and trust our bodies again. Our bodies communicate to us clearly and specifically, if we are willing to listen to them.

"Healing the Physical Level," Ibid.

4 I am convinced that life in a physical body is meant to be an ecstatic experience.

Ibid.

3828. Natalie Goldberg (1948–)

1 Stress is an ignorant state. It believes that everything is an emergency.

Wild Mind: Living the Writer's Life 1990

3829. Tipper Gore (1948–)

1 Homelessness is a result of deinstitutionalization and urban redevelopment. We haven't provided enough mental-health services, and we allowed gentrification to make a lot of money for some people without paying enough attention to what was happening to others.

Quoted in "I Know There Is Help" by Colin Greer, *Parade Magazine 11 September 1994*

2 Denial can have a corrosive effect. It takes a toll. It's true when you deny problems inside your family, and it takes a toll on all of us when we deny problems in our society.

Ibid.

3 Youngsters have to know about the responsibility and rewards of parenting. They have to learn about relationships. Sex education alone is not enough. Parent education is the relationship part.

Ibid.

4 Our society is suffering from great trauma. As we reach toward the year 2000, we have to be honest about that. We have serious addictions to deal with. Even our consumption often reaches the point of addiction. When a person has to get more and more to feel good, you're reaching the point of illness. We know overconsumption is not good for the planet. It's not good for individual people either.

Ibid.

3830. Antonia Hernandez (1948–)

1 A court victory is important but just the beginning of the process. It must translate into empowerment. It is the people that have the power to give life to those court victories.

Remark (1991), Quoted in *The 50 Most Influential Women in American Law* by Dawn Bradley Berry* 1996

*See 4399.

2 Without an educated Latino community, our dramatic increase as a percentage of the US population is not going to result in policies that improve our lives as Americans. Wasn't it George Orwell who said "To be political, you first have to be well informed"? A solid education levels the playing field for everybody. It's the surest provider of equal opportunity.

"Antonia Hernandez: The Leading Latina Legal Eagle for Civil Rights," *Civil Rights Journal Fall 1998*

3 As someone who is bilingual and had to learn English, I can tell you I'm a much more valuable American by being bilingual. Latinos have to learn English; it's the language of economic progress. However, that doesn't have to mean we have to forget Spanish and lose an asset that others don't have.

Ibid.

3831. S. E. Hinton (1948–)

1 Of all of us, Dally was the one I liked least. He didn't have Soda's understanding or dash, or Two-Bit's humor, or even Darry's superman qualities. But I realized that these three appealed to me because they were like the heroes in the novels I read. Dally was real. I liked my books and clouds and sunsets. Dally was so real he scared me.

The Outsiders 1967

2 I'd read everything in the house about 50 million times, even Darry's copy of "The Carpetbaggers,"* though he'd told me I wasn't old enough to read it. I thought so too after I finished it.

Ibid.

*A popular 1961 novel by American writer Harold Robbins (1916–97), loosely based on the life of Howard Hughes (1905–76), American aviator, industrialist, film producer, and philanthropist.

3 Stay gold.

Catch-phrase, Ibid.

4 "You're just like a ball in a pinball machine. Getting slammed back and forth; and you never think about anything, about where you're going or how you're going to get there . . ."

Rumble Fish 1975

3832. Nancy Horan (1948–)

1 Frank Lloyd Wright* was converting them—almost to the Woman—before her very eyes. For all she knew five minutes ago, they could just as well have booed. Now the room had the feeling of a revival tent. They were getting his religion, throwing away their crutches. Every one of them thought his disparaging remarks were aimed at someone else.

Ch. 1, Loving Frank 2007
*Frank Lloyd Wright (1869–1959), Am. architect.

2 "The human race will evolve to a higher plane where there won't be a need for laws regulating marriage and divorce."
"So if we can just hang on for a millennium or two, it'll all work out."

Ibid.

3 Ornament is not about prettifying the outside of something, he was saying. It should possess "fitness, proportion, harmony, the result of all of which is repose."

Ibid.

3833. Mardy Ireland (1948–)

1 I think it is exciting to decide not to have a baby, and really to try to make room for your own creative self, but I also think it's really hard. I don't think it is easy. I think there are agonies involved. But I also think that there are agonies involved in being a mother, many of which are never spoken. . . .

Reconceiving Women 1993

3834. Sheila Jeffreys (1948–)

1 The skills that all prostituted women must develop are those which allow them to *survive,* such as dissociation, being alert to danger and limiting the activities that the customers request to those [she is] prepared to accept without too much damage to her health and sense of self.

The Idea of Prostitution 1997

2 Prostituted women are being paid to receive exactly the treatment as sexual objects that other women workers are seeking to abolish.

Ibid.

3 We do think . . . that all feminists can and should be lesbians. Our definition of a political lesbian is a woman-identified woman who does not fuck men. It does not mean compulsory sexual activity with women.

Quoted in interview by Julie Bindel, *The Guardian* (London) *2 July 2005*

3835. Fatima Jibrell (1948–)

1 Because African political leaders have delegated their economic planning to the International Monetary Fund and the World Bank, they no longer have the power to protect their citizens or environment from being exploited by the First World.

Quoted in "Fatima Jibrell: Nursing Nature" by Tekla Szymanski, *World Press Review,* vol. 49, no. 7 *July 2002*

2 It is important to know that we are all human world citizens and belong to this fragile, limited space. If we go too far, we can't repair it.

Ibid.

3 We lived in this environment where we did not really need money. But the invention of money has created greedy mega-companies in Europe to come—and the European Union subsidizes these ships—to come to our coasts to suck out the marine resources, destroy the reefs. They are also doing waste-dumping.

Quoted in "Somalia: One Woman's Fight to Rescue the Environment" by Akwe Amosu, *AllAfrica.com 13 January 2003*

4 We are busy surviving. We are busy like chickens eating each other. If you make chickens hungry, they pick on each other. And that's what we are doing. We are picking on each other.

Ibid.

3836. Donna Karan (1948–)

1 I was so turned on when I was in Indonesia, to Bali, Thailand, Vietnam, Cambodia and how to interpret that kind of sensibility into a modern way. Taking the sensibility and the earthiness and the hand that's used in the East and connecting it to what we can do here in the West . . . I tried to put those two worlds together in a very sensual way.

Quoted in "Karan's spring accessories are pure and simple" by Elsa Klensch, CNN Interactive *7 March 1997*

2 I think of an evening bag as what I put on top of the table . . . almost like a piece of jewelry, not a bag.

Ibid.

3 Everything I do is a matter of heart, body and soul. For me, designing is an expression of who I am as a woman, with all the complications, feelings and emotions.

Quoted in *The Huffington Post 29 June 2008*

3837. Judy Kaye (1948–)

1 I approach Broadway music in a light way and fudge on the belting, which is the quickest way to shorten your vocal life. Most of the great songs don't have to be done that way—what gets people excited is if you get the words across.

"Kaye's Career Spans 'Grease' to 'Boheme'" by Richard Dyer, *Boston Globe 19 August 1990*

2 The thing that I find fun about performing is telling stories and creating characters.

Quoted in "Broadway's Favorite Diva" by Sheryl Flatow, *Playbill Magazine n.d.*

3 All I ever wanted to be was a working actress, and I thought that was the most romantic concept, and that's what I am, a working actress. The rest is gravy after that.

Quoted in "Meet Judy Kaye—The Phantom's Diva" by Maryann Lopinto, *Show Music Magazine n.d*

3838. Sara Keays (1948–)

1 We teach our children to be honourable, to own up when they are wrong, to take responsibility for their mistakes—it is increasingly difficult when the Government won't do that, financially or sexually . . .

"The curse of Keays," The *Times* (London) *14 January 1994*

2 The Government has decided there are valid families and others which are not valid, and which must disappear . . .*

Ibid.

*Keays was involved in a notorious affair with Cecil Parkinson (1931–), British politician and former cabinet minister.

3839. Margot Kidder (1948–)

1 Abortion might be killing a life; I don't know. That to me is not an issue. If there is a sin, it is the sin that we adults perpetrate on the children of the earth who truly are innocent and defenseless by bringing those children into the world when they will not be cared for . . . There are all over the globe children starving, being raped, dying, being beaten up because they're unwanted. They suffer abuses from which they never recover . . .

The Choices We Made, Angela Bonavoglia, ed. and intro. *1991*

3840. Ynestra King (1948?–)

1 Nature-hating and woman-hating are particularly related and associated and are mutually reinforcing.

Quoted in "The Goddess Revived, the Rise of Ecofeminism" by Kitty Mattes, *The Amicus Journal Fall 1990*

2 The wish that the body should be irrelevant has been one of my most fervent lifelong wishes. The knowledge that it isn't is my most intense lifelong experience.

"The Other Body," *Ms.* (New York) *March/April 1993*

3 The mythology of autonomy perpetuates in terrible ways the oppression of the disabled. It also perpetuates misogyny—and the destruction of the planet.

Ibid.

4 . . . the potential for human growth and creativity is infinite—but it is not groundless. The common ground for the person—the human body—is a place of shifting sand that can fail us at any time. It can change shape and properties without warning; this is an essential truth of embodied existence.

Ibid.

5 Most of us will do anything to our bodies to appear closer to norms of physical beauty which come naturally to about two percent of the female population. The rest of us struggle to be skinny, hairless, and lately muscular; we lie in the sun to get tan even when we know we're courting melanoma; we submit ourselves to extremely dangerous surgery. We primp, prune, douche, deodorize, and diet as if our natural bodies were our mortal enemies—and to the extent to which we make our own flesh an enemy, we are participating in the domination of nature.

Quoted in "It's Not Nice to Mess With Mother Nature— Ecofeminism 101 (1989)" by Lindsey Van Gelder, *Ms.* (New York) *Spring 2002*

3841. Gina Kolata (1948–)

1 The genes that make people fat need an environment in which food is cheap and plentiful.

Rethinking Thin, The New Science of Weight Loss—and the Myths and Realities of Dieting 2007

3842. Ross Shepard Kraemer (1948–)

1 Self-determination for women is only available at the cost of psychic self-destruction, at the cost of the repudiation of the feminine.

Her Share of the Blessings: Women's Religions Among Pagans, Jews, and Christians in the Greco-Roman World 1992

3843. Hermione Lee (1948–)

1 The life-writer must explore and understand the gap between the outer self . . . and the secret self.

Virginia Woolf 1997

2 Woolf's* story is reformulated by each generation.

Ibid.

*See 3841.

3844. Mary Jean LeTendre (1948–)

1 America's future walks through the doors of our schools each day.

Speech (University of Massachusetts) *15 November 2006*

2 Let us not confuse stability with stagnation.

Ibid.

3845. Emily Levine (1948?–)

1 *Re a Total Woman course:* A revolutionary new idea whereby women give up their entire lives and can stay home and devote themselves to their husbands, whether they like them or not.

Quoted in "Rising Stars," *Funny Women, American Comediennes, 1860–1985* by Mary Unterbrink *1987*

2 Old people can be fun if they're not yours.

Ibid.

3 There are even born-again bikers. They're the ones with the chains and tattoos that say "Born Again to Lose."

Ibid.

3846. Catherine Malfitano (1948–)

1 The mystery of love is greater than the mystery of death.

Quoted in "In the Kitchen with Catherine Malfitano" by Ralph Blumenthal, *The New York Times 27 March 1996*

2 She's not a victim [Madame Butterfly*] at all, she *chooses* her destiny. It's a very strong choice, and the way things turn out there is unfortunately no escape for her.

Quoted in *Diva, The New Generation: The Sopranos and Mezzos of the Decade Discuss Their Roles* by Helena Matheopoulous *1998*

*Eponymous character of opera by Giacomo Puccini, Italian composer (1858–1924).

3847. Mizuko Masuda (1948–)

1 A bag of memories is not as sturdy as you might think. A small rip from an insignificant newspaper article quickly becomes large enough to expose the bag's contents.

"Sinking Ground," *Unmapped Territories, New Women's Fiction from Japan,* ed. and tr. *1991*

2 Rather than being shocked at his quick transformation, she was impressed by his toughness.

That energy in men—who pursue wars, create orders and construct neon-filled cities, and who boast of their accomplishments—must come from this toughness . . .

Ibid.

3 As if she believed she could keep reinventing her life, she had allowed herself to make her present life unbearable.

Ibid.

3848. Christa McAuliffe (1948–1986)

1 What are we doing here? We're reaching for the stars.

Remark upon entering astronaut program,* quoted in *Time* (New York) *10 February 1986*

*Killed in explosion of spacecraft *Challenger,* 28 January 1986.

2   I touch the future. I teach.

          Speech (August 1985), Ibid.

3849. Heather McHugh (1948–   )

1   His crime was his belief
   the universe does not revolve around
   the human being: God is no
   fixed point or central government
   but rather is poured in waves, through
   all things: all things
   move.

      "What He Thought," St. 7, *Hinge & Sign: Poems 1968–1993*
      1994

2   I loved pencils. I loved their long hexagons. I loved their yellow
   paint (leaded) and their black lead (unleaded). I loved the little
   lines on the metal strip that held so fast to the stubborn flesh
   of the eraser. . . . Given a pencil, I wanted to leave my mark; I
   necklaced those metal strips with toothprints. For every tooth-
   mark, there was a thought. For every thought, a music. That's
   why I BEGAN writing.

      Interview, Amazon.com *July 1998*

3   What's done by heart to day can still
   be done to night by mind.

      "Ein Ander," *The Father of the Predicaments 1999*

4   Too volatile, am I? too voluble? too much a word-person?
   I blame the soup: I'm a primordially
   stirred person.

      "Ghazal of the Better-Unbegun," St. 1, Ibid.

5   Given an airplane, chance encounters always ask, So what are
   your poems about? They're about their business, and their
   father's business, and their monkey's uncle, they're about how
   nothing is about, they're not about about.

      "20–200 on 747" *n.d.*

3850. Pauline Melville (1948–   )

1   . . . stories are told for revenge or tribute.

      The Ventriloquist's Tale 1997

2   "I can do any voice: jaguar, London hoodlum, bellbird, 19th-
   century novelist, anteater, epic poet, a chorus of howler
   monkeys, urban brutalist, a tapir. The list is infinite."

      Ibid.

3   The odd thing was that even after he had been president for
   many years, he felt unsure of his position. He felt like a charlatan. And this was nothing to do with the rigged elections that
   had kept him in power for nearly two decades. He would have
   felt like a charlatan even if he had been fairly elected.

      "The President's Exile," *The Migration of Ghosts 1998*

4   "Was it the cancer that killed him like?" asked Scot Eddy nervously. None of them knew much funeral etiquette.
      "Oh no," said Mary. "He went to the lavvy and pulled the
   chain and the cistern fell down on his head."

      "Don't Give Me Your Sad Stories," Ibid.

5   During this time the bird was lost in thought. What he thought
   about was the written word. Books had become the truth. The
   written word had become proof. Laws were built on books
   which contained precedent. People were killed in their name.
   Confession, word of mouth, rumour, gossip, chattiness and

oratory had all lost their place in the hierarchy of power. Passports verified. Documents condemned. Signatures empowered.
Books were the storage place of memory. Books were written
to contradict other books.

      "The Parrot and Descartes," Ibid.

3851. Stephanie Mills (1948–   )

1   Being in the woods is being in church.

      "Fate and Faith," *Whatever Happened to Ecology? 1989*

2   Like it or not, we are entering a new era in Earth's history
   where wild Nature may persist at the macroscopic level only
   by human sufferance.

      Ch. 1, *In Service of the Wild: Restoring and Reinhabiting*
      Damaged Land 1995

3   There's a level of perception at which vegetation is generic. For
   most of us the landscape either has green things growing on it
   or not. It takes a while to begin to learn the difference between
   old-growth and second- and third-growth forest, or the difference between open land populated by exotic species—old
   fields—and open land like the tall grass prairie that is richly
   populated by a diversity of species.

      Ch. 6, Ibid.

4   The pleasures and riches of simplicity, it seems to me, arrive
   mainly through the senses, through savoring the world of a
   given moment.

      Ch. 1, *Epicurean Simplicity 2002*

5   Everywhere on earth, it seems, it is our species that needs to
   transform itself: to become as different from what we are now
   as the butterfly is from the leaf-chewing caterpillar, as different
   as the milkweed fluff is from the starry flowers whose nectar
   feasts the paper-thin airborne monarchs.

      Ch. 4, Ibid.

3852. Zoe Ann Nicholson (1948–   )

1   The Mother is just on the other side of thought waiting for you
   to find her. Although she is powerful enough to pierce through
   the veil of thought by herself, she does not seek to force her
   way into your consciousness, to your life, to the planet. She
   wants to be invited and welcomed through the practice of
   meditation and mindfulness by the women living and working
   on earth. As she flows into your life, you will discover who you
   really are and who you are intended to be.

      Introduction, *Matri, Letters from the Mother 2003*

2   A passionate soul must create a life that never seeks rest from
   their spirit. The body must dance and the mind must spin in
   deference to the spirit. The spirit is ruler, supreme choreographer, beloved whisperer. The passionate heart always chooses
   to listen. Do not be fooled. It is not that they have no choice.
   They have every choice and they choose spirit.

      Afterword, *The Passionate Heart 2003*

3   Why do Christians want to think of their founder in agony and
   pain. Why not in triumph and glory? And why is the man in
   the classroom posters so wimpy? Are these people reading the
   same gospels that I studied? I read about a revolutionary Jew
   who was killed for his dissent.

      Tuesday, May 18, Day 1, *The Hungry Heart: A Woman's Fast*
      for Justice 2004

4   Does the radical always dissolve into the conventional? Is it
   just a matter of time before the masses reduce a revolution and

use it as a form of control? Once gender equality is the convention, will society find another group to oppress?

Ibid.

5 I am fasting for equality of rights under the law in the U.S. I am fasting to legislate treating adults without regard to gender. I am fasting to criminalize discrimination. But my heart wants so much more.

I want a life built on trusting, intimate and integrated relationships. I want humans to meet without judgment, to join without conditions, to not require safeguards. I want danger and oppression relegated to fiction. I want limitless welcome, boundless potential and open communication. I want food for the body and the mind and soul to be equally important.

June 16, 1982, Day 30 of the Fast, Ibid.

3853. Sharon Niederman (1948–)

1 It's difficult to become a writer, a woman writer. To arrange one's life for writing, often at sacrifice; to believe in one's work when there may be little or no support; to commit to one's own imaginative processes when real life pushes women toward committing far more strongly toward other people's endeavors—these acts essential to becoming serious about one's work require a strength that few writers believe they possess and that they must improvise, like their stories, as they go along.

Introduction, *Shaking Eve's Tree, Short Stories of Jewish Women*, Sharon Niederman, ed. *1990*

2 Brainy women had a special obligation to look particularly chic and sexy, she believed, and she prided herself on never looking like a teacher or a librarian.

"A Gift for Languages," 1, Ibid.

3 Out of rebellion and hope, her parents had been leftists. All that remained of their youthful idealism was their disbelief in God.

Ibid.

4 Falling in love was the worst thing that could happen to a woman. Hadn't she seen this disaster repeated often enough? No matter how gifted or accomplished the woman . . . love provided a socially condoned route to self-destruction. Love automatically took precedence over work, money, reputation, ambition—the entire professional life that a woman had struggled so hard and honorably to create. Love succeeded where the world had failed to knock you out of the game.

5, Ibid.

3854. Janet Peery (1948–)

1 I was born in Kansas and lived there forty-five years. I didn't know how much I loved it, though, until I left it. I knew that in this place in order to see its beauty you had to look deep, to look closely, that in its seeming emptiness—the sky itself seems a landmark—there are riches not apparent to the eye accustomed to more flamboyant sights.

Interview, Amazon.com *July 1999*

2 He was dying faster than he could live, that much was clear.

What the Thunder Said: A Novella and Stories 2008

3 His desire had been to leave his sin behind and never have to tell it. Whether his act had been an accident or not, he had committed it, and though there was atonement, there was no forgiveness.

Ibid.

3855. Faith Popcorn (1948–)

1 America is a consumer culture, and when we change what we buy—and how we buy it—we'll change who we are.

"Prediction: Socioquake!" *The Popcorn Report 1991*

2 Anticipating a new reality is the beginning of the process of creating it.

"Brailing the Culture," Ibid.

3 When the first Ford automobiles came rolling off the assembly line—shiny, smooth, and, above all, *all the same*, the world came to see uniformity—mass quantities of uniformity—as the mark of excellence for the modern age. Handmade seemed unbelievably crude in comparison. Now the very reverse is coming to be true.

"Egonomics," Ibid.

4 We don't want more *anything* anymore. What we want now is less. More and more less.

"99 Lives," Ibid.

5 It's the new millennium. It's time to *think link*.

Ch. 2, *EVEolution: Understanding Women . . . 2000*

3856. Emily Prager (1948–)

1 Beauty is the still birth of suffering, every woman knows that.

"A Visit from the Footbinder," *Close Company: Stories of Mothers and Daughters*, Christine Park and Caroline Heaton, eds. *1987*

2 Beneath her dolly exterior lurked a raging little animal that bit and clawed and threw itself around rooms, causing destruction.

Clea & Zeus Divorce 1987

3 One night last month . . . she had a momentary resurfacing of longing for her Chinese mother, the first in two years, and we wept together again. But there is a location for this grief now, and it no longer sweeps over her being, an incomprehensible maelstrom that threatens her very identity and her attachments.

Wuhu Diary: On Taking My Adopted Daughter Back to Her Hometown in China 2001

3857. Melissa Pritchard (1948–)

1 All he knows is my soul appears salvageable, and for all my college education, I prove remarkably easy to fool.

The Instinct For Bliss 1997

2 Someday she'd figure out how she could let herself have great sex with such a lousy individual.

"Hallie," Ibid.

3858. Nora Räthzel (1948–)

1 A faint suspicion about the degree to which we have subordinated ourselves to structures of domination might, therefore, be the rational source of "irrational" anxieties towards "Ausländer" [foreigners].

"Harmonious 'Heimat' and Disturbing 'Ausländer'," *Feminism and Psychology*, Vol. 4, No. 1 *February 1994*

3859. Lyudmila Razumovskaya (1948–)

1 Watching you from our childhoods on, we learned to be hypocrites, to deceive, to make pretty facades.

Dear Yelena Sergeyevna, Curt Columbusm, tr. *1980*

3860. Erika Ritter (1948–   )

1   NICK. I don't get it. . . . If I can do you a favour, why not? What is it, you've got your life in ledger columns? "Business." "Romance."

   CHARLIE. That's right. Just don't mix me in with business, that's all. This town is one giant office. Casting done in bars. Contracts ratified on waterbeds. People sucking up to power because it might rub off. Those macrobiotic people had it all wrong. Around here, you are *who* you eat.

   Act I, Sc. 3, *The Automatic Pilot* 1978

3861. Pamela Jean Roach (1948–   )

1   If it's been a career woman, who's never been at home, never had children, never been involved in the education world, the PTA, if it's a person who's never been out there with the people, working with them, if they've never had children and stayed home with them, they're in the same position as a man.

   Quoted in "Cleaning house in government . . ." by Carol M. Ostrom, *Seattle Times*, A1-9 *2 August 1992*

3862. Wendy Rose (1948–   )

1   I am hungry enough
   to eat myself and you
   "The Indian Women Are Listening: To the Nuke Devils," St. 2,
   A Gathering of Spirit, Beth Brant,* ed. *1984*
   *See 3246.

2   the hope or the lie
   all the gods gave us that
   pain is a vitamin
   to make us grow.
   "Well You Caught Me Unprepared," St. 4, Ibid.

3   Nothing is old
   about us yet;
   we are still waiting,
   "Walking on the Prayerstick," St. 1, *That's What She Said*,
   Rayna Green,* ed. *1984*
   *See 3338.

4   It's our blood that gives you
   those southwestern skies.
   "Long Division: A Tribal History," Ibid.

3863. Friederike Roth (1948–   )

1   SHE (raging). Until the day I die I will insist absolutely that shared joy is half-joy. That love sings and swings and makes you uncritical and doesn't deal in accounts paid in advance, like a greedy, shriveled-up old woman.
   Sc. 12, *Piano Plays (Klavierspiele)*, Andrea Weddington, tr. *1980*

3864. Kathleen Sebelius (1948–   )

1   I don't believe allowing people to carry concealed handguns into sporting events, shopping malls, grocery stores, or the workplace would be good public policy. And to me the likelihood of exposing children to loaded handguns in their parents' purses, pockets and automobiles is simply unacceptable.
   "Sebelius vetoes concealed carry bill," Associated Press *16 April 2004*

2   The American people—folks like you and me—are not nearly as divided as our rancorous politics might suggest.
   (Speech, January 2008), Quoted in "Obama veepstakes: The other woman" by Walter Shapiro, *Salon.com 7 July 2008*

3   People bring their own life experiences, and women's life experiences are different than men's—not better, not worse, different. And 51,52 percent of the population is women. And so having people at the table who make decisions based on their life experiences, their lens—whether it's as a mother, a daughter, a spouse, somebody who's in the workplace—I think we get better policies, a better dynamic.
   Quoted in Ch. 4, *Why Women Should Rule the World: A Memoir* by Dee Dee Myers* 2008
   *See 4590.

3865. Ntozake Shange (1948–   )

1   TOUSSAINT L'OVERTURE*
   became my secret lover at the age of 8
   i entertained him in my bedroom
   widda flashlight under my covers

   way inta the night
   we discussed strategies
   how to remove white girls from my hopscotch games
   & etc.
   "toussaint," *for colored girls who have considered suicide/ when the rainbow is enuf* 1977
   *Leader of Haitian independence and emancipator of black slaves (ca. 1743–1803).

2   i found god in myself
   & i loved her/i loved her fiercely
   "a laying on of hands," Ibid.

3   I am gonna write poems til i die and when i have gotten outta this body i am gonna hang round in the wind and knock over everybody who got their feet on the ground.
   "advice," *Nappy Edges* 1979

4   Where there is a woman there is magic. If there is a moon falling from her mouth, she is a woman who knows her magic, who can share or not share her powers. A woman with a moon falling from her mouth, roses between her legs and tiaras of Spanish moss, this woman is a consort of the spirits.
   Sassafras, Cypress and Indigo 1982

5   I am a war correspondent after all . . . because I'm involved in a war of cultural and esthetic aggression. The front lines aren't always what you think they are.*
   Interview with Stella Dong, *Publishers Weekly 3 May 1985*
   *One of Shange's youthful goals was to be a war correspondent.

6   Maybe it's not the silences.
   Not the silences that bother me.
   It's just the noise like a roar inside my head takes over when it's silent.
   "Room in the Dark," I, *Liliane* 1994

3866. Leslie Marmon Silko (1948–   )

1   I will tell you something about stories,
   They aren't just entertainment.
   don't be fooled.
   They are all we have, you see,
   all we have to fight off
   illness and death.
   Ceremony 1977

2   Stolen rivers and mountains
   the stolen land will eat their hearts

and jerk their mouths from the Mother.
The people will starve.

(p. 132), Ibid.

3   . . . storytelling for Indians is like a natural resource.
*The Third Woman: Minority Women Writers of the United
States* (p. 118), Dexter Fisher, ed. *1980*

4   Corn cobs and husks, the rinds and stalks and animal bones
were not regarded by the ancient people as filth or garbage.
The remains were merely resting at a midpoint in their journey
back to dust. Human remains are not so different. They should
rest with the bones and rinds where they all may benefit living creatures—small rodents and insects—until their return is
completed.
"Landscape, History, and the Pueblo Imagination,"
*The Woman That I Am, The Literature and Culture of
Contemporary Women of Color,* D. Soyini Madison,* ed. *1994*
*See 3912.

5   Implicit in the Pueblo oral tradition was the awareness that
loyalties, grudges, and kinship must always influence the narrator's choices as she emphasizes to listeners this is the way
she has always heard the story told. The ancient Pueblo people
sought a communal truth, not an absolute. For them this truth
lived somewhere within the web of differing versions, disputes
over minor points, outright contradictions tangling with old
feuds and village rivalries.

Ibid.

6   After the rains, they tended the plants that sprouted out of the
deep sand; they each had plants they cared for as if the plants
were babies. Grandma Fleet has taught them this too. The
plants listen, she told them. Always greet each plant respectfully. Don't argue or fight around the plants—hard feelings
cause the plants to wither.

Part One, *Gardens in the Dunes 1999*

3867. Svetlana Slapsak (1948–)
1   All the bestialities of war were triggered by words—cliches put
forward by intellectuals and eagerly appropriated by politicians.
"Bosnia proves words can kill," *Seattle Post-Intelligencer,* Op-
Ed, A11 *27 May 1993*

2   Those writings by intellectuals were recycled by journalists;
soon, draftees were sent to be killed with writers' words on
their lips.

Ibid.

3   Fear, repulsion, concern for our careers—there were any
number of reasons why many did not act to thwart the false
prophets who have destroyed public discourse and civilization
in Serbia, not to mention the destruction they caused in Bosnia
and Croatia.
   We should have taken out the garbage when we first noticed the stench.

Ibid.

3868. Nancy Springer (1948–)
1   "I hate being a woman." He had surprised bottom-line truth
out of her, and it shocked her so that she burst out to defend it,
"Well, of course I do! Every book I read the whole time I was
growing up, men did the important things and women brought
drinks on trays."

Larque on the Wing 1994

3869. Meryl Streep (1948–)
1   We are the choices we have made.
Interview with Katie Couric,* *The Today Show* (NBC-TV) *2
June 1995*
*See 4402.

2   It's insane to have winners and losers in art. We live in a society
plagued by sports mania. To say that one performance is better
than another is just plain dumb.
Quoted in "What Makes Meryl Magic" by John Skow, *Time*
(New York) *7 September 1981*

3   I haven't felt young since I was 13.

Ibid.

4   It would be nice to have a woman President. I think half the
Senate should be women, half of Parliament, half the ruling
mullahs. But that will never happen, darling!
Quoted in *Time* (New York) *22 October 2007*

3870. Judy Syfers (1948?–)
1   My God, who *wouldn't* want a wife?
"I Want a Wife," *The First Ms. Reader,* Francine Klagsbrun,
ed. *1972*

2   The problems of an American wife stem from the fact that we
live in a society which is structured in such a way as to profit
only a few at the expense of the many. As long as we women
tolerate such a capitalist system, all but a privileged few of us
must necessarily be exploited as workers and as wives.

Ibid.

3871. Luisah Teish (1948–)
1   The millennium measures time by the solar calendar and the
birth of Christ. This is a mythological reference point. The assumption that "the solar millennium" reflects *universal truth* is
simply another manifestation of the Christian paradigm which
has been imposed upon the world. There are other cultures
with different spiritual traditions and calendars.
"Sister, Can You Paradigm? Or, Whose Millennium Is It?" *The
Fabric of the Future: Women Visionaries of Today Illuminate
the Path to Tomorrow,* M. J. Ryan, ed. *1998*

2   I maintain that the biggest challenge in the new millennium
could be a change of habit. We could change from a dominating commodity culture into one of true exchange in which we
learn from each other in humility and respect.

Ibid.

3   Every time a sister learns that she is not born to live in a world
of fear, to be dominated, every time a sister sits down with
a glass of water in front of her and understands that she is
intimately tied to water and that all life is tied to water she is
gradually building an inner strength that gives her armor to go
out and fight the world.
Quoted *in Feminism and Ecological Communities: An Ethic of
Flourishing* by Christine Cuomo* *1998*
*See 4674.

3872. Judith Thurman (1948?–)
1   If Colette's* militancy is limited to the boudoir, she is also one
of the first modern writers to suggest that "male" and "female"
are subjective assignments, and that a society which grants

the privilege of "doing" or "being done to" exclusively to one sex or the other warps its young. A child of either sex, she perceives, has urges to penetrate, devour, and possess; to be cherished, dominated, and contained.

> Introduction (2000 ed.), *The Pure and the Impure 1995*
> *See 1409.

2 I think we're really passing through a transitional period right now, and I don't know whether books as we know them and readers as we know them will come out on the other end. . . . There will always be people who really love the word, but we are definitely at the end of something.

> Quoted in "A Moment With . . . Judith Thurman, literary critic" by Travis Nichols, *Seattle Post-Intelligencer 27 November 2007*

3 It's very hard to make that distillation but that is actually what your job is. Without trying to pin the person like a butterfly to the wall, to sum it up. If I can do that, then I feel satisfied. To give the subject a reality in the form of a sentence that is like a piece of rock crystal or a prism.

> Ibid.

4 Disbelief is essential to good writing.

> *Cleopatra's Nose: 39 Varieties of Desire 2007*

3873. Bonnie Tiburzi (1948–)

1 Flying jets is exhilarating. . . . The airplane is . . . a world above a world—and you are in it . . . looking out and down at miracles.

> *Takeoff! 1984*

2 I'm not trying to make a statement, I'm just trying to make a living.

> Quoted *in Ladybirds—The Untold Story of Women Pilots in America* by Henry M. Holden with Capt. Lori Griffith *1991*

3874. María Suárez Toro (1948–)

1 Doing feminist radio is having one ear covered, in order to listen to what's inside, and the other ear open, to listen to other.

> *Women's Voices on FIRE 2000*

2 [Radio is the] venue closest to women because it's cheap and women are the poorest of the poor and there's also an intimacy about it. There's also a better chance for women to be heard for what they have to say, and not by how they look. They can also listen to the radio and do 20 things at the same time, and women are the busiest of the busy.

> Quoted in "Fire in Her Belly" by Judith Colp Rubin, *WIN (Women's International Net Magazine),* Issue 32 (Part A) winmagazine.org *May 2000*

3 Feminism is about women speaking out on all issues for everybody to hear. It's also to tell the men that not only do women have a right to be half of the voices heard, but when men don't have the right to listen to women's voices a right is being taken away from them. Because then they only get the perspective of half of the world.

> Ibid.

4 The domination of mechanistic science since the epoch of Descartes and Newton three hundred years ago has helped legitimize a vision of the world and of nature as being like a machine, and therefore subject to control by humans. This same mechanistic paradigm equates women with nature—therefore subject to the same masculine or patriarchal control—and views science as a means to dominate and control the environment.

> "Wings of the Butterfly": Employing Women's Art to Shift Modern Paradigms, *The Women's International Perspective* (thewip.net) *7 June 2007*

3875. Sherezada Vicioso (1948–)

1 If you stay in New York too long, you begin to get worn down by it.

> "An Oral History," Nina M. Scott, tr., *Breaking Boundaries: Latina Writing and Critical Readings,* Asuncion Horno-Delgado, Eliana Ortega, Nina M. Scott, and Nancy Saporta Strernbach, eds. *1989*

2 By dint of having lived in the United States, I am considered a "liberated woman," which means that the men feel they have a green light to harass me sexually while the women distrust me.

> Ibid.

3876. Carol Williams (1948–)

1 [My garden is] like a beach at which the tide goes in and out. Sometimes the tide of weeds is out, and the plants stand clear and lovely. Sometimes the tide is in, bringing its wrack of pigweed, nettle, mallows, and wild roses. This is lovely in another way.

> *Bringing a Garden to Life 1998*

2 [Gardening is] not just science but art, and not just law but lore.

> Ibid.

3 . . . flowers engage the heart's affections and unlock the deepest associations.

> Ibid.

4 An hour before work with the dew on the ground and green leaves translucent in the long rays of dawn, half an hour while a baby naps in the afternoon, twenty minutes after dinner as colors fade to dusk. Such brief interludes can be all that is needed for there to be something to pick for supper, month after month. They can redeem the whole day.

> Ibid.

3877. Marie C. Wilson (1948–)

1 We have to change the climate in order to get Americans thinking seriously about a woman candidate. If you are a democracy, you want an opportunity for everyone to participate, and women are the untapped national resource at this level of government. It's about wanting a democracy to mirror women's voices and visions.

> Quoted in "Women Who Could Be President" by Jane Ciabattari, *Parade Magazine 7 February 1999*

2 Historically, women have been the "government in exile"—leading at the foot of the table as a marginalized constituency. Yet to address the myriad of issues which confront women—from poverty and domestic violence to healthcare and work-life balance—women must be represented in the upper echelons of government where such issues are tackled and policy is enacted.

> "The Government in Exile: What Obama Can Do for Women," *The Huffington Post 6 November 2008*

3878. Christine Wiltz (1948–   )

1 He was saying to her, It's been done to us too, now we understand, now we know what's like to be a victim, to be connected to death by violence . . .

Glass House 1994

2 When somebody's that afraid, I guess they be pretty scary themselves.

Ibid.

3879. Robin Wright (1948–   )

1 To the outside world, the revolution and the theocracy born out of it were one and the same. But most sectors of Iranian society . . . made a distinction: The political upheaval aimed at ending autocratic rule and redistributing power was one thing. The subsequent Islamic government that eventually replaced the monarch—and then imposed its own restrictions—was quite another.

The Last Great Revolution, Turmoil and Transformation in Iran 2000

2 Since [the 1983 bombing of the U.S. Embassy in Beirut], Islamic extremism has progressively grown into the most energetic force in the Middle East—and the gravest threat to Western interests. . . . [It is a] new form of sacred rage that has since redefined the world's political divide. Fear of its explosive potential will define American foreign policy for years, potentially decades, to come. Al Qaeda and a growing array of offshoots continue to push their tentacles deeper throughout the region—and beyond.

Dreams and Shadows: The Future of the Middle East 2008

3880. Dorothy Allison (1949–   )

1 . . . get out there and do things, girl. Make people nervous and make your old aunt glad."

Bastard Out of Carolina 1992

2 Behind the story I tell is the one I don't . . . Behind the story you hear is the one I wish I could make you hear.

Talking About Sex, Class & Literature 1993

3 Change, when it comes, cracks everything open.

Two or Three Things I Know for Sure 1995

4 Way way down three or four corridors, around a turn, I hit a wall. My story was on this wall. I stood in front of my wall. . . . words were peeling across the wall, and every word was a brick. I touched one. . . . The brick fell away and a window opened. . . .

Ibid.

5 "My daddy always said that white folks are simply crazy. He also said that black folks are crazy too, but we aren't simple."

Cavedweller 1998

3881. Aida Alvarez (1949–   )

1 I realized that that was what power was about. If you stood up for your rights, you had moral authority. People actually respect you when you stand up for what you think is right.

Quoted in "She's Determined That Everyone Gets A Chance," *Parade Magazine 22 November 1998*

2 Everything you do has a price. Whatever you accomplish on one side, you have given something else up.

Ibid.

3 Affirmative action is about giving people who have demonstrated that they're successful an opportunity to continue to succeed.

Ibid.

3882. Terri Apter (1949–   )

1 The arguments [between mothers and daughters] were sometimes more and sometimes less hostile. They were often filled with love and delight. They were often filled with anger and frustration. But the aim of the argument was never to separate; it was always characterized by the underlying demand, "See me as I am, and love me for what I am."

Altered Loves: Mothers and Daughters During Adolescence 1990

2 One of the main tasks of adolescence is to achieve an identity— not necessarily a knowledge of who we are, but a clarification of the range of what we might become, a set of self-references by which we can make sense of our responses, and justify our decisions and goals.

Ibid.

3 . . . it's common for them [18 to 24 year-olds] to have been oversupervised and overscheduled as children, and they are likely to have had much more pressure put on them to excel and succeed, not just in school but in ballet, football, pony club, piano, gym, and so on. They have much less experience with managing their own time. And because they're much less likely to have been roaming free and playing outside from an early age, they start out with much less street sense

The Myth of Maturity: What Teenagers Need from Parents to Become Adults 2001

4 Thresholders* . . . have a lot of empathy for their parents. They speak a lot about wanting to protect them. They know about their financial difficulties and don't want to add to them by messing up. They're very ashamed if they drop out of university or don't make it in their first job. If parents can take on board that these are not the best years of their children's lives, that can help a lot. Also, if they realise how vulnerable these kids are, they will pick up the signs early. Withdrawal, lethargy, changes in eating habits, these are all danger signs.

Ibid.

*Apter's term for 18 to 24 year-olds.

3883. Bettina "Tina" Arndt (1949–   )

1 Today oral sex is on the menu, not as some exotic desert to be enjoyed long after the meat and potatoes but for a growing number of teenagers, a mere hors d'oeuvre.

"A Kiss Is Just A Kiss," *Sydney Morning Herald 18 August 2003*

2 My baby boomer generation is now in the thick of it. As our ageing parents grow frail and die, many of us have been forced to witness awful, undignified ends for the people we love most. We have watched helplessly as they died in mental and physical agony. . . . Most of us (over 70 per cent) want laws changed to allow doctors to provide assistance to terminally ill patients to commit suicide and to be able, where appropriate, to give lethal doses to such patients. Yet we continue to allow a noisy minority to lean on politicians and prevent Australia from providing the legal support for assisted suicide available in other parts of the world . . . The shameful result is old people in Australia are choosing to end their lives in the most horrific ways.

"Reject Gag on Euthanasia Debate," *West Australian 20 February 2006*

3 So, where's our pink Viagra? It's been seven long years since Viagra put new life into sexually ageing men, but there's still no magic pill for women.

"Where's Our Pink Viagra?" *Australian Women's Weekly April 2006*

4 The belief was that sex must wait until women are well and truly in the mood. But that was where we went wrong. The assumption that women need to want sex to enjoy it has proven a really damaging sexual idea, one that has wrought havoc in relationships for the past forty years.

Ch. 5, p. 76, *The Sex Diaries: Why Women Go Off Sex and Other Bedroom Battles 2009*

5 But it is certainly true that illicit liaisons can offer amazing emotional intensity, heart-fluttering human drama—excitement beyond the wildest of whitewater rafting trips or knee-trembling bungee jumps. The attraction of the sexually illicit will always glitter and good intentions fall by the wayside.

Ch. 7, p. 153, Ibid.

6 But when a man—or indeed a woman—wants to be wanted, yearns to see lust in their partner's eyes, longs for the ultimate connection that lovemaking can provide, then this is a basic need that should not be ignored. Very few relationships can weather the devastating effects of constant rejection.

Ch. 15, Ibid.

3884. Nora Astorga (1949–1989)

1 I want it to be known that I participated in the operation of bringing to justice the bloody henchman.*

Quoted in "Nora and the Dog," *Time 2 April 1984*
*Reference to assassination of General Reynaldo Perez Varga (1978).

3885. Michèle Barrett (1949–)

See also Anne Phillips: 4426:2–3.

1 Caring, sharing and loving would be more wide-spread if the family did not claim them for its own.

The Anti-Social Family, with Mary McIntosh* 1982
*See 2992.

3886. Esmeralda Bernal (1949–)

1 my womb
a public domain
erotica a doormat
trampled on by
birthright

"My Womb," St. 1 (1986), *The Woman That I Am, The Literature and Culture of Contemporary Women of Color* D. Soyini Madison,* ed. 1994
*See 3912.

2 never teach others
that hate is good.
never bear arms
for that is doom.
never envy or steal
for that is self-loss.
never teach what you do not
want at your doorstep.

"Never," *Wombcentric 2001*

3887. Victoria Bond (1949–)

1 The conductor traditionally has been anything but a mother figure. The conductor is much more like a general than a mother or a teacher. It's a kind of enforced leadership, the kind of leadership more likely to be expected of men than women. A woman conductor, because of those traditions, must rely completely on being able to transmit authority purely on the grounds of her musical ability.

Quoted in *Women at Work* by Betty Medsger 1975

3888. Anita Borg (1949–2003)

1 The technology of the future is going to be so pervasive and have such a significant impact on every domain. And it's going to have that impact either because we're part of it, we're just hit by it, or we're outside of it.

Quoted in "Tech revolutionary pushes equality" by Cliff Edwards, Associated Press *14 March 2000*

2 We really have to think about supporting efforts to recruit people at a whole lot of different places, and we have to think about the full diversity of experience that people have.

Ibid.

3 . . . every day, every single day, I remember that the world is not Silicon Valley, that there are places where so many people have so much to offer if just given a chance.

Ibid.

3888.1. Alida Brill (1949–)

1 What Marilyn [French*] hated was the injustice of a system that was based on one sex getting all the advantages while the other sex did the cleaning up, suffered the most betrayals, raised children, fixed broken lives, worked for less pay, witnessed their invisibility in historical texts. The fact we did not have a fully recorded history, despite the fact women had existed just as long as men angered her and motivated her to write women's history.

"The Marilyn French I knew," *The Guardian* (London; guardian.co.uk) *11 May 2009*
*See 2658.

2 Women don't decide to have an abortion the way we decide to have a haircut or a manicure. The movement is Pro-Choice, not Pro-Abortion. The other side is not Pro-Life—witness the corpse of George Tiller, if only in your mind. They are Anti-Choice.

The choice to terminate a pregnancy at any juncture is painful. It is an imprint on the heart of the history of your life. But a woman, wholly formed and informed, must and does have the right to the control of her womb and her body.

"On Dr. Tiller's* Death," The Women's Media Center (womensmediacenter.com) 3 June 2009
*(1941–2009), American physician, pro-choice advocate, abortion provider; murdered.

3 This is not only the death of a man who believed he had to do the right thing, indeed a very hard thing, a thing that probably shattered him on some days. It is a public announcement written in his blood of how frayed our system of honorable dissent has become. And how robust the campaign, media fed and financed, against the rights of all women at all times.

Ibid.

4 I became a girl-feminist because I knew I wasn't crazy and the doctors only believed me when they could see something. They

did not believe me when I told them in my own words exactly what happened in carefully detailed language taken from my diary that I used to record my journey of illness.

Dancing at the River's Edge 2009

3889. Victoria Castle (1949–)

1 Receiving means being available in the fullest sense of the word—allowing the precious moments of life to touch us deeply. Receiving has nothing to do with being worthy, but it has everything to do with being open. Receiving is the depth of inhalation.

p. 87, *The Trance of Scarcity 2007*

2 If you want to dominate people and keep them in fear, teach them to see only what's missing and what's not possible. Program them to believe in scarcity as the only reality. Keep them hoping for little and expecting even less. Soon they will become disheartened and docile, or remote and disengaged.

p. 141, *Ibid.*

3 A tribal species, we're hardwired with certain desires. Among those are the need to be safe, to belong (or to be included), to be known, to be loved, and to contribute. The ability to contribute, to bring value, is a source of deep fulfillment. It's more than just seeking approval; it's knowing that our lives matter. If we cannot bear to give of ourselves or our possessions, we suffocate under the burden of accumulation.

p. 164, *Ibid.*

3890. Jane Danowitz (1949?–)

1 We have a whole Congress full of heroes, astronauts, basketball stars, Rhodes scholars. . . . Who's to say that raising five children and holding down a job isn't as courageous as being a prisoner of war?

Quoted in "Cleaning house in government . . ." by Carol M. Ostrom, *Seattle Times, A1–9 2 August 1992*

2 Think about one woman on the Senate Judiciary Committee. Think about what a difference that would have made.*

Ibid.

*Referring to Anita Hill (see 4369) and Clarence Thomas (1948–); associate justice of the Supreme Court of the United States, 1991–), sexual harassment hearings held by the U.S. Senate Judiciary Committee, October 1991.

3 . . . the Bush Administration* has climbed into bed with industry at the expense of protecting the nation's environment.

E-wire news (ewire.com) *17 March 2001*

*George W. B- (1946–), Am. politician; 43rd president of the United States (2001–09).

4 Senators may cross the aisle—but they rarely cross the Capitol to testify.

News release, The Pew Campaign for Responsible Mining *26 July 2007*

5 Our national parks are threatened by a law written before the light bulb was invented. The surge of new claims within a stone's throw of the Grand Canyon and other national treasures should serve as a wake-up call to Congress that it's high time to modernize this antiquated law.*

"More Than 800 New Mining Claims Crowd Border of Grand Canyon National Park," Environmental Working Group (ewg.org) *16 August 2007*

*Re the 1872 Mining Act, signed into law by Ulysses S. Grant (1822–85), 18th president of the United States (1869–77).

6 The production of just one gold ring generates about 20 tons of waste, according to one mining policy organization, much of it left to litter the landscape as well as polluting rivers and streams.

"The Price of Gold," *Los Angeles Times 11 December 2007*

3891. Doris Davenport (1949–)

1 it is not your business,
how i came and i can't stand
nosey people but
this is your business.

i am not going back.
so here i am.
but what
i am, really,
ain't your business.

"To the 'Majority' from A 'Minority'," Sts. 2 & 3, *Eat Thunder and Drink Rain 1982*

2 when will the reall wimmin
appear

"Dogmatic Dykes," *Ibid.*

3892. Paula DiPerna (1949–)

1 I do not believe meat-eating to be an environmental threat on a par with ozone depletion, nor that violence toward women is no better or worse than violence toward animals, even though there may be a common source.

"Who can save the earth?," *The Women's Review of Books,* Vol. XI, No. 1 *October 1993*

2 Philanthropy itself is not "man bites dog"; it's very much "dog bites man."

Interview, *Philosophy News Digest 10 September 2003*

3893. Nancy E. Dowd (1949–)

1 There has been an amazing continuation of the common law tradition that an unmarried putative father owes no legal duty to [parent] his child and in effect is a "stranger" to the child.

In Defense of Single Mothers 1997

3894. Slavenka Drakulíc (1949–)

1 They [refugees] have nothing to do but wait. When I ask them what they're waiting for, they are not certain. Three of the men are waiting for a foreign country to accept them as immigrants; the others do not know what they are waiting for. One woman waits for a sign that her husband is alive, another just cries.

"Women Hide Behind A Wall of Silence," *The Nation* (New York) *1 March 1993*

2 Rape is an instrument of war, a very efficient weapon for demoralization and humiliation.

Ibid.

3 . . . the last taboo; the sexual mother.

Marble Skin (1987), Greg Mosse, tr. (from French) *1994*

4 The man's touch weaves bonds between us.

Ibid.

3895. Lynn Emanual (1949–)

1 I am a conceptual storyteller. In fact, I'm a conceptual liver. I prefer the cookbook to the actual meal. Feeling bores me.

That's why I write poetry. In poetry you just give the instructions to the reader and say, "Reader, you go on from here."

"The Politics of Narrative: Why I Am A Poet," St. 4, *Then, Suddenly—* 1999

2 My father drops in like baggage into a hold.

"The Burial," St. 4, Ibid.

3 So, I am inside
gertrude; we belong to each other, she and I, and it is so wonderful because I have always been a thin woman inside of whom a big woman is screaming to get out, and she's out now and if a river could type this is how it would sound, pure and complicated and enormous.

"inside gertrude stein,"* St. 1, Ibid.

*See 1450.

4 It is nearly dawn; the sun
is a fox chewing her foot from the trap;
every bite is a wound and every wound
is a red window, a red door, a red road.

"Homage to Sharon Stone,"* St. 2, Ibid.

*See 4472.

3896. Leslie Feinberg (1949–)

1 My parents worried that I was a lightning rod that would attract a dangerous storm.

Transgender Warriors 1996

2 Why was I subject to legal harassment and arrest at all? Why was I being punished for the way I walked or dressed, or who I loved? Who wrote the laws used to harass us, and why? . . . Who decided what was normal in the first place? . . . Have we always existed? Have we always been so hated? Have we always fought back?

Ibid.

3 I don't see why I should have to legally align my sex with my gender expression, especially when this policy needs to be fought. Why am I forced to check off an *F* or an *M* on these documents in the first place? For identification? Both a driver's license and a passport include photographs! . . . Why is the categorization of sex a legal question at all?

Ibid.

3897. Elizabeth George (1949–)

1 Her blood heated in the presence of this stiff-upper-lip attitude which she'd always found so contemptible in the men she knew, as if schooling and breeding and generations of reserve condemned each of them to a life of feeling nothing.

Ch. 28, *A Suitable Vengeance* 1991

2 She thought about how it was so simple with animals. They gave their hearts without question or fear. They had no expectations. They were so easy to love. If people could only be like that, no one would ever be hurt, she thought. No one would ever need to learn how to forgive.

Ibid.

3 "Isn't it always Madonna and Child? . . . Or Virgin and Child. Or Mother and Child. Or Adoration of the Magi with a cow and an ass and an angel or two. But you rarely see Joseph. Have you never wondered why?"

"November: The Rain," *Missing Joseph* 1993

4 "As a culture, we expect too much of men, I think, and not enough of women."

Ch. 16, *In the Presence of the Enemy* 1996

5 A father's dreams shouldn't become his son's nightmares.

Ch. 30, Ibid.

6 "We carry such baggage, don't we darling? And just when we think we've finally unpacked, there it all is again, waiting in front of our bedroom door, ready to trip us when we get up in the morning."

Ch. 30, *In Pursuit of the Proper Sinner* 1999

3898. Mary Catherine Gordon (1949–)

1 A fatherless girl thinks all things possible and nothing safe.

The Company of Women 1980

2 He is my husband, I say slowly, swallowing a new exotic food. Does this mean everything or nothing? I stand with him in an ancient relationship, in a ruined age, listening beyond my understanding to the warning voices, to the promise of my own substantial heart.

"Now I Am Married," *Temporary Shelter* 1987

3 I know that I must live my life now knowing it is not my own. I can keep them from so little; it must be the shape of my life to keep them at least from the danger I could bring them.

"Safe," Ibid.

4 For Catholic women, priestly celibacy scumbled the matte palette of wistful spinster dreams. Because there was no possibility of marriage as the end of this romance . . . the dance was performed on a small, intricate set of parquets

Circling My Mother 2007

5 For a writer with my temperament, there is no such thing as a statute of limitations.

Ibid.

3899. Lynn Gottlieb (1949–)

1 God has a female presence, [but] the female presence is in exile. It is not until we redeem Her and bring Her home to rest in us that the entire world will be redeemed.

Quoted in *Jewish Heroes & Heroines of America* by Seymour "Sy" Brody 1996

3900. Amy Gutmann (1949–)

1 Does justice demand that citizens be educated to suit the constitution of their society if that constitution supports cruelty and injustice? The strongest formulation of educational relativism suggests not, or at least not necessarily. Education must be guided by the *principles*, not the practices, of a regime.

Ch. 1, *Democratic Education*, rev. 1999

2 Schooling that is publicly mandated and subsidized by democratic citizens may legitimately pursue civic purposes, which include the teaching of literacy, numeracy, veracity, toleration, and mutual respect.

Epilogue, Ibid.

3 I am now professionally married to Penn. Only metaphorically speaking, of course.

Quoted in "Gutmann adjusts to life at Penn" by Chanakya Sethi, *The Daily Princetonian* 13 January 2005

3901. Jessica Hagedorn (1949–)

1 NARRATOR. As he often told his friend, the painter Frisquito: "I can no longer tolerate contradiction. This country is full of contradiction. If I stay, I shall go crazy." *(Pause)* Frisquito told Bongbong: "There's nothing wrong with being crazy. Being crazy is good for art. The thing to do is to get comfortable with it."

Tenement Lover: no palm trees/in new york city 1981

2 In all my writing there are always these characters who have a sense of displacement, a sense of being in self-exile, belonging nowhere—or anywhere. I think these themes are the human story. When it comes down to it, it's all about finding shelter, finding your identity.

Between Worlds, Contemporary Asian-American Plays, Misha Berson, ed. *1990*

3 Whenever she looks in any of her mirrors it is always night and she is always beautiful.

Dogeaters 1990

4 hey girl, how long you been here?
did you come with yr daddy in 1959 on a second-class boat
cryin' all the while cuz you didn't want to leave the barrio
"Motown/Smokey Robinson," St. 1 (1983), *The Woman That I Am, The Literature and Culture of Contemporary Women of Color,* D. Soyini Madison,* ed. *1994*

*See 3912.

3902. Gayl Jones (1949–)

1 "My great-grandmama told my grandmama the part she lived through that my grandmama didn't live through and my mama told me what they all lived through and we were supposed to pass it down like that from generation to generation so we'd never forget."

Corregidora 1975

2 It was as if the words were helping her, as if the words repeated again and again could be a substitute for memory, were somehow more than the memory.

Ibid.

3 "I'm leaving evidence. And you got to leave evidence too. And your children got to leave evidence. And when it come time to hold up the evidence, we got to have evidence to hold up. That's why they burned all the papers, so there wouldn't be no evidence to hold up against them."

Ibid.

4 "Am got a few of them cactus plants along Dairy Mart Road, though they ain't the archetypal cactus. I think it's Dairy Mart Road and some of that poverty grass. I guess it called poverty grass 'cause it the Southwest, you know. I'm going to have to find out the names of these grasses and plants and trees so's I can tell y'all what they is. I guess that's what I likes about the Southwest, though, the landscape. Well, I likes the people that I likes (the Perfectability Baptist Church would want me to say more about the likability of peoples and us commandments to love), but when you gets to the Southwest it got it own distinctive landscape."

Mosquito 1999

5 [Nadine imagines] . . . a true jazz story, where the peoples that listen can just enter the story and start telling it theyselves while they's reading.

Ibid.

3903. Linda S. Kauffman (1949?–)

1 Writing about yourself does not liberate you, it just shows how ingrained the ideology of freedom through self-expression is in our thinking.

"The Long Goodbye: Against the Personal Testimony or, An Infant Grifter Grows Up," Quoted in *Changing Subjects: The Making of Feminist Literary Criticism* by Gayle Greene* and Coppélia Kahn *1993*

*See 3416.

2 To these people [the religious Right], homosexuality, drugs, child abuse, and blasphemy are all synonymous, the moral equivalent of the Anti-Christ.

Part One, Contemporary Art Exhibitionists, *Bad Girls and Sick Boys: Fantasies in Contemporary Art and Culture 1998*

3 A danger exists in turning any new technology into a false utopia.

"Pulling the Plug on the Internet" by Pat Holt, Northern California Independent Booksellers Assoc. (holtuncensored. com) *18 January 2000*

4 The point of America . . . to allow what you hate to exist.

Ibid.

3904. Katherine Ketcham (1949–)
See Elizabeth Loftus, 3522:1–2.

3905. Baleka Kgositsile (1949–)

1 Rhythm
feet so precise
to the left
to the right
to the songs
we sing now
our voices beckoned
from the past of the future
will be pronounced
medicine or poison
rhythm
this dance is our future.
"Umkhonto," *A Poetics of Resistance: Women Writing in El Salvador, South Africa, and the United States* Mary K. DeShazer, ed. *1994*

3906. Jamaica Kincaid (1949–)

1 And what do I regret? Surely not that I stand in the knowledge of the presence of death. For knowledge is a good thing; you have said that. What I regret is that in the face of death and all that it is and all that it shall be I stand powerless, that in the face of death my will, to which everything I have ever known bends, stands as if it were nothing more than a string caught in the early-morning wind.

"At the Bottom of the River," *At the Bottom of the River 1984*

2 . . . since you are a tourist, the thought of what it might be like for someone who had to live day in, day out in a place that suffers constantly from drought, and so has to watch carefully every drop of fresh water used (while at the same time surrounded by a sea and an ocean—the Caribbean Sea on one side, the Atlantic Ocean on the other), must never cross your mind.

A Small Place 1988

3 My mother died at the moment I was born, and so for my whole life there was nothing standing between myself and eternity.

The Autobiography of My Mother 1996

4   She was very pleased to be who she was, and by that she meant she was pleased to be of the English people, and that made sense, because it is among the first tools you need to transgress against another human being—to be very pleased with who you are.

Ibid.

5   . . . [his life, so] like the bud that sets but, instead of opening into a flower, turns brown and falls off at your feet.

My Brother 1997

6   And now I started a new series of betrayals of people and things I would have sworn only minutes before to die for.

Annie John 1997

7   The undergarments that I wore were all new, bought for my journey, and as I sat in the car, twisting this way and that to get a good view of the sights before me, I was reminded of how uncomfortable the new can make you feel.

"Poor Visitor," *Lucy 2002*

8   What a surprise this was to me, that I longed to be back in the place that I came from, that I longed to sleep in a bed I had outgrown, that I longed to be with people whose smallest, most natural gesture would call up in me such a rage that I longed to see them all dead at my feet.

Ibid.

3907. Katarina Kruhonja (1949–   )

1   We accepted that we could not stop the war, that we could not influence what was going on, but we were responsible for the future, for our children and for the generations that were coming, and for a new State that was just beginning. We were disappointed in our parents and teachers who had not taught us adequately about the reality of war and its lessons, and also disappointed with ourselves because we had been so passive before.

Sign of Hope: The Center for Peace, Nonviolence and Human Rights in Osijek by Sr. Mary Evelyn Jegen *1996*

2   When the war [between Serbia and Croatia] started, I was a witness [to] the hatred which, in a very tangible way, was visited upon us by shelling, by bombs falling directly on our town . . . At the same time I was also the witness [to] the way this hatred was spreading quickly and damaging people much more than the bombs were damaging them.'

Acceptance Speech, Right Livelihood Awards (Stockholm) *9 December 1998*

3   But we also realised that we can resist the general belief that the best way to respond to violence was with still more violence and that we can preserve and nourish basic principles needed for long-term efforts aimed at transforming a totalitarian and war-torn society into a democratic one.

That future society would be based on common security and reconciliation, on the participation of citizens, on tolerance and human rights—a society more resistant to threats of war and more creative in building peace, justice and harmony.

Ibid.

4   But, we all suffer existential insecurity coming from oppression through poverty, economic injustice and political crisis—at this moment around the question "Should citizens and parliament be controlled by the secret police or should the secret police be controlled by parliament elected by citizens"?

Ibid.

3908–3909. Alicia Bay Laurel (1949–   )

1   When we depend less on industrially produced consumer goods, we can live in quiet places. Our bodies become vigorous; we discover the serenity of living with the rhythms of the earth. We cease oppressing one another.

Living on the Earth 1971

2   Let's all go out into the sunshine, take off our clothes, dance and sing and make love and get enlightened.

Quoted in *Contemporary Authors 1974*

3910. Annie Leibowitz (1949–   )

1   I don't have two lives. This is one life, and the personal pictures and the assignment work are all part of it.

Annie Leibovitz: A Photographer's Life, 1990–2005 2006

2   I think it would look better without the crown, less dressy.

Remark to Queen Elizabeth II* *A Year With the Queen* (BBC documentary) *2007*

*See 2549.

3   There are good deaths and bad deaths. And Susan's* was a bad death.

"Annie Leibovitz: Nothing left to hide" by Cathy Galvin, *The Sunday Times* (London) *5 October 2008*

*Re: her partner, Susan Sontag; see 2866.

4   As soon as you say it's over, the subject will feel relieved and suddenly look great. And then you keep shooting.

Annie Leibovitz At Work 2008

5   There certainly are people who are a pain to work with. I'd be crazy to name them. You can't be indiscreet in this business.

Ibid.

3911. Nan Levinson (1949–   )

1   To move, to go, to travel; the need can be so great as to be almost a sickness, away-sickness, maybe, an untamably sweet longing to go somewhere that will never be your home among people you'll never know well enough to belong to.

"Out of Place," *The Women's Review of Books*, Vol. XV, No. 10–11 *July 1998*

2   We travel to look at people who have stayed put.

Ibid.

3   To know how a society functions, transact business at the post office. To know how a society falls apart, fall in love.

Ibid.

4   American culture has never made peace with the erotic, but these days we seem able to talk about sex only at a fever pitch, as if whatever it touches has a special shimmer, as if we can imagine nothing more perilous, especially to women and children.

"That Special Shimmer," *Outspoken: Free Speech Stories 2003*

5   We do indeed live in a time of talk: rap, memoir, news headlines that read like experimental fiction, conversations that erupt into blame-mongering and moral certitude. When this logorrhea spills over into the public arena, we turn ourselves into a nation of button-holers, all insisting that attention be paid to our story, our beliefs, our gripe. This, we tell ourselves, is democracy: one big call-in show where fervor is a guarantee of truth and having an opinion is practically a civic duty.

"A Democracy of Voices," *Ibid.*

3912. D. Soyiini Madison (1949–)

1 As women of color the Native, Latina, African, and Asian in us has positioned us as "Other," as a "minority" sometimes ambiguously inside and sometimes threateningly outside dominant society. This reality constantly confronts us shaping our worldview and identity. We are "colored" women, and the "coloredness" of our skin is ingrained in our consciousness.

Introduction, The Woman That I Am, The Literature and Culture of Contemporary Women of Color 1994

3913. Marjorie Magner (1949–)

1 I have yet to meet a woman who, when presented with a stretch assignment, will not have the first thing out of her mouth be along the lines of "I don't know if I'm ready." That causes doubt about her. No man would say that. He would say, "Absolutely, sign me up."... My advice is "Zip it." The urge to doubt yourself will pass. Say "Thank you." You have to push yourself past your comfort zone.

Quoted in "Players: Marjorie Magner" by Judith H. Dobrzynski, Forbes.com 24 November 2008

2 I would walk into meetings [uninvited] and say, "I know you meant for me to be here."

Ibid.

3914. Stephanie Marston (1949–)

1 Every family should extend First Amendment rights to all its members, but this freedom is particularly essential for our kids. Children must be able to say what they think, openly express their feelings, and ask for what they want and need if they are ever to develop an integrated sense of self.

Ch. 1, The Magic of Encouragement: Nurturing Your Child's Self-Esteem 1990

2 Because children see parents as authority figures and gods, they think that the way you treat them is the way they deserve to be treated.... Consequently, when children are treated with respect, they conclude that they deserve respect and hence develop *self*-respect.

Ibid.

3 From the vantage point of midlife, we can look back and take stock of where we have been, what we've done, and where we want to go from here. It's not uncommon for a woman to feel that she wants to step free of the scripted life and roles she has been living and search for who she is in the depth of her being.

Ch. 1, If Not Now When: Reclaiming Ourselves at Midlife 2001

4 Maybe life is less about what we achieve and more about how we live moment to moment, day to day.

Ch. 6, Ibid.

5 Each time we choose to trust—and it's not always easy—our faith grows incrementally stronger.

Ibid.

3915. Baleka Mbete-Kgositsile (1949–)

1 Rhythm
feet so precise
to the left
to the right
to the songs
we sing now

our voices beckoned
from the past of the future
will be pronounced
medicine or poison
rhythm
this dance is our future.

"Umkhonto," A Poetics of Resistance: Women Writing in El Salvador, South Africa, and the United States, Mary K. DeShazer, ed. 1994

3916. Deepa Mehta (1949–)

1 Whether it's an interracial marriage, which religion to follow, or which sex to be with, when people make choices that do not harm anybody else, their choice should be respected.

Quoted in "Playing with Fire" by Bapsi Sidhwa, Ms. (New York) November/December 1997

2 When *Fire* was banned in Kenya, they said, "It will give our women ideas." Of course we have ideas. We aren't puppets.

Ibid.

3 For me, what you don't see is far more erotic than what you see.

Ibid.

3917. Ann S. Moore (1949–)

1 I have always believed in continuous improvement as a core value.

Quoted in "Amid tough times at Time Inc., its chairman-CEO discusses the media biz and trust" by Nat Ives, Advertising Age 9 October 2006

2 The days of selling a single media are seriously waning. Having a robust digital strategy is critical for every media brand.

Ibid.

3 When people trust each other and their leaders, they are able to work through problems, take smarter risks and accomplish more than anyone has the right to ask.

Ibid.

3918. Mary Mannin Morrissey (1949–)

1 Intuitively, I knew something that my mind could not as yet cognitively process into words. I knew that without dreams, the soul withers and dies.

Building Your Field of Dreams 1997

2 We grow a crop of life through the thoughts we hold.

Ch. 1, Ibid.

3 When our action is governed by habit, our attention is elsewhere: on the past, on the future, on other people's responses. When it is intentionally chosen, our attention is with the experience of the present moment.

Ch. 1, Guidance from the Darkness: The Transforming Power of the Divine Feminine in Difficult Times 2000

4 Adventure, by definition, requires us to embark on unknown territory. We don't know every step of the way, or what we will find when we get there. As we take our adventure in faith, we go to a whole new place in Spirit, beyond our present boundaries. We may have moments of uncertainty and discomfort, but what we discover can change our entire life.

Sermon, "Thoughts for Reflection," Seventh Avenue Presbyterian Church (San Francisco) 20 March 2005

3919. Jacqueline Moscou (1949–)

1 You come back to your roots. As I approach my 50th year, I'm increasingly interested in the African American tradition of spirituality. And believe me, that was not the way I was raised. I was raised on the picket line.

> Quoted in "'Black Nativity'* draws on tradition of spirituality" by Joe Adcock, *Seattle Post-Intelligencer,* What's Happening *11 December 1998*

*A staged retelling of the New Testament Christmas story from an African-American perspective, originally created by poet, essayist, novelist, and playwright Langston Hughes (1902–67).

3920. Janet Museveni (1949–)

1 Thirty years of instability, bad governance, and civil wars made Uganda one of the poorest countries in the world. And yet Uganda could easily be the bread basket of our region. So endowed was it by God that it was referred to as the "Pearl of Africa" by the great Winston Churchill.

> Speech, Hunger Project (New York) *3 October 1998*

2 The important role of voluntarism to the development of societies cannot be over emphasised. Volunteerism makes important economic, social, political and cultural contributions to society.

> Speech, National Launch of the International Year of Volunteers 2001 Initiative (Kampala), *5 December 2000*

3921. Holly Near (1949–)

1 Get off me baby, get off and leave me alone
I'm lonely when you're gone but I'm lonelier when you're home. . . .

> "Get Off Me Baby" *1973*

2 Well if you think travelling three is a drag
Pack up loner
I've got my own bag full of dreams for this little child of wonder
and you can only stay if you start to understand. . . .

> "Started Out Fine" *1973*

3 You were being Isadora,* I was being you
Did I know I'd grow to say:
You've got me flying, I'm flying . . .
You inspired a sister song . . .

> "You've Got Me Flying" *1976*

*I—Duncan; see 1512.

4 Why do we kill people who kill people to show that killing people is wrong?

> "Foolish Notion" *1980*

5 First he'll want to talk about it
Then he'll want to fight
Then he'll want to make love to me all night
my man's been laid off got, trouble, got
trouble . . .

> "Laid Off" *n.d.*

3922. Diana Nyad (1949–)

1 . . . the reason I keep doing it* is for the tremendous rush I get at the end of any great swim. . . . there is . . . nothing greater than touching the shore after crossing some great body of water knowing that I've done it with my own two arms and legs. . . . I'm overwhelmed by the strength of my body and the

power of my mind. For one moment, just one second, I feel immortal.

> Quoted in *WomenSports March 1976*

*Re marathon swimming.

2 From age eleven to age sixteen I lived a spartan life without the usual adolescent uncertainty. I wanted to be the best swimmer in the world, and there was nothing else.

> Ch. 2, *Other Shores 1978*

3 I want to see all the countries in the world and learn all the languages. I want to have thousands of friends and I want all my friends to be different. I want to play six instruments. I want to be the best in the world at two things. I want to be a great athlete and I want to be a great surgeon. I need to practice very hard every day. I need to sleep as little as possible. I need to read at least one major book every week. And I need to remember that my seventy years are going to go by too quickly.

> "What I Will Do for the Rest of My Life" (1959), Ch. 4, Ibid.

4 If you want to touch the other shore badly enough, barring an impossible situation, you will. If your desire is diluted for any reason, you'll never make it.

> Ch. 8, Ibid.

3923. Christine Dorothy Overall (1949–)

1 In a culture where women's sexuality is used to sell, and women learn that sex is our primary asset, sex work is not and cannot be just a private business transaction, an exchange of benefits between equals, or an egalitarian trade.

> "What's Wrong with Prostitution?" *Signs: A Journal of Women in Culture and Society,* Vol. 17 *Summer 1992*

2 Whether we should try to prolong our lives and postpone our deaths for as long as we can is a genuine, difficult, and significant question.

> Ch. 1, *Aging, Death, and Human Longevity: A Philosophical Inquiry 2003*

3 To keep directly before one's mind the observation that human beings are mortal, that most obvious and banal fact of human existence, and to further remind oneself that one is included within that most dreadful generalization, is a stimulus to ongoing reflection about the nature and purpose of one's life.

> Ibid.

3924. Constance Penley (1949–)

1 The corresponding lesson the fans taught me was that there is no better critic than a fan. No one knows the object better than a fan and no one is more critical.

> "Popular Science," *NASA/Trek: Popular Science and Sex in America 1997*

2 I grew up in space, enthralled by the sight of rockets taking off from Cape Canaveral.

> Ibid.

3 Science is popular in America. An astonishing number of ordinary Americans take an extraordinary interest in exploring the human relation to science and technology. In turn, the institutions of science and technology increasingly strive to be popular, that is, to try to find ways to communicate their ideas and endeavors in such a way that people (in government, the media and everyday life) feel they are sufficiently part of those ideas and endeavors to want to lend their enthusiastic support.

> Ibid.

3925. Katha Pollitt (1949–   )

1 Opponents often argue as if the widespread use of abortion were a modern innovation, the consequence of some aspect of contemporary life of which they disapprove (feminism, promiscuity, consumerism, Godlessness, permissiveness, individualism), and as if making it illegal would make it go away.
"Abortion in American History," *The Atlantic Monthly* (Boston) *May 1977*

2 Legalizing abortion was a public-health triumph that for pregnant women ranked with the advent of antisepsis and antibiotics.*
Ibid.

*Decriminalized in 1973 by the U.S. Supreme Court in its landmark ruling in *Roe v. Wade,* which allows medical abortion; see Sarah Weddington, 3622.

3 . . . lack of information rarely explains why people, and not just Presidents, fail to do the right thing.
"Subject to Debate," *The Nation* (New York) *18 December 1995*

4 The flag stands for jingoism and vengeance and war.
"Put Out No Flags," *The Nation 2001*

5 For decades, all around me, women were laying claim to forbidden manly skills—how to fix the furnace, perform brain surgery, hunt seals, have sex without love. Only I, it seems, stood still, growing, if anything, more helpless as the machines in my life increased in both number and complexity.
"Learning to Drive," *Learning to Drive and Other Life Stories 2008*

6 He believed that Jesus Christ was a space alien, which would explain a lot—the star of Bethlehem, the walking on water, the Resurrection.
Ibid.

7 The important thing is to live, to be yourself, this moment, now. To be the captain of your soul, and know that sooner or later the captain goes down with the ship.
Last lines, Ibid.

3926. Donna Powers (1949–   )

1 I'm of the belief that if American women had not joined the work force in World War II . . . it's very likely that we would not have won World War II.
Quoted in "A 'riveting' tale" by Andrew Dunn, *Tallhassee Democrat 7 December 2002*

3927. Sheila Radford-Hill (1949–   )

1 Black women now realize that part of the problem within the movement was our insistence that white women do for/with us what we must do for/with ourselves: namely, frame our own social action around our own agenda for change. . . . Critical to this discussion is the right to organize on one's own behalf.
"Considering Feminism as model for Social Change" (p. 160), Quoted in *Drylongso, A Self-Portrait of Black America,* Teresa de Lauretis, ed. *1986*

2 If feminism is to survive in the twenty-first century, its greatest challenge is to reclaim its core values and restore its activist roots. Feminist authenticity depends on the capacity of feminist theory to construct new paradigms that place its fundamental values at the center of both discourse and social activism.
Ch. 1, *Further to Fly: Black Women and the Politics of Empowerment 2000*

3 The unprecedented complexity of the social, political, cultural, and economic landscape is driving change in all forms of human thought. As knowledge itself is reconstituted, all feminisms must recognize that women are historically distinct, culturally different, economically diverse, and politically varied.
Ibid.

3928. Shulamit Ran (1949–   )

1 On the whole I would say that I am a very intuitive composer. But, just as I said I am intuitive, I would also have to say that I place high demands on that inner ear of mine and at every step of my composing I always . . . really stay in touch with how a moment in time relates to the entire span of the composition. I work very carefully at the detail level and very carefully at making that detail a part of the larger context.
Quoted in *Shulamit Ran: Her Music and Life* by Ann M. Guzzon *1996*

2 I really get into the depth of the instrument's soul and try to tap it and find ways of making new music and the instrument come together in a manner that is meaningful and beautiful.
Ibid.

3929. Barbara Ras (1949–   )

1 The landscape of one's homeland becomes so deeply ingrained in one's heart and soul and mind.
Quoted in "New Bedford native earns poetry award" by Robert Lovinger, *The Standard-Times* (New Bedford, Connecticut) *17 October 1998*

2 Days the wind uses them to write on air, a score in 3-D, arpeggios, tremolos, paradiddles, every appendage waving, hither, there, until night when they settle down
"The Sadness of Insects," *Bite Every Sorrow 1998*

3 You can't bring back the dead, but you can have the words forgive and forget hold hands as if they meant to spend a lifetime together.
"You Can't Have It All," Ibid.

4 You can have the touch of a single eleven-year-old finger on your cheek, waking you at one a.m. to say the hamster is back.
Ibid.

3930. Janice G. Raymond (1949–   )

1 . . . liberal speak—the language of reproductive choice and sexual liberation—pervades not only the sex and reproductive industries but progressive feminist theory and practice as well.
"Connecting Reproductive and Sexual Liberalism," *Radically Speaking: Feminism Reclaimed,* Diane Bell and Renate Klein, eds. *1996*

2 Governments that legalize prostitution as "sex work" will have a huge economic stake in the sex industry. Consequently, this will foster their increased dependence on the sex sector. If women in prostitution are counted as workers, pimps as businessmen, and buyers as consumers of sexual services, thus legitimating the entire sex industry as an economic sector, then governments can abdicate responsibility for making decent and sustainable employment available to women
"10 Reasons for Not Legalizing Prostitution," Coalition Against Trafficking in Women International (CATW) *25 March 2003*

3 Prostitution is commercial sexual exploitation posing as commercial sexual entertainment. It depends upon women's inequality and the sexual objectification of women, where women are viewed and treated as sexual commodities for men's pleasure.
> Speech, "The Consequences of Legal Policy on Prostitution and Trafficking in Women," Coalition Against Trafficking in Women International (CATW) *28 May 2004*

3931. Judith Resnik (1949–1986)

1 I think something is only dangerous if you are not prepared for it or if you don't have control over it or if you can't think through how to get yourself out of a problem.
> Quoted in *Time* (New York) *10 February 1986*

3932. Michele B. Roberts (1949–)

1 It was a changeable house. Sometimes it felt safe as a church, and sometimes it shivered then cracked apart.
> "The Wall," *Daughters of the House 1993*

2 . . . she struggled for years to get the hang of how she was supposed to be holy.
> *Impossible Saints 1998*

3933–3934. Deborah Rozman (1949–)

1 The ability to concentrate (or to focus the attention on any one thing for a duration of time) is directly proportional to the amount of true learning that takes place in an individual.
> Ch. 1, *Meditating with Children 1994*

2 Love is what increases emotional maturity and helps you develop intuitive intelligence, allowing you to maintain your balance and poise in challenging times. Love regenerates hope, allowing you to see what the future can be as people shift to deeper care and actualize the core values of the heart.
> Ch. 11, *Transforming Anger 2003*

3 Recalling or re-experiencing a positive emotion creates [new] positive emotions. Experiencing genuine feelings of joy or care creates coherence between your breathing and your heart. Then, the heart's power over the brain [kicks in]. It tells the brain what to do. There's more nerves going from the heart to the brain than the other way around.
> Quoted in "The Power of the Heart" by Julie Scelfo, *Newsweek 5 April 2005*

4 Emotions are managing people more than people are managing emotions.
> Ibid.

5 Genuine care is a powerful weapon against galloping stress.
> Introduction, *Transforming Stress 2005*

3935. Stephanie Salter (1949–)

1 Once in awhile, human beings still need to feel as though they have gotten away with something they shouldn't have.
> "Day game sinfully pleasant. . . ," *Seattle Post-Intelligencer,* Op-Ed, A11 *27 May 1993*

2 *Re Hein v. Freedom From Religion Foundation:* The [U.S. Supreme] court agrees that taxpayers should be able to sue when the government seems to be giving money to support religious endeavors—but only when it's Congress, not the White House, doing the giving.
> "The Supreme 5: Only Congress can be sued, not White House," *The Tribune-Star* (Terre Haute, Indiana) *10 July 2007*

3 Millions of born-and-bred citizens haven't a clue as to how the flag of the United States should be properly cared for and displayed. They disrespect the flag out of ignorance or laziness, flying it in rainstorms, at night without illumination, or backward when it hangs vertically. Against every rule of flag etiquette, people allow their flags to get filthy, tattered or to just fade into yellow-white.
> And yet, many of these same millions think it's worth amending the Constitution to make it a federal crime to rip or burn the flag in social or political protest.
> "Vexing topic for vexillologists: Americans and their flag," *The Tribune-Star* (Terre Haute, Indiana) *22 July 2008*

3936. Georgia Sassen (1949–)

1 . . . [I'd gained] a heightened perception of the "other side" of competitive success, that is, the great emotional costs at which success achieved through competition is gained—an understanding which, though confused, indicates some underlying sense that something is rotten in the state in which success is defined as having better grades than everyone else.
> "Success Anxiety in Women: A Constructivist Interpretation of Its Sources and Its Significance," *Harvard Educational Review,* No. 50 *1980*

3937. Susan Savage-Rumbaugh (1949?–)

1 . . . there is a huge capacity on the part of apes and probably all kinds of other animals that's being ignored.
> Quoted in article by Wendy Jewell, *Science Heroes* (myhero. com) *20 June 2006*

2 We haven't begun to study how language functions as a social regulator, how language establishes rules for social interaction.
> "A Talk on the Wild Side," *The Paula Gordon Show* (paulagordon.com) *n.d.*

3 Language is the home of the mind. It's humankind's tool. We apply it to everything. But research is bound by the current constraints of our science. Traditional scientific approaches do not work when studying relationships. No interaction ever repeats itself, not between humans and chimpanzees, not between two humans.
> Ibid.

4 If we restrict ourselves to requiring other primates to think like humans do, we won't learn about them or ourselves. Bonobos are not object-oriented like humans. We must approach interactions and relationships with and between Bonobos the way we approach any other culture we do not understand . . . before it's too late.
> Ibid.

3938. Patrizia Sentinelli (1949–)

1 I believe in a kind of cooperation that does not come from the top, as it frequently happened in the past, but listens to Africa's voice; an alternative to the competitive concept imposed by the liberal model, which can ultimately turn into cooperation among peoples and not only among governments.
> Address, Nairobi, Kenya, World Social Forum *22 January 2007*

2 To fight poverty we must start from local communities, by offering peoples in many regions of the African continent the possibility of holding a leading role in their own recovery.
> Ibid.

3 Africa is a politically significant continent, with an active and organized civil society, which after centuries of submission—first to colonialism and then to liberal policies—wants to walk with its own legs and hold its own position in the global context, which it could not have so far.

Ibid.

3939. Jane Smiley (1949–)

1 The one thing . . . maybe no family could tolerate was things coming out into the open.

A Thousand Acres 1991

2 With preference came point of view; with point of view, personality; with personality, uniqueness; with uniqueness, grief.

Moo 1995

3 In K.T. [Kansas Territory], it was often the case that every version of every story was equally true and equally false.

The All-True Travels and Adventures of Lidie Newton 1998

4 Shoppers, especially wealthy woman shoppers, got very little respect, but it was clear to Rosalind that shopping made the world go round. . . . What was now resting, in windows and on counters, would soon take flight, borne, like all objects, upon the current of money. The current of money had a little vortex right in her house with Al, right in their bank account. So much came in and so much went out that their bank account generated a little Gulf Stream, a warming current of consumption that eddied around the world.

Book Three, Ch. 51, *Horse Heaven 2000*

5 Actually, it was something of a miracle. You could explode your life into unrecognizable fragments just by not answering the phone and not returning calls. Two months in Bali, two months on the moon would have done a far less thorough job than he had done by not answering the phone.

Ch. 57, *Ibid.*

6 "Suffice it to say that the past is as variable as the future, otherwise we wouldn't disagree about it."

Ibid., Ch. 59

7 Other people could understand the war and explain it—there was, indeed, something reasonable about the war that other people seemed able to comprehend—but for Elena the war was entirely counterintuitive.

Day One, *Ten Days in the Hills 2007*

8 . . . if marriage was like a thousand-dollar bill, rare but tangible and possessable, and going steady was like a hundred-dollar bill—more common than you thought when you didn't have one—then kisses were like pennies, easily disregarded, hard to remember, or even inconvenient and annoying.

Ibid.

9 The root problem of conservatism is that it is tribal—conservatives cannot or will not believe in such basic concepts as epidemiology, ecology, or even Keynesian* economics (not to mention brotherly love).

"Conservatives Cost a Lot of Money," AlterNet.org *22 March 2007*

*Of or relating to the economic theories of John Maynard Keynes (1883–1946, British economist), especially those theories advocating government monetary and fiscal programs designed to increase employment and stimulate business activity.

10 Liberals assume that our nation is a place where work, citizenship, and simple humanity can claim certain rights and where no single group should predominate under the law. They assume that the world is never going to be a uniform place, but that other nations don't lose their humanity just because they disagree with or distrust us.

Ibid.

3940. Marianna Torgovnick (1949–)

1 The white man's burden—but also his fate and glory—is the individuated self.

"Men," *Primitive Passions: Men, Women, and the Quest for Ecstasy 1997*

2 Bad white people usurp the Indians' physical space; but good whites move into their mental and spiritual space.

"Movements and Trends," *Ibid.*

3 . . . the most startling feature of O'Keeffe's* [art] is the absence of people.

"Women," *Ibid.*

*Georgia O—; see 1670.

3941. Dubravka Ugresic (1949–)

1 I am 45. I am learning an alphabet. I am dealing with the first letter N, as in Nobody.

"ABCs of Exile," *The Suitcase: Refugee Voices from Bosnia and Croatia,* Julie Mertus, Jasmina Tesanovic, Habiba Metikos, and Rada Boric, eds. *1997*

2 The city [Amsterdam], which was like a snail, a shell, a spider's web, a piece of fine lace, a novel with an unusually circular plot and hence no end, never ceased to baffle me.

Ch. 1, *The Ministry of Pain 2006*

3 Not until I found myself abroad did I notice that my fellow countrymen communicate in a kind of half language, half swallowing their words, so to speak, and uttering semi-sounds. I experience my native language as an attempt by a linguistic invalid to convey even the simplest thought through gestures, grimaces, and intonations.

Ibid.

3942. Linda Susan Vance (1949–)

1 . . . the domination of women and the domination of nature go hand in hand.

"Ecofeminism and the Politics of Reality," *Ecofeminism: Women, Animals, Nature,* Greta Gaard, ed. *1993*

2 Save the rainforest in case valuable medicinal plants lie undiscovered there. Preserve wilderness as part of our "national heritage." Conserve resources for future generations. This is the rhetoric of property and progeny: the two things that matter most to a privileged few.

Ibid.

3943. Ann M. Veneman (1949–)

1 We simply will not be able to feed the world without biotechnology.

Quoted in "No Friend of the Farmer" by John Nichols, *The Nation 11 January 2001*

2 When you talk to agriculture people about what government can do to help, it's "help us open markets that are closed to us," I think that's a real legitimate role that we can play.

Interview (1995), Quoted in "New USDA Head, Ann Veneman, A Cheerleader for Biotech & Globalization" by Al Krebs, *Agribusiness Examiner, #100 2001*

3944. Minette Walters (1949–)

1 Only children know how to be happy.

Ch. 9, *The Dark Room* 1996

2 "If I'm remembered for just one photograph, then that will be immortality enough. I don't need any other. It's a birth of sorts, you know. Your creation emerges from the darkness of the developing room with just the same sense of achievement as a baby emerging from the womb."

Ibid.

3 "Works of art, be they children or photographs, can never be perfect."

Ibid.

4 For there was an intrinsic absurdity about forcing the police to follow every rule, when criminal behavior, which was dedicated to rule breaking, remained unchanged.

Ch. 10, Ibid.

3945. Stephanie M. Wildman (1949–)

1 A fundamental tension exists whenever analogies are used to compare other oppressions to racism. The comparison perpetuates racism/ white supremacy, but is also a necessary tool to teach about the oppression being compared. Any analogy to race must be used ethically and with care. We must always consider whether we are perpetuating or deconstructing societal racism at the conclusion of any analogy of discussion.

"Obscuring the Importance of Race," with Trina Grillo,
Privilege Revealed: How Invisible Preferences Undermines America 1996

2 Meeting needs and keeping people happy are tasks women do outside the workplace, in the home. When women arrive in the workplace, the gendered expectation is that they will still perform that caretaking role.

"Privilege in the Workplace: The Missing Element in Antidiscrimination Law," Ibid.

3946. Ann Claire Williams (1949–)

1 I've written on thousands of cases across the board, and I think it would be hard to type me. I don't think there is a type. I am not in Congress. We don't legislate in the courts.

Quoted in *Chicago Tribune* 11 December 1999

2 It takes no great leap of logic to see that within the cluster of constitutionally protected choices that includes the right to have access to contraceptives, there must be included within that cluster the right to submit to a medical procedure that may bring about, rather than prevent, pregnancy.

Opinion, Quoted in Ch. 1, *The Clone Age: Adventures in the New World of Reproductive Technology* by Lori B. Andrews 1999

3 There is this assumption that because our constitution provides for due process of law . . . there is this belief that we all have equal access to justice in our court system. When we look at legal education today, its cost, the consequences of the costs, the salaries paid in the profession, the demands placed on lawyers, we can see the direct impact on lifestyle choices and what lawyers do in the practice.

Speech, Wake Forest University Symposium (Winston-Salem, N.C.) 19 October 2005

3947. Iris Marion Young (1949–2006)

1 For every oppressed group there is a group that is privileged in relation to that group.

Ch. 2, *Justice and the Politics of Difference* 1990

2 Women's oppression consists not merely in an inequality of status, power, and wealth resulting from men's excluding them from privileged activities. The freedom, power, status, and self-realization of men is possible precisely because women work for them. Gender exploitation has two aspects, transfer of the fruits of material labor to men and transfer of nurturing and sexual energies to men.

Ibid.

3 Today the exclusion of dependent persons from equal citizenship rights is only barely hidden beneath the surface. Because they depend on bureaucratic institutions for support or services, the old, the poor, and the mentally or physically disabled are subject to patronizing, punitive, de-meaning, and arbitrary treatment by the policies and people associated with welfare bureaucracies

Ibid.

4 Gynocentric feminism defines women's oppression as the devaluation and repression of women's experience by a masculinist culture that exalts violence and individualism.

Quoted in *Who Stole Feminism? How Women Have Betrayed Women* by Christina Hoff Sommers* 1994

*See 4007.

5 Anyone interested in justice today must face the project of undoing the legacies of colonialism.

Ch. 1, *Global Challenges: War, Self-Determination and Responsibility for Justice* 2007

3948. Yosepha Alomang (1950–)

1 We have to gather our strength, work together. By working together we could face anything in our way. We also have to learn and understand and make peace with other people outside Papua. We don't want Papuan women to be threatened, killed or excluded.

PeaceWomen across the Globe (1000peacewomen.org) 2006

2 I still work to defend the indigenous people's rights. I've seen many other organizations emerging here, but not a single person dares to go against the government like me. But I am not going to be here forever. Somebody has to replace me later. We all have dreams to follow, but we have to be strong and stand up for our rights.

Ibid.

3 Many people speak of freedom. But what is freedom for Papuans? Freedom is when people are educated, when people are free from poverty and sufferings. That is freedom in our language.

Ibid.

3949. Cecilia Alvarez (1950–)

1 "If I don't like the art, the culture of these 'deviants,' I'm not going to allow anyone else to see it, to make their own decisions."
One of the tools to manipulate history and how we view ourselves is censorship.

Quoted in "Defining obscenity . . ." by Melinda Bargreen,
Seattle Times 27 September 1992

3950. Julia Alvarez (1950–)

1 All my childhood I had dressed like an American, eaten American foods and befriended American children. I had gone to an American school and spent most of the day speaking and reading English. At night, my prayers were full of blond hair and blue eyes and snow. All my childhood I had longed for this moment of arrival. And here I was, an American girl, coming home at last.*

   Comment to Brujula Compass, *American Scholar Winter 1987*
   *Describing her family's arrival in America.

2 I believe stories have this power—they enter us, they transport us, they change things inside us, so invisibly, so minutely, that sometimes we're not even aware that we come out of a great book as a different person from the person we were when we began reading it.

   Convocation speech, Appalachian State University *1994?*

3 I am a Dominican, hyphen, American. As a fiction writer, I find that the most exciting things happen in the realm of that hyphen—the place where two worlds collide or blend together.

   "Las Mariposas" by Ian Stevens, *Nations (552–556) 7 November 1994*

4 I write to find out what I'm thinking. I write to find out who I am. I write to understand things.

   "The Politics of Fiction" by Marny Requa, fronteramag.com *3 November 1997*

5 Often she has wondered if destiny has not played a trick and given her a perfect companion as a brother instead of a lover.

   In the Name of Salomé 2000

3951. Katherine Ashenburg (1950?–)

1 [We are still] as repulsed by our real bodies as were the medieval saints, although without their religious motivation.

   The Dirt on Clean 2007

2 As more of the world spins out of control, it seems there is a greater drive to manage what we can, however pointless it may be.

   Ibid.

3 The archetypal link between dirt and guilt, and cleanliness and innocence [is] built into our language—perhaps into our psyches.

   Ibid.

3952. Virginia Ayllón Soria (fl. 1950s–1990s)

1 And I put in my prayers, day and night, clasping my hands together to keep them from stealing, sealing off my mouth and my rage to keep from drinking and drinking not knowing where I'll end up. I go to church every Sunday, and I take the children, too, doing everything that the Bible says to do, that the priest and the sisters say to do, but nothing happens.

   "Prayer to the Goddesses," Kathy S. Leonard, tr., *Fire from the Andes: Short Fiction by Women from Bolivia, Ecuador and Peru*, Kathy S. Leonard and Susan Benner, eds. *1998*

3953. Judy Baca (1950–)

1 We transport the "World Wall" project to a site, then work with participants to help them image the transformation of our society to peace—both spiritual and material—which ends in balance. It's a Hopi concept that we're in the situation we're in because the world has gotten too male. So this is the male and

female back in balance. Many Native Americans have been talking about the teachings of the Grandmothers and there's a lot of interest in what happens when the world gets so rational and linear that we lose the ability to make intuitive leaps and imagine other ideas, dreams. We've forgotten our dreams.

   Quoted in "Judy Baca," *Exposures, Women & Their Art* by Ann Brown and Arlene Raven* *1989*
   *See 3533.

3954. Kate Braverman (1950–)

1 Except for a small group of organically damaged individuals, doing nothing at all indefinitely is quite rare. For one thing, fate and external circumstances usually don't leave us completely alone. There are always some new demands from that place out there. Sometimes the demands can be quite minimal, like getting yourself together enough to pick up your unemployment check.

   "Dropping What," *Dropping In, Putting It All Back Together 1973*

2 We've been raised by books which told our parents when we were supposed to move, sit, walk, read, stop hitting the kid next door and start making out instead. We grew up with them watching to see if we were on the right page at the right age.

   "Splitting," Ibid.

3 To be one woman, truly, wholly, is to be all women. Tend one garden and you will birth worlds.

   Palm Latitudes 1988

4 Los Angeles is a new cosmopolitan refugee city for the world. It's a city of confluences.

   Quoted in "From the Tropic of L.A." by Cristina Garcia,* *Time (New York) 20 November 1989*
   *See 4449.

5 California is looked at the way Italy used to be viewed in England. It's sexual and dangerous. Something could happen. A person could change.

   Ibid.

3955. Barbara E. Breitman (1950–)

1 It is a mystery to me
   that we arrive so often on similar terrain
   when our journeys
   seem so different.

   "For Sheila," St. 2, *Four Centuries of Jewish Women's Spirituality*, Ellen M. Umansky* & Dianne Ashton, eds. *1992*
   *See 4011.

3956. Katie Geneva Cannon (1950–)

1 . . . throughout the history of the United States, the interrelationship of white supremacy and male superiority has characterized the Black woman's reality as a situation of struggle—a struggle to survive in two contradictory worlds simultaneously, one white, privileged, and oppressive, the other black, exploited, and oppressed.

   "The Emergence of a Black Feminist Consciousness" (pp. 30–40), *Feminist Interpretations of the Bible*, Letty M. Russell, ed. *1985*

3957. Anne Regina Carson (1950–)

1 Whenever I visit my mother
   I feel I am turning into Emily Brontë. . . .

   "The Glass Essay," *Glass, Irony and God 1995*

2 I can hear little clicks inside my dream.
Night drips its silver tap
down the back.

Ibid.

3 I will do anything to avoid boredom . . .
"Short Talks," *Plainwater: Essays and Poetry 1996*

3958. Helen Clark (1950–)

1 I think legal marriage is unnecessary, and I would not have formalised the relationship except for going into Parliament.
Quoted in *Head and Shoulders* by Virginia Myers *1999?*

2 I think it's inevitable that New Zealand will become a republic and that would reflect the reality that New Zealand is a totally sovereign-independent 21st century nation 12,000 miles from the United Kingdom.
Quoted in "Republic 'inevitable' says Clark" by Vernon Slmall,
The Evening Post (Wellington, NZ) *23 February 2002*

3 I'm not aware I have ever described myself as an atheist. I describe myself as an agnostic.
Quoted in "Insults get personal between Clark and Brash" by
Audred Young, *The New Zealand Herald 8 July 2007*

3959–3960. Jan Clausen (1950–)

1 It is a powerful act, this absolute disowning of someone with whom one has shared a bed and so much of consciousness over many years.
Apples and Oranges: My Journey to Sexual Orientation 1999

2 What's got to stop is the rigging of [sexual] history to make the either/or look permanent and universal.

Ibid.

3961. Sarah Dunant (1950–)

1 Purity was coming back into fashion, and the blind eye of authority was getting back its vision.
Ch. 7, *The Birth of Venus 2003*

2 Why, I thought, must there always be two conversations, one that women have when there are men present and one we have when we are alone?

Ch. 10, Ibid.

3 My childhood was all here in the smells and tastes of this kitchen: black and red pepper, ginger, cloves, saffron, cardamom, and the pungent sweetness of our own crushed basil. An empire of trade on the chopping block.

Ch. 29, Ibid.

4 With so much religion abroad, holy madness was on the increase: people who lived so much with God that they didn't know any longer how to be with humans.

Ch. 30, Ibid.

5 Innocence can spring more traps than knowledge.

Ch. 36, Ibid.

6 The plague arrived as it always did, with no rhyme or reason, no forewarning, and no hint of the level of damage it might cause or how long it would rage. It was like a fire that could destroy five houses or five thousand, depending on which way the wind blew.

Ch. 38, Ibid.

3962. Irina Dunn (1950?–)

1 A woman needs a man like a fish needs a bicycle.*
Catchphrase *n.d.*
*Parodying "A man needs God like a fish needs a bicycle," it was later popularized by and incorrectly attributed to Gloria Steinem.

3963. Jo Ann Emerson (1950–)

1 Had I kept my old job, I wouldn't have gone to the office every day and talked about my late husband and worked through my feelings—the campaign allowed me to do that. Everywhere I went, people expressed their sorrow over Bill's* death and wanted to talk about him. It was the healthiest thing I could have done.
"Widows of Bono, Capps Are on Well-Worn Path to Office"
by Jodi Wilgoren, *Los Angeles Times 26 January 1998*
*Norvel William "Bill" Emerson (1938–96), United States Representative (R-MO; 1981–96).

2 Times of celebration and mourning, worries and reliefs—all the joys and burdens of life which only family share—are made less joyful or more difficult by the Code of Federal Regulations.*
Speech before Committee on Foreign Affairs, House of
Representatives *18 September 2008*
*Code restricting visitation rights from U.S.A. to Cuba.

3 Our nation, our communities and most importantly our families come together to respond to this scale of tragedy. Americans will risk their health, safety and property to look these loved ones in the eye, hug them, and help start the healing process.

Ibid.

3964. Laura Esquivel (1950–)

1 ". . . remember that the lazy man and the stingy man end up walking their road twice."
Ch. 1, *Like Water for Chocolate*, Carol Christensen and
Thomas Christensen, trs. (1992) *1989*

2 Naked as she was, with her loosened hair falling to her waist, luminous, glowing with energy, she might have been an angel and devil in one woman. The delicacy of her face, the perfection of her pure virginal body contrasted with the passion, the lust, that leapt from her eyes, from her every pore. These things, and the sexual desire Juan had contained for so long while he was fighting in the mountains, made for a spectacular encounter.

Ch. 3, Ibid.

3 "My grandmother had a very interesting theory; she said that each of us is born with a box of matches inside us but we can't strike them all by ourselves . . . Each person has to discover what will set off those explosions in order to live, since the combustion that occurs when one of them is ignited is what nourishes the soul."

Ch. 6, Ibid.

4 When the talk turns to eating, a subject of the greatest importance, only fools and sick men don't give it the attention it deserves.

Ch. 8, Ibid.

5 "The truth! The truth! Look, Tita, the simple truth is that the truth does not exist; it all depends on a person's point of view."

Ch. 10, Ibid.

3965. Lilian Faschinger (1950–)

1 It's a matter of you listening quietly without interrupting me. . . . If you're constantly interrupted you never get past the babble stage, a frustrating condition that results in terrible anxiety, making the one who is thinking or talking, respectively, highly unpredictable.

*Magdalena the Sinner** (1995), Edna McCown, tr. *1997*
*See 81.

2 . . . the majority of Austrian Catholic men and women are of the opinion that a woman should accept the suffering, the foreordained unhappiness that nature has allotted her, with masochistic joy. . . . Should women who want to sing and dance remain in Catholic Austria, they probably will end in the madhouse, in prison, or in suicide. For women who want to sing and dance, Catholic Austria is the most unsuitable country on earth.

(p. 85), Ibid.

3 Her act made me think of St. George slaying the dragon. She had crossed the line, of course, drawn for a Christian, a Catholic woman, but . . . in doing so she had saved others from sure death, just as St. George had saved many others from a terrible end by slaying the dragon. . . . What a woman!

(pp. 184–185), Ibid.

3966. Kathy E. Ferguson (1950–)

1 Feminism does not question the efficiency or effectiveness of business practices but the moral and political legitimacy of these practices: not how best to use the power that business accords certain groups of people (owners and managers, for example) but *why* these people are thus empowered.

"Postmodernism, Feminism, and Organizational Ethics: Letting Difference Be," *Women's Studies and Business Ethics*, Andrea Larson and R. Edward Freeman, eds. *1997*

2 The field of business has a tendency to co-opt its critics by absorbing them into its orthodoxies.

Ibid.

3 We make up our claims to truth . . . then we forget we made them up, then we forget that we forgot.

Ibid.

3967. Elizabeth Fishel (1950?–)

1 The five years of unlimited parental favor I had accrued before Annie was born had left me with an inflated view of my powers that I was not easily going to trade in. (Only years later did I realize, chastened, that her presence taught me how to share, how to hammer out a settlement of differences, how, in short, to enter into the human race.)

Ch. 1, *Sisters: Shared Histories, Lifelong Ties* 1979

2 Sisters define their rivalry in terms of competition for the gold cup of parental love. It is never perceived as a cup which runneth over, rather a finite vessel from which the more one sister drinks, the less is left for the others.

Quoted in *Woman to Woman* by Julia Gilden and Mark Riedman *1994*

3 Both within the family and without, our sisters hold up our mirrors: our images of who we are and of who we can dare to become.

Quoted in *People* (New York) *2 June 1980*

4 Comparison is a death knell to sibling harmony.

Ibid.

3968. Karen Joy Fowler (1950–)

1 Lizzie disliked being thought selfish, mainly because it was so likely true.

Sister Noon 2001

2 "If only she would stop speaking French. Or go to France, where it would be less noticeable."

The Jane Austen Book Club 2004

3 It occurred to her belatedly that Oliver's judgments were not a sound foundation for her own actions. He was, after all, in a spectacular lapse of judgment, dead.

Ibid.

4 It's hard to capture a dog's personality in a photograph; dogs suffer more from the flattening than people do, or cats even. Birds photograph well because their spirits are so guarded, and anyway, often the real subject is the tree.

Ch. 1, Ibid.

5 Never title a book as if you were playing straight man to the reviewers.

Wit's End 2008

3969. Laura Geller (1950–)

1 God is present at every moment; it is up to us to acknowledge God's presence.

Address, "Encountering the Divine Presence" (Central Conference of American Rabbis, 1986), *Four Centuries of Jewish Women's Spirituality* Ellen M. Umansky* and Dianne Ashton, eds. *1992*
*See 4011.

2 A blessing would have gently taught me what it means to be a woman, would have invisibly instructed me how miraculous the human body is, would have drawn me closer to my mother, my grandmothers and all the women whose lives made mine possible. A blessing would have named the divinity present in this moment of transformation, this moment of connection.

Ibid.

3 Wrestling with Torah is like making love. I get close enough to be wounded—and the texts often hurt. But I've gotten close enough to be blessed—the astonishing moment of blinding insight when the world suddenly looks forever different, when we discover wholeness in what had seemed to be disparate and unconnected.

Ibid.

4 Just as it took our people forty years of wandering in the desert to reach a rich and fertile promised land, the journey toward the promised land of an egalitarian Judaism is far from over. But the years of wandering have provided a glimpse into the future, the opportunity to revolutionize old ways of thinking, and to begin to shift the paradigm from equality between men and women to the transformation of Judaism itself.

"From Equality to Transformation: The Challenge of Women's Rabbinic Leadership," *Gender and Judaism: The Transformation of Tradition* T. M. Rudavsky, ed. *1995*

3970. Marita Golden (1950–)

1 We black women must forgive black men for not protecting us against slavery, racism, white men, our confusion, their doubts. And black men must forgive black women for our own sometimes dubious choices, divided loyalties, and lack of belief in their possibilities. Only when our sons and our daughters

know that forgiveness is real, existent, and that those who love them practice it, can they form bonds as men and women that really can save and change our community.

> p. 188, *Saving Our Sons 1995*

2   My mother, in a rare mood of satisfaction with my father, tells me, *"Your daddy is black, but he sure is handsome."*

> "Scenes from the Color Complex: (My Own)," *Don't Play in the Sun: One Woman's Journey Through the Color Complex 2004*

3   In the first seconds after the shattering sound of the bullets subsides, he would say, if asked right then, that he had fired every bullet in his gun. Never before has his gun been so large. Never before has it weighed so much. He's dizzy and breathless. His heart beats so fast, he can't believe he is still standing.

> Ch. 1, *After 2006*

3971. Patricia Gonzalez (195?–)

1   [Art is] a journey of self-discovery. It's finding out what it is that you're truly interested in, what really moves you, really touches you, so you can focus more on those things.

> Quoted in "Patricia Gonzalez," *Exposures, Women & Their Art* by Ann Brown and Arlene Raven* 1989
> *See 3533.

2   Everything that happens in your life somehow filters through into your work. If you're being honest, it's bound to. That's the essence of creativity: Things flow through you, are transformed, reformed and then come out of you.

> Ibid.

3972. Jorie Graham (1950–)

1   poor secret, did you need us?
    did you need us to find you?

> "Studies in Secrecy," *The Errancy 1997*

2   Nobody gets
    what they want. Never again are you the same. The longing
    is to be pure. What you get is to be changed.

> "Prayer," *Never 2002*

3   Me. Driven half mad but still in biography.
    By the shared misery of. Hatred. Training. Trust. Fear.
    Listening to the chatter each night of those who survived the day.

    There is no other human relationship like it.
    At its heart comradeship is an ecstasy.
    You will die for an other.

> "Spoken From the Hedgerows," sts. 9–10, *Overlord 2005*

4   They leapt up falls, ladders,
    and rock, tearing and leaping, a gold river
    and a blue river traveling
    in opposite directions.
    They would not stop, resolution of will
    and helplessness

> "Salmon" *n.d.*

3973. Madden Harkness (195?–)

1   The art in Europe overwhelmed me; it disrupted my inner chords, my relationship with life.

> Quoted in "Madden Harkness," *Exposures, Women & Their Art* by Ann Brown and Arlene Raven* 1989
> *See 3533.

2   I owe a real debt to my [high school] art teacher Mrs. Peterkin. I still keep in touch with her. The courses I took in college afterward didn't compare to what she taught and how she taught it. She really encouraged me, which was one of the first times I felt personal encouragement.

> Ibid.

3974. Saidiya Hartman (195?–)

1   On the really bad days, I felt like a monster in a cage with a sign warning: 'Danger, snarling Negro. Keep away'.

> *Lose Your Mother, A Journey Along the Atlantic Slave Route 2007*

2   I had come to Ghana too late and with too few talents. I couldn't electrify the country or construct a dam or build houses or clear a road or run a television station or design an urban water system or tend to the sick or improve the sanitation system or revitalize the economy or cancel the debt. No one had invited me. I was just . . . about as indispensable as a heater in the tropics.

> Ibid.

3   The domain of the stranger is always an elusive elsewhere.

> Prologue, Ibid.

4   In order to betray your race, you had first to imagine yourself as one. The language of race developed in the modern period and in the context of the slave trade.

> Ibid.

5   Slavery had established a measure of man and a ranking of life and worth that has yet to be undone. If slavery persists as an issue in the political life of black America, it is not because of an antiquarian obsession with bygone days or the burden of a too-long memory, but because black lives are still imperiled and devalued by a racial calculus and a political arithmetic that were entrenched centuries ago.

> Ch. 1, Ibid.

3975. Marie Howe (1950–)

1   It will take you
    as you like it best, hard and fast as a slap across your face,
    or so sweet and slow you'll scream give it to me give it to me
    until it does.

> "Death, the last visit," St. 4, *The Good Thief: Poems 1988*

2   I say that what he might mean by love is desire.
    Love is not a feeling, I say. And Michael says, Then what is it?

> "After the Movie," St. 6, *The Kingdom of Ordinary Time 2008*

3976. Arianna Huffington (1950–)

1   Liberation is an evershifting horizon, a total ideology that can never fulfill its promises. . . . It has the therapeutic quality of providing emotionally charged rituals of solidarity in hatred—it is the amphetamine of its believers.

> "The Liberated Woman? . . . And Her Liberators," *The Female Woman 1973*

2   Not only is it harder to be a man, it is also harder to become one.

> "The Male Man," Ibid.

3   In cyberspace, nobody can hear your accent.

> Motto, quoted in *Modern Maturity July-August 2000*

4 America is a country ready to be taken—in fact, longing to be taken—by political leaders ready to restore democracy and trust to the political process.

"The Quest for Leaders," *How to Overthrow the Government 2000*

5 . . . our leaders . . . stand on the bridge making theatrical gestures they claim will steer us in a new direction while, down in the control room, the autopilot, programmed by politicians in the pocket of special interests, continues to guide the ship of state along its predetermined course.

"A democracy on corporate autopilot," Tribune Media Services *11 August 2002*

6 Here we are in the middle of a vicious vortex. Pollsters conduct their increasingly inaccurate polls; the media then report the results as if Moses has just brought them down from the mountaintop; and our politicians tailor their messages to suit phantom voters. All the players involved in this charade understand they are acting on the flimsiest of pretenses—it's just that relying on polls is so much easier than actually reporting or leading.

"The pollsters can't hear America's silent majority," Tribune Media Services *15 November 2002*

7 When your house is burning down, you don't worry about the remodeling.

The Daily Show with Jon Stewart n.d.

3977. Beverly Hungry Wolf (1950–)

1 By tribal custom, all the old women of the past are my grandmothers.

The Ways of My Grandmothers 1980

2 Prejudice and lack of understanding among differing people and differing generations are the greatest challenges in trying to bridge my tribal culture with others. The problem exists on both sides. Through my work and writings I hope I'm contributing to a very slow improvement.

Children of the Sun: Stories by and About Indian Kids 1987

3978. Swanee Hunt (1950–)

1 1) Long-term planning is entertaining and immediately calming, but there's virtually no chance life will unfold accordingly;
2) My kids are the most precious, rewarding, infuriating, and humbling elements of my life—and I will never fully satisfy them, nor myself, in my mothering while I'm "out there" in the world;
3) One can think creatively, act boldly, and cry inconsolably at the same time;
4) Staying rooted in the "why" is essential when spreading out across the "how";
5) Life is not a jig-saw puzzle; the pieces don't fit.
Blessings on the reader. Go, if not in peace, then in purposeful passion.

"Career Moves: Kennedy School Faculty Describe the Ins and Outs of Their Careers," Harvard College *11 December 2000*

2 Real security requires more than bombs and bullets. In an increasingly dangerous world, we won't be safe until we cultivate an understanding that every person's tears are the same color. . . , and every dream carries the same weight.

Half-Life of a Zealot 2006

3 The value of adding women to parliaments is supported by research disseminated by the World Bank, which says that a higher number of women correlates to lower graft. That research has been corroborated in my conversations with U.S. diplomats around the world.

"The New Genghis Khan," Scripps Howard News Service *15 February 2006*

4 Women's energy can fuel reconstruction. The international community would do well to redesign its programs, creating not only employment for demobilized militias, but a leadership development program for women.

"Ma Ellen is Delivering Liberia," *International Herald Tribune 14 March 2007*

5 Women's community-based wisdom, fresh ideas, and commitment to the social good may be the best news in domestic policy today. They have much to contribute to decisions regarding the environment, health care, finance, and education. In foreign policy as well, the world could use more sway.

Foreign Affairs May/June 2007

3979. Carolyn R. Jabs (1950–)

1 If you keep doing little things about it, your dream, which was amorphous at first, will begin to take shape, like a statue emerging from a chunk of marble.

Quoted in "How to Kick a Dream Into Action," *Self* (May 1986), Ch. 8, *Working from the Heart* by Jacqueline McMakin with Sonya Dyer *1993*

3980. Bianca Jagger (1950–)

1 How many times has the United States been successful in exporting democracy to other countries?

Quoted on "Bianca Jagger: Champion of peace" by Bob Chaundy, *BBC News 14 February 2003*

2 Individuals can make a difference. I feel that one of the failings of our society today is that people have begun to lose the belief that you can influence the decision-makers.

Ibid.

3 But for every victim of oppression we can save, there are hundreds whose names we will never know. For every child . . . we can rescue, there are millions who die in obscurity, with no one to name, no one to care about their lives.

Acceptance Speech, Right Livelihood Awards (Stockholm) *9 December 2004*

4 I take as my role model one of the greatest and most courageous American leaders, Eleanor Roosevelt.* As first lady, and after her husband's death, she did not speak for any one cause or commitment—we do not remember and revere her for her work on child literacy, or her work with the hungry. We remember her simply as a crusader for justice—a woman who knew that ignorance, indigence, violence and fear were not different isolated problems. They were all children of the same neglect—they were all products of the same indifference to the world around us.

Ibid.

*See 1618.

5 We are at a dangerous juncture in the history of mankind. Since President George W. Bush* declared the war on terror, human rights and civil liberties are threatened, since he appears to regard human rights and civil liberties in direct conflict with security.

Ibid.

*Amer. politician; 43rd president of the United States (2001–09).

669

6 Until ChevronTexaco addresses the environmental damage it has caused in Ecuador,* it should be treated as an outlaw company that does not deserve the right to do further business or make further investments in any country anywhere in the world.

Speech (Ecuador) 2004
*Re the destruction of the Oriente Region in Ecuador over 20 years.

3981. Wendy Kaminer (1950–)

1 People find victimhood appealing because they believe it absolves them of their own misdeeds; it imbues them with a sense of righteousness.

It's All the Rage 1995

2 Debates about crime control are rarely sensible. They're ruled by politics and fear and the mindless exchange of attitudes that dominates the worst talk shows, where people never exchange ideas.

Ibid.

3 If the Menendez brothers are innocent because they were abused, so are many inmates on death row. Death row is filled with people who have had worse childhoods than Erik and Lyle Menendez,* in addition to worse lawyers.

Ibid.

*American teenagers tried in Los Angeles for the murder of both their parents.

4 With varying degress of success, virtuecrats ... have tried to capitalize politically on a sense of moral decay reflecting a much-lamented decline of religion and consequent rise in cynicism. Considering the ubiquity of religious belief, their complaints reflect a cognitive dissonance matched by the popularity of pornography in a society that deplores it.

Ch. 1, *Sleeping with Extra-Terrestrials: The Rise of Irrationalism and Perils of Piety 2000*

5 The taboo on dissent in the months following September 11 promoted a debased vision of patriotism as a promise to root for your team; it imagined the citizen as merely a fan. This undemocratic notion of citizenship has perennial appeal; it demands very little of us.

"Patriotic Dissent," *Free For All: Defending Liberty in America Today 2002*

6 Patriotism does not oblige us to acquiesce in the destruction of liberty. Patriotism obliges us to question it, at least.

Ibid.

3982. Michele Kort (1950–)

1 Mitchell* and Nyro, the primary goddesses of the singer-songwriter pantheon, became beacons of permission for other women musicians. These two women weren't just allowed to be confessional, but encouraged to be so by their listeners, who yearned to identify their own feelings in the songs. Mitchell's and Nyro's work thus became part and parcel of second-wave feminism, which craved personal expression as a tool to break down decades of the feminine mystique.

p. 98, *Soul Picnic: The Music and Passion of Laura Nyro 2002*
*Joni M— ; see 3443.

2 Fortunately, as long as recordings exist, a great singer never dies. Judy Garland,* Billie Holiday,** Dusty Springfield—the moment we hear their voices, they're beside us. The same, too,

with Laura Nyro.*** Every time her songs are played, if only for those moments when we're embraced by the plangent timbre of her voice, she is alive once again.

p. 274, Ibid.
*See 2428. **See 2244. ***See 3779.

3 Economics and politics and even social conscience aside, we know that only by empowering *all* women can we ensure the future of the world.

"Are U.S. Policies Killing Women," *Ms.* (New York) *Winter 2008*

4 ... the global gag rule ... only thwarts *safe* abortions, while reducing the already limited availability of other family-planning services.

Ibid.

3983. Marcela Lagarde (1950?–)

1 Machismo, which defines men as naturally superior, violent, oppressive and destructive beings, is no longer acceptable as a component of masculine identity.

"Toward a New Social Code Elaborated by Women," *La Jornada 6 August 1994*

2 If we do not deconstruct the social and mental patriarchy, we recreate it.

Ibid.

3 We women are called upon to repudiate patriarchal violence and other kinds of violation incurred in times of rebellion and insurgency, even when it occurs in the guise of liberation, and to demand our thought, voice, and presence as the minimal condition for personal and collective dialogue. We require, furthermore, a profound reconstruction of daily life, of society, of the State and of the culture, in order to eradicate violence as a method of history, of our history, of daily life and of utopias.

Ibid.

4 [Women] are against violence against women and for this, we should never mistreat another woman, never hit a girl, never educate women by punishing them, never denigrate the feminine world even if we disagree with something, but rather, we should value their contributions to society, solidarity, their coexistence, and their meeting together.

Speech (Barcelona), Living and Living Together: Women's World Forum *July 2004*

5 The fight against patriarchy started three centuries ago, with the betrayal of men from the first democratic state [the French revolution] that excluded women from the democratic pact because they didn't consider them to be citizens.

Ibid.

3984. Fran Lebowitz (1950–)

1 All God's children are not beautiful. Most of God's children are, in fact, barely presentable.

"Manners," *Metropolitan Life 1978*

2 There is no such thing as inner peace. There is only nervousness or death. Any attempt to prove otherwise constitutes unacceptable behavior.

Ibid.

3 Nothing succeeds like address.

"The Nail Bank: Not Just Another Clip Joint," Ibid.

4　If you're going to America, bring your own food.

　　　　　"Fran Lebowitz's Travel Hints," *Social Studies 1981*

5　The opposite of talking isn't listening. The opposite of talking is waiting.

　　　　　"People," Ibid.

6　To put it rather bluntly, I am not the type who wants to go back to the land; I am the type who wants to go back to the hotel.

　　　　　"Things," Ibid.

7　I never met anyone who didn't have a very smart child. What happens to these children, you wonder, when they reach adulthood?

　　　　　Quoted by Bob Morris in *The New York Times 10 August 1994*

8　This hideous religion that's all over the country—these huge church-malls—that's what substitutes for these lost towns. But that's not a town. That's a cult. A town is diverse, in a real way, not in this fake way we have now. A community is a butcher and a doctor, a minister, a town troublemaker. A "community" is not a bunch of people united by some grievance. That's just self-righteousness—incredibly dangerous and antidemocratic.

　　　　　Quoted by Susannah McNeely, *Ruminator* magazine *August/ September 2005*

3985. Birsel Lemke (1950–)

1　The Pergamon* village inhabitants ran unclothed in the demonstrations, bearing signs with the slogan, "Before EURO-GOLD strips us, we'll strip." The women, who always were at the head of the demonstrations and campaigns, denied themselves to their husbands until the former had expelled the gold mining companies.

　　　　　Acceptance Speech, Right Livelihood Awards (Stockholm) *9 December 2000*

　　*A village in Turkey.

2　But I would also like to thank all my friends who stopped wearing their gold jewellery for my sake.

　　　Because who really knows the story behind this glittering and allegedly valuable element? Isn't gold prospected for or panned or something like that? That is at least the widespread opinion. Wrong: Gold is (chiefly) extracted using tons of highly-poisonous cyanide.

　　　The famous nuggets no longer exist or cannot be found. There are tiny gold particles in many places . . . Such gold particles are sufficient for modern industry. It extracts from one ton of soil one to four grams of gold in a simple process—in a chemical process—namely with sodium cyanide.

　　　Gold production is wrongly classified as mining. Strictly speaking, these companies are part of the chemical industry.

　　　　　Ibid.

3　I regard our resistance as a triumph of friendship and of love of one's native country and culture over the plans of a billionaire industry, which we would have liked to persuade to grow olives instead of mining gold.

　　　　　Quoted in *Planet Savers: 301 Extraordinary Environmentalists: 1991–1997* by Kevin Desmond *2008*

3986. Werewere Liking (1950–)

1　How many lives collide with this same question and never find an answer? . . . Placating you to stay there and submit, without daring to envision anything else at all. And you scrape along in melancholy for the rest of your life. You, for instance, you who are reading me at this very moment, can you truly declare that you are where you wanted to be all along?

　　　　　The Amputated Memory: A Song Novel, Marjolijn de Jager, tr. *2008*

3987. Sara Louise Maitland (1950–)

1　Once dualistic thought gained ascendancy within Christianity, women were increasingly associated with nature and with the body, while men identified themselves happily with mind and spirit.

　　　　　Sex and God: Some Varieties of Women's Religious Experience, Linda Hurcombe, ed. *1987*

2　Hagiography [the study of saints] is littered with individuals of both sexes who seem to have organized their whole lives around the greed for violence and death as the way of proving their commitment.

　　　　　"Passionate Prayer: Masochistic Images in Women's Experience," Ibid.

3988. Silvia A. Malagrino (1950–)

1　The culture of domination cannot survive without censorship and the manipulation of consciousness.

　　　　　Lecture, "Latin American Women Photographers. The Practice of Freedom," American Photography Institute (New York) *24 May–25 June 1991*

2　At a time of institutionalized repression, persecution and murder, I turned to photography as a way of resistance.

　　　　　"Seven Latino artists and the narrative tradition" by Victor M. Cassidy, *artnet.com 20 May 1998*

3989. Helen Manos (1950–)

1　Samsara Dog lived many lives. Some of his lives were very long, some lasted only a few days. . . . Dog lived each life as it came until, finally, he learned the most important lesson of all.

　　　　　Samsara Dog 2007

3990. Sue Margolis (1950?–)

1　"The male morning-after pill, yeah. The moment the paternity suit's filed, it changes their blood group."

　　　　　Ch. 1, *Spin Cycle 2001*

2　"Practically all my boyfriends have missed the things that are really important to me—my birthday, the anniversary of when we met . . . My clitoris."

　　　　　Ibid.

3　"I daren't give your father the Danish or the cream cheese—he's actually dropped two or three pounds in the last week."

　　　"Yeah," Jack said dolefully, as he put the Danish and bagels into Shelley's bread bin, "I'm starving myself to death so that I can live a little longer."

　　　　　Ch. 14, Ibid.

4　"I've had so many failed blind dates, my mates joined to buy me a guide dog."

　　　　　Ibid.

5　He did what he always did when he thought he was terminally ill: he began to pray. Of course it wasn't real prayer, it was more like some kind of sacred trade-union negotiation in which the earthly official, Dan, set out his position—I.e., dying—and demanded that celestial management, God, put an acceptable offer on the table—i.e., cure him.

Ch. 1, Neurotica 1999

6 "The woman ate like a sparrow. If it wasn't for her nose she'd have had no shape at all."

Ch. 1, Apocalipstick 2003

3991. Colleen McCrory (1950–2007)

1 Canada is the Brazil of the North. Brazil is losing one acre of forest every nine seconds. We're losing one acre every twelve seconds.

goldmanprize.org 1992

2 Where else in the world do you still have so many grizzlies, black bear, caribou—and pure water you can drink right off a mountain slope? If we didn't have a campaign on, it would all be clear-cut.

Quoted in "A Campaigner against Clear-Cutting" by Ruth Abramson, *Time* (New York) *18 January 1999*

3992. Laura Miller (1950–)

1 Unable to grasp even the basic principles of statistics or the scientific method, Americans gullibly buy into a cornucopia of bogus notions, from recovered memory syndrome to intelligent design to the anti-vaccination movement.

"America closes the book on intelligence," *Salon.com 15 February 2008*

2 Wikipedia, for all its faults, aims to arrive at a consensus view on every subject people care enough to post about.

"The road to Wikipedia," *Salon.com 28 August 2008*

3 Philosophers proved themselves in dialogue with other philosophers, and Socrates himself denigrated writing as untrustworthy; you couldn't quiz a written text about what it meant and you couldn't see and evaluate the man who wrote it.

Ibid.

4 When the world feels random, cruel and pointless, Bach persuades me that there is a ravishing order underneath, beyond and above it all.

"20 questions for a critic," *PopMatters.com 1 December 2008*

5 Most critics write about writing. I wanted to write about reading and the relationship between reader and author, so intimate and remote all at once. In what other circumstances do we allow the thoughts of a total stranger to enter the privacy of our own minds?

Ibid.

6 Can a book win over a soul who is fundamentally disinclined to believe? If any books could have persuaded me, it would have been these, yet I didn't budge.

The Magician's Book: A Skeptic's Adventures in Narnia 2008

7 The author who can make a world for a reader—make him believe that the people, places and events he describes are, if anything, truer than his real immediate surroundings—that author is someone with a mighty power indeed.

Ibid.

8 First love . . . shapes us forever. The meeting of author and reader has a similar soul-shaping potential.

Ibid.

3993. Catherine Risingflame Moirai (195?–)

1 Every morning touch the earth.
Every night praise the worms.
Listen.

"How to Make a Garden in the City," St. 2, *Fominary*, Vol. 12, No. 1 *1982*

3994. Patty Murray (1950–)

1 History would not look very kindly at a moralistic Senate that went so far as to say that having an affair and trying to keep your family and friends and the country from the embarrassment of it was an impeachable offense.

"Murray urges trial dismissal . . . ," *Seattle Times*, A20 *24 January 1999*

2 Mr. President, if we do take action in Iraq, there is no doubt that our armed forces will prevail. We will win a war with Iraq decisively, and, God willing, we will win it quickly. But what happens after the war? That will have as big an impact on our future peace and security. Will we be obligated to rebuild Iraq? If so, how? Our economy is reeling, our budget is in deficit, and we have no estimate of the cost of rebuilding.*

Speech from Senate floor, *October 2002*
*Murray voted against the War Authorization for invading Iraq.

3 We've got to ask, why is [bin Laden] so popular around the world? Why are people so supportive of him in many countries that are riddled with poverty? . . . How would they look at us today if we had been there helping them . . . rather than just being the people who are going to bomb in Iraq and go to Afghanistan.

Speech, High school honors class (Seattle), *18 December 2002*

3995. Gloria Naylor (1950–)

1 Geometry forgotten, they sat in Lester's room for hours, reciting to each other the lines that helped to harness the chaos and confusions in their fourteen-year-old worlds. Bloody noses had made them friends, but giving sound to the bruised places in their hearts made them brothers.

"December 19th," *Linden Hills 1985*

2 Willie had left school after the ninth grade. He said there was really nothing more they could teach him. He knew how to read and write and reason. And from here on in, it was all propaganda. He was not free to read the books that were important to him, not to some rusty-minded teacher. And if you wanted to write about life, you had to go where life was, among the people.

Ibid.

3 Xavier Donnell was falling in love with a black woman. It was one of the most terrifying experiences of his life.

"December 21st," *Ibid.*

4 Maxwell had discovered long ago that he doubled the odds of finishing first if he didn't carry the weight of that milligram of pigment in his skin. There was no feasible reason why it should have slowed him down since in mass it weighed so little, and even that was consistently distributed over his six-foot frame. But the handicap had been set centuries before it was his turn at the gate. And since he knew no tract of ground but the planet earth and no competition but the human race, he had to use the rules as written and find a way to turn a consequence into an inconsequence in his struggle to reach the finish line as a man.

Ibid.

5   "You there, Sister?"

Mama Day 1988

6   Six months of looking for a job had made me an expert at picking out the people who, like me, were hurrying up to wait—in somebody's outer anything for a chance to make it through their inner doors to prove that you could type two words a minute, or not drool on your blouse while answering difficult questions about your middle initial and date of birth.

Ch. 1, Ibid.

7   The way a man chews can tell you loads about the kind of lover he'll turn out to be. Don't laugh—meat is meat.

Ibid

3996. Peggy Noonan (1950–)

1   Great speeches have always had great soundbites. The problem now is that the young technicians who put together speeches are paying attention only to the soundbite, not to the text as a whole, not realizing that all great soundbites happen by accident, which is to say, all great soundbites are yielded up inevitably, as part of the natural expression of the text. They are part of the tapestry, they aren't a little flower somebody sewed on.

Ch. 5, *What I Saw at the Revolution 1990*

2   A speech is poetry: cadence, rhythm, imagery, sweep! A speech reminds us that words, like children, have the power to make dance the dullest beanbag of a heart.

Ibid.

3   I love eulogies. They are the most moving kind of speech because they attempt to pluck meaning from the fog, and on short order, when the emotions are still ragged and raw and susceptible to leaps.

Ch. 13, Ibid.

4   Most people aren't appreciated enough, and the bravest things we do in our lives are usually known only to ourselves. No one throws ticker tape on the man who chose to be faithful to his wife, on the lawyer who didn't take the drug money, or the daughter who held her tongue again and again. All this anonymous heroism.

Ibid.

5   The battle for the mind of Ronald Reagan was like the trench warfare of World War I: never have so many fought so hard for such barren terrain.*

Ch. 14, Ibid.

*From 1984 to 1988, Noonan worked as a special assistant and speechwriter to Reagan, American politician and actor (1911–2004), 40th president of the United States (1981–89).

6   Beware the politically obsessed. They are often bright and interesting, but they have something missing in their natures; there is a hole, an empty place, and they use politics to fill it up. It leaves them somehow misshapen.

"Another Epilogue," Ibid.

3997. Roselyn O'Connell (1950?–)

1   There are fewer women in the pipeline than we want to have and we need to have. . . . We're going to see fewer women serving. And we're going to have fewer women running for positions like lieutenant governor or governor, because they haven't moved through that pipeline.

"Fewer women in legislatures, other offices," *USA Today 30 January 2003*

2   *Re why so few women head Fortune 500 companies:* One word: entitlement. Men feel entitled. . . . We need to help women start to see themselves as leaders.

Quoted in Introduction, *Some Leaders Are Born Women! Stories and Strategies for Building the Leader Within You* by Joan Eleanor Gustafson 2003

3   Whether we're Republican or Democratic, Greens or whatever, we're women first.

Quoted in "The Razor's Edge: Janet Napolitano"* by Alexis Jetter, *More Magazine March 2008*

*See 4423.

3998. María Otero (1950–)

1   Being a woman makes me a better manager. We reinforce each other. In some ways, being able to develop a management-leadership style that is based on forming a team is very much in line with the way I interact with my sisters or other women. We're all in it together.

Quoted in *Latin Finance March 2006*

2   Lending to the poor is both sustainable and profitable. It enables the poor to create wealth.

Ibid.

3998.1. Loyola de Palacio (1950–2006)

1   Dependence on external oil supplies is an Achilles' heel for our economies and it is more important than ever that oil consuming countries are ready to face threats to their external oil supplies.

Speech, World Economic Forum (New York), *Europa* (Brussels) *3 February 2002*

2   I have always supported the Kyoto Protocol and its objectives . . . [but] I believe that politics must be based on reality. And I have deep concerns about the Russian intentions to ratify, following tough declarations made by various Russian high representatives. I consider that European industry cannot commit itself to a plan in which it will be the only industrialised part of the world to add a burden to its industry and discover by 2008 that Russia might finally not ratify.

"EU/Russia: Loyola De Palacio Wants Deadline for Moscow to Ratify Kyoto Protocol," *European Report 28 February 2004*

3999. Gigliola Pierobon (1950?–)

1   It is horrible to listen to men in black togas (in court) having discussions about your morals, your cystitis, your feelings, your womb, the way you straddled your legs.

"Gazette News: Abortion in Italy," *Ms. October 1973*

4000. Diana Postlethwaite (1950–)

1   In the Victorian age, the humanist and the scientist still spoke a common language. A logician could read contemporary poetry; a novelist could debate the latest development in evolutionary theory. . . . Today, the literary critic and the historian of ideas often move in different worlds; the investigator of popular culture may be given short shrift by the more traditional his-

torian of the period; science and literature share little common ground.

> Preface, *Making It Whole: A Victorian Circle and the Shape of Their World 1984*

2 Like all of her Victorian compatriots, George Eliot* is a visionary who insists on remaining an empiricist.

> "Finale," Ibid.

See 955.

3 Gossip is a guilty pleasure—the guilt, of course, making it all the more pleasurable.

> "Buffalo Harlots!" *The Nation 11 May 1998*

4001. Marilyn Quayle (1950–)

1 I'm a great devil's advocate. I can pierce holes through anything.

> Quoted in "The Best Days of their Wives" by Michael Duffy, *Time* (New York) *24 August 1992*

2 I was brought up and firmly believe that one must have compassion for all people. You have to love everyone. But you don't have to love what they do.

> Quoted in "Being Tested Made us Stronger" by James Zumwalt, *Parade Magazine 5 June 1994*

4002. Sapphire (1950–)

1 "Precious what's on your mind?" I say, "What?" She say, "What you was thinking just then." I go to open my mouf. She say, "Don't say it, *write* it." I say, "I can't." She say, "Don't say that." She say, "Do what I say, write what you was thinking."

> *Push 1996*

2 I don't know what "realism" means but I do know what RE-ALITY is and it's a mutherfucker, lemme tell you.

> Ibid.

3 Ms Rain say
walk on
go into the poem
the HEART of it
beating
like
a clock
a virus
tick
tock.

> Ibid.

4003. Eve Kosofsky Sedgwick (1950–2009)

1 To the fine antennae of public attention the freshness of every drama of (especially involuntary) gay uncovering seems if anything heightened in surprise and delectability, rather than staled, by the increasingly intense atmosphere of public articulations of and about the love that is famous for daring not speak its name.

> Ch. 1, *Epistemology of the Closet 1990*

2 In twentieth-century Western culture gender and sexuality represent two analytic axes that may productively be imagined as being as distinct from one another as, say, gender and class, or

class and race. Distinct, that is to say, no more than minimally, but nonetheless usefully.

> p. 30, Ibid.

3 What I am proudest of is having a life where work and love are impossible to tell apart.

> *A Dialogue of Love 2000*

4004. Maurya Simon (1950–)

1 So devoted
to moving on, we move on; except now
and then, oh, the sighs in our hinges.

> "A Door in the Wind," St. 3, *The Enchanted Room 1986*

2 My daughters recede into my future like stars
shining above my life; my parents rekindle
subterranean lamps, their hearts live coals.

> "Forty-fifth Birthday," St. 2, *Calyx,* vol. 17, no. 3 *1998*

3 Brooklyn delivers itself over to winter
like a novice taking the veil.

> "Snow," 4. New York, Ibid.

4 *Seizure World,* your son calls it, this place
of palm-treed gentility, Southern California's oasis
for grey-haired denizens, for the Living.

> 5. Laguna Hills, Ibid.

4005. Meredith Small (1950–)

1 . . . the sperm is actually an unwilling participant in the reproductive process. . . . They are . . . reluctant to contact anything, and it's the egg that must pull them toward fertilization. . . . Contrary to popular belief, the egg is actually the aggressor.

> *Female Choices: Sexual Behavior of Female Primates 1993*

2 Feel the strands of DNA unravel and connect you and those brown eyes that stare back through the bars of the cage. And acknowledge that primateness, and sisterhood, extends beyond one family, one community, one race, one species.

> Ibid.

3 Most cities have integrated red light districts into their tourist maps much better than most people have integrated sexuality into their persona.

> Ch. 1, *What's Love Got to Do with It? 1995*

4 Human babies, and human adults for that matter, are animals. We are primates, a kind of mammal, and our babies are animal babies.

> Ch. 1, *Our Babies, Ourselves: How Biology and Culture Shape the Way We Parent 1998*

4006. Anna Deavere Smith (1950–)

1 MRS. YOUNG-SOON HAN (former liquor store owner). At leasteh they got something back, you know. Just let's forget Korean victims or other victims who are destroyed by them. They have fought for their rights over two centuries and I have a lot of sympathy and understanding for them. Because of their effort and sacrificing, other minorities, like Hispanics or Asians, maybe we have to suffer more by mainstream. You know that's why I understand, and then I like to be part of their 'joyment. But . . . That's why I had mixed feeling as soon as I heard the

verdict. I wish I could live together witheh Blacks, but after the riots there were too much differences.*

"Swallowing the Bitterness," *Twilight, Los Angeles, 1992* 1994
*Re the civil insurrection in Los Angeles after the announcement of the verdict in the Rodney King trial (1992).

2 The spirit of acting is the travel from the self to the other.
Article, Quoted in *Newsday October 1994*

3 My work is both political and personal. I'm trying to resolve this problem of strangeness and closeness in our world that's getting closer and closer. I'm interested in telling every side of the story.
"The Beauty of Black Art," *Time 10 October 1994*

4 Acting isn't nice. It's giving but it's also stealing.
Quoted in "Brilliant Careers: 0005" by Carol Lloyd, *Salon.
com 8 December 1998*

4007. Christina Hoff Sommers (1950–   )

1 American feminism is currently dominated by a group of women who seek to persuade the public that American women are not the free creatures we think we are. The leaders and theorists of the women's movement believe that our society is best described as a patriarchy, a "male hegemony," a "sex/gender system" in which the dominant gender works to keep women cowering and submissive.
Preface, *Who Stole Feminism? How Women Have Betrayed Women* 1994

2 The presumption that men are collectively engaged in keeping women down invites feminist bonding in a resentful community.
Ch. 1, Ibid.

3 Most American women subscribe philosophically to that older "First Wave" kind of feminism whose main goal is equity, especially in politics and education. A First Wave, "mainstream," or "equity" feminist wants for women what she wants for everyone: fair treatment, without discrimination.
Ibid.

4 The National Science Foundation spends millions each year to offer remedial programs to help girls with their science and math skills. The idea of special reading and writing classes for boys rarely surfaces. In schools, boys are the gender at risk. But no one is asking for money to cope with their academic shortfalls.
Ch. 1, *The War Against Boys: How Misguided Feminism is Harming Our Young Men* 2000

5 Departments of physics, math, chemistry, engineering, and computer science have remained traditional, rigorous, competitive, relatively meritocratic, and under the control of no-nonsense professors dedicated to objective standards. All that may be about to change. Following years of meticulous planning by the activists gathered for the hearing,* the era of academic détente is coming to an end.
"Why Can't a Woman Be More Like a Man?" *The American March/April 2008*
*October 17, 2007 hearing by a subcommittee of the House Committee on Science and Technology.

6 Few academic scientists know anything about the equity crusade. Most have no idea of its power, its scope, and the threats that they may soon be facing. The business community and citizens at large are completely in the dark. This is a quiet revolution. Its weapons are government reports that are rarely seen; amendments to federal bills that almost no one reads; small, unnoticed, but dramatically consequential changes in the regulations regarding government grants; and congressional hearings attended mostly by true believers.

American scientific excellence is a precious national resource. It is the foundation of our economy and of the nation's health and safety. . . . Will an academic science that is quota-driven, gender-balanced, cooperative rather than competitive, and less time-consuming produce anything like these results? So far, no one in Congress has even thought to ask.
Ibid.

4008. Debbie Stabenow (1950–   )

1 I've gotten more and more frustrated [with the drug industry] because they fight everything. I would love to find a way to work together on something meaningful. But they have the financial capacity, and a financial incentive, to fight everything, because so much money is at stake.
"Michigan Senator Who Ran on Drug Issue Will Lead Democrats in Debate" by Robert Pear, *The New York Times 15 July 2002*

2 We have an industry that is the most profitable in the world. And I don't begrudge that in any way. But when an industry is allowed to make 18 to 20 percent a year, at the same time it's raising prices three times the rate of inflation, and people who need life-saving medicine cannot afford it, I think it's time to ask where the corporate responsibility is.
Ibid.

3 The hard-working men and women of Michigan helped build America's middle class, and they deserve a president who will fight to keep good jobs here at home.
Speech, Democratic National Convention (Denver) *26 August 2008*

4009. Carol Sternhell (1950?–   )

1 *This* child, through some accident of fate, this particular child and no other has become mine. He could be living anywhere, not just in Iowa; if his birthmother had chosen someone else, or I had looked somewhere else, he could be the child of Republican bankers in Southern California or Christian evangelists in Mississippi or old hippies in Vermont. Benjamin, my son, would be a different person—and the miracle is, so would I.
"Maternal triangle," *The Women's Review of Books,* vol. 11, no. 1 *October 1993*

2 I believe reproductive technologies . . . are good because they help women who want children desperately to have them, they enable single women and lesbian and gay couples to become parents, they give us more control over our bodies, not less, and most of all because they turn all our ideas about "proper" families and acceptable social arrangements inside out. They're good because they help us use our biology to challenge biology And adoption, I believe, is good because it moves us beyond the constraints of biology, expands our notions of love, and places us in a much broader human community.
Ibid.

3 Why is it that some feminists who are militantly prochoice when it comes to abortion suddenly become antichoice when the subject turns to adoption, surrogacy, or technology? Why

is ending an unwanted pregnancy liberating, but proceeding with it and yet choosing not to mother so disturbing? Many anti-abortion activists strongly believe that no woman who has had an abortion ever ceases to mourn her lost child. That's exactly what anti-adoption activists believe about birthmothers. But—in both cases—it simply isn't true.

Ibid.

4   Difference causes problems in a society that fears it.

Ibid.

5   Just like motherhood, feminism was all-consuming; like motherhood, it changed—transformed, exploded—my life.

"Motherhood is powerful," *The Women's Review of Books,*
Vol. XIV, No. 7 *April 1997*

6   So far, I've loved everything about motherhood except chicken pox. . . . I love re-experiencing all the little corners of the world I'd forgotten to notice for decades.

Ibid.

4010. Jean Thompson (1950–   )

1   She hated her mother and she hated her father too, at least when he was around to be hated.

"The Brat," *Throw Like a Girl 2007*

2   The sadness had gotten too deep inside of me. That first sadness, which comes from family, and never entirely goes away.

"The Family Barcus," *Ibid.*

3   He was narrow-chested and his hips were so skinny that they seemed only a kind of attachment mechanism for his penis.

"Holy Week," *Ibid.*

4   Had she ever done mother things, held and rocked her, sung songs, counted her fingers and toes? It's nothing Leslie can call to mind, but she thinks it must have happened. You had to know a thing in order to miss it. Her mother is the thing lost, the shape of her hunger.

"Hunger," *Ibid.*

5   At the outset of an affair you look at crowds of dreary people, and you know you seem just as ordinary as any of them, and yet you have this whole hidden life blazing up inside you. And maybe they do too, maybe the world is full of jolly secrets, and people are more interesting than you believed. But they aren't.

"A Woman Taken in Adultery," *Ibid.*

4011. Ellen M. Umansky (1950–   )

1   Traditionally, they knew, only men said *kaddish.* Women could grieve, but only men could pray.

"Reclaiming the Covenant: A Jewish Feminist's Search for Meaning," *Four Centuries of Jewish Women's Spirituality*
Ellen M. Umansky & Dianne Ashton, eds. *1992*

2   Those who argue that liturgy cannot be changed have lost sight of Judaism as a living religion.

Ibid.

4012. Alice Vachss (1950–   )

1   We aid and abet rapists every time we settle for "treatment" (instead of prison) for the priest or the basketball coach who molests our children; every time we applaud a college football star even though we know he routinely beats up his girlfriend; every time we euphemize incest as "family dysfunction"; every

time we acquit a rapist because his victim had too much to drink or asked him to use a condom.

"All Rape Is 'Real' Rape," *The New York Times 11 August
1993*

2   Anyone who finds sexual gratification in the degradation, humiliation and pain of another human being is a predatory sadist. Whether or not he knew the victim, whether or not he used a weapon, if he used force (including extortion) to achieve sex, he crossed a line—a line collaborators would have us believe is blurred to the point of invisibility.

Ibid.

3   Rape seems to be the only crime that establishes performance criteria for victims.

Ibid.

4   . . . what we need to know about rapists is how to interdict them, and how to put them down for the count once they are finally captured.

(p. 281), *Sex Crimes: Ten Years on the Front Lines Prosecuting
Rapists and Confronting Their Collaborators 1993*

4013. Wendy Wasserstein (1950–2006)

1   PAUL STUART. Now you girls have careers and *you* want a wife.

Isn't It Romantic 1984

2   LILLIAN. You tell me who has to leave the office when the kid bumps his head or slips on a milk carton.

Ibid.

3   The real reason for comedy is to hide the pain.

"Wendy Wasserstein," *Interviews with Contemporary Women
Playwrights,* Kathleen Betsko* and Rachel Koenig *1987*
*See 3125.

4   We're all concerned, intelligent, good women. It's just that I feel stranded. And I thought the whole point was that we wouldn't feel stranded. I thought the point was that we were all in this together.

The Heidi Chronicles 1988

5   Life is a negotiation.

Ibid.

6   The worse the boyfriend, the more stunning your American Express bill.

Bachelor Girls 1990

7   In the forties emulating an ideal woman meant bobbing your hair like Betty Grable's.* In the eighties, because of Jessica Lange,** women have to get a Pulitzer Prize-winning actor-playwright to fall in love with them, have a child by one of the world's great dancers, be nominated for two Academy Awards, and enjoy doing the laundry alone on a farm.

Ibid.

*American musical film actor (1916–73). **American film actor (1949–   ).

8   GEOFFREY. You don't know what it's like to have absolutely no idea who you are!

The Sisters Rosensweig 1992

4014. Jody Williams (1950–   )

1   It wasn't until the voice of civil society was raised to such a high degree that governments began to listen, that change

began to move the world, with lightning and unexpected speed.

> Address, "A Global Ban On Landmines," Treaty Signing Conference (Ottawa, Canada) *3 December 1997*

2 It's sort of easy to make a challenge. It's very hard to put the full fate of your government behind the challenge and make it happen. That's real leadership.

> Ibid.

3 They challenged the world to work openly with civil society, to perhaps show the world that we no longer had to see each other as adversaries, that actually governments and civil society should dialogue, that we actually are part of the same world community and should work together for change. Thank you, Canada, for that leadership.

> Ibid.

4 But here we have 125 governments recognizing that the tide of history has changed, recognizing that together we are a super power. It's a new definition of super power: It is not one; it is everybody. You are all part of being a super power!

> Ibid.

5 . . . But I'm still Jody Williams who didn't go to her own graduation. I'm still Jody Williams, who doesn't know what my next job's going to be. . . .

The only thing I do know is that I still, every single day of my life, get up with joy and excitement and wonder about what am I going to do today that's going to make a difference. Nobody can define what makes a difference for you. You have to figure out what makes a difference for you. . . . What matters is that it gives you joy.

> Speech, University of Vermont (17 May 1998) *Christian Science Monitor 12 June 1998*

4015. Barbara Wilson (1950–)

1 My cat had come over to look at me, but she didn't seem alarmed. She sniffed my head and pronounced me still alive. I had seen the face of madness. I had felt her devouring breath . . . I had become her for just a millisecond. But afterwards I had returned to being me.

> *Blue Windows: A Christian Science Childhood 1997*

2 The world is an achingly beautiful and awful place. There is meaning and even pleasure sometimes in melancholy and in wrenching, reverent grief.

> Ibid.

3 A wound will never disappear, but it will fade and become part of a beloved body, a laugh line perhaps or a visible reminder of pain long gone.

> Ibid.

4016. Rolanda Young (1950–)

1 She [Maya Angelou]* told me that all you have to do [to write] is take an adjective and a noun, a verb and a couple of conjunctions, then ball them up, throw them against the wall and watch them sing.

> Quoted in "Rolanda Takes Her Show on the Road," *Parade Magazine September 1994*

*See 2618.

4017. Zhang Kangkang (1950–)

1 People can trace the causes and effects of the human comedies and tragedies of their times by studying history. On the other hand history is history, a pile of classical files, a science with no material benefits. Who would be interested in studying it?

> "The Wasted Years," Shen Zhen, tr., *Seven Contemporary Chinese Women Writers*, Gladys Yang,* ed. *1982*

*See 2358.

2 "But I think history is like a mirror reflecting the truth. We understand many things better after studying it."

> Ibid.

4018. Linsey Abrams (1951–)

1 We went to the party as prostitutes, the only women who got out of the house in ancient Rome.

> *Our History in New York 1995*

2 I think it was just one of those crazy things, as if suddenly you had lived two hours out of time.

Desire is like that; it has nothing to do with anything, but is like some lighted circle of the mind into which you step with another person, leaving the rest of life behind.

> Ibid.

4018.1. Carol J. Adams (1951–)

1 The serving of animal flesh at feminist conferences requires that feminist traffic in animals—that is, buy and consume animal parts—and announces that we endorse the literal traffic in animals: the production, transportation, slaughter and packaging of animals' bodies.

> Essay (p. 197), *Ecofeminism: Women, Animals, Nature*, Greta Gaard, ed. *1993*

4019. Christina Anyanwu (1951–)

1 Once you're a journalist, you go places that the ordinary Nigerian woman wouldn't go or wouldn't have much access. You see history in the making, you see people at their most intimate moments or making their mistakes.

> "Nigerian Women Speak Out," *Frontline World* pbs.org *January 2003*

2 I am passionate about this place [Nigeria] because I see the potential. And the potential is not just in the oil and gas, it's in human beings. This place is unexplored. What nature has given this place is untapped. Its people have not yet started their development. Their potential individually, nobody is fulfilling it.

> Ibid.

3 Over here, you want to build an institution, you build it from scratch. You want to be self-sufficient, so you create your own environment. You put up your own transmission tower.

> "Fifteen Years of Courage: Chris Anyanwu" by Peggy Simpson, *International Women's Media Foundation* iwmf.org *n.d.*

4 You have to speak truth to power.

> Ibid.

4020. Rilla Askew (1951–)

1 The brotherness that would not let them love one another nor unbind themselves.

> *The Mercy Seat 1997*

2 Oklahoma is a microcosm of the nation. Our state history is a microcosm of what's happened on the whole continent. We can't separate it from the past.

> *Fire in Beulah 2001*

3 Too Southern to be Midwestern, too Western to be Southern, too Midwestern to be purely Southwest, Oklahoma has kept the secret of its identity as a chameleon does.

Essay 2005

4 God enters us through sin, through the holes we cut in our souls by our own imperfection.

Harpsong 2007

5 "Truth is, some left, but most stayed, dumb as lambs to the slaughter maybe, but we were determined to live with the devil we knew."

Ibid.

6 "A hopeless man don't ask for forgiveness, on account of a hopeless man don't believe in it. He don't care. About that or anything else. He don't see the point in living. That's a kick in God's teeth, innit?"

Ibid.

4021. Kate Atkinson (1951–)

1 Once, the eye of God watched people, now it was the camera lens.

One Good Turn 2006

2 What were the true crimes? Capitalism, religion, sex? Murder—usually, but not necessarily. Theft—ditto. But cruelty and indifference were also crimes. As were bad manners and callousness. Worst of all was indifference.

Ibid.

3 A coincidence is just an explanation waiting to happen.

When Will There Be Good News? 2008

4 [He] couldn't rest until the flock was accounted for, all gathered safely in. It was his calling and his curse. Protect and serve.

Ibid.

4022. Michelle Bachelet (1951–)

1 [My inauguration] was not only the change from a great president [Richard Lagos] to a woman president. It's about putting an entire government to your service.

Quoted in "Chile inaugurates its first woman president" by Federico Quilodran, Associated Press *12 March 2006*

2 I want a government in which citizens will have an active participation, a government at the service of people.

Ibid.

3 The world looks different from the far distant south, and this is the viewpoint that my country wishes to bring. A viewpoint that is optimistic about the opportunities of globalization, but cautious about its risks. We can and must steer the course of the planet. Humans cannot and must not avoid being the instrument of their own advancement.

Address to the United Nations General Assembly *20 September 2006*

4 To our developed friends, I say this: opening your markets to products from the South is a requirement of justice. This will represent a huge step towards the elimination of poverty.

Ibid.

5 Whenever we restrict constitutional guarantees and yield to the temptation to employ illegal means to fight terrorism, we are handing a victory to its proponents, because only then do they succeed in threatening the spirit of our democracies.

Ibid.

6 Nothing justifies the violation of human rights.

Ibid.

4023. Robin Becker (1951–)

1 I'll do what my mother did
after she buried my sister:
outfitted herself in an elegant suit
for the rest of her life.

"Shopping," St. 3, *All American Girl 1996*

2 Oh, New World, we drift
from eviction to eviction, go underground,
emerge in a bark on a canal, minister to kings, adapt to extreme
weather, peddle our goods and die into the future.

"The Crypto-Jews," Ibid.

3 Worry calcifies
my ears against music; it stoppers my nose
against barbecue.

"Against Pleasure," St. 2, *Domain of Perfect Affection 2006*

4 This man who makes up half of who I am,
    this blusterer
who tricked the rich, outsmarting smarter men,

gave up his Army life insurance plan
    (not thinking of the future
wife and kids) and brokered deals with two-faced

rats who disappeared his cash but later overpaid
    for building sites

"Man of the Year," Sts. 3–5, Ibid.

4024. Christine Bell (1951–)

1 If heat had a smell, it would smell like this: layers upon layers of rotting vegetation steaming on the jungle floor. . . . If heat had a sound, it would be this manic staccato of unseen birds and the on-again, off-again static of insects.

Saint 1985

2 And Rosa . . . she is far from idle and far from sulking. She is sweating with responsibility. She is everywhere at once and nowhere at all. She supervises, directs, organizes, aids, like a saint in religious heat. Even when she just sits and sweats, the wheels of responsibility are turning in her head. Sometimes I hear a cluck of her tongue when the wheel hits a rut. If sweat had a sound, it would be Rosa's tongue clucking.

Ibid.

4025. Phyllis Bennis (1951–)

1 For Palestinians under occupation and in exile, the harsh image of the hundreds of men, wrapped in thick blankets against the bitter cold and trudging across the border with Israeli Uzis and mortars at their backs, resonated with a collective national memory of earlier expulsions.

"Death Blow to The Peace Talks," *The Nation 1 March 1993*

2   Palestinian violence is the violence of resistance, and has escalated as conditions of life and loss of hope breed greater desperation.

> Part One: The Crisis, *Understanding the Palestinian-Israeli Conflict: A Primer* 2007

3   In the real world, historical injustices sometimes become permanent. They do not become just or fair because time passes or power consolidates, but some parts of them do remain.

> Part Five: The Future, Ibid.

4026. Rochelle "Shelley" Berkley (1951–)

1   There isn't anybody further to the right in Congress than me when it comes to issues that affect the state of Israel.

> "Pro-Israel Hawk On Obama's Congressional Team" by James Besser, *The Jewish Week* 28 August 2008

2   The survival of Israel is the seminal issue upon which the Jewish community votes.

> Quoted in "Convention chatter Jewish pols confident of community vote for Obama" by Shani McManus, *South Florida Sun-Sentinel* 4 September 2008

4027. Jill Biden (1951–)

1   I wanted my own money, my own identity, my own career.

> Quoted in "Jill Biden has a low-key appeal" by Nicole Gaouette, *Los Angeles Times* 27 August 2008

2   I feel like I can make a greater difference in their lives. I just love that population [community college]. It just feels really comfortable to me. I love the women who are coming back to school and getting their degrees, because they're so focused

> Quoted in "Campaign Curriculum" by Libby Copeland, *The Washington Post* 25 October 2008

3   I buy my own clothes. I have a teacher's salary.

> "Jill Biden, teacher who avoids 'Washington scene'" by Sue Pleming, Reuters 3 November 2008

4   I think it is a strength that he* says what is on his mind. You don't have to second guess how he feels. He does not give the sound-bite answer.

> Ibid.

*Her husband, Joe Biden (1942–), 47th vice president of the United States.

5   He said Delaware could get another senator but his sons could not get another father.*

> Ibid.

*Biden was tempted to give up his Senate seat after his first wife and infant daughters were killed in a car wreck and his two sons were injured.

4028. Susan Jane Blackmore (1951–)

1   Just as the design of our bodies can be understood only in terms of natural selection, so the design of our minds can be understood only in terms of memetic* selection.

> *The Meme Machine* 1999

*A contagious information pattern replicated by parasitically infecting human minds and altering their behavior, causing them to propagate the pattern (as with icons, melodies, etc.).

4029. Nora Brooks Blakely (1951–)

1   Night sits inside and defeats the sun.

> "To Grandmother's House We Go," St. 3 (1984), *The Woman That I Am, The Literature and Culture of Contemporary Women of Color*, D. Soyini Madison,* ed. 1994

*See 3912.

4030. Phyllis Burke (1951–)

1   In our early gender training, we are taught that there is something we are able to do, but are forbidden, because of our sex. A boy is told that boys do not skip, or jump rope, but he knows that his body is capable of skipping. A girl is told not to physically fight because she is a girl, but she knows that her anger is as real as her fist.

> *Gender Shock: Exploding the Mythos of Male and Female* 1996

2   Like feminism, gender independence simply means that an individual is not precluded from feeling or doing anything because of their body.

> Ibid.

4031. Anne Campbell (1951–)

1   The denial of human universals is central to the liberal agenda because of critics' erroneous acceptance of the naturalistic fallacy and their mistaken belief that biology is destiny. If something is universal it may reflect fundamental human nature and if such a thing exists at a biological level then attempts to ameliorate the status quo are doomed.

> Ch. 1, *A Mind of Her Own: The Evolutionary Psychology of Women* 2002

2   Under monogamy, then, both sexes are selective about their partners but each sex wants the same set of sex-specific attributes. Inevitably, some are bound to be disappointed. But what you receive is inevitably connected to what you can offer.

> Ch. 6, Ibid.

3   Although research suggests that men disclose more when they talk to women than when they talk to other men, it seems that disclosure is not something that men look for in a friendship. They are quite happy with the status quo in general. They like the cut-and-thrust of banter and jokey one-upmanship most of the time. But when they have serious personal problems that make them vulnerable, they are more likely to discuss them with a woman than a man.

> Quoted in "Be girly, live longer" by Lisa Reich, *The Telegraph* (London) 12 August 2004

4   It's not that female friendships are better or worse—they are just different. Women tend to have fewer but more intimate friends than men. They disclose more personal information to them. Men are more judicious about disclosing information that makes them vulnerable.

> Ibid.

4032. Mary Ellen S. Capek (1951?–)

1   Fathers, especially, are . . . perhaps uncomfortable giving daughters trucks but distinctly uncomfortable giving sons dolls.

> "From molehills to mountains," *The Women's Review of Books,* Vol. XVI, No. 2 November 1998

2   As we are finding, now that a generation of feminist leaders approaches retirement, the organizations they worked so hard to transform all too easily revert back to their old shapes.

> Ibid.

3 Our culture spends an inordinate amount of time and energy making sure girls become girls and boys become boys.

Ibid.

4033. Theresa Hak Kyung Cha (1951–1982)

1 Truth embraces with it all other abstentions other than itself.

Dictée 1982

2 Let the one who is diseuse, Diseuse de bonne aventure.* Let her call forth. Let her break open the spell cast upon time upon time again and again.

Ibid.

*Fortune-teller.

3 The ink spills thickest before it runs dry before it stops writing at all.

Ibid.

4034. Susan Taylor Chehak (1951–)

1 She was dancing on a skylight; she was turning on a floor that was made out of glass. . . . And then there was only the gentlest murmur, as a chink took root, and it splintered, and there was the cruelest crackle of shattering glass, greedy fingers, a myriad of slivers, glittery cracks, eagerly branching, multiplying, radiating away in every direction, like intricate lace, a spider's web, and an explosion of crystal, smashed.

Dancing on Glass 1994

2 [Bader] rolls his fingertip over the raised flesh, and he thinks of how, over the years, he's allowed the blame for what happened to Lee and to Katherine, too, to become a part of him, like this scar. How it's attached itself to him, like an extra organ, or a tumor, not growing and taking on shape inside him, but around which he himself has grown and molded the contour of his life. . . . It's his guilt that has come to define him.

Ibid.

4035. Alice Cohan (1951–)

1 Many people now realize that Bush* could actually succeed in banning abortion. We've got to remind people of what life was like before, when women died from illegal abortions.

Quoted in "Bush mobilizes women" by Ruth Rosen, *San Francisco Chronicle 19 April 2004*

*George W. B- (1946–), Am. politician; 43rd president of the United States (2001–09).

2 The issues are so related when we think about control over our own bodies. Sexual activity without reproduction gives gays and lesbians a fundamental tenet on which they base their legitimacy.

"Gay organizations join abortion rights march" by Adrian Brune, *Washington Blade 23 April 2004*

4036. Lindsey Collen (1951–)

1 Another day of being colonized.

The Rape of Sita 1993*

*Banned by the Mauritian prime minister Sir Aneerood Jugnauth.

2 Wait for the silence, girls. For the gods if they ever spaketh in the past, hath stopped in the present.

Ibid.

3 ". . . the police suspect me, but they don't know what of."

Getting Rid of It 1997

4 She just goes on looking straight ahead of her. Her make-up holding her in place. Like a corpse.

Ibid.

4037. Robbie Davis-Floyd (1951–)

1 [The experience of childbirth was] irrevocably altered by the Pitocin that made the contractions too painful to bear, by the Demerol that made me woozy and unable to cope, by the institutional policy that would not let me eat even though I was starving, by the long steel hook that broke my waters and made it essential that the birth happen within a certain amount of time, by the deadly cold metal table on which I now lay, by the epidural anesthesia that cut me off from all sensation below my upper chest, and by the green curtain that cut me off from even visual contact with my huge belly and my emerging child.

"technobirth," *Cyborg Babies: From Techno-Sex to Techno-Tots*, Davis-Floyd and Joseph Dumit, eds. *1998*

2 The IV, for example, is the umbilical cord to the hospital, mirroring in microcosm the fact that we are all umbilically linked to the technocracy, dependent on society and its institutions for our nurturance and our life.

Ibid.

3 The fact that the baby's image on the ultrasound screen is often more real to the mother than its movement inside her reflects our cultural fixation on experience one step removed on TV and computer screens.

Ibid.

4038. Anita Diamant (1951–)

1 If you want to understand any woman you must first ask about her mother and then listen carefully.

Prologue, *The Red Tent 1997*

2 The more a daughter knows about her mother's life—without flinching or whining—the stronger the daughter.

Ibid.

3 Leah grabbed her sister by the shoulders. "Better to put your trust in my hands and Jacob's than in stories made out of wind and fear."

Pt. 2, Ch. 2, Ibid.

4 Why had no one told me that my body would become a battlefield, a sacrifice, a test? Why did I not know that birth is the pinnacle where women discover the courage to become mothers?

Pt. 3, Ch. 1, Ibid.

5 In the moment before I crossed over, I knew that the priests and magicians of Egypt were fools and charlatans for promising to prolong the beauties of life beyond the world we are given. Death is no enemy, but the foundation of gratitude, sympathy, and art. Of all life's pleasures, only love owes no debt to death.

Pt. 3, Ch. 5, Ibid.

6 There is no magic to immortality.

Ibid.

4039. Becky Norton Dunlop (1951–)

1 People are our most important natural resource. I am a strong advocate of people-based solutions to environmental problems.

Speech, Environmental Education Conference (Wintergreen, Va.) *10 August 1994*

2 Technology is the future of environmental protection. We need to champion the innovation that America's free-enterprise system promotes, not stifle it.
Ibid.

3 Common sense is no longer enough to thwart the aims of those who put the Earth First and people about seventh—after snail darters. What we need is a restoration of the legal precept that regulations, environmental or otherwise, must produce some benefit for human beings.
"Coming Down to Earth Day," Associated Press *22 April 1999*

4 [Environmentalists] no longer say environmental regulations save lives. They say such regulations are necessary to protect fundamental rights—not human rights but the rights of animals, trees and even majestic purple mountains.

To dismiss such thinking as bizarre would be a mistake. Many who harbor such ideas are serious people with serious objectives. They mean to alter core legal precepts and thereby restrict human freedoms traditionally protected by law.
Ibid.

5 Ronald Reagan's* principled vision to advance liberty for all, to end the march of Communism, to free America's economy to produce wealth and jobs for all— and his unwavering faith in God and the innate decency and judgment of the American people—truly changed the nation and the world for the better.
Ibid.

*(1911–2004), 40th president of the United States (1981–89), actor.

6 Is our country still the "melting pot" that it was once labeled or has it become a "mosaic?" Are we all Americans who bring with us customs of a distant land but forge new customs as Americans or are there those determined to fashion little nation-states within the borders of the United States divided by culture, religion, language and social customs. What is it that unites us? Will we continue to be a nation that truly lives our motto "E pluribus Unum," out of many, one?
Ibid.

4040. Esther Dyson (1951–)
1 Advertising has a poor reputation in many quarters because most advertising is designed for a broad market. But in the one-to-one world the Net promises, advertising will often be tailored and of higher quality.
"Intellectual Value," *Wired,* Issue 3.07 *July 1995*

2 The Net dramatically changes the economics of content. Because it allows us to copy content essentially for free, the Net poses interesting challenges for owners, creators, sellers, and users of intellectual property. In this new world of the Net, it is easy to copy information but hard to find it.
Ibid.

3 Knowledge will not set us free; it will make us take on and acknowledge responsibility for what was once left to local decision-makers, chance, markets and other less explicit forces.
"Knowledge Forces Responsibility," *The Huffington Post 23 August 2007*

4 Consumers themselves are changing—not in nature, but through nurture. In particular, Facebook and its ilk are letting individuals learn the habit of describing themselves and spreading their "presence" across the net. They are also learning how to block some of their friends, and how to control which of their friends get to see which parts of their profile. Right now is just the beginning. They will get much better at it . . .
"Disclosure 2.0," Ibid. *4 November 2007*

4041. Barbara Ettore (1951?–)
1 The other line moves faster. This applies to all lines—bank, supermarket, tollbooth, customs, and so on. And don't try to change lines. The Other Line—the one you were in originally—will then move faster.
Quoted in *The Official Rules* by Paul Dickson *1978*

2 It is one of the ironies of doing business today that, while companies are being asked to do more with less, they are also being told to do so under stricter legal and ethical guidelines. In a time of tighter rules, the days of tolerance for cutting corners, looking-the-other-way and one-hand-washing-the-other are rapidly fading. But the experts say that most companies haven't yet learned how to cope with changing paradigms.
"Crime and Punishment: A Hard Look at White Collar Crime" *ca. 1992*

3 By 2024, baby boomers' pension funds could become net sellers in the stock market, reducing the savings available for economic growth. This will inevitably impact the federal government's ability to generate revenues required to support defense programs, among other federal programs.
"Baby Boomers Threaten Entire Pension System," *USA Today April 1995*

4 Current projections are that future employees face dire tax increases unless changes are made to the pension, Social Security, and Medicare systems before the baby boomers retire.
"Heads You Lose. Tails, You Don't Win," *Management Review August 1995*

4042. Adrian Fogelin (1951–)
1 "You pay for an education one time. You pay for ignorance your whole life long."
Ch. 6, *Crossing Jordan 2000*

2 Gotta whole lotta history and a whole lotta family stitched into this quilt. What we forget, the quilt remembers.
Ibid.

3 Miss Rosa* wasn't trying to cause a fuss. She was just tired. Tired from work and tired from the way things was, I guess. Seemed like no big thing, one black woman on one bus wouldn't give up her seat. But what Rosa Parks did was like holdin' a match to tinder. Seemed for a time like the whole South might go up.
Ch. 7, Ibid.

*Re Rosa Parks; see 2206.

4 My dad used to say that being black was like carrying something heavy all the time, something you couldn't set down. If you're black, he said, you could work hard, but at the end of the day all you got was tired.
Ch. 8, Ibid.

5 If you want butterflies you have to feed caterpillars.
Ch. 18, *Anna Casey's Place in the World 2001*

6 When all else fails, think.
Ch. 11, *My Brother's Hero 2002*

7   "In my family, stories never end. They keep flopping around. You want to shoot them to put them out of their misery, only you can't."
Ch. 22, Sister Spider Knows All 2003

8   Even Beethoven wasn't Beethoven when he started out. He was just a kid with a few tunes in his head—kind of like you.
Friday, February 21, The Big Nothing 2004

9   Talent isn't common—but it's not uncommon either. What is uncommon is the will to do the work necessary to use a talent.
Friday, March 21, Ibid.

10   Reading isn't about taking tests. It's about—flying.
Ch. 2, The Real Question 2006

11   To find a friend fast, look around for a leftover person—someone no one is hanging out with—and talk to them.
Ch. 10, The Sorta Sisters 2007

4043. Terry Gross (1951–   )

1   Questions are my stock in trade, not answers.
Speech, Columbia University Graduate School of Journalism 21 May 2008

2   And as for letting someone in politics tell me a question is too personal—well, if someone is attempting to legislate our personal lives in ways inconsistent with their own, I feel I have a right, even a responsibility, to ask about it.
Ibid.

3   By respecting a guest's right to decline to answer a personal question, by giving him or her the responsibility to define what's going too far, I'm giving myself the freedom to ask absolutely anything.
Ibid.

4   Anyone who agrees to be interviewed must decide where to draw the line between what is public and what is private. But the line can shift, depending on who is asking the questions. What puts someone on guard isn't necessarily the fear of being 'found out.' It sometimes is just the fear of being misunderstood.
Quoted in Biography, NPR.org n.d.

4044. Mary Ann Gwinn (1951–   )

1   I'm fascinated with the notion that what we read says a great deal about the mind-set of our time. For better or worse, what we read defines who we are . . .
Quoted in "Inside the Times" by Michael R. Fancher, Seattle Times 18 October 1998

4045. Joy Harjo (1951–   )

1   i am a dangerous woman
but the weapon is not visible
security will never find it
they can't hear the clicking
of the gun
   inside my head.
"I Am a Dangerous Woman," St. 4, That's What She Said, Rayna Green,* ed. 1984

   *See 3338.

2   Remember the earth whose skin you are.
Red earth yellow earth white earth brown earth
black earth we are earth.
Remember the plants, trees, animal life who all have their

tribes, their families, their histories, too. Talk to them, listen to them. They are alive poems.
"Remember," Ibid.

3   The woman hanging from the 13th floor window
on the east side of Chicago is not alone.
. . . .
She is all the women of the apartment
building who stand watching her, watching themselves.
"The Woman Hanging From the 13th Floor Window," St. 3, Ibid.

4   At three my mother told me this story:

*God decided to make people. He put
the first batch in the oven, kept them in too
long. They burned. These were the black
people. God put in the next batch. They
were uncooked, not done. These were the
white people. But the next batch he cooked
just right, and these were the Indian
people, just like you.*
"Autobiography," Sts. 3–4, In Mad Love and War 1990

5   To pray you open your whole self
To sky, to earth, to sun, to moon

To one whole voice that is you
And know there is more
"Eagle Poem," Ibid.

6   I think of Wind and her wild ways the year
we had nothing to lose and lost it anyway . . .
"Grace," Ibid.

7   But come here, fear
I am alive and you are so afraid
   of dying.
"I Give You Back," St. 10 (1983), The Woman That I Am, The Literature and Culture of Contemporary Women of Color, D. Soyini Madison,* ed. 1994

   *See 3912.

8   The world begins at a kitchen table. No matter what, we must eat to live.
"Perhaps The World Ends Here," St. 1, The Woman Who Fell From The Sky 1994

9   All acts of kindness are lights in the war for justice.
"Reconciliation—A Prayer," III, Ibid.

4046. Amy Hempel (1951–   )

1   What seems dangerous often is not—black snakes, for example, or clear-air turbulence. While things that just lie there, like this beach, are loaded with jeopardy.
"In the Cemetery Where Al Jolson Is Buried" (1983), The Collected Stories of Amy Hempel 2006

2   I work with these dogs every day, and their capability, their decency, shames me.
"The Dog of the Marriage," Ibid.

3   Warren says, when he is angry, that he's as mad as all outdoors. He says do I want to meet him after dinner and chew the rug? He says he can't always follow the threat of my conversation.
"Tom-Rock Through the Eels," Ibid.

4 The only time the word baby doesn't scare me is the time that it should, when it is what a man calls me.

"Tumble Home," Ibid.

4047. Brenda Hillman (1951–)

1 My girl came to the study
and said Help me;
I told her I had a time problem
which meant:
I would die for you but I don't have ten minutes.

"Time Problem," *Loose Sugar* 1997

4048. Barbara Holland (1951–)

1 Speech that is but percussion under melody is bones to music. I do not understand a word you say, and yet you tell me in your rhythms, your harmonies, and richness of their structure.

"Translation," St. 1, *The East Side Scene*, Allen de Loach, ed. 1968

2 Agriculture, drink, and social life walked in holding hands. We stopped living in mutually hostile family groups, scouring the brush for berries and beetles and throwing rocks at other families, and clustered together into tribes to grow and ferment crops. Having discovered conviviality, we moved our living quarters closer together and quit trying to kill each other on sight. Visited the neighbors. Shared a few drinks. Learned to work and play together. Had a few beers.

The Joy of Drinking 2007

3 [Winston Churchill*] poured the gin into a pitcher and then nodded ritually at the bottle of vermouth across the room.

Ibid.

*(1874–1965) British politician and writer; prime minister (1940–45 and 1951–55).

4 [In Shakespeare's* day] coffeehouses sprang up to challenge the taverns. The authorities were suspicious of the whole thing and sent spies to eavesdrop. In the taverns all was amiable and easy, but the coffeehouses were cauldrons of edgy malcontents.

Ibid.

*(1564–1616) English playwright and poet.

4049. Anjelica Huston (1951–)
See Lillian Ross, 2611:1.

4050. Janis Ian (1951–)

1 My teachers all laugh, their smirking stares
Cutting deep down in our affairs
Preachers of equality
Think they believe it
Then why won't they just let us be?

"Society's Child" 1966

2 How do you do
would you like
to be friends?
No I just want a bed for the night
someone to tell me they care.
You can fake it, that's all right
In the morning I won't be here.

"The Come On" 1974

3 To those of us who knew the pain
of valentines that never came

and those whose names were never called
when choosing sides for basketball
It was long ago and far away
The world was younger than today
when dreams were all they gave for free
to ugly duckling girls like me

"At Seventeen" 1975

4 Halfway measures go unsung/
Take your pleasures while you're young

"You Are Love (Toujours Gai, Mon Cher)" 1980

4051. Patricia Jones (1951–)

1 I been thirsty so long that my mouth feels
like parchment/ got words written cross it/. Dead
stories bout dead feelings/ dried up/ dead

"I Done Got So Thirsty That My Mouth Waters at the Thought of Rain," St. 2 (1981), *The Woman That I Am, The Literature and Culture of Contemporary Women of Color*, D. Soyini Madison,* ed. 1994

*See 3912.

4052. Brigit Pegeen Kelly (1951–)

1 There
Would be a whistle, a hum, a high murmur, and, at last, a song,/
The low song a lost boy sings remembering his mother's call./
Not a cruel song, no, no, not cruel at all. This song/
Is sweet. It is sweet. The heart dies of this sweetness.

"Song," l.l., *Songs* 1995

4053. Natsuo Kirino (1951–)

1 My armor during the day was a flowing cape; at night it became Superman's cape. By day a businesswoman; by night a whore. . . . I was capable of using both my brains and my body to make money. Ha!

Grotesque, Rebecca Copeland, tr. 2007

2 But what if, when the sperm and the egg unite, they are full of animosity for each other? Wouldn't the creature they produce be contrary to expectation and abnormal as a result?

Ibid.

4054. H. Asuman Kiyak (1951–)
See Nancy Hooyman, 3582:1–2.

4055. Sharman MacDonald (1951–)

1 MORAG. A woman's body is a clock that runs down very rapidly.

When I Was a Girl, I Used to Scream and Shout 1984

2 Just because you're old you don't stop wanting.

The Girl With Red Hair 2005

4056. Meredith Maran (1951–)

1 I'd marched for reproductive rights, but I still mourned the baby I aborted when I was twenty. I'd been in a lesbian relationship for eleven years, but when my car broke down I still longed for a husband. I'd picketed beauty pageants, but I'd been secretly dieting for fifteen years . . .

Notes from an Incomplete Revolution 1997

2   Welcome to America, where on any given day, one million people are in treatment for drug or alcohol abuse.
> Introduction, *Dirty: A Search for Answers Inside America's Teenage Drug Epidemic 2003*

3   America's drug crisis is a runaway train. Keeping teenagers from jumping on board—or being flattened on the tracks—is the linchpin of the nation's efforts to stop it.
> Ibid.

4   I've long believed that teenagers are the canary in America's mine: old enough to know what's wrong around them, young enough to name and condemn it unreservedly. Their alienation and anger mirror and exacerbate our own.
> Ibid.

4057. Mary McAleese (1951–)

1   The experience of the Jewish community should humble us. They met terrible acts of anti-Semitism in Ireland, but they met many acts of kindness, too. They have contributed to Ireland way in excess of their size, in the arts, business, politics. Of all nations, we should be capable of giving the dispossessed the time and space to prove themselves.
> Quoted in "A maverick who's mellowed . . ." by Kevin Cullen, *The Boston Globe 15 October 1998*

2   The enduring freshness of Saint Patrick as symbol and icon is remarkable but not surprising. His life, lived a millennium and a half ago, is a story of emigration and exile familiar to many Irish right up to recent times and it is the story of so many exiled peoples in our modern world.
> Speech, Challenges & Opportunities Facing Ireland, Presidents & Prime Ministers *17 March 2000*

3   I'll be thinking of the fact that people from every ordinary walk of life—bank clerks, shop assistants, doctors, lawyers—transformed themselves into the most extraordinary killing machine, driven by an utterly evil ideology that seemed to captivate the minds, not just of German people, it has to be remembered, but of many people, right across Europe. Tragically, with outrageous consequences for those who died, and those who suffered for, and still continue to suffer all that abject loss, all that pitiless misery.*
> Quoted in Interview, "Mourning Ireland" with Aine Lawlor 27 *January 2005*
> *Re Ceremony of Remembrance at Auschwitz Camp on Holocaust Memorial Day she attended later that day.

4   It's a toxin you see, it's a poison, and it can be in weak and diluted form, but even in that weak and diluted form, it's still capable of surviving long enough for a Nazi-type era to come along, and to force it into concentrated form, and in concentrated form you get Auschwitz, you get Birkenau, you get Darfur, you get Rwanda. That's what you get when you don't stop the toxin.
> Ibid.

4058. Deborah E. McDowell (1951–)

1   . . . once a man keeps company with an alley cat, you can be sure that prowling is all he's got on his mind.
> *Leaving Pipe Shop: Memories of Kin 1997*

2   . . . men . . . run the streets with good-time women and then go home to their wives.
> Ibid.

3   If the outer rim [of the ear] hadn't turned dark by a certain month, then the child was sure to be fair-skinned and marked for success and the pain and satisfaction of others' envy.
> Ibid.

4   Don't never let no man see you low, 'cause then he'll sho'nuff try to walk all over you, and sometimes, you can't get up from it . . .
> Ibid.

5   . . . a part of me still detested the very idea of her scrubbing, scouring, bleaching, and buffing, while her "boss lady" went for her Saturday manicure.
> Ibid.

4059. Lynne McTaggart (1951–)

1   One of the coziest of certainties we've grown up with is that modern medicine works miracles and doctors cure diseases.
> Ch. 1, *What Doctors Don't Tell You: The Truth About the Dangers of Modern Medicine 1999*

2   With all the fancy chemicals and computerized testing equipment we have at hand, asthma, arthritis, diabetes, cancer—virtually all the chronic degenerative diseases known to mankind—are thriving, and medicine hasn't affected their incidence one tiny bit.
> Ibid.

3   Many of your doctor's arsenal of treatments don't work—indeed, have never been proven to work, let alone to be safe. It is a false science, built upon conjuring tricks, supposition, and blind preconception, whose so-called scientific method is a vast amount of stumbling in the dark.
> Ibid.

4060. Diane McWhorter (1951–)

1   Sometimes it seemed that all the profanity of industrial enterprise had collected in Birmingham.
> Ch. 1, *Carry Me Home: Birmingham, Alabama: The Climactic Battle of the Civil Rights Revolution 2001*

2   The relevance of Third Reich Germany to today's America is not that Bush* equals Hitler** or that the United States government is a death machine. It's that it provides a rather spectacular example of the insidious process by which decent people come to regard the unthinkable as not only thinkable but doable, justifiable. Of the way freethinkers and speakers become compliant and self-censoring. Of the mechanism by which moral or humanistic categories are converted into bureaucratic ones. And finally, of the willingness with which we hand control over to the state and convince ourselves that we are the masters of our destiny.
> "The N-Word, Unmentionable Lessons of the Midterm Aftermath," *Slate.com 28 November 2006*
> *George W. B— (1946–), Am. politician; 43rd president of the United States (2001–09). **Adolf Hitler (1889–1945), a.k.a. "Der Führer"; Austrian-born founder of the German Nazi Party and chancellor of the Third Reich (1933–45).

3   Thus, in the week before the election, hardly a ripple answered the latest decree from the Bush administration: Detainees held in CIA prisons were forbidden from telling their lawyers what methods of interrogation were used on them, presumably so they wouldn't give away any of the top-secret torture methods that we don't use. Cautiously, I look back on that as the crys-

tallizing moment of Bushworld: tautological as a Gilbert and Sullivan* libretto, absurd as a Marx Brothers** movie, and scary as a Kafka*** novel.

Ibid.

*W. S. G— (1836–1911) and Arthur S— (1842–1900), collaborators on 14 comic operas. **Five brothers, the most famous of whom is Groucho M— (1890–1977), vaudevilleans noted for their zany comic films. ***Franz K— (1883–1924), Austrian symbolic writer.

4061. Marlane Meyer (1951–)

1 SHERMAN. Pornography in its focus on the genital experience creates an ultimately carnal mind that is necessarily death-oriented since the body is always in a progressive state of decay. The earth begins to crawl up inside you.
SHERI. Ugh.
ETTA. We're dying anyway, who cares?

Etta Jenks 1986

4062. Shira Milgrom (1951–)

1 If logic tells you that life is a meaningless accident, don't give up on life. Give up on logic.
Sermon, Yom Kippur 5749 (1988; White Plains, New York), *Four Centuries of Jewish Women's Spirituality* Ellen M. Umansky* & Dianne Ashton, eds. *1992*
*See 4011.

2 There must be a limit to our grief. Yes, it is life affirming to allow ourselves to feel—to feel pain. But it is antilife to mourn without limit—to consume one's life in sadness.

Ibid.

3 But suppose we viewed life not as using up our limited supply but as the accumulation of moments—moments like treasures . . .

Ibid.

4063. Barbara "Barb" Morgan (1951–)

1 You know, there's a great sense of pride to be able to be involved in a human endeavour that takes us all a little bit farther. When you look down and see our Earth, and you realize what we are trying to do as a human race, it's pretty profound.
"Teacher-Astronaut, Crewmates Glad to be Home," space.com
22 August 2007

2 My first surprise was how black space really is. Pictures don't capture the depth and breadth of the color. It's the softest, smoothest, creamist black.
"Ten Who Inspire," *AARP Magazine January/February 2008*

4064. Khawar Mumtaz (1951?–)
See Farida Shaheed, 4208: 1–2.

4065. Cristina Narbona Ruiz (1951–)

1 Unfortunately, economic growth in recent years has been accompanied by over-exploitation of natural resources and an acceleration of our ecosystems' destruction. We must therefore show that we are able to change our mode of growth. Biosphere reserves are an incalculable treasure in terms of landscapes and biological diversity; they represent enormous potential because they can serve as laboratories to implement sustainable development policies and conservation of this biological diversity.
UNESCO.org, *28 January 2008*

4066. Noor Al-Hussein (1951–)

1 Growing up in Washington while my father* worked in the Kennedy Administration** established my ideals early in life. It was not my dream to be a movie star or even a Queen, but to join the Peace Corps. I did not achieve that dream—my life has moved in rather a different direction—but what I have tried to achieve reflects the same concerns and owes a great deal to that early inspiration.
Speech, Greater Washington Society of Association Executives (Kennedy Center, Washington, D.C.), *4 March 1996*
*Najeeb Elias Halaby (1915–2003), American businessman and government official. ** John F. Kennedy (1917–63), 35th president of the United States (1961–63); assassinated.

2 My life journey among American and Middle Eastern cultures has taught me that the foundation for constructive partnership already exists, embedded in our common moral heritage—in the teachings of the Muslim, Christian and Jewish faiths. We must be aware, however, that Arabs and Americans express common moral values with different cultural voices and vocabularies.

Ibid.

3 I recognized the familiar free spirit of the aviator in King Hussein* . . . a gravity-defying spirit, transcending constraining and narrow boundaries of convention and political strife, to reach for a higher and larger view and perspective.

Ibid.

*(1952–99), king of Jordan, her late husband.

4 But true peace is not merely the absence of hostility. Rather, it requires bonds of cooperation to nourish the acceptance and appreciation of coexistence.

Ibid.

5 Far too often, women have been commended in public for their commitment to peace, just before the doors to the negotiating room slammed shut in their faces.
Commencement Address, Mt. Holyoke College (So. Hadley, Mass.), *26 May 2002*

6 Now it is time [women] took their rightful place as the makers of peace, in the negotiating and legislative chambers, using their all too intimate experience with war and their expertise in coalition-building to create a new world community. To the men—or anyone—who says we must continue as we always have, it is time to say, "Sir, your hundred—or thousand, or ten thousand—years are up!"

Ibid.

4067. Sigrid Nunez (1951–)

1 Everything about the world of ballet responds to the young girl looking to escape real life.
A Feather on the Breath of God 1995

2 Being poor meant you could never relax.
p. 12, *Ibid.*

3 The sound of a pen scratching in the night is a holy sound.
p. 118, *Ibid.*

4 They were carried away not by love but by the vocabulary of love, the adjectives and verbs of love, one smooth golden word following another, like honey dripping from a spoon.
The Last of Her Kind 1996

5 She has become what memory often makes the dead: more sinned against than sinning.

p. 21, Ibid.

6 I believe you have to reach a certain age before you understand how much life really is like a novel, with patterns and leitmotivs and turning points, and guns that must go off and people who must return before the ending.

p. 196, Ibid.

7 Background is important. Things happen in the country that would never happen in the city. Things happen to people in strange places that would not happen to them at home. It isn't true that people who cross the sea change their skies but not their natures. We are different, depending on where we are.

Prologue, *Naked Sleeper* 1996

8 When writers say that it doesn't get easier what they mean is that is that it is always hard. That writing is always hard.

Interview with Robert Birnbaum, *The Morning News 29 March* 2007

9 If you are a novelist you need to pay attention to the culture. So it's part of your job to take in as much as you can. And it's a challenge, it really is.

Ibid.

4068. Jeannie Gayle Poole (1951–)

1 She [Zenobia Perry*] is a national treasurer and by honoring her and telling her story, we can raise the public's awareness of the lack of support and encouragement many women and minorities face.

"Xenia to Honor Zenobia" by Meth Michaels, *Dayton Daily News 11 July* 2002

*See 2099.

4069. Sally Ride (1951–)

1 The rockets light! The shuttle leaps off the launch pad in a cloud of steam and a trail of fire.

To Space and Back, with Susan Okie 1986

2 I can't remember a single time [my parents] ever told me not to do something I wanted to do.

Quoted in *Women Aviators* by Lisa Yount 1995

3 The best part of being in space is being weightless. It feels wonderful to be able to float without effort; to slither up, down, and around the inside of the shuttle just like a seal.

Ibid.

4 [I hope to see the United States] gain routine access to space, make it an extension of the Earth's environment, not just for exploration and national pride but for things the country can actually use—medicines, improved materials.

Ibid.

4070. Jamie Sams (1951–)

1 Our traditional Native American greeting in the Seneca language is *Na:weh Skennio*—thank you for being! Whether you know it or not, each of you represents a spark of inspiration within the Great Mystery. You are needed. You touch the lives of many and are responsible for changing the lives of others

for the better. For all that you do and for who you are, I thank you for being.

"Messages for the Men of the Millennium," *The Fabric of the Future: Women Visionaries of Today Illuminate the Path to Tomorrow*, M.J. Ryan, ed. 1998

2 When we are inspired, we funnel our creativity into fashioning something of beauty, whether it is dance, art, music, or making a meal for our families. When we finish, we exhale our creations, sending them into the world to be shared with others. Creativity is present in everything we do and is fueled by the amount of life-force we are willing to embrace.

Ibid.

3 Reclaiming the belly-laugh can cure a world of woes.

Ibid.

4071. Patricia Spallone (1951–)

1 Clearly, the [reproductive] technologies were not invented to serve *women's* needs, but the various needs and desires of medical scientists, research scientists, and the state, to further technological "progress" and to aid population control aims, all of which requires the use of women to those ends.

(p. 2), *Beyond Conception: The New Politics of Reproduction* 1989

4072. Starhawk (1951–)

1 Ritual is the original womb of art; its waters continue to nourish creativity.

Truth or Dare 1987

2 Language shapes consciousness, and the use of language to shape consciousness is an important branch of magic.

Dreaming the Dark: Magic, Sex, and Politics 1997

3 To be a Witch, to practice magic, we can't simply honor nature's cycles *in the abstract*. We need to know them intimately and understand them in the physical as well as the psychic world. A real relationship with nature is vital for our magical and spiritual development, and our psychic and spiritual health.

Ch. 1, *The Earth Path: Grounding Your Spirit in the Rhythms of Nature* 2004

4 The Goddess is the name we put on the great process of birth, growth, death, and regeneration that underlie the living world. The Goddess is the presence of consciousness in all living beings; the Goddess is the great creative force that spun the universe out of coiled strings of probability and set the stars spinning and dancing in spiral that our entwining DNA echoes as it coils, uncoils, and evolves.

Ibid.

4073. Vicky Stifter (1951?–)

1 I understand the logic behind, "Let's build the gate, shut the doors, keep them [immigrants] out and we'll all be better off." . . . If we build the gate and we consume resources from within our gate, that's one thing. But the reality is that . . . we're consuming resources from all over the world. We're consuming gas, coffee, food that's grown in the countries people are coming from. They're not able to survive because their land has been turned into places for exporting bananas. So they come here because they need to feed their children. . . . To say, "We can come to your countries to get your resources, but you can't

come here," I think it's immoral. I think it goes to the very soul of who we are as a nation.

> "Growth: enough already," *Seattle Times*, A17 *22 November 1998*

4074. Tatyana Tolstaya (1951–)

1   In Russia, people suffer from the stillness of time.

> *Independent* (London) *31 May 1990*

2   Already the writers are complaining that there is too much freedom. They need some pressure. The worse your daily life, the better your art. If you have to be careful because of oppression and censorship, this pressure produces diamonds.

> Ibid.

3   To retell a life you need an entire life. We'll skip it. Later, perhaps, sometime or another.

> "Yorick," *The New Yorker*, Jamey Gambrell, tr. *26 December 2005*

4   Because we are just as blind—no, a thousand times blinder than that old man in the wheelchair. We hear whispers but we plug our ears; we are shown but we turn away. We have no faith: we're afraid to believe, because we're afraid that we'll be deceived. We are certain that we're in the tomb. We are certain that there's nothing in the dark. There can't be anything in the dark.

> "See the Other Side," *The New Yorker*, Jamey Gambrell, tr. *12 March 2007*

4075. Linda Vallejo (1951–)

1   The sweat ceremony is like an art-making space. To make art, you have to be open, giving, honest with yourself. You get that same feeling in a good sweat ceremony. The feeling spreads out from your heart. You can open up and say whatever you want with total confidence and trust.

> Quoted in "Linda Vallejo," *Exposures, Women & Their Art* by Ann Brown and Arlene Raven* 1989

*See 3533.

2   In indigenous traditions, if you receive a vision—one of those spectacular moments of understanding—you have to share it with others through music, dance, poetry or art in order for it to work its wonder.

> Ibid.

3   I make art like some people make cookies. I'm always compulsively busy. I know that I can't quit.

> Ibid.

4076. Paula A. Vogel (1951–)

1   CECIL. Never forget that every single organic being around us strives to increase in numbers; that each lives by a struggle at some period in its life; that heavy destruction inevitably falls either on the young or the old.

> *And Baby Makes Seven* 1986

2   PECK. It [the car] doesn't have to be a 'she'—but when you close your eyes and think of someone who responds to your touch—someone who performs just for you and gives you just what you ask for—I guess I always see a 'she.' You can call it what you like

> *How I Learned to Drive* 1997

4077. Timberlake Wertenbaker (1951–)

1   CHORUS. They say a woman is a man turned inside out. Most evident in the genitals, his turned out, hers turned in, hers waiting for his, waiting for completion, that's what they say.

> *Inside Out* 1982

2   CHORUS. What is the anatomy of a woman?
LI. Not what you imagine through your genitals.

> Ibid.

3   PHILLIP. The Greeks believed that it was a citizen's duty to watch a play. It was a kind of work in that it required attention, judgement, patience, all social virtues.
TENCH. And the Greeks were conquered by the more practical Romans, Arthur.
COLLINS. Indeed, the Romans built their bridges but they also spent many centuries wishing they were Greeks.

> Act I, Sc. 6, *Our Country's Good* (adapt. of Thomas Keneally's* *The Playmaker*) 1989

*Austrian novelist (1935–).

4078. Kate Wheeler (1951?–)

1   There was a difference between telling lies and living them: one was permissible in order to prevent the other, she decided.

> *When Mountains Walked* 2000

2   Which was more dangerous, Maggie wondered, loving an idea or loving a person? Or loving a person who loved an idea?

> Ibid.

4079. Patricia Williams (1951–)

1   So-called formal equal opportunity has done a lot but misses the heart of the problem . . . the rules may be color-blind, but people are not.

> "The Obliging Shell: An Informal Essay on Formal Equal Opportunity," *Michigan Law Review* 87 *1989*

2   There's a security guard in the foyer of the building now; they hired an old black man in a blue suit with a badge, to keep out other old tired black people.

> "Fire and Ice," *The Alchemy of Race and Rights: Diary of a Law Professor* 1991

3   Cultural needs and ideals change with the momentum of time; the need to redefine our laws in keeping with the spirit of cultural flux is what keeps a society alive and humane.

> Ibid.

4   If our laws are thus piano-wired on the exclusive validity of literalism, if they are picked clean of their spirit, then society risks heightened irresponsibility for the consequence of abominable actions.

> Ibid.

5   Yet being ruled by the cool formality of language is surely as bad as being ruled solely by one's emotions.

> Ibid.

4080. Angie Zelter (1951–)

1   There are more and more people who define themselves as global citizens, who know that life is intimately interconnected, and that we can never be fully human whilst others continue to suffer, and who know that love, justice and nonviolence is the very essence of life.

> Acceptance Speech, Right Livelihood Awards (Stockholm), *9 December 2001*

2 We have all learnt by now that if we want nuclear disarmament then it is no good waiting for our Governments to do it.

Ibid.

3 Nuclear weapons are weapons of mass destruction and thus cannot be used with any precision or any pretence at righting any wrong. Their use is basically mass murder on a catastrophic scale with the potential for escalation to the use of thousands of nuclear weapons, which could put an end to all life on earth.

Ibid.

4 Law is based upon ethical values and is respected in so far, and only in so far, as it conforms to common human morality.

Ibid.

5 This is our message—killing is wrong. Mass killing is wrong. Threatening mass destruction is a denial of our own humanity and is suicidal. When something is wrong we have to stop it. Dismantling the machinery of destruction is thus a practical act of love that we can all join in. Please join us—together we are unstoppable.

Ibid.

4081. Shoshana Zuboff (1951–   )

1 Technological change defines the horizon of our material world as it shapes the limiting conditions of what is possible and what is barely imaginable. It erodes . . . assumptions about the nature of our reality, the "pattern" in which we dwell, and lays open new choices.

Conclusion, *In the Age of the Smart Machine 1988*

2 I've lived in a preindustrial (rural Argentina) as well as an industrial world. You experience a different sense of time in a community that works the land. Human relationships aren't professionalized or contractualized; family and friends take primacy. Life has much more continuity than discontinuity. There's a great deal of poetry in everyday life.

Interview (pp. 66–94), *Omni April 1991*

3 The dream of automation remains a powerful one—the idea of a clockwork world running without human intervention but generating enough wealth that everyone can go fishing, read books, and study art.

Ibid.

4 Computerization is part of a long-term historical process in which work has become increasingly abstract.

Ibid.

5 Managers, right up to the very top of the company, will be getting their personal rewards not from giving commands and eliciting obedience but from educating and nurturing the people under them.

Ibid.

6 Learning is the new form of labor.

Ibid.

7 In a world where authority is equated with ownership of information, sharing that information becomes very threatening.

Ibid.

4082. Jeri Allyn (1952?–   )

1 I see the restaurant as a symbol for the world. How do you feed and house a soul with work that's important?

Quoted in "Jeri Allyn," *Exposures, Women & Their Art* by Ann Brown and Arlene Raven* 1989

*See 3533.

2 My mother's most profound legacy was her death.* I learned I could continue living—and laughing.

Ibid.

*Allyn's mother died from cancer at the age of 43.

4083. Linda G. Alvarado (1952–   )

1 Values are a strong factor in success in business—sustained success; not just money. How one works with people and how we conduct everyday business says volumes on how a company survives and thrives.

Quoted in "A Hands-On Dream Builder" by William Plasencia, *Hispanic Magazine October 2002*

2 I think that Hispanics have to contribute back to their communities. What are we creating for our legacy?

Ibid.

3 The competitive environment with my brothers taught me about teamwork and the importance of taking risks. You can never get to second base if you keep your foot safely on first. I also realized that even if you strike out, you still get another turn at bat. This applies to professional life, too—a lot of great careers are unplanned.

"Ahead of Her Time," WomenWorking.com *March 2007*

4084. Nevada Barr (1952–   )

1 There hadn't been a god for many years. Not the nightgown-clad patriarch of Sunday school coloring books; not the sensitive young man with the inevitable auburn ringlets Anna had stared through in the stained-glass windows at Mass; not the many-armed and many-faceted deities of the Bhagavad Gita that she'd worshipped alongside hashish and Dustin Hoffman in her college days. Even the short but gratifying parade of earth goddesses that had taken her to their ample bosoms in her early thirties had gone, although she remembered them with more kindness than the rest.

God was dead. Let Him rest in peace. Now, finally, the earth was hers with no taint of Heaven.

(p. 1), *Track of the Cat 1993*

2 Nature was taking back what had once been hers. . . .

Liberty Falling 1999

3 Free money was never free.

Ch. 1, *Winter Study 2008*

4 She'd been around animals enough to know humans might know how much Jupiter weighs and where stars come from, but they remain in total ignorance about what the cat in their lap is thinking or who their dog tells their secrets to.

Ch. 2, Ibid.

5 He wasn't afraid now, Anna realized, and that made him brave. Except brave didn't count if one wasn't afraid. Without fear to burn away the dross and transform it from baser metal, bravery was merely stupidity or poor impulse control.

Ch. 11, Ibid.

6 It was said DNA didn't lie, but it has also been said pictures didn't lie until computers put the lie to that. What lied was people and they lied all the time, and for every reason under the sun. People lied with words and pictures, and, if it were possible, they would like with DNA.

Ch. 26, Ibid.

7 "So we play God?" Jonah asked.
"People always play God," Anna said. "There's nobody else to do it."

Ch. 37, Ibid.

4085. Roseanne Barr (1952–   )

1 ... I used to think that communing with nature was a healing, positive thing. Now, I think I'd like to commune with other things—like room service and temperature control.

Introduction, *My Life as a Woman* 1989

2 Many people accuse Jews of loving money. ... Let me set you straight. Jews do not love money, Jews love food and Jews love stories and Jews love life. The food and life parts are the reason we acquire money because we comprehend that those piles of quarters may buy us our lives at any given time in any given country with any given peoples who really believe that money and God are the same thing.

Ch. 2, Ibid.

3 "Housewives" is a term I employ that means anybody who has ever had to clean up somebody else's shit and not been paid for it. ...

Ch. 15, Ibid.

4 It was no accident that Lenny [Bruce*] had chosen comedy. It is the last "free speech" art form and, like my father said, it is mightier than the pen *and* the sword.

Ch. 19, Ibid.

*Lenny Bruce (1926–66), American comedian.

5 My breasts have fed three children, nurtured and sustained their bodies and built them up in twelve ways. If they wanna lay down after that, by god they deserve the rest.

Ibid.

6 Hollywood is where, as my husband says, people who were somebody someplace else come to be a nobody.

Ch. 21, Ibid.

7 I figure when my husband comes home from work, if the kids are still alive, then I've done my job.

Quoted in "Kosher at Last," *The Haunted Smile, The Story of Jewish Comedians in America* by Lawrence J. Epstein 2001

8 My husband said he needed more space, so I locked him out of the house.

Ibid.

4086. Sydney Biddle Barrows (1952–   )

1 A call girl is simply someone who hates poverty more than she hates sin.

Mayflower Madam 1986

4087. Medea Benjamin (1952–   )

1 When most Americans hear of human rights abuses, they likely think of atrocities in some far-off country in a forgotten corner of the globe. [But] abuses against individuals' basic rights also occur regularly here in the United States, and our money-saturated political system hardly deserves the title 'democracy.'

Quoted on *DiscoverTheNetworks.org 2006*

2 There are few countries where everyday people actually receive the benefits of cooperation with multinationals: a redistribution

of oil profit, a guarantee for healthcare written into the constitution, and record-breaking achievements in education. ... Venezuela has embarked upon some of the most innovative regional programs that Latin America has ever seen.

Ibid.

3 We must insist that governments stop taking innocent lives in the name of seeking justice for the loss of other innocent lives.

Speech (2002), Ibid.

4088. Julia Bonds (1952–   )

1 What I've seen happening in the coalfields is the total destruction of what God put on Earth to help humans and wildlife, the complete annihilation of the communities and culture of Appalachia.*

"Coal Miner's Slaughter" by Michelle Nijhuis, *grist.org 14 April 2003*

*A cultural region in the United States along the Appalachian Mountains that stretches from southern New York to northern Alabama, Georgia and Mississippi.

2 You don't have to be very smart to understand that once you remove soil and vegetation from the top of a very steep mountain valley, you're going to increase runoff from rain events. We've seen extensive flooding in Appalachia, and there's much more to come—and when disasters occur here, the taxpayers pay for it. It comes out of your pocket. It's insane, just insane.

Ibid.

3 If it blasts, oozes, or gushes, it's done near poor, oppressed, rural communities or minority communities. This is a dirty little secret that people are now speaking out about.

Ibid.

4 When powerful people pursue profits at the expense of human rights and our environment, they have failed as leaders. Responsible citizens must step forward, not just to point the way, but to lead the way to a better world.

goldmanprize.org 2003

4089. Elayne Boosler (1952–   )

1 Hookers! How do they do it? How could any woman sleep with a man without having a dinner and a movie first?

Quoted in "The 1960's to the 1980's," *Women in Comedy* by Linda Martin & Kerry Segrave 1986

2 Men want you to scream "You're the best" while swearing you've never done this with anyone before.

Ibid.

3 President Reagan* is a lot like E.T. He's cute, he's lovable, and he knows nothing about how Americans live.

Quoted in "Rising Stars," *Funny Women, American Comediennes, 1860–1985* by Mary Unterbrink 1987

*Ronald R- (1911–2004), 40th president of the United States (1981–89), actor.

4 The Vatican came down with a new ruling. They said no surrogate mothers ... A good thing they didn't make this rule before Jesus was born.

Quoted in "Kosher at Last," *The Haunted Smile, The Story of Jewish Comedians in America* by Lawrence J. Epstein 2001

4090. Denise M. Boudrot (1952–)

1 I don't ride to beat the boys, just to win.

> Quoted in *Women at Work* by Betty Medsger *1975*

4091. Helen Mack Chang (1952–)

1 A generalized clamor for justice was filled by voices of encouragement that strengthened our hopes and made me feel plural: to be myself among many and to experience within me the voices of many persons from many different backgrounds who, for the most noble ideals, supported our faith and our certainty.

> Acceptance Speech, Right Livelihood Award (Stockholm) 9 *December 1992*

2 . . . life has no meaning unless we make an effort to live together in justice and with dignity.

> Ibid.

3 The Government arrogantly assumes that the reasons, desires and interests which they imposed on the population represent the benefit and consensus of the majority.

> Ibid.

4 We are putting on trial the policy of terror in Guatemala of the past 30 years. We are not looking for reprisals but for justice. What we want is justice as proof that governmental arbitrariness will not continue; justice as a condition for the development of democratic relations free of fear and coercion.

> Quoted in *Newsweek November 2003*

4092. Jung Chang (1952–)

1 Without power or money, no Chinese could feel safe from the depredations of officialdom or random violence. There had never been a proper legal system. Justice was arbitrary, and cruelty was both institutionalized and capricious. An official with power was *the law*.

> Ch. 1, *Wild Swans: Three Daughters of China 1992*

2 When she pleaded with her mother to untie the bindings, her mother would weep and tell her that unbound feet would ruin her entire life, and that she was doing it for her own future happiness.
In those days, when a woman was married, the first thing the bridegroom's family did was to examine her feet. Large feet, meaning normal feet, were considered to bring shame on the husband's household.

> Ibid.

3 *Re death of Mao-Zedong:** People had been acting for so long they confused it with their true feelings. I wondered how many of the tears were genuine.

> Ch. 17, Ibid.

*(1893–1976; a.k.a. Mao Tse-tung), Chinese founder of the People's Republic of China.

4 Mao tse-tung, who for decades held absolute power over the lives of one-quarter of the world's population, was responsible for well over 70 million deaths in peacetime, more than any other twentieth-century leader.

> *Mao, The Unknown Story,* with Jon Halliday *2005*

4093. Catherine Clinton (1952–)

1 The female head of household had a full plate of daily and weekly domestic duties from baking bread to churning biographer. Mary Lincoln* did not have to make her own soap and candles like her foremothers, but was still likely to beat her own carpets, air her own linens, and restuff her own pillows for freshness.

> *Mrs. Lincoln/A Life 2008*

*See 950.

2 Her unconditional love sustained Lincoln's* growth to greatness. She was a woman of intense intellect and passion who stepped outside the boundaries her time prescribed and suffered for it.

> Ibid.

*Abraham Lincoln (1809–1965), 16th president of the United States (1861–65); assassinated.

4094. Judith Oritz Cofer (1952–)

1 So far has she gone
into herself,
that the taunting voices
from the outside calling
her *Loca, Loca*
reach her as bright beams
of light lining the road
to the kingdom where
she is the sole ruler.

> "Una Mujer Loca" (1986), *The Woman That I Am, The Literature and Culture of Contemporary Women of Color*, D. Soyini Madison,* ed. *1994*

*See 3912.

2 I was deliciously afraid of all
the invisible creeping, crawling dangers inhabiting
the luscious ground where I squatted to pee,
allowing impulse and need to fully overtake me,
inviting all the demons that reside in dark damp
hiding places into my most secret self.

> "The Pleasures of Fear," St. 2, *A Love Story Beginning in Spanish 2005*

4095. Judith G. Coffin (1952–)

1 Wage policy is also family policy and gender policy.

> *The Politics of Women's Work: The Paris Garment Trades, 1750–1915 1996*

2 Work is the people's patrimony.

> Ibid.

4096. Lisa Collier Cool (1952–)

1 The best way to get a reader's attention is to punch him in the nose—with your first paragraph.

> *How to Write Irresistible Query Letters 1987*

2 Finding a new idea is like falling in love—the excitement is highest when you first meet.

> Ibid.

4097. Vicki Covington (1952–)

1 Southerners love a story, even when it wounds them and ruins their reputation, wrecks their economy and sets fire to things.

> *The Last Hotel for Women 1996*

2 "Birmingham . . . you people, I see have changed." . . . His anger is being converted; he can taste it. It's a metal, a very

hard metal burning his tongue, gums, throat. He thinks of molten pig iron being tapped from the furnace, how slag floats to the top. "By-products," he says, staring at them all. "By-products of the Kennedys."*

Ibid.

*Re: the Civil Rights Act of 1964, enacted shortly after the assassination of John F. Kennedy (1917–63), 35th president of the United States (1961–63).

4098. Tuenjai Deetes (1952?–)

1 I cannot change the governments of the world on my own. With small groups, we can change the world and steer it in a positive direction.

"A Life in the Hills," *The Courier* (UNESCO) *October 2000*

2 Little by little, cultural identity is eroded by materialism.

"Tuenjai Deetes: a bridge to the hill tribes" by Ethirajan Anbarasan, Ibid.

3 The tourists tend to treat the indigenous people as some kind of exotic specimen. Instead of coming to the hills to take photos, they should learn to respect the local people and their culture.

Ibid.

4099. Lisa Dodson (1952–)

1 In the face of stigma, irrational regulations, peril to children, and a woman's despair, [a researcher's] neutrality is known only as collusive silence.

Don't Call Us Out of Name: The Untold Lives of Women and Girls in Poor America 1998

2 More than anything, they spoke of little erosions which finally wear you down into someone you don't want to be. They spoke of chronic exhaustion. They spoke of having no car, no warm coats, no baby clothes, no functioning laundry in the building no elevator and many stairs, no heat sometimes, no Pampers, no tampons, of long lines at clinics, and of being able to go only to stores which accept food stamps, and, above all, of having no one to "offer a kind word."

Ibid.

4100. Amy Domini (1952–)

1 In Europe there is a willingness at the highest levels of government and corporate leadership to talk about issues of ethics, sustainability, the right to do, and the goal of civilization. These are ideas to which a politician in America may occasionally give lip service. But you rarely hear a corporate leader even mention them.

"Empowering the Socially Responsible Investor," *Investing in Responsibility 1999*

2 I believe that Europe has a soul that can enrich the social investment industry in America and a leadership capacity, coming from the top, that is void in America.

Ibid.

3 Finance was originally created as a means of stimulating economics, not as a means of enriching individuals.

Ibid.

4 My belief is that if we can build the constituency to 10% socially responsible shareholders, we will be an important enough voice to alter the equation. We will be able to say: "Yes, make profit at any price" with one caveat: "Make the world better

for the next generation." And better not only in terms of clean water and clean air, but also in terms of human dignity. These are the goals of socially responsible investing and that's why I am so passionately dedicated to this field.

Ibid.

5 The Internet . . . is a great feedback loop. It is an absolutely wonderful place to test your assumptions. I see it as a model of what society is becoming—a rapidly evolving segmentation of different groups that are nevertheless able to co-exist because of some shared connectivity.

Ibid.

4101. Rita Dove (1952–)

1 You have to decide whether you're going to be *in* life or if you're going to stand by and watch it.

Quoted in "Author Dove reaches . . ." by Lynne K. Varner, *Seattle Post-Intelligencer,* C1, 4 *3 November 1992*

2 "Do you know what you're telling us? Your grandmother goes half across town to buy you the first Negro baby doll and you throw a fit, you throw her down the stairs like dirty laundry. You don't like it? You don't like being a Negro?"

Virginia stared at it—the bulging eyes, the painted head. She didn't look like that. And if she did, how could her own parents stand there and tell her so? How could they love her and show her at the same time that she was ugly?

Through the Ivory Gate 1992

3 don't think you can ever forget her
don't even try
she's not going to budge

"Lady Freedom Among Us," St. 8 (1993), *On the Bus with Rosa Parks* 1999*

*See 2206.

4 I prefer books to moonlight, statuary to trees.

"Reverie in Open Air," St. 1, *American Smooth 2004*

5 I've walked there, too: he can't give
you up, so you give in until you can't live
without him. Like these blossoms, white sores
burst upon earth's ignorant flesh, at first sight
everything is innocence—
then it's itch, scratch, putrescence.

"Afield," St. 2 *n.d.*

6 There's a way to study freedom but few have found
it; you must talk yourself to death and then beyond,
destroy time, then refashion it.

"Political," St. 1 *n.d.*

4102. Maureen Dowd (1952–)

1 It would be a waste of time trying to embarrass the Republicans on sex when they are doing such a fine job of embarrassing themselves.

"Like '50s film heroine, Monica managed to get herself a man," *The New York Times 8 October 1998*

2 People keep talking about redemption when they just want revenge.

This great capital, once a place of gravity, has been reduced to a keyhole.

"Ah, for a parallel universe, far from this nasty business," Ibid. *15 October 1998*

3 It's not that we don't want moral character in our leaders. We'd love it. But the great maw of entertainment has worn us down. We'll settle for the good policies of flawed people.
                    "No Grand Illusion," Ibid. *21 May 2000*

4 Sports was one of the last bastions where you could still sell tickets on pure ability. . . . [now] eroticism trumps athleticism.
                    "Nymphet at the Net," Ibid. *4 June 2000*

5 W.* believes in self-determination only if he's doing the determining.
                    "Didn't See It Coming, Again," Ibid. *1 February 2006*
    ** W. refers to George W. Bush, 43rd president of the U.S.

6 W. decided there was no need to be president of the whole country. He could just be president of his base. Obama is determined to be president of as much of the country as possible.
                    "The Long, Lame Goodbye," Ibid. *17 January 2009*

7 The exiting and entering presidents are opposite poles—one the parody of a monosyllabic Western gunslinger who disdains nuance, and one a complex, polysyllabic professor sort who will make a decision only after he has held it up to the light and examined it from all sides.
                    Ibid.

4103. Ferron (1952–   )

1 But by our light be we spirit,
   And by our hearts be we women,
   And by our eyes be we open,
   And by our hands be we wide.
                    "Testimony" *1980*

4104. Lynn Freed (1952?–   )

1 . . . homesickness, that crippling legacy of familiar sounds and smells and tastes now out of reach.
                    "Foreign Student" (1989), *Shaking Eve's Tree, Short Stories of Jewish Women* Sharon Niederman,* ed. *1990*
    *See 3855.

2 There was none of the chaos of our own services—women waving and talking in the balconies, men swaying and chanting and beating their breasts below. This service was orderly. It didn't seem Jewish at all.
                    Ibid.

4105. Alice Fulton (1952–   )

1 Everyday was all there was on the farm.
                    "Happy Dust," *The Missouri Review* 198-?

2 In my experience, it is better to keep away from saints unless you have business with them.
                    Ibid.

3 This long path wound grandly up through massive gates and meadows toward the sky. I suspected many pilgrims from the city never knew there could be such earth on earth.
                    Ibid.

4 Suddenly it seemed my little shut-in had been cooped up long enough. Suddenly it wanted liberty. It was coming like a loco-motive headlight. It was coming quick as scat. God Almighty! Now this baby was helping. Now this baby wanted to be born.
                    Ibid.

5 Nuns always want some little selfless thing in exchange for their favors, I find. God's the same way when you think about it.
                    Ibid.

6 Are we making love yet?
                    "The Expense of Spirit," St. 2, *Powers of Congress 19*

7 Because life's too short to blush,
   I keep my blood tucked in.
                    "About Face," St. 1, *Sensual Math 1995*

8 The natural is what
   poetry contests. Why else the line == why stanza == why meter and the rest.
                    "==," St. 7 (1994), Ibid.

4106. Lois Marie Gibbs (1952–   )

1 Average people and the average community can change the world. You can do it just based on common sense, determination, persistence and patience.
                    goldmanprize.org 1990

2 In seeking to reduce dioxin exposure, we could blame the vic-tim and get everybody to stop eating milk, fish, and meat and to stop breast-feeding their babies. Or we can use the same energy to stop the corporations who are filling our food and our bodies with dioxin.
                    Preface, *Dying from Dioxin: A Citizen's Guide to Reclaiming our Health and Rebuilding Democracy 1995*

3 There are no magic facts. There are no perfect heroes to give perfect speeches that will convince the polluters to stop pollut-ing. There is only the dogged determination of people working together to protect their own health, their families' health, and the health of their communities.
                    Ch. 9, Ibid.

4 People in grassroots environmental organizations do not be-lieve that the environmental and public health threats they face are due to random placement of industrial complexes or waste-disposal facilities. Communities at risk believe their neighborhoods were targeted, chosen deliberately by corpo-rations to be sacrificed in the name of economic growth and profits. This is a movement which is as much about human rights and justice as it is about public health and the environ-ment.
                    Prologue, *Love Canal: The Story Continues 1998*

5 The crisis at Love Canal* awoke a nation, and to a lesser extent the world, to the hazards of toxic chemicals in our environ-ment.
                    Ibid.
    *Chemical dump site near Niagara Falls, N.Y., that became the nexus of a protest in 1978.

6 . . . I believe that ordinary citizens—using the tools of dignity, self-respect, common sense, and perseverance—can influence solutions to important problems in our society.
                    Ch. 1, Ibid.

4107. P. J. Gibson (1952–   )

1 If I live to be 150, I still won't have enough time to write about all the black women inside of me.
                    Quoted in *9 Plays by Black Women*, Margaret Wilkerson, ed. and intro. *1986*

4108. Lala Shovket Hajiyeva (1952–)

1 I don't accept the male-female division in politics. I support politicians of high moral standards.

> Quoted in "A Limited Legacy" by Konul Khalilova, *WIN (Women's International Net Magazine)*, Issue 32 (Part A) winmagazine.org *May 2000*

2 There are no eternal friends nor eternal enemies in life.

> Ibid.

4109. Beth Henley (1952–)

1 CHICK. They say each cigarette is just a little stick of cancer. A little death stick.
MEG. That's what I like about it, Chick—taking a drag off of death. Mmm! Gives me a sense of controlling my own destiny. What power! What exhilaration! Want a drag?

> Act I, *Crimes of the Heart 1979*

2 BABE. He started hating me, 'cause I couldn't laugh at his jokes. I just started finding it impossible to laugh at his jokes the way I used to. And then the sound of his voice got to where it tired me out awful bad to hear it. I'd fall asleep just listening to him at the dinner table.

> Ibid.

3 CARNELLE. I just don't know what you can, well, reasonably hope for in life.
MacSAM. There's always eternal grace.

> *The Miss Firecracker Contest 1980*

4 . . . I find it fascinating to think about what the world is going to be like when people won't talk anymore. There are probably brilliant people, geniuses, alive today who don't even know how to say, "Hello, how are you?" because their minds are absorbed with electronic images.

> "Beth Henley," *Interviews with Contemporary Women Playwrights*, Kathleen Betsko* and Rachel Koenig *1987*
> *See 3125.

5 And all writing is creating or spinning dreams for other people so they won't have to bother doing it themselves.

> Ibid.

4110. Jeannie Hinck (1952–)

1 Wayne Cryts* you're a farmer's hero
and long may your story be told
here's to your grit and your courage
worth more than all of their gold
That's worth more than all of their gold

> "The Wayne Cryts Song/The Battle of the Beans" (lyrics), Capetown Records *1982*
> *Farmer and leader of the militant American Agriculture Movement who led a daring raid on court protected property to retrieve 31,000-bushels of soybeans he'd grown.

2 Friends shall rally his freedom gathering strength and support
They faithfully tie yellow ribbons and symbols of similar sort

> "Political Prisoner" (lyrics), Ibid.

3 I hear the cries of the weak and the dying
Oh despair, oh despair
for the Whiteman had wanted our forests
They led us here, led us here
The Spirit Of Death is heavy among us
A Trail Of Tears, Trail Of Tears

> "A Trail of Tears," St. 3, U.S. Congressional Record *28 February 1989*

4111. Deborah Jacobs (1952–)

1 The library is about rugged independence. You can come in as an independent learner and learn anything. . . . *That's* what makes my heart pound. The doors are open. This is where you can grow.

> "Deborah the Librarian" by Paula Bock, *Seattle Times, Northwest Living 7 February 1999*

2 Libraries are the core of our community and our democracy. I believe if you have strong libraries, you have strong communities.

> Ibid.

3 When I was in library school, I used to think if I could help one child as a librarian, I'd forever affect the quality of life for everybody in the universe. I still think that.

> Ibid.

4 How can I defend the library to a Christian parent who doesn't like Madonna's "Sex" if I don't have a book for them on curing homosexuality or teaching sexuality in a Christian home?

> Ibid.

4112. Asma Jehangir (1952–)

1 There have to be principles, justice. Otherwise, we fall into a cycle of revenge.

> Quoted in "Asma Jahangir, The pocket protector," by Tim McGirk, *Time* (New York) *28 April 2003*

2 Leadership that brings peace is far more courageous than the one which opens fire and goes for war.

> Ibid.

4113. Anodea Judith (1952–)

1 To lose our connection with the body is to become spiritually homeless. Without an anchor we float aimlessly, battered by the winds and waves of life.

> Ch. 1, *Eastern Body, Western Mind 1996*

2 Human civilization, birthed from the primal world of nature, has matured from the infancy of cave dwellers, to the teeming toddlerhood of early civilizations, and endured the sibling rivalry of 5000 years of warring empires to emerge at the present time in the throes of adolescence, undergoing a rite of passage into the next age. Like initiatory rites of tribal cultures—where failure can indeed bring death—this passage will either destroy us or deliver us.

> Speech, "Bridge to the Future" (Irvine, CA), Planetary Healing Conference *18 October 2002*

3 To touch is to be in touch. To be in touch is to be aware and awake. To touch each other is to begin to break down the barriers that keep people apart, bound by the illusion of separation. It is nature's most basic way of healing. And it's very touching.

> Ibid.

4 The human drama is nearing its denouement. The great unveiling is approaching, a time when the power structures of the world begin to crumble and people of the heart sing out a new truth.

> Ch. 1, *Waking the Global Heart 2006*

5 The cultural transformation from the *love of power* to the *power of love* is the drama of our time.

> Ibid.

4114. Nancy Keenan (1952–)

1 I was raised Catholic and my faith is extremely important to me, but my position on choice has been—and remains to be—compelled by my conscience and my values, not by my church's policy.

"Strong Faith, Strong Choice," *The Huffington Post* 12 *September 2006*

2 The same woman who wants a president to address the difficulty of paying to put gas in the car while other bills pile up on the kitchen counter also wants a president who respects her ability to make the personal, private medical decisions that are best for her and her family.

"Mocking Women's Health and Losing Their Votes (with "Air Quotes")," *The Huffington Post* 16 October 2008

4115. Faye Kellerman (1952–)

1 Darkness in the woods was more than just lack of light; it was something tangible. It enveloped and smothered.

Ch. 10, *Stalker 2000*

2 We Americans seem to be obsessed with the brilliance of the devious criminal mind. In reality, most felons are just plain dumb.

Ibid.

3 Always been my downfall . . . underestimating the gray matter of women. That's why my ex has a new Mercedes and I'm driving a ten-year-old Plymouth.

Ch. 33, Ibid.

4116. Laurie R. King (1952–)

1 "Women are quite mad when it comes to hospitality."

Ch. 3, *The Moor 1998*

2 For several weeks over the summer I had lived with the fact that debts to the dead are heavier than those owed the living because there is no negotiation, no forgiveness, only the stark knowledge that failure can never be recompensed, that even success can only restore balance.

Ch. 9, Ibid.

3 It is an amazing thing, the difference to one's powers of concentration a pair of comfortable shoes can make.

Ch. 4, *O Jerusalem 1999*

4 "I am not a Christian, Abbot Mattias."
"God does not mind, my child. He was, after all, your God before He was ours."
"In that case I accept your blessing, with thanks."

Ch. 17, Ibid.

5 She is a jewel, that city [Jerusalem], small and brilliant and hard, and as dangerous as any valuable thing can be. . . . It was 401 years since the Turks took the city, 820 years since the Crusaders under Godfrey of Bouillon had slaughtered every Moslem and Jew within the walls (and a good number of unrecognised native Christians as well), eighteen and a half centuries since the Romans had last razed her stones to the ground, and still she rose up within her snug, high walls, a nest of stone set to nurture the holy places of three faiths . . .

Ch. 18, Ibid.

6 "Using insult instead of argument is the sign of a small mind . . ."

Ibid.

7 "And treachery being what it is, it is always the person closest to one's heart who can wield a dagger with impunity."

Ch. 20, Ibid.

8 . . . it's God's true blessing that we cannot see our future, because we'd never be able to bear it, if we had any warning.

Ch. 9, *A Darker Place 1999*

9 There were times when the expedient solution was not the right one, when only faith justified an action—educated and open-eyed faith if possible, but if that failed, blind faith would have to do.

Ch. 30, Ibid.

10 "Well, there's two kinds of trying. One is going after something with both hands, the other is just leaving the door open in case it decides to come after you."

Ch. 14, *Keeping Watch 2003*

11 "Violent men are made, not born. Abuse permeates their image of what it is to be an authority figure—what other role model do they have?"

Ch. 33, Ibid.

12 Travel broadens, they say. My personal experience has been that, in the short term at any rate, it merely flattens, aiming its steam-roller of deadlines and details straight at one's daily life, leaving a person flat and gasping at its passage.

Ch. 1, *The Game 2004*

13 "Pride is a sweetmeat, to be savoured in small pieces; it makes for a poor feast."

Ch. 26, Ibid.

4117. Elizabeth Lesser (1952–)

1 Seeing life from the heights of spiritual insight makes everything more *real*. It's not so much that anything changes; rather, things become more fully what they already are. We don't transform ourselves; we become ourselves. And the more fully we step into reality, the more we want to defend the life we have be given; we want to respect and protect each other and the earth itself—not because we *should,* but because we have finally seen life for what it truly is: a sacred gift.

The Seeker's Guide 1999

2 During times of transition, amid everyday stress, and even when we face seemingly insurmountable adversity, life offers us a choice: either to turn away from change or to embrace it; to shut down or to be broken open and transformed.

Broken Open: How Difficult Times Can Help Us Grow 2005

3 How strange that the nature of life is change, and yet the nature of human beings is to resist change. And how ironic that the difficult times we fear might ruin us, are the very ones that can break us open and help us blossom into who we were meant to be.

Ibid.

4 I have shut down to my soul enough times to know what it feels like when the river is dammed. I know the feeling of deadness; I know how the river diverts itself and breaks through in other ways—as a desire to blame, as an emotion of anger, as physical illness, as restlessness, or weariness, or as self-destruction. The soul always speaks, and sometimes it speaks the loudest when we block its flow, when we live only half of a life, when we stay on the surface.

Ibid.

5   Whenever there's about to be a big change in society, funda-
    mentalism arises to thwart the change. It seems to be almost
    a law of physics, that the winds of change awaken fear and
    fundamentalism.
        Interview with Marianne Schnall,* feminist.com 10 June 2008
        *See 4758.

6   Yoga, meditation, natural foods, acupuncture—things like
    these were seen as practically voodoo [thirty years ago]. And
    now you can go into any hospital and they'll have massage,
    and Chinese medicine, and therapy, and a prayer room.
                                                              Ibid.

7   To be spiritual is to be genuine in everything you say and do,
    come what may. That's the spiritual warrior—like I'm going to
    be in the truth of the moment. Without a spiritual connection,
    the social activist often tries to bend herself around the times,
    and the politics.
                                                              Ibid.

8   Life's always changing. We always are being called to adapt.
                                                              Ibid.

4118. Judith Levine (1952–   )

1   The task of misogyny, and of stereotyping women, is main-
    tenance. Men both magnify woman's threat and devalue her
    to justify keeping her under the boot. Women have a tougher
    lot: they want to lift the boot from their necks, or, failing that,
    make sense of the fact that they can't.
        "Naming the Enemy," My Enemy, My Love: Women,
        Masculinity, and the Dilemmas of Gender 1992

2   While cutting the taxes of the wealthiest Americans, politicians
    of both parties have whittled public support for the institutions
    that help and unite all citizens, such as schools and universities,
    libraries, mass transit, day care, and hospitals; the government
    has even gotten out of the "business" of running its own pris-
    ons.
        Introduction, Harmful to Minors: The Perils of Protecting
        Children from Sex, Jocelyn M. Elders,* coauthor 2003
        *See 2843.

3   When the sexual revolution collided with the boom in media
    technologies, media sex mushroomed.... Sexual imagery pro-
    liferated like dirty laundry: the minute you washed it and put it
    away, there was more.
                                        Ch. 1, "Censorship," Ibid.

4   As the economy moves from the Steel Belt to Silicon Valley, the
    boundary between the symbolic and the real is disappearing.
    Representation is no longer just a facsimile of a thing: it is the
    thing itself.
                                                              Ibid.

5   Since September 11, the consumer in chief* has been exhorting
    us to keep our chins up by keeping our wallets open.
        "December 2003: Panic," Not Buying It: My Year Without
                                                     Shopping 2006
        *George W. Bush (1946–   ), Am. politician; 43rd president of the
        United States (2001–09).

4119. Nancy Lord (1952–   )

1   People in traditional cultures consider time differently from
    those of us raised on Western standards, who learned to be
    "on time," not to waste time, and sometimes to "kill" time.

These concepts have no meaning in Native cultures, where
time just is.
                    (p. 14), Fishcamp: Life on an Alaskan Shore 1997

2   Tonight the moon, tugging quiet water down the inlet, has me
    in its hold. Millions of years after the ancestors of land dwell-
    ers first crawled ashore, my blood remains as salty as the sea. I
    am eighty percent water, and my cells bulge toward the moon.
                                                        (p. 87), Ibid.

3   I want people to know that salmon exist, as food and more
    than food. I fear less the future of individual fishermen, my-
    self included, than I do a future in which people don't know
    or care what a wild salmon requires, a future in which we
    don't do what we must to ensure that rives run clean and un-
    impeded, that oceans be nurseries instead of strip mines and
    dumps. Only when we provide for salmon will they provide
    for us—will we live in a world where it's possible to continue.
                                                       (p. 258), Ibid.

4   ... there's no picking out any one thing without finding it
    hitched to absolutely everything else.
                                                              Ibid.

4120–4121. Emily Mann (1952–   )

1   ANNULLA. If women would only start thinking, we could
    change the world.
        Annulla Allen: An Autobiography of a Survivor (play) 1977

2   There is a network of caring people in theater all over the
    country, and outside this country, who don't care about New
    York reviews, but rather, care about important voices.
        Quoted in Interviews with Contemporary Women Playwrights
                        by Kathleen Betsko* and Rachel Koenig 1987
        *See 3125.

4122. Gwendolyn Mink (1952–   )

1   ... poor single mothers [on welfare are compelled] to surren-
    der basic constitutional rights of associational freedom and
    reproductive privacy as a condition of receiving economic as-
    sistance.
                                                Welfare's End 1998

2   ... all caregiving is work, whatever the racial, marital or class
    status of the caregiver ...
                                                              Ibid.

3   Dependency—as in "the deep, dark pit of welfare depen-
    dency"*—is the dirtiest word in the United States today.
    Choice—as in the choice to get an abortion—is not so gener-
    ally reviled as dependency, though it does spark more violent
    controversy. These two words—these groaningly laden con-
    cepts—dependency and choice—may be the two most powerful
    abstractions governing women's lives in the United States.
                                           Ch. 1, Whose Welfare? 1999
        *Quoting Orrin Hatch (1934–   ), U. S. senator (R-Utah; 1977–   ),
        from "Women in Transition" hearing before the Committee on
        Labor and Human Resources (8 November 1983).

4   When the law's putative champions deprive even one sexually
    harassed woman of its protections, they betray all sexually
    harassed women. When they redefine the law to exclude even
    one woman's injury, they betray feminism's signal legal accom-
    plishment and compromise its future.
        Ch. 1, Hostile Environment: The Political Betrayal of Sexually
                                                Harassed Women 2000

4123. Mayra Montero (1952–)

1 Each day in the batey* Papa Luc learned something different. And that night he had learned that great secrets did not exist in the lives of men, only small snares waiting at each step, the bait lying right there on the ground.

The Red of His Shadow 1996

*A native Caribbean plaza.

2 My mother always said you had to look at life as if it were the suspicious start of a crime: tying up loose ends, finding clues, following the trail coldly, as if it didn't even concern you.

p. 20, *In the Palm of Darkness,* Edith Grossman, tr. *1997*

3 What you love, he said, you must respect, and the principle of all love is memory.

p. 74, Ibid.

4 . . . signs create and rule, what is not marked is not sacred.

pp. 127–128, Ibid.

5 A man repeats all his roads, he repeats them without realizing it, his illusion is that they're new.

pp. 180–181, Ibid.

6 The city had an imaginary face, more or less its everyday face, with clerks leaving offices, people going into stores, crowded movies, and another hidden face, the face of landings, secret transmissions, homemade bombs, and disfigured corpses on the sidewalks. Between the imaginary face and the hidden face was shifting ground, insidious quicksand that swallowed up everything.

Dancing to "Alemendra," Edith Grossman, tr. *2007*

7 A madman with information is a hand grenade: pull the pin and you can explode along with him.

Ibid.

8 Lucy was his third son packed into a robust female body. A misfortune like any other.

Ch. 1, Ibid.

4124. Patricia A. Moore (1952–)

1 In small towns . . . There isn't the infrastructure of services for elders that you find in cities. I could walk for six blocks without being able to find a restroom.* Rural elders are suffering.

Quoted in "Undercover Among the Elderly" by Michael Ryan, *Parade Magazine 18 July 1993*

*Reference to three years traveling to 116 big cities and small towns disguised as an elderly woman.

2 We have made the point, very subtly, in our society that when you age, somehow you're not as good as you were. We need to understand aging is a natural, evolutionary process. Why is younger necessarily better? We have to learn to age well in our hearts.

Ibid.

4125. Cherríe Moraga (1952–)

1 A theory of the flesh means one where the physical realities of our lives—our skin color, the land or concrete we grew up on, our sexual longings—all fuse to create a politic born out of necessity. Here we attempt to bridge the contradictions in our experience:
      We are the colored in a white feminist movement.
      We are the feminists among the people of our culture.
      We are often the lesbians among the straight.

We do this bridging by naming our selves and by telling stories in our own words.

Introduction, *This Bridge Called My Back: Writings by Radical Women of Color,* co-author, Gloria Anzaldúa* *1984*
*See 3321.

2 In this country, lesbianism is a poverty—as is being brown, as is being a woman, as is being just plain poor. The danger lies in ranking the oppressions.

"La Güera," Ibid.

3 The real power, as you and I well know, is collective. I can't afford to be afraid of you, nor you of me. If it takes head-on collisions, let's do it: this polite timidity is killing us.

Ibid.

4 Smell is very important. Your eyes can fool you. You can see things that aren't there. But not smell. Smell remembers and tells the future. No lying about that.
      Smell can make your heart crack open no matter how many locks you have wrapped 'round it.

"La Ofrenda," *OUT/LOOK* No. 10 *Fall 1990*

5 But being a sister ain't no part-time occupation.

Ibid.

6 It is the intimacy of steel melting
into steel, the fire of our individual
passion to take hold of ourselves
that makes sculpture of our lives,
builds buildings.

"The Welder," St. 5, *The Woman That I Am, The Literature and Culture of Contemporary Women of Color,* D. Soyini Madison,* ed. *1994*
*See 3912.

4126. Caroline M. Myss (1952–)

1 We do indeed weave our spirits into the events and relationships of our lives. Life is as simple as that.

Introduction, *Anatomy of the Spirit: The Seven Stages of Power and Healing 1996*

2 Power is at the root of the human experience. Our attitudes and belief patterns, whether positive or negative, are all extensions of how we define, use, or do not use power. Not one of us is free from power issues. . . . Our relationship to power is at the core of our health.

Pt. I, Ch. 1, Ibid.

3 The truths contained in the scriptural teachings of the different religious traditions are meant to unite us, not separate us. Literal interpretation creates separation, whereas symbolic interpretation—seeing that all of them address the identical design of our spiritual natures—brings us together.

Ch. 2, Ibid.

4 All spiritual teachings are directed toward inspiring us to recognize that the power to make choices is the dynamic that converts our spirits into matter, our words into flesh. Choice is the process of creation itself.

Pt. II, Ch. 2, Ibid.

5 Prostitution of one's energy is a more common violation than is physical prostitution, for countless women and men remain in situations that represent physical security while feeling that they are selling a part of themselves in the process.

Ibid.

6   The belief that God blesses those who strive to do good by giving them financial rewards is extremely prevalent, as is the belief that helping others out financially through charity serves to ensure that we ourselves will be protected from poverty. These and many other beliefs of the same genre reflect the grander notion that God communicates with us through our finances and, conversely, that we communicate with God by our financial actions.

> Ibid.

4127. Jill Nelson (1952–   )

1   There is between black women a language all our own, sometimes spoken, oftentimes not. We communicate with each other through a tilt of the head, a quick cutting of eyes, a heartfelt exhalation of breath, a quiet sucking of teeth, a fleeting smile that can transform the tenor of a bad day.

It is a feminine, coded, unwritten language. It is complex in its simplicity. Black women's language grows out of our particular experience of oppression because of our race and our gender.

> *How I Became a Grown-Up Black Woman 1977*

2   I used to try to escape from my rage in notions of love, sex, orgasm, but my rage's appetite has become more specific. Now, it can only be satisfied by action, and not the pelvic kind.

> Ibid.

3   Two white males running the Metropolitan desk in a 70-percent-black city that is also the nation's capital are probably in a constant state of intrigue. Mostly involving how to parlay that job into a better, whiter one.

> Ch. 1, *Volunteer Slavery: My Authentic Negro Experience 1993*

4   Having given up the cornerstone of my coming-of-age and become a journalist, but still in possession of an addictive personality, I simply found another drug of choice: I mainlined information.

> "Fighting the Right," *The Women's Review of Books*, Vol. XII, Nos.10–11 *July 1995*

5   We would swim all day, stand holding hands in the surf and dare the waves to tumble us, happy when they did. We pulled our knees up to our chests, held our breath, and went under, the only sound that of the water roaring and crashing around us, the curl of the wave stirring up sand and pebbles that bombarded our bodies until the wave finished breaking and we could stumble to our feet, laughing and looking around to make sure everybody was okay, quickly grabbing someone's hand and holding tight before the next wave came.

> "What We Found Here," *Finding Martha's Vineyard: African Americans at Home on an Island 2005*

4128. Martha Nelson (1952–   )

1   It's amazing to run one of the most influential magazines in the world, with one of the broadest readerships and the greatest breadth of subject matter that you will encounter. The mix of the entertainment-industry and celebrity news, combined with hard news and human interest, basically means that every topic I am interested in I can find a way to cover in *People*.

> "So What Do You Do, Martha Nelson?" by Jennifer Baker, mediabistro.com *19 August 2003*

2   We certainly see and hear a lot of stuff out there based on rumors, and we have a lot of reporters allowing us to hear every kind of news and non-news, but in the end, we don't run on rumor. We run on fact.

> Ibid.

4129. Charity Kaluki Ngilu (1952–   )

1   He is a leader of darkness and death. . . . You can see his cowardice. Moi* is playing a game alone. He is player and referee.

> Quoted in "Kenya's First Woman President?" by Andrea Useem, *Ms. November/December 1997*

*Re Daniel Arap Moi, Kenyan politician (1924–   ), president of Kenya (1978–   ).

2   I had to carry water on my back, and my daughter will have to do the same.

> *The New York Times* interview, Quoted by Andrea Useem in "Kenya's First Woman President?," Ibid.

3   For how long are the other nations of the world going to fear America? Maybe this is the person who the world has been waiting for, to bridge the gap.

> Quoted in "Kenyan Politicians to America: Don't Be Afraid of Obama" by Andrew Rice, *The New York Observer 28 August 2008*

*Barack Obama (1961–   ), 44th president of the United States.

4   It's so interesting to see how democracy has evolved in America. It's very mature, it's peaceful and they are mostly talking about the issues.

> Ibid.

4130. Naomi Sihab Nye (1952–   )

1   "How do you know if you are going to die?"
I begged my mother.
We had been traveling for days.
With strange confidence she answered,
"When you can no longer make a fist."

> "Making a Fist," St. 2, *Words Under the Words: Selected Poems 1995*

2   Love means you breathe in two countries.

> "Two Countries," St. 2, Ibid.

3   I drive into the country to find sheep, cows,
to plead with the air:
Who calls anyone civilized?
Where can the crying heart graze?
What does a true Arab do now?

> "Blood," St. 5, *19 Varieties of Gazelle: Poems of the Middle East 2002*

4131. Suze Orman (1952–   )

1   . . . it takes courage to be rich. Why? Because choosing wealth as a goal requires facing everything about your money bravely, honestly, with courage—which is a very, very hard thing for most of us to do. But it can be done.

> *The Courage to Be Rich 1999*

2   Money doesn't bring courage, I learned. It's the other way around. Once I took that lesson to heart, I began to rebuild my life.

> Ibid.

3   Power attracts money; powerlessness repels it.

> Speech (Seattle), Women of Power Conference *6 April 2000*

4 Broke is not having one penny saved, even though you have a good job. If your car breaks down, so will you. You don't have the money for repairs, but you need the wheels to get to work.
The Money Book for the Young, Fabulous & Broke 2007

4132. Brenda Petersen (1952–)

1 The wolf is anything but lonely as he or she raises a shaggy head to howl; and yet our myths have imprisoned this creature into a symbol of isolation and separation. I suggest that it is we who are lonely, not the wolves—we who have hunted the wolf to extinction so that it is a very rare few of us who have ever even heard the call of the wolf in the wild.
"Wolves, wild women and wild men," *Seattle Times*, A17 20 *December 1992*

2 When we recognized that our fate was directly linked to the land, trees were holy.
"Killing Our Elders," *Finding Home* (quarterly) *n.d.*

3 Old trees like old people survive the ravages of middle-age competition for light, or limelight; they give back to their generations more oxygen, more stories; they are tall and far-sighted enough to see the future because they are so firmly rooted in the past. Old-growth trees or persons are nurturers; the young saplings planted to replace them need nurturing.
Ibid.

4133. Jayne Anne Phillips (1952–)

1 People don't always understand how babies can be a help, why seemingly beleaguered women might want another child, and another. If they can have them, if they can nurse them through what was once called childbed, and raise them. People forget, even women forget, how mothers fall in love with their babies.
"Callie," *Fast Lanes 1987*

2 Her milk let down with a flush and surge, and she held a clean diaper to one breast as she put him to the other. Now she breathed, exhaling slowly. The intense pain began to ebb; he drank the cells of her blood, Kate knew, and the crust that formed on her nipples where the cuts were deep-est. He was her blood. When she held him he was inside her; always, he was near her, like an atmosphere, in his sleep, in his being. She would not be alone again for many years, even if she wanted to, even if she tried. In her deepest thoughts, she would approach him, move around and through him, make room for him. In nursing there would be a still, spiral peace, an energy in which she felt herself, her needs and wants, slough away like useless debris. It seemed less im-portant to talk or think; like a nesting animal, she took on camouflage, layers of protective awareness that were almost spatial in dimension.
Ch. 2, *MotherKind 2000*

3 Fear and anger turn in his gut like a yin-yang eel, slippery and fishlike but dimly human in its blunt, circular probing, turning and turning, no rest.
Lark & Termite 2008

4 He commands a platoon now and he sees that war never ends; it's all one war despite players or location, war that sleeps dormant for years or months, then erupts and lifts its flaming head to find regimes changed, topography altered, weapons recast.
Ibid.

5 I think it's heroic to become a writer. Writers are the vanguard of the reading public.
Quoted in "The Writing Life" by Susan Salter Reynolds, *The Los Angeles Times 11 January 2009*

4134. Claudia Roth Pierpont (1952–)

1 Sex was her subject, not her effect.*
Passionate Minds, Women Rewriting the World 2000
*Re Mae West; see 1790.

2 In the course of a long and proud career, an intrepid explorer turned herself into a perfect lady.*
Ibid.
*Re Eudora Welty; see 2117.

3 The real and bottomless subject of Nin's diary* is not sex, or the flowering of womanhood, but deceit.
Ibid.
*Re Anais Nin; see 1979.

4 [*We the Living** is] a triumph of English as a second language, if not of English itself.
Ibid.
*Novel by Ayn Rand; see 2032.

4135. Christine A. Poon (1952–)

1 I ask a lot of questions. I have tried to restrain myself and to learn through the years that telling people is not as effective as asking. By asking you get a lot more out of folks. It's cer-tainly less threatening. But more important, I think it brings out ideas, and it begs other questions. From a leadership style, I probably do more questioning than telling. Although, some people will say that by my questions, I'm telling them.
Quoted in "Standing Out, Fitting In" by Elaine Paoloni, *Pharmaceutical Executive Magazine 1 April 2004*

2 Diversity isn't just because you are Asian or African-American, because you are a woman or a man. It's the individuality and the differences that you bring, the perspectives you bring to the job that is really the essence of diversity.
Ibid.

3 I loved the idea of science advancing healthcare and being able to cure many of the diseases that 50 years ago we took for granted people would die from.
Ibid.

4136. Anna Quindlen (1952–)

1 There are currently as many Americans in jail as in New Hamp-shire, but we have no coherent idea of the point of crime and punishment in our society. Rehabilitation? Interesting ideal, no reality. Deterrence? The recidivism rate and swelling prison population suggest otherwise.
Simple punishment? In an age of serial stranglings, serial cannibalism and serial pedophilia it becomes increasingly dif-ficult to figure out the appropriate punishment for tax evasion or even for a single crime of passion . . .
"Jean Harris* gives new meaning to 'doing time,'" *The New York Times 12 March 1992*
*See 2548.

2 Shell-shocked by horrors, we want the bars and the locks, never thinking about spending wisely and well. We invest a fortune on a college for criminals, where people learn they are

subhuman and act accordingly, a system called corrections that doesn't correct.

Ibid.

3   The child welfare system in this country is driven by . . . the ideal that biological is always better . . . and, because of it we are victimizing thousands of children who wait in foster homes and group homes and treatment centers for parents who, like Godot, somehow never come. We demand that young children sacrifice for the sake of their parents. It's supposed to be the other way around.

"Biological might not be better," *The New York Times*
1 October 1992

4   Testosterone does not have to be toxic.
"Bad guys give good bad name," *The New York Times*
13 April 1993

5   Stereotypes fall in the face of humanity.
"We human beings are best understood one at a time,"
The New York Times 30 April 1993

6   But a veneer of tolerance atop a deep pool of hatred, distrust and estrangement is no more than a shiny surface, as civil rights leaders can testify from decades of experience.

Ibid.

7   But nothing important, or meaningful, or beautiful, or interesting, or great ever came out of imitations. The thing that is really hard, and really amazing, is giving up on being perfect and beginning the work of becoming yourself. More difficult, because there is no zeitgeist to read, no template to follow, no masks to wear.

Commencement speech, Mount Holyoke College *23 May 1999*

8   Look inside. That way lays dancing to the melodies spun out by your own heart. This is a symphony. All the rest are jingles.

Ibid.

9   . . . the straight and narrow path that often leads absolutely nowhere.

Ibid.

10 One sentence and I can hear his voice in my head, that butterscotch-syrup voice that made goose bumps rise on my arms when I was young, that turned all of my skin warm and alive with a sibilant *S*, the drawling vowels, its shocking fricatives. It always sounded like a whisper, the way he talked, the intimacy of it, the way the words seemed to go into your guts, your head, your heart. "Jeez, Bob," one of the guys would say, "you should have been a radio announcer. You should have done those voice-over things for commercials." It was like a genie, wafting purple and smoke from the lamp, Bobby's voice, or perfume when you took the glass stopper out of the bottle.

Black and Blue 1998

11 How huge was his rage. It was like a twister cloud; it rose suddenly from nothing into a moving thing that blew the roof off, black and strong.

Ibid.

12 I have a warm personal relationship with God; I often picture her smiling wryly and saying, in the words of Shakespeare's Puck, "Lord, what fools these mortals be!"*

Newsweek 8 July 2001
*Re the Pledge of Allegiance legal controversy over the "under God" clause.

13 If the job of a good reporter is, as H. L. Mencken* once said, "to afflict the comfortable and comfort the afflicted," then you can easily do both at once by writing about how tough society can be on its youngest members.

Ch. 1, *Loud and Clear 2004*
*(1880–1956) American editor and critic; a founder and editor (1924–33) of the *American Mercury*.

4137. Deborah L. Rhode (1952–   )

1   The bar's ethical code miscasts professional self-interests as moral necessities.

"Ethical Perspectives on Legal Practice," *37 Stanford Law Review 589 January 1985*

2   Lawyers like to leave no stone unturned, provided they can charge by the stone.

Ibid.

3   We fail to see sexual abuse as a strategy of dominance and exclusion—a way of keeping women in their places and out of men's.

"Harassment Is Alive and Well and Living at the Water Cooler," *Ms.* (New York) *November/December 1997*

4   When men harass, it should not be women's characters that are on trial.

Ibid.

5   Americans dislike the fact that legal access is for sale, but they also dislike efforts to remedy it. Justice is what we proclaim on courthouse entrances, not in redistributed policies. As a result, most Americans end up with all—and only—the justice money can buy.

Professional Responsibility: Ethics by the Pervasive Method 1998

6   We have disputes that are too big for the courts, disputes that are too small, and disputes that should not have been disputes at all.

Ibid.

4138. Rebecca Roe (1952–   )

1   If a guy gets hit over the head on the street and reports it, he's looking for justice. If a woman gets raped or assaulted and reports it, then she's looking for vengeance.

Quoted in "On A Crusade" by Linda Keene, *Seattle Times,* Pacific Northwest section *26 July 1992*

2   If you're a male prosecutor and you're strong and assertive, you're seeking justice. If you're a woman and you're strong and assertive, you're seeking vengeance.

Ibid.

4139. Susan Seidelman (1952–   )

1   Failure is a luxury not yet afforded to women.

Quoted in "Calling Their Own Shots" by Richard Corliss, *Time 24 March 1986*

4140. Venda Sendzimir (1952–1996)

1   I loved and hated him, admired and resented him. In my most bitter moments I would explain to my friends that "my father's

real children are his inventions. My brothers and I are just his biological children."

"My Father* the Inventor," *American Heritage*, vol. 11, no. 3
Fall 1995

*Tadeusz Sendzimir (1894–1989), Pol./Am. engineer, inventor.

2 Independent inventive geniuses are getting scarce. Creative young minds are swallowed up by corporate research laboratories, while lone inventors struggle in obscurity or fold for lack of capital or stamina.

Ibid.

3 In the United States more than 40,000 people every year lose their lives in highway accidents. The toll in the skies is a tiny fraction of that figure. But airline passengers perish dramatically, in large numbers all at once, and these figures give aviation accidents a grim fascination that icy roads, drunk drivers, and sleepers at the wheel lack. We want to know what happened and whether it could happen to us. The "black box" was invented to answer those questions.

"Black Box," Ibid. vol. 12, issue 2 *Fall 1996*

4141. Vandana Shiva (1952–   )

1 It is the combination of the urge for free enquiry and my concern for nature and people, that made me leave the narrow confines of academia where disciplines are fragmented from each other, where knowledge is separated from action but linked intimately to power.

Acceptance Speech, Right Livelihood Awards (Stockholm) *9 December 1993*

2 Monocultures first inhabit the mind, and are then transferred to the ground. Monocultures of the mind generate models of production which destroy diversity and legitimise that destruction as progress, growth and improvement. From the perspective of the monoculture mind, productivity and yields appear to increase when diversity is erased and replaced by uniformity. However, from the perspective of diversity, monocultures are based on a decline in yields and productivity. They are impoverished systems, both qualitatively and quantitatively. They are also highly unstable and non-sustainable systems. Monocultures spread not because they produce more, but because they control more.

Ibid.

3 The seed too is small. It embodies diversity. It embodies the freedom to stay alive. And seed is still the common property of small farmers in India. Seed freedom goes far beyond freedom for the farmer from corporations. It indicates freedom of diverse cultures from centralised control.

Ibid.

4 Democracy begins with freedom from hunger, freedom from unemployment, freedom from fear, and freedom from hatred.

Quoted in "In the Footsteps of Ghandi," interview by Scott London, *Insight & Outlook* (radio) *February 1998*

5 We will rebuild society, we will rebuild local economies, we will rebuild human aspirations.

Ibid.

6 Humanity seems to be in a free fall towards disaster. The ecological fabric of our existence is being torn apart, as the violence of corporate globalisation combines with the violence of war.

"Paradigm Shift," *Resurgence*, #214 *September/October 2002*

7 'Development' had become the fig leaf for the fading promise of free trade.

"In the Name of Development," *Resurgence*, #236 *May/June 2006*

8 Industrialization is desacralization. Industrialization is a project of hubris which basically assumes that there is nothing like life processes, nature doesn't have its self-organizing capacities, people don't have their self-organizing capacities, women have no potential, they are merely the second sex, Third World peasants have no brains, therefore intellectual properties are in the industrialized North. All of these arrogant assumptions come out of a denial of reverence for life and the lack of recognition of that which makes life possible.

"Vandana Shiva In Her Own Words," interviewed by Paolo Scopacasa, EcoWorld.com *6 March 2004*

9 And another means for stealing the harvest from the people and from nature is this amazing invention of calling life itself an invention, the patenting of life.

Ibid.

10 Soil is my teacher, seeds are my teacher, nature is my teacher.

Ibid.

11 I defend the farmers' dignity and their right to survival, because for me peasants are the most creative and productive individuals on this planet, not the people who gamble on Wall Street and make billions overnight. I think the real wealth is created on the land by people who soil their hands, by people who work in cooperation with nature and give us the nourishment we need as humans.

Ibid.

12 Earth Democracy connects people in circles of care, cooperation, and compassion instead of dividing them through competition and conflict, fear and hatred.

Earth Democracy; Justice, Sustainability, and Peace 2005

4142. Champa Devi Shukla (1952–   )

1 Hindus and Muslims don't face different problems. On a fundamental level, they suffer equally regardless of religion.

Quoted in "Beating Dow with a Broomstick" by Sarita Sarvate, *India Currents 13 July 2004*

2 We have been fighting for many years now.* Every day more and more people are lending support to our struggle. We are sure that we will soon have the support we need to bring Dow to its knees.

goldmanprize.org *2004*
*Re 1984 Union Carbide gas leak that killed more than 20,000 people in Bhopal, India.

4143. Janna Malamud Smith (1952–   )

1 Publicly humiliating anyone for consensual adultery is draconian, and wrong. It teaches children cynicism. What they see is how little respect there is for privacy, and how gratuitously and harshly adults will harm one another to gain a little power . . .

You might say that how and why we disapprove of adultery is as important as whether we do.

"National politics: Debasing weapons fired in adultery wars," Op-Ed Page, *Seattle Post-Intelligencer 22 December 1998*

2 Child love makes mothers vulnerable, raises all stakes, and defines much about how we live—and have lived—in the world.

Ch. 1, *A Potent Spell: Mother Love and the Power of Fear 2003*

3 Mothers are contradictions: we are individuals, and yet we also function as the nerve-linked command centers of interdependent groups.

Ibid.

4144. Phoebe Snow (1952–)

1 I'd like to be a willow, a lover, a mountain
Or a soft refrain
But I'd hate to be a grown-up
And have to try to bear
My life in pain.

"Harpo's Blues," *Phoebe Snow* 1973

2 Sometimes this face looks so funny
That I hide it behind a book
Sometimes this face has so much class
That I have to sneak a second look.

"Either or Both," Ibid.

3 It must be Sunday
Everybody's telling the truth. . . .

"It Must Be Sunday," Ibid.

4145. Banu Subramaniam (1952–)

1 I grew to understand scientific culture as a set of practices and behaviors bound by the historical roots of science in Western, anglo, male, heterosexual culture. Graduate school was a gateway to these credentials and was about policing these boundaries—the weeding out of those who cannot and will not participate in these cultural practices.

"A contradiction in terms," *The Women's Review of Books,*
Vol. XV, No. 5 February 1998

2 A feminist scientist, not one who merely believes in women's rights, but one who wishes her science to be informed by feminism, is a contradiction in terms.

Ibid.

3 If the sciences have developed as a world without women, then women's studies, it would seem, has developed as a world without the sciences.

Ibid.

4 And yet it would seem that through years of institutionalization, women's studies finds itself just another discipline, with its own center, culture and practices, policing its own boundaries of sacred scholarship. As our theories grow, as our jargons multiply, we find at our disposal an ever more sophisticated vocabulary to lull us back into the self-serving, self-fulfilling world of the academy.

Ibid.

4146. Amy Tan (1952–)

1 To despair was to wish back for something already lost. Or to prolong what was already unbearable.

The Joy Luck Club 1989

2 "If she had as much talent as she has temper, she would be famous now."

"Two Kinds," Ibid.

3 "Only two kind of daughters," she shouted in Chinese. "Those who are obedient and those who follow their own mind!

Only one kind of daughter can live in this house. Obedient daughter!"

"Then I wish I wasn't your daughter. I wish you weren't my mother," I shouted. As I said these things I got scared. I felt

like worms and toads and slimy things were crawling out of my chest, but it also felt good, as if this awful side of me had surfaced, at last.

"Too late change this," said my mother shrilly.

Ibid.

4 We had hot and cold running servants.

The Kitchen God's Wife 1992

5 Mom calls herself "American mixed grill, a bit of everything white, fatty, and fried."

"The Girl With Yin Eyes," *The Hundred Secret Senses* 1995

6 The air I had breathed, I now knew, was composed not of gases but of the density and perfume of emotions. The body had been merely a filter, a censor. I knew this at once, without question, and I found myself released, free to feel and do whatever I pleased. That was the advantage of being dead: no fear of future consequences. Or so I thought.

"A Brief History of My Shortened Life," *Saving Fish from
Drowning* 2005

4147. T. Minh-Ha Trinh (1952–)

1 I write to show myself showing people who show me my own showing.

Woman, Native, Other 1989

2 Every griotte* who dies is a whole library that burns down.

"Grandma's Story," Ibid.
*French term for storyteller, often used in place of African "traditionalist."

3 Diseuse, Thought-Woman, Spider-Woman, griotte, storytalker, fortune-teller, witch. If you have the patience to listen, she will take delight in relating it to you. An entire history, an entire vision of the world, a lifetime story. . . . The world's earliest archives or libraries were the memories of women.

Ibid.

4 Speech is the materialization, externalization, and internalization of the vibrations of forces.

Ibid.

5 Whether a house is lively or not depends on the way it breathes.

"*Naked Spaces—Living is Round*" (screenplay, 1985), *Framer
Framed: Film Scripts and Interviews* 1992

6 A body resonates to music as does a string.

Ibid.

7 The civilized mind qualifies many of the realities it does not understand as untrue, superstitious, supernatural.

Ibid.

8 With digital systems taking part in our everyday thought and work, and with the advent of virtual reality, we are witnessing a profound reality shift, one that radically impacts upon the foundations of our knowledge, and upon our perception of the world.

"Still Speed," Elizabeth Dungan, coauthor, *The Digital Film
Even* 2005

4148. Theodora van den Beld (1952–)

1 The only thing you can control is your own effort.

Quoted in "Food Talk" by Lynn Steinberg, *Seattle Post-
Intelligencer,* C1 3 February 1999

2   A house has to have soul, just like a restaurant has to have soul. How you get it is hard to explain. It has to have someone with passion behind it.

> Ibid.

4149. Michelle Wallace (1952–   )

1   On April 4 King* was shot and the rioting began again, worse than ever. Praying, waiting, singing, and everything white were out. Rioting was viewed as urban guerrilla warfare, the first step toward the complete overthrow of the honky, racist government. On the cultural level everything had to be rehauled. Black poems, plays, paintings, novels, hairstyles, and apparel were springing up like weeds in Central Park. Brothers, with softly beating drums in the background, were talking about beautiful black Queens of the Nile and beautiful full lips and black skin and big asses.

> Pt. I, Ch. 1, *Black Macho and The Myth of the Superwoman* 1978

*Martin Luther King, Jr., American civil rights leader and minister (1929–68); Nobel Peace Prize (1964); assassinated.

2   The driving force behind the [Black Power] movement had really very little to do with bread and butter needs. The motive was revenge. It was not equality that was primarily being pursued but a kind of superiority—black manhood, black macho
        . . . And when the black man went as far as the adoration of his own genitals could carry him, his revolution stopped. A big Afro, a rifle, and a penis in good working order were not enough to lick the white man's world after all.

> Ch. 2, Ibid.

3   From the intricate web of mythology which surrounds the black woman, a fundamental image emerges. It is of a woman of inordinate strength, with an ability for tolerating an unusual amount of misery and heavy, distasteful work. This woman does not have the same fears, weaknesses, and insecurities as other women, but believes herself to be and is, in fact, stronger emotionally than most men. Less of a woman in that she is less "feminine" and helpless, she is really more of a woman in that she is the embodiment of Mother Earth, the quintessential mother with infinite sexual, life-giving, and nurturing reserves. In other words, she is a superwoman.

> Pt. II, Ch. 1, Ibid.

4150. Rebecca Wells (1952–   )

1   I am her mother, though, and it is my job to teach her that you cannot escape from life. Life is not a book. You can't just set it down on the coffee table and walk away from it when it gets boring or you get tired.

> "Bookworms," *Little Altars Everywhere* 1992

2   "It be good to know your children done turn out sweet. It make ever'thing less bitter. It be one of the savin things."

> "Playboys' Scrapbook," Ibid.

3   "That is just the way life happen. We done lived down the road from sadness all our lives. But you gotta know what sadness be yours and what be somebody else's, is what I say."

> Ibid.

4   "Something just cracked in Vivi. Maybe people are more like the earth than we now. Maybe they have fault lines that sooner or later are going to split open under pressure."

> Ch. 27, *Divine Secrets of the Ya-Ya Sisterhood* 1996

5   It was the biggest parking lot I'd ever seen. I had to blink and rub my eyes; I was disoriented to see stores and pavement where all my life there had been nothing but cotton. I'd never seen a field disappear before. I didn't know such a thing could happen. I thought a field was forever. At that age I thought that everything was forever.

> Ch. 29, Ibid.

4151. Marianne Williamson (1952–   )

1   God is definitely out of the closet.

> Quoted in *Vanity Fair* (New York) *June 1991*

2   Physical incarnation is highly overrated; it is one corner of universal possibility.

> Ibid.

3   Our deepest fear is not that we are inadequate. Our deepest fear is that we are powerful beyond measure. It is our light, not our darkness that most frightens us.

> *A Return to Love: Reflections on the Principles of a Course in Miracles* 1996

4   The love so many of us would like to see injected into the veins of civilization must first pour into us. Society will not transform until we transform; what's wrong "out there" is but a mere reflection of what's wrong "in here". This is liberating news if we see it that way. Once we recognize that our minds are the causal level of worldly events, then we are free to seek to change the world by changing our thoughts about the world.

> *Healing the Soul of America* 2000

4152. Brenda Wineapple (1952?–   )

1   The feminist icon need not, after all, be a feminist herself.

> "Gertrude Stein* reads JAMA," *Journal of the American Medical Association,* 276:1132 1996

*See 1450.

4153. Jeana L. Yeager (1952–   )

1   Dick* [flew] the airplane and I flew him. . . . We were really one pilot. We became an extension of one another, complementing each other.

> Quoted in *Women Aviators* by Lisa Yount 1995

*Dick Rutan, highly decorated air force pilot. Reference to their 10-day journey around the world in *Voyager,* the first aircraft to make the trip without stopping and without refueling.

2   [Running gave me] a feeling of sharing the beauty and strength of horses and the ease with which they flew across the land.

> Ibid.

4154. Talat Abbasi (1953?–   )

1   It's the eyes of course under those fantastic long eyelashes they were all set to coo over. They're not blind eyes seeing nothing. They're seeing as well as you and I but what they're seeing is nothing you and I can understand. That much they tell you as they confront you in one long unblinking stare before they go back to darting constantly, nervously, from left to right and back again, never at rest.

> "Mirage," *Bitter Gourd and Other Stories* 2001

2   Cooped up with the hyperactive frustrated boy in the bare two-room apartment. I lined the floor with mattresses, quilts

and foam after receiving warnings from the landlord about the neighbours complaining of "a herd at least of thumping, marauding elephants up there." They too were wrong of course. No threatening elephants. Just a small exquisite bird trapped in the room, flying in panic from wall to wall, hurling itself against them, hurting only itself, incapable of harming others. Watched in silence by the mother.

Ibid.

3   "I'm wanting to know just what good all this reading and writing which I'm hearing about will do. Will it get her a husband I'm wanting to know. Will it get her a male child I'm wanting to know. Will it even get her a dowry I'm wanting to know."

"Simple Questions," Ibid.

4155. Penina V. Adelman (1953–   )

1   I've always thought that the wombs of women form a secret, silent network of communication all over the world.

Torah Study, *Miriam's* Well: Rituals for Jewish Women Around the Year 1986*

*See 16.

2   If I can't give birth to a live human being, I can give birth to the ideas and struggles within me.

"Ballad of Hannah,"* 2, St. 3, Ibid.

*See 30.

3   Ritual places personal experience in the public realm where it may be witnessed, dealt with, and shared.

"The Womb and the Word: A Fertility Ritual for Hannah," *Four Centuries of Jewish Women's Spirituality* Ellen M. Umansky* & Dianne Ashton, eds. *1992*

*See 4011.

4156. Lori B. Andrews (1953–   )

1   We're approaching space-age technology with Model-T statutes and cases.*

The New York Times 27 June 1984

*Describing infertility cases and the law.

2   This was why the law had not kept up with the changes in reproductive medicine. If a lawyer from a hundred years ago were set down in a modern courtroom, he—and, of course, it would be a *he*—would feel completely at home. But if a doctor from the 1800s were to find himself among . . . liquid nitrogen tanks, laparoscopy equipment, and ultrasound, he wouldn't have the foggiest idea of what to do.

Ch. 1, *The Clone Age: Adventures in the New World of Reproductive Technology 1999*

3   The law addresses any new question by relying on precedent. When cars were introduced, the wisdom from cases dealing with horses and buggies governed. But . . . it was difficult to find precedents to deal with human embryos. Were they property or people? Where could we turn to learn if they could be frozen—or "enhanced" through genetic manipulation?

Ibid.

4   Genetic technologies could be applied in attempts to create "perfect" people. But moving in that direction entails such high psychological and social costs that the society we would be creating would be far from perfect.

Ch. 1, *Future Perfect 2001*

4157. Zainah Anwar (1953?–   )

1   It pains me that our religious leaders and Islamist activists, while bemoaning Islamophobia, and declaring that Islam is a religion of peace and tolerance, themselves utter statements that just feed the prejudices of others against Islam and Muslims.

"Making taboo a cherished tradition," *New Straits Times 16 June 2006*

2   Why should we continue to be discriminated against by a government that is committed to law reform, that's committed to recognizing equality between men and women. But in the name of Islam, Muslim women continue to be kept backwards. So for us, this is unacceptable.

Quoted in *Democracy Now! with Amy Goodman** (Carter Center) *7 September 2007*

*See 4408.1.

3   We offer alternative interpretations, alternative opinions within Islam, to locate our demand for rights, for justice, for equality for Muslim women.

Ibid.

4   In many countries where conflicts—where violence have broken out, the media played a very, very important role in enflaming public opinion and inciting hatred and the use of hate language, demonizing the other . . .

Ibid.

5   I wasn't a born leader. I was a born rebel.

"A sister steps out," *The Star 30 March 2008*

4158. Janette Barber (1953–   )

1   Whatever is going wrong jump on it because that might be the answer.

Quoted in *If Not Now . . . Then When?* by Peter J. Fogel *2005*

2   If you had a rotten enough life, you really ought to go into comedy.

Ibid.

3   I refuse to think of them as chin hairs. I think of them as stray eyebrows.

Stand-up routine *n.d.*

4159. Suzanne Benton (1953?–   )

1   The purpose of art is to explore humanity . . . art comes alive as it relates to people's lives . . .

Artists Section, Veteran Feminists of America vfa.us *2007*

4160. Benazir Bhutto (1953–2007)

1   Every dictator uses religion as a prop to keep himself in power.

Interview, *60 Minutes*, CBS-TV *8 August 1986*

2   A ship in port is safe, but that is not what ships are built for.

Ibid.

3   When a government is run at gunpoint, the youth of the country get the impression that real power comes from holding a gun, not from laws. With the restoration of free debate, students' minds will automatically switch from guns to books.

Inaugural Speech, Quoted by Barbara Crossette in, *The New York Times 3 December 1988*

4 What is not recorded is not remembered.

Daughter of Destiny 1989

5 You can't be fueled by bitterness. It can eat you up, but it cannot drive you.

Ibid.

6 I didn't choose this life; it chose me.

Daughter of the East 2007

7 On the day my father was arrested [in 1977], I changed from a girl to a woman. He would guide me over the next two years, cautioning me to remain focused and committed and never bitter. On the day he was murdered I understood that my life was to be Pakistan, and I accepted the mantle of leadership of my father's legacy and my father's party.

Reconciliation 2008

8 The hijackers of September 11 seemed to touch a nerve of Muslim impotence. The burning and then collapsing towers represented, to some, resurgent Muslim power, a perverse Muslim payback for the domination of the West.

Ch. 1, Ibid.

9 Within the Muslim world there has been and continues to be an internal rift, an often violent confrontation among sects, ideologies, and interpretations of the message of Islam. This destructive tension has set brother against brother, a deadly fratricide that has tortured intra-Islamic relations for 1,300 years. This sectarian conflict stifled the brilliance of the Muslim renaissance that took place during the Dark Ages of Europe, when the great universities, scientists, doctors, and artists were all Muslim. Today that intra-Muslim sectarian violence is most visibly manifest in a senseless, self-defeating sectarian civil war that is tearing modern Iraq apart at its fragile seams and exercising its brutality in other parts of the world, especially in parts of Pakistan.

Ibid.

10 One billion Muslims around the world seemed united in their outrage at the war in Iraq . . . but there is deadly silence when they are confronted with Muslim-on-Muslim violence. . . . Even regarding Darfur, where there is an actual genocide being committed against a Muslim population, there has been a remarkable absence of protests.

Ibid.

11 Like most women in politics, I am especially sensitive to maintaining my composure, to never showing my feelings. A display of emotion by a woman in politics or government can be misconstrued as a manifestation of weakness, reinforcing stereotypes and caricatures.

Ibid.

4161. Wendy Sue Bishop (1953–2003)

1 My lives line up like clothes on a clothesline.

"Autobiography," mid-passage 1997

2 Let my last door be a familiar shape, but slightly reworked: perhaps
An entrance, perhaps an exit . . .

"My Last Door," *My Last Door 2007*

3 What if we all could "un" everything?
Undate the person who bored us, undo
certain words? Our affairs undone, no one hurt.

"Omnivores," Ibid.

4 Good bones
allow for good revisions

"House/Home," Ibid.

4162. Kathleen M. Blee (1953–)

1 "Good" motherhood can provoke reactionary politics when, as for many in the twentieth century United States, it is defined fairly narrowly, as protecting and providing for one's own children, rather than as having a responsibility toward all children.

"Mothers in Race-Hate Movements," *The Politics of Motherhood: Activist Voices from Left to Right,* Alexis Jetter, Annelise Orlecks, and Diana Taylor, eds. 1996

4163. Amy Bloom (1953–)

1 In the middle of the eulogy at my mother's boring and heartbreaking funeral, I began to think about calling off the wedding.

"Love Is Not a Pie," *Come to Me 1993*

2 It was like nothing else in my life, that river of love that I could dip into and leave and return to once more and find it still flowing.

"Sleepwalking," Ibid.

3 Elizabeth knew that the bad things that had happened to her were no worse than other people's bad things; they were pretty small potatoes, in fact, compared to terminal cancer, death by famine, incest, quadriplegic paralysis . . .

(p. 132), *Love Invents Us 1997*

4164. Dionne Brand (1953–)

1 They loved grief and spent every penny on it and thought it made them holy, they had each a parched well inside their chests, sacred and hungry, they went to funerals of people they did not know, they stood at grave sides looking into the despair of the mourners, their eyes became ashy with passion.

In Another Place, Not Here 1997

2 They have come here to get away from Black people, to show white people that they are harmless, just like them. This lie will kill them.

Ibid.

3 She wants to be the kind of Black girl that is dangerous. Bigmouthed and dangerous.

Ibid.

4165. Tina Brown (1953–)

1 *Vanity Fair* is for the thinking rich, and *Town & Country* is for the *stinking* rich.

Quoted on p. 10, *NewHouse: All the Glitter, Power, and Glory of America's Richest Media Empire and the Secretive Man Behind It* by Thomas Maier 1994

2 I have come to think that being looked at obsessively by people you don't know actually changes the way your face and body are assembled—not just in the obvious ways of enhanced fashion sense or tricks of charm and self-possession, but in the illusion of size.

Ch. 1, *The Diana Chronicles 2007*

4166. Nina Beth Cardin (1953–)

1 We don't have to like everything we find in women's history, but we should *know* everything.

> Quoted in Ch. 4, *Deborah, Golda, and Me* by Letty Cottin Pogrebin* 1991

*See 3154.

2 The sun streams through my eastern window, and there they are—shimmering particles of dust, high-riding renegades floating aimlessly, leisurely, in the air about me, kicked up by the vitality of life the morning has witnessed.

I have two thoughts about this dust, one common, the other ethereal. The common thought is this: If the dust is floating now, it will come down later. My kitchen will once again be dirty.

A more noble, enduring, even transforming thought pushes that mundane thought aside: The dust, of course, is always there, but I do not always see it. It takes a certain light, a certain attentiveness and a certain moment of stillness to see it.

> Ch. 1, *The Tapestry of Jewish Time: A Spiritual Guide to Holidays and Lifecycle Events* 2000

3 People find it preferable to believe that we are responsible for our own suffering than to imagine that suffering is random and meaningless. It is tempting to choose a world of guilt and punishment over a world of capriciousness, in which there is no apparent moral relationship between our actions and our suffering or our rewards.

> "Spiritual Rehabilitation," *Ibid.*

4167. Elaine Chao (1953–)

1 My parents taught me the founding principles of this country, the principles of freedom and opportunity, the value of hard work, the need to ensure that every man and woman is compensated fairly for their hard work.

> "Bus taps replacement for Chavez," *Seattle Post-Intelligencer* 12 January 2001

4168. Jill Ciment (1953–)

1 With every exhalation, he watched the smoke fly out of his mouth in the shape of his soul.

> Ch. 1, *Teeth of the Dog* 1999

2 . . . the sheer newness, the unrelenting beauty, the intrigue of an unprobed culture, the mere fact of their traveling together again, would make him, if not exactly well, at least himself.

> *Ibid.*

3 She needed to be so shamelessly desired.

> *Ibid.*

4 In Vanduuan lore,* a boat tugs a whole new ocean behind it. Ocean eats ocean. New world devours old. The foam is the mark of its voracious appetite. Teeth of the dog, the natives call it.

> *Ibid.*

*A fictional island people.

4169. Marcia Clark (1953–)

1 Being called a bitch by some old-time gender bigot doesn't bother me. In context, it's a compliment. It means I've stood up to him, I haven't let him have his way, and now he's throwing his little tantrum. *But from women?*

> *Without a Doubt,* with Teresa Carpenter 1997

2 We lost because American justice is corrupted by celebrity.*

> *Ibid.*

*Reference to O. J. Simpson, American athlete (football) (1947–), who was tried and acquitted for the murder of his estranged wife and her friend (1994); Clark was the prosecuting attorney.

3 As a matter of principle, I don't feel that the government should be in the position of market-testing its arguments.

> *Ibid.*

4170. Deborah A. Coleman (1953–)

1 I feel almost predestined to run General Electric. I know it's partly irrational, but it's like training for the Olympics. You may never make it, but you want to aspire to something.

> Business Watch (p. 87), *Working Woman May 1987*

2 I've got to overcome the problem of my own self-management.

> Quoted in "Apple Computer Official To Take 5-Month Leave" by Lawrence M. Fisher, *Business People 8 December 1988*

4171. Rosalind Coward (1953–)

1 One of the reasons for the failure of feminism to dislodge deeply held perceptions of male and female behaviour was its insistence that women were victims, and men powerful patriarchs, which made a travesty of ordinary people's experience of the mutual interdependence of men and women.

> Ch. 9, *Our Treacherous Hearts 1992*

4172. Janet Davey (1953–)

1 Someone always wanted a drink. Someone always wanted the toilet. It seemed to her hopeless that she was still occupied with these wants. Other things came to an end. But children's demands continued.

> *First Aid 2006*

4173. Jessie Duarte (1953–)

1 Now we use it to wipe
arses, then to blow noses
or to write a poem on..
or better still . . .
we use it to write
an impassioned plea for
release to minister of law and order
who then stuffs it in
his ear!

> "Toilet Paper," *A Poetics of Resistance: Women Writing in El Salvador, South Africa, and the United States* Mary K. DeShazer, ed. 1994

4174. Eve Ensler (1953–)

1 If your vagina could speak, what would it say?

> *The Vagina Monologues 1995*

2 I was worried about vaginas. I was worried about what we think about vaginas, and even more worried that we don't think about them.

> *Ibid.*

3 Be bold and LOVE YOUR BODY. STOP FIXING IT. It was never broken.

> Preface, *The Good Body* (play) 2004

4 But whatever the cultural influences and pressures, my preoccupation with my flab, my constant dieting, exercising, worrying, is selfimposed. I pick up the magazines. I buy into the ideal. I believe that blond, flat girls have the secret. What is far more frightening than narcissism is the zeal for self-mutilation that is spreading, infecting the world.

Ibid.

5 . . . I see a government that is ruining this country, dominating the world, absolutely destroying the planet. A government that has birthed a mentality of occupation, invasion, domination, that has literally bombed the heart out of Iraq in the name of security, and escalated terrorism triple-fold.

"Conversations with Amazing Women: Eve Ensler" by
Marianne Schnall,* feminist.com 3 *October 2006*
*See 4758.

6 I'm seeing there is a new way, the third way. It's not left or right. It's not Democrat or Republican. It's a third way. And the third way to me is a shift in these principles where dominance, occupation, invasion and violence are the tools on which the whole planet turns and operates. The new tools would be cooperation, invitation, dialogue, and care. Care would be fundamental to the principles of the world.

Ibid.

7 It's not accidental that we grow up and don't question the President. It's not accidental we grow up and we don't question doctors. It's not accidental that we grow up and we don't question the media. We've been taught to relinquish our authority from a very young age. And in many circumstances we've been forced to because of violence.

Ibid.

8 When you give what you need the most, you heal whatever is broken.

Ibid.

9 But were you to give up that impossible idea [of security] and focus on freedom, on connection, on compassion—I tell you, it's a glorious life! It's a glorious life. It is amazing here in vulnerable land. It just occurred to me; it's another "v" word— "vulnerable land." You know? It's beautiful here in vulnerable land.

Ibid.

10 Why are we suddenly a nation and a people who strive for security above all else?

In fact, security is essentially elusive, impossible. We all die. We all get sick. We all get old. People leave us. People surprise us. People change us. Nothing is secure. And this is the good news. But only if you are not seeking security as the point of your life.

"Introduction: Worried About Security," *Insecure At Last:
Losing It in Our Security-Obsessed World 2006*

11 When you rape, beat, maim, mutilate, burn, bury, and terrorize women, you destroy the essential life energy on the planet. You force what is meant to be open, trusting, nurturing, creative, and alive to be bent, infertile, and broken.

Quoted in "Making Women's Health an International
Priority" by Lucinda Marshall,* Alternet.org 8 *March 2007*
*See 4381.

12 Its hard to be outspoken. People don't like loud, in your face, insistent women. We're programmed to think, do you like me?

Do you like me? Who cares! Sometimes I wake up and think, wow, they really don't like me.

Quoted in "The Vagina Monologues turns ten" by Karen
Bartlett, *The Times* (London) 15 *April 2008*

13 But when God and Guns come together in the public sector, when war is declared in God's name, when the rights of women are denied in God's name, that is the end of separation of church and state and the undoing of everything America has ever tried to be.

"Drill, Baby, Drill," *Huffington Post* 5 *September 2008*

14 Do we want a future of drilling? More holes in the ozone, in the floor of the sea, more holes in our thinking, in the trust between nations and peoples, more holes in the fabric of this precious thing we call life?

Ibid.

4174.1. Bonnie Erbe (1953?–)

1 Yes, it's sad that this unwed, pregnant mother of three had no money for bus fare. It's terrible that her boyfriend lost his job. It is heart-wrenching that she fell to tears in the doctor's office. But in the long run, can we agree that this unwed couple's decision not to bring a fourth child into the world when they are having trouble feeding themselves and three children is no tragedy? It's actually a fact-based, rational decision that in the end benefits the three children they already have and society as well.

"Abortion is not a tragedy," *Scripps Howard News* 1 *April
2009*

2 *Playboy* [magazine] is past its time and should just fold up and go away.

"Playboy Mix of Sex, Hate, and Politics Demeans
Conservative Women," *U.S. News & World Report* 3 *June
2009*

3 Granting amnesty to people who broke U.S. law turns our laws upside down and sends a message that U.S. laws can be broken with impunity.

"Illegal Immigration Is Bad for the Environment," Ibid. 25
June 2009

4175. Anne Fadiman (1953–)

1 What the doctors viewed as clinical efficiency the Hmong* viewed as frosty arrogance.

The Spirit Catches You and You Fall Down 1997
*An Asian ethnic group in the mountainous regions of Southeast Asia.

2 The more I've read about plagiarism, the more I've come to think that literature is one big recycling bin . . .

Ex Libris: Confessions of a Common Reader 1998

3 When you read silently, only the writer performs. When you read aloud, the performance is collaborative.

Ibid.

4 In my view, nineteen pounds of old books are at least nineteen times as delicious as one pound of fresh caviar.

"The Joy of Sesquipedalians,"* Ibid.
*Long, polysyllabic words.

5 After five years of marriage and a child, George and I finally resolved that we were ready for the more profound intimacy of

library consolidation. It was unclear, however, how we were to find a meeting point between his English-garden approach and my French-garden one.

"Marrying Libraries," Ibid.

4176. Patricia Ferguson (1953–)

1 Her heartbeat is slow. All the processes of her body are calmed. Within she feels the great lively peace of creativity.

Peripheral Vision 2008

2 She thought she had decided only not to decide. It had not occurred to her consciously, somehow, that this might be the same as deciding to try to get pregnant. At no point in all the long months of gestation was Sylvia able to recognize the fact that she had been trying to get pregnant, and had merely succeeded in doing so.

Ch. 1, Ibid.

3 "Are you terribly tired tonight?" Adam might ask her, mock-roguishly, for this had quickly become code.

"Yes," uttered flatly, of course meant No, whereas "No," even spoken consideringly or wryly or doubtfully, meant Yes.

Ibid.

4177. Vanessa Northington Gamble (1953–)

1 There is no healing in silence.

"The political is the personal," *The Women's Review of Books,* vol. 11, no. *1 October 1993*

2 Research has clearly demonstrated that cultural background influences health-seeking behavior, health beliefs, access to care, medical decision-making, and expectations of care.

Testimony, Institute of Medicine Committee for Guidance in Designing a National Health Care Disparities Report *20 March 2002*

4178. Janet Gibson (1953–)

1 Reef, mangroves, sea grass—they're all linked. If you touch one part, it affects the whole.

"Earth Day Defenders of the Planet," *Time 23 April 1990*

4179. Linda D. Hallman (1953?–)

1 Education is not a net-zero-sum game here. Basically, if girls were getting better at boys' expense, then we'd be at zero again, wouldn't we?

"Report Aims to Debunk Myths on Gender and Education" with Ray Suarez, *PBS News Hour 21 May 2008*

2 There are some boys that are in crisis and there are some girls that are in crisis [in education], and they're the ones that we have to target. Our education resources are precious, and we have got to find ways to start targeting and really strategically looking at how to lift the groups that need to be lifted.

Ibid.

3 As I said, our education resources are so small, and we have got to start targeting our dollars into the areas that we already know work: small class sizes, getting teachers to be ready to teach diverse populations, all of those types of areas.

This is where the targeted dollars need to go. That's strategic. That's the only way that the United States can remain competitive in the 21st century, and it's really a workforce issue.

Ibid.

4180. Jane Hirshfield (1953–)

1 . . . life is short.
But desire, desire is long.

"Heat," *Gravity and Angels 1988*

2 What empties itself falls into the place that is open.

"A Hand," *Given Sugar, Given Salt 2001*

3 It is time to consider a cat, the cultivation of African violets or flowering cactus.

"This Was One a Love Poem," Ibid.

4 A knife cannot cut itself open,
yet you ask me both to be you and to know you.

"Instant Glimpsable Only for an Instant," St. 8, *After 2006*

4181. Nancy Huston (1953–)

1 . . . *Lead us not into temptation.*

Ah but wouldn't it be terrific I can't help thinking if this grey and grimly smiling lady could allow herself to be led into temptation for a change—what would it be? A rhumba, a tango a cha-cha-cha a glass of Cuban rum an amber-skinned stranger shining ember eyes into her? What is she worried about now she's almost home free what could possibly happen to her at eight-odd that is the temptation?

Ch. 1, *Plainsong 1993*

2 I'm like sunlight, all-powerful, instantaneous and flowing effortlessly into the darkest corners of the univers . . . capable at six of seeing . . . illuminating . . . understanding everything.

Ch. 1, *Fault Lines 2006*

4182. Michiko Itatani (1953–)

1 We are on this seemingly insignificant planet in this insignificant location in the galaxy. Being confined to this small dot, the human mind travels around the universe. Even before we could circle the earth, we started to search the inner and outer space of the universe.

Quoted in "Michiko Itatani," *Exposures, Women & Their Art* by Ann Brown and Arlene Raven* *1989*
*See 3533.

2 For me, to be an artist is an intellectual choice and a carefully chosen commitment. There is no intoxication. My painting is a painterly diagram of my cosmology. It's incomplete, fragmented and under inquiry.

Ibid.

4183. Sandra Jackson-Opoku (1953–)

1 Much more than just one woman,
there are endless spirits
roaming inside me
River Mothers
moving, and
memory much
older

"Ancestors: In Praise of the Imperishable," *The Woman That I Am, The Literature and Culture of Contemporary Women of Color* D. Soyini Madison,* ed. *1994*
*See 3912.

2 Our names are unimportant. Though we are known by many names, we have but one purpose. The head itself has two ears,

but it does not hear in twos. We watch over our blood in the land of the living, helping where we can. Waiting to find the daughter of deepest memory and bring her home to us one day. We can reach through from the spirit world as you just have my dear. Touching the souls of those descendants who seem lost.

The River Where Blood Is Born 1997

4184. Rheta Grimsley Johnson (1953–)

1 And I swear, I can't see a cypress Santa or an alligator-drawn sleigh without thinking of how my Montgomery, Ala., mother whipped up a Christmas.

"Visions of mother whipping up Christmas dance in my head," *Seattle Post-Intelligencer 9 December 1998*

4185. Wahu Kaara (1953–)

1 We are witnessing a historical moment and building linkages with the people of the world, creatively and energetically. We are UNSTOPPABLE!"

Comments, G8 Conference (Edinburgh, Scotland) *2005*

2 African women are not dying for Africa anymore, they want to live for Africa.

Ibid.

3 The greatest challenge in our pursuit of justice is to stand up and speak to power.

Speech, "Justice for All! Our Only Way Out!," United Methodist Women's Assembly (Anaheim, California) *5 May 2006*

4 Life is no longer a manifestation of the Glory of God but a manifestation of Economic might with the safeguards of the military/industrial complex.

Ibid.

5 We neither want a world of hunger for some, nor one of excesses for others. God has provided enough for all us.

Ibid.

4186. Nancy Killefer (1953–)

1 Sit on your hands if you have to, but consulting is 75% listening.

Speech, Harvard Business School, *HARBUS 15 March 2004*

2 If we want our government to do more and do better, we must take public management and productivity more seriously. Otherwise, citizen demands for effective government in the future will go unheeded.

Article, *Business Week 14 March 2006*

3 If you are willing to embrace significant change, then you're looking at the right person. But if you just want to keep the trains running on time, don't ask me to do this job.*

Quoted in *The Washington Post 7 January 2009*
*Re having been offered Asst. Sec. of Treasury post in 1997.

4187. Cristina Kirchner (1953–)

1 The present time Latin America is going through, with its impressive natural and human resources, devoid of racial and religious conflicts, is a unique moment, and I believe that Argentina and Argentines are at the doorstep of an unprecedented opportunity.

Article, Telam.com *29 October 2006*

2 Women bring a different face to politics. We see the big geopolitical picture but also the smaller, daily details of citizens' lives.

Quoted in "The Latin Hillary" by Tim Padgett, *Time 8 October 2007*

3 There will be no definite triumph as long as there is poverty.

Inauguration speech *3 December 2007*

4 You can be sure that all and each one of us who have institutional responsibilities will raise not only our voice but will take concrete action against any sign of anti-Semitism. We are not willing to give away what has been a historic tradition in Latin America.

Quoted in "Argentina-Venezuela: Cristina Fernández triunfa en 15 minutos" by Humberto Márquez, Inter Press Service (ipsnoticias.net) *23 March 2008*

4188. Andrea Lee (1953–)

1 I had hoped to join the *rank* of dreaming expatriates for whom Paris can become a self-sufficient universe, but my life there had been no more than a slight hysteria, filled with the experimental naughtiness of children reacting against their training. It was clear, much as I did not want to know it, that my days in France had a number, that for me the bright, frank, endlessly beckoning horizon of the runaway had been, at some point, transformed into a complicated return.

(p. 15), *Sarah Phillips 1984*

2 The town was green and pretty, but had the constrained, slightly unreal atmosphere of a colony or a foreign enclave, that was because the people who owned the rambling houses behind the shrubbery were black. For them—doctors, ministers, teachers who had grown up in Philadelphia row houses—the lawns and tree-lined streets represented the fulfillment of a fantasy long deferred, and acted as a barrier against the predictable cruelty of the world.

(p. 39), Ibid.

3 For as long as I could remember, the civil rights movement had been unrolling like a dim frieze behind the small pleasures and defeats of my childhood; it seemed dull, a necessary burden on my conscience, like good grades or hungry people in India.

(pp. 39–40), Ibid.

4189. Linda Lingle (1953–)

1 Elections are about candidates and competing philosophies, governing is about helping the public achieve its hopes and dreams for the future.

Inaugural address *4 December 2006*

2 The magnitude and speed of change and innovation in the world today is so great, that if we fail to move forward, by definition, we will be going backwards.

Ibid.

3 But, hard or not . . . change will happen.
The question for us to answer is, will we just let change happen to us in the coming years . . . or will we create the change we want to see. . . ?

State of the Union address *22 January 2007*

4 A person dressed in shorts and slippers can shake the political world with a blog that he writes from his lanai.

Ibid.

4190. Julianne Malveaux (1953–)

1 If I were rich, I would send every child out of the country before they were 15 years old. You see yourself differently.

> Speech, "Covering diverse communities in the news" (Belmont University, Nashville, Tenn.) *January 2004*

2 African Americans are ultimate Americans. We were fighting for the right to fight in World War II.

> Ibid.

3 Compromise isn't in my vocabulary.

> Ibid.

4 *Re the diaspora of Hurricane Katrina* victims:* What are black folks doing in Utah? Nobody is trying to make them whole. Part of making them whole is allowing them to return

> "Black leaders say Katrina forcing dialogue on poverty," Associated Press *26 February 2006*

*On 25 August 2005, Hurricane Katrina devastated New Orleans and surrounding areas, as far as Mississippi; more than 1800 people lost their lives. The Federal Emergency Management Agency (FEMA) was controversially slow to respond.

5 If you keep doing what you are doing, you'll keep getting what you are getting—or so I heard growing up, whenever I made the same mistake twice.

> "Jobs, Jobs, Jobs!," *Ms.* (New York) *Fall 2008*

6 There are often *good* reasons to assume debt. Each of us does it when we don't pay the full price for a house or an automobile, and our nation can do it when we anticipate that investment will yield both human and economic returns. The bottom line is that we can drift into a second-class world status, or engage all of our citizens in a productive economy.

> Ibid.

4191. Makaziwe "Maki" Mandela (1953–)

1 From the cradle to the grave, blacks are aliens, are prisoners. From the day you're born, your future is determined by apartheid laws. Where you are going to be born, which schools you will attend, where you can work, where you can die and be buried.

> Quoted in "South African cruelty rampant . . ." by James Hodge, *Times Picayune* (New Orleans) *20 April 1988*

2 He [Tutu*] will not sing the song of the administration, but the songs of the oppressed people of South Africa.

> Ibid.

*Desmond Tutu, South African prelate and antiapartheid leader (1931–); Nobel Peace Prize (1984).

3 Black women take care of white children, but no one takes care of their children.

> Ibid.

4192. Deborah Mathis (1953–)

1 Sport hunting these days is as likely to occur on a playground as in the forest and young hunters are armed not only with semi-automatic weapons . . . but with warped designs on power; a hellish fascination with getting even; and the need to prove themselves to people utterly unworthy of the effort.

> Serial failures provide the ammunition.

> "'Pork' in crime bill. . . ," *Seattle Post-Intelligencer,* A10 *7 September 1994*

2 The homeward-bound trend is a logical product of the [women's] movement. Women have been to the men's only frontier and, in large measure, tamed it. Now, some of them are reversing course. For free-minded women, for feminists, there is no disappointment in this because it is happening as a matter of choice. Women are not being driven back to Apronland.

> "Liberation gives women the freedom to choose to stay home," *Seattle Post-Intelligencer,* Op-Ed *22 October 1998*

3 I love the old girl despite her nasty ways. I know she needs me. I think she knows it too. Still, she can be so difficult at times. So ornery and ungrateful. Cruel on occasion. Wicked. . . . I am determined to get her well . . . Her mercurial nature repels me today, attracts me tomorrow, but always, always intrigues. Of course I realize her neurosis is dangerous and I should probably run off. That would show her. But I am a sucker for the good in her, which is a good too good to leave. So here I stay, battered but bewitched. What can I say? She is my country, my home.

> Ch. 1, *Yet a Stranger: Why Black Americans Still Don't Feel at Home* 2002

4 Today it's not at all unusual for the Wham Bam to take place without even so much as a Thank You, Ma'am.

> Ch. 1, *Sole Sisters: The Joys and Pains of Single Black Women* 2007

4193. Alice McDermott (1953–)

1 "Aren't you glad that you only have to see your relatives at weddings and wakes?"

> *At Weddings and Wakes* 1992

2 Everyone loved him . . . and if you loved him, we all knew, you pleaded with him at some point. Or you drove him to AA, waited outside the church until the meeting was over, and drove him home again. Or you advanced him whatever you could afford so he could travel to Ireland to take the pledge. If you loved him, you took his car keys away, took his incoherent phone calls after midnight. You banished him from your house until he could show up sober. You saw the bloodied scraps of flesh he coughed up in his drinks. If you loved him, then you told him at some point that he was killing himself and felt the way his indifference ripped through your affection.

> *Charming Billy* 1998

3 With so many other forces at work in the world, brutal, sly, deceiving, unstoppable forces, what could be more foolish than staking your life on an ephemeral feeling, no more than an idea, really, a fancy, the culmination of which is a clumsy bit of nakedness, a few minutes of animal grunting and bumping, a momentary obliteration of thought, of conscience?

> Ibid.

4 But the child was light as a feather in his hands and the lightness took his breath away. The baby wore a seersucker sunsuit that left his tiny arms and shoulders bare and Billy covered these with a cupped palm as he rested the child against his chest. The flesh was as sweetly warm as if the hand of God had just formed it. He blew softly across the child's downy hair and closed his eyes to say, "Now, now, little fellow. Now now."

> Ibid.

5 [There were] . . . long stretches when nothing happened except that one's ties to home were imperceptibly dissolved and one became a stranger to one's life.

> *The Voyage of Narwhal* 1998

6 It was either God's reply or just April again, in the wind tunnel that was midtown Manhattan.

> Ch. 1, *After This* 2006

4194. Alyce Miller (1953–)

1 Words! My greatest fear is how wrong they can be.

> Title story, *The Nature of Longing* 1995

2 When they talked about white people, she knew they didn't really mean her, but then, where did that put her? Sometimes she felt great relief; sometimes it just about broke her heart.

> *Stopping for Green Lights* 1999

3 Weighted down for so long by low-grade despair I did not myself know, I had forgotten my own longings and desires. But now plunged into the mundane specifics of my outwardly respectable husband's pathetic love affair, I almost laughed. For this I have been so melancholy? For this I have wept over nameless woes?

> "Dimitry Gurov's Dowdy Wife," *Water* 2008

4 Over the years she observed various pregnant friends with a mixture of envy and repugnance: hands clasped smugly over burgeoning bellies, wearing the slightly vain expression of the expectant and the undeniable look of achievement.

> "Swimming," Ibid.

4195. Vera Mischenko (1953–)

1 We have good environmental laws in Russia, but enforcement is nil. Corruption is the rule. Officials can be bribed to issue illegal permits for resource exploitation—it's incredibly difficult to stop.

> Quoted in "Goldman Prize: The Year's 7 Environmental Heroes Honored" by Glen Martin, *San Francisco Chronicle* 17 *April 2000*

2 This is like letting the cat guard the cream. The Natural Resources Ministry [of Russia] disregards environmental laws all the time, and has consistently refused to conduct environmental impact assessments as is legally required when issuing mining and other resource extraction licenses.

> "Russian Environmentalists Sue President Putin Over Dissolution of Environmental Regulatory Agency," earthjustice.org *22 August 2000*

3 When we discovered several cases of briberies of very high government officials, we sent huge files to the prosecutor general's office, trying to force them to investigate some officials and multinationals. But instead we got investigations of ourselves.

> Quoted in "The Green Menace" by Paul Rauber, *Sierra November 2000*

4196. Bernadette Mosala (1953?–)

1 When men are oppressed, it's a tragedy. When women are oppressed, it's tradition.

> "A Notion of Sisterhood, *Sometimes When It Rains,* Ann Oosthuizen, ed. 1987

2 You are white and I am black. That's what matters in this country and it looks like life can never be lived on a human level in this land.

> Ibid.

4197. Harryette Romell Mullen (1953–)

1 By the way, my computer was stolen. Now I'm unable to process words.

> "All She Wrote," *Santa Monica Review Fall 1977*

2 I regret to say I'm unable to reply to your unexpressed desires.

> Ibid.

3 Please page our home and visit our sigh on the wide world's ebb. Just point and cluck at our new persuasion shoes.

> "Black Nikes," Ibid.

4 And I'm blinking off old eyelids
for a new way of seeing

> "Shedding Skin," St. 4, *Blues Baby: Early Poems* 1981

5 the souls ain't got a stray word
for the woman who's wayward

> "Page 39 / arrives early for the date," St. 3, *Muse & Drudge* 1995

4198. Tahira Naqvi (1953–)

1 The immensity of the sea on film was reduced to a mere blue splash of color, its place usurped by a vastness she could scarce hold within the frame of her vision; a window opened in her head, she drew in the wonder of the sea as it touched the hem of the heavens and, despite the heat, Sakina Bano shivered involuntarily. God's touch is upon the world, she silently whispered to herself.

> "Paths Upon Water," *The Forbidden Stitch: An Asian American Women's Anthology,* Shirley Geok-lin Lim,* Mayumi Tsutakawa, and M. Donnelly, eds. 1989

*See 3521.

2 Sakina Bano couldn't understand why these men and women wished to scorch their bodies, and why, if they were here by the shore of an ocean which seemed to reach up to God, they didn't at least gaze wide-eyed at the wonder which lay at their feet. Why did they choose instead to shut their eyes and merely wallow in the heat. Their skins had rebelled, the red and darkly-pink blotches spoke for themselves. Perhaps this is a ritual they must, of necessity, follow, she mused. Perhaps they yearn to be brown as we yearn to be white.

> Ibid.

3 Sometimes they also made love in the dark, if that is what one could call it, for their performance, devoid of passion or ardor, was as routine to him as the perusal of the paper, or watching the Six-Thirty News on CBS, or taking his blood pressure pills after his one cup of tea in the morning.

> "The Good Wife," *Monsoon Magazine* 2000

4 Finally spring wafted over, slowly at first, seemingly hesitant of its reception as the ground heaved and swelled with the weight of dead leaves and melting snow, and then with flagrant ardor; suddenly nature began its coupling, intense, fervidly orgasmic, perpetual, unmindful of the petty uncertainty of human life.

> Ibid.

4199. Donna J. Nelson (1953–)

1 It's hard to know what you can do or even what you want to do if you don't know where you are.

> Quoted in "Donna J. Nelson, Scientist of Gender Bias" by Allison Stevens, Women's Enews *3 January 2006*

2   Bench chemistry is my job and diversity is my hobby, and I think my hobby is taking over my life!
> Quoted in "Diversity 2007" by Damaris Christensen, *The Scientist* 2007

4200. Pippa Norris (1953–)

1   Recent years have seen growing tensions between the ideals and the perceived performance of democratic institutions. While there is no 'crisis of democracy,' many believe that all is not well with the body politic.
> Ch. 1, *A Virtuous Circle: Political Communications in Post-Industrial Societies* 2000

2   Info-tech has become a vital engine of growth for the world economy enabling many enterprising firms and communities to address economic and social challenges with greater efficiency. In poorer villages and isolated communities, a well-placed computer, like a communal well or an irrigation pump, may become another development tool, providing essential information about storm warnings and crop prices for farmers, or medical services and legal land records for villagers.
> Ch. 4, Ibid.

3   Yet representative democracy requires two-way communication as well as information, at regular intervals beyond elections, so that political leaders receive feedback and maintain contact with the grassroots.
> Ch. 6, Ibid.

4   The importance of *transparency* in government is widely acknowledged, both to promote greater public confidence in the policymaking process and to maximize accountability.
> Ibid.

5   The cyberculture provides a public space particularly conducive to progressive networks and alternative social movements, the insurgents challenging the authorities.
> Ch. 10, Ibid.

6   Protest politics did not disappear with afghan bags, patchouli oil and tie-dyed T-shirts in the sixties, instead it has moved from margin to mainstream. New social movements, transnational policy networks, and Internet activism offer alternative avenues of engagement.
> Ch. 1, *Democratic Phoenix: Political Activism Worldwide* 2003

7   There is nothing novel about concern for wildlife, biodiversity and preservation of natural habitats. . . . But the late twentieth century witnessed a dramatic rise in public concern about environmental issues, membership in environmental groups, the formation of government environmental agencies, and the number of environmental regulations and international treaties, making this movement one of the most important forces in the policy process. The diverse organizational structure of environmental groups, and the emphasis on "life-style politics" and direct action for recycling and environmental protection of local areas, exemplifies many of the defining features of new social movements.
> Ch. 10, Ibid.

8   The free press is one of the major institutions buttressing democratic transitions and consolidation.
> Ch. 9, *Driving Democracy: Do Power-Sharing Institutions Work?* 2008

4201. Vanessa L. Ochs (1953–)

1   I do believe that women must open Torah wide and seize it for themselves, though they know full well that the consequences may even be dangerous.
> Afterword, *Words on Fire: One Woman's Journey into the Sacred* 1999

2   To make your spiritual yearning public, I thought, was to announce that you were wounded. To turn deeply into religion was to admit that your own resources were so weak you had to resort to magic and miracle cures for healing. To acquire faith was to mobilize the powers of an overly active imagination.
> Ch. 1, Ibid.

3   I always found myself more drawn to each religious milieu than I would have anticipated, but in time, a ghoulish threat of being absorbed in alien territory always sent me retreating to the blander and safer ground of home.
> Ch. 8, Ibid.

4   Americans of all faith traditions are expressing a preference for "seeker-oriented spirituality." Few are persuaded to carry on religious traditions by guilt toward ancestors, the fear of censure by peers, the loss of religious institutions as a home away from home, or the threat of punishment in the afterlife.
> Ch. 1, *Inventing Jewish Ritual* 2007

4202. Maureen O'Hara (1953–)

1   Determining the optimal level of transparency is complicated because of the complex role that information plays in markets. On a basic level, information availability levels the playing field between participants, and thus it makes markets fairer. Viewed from this perspective, the best markets are those that are the most transparent. . . . Yet while transparency has obvious benefits, it has less obvious, but substantial costs. Problems arise because . . . If transparency reveals a complex trading strategy to the market, then traders can free-ride off the efforts of others, or, more perniciously attempt to manipulate the market to gain at the other traders' expense.
> "Designing Markets for Developing Countries," *International Review of Finance*, 2:4 2001

2   If I can make culture I must act responsibly. If I can only ever be part of the creation I must act humbly.
> *Constructing Emancipatory Realities n.d.*

4202.1. Terry O'Neill (1953?–)

1   NOW is the organization that fights for the rights of all women no matter the circumstances of their birth, their race or sexual orientation, no matter if they live in poverty or are trying to escape violence.
> Acceptance Speech, NOW Conference (Indianapolis, IN) 20 June 2009

2   My experience with domestic violence, as an abused wife left me humiliated and embarrassed. I only began to talk about this publicly five years ago as I realized that to keep quiet was to continue the abuse. I want to empower women and telling my story does just that. Women are fed up with persistent inequality and are ready for change. I am honored and eager to lead NOW in making that change.
> Ibid.

4203. Kathy Peiss (1953–)

1 Over the decades, mothers and daughters have taught each other about cosmetics, cliques have formed around looks, women have shared their beauty secrets and, in the process, created intimacy. Not only tools of deception and illusion, then, these little jars tell a rich history of women's ambition, pleasure, and community.

Introduction, *Hope in a Jar, The Making of America's Beauty Culture* 1998

2 The fashionable ideal has changed many times in recent decades, but the 1920s marked the moment when mass-produced images distinctly and powerfully began to influence female self-conceptions and beauty rituals.

Ch. 5, Ibid.

3 Makeup promised personal transformation, a pledge that sounded deeply in American culture—from conversion experiences and temperance oaths to the appeals of medicine men and faith healers. Beauty culturists had proclaimed the mutual transformation of external appearance and inner well-being.

Ibid.

4 The commercialization of men's appearance was often explained, paradoxically, by men's need for a sharp look in corporate America *and* by a new hedonism that rejected the conformity demanded by the business world.

Ch. 8, Ibid.

5 When women put on a face, they continue to express ideas of naturalness and artifice, authenticity and deception, propriety and danger, modernity and tradition. Making up remains a gesture bound to perceptions of self and body, the intimate and the social—a gesture rooted in women's everyday lives.

Ibid.

4204. Susan Pinkard (1953–)

1 Cuisine [of the ancient Mediterranean] *was* artifice: perfection was achieved when flavors fused so completely that it was hard to guess what the individual components were.

Ch. 1, *A Revolution in Taste: The Rise of French Cuisine, 1650–1800* 2008

2 Mexican kitchen lore claims that if one can identify a recipe's ingredients by smelling the steam rising from the pot, the mixture must cook longer to achieve a perfect blend of flavors.

Ibid.

4205. Pamela Redmond Satran (1953–)

1 A WOMAN SHOULD HAVE . . .
enough money within her control to move out
and rent a place of her own,
even if she never wants to or needs to . . .

St. 1, "30 Things a Woman Should Have and Should Know by the Time She's 30," St. 1, *Glamour Magazine* May 1997

2 A WOMAN SHOULD HAVE . . .
a set of screwdrivers, a cordless drill, and a black lace bra . . .

St. 5, Ibid.

3 EVERY WOMAN SHOULD KNOW. . . .
that her childhood may not have been perfect . . . but it's over . . .

St. 14, Ibid.

4206. Cathleen Schine (1953–)

1 June was the month that couldn't last, the breezes so scented with blossoms that the flowers themselves trembled and swayed, intoxicated.

Ch. 1, *The Love Letter* 1995

2 She loved her mail when she saw it lying there, so promising, such bounty, a cornucopia of greetings and checks and invitations and information, fruit spilling from the bowl, the daily harvest of daily life . . .

Ibid.

3 Have you ever lost a friend? It is the saddest and most baffling experience. No one sympathizes, unless the friend dies, which she did not. I lost my best friend many years ago. She had been my best friend for a decade, for more than half my childhood, and then she evaporated, as though she had never really existed at all.

The Evolution of Jane 1998

4 "Boredom is simply a failure of imagination."

Ch. 1, *The New Yorkers* 2007

4207. Miranda J. Seymour (1953?–)

1 Regarding the past, it is not a subject on which I am ever likely to achieve a settled view. It doesn't do to depend on love. Let me leave it at that for the moment.

Ch. 1, *The Summer of '39* 1995

2 Living to an old age has become a kind of victory over circumstances, but I haven't yet learned to behave as the old should. I'm not grateful, and I'm not tolerant, and I don't like small talk. That should be enough to keep away those well-meaning souls, newcomers all, who make a vocation out of doing good to those who never did enough harm to deserve it.

Ibid.

3 That was the trouble with babies: swathed in bonnets and shawls, they all looked alike.

Ch. 1, *The Bugatti Queen: In Search of a Motor-Racing Legend* 2004

4 A man came to no harm by knowing the landmarks of his own horizon.

Ibid.,

5 The House couldn't give more than it was. It couldn't confer friendship, or success. This was a source of bewilderment, sadness and disappointment

Thrumpton Hall: A Memoir of Life in My Father's House 2008

4208. Farida Shaheed (1953–)

1 . . . transforming the educational system requires a two-pronged approach: one led by mainstream educators and the other led by mobilized communities. And, given the powerfully patriarchal nature of the society, special efforts on every level must be made for women.

"Women's Education in Pakistan," with Khawar Mumtaz,* Quoted in *The Politics of Women's Education: Perspectives from Asia, Africa, and Latin America* by Jill Ker Conway and Susan C. Bourque 1993

*See 4064.

2 Pakistan's educational system is a poor imitation of the one the colonial powers left behind.

Ibid.

3 I am very conscious that language is an important source of power. I object to the term "Fundamentalism" because often it is not indigenous to where so-called fundamentalist projects exist. Its use and translation become problematic. In my country, Pakistan, the term has been imported from the West and has been translated into the local language as "those who love the fundamentals," those who stand up for the basics. In its translation the term is therefore giving legitimacy to precisely those forces that we are trying to combat.

> Quoted in interview, Association for Women's Rights in
> Development (awid.org) *12 February 2008*

4209. Gail Berkeley Sherman (1953–)

1 Whether converts leave their traditions in anger, bitterness, indifference, or disappointment, in our conversions we promise to wrestle with new terms in defining our lives and our relation to spiritual absolutes.

> "A Convert's Road to Prayer," *Response: A Contemporary
> Jewish Review Fall-Winter 1982*

2 A congregation did not merely collect the individual supplications of souls in varying states of grace; a community reaffirmed the existence of God to whom praises are due.

> Ibid.

4210. Barbara Smaller (1953–)

1 "Up a hundred and sixteen points! If only we'd had the foresight to invest ten minutes ago."

> *The New Yorker 24 August 1998*

2 "I thought I liked babies, but, as it turned out, I mainly like baby clothes."

> Ibid., *21 September 1998*

3 "My favorite part of being a stay-at-home mom is when they're at school."

> Ibid., *14 October 2002*

4 "If we take a late retirement and an early death, we'll just squeak by."

> Ibid., *7 July 2003*

5 . . . I, like many of my comrades who toil as art workers, keep a pad of paper, a pen, and a flashlight on my bedside table, ready to grasp at any straws my R.E.M. cycle might provide.

> "In which we have a restless night," Ibid. *19 March 2008*

4211. Ellen Snortland (1953–)

1 [My dog is] faithful, loving, valuable, warm, nurturing, intelligent, affectionate, and capable of ripping someone who attacks me or my loved ones to ribbons. She's a bitch and, except for the way she drools and sheds, I want to be just like her.

> "Unfurl Your Bitch Flag," *Beauty Bites Beast: Awakening the
> Warrior Within Women and Girls 2001*

2 Santa is so old hat. A Madison avenue puppet, he's also sexist, racist, runs a male-only sweatshop, abuses reindeer, ignores borders with impunity and is a poster child for gluttony. Is there anything admirable about him? For goodness' sake, he's a break-and-enter artist, which at the very least must be an impeachable offense.

> "Impeach Santa!" *Pasadena Weekly
> 20 December 2007*

3 This country does not take kindly to liberals, remember? They actually get shot and killed if you'll recall our pantheon of assassinated leaders. Not a conservative among them.

> "A Delicate Balance," Ibid. *17 January 2008*

4 "Y" is for the Y chromosome. Hmm. Why indeed?

> "Eliot's Alphabet," Ibid. *2 March 2008*

5 I assert that if and when the females of our species could learn how-to stop violence WHILE it's happening to them, we'd see a transformation of women's potential and participation in problem-solving on the planet within a remarkably short amount of time. The adage "Think Globally, Act Locally" is perfect. There is nothing more local than one's body, and if a critical mass of women could protect their own bodies, the globe would benefit.

> "My Unlikely Life Mission, Self-defense as Physical Literacy,"
> Women's International Perspective (thewip.net) *April 2008*

6 I realized when I was 10 that there was no rehearsal for courage.

> *Now That She's Gone: Unraveling the Mystery of
> My Mother* (play) *2008*

4212. Susan Spicer (1953–)

1 From the get-go, I found cooking mesmerizing. I was captivated by the colors, aromas, textures, and tastes, and found the process both sensual and fascinating.

> Introduction, *Crescent City Cooking 2007*

2 That story ["Stone Soup"] made me understand the power of food and community, of sharing, of being clever and resourceful—and of making the whole process fun.

> "The Spicer Pantry," Ibid.

4213. Suzy Szasz (1953–)

1 Life really is a crapshoot.

> *Living With It: Why You Don't Have to Be Healthy to Be
> Happy 1991*

2 I have noticed that in virtually all medical situations . . . rarely does a physician or paraprofessional address a patient by his last name. . . . It thus recreates the relationship between an adult and a child—the one dominant, intelligent, and important, the other submissive, unintelligent, and unimportant. The fact that people go along with this arrangement illustrates how willing most of us are to act like children when we are sick.

> Ch. 1, Ibid.

3 Some misfortunes we bring upon ourselves; others are completely beyond our control. But no matter what happens to us, we always have some control over what we do about it.

> Ch. 4, Ibid.

4214. Luci Tapahonso (1953–)

1 It is said that the wind enters each newborn,
a whoosh of breath inside, and the baby gasps

> Untitled poem, *Saanii Dahataal, The Women Are Singing 1993*

2 His voice a white cloud,
plumes of chimney smoke suspended in the dark

> Ibid.

4215. Lisa St. Aubin de Terán (1953–)

1 Travelling is like flirting with life. It's like saying, "I would stay and love you, but I have to go; this is my station."

Ch. 2, *Off the Rails* 1989

2 A solitary traveller can sleep from state to state, from day to night, from day to day, in the long womb of its controlled interior. It is the cradle that never stops rocking after the lullaby is over. It is the biggest sleeping tablet in the world, and no one need ever swallow the pill, for it swallows them.

Ch. 15, Ibid.

4216. Iyanla Vanzant (1953–)

1 When you are not happy where you are and you are not quite sure if you want to leave or how to leave, you are in the meantime.

In the Meantime: Finding Yourself and the Love You Want 1998

2 If you know who walks beside you, you can never be afraid.

One Day My Soul Just Opened Up: 40 Days and 40 Nights Towards Spiritual Strength and Personal Growth 1998

3 Life is about cleaning up the crap and, while you're doing it, being okay with the fact that you have to do it. . . . A word of caution. You can't get caught up in the crap! If you do, you will surely lose sight of the real meaning of life and lose your Self.

Ibid.

4217. Marilyn Waring (1953–)

1 What I find so offensive about it [the Moral Majority] in terms of Christian dogma is that it plays on fear, not love.

Quoted in "Gazette News: Marilyn Wang—New Zealand's Feisty M.P." by Robin Morgan*, *Ms.* (New York) *December 1981*

*See 3284.

2 I don't use all the operative academic words, but it seems you can have power *to,* or you can have power *for,* or you can have power *over,* or you're power-*less.*

Ibid.

3 Since the patriarchy has designated to us power as consumers, then let's do actions that break down national boundaries.

Ibid.

4218. Lucinda Williams (1953–)

1 Mr. Johnson sings over in a corner by the bar
Sold his soul to the devil so he can play guitar.

"2 Kool 2 Be 4-Gotten," 1st Verse, *Car Wheels On A Gravel Road* (album) 1998

2 Some kind of savior singin' the blues
A derelict in your duct tape shoes

"Drunken Angel," Ibid.

3 I think I lost it
Let me know if you come across it
Let me know if I let it fall
Along a back road somewhere

"I Lost it," chorus and 2nd Verse, Ibid.

4219. Margaret Willson (1953–)

1 We use boundaries to give our world definition—boundaries of space, of time, of dimension, of the inanimate and animate, of the living and the dead. Boundaries also influence the way we construct our identity; with them we mark private and public space. They allow the entire concept of possession to exist: our nation, our home, our family, our traditions, our ethnicity.

p. 99, *Dance Lest We All Fall Down (A Journey of Friendship, Poverty, Power and Peace)* 2007

2 In the United States, one is not supposed to get depressed. If depression approaches, one should immediately do something to get rid of it. Take drugs perhaps, go into trance. Our separate and individual responsibilities are to achieve and maintain constant states of happiness. Depression is antisocial and perhaps even deviant. The national emotional standard is set by drawings of smiling faces and a ritualized directive to "have a nice day."

pp. 111–112, Ibid.

3 In London, however, my friends regarded depression as a sign of emotional depth. According to them, given the current state of the world, a person who is continually happy must be ignorant, superficial, and entirely lacking in a social conscience. Even more demeaning, an incessantly happy person is boring.

p. 112–113, Ibid.

4220. Alla Yaroshinskaya (1953–)

1 Human Life—unique and individual—is only a moment in the eternal universe. Humanity should never forget this. We are floating through worlds and stars in order to finally create a life which is worthy of Man.

Acceptance Speech, Right Livelihood Award (Stockholm) 9 *December 1992*

2 Russia defends the international values of peace, cooperation and international security.

"American National Missile Defence: A Russian Perspective," The Bertrand Russell Peace Foundation (russfound.org) *July 2001*

3 The situation we have now in Russian-American affairs may be classified as a journey from "cold" war to peace and back to "cold" peace.

Ibid.

4221. Andi Zeisler (1953–)

1 Whatever their individual insecurities, there's no question that boys come of age with an entitlement so vast that displaying their boners in public is the least of it.

"Growing Up Norma," *Bitch,* Vol. 3, No. 1, *1998*

2 . . . the third wave is not really that far removed from the second wave (i.e., the women's movement of the 1970s; the first wave was the Suffragettes). The fight focuses on the same issues, since they haven't been fully resolved. Although the media likes to portray a conflict between the ideals of these two waves, in truth there is no fundamental disagreement.

Quoted in "Feminism is alive and well—and so are the issues" by Beth Fredericks and Tina Kozik, eons.com *October 2006*

3 Bitch is a word we use culturally to describe any woman who is strong, angry, uncompromising and, often, uninterested in pleasing men. We use the term for a woman on the street who doesn't respond to men's catcalls or smile when they say, "Cheer up, baby, it can't be that bad." We use it for the woman who has a better job than a man and doesn't apologize for it.

We use it for the woman who doesn't back down from a confrontation.

"The B-Word? You Betcha." *The Washington Post* 18
November 2007

4222. Jill Abramson (1954–)
See Jane Mayer, 4317:1–2.

4223. Kim Addonzio (1954–)
1 your face
is the bright lure I look for, love's hook
piercing me, hauling me cleanly up.

"Mermaid Song," *Tell Me* 2000

2 I want to walk like I'm the only
woman on earth and I can have my pick.

"What Do Women Want?," Ibid.

3 You don't know what love is
but you know how to raise it in me
like a dead girl winched up from a river.

"You Don't Know What Love Is," Ibid.

4224. Candace Allen (1954?–)
1 The trumpet slides back comfortably into its blue plush womb.
There was a time the womb was red, but it's been blue now for
quite a while. Cool blue. Cooler styles, cooler thoughts, cooler
notes, cooler times. Softer, mellower. Cool. But hot too, staccato heat. Focused, intense, like a blowtorch flame.

Ch. 1, *Valaida** 2004
*Valaida Snow (1904–56), famed jazz trumpeter and bandleader.

2 Thumbs up and under to adjust those rolls, wrestle that elastic,
straighten those stays. Welcome to the world of being almost
fifty-. . . well, who's to know, and who's to say? On a good
day, Time's a righteous trouper and telling no tales.

Ibid.

3 Strange things can take hold of the most civilized men on
ships.

p. 268, Ibid.

4225. Janine Maria Allwine (1954–)
1 The police actions on 9/26/06* were designed to do nothing
more than prevent us from doing the very thing this country
came into existence for—to protect the people from tyrants
and to guarantee the right of people like myself to speak out
against them when we see them.

The Honorable Rufus G. King, III** (Feb 16, 2007),
dissidentvoice.org March 2007
*Allwine and others were arrested during a protest. **Chief judge
of the Superior Court of the District of Columbia (2000–).

4226. Mary Kay Andrews (1954–)
1 They had half a bottle of Tanqueray. They had limes. Plenty
of ice. Plenty of time. It was only the Tuesday after Memorial
Day, so the summer still stretched ahead of them, as green and
tempting as a funeral home lawn. The hell of it was, they were
out of tonic water.

Ch. 1, *Little Bitty Lies* 2004

2 She couldn't stand it the way some women over thirty-five paraded around half naked in public—as if the world wanted to

see their goods. She kept her goods tucked neatly away, thank
you very much.

Ibid.

3 She can drink beer and wine all day and all night and not bat
an eyelash, but give her a mai-tai or, God forbid, a margarita,
and you are asking for trouble.

Ch. 1, *Hissy Fit* 2005

4 Enough! Enough parties. Enough presents. Enough luncheons
and teas, enough sappy wedding showers, enough family and
friends oohing and aahing over the perfect couple.

Ibid.

5 He's just a stray, but he almost never lies to me, which is more
than I can say for any other male I've ever been involved with.

Ch. 1, *Savannah Blues* 2007

6 "These recipes should look so easy, a trained chimp could fix
'em blindfolded."

Ch. 1, *Deep Dish* 2008

4227. Susan E. Arnold (1954–)
1 My company has not been perfect. No company has. We all
need to improve. But anyone who doesn't play fair hurts everyone who does. I challenge my company, my competitors and all
of our partners to work together to set the bar high.

"Arnold declares it's time to listen" by Andrea Nagel, *WWD*
26 May 2006

2 Beauty has seen an explosion in new products and solutions,
from nanotechnology and cosmeceuticals to natural oils and
herbs. More companies are offering and promising more stuff.
Sadly, that means more snake oil, and we all know that's true.

Ibid.

3 Apple was certainly paying attention when the record industry
wasn't. They paid attention to the way people were using the
Internet and how it was changing their relationship with music.
People no longer wanted to hear an entire CD, they wanted to
download individual songs and then burn their own personal
mixes. Now, 42 million iPods, about a billion songs and over
$9 billion later, iPod is bigger than music.

Ibid.

4228. Constance Avery-Clark (1954?–)
1 . . . professional women have less difficulty being orgasmic
than other women, because they do a better job of letting their
partner know what they need.

Quoted in "Making Time for Love" by Carin Rubenstein,
Working Woman October 1985/87

2 Sit down the first of every week and schedule in some physical
time together—at least 15 minutes three times a week—aimed
at increasing sensual awareness of one another.

"Personal Health" by Jane E. Brody, *The New York Times* 8
October 1986

4229. Sheila C. Bair (1954–)
1 The FDIC* remains committed to achieving what has been our
core mission for the past 75 years—protecting depositors and
maintaining public confidence in the financial system.

Testimony before Senate Committee on Banking, Housing and
Urban Affairs, *23 October 2008*
*Federal Deposit Insurance Corporation, which protects the first
$250,000 of deposits that are payable in the United States.

2 Despite what we hear about the credit crisis and the problems facing banks, the bulk of the U.S. banking industry is healthy and remains well-capitalized.

Ibid.

3 Minimizing foreclosures is important to the broader effort to stabilize global financial markets and the U.S. economy. Foreclosure is often a very lengthy, costly and destructive process that puts downward pressure on the price of nearby homes. While some level of home price decline is necessary to restore U.S. housing markets to equilibrium, unnecessary foreclosures perpetuate the cycle of financial distress and risk aversion, thus raising the possibility that home prices could overcorrect on the downside.

Ibid.

4230. Dora Bakoyannis (1954–)

1 The financial crisis and its effects, which our children are confronted with on a daily basis, have triggered insecurities and fears of the future. This heightens their feelings of unease with regard to the state—and young people have reacted.

Quoted in "I Expected Something Like This Would Happen," *Spiegel Online International* (spiegel.de/international/europe) *15 December 2008*

2 I think we all agree that Europe is the guardian of thought and mind. We therefore need more cooperation between us and we need to exchange views in this sector too. We are faced with major challenges. All these people have offered a great deal to European thought, and I think that closer cooperation between us and with all of the world's Academies might become a strong basis for us to move a step further, to take the step forward needed right now.

Statement re: meeting with French prime minister François Fillon,* ypex.gov.gr/mfa.gr/Articles/en-US/09032009_KL2004. htm *9 March 2009*
*(1954–), prime minister of France (2007–).

3 The International Community has embarked on an unprecedented commitment to Afghanistan's security, stabilization and development on a long-term basis.

In other words, the political will is there, the effort is there, the money is there but the desired end-result is still elusive, proving that the enormity of the international involvement may not be, after all, enough.

What we feel is still missing is the implementation of a truly concerted approach, a synergy of civil and military efforts, focused on a clear and realistic set of priorities that meets the needs of the Afghan people.

Speech, International Conference on Afghanistan (The Hague) *31 March 2009*

4231. Cherie Booth (1954–)

1 As long as young people feel they have no hope but to blow themselves up, we're never going to make progress, are we?

"PM's wife 'sorry' in suicide bomb row," *BBC News 18 June 2002*

2 It is not fair to Tony* or to the Government that the entire focus of political debate at the moment is about me. I know I'm in a very special position, I'm the wife of the Prime Minister, I have an interesting job and a wonderful family, but I also know I am not Superwoman. The reality of my daily life is that I'm juggling a lot of balls in the air. Some of you must experience that.**

"Maybe I should have asked more questions," *The Times* (London) *11 December 2002*
*Anthony "Tony" Charles Lynton Blair (1953–), British politician who served as prime minister (1997–2007). **Re: the scandal caused by her involvement with convicted fraudster Peter Foster to help buy two apartments.

3 We need more women lawyers, and more women judges. . . I am extremely confident that there are qualified women around, but that is not an application by me for any job.

Quoted in "Me a top judge? Maybe, says Cherie" by Steve Doughy, *Mail Onine 14 November 2007*

4232. Somer Brodribb (1954–)

1 As for the idea that feminists should be ragpickers in the bins of male ideas, we are not as naked as that.

"Radical Feminists 'Interrogate' Post-modernism," *Radically Speaking: Feminism Reclaimed*, Diane Bell and Renate Klein, eds. *1996*

2 Postmodernism is an addition to the masculinist repertoire of psychotic mind/body splitting and the peculiar arrangement of reality as Idea.

Ibid.

4233. Maria Burks (1954?–)

1 Every time you dial your cell phone, every time you turn on the car radio and hear a reporter broadcasting live via satellite from Saudi Arabia—all of that was made possible by what Marconi* did. That's how far we've come in 100 years.

Speech, Centennial Marconi Celebration (Wellfleet, Mass.), *17 January 2003*
*Guglielmo Marconi, Italian inventor of wireless transmission (1875–1937).

4234. Lorna Dee Cervantes (1954–)

1 Maybe it's here
en los campos extraños de esta ciudad
where I'll find it, that part of me
mown under
like a corpse
or a loose seed.

"Freeway 280," St. 4, *Emplumada 1981*

2 I believe in revolution
because everywhere the crosses are burning,
sharp-shooting goose-steppers round every corner,
there are snipers in the schools . . .

"Poem For The Young White Man Who Asked Me How I, An Intelligent, Well-Read Person, Could Believe In The War Between Races," St. 4 (1981), *The Woman That I Am, The Literature and Culture of Contemporary Women of Color*, D. Soyini Madison,* ed. *1994*
*See 3912.

3 This world
could be a dream, this
dream, a universe.

"Lápiz Azul," *¡Floricanto Sí! A Collection of Latina Poetry*, Bryce Milligan and Mary Guerrero-Milligan, trs. *1998*

4235. Roz Chast (1954–   )

1 Bad Housekeeping—The Magazine For Women Who Couldn't Care Less.

The New Yorker 30 May 1988

2 The World's First Genetically Engineered Human Hits Adolescence: 'We buy you the best genes in the world—for this?'

Ibid. *13 December 1993*

3 Required Seventh Grade Reading List: "The Red Badge of Boredom, Death Be Not Monotonous, The Tedious Pimpernel, Silas Yawnfest, All Humdrum on the Western Front, Ennui Pond, The Dull Man and The Sea."

Ibid. *23 December 2003*

4 Tuned In, Turned On, Dropped Out, Dropped In, Worked Out, Saved Up, Dropped Dead.

Cartoon caption, *Theories of Everything, Selected, Collected, Health-Inspected, Cartoons 1978–2006 2006*

5 What is your problem? Why did you run? If it weren't for you, Gore would have won.

"Thank You Card for Ralph Nader," Ibid.

6 When I carry a gun, I feel, and the bigger the gun the more I feel.

"The NRA's* Written Test for a Gun License," Ibid.
*National Rifle Association.

4237. Sandra Cisneros (1954–   )

1 Never marry a Mexican, my ma said once and always. She said this because of my father. She said this though she was Mexican too. But she was born here in the US., and he was born there, and it's *not* the same, you know.

"Never Marry a Mexican" (1991), *Woman Hollering Creek 1991*

2 Your body doesn't lie. It's not silent like you.

Ibid.

3 The house was immaculate, as always, not a stray hair anywhere, not a flake of dandruff or a crumpled towel. Even the roses on the dining-room table held their breath. A kind of airless cleanliness that always made me want to sneeze.

Ibid.

4 Human beings pass me on the street, and I want to reach out and strum them as if they were guitars. Sometimes all humanity strikes me as lovely. I just want to reach out and stroke someone, and say There, there, it's all right, honey. There, there, there.

Ibid.

5 When I see la *Virgen de Guadalupe* I want to lift her dress as I did my dolls' and look to see if she comes with *chones* [underwear], and does her *panocha* look like mine, and does she have dark nipples too? Yes, I am certain she does.

"Guadalupe, the Sex Goddess," *Goddess of the Americas/La Diosa de las Américas: Writings on the Virgin of Guadalupe,* Ana Castillo,* ed. *1996*
*See 4354.

6 Guadalupe the sex goddess, a goddess who makes me feel good about my sexual power, my sexual energy . . . My *Virgen de Guadalupe* is not the mother of God. She is God.

Ibid.

4238. Carolyn Clancy (1954?–   )

1 It occurs to me that there's more double-checking and systematic avoidance of mistakes at Starbucks than at most health care institutions.

Quoted by Ellen Goodman* in "The 'banality of screw-ups' haunts medicine," *Boston Globe 1 March 2003*
*See 3264.

4239. Beth Ann Conklin (1954–   )

1 Traditional beliefs in every continent associate female reproductive cycles with the moon.

"Lunar Cycles and Reproductive Rhythms," *thesis for master's in anthropology, University of Iowa May 1980*

4240. Joan Breton Connelly (1954–   )

1 There may be no finer tribute to the potency of the Greek priestess than the discomfort that her position caused the church fathers.

Portrait of a Priestess: Women and Ritual in Ancient Greece 2007

2 Modern Western theories of priesthood generally define a priest as one who mediates between gods and human beings. But in ancient Greece, all individuals had direct access to their gods. Private people could offer prayers, requests, thanks, and gifts and even perform sacrifice directly to divinities without the intervention of a priest.

Introduction, Ibid.

3 By marginalizing the importance of sacred-office holding, interpreters persist in presenting a pessimistic picture of the possibilities for Athenian women, subjected to utterly passive roles in an entirely secondary status.

Ibid.

4241. Amy Eilberg (1954–   )

1 The real director is God. A midwife sits with a woman in labor; she doesn't make a baby come out.

"Rabbi Amy Eilberg teaches women to be spiritual guides" by Marina Krakovsky, *The Jewish News Weekly 17 January 2003*

4242. Louise Erdrich (1954–   )

1 The drum breaks. There will be no parlance.
Only arrows whining, a death-cloud of nerves
swarming down on the settlers
who die beautifully, tumbling like dust weeds
into the history that brought us all here
together: this wide screen beneath the sign of the bear.

"Dear John Wayne,"* St. 3, *That's What She Said*, Rayna Green,** ed. *1984*
*American film actor (1907–79). **See 3338.

2 Our tribe unraveled like a coarse rope, frayed at either end as the old and new among us were taken.

Tracks 1988

3 Land is the only thing that lasts life to life. Money burns like tinder, flows off like water. And as for government promises, the wind is steadier.

Ibid.

4 Even when you plan to have a family, you never know who the person is going to be that you decide to become a parent to. We're accidentally born to our own parents.

Quoted in *A World of Ideas* by Bill Moyers *1989*

5   Columbus* only discovered that he was in some new place. He didn't discover America.

Ibid.

*Christopher Columbus (1451?–1506), Italian navigator and explorer who, in 1492, opened the path from the Old World to the New.

6   The ordained push West was supposed to clear the land of the native inhabitants. They were supposed to vanish before progress. That never happened. There are over three hundred tribes surviving and somehow managing to keep together language, culture, and religion. These are not visible people.

Ibid.

7   Our reservation is not real estate, luck fades when sold.

The Bingo Palace 1994

8   "There are names that go on through the generations with calm persistence. Names that heal a person just for taking them, and names that destroy. Names that travel, names that bring you home, names you only mutter in the deep water of your sleep. . . . Names to fear."

Off the Reservation 2004

9   Once we were a people who left no tracks. Now we are different. We print ourselves deeply on the earth. We build roads. . . . Where we go it is easy to follow. I have left my own tracks, too. I have left behind these words. But even as I write them down I know they are merely footsteps in snow.

Ibid.

10 The music was feeling itself. The sound connected instantly with something deep and joyous. . . . No, we can't live at that pitch. But every so often something shatters like ice and we are in the river of our existence . . . and this realization was in the music.

The Plague of Doves 2007

4243. Chris Evert Lloyd (1954–   )

1   Once you're been No. 1, you can never be satisfied with less.

Quoted in "Fire Over Ice" by Tom Callahan, *Time* (New York) *15 July 1985*

2   My whole career, people have been talking about how tough I am. Now that I'm losing some, I can see how tough I was—the killer instinct, the single-mindedness, playing like a machine. Boy, that's what made me a champion.

Quoted in "I Can See How Tough I Was" by William A. Henry III, *Time 11 September 1989*

3   Wherever there's more money, there's going to be more downfall.

Cited by Anna Quindlen* in "Behind the double axels. . . ," *The New York Times 25 January 1994*

*See 4136.

4244–4245. Cara Carleton "Carly" Fiorina (1954–   )

1   Leadership is all about unlocking the potential in others.

Speech, University of Maryland, *C-Span 10 October 2003*

2   There is no job that is America's God-given right anymore. We have to compete for jobs as a nation. Our competitiveness as a nation is not inevitable. It will not just happen.

Comment to Congressional committee, Quoted in" Coalition of High-Tech Firms to Urge Officials to Help Keep U.S. Competitive" by Jim Puzzanghera, *Knight Ridder Tribune 8 January 2004*

3   The worst thing I could have imagined happened. I lost my job in the most public way possible, and the press had a field day with it all over the world. And guess what? I'm still here. I am at peace and my soul is intact. I could have given it away and the story would be different.

Commencement address, North Carolina A&T State University 7 May 2005

4   Never sell your soul—because no one can ever pay you back.

Ibid.

5   One day at church, my mother gave me a small coaster with a saying on it. During my entire childhood, I kept this saying in front of me on a small desk in my room. In fact, I can still show you that coaster today. It says: "What you are is God's gift to you. What you make of yourself is your gift to God."

Those words have had a huge impact on me to this day.

Ibid.

4246. Mary Gaitskill (1954–   )

1   The photograph loomed over the toiling shoppers like a totem of sexualized pathology, a vision of feeling and unfeeling chafing together. It was a picture made for people who can't bear to feel and yet still need to feel. It was a picture by people sophisticated enough to fetishize their disability publicly. It was a very good advertisement for a product called Obsession.

Because They Wanted To: Stories 1997

2   "I fixed it so I wouldn't have to wash my face off at night," she said. She said it with brisk self-deprecation, as if her face, everybody's face, was a vaguely ridiculous thing that could come off at any moment. She also said it with pride that she'd acknowledged the problem and then gone right in there to fix it.

"Because They Wanted To," Ibid.

3   . . . he felt helplessness move through his body the way a swimmer feels a large sea creature pass beneath him.

"Tiny, Smiling Daddy," Ibid.

4247. Kim Gandy (1954–   )

1   We will not be the generation that both won and lost reproductive rights in our lifetime.

Quoted in "Protests display new vigor" by Laurie Kellman, Associated Press *23 January 2003*

2   We should remind the Decider* that presidents don't get moral waivers.

"Below the Belt," NOW** *Newsletter 9 January 2007*
*Re President George W. Bush's imperative to allow records to be waived for medical, moral or criminal issues such as drug problems and drunk driving arrests in order to increase recruitments for the Iragi war. **National Organization for Women.

3   The right to civil marriage for same-sex couples is an essential step on the road to full equality. Every person, regardless of their sexual orientation, deserves access to the more than a thousand legal protections and benefits in state and federal law that legal marriage brings.

"California Supreme Court Rules Ban on Same-Sex Marriage Unconstitutional," NOW *Newsletter 16 May 2008*

4   Women will not be fully equal until we break every last glass ceiling. Hillary Clinton proved that electing a woman president is within our grasp. Having her delegates tallied at the

convention will ensure that this important step in history will never be forgotten.

> NOW News release *14 August 2008*

5 George W. Bush* and Dick Cheney** were the opposite of hope. They were cynicism and fear and greed and destruction. Bush and Cheney wore the people down, sapped their spirit. They (and their "decider effect") are the reason people lack faith in government and the political process.

> "Below the Belt," *NOW Newsletter 19 November 2008*
> *George W. B— (1946–), Am. politician; 43rd president of the United States (2001–09). **Richard Bruce "Dick" C— (1941–), 46th vice president of the United States (2001–09).

6 The recovery plan [American Recovery and Reinvestment Act] isn't just about stimulating the economy, it's about recovering, and that means helping real people who are suffering. It includes helping families weather these difficult economic times by expanding safety net programs like food stamps and unemployment benefits, and yes, family planning, which is basic health care for women.

> Ibid. *31 January 2009*

4248. Cheri Gaulke (1954–)

1 Working collaboratively is not only part of who I am personally, but it's part of my politics. It's what I believe in—that people are equal, that everyone has something to contribute.

> "Cheri Gaulke," Quoted in *Exposures, Women & Their Art* by Ann Brown & Arlene Raven* *1989*
> *See 3533.

2 I think our sexuality is very earth-oriented and we can't really feel that connection with the earth if our feet are lifted up on high heels, if we're off balance.

> Ibid.

4249. Sylvie Germain (1954–)

1 Thousands of tiny insects of a bright phosphorescent green burst from Juliette's gaping body. They flew out of the open window in a whirl and descended on the cornfields, of which there was almost immediately nothing left but completely empty dried husks.

> *The Book of Nights,* Christine Donougher, tr. *1993*

4250. Nanci Griffith (1954–)

1 This heart was almost taken
this heart had a love of its own
This heart was reawakened
When you came along . . .
This heart hears the telephone ringin'
This heart is gonna let it go.

> "This Heart," *Flyer* (album) *1994*

2 And when he dies he says he'll catch
Some blackbird's wing
then he will fly away to Heaven
come some sweet blue-bonnet spring.

> "Gulf Coast Highway," Ibid.

3 . . . when the bankers swarm like locusts out there, turning away our yield.

> "Trouble in the Fields," Ibid.

4 I think of my songs as little gifts that I reach out and grab. They just happen.

> "Little Gifts . . ." by Michael Walsh, *Time 3 October 1994*

4251. Carol K. Howell (1954–)

1 "If we forget the Jews in Auschwitz, they died for nothing. If we forget the Jews in Russia, they suffer for nothing. That is what makes a Jew a Jew. He remembers."

> "Saving Soviet Jewelry," *Nebraska Review Spring 1988*

2 A family is a little civilization unto itself, with its own history, laws, codes, and discontents.

> "The Cutting," *River City Fall 1990*

3 . . . The shul needed a new roof. It needed a lot of other things besides, primarily new blood, but a roof was easier to find.

> "Tornado Watch Cookbook" (1986), *Shaking Eve's Tree, Short Stories of Jewish Women* Sharon Niederman, ed. *1990*

4 "Let's put it this way. You'd better hope there is no God. Because a God who presides over Auschwitz is either evil himself or psychotic."

> *Defying Gravity 1995*

5 "What does He want? Blindly obedient and faithful pets? Why didn't He just populate the earth with golden retrievers?"

> "The Islands Laugh Exultant," *Other Voices Spring 2001*

6 If life is the problem—short, arbitrary, unfair—then life is also the solution: life is what distracts you from the awful and essential fact of life.

> "The Unveiling," *Oxford Magazine,* Vol XVI *2002*

7 All you know is what you remember; pardon me, what you think you remember; pardon me, what you've been telling yourself you remember. All this time you've been talking to yourself. That's what you know.

> *A Fool at the Feast n.d.*

8 Avram said no cosmetics, but I smuggled in a few little things. This pot of concealer would just about erase those ugly marks. Just a dab, see? Gone! We give thanks, O Lord, for Estee Lauder: her price is above rubies!

> *The Make-up Lesson n.d.*

4252. Rickie Lee Jones (1954–)

1 Ask me if you want to know
The way to Coolsville

> "Coolsville," *RLJ 1979*

2 And if she don't know your name
She knows what you got
From your matzoh balls
To the chicken-in-the-pot

> "Danny's All-Star Joint" (1978), Ibid.

3 There are wounds that stir up the force of gravity:
a cold that will wipe the hope from your eyes.

> "Gravity" (1983), *The Magazine 1984*

4 Draw the Weird Beast
everywhere you go.
Death speaks the foreign
language we don't know.

Make sure they hear him
breathing.
"Rorschachs B. The Weird Beast" (1984), Ibid.

4253. Norma Kassi (1954–)

1 For thousands of years the Gwich'in* have safeguarded the sacred calving grounds of the Porcupine Caribou, which sustains our existence. Is it right that the fate of yet another indigenous culture will be determined by the U.S. government?

goldmanprize.org 2002

*(a.k.a. Kutchin or Gwitchin), a First Nation Alaska Native people who live mostly above the Arctic Circle.

4254. Deborah K. King (1954?–)

1 Black feminism asserts self-determination as essential.

"Multiple Jeopardy, Multiple Consciousness: The Context of a Black Feminist Ideology" (p. 72), *Signs: A Journal of Women in Culture and Society*, vol. 14, no. 1 *1988*

4255. Anne Lamott (1954–)

1 . . . I thought the secret of life was obvious: be here now, love as if your whole life depended on it, find your life's work, and try to get hold of a giant panda.

Hard Laughter 1980

2 Hope begins in the dark, the stubborn hope that if you just show up and try to do the right thing, the dawn will come. You wait and watch and work: you don't give up.

Introduction, *Bird by Bird, 1994*

3 Because for some of us, books are as important as almost anything else on earth. What a miracle it is that out of these small, flat, rigid squares of paper unfolds world after world after world, worlds that sing to you, comfort and quiet or excite you. Books help us understand who we are and how we are to behave. They show us what community and friendship mean; they show us how to live and die.

"Getting Started," Ibid.

4 Perfectionism is the voice of the oppressor, the enemy of the people.

"Perfectionism," Ibid.

5 Life is like a recycling center, where all the concerns and dramas of humankind get recycled back and forth across the universe.

"Writer's Block," Ibid.

6 It's so awful, attacking your child. It is the worst thing I know, to shout loudly at this 50-pound being with his huge trusting brown eyes.

Traveling Mercies 1998

4256. Annie Lennox (1954–)

1 There are two kinds of artists left: those who endorse Pepsi and those who simply won't.

The Guardian (London) *November 1990*

2 Together our voices will ring out across the world to tell politicians that millions of people dying of poverty is intolerable. Do nothing at your peril!

Live 8 Concert speech (Edinburgh, Scotland) *2005*

3 It Takes Strength To Live This Way
The Same Old Madness Every Day

I Wanna Kick These Blues Away
I Wanna Learn To Live Again . . .
"Dark Road," *Songs of Mass Destruction* (album) *2007*

4 You Could Be The Best Damn Thing
That Hasn't Happened Yet To Me

"Womankind," Ibid.

5 Throughout time immemorial, we can all connect through music across the cultural divide. It doesn't matter which language you speak, which race or tribe you come from. Music is a common language, a beautiful tool to raise awareness.

Quoted in "Annie Lennox Raises Her Voice" by Marianne Schnall,* *The Huffington Post* (huffingtonpost.com) *14 August 2008*

*See 4758.

6 I think the whole industry of celebrity and fame is really Faustian. I have had to really watch that dragon very carefully, so it didn't eat me up. I didn't want to be cannibalized by the industry of fame. And I don't look at myself as a celebrity, I see myself as a musician, an artist, a writer, a communicator.

Ibid.

7 We need to start to value humane and alternative means of conflict resolution. Warfare should be avoided at all costs. The ancient machismo culture of bloodshed and killing should be regarded as the barbarity it is, and prevented wherever possible. "Peace" needs to be valued and respected above anything else.

Ibid.

4257. Andrea Levy (1954?–)

1 My dad was a man and men didn't talk about their work. It was a secret between him and his wage packet. If you asked him what he did at work, he'd shrug and say that he worked for the Post Office.

Every Light in the House Burnin' 1994

2 "Child, everyone should know where they come from."

Fruit of the Lemon 1999

3 This was war. There was hardship I was prepared for—bullet, bomb and casual death—but not for the torture of missing cow-foot stew, not for the persecution of living without curried shrimp or pepper-pot soup. I was not ready, I was not trained to eat food that was prepared in a pan of boiling water, the sole purpose of which was to rid it of taste and texture. How the English built empires when their armies marched on nothing but mush should be one of wonders of the world.

Small Island 2004

4258. Jadwiga Lopata (1954?–)

1 Just as we warned, EU* bureaucracy is beginning to destroy our way of farming. We still have 1.5 million farms, more than any other European country. Most of our farms are tiny by European standards—about 7 hectares—and they play a huge role in protecting our biodiversity, as well as providing us with fantastic food. Most farms are mixed. Our farmers both plant crops and rear animals—one or two cows, a few goats, a few pigs and some chickens. And now they are facing more and more problems with EU bureaucracy. Polish farmers are finding that the practices they adopted hundreds of years ago are now illegal. It's become a nightmare.

"Polish farmers defy EU bureaucracy," *Seedling* (Barcelona) *July 2008*

*European Union.

2   When I was a child, I drank milk that farmers had hand-milked from their cows. I can't remember anyone ever getting ill as a result. But now it's illegal to milk by hand and sell it.

Ibid.

3   Many are changing the way they farm in order to survive. They are becoming less diverse. For instance, if you get rid of your animals and just cultivate fruit trees, the bureaucracy isn't so bad. But we're losing a lot of biodiversity as a result.

Ibid.

4   When supermarkets finally arrived, after the collapse of communism, people at first flocked to them. About 90 per cent of the food came from Western countries. It looked attractive as it was so well packaged. But quite soon people found that the food didn't taste as good as it looked and actually was often quite awful. So some people have gone back to buying local food, but a lot of people still buy in supermarkets because the food is so cheap there.

Ibid.

4259. Patricia Marx (1954?–)

1   My grandmother also told me that she—my grandmother—believes everyone has a determined number of footsteps to use up in a lifetime, and, therefore, it is foolhardy to exercise since you will only exhaust your quota sooner and die.

Ch. 1, *Him Her Him Again the End of Him 2006*

2   Those were the days when a person with a knapsack might knock on your door, say he was a friend of a friend of a cousin of an ex-girlfriend of a guy he had hiked with in Australia, and you then invited this person to sleep on your sofa and eat your food for as long as he felt like it.

Ibid.

3   I must have intuitively known even then, though, that if you ask a certain type of guy about himself, it's as good as winding a wind-up toy. For a given amount of time, said guy is in motion and requires only minimal attention from you. In this way, men are easier than plants.

Ibid.

4260. Cindy McCain (1954–)

1   The best thing I've ever done is go into recovery and stay drug-free.

Interview, *Dateline*, NBC-TV *1999*

2   My biggest goal is to hopefully inspire more people to get involved in their communities, to focus on, as my husband* has said, causes greater than themselves.

Quoted in "Two wives, two styles" by Lloyd and Mary Beth Brown, *Tallahassee Democrat 17 July 2008*
*John Sidney McCain III (1936–), United States senator (R-AZ, 1987–) and former candidate for president (2008).

4261. Angela Dorothea Merkel (1954–)

1   Almost everything in life looks slightly different from the inside than it does from the outside, as we well know. That goes for all houses, and it is also the case with Europe. From the outside, the European Union is a historic success story without precedent. The European Union is one of the most impressive works of peace on Planet Earth. European unification is a happy achievement for the people of Europe. It safeguards their freedom and paves the way for prosperity.

Speech to the European Parliament (Strasbourg), *17 January 2007*

2   Europe's soul is tolerance. Europe is the continent of tolerance.

Ibid.

3   Tolerance sounds its own death knell if it does not protect itself from intolerance. In the words of Thomas Mann,* "Tolerance becomes a crime when applied to evil." Tolerance without acceptance of intolerance is what makes us humane.

Ibid.
*(1875–1955), German writer, social critic, philanthropist; Nobel laureate, 1929.

4   The question is, "What makes Europe's diversity possible?" I believe the answer to this question is clear. Freedom is what makes our diversity possible. Freedom is the prerequisite for our diversity—freedom in all its manifestations: The freedom to express our opinions freely, even when others do not like them. The freedom to believe or not to believe. The freedom of enterprise. The freedom of artists to create their work as they see fit.

Europe needs this freedom just as much as we need air to breathe. Where it is restricted, we wither away.

Ibid.

4262. Karen Gordon Mills (1954?–)

1   The Small Business Administration provides an opportunity for the federal government to serve as a partner with small business—to help these businesses access capital and counseling, and to provide aid in times of natural disasters.

Chicago press conference, Associated Press *19 December 2008*

2   Small business will be at the table as we work our way through these difficult economic times—and as we grow the economy in the future.

Ibid.

3   America's spirit of entrepreneurship is one of our greatest assets as we compete in this global economy.

Ibid.

4263. Martha Minow (1954–)

1   Contemporary identity politics seems to offer people life rafts in the turbulent search for meaning, home, acknowledgment and redress . . . Recognition, of course, is not the only stake. Physical safety, when you are gay, or brown-skinned, or female, in the contemporary United States, is definitely at stake . . . when some people have specifically targeted others because of their race, or gender, or sexual orientation, or religion, or disability, demanding redress and acceptance *on those very grounds* is the only way not to concede those are natural or legitimate targets for injury. Hence, out of this arises identity politics.

Not Only For Myself: Identity, Politics, and the Law 1997

2   Perhaps there simply are two purposes animating societal responses to collective violence: justice and truth. Justice may call for truth but also demands accountability. . . . Then the question becomes: Should justice or truth take precedence? Of what value are facts without justice?

Ch. 2, *Between Vengeance and Forgiveness: Facing History after Genocide and Mass Violence 1999*

3   Traumatized people imagine that revenge will bring relief, even though the fantasy of revenge simply reverses the roles of perpetrator and victim, continuing to imprison the victim in

horror, degradation, and the bounds of the perpetrator's violence. By seeking to lower the perpetrator in response to his or her infliction of injury, does the victim ever master the violence or instead become its tool?

Ibid.

4   There are often powerful incentives against moving up the chain of command in holding people accountable for military abuses. Loyalty, hopes for promotion, fears of retaliation, and solidarity with those in authority explain some of the reasons why prosecutions of higher authorities so seldom follow military atrocities, even though the doctrine of command responsibility obviates the difficulties in establishing orders or actual knowledge in advance of the violations. Yet, precisely because there is a chain of command, responsibility for failing to prevent or halt abusive practices can and must be asserted.

"Living Up to Rules: Holding Soldiers Responsible for
Abusive Conduct and the Dilemma of the Superior Orders
Defense," *McGill Law Journal*, vol. 52 2007

5   Soldiers will not only be unlikely to resist a commander or peer group authorizing or engaging in atrocities but will also be prompted to join in with abusive behavior started by peers or prodded by superiors. Reducing the risk of military atrocity requires the direct engagement of the entire military, civilian authorities, and its citizens in designing the organization, the norms, and a culture that demand lawful and ethical conduct. Otherwise, atrocities will recur—and we will all be responsible.

Ibid.

4264–4265. Lepa Mladjenovic (1954–)
See Vera Litrichin, 3437.

4266. Medha Patkar (1954–)

1   Today it's the voice of the struggle, singing; tomorrow it will be the death bell ringing,

Acceptance Speech, Right Livelihood Awards (Stockholm), 9
December 1991

2   We look forward to the twenty-first century and the world economy but unfortunately not the hungry thirsty millions dragging behind. We have a growing chain of five star hotels with queues in their backyards of ill fed children, the pillars of our future.

Ibid.

3   While every political party has promised this in their election manifestos over the years, this is not in sight. Rainwater harvesting and decentralized water management is yet to get the due priority, political support, and budget allocation. As a result, the large dams are still looked at for all water needs and have proven to be a mirage . . .

"The Damned: To Build or Not to Build?" *Wide Angle (PBS)*
18 September 2003

4   There are viable options in terms of energy. Hydropower has proved not to be cheap and clean. The other options can be solar, wind, micro hydel,* and vast human power by using labor-intensive technology in a country like India.

Ibid.

*Small hdyro power systems adapting modern technology to the ancient water mill.

5   In spite of India having built over 3,600 large dams to date, the drought problem is not only unsolved, but has also worsened over the years.

Ibid.

4267. Deborah Prothrow-Stith (1954–)

1   Violence is a learned behavior that's preventable. But from the first cartoon to the latest super hero movie, violence is rewarded as a great way to handle anger.

Quoted in "Finding alternatives . . ." by Don Williamson,
Seattle Times, Op-Ed 8 November 1992

2   I've been around long enough to see zero tolerance go from a good idea to a horrible, horrible, mean implementation within the context of the school. We can't legislate this. We have to behave this way. We can't dictate to our children 'be nice.' We have to be nice. We have to show being nice on television and reward being nice.

"Deborah Prothrow-Sith Seeks End to Waves of Your
Violence," *Harvard Public Health NOW 25 May 2001*

3   We can learn some important lessons from dueling: The major lesson is that culture trumps laws. It matters what we say to our children. It matters how we're entertained. It matters when we watch superheroes solving problems violently.

"Dueling and youth violence," *The Boston Globe 30 April
2007*

4268. Condoleezza Rice (1954–)

1   Punish France, ignore Germany, and forgive Russia.

Quoted in *Washington Post 13 April 2003*

2   I remember the bombing of that Sunday School at 16th Street Baptist Church in Birmingham in 1963. I did not see it happen, but I heard it happen, and I felt it happen, just a few blocks away at my father's church. It is a sound that I will never forget, that will forever reverberate in my ears. That bomb took the lives of four young girls, including my friend and playmate, Denise McNair. The crime was calculated to suck the hope out of young lives, bury their aspirations. But those fears were not propelled forward, those terrorists failed.

Commencement address, Vanderbilt University *13 May 2004*

3   People may oppose you, but when they realize you can hurt them, they'll join your side.*

Quoted in *Rise of the Vulcans* by James Mann *2004*
*Advice given to her protégée, Kiron Skinner, while serving as provost at Stanford University.

4   When are we going to stop making excuses for the terrorists and saying that somebody is making them do it? No, these are simply evil people who want to kill.

Interview, PBS-TV *28 July 2005*

5   We tend to forget how daily and in some ways ordinary the U.S.-Canada relationship is. Our people are always going back and forth. We're in constant trade. It is just the most active of relationships at the level of people to people, not just government to government.

Quoted on meetmeattheborder.com *12 September 2006*

6   It's bad policy to speculate on what you'll do if a plan fails when you're trying to make a plan work.

Testimony, Senate Foreign Relations Committee *11 January
2007*

4269. Darlene Marie Ricker (1954–)

1   Just like in Hollywood, image is everything in the courtroom . . .

Lawyer's Wit and Wisdom, Bruce Nash, Allan Zullo, eds.;
Kathryn Zullo, compiler *1995*

2 Judges are, in many respects, like parents. You have to give them a good enough reason to do what you want.

Ibid.

4270. Mary Jo Salter (1954–)

1 [It] does you no justice if we call
   your death the death of anything but you.

"John Lenon,"* St. 5, *Henry Purcell*** *in Japan 1984*
*(1940–80), English rock musician, singer, songwriter; founding member of The Beatles; murdered. **(1659?–95), English Baroque composer.

2 a matched set, they differ
   almost imperceptibly—
   like salt and pepper shakers.

"Two Pigeons," St. 2, *Ibid.*

3 And now love's pain, your curse,
   is all I have. Forgive me . . . What worse
   punishment for suicide
   than having died?

"Elegies for Etsuko," *Unfinished Painting 1989*

4271. Yashodhara Raje Scindia (1954–)

1 If you visit the villages of India, you will weep at the poverty. I may not be made minister or get a Padma Shri, or even get voted back for the work I do, but I have the satisfaction of knowing I have made a few lives better.

Quoted in "The Princess Diaries" by Malavika Sangghvi, *The Times of India 29 May 2005*

2 But I have not disappeared, or run away or been cowed down. I've met life head on. You are dealt certain cards and you jolly well learn to work with them.

Ibid.

4272. Susan Seacrest (1954–)

1 Is it right that people in rural communities should have to buy bottled water? What kind of a world are we going to be living in?

Quoted in "Are the Wells Poisoned?" by Christopher Hallowell, Time.com *9 August 1999*

2 *Re aquifers:* [Like trustfunds] you want to use the interest responsibly but not deplete the principle.

Quoted in "Aquifer an unseen sea that quenches our thirst" by Andrew Moseman, *Lincoln Journal Star (Nebraska) 24 September 2007*

4273. Joni Seager (1954–)

1 Machismo has given us a design ethos of buildings and cities that are shaped by metaphors of machines; large-scale public buildings that are inhumane, confusing and intimidating; dwelling and working environments that are ecologically unsustainable.

"Blueprints for inequality," *The Women's Review of Books,* Vol. X, No. 4 *January 1993*

2 It may well be true that we cannot change society only by reforming our built environment; but it is just as true that we cannot change society if we leave its spatial conventions unexamined and intact.

Ibid.

3 Wherever you find women who are deprived of basic human rights, you are not going to have great social structures.

Quoted in "Joni Seager To Speak On Women's Role In History," *The Vermont Cynic 25 February 2003*

4 As a broad political observation, we might say that women everywhere face *de facto* restrictions on their public presence, dress, and private and public behavior.

Ch. 2, *The Penguin Atlas of Women in the World 2003*

4273.1. Sonia Sotomayor (1954–)

1 I saw [my mother] working, being the emotional and spiritual leader in our family. She had almost a fanatical emphasis on education. We got encyclopedias, and she struggled to make those payments. She kept saying, "I don't care what you do, but be the best at it."

Quoted in "A Breakthrough Judge: What She Always Wanted" by Jan Hoffman, *The New York Times 25 September 1992*

2 I don't get paralyzed by making decisions, but I fear the extent to which I'll be tortured by the difficult decisions I'll have to make.

Ibid.

3 I hope that none of you assumed on Monday that my lack of knowledge of any of the intimate details of your dispute meant that I was not a baseball fan. You can't grow up in the South Bronx without knowing about baseball.*

Quoted in "Strike-Zone Arbitrator—Sonia Sotomayor" by James McKinley, Jr., *The New York Times 1 April 1995*
*Comment at hearing on 1995 baseball strike.

4 O]ur experiences as women and people of color affect our decisions. The aspiration to impartiality is just that—it's an aspiration because it denies the fact that we are by our experiences making different choices than others. As recognized by legal scholars, whatever the reason, not one woman or person of color in any one position but as a group we will have an effect on the development of the law and on judging. . . . The people who argued [seminal decisions in race and sex discrimination] cases before the Supreme Court which changed the legal landscape ultimately were largely people of color and women.

Lecture, University of California Berkeley School of Law *2001*

5 I would hope that a wise Latina woman with the richness of her experiences would more often than not reach a better conclusion [as a judge] than a white male who hasn't lived that life.

Ibid.

4274. JoAnn Tall (1954?–)

1 The whole focus that I've always worked on as a grassroots environmentalist is that you do not tear up Mother Earth.

goldmanprize.org *1993*

4275. Elizabeth Tallent (1954–)

1 She did not bring seven children from Nicaragua in order for them to choose the doomed American existence of nerves rubbed raw by divorce, of quarrels, mutual contempt and lawyers' costly ministrations.

"Honey," *Honey 1993*

2 James is neither brutal nor about to be, but his circumstances confuse him, and he wishes that the gun wasn't all willingness to the hand that holds it.

"James Was Here," *Ibid.*

4276. Kathleen Turner (1954–)

1 Being a sex symbol has to do with an attitude, not looks. Most men think it's looks, most women know otherwise.

Quoted in *Observer* (London) *27 April 1986*

4277. Greta Van Susteren (1954–)

1 Washington is an extremely conservative place. Anything that starts to go out of the ordinary in one's personal life doesn't make it.

"High profile couple never pairs church and state" by Mary Jacoby, *St. Petersburg Times* (Florida) *13 December 1998*

2 I have said over and over and over again, it is our job in journalism to be aggressive in challenging politicians . . . but it is not right to gratuitously trash someone. . . . and worse, it becomes "conventional wisdom" giving some journalists blinders—meaning they don't step back and investigate for themselves but rather go with the so called conventional wisdom . . . that is not fair to the politician and is not a good for journalism or the First Amendment . . . our goal is to get information and let the people decide.

"The Trashing of Gov. Palin," gretawire.foxnews.com *7 November 2008*

4278. Vivienne Verdon-Roe (1954?–)

1 What would help in prisons would be educational opportunity for cooperative prisoners in a meditative environment, with job programs and small-business support in the communities on the outside. Instead we pay rich contractors to build enormously expensive kennels, with jobs for guards from the middle class.

Letter to the editor, *The New York Times 4 November 1994*

2 Since we are in a state of ignorance concerning the long term effects of LFA* sonar on marine life, and since the Navy has safer technology available, doesn't it seem to you that it's a needless risk to deploy this technology?

Letter to Senator Daniel K. Inouye** *11 June 2001*
*Re "Low-Frequency Active" (LFA) sonar program. **(1924–), United States senator (D-HI, 1963–).

3 It's amazing how something written 3000 years ago* is so appropriate today!?* And it's funny too.

Letter re: Lysistrata Project** *1 March 2003*
*Re Aristophanes' play "Lysistrata," in which women revolt against war by refraining from sexual activities with their husbands. **Founded in June 2002, it is dedicated to "the growing global consciousness of *being* Peace . . ."

4 We have a profound reverence for life. . . . The kind of world we're going to create really depends on our behavior in our daily life. We really encourage people to have the time to walk by the ocean and appreciate the things they're trying to save.

Quoted in "The roaring tide" by Jim Doyle, *San Francisco Chronicle 8 October 2004*

4279. Helena María Viramontes (1954–)

1 The only way Champ knows her mother's true hair color is by her roots which, like death, inevitably rise to the truth.

"Miss Clairol" (1987), *The Woman That I Am, The Literature and Culture of Contemporary Women of Color,* D. Soyini Madison,* ed. *1994*
*See 3912.

2 She is too busy thinking of things people otherwise dismiss like parentheses, but sticks to her like gum, like a hole on a shirt, like a tattoo, and sometimes she wishes she weren't born with such adhesiveness.

Ibid.

4280. Wang Anyi (1954–)

1 How a comfortable life can improve one's tolerance of others!

"Life in a Small Courtyard," Ch. 1, Hu Shihui, tr., *Seven Contemporary Chinese Women Writers,* Gladys Yang,* ed. *1982*
*See 2358.

2 "Our life was so beautiful and we were so deeply in love. So we're not poor at all."

"We're only short of money," Ziao Ji added dryly. We all laughed.

Ch. 4, Ibid.

3 It is very normal that serious literature is a bit lonely, but what worries me is the marketable and fashionable mass literature, which has influenced the young people's attitude towards literature. They don't really see the delight, attitude, and aesthetic pursuit of real literature.

"Wang Anyi—a Female Writer of Constant Innovations," chinaculture.org *19 September 2005*

4 While we stick to our own experience and conclusion, we should understand sincerely and observe other people's views on life, and enjoy the infinite spiritual landscape in people. When we read books with the trust we have in ourselves, the books will integrate with us, meaning we will in fact be reading about ourselves as well.

Ibid.

5 . . . after her eyes had adjusted to the darkness, she saw that the little world inside had barely changed; it was as if the little room had been encased in a time capsule. . . . Wang Qiyao failed to understand that it is precisely this myriad of unchanging little worlds that serves as a counterfoil to the tumultuous changes taking place in the outside world.

The Song of Everlasting Sorrow, Michael Berry & Susan Chang Egan, trs. *2008*

6 . . . even melancholy is noisy and clamorous. When it drizzles, raindrops write the word 'melancholy' on the window. The mist in the back longtang* is melancholic in an ambiguous way—it unaccountably hastens people along. It nibbles away at the patience she needs to be a daughter, eats away at the fortitude she must have to conduct herself as a woman. . . . Every day is more difficult to endure than the last, but, on looking back, one rues the shortness of the time.

Ibid.
*In Shanghai, a narrow alleyway that denotes the border of a neighborhood.

4281. Wang Yongchen (1954–)

1 While many people see a conflict between economic development and environmental protection, I believe that when you come closer to nature to learn more about it, you will find no real conflict between the two. On the contrary, a deteriorating environment makes economic development a 'mission impossible.' It is just like when people sacrifice health to make money and then have to spend that money to recover their health.

"Wang Yongchen Online: Environmentalist with a Dream," *Friends of Nature Spring 2006*

2   I felt that if we really want to have environmental protection, then people have to learn about the environment. . . . When [children] grow up to become bosses and have to weigh growing the economy and protecting the environment, they'll have a different response than people who haven't experienced nature.

Quoted in "Heros of the Environment: Wan Yongchen" by Austin Ramzy, *Time 2008*

4282. Sharon E. Watkins (1954?–   )

1   There are crises banging on the door right now, pawing at us, trying to draw us off our ethical center—crises that tempt us to feed the wolf of vengefulness and fear. . . . We need you to feed the good wolf within you, to listen to the better angels of your nature, and by your example encourage us to do the same.

Sermon, "Harmonies of Liberty" (Washington National Cathedral) *21 January 2009*

2   In times, such as these, we the people need you, the leaders of this nation, to be guided by the counsel that Isaiah gave so long ago, to work for the common good, for the public happiness, the wellbeing of the nation and the world, knowing that our individual wellbeing depends upon a world in which liberty and justice prevail.

Ibid.

3   America's true character, the source of our national wisdom and strength, is rooted in a generous and hopeful spirit.

Ibid.

4   At times like these—hard times—we find out what we're made of. Is that blazing torch of liberty just for me? Or do we seek the "harmonies of liberty," many voices joined together, many hands offering to care for neighbors far and near?

Ibid.

4283. Sheila Watt-Cloutier (1954–   )

1   Most people can't relate to the science, to the economics and to the technical aspects of climate change. But they can certainly connect to the human aspect.

Quoted in "Heroes of the Environment: Sheila Watt-Cloutier" by Laura Blue, *Time 2008*

4284. Sarah Willis (1954–   )

1   "From up close, the country is a deadly boring place, where people rust like old cars."

Some Things That Stay 2000

4285. Oprah Winfrey (1954–   )

1   Our prisons are filled with older men who, as young men, had the living hell beat out of them. Every parent who beat them said, "I'm doing this because I love you." When my grandmother used to whip my behind, she'd say "I'm doing this because I love you." And I'd want to say, "If you loved me, you'd get that switch off my butt." I still don't think that was love.

Quoted in Ch. 1, *Oprah!* by Robert Waldron *1987*

2   I understand that there are a lot of sick people in the world. I understand that many people are victimized, and some people certainly more horribly than I have been.* But you do have to be responsible for claiming your own victories, you really do.

If you live in the past and allow the past to define who you are then you never grow.

Ch. 2, Ibid.

*Winfrey was raped several times during her childhood, the first occurring when she was nine.

3   Sofia* teaches us that there is a great will and power inside us all, and that you can overcome anything. You can be down, you can even be broken, but there's always a way to mend.

Ch. 13, Ibid.

*The character portrayed by Winfrey in the film *The Color Purple* (based on Alice Walker's book; see 3029:11–20).

4   The great thing about attaining some level of success in your life is being spiritually in a place where you accept it and feel good about it and know why you are there, and not be afraid that tomorrow it's going to end.

Ch. 16, Ibid.

5   But somewhere I have always known that I was born for greatness in my life. Somewhere I have always felt it. I didn't mean it from an . . . an arrogant point of view, or greatness in terms of notoriety and money. Because who could have ever imagined this life that I'm living now, or that you could even make this much money? I couldn't have imagined it. But I did think that I would be able to use my life, and that my life could somehow be a force for good. I always did think that.

"100 Years of Great Women," *ABC News Special with Barbara Walters 30 April 1999*

6   Life is about becoming more than we are.

Interview with Charlie Rose, PBS-TV *29 October 1998*

7   Success is a magnifying glass on your personality.

"How I Got There," *Newsweek 14 November 2005*

8   I understand that the common denominator in the human experience, from the thousands of people that I've talked to, is that everybody just wants to be heard. Having that understanding and that connection has really given me wings to fly because I know that I can talk about anything to anybody with a sense of respect and integrity.

Ibid.

9   For me, doubt normally means don't. Doubt means do nothing until you know what to do.

Ibid.

10   Your calling isn't something that somebody can tell you about. It's what you feel. It's a part of your life force. It is the thing that gives you juice. The thing that you are supposed to do. And nobody can tell you what that is. You know it inside yourself.

Commencement speech, Howard University (Washington, D.C.) 12 May 2007

11   What other people label or might try to call failure, I have learned is just God's way of pointing you in a new direction.

Ibid.

12   Your integrity is not for sale.

Ibid.

13   There are those who say it's not his time,* that he should wait his turn. Think about where you'd be in your life if you'd waited when people told you to.

Speech, University of South Carolina *9 December 2007*

*Re: Senator Barack Obama's run for the presidency.

4286. Terry Wolverton (1954–)

1 I know the way your mind works.

You think because I say "I," I am revealing myself to you. You assume that the first person is personal. You believe you know something about me. This is how you get your power. You feel free to pass judgments; you decide that I'm tough or smart, wounded or seriously disturbed.

This is how Freud* ruined literature.

Bailey's Beads 1996
*Austrian physician and founder of psychoanalysis (1856–1939).

2 Recovery is so difficult to navigate because one is required to travel simultaneously in two directions: to walk again through the familiar landscapes of the past and to journey at the same time into unknown territory, to live as one has never before lived.

"Landmarks," *Calyx,* Vol. 17, No. 3 *1998*

3 Since my mother and stepfather were going out, I dropped a tab of mescaline and spent the evening on that glorious chemical edge, limbs turned to Jell-O, brain racing after a scattering of elusive thoughts, eyes staring at the patterns of energy in the air.

Ibid.

4 Whispered subterfuge, the miasma of the double life, a blur of truth and lies, a constant fear of discovery: these things too affect the body's chemistry, jolt the nervous system. Even the daily ritual of rolling joints—smoking before breakfast on the way to work, in the parking lot on break, on the drive home, after dinner, before bed—pales before the adrenaline rush of infidelity.

Ibid.

5 She switched from gin to wine, her solution to the problem she believes she doesn't have.

Ibid.

4287. Isabelle Adjani (1955–)

1 I'm a fanatic, a very dangerous person. Intensity is all that counts for me. When work keeps me busy, I feel like I'm drunk. It's my kind of eroticism.

"Isabelle Adjani," *People* (New York) *9 May 1990*

2 I think that people we have loved we always love.

"Mere Apparent," *Ibid. 12 December 1994*

4288. Randy Albelda (1955–)

1 Without an adequate understanding of the material basis of women's inequality, there is little hope for achieving gender equality.

Economics and Feminism: disturbances in the field 1997

2 To twist one of neoclassical economics' most popular metaphors, the theory's invisible hand has kept a very tight grip—if not a stranglehold—on the credibility of feminist explanations of women's unequal status in the marketplace of economic ideas.

Ibid.

4289. Sandra Bernhard (1955–)

1 I am of the philosophy that it's always wise to be nice to working-class people because they're the ones who can make you or break you—your mechanic, electrician, gardener, plumber.

May I Kiss You on the Lips, Miss Sandra? 1998

2 Southern California has been so overdeveloped that they might as well just build the entire coastline into one huge strip mall. At this point, we should just be able to walk from one strip mall to the other without interruption. There's no point to space—why should we have empty spaces? We don't want it. Empty space just scares us.

Ibid.

3 I wish you had, but I'm glad you didn't.

Ibid.

4 There's nothing worse than feeling dumb and having millions.

Ibid.

5 Life is a series of delicate meetings held together by a spider's thread strong as a steel span, tender as the wind blowing it all away.

Ibid.

4290. 'Asta Bowen (1955–)

1 The 20th century problem with creation spirituality, like the 17th century problem with the Copernican universe, is that it spells the end of business as usual. If the Earth is holy, we lose the right to subdue it; if the human spirit is mystical, our materialism must go; if the meek are truly blessed, our concept of power has to change. If we are the product of "original blessing" and not original sin, maybe up is down and down, up; anything is possible. Maybe the Earth is round after all.

"Can today's heretic be tomorrow's prophet?" *Seattle Post-Intelligencer,* Op-Ed *18 March 1993*

2 What we have forgotten in our zeal for equal rights, is that there are two ways to achieve equality; bringing the bottom up and bringing the top down.

"The ultimate in equal opportunity," *Seattle Post-Intelligencer,* Op-Ed *18 May 1993*

3 The problem with the health care industry is that it's an industry, not service. The bottom line is the profit of the owners, not the benefit of the consumers.

"Nation's health care system. . . ," *Seattle Post-Intelligencer,* Op-Ed, A11 *27 May 1993*

4 The world is changing, and the women's movement will change with it.

What happens to feminism matters because at long last, what happens to women matters. A paradigm shift has taken place in our society, and it is a sign of great hope. If women matter, then men may also matter one of these days, and then who knows? Little children, or even old people, might also begin to matter. We could leave behind the -isms and -ocracies and work together, women and men, old and young, to make the next days good days for everyone.

"Good days for women . . . ," *Seattle Post-Intelligencer 21 January 1994*

5 The adulation we shower on movie stars and filmmakers differs little from the honor given to the shamans and storytellers of time gone by.

By whatever medium stories are transmitted, be it celluloid in a multiplex theater or a dog-eared book on a beach, the fact remains that some kind of "telling" remains fundamental to human beings.

"The power of story . . . ," *Seattle Post-Intelligencer,* Op-Ed 6 *April 1994*

4291. Ann Deborah Braude (1955–)

1   From Biblical bans on women's voices to the attempted silencing of Hillary Clinton,* the control of women's speech has been a pillar of patriarchy.

"Language Barrier," *The Women's Review of Books*, Vol. XV, No. 12 *September 1998*

*See 3731.

2   Puritans' obsession with the efficacy of words grew out of their faith in The Word. They departed from the Catholic church and the Church of England over their conviction that human access to God resided in the words of the Bible rather than in the church and its sacraments. . . . Yet Puritans hoped that these unique individual encounters with the divine would reflect and support religious uniformity, as well as the hierarchies of a well-ordered society. This created an inherent conflict between a desire for freedom of expression and a desire for well-governed tongues.

Ibid.

4292. Geraldine Brooks (1955–)

1   One of the Koran's many descriptions of paradise reads like a brochure for a heavenly whorehouse. In a fertile garden with fountains and shade, male believers will be entertained by gorgeous supernatural beings with 'complexions like rubies and pearls', whose eyes will be incapable of noticing another man . . .

Nine Parts of Desire: The Hidden World of Islamic Women 2005

2   Many Muslims are content to claim that honor killings and clitoridectomy are not Islam; that they are customs that come from the national cultures and have nothing to do with the faith. With this assertion, many mainstream Muslims wash their hands of the twin brutalities that shape the lives of perhaps a quarter of the women of Islam

Ibid.

3   At some point every religion, especially one that purports to encompass a complete way of life . . . has to be called to account for the kind of life it offers people in the lands where it predominates.

"Beware of Dogma," Ibid.

4   Being Jewish remained an abstraction: something that had defined the kind of wedding I'd had . . . a certain awkwardness at Christmastime, and a label . . .

"Converts," Ibid.

4293. Carol M. Browner (1955–)

1   Time and time again, when the nation has set a new environmental standard, the naysayers have warned that it will cost too much, that it will impose an enormous economic burden on the American people. But, once we have set those standards, American ingenuity and innovation have found a solution at a far lower cost than predicted. . . . American businesses have risen to these challenges before, and they will do it again; all they need is predictability and flexibility.

Testimony, U.S. House Ways and Means Committee (Washington, D.C.), *18 September 2008*

4294. Roseanne Cash (1955–)

1   I'm not looking for your answers,
Just to know the question
Is good enough for me.

"The Wheel," *The Wheel* (album) *1993*

2   If there's a God on my side,
Why don't she show me her face?

"If There's a God on My Side," Ibid.

4295. Marilyn Chin (1955–)

1   for we all know
lust drove men to greatness,
not goodness, not decency.

"How I Got That Name," St. 1, *The Phoenix Gone, The Terrace Empty 1994*

2   survived by everybody and forgotten by all.

St. 4, Ibid.

3   We are Americans now, we live in the tundra
Of the logical, a sea of cities, a wood of cars.

"We Are Americans Now, We Live in the Tundra," St. 9 (1989), *The Woman That I Am, The Literature and Culture of Contemporary Women of Color*, D. Soyini Madison,* ed. *1994*

*See 3912.

4296. Darrah Cloud (1955–)

1   SONG. Those who love and understand this country are the only ones who ever really own it.

*O Pioneers!** 1992

*Adaptation of a novel by Willa Cather; also screenplay (see 1408:2–4).

2   I have found a language writing my own gender that is secret and which I want to reveal, so that it becomes part of the norm. For in language is perspective, and in perspective is a whole new way of looking at things.

Quoted by John Istel in *Contemporary Dramatists*, 5th ed., K.A. Berney, ed. *1993*

4297. Liza Donnelly (1955–)

1   "I'd invite you in, but my life's a mess."

Cartoon caption, *The New Yorker* 20 *January 1997*

2   "This is our son, Eddy. He's just graduated from school and is entering a void this fall."

Ibid. *18 August 2003*

3   Cartoonists usually are drawn to it as children and never grow out of it (or they never grow up, is another way to put it); the lucky ones get published and can make a living, the unlucky ones probably become axe murderers.

Quoted in "Interview with NYer Cartoonist Liza Donnelly" by Bob Eckstein, *Open.Salon.com* 4 *February 2009*

4   Why is it that women haven't typically gone into cartooning? I think there are a lot of answers to that, not one. The overriding thing is women have not traditionally been encouraged to be funny. That's changing, but for many years it was not ladylike to crack a joke, and it was not cool to take the spotlight away from a man by being humorous. Humor is powerful. But this is really not so true anymore, and more and more women are going into comedy, cartoons, comics.

Ibid.

4298. Carol Ann Duffy (1955–)

1   Today I am going to kill something. Anything.
I have had enough of being ignored and today
I am going to play God

"Education for Leisure," *Standing Female Nude 1985*

2　We three play poker while outside the real world shrinks to a
joker
"Poker in the Falklands with Henry and Jim," *Ibid.*

3　Some days, although we cannot pray, a prayer
utters itself
"Prayer," *Mean Time* 1994

4　The last hair on his head
floated out from a book. His scent went from the house.
The will was read. See, he was vanishing
to the small zero held by the gold of my ring.
"Mrs Lazarus," St. 4, *The World's Wife* 1999

5　Childhood is like a long greenhouse where everything is grow-
ing, it's lush and steamy. It's where poems come from.
Quoted in "Winning lines" by Peter Forbes, *The Guardian*
(London) *31 August 2002*

6　When you have a child, your previous life seems like someone
else's. It's like living in a house and then suddenly finding a room
that you didn't know was there, full of treasure and light. Every
day is a gift with a child, no matter what problems you have.
Quoted in "Christmas Carol" by Hephzibah Anderson, *The
Observer* (London) *4 December 2005*

7　Poetry and prayer are very similar. I write quite a lot of sonnets
and I think of them almost as prayers: short and memorable,
something you can recite.
Ibid.

8　Our abuse of the planet and our resources is an anxiety—childhood for children yet to be born will be darkened in ways we
can't imagine.
Ibid.

4299. Nancy L. Etcoff (1955–　)

1　. . . men are evaluated by their income and professional status
as harshly as women are evaluated by their looks.
Survival of the Prettiest 1999

2　Rather than denigrate one source of women's power, it would
seem far more useful for feminists to attempt to elevate all
sources of women's power.
Ibid.

4300. Annie Laurie Gaylor (1955–　)

1　Let's forget about the mythical Jesus and look for encouragement, solace, and inspiration from real women. Two thousand
years of patriarchal rule under the shadow of the cross ought
to be enough to turn women toward the feminist's salvation of
the world.
"Feminist salvation," *The Humanist* 1988

2　The "heretical" thoughts and often eloquent writing of women
without superstition should not be forgotten in the musty corridors of . . . libraries. One should not have to spend hours of
often discouraging labor at the computer terminal, or tramp
through university libraries, or experience eyestrain in front
of microfilmed documents just to be able to read some of the
views of women freethinkers! Ideas and accomplishments, not
just names, should be remembered. In many cases even their
names have been forgotten.
Preface, *Women Without Superstition, "No gods—No
Masters!"* 1997

3　Women freethinkers have worked to break the ties that bind
women and restrain intellect. They eschew superstition—a belief inconsistent with the known laws of science and reason.
Among the pioneers of social change striving to move humankind forward, they have directed their energies to this world,
not toward an unseen, improvable and unknowable one.
Ibid.

4301. Whoopi Goldberg (1955–　)

1　An actress can only play a woman. I'm an actor, I can play
anything.
Letter to Alice Walker,* *Today,* NBC-TV *13 January 1986*
*See 3547.

2　I wanna thank everybody who makes movies . . . I come from
New York; as a kid, I lived in the projects and you're the peo-
ple I watched . . . you're the people that made me wanna be an
actor . . . I'm so proud to be here, I'm proud to be an actor and
I'm gonna keep on acting, and thank you so much!
Acceptance speech, Best Supporting Actress, Academy Awards
(Los Angeles) *April 1990*

3　Most of all, I dislike this idea nowadays that if you're a black
person in America, then you must be called African-American.
Listen, I've visited Africa, and I've got news for everyone: I'm
not an African. The Africans know I'm not an African. I'm an
American. This is my country. My people helped to build it and
we've been here for centuries. Just call me black, if you want to
call me anything.
Quoted in *The Daily Telegraph* (London) *20 April 1998*

4302. Susan C. Grossman (1955–　)

1　It is almost difficult to remember God amid all the rules and
bustle of everyday Jewish life. We have appropriated Jewish
observance so well that we take it for granted, just as we often
take the ones we hold most dear for granted because we are
already comfortable with them.
"On *Tefillin*" (1986), *Four Centuries of Jewish Women's
Spirituality* Ellen M. Umansky* & Dianne Ashton, eds. 1992
*See 4011.

4303. Jeanette D. Gurung (1955?–　)

1　We have to come to terms with the fact that the face of the
farmer is female.
Speech, U.N. Commission on Sustainable Development *8 May
2008*

2　If we took as the reality that women are at the center of agriculture and the environment and then created institutions,
policies, programs, extension services around that reality we
would have a very different system.
Quoted in "Farm Women, an Unsung World Treasure"
by Regina Cornwell, The Women's Media Center
(womensmediacenter.com) *13 June 2008*

4303.1. Margaret "Peggy" Hamburg (1955–　)

1　I think that's an investment worth making. Clearly it's not off
the scale compared to other investments we routinely make for
national security and defending the health and well-being of
our nation.
Interview, CNN-TV *10 November 2001*

2　I believe that in this age of terror, the only thing that can stop a
small group of committed individuals is a large group of com-

mitted individuals. Only all of us acting together, with wise policies and sound judgments, can make our world safer.

Speech, Bowdoin College *May 2003*

4304. Peggy Hollman (1955–)

1   . . . what is deeply *personal*, what means most to us individually is also *universal*.

The Change Handbook 2007

2   Take responsibility for what you love as an act of service.

Address, "Towards a New News Ecology," Journalism that Matters-Poynter Institute (St. Petersburg, Fla.) *2 March 2009*

4305. bell hooks (1955–)

1   To me feminism is not simply a struggle to end male chauvinism or a movement to ensure that women will have equal rights with men; it is a commitment to eradicating the ideology of domination that permeates Western culture on various levels—sex, race, and class, to name a few—and a commitment to reorganizing U.S. society so that the self-development of people can take precedence over imperialism, economic expansion, and material desires.

(p. 194), *Ain't I A Woman: Black Women and Feminism 1981*

2   To be in the margin is to be part of the whole but outside the main body. As black Americans living in a small Kentucky town, the railroad tracks were a daily reminder of our marginality. Across those tracks were paved streets, stores we could not enter, restaurants we could not eat in, and people we could not look directly in the face. Across those tracks was a world we could work in as maids, as janitors, as prostitutes, as long as it was in a service capacity. We could enter that world but we could not live there. We had always to return to the margin, to cross the tracks to the shacks and abandoned houses on the edge of town.

Preface, *Feminist Theory: From Margin to Center 1984*

3   She eases her pain in poetry, using it to make the poems live, using the poems to keep on living.

"Black Is a Woman's Color" (1988), *Callaloo*, Vol. 12, No. 2 *Spring 1989*

4   They catch his angry words in their hands like lightning bugs. They store them in a jar to sort them out later.

Ibid.

5   Silenced. We fear those who speak about us, who do not speak to us and with us. We know what it is like to be silenced. We know that the forces that silence us, because they never want us to speak, differ from the forces that say speak, tell me your story. Only do not speak in a voice of resistance. Only speak from that space in the margin that is a sign of deprivation, a wound, an unfulfilled longing. Only speak your pain.

"Choosing the Margin as a Space of Radical Openness," *Yearning: Race, Gender, and Cultural Politics 1990*

6   We can no longer act as though sexism in black communities does not threaten our solidarity; any force which estranges and alienates us from one another serves the interests of racist domination.

"Homeplace (a site of resistance)," Ibid.

7   . . . no level of individual self-actualization alone can sustain the marginalized and oppressed. We must be linked to collective struggle, to communities of resistance that move us outward into the world.

Sisters of the Yam: Black Women and Self-Recovery 1993

8   The moment we choose to love we begin to move against domination, against oppression. The moment we choose to love we begin to move towards freedom, to act in ways that liberate ourselves and others.

Outlaw Culture—Resisting Representations 1994

9   As we search as a nation for constructive ways to challenge racism and white supremacy, it is absolutely essential that progressive female voices gain a hearing.

Killing Rage—Ending Racism 1995

10   To counter the fixation on a rhetoric of victimhood, black folks must engage in a discourse of self-determination.

Ibid.

4306. Debbie Horsfield (1955–)

1   We don't quarrel with a good review—except to ask why it's assumed that a woman can't write a play about football without wielding a sledge hammer and aiming it in the general direction of the male.

Introduction, *Plays by Women*, Vol. 1, Michelene Wandor,* ed. *1982*

*See 3237.

2   PHIL. Oh, we're all dead ignorant up North, aren't we? It's dead embarrassing. How d'y'admit y've never been windsurfing—never read Gormenghast—never heard of David Hockney? I've missed out. I'm not a Feminist, Friend-of-the-Earth, Ban-the-Bomber, Real Ale Freak. What am I? I don't know anything. Y'go to school, y'sit exams—nobody tells yer about Jean-Luc Godard or reading the *The Guardian*. Football? Oh but you don't actually go? Oh no, not me. Not much. What d'y'do if y'can't stand yoga, despise *The Hobbit*—an' thought that Donizetti was a cheap martini? How can y'be taken seriously if yer favorite film's *The Jungle Book*?

True Dare Kiss 1983

4307. Siri Hustvedt (1955–)

1   What used to be doesn't leave us.

The Sorrows of an American 2008

2   It's odd that we're all compelled to repeat pain, but I've come to regard this as a truth.

Ibid.

3   The work of psychoanalysis can turn ghosts into ancestors.

Ibid.

4   My solitude had gradually begun to alter me, to turn me into a man I had not expected. . . . I've often thought that none of us is what we imagine, that each of us normalizes the terrible strangeness of inner life with a variety of convenient fictions.

Ibid.

4308. Gwen Ifill (1955–)

1   We're very lazy when we think about race in this country. We try to put it in a box. It's Jesse [Jackson] versus Al [Sharpton], or Jesse and Al versus everyone else. We love simplistic conflict.

Quoted in "Controversy brews up around VP debate moderator Ifill" from Ed Hornick and Rebecca Sinderbrand, CNN-TV *2 October 2008*

2 [The new generation of black politicians was] raised to believe they could do anything. Their schools were integrated, and Ivy League colleges came looking for them. . . . They lived in a world shaped by access instead of denial.
Breakthrough: Politics and Race in the Age of Obama 2008

3 Those who marched back then often turn out to be the biggest critics of those who are poised to take over now.
Ibid.

4 . . . of the scores of black achievers interviewed for this book, none was willing to say race had not in some way enhanced or hampered the voters' perception of his or her political fitness. . . . The candidate may be judged not black enough or too black, but one way or another, race counts.
Ibid.

4309. Alice A. Jardine (1955?–   )
1 Men's relation to feminism is an impossible one.
Ch. 1, *Men in Feminism 1987*

2 The ceiling isn't glass; it's a very dense layer of men.
The New Yorker 1996

4310. Mary Karr (1955–   )
1 . . . a dysfunctional family is any family with more than one person in it. In other words, the boat I can feel so lonely in actually holds us all.
Introduction, *The Liars' Club, A Memoir 1995*

2 Out in West Texas, the sky is bigger than other places. There are no hills or trees. The only building is an occasional filling station, and those are scarce. How the westward settlers decided to keep moving in the face of all that nothing, I can't imagine. The scenery is blank, and the sky total. Even today you can drive for hours with nothing but the hypnotic rise and slope of telephone lines to remind you that you're moving.
Ch. 2, Ibid.

3 The newly dead do, after all, rent a lot of skull space from us.
Ch. 5, Ibid.

4 I think about the story of Job I heard in Carol Sharp's Sunday school. How he sort of learned to lean into feeling hurt at the end, the way you might lean into a heavy wind that almost winds up supporting you after a while. People can get behind pain that way, if they think it derives from powers larger than themselves.
Ch. 7, Ibid.

5 Mother didn't believe in Green Stamps or coupons. They were a trick to keep women hunched over their kitchen tables after their kids were asleep, not unlike darning and embroidery—things Mother excelled at but refused to do. Nor would she drive a block out of her way to get gas for two cents cheaper. Mother had transcended thrift, even before she got Grandma's money.
Ch. 10, Ibid.

6 I've heard it said that caring for an invalid is like caring for a baby. And I suppose it's the same basic deal, but a baby rewards you each day with change, sprouting a tooth or discovering that the object randomly waggling before its eyes is, in fact, its own hand. But an invalid is a hole you pour yourself into. Every day he fixes you with a glance more gnawed-out

tired than yours, more hurt. If life is suffering (as the Buddha says), some endless shit-eating contest, then the invalid always wins, hands. Down.
Ch. 14, Ibid.

4311. Cynthia Kenyon (1955–   )
1 No desserts. No sweets. No potatoes. No rice. No bread. No pasta. When I say 'no,' I mean 'no, or not much,' she notes. Instead, eat green vegetables. Eat the fruits that aren't the sweet fruits, like melon. Bananas? Bananas are a little sweet. Meat? Meat, yes, of course. Avocados. All vegetables. Nuts. Fish. Chicken. That's what I eat. Cheese. Eggs. And one glass of red wine a day. . . . I have a fabulous blood profile. My triglyceride level is only 30, and anything below 200 is good.
Quoted in "In Methuselah's Mould" by Bill O'Neill, *PLoS Biology*, Vol. 2, No. 1 (Public Library of Science) *20 January 2004*

2 On aging: People thought you just wore out, like an old car. And I thought, "No, there's going to be something beautiful here."
"Ten Who Inspire," *AARP Magazine January/February 2008*

3 The big, big, big payoff will be going after all the age-related diseases at once, just by going after the genes that control aging.
Ibid.

4312. Barbara Kingsolver (1955–   )
1 Those times made bonds among people. The clotheslines ran from house to house and the wash ran between families like the same drab flag repeated over and over, uniting them all in the nation of washtubs and rough knuckles. There was love in that life, a kind of solid hope. Children ran heedless under the flapping laundry in a nation of their own. But it's Alice's impression that most of them grew up with hungry hearts, feeling sure that one day they would run out of everything again.
Pigs in Heaven 1993

2 May Africa talk back? Might those pagan babies send *us* to hell for living too far from a jungle? Because we have not tasted the sacrament of palm nuts?
The Poisonwood Bible 1998.

3 That is the story of Congo they are telling now in America: a tale of cannibals. I know about this kind of story—the lonely look down upon the hungry; the hungry look down upon the starving. The guilty blame the damaged. . . . It makes everyone feel much better.
Ibid.

4 [Voodoo] . . . embraces death as its company, not its enemy.
Ibid.

5 Six months is a long time for a family to tolerate itself without any outside distractions.
Book Two: The Revelation: "Orleanna Price," Ibid.

6 Downstream is always someone else's up.
Ibid.

7 I could never work out whether we were to view religion as a life-insurance policy or a life sentence. I can understand a wrathful God who'd just as soon dangle us all from a hook. And I can understand a tender, unprejudiced Jesus. But I could never quite feature the two of them living in the same house.
Ibid.

8 God doesn't need to punish us. He just grants us a long enough life to punish ourselves.

> Book Four, Bel and the Serpent: "What We Lost," Ibid.

9 On the wings of an owl the fallen Congo came to haunt even our little family, we messengers of goodwill adrift on a sea of mistaken intentions.

> "Orleanna Price," Ibid.

10 If I'd known what marriage was going to be like, well, heck, I probably would have tied all those hope-chest linens together into a rope and hung myself from a tree!

> Book Five, Exodus: "What We Carried Out," Ibid.

11 "Friends, there is nothing like your own family to make you appreciate strangers!"

> Ibid.

12 There's nothing like living as a refugee in one's own country to turn a generous soul into a hard little fist.

> Ibid.

13 The substance of grief is not imaginary. It's as real as rope or the absence of air, and like both those things it can kill.

> "Orleanna Price," Ibid.

14 *Conquest* and *liberation* and *democracy* and *divorce* are words that mean squat, basically, when you have hungry children and clothes to get out on the line and it looks like rain.

> Ibid.

15 Manners had not been her long suit to begin with, even a life long ago when she lived in a brick house, neatly pressed between a husband and neighbors.

> "Predators," *Prodigal Summer* 2001

4313–4314. Jan Lesher (1955?–)

1 I think it's important to enjoy what you do at the time you are doing it, and take away experiences that you will carry with you forever

> Quoted in *AzBusiness Magazine* June 2008

2 *On being asked for advice for working in government:* Work hard, listen, allow for constructive criticism, be open to suggestions and be honest with yourself and the people around you. Don't make promises you can't keep, and if you don't know the answer to a question, don't be afraid to say so. Be willing to compromise, assist in finding solutions and learn to pick your battles.

> Ibid.

4315. Judith "Judy" Perez Martinez (1955–)

1 I hope we're moving not toward focusing more on how women can conform to the [law] profession as it exists, but how we can bring women's characteristics and qualities to better the profession.

> "Back to the Future," *Perspectives* Fall 1997

4316. Toni Marie Massaro (1955–)
Also see Barbara Allen Babcock, 3071:2.

1 The disagreements and fallibilities among us do mean, however, that, to the extent that education seeks to pass on the current state of our national knowledge, it should "teach the conflicts" along with the consensus. "Teaching the conflicts"

means that reformers must take seriously both the force of E. D. Hirsch's* lament that our students suffer from profound fact gaps in traditional subjects and the multiculturalists' arguments for an expanded American anthology.

> Ch. 6, *Constitutional Literacy: A Core Curriculum for a Multicultural Nation* 1993

*(1950–) Am. poet, academic; pres. John Simon Guggenheim Memorial Fdn.

4317. Jane Mayer (1955–)

1 The full story of his* confirmation thus raises questions not only about who lied and why, but, more important, about what happens when politics becomes total war and the truth—and those who tell it—are merely unfortunate sacrifices on the way to winning.

> *Strange Justice; The Selling of Clarence Thomas* coauthor, Jill Abramson* 1994

*Clarence Thomas (1928–), Am. Supreme Court justice, 1991.
**See 4222.

2 Historically, many black men felt that black women had succeeded at their expense and so owed them special deference.

> Ibid.

3 The Bush* Administration's redefinition of the standards of interrogation took place almost entirely out of public view.

> "Outsourcing Torture," *The New Yorker* 14 February 2005

*George W. B— (1946–), Am. politician; 43rd president of the United States (2001–09).

4 Scientific research on the efficacy of torture and rough interrogation is limited, because of the moral and legal impediments to experimentation.

> Ibid.

4318. Susan McDougal (1955–)

1 Finding that someone I cared about was in deep trouble, physically or emotionally, had always been a catalyst for me. When I was younger, I remember a friend saying, as we drove by a homeless person, "There's Susan's dream date—no home, no car, no job."

> Ch. 17, *The Woman Who Wouldn't Talk* 2003

4319. Candia McWilliam (1955–)

1 A man that unironic would be valuable in war.

> *Debatable Land* 1995

2 At the bow of the boat the anchor chain girned with a faint but surprisingly serious sound, as though the stone knight on a tomb were waking and beginning heavily to stir in his burdensome carapace, the stone conjunctions of his armour beginning painfully to grate into articulation.

> Ibid.

4320. Azar Nafisi (1955–)

1 . . . What we search for in fiction is not so much reality but the epiphany of truth.

> Part I, Lolita, 1, *Reading Lolita in Tehran* 2003

2 It is amazing how, when all possibilities seem to be taken away from you, the minutest opening can become a great freedom.

> Part I, Lolita, 9, Ibid.

3 The worst crime committed by totalitarian mind-sets is that they force their citizens, including their victims, to become complicit in their crimes.

> 22, Ibid.

4 This is how you read a novel: you inhale the experience.

> Part II, Gatsby, 12, Ibid.

5 Just over a year after I had returned to my country, my city, my home, I discovered that the same decree that had transformed the single word *Iran* into the *Islamic Republic of Iran* had made me and all that I had been irrelevant. The fact that I shared this fate with many others did not help much.

> Part II, Gatsby, 26, Ibid.

4321. Susan Neiman (1955–)

1 What occurred in Nazi death camps was so absolutely evil that, like no other event in human history, it defies human capacities for understanding.

> Preface, *Evil in Modern Thought* 2002

2 How could a good God create a world full of innocent suffering? Such questions have been off-limits to philosophy since Immanuel Kant* argued that God, along with many other subjects of classical metaphysics, exceeded the limits of human knowledge.

> Ibid.

*(1724–1804), German philosopher.

3 Modern conceptions of evil were developed in the attempt to stop blaming God for the state of the world, and to take responsibility for it on our own. The more responsibility for evil was left to the human, the less worthy the species seemed to take it on.

> Ibid.

4 What if the world were created by a Being whose whole purpose was to cause us torment and illusion? God knows it sometimes looks that way.

> Ibid.

5 Religion is not the source of ideas of good and evil, but one way to respond to them; it makes more sense to say the fact of evil gave rise to religion than that religion gave rise to the idea of evil . . . Religion is rather a way of trying to give shape and structure to the moral concepts that are embedded in our lives.

> *Moral Clarity, A Guide for Grown-up Idealists* 2008

4322. Indra Nooyi (1955–)

1 I am a global thinker in everything I do.

> Quoted in "Indra Nooyi" by Bill Saporito, *Time* 2008

2 The world has gone through a radical shift. There's incredible macroeconomic stability. That hasn't happened in the last 35 years.

> Ibid.

3 I need a healthy consumer out there. The only way I can do that is sustainability.

> Ibid.

4323. Urszula Nowakowska (1955?–)

1 Catholic fundamentalism and the ideology of a free-market economy constitute the biggest threat to women's rights and their status in society. Women are the most visible victims of

the period of transition, and they are going to pay the biggest price.

> *Ana's Land: Sisterhood in Eastern Europe*, Tanya Renne,* ed.
> 1996

*See 4830.

2 A law can be a powerful tool, which we must learn to use to our advantage. We must also learn to use any means at our disposal to change a law that is not satisfactory and that fails to provide us with adequate and sufficient guarantees.

> "Under Law in Poland," United Nations Development Fund
> for Women (unifem.org) 24 November 2000

4324. Susan Orlean (1955–)

1 The flat plainness of Florida doesn't impose itself on you, so you can impose upon it your own kind of dream.

> *The Orchid Thief* 1998

2 I was starting to believe that the reason it matters to care passionately about something is that it whittles the world down to a more manageable size. It makes the world seem not huge and empty but full of possibility. If I had been an orchid hunter I wouldn't have seen this place as sad-making and vacant—I think I would have seen it as acres of opportunity where the things I loved were waiting to be found.

> Ibid.

3 At the concerts I saw men wearing spats and women wearing hats such as I'd never seen before: a black porkpie with a turquoise veil and bow; a midshipman's white cap with little pearls sewn along the rim; a tricorne of orange faille; a green beanie; a purple derby, worn at a slant; a red saucer that had netting looped around the edge and a piece of stiff fabric shaped like a Dorito sticking straight up from the crown; a fuchsia-colored ten-gallon with an ostrich feather drooping from the hatband. The hats were on elderly ladies, who moved through the crowds like cruise ships.

> "Devotion Road," *The Bullfighter Checks Her Makeup* 2001

4 Taxidermists seem to make little distinction between loving animals that are alive and loving ones that are not.

> "Life Like," *My Kind of Place: Travel Stories from a Woman
> Who's Been Everywhere* 2004

5 An ad might have claimed that it was nestled in the Oregon mountains—in fact, an ad did claim that it was nestled in the Oregon mountains—but would fail to mention that it was nestled in what was possibly the only cramped, cluttered, suburban subdivision in the Oregon mountains.

> "Out of the Woods," *The New Yorker* 14 June 2004

4325. Louise Page (1955–)

1 [She] wrecked her life trying to keep her body whole. I did not ask her to be beautiful but to be there.

> *Tissue* 1978

2 LEONARD. You expect everything in you to shrivel [when you get old]. All the hate and the longing. The lust. You don't expect to have them any more. But there isn't much else so you have them all the more. I could kill now. If I had the strength. . . . That's not what you expect.

> *Salonika* 1982

4326. Nurit Peled-Elhanan (1955?–)

1 But I, who lost my only daughter, know that the death of any child means the death of the whole world. "Satan has not yet de-

vised a Vengeance for the death of a young child" said the Jewish poet Bialik, and that is not because Satan has no means to do so, but because after the death of a child there is no more death for there is no more life. The child takes the war and the future of the war into his little grave to rest with his little bones.

Speech, Women in Black (Evanston, Illinois) *1 June 2001*

2   Some people are willing to modify their system of classifications, unfortunately in Israel this is not the case. Israel is a nation state and its discourse is monologic to the extreme. It is a multicultural and multilingual society that behaves like a monolingual and monocultural society. Its system of classification is racist and immutable. People are either Jews or non-Jews, and it doesn't matter what they are if they are non-us. They are worth less, not to say worthless. Their blood is cheaper.

Lecture, "Language and Education," Women's International League for Peace and Freedom (Geneva) *2001*

3   I think that motherhood is the only common denominator that overcomes nationality and race and religion and I think mothers are the only ones who can stand up to politicians and generals.

Ibid.

4   And we know that today's school children are tomorrows politicians, and today's politicians are yesterdays school children
Ibid.

5   People who do not accept differences and are not ready to make room in themselves for differences, cannot speak to each other. Very much like Alice and the caterpillar, they can argue and fight and humiliate each other, but they cannot speak. People who cannot, or who would not accept difference and the fact that conversation is an ongoing negotiation about different classifications have a monolithic approach to conversation, namely, they want to win and conquer and dominate.

Ibid.

6   The blood of children has become the cheapest merchandise in the murderous game. And the so called leaders trade in it freely, easily, because for politicians and generals, children are abstract entities, and blood is a chip in the bargain.

Ibid.

7   To me, people are not divided into Palestinians and Jews. For me people are divided into peace lovers and war criminals.

Ibid.

8   The so-called free world is afraid of the Muslim womb.

Great France of "la liberte égalite et la fraternite" is scared of little girls with head scarves. Great Jewish Israel is afraid of the Muslim womb which its ministers call a demographic threat.

Almighty America and Great Britain are infecting their respective citizens with blind fear of the Muslims, who are depicted as vile, primitive and blood-thirsty, apart from their being non-democratic, chauvinistic, and mass producers of future terrorists.

Speech, "Women," European Parliament (Strasbourg) *8 March 2006*

4327. Joyce Radtke (1955–)

1   Like Persephone, the Greek goddess of eternal spring, I journeyed into the dark realms and used the seeds of creativity to find my way home. By imaging myself as Persephone, I was able to escape from the pain, the grieving, the dark and bar-ren landscape the doctors painted for me. I have returned to the light, to living moments as they come and embracing every second I have.

Artist's Statement, Art.Rage.Us exhibit, Los Angeles Public Library *March 1999*

4328. Maureen Reddy (1955–)

1   It was only when I stopped being white, in some sense, that I began to understand what whiteness means in America. . . . [making] whiteness visible, becoming aware of whiteness as a social construction, moves out of the mainstream of whiteness. . . . In all-white groups, I feel like a secret spy.*

Crossing the Color Line: Race, Parenting, and Culture 1994
*Re to her marriage to an African-American man.

2   . . . white people in responsible positions are usually unwilling to admit that racism exists in their environment in any form. And if the racism isn't overt—in other words, if no one is running down the halls screaming "nigger" and wearing a Klan hood—you can count on a long, uphill struggle.

Ibid.

4329. Adi Roche (1955–)

1   No army can be sent against an enemy you can't see, the invisible enemy of radiation.

Quoted in "Chernobyl charity founder Adi Roche gets top award" by Sean O'Riordan, *Irish Examiner 1 February 2003*

2   Children are our very special investment in the future; they are the nation's bequest to future generations; to deny them a future is a form of genocide. What greater arrogance is there than to deny any child a future?

Speech, United Nations General Assembly *April 2004*

3   . . . the day we cannot shed a tear for another human being or feel an emotion about the suffering or the agony of another human being, no matter what part of the world they are in, is the day I think we switch the light off on the planet because we have lost who we are as a species and we have lost our sense of responsibility of being part of the human family.

Interview with John LeKay, heyokamagazine.com *March 2007*

4   As long as we continue to seek only logical neat answers, we will be diverted from the truth and from that picture of human and ecological frailty which is showing us how delicately balanced the inter-relationship between man and nature really is. How precarious that balance has become in the hands of man. The reality will continue to allude us until we face up to this new understanding which really does require a new courage, a new bravery and a new open heart.

Ibid.

4330. Sara Roy (1955–)

1   Perhaps the greatest and most painful loss to the [Palestinian] movement has been the destruction of its ties to the majority of women at the grassroots level, who now feel abandoned and betrayed by their leadership at a time of acute need and unprecedented hardship.

"Conflicts, challenges and changes," *New Directions for Women*, Vol. XIV, No. 4 *January 1997*

2   As I think of the women in this [Palestinian] family . . . it is clear that it is not just the kitchen that constrains them but, perhaps more tragically, the lack of food to prepare in it.

"One step forward, two steps back," *The Women's Review of Books*, Vol. XVI, No. 3 *December 1998*

3   Today, there is a war against dissent, a dangerous war that not only threatens what we think but how we construct our thoughts and who, in the end we become. Whether we are talking about the Palestinian-Israeli conflict, the war in Iraq or global terrorism, our right to oppose is being stigmatized and invalidated.

Ch. 1, *Failing Peace: Gaza and the Palestinian-Israeli Conflict*
2006

4331. Milcha Sánchez-Scott (1955–   )

1   CUBANA. I'm human. I have a green card.

Latina 1980

2   SARITA. See, what I actually want to be . . . I mean, what I really am is an actress. . . . I'll give you my credits. I was a barrio girl who got raped by a gang in *Police Story*, a young barrio mother who got raped by a gang in *Starsky and Hutch*, a barrio wife who got beat up by her husband who was in a gang in *The Rookies*. I was even a barrio lesbian who got knifed by an all-girl gang called the Mal-flores . . . that means Bad Flowers. It's been a regular barrio blitz on television lately. If this fad continues, I can look forward to being a barrio grandmother done in by a gang of old Hispanics called Los Viejitos Diabilitos, the old devils.

Act I, Ibid.

3   CHATA (recalling her grandmother's words). "Ah! So you're a woman now. Got your own cycle like the moon. Soon you'll want a man. Well this is what you do. When you see the one you want, you roll the tortilla on the inside of your thigh and then you give it to him nice and warm. Be sure you give it to him and nobody else." Well, I been rolling tortillas on my thighs, on my nalgas, and God only knows where else, but I've been giving my tortillas to the wrong men . . .

Roosters 1987

4332. Mary L. Schapiro (1955–   )

1   Government has never really been very good outside of the intelligence and defense area at deploying massive technologies . . .

Interview with Kenneth Durr, SEC* Historical Society 2
November 2005
*U.S. Securities and Exchange Commission.

2   Investors can understand and accept a tech bubble or a recession—they go with the territory of a free market. What they won't accept is a system they can't trust. That's why it's so important for all of us to work together to safeguard that sense of trust and foster confidence among investors.

Ethics and Leadership Lecture, Dominican University (River Forest, Ill.) *14 October 2008*

3   . . . individuals have allowed the pursuit of wealth to become mere sport, devoid of any ethical meaning or moral obligation to others.

Speech, Dominican University *October 2008*

4333. Cathy Song (1955–   )

1   How poised it is!
Petal and leaf
curving like a fan,
the stem snipped and wedged
into the metal base—
to appear like a spontaneous accident.
"Ikebana," St. 5, *Picture Bride 1983*

2   My hair, freshly washed
like a measure of wealth,
like a bridal veil.
"The White Porch," St. 3, Ibid.

3   Like scooping water by the handful
out of a lake,
you write a poem
"Handful," *Free Lunch*, #21 *Spring 1998*

4   In proportion to what is taken
what is given multiplies.
"The Man Moves Earth," *Cloud Moving Hands 2007*

4334. Véronique Tadjo (1955–   )

1   Be wary of your guiding star. It may fall from the heavens and disintegrate into dust and ash.
Ch. LIX, *A vol d'oiseau* (As the crow flies, or In a straight line)
1986

2   Need one be blind not to see?
Deaf not to hear?
Mute not to cry?
Ibid. Ch. LX

4335. Debbie Taylor (1955?–   )

1   Who will undo all the HARM that's been done to us?
Will you hold—one more summit?
Will you write—one more report?
Will you hold—another decade?
LISTEN TO ME! THE WOMAN—OF AFRICA.
"Africa, My Africa," St. 16, *Moto* (African newspaper) *April 1985*

4336. Cynthia Tucker (1955–   )

1   We mix admiration for Star Trek-like scientific advances with a Victorian-era sexual prudishness. Go figure.
"Frank talk about birth control. . . ," *Atlanta Constitution 25 January 2003*

2   It's hard to run as an insurgent if you've been part of the establishment.
"McCain* relies on his image, avoids issues," *The Atlanta Journal-Constitution 7 September 2008*
*John Sidney McCain III (1936–   ), United States senator (R-AZ, 1987–   ) and Republican presidential nominee (2008).

4337. Donatella Versace (1955–   )

1   Plus-sized women shouldn't think of themselves as a size. They should think of themselves as women with rich goals in life.
"10 Questions," *Time 31 March 2008*

2   He [Gianni V— *] taught me everything I know. Even if my fashion changes, evolves with the millennium, the DNA is the same.
Ibid.
*Gianni V— (1946–97), Ital. fashion designer; her brother.

3   Gianni invented glamour.
Ibid.

4338. Cath Wallace (1955?–   )

1   I simply believe that nature does have rights and that humanity has got some obligation to be a good neighbor on the planet.
Quoted on goldmanprize.org *1991*

2   It is plain that we must get busy reducing our emissions very substantially and that the sooner we start, the easier and cheaper it will be to reduce enough to limit the amount of serious harm from global warming and climate and ice cap destabilisation.

"The green test: Cath Wallace," *New Zealand Herald 24 March 2008*

3   The ETS* combined with the moratorium on large new thermal generation would have for the first time placed a price on carbon and have provided investors in cleaner technology with some degree of certainty.

"ETS Review Comes Under Fire," guide2.co.nz *17 November 2008*

*Emissions trading scheme.

4339. Terry Tempest Williams (1955–)

1   . . . what might a different kind of power look like, feel like, and can power be redistributed equitably even beyond our own species?

Refuge: An Unnatural History of Family and Place 1991

2   Writing becomes an act of compassion toward life, the life we so often refuse to see because if we look too closely or feel too deeply, there may be no end to our suffering. But words empower us, move us beyond our suffering and set us free. This is the sorcery of literature. We are healed by our stories.

An Unspoken Hunger: Stories from the Field 1994

3   Where I live, the open space of desire is red. The desert before me is red is rose is pink is scarlet is magenta is salmon. The colors are swimming in light as it changes constantly, with cloud cover with rain with wind with light, delectable light, delicious light.

Red: Passion and Patience in the Desert 2001

4   In the open space of democracy, we are listening—ears alert—we are watching—eyes open—registering the patterns and possibilities for engagement. Some acts are private; some are public. Our oscillations between local, national, and global gestures map the full range of our movement. Our strength lies in our imagination, and paying attention to what sustains life, rather than what destroys it . . . Open lands open minds.

The Open Space of Democracy 2004

4340. Deborah Winger (1955–)

1   I was never afraid of failure after that* because, I think, coming that close to death, you get kissed. With the years, the actual experience of course fades, but the flavor of it doesn't.

Quoted in "What Choice Do I Have But To Live Fully" by Lisa Birbach, *Parade Magazine 6 March 1994*

*Of her brush with death.

2   I don't believe in careers. I believe in work.

Ibid.

4341. Lisa Zeidner (1955–)

1   I was a hard-core wage earner of the type hotel ads target. My husband was a cardiothoracic surgeon. My wallet was a garden of credit cards budding possibility, the holographic birds' wings glinting as if poised for flight.

Layover 1999

2   The best sex with wives is often had pretending they are strangers.

"Fact of the Act," nerve.com *2000*

3   They met by email and agreed within a dozen wry, decisive volleys that they should become lovers. Windows of opportunity were assessed, an equidistant hub city selected. They decided not to provide identity clues or fax through scanned photos, but instead unite blind, trusting the power of their mutual hunger . . .

Ibid.

4   Life is not a pie. A writer can't serve up tidy "slices of life," ingredients measured and premixed. Life is a volatile mess . . .

"'Last Night': The Middle of the Journey," *The New York Times 12 June 2005*

4342. Thalia Zepatos (1955–)

1   If you've been waiting to find the right person to go along on your trip, look in the mirror and then get out your passport. By traveling alone, you can follow your heart and move in your own rhythms . . .

"Traveling Alone or with Others?" *A Journey of One's Own 1992*

2   . . . hard work has always been an equal opportunity employer.

"Galleries and gamelans," *The Women's Review of Books,* Vol. XII, Nos. 10–11 *July 1995*

4343. Lisabeth Hughes Abramson (1956?–)

1   Our world is full of inconvenient truths. We accomplish nothing for families, the broader community and our justice system when we deny those truths.

"What's a father? Ky. Supreme Court has its say," *Kentucky Courier-Journal 25 April 2008*

4344. Marin Alsop (1956–)

1   Conducting's all body language. When a woman makes a gesture, the same gesture as a man, it's interpreted entirely differently. The thing I struggled with the most was getting a big sound from the brass because you really have to be strong. But if you're too strong, you're a b-I-t-c-h. As a woman, you have to be careful that it's not too harsh. It's a subtle line.

"*How I Got There,*" Newsweek *14 November 2005*

2   All through my childhood I would always end up being the captain of the team even if I wasn't a very good player. It's all about the thrill of being able to galvanize people to a unified endgame.

Ibid.

3   [Leonard] Bernstein* was more than a teacher; he coaxed the essence out of people.

Ibid.

*(1918–90), American award-winning conductor, composer, author, pianist, and lecturer.

4   The Four Symphonies of Johannes Brahms* provide the perfect universe for any conductor. Each symphony is a small planet, with its own unique ecosystem. Yet each of the symphonies is transformed and informed by the others, thereby creating a mini symphonic solar system.

It's a universe that I happily inhabit whenever possible . . .

"Orbiting the Symphonies of Brahms," National Public Radio (npr.org) *14 July 2007*

*German composer (1833–97).

5   For me as conductor, getting to know the composer on many levels is the key to understanding the music. That's my first and

main priority. I'm simply the messenger, and for that I need a personal understanding of what motivated him, what moved and touched him, and what led him to write the notes he chose to write.

"Marin Alsop's Symphonic Sleuthing," Ibid. *2 February 2008*

4345. Florencia Aróstica (1956?–   )

1　When the government says that Chile should be a great power in the food industry, they don't mean small family farms but the big exporting companies.

Speech, First Congress (Santiago), National Association of
Rural and Indigenous Women *23 March 2007*

2　When civil society sets forth proposals they are not taken fully into account, or they are converted into something different. That's not citizen participation. Government proposals have to be consistent with people's demands.

Ibid.

3　The current economic system only benefits big corporations. . . . One of the most important issues addressed by the Congress, which we understand to be an essential principle underlying every other aspect, was food sovereignty. We believe that no one in this country is showing proper concern about it.

Quoted in "Chile: Indigenous and Rural Women Make Their
Voices Heard" by Daniela Estrada, IPS-Inter Press Service *23
March 2007*

4346. Lynda Barry (1956–   )

1　The only thing I want to be famous for is inventing a nervous-breakdown gun. You could just shoot it at someone and they'd have a nervous breakdown and start sobbing, in fetal position. Someone like Slobodan Milosevic*—we don't have to kill him. Just give him a nervous breakdown.

Quoted in "Barefoot on the Stage" by Pamela Grossman,
Salon.com 21 May 1999
*(1941–2006), President of Serbia (1989–97) and Yugoslavia
(1997–2000); tried by United Nations tribunal for war crimes.

2　Well I had a song too. Probably everybody did. It's the first song you would really sing, the one your parents made you do over and over to show all your relatives how above average you were. And you can't ever change your song. Once a song is yours, it's yours for life.

The Good Times Are Killing Me 2002

3　When you come to a new place, you want to know *who are the dogs,* right?

The Greatest of Marlys 2002

4347. Rashida Bee (1956–   )

1　People are always surprised at the things I do—they wonder how a woman with no education and a background of poverty does what she does—but they have come to appreciate that what I am doing is not just for Bhopal but has meaning for the whole world. Now I am hopeful that more people from Muslim families, at least in my neighborhood, will realize that they should not keep women in the confines of the house.

Quoted in "She's the Bee's Knees" by Michelle Nijhuis, grist.
org *19 April 2004*

2　If there is exemplary punishment of the corporation and its officials, then other corporations will think twice before imposing risks on the life and health of ordinary people. We must spread

the word of Bhopal,* and make sure that legal responsibility for the disaster is fixed on the corporation that is responsible.

Ibid.
*Capital of Indian state of Madhya Pradesh and site of deadly disaster resulting when Union Carbide (now part of Dow Chemical) leaked deadly methyl isocyanate gas during the night of 3 December 1984, killing more than 20,000 people.

3　Dow* has been trying to portray us as a fringe group with unreasonable demands. This award nails that lie, and shows that our campaign and demands are based in truth.

Ibid.
*Dow Chemical Company, an American multinational corporation headquartered in Midland, Michigan.

4　We are still finding children being born without lips, noses or ears. Sometimes complete hands are missing, and women have severe reproductive problems.

Quoted on *goldmanprize.org 2004*

5　A woman's life involves discarding relationships that she has known from infancy and adopting strangers as her own.* If she can face the world outside at such a fundamental level, then why should any other struggle for empowerment scare her?

Quoted in "Recognition for Bhopal campaigners" by Tarun
Jain, *India Together April 2004*
*Re the cultural tradition of brides leaving their families to marry into those of their husbands.

4348. Sharon Begley (1956–   )

1　The mind can store an estimated 100 trillion bits of information—compared with which a computer's mere billions are virtually amnesiac.

"Memory: Science Achieves Important New Insights into the
Mother of the Muses," *Newsweek 29 September 1986*

2　The mind's cross-indexing puts the best librarian to shame.

Ibid.

3　During the winter, windows in the United States leak about as much heat as is provided by the oil flowing through the Alaskan pipeline every year.

"Fighting the Greenhouse," Ibid. *18 June 1990*

4　Human nature being what it is, scientists realize that if we depend on a penchant for sacrifice to forestall the greenhouse effect, we might as well start building sea walls to hold back the waters that will rise along with the thermostat.

Ibid.

5　In the last years of the twentieth century, a few iconoclastic neuroscientists challenged the paradigm that the adult brain cannot change and made discovery after discovery that, to the contrary, it retains stunning powers of neuroplasticity. The brain can indeed be rewired.

Ch. 1, *Train Your Mind, Change Your Brain: How a New
Science Reveals Our Extraordinary Potential to Transform
Ourselves 2007*

6　When politicians do it, they're tarred as flip-floppers. When lovers do it, we complain they're fickle. But scientists are supposed to change their minds. Having adopted their views on scientific questions—What killed the dinosaurs? Is the universe infinite?—based on a dispassionate evaluation of empirical evidence, they are expected to willingly, even eagerly, abandon cherished beliefs when new evidence undercuts them.

"On Second Thought. . . ," *Newsweek 3 January 2009*

4349. Barbara Bonney (1956–)

1   She [Ilia in Mozart's* opera *Idomeneo*] is a true blue female in the best sense of the word: the tender, nurturing sense that can make such women the salt of the earth. She is the Mother Teresa** of operatic characters because she gives without wanting anything back. It's all in one direction, it's all give. And that is something very, very special.

> Quoted in *Diva, The New Generation: The Sopranos and Mezzos of the Decade Discuss Their Roles* by Helena Matheopoulous *1998*
> *Wolfgang Amadeus Mozart, Austrian composer (1756–91).
> **See 2142.

4350. Gloria Bowles (1956?–)

1   . . . Western thought denies feeling as part of knowing, and . . . women are devalued because they are associated with feeling. She struggles to relocate and define the personal, which she has carefully suppressed in order to succeed in a male-dominated academic world. She decides that it must be *"what is important, answers one's needs, strikes one as immediately interesting."**

> "Constructive criticism," *The Women's Review of Books,* Vol. XI, No. 1 *October 1993*
> *Re the essay "Me and My Shadow" by Jane Tompkins (see 3234:1) in *The Intimate Critique.*

2   We thought the study of women would be a temporary phase; eventually we would all go back to our disciplines.

> Afterword, *Women's Studies on Its Own: A Next Wave Reader in Institutional Change* by Robyn Wiegman *2003*

4351. Rose Brady (1956–)

1   The task, then, was to dismantle the machine. He* had come up against fierce opponents of reform, and in the political-economic game that ensued he had not always played clean. But he kept his eye on the prize. The prize was a non-Communist Russia in which private property dominated the economy.

> *Kapitalizm: Russia's Struggle to Free Its Economy 1999*
> *Re Anatoly Chubais, aide to Boris Yeltsin, Soviet and Russian political leader (1931–   ); president of Russia (1991–2000).

4352. Lucie Brock-Broido (1956–)

1   Sometimes I think I will be broken by your lukewarm Hand
> "Into Those Great Countries of the Blue Sky of Which We Don't Know Anything," *The Master Letters 1995*

2   *Should you, before this reaches you, experience Immortality, Who will inform me of the exchange?*
> Ibid.

3   My world is as ordered as if—as if I
had stacked the stars in the nightsky's
orchard, senseless as crates of fish
stacked glimmering, one-eyed &
blank, one atop the other of them, cold
as Rome apples or a new moon.
> Ibid.

4353. Margaret Casey (1956–1985)

1   It hurts not being a contender.
> Quoted in *Time* (New York) *10 June 1985*

4354. Ana Castillo (1956–)

1   Love me withered as you loved me new.
Love me as if I were forever—
and I, will make the impossible
a simple act,
by loving you, loving you as I do
> "I Ask The Impossible," *Berkeley Poetry Review, #26 1990*

2   . . . the feminine principle to which I refer is concerned with preservation, protection—especially of the young and less fortunate—and affiliations of communities for the common good.
> *Massacre of the Dreamers: Reflections on Mexican-Indian Women in the United States 500 Years After the Conquest 1992*

3   But those two will probably grow old together because they really know how to be mad at each other, while me and my loverboy who didn't have a bad moment together have already gone up in smoke . . .
> Ch. 1, *Loverboys 1996*

4   I'm really a creature of habit, no doubt about it. There's only one place where I go for tacos and only one place where I go to get loaded. And there's my store. In between is home and sleep.
> Ibid.

4355. Lica Cecato (1956–)

1   We never give up. Everyday. Anywhere. When every woman refuses to stay silent [about violence], the situation is going to change.
> Speech, 10th anniversary of United Nations Trust Fund, *16 February 2007*

4356. Pauline W. Chen (1956?–)

1   That great passing of life was too sacred; it was nearly magical. Death was an immutable moment in time, locked up as much in our particular destiny as in the time and date of our birth.
> *Final Exam, A Surgeon's Reflections on Mortality 2006*

2   In the human anatomy course, cadavers are laid before fledgling physicians, and the familiarity of their form reminds us that each lived lives not unlike our own. For those of us who wince from simple paper cuts, running a scalpel against skin and definitively dividing the essential structures that once powered a fellow human are acts that require a leap of faith. While all aspiring physicians fully expect to perform a human cadaver dissection in medical school, the expectation hardly tempers the brutal reality.
> Ibid.

3   What many of us [med students] did not realize was that despite those dreams, our profession would require us to live among the dying. Death, more than life, would become the constant in our lives.
> Ibid.

4357. C. Hope Clark (1956–)

1   Your confidence is all it takes for someone to believe you.
> Newsletter, fundsforwriters.com *2 March 2008*

2   Money isn't a cure . . . it's a vitamin. It's a way to energize what you're already doing . . .
> Ibid.

4358. Susanna J. Coffey (1956?–)

1   Beauty is not only in the eye of the beholder, but totally within the form history has provided.

> Quoted in "Susanna Coffey," *Exposures, Women & Their Art*
> by Ann Brown and Arlene Raven* 1989
> *See 3533.

2   I had no way of visualizing anything without a mirror and the [women's] movement gave me a mirror.

> Ibid.

4359. Eileen Collins (1956–)

1   Because of [Amelia Earhart],* we had more women available to fly in the 1940s to help us get through World War II. And because of these women, women of my generation are able to look back and say, "Hey, they did it. They even flew military airplanes, we can do it, too."

> "100 Years of Great Women," *ABC News Special with Barbara Walters*** 30 April 1999
> *See 1847. **See 2687.

2   I'm a firm believer in getting people off the planet.

> Quoted in "Leader of the next shuttle ready" by Allen G. Breed, Associated Press *14 February 2003*

4360. Sarah Daniels (1956–)

1   MARY (suicide note to her husband). Your dinner and my head are in the oven.

> *Ripen Our Darkness 1981*

4361. Laura Davis (1956–)

Also see Bass, Ellen, 3720:1.

1   When you begin to talk honestly about your life in a safe environment, healing naturally begins to happen.

> "Creating Safety," *The Courage to Heal Workbook 1990*

4362. Lucy Ellman (1956–)

1   Writing a novel without being asked seems a bit like having a baby when you have nowhere to live.

> *The Guardian* (London) *16 January 1992*

2   [She had] the perfect face for her era: tight-lipped, pointy-nosed, pink-skinned, blonde-haired.

> *Dot in the Universe 2003*

4363. Karen Finley (1956–)

1   [I had a hero complex] enabled by my relationship with New York City, because New York is so self-important. I looked at New York and fell out of love.

> *A Different Kind of Intimacy 2000*

2   I couldn't stand being the Joan of Arc* of the art world anymore. Internally, I was burning at the stake from the constant battles of defending the First Amendment. The icon of free speech was becoming a pile of ashes. I had to rethink my career, my persona, my work. I needed an archetype makeover.

> Ibid.
> *See 252.

4364. Carrie Fisher (1956–)

1   Actors may know how to act, but a lot of them don't know how to behave.

> *Postcards From the Edge 1987*

2   I was into pain reduction and mind expansion, but what I've ended up with is pain expansion and mind reduction.

> Ibid.

3   Instant gratification takes too long.

> Ibid.

4   Relationship—that silk purse turned sow's ear . . .

> Ibid.

5   The message about sex and relationships that she had gotten as a child . . . was confused, contradictory. Sex was for men, and marriage, like lifeboats, was for women and children.

> *Surrender the Pink 1990*

4365. Anne Geddes (1956–)

1   I don't keep babies waiting. They have the biggest egos of all. They think the world revolves around them—and it does.

> Quoted in "Photographer prefers young models" by Samantha Critchell, Associated Press *14 January 2003*

4366. Bette Gordon (1956–)

1   . . . the ideas behind pornography are seduction, desire and voyeurism, which are also the basic components of cinema.

> Quoted in "On the Road with an Eccentric, Provocative Mom" by David Sterritt, *The New York Times 14 May 2000*

4367. Josephine Hart (1956?–)

1   I've always kept my name. A lot of my identity is in it, and I just didn't want to change it. It's quite a loss when a girl gives up her name.

> Quoted in "The Dark Side of the Upbeat Author" by Judith Weinraub, *The Washington Post 22 May 1991*

2   There is an internal landscape, a geography of the soul; we search for its outlines all our lives.

> Ch. 1, *Damage 1991*

3   Damaged people are dangerous. They know they can survive.

> Ch. 12, Ibid.

4   The poet in Ireland is an iconic figure . . .

> "Making poetry a vital part of life," *The Times* (London) *7 November 2008*

5   To some extent it's much more politically acceptable to go to football matches. If a major politician spends his free time in cultural activities, a mood has grown up which implies that there's something wrong with that. In fact, it's what would inform his mind.

> Ibid.

6   [Listening to poetry is] allowing yourself to stop depriving yourself of what is incandescently beautiful in life. To deny yourself that is voluntarily to starve your soul. And if your soul is starved it is impossible to be happy. Modern life makes it hard for people to feed their souls, and that's what people find there. They're on a starvation diet and they come out and they suddenly think: "My god! This is a feast!"

> Ibid.

7   After all, what is it that makes us human? It is language. And poetic language is the most rare form. It's like a gem because the wisdom and insight of the poet is compressed into it.

> Ibid.

4368. Susannah Heschel (1956–)

1 Words create worlds. If God is male then the male is God.
> Quoted in Ch. 4, *Deborah, Golda, and Me, Being Female and Jewish in America* by Letty Cottin Pogrebin* *1991*
> *See 3154.

2 When my father came back from Selma* and told us about the march, he said he felt a sense of the holy, a sense of holiness walking arm and arm with Doctor King.** He said, "I felt my legs were praying."
> Speech, Lawrence Family Jewish Community Center (San Diego) *10 March 2006*
> *City in Alabama best known for three civil rights marches that started there.**(1929–68), American clergyman, activist, and icon of the civil rights movement; assassinated.

3 The idea of judging a person by black, brown or white—it is an eye disease!
> Ibid.

4369. Anita Hill (1956–)

1 I had to tell the truth.
> Quoted in "A Moment of Truth," *Newsweek 21 October 1991*

2 . . . we need to turn the question around to look at the harasser,* not the target. We need to be sure that we can go out and look anyone who is a victim of harassment in the eye and say, "You do not have to remain silent anymore."
> Speech, Hunter College (New York City, 25 April 1992), Cited by Deborah Sontag, *The New York Times 26 April 1992*
> *Re Clarence Thomas (1948– ; Am. jurist and Supreme Court associate justice) and the issue of sexual harassment raised at a hearing held by the U.S. Senate Judiciary Committee, October 1991.

3 The possible violation of a woman's civil rights is not the same as the emotional pain and loss of trust that result from extramarital affairs. Equating the two promotes a form of moral fundamentalism that devalues women and the issues they face and offers only a formulaic approach to addressing them.
> "Clinton-Lewinsky Is Not Thomas-Hill," *Seattle Post-Intelligencer*, Op-Ed, A7 *29 September 1998*

4370–4371. Karen Hughes (1956–)

1 I think after September 11th* the American people are valuing life more and realizing that we need policies to value the dignity and worth of every life. And President Bush** has worked to say, let's be reasonable, let's work to value life, let's try to reduce the number of abortions, let's increase adoptions. And I think those are the kind of policies that the American people can support, particularly at a time when we're facing an enemy, and really the fundamental difference between us and the terror network we fight is that we value every life. It's the founding conviction of our country, that we're endowed by our creator with certain unalienable rights, the right to life and liberty and the pursuit of happiness. ***
> Interview, CNN *24 April 2004*
> *Day of al-Qaeda suicide attacks on, among others, the World Trade Center in New York in 2001; 2,794 victims, plus the hi-jackers. **George W. B— (1946–), Amer. politician; 43rd president of the United States (2001–09). ***In answer to a question about that day's pro-choice March for Women's Lives rally.

2 My most important responsibility is to my family and to the child I chose to have. My job is going to have to allow me to fulfill that responsibility, or I need to look at a different job.
> "How I Got There," *Newsweek 14 November 2005*

4372. Carrie Hunt (1956?–)

1 The more I get to know bears, the more I realize how gentle and willing to avoid trouble they are.
> "Bear Scarer," *People 15 June 1998*

2 Wonderful, gentle bears would die because nobody taught them the rules, and that's why I do this . . .*
> "Hunt's Dog-and-Bear Show," Time.com *27 March 2000*
> *Re her technique to teach bears to stay away from humans.

3 In all my work in national parks, I've never seen a park commit like this. They've been pioneers with us. They knew that this was this bear's last chance, and they did it right.*
> Quoted in "Carrie Hunt teaches bears 'to do the right thing' with help of her Karelians" by Michael Jamison, *The Missoulian 2005*
> *Re Glacier National Park in northwestern Montana.

4373. Valerie Bowman Jarrett (1956–)

1 I was just unbelievably bowled over by how impressive she [Michelle Obama] was. . . . Michelle* was so mature beyond her years, so thoughtful and perceptive. She really prodded me about what the job would be like because she had lots of choices. I offered it to her on the spot, which was totally inappropriate because I should have talked to the mayor** first. But I just knew she was really special.
> Quoted in "Barack's Rock" by Jonathan Van Meter, *Vogue October 2008*
> *M— Obama; see 4648. **Richard M. Daley (1942–), mayor of Chicago, Illinois (1989–).

2 [My childhood] required me to be able to straddle a bunch of different cultures and worlds. It made me comfortable talking to anybody at a very young age, and because I was an only child I spent a lot of time with adults.
> Ibid.

3 Barack* never grills. That's part of what is so effective about him: He puts you completely at ease, and the next thing you know he's asking more and more probing questions and gets you to open up and reflect a little bit.
> Ibid.
> *B— Obama (1961–), 44th president of the United States (2009–).

4374. Mae Jemison (1956–)

1 A woman who strives to be like a man lacks ambition.
> Speech, Women of Power Conference (Seattle) *6 April 2000*

2 At the heart of science are the words: I think, I wonder, and I understand.
> Ibid.

3 A right is not something that someone gives you, but something that no one can take away.
> Ibid.

4 Nothing will happen till we risk putting an idea into motion.
> Ibid.

4375. Rebecca L. Johnson (1956–)

1 The dirt in Boston is nothing like the good Ohio soil back home.
> "New Moon Over Roxbury," *Ecofeminism and the Sacred*, Carol J. Adams, ed. *1993*

4376. Carol Leifer (1956–)

1 I was part of a mixed marriage. I'm human; he's a Klingon.
> Quoted in "Kosher at Last," The Haunted Smile, *The Story of Jewish Comedians in America* by Lawrence J. Epstein 2001

2 Sex when you're married is like going to a 7-Eleven. There's not much variety, but at three in the morning, it's always there.
> Quoted in *The New Comedy Writing Step by Step* by Gene Perret 2007 *rev. ed.*

3 People who are against gay marriage are people who don't have any gay people in their lives. And when they do get to know gay people, they realize gay marriage doesn't have any impact on their lives. I do think we'll have the right soon that we didn't have before.
> Quoted in "Successful Women: Carol Leifer" by Danielle Cantor, *Jewish Woman Spring* 2009

4 See, that's the thing that truly sucks about death—no forwarding address.
> "But This One's Eating My Popcorn," *When You Lie About Your Age, the Terrorists Will Get You* 2009

5 We accept "the end" with so many other aspects of our lives— work deadlines, "must remit by" bills, "the end" as the last credit on a movie. But for some reason we still think somewhere that we're supposed to be here forever.
> "Shea Stadium and Its Effect on the Aging Process," Ibid.

6 You are the architect of this aging plan. You're the boss, and there is so much you can do without bringing in outside vendors.
> "When You Lie About Your Age, the Terrorists Win," Ibid.

4377. Naomi Littlebear Morena (1956?–)

1 You can't kill the spirit
It's like a mountain
old and strong; it lives on and on.
> "Like a Mountain" 1976

2 Complacency is a far more dangerous attitude than outrage.
> "The Dark of the Moon," quoted in *Light One Candle: Quotes of Hope and Action* by Arrington Chambliss 1991

4378. Jane Holl Lute (1956?–)

1 I don't think enough is known about UN peacekeeping. I think most people, what they don't know about peacekeeping may be actually more significant than what they do know. They may recognize the blue helmet but they may not know that peacekeeping, for example, is the second largest deployed military presence in the world, directly affecting the lives of 200 million people around the world, to the good. There have been a number of studies that said that UN peacekeeping, it's not perfect, it's not fault free, it can be uneven, uncertain at times, it can be late in coming, it can leave too early, but unmistakably, peacekeeping makes a circumstance better off than were it not there.
> "Global Connections with Bill Miller," UNA-USA TV *October 2006*

2 The US will spend more money in Iraq this week than on UN peacekeeping all year long. And we are in 18 places around the world, and those are not just random places, but places where the US has key interests.
> Ibid.

3 Every idea whose time has come began as an idea ahead of its time.
> "Tell Me More with Michel Martin," NPR-Radio *2 October 2008*

4 Peacekeepers ought to reflect the highest standards and aspirations that humanity has. That's the tradition that every new peacekeeper inherits.
> Ibid.

4379. Emily Lyon (1956–)

1 It has been 26 years since *Roe vs. Wade.** We thought that was all that would be necessary, but now we have to continually protect that right, day after day.
> Quoted in "Bombing victim builds a life . . ." by Rheta Grimsley Johnson,** *Seattle Post-Intelligencer*, A9 *6 February 1999*

*Supreme Court decision legalizing abortion (1973); also see Sarah Weddington, 3622. **See 4184.

4380. Sofia Macher (1956?–)

1 Fujimori* built his whole government on terrorism, using terrorism to keep his government in power. He used fear of terrorism to maintain a culture of secrets, behind which he hid the systematic corruption he cultivated. Ultimately, they have to admit that theirs was an anti-subversive strategy that systematically violated human rights.
> Address, Rights & Democracy (Montreal) *24 October 2002*

*Alberto Ken'ya F— (1939–), president of Peru, 1990–2000.

2 The international community should make sure in its intervention that there is an appropriate balance between the investment granted to deal with the past and that granted to build the future.
> Report for "Building a Future on Peace and Justice" Conference (Nuremberg) *25–27 June 2007*

4381. Lucinda Marshall (1956–)

1 Forgive my cynicism about Mother's Day. After all, what kind of ungrateful mother wouldn't want to be honored with pesticide-laced flowers, chocolate that depends on children in slavery for its production and cards that deplete our forests and litter Mother Earth? Truly, it is the ultimate insult to honor life-giving with such toxic offerings.
> Mothering in a world where damaging behavior is the revered norm is an oxymoron.
> "Personal Voices: A Mother's Day Manifesto," AlterNet.org *9 May 2003*

2 It is unfortunate when the media continues, with all its damaging and misogynist implications, to insist by inclusion that what women wear or how they look is related to their capability.
> "What She Wore: The Prevalence of Gender Bias in Reporting," AlterNet.org *14 December 2006*

3 It has been said that the health of a society is measured by how it treats women. Judging from global statistics, it is safe to say that society is in crisis.
> "International Women's Day 2007: We Stand With The Women of the World," *Counterpunch 8 March 2007*

4 Rape, a cheap alternative to bullets, has always been a de facto weapon of war.
> "Making Women's Health an International Priority," AlterNet.org *8 March 2007*

4382. Elizabeth Perle McKenna (1956–)

1   Live by what you treasure. Nothing is going to change if women don't live by their convictions. Get over the thrall of the macho marathon work schedule and put what is important to you on the agenda.

When Work Doesn't Work Anymore: Women, Work and Identity 1997

2   Don't be such a good girl. Women are trapped in unhappy situations at work because they want to fit in. Don't remain silent and swallow the unpalatable. Speak up!

Ibid.

4383. Lilian Nattel (1956–)

1   "A real writer tells the truth, and that's how he changes the world."

The River Midnight 1999

2   "I'm telling you plain, everything is God. Are you looking, Hayim? Are you using your eyes? The Baal Shem Tov,* of blessed memory, spent days in the fields and the woods, and there he saw the Holy One arising from every living thing and also the stones."

Ibid.

*Originally Israel ben Eliezer (1700?–60), Polish-born Jewish religious leader, and mystic, who founded Hasidism.

4384. Mariah Burton Nelson (1956–)

1   By playing sports, women are challenged to see themselves not as the same as men but as equally entitled to define the nature of the games and the relationships between and among players.

Are We Winning Yet? How Women are Changing Sports and Sports are Changing Women 1991

2   The story of women in sports is a personal story, because nothing is more personal than a woman's bone, sinew, sweat and desire, and a political story, because nothing is more powerful than a woman's struggle to be free.

Introduction, *Nike Is a Goddess*, Lissa Smith, ed. *1999*

3   Think of yourself as an athlete. I guarantee you it will change the way you walk, the way you work, and the decision you make about leadership, teamwork, and success.

"A is for Athlete," *We Are All Athletes 2002*

4385. Fae Myenne Ng (1956–)

1   Fault. In English or Cantonese that was the word we were all afraid of. I held it like a seed in my mouth. As kids, the three of us loved to suck on dried plums. Long after the sour and salty fruit dissolved, the seed stayed sweet, the true secret. Now I was afraid my secret guilt would start to grow sweet, and I would never want to spit it out.

Bone 1992

2   *The heart never travels.*
    I believe in holding still. I believe that the secrets we hold in our hearts are our anchors, that even the unspoken between us is a measure of our every promise to the living and to the dead. And all our promises, like all our hopes, move us through life with the power of an ocean liner pushing the sea.

Ibid.

3   I was a butcher. What a man did with his hands spoke his worth, so I tell my livelihood before I tell my name.

Ch. 2, *Steer Toward Rock 2008*

4   If there was a promise I could not fulfill, I did not inconvenience others by talk. No man wanted to taste another man's swallowed desire.

Ibid.

5   I wanted to be like the rooster, common as salt, but glorious with his five virtues. The rooster wears a crown, he has dignity. His spurs are sharp; he is a hero. He is brave; he faces his foe. He is generous and communicates when he finds food. A rooster is trustworthy; he tells perfect time.

Ibid.

4386. Achy Obejas (1956–)

1   To me, she was like the purest, blackest earth—that rich, sweet soil in which sugarcane grows. I always imagined her as hills in which I would roll around, happy and dirty, as if I were back in Cuba.

Memory Mambo 1996

2   I've always thought of the Virgin of Charity as the perfect mentor for Cuba: Cradling her child in her arms, she floats above a turbulent sea in which a boat with three men is being tossed about. One of the men is black and he is in the center of the boat, kneeling in prayer while the other two, who are white, row furiously and helplessly. (It's unspoken but understood that it's the entreaties of the black man, not the labor of the white rowers, that provides their deliverance.)

Ch. 1, *Days of Awe 2001*

4387. Susan C. Pearce (1956?–)
See Natalie J. Sokoloff, 3542:2–3.

4388. Carol Polowy (1956–)

1   Educational institutions mirror the stereotypes of the larger society. The fact that education has become known as a "woman's field" stems at least in part from the identification of childcare and child-rearing as woman's work. Men frequently view teaching as a stepping stone to educational administration while women look to careers as classroom teachers.

Address, "Sex Discrimination: The Legal Obligations of Educational Institutions," *Vital Speeches of the Day 1 February 1975*

2   When textbooks are examined in terms of their presentation and reinforcement of a social order, women and minority groups are dissatisfied with the lack of reality in the presentation.

Ibid.

4389. Dorothy E. Roberts (1956–)

1   American culture reveres no Black madonna. It upholds no popular image of a Black mother tenderly nurturing her child.

Killing the Black Body: Race, Reproduction, and the Meaning of Liberty 1997

2   The social order established by powerful white men was founded on two inseparable ingredients: the dehumanization of Africans on the basis of race, and the control of women's sexuality and reproduction.

Ibid.

4390. Rita Rudner (1956–)

1   Plastic surgery must be like childbirth without the child, Eva reasoned. After a while, if you're satisfied with the results, you forget the pain and want to do it again.

Pt. II, "All About Eva," *Tickled Pink 2001*

2 *Spin,* incidentally, was a relatively new term for what Leonard used to call bullshit.

> Pt. III, "A Yen for Change," Ibid.

3 Although she still had three months to go, Mindy already felt the hefty, protective tug of maternal obligation. Indeed, the bond was so strong she was considering not having the umbilical cord cut right away, but leaving it intact so she could keep track of her child's whereabouts until he or she was at least twenty-one.

> Pt. III, "New York State of Mindy," Ibid.

4 "You must live in the present, be conscious of the past, and not be more than thirty-five minutes late for the future."

> Pt. III, "Santas and Mantras," Ibid.

5 Individuality in dressing is not important to men. If they all look alike it means they haven't made a mistake.

> "Suite of Kharma," *ritafunny.com 2003*

6 I read recipes the same way I read science fiction. I get to the end and think, "Well, that's not going to happen."

> "Waist Management," Ibid.

7 My husband and I are either going to buy a dog or have a child. We can't decide to ruin our carpet or ruin our lives.

> haruth.com/WomenToWomen.htm *n.d.*

4391. Kathy Rudy (1956–)

1 Repeal of abortion laws will not end the abortion wars, it will give them a critically different inflection. That is, we will no longer be fighting about whether the procedure should or shouldn't be legal; we will be fighting about the fundamental differences between worldviews and communities.

> *Beyond Pro-Life and Pro-Choice: Moral Diversity in the Abortion Debate 1996*

4392. Habiba Sarabi (1956–)

1 I am doing this for the future of my people.* They may not understand now why it is so important, but if we can preserve the environment and our natural resources it will bring wealth for our children.

> Quoted in "Heroes of the Environment: Habiba Sarabi" by Aryn Baker, *Time 2008*
> *Establishing Afghanistan's first national park.

4393. Christina "Tina" M. Tchen (1956–)

1 I cannot imagine life on the sidelines, merely going home each night, perhaps clucking about our school system or the sorry state of healthcare, without being involved somehow in the work that addresses these issues.

> Quoted in "Skadden Partner to Take White House Post" by Molly McDonough, *ABA Journal 5 December 2008*

4394. Lilly Walters (1956–)
See Dottie Walters, 2538:1–2.

4395. Meg Whitman (1956–)

1 We went from start-up to grown-up. We made business history. At its core, eBay helped people make a living doing what they love.

> Article by Jon Swartz, *USA Today 21 September 2008*

2 The eBay model is very Republican in its essence—it's about making a small number of rules and getting out of the way.

> Ibid.

3 We [eBay] are far and away the largest marketplace. Sellers want to be where the buyers are, and buyers want to be where the sellers are. That's where being the largest helps.

> "The New Auctioneer," *Time Digital 50 n.d.*

4396. Marcia Wieder (1956–)

1 Most people think of dreams either as some unattainable fantasies or as something they do in their sleep. Neither definition is what I mean when I speak of dreams.

I define dreams as the aspirations, desires, goal, and hopes that you most want for yourself. These are the dreams you have while you are wide awake.

> Ch. 1, *Making Your Dreams Come True 1993*

2 You can learn whether you're on the right path to where you want to be by facing fear and acknowledging it as a landmark for change. . . . Fear is actually a measurement tool; it means that you're leaving the old behind; it's a gift that indicates you are closer to your dream.

> Ch. 7, Ibid.

3 The ideal way to experience a life of ease is to meet it with all of the above: open-armed, open-minded, and, most important, open-hearted.

> Ch. 1, *Doing Less and Having More: Five Easy Steps for Achieving Your Dreams 1998*

4 What does it mean to you to have more? Exactly what do you want more of? Do you even know?

> Ibid.

4397. Ellen Alderman (1957–)

1 There is simply no comprehensive body of law established to deal with all of the privacy concerns arising in the digital age.

> *The Right to Privacy,* coauthor, Caroline Kennedy* *1995*
> *See 4417.

2 Even if you don't cruise the superhighway, your personal profile will. A portrait of you in 1's and 0's, the language of computers, will exist in cyberspace.

> Ibid.

4398. Oral Ataniyazova (1957–)

1 We're finding an increasing rate of diseases in our country,* including birth abnormalities, cancer, kidney disease and allergies. The influence of environmental factors is clear.

> Quoted in "Goldman Prize: The Year's 7 Environmental Heroes Honored" by Glen Martin, *San Francisco Chronicle 17 April 2000*
> *Uzbekistan.

2 Many developing countries aren't protected from the importation of low-quality products and toxic waste. The ecologic illiteracy of political leaders and economic corruption worsens the difficult position of people in these developing countries . . . it is very important that governments fulfill their obligations to their citizens—

> Interview, *Global Fund for Women 2005*

3 I think that the role of women in this is very important because women carry a large responsibility for their children, and

without solutions for ecological and economic problems, there won't be a future for our children.

Ibid.

4399. Dawn Bradley Berry (1957–)

1 Female attorneys today still face the paradox that traits considered most desirable in a male attorney—self-assurance, a competitive and aggressive nature, and high ambition—are considered by many to be "unfeminine."

Quoted in *The 50 Most Influential Women in American Law* by Dawn Bradley Berry *1996*

4400. Cynthia Bond (1957?–)

1 She wore gray like rain clouds, like shapeless rain clouds before the bursting. She wrapped them about her skeleton body, her acres of sheathed legs, her arms swaying like a loose screen. That is how she moved. Her curved bow lips jerking slightly. Her eyes a misting glaze before the storm.

That is how Ruby walked in the crazy years . . .

"Ruby," *Afrekete: An Anthology of Black Lesbian Writing*, Catherine E. McKinley & L. Joyce DeLaney, eds. *1995*

4401. Rosemary Breslin (1957–)

1 Once in my life, off the coast of Maine, I dived off a high rock and from the moment my toes pushed off from the boulder it felt perfect . . .

Not Exactly What I Had in Mind: An Incurable Love Story 1997

2 . . . Tony* figured if I was good with all my scams, and now with the responsible repayment of my debts, he could get this to work for him. He ignited my newfound pride in doing the best job possible. And he employed it to make me a solid citizen, something I had sneered at my whole life. Tony set me up and I fell for it.

Ibid.

*Her husband, Tony Dunne.

4402. Katie Couric (1957–)

1 Grief is a strange animal. It creeps up on you at strange times.
"Whatever Katie Wants" by Cable Neuhaus, *Modern Maturity Nov/Dec 2005*

2 Nobody enjoys being trashed. But it comes with success, with an increasingly snarky environment in the world today.

Ibid.

4403. Jill Dolan (1957–)

1 How do you locate yourself on the edge of an issue? How do you not impose ethical answers but, instead, open a discussion of where the edge is and how it shifts?

Presence and Desire: Essays on Gender, Sexuality, Performance 1993

2 Feminism . . . never held my hand and comforted me. [It] has strengthened me . . . but it's also made me realize how dangerous I am and that my position, however it shifts historically, will never be safe. . . . Feminism has given me theory, and that is where I live.

(p. 82), Ibid.

3 The explicitness of pornography seems the most constructive choice for practicing cultural disruptions.

(p. 201), Ibid.

4404. Fran Drescher (1957–)

1 My first words . . . "Can I take it back if I wore it?"
Quoted in "Kosher at Last," *The Haunted Smile, The Story of Jewish Comedians in America* by Lawrence J. Epstein *2001*

2 Often, the truly great and valuable lessons we learn in life are learned through pain. That's why they call it "growing pains." It's all about yin and yang. And that's not something you order off column A at your local Chinese restaurant.

Prologue, *Cancer, Schmancer 2002*

3 How sad it is that a turtle can live to 150, or a parrot can live as long as a human, but man's best friend can only live for a decade or two. With some things there's little justice.

"Chester Drescher, Ibid.

4 I love walking my feet off. Gimme a map and a box of Band-Aids and I'm all set!

"Paris," Ibid.

5 I read for the part of Elizabeth, the virgin queen. I thought they said they were looking for a virgin from Queens. Whatever, the only virgin in my house is the olive oil.

perfectpeople.com 2003

6 Sometimes people come into your life for a season and other times for a lifetime.

TV.com n.d.

4405. Katherine Ellison (1957–)

1 It might not be a mass movement quite yet, but what the emerging grassroots effort to combat climate change lacks in numbers and unity, it's making up for in diversity, and, increasingly, respectability.

"Kyoto, U.S.A.," grist.org *31 July 2002*

2 Lacking overall direction by professional environmentalists, the climate change movement has been led from the ground up, by a strikingly diverse set of people . . . Some of these grassroots activists are motivated by empathy for the world's poor, who are likely to feel the first and worst impacts of meteorological turmoil. Others are driven by the desire to stem the species extinctions hastened by a warming Earth. Still others worry about their own children's futures.

Ibid.

3 It may seem farfetched as you're schlepping groceries or dragging your screaming 4-year-old to the time-out chair, but dedicated moms, you may have something important in common with meditating Buddhist monks.

It's the neurology of love and compassion—a little-understood aspect of parenting. . . . The basic theory uniting nerve-wracked U.S. suburbs with Himalayan mountain monasteries is that love, compassion and equanimity can be thought of as "skills" that can be improved with practice and are capable of changing neural circuitry.

"Inside the minds of monks and moms," *Los Angeles Times 23 October 2005*

Ibid.

4 The 1990s' "Decade of the Brain" revealed that human brains change and grow throughout our lifetime and that experience can rewire them. A violinist's brain is demonstrably different from someone who doesn't practice. A London taxicab driver, who must memorize that huge city's maze, has on average a

larger hippocampus—the brain's seat of memory—than workers in other occupations.

Ibid.

5 Now, few moms would deny that children challenge our mental resources. The hormonal roller-coaster, sleep deprivation, biased bosses, brainless chores, and too much Raffi* are just part of the toll. Because men, despite some notable recent progress, still aren't equitably sharing these burdens, we're left with a mostly female predicament. But what makes it all harder is a residue of feminism.

Ch. 1, The Mommy Brain: How Motherhood Makes Us
Smarter 2005

*R- Cavoukian (1948–), Canadian children's singer.

6 Here's the truly inconvenient truth: Scientists have long been warning that the world must cut back on greenhouse-gas emissions by as much as 70 percent, as soon as possible, if we're to have a fighting chance of stabilizing the climate. Yet even with full participation by the United States, the controversial Kyoto Protocol—the only global plan in the works—would hardly begin to do that.

"Turned Off by Global Warming," The New York Times
20 May 2006

4406. Claudia Emerson (1957–)

1 We didn't know what woke us—just something/
   moving, lighter than our breathing.

"The Bat," St. 1, Blackbird, vol. 2, no. 1 Spring 2003

2 You never tired, you told me, of the tangible/
   past you could admire, turn over /
     and over in your hand—

"Surface Hunting," St. 4, Ibid.

3 You see, aftermath is easier, opening/
again the wound along its numb scar

"Aftermath," St. 10, Late Wife: Poems 2005

4 and spiders—seasonless—survived the broom
to live in every corner, their egg sacs hung/
   like soft, spun pearls.

"Rent," St. 5, Ibid.

5 For three years you lived in your house/
just as it was before she died: your wedding/
portrait on the mantel, her clothes hanging/
in the closet, her hair still in the brush.

"Artifact," St. 1, Ibid.

4407. Laura Farabough (1957?–)

1 A strong woman artist who is not afraid of herself, her sexuality, passion, symbols, language, who is fearless, willing to take any and all risks, often produces work that is staggeringly beautiful and at the same time frightening, dangerous, something to be reckoned with.

"Laura Farabough," Interviews with Contemporary Women
Playwrights, Kathleen Betsko* and Rachel Koenig 1987

*See 3125.

4408. Amy Goodman (1957–)

1 The Financial Times describes the Bush administration's financial analysis as "a piece of fiction."

Quoted in "Peace Correspondent 'Democracy Now!' Host
Amy Goodman Is Making Her Voice Heard on Iraq" by
Michael Powell, The Washington Post 10 March 2003

2 You* are calling radio stations telling people to vote. What do you say to people who feel the two parties are bought by corporations and that at this point their vote doesn't make a difference?

Ibid.

*William Jefferson Clinton (1946–), 42nd president of the United States (1993–2001).

3 Go where the silence is and say something.

Ibid.

4 Steal our stories—please.

Ibid.

4409. Denise W. Gürer (1957?–)

1 The pipeline shrinkage problem for women in science is a well known and documented phenomenon. It is particularly evident in the computer science (CS) fields where the ratio of women to men involved in computing from high school to graduate school shrinks dramatically.

Introduction, "Investigating the Incredible Shrinking
Pipeline for Women in Computer Science," National Science
Foundation Report—Project 9812016, coauthor, Tracy
Camp* June 2002

*See 4671.

2 In looking at preschool and elementary level students, most seem to have positive attitudes towards computers without assuming any gender differences. It is not until later years that gender differences become pronounced. Thus, it is crucial that children at this young age are given equal exposure to computers and have positive experiences to carry through to their later years. Teachers should be careful to ensure all students have equal time and opportunity with the computers and most importantly, ensure that students at such a young age have fun.

Ibid.

3 Computer games are usually a child' s first experience with computers. This introduction plays a large role in determining a child' s future interest and enjoyment in using computers.

Ibid.

4 Creating software games for girls is not as easy as it sounds. Gender biases exist among software designers which prevent them from making games that girls will really enjoy. Many girl games on the market tend to create games that focus on shopping or putting on makeup, rather than the interactive storytelling or educational games that girls crave. In addition, creating an interactive storytelling game is potentially more technically difficult than a standard shoot 'em up game.

Ibid.

5 Women role models demonstrate the presence, the participation, and the continuing prospects of women in the CS fields. When young women think about computing as a career choice, the presence of successful women in CS is an encouraging signal. Not only do senior women scientists serve as role models in terms of scientific excellence; but young women also appreciate models of balancing a CS career with family and other aspects of life.

Ibid.

6 Industry still has a way to go to provide appropriate environments that allow a new mother to also be productive at her job (e.g., on-site daycare, expressing private rooms, flexible hours, and so on). Few people will argue that although our society is making progress toward becoming a culture in which women

are afforded the same opportunities as men, the progress is slow. Gender biases in relation to technology and technically oriented careers still permeate family life, our educational system, and the media.

Ibid.

4410. Tessa Hadley (1957?–)

1 Pearl doesn't really like her mother's clothes. They're much too sober and sensible, and they still have the stamp of the style that must have stood for political radicalism in her youth and now makes Pearl wince . . .

Everything Will Be All Right 2003

2 The next day she went, and he suffered. For the first time like an adult, secretly.

"Phosphorescence," *Sunstroke 2007*

3 In thinking that I was less naïve, I was merely being naïve in a different way, since one is naïve at every age. And the naïvety of old age is not the least of them.

"The Devil in the Flesh," *Ibid.*

4 All Pam's conversations began as if you hadn't stopped talking since you last saw her; they were as cluttered as her car.

"Friendly Fire," *The New Yorker 4 February 2008*

4411. Jane Hamilton (1957–)

1 I used to think if you fell from grace it was more likely than not the result of one stupendous error, or else an unfortunate accident. I hadn't learned that it can happen so gradually you don't lose your stomach or hurt yourself in the landing.

A Map of the World 1994

2 . . . the grass was so green it hurt to look at it, the air so overpoweringly sweet you had to go in and turn on the television, just to dull your senses.

Ibid.

3 I might have told him that our mission in life is . . . to fill up the endless gray void that is time.

Ibid.

4 Sometimes people get so confused by how fast everything's moving they have to throw somebody out, to make them feel better.

Ibid.

4412. Karen Heller (1957?–)

1 The simple life works in the two-dimensional world of magazines big on nubby sweaters (and free of moth holes) and high thread-count linens (with nary a wrinkle or peanut-butter stain). It doesn't work in the real world. Some reasons:
1. Children
2. Dirt
3. Work

"Simplicity sounds good. . . ," *Philadelphia Inquirer 9 January 2003*

2 The simplicity movement has a curious way of making everything about shopping . . .

Ibid.

3 War has long been a marketer's dream. An enduring poster, a snappy song, a bestseller, an action figure, a return to civil-

ians in epaulets and khaki. You have to be sold something this horrible, even if the pitchmen are a president* and vice president** who did their best to avoid Vietnam.

"When firefighters were No. 1," *Philadelphia Inquirer 26 January 2003*
*George W. Bush (1946–), Am. politician; 43rd president of the United States (2001–09). **Richard Bruce "Dick" Cheney (1941–), 46th vice president of the United States (2001–09).

4 Americans lease their lives to a Lexus and the illusion of a better life, but most people are not enjoying one. They're just driving personal debt higher.

"Projecting ourselves into the dream," *Philadelphia Inquirer 16 February 2003*

4413. Velina Hasu Houston (1957–)

1 FUMIKO. Ha. First our women put on dresses, then cut their hair, and smoke like men. . . .
KIHEIDA. You see what your Yankee freedom has done? You live in Kobe, a beautiful city ravaged by Yankee fire bombs, your own parents victims of them. How can you strut about in American clothes as Yankees walk in their ashes?
FUMIKO. (somberly). I do not look back, Obisan.

Sc. 3, *Asa Ga Kimashita* (Morning Has Broken) *1981*

2 FUSAE SHIMADA. There is nothing but the present moment— the one we can grasp in our fists and feel.

American Dreams 1984

3 The kinds of plays that are important to me are plays that give something to the world in which we live, that recycle our emotions, spirits, and intellect to refuel and improve the world—not destroy it. Important plays are rich with cultural and political substance. They reflect a social consciousness without losing a sense of the personal. Their vision remains inextricably tied to the never-ending exploration and excavation of the human condition. For theater should not only entertain but also enlighten.

Introduction, *The Politics of Life, Four Plays by Asian American Woman 1993*

4414. Shahieda Issel (1957–)

1 I said to myself, "The only thing they can do is kill my body. They are not going to get my mind, and my soul will live on in my children and in other people."

Quoted in Ch. 4, *Lives of Courage* by Diana E. H. Russell* *1989*
*See 3104.

4415. Tama Janowitz (1957–)

1 Long after the bomb falls and you and your good deeds are gone, cockroaches will still be here, prowling the streets like armored cars.

"Modern Saint 271," *Slaves of New York 1986*

2 I was like a social worker for lepers. My clients had a chunk of their body they wanted to give away; for a price I was there to receive it. Crimes, sins, nightmares, hunks of hair: it was surprising how many of them had something to dispose of. The more I charged, the easier it was for them to breathe freely once more.

Ibid.

3 With publicity comes humiliation.

International Herald Tribune (Paris) 8 September 1992

4416. Terri Jentz (1957–)

1 It seemed to me that it was a great risk to inhabit a body. Often I felt flashes of panic just to find myself encased in one.
Strange Piece of Paradise 2006

2 Back then [1977], all of America was in a drought. The fever dream of the sixties had simmered down and the country had lost its way. The national mood was dispirited, in recovery from shocks and traumas, pinched by stagnation and inflation. Fatalism shadowed sunny American optimism.
"A Dangerous Summer's Night," Ibid.

3 How could I get the recurring dreams to stop, the ones that haunted me through the years—dreams in which I was captive at the age of twenty, unable to progress to another stage of life? What dislocation of spirit had arrested a part of my psyche?
"Its Long Life," Ibid.

4417 Caroline Kennedy (1957–)
Also see Ellen Alderman, 4397:1–2.

1 I have never had a president who inspired me the way people tell me that my father inspired them. But for the first time, I believe I have found the man* who could be that president — not just for me, but for a new generation of Americans.
"A President Like My Father," *The New York Times* 27 *January 2008*
*Barack Obama (1961–   ), 44th president of the United States (2009–   ).

2 Knowing the impact my parents* had, and have, has always given me a continuing sense of their presence, as well as an understanding of the power every individual has to make a difference.
"Ten Who Inspire," *AARP Magazine Jan/Feb 2008*
*John F. Kennedy (1917–63), 35th president of the United States (1961–63), and Jacquelyn K— Onassis; see 2676.

3 I have lived a very advantaged life, and I am very fortunate. But our family tradition has been always to work for working people.
"As a Candidate, Kennedy Is Forceful but Remains Elusive," *The New York Times* 27 *December 2008*

4418. Myung Mi Kim (1957–)

1 One gives over to a language and then

What is given, given over?
"Into Such Assembly" 2, *The Woman That I Am, The Literature and Culture of Contemporary Women of Color*, D. Soyini Madison,* ed. *1994*
*See 3912.

4419. Sung-Joo Kim (1957–)

1 Asia is becoming the major market in the world and it's a natural trend that Asian companies will take over the luxury brands—after all we are the major buyers of the brands.
"Sung-Jo Kim plans great Asian powerhouse," *The Moodie Report October/November 2006*

2 You can't ignore half of the population's brain power. Unless you listen to what women want you will fail.
Ibid.

3 I was kicked out of the family because I did not follow their tradition and marry into another big family. I was left penniless.
Ibid.

4 If I had got a billion dollars like my brothers I would probably not be here today. Out of these hardships I have made my own way, and I now have the privilege of representing women in Korea regardless of their background.
Ibid.

4420. Valerie Matsumoto (1957–)

1 In the evening the air was thick with mosquitoes, gnats and moths. The cicadas buzzed in deafening chorus from every tree. They danced in frenzied legions around the porch light and did kamikaze dives into the bath water. All of them came in dusty gray hordes, as though the desert had sapped the color from them, but not their energy.
"Two Deserts" (1986), *The Forbidden Stitch: An Asian-American Women's Anthology*, Shirley Geok-lin Lim,* Mayma Tsutakawa, and M. Donnelly, eds. *1989*
*See 3521.

2 To Mattie, [a garden] was the true world of the heart, with no room for ungentle or impatient hands. It was a place of deeply sown hopes, lovingly nurtured, and its colors were the colors of unspoken dreams.
Ibid.

3 The modern imagination is more apt to see the urban face of California, with its burgeoning technological industries and Hollywood dream factories, than the agricultural bounty of its heartland.
Ch. 1, *Farming the Home Place: A Japanese American Community in California, 1919–1982 1994*

4 The hegemony of large-scale corporate farming and the style of cooperative marketing have . . . obscured the vital role that Asian immigrants and other racial ethnic people have played—and continue to play—in the cultivation of California's billion-dollar agricultural industry.
Ibid.

4421. Lorrie Moore (1957–)

1 When you were six you thought *mistress* meant to put your shoes on the wrong feet. Now you are older and know it can mean many things, but essentially it means to put your shoes on the wrong feet.
"How to Be the Other Woman," *Self-Help 1985*

2 "Fathers and sons," she said, "they're like governments; always having sword fights with their penises."
Ch. 1, *Anagrams 1996*

3 Faced with the large questions of life and not finding large answers, one must then settle for makeshift, little answers, just as on any given day a person must at least eat *something*, even if it was not marvelous and huge.
Ibid.

4 Wives are like cockroaches. They will survive you after a nuclear attack.
Birds of America 1998

5 [She was a] minor movie star once nominated for a major award.
Ibid.

6 In this culture we have this idea of mother love being different from romantic love. The great love you have for your children isn't a separate kind of love It is a romance. You are in love,

physically in a similar state, and you want this person's presence all the time.

> Quoted in "A generation of skeptics tunes in to Moore" by Hillel Italie, *Seattle Post-Intelligencer*, What's Happening 22 *January 1999*

4422. Mira Nair (1957–)

1 . . . I know what it's like to be in one place and dream of another. I also know what it's like to feel that nostalgia is a fairly useless thing because it is stasis. It does not take you many places.

> Quoted by Bonnie Greer in *The Guardian* (London) *12 June 2002*

2 I often begin movies with music in my head; it's a very important dimension to me. Not just the music itself, but how to use music in film: when and how and subtlety.

> Quoted by Amaya Rivera in *Mother Jones March/April 2007*

3 I make images in my work. I don't pen words.

> Ibid.

4423. Janet Napolitano (1957–)

1 He is a powerful persuader. He really is. As good as he is at motivating a large hall, he's as good or better one on one.

> Quoted in "Napolitano Cites Need For 'Fresh Voices' in Obama* Pick" by Dan Balz and Shailagh Murray, *The Washington Post 11 January 2008*
> *Barack Obama (1961–), 44th president of the United States (2009–).

2 You start off wanting to do everything through cooperation, but I'm not a potted plant.

> Quoted in "The Razor's Edge: Janet Napolitano" by Alexis Jetter, *More Magazine March 2008*

3 Fifty is the new 30. I have so much left I want to do.

> Ibid.

4 You show me a 50-foot wall and I'll show you a 51-foot ladder at the border.

> Remark (2005), Quoted in "Obama Tasks Napolitano with Homeland Security Overhaul" by Mimi Hall, *USA Today 2 December 2008*

4424. Martina Navratilova (1957–)

1 In Czechoslovakia there is no such thing as freedom of the press. In the United States there is no such thing as freedom from the press.

> Quoted in *Sportswit* by Lee Green *1984*

2 I came to live in a country I love; some people label me a defector. I have loved men and women in my life; I've been labelled "the bisexual defector" in print. Want to know another secret? I'm even ambidextrous. I don't like labels. Just call me Martina.

> Ch. 1, *Being Myself 1985*

3 Being blunt with your feelings is very American. In this big country, I can be as brash as New York, as hedonistic as Los Angeles, as sensuous as San Francisco, as brainy as Boston, as proper as Philadelphia, as brawny as Chicago, as warm as Palm Springs, as friendly as my adopted home town of Dallas, Fort Worth, and as peaceful as the inland waterway that rubs up against my former home in Virginia Beach.

> Ibid.

4 The moment of victory is much too short to live for that and nothing else.

> *The Guardian* (London) *21 June 1989*

5 Wimbledon is like a drug—once you win it, you've just got to do it again.

> "3rd time is charm," Reuters and AP *8 July 1990*

4425. Linda Olga Nghatsane (1957–)

1 Agriculture is a given platform for women. And so that's why it's very close to my heart to mobilize women to discover their talent for farming and the potential that is there for them. After all we are feeding families. We can just as well feed the nation.

> Quoted in "Making Women Farmers 'Visible' As They Feed Nations" by Regina Cornwell, Women's Media Center (womensmediacenter.com) *14 August 2008*

4426. Anne Phillips (1957?–)

1 Early feminist arguments . . . often conceived political priorities in terms of extending to women those rights and equalities that were being asserted as the birthright of men. Women applied to themselves rules that were originally formulated for a more limited constituency, and insisted on making universal what had started out far more particular.

> Ch. 2, *Destabilising Theory: Contemporary Feminist Debates*, coauthor, Michèle Barrett* *1992*
> *See 3885.

2 My object, however, is a multiculturalism without culture: a multiculturalism that dispenses with the reified notions of culture that feed those stereotypes to which so many feminists have objected, yet retains enough robustness to address inequalities between cultural groups; a multiculturalism in which the language of cultural difference no longer gives hostages to fortune or sustenance to racists, but also no longer paralyses normative judgment.

> Introduction, *Multiculturalism without Culture 2007*

3 People not previously marked by their ardent support for women's rights seemed to rely on claims about the maltreatment of women to justify their distaste for minority cultural groups, and in these claims, cultural stereotypes were rife.

> Ibid.

4427. Susan Powter (1957–)

1 Food=joy . . . guilt . . . anger . . . pain . . . nurturing . . . friendship . . . hatred . . . the way you look and feel. . . . Food=everything you can imagine.

> p. 15, *Food 1995*

2 Stop the Insanity!

> Catch-phrase *n.d.*

4428. Karen Propp (1957–)

1 In my experience, when wanting a child is a long-term, aching pain and trying to have one involves heroic medical measures, the narcissism inherent in parenting is often exacerbated. The inability to become pregnant easily becomes a devastating female failure.

> "The end and the means," *The Women's Review of Books*, vol. 15, no. 12 *September 1998*

2 I returned to Boston to meet Sam or someone like him: someone who does not find me strange, as did the Mormons, for

having education instead of children and dark unruly hair instead of a blond shiny coif

Ch. 1, *In Sickness and In Health: A Love Story 2002*

4429. Karambu Ringera (1957–   )

1   Some spoke of the biblical analogy that men are the head and women the neck. I always added that if the neck refused to move or was stiff, the head could not turn!!

"An End, a Beginning. . . ," Karambu.com *2007*

2   For me, the end merely does not justify the means, the means is a critical part of the process. I seek power with others, not power over others. I work to be a leader who inspires others to find the best in themselves . . .

Ibid.

3   Today's world needs leaders who inspire and empower others to step into their own power. Change can only come from within—we are all leaders, and if we endeavor to empower others, we can create strong partners for change in our communities.

"When Elephants Fight, the Grass Below Suffers," *World Pulse* (worldpulsemagazine.com) *15 February 2008*

4   In times of crisis, we must recognize that the assistance that meets the needs of men does not always meet the needs of women and children.

Ibid.

4430. Sima Samar (1957–   )

1   I've always been in danger, but I don't mind. I believe we will die one day so I said let's take the risk and help somebody else.

"Profile: Sima Samar," BBC News *6 December 2001*

2   I began seeing patients immediately [upon graduation], but I often had to run to my book to identify symptoms and treatments, and then I had to find out whether the necessary medicine was even available. I saw women die every day because of incomplete abortion or shoulder presentation of the fetus at delivery: we did not have the proper equipment to deal with these sorts of problems.

Article, *The New England Journal of Medicine 2004*

3   I believe that there is no full justice anywhere. One of the reasons the war became so violent, and lasted so long, was the lack of education, as well as poverty and joblessness. To overcome these things, I insist on education. I don't believe in any kind of development without the involvement of women.

Quoted in "Sima Samar: safeguarding human rights in Afghanistan" by Ivan Oransky, *The Lancet,* vol. 368, no. 9552 *9 December 2006*

4   While there have been some positive steps in Afghanistan, there is still a long road ahead. We did adopt a new Afghan Constitution, and it includes an equal-rights provision for women and guarantees women's representation in the Afghan parliament.

Quoted in "A Voice for the Voiceless" by Katherine Spillar, *Ms. Winter 2007*

5   Suicide bombers, who were never present in Afghanistan before, are now killing innocent people throughout the country, even in the streets of Kabul. These tactics of intimidation and outright violence prevent the social, economic and political participation of many Afghans, particularly women.

Ibid.

4431. Cindy Sheehan (1957–   )

1   How can you finish imperialism? It doesn't end, it just spreads. Some people think that we're fighting terrorism over there.* But when is that job ever going to be complete? Terrorism is just a new "ism." It was "communism" when I was growing up.

"Grieving military mom . . ." by Ron Hutcheson, *Knight Ridder Tribune 12 August 2005*
*Re the Iraq War, a.k.a. the Second Persian Gulf War, (20 March 2003–   ).

4431.1. Lee Sinclair (1957–   )

1   Self Defense is yours for life. No one can ever take it away from you.

Address, Kilimambogo School (Kenya) *2006*

2   One may say that I place too much stock in self defense. That it is not the end all be all, in the realm of violence prevention. Well, so far so good in my life and the lives of many, many women in Nairobi and beyond. If a 15 year old girl can escape a gang of 4 boys while one is holding a knife in her side, well, I'm just not willing to write off anyone as beyond help.

Thrive House December 2008

3   Women and children can't wait for legislation to be passed and sporadically enforced. They need help now! The best form of rape prevention is self defense. If not us, who? If not now, when?

Dialogue with former MP Njoki Ndugu (Kenya) *February 2009*

4   One day, all of us survivors will get this right. We will form our strongest alliances out of our most vulnerable moments. And we won't apologize about it ever again . . . and we won't blame ourselves and wonder what we could have done to have prevented it. And that will be the wind that fills the sails of the world.

Imworthdefending.org *n.d.*

4432. Hilda Solis (1957–   )

1   As the daughter of a union family—my father was a Teamster and my mother worked tirelessly for 25 years—I know that my seven siblings and I would not be where we are today without the wages and other protections my parents earned with the help of their union.

Article re Employee Free Choice Act, *Huffington Post 2 March 2007*

2   It's time to stop sending our money to foreign countries to buy oil when we have all the sun and wind we need right here at home. Barack Obama* will lead the transition to home-grown renewable fuels that will lower gas prices and create good-paying, green jobs. Big oil and John McCain** want more of the same . . .

No podemos seguir con lo mismo! Necesitamos un cambio! (We can't continue this way. We must have change!)

Speech, Democratic Convention *27 August 2008*
*Barack Obama (1961–   ), 44th president of the United States (2009–   ). **John Sidney McCain III (1936–   ), U. S. senator (R-AZ, 1987–   ) and Republican presidential nominee (2008).

3   Folks in my district want to see more restrictions on guns. They feel afraid at night when they hear gunshots. These are real stories. We know people die.

"Online NewsHour: At the Capitol: the 107th Congress," *PBS-TV 27 August 2008*

4433. Terri Swearingen (1957?–   )

1   This isn't a tragedy in the making;* the tragedy has already begun. . . . Our children are the "mine canaries."

"The World Infamous WTI** Incinerator," *Synthesis/ Regeneration 7–8 Summer 1995*
*Re location of school near toxic waste dump. **Waste Technologies Inc.

2   The failure of the EPA* to stop WTI is being seen as an important indication of how much influence special interests still retain on environmental matters.

Ibid.

*Environmental Protection Agency.

3   The sad and frustrating realization is that many parts of our "democratic" system are nothing more than tools to use if necessary when the public learns that they have been cheated. They use EPA public hearings, GAO* investigations, meetings with elected officials and congressional hearings in an attempt to out-wait us, wear us down and cause us to retreat, hoping we will just "give up."

Ibid.

*Government Accounting Office.

4434. Anne Sweeney (1957–   )

1   It's very important to me that the people I work with have a life and have interests and passions and the ability to fully realize them. It makes them more interesting people, more fun to work with, more innovative, and it means they're out in the world participating in it. We're a media company. We rely on people who can translate those experiences because they have them themselves.

Quoted in "The Wonderful World of Sweeney" by Anne Becker, *Broadcasting & Cable 25 February 2008*

2   It's hard to believe that just three years ago we were still debating the possibility—and wisdom—of putting TV content on other platforms.

Quoted in "Disney's Anne Sweeney: 'Can't Just Build It And Hope Viewers Come'" by Staci d. Kramer, WashingtonPost. com *9 January 2009*

4435. Mia Törnqvist (1957–   )

1   THE CHILD.* Nora Schahrazade is not lonely. You on the other hand could use some company. . . . You have to understand that she can't hold her mother's hand her whole life.

The Dreamed Life of Nora Schahrazade 1994
*An "angel-child," not on this plane.

4436. Melinda Wagner (1957–   )

1   It's always a complete thrill when I first hear my music. There are surprises and there are some things that happen exactly as I expected them. And it's one of the things that's so exciting about being a composer.

Online NewsHour with Elizabeth Farnsworth, PBS-TV *19 April 1999*

2   I think every time you listen to a piece of music, it reveals something more of itself.

Ibid.

3   Sometimes I feel that the melody is leading me by the nose. Some days I can control what it's going to do. But some other days, it wants to go in a different direction. And I go with it.

Ibid.

4437. Leyla Yunusova (1957?–   )

1   He is a classic Soviet leader.* He perfectly understands our people and the slave mentality we have fallen into over the last 70 years. His tools are control over people's livelihood, blackmail, corruption, propaganda and, if nothing else works, police repression.

Quoted in "In Post-Soviet Era, the Old Style Works" by Stephen Kinzer, *The New York Times 21 September 1997*
*Heydar Aliyev (1923–2003), president of Azerbaijan, 1993–2003.

2   There will be parliamentary elections in Azerbaijan on 6 November 2005. Since the collapse of the Soviet Union there have never been free and democratic elections in the republic—each election has been accompanied by falsification, police violence and numerous arrests of opposition supporters.

Frontline (frontlinedefenders.org) *October 2005*

4437.1. Christiane Amanpour (1958–   )

1   We thrived as I said on the pioneer spirit of CNN. We adored being the little network that could. It was called Chicken Noodle News, we thought that was cute, that was funny, we loved that fact. We loved the fact that we were mocked as we kicked ass all over the world. We were thrilled. We were thrilled and we were privileged to be part of a revolution, because make no mistake about it, Ted Turner changed the world with CNN. Not only did he create 24-hour news, and all that that has meant, but he truly created the global village. And as corny as that sounds, nothing has been the same since.

Acceptance speech, 2000 Edward R. Murrow Awards Ceremony (Minneapolis) *13 September 2000*

2   Our parent companies and corporations are raking in the profits, but let me throw down this challenge: what is the point of having all this money and this fancy new technology and being able to go anywhere and broadcast everywhere, if we are simply going to drive ourselves and our news operations into the ground? It really makes you wonder about mega-mergers. Yes, you are running businesses, and yes, we understand and accept that, but surely there must be a level beyond which profit from news is simply indecent.

Ibid.

3   In emerging democracies like Russia, in authoritarian states like Iran or even Yugoslavia, journalists play a vital role in civil society. In fact, they form the very basis of those new democracies and civil societies.

Ibid.

4   I believe that good journalism, good television, can make our world a better place. And I really believe good journalism is good business.

Ibid.

4438. Natalie Angier (1958–   )

1   Ah, romance. Can any sight be as sweet as a pair of mallard ducks gliding gracefully across a pond, male by female, seem-

ingly inseparable? Or, better yet two trumpeter swans, the legendary symbols of eternal love, each ivory neck one half of a single heart, souls of a feather staying coupled together for life?

Couple for life—with just a bit of adultery, cuckoldry, and gang rape on the side.

Alas for sentiment and the greeting card industry, it turns out that, in the animal kingdom, there is almost no such thing as monogamy.

Ch. 1, The Beauty of the Beastly 1995

2   Dolphins are turning out to be exceedingly clever, but not in the loving, utopian-socialist manner that sentimental Flipperophiles may have hoped. Researchers . . . have discovered that the males form social alliances that are far more sophisticated and devious than any seen in animals other than human beings.

Ch. 6, Ibid.

3   Put a few adults in a room with a sweet-tempered infant, and you may as well leave a tub of butter sitting out in the midday sun.

Ch. 1, Woman: An Intimate Geography 1999

4   We can't replicate men—and who would want to?

Quoted by Maureen Dowd* in "Freud** Was Way Wrong,"
The New York Times 11 June 2000
*See 4102. **Sigmund F- (1856–1939), Austrian psychiatrist; founder of psychoanalysis.

5   Female primates have two goals. They want control over their reproduction and access to resources.

Ibid.

6   Science is not a body of facts. Science is a state of mind. It is a way of viewing the world, of facing reality square on but taking nothing on its face. It is about attacking a problem with the most manicured of claws and tearing it down into sensible, edible pieces.

Ch. 1, The Canon: A Whirligig Tour of the Beautiful Basics of Science 2007

4439. Kaisha Atakhanova (1958–   )

1   So the government received a very well-thought-out campaign.

Sometimes it's not very productive to yell and scream—we had a very strong argument, with very good background on the issue.

Quoted in "Out of the Lab, Into the Fire" by Michelle Nijhuis,
grist.org 18 April 2005

2   The majority of our problems are coming from our use of natural resources—gas, oil, uranium. A lot of problems are coming from the fact that we're seen as a resource country [Kazakhstan], that people are taking resources from the land without thinking of the environmental impacts.

Ibid.

4440. Sophie Cabot Black (1958–   )

1   [Trying to get pregnant] becomes a lot like applying for a grant from the National Endowment for the Arts; you'd wait and wait and wait, but as soon as you got rejected, you could reapply.

Quoted in "The Boys," *Quests for Parenthood in a High-Tech Age*, Jill Bialosky* and Helen Schulman, eds. *1998*
*See 4603.

2   Once again I was trying to sneak a four-foot tank containing the essence of six hundred million California boys around a community that had never been outside of a thirty-mile radius of itself.

Ibid.

4441. Susannah "Susie" Bright (1958–   )

1   What I find, more and more, is that some people don't want to switch to their genital opposite—no, they want to liberate themselves from gender entirely. They are coming to this place not out of a childhood wish or identity, but from the cumulative process of living as a woman, a man, a dyke, a fag, a straight girl, a bi man. They have been all those places and their identity lies in the mosaic, not in any fixed spot.

"I Love Being a Gender," *The Sexual State of the Union 1997*

2   I had . . . all the elements of a pornographic experience. I felt the secrecy, the excess, the fear of violent reactions, the quease of perversion.

"My First Dirty Picture," Ibid.

3   The finest erotic authors are the great tease artists. They get the readers hanging by their short hairs, then they spin them around and make them forget what they came for—only to pull them in again like so much taffy.

"The Erotic Reader's Bill of Rights," *How to Write a Dirty Story: Reading, Writing, and Publishing Erotica 2002*

4442. Valda Jean Combs (1958?–   )

1   When black women press for inclusion, white women have historically been hard of hearing. As a result, far from viewing white women as partners in the struggle, women of color have the historical knowledge of white women in partnership with their men as oppressors.

"Barack Obama* Wins the Sojourner Truth** Vote," Women's
E-news (womensenews.org) *16 May 2008*
*Barack Obama (1961–   ), 44th president of the United States (2009–   ). **See 860.

2   But when we raised the problematic irony of women of color working outside their own homes in the homes of white women—where they were paid low wages with no benefits—this was often lost on white feminists. They seemed more riveted on breaking down the gender barriers to elite schools and high-paying professions.

Ibid.

3   Black women supporting Obama now dare to believe that change can come in our time. A change that offers our boys hope that they, too, can become president; a change that offers our community hope that black families can survive and thrive; and change that says out of oppression can come liberation for not just some of us, but all of us.

Ibid.

4   If anger and disappointment cause some women to sit out this election, other women will pay the price.

"Sisters, This Is an Election We Can't Sit Out," Ibid.
13 August 2008

4443. Jamie Lee Curtis (1958–   )

1   People get real comfortable with their features. Nobody gets comfortable with their hair. Hair trauma. It's the universal thing.

Quoted in *U.S.A. Today 21 February 1991*

2   I'm gonna like me when my answer is wrong,
like thinking my ruler was ten inches long . . .
I'm gonna like me 'cause I'm loved and I know it,
and liking myself is the best way to show it.
I'm Gonna Like Me: Letting Off a Little Self-Esteem 2002

3   Is there really/ a human race?
Is it going on now all over the place?
When did it start?/
Who said, "Ready, Set, Go"?
Did it start on my birthday?
I really must know
Is There Really a Human Race? 2006

4444. Michelle de Kretser (1958?–   )

1   "It is one thing to believe in equality, and quite another to find yourself fraternizing with your footman."
The Rose Grower 2000

2   While we might dread what justice requires of us, our fear cannot be allowed to interfere with the benefit to society.
The Hamilton Case 2003

3   The British made a fatal error when they brought in universal suffrage. It might be plausible in Europe, but here, with our ignorant masses, what can it lead to but the disasters we've seen since independence?
Ibid.

4   The past is not what is over but what we wish to have done with.
The Lost Dog 2008

5   Euphemisms are symptomatic of shame.
Ibid.

6   Reality is an effect produced by the accrual of detail.
Ibid.

4445. Ellen DeGeneres (1958–   )

1   If we don't want to define ourselves by things as superficial as our appearances, we're stuck with the revolting alternative of being judged by our actions, by what we do.
My Point . . . And I Do Have One 1995

2   Now we have hands-free phones, so you can focus on the thing you're really supposed to be doing . . . chances are, if you need both of your hands to do something, your brain should be in on it too.
Ellen DeGeneres: Here and Now (TV special) 2003

3   My grandmother started walking five miles a day when she was sixty. She's ninety-seven now, and we don't know where the hell she is.
Stand-up routine *n.d.*

4446. Luísa Dias Diogo (1958–   )

1   The broad goals of sustainable development call, today, for a wide range of partnership between member states, the United Nations, and the society as a whole, so as to drive our countries on the path to sustained growth and improved living conditions for its people.
The challenges of long-term sustainable employment require a concerted and coordinated approach that draws on the strengths of all countries and explores different alternatives.
Keynote address, "Working Out of Poverty" (Economic and Social Council of the United Nations, Geneva) *3 July 2006*

2   I will tell you a secret: if you want to cut defence spending, there is only one way: do it immediately and in a radical, draconian manner. There is no reasoning with the military!
Address, "My Country, On the Road to Development" (Terzo Festival dell'Economica, Trento, Italy) *29 May-2 June 2008*

4447. Heather Roote Faller (1958?–   )

1   How is time so fluid and so fine
that as moonlight filters down through the trees,
winding around the branches and spiraling down the trunk
to the furthest reaches of every hungry root,
so love trickles down and in to the smallest spaces and furthest time
to where I floated alone in silent expectation,
waiting for all this to happen?
"On Love and Moonlight," *Theology Today* October 2002

4448. Bonnie Friedman (1958–   )

1   An unhurried sense of time is in itself a form of wealth.
"Bit and Pieces of an Alter Ego," *The New York Times,* Travel *14 March 1999*

2   Is the whole of life stripping ourselves of cliché after cliché?
Ibid.

3   Traveling, each day is several.
Ibid.

4   The secret of the razor wall compelled me as a girl. I pulled open the mirror to see the hidden mouth [of the medicine chest where her father inserted razor blades], which was like the narrow backstairs near the incinerator or the gold medallions on the corridor walls or the blue gas haloes my mother showed me behind the dryers in the basement near the milk machine, or even the skittering hard-shelled waterbugs that wandered fat as stopwatches over the painted green floor, part of an empire I inherited with a checkerboard lobby and murky chandelier.
p. 264, *The Thief of Happiness* 2003

4449. Cristina García (1958–   )

1   Pilar, her first grandchild, writes to her from Brooklyn in a Spanish that is no longer hers. She speaks the hard-edged lexicon of bygone tourists itchy to throw dice on green felt or asphalt. Pilar's eyes, Celia fears, are no longer used to the compacted light of the tropics, where a morning hour can fill a month of days in the north, which receives only careless sheddings from the sun. She imagines her granddaughter pale, gliding through paleness, malnourished and cold without the food of scarlets and greens.
p. 7, *Dreaming in Cuban* 1992

2   If it were up to me, I'd record other things. Like the time there was a freak hailstorm in the Congo and the women took it as a sign that they should rule. Or the life stories of prostitutes in Bombay. Why don't I know anything about them? Who chooses what we should know or what's important. I know I have to decide these things for myself. Most of what I've learned that's important I've learned on my own, or from my grandmother.
p. 28, Ibid.

3   The familiar is insistent and deadly. I study the waves and keep time on my wicker swing. If I was born to live on an island, then I'm grateful for one thing: that the tides rearrange the borders. At least I have the illusion of change, of possibility. To

be locked within boundaries plotted by priests and politicians would be the only thing more intolerable.

Don't you see how they're carving up the world, Gustavo? How they're stealing our geography? Our fates? The arbitrary is no longer in our hands. To survive is an act of hope.

p. 99, Ibid.

4 Lourdes enjoys patrolling the streets in her thick-soled black shoes. These shoes, it seems to her, are a kind of equalizer. She can run in them if she has to, jump curbs, traverse the buckled, faulted sidewalks of Brooklyn without twisting an ankle. These shoes are power. If women wore shoes like these, she thinks, they wouldn't worry so much about more abstract equalities.

p. 127, Ibid.

5 I resent the hell out of the politicians and the generals who force events on us that structure our lives, that dictate the memories we'll have when we're old. Every day Cuba fades a little more inside me, my grandmother fades a little more inside me. And there's only my imagination where our history should be.

p. 138, Ibid.

4450. Salima Ghezali (1958–)

1 We must remember the principles that form the foundations of human society and exercise vigilance. This is the best way to ensure that civilization triumphs barbarism.

Comment on the banning of *La Nation* (Algeria) newspaper
1996

4451. Dina Goren-Bar (1958?–)

1 We shouldn't have to choose between women's freedom and national freedom. A mother of two children doesn't have to choose which one is more precious. All children and all freedoms are precious.

Quoted in Ch. 10, *Deborah, Golda, and Me* by Letty Cottin Pogrebin* 1991

*See 3154.

4452. E. J. Graff (1958–)

1 Marriage, in other words, turns out to be a kind of Jerusalem, an archaeological site on which the present is constantly building over the past, letting history's many layers twist and tilt into today's walls and floors. . . . [M]any people believe theirs is the one true claim to this holy ground. But like Jerusalem, marriage has always been a battleground, owned and defined first by one group and then another. While marriage . . . may retain its ancient name, very little else in this city has remained the same—not its boundaries, boulevards, or daily habits—except the fact that it is inhabited by human beings.

Introduction, *What Is Marriage For? The Strange Social History of Our Most Intimate Institution* 1999

2 Marriage has not been one revered, immutable, monogamous thing for 6000 years. Rather, marriage has always been hot political territory, constantly redefined to fit every time societies change.

Article, *New England Law Review* 38 2004

3 If journalism repeatedly frames the wrong problem, then the folks who make public policy may very well deliver the wrong solution.

"The Opt-Out Myth," *Columbia Journalism Review March/April* 2007

4 Here's what feminism hasn't yet changed: the American idea of mothering is left over from the 1950s, that odd moment in history when America's unrivaled economic power enabled a single breadwinner to support an entire family. Fifty years later we still have the idea that a mother, and not a father, should be available to her child at every moment.

Ibid.

4453. Jane Gross (1958?–)

1 Over and over, these men cry out against the weight of so many losses—not just a lover dead, but friends and friends of friends, dozens of them, until it seems that AIDS is all there is and all there ever will be.

"AIDS: The Next Phase," *The New York Times* 16 March 1987

2 Since the late 1960s and early 1970s, when working women made child care benefits a key part of the feminist agenda, it has become routine for companies to provide maternity leaves, job sharing and pre-tax accounts to pay for child care. These days, the accommodations offered to those of us caring for elderly parents often are modeled on these kinds of child care benefits. But the so-called "mommy track" and "daughter track" are more dissimilar than similar, and the child care paradigm does not always work to benefit adult caregivers.

"Where the Mommy Track Crosses the Daughter Track," *The New York Times* 28 October 2008

3 But nothing made her sparkle more those last few years than my brother's Westie. Oh, she was always glad to see one of us. But only Calpurnia sent my mother into gales of laughter, until tears rolled down her face, as the little pooch slobbered her with kisses and licked clean every last crumb that had fallen on her wheelchair.

"Another Nursing Home Thanksgiving," *The New York Times* 1 December 2008

4 . . . infancy and frail old age are exactly the same . . . and also completely different. What they share is utter dependence. But infancy, in the normal order of things, is a hopeful beginning; while senescence is the dimming of the light.

"Dreaming of Benjamin Button,"* *The New York Times* 5 January 2009

The Curious Case of Benjamin Button, a 2008 motion picture based on an F. Scott Fitzgerald (1896–1940, American writer) story about reverse aging.

4454. Claudia Henrion (1958–)

1 . . . the identification of mathematics with formal deductive proofs fuel[s] an image of mathematics as non-human and impersonal. Because the final product, rather than the process of doing mathematics, is what is highlighted, people are seen as almost irrelevant.

Women in Mathematics: The Addition of Difference 1997

4455. Martha Kegel (1958–)

1 The proponents of this law [scientific creationism] are trying to sneak religion into the public schools. They are trying to disguise the religious nature of the doctrine of creationism. They have dressed this law with verbal fig leaves, nice-sounding phrases like "equal time" and "non-discrimination." But the fact remains that creationism is a Bible story and teaching it as science in public schools violated the rights of religious minorities.

Quoted in *Daily Star* (Hammond, Louisiana) 3 December 1981

2 At least when they openly outlawed homelessness, they were being honest. In a way, they've now created a new crime—walking while homeless.

"Walking While Homeless" by Katy Reckdahl, *Gambit Weekly*
24 September 2002

3 The problem now is not so much chronic homelessness but an acute homeless epidemic, people suddenly made homeless as opposed to people who are homeless long term because of disability.

"Homeless population in New Orleans rapidly expands" by
Richard A. Webster, *New Orleans City Business*
13 March 2006

4456. Janice King (1958–)

1 If you continue to make people feel that their lifestyles are going to make them go to hell, without showing any love, then you'll lose this generation. The church as a whole has come to the revelation that the old way of trying to get the gospel out don't work for the younger generation.

Quoted in "It's *Soul* Mag" by Katherine Corcoran, *Knight*
Ridder Tribune 10 September 2005

4457. Sarah Lindsay (1958–)

1 The world is large
and without a fuss has absorbed stranger things than this.

"Cheese Penguin," *Primate Behavior 1997*

2 She doesn't know
why this time she pushes past the surface tension
and wimples up the minute incline
on jellied stumps . . .
She feels a pocket
flex inside her neck, she gapes
at the scoured entry of demanding air.

"Lungfish Conquers Depression," Ibid.

4458. Tzipora "Tzipi" Malka Livni (1958–)

1 Somebody who is fighting against Israeli soldiers is an enemy and we will fight back, but I believe that this is not under the definition of terrorism, if the target is a soldier.

Interview, *Nightline 28 March 2006*

2 In convincing the other, I try to start from their point of view, so it's easier for me to find a common denominator.

Quoted in "Her Jewish State" by Roger Cohen,
The New York Times 8 July 2007

3 Israelis must know that the international community does understand we are under attack. It is so important to Israel to know that our right to defend ourselves is supported and that you understand that there is suffering here, and not just among Palestinians.

Ibid.

4 Each of us can live with our narrative, so long as we are pragmatic when it comes to the land. I still believe in our right to the whole land, but felt it was more important to make a compromise. We cannot solve who was right or wrong in 1948 or decide who is more just. The Palestinians can feel justice is on their side, and I can feel it is on my side. What we have to decide about is not history but the future.

Ibid.

5 In order for us to be a democratic and a Jewish state, in the long run, we'll have to give away some of the land.

Quoted in "Mrs. Clean" by Tim McGirk, *Time 16 June 2008*

4459. Madonna (1958–)

1 Catholicism is not a soothing religion. It's a painful religion. We're all gluttons for punishment.

Interview in *Rolling Stone 23 March 1989*

2 Everyone probably thinks that I'm a raving nymphomaniac, that I have an insatiable sexual appetite, when the truth is I'd rather read a book.

Q Magazine (London) *June 1991*

3 I always thought of losing my virginity as a career move.

Epilogue, Quoted in *Madonna Unauthorized* by Christopher
Andersen *1991*

4 I wouldn't have turned out the way I was if I didn't have all those old-fashioned values to rebel against.

Time (New York, 17 December 1990), Ch. 11, *Madonna:*
Blonde Ambition 1992

4460. Yvonne Margarula (1958?–)
Also see Jacqui Katona, 4724.

1 It is a very large number of people who see this [uranium] mine as a bad thing. The agreement was arranged by pushing people and does not accurately reflect the wishes of Aboriginal people who own that country. We all stand together on that.

Quoted on goldmanprize.org n.d.

4461. Ceci Miller (1958–)

1 The purpose of a sacred visitation, or spiritual experience, if you like, is to change us, to move us deeper into living as our true self.

"What Is a Sacred Visitation?" *Sacred Visitations: Gifts of*
Grace That Transform the Heart and Awaken the Soul 2006

4462. Maria Elena Moyano (1958–1992)

1 This is my life. If they're going to kill me, they're going to kill me.
I'm going to be dead one day. . . . Death is always present. . . . And if my death can serve a purpose, so be it.

Quoted in "Shining Path* slays leader . . ." by Kevin Galvin
(AP), *Seattle Times*, A16 *23 February 1992*
*A Peruvian guerrilla group dedicated to overthrowing the government.

2 We're not with those who kill popular leaders, who massacre leaders of soup kitchens and the Glass of Milk program. We are not with those who . . . want to impose themselves by force and brutality.

Speech (14 February), Ibid.

4463. Naomi Oreskes (1958–)

1 If the history of science teaches anything, it is humility, and no one can be faulted for failing to act on what is not known. But our grandchildren will surely blame us if they find that we understood the reality of anthropogenic climate change and failed to do anything about it

"Beyond the Ivory Tower: The Scientific Consensus on
Climate Change," *Science 3 December 2004*

2   Earth scientists long believed that humans were insignificant in comparison with the vastness of geological time and the power of geophysical forces. For this reason, many were reluctant to accept that humans had become a force of nature, and it took decades for the present understanding to be achieved. Those few who refuse to accept it are not ignorant, but they are stubborn. They are not unintelligent, but they are stuck on details that cloud the larger issue. Scientific communities include tortoises and hares, mavericks and mules.

"Global Warming—Signed, Sealed and Delivered,"
The Los Angeles Times 24 July 2006

3   In any scientific community, there are always some individuals who simply refuse to accept new ideas and evidence. This is especially true when the new evidence strikes at their core beliefs and values.

Ibid.

4   Scientists and journalists focus on novelty, because both are largely about discovery.

"The Long Consensus On Climate Change," *The Washington Post 1 February 2007*

4464. Anna Politkovskaya (1958–2006)

1   For our new rich, freedom has nothing to do with political parties. Freedom is the freedom to go on great vacations. The richer they are, the more often they can fly away, and not to Antalya in Turkey, but to Tahiti or Acapulco. For the majority of them, freedom equals access to luxury.

Ch. 1, *A Russian Diary*, Arch Tait, tr. 2007

2   . . . Putin* went so far as to inform us that Parliament was a place not for debate, but for legislative tidying up. He was pleased that the new Duma would not be given to debating.

Ibid.
*Vladimir P— (1952–), second president of Russia (1999–2008); prime minister (2008–).

3   Here is the real cost of political cynicism—rejection by the younger generation.

Ibid.

4   In a corrupt country, business is even more unscrupulous than in countries where corruption has at least been reduced to a tolerable level and where it is not regarded as socially acceptable.

Ibid.

4465. Margie Profet (1958–)

1   No matter what aspect of physiology you look at, the core question is: what's it there for? Maybe it is just a fluke or a by-product. But maybe it has a function. You have to know that. Otherwise you're doing blind medical intervention.

Quoted in "Darwinian Medicine" by Terry McDermott, *Seattle Times*, Pacific Northwest section *31 July 1994*

2   I had this phobia of libraries. They were dusty and old, and I was afraid of going to the stacks and finding some old 18th-century scholar rotting there. Now I love them. They're like my sanctuaries.

Ibid.

3   Physicians don't look at function. Physicians seem to think if you ask what's the function of something, it's teleological. It's an intellectual theory, and there's no practical utility.

It's not important? It's the basis, it's the foundation for understanding physiology. And physiology is the basis for understanding medicine. . . .

Say we have two theories about the function of the heart. One is that it pumps blood. The second theory is that it's there to give us love and heartbreak.

In the second case it's removable. You had a bad loveship, take out your heart.

Ibid.

4   Science isn't a democracy.

Ibid.

4466. Cecile Richards (1958?–)

1   No one does more to reduce the need for abortions in this country than Planned Parenthood. I would welcome legislators, including those from South Dakota, to work with us on family planning instead of focusing on making doctors and women criminals.

Quoted in "Anti-Abortion Advocates? Bring 'Em On, Texan Says" by Robin Finn, *The New York Times 10 March 2006*

2   We are at a pivotal moment in the fight for women's rights and if we allow the anti-choice movement to continue to chip away at these rights, we, as a nation, stand to loose some of the basic freedoms protected by our Constitution.

"The Heart of the Heartland, 2006," *The Huffington Post 23 October 2006*

3   It's hard to imagine a more stinging indictment of the Bush* administration policy that supports a "just say no" approach to sex education than the current collision of popular culture and real life. Teen sex and unintended pregnancy are everywhere— from television to movies to the cover of People magazine. In fact, the only place these topics aren't being discussed are in health classes in high schools.

"Jamie Lynn Spears, *Juno* and *Knocked Up*: Can You Hear Me Yet?," *The Huffington Post 28 December 2007*

4   Elections are about choices, and Mom* would have said that women voting for John McCain would be like chickens choosing to vote for the Colonel.

"What Would Ann Do?" *The Huffington Post 10 June 2008*
*Re Ann Richards; see 2861.

5   . . . five men in black robes don't know better than women what's best for them.*

Quoted in "Daughter calls Sen. McCain** an enemy of women's health care . . ." by W. Gardner Selby, *American-Statesman 27 August 2008*
*Re conservative U.S. Supreme Court justices. **John Sidney McCain III (1936–), United States senator (R-AZ, 1987–) and Republican presidential nominee (2008).

4467. Miranda Richardson (1958–)

1   Insecurity, commonly regarded as a weakness in normal people, is the basic tool of the actor's trade.

The Guardian (London) *5 December 1990*

4468. Christina D. Romer (1958–)

1   Legislatures and central banks throughout the world now routinely attempt to prevent or moderate recessions. Whether such a change would have occurred without the Depression is again a largely unanswerable question. What is clear is that this change has made it unlikely that a decline in spending will

ever be allowed to multiply and spread throughout the world as it did during the Great Depression of the 1930s.

"Great Depression," *Encyclopædia Britannica 2004*

2 [The] Great Depressesion [was a] worldwide economic downturn that began in 1929 and lasted until about 1939. It was the longest and most severe depression ever experienced by the industrialized Western world. Although the Depression originated in the United States, it resulted in drastic declines in output, severe unemployment, and acute deflation in almost every country of the globe. But its social and cultural effects were no less staggering, especially in the United States, where the Great Depression ranks second only to the Civil War as the gravest crisis in American history.

Ibid.

3 Faced with what could have turned into a panic in 2008, the Fed responded aggressively. It's exactly the textbook description of what they should have done. Now the innovative things, such as lending to investment banks, raise big regulatory issues that I think someone needs to be thinking about a lot—making sure they're dealing with them correctly. But again the big picture was, don't let the New York financial market go under because it would have devastating real economic consequences. That was exactly the right focus for policy.

Interview, *The Region September 2008*

4 Just as there is no regularity in the timing of business cycles, there is no reason why cycles have to occur at all. The prevailing view among economists is that there is a level of economic activity, often referred to as full employment, at which the economy could stay forever.

"Business Cycles," *The Concise Encyclopedia of Economics 2008*

4469. Marina Silva (1958–)

1 All of our technical and scientific capacity will have to be used to reverse the process of destruction we have created. I am proud to be from Amazônia where we still have a chance to start a sustainable history.

Quoted on goldmanprize.org *1996*

2 There is no longer a way of thinking about growth for growth's sake. Growth is important, but it needs to be growth with development and sustainability, in all of its senses: social, environmental, economic, cultural.

Quoted in "I'd lost the strength to carry on" by Thom Phillips, *China Dialogue 20 June 2008*

3 Without the support of society it would have been impossible to have put 600 people involved in environmental crimes in the Amazon in jail. This is something that is achieved by a new social pact that is appearing inside and outside of the country.

Ibid.

4 Those who celebrated the industrial revolution never thought that we were injuring the planet, almost fatally. We didn't have this knowledge. Today we know.

Ibid.

4470. Mary Decker Slaney (1958–)

1 I've always got such high expectations for myself. I'm aware of them, but I can't relax them.

Sports Illustrated 29 July 1991

2 I think I've been good, but I want to be better. I think women reach their peak in their mid-thirties.

Ibid.

4471. Anne-Marie Slaughter (1958–)

1 It's very striking that Obama talks about a common security for our common humanity—now that is really engaged. He is really grasping that we are an interdependent world and the only way to address our problems is to embrace it . . .

"Hot Policy Wonks For The Democrats: The New Realists" by Jason Horowitz, *The New York Observer 14 August 2007*

4472. Sharon Stone (1958–)

1 If you have a vagina *and* an attitude in this town, then that's a lethal combination.

Empire (London) *June 1992*

4473. Elizabeth Strout (1958?–)

1 Besides, another thing to consider is how much Fat Bev loved to talk. She said so herself. "I can't shut up for five minutes," she said, and Amy, keeping an eye on the clock one day, had found this to be true. "I *need* to talk," Fat Bev explained. "It's a kind of physical thing." It seemed she had a point. It seemed her need to talk was as persistent as her need to consume Life Savers and cigarettes, and Amy, who loved Fat Bev, was sorry her own reticence must provide a disappointment.

Ch. 1, *Amy and Isabelle 1998*

2 "Honey," she said, nodding, "you marry a man whose mother is dead."

Ibid.

3 But Tyler was wary of shortcuts, and he was really afraid of cheap grace. He often thought of Pasteur's remarks that chance only helped those minds well prepared, and he hoped these days to have a moment of exalted understanding come to him as the "chance" result of his disciplined prayer.

Ch. 1, *Abide With Me 2006*

4 Bonnie was the central heating of his life.

"Starving," *Olive Kitteridge 2008*

4474. Margaret Wertheim (1958–)

1 The priestly culture of physics is not only a matter of concern for women, but for all those who care about science. In a time when so many physicists are talking about God, and when quasi-religious arguments are increasingly being brought to bear. . . , there is a pressing need for some clarity about the relationship between physics and religion.

Foreword, *Pythagoras' Trousers: God, Physics, and the Gender Wars 1997*

2 Around 600 B.C., the idea was born that natural phenomena were effected not by gods, but by processes inherent in nature itself—processes that could be comprehended, and predicted. A mechanistic mode of thinking began to cut through the rich layers of myth as people turned to nature itself to ask: What are you?

Ibid., Ch. 1

3 When significant numbers of women participate in science they alter the intellectual climate so that some practitioners of *both* sexes are enabled to see in new ways.

Ibid., Ch. 10

4 All gradients of reality, all existential distinctions, have finally been annihilated.

The Pearly Gates of Cyberspace 1999

4475. Lynda Williams (1958?–   )

1 Some boys kiss me, some boys hug me
  I think they're passe
  if they can't talk about quantum theory
  I just walk away.

"Hi-Tek Girl," St. 1 (sung to tune of "Material Girl"),
scientainment.com *1998*

2 We are living in a high-tech world
  and I am a high-tech girl.

Chorus, Ibid.

3 But I've discovered a new force
  that rules from high above.
  Let me propose to you
  a Unified Theory of Love!

"Love Boson," St. 1 Ibid.

4 The Cosmic soup expanded and cooled
  the particle zoo was born in the goo
  photons, bosons, gluons, gravitons
  Energy radiation-Watch Out!
  Inflation

"Big Bang," St. 2, Ibid. *1999*

5 Some like quantum gravity, pulling super strings from the cosmic soup.
  But I'm pointing my laser, at an earthly crystalline.
  I'm in a Solid State of Mind.

"Solid State of Mind," st. 1 (sung to tune of "New York State
of Mind," Ibid.

4476. Jennifer Ackerman (1959–   )

1 Our ears are made not for the stinging scream of sirens but for the sly scratch of a predator's paws and the whistle of wind that warns of impending weather. Our eyes evolved to tease apart not the monotonous grays of cityscapes but the subtle gold, olive, and burgundy hues that signaled ripe fruit and tender leaves, and our brains to reward our sensory efforts with feelings of deep pleasure.

"Paris: Space for the Soul," *National Geographic October
2006*

2 The benefit of laughter to blood vessel health is nearly equal to that of aerobic activity.

Sex Sleep Eat Drink Dream 2007

4477. Kim Suzanne Bridgford (1959–   )

1 I was forty-one years old and had just had a miscarriage; Mark was forty-five. We had waited eleven years to have a baby, but now I couldn't remember exactly what we had been waiting for.

"Seeing Angels," *Calyx*, vol. 17, no. 3 *1998*

2 Like a sword swallowed, I ate pain for a living; I coughed pain; I slept pain.
    Anything to fill the hole there.

Ibid.

3 "Children are there to listen to what you have to say."

Ibid.

4478. Cynthia Carr (1959?–   )

1 Finley* represents a frightening and rare presence—an unsocialized woman.

*On Edge: Performance at the End of the Twentieth Century
1994*

*Karen Finley; see 4363.

2 Bohemia was always part of the exile tradition, the place where the lost ones went to find each other. But it was exile from one tangible place to another. Now that there is no place, the exiles have become nomads, and there's a whole culture of the disappeared.

Ibid.

3 As a media creature since childhood, [Michael Jackson]* thinks he's all image. He has, in fact, abandoned his body, in order to inhabit its simulacrum. I think of him as a sort of radical "body artist." He doesn't want to be black, yet I don't think he wants to be white.
    And I don't think he wants to have a gender . . .

(p. 244), Ibid.

*American singer and composer (1958–2009).

4 The fact was, I was afraid and disturbed about the ways in which I might be "one of them" [a Klan member]. I wasn't just there as a journalist, after all, but as someone with a certain inheritance to confront. A grandfather I loved in the Klan. A town I loved responsible for the lynching. It didn't matter that my grandfather was so different from the wizard. That I was, too. I would be "one of them" unless I worked on it. I couldn't just anoint myself their opposite—the "good white person."

*Our Town: A Heartland Lynching, a Haunted Town, and The
Hidden History of White America 2006*

4479. Anne-Christine d'Adesky (1959–   )

1 "Why do these people from the outside only care what's happening to us after someone dies or is murdered?"

Under the Bone 1994

2 I who am left here as witness, passive eye in the center of a terrible storm.

Ibid.

4480. Tsitsi Dangarembga (1959–   )

1 Words like "always" and "never" were meaningless to my father, who thought in absolutes and whose mind consequently made great leaps in antagonistic directions when it leapt at all.

Ch. 2, *Nervous Conditions 1988*

2 "Money is a difficult thing to keep, especially when it is scarce."

Ibid.

3 The victimization, I saw, was universal. It didn't depend on poverty, on lack of education or on tradition. It didn't depend on any of the things I had thought it depended on. Men took it everywhere with them. Even heroes like Babamukuru did it. And that was the problem. . . . Femaleness as opposed and inferior to maleness.

Ch. 6, Ibid.

4481. Susan Faludi (1959–   )

1 It has not been unusual that during periods when women have made great social strides they have been ignored or vilified.

*Backlash: The Undeclared War Against American Women
1991*

2 What has made women unhappy in the last decade is not their "equality"—which they don't yet have—but the rising pressure to halt, and even reverse, women's quest for that equality.

Ch. 1, Ibid.

3 The backlash against women's rights would be just one of several powerful forces creating a harsh and painful climate for women at work. Reaganomics,* the recession, and the expansion of a minimum-wage service economy also helped, in no small measure, to slow and even undermine women's momentum in the job market.

But the backlash did more than impede women's opportunities for employment, promotions, and better pay. Its spokesmen kept the news of many of these setbacks from women. Not only did the backlash do grievous damage to working women—it did it on the sly.

Ch. 13, Ibid.

*Ronald Reagan (1911–2004), 40th president of the United States (1981–89), actor.

4 Because women's hour on the stage is long, long overdue. Because, whatever new obstacles are mounted against the future march toward equality, whatever new myths invented, penalties levied, opportunities rescinded, or degradations imposed, no one can ever take from the American woman the justness of her cause.

Epilogue, Ibid.

5 Their nation had come into his own, powerful, wealthy, dominant, in control of the greatest destructive force ever imagined. The fathers had made their sons masters of the universe and it felt, as in the time of Alexander, that what they had created would last forever.

Ch. 2, *Stiffed: The Betrayal of the American Man* 1999

6 Forgiveness was Jesus' overriding message. But whether Jesus was instructing men to forgive their earthly fathers or flout them is less clear. His statements on the subject do not exactly add up to a ringing endorsement of filial piety. He expected his disciples to abandon their fathers without hesitation, even when they were desperately needed apprentices in their fathers' trades.

Ch. 5, Ibid.

7 No matter what reasons brought men to the barricades, a man refusing to go to war could in no case avoid a societal verdict on his masculinity. Those adolescents could either go to war or stay home; but either way, the would be enlisted in a battle for male identity, a battle that would in the end be fought largely on the fathers' terms.

Ch. 6, Ibid.

4482. Maria Elena Foronda Farro (1959–)

1 I reviewed the environmental laws of my country—many people don't even know about them, much less exercise them. Discovering these laws, and putting them at the service of the people, was really inspiring. The people became leaders, and started to care about their struggle and their future.

Quoted in "How Do You Solve a Problem Like Maria?" by Michelle Nijhuis, grist.org *18 April 2003*

2 You only need a tiny spark of social consciousness to become an activist.

Ibid.

3 Environmental protection is recognized as a basic human right. But the most important thing is that the people believe in what

they do. And, this work has given our people back their dignity and self esteem.

Quoted in "Environmental Heroes: Peru's Maria Elena Foronda" by Rosanne Skirble, *Voice of America News 9 June 2003*

4483. Sarah "Fergie" Ferguson (1959–)

1 They [British royalty] took them [Secret Service Agents] away after I got separated. My daughters still have them. It gets difficult when I'm with them, because they work for my daughters, not me. Sometimes they forget who's the mother.

Quoted in Intelligence Report by Jane Ciabattari, *Parade Magazine 3 May 1997*

4484. Leslie Forbes (1959?–)

1 My sister was simply one language I no longer spoke, another country I'd lost.

Bombay Ice 1998

2 "Facts are like butterflies, madam. Most difficult to catch, and often lacking in beauty when finally pinned down."

Ibid.

3 . . . the precision of all men whose souls do not exceed the limits of their uniforms.

Ibid.

4485. Lisa Fugard (1959?–)

1 In the past she'd have handled them with a certain confidence, an ongoing rapid discernment—trust this one, have nothing to do with that character—her white skin at least giving her the illusion of security. Now she felt uncertain of herself.

Skinner's Drift 2006

2 "It's a cruel country. . . . My sometimes cruel husband loves this miserable, rotten, and yes, beautiful country."

Ibid.

3 Murdering a carpet was a deeply satisfying chore.

Ibid.

4 The monkeys are truly desperate. This morning I saw them sucking the corners of the wet sheets that Grace had hung on the washing line.

Ibid.

4486. Jennifer M. Granholm (1959–)

1 Often those who cloak themselves in a cape of religiosity happen to be some who are the biggest [budget] cutters. Now, some of that can balance out. But when you get to cutting the services for the least of these—in the 25th chapter of Matthew in the 37th verse the Lord says, "Whatsoever you do to the least of these, so also you do unto me"—that's when I question whether somebody is really living out the faith that they profess.

"On cut, Granholm cites Bible, draws wrath," *Detroit Free Press 29 January 2002*

2 No other state is the automotive capital of the world.

Quoted in "In the Race for Governor of Michigan, the Struggling Economy Is Topic A" by Monica Davey, *The New York Times 9 October 2006*

3   [President Bush]* has sat idly by while the [automobile] industry reels.

Ibid.

*George W. B- (1946–   ), Am. politician; 43rd president of the
United States (2001–09).

4487. Florence Griffith Joyner (1959–1998)

1   I don't think a person has to use drugs [to excel in athletics].
There is no substitute for hard work.

Quoted in "For Speed and Style, Flo with the Go" by Ellie
McGrath, *Time* (New York) *19 September 1988*

4488. Emmy Hafild (1959–   )

1   Natural resources are all we have now [in Indonesia]. Palm oil
is big. There will be big new plantations. I am very pessimistic,
but we have to do something. We have to stop the destruction.

Quoted in "Crusader for Indonesia's Enchanted Forests" by
David Liebhold, *Time* (New York) *11 January 1999*

2   Some of the best known brands in the world are literally cooking the climate.

"Greenpeace urges Indonesia to stop burning forest," Yahoo
News *8 November 2007*

4489. Christina Herrström (1959–   )

1   Seduce the audience. Seduce them and make them think as
well.

Correspondence with the author *1994*

2   . . . something very like love and care can be a way to keep sons
and daughters and growing forces of curiosity and liveliness in
control.

Ibid.

4490. Sharon Kleinbaum (1959–   )

1   We want a Jewish community where people participate, one
that truly welcomes all people, and different people, in our
midst. The Torah tells us over and over . . . About the stranger
in Egypt. . . . For us, exile is not a literary metaphor or a convenient refrain. It has genuine meaning every day in our lives.

Quoted in "'Luckiest Rabbi in America' Holds Faith Amid the
Hate" by Alex Witchel, *The New York Times 5 May 1993*

2   We have an obligation to do this, offering a place where homosexuals and their families can worship. Critics say that
homosexuality destroys the family, but we reconstruct families
that have been shattered.

Quoted on p. 305, *The Journey Home, How Jewish Women
Shaped Modern America* by Joyce Antler* *1997*

*See 3320.

3   Hatred and violence against anyone is an evil that we as a
moral and religious people must work our whole lives to eradicate.

Quoted on religionandpluralism.org *2007*

4491. Anne Landsman (1959–   )

1   People aren't nice, they look at you askew and their breath
singes you.

The Devil's Chimney 1997

2   Death is fierce after all.

The Rowing Lesson 2007

3   I'm in the sea up to my waist and I'm waving like mad but of
course you can't see me. I'm smaller than a pin, a memory of
yesterday, a part of your life that isn't now, that isn't in the sun
on a beach . . .

Ch. 1, Ibid.

4492. Maya Lin (1959–   )

1   You really can't function as a celebrity. Entertainers are celebrities. I'm an architect. I'm an artist. I make things.

Quoted in "First She Looks Inwards" by Jonathan Coleman,
Time (New York) *6 November 1989*

2   Architecture is like a mythical fantastic. It *has* to be experienced. It can't be described. We can draw it up and we can
make models of it, but it can only be experienced as a complete
whole.

Ibid.

3   If you don't remember history accurately, how can you learn?

Ibid.

4493. Laura Lippman (1959–   )

1   Oh well, anyone who had a job had to brownnose now and
then. She did it, too, and hated herself in the morning—until
she made her bank deposit.

Ch. 1, *The Sugar House 2000*

2   "I was married once," he liked to say, in a tone suggesting it
was a childhood communicable disease, like measles or chicken
pox. Once you had it, you had it.

Ch. 4, Ibid.

3   Besides, she had fallen a little in love with her Smith & Wes-
son. It felt good in her hand and it was much more reliable
than other tools of her trade—the cell phone, the computer, her
instincts.

Ch. 6, Ibid.

4   But this was a world where numbers mattered more than
anything, a place of ceaseless top 10 lists, top 100 lists, the
Forbes 500 and the *Fortune* whatever. Homeless men knew
how high the Dow closed yesterday, and everyone wanted
to be number one. All Tess had wanted was to weigh 120
pounds.

Ch. 8, Ibid.

4494. Lydia Lunch (1959–   )

1   Women are denied masturbation even more severely than men
and that's another method of control—they're not taught to
please themselves. . . . Most women—it takes them a while
to warm up to the "situation," but once they get into it, I'm
sure they're going to get just as hooked as—well, everyone I
know is!

Interview in *Re/Search*, No. 13, *Angry Women* (San Francisco)
1991

4495. Rigoberta Menchú (1959/60–   )

1   Perhaps for the first time, the world is looking at our land.
They now know its name.

Speech* (San Marcos, Guatemala), Cited in "Guatemalan wins
Peace Prize," *Seattle Post-Intelligencer*, A1 *17 October 1992*

*Made before her townspeople, upon hearing she'd won the Nobel
Peace Prize.

2 I consider this prize not as an award to me personally, but rather as one of the greatest conquests in the struggle for peace, for human rights and for the rights of the indigenous people who, along all the 500 years* have been . . . the victims of genocides, repression and discrimination.

Acceptance speech, Nobel Peace Prize (Oslo) *10 December 1992*

*The award coincided with the 500th anniversary of Christopher Columbus's arrival in the West Indies.

3 The indigenous community absorbs differences, be they sexual, mental, or physical.

"The Quincentenary and the Earth Summit," *Crossing Borders: An Autobiography,* Ann Wright, ed. and tr. *1998*

4 Culture isn't pure, it is dynamic, it is a kind of dialectic, it is something that progresses and evolves. As for purity, who can determine what that means?

Ibid.

5 Our experience, as indigenous peoples, is that religion was used as a powerful shotgun, a powerful machine gun, a powerful arrow, to try to dismantle our cultures. . . . I want to distinguish, however, between religion as a doctrine and as the beliefs of a people.

Ibid.

6 All refugees know the immense solitude you feel. . . . Not physical . . . but spiritual and cultural solitude. . . . When I was in exile, I felt I was a nomad because I could never put down roots.

"Coming Home to Guatemala, 1988 and 1994," Ibid.

4496. Connie Mofokeng (1959–)

1 I didn't think I'd come out alive; in fact, I was seeing death. But I was prepared to die as long as I died for the truth, and I knew that people would know that this was the case.*

(1987), quoted in Ch. 2, *Lives of Courage* by Diana E. H. Russell** *1989*

*Re the torture she experienced as a political prisoner. **See 3104.

4497. Rona Munro (1959–)

1 FIIONA. I don't know what I'm going to end up looking like. I feel like I'm not born yet.

Piper's Cave 1985

2 What happens if women no longer define their sexuality in response to male sexuality? What happens if we acknowledge our own potential for physical strength, for violence, for aggression? What do we do then?

Introductory note, *Plays by Women,* Vol. 8, Mary Remnant, ed. *1990*

3 I used to resist . . . [the] expectation that I would be concerned with "women's issues" . . . messy, sticky, biological things, babies and blood and gingerbread with no relevance, interest, or importance in the "real world." But then I came to think that sticky, biological things actually define what we are and that attempts to evade that realization lead us down the blind alleys where a large part of our culture has taken us.

Correspondence with Elaine Bernstein Partnow* *1995*

*See 3291.

4498. Jody Newman (1959?–)

1 When women run for office, they win as often as men do.

"Women Candidates Can Win . . . When They Run," *Perception and Reality (NWPC) 1994*

2 The gender gap does not and cannot ever elect anyone: It is simply the difference between the way women and men vote.

Quoted in "Gender gap not deep enough to trip a fall" by Lisa Leiter, Bnet.com *30 September 1996*

4499. Shannon O'Brien (1959–)

1 I don't think anyone should be terrified by what I perceive as a blip.* Women need to take some pride in the fact that so many women take on these challenges, and a number of women did win. And we go on from there.

"Fewer women in legislatures, other offices," *USA Today 30 January 2003*

*Re: her loss to Mitt Romney (1947– ; businessman, politician) in the Massachusetts governors race.

4500. Ann Packer (1959–)

1 How much do we owe the people we love?

The Dive From Clausen's Pier 2002

2 "But it's not very helpful to regard your choices as a series of right or wrong moves."

Ibid.

3 There was this sisterhood out there, a sisterhood of eye rolling and head shaking and sighing over the helplessness of husbands.

Ch. 1, *Songs Without Words 2007*

4501. Laurence Parisot (1959–)

1 Life, health and even love are precarious. So, why shouldn't work abide by this [natural] law?

Quoted in *Le Figaro 30 August 2005*

2 Precariousness is part of human condition.

Quoted in *France Inter 3 September 2005*

3 We don't have a great economic culture in France. We have a culture of politics and of sociology, but not of economics. We don't have an entrepreneurial culture at all. My priority is to change that cycle.

"How I Got There," *Newsweek 14 November 2005*

4502. Dana Priest (1959–)

1 The Defense Department's new leadership treated the Joint Staff like shop stewards in a unionized corporation. Rumsfeld* treated Shelton** and the senior military leadership as major impediments to his plans for a twenty-first-century "transformation" of the military.

Ch. 1, *The Mission: Waging War and Keeping Peace with America's Military 2004*

*Donald H. R— (1932–), businessman, politician; 13th and 21st U.S. Secretary of Defense. **Henry H. S— (1942–), chairman of the Joints Chiefs of Staff (1997–2001).

2 Civilians had suffered much more than combatants had in this cauldron of military and paramilitary violence, of guerrilla and drug-dealer choas.

Ch. 9, Ibid.

4503. Yasmina Reza (1959–)

1   "I'd like you to explain the word *happy*."

Desolation 2002

2   You can understand nothing about my life because you, Marie-Thérèse, were damned from the start. You accepted this damnation and you live with it. You've blended into the mass, you've ironed out all the discords between the world and yourself, and made your nest there, you say bottom line, you talk about the image of a washing machine, you say I have positively bloomed, a woman who talks about my business with that fervor is forever alien to me.

Adam Haberberg 2006

4504. Desiree Rogers (1959?–)

1   This is not just going to be about the culture and the arts. Part of this is reaching out to all Americans.

Quoted in "Desiree Rogers to be party planner for White House social events" by John McCormick, *Chicago Tribune* 25 November 2008

4505. Mona Sandoval Ruiz (1959–)

1   Death seemed to be everywhere and, sadly, a lot of the homeboys didn't seem to care. I didn't know if they thought it made them seem heroic or if the future was such a dim prospect they resigned themselves. Many talked as if they expected to die by twenty-one.

Two Badges: The Lives of Mona Ruiz 1997

2   The abusive marriage is the ebb and flow of the hatred it breeds. In some ways, the bad times, the worse valleys, make the good times and reconciliations seem stronger, more meaningful.

Ibid.

4506. Heffa Schücking (1959–)

1   We are witnessing a war. Although this war has not been declared, it is nonetheless global. It is a war against nature and those societies that still live close to nature.

Quoted on goldmanprize.org 1994

2   The only area, where the corporation feels bound to demonstrate an environmental conscience, seems to be the public relations area.

"NHPC:* People Don't Matter," urgewald.de *April 2008*
*National Hydroelectric Power Corporation.

3   As a perennial river, Narmada was once known for its predictable nature even in the monsoon. For centuries, it has been the centre of life, economy and culture for the communities along its banks.... Now ... the regime of water flow has been drastically altered.

Ibid.

4   Dams can kill.*

Ibid.
*On April 7, 2005, unannounced water releases of the Indira Sagar dam took place where more than 50,000 people were assembled for a religious festival; more than 200 were killed.

5   If there were an international competition for the title of "Most Ruthless Corporation," India's entry should undoubtedly be the National Hydroelectric Power Corporation [of India].

Ibid.

4507. Martha Sherrill (1959–)

1   The Buddha's mind is just a monolith, really—an obelisk with a pagoda roof and a spire. At the highest point, there was a crystal ball pointing to the sky.

The Buddha from Brooklyn 2001

2   And when he'd smiled, it was a burst of fireworks—as if he had searched the world over and finally found a girl he liked most of all.

The Ruins of California 2006

3   There are mountain villages and green valleys throughout Japan, and very few people live in them. The cities teem and buzz with life. But far away, the snow country world moves quietly, almost forgotten except as a dream.

Dog Man: An Uncommon Life on a Faraway Mountain 2008

4   There was a reason it was called the snow country. There weren't just mounds of snow or piles of snow.... There were avalanches, fortresses, ramparts, steep towering walls of snow. In the village, the drifts were so high that children jumped out of second-story windows into them and slid down to the street.

Ibid.

4508. Jill Bolte Taylor (1959–)

1   Find the key to unlock this thing we call insanity
Just dial 1-800-BRAIN-BANK for information, please.

"1-800-BRAIN-BANK" jingle, *My Stroke of Insight: A Brain Scientist's Personal Journey* 2006

2   Wow, what a strange and amazing thing I am. What a bizarre living being I am. Life! I am life! I am a sea of water bound inside this membranous pouch. Here, in this form, I am a conscious mind and this body is the vehicle through which I am ALIVE! I am trillions of cells sharing a common mind. I am here, now, thriving as life. Wow! What an unfathomable concept! I am cellular life, no—I am molecular life with manual dexterity and a cognitive mind!

Ch. 4, "Morning of the Stroke," Ibid.

3   I realized that the blessing I had received from this experience was the knowledge that deep internal peace is accessible to anyone at any time ... My stroke of insight would be: Peace is only a thought away, and all we have to do to access it is to silence the voice of our dominating left mind.

Ch. 15, "My Stroke of Insight," Ibid.

4   The effort it took for me to pay attention to what someone was saying was like the effort it takes to pay attention to someone who is speaking on a cell phone with a bad connection. You have to work so hard to hear what the person is saying that you may become impatient, frustrated, and hang up the phone.

Ibid.

4509. Suzanne Vega (1959–)

1   Today I am
a small blue thing
Like a marble
or an eye

"Small Blue Thing," *Suzanne Vega* (album) 1985

2   Solitude stands by the window
She turns her head as I walk in the room

I can see by her eyes she's been waiting
Standing in the slant of the late afternoon
"Solitude Standing" *1987*

3   I believe right now if I could
I would swallow you whole
I would leave only bones and teeth
We could see what was underneath
And we could be free then.
"The Undertow" *n.d.*

4510. Jeanette Winterson (1959–   )

1   We gamble with the hope of winning. But it's the thought of what we might lose that excites us.
The Passion 1987

2   However it is debased or misinterpreted, love is a redemptive feature. To focus on one individual so that their desires become superior to yours is a very cleansing experience.
Times (London) *26 August 1992*

3   I have no father. There's nothing unusual about that—even children who do have fathers are often surprised to see them.
Lighthousekeeping 2004

4   . . . wherever found, Civilized or Savage, [man] cannot keep to any purpose for much length of time, except the purpose of destroying himself.
The Stone Gods 2008

5   Far out, too far to see with the human eye or to hear with the human ear, is everything we have lost. . . . Sometimes, in our dreams, we see the boxed-up miseries and fears, orbiting two miles up, outside our little world.
Ibid.

6   The great thing about robots, even these Robo sapiens, is that nobody feels sorry for them. They are only machines.
Ch. 1, *Ibid.*

7   This is a great day for science. The last hundred years have been hell. The doomsters and the environmentalists kept telling us we were as good as dead and, hey presto, not only do we find a new planet, but it is perfect for new life. This time, we'll be more careful. This time we will learn from our mistakes. The new planet will be home to the universe's first advanced civilization. It will be a democracy—because whatever we say in public, the Eastern Caliphate isn't going to be allowed within a yatto-mile of the place. We'll shoot 'em down before they land.
Ibid.

8   He's the kind of man who was born to rise and rise: a human elevator.
Ibid.

4511. Meg Wolitzer (1959–   )

1   Feminism had recently landed in Canada; apparently the longing and ability to write historical fiction had always been inside Antonia, but it had taken a political upheaval to disgorge it.
The Ten-Year Nap 2008

2   . . . fragility always increases the price of a thing of beauty.
Ibid.

3   The rent battered and shook them; it sucked the money away from them each month as if it were stored in the wind tunnel of the lobby.
Ibid.

4512. Eimi Yamada (1959–   )

1   Confidence and disillusionment are always warring inside me when it comes to my talent. When people applaud my finished work, I find myself a likeable person; when I paint in solitude, however, I often suffer from anxiety attacks and have to just sit on the floor, waiting for help. What help? Help from a God who would make me paint, I suppose. I don't think about God most of the time, but when I feel such helplessness, I want to put myself in the hands of something absolute. It is at such moments that I sincerely wish I were not an artist.
"When A Man Loves A Woman," *Unmapped Territories, New Women's Fiction from Japan*, ed. and tr. *1991*

2   "Having sex doesn't mean love. You can sleep with a woman just for fun, or to make money. You shouldn't worry about our having had sex once, but you should be concerned about the fact that we're in bed without making love."
Ibid.

4513. Cynthia Rebecca Zarin (1959–   )

1   Skating backwards tells another story—
the risky star above the freezing town,
a way to walk on water and not drown.
"Skating in Harlem, Christmas Day," St. 5, *The Watercourse 2002*

2   When at night you woke
I sang to you, light in my arms
and your cheek wet, and the shore
we rowed toward was sleep.
"Michael's Boat," St. 1, *Ibid.*

4514. Ishrat Aafreen (1960?–   )

1   Such barren tales, such bitter talk/
Such beautiful, tender, red, and luscious lips

If you talk so much, what will people think?
The custom here is this: Girl, sew up your
lips.
"Ghazal," *We Sinful Women, Contemporary Urdu Feminist Poetry*, Rukhsana Ahmed, ed. and tr. *1990*

2   Scattering into shattered mirrors, broken bits
Gathering into the face of a flower, this girl.

The masters of the haveli* wanted simply this
She stay within the house, this household's girl.
"Shattered Mirrors, Broken Bits," sts. 4–8, *Ibid.*
*Hindi word for private mansions.

4515. Edith Anderson (fl. ca. 1960–90)

1   If a woman has learned before the last day of her life to cast off alien definitions and define herself, it is not too late.
Love in Exile, An American Writer's Memoir . . . 1999

2   Our world was cleft by unjust, unseen powers whose doings . . . we were too ignorant and hopeful to imagine.
Ibid.

3 What right have you to deprive her of the Socialism for which so many people died or went into exile? It may be imperfect but something can be made of it.

Ibid.

4516. Geneviève Antoine-Dariaux (fl. 1960s–d. 1973)

1 [Habit]
  is the chloroform of love.
  is the cement that unites married couples.
  is getting stuck in the mud of daily routine.
  is the fog that masks the most beautiful scenery.
  is the end of everything.

The Men in Your Life 1968

2 The stranger loses his charm the day he is no longer a stranger.

Ibid.

3 I have had sufficient beaux to feel no regret, but not so many as to feel remorse . . .

Ibid.

4 She began to think about her friends' happy tranquility, of their affection, of their two non-problem children: the boy wasn't on drugs; the girl wasn't a nymphomaniac; they weren't even quarrelsome. The kind of children nobody had any more.

Ch. 1, *The Fall Collection* 1973

5 Elegance has become so rare today that a well-cut black jersey cape makes heads turn. It isn't chic to be chic anymore!

Ch. 3, Ibid.

4517. Karen Baker-Fletcher (1960?–)

1 Our task is to grow large hearts, large minds, reconnecting with earth, Spirit, and one another. Black religion must grow ever deeper in the heart.

Sisters of Dust, Sisters of Spirit: Womanist Wordings on God and Creation 1998

2 . . . those who lament evil and suffering are not irrational. They are imbued with reason. This reason is integrated with *feeling*, which is the experience of reality. Such is the intelligence of the spirituals, the blues, jazz, and hip hop. Filled with the pathos of an infant's cry at times, it quickly moves beyond pure sound to articulate meaning in the midst of suffering and joy through its tonality, rhythms, and sometimes lyrics. Certain experiences of evil and of goodness reduce humanity to naught but a cry of lament or joy.

Ch. 1, *Dancing with God: The Trinity from a Womanist Perspective* 2007

4518. Melissa Bank (1960–)

1 My mother told the same stories over and over—maybe twenty-five in all; if you added them up, there were only about two hours of her life that she wanted me to know about.

The Wonder Spot 2005

2 "As soon as I'm in a relationship, I promote fear from clerk to president, even though all it can do is sweep up, turn off the lights and lock the door."

Ibid.

4519. Alison Bechdel (1960–)

1 My father . . . could conjure an entire, finished period interior from a paint chip. He was an alchemist of appearance, a savant of surface, a Daedalus* of décor.

Ch. 1, *Fun Home: A Family Tragicomic* 2006
*In Greek mythology, a craftsman and inventor.

2 We ate together, but otherwise were absorbed in our separate pursuits.

Ibid.

3 In the hot August afternoon, the city was reduced, like a long-simmering demiglace, to a fragrance of stunning richness and complexity.

Ch. 4, Ibid.

4520. Christine Billson (fl. ca. 1960)

1 I am admired because I do things well. I cook, sew, knit, talk, work, and make love very well. So I am a valuable item. Without me he would suffer. With him I am alone. I am as solitary as eternity and sometimes as stupid as clotted cream. Ha ha ha! Don't think! Act as if all the bills are paid.

You Can Touch Me 1961

4521. Linda J. Bilmes (1960–)

1 While companies pay lip service to the importance of their people, in reality they invest in almost anything else—sales, marketing, brands, customers, distribution, IT, finance—to enhance performance. Yet the most obvious, and overlooked, source of strategic advantage is to use people better.

The People Factor 2002

2 The people factor is a simple concept: investing in human creativity delivers high returns in terms of job satisfaction and shareholder returns.

Ibid.

3 The actual costs of disasters have a way of creeping well beyond initial estimates.

"Disasters and the Deficit," *The Atlantic Monthly* (Boston) December 2005

4 It is difficult to imagine a trillion dollars. People have difficulty with the scale of it. I explain to my students that one billion seconds = 32 years; one trillion seconds = 300 centuries. We spend $10 billion a month in Iraq—which is the same amount as the total annual United Nations budget (of which the US pays only about one-fifth). We spend about $5 billion per year on cancer research.

"Total economic cost of the war in Iraq," *Nieman Watchdog* (neimanwatchdog.org) 21 September 2006

5 The VA [Veterans Affairs] is also in a disadvantageous position compared with the Pentagon—the Pentagon budget is in its own orbit, but the VA has to compete for scarce discretionary funds.

Ibid.

4522. Erin Brockovich (1960–)

1 "Ralph Nader* with cleavage," they called me. I don't want to picture that.

"Erin Brockovich, The Brand" by Austin Bunn, *The New York Times* 28 April 2002
*(1934–), American attorney, author, consumer advocate, politician.

2 Don't be intimidated by authority. When it comes to your children and it comes to the safety of your family and you have a question and you're not getting an answer, demand it and keep after it until you get an answer.

Quoted in *Planet Savers: 301 Extraordinary Environmentalists: 1991–1997* by Kevin Desmond 2008

4523. Lisa Brown (1960–)

1 Conservatives have captured the intellectual initiative in popular and even much elite discourse. Their success in framing and communicating fundamental conservative principles has contributed to real legal and political change over the last two decades. Will we allow narrow and sterile conservative interpretations of our Constitution's vital principles and protections to reshape our national character and control our daily lives? Our answer, on this weekend and on every day of the coming years, is a resounding No.

"Constitution 2020" Conference (Yale Law School) 5 April 2005

4524. Julie Burchill (1960–)

1 A woman who looks like a girl and thinks like a man is the best sort, the most enjoyable to be and the most pleasurable to have and to hold.

"Born Again Cows," Damaged Gods: cults & heroes reappraised 1986

2 The freedom that women were supposed to have found in the Sixties largely boiled down to easy contraception and abortion; things to make life easier for men, in fact.

Ibid.

3 What Mrs. Thatcher* did for women was to demonstrate that if a woman had enough desire she could do what she wanted, do anything a man could do. . . . Mrs. Thatcher did not have one traditional feminine cell in her body.

Ibid.

*See 2537.

4 A good part—and definitely the most fun part—of being a feminist is about frightening men.

Quoted in Time Out (London) 16 November 1989

5 It has been said that a pretty face is a passport. But it's not, it's a visa, and it runs out fast.

"Kiss and Sell," Mail on Sunday (London, 1988), Sex and Sensibility 1992

4525. Sampat Pal Devi (1960–)

1 Nobody comes to our help in these parts. The officials and the police are corrupt and anti-poor. So sometimes we have to take the law in our hands. At other times, we prefer to shame the wrongdoers.

Quoted in "India's 'pink' vigilante women" by Soutik Biswas, BBC News 26 November 2007

2 We are not a gang in the usual sense of the term. We are a gang for justice.

Ibid.

3 Village society in India is loaded against women. It refuses to educate them, marries them off too early, barters them for money. Village women need to study and become independent to sort it out themselves.

Ibid.

4526. Jane Eaglen (1960–)

1 To be honest, making the voice seamless throughout its entire range takes a lot of physical strength. Not stamina, but sheer physical strength. The strength to use your muscles, and the diaphragm and the rest of the body in the right way—never the throat. There must never be an inkling of tension in the throat. I very much use all my body to sing. I use my legs, bottom, everything.

Quoted in Diva, The New Generation: The Sopranos and Mezzos of the Decade Discuss Their Roles by Helena Matheopoulous 1998*

*See 3675.

4527. Anita Perez Ferguson (1960?–)

1 The gender gap is often miscommunicated as the difference that women feel between one candidate and another. In actuality, it is a measure of the margin between the favorable votes of women for a candidate and the favorable votes of men for the same candidate.

Quoted in "Gender gap not deep enough to trip a fall" by Lisa Leiter, Bnet.com 30 September 1996

2 All widows are not created equal. Some widows make good candidates and good legislators. Others have not thought of themselves that way, haven't prepared for it, and probably will not do a good job for their constituents.

Quoted in "Widows of Bono, Capps Are on Well-Worn Path to Office" by Jodi Wilgoren, Los Angeles Times 26 January 1998

3 What we are really here to talk about is not the abstract concept of "diversity" as it relates to affirmative action programs or fears about quotas, but rather to changes in our population and workforce brought about by families in transition—families like those represented by me and you.

Women Seen and Heard: Lessons Learned from Successful Speakers, coauthor Lois Phillips 2003*

*See 3222.

4 You don't need to be an heiress, a CEO, or an elected official to have power and authority. You can leverage the personal power you have and move groups and audiences to action by being articulate and eloquent.

Ch. 1, Ibid.

5 Men don't have an edge on reason. Judging from the way in which male leaders have historically rationalized political actions that were impulsive, expedient, self-serving, and often violent, some would argue that women are more reasonable than men.

p. 123, Ibid.

4527.1. Tina Fey (1960–)

1 Improv helped to distract me from my usual stage bullshit and put my focus somewhere else so that I could stop acting. I guess that's what method acting is supposed to accomplish anyway. It distracts you so that your body and emotions can work freely. Improv is just a version of method acting that works for me.

Interview by Eric Spitznagel, The Believer November 2003

2 Despite the fact that Martha Stewart* has disgraced herself too much to hold an official position at Omnimedia, the company may still use her name and images to sell their products. You know, sort of like Clinton and the Democrats.

Episode 15, Saturday Night Live, Season 29 2003–04

*See 3307.

3 This week, penny collector Gene Sukie went to the bank and cashed in 10,000 pounds of pennies he had collected over 34

years, which were worth over 14,000 dollars. And, of course, I was in line behind him.

> Episode 6, Ibid. *2004–05*

4528. Cecilia Flores-Oebanda (1960–)

1 Life wasn't easy in the movement. But I did not see weariness in my comrades nor did I hear complaints. They were still happy, we were all happy. At the end of the day, you would sit down together. You talk, you laugh, you dream. Maybe that's the very important thing—not only dreaming, but willing to give yourself to your country.

> Article, *The Investigative Reporting Quarterly Jan–Feb 2006*

2 I helped sell fish and I was also a scavenger along with my siblings. Until now when I talk of hardship, I can still feel the warm drippings down my face from the basket of fish that I carried on my head. I can still smell the stench of the garbage that clung to my clothes and my skin. That's my history, that gives me all the reflection that no matter how hard you work, if you come from a very poor family, you have a very slim chance of getting out of that situation.

> Ibid.

3 During my days in the mountains, I carried a gun wherever I went—now I am armed with genuine commitment and undaunted bravery to fight for what I believe.

> "Surviving the Pains, Reaping the Gains," *World Pulse Magazine* (worldpulsemagazine.com) *14 May 2008*

4 In the Philippines, human trafficking is not a simple problem of illegal recruitment—traffickers operate in a very intricate underground network and often have strong connections with corrupt public officials and transport operators. Motivated by easy profits and the demand for laborers, traffickers exploit the vulnerable.

> Ibid.

4529. Greta Gaard (1960–)

1 Ecofeminism calls for an end to all oppressions, arguing that no attempt to liberate women (or any other oppressed group) will be successful without an equal attempt to liberate nature.

> "Living Interconnections with Animals and Nature" (p. 1), *Ecofeminism: Women, Animals, Nature,* ed. *1993*

2 . . . ecofeminism rests on the notion that the liberation of all oppressed groups must be addressed simultaneously.

> Ibid.

4530. Kaye Gibbons (1960–)

1 [She was] the first woman anybody knew with the courage not only to possess a toilet but to use it.

> *Charms for the Easy Life 1993*

2 "I still hold that it [the Civil War] was a conflict perpetrated by rich men and fought by poor boys against hungry women and babies."

> *On the Occasion of My Last Afternoon 1998*

4531. Nancy Gibbs (1960–)

1 Over the past 30 years, all that was orthodox has become negotiable.

> "The Dreams of Youth," *Time Special Issue* (New York) *Fall 1990*

2 If there is a theme among those coming of age today . . . it is that gender differences are often better celebrated than suppressed. Young women do not want to slip unnoticed into a man's world; they want that world to change and benefit from what women bring to it.

> Ibid.

3 Today's young adults dismiss old gender stereotypes and limitations. They expect equal opportunities but want more than mere equality. It is their dream that they will be the ones to strike a healthy balance at last between their public and private lives: between the lure of fame and glory, and a love of home and hearth.

> Ibid.

4532. Annette Gordon-Reed (1960?–)

1 There is, apparently, nothing like a story involving race, sex and interracial family lines to capture the American imagination.

> Conference paper, cited in "Taking New Measurements for Jefferson's Pedestal" by Nicholas Wade, *The New York Times,* National *7 March 1999*

2 Women harvested his [Thomas Jefferson's*] crops while he sat writing letters and thinking great thoughts. When he died penniless, the majority of them were scattered to the four winds, losing family, home and friends. All these activities—all of these things done to black women—have been taken in and washed clean of their import for those who style themselves as the keepers of Jefferson's flame.

> Ibid.

*American philosopher, educator and architect (1743–1826), 3rd president of the United States (1801–09). Reference to recent discovery that he fathered children with his African-American house slave-mistress.

4533. Melissa Green (1960?–)

1 Everything the woods could teach, my father taught:
Delight, exactitude, a faith, his journeyman's doubt.

> "August, iv," *The Squanicook Ecologues 1987*

2 We become the people we are because of what happens to us and how our memory of it charges the rest of our lives with meaning. It is not only that we make metaphor; metaphor makes us. Language is what we own to be greater than ourselves.

> Preface, *Color is the Suffering of Light: A Memoir 1994*

3 A tiny, formless child lying wrapped in white sheets in an incubator like some hothouse flower whose bloom would wither and die if touched by human hands. . . . No one held her in their arms, no one stroked her deathly pale skin. She was alone in the universe.

> (p. 3), Ibid.

4 There didn't seem to be any difference between what was terrible in the world and what was terrible in me. I had no skin, there was no buffer, I was a spongy mass of tissue that soaked up pain, terror, suffering, despair, and defeat from everything around me. The razor made a safe, straight mark, and suddenly, because I had cut myself, there was a membrane between me and the world, and it was bleeding.

> (p. 257), Ibid.

5 Illness married me, first and forever, put me to bed like a bad child.

> "A Saltbox in Vermont," *Fifty-Two 2007*

6 My fingers hold the very dress I loved
   to dance in, when dancing mattered—and it did.
                                    "Daphne in Mourning," St. 3 *n.d.*

4534. Nicola Griffith (1960–   )

1 There is a silence at the table and from that silence Lore understands that she is the chosen battleground of her parents, that
   whatever she does, however hard she tries, one of then will feel
   betrayed. But she is not even eleven, and she cannot help but try.
                                                    Slow River 1995

4535. Kimberly Willis Holt (1960–   )

1 Some people in Saitter say Momma and Daddy should have
   never been allowed to get married because they're different.
   Folks around here call it retarded, but I like "slow" better.
                                        Ch. 1, *My Louisiana Sky* 1998

2 Nothing ever happens in Antler, Texas.
                                                            Ibid.

3 I kept my eye on the ball, slowing the spin down in my mind,
   seeing each rotation until it came to the place I knew well. The
   place I called Baseball Heaven. I knew if I swung the bat right
   then, it would be all glory for me.
                                                    p. 81, Ibid.

4535.1. Michelle J. Howard (1960–   )

1 My top priority right now is to deter piracy here in the Gulf
   of Aden. I want to continue the extensive international co-
   ordination Admiral McKnight started. That's the true key to
   defeating piracy. Piracy is a problem that affects all maritime
   nations and requires an international solution. I'm looking
   forward to working with naval professionals from around the
   world on this vital mission.
                    Quoted in "Rear Adm. Michelle Howard Assumes Command
                    of Counter-Piracy Task Force CTF" by Lt. John Fage, *The
                    Tension 5 April 2009*

4536. Elena Kagan (1960–   )

1 I have a great love for this institution, and I think Harvard
   Law is an institution that can have a profound effect on the
   legal profession, and thus, through that, also on the nation and
   the world. . . . Leading an institution of that caliber is not only
   challenging, but also very important and very appealing.
                    Quoted in "People in the News" by Lauren A. E. Schuker, *The
                    Harvard Crimson 5 June 2003*

2 We don't look at politics. We figure that if we really go for
   the people who are doing the most interesting scholarship
   and who are the best teachers, we'll get a pretty wide political
   cross-section—and indeed we have. We're just looking for the
   best people, the best scholars, the best teachers.
                    Quoted in "Harvard Law On A Heterodox Spree, Listing To
                    Right" by Anna Schneider-Mayerson, *The New York Observer
                    4 December 2005*

3 When I got here [Harvard Law School] I looked around for little things I could do: things that don't cost much money, don't
   take much time, that you don't have to have a faculty meeting
   to do. As it turns out, you can buy more student happiness
   per dollar by giving people free coffee than anything else I've
   discovered.
                    Quoted in "Crimson tide" by Drake Bennett, *Boston Globe 19
                    October 2008*

4537. Charlotte Keatley (1960–   )

1 MARGARET. My parents are called, my parents are called. . . .
   Guilt, and . . . Duty. Wonderful, how they keep the family together . . .
                        Act III, Sc. 4, *My Mother Said I Never Should* 1987

4538. Beth Kephart (1960–   )

1 What, in the end, are you fighting for: Normal? Is normal possible? Can it be defined? . . . . And is normal superior to what
   the child inherently is, to what he aspires to, fights to become,
   every second of his day?
                            A Slant of Sun: One Child's Courage 1998

2 Nothing erodes it [a mother's love]. It is not sand on a beach. It
   is the nuclear heart of things—hard as the rock of this earth.
                                                            Ibid.

3 [Our son is] different in a million wonderful ways, and also
   different in ways that need our help.
                                                            Ibid.

4539. Celia Kitzinger (1960?–   )

1 In casting woman and serpent as evildoers, Judaic writers over-
   turned a powerful earlier tradition which associated both with
   wisdom and fertility.
                        "Why men hate women," *New Internationalist,* issue 212
                        October 1990

2 Projecting all guilt upon women, branding them as lustful allies
   of the Devil who wean men from God and lead them from the
   path of virtue, the Genesis story enshrines the myth of feminine evil as a justification for female oppression.
                                                            Ibid.

3 At last count the English language had 220 words (almost all
   derogatory) for a sexually promiscuous female and only 20 for
   a sexually promiscuous male (most of these complimentary).
                                                            Ibid.

4 Organized predatory violence has always been a male monopoly, whether practised against animals or women.
                        "Sex, beauty and beasts," *New Internationalist,* issue *215
                        January 1991*

5 Men's power over animals is virtually absolute. Over women,
   men have less control. In pornographic depictions of women
   as animals, the fantasy of total male dominance is made explicit. Woman becomes the inferior animal, captured, cut up
   into pieces, displayed as a trophy to masculine power.
                                                            Ibid.

4540. Amy Klobuchar (1960–   )

1 So what's the cost of the culture of corruption? Of people
   giving breaks to the oil companies and giving giveaways and
   Christmas presents to the drug companies and the insurance
   companies? The cost is $90 billion a year. There you go. Quan-
   tifiable.
                    Interview with Jonathan Singer, MyDD.com *23 February 2006*

2 We are basically losing our middle class with these wrongheaded policies where we are having the wrong priorities, we
   are giving tax cuts to the wealthiest, giving loopholes to the
   big corporate special interests, and it's becoming harder and
   harder for people to get by.
                                                            Ibid.

3 I always tell the story of a diner in my neighborhood. It's called Betty's Bikes and Buns. They've got this business card that says, "Betty's Bikes and Buns: Where Lies Become Legends." Well the people in our state are beginning to see the lies beneath the legends of the leadership in Washington, DC. They told us there were weapons of mass destruction; there weren't. They told us they'd leave no child behind; they left behind millions. They told us they'd unite this country, and they've divided us as never before. They told us that we'd be ready for any national disaster, and you just ask that mom stranded on the roof in New Orleans for three days with her three kids if that was true and she'll tell you the truth.

Ibid.

4541. Nigella Lucy Lawson (1960–)

1 The Great Culinary Renaissance we have heard so much about has done many things—given us extra virgin olive oil, better restaurants, and gastroporn—but it hasn't taught us how to cook.

"Basics," *How to Eat: The Pleasures and Principles of Good Food* 2002

2 There are no rules in my kitchen.

Quoted in "British sensation Lawson says cooking should be about fun, family" by Beth Cooney, *Oakland Tribune 4 June 2003*

3 And in a curious way, despite the fact that we're talking about Christmas and ham, it's a very Jewish thing to want to provide a huge spread. I always cook for eight, but make enough to feed 30 . . .

Quoted in "The big issue" by Shane Watson, *The Times (London) 2 December 2007*

4542. Margaret McMullan (1960–)

1 The home economics class cooked for the school and at eleven o'clock every day you could smell them burning lunch.

"Genevieve," *In My Mother's House* 2003

2 I know what to do when Momma has a cold or the stomach cramps. I fix her up with a nice cup of life-everlasting tea the way she taught me. And if the chills or fevers come, I dig up some horsemint to add to the tea. But I can't heal this hurt she's had since pappy left us, and she hasn't even asked me to try. I wish for once she would just ask me.

Ch. 1, *When I Crossed No-Bob* 2007

3 There had to come a time when all this mess would be over. This was America, for Christ's sake. Things got done.

"The Aftermath Lounge," *The Sun December 2008*

4 "These volunteers, they're just tourists," she said, leaning in closer to him. "They come and want to eat seafood and drink all night, and I'm thinking, Now wait a minute. You can't come here and act like nothing happened. Fix it, paint it, move on. You know? Like, the world can't just keep going—not after this."

Ibid.

4543. Jenny McPhee (1960?–)

1 "Be everywhere, do everything, and never fail to astonish."

Ch. 1, *The Center of Things* 2002

2 "For all I know, eternity could be time on an ego trip."

Ibid.

3 It wasn't that she felt manipulated, it was that she hadn't been manipulated well enough.

No Ordinary Matter 2004

4 I didn't exactly know why I wanted to die. I didn't think it was solely because I couldn't bear the pain and humiliation of being alive, although that certainly was a challenge.

A Man of No Moon 2007

4544. Susanna Millar (fl. 1960s)

1 If animals play, this is because play is useful in the struggle for survival; because play practices and so perfects the skills needed in adult life.

Ch. 1, *The Psychology of Play* 1968

2 For the healthy, a monotonous environment eventually produces discomfort, irritation and attempts to vary it.

Ch. 4, Ibid.

3 The social life of a child starts when he is born.

Ch. 7, Ibid.

4 Reading has been called "visible language" or "visible speech." The phrase is interesting, because it emphasizes the linguistic nature of reading. But it also suggests that to read is to understand language by means of vision. There is no comparable phrase such as "tactile language" or "felt speech," although reading by touch is the most important means of written communication for blind people.

Ch. 1, *Reading by Touch* 1997

4545. Florence Mpaayei (1960–)

1 Sustainable peace in Kenya, our region and the rest of our continent will only be realized when we each discover that our individual and collective actions constitute choices either for peace or violence. Peace education, while not offering all the answers, holds the possibility that we can begin to build foundations for peace in our young school-going people. I hope that this conference will be remembered for having spurred the region towards embracing peace education in our schools.

Remarks, Peace Conference (Nairobi) *December 1985*

2 Peace is more than just the absence of war. Peace means people having enough food, adequate health services, education, transportation facilities and a conducive atmosphere to reach their goals. If people don't have these things, there is unrest.

Speech, Global Network of Religions for Africa (Zanzibar) *16 February 2008*

3 The moral authority of leaders is an essential ingredient to human security. Our attitudes will determine whether we are able to resolve conflict. It requires real listening and a readiness to consider new ways. And if we are to be a bridge, we have to be willing to be walked on.

Remarks, Caux Forum (Switzerland) *July 2008*

4546. Gina Barkhordar Nahai (1960–)

1 I never knew that Jews weren't allowed out of the ghetto [in Iran]—or that there *was* a ghetto. I thought that it was just another neighborhood.

Quoted in "Revealing 'Peacock' is an emotional adventure" by Michelle Bisson, *Seattle Times*, L3 *9 June 1991*

2 Iranians do have incredible resilience, considering all they've been through.

Ibid.

3 Writing is my answer, my emotional reaction to all the injustices of the world.

Ibid.

4547. Vera Naufal (fl. 1960s)

1 The Palestinian woman carries all the burden. There are periods when men disappear, get jailed, killed, and the Palestinian woman is up to the challenge. I mean the traditional woman. She does everything in the house and for the children. She gets pregnant, gives birth, she builds houses and defends the camp, and goes to the first demonstration that goes out of the camp. . . . When water is cut off [to] the camp that is a woman's issue.

Remark* (1969), Quoted in *Daughters of Palestine: Leading Women of the Palestinian National Movement 1996*
*Made after witnessing the 1969 camp uprising in Lebanon.

4548. Mary Orr (1960–)

1 Journal writing and travel go together like chai and samosas. Each can stand alone, but both are enhanced by the other.

"Passages in India," *The Women's Review of Books*, Vol. XII, Nos. 10–11 *July 1995*

2 I asked the waiter what kind of fish they had: "Sorry madame, no fish today."

No problem. I had my alternative. I asked what they put in their noodles, knowing perfectly well I'd order them even with the tedious carrots and cabbage. "Sorry madame, no noodles today."

This surprised me. Too hungry to look further, long past the ability to make a decision, I grasped for the old standby: *biryani:* "Sorry madame, no *biryani.*"

I gave up. "What *do* you have, then?"

"Sorry, madame, no food today."

Ibid.

3 Standing behind me, the room boy placed his hands at the base of my neck, applying pressure. "Massage, madame?"

I showed him the door. I barricaded it with the other bed in the room. Then I angrily bolted the doors to the balcony, which connected with the rooms on either side of mine. Because of this Lothario I had to sleep in a stuffy cell. Land of the Buddha indeed.

Ibid.

4549. Silvana Paternostro (1960?–)

1 Each light is a crowded house with no sewage system but with a color TV, an abusive husband, a frigid wife, and a desperate daughter like Mariana, who wishes she could swim across to the other side where the rich women wear thongs, live in condominiums with smoky mirrors, and where Cytotec [a chemical abortifacient] is available.

In the Land of God and Man: Confronting Our Sexual Culture 1998

2 Colombians don't vote for human beings, they vote for saviors.

My Colombian War 2007

4550. Mary Proctor (1960–)

1 You're thoughts aren't worth a penny till you put them to use—and pennies make dollars.

Inscribed on artwork *n.d.*

4551. Sophia Rabliauskas (1960?–)

1 Creator gave us the responsibility to care for the land, the land that sustains our life. Our Elders have always believed that how we treat our land today will affect the health of the planet and the lives of many generations to come. It is critical now more than ever, that we fulfill that responsibility that was passed down to us from our ancestors.

Quoted on *goldmanprize.org 2007*

2 We wanted to have control of what happens in our territory— we didn't want any development that would destroy our land. Over the years the whole community has been involved in developing the land-management plan, and it's finally completed. To us this was a historic thing, to work with the government and get them to recognize and help us get the protection we needed.

Quoted in "First Things First" by Michelle Nijhuis, grist.org *25 April 2007*

3 We strongly believe that the land is very much alive, and that we do get the wisdom and the knowledge that we need from it.

Ibid.

4552. Sue Riddlestone (1960–)

1 An eco-community can recycle up to 65% of its waste. And what's left shouldn't go to landfill—you can find other ways to recover energy from that as well.

Quoted in "Making your home a green house" by Victoria Bone, BBC News (London) *14 May 2007*

2 It's no good saving energy in the home if you then get in the car every time you need to go shopping.

Ibid.

3 The UN's call to action is that in this year of food, fuel and financial crises we can bring a similar vision* to meet an even greater global challenge of our time. We can divert our actions, funds and political decisions to accelerate the transition to a sustainable and just society.

"New Deals, carbon emissions and Achim Steiner," *BioRegional (opal.bioregional.com) 2008*
*Re Roosevelt's New Deal (Franklin Delano R- 1882–1945), 32nd President of the United States (1933–45).

4553. Tina Rosenberg (1960–)

1 The sicario [hired killer] did for murder in Medellin what the transistor did for the radio. Killing is easy, cheap and popular. . . .

Children of Cain: Violence and the Violent in Latin America 1991

2 Unlike authoritarianism, totalitarianism is a conspiracy of the whole of society; "We are all guilty," Vaclav Havel* says. But of course not all should be punished. Distinctions must be made. A list of those to be punished will be drawn up, and those not on the list can then declare themselves innocent. They can erase their own history of complicity with dictatorship in their own ritual purification. But who, using what criteria, will draw up that list?

Pt. I, Ch. 1, *The Haunted Land: Facing Europe's Ghosts After Communism 1995*
*(1936–), Czech playwright, essayist; president of Czechoslovakia (1989–92) and the Czech Republic (1993–2003).

4554. Joanna Scott (1960–)

1 *You should let a storm take you where it will, the bird knows—warp and spin across the sky with the wind instead of trying to resist it. But the squall threatens to pull her downward into the turbulent lake, so she beats her powerful wings against the gusts, hovering while the rain swirls around her. All reason is swept away by the storm, leaving only the frenzied effort of life protecting itself and an insidious, creeping exhaustion.*

Ch. 1, *The Manikin 1996*

2 And so in November of 1974, on a day much like today, in the wake of a rainstorm, he climbed over the rail of the bridge and jumped, and as he fell he had enough time to acknowledge that if he'd had the wherewithal to consider other options he could have spared himself from the impending impact, which he must have felt in anticipation, with horrible, vivid clarity, before he experienced it as a distinct physical sensation, his body shattering the surface of the river right at the moment when he was probably condemning himself for being such a stupid fucking idiot, and wasn't it just so fucking typical for him to realize this too late!

November 6, 2006, *Follow Me 2009*

3 She turns toward her weariness as she might turn toward the sun on the first warm day of spring, basks in it, retaining just enough strength to drag herself up the two flights of stairs to her bedroom.

Ibid.

4 And the rest of them—what had they been up to these past years?

Doing and doing and doing. You know, the same old thing. They always liked best doing as close to nothing as they could get away with.

March 15, 2007, Ibid.

5 Like as not, folks won't be noticed until they generate a folder stuffed with unnecessary forms, my grandmother would grumble. You'd think life begins and ends on paper.

Ibid.

4555. Melissa Scott (1960–)

1 Trouble's on the nets tonight, riding the high data like a cowboy, the plains of light stark around her. The data flows and writhes like grass in the virtual wind, and she glides along the shifts and shadows, a shadow herself against their virtual sun.

Trouble and Her Friends 1994

2 Text was a necessary thing, in whatever form it was stored and accessed: it was a bridge and a barrier between the visible and invisible worlds, between places and peoples and the worlds of the metagovernments.

Ch. 1, *Night Sky Mine 1996*

4556. Shamima Shaikh (1960–1998)

1 In Islam the Qur'an applies to all . . .

Speech, "Women & Islam—The Gender Struggle in South Africa: The Ideological Struggle," *21 December 1997*

2 Despite the overwhelming and strong position of Muslims that Islam liberated women 1400 years ago, you still find there's a problem. Some thought and practice within Muslim society does not reflect this conviction, giving rise to the accusation that Islam oppresses women, to which the Muslim community reacts emotionally with denial and animosity, without reflecting inwardly and addressing the existing problems.

Ibid.

4557. Yulia Volodymyrivna Tymoshenko (1960–)

1 I'm very glad that people fell in love with my idealism. It is much worse when people fall in love with cynicism.

Quoted in "Crowning glory awaits the Orange heir apparent" by Andrew Billen, *The Times* (London) *20 May 2006*

2 I read my press cuttings every day and it is all negative material: all politicians are monsters!

Ibid.

4558. A. J. Verdelle (1960–)

1 I did not want the girls' jobs. Rather than walk with the girls holding banners that said CHRIST, THE OPEN DOOR, I wanted to be where my brothers belonged. I wanted to hit a big drum with sticks.

The Good Negress 1995

2 . . . history complicates things . . .

Ibid.

3 She tell me I ain't ig'nant, that I shouldn't let nobody make me think I'm ig'nant, that my problem is my language. That I live in a country where English is spoke and I don't know how to speak it. . . . Nobody who sounds dumb will ever be important, she say, no matter how much potential they have. Nobody will ever understand you, nobody who can help you rise, unless you can speak the language of the nation.

Ibid.

4559. Velma Wallis (1960–)

1 "We have learned much during our long lives. Yet there we were in our old age, thinking that we had done our share in life. So we stopped, just like that. No more working like we used to, even though our bodies are still healthy enough to do a little more than we expect of ourselves."

Ch. 2, *Two Old Women 1993*

2 They all depended on the land, and if its rules were not obeyed, quick and unjudgemental death could fall upon the careless and unworthy.

Ch. 3, Ibid.

3 The body needs food, but the mind needs people.

Ch. 4, Ibid.

4 The chief had known that a drastic change in leadership would have proved more damaging than the hunger, for in times when a band is starving, bad politics lead only to further disaster.

Ch. 6, Ibid.

4560. Becky Weed (1960?–)

1 Old-timers talk about how great the Montana country is, but you've got to take care of it. Killing [animals] just doesn't seem to fit.

Quoted in "The Best Coyote Defense Since the Road Runner" by Richard Woodbury, Time.com *27 March 2000*

2 We're all suffering because the public is trained to think that all ranchers hate the environment. We have to prove that we're good custodians. There are plenty of buyers who will seek out ranchers doing things in a responsible manner.

Ibid.

4561. Heather Wilson (1960–   )

1   We won't be safe if we pick up our ball and go home* . . . It's a choice between resolve and retreat, and . . . I choose resolve.

Quoted in "Race tests value, or cost, of loyalty" by Andrea Stone, *USA Today* 30 August 2006

*Re war in Iraq.

2   One of the greatest things about Senator Obama* is that he talks about the importance of being a father and a parent, but nobody asks whether he can do both at the same time. We need to end the double standard.

Quoted in "GOP Women Defend Palin . . ." by Gwin Ifill,** *The News Hour,* PBS-TV 2 September 2008

*Barack Obama (1961–   ), 44th president of the United States (2009–   ). **See 4308.

4562. Jane Akre (1961?–   )

1   Every parent and every consumer has the right to know what they're pouring on their children's morning cereal. We set out to tell Florida consumers the truth about a giant chemical company and a powerful dairy lobby. That used to be something investigative reporters won awards for. As we've learned the hard way, it's something you can be fired for these days . . .

Press conference (2 April 1998; Tallahassee), *In Motion Magazine* 28 April 1998

2   There is no justification for the five [television] stations not to support us. Attaching legal fees to whistleblowers is unprecedented, absurd. The "business" of broadcasting trumps it all. These news organizations must ensure they are worthy of the public trust while they use OUR airwaves, free of charge. Public trust is alarmingly absent here.

Quoted in "Court Ruled That Media Can Legally Lie" by Liane Casten, *CMW Report Spring 2003*

4563. Trezza Azzopardi (1961–   )

1   My father will gamble on anything that moves. He won't do Bingo or fruit machines or snow on Christmas Day, but horses and pontoon and poker and dogs. My father's love is Chance. Look at that roulette wheel! Bet red, bet black, bet red, bet black. If he could place his bet Under Starter's Orders he would still change his mind over every fence.

The Hiding Place 2000

2   "There's not a lot of wisdom in old age, despite what they say. Truth is, as you get older, things get further away. Objects—like telephone boxes and shops."

Remember Me 2003

3   "I went outside and had a shout. Don't ask me what the words were, it's letting them out that counts."

Ibid.

4   "No one comes back."

Ibid.

4564. Fatou Bensouda (1961–   )

1   The problem of child soldiers is very, very serious. Some are turned into killers, others are used as sex slaves. It is affecting a whole generation of children who are very difficult to re-integrate into society. Fighting is often all they know. It's a problem in many places, and we want to highlight this here.

"A Hague prosecutor focuses on her native Africa" by Marlise Simons, *Herald Tribune: Europe 25 February 2007*

4565. Suzanne Berne (1961–   )

1   Watch yourself—it's still the best advice anyone ever gave me.

A Crime in the Neighborhood 1997

2   I glimpsed the true power of mendacity: you can always be persuaded to doubt your own certainties but never your own lies.

The Ghost at the Table 2006

3   ". . . the minute you think you've got the last word on someone—well, that's exactly when he gets away from you, isn't it?"

Ibid.

4   Blood is bloody.

Ibid.

4566. Mary Bono (1961–   )

1   I used to tease him* that he would build condos at the base of Half Dome in Yosemite if he could. That's how extreme he was.

"The Widow's Run" by Frank Bruni, *The New York Times 29 March 1998*

*Re Sonny Bono (1935–98; American record producer, singer, actor, politician), her deceased husband.

2   I support the ban on partial-birth abortions. I oppose Federal funding. And I support parental notification. But in the end, it's between a woman, her family and her God. It's a moral decision, and she has to make it on her own. The Federal Government does not belong in it.

Ibid.

3   Video games are addictive—the more violent, the more so—and that's reason enough to quell any doubt over studies that find peripheral positive effects.

"Gaming Pros and Cons," Ibid. *12 June 2003*

4   With great respect to Steve Jobs, he's trying to sell hardware, first and foremost. I wonder if he would feel the same way about his patents being on the Internet free of patent protection.

Quoted in "Berners-Lee: Congress should consider net neutrality" by Grant Gross, *MacWorld 1 March 2007*

4566.1 Susan Boyle (1961–   )

1   Modern society is too quick to judge people on their appearances. [. . .] There is not much you do do about it; it is the way they think; it is the way they are. But maybe this could teach them a lesson, or set an example.

Quoted in "The Scot Heard Round the World" by Mary Jordan, *The Washington Post 14 April 2009*

2   I know what they were thinking, but why should it matter as long as I can sing? It's not a beauty contest.

Quoted in "She who laughs last—songstress Susan Boyle" by Gillian Harris, *The Sunday Times 19 April 2009*

4567. Ann Coulter (1961–   )

1   The ethic of conservation is the explicit abnegation of man's dominion over the Earth. The lower species are here for our use. God said so: Go forth, be fruitful, multiply, and rape the planet—it's yours. That's our job: drilling, mining and stripping. Sweaters are the anti-Biblical view. Big gas-guzzling cars with phones and CD players and wet bars—that's the Biblical view.

"Oil good; democrats bad," Townhall.com *12 October 2000*

2   Not all Muslims may be terrorists, but all terrorists are Muslims.

> Syndicated column, Universal Press Syndicate *28 September 2001*

3   Taxes are like abortion, and not just because both are grotesque procedures supported by Democrats. You're for them or against them. Taxes go up or down; government raises taxes or lowers them. But Democrats will not let the words abortion or tax hikes pass their lips.

> *Ibid., 2 February 2002*

4   I think the government should be spying on all Arabs, engaging in torture as a televised spectator sport, dropping daisy cutters wantonly throughout the Middle East and sending liberals to Guantanamo.

> *Ibid., 21 December 2005*

5   This year's Democratic plan for the future is another inane sound bite designed to trick American voters into trusting them with national security. To wit, they're claiming there is no connection between the war on terror and the war in Iraq, and while they're all for the war against terror—absolutely in favor of that war—they are adamantly opposed to the Iraq war. You know, the war where the U.S. military is killing thousands upon thousands of terrorists (described in the media as "Iraqi civilians," even if they are from Jordan, like the now-dead leader of al-Qaida in Iraq, Abu Musab al-Zarqawi). That war.

"What part of the war on terrorism do they support?" *Ibid. 23 August 2006*

4568. Diana, Princess of Wales (1961–1997)

1   Everywhere I go I smell fresh paint.

> Quoted in *The Daily Telegraph* (London) *28 January 1988*

2   I'd like to be a queen of people's hearts, in people's hearts, but I don't see myself being Queen of this country. I don't think many people will want me to be Queen.

> Interview with Martin Bashir, *BBC Panorama 20 November 1995*

3   Well there were three of us in this marriage, so it was a bit crowded.*

> Ibid.

*Re her husband's affair with Camilla Parker-Bowles, whom he married after Diana's death.

4   Anywhere I see suffering, that is where I want to be, doing what I can.

> Quoted by Andrew Morton in *The Sun 1 September 1997*

4569. Brigit Dressel (1961–1987)

1   These are all harmless drugs.* All athletes take them. It's really nothing special.

> Comment to mother, Quoted in "An Athlete Dying Young," *Time* (New York) *10 October 1988*

*Re use of steroids.

4570. Andrea Dunbar (1961–1991)

1   GIRL. It's not that I don't like you. I just want to be alone.
SAM. How long for? How long do you need?
GIRL. It could be a week, it could be a month, I don't know, it could be longer. I just couldn't say at this time.

SAM. But why do you need so long?
GIRL. I need that time. I gotta have it. And I'm going to get it at all costs.

> Act II, Sc. 8, *The Arbor 1980*

4571. Margaret Edson (1961–)

1   VIVIAN BEARING, PH.D. I have been asked "How are you feeling today?" while I was throwing up into a plastic washbasin. I have been asked as I was emerging from a four-hour operation with a tube in every orifice, "How are you feeling today?"

I am waiting for the moment when someone asks me this question and I am dead.

I'm a little sorry I'll miss that.

> (Opening), *Wit 1999*

2   VIVIAN BEARING, PH.D. It is not my intention to give away the plot, but I think I die at the end. They've given me less than two hours.

> Ibid.

3   VIVIAN BEARING, PH.D. Once I did the teaching, now I am taught. This is much easier. I just hold still and look cancerous. It requires less acting every time.

> Ibid.

4572. Yakin Ertük (1961?–)

1   There has always been a Nicole* throughout history, women [who have] fought patriarchy but who most often got victimized and crushed because the system is strong. What is unique in the Nicole story is the mobilized reaction [to it].

> Quoted in "'Nicole' rape case may yet reach UN" by Pennie Azarcon dela Cruz, Inquirer.net *18 September 2007*

*Pseudonym for Filipina whose rape in November 2005 resulted in the conviction of Daniel Smith.

2   One of the greatest barriers to overcome is the silence that surrounds the issue [of violence against women]. . . . We must create a culture of zero tolerance for one of the most pervasive yet least punished human rights violations in the world.

> Letter to Zonta International Officials *28 November 2007*

4573. Melissa Etheridge (1961–)

1   Now I am throwing off the carelessness of youth
To listen to an inconvenient truth

That I need to move, I need to wake up
I need to change, I need to shake up
I need to speak out, something's got to break up
I've been asleep and I need to wake up now

> "I Need to Wake Up," *Greatest Hits: The Road Less Traveled* (album) *2005*

2   Mostly I have to thank Al Gore,* for inspiring us, for inspiring me, showing that caring about the Earth is not Republican or Democrat; it's not red or blue, it's all green.

> Acceptance speech, Academy Awards, *2006*

*(1948–), American environmentalist, politician; 45th vice president of the United States (1993–2001).

3   You know what happens if you're completely still? Your mind eventually—that little tape that's running—bup, bup, bup—all the noise? It eventually runs off the reel. And you have nothing left to think. And all of a sudden, the answers are just there. It's

like someone just removed a big cloud. And I could see completely clearly.

> Interview with Marianne Schnall,* feminist.com *16 August 2007*

*See 4758.

4 And of course I just kept doing what I do and writing my own experience. And then my experience was one of my own personal break-ups and all this stuff. And then there's cancer—and then in the middle of cancer and chemotherapy, there's an awakening, there's an enlightenment of what life really is. And this sort of whole dream of success and this dream of "I've got to have a hit song," "I've got to do this"—it wasn't mine—I don't wish to dream that anymore. I wish to create—I believe that there's a world out there, who wants to hear music like this, who wants to put music on to be fed, to be nourished, to be held up and enlightened and excited. And I believe that artists do that for people, and that I can do that for people.

> Ibid.

4574. Suzanne Fields (1961?–)

1 Parents who think textbooks are written by fair but tough-minded scholars are unaware of how political process, not scholarship, produces their children's textbooks.

> "Radical Islam is sanitized for American textbooks," *Washington Times 21 February 2003*

2 Nothing galvanizes the public like the threat of terrorism.

> "It's the culture, stupid," *Washington Times 9 July 2007*

4575. Laura Flanders (1961–)

1 George W. Bush* might never have snagged the White House if one woman had been laughed at less: Katherine Harris,** Secretary of State of Florida. No one did more, more carefully, to use the power of her public office to steal the presidency for her candidate; no one was made more fun of in the media.

> Introduction, *Bushwomen: Tales of a Cynical Species 2004*
> *George W. B- (1946–), Am. politician; 43rd president of the United States (2001–09). **(1957–) Am. Politician, public servant.

2 Bushwomen: they're the one thing Bush has that Ronald Reagan* didn't, and they ease his way to accomplish things that Reagan never could.

> Ibid.
> *(1911–2004), 40th president of the United States (1981–89), actor.

4576. Michèle A. Flournoy (1961–)

1 Talking with the countries in the [Middle Eastern] region is long overdue. That said, given the passage of time, we should have limited expectations. Positions have hardened and a lot of feelings of distrust have increased. As an example, Iran was actually quite helpful to us in the immediate aftermath of Sept. 11. But rather than building on that dialogue, we characterized them as part of the axis of evil.

> "Next Steps: Experts React to Iraq Report," *The Wall Street Journal 6 December 2006*

4576.1. Margaret Flowers (1961?–)

1 ... single-payer health care would create a national health system. We don't have a system right now. Everything is very fragmented and very confusing. It would create a single sys-

tem where every person is included, and it covers all medically necessary care. It frees doctors and patients to make medical decisions without interference from the insurance companies, insurance companies who are only trying to profit off of this situation and are making it very, very difficult to provide quality care in this country.

> Quoted in "Baucus's Raucous Caucus: Doctors, Nurses and Activists Arrested Again for Protesting Exclusion of Single-Payer Advocates at Senate Hearing on Health Care" by Amy Goodman,* Democracy Now! *13 May 2009*
> *See 4408.1.

2 We need to change the conversation and stop talking about health insurance and start talking about creating a system that provides health care.

> Ibid.

4577. Suzanne Gardinier (1961–)

1 ... words are the bridges between our separatenesses and are sacred ...

> *A World That Will Hold All the People 1996*

2 Somehow Neruda's* sturdy aversion to bowing before kings weakens before patriarchs; his view of history is often through the eyes of Great Men. ... In this telling, the American continent has no mothers nor daughters; the Canto is not a "song of all" but of fathers, brothers, and sons.

> "Pablo Neruda," Ibid.
> *Chilean poet, diplomat (1904–73); Nobel Prize for Literature (1971), Lenin Prize for Peace (1953).

3 There are voices in the *Iliad* we do not hear at length, and faces we do not see, or glimpse only briefly: Those of the people who bind the battle wounds; those of the slaves in Troy and in the Achaean camp; and those of women, who may also be the nurses and the slaves, who are ignored and derided and raped and given as prizes in athletic contests.

> "Two Cities," Ibid.

4578. Libia Grueso (1961?–)

1 The jungle makes our lifestyle, and our natural vision, possible. The most important thing is that the [Afro-Colombian] community has a different lifestyle, a different kind of relationship with nature, a different sense of life and death. That is what we have to offer the rest of the world.

> Quoted in "Roll on, Colombia" by Michelle Nijhuis, grist.org *22 April 2004*

2 War in this region [Colombia's Pacific Coast region] is clearly about territory, about the land we have conserved for more than 400 years.

> Ibid.

3 If some of us have to die, that means that some of us have to continue—and in that persistence one finds the strength for the struggle.

> Ibid.

4579. Kathryn Harrison (1961–)

1 My father is an absence, a hole like one of those my grandmother cuts out of family photographs. Rather than discard the entire picture of an event that includes someone she dislikes, she snips the offender out with untidy haste, using her manicure scissors.

> *The Kiss 1997*

2   The tiny foot in his hand shape-shifted. One minute it repelled him, the next it seemed suddenly to express the beauty of the whole female body. Wasn't it all there, in May's foot? The smooth white of her neck, the curve of her breast and hip, the crook of her smallest finger, the delicate, mauve folds of her most intimate places.

The Binding Chair 2000

3   Yes, he's obsessed with sex. How else could he escape the inside of his head, where every thought refuses to be fleeting and instead waits its turn to be hyperarticulated, edited, revised and then annotated like some nightmare hybrid of Talmudic commentary and Freudian case study?

Envy 2005

4   Ironic that she'd become a dermatologist. She'd always had a personality like a rash, itchy, chafing, the kind of woman who just won't let you get comfortable.

Ibid.

4580. Judy Horacek (1961–   )

1   In Hell all the messages you ever left on answering machines will be played back to you.

Life on the Edge: Cartoons 1992

2   My life has been a quest to find new and better places to stick cartoons.

Quoted in "A new lease on life" by Kathryn Favelle, *National Library of Australia News,* XV (12)

4581. Hou Xiaotian (1961–   )

1   I was not part of Tiananmen,* but Tiananmen changed me.

Cited in Close-up by Jennifer Lin, *Seattle Times,* A3 *13 February 1994*

*Re the government massacre of demonstrators in Tiananmen Square in Beijing, China on 4 June 1989.

4582. Abigail Johnson (1961–   )

1   Retirement is fundamentally at the heart of our business* and we continue to focus significant resources on the financial needs of Americans preparing for, entering, or in retirement. . . . our goal is to empower people to be more productive at work and prosperous in life.

Quoted in "For Abigail Johnson, a leadership test" by Ross Kerber, *The Boston Globe 21 August 2007*

*Fidelity Employer Services Co. (Fesco).

4583. Jackie Kay (1961–   )

1   I want my waters to break
like Noah's flood

Ch. 1: The Seed, *Adoption Papers 1991*

2   I am a stranger visiting
Myself occasionally

"That Distance Apart," Pt. IV, St. 5, *That Distance Apart 1991*

3   That's what I liked about the blues, they told stories. The opposite of fairytales; these were grimy, real, appalling tragedies. There were people dying in the blues; people coming back to haunt the people who were living in the blues; there were bad men in the blues; there were wild women in the blues.

"In the House of Blues," *Bessie Smith 1997*

4   Our own pasts constantly rejuvenate themselves. It's not something that has happened and that was it. It's open to reinterpretation. I find it fascinating that we can't even say we've lived what we've lived.

Quoted in "Don't tell me who I am" by Libby Brooks, *The Guardian* (London) *12 January 2002*

5   You would never dream of asking a heterosexual writer how being heterosexual affected their writing, yet it's often asked of a lesbian writer.

Ibid.

6   . . . even in the early sixties there was something
Scandalous about adopting
Telling the world your secret failure
Bringing up an alien child
Who knew what it would turn out to be?

"The Mother Poem (two)," St. 1 n.d.

4584. Elizabeth Kolbert (1961–   )

1   Of all the examples of wrongheaded liberal social engineering that conservatives love to rail about, rent control has got to rank near the top . . .

"The Charisma of No Charisma," *The Prophet of Love: And Other Tales of Power and Deceit 2004*

2   Between the fawning and the gloating, the self-promotion and the perfunctory humility, victory celebrations are rarely tasteful affairs.

"The Long Campaign," Ibid.

4585. Annie Leonard (1961?–   )

1   Have you ever wondered where all the stuff we buy comes from and where it goes when we throw it out?

The Story of Stuff (documentary film) *2007*

2   But the truth is [the materials economy] is a system in crisis. And the reason it is in crisis is that it is a linear system and we live on a finite planet and you can not run a linear system on a finite planet indefinitely.

Ibid.

3   Now, the reason the corporation looks bigger than the government is that the corporation is bigger than the government. Of the 100 largest economies on earth now, 51 are corporations.

Ibid.

4   If everybody consumed at U.S. rates, we would need 3 to 5 planets. And you know what? We've only got one.

Ibid.

5   We have become a nation of consumers. Our primary identity has become that of consumer, not mothers, teachers, farmers, but consumers. The primary way that our value is measured and demonstrated is by how much we . . . consume. And do we!

Ibid.

6   Have you ever wondered why women's shoe heels go from fat one year to skinny the next to fat to skinny? It is not because there is some debate about which heel structure is the most healthy for women's feet. . . . It's to keep buying new shoes.

Ibid.

4586. Wendy Liebman (1961–)

1 I'm flying, and there's a guy sitting next to me, and I could tell he really wanted me . . . to shut up.

    Quoted in "Not the Last Laugh," *The Haunted Smile, The Story of Jewish Comedians in America* by Lawrence J. Epstein *2001*

2 Timing is everything. Time is everything else.

    "What I've Learned Doing Stand-up Comedy," wendyliebman. com *2002*

3 My HMO is so expensive, they charge me for a self-breast exam. It's a flat fee.

    glee mail, Ibid. *9 June 2003*

4587. Rosemary Mahoney (1961–)

1 They made drinking seem more an obligation than a pleasure.

    "The Animal Show," *Whoredom in Kimmage: The Private Lives of Irish Women 1993*

2 Belief, whether blind or examined, divinely guided or superstitiously misguided, had made those pilgrims singular and bold, strange and determined.

    Introduction, *The Singular Pilgrim: Travels on Sacred Ground 2003*

3 Marriage was nothing but a burden and a greased chute to nowhere. A woman was better off alone.

    "Hoda and the Women," *Down the Nile: Alone in a Fisherman's Skiff 2007*

4588. Catherine Mavrikakis (1961–)

1 I haven't gotten used to death. I never see it coming. Hervé's death goes splash! Just splash and it's over . . . A splash that keeps making me jump. One repetitious splash.

    A Cannibal and Melancholy Mourning, Nathalie Stephens, tr. *2000*

2 Before our dead we must be ravenous, we must be cannibals and swallow them whole or tear them apart with our voracious teeth.

    Ibid.

4589. Jackie Morris (1961–)

1 From the beginning of time, out of the silence, Snow Leopard sang the stars to life, the sun to rise and the moon to wax and wane. High above the hidden valley, her song clothed the world in white and built a crackling fortress of snow, buttressed with ice, to keep all things safe and secret.

    The Snow Leopard 2007

4590. Dee Dee Myers (1961–)

1 When you measure various qualities of both men and women—height, weight, intelligence, likelihood to become criminals, aptitude in science and math—men tend to differ more from each other than women do.

    Ch. 3, *Women Should Rule the World 2008*

2 When men are stressed, they get in someone's face—or retreat into their proverbial caves. . . . [but] women were more likely to respond to stress in their own way: by hanging out with their kids or talking things over with a friend or family member, a pattern of behavior which [researchers Taylor and Klein*] called "tend and befriend."

    Ch. 4, Ibid.

*Drs. Shelley E. Taylor and Laura Cousin Klein.

3 New research on women's brains suggest that motherhood literally alters a woman's brain . . . [improving] women's senses such as smell, taste, and touch; sharpen their social skills; and make them more efficient, resilient, and motivated.

    Ibid.

4 If our family tree suggests that violence in humans is innate, it may also suggest a strategy for controlling that violence. Bonobos, the "peaceful apes," look very much like chimpanzees. . . . But when it comes to their social lives, bonobos are a world apart. They have reduced the level of violence in relations between the sexes, in relations among males, and in relations between communities.

    Ch. 5, Ibid.

4591. Antonya Nelson (1961–)

1 We watched the creamy portion [of the Guinness] roil into the deep brown, mesmerizing as a gelogic event.

    Some Fun 2006

2 If she could suck it [the gin] back from the drain, she would, recant, let it flow in reverse, upward to its bottle where it belongs, solid vessel, noble kilted Brit on the label, standing in the freezer all day waiting for his date with her mother, waiting for nightfall, sweatclothes, ice and lime and bristling tonic. "I'm sorry," Claire concedes.

    "Some Fun," Ibid.

3 My love for my husband had burst into descrete pieces when he himself had come undone. I could name them—concern, fear, fondness, pity—all separate, like parts of a broken object it was my job to reassemble, an object whose linchpin I seemed to have misplaced.

    "Rear View," Ibid.

4592. Josephine Ojiambo (1961–)

1 There is nothing as satisfying to me as seeing a mother with a smile.

    Quoted in "Community health her goal" by Dan Teng'o and Phares Mutembei, *Lifestyle Magazine 6 January 2002*

2 Women have special gifts in constructing social harmony. We are more able to sacrifice personal ego for the greater good of the community.

    Speech, Quoted in *Kenya Times* (timesnews.co.ke) *29 December 2005*

3 For an understanding of the impact of conflict on women, their voices must be heard and their work on the ground recognized, valued and supported. Decisions on conflict management should be made with women, not for women.

    Ibid.

4593. Susan Power (1961–)

1 Too many people don't believe in their souls, don't recognize them when they feel the spirit twist against their heart or snap across their brain. And some that do believe hand their spirits over to the care of others, just give them blithely away, though they may be tight-fisted when it comes to their coins.

    The Grass Dancer 1994

2 Dad burned tobacco on Columbus Day to mourn the arrival of the man who pressed Indians into slavery; fasted on Thanksgiving Day to show his solidarity with all those eastern tribes

the Pilgrims killed off with their European strain of germs, and set off fireworks on June 26 to celebrate the anniversary of the Little Big Horn battle, when our ancestors crushed Custer like a wood tick.

"Roofwalker," *Roofwalker* 2002

4594. Marina Rikhvanova (1961–)

1 If Russia spent the state subsidies for nuclear energy on saving energy and alternative energy sources, the effect would be much better.

Quoted in "Brave Environmentalist Wins 'Green Nobel'" by Irina Titova, *The St. Petersburg Times* (Russia) *22 April 2008*

2 People can change the decisions of government.

Quoted in "Heroes of the Environment: Marina Rikhvanova" by Krista Mahr, *Time* 2008

3 It's huge, tremendous, mysterious, beautiful. It's 25 million years old, and every organism, every being, in Lake Baikal is a witness to this history.

Quoted in "Russian champion of Siberia's Lake Baikal has tough fight" by Megan K. Stack, *Los Angeles Times 18 January 2009*

4 We are preventing them from doing very quietly what they want to do very quietly.*

Ibid.

*Re: Vladimir Putin (1952– ; second president of Russia, 1999–2008; prime minister, 2008–) and his administration.

4595. Arundhati Roy (1961–)

1 Rahel froze. She was desperately sorry for what she had said. She didn't know where those words had come from. She didn't know that she'd had them in her. But they were out now, and wouldn't go back in. They hung about that red staircase like clerks in a government office.

Ch. 4, *The God of Small Things* 1997

2 Her belly button protruded from her satiated satin stomach like a domed monument on a hill. Chacko laid his ear against it and listened with wonder at the rumblings from within. Messages being sent from here to there. New organs getting used to each other. A new government setting up its systems. Organizing the division of labor, deciding who would do what.

Ibid.

3 The Great Stories are the ones you have heard and want to hear again. the ones you can enter anywhere and inhabit comfortably. They don't deceive you with thrills and trick endings. They don't surprise you with the unforeseen. They are as familiar as the house you lived in. Or the smell of your lover's skin. You know how they end, yet you listen as though you don't. In the way that although you know that one day you will die, you live as though you won't. In the Great Stories you know who lives, who dies, who finds love, who doesn't. And yet you want to know again.

Ch. 11, Ibid.

4 With a street-fighter's unerring instincts, Comrade Pillai knew that his straitened circumstances (his small, hot house, his grunting mother, his obvious proximity to the toiling masses) gave him a power over Chacko that in those revolutionary times no amount of Oxford education could match.
He held his poverty like a gun to Chacko's head.

Ch. 14, Ibid.

5 There is something precious about living in a place where literature actually affects lives, creates arguments, fierce debate—it isn't just a clubhouse activity. Living and writing from here [India] calls for a great deal of maturity. You can't just play at being a cool radical. You have to be aware of the consequences of what you say.

Quoted in "Arundhati Roy: A Forceful, Daring Debut" by Jordana Hart, *Ms.* (New York) *November/December 1997*

6 It is the writers, the poets, the artists, the singers, the filmmakers who can make the connections. . . . Who can translate cash-flow charts and scintillating boardroom speeches into real stories about real people with real lives. Stories about what it's like to lose your home, your land, your job, your dignity, your past, and your future to an invisible force. To someone or something you can't see. You can't hate. You can't even imagine.

Power Politics 2001

4596. Sarah Sewall (1961?–)

1 Breathing space for this Iraqi government may provide life support, but not a cure. Only a soup-to-nuts overhaul focused on carefully vetting and training personnel and holding them accountable—for years—could realistically stem the rot. Given limitations in U.S. capacity and will, this is not feasible.

"He Wrote the Book. Can He Follow It?" *The Washington Post 25 February 2007*

2 Petraeus* may provide the ultimate service to the troops and the nation—and seal his legacy—not by winning, but by speaking the truth about Iraq.

Ibid.

*David Howell P- (1952–), commanding general of U.S. Army.

3 We must renew America's image and show a new face to the world after eight years of alienating our allies and refusing to engage our enemies.

"The Judgment to Lead," *Daily Kos 26 November 2007*

4 We must proactively and patiently use all of our nation's strength—diplomatic, economic, and intelligence—to lead the world instead of relying solely upon military power because we ignored or rejected other options.

Ibid.

4597. Elma Softic-Kaunitz (1961–)

1 If the meaning of life is not the search for meaning, then what is it?

Sarajevo Days/Sarajevo Nights, Nada Conic, tr. 1996

2 They're exterminating the Muslims as though they were vermin or pestilence . . . setting living people on fire, roasting children alive, raping little girls, torturing men to death.

Ibid.

3 I want to remember everything. Simply so that nothing that human beings can do will ever surprise me again.

Ibid.

4 Truly it terrifies me to think that I may, by choosing to stay here, find myself in a foreign land. In an enemy land. In a very new world where there will be no place for me.

Ibid.

4598. Debbie Tomassi (1961–)

1 If the human body is a work of art . . . I must have been designed by a cartoonist.

Quoted in "A character named Gladys . . ." by Melinda Bargreen, *Seattle Times*, M1 *26 June 1994*

2 I don't need a man in my life . . . If I wanted something to sit around on the couch all day, I'd buy a couple of throw pillows.

Ibid.

4598.1. Kate Walbert (1961–)

1 The eyeliner she licked to draw has smudged in the slack, creased skin that fans her eyes, wrinkles she could not honestly attribute to laughter, or to a strong farm sun. Tennis, more likely. Or bourbon.

Our Kind 2004

2 She has never had any choice; it has been laid out for her, encoded in her cells like the pattern on the bone china handed down and handed down, again. Life as it will be for women: first the husband . . . and then the children.

Ibid.

3 Caroline's daughter, little Dorothy, is elsewhere, having reached the age of the disappeared—her voice shouting orders from behind the locked door of her bedroom or even standing present, her body a studded cast of her former self; if she is somewhere within it she is very, very deep.

Ch. 1, *A Short History of Women 2009*

4 "Mum starved herself for suffrage, Grandmother claiming it was just like Mum to take a cause too far."

Ibid.

4599. Leyla Zana (1961–)

1 Everywhere in the world women are ill treated by men but amongst the Kurds it is especially bad. A woman is not even treated as a servant, she is a thing, almost an animal.

Interview with Chris Kutschera, *The Middle East Magazine October 1993*

2 I no longer believe in the Turkish parliament. Its role is to cover up the action of the State, to conceal the misdeeds of the army and the police. The people who take the decisions in Turkey are the members of the national security council. Members of parliament are like notaries, they merely register the decisions. In fact, it is against everything I believe in, I do not have a voice. No, I will not run again.

Ibid.

4600. Naima Ahmed (1962–)

1 Everybody go to the bank [in Mogadishu] with big sack on their back like Santa Claus. They come out with their money, and somebody outside is waiting with a machine gun: BOOM boom boom! I say, Hello! OK, I don't need the bank money.

Quoted in "Naima's Song" by Paula Bock, *Seattle Times*, Pacific Northwest section *10 January 1999*

2 We're gonna sing songs about love, stories, make a show for the people because everybody, everybody has a break in their heart. When we sing, the people are gonna feel UP! Feel Good! Good! And we have power now. We have a heart now. We wake UP now!

Ibid.

4601. Elizabeth Alexander (1962–)

1 Even
my poems are lazy. I use
syllabics instead of iambs,
prefer slant to the gong of full rhyme,
write briefly while others go
for pages.

"Blues," St. 1, *Body of Life 1996*

2 The color of Washington's buildings represents who runs them: it is beautiful, what the family members have come to see, but it is also what they are up against and what they are not, for when they stop on the hot summer day for vanilla ice cream (more blinding whiteness) they are not allowed to eat at the counter.

"'Coming Out Blackened and Whole': Fragmentation and Reintegration in Audre Lorde's* *Zami* and *"The Cancer Journals," Power and Possibility: Essays, Reviews, and Interviews* (Poets on Poetry) *2007*

*See 2901.

3 I think, actually, that noticing and loving these shifts in diction are what made me a poet, growing up around my mother's Sugar Hill Harlem queen's English; my grandfather's Jamaican music and vocabulary, use of figurative language; my grandmother's soft, drawn-out Alabama vowels mixed with etymological wizardry and syntactic starch shaped by her teachers in the 1920s at Paul Laurence Dunbar High School in Washington, D.C.; my father's magnificent Harlem vernacular; the Yiddish inflections and improvisational suffixing and wry humor of my parents' Jewish New York City school-teachers; and then, how, how can I forget, the fluent Cackalacka spoken on the streets and front stoops of Washington, D.C., where I was reared in its eternal springtime.

"Dunbar* Lives!," Ibid.
*Re Paul Laurence D— (1872–1906), African-American poet, writer.

4 She gave the impeccable short lyric to the city, she went inside their homes, she wrought tableaux of their intimate lives, she venerated their intimate lives, she showed us the inside of a brown girl's head. She sings the song of the Southside of Chicago, that mighty city and its mighty black people.

"Ode to Miss Gwendolyn Brooks* (Ten Small Serenades)," Ibid.

*See 2281.

5 Say it plain, that many have died for this day. Sing the names of the dead who brought us here, who laid the train tracks, raised the bridges, picked the cotton and the lettuce, built brick by brick the glittering edifices they would then keep clean and work inside of.

"Praise song for the day," St. 8, Inaugural Poem *20 January 2009*

4602. Karrin Allyson (1962–)

1 Don't have to call Betty Crocker
Don't have to call Sara Lee
This man has done his homework
He makes his own recipe.

"My Sweet Home Cookin' Man," *My Sweet Home Cookin' Man* (album) *1994*

2 He's a chef of fine distinction—yes—
He comes complete with pots and pans
I've got a nick-name for him—I call him my
—Sweet home cookin' man.

Ibid.

4603. Jill Bialosky (1962?–)

1 How do you explain that once you've felt life inside you, the child has been permanently imprinted on the soul?

Essay, Quests for Parenthood in a High-Tech Age, Jill Bialosky and Helen Schulman, eds. 1998

2 Now I'm aware that a day can be a lifetime. In the three days that mark our son's life, he held his father's pinkie. He felt his mother caress his face.

Ibid.

3 She had awoken to his particular smell for over twelve years. And each morning she took it in newly, never tiring of the comfort and warmth of his body beside her.

Ch. 1, The Life Room 2007

4 Something has been brewing inside me and I can't look away from it any longer: I see myself as I truly am, rife with deep, complicated desires.

Ibid.

4604. Sarah Chayes (1962–)

1 "Taliban" is not the word most Kandaharis use for the militants mounting the current violence in southern Afghanistan. I have heard them called "enemies"—or sometimes, more poetically, "the spirits that come at night."

A Voice from Kandahar, "Care and Feeding of the Taliban," The New York Times Blog 9 July 2006

2 If we can't clean up Afghanistan, or effectively encourage its democracy outside our gates, at least we can take pleasure in creating something beautiful inside.

"Guns and Roses," Ibid. 17 July 2006

3 Opium eradication campaigns target the lowest rung of the opium economy, the struggling farmers. Yet well-known traffickers strut around town, flaunting their connections with senior officials.

"Why Farmers Grow Poppies," Ibid. 20 July 2006

4 Kandahar has been the cusp. You can see this place as an implacable barrier, or you can see it as the place where the barrier is pierced, a valve that channels a flow of people, ideas, merchandise and wisdom. That is the role I would choose for Kandahar and Afghanistan.

"Drawing Hope from History," Ibid. 1 August 2006

4605. Amy Chua (1962–)

1 In the numerous countries around the world that have pervasive poverty and a market-dominant minority, democracy and markets—at least in the form in which they are currently being promoted—can proceed only in deep tension with each other. In such conditions, the combined pursuit of free markets and democratization has repeatedly catalyzed ethnic conflict in highly predictable ways. This has been the sobering lesson of globalization in the last twenty years.

World on Fire 2002

2 That ethnicity can be at once an artifact of human imagination and rooted in the dark recesses of history—fluid and manipulable yet important enough to kill for—is what makes ethnic conflict so terrifyingly difficult to understand and contain.

Ibid.

3 To attain and maintain dominance on a global scale, coercion is simply too inefficient, persecution too costly, and ethnic or religious homogeneity, like inbreeding, too unproductive.

Day of Empire, How Hyperpowers Rise to Global Dominance—and Why They Fall 2007

4606. Nadia Comaneci (1962–)

1 I heard a lot of noise before I had a chance to see the scoreboard. And when I turned my head, I saw my number, 073, and under that there was 1.00. And I thought, "No, it can't be a one! I think I did better than one." I didn't know what that meant.* And after that, they put four digits, so now they can make a 10. I like to be remembered very simply, like the first perfect 10.

"100 Years of Great Women," ABC News Special with Barbara Walters 30 April 1999

*The scoreboard did not have enough digits to record a perfect score of 10, a first in Olympic history.

4607. Daljit Dhaliwal (1962–)

1 The whole thing about news and celebrity is bizarre. They're not natural bedfellows.

Quoted in "She's news to America" by Rachel Cooke, The Guardian (London) 23 June 2002

2 If you are somebody who takes the [news] industry seriously, I think it will take you seriously.

Ibid.

4608. Cindy Duehring (1962–1999)

1 Short-term profits can short-change our future. The economic cost of change is high, but the cost of ignoring chemical effects on human health is quietly but steadily growing even higher, creating a dangerous risk to the very underpinnings of society. A sustainable future includes human health.

Acceptance Speech, Right Livelihood Awards (Stockholm) 9 December 1997

2 Indoor air pollution is quietly taking a tremendous toll on society both economically and physically.

Ibid.

4609. Jennifer Egan (1962–)

1 Being somewhere but not completely: that was home for Danny. . . . All he needed was a cellphone or I-access, or both at once, or even just a plan to leave wherever he was and go someplace else really really soon.

The Keep 2006

2 "What's real, Danny? Is reality TV real? Are the confessions you read on the Internet real? . . . Who are you talking to on your cellphone? . . . We're living in a supernatural world, Danny. We're surrounded by ghosts."

Ibid.

4610. Nawal El Moutawakel (1962–)

1 Sport has given me so much that whatever I give back it will never be enough.

Quoted in "Nawal El Moutawakel is still a running light" by Gareth A. Davies, The Telegraph (London) 25 December 2007

2 My athletic race was the 400m hurdles but it has been a metaphor for my life. It has been up and down, there are sometimes

obstacles in the way. You have to get over the hurdles and keep running.

Ibid.

3 The school has changed, the kids have changed, the community has changed. Sport has taught the girls what to eat, how to stay clean, how to be aware of their body, how to dance—it is all part of their wider education.

If we can break the mould that inhibits so many young people, we can make a profound change both in my country and around the world. It's not a revolution, it's a celebration

Ibid.

4611. Anne Enright (1962–)

1 Neither childhood nor the future will diminish.

What Are You Like? 2000

2 We walked under a high, pale sky and we felt, in this landscape, so small, and there was no one to judge. That's all. There was an immense feeling of godlessness about it.

The Gathering 2007

3 The world will never know what has happened to you, and what you carry around as a result of it.

Ibid.

4 What do they want, men? It's the great mystery, isn't it? What men "want." And the damage they might do to get it.

"Until the Girl Died," *Yesterday's Weather 2008*

5 I think that many couples are happy in bed— strange, mismatched couples that you see on the metro; ugly ones too. What a great secret!

"Here's to Love," *Ibid.*

6 . . . the whole world has turned American.

"Yesterday's Weather," *Ibid.*

7 I don't want to drift away. I want to splatter.

"Felix," *Ibid.*

4612. Lisa Biank Fasig (1962–)

1 If a girl had a hammer, she'd probably use it to build some relationships.

"Sugar and spice and fantasy," *Providence Journal* (Rhode Island) *19 February 2003*

4613. Carolyn Ferrell (1962–)

1 I am a girl made out of brown peel, not iron and steel.

Don't Erase Me 1997

2 You could say that the fun stopped when I hit the end of my teenage years at fourteen.

Ibid.

4614. Isabel Fonseca (1962–)

1 Nostalgia is the essence of Gypsy song, and seems always to have been. But nostalgia for what? Nostos is the Greek for a "a return home"; the Gypsies have no home, and, perhaps uniquely among peoples, they have no dream of a homeland. Utopia—ou topos—means "no place." Nostalgia for utopia: a return home to no place. O lungo drom. The long road.

Bury Me Standing 1995

2 Walking downtown towards the wreck, I pause at Canal Street and think how much more representative this strip is of our city and our world than the twin towers. It is teeming with gadgets and bargains and, of course, life. Groaning from stores and laid out on the pavement it's all here: the some-of-what-you-fancy and the who'd'a' thunk it, the rip-off designer gear, the dozens of different kinds of hinges, the dazzling array of plumbers' "jewellery," the treasure trove of junk that is the Chinese department store; the world's biggest paint store, the smell of a dozen different cuisines cooking right here and now; red, white and blue T-shirts and flags in all sizes for sale. For every odd item there is an odd buyer: the exoticism and the internationalism are overwhelming.

"Back to the harsh reality," *The Guardian* (London) *11 October 2001*

3 Jean plunged the prawns into the boiling water and watched as they turned, almost instantly, from gray to pink. That must be what it's like, she thought. Having an affair.

Attachment 2008

4 But if I moved here would I stop feeling homesick? Probably not. It's more an idea than anything else. Now New York is here whenever I want it, and that's probably ideal. It's handy living in the wrong place.

Quoted in "A Novelist With a Story Attached" by Charles McGrath, *The New York Times 20 April 2008*

5 One of the lucky things about living with another writer is that they really understand what it's like to be preoccupied . . .

Ibid.

4615. Jodie Foster (1962–)

1 . . . my mother Brandy . . . taught me that all my finger paintings were Picasso's and that I didn't have to be afraid. And, mostly, that cruelty might be very human, and it might be very cultural, but it's not acceptable.

Acceptance Speech, Academy Awards *1989*

2 Ninety-five percent of women's experiences are about being a victim. Or about being an underdog, or having to survive . . . women didn't go to Vietnam and blow things up. They are not Rambo.

p. 19, *The New York Times Magazine 6 January 1991*

3 Normal is not something to aspire to, it is something to get away from.

Quoted by James J. Mapes, "Quantum Leap Thinking," *Brooks Community Newspapers* (Norwalk, Conn.) *January 2005*

4615.1. Lisa Gaeta (1962–)

1 YOU are the only one who can defend your life; if you don't think your life is important enough, why should anyone else?

IMPACT Personal Safety (ImpactPersonalSafety.com) *n.d.*

4616. Galina Gorchakova (1962–)

1 They (the women in Puccini's* operas) are disposed to take their fate in their own hands, whereas Verdi** heroines tend to surrender themselves to it. Of course, in Puccini's day the emancipation of women was beginning, and this made a huge difference to the way women came to be perceived.

(p. 100), Quoted in *Diva, The New Generation: The Sopranos and Mezzos of the Decade Discuss Their Roles* by Helena Matheopoulous *1998*

*Giacomo Puccini, Italian operatic composer (1858–1924). **Giuseppe Verdi, Italian composer (1813–1901).

4617. Faezeh Hashemi Rafsanjani (1962–)

1 In most of the Islamic world, women have cultural problems. They are regarded as a commodity, often forced into domesticity. For Iranian women, the values have changed.
"Iran Offers an Islamic Way to Improve the Lot of Women,"
The New York Times 21 December 1994

2 As the progressive trend of Olympism goes on, 500 million Moslem women are ignored because they maintain the moralities as stated in their holy religion Islam. This isolation is in contrast to the Olympic movement. There has been nothing done to help include Moslem ladies during the past 100 years of IOC activities. You can no longer neglect 500 million Moslem ladies of the world.
Address, World Conference on Woman and Sport (Lausanne, Switzerland) *1996*

3 The growing number of women who choose to wear the veil are actually being radical, not kowtowing to some patriarchal tradition. They are choosing to defy our western sexualised customs by not flaunting their bodies. They may not choose to wander about in mini skirts and high heels, but that doesn't mean they wag their finger at young women who do.
"Drawing a veil over choice. . . ," *Press and Journal, The Aberdeen* (UK) *20 December 2006*

4618. Bernice L. Hausman (1962–)

1 Gender was originally produced as a theoretical concept to guide clinicians treating intersexual subjects whose physiological sex transgressed the expected binary opposition between male and female. The identification of a gender role aided the clinician in designating a correct sex to which to assign the patient.
Changing Sex: Transsexualism, Technology, and the Idea of Gender 1995

4619. Lisa P. Jackson (1962–)

1 When it comes to the auto industry, the E.P.A.* apparently is the Emissions Permissions Agency.
Oft quoted public remark** *December 2007*
*Environmental Protection Agency. **In response to the Bush (George W. B-, 1946– , Am. politician; 43rd president of the United States, 2001–09) administration's attempt to prevent states from enacting tougher fuel efficiency standards.

4620. Dawn Johnsen (1962–)

1 . . . whenever any government or people act lawlessly, on whatever scale, questions of atonement and remedy and prevention must be confronted. And fundamental to any meaningful answer is transparency about the wrong committed.
"Restoring Our Nation's Honor," Slate.com *18 March 2008*

2 I'm afraid we are growing immune to just how outrageous and destructive it is, in a democracy, for the President to violate federal statutes in secret.
"NYT? What's Bush's* Excuse for Keeping Law Violations Secret?," Slate.com *27 March 2008*
*George W. B- (1946–), Am. politician; 43rd president of the United States (2001–09).

3 But we must regain our ability to feel outrage whenever our government acts lawlessly and devises bogus constitutional arguments for outlandishly expansive presidential power.
"Outrage at the Latest OLC Torture Memo," Slate.com *3 April 2008*

4 . . . recall that the last President who took the view that "when the President does it that means that it is not illegal" was forced to resign in disgrace.*
Ibid.
*Richard M. Nixon - (1913–94), 37th U.S. president.

4621. Jacqueline Joyner-Kersee (1962–1998)

1 Ask any athlete: we all hurt at all times. I'm asking my body to go through seven different tasks. To ask it not to ache would be too much.
Quoted in "Regal Masters of Olympic Versatility" by Tom Callahan, *Time 19 September 1988*

2 Jumping has always been the thing to me. It's like leaping for joy. . . .
Ibid.

3 I don't think being an athlete is unfeminine. I think of it as a kind of grace.
Ibid.

4 What Babe* did, she was able to capture the world with her talent. . . . Babe opened the door, and Wilma** continued to push the door open a little further.
"100 Years of Great Women," *ABC News Special with Barbara Walters 30 April 1999*
*Babe Didrickson; see 2218. **Wilma Rudolph, see 3226.

4622. Ginu Kamani (1962–)

1 "A modern girl. And how do you propose to find a man on your own?"
Daya narrowed her eyes and sneered, "By kidnapping and raping him, how else?" She cut into her samosa with an exaggerated swing of her knife, then licked the blade clean.
"Just Between Indians," *Junglee Girl 1995*

2 I am feeding her with the only food I can give. Blood and milk.
"Shakuntala," Ibid.

3 When I grow up I will smell the meat on men and the smell will keep me hungry.
"The Smell," Ibid.

4623. Julia Spicher Kasdorf (1962–)

1 We do not drink; we sing. Unaccompanied on Sundays, those hymns in four parts, our voices lift with such force that we lift, as chaff lifts toward God.
"Mennonites," l.l., *Sleeping Preacher 1992*

2 Aging,
our bodies collect wrinkles and scars
for each place the world would not give
under our weight.
"First Gestures," St. 2, *Eve's Striptease 1998*

3 As a gosling will claim for a parent whatever barn cat wanders into view, I fixed my gaze on the land that had fed, sheltered, worried, and buried the bodies of my ancestors for generations.
Ch. 1, *The Body and the Book: Writing from a Mennonite Life 2001*

4 As the infant learns her name from others, so we continuously depend on others to give us information about ourselves . . .
Ch. 6, Ibid.

4624. Peggy Liu (1962–)

1 It's the do-good, save-the-world, on-the-edge, it's-OK-nobody-has-figured-it-out-before mentality.
> Quoted in "China: A clean-tech gold rush?" by John Boudreau, *San Jose Mercury News 18 June 2007*

2 China doesn't have an energy policy problem, rather, it has an energy workforce problem. We can have all the solar panels we need free of charge and that will not be enough if we don't have the necessary skilled people to install these systems and maintain them. So, we believe that people matter . . . Education and skills building are very important.
> "Energy Efficiency: Getting more JUCCCE* per unit of GDP," The Green Leap Forward (greenleapforward.com) *25 June 2008*

*Joint US-China Cooperation on Clean Energy.

3 [I want to teach big business] how to make green by going green.
> *Forecast Earth*, The Weather Channel *2008*

4625. Marisa Acocella Marchetto (1962?–)

1 "You chant for inner peace. I'm chanting for a development deal."
> Cartoon caption, *The New Yorker 17 August 1998*

2 "Believe me when I tell you that I'm not that honest."
> Ibid. *5 March 2001*

3 "He's exactly the kind of man I've always wanted to change."
> Ibid. *5 August 2002*

4 "How stylish is that Pucci headwrap. Maybe I should've gotten the heavier chemo."
> "Cancer Vixen," *Glamour April 2005*

4626. Fanta Régina Nacro (1962–)

1 An African female filmmaker works in a society where women occupy a certain traditional position. So when a woman makes a film, people will gossip, and spread lies about her film. I still have not overcome these difficulties, but film is my passion and when I decided to become a filmmaker, I knew I would face these challenges.
> Quoted in "Festival Brings Attention to Female Filmmakers' Challenges in Africa" by Phuong Tran, voanews.com *28 February 2007*

4627. Taslima Nasrin (1962–)

1 During these days in hiding I felt I was dying every moment. I was not allowed to use the telephone, and I lived in a dark room. . . . It was like living in a jail cell or in exile.*
> Quoted in "Bangladesh writer surrenders" by Faris Hossaid (AP), *Seattle Times 4 August 1994*

*Bangladesh Islamic fundamentalists called for Nasrin's execution for suggesting the Koran be revised.

2 Every religion oppresses women. I talk about the Koran because I know this book best. It allows for torture and other mistreatment, especially for women. And I despise the Sharia laws. They cannot be changed. They must be thrown out, abolished.
> Quoted in "Writer with price on her head . . ." by Barry Bearak, *Seattle Post-Intelligencer 28 October 1998*

3 Whom she will approach to ask back these days for?
Facing darkness the poet ponders
Who will restore sunrays into her life?
Who is there to bring her back the song of life?
> "Was a poet ever kept in house arrest?," St. 4, Faizul Latif Chowdhury, tr., *The Statesman 20 January 2008*

4628. Rosie O'Donnell (1962–)

1 Lucille Ball* paved the way for every female performer, I think, today. You have to honor those who came before you and give a hand to those who are coming up after you, I think. Because we're all in it together.
> "100 Years of Great Women," *ABC News Special with Barbara Walters** 30 April 1999*

*See 2150. **See 2687.

4629. Anita Renfroe (1962–)

1 Everything is not going to get fixed and healed in this lifetime. That's what Heaven is for.
> *If It's Not One Thing, It's Your Mother 2006*

2 Each day you have a choice—hilarity or insanity.
> Stand-up routine, Women of Faith conference *2007*

3 Make a friend
Don't forget to share
Work it out
Wait your turn
Never take a dare
Get along
Don't make me come down there
> "Total Momsense" (to the tune of "The William Tell Overture") *2007*

4 Get an A, Get the door
Don't get smart with me
Get a Grip
Get in here I'll count to 3
Get a job
Get a life
Get a PhD
> Ibid.

5 I don't even know what the term "conservative" means anymore. It's become politicized to the point that it is almost synonymous with "Please check your brain at the door." It's almost like if you're an evangelical, you immediately get lumped in with the religious right or the fundamentalists.
> "Did You Hear the One About the Christian Comedian?" by Mimi Swartz, *The New York Times Magazine 24 February 2008*

6 The "William Tell" song took 24 years to live and two hours to make it rhyme.
> Ibid.

4630. Alice Sebold (1962–)

1 Dead or alive, a mother or the lack of a mother shaped one's whole life.
> *The Almost Moon 2007*

4631. Michelle Shocked (1962–)

1 If love was a train
I think I would ride a slow one
One that would ride thru the night

Making every stop
If love was a train
I would feel no pain and
I would never get off
    "If Love Was A Train," St. 1, *Short Sharp Shocked* (album) *1988*

2   Send me a dozen long stemmed roses
I'll tell you what I will do
I'll bend them into a crown of thorns
Then send them right back to you
    "On the Greener Side," *Captain Swing* (album) *1989*

3   The secret of a long life is knowing when it's time to go.
    "The Secret of a Long Life," *Campfire Tapes* (album) *1992*

4   You've got to learn some day my friend
That the means ain't justified by the ends
Sometimes you win sometimes you lose
But one thing will never change
It's how you play the game
    "How You Play the Game," *Don't Ask Don't Tell* (album) *2005*

4632. Nancy Sutley (1962–)

1   Cities are the first responders. If climate change causes more local forest fires, we have to deal with that on a city level. We can't afford to wait for national or international action.
    Interview, worldchanging.com *2007*

4633. Vesna Terselic (1962–)

1   For kids violence is not something repelling in itself, but comes mostly as part of the story about "winners and losers." Their levels of sensitivity regarding violent acts of kids and adults is then challenged. With diminished sensitivity there also comes the accepting of severe murder, torture and mutilation as something acceptable—just because of the simple fact that this happens so often.
    Acceptance Speech, Right Livelihood Awards (Stockholm) *9 December 1998*

2   Who can afford not to deal with violence? Who can afford to close their ears when a neighbour is beating his wife? Who can afford to look on while refugees are being bombed in Kosovo? Who can afford not to act when a woman in Stockholm does not dare to walk out of her house after dark? Who can afford to look on silently when ancient forests are destroyed in order to satisfy our consumer passion?
    Ibid.

3   Women are usually the first to go in to risk communication and who dare to do such things in order to rebuild the broken links in society.
    Ibid.

4634. Harriet A. Washington (1962?–)

1   In the South, rendering black women infertile without their knowledge during other surgery was so common that the procedure was called a "Mississippi appendectomy."
    Medical Apartheid: The Dark History of Medical Experimentation on Black Americans From Colonial Times to the Present 2006

2   First of all, it's important to understand that there was a scientific animus called "scientific racism," which at that time was simply science, and it posited that black people were very,

very different from whites, medically and biologically. And this provided a rationale and an underpinning not only for the institution of slavery—slavery probably could not have persisted if there hadn't been this medical underpinning—but also for the use of blacks in research.
    Interview by Amy Goodman* and Juan Gonzales, *Democracy Now!* (TV/radio news; democracynow.org) *19 January 2007*
    *See 4408.

4635. Naomi Wolf (1962–)

1   We are in the midst of a violent backlash against feminism.
    The Beauty Myth 1990

2   To ask women to become unnaturally thin is to ask them to relinquish their sexuality.
    "Hunger," Ibid.

3   The beauty myth moves for men as a mirage; its power lies in its ever-receding nature. When the gap is closed, the lover embraces only his own disillusion.
    "Sex," Ibid.

4   Pain is real when you get other people to believe in it. If no one believes in it but you, your pain is madness or hysteria.
    "Violence," Ibid.

5   Women have face-lifts in a society in which women without them appear to vanish from sight.
    Ibid.

6   There are and always have been two different approaches within feminism. One—"victim feminism," as I define it—casts women as sexually pure and mystically nurturing, and stresses the evil done to these "good" women as a way to petition for their rights. The other, which I call "power feminism," sees women as human beings—sexual, individual, no better or worse than their male counterparts—and lays claim to equality simply because women are entitled to it.
    Fire With Fire, The New Female Power and How It Will Change the 21st Century 1993

4636. Suha Arafat (1963–)

1   Let it be known to the honest people of Palestine that a gang of would-be inheritors are coming to Paris. You have to understand the scope of this conspiracy. I tell you, they are trying to bury alive Abu Amr.*
    "Arafat's Wife Now His Gatekeeper" by Laura King, *Los Angeles Times 9 November 2004*
    *Abu Amr was the nom de guerre of Yasser Arafat (1929–2004), first president of the Palestinian National Authority (1996–2004).

2   Every beautiful flower ends up surrounded by weeds.
    Ibid.

4637. Sandy Carter (1963–)

1   The space of "free time" is where the physical and emotional damage of work is repaired, the place where people relieve all the piled up unmet needs of rest, fun, creativity, critical thinking, and social connection. In sum, leisure is the location of a struggle to become more fully human.
    "Pop Music and the Left," *Zeta Magazine October 1988*

2   Seeing the world today involves multiple perspectives and requires not just data but insight from multiple angles.
    Ch. 1, *The New Language of Marketing 2.0 2009*

3   Globalization means that companies have to learn to be global AND local.

Ch. 2, Ibid.

4   Serious gaming is no longer an oxymoron.

Ch. 15, Ibid.

4638. Alison Leigh Cowan (1963?–)

1   Wall Street, where enough is never enough.

"Divorce, Wall Street Style," *The New York Times* 22 January 1989

2   What began four years ago as a tiny, grass-roots experiment to beautify the unsightly boxes that control traffic signals around town has become an unexpectedly impressive public art collection, with head-turning installations cropping up constantly to transform drab streetscapes into outdoor galleries.

"On Traffic-Signal Boxes, Art That Stops Traffic," *The New York Times* 25 November 2006

4639. Connie May Fowler (1963?–)

1   But Rose said, "My husband always says what people don't know won't hurt them."

I paused from my cleaning for a second. "Well, ma'am, my mama always said what people don't know may very well come up and bite them on the butt."

Ch. 1, Sugar Cage 1992

2   Could it be that my deep yearning was caused by a sadness bred in the womb, a dark past we're helpless to undo or make right, a history we have no memory of once we're birthed into this world? Are there events so ancient and awful that our fresh lives are spoiled even before the cord is cut, so we keep craving?

Ch. 1, Before Women Had Wings 1996

3   All evidence of him kaput, except for me—that part of him she couldn't erase. My presence was a constant, painful annoyance, the rock in the shoe that wouldn't let her forget.

But she tried. By God, did she ever.

Ch. 1, Remembering Blue 2000

4   Mother viewed anything remotely associated with the English language as a mortal sin—grammar, spelling, literature, punctuation. That's because in the arms of a good book, I could be lost to the world for days.

Ibid.

5   So come visit before you get involved in all your books and God again. Besides, you know as well as I do, God isn't up there. She left Boston ages ago.

The Problem with Murmur Lee 2005

4640. Glenda Elizabeth Gilmore (1963?–)

1   The South could remain the South only by chasing out some of its brightest minds and most bountiful spirits, generation after generation.

Gender and Jim Crow: Women and the Politics of White Supremacy in North Carolina, 1896–1920 1996

2   African American women embraced southern white progressivism, reshaped it, and sent back a new model that included black power brokers and grass roots activists . . . a feat they accomplished without financial resources, without the civic protection of their husbands, and without publicity.

"Diplomatic Women," *Ibid.*

4641. Jane Kamensky (1963–)
Also see Jill Lepore, 4725:2–4.

1   Increasingly after 1789, the proper deployment of the spoken word would be understood less as a way of dividing the saved from the damned or the criminal from the law-abiding than as a code distinguishing the refined from the vulgar.

Governing the Tongue: The Politics of Speech in Early New England 1998

2   . . . we have accepted, even embraced, the debasement of public discourse.

Ibid.

3   The gospel of ascent seeped into every sphere of life in the early republic, from farm house to schoolhouse to courthouse to countinghouse to meetinghouse. And wherever it touched, aspiration took shape. In the slaveholding south and the rural north and the ever-expanding western backcountry, aspiration pushed relentlessly at the horizontal: a hunger for more acres, father shores. But in the coastal port towns—especially in older, tightly bounded cities like Boston—the axis of aspiration was vertical.

Prologue, The Exchange Artist: A Tale of High-Flying Speculation and America's First Banking Collapse 2008

4642. Rita Katz (1963–)

1   The leadership of al-Qaeda* is very concerned about the wide support that Obama has been receiving from Arab and Muslim countries. To combat this threat, al-Qaeda has embarked on a propaganda campaign against Obama, not only by linking him to the policies of the Bush administration, including the occupation of Iraq and Afghanistan, but also by accusing him of actions in which he had no part.

Quoted in "To Combat Obama,** Al-Qaeda Hurls Insults" by Joby Warnick, *The Washington Post* 25 January 2009
*(a.k.a. al-Qaida) Islamist group founded ca. 1988 that has attacked civilian and military targets in various countries. **Barack O— (1961–), 44th president of the United States (2009–).

4643. Marian Keyes (1963–)

1   February the 15th is a very special day for me. It is the day I gave birth to my first child. It is also the day my husband left me. As he was present at the birth I can only assume the two events weren't entirely unrelated.

Watermelon 1998

2   Himself likes football. That's because he's a man. I don't like football. That's because I'm a woman. Although I pretend I like it. That's because I'm a modern woman.

Under the Duvet 2001

3   I hate jazz and make no bones about it. What's wrong with a rhythm? I want something I can tap my foot to without seeming as if I'm trying to send a message in Morse code.

Ibid.

4   Historically, the concerns of women wanting to talk about relationships and emotions were dismissed. Just because these things are important to women, men have made it their business to laugh at them or roll their eyes and say something like "You girls!" in that indulgent way of theirs. It's that whole thing of "women gossip, men talk," isn't it?

Quoted in "Be girly, live longer" by Lisa Reich, *The Telegraph* (London) 12 August 2004

4644. Jenny Kitzinger (1963–)

1 Assertiveness training is a start but it is not a solution . . . training individuals to be assertive . . . is no more "preventative" of child sexual abuse that building nuclear bunkers is "preventative of nuclear war."
"Defending Innocence: Ideologies of Childhood," *Feminist Review,* No. 28 *Spring 1988*

2 The twin concepts of innocence and ignorance are vehicles for adult double standards. A child is ignorant if she doesn't know what adults want her to know, but innocent if she doesn't know what adults don't want her to know.
"Who Are You Kidding?: Children, Power and the Struggle Against Sexual Abuse," *Constructing and Reconstructing Childhood,* A. James and A. Prout, eds. *1990*

3 The tenaciousness of terms such as slag [and other derogatory terms for "promiscuous" women] speak, in part, of the continuing absence of a discourse of female desire . . . But also reflects . . . the absence of a discourse about power.
"I'm Sexually Attractive But I'm Powerful": Young Women Negotiating Sexual Reputation, *Women's Studies International Forum* 18(2): 187–196 *1995*

4645. Julie Krone (1963–)

1 I've been in one Derby, and this is my third Belmont. But I've never thought of the fact that I haven't won a Triple Crown race. I'm not like that. I always look at the sunshine of things.*
Quoted in *The New York Times 6 June 1993*
*Said before she won the prestigious Triple Crown.

2 His nature just speaks to me. I didn't want him too far back to get dirt in his face, to get discouraged.*
Ibid.
*Re Colonial Affair, the horse with which she won the Triple Crown.

Quoted in *The New York Times Magazine 15 July 1993*

3 I don't think the question needs to be genderized.* It would feel great to anyone. But whether you're a girl or a boy or a Martian, you still have to go out and prove yourself again every day.
*Re: being the first woman jockey to win the Triple Crown.

4646. Naomi Levy (1963–)

1 But how many of us ever enter into *real* rest—not going on vacations or spending time on hobbies but practicing a regular discipline that can change our very selves?
To Begin Again: The Journey Toward Comfort, Strength and Faith in Difficult Times 1998

2 Celebrating a Sabbath day is a way to take one day out of each week and live it differently. In peace. It is not only a time to stop work, it is also a time to stop thinking about work. It is not a restriction, it is a freedom.
Ibid.

4647. Leisa D. Meyer (1963?–)

1 Women's entrance into the military raised questions about exactly what a "woman" is, what a "soldier" is, and what a "female soldier" could possibly be.
Creating G.I. Jane: Sexuality and Power in the Women's Army Corps During World War II 1998

4648. Michele Obama (1963–)

1 I wanted to have a career motivated by passion and not just money.
Quoted in "After Attacks, Michelle Obama Looks for a New Introduction" by Michael Powell and Jodi Kantor, *The New York Times 18 June 2008*

2 Home never feels dangerous.
Ibid.

3 Barack* will never allow you to go back to your lives as usual—uninvolved, uninformed.
Ibid.
*Her husband, Barack O- (1961–), 44th U.S. president.

4 Barack and I were raised with so many of the same values: that you work hard for what you want in life; that your word is your bond and you do what you say you're going to do; that you treat people with dignity and respect, even if you don't know them, and even if you don't agree with them.
Speech, Democratic National Convention (Chicago) *25 August 2008*

5 All of us driven by a simple belief that the world as it is just won't do—that we have an obligation to fight for the world as it should be.
Ibid.

6 I wanted to be able to bring what I learned to a broader base of people. And what better way to do it than to plant a vegetable garden in the South Lawn of the White House?
Quoted in "Obamas to Plant Vegetable Garden at White House" by Marian Burros, *The New York Times 19 March 2009*

7 I love clothes. First and foremost, I wear what I love. That's what women have to focus on: what makes them happy and what makes them feel comfortable and beautiful.
Quoted by Andre Leon Talley, *Vogue March 2009*

8 We learned in our household that there was nothing you couldn't talk about and that you found humor in even some of the toughest times. I want to bring that spirit of warmth, openness, and stability to my task.
Ibid.

9 This new policy [of the U.S. Mission to the United Nations] recognizes that America's future is intricately linked to the rest of the world, that the threats facing the global community know no borders, and no single country can tackle them alone.
Speech, U.S. Mission to the United Nations *6 May 2009*

10 There was never anything that I could imagine that I would need that they [my parents] wouldn't bend over backward to make sure that we had. There is just a sense of security that allows you to take risks. People think that it comes from wealth or generations of access and success, but it doesn't. The security of your parents' love really gives you the foundation to think that you can fly. And then you do.
"A Mother's Love: First Lady & Mom," *Essence May 2009*

4649. Suzan-Lori Parks (1963–)

1 BLACK MAN WITH WATERMELON. There is uh Now and there is uh Then. Ssall there is. (I bein in uh Now: uh Now bein in uh Then: I bein, in Now in then, in I will be. I was be too but that's uh Then that's past. That me that was be is uh me-has-been. Thuh Then that was be is uh has-been-Then too.

Thuh me-has-been sits in thuh be-me: we sit on this porch. Same porch. Same me. Thuh Then that's been somehow sits in thuh Then that will be: same Thens. I swing from uh tree. You cut me down and bring me back. Home. Here. I fly over thuh yard. I fly over thuh yard in all over. Them thens stays fixed. Fixed Thens. Thuh Thems stays fixed too. Thuh Thems that come and take me and thuh Thems that greet me and then them Thems that send me back here. Home. Stays fixed, Them do.

The Death of the Last Black Man in the Whole World 1990

4650. Ann Patchett (1963–)

1 Vice presidents were merely calling cards, things sent in lieu of things desired. They were replaceable, exchangeable. No war was fought or won over the inspiring words of a vice president . . .

Ch. 2, *Bel Canto 2001*

2 Warfare should not include cellular phones, it made everything seem less serious.

Ch. 3, Ibid.

3 Girls were like kittens in this way, if you got them right at the nape of their neck they went easily limp. Then he would whisper his suggestions, all the things they might do together, the wonderful dark explorations for which he was to be their guide. His voice traveled like a drug dripped down the spiraling canals of their ears until they had forgotten everything, until they had forgotten their own names, until they turned and offered themselves up to him, their bodies sweet and soft as marzipan.

Ch. 4, Ibid.

4 A daughter was a battle between fathers and boys in which the fathers fought valiantly and always lost.

Ibid.

5 There was such an incredible logic to kissing, such a metal-to-magnet pull between two people that it was a wonder that they found the strength to prevent themselves from succumbing every second. Rightfully, the world should be a whirlpool of kissing into which we sank and never found the strength to rise up again.

Ch. 8, Ibid.

6 Politicians would always be talking. They had been talking forever. If Tip had chosen to listen to them every time they chose to tell him something he would have gone out of his mind by the seventh grade.

Ch. 2, *Run 2007*

7 What a shame it would have been to miss God while waiting for Him.

Ch. 6, Ibid.

8 By telling them they had to stay home, Doyle had made them feel younger than they were, and that, oddly enough, made them think how nice it would be to be younger again. They had liked being the little boys. There was an ease in obedience, never thinking past their father's instruction.

Ch. 7, Ibid.

9 She was a swimmer, a gymnastics star, she was a superhuman force that sat outside the fundamental law of nature. Gravity did not apply to her. "Meditation in motion," her coach would say.

Ch. 9, Ibid.

4651. Alexandra Richie (1963?–)

1 . . . that bizarre mixture of cynicism, self-interest, political naiveté and sheer petulance which has, throughout [Berlin's] entire history, stood in the way of clear-headed political decisions.

Faust's* Metropolis: A History of Berlin 1998
*Reference to *Faust,* the play by German poet, novelist, and dramatist Johann Wolfgang von Goethe (1749–1832).

2 Rather than . . . claiming that Berlin was traditionally a city of immigrants they might protect its minorities from increasingly frequent attacks; rather than trying to remove the Soviet war memorial at Treptow they might ask why so little is known about the war-time treatment of Russian prisoners, over 3 million of whom were killed by the Nazis. Rather than . . . complain about how much is written about the concentration camps they might ask how it was that in 1991 Ravensbrück, only 35 miles from Berlin, barely escaped being transformed into a shopping mall and car park.

Ibid.

4652. Cecilia Rouse (1963?–)

1 Education is not a homogenous good. While competition for students may make schools more responsive to parents, this may be achieved through changes in other dimensions, such as religious education or nicer gymnasiums, rather than academic achievement.

"School Vouchers and Student Achievement: Recent Evidence, Remaining Questions" (6 August 2008), *Annual Review of Economics*, vol. 1 Lisa Barrow,* coauthor 2009
*See 4669.

2 The best research to date finds relatively small achievement gains for students offered education vouchers, most of which are not statistically different from zero.

Ibid.

3 There's some evidence if you look at an African-American and a white student with the same SAT scores coming into college, the [black] student's more likely to drop out. Why? They're coming in equally prepared. There's this great unknown the country hasn't come to terms with, which is the legacy of slavery and racism in society. It comes into play in a way we don't fully understand.

Quoted in "Celebrating Black History Month" by Harry Allen, *USA Weekend Magazine 11 February 2001*

4 I want an institution to [teach] the love of learning, the importance of independent thought, respecting what others believe and, therefore, promoting informed dialogue.

Ibid.

4653. Christina Schwarz (1963?–)

1 People want to hear everything, don't they? Spy every strap and pin and hem. It's not enough for them to run a finger along the scar or even to see the knife slice the skin, they must hear the blade purring against the whetstone.

Ch. 4, *Drowning Ruth 2000*

2 You have to be careful with your feelings, I think. It's a mistake to let them go just because they're summoned.

Ibid.

3 Keeping things whole, she reflected, rubbing the base of her thumb, demanded a great deal of concentration.

Ch. 14, Ibid.

4 But a sense that there might also exist some entirely different destination, one that he couldn't yet see but which lay just beyond the obscuring undergrowth of long habit and expectations, troubled him and kept him from moving forward. He had no idea how to hack through that foliage, nor whether whatever he uncovered would please him, but neither did he want to follow blindly the manicured course on which his feet were already set.

Ibid.

5 On a farm, the earth has secrets, and the weather has passions, but people don't matter so much.

Ch. 20, Ibid.

6 Of course, I knew it would take some application, but I imagined it would be the sort of labor demanded by the projects of my childhood, an absorbing concentration, more entertainment than work. Writing a novel, I believed, would be a way to achieve glittering success without the painful and humiliating apprenticeship other well-regarded careers required, and which I ought to have undergone in my twenties. Too late for that. I needed quick results.

All Is Vanity 2002

7 "But Ted, it's not like type, type, type, type, done! You make it sound like if only I applied myself I'd be sliding into the denouement around now."

Ibid.

4654. Helen Sharman (1963–)
1 There is very little difference between men and women in space.

Independent on Sunday (London) *9 June 1991*

4655. Lauren Slater (1963–)
1 . . . the blurry line between novels and memoirs. Everyone knows that a lot of memoirs have made-up scenes; it's obvious. And everyone knows that half the time at least fictions contain literal autobiographical truths. So how do we decide what's what, and does it even matter?

Lying, A Metaphorical Memoir 2000

4656. Jean M. Taylor (1963?–)
1 I fetched my car from the garage at City Hall and drove it to the garage near my office. A space alien analyzing my day would likely conclude that I was a drone that lived only to transport my queen, the Toyota, from one large cement box to another.

We Know Where You Live 1995

4657. Alice Thomson (1963–)
1 Inter-railers are the ambulatory equivalent of McDonalds, walking testimony to the erosion of French culture.

"Ticket to Ride the Rails of France," *Times* (London) *16 July 1992*

2 Once a prime minister has left office and given up his seat, he should be free to do whatever he wants as long as his snout isn't in the People's trough.

"Tony Blair* still works unpaid to save the world," *The Times* (London) *30 October 2008*
*(1953–), British prime minister, 1997–2007.

4658. Nayereh Tohidi (1963?–)
1 Iranians have become increasingly disillusioned with the "Islamist utopia" as they watch Islamists' efforts to eliminate corruption, drug addiction and prostitution fail and unemployment and class disparity rise. Ironically, large numbers of women learned to assert their political power during the Islamic Revolution—so they had rudimentary tools of resistance when the revolution's Islamic government promptly ordered sex segregation and mandatory veiling, and lifted restrictions on polygamy.

"Revolution? What's in it for them?," *The Los Angeles Times 31 July 2005*

2 Despite the hostility between the U.S. government and Iran, Iranians are among the most pro-American people in the world, and Iranian Americans make up more than one-third of the 3 million or so Iranians who live outside Iran.

Ibid.

3 In the midst of all the horrible and worrisome news of violence, war and massacres coming from the Middle East these days, it is news about women whose humane creativity, civic movements, and life-promoting and peace-seeking activities that bring hope for the future of this bloody and turbulent region.

"Beacons of hope," iranian.com, Taraneh Amin, tr. *23 December 2006*

4 . . . the women's movement has neither the intention of overthrowing the government, nor of seizing the state power. They reach beyond governments and aim at transforming the dominant cultural, social, economical, and political relations to achieve greater equality.

Ibid.

5 Just as slavery was once considered a natural and even divinely ordered phenomenon, but today belongs to a dark and embarrassing chapter of history, the era of patriarchy and sexism (in modern as well as traditional pre-modern forms) will come to an end sooner or later.

Ibid.

4659. Nualnoi Treerat (1963?–)
1 Those who put the government into power and those who end its life are not the same people.

Address, Institutions, Political Power and Rent-Seeking in Thailand, JSPS-NRCT Core University Program Workshop (Kyoto, Japan) *12–13 March 2007*

2 Concentration of wealth can easily lead to concentration of political power, and vice versa.

Ibid.

4660. Vanessa Williams (1963–)
1 [Botox is] a miracle drug, no cutting, nothing, and I love it. But I also want to act so I don't do it to freeze my face.

Interview, *The Barbara Walters* Special 24 February 2008*
*See 1929

2 The past just came up and kicked me.*

Quoted in *People 6 August 1984*
*Re loss of Miss America title after *Penthouse* publication of nude pictures.

4661. Cathy Young (1963–)
1 My discovery of America was also the discovery of a culture where female independence was celebrated; where it was not

a compliment to tell a woman she thought like a man; where it was not beneath a man's dignity to push a stroller; where an easy camaraderie seemed to reign between young men and women on college campuses.

Ceasefire! Why Women and Men Must Join Forces to Achieve True Equality 1999

2 This shift from women's rights to women's wrongs has far-reaching implications, besides making victimhood central to feminism.

Ibid.

4662. Dekha Ibrahim Abdi (1964–)

1 The participation in a peace process is not about the mathematics of numbers and percentages in relation to who is in majority or minority. It is about plurality, diversity, participation and ownership of all affected by the conflict . . .

Acceptance Speech, Right Livelihood Awards (Stockholm), 9 December 2007

2 It is not enough to work on your own Peace. In fact to sustain your peace you have the responsibility to work in your neighbour's house, in the next district.

Ibid.

3 I learnt that Peace is not an event, an end, but the peace is the way, though the journey is long and the road winding and difficult.

Ibid.

4663–4664. Leila Aboulela (1964–)

1 I like being part of a family, touching their things, knowing what they ate, what they threw in the bin. I know them in intimate ways while they hardly know me, as if I am invisible. It still takes me by surprise how natural I am in this servant role.

Ch. 10, *Minaret 2005*

2 *Sorry, no prams or pushchairs allowed, sorry, no dogs allowed, opening hours 9:30 till dusk.* In this country everything was labelled, everything had a name.

Ch. 1, *The Translator 2006*

3 She had given the child to Mahasen and it had not meant anything, nothing, as if he had not been once a piece of her, with her wherever she walked. She was unable to mother the child. The part of her that did the mothering had disappeared.

Ibid.

4 It had seemed strange for her when she first came to live here, all that privacy that surrounded praying. She was used to seeing people pray on pavements and on grass. She was used to praying in the middle of parties, in places where others chatted, slept or read.

p. 75, Ibid.

4665. Anne Applebaum (1964–)

1 If the nature of the Bolsheviks was mysterious, their leader, Vladimir Ilyich Ulyanov—the man the world would come to know by his revolutionary pseudonym, "Lenin"*—was even more so. During his many years as an émigré revolutionary, Lenin had been recognized for his brilliance, but also disliked for his intemperance and his factionalism. He picked frequent fights with other socialist leaders, and had a penchant for turn-

ing minor disagreements over seemingly irrelevant matters of dogma into major arguments.

Ch. 1, *Gulag: A History 2003*
*(1870–1924), Russian revolutionary; chairman of the Council of People's Commissars (1917–24).

2 In the early days, slovenliness, chaos, and disorder caused many unnecessary deaths. Even without outright sadism, the unthinking cruelty of guards, who treated their prisoners as domestic animals, led to much misery.

p. 88, Ibid.

3 It is often alleged that we now live in a thoroughly globalized world, a world where everyone knows everything in real time, where everyone has instant access to all information, where the man who answers Microsoft's help line is in Bangalore and the grapes at the Chevy Chase supermarket come from Chile. Yet even so, Washington—the metaphoric capital of this globalized world—still retains a streak of the small-town provincialism it had when I was a child.

"So Long, Washington (for Now)," *The Washington Post 24 May 2006*

4 . . . I'm not voting for McCain*—and, after a long struggle, I've realized that I can't—maybe it's worth explaining why, for I suspect there are other independent voters who feel the same. Particularly because it's not his campaign, disjointed though that has been, that finally repulses me: It's his rapidly deteriorating, increasingly anti-intellectual, no longer even recognizably conservative Republican Party.

Ibid.
*John Sidney McCain III (1936–), United States senator (R-AZ, 1987–) and Republican presidential nominee (2008).

4666. Yareli Arizmendi (1964–)

1 Let us not forget we're multiple personalities in a sense. We are Latino, but we're women. Being women we fall into one kind of discrimination, and being Latino we fall into another. Identity, I think, is multi-faceted.

Quoted in "A woman of the theater, a woman of film" by Fred Salas, *Motion Magazine 11 December 1999*

2 I always felt that I was born to be an actress in the sense that an actor is called upon to put her feelings at the service of making others understand the situation—think, but more than anything feel situations.

Ibid.

3 Latin America is a culture that is based on class—and it makes no bones about it.

Ibid.

4 How do you make the invisible, visible? You take it away.

A Day Without a Mexican (film,) Sergio Arau, co-writer *2004*

4667. Carol Azadeh (1964–)

1 Maybe more than one life is possible after all . . . if you have the courage to go after it.

"Bronagh," *The Marriage at Antibes 2000*

2 . . . surely life couldn't go full circle so quickly. Something else had to happen before she turned into one of the teaching instead of the taught.

Ibid.

3 . . . the forces of history or society can pick up your life and set it down impersonally, and this sometimes without your even having realized anything had been going on.

Ibid.

4 The past is not just another country, it's another culture.

"A Banal Stain," Ibid.

4668. Melody C. Barnes (1964–)

1 If we had a newly elected progressive President, below is the kind of State of the Union address he or she might give.

"My fellow Americans, let us tonight put aside our partisan interests and picture an America where citizens once again enjoy an open, honest, competent government. A government that turns away from reckless military adventures and concentrates on the genuine external threats we face as a nation. A government that works to ensure economic opportunity, affordable healthcare and a secure retirement for all."

"What a Progressive President Might Say," The Washington Post 22 January 2007

2 If we had a newly elected progressive President, below is the kind of State of the Union address he or she might give. . . .

"The potential for the United States to pursue a course of innovation that would create good, high-wage jobs has been largely abandoned, leaving our economy dangerously vulnerable to price shocks and upheavals that dampen economic growth and burden middle-class families with unpredictable gas and utility bills. It is time to change course."

Ibid.

3 If we had a newly elected progressive President, below is the kind of State of the Union address he or she might give. . . .

"In the area of science, I pledge to liberate our scientific community in its quest to improve the lives of people around the globe."

Ibid.

4 The best life advice I've received is also the best fashion advice: Be authentic. You shouldn't wear it just because it's in style or looks good on somebody else. You have to know who you are and honor that.

Quoted in "Ten Well Dressed Women: Melody Barnes" by Leslie Milk, The Washingtonian 1 October 2007

4669. Lisa Barrow (1964?–)
See Cecilia Rouse, 4652:1–2.

4670. Mairo Bello (1964?–)

1 Everyone in the bush . . . they have a radio around (their) arm. . . . It gives enlightenment to a lot of people. . . . It gets to people more than any other kind of media. Because the print media is for the educated . . . and the television media is for people who have lights in our community. It's not everywhere you go that you get electricity. . . .

"Nigerian Women Speak Out," Frontline World (pbs.org) January 2003

2 It's important to understand the dynamics of the culture and work within it. I told them 'I'm a foolish girl. I have no knowledge. I need your wisdom.'

Quoted in "The winning lawyer discusses death-by-stoning adultery case" by Linda Myers, Cornell Chronicle 6 May 2004

3 Case by case, we make a little difference, and little differences make the world a better place.

Ibid.

4 The more the authorities devise new strategies, the more sophisticated the traffickers become in running their trade.

"Nigeria: Porous Border Aids Human Trafficking," all.Africa. com 21 May 2008

5 The journey to women's health is not straightforward, and can be difficult for advocates, program planners, and beneficiaries alike. . . . We must ensure that girls and women can exercise their human rights, including their right to make informed and healthful choices about their sexuality and reproduction, without fear of violence or coercion.

International Women's Health Coalition ca. 2004

4671. Tracy Camp (1964–)
See Denise Gürer, 4409:1–6.

4672. Marina Carr (1964–)

1 GRANDMOTHER. There's two types of people in this world, from what I can make out: them that puts their children first and them that puts their lover first. And for what it is worth, the nine-fingered fisherman and myself belongs to the latter of these. I would gladly have hurled all seven of you down the slopes of hell for one more night with the nine-fingered fisherman and may I rot eternally for such unmotherly feelings.

The Mai 1994

2 There's the word, and there's the word processor.

Quoted in "A Playwright's Post-Beckett Period" by James Larity, The New York Times 3 November 1994

3 RED. D'ya know whah ud manes to be young. . . ? Do ya? Manes your slate is clane, manes the muck on your boots stays on your boots and don't sape up to your unploughed soul. Manes ya know . . . all abouh the dirty world, how and why men and women fall.

On Raftery's Hill 1999?

4673. Tracy Chapman (1964–)

1 I love you
is all that you can't say

"Baby Can I Hold You" (1982), Tracy Chapman (album) 1988

2 It won't do no good to call
The police
Always come late
If they come at all

"Behind the Wall" (1983), Ibid.

3 And those whose sole misfortune
Was having mountains o' nothing at birth.

"Mountains O' Things" (1987), Ibid.

4674. Chris J. Cuomo (1964–)

1 But which women's lives matter to feminism, and ought to matter in the creation of feminist sciences and technologies? Western feminism has itself been "local," disproportionately concerned with the interests of privileged European and American women. It has all but ignored the extent to which colonialism has fed the privileged at the expense of poor

women, women of color and women in Southern nations and cultures.

"Fertile hybrids," *The Women's Review of Books,* Vol. XVI, No. 3 *December 1998*

2 . . . both women and nature are considered and constructed as feminine, . . . [but] the inextricability of masculinity and femininity as concepts and as cultural products make it impossible to reclaim one without assuming the other . . .

Ch. 1, *Feminism and Ecological Communities: An Ethic of Flourishing 1998*

4675. Lisa W. Foderaro (1964?–)

1 In the job world, especially, clothes often say more than words. They can communicate confidence, attention to detail and creativity—or self-doubt and carelessness.

"First Impressions Can Have a Lasting Effect," *The New York Times 13 October 1985*

2 Amid their pride in their children's zeal for all things green, the grown-ups sometimes end up feeling like scofflaws under the watchful eye of the pint-size eco-police, whose demands grow ever greater, and more expensive.

"Pint-Size Eco-Police, Making Parents Proud and Sometimes Crazy," *The New York Times 9 October 2008*

4676. Kathy Freston (1964–)

1 Being part of the solution can be a whole lot simpler—and cheaper—than going out and buying a new hybrid. We can make a huge difference in the environment simply by eating a plant-based diet instead of an animal-based one.

"You Call Yourself a Progressive—But You Still Eat Meat?," *AlterNet.org 14 March 2007*

2 If we are to continue evolving—physically, emotionally, and spiritually—we really do have to look at how our dinner choices affect not only the environment but, even more importantly, the well-being (or intense suffering) of other creatures.

Ibid.

4677. Joanne Harris (1964–)

1 "Chocolate, I am told, is not a moral issue."

Chocolat 1998

2 People who know nothing of real magic imagine it to be a flamboyant process. . . . And yet the real business is very undramatic; simply the focusing of the mind toward a desired objective. There are no miracles, no sudden apparitions.

Ibid.

3 "There is a kind of sorcery in all cooking."

Ibid.

4 Wine talks; ask anyone. The oracle at the street corner; the uninvited guest at the wedding feast; the holy fool. It ventriloquizes. It has a million voices. It unleashes the tongue, teasing out secrets you never meant to tell, secrets you never even knew.

Ch. 1, *Blackberry Wine 2001*

5 Food was her nostalgia, her celebration, its nurture and preparation the sole outlet for her creativity.

Ch. 1, *Five Quarters of the Orange 2002*

6 But the past is a sly sickness. It may be carried on a breath of wind; in the sound of a flute; on the feet of a dancer.

Ch. 1, *Holy Fools 2005*

4678. Cynthia Hess (1964?–)

1 It was obvious that the size of your chest was in direct proportion to the size of your salary.

Quoted in *Newsweek 25 April 1994*

*Re her successful bid at declaring her 56FF breast implants a tax-deductible business expense.

4679. Maggie Jackson (1964?–)

1 The very bones of the apartment enable the fusion of home and work—a goal that Americans increasingly share.

Ch. 1, *What's Happening to Home: Balancing Work, Life and Refuge in the Information Age 2002*

2 How we build and design our homes speaks volumes about our identity and values.

Ibid.

3 As the lines fade between home and work, our innermost thoughts, our spiritual lives, and our social connections are increasingly ending up in the office.

Ch. 4, Ibid.

4 With our primary homes increasingly becoming public, frenzied places of busyness—headquarters or base camps of living—people are searching with a new urgency for a retreat. With the lines between work and home, public and private, strangers and intimates blurring, they are rediscovering the boundary of landscape as a shelter from the world.

Ch. 5, Ibid.

5 Banks, even big banks, go under. And now, once again, the popular wisdom that banks cannot fail has been temporarily replaced by the knowledge that banks can fail.

"Boom and bust: It's the American way," *The Los Angeles Times 20 July 2008*

4680. Christina Baker Kline (1964–)

1 "Did you ever do something—and you know that even if it didn't seem so weird at the time, someday it would change everything about you?"

Desire Lines 1999

2 I'm inclined to believe that the whole concept of a soul mate is like Sasquatch, the giant hairy ape-man of legend who turned out to be nothing more than a guy in a monkey suit running through a forest.

Ch. 1, *The Way Life Should Be 2008*

4680.1. Samira Al Kuwaiz (1964–)

1 In the beginning they are not used to seeing women in meetings here. In the beginning they don't even look at you, as a Saudi woman because they don't know how to deal with it. But later on, throughout the meeting, you see how it evolves, you see how they look at you, the look at you evolves. So you become a capable person more than you are a woman or a man.

Quoted in "Saudi Arabia's First Female CFO" by Lara Setrakian, *ABC News* (abcnews.go.com) *14 August 2008*

2 What we're doing, as women in the workforce, we are trying to ask for that change but we don't push for that change, because pushing for that change will end it for all of us. So what we are doing, we are in our own stride, in our own steady stride, we are pushing but very slowly.

Ibid.

3   Of course, being a working mother has its pros and it has its cons. You can't have everything. You can't be a complete working mother and put 100 percent in your work and you can't be a mother at home and a wife, and give all to your home. But what happens is, this equilibrium that I'm trying to reach, has given my daughters a kind of confidence in women.

Ibid.

4681. Courtney Love (1964–   )

1   We all get our glory
A little bit of fame
But there's no truth at the heart of any of it
Just the brilliance and the passion
And the bitterness remains
"Hold Onto Me," St. 3, *America's Sweetheart* (album) 2004

2   I'm overrated, desecrated
Still somehow illuminated
I know I've got a screw loose
"But Julian, I'm A Little Older Than You," St. 4, Ibid.

3   Well they say that rock is dead
And they're probably right
"Monologue," St. 1, Ibid.

4682. Jill Matthews (1964–   )

1   *Re the achievement of her championship:* Tell that to my in-laws. They say, big deal, so when am I getting pregnant?
Quoted in "Let Me Entertain You," *The Complete Idiot's Guide to Jewish History and Culture* by Rabbi Benjamin Blech
1999

4683. Martha S. McPhee (1964–   )

1   . . . I don't like to have a plan. I don't want to be pinned down. I like to wander, to drift from one notion to the next, from here to there and not know where there is.
Gorgeous Lies 2002

2   Somewhere in the deepest part of him, he wanted to be a part of the bigness of all that was America—big musicians and big poets and big plans and big trips and big presidents and big protests and big failures and big wars and big dreams.
L'America 2006

3   The illusion of immortality for an instant blooms, a beautiful flower, and everything that is here is here and all that is, truly is.
Ibid.

4   [He] . . . wanted to steal Beth, protect her from her dreams, make her his own. A thief, he had wanted to rob her of ambition and desire.
Ibid.

4683.1. Lynn Nottage (1964–   )

1   They say we are the renegades. We don't respect the rule of law . . . but how else do we protect ourselves against their aggression? How do we feed our families? They bring soldiers from Uganda, drive us from our land and make us refugees . . . and then turn us into criminals when we protest or try to protect ourselves. How can we let the government carve up our most valuable land to serve to companies in China?
Ruined (play) 2008

4684. Sarah Palin (1964–   )

1   Do you know the difference between a hockey mom and a pit bull? Lipstick.
Speech, Republic National Convention *27 August 2008*

2   Drill, baby, drill.
Ibid.

3   They're our next-door neighbors and you can actually see Russia from land here in Alaska, from an island in Alaska.
Interview with Katie Couric, *CBS News 25 September 2008*

4   . . . I know at the end of the day putting this in God's hands, the right thing for America will be done, at the end of the day on Nov. 4.
Ibid.

5   Teach both. You know, don't be afraid of information. . . . Healthy debate is so important and it's so valuable in our schools. I am a proponent of teaching both. And you know, I say this too as the daughter of a science teacher. Growing up with being so privileged and blessed to be given a lot of information on, on both sides of the subject—creationism and evolution.
Quoted in "'Creation science' enters the race" by Tom Kizzia,
Anchorage Daily News 27 October 2006

4685. Patricia Pearson (1964–   )

1   Women commit the majority of child homicides in the United States, a greater share of physical child abuse, an equal rate of sibling violence and assaults on the elderly, about a quarter of child sexual abuse, an overwhelming share of the killings of new-borns, and a fair preponderance of spousal assaults.
When She Was Bad: Violent Women and the Myth of Innocence 1997

2   New life announces itself as a mystery that a mother cannot solve.
Ch. 1, *Playing House 2003*

3   Life in a city as opportunistic and exuberant as New York always felt busy, even if nothing got done.
Ibid.

4   It is my job, my calling, my necessity and pleasure, to guide my two children through the shoals of a childhood filled with fast-flowing traffic and pedophiles, pesticide residues, asbestos-lined walls and lead-infused condiments to a safe footing on the shore of adulthood.
"Hemp Waffles: Betcha Can's Eat *Just One*," *Area Woman Blows Gasket: And Other Tales from the Domestic Frontier 2005*

4686. Lady Pink (1964–   )

1   Teenagers have lots of energy and are looking for something to do. Some kids turn to drugs or crime. I turned to art. I saw myself as an adventurer, a pioneer woman.
Quoted in "Lady Pink Graffiti with Feminist Intent" by Fern Siegel, *Ms.* (New York) *March/April 1993*

2   We were like sixties radicals, rebelling against the system. I was dodging bullets in the service of folk art, bringing art to the people.*
Ibid.

*Pink was the first female grafitti artist in the world to be exhibited.

3   If you're not harming anyone, all sexual preferences are cool.

Ibid.

4687. Susan E. Rice (1964–)

1   I swore to myself that if I ever faced such a crisis again, I would come down on the side of dramatic action, going down in flames if that was required.*

Article, *The Atlantic Monthly 2001*

*Re American policy toward Rwanda during the 1994 genocide.

2   To allow another state to deter the U.S. by threatening terrorism would set a terrible precedent. It would also be cowardly and, in the face of genocide, immoral.*

Testimony, Senate Foreign Relations Committee (Washington, D.C.) *11 April 2007*

*Re the genocide in Darfur perpetrated by Sudanese militia.

3   Still others insist that, without the consent of the U.N. or a relevant regional body, we would be breaking international law.* But the Security Council last year codified a new international norm prescribing "the responsibility to protect." It commits U.N. members to decisive action, including enforcement, when peaceful measures fail to halt genocide or crimes against humanity.

Ibid.

*Re the genocide in Darfur perpetrated by Sudanese militia.

4688. Christine Stevens (1964–)

1   Drum circles seem to tap into the primal need to share and support one another through one of the simplest and most beautiful ways to connect without words; music.

Ch. 1, *The Art and Heart of Drum Circles 2003*

4689. Stasa Zajovic (1964?–)

1   Has the body of a woman ever belonged to herself?

Ana's Land: Sisterhood in Eastern Europe, Tanya Renne,* ed.
1996

*See 4830.

4690. Lijia Zhang (1964–)

1   Yet I would have loved to have stayed on at school and later tried my luck entering university, as I was a good student. But I was tinghua too—obedient, the most desirable quality among Chinese children. Ting means listen and hua, words. Since I was little, I had been trained to listen to the words of parents, teachers and our Communist Party.

Socialism is Great! 2008

2   Privacy had no place in our society. After penetrating the factory gate, I had learnt that even one's period was not private. Once a month every woman reported to the hygiene room to face the "period police." If satisfied with the bloody evidence, the nurse would issue a pack of sanitary towels as part of a woman's welfare package; failure to bleed would invite a visit from the dreaded family planning officers.

Ibid.

4691. Helen Alfredsson (1965–)

1   To reach a point where you can really enjoy life, you need to find things out early. Do you know how many 55-year-old people are out there who haven't done anything but strive for success and money?

"One of a kind," *Golf Digest April 1999*

2   *Of an affair with a university soccer coach:* Very illegal. Isn't love more fun that way?

Ibid.

3   The harder you have it early, the tougher you get later.

Ibid.

4692. Andrea Barrett (1965–)

1   His people had a name for Zeke, a chain of soft syllables that meant *The One Who Is Trouble.*

The Voyage of Narwhal 1998

2   . . . there are continents and seas in the moral worlds, to which every man is an isthmus or an inlet, yet unexplored by him, but that it is easier to sail many thousand miles through cold and storm and cannibals . . . than it is to explore the private sea, the Atlantic and Pacific Ocean of one's being alone.

Ibid.

4693. Cassandra Quin Butts (1965–)

1   Barack* has an incredible ability to synthesize seemingly contradictory realities and make them coherent. It comes from going from a home where white people are nurturing you, and then you go out into the world and you're seen as a black person. He had to figure out whether he was going to accept this contradiction and be just one of those things, or find a way to realize that these pieces make up the whole

Quoted in *The New Yorker May 2007*

*B— Obama (1961–), 44th president of the United States (2009–).

4694. Christine Schuler Deschryver (1965?–)

1   The world should wake up and do something before it's too late, because maybe one day, we'll talk about women in Congo like a species that is in the process of disappearing.

Quoted in "A Conversation with Eve Ensler: Femicide in the Congo" by Michele Kort,* *Lumo, PB 17 September 2007*

*See 3982.

2   I don't want to compare, you know, problems we have in this world, but Congo, it started almost eleven years ago, and nobody's talking about this femicide, this holocaust. . . . Yeah, it's a femicide, because they are just destroying the female species, if I can talk like this, because can you imagine now—in Africa, woman is the heart of family. She is doing everything, babies, looking for food, looking for the whole family. And now they're destroying this resource.

Quoted in "They Are Destroying the Female Species in Congo" by Amy Goodmanm,* *Democracy Now!* (democracynow.org)
8 October 2007

*See 4408.1.

3   Darfur is nothing compared to what's going on in the Congo. My father was the founder of the National Park in Rwanda, which is home to rare silver back gorillas. During the war here, just one silver back was killed. And when it happened, within 48 hours millions in funding was sent to ensure the rest of the gorilla population was protected. Why isn't the same done with our women? I'll tell you why, because in the eyes of the international community animals have more value than humans in this part of the world.

Quoted in "The world continues to look away. Don't" by Brian O'Connell, *The Sidney Morning Herald 24 November 2007*

4   We've had so many celebrities passing through. They cried a lot but all they left behind was their business cards.

> Quoted in "The Vagina Monologues turns ten" by Karen Bartlett, *The Times* (London) *15 April 2008*

4695. Waris Dirie (1965–)

1   As we traveled throughout Somalia, we met families and I played with their daughters. When we visited them again, the girls were missing. No one spoke the truth about their absence or even spoke of them at all.

> *Desert Flower,* with Cathleen Miller *1998*

4696. Deborah Garrison (1965–)

1   a vamp on the rise through the ranks
of literary Gods and military men
who wouldn't stop at the President:
she'd take the Pentagon by storm
in halter dress and rhinestone extras.

> "An Idle Thought," *A Working Girl Can't Win 1998*

2   The good schoolgirl turns thirty,
forty, singing the song of time management
all day long, lugging the briefcase
home

> "The Second Child," *The Second Child 2007*

3   Goodbye, good boy.
What love, what sorrow,
to give you the heave-ho:
I'll have to wean you
starting tomorrow

> "Goodbye, New York," Ibid.

4   When I was unhappy
words slipped ceaselessly
from my pen,
arrows down the page,
tears run together,
running to tell.

> "Above the Roar," Ibid.

4697. Anna Giordano (1965?–)

1   The [rehabilitated birds] can't say thanks, but the best thanks is watching them fly free again.

> Quoted in "Making the Skies Safer" by Thomas Sancton, Time.com *13 March 2000*

2   If you witness something that is wrong, you can't close your eyes and turn your head. Your energy comes from the conviction that life is a treasure which nobody should destroy. Your will becomes the only thing that can turn hope into reality.

> Ibid.

4698. Evelyn Glennie (1965–)

1   I have perfect pitch, the ability to hear a note in my head and place it exactly in relation to other notes. And I learned to read music vertically, to look at the full score. If I'm playing a concerto, I must know what the clarinets and trumpets are doing. When I learn a piece of music, often I listen to it by placing a tape recorder between my knees and playing it.

> Quoted in "I Hear the Notes in My Head" by Gail Buchalter, *Parade Magazine 13 February 1994*

2   My deafness is something unique and I treasure it, and I don't want it to be taken away. I want to stay as I am. Sometimes, it has even helped me.

> Ibid.

3   People have the wrong idea about deafness. They think you live in a world of total silence, but that isn't the way it works.

> Quoted in "A Different Drummer" by Michael Walsh, *Time* (New York) *21 March 1994*

4   I don't think in terms of loud and soft. Instead I think of sounds as thin or fat, strong or weak. The amount of sounds you can create with just one cymbal are infinite.

> Ibid.

4699. Jennifer Michael Hecht (1965–)

1   The essence of the philosophical experience, the active verb of doing philosophy, is unlearning what you think you know.

> Ch. 1, *The Happiness Myth, Why What We Think Is Right Is Wrong: A History of What Really Makes Us Happy 2007*

2   We live in little cognitive comas. Or rather, we cavort in cognitive fields surrounded by electric fences: we all think we are free to go where we wish, but we are struck by a lot of pain when we try to think past our boundaries.

> Ibid.

3   Maybe we can stop feeling so conflicted about shallow American culture and recognize that we are lucky to have something shallow to share.

> Ch. 20, Ibid.

4700. Tracy E. Higgins (1965?–)

1   Although women have had the franchise now for over seventy-five years, few feminists (indeed perhaps few women) would conclude that women as a group have experienced the full measure of their potential political power.

> "Democracy and Feminism" (p. 110), *Harvard Law Review 8 1997*

2   Historically, the line between the home as private and the rest of civil and political society as public was defined by social norms as well as law, and that line was clearly gendered. Legislative classifications that excluded women from public activities ranging from lawyering to bartending to voting reinforced the notion that women's proper place was the private sphere of home and family.

> "Reviving the Public/Private Distinction in Feminist Theorizing," *Kent Law Review n.d.*

3   The deconstruction of the public/private dichotomy is elegant and powerful and addresses (albeit at a fairly abstract level) a broad range of feminist concerns. It exposes the way an apparently neutral concept like state action operates to entrench existing hierarchies of private power while simultaneously reinforcing the equation of private action with freedom. At the same time, the critique has yielded very few concrete results.

> Ibid.

4700.1. Lesley A. Hyatt (1965–)

1   Even before stepping onto the snow I heard the wind. A bellowing breath tinged with a sweet tinkling—the air blowing granules of snow across the treeless landscape. To step into that holy sound was to step into a kind of simultaneous ecstasy and misery: The wild exhilaration of the highest height; the

burning cold engulfing my whole body; the thrill and terror of moving forward.

In that moment there was me and not me: I was the wind—the sound of it; the feel of it; I was the mountain and everything its peak offered me—miles and miles of mountains; that perfect blue sky. I was the snow, white and cold. I was the rocky ground beneath that snow. I was the experiential Divine.

Commentary, "On Jonah, Yom Kippur" (Shtibl Minyan, Los Angeles) *October 2007*

2 Stand here under the sky.
Open your hands.
Cup them like a bowl.
Wait. Seeds will fill them.
Wait. They will fill again.
Dig holes.
Plant.

Commentary, "Beresheit," 3 (Shtibl Minyan, Los Angeles) *January 2009*

4701. Hauwa Ibrahim (1965–)

1 You find the men of the North trying to ensure that the women are possibly under their armpit so that they can control them. . . . They don't want any challenge, they want to feel they are the men and the women are women. The position of the woman here is to be in the house and to rear the children, not for her to be out, working. . . .

"Nigerian Women Speak Out," *Frontline World* (pbs.org) *January 2003*

2 When it comes to the issue of death, the moment you stone the first woman, there may be no stopping of it. And I cannot live with that. Because of that, I fight it. I fight my fear. . . .

Ibid.

4702. Pramila Jayapal (1965–)

1 True leadership in foreign or domestic policy, in issues of the environment, immigration or poverty shines through only when we think from a place of expansiveness, not of fear.

"Mother of Exiles," *Yes! Summer 2004*

2 Nominally, we celebrate America the melting pot, but in practice, we're not so sure who we want to allow into the pot.

Ibid.

3 As we've seen in our history, combining fear with patriotism is one of the most effective ways to silence dissent.

Speech, "Standing for Justice in Challenging Times," National Immigration Law Center *17 June 2005*

4 As much as the media and conservative talk show hosts tried to make the immigration debate only about undocumented Mexican immigrants, the truth is that the immigration debate is about America. It's about Mexicans, Haitians, Africans, Chinese and Indians. It's about undocumented and documented people. It's about what our construction industry and agricultural industry and service industries need to survive. It's about how we take care of each other, about the increasing gap between rich and poor. It's about immigrants, willing and unwilling, who built this country's railroads and highways. It's about the United States' responsibility to house and shelter those escaping war and political chaos—often brought on by US foreign policy. Ultimately, the immigration debate is really a debate about what kind of a country we want to be and what we are willing to stand up for.

Speech, South Asian Bar Association *12 October 2007*

5 Dream with me about immigrants walking proudly over the borders, being encouraged to stay legally and bring their families with them, because we openly acknowledge that this nation's economy depends on the hard work and labor of immigrants.

Ibid.

6 We need solutions that are grounded in those Constitutional protections of due process and that preserve America's standing in the world as a place of refuge from war and persecution. We need solutions that reflect the reality that our current system is outdated with quotas for immigrant entry that don't match our needs, and a bureaucracy that has no accountability to ensuring that even legal applications are processed in a timely fashion. We need solutions that look honestly, too, at the impact of globalization and free trade policies and how we can build the economies of poor countries around the world.

"Immigration: Waiting for Leadership," Women's Media Center (womensmediacenter.com) *6 August 2008*

4703. A. L. Kennedy (1965–)

1 I always end up asking for answers I can't have.

So I Am Glad 1995

2 Sex. I don't know what it means. I haven't approached it in quite a while, but I'm afraid my lack of understanding has to stay in the present tense. I can only remain bemused when I consider that on a depressingly regular basis I would render myself, and perhaps my companion, insensible with fatigue for no reason I could ever ascertain.

Ibid.

3 "Our interior lives have seismic effects on our exterior world. We have to wake up and think about that if we want to be really alive."

Original Bliss 1997

4 Gluck talked a great deal about himself—he put his inside on his outside with a kind of clinical delight.

Ibid.

5 It is a strange thing to watch [bullfighting]: an elaborately prepared transgression, a sacrifice and a sin, ugly and peculiarly moving.

On Bullfighting 1999

4704. Lisa Marcus (1965–)

1 And it would be romantic of me to imagine that feminism could remain unpolluted by the lures of institutional power and star systems. But feminism has also changed institutions—productively calling into question power/knowledge formations even as it was sometimes being seduced by them.

"Feminism's Daughter," *The Women's Review of Books,* Vol. XV, No. 5 *February 1998*

2 Feminism isn't finished. It did not fail to reproduce; it is being reinvented every day.

Ibid.

4705. Lisa Margonelli (1965–)

1 Oil diplomacy, long outsourced to oil companies, and increasingly to the U.S. military, needs attention and leadership. The special relationships the United States nurtured with countries like Venezuela and the security guarantees offered to Saudi

Arabia have lost their appeal; and the threats, which include sanctions and military intervention, have lost their effect.
Oil on the Brain, Adventures from the Pump to the Pipeline 2007

2 Winning, particularly in the politics of the petrostate, is little more than the start of a long war.
Ibid.

3 Think of a gas station as a crime scene before the fact, and you'll start to appreciate it as a maze engineered for belligerent rats.
Ibid.

4 The frozen landscape, hoping for equilibrium, was claiming the parts of my body that it could. Then waiting for the rest.
"Snow," anderbo.com

4706. Montgomery "Mitzi" McFate (1965–)

1 I'm very sympathetic to those [anti-war] concerns, but the fact is that the military is going to do its job one way or another. If you don't provide them with a set of alternative tools, they're going to fall back on the thing they know best, which is the M4.
"Leading the Charge for Change" by Anna Mulrine, *U.S. News & World Report 30 November 2007*

2 You can't just stand outside the Pentagon, holding up a sign that says, "You suck." Sometimes you actually need to do something.
Ibid.

4707. Karin Muller (1965–)

1 Dear Mom, I can't get a single, solitary soul to go down to the marketplace and try the roasted bugs with me. If only you were here.
Hitchhiking Vietnam: A Woman's Solo Journey in an Elusive Land 1998

2 There was nothing. No warbling birds, neither bullfrog nor scurrying rodent. Everything had been eaten in this overused land until the only sound left was the trill of uncooked insects.
Ibid.

4708. Asra Q. Nomani (1965–)

1 To them, the U.S.-led coalition attacks on Afghanistan is truly an attack on Islam, and these fundamentalist Pakistani cricket moms' sympathies lie mostly with the Taliban and even Osama bin Laden.*
"The Taliban's ladies auxiliary," Salon.com *25 October 2001*
*(1957–), Arabic founder of the terrorist organization al-Qaeda.

2 We are standing up for our rights as women in Islam. We will no longer accept the back door or the shadows, at the end of the day, we'll be leaders in the Muslim world. We are ushering Islam into the 21st century, reclaiming the voice that the Prophet gave us 1400 years ago.
Speech, "Death of a Muslim Joan of Arc" (Morgantown, West Virginia) *15 March 2005*

3 I, a daughter of Islam, was in the midst of the Hindu pilgrimage. I had grown up with a mocking understanding of the deities to which Hindus bow their heads, but sitting in a retreat

colony amid simple devotees . . . I understood that the spiritual intention of a polytheist is no different from that of a monotheist who prays in a synagogue, church, or mosque.
"The Dalai Lama and the Seeds of Pilgrimage," *Standing Alone in Mecca: An American Woman's Struggle for the Soul of Islam 2005*

4 . . . Islam isn't practiced one singular way—no matter how much any one Islamic ideology insists that its path has a monopoly on virtue. From our *adab* (culture) to the way we pray, Muslims have many paths to Mecca.
"Sex, Lies, and Truth," Ibid.

4709. Rosemary Okello-Orlale (1965–)

1 Biblical David felled a giant with a catapult, and Moses had only a shepherd's staff to deliver Israelites from slavery. We, the media women, have a pen. Through this pen we will bring peace to this country.
"Kenya: Senior Women Editors Campaign For Peace" by Kwamboka Oyaro, IPSNews.net *6 March 2008*

2 We all know that the media is assigned a special watchdog role in a democracy. This means that the independence of the media—freedom of speech and freedom of information is sacrosanct.
Introduction, *The Role of Media in Promoting Access to Information and Serving as a Public Watchdog 2008*

3 Powered by awesome and fast changing technology with its vast reach; the media is, quite simply, one of the most powerful forces on earth today for shaping the way people think.
Ibid.

4 There's an agreement that power is no longer wielded through the barrel of the gun but by those who control information.
"The 'demassified' and 'globalized' reality," Ibid.

4710. Julie Phillips (1965–)

1 Science fiction . . . has been seen as a masculine genre. And yet, with its metaphors for alienation and otherness, its unruly imagination, and its power to predict change, it is highly suited to talking about women's experience.
Ch. 1, *James Tiptree, Jr.: The Double Life of Alice B. Sheldon 2006*

4711. J. K. Rowling (1965–)

1 After all, to the well-organized mind, death is but the next great adventure.
"The Man with Two Faces," *Harry Potter and the Sorcerer's Stone 1997*

2 Nothing is more unnerving to the truly conventional than the unashamed misfit!
Salon.com *31 March 1999*

3 Never trust anything that can think for itself if you can't see where it keeps its brain.
"Dobby's Reward," *Harry Potter and the Chamber of Secrets 1999*

4 "It is our choices, Harry, that show what we truly are, far more than our abilities."
Ch. 18, Ibid.

5 "Lord Voldemort's gift for spreading discord and enmity is very great. We can fight it only by showing an equally strong bond of friendship and trust. Differences of habit and language are nothing at all if our aims are identical and our hearts are open."
Ch. 37, *Harry Potter and the Goblet of Fire 2000*

6 "Curiosity is not a sin. . . . But we should exercise caution with our curiosity . . . yes, indeed."
"The Pensieve," Ibid.

7 It's a strange thing, but when you are dreading something, and would give anything to slow down time, it has a disobliging habit of speeding up.
"The Hungarian Horntail," Ibid.

8 According to Madam Pomfrey, thoughts could leave deeper scarring than almost anything else . . .
"The Second War Begins," *Harry Potter and the Order of the Phoenix 2003*

9 It is the unknown we fear when we look upon death and darkness, nothing more.
"The Cave," *Harry Potter and the Half-Blood Prince 2005*

4712. Albena Simeonova (1965–)
1 We have to stand together, hand-in-hand, fighting against the destruction of the environment, fighting for the survival of the planet, and for all its people.
"Don Quixotes of the environment," *San Diego Earth Times February 1998*

2 This is not only a serious threat against my life, it represents a threat to all who campaign against nuclear plants trying to protect their lives and the local environment.
"Bulgarian Green Leader Threatened With Death," Environment News Service *8 March 2005*

4713. Norah Vincent (1965?–)
1 You see, we don't like to admit to ourselves that the expedient thing is almost always more appealing than the right thing. And since it's rare that the expedient thing and the right thing turn out to be the same thing, we tend to choose the expedient thing and then try to justify it after the fact. That's what we've been doing with abortion all along, because, well, unwanted babies are just too damned inconvenient. So we've had to find a way to kill them without feeling bad about it. And how have we done that? Simple. A fertilized egg isn't human until, umm, until we decide it is—yeah that's it—which may or may not be when it has a heartbeat, or brain waves, or, alas, in the case of partial-birth abortion, not until it passes the lips of the vagina and plops out onto the table for all to see. Yes, that should work nicely. Good. Done.
  Denial is a beautiful thing.
"Send in the clones," Salon.com *30 November 2001*

2 Sex is most powerful in the mind, and to men, in the mind, women have a lot of power, not only to arouse, but to give worth, self-worth, meaning, initiation, sustenance, everything.
Self-Made Man: One Woman's Journey Into Manhood and Back Again 2006

3 If you have never been sexually attracted to women, you will never quite understand the monumental power of female sexuality, except by proxy or in theory, nor will you quite know the immense advantage it gives us over men.
Ibid.

4 I passed in a man's world not because my mask was so real, but because the world of men was a masked ball.
Ibid.

5 Real lives and lived experience are the laboratory of the immersion journalist, and the journalist herself is the guinea pig. Consequently, a lot can change between the proposal and the finished book, and always does.
Voluntary Madness 2008

6 And what is 'mentally ill,' anyway? What can it mean to say that someone is mentally ill when the DSM *[Diagnostic and Statistical Manual of Mental Disorders]*, the psycho-bible, is, in my and many other far more qualified people's estimation, not a scientific document, but rather an entirely subjective and seemingly infinitely amendable and expandable laundry list of catchall terms for collections of symptoms.
Ibid.

4714. Cheryl L. West (1965–)
1 MADEAR. Some folks wear dey scars on de inside . . . you jus wearin' yours on de outside. . . . You show me a woman dat ain't got a scar somewhere an I'll show you a woman dat ain't lived nuttin' but a lie.
Jar the Floor 1991

2 REBA. I made you. My son! And I took such pride . . . but last night you made me realize I hadn't made nothing, not a damn thing . . . been walking around fooling myself . . .
Before It Hits Home 1991

3 We [blacks] want only positive images of ourselves . . . We have the right to be suspicious of anything that makes us look anything less than pristine, because there have been so many images out there that have been negative and false . . . [but] I'm going to write about—boils, warts and all . . .
Program notes for Seattle Repertory Theatre production of *Holiday Heart 1994*

4714.1. Shahla Ata (1966?–)
1 I want to achieve the unaccomplished goals of Mohammad Daud Khan.*
Quoted in "Madam President in Afghanistan?," AFP.com *17 May 2009*
*(1909–78), Afghan prince, politician; president of Afghanistan (1973–78); assassinated.

2 The people have tested men, but they did not get anything. Now, why not see what a woman can do?
Ibid.

4715. Cecilia Bartoli (1966–)
1 I wasn't born with my voice placed in the right position . . . [We] had to work on it endlessly and painstakingly, sometimes working on a single note for days or even weeks . . . Until slowly, with time, study, hard work and the mellowing that comes with growth, I expanded my vocal range and acquired agility.
Quoted in *Diva, The New Generation: The Sopranos and Mezzos of the Decade Discuss Their Roles* by Helena Matheopoulous *1998*

4716. Edie Brickell (1966–)
1 Philosophy is the talk on a cereal box.
"What I Am" *n.d.*

2   There's nothing I hate more than nothing
Nothing keeps me up at night
I toss and turn over nothing
Nothing could cause a great big fight.
"Nothing" *n.d.*

4717. Deana Carter (1966–)

1   Well it's perfectly clear, between the TV and beer
I won't get so much as a kiss
As I head for the door I turn around to be sure
Did I shave my legs for this?
"Did I Shave My Legs for This?," *Did I Shave My Legs for This??* (album) 1996

2   Thanks to Elvis and Kurt Cobain, the world will never be the same
You gotta make history one day at a time
"One Day at A Time," *The Story of My Life* (album) 2005

3   Oh wouldn't be scary
Just being ordinary?
"Ordinary," Ibid.

4718. Mary Beth Caschetta (1966–)

1   Lucy had to press down hard in her daily planner to scratch out the names of the missing and the dead; otherwise it seemed like nothing more than lunch being canceled.
"Lucy on the West Coast," *Lucy on the West Coast and Other Lesbian Short Fiction* 1996

2   I picture Judgment Day like this: a cup of coffee, the kitchen table, my mother seated across from me.
"Bride of Christ," *A Woman Like That: Lesbian and Bisexual Writers Tell Their Coming Out Stories*, Joan Larkin, ed. 1999

3   In some ways, I think, a relationship is like childhood: You can't assess the damage or success until it is long over. And even then, the facts are hazy.
"The Rest of the Party," *Women on the Verge*, Susan Fox Rogers, ed. 1999

4   "It's like letting go of everything when your mother dies," Violet said, somewhat mournfully.
"Wonderful You," *Eclectica Magazine*, v. 11, no. 3 *July/August 2007*

5   The thing about inspiration is it doesn't let you nap for very long.
"Four Days in Silence: A Writer's Search for Meaning, or Get Me To A Nunnery," *Women's Wonderlands*, Gillian Kendall, ed. 2008

4719. Helene Cooper (1966?–)

1   Liberian society rivaled Victorian England when it came to matters of social correctness. In Liberia, we cared far more about how we looked outside than about who we were inside.
Ch. 1, *The House at Sugar Beach* 2008

2   But rogues and thieves were very different animals. Rogues broke into your house while you were sleeping and made off with the fine china. Thieves worked for the government and stole money from the public treasury.
Ibid.

3   None of that American post-Civil War/civil rights movement baggage to bog me down with any inferiority complex about whether I was as good as white people. No European garbage to have me wondering whether some British colonial master was somehow better than me. Who needs to struggle for equality? Let everybody else try to be equal to me.
Ibid.

4720. Kirsten Gillibrand (1966–)

1   I don't think clients you represented as an associate are relevant . . . I think how you vote is relevant.*
AlbanyTimes-Union 15 November 2005
*Re her work as an attorney for Philip Morris Tobacco Co.; as a NY representative, she consistently voted for antismoking bills.

2   What I'd like to do legislatively, on the federal level—and I think we'll be able to do this with the new president—is actually make civil unions legal in all 50 states, make it the law of the land. . . .
Because what you want to fundamentally do is protect the rights and privileges of committed couples, so that they can have Medicare benefits, visit in the hospitals, have adoption rights. All [the] things that we give to married couples, committed gay couples should be eligible for. And then the question of whether you call it a marriage or not, what you label it, that can be left to the states to decide.
InsideOut Hudson Valley (New York) *January/February 2009*

3   The Senate is extremely slow: They have enormous difficulty passing the bills that even get through the House. That's the reality that I've recognized in my two years: that it takes time to change the world.
Ibid.

4721. Julie Greenberg (1966?–)

1   You can just imagine how many rituals there would be if men had babies!
Quoted in Ch. 4, *Deborah, Golda, and Me* by Letty Cottin Pogrebin* 1991
*See 3154.

2   Partnerships are not hard and fast contracts; rather they are spiritual covenants that allow for fluidity in relationship.
"Can I Trust That My Interfaith Partner Will Really Raise the Kids Jewish?" InterfaithFamily.com 2007

4722. Sheri Holman (1966–)

1   Ask for the right to vote and just see how the government answers: with doctors and poisons and frogs; with poor laws and anatomy acts and Thomas Malthus.*
The Dress Lodger 2000
*(1766–1834), English economist, sociologist, and pioneer in modern population study.

2   The poor cannot help but know they are worth more to us dead than alive.
Ibid.

4723. Janet [Damita Jo] Jackson (1966–)

1   The decision to have a costume reveal at the end of my halftime show performance was made after final rehearsals. MTV was completely unaware of it. It was not my intention that it go

as far as it did. I apologize to anyone offended—including the audience, MTV, CBS and the NFL.*

"Apologetic Jackson says 'costume reveal' went awry," *CNN.com 3 February 2004*

*Re: her right breast being exposed during the halftime show at the Super Bowl.

4724. Jacqui Katona (1966–)
Also see Yvonne Margarula, 4460.

1   Now any community that suffers from poverty, there's going to be crime taking place because people are desperate to try to survive and crime is often part of that. So once you're living in those circumstances, yes, it's inevitable that ultimately institutions will determine what happens in your life . . .

Quoted on "The Wisdom Interview" with Peter Thompson, *ABC Radio National* (abc.net.au) *3 April 2005*

2   Living in Kakadu [National Park, Australia] is draining; it's horrible to see people who are living in poverty; it's horrible to see children who are nutritionally deprived, verging on malnutrition; it's horrible to know that people are drinking themselves to death.*

Ibid.

*Due to uranium mining.

3   Now 100 years ago, people might have been shot for challenging authority, now people are incarcerated for challenging authority.

Ibid.

4725. Jill Lepore (1966–)

1   People have always made maps, whether drawn on paper, etched into bark, or traced in the sand. However they are made, maps are an attempt to describe the world or some part of it, but maps do other things, too: they delineate nations, mark off territory, and characterize a land's inhabitants. Sometimes, deliberately or not, maps lie.

Ch. 1, *Encounters in the New World: A History in Documents* 2002

2   Twould be an even greater sorrow to leave Edinburgh, that nursery of enlightened genius, did not each degree of longitude stretch the distance betwixt me and my creditors, to whom I owe so much gold, and so little gratitude . . .

Ch. 1, *Blindspot: A Novel*, Jane Kamensky,* coauthor 2008
*See 4641.

3   Had Columbus my gut, the world would be a smaller place. And maybe the better for it. O brave new world: wild, rebellious, mysterious, and strange. And distant. God above, who knew it could be so bloody far?

Ibid.

4   "Tis proved: a merchant measures his prospects by a port's fathoms and not by its people's piety, just as a whore measures a man's parts by the bulge of his purse and not of his breeches."

Ch. 2, Ibid.

4726. Martha McCaughey (1966–)

1   If women abdicate violence without being capable of it anyhow, it makes less of an impact than if that abdication were a real choice.

Real Knockouts: The Physical Feminism of Women's Self-Defense 1997

2   Because gender is not really natural it requires constant enforcement and repetition.

Ibid.

3   Self-defense enables women to internalize a different kind of bodily knowledge. As such, self-defense is feminism in the flesh.

Ibid.

4   In a marketplace of masculine identities, the caveman ethos is served up as Viagra for the masculine soul.

Introduction, *The Caveman Mystique: Pop-Darwinism and the Debates over Sex, Violence, and Science* 2007

4727. Elizabeth McCracken (1966–)

1   Library books are promiscuous, ready to lie in the arms of anyone who asked.

The Giant's House 1996

2   I thought I would be better than I am.

The River Beyond the World 1996

3   I've never gotten over my discomfort at other people's discomfort.

An Exact Replica of a Figment of My Imagination—A Memoir 2008

4   And so in my grief I understand that mourning is a kind of ventriloquism; we put words into the mouths of our bereavers, but of course it's all entirely about us, our wants, our needs, the dead are satisfied, we are greedy, greedy, greedy, unseemly, self-obsessed.

Ibid.

4728. Bernice L. McFadden (1966–)

1   There's a little bit of hooker in every woman. A little bit of hooker and a little bit of God.

Sugar 2000

2   People slammed dollar after hard-labored dollar on the bar, pushing further and further back the consequences of their pleasure. Eviction, screaming wives, hostile husbands and hungry babies. They would deal with that when the sun fulfilled the promise of another day. For now there were good times to be had, and good times cost.

Ibid.

3   [I didn't] want to talk about forgiveness with a woman who'd forgiven her life away, and mine right along with it.

The Warmest December 2001

4   One day last week I forgot that I hated my father, forgot that I even thought of him as a monster.

Ibid.

4729. Claire Messud (1966–)

1   It was an awesome, a fearful thought: you could make something inside your head, as huge and devastating as this, and spill it out into reality, make it really happen. You could—for evil, but if for evil, then why not for good, too?—change the world.

The Emperor's Children 2006

2   The apartment was entirely, was only, for her: a wall of books, both read and unread, all of them dear to her not only in themselves, their tender spines, but in the moments or periods they evoked.

Ibid.

3   He was aware that at thirty he stretched the limits of the charming wastrel, that some actual sustained endeavor might be in order were he not to fade, wisplike, away: from charming wastrel to needy, boring failure.

Ibid.

4730. Denise Mina (1966–   )

1   She remembered a time when she would watch him sleep, his eyes fluttering behind the lids, and she found the sigh so beautiful that it winded her. But on Monday night she woke up and looked at him and knew it was over. Eight long months of emotional turmoil had passed as suddenly as a fart.

Ch. 1, *Garnethill 1998*

2   January is the despairing heart of the Scottish winter and black clouds brooded low over the city, pregnant with spiteful rain.

Ch. 1, *Exile 2001*

3   London is a savage city . . .

Ch. 2, Ibid.

4   She had stumbled on a talent for articulating nationwide annoyances.

Slip of the Knife 2008

4731. Susan D. Moeller (1966?–   )

1   The Americanization of events makes the public feel the world subscribes, and must subscribe, to American cultural icons—and if it doesn't or can't it is not worth the bother . . .

Compassion Fatigue: How the Media Sell Disease, Famine, War and Death 1998

2   Like emergency-room triage, triage of emergencies does not necessarily mean that the sickest case gets the first and most help. Sometimes the sickest case is the most hopeless case, and receives little more than a Band-Aid of care—just enough so the hemorrhaging is not embarrassing.

Ch. 1, Ibid.

3   We can't respond to every appeal. And so we've come to believe that we don't care. If we turn the page originally because we don't want to respond to what is in actuality a fund-raising appeal, although in the guise of a direct humanitarian plea, it becomes routine to thumb past the pages of news images showing wide-eyed children in distress.

We've got compassion fatigue, we say, as if we have involuntarily contracted some kind of disease that we're stuck with no matter what we might do.

Ibid.

4   Americans seem to have an appetite for only one crisis at a time.

Ibid.

5   Managing images to elicit a supportive public opinion in wartime was understood as essential long before World War II—it's simply the method of management that has changed.

"The Power Joe Rosenthal* Knew," *The Washington Post 26 August 2006*

*The photographer (1912–2006) responsible for the famed World War II image of five Marines and Navy corpsman raising the flag over Iwo Jima.

6   Images are powerful indicators of victory and defeat.

Ibid.

4732. Ellen Moran (1966–   )

1   For so many of us who worked really hard to try to elect Hillary Clinton,* these are some tough times. If you want to end the war in Iraq, if you want to try to dig our way out of the hole that we're in in this economy, an economy that is punishing women in much larger numbers, the choice is very clear. Senator Obama** certainly offers the new direction for this country that we so desperately need, that women voters need.

Interview on *Larry King Live*, CNN-TV *June 2008*
*See 3731. **Barack O- (1961–   ), 44th president of the United States (2009–   ).

4733. Holly Morris (1966–   )

1   Feminism has been all about reacting. Now it's time to be proactive.

"Divas, not darlings" by Hugo Kugiya, *Seattle Times*, Pacific Northwest section *15 June 1997*

2   You don't have to be a martyr to do good things.

Ibid.

3   I have a perverse attraction to not knowing what's going to happen next.

Ibid.

4734. Inga Muscio (1966?–   )

1   "Cunt" is very arguably the most powerful negative word in the American English language. "'Cunt' is the ultimate one-syllable covert verbal weapon any streetwise six-year-old or passing motorist can use against a woman. "Cunt" refers almost exclusively to women, and expresses the utmost rancor. There's a general feeling of accord on this.

Cunt: A Declaration of Independence 1998

2   The only bush you can trust is your own.

Ibid.

3   Crows are born into this world.
I was not.
I was born into an environment of white supremacist racism, imperialism, and male domination.

Pt. 2, Introduction, *Autobiography of a Blue-Eyed Devil 2005*

4   There are many ways to procure goods in satisfying ways that do not require money. Knowing this, however, requires a shift in perspective, a slight—yet crucial—movement into the world, utilizing the vastly underestimated biological gift that can never truly be taken away from anyone: *the glorious human imagination*. Admitting that your imagination has been colonized and then doing something about it is by no means an easy thing to do, but it is very much a thing that can be done, no matter how little economic latitude you may have.

Ibid.

4735. Jodi Picoult (1966–   )

1   When people see my pictures, they seem fascinated. They ask me if I know what these things mean, but I never do. I can draw the image, but people have to face their own demons.

Prologue, Paige, *Harvesting the Heart 1995*

2   He blamed his faulty sense of direction on his *wasicun* blood. All his life he'd heard stories of his grandfather's father, who tracked the goddamned buffalo by the slightest rising of the wind. And when the woman his father loved had left without a word, hadn't he ridden for miles using ony his intuition to find

her? Compared to that, how difficult could it be to find the San Diego Freeway?

Ch. 1, Picture Perfect 2001

3 We live in a country where American kids are dying because we're sending them overseas to kill people for oil. But when one sad, distraught child who doesn't see the beauty in life goes and wrongly acts on his rage by shooting up a school, people start pointing a finger at heavy metal music. The problem isn't with rock lyrics, it's with the fabric of this society itself."

Nineteen Minutes 2007

4 Not that Jesus wasn't a really cool guy—great teacher, excellent speaker, yadda yadda yadda. But . . . Son of God? Where's the proof?

Change of Heart 2008

5 I don't even know my real dad; he and my mother split up before I was even born, and she swears that his absence is the best gift he could ever have given me.

Handle With Care 2009

4736. Belinda Stronach (1966–)
1 I've been uncomfortable for some time with the direction the Conservative party was taking. I regret to say that I do not believe the party leader is truly sensitive to the needs of each part of the country and just how big and complex Canada really is.

"Belinda Stronach—Newly Liberal," CBC-TV *17 May 2005*

4737. Natasha Trethewey (1966–)
1 A risky job, its only
guarantee the consolation check
for a dead man's family.

"At the Owl Club, North Gulfport, Mississippi, 1950," st. 6,
Domestic Work 2000

2 Do I deceive
anyone? Were they to see my hands, brown
as your dear face, they'd know I'm not quite
what I pretend to be. I walk these streets
a white woman, or so I think, until I catch the eyes
of some stranger upon me, and I must lower mine,
a *negress* again.

"Letter Home," St. 2, *Bellocq's Ophelia 2002*

3 bound only
for whatever awaits us, the sun now
setting behind us, the rails humming
like anticipation, the train pulling us
toward the end of another day.

"The Southern Crescent," 2, *Native Guard: Poems 2006*

4 This whole city is a grave. Every spring—
Pilgrimage—the living come to mingle

with the dead, brush against their cold shoulders
in the long hallways, listen all night

to their silence and indifference, relive
their dying on the green battlefield.

"Pilgrimage," Sts. 10–12, Ibid.

4738. Sherry Turkle (1966?–)
1 Technology catalyzes changes not only in what we do but in how we think.

The Second Self 1994

2 Terrified of being alone, yet afraid of intimacy, we experience widespread feelings of emptiness, of disconnection, of the unreality of self. And here the computer, a companion without emotional demands, offers a compromise. You can be a loner, but never alone. You can interact, but need never feel vulnerable to another person.

Ch. 9, Ibid.

3 Windows have become a powerful metaphor for thinking about the self as a multiple, distributed system. The self is no longer simply playing different roles in different settings at different times. The life practice of windows is that of a decentered self that exists in many worlds, that plays many roles at the same time.

Life on the Screen: Identity in the Age of the Internet 1995

4 The computer's holding power is a phenomenon frequently referred to in terms associated with drug addition. It is striking that the word "user" is associated mainly with computers and drugs. The trouble with that analogy, however, is that it puts the focus on what is external (the drug). I prefer the metaphor of seduction because it emphasizes the relationship between person and machine.

Ch. 1, Ibid.

5 The danger of technology is that it demands to be fed.

Ch. 4, Ibid.

4739. Marilyn Wann (1966–)
1 So there's nothing wrong with being fat. Just like there's nothing wrong with being short or tall, or black or brown. These are facts of identity that cannot and should not be changed. They are birthright. They're beyond aesthetics. They provide the diversity we need to survive.

Fat!So? Manifesto, *Fat!So? 1998*

2 I'm not interested in people accepting my fat, but in fat people's rights.

Ibid.

4740. Sarah Waters (1966–)
1 Although I didn't long believe the story told to me by Mother—that they had found me as a baby in an oyster-shell, and a greedy customer had almost eaten me for lunch—for eighteen years I never doubted my own oysterish sympathies, never looked far beyond my father's kitchen for occupation, or for love.

Ch. 1, Tipping the Velvet 1998

2 Pa used to say that any piece of history might be made into a tale: it was only a question of deciding where the tale began, and where it ended.

24 September 1874, *Affinity 1999*

4741. Beatrice Were (1966?–)
1 AIDS is now being looked at as a moral issue, not a public health issue, not a human rights issue, and the way that it's being handled is more ideological than anything else.

Quoted in "Beatrice Were: Fighting a Deadly U.S. AIDS Policy in Uganda" by Christopher Hayes, InTheseTimes.com *9 December 2005*

2 How do you talk about morals instead of condoms for sex workers? Or for married women?

Quoted in "Uganda's Shift in AIDS Policy Tied to U.S." by Anna Louie Sussman, womensnews.org *21 February 2006*

3   As a woman living with HIV, I am often asked whether there will ever be a cure for HIV/AIDS, and my answer is that there is already a cure. It lies in the strength of women, families and communities who support and empower each other to break the silence around AIDS and take control of their sexual lives.

Quoted in The Invisible Cure: Africa, the West, and the Fight Against AIDS by Helen Epstein* 2007

*See 3740.

4742. Denita Willoughby (1966?–)

1   . . . in corporate America at least, if you go out looking for racism you are always going to find it. So my guiding principle is to stay focused on those things you can control and remain clear in your mission. If you compare that to life as an entrepreneur, those same guiding principles exist.

Quoted in "Celebrating Black History Month" by Jeanine Amber, USA Weekend Magazine 11 February 2001

2   The main difference between pursuing a corporate route and an entrepreneurial route is financing. To be a successful entrepreneur, you also need that financing component. And unfortunately, most African Americans don't come from wealthy families. We don't have a directory of black venture capital companies willing to provide seed capital.

Ibid.

3   When you have black senior executives leading major corporations, it sets a path.

Ibid.

4743. Monica Ali (1967–)

1   The small edifice of their savings was reduced to dust.

Brick Lane 2003

2   She looked like the kind of woman who would never leave her cereal bowl in the sink all day. The sound of her heels on the cobbles made me feel lazy and rather disorganized. I fussed inside my bag, but why I should pretend to be busy, goodness only knows.

Alentejo Blue 2006

3   You can always defeat sarcasm in the end with cheeriness. It's quite a good weapon, actually; a blunt instrument but a strong one.

Ibid.

4   A bird, thought João, never has to think about what to do next. . . . A bird always knows how he feels.

Ibid.

4744. Leah Hager Cohen (1967–)

1   It seems to me that during my childhood, the fact that I was hearing was kindly overlooked.

Train Go Sorry: Inside a Deaf World 1994

2   For the longest time I never fully believed that I wouldn't eventually become deaf . . . I played at signing the way other children play dress-up . . . practicing for the future . . . I wanted to grow up and be deaf, be a Lexington student, with all the accoutrements: hearing aids, speech lessons, fast and clever hands

Ibid.

3   The disgusting thing about us Fisher-Harts was that there were only three of us in the world, and we had mythologized ourselves preciously.

House Lights 2007

4   Maybe it's the old problem of the fallible god. Maybe my love for him was too worshipful in nature to survive such a fall. My mother's love survived it, how? It was of a tougher, scrappier variety. . . . Suddenly, right now, I wish I could ask her the secret. Because try as I might, I cannot make myself love my father again.

Ibid.

5   He broke our trust by falling from iconic status. I broke our trust by seeing him plainly. For the first time it occurs to me that this might not be all bad. For the very first time it dawns: this might actually place us at an advantage.

Ibid.

4745. Janine Davidson (1967?–)

1   A woman whose job it is to pay attention to carrier battle groups and weapons platforms will—and should be—as knowledgeable as her male counterparts. And the ones I know in that line of work most certainly are.

Quoted in "Women Prominent in Defense Movement" by Spencer Ackerman, The Washington Independent 8 July 2008

2   COIN [counterinsurgency] blends the various fields of security, economic development, conflict resolution, rule of law, human rights and state/nation building—fields in which women were already working through academia, law, [nongovernmental organizations] and in the policy community. . . . So it makes sense to see more women trying to figure out this complex, interdisciplinary puzzle we call COIN. For me, this is the most interesting aspect. I think we have a long way to go in understanding how our theoretical constructs and conventional wisdom in these myriad fields may or may not link together in COIN and state-building, or the limitations on our role as an intervening force. So we need more diverse perspectives on the problem.

Ibid.

4746. Gail Devers (1967–)

1   I have a message for people. If there are times when you feel the walls are closing in on you, when you feel there's no way out, use me as an example. If you have faith in yourself and you never give up on your dreams, or your goals, anything's possible.*

Quoted in "A testament to courage" by Steve Kelley, Seattle Times, C1, 7 2 August 1992

*From 1988 to 1990, Devers suffered from Graves' disease; she came close to having her feet amputated.

2   I wouldn't wish my disease on anyone, but I feel thankful that I've gone through it. It's changed me as a person. I'm more determined. I'm a stronger person.

Ibid.

4747. Mona Eltahawy (1967–)

1   The presence of all these Muslim women at the Olympics is a clear message to the world—and the conservative clerics—that there is nothing in Islam that stops them from competing in the sports they love.

"Ain't No Sisters on the Team," Middle East Online (middle-east-online.com) 13 August 2008

2   . . . that year in Israel was essentially an early lesson that fundamentalists are the same everywhere and in every religion.

"On Being a Bumble Bee," The Jerusalem Report, #15 10 November 2008

3 Here's our deal—NYC is the ultimate understanding lover. The more she understands my need to stray the more likely I will return to her, my perfect honeycomb.

Ibid.

4748. Masha Gessen (1967–)

1 My body had turned against me. All I could do now was declare war on it myself.

Blood Matters: From Inherited Illness to Designer Babies, How the World and I Found Ourselves in the Future of the Gene 1998

2 *On medical advice of having an oophorectomy**: I politely suggested I could just shoot myself tomorrow: That would prevent my death from cancer with a 100 percent probability. The joke remained suspended in the thin air between us and the counselors, and with it, our disengagement from one another was complete.

Ibid.

*An oophorectomy is a surgical procedure to remove the ovaries.

3 DNA-testing equipment tends to fall into two categories: things that look like printers and things that look like toasters.

Ibid.

4749. Allegra Goodman (1967–)

1 He had been spared, and he was chastened, humbled by the victory. As one who survives a shipwreck, or a terrible disease, he asked God for strength and wisdom, and resolved to make a better start.

Intuition 2006

4750. Nicole Kidman (1967–)

1 When you've been blessed with a fortunate life, it is very much your duty to find the places where you can give back.

Speech, UNIFEM* 30th anniversary gala *13 May 2006*
*United Nations Development Fund for Women.

2 We all know in our heads and our hearts that every woman is entitled to a life free of violence. Let's make that a reality. Let's end violence against women.

Speech, 10th anniversary of UN Trust Fund *16 February 2007*

3 Addiction is very prevalent in our society, and it can be shattering to both people in the relationship.

But working through it together was an extraordinary path. It's very easy for a couple to experience joy together. But when you experience pain together, it can lead to such depth and such union. That is when you fuse.

Quoted by Anita Singh, *The Telegraph* (London) *5 November 2008*

4751. Vendela Kirsebom (1967–)

1 I was so lucky being born in a country where there's no war and every child has the right to be a child. I realize this is not a privilege that all children have in the world.

"The Power of Caring," *Time* (New York) *10 November 1998*

4752. Jhumpa Lahiri (1967–)

1 "You're always welcome here, Baba," she'd told her father on the phone. "You know you don't have to ask." Her mother would not have asked. "We're coming to see you in July," she would have informed Ruma, the plane tickets already in hand.

There had been a time in her life when such presumptuousness would have angered Ruma. She missed it now.

"Unaccustomed Earth," *Unaccustomed Earth 2008*

2 She [his daughter] now resembled his wife so strongly that he could not bear to look at her directly.

Ibid.

3 Somehow, she feared that any difference of opinion would chip away at the already frail bond that existed between them.

"A Choice of Accommodations," Ibid.

4 Bombay had made them more American than Cambridge had.

"Once in a Lifetime," Ibid.

5 I didn't think such violent things could happen to ordinary people.

"Brief Encounter," Ibid.

4753. Laura Mary Oaks (1967–)

1 In Ireland, reproduction is a medium through which competing national origin stories that focus on Irish national identity and cultural self-determination, indeed visions of "Irishness" itself, are imagined and expressed. An emphasis on women's right to control their bodies invokes narratives of independence, struggles that resulted in Irish citizens' self-governance, whereas attention to the "rights of the unborn" perpetuates a literary-mythical image of a natural, innocent Erin or motherland threatened by hostile outsiders and in need of protection.

Essay (p. 133), *Reproducing Reproduction: Kinship, Power, and Technological Innovation*, Sarah Franklin and Helena Ragoné, eds. *1998*

4754. Catherine Orenstein (1967?–)

1 Old stories can be reinvented. And heroines can always be reclaimed.

Little Red Riding Hood Uncloaked: Sex, Morality and the Evolution of a Fairy Tale 2002

2 Op-ed pages are so enormously powerful. It's one of the few places open to the public. Where else is someone like me going to get access?

Quoted in "Stop the Presses, Boys! Women Claim Space on Op-Ed Pages" by Patricia Cohen, *The New York Times 15 March 2007*

3 Personal and the public interests are not at odds. The belief that they are mutually exclusive has kept women out of power.

Ibid.

4755. Liz Phair (1967–)

1 I bet
you fall in bed too easily
with the beautiful girls who are shy and brave
and you sell yourself as a man to save
but all the money in the world is not enough

Verse 1, *Exile in Guyville 1993*

2 The fire you like so much in me
Is the mark of someone adamantly free
But you can't stop yourself
from wanting worse
Cause nothing feeds a hunger
like a thirst.

"Strange Loop?" Verse 1, Ibid.

3 and I never met a man
who was so pretty inside
he's got diamonds on the bed of his thumbnails . . .
and I liked it
let me tell you I liked it more and more
"Johnny Feelgood," 1st Verse, *White Chocolate Space Egg*
1998

4756. Shiva Rea (1967–)

1 [Happiness is] The inherent, all-permeating satisfaction that is always present. It's our birthright, independent of any external conditions. It needs to be nurtured and cultivated even though it's within us.
Quoted in "Viva Shiva!" by Colleen Morton Busch, *Yoga Journal July/August 2005*

2 Parenting makes you so creative. There are 101 games you can play with the sugar packets at restaurants. In both teaching and parenting, you have to work with whatever situation you're given.
Ibid.

4757. Julia Roberts (1967–)

1 I'm not a big regretter. I always say, "Worries many. Regrets none."
Quoted in "Julia Roberts, After the Layoff and With Lyle" by Timothy Egan, *The New York Times 12 December 1993*

2 How this woman* has kept her composure, with what the tabloid shows have done to John F. Kennedy, is unbelievable. This woman is nobility personified.
Ibid.

*Jacqueline Kennedy Oassis; see 2676.

3 You know, it may be too much to ask to be in a harness and creative at the same time.*
Ibid.

*Re her role as Tinkerbell in Steven Spielberg's film *Hook*.

4758. Marianne Schnall (1967–)

1 [Cameron Diaz]* flips the stereotype of environmentalists as being boring, serious and un-glamorous, and reinforces the concept that being green is instead becoming fashionable and hip—as well as a rewarding experience for humanity and the Earth.
"Talking Green with Cameron Diaz," *The Huffington Post 9 April 2008*

*See 4857.

2 There seems to be greater awareness about the serious issues we are facing, such as world poverty and global warming, which is spurring a growing, hopeful movement for change.
"Natalie Portman* on Her New Role: Giving Women Hope," *The Huffington Post 4 July 2008*

*See 4948.

3 There is another face of feminism, which is as equally individually defined and significant as the external face yet goes hand in hand with it—the internal face of feminism. Whereas the external aspect relates to the world outside of the woman, the world in which she lives, the internal landscape of feminism represents a woman's inner reality, the world that lives within her. . . . We can become so busy tending to all our duties, and

the needs of others, that we forget that we must first take care of ourselves.
"Reflections," feminist.com *2008*

4 Behind the headlines heralding potentially positive developments in the Democratic Republic of Congo (DRC), women and girls continue to be at risk. . . . [They] have been savagely raped and mutilated and remain traumatized.
With all the bad news facing the world right now, you might prefer not knowing the horrific details of these women's stories.
"Turning Pain to Power," WomensMediaCenter.com *2 February 2009*

4759. Tabitha Soren (1967–)

1 Of all consumer goods, only cars cause more deaths than guns. And you have to license and register your car. And you have to be trained to drive.
Why shouldn't the same rules apply to guns?
"Gun violence . . ." *Seattle Post-Intelligencer,* A15 *23 February 1994*

2 Gun violence is as misunderstood as the Second Amendment.
Ibid.

3 When I was a freelancer, I thought this journalism thing was a racket, and now that I'm where I am now, I know it's a racket.
"This Week in Rock," *MTV News n.d.*

4 Gossip is easy, politics is hard.
Ibid.

4760. Mona Sutphen (1967/68–)

1 Washington should welcome the pivotal powers into a vigorous international order to share the burden of solving pressing global issues of peace, climate, health, and growth.
"How America Can Thrive as Other Powers Rise," *Mount Holyoke Alumnae Quarterly Summer 2008*

2 The rise of other global powers is most often posed as a sorry tale, full of threats to American primacy, prosperity, and way of life. The potential loss of our #1 status implies a blow to our safety, economy, and prestige.
But this is a rare moment in history—none of the world's big powers is our adversary. The "pivotal powers"—China, Europe, India, Japan, and Russia—seek greater influence, but each also has an enormous stake in global stability and the world economy. As a result, they share our desire to combat the "rotten fruit" of globalization—terrorism, pandemic disease, the climate crisis, and nuclear proliferators like Iran and North Korea—which pose the greatest threats to America's way of life.
Ibid.

3 If an Indian researcher finds a cure for Alzheimer's, that is great news for everyone. What is problematic is failing to educate our own children and letting our innovation lead slip—the very innovation that has been a key driver of US economic growth.
Ibid.

4761. Nathalie Tauziat (1967–)

1 Aesthetics and charisma are seen as more important than sporting performance, and it won't change as long as the box office

puts [Anna] Kournikova* ahead of Lindsay Davenport** just because she is prettier . . .

The Hidden Side of Tennis 2001

*(1981–), Russian tennis pro and model. **(1976–), American tennis pro.

4761.1. Gillian Tett (1967?–)

1 I happen to think anthropology is a brilliant background for looking at finance. Firstly, you're trained to look at how societies or cultures operate holistically, so you look at how all the bits move together. And most people in the City don't do that. They are so specialised, so busy, that they just look at their own little silos. And one of the reasons we got into the mess we are in is because they were all so busy looking at their own little bit that they totally failed to understand how it interacted with the rest of society.

Quoted in "On the money" by Laura Barton, *The Guardian* (London) *31 October 2008*

2 People who come from a background of arts and humanities and social studies tend to think that money and the City is boring and somehow dirty. But if you don't look at how money goes round the world you don't actually understand the world at all. When you try and join up the dots about how money can be linked to politics, can be linked to culture, then it's electrifying.

Ibid.

3 Generally finance, maths, numbers, money, traditionally have not been seen as a female thing. That's all about the culture of power. And one way that you keep women away from the power traditionally is that not only do they not own the money, control the money, but they don't understand the money. I feel very strongly about educating women about finance.

Ibid.

4 The J.P. Morgan* derivatives team was engaged in the banking equivalent of space travel. Computing power and high-order mathematics were taking finance far from its traditional bounds, and this small group of brilliant minds was charting the outer reaches of cyberfinance. Like scientists cracking the DNA code or splitting the atom, the J.P. Morgan swaps team believed their experiments in what bankers refer to as "innovation"—meaning the invention of bold new ways of generating returns—were solving the most foundational riddles of their discipline.

Ch. 1, *Fool's Gold: How the Bold Dream of a Small Tribe at J.P. Morgan Was Corrupted by Wall Street Greed and Unleashed a Catastrophe 2009*

*J.P. Morgan & Co., a commercial and investment banking institution founded in 1871; defunct, 2000.

5 The financiers had created a vast "shadow banking" system that was running out of control.

As the pace of innovation heated up, credit products were spinning off into a cyberworld that eventually even the financiers struggled to understand. The link between the final product and its underlying assets was becoming so complex that it appeared increasingly tenous. Bankers were becoming like the inhabitants of the cave in Plato's tale, who—at best—could see only shadows, not tangible reality.

Ch. 6, Ibid.

4761.2. Debbie Wasserman Schultz

1 Being young was more difficult than being a woman. Most of the members [of the House of Representations] were old enough to be my parents or grandparents.

Quoted in "New Political Woman" by Scott S. Greenberger, *Moment Magazine* (Washington, D.C.) *May/June 2009*

2 [There is a] double standard for moms who are trying to do any professional job and balance family. It's very difficult for any of us.

Ibid.

3 The American voter has now evolved to a point where they don't choose their candidate based on color, creed or gender. They choose based on quality and what they'd like to see happen. I'm incredibly hopeful about the possibility of electing a woman—or a Jewish—president.

Ibid.

4762. Elizabeth Wurtzel (1967–)

1 *Depression is all about* If you loved me you would.

"I Hate Myself and I Want to Die," Prologue, *Prozac Nation 1994*

2 It is a girl who is exquisite, or preternaturally sexy, or possessed of a talent that makes her beautiful—it is a girl who is special, radiant, a sensitive artist, a delicate flower; it is a girl whose loss to the world would be viewed as the greatest tragedy . . . she is precisely the one who is most likely to mistake her own delicacy for invincibility.

Bitch 1998

4763. Debby Applegate (1968–)

1 When Henry* was a boy, his faith in his father was so deeply ingrained that it never occurred to him to ask why they did not celebrate Christmas. If he had, Lyman's answer would have been unequivocal. As an orthodox Calvinist, Lyman Beecher** interpreted the Bible literally, as solid fact, and there was nothing in the Scriptures to suggest that Christ was born on December 25. And even if there were, the day would be an occasion for solemn prayer, not sensual frivolity. Why, the Beechers didn't even celebrate their own birthdays.

Ch. 1, *The Most Famous Man in America: The Biography of Henry Ward Beecher 2007*

*H— Ward Beecher (1813–87) American Congregationalist minister, social reformer, and abolitionist. **(1775–1863) American Presbyterian minister, temperance movement leader, and father to several famous offspring.

2 . . . Connecticut, the Land of Steady Habits, where clocks, granite, and schoolteachers were its chief exports, and the specter of Puritanism still stalked every crevice of its rocky hills.

Ibid.

3 But Connecticut Yankees were a wily, peculiar breed, according to early American folklore, with a slippery shrewdness that could confound even Satan himself.

Ibid.

4 But in 1869, when outraged women demanded to know why they were not included in the right to vote [passage of the Fourteenth Amendment], they were informed by their allies in Congress that public opinion left room for just one minority group to make it through the door of suffrage and that this was "the Negro's hour."

"Two Can Make History," *The New York Times 25 May 2008*

5 But if history offers a lesson here, it is not that Americans cannot handle too much change at one time or that we must inch our way, one by one, through the door of equality. Rather, it is that opportunities for genuine change are rare and when they occur we must kick the door off the hinges while we can. It is

much harder to pry open the public mind once it has shut itself up again.

Ibid.

4764. Rebecca Barry (1968–)

1 People don't really want good advice. Good advice is: Eat bananas. Use condoms. Break up with the beautiful, terrible woman who will never stay with you. Bad advice is: Drink three bourbons a day. Sleep with your ex-boyfriend. Go look for a husband in a bar.

Later, At the Bar 2007

2 To her, the bar was like a good wedding, where love, sex, hope, and grief were just in the air and everyone who breathed it in was drunk not just on booze but the smoky haze around them.

Ibid.

3 Heartache, to her, coursed through everything—which was as it should be, since people needed it to make them kind.

Ibid.

4765. Iris Chang (1968–2004)

1 The chronicle of humankind's cruelty to fellow humans is a long and sorry tale. But if it is true that even in such horror tales there are degrees of ruthlessness, then few atrocities in world history compared in intensity and scale to the Rape of Nanking* during World War II.

Introduction, *The Rape of Nanking: The Forgotten Holocaust
of World War II 1997*

*The Imperial Japanese Army, which referred to it as the Nanking Incident, attacked Nanking (Nanjing) killing more than a quarter of a million Chinese in a six-week period.

2 America of today would not be the same America without the achievements of its ethnic Chinese.

The Chinese in America 2007

3 China's true grandeur, however, is not vested in its size or distance, but in its age—in five thousand years of continuous civilization and intact practices and traditions. The Chinese state is considered by many historians to be the oldest functioning organization on earth.

Ch. 1, *Ibid.*

4 When you believe you have a future, you think in terms of generations and years. When you do not, you live not just by the day—but by the minute. It is far better that you remember me as I was—in my heyday as a best-selling author—than the wild-eyed wreck who returned from Louisville . . . Each breath is becoming difficult for me to take—the anxiety can be compared to drowning in an open sea. I know that my actions will transfer some of this pain to others, indeed those who love me the most. Please forgive me. Forgive me because I cannot forgive myself.*

Suicide note, Quoted in "Historian Iris Chang won many
battles/The war she lost raged within," *San Francisco Gate
17 April 2005*

*Chang, who struggled with depression, committed suicide on 9 November.

4766. Céline Dion (1968–)

1 I feel like I'm at the bottom of the ladder, finally. I started at the top. I came down. Maturity is being grounded. When you feel grounded you feel strong. I know what I want.

People Magazine 3 December 2007

2 My life is to be a mom. It is what I enjoy the most. It is my most amazing reward. I will take a chance with my music. I don't take risks with my family.

Ibid.

4767. Heidi Julavits (1968–)

1 "Your passive-aggressive commentary is not desired at this moment," she said.
   "What's passive-aggressive about insincere curiosity?"

The Effect of Living Backwards 2005

2 Amnesia was not a disease, it was a practical use of storage space.

The Uses of Enchantment 2006

4768. Laura Cousino Klein (1968?–)

1 There's no doubt that friends are helping us live longer.

Quoted in "Be girly, live longer" by Lisa Reich, *The Telegraph*
(London) *12 August 2004*

2 There was this old joke that when the women who worked in the lab were stressed, they came in, cleaned the lab, had coffee, and bonded. When the men were stressed, they holed up somewhere on their own.

Quoted in Ch. 4, *Why Women Should Rule the World: A
Memoir* by Dee Dee Myers* 2008

*See 4590.

4769. Rachel Kushner (1968–)

1 Servants have their funny ways—superstitions—and you never know what they're up to.

Ch. 1, *Telex From Cuba 2008*

2 It was Daddy's idea to give the cane cutters plots of land so they could feed themselves, grow yucca and sweet potatoes. He believed in self-sufficiency. He brought over Rev. Crim, who ran United Fruit's agricultural school. The cane cutters' kids were mostly illiterate. They studied practical things: farming, housekeeping, Methodist values.

Ibid.

3 Mother said elegance was taking a plain outfit and accenting it with one flashy detail—a tie, maybe. I still think of her when I get dressed up.

Ibid.

4770. Lucy Lawless (1968–)

1 Television itself is obviously a powerful medium, reaching the wide world. The Internet covers the same territory but offers something else. It's not just a one-way thing anymore. They're all connecting up. They're diverse and widespread, but it's a tight-knit community.

Quoted in "Zena, Web Princess" by David Sheff, *Yahoo!
Internet Life May 1997*

2 All television is at least 5 percent eye candy.

Ibid.

3 It should be understood that New Zealand's shunning of [nuclear] vessels is not isolationist . . . It is not hostile atavism but an act of courage, hope for the future and love for our children's children.

"Albright role model . . ." Agence France Presse *4 August 1998*

4771. Maya MacGuineas (1968–   )

1   With the stimulus and growth components of the president's* economic proposals canceling each other out, the budget plan is likely to accomplish neither.

"An Economic Plan That Cancels Itself," *Los Angeles Times 7 February 2003*

*George W. Bush (1946–   ), Amer. politician; 43rd president of the United States (2001–09).

2   We have become accustomed to thinking that taxes, like hemlines, can only go up or down. This isn't true. Over the centuries changes in the form of U.S. taxes have been at least as dramatic as changes in the rate of taxation.

"Radical Tax Reform," *The Atlantic Monthly* (Boston) *January/February 2004*

3   If fairness means taxing people in accordance with their ability to pay, it is unfair to shift taxes away from the few who have benefited most from the New Economy and toward the many who have benefited much less (or even been hurt). But that is exactly what many of the tax reforms of the past several decades have done.

Ibid.

4   Globalization has made it easier for multinational corporations to follow the lowest labor costs and tax rates around the world; countries that can keep their tax burdens low have a competitive advantage over those that can't.

Ibid.

5   There are times when you need to run up the deficit and this is one of them. But we ran them up when we did not need to, and we have no plan to stop running them up. We have become serial deficit spenders.

"US Stares at a $1 Trillion Deficit," *Christian Science Monitor 16 October 2008*

6   There's a huge risk of another economic crisis, a debt crisis, once we get on the other side of this one.

Quoted in "Heavy spending to battle the financial crisis is unlikely to abate soon" by Jim Puzzanghera, *Los Angeles Times 30 November 2008*

4772. Irshad Manji (1968–   )

1   In Islam's golden age, so much progress was made that it became the basis of the European Renaissance. We Muslims have to change ourselves, that's the main difference. We can't keep blaming America or Israel for our misery.

The Trouble with Islam Today: A Muslim's Call for Reform in Her Faith 2003

2   Through our screaming self-pity and our conspicuous silences, we Muslims are conspiring against ourselves. We're in crisis, and we're dragging the rest of the world with us. If ever there was a moment for an Islamic reformation, it's now.

Ibid.

3   In the last 100 years alone, more Muslims have been tortured and murdered at the hands of other Muslims than at the hands of any former imperial power.

Interview by Beth Duff-Brown, Associated Press *1 May 2005*

4773. Sarah McLachlan (1968–   )

1   Oh my brother my sister my mother
your [sic] losing your identity

can't you see that it's you in the window
shining with intensity

"Circle," *Fumbling Towards Ecstasy 1993*

2   I love the time & in between the calm inside me
in the space where I can breathe
I believe there is a distance I have wandered
to touch upon the years of reaching out & reaching in
holding out holding in.
I believe this is heaven to no one else but me

"Elsewhere," Ibid.

3   . . . your angels speak with jilted tongues
the serpent's tale has come undone
you have no strength to squander.

"Ice," Ibid.

4   . . . every generation yields
a new born hope unjaded by their years.

"Wait," Ibid.

4774. Anuradha Mittal (1968–   )

1   Think about the courage of the poor who continue to occupy the land that the rich have stolen from them, even in the face of severe repression by private armies and police forces and death squads. We call them the "landless," but they are the ones who have earth in the cracks of their heels and under their fingernails. Their smell is of the land, and their blood washes the land for which they are killed. Look at them and tell me who has a right to the land.

Quoted in "Amid Plenty: Anuradha Mittal on the true cause of world hunger" by Derrick Jensen, *The Sun*, #314 *6 February 2002*

2   I wish it were true that U.S. aid came from a generosity of spirit, but it has always been a political tool used to control the behavior of Third World countries, to forge dubious alliances, and to buy cooperation during the Cold War.

Ibid.

3   Whoever controls the seed controls the food system.

Ibid.

4   The rich get richer at the expense of the poor. This mechanism is built into the capitalist system, around which our societies and our economies are organized. You know capitalism's "golden rule": whoever has the gold makes the rules. This system rewards greed and a complete lack of accountability on the part of ceos, investors, and transnational corporations.

Ibid.

5   Hunger is a social disease linked to poverty, and thus any discussion of hunger is incomplete without a discussion of economics.

Ibid.

6   Personally, I think that there should be a ban on the commercial usage of genetically engineered products until they have gone and they have proven to be safe for human health, for the environment and the livelihoods of farmers.

Quoted in "Hot Action" by Julie Sabatier, *Willamette Week* (Portland, Oreg.) *12 February 2007*

7   This industry [agri-biotech] has been using the PR tactics of green-washing, poor-washing and hope-dashing—by which I mean, these crops are good for the environment, or we need

these crops to feed the hungry, the poor, or we have to depend on this technology if you're going to feed the people because there is no other alternative.

> Quoted in "It Is Upon Us to Pave the Way for Sustainability" by Rajiv Fernando, IPS News *24 January 2008*

8   In countries like India or Brazil, hunger is caused by the failure to implement comprehensive agrarian reform where farmers have control and access over resources such as water, land, seeds.

> Ibid.

4775. Ann Wairimu Njogu (1968?–)

1   I needed new challenges. I had risen to the highest level in the company. Being young and energetic, I needed an occupation that could bring smiles to disadvantaged members of society.

> Quoted in "Born to fight—Healing the needy in society" by Evelyne Ogutu, Africanpress.com *3 May 2008*

2   America is ripe for that real change. It presents a very big opportunity for Americans to really embrace growth. Because you can only grow when you move from your comfort zone.

> Quoted in "Kenyan Politicians to America: Don't Be Afraid of Obama" by Andrew Rice, *The New York Observer 28 August 2008*

3   Kenyans like the rest of the world are indeed proud of the Barack Obama* candidature—not because of his origin, but because of the kind of change that he portrays and intends to bring to the world scene on foreign policy. I am curious though to know what the real motivation of the American press is in really emphasizing on the American and African roots of Barack Obama as opposed to seeking to advance the real change that he would be standing for.

> Ibid.

*Barack Obama (1961–), 44th president of the United States (2009–); his biological father was from Kenya.

4776. Mahboba Rawi (1968–)

1   So many Muslim women love to wear a scarf, and people don't realize this. You look colorful, it's our fashion, it's our identity, it's our culture, it's our religion.

> Quoted in "Down Under the Veil, Australia's Muslim Women Face a Rising Tide of Xenophobia" by Marianna Leishman, commonlanguageproject.net *12 March 2007*

2   I went back to my country, but 75% of the buildings were demolished, all there is was this horrible war, there is no house for me. I don't have a home to go to. This is my home!

> Ibid.

4777. Katie Roiphe (1968–)

1   As we are settling into our new surroundings, there are fliers and counselors and videotapes telling us how not to get AIDS and how not get raped, where not to wander and what signals not to send. By the end of freshman week, we know exactly what not do do.

> "The Blue-Light System," *The Morning After: Sex, Fear, and Feminism 1993*

2   In this era of Just Say No and No Means No, we don't have many words for embracing experience. Now instead of liberation and libido, the emphasis is on trauma and disease.

> Ibid.

3   Freedom from fear is a mythical premise and a state of mind.

> "Taking Back the Night," Ibid.

4   Allowing verbal coercion to constitute rape is a sign of tolerance toward the ultrafeminine stance of passivity.

> "The Morning After," Ibid.

5   Everything that flickered could be made permanent. That was what drew him to photography, what made every painstaking step worth it: the permanence of the image.

> Ch. 1, *Still She Haunts Me 2001*

4778. Jennifer Aniston (1969–)

1   It's unfortunate, but we live in a very disposable society. Those moments where it looks like 'Uh-oh, this isn't working!'— those are the most important, transformative moments. Most couples draw up divorce papers when they're missing out on an amazing moment of deepening and enlightenment and connection.

> Quoted in "The Unsinkable Jennifer Aniston" by Leslie Bennetts, *Vanity Fair September 2005*

2   When things happen, the tribe gathers around and lifts you up.

> Ibid.

3   A man divorcing would never be accused of choosing career over children.

> Ibid.

4779. Aviel Barclay (1969–)

1   It's a very strong statement for women to be empowered to tell the story of our people. . . .* This, I hope, will have permanent, long-term, positive impact on the role of women not only within traditional Judaism but globally, God willing.

> Quoted in "Black Fire on White Paper" by Leah Eichler, *Moment, A Conversation on Jewish Culture, Politics and Religion* (momentmag.com) *2003*

*Barclay is the first female Sofer Stam (Jewish ritual scribe).

4780. Emily Barton (1969–)

1   Men's faculties may have been as well developed as ours, but they spent so much effort scratching their existence from the soil that they had no time for ideas or contemplation. What sufficed sufficed; and however much men might have profited from introspection, their days were full of drudgery that kept it at bay.

> Ch. 1, *The Testament of Yves Gundron 2000*

2   *-Mannahata!* I'd whisper to the city, straining ever northward against her dense forest, and *-Scheyichibi!* to the green hummocks of Jersey, stretched out before me in a broad, flat band. *-Ihpetonga!* I'd think passionately, feeling the resonating power of the rocky heights on which I stood as I called it by its ancient name. The natives of the place had been driven east into Nassau and Suffolk generations before my parents had arrived . . . but I still liked to let their words roll round my mouth, like smooth river stones. These were clearly the names by which the places knew themselves. I felt them respond to my call, however quietly I voiced it; and I half expected the ground to tremble and send forth some spirit, either to squash me like a bug or to do my bidding.

> Ch. 1, *Brookland 2006*

3 But distance changes much;-I have missed you with a pain very like that of yearning for the dead since you've been gone.

Ibid.

4 ... there was no man among them so loyal he could not be tempted by a small gift of money and a monthly allotment of good gin.

Ibid.

4781. Sarah Boxer (1969?–)

1 The contraceptives that ... guard against disease are the least reliable at birth control.

"Contraception Conundrum: It's Not Just Birth Control Anymore," *The New York Times* 22 *June 1997*

2 Some songs have all the luck. They lead double, even triple lives, meaning everything to everyone, and meaning it passionately.

"Art of the Internet: A Protest Song, Reloaded," *The New York Times* 24 *September 2005*

3 Oh, if only children's books had no words! Then you could make up whatever you wanted to go with the pictures and speed along as you wished, guilt-free.

"Moving Experiences," *The New York Times* 12 *November 2006*

4 I don't have a blogging bone in my body. I am not an exhibitionist. I do not crave friends I've never met. I hate gossip. The ding of new e-mail hitting my in-box fills me with dread. Instant messaging makes me feel like I've been cornered at a party with no drink.

Introduction, *Ultimate Blogs: Masterworks from the Wild Web 2008*

4782. Leslie T. Chang (1969–)

1 For China's emerging middle class, this is an age of aspiration—but also a time of anxiety. Opportunities have multiplied, but each one brings pressure to take part and not lose out, and every acquisition seems to come ready-wrapped in disappointment that it isn't something newer and better.

"Gilded Age, Gilded Cage," *National Geographic May 2008*

2 ... you could say that the story of people leaving home in search of a better life is really the story of all nations and all people.

"In Conversation with Leslie T. Chang," BoowBrowse.com *2008*

3 Getting into a factory was easy. The hard part was getting out.

Ch. 1, *Factory Girls—From Village to City in a Changing China 2008*

4 If it was an ugly world, at least it was their own.

End, *Ibid.*

4783. Tina Chang (1969–)

1 The woman who wears
these shoes will be a warrior, will not think
about how wrong she is, how her calculations
look like the face of a clock with hands
ticking with each terrorizing minute.

"Duality," St. 3, *2007*

4784. Edwidge Danticat (1969–)

1 There are two ways to go to the cemetery. One is on your two feet, the other is in a box. Either way, it is a large travail.

Breath, Eyes, Memory 1994

2 According to Tante Atie, each finger had a purpose. It was the way she had been taught to prepare herself to become a woman. Mothering. Boiling. Loving. Baking. Nursing. Frying. Healing. Washing. Ironing. Scrubbing. It wasn't her fault, she said. Her ten fingers had been named for her even before she was born. Sometimes, she wished she had six fingers on each hand so she could have two left for herself.

Ibid.

4785. Emma Donoghue (1969–)

1 Insomniac at 4 a.m., the writer fantasized about going one step further and speaking the plain truth. No, Jonas, he might say to the spotty boy, this isn't a poem. These are pretentious words from an online thesaurus, typed out in no particular order.

"WriteOr," *Touchy Subjects 2006*

2 Appalled by his credit card debts, the writer succumbed to a one-year writer-in-residence job at a small college in the mountains.

Ibid.

3 The day he was 43, he accepted Jesus Christ as his Lord and Personal Savior. It was quite a shock to his system.

"The Man Who Wrote on Beaches," *Ibid.*

4786. Caroline Elkins (1969–)

1 The hypocrisies, the exploitations, the violence, and the suffering were all laid bare in the Pipeline.* It was there that Britain finally revealed the true nature of its civilizing mission.

Imperial Reckoning: The Untold Story of Britain's Gulag in Kenya 2006

*The British detention system in Kenya, a pipeline of overflowing prison camps where inmates routinely died.

2 'Mau Mau became for many whites in Kenya, and for many Kikuyu loyalists as well, what the Armenians had been to the Turks ... and the Jews to the Nazis. As with any incipient genocide, the logic was all too easy to follow.

Ibid.

3 [The British in Kenya believed they] had a duty, a moral obligation, to redeem the "backward heathens" of the world. The British were going to bring light to the Dark Continent. This was cultural imperialism par excellence. This was the "White Man's Burden."*

Ibid.

*Title of 1899 poem by English poet Rudyard Kipling (1865–1936).

4 Far from leaving behind democratic institutions and cultures, Britain bequeathed to its former colonies corrupted and corruptible governments. Colonial officials hand-picked political successors as they left in the wake of World War II, lavishing political and economic favors on their proteges. This process created elites whose power extended into the post-colonial era.

"What's Tearing Kenya Apart? History, for One Thing," *The Washington Post 6 January 2008*

4787. Ruth Forman (1969?–)

1 we don have no backyard
frontyard neither
we got black magic n brownstone steps
when the sun go down

"Young Cornrows Callin Out the Moon," *We Are the Young Magicians 1993*

2 . . . poetry should ride the bus
in a fat woman's Safeway bag
between the greens n chicken wings
to be served with Tuesday's dinner . . .
"Poetry Should Ride the Bus," Ibid.

3 . . . it is not your pen you are looking for. . . .

it is your tongue. . . .

it will not matter if your pockets are empty
if you write with a green Bic or a black Bic
or the blood of your finger
you will write
you will write
"If You Lose Your Pen," Ibid.

4788. Elizabeth Gilbert (1969–)

1 "Crosby says the first job of a horse is to figure out who's riding it and who's in charge."
"That's my old man's line. He says it to scare dudes. If horses were that smart, they'd be riding us."
"That's Crosby's line."
"No." I took another drink. "That's my old man's line, too."
"Pilgrims," *Pilgrims* 1997

2 Certainly other women had produced as many children in the island's history, but only over decades and only with evident reluctance. Seven babies born to a single exuberant family in just under six years seemed almost epidemic.
Ch. 1, *Stern Men* 2000

3 Briefly, the history of America goes like this: there was a frontier, and then there was no longer a frontier. It all happened rather quickly. There were Indians, then explorers, then settlers, then towns, then cities. Nobody was really paying attention until the moment the wilderness was officially tamed, at which point everybody wanted it back.
Ch. 1, *The Last American Man* 2002

4 If I lived somewhere cheaper than New York, maybe I could afford an extra bedroom and then I could have a special meditation room! That'd be nice. I could paint it gold. Or maybe a rich blue. No, gold. No, blue. . . . Finally noticing this train of thought, I was aghast. I thought: . . . How about this, you spastic fool—how about you try to meditate right here, right now, right where you actually are?
Eat, Pray, Love 2006

4789. Ayaan Hirsi Ali (1969–)

1 Life on earth is a test, and I was failing it, even though I was trying as hard as I knew how to. I was failing as a Muslim.
Infidel 2006

2 I was on a psychological mission to accept living without a God, which means accepting that I give my life its own meaning.
Ibid.

3 It takes a long time to dissolve the bars of a mental cage.
Ibid.

4 Islam is not a race . . . Islam is simply a set of beliefs, and it is not 'Islamophobic' to say Islam is incompatible with liberal democracy.
"Never confuse Islamic Sharia and the Muslims who really mean it with those extremist Christians who live in the United States," *Jihad Watch 13 July 2007*

5 Where there is no freedom of speech, there is no conscience.
Speech, European Parliament *14 February 2008*

4790. Ilyse Hogue (1969?–)

1 . . . the actions of increasingly large and unaccountable corporations are destroying the life-support systems of the Earth.
Quoted in "We Can Do It . . ." by Gregory Dicum, *San Francisco Chronicle 8 March 2006*

2 I think women are naturally inclined to think further out. Evolutionary biology has made certain that we instinctively nurture a safe, clean home, because we are responsible for care taking new life on a day-to-day basis in a different way than men. It might not sound super feminist, but thinking that way is a vision of a new world. The environmental movement is inherently transformative. It is a more feminine paradigm that is based on recognizing the connection that we all share as human beings.
Ibid.

3 For a long time, feminism was defined as women achieving in a male system. If you could go toe-to-toe with the guys and sit with your brandy and your cigar and at the end of the day have raked in more bucks or leveraged more power, then you were an accomplished woman. . . . [But now] We're after a world in which we actually become the archetype. That doesn't mean being good at what men have already done. It means it's time to draw up new plans and implement them. It's our turn.
Ibid.

4791. Olivia Judson (1969–)

1 We are engaged in only a small part of the sexual behaviour on the planet. In fact, ours is rather pedestrian when you look at other species. If it wasn't for the fact that it's ours, I doubt that we'd give it much attention.
Dr. Tatiana's Sex Advice to All Creation, The Definitive Guide to the Evolutionary Biology of Sex 2002

2 Monogamy is one of the most deviant behaviors in biology.
Ibid.

3 Boys are promiscuous and girls are chaste, right? Wrong. The battle of the sexes erupts because, in most species, girls are wanton.
Introduction, Ibid.

4 Studying evolution has changed the way I look at nature. For knowing that all of us—oak trees and venus fly traps, starlings and brush turkeys, humans and sea urchins, not to mention bacteria harvesting light from the glowing vents at the bottom of the sea—are the products of the same ancient forces is something that brings me enormous pleasure, awe and a sense of peace. As I have learned more about other organisms, I have come to regard them (and us!) with increasing amazement and delight.
The Wild Side, "Why I Study Evolution," *The New York Times* Blog *29 June 2006*

5 A male [starling] came back from the river, a feather in his beak, and perched on the roof of a shed. A light gust of wind blew the feather from his grasp—and he began to run along after it, like a man chasing a 10 pound note.
Ibid.

6 When we come to a difficult problem—something, say, that appears so complicated it is hard to imagine the steps through

which it could have evolved—the solution isn't to throw up one's hands and invoke deus ex machina. It's to imagine, to dream, to wonder: how? And then, to start to work it out.

Ibid.

4792. Paola Kaufman (1969–2006)

1 We had, how do I say it, the certainty of being loved, but never the feeling of love. Father's love, and also Mother's, was something that passed over one quickly, like the wind passes over the dry branches of the trees in winter, unaffected by them, passing on and leaving the only proof of its affection a few small piles of snow on the ground.

Ch. 1, The Sister 2003

2 To define home is to define God.

Ch. 6, Ibid.

3 Then, one morning, I discovered just that: that life would be like that day for ever. Just as it had been the day before so it would be the following day, and so would it be from then onwards. I discovered, not unhappily, that there was an order, a routine, to the things of each day, a measured rhythm that reflected life itself, in the same way that the cogs and wheels of a watch always work in the same way and are intrinsic to the passing of time.

Ch. 7, Ibid.

4 I suppose that having lost true love once, I never wanted to replace it with a lukewarm approximation that would only serve to make me remember it for ever.

Ibid.

5 Perhaps in the future world they'll find the way to prevent memory becoming a burden, to prevent all one's memories weighing as much as one's own bones, deforming them like my arthritic fingers are deformed every morning.

Ch. 14, Ibid.

4793. Nancy Kerrigan (1969–)

1 Why me? Why, why, why?*

Widely quoted remark (Detroit, Mich.) 6 January 1994

*On her foot being deliberately clubbed shortly before the 1994 Winter Olympics.

4794. Min Jin Lee (1969–)

1 The parishioners at my father's church called my mother a saint, and I suppose she was. But as her daughter, I didn't feel like I knew her very well, because she was so busy serving others.

"Axis of Happiness," Narrative Magazine 2004

2 She came to believe that the penalties incurred for the mistakes you made had to be paid out in full to the members of your family. But she didn't believe that she could ever discharge these sums.

"Motherland," The Missouri Review 2004

3 Competence can be a curse.

Ch. 1, Free Food for Millionaires 2007

4 A brilliant student of both physics and philosophy, Tina had once scolded Casey when she was on Weight Watchers: "The world is awash in hunger. How could you cause your own?"

Ibid.

5 "I'm sick of hearing how bad I am, when I'm not. You won the sweepstakes with kids like us. Why aren't we good enough?"

Ibid.

4795. Nora Bermúdez Méndez (1969–)

1 We believed
before they tortured us
that we carried
all the sensitivity of the world
in the soft plains of our skin.
And now we understand,
compañeros,
that conviction and faith
can't be carried on the skin
because if this were so
they would have killed us
a long time ago.

"Testimonies," A Poetics of Resistance: Women Writing in El Salvador, South Africa, and the United States Mary K. DeShazer, ed. 1994

4796. Binta S. Mohammed (1969?–)

1 Standing all alone, solitary
Smiling my sad smile
Inward is the only asylum

"Solitude" 1999

2 Feminism is a relative term. It can be interpreted with varying levels of emphasis. As far as I am concerned, feminism is concerned with the issues of women. It doesn't mean that you hate men or you are against them. But you are just discussing women's problems in search of befitting solutions.

Quoted in "There's Nothing Wrong With Feminism" by Muhammad Kabir Yusuf, allAfrica.com 16 September 2008

3 When I say man is naturally polygamous, I want us to look at the history of humanity. Throughout history, and whether through formal marriage or not, man would naturally want to have more than one woman. Either he would have one wife and many girlfriends out there or he would have many wives through formal marriage. What I was actually saying is that it is more honest to make it formal.

Ibid.

4 There is nothing wrong with censorship as long as it is done to protect public morality and advance the cause of creativity.

Ibid.

4797. Kathleen Parker (1969?–)

1 There are certain things you don't kid around with, and hormonally charged teenage boys and loaded guns are among the top two.

"Rape California-style. . . ," Orlando Sentinel (Florida) 14 January 2003

2 Art is not literal nor is it a policy statement. If it makes us stop and think, swear and weep, crash our cymbals and rage against the night—or question our point of view—then art will have done its best work. If only we would let it.

"We cheat ourselves by censoring challenging art," Ibid. 6 March 2003

3 The man at the top of the food chain does not have to play by bureaucracy's rule.

"Leader didn't rise to the occasion," Ibid. 8 September 2005

4 We love to boast that we are a nation of immigrants—and we are. But there's a different sense of America among those who trace their bloodlines back through generations of sacrifice.
"Getting Bubba," *Jewish World Review 14 May 2008*

5 If BS were currency, Palin* could bail out Wall Street herself.
   If Palin were a man, we'd all be guffawing, just as we do every time Joe Biden tickles the back of his throat with his toes. But because she's a woman—and the first ever on a Republican presidential ticket—we are reluctant to say what is painfully true.
"Palin Problem: She's out of her league," *National Review Online 26 September 2008*
   *Sarah P- ; see 4684.

4798. Joy Pincus (1969–   )

1 Coaches are hired to help people deal with any number of issues: finding a spouse, earning more money, changing career direction—challenges that people have faced for a long time. The methods used, however, are quite revolutionary: Unlike a consultant, who comes as an authority on an issue, a coach is not there to give advice or answers, but rather to ask questions and be a good listener.
"Coaching for Life," *Jerusalem Post 24 August 2004*

2 Knowing that something may or may not be very wrong with one's unborn child demands a precarious psychological balance. One has to walk a very thin line between expectation and resignation; simultaneously hoping for the best and preparing for the worst.
"An Abortion Sets Major Milestone in Her Life," *Women's E-News 14 August 2008*

3 So many things we meet in life are beyond our control, how we respond to them is not. In fact, our ability to choose how we respond may be the greatest gift we have as humans, and one of the most powerful things we have to offer others.
Ibid.

4799. Nina Revoyr (1969–   )

1 . . . it was as if she feared that if she stopped playing well and receiving recognition, she would somehow cease to exist.
The Necessary Hunger 1997

4800. B. Ruby Rich (1969?–   )

1 The global context of contemporary life rarely enters into the theoretical debates, as though to indicate that sexuality is not really as socially constructed as claimed, as though sexual issues were not so deeply affected, after all, by history, the economy, the cold war, disease, the new conservatism, or even fashion.
"Feminism and Sexuality in the Eighties" (1986), *Chick Flicks: Theories and Memories of the Feminist Film Movement 1998*

2 I really do believe film is the literature of our time. Ideas get played out on screen, and we identify with the characters we see. Film today is a secular religion. People's experience of the world is often mediated through movies.
"Films can make a difference, says critic B. Ruby Rich" by Jennifer McNulty, *Currents* (Univ. of Calif. at Santa Cruz), vol. 9, no. 27 *7–13 March 2005*

4801. Christina Salvatore (1969–   )

1 A better world for women is a better world for everyone.
UNIFEM End VAW Campaign Letter to District 11, Zona International, *28 November 2007*

4802. Marjane Satrapi (1969–   )

1 The Iraqis have always been our enemies. They want to invade us. That would be bad enough, but their driving is atrocious.
Persepolis 2003

2 If only my parents had known that their daughter was made up like a punk, that she smoked joints and had seen men in underpants—while they were being bombed, every day.
Ibid.

3 *Of her status as a princess:* . . . the kings of the Qajar dynasty . . . had hundreds of wives. They made thousands of kids. If you multiply these kids by generation you have, I don't know, ten to fifteen thousand princes and princesses. There's nothing extremely special about that.
Quoted in "A life in graphic detail" by Vanessa E. Jones, *Boston Globe 4 October 2004*

4 I have problems with authority. I wasn't made to take orders. My grandmother used to tell me: "Laws are for idiots." She was right.
Quoted in "Marjane Satrapi: Princess of darkness" by Robert Chalmers, *The Independent* (London) *1 October 2006*

5 When you're dropped in a pile of shit, so to speak, you have to decide—either add to the pile, or use it as fertiliser, and grow flowers.
Ibid.

4803. Deborah Siegel (1969–   )

1 As a result, in part, of the media's coverage of our candidates, the fracturing of our identities into gender, race, class, and age has been so thorough that the main task we have as a nation now is pulling ourselves together into a whole. If we're lucky, this new nation will be an improvement on what we had. If we don't exert every effort at reconciliation, these historic breakthroughs in political participation will be for naught. Media's involvement in our division—and its responsibility in the healing—cannot be underestimated.
"Bias, Punditry, and The Press: Where Do We Go From Here?" womensmediacenter.com *2008*

4804. Tanita Tikaram (1969?–   )

1 Look my eyes are just holograms
"twist in my sobriety" *n.d.*

2 Chance, changes are all that you have
"i love you" *n.d.*

4805. Irene Vilar (1969–   )

1 The Nation is a mother and Lolita,* who may have had trouble in being a mother before, now would not hesitate to die for that Nation.
A Message from God in the Atomic Age, Gregory Rabassa, tr. *1996*
   *L—Lebron; see 2605.

2 Soon she began to look for herself in the mirrors of motherhood. Each new pregnancy . . . must have been another way of filling hollow places.
Ibid.

4806. Rebecca Walker (1969–   )

1 Where are the stories that challenge the notion that perfect happiness can be found in a "perfect" body? Where are the anecdotes about learning to love parts of ourselves not because of how they look or how they measure up to Cindy Crawford,* but because of how they feel to us, or how they tell a unique part of our personal history.

> Foreword, *Adiós, Barbie: Young Women Write about Body Image and Identity*, Ophira Edut, ed. *1998*
> *American fashion model.

2 They say that love is the tie that binds, and not blood. In a photograph from their wedding day, they stand, brown and pale pink, inseparable, my mother's tiny five-foot-one-inch frame nestled birdlike within my father's protective embrace. Fearless, naive, breathtaking, they profess their shiny, outlaw love for all the world to see.

> *Black, White, and Jewish: Autobiography of a Shifting Self* *2000*

3 A nurse walks into Mama's room, my birth certificate in hand. At first glance, all of the information seems straightforward enough: mother, father, address, and so on. But next to boxes labeled "Mother's Race" and "Father's Race," which read Negro and Caucasian, there is a curious note tucked into the margin. "Correct?" it says. "Correct?" a faceless questioner wants to know. Is this union, this marriage, and especially this offspring, correct?

A mulatta baby swaddled and held in loving arms, two brown, two white, in the middle of the segregated South. I'm sure the nurses didn't have many reference points. Let's see. Black. White. Nigger. Jew. That makes me the tragic mulatta caught between both worlds like the proverbial deer in the headlights.

> Ibid.

4807. Aye Aye Win (1969?–   )

1 No one knows better about poverty than the billions of women, men, boys and girls living in the most deprived conditions, not knowing where the next meal will come from, or how long they will be living in a shed they call their home. No one knows better about exclusion than those who are constantly marginalized because of their social or physical status. No one knows better about injustice than those who are daily facing injustice. No one has greater self-interest to transform the situation than the affected communities themselves.

> Address, "Globalising from Below," World Social Forum (Nairobi) *January 2007*

2 What we need is nothing less than a local-global social transformation.

> Ibid.

4808. Michele Wucker (1969–   )

1 Haiti is a place where reality sometimes seems far away. To explain their world, Haitians often speak in proverbs, translating their daily life into symbols and images rather than attempting the impossible task of dissecting it. Analyses of Haiti's labyrinthine politics, of its shifting alliances and the personages that change on the surface of the country's leadership but nothing more, tend to collapse under their own weight.

> Ch. 1, *Why the Cocks Fight: Dominicans, Haitians, and the Struggle for Hispaniola* *2000*

2 At Carnival, the loudest voices are those of the ones who are usually silent: the strongman president is transformed into a smiling, wizened old man who provokes only laughter, while those who represent the Tainos, the slaves and the misfits are the most powerful and admired paraders. For a short time, the masses are more powerful than the Great Man. And men, who the rest of the year pride themselves on their machismo, can show off as women at Carnival. Briefly, traditional roles are reversed.

> Ch. 9, Ibid.

3 America's greatest economic asset is its ability to attract the world's ablest and most talented individuals to a system that can harness their abilities better than any other in the world. It is the combination of these individuals and the system that has made this country the world's engine of innovation and economic growth.

> "On the importance of skilled immigration to the U.S. economy," *LOCKOUT: Why America Keeps Getting Immigration Wrong When Our Prosperity Depends on Getting It Right* *2006*

4 In immigration policy, as in drug policy, enforcement too often is directed against the victims but fails to punish those who benefit . . .

> "On enforcing immigration laws," Ibid.

5 The only way to slow desperation-driven migration is to reduce desperation.

> "On designing laws that work," Ibid.

4809. Renée Zellweger (1969–   )

1 It does make things awkward, being constantly recognised. It's like being in a permanent state of adolescence. You know, when you're 13 and you start to get uncomfortable in your body, aware of the changes, and you're worried about your hair and your clothes. Then you go into the school lunchroom and you think they are all turning to see if there's something up your nose or in your teeth. Well, that's what it's like being famous.

> "Lone Star," *The Telegraph* (London) *28 October 2004*

4810. Rania Al-Abdullah (1970–   )

1 Today's events are a clear reminder that both sides of the conflict are suffering. It is also clear that the suffering cannot continue*.

> Quoted in "PM's Wife 'Sorry' in Suicide Bomb Row," BBC News *18 June 2002*
> *Re the death of Israeli citizens by a Palestinian suicide bomber.

2 A lens is something through which you can really reach out to people and get your message across.

> Quoted in "Queen Rania Takes on Stereotypes" by Beth Jones, BBC News *25 July 2008*

3 I do feel that our world is in a bit of a crisis at the moment. Violence has overtaken dialogue and compassion has lost out to anger. I'm hoping this [her YouTube V-log] will become a channel of communication between east and west because I very much think our world is in dire need of that.

> Ibid.

4811. Meltem Agduk Agduk (1970?–   )

1 If you want to change the mentality of a country, you need to involve many social actors . . . You need the government to enact and implement legislation, you need NGOs and other civil society and social actors, and you need the support of the private sector.

> "It Takes a Country: Turkey's Concerted Efforts to Stop Violence Against Women," UNFPA.org/News *26 February 2007*

2 Music is a language that all people can understand.
Ibid.

4812. Erin J. Aubry (1970?–)

1 My butt has a reserve of esteem and then some; like the brain, it may even have profound, uncharted capacities to heal.
"The Butt: Its Politics, Its Profanity, Its Power," *Adiós, Barbie: Young Women Write about Body Image and Identity,* Ophira Edut, ed. *1998*

2 Perhaps the secret of Oprah's* success lies in her ability to align worthy ideals with canny marketing.
"The Oprah Effect," *LA Weekly 27 May 1998*
*O- Winfrey; see 4285.

3 This is about no leaders. This is about the utter failure of collective reason in an age of fevered individualism. This is about the powder keg of racial frustration that keeps blowing up at odd and seemingly inappropriate moments because, 35 years after it relinquished its last legal claims as enforcer of a social and economic apartheid that was birthed in slavery, white America is content to live in a state of perilous ignorance about the persistent inequities of black and white.
"Unsocial Studies," Ibid. *12 May 1999*

4813. Mariah Carey (1970–)

1 You look at me and see the girl,
who lives inside the golden world,
but don't believe, that's all there is to see,
you'll never know the real me.
"Looking In," *Daydream* (album) *1995*

2 blindly I imagined I could keep you under glass,
now I understand to hold you I must open my hands, and watch you rise.
"Butterfly," *Butterfly* (album) *1997*

3 I can make it through the rain,
I can stand up once again,
on my own, and I know,
that I'm strong enough to mend
"Through The Rain," *Charmbracelet* (album) *2002*

4 Who's gonna love you when it all falls down?
Who's gonna love you when your bankroll runs out?
Who's gonna care when the novelty's over?
When the star of the show isn't you anymore.
"Clown," Ibid.

5 See, I'm looking for a man that'll rub me slow,
Make me sing real high when he goes down low.
"One & Only," *The Emancipation of Mimi* (album) *2005*

4814. Meghan Daum (1970–)

1 Most people now accept that women, especially teenagers, often make decisions regarding abortion based on educational and career goals and whether the father of the unborn child is someone they want to hang around with for the next few decades. The "choice" in this equation is not only a matter of whether to carry an individual fetus to term but a question of what kind of life the woman wishes to lead.
But what about the kind of life men want to lead?
"Shouldn't men have 'choice' too?" *Los Angeles Times 10 December 2005*

2 Everyone loves Evite.* Before this great innovation came our way, party hosts had the laborious task of writing up an e-mail announcing their events and then, gasp, typing people's addresses in the recipient field and sending it from their own accounts. And if you think that sounds medieval, I've heard there was a time when people called their friends on the phone to invite them to a party or, get this, wrote invitations by hand and distributed them through the U.S. mail!
"Eviting trouble," Ibid. *18 November 2006*
*On-line service for event and party invitations and r.s.v.p.'s.

3 For every wife who complains about dirty socks, there's another whose husband insists on neurotically folding them into perfect spheres. For every fading ingenue whose self-loathing and insecurity (or is it self-entitlement and ego?) drive her to the plastic surgeon's office, there's one (actually, more than one) who sees no shame in extra-large sweatpants. And for every marriage that looks like a tour through hell, there's one that looks like stratospheric bliss—sometimes these poles can exist within the same marriage on the same day.
"The books that read women," Ibid. *6 January 2007*

4815. Louise Dean (1970–)

1 Before he'd had cancer he'd been bored with life. Since he'd taken dying seriously, he'd been busy.
First line, *Becoming Strangers 2004*

2 It was not the British who have the stiff upper lips anymore, she thought . . . it's the Americans. She found them proud and complete. Other people suffered openly, like fish held up in the air, lips with hooks in them, gasping.
Ibid.

3 It was too hard to bear if you thought about it as a whole, you had to divide the awful task of raising children into days of trials and tempers, minutes of love, seconds of comprehension.
This Human Season 2007

4 There was no one who could rescue her from what she loved.
Ibid.

5 Terrorists, men and boys, all thinking their thoughts, minds like clocks that needed no winding. What were they remembering, what were they learning? Was killing educational? Perhaps, as a generation is brief. The young sowed horror in their springtime with high hopes for the crop and it rotted down through a long summer. They harvested grief in the autumn of their lives. And did they believe, even as they held their grandchildren, that there would be an end to it all? After a hard winter killed what was left of them off, it came again, this human season, this springtime of hatred. The young went to it because it was in their nature. Could a father teach his son to go against his nature? Could a son learn such a thing from his father? He didn't know.
Ibid.

6 [The evening news] . . . a chance to relax with a cup and a fag, listening to the killings.
Ibid.

4816. Ani DiFranco (1970–)

1 i got the answer here
i wrote it down somewhere
i just gotta find it
"Coming Up," Verse 1, *Imperfectly* (album) *1992*

2 every time i say something
they find hard to hear
they chalk it up to my anger
never to their own fear
"Not A Pretty Girl," Verse 2, *Not A Pretty Girl* (album) 1995

3 the river has more colors at sunset
than my sock drawer ever dreamed of
"Tiptoe," Ibid.

4 and you won't see me surrender
you won't hear me confess
'cuz you've left me with nothing
but i've worked with less
"Dilate," Verse 3, *Dilate* (album) 1996

5 i found religion in the greeting card aisle
now i know hallmark was right
"Superhero," Verse 1, Ibid.

6 art may imitate life
but life imitates t.v.
Ibid.

7 and i wonder who's gonna be president
tweedle dumb or tweedle dumber?
"Fuel," Verse 2, *Little Plastic Castle* (album) 1998

8 i've gotten out of everything
i've gotten into so far
"Virtue," *Up, Up, Up, Up, Up, Up* (album) 1999

4817. Susan Dworkin (fl. 1970s–1990s)

1 We are genetically programmed to be too fat for American fashion. Let down your guard and you can easily look like Mrs. Khrushchev, who comes from the same basic gene pool . . .
The Book of Candy 1996

2 . . . he had entered into his compact with Candy with so much pre-existing hatred for her breed and class of woman that there was never really any chance for survival.
Ibid.

3 [The JAP*] . . . comforter, guardian, caretaker, supporting the whole Jewish nation on her soft shoulders, cushioning the descent of his soul with her plump arms and plucking him out of the nightmares, protecting his sacred work, always waiting up, always worrying.
Ibid.

*Pejorative acronym for Jewish American Princess.

4818. Jennifer Gilmore (1970–)

1 If Seymour was to leave me, where would all my anger go?
Golden Country 2006

4819. Adele Griffin (1970–)

1 "I'm a ghost story, too. Geneve and me both. And our story is so awful that it crowds out everything else about us."
The Other Shepards 1998

2 . . . long limbs as delicately hinged as japanese brushtrokes . . .
Ibid.

4820. Tonya Harding (1970–)

1 To be perfectly honest, what I'm really thinking about are dollar signs.*
Quoted in *The New York Times* 15 January 1994
Re her wished-for product-endorsement contracts; they never materialized due to her involvement in a physical attack on rival Nancy Kerrigan; see 4793

4821. Anne Kajir (1970/74–)

1 Papua New Guinea is famous for its corruption, which permeates all levels of society. This corruption is fuelled by greed of multinational corporations who are hell bent on stealing resources from its traditional custodians.
Acceptance Speech, Goldman Award (San Francisco) 2006

2 How can anyone call it development when the land is raped for profit and the benefits of a few?
Ibid.

3 Landowners depend entirely on their forests as a means of survival so they must be properly informed on the impacts of logging on their land before signing away their customary birth given rights to these natural resources. It will be genocide if the robber barons continue to roam at will or plunge deeper into our last remaining rainforests.
Quoted on goldmanprize.org 2006

4822. Malalai Kaker (1970–2008)

1 You have long moustaches but you have no bravery.
Remark to fellow officers who abandoned an insurgency, quoted in "Trailblazing detective pays with her life" by Rosie DiManno, *The Star* (Toronto) 29 September 2008

2 People have small, narrow minds. It will take a long time for many people to accept (females) in this position. But I want to show other women that it can be done, even here in Kandahar (Afghanistan).
Ibid.

4823. Naomi Klein (1970–)

1 Countries are shocked—by wars, terror attacks, coups d'état and natural disasters. . . . they are shocked again—by corporations and politicians who exploit the fear and disorientation of this first shock to push through economic shock therapy.
The Shock Doctrine, The Rise of Disaster Capitalism 2007

2 Washington's game plan for Iraq . . . Shock and terrorize the entire country, deliberately ruin its infrastructure, do nothing while its culture and history are ransacked, then make it all O.K. with an unlimited supply of cheap household appliances and imported junk food.
Ibid.

4824. Jennifer Lopez (1970–)

1 The number of women and children who live in an environment without access to quality health care or health education is far too great for us to ignore. After the birth of my newborns, whom I realized were receiving fantastic medical care, I also realized that my passion was not to just try to increase the access to healthcare for underserved women and children, but to try to improve the quality of this care for everyone, regardless of their ability to pay.
News & Blog, jenniferlopez.com *16 August 2008*

4825. Annette Motley (fl. 1970s–1980s)

1 "Ah, Second Daughter, your imagination takes you journeying as far as any traveler."

"Is that a curse, or a blessing, do you think?"

"A blessing, surely as long as imagination outstrips desire."

Pt. I, Ch. 3, *Green Dragon, White Tiger* 1986

2 How the Chinese man loved to build such walls. It was part of his temperament. He built them around his cities and his houses; around his women; and most of all around his innermost thoughts.

Ch. 4, Ibid.

4826. Hannah Nelson (fl. 1970s)

1 I have grown to womanhood in a world where the saner you are, the madder you are made to appear.

(p. 7), Quoted in *Drylongso, A Self-Portrait of Black America* by John Langston Gwaltney 1980

4827. Beth Orton (1970–)

1 Why must people always want what they can't have?

"Blood Red River," *Central Reservation* (album) 1999

2 You might as well smile
Because tomorrow you just don't know.

"Pass in Time," Ibid.

3 Why should I know better by now
When I'm old enough not to?

"Stolen Car," Ibid.

4828. Shailja Patel (1970–)

1 Their names will not be remembered,
they are not American.
Museums will not hold their relics, they are not
American. No other mother's
children will be slaughtered
in their memory, they are not
American.

"Eater of Death," Four, *What If? A Journal Of Radical Possibilities*, Issue 2 2002

2 Something / is bursting the walls of my arteries something / is pounding its way up my throat like a volcano / rising / finally / I understand / why I'm a poet

Because I was born to a law / that states / before you claim a word you steep it / in terror and shit / in hope and joy and grief / in labour endurance vision costed out / in decades of your life / you have to sweat and curse it / pray and keen it / crawl and bleed it / with the very marrow / of your bones / you have to earn / its / meaning

"Shilling Love," Two, Sts. 16–17, *Lodestar Quarterly*, Issue 9 *Spring 2004*

3 And if I believe one thing / on this scarred and silenced earth / it is the fire in your throats just waiting / for a match.

"For the Women of Project Pride," St. 6 2006

4 How many ways can you splice a history? Price a country? Dice a people? Slice a heart? Entice—what's been erased—back into story?

"How Ambi Became Paisley," *Migritude, An Epic Journey In Four Movements* 2008

5 The most telling—and compelling—line of a man's body is that place where his neck joins his shoulder. From which the head extends, retracts, responds. It can be beautiful in its cleanness and purpose. Its strength and flexibility, its balance and alignment. It can disturb in its distortion and strain, its rigidity or collapse.

I like to think that if I could see that line in its entirety, if I could enter the living braid of muscles beneath—trapezius, levator scapulae, sterno-cleido-mastoid—it would tell me everything about a man. Where he intersects with his reality. How he meets, receives, and inserts himself into the world.

Bwagamoyo (The Father), Pt. II, Ibid.

4829. Samantha Power (1970–)

1 The United States had never in its history intervened to stop genocide and had in fact rarely even made a point of condemning it as it occurred.

"A Problem from Hell": America and the Age of Genocide 2003

2 The fact that genocide or concentration camps or the deaths that are now occurring in Darfur could be the subject for domestic politics is a sign of how education has changed, how course curriculums are changing, and how, to an extent, media has helped educate and bring into the living rooms suffering that for the better part of the twentieth century was so far off limits that it remained very abstract.

Discussion, DePauw University (depauw.edu/news) *16 September 2005*

3 Another longstanding foreign policy flaw is the degree to which special interests dictate the way in which the "national interest" as a whole is defined and pursued. . . .

Quoted in "Samantha Power on U.S. Foreign Policy" by Molly Lanzarotta, Harvard University, John F. Kennedy School of Government *14 March 2007*

4830. Tanya Renne (1970–)

1 . . . decades of mono-ideology had left the people without a structure to create or deal with choice. "Options" as a concept had disappeared from social memory . . .

Introduction, *Ana's Land: Sisterhood in Eastern Europe*, intro. and ed. 1996

2 For feminism, the fall of communism has meant categorical rejection. It is seen either as an imported Western ideology to be rejected out of hand or as an old communist principle to be proudly refused . . .

Ibid.

4831. Amy Richards (1970–)

1 For many women, our bodies have become the canvasses upon which our struggles paint themselves. Body image, in fact, may be the pivotal third wave issue—the common struggle that mobilizes the current feminist generation.

Essay, *Adiós, Barbie: Young Women Write about Body Image and Identity*, Ophira Edut, ed. 1988

2 The initial tension between feminism and motherhood developed because the former advocates the pursuit of independence, while the latter is based on dependence. In its most basic definition, feminism is about self-worth and dignity, which mothers need in order to parent effectively—even if they don't think

they need it for themselves, they should be giving that example to their children.

Introduction, *Opting In: Having a Child Without Losing Yourself 2008*

3 . . . motherhood's relationship to feminism has been reduced to right and wrong answers. Did you have a home birth, are you a member of La Leche League, and do you let your daughter play with Barbie? The polar extremes receive the most attention—home births or hospitals; PTA mom or latchkey kid . . .

Ibid.

4832–4833. Sally Park Scattergood (fl. 1970s–1990s)

1 . . . childrearing, which is probably the most important task that most human beings will ever undertake, and one of vital importance for society, is ignored in our school curriculum.

Quoted in *Boys Will Be Boys* by Myriam Miedzian *1991*

4834. Danzy Senna (1970–)

1 Before I ever saw myself, I saw my sister. When I was still too small for mirrors, I saw her as the reflection that proved my own existence. . . .

In those days, I rotated around Cole. Everything was her. I obeyed her, performed for her, followed her, studied her the way little sisters do. We were rarely far apart. We even spoke our own language. Cole insists that it began before I was born, when I was just a translucent ball in my mother's womb.

"face" (p. 5), *Caucasia 1998*

2 Have you ever seen the end of a story before it even begins? Not like a psychic. But like somebody who keeps making the same mistake, because it feels good for a while, and even when it starts to feel bad it's a familiar kind of bad. A problem you can call your own.

Ch. 1, *Symptomatic 2004*

4835. Tiffany Shlain (1970?–)

1 It's an honor to honor.*

Quoted in "Webby Awards Founder Predicts Trends" by David Wilson, *South China Morning Post 14 February 2006*
*Her response to her own challenge to make an acceptance speech for the Webby Awards in five words.

2 I hope to not contribute to the technological jungle where ring tones become wild beasts that disrupt serene moments.

Ibid.

3 Jews are so connected, all around the world. The fact that we're reinventing and reinterpreting, it's all about evolving. And that's how Jews have survived.

Quoted in "A Jewish girl in a Barbie world" by Sue Fishkoff, *The Jerusalem Post 27 May 2006*

4836. Loung Ung (1970–)

1 It seems to me we are living in a time in which fear is used as a tool in the media, entertainment, culture, and politics. I think right now, it takes courage to live a life of hope. A life of insights. A life of family. And to not buy into this fear that we're being sold.

Conversation with Marianne Schnall*, feminist.com *7 July 2008*
*See 4758.

2 Activism is like a muscle, the more you use it, the stronger it'll become.

Ibid.

3 The myth of the rugged individualism, the pull yourselves up by your bootstraps mentality breeds this belief that success achieved alone is sweeter than success achieved as a group. Says who?

Ibid.

4838–4839. Dorothy Wright Wilson (fl. 1970s)

1 If criminals wanted to grind justice to a halt, they could do it by banding together and all pleading not guilty. It's only because we have plea-bargaining that our criminal justice system is still in motion. That doesn't say much for the quality of justice.

Quoted in *The Los Angeles Times 11 August 1974*

4840. Claire Bayliss (1971?–)

1 Female friendships have always been special. But I think female friendship groups have become like a second, or extended, family for many women.

Quoted in "Be girly, live longer" by Lisa Reich, *The Telegraph* (London) *12 August 2004*

2 Perhaps men find our ability to talk openly about emotions and relationships a little intimidating. Or maybe they're just worried that we're talking about them. Which, let's face it, we just might be.

Ibid.

4841. Amy O. Charkowski (1971–)

1 Bacteria and fungi and archaea and viruses: they're the most abundant types of life on Earth. They're everywhere. They're on us, inside us. They're on leaves, on roots, in the soil. And they're important for all sorts of processes. They're required to keep life going on the planet. Basically, they recycle everything.

Quoted in "Amy Charkowski describes the human world" by Abby Frank, *Earth & Sky* (earthsky.org) *12 February 2007*

2 It's hard to know what agriculture is going to look like in 100 years.

Ibid.

4842. Seema Chowdhury (1971–)

1 And that gift is certainly rare/
That needs lots of love and care/
That brings laughter and fun to all/
And that's the gift of a baby small/

"A Baby Small" *n.d.*

4843. Kiran Desai (1971–)

1 "He has not progressed. Colonial neurosis, he's never freed himself from it."

The Inheritance of Loss 2005

2 Profit could only be harvested in the gap between nations, working one against the other.

Ibid.

3 Old hatreds are endlessly retrievable, . . . [they are] purer . . . because the grief of the past was gone. Just the fury remained, distilled, liberating.

Ibid.

4 "... chicken tikka masala has replaced fish and chips as the No. 1 takeout dinner."

Ibid.

4844. Jill Alexander Essbaum (1971–)

1 Relentless
death, you have withered shut my heart
like an old rose closing, pungent and motionless
"Wednesday, Ash," St. 7, *Heaven* 1999

2 We've just this single hour, so let's not waste
it ratcheting what cannot be repaired.
Untitled sonnet, *Oh Forbidden* 2003

3 She's the fiction invented for your arousal,
The serpent you take up and the poison you suckle,
A frivolous income at your disposal
"Harlot," St. 15, *Harlot* 2004

4 Like: I would have killed myself for you.
Like: I may already have.
"A Force is a Push or a Pill," St. 9, *MiPOesias Magazine*
(mipoesias.com) 2006

5 How ours is a union that begins and ends in pain.
When it is over we do it again.
"The Thirty-four Sorrows and a Solitary Anguish of
Irreparable Regret," St. 28, Ibid.

4845. Olga Grushin (1971–)

1 Geniuses are human. Humans quit.
The Dream Life of Sukhanov 2006

2 He was being assailed by his past. His own dreadful fate had
caught up with him after all.
Ibid.

3 Summer seemed to have tiptoed out of Moscow while no one
was looking.
Ibid.

4846. Wajeha al-Huwaider (1971?–)

1 Nothing can make you feel shame in spinsterhood, or to regret
the years you spend alone ... No! ... It is a thousand times
better to be an old maid than to marry a man in this miserable
East ...
"Better to Be an Old Maid than to Marry an Arab Man,"
MiddleEastTransparent.com *1 May 2004*

2 In Arab countries, and particularly in the Gulf countries, the
cycle of discrimination against the woman begins when she is
a fetus in her mother's womb; [it continues] when she emerges
into the air of the world, and goes on until her death. According to men's interpretation, the woman is always 'lewdness'
and sometimes 'impure' ... The woman is [flawed in mind and
in religion]—yet it was the Muslim mothers [i.e. the wives of
the prophet Muhammad] who taught the people a great deal
about the commandments of the religion and its foundations.
"Discrimination Against Arab Women Begins in the Womb,"
Elaph.com *5 February 2006*

3 Any natural distribution of kinds of creatures on the earth
includes five percent of those called pathfinders, pioneers,
or elites. They have a penetrating glance, and the capability
to push societies forward. This special trait is not limited to
human societies ... it is also found among animals, birds, and

even tiny insects ... The existence of this five percent is inescapable; it plays a real part among the members [of the group
to which it belongs] in the continuation of the life of every species, and in dealing with the challenges that these groups face
from time to time ... Where are the pathfinders of the Arab
peoples, and where are their elites? Why have the Arab peoples
become herds and rabble? Where is someone to direct them
and drive the train of revival forward?
"The Vital Pathfinding Arab Elite is Persecuted and Cannot
Advance Arab Society," MiddleEastTransparent.com *15 July
2006*

4 When all the years of your life are stolen from you ... and
your vitality, your mind, and your soul are wrested away, all in
the name of religion, customs, traditions ... and an outmoded
heritage—and you know that this has usurped your right to
life—don't weep and don't cry, and don't imagine that this is a
Western conspiracy against you; these are actions and behaviors that are a product of your own country.
"This is not a Western Conspiracy" (prose poem) *n.d.*

5 When religion has control over science—you can be sure that
you are in an Arab country.
"When" (prose poem) *n.d.*

4847. Gwyneth Paltrow (1971–)

1 Sometimes people fall in love with people they shouldn't
marry.
Quoted in "It was a real awakening for me" by Dotson Rader,
Parade Magazine 17 January 1999

2 You'll never be happy if you can't figure out that loving people
is all there is. And that it's more important to love than to be
loved. Because that is when you feel love, by loving somebody.
Ibid.

3 My dad took me to Paris for the weekend. We had the most
amazing time. On the plane back to London, he asked me, "Do
you know why I took you to Paris—only you and me?" And I
said, "Why?" And he said, "Because I wanted you to see Paris
for the first time with a man who would always love you."
Ibid.

4848. Stephanie Danielle Roth (1971?–)

1 The greatest victory for the local people was when, for the
first time in history, all the churches of Romania united and
made the official declaration that property in Rosia Montana
was not for sale, and that they would refuse to relinquish their
property for the mining project. The church is a symbol of the
living community, so that was very important to the locals.
"Mine Sweeper" by Michelle Nijhuis, grist.org *21 April 2005*

2 Since the World Bank pulled out of the mine project, the mining
company is like a dead person being kept alive by its shareholders. It's time to pull the plug.
Ibid.

4849. Sarah Silverman (1971–)

1 Frankly, I think it's a good law [24-hour waiting period before
getting an abortion]. The other day I wanted to go get an abortion. I really wanted an abortion, but then I thought about it
and it turned out I was just thirsty.
Saturday Night Live (TV) 1993

2 I saw my father naked once ... But it was okay ... Because I
was soooo young ... and sooo drunk.
Stand-up routine *n.d.*

4850. Renee Swindle (1971?–)

1 Don't let anyone tell you any different, sometimes love isn't about nothing but a crooked tooth, the curl of an eyebrow, the hairs on a wrist, a gold chain, or one small mole.

Ch. 1, *Please Please Please* 1999

2 If I were ever to make a list of all the men I'd been with I'd have to write their names under two headings: "Men I Almost Loved" and "Men Who Have Gotten on My Nerves." The list under men who have gotten on my nerves would be endless.

Ch. 8, Ibid.

4851. Lara Vapnyar (1971–)

1 Apollinaria Suslova didn't succeed at anything, except immortality. But what good has immortality ever done anyone?

Ch. 1, *Memoirs of a Muse* 2006

2 "The best way to deal with death is to ignore it."

Ch. 2, Ibid.

3 Most of the wars were as senseless as they were ugly, and yet they took up almost all the space in our history books. Foreign wars, civil wars, territorial wars, religious wars, political wars. Chapters and chapters of wars. And only a small, unimpressive appendix at the end of the textbook was devoted to the important scientific discoveries, cultural changes, or artistic achievements of a certain period.

Ch. 4, Ibid.

4 I admitted that it was possible to have money and no culture— I'd seen all too many examples of that—but not vice versa.

Ch. 10, Ibid.

5 Like a stubborn mosquito, my mother's voice seemed to hover around, invisible and malicious. I wished that the voice were a real mosquito and I could just smash it against the wall.

Ibid.

4852. Vendela Vida (1971–)

1 Going to college has always struck me as the quintessential American experience—that is, of officially leaving behind what you once were and starting over somewhere else. Yet I've never understood why people who have just arrived at college would renounce their freedom by joining a fraternity or sorority so early in the game.

Ch. 1, *Girls on the Verge: Debutante Dips, Drive-bys, and Other Invitations* 1999

2 When you believe anyone could be your mother, you begin to think anyone could be your brother, your lover, your son.

Let the Northern Lights Erase Your Name 2007

3 Recently, everything around me felt familiar yet amiss, like the first time you ride in the back seat of your own car.

Ch. 1., Ibid.

4853. Celeste M. Ward (1971?–)

1 Organizing, training, equipping, and advising indigenous armies and police have become key missions for the military as a whole and no longer niche missions for our Special Operations Forces.

Testimony, HASC O&I Subcommittee Hearing, *30 October 2007*

4854. Anne Pierson Wiese (1971?–)

1 the heartprick of longitude and latitude
to home in on, the conviction that life
depends, every day, on what outlasts you.

"Profile of the Night Heron," *Floating City* 2006

2 Whatever you've done or undone, there's a dish for you/
to take out or eat in: spice for courage, sweet for chagrin.

"Columbus Park," Ibid.

3 The old maples and oaks,
roots plumbing the hill as humans could not,
whisper of what's below: more rock—more rock—more rock.

"Mica Schist," Ibid.

4 Love displaces
everything.

"In the beginning," sts. 1 & 2, Ibid.

4854.1. Shukria Barakzai

1 Eight years ago women were not allowed to get a job or leave the house alone. Eight years ago we were not just second-class citizens; we were ignored in the community. In a situation where we see women being attacked, violence against women, acid attacks, political discrimination—still women are doing something, they are campaigning, we can see their pictures.

"Madam President in Afghanistan?" *AFP* (afp.com)
17 May 2009

4855. Bernardina Guervara Corvera (1972–)

1 Ants don't need money to eat.
The earth belongs to them,
and their fortresses bulge with food
for these nameless days of rain.

"My Commandante Federico" (1981), *A Poetics of Resistance: Women Writing in El Salvador, South Africa, and the United States,* Mary K. DeShazer, ed. 1994

4856. Ana Marie Cox (1972–)

1 "Now, though, McDonnell calls herself a 'blog fanatic,' checking in on the irreverent, sometimes saucy—and often wrong—'Web logs' as much as two or three hours a day. 'I've stopped watching television and knitting,' she says, petting her Dell keyboard. 'Forget scrapbooking. I'm hooked.'"

Dog Days 2005

2 "This is what happens when Republicans get bored with buying up riverfront property. They write checks to muddy the reputation of a good man who is trying to help the lives of people who don't have private planes."

Ibid.

3 "[Asperger syndrome]. You know, like autism, but functional. You can dress yourself and whatnot, but you can't actually interact with people. It's what everyone here has."

Ibid.

4857. Cameron Diaz (1972–)

1 We didn't create those things to ruin the world. We didn't do it consciously—like, "Oh, let's make cars so that we can burn ourselves up"—you know? That wasn't a conscious decision but now that we know what it does do, now it's our responsibility to make the changes.

Quoted in "Talking Green with Cameron Diaz" by Marianne Schnall,* *The Huffington Post 9 April 2008*

*See 4758.

2 It does just start with the basics—it starts with being aware of your consumption, your energy consumption, everything from the products you buy—there are a slew of products as far as recycling. I mean, toilet paper—recycled paper is a really great thing—everybody wipes their butt every day. And those are trees—I mean there are entire forests being cut down so we can wipe our butt.

Ibid.

3 Don't you feel like in the last few years the global community, all of sudden we have this language we didn't have before? We're a global society, we're a global community.

Ibid.

4 But even if we don't survive, it's such a better way to spend our time. I'd rather be leaving this planet laughing—I'd rather do it that way—we may as well have fun when you're trying to create something good. Even if it is a struggle, you may as well have a laugh while you're doing it.

Ibid.

4858. Camille T. Dungy (1972–)

1 What gruesome genius invents our brutal hearts?
"Daisy Cutter," St. 12, From the Fishhouse: An Anthology of Poems . . . 2004

2 but you won't give me more
than your body tuned for walking out my door
"blackspoon," Ibid.

3 long time gone. Long time gone and don't know
when I'm coming back but see me there.
"long time gone, long time yet to come," St. 2, What to Eat, What to Drink, What to Leave for Poison 2006

4859. Mia Hamm (1972–)

1 Many people say I'm the best women's soccer player in the world. I don't think so. And because of that, someday I just might be.
Go for the Goal: A Champion's Guide to Winning in Soccer and Life 1999?

2 There is no me in Mia.

Ibid.

4860. Caroline Heldman (1972–)

1 What would disappear from our lives if we stopped seeing ourselves as objects? Painful high heels? Body hatred? Constant dieting? Liposuction? It's hard to know. Perhaps the most striking outcome of self-objectification is the difficulty women have in imagining identities and sexualities truly our own. In solidarity, we can start on this path, however confusing and difficult it may be.
"Out-of-Body Image: Women See Themselves Through Eyes of Others," Ms. (New York) Spring 2008

2 In one sense, it is great to see young women displaying flagrant sexuality in ways they would never have done a generation ago, and it would be marvelous if these appearance choices reflected the female sexual freedom that feminists have fought so hard for. But they do not. Girls and women are being taught to eroticize male sexual pleasure as though it is their own, instead of exploring sexuality in truly empowering and satisfying ways.
"Love Your Body Day," The Huffington Post 14 October 2008

3 The idea of empowerment through object status is illogical for the simple fact that subjects act, while objects are acted upon. By participating in their own objectification, girls/women place themselves in a position to be acted upon. The real power in this arrangement lies with boys and men who are socialized to believe that they are entitled to consume women as objects, in media and in "real life."

Ibid.

4861. Heather A. Higginbottom (1972?–)

1 Working in the White House is an incredible privilege, but you start early and end late.
Quoted in "CV grad joins team advancing Obama agenda" by George Basler, pressconnects.com 15 December 2008

4862. Rani Hong (1972–)

1 I have always said if we survivors come forth and tell our story—reveal the truth of what happened to us—it will help people understand the realities of human trafficking. We can't stay silent. If we do, we stay in the dark and allow the traffickers to continue the destruction of innocent lives.
Quoted in "I Am Like So Many" by Rhyen Coombs, World Pulse Magazine (worldpulsemagainze.com) 14 May 2008

2 When you start stepping out and helping others—when you start being a voice—you can begin the process of healing. It is very difficult, but it is beneficial to our own self-worth and self-image. We are overcomers, and we are survivors, and we can make a difference.

Ibid.

4863. Manana Kochladze (1972–)

1 Public opinion is one of the strongest tools we have in our negotiations with the company [BP].*
Quoted in "Georgia On Her Mind" by Michelle Nijhuis, grist. org 23 April 2004
*BP Global, an international oil and gas corporation.

2 The BP pipeline has militarized the country [Georgia].
"Apocalypse Palin," The Nation 15 September 2008*
*Sarah P— ; see 4684.

4864. Lisa Leslie (1972–)

1 I think our country is so far behind relative to other countries and their respect for women in sports. Other countries treat their women's teams so much better and that is why a lot of women go play overseas. Russia, Spain—you can name so many other countries that respect women's sports. Women are on the front page of their sports news. They have headlines and are a major part of the news like any other sport.
Quoted in "Oh, Baby! Leslie's Regained the Spark" by Dave Hollander, AOL Sports 18 May 2008

2 My road to roundball was more of an obstacle course than an expressway.
Ch. 1, Don't Let The Lipstick Fool You: The Making of a Champion, with Larry Burnett 2008

4865. Mariam Matossian (1972–)

1 Oh my beautiful dear Mom
I love the sound of your sweet voice
Oh my beautiful dear Mom

You are precious to me
There is no one like you
You are gift from God

"Nverus" (My Gift), *In the Light* (album) 2007

2 You filled my hungry soul
With hope
And You put sweet, new songs
In my heart

"Nor Yerk" (New Song), Ibid.

4866. Dana Perino (1972–)

1 I have grown a thicker skin than I had when I came to Washington.

Quoted in "The Dog Handler" by Massimo Calabresi, *Time* (New York) *29 October 2007*

2 The relationship between the press secretary and the media is always going to be adversarial.

Ibid.

3 Both the president and the vice president have long believed, and it's a part of what has made them the leaders that they are, which is not to chase popularity polls but to hold themselves to a standard that requires people not to like them.

"Perino: President Unpopular On Purpose," Associated Press *20 March 2008*

4867. Nomi Prins (1972–)

1 Then there's your Social Security card. If it's anything like mine, it's frayed around the edges from having been stuck behind the other cards. So is the system it represents.

Introduction, *Jacked: How "Conservatives" Are Picking Your Pocket 2006*

2 Wallets are roadmaps of our daily realities: they hold photos of the people we love, chunks of our identity, and plastic cards that evoke our financial worries. The cards inside your wallet tell a story. They also tell the tale of the government's impact on you.

Ibid.

3 Wall Street will continue to battle for fewer restrictions under the political guise of American global competition, while Americans bear the brunt of the consequences.

"Why the Economy Went South," *Mother Jones 7 July 2008*

4 The current financial crisis—and the debate over the bailout package—provided an opportunity to shine a light under the hood of the industry, remove its engine, and reinstall a more efficient one.

Ibid.

5 Ultimately, Wall Street and investors were rolling the dice in a real-life version of Risk—only the "game of global domination," as it has long billed itself, became a game of global diminution.

"The risk fallacy," *Fortune 28 October 2008*

4868. Alyson M. Richman (1972–)

1 I wore my destiny like a too-tight robe in which I could not breathe. Each thread of fabric was woven by an ancestor.

The Mask Carver's Son 2000

2 Salomè had always believed that God had made women with wombs so that, after they had children, they had a place to store their secrets.

Pt. I, Ch. 1, *Swedish Tango 2005*

3 Papa had written his dissertation on melancholia, taking the position that, historically, all great men—the great philosophers, poets, and artists of the world—suffered from that illness. Thus, he always had a sympathetic ear for those artists who considered themselves depressed or affected by a malady . . .

Ch. 1, *The Last Van Gogh 2006*

4869. Cristina Sanchez (1972–)

1 The bullfighting world is made by and for men, but I still have the pride that I've made history. I've written golden pages in the bullfighting world.

"Woman bullfighter quits the ring in macho Spain" by Mar Roman, Associated Press *21 May 1999*

2 It's a lovely profession, and if I was born again I would do it again.

Ibid.

4870. Wendy Shanker (1972–)

1 The word that I like the most, and the one that I think aptly describes my body, is "fat." The opposite of thin. I like it. It's short, it's sweet, it's surprisingly compact.

Ch. 1, *The Fat Girl's Guide to Life 2004*

2 Plenty of research suggests that obesity—at least as it's clinically defined—is not nearly the death sentence that most media outlets and weight-loss companies would have you believe.

Ch. 7, Ibid.

3 A bagel-free life is not worth living. A brunch is not a brunch without French toast. How much are fat people supposed to give up to fit in?

Ibid.

4871. Dalia Sofer (1972–)

1 Summer is leaving, and with it the buzz of ceiling fans, the smell of wet dust rising through the air-conditioning vents, the clink of noontime dishes heard through open windows, the chatter of families passing long, muggy afternoons in courtyards, eating pumpkin seeds and watermelon.

The Septembers of Shiraz 2007

2 Absence, Shirin thinks, is death's cousin. One day something is there, the next day it isn't. Abracadabra.

Ibid.

3 These objects, she had always believed, are infused with the souls of the places from which they came, and of the people who had made or sold them. On long, silent afternoons . . . she would sit in her sun-filled living room and look at each one—the glass vase, a reminder of Francesca, in Venice; the copper plate, a souvenir of Ismet, in Istanbul; the silver teapot, a keepsake from Firouz, in Isfahan.

Ibid.

4872. Dana Spiotta (1972?–)

1 No matter how long she had lived here, no matter how many summers she had spent here as a child, she never failed to become momentarily unnerved by palm trees. They seemed to

say, This isn't a real place where things count, this is exotic, this is tropical, this is a vacation! And she got a kind of thrill from it, living here was a sort of faux living, it's what gave her so much license with time.

Lightning Field 2001

2   She sometimes thought that if someone saw all the movies she had seen, the number of times she had seen them and in the order she had seen them, that person might know exactly who she was. That couldn't really be true, but it was half true, it felt that crucial, as if her identity were a collection of references.

Ibid.

3   It is easy for a life to become unblessed.

Ch. 1, *Eat the Document 2006*

4   She discovered, despite what people may imagine, having nothing to lose is a lot like having nothing.

Ibid.

5   "If you want to change your life, first you change your name."

Ibid.

4873. Janelle S. Taylor (1972?–   )

1   ... the public may form a relationship with the fetus that is equally emotionally profound as that of the pregnant woman—or indeed *more* profound, if the viewers have "succeeded" in bonding with the fetus and the pregnant woman has, for whatever reason, "failed."

Essay, *Reproducing Reproduction: Kinship, Power, and Technological Innovation*, Sarah Franklin and Helena Ragoné, eds. *1998*

4874. Hannah Tinti (1972–   )

1   He said jumping into the ocean after dark is like stepping down into a graveyard, falling through the earth, bumping into coffins and bodies, and feeling all of the lost bits and pieces of souls that have seeped into the soil come looking for you. He said he'd never do it again.

"Animal Crackers," *Animal Crackers 2008*

2   "Is that what you wanted to hear?"
"No."
The man reached over, took hold of the lantern, and blew it out. Night enveloped the barn. "Well," he said at last to the darkness between them, "that's when you know it's the truth."

The Good Thief 2008

3   Much of what the boys had learned had been transferred from child to child like a disease ...

Ibid.

4   It had been decided that the brothers must give the children some knowledge; at the very least enough language to read the Bible, and enough arithmetic so that the Protestants could not cheat them.

Ibid.

5   He was missing a hand. ... Somewhere between his entry into the world and his delivery through the door of Saint Anthony's, Ren had lost it. He wondered where the hand was now. He closed his eyes and saw it clearly, palm open, the fingers slightly curled. He imagined it behind a dustbin, inside a wooden box, hidden in the grasses of a field. He did not consider size. He did not think that it would no longer

fit him. Ren simply looked at his right and thought about its match, waiting patiently somewhere in the world for him to retrieve it.

Ch. 1, Ibid.

4875. Marianne Apostolides (1973?–   )

1   I looked in the mirror and saw flabby arms, fatty hips, a rounded belly. I saw myself piece by piece by piece. I didn't see a form composed of curves and straight edges, of soft tissue and strong muscles. I didn't see *me*. My body image reflected my self-image: I hated my body because I hated myself, I doubted my body because I doubted myself, I was angry at my body because I was angry at myself. Hate, doubt, anger. That's what I saw when I looked in the mirror.

Inner Hunger: A Young Woman's Struggle through Anorexia and Bulimia 1998

2   In certain common subcultures for girls—ballet, gymnastics, modeling, acting, etc.—a thin body is the standard for success and approval. Girls become aware of this standard through the comments of coaches, the gravitation of coaches toward those who have the "ideal" bodies, and the example set by older girls thriving in these activities. When puberty makes a girl's body more curved and less like the subculture's ideal, that body becomes an obstacle—one that some try to eliminate through dieting.

Ch. 1, Ibid.

4876. Matthea Harvey (1973–   )

1   We were tired of hard news—
it helped to turn down our hearing aids.

"The Future of Terror/1," *Modern Life 2008*

2   Happy-go-lucky is just a decision to proceed
with an assumption of happiness and luck.

"The Future of Terror/2," Ibid.

3   Form may define external appearance but there is room
For improvement within ...

"Pity the Bathtub Its Forced Embrace of the Human Form," Ibid.

4877. Monica Lewinsky (1973–   )

1   ... no one ever asked me to lie, and I was never promised a job for my silence.

The Starr Report: The Independent Counsel's Complete Report to the Congress on the Investigation of President Clinton 9 September 1998

2   He [William J. Clinton]* reminded me of my mom because like her, he was an ostrich, putting his head in the sand because he didn't like confrontation.

Quoted in *Monica's Story* by Andrew Morton *1999*
*American politician and lawyer (1946–   ), 42nd president of the United States (1993–2001).

3   Sex is like eating ... Sometimes you have fast food, and sometimes you eat a gourmet meal.

Time (New York) *22 March 1999*

4878. Ellen Litman (1973–   )

1   I think a supermarket is a poor place for a romance to begin.

first line, *The Last Chicken in America 2007*

2 Alick smiles at me, and it's the unpleasantly wholesome American smile. It emanates charm and flouride, good fortune and good breeding, and you either know it's fake and don't trust it, or you trust it too much.

Ibid.

4878.1. Rachel Maddow (1973–)

1 If you want a left-right fight, in 2004 or today, there's this roster of dozens, if not hundreds, of conservative talk-show hosts to book. On the left there's Alan Colmes. Oh, wait a minute, he's taken. I think I got booked, initially, by default.

Quoted in "Now in Living Rooms, the Host Apparent" by Jaques Steinberg, *The New York Times* 17 July 2008

2 I'm a national security liberal, which I tell people because it's meant to sound absurd.

Ibid.

4879. Karen Rosenberg (1973?–)

1 What makes identity politics so tenacious? I think much of its appeal lies in its neo-Victorian sentimentalization of home as the site of safety, intimacy and reinvigoration. Studies of Romanticism constantly point out that it's precisely that which is perceived as lost which is often most lovingly cherished. And the tremendous longing invested in the word "home" suggests nostalgia for an *absent* ideal.

"Identity crisis," *The Women's Review of Books*, Vol XIV, No. 5 February 1997

2 To speak of history does not necessarily mean to be weighed down by it; to pay attention to power need not imply to give in to it.

Ibid.

4880. Katherine Taylor (1973–)

1 "Look," I said, "if you don't want me to go because you don't think it's best for me, that I understand. But if you don't want me to go because you don't think it's best for you, that's not quite fair, is it."

Rules for Saying Goodbye 2007

4880.1. Rebecca Traister (1973?–)

1 That two people who stand on opposing sides of the many political canyons facing the country could successfully couple may be beyond the ken of many of us. And yet, the country—red and blue—is dotted with pairs who cheerfully cancel each other out at the polls, who spend news hours and election years raging, bickering, throwing their hands up in frustration, and perhaps even getting off on the fact that never shall their ideologies meet.

"Strange bedfellows," Salon.com 23 January 2004

2 . . . we feel obligated to acknowledge that of course motherhood is a sacrifice, of course there are consequences, of course for many women and men, choosing to have children and become less self-obsessed is a pleasure. But so much of what pro-life advocacy is about—whether it denies people sex education or contraception or access to abortion—is in valuing the cells that make up a fetus (or baby) more than the woman in whose body those cells have grown.

"Bristol Palin stammers the truth," Salon.com 18 February 2009

3 Of course there are men and women who are actively looking for a spouse. But in college, and beyond, what most people are seeking is connection—romantic, sexual, long-lasting, brief, whatever. The idea that "mating," whether you are 20 or 40 or 60, is all about securing a walk down an aisle is more than a little stale in a world in which divorce is common, cohabitation is both a norm and a serious commitment, and marriage between same-sex couples remains illegal in most states.

"Engaged and underaged," Salon.com 28 April 2009

4881. Danielle Anne Trussoni (1973–)

1 My father was running from the police, from his first ex-wife, his creditors, and his dreams. He was running from his second ex-wife (my mother), his illegitimate children, and his past. He was running from himself, and I was right there with him, an eleven-year-old accomplice to his evenings of escape.

Ch. 1, *Falling Through the Earth: A Memoir* 2006

4882. Heather Whitestone-McCallum (1973–)

1 The most handicapped [person] in the world is a negative thinker.

People, *Seattle Post-Intelligencer* September 1994

4883. Rebecca Curtis (1974–)

1 . . . once my sister's [fortune] cookie had said, "You will discover great wealth," and then in the parking lot she found a dime and for years after that I waited for my cookies to come true.

"Hungry Self," *Twenty Grand, and Other Tales of Love and Money* 2007

2 I was terribly in love with him, but we were separated by race and by the fact that he hated me.

Ibid.

4884. Nicole Krauss (1974–)

1 No matter how often I imagined the possible failure of my organs, I found the consequences inconceivable. That it could happen to me. I forced myself to picture the last moments. The penultimate breath. A final sigh. And yet. It was always followed by another.

"Until the Writing Hand Hurts," *The History of Love* 2005

2 So many words get lost. They leave the mouth and lose their courage, wandering aimlessly until they are swept into the gutter like dead leaves.

"The Trouble with Thinking," Ibid.

3 Perhaps this is what it means to be a father—to teach your child to live without you. If so, no one was a greater father than I.

"Die Laughing," Ibid.

4 I've always arrived too late for my life.

"A Joy Forever," Ibid.

5 Because wasn't that what wives of artists were meant to do? Husband their husbands' work into the world, which, without them, would be lost to obscurity?

"The Last Page," Ibid.

6 There are so many ways to be alive, but only one way to be dead.

"A + L," Ibid.

4885. Tania Lienert (1974?–)

1 Radical feminists . . . are not hesitant about naming men and male supremacy as a problem. However, many other feminists do not think it is a good strategy to be so explicit—it might offend men and get them offside. So radical feminist theories are dismissed or trivialized as being biologically determinist—and hence not really feminist—and theories that are less threatening to the status quo are put forward in their place. These include socialist feminism, where capitalism is faulted rather than men themselves.

"On Who Is Calling Radical Feminists 'Cultural Feminists' and Other Historical Sleights of Hand," *Radically Speaking: Feminism Reclaimed,* Diane Bell and Renate Klein, eds. *1996*

4886. Natalie Louise Maines (1974–)

1 Just so you know, we're on the good side with y'all. We do not want this war, this violence, and we're ashamed that the President of the United States is from Texas.

Quoted in "The Dixie Chicks" concert review by Betty Clarke, *Guardian Unlimited 12 March 2003*

2 I feel the president* is ignoring the opinions of many in the U.S. and alienating the rest of the world . . . My comments were made in frustration and one of the privileges of being an American is you are free to voice your own point of view . . . While we support our troops, there is nothing more frightening than the notion of going to war with Iraq and the prospect of all the innocent lives that will be lost.

"Dump Dixie Chicks," *TheBostonChannel.com 12 April 2007*
*George W. B- (1946–), Am. politician; 43rd president of the United States (2001–09).

4887. Tammy S. Schultz (1974?–)

1 Our diplomats are not used to laying their lives on the line in operational roles. . . . Our diplomats have been the conveyer belts of policy—not the engines of policymaking or operations.
"Diplomatic Infighting," *The Washington Post 2 November 2007*

2 The country cannot continue fighting the wars of the 21st century with the civilian tools of the 20th.
Ibid.

3 . . . these type of operations require very perceptive and deep emotional IQs. That's not to say men don't have those, but the studies I've seen suggest women have a more collaborative style. And if you look at what you're trying to build with COIN [counterinsurgency], at end of the day, it's about building host-nation capacity.
Quoted in "Women Prominent in Defense Movement" by Spencer Ackerman, *The Washington Independent 8 July 2008*

4888. Hwee Hwee Tan (1974–)

1 I'm at the top of the food chain, but I feel nothing.
Foreign Bodies 1998

2 I didn't want to believe. Faith is so unhip. Atheism is much more glamorous.
Ibid.

4889. Nika Turbina (1974–2002)

1 What a shame that
I'm not a fortune teller.
I would tell fortunes

only with flowers
and I would heal
the earth's wounds
with a rainbow.
"Telling Fortunes," Ljubov v. Kuchkina, tr., *First Draft 1983*

2 It is the solitude of night I love
being alone
on my own.
I talk about
whatever I want then,
and everything that fate doesn't allow.
Untitled (1982), Ibid.

3 Like a flock of birds
all the days
have gathered at our feet.
I don't know what to feed them,
there are no lines left.
"Remembrance" (1981), Ibid.

4 You and I
live on different
islands, even though
we are in the same apartment.
Untitled, Ibid.

5 What frightens me is indifference. It can devour the world, our tiny little planet, the little heart that beats in the universe.
"People" (p. 65), *Time* (New York) *23 November 1987*

4890–4891. Dominika Dery (1975–)

1 She hoped until she believed, and then she believed until she knew.
Ch. 1, *The Twelve Little Cakes 2004*

2 Life under communism was difficult but not impossible. The system was unfair but the human spirit triumphed on a daily basis, and if there was one thing my parents knew for certain in a time of great social and political upheaval, it was this: they loved each other with all their hearts.
Ibid.

4892. Nell Freudenberger (1975–)

1 As you got older, Zubin noticed, very occasionally a fantasy that you'd been having forever came true.
"The Tutor," *Lucky Girls: Stories 2003*

2 It seemed possible that people who were leading particularly honest, clearheaded lives would radiate peace: a kind of human feng shui.
The Dissident 2006

4893. Rachel Harris (1975?–)

1 Our presidential candidates have to recognize climate change as an urgent human rights issue—not just a market issue. They might start by recognizing the gender-specific impacts of climate change—and that the solution, as well as the most impacted, will have a woman's face.
"Climate Change is a Human Rights Challenge," *Women's Media Center* (womensmediacenter.com) *12 August 2008*

2 Those impoverished persons around the world who contribute very little to global warming are the most vulnerable to the negative effects of climate change. Therefore, the United States

and other developed nations contributing must help poorer nations to cope with their current and future climate change issues, as well as drastically reduce emissions to non-dangerous levels.

Ibid.

4894. Lauryn Hill (1975–)

1 My mother always thought I'd be a star
But way before the record deal
The streets that nurtured Lauryn Hill
Made sure that I'd never go too far
"Every Ghetto Every City," 1st Verse, *The Miseducation of Lauryn Hill* (album) 1998

2 Loving you is like a battle
And we both end up with scars
"Ex-Factor," 1st Verse, Ibid.

3 He was the ocean and I was the sand
"I Used to Love Him," Verse 1, Ibid.

4 Now don't you understand man universal law
What you throw out comes back to you, star
Never underestimate those who you scar
Cause karma, karma, karma comes back to you hard
"Lost Ones," last Verse, Ibid.

4895. Angelina Jolie (1975–)

1 We cannot close ourselves off to information and ignore the fact that millions of people are out there suffering. I honestly want to help. I don't believe I feel differently from other people. I think we all want justice and equality, a chance for a life with meaning. All of us would like to believe that if we were in a bad situation someone would help us.
"Angelina Jolie named UNHCR Goodwill Ambassador for refugees," unhcr.org *23 August 2001*

2 To be intimate with a married man, when my own father* cheated on my mother, is not something I could forgive. I could not look at myself in the morning if I did that. I wouldn't be attracted to a man who would cheat on his wife.
"Angelina, saint vs. sinner," *Daily News 2 February 2006*
*The actor Jon Voigt (1938–).

3 As much as I would love to never have to visit Washington, that's the way to move the ball.
"Bad Girl Interrupted," *Forbes Magazine 12 June 2006*

4 Accountability is a powerful force. It has the potential to change behavior—to check aggression by those who are used to acting with impunity. . . . When crimes against humanity are punished consistently and severely, the killers' calculus will change.
"Justice for Darfur," *Washington Post 28 February 2007*

4896. Imane Khalifeh (1975–)

1 We want simply to live in peace
We want to raise up our children
And save our brothers and sisters . . .
We want our families to remain whole
Let us walk out of our isolation and join one another.
Let us walk out of our tears and screams of pain.
Poem that launched the Lebanese peace movement *1984*

4897. Jensine Larsen (1975–)

1 I am convinced that there is a potent and sophisticated global movement rising from all corners of the earth. It is a movement focused on creating innovative solutions for our children, for our future. This rising lifeforce—this pulse—is bravely moving beyond patterns of blame and victimization to harness the vast power of human potential.
"News with a Future," *World Pulse Magazine,* Premier Issue (worldpulsemagazine.com) *2003*

2 Our greatest untapped resource is the potential of women and youth. Here lies the earth's true gems—our rubies, our salt, our diamonds, and our black gold.
Ibid.

3 When we are the active embodiment of equality, love, and integrity and when we have the guts to speak a language of inclusiveness and partnership . . . we will be completely irresistible.
"Boundless Courage," Ibid. *2003*

4 Water is most alive when it moves. Coursing through our bodies and across the earth, this liquid life force has its own voice and its own path. Yet, when we block, force, and contaminate water it becomes sluggish and deadly. Its death is our death.
"The Movement of Water," Ibid. *21 March 2008*

5 Just as water activists have a profound opportunity to realize the untapped leadership of women, women's rights activists must realize how essential water is to women's lives. Access to safe, pure and abundant water is one of the greatest—and most overlooked—sources of freedom and empowerment for women and their communities across the globe.
Ibid.

4898. Nora Manjaa (1975?–)

1 People in Mongolia are tired of the old politics and they're looking for new leadership. That's why I want to mobilize a new generation of leaders for the next elections and develop strategies to really empower the public.
Quoted in "The New Genghis Khan" by Swanee Hunt*, Scripps Howard News Service *15 February 2006*
*See 3978.

2 If I, an educated person, can be abused, how will ordinary people know their rights and defend themselves?
Ibid.

4898.1. Danica McKellar (1975–)

1 I'm sorry, but "integer" has got to be the most boring, sterile word I've ever heard. Doesn't it remind you of, I don't know, some type of medical instrument used in a hospital? Some doctor says to her intern: "Quick, pass me the integer. We have to operate." Actually, that's already sounding more exciting.
Ch. 1, *Math Doesn't Suck: How to Survive Middle-School Math Without Losing Your Mind or Breaking a Nail 2007*

2 I was terrified of math.
I remember sitting in my seventh grade math class, staring at a quiz as if it were written in Chinese—it might as well have been a blank sheet of paper. Total brain freeze.
"Math Used to Totally Suck," *Kiss My Math: Showing Pre-Algebra Who's Boss 2008*

3 But math is actually a good thing. Here are a few reasons why: Math builds confidence, keeps you from getting ripped off, makes you better at adjusting cookie recipes, understanding sports scores, budgeting and planning parties and vacations, interpreting how good a sale really is, and spending your allowance.

Ibid.

4899. Mildred Ngesa (1975–)

1 We twist news for politicians . . . and smile at chaos as it makes us sell newspapers and attract more viewers and listeners to our broadcast media.

Quoted in "Kenya: Senior Women Editors Campaign For Peace" by Kwamboka Oyaro, IPSNews.net *6 March 2008*

4900. Wendy Shalit (1975–)

1 Today men expect to be able to treat all women like prostitutes, only without just compensation, and the virgins are the ones who are now stigmatized, told that no man will have them.

A Return to Modesty 1998

2 I see so many young women around me spending half of their time sleeping with all these men, and the other half telling me how heartbroken they are. I wonder who gave them the idea that this is what they had to do in the first place?

Ibid.

4901. Curtis Sittenfeld (1975–)

1 Money is not discussed. People have so much, so it's like nobody needs to mention it.

Prep 2005

2 "I'm from Idaho, and I was the biggest hayseed when I got here," she was saying. "I practically arrived on a tractor."

Ch. 1, Ibid.

3 "The teachers here have seen everything. We imagine ourselves as distinct entities, but in their eyes, we merge into a great mass of adolescent neediness. You know what I mean?"

Ibid.

4902. Zadie Smith (1975–)

1 . . . he was overcome by the sensation that Life was an enormous rucksack so impossibly heavy that, even though it meant losing everything, it was infinitely easier to leave all baggage here on the roadside and walk on into the blackness.

White Teeth 2000

2 "We're not licensed for suicides around here. This place halal. Kosher, understand? If you're going to die round here, my friend, I'm afraid you've got to be thoroughly bled first."

Ibid.

3 This is what divorce is: taking things you no longer want from people you no longer love.

Ibid.

4 The shit is not the shit (this was Mo's mantra); the pigeon is the shit.

Ibid.

5 [The priority at faculty meetings] is to try to get a chair as near the exit as possible, so as to enable discreet departure halfway through.

On Beauty 2005

6 [Howard] could identify 30 different ideological trends in the social sciences, but did not really know what a software engineer was.

Ibid.

7 [Monty is] a man constantly on the lookout for the camera he knew must be filming him . . .

Ibid.

8 The elderly wilt when transplanted.

"Judith Castle," *The Book of Other People 2007*

4903. Khulood Badawi (1976–)

1 Despite the doubts about their effectiveness and necessity, there is always a need to demonstrate and express a collective cry of protest. The demonstration is an old and traditional method, but it is irreplaceable and we are determined to preserve it.

Interview, justvision.org *7 February 2005*

2 I think that every nation fears for its existence, but the way the Israelis have dealt with it has created a psychological barrier that prevents them from dealing with facts on the ground. They feel the need to continuously remind themselves of those fears. Israeli policies and education are centered on the catastrophe that hit them. This leads them to constantly feel threatened and that's why they are always afraid of the Arab world, which they have difficulty perceiving in any other way than as the enemy. It's not that the Jews' fears are illegitimate. As a Palestinian I have my own fears, too; I've been through the Nakba,* the Naksa,** the occupation, and attempts—which are failing—to wipe out my identity, but my past does not hold me back. One must move on.

Ibid.

*"Day of catastrophe," marking the creation of Israel and the beginning of the Palestinian exodus and defeat in the 1948 Arab-Israeli War. ** "Setback," commemorates the mass displacement and dispossession of Palestinians during and after the 1967 Six-Day War between Israel, Egypt, Jordan, and Syria.

3 One of the most important lessons I learned is that my personal identity is more important than my national identity, and that one should never divide his personal identity under any circumstances.

Ibid.

4904. Maysa Baransi-Siniora (1976–)

1 [My daughter] doesn't understand why three religions are necessary. I told her—There was the first prophet, Moses, and people didn't listen to him and then God took the second prophet, Jesus, and he wasn't listened to either, and then God took the third prophet, Mohammed, and people don't listen to him. But God is the same God.

Quoted in "Making waves" by Neri Livneh, haaretz.com 22 *February 2007*

2 As a woman, I believe in women. I believe that if there is a rise in the power of both Jewish and Palestinian women, there will be a better chance for peace.

Ibid.

3 If you want to punish me, send me to a mall.

Ibid.

4 It's very sad the way the whole world is turning fundamentalist.

Ibid.

4905. Olena Kalytiak Davis (1976?–)

1 Who can your love ignite,
like this, like kerosene?

"Like Kerosene," St. 4, *Her Soul Out of Nothing* 1997

2 dear reader—
dear void—
dear reader devoid
of anything better
to do . . .

i.e. "who's there?"
"stand and unfold yourself"

"Dispatches: Journals," opening lines, poetryfoundation.
org/dispatches *3 February 2006*

4906. Kris Delmhorst (1976?–)

1 After the darkness
unspeakable high processions
sun and moon and countless teeming stars.
We came down from the garden
wandering with our questions,
Where is this life? Oh why this restless soul?

"Light of the Light" (adapted from Walt Whitman's* "Passage
to India," *Strange Conversation* (album) 2006
*(1819–92), American poet, journalist, humanist.

2 so no more I'll be your keeper, or sing these songs for you.
Take all these useless verses and please take this useless body
too.
Let it burn.

"Strange Conversation," Ibid.

3 in twilight and blindness
all our work is done
we fumble and flail, we try and we fail
we only are what we almost become

"The Drop & the Dream," Ibid.

4 I want to live after I die
I want to make a bit of beauty
and leave a little light behind

"Invisible Choir" (inspired by George Eliot*), Ibid.
*See 955.

5 Water water bring me more
Douse the rafters and the floor
Throw your bucket, take your turn
Or just stand back and let the damn thing burn

"Water Water" (adapted from "The Scare-Fire" by Robert
Herrick,* 148), Ibid.
*(1591–1674), Eng. poet.

6 Today you wake up sad and empty, don't go back to sleep.
There's a million ways to kneel and kiss the ground.

"Everything Is Music" (adapted from Rumi*), Ibid.
*a.k.a. Mawlana Jalal ad-Din Muhammad Balkhi (1207–73), Per-
sian poet and mystic.

4907. Rivka Galchen (1976–)

1 "I could never be an analyst, those people are too unpleasant,
too passive-aggressively authoritarian, and yes, all crazy and
out of fashion to boot."

Atmospheric Disturbances 2008

2 Who can ever really know about anyone's happiness, even
one's own?

Ibid.

4908. Jean Grae (1976–)

1 Listen, there's nothing like knowin' yourself
Like the way I know that smokin's kind of broken my health
Like the way I know my flow don't make appropriate wealth
I can't change that
But funny I'm sayin' that when it's money I'm aimed at
I give a fuck if you frame that or quote it
I meant what I said cuz I wrote it, point noted
I know I'm overly sensitive when it comes to, well/
ust about everything.

"Don't Rush Me," *Jeanius* (album) 2008

4909. Sara Gruen (1976?–)

1 Age is a terrible thief. Just when you think you're getting the
hang of it, it knocks your legs out from under you and stoops
your back.

Ch. 1, *Water for Elephants* 2006

2 Actually, it's not so much that I've forgotten. It's more like I've
stopped keeping track.

Ibid.

3 Keeping up the appearance of having all your marbles is hard
work but important. Anyway, I'm not really addled. I just have
more facts to keep track of than other people.

Ch. 5, Ibid.

4 I try to brush the hairs flat with my hand and freeze at the sight
of my old hand on my old head. I lean close and open my eyes
very wide, trying to see beyond the sagging flesh.
It's no good. Even when I look straight into the milky blue
eyes, I can't find myself anymore. When did I stop being me?

Ch. 8, ibid.

4910. Marion Jones (1976–)

1 I feel in my heart I can jump far.

"Marion Jones looks to win gold," by Jim Caple, *Seattle Post-
Intelligencer 10 July 2000*

4911. Jennifer 8. Lee (1976–)

1 Passions seem lively and motivating, while obsessions sound
dark and vaguely deviant. But the line between passion and
obsession is a wobbly one. Obsessions pick us more than
we pick them. They control us more than we control them.
Why do people become obsessed with bird-watching, solving
mathematical proofs, making money? Maybe they're trying
to complete themselves, to fill a void, whether it be through
beauty, truth, or security.

"Wok On," *The Fortune Cookie Chronicles* 2008

4912. Fiona Maazel (1976–)

1 Pornography's . . . heroes bring no hang-ups or baggage to bear
on the sexual act; mental warfare is written out of the story.
What's left is a vacuum that can only be filled by sex. Nonstop
sex. Sex in every other paragraph if not in each one. Dull the
mind and the body will come to life. And it's true: Pornography is the great equalizer. It makes simian brutes of us all.

"I was a bad pornographer," Salon Books 2000

2 Just the sight of him reduces me to the basics. I need food,
water, shelter, Eric. I'd like to crawl under his shirt and stay
there. I'd like to pitch a cot under his shirt and live there.

Last Last Chance 2008

3   When the plague got here, and it would, who would I have to hole up with? Whose life would I have to fear for the most? . . . When the bomb drops, your first thought is: How can I get to him? But for me, I'd have no one. No one to curl up and die with.

Ibid.

4913. Aimee Mullins (1976–   )

1   Confidence is the sexiest thing a woman can have. It's much sexier than any body part.

Quoted in "Confidence . . ." by Elizabeth Shepard, *Parade Magazine 21 June 1998*

2   Let me be the one who changes fear into understanding and makes people comfortable with amputees. Who knows? Maybe, little by little, I can change the world.

Ibid.

3   The truth is, I'm sort of lucky to have this body because it forced me to find my strength and beauty within.*

Ibid.

*Mullins's legs were amputated below the knee on her first birthday.

4914. Marie Phillips (1976–   )

1   "We were . . . famous once. Everyone knew who we were. People were different then. They believed. The adulation, the fame, it was like—well, it was worship, really."

Gods Behaving Badly 2007

4915. Chimamanda Ngozi Adichie (1977–   )

1   Whenever he drained a pot of boiled beans, he thought of the slimy sink as politician.

Half of a Yellow Sun 2006

2   "The benefit of being the ugly daughter is that nobody uses you as sex bait."

Ibid.

3   "The irony, of course, is that we in the Commonwealth can't control the British moving to our countries."

Ibid.

4916. Taghred Chandab (1977–   )

1   Muslim women are not the prisoners that people in the west would like to have you believe—I am a journalist, author, mother, wife and daughter: everything I have ever wanted.

Quoted in "Down Under the Veil, Australia's Muslim Women Face a Rising Tide of Xenophobia" by Marianna Leishman, commonlanguageproject.net *12 March 2007*

2   [Wearing the hijab is a] spiritual decision between myself and God.

Ibid.

4917. Marisa Handler (1977?–   )

1   When I was new to this country, commercials were my best teachers, my earliest friends. They educated me effectively, smilingly, on the mores of my new culture. But over the past few years, my attitude toward the parade of friendly faced commodities has changed.

Loyal to the Sky, Notes from an Activist 2007

2   Panic stabs through the crowd, and the pace picks up. Somewhere in the conjoined brain of this terrorized animal the primal impulse to flee has been slumbering; once aroused it is overwhelming, irresistible, familiar.

Ibid.

4918. Roxana Saberi (1977–   )

1   Many Lebanese Christians say they feel caught in the middle of a war in which they have a lot to lose and little to gain.

"Lebanese Christians Caught in Political Crossfire," Inter Press Service *9 August 2006*

2   They [the Iranian government] are generally—they at least show themselves to be—very suspicious of people who have contact with the outside world.

Interviewed on *All Things Considered* by Melissa Block, NPR Radio *28 May 2009*

3   At first, I just felt very afraid. But then I realized that I need to turn this challenge into an opportunity, and maybe this challenge can make me stronger, mentally and spiritually. And when I made the false confession, after that, I realized that I had made a mistake and I needed to try to right my wrongs, even if it meant that I would suffer. As long as I did the right thing, in the long run, in the end, I would be victorious.*

Ibid.

*Arrested and imprisoned for two months, she endured severe psychological pressure from her interrogators.

4   So I think these experiences, they taught me a lot and I learned a lot from the other political prisoners there, too— the other women—because after several weeks, I was put into a cell with them. Many of those women were there because they are standing up for human rights or the freedom of belief or expression.

Many of them are still there today; they don't enjoy the kind of international support that I did. And they're not willing to give in to pressures to make false confessions or to sign off to commitments not to take part in their activities once they're released; they would rather stay in prison and stand up for those principles that they believe in.

Ibid.

4919. Shakira (1977–   )

1   This is pathetic and sardonic
It's sadistic and psychotic
Tango is not for three
Was never meant to be

"Tango," *Laundry Service* (album) *2001*

2   Love has always been full of patience, hasn't it? And patience is the privilege of those who truly love, right?

Quoted in "Shakira pauses for poetry" by Agustin Gurza, *Los Angeles Times 28 November 2007*

3   Let's not forget that at the end of this day when we all go home, 960 children will have died in Latin America.

Speech, U.N. ceremony *3 April 2006*

4920. Riham Shebl (1977?–   )

1   I believe there isn't enough political commitment to eradicating FGM/C.* When the government focused on family planning, television advertising was in great abundance. So why did it take them till 2003 to talk about it on television, listing it on

the national agenda? Sexual education is also an important missing link because people don't realise that desire begins in the brain, not the genitals.

Quoted in "Rallying for Ms Nadia" by Amira El-Noshokaty,
Al-Ahram Weekly 25–31 January 2007
*Female genital mutilation and/or cutting.

2 For a long time FGM/C was associated with lack of education, a lower socio-economic background. This made it worse for upper- and middle-class women, because it became a double stigma; they were not only circumcised, but are also like the poor and the uneducated. That's why I dedicated this film to my own social class.

Ibid.

4921. Kerry Washington (1977–)

1 We have to heal the violence within ourselves as we heal the violence in the world. We have to be aware of the violence that we're inflicting on our little girls, at the same time as we are being aware of the violence that we are perpetuating as a nation—that all of these things are important. And I like that kind of thorough exploration of violence and what it means—our psychic violence, our physical violence, our political violence. And the violence that we perpetuate against each other as women.

Interview with Marianne Schnall,* feminist.com
16 September 2007
*See 4758.

2 But there's a vested interest, economically, politically, emotionally, for a lot of people, to silence us. And to make us silence ourselves. And so I don't even think that it's all the time done on purpose, I think that there are certain people, let's call them the "haves", who like what they have, and they don't want to talk about change. They don't want to go any deeper. They don't want to dig deeper. They don't want to acknowledge the evolutionary, new paradigm of power.

Ibid.

4922. Ather Zia (1977?–)

1 The mere mention of Kashmir, brings about an inevitable gush of emotions, a slew of stanched resolutions, sterile accords and pacts, impulsive wars and the incessant violence.

"Wither Kashmir: Short-term glory or long-term solution,"
The Kashmiri Times 3 August 2007

4923. Olga Gerasymyuk (1978?–)

1 Women [in the Ukraine] take the role of savior—they try to save themselves, their family.

"After the Fall, Traffic In Flesh, Not Dreams" by Alison Smale,
The New York Times 11 June 2000

4924. Porochista Khakpour (1978–)

1 ... when life said Ha, you find me boring, do you, then take this, O bored ones, I'll show you what boredom looks like with its entrails pulled out of its anus with a neon stick, take that, you want boredom, I'll smear you in the toxic shit of adventure, you want that, I'll give you a supersonic nuclear urine flushed swirlie down to the scatophiled-dream-depths of thrillsville, O too-content human—after that night, should the night have truly transpired, he was destined to long for the comfortable vacuum of anti-event for the rest of his life.

Sons and Other Flammable Objects 2007

2 He had imagined it because it could happen, because it was inevitable even, because why not? Probability dusts the glitter off coincidence's shoulders.

Ibid.

3 I'm trying to find myself, an identity outside yours, outside nationality, outside ethnicity, outside family, outside history. . . . foreign to them and to you and to everything, wholly my own lone person.

Ibid.

4925. Halima Bashir (1979–)

1 Darfur. I know to you this must be a word soaked in suffering and blood. A name that conjures up terrible images of a dark horror and an evil without end. Pain and cruelty on a magnitude inconceivable in most of the civilized world. But to me Darfur means something quite different: It was and is that irreplaceable, unfathomable joy that is home.

Ch. 1, *Tears of the Desert: A Memoir of Survival in Darfur 2008*

2 It was almost as if they were *intimate* together, and Grandma was . . . well . . . she was *Grandma,* and far too old and wizened for that sort of thing.

Ch. 4, Ibid.

3 As I looked around at Aisha's beautiful house, I realized that we inhabited separate worlds and lives, ones that only ever collided at the school. . . . I wondered why these houses seemed reserved for Arab families. They were a minority in Sudan, so how was it that the best homes and the best jobs were reserved for them?

Ch. 8, Ibid.

4926. Kory Johnson (1979–)

1 I see how [poor people] get dumped on, and I know dirty industry goes into the poor neighborhoods. These communities rarely have the technology to fight back. They have to hold a bake sale just to buy posterboard.

Quoted in "Toxic Avenger" by Kristen Arant, *Hues 38 September-October 1998*

2 Young people everywhere are entitled to environmental justice, no matter what their color or socioeconomic status.

Quoted on goldmanprize.org 1998

4927. Malalai Joya (1979–)

1 Countries like the US have their own strategic policies in Afghanistan . . . As long as they support the Northern Alliance with the mask of democracy, there will never be improvements in Afghanistan.

Quoted in "Afghan MP says she will not be silenced" by Tom Coghlan, Kabul, BBC News *27 January 2006*

2 They will kill me but they will not kill my voice, because it will be the voice of all Afghan women. You can cut the flower, but you cannot stop the coming of spring.

Ibid.

3 The Afghan parliament is the most disgusting and corrupt parliament in the world. Over 85 percent of the MPs [members of parliament] are those who should first of all appear in the court for their crimes against our people. . . . I am very fed up with the parliament and have no hope for it to do anything for

our people. It is a parliament of killers, murderers, drug-lords and traitors to the motherland.

> Interview with Malalai Joya by NOW, *pbs.org 2 March 2007*

4 I think that no nation can donate liberation to another nation. Liberation is not money to be donated; it should be achieved in a country by the people themselves.

> Ibid.

4928. Caille Millner (1979–   )

1 What I learned at Harvard was how to behave as though I had gone to Harvard.

> *The Golden Road, Notes on My Gentrification 2007*

2 I smoked clove cigarettes, and read obscure books, and wore dark currant lipstick that didn't suit my complexion. I refused to show surprise, interest or delight.

> Ibid.

4929. Marisha Pessl (1979–   )

1 "When it comes to certain human miseries, the only eyewitnesses should be the pavement and maybe the trees."

> *Special Topics in Calamity Physics 2006*

2 It really wasn't so much the tragic event itself, but others having knowledge of it that prevented recovery.

> Ibid.

3 "Dad picked up women the way certain wool pants can't help but pick up lint."

> Ibid.

4 "Everyone is responsible for the page-turning tempo of his or her Life Story."

> Ibid.

5 "Life hinges on a couple of seconds you never see coming."

> Ibid.

4930. Aparna Basu (fl. 1980s–2000s)

1 History is no longer just a chronicle of kings and statesmen, of people who wielded power, but of ordinary women and men engaged in manifold tasks. Women's history is an assertion that women have a history.

> Web site, *Women in World History Curriculum* (womeninworldhistory.com) *1996–97*

2 The history of science and technology is a neglected area.

> "Research in History of Education, a Trend Report," *Fourth Survey of Research in Education 1983–88*, Vol. I *n.d.*

4931. Gisele Bundchen (1980–   )

1 Today, no one is a virgin when they get married. To prohibit condoms is ridiculous, just think of all the diseases transmitted without them. How is it possible to not want people to use condoms and also not have abortions? It's impossible, I'm sorry.

> Quoted by Associated Press *6 June 2007*

4932. Zlata Filipovic (1980–   )

1 War has crossed out the day and replaced it with horror, and now horrors are unfolding instead of days.

> *Zlata's Diary 1994*

4933. Lenore Friedman (fl. 1980s–   ) (b. ca. 1942)

1 For many women practicing [Buddhism] today, one of the greatest obstacles remains the absence of clear female role models and foremothers in Buddhist literature and scripture. It is still a truism that all major teachers, lineage holders, and masters down the ages have been men.

> *Meetings with Remarkable Women: Buddhist Teachers in America 1987*

4934. Molly Jong-Fast (1980–   )

1 Art—what a mistake.

> *Normal Girl 2000*

2 Smoking heroin after snorting coke is a bit like having a Tasti-D-Lite on the way home from the gym.

> Ibid.

3 Children of famous people are like Communism—better in concept than in practice.

> Ibid.

4935. Melinda Kramer (1980–   )

1 Women are inextricably linked to issues of environmental sustainability, as mothers, as caretakers, as food producers, as consumers and as nurturers. . . . In order to ensure their own health, and that of their family and communities, women really need to manage and influence environmental policies. For a lot of women, environmentalism is too narrow a term for their work—social justice and human rights have a lot to do with women's everyday responsibilities.

> Quoted in "We Can Do It . . ." by Gregory Dicum, *San Francisco Chronicle 8 March 2006*

2 Unfortunately, even though women are key to water sustainability and have been the water keepers across cultures and across generations, there are barriers—political, social and economic barriers—for women as they attempt to bring and usher in clean water to their communities.

> Quoted in "On the Front Lines with Melinda Kramer" by Rhyen Coombs, *World Pulse Magazine* (worldpulsemagazine.com) *21 March 2008*

4936. Olya Melen (1980?–   )

1 I have been to the [Danube] delta many times, and every time it's like an adventure to paradise. The nature there—it's incredible, it's like a fairy tale.

> Quoted in "The Blew Danube" by Michelle Nijhuis, grist.org *25 April 2006*

2 As a public interest environmental lawyer, my goal is to seek the rule of law to preserve nature for present and future generations. Our fragile Mother Earth badly needs legal defenders.

> Quoted on goldmanprize.org *2006*

4937. Debora Phillips (fl. 1980s–   )

1 Lovemaking is relegated to a time when both are exhausted—the North American mating hour is at 11:30, right after the nightly news.

> "Personal Health" by Jane E. Brody, *The New York Times 8 October 1986*

2 Sex becomes as routine as tying one's shoes. When a couple has sex at the same time in the same place and in the same way

week after week, year after year, sex becomes very unexciting, which in itself can lead to a loss of sexual desire.

Ibid.

3   Sex needs an investment of time, energy and creativity. It is not just the result of falling into bed.

Ibid.

4938. Rebecca Ray (1980–)

1   I sort of liked him hating me. I knew exactly where I stood: right at his feet.

Pure 2000

2   She was the kind of person who warned everyone she was going to fart and gangs of blokes flocked around her, just to get a whiff.

Ibid.

4939. Graciela "Chely" Rodriguez (1980?–)

1   I've decided to become my own role model by reminding myself who I am every day. I am an eighteen-year-old Latina, a full-figured former model. I have survived an eating disorder. And I'm learning to love my body.

Essay, *Adiós, Barbie: Young Women Write about Body Image and Identity,* Ophira Edut, ed. *1998*

2   Girls Inc. didn't change the circumstances in my life. But it did teach me what I could do to take control of my life.

"Girls Inc. Luncheon Celebrates Guiding Young Lives," *Santa Barbara News-Press 6 February 2008*

4940. Georgiana Valoyce Sanchez (fl. 1980s)

1   For a moment we were equals, looking into each other's eyes, acknowledging our separateness. If not understanding, at least accepting the other's stand. It was a brief moment of union. Before the eyes looked away. Before we fell back into the hurting bones of ourselves, of our roles as husband and wife.

"The Heart of the Flower," *The Stories We Hold Secret: Tales of Women's Spiritual Development,* Linda Hogan,* Carol Bruchac and Judith McDaniel, eds. *1986*

*See 3753.

2   My mind was like a small alert bird perched atop the headboard, watching.

Ibid.

3   A long, long time ago, the Creator, and who knows how many Great Beings—gave the People language. At this time stories were born.

. . . Stories mirror our world, at the same time they are like rays of sunlight illuminating the dark places so that we can see more clearly.

. . . Without our stories . . . we would be lost.

"Chumash/Tohono-O'Odham," California Indian Storytellers Association *n.d.*

4941. Nishita Shah (1980–)

1   My dad said I could study anything I wanted, as long as it was business.

"Indian origin Nishita Shah 19th richest in Thailand" by Bupha Ravirot, TahiIndian.com *12 July 2008*

4942. Sarah Stuteville (1980–)

1   The landscape is all dust and smoke and heat. In the parched countryside the fields smolder and burn under a brutal sun.

March is the height of Cambodia's dry season and all over the country peasants are clearing and preparing the land for planting rice when the rains come.

"Dismantling a Dangerous Past," *Common Language Project* (clpmag.org) *14 March 2006*

2   Despite its distress, Lake Victoria is stunning at dawn as the day begins along her shores. Fishermen hoist the patchwork canvas sails of their handmade boats to a riot of bird calls. Hippos break the water's glassy surface with their broad snouts and snowy white egrets swoop gracefully in the rich golden light.

But beneath the scenic beauty a grim future looms for this great lake.

"Troubled Waters, The Coming Calamity on Lake Victoria," Ibid. *24 June 2008*

3   Women in this part of the world [Pakistan] are often cast as an exotic political side note in the U.S. When I promised myself that I would pursue "more gender diversity in my reporting" I was imagining occasional context to the real war news of this region. Instead women are in many ways at the forefront of the conflicts here and their voices aren't a footnote to the politics of this country, I'm realizing they are the politics of Pakistan.

"Hanging with the Ladies," Ibid. *9 April 2009*

4943. Ba Tam (fl. 1980s)

1   I was happy! It is just like heaven! Because people live here in freedom.*

(p. 425), Quoted in *Hearts of Sorrow: Vietnamese American Lives* by James Freeman *1989*

*Upon her arrival in the United States.

2   In Vietnam, in a village, from one end to another, everybody knows each other. Even in the city where I lived, we knew each other and visited one another. If I was sick, my friends visited me, and I did the same for them. I would see my friends at the market. When I think of that, I miss not having people I know nearby. It's very sad. Over here I live at home, and I cannot go anywhere.* In Vietnam, if I felt sad, I'd go to visit my friends, my fellow "sisters" . . . I am very sad and I have nowhere to go.

(p. 426), Ibid.

*One month after her arrival.

4944. Venus Williams (1980–)

1   It had to be hard [for Althea Gibson*] because people were unable to see past color. Still, these days, it's hardly any different because you realize it's been only 40 years. How can you change years and centuries of being biased in 40 years?

Quoted in "Venus Williams Wins Wimbledon . . ." by Selena Roberts, *The New York Times 9 July 2000*

*See 2958.

4945. Natasha Bedingfield (1981–)

1   Drench yourself in words unspoken/
Live your life with open arms wide open/
Today is where your book begins/
The rest is unwritten.

"Unwritten", *Unwritten (album) 2004*

4946. Lily Koppel (1981–)

1   But the diary seems a particularly eloquent survivor of another age. It was as if a corsage once pinned to a girl's dress were preserved for three quarters of a century, faded ribbons intact,

the scent still lingering on its petals. Through a serendipitous chain of events, the diary was given the chance to tell its story.
Ch. 1, The Red Leather Diary 2008

2 Since setting foot in the celebrity world, I had abandoned the novel I was working on. Fiction seemed strange when my reality felt so unreal.
Ibid.

4947. Jessica Partnow (1981–)

1 What I've found is that traveling and reporting here [in India] only become impossible when I insist that things should work in a certain way. When I slip, and expect that the internet connection should work, or there should be at least one restaurant serving beer in any given city, or that the name of the train I'm trying to catch should be written in English characters, I'm disappointed every time. When I remember that I have no idea what to expect at any given moment, and instead focus on listening carefully and being ready to change my plans at any given moment, I do just fine.
"Why Can't They Just Play Baseball?" The Common Language Project (clpmag.org) 3 April 2006

2 On my 25th birthday there were a lot of things I'd never done.... I had never spent time in a third world slum. I had never walked through a minefield. I had never talked to a prostitute.
"Reporting from the Red Light," Ibid. 8 May 2006

3 When you first see an elephant carcass, it's so big it looks more like a boulder than an animal.
"Kenya's Elephant Problem," PRI's The World 13 May 2008

4 When you move to New York City your address quickly becomes your most important identifying characteristic. Forget race, gender, religion, politics: what people really want to know is whether you live above 14th street and below 96th.
"Out of the Melting Pot and Into the Fire," The Common Language Project (clpmag.org) 14 August 2006

5 Conventional wisdom says that native people disappeared with the move to reservations. But really it's their history that has been hidden from view.
"First Peoples of the Duwamish," KUOW-Radio News (NPR affiliate) 25 September 2007

6 Seattle recently re-branded itself Metronatural. And we think of ourselves as a green city. But we're also home to one of the most contaminated industrial waste sites in the country.
"Surviving on the Duwamish," Ibid. 28 September 2007

4948. Natalie Portman (1981–)

1 There's so much goodness there [in Israel], and such a value placed on education, which is sort of universal among Jews around the world. I appreciate that obviously, to be a part of that.
Interview, Jewish Chronicle 6 July 2007

2 But I do think there is a sort of natural balance in nature between men and women, and that it's being thrown off-balance by the social and economic inequities between men and women.
"Natalie Portman on Her New Role: Giving Women Hope" by Marianne Schnall,* The Huffington Post 4 July 2008
*See 4758.

3 I'm trying to use whatever attention is focused on me and divert it to something that really deserves the attention and try and sort of stay out of the way of the rest of the stuff.
Ibid.

4 It's sort of shocking to me when politicians decide to spend money building walls between such places, instead of economically developing inside—it's so costly to do all this crazy security walls and building walls between human beings. No one wants to leave their homes—people want to stay where they live, with their families. You just want to create economic opportunity in those places and this is really what microfinance is about—it's really just about spreading the luck.
Ibid.

4949. Robyn Scott (1981–)

1 Grandpa said that in Botswana going to funerals was practically a national pastime. Not actually knowing the deceased did not, moreover, prevent people attending a funeral.
Twenty Chickens for a Saddle: The Story of an African Childhood 2008

2 Now, as always, the past and its possibilities were soon banished by the excitement of what lay ahead: the temptation to dwell and regret no match for the love of change that Mum and Dad both lived and breathed so infectiously into the family.
Ibid.

3 Heat overwhelmed me as I stood, stunned, in the fierce, dry, completely still air. It was unfairly, unbelievably hot, heat like nothing I had ever felt before. Normal thought, in this temperature and blinding light, was suddenly impossible. Mesmerized, I watched shimmering waves float above the dark tar. Beyond the runway fence posts, the flat green scrub seemed frozen behind the wobbling veil of heat. The almost white sky was empty; nothing stirred in the bushes: a few black cows stood motionless, sleeping beside the fence.
Heat was the only thing moving.
Ch. 1, Ibid.

4950. Britney Spears (1981–)

1 Sundance [Film Festival] is weird. The movies are weird—you actually have to think about them when you watch them.
Quoted in The Washington Post 31 January 2003

2 Honestly, I think we should just trust our president in every decision he makes and should just support that, you know, and be faithful in what happens.
CNN-TV Interview 3 September 2003

4951. Eisa Davis (1983?–)

1 this time we uplift the human race/
and I know the rainbow might be/
but is poetry enuf?
Letter to Ntozake Shange,* Letters of Intent: Women Cross the Generations to Talk about Family, Work, Sex, Love, and the Future of Feminism Anna Bondoc and Meg Daly, eds. 1999
*See 3865.

4952. Neema "Ngwatilo" Mawiyoo (1983–)

1 She looks at her child asleep in his cot
resolves to forge a home for him; even steal

828

a path to widen, in which to place cobblestones
or some other rock she can own.
"Heirloom" *2006*

2 there is no peace
that we fight to create.
"at stake//our mistake//softly spake," St. 1 *2007*

3 If my heart is spread across lands,
divided more by immigration officers / than by mountains and
oceans
"Thot, before the first note sounds," St. 1 *2007*

4 every temple hot and righteous
vengeful fists on freedoms fields
"Flag and Future," St. 3 *2008*

5 Did my ancestors kiss
to share love and passion
that warmed, pulsated
between them?
"Hybrid Love," St. 1 *2008*

4953. Amy Winehouse (1983–)

1 You can't sit down right,
Cause your jeans are too tight
"Fuck Me Pumps," *Frank* (album) *2003*

2 You've got a degree in philosophy,
So you think you're cleverer than me.
But I'm not just some drama queen,
Cos it's where you're at not where you've been.
"Help Yourself," Ibid.

3 I'll be some next man's other woman soon.
"Tears Dry On Their Own," *Back to Black* (album) *2006*

4954. Liz Moore (1984?–)

1 But how he dwells on it now, walking about New York; how
the longing to be sixteen again hits him sometimes between
the eyes and coaxes ridiculous guttural sounds from him, especially when he is drunk; how it comes crashingly down about
him when he sees himself in storefront windows, when his reflection catches him off guard!
Ch. 3, *The Words of Every Song* *2007*

2 Crying makes him think of hot, angry embarrassment: how liquids appear so suddenly, how the throat aches, how the tears
themselves fall, terribly loud and hot, onto the pillow one after
another, leaking over the bridge of the nose.
Ch. 4, Ibid.

3 It was 1997. The fashion was to look as if you had just gotten
into a fight and had emerged stylishly abused.
Ch. 5, Ibid.

4955. Melody Gardot (1985–)

1 The world has kissed me.
Quoted in "Beginning her career purely by accident" by
Siddhartha Mitter, *The Boston Globe 8 August 2008*

2 I would be lucky to find me a man who could love me the way
that I am
"Worrisome Heart," *Worrisome Heart* (album) *2008*

4956. Thembi Ngubane (1985–)

1 My mother, she clothed me, fed me, raised me, and now, at the
end of the day, she must also bury me. I was supposed to be the
one who was going to look after her. . . . That is not right.
Audio Diary (2005), *All Things Considered*, NPR *2005*

4957. Maria Sharapova (1987–)

1 I think Russians might be tougher than other people. When
I arrived in America I was young, but I already knew what I
wanted. I think that when you start from nothing, when you
come from nothing, it makes you hungry. I am proud of where
I came from and I know what I want. I want to win.
"Maria Sharapova," JockBio.com *2003*

2 Tennis has never been the most important thing in my life. My
family, my health, my happiness . . . they are more important
to me. On court, I want to win. Off court, I want to be a better
person. Tennis is a path to my future.
Ibid.

3 *When questioned about her on-court grunting at the 2006
Australian Open:* I know this is your job. But take your
notepads, take your pencils down, take your grunt-o-meters
down, the fashion police, put it all away and just watch the
match.
"Beaten Sharapova turns on media," BBC 26 *January 2006*

4958. Haifa Abdul Rahman (fl. 1990s–)

1 We see feminism in America as dividing men from women—
separating women from the family. This is not good for
anyone.
Quoted in *In Search of Islamic Feminism: One Woman's
Global Journey* by Elizabeth Warnock Fernea *1998*

4959. Lucia Annunziata (fl. 1990s)

1 A haze of sentiment has traditionally clouded America's perception of Italy: Americans love the country, but it is a love
based on cliché.
"The Fall of the Cold War Order," *The Nation* (New York) *5
April 1993*

2 But this is exactly the nature of the Italian political system: It
has worked by being both in turmoil and unchangeable, corrupt yet efficient. For almost five decades, paralysis and farce
have been not the "underdeveloped" face of a modern nation
but two faces of the same coin. This paradox has been our
Berlin wall.
Ibid.

4960. Margalynne Armstrong (fl. 1990s)

1 . . . white people have the privilege of escaping people of color,
and . . . anyone who can afford to is entitled to abandon the
urban poor.
"Privilege in Residential Housing," quoted in *Privilege
Revealed: How Invisible Preference Undermines America* by
Stephanie M. Wildman* *1996*
*See 3945.

2 The lesson our society must learn from the rising that followed
the Simi Valley*acquittals is that those to whom the pledge of
equality was made have not forgotten America's promises and
refuse to allow themselves to be forgotten.
Ibid.

*Re to the Simi Valley, California jury acquittal of the police officers accused of beating Rodney King that led to the 1992 uprising in the Watts district of south central Los Angeles.

3 Our system allows easy circumvention of fair housing law when discrimination takes the form of financial requirements or if exclusion is attributed to protection of property interests.

Ibid.

4961. Atsango Chesoni (fl. 1990s)

1 I actually consider certain depictions and portrayals of women in the media to be violence against women by perpetuating the objectification of women's bodies. We have limited control over how our images are used.

The language used when incidents of violence against women are reported is also a problem, because it often trivialises abuse.

"Putting Gender on the News Agenda," Sapa-IPS *19 August 1996*

4962. Mary Clyde (fl. 1990s)

1 Nicole wore clear bags.* Anne worse flesh-colored bags. She said she thought they were feminine . . .

"Krista Had a Treble Clef Rose," *Survival Rates 1999*
*Re ostomy bags, necessary after removal of cancerous colon.

2 Nicole says, "The anesthesia made my hair fall out. I've got three hairs left. I'm playing up my eyes."

Ibid.

3 He saw disappointment slip from their eyes, coming to rest at the corners of their mouths.

"Pruitt Love," Ibid.

4 Dr. Rodgers, insisting that cancers have personalities, has told them thyroid cancer lacks any real oncological ambition. He's called it shiftless, an embarrassment to the whole cancer community.

"Survival Rates," Ibid

4963. Diane DiPerna (fl. 1990s)

1 When the heads of state assembled for their group photo, they no longer seemed agents of progress but rather mere wooden soldiers, impotent from a lack of courage or penetrating ideas.

"Thinking globally, acting locally," *The Women's Review of Books*, vol. 10, no. 4, pp. 6–7 *January 1993*

2 Route 20, the arrow-straight road that once took American pioneers west across New York, traverses what would have been my Congressional district. At night, only blackness fills the rearview mirror; one can feel like an astronaut alone in the void except for an occasional flash of red, a deer or raccoon's eye, or the face-on too-bright headlights of some other late night space traveler.

Ibid.

3 But people will choose change only if they believe things can change for them . . .

Ibid.

4 In the end, politics is only as remote and as tarnished as we ordinary citizens let it become.

Ibid.

4964. Elizabeth Haiken (fl. 1990s–2000s)

1 . . . the surgical solution has allowed us to hold on to an idealized self-image:. . . . We are realists, pragmatists . . . bent on creating and recreating ourselves in the most modern of all possible ways.

Venus Envy: A History of Cosmetic Surgery 1997

2 Imagine a (perhaps) not too distant future, in which babies are made to order, down to the size of their noses and the longevity of their hairlines, a future in which "post-birth alteration" is remembered nostalgically as the primitive practice of well-meaning but technologically handicapped medical practitioners. If the market has its way with those accomplishments, cosmetic surgery as a way of altering the configuration of the face will become obsolete. But then, of course, we will face a new set of equally troubling questions about the complex relationship between culture, appearance, and human identity.

"Making of the Modern Face: Cosmetic Surgery," *Social Research Magazine* (New School for Social Research) *2002*

3 As a practice, cosmetic surgery is contemporaneous with reconstructive surgery, which means that plastic surgery emerges out of culture, as well as medicine. The drive toward technical and technological advancement is given impetus by consumer conviction that certain features are not advantageous and thus desirable of improvement, and by the whiff of money.

Ibid.

4 If cosmetic surgery is not about identity—if, in other words, it's only about changing external appearance—then it's not deep and meaningful but superficial; it may not even be medicine.

Ibid.

4965. Sally Halprin (fl. 1990s)

1 [Being on the antidepressant Prozac] is not at all like being on cruise control. It's more like driving a car with an unreliable fuel gauge on a long trip on an unfamiliar highway with no signs to indicate the distance to the next gas station or rest stop—and not minding.

"Life with Prozac," *San Francisco Chronicle 15 August 1993*

4966. Sarah Kerr (fl. 1990s)

1 Certain economic crises, precisely because they occur at an abstract remove, have some of the sickening allure of a horror story, or of a myth in which a merciless god threatens to wipe out a city at some unspecified date in the future.

"The Confidence Men," *The New York Review of Books 10 August 1995*

2 That the market-based approach works best of all is a given. Therefore the market-based approach deserves our confidence. And only if we trust in the market-based approach, as it deserves, will it show you doubters that it works best of all. A roundabout piece of reasoning, requiring an almost religious faith.

Ibid.

3 So while credibility is reassuring it can also be callous.

Ibid.

4967. Natalie Nenadic (fl. 1990s)

1 Serbian fascists . . . use rape as a public spectacle to induce women to leave their homes and never return. These sexual atrocities . . . are filmed as they are taking place [and] used as

propaganda in which the ethnicities of the victims and the aggressor are switched . . .

"Femicide: a Framework for Understanding Genocide," *Radically Speaking: Feminism Reclaimed* Diane Bell and Renate Klein, eds. *1996*

2 Survivors chose to speak out and let the world know about genocidal sexual atrocities so that they could thereby stop them and maybe save the women who were left behind and so that this would never happen again. . . . [International visibility] will make it more possible to guard the memory of what they suffered from the slander and revisionism which silences survivors' speech and lessen chances for survival. It can give women, as a group, something to remember.

Ibid.

4968–4969. Martha Nichols (fl. 1990s)

1 . . . we no longer see the zeroes and ones of machine code, but the logic of programming still rules what hackers create. Computer interaction forces users into an analytical, problem-solving mode, which is why the adventure-game format . . . was such a good match for early computer stories. There's just one hitch: problem-solving, especially in a binary universe, is not the only thing we do in life or art.

"Cyber, cyber, burning bright," *The Women's Review of Books,* Vol. XV, No. 4 *January 1998*

2 The conservative politics that now hold sway are a good first for cyberspace's love of anarchy and individualism, and its sense of boyish rebellion.

Ibid.

4970. Alyson Singer (fl. 1990s)

1 The law is so phallic! It doesn't leave much room for sensitivity, which must be why so many guys are happy in it.

Quoted in *Lawyer's Wit and Wisdom* Bruce Nash, Allan Zullo, eds.; Kathryn Zullo, comp. *1995*

4971. Yelena Tarasova (fl. 1990s)

1 Plastic surgery can correct a horrible nose, but the soul carries the scars from the operation. Everything that heals in the body continues to bleed and fester in the soul. That's what she thought when she was young, and if she were to remember everything now the way it happened, she would see her soul: a fat, melancholy blob, always sighing heavily.

"She Who Bears No Ill," *Half a Revolution: Contemporary Fiction by Russian Women,* Masha Gessen, ed. and tr. *1995*

4972. Cathy Rindner Tempelsman (fl. 1990s–   )

1 Whenever parents become overly invested in a particular skill or accomplishment, a child's fear of failure multiplies.

Ch. 1, *Child-Wise 1994*

2 The child who acts unlovable is the child who most needs to be loved.

Ch. 5, Ibid.

3 Children are as destined biologically to break away as we are, emotionally, to hold on and protect.

Ch. 14, Ibid.

4 When words fail us or, quite the opposite, when they rush from our mouths faster than we would like, we can console ourselves

that if no single moment is going to define our relationship with a child, neither can a single lapse of good judgment or patience destroy it.

Last ch., Ibid.

4973. Jelica Todosijevic (fl. 1990s)

1 Now we are no longer imprisoned by state limitations and censorship. . . . since we are receiving so much information, we have a wonderful opportunity to collect other people's experiences and apply it in our work. Sometimes it introduces revolutionary ideas, which makes our work much easier . . . Most of the time, though, learning about the successes of women-in-struggle itself gives us a lot of positive energy to go on.

NEWW On-line, Cited by Sonia Jaffe Robbins in "Lost in cyberspace," *The Women's Review of Books,* Vol. XIV, No. 2 *November 1996*

4974. Geraldine Heng (fl. 1993–2003)

1 . . . no variety of feminism is secure from the intervention of the state, nor from the power of any who are able to wield the discourse of nationalism.

Essay, *Feminist Genealogies, Colonial Legacies, Democratic Futures,* M. Jacqui Alexander and Chandra Talpade Mohanty, eds. *1997*

2 The evolution of romance . . . through the Middle Ages and beyond, attests to the successful tenacity of the genre in harnessing the characteristic resources of a literary empire of fantasy, so that in the hands of able manipulators romance may offer a ready and—equally important *safe* language of cultural discussion, and cultural transformation, in the service of crisis and urgent contingency.

Ch. 1, *Empire of Magic 2003*

4975. Elena Ferrante (fl. 2000s)

1 "Women without love lose the light in their eyes, women without love die while they are still alive."

The Days of Abandonment, Ann Goldstein, tr. *2005*

2 "Locks become habituated. They have to recognise the hand of their master."

Ibid.

3 They behaved with that man the way my father imagined women behaved, the way he imagined his wife behaved as soon as he turned his back, the way Amalia, too, perhaps, had for her whole life dreamed of behaving: a woman of the world who bends over without having to place two fingers at the centre of her neckline, crosses her legs without worrying about her skirt, laughs coarsely, covers herself with costly objects, her whole body brimming with indiscriminate sexual offerings, ready to joust face to face with men in the arena of the obscene.

Ibid.

4 When one writes one never needs to lie.

Interview, *Unità ca. 2005*

5 I had forgotten nothing, but I didn't want to remember.

Troubling Love, Ann Goldstein, tr. *2006*

6 Rats and dogs are the kings of the town during the night. The rubbish, piled as high as the second floor of buildings, comes alive in the dark. . . . During the day, the rats disappear and the

dogs calm down, men, women and children reappear.... And this city with its population of one million individuals goes on.

"Elena Ferrante on the waste disposal crisis in Naples," *La Repubblica 16 January 2008*

4976. Hanaa Hajar (fl. 2005)

1   ... the absence of women from this field [cartooning] stems from men's monopolization of it.... We have to prove that we are not afraid of politics and to take over in this field ...

Quoted in "Danger, female cartoonist" by Zvi Bar'el, *Haaretz. com 13 March 2007*

4977. Judy Goldberg Dey (Contemporary)

1   Women are much more likely than men to be single parents, and many mothers shoulder the full responsibility for the care of their children with little or no financial assistance from fathers. In this way, pay equity for women is a children's issue as well as a women's issue.

Ch. 1, *Behind the Pay Gap* (AAUW Educational Foundation) coauthor, Catherine Hill* 2007

*See 4979.

2   Gender pay discrimination can be overt or subtle. It is difficult to document discrimination because gender is usually easily identified by name, voice, or appearance.

Ch. 4, Ibid.

3   Leadership is critical to changing pay inequities within an organization. Without a concerted commitment at the top, policies and changes are unlikely to be taken seriously by managers and employees

Ibid.

4978. Rosie DiManno (Contemporary)

1   Men are from another planet, sent here by spaceships to copulate with female earthlings and propagate the species—a task for which science has rendered them all but redundant. We need keep only a handful of donors on a sperm farm for that purpose, where they can subsist on pizza and beer and Playboy magazine

Column, *The Star* (Toronto) *11 January 1999*

2   Most Americans don't know hockey. They don't get hockey. It's a yuk-yuk under-appreciated sport, an entry-level beat for

sports writers on U.S. papers. Palin, journalism degree from the University of Idaho in hand, never had the reporting chops to be a genuine sports scribe, of course, but she did put in a couple of years as a sportscast babe—no doubt where she learned to read a teleprompter with such gusto, before transforming into a broodmare hockey mom and, ultimately, veep nominee.

"Hockey moms drafted into politics," *The Star* (Toronto) 6 *September 2008*

4979. Catherine Hill (Contemporary)
Also see Judy Goldberg Dey, 4977:1–3.

1   In our report, AAUW* found that just one year after college graduation, women earn only 80 percent of what their male counterparts earn. Even women who make the same choices as men in terms of fields of study and occupation earn less than their male counterparts. Ten years after graduation, women fall further behind, earning only 69 percent of what men earn. After controlling for factors known to affect earnings, a portion of these pay gaps remains unexplained and is likely due to discrimination.

Testimony, U.S. House Committee on Education and Labor (Washington, D.C.) *24 April 2007*

*American Association of University Women.

2   Most companies do the right thing anyway, but some will only do the right thing when they see laws on the books. And some companies have to be taken to court. Without (punitive) damages for discrimination, there really is no way to make them take the issue seriously.

Quoted in "Senate approves landmark equal pay legislation" by David Lightman & Tony Pugh, McClatchy Newspapers 22 *January 2009*

4980. Wilina Lim Wei-ling (Contemporary)

1   I have a team of 45 technical staff, eight science staff, three medical staff. Most of my staff are women. I don't know what happens to the men. I guess they go into finance.

"How I Got There," *Newsweek 14 November 2005*

2   For me, my greatest achievement is that during difficult times like bird flu and SARS, no one from my team said: 'I don't want to work.' No one called in sick and they all worked hard.

APO News, vol. 36, no. 2 February 2006

Biographical Index

Every contributor is listed alphabetically and her contributor number given (these numbers will be found in page headings throughout the quotations section). Women well known by a name other than the one used as the heading of their entries in the quotation section are cross-indexed here. All coauthors are listed except "as told to" authors.

Brief biographical information is given for each woman: her full name (those parts of her name not commonly used are in brackets) and any hereditary or honorary title she is known to hold or to have held; her nationality and—if different—her country (or countries, when each has been substantial) of residence (e.g., Austrian/Cuban/Amer., as is the case of Riane Eisler, indicates she was born in Austria, lived a substantial portion of her life in Cuba, but now resides in the United States). Nationality is followed by other appellations by which the quoted woman has been known—everything from nicknames to pseudonyms to birth names. Next come notable family relations, if any, including brief biographical data on those relations, when available. If another woman included in that citing is also listed in the book, her name is marked with an asterisk (*). Notable achievements, including "firsts," discoveries, inventions, record settings, and so on, follow, after which come major awards and honors. The latter is by no means comprehensive or, when it comes to European and Asian countries, consistent; it is simply meant as an indicator of the woman's status in her profession.

A word about alphabetization of names: many women nobles, women of the Middle Ages, and some Asian women are alphabetized by what may not be a surname. Letter-by-letter alphabetization is used.

Abbreviations for relatives of the woman being quoted are in relation to her—the *contributor's* relationship to the other rather than the other's relationship to her (e.g., "*daughter* of . . . " rather than "father . . .")—and are as follows:

w.	wife	m.	mother
gm.	grandmother	s.	sister
d.	daughter	gd.	granddaughter
p.	partner	a.	aunt
ga.	grandaunt	mn.	married name
gn.	grandniece	m.-in-law	mother-in-law
c.	cousin	d.-in-law	daughter-in-law
n.	niece		

All other kinship terms are spelled out in full. Other names may be indicated by a.k.a. (*also known as,* for aliases), a.s.a. (*also seen as,* for different spellings), and pseud. (*pseudonyms,* or pen names).

The term *educator* encompasses teachers, professors (whether full, associate or assistant) and other instructors. The term *composer* designates one who writes classical music; *songwriter* is used for popular music. The term *theatrician* (first coined in the first edition of *The Quotable Woman* in 1978 and since in wider use) connotes one who has worked in almost every capacity in theater (producer, director, actor, designer, etc.).

Various organizations and affiliations that are often repeated are abbreviated, as follows:

AAP: Academy of American Poets

AAAL: American Academy of Arts and Letters

ABA: American Book Award, Before Columbus Foundation

AC: Companion in the Order of Australia

ACTRA: Alliance of Canadian Cinema, Television and Radio Artists

ASL: American Sign Language

Blackburn: Susan Smith Blackburn Prize

Bollingen: Bollingen Prize in Poetry

C.B.E.: Commander of the Order of the British Empire

DCA: Dramalogue Critics Award GFN

DCCA: Drama Critics Circle Award

DDA: Drama Desk Award

Ford: Ford Foundation (grants and awards)

Fulbright: Fulbright scholarship

Golden Globe: Golden Globe award for excellence in film and television (Hollywood Foreign Press Association)

Goldman: Goldman Environmental Prize

Grammy: Statuette awarded by National Academy of Recording Arts and Sciences

Guggenheim: Guggenheim Foundation (grants and awards)

Hugo: Hugo Award from the World Science Fiction Convention

IWSHF: International Women's Sports Hall of Fame

Emmy: Statuette awarded by Academy of Television Arts and Sciences

MacArthur: John D. and Catherine T. MacArthur Foundation Fellowship

McKnight: McKnight Composer Fellowship

MP: Member of Parliament

NAACP: National Association for the Advancement of Colored People

NASA: National Aeronautics and Space Administration

NBA: National Book Award

NBCCA: National Book Critics Circle Award

NEA: National Endowment for the Arts fellowship or grant

Nebula: Nebula Award from the Science Fictions Writers of America

NEH: National Endowment for the Humanities fellowship or grant

Newbery: Newbery Medal for American literature for children

NOW: National Organization for Women

NIAL: National Institute of Arts and Letters

NSF: National Science Foundation fellowship or grants

NWHF: National Women's Hall of Fame

NWPC: National Women's Political Caucus

NYDCCA: New York Drama Critics Circle Award

ODCCA: Outer Drama Critics Circle Award

Obie: Village Voice Award for exceptional achievement in off-Broadway theater

Oscar: Statuette awarded by the Academy of Motion Picture Arts and Sciences

PEN: Award from PEN international literary organization

Pushcart: Pushcart Press Prize

Right Livelihood: Right Livelihood Award (Stockholm)

Rockefeller: Rockefeller Foundations fellowships and grants

RRHF: Rock and Roll Hall of Fame

SHF: Songwriters Hall of Fame

Tony: Antoinette Perry Award sponsored by the American Theatre Wing for outstanding Broadway theater

UNICEF: United Nations International Children's Fund

Lastly, in the interest of book length, several common and frequently used words have been abbreviated, to wit:

Assn.	association
Intl.	International
Ctr.	Center
Dir.	Director
Exec.	Executive
Fed.	Federation
Fdn.	foundation
fdr.	Founder
fdg. mbr.	Founding member
genl.	general
inst.	Institute
mbr.	member
Natl.	National
Pres.	President.
Rep.	Representative
Sec.	Secretary.
U.N.	United Nations
U.S.	United States of America
Univ.	university

(All U.S. states are given Post Office abbreviations.)

&

A

Aafreen, Ishrat (1960?–)   4514
Pakistani/Amer. Poet

Abbagnano, Nicola (1901–1990)   1924
Ital. Philosopher

Abbasi, Talat (1953?–)   4154
Pak./Amer. Writer

Abbot, Sidney (1934–)   3015
Amer. writer, editor, historian

Abbott, Berenice (1898–1991)   1859
Amer. photographer, writer; technical pioneer of photographic equipment

Abbott, Patsy (fl. 1930s–50s)   2690
Amer. Comedian; née Goldie Schwartz

Abbott, Shirley [Jean] (1934–)   2875
Amer. historian, editor, writer; w. Alexander Tomkievicz, illustrator

Abbott, Wenonah Stevens (1865–1950)   1307
Amer. journalist, poet

Abdellah, Faye Glenn (1919–) 2335
Amer. nurse, military officer; first nurse office to receive the rank of a two-star rear admiral; NWHF, 2000

Abdi, Dekha Ibrahim (1964–)   4662
Kenyan peace activist; Right Livelihood, 2007

Al-Abdullah, Queen of Jordan, Rania (1970–)   4810
Kuw./Jor. queen, woman's rights activist, philanthropist;

née Al-Yassin; w. King Abdullah II of Jordan (1962–)

Abdul Rahman, Haifa (fl. 1990s)   4958
Iraqi civil servant; deputy sec., Genl. Fed. of Iraqi Women

Abel of Beth-maacah, Woman of (fl. 1040s–970s B.C.E.)   29
Isr. peacemaker

Abigail (fl. 990s B.C.E.)   34
Judaean biblical figure; w. Navah (1) and David (2), m. Chileah

Aboulela, Leila (1964–)   4663
Egypt./Sudanese novelist

Abrams, Linsey (1951–) 4018
Amer. novelist

Abramson, Jill (1954–) 4222
Amer. author, journalist

Abramson, Lisabeth Hughes
(1956?–) 4343
Amer. Judge, attorney; State
Supreme Court Justice-KY,
2007–

Aburdene, Patricia (1947?–) 3709
Amer. social forecaster, au-
thor; w. John Naisbitt (writer);
Medal of Italy from Senate of
Italy, 1990

Abutsu (?–1283?) 227
Jap. nun, poet

Abzug, Bella (1920–1998) 2360
Amer. lawyer, politician,
activist; née Savitsky; U.S.
congresswoman (D-N.Y.),
1971–1977; cofounder, Natl.
Women's Political Caucus;
2nd Jewish woman in Con-
gress (1970); cofounder,
Women's Strike for Peace;
cofounder, Coalition for
a Democratic Alternative;
NWHF, 1994

Ace, Jane (1905–1974) 2009
Amer. comedian, radio
personality; neé Epstein; w.
Goodman A— (TV & radio
comedy writer, 1899–1982)

Acker, Kathy (1947–1997) 3710
Amer. writer

Ackerman, Diane (1948–) 3808
Amer. nonfiction writer,
journalist, naturalist, poet;
AAP Poetry Prize, 1972;
Rockefeller 1974–1976; NEA,
1976, 1986

Ackerman, Jennifer (1959–) 4476
Amer. Science writer; w. Karl
A— (novelist)

Adams, Abigail (1744–1818) 646
Amer. first lady, letter writer,
feminist; née Smith; w. John
A— (1735–1826; 2nd U.S.
president), m. John Quincy
A— (1767–1848; 6th U.S.
president), m.-in-law Louisa
Catherine A—,* s. Elizabeth
Peabody*; NWHF, 1976

Adams, Carol J. (1951–) 4018.1
Amer. activist, environmental;
Mbr. of Board of Directors
of the Natl. Low Income
Housing Coalition, 1981;
Natl Chairperson of NY
State Governor's Commis-
sion on Domestic Violence,
1983–1987; Rockefeller,
1972–1973; English Speaking
Union Grant 1974

Adams, Grace (1900–?) 1893
Amer. psychologist; née
Kinckle

Adams, Léonie (1899–1988) 1880
Amer. poet, educator, poetry,
editor, poetry; Guggenheim,
1928, 1929

Adams, Louisa Catherine
(1775–1852) 766
Eng./Amer. first lady; née
Johnson; w. John Quincy A—
(1767–1848; 6th U.S. pres.),
d.-in-law Abigail A—,* gm.
Henry B. A— (1838–1919;
historian)

Adams, Maude (1872–1953) 1396
Amer. actor; famed for portrayal of Peter Pan

Adams, Sarah Flower
(1805–1848) 888
Eng. hymnist

Adamson, Joy (1919–1980) 2336
Aust./Kenyan naturalist, photographer, painter, author; née
Joy-Friederike Victoria Gess-
ner; w. George A— (naturalist)

al-Adawiya, Rabi'a
(712/17–801) 136
Persian poet, slave, Sufi
mystic, Islamic saint, scholar;
a.k.a. R— the mystic; pivotal
figure in the early development of Sufism

Addams, Jane (1860–1935) 1251
Amer. social worker; founder
of Hull-House, Chicago;
Nobel Peace Prize, 1931; Hall
of Fame, 1965; NWHF, 1973

Addison, Mrs. (fl. 1810s) 909
Poet

Addonzio, Kim (1954–) 4223
Amer. poet, educator; NEA;
Pushcart

Adelman, Penina V. (1953–) 4155
Amer. storyteller, social worker

Adelwip see HADEWIJCH OF
BRABANT

Adichie, Chimamanda Ngozi
(1977–) 4915
Nig./Amer. writer

Adjani, Isabelle (1955–) 4287
Fr. actor, singer; César Award
(4)

Adler, Freda (1934–) 2876
Amer. nonfiction writer,
educator

Adler, Margot [Carole]
(1941–) 3238
Amer. writer

Adler, Polly (1900–1962) 1894
Pol./Amer. author, madam

Adler, Rachel (1943–) 3387
Amer. theoretician

Adler, Renata (1938–) 3068
Ital./Amer. writer, philosopher,
film critic; AAAL (1987)

Adnan, Etel (1925–) 2505
Lebanese/Fr./Amer. poet,
novelist, documentary filmmaker

Agata, Hikari (1943–) 3388
Jap. writer; New Writers'
Prize, 1982

Agduk Agduk, Meltem
(1970?–) 4811
Turk. public servant

Agnes the Martyr (1500–1535) 295
Eng. Protestant martyr

Agnesi, Maria Gaëtana
(1718–1799) 581
Ital. scholar, mathematician;
established a hospice for
elderly infirm women; cubic
curve known as the "witch
of Agnesi" named for her
careful description of it

Agreda, María de
(1602–1664/65) 415
Span. abbess, essayist, philosopher, mystic;
née Maria Fernandez Coronel,
a.k.a. Sister Maria de Jesús

Agrippina the Younger, [Empress]
(14–59 C.E.) 80
Roman royalty; d. A— the
Elder, s. Emperor Caligula, w.
Gneus Dominitus (1) and Em-
peror Claudius (2), m. Nero

Aguilar, Grace (1816–1847) 932
Eng. Poet, teacher

Aguirre, Isidora (1919–) 2337
Chilean novelist, illustrator,
educator, playwright; Golden
Laurel Prize, 1960

Ahmed, Leila (1940–) 3169
Egyp./Amer. women's studies
and religion educator

Ahmed, Naima (1962–) 4600
Somalian/Amer. singer,
actor; m. Malika (recording
star)

Ai, (1947–) 3711
Amer. Poet, educator; née
Florence Anthony; NBA, 1999

Aidoo, (Christina) Ama Ata
(1942–) 3316
Ghanian/Zimb. poet, play-
wright, scholar, educator

Aiken, Joyce (1931–) 2750
Amer. Artist, art educator,
feminist

Aiken, Lucy (1781–1864) 785
Eng. letter writer, histo-
rian, poet; n. Anna Letitia
Barbauld*

Aimée, Anouk (1932–) 2782
French screen actor; née Françoise Sorya Dreyfus; ex-w.
Albert Finney (1936– ; Eng.
screen actor,)

Ainge de Vere, Mary see BRIDGES,
MADELINE

Airlie, Catherine see MACLEOD,
JEAN

'Aisha bint Ahmad al-Qurtubiyya
(fl. 960s–d. 999) 161
Span. poet

Aissé, Charlotte Elizabeth
(1694/95–1733) 540
Fr. beauty, letter writer

Ajax see BESANT, ANNIE

Akalaitis, JoAnne (1937–) 3016
Amer. playwright, educator,
stage director; ex-w. Philip
Glass (composer); founding
member of Mabou Mimes
(Chicago); Drama Desk
Award; Obie (4); Guggenheim;
NEA; Rockefeller; head of the
New York Shakespeare Festi-
val 1991

Akers, Elizabeth Chase
(1832–1911) 1043
Amer. poet; née Strong; pseud.
Florence Percy; w. Allen

Akhmatova, Anna
(1899–1966) 1692
Russ. poet; née A— An-
dreevna Gorenko; w. Nikolai
Gumilev (d. 1921; poet and
critic); with Gumilev, leader
of Acmeism, a movement that
praised the virtues of lucid,
carefully crafted verse

Akhyaliyya, Laila
(fl. 660s–699/704) 122
Iraqi poet; a.s.a. Layla al-
Akhyaliyya

Akins, Zoë (1886–1958) 1646
Amer. playwright, screen-
writer, writer, poet; w.
Rumbold; Pulitzer, 1935

Alais (fl. 12th century) 202
Fr. trobairitz, nun?

Alam, Glynn Marsh (1943–) 3389
Amer. writer

Alamanda (fl. 1165–1199) 194
Fr. trobairitz

Albelda, Randy [Pearl]
(fl. 1955–90s) 4288
Amer. nonfiction writer, economics; educator, economics

Albers, Anni [Annelise]
(1899–1994) 1881
Ger./Amer. Printmaker, textile
artist; née Else Frieda Fleis-
chmann; w. Josef A—, painter
and color theorist

Albert, Octavia Victoria Rogers
(1853–1889/90) 1196
Amer. freedwoman, novelist

Albery, Nobuko (1940?–) 3170
Jap./Monacan novelist, his-
torian; née Uenishi; a.k.a.
N— Morris; w. Sir Donald
A— (d. 1988; theatrical pro-
ducer)

Albrecht of Johannsdorf, Mistress of
(fl. 13th century) 229
Ger. courtesan

Albret, Jeanne d' [Queen of Na-
varre] (1528–1572) 327
Fr. royalty; d. Marguerite
of Navarre,* m. Henry IV

(1553–1610; king of France, 1589–1610) and Charlotte de Bourbon

Albright, Madeleine [Korbel] (1936–) 2959
Amer. public servant; Secretary of State, 1997–2001; first highest ranking woman ever to serve in the U.S. government; NWHF

Alcoforado, Mariana (1640–1723) 471
Port. nun

Alcosser, Sandra [B.] (1944–) 3472
Amer. educator, poet; NEA, 1985, 1991

Alcott, Louisa May (1832–1888) 1044
Amer. editor, writer; pseud. A. M. Barnard; NWHF

Alden, Ada (1857–1936) 1215
Amer. poet; pseud. Ada Foster Murray

Alden, Paulette Bates (1947–) 3712
Amer. author

Alden, Priscilla (1602?–pre-1687) 416
Eng./Amer. pilgrim; née Mullins; w. John A—, related to Sarah A— Ripley*

Alderman, Ellen (1957–) 4397
Amer. attorney

Aldis, Mary Reynolds (1872–1949) 1397
Amer. playwright, poet, artist

Aldrude (fl. 1170s) 196
Ital. noble; a.k.a. countess de Bertinora

Alexander, Elizabeth (1962–) 4601
Amer. poet, literary critic, book editor, poetry educator; NEA, Pushcart

Alexander, Jane (1939–) 3117
Amer. arts administrator, actor; née Quigley; w. Robert A— (1; actor, director); Ed Sherin (2; producer, director); Tony, 1968; chair NEA, 1993–1997

Alexander, Mrs. (1825–1902) 997
Amer. writer; pseud. Annie Hector

Alexander, Mrs. Cecil Frances (1818–1895) 943
Ir. hymnist, poet; née Humpheys

Alexander, Shana (1926–2005) 2540
Amer. writer, editor; née Ager

Alfredsson, Helen (1965–) 4691
Swed. golf pro; w. Kent Nilsson, hockey player; step. Robert N—, hockey player

Alger, Abby Langdon (1850–?) 1170
Amer. writer

Ali, Monica (1967–) 4743
Bangl./Eng. writer

Allen, Candace (1954?–) 4224
Amer./Eng. ; ex-w. Sir Simon Rattle, British conductor; first African-American female member of the Director's Guild of America; fdg. mbr & leader of Reel Black Women

Allen, Charlotte Vale (1941–) 3239
Can./Amer. novelist, actress

Allen, Dede (1925–) 2506
Amer. film editor; Oscar (3)

Allen, Florence Ellinwood (1884–1966) 1603
Amer. suffragist, author, attorney, jurist; descendant of Ethan Allen (Revolutionary hero; 1738–89); first woman jurist in the world to sit on a high court; first woman to sit on a federal bench (U.S. Court of Appeals, 6th Circuit, 1934–1959); NWHF, 2005

Allen, Mary Wood (1841–1908) 1099
Amer. lecturer, physician

Allen, Paula Gunn (1939–) 3118
Amer. critic; poet, novelist, Native American studies educator, antiwar activist; s. Carol Lee Sanchez*

Allen, Susan Au (1946–) 3625
Amer. politician, legislator

Allende, Hortensia Bussi de (1915–) 2234
Chilean first lady; widow of Salvador A— (1908–1973; Marxist president of Chile, 1970–1973), a. Isabel A—*; Int. Lenin Peace Prize, 1976

Allende, Isabel (1942–) 3317
Chilean/Amer. journalist, novelist; nc. Salvador A— (1908–1973; president of Chile 1970–1973) and Hortensia Bussi de A—*

Allen's Wife, Josiah   see HOLLEY, MARIETTA

Allerton, Ellen Palmer (1835–1893) 1060
Amer. poet

Allfrey, Phyllis Shand (1915–1986) 2235
Dominican writer

Alliluyeva, Svetlana (1925–) 2507
Russ. writer; d. Joseph Stalin (1879–1953; communist revolutionary and political leader)

Allingham, Margery (1904–1966) 1987
Eng. writer

Allison, Dorothy E. (1949–) 3880
Amer. novelist

Allred, Gloria [Rachel Bloom Bray] (1941–) 3240
Amer. feminist, attorney, radio talk show host, author; m.

Lisa Bloom (1961–), lawyer & TV host

Allwine, Janine Maria (1954–)4225
Amer. activist, political

Allyn, Jeri (1952?–) 4082
Amer. conceptual artist

Allyson, Karrin (1962–) 4602
Amer. singer, songwriter

Almucs de Castelnau (1140–?) 188
Provençal trobairitz; patron of troubadours

Alomang, Yosepha (1950–) 3948
Indones. activist, environmental; a.k.a. Mama Yosepha; Goldman, 2001

Aloni, Shulamit (1929–) 2650
Pol./Isr. educator, politician, lawyer, feminist, writer

Alonso, Dora (1910?–) 2118
Cub. writer

Alsop, Marin (1956–) 4344
Amer. conductor; first conductor ever to receive the MacArthur

Alston, Theodosia Burr (1783–1813) 793
Amer. social leader; d. Aaron (1756–1836; politician, U.S. vice president, 1801–05) and Theodosia DeVisme Burr,* w. Joseph A— (governor of South Carolina), great-gd. Sarah Pierpont Edwards*

Alta (1942–) 3319
Amer. poet, feminist; a.k.a. Alta Gerrey; fdr., Shameless Hussy Press

Alther, Lisa Reed (1944–) 3473
Amer. novelist

Alvarado, Linda G. (1952–) 4083
Amer. business executive, philanthropist; NWHF, 2003

Alvarez, Aida (1949–) 3881
Puerto Rican/Amer. civil servant, journalist

Alvarez, Cecilia [Concepcion] (1950–) 3949
Amer. installation artist, illustrator

Alvarez, Julia (1950–) 3950
Domin./Amer. novelist, poet, educator

Amanpour, Christiane (1958) 4437.1
Eng./Iran./Amer. journalist; w. James Rubin, former US State Department spokesman; CNN Chief Intl. Correspondent; CBE, 2007; Emmy (9)

Ambapali (fl. 560s–d. 480 B.C.E.) 54
Ind. poet, courtesan, Buddhist nun

Ambrose, Mary, Mother (1892–?) 1737
Roman Catholic nun; née Mulholland

Amelia, [Princess] (1783–1810) 794
Eng. poet; d. George III of Britain (1738–1820)

American, Sadie (1862–1944) 1281
Amer. reformer, social worker; cofounder. & exec. sec., Natl. Council of Jewish Women, 1894–1914

Amir, Anda (1902–1980?) 1944
Pol./Isr. poet; née Pinkerfield; m. Pinkerfield

Anastasi, Anna (1908–2001) 2076
Amer. educator, psychologist, author; a.s.a. Anna; a.k.a. "the test guru"; w. John Porter Foley, Jr., psychologist

Ancelot, Virginie [Marguerite Louise] (1792–1875) 829
Fr. novelist, dramatist; née Chardon

Andal (fl. 10th century) 167
Ind. poet

Anderson, Catherine (1947–) 3713
Amer. poet

Anderson, Edith (fl. 1960s–90s) 4515
Amer./Ger. translator, novelist

Anderson, Judith, Dame (1898–1992) 1841
Aust./Amer. actor; née Frances Margaret Anderson-Anderson; Emmy, 1954, 1961; Tony, 1948; DBE, 1960; AC, 1991

Anderson, Laurie (1947–) 3714
Amer. composer, songwriter, performance artist; NEA, 1977, 1979; Guggenheim, 1983

Anderson, Margaret [Caroline] (1886–1973) 1647
Amer. writer, musician

Anderson, Marian (1902–1993) 1945
Amer. concert singer; first African-American member of the Metropolitan Opera Company, 1955; U.S. delegate to the United Nations, 1958–1959; Spingarn Medal, 1939; Presidential Medal of Freedom, 1963; Grammy Lifetime Achievement, 1991; NWHF, 1973

Anderson, Ruth Ann (1945?–)3553
Amer. artist (sculptor & drawer), social worker

Andrews, Corinne   see WEST, REBECCA

Andrews, Lori B.(1953–) 4156
Amer. Attorney, law professor, writer

Andrews, Mary Kay (1954–) 4226
Amer. novelist, journalist; née Kathy Hogan Trocheck

Andrus, Ethel Percy (1884–1967) 1604
Amer. teacher, administrator; fdr., Natl, Retired Teacher's Assn., 1947; fdr., The American Assn. of Retired Persons, 1958; NWHF, 1967

Anduza, Clara d' (1200–1235) 203
Fr. trobairitz
Angela of Foligno
(1250–1309) 219–220
Ital. religious figure, mystic;
beatified, 1693
Angelou, Maya (1928–) 2618
Amer. activist, storyteller,
producer, dancer, screenwriter,
poet, actor; née Marguerite
Johnson; Inaugural poet, 20
Jan. 1993; Rockefeller, 1975;
NWHF
Anger, Jane (fl. 1580s) 383
Eng. feminist, pamphleteer;
pseud. only; author of the first
published English defense of
women written by a woman
Angier, Natalie (1958–) 4438
Amer. science journalist; Pulit-
zer, 1991
Anguissola, Sofonisba
(1535/40?–1625) 335
Ital. painter; a.s.a. So-
phonisba Anguisciola; s.
Elena, Lucia, Minerva, and
Anna (all Ital. painters);
protégée of Michelangelo
(artist, 1475–1564); first dis-
tinguished woman painter of
the Renaissance
Angus, Rita (1908–1970) 2077
N.Z. artist, painter
Aniston, Jennifer (1969–) 4778
Amer. actor; d. John A— ,
actor, and Nancy Dow, actor;
ex-w. Brad Pitt, actor; Emmy,
2002; Golden Globe, 2003
Ankhesenpaton (fl. 1390s B.C.E.) 15
Egyp. queen; née Ankhe-
senpaaten; d. Akhenaton
(1375?–1358?; king of Egypt)
and Nefertiti (c.1372–1350
B.C.E.; queen of Egypt), w. Tu-
tankhamun (fl. ca.1350 B.C.E.,
Egyptian king of the XVIII
Dynasty)
Anna (fl. 720s B.C.E.) 43
Hebrew biblical figure; w.
Tobit, m. Tobias
Anna of Saxony (fl. 1580s) 384
Ger. medical practitioner; w.
Elector Augustus; founded a
school for midwives
Anna Maria of Braunschweig
(fl. 1540s) 337
Ger. royalty; d. Elisabeth of
B—*
Annan, Annie Rankin
(1848–1925) 1157
Amer. poet; w. Glenny
Anne of Austria (1601–1666) 414
Aus./Fr. queen of France,
letter writer
Anne of England, Queen
(1665–1714) 504
Eng. royalty, queen; a.k.a.
Good Queen Anne; d. king

James II (1633–1701); s. Mary
II of England* and James,
the Old Pretender, s.-in-law
King William III of England
(1650–1702); w. George,
prince of Denmark; originated
the practice of racing horses
for money
Annunziata, Lucia (fl. 1990s) 4959
Ital. journalist
An Old Man see MARSH, ANNE
Anthony, Katharine [Susan]
(1877–1965) 1487
Amer. writer, educator
Anthony, Susan B. (1820–1906) 963
Amer. editor, suffragist;
founder of Woman's State
Temperance Society of New
York; Hall of Fame, 1950;
NWHF
Antin, Mary (1881–1949) 1563
Russ./Amer. writer, patriot;
w. Amadeus William Grabau,
geologist
Antler, Joyce (1942–) 3320
Amer. educator, author; m.
Lauren A— , comedian
Antoine-Dariaux, Geneviève (fl.
1960s–1973) 4516
Fr. fashion designer, writer
Antrim, Minna [Thomas]
(1861–1950?) 1262
Amer. writer
Anwar, Zainah (1953?–) 4157
Malay. feminist, journalist; d.
Tan Sri Anwar Malik (1887–
1997), leader of UMNO; s.
Ahmad Zakii A— , artist;
dir., Sisters in Islam (SIS),
1987–1997
Anyanwu, Christina (1951–) 4019
Nig. radio producer,
publisher, journalist; Interna-
tional Press Freedom Award,
1997
Anyte of Tegea (fl. ca. 300 B.C.E.) 66
Greek poet
Anzaldúa, Gloria [Evangelina]
(1942–2004) 3321
Amer. educator, writer, edi-
tor, poet
Apostolides, Marianne
(1973?–) 4875
Can. writer, activist, editor
Appignanesi, Lisa (1946–) 3626
Pol./Eng. novelist, TV producer; née Elsbieta Borenztejn;
m. Josh A—, filmmaker
Applebaum, Anne [Elizabeth]
(1964–) 4665
Amer./Pol. journalist, author;
w. Radoslaw Tomasz Sikor-
ski (1963–), Pol. politician,
journalist; Minister of Foreign
Affairs, 2007-; Pulitzer, 2004
Applegate, Debby (1968–) 4763
Amer. biographer; Pulitzer,
2007

Apter, Terri (1949–) 3882
Brit. writer, psychologist,
educator
Aquino, Corazon
(1933–2009) 2830
Filipina political leader;
née Maria C— Cojuangco;
w. Benigno "Ninoy" A—
(1932–1983; journalist and
politician; assassinated); Phil-
ippine president, 1986–92
Arafat, Suha (1963–) 4636
Pal. pubic figure; d. Raymond
Hawa Tawil*; w. Yasser Ara-
fat (1929–2004), Chairman
of Palestine Liberation Orga-
nization
d'Aragona, Tullia (1510–1556) 301
Ital. courtesan, writer, poet
Arblay, Madame d' see BURNEY,
FANNY
Arbour, Louise (1947–) 3715
Can. justice; U.N. High Com-
missioner for Human Rights,
2004–2008; Justice, Supreme
Court of Canada (1999–
2004); OC, 2007
Arbus, Diane (1923–1971) 2444
Amer. photographer; w. Allan
A— (actor, photographer)
Ardagh, Susan Hamilton
(1854–1935) 1200
Eng. advice writer; a.k.a.
countess of Malmesbury
Ardelia see FINCH, ANNE
Arden, Elizabeth (1878–1966) 1503
Can./Amer. businesswoman;
fdr./developer of Elizabeth
Arden Cosmetics
Arditti, Rita (1934–) 2877
Argen./Amer. activist (human
rights), geneticist; cofounder,
New Words and Women's
Community Cancer Project
Arendt, Hannah
(1906–1975) 2036
Ger./Amer. historian, phi-
losopher
Arensberg, Ann (1937–) 3017
Amer. novelist
Ariadne (fl. 1690s) 535
Eng. playwright
Arizmendi, Yareli (1964–) 4666
Mex./Amer. actor, screen-
writer, producer, activist;
w. Sergio Arau, musician,
painter; f.-in-law, Alfonso
Arau, Mex. Film director,
actor
Arizpe, Lourdes (1943/46–) 3390
Mex. anthropologist, admin-
istrator
Armantrout, Rae (1947–) 3716
Amer. poet, educator, poetry
Armstrong, Cora Harvey
(1937?–) 3018
Amer. singer, gospel, song-
writer; The Cora Harvey

Armstrong And Full Deliver-
ance
Armstrong, Karen (1944–) 3474
Eng. nun, former, writer, reli-
gious, lecturer
Armstrong, Margalynne
(fl. 1990s) 4960
Amer. activist
Armstrong, Mary F[rances]
(fl. 1880s–1903) 1539
Amer. social commentator,
teacher
Armstrong, Sue (1942–) 3322
S. Afr. journalist
Arndt, Bettina "Tina" (1949–) 3883
Eng./Aust. sex therapist,
psychologist, clinical,
commentator; d. H.W. A—
(1915–), Ger./Aust. Economist
Arnim, Bettina von
(1785–1859) 798
Ger. sculptor, writer, musi-
cian; née Elizabeth Katharina
Ludovica Magdalena; s.
Clemens Bretano (musician);
friend of Johann Wolfgang
von Goethe (1749–1832;
German poet, dramatist,
scientist)
Arnim, Mary Elizabeth, countess
von (1866–1941) 1322
Aust./Eng. writer; née Beau-
champ, pseud. Elizabeth; w.
Count Russell
Arnold, Margaret Shippen
(1760–1804) 704
Amer./Eng. letter writer; w.
Benedict A— (1741–1801;
American revolutionary
general)
Arnold, Mary Augusta see WARD,
MARY
Arnold, Susan E. (1954–) 4227
Amer. business executive
Arnould, Sophie
(1740/44–1802) 628
Fr. actor, opera star; née Anne
Madeleine
Arnow, Harriette [Simpson]
(1908–1986) 2078
Amer. writer
Aronson, Muriel Fox see FOX,
MURIEL
Aróstica, Florencia (1956?–) 4345
Chilean administrator; presi-
dent, Natl. Assn. of Rural
and Indigenous Women
(ANAMURI)
Arria the Elder (?–42 C.E.) 87
Roman hero; w. Caecina
Paetus
Arrien, Angeles (1935–) 2920
Amer. consultant, corporate,
anthropologist, educator,
nonfiction writer; founder,
Angeles Arrien Foundation for
Cross Cultural Education and
Research

Arroyo, Gloria Macapagal (1947–) 3717
Filipina politician, economist, educator; a.k.a. G.M.A.; d. Diosdado Macapagal (pres. Philippines); 14th Pres. of the Republic of the Philippines (2001– ; second female pres.); first female vice pres.

Arslan, Antonia (1938–) 3069
Ital. educator, archaeologist, writer

Artemisia (fl. 480s B.C.E.) 60
Carian/Turk. queen of Halicarnassus, military leader

Artois, Mahuat d' (1285–1319) 228
Fr. noble; a.k.a. Matilda; m. Jeanne of Navarre*

Arundel, duchess of see HOWARD, ANNE

Arzner, Dorothy (1900–1980) 1895
Amer. film director

Ascarelli, Devorah (fl. 1600s) 409
Ital. poet, translator

Ascher, Barbara Lazear (1947?–) 3718
Amer. author, attorney, columnist

Ash, Mary Kay (1918–2001) 2306
Amer. business executive, author; née Wagner; fdr., Mary Kay Cosmetics, Inc.; Horatio Alger Award, 1978

Ashenburg, Katherine (1950?–) 3951
Can. writer, educator, public speaker

Ashford, Daisy (1890?–1972) 1704
Eng. writer

Ashmun, Margaret Eliza (1875–1940) 1452
Amer. writer

Ashrawi, Hanan (1946–) 3627
Palestinian/Isr. public servant, educator, scholar; a.s.a. Mikhail-Ashrawi; d. Daoud Mikhael, physician and cofounder. of PLO; fdr., Palestinian Independent Commission for Citizens' Rights; dean of humanities at Bir Zeit University (1991)

Ashton, Winifred see DANE, CLEMENCE

Ashton-Warner, Sylvia [Constance] (1908–1984) 2079
N.Z. writer, teacher; w. Henderson; developed Creative Capital Teaching Scheme

Askew, Anne (1520–1546) 313
Eng. martyr; d. Sir William A—, w. Thomas Kyne

Askew, Rilla (1951–) 4020
Amer. writer

Aspasia (fl. 420s B.C.E.) 62
Greek teacher; a.k.a. Princeps Gracia; teacher of Socrates; counselor to Pericles

Asquith, Margot (1864–1945) 1301
Eng. writer, socialite; a.k.a. countess of Oxford and Asquith; w. Herbert Henry A— (1852–1928; British Liberal politician and prime minister)

Assad, Maríe B[assilli] (1923–) 2445
Egyp. anthropologist, activist, women's rights; head of Task Force to Fight the Circumcision of Girls

Astell, Mary (1666/68–1731) 507
Eng. pamphleteer; first self-avowed feminist writer in English

Astor, Brooke (1902–2007) 1946
Amer. foundation executive, writer, civic worker; née Russell

Astor, Madeline Talmage (1893–1940) 1760
Amer. social leader; née Force; w. (1) John Jacob A— (1763–1848; German-born American fur trader and capitalist); (2) William K. Dick; (3) Enzo Fiermonte, boxer

Astor, Mary (1906–1987) 2037
Amer. actor, novelist; née Lucile V. Langhanke; Oscar, 1941

Astor, Nancy [Witcher Langhorne], Lady (1879–1964) 1519
Amer./Eng. politician; first woman to sit in British House of Commons; Lord Mayor of Plymouth; leader of women's and children's rights

Astorga, Nora (1949–1989) 3884
Nicaraguan attorney, revolutionary, diplomat

Astrea see BEHN, APHRA

Ata, Shahla (1966?–) 4714.1
Afghan politician

Atakhanova, Kaisha (1958–) 4439
Kaz. biologist, activist, environmental; fdr., Karaganda Ecological Center; Goldman, 2005

Ataniyazova, Oral (1957–) 4398
Uzb. obstetrician, medical scientist, environmental activist; fdr., Perzent; Goldman, 2000

Atherton, Gertrude [Franklin] (1857–1948) 1216
Amer. writer; pseud. Frank Lin; great-grandn. Benjamin Franklin (1706–1790; American statesman and writer); grandn. of Sarah Bache*

Atkins, Eileen (1934–) 2878
Brit. stage & screen actor

Atkinson, Kate (1951–) 4021
Eng. playwright, novelist; 1995 Whitbread Book of the Year

Atkinson, Ti-Grace (1938–) 3070
Amer. writer, feminist

Atlan, Liliane (1932–) 2783
Fr. playwright; Légion d'Honneur

Atwood, Margaret [Eleanor] (1939–) 3119
Can. essayist, novelist, poet; w. Graeme Gibson (writer); Governor General's Award, 1966, 1986; Radcliffe Medal 1980; Guggenheim, 1981; Booker Prize, 2000

Auber, Harriet (1773–1862) 761
Eng. poet, hymnist

Aubin, Penelope (1679–1731) 521
Eng. author

Aubry, Erin J. (1970?–) 4812
Amer. journalist

Auclert, Hubertine (1848–1914) 1158
Fr. feminist

Audeley, Eleanor (fl. 1620s–d. 1651) 436
Scot. prophet, Protestant pamphleteer; a.k.a. Davies, Douglas

Auel, Jean M[arie] (1936–) 2960
Amer. novelist

Augusta (1757–1831) 689
Ger. diarist; a.k.a. Duchess of Saxe-Coburg-Saafeld; grandm. Queen Victoria*

Augustín, María (1786–1857) 800
Span. military hero; a.k.a. Agostina, the Maid of Saragossa (a.s.a. Zaragosa); described in Byron's "Childe Harold"

Aung San Suu Kyi (1945–) 3554
Burmese peace and human rights activist, politician; d. General A— S— (d. 1947; activist and hero; assassinated) and Khin Kyi (ambassador to India); m. Khin Kyi (ambassador to India); cofounder, Natl. League for Democracy, 1988; Sakharov Prize for Freedom of Thought, 1990; Nobel Peace Prize, 1991

Aury, Dominique (1907–1998) 2059
Fr. translator, editor, literary critic, writer; née Anne Desclos; pseud. Pauline Reage; l. Jean Paulhan (1884–1968, Fr. writer, literary critic, publisher; Légion d'Honneur

Austen, Jane (1775–1817) 767
Eng. novelist

Austin, Mary Hunter (1868–1934) 1346
Amer. suffragist, lecturer, writer

Austin, Sarah Taylor (1793–1867) 836
Eng. author; d. Susannah Cook Taylor, w. John A— (jurist), m. Lucie A— Duff Gordon (1821–1869; writer and translator)

Auvaiyar (fl. third century?) 102
Ind. poet

Ava, Frau (?–1127) 185
Ger. nun, composer, poet, sacred singer; first woman known to compose biblical and religious songs

Avary, Myrta Lockett (1857–1946) 1217
Amer. book editor; a.k.a. M— Harper L—

Avery, Byllye Y. (1937–) 3019
Amer. health activist, author, lecturer, educator; fdr., Natl. Black Women's Health Project, 1983; fdr., Avery Inst. for Social Change; MacArthur Fdn.

Avery-Clark, Constance (1954?–) 4228
Amer. psychologist

Axline, Virginia Mae (1911–1988) 2149
Amer. psychologist

Ayer, Harriet Hubbard (1849–1903) 1163
Amer. entrepreneur, columnist, beauty advice

Ayllón Soria, Virginia (fl. 1950s–1990s) 3952
Bolivian literary critic, essayist

Ayscough, Florence (1878–1942) 1504
Chin./Amer. translator, lecturer, librarian; née Wheelock

Azadeh, Carol (1964–) 4667
Ir./Fr. novelist

Azalais de Porcairages (1140?–?) 188
Provençal trobairitz

Azara, Nancy (1939–) 3120
Amer. author, feminist, sculptor; partner, artist Darla Bjork

az-Zabba, (see ZENOBIA OF PALMYRA)

Azzopardi, Trezza (1961–) 4563
Ital./Eng. novelist

B

B. B., Mrs. Bogan of Bogan see NAIRNE, CAROLINA

Babbitt, Natalie (1932–) 2784
Amer. illustrator, writer, children's; w. of Samuel Fisher

(Zane Moore) Babbitt, vice-President of Brown University; Newbery, 1971

Babcock, Barbara Allen (1938–)   3071
Amer. lawyer, educator, author; U.S. asst. attorney general (1977–1981)

Babitz, Eve (1943–)   3391
Amer. writer

Baca, Judy (1950–)   3953
Amer. artist, painter; created *The Great Wall of Los Angeles* (1976); *World Wall* (1988)

Bacall, Lauren (1924–)   2476
Amer. screen actor, author; née Betty Joan Perske; widow of Humphrey Bogart (actor), ex-w. Jason Robards (actor); Tony, 1970

Bache, Sarah Franklin (1744–1808)   647
Amer. letter writer; d. Benjamin Franklin (American statesman and writer, 1706–1790), great-a. Gertrude Atherton*

Bachelet, [Verónica] Michelle (1951–)   4022
Chilean politician, pediatrician, epidemiologist; Pres. of Chile, 2006– (first woman)

Bachman, Moira (fl. 1940s)   3171
Amer. labor activist

Bachmann, Ingeborg (1926–1973)   2541
Ger. writer, novelist

Backus, Bertha Adams (fl. 1910s)   2119
? poet

Bacon, Anne Cooke (1528?–1610?)   328
Eng. translator, author; d. Anthony Cooke, s. Elizabeth Hoby Russell,* Catherine Killigrew* and Lady Mildred Burleigh, m. Frances B— (1561–1626; English philosopher, essayist and statesman) and Anthony B—

Bacon, Josephine Dodge (1876–1961)   1468
Amer. writer, humorist, poet

Bacon, Martha (1917–1981)   2280
Amer. poet, novelist, educator, English

Badawi, Khulood (1976–)   4903
Pal./Isr. peace activist

Baez, Joan (1941–)   3241
Amer. songwriter, singer, civil rights activist; founder of Institute for the Study of Nonviolence (California)

Bagnold, Enid (1889–1981)   1693
Eng. playwright, screenwriter; w. Lord Jones

Bai, Lakshmi (1828–1858)   1016
Ind. military hero, royalty, head of state; w. Gangadhar Rao, Raja of Jhansi (d. 1853)

Bai, Mukta (fl. 13th century)   230
Ind. beggar, poet

Bai Fengxi (1932?–)   2785
Chin. playwright, actor

Bailey, Pearl [Mae] (1918–1990)   2307
Amer. singer, diplomat, writer; mn. Bellson

Bailey, Urania Locke [Stoughton] (1820–1882)   964
Amer. writer, evangelist; pseud. Julia Gill, Una L—

Baillie, Grisell see HOME, GRISELL

Baillie, Joanna (1762–1851)   713
Scot./Brit. poet, playwright

Baillie, Margaret see SAUNDERS, MARGARET

Bainbridge, Beryl Margaret (1933–)   2831
Eng. novelist, columnist

Bair, Sheila C. (1954–)   4229
Amer. lawyer, educator, economist; chair, FDIC (2006–)

Baizley, Doris (1945–)   3555
Amer. playwright; founding member of L.A. Theatreworks

Baker, Dorothy [Dodds] (1907–1968)   2060
Amer. writer

Baker, Dorothy Gillam (1906–1990)   2038
Amer. educator, peace activist, scholar; née Gillam

Baker, Elizabeth (1876–1962)   1469
Eng. playwright

Baker, Ella J. (1903–1986)   1962
Amer. civil rights activist; founding member of Young Negroes Cooperative League, 1932, Student Nonviolent Coordinating Committee (SNCC), 1960, and Mississippi Freedom Democratic Party, 1964; NWHF

Baker, Josephine (1906–1975)   2039
Amer./Fr. exotic dancer, singer

Baker, Mary (1892–197-?)   1738
Scot./Scot. attorney, activist; a.k.a. Sheila Stuart

Baker, Sara Josephine (1873–1945)   1407
Amer. inventor, physician health researcher; pioneer in the field of public health; invented measured-dose dropper (1908), safe baby clothes (1908); first woman to earn a doctorate in public health (1917); first chief of newly formed Division (later "Bureau") of Child Hygiene, New York City (1908); Established

"Baby Health Stations" and "Little Mothers League"

Baker-Fletcher, Karen (1960?–)   4517
Amer. educator (theology)

Bakke, Kit (1946–)   3628
Amer. writer, activist, nurse, health care consultant

Bakoyannis, Dora (1954–)   4230
Greek politician; minister for foreign affairs (2006–); mayor of Athens (2002–2006), first woman; World Mayor Award, 2005

Balch, Emily Greene (1867–1961)   1333
Amer. peace activist, social economics educator; Sec.-Genl, Women's Int. League for Peace & Freedom; Nobel Peace Prize, 1946

Baldwin, Christina (1946–)   3629
Amer. writer, teacher, facilitator; cofounder, PeerSpirit. com, 1995; Storycatcher.net, 2005

Baldwin, Faith (1893–1978)   1761
Amer. writer; mn. Cuthrell

Baldwin, Monica (1893–1975)   1762
Eng. writer, ex-nun; n. British P.M. Stanely B—

Ball, Lucille (1911–1989)   2150
Amer. television producer, comedian, actor; w. Desi Arnaz (actor); Emmy, 1952, 1955, 1967, 1968; NWHF

Ballard, Bettina (1903–1961)   1963
Amer. magazine editor

Bambara, Toni Cade (1939–1995)   3121
Amer. novelist, writer, lecturer, anthologist, civil rights activist, educator, screenwriter; founder and director of Pamoja Writers Collective 1976–85; ABA, 1981

Bamber, Helen (1925–)   2508
Eng. human rights activist; founder, the Medical Foundation for the Care of Victims of Torture; Helen Bamber Fdn., 2005

Bancroft, Anne (1932–2005)   2786
Amer. actor; née Anna Maria Louíse Italiano; w. Mel Brooks, comedian-director-producer; Antoinette Perry; NWHF Award (2); Oscar

Bandler, Faith [Ida Lessing] (1920–)   2361
Austral. civil rights activist, novelist; née Mussing; cofounder, Aboriginal Australian Fellowship; founding member, Australian Republican Movement

Bang, Mary Jo (1946–)   3630
Amer. poet, educator, English; NBCC, 2008; Guggenheim, 2004; Pushcart, 2003

Bank, Melissa (1960–)   4518
Amer. novelist

Bankhead, Tallulah (1903–1968)   1964
Amer. actor, stage & screen

Bank-Smith, Nancy (1930?–)   2691
Brit. columnist

Bannerman, Helen (1862–1946)   1282
Amer. writer

Banning, Margaret Culkin (1891–1982)   1721
Amer. writer

Bara, Theda (1885–1955)   1623
Amer. actor; née Theodosia Goodman

Barakzai, Shukria (1972–)   4854.1
Afghan lawyer, newspaper publisher; MP; established Aina-E-Zan (Women's Mirror), a weekly newspaper (Kabul)

Baransi-Siniora, Maysa (1976–)   4904
Pal./Isr. radio producer, political activist; codirector, Radio All For Peace.

Barbauld, Anna Letitia (1743–1825)   642
Eng. editor, poet, essayist; née Aiken; a. Lucy Aiken*

Barber, Janette (1953–)   4158
Amer. comedian, television producer, writer; Emmy (6)

Barber, Lynn (1944–)   3475
Eng. editor, journalist

Barber, Margaret Fairless (1869–1901)   1355
Eng. writer; pseud. Michael Fairless

Barber, Mary (1690?–1757)   536
Ir./Eng. poet; a.k.a. Sapphira

Barclay, Aviel (1969–)   4779
Can. torah scribe; first female Sofer Stam (Jewish ritual scribe)

Bard, Ann Elizabeth Campbell see MACDONALD, BETTY

Bardot, Brigitte (1934–)   2879
Fr. animal rights advocate, screen actor; founder, Brigitte Bardot Foundation (animal welfare)

Bardwick, Judith M. (1933–)   2832
Amer. writer, speaker, management consultant, psychologist

Barfoot, Joan (1946–)   3631
Can. journalist, novelist

Barker, Elsa (1869–1954)   1356
Amer. writer, poet

Barker, Jane (fl. 1680s–d. 1715)   523
Eng. poet, novelist

Barker, Patricia (1943–)   3392
Eng. poet, novelist; Booker, 1995

Barley, Mary [Lynn] (1946–) 3632
Amer. nonprofit administrator, environmental activist; w. George B—, (1934–1995) environmentalist; dir., Everglades Fdn., 1995–

Barlow, Maude [Victoria] (1947–) 3719
Can. author, civil rights activist; Chairperson, Council of Canadians; cofounder, Blue Planet Project; Right Livelihood Award, 2005

Barnard, A. M. see ALCOTT, LOUISA

Barnard, Anne, Lady (1750–1825) 659
Scot. letter writer, poet; née Lindsay

Barnard, Charlotte Alington (1830–1869) 1022
Eng. ballad writer; pseud. Claribel

Barnard, Jessie (1903–1986) 1965
Amer. educator, sociologist, feminist

Barnebey, Faith (1934–) 2880
Amer. newspaper reporter

Barnes, Djuna (1892–1982) 1739
Amer. journalist, writer, artist, playwright, illustrator; pseud. Lydia Steptoe

Barnes, Juliana see BERNERS, JULIANA

Barnes, Margaret Ayer (1886–1967) 1648
Amer. writer; Pulitzer, 1931

Barnes, Melody C. (1964–) 4668
Amer. lawyer, public servant; White House Dir. Domestic Policy, 2009–

Barney, Natalie Clifford (1876–1972) 1470
Amer./Fr. essayist, author, translator

Barnhouse, Ruth Tiffany (1923–1999) 2446
Amer. psychiatrist, Episcopal priest, educator; mn. Beuscher

Barnwell, Ysaye [Maria] (1946–) 3633
Amer. ASL interpreter, speech pathologist, community activist, singer; member, Sweet Honey in the Rock (vocal group)

Barolini, Helen (1925–) 2509
Amer. writer, editor, translator; née Mollica; w. Anthony B— (Ital poet and journalist)

Baron, Marie le see LE BARON, MARIE

Barr, Amelia [Edith Huddleston] (1831–1919) 1033
Eng./Amer. novelist

Barr, Mary A. (1852–?) 1188
Scot. poet

Barr, Nevada (1952–) 4084
Amer. writer, novelist, performer, park ranger

Barr, Roseanne (1952–) 4085
Amer. actor, comedian

Barreno, Maria Isabel (1939–) 3122
Portuguese writer, poet

Barrett, Andrea (1965–) 4692
Amer. novelist; NBA, 1996

Barrett, Michèle (1949–) 3885
Amer. nonfiction writer, sociology professor

Barrett, Rona (1936–) 2961
Amer. columnist, television personality; fdr., Rona Barrett Fdn.

Barrington, Judith [M.] (1944–) 3476
Eng./Amer. Poet

Barrow, Lisa (1964?–) 4669
Amer. economist, educator

Barrows, Sydney Biddle (1952–) 4086
Amer. brothel-keeper; a.k.a. Sheila Devin

Barry, James Stuart Miranda (1792/95?–1865) 830
Irish physician, military officer; née Margaret Ann Bulkley; n. James Barry, artist; Inspector Genl. of Hospitals, 1865?; performed first successful caesarean section in British Empire, 1926

Barry, Kathleen (1939?–) 3123
Amer. educator, activist, women's rights, author; cofounder, The Coalition Against Trafficking in Women, 1988; Fdr., Int. Feminist Network Against Female Slavery, 1983

Barry, Lynda (1956–) 4346
Amer. cartoonist, author

Barry, Rebecca (1968–) 4764
Amer. novelist; née Margaret Ann Bulkley; great-great-grandd. Henry Ward Beecher; great-great n. Harriet Beecher Stowe*; n. Roxana Robinson, author

Barrymore, Ethel (1879–1959) 1520
Amer. stage & screen actor; Academy Award, 1944

Barth, Belle (1911–1971) 2151
Amer. comedian; née Annabelle Salzman; a.k.a. the female Lenny Bruce

Bartholet, Elizabeth (1940–) 3172
Amer. educator, law, attorney

Bartoli, Cecilia (1966–) 4715
Ital./Amer. opera singer

Barton, Clara [Harlowe] (1821–1912) 980
Amer. writer, nurse; a.k.a. "The Angel of the Battlefield";

founder, American Red Cross; Hall of Fame, 1976; NWHF

Barton, Emily (1969–) 4780
Amer. writer, fiction; w. Thomas Hopkins, writer

Bar-Yosef, Rivka Weiss (1942?–) 3323
Isr. educator (sociology), women's rights activist

Bashir, Halima (1979–) 4925
Sud./Brit. physician, women and children's rights activist

Bashkirtseff, Marie [Konsantinovna] (1858/60–1884) 1230
Russ./Fr. diarist, artist

Basine (fl. 460s) 111
Thuringian/Fr. queen; w. Basin, king of Thuringia (1) and Childeric, king of France (2), m. Clovis (first Christian king of France)

Basinger, Jeanine (1936–) 2962
Amer. writer, educator (film studies), historian (film)

Bass, Ellen (1947–) 3720
Amer. poet

Bassoff, Evelyn S[ilten] (1944–) 3477
Amer. psychologist, author

Basu, Aparna (fl. 1980s–2000s–) 4930
Ind. history professor

Bat-Miriam, Yocheved (1901–1980) 1925
Isr. poet; née Zhelezniak

Bates, Katherine Lee (1859–1929) 1241
Amer. poet, educator

Bateson, Mary Catherine (1939–) 3124
Amer. scholar, author, educator, anthropologist; d. Margaret Mead* and Gregory B— (anthropologist, 1904–1980)

Bathsheba (fl. 1000s–970s B.C.E.) 33
Judaean queen; w. Ukiah (1) and David, king of Israel (2), m. Solomon

Bathurst, Elizabeth (1655?–1685/91) 491
Eng. religious figure (Quaker)

Battelle, Phyllis (1922–) 2417
Amer. syndicated columnist

Baudonivia (fl. 6th century) 117
Frankish nun, biographer; founder, Abbey of the Holy Cross

Baum, Vicki (1888–1960) 1674
Ger./Amer. novelist, screenwriter, playwright; a.k.a. Hedwig Baum

Bawden, Nina (1925–) 2510
Eng. Children's writer, novelist; a.k.a. N— Mary Mabey Kark; Booker, 1987

Bayes, Nora (1880–1928) 1540
Amer. comedian, lyricist; née Dora Goldberg; ex-w. Jack Norworth, composer, song and dance man; SHF

Bayliss, Claire (1971?–) 4840
Brit. magazine editor

Bayly, Ada Ellen see LYALL, EDNA

Baynard, Anne (1672–1697) 516
Eng. scholar

Bazan, Emilia Pardo, condesa de (1852–1921) 1189
Span. novelist, feminist, educator, stateswoman

Beale, Frances M. (1940–) 3173
Amer. journalist, civil rights activist, feminist; m. Lisa B—,* environmenatlist; fdg. mbr., Third World Women's Alliance

Beals, Jessie Tarbox (1870–1942) 1370
Amer. photographer; first woman press photographer in U.S.

Beard, Mary Ritter (1876–1958) 1471
Amer. historian; w. Charles Austin B— (1874–1948; Amer. historian and education); m. Miriam B—*

Beard, Miriam (1901–1983) 1926
Amer. feminist, historian, writer; d. Charles and Mary B—,* historians; w. Dr. Alfred Vagt, historian

Beatrijis of Nazareth (ca. 1200–1268) 204
Belgian prioress, scholar, essayist; a.s.a. Beatrice; a.k.a. Beatrijs van Tienen

Beatriz de Dia (1140?–post-1189?) 190
Provençal trobairitz; a.s.a. Beatrice, a.k.a. countess of Die; d. Marguerite de Bourgogne and Comte Guigues IV (dauphin of the Viennois and count of Albon), w. Guillem de Poitiers (count of Valentinois?), m. Aymar (count of Dia), lover of Raimbaut

Beatrix, Queen of the Netherlands, (1938–) 3072
Dutch royalty; née B— Wilhelmina Armgard; d. Juliana*; s. Princess Irene; m. Princes Willem-Alexander, Johan-Friso, Constantijn

Beauveau, Marie de (1711–1786) 571
Fr. poet; a.k.a. Françoise Catherine, marquise de Boufflers

Beauvoir, Simone de [Lucie Ernestine Marie Bertrand] (1908–1986) 2080
Fr. feminist, philosopher, writer; lover of Jean Paul Sartre

(1905–1980; philosopher, playwright); Prix Goncourt, 1954

Bechdel, Alison (1960–) 4519
Amer. cartoonist

Beck, Evelyn Torton (1933–) 2833
Amer. writer, educator

Becker, Robin (1951–) 4023
Amer. poetry editor, poet, English and women's studies educator; NEA

Bedford, countess of see HARINGTON, LUCY

Bedford, Sybille von Schoenbeck (1911–) 2152
Ger./Eng. writer, essayist, biographer, novelist; C.B.E., 1981

Bedingfield, Natasha (1981–) 4945
Eng. singer, songwriter, philanthropist; s. Daniel B— (1979–) singer-songwriter, and Nikola Rachelle (1983–) singer-songwriter

Bee, Rashida (1956–) 4347
Ind. environmental activist, labor activist; Goldman, 2004

Beecher, Catharine Esther (1800–1878) 865
Amer. writer, educator; s. Harriet B— Stowe,* Henry Ward B— (1813–1887), famed cleric newspaper editor, abolitionist

Beers, Ethel Lynn (1827–1879) 1011
Amer. poet; née Eliot, pseud. Ethelinda Eliott

Beeton, Isabella [Mary] Mayson (1837–1865) 1074
Eng. writer (domestic arts)

Begbie, Janet (fl. 1910s–d. 1970?) 2120
Eng. poet

Begley, Sharon (1956–) 4348
Amer. science journalist, magazine editor

Behn, Aphra (1640–1689) 472
Eng. translator, novelist, spy, poet, playwright; née Amis; a.s.a. Afra, Aphara, Ayfara, a.k.a. Astrea; first woman in history to have earned a living as a writer

Belcher, Jennifer M. (1945?–) 3556
Amer. public servant; State Legislator, WA (1982–92)

Belenky, Mary Field (1933–) 2834
Amer. author, educator, researcher

Bell, Acton see BRONTË, ANNE

Bell, Christine (1951–) 4024
Amer. writer

Bell, Currer see BRONTË, CHARLOTTE

Bell, Ellis see BRONTË, EMILY

Bell, Florence [Evelene Eleanore] (1851–1930) 1182
Eng. writer, social reformer; née Olliffe; stepm. Gertrude B—*

Bell, Gertrude (1868–1926) 1347
Eng. writer, archaeologist, public servant, political analyst; granddd. Sir Isaac Lowthian B— (1816–1904–), chemist, industrialist; stepd. Florence B—*; 1st woman officer in the history of British military intelligence (Major, 1917)

Bell, Helen Olcott (1830–1918) 1023
Amer. writer; d. Rufus Choate (1799–1859; politician)

Bellamy, Carol (1942–) 3324
Amer. lawyer, public servant, investment banker; dir., Peace Corps (1993–95); exec. Dir., UNICEF (1995–2004)

Bello, Mairo (1964?–) 4670
Nig. administrator, activist (reproductive health); fdg. dir., Adolescent Health and Information Project (AHIP; Kano, Nigeria)

Bellows, Laurel Gordon (1948–) 3809
Amer. attorney

Belmont, Eleanor Robson (1878–1979) 1505
Amer. actor, socialite; fdr., Metropolitan Opera Guild (NYC)

Bender, Marilyn (1925–) 2511
Amer. journalist; w. Altschul

Bender, Sheila (1948–) 3810
Amer. writer, poet, workshop facilitator

Benedict, Agnes E[lizabeth] (1889–1950) 1694
Amer. educator

Benedict, Ruth [Fulton] (1887–1948) 1659
Amer. anthropologist, biographer, poet; pseud. Anne Singleton; née Fulton; NWHF

Benes, Francine M. (1945?–) 3557
Amer. psychiatrist, physician; dir., Harvard Brain Tissue Resource Center

Benét, Laura (1884–1979) 1605
Amer. biographer, writer, poet

Benet, Mother (fl. 1550s–) 347
Eng. commoner

Benet, Sula (1903–1982) 1966
Pol. anthropologist, etymologist; née Sara Benetowa

Bengis, Ingrid (1944–) 3478
Amer. writer

Benítez, Sandra Ables (1941–) 3242
Amer. novelist; d. James Q. B— (diplomat and writer), and Marta A. B— (executive secretary and translator)

Benjamin, Medea (1952–) 4087
Amer. author, political activist; née Susan B—; cofounder, Global Exchange; cofounder, Code Pink: Women for Peace

Benmussa, Simone (1931–2001) 2751
Tunisian/Fr. playwright, radio producer, literary manager, journalist

Bennett, Georgette (1946–) 3634
Hung./Amer. TV correspondent, criminologist, sociologist, nonfiction writer

Bennis, Phyllis (1951–) 4025
Amer. private investigator, nonfiction writer, journalist, radio, organizer-agitator; n. Warren B— (1925–), scholar, author, pioneer of field of Leadership Studies

Benson, Stella (1892–1933) 1740
Eng. poet, writer

Bensouda, Fatou (1961–) 4564
Gambia/Dutch lawyer; Deputy Prosecutor, Head of Prosecutions, for the International Criminal Court

Benston, Margaret Lowe (1937–) 3020
Amer. educator, physical chemist

Benton, Suzanne (1953?–) 4159
Amer. feminist, sculptor

Berberova, Nina (1901–1993) 1927
Russ. poet, writer, literary critic

Berenson, Mary (1864–1945) 1302
Amer. art historian, writer; w. Bernard B— (1865–1959; Lithuanian-born American art critic and historian)

Berg, Elizabeth (1948–) 3811
Amer. novelist

Berg, Gertrude (1899–1966) 1882
Amer. radio writer, playwright, actor; Emmy, 1950; Tony, 1959

Bergen, Candice (1946–) 3635
Amer. screen actor, photographer; writer, playwright; d. Edgar Bergen (d. 1978; ventriloquist), w. Louis Malle (1932–1995; Fr. film director)

Bergman, Ingrid (1915–1982) 2236
Swed. screen actor; w. Roberto Rosselini (1906–1977; Ital. film director); Academy Award, 1944, 1956, 1974; Tony, 1947; Emmy, 1960

Berkley, Rochelle "Shelley" (1951–) 4026
Amer. political activist, lawyer; née Levine; U.S. Rep (D-Nev), 1999–

Berman, Ellen (1946–) 3636
Amer. artist, painter; NEA

Bern, Sandra Lipsitz (1944–) 3479
Amer. feminist scholar

Bernadette, St. (1844–1923) 1121
Fr. Roman Catholic saint; née Marie-Bernard Soubirous

Bernal, Esmeralda (1949–) 3886
Amer. nurse, poet

Bernard, Jessie Shirley (1903–1996) 1967
Amer. sociologist, author; w. L. L. B— (1881–?; her collaborator)

Berne, Suzanne (1961–) 4565
Amer. novelist; Great Britain's Orange Prize; NEA

Berneri, Marie Louise (1918–1949) 2308
Ital. anarchist

Berners, Juliana, Dame (1460?–?) 266
Eng. prioress, poet; a.s.a. Bernes, a.k.a. Julians Barnes; first known female English poet and author

Bernhard, Sandra (1955–) 4289
Amer. comedian

Bernhardt, Sarah (1844–1923) 1122
Fr. writer, actor; a.k.a. "The Divine Sarah"

Bernikow, Louise (1940–) 3174
Amer. poet, journalist

Berresford, Susan V[ail] (1943?–) 3393
Amer. business executive; pres., Ford Fdn.

Berriault, Gina (1926–) 2542
Amer. writer; NBCCA, 1996; Pen/Faulkner Award 1997

Berry, Dawn Bradley (1957–) 4399
Amer. attorney

Berry, Dorothy (fl. 1630s) 456
Eng. poet

Berry, Mary Frances (1938–) 3073
Amer. attorney, educator

Berssenbrugge, Mei-mei (1947–) 3721
Chin./Amer. poet, educator; NEA Fellowship (2), American Book Award (2)

Bertana, Lucia dall'Orno (1521–1567) 318
Ital. poet, writer; w. Gerone B—

Bertegund (fl. 530s) 115
Merovingian nun?

Bertell, Rosalie (1929–) 2651
Can. health activist, nun, statistician, author; Right Livelihood Award (Stockholm; 1986)

Berthold, Ernst see ROBINSON, THERESE

Bertinora, countess de see ALDRUDE

Bertken, Sister (1427?–1514?) 257
Dutch nun, poet, mystic; a.k.a. Bertha Jacobs

Beruriah (fl. 1210s–d. 1280) 216
Isr. author, biblical scholar; w. Rebbe Meir

Besant, Annie Wood (1847–1933) 1148
Eng./Ind. religious leader, political activist, philosopher; pseud. Ajax; active exponent of Theosophy; founder, Central Hindu College, 1898, and Indian Home Rule League, 1916; president, Indian National Congress, 1917

Bethune, Mary McLeod (1875–1955) 1453
Amer. writer, educator, organizer, lecturer; founder, Bethune-Cookman College, 1904; cofounder, National Association of Colored Women's Clubs; Spingarn Medal, 1935; NWHF

Betsch, MaVynée (1935–2005) 2921
Amer. opera singer, environmental activist, philanthropist; née Marvyne B—; a.k.a. the Beach Lady; great-grandd. A. L. Lewis, entropeneur, philanthropist; fdr. American Beach, 1935; s. Johnetta Cole*

Betsko, Kathleen (1939–) 3125
Eng. theater historian, editor, playwright

Bettencourt, Liliane Schueller (1922–) 2418
Fr. foundation executive, business executive; d. Mr. Eugène Schueller, founder of L'Oréal; 2nd richest person in France; 12th wealthiest in the world; fdr., Bettencourt Schueller Foundation, which awards the "Liliane Bettencourt Prize for Life Sciences"

Bhatt, Ela (1933–) 2835
Ind. social worker, lawyer; established Self-Employed Women's Association (SEWA), 1972; Right Livelihood, 1984

Bhutto, Benazir (1953–2007) 4160
Pak. political leader; d. Zulfikar Ali B— (1928–1979; politician, first elected president and prime minister of Pakistan; executed), and Nusrat (MP and deputy prime minister); m. Nusrat Ispahani B— (co-leader of People's Party); prime minister of Pakistan, 1988–90 and 1993–96; first woman in modern history to lead a predominantly Muslim nation

Bialosky, Jill (1962?–) 4603
Amer. editor, writer, poet

Bianchi, Martha [Gilbert] Dickinson (1866–1943) 1323
Amer. writer, poet, editor; n. and literary heir of Emily Dickinson*

Bibesco, Elizabeth Asquith, Princess (1897–1945) 1842
Eng./Rom. poet, writer

Biddle, Flora Miller (1947?–) 3722
Amer. museum director; grandd. Gertrude Vanderbilt Whitney, sculptor and founder of the Whitney Museum of American Art, 1930; pres., Whitney Museum of American Art (1977–1995)

Biden, Jill [Tracy Jacobs] (1951–) 4027
Amer. English teacher, pubic figure; w. Joe Biden, 44th V.P. of U.S.A.

Bieber, Margarete (1879–1978) 1521
Prussian/Amer. archaeologist, educator

Bieiris de Romans (1200–1235) 205
Fr. trobairitz

Billings, Victoria (1945–) 3558
Amer. journalist, writer

Billington-Greig, Teresa (1877–1964) 1488
Eng. suffragist, nonfiction writer

Billson, Christine (fl. 1960s) 4520
Eng. writer

Bilmes, Linda J. (1960–) 4521
Amer. economist, professor of economics, public administrator

Bingen, Hildegarde von see HILDEGARDE VON BINGEN

Bingham, Anne Willing (1764–1801) 719
Amer. social figure; w. William B— (U.S. Congressman)

Bingham, Charlotte (1942–) 3325
Eng. scenarist, novelist; d. Madeleine* and John B—, a.k.a. Lord and Lady Clanmorris; w. Terence Brady, writer

Bingham, Madeline (1912–1988) 2172
Eng. playwright, writer; pseud. Julia Mannering; w. Baron Clanmorris, m. Charlotte B—*

Bingham, Sallie (1937–) 3021
Amer. writer; w. Ellsworth

Bingham, Sally (1941–) 3243
Amer. priest, environmental activist; fdr., Regeneration Project, 1993

Binh, Nguyen Thi (1930–) 2692
Viet. politician; foreign minister of the South Vietnamese National Liberation Front

Birch, Alison Wyrley [Greenbie] (1922–) 2419
Amer. writer, journalist

Bird, Carmel (1940–) 3175
Austral. writer

Bird, Caroline (1915–) 2237
Amer. lecturer, social critic, writer; d. Hobart B—, lawyer, journalist, civil rights activist

Bird, Rose [Elizabeth] (1936–1999) 2963
Amer. lawyer, jurist

Birkeland, Janis Lynn (1945–) 3559
Amer. environmental activist

Bishop, Elizabeth (1911–1979) 2153
Amer. poet, writer; Guggenheim, 1947; AAP 1955; Pulitzer, 1956; Rockefeller, 1967; NBA, 1970; NBCCA, 1977

Bishop, Wendy Sue (1953–2003) 4161
Amer. essayist, educator, poet

Bisset, Jacqueline (1946–) 3637
Eng. actor

Black, Barbara Aronstein (1933–) 2836
Amer. educator, legal history, college dean, legal historian; w. Charles L. B—, Jr., law professor, author; Dean, Columbia Law School (1st woman to head an Ivy League law school), 1986; fellowship & lecture series named in her honor at Columbia

Black, Shirley Temple (1928–) 2619
Amer. screen actor, diplomat; first woman appointed Chief of Protocol in U.S. State Dept.; Special Academy Award, 1934

Black, Sophie Cabot (1958–) 4440
Amer. poet, essayist

Blackburn, Julia (1948–) 3812
Brit. biographer; d. Thomas B— (1916–1977), poet, & Rosalie de Meric (1917–1999), artist

Blackmore, Susan Jane (1951–) 4028
Eng. nonfiction writer, educator (psychology)

Blackwell, Antoinette Brown (1825–1921) 998
Amer. minister, writer, feminist; s.-in-law Elizabeth* and Emily* B—; NWHF

Blackwell, Elizabeth (1821–1910) 981
Amer./Eng. physician, feminist, writer; s. Emily B—,* s.-in-law Antoinette Brown B—* and Lucy Stone*; first woman physician in U.S.; cofounder, New York Infirmary for Women (first women's health center), 1857; NWHF

Blackwell, Emily (1826–1911) 1005
Amer. feminist, physician, writer; s. Elizabeth B—*, s.-in-law Antoinette Brown B—*, and Lucy Stone*; cofounder, New York Infirmary for Women (first women's health center), 1857; NWHF

Blackwell, Helen see DUFFERIN, HELEN

Blais, Madeleine (1947/9–) 3723
Amer. educator (journalism), journalist; Pulitzer, 1980, 1992

Blake, Lillie Devereux (1833–1913) 1049
Amer. suffragist, political activist, writer

Blakely, Mary Kay (1948–) 3813
Amer. journalist; cofounder of Cathryn Adamsky Women in Née d Fund

Blakely, Nora Brooks (1951–) 4029
Amer. theatrician, poet, writer; d. Gwendolyn Brooks* and Henry B—, (writer); founder and director, Chocolate Chips Theatre Company, Chicago

Blamire, Susanna (1747–1794) 653
Eng./Scot. poet

Bland, Mrs. Hubert see NESBIT, EDITH

Blavatsky, Elena Petrovna (1831–1891) 1034
Russ. religious leader, writer; née Hahn; founder, Theosophical Society in U.S. and India

Blee, Kathleen M. (1953–) 4162
Amer. activist, sociologist, educator

Bleecker, Ann Eliza (1752–1783) 670
Amer. author; née Schuyler, a.s.a. Bleeker; m. Margaretta Van Wyck Faugères*

Blessington, Marguerite, Lady (1789–1849) 808
Ir. novelist, salonist, poet; d. Edmund Power, w. Capt. Maurice St. Leger Farmer (1) and Charles John Gardener, 1st earl of Blessington (2)

Blind, Mathilde (1841–1896) 1100
Ger./Eng. poet, biographer; née Cohen

Blixen, Karen, Baroness see DINESEN, ISAK

Blodgett, Katharine "Katie" Burr (1898–1979) 1860
Amer. scientist, chemist; invented color gauge to measure thickness of monomolecular layers (1933), nonreflective

glass (1938), and smokescreen (for U.S. military, 1941); first woman scientist to work for General Electric (1918); first woman to receive Ph.D. in physics from Cambridge (1926)

Bloom, Amy [Amelia] (1953–) 4163
Amer. writer (short story), psychotherapist; d. Murray (journalist, writer), and Sydelle B— (writer)

Bloomer, Amelia Jenks (1818–1894) 944
Amer. reformer, writer, temperance leader; founded and published *The Lily*, 1849–55 (first newspaper published by and for women in U.S.); first woman Deputy Postmaster; introduced "bloomers"; NWHF

Blume, Judy (1938–) 3074
Amer. fiction writer; née Sussman

Blunt, Anne (1837–1917) 1075
Eng./Arab. horse breeder, water colorist; d. Ada Byron Lovelace* and William King, first earl of Lovelace; grand. Lord Byron, poet; w. Wilfrid Scawen B—, poet

Boadicea (fl. 40s–65 C.E.) 86
Eng. queen; w. Prasutagas (king of Iceni, i.e., Norfolk, Suffolk, Cambridge and Huntingdonshire)

Boesing, Martha Gross (1936–) 2964
Amer. stage director, actor, playwright; founder the Fourth Street Players, the Moppet Players (later, the Minneapolis Children's Theatre), At the Foot of the Mountain; NEA, 1979; Ford, 1983

Bogan, Louise (1897–1970) 1843
Amer. literary critic, writer, poet; w. Raymond Holden (poet)

Boggs, [Corinne] Lindy [C.] (1916–) 2262
American politician, women's rights activist; née Corinne Morrison Claiborne; w. Hale B—; U.S. Representative (1915–1972); U.S. Representative (1973–1990)

Bok, Sissela Ann (1934–) 2881
Swed./Amer. writer, philosopher, author; d. [Karl] Gunnar Myrdal (1898–1987; Swedish economist who won Nobel Prize in economics, 1974), and Alva Reimer Myrdal*

Boland, Eavan (1944–) 3480
Ir. poet; d. Frederick (diplomat) and Frances (painter), w.

Kevin Casey (novelist); Irish Arts Council Macauley Fellowship, 1967; Poetry Book Society Choice 1987

Bolen, Jean Shinoda (1936–) 2965
Amer. author, Jungian psychoanalyst

Boleyn, Anne (1507–1536) 300
Eng. queen; a.s.a. Bullen, Bulleyne; second w. Henry VIII, m. Elizabeth I*

Bolgar, Hedda (1909–) 2106
Aus./Amer. psychoanalyst, psychologist; fdr., Los Angeles Institute and Society for Psychoanalytic Studies, 1970; Wright Inst., Los Angeles, 1974

Bolt, Carol (1941–) 3244
Can. playwright, dramaturg; née Johnson; grants from Canada Council 1967, 1972; grants from Ontario Arts Council 1972, 1973, 1974, 1975; Silver Jubilee Award 1978

Bolton, Sarah Knowles (1841–1916) 1101
Amer. social reformer, poet, editor

Bombeck, Erma (1927–1996) 2586
Amer. author, humorist, columnist; née E— Louise Fiste

Bonal, Denise (1921–) 2396
Algerian/Fr. playwright, actor; pseud. Luis Aftel

Bonaparte, Marie L., Princess (1881–1962) 1564
Fr. sexologist, educator, writer, psychoanalyst; founder of Paris Psychoanalytical Society, 1926

Bonaparte, Marie Letitia (1748–1836) 655
Corsican noble; née Ramolino, a.s.a. Buonaparte, a.k.a. Madame Mère; w. Carlo Bonaparte, m. Napoleon I (1769–1921; Emperor of the French)

Bond, Carrie Jacobs (1862–1946) 1283
Amer. composer, songwriter

Bond, Cynthia (1957?–) 4400
Amer. writer; fdr., Words Changing Worlds

Bond, Victoria (1949–) 3887
Amer. orchestra conductor

Bonds, Julia (1952–) 4088
Amer. environmental activist; dir. Coal River Mountain Watch; Goldman, 2003

Bonham-Carter, Violet, [Baroness] (1887–1969) 1660
Brit. politician; a.k.a. Asquith; d. Herbert Henry Asquith (1852–1928; 1st earl of Oxford and Asquith; prime minister of Great Britain,

1908–16); grandm. Jane B—, politician, and Helena B—, actor

Bonner, Ylena Georgievna (1923–) 2447
Russ. Soviet dissident, physician; w. Andrei Sakharov (dissident, scientist, 1921–1989; Nobel Peace Prize, 1975)

Bonney, Barbara (1956–) 4349
Amer. opera singer

Bonny, Anne (1700–1782) 548
Ir./Amer. pirate

Bono, Mary (1961–) 4566
Amer. politician; née Whitaker; w. Sonny B— (1935–1998), Amer. Actor, singer, politician; w. Congressman Connie Mack IV (3); U.S. Representative (R-CA), 1998–

Boosler, Elayne (1952–) 4089
Amer. comedian

Booth, Cherie (1954–) 4231
Eng. barrister, public figure; mn. Blair; w. Tony Blair (1953–), British prime minister, 1997–2007

Booth, Evangeline [Cory] (1865–1950) 1308
Eng./Amer. reformer, composer, lecturer, musician; first woman general in Salvation Army

Boothby, Frances (fl. 1660s) 493
Eng. playwright; first English woman to have an original play produced on the public stage

Boothroyd, Betty (1929–) 2652
Eng. politician, dancer; MP, 1973– ; 155th Speaker of House of Commons, 1994–

Borg, Anita (1949–2003) 3888
Amer. computer scientist; née Naffz; fdr., Institute for Women and Technology, 1997; fdr. SystersList; cofounder, the Grace Hopper* Celebration of Women in Computing

Borgia, Lucrezia (1480–1519) 281
Ital. noble; d. Pope Alexander VI, s. Cesare Borgia (1478–1507; adventurer), w. Giovanni Sforza (1, annulled), Alfonso, duke of Bisceglie (2, assassinated) and Alfonso d'Este (3, son of Ercole, duke of Ferrara), s.-in-law Isabella d'Este*

Borysenko, Joan (1946?–) 3638
Amer. educator, psychotherapist, yoga instructor, biologist

Botta, Anne [Charlotte] (1815–1891) 926
Amer. hostess, poet, educator, writer; née Lynch

Bottome, Phyllis (1884–1963) 1606
Eng./Amer. novelist; a.k.a. P— Forbes-Dennis

Botume, Elizabeth [Hyde] (fl. 1870s) 1371
Amer. educator, writer

Boucher, Sandy (1936–) 2966
Amer. writer

Boudrot, Denise M. (1952–) 4090
Amer. jockey

Boufflers, marquise de see BEAUVEAU, MARIE DE

Boulbie, Judith (?–1706) 556
Eng. prophet, religious figure (Quaker), writer; a.s.a. Boulby

Boulding, Elise M. (1920–) 2362
Nor./Amer. sociologist, author, peace activist, scholar; née Biorn-Hansen; w. Kenneth B— (1910–1993), Eng. Economist, poet

Boumi Pappa, Rita (1906–1984) 2040
Greek translator, poet; a.s.a. Pappas

Bourbon, Catherine de (1559–1604) 362
Fr. noble; d. Jeanne d'Albret,* s. Henry IV (1553–1610; king of France, 1589–1610), w. Henri de Lorraine, duc de Bar

Bourke-White, Margaret (1906–1971) 2041
Amer. writer, war correspondent, photographer; NWHF

Bouza, Erica (1941?–) 3245
Brit./Amer. political activist, secretary; w. Tony B—, Sp./Amer. public administrator

Bovasso, Julie Anne (1930–1991) 2693
Amer. educator, playwright, theatrician; organizer, Women's Theater Council; Obie, 1956 (2), 1969 (3); Rockefeller; Guggenheim

Bovey, Shelley (1947–) 3724–3725
Welsh/Eng. writer, broadcaster

Bowditch, Katherine (1894–1933) 1791
Amer. poet

Bowen, Asta (1955–) 4290
Amer. writer, columnist, educator

Bowen, Catherine Drinker (1897–1973) 1844
Amer. writer, historian; NBA, 1958

Bowen, Elizabeth (1899–1973) 1883
Ir./Eng. writer; mn. Camerson

Bowen, Louise de Koven (1859–1947) 1242
Amer. civic leader, social worker

Bowen, Marjorie (1888–1952) 1675–1676
Eng. writer, playwright, historian; née Gabrielle Margaret

Vere Campbell; pseud. George
Runnell Preedy, Joseph Shear-
ing; mn. Long
Bower, B. M.
(1871–1940)   1385
Amer. novelist; née Muzzy;
a.k.a. Bertha M-Sinclair, Sin-
clar-Cowan
Bowes, Elizabeth (fl. 1550s)   348
Scot. commoner; m. Marjorie
B—, m.-in-law John Knox
(1514?–72; founder of Scot-
tish Presbyterianism)
Bowles, Gloria (1956?–)   4350
Amer. magazine editor,
nonfiction writer, educator
(women's studies); coord.,
Women's Studies, UC
Berkeley
Bowman, Meg (1929–)   2653
Amer. feminist, educator,
author
Boxer, Barbara (1940–)   3176
Amer. stateswoman; née Levy;
Senator (D), CA (1992–); Rep
(D), CA (1983–1992)
Boxer, Sarah (1969?–)   4781
Amer. journalist, photography
critic, author
Boyd, Nancy see MILLAY, EDNA
Boylan, Helen see MARTIN, MAR-
THA
Boyle, Kay (1902–1992)   1947
Amer. writer, educator, politi-
cal activist; p. Ernest Walsh
(d. 1926), literary editor;
Guggenheim (2); Lifetime
Achievement, NEA
Boyle, Sarah [Roberts]
(1812–1869)   917
Amer. poet
Boyle, Susan (1961–)   4566.1
Scot. singer, homemaker
Bracken, Peg (1918–)   2309
Amer. humorist, writer
Brackett, Anna C[allender]
(1836–1911)   1070
Amer. teacher, writer, admin-
istrator
Brackley, Elizabeth [Cavendish]
(1623?–1663)   445
Eng. playwright; d. Wil-
liam Cavendish, duke of
Newcastle, stepd. Margaret
Cavendish,* s. Jane Caven-
dish*
Braddon, Mary Elizabeth
(1837–1915)   1076
Eng. writer; pseud. M— E—
Maxwell
Bradford, Cornelia
(1695?–1755)   542
Amer. journalist, publisher,
printer; née Smith; d.-in-law
William B— (1663–1752;
pioneer printer), w. Andrew
B—

Bradford, Elizabeth
(1663–1731)   500
Eng./Amer. poet
Bradford, Mistress (fl. 1580s) 385
Eng. commoner; m. John
B— (executed ca. 1581/82)
Bradley, Katharine
(1846–1914)   1141
Eng. poet; pseud. Michael
Field
Bradley, Marion Zimmer
(1930–1999)   2694
Amer. novelist, teacher
Bradley, Mary [Emily]
(1835–1898)   1061
Amer. poet
Bradstreet, Anne
(1612?–1672)   430
Eng./Amer. poet, essayist; née
Dudley, a.k.a. The Tenth Muse;
d. Thomas Dudley (governor
of Massachusetts, 1634–1650),
w. Simon B— (1603–1697;
governor of Massachusetts);
author of first volume of poetry
published in the U.S.
Bradwell, Myra R.
(1831–1894)   1035
Amer. suffragist, attorney,
editor, nurse; née Colby; first
woman to be admitted to Il-
linois Bar; NWHF
Brady, Rose (1956–)   4351
Amer. historian
Braid, Bernice (1933–)   2837
Amer. educator; w. Paul
Witkovsky (1937–), research
scientist; s.-in-law, Sue Wit-
kovsky*
Brainard, Mary Gardiner
(fl. 1860s)   1252
Amer. Poet
Bramble, Tabitha see ROBINSON,
MARY
Branch, Anna Hempstead
(1875–1937)   1374
Amer. social worker, poet
Branch, Mary [Lydia Bolles]
(1840–1922)   1091
Amer. writer, poet
Brand, Dionne (1953–)   4164
Trinidadian/Can. poet, essayist,
novelist, filmmaker; Canada
Council Arts Grant, 1980; On-
tario Arts Council Grant, 1982
Brandenburg, Elizabeth of see
ELISABETH OF BRANDENBURG
Brant, Beth (1941–)   3246
Can./Amer. writer, poet, edi-
tor, anthologist
Bratton, Martha
(fl. 1770s–d. 1816)   746
Amer. patriot; w. Colonel B—
Braude, Ann Deborah
(1955–)   4291
Amer. administrator, uni-
versity, nonfiction writer; d.
Marvin (politician)

Braun, Carol Moseley (see MOSE-
LEY, CAROL BRAUN)
Braunschweig, duchess of see
ANNA MARIA OF BRAUNSCHWEIG
and ELISABETH OF BRAUNSCHWEIG
Braverman, Kate (1950–)   3954
Amer. poet, novelist, perfor-
mance artist
Bray, Ann Eliza (1790–1883)   815
Eng. novelist; née Kemp; mn.
Stothard
Breckinridge, Mary
(1881–1965)   1565
Amer. nurse; founder of Fron-
tier Nursing Service, 1925;
NWHF
Breckinridge, Sophonisba Preston
(1866–1948)   1324
Amer. lawyer, social worker;
d. Wm. B— , KY Congress-
man; first woman admitted to
the Kentucky bar
Bregy, Charlotte (1619?–1693) 435
Aus. letter writer, poet; née
Saumaise de Chazan
Breillat, Catherine (1948–)   3814
Fr. filmmaker, novelist, screen-
writer
Breitman, Barbara E. (1950–) 3955
Amer. poet, psychotherapist
Bremer, Frederika (1801–1865) 868
Swed. writer
Brennan, Maeve
(1916–1993)   2263
Ir. writer
Brenner, Antonia (1926–)   2543
Amer. nun, prison reform ac-
tivist; née Mary Clark, a.k.a.
La Sister, "angel de la carcel"
(the prison angel)
Brent of Bin Bin see FRANKLIN,
MILES
Brent, Linda see JACOBS, HARRIET
Brereton, Jane (1685–1740)   529
Eng. poet; née Hughes, a.k.a.
Melissa
Breslin, Rosemary (1957–)   4401
Amer. screenwriter, journalist;
d. Jimmy B— (journalist)
Brett, Dorothy (1883–1977)   1591
Eng./Amer. biographer,
writer, painter; d. Viscount
Esther
Breuer, Bessie (1893–1975)   1763
Amer. writer
Brewster, Martha
(fl. 1740s–1757)   629
Amer. poet; née Wadsworth
Breze, countess de see POITIERS,
DIANE DE
Brice, Fanny (1891–1951)   1722
Amer. singer, comedian; SHF
Brickell, Edie (1966–)   4716
Amer. songwriter, singer
Bricker-Jenkins, Mary
(1942–)   3326
Amer. author, farmer, feminist,
social worker

Bridges, Madeline
(1844–1920)   1123
Amer. poet; a.k.a. Mary Ainge
de Vere
Bridget of Sweden, Saint
(1303–1373)   234
Swed. mystic, author, nun;
a.s.a. Brigit, Birgitta, Brigitta,
a.k.a. Sibyl of the North;
d. Sir Birger, w. Prince Ulf
Gudmarsson of Nericia, m.
St. Katherine of Sweden;
founded religious order of
the Bridgettines; her vision
of the nativity supplanted the
accepted Pseudo–Bonaven-
tura version and influenced
Western art, music, and
literature
Bridgford, Kim Suzanne
(1959–)   4477
Amer. writer; educator, writing
Briggs, Dorothy Corkille
(1924–)   2477
Amer. child rearing educator,
child counselor
Bright, Chris (fl. 1990s)   3623
Amer. environmental re-
searcher, nonfiction writer
Bright, Susannah "Susie"
(1958–)   4441
Amer. blogger, lecturer, radio
& TV host, feminist; a.k.a.
Susie Sexpert, Sue Daniels;
cofounder, Teamsters for
a Democratic Union; co-
founder -ed., On Our Backs
magazine
Brightman, Carol (1939–)   3126
Amer. biographer, writer, ac-
tivist, antiwar
Brigid of Kildare, Saint
(453–523)   110
Ir. nun, poet; a.s.a. Bridget,
Brigit, Brighid, Bride, a.k.a.
the Mary of the Gaels;
founder and abbess of
Convent of Cill-Dara (now
Kildare), first Irish nunnery
Brill, Alida (1949–)   3888.1
Amer. author, social critic,
advocate for women and girls;
a.k.a. Brill-Scheuer
Brine, Mary Dow
(1816–1913)   933
Amer. poet, writer
Brinker, Ruth (1922–)   2420
Amer. social activist; fdr., Proj-
ect Open Hand, 1985
Brittain, Vera (1893–1970)
1764–1765
Eng. writer, poet
Brock-Broido, Lucie (1956–) 4352
Amer. Poet
Brockovich, Erin (1960–)   4522
Amer. environmental activist,
legal clerk; née Pattee

Brodie, Fawn M[cKay]
(1915–1981)   2238
   Amer. biographer; w. Bernard
   B— (editor and collaborator)
Brodine, Karen [Harriet]
(1947–)   3726
   Amer. poet
Brodribb, Somer (1954–)   4232
   Can. radical feminist
Bronaugh, Anne (1876–1961) 1472
   Amer. actor, poet; famed for
   role of Rosemary in Abie's
   Irish Rose
Broner, E. M. (1930–)   2695
   Amer. writer, playwright; née
   Esther Masserman
Brontë, Anne (1820–1849)   965
   Eng. poet, novelist; pseud.
   Acton Bell, Alexander Hy-
   bernia; s. Charlotte B—* and
   Emily B—*
Brontë, Charlotte
(1816–1855)   934
   Eng. novelist, poet; pseud.
   Currer Bell; s. Anne B—* and
   Charlotte B—*
Brontë, Emily (Jane)
(1818–1848)   945
   Brit. novelist, poet; pseud.
   Ellis Bell; s. Anne B—* and
   Charlotte B—*
Brooke, Frances
(1724–1789)   593
   Eng. editor, librettist, transla-
   tor, playwright, historian,
   writer; née Moore, a.k.a.
   Mary Singleton; w. Rev. John
   B—
Brookner, Anita (1928–)   2620
   Brit./Eng. novelist, art histo-
   rian, educator; Booker, 1984;
   Royal Society of Literature
   Fellow 1983; C.B.E., 1990
Brooks, [Mary] Louise
(1906–1985)   2042
   Amer. actor, dancer, model
Brooks, Gwendolyn
(1917–2000)   2281
   Amer. novelist, poet; w.
   Henry Blakely, m. Nora
   B— Blakely*; Poet Laureate of
   Illinois, 1968; Pulitzer, 1950;
   NWHF
Brooks, Maria (1795–1845) 845
   Amer. poet; née Gowen, a.k.a.
   Maria del Occidente
Brothers, Joyce [Diane]
(1927–)   2587
   Amer. journalist, psychologist;
   mn. Bauer
Brotherton, Alice Williams
(1848–1930)   1159
   Amer. poet, writer, lecturer
Brown, Abbie Farwell
(1875–1927)   1455
   Amer. lyricist, writer, poet
Brown, Alice (1857–1948)   1218
   Amer. poet, writer

Brown, Anna Gordon
(1747–1810)   654
   Scot. balladeer
Brown, Barbara B.
(1928–1999)   2621
   Amer. lecturer, pharmacologist, science researcher,
   author; pioneer in field of
   biofeedback
Brown, Charlotte [Hawkins]
(1882–1961)   1577
   Amer. civil rights activist, edu-
   cator, lecturer
Brown, Clara (1803–1885)   875
   Amer. slave, pioneer; coestab-
   lished St. James Methodist
   Church, first in Denver, Colo-
   rado (1860)
Brown, Eileen Kampakuta
(1930?–)   2696
   Aust. environmental activist;
   cofounder, Kupa Piti Kungka
   Tjuta, 1995; Goldman, 2003
Brown, Frances
(1816–1879)   935
   Amer. poet
Brown, Helen Gurley
(1922–)   2421
   Amer. writer, magazine editor
Brown, Kathleen (1946–)   3639
   Amer. politician; d. Pat B—, s.
   Jerry B— (both former gover-
   nors of California)
Brown, Lisa (1960–)   4523
   Amer. lawyer, Constitutional,
   civil rights activist; w. Kevin
   Cullen, oncologist, hospital
   administrator; White House.
   staff sec.
Brown, Mary Elizabeth
(1842–1917)   1108
   Amer. Hymnist
Brown, Maxine (1939–)   3127
   Amer. singer
Brown, Olympia (1835–1926) 1062
   Amer. suffragist, minister
   (Universalist); m. Gwendolyn
   Willis*; first woman ordained
   in U.S., 1863 (Universalist)
Brown, Ophelia Guyon
(fl. 1880s)   1541
   Amer. writer, poet; mn. Adams
Brown, Rachel Fuller
(1898–1980)   1861
   Amer. bacteriologist, chem-
   ist; with Elizabeth Hazen,*
   invented Lystatin, the first
   fungicide safe for human use;
   Chemical Pioneer Award of
   American Institute of Chem-
   ists (first woman honoree,
   1975); National Inventors
   Hall of Fame (1994)
Brown, Rita Mae (1944–)   3481
   Amer. feminist, educator,
   writer, poet
Brown, Rosellen (1939–)   3128
   Amer. poet, writer

Brown, Rosemary
(1920–2003)   2697
   Jamaican/Can. politician
Brown, Tabitha Moffatt
(1780–1858)   779
   Amer. public school educa-
   tor, pioneer, letter writer;
   founder, Orphan Asylum in
   Forest Grove, Oregon (later
   Tualatin Academy, then
   Pacific University); named
   "Mother Of Oregon" in
   1987
Brown, Tina (1953–)   4165
   Eng./Amer. magazine editor,
   biographer, talk show host;
   née Christina Hambley B— ;
   a.k.a. Lady Evans; w. Sir Har-
   old Evan (1928–), Brit./Amer.
   Journalist, writer
Brown, Trisha (1936)   2967
   Amer. arts administrator,
   dancer, choreographer;
   founded The Trisha Brown
   Company (1970); cofounder,
   Judson Dance Theater
   (1960s); MacArthur, 1991
Browner, Carol M. (1955–) 4293
   Amer. lawyer, environmental,
   management consultant; w.
   Thomas J. Downey, U.S. Rep.;
   W.H. Coord. of Energy &
   Climate Policy, 2009–
Browning, Elizabeth Barrett
(1806–1861)   892
   Eng. poet; née Moulton;
   w. Robert B— (Scot. poet,
   1812–1889)
Brownmiller, Susan (1935–) 2922
   Amer. feminist, writer
Brubaker, Pamela K. (1946–) 3640
   Amer. educator, religion writer
Bruce, Mary Grant
(1878–1958)   1506
   Aust. novelist
Brumberg, Joan Jacobs
(1944–)   3482
   Amer. nonfiction writer, his-
   torian
Brundtland, Gro Harlem
(1939–)   3129
   Nor. physician, pediatrician,
   politician; a.k.a. Mother
   Norway; w. Arne B— (1936–
   ; physician, journalist); first
   woman prime minister of
   Norway, 1981, 1986–96
Brunet, Marguerite
(1730–1820)   606
   Fr. theater manager, director;
   a.k.a. La Montansier
Brunton, Mary (1778–1818) 775
   Scot. novelist, poet; née
   Balfour
Bryan, Margaret, Lady
(fl. 1530s)   329
   Eng. courtier

Bryan, Mary E[dwards]
(1838/46–1913)   1081
   Amer. clubwoman, journalist,
   poet, editor, author
Bryant, Anita Jane (1940–) 3177
   Amer. activist, singer; née
   Green; Miss Oklahoma 1959
Bryant, Castell (1948–)   3815
   Amer. educator, administrator;
   Interim President of Florida
   A&M University (1st woman)
Buck, Lillie West Brown   see LES-
   LIE, AMY
Buck, Pearl S. (1892–1973) 1741
   Amer. children's activist,
   novelist; née Sydenstricker;
   a.k.a. P. Walsh, pseud. John
   Sedges; Pulitzer Prize, 1932;
   first American woman to
   win Nobel Prize, 1938;
   NWHF
Budiardjo, Carmel (1925–) 2512
   Brit./Indones. administrator,
   activist (human rights); co-
   founder, TAPOL, 1973; Right
   Livelihood Award, 1994
Buell, Mary E. (1871–1972) 1386
   Amer. poet
Bunch, Charlotte (1944–) 3483
   Amer. editor, writer, educa-
   tor, feminist; founder of
   Quest magazine; exec. dir.,
   Ctr. for Women's Global
   Leadership (Rutgers Univer-
   sity); NWHF
Bundchen, Gisele [Caroline Non-
   nenmacher] (1980–)   4931
   Braz./Amer. model, social
   activist, philanthropist, busi-
   nesswoman
Bunting, Mary Ingraham
(1910–1998)   2121
   Amer. educator, microbiolo-
   gist, bacteriologist
Burbidge, E. Margaret
(1919–)   2338
   Eng./Amer. astronomer; née
   Green; w. Geoffrey B— (physi-
   cist, astronomer); first woman
   president of the American
   Association for Advancement
   of Science, 1980–
Burchill, Julie (1960–)   4524
   Brit. author, journalist
Burgos, Julia de
(1914–1953)   2214
   Puerto Rican poet
Burk, Martha Gertrude
(1941–)   3247
   Amer. civic administrator,
   newsletter editor
Burke, Billie (1885–1970) 1624
   Amer. stage & screen actor;
   a.k.a. Mary William Ethelbert
   Appleton B—; w. Florenz
   Ziegfeld Jr. (theatrical pro-
   ducer, 1869–1932)
Burke, Fielding   see DARGAN, OLIVE

Burke, (Martha) Jane (1852–1903) 1190
Amer. adventurer, scout, sharpshooter; pseud. Calamity Jane, Martha Jane Canary

Burke, Phyllis (1951–) 4030
Amer. nonfiction writer, lesbian rights activist, novelist

Burkett, Elinor (1943?–) 3394
Amer. journalist, writer, educator (journalism)

Burks, Maria (1954?–) 4233
Amer. public servant

Burlend, Rebecca Burton (1793–1872) 837
Eng./Amer. pioneer, homesteader

Burlingame, Lettie (1859–1890) 1243
Amer. attorney

Burnell, Jocelyn Bell (1943–) 3395
Brit. educator (physics), astrophysicist; discovered the first four pulsars (rotating neutron stars); Herschel Medal from the Royal Astronomical Society, London 1989

Burnett, Carol (1933–) 2838
Amer. comedian, film & TV actor; née Creighton; Emmy (4), Golden Globe (7)

Burnett, Frances [Eliza] (1849–1924) 1164
Amer. writer; née Hodgson

Burney, Fanny (1752–1840) 671
Eng. novelist, playwright; a.k.a. Frances, Mme. d'Arblay; d. Charley B— (noted musicologist); Second Keeper of the Robes to Queen Charlotte (1786–91)

Burr, Amelia [Josephine] (1878–1940?) 1507
Amer. poet, writer; mn. Elmore

Burr, Theodosia see ALSTON, THEODOSIA

Burr, Theodosia De Visme (1736–1794) 620
Swiss/Amer. householder; née Bartow; w. Prevost (1), Aaron B— (2; 1756–1836; politician; U.S. vice president, 1801–05); m. Theodosia Burr Alston*

Burrell, Sophia, Lady (1750?–1764) 660
Eng. poet, dramatist; née Raymond; mn. Clay (2)

Burroughs, Nannie Helen (1883–1961) 1592
Amer. organizer, educator, journalist

Burton [of Coventry], Elaine Frances, Baroness (1904–1991) 1988
Eng. lecturer, writer, politician

Burton, Harriet Emma (1874–?) 1424
Brit. poet; a.k.a. H.B. Laidlaw

Burton, Isabel, Lady (1831–1896) 1036
Eng. diarist, writer; née Arundel; w. Sir Richard B— (British explorer and Orientalist, 1821–90)

Burton, Sala (1925–1987) 2513
Pol./Amer. politician; née Galante; w. Phillip B— (1926–1983), U.S. Rep.; U.S. Rep. (D-CA), 1983–87

Burton, Sandra (1934?–) 2553
Amer. news bureau chief, journalist

Busfield, Joan (1939?–) 3130
Brit. Ssociologist, educator

Bush, Barbara (1925–) 2514
Amer. social activist, literacy advocate, first lady, writer; née Pierce; w. George Herbert Walker B— (1924– ; 41st U.S. pres., 1989–92); m. George W. (1946– ; 43rd U.S. pres.), John (Jeb) B— (1953– ; governor of Florida); d. Marvin Pierce (publishing executive)

Bush, Laura (1946–) 3641
Amer. public figure, educator, librarian; née Welch; w. George W. B— , pres. of U.S.A. (2001–2009)

Butler, Mrs. see KEMBLE, FANNY

Butler, Octavia [Estelle] (1947–1970) 3727
Amer. novelist; Hugo, 1984; Nebula, 1987

Butts, Cassandra Quin (1965–) 4693
Amer. lawyer, policy consultant; Deputy White House counsel, 2009–

Butts, Mary Frances (1836–1902) 1071
Amer. poet

Buxton, Bertha (1844–1881) 1124
Eng. writer

Byatt, A[ntonia] S[usan] (1936–) 2968
Brit. novelist, literary critic; s. Margaret Drabble*; Booker Prize, 1990

Byron, Beverly Butcher (1932–) 2787
Amer. politician; w. Goodloe B— (politician, d. 1978); U.S. House of Representatives, D-Maryland, 1979–1993

Byron, Lady see MILBANKE, ANNE

Byron, Mary (1861–1936) 1263
Eng. poet

C

Cabeza de Baca, Fabiola (1895–?) 1806–1807
Amer. teacher, home economics, writer, nutritionist; a.k.a. F— C. Gilbert

Cabrini, Frances Xavier, Saint (1850–1917) 1171
Amer. Roman Catholic saint; a.k.a. Mother Francesca C—; first American canonized; founder, Missionary Sisters of the Sacred Heart; NWHF

Caccini, Francesca (1587–1640?) 394
Ital. singer, composer; friend of Michelangelo Buonarroti, the younger

Cadden, Vivian (1916–1995) 2264
Amer. writer, magazine editor; a.k.a. V— C—Schuman

Cade, Toni see BAMBARA, TONI

Caesaria, Saint (fl. 6th century) 118
Fr. abbess of St. Jean of Arles

Cahill, Susan [Jane Neunzig] (1940–) 3178
Amer. anthologist, educator, English

Caine, Lynn (1927–1987) 2588
Amer. publicist, writer

Calamity Jane see BURKE, MARTHA JANE

Calderón, Sila María (1942–) 3327
P. R. politician, business executive; first woman governor of Puerto Rico, 2001–2005

Calderone, Mary Steichen (1904–1998) 1989
Amer. physician, public servant, sex educator, feminist; d. Edward Steichen (1879–1973; photographer) and Joanna S—*; w. Frank C— (public health official); n. Carl Sandburg (1878–1967; poet, biographer); medical director, Planned Parenthood Federation of America; cofounder, Sex Information and Education Council of the United States (SEICUS); pioneer in sex and birth control education; NWHF

Caldicott, Helen [Mary] (1938–) 3075
Aust./Amer. author, physician, social activist; founder, Physicians for Social Responsibility; fdr., Women for Nuclear Disarmament (WAND), 1980; fdg pres., STAR Fdn. (Standing for Truth About Radiation)

Caldwell, [Janet Miriam] Taylor [Holland] (1900–1985) 1896
Eng./Amer. novelist; pseud. Max Reinor; mn. Reback

Caldwell, Sarah (1924–) 2478
Amer. opera director, orchestra conductor, impresario; founder, Opera Company of Boston

Calisher, Hortense (1911–2009) 2154
Amer. educator, novelist; a.k.a Mrs. Curtis Harnack; pseud.

Jack Fenno; Guggenheim 1952, 1955; AAAL 1967

Calvin, Idelette de Bure (?–1549) 346
Belg./Swiss householder; w. Jean Stordeur (1) and John C— (2; 1509–1564, founder of Calvinism)

Cam, Helen M. (1885–1968) 1625
Eng. historian, educator

Camerino, Duchess of see CIBO, CATERINA

Cameron, Julia Margaret (1815–1879) 927
Eng. photographer; née Pattle

Camp, Tracy (1964–) 4671
Amer. educator, computer science and math, computer scientist; Fulbright

Campan, Jeanne Louise [Henriette] (1752–1822) 672
Fr. writer, diarist, educator; née Genet; first lady of the bedchamber to Marie Antoinette*

Campbell, Anne (1951–) 4031
Eng. psychologist, author, educator, psychology

Campbell, Beatrix (1947–) 3728
Brit. author, journalist

Campbell, Dorothea Primrose (1792–1863) 831
Scot. poet, novelist

Campbell, Jane Montgomery (1817–1879) 941
Ger. poet

Campbell, Kim (1946–) 3642
Can. politician, judge, lawyer; née Avril Phaedra C—; first woman prime minister of Canada (1993)

Campbell, Maria (1940–) 3179
Can. writer, social reformer

Campbell, Patrick, Mrs. (1865–1940) 1309
Eng. actor; née Beatrice Stella Tanner

Canaan, Andrea R. (1947?–) 3729
Amer. poet, writer, social worker

Canary, Martha Jane see BURKE, (MARTHA) JANE

Canfield, Dorothy see FISHER, DOROTHY

Cannon, Annie Jump (1863–1941) 1293
Amer. suffragist, scientist, astronomer; a.k.a. "The Census Taker of the Sky"; d. Wilson Lee C— (Lt. Gov. Delaware); developed the first standard procedure to classify stars; first woman awarded an honorary doctorate by Oxford University, England (1925); established the A— J— C— Prize for women astronomers; Draper Medal,

Natl. Academy of Sciences, 1931; NWHF

Cannon, Katie Geneva (1950–) 3956
Amer. writer, feminist

Canth, Minna (1844–1897) 1125
Finn. playwright, journalist, shopkeeper; née Ulrika Wilhelmina Johnsson

Cantwell, Mary (1930–2000) 2698
Amer. writer, journalist

Capek, Mary Ellen S. (1951?–) 4032
Amer. nonprofit consultant, researcher, writer; founder, National Council for Research on Women, 1981

Capps, Lois (1938–) 3076
Amer. politician, nurse, educator; née Grimsrud; w. Walter C— (1934–1997), U.S. Rep; U.S. Rep. (D-CA), 1998–

Carabillo, Toni [Virginia Anne] (1926–1997) 2544
Amer. writer, graphic designer, feminist, editor; national vice president of NOW, 1971–1997 (cofounder, Los Angeles chapter)

Caraway, Hattie Wyatt (1878–1950) 1508
Amer. politician; w. Thaddeus H. C— (1871–1931), U.S. Rep., 1913–1921; U.S. Senator, 1921–1931; U.S. Senator (D-AR), 1931–1945

Cardin, Nina Beth (1953–) 4166
Amer. rabbi, writer

Carew, Elizabeth (1585?–1639) 391
Eng. poet, linguist, teacher, writer; née Tanfield, a.s.a. Carey, Cary, Carye; a.k.a. viscountess of Falkland or Lady Falkland; first known female playwright of the English language

Carey, Mariah (1970–) 4813
Amer. singer, songwriter, actor

Carleton, Emma [Nunemacher] (1850–1927) 1172
Amer. writer, journalist

Carlisle, Andrea (1944–) 3484
Amer. writer

Carlisle, countess of see HAY, LUCY and HOWARD, ISABELLA

Carlyle, Jane [Baillie] Welsh (1801–1866) 869
Scot. poet, letter writer; w. Thomas C— (Eng. writer, 1795–1881)

Carmo, Isabel do (1940–) 3180
Portuguese revolutionary

Carney, Julia A. (1823–1908) 986
Amer. educator, poet; mn. Fletcher

Carol, Kate Fletcher see OSGOOD, FRANCES

Caroline Matilda (1751–1775) 667
Danish/Nor. queen

Carpenter, Liz (1920–2010) 2363
Amer. feminist, author; née Elizabeth Sutherland; cofounder, National Women's Political Caucus, 1971

Carpio de San Feliz, Marcela de, Sister (1605–1688) 420
Span. nun, poet; d. Lope de Vega (dramatist, 1562–1635)

Carr, Cynthia (1959?–) 4478
Amer. columnist; a.k.a. C. Carr

Carr, Emily (1871–1945) 1387
Can. painter, writer

Carr, Marina (1964–) 4672
Ir. playwright

Carriera, Rosalba (1675–1757) 519
Ital. painter; elected to French Academy of Painting, 1720

Carrigan, Ana (1944?–) 3485
Ir./Amer. film maker, lecturer, essayist, nonfiction writer

Carrington, Dora [de Houghton] (1893–1932) 1648
Eng. artist, interior designer, artist, media

Carrington, Leonora (1917–) 2282
Brit. writer, painter

Carroll, Jean (1911–) 2155
Fr./Amer. comedian; née Celine Zeigman; w. Buddy Howe, comic

Carroll, Mrs. see CENTLIVRE, SUSANNA

Carroll, Vinnette [Justine] (1922–2002) 2422
Amer. social worker, director, playwright, actor; founder of Urban Arts Corps, NYC (1967); founder of Vinette Carroll Repertory Co., Fort Lauderdale, Florida; DCCA (direction), 1972; Obie, 1962; Ford, 1960; Emmy, 1964; DDA, 1972

Carson, Anne Regina (1950–) 3957
Can. essayist, classicist, poet; w. David Price (anthropologist and author)

Carson, Norma (fl. 1940s–1950s–) 3181
Amer. trumpeter

Carson, Rachel [Louise] (1907–1964) 2061
Amer. environmentalist, marine biologist, zoologist, nonfiction writer; NBA, 1952; Presidential Medal of Freedom, 1980; NWHF

Carswell, Catherine (1879–1946) 2061
Scot. writer; née MacFarlane

Carter, Angela (Olive) (1940–1992) 3182
Eng. journalist, writer; née Stalker

Carter, Deana (1966–) 4717
Amer. singer, songwriter; d. Fred Carter Jr., musician

Carter, Elizabeth (1717–1806) 578
Eng. poet, letter writer, bluestocking, diarist, translator; née Deal, a.k.a. Eliza

Carter, [Bessie] Lillian (1898–1983) 1862
Amer. public figure, author, nurse, volunteer; née Gordy; m. James Earl "Jimmy" C— (1924–), 39th U.S. president

Carter, [Eleanor] Rosalyn Smith (1927–) 2589
Amer. first lady, author; w. Jimmy C— (politician, 1924– ; U.S. president, 1977–1981); NWHF

Carter, Sandy (1963–) 4637
Amer. author, internet marketer

Cartland, Barbara (1901–2000) 1928
Eng. lecturer, TV personality, biographer, novelist; a.k.a. Barbara McCorquodale; Guinness Book of World Records for largest number of books sold in the world, 750 million by 1999; Dame O.B.E.

Cartwright, Johanna (fl. 1640s) 473
Eng. civil rights activist

Cary, Alice (1820–1871) 966
Amer. poet; s. Phoebe C—*

Cary, Phoebe (1824–1871?) 992
Amer. poet; s. Alice C—*

Caschetta, Mary Beth (1966–) 4718
Amer. writer, novelist

Case, Elizabeth York (1840?–1911) 1092
Amer. poet, writer

Case, Phila Henrietta see MACLEOD, JEAN

Case, Sue-Ellen (1942–) 3328
Amer. theater historian, journal editor, educator (English), author

Casey, Margaret (1956–1985) 4353
Amer. activist for the disabled

Cash, Roseanne (1955–) 4294
Amer. songwriter, singer; d. Johnny C— (singer, 1932–)

Cashman, Nellie (1851–1904) 1183
Ir. adventurer

Cassatt, Mary [Stevenson] (1844–1926) 1126
Amer./Fr. painter; NWHF

Cassian, Nina [Renée Annie Stefanescu] (1924–) 2479
Romanian musician, poet

Castedo-Ellerman, Elena (1937–) 3022
Chilean writer

Castellani, Maria (fl. 1930s–1990–) 2699
Ital. writer, educator

Castellanos, Rosario (1925–1974) 2515
Mex. diplomat, poet, writer; Premio Chiapas, 1958; Premio Xavier Villaurrutia, 1960; Premio Sor Juana Inés de la Cruz,* 1962; Sourasky Prize for Literature, 1971

Castelloza (1200?–?) 206
Provençal trobairitz; w. Turc de Mairona; lover of N'Arman de Breon

Castiglione, Ippolita (?–1521) 319
Ital. poet; née Torella; w. Baldassare C— (1478–1529; author)

Castillo, Ana (1956–) 4354
Amer. poet, novelist, essayist; cofounder, Third Woman magazine

Castillo, Aurora (1914–1998) 2215
Amer. environmental activist; cofounder, The Mothers of East Los Angeles (MELA), 1984; Goldman Environmental Prize, 1995

Castillo y Guevara, Francisca Josefa del (1691?–1743) 537
Colombian writer (religion), abbess, poet; a.k.a. Sister Francisca Josepha de la Concépcion, La Madre Castillo

Castle, Barbara (1910–2002) 2122
Eng. politician, MP, cabinet minister; a.k.a. Baroness Castle of Blackburn

Castle, Victoria (1949–) 3889
Amer. leadership teacher, author, mixed media artist, human rights and environmental activist, executive coach, somatic instructor; cofounder, HotWomenForACoolPlanet.com, 2007

Castro, Rosalia de (1837–1885) 1077
Span. poet

Castro, Susan Witkovsky see WITKOVSKY, SUSAN

Catalani, Angelica (1779–1848) 778
Ital. singer

Cather, Katherine Dunlap (1877–1926) 1489
Amer. writer, educator

Cather, Willa [Sibert] (1873–1947) 1408
Amer. editor, journalist, poet, writer; Pulitzer, 1923; NWHF

Catherine II of Russia (1729–1796) 604
Ger./Russ. empress; née Sophia Augusta Frederica of Anhalt-Zerbst, a.k.a. Catherine the Great; w. Peter III

Catherine of Aragon (1485–1536) 283
Span. queen of England; d. King Ferdinand and Isabella I* of Spain, w. Arthur (1; first son of Henry VII) and (2), first w. Henry VIII, m. Mary I of England*

Catherine of Bologna (1413–1463) 253
Ital. abbess, hymnist, essayist

Catherine of Genoa, Saint (1447–1510) 263
Ital. mystic; née Caterina Fieschi; w. Giuliano Adorno

Catherine of Siena, Saint (1347–1380) 237
Ital. mystic, diplomat; née Caterina Benincasa; patron saint of the Dominicans

Catherwood, Mary [Hartwell] (1847–1901) 1149
Amer. writer

Catt, Carrie Chapman (1859–1947) 1244
Amer. columnist, educator, newspaper editor, public education administrator, suffragist; née Lane; founder, Committee for the Cause and Cure of War, 1925; early organizer of United Nations, 1943; sponsored first international study on the status of women; cofounder, International Woman Suffrage Alliance, 1904; cofounder, League of Women Voter, 1919; NWHF

Caulkins, Frances Manwaring (1795–1869) 846
Amer. educator, author, historian; first woman elected to membership in Massachusetts Historical Society, 1849

Cavell, Edith Louisa (1865–1915) 1310
Eng. nurse, patriot; worked in underground during World War I; executed

Cavendish, Georgiana (1757–1806) 690
Eng. poet, society leader, art patron; a.k.a. duchess of Devonshire; d. John, 1st earl of Spencer; a. Caroline Lamb*; friend of Dr. Samuel Johnson (1809–84; Eng. writer and lexicographer) and Richard Brinsley Sheridan (1751–1816; British playwright and politican); painted by both

Thomas Gainsborough (1717–88; portrait and landscape painter) and Sir Joshua Reynolds (1724–92; painter)

Cavendish, Jane (1621–1669) 441
Eng. playwright; d. Willam C—, duke of Newcastle; stepd. Margaret C—;* s. Elizabeth Brackley*

Cavendish, Margaret (1623/24–1673/74) 446
Eng./Fr. poet, writer, playwright; a.k.a. duchess of Newcastle, Mad Madge, née Lucas; d. Thomas Lucas and Elizabeth Leighton, w. Sir William C—, earl of Newcastle (patron of the arts); stepm. Elizabeth Brackley* and Jane C—*; England's first feminist playwright; first woman to publish a collection of plays [NOTE: Cavendish's plays were written as closet dramas, to be read rather than staged]; first woman to publish her autobiography; first woman to publish a biography of her husband; first woman to write about science

Cazalla, Maria (fl. 1530s) 330
Span. commoner; tried before the Spanish Inquisition, 1531–34

Ceballos, Jacqui Michot (1925–) 2516
Amer. feminist; s. Louis Michot, LA Congressman; cofounder, NWPC and Women's Forum; founder and pres., VFA

Cecato, Lica (1956–) 4355
Braz. singer, graphic artist, social activist

Cedering, Siv (1939–) 3131
Swed./Amer. writer, poet, translator, artist

Celle, Princess of see SOPHIA DOROTHEA OF CELLE

Cenci, Beatrice (1577–1599) 381
Ital. noble; heroine of Shelley's tragedy The Cenci (Eng. poet, 1792–1822); committed patricide

Centlivre, Susanna (1667–1723) 511
Ir./Eng. playwright, actor; née Freeman, a.k.a. Mrs. Carroll; w. Joseph C— (Yeoman of the Mouth to Queen Anne; i.e., the cook)

Cereta, Laura (1469–1499) 273–274
Ital. scholar

Cervantes, Lorna Dee (1954–) 4234
Amer. nonfiction writer, poet, educator; founder and editor

in chief, Mango Publications; NEA, 1979

Ceschina, Yoko Nagae (1932–) 2788
Jap./Ital. harpist, philanthropist; w. Count Renzo C—, businessman

Céu, Violante do (1602?–1693) 417
Portuguese nun, playwright, poet, musician; née Montesino, a.s.a. Ceo

Cha, Theresa Hak Kyung (1951–1982) 4033
Kor./Amer. writer, performance artist

Challans see RENAULT, MARY

Chamber, Anna (?–1777) 774
Eng. poet; a.k.a. countess Temple

Chamberlin, Judi (1944–) 3486
Amer. author, psychiatric consultant, anti-psychiatry activist, lecturer; Distinguished Service Award of the Pres. of the U.S.A., 1992

Chambers, [Carolyn] Jane (1937–1983) 3023
Amer. playwright, TV & radio producer; DCCA (1980); Jane Chambers Playwriting Award established in her honor by Women in Theatre

Chambers, Jessie (1887–1965) 1661
Eng. biographer, writer; mn. Wood

Chamorro, Violeta Barrios de, Doña (1929–) 2654
Nicaraguan political leader, newspaper editor; w. Pedro Joaquin C— (d. 1978; newspaper publisher; assassinated); first woman president of Nicaragua, 1990–1995

Chamrond, Marie Anne de Vichy see DEFFAND, MARIE

Chandab, Taghred (1977–) 4916
Aust. writer

Chandidas, (ca. 1375–1450) 246
Beng. poet

Chandler, Loma (1905–1988) 2010
Amer. writer

Chandler, Mary (1687–1745) 531
Eng. poet, milliner

Chanel, Coco (1883–1971) 1593
Fr. fashion designer; née Gabrielle Bonheur C–

Chang, Diana (1934–) 2882
Amer. poet, painter, novelist, book editor

Chang, Helen Mack (1952–) 4091
Guatamalen human rights activist, businesswoman; s. Myrna Mack, anthropologist, human rights activist; assassinated, 1990; fdr., Myrna Mack Foundation, 1992; Right Livelihood Award,

1992; Notre Dame Prize for Distinguished Public Service in Latin America, 2005

Chang, Iris (1968–2004) 4765
Amer. historian, journalist

Chang, Jung (1952–) 4092
Chin./Brit. writer; w. Jon Halliday, British historian

Chang, Leslie T. (1969–) 4782
Amer. journalist, author; w. Peter Hessler, author

Chang, Tina (1969–) 4783
Amer. poet, educator

Chang, Ts'ai-t'ien (1862–1945) 1283.1
Chin. political activist, communist

Chao, Elaine (1953–) 4167
Amer. civil servant; w. Senator Mitch McConnell, R-KY; pres. & chief exec., United Way of America, 1992–96; dir., Peace Corps, 1991–92; deputy secy., DOT, 1989–91

Chao Li-hua (fl. 1360s–d. 1644) 240
Chin. poet

Chao Luan-luan (fl. 8th century) 144
Chin. poet, courtesan

Chapman, Maria Weston (1806–1885) 893
Amer. editor, abolitionist; s. Caroline and Anne C—, abolitionists; w. Henry Grafton C—, abolitionist, merchant; cofounder, Boston Female Anti-Slavery Society, 1834; ed., Non-Resistant (1839–1842)

Chapman, Tracy (1964–) 4673
Amer. singer, songwriter

Chapone, Hester (1727–1801) 598
Eng. essayist, bluestocking, poet; née Mulso, a.s.a. Champone, a.k.a. The Little Spitfire

Chard, Sylvia C. (1938–) 3077
Eng./Can. early childhood educator, author

Charke, Charlotte (?–1760) 705
Eng. playwright, actor; gd. Caius Gabriel Cibber (sculptor); d. Colley Cibber (1671–1757; actor, manager, playwright, Poet Laureate)

Charkowski, Amy O. (1971–) 4841
Amer. educator, microbiologist

Charles, Elizabeth [Rundle] (1828–1896) 1017
Eng. writer

Charlotte Elizabeth see TONNA, CHARLOTTE

Charrière, Madame de (1740–?) 630
Dutch/Fr. novelist; née Isabelle van Tuyll van Serooskerken, a.k.a. Belle van Zuylen

Chase, Ilka (1905–1978) 2011
Amer. writer, actor; mn. Brown

Chase, Mary (1907–1981)   2062
Amer. playwright, newspaper reporter, community activist; née Coyle; founder of House of Hope (home for alcoholic women); Pulitzer, 1945; NYDCC, 1945

Chase-Riboud, Barbara [Dewayne Tosi] (1939–)   3132
Amer./Fr. poet, novelist, sculptor; NEA, 1973

Chast, [Rosaline] Roz (1954–)   4235
Amer. cartoonist; w. Bill Franzen, humorist

Châtelet, Émilie du (1706–1749) 557
Fr. translator, mathematician, physicist; née Gabrielle-Émilie Le Tonnelier de Breteuil; lover of Voltaire

Chávez, Denise Elia (1948–)   3816
Amer. writer, playwright; NEA, 1981, 1982; Rockefeller, 1984

Chayes, Sarah (1962–)   4604
Amer. reporter, social activist

Cheever, Susan (1943–)   3396
Amer. biographer, novelist; d. John C— (1912–1982), Amer. Pulitzer Prize-winning writer; s. Benjamin C— (1948–), writer

Chehak, Susan Taylor (1951–)   4034
Amer. novelist

Chen, Pauline W. (1956?–)   4356
Amer. physician, writer

Cheney, Gerturde Louise (1918–)   2310
Amer. poet

Cheney, Lynne Ann (1941–)   3248
Amer. novelist, talk show host, scholar; née Vincent; w. Dick Cheney, 43rd U.S. vice president

Cheng, Nien (1915–?)   2239
Chin./Amer. author, business executive, political activist; m. Meiping C—, Shanghai film actress; assassinated

Cher (1946–)   3643
Amer. singer, fitness consultant, actor; née Cherilyn Sarkisian (a.s.a. Sakisian); a.k.a. Cherilyn La Piere; ex-w. Sonny Bono (singer, actor, politician, 1935–1997)

Chernin, Kim (1940–)   3183
Amer. editor, writer; née Kusnitz

Chesler, Phyllis (1940–)   3184
Amer. educator, writer, psychiatrist

Chesnut, Mary Bokin (1823–1886)   987
Amer. diarist

Chesoni, Atsango (fl. 1990s–) 4961
Kenyan lawyer, activist, women's rights

Chess, Stella (1914–2007)   2216
Amer. child psychiatrist; w. Alexander Thomas (d. 2003), researcher, author; pioneer in child development

Chiang Kai-shek, Madame (1898–2003)   1863
Chin. reformer, educator, sociologist; née Soong Mei-ling; w. Chiang Kai-shek (1887–1975; military and political leader), s. Mme. Sun Yat-sen*

Chiang Ping-tzu   see TING LING

Chicago, Judy (1939–)   3133
Amer. artist, painter, lecturer, writer; née Gerowitz or Cohen; mn. Hamrol; cofounder, Woman's Building, Feminist Studio Workshop/College, Los Angeles, 1973

Chien Shiung Wu (1912–1997)2173
Chin./Amer. physicist; d. Wu Zhong-Yi (opened the first school for girls in China); first women to receive Comstock Award from the National Academy of Sciences, 1964 (member since 1958); first woman to be elected president of The American Physical Society, 1975; ; NWHF

Child, Julia [Carolyn] (1912–2004)   2174
Amer. chef, author, TV personality; née McWilliams; Emmy, 1966; NBA, 1980; NWHF

Child, Lydia Maria (1802–1880)   870
Amer. writer, editor, abolitionist; NWHF

Childe-Pemberton, Harriet L. (fl. 1891–1912–)   1723
Eng. playwright, poet; a.k.a. H. L. C. P—

Childress, Alice (1920–1994) 2364
Amer. novelist, playwright, columnist, actor, writer; cofounder, American Negro Theater; Obie, 1956; Newbery; NBA, 1974; Rockefeller, 1967

Childs, E. Kitch (1937–1993) 3024
Amer. feminist psychotherapist, gay and lesbian rights activist; Chicago Gay and Lesbian Hall of Fame, 1993

Chin, Ann-ping (1948–)   3817
Taiwan./Amer. historian, educator, writer; w. Johnathan Spence, professor

Chin, Marilyn [Mei Ling] (1955–)   4295
Amer. translator, educator (creative writing), poet; NEA, 1984–85; PEN, 1994, 1995; Pushcart, 1994, 1995, 1997

Ch'in Chia, Wife of (fl. 1st century B.C.E.)   72
Chin. poet

Chip, Will   see MORE, HANNAH

Chisholm, Shirley [Anita] (1924–2005)   2480
Amer. author, politician, educator; née St. Hill; U.S. Congresswoman (D-NY), 1969–1983; first African-American woman elected to Congress; first major African-American party candidate for office of U.S. president; cofounder, National Political Congress of Black Women; NWHF

Chittick, Elizabeth L. (1908–2008)   2081
Amer. feminist activist, commentator, civil servant; Pres., Natl. Woman's Party, 1971–89; first woman civilian administrator of the US Naval Air Station, the first woman registered representative of the New York Stock Exchange (Bache & Co., 1950–1962) and first woman revenue collections officer with the IRS

Chittister, OSB, Joan (1936–)   2969
Amer. author, activist, peace, nun; founder and executive director of Benetvision: A Resource and Research Center for Contemporary Spirituality

Ch'iu Chin (1874–1907)   1425
Chin. revolutionary, feminist; executed by Manchu regime

Chiyoni   see FUKUZOYO CHIYO

Chloris   see WHARTON, ANNE

Chodorow, Nancy Julia (1944–)   3487
Amer. social scientist; NSF Fellowship 1970–72; NEH, 1982–86, 1995–96; Guggenheim, 1995–96

Choiseul, Louise Honorine de (1734–1801)   616
Fr. letter writer; née Crozat du Châtel; w. duc de C— (1719–1785; foreign minister, minister of war)

Chona, Marie (1845?–1937?) 1134
Amer. writer

Chopin, Kate [O'Flaherty] (1851–1904)   1184
Amer. writer

Chowdhury, Seema (1971–) 4842
Bangl. poet

Christian, Barbara T. (1943–2000)   3397
Amer. literary critic, educator (Afro–American studies), nonfiction writer; ABA, 1983

Christian, Meg (1946–)   3644
Amer. songwriter, folk singer

Christie, Agatha [Mary Clarissa], Dame (1891–1975)   1724
Eng. mystery writer, playwright; née Miller; w. Sir Max Mallowan, archaeologist (1904–1978; outsold only by Shakespeare & Bible

Christina, Leonora (1621–1685)   442
Danish diarist, poet; d. Christian IV of Denmark, w. Corfits Ulfeldt (statesman)

Christina of Sweden (1626–1689)   450
Swed. intellectual, queen, author; d. Gustavus Adolphus (king of Sweden, 1611–1632)

Christine de Pisan (1363/65–1430/31)   244
Ital./Fr. scholar, feminist, author, poet, balladeer; née Pisani; w. Etienne de Castel; first professional female author in western Europe

Chu Shu-chên, (fl. 1180s–1200) 197
Chin. poet

Chua, Amy (1962–)   4605
Amer. educator (law), lawyer, writer

Chudleigh, Lady   see LEE, MARY

Chuo Wên-chün (179?–117 B.C.E.)   69
Chin. poet, legendary lover; a.s.a. Cho; w. Su-ma Hsiang-ju (poet)

Churchill, Caryl (1938–)   3078
Eng. playwright; Obie, 1990

Churchill, Jennie Jerome (1854–1921)   1201
Amer./Eng. editor, society leader, playwright; w. Sir Randolph C— (1849–95; British politican), m. Sir Winston C— (British statesman, 1874–1965; prime minister, 1940–45, 1951–55)

Chute, Carolyn (1947–)   3730
Amer. writer, political activist

Cibo, Caterina (1501–1557)   297
Ital. religious reformer; a.k.a. duchess of Camerino; n. Pope Clement VII (née Giulio de' Medici, 1475?–1534; pope, 1523–1534), w. Giovanni Maria Varano; saved the Order of Friars Minor Capuchin, an independent order of Franciscans, from suppression

Ciment, Jill (1953–)   4168
Can. novelist; NEA, 1995

Cinciotta, Linda Ann (1943–) 3398
Amer. attorney, public servant

Cisneros, Sandra (1954–)   4237
Amer. educator, poet, writer; NEA, 1982, 1988; ABA, 1985; MacArthur, 1995

Cixous, Hélène (1937–) 3025
Fr. poet, educator, philosopher, playwright

Claflin, Tennessee
(1845–1923) 1135
Amer. feminist, writer, editor; a.k.a. Tennie C., Lady Cook; s. Victoria C— Woodhull*; first woman stockholder in U.S.; cofounder, *Woodhull and Claflin's Weekly*, 1870

Claiborne, Liz (1929–2007) 2655
Amer. fashion designer, entrepreneur; née Anne Elisabeth Jane C—; cofounder, The Liz Claiborne and Art Ortenberg Foundation, dedicated to the conservation of nature and the amelioration of human distress

Clampitt, Amy Kathleen
(1920–1994) 2365
Amer. poet; Guggenheim, 1982; MacArthur, 1992

Clancy, Carolyn (1954?–) 4238
Amer. administrator, activist, health, physician

Clappe, Louise Amelia
(1819–1906) 954
Amer. public school educator, letter writer, pioneer; née Knapp Smith; pseud. Dame Shirley

Clare of Assisi, Saint
(1193/94–1253) 201
Ital. nun; founder, Order of the Poor Clares

Clarenbach, Kathryn [Frederick]
(1920–1994) 2366
Amer. feminist, educator, political scientist; founding mbr. & first chair, NOW

Claribel see BARNARD, CHARLOTTE

Clarinda see CRAIG, AGNES

Clark, C. Hope (1956–) 4357
Amer. editor, writer; founder, FundsForWriters.com

Clark, Eleanor (1913–1996) 2195
Amer. literary critic, novelist; w. Robert Penn Warren (poet and novelist, 1905–89); NBA, 1965

Clark, Eugenie (1922–) 2423
Amer. marine biologist, author

Clark, Helen [Elizabeth]
(1950–) 3958
N.Z. politician; w. Peter Davis (1947–), Eng./NZ educator, sociologist; Prime Minister of New Zealand, 1999–2008

Clark, Marcia [Rachel]
(1953–) 4169
Amer. lawyer

Clark, Margaret D. (1943–) 3399
Aust. juvenile novelist; a.k.a. Lee Striker

Clarke, Edith (1883–1959) 1594
Amer. mathematician, educator, physics, electrical engineer

Clarkstone, Bessie (?–1625) 448
Eng. householder

Clausen, Jan (1950–) 3959–3960
Amer. writer

Clayton, Eva M. (1934–) 2883
Amer. politician; U.S. Representative-D-NC (1993–2003)

Cleage, Pearl [Michelle]
(1948–) 3818
Amer. playwright, journalist, actor, writer; a.k.a. P— Lomax; NEA (5)

Cleghorn, Sarah Norcliffe
(1876–1959) 1473
Amer. poet, socialist, pacifist

Clemence see MICHEL, LOUISE

Clementine see HOWARTH, ELLEN

Clements, Marcelle (1948–) 3819
Fr./Amer. writer

Clemmer, Mary
(1839–1884) 1087
Amer. poet, writer; mn. Hudson

Clendinnen, Inga (1934–) 2884
Aust. nonfiction writer, anthropologist; Conference on Latin American History Prize, 1981; Herber Eugene Bolton Memorial Prize, 1988

Cleopatra VII (69 B.C.E.–30 C.E.) 75
Egyp. queen; d. Ptolemy XII, s. and w. Ptolemy XIII (1; both Egyptian kings), lover of Julius Caesar (100–44 B.C.E; Roman general, statesman, and historian), w. Mark Antony (2, c.83 –30 B.C.E.; Roman politician and soldier), m. Cleopatra Selene (queen of Mauretania)

Cleora see THRYNNE, FRANCES

Clere, Elizabeth (fl. 1450s) 259
Eng. householder; related to the Pastons of England

Cleyre, Voltairine de
(1866–1912) 1325
Amer. anarchist, educator, feminist, writer, poet

Cliff, Michelle (1946–) 3645
Jamaican writer; partner, Adrienne Rich*

Clifford, Anne, Lady
(1590–1676) 396
Eng. letter-writer, diarist, patron of literary arts; a.k.a. Diana Primrose (?); gd. Francis Russell, 2nd earl of Pembroke; d. Margaret Russell and George C—, 3rd earl of Cumberland; w. Richard Sackville, earl of Dorset (1) and Phillip Herbert, earl of Bedford (2), n. Ann, countess of Warwick

Clifton, [Thelma] Lucille
(1936–) 2970
Amer. children's writer, poet, educator (poetry); née Sayles

Clinchy, Blythe M. (1930–) 2700
Amer. educator (psychology), author

Clingerman, Mildred McElroy
(1918–1997) 2311
Amer. writer

Clinton, Catherine (1952–) 4093
Amer./Ir. biographer, educator, history

Clinton, Elizabeth
(1574–1630?) 379
Eng. noble, author; a.k.a. countess of Lincoln; w. Thomas C—, 3rd earl of Lincoln

Clinton, Hillary Rodham
(1947–) 3731
Amer. children's rights advocate, diplomat, lawyer, health care activist, first lady, U.S. senator (D-NY); w. William J. C— (1946– ; 42nd U.S. president, 1993–2001); m. Chelsea C—; d.-in-law, Virginia Cassidy Kelley*; U.S. Senator (D-NY), 2001–2008; Sec. of State, 2009– ; NWHF

Clitherow, Margaret
(1556?–1586) 358
Eng. Catholic martyr; née Middleton, a.s.a. Clitheroe; a.k.a. "the Pearl of York"; d. Thomas Middleton (1570?–1627; playwright), w. John C—; canonized, 1970

Clive, Catherine (1711–1785) 572
Eng. actor, playwright; née Rafter, a.k.a. Kitty C—

Cloud, Darrah (1955–) 4296
Amer. screen & TV writer, playwright; w. Dave Owens (actor-director); Rockefeller; NEA

Clyde, Mary (fl. 1990s–) 4962
Amer. writer, fiction

Coates, Florence Earle
(1850–1927) 1173
Amer. poet

Coatés, Grace Stone (1881–?) 1566
Amer. writer

Coatsworth, Elizabeth [Jane]
(1893–1986) 1766
Amer. novelist, poet; Newbery, 1931

Cobb, Geraldyn (1931–) 2752
Amer. aviator; first woman to take, and pass, astronaut tests for NASA

Cobbe, Frances Power
(1822–1904) 983
Eng. writer

Coblentz, Catherine Cate
(1897–1951) 1845
Amer. writer

Cochran, Jacqueline
(1906–1980) 2043
Amer. aviator, businesswoman, inventor; mn. Odium; founder and director, Women's Airforce Service Pilots (WASP, 1943); first woman to break the sound barrier; first woman to test-fly a jet fighter; first woman to fly a warplane across Atlantic; Distinguished Service Medal, 1945; Distinguished Flying Cross, 1969; Aviation Hall of Fame, 1971; Order of Merit, 1970; NWHF

Cockburn, Alicia (1713–1794) 574
Scot. poet, society leader, songwriter, playwright; née Rutherford, a.k.a. Alison

Cockburn, Catherine see TROTTER, CATHERINE

Cocroft, Susan (1862–?) 1284
Amer. beauty culturist

Cofer, Judith Oritz (1952–) 4094
Puerto Rican/Amer. poet

Coffee, Lenore J. (1896–1984) 1820
Amer. screenwriter, playwright, novelist; w. William J. Cowen, Amer. writer-director

Coffey, Susanna J. (1956?–) 4358
Amer. artist, painter, educator; s. Jane C— , writer; Guggenheim, NEA

Coffin, Judith G. (1952–) 4095
Amer.? historian

Cohan, Alice (1951–) 4035
Amer. feminist, organizer; p. Jan Welch (1939–2008), Amer. Feminist; political dir., Feminist Majority

Cohen, Amy (1942–) 3329
Amer. educator, mathematician

Cohen, Charlotte Bonny
(1943–) 3400
Amer. political activist

Cohen, Deborah S. (1948–) 3820
Amer. educator, history, writer

Cohen, Leah Hager (1967–) 4744
Amer. writer

Cohen, Mary M. (1854–1911) 1202
Amer. poet, essayist, teacher

Cohen, Sherry Suib (1934–) 2885
Amer. author, teacher, lecturer, journalist

Coignard, Gabrielle de
(1552?–d. 1594) 354
Fr. poet

Colborn, Theodora ""Theo"
(1928–) 2622
Amer. ecologist, pharmacist, zoologist, rancher (sheep); a.k.a. "the Rachel Carson of the '90s"; 2nd Annual Rachel Carson Award for Integrity in Science

Cole, Johnnetta B. (1936–) 2971
Amer. educator, anthropology, nonprofit administrator;

s. MaVynée B—*; pres., Spelman College, 1989–97 (1st female); pres. Bennett College, 2002–07

Cole, Mary (fl. 1790s)   816
Amer. author

Coleman, Bessie (1892–1926)   1742
Amer. aviator; first person of African descent in the world to receive a pilot's license; NWHF; IWSHF, 1992

Coleman, Deborah A. (1953–) 4170
Amer. businesswoman

Coleridge, Mary [Elizabeth] (1861–1907)   1264
Eng. poet, educator, biographer, writer

Coleridge, Sara (1802–1852)   871
Eng. author, translator, poet; d. Samuel C— (1772–1834), Eng. poet, man of letters

Colette (1873–1954)   1409
Fr. writer; née Sidonie Gabrielle C—; first president of Goncourt Academy

Cole-Whittaker, Terry (1939–)   3134
Amer. minister, nonfiction writer

Coligny, Henriette de (1613?–1673)   431
Fr. poet; a.k.a. countess de la Suze; mn. Hamilton (1), Suze (2)

Colins, Janet (1917–2003)   2283
Amer. dancer, ballet, choreographer, painter; c. Carmen de Lavallade*; first black artist to perform at the Metropolitan Opera House, 1951

Colledge, Cecilia (1920–2008)   2367
Brit./Amer. figure skater, skate coach; Olympic silver, 1936

Collen, Lindsey (1951?–)   4036
S. Afr. novelist, political activist

Collier, Mary (1689/90– ca. 1762)   532
Eng. poet, laundress, writer

Collins, Anne (fl. 1650s)   485
Eng. poet

Collins, Eileen, Lt. (1956–)   4359
Amer. astronaut; NWHF

Collins, Emily (1818?–1879?)   946
Amer. suffragist

Collins, Joan [Henrietta] (1933–)   2840
Eng. actor, author; ex-w. Anthony Newley, singer, actor, film composer; OBE, 1997; Golden Globe, 1983

Collins, Judy [Marjorie] (1939–)   3135
Amer. folksinger, songwriter; Grammy, 1968

Collins, Kathleen (1931–1988) 2753
Amer. playwright; a.k.a. K— Kranidas

Collins, Marva Nettles (1936–)   2972
Amer. educator; née ; fdr., Westside Preparatory School, Chicago, 1975

Collins, Patricia Hill (1948–) 3821
Amer. educator (Afro-American studies), nonfiction writer

Colonna, Vittoria da (1490–1547)   287
Ital. poet; a.k.a. marchesa de Pescara; d. Fabrizio C— (Roman noble, d. 1520), w. Ferrante Francesco d'Avalos; friend of Michelangelo (1475–1564; Ital. sculptor, painter, poet)

Colquhoun, Janet (1781–1846) 786
Scot. writer, philanthropist, diarist; née Sinclair, a.k.a. Lady of Rossdhu, Scotland; founder, School of Industry (near Rossdhu, Scotland)

Colum, Mary "Molly" (1884–1957)   1607
Ir./Amer. literary critic; née M— Gunning Maguire; w. Padraic C— (1881–1972), Ir. poet, novelist, dramatist; Guggenheim

Colvin, Claudette (1940–)   3185
Amer. civil rights activist

Colwin, Laurie (1944–1992)   3488
Amer. writer

Comaneci, Nadia (1962–)   4606
Romanian gymnast; Olympic gold, 1976 (3) ; IWSHF, 1990

Combs, Valda Jean (1958?–)   4442
Amer. minister, lawyer, activist, AIDS, journalist

Comden, Betty (1919–2006)   2339
Amer. screenwriter, playwright, lyricist; née Elizabeth Cohen; Tony (5); Grammy, 1992; Obie, 1959

Comini, Alessandra (1938?–)   3079
Amer. nonfiction writer, educator, art history, musicologist

Commire, Anne (1940?–)   3186
Amer. playwright; Rockefeller

Comnena, Anna (1083–1153)   176
Byzantine historian; pseud. Ben Sonnenberg; d. Alexius Comnenus (1081–1118; emperor of Constantinople); world's first female historian

Compiuta Donzella, La (fl. 13th century)   231
Ital. poet; a.k.a. Accomplished Maid of Tuscany, The Divine Sibyl, The Perfect Maid

Compton, Elizabeth, Lady (fl. 1590s)   397
Eng. maid of honor; d. John Spencer (mayor of London,

1584/85), w. William, 2nd Lord C— (later earl of Northampton); maid of honor to Elizabeth I*

Compton, Lynn D. (1921–)   2181–2182
Amer. attorney

Compton-Burnett, Ivy, Dame (1892–1969)   1743
Eng. satirist, writer

Conant, Isabel La Howe [Fiske] (1874–?)   1426
Amer. poet

Concépcion, Francisca Josepha de la, Sister   see CASTILLO Y GUEVARA, FRANCISCA

Condé, Maryse (1937–)   3026
Guadeloupean playwright, writer (children), literary critic, novelist

Cone, Helen Gray (1859–1934)   1245
Amer. educator, poet

Cones, Nancy Ford (1869–1962)   1357
Amer. photographer

Conklin, Beth Ann (1954–)   4239
Amer. anthropologist, educator

Conkling, Grace [Walcott] H. (1878–1958)   1509
Amer. writer, poet, lecturer; née Hazard; m. Hilda C—*

Conkling, Hilda (1910–1986) 2123
Amer. poet; d. Grace C—*

Connelly, Joan Breton (1954–)4240
Amer. archaeologist, historian, educator

Connolly, Olga (1932–)   2789
Cuban/Amer. athlete; née Fikotova; Olympic medalist, discus throwing

Conrad, Beatrice (1927–)   2590
Amer. social worker, poet, writer, educator; née Freedman

Conran, Shirley (1932–)
social worker, poet, writer, educator; née Freedman
Eng. designer, journalist

Constantia   see MORTON, SARAH; MURRAY, JUDITH

Cook, Blanche Weisen (1941–)3249
Amer. poet, journalist, professor of history, author

Cook, Eliza (1818–1889)   947
Eng. poet

Cooke, Rose Terry (1827–1892)   1012
Amer. poet

Cookson, Catherine [McMullen] (1906–1998)   2044
Eng. writer; a.k.a. Catherine Marchant

Cool, Lisa Collier (1952–)   4096
Amer. journalist, writer, literary agent; d. Oscar C— , literary agent; generational descendent of Worthington

Whitridge, 19th century painter, and John Perrin, fdr. Rohoboth, MA, 1645; pres., American Society of Journalists and Authors (2003–05)

Coolbrith, Ina [Donna] (1841–1928)   1102
Amer. poet, librarian, writer; née Josephine Donna Smith

Coolidge, Grace Goodhue (1879–1957)   1523
Amer. hostess, first lady; w. Calvin C— (1872–1933; politician; U.S. president, 1923–29)

Coolidge, Susan (1845–1905) 1136
Amer. writer; née Sarah Chauncey Woolsey

Coombs, Mary (1944–)   3489
Amer. professor of law

Coontz, Stephanie (1944–)   3490
Amer. writer

Cooper, Anna Julia [Haywood] (1858–1964)   1231
Amer. scholar, educator, writer

Cooper, Diana, Lady (1892–1986)   1744
Eng. nurse, society leader, writer, actor; née Manners, a.k.a. viscountess of Norwich; w. Alfred Duff C— (diplomat, politician d. 1952)

Cooper, Edith [Emma] (1862–1913)   1285
Eng. writer

Cooper, Elizabeth (fl. 1730s)   607
Eng. playwright, anthologist

Cooper, Helene (1966?–)   4719
Liber./Amer. writer, journalist

Cooper, Jane (1924–2007)   2481
Amer. poet, educator; New York State Poet, 1996–97; NEA; Guggenheim

Cope, Wendy Mary (1945–)   3560
Brit. poet

Copley, Mary Singleton   see PELHAM, MARY

Copley, Susannah Farnum (fl. 1760s–d. 1836)   706
Amer./Eng. letter writer, householder; née Clarke; w. John Singleton C— Jr., Baron Lyndhurst (statesman)

Corbett, E. T., Mrs. (fl. 1880s) 1542
Brit. poet

Corbin, Alice (1881–1949)   1567
Amer. editor, poet; w. Henderson

Corday, Charlotte (1768/69–1793)   736
Fr. noble, intellectual; née Maria-Anne Charlotte C— d'Armont; assassin of Jean-Paul Marat (1743–93; Fr. revolutionary)

Corey, Martha (?–1692)   538
    Eng./Amer. alleged witch
Corey, Shirley Trusty
(1935–)   2923
    Amer. arts-in-education spe-
    cialist, educator
Cori, Gerty (1896–1957)   1821
    Aus./Amer. scientist, bio-
    chemist; née Radnitz; w. Carl
    Ferdinand C— (1896–1984;
    scientist); discovered Cori-
    ester (1936); first woman
    to receive Nobel Prize in
    medicine and physiology;
    third w Noblest; first Jewish-
    American. Natl. Science Board
    of the Natl. Science Fdn.,
    1952 (named to); Nobel Prize
    (1947) with her husband,
    Carl Ferdinand C—, for their
    discovery of the course of the
    catalytic conversion of glyco-
    gen; NWHF
Corinna (fl. 520s–d. 420 B.C.E.)   55
    Greek lyric poet; a.s.a. Crinna,
    Korinna, Korina, a.k.a. The
    Lyric Muse, The Fly, The
    Boeotian Sow; d. Ache-
    loodoros and Hipokrateia
    (contemporaries of Pindar,
    lyric poet)
Corinna   see THOMAS, ELIZABETH
Cornelia (fl. 160s–140 B.C.E.)   71
    Roman letter writer, scholar;
    a.k.a. Mother of the Grac-
    chi; w. Tiberius Sempronius
    Gracchus II (statesman), m.
    Tiberius Sempronius Gracchus
    III, Gaius IV and Sempronia
    (w. Scipio Africanus the
    Younger)
Cornelia   see HALE, SARAH
Cornford, Frances Darwin
(1886–1960)   1649
    Eng. Poet; d. Francis D—,
    Brit. botanist; grandd. Charles
    D—
Cornuel, A. M. Bigot de
(1605/14?–1694)   421
    Fr. wit, letter writer
Corpi, Lucha (1945–)   3561
    Mex./Amer. poet, novelist; co-
    ordinator of Chicano Studies
    Library, 1970–72; founding
    member of Aztlan Cultural
    1971 and Centro Chicano
    de Escritores 1980; NEA
    1979–80
Corrigan, Maireád (1944–)   3491
    Ir. peace activist; cofounder,
    Northern Ireland Peace
    Movement (later renamed
    Community of Peace People);
    co-recipient with Betty Wil-
    liams,* Nobel Peace Prize,
    1976
Cortissoz, Ellen Mackay   see
HUTCHINSON, ELLEN

Corvera, Bernardina Guervara
(1972–)   4855
    El Salv./Guatamalen poet
Costa, Maria Fatima Velho da
(1940?–)   3080
    Portuguese writer
Cota-Cárdenas, Margarita
(1941–)   3250
    Amer. novelist, poet; co-
    founder.-ed., Scorpion Press
Cottin, Sophie (1773–1807)   762
    Fr. author; née Ristaud
Cotton, Elizabeth (1893–1987)   1767
    Amer. guitarist, songwriter;
    a.k.a. "Sis" Cotton
Cotton, Nancy (1944?–)   3492
    Brit./Amer. educator, author
Coulter, Ann [Hart] (1961–)   4567
    Amer. political commentator,
    syndicated columnist, author,
    lawyer
Countess of Oxford and Asquith
(see ASQUITH, MARGOT)
Countess Temple, (see CHAMBER,
ANNA)
Couric, Katie (1957–)   4402
    Amer. journalist, TV person-
    ality
Covington, Vicki (1952–)   4097
    Amer. novelist; w. Dennis
    C- (writer); NEA, 1988
Cowan, Alison Leigh
(1963?–)   4638
    Amer. journalist
Coward, Rosalind (1953–)   4171
    Brit. author
Cowley, Hannah (1743–1809)   643
    Eng. playwright, poet; née
    Parkhouse, a.k.a. Anna
    Matilda
Cox, Ana Marie (1972–)   4856
    Amer. author, blogger, editor,
    newspaper; a.k.a. Ann O'Tate;
    w. Chris Lehmann, journalist;
    fdr., Wonkette
Craig, Agnes (1759–1841)   696
    Scot. poet; a.k.a. Clarinda
    (heroine of songs by Robert
    Burns, 1759–96; poet); mn.
    McLehose
Craighead, Meinrad (1936–)   2973
    Amer. visual artist, scholar;
    Fulbright, 1965
Craigie, Pearl [Mary Teresa]
(1867–1906)   1334
    Amer./Eng. playwright, writer;
    pseud. John Oliver Hobbes
Craigin, Elisabeth (fl. 1930s)   2701
    Amer. writer
Craik, Dinah [Maria] Mulock
(1826–1887)   1006
    Eng. poet, writer
Cram, Mildred (1889–1985)   16
    Amer. writer
Crane, Nathalia [Clara Ruth]
(1913–1998)   2196
    Amer. poet, novelist, educator
    English; mn. Black

Crapsey, Adelaide (1878–1914)   1510
    Amer. poet, educator
Craster, Edmund, Mrs.
(?–1874)   1427
    Eng. poet
Craven, Margaret (1901–1980)   1929
    Amer. fiction writer, journalist
Crawford, Julia (1800–1885)   866
    Ir. poet
Crawford, Louisa Macartney
(1790–1858)   817
    Eng. poet, songwriter
Creech, Sharon (1945–)   3562
    Amer. novelist, children's;
    Newbery Medal, 1995
Crespi, Camilla T. (1942–)   3330
    Czech./Ital./Amer. novelist;
    née Trinchieri; a.k.a. Trella
    Crespi
Cresson, Édith (1934–)   2886
    Fr. politician, government
    official; née Campion; French
    Prime Minister, 1991–92 (first
    woman to hold such office)
Crist, Judith (1922–)   2424
    Amer. film critic; née Klein
Crittenden, Ann (1937–)   3027
    Amer. journalist, author,
    lecturer
Croce, Arlene (1934–)   2887
    Amer. editor, writer, dance
    critic; founded Ballet Review
    Magazine (1965)
Crocker, Hannah Mather
(1752–1829)   673
    Amer. author; great-gd. In-
    crease Mather (1639–1723;
    clergyman and writer), gd.
    Cotton Mather (1663–1728;
    Puritan minister), n. Thomas
    Hutchinson (1711–80; royal
    governor of Massachusetts)
Cromwell, Gladys
(1885–1919)   1626
    Amer. poet
Cronan, Sheila (1946?–2003)   3646
    Amer. feminist, lawyer
Crosby, Sarah (1729–1804)   605
    Eng. Methodist leader
Cross, Amanda   see HEILBRUN,
CAROLYN
Cross, Mary Ann   see ELIOT,
GEORGE
Crothers, Rachel (1878–1958)   1511
    Amer. community activist,
    actor, stage director, play-
    wright; founder of Stage Relief
    Fund (1932) and the Ameri-
    can Theater Wing for War
    Relief (1940); organized Stage
    Door Canteen, NY (1945);
    NIAL, 1933; Natl. Achieve-
    ment Award, 1938
Crouse, Mary Elizabeth
(1873–?)   1410
    Amer. writer, poet
Crowe, Catharine (1790–1872)   818
    Eng. author; née Stevens

Crowe, F. J.   see JOHNSTON, JILL
Crowe, Frances (1919–)   2340
    Amer. Quaker activist; co-
    founder, Traprock Peace
    Center, 1979
Crowell, Grace Noll
(1877–1969)   1490
    Amer. poet, writer
Crowley, Candy (1948–)   3821.1
    Amer. political correspondent
Cruz, Juana Inés de la, Sor
(1651–1695)   487
    Mex. poet, scholar, nun,
    feminist; née Juana Inés
    de Asbaje y Ramirez de
    Santillana, a.k.a. Sor Juana,
    The Tenth Muse, Phoenix of
    Mexico, The Mexican Nun;
    first important literary figure
    of the New World
Cryer, Gretchen (1935–)   2924
    Amer. singer, lyricist, actor,
    playwright; Obie (4), 1970
Culross, Lady   see MELVILL, ELIZA-
BETH
Cumming, Anne (1917–)   2284
    Brit. author
Cumming, Patricia [Arens]
(1932–)   2791
    Amer. educator, poet, play-
    wright
Cunard, Nancy (1896–1965)   1822
    Eng./Fr. activist, human
    rights, poet, society figure,
    publisher, journalist; d. Sir
    Bache Cunard, shipping
    magnate
Cunningham, Agnes "Sis"
(1909–2004)   2107
    Amer. musician, songwriter,
    political activist, music pub-
    lisher; w. Gordon Friesen,
    music publisher; fdr., Broad-
    side (folk-song magazine)
Cunningham, Imogen
(1883–1976)   1595
    Amer. photographer
Cuomo, Chris[tine] J. (1964–)   4674
    Amer. author, educator (phi-
    losophy)
Curie, Ève (1904–2007)   1990
    Fr./Amer. writer, pianist, lec-
    turer, war correspondent; d.
    Pierre (1859–1906; physical
    chemist) and Marie C—*; s.
    Irène Joliot-C—*
Curie, Marie (1867–1934)   1335
    Fr. physicist; née Sklodowska;
    w. Pierre C— (1859–1906;
    physical chemist), m Ève C—
    * and Irène Joliot-C—*; the
    first woman ever appointed
    to teach at the Sorbonne,
    1906; w/husband, discov-
    ered radium;first woman
    member of French Academy
    of Medicine; director of Ra-
    dium Institute at University

of Paris; Nobel Prize, 1903, 1911

Currie, Mary Montgomerie, Lady   *see* FANE, VIOLET

Curtis, Jamie Lee (1958–)   4443
Amer. actor, author; d. Tony Curtis & Janet Leigh, actors; w. Christopher Guest (a.k.a. Lord Haden-Guest), actor; Golden Globe, 1989, 1994

Curtis, Rebecca (1974–)   4883
Amer. writer, educator

Curtiss, Ursula Reilly (1923–1984)   2448
Amer. writer

Cushman, Charlotte Saunders (1816–1876)   936
Amer. actor; first theatrician in Hall of Fame, 1915

Custance, Olive [Eleanor] (1874–1944)   1358
Eng. poet; a.k.a. Lady Alfred Douglas

D

Daché, Lilly (1904–1989)   1991
Fr./Amer. writer, business executive, fashion designer

Dacier, Anne (1651–1720)   488
Fr. translator, author, scholar; née Lefevre; w. Lesnier (1), w. André D— (2, frequent collaborator)

d'Adesky, Anne-Christine (1959?–)   4479
Haitian Amer. novelist, journalist, activist; founder and co-executive director of the Women's Equity in Access to Care and Treatment (WE-ACTx)

Daisy, princess of Pless (1873–1943)   1411
Ir./Ger. actor, writer, princess; née Cornwallis-West

Dai, Qing (1941–)   3250.1
Chin. journalist, environmental activist, engineer; d. Fu Daqing (1900–1944?) translator, organizer; executed.; Goldman, 1993

Dall, Caroline [Wells Healey] (1822–1912)   984
Amer. writer

Dalla Costa, Mariarosa (1938?–)   3081
Ital. feminist, educator, eco-feminism activist

Daly, Mary (1928–)   2623
Amer. educator, writer, theologian, feminist philosopher

Dane, Clemence (1888–1965) 1677
Eng. playwright, novelist, writer, actor; née Winifred Ashton; a.k.a. Diane Cortis; Academy Award, 1946

Dangarembga, Tsitsi (1959–) 4480
Zimb. playwright, writer

Danieli, Cecilia (1943–2008)   3401
Ital. business executive

Daniels, Sarah (1956–)   4360
Eng. playwright; London Theatre Critics Award, 1983; Bursary, Arts Council of Great Britain, 1985

Danielsson, Marie-Thérèse (1923–2003)   2449
Fr. writer, activist (anti-nuclear), activist (women's rights); w. Bengt D— (1921–1997), adventurer, anthropologist, writer, activist; Right Livelihood Award, 1991

Dann, Carrie (1928?–)   2624
Amer. rancher, activist (Native American rights); s. Mary D—*; Right Livelihood Award, 1993

Dann, Mary (1923–2005)   2450
Amer. activist (Native American rights), rancher; s. Carrie D—*; Right Livelihood Award, 1993

Danowitz, Jane (1949?–)   3890
Amer. political activist, nonprofit administrator; exec. dir., Women's Campaign Fund; director, Heritage Forests Campaign

Danticat, Edwidge (1969–)   4784
Haitian/Amer. novelist

D'Arcy, Margaretta (Ruth) (1934–)   2888
Ir. playwright; w. John Arden (playwright, author)

Dargan, Olive (1869–1968)   1358
Amer. poet, writer; née Tilford, pseud. Fielding Burke

D'Arusmont, Frances   *see* WRIGHT, FRANCES

Dashkova, Ekaterina Vorontsova, Princess (1743–1810)   644
Russ. civil servant, memoirist; companion to Catherine the Great*; first non-royal European woman to hold major public office; director of St. Petersburg Academy of Sciences, 1782–96; founder and president, Russian Academy of Sciences

Dasi, Binodini (1863–1941)   1294
Ind./Beng. actor, writer

Datini, Margherita (1360–1423)   241
Ital. letter writer; w. Francesco de Marco D—

Dauenhauer, Nora [Marks] (1927–)   2591
Amer. teacher, poet, cultural preservationist, scholar, dancer, linguist

Daughtrey, Martha Craig (1942–)   3331
Amer. jurist?, attorney

Daum, Meghan (1970–)   4814
Amer. journalist, novelist, public speaker

Davenport, Doris (1949–)   3891
Amer. poet, writer, educator, performance artist

Davey, Janet (1953–)   4172
Brit. writer

David-Néel, Alexandra (1868–1969)   1348
French author, lecturer, explorer, singer

Davidson, Janine (1967?–)   4745
Amer. defense theorist, aviator, educator, national security studies

Davidson, Laura Lee (1807–1949)   1372
Amer. educator, nature writer

Davidson, Lucretia Maria (1808–1825)   903
Amer. poet; s. Margaret D—*

Davidson, Margaret (1823–1838)   988
Amer. poet; s. Lucretia Maria D—*

Davidson, Sara (1947–)   3732
Amer. writer, journalist, screenwriter, radio host

Davies, Douglas *see* AUDELEY, ELEANOR

Daviot, Gordon (1896–1952)   1823
Scot. novelist, playwright; née Elizabeth Mackintosh; a.k.a. Josephine Tey

Davis, Adelle (1904–1974)   1992
Amer. nutritionist, writer; pseud. Jane Dunlap

Davis, Angela [Yvonne] (1944–)   3493
Amer. writer, political activist, educator; Int. Lenin Peace Prize, 1978

Davis, Bette (1908–1989)   2082
Amer. actor, screen; Academy Award, 1935, 1938; Emmy, 1979

Davis, Dorothy Salisbury (1916–)   2265
Amer. writer

Davis, Eisa (1983?–)   4951
Amer. playwright, poet, actor

Davis, Elizabeth Gould (1910–1974)   2124
Amer. writer, librarian

Davis, Laura (1956–)   4361
Amer. abuse counselor

Davis, Lydia (1947–)   3733
Amer. writer, translator; w. (1) Paul Auster (1947–), author; (2) Alan Cote, painter; MacArthur Genius

Davis, Nancy   *see* REAGAN, NANCY

Davis, Olena Kalytiak (1976?–)   4905
Amer. poet

Davis, Rebecca Harding (1831–1910)   1037
Amer. social critic, writer

Davis, Thadious M. (1944–) 3494
Amer. poet; educator, English

Davis-Floyd, Robbie (1951–)   4037
Amer. midwife, anthropologist

Davys, Mary (1674–1732)   517
Ir./Eng. shopkeeper, novelist, playwright

Day, Dorothy (1897–1980)   1846
Amer. writer, pacifist, religious activist, social worker; cofounder, *The Catholic Worker*; created network of Houses of Hospitality, organizer, Catholic Worker Movement; NWHF

Day, Lillian (1893–1991)   1768
Amer. writer; a.k.a. L— D— Lederer

Dayan, Yaël (1939–)   3136
Isr. writer, war correspondent; d. Moshe D— (military and political leader, 1915–81)

Dean, Louise (1970–)   4815
Eng./Fr. novelist

De Bary, Anna Bunston (1869–?)   1359
Eng. Poet

Deborah (fl. 1070s B.C.E.)   27
Isr. leader, prophet, judge; d. Abinoam, s. Barak, w. Lapidoth, gm. Tobit; savior of Israel

De Chatte, Mme.   *see* DESJARDINS, MARIE-CATHERINE

Decter, Midge (1927–)   2592
Amer. social critic, writer, editor; née Rosenthal

Ded, Lal (fl. 14th century?)   248
Ind. poet

Deen, Paula (1947–)   3734
Amer. cook, restauranteur, television personality; Emmy (2), 2007

Deetes, Tuenjai (1952?–)   4098
Thai social activist; cofounder, Hill Area Development Foundation (HADF), 1986; Goldman Environmental Prize, 1994

Deffand, Marie Anne, marquise du (1697–1780)   544
Fr. salonist, letter writer; a.s.a. Du Deffand, a.k.a. Marie Anne de Vichy Chamrond

DeGeneres, Ellen [Lee] (1958–)   4445
Amer. comedian, actor, television host; Emmy (11)

De Groen, Alma (1941–)   3251
N.Z./Aust. TV writer, playwright; Australian Writers Guild Award (1985); Canada Council grant (1970)

de Hoyos, Angela (1940–)   3187
Mex./Amer. poet, painter;
World Poetry Society Intercontinental Distinguished Service
Citation, 1970–71

de Kretser, Michelle (1958?–) 4444
Sri Lankan/Aust. novelist;
founding editor, *Australian
Women's Book Review* (1989)

De La Cruz, Jessie Lopez
(1919–)   2341
Amer. farmworker, union
organizer; founding member,
National Land for People,
1974; award, League of
Mexican-American Women,
1977

Delaney, Shelagh (1939–)   3137
Eng. TV & screen writer, playwright; DCAA

Delany, A. Elizabeth "Bessie"
(1891–1995)   1725
Amer. dentist; s. Sarah D—*;
second black female dentist
licensed in New York City
(1925)

Delany, Mary (1700–1788)   549
Eng. poet, letter writer,
painter; née Granville; a.k.a.
Pendarves

Delany, Sarah "Sadie"
(1889–1999)   1696
Amer. educator, high school;
s. Elizabeth D—*; first black
home economics teacher in a
New York City high school
1925

de Lavallade, Carmen
(1931–)   2754
Amer. dancer, choreographer,
actor; c. Janet Collins*; w.
Geoffrey Holder, theatrician,
painter

Delilah (fl. 1080s B.C.E.)   24
Philistine biblical figure; second w. Samson

Delmar, Viña (1905–1990)   2013
Amer. playwright; writer; née
Alvina Croter; m. Gray D—,
Amer. TV director

Delmhorst, Kris (1976?–)   4906
Amer. singer, songwriter, musician; w. Jeffrey Foucalt, Amer.
singer/songwriter

Del Ponte, Carla (1947–)   3735
Swiss lawyer; prosecutor,
Int. Criminal Tribunal for
Yugoslavis and for Rwandans,
1999; atty. Gen., Switzerland

Demarest, Mary Lee
(1857–1888)   1219
Ir. poet

de Matteo, Donna (1941–)   3252
Amer. playwright

DeMille, Agnes [George]
(1905–1993)   2012
Amer. dancer, choreographer,
writer; d. Cecil B. D— (film-

maker, 1881–1959); Tony,
1947, 1962

Deming, Alison Hawthorne
(1946–)   3647
Amer. poet, essayist; NEA,
1990, 1995

Deming, Barbara
(1917–1984)   2285
Amer. feminist, pacifist,
writer

de Moor, Margriet (1941–) 3253
Dutch writer

Dench, Judi (1934–)   2889
Eng. actor; w. Michael Williams (d. 2001), actor; m.
Flinty Williams (1973–),
actor; DBE, 1988; Oscar,
1998; Golden Globe, 1998,
2001; Olivier (7)

Deneuve, Catherine (1943–) 3402
Fr. actor, human right's
activist, philanthropist;
née C— Fabienne Dorl,ac;
d. Maurice Dorl,ac, actor,
& Ren,e D—, actor; m.
Christian Vadim, Chiara
Mastroianni, actors; Cesar,
1980, 1991

Denham, Alice (1933–)   2841
Amer. model, society figure,
writer

Dennie, Abigail Colman
(1715–1745)   576
Amer. poet; a.k.a. Celia; s.
Jane Turrell*

Deroine, Jeanne-Françoise
(1805–1894)   889
Fr. feminist

Derricotte, Toi (1941–)   3254
Amer. poet, educator; cofounder, Cave Canem, 1996;
NEA, Guggenheim

Dery, Dominika
(1975–)   4890–4891
Cuban economist, writer, journalist; a.k.a. D— Furmanov

Desai, Kiran (1971–)   4843
Brit. writer; d. Anita D— ,
writer; Booker Prize (2006)

Desbordes-Valmore, Marceline
[Félicité Josèphe] (1786–1859) 801
Fr. poet, actor

Deschryver, Christine Schuler
(1965?–)   4694
Cong. human rights activist

Deshoulières, Antoinette
(1638–1694)   469
Fr. author, poet; née Du
Ligier de la Garde, a.k.a.
The Tenth Muse, the French
Calliope

Desjardins, Marie-Catherine
(1632–1683)   460
Fr. poet, actor; a.k.a. M—
Hortense de Villedieu, Mme
De Chatte; probably a member
of Molière's theater company
(dramatist, 1622–73)

Detourbey, Jean
(1837–1908)   1078
Fr. society leader, writer; a.k.a.
Comtesse de Luynes; lover of
Louis-Napoleon Bonaparte III,
Alexandre Dumas fils, (1824–
1895; Fr. dramatist), and
Gustave Flaubert (1821–1880;
Fr. writer)

Deutsch, Babette
(1895–1974)   1808
Amer. translator, poet, novelist, literary critic; w. Avraham
Yarmolinsky (d. 1976; writer,
literary scholar)

Deutsch, Helene (1884–1982) 1608
Pol./Amer. psychiatrist, psychoanalyst, writer

Devers, Gail (1967–)   4746
Amer. athlete (runner); Olympic medalist in 100-meter
hurdles

Devi, Indra (1899–?)   1884
Russ./Amer. yogini, writer; née
Petersen; mn. Knauer

Devi, Sampat Pal (1960–)   4525
Ind. activist (political), health
care worker; founder of
Gulbai Gang (Pink Gang)

De Vinck, Catherine (1922–) 2425
Belg./Amer. poet

Devlin, Bernadette [Josephine]
(1947–)   3736
Ir. activist, political, politician; m. Róisín McAliskey
(political activist, 1971–);
Nationalist M.P., 1969–
1974

Devonshire, duchess of *see* CAVENDISH, GEORGIANA

DeWit, Antoinette (1923–)   2451
Amer. cookbook author, artist; founder, Enabled Artists
Guild, Oregon

De Wolfe, Elsie (1865–1950) 1311
Eng. society leader, actor,
writer; a.k.a. Lady Mendel

Dey, Judy Goldberg
(Contemporary–)   4977
Amer. researcher

Dhaliwal, Daljit (1962–)   4607
Eng./Amer. television commentator, journalist

Diamant, Anita (1951–)   4038
Amer. writer, journalist

Diamond, Selma (1920–1985) 2368
Can./Amer. scriptwriter, comedian

Diana, princess of Wales
(1961–1997)   4568
Eng. princess; née Lady
D— Frances Spenser

Dias, Alonzo *see* ERAUSO, CATALINA DE

Diaz, Cameron (1972–)   4857
Amer. actor, fashion model;
Golden Globe, 1999

Dicciani, Nance K.
(1948?–)   3822
Amer. chemical engineer, business executive

Dickinson, Emily [Elizabeth]
(1830–1886)   1024
Amer. poet; NWHF

Didion, Joan (1935–)   2925
Amer. scenarist, journalist, writer; w. John Gregory
Dunne (writer)

Didrikson Zaharias [Mildred Ella],
"Babe" (1914–1956)   2217
Amer. athlete (track); first
American to win the British
Women's Championship,
1947; Olympic champion,
1932, Women's Sports Hall of
Fame, 1980; NWHF; IWSHF,
1980

Dia, countess of *see* BEATRITZ
DE DIA

Diehl, Guida (1868–?)   1349
Ger. political activist

Dietrich, Marlene (1901–1992)1930
Ger./Amer. screen actor, singer

DiFranco, Ani (1970–)   4816
Amer. songwriter, singer

Dilke, Emilia, Lady
(1840–1904)   1093
Fr. art critic, literary critic,
political activist, painter; née
Emily Francis Strong, a.k.a.
E. F. S. Pattison and Francis
Pattison; w. Sir Charles D—

Dillard, Annie (1945–)   3563
Amer. writer, poet, magazine
editor; née A— Doak; w.
Richard Henry Wilde D—
Amer. poet, critic, translator;
Pulitzer, 1975

Diller, Phyllis (1917–)   2286
Amer. writer, comedian,
pianist

DiManno, Rosie
(Contemporary–)   4978
Can. columnist, feminist

Dinesen, Isak (1885–1962)   1627
Danish/S. Afr. writer; a.k.a.
Baroness Karen Blixen,
Christentze D—; ex-w. Baron
Bror Blizen-Finecke; founding
member, Danish Academy;
Ingenio et Arti Medal from
King Frederick IX of Demark, 1950; The Golden
Laurels, 1952; Hans Christian Andersen Prize, 1955;
Danish Critics' Prize, 1957;
Henri Nathansen Memorial
Fund Award, 1957

Ding Ling *see* TING LING

Dinnerstein, Dorothy (1923–) 2452
Amer. author, psychologist,
educator, feminist

Diogo, Luísa Dias (1958–)   4446
Moz. politician, anti-poverty and health advocate,

economist; Prime Minister of Mozambique, 2004– (first woman to hold post)

Dion, Céline [Marie Claudette] (1968–)   4766
Can. singer; Grammy (5); Golden Globe (2); Oscar, 1992, 1998; Governor General's Award (1990)

DiPerna, Diane (fl. 1990s)   4963
Amer. journalist, politician, nonfiction writer, environmental activist

DiPerna, Paula (1949–)   **3215**
Amer. nonfiction writer; Ford, 1981

Di Prima, Diane (1934–)   2890
Amer. editor, playwright, writer, poet

Dirie, Waris (1965–)   4695
Somalian model, public servant, women's rights activist; special ambassador to United Nations

Dix, Dorothea [Lynde] (1802–1887)   872
Amer. humanitarian, reformer; NWHF, 1980

Dix, Dorothy (1861–1951)   1265
Amer. journalist, columnist; née Elizabeth Meriwether; mn. Gilmer

Dixon, Marlene (1936–)   2974
Amer. feminist, educator, sociology

Dobree, Henrietta [Octavia de Lisle] (1831–1894)   1038
? hymnist

Dodge, Mabel (1879–1962)   1524
Amer. arts patron, writer; née Ganson; mn. Luhan

Dodge, Mary [Elizabeth] Mapes (1831–1905)   1039
Amer. editor, writer

Dodge, Mary Abigail *see* HAMILTON, GAIL

Dodson, Lisa (1952–)   4099
Amer. researcher, educator (sociology); grand. Ella Reeve Bloor (a.k.a. Mother Bloor; 1862–1951), Am labor organizer

Dohm, Hedwig (1833–1919)   1050
Ger. feminist

Doi, Takako (1928–)   2625
Jap. politician, lawyer; first Japanese woman to lead a major political party; Chair Japan Socialist Party, 1986–1991

Dolan, Jill (1957–)   4403
Amer. critic, drama

Dole, Elizabeth Hanford (1936–)   2975
Amer. nonprofit administrator; w. Robert "Bob" D— (1923– ; lawyer and politician, U.S. senator); NWHF

Dolliver, Clara (fl. 1874–1891–)   1429
Amer. poet

Dolson, Hildegarde (1908–1981)   2083
Amer. fiction writer; a.k.a. Hildegarde Lockridge

Domini, Amy (1952–)   4100
Amer. financial advisor, human rights activist

Domna H. (fl. 12th century)   207
Fr. trobairitz

Donnelly, Liza (1955–)   4297
Amer. educator, cartoonist, author, illustrator; w. Michael Maslin, cartoonist

Donoghue, Emma (1969–)   4785
Ir./Can. writer

Doody, Margaret Anne (1939–)   3138
Can. educator, literature; Guggenheim, 1978

Doolittle, Hilda (1886–1961)   1650
Amer. poet; a.k.a. H.D. and Edith Gray; mn. Aldington

Doress-Worters, Paula B. (1938–)   3082
Amer. writer, feminist, social activist, educator, women's studies; m. Hannah Doress, activist, feminist, publicist; c. Frieda Forman, educator, editor, author; cofounder, Boston Women's Health Book Collective (Our Bodies, Our Selves)

Dorr, Julia [Caroline] (1825–1913)   999
Amer. poet, writer; née Ripley

Dorset, F. H. *see* LLEWELLYN-THOMAS, BEATRICE

Dostoevsky, Anna (1846–1918)   1142
Russ. diarist; w. Feodor D— (novelist, 1821–81)

Doten, Elizabeth (1829–?)   1013
Amer. poet; a.s.a. Lizzie D—

Doubiago, Sharon (1946–)   3648
Amer. essayist, poet, fiction writer

Doudney, Sarah (1843–1926)   1113
Eng. writer, poet

Douglas, Alford, Lady *see* CUSTANCE, OLIVE

Douglas, Anne *see* HOWARD, ANNE

Douglas, Eleanor *see* AUDELEY, ELEANOR

Douglas, Helen Gahagan (1900–1980)   1897
Amer. lecturer, politician, actor, writer; w. Melvyn D— (actor); U.S. delegate to United Nations, 1946; U.S. Representative, D-Calif, 1945–1951

Douvan, Elizabeth [Ann Malcolm] (1926–2002)   2545
Amer. psychologist

Dove, Rita Frances (1952–)   4101
Amer. novelist, educator (English), poet; w. Fred Viebahn (German novelist); Pulitzer (poetry), 1987; U.S. Poet Laureate, 1994–95; NBA, 1991

Dow, Dorothy [Minerva] (1903–1979)   1968
Amer. poet

Dowd, Maureen (1952–)   4102
Amer. columnist; Pulitzer Prize, 1999

Dowd, Nancy E. (1949–)   3893
Amer. educator (law), feminist

Dowling, Colette (1938–)   3083
Amer. writer

Dowriche, Anne (1550?–1638?)   349
Eng. poet; s. Pearse Edgecombe of Devon

Drabble, Margaret (1939–)   3139
Eng. writer; s. A. S. Byatt*

Drakulić, Slavenka (1949–)   3894
Yug. feminist, essayist; a.s.a. Drakulic-Ilic; cofounder of the first feminist group in Yugoslavia; Fulbright, 1990; Independent Foreign Fiction Award, 1990

Draper, Mary (1718?–1810)   582
Amer. patriot

Dreifus, Claudia (1944–)   3495
Amer. labor organizer, writer, lecturer, editor

Drescher, Fran (1957–)   4404
Amer. comedian, actor, TV producer

Dressel, Brigit (1961–1987)   4569
Ger. athlete

Dresselhaus, Mildred Spiewak (1930–)   2702
Amer. physicist, educator; w. Gene D— (physicist, educator); National Medal of Science, 1990

Dressler, Marie (1873–1934)   1412
Can. actor; née Koerber; Academy Award, 1931

Drew, Elizabeth (1887–1965)   1662
Eng./Amer. literary critic, writer

Drexler, Rosalyn (1926–)   2546
Amer. playwright, novelist, sculptor; a.k.a. Julia Sorel; cofounder, Women's Theater Council (1972); Obie, 1964, 1979, 1985; Emmy, 1974; Rockefeller, 1965; Guggenheim, 1970–1

Drinker, Sophie Hutchinson (1888–1968)   1678
Amer. musician, writer

Driscoll, Louise (1875–1957)   1456
Amer. poet, writer

Droste-Hülshoff, Anette Elizabeth von (1797–1848)   852
Ger. poet, novelist

Drouet, Juliette (1806–1883)   894
Fr. society leader; consort of Victor Hugo (1802–85; poet, dramatist, novelist)

du Maurier, Daphne (1907–1989)   2063
Eng. playwright, writer; gd. George d— (singer, author, artist); d. Gerald d— (actormanager) and Muriel (actor); C.B.E., 1969; NBA, 1938

Du Pré, Jacqueline (1945–1987)   3564
Brit. cellist; s. Hilary D— (musician, 1942–)

Duarte, Jessie (1953–)   4173
S. Afr. public servant, poet, political activist

DuBois, Ellen Carol (1947–)   3737
Amer. educator (history), nonfiction writer; Ford, 1974; Rockefeller, 1978

Duchess of Saxe-Coburg-Saafeld (*see* AUGUSTA)

Duclaux, Anges Mary Frances *see* ROBINSON, A[GNES] MARY

Dudar, Helen (1908–2002)   2084
Amer. writer, journalist

Dudevant, Baronness *see* SAND, GEORGE

Duehring, Cindy (1962–1999)   4608
Amer. activist (health); née Froeschle; founder and director, Environmental Access Research Network (EARN), 1986 (now a wing of the Chemical Injury Information Network (CIIN)

Duff, Esther Lillian (fl. 1910s)   2125
Eng. poet

Dufferin, Helen, Lady (1807–1867)   900
Ir. songwriter; née Blackwood, a.k.a. Helen Selina Sheridan, countess of Dufferin and Gifford; pseud. Impulsia Gushington

Duffy, Carol Ann (1955–)   4298
Scot./Eng. poet, playwright, writer; ex-p. Jackie Kay, poet; OBE, 1981; CBE, 2002

Duffy, Maureen (1933–)   2842
Eng. novelist, playwright

Dugaw, Dianne (1948–)   3823
Amer. educator, nonfiction writer

Dugdale, Bridget Rose (1941–)3255
Ir. revolutionary

Dukakis, Olympia (1931–)   2755
Amer. actor, theater producer; fdr., Actor's Company (Boston), Whole Theatre Company (Montclair, NY); Oscar, 1987; Golden Globe, 1988

Duke, [Anna Marie] "Patty" (1946–)   3649
Amer. actor, mental health activist; ex-w. (3) John Astin,

actor; Oscar, 1962; Emmy (3); Golden Globe, 1962, 1969

Dukes, Marie, Dame *see* RAMBERT, MARIE

Dunant, Sarah (1950–)   3961
Eng. broadcaster, novelist, critic

Dunayevskaya, Raya (1910–1987)   2126
Ukrainian/Amer. philosopher, author; founder of Marist Humanism philosophy in USA

Dunbar, Andrea (1961–1991) 4570
Eng. playwright

Dunbar, Roxanne (1939–)   3140
Amer. political activist, writer

Dunbar-Nelson, Alice [Ruth] (1875–1935)   1457
Amer. teacher, journalist, social worker, editor, author; née Moore; w. Paul Laurence D— (1872–1906; poet)

Dunbar-Ortiz, Roxanne (1938–)   3084
Amer. educator, writer, historian, activist (human rights)

Duncan, Isadora (1878–1927) 1512
Amer. dancer, dance teacher, writer; innovator of modern dance

Duncan, Sheena (1932–)   2792
S. Afr. anti-apartheid activist, public servant; d. Jean Sinclair, fdr. Black Sash; pres., Black Sash

Dungy, Camille T. (1972–)   4858
Amer. poet, educator, writing; NEA

Dunlap, Jane *see* DAVIS, ADELLE

Dunlop, Becky Norton (1951–)   4039
Amer. consultant, lecturer, author, public servant

Dunn, [Patricia] [Irene] Irina (1950?–)   3962
Aust. politician, prison reform activist, filmmaker, documentary, writer; China-born; Senator, 1988–90

Dunn, Jennifer (1941–2007) 3256
Amer. politician; congresswoman (R- Washington), 1993–2005

Dunn, Katherine "Karen" (1945–)   3565
Amer. writer; Rockefeller

Dunn, Lydia [Selina], Dame (1940–)   3188
Hong Konger stateswoman, business executive; a.k.a. "The Iron Lady of the East"; C.B.E., 1983

Dunn, Nell (1936–)   2976
Eng. playwright; Blackburn, 1981; Society of West End Theatre Award, 1981

Dupin, Amandine Aurore Lucile *see* SAND, GEORGE

Durant, Ariel (1898–1981)   1864–1865
Russ./Amer. author, historian; née Ada Kaufman; w. Will D— (historian, 1885–1981); Pulitzer, 1968; Presidential Medal of Freedom, 1977

Duras, Marguerite (1914–1996)   2218
Indochinese/Fr. playwright, TV & screen writer, novelist; née Donadieu; w. Robert Antelme (1; writer); Dionys Moscolo (2; philosopher and critic); Prix Jean Cocteau; Grand Prix and Académie du Cinema, 1992; Prix Goncourt, 1984)

Durham, Helen *see* HATHAWAY, HELEN

Durham, Jane Lazarre *see* LAZARRE, JANE

Durham, Judith (1943–)   3403
Aust. singer, songwriter, pianist; née Cock; w. Ron Edgeworth (d. 1994), pianist; OAM (Medal of the Order of Australia)

Duse, Eleanora [Guilia Amalia] (1859–1924)   1246
Ital. actor; lover of Gabriele D'Annunzio (1863–1938; novelist, poet, dramatist, soldier)

Dwight, Mary Ann (1806–1858)   895
Amer. writer

Dworkin, Andrea (1946–2005)3738
Amer. journalist, author, feminist, social critic; née Spiegel

Dworkin, Susan (fl. 1970s–90s)   4817
Amer. author

Dyer, Mary (fl. 1630s–d. 1660) 429
Eng./Amer. Quaker martyr; née Barrett, a.s.a. Dyre

Dyson, Esther (1951–)   4040
Swiss/Amer. journalist, entrepreneur, philanthropist, commentator, digital technology; d. Freeman D— , physicist, and Verena Huber-D—, mathematician; s. George D—, digital technology historian

E

Eaglen, Jane (1960–)   4526
Eng. opera singer

Eane, Elizabeth *see* ABERGAVENNY, FRANCES

Earhart, Amelia (1897–1937) 1847
Amer. writer, women's rights activist, pacifist, aviator, social worker; w. George P. Putnam (American publisher); first woman to fly across Atlantic (1928) and to fly solo across Atlantic (1932); first person to fly solo from Hawaii to San Francisco (1935); set cross-country speed record; cofounder Ninety-Nines, first women's aviator organization (1930); first woman to receive French Legion of Honor, Distinguished Flying Cross 1932; Women's Sports Hall of Fame, 1980; NWHF; IWSHF, 1980

Earle, Sylvia A. (1935–)   2926
Amer. nonfiction writer, marine biologist, explorer, environmental activist; a.k.a. Her Deepness; Conservation Service Award, U.S. Dept. of Interior, 1970

Earp, Josephine "Josie" Sarah "Sadie" (1861?–1944)   1266
Amer. dancer, actor; née Marcus; w. Wyatt E—

Eastman, Crystal (1881–1928) 1568
Amer. attorney; industrial safety pioneer; NWHF

Eastwood, Alice (1859–1953) 1247
Can./Amer. nonfiction writer, botanist, botany curator; honorary pres. of Seventh Int. Botanical Congress, 1950

Ebadi, Shirin (1947–)   3739
Iran. activist, human rights, lawyer, judge; Iran's first female judge; Nobel Peace Prize, 2003 (3rd Muslim and 1st female Muslim to have won); Nobel Peace, 2003

Eberhardt, Isabelle (1877–1904)   1491
Russ. adventurer

Eccles, Visxountess *see* HYDE, MARY

Eckenstein, Lina (1857–1931) 1220
Amer./Can. writer, educator

Eddy, Mary Baker (1821–1910) 982
Amer. pastor, writer, theologian; founder, Christian Science, 1866, and *The Christian Science Monitor*, 1908; NWHF

Edelman, Marian Wright (1939–)   3141
Amer. lawyer, children's rights advocate, nonprofit administrator; founder, Children's Defense Fund, 1973; Gandhi Peace Award 1989; MacArthur, 1985; NAACP Roy Wilkins Civil Rights Award 1984; Rockefeller, 1981; NWHF

Edelstein, Jean (1927–)   2593
Amer. painter, performance artist; w. Sy E—, graphic designer, photographer; m. Barbara E— , artist, sculptor, and Bruce E— , sculptor, painter; m-in-law, Jian-Jun Chang, artist; NEA, 1998

Eden, Emily (1797–1869)   853
Eng./Ind. novelist; a.k.a. Lady Auckland; d. William E—, 1st baron of Auckland, s. George E—, earl of Auckland

Ederle, Gertrude [Caroline] (1906–2003)   2045
Amer. athlete (swimmer); first woman to swim the English Channel, 1926; Olympic medallist (three medals at the 1924 Paris Olympics: a gold in the 4x100-meter relay and bronze in the 100 and 400 freestyle) ; IWSHF, 1980

Edgeworth, Maria (1767–1849) 734
Ir. essayist, novelist

Edna (fl. 720s B.C.E.)   44
Mede biblical figure; w. Raguel, m. Sarah

Edson, Margaret (1961–)   4571
Amer. playwright, educator, public school; Pulitzer,1999

Edwards, Amelia (1831–1889) 1040
Eng. writer, Egyptologist

Edwards, Anne (1927–)   2594
Amer. writer, scenarist

Edwards, Betty (1926–)   2547
Amer. author, researcher, artist

Edwards, Marie (1926?–)   2548
Amer. psychologist; née Babare

Edwards, Sarah Pierpont (1710–1758)   567
Amer. Puritan mystic, householder; great-gd. Rev. Thomas Hooker (English-born American colonizer and cleric, 1586?–1647; founder, city of Hartford, Conn., 1636), d. James Pierpont, a.s.a. Pierrepont (pastor and cofounder of Yale college), w. Jonathan Edwards (American theologian and philosopher, 1703–1758; president, College of New Jersey [now Princeton], 1703–1758)

Egan, Jennifer (1962–)   4609
Amer. novelist

Egburg (fl. 8th century)   137
Eng. nun

Egeria (fl. 380s–d. 384)   108
Span. abbess, writer (travel); a.k.a. Aetheria

Egeria *see* HEMANS, FELICIA

Egerton, Sarah F[yge Field] (1670–1723)   514
Eng. poet; possibly youngest feminist polemicist on record

Eglui, Ellen (fl. 1880s–)   1543
Amer. inventor; invented the clothes wringer for washing machines; sold the patent rights in 1888 for $18.00

Ehrenreich, Barbara (1941–) 3257
Amer. columnist, author; Guggenheim, 1987

Ehrlich, Emma (1893–?) 1769
Amer. secretary; long-time secretary to Henrietta Szold; considerably her junior

Eifuku, Empress (1271–1342) 225
Jap. poet, noble

Eilberg, Amy (1954–) 4241
Amer. rabbi; first woman rabbi ordained by Conservative movement (1993)

Eisenhower, Mamie [Geneva] Doud (1896–1979) 1824
Amer. society leader, first lady; w. Dwight "Ike" D. E— (American general and politician, 1890–1969; 34th U.S. president, 1953–61)

Eisler, Riane [Tennenhaus] (1931–) 2756
Aus./Cuban/Amer. author, social historian; w. David Loye (philosopher, author); founder, Center for Partnership Studies, International Partnership Network

Elders, Joycelyn "Minnie" (1933–) 2843
Amer. civil servant, pediatrician, endocrinologist; U.S. Surgeon General, 1993–1994

Eleanor of Aquitaine (1122?–1204) 183
Fr./Eng. queen; w. Louis VII of France (1) and Henry II of England (2), m. Richard I (the Lion Heart) and John of England

Elia, Bridget see LAMB, MARY
Elion, Gertrude B. (1918–1999) 2312
Amer. chemist & biologist; first woman elected to the National Inventor's Hall of Fame (1991); Nobel Prize in physiology and chemistry, 1988, with George Hitchens (1905–1998), for their discoveries of important principles for drug treatment; NWHF

Eliot, George (1819–1880) 955
Eng. writer; née Marian Evans; mn. Cross

Eliott, Ethelinda see BEERS, ETHEL
Elisabeth, Saint (fl. 20s B.C.E.–? C.E.) 78
Judean saint; w. Zechariah, m. John the Baptist, c. Virgin Mary*

Elisabeth of Brandenburg (1485–1545) 284
Ger. noble; s. Christian II of Denmark, w. Joachim I (elector of Brandenburg), m. Elizabeth of Braunschweig*

Elizabeth see ARNIM, MARY

Elizabeth I of England, Queen (1533–1603) 334
Eng. queen; a.k.a. Elizabeth Tudor; d. Henry VIII of England (1491–1597) and Ann Boleyn,* half s. Mary I of England* and Edward VI (1537–53; king of England, 1447–53), gd. Elizabeth of York,* first c. Mary, Queen of Scots*

Elizabeth II of Great Britain, Queen (1926–) 2549
Eng. queen, spokesperson; d. Queen Mother Elizabeth* and King George VI (1895–1952); w. Phillip Mountbatten, duke of Edinburgh (1921–)

Elizabeth, Caroline Amelia (1768–1821) 737
Ger./Eng. queen; second w. George IV of England (1762–1830), m. Charlotte Augusta (1762–1830)

Elizabeth, Helene Marie Phillipine (1764–1794) 720
Fr. noble, French; s. Louis XVI, king of France (1754–93)

Elizabeth, Queen Mother (1900–2002) 1898
Eng. queen; née Lady E— Angela Marguerite Bowes-Lyon; w. King George VI (1895–1952), m. Elizabeth II*

Elizabeth of Braunschweig (1510–1558) 302
Ger. noble; d. Elisabeth of Brandenburg*, w. Erich, duke of Braunschweig-Calenberg, m. Anna Maria of B—*

Elizabeth of Romania see SYLVA, CARMEN

Elizabeth of Thuringia, Saint (1206/07–1231) 214
Ger. queen, Franciscan tertiary; d. Andrew II of Hungary (1205–35), w. Ludwig (landgrave of Thuringia)

Elizabeth of York (1465/66–1503) 271
Eng. queen, poet; d. Edward IV, king of England (1442–83) and Elizabeth Woodville-Grey,* m. Henry VII, king of England (1485–1509), gm. Elizabeth I*

Elkins, Caroline (1969–) 4786
Amer. educator, history, author; Pulitzer, 2006

Ellerbee, Linda [Jane] (1944–) 3496
Amer. journalist; née Smith; Peabody Award, 1992

Elliot, Jean (1727–1805) 599
Scot. poet, songwriter; a.s.a. Jane E—

Elliott, Anna (fl. 1770s) 747
Amer. householder

Elliott, Charlotte (1789–1871) 809
Eng. hymnist

Elliott, Maxine (1871–1940) 1388
Amer. actor, theater owner-manager

Ellis, Alice Thomas (1932–2005) 2793
Brit. author; a.k.a. Anna Haycraft

Ellis, Sarah (1812–1872) 918
Eng. writer, missionary; w. William E—; cofounder, Rawdon House School for Girls

Ellison, Katherine (1957–) 4405
Amer. journalist, author, consultant; Pulitzer, 1986

Ellman, Lucy (1956–) 4362
Amer./Scot. novelist; d. Richard E—, biographer; w. Todd McEwan, Amer. Writer

Elmendorf, Mary J[ohnson] (fl. 1920s) 2369
Amer. poet

El Moutawakel, Nawal (1962–) 4610
Mor. athlete (hurdler); first Muslim, Arab and African woman to Olympic champion; minister of sports, 2007–; Olympic Gold, 1984; IWSHF, 2006

Elstob, Elizabeth (1683–1756) 528
Eng. governess, Anglo-Saxon scholar; a.k.a. The Saxon Lady; n. Rev. Charles E—

Eltahawy, Mona (1967–) 4747
Egyp./Amer. journalist, editor, lecturer, commentator

Elwell, Sue Levi (1948–) 3824
Amer. rabbi; cofounder & director, L.A. Jewish Feminist Center; assistant director of the Union of American Hebrew Congregations' Pennsylvania region

Emanual, Lynn (1949–) 3895
Amer. poet; NEA

Embree, Alice (1945?–) 3566
Amer. political activist, feminist

Emecheta, Buchi (1944–) 3497
Nigerian/Eng. novelist

Emerson, Claudia (1957–) 4406
Amer. poet, educator, magazine editor; Poet Laureate of VA, 2008; Pulitzer, 2006

Emerson, Jo Ann (1950–) 3963
Amer. politician; w. Bill Emerson (1938–1996), Amer. Politician; U.S. Representative (R-MO), 1996–

Emerson, Mary Moody (1774–1863) 763
Amer. intellectual; a. (and mentor) Ralph Waldo

E— (philosopher, essayist and poet, 1803–82)

Emilia see STOCKTON, ANNIS
Emon, Akazome (fl. 1000s–1010) 168
Jap. poet; d. Taira no Kanemori (poet, d. 990); w. Oe no Masahira (scholar, 952–1012); great-gm. Oe no Masafusa (scholar, 1041–1111)

Emshwiller, Carol (1921–) 2397
Amer. writer; née Fries

Enclos, Ninon de l' see LENCLOS, NINON DE

English, Deirdre [Elena] (1948–) 3825
Amer. editor, writer; d. Maurice English (poet and publisher); First Prize at the, Film Festival for Peace in Vietnam, 1972

Enheduanna (2354?— B.C.E.?) 4
Sumerian moon priestess; a.s.a. En Hedu'anna; d. King Sargon of Agade (2334–2279 B.C.E.); first writer whose name and work has been preserved

Enright, Anne (1962–) 4611
Ir. writer; Booker Prize, 2007

Ensler, Eve (1953–) 4174
Amer. actor, feminist, playwright; founder and artistic director of V-Day (www.vday.org); Obie, 1996; Guggenheim Fellowship, 1999; Obie, 1996

Ephelia (fl. 1640s–d. 1681?) 474
Eng. poet; possibly the daughter of Katharine Phillips*

Ephelia see PHILIPS, JOAN

Ephron, Delia (1944?–) 3498
Amer. writer, humorist; s. Nora E—*; d. Henry & Phoebe Ephron, screenwriters

Ephron, Nora (1941–) 3258
Amer. writer, screenwriter; w. Dan Greenberg, novelist (1), Carl Bernstein, investigative reporter (2), Nicholas Pileggi, crime journalist/screenwriter (3); s. Delia E—*; d. Henry & Phoebe Ephron, screenwriters

Epstein, Cynthia Fuchs (1933–) 2844
Amer. educator (sociology), researcher

Erauso, Catalina de (1585–post-1624) 392
Span. soldier, adventurer; a.k.a. Antonia de E— (?) and Alonzo Dias

Erbe, Bonnie (1953?–) 4174.1
Amer. Journalist, lawyer, TV host

Erde, Betty Skelton (1926–)   2550
Amer. auto racer, pilot; auto
industry's first female test
driver, in 1954; the first
woman to set a world land
speed record in 1956 (145
mph at Daytona Beach); and
then the world land speed
record for women in 1965,
hitting 315.72 mph at Bonn-
eville.; 5th woman inductee in
Motorsports Hall of Fame of
America; National Aviation
Hall of Fame, 2005

Erdrich, Louise (1954–)   4242
Amer. poet, newspaper
editor, novelist; née Karen
L— E—; w. Michael Dorris
(1945–1997; writer); NEA,
1982; NBCCA, fiction, 1984;
Guggenheim, 1985–86

Erinna (fl. 610s–d. 595 B.C.E.)   47
Greek poet

Eristi-Aya (1790?–1745 B.C.E.)   12
Mesopotamian letter writer; d.
Zimri-Lim

Ertük, Yakin (1961?–)   4572
Turk. government official,
activist (women's rights),
educator; Special Rapporteur
on Violence against Women
for UN

Eschenbach, Maria von Ebner
(1830–1916)   1025
Aus. novelist; née Dubsky

Escot, Pozzi (1933–)   2845
Peru. Composer

Espinosa, María (1939–)   3142
Amer. novelist, poet, translator, teacher; née Paula
Cronbach; w. (1) Mario Espinosa Wellmann, Chilean writer

Esquivel, Laura (1950–)   3964
Mex. novelist

Essbaum, Jill Alexander
(1971–)   4844
Amer./Swiss poet

Essex, Lady   see WALSINGHAM,
FRANCES

Estaugh, Elizabeth Haddon
(1680–1762)   524
Eng./Amer. Quaker activist,
proprietor; founder, city of
Haddonfield, New Jersey;
heroine of Longfellow's
"Tales of a Wayside Inn"
(Amer. poet and translator,
1807–82)

Este, Anne d'
(1531–post-1563)   333
Ital./Fr. noble; a.k.a. duchess of
Guise; grandn. Isabella* and
Beatrice* d'E—, gd. Lucrezia
Borgia* and Alfonso d'E—, d.
Renée of France* and Ercole
d'E—, w. François de Lorraine
(2nd duke of Guise), friend of
Olimpia Morata*

Este, Beatrice d' (1475–1497)   278
Ital. noble; a.k.a. duchess of
Milan; s. Isabella d'E—,* w.
Ludovico Sforza Il Moro,
duke of Milan; great a. Anne
d'E—*

Este, Isabella d' (1474–1530)   276
Ital. art patron, letter writer,
noble; a.k.a. marquise of
Mantua; d. Ercole I, duke
of Ferrara and Leonora of
Aragon, s. Beatrice d'E—,* w.
Francesco Gonzaga, marquise
of Mantua, s.-in-law Elisabetta Gonzaga* and Lucrezia
Borgia,* great aunt of Anne
d'E—*

Estés, Clarissa Pinkola
(1945–)   3567
Amer. storyteller, ethnologist,
writer, Jungian psychoanalyst,
poet

Esther (fl. 510s–d. 465 B.C.E.)   56
Isr./Persian queen; a.k.a.
Hadassah; d. Abihail, c. and
adopted d. Mordecai, second
w. Ahaseurus (519?–465
B.C.E., king of Persia, a.k.a.
Xerxes I)

Etcoff, Nancy L. (1955–)   4299
Amer. nonfiction writer, psychologist

Etessami, Parvin (1907–1940)   2064
Iran. poet; d. Etesamolmolk,
publisher

Etherell, Elizabeth   see WARNER,
SUSAN

Etheridge, Melissa (1961–)   4573
Amer. singer, human right's
activist, songwriter; Oscar,
2006; Grammy, 1992, 1994

Ettore, Barbara (1951?–)   4041
Amer. private investigator,
market researcher, financial
writer

Eugene-Richard, Margie
(1942–)   3332
Amer. environmental activist,
teacher, middle school; fdr.,
Concerned Citizens of Norco,
1989; Goldman Environmen-
tal Prize, 2004

Eusebia   see THRYNNE, FRANCES

Evans, Augusta [Jane]
(1835–1909)   1063
Amer. writer; w. Wilson

Evans, Edith [Mary], Dame (1888–
1976)   1679
Eng. actor; C.B.E.

Evans, Mari (1923–)   2453
Amer. educator, writer, poet

Evans, Marian   see ELIOT,
GEORGE

Evatt, Elizabeth (1933–)   2846
Aust. jurist; first female
judge of an Australian federal court

Eve (pre–4000 B.C.E.)   1
biblical figure; w. Adam; m.
Cain, Abel and Seth, ancestor
of Christ, gm. Enoch, child of
Cain; first woman

Evelyn, Mary (1634–1709)   464
Eng. writer

Evert Lloyd, Chris[tine Marie]
(1954–)   4243
Amer. athlete (tennis); w.
John L— (tennis player);
Wimbledon singles (1974,
1976, 1981); U.S. Open Singles (6; 1975–82) ; IWSHF,
1981

F

Fabien, Michèle (1945–1999)   3568
Belg. playwright

Fadiman, Anne (1953–)   4175
Amer. essayist, book editor,
journalist; d. Clifton F—
(writer, editor, 1904–99)

Fairless, Michael   see BARBER,
MARGARET

Fairley, Darlene (1943–)   3404
Amer. politician; Wash. State
Senator (D), 1994–

Fairstein, Linda A. (1947–)   3741
Amer. activist, attorney, crime
writer

Falconar, Harriet (1775–?)   768
Eng. poet; s. Maria F—*

Falconar, Maria (1772–?)   759
Eng. poet; s. Harriet F—*

Falk, Marcia [Lee] (1946–)   3650
Amer. poet, liturgist,
translator, painter, lecturer,
teacher of creative writing &
Jewish studies; Fulbright

Falkland, viscountess of   see
CAREW, ELIZABETH

Fallaci, Oriana (1929–2006)   2656
Ital. writer, journalist

Faller, Heather Roote
(1958?–)   4447
Amer. poet

Faludi, Susan (1959–)   4481
Amer. feminist, nonfic-
tion writer; Pulitzer, 1991;
NBCCA, 1991

Fane, Violet (1843–1905)   1114
Eng. poet; née Lamb, a.k.a.
Lady Mary Montgomery Currie

Fanshawe, Ann, Lady
(1625–1680)   449
Eng. author; née Harrison;
w. Sir Richard F— (diplomat,
author)

Fanshawe, Catherine Marie
(1765–1834)   726
Eng. painter, poet

Farabough, Laura (1957?–)   4407
Amer. playwright, stage designer, stage director, artist

Faraday, Ann (1935–)   2927
Amer. dream researcher, psychologist

Farenthold, Sissy [Frances]
(1926–)   2551
Amer. administrator, lawyer,
politician; née Tarlton; state
house of representatives, D-
Texas, 1968–1972

Farhoud, Abla (1945–)   3569
Lebanese/Can. playwright

Farmer, Fannie [Merritt]
(1857–1915)   1221
Amer. chef, writer; founder,
Miss Farmer's School of
Cookery, Boston, 1902

Farnese, Giulia (1476–1524)   277
Ital. noble; reputed to have
been the mistress of Pope Alexander VI

Farnham, Eliza (1815–1864)   928
Amer. writer, feminist; née
Burhans

Farrar, Eliza Ware
(1791–1870)   822
Fr./Amer. author; née Elizabeth
Rotch, a.k.a. Mrs. John F—

Farro, Maria Elena Foronda
(1959–)   4482
Peru. sociologist, environ-
mental activist; fdr., Natura;
Goldman Environmental
Prize, 2003

Farrokhzad, Forough
(1935–1967)   2928
Iran. poet

Faschinger, Lilian (1950–)   3965
Aus./Fr. poet, novelist, short
story writer

Fasig, Lisa Biank (1962–)   4612
Amer. reporter

Faugères, Margaretta Van Wyck
(1771–1801)   755
Amer. essayist, poet; née
Bleecker; d. Ann Eliza
Bleecker*

Faulks, Frederick, Mrs.   see GAR-
RISON, THEODOSIA

Faure, Elie (1875–1937)   1458
Fr. historian, art critic

Fauset, Crystal Bird
(1894–1965)   1792
Amer. civil rights activist, politician; the first black woman
to be elected to a state legislature (D-PA), 1938

Fausto-Sterling, Anne
(1944–)   3499
Amer. biologist, writer, educator; p. Paula Vogel*

Fawcett, Millicent Garrett, Dame
(1847–1929)   1150
Eng. economist, suffragist;
s. Elizabeth G— Anderson
(1836–1917), physician, hospital administrator

Fedele, Cassandra
(1465–1558)   272
Ital. scholar; w. Johannes
Maria Mapellus

Fee, Elizabeth (1946–)   3651
Ir./Amer. consultant, feminist
scholar, researcher, educator
(history)

Feinberg, Leslie (1949–)   3896
Amer. nonfiction writer

Feinstein, Dianne (1933–)   2848
Amer. politician; née Goldman; U.S. Senator (D-CA),
1992– , mayor of San
Francisco, 1978–1988; first
woman to represent California
in U.S. Senate

Feldt, Gloria (1942–)   3333
Amer. administrator (NGO);
pres., Planned Parenthood,
1995–

Felkin, Ellen Thorneycroft   see
FOWLER, ELLEN

Felton, Rebecca Latimer (1835–
1930)   1064
Amer. author, teacher,
reformer, politician; first
woman to serve in the U.S.
Senate (GA; for two days in
November 1922; she was also
the oldest entering freshman
senator)

Feng Meng-lung (1574–1645)   380
Chin. poet

Fenwick, Millicent [Hammond]
(1910–1992)   2127
Amer. politician, editor;
state general assembly,
1967–1973; U.S. House of
Representatives, (R-NJ),
1975–1983

Ferber, Edna (1887–1968)   1663
Amer. playwright, novelist,
scenarist; Pulitzer, 1925

Fergus, Pamelia Dillin
(1924–1987)   2482
Amer. homesteader, pioneer

Ferguson, Anita Perez
(1960?–)   4527
Amer. lecturer, journalist,
radio, public servant; pres.,
NWPC, 1995–99

Ferguson, Elizabeth Graeme
(1737–1801)   624
Amer. diarist, letter writer,
poet, translator, society leader;
a. Anna Young Smith*

Ferguson, Kathy E. (1950–)   3966
Amer. political scientist

Ferguson, Marilyn [Louise]
(1938–2008)   3085
Amer. author, newsletter
editor, public speaker; née
Grasso; cofounder, As-
sociation of Humanistic
Psychology

Ferguson, Patricia (1953–)   4176
Eng. nurse, novelist, midwife

Ferguson, Sarah "Fergie"
(1959–)   4483
Eng. spokesperson; ex.-w.
Prince Phillip, duke of York

Fermi, Laura Capon
(1907–1977)   2065
Ital./Amer. author; w. Enrico
F— , It./Amer. physicist;
Nobel Prize (1938)

Fern, Fanny (1811–1872)   914
Amer. novelist, columnist;
née Sara Payson Willis; mn.
Parton; 1st woman in U.S.A.
to have a regular newspaper
column

Fernandez, Irene (1946–)   3652
Malay. teacher, human right's
activist; fdg. Mbr., Asia Pacific
Women Law and Develop-
ment (APWLD); Fdr. and dir.,
Tenaganita, 1991; Right Livelihood, 2005

Fernea, Elizabeth Warnock
(1927–2008)   2595
Amer. writer, documentary
filmmaker, anthropologist,
educator; w. Robert A. F— ,
anthropologist

Ferrante, Elena (fl. 2000s–)   4975
Ital. novelist; pseud. (true
identity unknown)

Ferrara, duchess of   see RENÉE DE
FRANCE

Ferraro, Geraldine A. (1935–)   2929
Amer. politician; Congress
(D.-NY), 1979–1985; first
woman to receive Democratic
nomination for vice president;
NWHF

Ferrell, Carolyn (1962–)   4613
Amer. short story writer

Ferrier, Susan Edmonstone
(1782–1854)   790
Scot. novelist; a.k.a. Mary
F—

Ferris, Helene (1937–)   3028
Amer. rabbi

Ferron (1952–)   4103
Can. songwriter, singer, poet

Fey, Tina (1960–)   4527.1
Amer. actor, comedian, TV
writer & producer; née Elizabeth Stamatina F— ; Emmy
(5), Golden Globe (3)

Fiedler, Maureen (1942–)   3334
Amer. Roman Catholic nun,
religious rights activist, radio
host; codirector, Quixote
Center, a national faith-based
justice center (23 yrs)

Field, Connie (1948–)   3826
Amer. filmmaker

Field, Joanna (1900–1998)   1899
Eng. psychologist, writer;
née Marion Blackett; mn.
Milner

Field, Kate (1838–1896)   1082
Amer. actor, lecturer, writer; née
Mary Katherine Keemle F—

Field, Michael   see BRADLEY,
KATHARINE

Field, Rachel Lyman
(1894–1942)   1793
Amer. playwright, poet,
writer; mn. Pederson; Newbery, 1930

Field, Sally (1946–)   3653
Amer. actor; Oscar, 1979,
1984; Emmy (3); Golden
Globe, 1979, 1984

Fielding, Sarah (1710–1768)   568
Eng. author

Fields, Annie Adams
(1834–1915)   1055
Amer. biographer, poet

Fields, Dorothy (1905–1974)   2014
Amer. lyricist, playwright;
d. Lew Fields (of Weber and
Fields, vaudeville comedians),
w. Herbert F— (lyricist and
her frequent collaborator);
Academy Award, 1936; Tony,
1959; Songwriters Hall of
Fame, 1971

Fields, Gracie (1898–1979)   1866
Eng./Ital. actor, entertainer,
singer; née Stansfield; C.B.E.,
1979

Fields, Suzanne (1961?–)   4574
Amer. columnist

Fields, Totie (1931–1978)   2757
Amer. comedian; née Sophie
Feldman

Figes, Eva (1932–)   2794
Ger./Eng. novelist; née Unger

Figner, Vera (1852–1942)   1191
Russ. revolutionary; née Niko-
layevna

Filipovic, Zlata (1980–)   4932
Bosnian diarist

Filsinger, E. B., Mrs.   see TEASDALE,
SARA

Finch, Anne (1661–1720)   497
Eng. literary critic, poet, feminist, translator; née Kingsmill,
a.k.a. countess of Winchelsea,
Ardelia, Flavia

Fine, Sylvia (1913–1991)   2197
Amer. lyricist, humanitarian;
w. Danny Kaye, Amer. Actor,
comedian; Emmy, 1975; UNI-
CEF award

Fingerhut, Arden (1946–1994)   3654
Amer. stage lighting designer,
educator (theater); Obie, 1982

Finley, Karen (1956–)   4363
Amer. performance artist;
Obie, 1998; Guggenheim

Fiorenza, Elisabeth Schüssler
(1938–)   3086
Rum./Amer. educator (the-
ology), author, historian;
cofounder and co-ed., Journal
of Feminist Studies in Religion

Fiorina, Cara Carleton "Carly"
Snéed (1954–)   4244–4245
Amer. business execu-
tive; CEO (1999–2005) &
Chairman of the Board
(2000–2005), Hewlett-Pack-
ard; candidate for U.S. Senate
(R-CA)

Firestone, Shulamith
(1945–)   3570
Can./Amer. writer, editor,
feminist; founder, Notes from
the Second Year (periodical)

Fishback, Margaret
(1900–1985)   1900
Amer. poet, writer, advertising
executive; a.k.a. M— F—
Powers

Fishel, Elizabeth (1950?–)   3967
Amer. author, journalist

Fisher, Carrie (1956–)   4364
Amer. actor, novelist; d. Eddie
F— (singer) and Debbie Reyn-
olds (actor, dancer, singer)

Fisher, Dorothy Canfield
(1879–1958)   1525
Amer. writer

Fisher, M. F. K. (1908–1992)   2085
Amer. writer (food); née Mary
Frances Kennedy; d. Rex
Brenton (newspaper editor
and publisher)

Fisher, Renée (1947–)   3743
Amer. writer, entrepreneur,
special ed teacher, poet, realtor

Fiske, Minnie [Maddern]
(1865–1932)   1312
Amer. actor, playwright; née
Davey

Fitzgerald, Frances (1940–)   3189
Amer. journalist; Pulitzer,
1973; NBA, 1973

Fitzgerald, Penelope
(1916–2000)   2266
Eng. novelist; d. Edmund
Valpy (editor) and Christina
[Hicks] Knox; NBCCA, 1997;
Booker, 1979

Fitzgerald, Zelda (1900–1948)   1901
Amer. adventurer, writer; née
Sayre; w. F. Scott F— (writer,
1896–1969)

Fitzpatrick, Sheila Mary
(1941–)   3259
Amer. educator, historian

Flagg, Fannie (1941–)   3260
Amer. novelist; née Patricia
Neal

Flanagan, Hallie (1890–1969)   1705
Amer. theater producer,
educator; head of the Federal
Theatre of the New Deal's
W.P.A., 1935–1938

Flanagan, Mary (1943–)   3405
Amer./Eng. writer

Flanders, Laura (1961–)   4575
Brit./Amer. journalist, televi-
sion commentator, author; d.
Michael F— (1922–1975),
Eng. Actor, comic singer; s.
Stephanie Hope F— (1968–),
journalist; grandd. Francis

Claud C— (1904–1982), Eng. journalist

Flanner, Hildegarde (1899–1987) 1885
Amer. poet, author; mn. Monhoff

Flanner, Janet (1892–1978) 1745
Amer. lecturer, war correspondent, journalist; pseud. Genêt; NBA, 1966

Flavia see FINCH, ANNE

Fleeson, Doris (1901–1970) 1931
Amer. columnist; mn. Kimball

Fleisser, Marie-Luise (1901–1974) 1932
Ger. playwright, writer; from 1924–29 collaborator and lover, Bertold Brecht (Ger. poet and playwright, 1898–1956)

Flekkøy, Målfrid Grude (193–?–) 2703
Nor. government worker, psychologist; Norway's first Barneombudet (Advocate for Children), 1981–1988; UNICEF consultant

Fleming, Amalia, Lady (1912–1986) 2175
Greek/Eng. political activist, bacteriologist; née Coutsouris-Voureka; w. Sir Alexander F— (bacteriologist who, in 1928, discovered penicillin, 1881–1955; Nobel, 1945)

Fleming, Joan [Margaret] (1908–1980) 2086
Eng. writer, playwright

Fleming, Marjory (1803–1811) 876
Scot. diarist

Fletcher, Bridget (1726–1770) 597
Amer. hymnist; née Richardson

Fletcher, Julia A. see CARNEY, JULIA

Fletcher, Lucille (1912–1973) 2176
Amer. writer, scenarist

Fletcher, Mary (1739–1815) 627
Eng. philanthropist; née Bosanquet, a.s.a. Basquet

Fleury, Maria de (fl. 1781–1791) 787
Amer. pamphleteer, poet

Flexner, Anne Crawford (1874–1955) 1430
Amer. suffragist, political activist, playwright; cofounder, American Dramatists

Flinders, Carol (1943–) 3406
Amer. educator, nonfiction writer, scholar; m. Mesh F—, co-creator of web-based video series "lonelygirl15"

Flint, Annie Johnson (1866–1932) 1326
Amer. poet

Flores-Oebanda, [Maria] Cecilia (1960–) 4528
Filipina activist (human rights), administrator; a.k.a. Commander Liway; founder

& director, Visayan Forum Foundation, 1991; coordinator, Global March Against Child Labor; 2005 Anti-Slavery Award by Anti-Slavery International

Flournoy, Michèle A. (1961–) 4576
Amer. public servant; fdr., Ctr. for a New American Security, 2007; Under Secretary of Defense for Policy, 2009–

Flowers, Margaret (1961?–) 4576.1
Amer. pediatrician, health care activist

Flynn, Elizabeth Gurley (1890–1964) 1706
Amer. writer, communist leader, civil rights activist; a.k.a. "The Rebel Girl"

Foderaro, Lisa W[hite] (1964?–) 4675
Amer. journalist

Fogelin, Adrian (1951–) 4042
Amer. children's writer, illustrator; d. Maria Bontempi F—, writer; grandd. Giuseepe Bontempi, inventor

Follen, Eliza Lee (1787–1860) 803
Ger./Amer. poet, author; née Cabott

Follett, Mary Parker (1868–1933) 1350
Amer. organizational manager, writer, sociologist, lecturer

Foltz, Clara Shortridge (1849–1934) 1165
Amer. reformer, lawyer; first female member of California Bar, 1915

Fonda, Jane [Seymour] (1937–) 3029
Amer. political activist, fitness expert, actor; d. Henry F— (actor, 1905–82), s. Peter F— (actor), ex-w. Roger Vadim (1, Fr. film director), Tom Hayden (2, activist, politician); w. Ted Turner (3, media mogul); Academy Award, 1971, 1978

Fonte, Moderata (1555–1592) 357
Ital. writer; a.k.a. Modesta Pozzo

Fonteyn, Margot, Dame (1919–1991) 2342
Brit. ballet dancer; née Peggy Hookham, a.k.a. M— F— de Arias; w. Dr. Roberto Arias (Panamanian diplomat, d. 1989); Benjamin Franklin Medal from Royal Society of the Arts, 1974

Forbes, Esther (1894–1967) 1794
Amer. writer; Pulitzer, 1943; Newbery Award, 1944

Forbes, Leslie (1959?–) 4484
Can. novelist, broadcaster, artist

Forbus, Lady Willie (1892–1993) 1746
Amer. lawyer; State Senate, D-Wash., 1942–46

Forcalquier, Garsenda de see GARSENDA DE FORCALQUIER

Ford, Anna (1943–) 3407
Brit. public speaker, journalist, television

Ford, Betty (1918–) 2313
Amer. civic leader, first lady; née Elizabeth Bloomer; w. Gerald R. F— (politician, 1913– ; 38th U.S. president, 1974–1977); fdr., Betty Ford Ctr

Ford, Lena Guilbert (1870–1916) 1373
Amer. poet, lyricist

Forman, Ruth (1969?–) 4787
Amer. poet

Fornés, Maria Irene (1930–) 2704
Cub./Amer. playwright, stage director; cofounder, Women's Theater Council, Theater Strategy; Obie (4); Rockefeller; NEA; AAIAL

Fossey, Dian (1932–1985) 2795
Amer. anthropologist

Foster, Doris Ann (1945/55–) 3571
Amer. prisoner, letter writer; a.k.a. Raven; life sentence for murder commuted in 1987

Foster, Hannah Webster (1759–1840) 697
Amer. novelist

Foster, Jodie (1962–) 4615
Amer. actor, director, producer; Oscar, 1988, 1991; Golden Globe, 1988, 1991

Fowler, Connie May (1963?–) 4639
Amer. novelist, screenwriter, memoirist

Fowler, Ellen Thorneycroft (1860–1929) 1253
Eng. writer; mn. Felkin

Fowler, Karen Joy (1950–) 3968
Amer. novelist

Fox, Margaret Askew Fell (1614–1702) 432–433
Eng./Amer. writer (religion), religious leader; a.k.a. Askew; the "mother" of the Friends; w. George F— (1624–1691; Eng. religious leader; founder, Society of Friends, or Quakers, 1647–1648)

Fox, Muriel (1928–) 2626
Amer. speech writer, publicist, business executive, feminist; mn. Aronson; cofounder, NOW

Fox, Paula (1923–) 2454
Amer. writer; d. Elsie De Sola Fox, Cuban-born screenwriter and Paul Hervey F—, novelist; grandm. Courtney Love*

(1964–), Amer. Rock musician; Newbery Medal, 1974

Fox, Robin Lane see LANE FOX, ROBIN

Fox-Genovese, Elizabeth (1941–2007) 3261
Amer. historian, women's studies scholar; d. Edward Whiting Fox, historian; w. Eugene D. G—, historian; Natl. Humanities Medal, 2003

Fradonnet, Catherine (1547–1587) 345
Fr. poet, playwright; a.k.a., with her mother, Les Dames des Roches; d. Madeleine F—*

Fradonnet, Madeleine (1520?–1587) 314
Fr. poet; née Neveu, a.k.a., with her daughter, Les Dames des Roches; w. André F— (1), François Eboissard (2), m. Catherine F—*

Fraiberg, Selma (1918–1981) 2314
Amer. child psychoanalyst, clinician, author, researcher; née Horwitz

Frame, Janet (1924–2004) 2483
N.Z. poet, writer

Franco, Veronica (1546–1591) 344
Ital. poet, courtesan; friend of Tintoretto (Venetian painter, 1518–94); founder of hospice for "fallen women"

Frank, Anne (1929–1945) 2657
Ger. diarist; executed by Nazis

Frank, Florence Kiper (1885–1976) 1628
Amer. poet, playwright

Frank, Ray (1865–1948) 1313
Amer. religious activist, journalist; m. Litman; first woman accepted at Hebrew Union College (Cincinnati)

Franken, Rose [Dorothy] (1895–1988) 1809
Amer. playwright, screenwriter, stage director, novelist; née Lewin, pseud. Margaret Grant, Franken Meloney

Franklin, Eleanor Anne (ca.1795–1825) 847
Eng. poet; née Porden

Franklin, Miles (1880–1956) 1544
Aust. novelist; a.k.a. Brent of Bin Bin

Franklin, Rosalind Elsie (1920–1958) 2370
Eng. physicist, research scientist; co-discoverer of DNA (noted for her work with X-ray crystallography on biological molecules which were essential to deciphering the structure of DNA)

Franks, Rebecca (1760–1823)   707
Amer./Eng. social figure; a.k.a.
Lady Johnson

Frantz, Marge (1918?–)   2315
Amer. educator

Franz, Marie-Louise von
(1915–1998)   2240
Swiss scholar, author, Jungian
analyst; founder, C. G. Jung
Institute, Zurich

Fraser, Antonia, Lady (1932–) 2796
Eng. biographer, historian,
novelist, social activist, TV
personality; née Antonia
Pakenham; d. Lord Longford
(1905– ; author, social reformer; former Labour cabinet
minister), w. Hugh Fraser (1;
politician), Harold Pinter (2;
1930– ; playwright)

Fraser, Arvonne (1925–)   2517
Amer. administrator, edi-
tor, feminist, public servant,
author

Fraser, Clara (1923–1998)   2455
Amer. feminist, civil rights
activist; cofounder, Radical
Women, Freedom Socialist
Party, 1967

Fraser, Kathleen (1937–)   3030
Amer. poet

Fréchette, Louise (1946–)   3655
Can. public servant

Fredriksson, Marianne
(1927–2007)   2595.1
Swed. novelist, journalist; née
Persson

Freed, Lynn (1952?–)   4104
S. Afr./Amer. writer, educator
(English)

Freeman, Jo (1945–)   3572
Amer. feminist, political sci-
entist, writer, lawyer; a.k.a.
Joreen

Freeman, Judith (1946–)   3656
Amer. novelist

Freeman, Mary [Eleanor] Wilkins
(1852–1930)   1192
Amer. poet, writer

Freer, Otto, Mrs.   see LEE, AGNES

Fremantle, Anne [Jackson]
(1909–2002)   2108
Brit./Amer. art critic, writer,
educator, editor, poet

Fremont, Helen (1945?–)   3573
Amer. writer, lawyer

French, Marilyn (1929–2009) 2658
Amer. novelist, writer; née
Mara Solwoska

Freston, Kathy (1964–)   4676
Amer. spiritual counselor,
author

Freud, Anna (1895–1982)   1810
Aus./Eng. psychoana-
lyst, author; d. Sigmund
F— (physician and founder of
psychoanalysis, 1856–1939);
founder, Hampstead Child

Therapy Clinic, London;
pioneer in the field of child
psychoanalysis; C.B.E., 1967

Freudenberger, Nell (1975–) 4892
Amer. writer, fiction

Friday, Nancy (1937–)   3031
Amer. writer; née Colbert

Friedan, Betty [Naomi]
(1921–2006)   2398
Amer. feminist, writer; née
Goldstein; founder, National
Organization for Women
(NOW), 1966; Humanist of
the Year Award, 1975; NWHF

Friedman, Bonnie (1958–)   4448
Amer. writer

Friedman, Lenore
(fl. 1980s–)   4933
Amer. author

Frietschie, Barbara (1766–1862)729
Amer. patriot; née Hauer,
a.s.a. Frietchie; subject of
Whittier's poem "Barbara Fritchie" (Amer. poet, 1807–92)

Frings, Ketti (1915–1981)   2241
Amer. writer, playwright,
screenwriter; née Katherine
Hartley; pseud. Anitaire; Pulitzer, 1958; NYDCCA, 1958

Frost, Frances (1905–1959)   2015
Amer. poet

Frucht, Abby (1957–)   4408
Amer. novelist

Fry, Elizabeth (1780–1845)   780
Eng. prison reform activist,
social reformer

Frye, Marilyn (1941–)   3262
Amer. nonfiction writer, philosopher

Fuentes, Sonia Pressman
(1928–)   2627
Ger./Amer. public speaker,
author, feminist, attorney;
cofounder, NOW; cofounder,
WEAL, Federally Employed
Women; inducted into Maryland Women's Hall of Fame

Fugard, Lisa (1959?–)   4485
S. Afr./Amer. writer, actor; d.
Athol F— , playwright, and
Sheila Meiring F—*

Fugard, Sheila [Meiring]
(1932–)   2797
Eng./S. Afr. writer; w. Athol
F— (playwright, 1932–)

Fukuzoyo Chiyo
(1701/03?–1775)   554
Jap. poet, painter; a.k.a. Chiyoni, Chiyojo, Kaga no Chiyo

Fulke-Greville, Frances   see GRE-
VILLE, FRANCES

Fuller, Loie (1862–1928)   1286
Amer./Fr. scenic designer, filmmaker, choreographer, modern
dancer

Fuller, Margaret (1810–1850)   910
Amer. journalist, translator,
social critic, editor, feminist,

educator; née Sarah M— F—,
a.k.a. Marchesa Ossoli; NWHF

Fuller, Margaret Witter
(1871–1954)   1389
Amer. writer, poet

Fulton, Alice (1952–)   4105
Amer. educator (English),
poet, short story writer;
Guggenheim 1986, 1987; MacArthur 1991

Furman, Laura (1945–)   3574
Amer. writer, educator, writ-
ing, book editor; Guggenheim,
NEA

Furness, Betty (1916–1994) 2266.1
Amer. columnist, government
official, TV reporter, actor

Fussell, Betty Harper (1927–) 2596
Amer. writer, food; ex.-w. Paul
F— (1924–), literary critic,
military historian

Fyleman, Rose (1877–1957)   1492
Eng. poet

G

Gaard, Greta (1960–)   4529
Amer. environmental activist,
book editor

Gabaldon, Diana (1950?–)   3259
Amer. writer

Gabor, Zsa Zsa (1917–)   2287
Hung./Amer. business ex-
ecutive, actor; ex-w. Conrad
Hilton (1, Amer. hotel chain
organizer, 1887–1979),
George Sanders (2, Brit-
ish-born Amer. actor); Miss
Hungary 1936

Gabrielli, Caterina (1730–1796) 608
Ital. singer

Gaeta, Lisa (1962–)   4615.1
Amer. teacher, writer, personal
safety expert

Gage, Frances Dana
(1808–1884)   904
Amer. lecturer, poet, social
reformer

Gage, Mathilda J. (1826–1898)1007
Amer. writer, suffragist;
NWHF

Gaitskill, Mary (1954–)   4246
Amer. writer

Galchen, Rivka (1976–)   4907
Can./Amer. novelist, physician, educator (writing)

Galdikas, Biruté M. F. (1946–)3657
Ger./Can. primatologist; estab-
lished Orangutan Foundation
Int., 1968

Gale, Zona (1874–1938)   1431
Amer. writer, playwright, poet;
mn. Breese; Pulitzer, 1921

Galinsky, Ellen (1943?–)   3408
Amer. author, photographer,
lecturer, researcher (work-
family issues); w. Norman
G—, artist; cofounder.-pres.,
Families and Work Institute

Gallagher, Mary (1947–)   3744
Amer. novelist, stage director,
actor, playwright; NEA, 1978;
Guggenheim, 1983; Blackburn
Prize, 1987

Gallagher, Tess (1943–)   3409
Amer. screenwriter, educator,
poet, writer; w. Raymond
Carver (writer); NEA,
1976, 1981; Guggenheim,
1978–1979

Gallaire-Bourega, Fatima
(1944–)   3500
Algerian/Fr. writer, playwright

Galland, China (1943?–)   3410
Amer. writer, naturalist

Gallant, Mavis [Leslie]
(1922–)   2426
Eng./Can. writer; née Young

Gallatin, Grace (see Seton-Thompson, Grace)

Galloway, Priscilla (1930–)   2705
Can. writer, poet, educator;
a.k.a. Anne Peebles; ALA, 1996

Gambara, Veronica
(1485–1550)   285
Ital. poet, governor; w. Gilberto
X, lord of Correggio, friend and
correspondent of Pietro Bembo
(1470–1547; It. poet)

Gambaro, Griselda (1928–) 2628
Argen. playwright, writer;
Premio del Fondo Nacional
de las Artes de la Argentina
(1963); Premio Emece

Gamble, Eliza Burt
(1841–1920)   1103
Amer. author

Gamble, Vanessa Northington
(1953–)   4177
Amer. educator (medicine),
physician, historian (medicine)

Gandhi, Indira (1917–1984) 2288
Ind. politician, leader, political; née I— Priyadarshini
Nehru; d. Jawaharlal Nehru
(1889–1964; statesman;
first prime minister of India,
1947–64); pres., National
Congress Party, 1959–60;
minister of information, 1964;
first woman prime minister
of India, 1966–77, 1980–84;
assassinated; m. Rajiv G—
(1944–1991; prime minister
of India, 1984–1989)

Gandhi, Sonia (1946–)   3658
Ital./Ind. politician; née Edvige
Antonia Albina Maino; w.
Rajiv Gandhi (1944–1991),
Prime Minister of India;
Pres., Indian Natl. Congress,
2004–2006

Gandy, Kim (1954–)   4247
Amer. activist, women's
rights, lawyer; Pres., NOW
(2001–2009)

Gao Yaojie, (1927–)   2597
Chin. gynecologist, researcher (AIDS); Female Global Leadership Award from Vital Voices Global Partnership (2006); Ramon Magsaysay Award for Public Service, 2003

Garber, Marjorie B. (1944–)   3501
Amer. writer, educator (literature)

Garbo, Greta (1905–1990)   2017
Swed./Amer. actor

García, Cristina (1958–)   4449
Cub./Amer. novelist, journalist

Gardam, Jane (1928–)   2629
Eng. writer, dramatist; Whitbread (2); Booker, 1978

Garden, Mary (1874–1967)   1432
Scot./Amer. opera singer; a.k.a. "the Sarah Bernhardt of opera"

Gardiner, Lisa (1900–1956)   1902
Amer. dancer, choreographer, educator; founder, Washington School of Ballet

Gardinier, Suzanne (1961–)   4577
Amer. poet, essayist

Gardner, Ava (1922–1990)   2427
Amer. screen actor; née A— Lavinia G— ; w. Artie Shaw (1, band leader, 1910–?), Mickey Rooney (2, screen actor, 1920–), Frank Sinatra (3, singer, actor, 1944–1998)

Gardot, Melody (1985–)   4955
Amer. singer, songwriter

Garfield, Lucretia Rudolph (1832–1918)   1045
Amer. society leader, first lady; w. James G— (politician, 1831–81; 20th U.S. president, 1981; assassinated); s. Lucy Hayes*

Garland, Judy (1922–1969)   2428
Amer. singer, screen actor; née Frances Gumm; David Rose (1; 1910–?; orchestra leader), Vincente Minnelli (1910–?; 2; film director), Sidney Luft (3; talent manager), Mark Herron (4; actor), Mickey Deans (5; discotheque manager); m. Liza Minnelli,* Lorna Luft (1952– ; singer); Academy Award, 1939; Grammy, 1961; SHF

Garrick, Eva Maria (1725–1822)   596
Ital./Eng. actor, dancer; née Viegel, a.k.a. Violette; w. David Garrick (1717–79; Eng. actor, manager, dramatist)

Garrison, Deborah (1965–)   4696
Amer. poet, editor

Garrison, Theodosia (1874–1944)   1433
Amer. writer, poet; a.k.a. Mrs. Frederick Faulks

Garsenda de Forcalquier (ca. 1180–ca. 1242)   198
Provençal trobairitz; w. Alphonse II, lord of Provence

Garson, Barbara (1942–)   3335
Amer. playwright; Obie, 1977

Garthwaite, Terry (1939–)   3143
Amer. lyricist, singer

Garvey, Jane F. (1944–)   3502
Amer. public servant, business administrator; admin., F.A.A. (first woman)

Gaskell, Elizabeth [Cleghorn] (1810–1865)   911
Eng. novelist; née Stevenson

Gates, Ellen [Huntington] (1835–1920)   1065
Amer. writer, poet

Gauhari, Farooka (1947–)   3745
Afghan writer

Gaulke, Cheri (1954–)   4248
Amer. video & performance artist; cofounder, Feminist Art Workers (1976); cofounder, Sisters of Survival (1981)

Gawain, Shakti (1948–)   3827
Amer. workshop leader, therapist, dance teacher, writer

Gaylor, Annie Laurie (1955–)   4300
Amer. editor, feminist, author, radio & TV host; cofounder, Freedom From Religion Fdn.

Gearhart, Sally [Miller] (1931–)   2758
Amer. political, lesbian and animal rights activist, educator (speech), writer

Geddes, Anne (1956–)   4365
Amer. photographer

Gee, Shirley (1932–)   2798
Eng. playwright; née Thieman; w. Donald G— (actor); Blackburn, 1985

Gelfant, Blanche H[ousman] (1922–)   2429
Amer. teacher, literary scholar

Geller, Laura (1950–)   3969
Amer. rabbi

Gellhorn, Martha [Ellis] (1908–1998)   2266.1
Amer. author, journalist

Gelpi, Barbara C[harlesworth] (1933–)   2849
Amer. educator, author, scholar

Gems, Pam[ela Iris] (1925–)   2518
Eng. radio & TV writer, playwright, translator

Genefke, Inge (1944?–)   3503
Danish activist (human rights), physician; medical dir., Rehabilitation and Research Centre for Torture Victims (RCT; Copenhagen), 1982; Honorary Right Livelihood Award, 1988

Genêt   see FLANNER, JANET

Geniesse, Jane Fletcher (1936–)   2977
Amer. biographer, columnist, novelist; d. Rev. Joseph Francis F— (1904–1991), theologian, and Forrest Hatfield F— (1905–1988), poet, painter, activist; s. Joseph F— (1935–1984), historian, linguist

Genlis, Stephanie Félicité, countess (1746–1830)   650
Fr. tutor, writer, musician, harpist; née Du Crest de St. Aubin

Gentileschi, Artemisia (1593–1651/53)   403
Ital. painter; d. Orazio G— (1563–1639; painter); m. Palerma G— (painter)

Geoffrin, Marie Thérèse Rodet (1669–1757)   513
Fr. wit, salonist

Geonzon, Winefreda Estanero (1930?–1990)   2706
Filipina lawyer, civil rights activist; founded Free Legal Assistance Volunteers Association (FREELAVA); Right Livelihood Award, 1984

George, [Susan] Elizabeth (1949–)   3897
Amer. novelist

Gera, Bernice (1931–1992)   2759
Amer. sports figure; first woman umpire, 1972

Gerasymyuk, Olga (1978?–)   4923
Ukrainian television host

Gerber, Merrill Joan (1938–)   3087
Amer. educator (writing), writer; Ribalow Award, The Kingdom of Brooklyn

Germain, Sylvie (1954–)   4249
Fr./Cuban educator (philosophy), novelist

Gerould, Katherine (1879–1944)   1526
Amer. writer; née Fullerton

Gerson, Kathleen (1947–)   3746
Amer. educator, sociology, author

Gerstenberg, Alice (1885–1972)   1629
Amer. playwright, community activist; cofounder, Chicago Jr. League Theater for Children (1921); founder, Playwrights Theatre of Chicago

Gertrude the Great (1256–1302)   221
Ger. Benedictine mystic, author; a.k.a. Saint Gertrude of Hefta

Gervitz, Gloria (1943–)   3411
Mex. poet, translator; fellowship, Fondo Nacional de Creadores Artisticos (FONCA), 1992–93

Gessen, Masha (1967–)   4748
Russ. journalist, author; d. Yoka G, writer, tr.

Geyer, Georgia Anne (1935–)   2930
Amer. educator, columnist, author

Ghaaem-Maghami, Aalamtaaj (1884–1947)   1609
Iran. poet; a.k.a. Jaleh

Ghezali, Salima (1958–)   4450
Alger. journalist, editor, activist (women's rights); Sakharov Prize for Freedom of Thought, 1997

Ghoratolain, Tahereh (1817–1853)   942
Iran. poet; a.s.a. Zareen-Taaj

Gibbons, Kaye (1960–)   4530
Amer. novelist; AAAL; NEA

Gibbons, Stella [Dorotea] (1902–1995)   1948
Eng. writer, poet; mn. Weber

Gibbs, Lois Marie (1952–)   4106
Amer. environmental activist, author; fdr., Center for Health, Environment and Justice (CHEJ), 1980; Goldman Environmental Prize, 1990

Gibbs, Nancy Reid (1960–)   4531
Amer. journalist

Gibson, Althea (1927–2003)   2598
Amer. athlete (golf & tennis); first black woman to win both the U.S. Open, 1950, and Wimbeldon, 1957; Olympic champion; Women's Sports Hall of Fame, 1980; Florida Women's Hall of Fame, 1999; NWHF; IWSHF, 1980

Gibson, Janet [Patricia] (1953–)   4178
Beliz. biologist, zoologist, environmental activist; Goldman, 1990

Gibson, Margaret (1944–)   3504
Amer. poet, educator

Gibson, P.J. [Patricia Joann] (1952–)   4107
Amer. playwright, educator (English)

Gideon, Lillian (1908–?)   2088
Amer. medical and psychiatric social worker, travel agent; w. Russell G— (civil rights activist, d. 1985)

Gilbert, Elizabeth (1969–)   4788
Amer. writer, biographer; Pushcart, 1997

Gilbert, Mrs.   see TAYLOR, ANN

Gilbert, Peggy (1905–2007)   2018
Amer. saxophonist, band leader, columnist; née Knechtges; pioneer of equal rights for female musicians

Gilbert, Sandra [Mortola] (1936–)   2978
Amer. educator, poet, writer

Gilbreth, Lillian Moller (1878–1962) 1513 Amer. engineer, inventor, author; w. Frank G— (1868–1924), Amer. engineer; "First Lady of Engineering"; with her husband Frank, a pioneer in ergonomics; NWHF

Gilchrist, Ellen (1935–) 2931 Amer. writer; NEA, 1979; Pushcart, 1979–80, 1983

Gilchrist, Marie [Emilie] (1893–1989) 1770 Amer. researcher, writer

Gildersleeve, Virginia [Crocheron] (1877–1965) 1493 Amer. author; diplomat; educational administrator; dean, Barnard College, 1911–47; U.S. delegate to United Nations, 1945

Gill, Julia see BAILEY, URANIA

Gill, Sarah Prince (1728–1771) 601 Amer. poet, diarist; s. Deborah Prince (poet)

Gillan, Maria Mazziotto (1940–) 3190 Amer. poet, educator

Gillespie, Marcia [Ann] (1944–) 3505 Amer. editor; ed.-in-chief, Ms. Magazine

Gilliatt, Penelope [Ann Douglass] (1932–) 2799 Eng. scenarist, writer, film critic

Gillibrand, Kirsten [Elizabeth Rutnik] (1966–) 4720 Amer. politician, lawyer; U.S. Senator, D-NY (2009–)

Gilligan, Carol (1936–) 2979 Amer. psychologist, author, feminist; née Friedman

Gilman, Caroline (1794–1888) 843 Amer. educator, poet, author; née Howard, pseud. Clarissa Packard; w. Samuel G— (poet), m. C— Howard (author)

Gilman, Charlotte [Anna] Perkins [Stetson] (1860–1935) 1254 Amer. lecturer, poet, publicist, writer, social critic; greatn. Harriet Beecher Stowe*; NWHF

Gilmer, Elizabeth Merriwether see DIX, DOROTHY

Gilmore, Glenda Elizabeth (1963?–) 4640 Amer. nonfiction writer, historian, educator; w. Ben Kiernan (1953–) Austral./Amer. Scholar

Gilmore, Jennifer (1970–) 4818 Swiss/Amer. writer; s. Kate G-, performance artist; w. Pedro Barbeito (1969–) Sp./Amer. Artist

Gilpin, Laura (1891–1979) 1726 Amer. photographer

Gilson, Mary Barnett (1877–1959) 1494 Amer. industrial relations consultant, economist, educator; Guggenheim, 1939

Giltinan, Caroline (1884–?) 1610 Amer. poet; a.k.a. Mrs. Leo P. Harlow

Gimbutas, Mirija Alseika (1921–1994) 2399 Lithuanian/Amer. archaeologist; NSF 1956–60, 1968–69, 1973–74; NEH, 1967

Gingold, Hermione [Ferdinanda] (1897–1987) 1848 Eng. actor, comedian; Grammy, 1976

Ginsburg, Ruth Bader (1933–) 2850 Amer. educator, lawyer; 2nd woman appointed as U.S. Supreme Court justice, 1993; NWHF

Ginzburg, Eugenia [Semyonovna] (1904–1977) 1994 Russ. social critic, author; m. Vasily Aksyonov, writer

Ginzburg, Natalia [Levi] (1916–1991) 2267 Ital. writer, politician, playwright; pseud. Alessandra Tornimparte; w. Leone G— (1, d. 1944; Russ. intellectual and hero of the Resistance); Gabriel Boldine (2); Premio Strega, 1964

Giordano, Anna (1965?–) 4697 Ital. ornithologist, animal rights advocate; Goldman, 1998

Giovanelli, Elettra Marconi (1930–) 2707 Ital. public figure; d. Guglielmo Marconi (1874–1937), Italian inventor

Giovanni, Nikki (1943–) 3412 Amer. educator, poet

Girardin, Delphine de (1804–1855) 885 Fr. writer; née Gay; pseud. Vicomte Charles de Launay

Giroud, Françoise (1916–2003) 2268 Swiss/Fr. journalist, politician, editor; cofounder of Elle and L'Express magazines

Girsh, Faye Joan (1933–) 2851 Amer. civil rights activist, nonprofit administrator; exec. dir., Hemlock Society USA

Gish, Lillian [Diana] (1893–1993) 1771 Amer. actor; s. Dorothy G— (1898–1968), actor; Academy Lifetime Achievement Award, 1971

Glancy, Diane (1941–) 3263 Amer. novelist, poet; née Hall

Glaser, Lulu (1874–1958) 1434 Amer. musical comedy actor; née Lillian G—; w. (1) Ralph C. Herz, actor, comic; (2) Tom Richards, actor; (3) DeWolf Hopper, Sr., actor

Glasgow, Ellen [Anderson Gholson] (1874–1945) 1435 Amer. writer; Pulitzer, 1942

Glasgow, Maude (1868–1955) 1351 Amer. writer, physician

Glaspell, Susan (1876/82–1948) 1474 Amer. writer, playwright; w. George Cram Cook (1; d. 1922; editor, critic, novelist, poet, educator, stage producer; cofounder, Provincetown Players; Pulitzer, 1931

Glassman, Carol (1942?–) 3336 Amer. judge, civil rights activist

Glenconnor, Pamela [Wyndham], Lady (1871–1928) 1390 Eng. writer; née Gray

Glendon, Mary Ann (1938–) 3088 Amer. lawyer, author, educator

Glennie, Evelyn (1965–) 4698 Scot. musician (classical percussionist)

Gloriana see MORGAN, SYDNEY

Glück, Louise Elisabeth (1943–) 3413 Amer. poet, educator; Chancellor, AAP, 1999–; Pulitzer, 1993; NBCCA for Poetry, 1985; Guggenheim, 1975, 1987–88; Rockefeller, 1967; NEA 1969, 1979 and 1988–1989; Library of Congress Poet Laureate (03/04)

Glückel of Hameln (1646–1724) 479 Ger. diarist

Glyn, Elinor (1864–1943) 1303 Eng. writer; née Sutherland

Goddard, Mary Katherine (1736/38?–1816) 621 Amer. printer, postmaster, newspaper publisher; d. Sarah Updike G—,* s. William G— (publisher, postmaster); first printed copy of Declaration of Independence came from her press; probably first woman postmaster in American colonies

Goddard, Sarah Updike (1700?–1770) 550 Amer. printer; m. Mary Katherine G—* and William G— (printers)

Godolphin, Margaret [Blagge] (1652–1678) 489 Eng. maid of honor, letter writer

Godwin, Gail (1937–) 3032 Amer. educator, lecturer, novelist, journalist

Godwin, Hannah (fl. 1790s) 819 Eng. letter writer; s. William G— (1756–1836; writer and political theorist); s.-in-law, Mary Wollstonecraft*; a. Mary Shelley*

Goedicke, Patricia [McKenna] (1931–2006) 2760 Amer. poet; NEA, 1968, 1976, 1977.

Goeppert Mayer, Maria see MAYER, MARIA

Goetz, Cecelia Helen (1918?–)2316 Amer. jurist

Goitschel, Marielle (1946–) 3659 Fr. skier; s. Christine G— (skier, 1945–); Olympic gold and silver medals, 1964

Golan, Galia (1939?–) 3143.1 Amer./Isr. educator, writer, peace activist

Goldberg, Leah (1911–1970) 2156 Lith./Isr. Poet

Goldberg, Natalie (1948–) 3828 Amer. author, educator (writing), poet, painter

Goldberg, Whoopi (1955–) 4301 Amer. actor, comedian, TV host; née Caryn Elaine Johnson; Oscar, 1990; Emmy, 2002; Golden Globe, 1986, 1991; Grammy, 1985; Tony, 2002

Goldberger, Nancy Rule (1934–) 2891 Amer. author, professor of psychology

Golden, Marita (1950–) 3970 Amer. novelist, educator, poet

Goldman, Emma (1869–1940) 1360 Russ./Amer. lecturer, political organizer, editor, anarchist, political agitator; founder, Mother Earth, 1906

Gonzaga, Elisabetta (1471–1526) 275 Ital. art & literary patron; a.k.a. duchess of Urbino; s. Francisco G—, marquis of Mantua, s.-in-law Isabella d'Este,* w. Guidobaldo da Montefeltro, duke of Urbino; cultivated a genteel court that inspired Castiglione's book The Courtier (1478–1529; Baldassare C—, Ital. author and statesman)

Gonzaga, Giulia (1513–1566) 306 Ital. art patron; s.-in-law Pico della Mirandola (philosopher), w. Vespasiano Colonna

Gonzaga, Lucrezia [di Bozzolo e Sabbioneta] (?–1552?) 355 Ital. letter writer; cousin Ippolita G—, w. Gianpaolo Manfrone

Gonzales, Sylvia Alicia
(1943–)   3414
    Amer. artist, poet
Gonzalez, Patricia (195-?–)   3971
    Colombian/Eng. artist, painter
Goodale, Dora Read
(1866–1915)   1327
    Amer. poet; s. Elaine G—*
    (poet)
Goodale, Elaine (1863–1953) 1295
    Amer. poet; mn. Eastman; s.
    Dora Read G—* (poet)
Goodall, Jane (1934–)   2892
    Eng./Tanz. biologist, primatol-
    ogist, conservationist, activist
    (animal rights), author; née
    Valerie J— Morris G—;
    founder, The Jane Goodall
    Institute for Wildlife Research,
    Education and Conservation;
    DBE, 2004
Goodenough, J[udith] B.
(1942–)   3337
    Amer. poet; née Beach
Goodison, Lorna (1947–)   3747
    Jamaican poet, educator,
    painter
Goodman, Allegra (1967–)   4749
    Amer. novelist
Goodman, Amy (1957–)   4408.1
    Amer. broadcast journalist,
    syndicated columnist, author
Goodman, Carolyn [Elixabeth
Drucker] (1915–2007)   2242
    Amer. civil rights activist,
    psychologist; fdr., Andrew
    Goodman Foundation, 1966
Goodman, Ellen H. (1941–)   3264
    Amer. columnist; Pulitzer, 1980
Goodman, Linda (1925–
1995)   2519
    Amer. astrologer, writer
Goodwin, Doris Kearns
(1943–)   3415
    Amer. historian, author, po-
    litical commentator; Pulitzer,
    1995
Gorbachev, Raisa Maxima
(1932–1999)   2800
    Russ. Soviet first lady, educa-
    tor (sociology); w. Mikhail
    Sergeyevich G— (1931– ;
    politician; general secretary of
    Communist Party, 1985–91;
    president, U.S.S.R., 1989–91;
    Nobel Peace Prize, 1990)
Gorbanevskaya, Natalya
(1936–)   2980
    Russ. political activist, poet
Gorchakova, Galina [Aleksandrova]
(1962–)   4616
    Russ. opera singer
Gordimer, Nadine (1923–)   2456
    S. Afr. lecturer, writer; Booker,
    1974; Nobel, 1991
Gordon, Bette (1956–)   4366
    Amer. educator, filmmaker

Gordon, Mary Catherine
(1949–)   3898
    Amer. novelist, literary critic,
    educator (writing); d. David
    G— (writer and publisher)
Gordon, Ruth (1896–1985)   1825
    Amer. actor, screenwriter,
    playwright; née Jones; w.
    Garson Kanin (1912– ; screen-
    writer, producer); s.-in-law,
    Michael (screenwriter) and
    Fay Kanin*; Academy Award,
    1968; Emmy, 1979
Gordon-Reed, Annette
(1960?–)   4532
    Amer. lawyer, educator
Gordy Edwards, Esther
(ca. 1920–)   2370.1
    Amer. personal manager; s.
    Berry G— (1929–) American
    record producer; founder of
    Motown record label; fdr., Mo-
    town Historical Museum, 1985
Gore, Catherine [Grace Frances]
(1799–1861)   863
    Eng./Fr. novelist, poet, play-
    wright, composer; née Moody
Gore, Tipper (1948–)   3829
    Amer. photographer, social
    care advocate; née Mary Eliza-
    beth Aitcheson; w. Albert G—,
    Jr. (1948– ; politician; U.S.
    vice president, 1993–2001)
Gore-Booth, Eva (1872–
1949)   1398
    Ir. poet
Goren-Bar, Dina (1958?–)   4451
    Isr. educator, computer sci-
    entist
Gorenko, Anna Andreevna   see
AKHMATOVA, ANNA
Gormley (fl. 10th century)   169
    Ir. queen, poet; a.s.a. Gorm-
    phley
Gornick, Vivian (1935/8–)   2932
    Amer. writer, essayist, journalist
Gossamer, Lady   see MICHITSUNA,
MOTHER OF
Gottleib, Linda (1941?–)   3265
    Amer. writer, film producer
Gottlieb, Lynn (1949–)   3899
    Amer. storyteller, rabbi; or-
    dained in 1981
Gottschewski, Lydia
(fl. 1930s)   2708
    Ger. political activist (Nazi)
Goudge, Elizabeth [de Beauchamp]
(1900–1984)   1903
    Eng./Amer. writer
Gouges, Olympe de
(1748–1793)   656
    Fr. feminist; author of Decla-
    ration of Rights of Women,
    1791
Gould, Hannah Flagg
(1789–1865)   810
    Amer. poet

Gould, Lois (1937–2002)   3033
    Amer. editor, writer
Goulianos, Joan [Susan]
(1939–)   3144
    Amer. editor, writer, literary
    critic; née Rodman
Gourielli-Tchkonia, Princess   see
RUBINSTEIN, HELENA
Gournay, Marie le Jars de
(1565–1645)   369
    Fr. writer, editor, book
Gowdie, Isobel (fl. 1660s)   494
    Scot. witch
Gracia, Princeps   see ASPASIA
Grae, Jean (1976–)   4908
    S. Afr./Amer. singer, song-
    writer; née Tsidi Ibrahim;
    d. Abdullah Ibrahim a.k.a.
    Adolph Johannes Brand a.k.a.
    Dollar Brand, jazz pianist,
    and South African jazz singer
    Sathima Bea Benjamin
Graff, E.J. (1958–)   4452
    Amer. researcher, journalist
Grafton, Sue (1940–)   3191
    Amer. novelist
Graham, Bette Clair
(1924–1980)   2484
    Amer. businesswoman, inven-
    tor; née McMurray; inventor
    of correction fluid; founder,
    Liquid Paper
Graham, Isabella (1742–1814) 638
    Scot./Amer. letter writer, edu-
    cator, philanthropist, poet;
    née Marshall; founder, N.Y.
    Widow's Society, N.Y. Or-
    phan's Asylum, N.Y. Society
    for the Promotion of Industry
Graham, Janet (1723/24–1805) 592
    Scot. poet
Graham, Jorie (1950–)   3972
    Amer. poet; chancellor, AAP,
    1997; Pulitzer, 1995; Mac-
    Arthur, 1990; Guggenheim,
    1983; NEA, 1985
Graham, Katherine
(1917–2001)   2289
    Amer. newspaper publisher,
    editor; née Meyer; widow,
    Philip L. G— (newspaper
    publisher, 1915–63); Pulitzer,
    1998; NWHF
Graham, Laurie (1940–)   3192
    Amer. book editor
Graham, Margaret Collier
(1850–1910)   1174
    Amer. writer
Graham, Martha
(1894–1991)   1795
    Amer. dancer, choreographer,
    educator; direct descendant of
    Miles Standish (1584–1650;
    colonist); founder, Martha
    G— Dance Company; pioneer
    of modern dance; Presidential
    Medal of Freedom, 1976

Graham, Sheilah
(1904–1988)   1995
    Eng./Amer. writer, columnist
Graham, Virginia
(1912–1998)   2177
    Amer. writer, TV & radio
    commentator, playwright
Grahn, Judy (1940–)   3193
    Amer. feminist, poet
Grandin, Temple (1947–)   3748
    Amer. zoologist, author,
    educator
Granholm, Jennifer M.
(1959–)   4486
    Can./Amer. politician, law-
    yer; Gov. (D-MI), 2003– (1st
    female)
Grant, Anne (1755–1838)   680
    Scot./Amer. poet, author; née
    MacVicar, a.k.a. Anne Grant
    of Loggan (or Laggan)
Grant, Lee (1927–)   2599
    Amer. actor, director; née
    Lyova Haskell Rosenthal;
    Obie, 1964; Emmy, 1966,
    1971; Academy Award, 1975
Grant, Toni [Gale]
(1941–)   3266–3267
    Amer. psychologist, radio
    commentator
Granville-Barker, Helen   see HUN-
TINGTON, HELEN
Grasso, Ella (1919–1981)   2343
    Amer. politician; née
    Tambussi; U.S. House of
    Representatives, 1971–1975;
    governor, 1975–1980, D-Con-
    neticut; NWHF
Gratz, Rebecca (1781–1869) 788
    Amer. educator, humanitarian;
    founder, Philadelphia Orphan
    Society, 1815; founder, He-
    brew Sunday School Society,
    first of its kind in America and
    the model for all Jewish edu-
    cation in America
Grau, Shirley Ann (1929–)   2659
    Amer. writer; stepm. Peter Fei-
    belman (writer); Pulitzer, 1965
Graves, Clarissa (1892–1985?) 1747
    Brit. poet, translator; s. Rob-
    ert G— , poet
Gray, Agnes Kendrick (1894–?)1796
    Ir. poet
Gray, Elizabeth Dodson
(1929–)   2660
    Amer. writer
Gray, Francine Du Plessix
(1930–)   2709
    Pol./Amer. writer
Gray, Kimi (1946–)   3660
    Amer. social activist
Gray, Madeline (1902–?)   1949
    Amer. writer
Green, Anna [Katherine]
(1846–1935)   1143
    Amer. writer

Green, Constance McLaughlin (1897–1975) 1849
Amer. historian, educator; d. Andrew Cunningham M—, Pulitzer Prize–winning historian; Pulitzer, 1963

Green, Edith Starrett (1910–1987) 2128
Amer. politician; a.k.a. Mrs. Education; U.S. representative (D-OR), 1955–75

Green, Hannah (see Joanne Greenberg)

Green, Mary A. E. (1818?–1895) 948
Eng. historian, writer, editor; née Everett

Green, Melissa (1960?–) 4533
Amer. writer, poet

Green, Rayna (1942–) 3338
Amer. historian, poet, editor, writer

Greenberg, Blu (1936–) 2981
Amer. writer, educator, poet; née Blanche G—

Greenberg, Joanne (1932–) 2801
Amer. writer; née, a.k.a. Hanna Green

Greenberg, Julie (1966?–) 4721
Amer. rabbi, psychotherapist

Greene, Bella da Costa (1883–1950) 1527
Amer. librarian, bibliographer; personal librarian to J. Pierpont Morgan (1837–1913; financier and philanthropist)

Greene, Catharine (1753–1815?) 3675
Amer. householder; née Littlefield; w. Genl. Nathanael G— (1), Miller (2); patron of Eli Whitney (1765–1825; inventor of cotton gin)

Greene, Gayle (1943–) 3416
Amer. literary critic, educator

Greene, Jeanette (1929–) 2661
Amer. politician, educator; Alabama state representative (R), 1993–

Greene, Jennifer (1945–) 3575
Amer. lecturer, organic farmer, educator, scientific researcher, author; fdr.-dir., Water Research Institute of Blue Hill (WRI), 1991

Greenfield, Meg (1930–1999) 2710
Amer. journalist; Pulitzer, 1978

Greer, Germaine (1939–) 3145
Aust. writer, feminist, educator

Gregg, Linda [Alouise] (1942–) 3339
Amer. poet, educator (poetry)

Gregoria, Francisca (1653–1710) 490
Span. nun, poet

Gregory, Augusta, Lady (1852–1932) 1193
Ir. writer, director, playwright; née Persse; cofounder, Irish National Theatre Society, 1902; director, Abbey Theatre

Greiffenberg, Catharina Regina von (1633–1694) 463
Ger. poet

Grenfell, Joyce Phipps (1910–1979) 2129
Eng. writer, actor

Greville, Frances [Evelyn Maynard] (1861–1938) 1267
Eng. writer; a.k.a. countess of Warwick

Greville, Frances Fulke (1720–1789) 583
Eng. poet; née M'Cartney, a.k.a. Fanny

Grey, Elizabeth Woodville, Lady (1437?–1492) 260
Eng. queen; d. Sir Richard Woodville, w. Sir John G— (1), Edward IV (2; 1442–83; king of England, 1461–83); s.-in-law Richard III (1452–85; king of England, 1483–85), m. Elizabeth of York,* gm. Henry VIII (1491–1547; king of England, 1509–47)

Grey, Jane, Lady (1537–1554) 336
Eng. queen; grandn. Henry VIII (1491–1547; king of England, 1509–47), second cousin Mary I* and Elizabeth I*, d. Henry G—, duke of Dorset and Suffolk, gd. Mary of France,* w. Guildford Dudley (d. 1554; he and Lady Jane were executed), d.-in-law duke of Northumberland, s. Mary Grey*

Grey, Mary (1543/44–1578) 343
Eng. maid of honor; s. Lady Jane* and Lady Catherine G—, w. Keyes (sergeant-porter to Elizabeth I); maid of honor to Elizabeth I*

Grey, Pamela see GLENCONNOR, PAMELA

Grierson, Constantia (1706?–1733) 559
Ir. editor, linguist, poet

Griffin, Adele (1970–) 4819
Amer. writer, children's

Griffin, Susan (1943–) 3417
Amer. poet, educator, writer; NEA, 1976; Malvina Reynolds* Award for Cultural Achievement, 1982

Griffith, Aline (1923–) 2457
Amer./Span. social figure, spy; a.k.a. Countess of Romanones

Griffith, Nanci (1954–) 4250
Amer. singer, songwriter

Griffith, Nicola (1960–) 4534
Eng./Amer. novelist

Griffith Joyner, Florence (1959–1998) 4487
Amer. athlete; a.k.a. Flo-Jo; w. Al Joyner (Olympic Medalist); s.-in-law Jackie Joyner-Kersee*; Olympic Medalist, 1984, 1988; IWSHF, 1998

Griffiths, Martha Wright (1912–2003) 2178
Amer. activist, women's rights, politician, lawyer, judge; a.k.a. Mother of the ERA; U.S. House of Representatives, D-MI, 1955–75; Lt. Gov., 1983–90; NWHF

Griffitts, Hannah (1727–1817) 600
Amer. essayist, poet, letter writer; a.k.a. Fidelia

Grignan, Françoise, comtesse de (1646–1705) 480
Fr. letter writer; née Françoise Marguerite de Sévigné; d. Marie de Sévigné*

Grimes, Martha (1931–) 2761
Amer. detective novelist

Grimké, Angelina [Emily] (1805–1879) 890
Amer. feminist, writer, abolitionist, reformer; s. Sarah Moore G—*, Thomas Smith G— (South Carolina state senator) and Frederick G— (South Carolina Supreme Court judge), a. Archibald Henry G— (lawyer and NAACP leader), c. Robert Barnwell Rhett (editor, secessionist); NWHF

Grimké, Sarah Moore (1792–1873) 832
Amer. author, women's rights pioneer, teacher, abolitionist; s. Angelina Emily G—,* Thomas Smith G— (South Carolina state senator) and Frederick G— (South Carolina Supreme Court judge), a. Archibald Henry G— (lawyer and NAACP leader), c. Robert Barnwell Rhett (editor and secessionist); NWHF

Gripenberg, Alexandra, Baroness (1857–1913) 1222
Finn. women's rights activist

Gross, Jane (1958?–) 4453
Amer. journalist

Gross, Rita M (1944?–) 3506
Amer. scholar, educator, author

Gross, Terry (1951–) 4043
Amer. radio host, radio producer, author; w. Francis Davis (jazz critic; host of Fresh Air since 1975; Peabody, 1993

Grossman, Chaika (1919–1991?) 2344
Pol./Isr. activist, educator, author, public servant; deputy speaker of the Knesset, head of the Labor and Social Affairs Committee (retired 1988)

Grossman, Susan C. (1955–) 4302
Amer. rabbi, author

Grote, Harriet (1792–1878) 833
Eng. biographer

Gruber, Ruth (1911–) 2157
Amer. journalist, immigrant activist, author, poet; a.k.a. Mother Ruth

Gruen, Sara (1976?–) 4909
Can./Amer. novelist, animal rights activist

Grueso, Libia (1961?–) 4578
Colo. social worker, civil rights activist, environmental activist; cofounder, Process of Black Communities (PCN); Goldman, 2004

Grumbach, Argula von (1492–1564/1568) 288
Ger. Lutheran reformer, noble; née von Stauff

Grumbach, Doris Isaac (1918–) 2317
Amer. writer, novelist, literary critic

Grushin, Olga (1971–) 4845–4846
Russ./Amer. novelist

Grymeston, Elizabeth (1563?–1603) 367
Eng. author; w. Christopher G— (Bursar of Caius College, Cambridge)

Gubar, Susan [David] (1944–) 3507
Amer. educator, author

Guercheville, Antoinette de Pons, Marchioness (1570–1632) 374
Fr. noble

Guest, Barbara (1920–2006) 2371
Amer. writer, poet, painter, editor

Guest, Judith (1936–) 2982
Amer. educator, writer

Guevara, Marina de (1510?–1559) 303
Span. nun; burned as a heretic by the Spanish Inquisition

Guffy, Ossie (1931–) 2762
Amer. writer, civil rights organizer

Guidon, Niède (1933–) 2852
Braz. archaeologist; est. Musée de l'Homme Américain

Guilbert, Yvette (1865–1944) 1314
Fr. entertainer, actor; née Emma Laure Esther G—

Guillelma de Rosers
(fl. 1230s–d. 1265)   217
Fr. trobairitz; beloved of
Lanfrances Cigala (Genoese
lawyer and troubador)

Guillet, Pernette du
(1520?–1545)   315
Fr. poet, musician, linguist;
subject of Maurice Scève sonnet sequence *Delie*

Guinan, [Mary Louise Cecilia]
Texas (1884–1933)   1611
Amer. nightclub entertainer,
circus performer, actor

Guiney, Louise Imogen
(1861–1920)   1268
Amer./Eng. writer, poet

Guise, duchess of   *see* ESTE,
ANNE D'

Guitar, Mary Anne (1920?–)   2372
Amer. writer

Gullette, Margaret Morganroth
(1941–)   3268
Amer. critic, cultural,
scholar; w. David G— , author, actor, poet, professor;
cofounder, *Ploughshares*
magazine; m. Sean G— ,
actor, screenwriter; m-in-law.
Yto Barrada G—, photogra-
pher; c. Judith M- Schneider,
professor, author; c. Robert
Eisner, economist; c. Peter
Schnall, physician, scholar,
author

Guppy, Shusha (1935–2008)   2933
Iran./Eng. editor, writer,
songwriter, singer; née Assar;
d. Mohammad Kazem Assar,
Shia theologian and philosopher

Gur, Batya (1947–2005)   3749
Isr. novelist, educator (writing), social activist, literary
critic

Gürer, Denise W. (1957?–)   4409
Amer. computer scientist; co-
chair, Assoc. of Computing
Machinery's Committee on
Women in Computing

Gurney, Dorothy [Frances]
(1858–1932)   1232
Eng. Poet

Gurung, Jeanette D. (1955?–) 4303
Amer. organizer, activist,
women's rights, administrator; fdr., Women Organizing
for Change in Agriculture and
Natural Resources Manage-
ment (WOCAN)

Gutmann, Amy (1949–)   3900
Amer. political theorist, educator, university administrator;
Pres., Univ. of Pennsylvania,
2004–

Gutmans, Sarel (fl. 1620s–)   437
Bohemian householder

Guyon, Jeanne-Marie [Bouvier] de
la Motte (1648–1717)   482
Fr. author, poet, biblical
scholar, Quietist mystic; introduced Quietism into France

Gwinn, Mary Ann (1951–)   4044
Amer. book critic, journalist,
newspaper editor; Pulitzer (for
natl. reporting), 1990

Gwyn, Nell (1650–1687)   486
Eng. actor; née Eleanor G—,
a.s.a. Gwynne, a.k.a. "pretty
witty Nell"; mistress of Charles
II (1630–85; king of England,
1660–85), m. Charles Beauclerk, duke of St. Albans, and
James, Lord Beauclerk

H

Hacker, Marilyn (1942–)   3340
Amer. poet, literary editor;
Guggenheim; NBA, 1975

Hadassah   *see* ESTHER

Hadewijch of Brabant
(fl. 1230s–d. 1260/65)   218
Dutch poet; a.k.a. Adelwip;
head of a *beguinage*; greatest name in Medieval Dutch
literature

Hadley, Tessa (1957?–)   4410
Eng. writer, educator

Hafild, Emmy (1959–)   4488
Indones. environmental activist, administrator, agronomist;
dir., Greenpeace Southeast Asia

Hagar (2300?–ca. 1850 B.C.E.)   5
Egyp. maidservant; mistress
of Abraham (first patriarch
and progenitor of Hebrews),
m. Ishmael (considered the
forbear of Arabs)

Hagedorn, Jessica Tarahata
(1949–)   3901
Filipina/Amer. poet, playwright, performance artist,
novelist, radio commentator;
ABA

Hagen, Uta (1919–2004)   2345
Ger./Amer. actor, teacher
(acting), author; w. Herbert
Berghof (Austrian-born Amer.
actor, director, teacher, 1909–
?); cofounder, Herbert Berghof
Studios, New York; Tony,
1951, 1963; London Critics
Award, 1963, 1964

Haggerty, Joan (1940–)   3194
Can. writer

Hahn, Emily "Mickey"
(1905–1997)   2019
Amer./Chin. environmental activist, spy, writer, adventurer;
m. Charles Boxer, British army
officer; staff writer for *The
New Yorker* (1925–1995)

Haiken, Elizabeth
(fl. 1990s–2000s)   4964
Amer. nonfiction writer

Hainstock, Elizabeth G.
(1928?–)   2630
Amer. author, educational
consultant

Hajar, Hanaa (fl. 2005–)   4976
Saudi cartoonist; a.s.a. Hannah Hajjar

Hajiyeva, Lala Shovket
(1952–)   4108
Azeri politician

Hale, Clara Mcbride
(1905–1992)   2020
Amer. child care worker; fdr.,
Hale House, 1973

Hale, Lucretia Peabody
(1820–1900)   967
Amer. writer; s. Edward Everett H— (1822–1909; author,
Unitarian minister and social
reformer; chaplain of the U.S.
Senate, 1903–9)

Hale, Nancy (1908–1988)   2089
Amer. writer, editor

Hale, Sarah Josepha
(1788–1879)   807
Amer. writer, editor, poet;
née Buell, a.k.a. Cornelia;
first woman magazine editor
in U.S.; established Thanksgiving as national holiday;
established Mount Vernon as
national shrine

Haley, Gail E. (1939–)   3146
Amer. children's writer, illustrator; w. Joseph A. Haley,
mathematician; Caldecott,
1970

Halifax, Joan (1942–)   3341
Amer. anthropologist, ecologist, civil rights activist, Zen
teacher, hospice caregiver;
ex-w. Stanislav Grof (1931–),
Czech./Amer. Pioneer in
transpersonal psychology; fdr.,
Ojai Foundation (CA, 1979),
Project on Being with Dying;
Upaya Institute and Zen Center (NM, 1990)

Hall, Hazel (1886–1924)   1651
Amer. poet

Hall, Daniel, Mrs.
(fl. 1770s–80s)   748
Amer. householder

Hall, Hazel (1886–1924)   1651
Amer. poet

Hall, Radclyffe (1880–1943)   1545
Eng. writer, poet; née Mar-
guerite R— H—; pseud. John
R— H—

Hall, Sharlot Mabridth
(1870–1943)   1374
Amer. editor, writer, poet

Hallack, Cecily R.
(1898–1938)   1866.1
Eng. writer, poet

Hallman, Linda D. (1953?–) 4179
Amer. foundation administrator; exec. dir., AAUW

Halonen, Tarja Kaarina
(1943–)   3418
Finn. lawyer, politician; President of Finland, 2000– ; first
woman to hold the office

Halprin, Anna (1920–)   2373
Amer. choreographer,
dance therapist, author; w.
Lawrence H— , landscape
architect, city planner, author,
painter; fdr., San Francisco
Dancer's Workshop, 1955;
cofounder. Tamalpa Institute,
1978

Halprin, Sally (fl. 1990s–)   4965
Amer. journalist

Halsey, Margaret [Frances]
(1910–1997)   2130
Amer. writer; mn. Stern

Halsted, Anna Roosevelt
(1906–1975)   2046
Amer. women's rights &
civil rights activist, editor;
d. Eleanor* and Franklin
D. R— (1882–1945; politi-
cian; 32nd U.S. president,
1933–45); grandn. Theodore
R— (1858–1919; military
hero and politician; 26th
U.S. president, 1901–09) and
Corinne R. Robinson,* n.
Edith Carow R—*

Hamburg, Margaret "Peggy" [Ann]
(1955–)   4303.1
Amer. physician, public health
administrator; d. Beatrix
H— , first African-American
woman to attend Vassar
College and earn a degree
from Yale University School
of Medicine; David H— ,
president of the Institute of
Medicine; dir, Food and Drug
Administration (2009–)

Hamer, Fannie Lou
(1917–1977)   2290
Amer. farmer, civil rights
activist; founder of the Mississippi Freedom Democratic
Party; NWHF

Hamill, Janet (1945–)   3576
Amer. poet, writer, painter,
performance artist

Hamilton, Alice (1869–1970) 1361
Amer. bacteriologist, physician; founder of the science
of industrial medicine in the
U.S.A.; first woman faculty
member at Harvard Univer-
sity; NWHF

Hamilton, Anna (1843–1875) 1115
Ir. poet

Hamilton, Edith (1867–1963) 1336
Amer. translator, classical
scholar, writer

Hamilton, Eleanor (1909–?)   2109
Amer. sex therapist, marriage
counselor, author; née Poorman

Hamilton, Elizabeth
(1758?–1816)   691
Ir./Scot. governess, poet,
author

Hamilton, Emma, Lady
(1765–1815)   727
Eng. beauty, adventurer; née
Emily Lyon, a.k.a. Emily
Hart; w. Sir William H—,
mistress of Horatio Nelson
(1758–1805; Brit. admiral),
m. Horatia Nelson

Hamilton, Gail (1833–1896)   1051
Amer. humorist, writer; née
Mary Abigail Dodge

Hamilton, Jane (1957–)   4411
Amer. novelist

Hamm, Mia (1972–)   4859
Amer. athlete (soccer); U.S.
National soccer team; Olym-
pic gold medalist; World Cup
champion; five-time National
Player of the Year

Hammond, Eleanor Prescott
(1866–1933)   1328
Amer. scholar, writer

Hampl, Patricia (1946–)   3661
Amer. essayist

Hampson, Daphne (1944–)   3508
Brit. philosopher

Handle, Irene (1901/02–1987) 1806
Eng. author, actor

Handler, Marisa (1977?–)   4917
S. Afr./Amer. journalist, activist, musician

Handler, Ruth (1916–)   2269
Amer. businesswoman,
advocate for breast can-
cer survivors, inventor;
cofounder, Mattel Corp.,
1944; designed "Barbie" doll,
1956; designed "Ken" doll,
1961; designed "Nearly Me"
artificial breast for mastectomy patients, 1976

Hanim, Leylâ (1850–1936)   1175
Turk. poet

Hankey, Katherine
(1834–1911)   1056
Eng. hymnist

Hannah (1040 B.C.E.?–?)   30
Hebrew biblical figure; w.
Elkanah, son of Jeroham; m.
Samuel (judge and prophet,
11th century B.C.E.)

Hansberry, Lorraine
(1930–1965)   2711
Amer. playwright; w. Robert
Nemiroff (songwriter, publisher); NYDCCA, 1959

Hansen, Grace (1913–1985)   2198
Amer. politician, dance director

Han Suyin, (1917–)   2291
Chin./Fr. physician, writer,
researcher; a.k.a. Elizabeth
Comber, née Rosalie Elisabeth
Kuangchu Chow

Han Ts'ui-p'in, (fl. 850s–)   153
Chin. courtier, poet

Hapsburg, Maria   see MARIA OF
HUNGARY AND BOHEMIA

Harding, Florence Kling
(1860–1924)   1255
Amer. first lady, society leader;
w. Warren G. H— (1865–
1923; politician; 29th U.S.
president, 1921–23)

Harding, M. Esther
(1888–1971)   1680
Amer. psychoanalytic writer,
author, psychologist

Harding, Sandra G. (1935–) 2934
Amer. feminist philosopher of
science; NSF fellowship, 1983;
named Woman Philosopher of
the Year, 1990

Harding, Tonya [Maxene]
(1970–)   4820
Amer. ice skater; mn. Gillooly;
1st pl., U.S. Figure Skating
Championships, 1991

Hardwick, Elizabeth
(1916–2007)   2270
Amer. writer, literary &
drama critic, educator; w.
Robert Lowell (Amer. Poet,
1917–1977); cofounder, New
York Review of Books; first
woman to receive George
Jean Nathan Award for theater criticism

Hari, Mata (1876–1917)   1475
Dutch spy, dancer; née Mar-
garetha Geertruida Zelle,
a.k.a. "The Red Danger"; mn.
MacLeod

Harima, Young Woman of
(fl. 710s–719)   134
Jap. poet

Harington, Lucy (1581–1627)   389
Eng. poet, patron of poets;
a.k.a. countess of Bedford,
Lady Russell, Selena; d. Sir
John H— (translator), w. Ed-
ward Russell, earl of Bedford

Harjo, Joy (1951–)   4045
Amer. filmmaker, educator
(creative writing), saxophonist, poet, screenwriter, editor;
NEA; NEH

Harkness, Madden (195-?–)   3973
Amer. painter

Harley, Brilliana, Lady
(1600–1643)   411
Eng. letter writer; d. Sir
Edward Conway, baron of
Ragley; third w. Sir Robert
H— (Member of Parliament)

Harlow, Leo P., Mrs.   see GILTI-
NAN, CAROLINE

Harper, Frances Ellen Watkins
(1825–1911)   1000
Amer. poet, novelist, activist,
essayist, orator; Underground
Railroad Worker, 1853–54;

founding member and vice-
president, National Association
of Colored Women, 1897

Harper, Martha Matilda
(1857–1950)   1223
Can./Amer. servant, entrepreneur; created the first
business format franchising
system in the United States
(beauty salons); invented
first reclining shampoo chair;
NWHF, 2003

Harriman, Florence [Jaffray] Hurst
(1870–1967)   1375
Amer. public servant; U.S.
Minister to Norway, 1937–
1940

Harris, Barbara (1935–)   2935
Amer. actor; Tony, 1967

Harris, Barbara Clementine
(1930–)   2712
Amer. priest; first woman
bishop in Anglican Communion

Harris, Corra May
(1869–1935)   1362
Amer. writer; née White

Harris, Janet [Dorothea]
(1915–)   2243
Amer. educator, civil rights
activist, writer; official of
NOW and CORE (Congress
of Racial Equality)

Harris, Jean (1923–)   2228
Amer. school administrator,
nonfiction writer, teacher; née
Struven

Harris, Joanne [Michèle Sylvie]
(1964–)   4677
Brit. writer

Harris, Julie (1925–)   2520
Amer. stage & screen actor;
NYDCCA, 1951; Tony (4);
Emmy, 1958, 1961

Harris, Marguerite
(1899–1978)   1886
Amer. poet; founder of Woodstock Poetry Festival

Harris, Maureen [Scott]
(1943–)   3419
Can. poet

Harris, Patricia Roberts
(1924–1985)   2485
Amer. educator, lawyer,
politician; U.S. Ambassador
to Luxembourg, 1965–67;
Secretary, U.S. Dept. of Housing and Urban Development,
1977–79; Secretary, U.S. Dept.
of Health, Education & Welfare, 1979–1980; first black
woman Cabinet member in
U.S.A.; NWHF

Harris, Rachel (1975?–)   4893
Amer. environmentalist; co-
ordinator of the U.S. Climate
Change Campaign of the
Women's Environment & De-
velopment Organization

Harris, Ruth Mae (1940–)   3195
Amer. teacher, civil rights ac-
tivist, singer; one of the 1960's
"Freedom Singers"

Harrison, Barbara Grizzuti
(1934–2002)   2893
Amer. journalist, writer; ABA

Harrison, Jane [Ellen]
(1850–1928)   1176
Eng. writer, classical scholar,
archaeologist

Harrison, Kathryn (1961–)   4579
Amer. writer; w. Colin H—
(1960–), author, editor

Hart, Emily   see HAMILTON,
EMMA

Hart, Frances [Newbold] Noyes
(1890–1943)   1707
Amer. writer

Hart, Josephine (1956?–)   4367
Ir./Eng. novelist, theater producer, poetry advocate; w.
Maurice Saatchi, advertising
magnate, political adviser

Hart, Louise (1937–)   3034
Amer. lecturer, author

Hart, Nancy (1735?–1830)   618
Amer. revolutionary hero;
née Ann Morgan, a.k.a.
"Aunt Nancy"; possibly c.
Daniel Boone (frontiersman,
1734–1820) and Gen. Daniel
Morgan (Amer. Revolutionary
general, 1836–1802)

Hartigan, Grace (1922–)   2430
Amer. painter

Hartman, Saidiya (195-?–)   3974
Amer. author, educator (African American studies)

Harvey, Alice
(fl. 1580s–d. 1600)   386
Eng. noble; s. Gabriel H—

Harvey, Matthea (1973–)   4876
Amer. poet, educator, poetry

Hashemi Rafsanjani, Faezeh
(1962–)   4617
Iran. political scientist, newspaper publisher, women's
rights activist; d. Akbar
Hashemi Rafsanjani (1934–),
politician, businessman; former
President (1989–1997); MP

Hasina Wajed, Sheikh
(1947–)   3749.1
Bangladesh politician; d.
Sheikh Mujibur Rahman
(1920–1975), fdg. father &
first pres. of Bangladesh; w.
M. A. Wazed Miah (1942–
2009), nuclear scientist; prime
minister, 1996–2001; 2009–

Haskell, Molly (1940–)   3147
Amer. film critic, writer; w.
Andrew Sarris, Amer. film
critic

Haskins, Minnie [Louise]
(1875–1957)   1459
Eng. educator, writer

Hastings, Flora [Elizabeth], Lady (1806–1839)   896
Eng. poet

Hastings, Selina (1707–1791)   562
Eng. Methodist leader; a.k.a. countess of Huntingdon

Hathaway, Helen [Durham] (1893–1932)   1772
Amer. writer, satirist

Hathshepsut (fl. 1500s–d. 1482 B.C.E.)   14
Egyp. queen, poet; w. Thutmose II; one of five women in Egyptian history crowned as king

Hatun, Mihri (1440–1506)   261
Turk. poet; a.k.a. Mihrinisa or Fahrunnisa

Hauser, Ewa (1946–)   3662
Cuban novelist, educator (political science)

Hausman, Bernice L. (1962–)   4618
Amer. nonfiction writer, educator (English)

Hausset, Madame du (fl. 1750s–1764)   661
Fr. courtier; royal bed-chamber attendant to Mme. de Pompadour*

Havergal, Frances Ridley (1836–1879)   1072
Eng. poet

Hawes, Elizabeth "Babe" (1903–1971)   1969
Amer. fashion designer, author

Hawkes, Jacquetta [Jessie] [Hopkins] (1910–1996)   2131
Eng. writer, archaeologist; d. Sir Frederick Gowland (biochemist); w. J.B. Priestley (1894–1984; playwright, novelist); principal, founder and secretary of United Kingdom Commission for UNESCO 1943–48; C.B.E., 1952

Hawn, Goldie [Jean] (1945–)   3577
Amer. actor, producer; partner, Kurt Russell, actor (1951–); Golden Globe (1969); Oscar (1969)

Hawthorne, Sophia Amelia Peabody (1809–1871)   906
Amer./Eng. painter, illustrator; w. Nathaniel H— (1804–1864), Amer. Author

Hay, Lucy (1599–1660)   406
Eng. wit; a.k.a. countess of Carlisle

Hayashi Fumiko (1904–1951)   1993
Jap. poet, writer; Women's Prize for Literature, 1948

Hayden, Anna Tompson (1648?–1720?)   483
Amer. poet; a.s.a. Haiden; half-s. Benjamin Tompson (poet)

Hayden, Esther (1713?–1758)   575
Amer. poet

Hayes, Elinor [Rice] (1901–1994)   1933
Amer. writer

Hayes, Helen (1900–1992)   1904
Amer. writer, actor; née Brown; w. Charles MacArthur (playwright, 1895–1956); m. James MacArthur (1937– ; actor); Academy Award, 1931, 1932, 1970; Tony, 1947, 1958, 1980 for "distinguished lifetime achievement"; Emmy, 1952; Grammy, 1977; NWHF

Hayes, Lucy Webb (1831–1889)   1041
Amer. society leader, first lady; w. Rutherford B. H— (1822–93; politician, lawyer, soldier; 19th U.S. president, 1877–81); s. Lucretia Garfield*

Haywood, Eliza (1693?–1756)   539
Eng. poet, editor, novelist, playwright, actor; née Fowler, a.s.a. Heywood; produced *The Female Spectator* (1722–46), the first magazine created by and for women

Hazan, Marcella (1924–)   2486
Ital./Amer. cook, researcher, author, biologist, geologist-paleontologist, teacher

Hazleton, Lesley (1945–)   3578
Brit./Amer. educator, political journalist, nonfiction writer; founding teacher and counselor at Jerusalem Experimental High School, 1972–75

Hazzard, Shirley (1931–)   2763
Aust./Amer. writer; w. Francis Steegmuller (scholar)

H. D. see DOOLITTLE, HILDA

Head, Bessie [Amelia Emery] (1937–1986)   3035
S. Afr./Bots. novelist

Head, Edith (1897–1981)   1850
Amer. author, costume designer; Academy Award (8)

Healy, Bernadine (1944–)   3509
Amer. cardiologist, administrator, journalist; dir., NIH (1991–93); dir., American Red Cross (1999–2001)

Hearne, Mary (fl. 1710s–20s)   569
Eng. novelist

Heathorn, Henrietta [Anne] (1825–1915)   1001
Eng. writer, poet; w. Thomas Henry Huxley (1825–95; biologist and educator)

Heaton, Rose Henniker (1884–?)   1612
Eng. poet, writer; mn. Porter

Hebard, Gracy [Raymond] (1861–1936)   1269
Amer. educator, historian

Hebblethwaite, Margaret (1954?–)   4250.1
Eng./Par. missionary, author, teacher, journalist, feminist

Hecht, Jennifer Michael (1965–)   4699
Amer. poet, historian, educator

Heckler, Margaret [O'Shaughnessy] (1931–)   2764
Amer. lawyer, politician; U.S. Congresswoman (R-Massachusetts), 1967–1983; cofounder, Congressional Caucus for Women's Issues, 1977

Hector, Annie   see ALEXANDER, MRS.

Hedrick, Joan D. (1944–)   3510
Amer. biographer, educator; Pulitzer, 1996

Hedström, Barbro (1943–)   3420
Swed. sculptor, actor; great-great grandn. Emily Nomen (ca. 1830; painter, author); chair, Varmland Artist Union, 1986–

Heelis, Helen   see POTTER, BEATRIX

Hegi, Ursula (1946–)   3663
Ger./Amer. novelist

Heide, Wilma Scott (1921–1985)   2400
Amer. nurse, feminist; 3rd president of NOW, 1971–74

Heilbrun, Carolyn G. (1926–2003)   2552
Amer. social critic, educator (English), novelist, nonfiction writer; née Gold; pseud. Amanda Cross

Heimel, Cynthia (1947–)   3750
Amer. humorist, writer, playwright

Hejinian, Lyn (1941–)   3269
Amer. poet, translator, essayist; w. Larry Ochs (1949–), Amer. Jazz saxophonist and composer

Heldman, Caroline (1972–)   4860
Amer. educator, political science, activist, political, reporter; 4th degree black-belt in Tae Kwon Do

Heldman, Gladys (1922–2003)   2431
Amer. publicist, writer; cofounder, Virginia Slims Women's Pro Tennis Tour; fdr., *World Tennis* magazine

Helfenstein, Ernest   see SMITH, ELIZABETH

Heller, Karen (1957?–)   4412
Amer. columnist, writer

Hellman, Lillian (1905–1984)   2021
Amer. writer, political activist, playwright; ex-w. Arthur Kober (playwright), lover, Dashiell Hammett (1894–1961; detective fiction writer);

NYDCC, 1941, 1960; NBA, 1969/1970

Helmsley, Leona (M) (1920–2007)   2374
Amer. hotel owner; née Rosenthal; a.k.a. Queen of Mean; w. Harry H— (1910– ; real estate magnate)

Héloïse (1098?–1164)   178
Fr. abbess, letter writer; w. Peter Abelard (1079–1142; theologian and philosopher)

Hemans, Felicia Dorothea (1793–1835)   838
Eng. poet, playwright, translator, illustrator; née Brown, a.k.a. Egeria

Hempel, Amy (1951–)   4046
Amer. writer, journalist, educator

Henderson, Hazel (1933–)   2853
Brit./Amer. economist, columnist, futurist, author

Heng, Geraldine (fl. 1993–2003)   4974
Singap./Amer. educator (women's studies); founder and codirector, the Global Middle Ages Project (G-MAP), the Mappamundi project, and the Scholarly Community for the Globalization of the Middle Ages (SCGMA)

Henley, Beth (1952–)   4109
Amer. playwright, actor; Pulitzer for Drama, 1981

Henley, Nancy [Eloise] M[ain] (1934–)   2894
Amer. psychologist, educator, author

Henrey, Robert, Mrs. (1906–2004)   2047
Fr. novelist, a.k.a. Madeleine Henry

Henrietta Maria, Queen (1609–1666)   424
Fr./Eng. queen; d. Maria de Medici and Henry IV (1553–1610; king of France, 1589–1610), w. Charles I (1600–49; king of England, 1625–49), m. Charles II (1630–85; king of England, 1660–85)

Henriksen, Louise Levitas (1912–1997)   2179
Amer. journalist; d. Anzia Yezierska*

Henrion, Claudia (1958–)   4454
Amer. mathematician, educator

Hepburn, Audrey (1929–1993)   2662
Belg./Eng. screen actor, children's rights advocate; née Edda van Heemstra H— Ruston; w. Mel Ferrer (1; Amer. actor, 1917–); UNICEF ambassador; Academy Award,

1953; Jean Hersholt Humanitarian Award, 1992

Hepburn, Katherine
(1909–2003)   2110
Amer. screen actor; Academy
Award (4); Emmy, 1975

Hepworth, Barbara [Jocelyn], Dame
(1903–1975)   1970
Eng. sculptor; C.B.E., 1965

Herbert, Marie (1941–)   3270
Ir. wilderness guide, writer,
psychotherapist; w. Sir Wally
H—

Herbert, Mary Sidney
(1561–1621)   365
Eng. translator, poet, patron
of literature; a.k.a. countess
of Pembroke; s. Sir Phillip Sidney (1554–86; poet,
soldier, politician), a. M— S—
Wroth*

Herchenfreda (fl. 600s)   119
Merovingian householder

d'Hericourt, Jenny P.
(1809–1875)   907
Fr. philosopher

Herman, Judith Lewis (1942–)3342
Amer. author; cofounder,
Cambridge Hospital Victims
of Violence (VOV) Program,
Mass. (1984); National Institute of Mental Heath Fellow,
1997; Guggenheim 1984, 1985

Herman, Susan J.
(1942–2009)   3343
Amer. educator, organizational
consultant; née Goldsmith;
mn. Kofinas; est., The Susan
J. Herman Leadership Award
in Holocaust and Genocide
Awareness, 2009

Hernandez, Aileen Clarke
(1926–)   2553
Amer. business executive, feminist, public affairs counselor;
president of NOW, 1970–71

Hernandez, Antonia (1948–) 3830
Amer. lawyer

Herndon, Rosanna Taylor
(1930–)   2713
Amer. author, educator, storyteller; m. Cici Miller*

Heron, Joan (1933–)   2854
Amer. psychiatric nurse, educator (nursing), social activist

Herron, Carolivia (1947–)   3751
Amer. writer

Herrström, Christina (1959–) 4489
Swed. playwright; w. Peter
Schildt (actor-director); Royal
Theatre Dramateus, 1987

Herschberger, Ruth
(1917–)   2292–2293
Amer. poet

Herschel, Caroline Lucretia
(1750–1848)   662
Ger./Eng. astronomer; s. Sir
William H— (1739–1822;

astronomer), a. John H—
(1792–1871; astronomer)

Heschel, Susannah (1956–)   4368
Amer. writer, educator (Jewish
studies); d. Abraham Joshua
H—, Pol./Amer. rabbi, philosopher, civil rights activist;
Rockefeller Fellow, Ford Fdn.
Grant

Hess, Cynthia (1964?–)   4678
Amer. dancer, exotic; a.k.a.
Tonda Marie, Chesty Love

Hewett, Dorothy Coade
(1923–2002)   2459
Aust. lyricist, playwright,
poet, novelist, political activist; Australian Writers Guild
awards 1974 and 1982;
International Women's Year
grant, 1976; Lifetime Emeritus grant, Australia Council
1997.

Hewitt, Mary Elizabeth
(1807–1894)   901
Amer. poet, editor

Hewlett, Sylvia Ann (1946–) 3664
Eng./Amer. author, economist

Heyward, Carter, Reverend
(1945–)   3579
Amer. Episcopal priest, educator (theology), book editor,
nonfiction writer

Heyward, Jane Screven
(fl. 1920s–1939)   2375
Amer. poet

Hibbard, [Helen] Grace
(1870?–1911)   1376
Amer. poet, writer; née Porter

Hickey, Emily [Henrietta]
(1845–1913)   1137
Ir. poet

Hickok, Lorena A.
(1893–1968)   1773
Amer. political journalist

Higginbottom, Heather A.
(1972?–)   4861
Amer. public servant

Higgins, Tracy E. (1965?–)   4700
Amer. lawyer, educator (law)

Higginson, Ella [Reeves]
(1862–1940)   1287
Amer. writer, poet, historian

Highbridge, Dianne (1945–) 3580
Aust./Jap. writer

Hildegarde von Bingen
(1098–1179)   179
Ger. composer, abbess, mystic,
poet, painter; a.k.a. Sibyl of
the Rhine

Hill, Anita [Faye] (1956–)   4369
Amer. educator (law), attorney; Ida B. Wells Award from
the National Coalition of 100
Black Women, 1991

Hill, Catherine
(Contemporary–)   4979
Amer. researcher; Dir. Of Research, AAUW Ed. Fdn.

Hill, Lauryn (1975–)   4894
Amer. songwriter, singer;
founder, The Refugee Camp
Youth Project

Hill, Ruth Beebe (1913–)   2199
Amer. historian, novelist

Hillesum, Etty (1914–1943)   2219
Dutch diarist, writer

Hillman, Brenda (1951–)   4047
Amer./Braz. poet

Hime, Iwa no   see IWA NO HIME

Himmelfarb, Gertrude
(1922–)   2432
Amer. educator, historian, author; w. Irving Kristol, Amer.
journalist, essayist; father of
neoconservatism; m. William
Kristol, editor

Hinck, Jeannie (1952–)   4110
Amer. songwriter, poet, singer

Hind bint Utba
(fl. 600s–d. 635)   120
Arab poet

Hine, Darlene Clark (1947–) 3752
Amer. educator, history, historian, African-American; Pres.,
Organization of American Historians (2002); pres., Southern
Historical Assn. (2004)

Hine, Lorraine (1930–)   2714
Amer. politician; state representative (D-Washington),
199?–

Hinkle, Beatrice [Mores]
(1874–1953)   1436
Amer. translator, writer,
psychiatrist; née Van Geisen;
developed first psychotherapeutic clinic in U.S. at Cornell
Medical College, 1908

Hinkson, Katharine Tynan
(1861–1931)   1270
Ir. writer, poet

Hinton, S[usan] E[loise]
(1948–)   3831
Amer. novelist

Hirshfield, Jane (1953–)   4180
Amer. poet, translator

Hirsi Ali, Ayaan (1969–)   4789
Som./Dutch screenwriter, feminist, politician; d. H- Magan
Ise, Somali scholar, politician,
revolutionary opposition
leader; MP, Dutch Parliament

Hite, Shere (1942–)   3344
Amer. sex educator, feminist;
née Shirley Diana Gregory

Hit-him-home, Joane
(fl. 1640s)   475
Eng. author (pseud. only)

Ho, Lady (fl. 300 B.C.E.)   67
Chin. poet

Hobbes, John Oliver   see CRAIGIE,
PEARL

Hobson, Laura Z[ametkin]
(1900–1986)   1905
Amer. publicist, journalist,
writer

Hoby, Elizabeth   see RUSSELL,
ELIZABETH

Hoby, Margaret, Lady
(1570–1633)   375
Eng. diarist; née Dakins; w.
Walter Devereaux (1; brother
of Robert, earl of Essex),
Thomas Sidney (2; brother of
Phillip Sidney, 1554–86; poet,
soldier and politician) and
Thomas Posthumous H— (3);
s. Thomas H— and Elizabeth
H— Russell*

Hochman, Sandra (1936–)   2983
Amer. poet, filmmaker; mn.
Leve

Hochschild, Arlie Russell
(1940–)   3196
Amer. educator, writer, researcher

Hocking, Anne (1890–1966)   1708
Brit. mystery novelist; a.k.a.
Mona Messer

Hodgkin, Dorothy Crowfoot
(1910–1994)   2132
Brit. physicist (crystallography); photographed for the
first time single crystals of a
protein — pepsin (1934, w/J.
D. Bernal); first person to determine the three-dimensional
structure of a complex bio-organic molecule, 1941;
determined the structure
of penicillin, 1944; Royal
Medal, The Royal Society of
London 1956; Nobel Prize
in chemistry, 1964; second
woman to receive Order of
Merit (U.K.), 1965; Lenin
Peace Prize, 1987

Hoffman, Eva (1945–)   3581
Pol./Amer. writer, editor; née
Wydra ;a.s.a. Ewa H–

Hoffman, Malvina
(1885–1966)   1630
Amer. sculptor; mn. Grimson

Hogan, Linda [K.] (1947–)   3753
Amer. writer, poet, storyteller,
environmental activist

Hoglah   see MAHLAH, NOAH,
HOGLAH, MILCAH AND TIRZAH,
FIVE DAUGHTERS OF ZELOPHEHAD

Hogue, Ilyse (1969?–)   4790
Amer. activist (environmental); Director, Rainforest
Action Network; Campaign
Director, MoveOn.org; co-founder, smartMeme.com

Holbrook, Ann [Catherine]
(1780–1837)   781
Eng. actor, author; née Jackson

Holford, Margaret
(1778–1852)   776
Scot. novelist, poet; née
Wrench; a.k.a. M- Hodson; d.
M- Wrench H—*

Holford, Margaret Wrench (1761?–1834) 711
Eng. poet, novelist; m. Margaret Hodson Holford*

Holiday, Billie (1915–1959) 2244
Amer. songwriter, singer; née Eleanora Fagan; Recording Academy Hall of Fame; RRHF, 2000

Holland, Barbara (1951–) 4048
Amer. poet

Holland, Elizabeth (1771–1845)756
Eng. salonist; née Vassall; w. Lord H—

Holland, Norah M. (1876–1925) 1476
Amer. poet

Hollander, Xaviera (1943–) 3421
Indones./Amer. brothel-keeper, prostitute; née de Vries

Holley, Marietta (1836?–1926)1073
Amer. humorist, writer; pseud. Josiah Allen's Wife

Holley, Mary [Phelps] Austin (1784–1846) 796
Amer. author, land speculator

Hollibaugh, Amber (1947?–) 3754
Amer. activist (AIDS), community organizer

Holliday, Judy (1921–1965) 2401
Amer. actor; née Tuvim; Oscar (1950)

Hollman, Peggy (1955–) 4304
Amer. writer, software designer, conference host

Holman, Sheri (1966–) 4722
Amer. novelist

Holmes, Marjorie (1910–2002)2133
Amer. author, artist, columnist

Holmes, Mary Jane [Hawes] (1828–1907) 1018
Amer. writer

Holt, Anne Haw (1934–) 2895
Amer. storyteller, novelist, poet, historian

Holt, Kimberly Willis (1960–) 4535
Amer. writer, children's; National Book Award, 1999

Holtby, Winifred (1898–1935) 1867
Eng. novelist, journalist, pacifist

Holtzman, Elizabeth (1941–) 3271
Amer. lawyer, politician; a.k.a. "Liz the Lion"; U.S. congresswoman (D-New York), 1973–81; youngest woman ever elected to Congress; cofounder, congressional Caucus for Women's Issues, 1977

Holtzman, Fanny Ellen (1903–1980) 1971
Amer. attorney

Home, Anne (1742–1821) 639
Scot. bluestocking, poet; a.k.a. A— Hunter; w. John Hunter, m. John Hunter of Glasgow (physiologist, anatomist)

Home, Grisell, Lady (1665–1746) 505
Scot. poet, author, spy; a.s.a. Hume, a.k.a. Grizel Baillie

Homespun, Prudentia see WEST, JANE

Ho Nansorhon (1563–1589) 368
Korean poet; s. Ho Kyun (novelist)

Hong, Rani (1972–) 4862
Ind./Amer. administrator, human rights activist; cofounder, Tronie Foundation

Honnamma (fl. 1660s–d. 1699) 495
Ind. poet

Honora or Honora–Maresia see MURRAY, JUDITH

Hooks, Bell (1955–) 4305
Amer. feminist theorist, poet, cultural critic, writer, educator; née Gloria Jean Watkins

Hooper, Ellen Sturgis (1816–1841) 937
Amer. poet

Hoover, Eleanor (1925?–) 2521
Amer. writer

Hoover, Louise "Lou" Henry (1874–1944) 1437
Amer. first lady, translator, society leader; w. Herbert H— (1874–1964; politician; 31st U.S. president, 1929–1933)

Hooyman, Nancy R. (1945–) 3582
Amer. educator (gerontology), college administrator, feminist, social worker

Hope, Laurence (1865–1904) 1315
Eng. poet; a.k.a. Adela Florence Nicolson

Hope, Lugenia Burns (1871–1947) 1390.1
Amer. black rights activist, social worker, educator

Hoper, Mrs. (fl. 1740s) 631
Eng. actor, playwright

Hopkins, Jane Ellice (1837–1915) 1079
Eng. social reformer, writer

Hopkins, Nancy (1944–) 3511
Amer. educator, biologist

Hopper, Grace Murray (1906–1992) 2048
Amer. mathematician, military officer, educator; née Brewster; helped program Mark I, first large scale automatic calculator; coined computer term "bug"; co-creator of COBOL, the computer language for business, and invented the language APT; Data Processing Management Association's first "Man of the Year" award, 1969; NWHF

Hopper, Hedda (1890–1966) 1709
Amer. writer, columnist

Horacek, Judy (1961–) 4580
Aust. cartoonist, illustrator

Horan, Nancy (1948–) 3832
Amer. writer

Horikawa, Lady (fl. 1130s–d. 1165) 186
Jap. poet; attendant of Empress Dowager Taiken

Horne, Lena (1917–2010) 2294
Amer. singer, actor, activist (civil rights); w. Lennie Hayton (2), Amer. Music conductor and arranger; NYDCC, 1980; Grammy(3) plus Lifetime Achievement, 1989

Horne, Marilyn (1934–) 2896
Amer. opera singer; Grammy (3); Gold Medal of Merit, NIAL, 1987; Abbiatti Premis for Best Operatic Interpretation of the Year, 1986

Horner, Matina (1939–) 3148–3149
Amer. educator, college administrator, psychologist, writer; née Souretis; pres., Radcliffe College (1972–1989)

Horney, Karen (1885–1952) 1631
Ger./Amer. psychiatrist, writer; née Danielson

Horsfield, Debbie (1955–) 4306
Eng. TV writer, playwright; Thames TV Award, 1983

Horta, Maria Teresa (1939–) 3036
Portuguese writer, poet

Hortensia (85 B.C.E.–?) 74
Roman orator, reformer; d. Quintus Hortensius (orator)

Hosain, Attia (1913–1998) 2200
Ind./Eng. writer, journalist, radio producer; great-aunt Kamila Shamsie (1973–), Ind. Novelist

Ho Shuang-ch'ing (1712–?) 573
Chin. poet

Hosmer, Harriet (1830–1908) 1026
Amer./Ital. sculptor

Hospital, Janette Turner (1942–) 3345
Aust. novelist, educator (writing); a.k.a. Alex Juniper

Houdetot, Sophie de la Briche, countess (1730–1813) 609
Fr. musician, poet, wit

Houston, Jean (1937–) 3037
Amer. nonfiction writer, philosopher; cofounder, Foundation for Mind Research

Houston, Jeanne Wakatsuki (1934–) 2897
Amer. writer; a.k.a. Toyo

Houston, Libby (1941–) 3272
Eng. poet, broadcaster; a.k.a. Elizabeth Maynard H—

Houston, Velina Hasu (1957–) 4413
Amer. writer, playwright; cofounder, Amerasian League; Lorraine Hansberry Playwriting Award, 1982, Blackburn; Rockefeller, 1984, 1987

Hou Xiaotian (1961–) 4581
Chin. political activist, educator; w. Wang Juntao (activist, 1959– ; political prisoner, 1989–)

Howar, Barbara (1934–) 2898
Amer. writer, society leader

Howard, Anne Dacre (1557–1630) 359
Eng. poet; a.k.a. duchess of Arundel; w. Phillip H—, earl of Arundel

Howard, Anne Douglas (1696–1764) 543
Eng. poet; a.k.a. A— Douglas; Viscountess Irwin

Howard, Isabella (1722?–1793/95?) 589
Eng. poet; née Byron, a.k.a. countess of Carlisle

Howard, Jane [Temple] (1935–1996) 2936
Amer. writer, editor, writer

Howard, Maureen [Keans] (1930–) 2715
Amer. writer; NBCCA, 1978

Howarth, Ellen [Clementine Doran] (1827–1899) 1014
Amer. poet; pseud. Clementine

Howe, Fanny (1940–) 3197
Amer. poet, novelist; NEA

Howe, Florence (1929–) 2663
Amer. author, public administrator, literary scholar, historian, educator; née Rosenfeld; cofounder, The Feminist Press, 1970

Howe, Julia Ward (1819–1910) 956
Amer. poet; civil rights, women's rights activist; suffragist; lecturer; writer; social reformer; founder, Mother's Day (orig. 2 June 1872), as a peace day; founder, Girl Scouts of America; NWHF

Howe, Louise Kapp (1934–1984) 2899
Amer. writer, editor

Howe, Marie (1950–) 3975
Amer. poet, educator; Guggenheim, NEA

Howe, Tina (1937–) 2678
Amer. playwright, educator; d. Quincy H— (news commentator, editor, historian); gd. Mark Antony DeWolf H— (poet and Pulitzer Prize–winning biographer); w. Norman Levy (a.s.a. Levi; historian and novelist); Obie and ODCCA, 1983; Rockefeller; Guggenheim; NEA; AAAL, 1982

Howell, Carol K. (1954–) 4251
Amer. writer, poet

Howell, Georgina (1942–) 3346
Eng. biographer, journalist

Howell, Margery Eldredge (1893–1946) 1774
Amer. poet

Howells, Mildred (1872–1966)1399
Amer. poet, painter; d. William Dean H—

Howitt, Mary (1799–1888) 864
Eng./Ital. essayist, translator, poet; née Botham; m. William H— (frequent collaborator); honored by Literary Academy of Stockholm for translation of works of Frederika Bremer*

Howland, Bette (1937–) 3039
Amer. poet, writer; McArthur "genius" grant; Guggenheim Fellowship (1978)

Howland, Robert Shaw, Mrs. see WOOLSEY, MARY

Ho Xuan Huong (fl. 1760s–1799) 708
Viet. poet

Hoyt, Helen (1887–1972) 1664
Amer. poet; a.k.a. Mrs. W. W. Lyman; Helen H- Lyman; mn. Lyman; d. Henry M. H—, gov. of PA; aunt, Elinor Wylie*

Hrdy, Sarah Blaffer (1946–) 3665
Amer. anthropologist, primatologist, educator

Hroswitha of Gandersheim (935?–1000) 158
Ger. nun, poet, playwright; née Helena von Rossen, a.s.a. Hrosvitha, Rosvitha, Hrotsvit; earliest woman poet of the middle ages whose works are preserved, first playwright and first female poet of Germany

Hsiang Chin-yu (fl. 1910s–1927) 2134
Chin. militant

Hsiao Hung (1911–1941) 2158
Chin. novelist; née Chang Nai-ying

Hsi-chün (fl. 100s B.C.E.) 73
Chin. poet; w. K'un Mo, king of Wu-sun

Hsieh Ping-ying (1906–2000) 2049–2050
Chin. political activist, novelist

Hsüeh T'ao (768–831) 140
Chin. singer, poet

Huang O (1498–1569) 292
Chin. poet; w. Yang Shen (poet)

Huang Zongying (1925–) 2522
Chin. actor, researcher, writer

Hubbard, Alice (1861–1915) 1271
Amer. writer; née Moore

Hubbard, Barbara Marx (1929–) 2664
Amer. futurist, social architect, speaker, author; pres., The Foundation for Conscious Evolution

Hubbard, Ruth (1924–) 2487
Amer. educator (biology), biologist

Huber, Catherine R. see RILLIET-HUBER, CATHERINE

Hudson, Helen (1920–) 2376
Amer. writer, political activist; née H— Lane

Huerta, Dolores (1930–) 2716
Amer. union organizer, farmworker; née Hernandez; vice president and founding member, United Farm Workers of America, 1962; NWHF

Huffington, Arianna [Stassinopoulos] (1950–) 3976
Greek/Amer. syndicated columnist, writer, public figure; s. Agapi, author, speaker performer; ex.-w. Michael H—, politician

Hufstedler, Shirley M. (1925–) 2523
Amer. public servant, lawyer, judge; U.S. secretary of education (1979–81)

Hughes, Karen (1956–) 4370–4371
Fr./Amer. political operative, government official; née Parfitt

Huldah (fl. 580s B.C.E.) 52
Judaean prophet; w. Shallum (son of Tikvah); adviser to King Josiah of Judah (640?–09? B.C.E.)

Hull, Jane Dee (1935–) 2937
Amer. politician, educator; Republican governor of Arizona, 1997–2003; Secy of State, 1994–1997

Hulme, Kathryn (1900–1981) 1906
Amer. writer

Hulme, Keri (1947–) 3755
N.Z. painter, writer; Booker, 1985; Pegasus Prize in literature, 1984

Hume, Anna (fl. 1640s) 476
Eng. poet

Huneberc of Heidenheim (ca. 778–786) 142
Eng./Ger. Benedictine nun

Hungerford, Margaret Wolfe (1855?–1897) 1205
Ir. writer; née Hamilton, pseud. The Duchess

Hungry Wolf, Beverly (1950–)3977
Amer. writer

Hunt, Carrie (1956?–) 4372
Amer. biologist, animal rights advocate; fdr., Wind River Bear Institute, 1995

Hunt, Helen Fiske see JACKSON, HELEN [MARIA]

Hunt, Lynn (1945–) 3583
Pan./Amer. historian, educator; d. Ruby H—, public servant; president, American Historial Assoc. (2002)

Hunt, Swanée (1950–) 3978
Amer. minister, public servant, photographer, composer,

social activist; w. Charles Ansbacher, conductor of the Boston Landmarks Orchestra; Natl. Women's Hall of Fame, 2007; fdr.-dir., the Women and Public Policy Program at Harvard's Kennedy School of Government (1999–); U.S. ambassador to Austria (1993–1997); NWHF

Hunter, Alberta (1895–1984) 1811
Amer. singer, songwriter, nurse

Hunter, Anne see HOME, ANNE

Hunter, Clementine (1886/1887–1988) 1652
Amer. painter; a.k.a. "the black Granda Moses"

Hunter, Kristin [Elaine] (1931–) 2765
Amer. writer, journalist; a.k.a. K- H- Lattany

Hunter-Gault, Charlayne (1942–) 3347
Amer./S. Afr. journalist; Peabody (2); Emmy (2)

Huntingdon, countess of see HASTINGS, SELINA

Huntington, Emily Clark see MILLER, EMILY

Huntington, Helen (1875?–1950) 1460
Eng. translator, writer; née Gates; pseud. H. H. Lynde; w. Harley Granville-Baker

Hurnscot, Loran (1900?–1970) 1907
Eng. writer; pseud. Gay Stuart Taylor

Hurst, Fannie (1889–1968) 1697
Amer. writer; mn. Danielson

Hurston, Zora Neale (1891–1960) 1727
Amer. anthropologist, essayist, folklorist, playwright, novelist; Guggenheim, 1936, 1938; NWHF

Huston, Anjelica (1951–) 4049
Amer. actor, director, film; d. John H—, director; ex-p. Jack Nicholson, actor; w. Robert Graham, Jr., sculptor; Golden Globe (2)

Huston, Nancy (1953–) 4181
Can. novelist, essayist

Hustvedt, Siri (1955–) 4307
Amer. essayist, poet, novelist

Hutchinson, Anne (1591–1643) 399
Eng./Amer. religious liberal; NWHF

Hutchinson, Ellen M[cKay] (fl. 1880s–1933) 1546
Amer. writer, editor, journalist; mn. Cortissoz

Hutchinson, Lucy (1620–1671) 438
Eng. diarist; née Aspley

Hutten, Bettina von, Baroness (1874–1957) 1438
Amer./Eng. writer; née Riddle

Hutton, Lauren (1943–) 3422
Amer. model, adventurer, business executive

al-Huwaider, Wajeha (1971?–) 4864
Saudi writer, poet, journalist, human rights activist

Huxley, Thomas Henry, Mrs. see HEATHORN, HENRIETTA

Huxtable, Ada Louise (1921–)2402
Amer. writer, architecture critic; née Landman; d. Michael Landman, playwright; Pulitzer, 1970

Hwang, Chin-I (1506?–1544) 299
Korean poet

Hyatt, Lesley A[nn] (1965–) 4700.1
Amer. writer, teacher; mn. Friedman; d. Judith P. Hyman*; n. Elaine B. Partnow,* Susan Partnow*; c. Jessica Partnow*; Fulbright

Hybernia, Alexander see BRONTË, ANNE

Hyde, Mary [Morley Crapo Eccles] (fl. 1940s–1982) 3198
Amer. writer

Hyman, Judith Partnow (1938–) 3089
Amer. psychotherapist, educator (psychotherapy); s. Elaine B. P—* and Susan Partnow*; a. Jessica Partnow* M. Lesley Hyatt*;

Hypatia (355–415) 107
Roman educator, mathematician, astronomer, philosopher; d. Theon (mathematician, philosopher); invented several tools: an instrument for distilling water, an instrument to measure the specific gravity of water, an astrolabe and a planisphere

I

Ian, Janis (1951–) 4050
Amer. singer, songwriter; née J- Eddy Fink; Grammy, 1975

Ibarbourou, Juana de (1895–1989) 1812
Urug. poet

Ibarruri, Dolores [Gomez] (1895–1989) 1813
Span./Sov. editor, revolutionary, government official, communist; pseud. "La Pasionaria" (The Passion Flower); Lenin Peace Prize, 1964; Order of Lenin, 1965

Ibrahim, Hauwa (1965–) 4701
Nig. educator (law), attorney, human right's activist; Sakharov Prize, 2005

Ifill, Gwen (1955–) 4308
Amer. political journalist, TV newscaster, author

Inanna (fl. 2300 B.C.E.) 6
Sumerian priestess

Inchbald, Elizabeth (1753–1821) 676
Eng. playwright, translator, author; née Simpson

Inés de la Cruz, Juana see CRUZ, JUANA INÉS DE LA

Ingelow, Jean (1820–1897) 968
Eng. poet, writer

Iola see WELLS, IDA

Iratsume, Kasa no (fl. 8th century–) 145
Jap. noble, poet; w. Otomo no Yakamochi (poet); n.-in-law Otomo no Sakano-e no Iratsume*

Iratsume, Otomo no Sakano-e no (700?–750) 128
Jap. courtier, poet; a.k.a. Lady Sakano, a.s.a. Sakano-e; s. Tabito (governor and poet), a. Otomo no Yakamochi (poet) and Kasa no Iratsume*

Ireland, Mardy Sanders (1948–) 3833
Amer. psychologist

Irigaray, Luce (1930–) 2717
Belg./Fr. feminist, philosopher, educator, writer, psychoanalyst

Iron, Ralph see SCHREINER, OLIVE

Irving, Minna (1857–1940) 1224
Amer. poet; mn. Michiner

Irwin, Viscountess see HOWARD, ANNE

Isaacs, Susan (1943–) 3423
Amer. scriptwriter, novelist

Isabella (1180?–?) 199
Roman trobairitz; friend of Elias Cairel (troubadour)

Isabella I (1451–1504) 264
Span. queen; d. John II of Castile and Isabella of Portugal; w. Ferdinand II, king of Aragon (a.k.a. Ferdinand V, 1452–1516; king of Castile); m. Catherine of Aragon*

Isasi-Diaz, Ada Maria (1943–)3424
Cub./Amer. theologian

Isaure, Clemence (1464–1515/16) 270
Fr. poet, nun; a.s.a. Clemenza, a.k.a. The Sappho of Toulouse; The Queen of Poetry; sponsored the Jeux Floreaux (Floral Games), annual May 1 poetry contest

Ise, Lady (875?–938?) 155
Jap. poet; d. Fujiwara no Tsugukage (governor of Ise), mistress of Emperor Uda, m. Prince Katsura and Lady Nakatsukasa*

Iselda (fl. 12th century) 208
Fr. trobairitz, nun

Ishikawa, Lady (fl. 780s–d. 800)143
Jap. poet

Isis (3100?– B.C.E.?) 3
Egyp. goddess and queen

Iskin, Ruth (1920–) 2377
Amer. art historian

Isma'il of Syria, Rabi'a bint (see Rabi'a bint Isma'il of Syria)

Issel, Shahieda (1957–) 4414
S. Afr. anti-apartheid activist

Itani, Frances [Susan] (1942–) 3348
Can. poet, novelist, essayist; Commonwealth Writers Prize, 2003

Itatani, Michiko (1953?–) 4182
Jap./Amer. educator (art), painter

Ivins, Molly (1944–2007) 3512
Amer. writer, syndicated newspaper columnist

Iwa no Hime (?–347) 106
Jap. empress, poet; w. Emperor Nintoku

Izumi Shikibu (974?–1030?) 165
Jap. courtier, diarist, poet; née Ōe Shikibu; d. Ōe no Masamune, lord of Echizen, w. Fujiwara no Yasumasa, lord of Tango (1), Tachibana no Michisada, lord of Izumi (2), mistress of Prince Tametaka and his brother, Prince Atsumichi, m. Ko–Shikibu no Naishi (female poet)

J

Jabs, Carolyn R. (1950–) 3979
Amer. writer

Jacker, Corinne (1933–) 2855
Amer. poet, playwright, writer; née Litvin; Emmy; Obie (2), 1975

Jackson, Elaine (1943–) 3425
Amer. playwright, educator; a.k.a. Gillian Freeman, Eliot George; Rockefeller, 1978; NEA, 1983; Langston Hughes Playwriting Award, 1979

Jackson, Glenda (1936–) 2984
Brit. actor, politician; Labour MP (1992–); CBE, 1978; Oscar, 1970, 1973; Emmy (2), 1972; Golden Globe, 1974

Jackson, Helen [Maria] Fiske Hunt (1830–1885) 1027
Amer. poet, writer; friend of Emily Dickinson*

Jackson, Jacquelyne (1932–) 2802
Amer. writer, educator, sociologist

Jackson, Janet [Damita Jo] (1966–) 4723
Amer. singer, actor; youngest of Jackson family of musicians

Jackson, Laura see RIDING, LAURA

Jackson, Lisa P[erez] (1962–) 4619
Amer. public servant, chemical engineer; U.S. Admin., EPA, 2009–

Jackson, Maggie (1964?–) 4679
Amer. educator, history, author

Jackson, Mahalia (1911–1972)2159
Amer. singer, gospel; founder, Mahalia Jackson Foundation; Grammy, 1961, 1962, 1976; RRHF, 1997

Jackson, Rachel Robards (1767–1828) 735
Amer. first lady; née Donelson; w. Lewis Robards (1) and Andrew J— (2; 1767–1845; politician, general; 7th U.S. president, 1829–37)

Jackson, Rebecca Cox (1795–1871) 848
Amer. Shaker religious leader; a.k.a. Mother J—

Jackson, Shirley (1919–1965) 2346
Amer. writer; w. Stanley Edgar Hyman (1919–1970; literary critic); NWHF

Jackson of Lodsworth, Baroness see WARD, BARBARA

Jackson-Opoku, Sandra (1953–) 4183
Amer. journalist, poet, TV writer

Jacobi, Kathryn (1947–) 3756
Amer. artist, painter

Jacobs, Bertha see BERTKEN, SISTER

Jacobs, Deborah (1952–) 4111
Amer. librarian

Jacobs, Harriet [Brent] (1818–1896) 949
Amer. slave, writer; a.k.a. Linda Brent

Jacobs, Jane (1916–2006) 2271
Amer./ Can. social critic, architectural writer, activist; née Butzner; Lifetime achievement, Natl Bldg Fdn, 2000

Jacobs, Rayda (1947?–) 3757
S. Afr./Can. novelist, filmmaker (documentary)

Jacobs, Rose Gell (1888–1975)1681
Amer. Zionist, businesswoman, journalist, civic leader; founding member of Hadassah, 1912

Jacobsen, Josephine [Winder] (1908–2003) 2090
Can./Amer. poet, author

Jacobson, Ethel (1905?–) 2022
Amer. writer, poet, literary critic

Jacobson, Sandra Weinstein (1930–) 2718
Amer. feminist

Jacoby, Susan (1945–) 3584
Amer. writer, columnist, scholar

Jacquet de la Guerre, Elisabeth-Claude (1664–1729) 502
Fr. composer, harpsichordist; w. Marin de la Guerre (organist)

Jael (fl. 1070s B.C.E.) 28
Kenite biblical figure; w. Heber; killed Sisera, captain of Jabin's army, and saved Israel from Jabin's oppression

Jaffe, Rona (1932–2005) 2766
Amer. novelist; founder, Rona Jaffe Foundation Writers' Awards, 1995

Jagan, Janet (1920–) 2378
Amer./Guyanese newspaper editor, political activist; w. Cheddi J— (d. 1972; Guyanese prime minister, 1971–1972); first female legislator in the Caribbean; first female Cabinet minister in the region; first woman prime minister and vice president, Guyana (1997–1999)

Jagger, Bianca (1950–) 3980
Nic./Eng. actor, human rights activist; née Bianca Pérez-Mora Macías; w. Mick J— (1943–) Eng. rock musician; married 1970–79; chair, World Future Council, 2007; founder, Bianca Jagger Human Rights Foundation, 2005; Right Livelihood Award, 2004

Jahan, Nur (1577–1645) 382
Ind. empress, poet; w. Emperor Jehan-gir (a.s.a. Jahangir)

Jain, Devaki (1933–) 2856
Ind. feminist, economist

James, Alice (1848–1892) 1160
Amer. diarist; s. William (1842–1920; psychologist, philosopher) and Henry (1843–1916; novelist) J—

James, Bessie Rowland (1895–1974) 1814
Amer. writer; pseud. Mary Waterstreet; w. Marquis J— (1891–1955) Pulitzer Prize winning author, journalist

James, P. D., Baroness (1920–) 2379
Eng. mystery novelist, civil servant; a.k.a. Phyllis Dorothy J— White; née White; OBE, 1983

James, Sarah (1944–) 3513
Amer. environmental activist; Goldman Environmental Prize, 2002

James, Selma (1930–) 2719
Amer. author, political activist; fdr., Int. Wages for Housework Campaign; coord., Global Women's Strike

James, Sibyl (1946–) 3666
Amer. poet, educator, writer

Jameson, Anna Brownwell (1794–1860) 844
Ir./Eng. art critic, author; née Murphy; d. Denis Murphy (miniature painter, ?–d. 1842)

Jamieson, Kathleen Hall (1946–) 3667
Amer. nonprofit administrator, educator (communications)

Jamison, Judith (1943–) 3426
Amer. dancer, choreographer; artistic director, Alvin Ailey American Dance Theatre (Alvin Ailey, 1931–89; African-American modern dancer and choreographer)

Jance, J. A. (1944–) 3514
Amer. writer, creative fiction; née Judith Ann J—

Janeway, Elizabeth [Hall] (1913–2005) 2201
Amer. literary critic, lecturer, sociologist, author; w. Eliot J— (economist); Pulitzer, 1971

Janis, Elsie (1889–1956) 1698
Amer. writer, composer, actor, poet; née Bierbower

Janowitz, Tama (1957–) 4415
Amer. author

Janvier, Margaret [Thomson] (1845–1913) 1138
Amer. poet; pseud. M— Vandegrift

Jardine, Alice A. (1955?–) 4309
Amer. scholar (feminist), educator; a.s.a. Jardim

Jardine, Lisa (1944–) 3515
Eng. historian; née L- Anne Bronowski; mn. Hare; d. Rita Coblenz, sculptor and activist

Jarrett, Valerie Bowman (1956–) 4373
Iran./Amer. lawyer, public servant, business consultant, civic leader; d. James B— , genetist, pathologist; grand. Robert Robinson Taylor, first black to grad. M.I.T., & Robert Rochon Taylor, 1st black to head Chicago Housing Authority; senior adviser to the president, 2009–

Jay, Karla (1947–) 3758
Amer. educator (English); née Berlin

Jay, W. M. L. see WOODRUFF, JULIA

Jayapal, Pramila (1965–) 4702
Ind./Amer. writer, consultant, development, activist, editor; fdr. and Exec. Dir. of OneAmerica (formerly Hate Free Zone)

Jeanne of Navarre (1271–1307/9?) 226
Fr. patron of arts and letters; w. Phillip V (1294–1322; king of France, 1316–22), d. Mahout d'Artois*; founded College of Navarre

Jeffreys, Sheila (1948–) 3834
Aust. political scientist, nonfiction writer, feminist

Jefimija (1348?–1405?) 238–239
Serb. poet, princess; née Jelena or Milica Hrebeljanović; a.s.a Jevgenija; d. Vojihna or Prince Vratko (ruler of province of Drama), w. Uglješa Mrnjavcević or Prince Lazar

Jeger, Lena May, Baroness (1915–2007) 2245
Eng. politician, civil rights activist, writer; née Chivers; MP (21 years).

Jehangir, Asma (1952–) 4112
Pak. human rights activist, lawyer, administrator; d. Malik Jilani, political activist; United Nations Special Rapporteur on Freedom of Religion or Belief of the Commission on Human Rights, 2004–; UN Special Rapporteur on Extrajudicial, Arbitrary and Summary Executions.

Jekyll, Gertrude (1843–1932) 1116
Brit. gardener, writer, designer (landscape)

Jellicoe, [Patricia] Ann (1927–) 2600
Eng. playwright, theatrician, translator; cofounder/director, Cockpit Theatre Club (1952–54); founder, Colway Theatre Trust, 1980–

Jemison, Mae (1956–) 4374
Amer. astronaut; NWHF

Jenkins, Carol (1944–) 3516
Amer. journalist, TV news anchor, women's rights activist; m. Elizabeth Gardner Hines; pres. & cofounder, Women's Media Center

Jenkins, Margaret (1947?–) 3759
Amer. choreographer, dancer; artistic director, Margaret Jenkins Dance Company, 1974–

Jennings, Elizabeth (1926–2001) 2554
Eng. poet

Jentz, Terri (1957–) 4416
Amer. writer, screenwriter; p. Donna Deitch, film director

Jephthah the Gileadite, Daughter of (fl 1140s B.C.E.) 21
Hebrew biblical figure; d. of Jephthah (ninth judge of Israel)

Jerusalem (mother of the dead child), Prostitute of (fl. 950s B.C.E.) 36
Hebrew biblical figure

Jerusalem (mother of the living child), Prostitute of (fl. 950s B.C.E.) 37
Hebrew biblical figure

Jessop, Violet (1887–1971) 1665
Argen./Eng. ship steward, nurse; survivor of the Titanic

Jesus, Carolina Maria de (1914–1977) 2220
Braz. Diarist

Jessye, Eva (1895–1992) 1815
Amer. choral director, civil rights activist; est. Eva Jessye African-American Music Collection (Univ. of MI)

Jewett, Sarah Orne (1849–1909) 1166
Amer. writer

Jewsbury, Geraldine (1812–1880) 919
Eng. novelist

Jewsbury, Maria Jane (1800–1833) 867
Eng. poet

Jezebel (fl. 870s–d. 853 B.C.E.) 40
Phoenician queen; w. Ahab, d.-in-law Omri, king of Israel (ca. 884–872 B.C.E.)

Jhabvala, Ruth Prawer (1927–) 2601
Ger./Eng. writer, screenwriter; Booker, 1983; MacArthur; AAAL; Academy Award (2); Guggenheim

Jiang Qing (1914–1991) 2221
Chin. public official; w. Mao Zedong (Tse-tung) (founder, People's Republic of China, 1892–1976)

Jibrell, Fatima (1948–) 3835
Som. environmental activist, documentary filmmaker; fdr.-dir., Horn of Africa Relief and Development Organization; fdr., Women's Coalition for Peace; cofounder, Sun Fire Cooking; Goldman Environmental Prize, 2002

Jiles, Paulette (1943–) 3427
Amer./Can. poet, novelist; Governor's Award, 1984

Joan of Arc, Saint (1412?–1431) 252
Fr. hero, patriot, martyr; a.k.a. The Maid of Orléans; led battles that turned the tide of the Hundred Years' War; saw Charles VII crowned; burned at the stake for heresy

Job, Wife of (fl. eighth century B.C.E.) 41
Edomite biblical figure

Joceline, Elizabeth (1566–1622) 371
Eng. householder, author; a.s.a. Jocelyn; d. Sir Richard Brooke

Johnsen, Dawn (1962–) 4620
Amer. lawyer, educator, constitutional law, nonprofit administrator; dir., W.H. Office of Legal Counsel, 2009–

Johnson, Abigail (1961–) 4582
Amer. business executive; d. Edward C. (Ned) Johnson III, investment giant

Johnson, Adelaide [Margaret McFadven] (1905–1960) 2023
Amer. psychiatrist, physician, lecturer

Johnson, Amy (1908?–1941) 2091
Eng. aviator

Johnson, Diane (1934–) 2900
Amer. novelist, screenwriter, educator

Johnson, Eleanor Murdock (1892–1987) 1748
Amer. author, editor, magazine publisher; creator and editor of the Weekly Reader, the most popular classroom newspaper in America (1928–61)

Johnson, Emily Pauline (1861–1913) 1272
Can. poet

Johnson, Georgia Douglas (1886–1966) 1653
Amer. poet

Johnson, Guion Griffis (1900–1989) 1908
Amer. writer, educator

Johnson, Josephine Winslow (1910–1990) 2135
Amer. novelist, poet, essayist, labor activist; Pulitzer, 1935; O. Henry (5)

Johnson, Kory (1979–) 4926
Amer. environmental activist; fdr., Children for a Safe Environment (CFSE), 1988; Goldman Environmental Prize, 1998

Johnson, [Claudia Alta] Lady Bird (1912–2007) 2180
Amer. cattle rancher, environmental activist, public figure; née Taylor; w. Lyndon B. J— (1908–73; politician; 36th U.S. president, 1963–1969); Presidential Medal of Freedom, 1977; Congressional Gold Medal, 1984

Johnson, Osa [Helen] (1894–1953) 1797
Amer. writer, explorer, filmmaker; née Leighty; w. Martin J— (explorer and filmmaker, 1884–1937)

Johnson, Pamela Hansford (1912–1981) 2181–2182
Eng. literary critic, novelist

Johnson, Rebecca L. (1956–) 4375
Amer. environmental activist

Johnson, Rheta Grimsley (1953–) 4184
Amer. columnist

Johnson, Shirbey (1941–) 3273
Amer. athletics director

Johnson, Shirley Childress (1947?–) 3760
Amer. lecturer, ASL interpreter, workshop leader; member, Sweet Honey in the Rock (vocal group)

Johnson, Sonia (1936?–) 2985
Amer. author, feminist

Johnson-Sirleaf, Ellen (1938–) 3090
Liber. politician; a.k.a. the Iron Lady; president, Liberia (2006–), Africa's first elected female head of state

Johnston, Annie Fellows (1863–1931) 1296
Amer. author, educator

Johnston, Henrietta (1665?–1728/29) 506
Ir./Amer. painter; née Deering; possibly the first professional woman artist in America

Johnston, Jennifer (1930–) 2429
Ir. novelist

Johnston, Jill (1929–) 2665
Eng./Amer. writer, feminist; pseud. F. J. Crowe

Johnston, Mary (1870–1936) 1377
Amer. novelist, women's rights activist

Johnstone, Wilhelmina Kemp (1900–1970) 1909
W. Ind. poet, writer

Jolie, Angelina (1975–) 4895
Amer. diplomat, actor; d. Jon Voight (1938–), actor, Marcheline Bertrand, actor; goodwill ambassador for the United Nations High Commission for Refugees, 2001–; Oscar, 1999; Golden Globe, 1997, 1998, 1999

Joliot-Curie, Irène (1897–1956) 1851
Fr. chemist; d. Marie* and Pierre C— (1859–1906; physical chemist), s. Ève C—*, w. Frédéric Joliot (physicist); Nobel Prize for Chemistry, 1935

Jones, Amanda Theodosia (1835–1914) 1066
Amer. teacher, poet, inventor, spiritualist, author; invented vacuum canning process, 1873; patented oil burner, 1880

Jones, Ann [Maret] (1937–) 3040
Amer. nonfiction writer

Jones, Beverly (1927–) 2602
Amer. feminist, writer

Jones, Emily Beatrix [Coursolles] (1893–1966) 1775
Eng. novelist; pseud. E. B. C. J—; mn. Lucas

Jones, Gayl (1949–) 3902
Amer. novelist

Jones, Lady   see BAGNOLD, ENID

Jones, Margo (1913–1955) 2202
Amer. director, theater producer; founder of Theater '47–'50, Dallas, Texas

Jones, Marion (1976–) 4910
Amer. track athlete

Jones, Mary (fl. 1750s– d. 1778)663
Eng. poet

Jones, Mother [Mary Harris] (1830–1930) 1028
Ir./Amer. humanitarian, labor organizer; née Harris; NWHF

Jones, Patricia (1951–) 4051
Amer. literary critic, poet

Jones, Rickie Lee (1954–) 4252
Amer. singer, songwriter; Grammy, 1979

Jong, Erica (1942–) 3349
Amer. poet, writer; née Mann; m. Molly Jong-Fast*; NEA, 1973–74

Jong-Fast, Molly (1980–) 4934
Amer. novelist; d. Erica Jong*

Joplin, Janis (1943–1970) 3428
Amer. songwriter, singer; RRHF, 1995

Jordan, Barbara [Charline] (1936–1996) 2986
Amer. politician, educator; state senator (D-Texas), 1966–72; U.S. congresswoman (D-TX), 1973–79; first black and first woman to give keynote address at Democratic National Conference, 1976; Eleanor Roosevelt* Humanities Award, 1984; Presidential Medal of Freedom, 1994; Best Orator of the year by Orators Hall of Fame, 1985; NWHF, 1990

Jordan, Dorothea (1762–1816) 712
Scot. poet

Jordan, June (1936–2002) 2987
Amer. biographer, environmental activist, filmmaker, essayist, political activist, children's writer, poet, educator; née Meyer; Rockefeller; NEA

Jordan, Sara Murray (1884–1959) 1613
Amer. gastroenterologist

Joreen (see Freeman, Jo)

Josefowitz, Natasha (1926–) 2555
Fr./Amer. consultant, syndicated columnist, author, lecturer; née Chapro

Joseph, Helen (1905–1992) 2024
Eng./S. Afr. anti-apartheid activist, social worker; first person in S.A. to be subjected to house arrest; cofounder, Congress of Democrats

Joseph, Jenny (1932–) 2803
Eng. fiction writer, poet

Josephine, Empress (1763–1814) 717
Fr. empress; née Marie-Josèphe Rose Tascher de la Pagerie; w. Alexandre, vis-comte de Beauharnais (1); first w. Napoleon I (2, 1769–1921; emperor of the French), m. Eugène and Hortense (by de Beauharnais)

Joshee, Anandabai (1865–1887) 1316
Ind. physician; née Yumna; first Hindu woman and first Indian woman to receive medical degree

Jotuni, Maria (1880–1943) 1547
Finn. playwright, writer; w. Vijo Tarkianen (historian and professor)

Joya, Malalai (1979–) 4927
Afghan educator, activist, politician; MP, 2005– ; director, Organisation for Promoting Afghan Women's Capabilities (OPAWC)

Joyner, Florence Griffith   see GRIFFITH JOYNER, FLORENCE

Joyner-Kersee, Jacqueline "Jackie" (1962–1998) 4621
Amer. athlete (track); s. Al Joyner (Olympic Medalist), s.-in-law Florence Griffith Joyner*; Olympic Gold (3), 1988; IWSHF, 2003

Judith (fl. 6th century–d. 495 B.C.E.) 48
Isr. hero; d. Merari (son of Ox); w. Manasseh; killed Holofernes (commander of Assyrian forces) and brought peace to Israel

Judith, Anodea (1952–) 4113
Amer. therapist, author, public speaker; née Judith Ann Mull

Judson, Ann Hasseltine (1789–1826) 811
Amer. missionary; a.k.a. Nancy J—; one of the first women to leave the U.S. for foreign missionary work

Judson, Olivia (1969–) 4791
Amer./Brit. biologist, journalist; a.k.a. Dr. Tatiana; d. Horace Freeland J—, American scholar

Judson, Sarah [Hall] B[oardman] (1803–1845) 877
Eng. poet

Julavits, Heidi (1968–) 4767
Amer. novelist

Juliana [Louise Emma Marie Wilhelmina], Queen (1909–2004) 2111
Dutch queen; d. Queen Wilhelmina, m. Beatrix Wilhelmina Armgard (1938– ; queen of the Netherlands, 1980–); queen of the Netherlands, 1948–1980

Juliana of Norwich (1342?–1416?) 236
Eng. author, mystic; a.k.a. Dame Julian; first Englishwoman of letters; retired in seclusion to Church of St. Julian

Jung, Emma (1882–1955) 1578
Swiss scholar, lecturer, writer; née Rauschenbach; w. Carl J— (1875–1961; psychiatrist who founded analytical psychology)

Justin, Dena (1912–) 2183
Amer. educator, lecturer, writer

K

Kaara, Wahu (1953–) 4185
Kenyan activist (social), educator; 2005 Nobel Prize nominée

Kael, Pauline (1919–2001) 2347
Amer. film critic, writer; NBA, 1974

Kaga no Chiyo   see FUKUZOYO CHIYO)

Kagan, Elena (1960–) 4536
Amer. administrator, lawyer, educator, public servant; dean, Harvard Law School, 2003–2008 (first woman); U.S. Solictor General, 2009–; Supreme Court nominee

Kahlil, Aisha (1940?–) 3199
Amer. performing arts administrator, singer; member, Sweet Honey in the Rock (vocal group); codirector, First World Productions

Kahlo [de Rivera], Frida (1907–1954) 2066
Mex. painter; w. Diego Rivera (muralist, 1886–1957)

Kahn, Florence Prag (1866–1948) 1329
Amer. politician, lawyer; w. Julius K— (actor, congressman, R-CA); U.S. House of Representatives (R-CA), 1925–1937 (first Jewish woman to have seat in House)

Kahn, Kathy (1945–) 3585
Amer. songwriter, musician, social worker, writer

Kajir, Anne (1970/74–) 4821
Papuan environmental activist, attorney; CEO, Environmental Law Centre; Goldman Environmental Prize, 2006

Kaker, Malalai (1970–2008) 4822
Afghan police officer; first female police detective; deputy commander of the

Kandahar city police department, the most senior female officer in all of southern Afghanistan

Kalisch, Shoshana (1928?–) 2631
Cuban/Amer. singer, songwriter, actor; survivor of Auschwitz

Kalish, Mildred Armstrong (1923–) 2460
Amer. educator (English), memoirist

Kallen, Lucille [Eve] Chernos (1922–1999) 2433
Amer. writer, attorney, dramatist

Kamal, Zahira (1945–) 3586
Jerusalemite teacher, women's rights activist; cofounder, Women's Work Committee

Kamamalu (1797?–1824) 854
Hawaiian queen; d. King Kamehameha I (ca. 1738–1819); s. and w. King Liholiho K— (both died from measles on a visit to Britain)

Kamani, Ginu (1962–) 4622
Ind./Amer. writer

Kamel, Laila Iskandar (1947–)3761
Egyp. environmental activist, education and development specialist; Goldman Environmantal Prize, 1994

Kamensky, Jane (1963–) 4641
Amer. writer, historian

Kaminer, Wendy (1950–) 3981
Amer. critic, social, lawyer; Guggenheim, 1993

Kanin, Fay (1917–) 2295
Amer. producer, playwright, screenwriter, actor, union activist; née Mitchell; w. Michael K— (screen writer), sister-in-law of Garson K— (1912–99, playwright, producer) and Ruth Gordon*; Academy Award, 1958; Emmy (3), 1974, 1979

Kanner, Barbara (1925–) 2524
Brit. historian

Kanter, Rosabeth Moss (1943–) 3429
Amer. writer, sociologist, educator

Kaplan, Gisela (1944–) 3516.1
Ger./Aust. veterinarian science, educator (animal behavior)

Kaplan, Louise J. (1929–) 2666
Amer. psychologist, author

Kaplan, Temma E. (1942–) 3350–3351
Amer. educator, feminist, historian; née Thane?

Kaptur, Marcy [Carolyn] (1946–) 3668
Amer. politician, congresswoman; U.S. representative (D-Ohio), 1983–

Karan, Donna [Ivy] (1948–) 3836
Amer. fashion designer, business executive, philanthropist; née Faske

Karmel, Marjorie (1933?–) 2857
Amer. writer; cofounder, American Society for Psychoprophylaxis in Obstetrics (ASPO), 1960

Karon, Jan (1937–) 3041
Amer. Christian novelist

Karr, Mary (1955–) 4310
Amer. poet, essayist, memoirist, educator

Kasdorf, Julia Spicher (1962–) 4623
Amer. poet, writer, educator, creative writing

Kasebier, Gertrude (1852–1934) 1194
Amer. photographer

Kasmuneh (fl. 12th–13th century) 209
Span. poet; d. Ishmael (poet)

Kassebaum, Nancy (1932–) 2804
Amer. politician; d. Alfred Mossman Landon (1887–1987; governor of Kansas); w. Howard Baker (2; former senator and); U.S. senator (R-Kansas), 1979–1997; first woman elected to the U.S. Senate who was not the widow of a congressman

Kassi, Norma (1954–) 4253
Can. environmental activist; Goldman Environmental Prize, 2002

Kassiane (804?–867?) 149
Byzantine poet, Eastern Orthodox nun; a.s.a. Kassia; founded a convent

Katie, Byron (1942–) 3352
Amer. workshop leader, author, speaker; née Byron Kathleen Reid; w. Stephen Mitchell, writer, translator

Katona, Jacqui (1966–) 4724
Aust. environmental activist, newspaper editor; Goldman Environmental Prize, 1999

Katz, Lilian G. (1932–) 2805
Eng./Amer. early childhood educator, author, columnist; fdr., Early Childhood Research Quarterly & Early Childhood Research & Practice Journal (1999)

Katz, Rita (1963–) 4642
Iraqi/Amer. spy; cofounder, SITE Intelligence Group

Kauffman, Linda S. (1949?–) 3903
Amer. author, lecturer, educator

Kaufman, Bel (1911–) 2160
Ger./Amer. writer, teacher, scenarist; m. Spiegalman; grandd. Sholom Aleichem

Kaufman, Paola (1969–2006) 4792
Argen. biologist, novelist, researcher (science); née Yannielli; The Devil's Golfcourse (winner of the Fondo Nacional de las Artes Prize), The Sister (winner of the Casa de las Americas Prize) and The Lake (winner of the Planeta Prize for fiction

Kaufman, Shirley (1923–) 2461
Amer./Isr. poet; International Poetry Forum United States Award, 1969

Kaufman, Sue (1926–) 2556
Amer. writer, editor; mn. Barondess

Kavanagh, Julia (1824–1877) 993
Ir. writer

Kawai Chigetsu-Ni (1632–1736)461
Jap. poet

Kay, Jackie (1961–) 4583
Scot. poet, novelist, educator, creative writing; ex.-p. Carol Ann Duffy*

Kaye, Carol (1925–) 2525
Amer. educator

Kazu-no-Michi, Princess (1846–1877) 1144
Jap. political activist, princess, poet

Kearney, Belle (1863–1839) 1297
Amer. lecturer, educator, writer

Keating, Sarah Sayward see WOOD, SALLY

Keatley, Charlotte (1960–) 4537
Eng. playwright, stage director, theater critic, actor, educator

Keays, Sara (1948–) 3838
Eng. political activist

Keenan, Nancy (1952–) 4114
Amer. politician, administrator (NGO); pres., NARAL, 2004–

Kegel, Martha (1958–) 4455
Amer. journalist, administrator, civil rights activist

Keith, Penelope (1940–) 3200
Eng. writer; née Hatfield

Kellems, Vivien (1896–1975) 1826
Amer. feminist, industrialist, lecturer

Keller, Evelyn Fox (1936–) 2988
Amer. nonfiction writer, educator, feminist, physicist

Keller, Helen [Adams] (1880–1968) 1548
Amer. lecturer, writer; student of Annie Sullivan*; deaf and blind from infancy; Presidential Medal of Freedom, 1964; NWHF

Kellerman, Faye (1952–) 4115
Amer. novelist

Kellett, Christine H. (1941–) 3274
Amer. attorney, administrator

Kelley, Edith Summers (1884–1956) 1614
Can./Amer. novelist

Kelley, Florence (1859–1932) 1248
Amer. civic reformer, writer, attorney; d. William D. K— , U.S. congressman

Kelley, Kitty (1942–) 3353
Amer. journalist, biographer

Kelley, Virginia Cassidy (1923–1994) 2462
Amer. nurse; m. William Jefferson Clinton (1946– ; lawyer and politician; 42nd president of U.S., 1993–2001), m.-in-law, Hilary Rodham Clinton*

Kellor, Frances Alice (1873–1952) 1413
Amer. lawyer, sociologist, public servant, activist, immigrant

Kelly, Brigit Pegeen (1951–) 4052
Amer. poet, educator (English)

Kelly, Emily "Pat" [Martha] (1872/3–1922) 1400
Brit. mountaineer

Kelly, Petra (1947–1992) 3762
Ger. activist, political; cofounder, Die Grünen (Green Party), 1979; Right Livelihood, 1982

Kelly-Gadol, Joan (1928–1982) 2632
Amer. historian; NEA, 1967–68

Kemble, Fanny [Frances Anne] (1809–1893) 908
Eng. writer, actor, poet; mn. Butler; n. Sarah Siddons* and John Kemble (actor- manager, 1757–1823)

Kemnitz, Mathilda von (1877–?) 1495
Ger. writer; a.k.a. Mathilde Spiess Ludendorff

Kempe, Margery (1373?–1438?) 245
Eng. author, mystic; née Burnham; w. John K—; author of first known English autobiography

Kempton, Sally [Durgananda] (1943–) 3430
Amer. journalist, writer, teacher (spiritual), feminist; d. Murray K— (writer, journalist, 1918–); descendent of George Mason, author of Virginia Bill of Rights

Kennard, Joyce L. (1941–) 3275
Indones./Amer. justice, lawyer; Assoc. Justice, California Supreme Court, 1989–

Kennedy, A. L. (1965–)   4703
Scot. novelist, educator (writing), screenwriter; née Alison Louise K—; Costa (2007)

Kennedy, Adrienne (1931–)   2767
Amer. playwright; cofounder, Women's Theater Council; Obie (1962); Rockefeller (3); Guggenheim; NEA

Kennedy, Caroline [Bouvier] (1957–)   4417
Amer. lawyer, writer; d. John F. Kennedy (1917–1963; 35th U.S. president, 1961–63; assasinated) and Jaqueline K– Onassis*; w. Edwin A. Schlossberg, designer; cofounder, Profiles in Courage Award

Kennedy, Florynce R[ae] (1916–2000)   2272
Amer. civil rights activist, lawyer, feminist

Kennedy, Jacqueline Bouvier see
ONASSIS, JACQUELINE

Kennedy, Marilyn Moats (1943–)   3431
Amer. career consultant, author, public speaker

Kennedy, Rose Fitzgerald (1890–1995)   1710
Amer. public figure; w. Joseph P. K—, Sr. (1888–1969; banker, industrialist, diplomat), m. John F. K— (1917–63; politician; 35th U.S. president, 1961–63; assassinated), Robert F. K— (lawyer and politician, 1925–68; assassinated), and Edward "Ted" K— (1932–2009; U.S. Senator, D-MA, 1962–2009)

Kennelly, Barbara B. (1936–)   2989
Amer. politician; née Bailey; d. John M. B—,(1904–1975), political figure; w. James J. K—, politician; U.S. Rep (D-CT), 1982–1999; pres. & CEO, Natl. Comm. To Preserve Social Security and Medicare

Kenney, Annie (1879–1953)   1528
Eng. suffragist

Kenny, Elizabeth (1880–1952) 1549
Aust. nurse; a.k.a. Sister K—; developed method of treatment for paralysis brought on by poliomyelitis

Kent, Corita (1918–1986)   2318
Amer. former nun, graphic artist

Kenyon, Cynthia [Jane] (1955–)   4311
Amer. molecular biologist

Kenyon, Jane (1947–1995)   3763
Amer. poet; w. Donald Hall, poet; New Hampshire poet laureate

Kephart, Beth (1960–)   4538
Amer. writer, poet

Keppel, Caroline, Lady (1735–?)   619
Scot. poet

Kerber, Linda Kaufman (1940–)   3201
Amer. nonfiction writer, educator, history; NEH, 1976, 1983–84, 1994; Guggenheim, 1990

Kerbis, Gertrude Lemp (1926–)   2557
Amer. architect

Kerr, Jean (1923–2003)   2463
Amer. author, playwright; née Collins; w. Walter K— (journalist, 1913–)

Kerr, Sarah (fl. 1990s)   4966
Amer. journalist

Kerr, Sophie (1880–1965)   1550
Amer. writer; mn. Underwood

Kerrigan, Nancy (1969–)   4793
Amer. ice skater; mn. Solomon; est. The Nancy Kerrigan Foundation (for blind); Olympic Bronze, 1992; Olympic Silver, 1994

Kesselman, Wendy (1940–)   3202
Amer. singer, writer, composer, playwright; Fulbright; NEA, 1982; Ford, 1979; Guggenheim, 1982; McKnight, 1985; Blackburn, 1980

Ketcham, Katherine (1949–) 3904
Amer. writer

Keuls, Eva Clara (1928–)   2633
Dutch/Amer. classical historian; NEH 1967, 1980–81; Guggenheim, 1974–75

Key, Ellen [Karolina Sofia] (1849–1926)   1167
Swed. writer, feminist

Keyes, Frances Parkinson (1885–1970)   1632
Amer. writer, editor

Keyes, Marian (1963–)   4643
Ir. writer

Keyserling, Mary [Dublin] (1910–1997)   2136
Amer. economist, government official

Kgositsile, Baleka (1949–)   3905
S. Afr. public servant, poet; w. Keorapetse K— , exiled writer poet

Khakpour, Porochista (1978–)   4924
Iran./Amer. novelist

Khalifeh, Imane (1975–)   4896
Leban./Fr. activist (peace), educator, poet; Honorary Right Livelihood Award, 1984

Al-Khansa, (600–670)   116
Middle Eastern poet; née Tumadir bint Amr ibn al Harith ibn al Sharid; a.k.a. Tumadir

al-Khansa; m. 'Amra (poet), related to Zuhair ibn Abu Sulma (poet)

Khatun, Jahan (fl. 14th century–)   249
Persian poet

Khatun, Padeshah (fl. 1269–1273)   224
Persian poet

Kidder, Margot (1948–)   3839
Amer. actor, anti-war activist

Kidman, Nicole (1967–)   4750
Aust./Amer. actor, humanitarian; ex-w. Tom Cruise, actor; w. Keith Urban, musician; Goodwill Ambassador of the United Nations Development Fund for Women (UNIFEM), 2006–; Oscar, 2002; Golden Globe (3)

Kieko, Yamamuro (1874–1915)   1439
Jap. evangelist, philanthropist

Kii, Lady (fl. 8th century)   146
Jap. poet

Kijewski, Karen (1943–)   3432
Amer. novelist

Kilbourne, Jean (1943–)   3433
Amer. filmmaker, documentary, social theorist

Kilgallen, Dorothy (1913–1965)   2203
Amer. columnist, radio & TV personality; w. Dick Kollmar (actor)

Killefer, Nancy (1953–)   4186
Amer. public servant, management consultant

Killigrew, Anne (1660?–1685)   496
Eng. lady-in-waiting, poet, painter; d. Dr. Henry K—, c. Charles and Thomas K— (playwrights)

Killigrew, Catherine (1530?–1583)   331
Eng. poet; d. Anthony Cooke, s. Anne Cooke Bacon*, Lady Mildred Burleigh and Elizabeth Hoby Russell*

Kilmer, Aline Murray (1888–1941/44)   1682
Amer. poet; w. Joyce K— (poet, 1886–1918)

Kim, Elaine Haikyung (1942–)3354
Amer. nonfiction writer, educator (Asian American studies), community activist

Kim, Myung Mi (1957–)   4418
Amer. poet, educator (ESL), translator

Kim, Sung-Joo (1957–)   4419
Kor./Eng. business executive; Chairperson and CEO of Sungjoo Group

Kimball, Harriet [McEwan] (1834–1917)   1057
Amer. poet

Kincaid, Jamaica (1949–)   3906
W. Ind./Amer. novelist, gardener; née Elaine Cynthia Potter Richardson

King, Billie Jean (1943–)   3434
Amer. athlete (tennis); pioneer in raising recognition and pay for professional women athletes; Sports Illustrated's first "sportswoman of the year"; founder and developer of World Tennis Team, 1976, and Women's Professional Softball League, 1975; cofounder, Virginia Slims Women's Pro Tennis Tour; Wimbledon (20); Women's Sports Hall of Fame, 1980; NWHF; IWSHF, 1980

King, Carole (1942–)   3355
Amer. songwriter, singer; Grammy, 1971

King, Coretta Scott (1927–2006)   2603
Amer. civil rights activist, concert singer, diplomat, lecturer, author; widow, Martin Luther King, Jr. (1926–1968; clergyman, civil rights leader, hero; assassinated); founder and president, Martin Luther King, Jr., Center for Non-Violent Social Change, 1971

King, Deborah K. (1954?–)   4254
Amer. feminist, sociologist, educator

King, Florence (1936–)   2990
Amer. novelist, essayist, columnist

King, Georgiana Goddard (1871–1939)   1391
Amer. poet, educator, scholar, art & literary critic; a.s.a. G. G. K—; founded art department at Bryn Mawr College, 1912

King, Harriet [Eleanor] (1840–1920)   1094
Eng. poet

King, Janice (1958–)   4456
Amer. care giver, publisher; publisher of Soul magazine

King, Laurie R. (1952–)   4116
Amer. novelist

King, Ynestra (1948?–)   3840
Amer. ecologist, environmental activist; pioneer of ecofeminism

King, Countess of Lovelace, Ada Byron (1815–1852)   929
Eng. scientist, computer, mathematician; d. Lord Byron, poet; m. Anne Blunt*; world's first computer programmer; programming language "Ada" named for her

King-Hammond, Leslie (1944–)   3517
Amer. educator (art), art curator

Kingsolver, Barbara (1955–) 4312 Amer. novelist

Kingston, Maxine [Ting Ting] Hong (1940–) 3203 Amer. editor, nonfiction writer

Ki no Tsurayuki, Daughter of (fl. 940s–d. 967) 159 Jap. Poet

Kinsky, Countess see SUTTNER, BERTHA

Kinsolving, Sally [Bruce] (1876–?) 1477 Amer. poet

Kintz, Linda (1945–) 3587 Amer. feminist academic

Kirchheimer, Gloria DeVidas (1942?–) 3356 Amer. editor, translator, folklorist, writer; a.k.a. G- Levy

Kirchner, Cristina [Elizabeth Fernandez de] (1953–) 4187 Argen. politician; w. Nestor K—, Pres. Argentina; President, Argentina, 2007– (first woman)

Kirino, Natsuo (1951–) 4053 Jap. novelist; née Mariko Hashioka

Kirk, Lisa (1925–1990) 2526 Amer. actor, singer; née Elsie Marie K—; w. Robert Wells (1922–1998), sketch artist

Kirkland, Winifred Margaretta (1872–1943) 1401 Amer. writer

Kirkpatrick, Jeane (1926–2006) 2558 Amer. public official, educator (political science); a.k.a. J— Duane Jordan K— ; U.S. representative to United Nations, 1981–

Kirsebom, Vendela [Maria] (1967–) 4751 Swed. model, fashion, diplomat, actor; ex-w. Olaf Thommessen, Norwegian politican

Kissling, Frances (1943–) 3435 Amer. pro-choice activist; née Romanski; Pres., Catholics for a Free Choice (1982–2007)

Kitt, Eartha (1927–2008) 2604 Amer. singer, dancer, actor, activist, children's; née E- Mae Keith; Emmy (2)

Kitzinger, Celia (1960?–) 4539 Eng. educator (psychology), writer, psychologist; d. Sheila K—*; s. Jenny K—*; partner, Sue Wilkinson, educator, author

Kitzinger, Jenny (1963–) 4644 Eng. educator (communications); d. Sheila K—*; s. Celia K—*

Kitzinger, Sheila [Helena Elizabeth] (1929–) 2667 Eng. educator (midwifery), lecturer, author, childbirth movement activist; m. Jenny K—*; m. Celia K—*; w. Uw Kitzinger CBE, fdg. pres., Templeton College, Oxford

Kiyak, H. Asuman (1951–) 4054 Amer. psychologist, educator (psychology)

Kizer, Carolyn (1925–) 2527 Amer. educator, poet, editor; née Ashley; founder, Poetry Northwest, 1959; chancellor, AAP; AAAL; Pulitzer (1985)

Klagsbrun, Francine (1931–) 2768 Amer. writer, editor, journalist, humanitarian; née Lifton

Klein, Laura Cousino (1968?–) 4768 Amer. medical psychologist, educator, behavioral health

Klein, Melanie (1882–1960) 1579 Aus./Brit. psychoanalyst, writer; née Reizes; an originator of psychoanalytic treatment of children

Klein, Naomi (1970–) 4823 Can. journalist, author, activist; w. Avi Lewis, documentary filmmaker, TV news anchor

Kleinbaum, Sharon (1959–) 4490 Amer. rabbi, gay and lesbian rights activist

Klepfisz, Irena (1941–) 3276 Pol./Amer. political activist, poet, essayist, translator, Yiddish, educator (women's studies); cofounder, Conditions (magazine)

Kline, Christina Baker (1964–)4680 Amer. writer

Klobuchar, Amy (1960–) 4540 Amer. attorney, politician; U.S. senator (MN), 110th Congress

Klopstock, Margaret (1728–1758) 602 Ger. author; née Meta Moller; w. Frederick Gottlieb K— (poet, 1724–1803)

Knesebeck, Eleonora von dem (fl. 1680s–d. 1713) 525 Ger./Eng. courtier; lady-in-waiting to Sophia Dorothea of Celle (Zelle)*

Knight, Sarah Kemble (1666–1727) 508 Amer. businesswoman, diarist, poet

Knollys, Lettice (1540–1634) 338 Eng. courtier; a.k.a. countess of Leicester; w. Walter Devereaux, first earl of Leicester (1), Robert Dudley, earl of Leicester (2), and Christopher Bount (3); m. Robert Devereaux, second earl of Essex

(favorite of Elizabeth I*) and Penelope Devereaux Rich*; maid of honor to Elizabeth I of England*

Knopf, Blanche Wolf (1894–1966) 1798 Amer. publisher; w. Alfred Knopf, Jr.

Knopf, Olga (1888–?) 1683 Aus./Amer. psychiatrist, writer

Knowles, Mary (1733–1807) 615 Eng. letter writer; friend of Samuel Johnson (1709–84; author, lexicographer) and James Boswell (1740–95; Scot. diarist, lawyer, biographer)

Kochladze, Manana (1972–) 4863 Georgian environmental activist, biologist; fdr., Green Alternative, 2000; Goldman, 2004

Kogawa, Joy (Nozomi) (1935–) 2938 Can. novelist, poet

Koghtnatsi, Khosrovidoukht (?–737) 138 Armen. poet; d. Khosrov (prince of the Koghten region)

Kohut, Rebekah Bettelheim (1864–1951) 1304 Hung./Amer. activist, human rights, teacher, writer; w. Alexander K—, leader of Jewish Conservative movement (d. 1894); co-led the first World Council of Jewish Women in Vienna (1923), from which sprang the International Council of Jewish Women

Koka, Stewardess of the Empress (fl. 12th century) 210 Jap. poet; a.k.a. Mon-in no Betto; d. Fujiwara no Toshitaka

Kolata, Gina (1948–) 3841 Amer. journalist (science); s. Judi Bari, environmental activist; d. Ruth Aaronson Bari, mathematician

Kolb, Barbara (1939–) 3150 Amer. composer; first woman composer to win the Prix de Rome

Kolbert, Elizabeth (1961–) 4584 Amer. journalist, author

Koller, Alice (1924–) 2488 Amer. philosopher

Kollontai, Aleksandra [Mikhailovna] (1872–1952) 1402 Russ. propagandist, writer, diplomat, government official; first commissar of Public Welfare for Bolshevik Government, 1917–1918; Order of Lenin

Kollwitz, Käthe (1867–1945) 1337 Ger. graphic artist, painter, sculptor; née Schmidt; first woman elected full member

of Prussian Academy of Arts, 1919

Kolmar, Gertrud (1894–1943) 1799 Ger. poet, interpreter; née Chodziesner

Komarovsky, Mirra (1906–1999) 1889 Russ./Amer. sociologist, college professor, editor, author; w. Marcus A. Heyman

Kometani, Foumiko (1930–) 2720–2721 Jap./Amer. writer, painter; w. Josh Greenfield (1928–), Amer. writer, playwright; Akutagawa Prize, 1986

Koontz, Libby [Elizabeth] [Duncan] (1919–1989) 2348 Amer. government official; director, Women's Bureau, 1969–73 (first black woman to hold position); first black pres. of Natl. Education Assoc.

Koppel, Lily (1981–) 4946 Amer. journalist

Kort, Michele (1950–) 3982 Amer. editor, journalist, author

Kouchak, Nahabed (?–1592) 401 Armen. poet; a.s.a. Kouchag

Kovalevskaya, Sofia Vasilyevna (1850–1891) 1177 Russ./Swed. scientist, mathematician; Prix Bordin of the French Academy of Sciences, 1886; Swedish Academy of Sciences, 1889

Kraemer, Ross Shepard (1948–) 3842 Amer. historian, nonfiction writer, educator (religions)

Kramarae, Cheris (1938–) 3091 Amer. writer, linguist

Kramer, Jane (1938–) 3092 Amer. writer

Kramer, Joyce (1942–) 3357 Amer. teacher, AIDS activist, writer, realtor, consultant

Kramer, Melinda (1980–) 4935 Amer. administrator, environmental activist; cofounder, Women's Global Green Action Network, 2005; founding director, Women's Earth Alliance

Krantz, Judith (1928–) 2634 Amer. novelist, editor; née Tarcher

Krásnohorská, Eliska (1847–1926) 1151 Czech social & literary critic, translator, librettist, children's writer, feminist; edited the first Czech women journal; cofounder, first Czech girls' gymnasium (college prep)

Krauss, Nicole (1974–)   4884
Amer. poet, novelist; w. Jonathan Safran Foer (1977– ; Amer. novelist)

Kreps, Juanita (1921–2010)   2403
Amer. educator, government official, administrator; née Morris; U.S. Secretary of Commerce, 1977–79 (first woman to hold position)

Krim, Mathilde (1926–)   2559
Ital./Swiss/Isr./Amer. biologist; w. Arthur K— (executive); founder, AIDS Medical Foundation, 1983 (later the American Foundation for AIDS Research)

Kristeva, Julia (1941–)   3277
Fr. author, psychoanalyst, philosopher, feminist; w. Philippe Soller, writer

Krone, Julie [Louise] (1963–)   4645
Amer. jockey; first woman jockey to win Triple Crown (Belmont Stakes, 1993); first woman inducted into the National Museum of Racing and Hall of Fame, 2000

Krudener, Juliana, Baroness (1764–1824)   721
Russ. mystic, novelist; a.k.a. Barbara J— von Vietinghoff

Kruhonja, Katarina (1949–)   3907
Yug. activist (human rights), physician; Director, Centre for Peace, Non-Violence and Human Rights; Right Livelihood, 1998

Krupskaia, Nadezhda Konstanitovna (1869–1939)   1363
Russ. women's rights activist; w. Vladimir Ilyich Lenin (Communist leader and founder of the Bolsheviks, 1870–1924)

Kshetrayya (fl. 17th century)   551
Ind. poet

Kuan Tao-shêng (1262–1319)   223
Chin. poet, calligrapher, painter

Kubatum (fl. 2030s B.C.E.)   7
Sumerian poet

Kübler-Ross, Elizabeth (1926–2004)   2560
Swiss/Amer. author, thanatologist, psychiatrist; NWHF

Kuhn, Maggie (1905–1995)   2025
Amer. author, civil rights activist; née Margaret E. K—; founder, Gray Panthers, 1970; NWHF

Kuklina, Ida (1925?–)   2528
Russ. human rights activist, attorney, researcher; cofounder, Human Rights Center of Russia

Kumaratunga, Chandrika Bandaranaike (1945–)   3588
Sri Lankan politician; d. Solomon West Ridgway Dias Bandaranaike, prime minister, Sri Lanka; assassinated, 1959; widow, Vijaya Kumaratunga, film star, politician; assassinated, 1988; first female Pres., Sri Lanka, 1994–2005

Kumin, Maxine [Winokur] (1925–)   2529
Amer. novelist, poet, children's writer, essayist; chancellor, AAP; Pulitzer, 1973; AAAL

Kummer, Clare [Rodman Beecher] (1888–1948)   1684
Amer. playwright, songwriter

Kushner, Rachel (1968–)   4769
Amer. editor, magazine, novelist

Al Kuwaiz, Samira (1964–)   4680.1
Saudi educator, financial analyst; 1st female CEO in Saudi Arabia

L

Labé, Louise (1520/22–1566)   316
Fr. feminist, poet, linguist, soldier; a.s.a. Labbé; a.k.a. La belle Amazone, La belle Cordière (The Beautiful Ropemaker), Captain Lays (title and pseud. while in the army); w. Ennemond Perrin

La Coste, Marie [Ravene] de (1849–1936)   1139
Amer. writer, poet

Lactilla   see YEARSLEY, ANNE

Lacy, Mary (fl. 1770s)   749
Brit. sailor; a.k.a. William Chandler

La Fayette, Marie Madeleine de, comtesse de (1634–1692/93)   465
Fr. salonist, novelist; a.k.a. M— Pioche de la Vergne; w. François Motier, comte de La Fayette

LaFollette, Suzanne (1893–1983)   1776
Amer. feminist, writer, editor; d. William L. L— (U.S. congressman)

Laforet, Carmen (1921–2004)   2404
Span. novelist

Lagarde [y de los Ríos], [Maria] Marcela (1950?–)   3983
Mex. educator (anthropology), politician, author, feminist; Mex. legislator (PRD), 2003–

Lagerlöf, Selma [Ottila Lovisa] (1858–1940)   1233
Swed. writer; first woman elected to and director of Swedish Academy; Nobel

Prize in literature, 1909 (first woman to receive award)

Lahiri, Jhumpa (1967–)   4752
Brit./Amer. writer; w. Alberto Vourvoulias-Bush, journalist; Pulitzer (2000)

Laing, Dilys (1906–1960)   2051
Can. poet, editor

Lais (?–340 B.C.E.)   65
Roman/Greek courtesan, musician

Lakich, Lili (1942–)   3358
Amer. painter; founder, Museum of Neon Art (MONA), Los Angeles (1982)

Lal Ded   see DED, LAL

Lalleswari (1317?–1391?)   235
Ind. poet, saint; a.k.a. Lalla

Lamb, Caroline, Lady (1785–1828)   799
Eng. novelist; d. Frederick Ponsonby, third earl of Bessborough, w. Sir William L—, second viscount Melbourne, mistress of Lord Byron (1788–1824; poet), n. Georgiana Cavendish*

Lamb, Mary Ann (1764–1847)   722
Eng. dressmaker, author, letter writer, poet; a.k.a. Sempronia, Bridget Elia; s. Charles L— (1775–1834; critic, essayist), with whom she wrote Tales from Shakespeare (1807)

Lamb, Myrna (1935–)   2599
Amer. playwright; Rockefeller, 1972; Guggenheim, 1973; NEA, 1974–5

Lambert, Angela (1940–2007)   3204
Brit. Journalist, art critic, author; née Helps

Lambrun, Margaret (fl. 1580s)   387
Scot. courtier; a.k.a. Anthony Sparke

Lamott, Anne (1954–)   4255
Amer. writer, political activist; d. Kenneth L— (writer); Guggenheim, 1985

Lanchester, Elsa (1902–1986)   1950
Brit./Amer. actor; née Elizabeth Sullivan; widow of Charles Laughton (1899–1962; screen actor)

Landers, Ann (1918–2002)   2319
Amer. columnist; née Esther "Eppie" Pauline Friedman; mn. Lederer, s. Abigail Van Buren*

Landon, Letitia [Elizabeth] (1802–1838)   873
Eng. poet, novelist; a.s.a. L. E. L—; mn. Maclean

Landowska, Wanda (1879–1959)   1529
Pol./Amer. music scholar, composer, harpsichordist; w. Henry Lew (writer, d. 1919);

founder, l'Ecole de Musique Ancienne; Recording Academy Hall of Fame

Landsman, Anne (1959–)   4491
S. Afr./Amer. novelist

Lane, Rose Wilder (1886–1965)   1654
Amer. novelist; d. Laura Ingalls Wilder*

Lange, Dorothea (1895–1965)   1816
Amer. photographer; NWHF

Langer, Felicia (1930–)   2722
Pol./Ger. lawyer, human rights activist, educator; Right Livelihood, 1990

Langer, Susanne K[nauth] (1895–1985)   1817
Amer. educator, philosopher, writer

Langley, Eve [Maria] (1908–1974)   2092
Aust. writer

Langston, [Laodicea] "Dicey" (1766–1837)   730
Amer. Revolutionary War hero

Langtry, Lillie (1853–1929)   1197
Eng. actor; née Emily Charlotte Le Breton; a.k.a. "The Jersey Lily"

Lansbury, Angela (1925–)   2530
Eng./Amer. actor; Tony (4); Golden Globe (6)

Lanyer, Aemilia (1569–1645)   372
Eng. poet; a.s.a. Emilia Lanier; d. Baptista Bassano (musician) and Margaret Johnson, w. Alphonso L— (musician), mistress of Henry Carey, Lord Hunsdon; probably the "Dark Lady" addressed in Shakespeare's sonnets #127–152

La Pasionaria   see IBARRURI, DOLORES

Lape, Esther [Everett] (1881–1949)   1569
Amer. social activist, author, researcher, educator, suffragist, editor

Lappé, Frances Moore (1944–)   3518
Amer. author, activist, ecologist; w. Marc L—; founder, Food First/Institute for Food and Development Policy, 1975; cofounded (with daughter Anna) Small Planet Institute, 2002; Right Livelihood, 1987

Laramore, Vivian Yeiser (1892?–1975)   1749
Amer. poet

Larcom, Lucy (1826–1893)   1008
Amer. editor, poet, mill worker

Larsen, Jensine (1975–)   4897
Amer. publisher, journalist; founder, World Pulse Magazine, online magazine, 2003

Lasker-Schüler, Else
(1869–1945)   1364
    Ger./Swiss playwright, poet;
    Kleist Prize for Literature,
    1931
La Suze, countess de   see COLIGNY,
HENRIETTE DE
Lathbury, Eva
(fl. early 1900s)   1910
    Eng. writer
Lathbury, Mary [Artemisia]
(1841–1913)   1104
    Amer. hymnist, poet; a.k.a.
    "The Chautauqua Laureate"
Lauder, Estée (1906–2004)   2052
    Amer. philanthropist, busi-
    ness executive; née Josephine
    E— Mentzer; founder and
    chair, Estée Lauder, Inc., 1946;
    Presidential Medal of Free-
    dom, 2004
Launay, Charles, vicomte de   see
GIRARDIN, DELPHINE DE
Launey, Mme. de (fl. 1820s)   969
    Fr. actor; a.k.a. Mlle Hopkins;
    friend of Marceline Des-
    bordes-Valmore*
Laurel, Alicia Bay
(1949–)   3908–3909
    Amer. illustrator, naturalist,
    writer
Laurence, [Jean] Margaret
(1926–1987)   2561
    Can. writer; née Wemyss;
    Governor General Award,
    1967, 1974
Laurencin, Marie
(1885–1956)   1633
    Fr. painter, illustrator, poet;
    lover of Guillaume Apollinaire
    (1880–1918; poet), w. Otto
    von Waltjen (Ger. painter)
Laut, Agnes C. (1871–1936)   1392
    Can. journalist, writer
Lavin, Mary (1912–1996)   2184
    Amer./Ir. writer
Lawless, Lucy (1968–)   4770
    N.Z. TV actor, singer; née
    Lucille Frances Ryan
Lawrence, Frieda
(1879–1956)   1530
    Ger./Eng. writer, literary
    figure; née Emma Maria
    F— Johanna Freiin von
    Richthofen; s. Manfred von
    Richthofen (Ger. aviator, sol-
    dier; shot down 1918; a.k.a.
    the Red Baron); w. D.H. L—
    (1885–1930; Eng. writer)
Lawrence, Gertrude
(1901–1952)   1934
    Eng. actor; née Getrude Alex-
    ander Dagmar L— Klassen
Lawrenson, Helen
(1904–1982)   1996
    Amer. writer, magazine edi-
    tor; née Brown; a.k.a. H— B.
    Nordon

Lawson, Nigella Lucy
(1960–)   4541
    Eng. food writer, journalist,
    broadcaster; d. Nigel L—
    (1932–), politician, journalist;
    British Book Award, 2000
Lays, Captain   see LABÉ, LOUISE
Layton, Elizabeth (1910–1993)2137
    Amer. artist
Lazarre, Jane D[urham]
(1943–)   3436
    Amer. journalist, Amer.
    educator (writing); m. Adam
    Lazarre-White, dramatist
Lazarus, Emma (1849–1887)   1168
    Amer. writer, poet
Lea, Fanny Heaslip
(1884–1955)   1615
    Amer. writer
Leach, Penelope (1937–)   3042
    Eng. child development spe-
    cialist, psychologist, author;
    d. Nigel Balchin (1908–1970),
    novelist
Leachman, Cloris (1926–)   2562
    Amer. actor; ex-w. George
    Englund (film producer);
    Academy Award, 1971;
    Emmy, 1973,1974, 1975 (2)
Leah (fl. 18th century B.C.E.)   9
    Haran/Hittite biblical figure;
    d. Laban, son of Habor, s.
    Rachel,* first w. Jacob, m.
    Reuben, Simeon, Levi, Judah,
    Zebulun, Issachar (six of the
    founders of the 12 tribes of
    Israel) and Dinah
Leapor, Mary (1722–1746)   590
    Eng. servant, playwright, poet
Lear, Moya Olson
(1915–2001)   2246
    Amer. businesswoman, phi-
    lanthropist; d. Ole Olson,
    vaudeville star; w. William
    L— , inventor who created the
    Lear jet; m. John L— , pilot
    and UFOlogist
Lease, Mary [Elizabeth]
(1850/53–1933)   1178
    Amer. writer, lecturer; a.k.a.
    "The Kansas Pythoness"; née
    Clyens
Le Baron, Marie (1842–1894) 1109
    Amer. suffragist, lyricist
Lebowitz, Fran (1950–)   3984
    Amer. humorist, journalist
Lebron, Lolita (1927–)   2605
    Puerto Rican political activist;
    gm. Irene Vilar*
Ledbetter, Lilly (1938–)   3093
    Amer. worker, equal pay
    activist; prime mover of the
    Lilly Ledbetter Fair Pay Act,
    2009
Leddy, Mary Jo (1946–)   3669
    Can. writer, speaker, theo-
    logian, social activist; fdr.,
    Catholic New Times

Leduc, Violette (1907–1972) 2068
    Fr. writer
Lee, Agnes (1868–1939)   1352
    Amer. poet; mn. Freer
Lee, Andrea (1953–)   4188
    Amer. writer
Lee, Ann (1736–1784)   622
    Eng./Amer. religious leader;
    mn. Standerin, a.s.a. Standley,
    Stanly; a.k.a. Mother Anna
    Lee, Mother of the New
    Creation; founder, American
    Shakers (United Society of
    Believers in Christ's Second
    Appearing), ca. 1774
Lee, Barbara (1946–)   3670
    Amer. politician, political
    fund-raiser; congresswoman
    (D-California), 1998– ; co-
    founder, The White House
    Project
Lee, Ettie (1885–1974)   1634
    Amer. humanitarian, teacher;
    founder of several boys'
    homes
Lee, Gypsy Rose (1914–1970) 2222
    Amer. burlesque entertainer,
    writer (mystery)
Lee, Hannah Farnham
(1780–1865)   782
    Amer. author
Lee, [Nellie] Harper (1926–) 2563
    Amer. writer; Pulitzer, 1961
Lee, Hermione (1948–)   3843
    Eng. educator (English), biog-
    rapher, literary critic
Lee, Jennifer (1976–)   4911
    Amer. reporter, writer
Lee, Malka (1904/05–1976)   1856
    Amer. writer
Lee, Mary Chudleigh, Lady
(1656–1710)   492
    Eng. author, poet; a.k.a.
    Marissa
Lee, Min Jin (1969–)   4794
    Kor./Amer. writer, lawyer
Lee, Sophia (1750–1824)   664
    Eng. educator, writer; s. Har-
    riet L— (writer)
Leech, Margaret [Kernochan]
(1893–1974)   1778
    Amer. biographer, writer; w.
    Ralph Pulitzer; Pulitzer, 1942,
    1960
Leek, Sybil (1917–1982)   2296
    Eng./Amer. business execu-
    tive, author, mystic, witch; née
    Fawcett
Leffland, Ella (1931–)   2769
    Amer. novelist
Le Gallienne, Eva (1899–1991)1887
    Eng./Amer. actor, translator,
    writer; founder and director,
    Civic (later American) Rep-
    ertory Theater, New York,
    1926; Emmy, 1978
Le Gallienne, Hesper (1893–?)1777
    Eng./Amer. writer, poet

Le Guin, Ursula K. (1929–) 2668
    Amer. writer; Nebula and
    Hugo Awards, 1969; NBA,
    1973
Lehman, Lotte (1888–1976)   1685
    Ger./Amer. writer, educator,
    opera singer; Viennese Cross
    of Honor, First Class, 1962;
    Legion of Honor
Leibowitz, Annie (1949–)   3910
    Amer. photographer, portrait;
    p. Susan Sontag*
Leicester, countess of   see KNOLLYS,
LETTICE
Leifer, Carol (1956–)   4376
    Amer. comedian, television
    writer, producer, actor
Leigh, Carolyn [Paula]
(1926–1983)   2564
    Amer. lyricist, composer; née
    Rosenthal
Leigh, Dorothy (?–1616?)   428
    Eng. author; née Kemp; w.
    Ralph L—
Leigh, Vivien (1913–1967)   2204
    Eng. actor; née Hartley; ex-w.
    Sir Laurence Olivier (1907–
    98; actor); Academy Award,
    1939, 1951
Leitch, Mary Sinton [Lewis]
(1876–1954)   1478
    Amer. poet
Leith, Prue (1940–)   3205
    S. Afr./Brit. writer, chef, TV
    personality, restauranteur;
    née Prudence Margaret L—;
    OBE, 1989
Lejeune, Caroline [Alice]
(1897–1973)   1852
    Brit. film critic, playwright
Lemke, Birsel (1950–)   3985
    Turk. environmental activ-
    ist; fdr., Citizen's Initiative
    HAYIR! (No!), 1990; Right
    Livelihood, 2000
L'Enclos, Ninon de
(1620–1705)   439
    Fr. courtesan; née Anne de L—
Lenéru, Marie (1875–1940)   1461
    Fr. screenwriter, playwright,
    writer
L'Engle, Madeleine
(1918–2007)   2320
    Amer. writer (children); née
    M— Camp L— Franklin;
    Newbery, 1962
Lennart, Isobel (1915–1971) 2247
    Amer. playwright, screenwriter
Lenngren, Anna Maria
(1755–1817)   681
    Swed. poet
Lennox, Annie (1954–)   4256
    Scot. singer, songwriter, AIDS
    activist, humanitarian; née
    Ann-Lynne Griselda L—;
    ex-w. Uri Fruchtmann, Israeli
    film and record producer;
    Grammy (4), Golden Globe,

& Oscar, 2004; BRIT Awards (8)

Lennox, Charlotte (1720–1804) 584
Amer./Eng. novelist, poet, playwright; d. James Ramsay (Lt. Governor of New York, 1720); possibly the first American novelist

Lenya, Lotta (1898–1981) 1868
Aus./Amer. singer, actor; née Karoline Wilhelmine Charlotte Blaumauer Teuschl; w. Kurt Weill (1900–1950; Ger. born-American composer); Tony, 1956

Leonard, Annie (1961?–) 4585
Amer. scholar, environmental activist

Lepore, Jill (1966–) 4725
Amer. educator, history, author, journalist

Lerner, Gerda (1920–) 2380
Aus./Amer. writer, lecturer, educator, historian; née Kronstein; founder of university-based women's history studies

Lerner, Harriet Goldhor (1944–) 3519
Amer. psychologist, workshop leader, lecturer

Le Row, Caroline Bigelow (1843–?) 1117
Amer. editor, poet

Le Shan, Eda J. (1922–2002) 2434
Amer. TV host, family counselor, columnist, educator, writer

Lesher, Jan (1955?–) 4313–4314
Amer. politician

Leslie, Amy (1860–1939) 1256
Amer. actor, drama critic; a.k.a. Lillie West Brown Buck

Leslie, Eliza (1787–1858) 804
Amer. humorist, author, cookery expert, editor; a.s.a. Elizabeth, Betsey, Miss L—; s. Charles Robert L— (painter)

Leslie, Lisa [Deshaun] (1972–) 4864
Amer. athlete (basketball), model; m. Lockwood; three-time Olympic gold medalist 1996, 2000, 2004

Lespinasse, Julie-Jeanne-Éléonore de (1732–1776) 614
Fr. salonist, author

Lesser, Elizabeth (1952–) 4117
Amer. author, educator, social activist; cofounder, Omega Institute

Lessing, Doris (1919–) 2349
Eng. novelist, playwright; née D— May Taylor; Nobel Prize, 2007

Le Sueur, Marian (1877–1954) 1496
Amer. lawyer, political activist; m. Meridel L—*

Le Sueur, Meridel (1900–1996) 1911
Amer. historian, poet, writer; d. Marian L—*

LeTendre, Mary Jean (1948–) 3844
Amer. educator, civil servant; founder, LeTendre Education Fund, 1998; Director, Compensatory Education Programs at the U.S. Department of Education

Letts, Winifred (1882–1972) 1580
Ir. poet, writer; mn. Verschoyle

Leveridge, Lillian (1879–1953) 1531
Can. poet

Leverson, Ada [Beddington] (1862–1933) 1288
Eng. novelist

Levertov, Denise (1923–1997) 2464
Eng./Amer. poet, translator, educator (poetry), poetry editor; w. Mitchell Goodman (American writer); Guggenheim

Levi-Montalcini, Rita (1909–) 2112
Ital./Amer. medical scientist; s. Gino L— (Ital. architect and educator, d. 1986) and Paola L— (Ital. painter); discovered nerve growth factor (NGF); Nobel Prize, 1986

Levin, Diane E. (1947–) 3764
Amer. educator, early childhood, psychologist, sociologist, author; w. Gary Goldstein, physics professor; m. Eli L—G—, D.J., music composer; fdr. SoulClap.us

Levine, Emily (1948?–) 3845
Amer. comedian

Levine, Judith (1952–) 4118
Amer. author, journalist, feminist, radical; cofounder, Natl. Writers Union and No More Nice Girls

Levinson, Nan (1949–) 3911
Amer. journalist, novelist, educator

Levy, Amy (1861–1889) 1273
Eng. poet

Levy, Andrea (1954?–) 4257
Brit. writer

Levy, Naomi (1963–) 4646
Amer. nonfiction writer, rabbi

Lewes, Joyce (?–1557) 360
Eng. Protestant martyr; mn. Appleby (1); w. Thomas L— of Mancetter (2)

Lewinsky, Monica (1973–) 4877
Amer. public figure

Lewis, Edith (1880?–1955?) 1551
Amer. biographer, editor; companion, Willa Cather*

Lewis, Sarah Anna (1824–1880) 994
Eng. poet

Lewitzky, Bella (1916–2004) 2273
Amer. ballet dancer, choreographer; founder, Bella Lewitzky Dance Company

L'Heritier, Marie Jeanne [de Villadon] (1664–1734) 503
Fr. poet, novelist, translator

Liadan (fl. 7th century) 129
Ir. nun, poet; a.s.a. Liadain

Lichtenstein, Tehilla (1893–1973) 1779
Jerusalemite/Amer. religious leader; née Hirschensohn; w. Rabbi Morris L—; cofounder, Society of Jewish Science (1922)

Liddell, Catherine [Fraser Tytler] (1848–1927) 1161
Eng. poet, writer

Lieberman, Alicia F. (1947–) 3765
Par./Amer. educator (early childhood), researcher

Liebman, Wendy (1961–) 4586
Amer. comedian; Best Female Stand-up, American Comedy Awards, 1997

Lienert, Tania (1974?–) 4885
Amer. radical feminist

Lightfoot, Sara Lawrence (1944–) 3520
Amer. educator, author, sociologist, writer

Lightner, Candy (1946–) 3671
Amer. realtor, reformer; founder of MADD (Mothers Against Drunk Driving), 1980

Liking, Werewere (1950–) 3986
Camer./Ivorian playwright, performance artist, novelist; fdr., Ki-Yi Mbock theatre troupe, 1980; fdr., Ki-Yi village, 1985 (for the artistic education of young people)

Liliuokalani, Lydia Kamekeha (1838–1917) 1083
Hawaiian queen of the Islands, songwriter

Liljeström, Rita (1928–) 2635
Swed. social researcher, writer, educator (sociology)

Lillie, Beatrice (1898–1989) 1869
Eng. actor, comedian; née Constance Sylvia Munston; a.k.a. Lady Peel

Lim, Genny (1946–) 3672
Amer. poet, playwright, anthologist; ABA, 1982; Rockefeller

Lim, Shirley Geok-Lin (1944–) 3521
Malaysian/Amer. educator (English & feminist theory), poet, scholar

Lim Wei-ling, Wilina (Contemporary) 4980
Indones./Chin. virologist

Lin, Frank see ATHERTON, GERTRUDE

Lin, Maya (1959–) 4492
Amer. sculptor, architect; p. Peter Boynton (sculptor); designed Vietnam Memorial, Washington, D.C., 1982; NWHF

L'Incarnation, Marie de (1599–1672) 407
Fr. nun; née Guyard; w. Claude Martin I (master silkworker), m. Claude Martin II (her biographer); founder and mother superior of the first Ursuline Mission in Canada

Lincoln, Abbey (1930–) 2723
Amer. actor, singer; née Anna Marie Wooldridge

Lincoln, countess of see CLINTON, ELIZABETH

Lincoln, Mary Todd (1818–1882) 950
Amer. first lady; w. Abraham L— (1809–65; lawyer, politician; 16th U.S. president; assassinated)

Lincoln, Victoria (1904–1981) 1997
Amer. novelist, biographer

Lind, Jenny (1820–1887) 970
Swed. opera singer; a.k.a. "The Swedish Nightingale"; mn. Goldschmidt

Lindbergh, Anne [Spencer] Morrow (1906–2001) 2053
Amer. nonfiction writer, poet, aviator; w. Charles L— (aviator, 1902–1974); d. Elizabeth Reed M—*; NWHF

Lindgren, Astrid [Anna Emilia] (1907–2002) 2069
Swed. writer, activist, screenwriter; gold medal of the Swedish Academy in 1971; Honorary Right Livelihood Award, 1994

Lindley, Mary Ann (1947–) 3766
Amer. newspaper editor, columnist, journalist

Lindsay, Anne, Lady see BARNARD, ANNE

Lindsay, Sarah (1958–) 4457
Amer. poet

Lingle, Linda (1953–) 4189
Amer. politician; Governor [R], Hawaii, 2002–

Lippman, Laura (1959–) 4493
Amer. novelist

Lipstadt, Deborah [Esther] (1947–) 3767
Amer. historian, educator

Lipton, Eunice (1941–) 3278
Amer./Fr. art historian, art critic; w. Ken Aptekar, artist

Li Qingzhao (1081/84–1140/51) 175
Chin. collector, poet, scholar; a.s.a. Li Ch'ing-chao; w. Chao Ming-ch'eng (poet, d. 1129)

Lisiewska-Therbusch, Anna Dorothea (1721–1782) 587
Ger./Fr. painter

Lisle, Honor, Viscountess (1500?–1550) 296
Eng. letter writer; w. Sir John Basset (1) and Arthur Plantagenet (2, son of Edward IV, 1442–83; king of England, 1461–83)

Lispector, Clarice (1920–1977) 2381
Russ./Braz. novelist, writer; Graca Aranha Prize, Brazilian PEN club; Jabuti Prize, Camara Brasileira do Livro

Litman, Ellen (1973–) 4878
Russ./Amer. educator, writer

Litman, Jane (194-?–) 3206
Amer. feminist, rabbi, educator (Jewish studies)

Litrichin, Vera (1943–) 3437
Serb. human rights and peace activist; cofounder, SOS Hotline and Center for Girls (Belgrade)

Littlebear Morena, Naomi (1956?–) 4377
Amer. songwriter

Littlewood, Joan [Maud] (1914–2002) 2223
Eng. theatrician, actor; w. Edwan MacColl (folk singer and political dramatist); cofounder, Theater of Action, Manchester (1934, with Mac-Coll); pioneered collaborative approach to theater making; cofounder, Theatre Union (1960s); cofounder, Theatre Workshop, Stratford; Best Production Award, Theater of the Nations, Paris (1955, 56, 57); Lifetime Achievement, Directors' Guild of Great Britain

Liu, Peggy (1962–) 4624
Chin./Amer. environmentalist, administrator (NGO), entrepreneur; fndr.-chair, Joint U.S.-China Cooperation on Clean Energy (JUCCCE)

Lively, Penelope [Margaret] (1933–) 2858
Egyp./Eng. novelist, historian; Booker, 1987

Livermore, Mary [Ashton] (1820–1905) 971
Amer. lecturer, writer, social reformer; née Rice

Livingstone, Belle (1875–1957) 1462
Amer. society leader, actor

Livni, Tzipora "Tzipi" Malka (1958–) 4458
Isr. lawyer, politician; Foreign Affairs Minister, Acting P.M.

Li Yeh (fl. eighth century) 147
Chin. poet, calligrapher, Taoist priestess, musician

Llewellyn-Thomas, Beatrice [Caroline] (1890–?) 1711
Eng. writer, poet; pseud. F. H. Dorset

Lloyd, Chris Evert see EVERT LLOYD, CHRIS

Lloyd, Marie (1870–1922) 1378
Eng. entertainer; née Mathilda Alice Victoria Wood

Locke, Anne (1530?–1590?) 332
Scot. translator; a.k.a. A—Dering, A— Prouse; friend of John Knox (1514?–72; founder of Scottish Presbyterianism); composed the first English sonnet sequence

Locke, Una see BAILEY, URANIA

Lockridge, Hildegarde see DOLSON, HILDEGARDE

Lockwood, Belva [Ann] (1830–1917) 1029
Amer. feminist, lawyer; née Bennett; NWHF

Loftus, Elizabeth Fishman (1944–) 3522
Amer. educator, psychologist, forensic consultant; NSF, 1977

Lombarda (1190?–?) 200
Fr. trobairitz

Longauex y Vasquez, Enriqueta (1945?–) 3589
Amer. civil rights activist

Longworth, Alice [Lee] Roosevelt (1884–1980) 1616
Amer. wit, society leader; d. Theodore Roosevelt (war hero, politician, 1858–1919; 26th U.S. president, 1901–09), w. Nicholas L— (politician, 1869–1931), s. Edith Carow Roosevelt,* n. Corinne R. Robinson*

Lonsdale, Kathleen Yardley (1903–1971) 1972
Brit. physicist; first woman president of the British Association for the Advancement of Science (1967); C.B.E., 1956

Loos, Anita (1888–1981) 1686
Amer. screenwriter, novelist, playwright, humorist; mn. Emerson

Lopata, Jadwiga (1954?–) 4258
Pol. administrator, environmental activist, organic farmer; fdr., European Center for Ecological Agriculture and Tourism-Poland (ECEAT-Poland), 1993; cofounder.-dir., International Coalition to Protect the Polish Countryside (ICPPC), 2000; Goldman Environmental Prize, 2002

Lopez, Jennifer (1970–) 4824
Amer. actor, singer, entrepreneur, TV producer; a.k.a. J.Lo

López de Córdoba, Leonor (1361?–1420) 243
Spanish courtier, memoirist

Lord, Betty Bao (1938–) 3094
Chin./Amer. writer, arts administrator, photographer

Lord, Nancy (1922–) 4119
Amer. fisher, writer, environmentalist; a.k.a. Eve Titus

Lorde, Audre [Geraldine] (1934–1992) 2901
Amer. poet, writer, feminist; cofounded (with Barbara Smith*and Cherrie Moraga*) the first publishing collective by women of color, Kitchen Table: Women of Color Press

Loren, Sophia (1934–) 2902
Ital. actor; née Sofia Villani Scicolone; w. Carlo Ponti (1913– ; film producer); Academy Award, 1961, 1991

Lorraine, duchess of (fl. 13th century) 232
Fr. poet

Lot's daughter (the elder) (fl. 18th century B.C.E.) 10
Semite/Mesopotamian biblical figure; grandn. Abraham (patriarch of the Hebrews), d. Lot, m. Moab (by Lot)

Lothrop, Amy see WARNER, ANNA

Lothrop, Harriet Mulford see SIDNEY, MARGARET

Loud, Pat (1926–) 2565
Amer. writer, TV personality

Lougee, Carolyn Chappell (1942–) 3359
Amer. historian, educator (history)

Louis, Minnie D. (1841–1922) 1105
Amer. writer, community activist, teacher; cofounder, NCJW; founder, Downtown Sabbath School (later the Hebrew Technical School for Girls (1880)

Love, Barbara J. (1937–) 3043
Amer. editor, writer

Love, Courtney (1964–) 4681
Amer. singer, songwriter; grandd. Paula Fox*

Lovell, Marie [Anne Lacy] (1803–1877) 878
Eng. playwright, actor

Low, Juliette (1860–1927) 1257
Eng./Amer. humanitarian; née Gordon; founder of Girl Scouts of America, 1912; NWHF, 1980

Lowell, Amy (1874–1925) 1440
Amer. poet, literary critic; Pulitzer, 1926

Lowry, Beverly (1938–) 3095
Eng. writer, educator (writing); née Fey

Lowry, Lois [Ann] (1937–) 3044
Amer. writer; née Hammersburg; Newbery, 1990, 1994

Lowry, Mary (1941?–) 3279
Amer. community activist; w. Mike L— (1939–), governor of Washington, 1993–1997

Loy, Mina Gertrude (1882–1966) 1581
Eng./Amer. poet, fiction writer, visual artist; née Lowry; w. Stephen Haweis (1; artist) and Arthur Cravan (2; writer)

Lu, Hsui-Lein Annette (1944–) 3523
Taiwan. lawyer, diplomat; founded the Taiwanese women's movement (ca. 1978) and the movement to regain United Nations membership for Taiwan (1991); World Peace Prize (2001)

Lubchenco, Jane (1947–) 3768
Amer. environmental scientist, marine ecologist, educator; admin., National Oceanic and Atmospheric Administration, 2009– (1st woman); MacArthur

Lucas, F. L., Mrs. see JONES, EMILY

Luce, Clare Boothe (1903–1987) 1973
Amer. writer, feminist, politician, diplomat, playwright; w. Henry Robinson L— (2; publishing tycoon, 1898–1967); U.S. congresswoman (R-CT), 1943–47; U.S. ambassador to Italy, 1953–57; Presidential Medal of Freedom, 1983

Luce, Gay Gaer (1930–) 2724
Amer. writer, researcher; founder, Nine Gates Mystery School

Ludendorff, Mathilde Spiess see KEMNITZ, MATHILDA

Ludwig, Paula (1900–1974) 1912
Aus./Ger. poet

Luhan, Mabel Dodge see DODGE, MABEL

Luker, Kristin Carol (1946–) 3673
Amer. nonfiction writer, sociologist, educator (sociology)

Lunch, Lydia (1959–) 4494
Amer. rock singer, poet, actor, writer; née Koch; a.k.a. "the Roseanne of Punk Rock"

Lupino, Ida (1918–1995) 2321
Eng./Amer. actor, film director & producer; ex-w. Howard Duff (1917–90; actor)

Lurie, Alison (1926–) 2566
Amer. writer, author; Pulitzer, 1985

Luscomb, Florence
(1887–1985)   1666
    Amer. organizer, pacifist,
    architect, suffragist
Lute, Jane Holl (1956?–)   4378
    Amer. military officer, public
    servant, political scientist,
    lawyer; w. Lt. Gen. Douglas
    E. L— (1953–); Homeland
    Security Deputy Secy., 2009–
Luxborough, Henrietta Knight
(1699–1756)   547
    Eng. poet, letter writer; half-s.
    Lord Bolingbroke (statesman,
    orator, writer, 1678–1751)
Luxemburg, Rosa (1870–1919)1379
    Pol./Ger. writer, socialist,
    revolutionary
Luynes, comtesse de   see DETOUR-
BEY, JEAN
Lyall, Edna (1857–1903)   1225
    Eng. writer; née Ada Ellen
    Bayly
Lydia (fl. 50s C.E.)   90
    Turk. merchant
Lydon, Susan (1943–2005)   3438
    Amer. feminist, political activist,
    writer; née Gordon; founding
    ed., Rolling Stone magazine
Lyman, W. W., Mrs.   see HOYT,
HELEN
Lynde, H. H.   see HUNTINGTON,
HELEN
Lynn, Loretta (1932–)   2806
    Amer. songwriter, singer; née
    Webb; Grammy (4); Country
    Music Hall of Fame (1988)
Lynx   see WEST, REBECCA
Lyon, Emily (1956–)   4379
    Amer. nurse
Lyon, Mary [Mason]
(1797–1849)   855
    Amer. administrator, teacher;
    founder, Mount Holyoke Fe-
    male Seminary for Girls (later
    Mount Holyoke College),
    1836; pioneer in the field of
    higher education for women;
    Hall of Fame, 1905; NWHF
Lyon, Mrs. (1762–1840)   714
    Ir. poet
Lyon, Phyllis (1924–)   2489
    Amer. writer, civil rights ac-
    tivist, feminist; cofounder of
    Daughters of Bilitis
Lytton, Constance
(1869–1923)   1365
    Eng. suffragist, noble; d. Rob-
    ert, the first earl of Lytton;
    adopted false identity (Jane
    Wharton), so as to avoid spe-
    cial treatment upon arrest

M

Maathai, Wangari Muta
(1940–)   3207
    Kenyan scientist, educator,
    social activist; first woman

in East and Central Africa to
    earn a doctorate degree; chair,
    National Council of Women
    of Kenya, 1981–87; fdr.,
    Green Belt Movement, 1976;
    2004 Nobel Peace laureate;
    Right Livelihood Award,
    1984; International Advocate
    for Peace Award, 2004; Gold-
    man Environmental Prize,
    1991
Maazel, Fiona (1976–)   4912
    Amer. novelist, editor
Mable, Jackie "Moms"
(1894–1975)   1800
    Amer. comedian; née Loretta
    Mary Aiken
Macartney, Frances   see GREVILLE,
FRANCES
Macatti, Okkur
(fl. first–third century)   95
    Ind. poet
Macaulay, Rose, Dame
(1881–1958)   1570
    Eng. writer
MacDonald, Betty
(1908–1958)   2093
    Amer. fiction writer; née &
    a.k.a. Ann Elizabeth Campbell
    Bard
Macdonald, Cynthia
(1928–)   2636
    Amer. poet
MacDonald, Sharman
(1951–)   4055
    Scot./Eng. playwright, actor;
    w. Will Knightley, actor; m.
    Keira Knightley, actor; Lon-
    don Evening Standard Award,
    1984
MacGuineas, Maya [Carol]
(1968–)   4771
    Amer. economist; w. Robin
    Jermyn Brooks (1970–), Brit.-
    Amer. Economist; cofounder,
    Centrists.Org
Macher, Sofia (1956?–)   4380
    Peru. human rights activist,
    government official; Com-
    missioner of the Truth and
    Reconciliation Commission
    (TRC); Notre Dame Prize for
    Distinguished Public Service in
    Latin America, 2004
Macivar, Anne   see GRANT,
ANNE
MacKay, Shena (1944–)   3524
    Scot./Eng. novelist
MacKinnon, Catherine A.
(1946–)   3674
    Amer. activist, author, scholar,
    attorney, educator
MacLaine, Shirley (1934–)   2903
    Amer. writer, actor, activist;
    née Beaty; s. Warren Beatty
    (screen actor, 1937–); Golden
    Globe, 1960, 1963, 1988;
    Oscar, 1983

MacLeod, Jean S[utherland]
(1908–)   2094–2095
    Eng. novelist, poet; pseud.
    Catherine Airlie, Phila Henri-
    etta Case
MacMurray, Rose [Chatfield-
Taylor] (1921–1997)   2405
    Amer. teacher, novelist, trans-
    lator, poet
MacPherson, Myra (1935?–)   2939
    Amer. journalist, author
Macuilxochitl (1435–1499?)   259
    Aztec poet; d. Tlacaelel
    (counselor to Itzcoatl)
Macy, Joanna [Rogers]
(1929–)   2669
    Amer. Buddhist scholar,
    nonfiction writer, workshop
    leader; Fulbright; Ford 1979,
    1980
Madan, Judith (fl. 1750s)   665
    Eng. poet; née Cowper; s.
    William Cowper (1664?–1723;
    jurist; Lord High Chancellor
    of England, 1707–10 and
    1714–18)
Maddow, Rachel (1973–)   4878.1
    Amer. TV host, political com-
    mentator
Madgett, Naomi [Cornelia] Long
(1923–)   2465
    Amer. poet, book editor,
    teacher
Madison, D. Soyiini (1949–)   3912
    Amer. activist, educator;
    Fulbright
Madison, Dolley (1768–1849)   738
    Amer. society leader, first
    lady; née Dorothea Payne;
    w. John Todd (1) and
    James M— (2; 1751–1836;
    politician; 4th U.S. president,
    1809–1849)
Madonna (1958–)   4459
    Amer. actor, singer; née
    M— Louise Veronica Ciccone;
    RRHF, 2008
Magdeburgh, Mechtild von   see
MECHTILD VON MAGDEBURG
Magdelene, Mary   see MARY MAG-
DALENE
Maggio, Rosalie (1943–)   3439
    Amer. writer
Magnani, Anna
(1918–1973)   2322
    Egyp./Ital. actor; Academy
    Award, 1955
Mahaadeviyakka
(fl. 12th century)   211
    Ind. poet, Hindu saint; a.s.a.
    Mahadevi; w. King Kausika
Mahler, Alma   see WERFEL, ALMA
Mahler, Margaret
(1897–1985)   1853
    Hung./Amer. psychiatrist,
    psychoanalyst, lecturer,
    nonfiction writer; née Schoen-
    berger

Mahler-Werfel, Alma
(1879–1964)   1532
    Aus./Amer. diarist, society fig-
    ure, composer; née Schindler;
    m. Anna M— (sculptor);
    widow of Gustav Mahler
    (1860–1911; 1, Aus. com-
    poser & conductor); Franz
    Werfel (1890–1945; 2, Aus.
    writer)
Mahodahi (fl. 7th–11th century)130
    Ind. poet
Mahoney, Rosemary (1961–)   4587
    Amer. writer, nonfiction; NEA
Mahsati Ganjavi
(fl. 12th century)   212
    Persian poet; a.s.a. Mhasti
    Ganjehi
Maines, Natalie Louise (1974–)
4886
    Amer. singer, songwriter; mn.
    Pasdar; Grammy (for Dixie
    Chicks), 13
Maintenon, Françoise de
(1635–1719)   466
    Fr. letter writer; née
    d'Aubigné, a.s.a. marquise
    or Mme de M—; w. Paul
    Scarron (1; 1610–60; writer),
    mistress and w. Louis XIV (2;
    1638–1715, king of France,
    1643–1715); founded school
    for daughters of impoverished
    noblemen at St.-Cyr, 1686
Mairs, Nancy (1943–)   3440
    Amer. writer, editor, technical,
    teacher; n. Jean Pedrick, poet
Maitland, Sara Louise (1950–)3987
    Eng. Writer (religion)
Makeba, Miriam [Zenzi]
(1932–2008)   2807
    S. Afr./Amer. political activist,
    singer; a.k.a. Mama Africa;
    ex-w. Stokely Carmichael
    (Amer. civil rights activist;
    a.k.a. Kwame Toure); w.
    Hugh Masekela (So.Af. Born
    jazz trumpeter); m. Bongi
    M— (1949–1985), singer-
    songwriter; Grammy (1966)
Makhfi (1639–1703)   470
    Ind. princess, poet, patron
    of poets, patron of scholars;
    a.k.a. Zibu'n-Nisa (a.s.a. Zeb-
    un-Nissa)
Makhubu, Lydia Phindile
(1937–)   3045
    Swazi chemist, research scien-
    tist, university administrator;
    first Swazi woman to earn a
    Ph.D.; founder, Royal Swa-
    ziland Society of Science and
    Technology, 1977; cofounder,
    Third World Organization of
    Women in Science (TWOWS),
    1989; first woman to head As-
    sociation of Commonwealth
    Universities

Makin, Bathsua (1600?–1675?) 412
Eng. author, tutor, scholar;
d. John Pell, s. John Pell II
(mathematician); royal tutor
to Princess Elizabeth and
other children of Charles II
(1630–85; king of England,
1660–85)

Malagrino, Silvia A. (1950–) 3988
Argen./Amer. photographer,
filmmaker, educator, artist,
multi-media; NEA

Malcolm, Janet (1934–) 2904
Cuban-born Amer. writer,
critic

Malfitano, Catherine (1948–) 3846
Ital. opera singer; d. Maria
Maslova, dancer

Mallicoat, Helen M.
(1907–1984) 2070
Amer. poet

Malmesbury, Countess of (see Ardagh, Susan)

Malone-Mayes, Vivienne
(1932–1995) 2808
Amer. mathematician, activist (civil rights); first Black
faculty member at Baylor
University

Malpede, Karen (1945–) 3590
Amer. theater historian, peace
activist, playwright, educator; w. George Bartenieff
(actor-producer); cofounder,
New Cycle Theatre, Brooklyn
(1976–84); with Bartenieff,
cofounder, Theater Three Collaborative

Malveaux, Julianne (1953–) 4190
Amer. economist, author,
college president, columnist,
commentator

Mamonova, Tatyana
(1938?–) 3096
Sov./Aus. critic, translator, painter, feminist, poet;
founder of modern Russian
women's movement

Mancini, Maria Anna
(1649–1714) 484
Ital./Fr. salonist; d. Michele
Lorenzo Mand Girolama
Mazzarino, s. Laure, Olympe,
Marie, and Hortense M—,
w. Godefroy Maurice de
la Tour, duc de Bouillon,
n. Jules Mazarin Ital.-born
French cardinal (1602–61);
patron of Jean de La Fontaine
(1621–95; Fr. writer), Pierre
Corneille (Fr. playwright,
1606–84), and Jean-Baptiste
Molière (1622–73; Fr. playwright)

Mandela, [Nomzamo] Winnie [Ma-
dikizela] (1934–) 2905
S. Afr. political activist, social
worker (medical), political

leader; a.k.a. Umama Wethu,
the Mother of the Nation;
ex-w. Nelson M— (1918–;
anti-apartheid activist and
leader; president, So. Africa,
1994– ; Nobel Peace Prize,
1993), m. Maki M—*

Mandela, Maki (1953–) 4191
S. Afr. political activist, sociologist; d. Nelson M— (1918– ;
anti-apartheid activist and
leader; president, So. Africa,
1994– ; Nobel Peace Prize,
1993) and Winnie M—*

Manjaa, [Ichinnorov] Nora
(1975?–) 4898
Chin. attorney, social activist;
fdr.-dir, Women's Leadership
Fdn. (Mongolia)

Manji, Irshad (1968–) 4772
Ugan./Can. feminist, journalist, educator; founder and
president of Project Ijtihad

Mankiller, Wilma Pearl
(1945–2010) 3591
Amer. social worker, Na-
tive American rights activist,
politician; chief of the Cherokee Nation of Oklahoma,
1987–95; first woman to head
a major Native American
tribe; NWHF

Manley, Delariviere
(1663/72–1724) 501
Eng. author, editor, playwright; a.k.a. (Mary)
D— M—; pseud. Mrs.
Crackenthorpe; née Daniels;
first Englishwoman to be a
political journalist, to author
a best-seller, and to be arrested
for her writings

Manley, Joan [Adele] (1932–) 2809
Amer. book publisher; née
Daniels; first woman pub-
lisher of Time-Life Books
(1970)

Mann, Emily (1952–) 4120–4121
Amer. playwright; w. Gerry
Banman (actor, writer); Guggenheim, 1983; NEA 1984,
1986; Tony, 1994; Obie,
1981

Mann, Erika (1905–1969) 2026
Ger. writer, lecturer, journalist; d. Thomas M— (writer,
1875–1955), w. W. H. Auden
(Eng./Amer. author, 1907–73)

Manner, Eeva-Liisa (1921–) 2406
Finn. playwright, writer, poet

Mannering, Julia see BINGHAM,
MADELINE

Manners, Diane see COOPER,
DIANA

Manners, Frances, Lady see ABER-
GAVENNY, FRANCES

Mannes, Marya (1904–1990) 1998
Amer. writer, journalist

Manoah, Wife of (fl. 1080 B.C.E.) 25
Hebrew biblical figure; w.
M— of Zorah, m. Samson
(Old Testament Isr. judge)

Manos, Helen (1950–) 3989
Aust. writer, children's,
teacher

Mansfield, Katherine
(1888–1923) 1687
N.Z./Eng. writer, literary
critic; née K— Beauchamp
Murry

Mantua, Marquise of see ESTE,
ISABELLA D'

Mara, Gertrude Elizabeth
(1749–1833) 657
Ger. singer; née Schmaling

Maraini, Dacia (1936–) 2991
Ital. feminist, political activist,
writer, playwright, poet; w. Al-
berto Moravia (né Pincherle;
1907–90; fiction writer); d.
Princess Topazia Alliata de
Salaparuta, artist, and Fosco
Maraini, ethnologist and
mountaineer; founder, La
Maddalena (feminist theater),
Rome, 1972

Maran, Meredith (1951–) 4056
Amer. writer

Marbury, Elisabeth
(1856–1933) 1211
Amer. theater manager,
literary agent, playwright,
translator

Marcelle, countess de (fl. 1540s) 339
Fr. nun

Marchant, Catherine see COOK-
SON, CATHERINE

Marchetto, Marisa Acocella
(1962?–) 4625
Amer. cartoonist, illustrator;
w. Silvano M—, restauranteur;
fdr., The Cancer Vixen FUNd

Marchocka, Anna Maria
(1603–1652) 418
Pol. Carmelite nun; a.k.a.
Sister Teresa

Marcos, Imelda (1929–) 2670
Filipina public figure; née
Romualdez; w. Ferdinand M—
(1917–89; politician; president
of Philippines, 1966–86); governor of metropolitan Manila,
1975–86; cabinet member,
1978–86; Miss Manila, 1953

Marcus, Lisa (1965–) 4704
Amer. educator (ethnic literature & feminist theory)

Margaret of Alençon see MARGUE-
RITE OF NAVARRE

Margaret of Angoulême see MAR-
GUERITE OF NAVARRE

Margaret of Anjou
(1430–1482) 258
Eng. military hero, queen; w.
Henry VI (1421–71; king of
England, 1422–61 & 1470–71)

m. Edward, prince of Wales
(1470–83?)

Margaret of Austria
(1480–1530) 282
Aus. regent of the Neth-
erlands; d. Maximilian of
Austria, w. Charles VIII (1;
1471–98; king of France,
1483–98), Don Juan of Castile
and Aragon (2), and Philibert,
duke of Savoy (3); Regent of
the Netherlands

Margaret of Nassau (fl. 1360s) 242
Ger. noble; friend of Matilda
of Cleves

Margarula, Yvonne (1958?–) 4460
Aust. environmental activist;
Goldman, 1999

Margolis, Sue (1950?–) 3990
Eng. novelist

Margonelli, Lisa (1965–) 4705
Amer. author, journalist

Margot see MARGUERITE OF
VALOIS

Margrethe II, (1940–) 3208
Danish queen, painter, il-
lustrator, translator; a.k.a.
Dronningen ("the queen");
pseud. Ingahild Grathmer; d.
King Frederik IX and Crown
Princess Ingrid; first female
Danish sovereign under the
new Act of Succession

Marguerite of Navarre
(1492–1549) 289
Fr. patron of literature,
scholar, author, religious reformer, poet; a.k.a. Margaret
of Angouleme, of Alençon,
The Tenth Muse, The Pearl,
Parlamente (her pseud. in
the Heptameron); s. Francis I
(1494–1547, king of France,
1515–47); w. duke of Alençon (1) and Henry d'Albret
(2; titular king of Navarre),
m. Jeanne d'Albret*,
gm Henry IV of France
(1553–1610; king of France,
1589–1610)

Marguerite of Valois
(1553–1615) 356
Fr. queen, diarist; a.k.a. Margot; d. Catherine de' Medici,*
s. Francis II of France, Charles
IX (1560–74; king of France)
and Henry III (1574–89; king
of France), first w. Henry
of Navarre (later Henry IV,
1553–1610; king of France,
1589–1610)

Maria de Jesus, Sister see AGREDA,
MARÍA DE

Maria, Grand Duchess of Russia
(1890–1958) 1712
Russ. duchess

Maria, Laura see ROBINSON,
MARY

Maria of Hungary and Bohemia
(1505–1558)   298
    Aus. royalty; a.k.a. Maria
    Hapsburg; s. Charles V
    (1500–58; Holy Roman Em-
    peror, a.k.a. Charles I, king of
    Spain), Ferdinand of Austria,
    Elizabeth (a.k.a. Isabel) of
    Denmark, and Eleanore of
    Portugal; w. Louis II of Bohe-
    mia and Hungary
Maria Theresa (1717–1780)   579
    Aus. letter writer, reformer,
    empress, philanthropist,
    queen; a.k.a. archduchess of
    Austria, queen of Hungary
    and Bohemia, empress of
    the Holy Roman Emperor;
    d. Charles VI of Austria, w.
    Francis of Lorraine (grand-
    duke of Tuscany, later Francis
    I, Holy Roman Emperor),
    m. Joseph II (1741–90, Holy
    Roman Emperor, 1765–90,
    king of Bohemia and Hun-
    gary, 1780–90), and Marie
    Antoinette*
Maribel, Mother (1887–1970) 1667
    Eng. nun, sculptor; Reverend
    Mother General of the Com-
    munity of St Mary the Virgin
    1940–1953
Marie-Antoinette (1755–1793) 682
    Aus./Fr. queen (1774–93); née
    Josephe Jeanne Marie-A—;
    d. Francis I, (Holy Roman
    Emperor) and Empress Maria
    Theresa,* w. Louis XVI
    (1754–93; king of France,
    1754–93), m. Louis, dauphin
    of France
Marie de France (1160?–1215?) 193
    Fr./Eng. noble, translator,
    author; first European female
    author of fiction
Marinda   see MONK, MARY
Marinella, Lucrezia
(1571–1653)   376
    Ital. author
Marion, Frances (1886–1973) 1655
    Amer. journalist, scenarist;
    Academy Award, 1932
Marissa   see LEE, MARY
Markham, Beryl (1902–1986) 1951
    Eng./Kenyan author, aviator,
    horse trainer, adventurer; née
    Clutterbuck; first woman to
    cross the Atlantic east-to-west
    solo
Markham, Lucia Clark
(1870–1967)   1380
    Amer. poet
Markova, Alicia (1910–2004) 2138
    Eng. ballet dancer; née Marks
Marlin, Alice Tepper (1944–) 3525
    Amer. economist, human
    right's activist; founder and
    exec.dir., Council on Eco-

nomic Priorities, 1968–1999;
    President and CEO of Social
    Accountability International
    (SAI),; Honorary Right Liveli-
    hood, 1990
Marsh, Anne (1791–1874)   823
    Eng. author; née Caldwell,
    pseud. "An Old Man"
Marshall, [Sarah] Catherine
(1914–1983)   2224
    Amer. writer, editor; née
    Wood
Marshall, Lucinda (1956–) 4381
    Amer. artist, feminist, writer;
    founder, Feminist Peace
    Network; fpn@feminist-
    peacenetwork.org (7/6/08)
Marston, Stephanie (1949–) 3914
    Amer. psychotherapist, author,
    public speaker, corporate
    consultant
Martin, Anne Henrietta
(1875–1951)   1463
    Amer. suffragist, reformer,
    educator
Martin, Del [Dorothy Louise]
(1921–2008)   2407
    Amer. writer, feminist, civil
    rights activist; née Taliaferro;
    p. Phyllis Lyon*; cofounder,
    Daughters of Bilitis
Martin, Elizabeth
(1745?–post-1776)   648
    Amer. patriot; née Marshall
Martin, Emily (1944–)   3526
    Amer. anthropologist,
    feminist, Sinologist; a.k.a.
    E— M— Ahern
Martin, Jane Roland (1929–) 2671
    Amer. educator (philosophy),
    scholar
Martin, Judith (1938–)   3097
    Amer. etiquette columnist,
    author; pseud. Miss Manners;
    née Perlman; n. Selig Perlman,
    economist, labor historian;
    National Humanities Medal,
    2005
Martin, Lynn [Morley]
(1939–)   3151
    Amer. civil servant, politician,
    educator, businesswoman;
    U.S. secretary of labor, 1991–
    1993; Congress (R-Illinois),
    1981–1991
Martin, Martha (1896–1959) 1827
    Amer. diarist, adventurer;
    a.k.a. Helen Boylan
Martin, Sarah (1791–1843) 824
    Eng. prison reform activist,
    dressmaker
Martin, Sarah Catherine
(1768–1826)   739
    Eng. poet
Martineau, Harriet
(1802–1876)   874
    Eng. writer, feminist, critic,
    social

Martinez, Judith "Judy" Perez
(1955–)   4315
    Honduran/Amer. lawyer
Martínez Sierra, María
(1874–1974)   1441
    Span./Argen. playwright,
    feminist, politician, so-
    cialist; née M— de la O
    Lejárraga García; w. Gregorio
    M— (novelist, poet, essayist,
    theatrician); cofounder, Eslava
    Theater (Madrid)
Marula (fl. 1150s)   191
    Ind. poet
Marx, Patricia (1954?–)   4259
    Amer. humorist, writer
Mary I of England
(1516–1558)   309
    Eng. queen; a.k.a. Bloody
    Mary, Mary Tudor; d. Henry
    VIII (1491–1547; king of
    England, 1509–47) and
    Catherine of Aragon,* half-
    s. Elizabeth I* and Edward
    VI (1537–53; king of En-
    gland, 1447–53), w. Phillip
    II (1527–98: king of Spain,
    1556–98)
Mary II of England
(1662–1694)   498
    Eng. queen; d. James II
    (1633–1701; king of England,
    1685–88) and Anne Hyde, s.
    Anne of England,* w. William
    II of Orange (1650–1702;
    later William III of England,
    1689–1702)
Mary, Queen Consort of Great Brit-
ain (1867–1963)   1338
    Brit. royalty; w. George V
    (1865–1936; king of England,
    1910–36)
Mary, Virgin
(fl. 7 B.C.E.–25 C.E.)   79
    Jerusalemite biblical figure;
    d. Anna and Joachim, w.
    Joseph, m. Jesus Christ, c. St.
    Elizabeth*
Maryam bint Abi Ya'qub al-Ansari
(fl. 1000s–d. 1035)   170
    Span. poet
Mary Magdalene (fl. 20s C.E.) 81
    Jerusalemite biblical figure;
    first person to learn of the
    resurrection
Mary of France (1496–1533) 290
    Eng. queen; a.k.a. The White
    Queen, Mary Tudor, duch-
    ess of Suffolk; d. Henry VII
    (1457–1509; king of England,
    1485–1509); s. Henry VIII
    (1491–1547; king of England,
    1509–47), w. Louis XII (1;
    1462–1514; king of France,
    1499–1515) and Charles
    Brandon, duke of Suffolk (2),
    gm. Lady Jane Grey*

Mary of the Gaels   see BRIGID OF
KILDARE
Mary of Warwick, countess
(1624–1678)   447
    Ir. society leader; née Mary
    Boyle, a.k.a. Mary Rich
Mary Queen of Scots
(1542–1587)   341
    Scot./Fr. poet, queen; a.k.a.
    Mary Stuart; d. James V
    (1512–42; king of Scotland,
    1513–42) and Mary of Guise
    (1515–60), w. Francis II of
    France (1), Henry Stuart (2;
    Lord Darnley), and James Hep-
    burn (3; 4th earl of Bothwell),
    m. James VI of Scotland (later
    James I [1566–1625; king of
    England, 1603–25]), first c. of
    Elizabeth I of England*
Mashinini, Emma (1929–)   2672
    S. Afr. labor activist, union
    administrator; fdr., Com-
    mercial Catering and Allied
    Workers' Union, 1975 (now
    second largest labor union
    in S.A.)
Mason, Bobbie Ann (1940–) 3209
    Amer. novelist, literary critic
Mason, Caroline [Atherton Briggs]
(1823–1890)   989
    Amer. poet
Mason, Viviane Carter
(1900–1982)   1913
    Amer. activist, civil rights,
    administrator; cofounder,
    Women's Council for Interra-
    cial Cooperation, 1945; pres.,
    National Council of Negro
    Women, 1953–
Massaro, Toni Marie (1955–) 4316
    Amer. lawyer, educator
Massie, Suzanne (1941?–)   3280
    Amer. lecturer, Russian his-
    torian, writer; w. Seymour
    Papert, MIT professor, math-
    ematician and pioneer of
    technology for learning
Masters, Mary (fl. 1730s–1755) 610
    Eng. letter writer, poet
Masterson, Martha Gay
(1837–1916)   1080
    Amer. memoirist, pioneer
Masuda, Mizuko (1948–)   3847
    Jap. writer
Matheopoulos, Helena
(1946?–)   3675
    Greek/Eng. journalist (fash-
    ion), historian, classical music
Mathews, Jessica Tuchman
(1946–)   3676
    Amer. research center execu-
    tive, environmental scientist;
    d. Barbara T—*
Mathilde, Princess (1820–1904) 972
    Fr. princess, writer; n. Na-
    poléon I (1729–1821; emperor
    of the French, 1804–14)

Mathis, Deborah (1953–)   4192
    Amer. columnist, writer (non-
    fiction)
Matilda (*see* Artois, Mahuat d')
Matilda of Magdeburg   *see*
MECHTILD VON MAGDEBURG
Matilda, Anna   *see* COWLEY,
HANNAH
Matilda, Queen (1100?–1135)   180
    Eng. queen
Matossian, Mariam (1972–)   4865
    Can./Amer. singer, songwriter,
    folklorist, teacher
Matraini, Chiara Cantarini
    (1514–post-1597)   307
    Ital. poet; a.s.a. Clara M—; w.
    Vicenzo Cantarini
Matsui, Doris Okada (1944–)   3527
    Amer. politician, public
    servant; widow, Bob Matsui
    (1941–2005), U.S. Rep; U.S.
    representative (D-CA), 2005–
Matsumoto, Valerie (1957–)   4420
    Amer. writer, educator (his-
    tory)
Mattern, Evelyn (1941–2003)   3281
    Amer. nun, activist, poet, au-
    thor, mystic
Matthews, Glenna C. (1938–)   3098
    Amer. historian, nonfiction
    writer
Matthews, Jill (1964–)   4682
    Amer. athlete (boxer); a.k.a.
    "The Zion Lion"; first woman
    to win a Golden Gloves
    competition (1995); Junior
    Flyweight Champion of the
    World, 1998
Matthews-Simonton, Stephanie
    (1940–)   3210
    Amer. psychotherapist; w.
    John S— ; with husband, pio-
    neers in cancer psychotherapy
Maule, Frances (1879–1966)   1533
    Amer. advertising copywriter,
    suffragist; mn. Björkman
Mavrikakis, Catherine
    (1961–)   4588
    Can. novelist, educator
Mawiyoo, Née ma "Ngwatilo"
    (1983–)   4952
    Kenyan writer, musician, poet;
    d. Janet Mawiyoo, public
    servant, and Rev. Canon Sam
    Mawiyoo, rel. leader
Maximilla (fl. 460s)   112
    Roman religious leader
Maxtone Graham, Joyce
Anstruther   *see* STRUTHER, JAN
Maxwell, Darcy, Lady
    (1742?–1810)   640
    Scot./Eng. philanthropist,
    courtier, religious leader; née
    Brisbane; friend of John Wes-
    ley (1703–91; Eng. clergyman;
    founder of Methodism, 1738)
Maxwell, Elsa (1883–1963)   1596
    Amer. writer, society leader

Maxwell, Mary Elizabeth   *see*
BRADDON, MARY
May, Elaine (1932–)   2810
    Amer. comedian, scenarist; née
    Berlin; d. Jack Berlin, writer-
    director-actor Yiddish theater;
    m. Jeannie B— , actor;
    Grammy (1960)
May, Julia Harris (1833–1912)1052
    Amer. poet
Mayberg, Maude (fl. 1892–)   1750
    Amer. lecturer (beauty), busi-
    nesswoman; a.k.a. Madame
    Yale
Mayer, Bernadette (1945–)   3592
    Amer. poet, writer, editor,
    magazine; w. Lewis Warsh,
    writer, publisher
Mayer, Jane (1955–)   4317
    Amer. journalist, author
Mayer, Maria Goeppert
    (1906–1972)   2054
    Ger./Amer. physicist; w. J. A.
    Jensen; discovered shell struc-
    ture of atomic nuclei; Nobel
    Prize, 1963; NWHF
Maysun (fl. 670s)   125
    Syr. poet; w. M-uawiya I
    (?–680, first Arab caliph to
    govern North Africa)
Mazuchelli, Elizabeth Sarah
    (1832–1914)   1046
    Eng./Ind. traveler
Mbete-Kgositsile, Baleka
    (1949–)   3915
    S. Afr. politician, poet; w.
    Keorapetse Kgositsile, writer;
    ANC MP; Speaker of Parlia-
    ment
McAleese, Mary (1951–)   4057
    Ir. politician, barrister, jour-
    nalist, educator; president of
    Ireland, 1997– ; second female
    to hold such office
McAuliffe, [Sharon] Christa [Cor-
    rigan] (1948–1986)   3848
    Amer. public school teacher,
    astronaut; died in U.S. space
    shuttle *Challenger* explosion
    (28 January)
McBride, Mary Margaret
    (1899–1976)   1888
    Amer. columnist, radio per-
    sonality, writer
McCain, Cindy [Lou Hensley]
    (1954–)   4260
    Amer. business executive,
    philanthropist; w. John M— ,
    U.S. senator (R-AZ); fdr.-dir.,
    American Voluntary Medical
    Team (1988–95)
McCall, Dorothy (1889–?)   1699
    Amer. political activist
McCallion, Hazel (1921–)   2408
    Can. politician, newspaper
    editor; Mayor of Mississauga,
    Ontario (1978–); Order of
    Canada, 2005; second place

in 2005 international World
    Mayor poll
McCarthy, Abigail
    (1915–2001)   2248
    Amer. columnist; née Quigley;
    ex-w. Eugene M— (politician,
    1916–2005)
McCarthy, Mary [Therese]
    (1912–1989)   2185
    Amer. writer, editor, drama
    and social critic; s. Kevin M—
    (actor); ex-w. Edmund Wilson
    (3; 1895–1972; literary &
    social critic), James West (4;
    diplomat)
McCarthy, Sarah J. (1942–)   3360
    Amer. writer, educator,
    activist; a.k.a. Sally M—
McCaslin, Mary (1946?–)   3677
    Amer. singer, songwriter
McCaughey, Martha (1966–)   4726
    Amer. educator (women's
    studies); Dir., Women's Stud-
    ies, Appalachian State Univ.
McClintock, Barbara
    (1902–1992)   1952
    Amer. geneticist, botanist, ed-
    ucator; pioneering research on
    the chromosomal structure of
    maize; identified two kinds of
    genes, functional or structural
    and controlling; especially
    noted for her theory of trans-
    position of chromosomes;
    National Medal of Science,
    1970; Nobel Prize (physiol-
    ogy), 1983 (first woman to
    receive Nobel unshared);
    NWHF
McClung, Nellie (1873–1951)   1414
    Can. writer, feminist
McCormick, Anne O'Hare
    (1882–1954)   1582
    Amer. journalist, writer; Pulit-
    zer, 1937
McCormick, Virginia Taylor
    (1873–1957)   1415
    Amer. poet
McCorquodale, Barbara   *see* CART-
LAND, BARBARA
McCorvey, Norma [Leah]
    (1947–)   3769
    Amer. entertainer, home-
    maker; a.k.a Jane Roe; née
    Nelson; plaintiff in infamous
    Supreme Court 1973 case
    Roe v. Wade, which legalized
    abortion.
McCoy, Rose Marie (1922–)   2435
    Amer. singer, songwriter
McCracken, Elizabeth (1966–)   4727
    Amer. writer; d. Samuel
    (writer) and Natalie
    M— (writer); NEA 1992;
    Guggenheim 1998
McCrory, Colleen (1950–2007)3991
    Can. environmental activist,
    administrator; fdr., Valhalla

Wilderness Society, 1975;
    Goldman, 1992
McCullers, Carson
    (1917–1967)   2297
    Amer. playwright, writer; née
    Smith; DCCA, 1950; Guggen-
    heim (2); NIAL, 1952
McDermott, Alice (1953–)   4193
    Amer. novelist, educator, writ-
    ing; NBA, 1996
McDougal, Susan [Carol]
    (1955–)   4318
    Ger./Amer. public figure,
    prison reform activist; née
    Henley; ex-w. Jim McDougal
McDougall, Joyce (1926–)   2567
    N.Z./Fr. author, psychoana-
    lyst; née Carrington
McDowell, Deborah E.
    (1951–)   4058
    Amer. literary critic, educator
McFadden, Bernice L. (1966–)4728
    Amer. novelist
McFate, Montgomery "Mitzi"
    (1965–)   4706
    Amer. defense theorist, cul-
    tural anthropologist; d. Mary
    M— (a.k.a. Mary Sapone),
    NRA spy
McFerren, Martha (1947–)   3770
    Amer. poet
McGill, Alice (1927–)   2606
    Amer. writer (children's),
    storyteller
McGinley, Phyllis (1905–1978)   2027
    Amer. writer, poet, humorist;
    Pulitzer, 1961
McGovern, Ann (1930–)   2725
    Amer. editor, writer
McGrory, Mary (1918–2004)   2323
    Amer. columnist; Pulitzer,
    1975
McHugh, Heather (1948–)   3849
    Amer. poet, educator (writ-
    ing); chancellor, AAP; NEA,
    1974, 1981; Guggenheim
McIntosh, Kinn Hamilton
    (1930–)   2726
    Eng. novelist; pseud. Cath-
    erine Aird
McIntosh, Maria (1803–1878)   879
    Amer. writer
McIntosh, Mary (1936–)   2992
    Eng. nonfiction writer, soci-
    ologist
McIntosh, Peggy (1934–)   2906
    Amer. feminist scholar, anti-
    racist activist; founder and
    co-director of the National
    S.E.E.D. Project on Inclusive
    Curriculum (Seeking Educa-
    tional Equity and Diversity)
McIntyre, Tami (1921–)   2409
    Chin./Amer. educator, writer
McKellar, Danica (1975–)   4898.1
    Amer. actor, mathematics au-
    thor, education advocate

McKenna, Elizabeth Perle (1956–) 4382
Amer. author, publisher

McKenney, Ruth (1911–1972) 2161
Amer. writer; w. Richard Bransten (a.k.a. Bruce Minton), writer; m. Eileen B—, State Supreme Court justice, NYC

McLachlan, Sarah (1968–) 4773
Can. songwriter, singer; founder, Lilith Fair

McLaughlin, Patricia (1945–) 3593
Amer. columnist, editor

McLeod, Irene Rutherford (1891–1964?) 1729
Aust. poet; w. Aubrey de Sélincourt (1894–1962), Eng. Writer, scholar, tr.

McLeod, Merikay (1947–) 3771
Amer. editor, author; mn. Silver

McMullan, Margaret (1960–) 4542
Amer. writer, educator, gardener

McNamara, Jo Ann [Kay] (1931–) 2770
Amer. nonfiction writer

McPartland, Marian (1918–) 2324
Eng./Amer. pianist, jazz, radio & TV host, writer, composer, band leader, record producer; née Turner; w. Jimmy M— (1907–1991), Amer. Cornetist; Grammy, 2004; National Radio Hall of Fame, 2007; Peabody Award, 1983

McPhee, Jenny (1960?–) 4543
Amer. novelist, translator; d. John M— (1931–) Amer. Writer; a pioneer of creative nonfiction; s. Martha M—, novelist

McPhee, Martha S. (1964–) 4683
Amer. novelist, educator; d. John M—, writer; Guggenheim; NEA

McPherson, Aimee Semple (1890–1944) 1713
Can./Amer. evangelist; a.k.a. Sister Aimee; founder, International Church of the Four-Square Gospel

McPherson, Sandra (1943–) 3441
Amer. educator (English), poet; NEA (3); Guggenheim, 1976, 1977; AAAL, 1987

McRae, Carmen (1920–1994) 2382
Amer. jazz singer, composer, pianist, actor

McTaggart, Lynne (1951–) 4059
Brit. journalist, author; w. Bryan Hubbard, publisher

McWhorter, [Rebecca] Diane (1951–) 4060
Amer. journalist; w. Richard Rosen, author; Pulitzer Prize, 2002

McWilliam, Candia [Francis Juliet] (1955–) 4319
Scot. novelist; d. Colin M— , architectural writer and academic

Mead, Margaret (1901–1977) 1935
Amer. editor, museum curator, writer, anthropologist; w. Gregory Bateson (1904–80; anthropologist), m. Mary Catherine Bateson* and Edward Sherwood M—; Presidential Medal of Freedom, 1979;

Meadows, Donella "Dana" (1941–2001) 3282
Amer. journalist, scientist; cofounder, Int. Network of Resource Information Centres (INRIC), 1981

Means, Marianne [Hansen] (1934–) 2907
Amer. political columnist;

Mechain, Gwerfyl (1460?–1500) 267
Welsh poet

Mechtild von Magdeburg (1207?–1282/97) 215
Ger. mystic, author, religious reformer; a.k.a. Matilda of Magdeburg; member of Beguines

Medici, Catherine de' (1519–1589) 310
Ital./Fr. queen; d. Lorenzo de' Medici, duke of Urbino; gd. Lucrezia de' Medici,* w. Henry III (1574–89; king of France), m. Marguerite of Valois,* Francis II of France, Charles IX (1560–74; king of France) and Henry III (1574–89; king of France)

Medici, Lucrezia de' (1425–1482) 255
Ital. poet, patron of the arts; née Tournabuoni; w. Piero de' Medici, m. Lorenzo de' Medici (the Magnificent), gm. Catherine de' Medici,* great gm. Marguerite of Valois*

Mee, Margaret [Ursula] (1909–1988) 2113
Eng. painter (botanical), environmental activist

Megaw, Helen Dick (1907–2002) 2071
Amer. physicist (crystallography)

Mehri (1404?–1447) 250
Iran. poet; a.k.a. Mihru'n-Nisa of Heart

Mehta, Deepa (1949–) 3916
Ind./Can. filmmaker; ex-w. Paul Saltzman (film producer)

Meir, Golda (1898–1978) 1870
Russ./Amer./Isr. politician; née Mabovitch; mn. Meyerson; Israel's first minister of labor, 1949–56; foreign minister, 1956–66 and prime minister, 1969–74

Meitner, Lise (1878–1968) 1514
Aus./Ger. physicist, educator, physics; Germany's first woman full physics professor; codiscovered, with Otto Hahn, proctactinium; codiscovered, with Otto Frisch, nuclear fission; Enrico Fermi Award, 1966

Melanie (1947–) 3772
Amer. singer, songwriter; née M— Safka

Melba, Nellie, Dame (1861–1931) 1274
Aust. opera singer; née Helen Porter Mitchell

Melen, Olya (1980?–) 4936
Ukrainian environmental activist, attorney; Goldman, 2006

Melvill, Elizabeth (1582?–1640) 390
Scot. poet; a.k.a. Lady Culross, Lady Colvill of Culross; d. Sir James M—, w. Colvill of Culross; earliest known Scottish woman writer to have her work appear in print

Melville, Pauline (1948–) 3850
Guyanese/Eng. writer, actor

Menchú, Rigoberta (1959–) 4495
Guateamalen Indian rights activist; Nobel Peace Prize, 1992

Mendel, Lady see DE WOLFE, ELSIE

Mendenhall, Dorothy Reed (1874–1964) 1442
Amer. physician, government official, civil rights activist; director of U.S. Children's Bureau; innovator in obstetrics; identified the Reed cell in Hodgkin's disease

Méndez, Nora Bermúdez (1969–) 4795
El Salv. poet

Mensah-Williams, Margaret (–)
Namibian politician, teacher; Senator & Deputy Speaker of Parliament, 1998–

Mercer, Margaret (1791–1846) 825
Amer. philanthropist, educator, abolitionist

Mercis see PHARAOH'S DAUGHTER

Mercouri, Melina (1925–1994) 2531
Greek political activist, actor, government official; w. Jules Dassin (Amer. film director, 1911–2008)

Mère, Madame see BONAPARTE, MARIE

Merian, Maria Sibylla (1647–1717) 481
Ger. painter, botanist, entomologist; mn. Graff

Merkel, Angela [Dorothea] (1954–) 4261
Ger. physicist, politician; née Kasner; Chancellor of Germany, 2005–

Mer-Khamis, Arna (1929–1995) 2673
Isr. peace activist; founder, the Defence of Children under Occupation/Care and Learning, 1987; Right Livelihood, 1993

Merman, Ethel (1908–1984) 2114
Amer. actor, singer; née E— Agnes Zimmerman; Tony, 1951; Grammy, 1959

Mernissi, Fatima (1940–) 3211
Mor. sociologist, feminist, author; a.s.a. Fatema

Merriam, Eve (1916–1992) 2274
Amer. playwright, feminist, writer, poet, director; Obie, 1977

Merry, Anne Brunton (1769–1808) 743
Eng./Amer. theater manager, actor; a.k.a. Mrs. Wignell, Mrs. Warren; w. Robert M— (1; poet, playwright, politician), Thomas Wignell (2; theater producer, manager), and William Warren (3; theater producer, manager)

Messud, Claire (1966–) 4729
Fr./Amer. writer

Mettika (fl. 6th century B.C.E.) 49
Chin. Buddhist nun

Metzger, Deena [Posy] (1936–)2993
Amer. poet, writer

Mew, Charlotte (1869–1928) 1366
Eng. writer, poet

Meyer, Agnes [Elizabeth Ernst] (1887–1970?) 1668
Amer. translator, social worker, writer, journalist

Meyer, Annie Nathan (1867–1951) 1339
Amer. writer, playwright; s. Maud N—*; great-grandd. Gershom Mendes Seixas, rabbi & American revolutionary hero; cousin, Benjamin N— Cardozo, second Jewish justice of U.S. Supreme Court;

Emma Lazarus*; cofounder, Barnard College (1889)

Meyer, Leisa D. (1963?–) 4647 Amer. educator, history

Meyer, Marlane (1951–) 4061 Amer. playwright, TV writer; née M— Emily Huapala Gomard; DCA, 1986; a.s.a. Marlene G— M—; Dramalogue Critics Award, 1986; Blackburn, 1990; NEA

Meynell, Alice Christiana (1847–1922) 1152 Eng. poet, literary critic; née Thompson

Meysenbug, Malwida von (1816–1903) 940 Ger. writer

Michaelis, Aline Triplett (1885–1958) 1635 Amer. poet, journalist; Poet Laureat of Texas (1934–36; first woman)

Michal (fl. 1010s–970 B.C.E.) 32 Hebrew queen; d. Saul, king of Israel, s. Merab (first betrothed of David), first w. David, king of Israel

Michel, Louise (1830–1905) 1030 Fr. revolutionary, teacher; pseud. Clemence; a.k.a. "the red virgin of Montmarte"

Michelman, Kate (1942–) 3361 Amer. civic organization administrator, women's rights activist; executive director, National Abortion Rights Action League (NARAL), 1985–2004

Michiel, Renier Giustina (1755–1832) 683 Ital. botanist, noble

Michiner, Harry, Mrs. see IRVING, MINNA

Michitsuna, Mother of (fl. 950s–d. 974) 160 Jap. diarist; a.k.a. Lady Gossamer; mistress of Fujiwara no Kane-iye (statesman), w. Regent Kaneie, m. Udaish? Michitsuna no haba

Midler, Bette (1945–) 3594 Amer. actor, singer, writer; a.k.a. The Divine Miss M; Grammy, 1973, 1980 (2); Tony, 1973; Emmy 1978

Mihru'n-Nisa of Heart see MEHRI

Mikulski, Barbara [Ann] (1936–) 2994 Amer. politician; U.S. House of Representatives (D-Maryland), 1977–1987; U.S. senator (D-MD), 1987– ; first woman to hold a Senate leadership post

Milan, duchess of see ESTE, BEATRICE D'

Milbanke, Anne Isabella (1792–1860) 834 Eng. poet; a.k.a. Lady Byron, Annabella; w. George Gordon (a.k.a. Lord Byron, poet, 1788–1824); m. Augusta Ada Byron

Milcah see ZELOPHEHAD, FIVE DAUGHTERS OF

Mildmay, Lady see SHERRINGTON, GRACE

Miles, Josephine (1911–1985) 2162 Amer. literary critic, educator, poet

Milgrom, Shira (1951–) 4062 Amer. educator, rabbi; w. David Elcott (1954–), U.S. director of interreligious affairs for the American Jewish Committee

Mill, Harriet Taylor (1807–1858) 902 Eng. suffragist, philosopher; w. John Stuart M— (1806–73; philosopher, economist) who credited her as his frequent co-author

Millar, Margaret Ellis (1915–1994) 2249 Can./Amer. fiction writer; née Sturm; w. Kenneth M— (pseud. Ross Macdonald; writer)

Millar, Susanna (fl. 1960s) 4544 Eng. writer, psychologist

Millay, Edna St. Vincent (1892–1950) 1751 Amer. poet, playwright, writer; pseud. Nancy Boyd; w. Eugene Boissevain; Pulitzer, 1923

Miller, Alice (1923–) 2466 Pol./Swiss author, painter, psychologist

Miller, Alice Duer (1874–1942) 1443 Amer. poet, novelist; mn. Wise

Miller, Alyce (1953–) 4194 Swiss/Amer. poet, writer, educator, English, attorney, animal law; Flannery O'Connor Award for Short Fiction, Mary McCarthy Prize for Short Fiction

Miller, Caroline [Pafford] (1903–1992) 1974 Amer. novelist; Pulitzer, 1934

Miller, Casey Geddes (1919–1997) 2350 Amer. etymologist; pioneer in study of non-sexist language

Miller, Ceci (1958–) 4461 Amer. author, public speaker, book editor, publishing consultant; d. Rosanna Taylor Herndon,* Amer. author, educator; pres., CeciBooks

Miller, Emily (1833–1913) 1053 Amer. poet, social reformer, writer, journalist, editor; a.k.a. E— Clarke Huntingdon

Miller, Helen [Day] Hill (1899–1995) 1889 Amer. biographer, journalist

Miller, Isabel see ROUTSONG, ALMA

Miller, Jean Baker (1927–2006) 2607 Amer. psychiatrist, psychoanalyst, editor, teacher, author

Miller, Laura (1950–) 3992 Amer. journalist, critic, literary, novelist; cofounder, Salon.com

Miller, Lee (1907–1977) 2072 Amer. model, photographer; w. Sir Roland Algernon Penrose (1900–84; Eng. art critic, collector, painter)

Miller, Sue (1943–) 3442 Amer. novelist

Miller, Susan (1944–) 3528 Amer. playwright, screenwriter; Obie, 1979; NEA, 1976, 1983; Rockefeller, 1975; Susan Smith Blackburn Prize (2002)

Millet, Kate (1934–) 2908 Amer. sculptor, writer, feminist

Millner, Caille (1979–) 4928 Amer. newspaper editor

Mills, Karen Gordon (1954?–)4262 Amer. business executive; w. Barry M— , college president; dir., SBA, 2009–

Mills, Stephanie (1948–) 3851 Amer. author, lecturer, ecologist, teacher

Mina, Denise (1966–) 4730 Scot. novelist

Miner, Dorothy Eugenia (1904–1973) 1999 Amer. librarian, scholar

Minh-ha, Trinh see TRINH, T. MINH-HA

Mink, Gwendolyn (1952–) 4122 Amer. community activist, educator (women's studies), writer; d. Patsy M—*; founding mbr., The Women's Committee of 100

Mink, Patsy [Matsu Takemoto] (1927–2002) 2608 Amer. lawyer, politician; m. Gwendolyn M—*; first Asian-American elected to Congress (D-HI), 1965–1977 and 1990– ; cofounder, National Women's Political Caucus; cofounder, Women USA; NWHF

Minnelli, Liza (1946–) 3678 Amer. singer, actor; d. Judy Garland* and Vincent

M— (film director, 1910–), s. Lorna Luft (singer, 1952–); Oscar, 1973; Emmy 1972; Grammy, 1989; Golden Globe, 1973, 1985

Minow, Martha (1954–) 4263 Amer. educator (law)

Mirabai (1498–1547) 293 Ind. Hindu saint, poet, princess

Miriam (fl. 1250s–30s B.C.E.) 16 Hebrew poet, prophet; d. Jochebed, s. Moses (Hebrew prophet, lawgiver) and Aaron, w. Hur

Mirikitani, Janice (1941–) 3283 Amer. poet, book editor, nonprofit administrator, activist, community; poet laureat of San Francisco (2000); founding pres., Glide Foundation

Mirrielees, Edith Ronald (1878–1962) 1515 Amer. editor, writer, educator

Mischenko, Vera (1953–) 4195 Russ. attorney, environmental activist; cofounder, Ecojuris; Goldman, 2000

Mistral, Gabriela (1889–1957) 1700 Chilean educator, diplomat, educational activist, poet; née Lucila Godoy y Alcayaga; Chilean consul in Naples, Madrid, and Lisbon; first Latina to win Nobel Prize, 1945

Mitchell, Helen Porter see MELBA, NELLIE

Mitchell, Joni (1943–) 3443 Can./Amer. singer, songwriter; née Roberta Joan Anderson; Grammy, 1969; RRHF, 1997

Mitchell, Juliet (1940–) 3212 N.Z./Eng. psychoanalyst, feminist, writer, educator

Mitchell, Margaret (1900–1949) 1914 Amer. novelist, journalist; mn. Marsh; Pulitzer, 1937

Mitchell, Maria (1818–1889) 951 Amer. astronomer, educator; first woman astronomer in U.S.; first woman member of American Academy of Arts and Sciences; discovered new comet, 1847; Hall of Fame, 1905; NWHF

Mitchell, Martha (1918–1976) 2325 Amer. public figure; née Jennings; w. John M— (1913–88; lawyer; attorney general of U.S., 1968–72)

Mitford, Jessica [Lucy] (1917–1996) 2298 Eng./Amer. social critic, writer; mn. Treuhaft

Mitford, Mary Russell (1787–1855) 805
Eng. author, playwright, poet; a.k.a. Sancho Panza in Petticoats

Mitford, Nancy (1904–1973) 2000
Eng./Fr. novelist, biographer; a.k.a. N— Freeman M— Rodd; d. David Bertram Ogilvy (second baron Redesdale)

Mittal, Anuradha (1968–) 4774
Ind./Amer. activist, human rights, political scientist; Co-director, Institute for Food and Development Policy (Food First); founder and director, The Oakland Institute

Mladjenovic, Lepa (1954–) 4264–4265
Yug./Serb. human rights activist, woman's counselor; cofounder, Belgrade Women in Black

Mock, Geraldine "Jerrie" Fredritz (1925–) 2532
Amer. aviator, radio & TV host; a.k.a. the flying housewife; first woman to fly alone around the world

Modjeska, Helena (1840–1920) 1095
Pol. actor; née Opid

Modotti, Tina (1896–1942) 1828
Ital./Amer./Mex. actor, revolutionary, photographer; companion to Edward Weston (1; 1850–1936; Eng/Amer. photographer), Julio Antonio Mella (2; Cuban revolutionary; assassinated, 1928)

Moeller, Susan D. (1966?–) 4731
Amer. journalist, administrator

Moffat, Mary Jane (1933–2004) 2859
Amer. actor, writer, educator

Mofokeng, Connie (1959–) 4496
S. Afr. political activist

Mohammed, Binta S. (1969?–) 4796
Nig. poet, novelist, educator

Moirai, Catherine Risingflame (195-?–) 3993
Amer. poet

Moïse, Penina (1797–1880) 856
Amer. Jewish hymnist, poet, educator

Mojtabai, A.G. [Ann Grace] (1937–) 3046
Amer. writer, librarian; née Alpher

Molesworth, Mary Louisa (1839–1921) 1088
Dutch/Eng. essayist, author; a.k.a. Ennis Graham

Molina de Pick, Gracia (1930–) 2727
Mex./Amer. educator, activist, chicano/a; a.k.a. G— M— En-

riquez; founder of several organizations the Natl. Council of La Raza

Molodowsky, Kadya (1894–1975) 1801
Russ./Amer. writer, poet

Mongella, Gertrude Ibengwe (1945–) 3595
Tanz. diplomat; a.k.a. Mama M—; Secretary General of United Nations Fourth Conference on the World's Women, 1995; pres., Pan-African Parliament

Monica (340–395) 105
Numidian letter writer; a.s.a. Monnica; w. Patricius, m. St. Augustine (354–430; theologian, bishop of Hippo), Navigius and Perpetuals

Monk, Karen (Contemporary) 4982
Amer. writer

Monk, Mary (?–1715) 577
Ir. noble, poet; née Molesworth, a.s.a. Monck, pseud. Marinda

Monroe, Anne Shannon (1877–1942) 1497
Amer. writer, lecturer

Monroe, Harriet (1860–1936) 1258
Amer. editor, poet

Monroe, Marilyn (1926–1962) 2568
Amer. screen actor; née Norma Jean Baker; ex-w. Joe DiMaggio (2, 1914–99; baseball hero), Arthur Miller (3, playwright, 1915–2005)

Montagu, Elizabeth (1720–1800) 585
Eng. essayist, letter writer; née Robinson; first Bluestocking

Montagu, Lily (1873–1963) 1416
Eng. religious figure, social worker, novelist, judge; a.k.a. Lillian Helen M—; fdr. Jewish Religious Union (1902); Int. JRU, 1926; proponent of Liberal Jewish movement

Montagu, Mary Wortley, Lady (1689–1762) 533
Eng. poet, essayist, letter writer; d. Evelyn Pierrepont (marquess of Dorchester and first duke of Kingston) w. Edward W— M— I, m. Edward W— M— II (writer, traveler)

Montansier, La see BRUNET, MARGUERITE

Montefiore, Judith (1784–1862) 797
Eng. diarist; née Cohen; w. Moses M—

Montero, Mayra (1952–) 4123
Cub./P. R. columnist, political activist, novelist

Montessori, Maria (1870–1952) 1381
Ital. physician, educator, writer; originator of Montessori Method of education; first Italian woman to receive M.D. from University of Rome

Montgomery, countess of see WROTH, MARY SIDNEY

Montgomery, Lucy Maud (1874–1942) 1444
Can. writer

Montgomery, Roselle Mercier (1874–1933) 1445
Amer. poet

Montolieu, Jeanne Isabelle (1751–1832) 668
Swiss novelist

Montpensier, duchess of see ORLÉANS, ANN-MARIE-LOUISE

Moodie, Susanna (1803–1885) 880
Can. writer, poet

Moody, Anne (1940–) 3213
Amer. writer, activist

Moore, Grace (1901–1947) 1936
Amer. actor, opera singer

Moore, Honor (1945–) 3596
Amer. playwright, poet; grandd. Margarett Sargent, painter; d. Paul M— (1919–2003), Episcopal bishop of NY (1972–89)

Moore, Julia A (1847–1920) 1153
Amer. poet; a.k.a. "Sweet Singer of Michigan"; née Davis

Moore, Liz (1922–) 2436
Amer. environmental & health activist; cofounder, Colorado Coalition for the Prevention of Nuclear War; founder, Solar Action Network of the American Solar Energy Society; creator of "The Ten Commandments for HMOs"

Moore, Liz (1984?–) 4954
Amer. musician, songwriter, novelist

Moore, Lorrie (1957–) 4421
Amer. educator (English), fiction writer; a.k.a. Marie Lorena M—

Moore, Marianne [Craig] (1887–1972) 1669
Amer. literary editor, poet; NBA, 1952; Pulitzer, 1952

Moore, Martha Milca (1740–1829) 632
Amer. poet, educator

Moore, Patricia A. (1952–) 4124
Amer. industrial designer, gerontologist, lecturer

Moore, Susanna (1945–) 3597
Amer. novelist; AAAL, 1983, 1999

Moore, Virginia [E.] (1903–1993) 1975
Amer. biographer, poet

Moorhead, Sarah Parsons (fl. 1740s) 633
Amer. poet

Mora, Elizabeth Catlett (1919–) 2351
Amer./ Mex. political activist, sculptor, printmaker, educator; w. Francisco Mora, Mex. artist

Moraga, Cherríe (1952–) 4125
Amer. educator, essayist, anthologist, playwright, poet; cofounded (with Audre Lorde* and Barbara Smith*) the first publishing collective by women of color, Kitchen Table: Women of Color Press; ABA, 1986; NEA

Moran, Ellen (1966–) 4732
Amer. campaign manager, nonprofit administrator, public servant; White House dir. of communications, 2009–

Morata, Olimpia (1526–1555) 325
Ital. poet, scholar

More, Hannah (1745–1833) 649
Eng. philanthropist, reformer, writer; a.k.a. The Laureate of the Bluestockings, Stella; pseud. Will Chip

Moreau, Jeanne (1928–) 2637
Fr. actor

Morgan, Angela (1874?–1957) 1446
Amer. poet, writer, lecturer

Morgan, Barbara [Brooks] (1900–1992) 1915
Amer. photographer

Morgan, Barbara "Barb" [Radding] (1951–) 4063
Amer. astronaut, teacher

Morgan, Elaine [Neville] (1920–) 2383
Welsh writer, educator, anthropologist, television writer

Morgan, Elizabeth (1947–) 3773
Amer. physician, prisoner, author

Morgan, Julia (1872–1957) 1403
Amer. architect; first woman awarded degree in architecture from L'Ecole des Beaux-Arts, Paris

Morgan, Marabel (1937–) 3047
Amer. self-help writer; née Hawk

Morgan, Marlo (1937–) 3048
Amer. health care professional, author

Morgan, Robin (1941–) 3284
Amer. poet, writer, anthologist, feminist, actor, editor; cofounder, New York Radical Feminists (1967); founder, WITCH (Women's

International Terrorist Conspiracy from Hell)

Morgan, Ruth (1920–1978) 2384
Amer. novelist

Morgan, Sydney Owenson, Lady (1776?–1859) 770
Ir./Eng. novelist, actor, historian, poet; a.k.a. Gloriana; first woman in Great Britain to receive a pension for service to the world of letters

Morgantini, Luisa (1940–) 3214
Ital. politician, peace activist; cofounder, Women in Black; Member, European Parliament, 1999–

Mori, Nobuko (1932–) 2811
Jap. politician, medical researcher

Morphonios, Ellen James (1929–2002) 2674
Amer. attorney, judge, radio talk show host; a.k.a. "Maximum" Morphonios

Morpurgo, Rahel (1790–1871) 820
Ital./Hebrew turner, seamstress, poet; née Luzzatto, a.s.a. Rachel; gd. Isaac Luzzatto (1729–?), c. Samuel David Luzzatto

Morra, Isabella da (1520–1546) 317
Ital. poet; d. Giovanni Michele di M—

Morris, Esther Hobart McQuigg Slack (1814–1902) 923
Amer. attorney, suffragist; first female justice of the peace in USA

Morris, Holly (1966–) 4733
Amer. publisher, TV host & producer, editor, feminist; d. Jeannie M— (sports writer, broadcaster) and Johnny M— (football player and sports broadcaster)

Morris, Jan (1926–) 2569
Welsh journalist, writer; née James Humphrey M—

Morris, Margaret (1737?–1816) 625
Amer. healer, diarist; née Hill

Morris, Mary [Elizabeth] (1913–1986) 2205
Amer. editor, nonfiction writer, author, columnist; née Davis

Morris, Nobuko see ALBERY, NOBUKO

Morrison, Toni (1931–) 2771
Amer. novelist, book editor; née Chloe Anthony Wofford; first black woman to win Nobel Prize, 1993; Pulitzer, 1988

Morrissey, Mary Mannin (1949–) 3918
Amer. minister, author

Morrow, Elizabeth Cutter (1873–1955) 1417
Amer. poet, writer; m. Anne Morrow Lindberg*, mn. Whitney

Mortimer, Penelope (1918–1999) 2326
Eng. writer; née Fletcher

Morton, Sarah Wentworth (1759–1846) 698
Amer. poet; née Apthorp; a.k.a. Constantia, Philenia, A Lady of Boston, The American Sappho, The American Montague

Mosala, Bernadette (1953?–) 4196
S. Afr. writer

Moscou, Jacqueline (1949–) 3919
Amer. stage director

Moseley Braun, Carol [Elizabeth] (1947–) 3774
Amer. politician, lawyer; U.S. Senator (D-IL), 1993–1999; ambassador to N.Z. (1999–2001); first African-American woman elected to U.S. Senate

Moses, Claire Goldberg (1941–) 3285
Amer. educator (women's studies), journal editor, nonfiction writer

Moses, Grandma (1860–1961) 1259
Amer. painter; née Anna Mary Robertson

Moskowitz, Faye S. (1930–) 2728
Amer. writer, radio commentator, educator, English

Moss, Cyntha (1940?–) 3215
Amer. journalist, animal rights advocate

Mossell, N[athan] F[rancis], Mrs. (1856–1946) 1212
Amer. writer

Motley, Annette (fl. 1970s–80s) 4825
Eng. novelist

Motoni, Nomura (1806–1867) 897
Jap. poet, political activist

Mott, Lucretia (1793–1880) 839
Amer. abolitionist, suffragist, Quaker minister; née Coffin; founder, The Female Anti-Slavery Society, 1833; with Elizabeth Cady Stanton,* organized the first women's rights convention, Seneca Falls, New York, 1848; NWHF

Moulton, Louise (1835–1908) 1067
Amer. poet, writer; née Chandler

Mountain Wolf Woman (1881–1960) 1571
Amer. autobiographer; née Kehachiwinga

Mowatt, Anna Cora (1819–1870) 957
Amer./Fr. public speaker, actor, playwright, poet; cofounder, Mount Vernon Association (first time a group of women was allowed to band together and purchase property)

Moyano, Maria Elena (1958–1992) 4462
Peru. politician, community activist

Mpaayei, Florence (1960–) 4545
Kenyan peace activist, administrator; d-in-law, Rev. John Tompo M—, educator, evangelist; Ex. Dir., Nairobi Peace Initiative

Mubarak, Suzanne (1941–) 3286
Egyp. activist, children's; née Saleh Sabet or Thabet; w. Hosni Mubarak, president of Egypt; fdr.-pre., EBBY, the Egyptian chapter of Int. Board on Books for Young People (IBBY)

Mueller, Lisel (1924–) 2490
Ger./Amer. poet; NBA, 1981; Pulitzer, 1997

Mukherjee, Bharati (1940–) 3216
Ind./Amer. educator (English), novelist; a.k.a. B— M— Blaise; Guggenheim, 1978, 1979; NEA 1986; NBCCA, 1988

Mullen, Harryette Romell (1953–) 4197
Amer. educator (Afro-American literature), poet; Rockefeller

Muller, Karin (1965–) 4707
Swiss/Amer. writer

Muller, Mary Ann (1820–1901) 973
Eng./N.Z. suffragist; a.k.a. Femimna; née Wilson

Mullins, Aimee (1976–) 4913
Amer. athlete (track), model; cofounder, HOPE (Helping Other People Excel), a nonprofit support for disabled athletes

Mumford, Ethel Watts (1878–1940) 1516
Amer. humorist, playwright, writer; mn. Grant

Mumtaz, Khawar (1951?–) 4064
Pak. human rights activist, writer

Munda, Constantina (fl. 1610s) 425
Eng. feminist; a.k.a. Moral Constancy

Munk, Erika (1939–) 3152
Amer. journalist, educator (theater), editor

Munro, Alice (1931–) 2772
Can. writer; Governor General's Literary Award (3)

Munro, Rona (1959–) 4497
Scot. actor, playwright; Blackburn, 1991; London Evening Standard Award, 1991; London Theater Critics Circle Prize, 1992

Murasaki Shikibu see SHIKIBU, MURASAKI

Murdoch, [Jean] Iris, Dame (1919–1999) 2352
Ir. novelist; w. John Bayley (poet, lecturer)

Murphy, Beatrice M. (1908–1992) 2096
Amer. poet, editor (book); a.k.a. Beatrice M. Campbell

Murphy, Sara (1883–1975) 1597
Amer. socialite; w. Gerald M— (1888–1964; painter)

Murphy, Virginia Backentoe (1834–1921) 1058
Amer. pioneer

Murray, Ada Foster see ALDEN, ADA

Murray, Janet Horowitz (1946–) 3679
Amer. technology scientist, educator, researcher, software designer

Murray, Judith Sargent (1751–1820) 669
Amer. feminist, author, playwright, poet; a.k.a. Constantia, Honora-Martesia, Honora; s. Winthrop M—, Jr. (first governor of Mississippi Territory, 1798)

Murray, Kathryn (1906–1999) 2055
Amer. radio & TV host, ballroom dancer; née Kohnfelder; w. Arthur M— (1895–1991; ballroom dancer & entrepreneur)

Murray, Patty (1950–) 3994
Amer. politician; a.k.a. "mom in tennis shoes"; U. S. Senate (D-Washington), 1993–

Murray, Pauli (1910–1985) 2139
Amer. feminist, lawyer, Episcopal priest, poet; a.k.a. Anna Pauline M—; first black woman in U.S. ordained as Episcopal priest; cofounder, NOW

Murry, Ann (fl. 1770s–1799) 750
Eng. author, poet

Murry, Kathleen Beauchamp see MANSFIELD, KATHERINE

Murungi, Kaari Betty (Contemporary) 4983
Kenyan lawyer, human rights, activist, human rights, administrator; dir., Urgent Action Fund-Africa; International

Advocate for Peace Award, 2005

Muscio, Inga (1966?–)   4734
Amer. feminist, public speaker, author; a.k.a. Inga La Gringa

Museveni, Janet (1949–)   3920
Ugan. activist (AIDS), First Lady; w. Yoweri M—, president of Uganda (1986–); fdr., Uganda Women's Effort to Save Orphans (UWESO)

Musgrave, Thea (1928–)   2637.1
Scot./Amer. composer, conductor, lecturer

Muske-Dukes, Carol (1945–)   3598
Amer. novelist, poet, educator; NEA, Guggenheim

Musser, Tharon (1925–)   2533
Amer. theater consultant, theatrical lighting designer; introduced the use of computers to Broadway; Tony, 1972, 1976, 1982; Theater Hall of Fame, 1985

Mutta (fl. sixth century B.C.E.)   50
Chin. Buddhist nun

Myerhoff, Barbara (1935–1985)   2940
Amer. educator, writer

Myers, Dee Dee [Margaret Jane] (1961–)   4590
Amer. political commentator, author; w. Todd Purdum, editor; White House Press Secretary, 1993–94; first woman to hold such office

Myers, Isabel Briggs (1898–1980)   1854
Amer. psychologist, author; d. Katharine Cook Briggs (1875–1968); co-creator, Myers-Briggs Type Indicator (MBTI)

Myerson, Bess (1924–)   2491
Amer. TV personality, government official, columnist; Miss America, 1945

Myrdal, Alva Reimer (1902–1986)   1953–1954
Swed. sociologist, family welfare advocate, diplomat, peace activist; w. Gunner M— (1898–1987; economist; Nobel Prize in economics, 1974), m. Sissela Ann Bok*; Nobel Peace Prize, 1982; West German Peace Prize

Myrrina   see PHARAOH'S DAUGHTER

Myrta (fl. first century)   96
Roman prophet

Myss, Caroline (1952–)   4126
Amer. medical intuitive, lecturer, nonfiction writer

N

Nacro, Fanta Régina (1962–)   4626
Burkinabe filmmaker; Burkina Faso (West African nation)

Nafisi, Azar (1955–)   4320
Iran./Amer. educator, writer; d. Ahmas N—, mayor of Tehran, and Nezhat N—, among first women to be elected to Iranian parliament

Nagako, Empress (1903–2000)1976
Jap. empress; w. Hirohito (1901–89; emperor of Japan, 1926–89), m. Akihito (1933– ; emperor of Japan, 1989–)

Nahai, Gina Barkhordar (1960–)   4546
Iran./Amer. novelist

Naidu, Sarojini [Chattopadhyay] (1879–1949)   1534
Ind. poet

Nair, Mira (1957–)   4422
Ind./Amer. filmmaker; Cannes Film Festival Award, 1988

Nairne, Carolina, Baroness (1766–1845)   731
Scot./Ir. author, poet; née Oliphant (a.s.a. Olifard); a.k.a. B.B. (Mrs. Bogan of Bogan), S.M. (The Scottish Minstrel), Flower of Strathearn; w. Major William Murray N—

Nakatsukasa, Lady (fl. 970s)   164
Jap. poet; d. Lady Ise*

Namir, Ora (1930–)   2729
Isr. politician; Member of Knesset; chair of Status of Women Commission; minister of labor and social affairs, 1992–96; ambassador to China, 1996–

Namjoshi, Suniti (1941–)   3287
Ind./Eng. civil servant, poet, educator, writer

Nannakaiya, Kaccipe (fl. 3rd century?)   103
Ind. poet

Naomi (fl. 1100s B.C.E.)   22
Isr. biblical figure; w. Elimelech, m.-in-law Ruth*

Napolitano, Janet (1957–)   4423
Amer. attorney, politician; Democratic attorney general, Arizona, 1999–2001; governor, 2002– ; Sec. of Homeland Security, 2009–

Naqvi, Tahira (1953?–)   4198
Pak./Amer. anthologist, writer, educator (English), translator

Narbona Ruiz, [María] Cristina (1951–)   4065
Span. environmental activist, public servant, economist; minister of the environment, 2004–2008

Nasrin, Taslima (1962–)   4627
Bangladeshan/ Ind. physician, poet, novelist, feminist; a.s.a. Nasreen; Sakharov Prize for Freedom of Thoughts from the European Parliament, 1994

Nathan, Maud (1862–1946) 1289–1290
Amer. social reformer; w. Frederick N—, broker, founder Internatl. Men's Suffrage League; s. Annie N— Meyer*; great-grandd. Gershom Mendes Seixas, rabbi & American revolutionary hero; cousin, Benjamin N— Cardozo, second Jewish justice of U.S. Supreme Court; cousin, Emma Lazarus*; cofounder, N.Y. Consumers' League (1891)

Nation, Carry [Amelia] (1846–1911)   1146
Amer. prohibitionist; née Moore

Nattel, Lilian (1956–)   4383
Can. writer, fiction

Naufal, Vera (fl. 1960s)   4547
Palestinian political activist

Navarre, Marguerite de   see MARGUERITE OF NAVARRE

Navratilova, Martina (1957–) 4424
Cuban/Amer. athlete (tennis); Wimbledon record (nine women's singles titles); IWSHF, 1984

Naylor, Gloria (1950–)   3995
Amer. fiction writer; Natl. Book Award, 1983

Neal, Patricia (1926–)   2570
Amer./Eng. screen actor; ex-w. Roald Dahl (writer); Tony Award, 1947; British Film Academy Award, 1963; Academy Award, 1963

Near, Holly (1949–)   3921
Amer. singer, songwriter, social change activist

Nearing, Helen (1904–1995)   2001
Amer. musician, farmer, activist (simplicity); née Knothe; w. Scott N— (1883–1983), American radical economist, educator, writer, political activist, and advocate of simple living.

Necker, Suzanne Chardon (1737–1794)   626
Fr. salonist, author; née Curchod; w. Jacques N— (minister of finance for Louis IV), m. Germaine de Stael*, a. Madame N— de Saussure*

Necker de Saussure, Madame (1768?–1847)   740
Fr. author, translator; n. Jacques N— (minister of finance for Louis XVI) and Suzanne N—*, c. Germaine de Stael*

Neel, Alice (1908–1984)   2097
Amer. painter

Neiman, Susan (1955–)   4321
Amer. essayist, cultural commentator, philosopher

Nelson, Antonya (1961–)   4591
Amer. writer

Nelson, Donna J. (1953–)   4199
Amer. educator, chemistry

Nelson, Hannah (fl. 1970s–)   4826
Amer. householder

Nelson, Jill (1952–)   4127
Amer. writer, journalist

Nelson, Mariah Burton (1956–)   4384
Amer. nonfiction writer, athlete (basketball), feminist

Nelson, Marilyn (1946–)   3680
Amer. educator (English), translator, poet; s. Mel N— (songwriter); NEA 1981, 1990; Fulbright 1995

Nelson, Martha (1952–)   4128
Amer. magazine manager; managing ed., *People* magazine, 2002–

Nelson, Paula (1945–)   3599
Amer. economist, business executive; founder, Joy of Money, Inc.

Nelson, Portia (1920–2001)   2385
Amer. nightclub entertainer, songwriter, writer, actor; née Betty Mae N—

Nemeth, Maria (1932–)   2812
Hung./Amer. journalist, psychologist; founder, Academy for Coaching Excellence and Mastering Life's Energies

Némirovsky, Irène (1903–1942)   1977
Russ./Fr. novelist

Nenadic, Natalie (fl. 1990s)   4967
Amer. radical feminist, educator, philosophy

Nesbit, Edith (1858–1924)   1234
Eng. writer, poet; w. Hubert Bland; cofounder, Fabian Society

Neuber, Friederika Karoline (1697–1760)   545
Ger. playwright, actor, theater manager; née Weissenborn, a.k.a. die Neuberin

Nevelson, Louise (1899–1988)   1890
Russ./Amer. sculptor, feminist; pioneer in environmental sculpture

Nevill, Dorothy (1826–1913)   1009
Eng. writer, hostess

Newbold, Frances   see HART, FRANCES [NEWBOLD]

Newcastle, Duchess of   see CAVENDISH, MARGARET

Newlin, Marjorie (1920–)   2386
Amer. weight-lifter; a.s.a. Morjorie N—

Newman, Frances (1883–1928)   1598
Amer. writer, librarian, translator, literary critic

Newman, Jody (1959?–) 4498
Amer. educator, counseling, feminist; Exec. Dir., NWPC, 1996

Newman, Naomi (1930–) 2730
Amer. playwright, actor, director; cofounder, A Traveling Jewish Theatre, 1978

Newton, Frances (fl. 1930s–1940s–) 2731
Amer. writer

Ng, Fae Myenne (1956–) 4385
Amer. novelist; w. Mark Coovalis (author); NEA

Ngesa, Mildred (1975–) 4899
Kenyan journalist; Female Award for Media Excellence (FAME) by the Forum for African Women Journalists (FAWE), 1988

Nghatsane, Linda Olga (1957–) 4425
S. Afr. farmer, consultant, agricultural

Ngilu, Charity Kaluki (1952–) 4129
Kenyan businesswoman, politician; Social Democrat, M.P.; first woman to run for president of Kenya; minister of health, 2003–07; minister of water and irrigation, 2008–

Ngubane, Thembi (1985–) 4956
S. Afr. AIDS activist

Nguyen Tih Binh see BINH, NGUYEN

Ní Chonaill, Eibhlín Dhubh (1743–1790) 645
Ir. poet

Nichols, Anne (1891–1966) 1730
Amer. playwright

Nichols, Martha (fl. 1990s) 4968–4969
Amer. writer, newspaper editor

Nichols, Mary D. (1945–) 3600
Amer. lawyer, environmental, administrator, journalist

Nichols, Ruth Rowland (1901–1961) 1937
Amer. aviator; first woman to pilot a passenger airplane; set women's world altitude, speed and long-distance records

Nicholson, Zoe Ann (1948–) 3852
Amer. speaker, author, feminist

Niedecker, Lorine (1903–1970)1978
Amer. writer, secretary, house cleaner

Niederman, Sharon (1948–) 3853
Amer. journalist, writer, educator, anthologist

Niemann, Linda [Grant] (1946–) 3681
Amer. freight conductor, writer

Niemi, Judith (1941–) 3288
Amer. wilderness guide, writer

Nien Cheng (see Cheng, Nien)

Nightingale, Florence (1820–1910) 974
Eng. nurse, writer; a.k.a. "The Lady with the Lamp"; founder of nursing profession; first woman to receive British Order of Merit

Nijo, Lady (1258–1306?) 222
Jap. diarist

Nijo, Empress (842–910) 151
Jap. poet, noble; w. Emperor Seiwa, m. Emperor Yozei

Nin, Anaïs (1903–1977) 1979
Fr./Amer. lecturer, writer, diarist

Nirmala, Sister (1934–) 2909
Ind. nun; née Joshi; head of the Missionaries of Charity, India (order founded by Mother Teresa*), 1996–

Nirmala Devi, Shri Mataji (1923–) 2467
Ind. spiritualist; née Nirmala Srivastava; w. Sir. C.P. Srivastava, Secretary General of the United Nations International Maritime Organization; fdr., Sahaja Yoga (1970); Nobel Peace Prize nominee

Nisa (1931–) 2773
Botswanan householder

Niven, James, Mrs. see VARDILL, ANNA

Nixon, [Thelma Catherine] Pat (1912–1993) 2186
Amer. first lady; née Ryan; w. Richard M. N— (1913–94; politician; U.S. president, 1969–74; resigned)

Njogu, Ann Wairimu (1968?–)4775
Kenyan lawyer, human right's activist, administrator; dir., Centre for Rights Education and Awareness

Noah see ZELOPHEHAD, FIVE DAUGHTERS OF

Noble, Vicki (1943?–) 3775
Amer. author, workshop leader; founder, Motherpeace Institute

Noddings, Nel (1929–) 2675
Amer. educator, author, philosopher

Nogarola, Isotta (1417–1461/8) 254
Ital. scholar, author; n. Angela N— (author)

Nomani, Asra Q. (1965–) 4708
Ind./Amer. author, journalist, feminist, educator, journalism; fdr., Muslim Women's Freedom Tour

Nonnen, Emily (1812–1905) 920
Eng./Ger. sculptor, translator; great-great aunt, Barbro Hedstrom*; first translation into Swedish of Alice In Wonderland

Noonan, Peggy (1950–) 3996
Amer. writer, speech, journalist

Noor Al-Hussein, (1951–) 4066
Amer./Jor. queen; née Lisa Najeeb Halaby; widow King Hussein (1935–1999); fdr., Noor Al Hussein Foundation (NHF)

Noor Inayat Khan, (1914–1944) 2225
Russ./Eng. war hero, children's writer, spy; née Noor-un-Nisa Inayat Khan; a.k.a. Nora Baker; d. Hazrat Inayat Khan, founder of Sufi Order Int.

Nooyi, Indra (1955–) 4322
Ind./Amer. business executive; CEO, PepsiCo, 2006–

Norberg-Hodge, Helena (1946–) 3682
Amer./Swed. anthropologist, linguist; a.k.a. H— Dolma; fdr., Int. Society for Ecology and Culture (ISEC); fdr., Int. Forum on Globalization; Right Livelihood, 1986

Norden, Helen B. see LAWRENSON, HELEN

Norman, Dorothy (1905–1997) 2028
Amer. photographer, writer, editor, social activist; née Stecker; p. Alfred Stieglitz, Amer. photographer; fdr., American Emergency Food Committee for India & The American Citizens' Committee for Economic Aid Abroad

Norman, Jessye (1945/6–) 3601
Amer. opera singer

Norman, Liane (1937–) 3049
Amer. educator, author

Norman, Marsha (1947–) 3776
Amer. arts administrator, playwright; ODCCA, 1977; Pulitzer; Blackburn; Tony, 1983, 1991; NEA; Rockefeller; AAAL; NIAL

Norris, Kathleen (1947–) 3777
Amer. novelist, poet, essayist

Norris, Kathleen Thompson (1880–1966) 1552
Amer. poet, essayist

Norris, Pippa (1953–) 4200
Brit./Amer. political scientist, political science educator, public administrator, author

Northern Mother (fl. 1350s) 236
Eng. poet

Norton, Caroline [Elizabeth Sarah] Sheridan (1808–1877) 905
Eng. writer, poet; gd. William Brinsley Sheridan

Norton, Eleanor Holmes (1937–) 3050
Amer. politician, civil rights activist, lawyer; House of

Representatives (D-D.C.), 1991–

Norton, Grace Fallow (1876–1926) 1479
Amer. poet

Norwich, Viscountess of see COOPER, DIANA

Notley, Alice (1945–) 3602
Amer./Fr. poet; w. (1) Ted Berrigan(1934–1983), poet; (2) Douglas Oliver, British poet

Nottage, Lynn (1964–) 4683.1
Amer. playwright; Pulitzer, 2009; Obie, 2004; Guggenheim, 2005; MacArthur, 2007

Novis, Emile see WEIL, SIMONE

Nowakowska, Urszula (1955?–) 4323
Pol. political activist, lawyer; dr. Women's Rights Center (Warsaw)

Nukada (fl. 660s–699) 123
Jap. poet, princess; w. Kobun (1) and Emperor Temmu (2), m. Prince Katsuragi and Princess Toichi

Nunez, Sigrid (1951–) 4067
Amer. novelist, educator, writing; Rome Prize in literature, Whiting Writer's Award, Berlin Prize in Literature.

Nussbaum, Hedda (1942–) 3362
Amer. editor

Nussbaum, Martha (1947–) 3778
Amer. philosopher, educator, classicist, author; née Craven

Nüsslein-Volhard, Christiane (1942–) 3363
Ger. biologist; Nobel Prize in chemistry & Physiology, with Edward B. Lewis (1918–) and Eric F. Wieschaus (1947), for their discoveries concerning the genetic control of early embryonic development, 1995

Nyad, Diana (1949–) 3922
Amer. long-distance swimmer, radio host; World record holder (as of 2005); NWHF, 1986; IWSHF, 2008

Nye, Naomi Sihab (1952–) 4130
Amer. songwriter, singer, writer (children), poet

Nyoho see SHIKISHI NAISHINNO

Nyro, Laura (1946–1997) 3779
Amer. songwriter, singer, musician

O

Oakley, Ann (1944–) 3529
Eng. sociologist, writer; née Titmuss

Oakley, Annie (1860–1926) 1260
Amer. frontier entertainer, markswoman; née Phoebe Ann

Mozee; w. Frank Butler (marksman, entertainer); NWHF

Oaks, Laura Mary (1967–) 4753
Ir. anthropologist

Oates, Joyce Carol (1938–) 3099
Amer. writer; NBA, 1970

Obama, Michele (1963–) 4648
Amer. first lady, lawyer; née Robinson; w. Barack O— , 44th U.S. President

Obejas, Achy (1956–) 4386
Cub./Amer. short story writer, novelist

O'Brien, Edna (1930–) 2732
Ir./Eng. writer, pacifist

O'Brien, Mary Mamie (1926–1998) 2571
Eng./Scot./Can. nurse, feminist philosopher, educator (women's studies), midwife; founding member, Feminist Party of Canada

O'Brien, Shannon [Patricia Elizabeth] (1959–) 4499
Amer. politician, lawyer; w. Emmet Hayes, politician; MA State Treasurer, 1999–2003

O'Brien, Virginia (1946–) 3683
Amer. nonfiction writer, executive coach

Ocampo, Victoria (1891–1979) 1731
Argen. writer, publisher; a.k.a. Queen of Letters; founder, *Sur* (avant-garde literary magazine)

O'Casey, Eileen [E. Kathleen Reynolds O.] (1903–1995) 1980
Ir./Eng. writer, actor; née Carey; w. Sean O— (Ir. playwright, 1880–1964)

Occident, Maria del *see* BROOKS, MARIA

Ochs, Vanessa L. (1953–) 4201
Amer. writer, educator (religious studies); Natl. Jewish Book Award, 2007; NEA

O'Connell, Roselyn (1950?–) 3997
Amer. activist, political; pres., Natl. Women's Political Caucus (NWPC), 1999–

O'Connor, Flannery (1925–1964) 2534
Amer. writer; NBA, 1972

O'Connor, Karen (1938–) 3100
Amer. abortion rights activist, writer; a.k.a. K— O— Sweeney

O'Connor, Sandra Day (1930–) 2733
Amer. lawyer, judge; first woman to serve on U.S. Supreme Court, 1981–2006; NWHF

Odetta, (1930–2008) 2734
Amer. singer, musician, civil rights activist; née O— Holmes; a.k.a. The Voice of the

Civil Rights Movement"; NEA Natl. Medal of Arts, 1999; Living Legend tribute (Library of Congress), 2003

O'Donnell, Rosie (1962–) 4628
Amer. TV personality, actor; established the For All Kids Foundation, 1997; founder, Rosie's Broadway Kids, 2003; Emmy Award f (11)

O'Faolain, Nuala (1940–2008) 3217
Ir. writer, journalist, TV producer; d. Terry O'Sullivan, journalist

O'Grady, Ellen (1867–1938) 1340
Amer. poet, police commissioner

O'Hara, Maureen (1953–) 4202
Amer. educator (finance), mathematician

Ohba, Minako (1930–) 2735
Jap. writer; Akutagawa Prize, 1969

Ojiambo, Josephine (1961–) 4592
Kenyan health activist, physician; chair, Kenya Medical Women's Assoc. (KEMWA)

O'Keeffe, Adelaide (1776–1855?) 771
Eng. novelist, poet

O'Keeffe, Georgia (1887–1986) 1670
Amer. painter; widow of Alfred Stieglitz (1864–1946; photographer; a.k.a. "father of modern photography"); Presidential Medal of Freedom, 1977; NWHF

Okello-Orlale, Rosemary (1965–) 4709
Kenyan administrator, social activist, journalist; Exec. Dir., African Woman and Child Feature Service; Best Female Reporter, African Information Society Initiative media awards, 2004

Okin, Susan Moller (1946–2004) 3684
N.Z./Amer. philosopher (feminist theory), educator

Oku (661–701) 124
Jap. poet, princess; d. Emperor Temmu; s. Prince Otsu

Olds, Sharon (1942–) 3364
Amer. poet, educator (poetry); New York State Poet, 1998–2000; NBCCA, 1983

Olesnicka, Zofia (fl. 1550s) 350
Pol. poet; w. or s. Mikolaj O—, lord of Pinczow; first poet in the Polish tongue

Oliphant, Carolina *see* NAIRNE, CAROLINA

Oliphant, Margaret (1828–1897) 1019
Scot. historian, writer; mn. Wilson

Oliver, Mary (1935–) 2941
Amer. nonfiction writer, creative, poet; Pulitzer, 1984; NBA, 1992; NEA 1972, 1973; Guggenheim 1980, 1981

Oliver, Ruth Law (1891–1970) 1671
Amer. aviator; a.k.a. R— Bancroft Law; first enlisted U.S. Army aviatrix and allowed to wear NCO Uniform; aviation pioneer

Oliveros, Pauline (1932–) 2813
Amer. accordionist, composer; fdr., The Deep Listening Inst., 1985

Olsen, Frances (1945–) 3603
Amer. educator, law

Olsen, Tillie (1912–2007) 2187
Amer. writer; née Lerner; Ford Foundaton Grant (1959); Guggenheim (1975); citation for distinguished contribution to American literature from the American Academy and NIAL, 1976

O'Malley, Mary (1941–2006) 3289
Eng. actor, playwright; née Hickey; cofounded Lyric Theatre, Belfast (1951)

Onassis, Jacqueline Kennedy (1929–1994) 2676
Amer. editor, photographer, first lady; née Bouvier; widow of John F. Kennedy (1; 1917–63; politician; 35th U.S. president, 1960–63; assassinated) and Aristotle O— (2; 1906?–75; Greek shipping magnate & financier); Emmy, 1962

O'Neill, Carlotta Monterey (1888–1970) 1688
Span./Amer. actor; w. Eugene O— (Amer. playwright, 1888–1953)

O'Neill, Henrietta (1758–1793) 692
Ir. poet; née Dungarvon

O'Neill, Moira (1864–1955) 1305
Ir./ Can. poet, lyricist; née Agnes Higginson Skrine; m. Molly Keane (Ir. Novelist, 1905–1996)

O'Neill, Rose [Cecil] (1874–1944) 1447
Amer. writer, poet, illustrator; created the Kewpie doll, 1909

Ono, Yoko (1933–) 2860
Jap./Amer. poet, painter, songwriter; widow of John Lennon (1940–80; Eng. singer, songwriter of Beatles fame; murdered)

Ono no Komachi (834–880) 150
Jap. poet; d. Yoshisada, lord of Dewa; legendary beauty of Japan

Opie, Amelia (1769–1853) 744
Eng. poet, novelist; née Alderson; second w. John O— (1761–1807; painter)

Orbach, Susie (1946–) 3685
Eng. psychotherapist, feminist, author

Orczy, [Emmunska], Baroness (1865–1947) 1317
Hung./Brit. novelist, playwright; mn. Barstow

O'Reilly, Jane (1936–) 2995
Amer. editor, writer

Orenstein, Catherine (1967?–) 4754
Amer. journalist, activist, author

Oreskes, Naomi (1958–) 4463
Amer. educator, geologist, college provost; s. Michael O— , newspaper editor; consultant to the U.S. Environmental Protection Agency and the U.S. Nuclear Waste Technical Review Board; NEH

Orinda *see* PHILIPS, KATHERINE

Orlean, Susan (1955–) 4324
Amer. writer, journalist

Orléans, Ann-Marie-Louise d' (1627–1693) 452
Fr. noble, author; a.k.a. La Grande Mademoisselle, duchesse de Montpensier; gd. Henry IV (1553–1610; king of France, 1589–1610), d. Gaston d'O—, n. Louis XIII (1601–43; king of France, 1610–43)

Orlova, Raisa Davydovna (1918–1989) 2327
Sov./Ger. literary critic, author, editor, diplomat

Orman, Suze (1952–) 4131
Amer. nonfiction writer, financial expert

Ormes, Cicely (1525–1557) 324
Eng. weaver, Protestant martyr; w. Edmund O—

Orr, Mary (1960?–) 4548
Can. public servant, laborer, radio producer, travel writer

Orr, Mary [Caswell] (1910–2006) 2140
Amer. actor, playwright, short story writer; w. Reginald Denham, director-playwright

Orred, Meta (1845/46–1925) 1140
Eng. lyricist, poet

Orsini, Isabella de' Medici (1542–1576) 342
Ital. noble; a.k.a. duchess of Bracciano; d. Cosimo I and Eleanora de Toledo, w. Paolo Giordano d'O—, duke of Bracciano

Ortese, Anna Maria (1914–1998) 2226
Ital. writer; Premio Viareggio Prize, 1953; Premio St. Vincent Prize, 1958

Orth, Maureen Ann (1943–) 3444
Amer. nonfiction writer, journalist; w. Tim Russert (1950–2008), TV journalist, lawyer

Orton, Beth (1970–) 4827
Eng. singer, songwriter

Osborne, Dorothy (1627–1695) 453
Eng. letter writer; a.k.a. Lady Temple

Osgood, Frances Sargent (1811–1850) 915
Amer. poet; née Locke; pseud. Kate Florence Carol

Ossoli, Marchesa *see* FULLER, MARGARET

Osten, Suzanne (1944–) 3530
Swed. writer, stage director, playwright; w. Etienne Glasser (actor-director); cofounder, Fickteatern (Pocket Theatre), 1967–71; cofounder & artistic director, Unga Klara (children's theater wing of Stockholm City Theater), 1975– ; Felix Award, 1990

Ostenso, Martha (1900–1963) 1916
Nor./Amer. writer, humorist, poet

Ostriker, Alicia Suskin (1937–) 3051
Amer. literary critic, poet; NEA 1976, 1977; Guggenheim 1984, 1985; Rockefeller 1982

Otero, Caroline (1868–1965) 1353
Span. actor, courtesan; a.k.a. "La Belle"; née Augustine O. Iglesias

Otomo no Sakano-e no Iratsume (*see* Iratsume, Otomo no Sakano-e no)

Otto, Louise (1819–1895) 958
Ger. novelist, feminist; a.k.a. Luise Otto-Peters

Ouida (1839–1908) 1089
Eng. writer; née Marie Louise de la Ramée

Overall, Christine Dorothy (1949–) 3923
Can. writer

Owen, Anita (fl. 1890s–1920s–) 1714
Amer. poet, songwriter

Owen, Jane (fl. 1610s–d. 1633?) 426
Eng. religious author

Owen, Mary A[licia] (1850–1935) 1179
Eng. nonfiction writer, folklorist

Owens, Rochelle (1936–) 2996
Amer. poet, educator, illustrator, playwright; née Bass; w. George Economou (professor); cofounder, Women's Theater Council, 1972; Rockefeller (2); Ford; Guggenheim; NEA; Obie Award, 1967, 1981

Owens, Vilda Sauvage (1875–1950) 1464
Welsh/Amer. poet

Oxlie of Morpet, Mary (fl. 1616–) 434
Scot. poet

Ozick, Cynthia (1928–) 2638
Amer. writer

P

Packard, Clarissa *see* GILMAN, CAROLINE

Packer, Ann (1959–) 4500
Amer. novelist

Paddleford, Clementine (1898–1967) 1871
Amer. food writer, aviator

Page, Geraldine (1924–1987) 2492
Amer. actor; w. Rip Torn, Amer. Actor; Oscar, 1985; Emmy, 1967, 1969; Golden Globe, 1962, 1963

Page, Louise (1955–) 4325
Eng. radio writer, playwright

Pagels, Elaine (1943–) 3445
Amer. educator, historian of religion, author; née Hiesey; NBA, 1980; NBCCA

Paglia, Camille [Anna] (1947–) 3780
Amer. educator, nonfiction writer, social critic

Paik, Younhee (1945?–) 36
Korean/Amer. artist, painter

Painter, Charlotte (1926–) 2572
Amer. educator, writer

Painter, Nell [Irvin] (1942–) 3365
Amer. historian, educator, author

Painter, Pamela (1941–) 3290
Amer. editor, fiction writer; founding editor, *Story Quarterly*, 1974; Pushcart Prizes (3)

de Palacio, Loyola (1950–2006) 3998.1
Span. politician, business executive, public servant; née L— d- y del Valle-Lersundi; s. Ana P— , public servant; fdg. Mbr., Alianza Popular, 1976

Paley, Barbara "Babe" (1915–1978) 2251
Amer. socialite, fashion editor, art collector; née Cushing; w. William S. P—, broadcasting tycoon

Paley, Grace [Goodside] (1922–2007) 2437
Amer. writer; Guggenheim 1961; NEA 1987

Paley, Vivian Gussin (1929–) 2677
Amer. educator, writer; founder, Sisters in Crime, 1987; MacArthur

Palin, Sarah [Louise Heath] (1964–) 4684
Amer. politician; Gov. (R-AK), 2006–2009

Palmer, Alice [Elvira] Freeman (1855–1902) 1206
Amer. poet, editor, college administrator; founder, American Assoc. of University Women; Hall of Fame, 1920

Palmer, Gretta Brooker (1905–1953) 2029
Amer. writer, journalist

Paltrow, Gwyneth (1971–) 4847
Amer. actor; d. Blythe Danner (stage & screen actor, 1943–) and Bruce P— (TV writer, director); Academy Award, 1999

Pan Chao (Lady Pan) (fl. 45) 8788

Pandit, Vijaya Lakshmi (1900–1990) 1917
Ind. government official, diplomat, pacifist; w. Jawaharlal Nehru (statesman and hero, 1889–1964; first prime minister of India, 1947–64), a. Indira Gandhi*; president, United Nations General Assembly, 1953

Pankhurst, Adela (1885–1961) 1636
Eng./Aust. suffragist, political activist, editor; w. Tom Walsh, d. Emmeline P—*, s. Christabel* and Sylvia P—*

Pankhurst, Christabel (1880–1958) 1553
Eng. writer, suffragist, evangelist; d. Emmeline P—*, s. Sylvia* and Adela P—*

Pankhurst, Emmeline [Goulden] (1858–1928) 1235
Eng. suffragist; m. Christabel,* Sylvia* and Adela P—*; founder, Women's Social and Political Union, 1905

Pankhurst, Sylvia (1882–1960) 1583
Eng. suffragist, social reformer, editor, historian, newspaper publisher; d. Emmeline P—,* s. Christabel* and Adela* P—

Panova, Vera Fedorovna (1905–1973) 2030
Russ. playwright, novelist, journalist; a.k.a. V— Veltman; Stalin Prize, 1947, 1948, 1950

Pappas, Rita Boumy *see* BOUMI PAPPA, RITA

Pappenheim, Bertha (1859–1936) 1249
Aus./Ger. dramatist, feminist, reformer, essayist, poet; a.k.a. Anna O; famous patient of Sigmund Freud's; director of orphanage; founder of Jewish feminist organization; reformer against sexual exploitation of women and children; fdr., Care for Women

Pardoe, Julia (1806–1862) 898
Eng. writer, historian

Parent, Gail (1940–) 3218
Amer. writer, scenarist; Emmy (2)

Paretsky, Sara (1947–) 3781
Amer. novelist

Parisot, Laurence (1959–) 4501
Fr. business lobbyist, government official; granddd. Jacques P— of Parisot group; Ordre national du Mérite

Parker, Dorothy (1893–1967) 1780
Amer. poet, humorist, writer; née Rothschild

Parker, Gail Thain (1943–) 3446
Amer. college administrator, educator, writer

Parker, Kathleen (1969?–) 4797
Amer. columnist

Parker, Pat (1944–1989) 3531
Amer. medical administrator, activist, poet; WIM Publications Memorial Poetry Award established in her name

Parker, Suzy (1933–2003) 2814
Amer. actor, model; née Cecilia Ann Renée P—; w. Bradford Dillman (3), actor

Parks, Rosa (1913–2005) 2206
Amer. civil rights activist; a.k.a. "Mother of the Civil Rights Movement"; Spingarn Medal, 1979; NWHF

Parks, Suzan-Lori (1963–) 4649
Amer. playwright, TV & screen writer; Pulitzer, 2002; Obie, 1990; NEA; Rockefeller

Parr, Catherine (1512/13–1548) 305
Eng. queen, author; w. Edward, Lord Brough of Gainsborough (1), third w. Sir John Nevill, Lord Latimer (2); sixth w. Henry VIII (3; 1491–1547; king of England, 1509–1547); w. Thomas Seymour, lord high admiral (4; 1508?–49; executed)

Parra, Violeta (1917–1967) 2299
Chilean political activist, songwriter, folklorist; née V— del Carmen P— Sandoval

Parry, Blanche (fl. 1560s) 363
Eng. astrologer, courtier; d. Henry P— of Newcourt and Herfordshire; chief gentlewoman to the privy chamber, keeper of jewels of Elizabeth I of England*

Partnow, Elaine Bernstein (1941–) 3291
Amer. public speaker, playwright, actor, anthologist, writer; s. Susan P—* and Judith P— Hyman*; w. Turner Browne (photographer, author, businessman, 1949–); a. Jessica P—*, Lesley A. Hyatt*

Partnow, Jessica [Leigh] (1981–)   4947
Amer. journalist; d. Susan P—*; n. Elaine P—* & Judith Hyman*; c. Lesley A. Hyatt*; cofounder, Common Language Project (clpmag.com), 2004

Partnow, Susan (1947–)   3161
Amer. management & organizational training consultant, peace activist, speech therapist, author; s. Elaine P—* and Judith P— Hyman*; m. Jessica P—*; a. Lesley A. Hyatt*; cofounder, Families for Peace (1982), Global Citizen Journey (2002), Conversation Cafés (2005)

Parton, Dolly [Rebecca] (1946–)   3686
Amer. songwriter, singer; Grammy, 1978, 1979

Parton, Sara Payson Willis   see FERN, FANNY

Partridge, Frances (1900–2004)   1918
Brit. translator, author, musician (violinist), scholar; née Marshall; CBE, 2000

Parturier, Françoise (1919–1995)   2353
Fr. writer, columnist, feminist

Pascalina, Madre (1894–1983) 1802
Bavarian/Ital. nun; née Josefine Lehnert; companion to Pope Pius XII (Ital. cleric, diplomat; née Eugenio Pacelli, 1876–1958; elected pope, 1939)

Pastan, Linda (1932–)   2815
Amer. poet, physician; Pushcart Prize

Paston, Agnes (?–1479)   280
Eng. householder, letter writer; w. William I, m. John I, Edmund I, Elizabeth, William II and Clement; m.-in-law Margaret Mautby P—*: gm. Margery Brews P—

Paston, Margaret Mautby (1441–1484)   262
Eng. householder; w. John I, m. John II, John III, Edmund II, Walter, William III, Margery and Anne, d.-in-law Agnes P—*

Patchett, Ann (1963–)   4650
Amer. novelist; PEN/Faulkner Award, 2002

Patel, Shailja (1970–)   4828
Kenyan/Amer. activist, poet, playwright, theatrician

Pateman, Carole (1940–)   3219
Eng./Amer. feminist, political theorist, educator (political science)

Paternostro, Silvana (1960?–) 4549
Colombian/Amer. journalist

Patkar, Medha (1954–)   4266
Ind. social scientist, environmental activist, educator; fdr., Save Narmada Movement; Right Livelihood, 1991; Goldman, 1992

Patterson, Eleanor [Medill] (1881–1948)   1572
Amer. newspaper editor; a.k.a. "Cissy"

Patterson, Martha Johnson (1828–1901)   1020
Amer. society leader; d. Andrew J— (1808–75; tailor, politician; 17th U.S. president, 1865–69)

Pattison, E. F. S. or Francis   see DILKE, EMILIA

Paul, Alice (1885–1977)   1637
Amer. suffragist, women's rights activist, attorney; established Congressional Union, 1913 (offshoot from NAWSA); cofounder, National Woman's Party, 1916; drafted ERA, 1923; founder, World Women's Party; NWHF, 1980; Congressional Gold Medal, 2008

Pavlova, Anna (1881–1931)   1573
Russ. ballet dancer

Payne, Ethel L. (1911–1991)   2163
Amer. journalist, columnist, lecturer, activist, civil rights, commentator; a.k.a. "First Lady of the Black Press"; first African-American woman radio and television commentator to be employed by a national network

Payne-Gaposchkin, Cecilia Helena (1900–1979)   1919
Eng./Amer. astronomer; first woman to become a full professor at Harvard

Peabody, Elizabeth (1750–1815)   666
Amer. householder; née Smith; mn. Shaw, s. Abigail Adams*

Peabody, Elizabeth Palmer (1804–1894)   886
Amer. educator, early education, writer; pioneered kindergarten in U.S.A., 1860

Peabody, Josephine Preston (1874–1922)   1448
Amer. playwright, poet, writer; mn. Marks

Peace Pilgrim, (1908–1981)   2098
Amer. pacifist, walker, philosopher; née Mildred Lisette Norman

Pearce, Susan C. (1956?–)   4387
Amer. educator, sociology

Pearson, Patricia (1964–)   4685
Can. journalist, novelist; grandd. Lester B. Pearson

(1897–1972), Can. Prime minister (1963–68), Nobel Peace Prize, 1957

Peebles, Anne   see GALLOWAY, PRISCILLA

Peel, Lady   see LILLIE, BEATRICE

Peelen, Jean (1941–)   3292–3293
Amer. attorney, civil rights, actor, writer, workshop facilitator, federal manager

Peery, Janet (1948–)   3854
Amer. novelist, literary critic, short story writer, teacher; NEA 1990

Peiss, Kathy [Lee] (1950?–)   4203
Amer. author, historian, educator; Guggenheim Fellow

Peled-Elhanan, Nurit (1955?–)4326
Isr. activist (peace), educator; d. Mattityahu P— , Arab general, scholar; w. Rami E— , cofounder of Parents' Circle/Families' Forum; cofounder, Bereaved Families for Peace; Sakharov Prize for Freedom of Thought, 2001

Pelham, Mary Singleton Copley (1710–1789)   570
Ir. shopkeeper; mn. Copley (1); w. Peter P— (2; limner and engraver), m. John S— C— (1738–1815; American artist)

Pelosi, Nancy (1940–)   3220
Amer. politician; Rep. CA (D), 1987– ; House minority Speaker; first female Speaker of the House of Reps. (2007–)

Pemberton, H. L. C.   see CHILDE-PEMBERTON, HARRIET

Pembroke, countess of   see HERBERT, MARY

Penelope (1214?–? B.C.E.)   20
Greek noble; a.k.a. Arnaea; w. Odysseus (king of Ithaca in Greek myth); m. Telemachus

Peng Peiyun, (1929–)   2678
Chin. politician, public servant; w. Wang Hanbin, politician; Chair, Red Cross Society of China, 1999–

Penley, Constance (1949–)   3924
Amer. educator, author, media scholar; fdr., Camera Obscura

Pennington, Mrs. (1734–1759)   617
Eng. poet

Percy, Florence   see AKERS, ELIZABETH

Perera, Sylvia Brinton (1932–) 2816
Amer. psychoanalyst, Jungian, feminist

Peri, Janis-Rozena (1940?–)   3221
Amer. educator, music, soprano; d. Zenobia Perry*

Perino, Dana [Marie] (1972–) 4866
Amer. public affairs consultant, public servant; White House Press Sec., 2007–09

Perkins, Frances (1882–1965) 1584
Amer. government official, writer; U.S. secretary of labor, 1933–44; chair, U.S. Civil Service Commission, 1946–53; first woman in U.S. cabinet; NWHF

Perl, Teri (1926–)   2573
Amer. mathematician, computer scientist, author, educator (technology); ex-w. Martin L. P—, 1995 Physics Nobel laureat; m. Jed P— , art critic; chair, Math-Science Network; cofounder, The Learning Company, 1980

Perón, [Marie] Eva Duarte (1919–1952)   2144
Argen. government official, lecturer, radio personality, political leader, actor; née E— M— Ibaguren, a.k.a. Evita; w. Juan Domingo P— (1895–1974; politician and soldier; president of Argentina, 1946–55, 1973–74); founder, Eva Perón Foundation, 1948; formed Peronista Feminist Party, 1949

Perovskaya, Sofia (1853–1881) 1198
Russ. revolutionary; assassin of Alexander II (1818–81; czar of Russia, 1855–81)

Perpetua, Vivia (180?–203)   99
Carthaginian Catholic martyr

Perry, Eleanor (1915–1981)   2252
Amer. screenwriter; Emmy, 1967, 1973

Perry, Nora (1831–1896)   1042
Amer. poet, writer

Perry, Zenobia Powell (1908–2004)   2099
Amer. composer, classical; m. Janis-Rozena Peri*

Pert, Candace B. (1946–)   3687
Amer. pharmacologist, researcher

Perutz, Kathrin (1939–)   2763
Amer. novelist, nonfiction writer

Pesotta, Rose (1896–1965)   1829
Russ./Amer. union activist, anarchist, laborer; v.p., Int. Ladies Garment Workers Union (ILGWU), 1933–44; first woman to hold position.

Pessl, Marisha (1979–)   4929
Amer. writer, playwright, actor

Petchesky, Rosalind (1942–) 3366
Amer. writer, health activist, researcher; cofounder, International Reproductive Rights Research Action Group

Peterkin, Julia (1880–1961)   1554
Amer. fiction writer; née Mood; Pulitzer, 1929; O. Henry, 1925, 1930

Peterson, Brenda [Carole]
(1952–)   4132
  Amer. writer
Peterson, Virgilia (1904–1966)
2002–2003
  Amer. writer, lecturer, transla-
  tor, TV personality, literary
  critic; mn. Paulding
Pethick-Lawrence, Emmeline,
Baroness (1867–1954)   1341
  Eng. suffragist; w. Baron Fred-
  erick William P— (1871–1961)
Petigny, Maria-Louisa Rose
(1768–1800)   741
  Fr. poet; née Levesque
Petröczi, Kata Szidónia
(1662–1708)   499
  Hung. poet
Petrushevskaya, Lyudmila
(1938–)   3101
  Russ. playwright, writer;
  a.k.a. the feminist Chekov
Petry, Ann [Lane] (1908–1997)2100
  Amer. journalist, novelist
Pfeiffer, Ida Laura (1797–1858) 857
  Aus. traveler, adventurer, col-
  lector, author; a.k.a. Madame
  P—
Phair, Liz (1967–)   4755
  Amer. songwriter, singer, musi-
  cian, guitarist; née Elizabeth
  Clark P—
Pharaoh's daughter
(fl. 1250s B.C.E.)   17
  Egyp. princess; a.k.a. Ther-
  muthis, Myrrina, Mercis; d.
  Ramses II (?); rescued Moses
  (Hebrew prophet and lawgiver)
  and raised him as her son
Pharr, Suzanne (1939–)   3153
  Amer. social justice activist,
  author; founder, the Women's
  Project (AR, 1981); cofounder
  of Southerners on New
  Ground (1984)
Phelps, Almira Lincoln
(1793–1884)   840
  Amer. poet, educator, author,
  botanist; née Hart; s. Emma
  Hart Willard*
Phelps, Elizabeth (1815–1852) 930
  Amer. writer; pseud. H. Trusta
Phelps, Elizabeth Stuart
(1844–1911)   1127
  Amer. writer; mn. Ward
Philenia see MORTON, SARAH
Philips, Joan (fl. 1670s–d. 1682)515
  Eng. poet; a.k.a. Ephelia; gd.
  Katherine P—* (?)
Philips, Katherine Fowler
(1631–1664)   459
  Eng./Ir. poet, translator,
  playwright; née Fowler, a.k.a.
  Orinda, The English Sappho;
  gm. Joan P—* (?)
Phillips, Angela Marie (1947–) 3783
  Brit. feminist, journalist, non-
  fiction writer

Phillips, Anne (1957?–)   4426
  Brit. educator (gender), author
Phillips, Bonnie (1942–)   3367
  Amer. environmental activist,
  administrator
Phillips, Debora (fl. 1980s–) 4937
  Amer. sex therapist, author,
  physician
Phillips, Jayne Anne (1952–) 4133
  Amer. educator, writer
Phillips, Julia (1944–2001) 3532
  Amer. film producer; Oscar,
  1973 (first woman producer
  to win Oscar)
Phillips, Lois (1940–)   3222
  Amer. lecturer, workshop
  leader, consultant (manage-
  ment & organizational
  training); fdg. exec. dir., An-
  tioch University Santa Barbara
  (1977–1988); fdg. co-dir.
  "The Everywoman Center" at
  Univ. of MA, Amherst
Phillips, Marie (1976–)   4914
  Brit. novelist
Philomela see ROWE, ELIZABETH
Philomela see WARREN, MERCY
Phinehas, Wife of
(1040?–d. 970 B.C.E.)   31
  Hebrew biblical figure; d.-
  in-law Eli (Israeli judge), m.
  Ichabod, gm. Ahijah
Phyrne (fl. 4th century B.C.E.) 64
  Greek model, beauty, cour-
  tesan
Pickford, Mary (1893–1979) 1781
  Can./Amer. writer, philanthro-
  pist, actor; née Gladys Marie
  Smith, a.k.a. "America's
  Sweetheart"; cofounder,
  Motion Picture Relief Fund;
  cofounder, Academy of Mo-
  tion Picture Arts and Sciences;
  cofounder, United Artists
  Corp., 1919; Academy Award,
  1929
Picon, Molly (1898–1992)   1872
  Amer. actor, lyricist; née
  Malka Opiekun
Picoult, Jodi [Lynn] (1966–) 4735
  Amer. novelist
Pierce-Baker, Charlotte
(1943–)   3447
  Amer. nonfiction writer,
  educator (women and gender
  studies)
Piercy, Marge (1936–)   2997
  Amer. magazine editor, poet,
  feminist, novelist, writer;
  founder, Movement for a
  Democratic Society (MDS)
Pierobon, Gigliola [Lola]
(1950?–)   3999
  Ital. feminist
Pierpont, Claudia Roth
(1952–)   4134
  Amer. journalist, educator
  (journalism); Guggenheim

Pilkington, Laetitia (1708–1750)563
  Ir./Eng. playwright, poet,
  printer; née Van Lewen
Pillay, Navanethem "Navi"
(1940–)   3223
  S. Afr. civil servant, lawyer,
  judge; cofounder, Equality
  Now (1985); first woman of
  color appointed as High Court
  judge in South Africa and Int.
  Criminal Tribunal for Rwanda
  (ICTR)
Pinar, Florencia del
(fl. 1460s–d. 1499)   268
  Span. poet
Pinckney, Eliza (1722?–1793) 591
  W. Ind./Amer. plantation
  manager; a.s.a. Elizabeth
  Lucas; d. George Lucas (Ital.
  governor of Antigua), w.
  Charles P— (Speaker of the
  South Carolina House of As-
  sembly, 1736–40, and chief
  justice, 1752); distinguished
  for her success in the cultiva-
  tion of indigo
Pincus, Joy (1969–)   4798
  Amer./Isr. writer, lecturer,
  workshop facilitator
Pincus, Lily (1898–1981)   1873
  Cuban/Eng. family relations
  counselor, nonfiction writer;
  founder, Institute of Marital
  Studies, London
Ping, Yang (see Yang Ping)
Pink, Lady (1964–)   4686
  Ecuad./Amer. graffiti art-
  ist; née Sandra Fabara; first
  woman graffiti artist in the
  world to be exhibited
Pinkard, Susan [K.] (1953–) 4204
  Amer. historian, educator
Piozzi, Hester Lynch
(1741–1821)   635
  Welsh/Eng. author; a.k.a. H—
  L— Thrale, née Salusbury; w.
  Henry Thrale (1) and Gabriel
  P— (2); friend of Dr. Samuel
  Johnson (1709–84; author,
  lexicographer)
Piper, Adrian (1946–)   3688
  Amer. philosopher, perfor-
  mance artist
Pipher, Mary [Bray] (1947–) 3784
  Amer. author, psychologist,
  radio commentator; a.k.a.
  M— Elizabeth P—
Pitter, Ruth (1897–1992)
1855–1856
  Eng. poet; first woman to re-
  ceive the Queen's Gold Medal
  for Poetry (1955); CBE, 1979
Pix, Mary Griffith
(1666?–1706/9?)   509
  Eng. novelist, playwright,
  translator
Plain, Belva (1919–)   2355
  Amer. novelist

Plaskow, Judith (1947–)   3785
  Amer. professor (religious
  studies), author
Plath, Sylvia (1932–1963)   2817
  Amer. writer, poet; pseud.
  Victoria Lucas; w. Ted
  Hughes (1930–98; Poet
  Laureate of England, 1984);
  Pulitzer, 1982
Plato, Ann (1820?–post-1841) 975
  Amer. poet, essayist, educa-
  tor; author of second volume
  of poetry by a black woman
  published in the United States
Pocahontas (1595?–1617)   404
  Amer. folk hero, princess;
  a.k.a. Mato (Snowfeather),
  Rebecca; the Nonpareil of
  Virginia; d. Chief Powhatan
  (1550?–1618; Algonquian
  leader, née Wahunsonacock),
  w. Kocoum (1) and John
  Rolfe (2); first American
  Christian convert, legend-
  ary savior of Captain John
  Smith of Jamestown (English-
  born American colonist, ca.
  1580–1631)
Pogrebin, Letty Cottin (1939–)3154
  Amer. columnist, writer,
  editor, peace and women's
  rights activist; cofounder, Ms.
  Magazine, 1971; cofounder,
  Natl. Women's Political Cau-
  cus, 1971
Poisson, Jeanne-Antoinette see
  POMPADOUR, JEANNE-ANTOINETTE
Poitiers, Diane de
(1499–1566)   294
  Fr. royal mistress; a.k.a. com-
  tesse de Brézé, duchesse de
  Valentinois; w. Louis de Breze,
  comte de Maulevrier (grand
  seneschal of Normandy);
  mistress of Henry II (1519–59,
  king of France, 1547–59)
Polier, Justine Wise
(1903–1987)   1981
  Amer. judge
Politkovskaya, Anna
(1958–2006)   4464
  Russ. journalist
Polk, Sarah Childress
(1803–1891)   881
  Amer. hostess, first lady; w.
  James P— (1795–1849; 11th
  U.S. president, 1845–49)
Pollard, "Sister" Evelyn
(1883?–1960?)   1599
  Amer. civil rights activist
Pollard, Josephine
(1834–1892)   1059
  Amer. hymnist, naturalist,
  writer
Pollitt, Katha (1949–)   3925
  Amer. journalist, poet, es-
  sayist; NBCCA, 1983; NEA,
  1984; Guggenheim, 1987

Pollock, [Mary] Sharon [Chalmers] (1936–) 2998
Can. actor, playwright, arts activist; Canada Council Senior Arts Grant, 1984; Alberta Playwriting Competition, 1971

Polowy, Carol (1956?–) 4388
Amer. educator

Polyxena (fl. 30s C.E.) 84
Greek biblical figure

Pompadour, Jeanne-Antoinette Poisson de, Madame (1721–1764) 588
Fr. patron of arts & literature, salonist; a.s.a. marquise de P—; d. François Poisson (equerry to the duke of Orléans), w. Lenormand d'Etoiles; mistress of Louis XV (1710–74; king of France, 1715–74)

Pompeia Plotina (80?–122 C.E.) 93
Roman empress; w. Emperor Trajan, m. Emperor Adrian

Ponsot, Marie Birmingham (1921–) 2410
Amer./Europ./N. Afr. poet, educator (poetry); NBCCA, 1998

Pool, Gail (1946–) 3689
Amer. educator, literary critic, columnist

Poole, Jeannie Gayle (1951–) 4068
Amer. musicologist, composer, filmmaker, author, producer; cofounder, The Int. Inst. for the Study of Women in Music

Poon, Christine A. (1952–) 4135
Amer. business executive

Popcorn, Faith (1948–) 3855
Amer. author, business consultant; née Plotkin; fdr., BrainReserve

Poppæa Sabina (fl. 50s–60 C.E.) 85
Roman courtier; mistress of Nero

Porcia (?–42 B.C.E.) 77
Roman noble; d. Marcus Porcius Cato (patriot, stoic philosopher), w. Decimus Junius Brutus (general, member of the conspiracy to assassinate Julius Caesar)

Porter, Adrian, Mrs. see HEATON, ROSE

Porter, Anne (1911–) 2164
Amer. poet; w. Fairfield Porter (1907–1975), Amer. Painter, art critic

Porter, Eleanor H. (1868–1920) 1354
Amer. writer; née Hodgman

Porter, Helen Grace see HIBBARD, [HELEN] GRACE

Porter, Jane (1776–1850) 772
Eng. novelist; s. Anna Maria P— (novelist) and Sir Robert Ker P— (artist, traveler)

Porter, Katherine Anne (1890–1980) 1715
Amer. writer; Pulitzer, 1966; NBA, 1966

Porter, Sylvia (1913–1991) 2207
Amer. economist, writer, columnist; née Feldman; a.k.a. Mrs. G. Sumner Collins

Portillo Trambley, Estela (1927/36–1998/99) 2609
Amer. writer, fiction, poet, playwright; Premio Quinto Sol award, 1972

Portman, Natalie (1981–) 4948
Isr./Amer. actor, activist; née Hershlag; Golden Globe, 2005

Post, Emily (1873–1960) 1418
Amer. society leader, writer; trendsetter of manners

Postlethwaite, Diana (1950–) 4000
Amer. educator, English, literary critic, author

Potor, Aurelia (1915–1999) 2253
Amer. physician

Potter, Beatrix (1866–1943) 1330
Eng. mycologist, writer (children), illustrator; a.k.a. Helen B— P— Heelis

Poulsson, Emilie (1853–1939) 1199
Amer. illustrator, editor, writer

Pounds, Jessie Brown (1861–1921) 1275
Amer. hymnist, missionary

Powell, Dawn (1897–1965) 1830
Amer. playwright, novelist, satirist; NIAL, 1964

Powell, Maxine (1924–) 2492.1
Amer. personal coach, actor; fdr., Maxine Powell Finishing and Modeling School, Detroit, 1951

Power, Samantha (1970–) 4829
Ir./Amer. journalist, lawyer, scholar (foreign policy), author; w. Cass Sunstein, legal scholar; fdg. exec. dir., Carr Center for Human Rights Policy (1998–2002); Pulitzer, 2003

Power, Susan (1961–) 4593
Amer. writer, educator

Powers, Donna (1949–) 3926
Amer. realtor, conservation activist; fdr., Rosie the Riveter Trust and Memorial (CA), 1991

Powter, Susan (1957–) 4427
Aust./Amer. motivational speaker, personal trainer, dietitian, author, TV host

Prager, Emily (1948–) 3856
Amer. writer, humorist

Pratt, Minnie Bruce (1946–) 3690
Amer. author, poet, essayist, educator (women's studies)

Praxilla (fl. 450s B.C.E.) 61
Greek poet

Preedy, George Runnell see BOWEN, MARJORIE

Prejean, Helen, Sister (1939–) 3155
Amer. activist, educator, nun; cofounder, Hope House, New Orleans, Louisiana

Prell, Riv-Ellen (1947–) 3786
Amer. anthropologist, educator (Jewish studies), author

Prentiss, Elizabeth Payson (1818–1878) 952
Amer. hymnist, poet, writer

Prest, Wife of (?–1558) 361
Eng. religious martyr

Preston, Ann (1813–1872) 921
Amer. physician, writer, educator

Preston, Margaret J[unkin] (1820–1897) 976
Amer. poet, writer

Previn, Dory (1929–) 2679
Amer. songwriter, singer; née Langan; ex-w. Andre P— (conductor, composer, pianist, 1929–)

Price, Leontyne (1927–) 2610
Amer. opera singer; Spingarn Medal, 1965; Grammy (11); Presidential Medal of Freedom, 1964

Priesand, Sally (1947–) 3787
Amer. rabbi; first woman rabbi

Priest, Dana (1959–) 4502
Amer. journalist, author; w. Wm. Goodfellow (1947–), fdr.-dir., Center for Int. Policy; Pulitzer, 2006, 2008; MacArthur, 2001

Priest, Ivy Baker (1905–1975) 2031
Amer. government official; m. Patricia Ann P— (1936–), actor; treasurer of the U.S. (1953–1961)

Primavera, Jurgenne (1945?–) 3605
Filipina scientist

Primrose, Diana (fl. 1630s) 457–458
patron of literary arts; Eng. poet

Prince, Lucy Terry see TERRY, LUCY

Prins, Nomi (1972–) 4867
Amer. journalist, author, investment banker, TV commentator; pseud. Natalia Prentice; w. Jack P—, renown statistician

Pritchard, Melissa (1948–) 3857
Amer. writer, poet; NEA, 1982; Pushcart, 1983, 1996

Proctor, Adelaide [Anne] (1825–1864) 1002
Eng. poet

Proctor, Edna Dean (1829–1923) 1021
Amer. poet

Proctor, Mary (1960–) 4550
Amer. folk artist

Profet, Margie (1958–) 4465
Amer. biologist, evolutionary theorist; d. Bob and Karen P— (physicists); MacArthur

Propp, Karen (1957–) 4428
Amer. writer, editor, educator

Prose, Francine (1947–) 3788
Amer. writer; Guggenheim

Prothrow-Stith, Deborah (1954–) 4267
Amer. physician, civil servant, author, educator

Proulx, E. Annie (1935–) 2942
Amer. short story writer, novelist; NBA, 1993; Pulitzer, 1994

Pryor, Sarah Agnes [Rice] (1830–1912) 1031
Amer. author, Civil War hero

Ptaschkina, Nelly (1903–1920) 1982
Russ. diarist

Pulcheria, Aelia (399–454) 109
Byzantine scholar, empress, saint; d. Arcadius (377?–408; emperor of the East, 395–408), s. Emperor Theodosius II (401–50, Roman emperor of the East, 408–50), w. General Marcian (396–457, Eastern Roman emperor, 450–57); canonized by the Greek Orthodox Church

Pulci, Antonia (1452–1501) 265
Ital. playwright, nun

Purim, Flora (1942–) 3368
Braz./Amer. singer, songwriter

Pursufull, Carmen M. (1930–) 2736
Amer. poet, poetry editor

Putnam, Emily James (1865–1944) 1318
Amer. college administrator, educator, writer; first dean of Barnard College, New York

Pym, Barbara (1913–1980) 2208
Brit. novelist

Pyper, Mary (1795–1870) 849
Scot. poet

Q

Qernertoq (fl. ca. ninth–14th century) 156
Can. poet

Quant, Mary (1934–) 2910
Eng. fashion designer; developed the miniskirt (also credited to Courreges); the hipster); OBE

Quayle, Marilyn (1950–) 4001
Amer. lawyer, novelist; w. James Danforth Q— (politician, 1947– ; 41st vice president of United States, 1989–93)

Quick-to-See Smith, Jaune (1940–) 3224
Amer. artist, painter, poet

Qui Jin (1875–1907)   1465
    Chin. writer, revolutionary
Quimby, Edith (1891–1982)   1732
    Amer. scientist, physicist, edu-
    cator, radiology; née Hinkley;
    a founder of radiation physics
Quin Guanshu (1929–)   2679.1
    Chin. botanist
Quindlen, Anna (1952–)   4136
    Amer. columnist, novelist;
    Pulitzer, 1992
Quinn, Jane Bryant (1939–) 3156
    Amer. economist, financial
    adviser
Quinn, Sally (1941–)   3294
    Amer. journalist
Qurrat al-'Ayn (?–1852)   1195
    Ind. Islamic saint, religious
    teacher (Babism), poet

R

Rabi'a bint Isma'il of Syria
(?–755)   139
    Arab poet
Rabi'a al-Adawiya,
(712/17–801)   136
    Persian poet, Sufi mystic,
    slave, saint, Islamic, scholar;
    a.k.a. R— the mystic; pivotal
    figure in the early develop-
    ment of Sufism
Rabi'a of Balkh
(fl. 10th century)   171
    Iran. poet; d. Ka'b, king of
    Balkh
Rabliauskas, Sophia (1960?–) 4551
    Can. environmental activist;
    Goldman, 2007
Rachel (?–1732 B.C.E.?)   13
    Hebrew biblical figure; d.
    Leban, s. Leah,* second w.
    Jacob, m. Benjamin; mother
    of two of the twelve tribes
    of Israel
Rachel (1890–1931)   1716
    Russ./Isr. poet; née Blaustein
    or Bluewstein
Radcliffe, Ann (1764–1823)   723
    Eng. poet, novelist; née Ward;
    w. William R— (editor)
Radegunda, Saint (518?–587)   114
    Frankish/Merovingian prin-
    cess, nun; w. Chlotar I (a.s.a.
    Clotaire)
Radford-Hill, Sheila (1949–) 3927
    Amer. black rights activist,
    feminist
Radner, Gilda [Susan]
(1946–1989)   3691
    Amer. actor, comedian; w.
    Gene Wilder (producer, actor,
    1934–); Emmy, 1978
Radtke, Joyce (1955–)   4327
    Amer. painter
Rahman, Aishah (1936/37–)   2999
    Amer. playwright, educator;
    cofounder, Blackberry Produc-
    tion Co.; Rockefeller, 1988

Raine, Kathleen Jessie
(1908–2003)   2101
    Eng. poet, literary critic,
    scholar; CBE, 2000
Rajalakshmi, R[amakrishnan]
(1926–)   2574
    Ind. nutritionist, biochemist,
    educator (nutrition); noted
    for her work in nutrition with
    UNICEF and other interna-
    tional organizations
Raleigh, Elizabeth
(1565–1647)   370
    Eng. noble; d. Sir Nicholas
    Throckmorton (1515–71), w.
    Sir Walter R— (1552?–1618;
    courtier, writer, navigator,
    colonizer)
Rambert, Marie, Dame
(1891–1982)   1733
    Pol./Eng. impresario, ballet
    teacher & director; a.k.a.
    Dame Marie Dukes; w.
    Ashley Dukes (playwright,
    director of Mercury Theater);
    founder of Ballet Rambert,
    1926 (later the Modern
    Dance Company); C.B.E.,
    1962
Rame, Franca (1928–)   2639
    Ital. playwright, theatrician;
    w. Dario Fo (Nobel Prize–win-
    ning playwright, 1926–); gd.
    Pio Rame (theatrician); co-
    founder, La Compagnia Dario
    Fo-Franca Rame (1959),
    Nuovo Scene (1968), Il Col-
    lectivo Teatrale La Comune
    (1970)
Ramée, Louise de la   see OUIDA
Ramey, Estelle R.
(1917–2006)   2300
    Amer. physiologist, bio-
    physicist, endocrinologist,
    educator; née Stella Rose-
    mary Rubin; founder and
    the second president of the
    American Women in Science
Ramos, Rosa Hilda
(1945?–)   3606
    P. R. environmental activist
Ramsay, Martha Laurens
(1759–1811)   699
    Amer. letter writer
Ran, Shulamit (1949–)   3928
    Isr./Amer. composer, music
    educator; Pulitzer/music, 1991
    (second woman); Guggen-
    heim (2)
Rand, Ayn (1905–1982)   2032
    Russ./Amer. novelist, philoso-
    pher, screenwriter; née Alissa
    Rosenbaum; mn. O'Connor;
    devised philosophy of "objec-
    tivism"
Randal, Vera (1922–)   2438
    Amer. writer

Randall, Margaret (1936–)   3000
    Cub./Amer. nonfiction
    writer, photographer, poet
Rank, Beata (1896–1967)   1831
    Amer. psychologist; née Hoff-
    man
Rankin, Jeannette [Pickering]
(1880–1973)   1555
    Amer. politician, suffragist,
    pacifist; U.S. congresswoman
    (R-MO), 1917–1919 and
    1941–1943; first woman
    elected to U.S. Congress or to
    any national government; co-
    founder, Women's International
    League for Peace and Freedom
    (WILPF), 1918; NOW Susan B.
    Anthony Hall of Fame, 1972;
    only person in congressional
    history to vote against U.S.
    entry into World Wars I and II;
    NWHF
Raphaël, Sally Jessy (1943–) 3447.1
    Amer. TV & radio personal-
    ity; Natl. Assn. of Radio Talk
    Show "Talk Show Host of
    the Year," 1992; Emmy, 1989
Ras, Barbara (1949–)   3929
    Amer. poet
Rascoe, Judith (1941–)   3295
    Amer. writer, scenarist
Rathbone, Eleanor
(1872–1946)   1404
    Eng. suffragist, politician
Räthzel, Nora (1948–)   3858
    Ger. cultural historian, nonfic-
    tion writer
Raven see FOSTER; DORIS ANN
Raven, Arlene (1944–2006)   3533
    Amer. feminist, art historian;
    cofounder, The Woman's
    Building and the Feminist
    Studio Workshop/College, Los
    Angeles, 1973; fdr., Women's
    Caucus for Art
Ravitch, Diane (1938–)   3102
    Amer. writer, educator; née
    Silvers
Rawalt, Marguerite
(1895–1989)   1818
    Amer. lawyer, feminist; co-
    founder, NOW, 1966
Rawi, Mahboba (1968–)   4776
    Afghan/Aust. political activist;
    fdr., Mahboba's Promise (Af-
    ghan women's refuge center)
Rawlings, Marjorie Kinnan
(1896–1953)   1832
    Amer. writer; Pulitzer, 1939
Ray, Dixy Lee (1914–1994)   2227
    Amer. government official,
    politician, marine biologist,
    educator; chair, U.S. Atomic
    Energy Commission,
    1973–75; governor (D-WA),
    1977–80; Guggenheim 1952;
    United Nations Peace Medal,
    1973

Ray, Rebecca (1980–)   4938
    Eng. novelist
Raymond, Janice G. (1949–) 3930
    Amer. feminist, educator
    (women's studies); co-exec.
    dir., Coalition Against Traf-
    ficking in Women (CATW)
Razovsky, Cecilia
(1886/1891–1968)   1656
    Amer. immigrant activist; mn.
    Davidson
Razumovskaya, Lyudmila
(1948–)   3859
    Lith. playwright; a.s.a. Lud-
    milla
Rea, Shiva (1967–)   4756
    Amer. yoga instructor
Reagan, Maureen
(1941–2001)   3296
    Amer. public servant;
    d. Ronald R— (1911– ;
    politician, actor; 40th
    president of U.S., 1981–89)
    and Nancy R—*
Reagan, Nancy (1921–)   2411
    Amer. first lady, actor; née B.
    Anne Frances Robbins, a.k.a.
    Nancy Davis; w. Ronald R—
    (1911– ; politician, actor; 40th
    president of U.S., 1981–89);
    m. Maureen R—*
Reagon, Bernice Johnson
(1942–)   3369
    Amer. singer, history curator;
    organizer, Sweet Honey in the
    Rock (vocal group)
Rebecca (fl. fifth century B.C.E.) 57
    Greek public figure
Rebekah (fl. 18th century B.C.E.) 11
    Mesopotamian biblical figure;
    d. Bethuel (son of Nahor), s.
    Laban, w. Isaac, m. Esau and
    Jacob; one of the four Jewish
    matriarchs
Rebolledo, Tey Diana
(1937–)   3052
    Amer. educator (women's and
    Latina literature), book edi-
    tor, administrator, nonfiction
    writer
Reddy, Helen (1941–)   3297
    Aust./Amer. songwriter, singer,
    public servant, hypnothera-
    pist; Grammy, 1972
Reddy, Maureen (1955–)   4328
    Amer. nonfiction writer
Reed, Donna (1921–1986)   2412
    Amer. pacifist, actor, civil
    rights activist; née D— Belle
    Mullenger; cofounder, An-
    other Mother for Peace;
    Academy Award, 1953
Reed, Esther De Berdt
(1746–1780)   651
    Eng./Amer. relief worker; w.
    Joseph R— (Amer. soldier and
    statesman, 1741–80)

Reese, Lizette [Woodworth] (1856–1935) 1213
Amer. poet, writer

Reeves, Nancy (1913–) 2209
Amer. writer, educator, lawyer; née Goldhaber

Rehm, Diane (1936–) 3001
Amer. radio host, author; née Aed; host of *The Diane Rehm Show* since 1979

Reid, Willa Mae (1939–) 3157
Amer. civil rights activist, politician

Reiner, Max *see* CALDWELL, JANET MIRIAM] TAYLOR

Reinharz, Shulamit (1946–) 3693
Dutch/Amer. sociologist, feminist

Reinisch, June Machover (1943–) 3448
Amer. psychologist

Reinshagen, Gerlind (1926–) 2575
Ger. playwright, radio writer, novelist

Reitz, Rosetta (1924–2008) 2493
Amer. historian, jazz, record producer, food columnist, feminist; cofounder, OWL (Older Women's Liberation)

Remington, Deborah (1935–) 2603
Amer. painter

Renard, Cecile (1774?–1794) 764
Fr. shopkeeper, royalist sympathizer

Renault, Mary (1905–1983) 20
Eng./S. Afr. novelist; née Eileen M— Challans

Rendell, Ruth (Barbara) (1930–) 2737
Eng. writer; a.k.a. Barbara Vine

Renée de France (1510–1575) 304
Fr./Ital. benefactor of Calvinists, patron of arts; a.k.a. duchess of Ferrara; d. Louis XII (1462–1514; king of France, 1499–1515), w. Ercole d'Este II, duke of Ferrara, m. Alfonso, Leonora and Ann d'Este*

Renfroe, Anita (1962–) 4629
Amer. comedian, lyricist, singer, author

Renne, Tanya (1970–) 4830
Slov. anthologist, political activist, web developer

Reno, Janet (1938–) 3103
Amer. civil servant; U.S. attorney general, 1993– (first woman to hold this office); NWHF

Repplier, Agnes (1858–1950) 1236
Amer. writer, social critic

Resnik, Judith (1949–1986) 3931
Amer. electrical and design engineer, astronaut

Resnik, Muriel (1917–1995) 2301
Amer. playwright, novelist

Revoyr, Nina (1969–) 4799
Amer. novelist

Reynolds, Malvina (1900–1978) 1920
Amer. political activist, songwriter, folk singer

Reza, Yasmina (1959–) 4503
Fr. actor, novelist, playwright, translator; Laurence Olivier Award, 1998; Tony, 1998; Molière Award, 1987, 1990

Rhode, Deborah L[ynn] (1952–) 4137
Amer. educator (law), nonfiction writer, attorney

Rhys, Jean (1890–1979) 1717
W. Ind./Eng. novelist, dancer; née Ella Gwendolen Rees William; C.B.E., 1977; Royal Society of Literature Award

Rice, Alice Caldwell [Hegan] (1870–1942) 1382
Amer. writer, humorist

Rice, Ann (1941–) 3298
Amer. novelist; née Howard Allen O'Brien; w. Howard R— , poet (?–2002)

Rice, Condoleezza (1954–) 4268
Amer. educator, public servant; 2nd woman to serve as Secretary of State

Rice, Ruth Mason (1884–1927) 1617
Amer. poet

Rice, Susan E. (1964–) 4687
Amer. political analyst, diplomat; U.S. ambassador to U.N., 2009–

Rice-Davies, [Marilyn] Mandy (1944–) 3534
Eng. model, mistress, showgirl, author

Rich, Adrienne [Cecile] (1929–) 2680
Amer. poet, educator, feminist; p. Michelle Cliff*; NEA, 1974

Rich, B. Ruby (1969?–) 4800
Amer. film critic & scholar, educator

Rich, Mary *see* MARY OF WARWICK

Rich, Penelope Devereaux (1562/63–post-1605) 366
Eng. noble; d. Lettice Knollys,* s. Robert, second earl of Essex (favorite of Elizabeth I*), w. Lord Rich (1), mistress (later wife) Lord Mountjoy, earl of Devonshire (2); inspiration for Sir Philip Sidney's sonnet sequence "Astrophel and Stella" (1554–86; poet, politician, soldier)

Richards, [Dorothy] Ann [Willis] (1933–2006) 2861
Amer. politician; m. Cecile R—*; governor of Texas, 1992–1995

Richards, [Amelia] Amy (1970–) 4831
Amer. abortion rights activist, journalist; cofounder, Third Wave Foundation

Richards, Beah (1920–2000) 2387
Amer. civil rights activist, playwright, actor, poet; Emmy (2), 1988; Tony, 1965; Black Filmmakers Hall of Fame, 1974

Richards, Cecile (1958?–) 4466
Amer. women's rights activist, journalist, administrator, labor organizer; d. Ann R—*; pres., Planned Parenthood Federation of America (PPFA), 2006–

Richards, Janet Radcliffe (1944–) 3535
Brit. bioethicist, philosopher, feminist

Richards, Laura [Elizabeth] Howe (1850–1943) 1180
Amer. writer; d. Julia Ward H—*; Pulitzer, 1917

Richardson, Dorcas (1741?–1834) 636
Amer. patriot; née Nelson; w. Capt. Richard R—

Richardson, Dorothy Miller (1873–1957) 1419
Eng. writer

Richardson, Margaret "Peggy" Milner (1943–) 3449
Amer. civil servant; U.S. Commissioner of Internal Revenue

Richardson, Miranda (1958–) 4467
Brit. actor; Golden Globe, 1993, 1995

Richie, Alexandra (1963?–) 4651
Can./Eng. historian

Richman, Alyson M. (1972–) 4868
Amer. novelist

Richman, Julia (1855–1912) 1207
Amer. writer, educator, lecturer, administrator; first female school superintendent in New York City; fndr, Young Women's Hebrew Assoc.; dir., Educational Alliance, Hebrew Free School, NYC

Richter, Gisela [Marie Augusta] (1882–1972) 1585
Eng./Amer. museum curator, art historian; Gold Medal, Archaeological Institute of America, 1968

Richthofen, Emma Maria Frieda Johanna Freiin von *see* LAWRENCE, FRIEDA

Ricker, Darlene Marie (1954–)4269
Amer. lawyer

Ricker, Marilla (1840–1920) 1096
Amer. lawyer, humanitarian, civil rights activist; a.k.a. "The Prisoner's Friend"

Riddlestone, Sue (1960–) 4552
Eng. environmentalist, nurse; w. Pooran Desai (1965–), environmentalist; cofounder-director, One Planet Living; cofounder, BioRegional Development Group, 1994

Ride, Sally [Kristen] (1951–) 4069
Amer. physicist, astronaut; w. Steven Hawley (astronaut); first American woman in space; director, California Space Institute; NWHF

Riding, Laura [Jackson] (1901–1991) 1938
Amer. poet, writer, literary critic; née Reichenthal; Guggenheim, 1973; NEA, 1979

Ridler, Anne Barbara (1912–2001) 2188
Eng. poet, librettist, playwright; née Bradby

Riedesel, Frederica de (1746–1808) 652
Ger./Can. diarist, letter writer; née F— Charlotte Louisa Massow; d. Massow (Prussian minister of state); established a military orphanage and poorhouse in Brunswick

Riefenstahl, Leni (1902–2003) 1955
Ger. scenarist, actor, filmmaker

Rieux, Renée de Chateauneuf (1550–1587) 351
Fr. noble; a.k.a. la Belle; favorite of duc d'Anjou

Rieux, Virginie des (fl. 16th century–) 410
Fr. writer

Rikhvanova, Marina (1961–) 4594
Russ. ecologist; co-chair, Baikal Ecological Wave (BEW); Goldman, 2008

Riley, Janet Mary (1915–) 2254
Amer. educator, civil rights activist, lawyer

Riley, Matilda White (1911–2004) 2165
Amer. sociologist

Rilliet-Huber, Catherine (1764–post-1810) 724
Ital./Fr. letter writer; friend of Germaine de Stael*

Rind, Clementina (1740?–1774) 634
Amer. printer, newspaper editor; w. William R , publisher; Virginia's first female printer

Rinehart, Mary Roberts (1876–1958) 1480
Amer. playwright, journalist, mystery writer

Ringera, Karambu (1957–) 4429
Kenyan peace activist, politician; fdr. & pres., Int. Peace Initiatives (IPI)

Ripley, Sarah Alden (1793–1867) 841
Amer. scholar; née Bradford; related to Priscilla Alden* and William Bradford (Eng. Puritan colonist, 1590–1657; governor of Plymouth Colony, 1621–51), a. Ralph Waldo Emerson (philosopher, author, 1803–82)

Rittenhouse, Jessie [Belle] (1869–1948) 1367
Amer. editor, poet, writer, literary critic; founder, Poetry Society of America

Ritter, Erika (1948–) 3860
Can. playwright, radio personality, radio, TV & short story writer, comedian; ACTRA Award (Canada); 1982)

Rivera, Marina (1942–) 2917
Amer. poet

Rivers, Caryl (1937–) 3053
Amer. journalist, educator (journalism)

Rivers, Joan (1933–) 2862
Amer. comedian, TV personality; née Molinsky; w. Edgar Rosenberg, producer (suicide); Emmy, 1990

Roach, Pam[ela Jean] (1948–) 3861
Amer. politician; state senator (R-Washington) 1990–

Roberts, Cokie (1943–) 3450
Amer. columnist, author, radio commentator; née Mary Martha Corinne Morrison Claiborne Boggs; d. Lindy B—* & Hale B—, Congressman; w. Steven V. R— , columnist; Emmy, 1991

Roberts, Dorothy E. (1956–) 4389
Amer. educator (law), nonfiction writer

Roberts, Elizabeth Madox (1885–1941) 1638
Amer. poet, novelist

Roberts, Julia [Fiona] (1967–) 4757
Amer. actor; w. Lyell Lovett, Amer. Singer; Academy, 2000; Golden Globe (3)

Roberts, Michele B. (1949–) 3932
Eng./Fr. poet, novelist, playwright

Robertson, Anna Mary see MOSES, GRANDMA

Robinson, A[gnes] Mary F[rances] (1857–1944) 1226
Eng./Fr. poet; mn. Darmesteter and Duclaux

Robinson, Barbara Paul (1941–) 3299
Amer. lawyer; first woman pres. of the Assn. of the Bar of the City of New York

Robinson, Corinne Roosevelt (1861–1933) 1276
Amer. poet; s. Theodore Roosevelt (1858–1919; war hero, politician, 26th U.S. president, 1901–09), a. Edith Carow Roosevelt* and Eleanor Roosevelt*

Robinson, Harriet [Hanson] (1825–1911) 1003
Amer. suffragist, writer, mill worker

Robinson, Jill (1936–) 3002
Amer. writer; d. Dore Schary (author, 1905–1980)

Robinson, Lillian [Sara] (1941–2006) 3300
Amer. nonfiction writer, educator

Robinson, Mabel Louise (1874–1962) 1449
Amer. educator, writer

Robinson, Marilynne (1943–) 3451
Amer. essayist, novelist; NBCCA, 2004; Pulitzer, 2005

Robinson, Mary (1758–1800) 693
Eng./Fr. teacher, actor, playwright, poet, novelist; a.k.a. Laura, Laura Maria, Perdita, La Belle Anglaise; pseud. Tabitha Bramble

Robinson, Therese Albertine Louise (1797–1870) 858
Ger./Russ./Amer. poet, translator, historian, novelist; née van Jacob; pseud. Talvi, Ernst Berthold

Roche, Adi (1955–) 4329
Ir. peace activist; fdr., Chernobyl Children's Project; Irish Person of the Year, European Person of the Year, et al

Rochefort, Christiane (1917–1998) 23
Fr. filmmaker, writer, scenarist

Rochlin, Harriet (1924–) 2494
Amer. writer, historian

Rockefeller, Lucy (1838–1878) 1084
Amer. socialist; mn. Briggs; s. John D. R—

Roddick, Anita (1942–2007) 3370
Eng. business executive, entrepreneur; established retail chain, The Body Shop

Rodgers, Carolyn M. (1945–) 3607
Amer. novelist, writer, poet; NEA, 1970; PEN

Rodriguez, Graciela "Chely" (1980?–) 4939
Amer. writer

Roe, Anne (1904–1991) 2004
Amer. writer, psychologist

Roe, Rebecca (1952–) 4138
Amer. lawyer

Roepke, Gabriela (1920–) 2388
Chilean playwright, educator; founder of El Teatro de Ensayo, Santiago

Rogers, Desiree (1959?–) 4504
Amer. businesswoman, public servant; White House social secretary, 2009–2010

Rogers, Estelle H. (Contemporary) 4984
Amer. attorney; exec. dir., Death with Dignity Natl. Ctr.,WA, D.C.

Rogers, Ginger (1911–1995) 2166
Amer. actor, ballroom dancer, singer; née Virginia Katherine McMath; d. Lela R— (1891–1977), reporter, scriptwriter, movie producer; fdr. Motion Picture Alliance for the Preservation of American Ideals; w. (2) Lew Ayres (1908–1996), actor; (4) Jacques Bergerac, lawyer, actor, CEO; (5) William Marshal, director-producer; Oscar, 1940

Rogers, Hester Ann (1756–1794) 687
Eng. Methodist leader

Rogers, Lesley [Joy] (1943–) 3452
Aust./Amer. scientist, physiologist, educator, physiology

Rogers, Pattiann (1940–) 3225
Amer. poet, educator; NEA 1982, 1988; Guggenheim 1984, 1985

Roiphe, Anne Richardson (1935–) 2943
Amer. novelist; m. Katie R—*

Roiphe, Katie (1968–) 4777
Amer. journalist, author, feminist; d. Anne R—*

Roland, Jeanne-Marie (1754–1793) 678
Fr. patriot, social figure, political activist; née Philipon; w. Jean Marie Roland de la Platière (1734–93; industrial scientist); executed by the Jacobins

Roland, Pauline (1805–1852) 891
Fr. feminist, writer, socialist

Rolf, Ida P. (1896–1979) 1833
Amer. biochemist, physical therapist; developer of Rolfing

Rollin, Betty (1936–) 3003
Amer. actor, editor, writer, TV reporter

Rolls, Mrs. Henry (fl. 1810s–1825) 912
Eng. poet

Romer, Christina D. (1958–) 4468
Amer. educator (economic history), economist; w. David H. R— , economics professor

Ronell, Ann (1908–1993) 2102
Amer. orchestra conductor, songwriter; first woman to conduct and compose for film

Ronstadt, Linda (1946–) 3694
Amer. singer; Grammy (4); SHF

Roosevelt, [Anna] Eleanor (1884–1962) 1618
Amer. lecturer, humanitarian, first lady, government official, writer; w. Franklin D. R— (1882–1945; politician; 32nd U.S. president, 1933–45), m. Alice R— Halsted,* n. Theodore R— (1858–1919; war hero, politician; 26th U.S. president, 1901–09), Corinne R— Robinson,* c. Edith Carow R—* and Alice R— Longworth*; U.S. delegate to United Nations, 1945–53, 1961; United Nations Prize, 1968; NWHF

Roosevelt, Edith Carow (1861–1948) 1277
Amer. society leader; d. Theodore R— (1858–1919; war hero, politician 26th U.S. president, 1901–09), n. Corinne R. Robinson,* a. Anna R— Halsted,* c. Eleanor R—*, s. Alice R— Longworth*

Rosaldo, Michelle Zimbalist (1944–1981) 3536
Amer. anthropologist

Rose, Ernestine [Potowski] (1810–1892) 913
Pol./Amer. socialist, feminist, abolitionist; NWHF

Rose, Phyllis (1942–) 3371
Amer. biographer, educator, literary critic; née Davidoff; w. Laurent de Brunhoff, author & illustrator of Babar books

Rose, Wendy [Elizabeth] (1948–) 3862
Amer. poet, artist, editor; née Bronwen Elizabeth Edwards

Rosen, Marjorie (1942–) 3372
Amer. writer, film historian

Rosen, Ruth (1945–) 3608
Amer. historian, educator (history), political columnist

Rosenberg, Ethel (1915–1953) 2255
Amer. public figure; née Greenglass; w. Julius R—; only U.S. citizen, with her husband, to be executed for treason

Rosenberg, Karen (1973?–) 4879
Amer. essayist, journalist

Rosenberg, Tina (1960–) 4553
Amer. nonfiction writer, political journalist, speech writer;

MacArthur, 1987; NBA, 1995; Pulitzer, 1996

Rosenfeld, Bobbie (1904–1969) 2005
Can. athlete, sports writer

Rosenstein, Harriet (1932?–) 2818
Amer. writer, teacher, psychotherapist

Rosenthal, Ida (1886–1973) 1657
Russ./Amer. dressmaker, political activist, inventor, philanthropist; née Kaganovich; invented the first modern brassiere, Maiden Form, 1922

Rosenthal, Rachel (1926–) 2576
Fr./Amer. performance artist; founder, director, Instant Theatre, Los Angeles, 1956–66; Obie, 1989

Ross, Lillian (1927–) 2611
Amer. writer, journalist; mistress, William Shawn American editor of The New Yorker, 1952–1987 (1907–1992)

Ross, Susan C. (1942–) 3373
Amer. civil rights activist, educator, writer, lawyer

Rossetti, Christina [Georgina] (1830–1894) 1032
Eng. poet, writer; pseud. Ellen Alleyne; s. Dante Gabriel R— (1828–82; poet, painter)

Rossi, Alice S. (1922–) 2439
Amer. author, educator, scholar, editor; w. Peter H. R— (1921–2006), sociologist, author, educator; cofounder, NOW.

Rossner, Judith (1935–2005) 2944
Amer. writer

Roth, Friederike (1948–) 3863
Ger. philosopher, translator, linguist, radio writer, playwright, poet

Roth, Stephanie Danielle (1971?–) 4848
Fr./Rum. journalist, environmental activist, editor; Goldman, 2005

Roulet, Elaine, Sister (1930–) 2738
Amer. nun, teacher, prison reformer; NWHF

Roumeau, Jacqueline (Contemporary) 4985
Chilean actor, administrator; dir., Cultural Corp. of Artists for Rehabilitation and Social Reinsertion through Art (CO-ARTRE), Chile

Rourke, Constance [Mayfield] (1885–1941) 1639
Amer. writer

Rouse, Cecilia [Elena] (1963?–) 4652
Amer. educator (economics and public affairs), economic analyst

Routledge, Katherine (1866–1935) 1331
Eng. archaeologist, author, explorer

Routsong, Alma (1924–1996) 2495
Amer. feminist, writer; pseud. Isabel Miller

Row, Amanda (1931–) 2774
Amer. writer, educator

Rowe, Dorothy (1930–) 2739
Aust./Brit. psychologist, author

Rowe, Elizabeth Singer (1674–1737) 518
Eng. poet, author; a.k.a. E— Singer; pseud. Philomena

Rowland, Helen (1876–1950) 1481
Amer. journalist, humorist, writer

Rowlandson, Mary [White] (1637?–1711) 468
Amer. pioneer, author

Rowling, J. K. (1965–) 4711
Eng. writer (juvenile); née Joanne "Jo" R—; OBE

Rowson, Susanna Haswell (1762–1824) 715
Eng./Amer. novelist, playwright, actor, poet, editor, textbook writer

Roy, Arundhati (1961–) 4595
Ind. screenwriter, novelist; w. Pradip Krishen (filmmaker); n. Prannoy R— , media mogul; Booker Prize, 1997

Roy, Gabrielle (1909–1983) 2115
Can. novelist; Governor General's Award (3)

Roy, Sara (1955–) 4330
Amer. scholar

Royall, Anne Newport (1769–1854) 745
Amer. author, newspaper publisher, traveler; née Newport; a.k.a. "Grandma of the Mudrakers"; sometimes called the first American newspaperwoman

Royden, [Agnes] Maude (1877–1956) 1498
Eng. religious leader

Rozman, Deborah (1949–) 3933–3934
Amer. psychologist, writer, educator; cofounder, Inst. of HeartMath; pres. & CEO of Quantum Intech, Inc

Ruarowna, Margareta (fl. 1620s) 440
Pol. author (religion), poet; d. Marcin Ruar

Rubenstein, Gillian (1942–) 3374
Eng./Aust. children's writer, playwright; pseud. Lian Hearn

Rubin, Vera C. (1928–) 2640
Amer. astrophysicist; w. Robert R— (mathematician); Gold Medal of the Royal Astronomical Society (London), the first woman to be awarded this medal since Caroline Herschel* in 1828; Natl. Medal of Science, 1993

Rubinstein, Helena (1870–1965) 1383
Pol./Amer. writer, cosmetic manufacturer, business executive; a.k.a. Princess Gourielli-Tchkonia

Ruckelshaus, Jill (1937–) 3054
Amer. civil servant, lecturer, business executive; née Strickland; w. William R— (1932–) public servant, business executive; officer, U.S. Commission of Civil Rights, 198?–?

Ruddick, Sara (1935–) 2607
Amer. teacher, pacifist, author, philosopher

Rudikoff, Sonya (1927–1997) 2612
Amer. writer, scholar

Rudman, Masha Kabakow (1933–) 2863
Amer. educator, education, author

Rudner, Rita (1956–) 4390
Amer. comedian

Rudolph, Wilma "Skeeter" (1940–1994) 3226
Amer. track and field athlete; fdr., Wilma Rudolph Foundation; polio survivor; triple gold Olympic medalist in track,1960; NWHF, 1994; IWSHF, 1980

Rudy, Kathy (1956–) 4391
Amer. educator (ethics & women's studies)

Ruether, Rosemary Radford (1936–) 3004
Amer. theologian, nonfiction writer, feminist, educator (theology)

Ruiz, Mona Sandoval (1959–) 4505
Amer. police officer

Rukeyser, Muriel (1913–1980) 2210
Amer. biographer, writer, civil rights activist, poet, translator, film editor; NIAL, 1942; AAAL, 1942

Rule, Jane (1931–2007) 2775
Amer./Can. writer

Runkle, Bertha (1878–1958) 1517
Amer. writer; mn. Bash

Rush, Florence (1918–2008) 2328
Amer. psychiatric social worker, activist, children's; cofounder, OWL

Russell, Anna (1911–2006) 2167
Eng./Amer. singer, comedian; née Russell-Brown

Russell, Countess see ARNIM, MARY

Russell, Diana E. H. (1938–) 3104
S. Afr./Amer. feminist, writer, educator, sociology

Russell, Dora [Winifred], countess (1894–1986) 1803
Brit. pacifist, author, feminist, campaigner; née Black; ex-w. Lord Bertrand R— (1872–1970; philosopher and mathematician); cofounder, Beacon Hill School, West Sussex, 1927 (progressive school); pioneer of women's rights

Russell, Elizabeth Hoby, Lady (1527–1609) 326
Eng. diarist, courtier; d. Anthony Cooke (1442–83; tutor to Edward IV; king of En-gland, 1461–83; s. Anne Cooke Bacon,* Lady Mildred Burleigh and Catherine Killigrew,* w. Sir Thomas H— (1; author, translator) and Lord John R— (2), m. Elizabeth, Ann and Thomas Posthumous H—, m.-in-law Lady Margaret H—*; earliest known English woman diarist

Russell, Lady see HARINGTON, LUCY

Russell, Rachel, Lady (1636–1723) 467
Eng. letter writer; née R— Wriothesley; w. Vaughn (1), Lord William R— (2)

Russell, Rosalind (1911–1976) 2168
Amer. philanthropist, screen actor; mn. Brisson; cofounder, Independent Artists, Inc., 1947; Tony, 1953

Ruth (fl. 1100s B.C.E.) 23
Moabite biblical figure; d.-in-law Naomi,* w. Mahlon (1) and Boaz (2), m. Obed, great-gm. David; founder, with Boaz, of the House of David

Rutherford, Alison see COCKBURN, ALICIA

Ru Zhijuan (1925–) 2535
Chin. editor, writer; m. Wang Anyi (1954–), writer

Ryan, Kay (1945–) 3609
Amer. poet

Ryan, Sarah (1724?–1768) 594
Eng. Methodist leader, school housekeeper; friend of John Wesley (1703–1791; preacher; founder of Methodism, 1784) and Mary Fletcher*

S

Saberi, Roxana (1977–) 4918
Amer./Iran. journalist; Tehran bureau chief, Feature Story News

Sabin, Florence [Rena] (1871–1953) 1393
Amer. writer, anatomist, public health scientist, educator; NWHF

Sablé, Madeleine de Souvré de, Marquise (1599–1678)　408
Fr. salonist

Sachs, Nelly (1891–1970)　1734
Ger./Swed. translator, poet, playwright; Prize of the Swedish Poets Association, 1958; Nobel Prize, 1966

Sackville, Margaret, Lady (1881–1963)　1574
Eng. poet

Sackville-West, Vita (1892–1962)　1752
Eng. writer

Sadik, Nafis (1929–)　2681
Pak. physician, civil servant

Safiya bint Musafir (fl. 670s)　126
Arab poet

Sagan, Françoise (1935–2004)　2945
Fr. writer

Sage, Lorna (1943–2001)　3453
Welsh author, literary critic

Sainte-Marie, Buffy (1941–)　3301
Can. songwriter, civil rights activist, singer; founder, North American Women's Association

Sakanoé, Lady　see IRATSUME, KASA NO

Salavarrieta, Policarpa (1791?–1817)　826
Colo. revolutionary, martyr, seamstress; a.k.a. La Pola

Salisbury, Joyce Ellen (1944–)　3537
Amer. historian, educator (history)

Salome (fl. 20s C.E.)　82
Judaean princess; d. Herodias* and Herod Philip, gm. Herod Antipas

Salter, Mary Jo (1954–)　4270
Amer. editor, poet, educator

Salter, Stephanie (1949–)　3935
Amer. journalist

Salvatore, Christina (1969–)　4801
Amer. accountant, tax specialist, women's rights advocate; grandd. Henry George Warren, MS state senator

Samalin, Nancy (1937–)　3055
Amer. author, parent education specialist, public speaker

Samar, Sima (1957–)　4430
Afghan physician, public servant; chair, Afghan Independent Human Rights Commission (AIHRC); 1st Hazara woman to obtain a medical degree; Asia Democracy & Human Rights Awards, 2008

Samaritan Woman (fl. 20s C.E.)　83
Samaritan biblical figure

Sameh, Catherine (1965–)　3530
Amer. businesswoman, activist

Samman, Ghada (1942–)　3318
Syr./Leb. writer

Sampson, Edith Spurlock (1898?–1979)　1874
Amer. lawyer, judge, civil servant; first African-American delegate to the U.N.; first woman to receive a law degree from Loyola Univ.; first black woman to be elected as a U.S. judge (Chicago Municipal Court, 1962)

Sampter, Jessie Ethel (1883–1938)　1600
Amer./Isr. poet, activist, political, Zionist

Sams, Jamie (1951–)　4070
Amer. nonfiction writer, humanitarian, artist

Samson, First wife of (fl. 1080s B.C.E.)　26
Philistine biblical figure; first w. Samson (1; Old Testament Isr. judge and warrior), Samson's best man (2)

Sanchez, Carol Lee (1934–)　2911
Amer. educator, painter, poet; s. Paula Gunn Allen*

Sanchez, Cristina (1972–)　4869
Span. matador

Sanchez, Georgiana Valoyce (fl. 1980s–2000s)　4940
Amer. writer, storyteller; a.k.a. Tohono-O'Odham (Chumash name)

Sanchez, Sonia (1934–)　2912
Amer. educator (English), poet, children's writer, playwright, activist; née Wilsonia Benita Driver

Sánchez-Scott, Milcha (1955–)　4331
Colombian/Indonesian/Chin./Dutch/Amer. playwright; DCCA, 1980

Sand, George (1804–1876)　887
Fr. writer; née Amadine Aurore Lucie Dupin; w. Baron Dudevant

Sandler, Bernice "Bunny" R[esnick] (1928–)　2641
Amer. scholar, educator, feminist, lecturer; a.k.a. "The Godmother of Title IX"

Sanger, Margaret (1883–1966)　1535
Amer. editor, civil rights activist, nurse, writer; née Higgins; pioneer of birth-control movement; founder, International Planned Parenthood Federation, 1948; organizer, first World Population Conference, 1927; NWHF

Sangster, Margaret E[lizabeth] (1838–1912)　1085
Amer. poet, writer, editor; née Munson

Sanu, Chigami (fl. 710s–d. 784)　135
Jap. civil servant, poet; w. Nakatomi Yakamori

Sapphira　see BARBER, MARY

Sapphire (1950–)　4002
Amer. novelist, poet, performance artist

Sappho (fl. 610s–d. 635 B.C.E.)　46
Greek choral teacher, poet, dance teacher; a.s.a. Sappha, Psappho, a.k.a. The Poetess, The Tenth Muse, The Pierian Bee; first lyric poet in recorded history

Sappington, Margo (1947–)　3789
Amer. choreographer

Sarabi, Habiba (1956–)　4392
Afghan politician, reformer, hematologist; a.s.a. Sarobi; née Mazari Sharif; Governor of Bamiyan Province, Afghanistan, 2005– ; est. Afghanistan's first national park; first woman governor in country

Saragossa, Maid of　see AUGUSTÍN, MARÍA

Sarah (1987?–1860 B.C.E.)　8
Chaldean/Canaanite biblical figure; a.s.a. Sarai; w. Abraham, m. Isaac

Sarah (fl. 720s)　45
Mede/Assyr. biblical figure; d. Raguel and Edna,* w. Tobias (8); first seven husbands killed by a demon on their wedding nights

Sarandon, Susan (1946–)　3695
Amer. actor, activist, civil rights; née S— Abigail Tomalin; partner, Tim Robbins (1958–) actor, screenwriter, director, producer, activist; UNICEF Goodwill Ambassador, 1999; Oscar, 1995

Sarashina, Lady (1008–1060?)　173
Jap. diarist; d. Takasue no Musume (court official), c. Michitsune (author)

Sarraute, Nathalie (1900–1999)　1921
Russ./Fr. playwright, essayist, novelist; née Tcherniak; Internatl. Prize for Literature, 1964

Sarton, [Eleanor] May (1912–1995)　2189
Belg./Amer. writer, poet, novelist, playwright; d. George S— (scholar; founder of Isis journal, 1912)

Saruhashi, Katsuko (1920–2007)　2389
Jap. research scientist; noted for her study of carbon dioxide in seawater and in radioactive fallout; founder, Society of Japanese Women Scientists, 1958; founder, Assoc. for the Bright Future of Women Scientists and the Saruhashi Prize, 1980; first woman to receive doctoral degree in chemistry from Tokyo University, 1957

Sassen, Georgia (1949–)　3936
Amer. psychologist, educator

Sasso, Sandy Eisenberg (1947–)　3790
Amer. rabbi; first woman ordained by Reconstructionist movement

Satran, Pamela Redmond (1953–)　4205
Amer. novelist, journalist, web developer; w. Richard S— , news editor; fdr., Montclair Editors & Writers (MEWS), 2001

Satrapi, Marjane (1969–)　4802
Iran./Fr. princess, graphic novelist, illustrator, film director; great-grandd. Nasser al-Din Sha, Sah of Persia (1848–1896); fdr., Cinema for Peace, 2008

Saunders, Cicely, Dame (1918–2005)　2329
Eng. physician, writer; w. Marian Bohusz-Szyszko (Pol. artist, 1901–); founder of St. Christopher's Hospice, London, 1967; OBE, 1965; DBE, 1979

Saunders, Margaret Baillie (1873–1949)　1420
Eng. writer

Savage-Rumbaugh, Susan (1949?–)　3937
Amer. linguist, primatologist, psychologist

Savitsky, Esther (1898?–197-?)　1875
Russ./Amer. retail clerk, homemaker; née Tanklefsky; m. Bella Abzug*

Sawyer, Diane (1945–)　3610
Amer. TV reporter; w. Mike Nichols (stage & film director, actor, comedian, 1931–)

Sawyer, Ruth (1880–1970)　1556
Amer. writer (children)

Sayers, Dorothy L[eigh] (1893–1957)　1782
Eng. writer; mn. Fleming

Scanlan, Susan (1947?–)　3791
Amer. administrator (NGO), activist, women's rights; chair, Natl. Council of Women's Organizations (NCWO)

Scarf, Maggie (1932–)　2819
Amer. author, scholar, journalist

Scattergood, Sarah "Sally" Park (fl. 1970s–90s)　4832–4833
Amer. educator, educational activist; founder, Education for Parenting, 1978

Schaeffer, Susan Fromberg (1941–) 3302
Amer. poet, educator, writer

Schapiro, Mary L. (1955–) 4332
Amer. economist, public servant, lawyer; chair, SEC (1st woman), 2009–

Schapiro, Miriam (1923–) 2468
Amer. collage artist, feminist, educator (art); w. Paul Brach (artist, arts administrator); developed "femmage," a form of collage using such media as lace and fabric

Schiaparelli, Elsa (1896–1973) 1834
Ital. fashion designer

Schine, Cathleen (1953–) 4206
Amer. novelist

Schirmacher, Kathe (1865–1930) 1319
Ger. feminist, author

Schlafly, Phyllis (1924–) 2496
Amer. writer, political activist; née Stewart; fdr., Eagle Forum (1972)

Schlessinger, Laura Catherine (1947–) 3792
Amer. radio host, author, commentator

Schmidt, Karen Anne (1945–) 3611
Amer. politician; state representative (D-WA), 199?–

Schnall, Marianne (1967–) 4758
Amer. writer, activist, women and environmental; fdr., Feminist.com, 1995 & EcoMall.com, 1993

Schnall, Susan (1943–) 3454
Amer. military rights activist, nurse, Navy; née Levine

Schneiders, Sandra Marie (1936–) 3005
Amer. theologian, author

Schneir, Miriam (1933–) 2864
Amer. scholar, writer, editor

Schreiner, Olive [Emile Albertina] (1855–1920) 1208
S. Afr. social critic, writer, feminist; pseud. Ralph Iron

Schroeder, Patricia (1940–) 3227
Amer. politician, lawyer, educator; née Scott; U.S. congresswoman (D-CO), 1973–1997; first woman elected to Congress from Colorado; first female member of Congress with young children; cofounder, Congressional Women's Caucus, 1977; NWHF

Schtok, Fradel (1890–193–?) 1718
Pol./Amer. writer

Schücking, Heffa (1959–) 4506
Ger. environmental activist; fdr.-dir., Urgewald, 1992; Goldman, 1994

Schulder, Dinae B. (1937–) 3056
Amer. lawyer, educator

Schultz, Tammy S. (1974?–) 4887
Amer. educator, national-security studies, defense theorist

Schumann-Heink, Ernestine (1861–1936) 1278
Aus./Amer. opera singer; née Roessler

Schurman, Anna Maria van (1607–1678) 422
Ger. letter writer, theological scholar, artist, author

Schutz, Susan Polis (1944–) 3538
Amer. poet, businesswoman, women's rights activist; m. Jared S— P— (1975–), philanthropist, politician; fdr., Blue Mountain Arts

Schutzinn, Katharina see ZELL, KATHERINE

Schwarcz, Vera (1947–) 3793
Romanian/Amer. China scholar, linguist, writer; Guggenheim, 1989–90

Schwarz, Christina (1963?–) 4653
Amer. writer, creative fiction, teacher

Schwimmer, Rosika (1877–1948) 1499
Hung./Amer. pacifist, suffragist

Scindia, Yashodhara Raje, Rajmata (1954–) 4271
Eng./Ind. political leader, royalty; d. Madhavrao Scindia, Maharajah, and Vijaya Raje, politician; MP; princess

Scofield, Sandra [Jean] (1943–) 3455
Amer. novelist

Scott, Blanche Stuart (1892–1970) 1753
Amer. adventurer; first woman in the U.S.A. to drive cross country in an automobile and to fly a plane; NWHF

Scott, Evelyn (1893–1963) 1783
Amer. writer

Scott, Hazel [Dorothy] (1920–1981) 2390
W. Ind./Amer. pianist, singer, actor, entertainer; ex-w. Adam Clayton Powell, Jr. (politician and clergyman, 1908–72); first black woman to have her own TV show (1950)

Scott, Joanna (1960–) 4554
Amer. novelist, educator; w. James Longenbach, poet, literary critic, professor; MacArthur; Guggenheim; Pushcart

Scott, Mary (fl. 1770s) 751
Eng. poet; a.k.a. Miss Scott of Ancram

Scott, Melissa [Elaine] (1960–) 4555
Amer. novelist; p. Lisa A. Barnett (writer); founder, Wavelengths (journal)

Scott, Robyn (1981–) 4949
Brit./Bots. journalist, author

Scott-Maxwell, Florida (1883–1979) 1601
Amer./Scot. actor, writer, psychologist, playwright, suffragist

Scudder, Janet (1873–1940) 1421
Amer. painter, writer, sculptor; née Neta Deweze Frazee S—

Scudéry, Madeleine de (1607–1701) 423
Fr. poet, novelist; a.s.a. Madeleine Scudéri, a.k.a. Sapho; s. George de S— (playwright, critic)

Seaberg, Rönnog (1932–2007) 2820
Swed./Amer. educator, novelist, poet; w. Steve S—, saxophonist; Noted for "acrobatic poetry" readings performed, clothed or unclothed, while her husband played the saxophone

Seacrest, Susan (1954–) 4272
Amer. environmental activist; fdr., Groundwater Fdn., 1985

Seager, Joni (1954–) 4273
Can./Amer. geographer, feminist, nonfiction writer, educator

Sears, Vicki (1941–) 2879
Amer. therapist, feminist, teacher, writer, consultant (gender and environment), educator (geography); Rockefeller, Ford

Sebelius, Kathleen (1948–) 3864
Amer. politician; née Gilligan; d. John J. G— (1921–), politician, former gov. Ohio; Gov. KA-D, 2003–09; Sec. of Health & Human Svcs., 2009–

Sebold, Alice (1962–) 4630
Amer. novelist

Sedges, John see BUCK, PEARL

Sedgwick, Catherine Maria (1789–1867) 812
Amer. novelist, author, educator; d. Theodore S— (U.S. representative and senator, Massachusetts state supreme court justice)

Sedgwick, Eve Kosofsky (1950–2009) 4003
Amer. literary critic, educator; pioneer of gender and queer studies

See, Carolyn [Penelope] (1934–) 2913
Amer. writer

Seeger, Ruth Crawford (1901–1953) 1939
Amer. composer, modernist, folk music specialist; w. Charlie S— (1886–1979), musicologist, composer, teacher; m. Mike S— (1933–), folk musician; Peggy S— (1935–), folk singer; stepm. Pete S— (1919–), folk singer, political activist

Seidelman, Susan (1952–) 4139
Amer. film director

Seiffert, Marjorie Allen (1885–1968) 1640
Amer. poet

Sei Shonagon see SHONAGON, SEI

Sekaquaptewa, Helen (1898–1990) 1876
Amer. autobiographer

Selby, Spring Mae (1955–) 3411
Amer. musician, comedian

Semenow, Dorothy (1930–) 2740
Amer. feminist, psychoanalyst

Semiramis (fl. 8th century B.C.E.) 42
Assyr. queen; a.k.a. Summuramat

Semmel, Joan (1932–) 2821
Amer. educator, art, artist, painter

Sempronia see LAMB, MARY

Sendzimir, Venda (1952–1996) 4140
Amer. antiwar activist, feminist, philanthropist, author; d. Tadeusz Sendzimir (1894–1989), Pol./Amer. Engineer, inventor; w. David Ludlow, photographer, social activist

Senesh, Hannah (1921–1944) 2413
Hung./Palestinian soldier, diarist, political activist; executed by Nazis

Sengers, Johanna [Maria Henrica] Levelt (1929–) 2682
Dutch/Amer. scientist, physicist; National Academy of Engineering, 1992; National Academy of Sciences, 1996

Senna, Danzy (1970–) 4834
Amer. novelist

Sentinelli, Patrizia (1949–) 3938
Ital. civil servant; deputy minister of foreign affairs

Seton, Anya (1904–1990) 2006
Amer. writer; a.s.a. Ann S—; d. Ernest Thompson S— (1860–1946) wildlife illustrator, naturalist & Grace Seton-Thompson*

Seton, Cynthia Propper (1926–1982) 2577
Amer. novelist

Seton, Elizabeth (1774–1821) 765
Amer. nun; née E— Ann Bayley, a.k.a. Mother S—; w. William Magee S—; founder, Society for Relief of Poor

Widows with Small Children (first charitable organization of New York); founder, Sisters of Charity of St. Joseph; first canonized American Saint; NWHF, 1980

Seton, Julia [Moss] (1889–1975) 1701
Amer. writer, lecturer, historian; née Buttree; w(2). Ernest Thompson S— (1860–1946) wildlife illustrator

Seton-Thompson, Grace (1872–1959) 1405
Amer. feminist, travel writer, poet, lecturer, designer; a.k.a. G— Gallatin; w(1). Ernest Thompson S— (1860–1946) wildlife illustrator, naturalist; m. Anya Seton*

Seuling, Barbara (1937–) 3057
Amer. children's writer

Seven Brothers, Mother of the (164?–161 B.C.E.) 70
Hebrew biblical figure

Severn, Jill (1947–) 3794
Amer. gardener, writer

Sévigné, Marie, marquise de (1626–1696) 451
Fr. salonist, letter writer; née M— de Rabutin Chantel; w. Marquis Henri de S—, m. Comtesse Françoise de Grignan*

Sewall, Harriet [Winslow] (1819–1889) 959
Amer. suffragist, philanthropist, abolitionist, poet

Sewall, Sarah (1961?–) 4596
Amer. scholar, defense theorist; w. Tom Conroy, politician; Rhodes scholar

Seward, Anna (1742–1809) 641
Eng. poet; a.k.a. the Swan of Lichfield

Sewell, Anna (1820–1878) 977
Eng. writer

Sewell, Sarah Ann (1844?–1920?) 1128
Eng. writer, social critic

Sexton, Anne (1928–1974) 2642
Amer. poet; née Harvey; Pulitzer, 1967

Seymour, Miranda J. (1953?–) 4207
Brit. critic, literary, novelist, biographer; w. (1) Andrew Sinclair, novelist, historian; (2) Anthony Gottlieb, editor, historian

Sforza, Caterina (1462–1509) 269
Ital. military leader, politician; d. Galeazzo Maria S— (duke of Milan), w. Girolamo Riario (1), Giacomo Feo (2), and Giovanni de 'Medici (3), m. Giovanni dalle Bande Nere

Sforza, Costanza Varano (1426–1447) 256
Ital. scholar; gd. Battista Montefeltro

Shaarawi, Huda (1879–1947) 1536
Egyp. writer, women's rights activist, philanthropist; founded the Intellectual Association of Egyptian Women, 1914

Shah, Nishita (1980–) 4941
Ind./Thai business executive

Shaheed, Farida (1953–) 4208
Pak. women's rights activist, sociologist, nonprofit administrator; dir., Shirkat Gah-Women's Resource Center

Shaikh, Shamima (1960–1998) 4556
S. Afr. feminist, editor, teacher; spearheaded Muslim Youth Movement

Shain, Merle (1935–1989) 2947
Can. writer, TV commentator, social worker

Shainess, Natalie (1915–) 2256
Amer. psychiatrist, writer, educator

Shakira, (1977–) 4919
Colo. singer, songwriter, music arranger, record producer, philanthropist; née S— Isabel Mebarak Ripoll; fdr., Pies Descalzos Fdn., 1995; UNICEF Goodwill Ambassador; Grammy (2)

Shalala, Donna Edna (1941–) 3304
Amer. civil servant; U.S. Secretary of Health and Human Services, 1993–2001

Shalit, Wendy (1975–) 4900
Amer. writer

Shalom, Imma (fl. 50 C.E.–) 91
Jerusalemite scholar; s. Rabbi Gamaliel II; w. Rabbi Eliezer ben Hyrcanus-both famous first century C.E. rabbis

Shalvi, Alice (1926–) 2578
Isr. feminist, civil servant, scholar; fdr., Israel Women's Network (1984)

Shane, Elizabeth (1877–1951) 1500
Ir. poet

Shange, Ntozake (1948–) 3865
Amer. theatrician, poet, playwright; Obie, 1977, 1980 (2)

Shanker, Wendy (1972–) 4870
Amer. writer, comedian

Sharapova, Maria (1987–) 4957
Russ./Amer. athlete (tennis); Grand Slam (3); Wimbledon, 2004; U.S. Open, 2006

Sharman, Helen (1963–) 4654
Brit. astronaut, scientist, broadcaster; Great Britain's first astronaut in space; OBE

Sharp, Joane (fl. 1610s) 427
Eng. poet

Shaw, Anna Howard (1847–1919) 1154
Eng./Amer. lecturer, suffragist, minister; NWHF

Shaw, Anna Moore (1898–1975) 1877
Amer. writer

Shaykh, Hanan (1945–) 3611.1
Leban./Eng. novelist, journalist (see al- Shaykh, Hanan)

Shaywitz, Sally E. (1942–) 3376
Amer. writer, pediatrician

Shear, Marie (1940–) 3228
Amer. writer, editor

Shearing, Joseph see BOWEN, MARJORIE

Sheba, Queen of (fl. 950s B.C.E.) 38
Arab queen; legendary m., by Solomon (wise king of Israel), of Menelek I (founder of Abyssinia)

Shebl, Riham (1977?–) 4920
Egyp. filmmaker, activist, women's rights

Sheehan, Cindy (1957–) 4431
Amer. activist, antiwar

Sheehan, Susan (1937–) 3058
Aus./Amer. journalist, author; née Margulies; w. Neil S— (1936–), Pulitzer journalist; Pulitzer, 1983

Sheehy, Gail (1937–) 3059
Amer. social critic, writer; née Henion

Sheepshanks, Mary (1945?–) 3612
Eng. novelist, poet; a.k.a. Mary Nickson

Sheindlin, Judy (1942–) 3377
Amer. lawyer, judge, TV personality, author; née Blum; a.k.a. Judge Judy

Sheldon, Alice "Alli" Bradley (1915–1987) 2257
Amer. writer; pseud. James Tiptree, Jr.

Sheldon, Karin P. (1945–) 3613
Amer. lawyer, environmental activist; exec. dir., Western Resource Advocates, 2007–

Shelley, Mary Wollstonecraft (1797–1851) 859
Eng. author; d. M— W—* and William Godwin (1756–1836; writer and political theorist), w. Percy Bysshe S— (1792–1822, poet); n. Hannah Godwin*

Shelley, Rebecca (1887–1984) 1672
Amer. pacifist; a.s.a. Shelly

Shelton, Charlotte (1947–) 3795
Amer. business consultant, educator (management), author; m. Laura S— , writer; cofounder, WiseWork; pres. & CEO, Unity, 2006–

Shen-ch'iung, Nieh (960–1279) 162
Chin. courtesan, poet

Shen Rong (1935–) 2948
Chin. translator, writer

Shepard, Alice M. (fl. 1930s) 2741
Amer. poet

Shepherd, Karen (1940–) 3229
Amer. politician; state senator, 1991–1993, U.S. congresswoman (D-UT), 1993–1995; second woman from Utah sent to Congress

Sherfey, Mary Jane (1933–) 2865
Amer. educator, psychiatrist, writer

Sheridan, Clare [Consuelo] (1885–1970) 1641
Eng. sculptor, writer; née Frewen

Sheridan, Frances (1724–1766) 595
Ir./Eng. poet, novelist, playwright; née Chamberlaine; m. Richard Brinsley S— (1751–1816; playwright)

Sheridan, Helen Selina see DUFFERIN, HELEN

Sherman, Gail Berkeley (1953–) 4209
Amer. educator

Sherman, Susan (1939–) 3158
Amer. editor, poet, playwright, educator; fdg. ed., IKON

Sherrill, Martha (1959–) 4507
Amer. journalist, novelist

Sherrington, Grace (1551/52–1620) 353
Eng. diarist; a.k.a. Lady Mildmay; d. Sir Henry S—, w. Anthony Mildmay, d.-in-law Mary M— (s. Sir Francis Walsingham)

Sherwood, Kate Brownlee (1841–1914) 1106
Amer. journalist, poet; a.k.a. "poetess of patriotism"; w. Isaac R. S— , congressman, army general

Sherwood, Margaret P[ollack] (1864–1955) 1306
Amer. poet, writer

Sherwood, Mary Martha (1775–1851) 769
Eng. author; née Butt

Shields, Carol (1935–2003) 2949
Amer./Can. novelist; Pulitzer, 1994; NBCCA, 1994; Governor General's Award, 1993

Shih Ming see YANG PING

Shikibu, Izumi, Lady see IZUMI SHIKIBU

Shikibu, Murasaki
(974–1031?) 166
Jap. poet, diarist, lady-in-waiting, novelist; great-gd. Fujiwara
no Kanesuke (poet), d. Tame-
toki, lord of Echigo; second
w. Fujiwara no Nabutaka, m.
Daini Sanmi (female poet); lady-
in-waiting to Empress Akiko;
reputed to have written the
world's first novel (*The Tale of
Genji*), 1001–1015

Shikishi Naishinno
(1151?–1201) 192
Jap. Buddhist priestess, poet,
painter, princess; a.k.a.
Nyoho; d. ex-emperor Go-
Shirakawa

Shipton, Ursula (1488–1561) 286
Eng. witch, seer; a.k.a.
Mother S—

Shiva, Vandana (1952–) 4141
Ind. physicist, activist, ecologist; dir., Bija Vidyapeeth, the
Intl. College for Sustainable
Living (Dehra Dun, India);
dir., Research Fdn. for Science, Technology and Natural
Resource Policy; Right Livelihood, 1993

Shivers, Louise (1929–) 2683
Amer. novelist; NEA, 1986

Shlain, Tiffany (1970?–) 4835
Amer. filmmaker; w. Ken
Goldberg, writer, robotics
wizard; fdr., The Webby
Awards

Shnall, Susan (1943–) 2969
Amer. military rights activist,
nurse, Navy; née Levine

Shocked, Michelle (1962–) 4631
Amer. singer, songwriter; née
Karen M— Johnston

Shonagon, Sei (966/67–1013?) 163
Jap. courtier, diarist, poet; née
Nakika; d. Kiyohara no Mo-
tosuke (poet and governor of
Province of Bingo); attendant
to Empress Temmu

Shore, Dinah [Frances Rose]
(1920–1994) 2391
Amer. actor, singer; ex-w.
George Montgomery (actor,
1916–); Emmy, 1954–1959;
SHF

Showalter, Elaine (1941–) 3305
Amer. literary critic, writer,
feminist; née Cottler

Shubrick, Mrs. Richard
(fl. 1770s–178-?) 752
Amer. householder

Shukla, Champa Devi
(1952–) 4142
Ind. environmental & labor
activist; Goldman, 2004

Shulman, Alix Kates (1932–) 2822
Amer. feminist, writer

Shur, Fanchon (1935–) 2950
Amer. dancer, choreographer,
movement therapist; w. Bonia
S— , Latvian/Israeli/Ameri-
can musician & composer;
fdr., Fanchon Shur Ceremonial Dance Theater, 1974

Sibyl, the Jewish
(fl. 190s–d. 165 B.C.E.?) 68
Egyp. evangelist, poet

Siddons, Sarah (1755–1831) 684
Eng. sculptor, actor; d. Roger
Kemble (actor, theater manager), s. John Phillip Kemble
(1757–1823; actor–manager),
w. William S— (actor, business manager), a. Fanny
Kemble*

Sidney, Margaret
(1844–1924) 1129
Amer. writer; née Harriet
Stone; mn. Mulford and
Lothrop

Sidqi (?–1703) 555
Turk. Sufi poet; d. Qamr Muhammad (scholar)

Siebert, Muriel "Mickie"
(1932–) 2823
Amer. feminist, securities
analyst; a.k.a. "the Woman
of Finance"; first woman to
hold seat on New York Stock
Exchange; NWHF, 1994

Siegel, Deborah (1969–) 4803
Amer. writer, women's rights
activist, workshop leader;
cofounder, The Scholar &
Feminist Online

Sigea, Luisa (1522–1560) 321
Portuguese scholar; tutor to
Maria, princess of Portugal

Signoret, Simone
(1921–1985) 2414
Fr. screen actor; née Ka-
minker; w. Yves Allégret (1),
Yves Montand (2; 1921– ;
actor); m. Catherine Allégret
(actress); Academy Award,
1959

Sigourney, Lydia Howard
(1791–1865) 827
Amer. magazine editor, author,
poet, teacher; née Huntley,
a.k.a. the Sweet Singer of Hartford, the American Hemans,
the Female Milton; second w.
Charles S— ; first professional
female poet in the U.S.

Sigurdardottir, Johanna
(1942–) 3378
Ice. politician, union organizer; p. Jonina Leosdottir,
writer, playwright; P.M.
Iceland, 2009– (first woman;
first gay)

Sila (fl. seventh–11th century) 131
Ind. poet

Silabhlaṭṭarika
(fl. seventh–11th century) 132
Ind. poet

Silko, Leslie Marmon (1948–) 3866
Amer. novelist, poet; NEA,
1974; Pushcart, 1977; MacArthur, 1983

Sill, Judee (1944–1979) 3539
Amer. songwriter, singer

Sills, Beverly (1929–2007) 2684
Amer. opera singer, arts
administrator; née Belle
Silverman; Grammy, 1976;
Presidential Medal of Free-
dom, 1980; NWHF

Silva, Marina [Osmarina da]
(1958–) 4469
Braz. environmental activist,
politician; Environment Minister, 2003–2008; Goldman,
1996

Silver, Joan Micklin (1935–) 2951
Amer. writer, film producer &
director

Silverman, Sarah (1971–) 4849
Amer. comedian, actor

Silvia of Sweden, Queen,
(1943–) 3456
Ger./Swed. interpreter, public
servant, human right's and
children's advocate, royalty;
née S— Renate de Toledo
Sommerlath; consort Carl
XVI Gustaf, King of Sweden
(1946–); cofounder, World
Childhood Foundation, 1999

Simeonova, Albena (1965–) 4712
Bulg. ecologist, antinuclear
activist; dir., Foundation for
Ecological Education and
Training; cofounder, Bulgar-
ian Green Federation, 1996;
Goldman, 1996

Simmons, Laura (1877–1949) 1501
Amer. poet

Simmons, Ruth (1945?–) 3614
Amer. educator, college dean;
first black pres. of Ivy League
inst. (Brown University,
2001–)

Simon, Carly (1945–) 3615
Amer. songwriter, singer; w.
James Taylor (1948– ; singer);
Grammy, 1971, 1990; Oscar,
1989; Songwriters Hall of
Fame, 1994

Simon, Kate [Grobsmith]
(1912–1990) 2190
Amer. writer, historian

Simon, Maurya (1950–) 4004
Amer. poet, educator (writing)

Simon, Patricia (1934–1993) 2914
Amer. writer

Simon, Rachel (1824–1900?) 995
Brit. diarist, community
activist; w. Oswald S—, fdr.
of "Sunday movement" (religious fellowship of Christian
theists and liberal Jews)

Simonson, Joy Rosenheim
(1919–2007) 2356
Amer. women's rights activist;
Chair, Natl. Advisory Council
on Women's Educational
Programs (1975–1982); initiated and organized the D.C.
Commission for Women,
1967–1982

Simonton, Stephanie see MAT-
THEWS-SIMONTON, STEPHANIE

Simos, Miriam see STARHAWK

Simpson, Becky (1936–) 3006
Amer. social activist; a.k.a..
"Mother Teresa of Appala-
chia"; fdg. dir., Cranks Creek
Survival Center (KY), 1982

Simpson, Nancy (1938–) 3105
Amer. poet

Sinclair, Lee (1957–) 4431.1
Amer. writer, activist, self-defense trainer

Singer, Alyson (fl. 1990s) 4970
Amer. lawyer

Singer, June K. (1918/20–2004) 2330
Amer. nonfiction writer, Jungian psychoanalyst; w. Dr. Iving
Sunshine (1910–2006), pioneering toxicologist

Singer, Maxine [Frank]
(1931–) 2776
Amer. biochemist

Sinha, Kabita (1931–1999) 2777
Bengalese poet, novelist

Sisulu, Nontsikelelo Albertina
(1919–) 2357
S. Afr. anti-apartheid activist;
widow, Walter Sisulu (1912–
2003), activist

Sittenfeld, [Elizabeth] Curtis
(1975–) 4901
Amer. novelist

Sitwell, Edith [Louisa], Dame
(1887–1964) 1673
Eng. editor, poet, literary
critic

Siunetsi, Sahakdoukht
(fl. eighth century) 148
Armen. teacher, poet, musician

Skinner, Cornelia Otis
(1901–1979) 1940
Amer. entertainer, actor,
writer; d. Otis S— (1858–
1942; actor)

Sklarek, Norma Merrick
(1928–) 2643
Amer. architect; first black
woman licensed as an architect in U.S.A. and to form her
own firm

Skram, Amalie (1846–1905) 1147
Nor./Danish novelist, feminist;
w. Erik Skram, Danish writer

Skrine, Agnes Higgenson see
O'NEILL, MOIRA

Slaney, Mary Decker (1958–) 4470
Amer. runner; w. Richard
S— , discus thrower; holds 7
Amercan records; Olympic
Gold (3)

Slapsak, Svetlana (1948–) 3867
Yug. novelist, linguist, historian, cultural

Slater, Lauren (1963–) 4655
Amer. memoirist, psychologist

Slaughter, Anne-Marie
(1958–) 4471
Amer. college administrator,
educator, author; dean, Princeton's Woodrow Wilson School
of Public & Intl. Affairs; dir.,
policy planning, U.S. State
Dept., 2009– (first woman)

Slave girl who was a soothsayer
(fl. 50s C.E.) 92
Greek slave

Sleigh, Sylvia (1916–) 2275
Welsh/Amer. artist, painter; w.
Lawrence Alloway, art critic

Slick, Grace (1939–) 3159
Amer. songwriter, singer,
visual artist; née Wing; Rock
and Roll Hall of Fame, 1996

Sloan- Hunter, Margaret [Bentson]
(1947–2004) 3796
Amer. civil rights activist;
cofounder, National Black
Feminist Organization

Slocumb, Mary (1760–1836) 709
Amer. patriot, plantation manager; née Hooks

S. M. [The Scottish Minstrel] see
NAIRNE, CAROLINA

Small, Meredith (1950–) 4005
Amer. anthropologist, educator (anthropology), science
journalist

Smaller, Barbara (1953–) 4210
Amer. cartoonist

Smart, Elizabeth (1913–1986) 2211
Can. poet, author

Smeal, Eleanor [Marie Cutri]
(1939–) 3160
Amer. feminist, nonprofit
administrator, civil rights
activist; president, NOW,
1977–87; fdg. pres., Feminist
Majority Fdn.

Smedley, Agnes (1892–1950) 1754
Amer. author, lecturer

Smiley, Jane [Graves] (1949–) 3939
Amer. writer, author; Fulbright, 1976–77; NEA, 1978,
1987; Pulitzer, 1991; NBCCA,
1991

Smith, Anna Deavere (1950–) 4006
Amer. educator, actor, play-
wright; MacArthur, 1996;
Obie, 1992; DCCA; DDA

Smith, Anna Young
(1756–1780?) 688
Amer. poet; pseud. Sylvia; n.
Elizabeth Graeme Ferguson*

Smith, Arabella [Eugenia]
(1844–1916) 1130
Amer. poet

Smith, Barbara (1946–) 3697
Amer. anthologist, poet; cofounded (w/ Audre Lorde*
and Cherríe Moraga*) the
first publishing collective
by women of color, Kitchen
Table: Women of Color Press

Smith, Bessie (1898–1937) 1878
Amer. songwriter, singer;
NWHF; SHF; RRHF, 1989

Smith, Betty (1896–1972) 1835
Amer. writer

Smith, Charlotte (1749–1806) 658
Eng. novelist, translator, poet;
née Turner; d. Catherine Dorset (poet)

Smith, Dodie (1896–1990) 1836
Eng./Amer. novelist, screen-
writer, playwright; pseud.
C. L. Anthony; née Dorothy
Gladys Beesley

Smith, Dorothy E[dith]
(1926–) 2579
Eng./Can. sociologist,
feminist; s. Ullin Place, brain
specialist; Milner Place, British
poet; founded discipline of
Institutional Ethnography

Smith, Elizabeth Oakes
(1806–1893) 899
Amer. lecturer, writer, suffragist, social reformer; née Prince,
pseud. Ernest Helfenstein

Smith, Evelyn Elizabeth
(1930?–2002?) 2742
Amer. writer

Smith, Hazel Brannon
(1914–1994) 2228
Amer. newspaper publisher,
editor, journalist; Pulitzer,
1964

Smith, Janna Malamud
(1952–) 4143
Amer. psychotherapist, writer;
d. Bernard M— (writer,
1914–86)

Smith, Laura Frost
(1893–1998) 1784
Amer. pacifist, nurse; oldest
known living (as of 1998)
American veteran of World
War I

Smith, Lee (1944–) 3540
Amer. writer

Smith, Liz (1923–) 2469
Amer. columnist; née Mary
Elizabeth S—; a.k.a. "the
Grand Dame of Dish"

Smith, Margaret Bayard
(1778–1844) 7777
Amer. journalist, author

Smith, Margaret Chase
(1897–1995) 1857
Amer. politician; U.S. congresswoman, 1940–49,

Senator (R-ME), 1949–73;
first woman elected to both
U.S. House and Senate; longest serving woman in Senate
history; NWHF

Smith, May Riley (1842–1927) 1110
Amer. writer, poet

Smith, Nora Archibald
(1859–1934) 1250
Amer. writer, poet, educator;
s. Kate Douglas Wiggin*

Smith, [Patricia Lee] "Patti"
(1946–) 3696
Amer. singer, poet, song-
writer, political activist; a.k.a.
"the Godmother of Punk";
Rock and Roll Hall of Fame,
2007

Smith, Robyn [Carolyn]
(1944–) 3541
Amer. jockey; w. Fred Astaire
(1899–1987; dancer, film
star); first woman jockey to
win a major stakes horse race

Smith, Sarah (1947–) 3797
Amer. writer, educator

Smith, Sophia (1796–1870) 851
Amer. philanthropist;
founder, Smith College
(Northampton, Massachu-
setts); NWHF

Smith, Stevie (1902–1971) 1956
Eng. writer, poet; née Florence
Margaret S—

Smith, Zadie (1975–) 4902
Eng. writer; s. Doc Brown,
rapper

Smyth, Ethel Mary, Dame
(1858–1944) 1237
Eng. feminist, conductor,
composer

Snitow, Ann (1943–) 3457
Amer. writer

Snortland, Ellen (1953–) 4211
Amer. playwright, performer,
writer, women's rights activist,
filmmaker, columnist

Snow, Helen Foster
(1907–1997) 2073
Amer. writer, educator, researcher; pseud. Nym Whales;
w. Edgar S—

Snow, Phoebe (1952–) 4144
Amer. songwriter, singer, mu-
sician, guitarist; née P— Ann
Laub

Snowe, Olympia (1947–) 3798
Amer. politician; née O—
Jean Bouchles; w. (1) Peter
S— (d. 1973), politician; (2)
John McKernon, politican;
U.S. Senator (R-ME), 1995–

Sofer, Dalia (1972–) 4871
Iran./Amer. writer

Sofía of Spain, Queen (1938–) 3106
Greek/Span. royalty, hu-
manitarian, human right's
activist; née Princess Sofía

of Greece and Denmark; d.
Paul of Greece & Frederika of
Hanover; consort King Juan
Carlos (1938–)

Sofola, Zulu Zulu
(1935–1995) 2952
Nigerian educator, play-
wright; first published and
established female Nigerian
dramatist; Ford, 1969–72;
Fulbright, 1988

Softic-Kaunitz, Elma (1961–) 4597
Serb. educator (philosophy),
diarist

Sokoloff, Natalie J(ean)
(1944–) 3542
Amer. nonfiction writer,
educator (sociology), prison
reform activist

Sokolow, Anna (1910–2000) 2141
Amer. dancer, choreographer;
Samuel H. Scripps American
Dance Festival Award, 1991;
Natl. Museum of Dance's
Dance Hall of Fame, 1998

Solanas, Valerie (1940–1988) 3230
Amer. feminist, actor, painter

Solis, Hilda (1957–) 4432
Amer. politician, government
analyst; U.S. Rep (D-CA),
2001–2008; U.S. Sec. Of
Labor, 2009–

Solomon, Hannah Greenebaum
(1858–1942) 1238
Amer. activist, religious;
fdr., Natl. Council of Jewish
Women (1893); NWHF

Somers, Helen [Matthews]
(1932–) 2824
Amer. politician, educator,
finance analyst; Wash. State
Rep. (D), 1973–2008

Somerset, duchess of see THYNNE,
FRANCES

Somerville, Mary (1780–1872) 783
Scot. translator, mathematician, astronomer, physical
geographer; née Fairfax;
w. William S— (2); first
women's college at Oxford
University was funded by and
named

Sommers, Christina Hoff
(1950–) 4007
Amer. author, educator, philosophy, lecturer

Song, Cathy (1955–) 4333
Amer. poet

Sonneschein, Rosa
(1847–1932) 1156
Hung./Amer. journalist, editor, religious activist; d. Rabbi
Hirsch-Baer Fassel (eminent
Hungarian); w. Rabbi Solomon Hirsch S—, d.; est. The
American Jewess, periodical
for Council of Jewish Women
(1895–99)

Sontag, Susan (1933–2004) 2866
Amer. screenwriter, essay-
ist, cultural critic; p. Annie
Leibovitz*; National Book
Critics Circle Award, 1978;
MacArthur Fellowship, 1990;
National Book Award, 2000

Soong Chin-ling see SUN YAT-SEN,
MADAME

Soong Mei-ling see CHIANG KAI-
SHEK, MADAME

Sophia Dorothea of Celle (Zelle)
(1666–1726) 510
Eng. queen; a.k.a. princess
of Celle, princess of Alden;
d. George William, duke of
Brunswick-Lünsberg-Zelle,
w. George I (1660–1727;
king of Great Britain and
Ireland, 1714–27), m. George
II (1683–1760; king of Great
Britain and Ireland, 1727–
60), and Sophia Dorothea
(w. Frederick Wilhelm I of
Prussia)

Soren, Tabitha (1967–) 4759
Amer. TV news anchor; née
T— Lee Sornberger; a.k.a.
T— Lee Lewis; w. Michael
Lewis, writer; Peabody,
1993

Sorrels, Rosalie (1933–) 2867
Amer. folksinger, songwriter

Sotomayor, Sonia (1954–) 4273.1
Amer. Supreme Court justice,
lawyer, law educator; federal
judge on the U.S. Court of Appeals for the Second Circuit

Southampton, countess of see
VERNON, ELIZABETH

Southern, Eileen Jackson
(1920–2002) 2392
Amer. writer, musicologist; first
black woman to be appointed
as a tenured full professor at
Harvard University; cofounder,
The Black Perspective in Music
(first musicological journal on
the study of African-American
music; 1973)

Southey, Caroline Anne
(1786–1854) 802
Eng. poet, letter writer; née
Bowles, a.k.a. Cowper of Our
Modern Poetesses; second
w. Robert S— (1777–1843);
poet, literary critic, biographer)

Sowerby, Githa (1876–1970) 1482
Eng. playwright, writer (chil-
dren); w. John Kendell, Eng.
Writer (pseud. Dum-dum)

Sowernam, Ester (fl. 1610s) 428
Eng. author

Spacks, Patricia [Ann] Meyer
(1929–) 2685
Amer. literary critic, editor,
educator

Spafford, Anna (1842–1923) 1111
Nor./Amer. missionary; née
Larssen (later Lawson); w.
Horatio S— (1828–1888, law-
yer, psalmist, missionary; m.
Bertha S—*; cofounder, The
American Colony (Jerusalem),
1881

Spafford, Bertha (1878–1968) 1518
Amer./Jerusalem nurse,
humanitarian, author;
mn. Vester; d. Horatio
Vester— (1828–1888), lawyer,
psalmist, missionary, & Anna
S—*; fdr., Spafford Children's
Ctr., 1925 (Jerusalem)

Spalding, Catherine
(1793–1858) 842
Amer. nun; first mother superior of the Sisters of Charity
of Nazareth; founder, St.
Vincent's Orphan Asylum,
founder, first Catholic infirmary in Kentucky (now St.
Joseph's Hospital)

Spallone, Patricia (1951–) 4071
Amer./Eng. reproductive activist, educator (science and
technology)

Spark, Muriel [Sarah]
(1918–2006) 2331
Scot. poet, writer; née Cam-
berg

Sparke, Anthony see LAMBRUN,
MARGARET

Speare, Dorothy
(1898–1951) 1879
Amer. scenarist, writer; a.k.a.
Mrs. Franklin Butler Christmas

Spears, Britney (1981–) 4950
Amer. singer, entertainer;
Grammy, 2005

Speght, Rachel (1597–1630?) 405
Eng. polemicist, poet; d.
Thomas S— (?); first English
woman to write a feminist polemic under her own name

Spellberg, Denise A.
(Contemporary) 4986
Amer. educator, history,
author

Spence, Jo (1934–1992) 2915
Eng. photographer, feminist

Spencer, Anna Garlin
(1851–1931) 1185
Amer. feminist, educator, minister, social reformer

Spencer, Lilly Martin
(1822–1902) 985
Amer. painter

Spender, Dale (1943–) 3458
Aust. feminist scholar, nonfiction writer, educator

Speranza see WILDE, JANE

Spero, Nancy (1926–) 2580
Amer. painter & printer; w.
Leon Golub (1922–2004),
artist

Spewack, Bella (1899–1990) 1891
Romanian/Amer. playwright,
screenwriter, librettist; née
Cohen; w. Samuel S— (col-
laborator)

Speyer, Leonora (1872–1956) 1406
Amer. poet, violinist, educator; née Von Stosch; Pulitzer,
1927

Spicer, Susan (1953–) 4212
Amer. chef, restauranteur

Spider Woman (3500?— B.C.E.?) 2
Amer. Hopi goddess; considered by Hopis to be creator
of life

Spiotta, Dana (1972?–) 4872
Amer. writer, fiction, restauranteur

Spofford, Harriet (1835–1921) 1068
Amer. writer, poet; née
Prescott

Spolin, Viola (1906–1994) 2056
Amer. producer, director,
educator (theatre), actor; m.
Paul Sills (1927–2008) Amer.
producer-director of Second
City

Spretnak, Charlene (1946–) 3698
Amer. cultural & social critic,
educator, environmental activist; cofounder, Green Party

Springer, Carol (1936–) 3007
Amer. politician, business-
woman; state treasurer
(R-AZ), 1999–2003; AZ State
Senator (R), 1990–98

Springer, Nancy (1948–) 3868
Amer. novelist

Sproat, Nancy Dennis
(1766–1826) 732
Amer. poet

Spyri, Johanna (1827–1901) 1015
Swiss writer; née Heusser

Stabenow, Debbie (1950–) 4008
Amer. politician, social
worker, leadership training
consultant; née Greer; w. Tom
Athans (1961–), political
activist, radio producer; U.S.
Senator (D-MI), 2001–

Staël, Germaine de, Madame
(1766–1817) 733
Fr./Swiss feminist, novelist,
literary critic; née Anna Louise G— de S—; d. Suzanne
Chardon* and Jacques Necker
(1732–1804; financier and
statesman; minister of finance
for Louis XVI); w. Baron Eric
Magnus de S— de Holstein (1;
Swed. ambassador), mistress
and w. Lt. John Rocca (2); m.,
by Vicomte Louis de Narbonne-
Lara, Auguste and Albert; c.
Mme Necker de Saussure*

Stafford, Jean (1915–1979) 2258
Amer. writer; w. Robert Lowell (1; poet, 1917–77), Oliver

Jensen (2; writer) and A. J.
Liebling (3; writer); Pulitzer,
1970

Stampa, Gaspara (1523–1554) 323
Ital. courtesan, poet, singer;
s. Baldassare S— (poet,
courtesan, singer), Cassandra
S— (poet, singer)

Stanford, Sally (1904–1982) 2007
Amer. brothel-keeper, civic
leader, author

Stanhope, Hester Lucy, Lady
(1776–1839) 773
Eng./Syr. astrologer, traveler;
a.k.a. White Queen of the
Desert; d. Charles, third earl
of S— (inventor)

Stannard, [Barbara] Una
(1927–2004) 2613
Amer. educator, writer; w.
John Backus (1924–2007),
Amer. computer scientist,
mathematician; Natl. Medal
of Science (1976)

Stannow, Lovisa
(Contemporary) 4987
Amer. health activist

Stanton, Elizabeth Cady
(1815–1902) 931
Amer. newspaper editor, abo-
litionist, suffragist, historian,
nonfiction writer; d. Daniel
C— (lawyer, congressman,
judge); co-organizer, Women's
Rights Convention in Seneca
Falls, N.Y. in 1848; cofounder,
Women's Loyal League, 1863;
cofounder, American Equal
Rights Association (AERA);
1866; cofounder, National
Woman Suffrage Association
(NWSA; 1869); cofounder,
National American Woman
Suffrage Society (NAWSA),
1890; NWHF

Stanwyck, Barbara
(1907–1990) 2074
Amer. actor; née Ruby McGee
Stevens; Emmys, 1961, 1966

Starbuck, Mary Coffyn
(1644/45–1717) 478
Amer. Quaker minister; a.k.a.
The Great Woman

Starhawk (1951–) 4072
Amer. lecturer, scriptwriter,
nonfiction writer, Wiccan minister; née Miriam Simos

Stark, Freya Madeline, Dame
(1893–1993) 1785
Fr./Eng. photographer, travel
writer

Starr, Hattie (fl. 1890s) 1719
Amer. songwriter

Stassinopoulos, Arianna see HUFF-
INGTON, ARIANA

St. Denis, Ruth (1880–1968) 1557
Amer. dancer, choreographer,
educator; née Dennis; w. Ted

Shawn (1891–1972; dancer and choreographer); cofounder, Denishawn Dance Company

Stead, Christina [Ellen] (1902–1983)　　1957
Aust. novelist; w. William J. Blake (Amer. writer, d. 1968)

Steel, Danielle [Fernande Dominique] (1947–)　　3799
Amer. novelist; née Schulein-Steel; fdr., Yo! Angel! (San Francisco); over 550 million copies of her books have been sold

Steele, Anne (1717–1778/79)　　580
Eng. hymnist, poet; pseud. Theodosia

Steichen, Joanna T(aub) (1933–)　　2868
Amer. psychotherapist, clinical teacher, author; w. Edward Steichen (1879–1973; photographer), m. Mary Calderone*

Stein, Edith (1891–1942)　　1735
Dutch nun, Carmelite, philosopher; a.k.a. Teresa Benedicta of the Cross; Saint Teresa, Blessed of the Cross; converted from Judaism to Catholicism in 1922; murdered at Auschwitz; canonized in 1998

Stein, Gertrude (1874–1946)　　1450
Amer./Fr. writer, playwright, art collector, librettist; p. Alice B. Toklas*; Obie, 1964

Stein, Linda (1943–)　　3459
Amer. sculptor, painter, feminist

Steinem, Gloria (1934–)　　2916
Amer. feminist, editor, writer; cofounder, New York magazine 1968 and Ms., 1972; cofounder, Natl. Women's Political Caucus, 1971; cofounder, Women's Action Alliance, 1971; cofounder, Coalition of Labor Union Women, 1974; fdr., Choice USA, 1991; Ceres Medal, United Nations; NWHF, Fame, 1993

Stella　see MORE, HANNAH

Stephenson, Isabella S. (1843–1890)　　1118
Eng. poet, hymnist

Steptoe, Lydia　see BARNES, DJUNA

Stern, Edith Mendel (1901–1975)　　1941
Amer. social critic, feminist, writer

Sternhell, Carol (195-?–)　　4009
Amer. educator (journalism), journalist, literary critic

Stevens, Christine (1918–2002)　　2332
Amer. animal rights advocate; a.k.a. "Mother of the Animal Protection Movement"; fdr., Animal Welfare Inst., 1951, &

Society for Animal Protective Legislation, 1955

Stevens, Christine (1964–)　　4688
Amer. drummer, music therapist, speaker, peace activist, social worker

Stevens, Nettie Maria (1861–1912)　　1279
Amer. teacher, librarian, biologist; NWHF

Stewart, Alice (1906–2002)　　2057
Eng. health activist, physician; Right Livelihood, 1985

Stewart, Elinore Pruitt (1876–1933)　　1483
Amer. homesteader, letter writer

Stewart, Eliza [Daniel] "Mother" (1816–1908)　　938
Amer. temperance leader

Stewart, Ella S[eass] (1871–?)　　1394
Amer. administrator, activist; née Phillips

Stewart, Maria [Frances] W. [Miller] (1803–1879)　　882
Amer. public speaker, educator, social reformer, writer, abolitionist

Stewart, Martha (1941–)　　3307
Amer. magazine editor, business executive, advice columnist, author, TV personality; née M— Helen Kostyra

Stewart, Mary [Florence Elinor Rainbow] (1916–)　　2276
Eng. novelist; née Rainbow

Stifter, Vicky (1951?–)　　4073
Amer. civil rights activist, nonprofit administrator; w. Rev. John Boonstra; exec. dir., NW Immigrant Rights Project, Seattle

Stiller, Nikki (Contemporary)　　4988
Amer. educator, poet, writer

Stimpson, Catharine R[oslyn] (1936–)　　3008
Amer. educator, writer, literary critic; dean of NYU's Graduate School of Arts and Science, 1998–

Stinson, Katherine (1891–1977)　　1736
Amer. architect, aviator; a.k.a. the Flying Schoolgirl; s. Marjorie, Eddie and Jack S— (aviators; all four siblings known as "the Flying Stinsons"); fourth American women to obtain pilot's license (1912); set time and distance record flying from San Diego to San Francisco, 1917

Stiver, Irene Pierce (1924–2000)　　2497
Amer. psychologist, activist, women's health, author, educator; pioneer of relational-cultural theory

St. James, Margo (1937–)　　3060
Amer. prostitute, activist; founder, Coyote (civil rights for prostitutes), 1975

St. Joan, Jacqueline (1945–)　　3616
Amer. judge, attorney, poet, women's rights activist

St. John, Christopher [Marie] (1875?–1960)　　1466
Eng. playwright, translator, novelist, suffragist, biographer; cofounder, Writers' Franchise League

St. John, Madeleine (1941–2006)　　3306
Aust./Eng. novelist

St. Johns, Adela Rogers (1894–1988)　　1804
Amer. journalist, writer; Presidential Medal of Freedom, 1970

Stockton, Annis (1736–1801)　　623
Amer. poet; née Boudinot, pseud. Emilia (a.s.a. Amelia)

Stoddard, Elizabeth (1823–1902)　　990
Amer. writer; née Barstow; mn. Holmes

Stokes, Rose Pastor (1879–1933)　　1537
Russ./Amer. civil rights activist, journalist; w. James Phelps Stokes (1872–1960)

Stone, Lucy (1818–1893)　　953
Amer. editor, abolitionist, suffragist, lecturer; w. Henry Brown Blackwell, s.-in-law, Antoinette Brown*, Emily* and Elizabeth* Blackwell; probably the first woman ever to speak on women's rights in public; cofounder, American Woman Suffrage Assoc. (AWSA; 1869); publisher, The Woman's Journal, 1870; NWHF

Stone, Merlin (1931–)　　2778
Amer. educator, nonfiction writer

Stone, Sharon (1958–)　　4472
Amer. screen actor; Emmy, 2004; Golden Globe, 1996

Stopes, Marie Carmichael (1880–1958)　　1558
Eng. poet, feminist, lecturer, botanist, educator

Storace, Nancy (1765–1815)　　728
Eng. singer; née Anna Selina S—

Storey, Violet Alleyn (1900–?)　　1922
Eng. poet

Storkey, Elaine (1943–)　　3460
Eng. philosopher, sociologist, theologian, author, media personality; née Lively; w. Alan S—, economist, writer, lecturer

Storni, Alfonsina (1892–1938)　　1755
Argen. poet

Stowe, Harriet [Elizabeth] Beecher (1811–1896)　　916
Amer. writer, social critic; s. Henry Ward Beecher (1813–87; clergyman, editor, writer), Catherine Esther S—*; great-a. Charlotte Perkins Gilman*; Hall of Fame, 1910; NWHF

Strand, Polly (1932–2003)　　2825
Amer. animal rights advocate, graphic artist, businesswoman; fdr., Gray Guerillas

Strasberg, Susan (1938–1999)　　3107
Amer. actor; d. Lee S—, director, drama coach, and founder Actors' Studio

Straus, Geneviève (1849–1926)　　1169
Fr. society leader; d. Jacques François Halévy (1838–75; composer), w. Georges Bizet (1838–75; composer); Emile S—

Streep, Meryl [Louise] (1948–)　　3869
Amer. actor; Oscar, 1979, 1982; Emmy, 1978, 2004; Golden Globe (6)

Streisand, Barbra (1942–)　　3379
Amer. filmmaker, actor, singer; w. Elliott Gould (1; 1938– ; actor), James Brolin (2; 1940– ; actor); Grammy (5); Emmy, 1964; London Critics Musical Award 1966; Oscar, 1968, 1976; Golden Globe, (7) ; SHF

Streshinsky, Naomi [Gottlieb] (1925–)　　2536
Amer. sociologist

Stronach, Belinda [Caroline] (1966–)　　4736
Can. politician, business executive, humanitarian; d. Frank S— (1932–), Austrian-Can. fdr. Maga Intl.; w. (2) Johann Olav Koss (1968–), Nor. speed skating champion; MP, 2004–08

Strong, Anna Louise (1885–1970)　　1642
Amer. journalist, writer

Strong, Harriet Williams Russell (1844–1926)　　1131
Amer. suffragist, inventor, agriculturalist, philanthropist, civic leader; primary innovator of dry land irrigation and water conservation techniques; NWHF, 2001

Strouse, Jean (1945–)　　3617
Amer. nonfiction writer, historian, administrator; NEA, 1976, 1979; Guggenheim, 1977, 1978; MacArthur, 2001

Strout, Elizabeth (1958?–)　　4473
Amer. educator, writing, writer

Strozzi, Alessandra de' Machingi (1406–1471)　　251
Ital. householder, letter writer; m. Lorenzo, Filippo and Matteo S—

Struther, Jan (1901–1953)   1942
Eng. poet, writer; née Joyce
Anstruther; w. Anthony Max-
tone Graham

Struven, Mildred Witte
(1896?–post-1983)   1837
Amer. householder; m. Jean
Harris*

Stuart, Mary see MARY OF SCOTS

Stubbes, Katherine
(1571–1591/92)   377
Eng. householder; w. Phillip
S—

Stuteville, Sarah (1980–)   4942
Amer. journalist; w. Alex
Stonehill, photojournalist; co-
founder, Common Language
Project (clpmag.org)

Suarez, Bibiana (195-?–)   3285
Puerto Rican/Amer. painter

Subramaniam, Banu (1952–)   4145
Ind./Amer. biologist, educator
(women's studies & biology)

Suckow, Ruth (1892–1960)   1756
Amer. writer; mn. Nuhn

Suffolk, duchess of see WIL-
LOUGHBY, CATHERINE

Sugawara no Takasue no Musume
(fl. 11th century)   181
Jap. poet, diarist, lady-in-waiting; d. Taira no Kanemore
(poet)

Sugimoto, Etsu Inagaki
(1874?–1950)   1451
Jap. educator, writer

Sukarnoputri, Megawati
(1947–)   3800
Indones. politician; née Diah
Permata M— Setiawati S—;
d. Sukarno (1901–1970), 1st
pres. of Indonesia & independence hero; Pres. of Indonesia,
2001–2004; first woman
president

Sullam, Sarah Copia
(1592–1641)   402
Ital. poet

Sullivan, Annie (1866–1936)   1332
Amer. educator for deaf and
blind; mn. Macy; tutored
Helen Keller*; inventor of
manual alphabet; NWHF

Sullivan, Leonor [Kretzer]
(1902–1988)   1958
Amer. politician; w. John B.
S— (U.S. congressman, 1944–
51); U.S. congresswoman
(D-Missouri), 1953–77

Sulpicia (80?–99 C.E.)   94
Roman poet; a.k.a. the
Roman Sappho

Sulpicia (fl. 60s B.C.E.–d. 14 C.E.) 76
Roman poet; n. Valerius Mes-
salla Corvinus (statesman,
patron of letters)

Sumangalamata
(fl. 6th century B.C.E.)   51
Chin. nun, Buddhist

Summerskill, Edith [Clara], Lady
(1901–1980)   1943
Eng. politician, women's
rights activist, author, physician; M.P.; cabinet minister

Summuramat see SEMIRAMIS

Sumner, Helen L. (1876–1933) 1484
Amer. children's rights advo-
cate, government official; mn.
Woodbury

Sun, Tao-hüsan
(fl. 1100s–d. 1135)   182
Chin. poet

Sun Bu-er (1124–?)   184
Chin. Taoist sage

Sun Tao-hüsan
(fl. 1100s–d. 1135)   181
Chin. poet

Sun Yat-sen, Madame
(1893–1981)   1786
Chin. civil rights activist,
lecturer, political leader;
née Soong Ch'ing-ling; w.
Sun Yat-sen (1866–1925;
physician and revolutionary
leader; father of the Republic
of China), s. Mme Chiang
Kai-shek*

Sun Yün-fêng (1764–1814)   725
Chin. poet; w. Ch'en
(scholar)

Suo, Lady (fl. 1030s–1065)   174
Jap. courtier, poet; d. Taira no
Tsugunaka (governor of Suo);
lady-in-waiting to Emperor
Go-Reizei

Susanna (fl. 580s–d. 538 B.C.E.)   53
Hebrew biblical figure; d.
Hilkiah, w. Joakim

Susman Ashkenazi, Rachel
(fl. 1560s)   364
Jerusalemite householder

Süssmuth, Rita (1937–)   3061
Ger. educator, politician;
president, Bundestag (German
parliament)

Sutcliffe, Ann
(fl. 1600s–d. 1630)   413
Eng. religious writer; w. John
S— (groom to His Majesty's
Privy Chamber)

Sutherland, Efua Theodora
(1924–1996)   2498
Ghanian theatrician, arts
administrator, playwright;
founder, Accra (experimental
theater group, 1958; be-
came Ghana Drama Studio);
founder, Ghana Society of
Writers (now the Writer's
Workshop in the Institute
of African Studies, Univ. of
Ghana, Legion); founder,
Kusum Sgoromba (children's
theater group)

Sutherland, Joan (1926–)   2581
Aust. opera singer; Grammy,
1961

Sutley, Nancy (1962–)   4632
Amer. environmental
administrator; Chair, W.H.
Council on Environmental
Quality

Sutphen, Mona (1967/68–)   4760
Amer. civil servant, author,
business consultant; W.H.
deputy chief of staff, 2009–

Suttner, Bertha Sophie Felicita von,
Baroness (1843–1914)   1119
Aus. writer, pacifist; née
Kinsky; hon. president Per-
manent International Peace
Bureau, Berne, Switzerland;
Nobel Peace Prize, 1905

Suu Kyi, Aung San see AUNG SAN
SUU KYI

Suyin, Han see HAN SUYIN

Suzman, Helen (1917–)   2303
S. Afr. politician, professor; née Gravonsky; M.P.,
1953–89; United Nations
Prize, 1978

Svirsky, Gila (1946–)   3699
Amer./Isr. translator, peace
activist; cofounder, Coalition
of Women for a Just Peace,
2000

Swallow, Ellen (1842–1911)   1112
Amer. engineer, mineralogist;
a.k.a. The first lady of Science; mn. Richards; developed
interdisciplinary science of
ecology; first woman admitted
to Massachusetts Institute of
Technology (MIT) and first
to receive degree; the first
woman mineralogist; founder,
first Women's Science Laboratory at MIT; NWHF

Swanson, Gloria [May Josephine]
(1899–1983)   1892
Amer. businesswoman, pro-
ducer, actor; née Svensson;
w. Wallace Beery (1; 1881–?;
actor), William Duffy (6;
writer); Golden Globe, 1950

Swearingen, Terri (1957?–)   4433
Amer. nurse, environmental
activist; cofounder, Tri-State
Environmental Council, 1990;
Goldman, 1997

Sweeney, Anne (1957–)   4434
Amer. business executive; w.
Lee Hsien Loong (1952–),
prime minister of Singapore;
co-chair, Disney Media Networks

Swenson, May
(1913/19–1989)   2212
Amer. poet; Bollingen Prize,
1981

Swerda, Patricia (1916–)   2277
Amer. artist, educator (gardening), horticulturist, author; née
Fine; first Anglo woman named
as Ikenobo ikebana master

Swerdlow, Amy [Miriam Galstuck]
(1923–)   2470
Amer. women's rights activist,
historian; cofounder, Women
Strike for Peace

Swetchine, Sophie-Jeanne Soymonof
(1782–1857)   791
Russ./Fr. letter writer

Swift, Kate (1923–)   2471
Amer. etymologist; see Casey
Miller; d. of Otis Peabody
& E. Longworth Swift (both
journalists)

Swindle, Renée (1971?–)   4850
Amer. novelist

Swit, Loretta (1939–)   3161
Amer. TV actor; Emmy, 1980

Syfers, Judy (1948?–)   3870
Amer. writer, women's rights
activist; m. Brady

Sykes, Roberta [Bobbi]
(1943–)   3461
Aust. writer, civil rights activist; Australian Human Rights
Medal, 1994

Sylva, Carmen (1843–1916)   1120
Ger./Romanian poet, writer;
née Pauline Elisabeth Ot-
tilie Luise, princess of Wied;
a.k.a. Elizabeth, queen of
Romania (1881–1916), w.
Carol I (1839–93?, king of
Romania, 1866–93); m. Carol
II (1893–1953, king of Romania, 1930–40); m. Carol II
(1893–1953; king of Roma-
nia, 1930–40)

Sylvia see SMITH, ANNA

Symes, Lillian (1895–?)   1819
Amer. suffragist, writer

Symonds, Caroline (1792–1803) 835
Eng. poet

Szasz, Suzy (1953–)   4213
Amer. librarian; d. Thomas
S— (1920–), Hung./Amer.
Psychiatrist, scholar

Szold, Henrietta (1860–1945) 1261
Amer. activist, religious; fdr.,
Hadassah, 1912; NWHF

Szymborska, Wislawa
(1923–)   2472
Pol. essayist, poet; w. Adam
Wlodek (1, poet); Kornel
Filipowicz (2, writer); Goethe
Prize, 1991; Herder Prize,
1995; Nobel Prize, 1996

T

Tadjo, Véronique (1955–)   4334
Ivorian/Eng. poet, writer,
illustrator, educator; 1993
UNICEF Prize

Taft, Helen Herron
(1861–1943)   1280
Amer. first lady; w. William
Howard T— (1857–1930;
politician, jurist; 27th U.S.
president, 1909–13; 10th

Supreme Court justice, 1921–30); m. Robert Alphonso T— (1889–1953; politician, 1938–53; U.S. senator, R—OH)

Tager, Marcia (194-?–2004) 3231
Amer. writer

Taggard, Genevieve (1894–1948) 1805
Amer. editor, educator, poet; mn. Wolf and Durrant

Táhirih, Fátimih Baraghání (1814/20–1852) 924–925
Iran. theologian, poet, feminist; Fátimih is pseud. (The Pure One); a.k.a. Qurratu'l-`Ayn (Comfort of the Eyes); the first act of public unveiling in Iranian history; 17th disciple, and only woman, of the Báb (of Bahá'í faith); executed

Tait, Katherine (1923–) 2473
Eng. public figure; d. Bertrand Russell (1872–1970; mathematician, philosopher)

Tall, JoAnn (1954?–) 4274
Amer. broadcaster, environmental activist; cofounder, Native Resource Coalition, 1989; Goldman, 1993

Tallent, Elizabeth (Ann) (1954–) 4275
Amer. writer; NEA, 1983

Talmadge, Betty Shingler (1924–2005) 2499
Amer. businesswoman, cookbook writer, meat broker; ex-w., Herman E. Talmadge (1013–2002), U.S. senator (1957–1981)

Talvi see ROBINSON, THERESE

Tam, Ba (fl. 1980s) 4943
Viet. diarist

Tamar (fl. 990s B.C.E.) 35
Hebrew princess; d. David (king of Israel) and Maacah, s. Absalom, half-s. Amnon

Tan, Amy [Ruth] (1952–) 4146
Amer. novelist, writer

Tan, Hwee Hwee (1974–) 4888
Singaporean novelist

Tanaka, Yukiko (1940–) 3232
Jap./Amer. translator, nonfiction writer, anthologist

T'ang Wan, Lady (fl. 12th century) 213
Chin. poet; w. Lu Yu (poet)

Tannen, Deborah F[rances] (1945–) 3618
Amer. nonfiction writer, linguist; NEH (3); Rockefeller, 1982–1983

Tanner, Beatrice Stella see CAMPBELL, PATRICK
Amer. scientist

Tapahonso, Luci (1953–) 4214
Amer. poet, writer; Southwestern Association

Indian Affairs Literature fellowship, 1981; New Mexico Eminent Scholar Award, New Mexico Commission of Higher Education 1989

Tapp, June L. (1930–) 2743
Amer. educator, psychologist

Tappan, Eva March (1854–1930) 1203
Amer. writer, poet, historian, editor

Tarabotti, Arcangela (1604–1652) 419
Ital. scholar, writer, nun; née Elana Cassandra T—; a.k.a. Galerana Baratotti

Tarasova, Yelena (fl. 1990s) 4971
Russ. Writer; w. Gennadi P. Terrasov, Rus. Diplomat?

Tarbell, Ida [Minerva] (1857–1944) 1227
Amer. historian, biographer, editor; NWHF

Tarule, Jill M[attuck] (1943–) 3462
Amer. educator, author, administrator; née Mattuck

Tattlewell, Mary (fl. 1640s) 477
Eng. author

Tauziat, Nathalie (1967–) 4761
Central African Republic/Fr. tennis champion, author

Tawil, Raymonda (1940?–) 3233
Pal. political organizer, journalist, poet; m. Suha Arafat*

Tax, Meredith (1946?–) 3700
Amer. feminist, writer; cofounder, Bread and Roses (Boston)

Taylor, Ann (1782–1866) 792
Eng. poet; a.k.a. Mrs. Gilbert; s. Jane T—*; developed, with her sister, the "awful warning" school of poetry

Taylor, Arie P. (1927–2003) 2614
Amer. military officer; first black noncommissioned officer in charge of women's Air Force training; first African-American woman legislator, CO (1973–84)

Taylor, Debbie (1955?–) 4335
Zimb. poet

Taylor, Elizabeth (1932–) 2826
Eng./Amer. actor, entrepreneur, AIDS activist; w. Conrad "Nicky" Hilton (1; 1926–78; hotel chain heir), Michael Wilding (2; 1912–79; actor), Mike Todd (3; 1907–58; film producer), Eddie Fisher (4; 1928– ; singer), Richard Burton (5; 1925–84; actor), John W. Warner (6; 1927– ; U.S. senator– Virginia), and Larry Fortenski (7; construction worker); Academy Award, 1960, 1966; Jean Hersholt

Humanitarian Award, 1992, C.B.E., 2000

Taylor, Jane (1783–1824) 795
Eng. poet; s. Ann T—*; developed, with her sister, the "awful warning" school of poetry

Taylor, Janelle S. (1972?–) 4873
Amer. socio-cultural anthropologist, educator

Taylor, Jean M. (1963?–) 4656
Amer. writer

Taylor, Jill Bolte (1959–) 4508
Amer. neuroanatomist, lecturer; a.k.a. "the Singin' Scientist"

Taylor, Katherine (1973–) 4880
Amer. novelist; Pushcart Prize & the McGinnis-Ritchie Award in fiction

Taylor, Mrs. (fl. 1680s) 526
Eng. poet

Taylor, Renée (1933–) 2869
Amer. screenwriter, director, actor; née Wexler; w. Joe Bologna (1934–), Amer. writer-actor-director

Tchen, Christina "Tina" M. (1956–) 4393
Amer. lawyer, public servant; Dir., White House Public Liaison (2009–)

Teasdale, Sara (1884–1933) 1619
Amer. poet; mn. Filsinger; Pulitzer, 1918

Teish, Luisah (1948–) 3871
Amer. performer, writer, priestess, teacher; fdr. & pres., Ile Orunmila Oshun; fnr., School of Ancient Mysteries/ Sacred Arts Center (Oakland CA, 1994)

Tekoa, Woman of (fl. 940s B.C.E.) 39
Hebrew biblical figure

Telesilla (fl. 5th century B.C.E.) 58
Greek military leader, poet, hero

Tempelsman, Cathy Rindner (fl. 1990s) 4972
Amer. journalist, author

Temple, Countess see CHAMBER, ANNA

Temple, Shirley see BLACK, SHIRLEY

Tencin, Claudine Alexandrine [Guerin] de (1685–1749) 530
Fr. salonist, author

Teng Ying-ch'ao (1903–?) 1983
Chin. public figure, government official; w. Zhou Enlai (Chou En-lai; 1898–1976); statesman

Tenneson, Joyce (1945–) 3619
Amer. photographer

Terán, Lisa St. Aubin de (1953–) 4215
Brit. author; w. George Macbeth (2), poet; Robbie Duff Scott (3), painter

Teresa [of Calcutta], Mother (1910–1997) 2142
Albanian/Ind. Roman Catholic nun, missionary; née Agnes Gonxha Bojaxhiu; founder, Missionaries of Charity, 1948; first Pope John XXIII Peace Prize; Nobel Peace Prize, 1979

Teresa of Ávila, Saint (1515–1582) 308
Span. nun, poet; née Teresa de Cepeda y Ahumada, a.s.a. Theresa, a.k.a. St. Teresa of Jesús; founded nine convents, reformed the Carmelite Order, with Saint James of Santiago, copatron saint of Spain

Teresa, Sister see MARCHOCKA, ANNA

Terracina, Laura (1519?–1577?) 311
Ital. poet

Terrell, Mary Church (1863–1954) 1299
Amer. public speaker, women's rights & black rights activist, educator; cofounder, Colored Women's League of Washington, 1892; cofounder & first president, National Association of Colored Women, 1896; founding member, NAACP, 1909

Terry, Ellen [Alice], Dame (1848–1928) 1162
Eng. actor

Terry, Lucy (1730?–1821) 611
Amer. poet, slave

Terry, Megan (1932–) 2827
Amer. playwright; née Marguerite Duffy; cofounder, Women's Theater Council (NY); Obie, 1970; NEA; Guggenheim

Terselic, Vesna (1962–) 4633
Croat. anti-war activist; cofounder, Croatian Anti-War Campaign (ARK), 1991; Right Livelihood, 1998

Tett, Gillian (1967?–) 4761.1
Eng. social anthropologist, journalist; British Business Journalist of the Year, 2008; Journalist of the Year, British Press Awards, 2009

Teubal, Savina J. (1926–2005) 2582
Argen./Amer. writer, biblical scholar

Thatcher, Margaret (1925–) 2537
Eng. scientist, chemist, attorney, tax, political leader; née M— Hilda Roberts; a.k.a. the Iron Lady; Baroness Thatcher of Kesteven; M.P., 1959; prime minister of Britain, 1979–1990; first woman to head a major government in modern Europe; took up

lifetime seat in House of Lords, 1992; Baroness Kesteven (1992)

Thaxter, Celia (1835–1894) 1069
Amer. poet; née Laighton

Theano (fl. 420s B.C.E.) 63
Greek priestess

Theodora, Empress
(508?–d. 547/48) 113
Byzantine empress, dancer, actor; w. Justinian I (483–565, emperor 527–65)

Theodosia see STEELE, ANNE

Therbusch, Anna Dorothea Lisiewka see LISIEWSKA-THERBUSCH, ANNA

Thérèse de Lisieux,
(1873–1897) 1422
Fr. nun; née Marie-Françoise T— Martin; a.k.a. The Little Flower of Jesus; canonized saint; Doctor of the Church

Thermuthis see PHARAOH'S DAUGHTER

Thomas, Aline (1910–?) 2143
Amer. songwriter

Thomas, Audrey Grace
(1935–) 2953
Amer./Can. writer, educator; née Callahan

Thomas, Edith [Matilda]
(1854–1925) 1204
Amer. poet

Thomas, Elizabeth
(1675/77?–1730/31) 520
Eng. letter writer, poet; pseud. Corinna

Thomas, Helen (1920–) 2393
Amer. journalist, author; first female officer of the Natl. Press Club; first female mbr. and pres., White House Correspondents Assn.; 1st female mbr., Gridiron Club

Thomas, Louisa [Carroll Jackson]
(1865–?) 1320
? poet

Thomas, Lynn M. (1947–) 3801
Amer. magazine editor, educator (history); née Massimino

Thomas, Marlo (1937–) 3062
Amer. actor, children's rights advocate; née Margaret Julia T—; d. Danny T— (1912–1991), Amer. Comedian, actor; w. Phil Donahue (1935–), Amer. Media personality, writer; Emmy (4); Golden Globe, 1967; Grammy, 2006

Thomas, Martha "Minnie" [Carey]
(1857–1935) 1228
Amer. college administrator, educator, suffragist, writer; cofounder, Bryn Mawr College, 1885

Thomas, Minnie (1933?–) 2870
Amer. social reformer

Thompson, Clara
(1893–1958) 1787
Amer. lecturer, physician, psychiatrist, writer, educator

Thompson, Dorothy
(1894–1961) 1676
Amer. writer, journalist; ex-w. Sinclair Lewis (novelist, 1885–1951)

Thompson, Jean (1950–) 4010
Amer. writer, educator, writing; Guggenheim, NEA

Thompson, Kay
(1911–1998) 2169
Amer. writer (children)

Thomson, Alice (1963–) 4657
Brit. journalist, writer, travel

Thorne, Barrie (1942–) 3380
Amer. professor (women's studies & sociology)

Thornton, Alice (1627–1707) 454
Eng. author, householder

Thorpe, Rose Hartwick
(1850–1939) 1181
Amer. songwriter, writer

Thrale, Hester Lynch or Mrs. Henry see PIOZZI, HESTER

Thundercloud, Katherine see WITT, SHIRLEY

Thurman, Judith (1948?–) 3872
Amer. critic, literary, biographer; NBA, 1983

Thynne, Frances (?–1754) 679
Eng. poet; a.k.a. duchess of Somerset; pseud. Cleora, Eusebia

Tibergeau, Marchioness de
(fl. 17th century) 552
Fr. poet, patron of literature; née Silery; n. La Rochefoucauld (1613–80; moralist)

Tibors (1130?–1182) 187
Provençal trobairitz; s. Raimbaut d'Orange (troubadour), w. Bertrand des Baux

Tiburzi, Bonnie [Linda]
(1948–) 3873
Amer. aviator; first woman to be hired as a pilot by a major U.S. airline

Tiefer, Leonore (1944–) 3543
Amer. activist, psychologist, writer

Tighe, Mary (1772–1810) 760
Ir. poet; née Blackford

Tikaram, Tanita (1969?–) 4804
Amer. songwriter, singer

Tilghman, Shirley M[arie]
(1946–) 3701
Can./Amer. molecular geneticist, university administrator, educator; pres., Princeton Univ. 2001– ; 1st woman to hold post

Tillman, Lynne (1947–) 3802
Amer. short story writer, educator (writing), novelist; p. David Hofstra, musician

Tillmon, Johnnie (1926–2001) 2583
Amer. welfare rights activist; w. Harvey Blackston ("Harmonica Fats"; 1917–2000), musician

Ting Ling (1906–1985/1986) 2058
Chin. feminist, writer, communist; née Jiang Weizhi, a.s.a. Ding Ling, pseud. Chiang Ping-tzu; Stalin Prize for Literature, 1951

Tinti, Hannah (1972–) 4874
Amer. writer, editor, magazine; cofounder, One Story magazine, 2002

Tipton, Billy (1914–1989) 2229
Amer. saxophonist; née Dorothy Lucille T—

Tipton, Jennifer (1937–) 3063
Amer. lighting designer; Tony, 1977; Obie, 1979

Tirzah see ZELOPHEHAD, FIVE DAUGHTERS OF

Tobias, Sheila (1935–) 2954
Amer. author, math and science consultant, feminist

Todd, Mabel Elsworth
(1880–1956) 1559
Amer. educator, dancer, writer

Todosijevic, Jelica (fl. 1990s) 4973
Yug. lesbian & AIDS activist, e-mail trainer

Tohidi, Nayereh (1963?–) 4658
Iran./Amer. educator (gender studies), human rights activist

Toklas, Alice B (1877–1967) 1502
Amer./Fr. writer, art & literary figure; p. and secretary to Gertrude Stein*

Tollet, Elizabeth (1694–1754) 541
Eng. poet, playwright

Tolstaya, Tatyana (1951–) 4074
Russ. writer, TV host, publicist; a.s.a. Tatiana; grandd. Aleksei Nikolaevich Tolstoi, novelist, & Natalia Krandievskaya T— , poet; s. Natalia T— , writer

Tolstoy, Sophie (1844–1919) 1132
Russ. diarist; née Behrs; w. Leo T— (novelist, 1828–1910)

Tomassi, Debbie (1961–) 4598
Amer. cartoonist

Tomioka, Taeko (1935–) 2955
Jap. poet, writer

Tomlin, Lily (1936–) 3009
Amer. comedian, actor; p. & collaborator, Jane Wagner*; Grammy, 1971; Emmy (3); Tony (2)

Tompkins, Jane P[arry]
(1940–) 3234
Amer. literary critic, educator (English and education)

Tonna, Charlotte Elizabeth
(1790–1846) 821
Eng. educator, poet, author; née Browne; mn. Phelan (1)

Tillmon, Johnnie (1926–2001) 2583

Torelli, Barbara (1475–1533) 279
Ital. poet; w. Bentivoglio (1), Ercole Strozzi (2); friend of Lucrezia Borgia*

Torgovnick, Marianna
(1949–) 3940
Amer. educator (English), nonfiction writer; a.k.a. M— DeMarco T—; ABA; NEH, 1977; Guggenheim, 1981

Tornimparte, Alessandra see GINZBURG, NATALIA

Törnqvist, Mia (1957–) 4435
Swed. playwright; d. Arne T— (playwright, poet, art critic); p. Christopher Torch (artistic & stage director); artistic director, Korsväg (cultural crossroads program); Government's Prize; Critic's Prize, 1995

Toro, María Sáurez (1948–) 3874
Puerto Rican/Costa Rican radio producer, educator, feminist, journalist; co-dir., FIRE (Feminist Intl. Radio Endeavor), 1991

Torrella, Ippolita see CASTIGLIONE, IPPOLITA

Torres, Amaryllis Tigalo
(1944?–) 3544
Filipina educator, university administrator, author

Torvik, Solveig (1939–) 3162
Amer. columnist, editorial writer

Toshiko Kishida
(1863–1901) 1300
Jap. public speaker, feminist, courtier; lady-in-waiting to the Empress

Toth, Emily (1944–) 3545
Amer. nonfiction writer, biographer, educator (English)

Towne, Laura [Matilda]
(1825–1901) 1004
Amer. educator

Townsend, Eliza (1789–1854) 813
Amer. poet

Townsend, Sue (1946–) 3702
Eng. playwright, novelist

Trachtenberg, Inge (1923?–) 2474
Ger./Amer. writer

Tracy, Honor [Lilbush Wingfield]
(1913–1989) 2213
Eng. writer, humorist

Traister, Rebecca (1973?–) 4880.1
Amer. journalist, TV commentator

Trapido, Barbara [Louise]
(1941–) 3308
S. Afr./Eng. novelist, teacher

Trapnel, Anna (1622?–?) 444
Eng. mystic

Treadwell, Sophie
(1885/90–1970) 1643
Amer. playwright, actor, journalist, war correspondent, novelist

Treerat, Nualnoi (1963?–)   4659
Thai educator, economics, economist

Trefusis, Elizabeth (1763–1808)   718
Eng. poet; s. Lord Clinton

Treichler, Paula Antonia (1943–)   3463
Amer. writer, linguist, scholar

Treiman, Joyce (1922–1991)   2440
Amer. painter

Tremain, Rose (1943–)   3464
Eng. teacher, lecturer, editor, novelist; née Rosemary Jane Thomson; d. Keith Nicholas Home (writer)

Trench, Melesina (1768–1827)   742
Eng./Ir. author, poet; née Chen-evix, a.k.a. Mrs. Rich-ard T— (2); mn. St. George (1)

Trethewey, Natasha (1966–)   4737
Amer. poet, educator, English; Pulitzer, 2007

Trevisan, Anna F. (1905–)   2034
Ital./Amer. drama critic, playwright

Trevor, Claire (1912–2000)   2191
Amer. actor

Trimmer, Sarah Kirby (1741–1810)   637
Eng. educator, author, editor; a.k.a. "Good Mrs. T."; introduced use of picture books for educating children

Trinh, T. Minh-Ha (1952–)   4147
Viet./Amer. writer, poet, filmmaker, playwright; a.s.a. Thi Minh Ha T—

Trinh, Trieu Thi (fl. 270s)   101
Viet. revolutionary

Tristan, Flora (1803–1844)   883
Peru./Fr. feminist, novelist; founder, *Union ouvrière*

Trollope, Frances Milton (1780–1863)   784
Eng. novelist; née Ternan; w. Thomas Anthony T— ; m. Anthony T— (novelist, 1815–52) and Thomas Adolphus T— (author, 1810–92)

Trollope, Joanna (1943–)   3465
Eng. novelist; Historical Novel of the Year Award, Romantic Novelists Association 1979; Elizabeth Goudge Historical Award, 1980

Trotter, Catherine (1679–1749)   522
Eng. poet, essayist, playwright; a.k.a. C— Cockburn

Trotula of Salerno, (?–1097)   177
Ital. medical professor, midwife; a.k.a. Dame Trott

Troubridge, [Laura Gurney], Lady (1865?–1946)   1321
Eng. writer; n. Julia Margaret Cameron*

Truman, Bess (1885–1982)   1644
Amer. first lady; née Elizabeth Virginia Wallace; w. Harry S T— (1884–1972; politician; 33rd U.S. president, 1945–53); m. Margaret T—*

Truman, Margaret (1924–2008)   2500–2501
Amer. writer, concert singer; d. Harry T— (1884–1972; politician; 33rd U.S. president, 1945–53) and Bess T—*; w. Clifrton Daniel (1912–2000), editor-reporter

Trussoni, Danielle Anne (1973–)   4881
Amer. writer

Trusta, H.   see PHELPS, ELIZABETH

Truth, Sojourner (1797?–1883)   860
Amer. author, lecturer, abolitionist, reformer, mystic, slave; née Isabella Baumfree, a.k.a. Isabella van Wagener (her slave name); first African-American woman to speak publicly against slavery; NWHF

Ts'ai Yen (162?–239?)   98
Chin. scholar, poet; d. Ts'ai I (scholar, poet); first great Chinese woman poet

Tsushima, Yūko (1947–)   3803
Jap. novelist; née Satoko T—; d. Osamu Dazai (1909–1948), novelist

Tsvetaeva, Marina [Ivanova] (1892–1941)   1757
Russ. poet, essayist, playwright

Tubman, Harriet (1820?–1913)   978
Amer. slave, abolitionist, emancipator; née Araminta Ross, a.k.a. "Moses", "The Conductor of the Underground Railroad"; NWHF

Tuchman, Barbara (1912–1989)   2192
Amer. author, historian; née Wertheim; first woman president of AAAL, 1979; Pulitzer, 1963, 1972; NBA, 1980

Tucker, Anne (1945–)   3620
Amer. editor, historian, photographic critic

Tucker, C[ynthia] DeLores (1930–)   2615
Amer. civil rights activist, civil servant; née Nottage; first African-American and first woman to serve as commonwealth secretary (state of Pennsylvania); fdr., Natl. Congress of Black Women (NCBW); first African-American secretary of state (PA, 1971–77)

Tucker, Cynthia (1955–)   4336
Amer. syndicated columnist, editor; Pulitzer Prize, 2007

Tucker, Sophie (1884–1966)   1620
Amer. singer; née Sonia Kalish; a.k.a. "The Last of the Red Hot Mamas"; pres., American Federation of Actors (1938) ; SHF

Tudor, Mary   see MARY I OF ENGLAND

Tuite, Marjorie (1922–1986)   2441
Amer. Dominican nun, human right's activist, feminist

Tunnell, Sophie (1884–?)   1621
Amer. poet

Turbina, Nika (1974–2002)   4889
Russ. poet

Turell, Jane Colman (1708–1735)   564
Amer. poet; a.s.a. Turrell; s. Abigail C— Dennie*

Turkle, Sherry (1966?–)   4738
Amer. psychologist, educator, author

Turnbull, Agnes Sligh (1888–1982)   1689
Amer. novelist

Turnbull, Margaret (1889?–1942)   1702
Scot./Amer. playwright, scenarist, writer

Turner, Kathleen (1954–)   4276
Amer. actor; Golden Globe, 1984, 1985

Turner, Nancy Byrd (1880–1971)   1560
Amer. editor, poet

Tusquets, Esther (1936–)   3010
Span. novelist, publisher; Premio Ciudad de Barcelona, 1979; Honorary Fellow of the Society of Spanish and Spanish-American Studies

Tussman, Malka Heifetz (1893–1987)   1788
Ukrainian/Amer. poet; Manger Prize for Yiddish Literature (1981)

Tuthill, Louisa Caroline (1798/99–1879)   862
Amer. poet, author, playwright; née Huggins

Tweedie, Jill (1932/36–1993)   2828
Eng. author, journalist, feminist, broadcaster

Tyler, Anne (1941–)   3309
Amer. fiction writer; w. Tahi Mohammad Modarressi (d. 1997), Iranian psychiatrist and novelist; NBCCA, 1985; Pulitzer, 1989

Tyler, Priscilla Cooper (1816–1889)   939
Amer. actor, society leader; d.-in-law John T— (1790–1862; lawyer, politician; 10th U.S. president, 1841–45)

Tyler, Robin (1942–)   3381
Can./Amer. comedian, producer, gay and lesbian rights activist; née Chernick; granddin-law Culbert-Levy Olson, first Dem. Gov. of CA; p. Diane Olson; exec. dir., The Equality Campaign; 1st lesbian plaintiffs in CA Supreme Court Same-Sex Marriage lawsuit

Tymoshenko, Yulia Volodymyrivna (1960–)   4557
Ukrainian politician, businesswoman; prime minister, 2007– (first female)

Tynan, Katharine   see HINKSON, KATHARINE

Tyrwhit, Elizabeth (fl. 1580s)   322
Eng. courtier, author; née Oxenbridge; w. Sir Robert Tyrwhit Knight (1508–1572)

Tzu Yeh, Tzu (fl. third–fourth century)   104
Chin. poet

U

Ueland, Brenda (1892–1985)   1758
Amer. writer

Ugresic, Dubravka (1949–)   3941
Croat. novelist

Uhlenbeck, Karen (Keskulla) (1942–)   3382
Amer. mathematician; MacArthur, 1983–1988; NSF fellow 1964–65

Uhnak, Dorothy (1933–2006)   2871
Amer. police officer, novelist; née Goldstein; Edgar Award, 1968

Ukeles, Mierle Laderman (1939–)   3163
Amer. performance artist, artist, multi-media

Ukon, [Lady] (fl. 860s–d. 899)   154
Jap. courtier, poet; w. Emperor Kogun

Ulinover, Miriam (1888/94–1944)   1690
Pol. poet

Ullman, Liv [Johanne] (1938–)   3108
Nor. actor, author; Grand Cross of St. Olav; Golden Globe, 1973

Ulrich, Laurel Thatcher (1938–)   3109
Amer. writer, biography; Pulitzer, 1991

Ulrich, Mabel (1882?–?)   1586
Amer. civil servant, physician

Umansky, Ellen M. (1950–)   4011
Amer. writer, educator, religions

Underwood, S. K., Mrs.   see KERR, SOPHIE

Undset, Sigrid (1882–1949)   1587
Danish/Nor. novelist; d. Ingvald U— (archaeologist); w. Anders Castus Svarstad (Nor.

painter); Grand Cross of St. Olav, 1945; Nobel, 1928

Ung, Loung (1970–) 4836 Camb. author, human rights activist, lecturer

Unsoeld, Jolene (1931–) 2779 Amer. politician; U.S. congresswoman (D-WA), 1989-95

Urbino, Duchess of see GONZAGA, ELISABETTA

V

Vachss, Alice (1950–) 4012 Amer. attorney, prosecutor, author; w. Andrew Henry Bachss (1942–), author, child protection consultant, attorney

Valdés, Gina (1943–) 3466 Amer. poet

Valentine, Jean (1934–) 2917 Amer. poet, educator, poetry; Guggenheim, NEA

Valentinois, duchess of see POITIERS, DIANE DE

Valenzuela, Luisa (1938–) 3110 Argen./Amer. scriptwriter, lecturer, journalist, novelist

Valian, Virginia (1942–) 3383 Amer. psychologist, educator, linguist

Valiente, Doreen (1922–1999) 2442 Eng. witch, author; née Dominy; a.k.a. "the mother of modern paganism"; leader of Wiccan and pagan movements in Britain

Vallana (fl. ninth–10th century) 157 Ind. poet

Vallejo, Linda (1951–) 4075 Amer. sculptor, printmaker

Valois, Marguerite see MARGUERITE OF VALOIS

Van Buren, Abigail (1918–2003) 2333 Amer. lecturer, advice columnist; née Pauline Esther Friedman; mn. Phillips; s. Ann Landers*

van den Beld, Theodora (1952–) 4148 Dutch/Amer. restauranteur, caterer, building contractor

Van Duyn, Mona [Jane] (1921–2004) 2415 Amer. poet, educator, editor; first woman Poet Laureate of the United States; chancellor, AAP; NBA, 1970; Pulitzer, 1970; NEA; Guggenheim; Bollingen, 1970

Van Horne, Harriet (1920–1998) 2394 Amer. columnist, TV & radio personality

Van Rensselaer, Mariana Griswold (1851–1934) 1186 Amer. art critic; first American-born woman to become a professional art critic

Van Runkle, Theadora (1940–) 3235 Amer. fashion designer

Van Susteren, Greta (1954–) 4277 Amer. journalist, TV personality, lawyer; s. Lisa V— , politician

van Wagener, Isabella see TRUTH, SOJOURNER

Van Zuylen, Belle see CHARRIÈRE, MADAME DE

Vance, Linda Susan (1949–) 3942 Amer. environmental activist

Vandegrift, Margaret see JANVIER, MARGARET

Vanderbilt, Amy (1908–1974) 2103 Amer. society leader, writer

Vanderbilt, Gloria [Laura] (1924–) 2502 Amer. actor, socialite, clothing designer, writer; née Morgan; member of Vanderbilt dynasty; m. Anderson Cooper, TV newscaster

Vanzant, Iyanla (1953–) 4216 Amer. writer (inspirational), public speaker, minister; née Ronda Eva Harris

Vapnyar, Lara (1971–) 4851 Russ./Amer. writer

Varda, Agnes (1928–) 2644 Fr. filmmaker; w. Jacques Demy

Vardill, Anna Jane (1781–1852) 789 Eng. poet, author; a.k.a. Mrs. James Niven

Varnhagen, Rachel Levin (1771–1833) 757 Ger. letter writer, salonist; s. Ludwig Robert, poet

Vasquez, Enriqueta Longauex y see LONGAUEX Y VASQUEZ, ENRIQUETA

Vassiltchikov, Marie (1917–1978) 2304 Russ./Ger. civil servant, translator, nurse; d. Prince Illarion & Princess Lydia V— of St. Petersburg

Vega, Suzanne (1959–) 4509 Amer. singer, songwriter

Velho da Costa, Marie Fatima see COSTA, MARIA

Vendela (196-?–) 3490 Swed. fashion model, actor, diplomat

Vendler, Helen Hennessy (1933–) 2872 Amer. lecturer, literary critic, educator (English), writer; w.

Zeno V—, philosopher, linguist, educator

Veneman, Ann M[argaret] (1949–) 3943 Amer. lawyer, public servant; U.S. Sec. of Agriculture (2001-2005), first woman to hold post; dir., UNICEF (2005–)

Venmanipputi (fl. first–third century) 97 Ind. poet

Ventadorn, Marie de (1165?–?) 195 Fr. trobairitz; w. Ebles V de V— (lord and patron of troubadours)

Verdelle, A. J. (1960–) 4558 Amer. novelist

Verdon-Roe, Vivienne (1954?–) 4278 Amer. documentary filmmaker, environmental activist; cofounder, The Video Project, 1983; cofounder, Seaflow, 2000; Academy, 1986

Vere, Mary Ainge de see BRIDGES, MADELINE

Vernon, Elizabeth (1572?–1648?) 378 Eng. noble; a.k.a. countess of Southampton; w. Henry Wriothesley, third earl of Southampton

Vernon, Lillian (1927–) 2616 Ger./Amer. entrepreneur, business executive

Verona, Virginia (1882–?) 1588 Amer. lobbyist, political activist

Versace, Donatella (1955–) 4337 Ital. fashion designer, business executive; s. Gianni V— (1946–1997), Ital. fashion designer

Verschoyle, W. H. Foster, Mrs. see LETTS, WINIFRED

Vestris, Eliza (1791/97–1856) 828 Eng. theater director, actor; née Lucia Elizabeth Bartolozzi; gd. Francisco Bartolozzi (1727–1815; artist, engraver), w. Auguste Armand V— (1) and Charles James Mathews (2; actor); the first female lessee of the English stage

Vicioso, Sherezada [Chiqui] (1948–) 3875 Dominican/Amer. poet, literary critic, educator

Victoria, Queen (1819–1901) 960 Eng. noble, diarist; queen of Great Britain & Ireland, 1837–1901, and empress of India 1876–1901)

Vida, Vendela (1971–) 4852 Amer. journalist, novelist, editor; w. Dave Eggers, writer, publisher

Vidya (fl. seventh–11th century) 133 Ind. queen, poet; a.s.a. Vijja; w. Candraditya (son of Pulakesin II)

Vigée-Lebrun, Elisabeth (1755–1842) 685 Fr. painter; née Marie Louise E—

Vilar, Irene (1969–) 4805 Puerto Rican memoirist, magazine editor, literary agent; gd. Lolita Lebron*

Villanueva, Alma Luz (1944–) 3546 Amer. poet, novelist

Villedieu, Marie Catherine Hortense de see DESJARDINS, MARIE-CATHERINE

Vincent, Norah (1965?–) 4713 Amer. journalist, author

Vincenzi, Penny (1939–) 3164 Eng. novelist, journalist

Vinck, Catherine de see DE VINCK, CATHERINE

Violette see GARRICK, EVA

Viorst, Judith (1931–) 2780 Amer. journalist, writer, poet; née Stahl; Emmy, 1970

Viramontes, Helena María (1954–) 4279 Amer. educator (literature), writer, literary editor; cofounder, Southern California Latino Writers and Film Makers group; NEA, 1989

Visconti, Valentine (fl. 1390s–1405) 247 Ital. noble; a.k.a. V— de Milan; w. Louis d'Orleans

Viva (1943–) 3467 Amer. writer, painter, model, actor; née Susan Hoffman

Vogel, Paula A(nne) (1951–) 4076 Amer. playwright, educator; artistic director, Theater with Teeth (New York, 1982–85), Theater Eleanor Roosevelt (Providence, Rhode Island, 1990–); NEA, 1979, 1980; Pulitzer, 1998

Volk, Patricia (1943–) 3468 Amer. writer; grandd. Jacob V— , inventor of wrecking ball

Voronel, Nina (1933–) 2873 Sov. poet, playwright, translator; w. Alexander V—, physicist

Vorse, Mary Heaton (1881–1966) 1575 Amer. writer

vos Savant, Marilyn (1946–) 3703 Amer. columnist, lecturer, author, playwright

Vostrá, Alena (1938–) 3111 Cuban playwright, theatrician; w. Jaroslav Vostry (critic); cofounder, Cinohern Klub (Drama Club)

Voznesenskaya, Yuliya (1940–) 3236
Sov./Ger. feminist, writer

Vreeland, Diana (1903–1989) 1984
Eng. Fr./Amer. museum curator, fashion critic, magazine editor; née Dalziel; Legion of Honor, France

Vreeland, Susan (1946–) 3704
Amer. novelist, teacher

W

Waddles, Charleszetta [Lina], Reverend Mother (1912–2001) 2193
Amer. preacher, writer, poverty activist; a.k.a. Mother Waddles; founder, Perpetual Mission for Saving Souls of All Nations, Inc.; Sojourner Truth Award

Wade-Gayles, Gloria Jean (1938–) 3112
Amer. civil rights activist, educator, feminist; NEH, 1975

Wagner, Jane (1935–) 2956
Amer. designer, scriptwriter, actor, director; p. & collaborator, Lily Tomlin*; Emmy, 1974, 1976

Wagner, Melinda (1957–) 4436
Amer. composer, music educator; Pulitzer/Music, 1999

Wagner, Sally Roesch (1942–) 3384
Amer. nonprofit administrator, women's studies educator, lecturer, biographer; exec. dir., Matilda Joslyn Gage* Fdn.

Waite, Mary (?–1689) 534
Eng. writer, religious; née Smith

Wakoski, Diane (1937–) 3064
Amer. poet; mn. Sherbell

Walbert, Kate (1961–) 4598.1
Amer. playwright, writer, writing teacher

Wald, Lillian D. (1867–1940) 1342
Amer. nurse, civil rights activist; cofounder, NAACP, the Federal Children's Bureau, the Women's League for Peace and Freedom, et al.; NWHF

Walders, Davi (1938?–) 3113
Amer. poet, consultant, educational; née Dubrow; Fullbright; NEH

Waldman, Anne (Lesley) (1945–) 3621
Amer. writer, anthologist; NEA, 1979–80

Waldo, Octavia (1929–) 2686
Amer. writer, educator, painter; a.k.a. Octavia Waldo Locke

Walker, Alice (1944–) 3547
Amer. civil rights activist, teacher, poet, novelist, essayist; founder, Wild Trees Press, 1984; Pulitzer, 1983; NBA,

1983; NIAL, 1974; Guggenheim, 1977–78

Walker, Barbara G[oodwin] (1930–) 2744
Amer. researcher, writer

Walker, C. J., Madam (1867–1919) 1343
Amer. philanthropist, entrepreneur, inventor; née Sarah Breedlove; invented first commercial personal care products for African Americans; first self-made American woman millionaire; NWHF

Walker, Katharine [Kent Child] (1840–1916) 1097
Amer. writer, activist (religion)

Walker, Margaret [Abigail] (1915–1998) 2259
Amer. educator, poet, novelist; a.s.a. M— W— Alexander (mn.)

Walker, Mary [Edwards] (1832–1919) 1047
Amer. physician, feminist; second woman graduate from a medical school in the U.S.; first woman to receive Congressional Medal of Honor, 1865; NWHF, 2000

Walker, Rebecca (1969–) 4806
Amer. writer, contributing editor, feminist; née Leventhal; d. Alice Walker*

Walker, Sarah Breedlove (1867–1919) 1344
Amer. washerwoman, philanthropist, entrepreneur; a.k.a. Madam C. J. Walker

Wallace, Cath (1955?–) 4338
N.Z. environmental activist, economist, educator (environmental economics); Goldman, 1991

Wallace, Michelle (1952–) 4149
Amer. writer, journalist; d. Faith Ringgold (feminist artist)

Wallada al-Mustakfi (fl. 1000s–d. 1035) 172
Arab/Span. princess, poet; a.s.a. Ouallada; d. Callif al-Mustkfi of Cordova, companion of Ibn Zaidun (court poet)

Wallbridge, Elizabeth (1770–1801) 753
Eng. servant, Methodist leader; a.k.a. The Diaryman's Daughter

Wallis, Velma (1960–) 4559
Amer. novelist

Walsh, Jill Paton (1937–) 3065
Amer. mystery & children's writer; née Gillian Bliss; a.k.a. Gillian P— W— ; CBE, 1996

Walsh, María Elena (1930–) 2745
Arg. poet, children's writer, songwriter, playwright

Walsingham, Frances (1569–1631) 373
Eng. noble; a.k.a. Lady Essex; d. Sir Francis W—; w. Sir Phillip Sidney (1; 1554–86; poet, soldier, politician) and Robert Devereaux, second earl of Essex (2; 1566–1601; noble; favorite of Elizabeth I*)

Walters, Anna Lee (1946–) 3705
Amer. administrator, educator, writer; ABA, 1986

Walters, Barbara (1929–) 2687
Amer. journalist, TV producer & commentator, writer; first woman network news anchor; Emmy

Walters, Dottie (1925–2007) 2538
Amer. workshop leader, nonfiction writer, public speaker; m. Lilly W—*

Walters, Lilly (1956–) 4394
Amer. public speaker, workshop leader, nonfiction writer; née Lillet W—; d. Dottie W—*

Walters, Minette (1949–) 3944
Eng. crime novelist

Walton, Meredith "Marty" (1936–) 3011
Amer. administrator

Wanatee, [Jean] Adeline [Morgan] (1910–1996) 2144
Amer. storyteller, author, educator

Wandor, Michelene (Dinah) (1940–) 3237
Eng. poet, theater historian, playwright, writer, anthologist; née Samuels; Emmy; Arts Council Awards, 1974, 1983; International Emmy from Thames TV 1987

Wang Anyi (1954–) 4280
Chin. editor, writer

Wang Ch'ing-hui (fl. 13th century) 233
Chin. poet; director of palace women's quarters

Wang Wei (fl. 17th century) 553
Chin. courtesan, priestess, poet; a.k.a. The Taoist Master in the Straw Coat

Wang Yongchen, (1954–) 4281
Chin. journalist, environmental activist; cofounder, Green Earth Volunteers (China)

Wann, Marilyn (1966–) 4739
Amer. writer, activist; fdr., Fat!So? Magazine, 1994

Ward, Barbara [Mary] (1914–1981) 2230
Brit. conservationist, economist, nonfiction writer,

letter writer; a.k.a. Baroness Jackson of Lodsworth; president (1973), chair (1980) International Institute for Environment & Development; first woman to address a Vatican assembly; C.B.E., 1974

Ward, Celeste M. (1971?–) 4853
Amer. defense theorist, public servant; Deputy Asst. Sec. of Defense for Stability Operations Capabilities

Ward, Mary (1585–1645) 393
Eng. nun; founded religious order of English women based on rules of the Society of Jesus

Ward, Mary Augusta (1851–1920) 1187
Eng. social worker, novelist, writer; a.k.a. Mrs. Humphry W—; née Arnold

Ware, Katharine Augusta (1797–1843) 861
Amer./Fr. poet; née Rhodes

Waring, Marilyn (1953–) 4217
N.Z. singer, politician; Nationalist M.P. (at age 22); only woman M.P. in the National Party (as of 1975)

Warner, Anna Bartlett (1820–1912) 979
Amer. poet, writer; pseud. Amy Lothrop; s. Susan W—*

Warner, Marina (1946–) 3706
Eng. novelist, nonfiction writer; w. William Shawcross (1; writer) and John Dewe Matthews (2; painter); Commonwealth Prize—Eurasia 1988

Warner, Susan [Bogert] (1819–1885) 961
Amer. writer; pseud. Elizabeth Etherell; s. Anna Bartlett W—*

Warner, Sylvia Townsend (1893–1978) 1789
Eng. poet, writer; p. Valentine Ackland

Warren, Mercy Otis (1728–1758) 603
Amer. historian, playwright, poet; née Otis, a.k.a. Philomena; s. James O— (1725–83; Amer. Revolutionary leader, publicist), w. Gen. James W— (member, Massachusetts legislature); NWHF

Warren, Mrs. see MERRY, ANNE

Warwick, countess of see GREVILLE, FRANCES

Washburn, Margaret Floy (1871–1939) 1395
Amer. behavioral scientist

Washington, Harriet A. (1962?–) 4634
Amer. journalist, bioethics, writer, educator; NBCCA, 2008

Washington, Kerry (1977–)   4921
Amer. actor, activist

Washington, Martha
(1731–1802)   613
Amer. first lady; née Dandridge; w. Daniel Parke Curtis (1) and George W— (2; 1732–99; military leader; 1st U.S. president, 1789–97), m. John Parke Curtis and M— (a.k.a. Patsy), greatgrandm.-in-law of Robert E. Lee (1807–70; Confederate general), d.-in-law of Mary W—*

Washington, Mary (1708–1789)565
Amer. patriot; née Ball; m. George W— (2; 1732–99; military leader; 1st U.S. president, 1789–97), m.-in-law Martha W—*

Wasserman Schultz, Debbie
(1967–)   4761.2
Amer. lawyer, politician; U.S. representative (D-FL); Florida's first Jewish congresswoman

Wasserstein, Wendy
(1950–2006)   4013
Amer. playwright, essayist, educator; Tony (first woman to be awarded prize for Best Play); Blackburn; NYDCCA; Pulitzer, 1989; Guggenheim; Obie

Waters, Alice (1944–)   3548
Amer. chef, restaurateur

Waters, Ethel (1896–1977)   1838
Amer. singer, actor; first black woman in a white Broadway show; NYDCCA, 1950; Grammy Hall of Fame, 1998

Waters, Maxine (1938–)   3114
Amer. politician; née M— Moore Carr; U.S. Representative (D-CA) - 1990–

Waters, Sarah (1966–)   4740
Welsh/Eng. novelist

Waterstreet, Mary   see JAMES, BESSIE

Watkins, Sharon E. (1954?–)   4282
Amer. minister; pres. and genl. minister of the Christian Church (Disciples of Christ), U.S. & Canada; first woman to lead U.S.Inaugural national sermon

Watt-Cloutier, Sheila (1954–)   4283
Can. politician, activist

Wattleton, Faye (1943–)   3469
Amer. administrator, midwife, nurse, women's & abortion rights activist; president, Planned Parenthood Federation of America (1978–1992); pres. Ctr. for the Advancement of Women; NWHF, 1993

Wauneka, Annie Dodge
(1910–1997)   2145
Amer. Indian rights & public health activist; first Native American to receive Presidential Medal of Freedom, 1963; NWHF

Wayne, June (1918–)   2334
Amer. artist, lithographer; founder, Tamarind Lithography Workshop

Wazed, Hasina (1947–)   3805
Bangl. politician; a.k.a. Sheik Hasina; d. Sheik Mujibur Rahman, first prime minister of Bangladesh; assassinated, 1975; prime minister, 1996–2001; pres. Awami League, 1981–

Weaver, Frances (1928?–2004) 2645
Amer. writer, public speaker

Webb, Beatrice Potter
(1858–1943)   1239
Eng. reformer, sociologist, writer, historian; w. Sidney W— ; cofounder, Fabian Society, 1883, and of the New Statesman, 1913

Webb, Mary [Gladys]
(1881–1927)   1576
Eng. religious leader, novelist, poet; née Meredith

Webster, Margaret
(1905–1972)   2035
Amer./Eng. actor, director, writer; d. Dame May Whitty

Weddell, Mrs. (fl. 1730s–40s)   612
Eng. playwright

Weddington, Sarah [Ragle]
(1945–)   3622
Amer. lawyer, pro-choice activist; attorney who won Roe vs. Wade, landmark U.S. Supreme Court case granting women the right to abortion; Margaret Sanger* Award, Planned Parenthood Federation of America, 1980

Weed, Becky (1960?–)   4560
Amer. rancher, geologist, animal rights advocate

Weil, Simone (1909–1943)   2116
Fr. scholar, philosopher, mystic, poet, playwright, journalist, revolutionary; pseud. Emile Novis

Weimer, Joan Myers (1936–) 3012
Amer. biographer, educator

Weinberg, Sheila Pelz (1946–) 3707
Amer. rabbi, peace activist, administrator, poet; cofounder, Inst. for Jewish Spirituality (IJS)

Weinraub, Sally (1924–)   2503
Eng. writer

Weinstock, Lotus (1943–1997) 3470
Amer. comedian, performance artist; née Marlena W—; d.

Lili Haydn, violinist; p. Lenny Bruce (1925–1966) American stand-up comic, social critic, satirist

Weisberg, Ruth (1942–)   3385
Amer. art educator, painter

Weisman, Leslie Kanes
(1945–)   3623
Amer. architect, public speaker, educator

Weisstein, Naomi (1939–)   3165
Amer. experimental psychologist, educator, writer, feminist, pianist, comedian

Welby, Amelia C. (1819–1852) 962
Amer. poet

Weldon, Fay (1933–)   2874
Eng. TV & screen writer, playwright, novelist; née Birkinshaw; s. Daniel W— (filmmaker)

Wells, Carolyn (1869–1942)   1368
Amer. writer, humorist; mn. Houghton

Wells, Ida B. (1862–1931)   1291
Amer. antilynching activist & abolitionist, writer, lecturer, educator; pseud. Iola; a.s.a. I— W-Barnett (mn.); cofounder, NAACP and National Association of Colored Women's Clubs; NWHF

Wells, Rebecca (1952–)   4150
Amer. actor, novelist, playwright

Wells-Witteman, Alisa
(1929–)   2688
Amer. photographer; née Andrews

Welty, Eudora (1909–2001)   2117
Amer. writer, photographer; Pulitzer, 1973; Presidential Medal of Freedom, 1980; ABA 1981, 1984; NIAL, 1972; NWHF

Wentworth, Anne (1630?–?)   455
Eng. religious figure, letter writer

Were, Beatrice (1966?–)   4741
Ugan. administrator (NGO), activist (AIDS); cofounder, Natl. Community of Women Living with AIDS (NACWOLA); InterAction Humanitarian Award in 2003; Human Rights Defender Award, the highest honor bestowed by Human Rights Watch.

Werfel, Alma   see MAHLER-WERFEL, ALMA

Wertenbaker, Timberlake
(1951–)   4077
Amer./Eng. translator, playwright; née Lael Louisiana T—; d. Charles W— (foreign correspondent); Olivier Award,

1989, 1992; NYDCCA, 1989; London Evening Standard Award, 1980

Wertheim, Margaret (1958–) 4474
Aust./Amer. science writer, fashion model, TV host

Wesley, Susanna
(1668?–1742)   512
Eng. Methodist leader, psalmist; a.k.a. Mother of Methodism; m. John (1703–1791) and Charles W— (1707–88; both clergymen; founders of Methodism, 1729)

West, Cheryl L. (1965–)   4714
Amer. playwright, social worker; Blackburn, 1990

West, Frances (1931–2007)   2781
Amer. Unitarian minister

West, Jane (1758–1852)   694
Eng. novelist, playwright, poet; pseud. Prudentia Homespun

West, Jessamyn (1902–1984)   1959
Amer. writer, novelist; née Ray; mn. McPherson

West, Mae (1893–1980)   1790
Amer. stage & screen actor, stage producer, screenwriter, playwright, nightclub entertainer

West, Rebecca, Dame
(1892–1983)   1759
Ir./Eng. novelist, literary critic, journalist, suffragist; née Cicely Isabel Andrews Fairfield, a.k.a. Lynx, Corinne Andrews, mn. Andrews; companion of, and parent with, H. G. Wells (1866–1946; writer) of Anthony W— (author, critic); C.B.E., 1959

Westergaard, Brita (1944?–) 3549
Nor. government official

Westheimer, Ruth [Karola]
(1928–)   2646
Ger./Amer. media personality, sex therapist, author; a.k.a. Dr. Ruth

Westwood, Vivienne
(1941–)   3310
Brit. fashion designer; OBE, 1992; DBE, 2006

Wetherell, Elizabeth   see WARNER, SUSAN

Whales, Nym   see SNOW, HELEN

Wharton, Anne, Countess
(1632?–1685)   462
Eng. translator, novelist, playwright, poet; née Lee, a.k.a. Cloris

Wharton, Edith [Newbold]
(1862–1937)   1292
Amer. writer; née Jones; Pulitzer, 1921; NWHF

Wheathill, Ann (fl. 1580s)   388
Eng. religious writer, noble

Wheatley, Margaret "Meg" (1941–) 3311
Amer. educator (management), social scientist, systems management consultant

Wheatley, Phillis (1753?–1784) 677
Amer. slave, poet; a.k.a. poet-laureate of Boston, the Negro Sappho; w. John Peters

Wheeler, Kate (1951?–) 4078
Peru./Amer. writer, nun, Buddhist

Wheeler, Mercy (1706–1733?) 560
Amer. poet

Whitbread, Jane (1914–?) 2231
Amer. writer, journalist; a.k.a. J— W— Levin

Whitehorn, Katharine [Elizabeth] (1928–) 2647
Eng. columnist, writer; w. Gavin Lyall (1932–2003), Eng. novelist

Whiteley, Opal [Stanley] (1897–1992) 1858
Amer. diarist, nature writer

Whiteman, Roberta Hill (1947–) 3806–3807
Amer. educator (literature), poet

Whitestone-McCallum, Heather (1973–) 4882
Amer. beauty, entrepreneur, author, public speaker; first deaf Miss America, 1994

Whitman, [Margaret Cushing] Meg (1956–) 4395
Amer. business executive; CEO of eBay, 1998–2008

Whitman, Marina von Neumann (1935–) 2957
Amer. economist, author, professor (economics); d. John v— (1903–1957), Hung./Amer. mathematician

Whitman, Sarah [Helen] Power (1803–1878) 884
Amer. writer, poet; fiancée of Edgar Allen Poe (poet, writer, 1809–49)

Whitney, Adeline Dutton (1824–1906) 996
Amer. writer, poet; née Train

Whitney, Isabella (1540?–1573) 340
Eng. poet; s. Geoffrey W— (poet)

Whitson, Beth Slater (1879–1930) 1538
Amer. songwriter, writer, poet

Whitton, Charlotte [Elizabeth] (1896–1975) 1839
Can. politician, writer; Mayor of Ottawa, Ontario, 1951–56 and 1960–64 (first woman mayor of Ottawa)

Whyte, Edna Gardner (1902–1993) 1960
Amer. nurse, aviator; Aviation Hall of Fame

Wickham, Anna (1884–1947) 1622
Eng. poet; née Edith Alice Mary Harper; mn. Hepburn

Widdemer, Margaret (1880–1978) 1561
Amer. poet, writer; Pulitzer, 1919

Wieder, Marcia (1956–) 4396
Amer. lecturer, author, business executive, dream coach; fdr., Dream University

Wiese, Anne Pierson (1971?–) 4854
Amer. poet; Walt Whitman Award, 2006

Wiggin, Kate Douglas (1856–1923) 1214
Amer. poet, writer, educator; née Smith; s. Nora Archibald Smith*; founder, California Kindergarten Training School

Wigman, Mary (1886–1973) 1658
Ger. dancer, choreographer

Wignell, Mrs. see MERRY, ANNE

Wilcox, Ella Wheeler (1855–1919) 1209
Amer. poet, journalist

Wilcox, Margaret R. (1910?–) 2146
Amer. civil rights activist, educator

Wilde, Jane Francesca, Lady (1826–1896) 1010
Ir. author, translator, poet; pseud. Speranza

Wilder, Laura Ingalls (1867–1957) 1345
Amer. writer

Wildman, Stephanie M[ay] (1949–) 3945
Amer. writer, educator (law)

Wiley, Doreen Gandy (1927–) 2617
Filipina/Amer. novelist, poet

Wilhelm, Gale (1908–1991) 2104
Amer. writer

Wilkinson, Eliza (1755?–?) 686
Amer. letter writer; née Yonge

Wilkinson, Jemima (1752–1819) 674
Amer. religious leader; a.k.a. the Publick Universal Friend; founded the Jerusalem Township, New York, 1794

Wilkinson, Marguerite (1883–1928) 1602
Amer. poet; née Bigelow

Willard, Emma Hart (1787–1870) 806
Amer. author, poet, educator, feminist; s. Almira Lincoln Phelps*, w. Dr. John W— (1) and Yates (2); founder, Troy Female Seminary, 1821 (later Emma Willard School, 1895); Hall of Fame, 1905

Willard, Frances [Elizabeth] (1839–1898) 1090
Amer. reformer, temperance leader; NWHF

Willard, Nancy (1936–) 3013
Amer. educator, historian, writer; w. Eric Lindbloom (photographer); NEA, 1976, 1987–88; Caldicott, 1982; Newbery, 1982, 1993

Willebrandt, Mabel Walker (1889–1963) 1703
Amer. lawyer

Williams, Ann Claire (1949–) 3946
Amer. judge, attorney; first African-American woman on the Federal Disctrict Court in IL (1985); first African American woman appointed to federal appeals court (1999)

Williams, Anna (1706–1783) 561
Eng. author, poet, translator

Williams, Bertye Young (1876–1951) 1485
Amer. editor, writer, poet

Williams, Betty (1943–) 3471
Ir./Amer. activist, peace; co-founder, The Peace People; Nobel Peace Prize, 1976

Williams, Carol (1948–) 3876
Amer. gardener, writer

Williams, E. Faye (1941–) 3312
Amer. lawyer, businesswoman, educator, minister, peace and human rights activist; chair, Natl. Congress of Black Women (NCBW)

Williams, Fannie Barrier (1855–1944) 1210
Amer. journalist, lecturer, teacher, social activist

Williams, Helen Maria (1762–1827) 716
Eng./Fr. politician, composer, poet, translator, novelist; member of Dr. Samuel Johnson's circle (1709–84; author, lexicographer)

Williams, Jody (1950–) 4014
Amer. peace activist; founding coordinator, International Campaign to Ban Landmines (ICBL), 1992; developed & directed Medical Aid for El Salvador, 1986–1992; co-coordinator, Nicaragua-Honduras Education Project, 1984–86; ICBL was awarded the Nobel Peace Prize, 1998

Williams, Joy (1944–) 3550
Amer. novelist, educator

Williams, Lucinda (1953–) 4218
Amer. singer, songwriter, poet

Williams, Lynda (1958?–) 4475
Amer. physicist, songwriter, educator; a.k.a. the Physics Chanteuse

Williams, Mary Lou (1910–1981) 2147
Amer. jazz pianist, composer, music arranger; née M— Elfrieda Scruggs

Williams, Patricia [Joyce] (1951–) 4079
Amer. educator (law), nonfiction writer, attorney

Williams, Pearl (1914–1991) 2232
Amer. comedian; a.k.a. Pearl Wolfe-Williams

Williams, Sarah Sadie (1841–1868) 1107
Eng. poet

Williams, Sherley Anne (1944–1999) 3551–3552
Amer. educator (literature), poet, writer

Williams, Shirley (1930–) 2746
Brit. politician; academician; née S— Vivien Teresa Brittain Catlin; a.k.a. Baroness W— of Crosby, PC; d. Sir George Catlin, political scientist and philosopher, and Vera Brittain*; w. Sir Bernard W— (1), philosopher; Richard E. Neustadt (2; d. 2003), historian and educator; MP; cofounder, Social Democratic Party, 1981

Williams, Terry Tempest (1955–) 4339
Amer. naturalist, educator, environmental activist

Williams, Vanessa (1963–) 4660
Amer. singer, songwriter, actor, beauty queen, gay rights activist; first black Miss America (1983); Oscar (song), 1995

Williams, Venus [Ebony Starr] (1980–) 4944
Amer. tennis professional; s. Serena W— , tennis champion; Wimbledon (5); Olympic Gold, 2000

Williamson, Marianne (1952–) 4151
Amer. philanthropist, spiritual activist, lecturer, author; fdr., The Peace Alliance

Willis, Gwendolen [Brown] (1876–1969) 1486
Amer. writer, professor; d. Olympia Brown*

Willis, Lydia Fish (1709–1767) 566
Amer. poet

Willis, Sarah (1954–) 4284
Amer. novelist, teacher; d. Kirk W— , actor, director of The Cleveland Play House (1924–1966)

Willner, Ann Ruth (1939?–) 3166
Amer. political scientist, educator (political science)

Willoughby, Catherine (1519/20–1580) 312 Eng. noble; a.k.a. duchess of Suffolk; d. William, Lord W— and Maria de Salinas (lady-in-waiting to Catherine of Aragon*), second w. Charles Brandon, duke of Suffolk (1), w. Richard Bertie (2)

Willoughby, Denita (1966?–) 4742 Amer. business executive

Willson, Dixie (1890–1974) 1720 Amer. poet, writer

Willson, Margaret (1953–) 4219 Amer. anthropologist, educator, educational activist, author; cofounder, Bahia Street, 1996

Wilner, Eleanor (1937–) 3066 Amer. poet, civil rights activist; NEA, 1976–77; MacArthur, 1991

Wilson, Augusta Jane see EVANS, AUGUSTA)

Wilson, Barbara (1950–) 4015 Amer. book publisher, short story writer, novelist

Wilson, Dorothy Wright (fl. 1970s) 4838–4839 Amer. educator, university administrator

Wilson, Elizabeth (1936–) 3014 Brit. journalist, author

Wilson, Harriette (1789–1846) 814 Eng. diarist

Wilson, Heather (1960–) 4561 Amer. politician, business consultant, foreign policy strategist; U.S. Rep. (R-NM), 1998–

Wilson, Margaret (1882–1973) 1589 Amer./Eng. novelist; Pulitzer, 1924

Wilson, Marie C. (1948–) 3877 Amer. women's rights activist, nonprofit administrator, author; fdr. & pres., The White House Project; co-creator, Take Our Daughters and Sons to Work Day

Wilson, Martha (1758–post-1848) 695 Amer. householder; née Stewart; friend of George Washington (1732–99; military leader; 1st U.S. president, 1789–97)

Wiltz, Christine (1948–) 3878 Amer. novelist

Win, Aye Aye (1969?–) 4807 Burmese human right's activist, nonprofit administrator; cofounder. & exec. dir., Dignity Intl.

Winchilsea, Lady see FINCH, ANNE

Windsor, Wallis Simpson, duchess of (1896–1986) 1840 Amer./Eng. public figure; née Warfield; w. duke of W— (1894–1972; king of Great Britain, 1936–37; abdicated)

Wineapple, Brenda (1952?–) 4152 Amer. biographer

Winegarten, Renée [Cecile] (1922–) 2443 Eng. literary critic, writer

Winfrey, Oprah (1954–) 4285 Amer. TV personality & producer, screen actor, philanthropist; Emmy, 2000, 2002; Peabody, 1995; NWHF

Winger, Deborah (1955–) 4340 Amer. actor; ex-w. Timothy Hutton (actor)

Wingfield, Eileen Wani (1930?–) 2747 Aust. environmental activist; cofounder, Kupa Piti Kungka Tjuta, 1995; Goldman, 2003

Winn, Marie (1938?–) 3115 Cuban/Amer. wildlife advocate, columnist, author, birder; s. Janet Malcolm, writer; w. Allan Miller, filmmaker & palindromist

Winn, Mary Day (1888–1965) 1691 Amer. writer

Winnemucca, Sarah (1844–1891) 1133 Amer. Indian rights activist, army scout, interpreter, lecturer, teacher; d. Old Chief W— (18??–1882); gd. Captain Truckee; NWHF

Winslow, Anna Green (1759–1780) 700 Can./Amer. diarist, poet

Winslow, Anne Goodwin (1875–1959) 1467 Amer. writer, poet

Winslow, Thyra Samter (1903–1961) 1985 Amer. literary & drama critic, scenarist

Winters, Shelley (1922–2006) 2395 Amer. stage, screen actor; née Shirley Shrift; ex-w. Vittorio Gassman, Ital. Actor (1952–54; 2), Anthony Franciosa, actor (1957–1960; 3); Academy Award, 1959, 1965; Emmy, 1964

Winterson, Jeanette (1959–) 4510 Eng. novelist, journalist, businesswoman; OBE, 2006

Winthrop, Margaret (1591?–1647) 400 Eng./Amer. letter writer; née Tyndal; w. John W— (1588–1649; colonial administrator; first governor of Massachusetts Bay Colony)

Winwar, Frances (1900–1985) 1923 Ital./Amer. writer, translator, literary critic; née Francesca Vinciguerra

Wiseman, Jane (fl. 1682–1717) 527 Eng. tavern keeper, playwright, servant, actor; mn. Holt

Witkovsky, Susan (1942–) 3386 Amer. pre-school consultant, adult education specialist; wrote model city program (San Francisco) for Headstart, 1971; s.-in-law, Bernice Braid*

Witt, Shirley Hill (1934–) 2918 Amer. Indian rights activist, anthropologist, educator, writer, poet; a.k.a. Katherine Thundercloud

Wittig, Monique (1935–2003) 2958 Fr. writer, educator, poet, social theorist

Woffington, Peg (1720–1760) 586 Eng. actor, author

Wohlstetter, Roberta (1912–2007) 2194 Amer. military intelligence historian, educator, lecturer; née Morgan; d. Edmund M—, law professor; w. Albert W— (1913–1997), nuclear strategist; Presidential Medal of Freedom, 1985

Wolf, Beverly Hungry see HUNGRY WOLF, BEVERLY

Wolf, Christa (1929–) 2689 Ger. pacifist, feminist, novelist, writer; née Ihlenfeld

Wolf, Naomi (1962–) 4635 Amer. feminist, nonfiction writer; Rhodes Scholar, 1986

Wolfe, Leslie (1944–) 3031 Amer. nonprofit administrator

Wolff, Charlotte (1904–1986) 2008 Ger./Eng. psychiatrist, writer

Wolitzer, Hilma (1930–) 2748 Amer. writer, educator (writing); m. Meg W—*

Wolitzer, Meg (1959–) 4511 Amer. educator, novelist; d. Hilma W—*

Wollstonecraft, Mary (1759–1797) 701 Eng. author, feminist; w. William Godwin (1756–1836; political philosopher), m. Mary W— Shelley*; s.-in-law, Hannah Godwin*

Wolverton, Terry (1954–) 4286 Amer. literary editor, writer, poet

Wong, Nellie (1934–) 2919 Amer. writer, feminist, poet, activist

Woo, Merle (1941–) 3313 Amer. poet, civil rights activist, educator

Wood, Ellen (1813–1887) 922 Eng. playwright, journalist, writer; née Price

Wood, J. R., Mrs. see CHAMBERS, JESSIE

Wood, Natalie (1938–1981) 3116 Amer. actor; née Natalia Nikolaevna Zakharenko; d. Nicholas (architect and set designer) and Maria G— (ballet dancer), s. Lana W— (actress, 1946–); w. Robert Wagner (1 & 3; 1930– ; actor), Richard Gregson (2; British producer); m. Natasha Wagner (actress)

Wood, Sally Sayward (1759–1855) 702 Amer. novelist; née Barrell, a.k.a. Sarah Sayward Keating

Woodhull, Victoria Claflin (1838–1927) 1086 Amer. spiritualist, actor, writer, political activist, editor, stock broker, feminist; s. Tennessee C—*; published The Woodhull & Claflin Weekly, 1870–1876; ran for U.S. president, 1870; formed Equal Rights Party, 1872; published The Humanitarian, 1892–1901; NWHF

Woodman, Marion (1928–) 2648 Can. Jungian analyst, author, feminist

Woodruff, Julia [Louise M.] (1833–1909) 1054 Amer. writer; pseud. W. M. L. Jay

Woods, Rose Mary (1917–2005) 2305 Amer. secretary; personal secretary to President Nixon, 1969–1974

Woodville-Grey, Elizabeth see GREY, ELIZABETH

Woodward, Joanne [Gignilliat Trimmier] (1930–) 2749 Amer. actor, environmental activist; w. Paul Newman (1925–2008), actor; m. Nell Potts Newman, actor; Oscar, 1957; Emmy (3); Golden Globe (3)

Woolf, Virginia (1882–1941) 1590 Eng./Eng. writer, literary critic; b. Adeline V— Stephen; a.k.a. V— Stephen, V— Adeline W—; d. Sir Leslie Stephen (biographer, ciritic, scholar); w. Leonard W— (economist, publisher, writer); with Leonard, founder and operator of Hogarth Press, 1917; with brother Thoby Stephen, founder of *Hyde Park Gate News*, 1891–1895

Woolley, Hannah (1621/23?–1675/76?) 443
Eng. governess, pioneer educator

Woolsey, Mary (1832–1864) 1048
Amer. poet, social worker; mn. Howland

Woolsey, Sarah Chauncey *see* COOLIDGE, SUSAN

Wordsworth, Dorothy (1771–1855) 758
Eng. diarist, naturalist; s. William W— (1770–1850; poet); s.-in-law of Mary W—*; a. Elizabeth W—*

Wordsworth, Elizabeth (1840–1932) 1098
Amer. poet; great-n. William W-(1770–1850; poet) and Mary W—*; n. Dorothy W—*

Wordsworth, Mary (1770–1859) 754
Eng. letter writer; née Hutchinson; w. William W— (poet, 1770–1850); s.-in-law Dorothy W—*, great-a. Elizabeth W—*

Wortham, Anne (1941–) 3314
Amer. scholar, sociologist

Worthington, Robin (1932–) 2829
Amer. writer

Wray, Fay (1907–2004) 2075
Amer. screen actor

Wright, Frances (1795–1852) 850
Scot./Amer. poet, lecturer, philanthropist, author, feminist, social reformer; a.s.a. Fanny W; w. William D'Arusmont; NWHF

Wright, Judith (1915–2000) 2260
Aust. poet, writer, activist, aboriginal rights; Queen's Gold Medal, 1992

Wright, Robin (1948–) 3879
Amer. author, commentator, journalist; Overseas Press Club Award, 1976; Natl. Press Club, 2004; MacArthur

Wright, Susanna (1697–1784) 546
Eng./Amer. painter, frontierswoman, poet, letter writer, scholar

Wroth, Mary Sidney (1587–1651/53) 395
Eng. poet, patron of poets; a.s.a. Wroath, a.k.a. countess of Montgomery; d. Robert, earl of Leicester, n. M— S— Herbert* and Sir Phillip S— (poets), c. Elizabeth Manners (poet, d. Sir Phillip S—)

Wu, Chien-Shiung *see* CHIEN SHIUNG WU

Wu Tse-t'ien (624–705) 121
a. s. Wu Zetian; Chin. empress, poet; only empress in

Chinese history to rule in her own right, 689–705

Wucker, Michele (1969–) 4808
Amer. nonprofit administrator, author; dir., World Policy Inst.; Guggenheim

Wurdeman, Audrey (1911–1960) 2170
Amer. poet, novelist; g-g-gd. Percy Bysshe Shelly; w. Joseph Auslander (1897–1970), 1st U.S. poet laureate; Pulitzer, 1935

Wurtzel, Elizabeth [Leigh] (1967–) 4762
Amer. rock and roll critic, writer, attorney, journalist

Wyatt, Edith Franklin (1873–1958) 1423
Amer. writer

Wylie, Elinor [Morton] (1885–1928) 1645
Amer. writer, poet; née Hoyt; w. William Rose Benét (1886–1950; writer and editor), s.-in-law, Stephen Vincent B— (1898–43; writer)

Wyse, Lois (1926–2007) 2584
Amer. advertising executive, columnist, author; née Wohlgemuth

X

Xanthippe (fl. fifth century B.C.E.) 59
Greek householder; w. Socrates (philosopher, 469–399 B.C.E.)

Xue Tao (768–831) 141
Chin. concubine, poet, calligrapher, hostess; ; a.s.a. Hsueh T'ao, Sie Thao, Hung-tu

Y

Yalow, Rosalyn (1921–) 2416
Amer. physicist; née Sussman; Nobel Prize, 1977; first woman to receive Albert Lasker Award, 1976; NWHF

Yamada, Eimi (1959–) 4512
Jap. cartoonist, painter, writer; Naoki Literary Prize

Yamada, Mitsuye [May] (1923–) 2475
Amer. book editor, poet; cofounder, Multi-Cultural Women Writers of Orange County; board of directors, Amnesty Int., 1988

Yamatohime (fl. 670s) 127
Jap. empress, poet; w. Emperor Tenjo

Yamauchi, Wakako (1924–) 2504
Amer. playwright, writer; d. Joy Y— (editor); Rockefeller, 1977, 1979, 1980

Yang, Gladys (1919–1999) 2358
Chin. translator, editor; née Tayler; w. Yang Xianyi (1915–), Chinese translator

Yang Jiang (1911–) 1985
Chin. educator (literature), writer, translator, playwright; née Y— Chi-k'ang; a.s.a. Chiang' w. Chi'ien Chungshu (a.s.a. Qian Zhongshu; 1910–1998), Ch. scholar-novelist; s. Yang Bi (1922–1968), translator

Yang Ping (1908–?) 2105
Chin. writer, journalist, political activist, editor; pseud. Shih Ming

Yankowitz, Susan (1941–) 3315
Amer. playwright, TV & screen writer, educator; w. Herbert Leibowitz (writer–editor); NEA, 1972, 1979, Rockefeller, 1973; Guggenheim, 1975

Yard, Molly (1914–2005) 2233
Chin./Amer. civil servant, political activist, feminist; w. Sylvester Garrett (labor arbitrator); president, NOW, 1987–1991

Yaroshinskaya, Alla (1953–) 4220
Ukrainian government official, journalist, writer, human rights activist; mbr., Supreme Soviet of USSR, 1989; adviser to Boris Yeltsin, 1993; fdr., Alla Yaroshinskaya Charitable Fund, 1993; Right Livelihood, 1992

Yeager, Jeana L. (1952–) 4153
Amer. draftsperson, aviator; copiloted *Voyager*, first aircraft to fly around the world without stopping or refueling; Presidential Citizens Medal, 1986

Yearsley, Anne (1760–1806) 710
Eng. novelist, poet; a.k.a. Lactilla, Bristol Milkwoman

Yee, Marian (Contemporary) 4989
Amer. writer, educator (literature), poet

Yener, Kutlu Aslihan (1946–) 3708
Turk./Amer. archaeologist

Yezierska, Anzia (1880/81–1970) 1562
Pol./Amer. author; a.k.a. Hattie Mayer

Yglesias, Helen (1915–2008) 2261
Amer. editor, writer; née Bassine

Yonge, Charlotte [Mary] (1823–1901) 991
Eng. author

York, Eva Rose (1858–1935?) 1240
Can. philanthropist, composer, musician, editor; née Fitch; founder, Redemption

Home and Bible School, Toronto, Ontario

Young, Cathy (1963–) 4661
Amer. nonfiction writer, journalist; née Ekaterina Jung

Young, Elizabeth (fl. 1550s) 352
Eng. protestant reformer

Young, Iris Marion (1949–2006) 3947
Amer. educator, political science, author

Young, Leontine [Ruth] (1910–1988) 2148
Amer. social worker, author, educator

Young, Louise B[uchwalter] (1919–) 2359
Amer. physicist, science writer; w. Hobart P. Y— (business executive)

Young, Rida Johnson (1869–1926) 1369
Amer. playwright, lyricist; Songwriters Hall of Fame, 1970

Young, Rolanda (1950–) 4016
Amer. TV reporter & anchor

Younger, Maud (1870–1936) 1384
Amer. suffragist, union activist, writer; a.k.a. "Mother of the Eight-Hour Law"

Yourcenar, Marguerite (1903–1987) 1986
Belg./Amer. essayist, writer; née M— de Crayencour; p. Grace Frick (translator); first woman to be elected to the French Academy, 1980; Grand Prix National des Lettres, Grand Prix de la Littérature de l'Académie Française

Yü Hsüan-chi (843?–868) 152
Chin. courtesan, Taoist priestess, poet

Yung, Judy (1939?–) 3167
Amer. historian, educator

Yunusova, Leyla (1957?–) 4437
Azeri politician, nonprofit administrator; chair, Inst. of Peace and Democracy; fdr., Azerbaijan Social Democratic Party (ASDP)

Z

az Zabba *see* ZENOBIA OF PALMYRA

Zaharias, Mildred *see* DIDRIKSON, ZAHARIAS [MILDRED ELLA] "BABE"

Zajovic, Stasa (1964?–) 4689
Serb. antiwar activist; cofounder, Women in Black

Zana, Leyla (1961–) 4599
Turk. human rights activist, politician; first Kurdish woman to win a seat in the Turkish parliament, 1991;

Sakharov Prize for Freedom of Thought, 1995

Zane, Elizabeth "Betty" (1759–1823)   703
Amer. frontier hero; a. Zane Grey (1872–1939) Amer. author

Zarin, Cynthia Rebecca (1959–)   4513
Amer. educator, writer, journalist, poet; NEA; Los Angeles Times Book Prize (2002)

Zassenhaus, Hiltgunt (1916–2004)   2279
Ger./Amer. political activist, physician; leader in underground resistance, World War II

Zaturenska, Marya (1902–1982)   1961
Russ./Amer. biographer, poet; w. Horace Gregory (1898–1982; poet, literary critic, translator); Pulitzer, 1938

Zayas y Sotomayor, Maria de (1590–1661/69)   398
Span. novelist

Zeidner, Lisa (1955–)   4341
Amer. novelist, poet, educator (English), screenwriter

Zeisler, Andi (1953–)   4221
Amer. writer, publisher, illustrator, women's rights activist; cofounder, Bitch Magazine: A Feminist Response to Pop Culture

Zell, Katherine (1497/98–1562) 291
Ger. hymnist, reformer, activist (religion); a.k.a. Katharina Schutzinn; w. Matthew Z— (Protestant minister)

Zelle, Gertrud Margarete see HARI, MATA

Zellweger, Renée [Kathleen] (1969–)   4809
Amer. actor; Oscar, 2003; Golden Globe (3)

Zelophehad, Five Daughters of (Mahlah, Noah, Hoglah, Milcah and Tirzah) (fl. 1240s–1200 B.C.E.)   18
Hebrew biblical figures; demanded right of father's inheritance if no son living; first women to win legal property rights

Zelter, Angie (1951–)   4080
Brit. peace activist; a.k.a. Angela Julian; fdr., Trident Ploughshares, 2000; Intl.

Women's Peace Service; Right Livelihood, 2001

Zenobia of Palmyra (240–300) 100
Syr. linguist, queen, military leader; née Bathzabbi; a.k.a. az-Zabba, Septimia Z—, queen of the East; w. Odaenathus, king of Palmyra; student of Longinus (Greek philosopher, rhetorician)

Zepatos, Thalia (1955–)   4342
Amer. travel writer, political activist

Zetkin, Klara (1857–1933)   1229
Ger. political activist; cofounder, Communist Party of Germany

Zetterling, Mai (1925–1994)   2539
Swed. actor, film director

Zhang, Lijia (1964–)   4690
Chin. journalist, laborer, activist

Zhang Jie (1937–)   3067
Chin. writer

Zhang Kangkang (1950–)   4017
Chin. writer

Zhivago, Um (contemporary)   4990
Pal. women's rights activist

Zia, Ather (1977?–)   4922
Ind./Amer. editor, journalist

Zia Rahman, Khaleda (1945–)   3624
Bangl. politician; a.k.a. Begum Zia; widow, Zia ur-Rahman, army general; assassinated, 1981; prime minister, 1991–1996, 2001–2006; first woman P.M. of Bangladesh; pres., Bangladesh Nationalist Party

Zipporah (fl. 1230s B.C.E.)   19
Hebrew biblical figure; d. Reuel (a.k.a. Jethro, priest of Midian); w. Moses (prophet, lawgiver) ; m. Gershom

Zolde, Henrietta (see Szolde, Henrietta)

Zong Pu (1928–)   2649
Chin. editor, writer; d. Feng Youlan (historian)

Zuboff, Shoshana (1951–)   4081
Amer. organizational consultant, educator, nonfiction writer

Zwilich, Ellen Taaffe (1939–) 3168
Amer. composer; Pulitzer/Music, 1983 (first woman)

Zygmuntowicz, Itka Frajiman (1926–)   2585
Pol./Amer. writer, poet, lecturer

Career and Occupation Index

Contributors have been indexed according to the major career paths their lives have taken and are listed alphabetically, within each category, with references to contributor numbers. Careers and Occupations are divided into the following divisions and categories:

A. ACADEMIA AND CRITICISM

Art Patrons and Collectors
Arts, Media, and Literary Critics
Biographers, Historians, Scholars, and Social or Cultural Critics
Education, Civic and Foundation/Association Administrators, and Consultants
Educators and Instructors
Librarians, Curators, and Preservationists
Philosophers

B. ARTS AND ENTERTAINMENT

Actors, Entertainers, and Performers
Comedians, Humorists, Cartoonists, and Wits
Courtesans, Brothel-Keepers, Mistresses, and Prostitutes
Dancers, Choreographers, and Dance Critics
Designers—Architectural, City, Industrial, and Interiors
Designers—Costume and Fashion
Designers—Graphic, Print, and Illustration
Directors—Stage, Film, and Television
Film, Television, Video, and Media Producers, Designers, Specialists, and Technicians
Lecturers, Public Speakers, and Workshop Leaders
Musicians, Singers, and Conductors
Painters, Sculptors, Artisans, and Other Visual Artists
Photographers
Radio and Television Personalities
Songwriters, Arrangers, Composers, and Lyricists
Theater Producers, Artistic Directors, Designers, et al.

C. POLITICAL, SOCIAL AND JUDICIAL ARENA

Activists, Reformers, and Revolutionaries
Criminologists, Police Workers, and Investigators
Diplomats, Civil Servants, Government Officials, and Spies
Feminists and Suffragists
Heads of State, Presidents, Premiers, Governors, et al.
Judges, Lawyers, and Legal Scholars
Labor Leaders
Politicians
Public Figures and Society Leaders

D. PRINTED WORD

Diarists and Letter Writers
Dramatists—Librettists, Playwrights, Scriptwriters, and Dramaturgs
Journalists, Bloggers, Columnists, Reporters, and Editors
Poets
Printed Media Publishers, Proprietors, Agents, et al.
Translators, Etymologists, Linguists, and Interpreters
Writers—Fiction and Nonfiction

E. SCIENCE AND MEDICINE

Computer Science and Technology
Engineers
Health Sciences—Physicians, Dentists, Psychiatrists, Midwives, Healers, et al.
Naturalists
Nutritionists, Chefs, Cookbook Writers, and Food Specialists
Psychotherapists, Analysts, and Counselors
Scientists—Biological
Scientists—Chemical
Scientists—Earth and Sky
Scientists—Physics
Social and Behavioral Science

F. OTHER
Adventurers, Frontier Settlers, Heroes, and Pilots
Athletes, Sports, and Fitness Figures
Business Executives, Entrepreneurs, Industrialists,
   and Consultants
Economists, Financial Specialists, and Bankers
Farmers, Ranchers, Horticulturists, and Agriculturists
Householders, Laborers, Office Workers, Slaves, and
   Miscellaneous

Inventors
Military Personnel, Soldiers, and Patriots
Occultists, Witches, and Prophets
Philanthropists and Humanitarians
Religious Figures, Leaders, and Theologians
Royalty and Courtiers

A. ACADEMIA AND CRITICISM

ART PATRONS AND COLLECTORS

Cavendish, Georgiana 690
Dodge, Mabel 1524
Este, Isabella d' 276
Gonzaga, Elisabetta 275
Gonzaga, Giulia 306
Harington, Lucy 389
Herbert, Mary Sidney 365
Jeanne of Navarre 226
Makhfi 470
Marguerite of Navarre 289
Medici, Lucrezia de' 255
Paley, Barbara "Babe" 2251
Pompadour, Jeanne-Antoinette
   Poisson de 588
Renée de France 304
Stein, Gertrude 1450
Tibergeau, Marchioness de 552
Wroth, Mary Sidney 395

ARTS, MEDIA, AND LITERARY CRITICS

Adler, Renata 3068
Alexander, Elizabeth 4601
Allen, Paula Gunn 3118
Aury, Dominique 2059
Ayllón Soria, Virginia 3952
Banks-Smith, Nancy 2691
Berberova, Nina 1927
Bogan, Louise 1843
Boxer, Sarah 4781
Byatt, A. S. 2968
Cassian, Nina 2479
Christian, Barbara T. 3397
Clark, Eleanor 2195
Colum, Mary "Molly" 1607
Condé, Maryse 3026
Crist, Judith 2424
Deutsch, Babette 1808
Dilke, Emilia 1093
Dolan, Jill 4403
Drew, Elizabeth 1662
Dunant, Sarah 3961
Faure, Elie 1458
Finch, Anne 497
Fremantle, Anne 2108
Gilliatt, Penelope 2799
Gordon, Mary Catherine 3898
Goulianos, Joan 3144
Greene, Gayle 3416
Grumbach, Doris Isaac 2317

Gullette, Margaret Morganroth
   3268
Gur, Batya 3749
Gwinn, Mary Ann 4044
Hardwick, Elizabeth 2270
Hart, Josephine 4367
Haskell, Molly 3147
Huxtable, Ada Louise 2402
Jacobson, Ethel 2022
Jameson, Anna Brownwell 844
Janeway, Elizabeth 2201
Johnson, Pamela Hansford 2181–
   2182
Johnston, Jill 2665
Jones, Patricia 4051
Kael, Pauline 2347
Keatley, Charlotte 4537
Kerr, Sarah 4966
King, Georgiana Goddard 1391
Krásnohorská, Eliska 1151
Lambert, Angela 3204
Lee, Hermione 3843
Lejeune, Caroline 1852
Leslie, Amy 1256
Lipton, Eunice 3278
Lowell, Amy 1440
Malcolm, Janet 2904
Mamonova, Tatyana Valentina 3096
Mansfield, Katherine 1687
Mason, Bobbie Ann 3209
McCarthy, Mary 2185
McDowell, Deborah E. 4058
Meynell, Alice Christiana 1152
Miles, Josephine 2162
Miller, Laura 3992
Newman, Frances 1598
Orlova, Raisa Davydovna 2327
Ostriker, Alicia Suskin 3051
Peery, Janet 3854
Peterson, Virgilia 2002–2003
Pool, Gail 3689
Postlethwaite, Diana 4000
Raine, Kathleen Jessie 2101
Rich, B. Ruby 4800
Riding, Laura 1938
Rittenhouse, Jessie 1367
Rose, Phyllis 3371
Sage, Lorna 3453
Seymour, Miranda J. 4207
Showalter, Elaine 3305
Sitwell, Edith 1673
Spacks, Patricia Meyer 2685
Spretnak, Charlene 3698
Staöl, Germaine de 733

Sternhell, Carol 4009
Stimpson, Catharine R. 3008
Tompkins, Jane P. 3234
Trevisan, Anna F. 2034
Tucker, Anne 3620
Van Rensselaer, Mariana Griswold
   1186
Vendler, Helen Hennessy 2872
Vicioso, Sherezada 3875
Vreeland, Diana 1984
West, Rebecca 1759
Winegarten, Renee 2443
Winslow, Thyra Samter 1985
Winwar, Frances 1923
Woolf, Virginia 1590
Wurtzel, Elizabeth 4762

BIOGRAPHERS, HISTORIANS, SCHOLARS, AND SOCIAL OR CULTURAL CRITICS

Abbott, Shirley 2875
Aburdene, Patricia 3709
Adler, Rachel 3387
Agnesi, Maria Gaōtana 581
Aidoo, Ama Ata 3316
Aiken, Lucy 785
Albery, Nobuko 3170
Applegate, Debby 4763
Arendt, Hannah 2036
Armstrong, Mary F. 1539
Ashrawi, Hanan 3627
Baker, Dorothy Gillam 2038
Basinger, Jeanine 2962
Bateson, Mary Catherine 3124
Baudonivia 117
Baynard, Anne 516
Beard, Mary Ritter 1471
Beard, Miriam 1926
Beatrijs of Nazareth 204
Bedford, Sybille von Schoenbeck 2152
Belenky, Mary Field 2834
Bell, Gertrude 1347
Benedict, Ruth 1659
Benét, Laura 1605
Berenson, Mary 1302
Bern, Sandra Lipsitz 3479
Bernal, Esmeralda 3886
Beruriah 216
Betsko, Kathleen 3125
Bird, Caroline 2237
Black, Barbara Aronstein 2836
Blackburn, Julia 3812
Blind, Mathilde 1100
Boulding, Elise M. 2362

Bowen, Catherine Drinker 1844
Bowen, Marjorie 1675–1676
Brady, Rose 4351
Brett, Dorothy 1591
Brightman, Carol 3126
Brodie, Fawn M. 2238
Brooke, Frances 593
Brookner, Anita 2620
Brown, Barbara B. 2621
Brown, Tina 4165
Brumberg, Joan Jacobs 3482
Cam, Helen M. 1625
Capek, Mary Ellen S. 4032
Carson, Anne Regina 3957
Carter, Elizabeth 578
Cartland, Barbara 1928
Case, Sue-Ellen 3328
Caulkins, Frances Manwaring 846
Chambers, Jessie 1661
Chang, Iris 4765
Chapone, Hester 598
Châtelet, Emilie du 557–558
Cheever, Susan 3396
Cheney, Lynne Ann 3248
Chin, Ann-ping 3817
Christina of Sweden 450
Christine de Pisan 244
Clarenbach, Kathryn 2366
Clinton, Catherine 4093
Coffin, Judith G. 4095
Coleridge, Mary 1264
Comnena, Anna 176
Connelly, Joan Breton 4240
Coontz, Stephanie 3490
Cooper, Anna Julia 1231
Corday, Charlotte 736
Cornelia 71
Craighead, Meinrad 2973
Cruz, Juana Inés de la 487
Dacier, Anne 488
Dauenhauer, Nora 2591
Davis, Rebecca Harding 1037
Decter, Midge 2592
Dey, Judy Goldberg 4977
Dodson, Lisa 4099
Dugaw, Dianne 3823
Dunbar-Ortiz, Roxanne 3084
Durant, Ariel 1864–1865
Dworkin, Andrea 3738
Edwards, Amelia 1040
Edwards, Betty 2547
Eisler, Riane 2756
Elstob, Elizabeth 528
Emerson, Mary Moody 763

Epstein, Cynthia Fuchs 2844
Faure, Elie 1458
Fedele, Cassandra 272
Fee, Elizabeth 3651
Ferguson, Kathy E. 3966
Fields, Annie Adams 1055
Fiorenza, Elisabeth Schüssler 3086
Fitzpatrick, Sheila Mary 3259
Flinders, Carol Lee 3406
Fraiberg, Selma 2314
Franz, Marie-Louise von 2240
Fraser, Antonia 2796
Freeman, Jo 3572
Fuller, Margaret 910
Galinsky, Ellen 3408
Gamble, Vanessa Northington 4177
Gelfant, Blanche H. 2429
Gelpi, Barbara C. 2849
Geniesse, Jane Fletcher 2977
Gilbert, Elizabeth 4788
Gilchrist, Marie 1770
Gilman, Charlotte Perkins 1254
Gilmore, Glenda Elizabeth 4640
Ginzburg, Eugenia 1994
Giroud, Françoise 2268
Goodwin, Doris Kearns 3415
Graff, E.J. 4452
Green, Constance McLaughlin 1849
Green, Mary A. E. 948
Green, Rayna 3338
Greene, Jennifer 3575
Gross, Rita M 3506
Grote, Harriet 833
Gulbadan Begam bint Babur
  Badshah 320
Gullette, Margaret Morganroth
  3268
Gutmann, Amy 3900
Guyon, Jeanne-Marie de la Motte
  482
Haiken, Elizabeth 4964
Hamilton, Edith 1336
Hammond, Eleanor Prescott 1328
Han Suyin 2291
Harrison, Jane 1176
Hazan, Marcella 2486
Hebard, Gracy 1269
Hecht, Jennifer Michael 4699
Hedrick, Joan D. 3510
Heilbrun, Carolyn G. 2552
Herron, Carolivia 3751
Higginson, Ella 1287
Hill, Catherine 4979
Hill, Ruth Beebe 2199
Himmelfarb, Gertrude 2432
Hine, Darlene Clark 3752
Hite, Shere 3344
Hochschild, Arlie Russell 3196
Holt, Anne Haw 2895
Home, Anne 639
hooks, bell 4305
Howe, Florence 2663
Howell, Georgina 3346
Huang Zongying 2522
Hubbard, Barbara Marx 2664
Hunt, Lynn 3583
Iskin, Ruth E. 2377
Jacobs, Jane 2271

Jacoby, Susan 3584
Jardine, Alice A. 4309
Jardine, Lisa 3515
Jeffreys, Sheila 3834
Jordan, June 2987
Jung, Emma 1578
Kamensky, Jane 4641
Kaminer, Wendy 3981
Kanner, Barbara "Penny" 2524
Kaplan, Temma E. 3350–3351
Kaufman, Paola 4792
Kelley, Kitty 3353
Kelly-Gadol, Joan 2632
Keuls, Eva Clara 2633
Kilbourne, Jean 3433
King, Georgiana Goddard 1391
Kraemer, Ross Shepard 3842
Kramarae, Cheris 3091
Krásnohorská, Eliska 1151
Kuklina, Ida 2528
Landowska, Wanda 1529
Lape, Esther 1569
Le Sueur, Meridel 1911
Lee, Hermione 3843
Leech, Margaret 1778
Leonard, Annie 4585
Lerner, Gerda 2380
Lewis, Edith 1551
Li Qingzhao 175
Lieberman, Alicia F. 3765
Liljestrvm, Rita 2635
Lim, Shirley Geok-Lin 3521
Lincoln, Victoria 1997
Lipstadt, Deborah 3767
Lipton, Eunice 3278
Lively, Penelope 2858
Lougee, Carolyn Chappell 3359
Luce, Gay Gaer 2724
Lute, Jane Holl 4378
MacKinnon, Catherine A. 3674
Macy, Joanna 2669
Makin, Bathsua 412
Malpede, Karen 3590
Marguerite of Navarre 289
Martin, Emily 3526
Martin, Jane Roland 2671
Martineau, Harriet 874
Massie, Suzanne 3280
Matheopoulos, Helena 3675
Matossian, Mariam 4865
Matthews, Glenna C. 3098
McCarthy, Mary 2185
McIntosh, Peggy 2906
Miller, Helen Hill 1889
Miner, Dorothy Eugenia 1999
Mitford, Jessica 2298
Mitford, Nancy 2000
Mittal, Anuradha 4774
Moore, Virginia 1975
Morata, Olimpia 325
Morgan, Sydney Owenson 770
Murray, Janet Horowitz 3679
Nogarola, Isotta 254
Norris, Pippa 4200
Nussbaum, Martha C. 3778
Oliphant, Margaret 1019
Owen, Mary A. 1179
Pagels, Elaine 3445

Paglia, Camille 3780
Painter, Nell 3365
Pankhurst, Sylvia 1583
Pardoe, Julia 898
Partridge, Frances 1918
Pateman, Carole 3219
Peiss, Kathy 4203
Penley, Constance 3924
Pert, Candace B. 3687
Petchesky, Rosalind Pollack 3366
Pinkard, Susan 4204
Poole, Jeannie Gayle 4068
Power, Samantha 4829
Profet, Margie 4465
Pulcheria, Aelia 109
Rabi'a al-Adawiya 136
Raine, Kathleen Jessie 2101
Räthzel, Nora 3858
Raven, Arlene 3533
Reitz, Rosetta 2493
Repplier, Agnes 1236
Rice, Susan E. 4687
Rich, B. Ruby 4800
Richards, Janet Radcliffe 3535
Richie, Alexandra 4651
Richter, Gisela 1585
Ripley, Sarah Alden 841
Robinson, Therese Albertine Louise
  858
Rochlin, Harriet 2494
Rose, Phyllis 3371
Rosen, Marjorie 3372
Rosen, Ruth 3608
Rossi, Alice S. 2439
Roy, Sara 4330
Rudikoff, Sonya 2612
Rukeyser, Muriel 2210
Salisbury, Joyce Ellen 3537
Sandler, Bernice "Bunny" R. 2641
Scarf, Maggie 2819
Schneir, Miriam 2864
Schreiner, Olive 1208
Schultz, Tammy S. 4887
Schurman, Anna Maria van 422
Schwarcz, Vera 3793
Seeger, Ruth Crawford 1939
Seton, Julia 1701
Sewall, Sarah 4596
Sewell, Sarah Ann 1128
Seymour, Miranda J. 4207
Sforza, Costanza Varano 256
Shalom, Imma 91
Shalvi, Alice 2578
Sheehy, Gail 3059
Sigea, Luisa 321
Simon, Kate 2190
Slapsak, Svetlana 3867
Snow, Helen Foster 2073
Sontag, Susan 2866
Southern, Eileen Jackson 2392
St. John, Christopher Marie 1466
Stanton, Elizabeth Cady 931
Stern, Edith Mendel 1941
Storkey, Elaine 3460
Stowe, Harriet Beecher 916
Strouse, Jean 3617
Swerdlow, Amy 2470
Tappan, Eva March 1203

Tarabotti, Arcangela 419
Tarbell, Ida 1227
Teubal, Savina J. 2582
Toth, Emily 3545
Treichler, Paula Antonia 3463
Ts'ai Yen 98
Tuchman, Barbara 2192
Tucker, Anne 3620
Ulrich, Laurel Thatcher 3109
Wade-Gayles, Gloria Jean 3112
Wagner, Sally Roesch 3384
Walker, Barbara G. 2744
Wandor, Michelene 3237
Ward, Celeste M. 4853
Warner, Marina 3706
Warren, Mercy Otis 603
Webb, Beatrice Potter 1239
Weil, Simone 2116
Weimer, Joan Myers 3012
Willard, Nancy 3013
Willner, Ann Ruth 3166
Wineapple, Brenda 4152
Wohlstetter, Roberta 2194
Wortham, Anne 3314
Wright, Susanna 546
Yung, Judy 3167
Zaturenska, Marya 1961

EDUCATION, CIVIC AND FOUNDATION/ASSOCIATION ADMINISTRATORS, AND CONSULTANTS

Alexander, Jane 3117
Andrus, Ethel Percy 1604
Aróstica, Florencia 4345
Astor, Brooke 1946
Barley, Mary 3632
Bello, Mairo 4670
Bettencourt, Liliane Schueller 2418
Biddle, Flora Miller 3722
Black, Barbara Aronstein 2836
Brackett, Anna C. 1070
Braude, Ann Deborah 4291
Brown, Trisha 2967
Bryant, Castell 3815
Budiardjo, Carmel 2512
Burk, Martha Gertrude 3247
Capek, Mary Ellen S. 4032
Catt, Carrie Chapman 1244
Clancy, Carolyn 4238
Cole, Johnnetta B. 2971
Danowitz, Jane 3890
Davenport, Doris 3891
Dole, Elizabeth Hanford 2975
Edelman, Marian Wright 3141
Feldt, Gloria 3333
Flores-Oebanda, Cecilia 4528
Fraser, Arvonne 2517
Gildersleeve, Virginia 1493
Girsh, Faye Joan 2851
Gurung, Jeanette D. 4303
Gutmann, Amy 3900
Hafild, Emmy 4488
Hale, Clara Mcbride 2020
Hallman, Linda D. 4179
Harris, Jean 2458
Healy, Bernadine 3509
Hollibaugh, Amber 3754

Hong, Rani 4862
Hooyman, Nancy R. 3582
Horner, Matina S. 3148–3149
Howe, Florence 2663
Jamieson, Kathleen Hall 3667
Jehangir, Asma 4112
Johnsen, Dawn 4620
Kagan, Elena 4536
Kahlil, Aisha 3199
Keenan, Nancy 4114
Kegel, Martha 4455
Kellett, Christine H. 3274
Kramarae, Cheris 3091
Kramer, Melinda 4935
Liu, Peggy 4624
Lopata, Jadwiga 4258
Lord, Betty Bao 3094
Lougee, Carolyn Chappell 3359
Makhubu, Lydia Phindile 3045
Malveaux, Julianne 4190
Martin, Jane Roland 2671
Mashinini, Emma 2672
Mason, Viviane Carter 1913
McCrory, Colleen 3991
Michelman, Kate 3361
Mirikitani, Janice 3283
Moeller, Susan D. 4731
Moran, Ellen 4732
Mpaayei, Florence 4545
Murungi, Kaari Betty 4983
Nichols, Mary D. 3600
Njogu, Ann Wairimu 4775
Norman, Marsha 3776
Okello-Orlale, Rosemary 4709
O'Neill, Terry 4202.1
Oreskes, Naomi 4463
Palmer, Alice Freeman 1206
Parker, Gail Thain 3446
Phillips, Bonnie 3367
Putnam, Emily James 1318
Richards, Cecile 4466
Richman, Julia 1207
Rogers, Lesley 3452
Roumeau, Jacqueline 4985
Scanlan, Susan 3791
Shaheed, Farida 4208
Shalala, Donna 3304
Sills, Beverly 2684
Simmons, Ruth 3614
Slaughter, Anne-Marie 4471
Smeal, Eleanor 3160
Stifter, Vicky 4073
Strouse, Jean 3617
Sutherland, Efua Theodora 2498
Sutley, Nancy 4632
Tarule, Jill M. 3462
Thomas, Martha "Minnie" 1228
Tilghman, Shirley M. 3701
Torres, Amaryllis Tiglao 3544
Tyson, Laura D'Andrea 3804
Wagner, Sally Roesch 3384
Walders, Davi 3113
Wattleton, Faye 3469
Weinberg, Sheila Pelz 3707
Were, Beatrice 4741
Wilson, Dorothy Wright 4838–4839
Wilson, Marie C. 3877
Win, Aye Aye 4807

Wucker, Michele 4808
Yunusova, Leyla 4437

EDUCATORS AND INSTRUCTORS

Adams, Léonie 1880
Addonzio, Kim 4223
Adler, Freda 2876
Adler, Rachel 3387
Aguilar, Grace 932
Aguirre, Isidora 2337
Ahmed, Leila 3169
Ai 3711
Aidoo, Ama Ata 3316
Aiken, Joyce 2750
Akalaitis, JoAnne 3016
Al Kuwaiz, Samira 4664
Albelda, Randy 4288
Alcosser, Sandra 3472
Alexander, Elizabeth 4601
Allen, Paula Gunn 3118
Aloni, Shulamit 2650
Alvarez, Julia 3950
Anastasi, Anne 2076
Andrews, Lori B. 4156
Andrus, Ethel Percy 1604
Anthony, Katharine 1487
Antler, Joyce 3320
Anzaldúa, Gloria Evangelina 3321
Apter, Terri 3882
Armantrout, Rae 3716
Armstrong, Mary F. 1539
Arrien, Angeles 2920
Arroyo, Gloria Macapagal 3717
Arslan, Antonia 3069
Ashenburg, Katherine 3951
Ashrawi, Hanan 3627
Ashton-Warner, Sylvia 2079
Aspasia 62
Avery, Byllye Y. 3019
Baca, Judy Francisca 3953
Bacon, Martha 2280
Bair, Sheila C. 4229
Baker, Dorothy Gillam 2038
Baker-Fletcher, Karen 4517
Balch, Emily Greene 1333
Baldwin, Christina 3629
Bambara, Toni Cade 3121
Bang, Mary Jo 3630
Barnard, Jessie 1965
Barnhouse, Ruth Tiffany 2446
Barrett, Michèle 3885
Barrow, Lisa 4669
Barry, Kathleen 3123
Bartholet, Elizabeth 3172
Bar-Yosef, Rivka Weiss 3323
Basinger, Jeanine 2962
Basu, Aparna 4930
Bates, Katherine Lee 1241
Bateson, Mary Catherine 3124
Bazan, Emilia Pardo 1189
Beck, Evelyn Torton 2833
Becker, Robin 4023
Beecher, Catharine Esther 865
Belenky, Mary Field 2834
Benedict, Agnes E 1694
Benston, Margaret Lowe 3020
Berry, Mary Frances 3073
Berssenbrugge, Mei-mei 3721

Bethune, Mary McLeod 1453
Biden, Jill 4027
Bieber, Margarete 1521
Bilmes, Linda J. 4521
Bishop, Wendy Sue 4161
Black, Barbara Aronstein 2836
Blackmore, Susan Jane 4028
Blais, Madeleine 3723
Blee, Kathleen M. 4162
Bonaparte, Marie L. 1564
Borysenko, Joan Z. 3638
Botta, Anne 926
Botume, Elizabeth 1371
Bovasso, Julie Anne 2693
Bowen, 'Asta 4290
Bowles, Gloria 4350
Bowman, Meg 2653
Boyle, Kay 1947
Brackett, Anna C. 1070
Bradley, Marion Zimmer 2694
Braid, Bernice 2837
Bridgford, Kim Suzanne 4477
Briggs, Dorothy Corkille 2477
Brookner, Anita 2620
Brown, Charlotte 1577
Brown, Rita Mae 3481
Brown, Tabitha Moffatt 779
Brubaker, Pamela K. 3640
Bryant, Castell 3815
Bunch, Charlotte 3483
Bunting, Mary Ingraham 2121
Burkett, Elinor 3394
Burnell, Jocelyn Bell 3395
Burroughs, Nannie Helen 1592
Busfield, Joan 3130
Bush, Laura 3641
Cabeza de Baca, Fabiola 1806–1807
Cahill, Susan 3178
Calderone, Mary Steichen 1989
Calisher, Hortense 2154
Cam, Helen M. 1625
Camp, Tracy 4671
Campan, Jeanne Louise 672
Campbell, Anne 4031
Capps, Lois 3076
Carew, Elizabeth 391
Carney, Julia A. 986
Case, Sue-Ellen 3328
Castellani, Maria 2699
Castle, Victoria 3889
Cather, Katherine Dunlap 1489
Catt, Carrie Chapman 1244
Caulkins, Frances Manwaring 846
Cervantes, Lorna Dee 4234
Chang, Tina 4783
Chard, Sylvia C. 3077
Charkowski, Amy O. 4841
Châtelet, Emilie du 557–558
Chesler, Phyllis 3184
Chiang Kai-shek 1863
Chin, Ann-ping 3817
Chin, Marilyn 4295
Chisholm, Shirley 2480
Christian, Barbara T. 3397
Chua, Amy 4605
Cisneros, Sandra 4237
Cixous, Hélène 3025
Clappe, Louise Amelia 954

Clarenbach, Kathryn 2366
Clarke, Edith 1594
Cleyre, Voltairine de 1325
Clifton, Lucille 2970
Clinchy, Blythe M. 2700
Clinton, Catherine 4093
Cofer, Judith Ortiz 4094
Coffin, Judith G. 4095
Cohen, Amy 3329
Cohen, Deborah S. 3820
Cohen, Mary M. 1202
Cohen, Sherry Suib 2885
Cole, Johnnetta B. 2971
Coleridge, Mary 1264
Colledge, Cecilia 2367
Collins, Marva Nettles 2972
Collins, Patricia Hill 3821
Comini, Alessandra 3079
Cone, Helen Gray 1245
Conklin, Beth Ann 4239
Connelly, Joan Breton 4240
Conrad, Beatrice 2590
Cook, Blanche Weisen 3249
Coombs, Mary 3489
Coontz, Stephanie 3490
Cooper, Anna Julia 1231
Cooper, Jane 2481
Corey, Shirley Trusty 2923
Cotton, Nancy 3492
Crane, Nathalia 2196
Crapsey, Adelaide 1510
Cumming, Patricia 2791
Cuomo, Chris J. 4674
Curtis, Rebecca 4883
Dalla Costa, Mariarosa 3081
Daly, Mary 2623
Dauenhauer, Nora 2591
Daughtrey, Martha Craig 3331
Davidson, Janine 4745
Davidson, Laura Lee 1372
Davis, Angela 3493
Davis, Thadious M. 3494
Delany, Sarah "Sadie" 1696
Derricotte, Toi 3254
Dinnerstein, Dorothy 2452
DiPerna, Paula 3892
Dixon, Marlene 2974
Dodson, Lisa 4099
Donnelly, Liza 4297
Doody, Margaret Anne 3138
Doress-Worters, Paula B. 3082
Dove, Rita Frances 4101
Dowd, Nancy E. 3893
Dresselhaus, Mildred Spiewak 2702
DuBois, Ellen Carol 3737
Dugaw, Dianne 3823
Dunbar-Nelson, Alice 1457
Dunbar-Ortiz, Roxanne 3084
Duncan, Isadora 1512
Dungy, Camille T. 4858
Eckenstein, Lina 1220
Edson, Margaret 4571
Elkins, Caroline 4786
Elstob, Elizabeth 528
Emerson, Claudia 4406
Epstein, Cynthia Fuchs 2844
Epstein, Helen 3740
Ertük, Yakin 4572

Escot, Pozzi 2845
Espinosa, María 3142
Eugene-Richard, Margie 3332
Evans, Mari 2453
Falk, Marcia 3650
Fausto-Sterling, Anne 3499
Fee, Elizabeth 3651
Felton, Rebecca Latimer 1064
Fernandez, Irene 3652
Fernea, Elizabeth Warnock 2595
Fingerhut, Arden 3654
Fiorenza, Elisabeth Schüssler 3086
Fitzpatrick, Sheila Mary 3259
Flanagan, Hallie 1705
Flinders, Carol Lee 3406
Frantz, Marge 2315
Freed, Lynn 4104
Fremantle, Anne 2108
Fuller, Margaret 910
Fulton, Alice 4105
Furman, Laura 3574
Galchen, Rivka 4907
Gallagher, Tess 3409
Galland, China 3410
Galloway, Priscilla 2705
Gamble, Vanessa Northington 4177
Garber, Marjorie B. 3501
Gardiner, Lisa 1902
Gawain, Shakti 3827
Gearhart, Sally Miller 2758
Gelfant, Blanche H 2429
Gelpi, Barbara C. 2849
Gerber, Merrill Joan 3087
Germain, Sylvie 4249
Gerson, Kathleen 3746
Geyer, Georgie Anne 2930
Gibson, Margaret 3504
Gibson, P.J. 4107
Gilbert, Sandra 2978
Gillan, Maria Mazziotto 3190
Gilman, Caroline 843
Gilmore, Glenda Elizabeth 4640
Gilson, Mary Barnett 1494
Ginsburg, Ruth Bader 2850
Giovanni, Nikki 3412
Glendon, Mary Ann 3088
Glück, Louise Elisabeth 3413
Godwin, Gail 3032
Goldberg, Natalie 3828
Goldberger, Nancy Rule 2891
Golden, Marita 3970
Goodison, Lorna 3747
Gorbachev, Raisa Maxima 2800
Gordon, Bette 4366
Gordon, Mary Catherine 3898
Gordon-Reed, Annette 4532
Goren-Bar, Dina 4451
Graham, Isabella 638
Graham, Martha 1795
Grandin, Temple 3748
Gratz, Rebecca 788
Green, Constance McLaughlin 1849
Greenberg, Blu 2981
Greene, Gayle 3416
Greene, Jeanette 2661
Greene, Jennifer 3575
Greer, Germaine 3145
Gregg, Linda 3339

Griffin, Susan 3417
Grimké, Sarah Moore 832
Gross, Rita M 3506
Grossman, Chaika 2344
Gubar, Susan 3507
Guest, Judith 2982
Gur, Batya 3749
Gutmann, Amy 3900
Hadley, Tessa 4410
Hagen, Uta 2345
Haiken, Elizabeth 4964
Hainstock, Elizabeth G. 2630
Halifax, Joan 3341
Hamilton, Elizabeth 691
Hardwick, Elizabeth 2270
Harjo, Joy 4045
Harris, Janet 2243
Harris, Jean 2458
Harris, Patricia Roberts 2485
Harris, Ruth Mae 3195
Hartman, Saidiya 3974
Harvey, Matthea 4876
Haskins, Minnie 1459
Hauser, Ewa 3662
Hausman, Bernice L. 4618
Hazan, Marcella 2486
Hazleton, Lesley 3578
Hebard, Gracy 1269
Hebblethwaite, Margaret 4250.1
Hecht, Jennifer Michael 4699
Hedrick, Joan D. 3510
Heilbrun, Carolyn G. 2552
Heldman, Caroline 4860
Hempel, Amy 4046
Heng, Geraldine 4974
Henley, Nancy M. 2894
Henrion, Claudia 4454
Herbert, Marie 3270
Herman, Judith Lewis 3342
Herman, Susan 3343
Herndon, Rosanna Taylor 2713
Herron, Carolivia 3751
Heyward, Carter 3579
Higgins, Tracy E. 4700
Hill, Anita 4369
Himmelfarb, Gertrude 2432
Hine, Darlene Clark 3752
Hite, Shere 3344
Hochschild, Arlie Russell 3196
hooks, bell 4305
Hooyman, Nancy R. 3582
Hope, Lugenia Burns 1390.1
Hopkins, Nancy 3511
Hopper, Grace Murray 2048
Horner, Matina S. 3148–3149
Hospital, Janette Turner 3345
Hou Xiaotian 4581
Houston, Velina Hasu 4413
Howard, Jane 2936
Howe, Florence 2663
Howe, Marie 3975
Howe, Tina 3038
Hrdy, Sarah Blaffer 3665
Hubbard, Ruth 2487
Hull, Jane Dee 2937
Hunt, Lynn 3583
Hyatt, Lesley A. 4700.1
Hyman, Judith Partnow 3089

Hypatia 107
Ibrahim, Hauwa 4701
Irigaray, Luce 2717
Isasi-Diaz, Ada Maria 3424
Itatani, Michiko 4182
Jackson, Elaine 3425
Jackson, Jacquelyne J. 2802
Jackson, Maggie 4679
James, Sibyl 3666
Jamieson, Kathleen Hall 3667
Jardine, Alice A. 4309
Jay, Karla 3758
Jemison, Mae 4374
Johnsen, Dawn 4620
Johnson, Diane 2900
Johnson, Guion Griffis 1908
Johnston, Annie Fellows 1296
Jones, Amanda Theodosia 1066
Jordan, Barbara 2986
Jordan, June 2987
Joya, Malalai 4927
Justin, Dena 2183
Kaara, Wahu 4185
Kagan, Elena 4536
Kalish, Mildred Armstrong 2460
Kamal, Zahira 3586
Kanter, Rosabeth Moss 3429
Kaplan, Gisela 3516.1
Kaplan, Temma E. 3351
Karr, Mary 4310
Kasdorf, Julia Spicher 4623
Katz, Lilian G. 2805
Kauffman, Linda S. 3903
Kaufman, Bel 2160
Kay, Jackie 4583
Kaye, Carol 2525
Kearney, Belle 1297
Keatley, Charlotte 4537
Keller, Evelyn Fox 2988
Kelly, Brigit Pegeen 4052
Kempton, Sally 3430
Kennedy, A. L. 4703
Kent, Corita 2318
Kerber, Linda Kaufman 3201
Keuls, Eva Clara 2633
Khalifeh, Imane 4896
Kim, Elaine Haikyung 3354
Kim, Myung Mi 4418
King, Deborah K. 4254
King, Georgiana Goddard 1391
King-Hammond, Leslie 3517
Kintz, Linda 3587
Kirkpatrick, Jeane 2558
Kitzinger, Celia 4539
Kitzinger, Jenny 4644
Kitzinger, Sheila 2667
Kiyak, H. Asuman 4054
Kizer, Carolyn 2527
Klein, Laura Cousino 4768
Klepfisz, Irena 3276
Kohut, Rebekah Bettelheim 1304
Kraemer, Ross Shepard 3842
Kramer, Joyce 3357
Kreps, Juanita 2403
Lagarde, Marcela 3983
Langer, Felicia 2722
Langer, Susanne K. 1817
Lape, Esther 1569

Lazarre, Jane D. 3436
Le Row, Caroline Bigelow 1117
Le Shan, Eda J. 2434
Lease, Mary 1178
Lee, Ettie 1634
Lee, Hermione 3843
Lee, Sophia 664
Lehman, Lotte 1685
Lepore, Jill 4725
Lerner, Gerda 2380
Lesser, Elizabeth 4117
LeTendre, Mary Jean 3844
Levertov, Denise 2464
Levin, Diane E. 3764
Levinson, Nan 3911
Lieberman, Alicia F. 3765
Lightfoot, Sara Lawrence 3520
Liljeström, Rita 2635
Lim, Shirley Geok-Lin 3521
Lipstadt, Deborah 3767
Litman, Ellen 4878
Litman, Jane 3206
Loftus, Elizabeth Fishman 3522
Louis, Minnie D. 1105
Lowry, Beverly 3095
Lubchenco, Jane 3768
Luker, Kristin Carol 3673
Lyon, Mary 855
Maathai, Wangari Muta 3207
MacKinnon, Catherine A. 3674
MacMurray, Rose 2405
Madgett, Naomi Long 2465
Madison, D. Soyiini 3912
Mairs, Nancy 3440
Malagrino, Silvia A. 3988
Malpede, Karen 3590
Manji, Irshad 4772
Manos, Helen 3989
Marcus, Lisa 4704
Martin, Anne Henrietta 1463
Martin, Lynn 3151
Matossian, Mariam 4865
Matsumoto, Valerie 4420
Mavrikakis, Catherine 4588
McAleese, Mary 4057
McAuliffe, Christa 3848
McCarthy, Sarah J. 3360
McCaughey, Martha 4726
McClintock, Barbara 1952
McDermott, Alice 4193
McDowell, Deborah E. 4058
McHugh, Heather 3849
McIntyre, Tami 2409
McKellar, Danica 4898.1
McMullan, Margaret 4542
McPhee, Martha S. 4683
McPherson, Sandra 3441
Meitner, Lise 1514
Mercer, Margaret 825
Meyer, Leisa D. 4647
Michel, Louise 1030
Miles, Josephine 2162
Milgrom, Shira 4062
Miller, Alyce 4194
Miller, Jean Baker 2607
Mills, Stephanie 3851
Mink, Gwendolyn 4122
Minow, Martha 4263

Mirrielees, Edith Ronald 1515
Mistral, Gabriela 1700
Mitchell, Juliet 3212
Mitchell, Maria 951
Moffat, Mary Jane 2859
Mohammed, Binta S. 4796
Moïse, Penina 856
Molina de Pick, Gracia 2727
Montessori, Maria 1381
Moore, Lorrie 4421
Moore, Martha Milcah 632
Mora, Elizabeth Catlett 2351
Moraga, Cherríe 4125
Morgan, Barbara "Barb" 4063
Morgan, Elaine 2383
Moses, Claire Goldberg 3285
Moskowitz, Faye S. 2728
Mukherjee, Bharati 3216
Mullen, Harryette Romell 4197
Munk, Erika 3152
Murray, Janet Horowitz 3679
Murray, Margaret Alice 1298
Murray, Pauli 2139
Myerhoff, Barbara 2940
Nafisi, Azar 4320
Namjoshi, Suniti 3287
Naqvi, Tahira 4198
Nelson, Donna J. 4199
Nelson, Marilyn 3680
Nenadic, Natalie 4967
Newman, Jody 4498
Niederman, Sharon 3853
Noddings, Nel 2675
Nomani, Asra Q. 4708
Norman, Liane 3049
Norris, Pippa 4200
Nunez, Sigrid 4067
Nussbaum, Martha C. 3778
O'Brien, Mary Mamie 2571
Ochs, Vanessa L. 4201
O'Hara, Maureen 4202
Okin, Susan Moller 3684
Olds, Sharon 3364
Oliver, Mary 2941
Olsen, Frances 3603
O'Neill, Terry 4202.1
Oreskes, Naomi 4463
Otero, María 3998
Overall, Christine 3923
Owens, Rochelle 2996
Pagels, Elaine 3445
Paglia, Camille 3780
Painter, Charlotte 2572
Painter, Nell 3365
Paley, Vivian Gussin 2677
Parker, Gail Thain 3446
Partnow, Susan 3782
Pateman, Carole 3219
Patkar, Medha 4266
Payne-Gaposchkin, Cecilia Helena 1919
Peabody, Elizabeth Palmer 886
Pearce, Susan C. 4387
Peery, Janet 3854
Peiss, Kathy 4203
Peled-Elhanan, Nurit 4326
Penley, Constance 3924
Peri, Janis-Rozena 3221

Perl, Teri 2573
Petchesky, Rosalind Pollack 3366
Phelps, Almira Lincoln 840
Phillips, Anne 4426
Phillips, Jayne Anne 4133
Phillips, Lois 3222
Pierce-Baker, Charlotte 3447
Pierpont, Claudia Roth 4134
Pinkard, Susan 4204
Plaskow, Judith 3785
Plato, Ann 975
Polowy, Carol 4388
Ponsot, Marie Birmingham 2410
Pool, Gail 3689
Postlethwaite, Diana 4000
Powell, Maxine 2492.1
Power, Susan 4593
Pratt, Minnie Bruce 3690
Prejean, Helen 3155
Prell, Riv-Ellen 3786
Preston, Ann 921
Propp, Karen 4428
Prothrow-Stith, Deborah 4267
Putnam, Emily James 1318
Quimby, Edith 1732
Qurrat al-'Ayn 1195
Rahman, Aishah 2999
Rajalakshmi, R. 2574
Rambert, Marie 1733
Ramey, Estelle R. 2300
Ran, Shulamit 3928
Ravitch, Diane 3102
Ray, Dixy Lee 2227
Raymond, Janice G. 3930
Rebolledo, Tey Diana 3052
Reddy, Maureen 4328
Reeves, Nancy 2209
Reinharz, Shulamit 3693
Rhode, Deborah L. 4137
Rice, Condoleezza 4268
Rich, Adrienne 2680
Richman, Julia 1207
Riley, Janet Mary 2254
Rivers, Caryl 3053
Roberts, Dorothy E. 4389
Robinson, Lillian 3300
Robinson, Mabel Louise 1449
Robinson, Mary 693
Roepke, Gabriela 2388
Rogers, Pattiann 3225
Romer, Christina D. 4468
Rose, Phyllis 3371
Rosen, Ruth 3608
Rosenstein, Harriet 2818
Rosenthal, Rachel 2576
Ross, Susan C. 3373
Rossi, Alice S. 2439
Roulet, Elaine 2738
Rouse, Cecilia 4652
Row, Amanda 2774
Rozman, Deborah 3933–3934
Rudman, Masha Kabakow 2863
Rudy, Kathy 4391
Ruether, Rosemary Radford 3004
Russell, Diana E. H. 3104
Sabin, Florence 1393
Salisbury, Joyce Ellen 3537
Salter, Mary Jo 4270

Samalin, Nancy 3055
Sanchez, Carol Lee 2911
Sanchez, Sonia 2912
Sandler, Bernice "Bunny" R. 2641
Sappho 46
Sassen, Georgia 3936
Scattergood, Sally 4832–4833
Schaeffer, Susan Fromberg 3302
Schapiro, Miriam 2468
Schroeder, Pat 3227
Schulder, Diane B. 3056
Schultz, Tammy S. 4887
Schwarz, Christina 4653
Seaberg, Rönnog 2820
Seager, Joni 4273
Sears, Vicki 3303
Sedgwick, Catherine Maria 812
Semmel, Joan 2821
Shaikh, Shamima 4556
Shainess, Natalie 2256
Shelton, Charlotte 3795
Sherfey, Mary Jane 2865
Sherman, Gail Berkeley 4209
Sherman, Susan 3158
Sigea, Luisa 321
Sigourney, Lydia Howard 827
Simmons, Ruth 3614
Simon, Maurya 4004
Sinclair, Lee 4431.1
Siunetsi, Sahakdoukht 148
Slapsak, Svetlana 3867
Slaughter, Anne-Marie 4471
Small, Meredith F. 4005
Smith, Anna Deavere 4006
Smith, Nora Archibald 1250
Smith, Sarah 3797
Snow, Helen Foster 2073
Sofola, Zulu 2952
Softic-Kaunitz, Elma 4597
Sokoloff, Natalie J. 3542
Somers, Helen 2824
Sommers, Christina Hoff 4007
Sotomayor, Sonia 4273.1
Southern, Eileen Jackson 2392
Spacks, Patricia Meyer 2685
Spellberg, Denise A. 4986
Spencer, Anna Garlin 1185
Spender, Dale 3458
Speyer, Leonora 1406
Spolin, Viola 2056
Spretnak, Charlene 3698
St. Denis, Ruth 1557
Stannard, Una 2613
Steichen, Joanna T. 2868
Sternhell, Carol 4009
Stevens, Nettie Maria 1279
Stewart, Maria W. 882
Stiller, Nikki 4988
Stimpson, Catharine R. 3008
Stiver, Irene Pierce 2497
Stone, Merlin 2778
Stopes, Marie Carmichael 1558
Strout, Elizabeth 4473
Subramaniam, Banu 4145
Sugimoto, Etsu Inagaki 1451
Sullivan, Annie 1332
Süssmuth, Rita 3061
Suzman, Helen 2303

Swerda, Patricia 2277
Tadjo, Véronique 4334
Taggard, Genevieve 1805
Tannen, Deborah F. 3618
Tapp, June L. 2743
Tarule, Jill M. 3462
Taylor, Janelle S. 4873
Teish, Luisah 3871
Terrell, Mary Church 1299
Thomas, Audrey Grace 2953
Thomas, Lynn M. 3801
Thomas, Martha "Minnie" 1228
Thompson, Clara 1787
Thompson, Jean 4010
Thorne, Barrie 3380
Tilghman, Shirley M. 3701
Tillman, Lynne 3802
Todd, Mabel Elsworth 1559
Tohidi, Nayereh 4658
Tompkins, Jane P. 3234
Tonna, Charlotte Elizabeth 821
Torgovnick, Marianna 3940
Toro, María Suárez 3874
Torres, Amaryllis Tiglao 3544
Toth, Emily 3545
Towne, Laura 1004
Trapido, Barbara 3308
Treerat, Nualnoi 4659
Tremain, Rose 3464
Trethewey, Natasha 4737
Trimmer, Sarah Kirby 637
Trinh, T. Minh-Ha 4147
Trotula of Salerno 177
Turkle, Sherry 4738
Tyson, Laura D'Andrea 3804
Uhlenbeck, Karen 3382
Ulrich, Laurel Thatcher 3109
Umansky, Ellen M. 4011
Valentine, Jean 2917
Valian, Virginia 3383
Van Duyn, Mona 2415
Vendler, Helen Hennessy 2872
Vicioso, Sherezada 3875
Viramontes, Helena María 4279
Vogel, Paula A. 4076
Vreeland, Susan 3704
Wade-Gayles, Gloria Jean 3112
Wagner, Melinda 4436
Wagner, Sally Roesch 3384
Walbert, Kate 4598.1
Waldman, Anne 3621
Waldo, Octavia Capuzzi 2686
Walker, Alice 3547
Walker, Margaret 2259
Wallace, Cath 4338
Walters, Anna Lee 3705
Wanatee, Adeline 2144
Washington, Harriet A. 4634
Wasserstein, Wendy 4013
Weimer, Joan Myers 3012
Weisberg, Ruth 3385
Weisman, Leslie Kanes 3623
Weisstein, Naomi 3165
Wells, Ida B. 1291
Wheatley, Margaret "Meg" 3311
Whiteman, Roberta Hill 3806–3807
Whitman, Marina von Neumann 2957

Wiggin, Kate Douglas 1214
Wilcox, Margaret R. 2146
Wildman, Stephanie M. 3945
Willard, Emma Hart 806
Willard, Nancy 3013
Williams, E. Faye 3312
Williams, Fannie Barrier 1210
Williams, Joy 3550
Williams, Lynda 4475
Williams, Patricia 4079
Williams, Sherley Anne 3551–3552
Williams, Shirley 2746
Williams, Terry Tempest 4339
Willis, Gwendolen 1486
Willner, Ann Ruth 3166
Willson, Margaret 4219
Wilson, Dorothy Wright 4838–4839
Winnemucca, Sarah 1133
Witkovsky, Susan 3386
Witt, Shirley Hill 2918
Wittig, Monique 2958
Wohlstetter, Roberta 2194
Wolitzer, Hilma 2748
Wolitzer, Meg 4511
Woo, Merle 3313
Woolley, Hannah 443
Yang Jiang 2171
Yankowitz, Susan 3315
Yee, Marian 4989
Young, Iris Marion 3947
Young, Leontine 2148
Yung, Judy 3167
Zarin, Cynthia Rebecca 4513
Zeidner, Lisa 4341
Zuboff, Shoshana 4081

LIBRARIANS, CURATORS, AND PRESERVATIONISTS

Ayscough, Florence 1504
Bush, Laura 3641
Coolbrith, Ina 1102
Dauenhauer, Nora 2591
Davis, Elizabeth Gould 2124
Eastwood, Alice 1247
Greene, Bella da Costa 1527
Hurston, Zora Neale 1727
Jacobs, Deborah 4111
King-Hammond, Leslie 3517
Li Qingzhao 175
Mead, Margaret 1935
Miner, Dorothy Eugenia 1999
Mojtabai, A.G. 3046
Newman, Frances 1598
Pfeiffer, Ida Laura 857
Reagon, Bernice Johnson 3369
Richter, Gisela 1585
Stevens, Nettie Maria 1279
Szasz, Suzy 4213
Vreeland, Diana 1984

PHILOSOPHERS

Abbagnano, Nicola 1924
Adler, Renata 3068
Agreda, María de 415
Arendt, Hannah 2036
Beauvoir, Simone de 2080
Besant, Annie Wood 1148
Bok, Sissela Ann 2881

Cixous, Hélène 3025
Daly, Mary 2623
Dunayevskaya, Raya 2126
Frye, Marilyn 3262
Hampson, Daphne 3508
Harding, Sandra G. 2934
d'Hericourt, Jenny P. 906
Houston, Jean 3037
Hypatia 107
Irigaray, Luce 2717
Koller, Alice 2488
Kristeva, Julia 3277
Langer, Susanne K. 1817
Mill, Harriet Taylor 902
Neiman, Susan 4321
Noddings, Nel 2675
Nussbaum, Martha C. 3778
O'Brien, Mary Mamie 2571
Okin, Susan Moller 3684
Peace Pilgrim 2098
Piper, Adrian 3688
Rand, Ayn 2032
Richards, Janet Radcliffe 3535
Roth, Friederike 3863
Stein, Edith 1735
Storkey, Elaine 3460
Weil, Simone 2116

B. ARTS AND ENTERTAINMENT

ACTORS, ENTERTAINERS, AND PERFORMERS

Abbott, Patsy 2690
Adams, Maude 1396
Adelman, Penina V. 4155
Adjani, Isabelle 4287
Ahmed, Naima 4600
Aimée, Anouk 2782
Alexander, Jane 3117
Allen, Charlotte Vale 3239
Anderson, Judith 1841
Anderson, Laurie 3714
Angelou, Maya 2618
Aniston, Jennifer 4778
Arizmendi, Yareli 4666
Arnould, Sophie 628
Astor, Mary 2037
Atkins, Eileen 2878
Bacall, Lauren 2476
Bai Fengxi 2785
Ball, Lucille 2150
Bancroft, Anne 2786
Bankhead, Tallulah 1964
Bara, Theda 1623
Bardot, Brigitte 2879
Barr, Nevada 4084
Barr, Roseanne 4085
Barrymore, Ethel 1520
Belmont, Eleanor Robson 1505
Berg, Gertrude 1882
Bergen, Candice 3635
Bergman, Ingrid 2236
Bernhard, Sandra 4289
Bernhardt, Sarah 1122
Bisset, Jacqueline 3637
Black, Shirley Temple 2619
Boesing, Martha Gross 2964

Bonal, Denise 2396
Bovasso, Julie Anne 2693
Braverman, Kate 3954
Bronaugh, Anne 1472
Brooks, Louise 2042
Bundchen, Gisele 4931
Burke, Billie 1624
Burnett, Carol 2838
Campbell, Patrick 1309
Carey, Mariah 4813
Carroll, Vinnette 2422
Centlivre, Susanna 511
Cha, Theresa Hak Kyung 4033
Chamberlin, Judi 3486
Charke, Charlotte 705
Chase, Ilka 2011
Cher 3643
Childress, Alice 2364
Cleage, Pearl 3818
Clive, Catherine 572
Collins, Joan 2840
Cooper, Diana 1744
Crothers, Rachel 1511
Cryer, Gretchen 2924
Curtis, Jamie Lee 4443
Cushman, Charlotte Saunders 936
Daisy, Princess of Pless 1411
Dane, Clemence 1677
Dasi, Binodini 1294
Davenport, Doris 3891
Davis, Bette 2082
Davis, Eisa 4951
de Lavallade, Carmen 2754
De Wolfe, Elsie 1311
DeGeneres, Ellen 4445
Dench, Judi 2889
Deneuve, Catherine 3402
Denham, Alice 2841
Desbordes-Valmore, Marceline 801
Desjardins, Marie-Catherine 460
Dietrich, Marlene 1930
Dirie, Waris 4695
Douglas, Helen Gahagan 1897
Drescher, Fran 4404
Dressler, Marie 1412
Dukakis, Olympia 2755
Duke, "Patty" 3649
Duse, Eleanora 1246
Earp, Josephine "Josie" Sarah "Sadie" 1266
Edelstein, Jean 2593
Elliott, Maxine 1388
Ensler, Eve 4174
Estés, Clarissa Pinkola 3567
Evans, Edith 1679
Fey, Tina 4527.1
Field, Kate 1082
Field, Sally 3653
Fields, Gracie 1866
Finley, Karen 4363
Fisher, Carrie 4364
Fiske, Minnie 1312
Fonda, Jane 3029
Foster, Jodie 4615
Fugard, Lisa 4485
Furness, Betty 2266.1
Gabor, Zsa Zsa 2287
Gallagher, Mary 3744

Garbo, Greta 2017
Gardner, Ava 2427
Garland, Judy 2428
Garrick, Eva Maria 596
Gaulke, Cheri 4248
Gingold, Hermione 1848
Gish, Lillian 1771
Glaser, Lulu 1434
Goldberg, Whoopi 4301
Gordon, Ruth 1825
Gottlieb, Lynn 3899
Grant, Lee 2599
Grenfell, Joyce Phipps 2129
Guilbert, Yvette 1314
Guinan, Texas 1611
Gwyn, Nell 486
Hagedorn, Jessica Tarahata 3901
Hagen, Uta 2345
Hamill, Janet 3576
Harris, Barbara 2935
Harris, Julie 2520
Hawn, Goldie 3577
Hayes, Helen 1904
Haywood, Eliza 539
Hedström, Barbro 3420
Henley, Beth 4109
Hepburn, Audrey 2662
Hepburn, Katherine 2110
Herndon, Rosanna Taylor 2713
Hinck, Jeannie 4110
Holbrook, Ann 781
Holliday, Judy 2401
Holt, Anne Haw 2895
Hoper, Mrs. 631
Horne, Lena 2294
Huang Zongying 2522
Huston, Anjelica 4049
Hutton, Lauren 3422
Jackson, Glenda 2984
Jackson, Janet 4723
Jagger, Bianca 3980
Janis, Elsie 1698
Jellicoe, Ann 2600
Jolie, Angelina 4895
Kahn, Madeline 3350
Kalisch, Shoshana 2631
Kanin, Fay 2295
Kaye, Judy 3837
Keatley, Charlotte 4537
Keith, Penelope 3200
Kemble, Fanny 908
Kidder, Margot 3839
Kirk, Lisa 2526
Kirsebom, Vendela 4751
Kitt, Eartha 2604
Lanchester, Elsa 1950
Langtry, Lily 1197
Lansbury, Angela 2530
Launey 969
Lawless, Lucy 4770
Lawrence, Gertrude 1934
Le Gallienne, Eva 1887
Leachman, Cloris 2562
Lee, Gypsy Rose 2222
Leigh, Vivien 2204
Lenya, Lotta 1868
Leslie, Amy 1256
Leslie, Lisa 4864

Liking, Werewere 3986
Lillie, Beatrice 1869
Lincoln, Abbey 2723
Littlewood, Joan 2223
Livingstone, Belle 1462
Lloyd, Marie 1378
Lopez, Jennifer 4824
Loren, Sophia 2902
Lovell, Marie 878
Lunch, Lydia 4494
Lupino, Ida 2321
Mable, Jackie "Moms" 1800
MacDonald, Sharman 4055
MacLaine, Shirley 2903
Madonna 4459
Magnani, Anna 2322
McCorvey, Norma 3769
McGill, Alice 2606
McKellar, Danica 4898.1
McRae, Carmen 2382
Melville, Pauline 3850
Mercouri, Melina 2531
Merman, Ethel 2114
Merry, Anne Brunton 743
Midler, Bette 3594
Miller, Lee 2072
Minnelli, Liza 3678
Modjeska, Helena 1095
Modotti, Tina 1828
Moffat, Mary Jane 2859
Monroe, Marilyn 2568
Moore, Grace 1936
Moreau, Jeanne 2637
Morgan, Robin 3284
Morgan, Sydney Owenson 770
Mowatt, Anna Cora 957
Mullins, Aimee 4913
Munro, Rona 4497
Neal, Patricia 2570
Nelson, Portia 2385
Neuber, Frïederika Karoline 545
Newman, Naomi 2730
Oakley, Annie 1260
O'Casey, Eileen 1980
O'Donnell, Rosie 4628
O'Malley, Mary 3289
O'Neill, Carlotta Monterey 1688
Orr, Mary 2140
Otero, Caroline 1353
Page, Geraldine 2492
Paltrow, Gwyneth 4847
Parker, Suzy 2814
Partnow, Elaine Bernstein 3291
Peelen, Jean 3292–3293
Perón, Eva Duarte 2354
Pessl, Marisha 4929
Phyrne 64
Pickford, Mary 1781
Picon, Molly 1872
Piper, Adrian 3688
Pollock, Sharon 2998
Portman, Natalie 4948
Radner, Gilda 3691
Reagan, Nancy 2411
Reed, Donna 2412
Reza, Yasmina 4503
Richards, Beah 2387

Richardson, Miranda 4467
Riefenstahl, Leni 1955
Roberts, Julia 4757
Robinson, Mary 693
Rogers, Ginger 2166
Rollin, Betty 3003
Rosenthal, Rachel 2576
Roumeau, Jacqueline 4985
Rowson, Susanna Haswell 715
Rudner, Rita 4390
Russell, Rosalind 2168
Sanchez, Georgiana Valoyce 4940
Sapphire 4002
Sarandon, Susan 3695
Scott, Hazel 2390
Scott-Maxwell, Florida 1601
Shore, Dinah 2391
Siddons, Sarah 684
Signoret, Simone 2414
Silverman, Sarah 4849
Skinner, Cornelia Otis 1940
Smith, Anna Deavere 4006
Snortland, Ellen 4211
Solanas, Valerie 3230
Soren, Tabitha 4759
Spears, Britney 4950
Spolin, Viola 2056
Stanwyck, Barbara 2074
Stone, Sharon 4472
Strasberg, Susan 3107
Streep, Meryl 3869
Streisand, Barbra 3379
Swanson, Gloria 1892
Swit, Loretta 3161
Taylor, Elizabeth 2826
Taylor, Renee 2869
Teish, Luisah 3871
Terry, Ellen 1162
Theodora 113
Thomas, Marlo 3062
Tomlin, Lily 3009
Treadwell, Sophie 1643
Trevor, Claire 2191
Tucker, Sophie 1620
Turner, Kathleen 4276
Tyler, Priscilla Cooper 939
Ukeles, Mierle Laderman 3163
Ullman, Liv 3108
Vanderbilt, Gloria 2502
Vestris, Eliza 828
Viva 3467
Wagner, Jane 2956
Wanatee, Adeline 2144
Washington, Kerry 4921
Waters, Ethel 1838
Webster, Margaret 2035
Weinstock, Lotus 3470
Wells, Rebecca 4150
Wertheim, Margaret 4474
West, Mae 1790
Williams, Pearl 2232
Williams, Vanessa 4660
Willson, Dixie 1720
Winfrey, Oprah 4285
Winger, Debra 4340
Winters, Shelley 2395
Wiseman, Jane 527

Woffington, Peg 586
Wood, Natalie 3116
Woodhull, Victoria Claflin 1086
Woodward, Joanne 2749
Wray, Fay 2075
Xue Tao 141
Zellweger, Renée 4809
Zetterling, Mai 2539

COMEDIANS, HUMORISTS, CARTOONISTS, AND WITS

Ace, Jane 2009
Bacon, Josephine Dodge 1468
Ball, Lucille 2150
Barber, Janette 4158
Barr, Roseanne 4085
Barth, Belle 2151
Bayes, Nora 1540
Bombeck, Erma 2586
Boosler, Elayne 4089
Bracken, Peg 2309
Brice, Fanny 1722
Burnett, Carol 2838
Carroll, Jean 2155
Chast, Roz 4235
Cornuel, A. M. Bigot de 421
DeGeneres, Ellen 4445
Diamond, Selma 2368
Diller, Phyllis 2286
Donnelly, Liza 4297
Ephron, Delia 3498
Fields, Totie 2757
Fey, Tina 4527.1
Geoffrin, Marie Thérèse Rodet 513
Gingold, Hermione 1848
Goldberg, Whoopi 4301
Hamilton, Gail 1051
Hay, Lucy 406
Heimel, Cynthia 3750
Holley, Marietta 1073
Houdetot, Sophie de la Briche 609
Lebowitz, Fran 3984
Leslie, Eliza 804
Levine, Emily 3845
Liebman, Wendy 4586
Lillie, Beatrice 1869
Longworth, Alice Roosevelt 1616
Loos, Anita 1686
Marchetto, Marisa Acocella 4625
Marx, Patricia 4259
May, Elaine 2810
McGinley, Phyllis 2027
Mumford, Ethel Watts 1516
Ostenso, Martha 1916
Parker, Dorothy 1780
Prager, Emily 3856
Radner, Gilda 3691
Renfroe, Anita 4629
Rice, Alice Caldwell 1382
Ritter, Erika 3860
Rivers, Joan 2862
Rowland, Helen 1481
Russell, Anna 2167
Shanker, Wendy 4870
Silverman, Sarah 4849
Smaller, Barbara 4210
Tomassi, Debbie 4598

Tomlin, Lily 3009
Tracy, Honor 2213
Tyler, Robin 3381
Weinstock, Lotus 3470
Weisstein, Naomi 3165
Wells, Carolyn 1368
Yamada, Eimi 4512

COURTESANS, BROTHEL-KEEPERS, MISTRESSES, AND PROSTITUTES

Albrecht of Johannsdorf, Mistress of 229
Ambapali 54
d'Aragona, Tullia 301
Barrows, Sydney Biddle 4086
Chao Luan-luan 144
Franco, Veronica 344
Hollander, Xaviera 3421
Jerusalem [mother of the dead child], Prostitute of 36
Jerusalem [mother of the living child], Prostitute of 37
Lais 65
L'Enclos, Ninon de 439
Otero, Caroline 1353
Phyrne 64
Poitiers, Diane de 294
Rice-Davies, Mandy 3534
Shen-ch'iung, Nieh 162
St. James, Margo 3060
Stampa, Gaspara 323
Wang Wei 553
Yü Hsüan-chi 152

DANCERS, CHOREOGRAPHERS, AND DANCE CRITICS

Angelou, Maya 2618
Baker, Josephine 2039
Boothroyd, Betty 2652
Brooks, Louise 2042
Brown, Trisha 2967
Colins, Janet 2283
Croce, Arlene 2887
Dauenhauer, Nora 2591
de Lavallade, Carmen 2754
de Mille, Agnes 2012
Duncan, Isadora 1512
Earp, Josephine "Josie" Sarah "Sadie" 1266
Fonteyn, Margot 2342
Fuller, Loie 1286
Gardiner, Lisa 1902
Garrick, Eva Maria 596
Graham, Martha 1795
Halprin, Anna 2373
Hari, Mata 1475
Hess, Cynthia 4678
Jamison, Judith 3426
Jenkins, Margaret 3759
Kitt, Eartha 2604
Lewitzky, Bella 2273
Markova, Alicia 2138
Murray, Kathryn 2055
Pavlova, Anna 1573
Rhys, Jean 1717
Rogers, Ginger 2166

Sappington, Margo 3789
Shur, Fanchon 2950
Sokolow, Anna 2141
St. Denis, Ruth 1557
Theodora 113
Todd, Mabel Elsworth 1559
Wigman, Mary 1658

Designers—Architectural, City, Industrial, and Interiors

Jekyll, Gertrude 1116
Kerbis, Gertrude Lemp 2557
Lin, Maya 4492
Luscomb, Florence 1666
Moore, Patricia A. 4124
Morgan, Julia 1403
Sklarek, Norma Merrick 2643
Stinson, Katherine 1736
Weisman, Leslie Kanes 3623
Yeager, Jeana L. 4153

Designers—Costume and Fashion

Antoine-Dariaux, Geneviève 4516
Chanel, Coco 1593
Claiborne, Liz 2655
Daché, Lilly 1991
Forbes, Leslie 4484
Hawes, Elizabeth "Babe" 1969
Head, Edith 1850
Karan, Donna 3836
Quant, Mary 2910
Schiaparelli, Elsa 1834
Van Runkle, Theodora 3235
Vanderbilt, Gloria 2502
Versace, Donatella 4337
Westwood, Vivienne 3310

Designers—Graphic, Print, and Illustration

Albers, Anni 1881
Alvarez, Cecilia 3949
Barry, Lynda 4346
Bechdel, Alison 4519
Carabillo, Toni 2544
Cecato, Lica 4355
Chast, Roz 4235
Conran, Shirley 2790
Donnelly, Liza 4297
Haley, Gail E. 3146
Hawthorne, Sophia Amelia Peabody 907
Hollman, Peggy 4304
Horacek, Judy 4580
Kent, Corita 2318
Kollwitz, Käthe 1337
Marchetto, Marisa Acocella 4625
Margrethe II 3208
Morris, Jackie 4589
Satran, Pamela Redmond 4205
Satrapi, Marjane 4802
Seton-Thompson, Grace 1405
Smaller, Barbara 4210
Strand, Polly 2825
Tadjo, Véronique 4334
Wagner, Jane 2956

Wayne, June 2334
Xue Tao 141
Zeisler, Andi 4221

Directors—Stage, Film, and Television

Akalaitis, JoAnne 3016
Arzner, Dorothy 1895
Boesing, Martha Gross 2964
Bovasso, Julie Anne 2693
Brunet, Marguerite 606
Caldwell, Sarah 2478
Carroll, Vinnette 2422
Crothers, Rachel 1511
Farabough, Laura 4407
Fernea, Elizabeth Warnock 2595
Forman, Ruth 4787
Fornés, Maria Irene 2704
Foster, Jodie 4615
Franken, Rose 1809
Gallagher, Mary 3744
Gordon, Bette 4366
Grant, Lee 2599
Gregory, Augusta 1193
Hansen, Grace 2198
Huston, Anjelica 4049
Jellicoe, Ann 2600
Jones, Margo 2202
Keatley, Charlotte 4537
Lupino, Ida 2321
Merriam, Eve 2274
Moreau, Jeanne 2637
Moscou, Jacqueline 3919
Nacro, Fanta Régina 4626
Nair, Mira 4422
Newman, Naomi 2730
Osten, Suzanne 3530
Poole, Jeannie Gayle 4068
Rambert, Marie 1733
Satrapi, Marjane 4802
Seidelman, Susan 4139
Spolin, Viola 2056
Vestris, Eliza 828
Wagner, Jane 2956
Webster, Margaret 2035
Zetterling, Mai 2539

Film, Television, Video, and Media Producers, Designers, Specialists, and Technicians

Adnan, Etel 2505
Allen, Dede 2506
Arizmendi, Yareli 4666
Ball, Lucille 2150
Baransi-Siniora, Maysa 4904
Barber, Janette 4158
Benmussa, Simone 2751
Brand, Dionne 4164
Breillat, Catherine 3814
Carrigan, Ana 3485
Chambers, Jane 3023
Dunn, Irina 3962
Fey, Tina 4527.1
Field, Connie 3826
Flanagan, Hallie 1705
Foster, Jodie 4615
Fuller, Loie 1286

Gaulke, Cheri 4248
Gottleib, Linda 3265
Gross, Terry 4043
Harjo, Joy 4045
Hawn, Goldie 3577
Hochman, Sandra 2983
Hosain, Attia 2200
Jacobs, Rayda 3757
Jibrell, Fatima 3835
Johnson, Osa 1797
Jones, Margo 2202
Jordan, June 2987
Kilbourne, Jean 3433
Lopez, Jennifer 4824
Lupino, Ida 2321
Malagrino, Silvia A. 3988
Mehta, Deepa 3916
Morris, Holly 4733
O'Faolain, Nuala 3217
Orr, Mary 4548
Phillips, Julia 3532
Poole, Jeannie Gayle 4068
Reitz, Rosetta 2493
Riefenstahl, Leni 1955
Rochefort, Christiane 2302
Rukeyser, Muriel 2210
Shakira 4919
Shebl, Riham 4920
Shlain, Tiffany 4835
Silver, Joan Micklin 2951
Snortland, Ellen 4211
Streisand, Barbra 3379
Tall, JoAnn 4274
Taylor, Renee 2869
Tipton, Jennifer 3063
Toro, María Suárez 3874
Trinh, T. Minh-Ha 4147
Tyler, Robin 3381
Varda, Agnes 2644
Verdon-Roe, Vivienne 4278
Walters, Barbara 2687
Winfrey, Oprah 4285

Lecturers, Public Speakers, and Workshop Leaders

Allen, Mary Wood 1099
Armstrong, Karen 3474
Ashenburg, Katherine 3951
Austin, Mary Hunter 1346
Avery, Byllye Y. 3019
Ayscough, Florence 1504
Baldwin, Christina 3629
Bambara, Toni Cade 3121
Bardwick, Judith M. 2832
Bender, Sheila 3810
Bethune, Mary McLeod 1453
Bird, Caroline 2237
Bonham-Carter, Violet 1660
Booth, Evangeline 1308
Bright, Susannah "Susie" 4441
Brotherton, Alice Williams 1159
Brown, Barbara B. 2621
Brown, Charlotte 1577
Burton, Elaine Frances 1988
Carrigan, Ana 3485
Cartland, Barbara 1928
Chamberlin, Judi 3486

Chicago, Judy 3133
Cohen, Sherry Suib 2885
Conkling, Grace H. 1509
Crittenden, Ann 3027
Curie, Ève 1990
Daum, Meghan 4814
David-Néel, Alexandra 1348
Douglas, Helen Gahagan 1897
Dreifus, Claudia 3495
Dunlop, Becky Norton 4039
Eltahawy, Mona 4747
Falk, Marcia 3650
Ferguson, Anita Perez 4527
Ferguson, Marilyn 3085
Field, Kate 1082
Flanner, Janet 1745
Follett, Mary Parker 1350
Ford, Anna 3407
Fuentes, Sonia Pressman 2627
Gage, Frances Dana 904
Galinsky, Ellen 3408
Gawain, Shakti 3827
Gilman, Charlotte Perkins 1254
Godwin, Gail 3032
Goldman, Emma 1360
Gordimer, Nadine 2456
Greene, Jennifer 3575
Harper, Frances Ellen Watkins 1000
Hart, Louise 3034
Hortensia 74
Howe, Julia Ward 956
Hubbard, Barbara Marx 2664
Janeway, Elizabeth 2201
Johnson, Adelaide 2023
Johnson, Shirley Childress 3760
Josefowitz, Natasha 2555
Judith, Anodea 4113
Jung, Emma 1578
Justin, Dena 2183
Kamel, Laila Iskandar 3761
Katie, Byron 3352
Kauffman, Linda S. 3903
Kearney, Belle 1297
Kellems, Vivien 1826
Keller, Helen 1548
Kennedy, Marilyn Moats 3431
King, Coretta Scott 2603
Kitzinger, Sheila 2667
Lease, Mary 1178
Leddy, Mary Jo 3669
Lerner, Gerda 2380
Lerner, Harriet Goldhor 3519
Livermore, Mary 971
Macy, Joanna 2669
Mahler, Margaret 1853
Mann, Erika 2026
Marston, Stephanie 3914
Massie, Suzanne 3280
Mayberg, Maude 1750
Miller, Ceci 4461
Mills, Stephanie 3851
Monroe, Anne Shannon 1497
Moore, Patricia A. 4124
Morgan, Angela 1446
Mowatt, Anna Cora 957
Muscio, Inga 4734
Musgrave, Thea 2637.1

Myss, Caroline M. 4126
Nicholson, Zoe Ann 3852
Nin, Anaïs 1979
Noble, Vicki 3775
O'Brien, Virginia 3683
Partnow, Elaine Bernstein 3291
Payne, Ethel L. 2163
Peelen, Jean 3292–3293
Perón, Eva Duarte 2354
Peterson, Virgilia 2002–2003
Phillips, Lois 3222
Pincus, Joy 4798
Powter, Susan 4427
Richman, Julia 1207
Roosevelt, Eleanor 1618
Ruckelshaus, Jill 3054
Samalin, Nancy 3055
Sandler, Bernice "Bunny" R. 2641
Seton, Julia 1701
Seton-Thompson, Grace 1405
Sharman, Helen 4654
Shaw, Anna Howard 1154
Shelton, Charlotte 3795
Smedley, Agnes 1754
Smith, Elizabeth Oakes 899
Sommers, Christina Hoff 4007
Starhawk 4072
Stevens, Christine 4688
Stewart, Maria W. 882
Stone, Lucy 953
Stopes, Marie Carmichael 1558
Sun Yat-sen, Madam 1786
Taylor, Jill Bolte 4508
Terrell, Mary Church 1299
Thompson, Clara 1787
Toshiko, Kishida 1300
Tremain, Rose 3464
Truth, Sojourner 860
Ung, Loung 4836
Valenzuela, Luisa 3110
Van Buren, Abigail 2333
Vanzant, Iyanla 4216
Vendler, Helen Hennessy 2872
vos Savant, Marilyn 3703
Wagner, Sally Roesch 3384
Walters, Dottie 2538
Walters, Lilly 4394
Weaver, Frances 2645
Weisman, Leslie Kanes 3623
Wells, Ida B. 1291
Whitestone-McCallum, Heather 4882
Wieder, Marcia 4396
Williams, Fannie Barrier 1210
Williamson, Marianne 4151
Winnemucca, Sarah 1133
Wohlstetter, Roberta 2194
Wright, Frances 850
Zygmuntowicz, Itka Frajman 2585

**MUSICIANS, SINGERS, AND
CONDUCTORS**
Adjani, Isabelle 4287
Ahmed, Naima 4600
Allyson, Karrin 4602
Alsop, Marin 4344
Anderson, Margaret 1647
Anderson, Marian 1945

Anduza, Clara d' 203
Armstrong, Cora Harvey 3018
Arnim, Bettina von 798
Arnould, Sophie 628
Ava, Frau 185
Baez, Joan 3241
Bailey, Pearl 2307
Baker, Josephine 2039
Barnwell, Ysaye 3633
Bartoli, Cecilia 4715
Bedingfield, Natasha 4945
Betsch, MaVynee 2921
Bond, Victoria 3887
Bonney, Barbara 4349
Booth, Evangeline 1308
Boyle, Susan 4566.1
Brice, Fanny 1722
Brickell, Edie 4716
Brown, Maxine 3127
Bryant, Anita Jane 3177
Caccini, Francesca 394
Caldwell, Sarah 2478
Carey, Mariah 4813
Carson, Norma 3181
Carter, Deana 4717
Cash, Roseanne 4294
Cassian, Nina 2479
Catalani, Angelica 778
Cecato, Lica 4355
Ceschina, Yoko Nagae 2788
Céu, Violante do 417
Chapman, Tracy 4673
Cher 3643
Christian, Meg 3644
Collins, Judy 3135
Comini, Alessandra 3079
Cotton, Elizabeth 1767
Cryer, Gretchen 2924
Cunningham, Agnes "Sis" 2107
Curie, Éve 1990
David-Néel, Alexandra 1348
Dietrich, Marlene 1930
DiFranco, Ani 4816
Diller, Phyllis 2286
Dion, Céline 4766
Drinker, Sophie Hutchinson 1678
Du Pré, Jacqueline 3564
Dugaw, Dianne 3823
Durham, Judith 3403
Eaglen, Jane 4526
Etheridge, Melissa 4573
Ferron 4103
Fields, Gracie 1866
Gabrielli, Caterina 608
Garden, Mary 1432
Gardot, Melody 4955
Garland, Judy 2428
Garthwaite, Terry 3143
Genlis, Stephanie Félicité 650
Gilbert, Peggy 2018
Glaser, Lulu 1434
Glennie, Evelyn 4698
Gorchakova, Galina 4616
Grae, Jean 4908
Griffith, Nanci 4250
Guillet, Pernette du 315
Guppy, Shusha 2933
Harjo, Joy 4045

Harris, Ruth Mae 3195
Hill, Lauryn 4894
Holiday, Billie 2244
Horne, Lena 2294
Horne, Marilyn 2896
Houdetot, Sophie de la Briche 609
Hsüeh T'ao 140
Hunter, Alberta 1811
Ian, Janis 4050
Jackson, Janet 4723
Jackson, Mahalia 2159
Jacquet de la Guerre, Elisabeth-
  Claude 502
Jessye, Eva 1815
Jones, Rickie Lee 4252
Joplin, Janis 3428
Kahlil, Aisha 3199
Kahn, Kathy 3585
Kalisch, Shoshana 2631
Kaptur, Marcy 3668
Kaye, Judy 3837
Kesselman, Wendy 3202
King, Carole 3355
King, Coretta Scott 2603
Kirchheimer, Gloria DeVidas 3356
Kirk, Lisa 2526
Kitt, Eartha 2604
Lais 65
Landowska, Wanda 1529
Lawless, Lucy 4770
Lehman, Lotte 1685
Lennox, Annie 4256
Lenya, Lotte 1868
Li Yeh 147
Lincoln, Abbey 2723
Lind, Jenny 970
Lopez, Jennifer 4824
Love, Courtney 4681
Lunch, Lydia 4494
Lynn, Loretta 2806
Madonna 4459
Maines, Natalie Louise 4886
Makeba, Miriam 2807
Malfitano, Catherine 3846
Mara, Gertrude Elizabeth 657
Matossian, Mariam 4865
Mawiyoo, Neema "Ngwatilo" 4952
McCaslin, Mary 3677
McCoy, Rose Marie 2435
McLachlan, Sarah 4773
McPartland, Marian 2324
McRae, Carmen 2382
Melanie 3772
Melba, Nellie 1274
Merman, Ethel 2114
Midler, Bette 3594
Minnelli, Liza 3678
Mitchell, Joni 3443
Moore, Grace 1936
Moore, Liz 4954
Musgrave, Thea 2637.1
Near, Holly 3921
Nearing, Helen 2001
Norman, Jessye 3601
Nye, Naomi Sihab 4130
Nyro, Laura 3779
Odetta 2734
Oliveros, Pauline 2813

Orton, Beth 4827
Parra, Violeta 2299
Parton, Dolly 3686
Partridge, Frances 1918
Peri, Janis-Rozena 3221
Phair, Liz 4755
Previn, Dory 2679
Price, Leontyne 2610
Purim, Flora 3368
Reagon, Bernice Johnson 3369
Reddy, Helen 3297
Renfroe, Anita 4629
Reynolds, Malvina 1920
Rogers, Ginger 2166
Ronell, Ann 2102
Ronstadt, Linda 3694
Russell, Anna 2167
Sainte-Marie, Buffy 3301
Schumann-Heink, Ernestine 1278
Scott, Hazel 2390
Shakira 4919
Shocked, Michelle 4631
Shore, Dinah 2391
Sill, Judee 3539
Sills, Beverly 2684
Simon, Carly 3615
Siunetsi, Sahakdoukht 148
Slick, Grace 3159
Smith, "Patti" 3696
Smith, Bessie 1878
Smyth, Ethel Mary 1237
Snow, Phoebe 4144
Sorrels, Rosalie 2867
Spears, Britney 4950
Speyer, Leonora 1406
Stampa, Gaspara 323
Stevens, Christine 4688
Storace, Nancy 728
Streisand, Barbra 3379
Sutherland, Joan 2581
Tikaram, Tanita 4804
Tipton, Billy 2229
Truman, Margaret 2500–2501
Tucker, Sophie 1620
Vega, Suzanne 4509
Waring, Marilyn 4217
Waters, Ethel 1838
Weisstein, Naomi 3165
Williams, Mary Lou 2147
Williams, Vanessa 4660
Winehouse, Amy 4953
York, Eva Rose 1240

**PAINTERS, SCULPTORS,
ARTISANS, AND OTHER VISUAL
ARTISTS**
Adamson, Joy 2336
Aguirre, Isidora 2337
Aiken, Joyce 2750
Albers, Anni 1881
Aldis, Mary Reynolds 1397
Allyn, Jeri 4082
Alvarez, Cecilia 3949
Anderson, Ruth Ann 3553
Anguissola, Sofonisba 335
Angus, Rita 2077
Arnim, Bettina von 798
Azara, Nancy 3120

Babbitt, Natalie 2784
Baca, Judy Francisca 3953
Barnes, Djuna 1739
Bashkirtseff, Marie 1230
Benton, Suzanne 4159
Berman, Ellen 3636
Blunt, Anne 1075
Brett, Dorothy 1591
Carr, Emily 1387
Carriera, Rosalba 519
Carrington, Leonora 2282
Cassatt, Mary 1126
Castle, Victoria 3889
Cedering, Siv 3131
Chang, Diana 2882
Chase-Riboud, Barbara 3132
Chicago, Judy 3133
Coffey, Susanna J. 4358
Colins, Janet 2283
Craighead, Meinrad 2973
de Hoyos, Angela 3187
Delany, Mary 549
DeWit, Antoinette 2451
Dilke, Emilia 1093
Drexler, Rosalyn 2546
Edelstein, Jean 2593
Edwards, Betty 2547
Falk, Marcia 3650
Fanshawe, Catherine Marie 726
Farabough, Laura 4407
Fukuzoyo Chiyo 554
Gentileschi, Artemisia 403
Goldberg, Natalie 3828
Gonzales, Sylvia Alicia 3414
Gonzalez, Patricia 3971
Goodison, Lorna 3747
Guest, Barbara 2371
Hajar, Hanaa 4976
Hamill, Janet 3576
Harkness, Madden 3973
Hartigan, Grace 2430
Hawthorne, Sophia Amelia Peabody 907
Hedström, Barbro 3420
Hemans, Felicia 838
Hepworth, Barbara 1970
Hildegarde von Bingen 179
Hoffman, Malvina 1630
Holmes, Marjorie 2133
Hosmer, Harriet 1026
Howells, Mildred 1399
Hulme, Keri 3755
Hunter, Clementine 1652
Itatani, Michiko 4182
Jacobi, Kathryn 3756
Johnston, Henrietta 506
Kahlo, Frida 2066
Killigrew, Anne 496
King-Hammond, Leslie 3517
Kollwitz, Käthe 1337
Kometani, Foumiko 2720–2721
Kuan Tao-shêng 223
Lakich, Lili 3358
Laurel, Alicia Bay 3908–3909
Laurencin, Marie 1633
Layton, Elizabeth 2137
Leibowitz, Annie 3910
Li Yeh 147

Lin, Maya 4492
Lisiewska-Therbusch, Anna Dorothea 587
Loy, Mina 1581
Malagrino, Silvia A. 3988
Mamonova, Tatyana Valentina 3096
Margrethe II 3208
Maribel, Mother 1667
Marshall, Lucinda 4381
Mee, Margaret 2113
Merian, Maria Sibylla 481
Miller, Alice 2466
Millett, Kate 2908
Mora, Elizabeth Catlett 2351
Morris, Jackie 4589
Moses, Grandma 1259
Neel, Alice 2097
Nevelson, Louise 1890
Nonnen, Emily 920
O'Keeffe, Georgia 1670
O'Neill, Rose 1447
Ono, Yoko 2860
Ormes, Cicely 324
Owens, Rochelle 2996
Paik, Younhee 3604
Parra, Violeta 2299
Pink, Lady 4686
Potter, Beatrix 1330
Poulsson, Emilie 1199
Proctor, Mary 4550
Quick-to-See Smith, Jaune 3224
Radtke, Joyce 4327
Randall, Margaret 3000
Rose, Wendy 3862
Sanchez, Carol Lee 2911
Schapiro, Miriam 2468
Schurman, Anna Maria van 422
Scudder, Janet 1421
Semmel, Joan 2821
Sheridan, Clare 1641
Shikishi Naishinno 192
Siddons, Sarah 684
Sleigh, Sylvia 2275
Slick, Grace 3159
Solanas, Valerie 3230
Spencer, Lilly Martin 985
Spero, Nancy 2580
Stein, Linda 3459
Stein, Linda 3459
Stone, Merlin 2778
Swerda, Patricia 2277
Toklas, Alice B. 1502
Treiman, Joyce 2440
Ukeles, Mierle Laderman 3163
Vallejo, Linda 4075
Vigée-Lebrun, Elisabeth 685
Viva 3467
Waldo, Octavia Capuzzi 2686
Wayne, June 2334
Weisberg, Ruth 3385
Wilson, Dagmar 2278
Wright, Susanna 546
Yamada, Eimi 4512

PHOTOGRAPHERS

Abbott, Berenice 1859
Adamson, Joy 2336
Arbus, Diane 2444

Beals, Jessie Tarbox 1370
Bergen, Candice 3635
Bourke-White, Margaret 2041
Cameron, Julia Margaret 927
Cones, Nancy Ford 1357
Cunningham, Imogen 1595
Galinsky, Ellen 3408
Geddes, Anne 4365
Gilpin, Laura 1726
Gore, Tipper 3829
Kasebier, Gertrude 1194
Lange, Dorothea 1816
Lord, Betty Bao 3094
Malagrino, Silvia A. 3988
Miller, Lee 2072
Modotti, Tina 1828
Morgan, Barbara 1915
Norman, Dorothy 2028
Onassis, Jacqueline Kennedy 2676
Spence, Jo 2915
Stark, Freya Madeline 1785
Tenneson, Joyce 3619
Wells-Witteman, Alisa 2688
Welty, Eudora 2117

RADIO AND TELEVISION PERSONALITIES

Ace, Jane 2009
Allred, Gloria 3240
Arndt, Bettina "Tina" 3883
Barrett, Rona 2961
Bennett, Georgette 3634
Bennis, Phyllis 4025
Bovey, Shelley 3724–3725
Bright, Susannah "Susie" 4441
Brown, Tina 4165
Cartland, Barbara 1928
Cheney, Lynne Ann 3248
Child, Julia 2174
Chittick, Elizabeth L. 2081
Coulter, Ann 4567
Couric, Katie 4402
Davidson, Sara 3732
Deen, Paula 3734
DeGeneres, Ellen 4445
Dhaliwal, Daljit 4607
Dunant, Sarah 3961
Eltahawy, Mona 4747
Erbe, Bonnie 4174.1
Fiedler, Maureen 3334
Flanders, Laura 4575
Forbes, Leslie 4484
Ford, Anna 3407
Fraser, Antonia 2796
Furness, Betty 2266.1
Gaylor, Annie Laurie 4300
Gerasymuk, Olga 4923
Goldberg, Whoopi 4301
Goodman, Amy 4408.1
Goodwin, Doris Kearns 3415
Graham, Virginia 2177
Grant, Toni 3266–3267
Gross, Terry 4043
Hagedorn, Jessica Tarahata 3901
Houston, Libby 3272
Ifill, Gwen 4308
Jenkins, Carol 3516
Kilgallen, Dorothy 2203

Lawson, Nigella Lucy 4541
Le Shan, Eda J. 2434
Leith, Prue 3205
Loud, Pat 2565
Maddow, Rachel 4878.1
Malveaux, Julianne 4190
McBride, Mary Margaret 1888
Mock, Geraldine "Jerrie" 2532
Morphonios, Ellen James 2674
Morris, Holly 4733
Moskowitz, Faye S. 2728
Murray, Kathryn 2055
Myers, Dee Dee 4590
Myerson, Bess 2491
Nyad, Diana 3922
O'Donnell, Rosie 4628
Payne, Ethel L. 2163
Perón, Eva Duarte 2354
Peterson, Virgilia 2002–2003
Pipher, Mary 3784
Powter, Susan 4427
Prins, Nomi 4867
Raphaël, Sally Jessy 3447.1
Rehm, Diane 3001
Ritter, Erika 3860
Rivers, Joan 2862
Rollin, Betty 3003
Sawyer, Diane 3610
Schlessinger, Laura Catherine 3792
Shain, Merle 2947
Sharman, Helen 4654
Sheindlin, Judith 3377
Stewart, Martha 3307
Storkey, Elaine 3460
Tolstaya, Tatyana 4074
Traister, Rebecca 4527.1
Tweedie, Jill 2828
Van Horne, Harriet 2394
Van Susteren, Greta 4277
Walters, Barbara 2687
Wertheim, Margaret 4474
Westheimer, Ruth 2646
Winfrey, Oprah 4285
Wright, Robin 3879
Young, Rolanda 4016

SONGWRITERS, ARRANGERS, COMPOSERS, AND LYRICISTS

Abbott, Patsy 2690
Adams, Sarah Flower 888
Alais 202
Alamanda 194
Alexander, Mrs. Cecil Frances 943
Allyson, Karrin 4602
Almucs de Castelnau 188
Anderson, Laurie 3714
Anduza, Clara d' 203
Armstrong, Cora Harvey 3018
Auber, Harriet 761
Ava, Frau 185
Azalais de Porcairages 189
Baez, Joan 3241
Barnard, Charlotte Alington 1022
Bayes, Nora 1540
Beatriz de Dia 190
Bedingfield, Natasha 4945
Bieiris de Romans 205
Bond, Carrie Jacobs 1283

Booth, Evangeline 1308
Brickell, Edie 4716
Brown, Abbie Farwell 1455
Brown, Anna Gordon 654
Brown, Mary Elizabeth 1108
Caccini, Francesca 394
Carey, Mariah 4813
Carter, Deana 4717
Cash, Roseanne 4294
Castelloza 206
Catherine of Bologna 253
Chapman, Tracy 4673
Christian, Meg 3644
Christine de Pisan 244
Cockburn, Alicia 574
Collins, Judy 3135
Comden, Betty 2339
Corinna 55 Cotton, Elizabeth 1767
Crawford, Louisa Macartney 817
Cryer, Gretchen 2924
Cunningham, Agnes "Sis" 2107
DiFranco, Ani 4816
Dobree, Henrietta 1038
Domna H. 207
Dufferin, Helen 900
Durham, Judith 3403
Elliot, Jean 599
Elliott, Charlotte 809
Escot, Pozzi 2845
Etheridge, Melissa 4573
Ferron 4103
Fields, Dorothy 2014
Fine, Sylvia 2197
Fletcher, Bridget 597
Ford, Lena Guilbert 1373
Gardot, Melody 4955
Garsenda de Forcalquier 198
Garthwaite, Terry 3143
Gore, Catherine 863
Grae, Jean 4908
Griffith, Nanci 4250
Guillelma de Rosers 217
Guppy, Shusha 2933
Hankey, Katherine 1056
Hewett, Dorothy Coade 2459
Hildegarde von Bingen 179
Hill, Lauryn 4894
Hinck, Jeannie 4110
Holiday, Billie 2244
Home, Grisell 505
Hunter, Alberta 1811
Ian, Janis 4050
Isabella 199
Iselda 208
Jacquet de la Guerre, Elisabeth-
    Claude 502
Janis, Elsie 1698
Jones, Rickie Lee 4252
Joplin, Janis 3428
Kahn, Kathy 3585
Kalisch, Shoshana 2631
Kesselman, Wendy 3202
King, Carole 3355
Kolb, Barbara 3150
Kummer, Clare 1684
La Coste, Marie de 1139
Landowska, Wanda 1529
Lathbury, Mary 1104

le Baron, Marie 1109
Leigh, Carolyn 2564
Lennox, Annie 4256
Liliuokalani, Lydia Kamekeha 1083
Littlebear Morena, Naomi 4377
Lombarda 200
Love, Courtney 4681
Lynn, Loretta 2806
Mahler-Werfel, Alma 1532
Maines, Natalie Louise 4886
Matossian, Mariam 4865
McCaslin, Mary 3677
McCoy, Rose Marie 2435
McLachlan, Sarah 4773
McPartland, Marian 2324
McRae, Carmen 2382
Melanie 3772
Mitchell, Joni 3443
Moïse, Penina 856
Moore, Liz 4954
Musgrave, Thea 2637.1
Near, Holly 3921
Nelson, Portia 2385
Norris, Pippa 4200
Nye, Naomi Sihab 4130
Nyro, Laura 3779
Oliveros, Pauline 2813
O'Neill, Moira 1305
Ono, Yoko 2860
Orred, Meta 1140
Orton, Beth 4827
Owen, Anita 1714
Parra, Violeta 2299
Parton, Dolly 3686
Perry, Zenobia Powell 2099
Phair, Liz 4755
Picon, Molly 1872
Pollard, Josephine 1059
Poole, Jeannie Gayle 4068
Pounds, Jessie Brown 1275
Prentiss, Elizabeth Payson 952
Previn, Dory 2679
Purim, Flora 3368
Ran, Shulamit 3928
Reagon, Bernice Johnson 3369
Reddy, Helen 3297
Renfroe, Anita 4629
Reynolds, Malvina 1920
Ronell, Ann 2102
Sainte-Marie, Buffy 3301
Seeger, Ruth Crawford 1939
Shakira 4919
Shocked, Michelle 4631
Sill, Judee 3539
Simon, Carly 3615
Slick, Grace 3159
Smith, "Patti" 3696
Smith, Bessie 1878
Smyth, Ethel Mary 1237
Snow, Phoebe 4144
Sorrels, Rosalie 2867
Starr, Hattie 1719
Steele, Anne 580
Stephenson, Isabella S. 1118
Thomas, Aline 2143
Thorpe, Rose Hartwick 1181
Tibors 187
Tikaram, Tanita 4804

Trinh, T. Minh-Ha 4147
Vega, Suzanne 4509
Ventadorn, Marie de 195
Wagner, Melinda 4436
Walsh, Maria Elena 2745
Wesley, Susanna 512
Whitson, Beth Slater 1538
Williams, Helen Maria 716
Williams, Lucinda 4218
Williams, Lynda 4475
Williams, Mary Lou 2147
Williams, Vanessa 4660
Winehouse, Amy 4953
York, Eva Rose 1240
Young, Rida Johnson 1369
Zell, Katherine 291
Zwilich, Ellen Taaffe 3168

THEATER PRODUCERS, ARTISTIC DIRECTORS, DESIGNERS, ET AL.

Angelou, Maya 2618
Blakely, Nora Brooks 4029
Bovasso, Julie Anne 2693
Bovasso, Julie Anne 2693
Brunet, Marguerite 606
Caldwell, Sarah 2478
Dukakis, Olympia 2755
Elliott, Maxine 1388
Farabough, Laura 4407
Fingerhut, Arden 3654
Fuller, Loie 1286
Hart, Josephine 4367
Jellicoe, Ann 2600
Kanin, Fay 2295
Littlewood, Joan 2223
Marbury, Elisabeth 1211
Merry, Anne Brunton 743
Musser, Tharon 2533
Neuber, Friederika Karoline 545
Patel, Shailja 4828
Rambert, Marie 1733
Rame, Franca 2639
Shange, Ntozake 3865
Spolin, Viola 2056
Sutherland, Efua Theodora 2498
Swanson, Gloria 1892
Vostrá, Alena 3111
West, Mae 1790

C. POLITICAL, SOCIAL, AND JUDICIAL ARENA

ACTIVISTS, REFORMERS, AND REVOLUTIONARIES

Abdi, Dekha Ibrahim 4662
Al-Abdullah, Queen of Jordan,
    Rania 4810
Abel of Beth-maacah, Woman of 29
Abzug, Bella 2360
Adams, Carol J. 4018.1
Aiken, Joyce 2750
Allen, Candace 4224
Allen, Paula Gunn 3118
Allwine, Janine Maria 4225
Alomang, Yosepha 3948
American, Sadie 1281
Angelou, Maya 2618
Anger, Jane 383
Anwar, Zainah 4157

Apostolides, Marianne 4875
Arditti, Rita 2877
Arizmendi, Yareli 4666
Armstrong, Margalynne 4960
Assad, Marie B. 2445
Astell, Mary 507
Astorga, Nora 3884
Atakhanova, Kaisha 4439
Ataniyazova, Oral 4398
Audeley, Eleanor 436
Aung San Suu Kyi 3554
Avery, Byllye Y. 3019
Azara, Nancy 3120
Baca, Judy Francisca 3953
Bachman, Moira 3171
Badawi, Khulood 4903
Baez, Joan 3241
Baker, Dorothy Gillam 2038
Baker, Ella J. 1962
Baker, Mary 1738
Bakke, Kit 3628
Balch, Emily Greene 1333
Bambara, Toni Cade 3121
Bamber, Helen 2508
Bandler, Faith 2361
Baransi-Siniora, Maysa 4904
Bardot, Brigitte 2879
Barley, Mary 3632
Barlow, Maude 3719
Barnard, Jessie 1965
Barnwell, Ysaye 3633
Barry, Kathleen 3123
Bar-Yosef, Rivka Weiss 3323
Bashir, Halima 4925
Beal, Frances M. 3173
Bee, Rashida 4347
Bell, Florence 1182
Bello, Mairo 4670
Benjamin, Medea 4087
Bennis, Phyllis 4025
Benton, Suzanne 4159
Berkley, Rochelle "Shelley" 4026
Berneri, Marie Louise 2308
Bertell, Rosalie 2651
Besant, Annie Wood 1148
Bethune, Mary McLeod 1453
Betsch, MaVynee 2921
Bingham, Sally 3243
Birkeland, Janis Lynn 3559
Blake, Lillie Devereux 1049
Blee, Kathleen M. 4162
Bloomer, Amelia Jenks 944
Boggs, Lindy 2262
Bolton, Sarah Knowles 1101
Bonds, Julia 4088
Bonner, Ylena Georgievna 2447
Booth, Evangeline 1308
Boulding, Elise M. 2362
Bouza, Erica 3245
Bowman, Meg 2653
Boyle, Kay 1947
Brenner, Antonia 2543
Bright, Susannah "Susie" 4441
Brightman, Carol 3126
Brill, Alida 3888.1
Brinker, Ruth 2420
Brockovich, Erin 4522
Brown, Charlotte 1577

Brown, Eileen Kampakuta 2696
Brown, Lisa 4523
Bryant, Anita Jane 3177
Buck, Pearl S. 1741
Budiardjo, Carmel 2512
Bundchen, Gisele 4931
Burke, Phyllis 4030
Burroughs, Nannie Helen 1592
Bush, Barbara 2514
Caldicott, Helen 3075
Campbell, Maria 3179
Cannon, Katie Geneva 3956
Carmo, Isabel do 3180
Carnahan, Jean 2839
Carter, Lillian 1862
Cartwright, Johanna 473
Casey, Margaret 4353
Castillo, Aurora 2215
Castle, Victoria 3889
Ceballos, Jacqui Michot 2516
Cecato, Lica 4355
Chang, Helen Mack 4091
Chapman, Maria Weston 893
Chase, Mary 2062
Chayes, Sarah 4604
Chesler, Phyllis 3184
Chesoni, Atsango 4961
Chiang Kai-shek, Madame 1863
Child, Lydia Maria 870
Childs, E. Kitch 3024
Chittick, Elizabeth L. 2081
Chittister, OSB, Joan 2969
Ch'iu Chin 1425
Chute, Carolyn 3730
Cibo, Caterina 297
Clancy, Carolyn 4238
Cleghorn, Sarah Norcliffe 1473
Cleyre, Voltairine de 1325
Clinton, Hillary Rodham 3731
Cohan, Alice 4035
Cohen, Charlotte Bonny 3400
Collen, Lindsey 4036
Combs, Valda Jean 4442
Corrigan Maguire, Maireád 3491
Cronan, Sheila 3646
Crothers, Rachel 1511
Crowe, Frances 2340
Cunard, Nancy 1822
Cunningham, Agnes "Sis" 2107
d'Adesky, Anne-Christine 4479
Dai Qing 3293
Dalla Costa, Mariarosa 3081
Danielsson, Marie-Thérèse 2449
Dann, Carrie 2624
Dann, Mary 2450
Danowitz, Jane 3890
Davis, Angela 3493
Day, Dorothy 1846
Deetes, Tuenjai 4098
Deming, Barbara 2285
Deneuve, Catherine 3402
Deschryver, Christine Schuler 4694
Devlin, Bernadette 3736
Diehl, Guida 1349
Dilke, Emilia 1093
DiManno, Rosie 4978
Dinnerstein, Dorothy 2452
Diogo, Luísa Dias 4446

DiPerna, Diane 4963
Dirie, Waris 4695
Dix, Dorothea 872
Domini, Amy 4100
Doress-Worters, Paula B. 3082
Duarte, Jessie 4173
Duehring, Cindy 4608
Dugdale, Bridget Rose 3255
Dunbar, Roxanne 3140
Dunbar-Ortiz, Roxanne 3084
Duncan, Sheena 2792
Dunn, Irina 3962
Earhart, Amelia 1847
Earle, Sylvia A. 2926
Ebadi, Shirin 3739
Edelman, Marian Wright 3141
Embree, Alice 3566
Ensler, Eve 4174
Ertük, Yakin 4572
Estaugh, Elizabeth Haddon 524
Etheridge, Melissa 4573
Eugene-Richard, Margie 3332
Evers-Williams, Myrlie 2847
Fairstein, Linda A. 3741
Farro, Maria Elena Foronda 4482
Fauset, Crystal Bird 1792
Felton, Rebecca Latimer 1064
Fernandez, Irene 3652
Fiedler, Maureen 3334
Figner, Vera 1191
Fleming, Amalia 2175
Flexner, Anne Crawford 1430
Flores-Oebanda, Cecilia 4528
Flowers, Margaret 4576.1
Flynn, Elizabeth Gurley 1706
Foltz, Clara Shortridge 1165
Fonda, Jane 3029
Frank, Ray 1313
Fraser, Antonia 2796
Fraser, Arvonne 2517
Fraser, Clara 2455
Fry, Elizabeth 780
Fuentes, Sonia Pressman 2627
Gaard, Greta 4529
Gage, Frances Dana 904
Gandy, Kim 4247
Gaylor, Annie Laurie 4300
Gearhart, Sally Miller 2758
Genefke, Inge 3503
Geonzon, Winefreda Estanero 2706
Gerstenberg, Alice 1629
Ghezali, Salima 4450
Gibbs, Lois Marie 4106
Gibson, Janet 4178
Gilligan, Carol 2979
Giordano, Anna 4697
Girsh, Faye Joan 2851
Glassman, Carol 3336
Goldman, Emma 1360
Goodall, Jane 2892
Goodman, Carolyn 2242
Gorbanevskaya, Natalya 2980
Gore, Tipper 3829
Gottschewski, Lydia 2708
Gray, Elizabeth Dodson 2660
Gray, Kimi 3660
Grebäck, Kerstin 3267

Griffiths, Martha Wright 2178
Grimké, Angelina 890
Grimké, Sarah Moore 832
Gripenberg, Alexandra 1222
Grossman, Chaika 2344
Gruber, Ruth 2157
Gruen, Sara 4909
Grueso, Libia 4578
Grumbach, Argula von 288
Guffy, Ossie 2762
Gur, Batya 3749
Gurung, Jeanette D. 4303
Hafild, Emmy 4488
Hahn, Emily "Mickey" 2019
Halifax, Joan 3341
Halsted, Anna Roosevelt 2046
Hamer, Fannie Lou 2290
Handler, Marisa 4917
Handler, Ruth 2269
Harper, Frances Ellen Watkins 1000
Harris, Barbara Clementine 2712
Harris, Janet 2243
Harris, Ruth Mae 3195
Hart, Nancy 618
Hashemi Rafsanjani, Faezeh 4617
Hebblethwaite, Margaret 4250.1
Heldman, Caroline 4860
Hellman, Lillian 2021
Hepburn, Audrey 2662
Hernandez, Antonia 3830
Hewett, Dorothy Coade 2459
Hite, Shere 3344
Hogue, Ilyse 4790
Hollibaugh, Amber 3754
Holtby, Winifred 1867
Hong, Rani 4862
Hope, Lugenia Burns 1390.1
Hopkins, Jane Ellice 1079
Horne, Lena 2294
Hortensia 74
Hou Xiaotian 4581
Howe, Julia Ward 956
Hsiang Chin-yu 2134
Hsieh Ping-ying 2049–2050
Hudson, Helen 2376
Hunt, Carrie 4372
al-Huwaider, Wajeha 4846
Ibarruri, Dolores 1813
Ibrahim, Hauwa 4701
Issel, Shahieda 4414
Jacobs, Jane 2271
Jacobs, Rose Gell 1681
Jacobson, Sandra Weinstein 2718
Jagan, Janet 2378
Jagger, Bianca 3980
Jain, Devaki 2856
James, Sarah 3513
James, Selma 2719
Jayapal, Pramila 4702
Jeffreys, Sheila 3834
Jeger, Lena May 2245
Jehangir, Asma 4112
Jessye, Eva 1815
Jibrell, Fatima 3835
Johnson, Lady Bird 2180
Johnson, Josephine Winslow 2135
Johnson, Kory 4926
Johnson, Rebecca L. 4375

Johnston, Mary 1377
Jordan, June 2987
Joseph, Helen 2024
Joya, Malalai 4927
Kaara, Wahu 4185
Kajir, Anne 4821
Kamal, Zahira 3586
Kamel, Laila Iskandar 3761
Kanin, Fay 2295
Kassi, Norma 4253
Katona, Jacqui 4724
Kazu-no-Michi 1144
Keays, Sara 3838
Kegel, Martha 4455
Keller, Evelyn Fox 2988
Kelley, Florence 1248
Kellor, Frances Alice 1413
Kelly, Petra 3762
Kennedy, Florynce R. 2272
Khalifeh, Imane 4896
Kidder, Margot 3839
Kim, Elaine Haikyung 3354
King, Coretta Scott 2603
King, Ynestra 3840
Kissling, Frances 3435
Kitt, Eartha 2604
Kitzinger, Sheila 2667
Klein, Naomi 4823
Kleinbaum, Sharon 4490
Klepfisz, Irena 3276
Kochladze, Manana 4863
Kohut, Rebekah Bettelheim 1304
Kollontai, Aleksandra 1402
Kramer, Joyce 3357
Kramer, Melinda 4935
Kristeva, Julia 3277
Kruhonja, Katarina 3907
Krupskaia, Nadezhda
    Konstanitovna 1363
Kuhn, Maggie 2025
Kuklina, Ida 2528
Lagarde, Marcela 3983
Lamott, Anne 4255
Langer, Felicia 2722
Lape, Esther 1569
Lappé, Frances Moore 3518
Lease, Mary 1178
Lebron, Lolita 2605
Ledbetter, Lilly 3093
Leddy, Mary Jo 3669
Lemke, Birsel 3985
Leonard, Annie 4585
Lesher, Jan 4313–4314
Lesser, Elizabeth 4117
Le Sueur, Marian 1496
Levine, Judith 4118
Lightner, Candy 3671
Lindgren, Astrid 2069
Litman, Jane 3206
Litricin, Vera 3437
Liu, Peggy 4624
Livermore, Mary 971
Longauex y Vasquez, Enriqueta
    3589
Lopata, Jadwiga 4258
Louis, Minnie D. 1105
Lowry, Mary 3279
Luscomb, Florence 1666

Luxemburg, Rosa 1379
Lydon, Susan 3438
Lyon, Phyllis 2489
Lytton, Constance 1365
Maathai, Wangari Muta 3207
Macher, Sofia 4380
MacKinnon, Catherine A. 3674
MacLaine, Shirley 2903
Madison, D. Soyiini 3912
Makeba, Miriam 2807
Malone-Mayes, Vivienne 2808
Malpede, Karen 3590
Mandela, Winnie 2905
Mandela, Makaziwe "Maki" 4191
Manji, Irshad 4772
Mankiller, Wilma Pearl 3591
Maraini, Dacia 2991
Margarula, Yvonne 4460
Marguerite of Navarre 289
Maria Theresa 579
Marlin, Alice Tepper 3525
Marshall, Lucinda 4381
Martin, Anne Henrietta 1463
Martin, Del 2407
Martin, Emily 3526
Martin, Sarah 824
Martínez Sierra, María 1441
Mashinini, Emma 2672
Mason, Viviane Carter 1913
Mattern, Evelyn 3281
McCall, Dorothy 1699
McCarthy, Sarah J. 3360
McCrory, Colleen 3991
McDougal, Susan 4318
McIntosh, Peggy 2906
McPartland, Marian 2324
Mechtild von Magdeburg 215
Mee, Margaret 2113
Melen, Olya 4936
Menchú, Rigoberta 4495
Mendenhall, Dorothy Reed 1442
Mercer, Margaret 825
Mercouri, Melina 2531
Mer-Khamis, Arna 2673
Mernissi, Fatima 3211
Michel, Louise 1030
Michelman, Kate 3361
Miller, Emily 1053
Mills, Stephanie 3851
Mink, Gwendolyn 4122
Mirikitani, Janice 3283
Mischenko, Vera 4195
Mistral, Gabriela 1700
Mitchell, Juliet 3212
Mittal, Anuradha 4774
Mladjenovic, Lepa 4264–4265
Modotti, Tina 1828
Mofokeng, Connie 4496
Molina de Pick, Gracia 2727
Montagu, Lily 1416
Montero, Mayra 4123
Moody, Anne 3213
Moore, Liz 2436
Mora, Elizabeth Catlett 2351
More, Hannah 649
Morgantini, Luisa 3214
Morris, Esther Hobart 923
Moss, Cyntha 3215

Motoni, Nomura 897
Mott, Lucretia 839
Moyano, Maria Elena 4462
Mpaayei, Florence 4545
Mumtaz, Khawar 4064
Murungi, Kaari Betty 4983
Museveni, Janet 3920
Myrdal, Alva Reimer 1953–1954
Narbona Ruiz, Cristina 4065
Nathan, Maud 1289–1290
Nation, Carry 1146
Naufal, Vera 4547
Near, Holly 3921
Nearing, Helen 2001
Ngubane, Thembi 4956
Njogu, Ann Wairimu 4775
Nomani, Asra Q. 4708
Norman, Dorothy 2028
Norton, Eleanor Holmes 3050
Nowakowska, Urszula 4323
O'Brien, Edna 2732
O'Connell, Roselyn 3997
O'Connor, Karen 3100
Odetta 2734
Ojiambo, Josephine 4592
Okello-Orlale, Rosemary 4709
O'Neill, Terry 4202.1
Orenstein, Catherine 4754
Otero, María 3998
Pandit, Vijaya Lakshmi 1917
Pankhurst, Adela 1636
Pankhurst, Sylvia 1583
Pappenheim, Bertha 1249
Parker, Pat 3531
Parks, Rosa 2206
Parra, Violeta 2299
Partnow, Susan 3782
Patel, Shailja 4828
Pateman, Carole 3219
Patkar, Medha 4266
Paul, Alice 1637
Payne, Ethel L. 2163
Peace Pilgrim 2098
Peled-Elhanan, Nurit 4326
Perovskaya, Sofia 1198
Pesotta, Rose 1829
Petchesky, Rosalind Pollack 3366
Pharr, Suzanne 3153
Phillips, Bonnie 3367
Pogrebin, Letty Cottin 3154
Pollard, "Sister" Evelyn 1599
Pollitt, Katha 3925
Pollock, Sharon 2998
Portman, Natalie 4948
Powers, Donna 3926
Prejean, Helen 3155
Pritchard, Melissa 3857
Qui Jin 1465
Rabliauskas, Sophia 4551
Radford-Hill, Sheila 3927
Ramos, Rosa Hilda 3606
Rankin, Jeannette 1555
Rawalt, Marguerite 1818
Rawi, Mahboba 4776
Razovsky, Cecilia 1656
Reagon, Bernice Johnson 3369
Reed, Donna 2412
Reid, Willa Mae 3157

Reitz, Rosetta 2493
Renard, Cecile 764
Renne, Tanya 4830
Reynolds, Malvina 1920
Rich, Adrienne 2680
Richards, Amy 4831
Richards, Beah 2387
Richards, Cecile 4466
Ricker, Marilla 1096
Riddlestone, Sue 4552
Riley, Janet Mary 2254
Ringera, Karambu 4429
Rizk, Sarah
Robinson, Lillian 3300
Roche, Adi 4329
Roland, Jeanne-Marie 678
Roland, Pauline 891
Rose, Ernestine Louise 913
Rosenthal, Ida 1657
Rosenthal, Rachel 2576
Ross, Susan C. 3373
Roth, Stephanie Danielle 4848
Roulet, Elaine 2738
Rukeyser, Muriel 2210
Rush, Florence 2328
Russell, Diana E. H. 3104
Russell, Dora 1803
Sainte-Marie, Buffy 3301
Salavarrieta, Policarpa 826
Salvatore, Christina 4801
Sampter, Jessie Ethel 1600
Sanchez, Sonia 2912
Sandler, Bernice "Bunny" R. 2641
Sanger, Margaret 1535
Sarabi, Habiba 4392
Sarandon, Susan 3695
Scanlan, Susan 3791
Scattergood, Sally 4832–4833
Schlafly, Phyllis 2496
Schnall, Marianne 4758
Schnall, Susan 3454
Schutz, Susan Polis 3538
Schwimmer, Rosika 1499
Seacrest, Susan 4272
Seaman, Barbara 2946
Sendzimir, Venda 4140
Senesh, Hannah 2413
Sewall, Harriet 959
Shaheed, Farida 4208
Shaikh, Shamima 4556
Shalvi, Alice 2578
Shebl, Riham 4920
Sheehan, Cindy 4431
Sheldon, Karin P. 3613
Shelley, Rebecca 1672
Shiva, Vandana 4141
Shukla, Champa Devi 4142
Silva, Marina 4469
Silvia of Sweden, Queen 3456
Simeonova, Albena 4712
Simon, Rachel 995
Simonson, Joy Rosenheim 2356
Simpson, Becky 3006
Sinclair, Lee 4431.1
Sisulu, Nontsikelelo Albertina 2357
Skram, Amalie 1147
Sloan-Hunter, Margaret 3796
Smeal, Eleanor 3160

Smith, "Patti" 3696
Smith, Elizabeth Oakes 899
Smith, Laura Frost 1784
Snortland, Ellen 4211
Sofía of Spain, Queen 3106
Sokoloff, Natalie J. 3542
Solomon, Hannah Greenebaum 1238
Sonneschein, Rosa 1156
Spallone, Patricia 4071
Spence, Jo 2915
Spencer, Anna Garlin 1185
Spretnak, Charlene 3698
St. James, Margo 3060
St. Joan, Jacqueline "Jackie" 3616
Stannow, Lovisa 4987
Stanton, Elizabeth Cady 931
Stein, Linda 3459
Stevens, Christine 2332
Stevens, Christine 4688
Stewart, Alice 2057
Stewart, Eliza "Mother" 938
Stewart, Ella Jane S. 1394
Stewart, Maria W. 882
Stifter, Vicky 4073
Stiver, Irene Pierce 2497
Stokes, Rose Pastor 1537
Stone, Lucy 953
Strand, Polly 2825
Summerskill, Edith 1943
Sumner, Helen L. 1484
Sun Yat-sen, Madam 1786
Suttner, Bertha von 1119
Suzman, Helen 2303
Svirsky, Gila 3699
Swearingen, Terri 4433
Swerdlow, Amy 2470
Syfers, Judy 3870
Sykes, Roberta 3461
Symes, Lillian 1819
Szold, Henrietta 1261
Táhirih, Fátimih Baraghání 924–925
Tall, JoAnn 4274
Tawil, Raymonda 3233
Tax, Meredith 3700
Taylor, Elizabeth 2826
Terrell, Mary Church 1299
Terselic, Vesna 4633
Thomas, Marlo 3062
Thomas, Minnie 2870
Tiefer, Leonore 3543
Tillmon, Johnnie 2583
Ting Ling 2058
Todosijevic, Jelica 4973
Tohidi, Nayereh 4658
Trinh, Trieu Thi 101
Truth, Sojourner 860
Ts'ai-t'ien Chang 1283.1
Tubman, Harriet 978
Tucker, C. DeLores 2615
Tucker, Sophie 1620
Tuite, Marjorie 2441
Tweedie, Jill 2828
Tyler, Robin 3381
Ung, Loung 4836
Vance, Linda Susan 3942
Verdon-Roe, Vivienne 4278
Verona, Virginia 1588
Waddles, Charleszetta 2193

Wade-Gayles, Gloria Jean 3112
Wald, Lillian D. 1342
Walker, Alice 3547
Walker, Katharine 1097
Walker, Rebecca 4806
Wallace, Cath 4338
Wang Yongchen 4281
Wann, Marilyn 4739
Ward, Barbara 2230
Washington, Kerry 4921
Watt-Cloutier, Sheila 4283
Wattleton, Faye 3469
Wauneka, Annie Dodge 2145
Webb, Beatrice Potter 1239
Weddington, Sarah 3622
Weed, Becky 4560
Weil, Simone 2116
Weinberg, Sheila Pelz 3707
Wells, Ida B. 1291
Were, Beatrice 4741
Wilcox, Margaret R. 2146
Willard, Frances 1090
Williams, Betty 3471
Williams, E. Faye 3312
Williams, Fannie Barrier 1210
Williams, Jody 4014
Williams, Terry Tempest 4339
Williams, Vanessa 4660
Williamson, Marianne 4151
Willson, Margaret 4219
Wilner, Eleanor 3066
Wilson, Dagmar 2278
Wilson, Marie C. 3877
Win, Aye Aye 4807
Wingfield, Eileen Wani 2747
Winn, Marie 3115
Winnemucca, Sarah 1133
Witt, Shirley Hill 2918
Wittig, Monique 2958
Wolf, Christa 2689
Wong, Nellie 2919
Woo, Merle 3313
Woodhull, Victoria Claflin 1086
Woodman, Marion 2648
Woodward, Joanne 2749
Wright, Frances 850
Wright, Judith 2260
Yang Ping 2105
Yard, Molly 2233
Yaroshinskaya, Alla 4220
Young, Elizabeth 352
Younger, Maud 1384
Zajovic, Stasa 4689
Zana, Leyla 4599
Zassenhaus, Hiltgunt Margaret 2279
Zeisler, Andi 4221
Zell, Katherine 291
Zelter, Angie 4080
Zepatos, Thalia 4342
Zetkin, Klara 1229
Zhang, Lijia 4690
Zhivago, Um 4990

CRIMINOLOGISTS, POLICE WORKERS, AND INVESTIGATORS

Bennett, Georgette 3634
Bennis, Phyllis 4025

Ettore, Barbara 4041
Griffith, Aline 2457
Kaker, Malalai 4822
Katz, Rita 4642
Loftus, Elizabeth Fishman 3522
Noor Inayat Khan 2225
O'Grady, Ellen 1340
Ruiz, Mona Sandoval 4505
Uhnak, Dorothy 2871

DIPLOMATS, CIVIL SERVANTS, GOVERNMENT OFFICIALS, AND SPIES

Abdul Rahman, Haifa 4958
Agduk Agduk, Meltem 4811
Albright, Madeleine 2959
Alvarez, Aida 3881
Ashrawi, Hanan 3627
Astor, Brooke 1946
Astorga, Nora 3884
Bailey, Pearl 2307
Barnes, Melody C. 4668
Bazan, Emilia Pardo 1189
Behn, Aphra 472
Belcher, Jennifer M. 3556
Bell, Gertrude 1347
Bellamy, Carol 3324
Bilmes, Linda J. 4521
Black, Shirley Temple 2619
Burks, Maria 4233
Butts, Cassandra Quin 4693
Calderone, Mary Steichen 1989
Castellanos, Rosario 2515
Catherine of Siena 237
Chao, Elaine 4167
Chittick, Elizabeth L. 2081
Cinciotta, Linda Ann 3398
Clinton, Hillary Rodham 3731
Cresson, Édith 2886
Dashkova, Ekaterina Vorontsova 644
Davidson, Janine 4745
Dirie, Waris 4695
Duarte, Jessie 4173
Duncan, Sheena 2792
Dunlop, Becky Norton 4039
Dunn, Lydia 3188
Elders, Joycelyn "Minnie" 2843
Ertük, Yakin 4572
Ferguson, Anita Perez 4527
Flekkøy, Målfrid Grude 2703
Flournoy, Michèle A. 4576
Fraser, Arvonne 2517
Fréchette, Louise 3655
Furness, Betty 2266.1
Garvey, Jane F. 3502
Gildersleeve, Virginia 1493
Goddard, Mary Katherine 621
Grossman, Chaika 2344
Hamburg, Margaret "Peggy" 4303.1
Hari, Mata 1475
Harriman, Florence Hurst 1375
Harris, Patricia Roberts 2485
Hernandez, Aileen Clarke 2553
Higginbottom, Heather A. 4861
Home, Grisell 505
Hufstedler, Shirley M. 2523

Hughes, Karen 4370–4371
Ibarruri, Dolores 1813
Jackson, Lisa P. 4619
Jacobs, Rose Gell 1681
James, P.D. 2379
Jarrett, Valerie Bowman 4373
Jiang Qing 2221
Jolie, Angelina 4895
Kagan, Elena 4536
Kellor, Frances Alice 1413
Keyserling, Mary 2136
Kgositsile, Baleka 3905
Killefer, Nancy 4186
King, Coretta Scott 2603
Kirkpatrick, Jeane 2558
Kirsebom, Vendela 4751
Kollontai, Aleksandra 1402
Koontz, Libby 2348
Kreps, Juanita 2403
Lee, Barbara 3670
Lesher, Jan 4313–4314
LeTendre, Mary Jean 3844
Lu, Annette 3523
Luce, Clare Boothe 1973
Lute, Jane Holl 4378
Macher, Sofia 4380
Majid, Friba 4981
Martin, Lynn 3151
Matsui, Doris Okada 3527
McFate, Montgomery "Mitzi" 4706
Mendenhall, Dorothy Reed 1442
Mercouri, Melina 2531
Mistral, Gabriela 1700
Mongella, Gertrude Ibengwe 3595
Moran, Ellen 4732
Myerson, Bess 2491
Myrdal, Alva Reimer 1953–1954
Namjoshi, Suniti 3287
Narbona Ruiz, Cristina 4065
Norris, Pippa 4200
Orlova, Raisa Davydovna 2327
Orr, Mary 4548
de Palacio, Loyola 3960
Pandit, Vijaya Lakshmi 1917
Parisot, Laurence 4501
Peelen, Jean 3292–3293
Peng Peiyun 2678
Perino, Dana 4866
Perkins, Frances 1584
Perón, Eva Duarte 2354
Pillay, Navanethem "Navi" 3223
Priest, Ivy Baker 2031
Prothrow-Stith, Deborah 4267
Ray, Dixy Lee 2227
Reagan, Maureen 3296
Reddy, Helen 3297
Reed, Esther De Berdt 651
Reno, Janet 3103
Rice, Condoleezza 4268
Rice, Susan E. 4687
Richardson, Margaret "Peggy" Milner 3449
Rogers, Desiree 4504
Roosevelt, Eleanor 1618
Ruckelshaus, Jill 3054
Sadik, Nafis 2681
Samar, Sima 4430
Sampson, Edith Spurlock 1874

Sanu, Chigami 135
Schapiro, Mary L. 4332
Sentinelli, Patrizia 3938
Shalala, Donna 3304
Shalvi, Alice 2578
Silvia of Sweden, Queen 3456
Solis, Hilda 4432
Sumner, Helen L. 1484
Sutphen, Mona 4760
Tchen, Christina "Tina" M. 4393
Teng Ying-ch'ao 1983
Tucker, C. DeLores 2615
Tyson, Laura D'Andrea 3804
Ulrich, Mabel S. 1586
Vassiltchikov, Marie 2304
Veneman, Ann M. 3943
Verona, Virginia 1588
Ward, Celeste M. 4853
Westergaard, Brita 3549
Yard, Molly 2233
Yaroshinskaya, Alla 4220

FEMINISTS AND SUFFRAGISTS

Adams, Abigail 646
Allen, Florence Ellinwood 1603
Allred, Gloria 3240
Aloni, Shulamit 2650
Alta 3319
Anger, Jane 383
Anthony, Susan B. 963
Atkinson, Ti-Grace 3070
Auclert, Hubertine 1158
Austin, Mary Hunter 1346
Bazan, Emilia Pardo 1189
Beard, Miriam 1926
Beauvoir, Simone de 2080
Billington-Greig, Teresa 1488
Blackwell, Antoinette Brown 998
Blackwell, Elizabeth 981
Blackwell, Emily 1005
Blake, Lillie Devereux 1049
Bradwell, Myra R. 1035
Bricker-Jenkins, Mary 3326
Brodribb, Somer 4232
Brown, Olympia 1062
Brown, Rita Mae 3481
Brownmiller, Susan 2922
Bunch, Charlotte 3483
Calderone, Mary Steichen 1989
Cannon, Annie Jump 1293
Carabillo, Toni 2544
Carpenter, Liz 2363
Catt, Carrie Chapman 1244
Ch'iu Chin 1425
Christine de Pisan 244
Claflin, Tennessee 1135
Clarenbach, Kathryn 2366
Cleyre, Voltairine de 1325
Collins, Emily 946
Cruz, Juana Inés de la 487
Deming, Barbara 2285
Deroine, Jeanne-Françoise 889
Dixon, Marlene 2974
Dohm, Hedwig 1050
Dowd, Nancy E. 3893
Drakulíc, Slavenka 3894
Dworkin, Andrea 3738
Embree, Alice 3566

Faludi, Susan 4481
Farnham, Eliza 928
Fawcett, Millicent Garrett 1150
Finch, Anne 497
Firestone, Shulamith 3570
Flexner, Anne Crawford 1430
Fox, Muriel 2626
Fraser, Clara 2455
Freeman, Jo 3572
Friedan, Betty 2398
Fuller, Margaret 910
Gage, Mathilda J. 1007
de Gouges, Olympe 656
Gournay, Marie le Jars de 369
Grahn, Judy 3193
Greer, Germaine 3145
Grimké, Angelina 890
Grimké, Sarah Moore 832
Heide, Wilma Scott 2400
Hernandez, Aileen Clarke 2553
Hirsi Ali, Ayaan 4789
hooks, bell 4305
Hooyman, Nancy R. 3582
Howe, Julia Ward 956
Irigaray, Luce 2717
Jenkins, Carol 3516
Johnson, Sonia 2985
Johnston, Jill 2665
Jones, Beverly 2602
Kaplan, Temma E. 3350–3351
Kellems, Vivien 1826
Kempton, Sally 3430
Kennedy, Florynce R. 2272
Kenney, Annie 1528
Key, Ellen 1167
King, Deborah K. 4254
Krásnohorská, Eliska 1151
Labé, Louise 316
LaFollette, Suzanne 1776
Lape, Esther 1569
le Baron, Marie 1109
Lienert, Tania 4885
Lockwood, Belva 1029
Lorde, Audre 2901
Luce, Clare Boothe 1973
Luscomb, Florence 1666
Lydon, Susan 3438
Lyon, Phyllis 2489
Mamonova, Tatyana Valentina 3096
Maraini, Dacia 2991
Martin, Del 2407
Martineau, Harriet 874
Martínez Sierra, María 1441
Maule, Frances 1533
McClung, Nellie 1414
Merriam, Eve 2274
Mill, Harriet Taylor 902
Millett, Kate 2908
Morgan, Robin 3284
Morris, Holly 4733
Mott, Lucretia 839
Muller, Mary Ann 973
Munda, Constantina 425
Murray, Judith Sargent 669
Murray, Pauli 2139
Muscio, Inga 4734
Nasrin, Taslima 4627
Nelson, Mariah Burton 4384

Nenadic, Natalie 4967
Nevelson, Louise 1890
Newman, Jody 4498
Orbach, Susie 3685
Otto, Louise 958
Pankhurst, Adela 1636
Pankhurst, Christabel 1553
Pankhurst, Emmeline 1235
Pankhurst, Sylvia 1583
Pappenheim, Bertha 1249
Parturier, Françoise 2353
Paul, Alice 1637
Perera, Sylvia Brinton 2816
Pethick-Lawrence, Emmeline 1341
Phillips, Angela Marie 3783
Piercy, Marge 2997
Pierobon, Gigliola 3999
Radford-Hill, Sheila 3927
Rankin, Jeannette 1555
Rathbone, Eleanor 1404
Raven, Arlene 3533
Raymond, Janice G. 3930
Reinharz, Shulamit 3693
Robinson, Harriet 1003
Roiphe, Katie 4777
Roland, Pauline 891
Rose, Ernestine Louise 913
Routsong, Alma 2495
Ruether, Rosemary Radford 3004
Russell, Dora 1803
Schapiro, Miriam 2468
Schirmacher, Kathe 1319
Schreiner, Olive 1208
Schwimmer, Rosika 1499
Scott-Maxwell, Florida 1601
Seager, Joni 4273
Semenow, Dorothy 2740
Sendzimir, Venda 4140
Seton-Thompson, Grace 1405
Sewall, Harriet 959
Shaarawi, Huda 1536
Shaw, Anna Howard 1154
Sheppard, Kate 1155
Showalter, Elaine 3305
Shulman, Alix Kates 2822
Siebert, Muriel "Mickie" 2823
Siegel, Deborah 4803
Smeal, Eleanor 3160
Smith, Dorothy E. 2579
Smith, Elizabeth Oakes 899
Smyth, Ethel Mary 1237
Solanas, Valerie 3230
Spencer, Anna Garlin 1185
Spender, Dale 3458
St. John, Christopher Marie 1466
Staöl, Germaine de 733
Stanton, Elizabeth Cady 931
Steinem, Gloria 2916
Stern, Edith Mendel 1941
Stone, Lucy 953
Stopes, Marie Carmichael 1558
Strong, Harriet Williams Russell 1131
Thomas, Martha "Minnie" 1228
Ting Ling 2058
Toshiko, Kishida 1300
Tristan, Flora 883
Tuite, Marjorie 2441

Voznesenskaya, Yuliya 3236
Wade-Gayles, Gloria Jean 3112
Walker, Mary Edwards 1047
Weisstein, Naomi 3165
West, Rebecca 1759
Willard, Emma Hart 806
Wolf, Christa 2689
Wolf, Naomi 4635
Wollstonecraft, Mary 701
Wong, Nellie 2919
Woodhull, Victoria Claflin 1086
Wright, Frances 850
Yard, Molly 2233
Younger, Maud 1384

HEADS OF STATE, PRESIDENTS, PREMIERS, GOVERNORS, ET AL.

Aquino, Corazon 2830
Bai, Lakshmi 1016
Bhutto, Benazir 4160
Brundtland, Gro Harlem 3129
Calderón, Sila María 3327
Campbell, Kim 3642
Chamorro, Violeta Barrios de 2654
Gambara, Veronica 285
Gandhi, Indira 2288
Meir, Golda 1870
Ray, Dixy Lee 2227
Richards, Ann 2861
Thatcher, Margaret 2537

JUDGES, LAWYERS, AND LEGAL SCHOLARS

Abramson, Lisabeth Hughes 4343
Abzug, Bella 2360
Alderman, Ellen 4397
Allen, Florence Ellinwood 1603
Allred, Gloria 3240
Aloni, Shulamit 2650
Andrews, Lori B. 4156
Arbour, Louise 3715
Ascher, Barbara Lazear 3718
Astorga, Nora 3884
Bair, Sheila C. 4229
Baker, Mary 1738
Barnes, Melody C. 4668
Bartholet, Elizabeth 3172
Bellamy, Carol 3324
Bellows, Laurel Gordon 3809
Bensouda, Fatou 4564
Berkley, Rochelle "Shelley" 4026
Berry, Dawn Bradley 4399
Berry, Mary Frances 3073
Bhatt, Ela 2835
Bird, Rose 2963
Booth, Cherie 4231
Bradwell, Myra R. 1035
Breckinridge, Sophonisba Preston 1324
Brown, Lisa 4523
Browner, Carol M. 4293
Burlingame, Lettie 1243
Butts, Cassandra Quin 4693
Campbell, Kim 3642
Chesoni, Atsango 4961
Chua, Amy 4605
Cinciotta, Linda Ann 3398
Clark, Marcia 4169

Clinton, Hillary Rodham 3731
Combs, Valda Jean 4442
Coulter, Ann 4567
Cronan, Sheila 3646
Daughtrey, Martha Craig 3331
Doi, Takako 2625
Eastman, Crystal 1568
Ebadi, Shirin 3739
Edelman, Marian Wright 3141
Erby, Bonnie 4174.1
Evatt, Elizabeth 2846
Fairstein, Linda A. 3741
Farenthold, Sissy 2551
Foltz, Clara Shortridge 1165
Forbus, Lady Willie 1746
Freeman, Jo 3572
Fremont, Helen 3573
Fuentes, Sonia Pressman 2627
Gandy, Kim 4247
Geonzon, Winefreda Estanero 2706
Gillibrand, Kirsten 4720
Ginsburg, Ruth Bader 2850
Glassman, Carol 3336
Glendon, Mary Ann 3088
Goetz, Cecelia Helen 2316
Gordon-Reed, Annette 4532
Granholm, Jennifer M. 4486
Griffiths, Martha Wright 2178
Halonen, Tarja Kaarina 3418
Harris, Patricia Roberts 2485
Heckler, Margaret 2764
Hernandez, Antonia 3830
Higgins, Tracy E. 4700
Hill, Anita 4369
Holtzman, Elizabeth 3271
Holtzman, Fanny Ellen 1971
Hufstedler, Shirley M. 2523
Ibrahim, Hauwa 4701
Jarrett, Valerie Bowman 4373
Jehangir, Asma 4112
Johnsen, Dawn 4620
Kagan, Elena 4536
Kahn, Florence Prag 1329
Kajir, Anne 4821
Kallen, Lucille Chernos 2433
Kaminer, Wendy 3981
Kegel, Martha 4455
Kellett, Christine H. 3274
Kelley, Florence 1248
Kellor, Frances Alice 1413
Kennard, Joyce L. 3275
Kennedy, Caroline 4417
Kennedy, Florynce R. 2272
Klobuchar, Amy 4540
Kuklina, Ida 2528
Langer, Felicia 2722
Le Sueur, Marian 1496
Lee, Min Jin 4794
Livni, Tzipora "Tzipi" Malka 4458
Lockwood, Belva 1029
Lu, Annette 3523
Lute, Jane Holl 4378
MacKinnon, Catherine A. 3674
Martinez, Judith "Judy" Perez 4315
McAleese, Mary 4057
Melen, Olya 4936
Mink, Patsy 2608

Mischenko, Vera 4195
Montagu, Lily 1416
Morphonios, Ellen James 2674
Morris, Esther Hobart 923
Moseley Braun, Carol 3774
Murray, Pauli 2139
Murungi, Kaari Betty 4983
Napolitano, Janet 4423
Nichols, Mary D. 3600
Njogu, Ann Wairimu 4775
Norton, Eleanor Holmes 3050
Nowakowska, Urszula 4323
Obama, Michelle 4648
O'Brien, Shannon 4499
O'Connor, Sandra Day 2733
O'Neill, Terry 4202.1
Otero, María 3998
Paul, Alice 1637
Peelen, Jean 3292–3293
Pillay, Navanethem "Navi" 3223
Polier, Justine Wise 1981
Power, Samantha 4829
Quayle, Marilyn 4001
Rawalt, Marguerite 1818
Reeves, Nancy 2209
Rhode, Deborah L. 4137
Ricker, Darlene Marie 4269
Ricker, Marilla 1096
Riley, Janet Mary 2254
Robinson, Barbara Paul 3299
Roe, Rebecca 4138
Rogers, Estelle H. 4984
Ross, Susan C. 3373
Sampson, Edith Spurlock 1874
Schapiro, Mary L. 4332
Schroeder, Pat 3227
Schulder, Diane B. 3056
Sheindlin, Judith 3377
Sheldon, Karin P. 3613
Singer, Alyson 4970
Sonneschein, Rosa 1156
Sotomayor, Sonia 4273.1
St. Joan, Jacqueline "Jackie" 3616
Tchen, Christina "Tina" M. 4393
Thatcher, Margaret 2537
Vachss, Alice 4012
Van Susteren, Greta 4277
Veneman, Ann M. 3943
Wasserman Schultz, Debbie 4761.2
Weddington, Sarah 3622
Willebrandt, Mabel Walker 1703
Williams, Ann Claire 3946
Williams, E. Faye 3312
Williams, Patricia 4079
Wurtzel, Elizabeth 4762

LABOR LEADERS
De La Cruz, Jessie Lopez 2341
Dreifus, Claudia 3495
Huerta, Dolores 2716
Jones, Mother 1028
Sigurdardottir, Johanna 3378

POLITICIANS
Abzug, Bella 2360
Allen, Susan Au 3625
Aloni, Shulamit 2650
Aquino, Corazon 2830

Arroyo, Gloria Macapagal 3717
Astor, Nancy 1519
Aung San Suu Kyi 3554
Bachelet, Michelle 4022
Bender, Sheila 3810
Bhutto, Benazir 4160
Binh, Nguyen Thi 2692
Boggs, Lindy 2262
Bonham-Carter, Violet 1660
Bono, Mary 4566
Boothroyd, Betty 2652
Boxer, Barbara 3176
Brown, Kathleen 3639
Brown, Rosemary 2697
Brundtland, Gro Harlem 3129
Burton, Sala 2513
Burton, Elaine Frances 1988
Byron, Beverly Butcher 2787
Campbell, Kim 3642
Capps, Lois 3076
Caraway, Hattie Wyatt 1508
Carnahan, Jean 2839
Castle, Barbara Anne 2122
Chamorro, Violeta Barrios de 2654
Chisholm, Shirley 2480
Clark, Helen 3958
Clayton, Eva M. 2883
Cresson, Édith 2886
de Palacio, Loyola 3960
Devlin, Bernadette 3736
Diogo, Luísa Dias 4446
DiPerna, Diane 4963
Doi, Takako 2625
Dole, Elizabeth Hanford 2975
Douglas, Helen Gahagan 1897
Dunn, Irina 3962
Dunn, Jennifer 3256
Emerson, Jo Ann 3963
Fairley, Darlene 3404
Farenthold, Sissy 2551
Fauset, Crystal Bird 1792
Feinstein, Dianne 2848
Felton, Rebecca Latimer 1064
Fenwick, Millicent 2127
Ferraro, Geraldine A. 2929
Gandhi, Indira 2288
Gandhi, Sonia 3658
Gillibrand, Kirsten 4720
Ginzburg, Natalia 2267
Giroud, Françoise 2268
Goldberg, Natalie 3828
Granholm, Jennifer M. 4486
Grasso, Ella 2343
Green, Edith Starrett 2128
Greene, Jeanette 2661
Griffiths, Martha Wright 2178
Gripenberg, Alexandra 1222
Hajiyeva, Lala Shovket 4108
Halonen, Tarja Kaarina 3418
Hansen, Grace 2198
Hashemi Rafsanjani, Faeze 4617
Hasina Wajed, Sheikh 3749.1
Heckler, Margaret 2764
Hine, Lorraine 2714
Hirsi Ali, Ayaan 4789
Holtzman, Elizabeth 3271
Hull, Jane Dee 2937
Jackson, Glenda 2984

Jeger, Lena May 2245
Johnson-Sirleaf, Ellen 3090
Jordan, Barbara 2986
Joya, Malalai 4927
Kahn, Florence Prag 1329
Kaptur, Marcy 3668
Kassebaum, Nancy 2804
Keenan, Nancy 4114
Kennelly, Barbara B. 2989
Kirchner, Cristina 4187
Klobuchar, Amy 4540
Kumaratunga, Chandrika
   Bandaranike 3588
Lagarde, Marcela 3983
Lee, Barbara 3670
Lingle, Linda 4189
Livni, Tzipora "Tzipi" Malka 4458
Luce, Clare Boothe 1973
Madgett, Naomi Long 2465
Mandela, Winnie 2905
Mankiller, Wilma Pearl 3591
Martin, Lynn 3151
Martínez Sierra, María 1441
Matsui, Doris Okada 3527
Mbete-Kgositsile, Baleka 3915
McAleese, Mary 4057
Meir, Golda 1870
Merkel, Angela 4261
Mikulski, Barbara 2994
Mink, Patsy 2608
Morgantini, Luisa 3214
Mori, Nobuko 2811
Moseley Braun, Carol 3774
Moyano, Maria Elena 4462
Murray, Patty 3994
Namir, Ora 2729
Napolitano, Janet 4423
Ngilu, Charity Kaluki 4129
Norton, Eleanor Holmes 3050
O'Brien, Shannon 4499
Palin, Sarah 4684
Pelosi, Nancy 3220
Peng Peiyun 2678
Perón, Eva Duarte 2354
Rankin, Jeannette 1555
Rathbone, Eleanor 1404
Ray, Dixy Lee 2227
Reid, Willa Mae 3157
Richards, Ann 2861
Ringera, Karambu 4429
Roach, Pam 3861
Sarabi, Habiba 4392
Schmidt, Karen Anne 3611
Schroeder, Pat 3227
Scindia, Yashodhara Raje 4271
Sebelius, Kathleen 3864
Sforza, Caterina 269
Shepherd, Karen 3229
Sigurdardottir, Johanna 3378
Silva, Marina 4469
Smith, Margaret Chase 1857
Snowe, Olympia 3798
Solis, Hilda 4432
Somers, Helen 2824
Springer, Carol 3007
Stabenow, Debbie 4008
Stronach, Belinda 4736
Sukarnoputri, Megawati 3800

Sullivan, Leonor 1958
Summerskill, Edith 1943
Sun Yat-sen, Madam 1786
Süssmuth, Rita 3061
Suzman, Helen 2303
Thatcher, Margaret 2537
Tymoshenko, Yulia Volodymyrivna
   4557
Unsoeld, Jolene 2779
Waring, Marilyn 4217
Wasserman Schultz, Debbie 4761.2
Waters, Maxine 3114
Watt-Cloutier, Sheila 4283
Wazed, Hasina 3805
Whitton, Charlotte 1839
Williams, Helen Maria 716
Williams, Shirley 2746
Wilson, Heather 4561
Yunusova, Leyla 4437
Zana, Leyla 4599
Zia Rahman, Khaleda 3624

PUBLIC FIGURES AND SOCIETY LEADERS
Adams, Abigail 646
Adams, Louisa Catherine 766
Aissé, Charlotte Elizabeth 540
Allende, Hortensia Bussi de 2234
Alston, Theodosia Burr 793
Arafat, Suha 4636
Asquith, Margot 1301
Astor, Madeline Talmage 1760
Belmont, Eleanor Robson 1505
Biden, Jill 4027
Bingham, Anne Willing 719
Blessington, Marguerite 808
Booth, Cherie 4231
Botta, Anne 926
Bowen, Louise de Koven 1242
Bryan, Mary E. 1081
Bush, Barbara 2514
Bush, Laura 3641
Carter, Lillian 1862
Carter, Rosalyn Smith 2589
Cavendish, Georgiana 690
Churchill, Jennie Jerome 1201
Clinton, Hillary Rodham 3731
Cockburn, Alicia 574
Coolidge, Grace Goodhue 1523
Cooper, Diana 1744
Cunard, Nancy 1822
De Wolfe, Elsie 1311
Deborah 27
Deffand, Marie Anne du 544
Denham, Alice 2841
Detourbey, Jean 1078
Drouet, Juliette 894
Eisenhower, Mamie 1824
Elizabeth II of England 2549
Ferguson, Elizabeth Graeme 624
Ferguson, Sarah "Fergie" 4483
Flynn, Elizabeth Gurley 1706
Ford, Betty 2313
Franks, Rebecca 707
Garfield, Lucretia Rudolph 1045
Geoffrin, Marie Thérèse Rodet 513
Giovanelli, Elettra Marconi 2707
Gorbachev, Raisa Maxima 2800

Gratz, Rebecca 788
Griffith, Aline 2457
Hamilton, Emma 727
Harding, Florence Kling 1255
Hayes, Lucy Webb 1041
Holland, Elizabeth 756
Hoover, Louise "Lou" Henry 1437
Howar, Barbara 2898
Huffington, Arianna 3976
Jackson, Rachel Robards 735
Jarrett, Valerie Bowman 4373
Johnson, Lady Bird 2180
Kennedy, Rose Fitzgerald 1710
La Fayette, Marie Madeleine de 465
Lespinasse, Julie-Jeanne-Eléonore de 614
Lewinsky, Monica 4877
Lincoln, Mary Todd 950
Livingstone, Belle 1462
Longworth, Alice Roosevelt 1616
Madison, Dolley 738
Mahler-Werfel, Alma 1532
Mancini, Maria Anna 484
Marcos, Imelda 2670
Mary of Warwick 447
Maxwell, Elsa 1596
McDougal, Susan 4318
McLaughlin, Patricia 3593
Mitchell, Martha 2325
Murphy, Sara 1597
Museveni, Janet 3920
Necker, Suzanne Chardon 626
Nevill, Dorothy 1009
Nixon, Pat 2186
Obama, Michele 4648
Onassis, Jacqueline Kennedy 2676
Paley, Barbara "Babe" 2251
Patterson, Martha Johnson 1020
Phyrne 64
Polk, Sarah Childress 881
Pompadour, Jeanne-Antoinette Poisson de 588
Post, Emily 1418
Reagan, Nancy 2411
Rebecca 57
Rockefeller, Lucy 1084
Roland, Jeanne-Marie 678
Roosevelt, Eleanor 1618
Roosevelt, Edith Carow 1277
Rosenberg, Ethel 2255
Sablé, Madeleine de Souvré de 408
Schlessinger, Laura Catherine 3792
Sévigné, Marie de 451
Stanford, Sally 2007
Straus, Geneviève 1169
Strong, Harriet Williams Russell 1131
Taft, Helen Herron 1280
Tait, Katherine 2473
Tencin, Claudine Alexandrine de 530
Teng Ying-ch'ao 1983
Truman, Margaret 2500–2501
Truman, Bess 1644
Tyler, Priscilla Cooper 939
Vanderbilt, Amy 2103
Vanderbilt, Gloria 2502
Varnhagen, Rahel Levin 757

Washington, Martha 613
Whitestone-McCallum, Heather 4882
Windsor, Wallis Simpson 1840
Xue Tao 141

D. PRINTED WORD
DIARISTS AND LETTER WRITERS

Adams, Abigail 646
Aiken, Lucy 785
Aissé, Charlotte Elizabeth 540
Anne of Austria 414
Arnold, Margaret Shippen 704
Augusta 689
Bache, Sarah Franklin 647
Barnard, Anne 659
Bashkirtseff, Marie 1230
Bregy, Charlotte 435
Brown, Tabitha Moffatt 779
Burton, Isabel 1036
Campan, Jeanne Louise 672
Carlyle, Jane Welsh 869
Carter, Elizabeth 578
Chesnut, Mary Bokin 987
Choiseul, Louise Honorine de 616
Christina, Leonora 442
Clappe, Louise Amelia 954
Clifford, Anne 396
Colquhoun, Janet 786
Copley, Susannah Farnum 706
Cornelia 71
Cornuel, A. M. Bigot de 421
Datini, Margherita 241
de Jesus, Carolina Maria 2217
Deffand, Marie Anne du 544
Delany, Mary 549
Dostoevsky, Anna 1142
Eristi-Aya 12
Este, Isabella d' 276
Ferguson, Elizabeth Graeme 624
Filipovic, Zlata 4932
Fleming, Marjory 876
Foster, Doris Ann 3571
Frank, Anne 2657
Gill, Sarah Prince 601
Glückel of Hameln 479
Godolphin, Margaret 489
Godwin, Hannah 819
Gonzaga, Lucrezia 355
Graham, Isabella 638
Griffitts, Hannah 600
Grignan, Françoise-Marguerite de Sévigné 480
Harley, Brilliana 411
Héloise 178
Hillesum, Etty 2220
Hoby, Margaret 375
Hutchinson, Lucy 438
Izumi Shikibu 165
James, Alice 1160
Knight, Sarah Kemble 508
Knowles, Mary 615
Lamb, Mary Ann 722
Lisle, Honor 296
López de Córdoba, Leonor 243
Luxborough, Henrietta Knight 547
Mahler-Werfel, Alma 1532
Maintenon, Françoise de 466

Marguerite of Valois 356
Maria Theresa 579
Martin, Martha 1827
Masters, Mary 610
Michitsuna, Mother of 160
Monica 105
Montagu, Elizabeth 585
Montagu, Mary Wortley 533
Montefiore, Judith 797
Morris, Margaret 625
Nijo, Lady 222
Nin, Anaïs 1979
Osborne, Dorothy 453
Paston, Agnes 280
Ptaschkina, Nelly 1982
Ramsay, Martha Laurens 699
Riedesel, Frederica de 652
Rilliet-Huber, Catherine 724
Russell, Elizabeth Hoby 326
Russell, Rachel 467
Sarashina, Lady 173
Schurman, Anna Maria van 422
Senesh, Hannah 2413
Sévigné, Marie de 451
Sherrington, Grace 353
Shikibu, Murasaki 166
Shonagon, Sei 163
Simon, Rachel 995
Softic-Kaunitz, Elma 4597
Southey, Caroline Anne 802
Stewart, Elinore Pruitt 1483
Strozzi, Alessandra de' Machingi 251
Sugawara no Takasue no musume 181
Tam, Ba 4943
Thomas, Elizabeth 520
Tolstoy, Sophie 1132
Victoria 960
Ward, Barbara 2230
Wentworth, Anne 455
Whiteley, Opal 1858
Wilkinson, Eliza 686
Wilson, Harriette 814
Winslow, Anna Green 700
Winthrop, Margaret 400
Wordsworth, Dorothy 758
Wordsworth, Mary 754
Wright, Susanna 546

DRAMATISTS—LIBRETTISTS, PLAYWRIGHTS, SCRIPTWRITERS, AND DRAMATURGS

Aguirre, Isidora 2337
Aidoo, Ama Ata 3316
Akalaitis, JoAnne 3016
Akins, Zoö 1646
Aldis, Mary Reynolds 1397
Allen, Candace 4224
Ancelot, Virginie 829
Angelou, Maya 2618
Ariadne 535
Arizmendi, Yareli 4666
Atkinson, Kate 4021
Atlan, Liliane 2783
Bagnold, Enid 1693
Bai Fengxi 2785
Baillie, Joanna 713

Baizley, Doris 3555
Baker, Elizabeth 1469
Bambara, Toni Cade 3121
Barnes, Djuna 1739
Baum, Vicki 1674
Behn, Aphra 472
Benmussa, Simone 2751
Berg, Gertrude 1882
Bergen, Candice 3635
Betsko, Kathleen 3125
Bingham, Madeline 2172
Boesing, Martha Gross 2964
Bolt, Carol 3244
Bonal, Denise 2396
Boothby, Frances 493
Bovasso, Julie Anne 2693
Bowen, Marjorie 1675–1676
Brackley, Elizabeth 445
Breillat, Catherine 3814
Breslin, Rosemary 4401
Broner, E.M. 2695
Brooke, Frances 593
Burney, Fanny 671
Burrell, Sophia 660
Canth, Minna 1125
Carr, Marina 4672
Carroll, Vinnette 2422
Cavendish, Jane 441
Cavendish, Margaret 446
Centlivre, Susanna 511
Céu, Violante do 417
Chambers, Jane 3023
Charke, Charlotte 705
Chase, Mary 2062
Chávez, Denise Elia 3816
Childe-Pemberton, Harriet L. 1723
Childress, Alice 2364
Christie, Agatha 1724
Churchill, Caryl 3078
Churchill, Jennie Jerome 1201
Cixous, Hélène 3025
Cleage, Pearl 3818
Clive, Catherine 572
Cloud, Darrah 4296
Cockburn, Alicia 574
Coffee, Lenore J. 1820
Collins, Kathleen 2753
Comden, Betty 2339
Commire, Anne 3186
Condé, Maryse 3026
Cooper, Elizabeth 607
Cowley, Hannah 643
Craigie, Pearl 1334
Crothers, Rachel 1511
Cryer, Gretchen 2924
Cumming, Patricia 2791
Dane, Clemence 1677
Dangarembga, Tsitsi 4480
Daniels, Sarah 4360
D'Arcy, Margaretta 2888
Davidson, Sara 3732
Daviot, Gordon 1823
Davis, Eisa 4951
Davys, Mary 517
De Groen, Alma 3251
de Matteo, Donna 3252
Delaney, Shelagh 3137
Delmar, Viña 2013

Di Prima, Diane 2890
Diamond, Selma 2368
Didion, Joan 2925
Drexler, Rosalyn 2546
du Maurier, Daphne 2063
Duffy, Carol Ann 4298
Duffy, Maureen 2842
Dunbar, Andrea 4570
Dunn, Nell 2976
Duras, Marguerite 2219
Dworkin, Susan 4817
Edson, Margaret 4571
Edwards, Anne 2594
Ensler, Eve 4174
Ephron, Nora 3258
Evans, Mari 2453
Fabien, Michèle 3568
Farabough, Laura 4407
Farhoud, Abla 3569
Ferber, Edna 1663
Fey, Tina 4527.1
Field, Rachel Lyman 1793
Fields, Dorothy 2014
Fiske, Minnie 1312
Fleisser, Marie-Luise 1932
Fleming, Joan 2086
Fletcher, Lucille 2176
Flexner, Anne Crawford 1430
Fornés, Maria Irene 2704
Fowler, Connie May 4639
Fradonnet, Catherine 345
Frank, Florence Kiper 1628
Franken, Rose 1809
Frings, Ketti 2241
Gale, Zona 1431
Gallagher, Mary 3744
Gallagher, Tess 3409
Gallaire-Bourega, Fatima 3500
Gambaro, Griselda 2628
Gardam, Jane 2629
Garson, Barbara 3335
Gee, Shirley 2798
Gems, Pam 2518
Gerstenberg, Alice 1629
Gibson, P.J. 4107
Gilliatt, Penelope 2799
Gilliatt, Penelope 2799
Ginzburg, Natalia 2267
Glaspell, Susan 1474
Gordon, Ruth 1825
Gore, Catherine 863
Graham, Virginia 2177
Gregory, Augusta 1193
Hagedorn, Jessica Tarahata 3901
Hansberry, Lorraine 2711
Harjo, Joy 4045
Haywood, Eliza 539
Heimel, Cynthia 3750
Hellman, Lillian 2021
Hemans, Felicia 838
Henley, Beth 4109
Herrström, Christina 4489
Hewett, Dorothy Coade 2459
Hirsi Ali, Ayaan 4789
Hoper, Mrs. 631
Horsfield, Debbie 4306
Houston, Velina Hasu 4413
Howe, Tina 3038
Hroswitha of Gandersheim 158

Hurston, Zora Neale 1727
Inchbald, Elizabeth 676
Isaacs, Susan 3423
Jacker, Corinne 2855
Jackson, Elaine 3425
Jackson-Opoku, Sandra 4183
Jellicoe, Ann 2600
Jentz, Terri 4416
Jhabvala, Ruth Prawer 2601
Johnson, Diane 2900
Jotuni, Maria 1547
Kallen, Lucille Chernos 2433
Kanin, Fay 2295
Kaufman, Bel 2160
Keatley, Charlotte 4537
Kennedy, A. L. 4703
Kennedy, Adrienne 2767
Kerr, Jean 2463
Kesselman, Wendy 3202
Krásnohorská, Eliska 1151
Kummer, Clare 1684
Lasker-Schüler, Else 1364
Lea, Fanny Heaslip 1615
Leapor, Mary 590
Lejeune, Caroline 1852
Lenéru, Marie 1461
Lennart, Isobel 2247
Lennox, Charlotte 584
Lessing, Doris 2349
Liking, Werewere 3986
Lim, Genny 3672
Lindgren, Astrid 2069
Loos, Anita 1686
Lovell, Marie 878
Luce, Clare Boothe 1973
MacDonald, Sharman 4055
Malpede, Karen 3590
Manley, Delariviere 501
Mann, Emily 4120–4121
Manner, Eeva-Liisa 2406
Maraini, Dacia 2991
Marbury, Elisabeth 1211
Marion, Frances 1655
Martínez Sierra, María 1441
May, Elaine 2810
McCullers, Carson 2297
Merriam, Eve 2274
Meyer, Annie Nathan 1339
Meyer, Marlane 4061
Millay, Edna St. Vincent 1751
Miller, Susan 3528
Mitford, Mary Russell 805
Moore, Honor 3596
Moraga, Cherríe 4125
Moreau, Jeanne 2637
Morgan, Elaine 2383
Mowatt, Anna Cora 957
Mumford, Ethel Watts 1516
Munro, Rona 4497
Murray, Judith Sargent 669
Neuber, Friederika Karoline 545
Newman, Naomi 2730
Nichols, Anne 1730
Norman, Marsha 3776
Nottage, Lynn 4683.1
O'Malley, Mary 3289
Orczy, 1317 Orr, Mary 2140
Osten, Suzanne 3530

Owens, Rochelle 2996
Page, Louise 4325
Panova, Vera Fedorovna 2030
Pappenheim, Bertha 1249
Parent, Gail 3218
Parks, Suzan-Lori 4649
Partnow, Elaine Bernstein 3291
Patel, Shailja 4828
Peabody, Josephine Preston 1448
Perry, Eleanor 2252
Pessl, Marisha 4929
Petrushevskaya, Lyudmila 3101
Philips, Katherine Fowler 459
Pilkington, Laetitia 563
Pix, Mary Griffith 509
Pollock, Sharon 2998
Portillo Trambley, Estela 2609
Powell, Dawn 1830
Pulci, Antonia 265
Rahman, Aishah 2999
Rame, Franca 2639
Rand, Ayn 2032
Rascoe, Judith 3295
Razumovskaya, Lyudmila 3859
Reinshagen, Gerlind 2575
Resnik, Muriel 2301
Reza, Yasmina 4503
Richards, Beah 2387
Ridler, Anne Barbara 2188
Riefenstahl, Leni 1955
Rinehart, Mary Roberts 1480
Ritter, Erika 3860
Roberts, Michele 3932
Robinson, Mary 693
Rochefort, Christiane 2302
Roepke, Gabriela 2388
Roth, Friederike 3863
Rowson, Susanna Haswell 715
Roy, Arundhati 4595
Rubenstein, Gillian 3374
Sachs, Nelly 1734
Sagan, Françoise 2945
Sanchez, Sonia 2912
Sánchez-Scott, Milcha 4331
Sarraute, Nathalie 1921
Sarton, May 2189
Scott-Maxwell, Florida 1601
Shange, Ntozake 3865
Sheridan, Frances 595
Sherman, Susan 3158
Smith, Anna Deavere 4006
Smith, Dodie 1836
Snortland, Ellen 4211
Sofola, Zulu 2952
Sontag, Susan 2866
Sowerby, Githa 1872
Speare, Dorothy 1879
Spewack, Bella 1891
St. John, Christopher Marie 1466
Starhawk 4072
Stein, Gertrude 1450
Sutherland, Efua Theodora 2498
Swenson, May 2212
Taylor, Renee 2869
Terry, Megan 2827
Tollet, Elizabeth 541
Törnqvist, Mia 4435
Townsend, Sue 3702

Treadwell, Sophie 1643
Trevisan, Anna F. 2034
Trinh, T. Minh-Ha 4147
Trotter, Catherine 522
Tsvetaeva, Marina 1757
Turnbull, Margaret 1702
Tuthill, Louisa Caroline 862
Valenzuela, Luisa 3110
Vogel, Paula A. 4076
Voronel, Nina 2873
vos Savant, Marilyn 3703
Vostrá, Alena 3111
Wagner, Jane 2956
Walbert, Kate 4598.1
Walsh, Maria Elena 2745
Wandor, Michelene 3237
Warren, Mercy Otis 603
Wasserstein, Wendy 4013
Weddell, Mrs. 612
Weil, Simone 2116
Weldon, Fay 2874
Wells, Rebecca 4150
Wertenbaker, Timberlake 4077
West, Cheryl L. 4714
West, Jane 694
West, Mae 1790
Wharton, Anne 462
Winslow, Thyra Samter 1985
Wiseman, Jane 527
Wood, Ellen 922
Yamauchi, Wakako 2504
Yang Jiang 2171
Yankowitz, Susan 3315
Young, Rida Johnson 1369
Zeidner, Lisa 4341

JOURNALISTS, BLOGGERS,
COLUMNISTS, REPORTERS, AND
EDITORS
Abbott, Shirley 2875
Abbott, Wenonah Stevens 1307
Abramson, Jill 4222
Ackerman, Diane 3808
Adams, Léonie 1880
Akre, Jane 4562
Alcott, Louisa May 1044
Alexander, Elizabeth 4601
Alexander, Shana 2540
al-Huwaider, Wajeha 4846
Allende, Isabel 3317
al-Shaykh, Hanan 3611.1
Alvarez, Aida 3881
Amanpour, Christiane 4437.1
Andrews, Mary Kay 4226
Angier, Natalie 4438
Annunziata, Lucia 4959
Anthony, Susan B. 963
Anyanwu, Christina 4019
Anzaldúa, Gloria Evangelina 3321
Apostolides, Marianne 4875
Applebaum, Anne 4665
Armstrong, Sue 3322
Ascher, Barbara Lazear 3718
Aubry, Erin J. 4812
Aury, Dominique 2059
Avary, Myrta Lockett 1217
Ayer, Harriet Hubbard 1163
Bainbridge, Beryl Margaret 2831

CAREER AND OCCUPATION INDEX

Ballard, Bettina 1963
Bambara, Toni Cade 3121
Banks-Smith, Nancy 2691
Barbauld, Anna Letitia 642
Barber, Lynn 3475
Barfoot, Joan 3631
Barnebey, Faith 2880
Barnes, Djuna 1739
Barolini, Helen 2509
Barrett, Rona 2961
Battelle, Phyllis 2417
Bayliss, Claire 4840
Beal, Frances M. 3173
Becker, Robin 4023
Begley, Sharon 4348
Bender, Marilyn 2511
Benmussa, Simone 2751
Bernikow, Louise 3174
Betsko, Kathleen 3125
Bialosky, Jill 4603
Bianchi, Martha Dickinson 1323
Billings, Victoria 3558
Birch, Alison Wyrley 2419
Blais, Madeleine 3723
Blakely, Mary Kay 3813
Bolton, Sarah Knowles 1101
Bombeck, Erma 2586
Bourke-White, Margaret 2041
Bowen, 'Asta 4290
Bowles, Gloria 4350
Boxer, Sarah 4781
Bradford, Cornelia 542
Bradwell, Myra R. 1035
Brant, Beth 3246
Breslin, Rosemary 4401
Bright, Susannah "Susie" 4441
Brooke, Frances 593
Brooks, Geraldine 4292
Brothers, Joyce 2587
Brown, Helen Gurley 2421
Brown, Tina 4165
Bryan, Mary E. 1081
Bunch, Charlotte 3483
Burchill, Julie 4524
Burk, Martha Gertrude 3247
Burkett, Elinor 3394
Burroughs, Nannie Helen 1592
Cadden, Vivian 2264
Cahill, Susan 3178
Campbell, Beatrix 3728
Canth, Minna 1125
Cantwell, Mary 2698
Carabillo, Toni 2544
Carleton, Emma 1172
Carr, Cynthia 4478
Carter, Angela 3182
Case, Sue-Ellen 3328
Cather, Willa 1408
Catt, Carrie Chapman 1244
Chamorro, Violeta Barrios de 2654
Chang, Diana 2882
Chang, Iris 4765
Chang, Leslie T. 4782
Chapman, Maria Weston 893
Chase, Mary 2062
Chayes, Sarah 4604
Chernin, Kim 3183
Child, Lydia Maria 870

Childress, Alice 2364
Churchill, Jennie Jerome 1201
Claflin, Tennessee 1135
Clark, C. Hope 4357
Cleage, Pearl 3818
Cohen, Sherry Suib 2885
Combs, Valda Jean 4442
Conran, Shirley 2790
Cook, Blanche Weisen 3249
Cool, Lisa Collier 4096
Cooper, Elizabeth 607
Cooper, Helene 4719
Corbin, Alice 1567
Coulter, Ann 4567
Couric, Katie 4402
Cowan, Alison Leigh 4638
Cox, Ana Marie 4856
Craven, Margaret 1929
Crittenden, Ann 3027
Croce, Arlene 2887
Crowley, Candy 3821.1
Cunard, Nancy 1822
Curie, Ève 1990
d'Adesky, Anne-Christine 4479
Daum, Meghan 4814
Davidson, Sara 3732
Dayan, Yaöl 3136
Decter, Midge 2592
Dery, Dominika 4890–4891
Dhaliwal, Daljit 4607
Di Prima, Diane 2890
Diamant, Anita 4038
Didion, Joan 2925
Dillard, Annie 3563
DiManno, Rosie 4978
DiPerna, Diane 4963
Dix, Dorothy 1265
Dodge, Mary Mapes 1039
Dowd, Maureen 4102
Dreifus, Claudia 3495
Dudar, Helen 2084
Dunbar-Nelson, Alice 1457
Dworkin, Andrea 3738
Dyson, Esther 4040
Ehrenreich, Barbara 3257
Ellerbee, Linda 3496
Ellison, Katherine 4405
Eltahawy, Mona 4747
Emerson, Claudia 4406
English, Deirdre 3825
Erbe, Bonnie 4174.1
Erdrich, Louise 4242
Ettore, Barbara 4041
Fadiman, Anne 4175
Fallaci, Oriana 2656
Fasig, Lisa Biank 4612
Fenwick, Millicent 2127
Ferguson, Anita Perez 4527
Ferguson, Marilyn 3085
Fern, Fanny 914
Fields, Suzanne 4574
Firestone, Shulamith 3570
Fishel, Elizabeth 3967
Fitzgerald, Frances 3189
Flanders, Laura 4575
Flanner, Janet 1745
Fleeson, Doris 1931
Foderaro, Lisa W. 4675

Fonseca, Isabel 4614
Frank, Ray 1313
Fraser, Arvonne 2517
Fredriksson, Marianne 2595.1
Fremantle, Anne 2108
Fuller, Margaret 910
Furman, Laura 3574
Furness, Betty 2266.1
Gaard, Greta 4529
García, Cristina 4449
Garrison, Deborah 4696
Gaylor, Annie Laurie 4300
Gellhorn, Martha 2087
Geniesse, Jane Fletcher 2977
Gessen, Masha 4748
Geyer, Georgie Anne 2930
Ghezali, Salima 4450
Gibbs, Nancy 4531
Gilbert, Peggy 2018
Gillespie, Marcia 3505
Giroud, Françoise 2268
Godwin, Gail 3032
Goldman, Emma 1360
Goodman, Amy 4408.1
Goodman, Ellen H. 3264
Gornick, Vivian 2932
Gould, Lois 3033
Goulianos, Joan 3144
Gournay, Marie le Jars de 369
Graff, E. J. 4452
Graham, Katharine 2289
Graham, Laurie 3192
Graham, Sheilah 1995
Green, Mary A. E. 948
Green, Rayna 3338
Greene, Bella da Costa 1527
Greenfield, Meg 2710
Grierson, Constantia 559
Gross, Jane 4453
Gruber, Ruth 2157
Guest, Barbara 2371
Guppy, Shusha 2933
Gwinn, Mary Ann 4044
Hacker, Marilyn 3340
Hajar, Hanaa 4976
Hale, Nancy 2089
Hale, Sarah Josepha 807
Hall, Sharlot Mabridth 1374
Halprin, Sally 4965
Halsted, Anna Roosevelt 2046
Handler, Marisa 4917
Harjo, Joy 4045
Harrison, Barbara Grizzuti 2893
Haywood, Eliza 539
Hazleton, Lesley 3578
Healy, Bernadine 3509
Hebblethwaite, Margaret 4250.1
Heldman, Caroline 4860
Heller, Karen 4412
Hempel, Amy 4046
Henderson, Hazel 2853
Henriksen, Louise Levitas 2179
Hewitt, Mary Elizabeth 901
Heyward, Carter 3579
Hickok, Lorena A. 1773
Hobson, Laura Z. 1905
Hoffman, Eva 3581
Holmes, Marjorie 2133

Holtby, Winifred 1867
Hopper, Hedda 1709
Hosain, Attia 2200
Howard, Jane 2936
Howe, Louise Kapp 2899
Howell, Georgina 3346
Huffington, Arianna 3976
Hughes, Karen 4370–4371
Hunter, Kristin 2765
Hunter-Gault, Charlayne 3347
Hutchinson, Ellen M. 1546
Ibarruri, Dolores 1813
Ifill, Gwen 4308
Ivins, Molly 3512
Jackson-Opoku, Sandra 4183
Jacobs, Rose Gell 1681
Jacoby, Susan 3584
Jagan, Janet 2378
Jayapal, Pramila 4702
Jenkins, Carol 3516
Johnson, Eleanor Murdock 1748
Johnson, Rheta Grimsley 4184
Josefowitz, Natasha 2555
Judson, Olivia 4791
Katona, Jacqui 4724
Katz, Lilian G. 2805
Kaufman, Sue 2556
Kelley, Kitty 3353
Kempton, Sally 3430
Kerr, Sarah 4966
Keyes, Frances Parkinson 1632
Kilgallen, Dorothy 2203
King, Florence 2990
Kingston, Maxine Hong 3203
Kirchheimer, Gloria DeVidas 3356
Kizer, Carolyn 2527
Klagsbrun, Francine 2768
Klein, Naomi 4823
Kolata, Gina 3841
Kolbert, Elizabeth 4584
Koppel, Lily 4946
Kort, Michele 3982
Kramer, Jane 3092
Krantz, Judith 2634
Kushner, Rachel 4769
LaFollette, Suzanne 1776
Laing, Dilys 2051
Lambert, Angela 3204
Landers, Ann 2319
Lape, Esther 1569
Larcom, Lucy 1008
Larsen, Jensine 4897
Laut, Agnes C. 1392
Lawrenson, Helen 1996
Lawson, Nigella Lucy 4541
Le Row, Caroline Bigelow 1117
Lebowitz, Fran 3984
Lee, Jennifer 8. 4911
Lepore, Jill 4725
Leslie, Eliza 804
Levertov, Denise 2464
Levine, Judith 4118
Levinson, Nan 3911
Lewis, Edith 1551
Lim, Genny 3672
Lindley, Mary Ann 3766
Love, Barbara J. 3043
Maazel, Fiona 4912

MacPherson, Myra 2939
Maddow, Rachel 4878.1
Madgett, Naomi Long 2465
Mairs, Nancy 3440
Malveaux, Julianne 4190
Manji, Irshad 4772
Manley, Delariviere 501
Mann, Erika 2026
Mannes, Marya 1998
Margonelli, Lisa 4705
Marion, Frances 1655
Marshall, Catherine 2224
Martin, Judith 3097
Matheopoulos, Helena 3675
Mathis, Deborah 4192
Mayer, Bernadette 3592
Mayer, Jane 4317
McAleese, Mary 4057
McBride, Mary Margaret 1888
McCarthy, Abigail 2248
McCarthy, Mary 2185
McCormick, Anne O'Hare 1582
McGovern, Ann 2725
McGrory, Mary 2323
McLaughlin, Patricia 3593
McLeod, Merikay 3771
McTaggart, Lynne 4059
McWhorter, Diane 4060
Mead, Margaret 1935
Meadows, Donella "Dana" 3282
Means, Marianne 2907
Meyer, Agnes 1668
Michaelis, Aline Triplett 1635
Miller, Ceci 4461
Miller, Emily 1053
Miller, Helen Hill 1889
Miller, Jean Baker 2607
Miller, Laura 3992
Millner, Caille 4928
Mirikitani, Janice 3283
Mirrielees, Edith Ronald 1515
Moeller, Susan D. 4731
Monroe, Harriet 1258
Montero, Mayra 4123
Moore, Marianne 1669
Moraga, Cherríe 4125
Morgan, Robin 3284
Morris, Holly 4733
Morris, Jan 2569
Morris, Mary 2205
Morrison, Toni 2771
Moses, Claire Goldberg 3285
Moss, Cyntha 3215
Munk, Erika 3152
Murphy, Beatrice M. 2096
Myerson, Bess 2491
Naqvi, Tahira 4198
Nelson, Jill 4127
Nelson, Martha 4128
Nemeth, Maria 2812
Ngesa, Mildred 4899
Nichols, Martha 4968–4969
Nichols, Mary D. 3600
Niederman, Sharon 3853
Nomani, Asra Q. 4708
Noonan, Peggy 3996
Norman, Dorothy 2028
Nussbaum, Hedda 3362

O'Faolain, Nuala 3217
Okello-Orlale, Rosemary 4709
Onassis, Jacqueline Kennedy 2676
O'Reilly, Jane 2995
Orenstein, Catherine 4754
Orlean, Susan 4324
Orlova, Raisa Davydovna 2327
Orth, Maureen Ann 3444
Painter, Pamela 3290
Paley, Barbara "Babe" 2251
Palmer, Alice Freeman 1206
Palmer, Gretta Brooker 2029
Pankhurst, Adela 1636
Pankhurst, Sylvia 1583
Panova, Vera Fedorovna 2030
Parker, Kathleen 4797
Partnow, Elaine Bernstein 3291
Partnow, Jessica 4947
Parturier, Françoise 2353
Paternostro, Silvana 4549
Patterson, Eleanor 1572
Payne, Ethel L. 2163
Pearson, Patricia 4685
Petry, Ann 2100
Phillips, Angela Marie 3783
Piercy, Marge 2997
Pierpont, Claudia Roth 4134
Pogrebin, Letty Cottin 3154
Politkovskaya, Anna 4464
Pollitt, Katha 3925
Pool, Gail 3689
Porter, Sylvia 2207
Poulsson, Emilie 1199
Power, Samantha 4829
Priest, Dana 4502
Prins, Nomi 4867
Propp, Karen 4428
Pursifull, Carmen M. 2736
Qing, Dai 3250.1
Quindlen, Anna 4136
Quinn, Sally 3294
Rebolledo, Tey Diana 3052
Reitz, Rosetta 2493
Renne, Tanya 4830
Richards, Amy 4831
Richards, Cecile 4466
Rind, Clementina Bird 634
Rinehart, Mary Roberts 1480
Rittenhouse, Jessie 1367
Rivers, Caryl 3053
Roiphe, Katie 4777
Rollin, Betty 3003
Rose, Wendy 3862
Rosen, Ruth 3608
Rosenberg, Tina 4553
Ross, Lillian 2611
Rossi, Alice S. 2439
Roth, Stephanie Danielle 4848
Rowland, Helen 1481
Rowson, Susanna Haswell 715
Ru Zhijuan 2535
Saberi, Roxana 4918
Salter, Mary Jo 4270
Salter, Stephanie 3935
Sanger, Margaret 1535
Sangster, Margaret E. 1085
Satran, Pamela Redmond 4205
Scarf, Maggie 2819

Schneir, Miriam 2864
Scott, Robyn 4949
Seaman, Barbara 2946
Shaikh, Shamima 4556
Shear, Marie 3228
Sheehan, Susan 3058
Sherman, Susan 3158
Sherrill, Martha 4507
Sherwood, Kate Brownlee 1106
Sigourney, Lydia Howard 827
Sitwell, Edith 1673
Slapsak, Svetlana 3867
Small, Meredith F. 4005
Smedley, Agnes 1754
Smith, Barbara 3697
Smith, Hazel Brannon 2228
Smith, Liz 2469
Smith, Margaret Bayard 777
Sonneschein, Rosa 1156
Soren, Tabitha 4759
Spacks, Patricia Meyer 2685
St. Johns, Adela Rogers 1804
Stanton, Elizabeth Cady 931
Steinem, Gloria 2916
Sternhell, Carol 4009
Stewart, Martha 3307
Stokes, Rose Pastor 1537
Stone, Lucy 953
Strong, Anna Louise 1642
Stuteville, Sarah 4942
Taggard, Genevieve 1805
Tanaka, Yukiko 3232
Tappan, Eva March 1203
Tarbell, Ida 1227
Tawil, Raymonda 3233
Tempelsman, Cathy Rindner 4972
Tett, Gillian 4761.1
Thomas, Helen 2393
Thomas, Lynn M. 3801
Thomson, Alice 4657
Thurman, Judith 3872
Tinti, Hannah 4874
Torvik, Solveig 3162
Traister, Rebecca 4527.1
Treadwell, Sophie 1643
Tremain, Rose 3464
Trimmer, Sarah Kirby 637
Tucker, Anne 3620
Tucker, Cynthia 4336
Turner, Nancy Byrd 1560
Tweedie, Jill 2828
Valenzuela, Luisa 3110
Van Buren, Abigail 2333
Van Duyn, Mona 2415
Van Horne, Harriet 2394
Van Susteren, Greta 4277
Vida, Vendela 4852
Vilar, Irene 4805
Vincent, Norah 4713
Vincenzi, Penny 3164
Viorst, Judith 2780
Viramontes, Helena María 4279
vos Savant, Marilyn 3703
Vreeland, Diana 1984
Waldman, Anne 3621
Walker, Rebecca 4806
Wallace, Michelle 4149
Walters, Barbara 2687

Wandor, Michelene 3237
Wang Yongchen 4281
Washington, Harriet A. 4634
Weil, Simone 2116
West, Rebecca 1759
Whitbread, Jane 2231
Whitehorn, Katharine 2647
Wilcox, Ella Wheeler 1209
Williams, Bertye Young 1485
Williams, Fannie Barrier 1210
Wilson, Elizabeth 3014
Winn, Marie 3115
Winterson, Jeanette 4510
Wolverton, Terry 4286
Wood, Ellen 922
Woodhull, Victoria Claflin 1086
Wright, Robin 3879
Wurtzel, Elizabeth 4762
Wyse, Lois 2584
Yamada, May 2475
Yang, Gladys 2358
Yang Ping 2105
Yaroshinskaya, Alla 4220
Yglesias, Helen 2261
York, Eva Rose 1240
Young, Cathy 4661
Zarin, Cynthia Rebecca 4513
Zeisler, Andi 4221
Zhang, Lijia 4690
Zia, Ather 4922
Zong Pu 2649

POETS

Aafreen, Ishrat 4514
Abbott, Wenonah Stevens 1307
Abutsu 227
Ackerman, Diane 3808
Adams, Léonie 1880
Addison, Mrs. R. 909
Addonzio, Kim 4223
Adnan, Etel 2505
Aguilar, Grace 932
Ai 3711
Aidoo, Ama Ata 3316
Aiken, Lucy 785
'Aisha bint Ahmad al-Qurtubiyya 161
Akers, Elizabeth Chase 1043
Akhmatova, Anna 1692
Akhyaliyya, Laila 122
Akins, Zoö 1646
Alcosser, Sandra 3472
Alden, Ada 1215
Aldis, Mary Reynolds 1397
Alexander, Elizabeth 4601
Alexander, Mrs. Cecil Frances 943
al-Huwaider, Wajeha 4846
Al-Khansa 116
Allen, Paula Gunn 3118
Allerton, Ellen Palmer 1060
Alta 3319
Alvarez, Julia 3950
Ambapali 54
Amelia 794
Amir, Anda 1944
Andal 167
Anderson, Catherine 3713
Angelou, Maya 2618

Annan, Annie Rankin 1157
Anyte of Tegea 66
Anzaldúa, Gloria Evangelina 3321
Armantrout, Rae 3716
Ascarelli, Devorah 409
Atwood, Margaret 3119
Auber, Harriet 761
Austin, Mary Hunter 1346
Auvaiyar 102
Ava, Frau 185
Backus, Bertha Adams 2119
Bacon, Josephine Dodge 1468
Bacon, Martha 2280
Bai, Mukta 230
Baillie, Joanna 713
Bang, Mary Jo 3630
Barbauld, Anna Letitia 642
Barber, Mary 536
Barker, Elsa 1356
Barker, Jane 523
Barker, Patricia 3392
Barnard, Anne 659
Barr, Mary A 1188
Barreno, Maria Isabel 3122
Barrington, Judith 3476
Bass, Ellen 3720
Bates, Katherine Lee 1241
Bat-Miriam, Yocheved 1925
Beauveau, Marie de 571
Becker, Robin 4023
Beers, Ethel Lynn 1011
Begbie, Janet 2120
Behn, Aphra 472
Benedict, Ruth 1659
Benét, Laura 1605
Benson, Stella 1740
Berberova, Nina 1927
Bernal, Esmeralda 3886
Berners, Juliana 266
Bernikow, Louise 3174
Berry, Dorothy 456
Berssenbrugge, Mei-mei 3721
Bertana, Lucia dall'Orno 318
Bertken, Sister 257
Bialosky, Jill 4603
Bianchi, Martha Dickinson 1323
Bibesco, Elizabeth Asquith 1842
Bishop, Elizabeth 2153
Bishop, Wendy Sue 4161
Black, Sophie Cabot 4440
Blakely, Nora Brooks 4029
Blamire, Susanna 653
Blessington, Marguerite 808
Blind, Mathilde 1100
Bogan, Louise 1843
Boland, Eavan 3480
Bolton, Sarah Knowles 1101
Botta, Anne 926
Boumi Pappa, Rita 2040
Bowditch, Katherine 1791
Boyle, Sarah 917
Bradford, Elizabeth 500
Bradley, Katharine 1141
Bradley, Mary 1061
Bradstreet, Anne 430
Brainard, Mary Gardiner 1252
Branch, Anna Hempstead 1454
Branch, Mary 1091

Brand, Dionne 4164
Brant, Beth 3246
Braverman, Kate 3954
Bregy, Charlotte 435
Breitman, Barbara E. 3955
Brereton, Jane 529
Brewster, Martha 629
Bridges, Madeline 1123
Brine, Mary Dow 933
Brittain, Vera 1764–1765
Brock-Broido, Lucie 4352
Brodine, Karen 3726
Bronaugh, Anne 1472
Brontö, Anne 965
Brontö, Charlotte 934
Brontö, Emily 945
Brooks, Gwendolyn 2281
Brooks, Maria 845
Brotherton, Alice Williams 1159
Brown, Abbie Farwell 1455
Brown, Alice 1218
Brown, Frances 935
Brown, Ophelia Guyon 1541
Brown, Rita Mae 3481
Brown, Rosellen 3128
Browning, Elizabeth Barrett 892
Brunton, Mary 775
Bryan, Mary E. 1081
Buell, Mary E. 1386
Burgos, Julia de 2214
Burr, Amelia 1507
Burrell, Sophia 660
Burton, Harriet Emma 1424
Butts, Mary Frances 1071
Byron, Mary C. G. 1263
Campbell, Dorothea Primrose 831
Campbell, Jane Montgomery 941
Canaan, Andrea R. 3729
Carew, Elizabeth 391
Carlyle, Jane Welsh 869
Carney, Julia A. 986
Carpio de San Feliz, Marcela de 420
Carson, Anne Regina 3957
Carter, Elizabeth 578
Cary, Alice 966
Cary, Phoebe 992
Case, Elizabeth York 1092
Cassian, Nina 2479
Castellanos, Rosario 2515
Castiglione, Ippolita 319
Castillo, Ana 4354
Castillo y Guevara, Francisca Josefa
    del 537
Castro, Rosalia de 1077
Cather, Willa 1408
Cavendish, Georgiana 690
Cavendish, Margaret 446
Cedering, Siv 3131
Cervantes, Lorna Dee 4234
Céu, Violante do 417
Chamber, Anna 774
Chandidas 246
Chandler, Mary 531
Chang, Diana 2882
Chang, Tina 4783
Chao Li-hua 240
Chao Luan-luan 144
Chapone, Hester 598

Chase-Riboud, Barbara 3132
Cheney, Gertrude Louise 2310
Childe-Pemberton, Harriet L. 1723
Chin, Marilyn 4295
Ch'in Chia, Wife of 72
Chowdhury, Seema 4842
Christina, Leonora 442
Christine de Pisan 244
Chu Shu-chên 197
Chuo Wên-chün 69
Cisneros, Sandra 4237
Cixous, Hélène 3025
Clampitt, Amy Kathleen 2365
Cleghorn, Sarah Norcliffe 1473
Clemmer, Mary 1087
Cleyre, Voltairine de 1325
Clifford, Anne 396
Clifton, Lucille 2970
Coates, Florence Earle 1173
Coates, Grace Stone 1566
Coatsworth, Elizabeth 1766
Coblentz, Catherine Cate 1845
Cockburn, Alicia 574
Cofer, Judith Ortiz 4094
Cohen, Mary M. 1202
Coignard, Gabrielle de 354
Coleridge, Mary 1264
Coleridge, Sara 871
Coligny, Henriette de 431
Collier, Mary 532
Collins, Anne 485
Colonna, Vittoria da 287
Compiuta Donzella, La 231
Conant, Isabel La Howe 1426
Cone, Helen Gray 1245
Conkling, Grace H. 1509
Conkling, Hilda 2123
Conrad, Beatrice 2590
Cook, Blanche Weisen 3249
Cook, Eliza 947
Cooke, Rose Terry 1012
Coolbrith, Ina 1102
Cooper, Jane 2481
Cope, Wendy Mary 3560
Corbett, E. T. 1542
Corbin, Alice 1567
Cornford, Frances Darwin 1649
Corpi, Lucha 3561
Corvera, Bernardina Guevara 4855
Cota-Cárdenas, Margarita 3250
Cowley, Hannah 643
Craig, Agnes 696
Craik, Dinah Mulock 1006
Crane, Nathalia 2196
Crapsey, Adelaide 1510
Craster, Edmund 1427
Crawford, Julia 866
Crawford, Louisa Macartney 817
Cromwell, Gladys 1626
Crouse, Mary Elizabeth 1410
Crowell, Grace Noll 1490
Cruz, Juana Inés de la 487
Cumming, Patricia 2791
Cunard, Nancy 1822
Custance, Olive 1428
d'Aragona, Tullia 301
Dargan, Olive 1358
Dauenhauer, Nora 2591

Davenport, Doris 3891
Davidson, Lucretia Maria 903
Davidson, Margaret 988
Davis, Eisa 4951
Davis, Olena Kalytiak 4905
Davis, Thadious M. 3494
De Bary, Anna Bunston 1359
de Hoyos, Angela 3187
De Vinck, Catherine 2425
Ded, Lal 248
Delany, Mary 549
Demarest, Mary Lee 1219
Deming, Alison Hawthorne 3647
Dennie, Abigail Colman 576
Derricotte, Toi 3254
Desbordes-Valmore, Marceline 801
Deshoulières, Antoinette 469
Desjardins, Marie-Catherine 460
Deutsch, Babette 1808
Di Prima, Diane 2890
Dickinson, Emily 1024
Dillard, Annie 3563
Dolliver, Clara G. 1429
Doolittle, Hilda 1650
Dorr, Julia 999
Doten, Elizabeth "Lizzie" 1013
Doubiago, Sharon 3648
Doudney, Sarah 1113
Dove, Rita Frances 4101
Dow, Dorothy 1968
Dowriche, Anne 349
Driscoll, Louise 1456
Droste-Hülshoff, Anette Elizabeth
    von 852
Duarte, Jessie 4173
Duff, Esther Lillian 2125
Duffy, Carol Ann 4298
Dungy, Camille T. 4858
Egerton, Sarah F. 514
Eifuku, Empress 225
Elizabeth of York 271
Elliot, Jean 599
Elmendorf, Mary J. 2369
Emanual, Lynn 3895
Emerson, Claudia 4406
Emon, Akazome 168
Ephelia 474
Erdrich, Louise 4242
Erinna 47
Espinosa, María 3142
Essbaum, Jill Alexander 4844
Estés, Clarissa Pinkola 3567
Etessami, Parvin 2064
Evans, Mari 2453
Falconar, Harriet 768
Falconar, Maria 759
Falk, Marcia 3650
Faller, Heather Roote 4447
Fane, Violet 1114
Fanshawe, Catherine Marie 726
Farrokhzad, Forough 2928
Faschinger, Lilian 3965
Faugéres, Margaretta Van Wyck 755
Feng Meng-lung 380
Ferguson, Elizabeth Graeme 624
Ferron 4103
Field, Rachel Lyman 1793
Fields, Annie Adams 1055

Finch, Anne 497
Fishback, Margaret 1900
Fisher, Renee 3743
Flanner, Hildegarde 1885
Fleury, Maria de 787
Flint, Annie Johnson 1326
Follen, Eliza Lee 803
Ford, Lena Guilbert 1373
Forman, Ruth 4787
Fradonnet, Catherine 345
Fradonnet, Madeleine 314
Frame, Janet 2483
Franco, Veronica 344
Frank, Florence Kiper 1628
Franklin, Eleanor Anne 847
Fraser, Kathleen 3030
Freeman, Mary Wilkins 1192
Fremantle, Anne 2108
Frost, Frances 2015
Fukuzoyo Chiyo 554
Fuller, Margaret Witter 1389
Fulton, Alice 4105
Fumiko, Hayashi 1993
Fyleman, Rose 1492
Gage, Frances Dana 904
Gale, Zona 1431
Gallagher, Tess 3409
Galloway, Priscilla 2705
Gambara, Veronica 285
Gardinier, Suzanne 4577
Garrison, Deborah 4696
Garrison, Theodosia 1433
Gates, Ellen 1065
Gervitz, Gloria 3411
Ghaaem-Maghami, Aalamtaaj 1609
Ghoratolain, Tahereh 942
Gibbons, Stella 1948
Gibson, Margaret 3504
Gilbert, Sandra 2978
Gill, Sarah Prince 601
Gillan, Maria Mazziotto 3190
Gilman, Caroline 843
Gilman, Charlotte Perkins 1254
Giltinan, Caroline 1610
Giovanni, Nikki 3412
Glancy, Diane 3263
Glück, Louise Elisabeth 3413
Goedicke, Patricia 2760
Goldberg, Lea 2156
Golden, Marita 3970
Gonzales, Sylvia Alicia 3414
Goodale, Dora Read 1327
Goodale, Elaine 1295
Goodenough, J. B. 3337
Goodison, Lorna 3747
Gorbanevskaya, Natalya 2980
Gore, Catherine 863
Gore-Booth, Eva 1398
Gormley 169
Gould, Hannah Flagg 810
Graham, Isabella 638
Graham, Janet 592
Graham, Jorie 3972
Grahn, Judy 3193
Grant, Anne 680
Graves, Clarissa 1747
Gray, Agnes Kendrick 1796
Green, Melissa 4533

Green, Rayna 3338
Greenberg, Blu 2981
Gregg, Linda 3339
Gregoria, Francisca 490
Greiffenberg, Catharina Regina
    von 463
Greville, Frances Fulke 583
Grierson, Constantia 559
Griffin, Susan 3417
Griffitts, Hannah 600
Gruber, Ruth 2157
Guest, Barbara 2371
Guillet, Pernette du 315
Guiney, Louise Imogen 1268
Gurney, Dorothy 1232
Guyon, Jeanne-Marie de la Motte
    482
Hacker, Marilyn 3340
Hadewijch of Brabant 218
Hagedorn, Jessica Tarahata 3901
Hale, Sarah Josepha 807
Hall, Hazel 1651
Hall, Radclyffe 1545
Hall, Sharlot Mabridth 1374
Hallack, Cecily R. 1866.1
Hamill, Janet 3576
Hamilton, Anna 1115
Hamilton, Elizabeth 691
Han Ts'ui-p'in 153
Hanim, Leylâ 1175
Harima, Young Woman of 134
Harington, Lucy 389
Harjo, Joy 4045
Harper, Frances Ellen Watkins 1000
Harris, Marguerite 1886
Harris, Maureen 3419
Harvey, Matthea 4876
Hastings, Flora 896
Hathshepsut 14
Hatun, Mihri 261
Havergal, Frances Ridley 1072
Hayden, Anna Tompson 483
Hayden, Esther 575
Haywood, Eliza 539
Heathorn, Henrietta 1001
Heaton, Rose Henniker 1612
Hecht, Jennifer Michael 4699
Hejinian, Lyn 3269
Hemans, Felicia 838
Herbert, Mary Sidney 365
Herschberger, Ruth 2292–2293
Hewett, Dorothy Coade 2459
Hewitt, Mary Elizabeth 901
Heyward, Jane Screven 2375
Hibbard, Grace 1376
Hickey, Emily 1137
Higginson, Ella 1287
Hildegarde von Bingen 179
Hillman, Brenda 4047
Hinck, Jeannie 4110
Hind bint Utba 120
Hinkson, Katharine Tynan 1270
Hirshfield, Jane 4180
Ho 67
Ho Nansorhon 368
Ho Shuang-ch'ing 573
Ho Xuan Huong 708
Hochman, Sandra 2983

Holford, Margaret 776
Holford, Margaret Wrench 711
Holland, Barbara 4048
Holland, Norah M. 1476
Holt, Anne Haw 2895
Home, Anne 639
Home, Grisell 505
Honnamma 495
hooks, bell 4305
Hooper, Ellen Sturgis 937
Hope, Laurence 1315
Horikawa 186
Horta, Maria Teresa 3036
Houdetot, Sophie de la Briche 609
Houston, Libby 3272
Howard, Anne Dacre 359
Howard, Anne Douglas 543
Howard, Isabella 589
Howarth, Ellen 1014
Howe, Fanny 3197
Howe, Julia Ward 956
Howe, Marie 3975
Howell, Carol K. 4251
Howell, Margery Eldredge 1774
Howells, Mildred 1399
Howitt, Mary 864
Howland, Bette 3039
Hoyt, Helen 1664
Hroswitha of Gandersheim 158
Hsi-chün 73
Hsüeh T'ao 140
Huang O 292
Hulme, Keri 3755
Hume, Anna 476
Hustvedt, Siri 4307
Hwang Chin-I 299
Ibarbourou, Juana de 1812
Ingelow, Jean 968
Iratsume, Kasa no 145
Iratsume, Otomo no Sakano-e no
    128
Irving, Minna 1224
Isaure, Clemence 270
Ise, Lady 155
Ishikawa 143
Itani, Frances 3348
Iwa no Hime 106
Izumi Shikibu 165
Jacker, Corinne 2855
Jackson, Helen Fiske Hunt 1027
Jackson-Opoku, Sandra 4183
Jacobsen, Josephine 2090
Jacobson, Ethel 2022
Jahan, Nur 382
James, Sibyl 3666
Janis, Elsie 1698
Janvier, Margaret 1138
Jefimija 238–239
Jennings, Elizabeth 2554
Jewsbury, Maria Jane 867
Jiles, Paulette 3427
Johnson, Emily Pauline 1272
Johnson, Georgia Douglas 1653
Johnson, Josephine Winslow 2135
Johnstone, Wilhelmina 1909
Jones, Amanda Theodosia 1066
Jones, Mary 663
Jones, Patricia 4051

Jong, Erica 3349
Jordan, Dorothea 712
Jordan, June 2987
Joseph, Jenny 2803
Judson, Sarah B. 877
Karr, Mary 4310
Kasdorf, Julia Spicher 4623
Kasmuneh 209
Kassiane 149
Kaufman, Shirley 2461
Kawai Chigetsu-Ni 461
Kay, Jackie 4583
Kazu-no-Michi 1144
Kelly, Brigit Pegeen 4052
Kemble, Fanny 908
Kenyon, Jane 3763
Kephart, Beth 4538
Keppel, Caroline 619
Kgositsile, Baleka 3905
Khalifeh, Imane 4896
Khatun, Jahan 249
Khatun, Padeshah 224
Ki no Tsurayuki, Daughter of 159
Kii, Lady 146
Killigrew, Anne 496
Killigrew, Catherine 331
Kilmer, Aline Murray 1682
Kim, Myung Mi 4418
Kimball, Harriet 1057
King, Georgiana Goddard 1391
King, Harriet 1094
Kinsolving, Sally 1477
Kizer, Carolyn 2527
Klepfisz, Irena 3276
Knight, Sarah Kemble 508
Kogawa, Joy 2938
Koghtnatsi, Khosrovidoukht 138
Koka, Stewardess of the Empress
    210
Kolmar, Gertrud 1799
Kouchak, Nahabed 401
Krásnohorská, Eliska 1151
Krauss, Nicole 4884
Kshetrayya 551
Kuan Tao-shjng 223
Kubatum 7
Kumin, Maxine 2529
Labé, Louise 316
Laing, Dilys 2051
Lalleswari 235
Lamb, Mary Ann 722
Landon, Letitia 873
Lanyer, Aemilia 372
Laramore, Vivian Yeiser 1749
Larcom, Lucy 1008
Lasker-Schüler, Else 1364
Lathbury, Mary 1104
Laurencin, Marie 1633
Lazarus, Emma 1168
Le Gallienne, Hesper 1777
Le Row, Caroline Bigelow 1117
Le Sueur, Meridel 1911
Lea, Fanny Heaslip 1615
Leapor, Mary 590
Lee, Agnes 1352
Lee, Mary Chudleigh 492
Leitch, Mary Sinton 1478
Lenngren, Anna Maria 681

Lennox, Charlotte 584
Letts, Winifred 1580
Leveridge, Lillian 1531
Levertov, Denise 2464
Levy, Amy 1273
Lewis, Sarah Anna 994
L'Heritier, Marie Jeanne 503
Li Qingzhao 175
Li Yeh 147
Liadan 129
Liddell, Catherine 1161
Lim, Genny 3672
Lim, Shirley Geok-Lin 3521
Lindbergh, Anne Morrow 2053
Lindsay, Sarah 4457
Llewellyn-Thomas, Beatrice 1711
Locke, Anne 332
Lorde, Audre 2901
Lorraine, Duchess of 232
Lowell, Amy 1440
Loy, Mina 1581
Ludwig, Paula 1912
Lunch, Lydia 4494
Luxborough, Henrietta Knight 547
Lyon, Mrs. 714
Macatti, Okkur 95
Macdonald, Cynthia 2636
MacLeod, Jean S. 2094–2095
MacMurray, Rose 2405
Macuilxochitl 259
Madan, Judith 665
Mahadeviyakka 211
Mahodahi 130
Mahsati Ganjavi 212
Makhfi 470
Mallicoat, Helen M. 2070
Mamonova, Tatyana Valentina 3096
Manner, Eeva-Liisa 2406
Maraini, Dacia 2991
Marguerite of Navarre 289
Markham, Lucia Clark 1380
Martin, Sarah Catherine 739
Marula 191
Mary of Scots 341
Maryam bint Abi Ya'qub al-Ansari 170
Mason, Caroline 989
Masters, Mary 610
Matraini, Chiara Cantarini 307
Mattern, Evelyn 3281
Mawiyoo, Neema "Ngwatilo" 4952
May, Julia Harris 1052
Mayer, Bernadette 3592
Maysun 125
Mbete-Kgositsile, Baleka 3915
McCormick, Virginia Taylor 1415
McFerren, Martha 3770
McGinley, Phyllis 2027
McHugh, Heather 3849
McLeod, Irene Rutherford 1729
McPherson, Sandra 3441
Mechain, Gwerfyl 267
Medici, Lucrezia de' 255
Mehri 250
Melvill, Elizabeth 390
Méndez, Nora Bermúdez 4795
Merriam, Eve 2274

Metzger, Deena 2993
Mew, Charlotte 1366
Meynell, Alice Christiana 1152
Michaelis, Aline Triplett 1635
Milbanke, Anne Isabella 834
Miles, Josephine 2162
Millay, Edna St. Vincent 1751
Miller, Alice Duer 1443
Miller, Alyce 4194
Miller, Emily 1053
Mirabai 293
Miriam 16
Mirikitani, Janice 3283
Mistral, Gabriela 1700
Mitford, Mary Russell 805
Mohammed, Binta S. 4796
Moirai, Catherine Risingflame 3993
Moïse, Penina 856
Molodowsky, Kadya 1801
Monk, Mary 577
Monroe, Harriet 1258
Montagu, Mary Wortley 533
Montgomery, Roselle Mercier 1445
Moodie, Susanna 880
Moore, Honor 3596
Moore, Julia A 1153
Moore, Marianne 1669
Moore, Martha Milcah 632
Moore, Virginia 1975
Moorhead, Sarah Parsons 633
Moraga, Cherríe 4125
Morata, Olimpia 325
Morgan, Angela 1446
Morgan, Robin 3284
Morgan, Sydney Owenson 770
Morpurgo, Rahel 820
Morra, Isabella da 317
Morrow, Elizabeth Cutler 1417
Morton, Sarah Wentworth 698
Motoni, Nomura 897
Moulton, Louise 1067
Mowatt, Anna Cora 957
Mueller, Lisel 2490
Mullen, Harryette Romell 4197
Murphy, Beatrice M. 2096
Murray, Judith Sargent 669
Murray, Pauli 2139
Murry, Ann 750
Muske-Dukes, Carol 3598
Naidu, Sarojini 1534
Nairne, Carolina 731
Nakatsukasa 164
Namjoshi, Suniti 3287
Nannakaiya, Kaccipe 103
Nasrin, Taslima 4627
Nelson, Marilyn 3680
Nesbit, Edith 1234
Ní Chonaill, Eibhlín Dhubh 645
Nijo, The Empress of 151
Norris, Kathleen 3777
Norris, Kathleen Thompson 1552
Norton, Caroline Sheridan 905
Norton, Grace Fallow 1479
Notley, Alice 3602
Nukada 123
Nye, Naomi Sihab 4130
O'Grady, Ellen 1340

O'Keeffe, Adelaide 771
Oku 124
Olds, Sharon 3364
Olesnicka, Zofia 350
Oliver, Mary 2941
O'Neill, Henrietta 692
O'Neill, Moira 1305
O'Neill, Rose 1447
Ono, Yoko 2860
Ono no Komachi 150
Opie, Amelia 744
Orred, Meta 1140
Osgood, Frances Sargent 915
Ostenso, Martha 1916
Ostriker, Alicia Suskin 3051
Owen, Anita 1714
Owens, Rochelle 2996
Owens, Vilda Sauvage 1464
Oxlie of Morpet, Mary 434
Palmer, Alice Freeman 1206
Pappenheim, Bertha 1249
Parker, Dorothy 1780
Parker, Pat 3531 Pastan, Linda 2815
Patel, Shailja 4828
Peabody, Josephine Preston 1448
Pennington, Mrs. 617
Perry, Nora 1042
Pétigny de Saint-Romain, Marie-Louise-Rose 741
Petröczi, Kata Szidónia 499
Phelps, Almira Lincoln 840
Philips, Joan 515
Philips, Katherine Fowler 459
Piercy, Marge 2997
Pilkington, Laetitia 563
Pinar, Florencia del 268
Pitter, Ruth 1855–1856
Plath, Sylvia 2817
Plato, Ann 975
Pollitt, Katha 3925
Ponsot, Marie Birmingham 2410
Porter, Anne 2164
Portillo Trambley, Estela 2609
Pratt, Minnie Bruce 3690
Praxilla 61
Prentiss, Elizabeth Payson 952
Preston, Margaret J. 976
Previn, Dory 2679
Primrose, Diana 457
Pritchard, Melissa 3857
Proctor, Adelaide 1002
Proctor, Edna Dean 1021
Pursifull, Carmen M. 2736
Pyper, Mary 849
Qernertoq 156
Quick-to-See Smith, Jaune 3224
Qurrat al-'Ayn 1195
Rabi'a al-Adawiya 136
Rabi'a bint Isma'il of Syria 139
Rabi'a of Balkh 171
Rachel (2) 1716
Radcliffe, Ann 723
Raine, Kathleen Jessie 2101
Raine, Nancy Venable 3692
Randall, Margaret 3000
Ras, Barbara 3929
Reese, Lizette 1213

Rice, Ruth Mason 1617
Rich, Adrienne 2680
Richards, Beah 2387
Riding, Laura 1938
Ridler, Anne Barbara 2188
Rittenhouse, Jessie 1367
Roberts, Elizabeth Madox 1638
Roberts, Michele 3932
Robinson, A. Mary F. 1226
Robinson, Corinne Roosevelt 1276
Robinson, Mary 693
Robinson, Therese Albertine Louise 858
Rodgers, Carolyn M. 3607
Rogers, Pattiann 3225
Rolls, Mrs. Henry 912
Rose, Wendy 3862
Rossetti, Christina 1032
Roth, Friederike 3863
Rowe, Elizabeth Singer 518
Rowson, Susanna Haswell 715
Ruarowna, Margareta 440
Rukeyser, Muriel 2210
Ryan, Kay 3609
Sachs, Nelly 1734
Sackville, Margaret 1574
Sackville-West, Vita 1752
Safiya bint Musafir 126
Salter, Mary Jo 4270
Sampter, Jessie Ethel 1600
Sanchez, Carol Lee 2911
Sanchez, Sonia 2912
Sangster, Margaret E. 1085
Sanu, Chigami 135
Sapphire 4002
Sappho 46
Sarton, May 2189
Schaeffer, Susan Fromberg 3302
Schutz, Susan Polis 3538
Scott, Mary 751
Scudéry, Madeleine de 423
Seaberg, Rönnog 2820
Sears, Vicki 3303
Seiffert, Marjorie Allen 1640
Seton-Thompson, Grace 1405
Sewall, Harriet 959
Seward, Anna 641
Sexton, Anne 2642
Shane, Elizabeth 1500
Shange, Ntozake 3865
Sharp, Joane 427
Sheepshanks, Mary 3612
Shen-ch'iung, Nieh 162
Shepard, Alice M. 2741
Sheridan, Frances 595
Sherman, Susan 3158
Sherwood, Kate Brownlee 1106
Sherwood, Margaret P. 1306
Shikibu, Murasaki 166
Shikishi Naishinno 192
Shonagon, Sei 163
Sibyl, the Jewish 68
Sidqi 555
Sigourney, Lydia Howard 827
Sila 131
Silabhlattarika 132
Silko, Leslie Marmon 3866

Simmons, Laura 1501
Simon, Maurya 4004
Simpson, Nancy 3105
Sinha, Kabita 2777
Sitwell, Edith 1673
Siunetsi, Sahakdoukht 148
Sloan-Hunter, Margaret 3796
Smart, Elizabeth 2211
Smith, "Patti" 3696
Smith, Anna Young 688
Smith, Arabella 1130
Smith, Barbara 3697
Smith, Charlotte 658
Smith, May Riley 1110
Smith, Nora Archibald 1250
Smith, Stevie 1956
Song, Cathy 4333
Southey, Caroline Anne 802
Spark, Muriel 2331
Speght, Rachel 405
Speyer, Leonora 1406
Spofford, Harriet 1068
Sproat, Nancy Dennis 732
St. Joan, Jacqueline "Jackie" 3616
Stampa, Gaspara 323
Steele, Anne 580
Stephenson, Isabella S. 1118
Stiller, Nikki 4988
Stockton, Annis 623
Stoddard, Elizabeth 990
Stopes, Marie Carmichael 1558
Storey, Violet Alleyn 1922
Storni, Alfonsina 1755
Struther, Jan 1942
Sugawara no Takasue no musume 181
Sullam, Sarah Copia 402
Sulpicia 76
Sulpicia 94
Sun, Tao-hüsan 182
Sun Yün-fêng 725
Suo 174
Sutherland, Efua Theodora 2498
Swenson, May 2212
Sylva, Carmen 1120
Symonds, Caroline 835
Szymborska, Wislawa 2472
Tadjo, Véronique 4334
Taggard, Genevieve 1805
Táhirih, Fátimih Baragháni 925
T'ang Wan 213
Tapahonso, Luci 4214
Tappan, Eva March 1203
Taylor, Ann 792
Taylor, Debbie 4335
Taylor, Jane 795 Taylor, Mrs. 526
Teasdale, Sara 1619
Telesilla 58
Teresa of Avila 308
Terracina, Laura 311
Terry, Lucy 611
Thaxter, Celia 1069
Thomas, Edith 1204
Thomas, Elizabeth 520
Thomas, Louisa 1320
Thrynne, Frances 679
Tibergeau, Marchioness de 552

Tighe, Mary 760
Tollet, Elizabeth 541
Tomioka, Taeko 2955
Tonna, Charlotte Elizabeth 821
Torelli, Barbara 279
Townsend, Eliza 813
Trefusis, Elizabeth 718
Trench, Melesina 742
Trethewey, Natasha 4737
Trinh, T. Minh-Ha 4147
Trotter, Catherine 522
Ts'ai Yen 98
Tse-t'ien Wu 121
Tsvetaeva, Marina 1757
Tunnell, Sophie 1621
Turbina, Nika 4889
Turell, Jane Colman 564
Turner, Nancy Byrd 1560
Tussman, Malka Heifetz 1788
Tuthill, Louisa Caroline 862
Tzu Yeh, Tzu 104
Ukon, Lady 154
Ulinover, Miriam 1690
Valdés, Gina 3466
Valentine, Jean 2917
Vallana 157
Van Duyn, Mona 2415
Vardill, Anna Jane 789
Venmanipputi 97
Vicioso, Sherezada 3875
Vidya 133
Villanueva, Alma Luz 3546
Viorst, Judith 2780
Voronel, Nina 2873
Wakoski, Diane 3064
Walders, Davi 3113
Waldman, Anne 3621
Walker, Alice 3547
Walker, Margaret 2259
Wallada al-Mustakfi 172
Walsh, Maria Elena 2745
Wandor, Michelene 3237
Wang Ch'ing-hui 233
Wang Wei 553
Ware, Katharine Augusta 861
Warner, Anna Bartlett 979
Warner, Sylvia Townsend 1789
Warren, Mercy Otis 603
Webb, Mary 1576
Weil, Simone 2116
Weinberg, Sheila Pelz 3707
Welby, Amelia C. 962
West, Jane 694
Wharton, Anne 462
Wheatley, Phillis 677
Wheeler, Mercy 560
Whiteman, Roberta Hill 3806–3807
Whitman, Sarah Power 884
Whitney, Adeline Dutton 996
Whitney, Isabella 340
Whitson, Beth Slater 1538
Wickham, Anna 1622
Widdemer, Margaret 1561
Wiese, Anne Pierson 4854
Wiggin, Kate Douglas 1214
Wilcox, Ella Wheeler 1209
Wilde, Jane Francesca 1010

Wiley, Doreen Gandy 2617
Wilkinson, Marguerite 1602
Willard, Emma Hart 806
Williams, Anna 561
Williams, Bertye Young 1485
Williams, Helen Maria 716
Williams, Lucinda 4218
Williams, Sarah "Sadie" 1107
Williams, Sherley Anne 3551–3552
Willis, Lydia Fish 566
Willson, Dixie 1720
Wilner, Eleanor 3066
Winslow, Anna Green 700
Winslow, Anne Goodwin 1467
Witt, Shirley Hill 2918
Wittig, Monique 2958
Wolverton, Terry 4286
Wong, Nellie 2919
Woo, Merle 3313
Woolsey, Mary 1048
Wordsworth, Elizabeth 1098
Wright, Frances 850
Wright, Judith 2260
Wright, Susanna 546
Wroth, Mary Sidney 395
Wurdeman, Audrey 2170
Wylie, Elinor 1645
Xue Tao 141
Yamada, May 2475
Yamatohime 127
Yearsley, Anne 710
Yee, Marian 4989
Yü Hsüan-chi 152
Zarin, Cynthia Rebecca 4513
Zaturenska, Marya 1961
Zeidner, Lisa 4341
Zygmuntowicz, Itka Frajman 2585

PRINTED MEDIA PUBLISHERS, PROPRIETORS, AGENTS, ET AL.

Anyanwu, Christina 4019
Benmussa, Simone 2751
Bradford, Cornelia 542
Cunard, Nancy 1822
Cunningham, Agnes "Sis" 2107
Goddard, Mary Katherine 621
Goddard, Sarah Updike 550
Graham, Katharine 2289
Gripenberg, Alexandra 1222
Hashemi Rafsanjani, Faezeh 4617
Johnson, Eleanor Murdock 1748
King, Janice 4456
Knopf, Blanche Wolf 1798
Larsen, Jensine 4897
Lawrence, Frieda 1530
Manley, Joan 2809
Marbury, Elisabeth 1211
McKenna, Elizabeth Perle 4382
Miller, Ceci 4461
Morgan, Robin 3284
Morris, Holly 4733
Ocampo, Victoria 1731
Pankhurst, Sylvia 1583
Pilkington, Laetitia 563
Rind, Clementina Bird 634
Royall, Anne Newport 745
Smith, Hazel Brannon 2228

Toklas, Alice B. 1502
Tusquets, Esther 3010
Vilar, Irene 4805
Wilson, Barbara 4015

TRANSLATORS, LINGUISTS, ETYMOLOGISTS, AND INTERPRETERS

Anderson, Edith 4515
Ascarelli, Devorah 409
Aury, Dominique 2059
Ayscough, Florence 1504
Bacon, Anne Cooke 328
Barney, Natalie Clifford 1470
Barnwell, Ysaye 3633
Barolini, Helen 2509
Behn, Aphra 472
Benet, Sula 1966
Boumi Pappa, Rita 2040
Brooke, Frances 593
Carew, Elizabeth 391
Carter, Elizabeth 578
Cassian, Nina 2479
Cedering, Siv 3131
Châtelet, Émilie du 557
Chin, Marilyn 4295
Coleridge, Sara 871
Dacier, Anne 488
Dauenhauer, Nora 2591
Davis, Lydia 3733
Deutsch, Babette 1808
Espinosa, María 3142
Falk, Marcia 3650
Ferguson, Elizabeth Graeme 624
Finch, Anne 497
Fuller, Margaret 910
Gems, Pam 2518
Gervitz, Gloria 3411
Gorbanevskaya, Natalya 2980
Graves, Clarissa 1747
Grierson, Constantia 559
Guillet, Pernette du 315
Hamilton, Edith 1336
Hejinian, Lyn 3269
Hemans, Felicia 838
Herbert, Mary Sidney 365
Hinkle, Beatrice 1436
Hirshfield, Jane 4180
Hoover, Louise "Lou" Henry 1437
Howitt, Mary 864
Huntington, Helen 1460
Inchbald, Elizabeth 676
Jellicoe, Ann 2600
Jemison, Mae 4374
Johnson, Shirley Childress 3760
Kim, Myung Mi 4418
Kirchheimer, Gloria DeVidas 3356
Klepfisz, Irena 3276
Kolmar, Gertrud 1799
Krásnohorská, Eliska 1151
Labé, Louise 316
Le Gallienne, Eva 1887
Levertov, Denise 2464
L'Heritier, Marie Jeanne 503
Locke, Anne 332
MacMurray, Rose 2405
Mamonova, Tatyana Valentina 3096

Marbury, Elisabeth 1211
Margrethe II 3208
Marie de France 193
McPhee, Jenny 4543
Meyer, Agnes 1668
Miller, Casey Geddes 2350
Naqvi, Tahira 4198
Necker de Saussure, Madame 740
Nelson, Marilyn 3680
Newman, Frances 1598
Norberg-Hodge, Helena 3682
Partridge, Frances 1918
Peterson, Virgilia 2002–2003
Philips, Katherine Fowler 459
Pix, Mary Griffith 509
Reza, Yasmina 4503
Robinson, Therese Albertine Louise 858
Roth, Friederike 3863
Rukeyser, Muriel 2210
Sachs, Nelly 1734
Savage-Rumbaugh, Susan 3937
Schwarcz, Vera 3793
Shen Rong 2948
Silvia of Sweden, Queen 3456
Slapsak, Svetlana 3867
Smith, Charlotte 658
Somerville, Mary 783
St. John, Christopher Marie 1466
Svirsky, Gila 3699
Swift, Kate 2471
Tanaka, Yukiko 3232
Tannen, Deborah F. 3618
Treichler, Paula Antonia 3463
Valian, Virginia 3383
Vassiltchikov, Marie 2304
Voronel, Nina 2873
Wertenbaker, Timberlake 4077
Wharton, Anne 462
Wilde, Jane Francesca 1010
Williams, Anna 561
Williams, Helen Maria 716
Winnemucca, Sarah 1133
Winwar, Frances 1923
Yang, Gladys 2358
Yang Jiang 2171
Zenobia of Palmyra 100

WRITERS—FICTION AND NONFICTION

Abbasi, Talat 4154
Abbot, Sidney 3015
Abbott, Berenice 1859
Abbott, Shirley 2875
Aboulela, Leila 4663
Abrams, Linsey 4018
Abramson, Jill 4222
Aburdene, Patricia 3709
Acker, Kathy 3710
Ackerman, Diane 3808
Ackerman, Jennifer 4476
Adamson, Joy 2336
Adichie, Chimamanda Ngozi 4915
Adler, Freda 2876
Adler, Margot 3238
Adler, Polly 1894
Adler, Renata 3068
Adnan, Etel 2505

Agata, Hikari 3388
Agreda, María de 415
Aguirre, Isidora 2337
Akins, Zoö 1646
Alam, Glynn Marsh 3389
Albelda, Randy 4288
Albert, Octavia V. 1196
Albery, Nobuko 3170
Alcott, Louisa May 1044
Alden, Paulette Bates 3712
Alexander 997
Alexander, Shana 2540
Alger, Abby Langdon 1170
al-Huwaider, Wajeha 4846
Ali, Monica 4743
Allen, Candace 4224
Allen, Charlotte Vale 3239
Allen, Florence Ellinwood 1603
Allen, Paula Gunn 3118
Allende, Isabel 3317
Allfrey, Phyllis Shand 2235
Alliluyeva, Svetlana 2507
Allingham, Margery 1987
Allison, Dorothy E. 3880
Allred, Gloria 3240
Aloni, Shulamit 2650
Alonso, Dora 2118
al-Samman, Ghada 3318
al-Shaykh, Hanan 3611.1
Alther, Lisa Reed 3473
Alvarez, Julia 3950
Anastasi, Anne 2076
Ancelot, Virginie 829
Anderson, Edith 4515
Anderson, Margaret 1647
Andrews, Lori B. 4156
Andrews, Mary Kay 4226
Anthony, Katharine 1487
Antin, Mary 1563
Antler, Joyce 3320
Antoine-Dariaux, Geneviève 4516
Antrim, Minna 1262
Anwar, Zainah 4157
Anzaldúa, Gloria Evangelina 3321
Apostolides, Marianne 4875
Appignanesi, Lisa 3626
Applebaum, Anne 4665
Apter, Terri 3882
Ardagh, Susan Hamilton 1200
Arensberg, Ann 3017
Armstrong, Karen 3474
Arnim, Bettina von 798
Arnim, Mary Elizabeth 1322
Arnow, Harriette 2078
Arrien, Angeles 2920
Arslan, Antonia 3069
Ascher, Barbara Lazear 3718
Ash, Mary Kay 2306
Ashenburg, Katherine 3951
Ashford, Daisy 1704
Ashmun, Margaret Eliza 1452
Ashton-Warner, Sylvia 2079
Askew, Rilla 4020
Asquith, Margot 1301
Astor, Brooke 1946
Astor, Mary 2037
Atherton, Gertrude 1216
Atkinson, Kate 4021

Atkinson, Ti-Grace 3070
Atwood, Margaret 3119
Aubin, Penelope 521
Auel, Jean M. 2960
Aury, Dominique 2059
Austen, Jane 767
Austin, Mary Hunter 1346
Austin, Sarah Taylor 836
Avery, Byllye Y. 3019
Ayllón Soria, Virginia 3952
Azadeh, Carol 4667
Azzopardi, Trezza 4563
Babbitt, Natalie 2784
Babitz, Eve 3391
Bacall, Lauren 2476
Bachmann, Ingeborg 2541
Bacon, Anne Cooke 328
Bacon, Josephine Dodge 1468
Bacon, Martha 2280
Bailey, Pearl 2307
Bailey, Urania Locke 964
Bainbridge, Beryl Margaret 2831
Baker, Dorothy 2060
Bakke, Kit 3628
Baldwin, Christina 3629
Baldwin, Faith 1761
Baldwin, Monica 1762
Bambara, Toni Cade 3121
Bandler, Faith 2361
Bank, Melissa 4518
Bannerman, Helen 1282
Banning, Margaret Culkin 1721
Barbauld, Anna Letitia 642
Barber, Janette 4158
Barber, Margaret Fairless 1355
Bardwick, Judith M. 2832
Barfoot, Joan 3631
Barker, Elsa 1356
Barker, Jane 523
Barker, Patricia 3392
Barlow, Maude 3719
Barnes, Djuna 1739
Barnes, Margaret Ayer 1648
Barney, Natalie Clifford 1470
Barolini, Helen 2509
Barr, Amelia 1033
Barr, Nevada 4084
Barreno, Maria Isabel 3122
Barrett, Andrea 4692
Barrett, Michèle 3885
Barry, Kathleen 3123
Barry, Lynda 4346
Barry, Rebecca 4764
Barton, Clara 980
Barton, Emily 4780
Basinger, Jeanine 2962
Bassoff, Evelyn S. 3477
Bateson, Mary Catherine 3124
Baum, Vicki 1674
Bawden, Nina 2510
Bazan, Emilia Pardo 1189
Beard, Miriam 1926
Beatrijs of Nazareth 204
Beauvoir, Simone de 2080
Beck, Evelyn Torton 2833
Bedford, Sybille von Schoenbeck 2152
Beecher, Catharine Esther 865

Beeton, Isabella Mayson 1074
Behn, Aphra 472
Belenky, Mary Field 2834
Bell, Christine 4024
Bell, Florence 1182
Bell, Gertrude 1347
Bell, Helen Olcott 1023
Bender, Sheila 3810
Benét, Laura 1605
Bengis, Ingrid 3478
Benítez, Sandra Ables 3242
Benjamin, Medea 4087
Bennett, Georgette 3634
Bennis, Phyllis 4025
Benson, Stella 1740
Berberova, Nina 1927
Berenson, Mary 1302
Berg, Elizabeth 3811
Bergen, Candice 3635
Bernard, Jessie Shirley 1967
Berne, Suzanne 4565
Bernhardt, Sarah 1122
Berriault, Gina 2542
Bertana, Lucia dall'Orno 318
Bertell, Rosalie 2651
Beruriah 216
Bethune, Mary McLeod 1453
Bialosky, Jill 4603
Bianchi, Martha Dickinson 1323
Bianco, Margery Williams
Bibesco, Elizabeth Asquith 1842
Billings, Victoria 3558
Billington-Greig, Teresa 1488
Billson, Christine 4520
Bingham, Charlotte 3325
Bingham, Madeline 2172
Bingham, Sallie 3021
Birch, Alison Wyrley 2419
Bird, Carmel 3175
Bird, Caroline 2237
Bishop, Elizabeth 2153
Bishop, Wendy Sue 4161
Black, Sophie Cabot 4440
Blackmore, Susan Jane 4028
Blackwell, Antoinette Brown 998
Blackwell, Elizabeth 981
Blackwell, Emily 1005
Blake, Lillie Devereux 1049
Blakely, Nora Brooks 4029
Blavatsky, Elena Petrovna 1034
Bleecker, Ann Eliza 670
Blessington, Marguerite 808
Bloom, Amy 4163
Bloomer, Amelia Jenks 944
Blume, Judy 3074
Bogan, Louise 1843
Bok, Sissela Ann 2881
Bolen, Jean Shinoda 2965
Bombeck, Erma 2586
Bonaparte, Marie L. 1564
Bond, Cynthia 4400
Botta, Anne 926
Bottome, Phyllis 1606
Botume, Elizabeth 1371
Boucher, Sandy 2966
Boulbie, Judith 556
Boulding, Elise M. 2362
Bourke-White, Margaret 2041

Bovey, Shelley 3724–3725
Bowen, 'Asta 4290
Bowen, Catherine Drinker 1844
Bowen, Elizabeth 1883
Bowen, Marjorie 1675–1676
Bower, B. M. 1385
Bowles, Gloria 4350
Bowman, Meg 2653
Boxer, Sarah 4781
Boyle, Kay 1947
Bracken, Peg 2309
Brackett, Anna C. 1070
Braddon, Mary Elizabeth 1076
Bradley, Marion Zimmer 2694
Bradstreet, Anne 430
Branch, Mary 1091
Brand, Dionne 4164
Brant, Beth 3246
Braude, Ann Deborah 4291
Braverman, Kate 3954
Bray, Ann Eliza 815
Breillat, Catherine 3814
Bremer, Frederika 868
Brennan, Maeve 2263
Brett, Dorothy 1591
Breuer, Bessie 1763
Bricker-Jenkins, Mary 3326
Bridget of Sweden 234
Bridgford, Kim Suzanne 4477
Brightman, Carol 3126
Brill, Alida 3888.1
Brine, Mary Dow 933
Brittain, Vera 1764–1765
Broner, E. M. 2695
Brontë, Anne 965
Brontë, Charlotte 934
Brontë, Emily 945
Brooke, Frances 593
Brookner, Anita 2620
Brooks, Geraldine 4292
Brooks, Gwendolyn 2281
Brotherton, Alice Williams 1159
Brown, Abbie Farwell 1455
Brown, Alice 1218
Brown, Barbara B. 2621
Brown, Helen Gurley 2421
Brown, Ophelia Guyon 1541
Brown, Rita Mae 3481
Brown, Rosellen 3128
Brownmiller, Susan 2922
Brubaker, Pamela K. 3640
Bruce, Mary Grant 1506
Brumberg, Joan Jacobs 3482
Brunton, Mary 775
Bryan, Mary E. 1081
Buck, Pearl S. 1741
Bunch, Charlotte 3483
Burchill, Julie 4524
Burke, Phyllis 4030
Burkett, Elinor 3394
Burnett, Frances 1164
Burney, Fanny 671
Burr, Amelia 1507
Burton, Isabel 1036
Burton, Elaine Frances 1988
Bush, Barbara 2514
Butler, Octavia 3727
Buxton, Bertha 1124

Byatt, A. S. 2968
Cadden, Vivian 2264
Caine, Lynn 2588
Caldicott, Helen 3075
Caldwell, Taylor 1896
Calisher, Hortense 2154
Campan, Jeanne Louise 672
Campbell, Anne 4031
Campbell, Beatrix 3728
Campbell, Dorothea Primrose 831
Campbell, Maria 3179
Canaan, Andrea R. 3729
Cannon, Katie Geneva 3956
Cantwell, Mary 2698
Capek, Mary Ellen S. 4032
Carabillo, Toni 2544
Cardin, Nina Beth 4166
Carew, Elizabeth 391
Carleton, Emma 1172
Carlisle, Andrea 3484
Carnahan, Jean 2839
Carpenter, Liz 2363
Carr, Emily 1387
Carrigan, Ana 3485
Carrington, Leonora 2282
Carson, Anne Regina 3957
Carson, Rachel 2061
Carswell, Catherine 1522
Carter, Lillian 1862
Carter, Angela 3182
Carter, Rosalyn Smith 2589
Carter, Sandy 4637
Cartland, Barbara 1928
Caschetta, Mary Beth 4718
Case, Elizabeth York 1092
Case, Sue-Ellen 3328
Castedo-Ellerman, Elena 3022
Castellani, Maria 2699
Castellanos, Rosario 2515
Castillo, Ana 4354
Castillo y Guevara, Francisca Josefa del 537
Castle, Victoria 3889
Cather, Katherine Dunlap 1489
Cather, Willa 1408
Catherine of Bologna 253
Catherwood, Mary 1149
Caulkins, Frances Manwaring 846
Cavendish, Margaret 446
Cedering, Siv 3131
Cervantes, Lorna Dee 4234
Cha, Theresa Hak Kyung 4033
Chamberlin, Judi 3486
Chambers, Jessie 1661
Chandab, Taghred 4916
Chandler, Loma 2010
Chang, Diana 2882
Chang, Jung 4092
Chang, Leslie T. 4782
Chapone, Hester 598
Chard, Sylvia C. 3077
Charles, Elizabeth 1017
Charrière, Madame de 630
Chase, Ilka 2011
Chase-Riboud, Barbara 3132
Chávez, Denise Elia 3816
Cheever, Susan 3396
Chehak, Susan Taylor 4034

Chen, Pauline W. 4356
Cheney, Lynne Ann 3248
Cheng, Nien 2239
Chernin, Kim 3183
Chesler, Phyllis 3184
Chicago, Judy 3133
Child, Julia 2174
Child, Lydia Maria 870
Childress, Alice 2364
Chin, Ann-ping 3817
Chisholm, Shirley 2480
Chittister, OSB, Joan 2969
Chona, Marie 1134
Chopin, Kate 1184
Christian, Barbara T. 3397
Christie, Agatha 1724
Christina of Sweden 450
Christine de Pisan 244
Chua, Amy 4605
Chute, Carolyn 3730
Ciment, Jill 4168
Cisneros, Sandra 4237
Claflin, Tennessee 1135
Clark, C. Hope 4357
Clark, Eleanor 2195
Clark, Eugenie 2423
Clark, Margaret D. 3399
Clausen, Jan 3959–3960
Cleage, Pearl 3818
Clements, Marcelle 3819
Clendinnen, Inga 2884
Cleyre, Voltairine de 1325
Cliff, Michelle 3645
Clifton, Lucille 2970
Clinchy, Blythe M. 2700
Clingerman, Mildred McElroy 2311
Clinton, Elizabeth 379
Clyde, Mary 4962
Coates, Grace Stone 1566
Coatsworth, Elizabeth 1766
Cobbe, Frances P. 983
Coblentz, Catherine Cate 1845
Coffee, Lenore J. 1820
Cohen, Deborah S. 3820
Cohen, Leah Hager 4744
Cohen, Mary M. 1202
Cohen, Sherry Suib 2885
Cole, Mary 816
Coleridge, Mary 1264
Coleridge, Sara 871
Colette 1409
Cole-Whittaker, Terry 3134
Collen, Lindsey 4036
Collier, Mary 532
Collins, Joan 2840
Collins, Patricia Hill 3821
Colquhoun, Janet 786
Colwin, Laurie 3488
Comini, Alessandra 3079
Compton-Burnett, Ivy 1743
Condé, Maryse 3026
Conkling, Grace H. 1509
Conrad, Beatrice 2590
Cook, Blanche Weisen 3249
Cookson, Catherine 2044
Cool, Lisa Collier 4096
Coolbrith, Ina 1102

Coolidge, Susan 1136
Coontz, Stephanie 3490
Cooper, Anna Julia 1231
Cooper, Diana 1744
Cooper, Edith 1285
Cooper, Helene 4719
Corpi, Lucha 3561
Costa, Maria Fatima Velho da 3080
Cota-Cárdenas, Margarita 3250
Cottin, Sophie 762
Cotton, Nancy 3492
Coulter, Ann 4567
Covington, Vicki 4097
Coward, Rosalind 4171
Cox, Ana Marie 4856
Craigie, Pearl 1334
Craigin, Elisabeth 2701
Craik, Dinah Mulock 1006
Cram, Mildred 1695
Crane, Nathalia 2196
Craven, Margaret 1929
Creech, Sharon 3562
Crespi, Camilla T. 3330
Crittenden, Ann 3027
Croce, Arlene 2887
Crocker, Hannah Mather 673
Crouse, Mary Elizabeth 1410
Crowe, Catharine 818
Crowell, Grace Noll 1490
Cumming, Anne 2284
Cuomo, Chris J. 4674
Curie, Ève 1990
Curtis, Rebecca 4883
Curtiss, Ursula Reilly 2448
Daché, Lilly 1991
Dacier, Anne 488
d'Adesky, Anne-Christine 4479
Daisy, Princess of Pless 1411
Dall, Caroline 984
Daly, Mary 2623
Dane, Clemence 1677
Dangarembga, Tsitsi 4480
Danielsson, Marie-Thérèse 2449
Danticat, Edwidge 4784
d'Aragona, Tullia 301
Dargan, Olive 1358
Dashkova, Ekaterina Vorontsova 644
Dasi, Binodini 1294
Daum, Meghan 4814
Davenport, Doris 3891
Davey, Janet 4172
David-Néel, Alexandra 1348
Davidson, Laura Lee 1372
Davidson, Sara 3732
Daviot, Gordon 1823
Davis, Adelle 1992
Davis, Angela 3493
Davis, Dorothy Salisbury 2265
Davis, Elizabeth Gould 2124
Davis, Lydia 3733
Davis, Rebecca Harding 1037
Davys, Mary 517
Day, Dorothy 1846
Day, Lillian 1768
Dayan, Yaël 3136
de Baca, Fabiola Cabeza 1806–1807

de Kretser, Michelle 4444
de Mille, Agnes 2012
de Moor, Margriet 3253
De Wolfe, Elsie 1311
Dean, Louise 4815
Decter, Midge 2592
Delmar, Viña 2013
Deming, Alison Hawthorne 3647
Deming, Barbara 2285
Denham, Alice 2841
Dery, Dominika 4890–4891
des Rieux, Virginie 410
Desai, Kiran 4843
Deshoulières, Antoinette 469
Detourbey, Jean 1078
Deutsch, Babette 1808
Deutsch, Helene 1608
Devi, Indra 1884
Di Prima, Diane 2890
Diamant, Anita 4038
Didion, Joan 2925
Dillard, Annie 3563
Diller, Phyllis 2286
Dinesen, Isak 1627
Dinnerstein, Dorothy 2452
DiPerna, Diane 4963
DiPerna, Paula 3892
Dodge, Mabel 1524
Dodge, Mary Mapes 1039
Dolliver, Clara G. 1429
Dolson, Hildegarde 2083
Donoghue, Emma 4785
Doolittle, Hilda 1650
Doress-Worters, Paula B. 3082
Dorr, Julia 999
Doubiago, Sharon 3648
Doudney, Sarah 1113
Douglas, Helen Gahagan 1897
Dove, Rita Frances 4101
Dowling, Colette 3083
Drabble, Margaret 3139
Drakulíc, Slavenka 3894
Dreifus, Claudia 3495
Drew, Elizabeth 1662
Drexler, Rosalyn 2546
Drinker, Sophie Hutchinson 1678
Driscoll, Louise 1456
Droste-Hülshoff, Anette Elizabeth
    von 852
du Maurier, Daphne 2063
DuBois, Ellen Carol 3737
Dudar, Helen 2084
Duffy, Carol Ann 4298
Duffy, Maureen 2842
Dugaw, Dianne 3823
Dunant, Sarah 3961
Dunayevskaya, Raya 2126
Dunbar, Roxanne 3140
Dunbar-Nelson, Alice 1457
Dunbar-Ortiz, Roxanne 3084
Duncan, Isadora 1512
Dunlop, Becky Norton 4039
Dunn, Irina 3962
Dunn, Katherine "Karen" 3565
Durant, Ariel 1864–1865
Duras, Marguerite 2219
Dwight, Mary Ann 895
Dworkin, Andrea 3738

Dworkin, Susan 4817
Earhart, Amelia 1847
Earle, Sylvia A. 2926
Eastwood, Alice 1247
Eckenstein, Lina 1220
Eddy, Mary Baker 982
Eden, Emily 853
Edgeworth, Maria 734
Edwards, Amelia 1040
Edwards, Anne 2594
Edwards, Betty 2547
Egan, Jennifer 4609
Egeria 108
Ehrenreich, Barbara 3257
Eisler, Riane 2756
Eliot, George 955
Elkins, Caroline 4786
Ellis, Alice Thomas 2793
Ellis, Sarah 918
Ellison, Katherine 4405
Ellman, Lucy 4362
Emecheta, Buchi 3497
Emshwiller, Carol 2397
English, Deirdre 3825
Enright, Anne 4611
Ephron, Delia 3498
Ephron, Nora 3258
Epstein, Helen 3740
Erdrich, Louise 4242
Eschenbach, Maria von Ebner 1025
Espinosa, María 3142
Esquivel, Laura 3964
Estés, Clarissa Pinkola 3567
Etcoff, Nancy L. 4299
Evans, Augusta 1063
Evans, Mari 2453
Evelyn, Mary 464
Evers-Williams, Myrlie 2847
Fadiman, Anne 4175
Fairstein, Linda A. 3741
Fallaci, Oriana 2656
Faludi, Susan 4481
Fanshawe, Ann 449
Farmer, Fannie 1221
Farnham, Eliza 928
Farrar, Eliza Ware 822
Faschinger, Lilian 3965
Faugéres, Margaretta Van Wyck
    755
Fausto-Sterling, Anne 3499
Feinberg, Leslie 3896
Felton, Rebecca Latimer 1064
Ferber, Edna 1663
Ferguson, Marilyn 3085
Ferguson, Patricia 4176
Fermi, Laura Capon 2065
Fern, Fanny 914
Fernea, Elizabeth Warnock 2595
Ferrante, Elena 4975
Ferrell, Carolyn 4613
Ferrier, Susan Edmonstone 790
Field, Joanna 1899
Field, Kate 1082
Field, Rachel Lyman 1793
Fielding, Sarah 568
Figes, Eva 2794
Fiorenza, Elisabeth Schüssler 3086
Firestone, Shulamith 3570

Fishback, Margaret 1900
Fishel, Elizabeth 3967
Fisher, Carrie 4364
Fisher, Dorothy Canfield 1525
Fisher, M. F. K. 2085
Fisher, Renee 3743
Fitzgerald, Frances 3189
Fitzgerald, Penelope 2266
Fitzgerald, Zelda 1901
Flagg, Fannie 3260
Flanagan, Mary 3405
Flanders, Laura 4575
Flanner, Hildegarde 1885
Fleisser, Marie-Luise 1932
Fleming, Joan 2086
Fletcher, Lucille 2176
Fleury, Maria de 787
Flinders, Carol Lee 3406
Flynn, Elizabeth Gurley 1706
Follen, Eliza Lee 803
Follett, Mary Parker 1350
Fonseca, Isabel 4614
Fonte, Moderata 357
Forbes, Esther 1794
Forbes, Leslie 4484
Foster, Hannah Webster 697
Fowler, Connie May 4639
Fowler, Ellen Thorneycroft 1253
Fowler, Karen Joy 3968
Fox, Margaret Askew Fell 432–433
Fox, Paula 2454
Fraiberg, Selma 2314
Frame, Janet 2483
Franken, Rose 1809
Franklin, Miles 1544
Franz, Marie-Louise von 2240
Fraser, Antonia 2796
Fraser, Arvonne 2517
Fredriksson, Marianne 2595.1
Freed, Lynn 4104
Freeman, Jo 3572
Freeman, Judith 3656
Freeman, Mary Wilkins 1192
Fremantle, Anne 2108
Fremont, Helen 3573
French, Marilyn 2658
Freston, Kathy 4676
Freud, Anna 1810
Freudenberger, Nell 4892
Friday, Nancy 3031
Friedan, Betty 2398
Friedman, Bonnie 4448
Friedman, Lenore 4933
Frings, Ketti 2241
Frucht, Abby 4408
Frye, Marilyn 3262
Fuentes, Sonia Pressman 2627
Fugard, Lisa 4485
Fugard, Sheila 2797
Fuller, Margaret Witter 1389
Fulton, Alice 4105
Fumiko, Hayashi 1993
Furman, Laura 3574
Fussell, Betty Harper 2596
Gage, Mathilda J. 1007
Gaitskill, Mary 4246
Galchen, Rivka 4907
Gale, Zona 1431

Galinsky, Ellen 3408
Gallagher, Mary 3744
Gallagher, Tess 3409
Gallaire-Bourega, Fatima 3500
Galland, China 3410
Gallant, Mavis 2426
Galloway, Priscilla 2705
Gambaro, Griselda 2628
Gamble, Eliza Burt 1103
Garber, Marjorie B. 3501
García, Cristina 4449
Gardam, Jane 2629
Gardinier, Suzanne 4577
Garrison, Theodosia 1433
Gaskell, Elizabeth 911
Gates, Ellen 1065
Gauhari, Farooka 3745
Gawain, Shakti 3827
Gaylor, Annie Laurie 4300
Gearhart, Sally Miller 2758
Gellhorn, Martha 2087
Gelpi, Barbara C. 2849
Geniesse, Jane Fletcher 2977
Genlis, Stephanie Félicité 650
George, Elizabeth 3897
Gerber, Merrill Joan 3087
Germain, Sylvie 4249
Gerould, Katherine 1526
Gerson, Kathleen 3746
Gertrude the Great 221
Gessen, Masha 4748
Geyer, Georgie Anne 2930
Gibbons, Kaye 4530
Gibbons, Stella 1948
Gibbs, Lois Marie 4106
Gilbert, Elizabeth 4788
Gilbert, Sandra 2978
Gilbreth, Lillian Moller 1513
Gilchrist, Ellen 2931
Gilchrist, Marie 1770
Gildersleeve, Virginia 1493
Gilliatt, Penelope 2799
Gilligan, Carol 2979
Gilman, Caroline 843
Gilman, Charlotte Perkins 1254
Gilmore, Glenda Elizabeth 4640
Gilmore, Jennifer 4818
Ginzburg, Eugenia 1994
Ginzburg, Natalia 2267
Girardin, Delphine de 885
Giroud, Françoise 2268
Glancy, Diane 3263
Glasgow, Ellen 1435
Glasgow, Maude 1351
Glaspell, Susan 1474
Glenconnor, Pamela 1390
Glendon, Mary Ann 3088
Glyn, Elinor 1303
Godwin, Gail 3032
Goldberg, Natalie 3828
Goldberger, Nancy Rule 2891
Golden, Marita 3970
Goodall, Jane 2892
Goodman, Allegra 4749
Goodman, Linda 2519
Goodwin, Doris Kearns 3415
Gordimer, Nadine 2456
Gordon, Mary Catherine 3898

Gore, Catherine 863
Gornick, Vivian 2932
Gottlieb, Linda 3265
Goudge, Elizabeth 1903
Gould, Lois 3033
Goulianos, Joan 3144
Gournay, Marie le Jars de 369
Grafton, Sue 3191
Graham, Margaret Collier 1174
Graham, Sheilah 1995
Graham, Virginia 2177
Grandin, Temple 3748
Grant, Anne 680
Grau, Shirley Ann 2659
Gray, Elizabeth Dodson 2660
Gray, Francine Du Plessix 2709
Gray, Madeline 1949
Green, Anna 1143
Green, Mary A. E. 948
Green, Melissa 4533
Green, Rayna 3338
Greenberg, Blu 2981
Greenberg, Joanne 2801
Greene, Jennifer 3575
Greer, Germaine 3145
Gregory, Augusta 1193
Grenfell, Joyce Phipps 2129
Greville, Frances 1267
Griffin, Adele 4819
Griffin, Susan 3417
Griffith, Nicola 4534
Griffitts, Hannah 600
Grimes, Martha 2761
Grimké, Angelina 890
Grimké, Sarah Moore 832
Gripenberg, Alexandra 1222
Gross, Rita M 3506
Gross, Terry 4043
Grossman, Chaika 2344
Grossman, Susan C. 4302
Gruber, Ruth 2157
Gruen, Sara 4909
Grumbach, Doris Isaac 2317
Grushin, Olga 4845–4846
Grymeston, Elizabeth 367
Gubar, Susan 3507
Guest, Barbara 2371
Guest, Judith 2982
Guffy, Ossie 2762
Guiney, Louise Imogen 1268
Guitar, Mary Anne 2372
Guppy, Shusha 2933
Gur, Batya 3749
Guyon, Jeanne-Marie de la Motte 482
Hadley, Tessa 4410
Hagedorn, Jessica Tarahata 3901
Haggerty, Joan 3194
Hahn, Emily "Mickey" 2019
Haiken, Elizabeth 4964
Hainstock, Elizabeth G. 2630
Hale, Lucretia Peabody 967
Hale, Nancy 2089
Hale, Sarah Josepha 807
Haley, Gail E. 3146
Hall, Radclyffe 1545
Hall, Sharlot Mabridth 1374
Hallack, Cecily R. 1866.1

Halprin, Anna 2373
Halsey, Margaret 2130
Hamill, Janet 3576
Hamilton, Edith 1336
Hamilton, Eleanor 2109
Hamilton, Elizabeth 691
Hamilton, Gail 1051
Hamilton, Jane 4411
Hammond, Eleanor Prescott 1328
Hampl, Patricia 3661
Han Suyin 2291
Harding, M. Esther 1680
Hardwick, Elizabeth 2270
Harper, Frances Ellen Watkins 1000
Harris, Corra May 1362
Harris, Janet 2243
Harris, Jean 2458
Harris, Joanne 4677
Harrison, Barbara Grizzuti 2893
Harrison, Jane 1176
Harrison, Kathryn 4579
Hart, Frances Noyes 1707
Hart, Josephine 4367
Hart, Louise 3034
Hartman, Saidiya 3974
Haskell, Molly 3147
Haskins, Minnie 1459
Hathaway, Helen 1772
Hauser, Ewa 3662
Hausman, Bernice L. 4618
Hawes, Elizabeth "Babe" 1969
Hawkes, Jessie 2131
Hayes, Elinor Rice 1933
Hayes, Helen 1904
Haywood, Eliza 539
Hazan, Marcella 2486
Hazleton, Lesley 3578
Hazzard, Shirley 2763
Head, Bessie 3035
Head, Edith 1850
Hearne, Mary 569
Heathorn, Henrietta 1001
Heaton, Rose Henniker 1612
Hebblethwaite, Margaret 4250.1
Hegi, Ursula 3663
Heilbrun, Carolyn G. 2552
Heimel, Cynthia 3750
Hejinian, Lyn 3269
Heldman, Gladys Medalie 2431
Heller, Karen 4412
Hellman, Lillian 2021
Hempel, Amy 4046
Henderson, Hazel 2853
Henley, Nancy M. 2894
Henrey, Robert 2047
Herbert, Marie 3270
Herman, Judith Lewis 3342
Herndon, Rosanna Taylor 2713
Herron, Carolivia 3751
Heschel, Susannah 4368
Hewett, Dorothy Coade 2459
Hewlett, Sylvia Ann 3664
Heyward, Carter 3579
Hibbard, Grace 1376
Higginson, Ella 1287
Highbridge, Dianne 3580
Hill, Ruth Beebe 2199
Hillesum, Etty 2220

Himmelfarb, Gertrude 2432
Hinkle, Beatrice 1436
Hinkson, Katharine Tynan 1270
Hinton, S. E. 3831
Hit-him-home, Joane 475
Hobson, Laura Z. 1905
Hochschild, Arlie Russell 3196
Hocking, Anne 1708
Hoffman, Eva 3581
Holbrook, Ann 781
Holford, Margaret 776
Holford, Margaret Wrench 711
Holland, Barbara 4048
Holley, Marietta 1073
Holley, Mary Austin 796
Hollman, Peggy 4304
Holman, Sheri 4722
Holmes, Marjorie 2133
Holmes, Mary Jane 1018
Holt, Anne Haw 2895
Holt, Kimberly Willis 4535
Holtby, Winifred 1867
Home, Grisell 505
hooks, bell 4305
Hoover, Eleanor 2521
Hopkins, Jane Ellice 1079
Hopper, Hedda 1709
Horan, Nancy 3832
Horner, Matina S. 3148–3149
Horney, Karen 1631
Horta, Maria Teresa 3036
Hosain, Attia 2200
Hospital, Janette Turner 3345
Houston, Jean 3037
Houston, Jeanne Wakatsuki 2897
Houston, Velina Hasu 4413
Howar, Barbara 2898
Howard, Jane 2936
Howard, Maureen 2715
Howe, Fanny 3197
Howe, Florence 2663
Howe, Julia Ward 956
Howe, Louise Kapp 2899
Howell, Carol K. 4251
Howitt, Mary 864
Howland, Bette 3039
Hsiao Hung 2158
Hsieh Ping-ying 2049–2050
Huang Zongying 2522
Hubbard, Alice 1271
Hubbard, Barbara Marx 2664
Hudson, Helen 2376
Huffington, Arianna 3976
Hulme, Kathryn 1906
Hulme, Keri 3755
Huneberc of Heidenheim 142
Hungerford, Margaret Wolfe 1205
Hungry Wolf, Beverly 3977
Hunter, Kristin 2765
Huntington, Helen 1460
Hurnscot, Loran 1907
Hurst, Fannie 1697
Hurston, Zora Neale 1727
Huston, Nancy 4181
Hustvedt, Siri 4307
Hutchinson, Ellen M. 1546
Hutten, Bettina von 1438
Huxtable, Ada Louise 2402

Hyatt, Lesley A. 4700.1
Hyde, Mary 3198
Ian, Janis 4050
Ifill, Gwen 4308
Inchbald, Elizabeth 676
Ingelow, Jean 968
Irigaray, Luce 2717
Isaacs, Susan 3423
Itani, Frances 3348
Ivins, Molly 3512
Jabs, Carolyn R. 3979
Jacker, Corinne 2855
Jackson, Helen Fiske Hunt 1027
Jackson, Jacquelyne J. 2802
Jackson, Maggie 4679
Jackson, Shirley 2346
Jacobs, Harriet 949
Jacobs, Jane 2271
Jacobs, Rayda 3757
Jacobsen, Josephine 2090
Jacobson, Ethel 2022
Jacoby, Susan 3584
Jaffe, Rona 2766
James, Bessie Rowland 1814
James, P. D. 2379
James, Selma 2719
James, Sibyl 3666
Jameson, Anna Brownwell 844
Jance, J. A. 3514
Janeway, Elizabeth 2201
Janis, Elsie 1698
Janowitz, Tama 4415
Jayapal, Pramila 4702
Jeffreys, Sheila 3834
Jeger, Lena May 2245
Jekyll, Gertrude 1116
Jentz, Terri 4416
Jewett, Sarah Orne 1166
Jewsbury, Geraldine 919
Jhabvala, Ruth Prawer 2601
Jiles, Paulette 3427
Joceline, Elizabeth 371
Johnson, Diane 2900
Johnson, Eleanor Murdock 1748
Johnson, Guion Griffis 1908
Johnson, Josephine Winslow 2135
Johnson, Osa 1797
Johnson, Pamela Hansford 2181–2182
Johnson, Sonia 2985
Johnston, Annie Fellows 1296
Johnston, Jill 2665
Johnston, Mary 1377
Johnstone, Wilhelmina 1909
Jones, Amanda Theodosia 1066
Jones, Ann 3040
Jones, Beverly 2602
Jones, Emily Beatrix 1775
Jones, Gayl 3902
Jong, Erica 3349
Jong-Fast, Molly 4934
Jordan, June 2987
Josefowitz, Natasha 2555
Joseph, Jenny 2803
Jotuni, Maria 1547
Judith, Anodea 4113
Julavits, Heidi 4767
Juliana of Norwich 236

Jung, Emma 1578
Justin, Dena 2183
Kael, Pauline 2347
Kahn, Kathy 3585
Kalish, Mildred Armstrong 2460
Kallen, Lucille Chernos 2433
Kamani, Ginu 4622
Kamensky, Jane 4641
Kanter, Rosabeth Moss 3429
Kaplan, Louise J. 2666
Kaplan, Temma E. 3350–3351
Karmel, Marjorie 2857
Karon, Jan 3041
Karr, Mary 4310
Kasdorf, Julia Spicher 4623
Katie, Byron 3352
Katz, Lilian G. 2805
Kauffman, Linda S. 3903
Kaufman, Bel 2160
Kaufman, Paola 4792
Kaufman, Sue 2556
Kavanagh, Julia 993
Kay, Jackie 4583
Kearney, Belle 1297
Keller, Evelyn Fox 2988
Keller, Helen 1548
Kellerman, Faye 4115
Kelley, Edith Summers 1614
Kelley, Florence 1248
Kemble, Fanny 908
Kemnitz, Mathilda von 1495
Kempe, Margery 245
Kempton, Sally 3430
Kennedy, A. L. 4703
Kennedy, Caroline 4417
Kennedy, Marilyn Moats 3431
Kephart, Beth 4538
Kerber, Linda Kaufman 3201
Kerr, Jean 2463
Kerr, Sophie 1550
Kesselman, Wendy 3202
Ketcham, Katherine 3904
Key, Ellen 1167
Keyes, Frances Parkinson 1632
Keyes, Marian 4643
Khakpour, Porochista 4924
Kijewski, Karen 3432
Kilmer, Aline Murray 1682
Kim, Elaine Haikyung 3354
Kincaid, Jamaica 3906
King, Coretta Scott 2603
King, Florence 2990
King, Georgiana Goddard 1391
King, Laurie R. 4116
Kingsolver, Barbara 4312
Kingston, Maxine Hong 3203
Kirchheimer, Gloria DeVidas 3356
Kirino, Natsuo 4053
Kirkland, Winifred 1401
Kitzinger, Celia 4539
Kitzinger, Sheila 2667
Klagsbrun, Francine 2768
Klein, Melanie 1579
Klein, Naomi 4823
Klepfisz, Irena 3276
Kline, Christina Baker 4680
Klopstock, Margaret 602
Knopf, Olga 1683

Kogawa, Joy 2938
Kohut, Rebekah Bettelheim 1304
Kolbert, Elizabeth 4584
Kollontai, Aleksandra 1402
Kometani, Foumiko 2720–2721
Kort, Michele 3982
Kraemer, Ross Shepard 3842
Kramer, Jane 3092
Kramer, Joyce 3357
Krantz, Judith 2634
Krásnohorská, Eliska 1151
Krauss, Nicole 4884
Kristeva, Julia 3277
Krudener, Juliana 721
Kübler-Ross, Elisabeth 2560
Kuhn, Maggie 2025
Kumin, Maxine 2529
Kushner, Rachel 4769
La Coste, Marie de 1139
La Fayette, Marie Madeleine de 465
LaFollette, Suzanne 1776
Laforet, Carmen 2404
Lagarde, Marcela 3983
Lagerlvf, Selma 1233
Lahiri, Jhumpa 4752
Lamb, Caroline 799
Lamb, Mary Ann 722
Lambert, Angela 3204
Lamott, Anne 4255
Landon, Letitia 873
Landsman, Anne 4491
Lane, Rose Wilder 1654
Langer, Susanne K. 1817
Langley, Eve 2092
Lape, Esther 1569
Lappé, Frances Moore 3518
Lathbury, Eva 1910
Laurel, Alicia Bay 3908–3909
Laurence, Margaret 2561
Laut, Agnes C. 1392
Lavin, Mary 2184
Lawrence, Frieda 1530
Lawrenson, Helen 1996
Lazarre, Jane D. 3436
Lazarus, Emma 1168
Lazarus, Josephine 1145
Le Gallienne, Eva 1887
Le Gallienne, Hesper 1777
Le Guin, Ursula K. 2668
Le Shan, Eda J. 2434
Le Sueur, Meridel 1911
Lea, Fanny Heaslip 1615
Leach, Penelope 3042
Leddy, Mary Jo 3669
Leduc, Violette 2068
Lee, Harper 2563
Lee, Andrea 4188
Lee, Gypsy Rose 2222
Lee, Hannah Farnham 782
Lee, Jennifer 8. 4911
Lee, Mary Chudleigh 492
Lee, Min Jin 4794
Lee, Sophia 664
Leech, Margaret 1778
Leek, Sybil 2296
Leffland, Ella 2769
Lehman, Lotte 1685
Leith, Prue 3205

Lenéru, Marie 1461
L'Engle, Madeleine 2320
Lennox, Charlotte 584
Lepore, Jill 4725
Lerner, Gerda 2380
Leslie, Eliza 804
Lespinasse, Julie-Jeanne-Eléonore
de 614
Lesser, Elizabeth 4117
Lessing, Doris 2349
Letts, Winifred 1580
Leverson, Ada 1288
Levin, Diane E. 3764
Levine, Judith 4118
Levinson, Nan 3911
Levy, Andrea 4257
Levy, Naomi 4646
L'Heritier, Marie Jeanne 503
Liddell, Catherine 1161
Lightfoot, Sara Lawrence 3520
Liking, Werewere 3986
Liljeström, Rita 2635
Lincoln, Victoria 1997
Lindbergh, Anne Morrow 2053
Lindgren, Astrid 2069
Lippman, Laura 4493
Lispector, Clarice 2381
Litman, Ellen 4878
Lively, Penelope 2858
Livermore, Mary 971
Llewellyn-Thomas, Beatrice 1711
Loos, Anita 1686
Lord, Betty Bao 3094
Lord, Nancy 4119
Lorde, Audre 2901
Loud, Pat 2565
Louis, Minnie D. 1105
Love, Barbara J. 3043
Lowry, Beverly 3095
Lowry, Lois 3044
Loy, Mina 1581
Luce, Clare Boothe 1973
Luce, Gay Gaer 2724
Luker, Kristin Carol 3673
Lunch, Lydia 4494
Lurie, Alison 2566
Luxemburg, Rosa 1379
Lyall, Edna 1225
Lydon, Susan 3438
Lyon, Phyllis 2489
Maazel, Fiona 4912
Macaulay, Rose 1570
MacDonald, Betty 2093
MacKay, Shena 3524
MacKinnon, Catherine A. 3674
MacLaine, Shirley 2903
MacLeod, Jean S. 2094–2095
MacMurray, Rose 2405
MacPherson, Myra 2939
Macy, Joanna 2669
Maggio, Rosalie 3439
Mahler, Margaret 1853
Mahoney, Rosemary 4587
Mairs, Nancy 3440
Maitland, Sara Louise 3987
Makin, Bathsua 412
Malcolm, Janet 2904
Malveaux, Julianne 4190

Manley, Delariviere 501
Mann, Erika 2026
Manner, Eeva-Liisa 2406
Mannes, Marya 1998
Manos, Helen 3989
Mansfield, Katherine 1687
Maraini, Dacia 2991
Maran, Meredith 4056
Margolis, Sue 3990
Margonelli, Lisa 4705
Marguerite of Navarre 289
Marie de France 193
Marinella, Lucrezia 376
Markham, Beryl 1951
Marsh, Anne 823
Marshall, Catherine 2224
Marshall, Lucinda 4381
Marston, Stephanie 3914
Martin, Del 2407
Martineau, Harriet 874
Marx, Patricia 4259
Mason, Bobbie Ann 3209
Massie, Suzanne 3280
Masterson, Martha Gay 1080
Masuda, Mizuko 3847
Mathilde 972
Mathis, Deborah 4192
Matsumoto, Valerie 4420
Mattern, Evelyn 3281
Matthews, Glenna C. 3098
Maule, Frances 1533
Mavrikakis, Catherine 4588
Mawiyoo, Neema "Ngwatilo"
4952
Maxwell, Elsa 1596
Mayer, Bernadette 3592
Mayer, Jane 4317
McBride, Mary Margaret 1888
McCarthy, Mary 2185
McCarthy, Sarah J. 3360
McClung, Nellie 1414
McCormick, Anne O'Hare 1582
McCracken, Elizabeth 4727
McCullers, Carson 2297
McDermott, Alice 4193
McDougall, Joyce 2567
McFadden, Bernice L. 4728
McGill, Alice 2606
McGinley, Phyllis 2027
McGovern, Ann 2725
McIntosh, Kinn Hamilton 2726
McIntosh, Maria 879
McIntosh, Mary 2992
McIntyre, Tami 2409
McKellar, Danica 4898.1
McKenna, Elizabeth Perle 4382
McKenney, Ruth 2161
McLeod, Merikay 3771
McMullan, Margaret 4542
McNamara, Jo Ann 2770
McPartland, Marian 2324
McPhee, Jenny 4543
McPhee, Martha S. 4683
McTaggart, Lynne 4059
McWilliam, Candia 4319
Mead, Margaret 1935
Mechtild von Magdeburg 215
Melville, Pauline 3850

Mernissi, Fatima 3211
Merriam, Eve 2274
Messud, Claire 4729
Metzger, Deena 2993
Mew, Charlotte 1366
Meyer, Agnes 1668
Meyer, Annie Nathan 1339
Midler, Bette 3594
Millar, Margaret Ellis 2249
Millar, Susanna 4544
Millay, Edna St. Vincent 1751
Miller, Alice 2466
Miller, Alice Duer 1443
Miller, Alyce 4194
Miller, Caroline 1974
Miller, Ceci 4461
Miller, Emily 1053
Miller, Jean Baker 2607
Miller, Laura 3992
Miller, Sue 3442
Millett, Kate 2908
Mills, Stephanie 3851
Mina, Denise 4730
Mink, Gwendolyn 4122
Mirrielees, Edith Ronald 1515
Mitchell, Juliet 3212
Mitchell, Margaret 1914
Mitford, Jessica 2298
Mitford, Mary Russell 805
Mitford, Nancy 2000
Moffat, Mary Jane 2859
Mohammed, Binta S. 4796
Mojtabai, A.G. 3046
Molesworth, Mary Louisa 1088
Molodowsky, Kadya 1801
Monk, Karen 4982
Monroe, Anne Shannon 1497
Montagu, Elizabeth 585
Montagu, Lily 1416
Montagu, Mary Wortley 533
Montero, Mayra 4123
Montessori, Maria 1381
Montgomery, Lucy Maud 1444
Montolieu, Jeanne Isabelle 668
Moodie, Susanna 880
Moody, Anne 3213
Moore, Liz 4954
Moore, Lorrie 4421
Moore, Susanna 3597
Moraga, Cherríe 4125
More, Hannah 649
Morgan, Angela 1446
Morgan, Elaine 2383
Morgan, Elizabeth 3773
Morgan, Marabel 3047
Morgan, Marlo 3048
Morgan, Robin 3284
Morgan, Ruth 2384
Morgan, Sydney Owenson 770
Morris, Jackie 4589
Morris, Jan 2569
Morris, Mary 2205
Morrison, Toni 2771
Morrissey, Mary Mannin 3918
Morrow, Elizabeth Cutler 1417
Mortimer, Penelope 2326
Mosala, Bernadette 4196
Moses, Claire Goldberg 3285

Moskowitz, Faye S. 2728
Mossell, N. F. 1212
Motley, Annette 4825
Moulton, Louise 1067
Mountain Wolf Woman 1571
Mukherjee, Bharati 3216
Muller, Karin 4707
Mumford, Ethel Watts 1516
Munro, Alice 2772
Murdoch, Iris 2352
Murray, Judith Sargent 669
Murry, Ann 750
Muscio, Inga 4734
Muske-Dukes, Carol 3598
Myerhoff, Barbara 2940
Myers, Dee Dee 4590
Myers, Isabel Briggs 1854
Myss, Caroline M. 4126
Nafisi, Azar 4320
Nahai, Gina Barkhordar 4546
Nairne, Carolina 731
Namjoshi, Suniti 3287
Naqvi, Tahira 4198
Nasrin, Taslima 4627
Nattel, Lilian 4383
Naylor, Gloria 3995
Necker, Suzanne Chardon 626
Necker de Saussure, Madame 740
Neiman, Susan 4321
Nelson, Antonya 4591
Nelson, Jill 4127
Nelson, Mariah Burton 4384
Nelson, Portia 2385
Némirovsky, Irène 1977
Nesbit, Edith 1234
Nevill, Dorothy 1009
Newman, Frances 1598
Newton, Frances 2731
Ng, Fae Myenne 4385
Nicholson, Zoe Ann 3852
Niedecker, Lorine 1978
Niederman, Sharon 3853
Niemann, Linda 3681
Niemi, Judith 3288
Nightingale, Florence 974
Nin, Anaïs 1979
Noble, Vicki 3775
Noddings, Nel 2675
Nogarola, Isotta 254
Nomani, Asra Q. 4708
Noonan, Peggy 3996
Noor Inayat Khan 2225
Norman, Dorothy 2028
Norman, Liane 3049
Norris, Kathleen 3777
Norris, Kathleen Thompson 1552
Norris, Pippa 4200
Norton, Caroline Sheridan 905
Nunez, Sigrid 4067
Nussbaum, Martha C. 3778
Nye, Naomi Sihab 4130
Oakley, Ann 3529
Oates, Joyce Carol 3099
Obejas, Achy 4386
O'Brien, Edna 2732
O'Brien, Virginia 3683
Ocampo, Victoria 1731
O'Casey, Eileen 1980

Ochs, Vanessa L. 4201
O'Connor, Flannery 2534
O'Connor, Karen 3100
O'Faolain, Nuala 3217
Ohba, Minako 2735
O'Keeffe, Adelaide 771
Oliphant, Margaret 1019
Oliver, Mary 2941
Olsen, Tillie 2187
O'Neill, Rose 1447
Opie, Amelia 744
Orbach, Susie 3685
Orczy, Baroness 1317
O'Reilly, Jane 2995
Orenstein, Catherine 4754
Orlean, Susan 4324
Orléans, Ann-Marie-Louise d' 452
Orlova, Raisa Davydovna 2327
Orman, Suze 4131
Orr, Mary 4548
Orr, Mary 2140
Ortese, Anna Maria 2226
Orth, Maureen Ann 3444
Osten, Suzanne 3530
Ostenso, Martha 1916
Otto, Louise 958
Ouida 1089
Overall, Christine 3923
Owen, Jane 426
Owen, Mary A. 1179
Ozick, Cynthia 2638
Packer, Ann 4500
Paddleford, Clementine 1871
Pagels, Elaine 3445
Paglia, Camille 3780
Painter, Charlotte 2572
Painter, Nell 3365
Painter, Pamela 3290
Paley, Grace 2437
Paley, Vivian Gussin 2677
Palmer, Gretta Brooker 2029
Pan Chao 8788
Pankhurst, Christabel 1553
Panova, Vera Fedorovna 2030
Pappenheim, Bertha 1249
Pardoe, Julia 898
Parent, Gail 3218
Paretsky, Sara 3781
Parker, Dorothy 1780
Parker, Gail Thain 3446
Parr, Catherine 305
Partnow, Elaine Bernstein 3291
Partnow, Susan 3782
Partridge, Frances 1918
Parturier, Françoise 2353
Patchett, Ann 4650
Peabody, Elizabeth Palmer 886
Peabody, Josephine Preston 1448
Peelen, Jean 3292–3293
Peery, Janet 3854
Peiss, Kathy 4203
Penley, Constance 3924
Perkins, Frances 1584
Perl, Teri 2573
Perry, Nora 1042
Pessl, Marisha 4929
Petchesky, Rosalind Pollack 3366
Peterkin, Julia 1554

Peterson, Brenda 4132
Peterson, Virgilia 2002–2003
Petrushevskaya, Lyudmila 3101
Petry, Ann 2100
Pfeiffer, Ida Laura 857
Pharr, Suzanne 3153
Phelps, Almira Lincoln 840
Phelps, Elizabeth 930
Phelps, Elizabeth Stuart 1127
Phillips, Angela Marie 3783
Phillips, Anne 4426
Phillips, Debora 4937
Phillips, Jayne Anne 4133
Phillips, Julie 4710
Phillips, Marie 4914
Pickford, Mary 1781
Picoult, Jodi 4735
Pierce-Baker, Charlotte 3447
Piercy, Marge 2997
Pincus, Joy 4798
Pincus, Lily 1873
Piozzi, Hester Lynch 635
Pipher, Mary 3784
Pix, Mary Griffith 509
Plain, Belva 2355
Plaskow, Judith 3785
Plath, Sylvia 2817
Plato, Ann 975
Pogrebin, Letty Cottin 3154
Pollard, Josephine 1059
Pollitt, Katha 3925
Poole, Jeannie Gayle 4068
Popcorn, Faith 3855
Porter, Eleanor H 1354
Porter, Jane 772
Porter, Katherine Anne 1715
Porter, Sylvia 2207
Portillo Trambley, Estela 2609
Post, Emily 1418
Postlethwaite, Diana 4000
Potter, Beatrix 1330
Poulsson, Emilie 1199
Powell, Dawn 1830
Power, Samantha 4829
Power, Susan 4593
Powter, Susan 4427
Prager, Emily 3856
Pratt, Minnie Bruce 3690
Prentiss, Elizabeth Payson 952
Preston, Ann 921
Preston, Margaret J. 976
Priest, Dana 4502
Prins, Nomi 4867
Pritchard, Melissa 3857
Prose, Francine 3788
Prothrow-Stith, Deborah 4267
Proulx, E. Annie 2942
Pryor, Sarah Agnes 1031
Putnam, Emily James 1318
Pym, Barbara 2208
Quayle, Marilyn 4001
Qui Jin 1465
Quindlen, Anna 4136
Radcliffe, Ann 723
Raine, Nancy Venable 3692
Rand, Ayn 2032
Randal, Vera 2438

Randall, Margaret 3000
Rascoe, Judith 3295
Räthzel, Nora 3858
Ravitch, Diane 3102
Rawlings, Marjorie Kinnan 1832
Ray, Rebecca 4938
Rebolledo, Tey Diana 3052
Reddy, Maureen 4328
Reese, Lizette 1213
Reeves, Nancy 2209
Rehm, Diane 3001
Renault, Mary 2033
Rendell, Ruth 2737
Renfroe, Anita 4629
Repplier, Agnes 1236
Resnik, Muriel 2301
Revoyr, Nina 4799
Reza, Yasmina 4503
Rhode, Deborah L. 4137
Rhys, Jean 1717
Rice, Alice Caldwell 1382
Rice, Ann 3298
Richards, Laura Howe 1180
Richardson, Dorothy Miller 1419
Richman, Alyson M. 4868
Richman, Julia 1207
Riding, Laura 1938
Rinehart, Mary Roberts 1480
Rittenhouse, Jessie 1367
Ritter, Erika 3860
Roberts, Dorothy E. 4389
Roberts, Elizabeth Madox 1638
Roberts, Michele 3932
Robinson, Harriet 1003
Robinson, Jill 3002
Robinson, Lillian 3300
Robinson, Mabel Louise 1449
Robinson, Marilynne 3451
Robinson, Mary 693
Robinson, Therese Albertine Louise 858
Rochefort, Christiane 2302
Rochlin, Harriet 2494
Rodgers, Carolyn M. 3607
Rodriguez, Graciela "Chely" 4939
Roe, Anne 2004
Roiphe, Anne 2943
Roiphe, Katie 4777
Roland, Pauline 891
Rollin, Betty 3003
Roosevelt, Eleanor 1618
Rosen, Marjorie 3372
Rosenberg, Karen 4879
Rosenberg, Tina 4553
Rosenfeld, Bobbie 2005
Rosenstein, Harriet 2818
Ross, Lillian 2611
Ross, Susan C. 3373
Rossetti, Christina 1032
Rossi, Alice S. 2439
Rossner, Judith 2944
Rourke, Constance 1639
Routledge, Katherine 1331
Routsong, Alma 2495
Row, Amanda 2774
Rowe, Dorothy 2739
Rowe, Elizabeth Singer 518
Rowland, Helen 1481

Rowlandson, Mary 468
Rowling, J. K. 4711
Rowson, Susanna Haswell 715
Roy, Arundhati 4595
Roy, Gabrielle 2115
Royall, Anne Newport 745
Rozman, Deborah 3933–3934
Ru Zhijuan 2535
Ruarowna, Margareta 440
Rubenstein, Gillian 3374
Rubinstein, Helena 1383
Rudikoff, Sonya 2612
Rudman, Masha Kabakow 2863
Ruether, Rosemary Radford 3004
Rukeyser, Muriel 2210
Rule, Jane 2775
Runkle, Bertha 1517
Russell, Diana E. H. 3104
Russell, Dora 1803
Sabin, Florence 1393
Sackville-West, Vita 1752
Sagan, Françoise 2945
Sage, Lorna 3453
Samalin, Nancy 3055
Sams, Jamie 4070
Sanchez, Georgiana Valoyce 4940
Sanchez, Sonia 2912
Sand, George 887
Sanger, Margaret 1535
Sangster, Margaret E. 1085
Sapphire 4002
Sarraute, Nathalie 1921
Sarton, May 2189
Satran, Pamela Redmond 4205
Satrapi, Marjane 4802
Saunders, Cicely 2329
Saunders, Margaret Baillie 1420
Sawyer, Ruth 1556
Sayers, Dorothy L. 1782
Scarf, Maggie 2819
Schaeffer, Susan Fromberg 3302
Schine, Cathleen 4206
Schirmacher, Kathe 1319
Schlafly, Phyllis 2496
Schlessinger, Laura Catherine 3792
Schnall, Marianne 4758
Schneiders, Sandra Marie 3005
Schneir, Miriam 2864
Schreiner, Olive 1208
Schtok, Fradel 1718
Schurman, Anna Maria van 422
Schwarcz, Vera 3793
Schwarz, Christina 4653
Scofield, Sandra 3455
Scott, Evelyn 1783
Scott, Melissa 4555
Scott, Robyn 4949
Scott-Maxwell, Florida 1601
Scudder, Janet 1421
Scudéry, Madeleine de 423
Seaberg, Rvnnog 2820
Seager, Joni 4273
Seaman, Barbara 2946
Sears, Vicki 3303
Sebold, Alice 4630
Sedgwick, Catherine Maria 812
See, Carolyn 2913
Sekaquaptewa, Helen 1876

Sendzimir, Venda 4140
Senna, Danzy 4834
Seton, Anya 2006
Seton, Cynthia Propper 2577
Seton, Julia 1701
Seton-Thompson, Grace 1405
Seuling, Barbara 3057
Severn, Jill 3794
Sewell, Anna 977
Sewell, Sarah Ann 1128
Seymour, Miranda J. 4207
Shaarawi, Huda 1536
Shain, Merle 2947
Shainess, Natalie 2256
Shalit, Wendy 4900
Shange, Ntozake 3865
Shanker, Wendy 4870
Shaw, Anna Moore 1877
Shaywitz, Sally E. 3376
Shear, Marie 3228
Sheehan, Susan 3058
Sheehy, Gail 3059
Sheepshanks, Mary 3612
Sheindlin, Judith 3377
Sheldon, Alice Bradley 2257
Shelley, Mary Wollstonecraft 859
Shelton, Charlotte 3795
Shen Rong 2948
Sherfey, Mary Jane 2865
Sheridan, Clare 1641
Sheridan, Frances 595
Sherrill, Martha 4507
Sherwood, Margaret P. 1306
Sherwood, Mary Martha 769
Shields, Carol 2949
Shikibu, Murasaki 166
Shivers, Louise 2683
Showalter, Elaine 3305
Shulman, Alix Kates 2822
Sidney, Margaret 1129
Siegel, Deborah 4803
Signoret, Simone 2414
Sigourney, Lydia Howard 827
Silko, Leslie Marmon 3866
Silver, Joan Micklin 2951
Simon, Kate 2190
Simon, Patricia 2914
Sinclair, Lee 4431.1
Singer, June K. 2330
Sinha, Kabita 2777
Sittenfeld, Curtis 4901
Skinner, Cornelia Otis 1940
Skram, Amalie 1147
Slapsak, Svetlana 3867
Slater, Lauren 4655
Slaughter, Anne-Marie 4471
Smart, Elizabeth 2211
Smedley, Agnes 1754
Smiley, Jane 3939
Smith, Betty 1835
Smith, Charlotte 658
Smith, Dodie 1836
Smith, Elizabeth Oakes 899
Smith, Evelyn Elizabeth 2742
Smith, Janna Malamud 4143
Smith, Lee 3540
Smith, Margaret Bayard 777
Smith, May Riley 1110

Smith, Nora Archibald 1250
Smith, Sarah 3797
Smith, Stevie 1956
Smith, Zadie 4902
Snitow, Ann 3457
Snortland, Ellen 4211
Snow, Helen Foster 2073
Sofer, Dalia 4871
Sokoloff, Natalie J. 3542
Sommers, Christina Hoff 4007
Sontag, Susan 2866
Southern, Eileen Jackson 2392
Sowerby, Githa 1482
Sowernam, Ester 428
Spark, Muriel 2331
Speare, Dorothy 1879
Speght, Rachel 405
Spellberg, Denise A. 4986
Spender, Dale 3458
Spiotta, Dana 4872
Spofford, Harriet 1068
Springer, Nancy 3868
Spyri, Johanna 1015
St. John, Christopher Marie 1466
St. John, Madeleine 3306
St. Johns, Adela Rogers 1804
Staöl, Germaine de 733
Stafford, Jean 2258
Stanford, Sally 2007
Stannard, Una 2613
Stanton, Elizabeth Cady 931
Starhawk 4072
Stark, Freya Madeline 1785
Stead, Christina 1957
Steichen, Joanna T. 2868
Stein, Gertrude 1450
Steinem, Gloria 2916
Stern, Edith Mendel 1941
Stewart, Maria W. 882
Stewart, Martha 3307
Stewart, Mary 2276
Stiller, Nikki 4988
Stimpson, Catharine R. 3008
Stiver, Irene Pierce 2497
Stoddard, Elizabeth 990
Stone, Merlin 2778
Storkey, Elaine 3460
Stowe, Harriet Beecher 916
Strong, Anna Louise 1642
Strouse, Jean 3617
Strout, Elizabeth 4473
Struther, Jan 1942
Suckow, Ruth 1756
Sugimoto, Etsu Inagaki 1451
Summerskill, Edith 1943
Sutcliffe, Ann 413
Sutherland, Efua Theodora 2498
Sutphen, Mona 4760
Suttner, Bertha von 1119
Swerda, Patricia 2277
Swetchine, Sophie-Jeanne Soymonof 791
Swindle, Renee 4850
Syfers, Judy 3870
Sykes, Roberta 3461
Sylva, Carmen 1120
Symes, Lillian 1819
Szymborska, Wislawa 2472

Tadjo, Véronique 4334
Tager, Marcia 3231
Tait, Katherine 2473
Tallent, Elizabeth 4275
Talmadge, Betty Shingler 2499
Tan, Amy 4146
Tan, Hwee Hwee 4888
Tanaka, Yukiko 3232
Tannen, Deborah F. 3618
Tapahonso, Luci 4214
Tappan, Eva March 1203
Tarabotti, Arcangela 419
Tarasova, Yelena 4971
Tarule, Jill M. 3462
Tattlewell, Mary 477
Tauziat, Nathalie 4761
Tax, Meredith 3700
Taylor, Jean M. 4656
Taylor, Katherine 4880
Teish, Luisah 3871
Tempelsman, Cathy Rindner 4972
Tencin, Claudine Alexandrine de
    530
Terán, Lisa St. Aubin de 4215
Teubal, Savina J. 2582
Thomas, Audrey Grace 2953
Thomas, Helen 2393
Thomas, Martha "Minnie" 1228
Thompson, Clara 1787
Thompson, Jean 4010
Thompson, Kay 2169
Thomson, Alice 4657
Thornton, Alice 454
Thorpe, Rose Hartwick 1181
Thurman, Judith 3872
Tiefer, Leonore 3543
Tillman, Lynne 3802
Ting Ling 2058
Tinti, Hannah 4874
Tobias, Sheila 2954
Todd, Mabel Elsworth 1559
Toklas, Alice B. 1502
Tolstaya, Tatyana 4074
Tomioka, Taeko 2955
Tonna, Charlotte Elizabeth 821
Torgovnick, Marianna 3940
Torres, Amaryllis Tiglao 3544
Toth, Emily 3545
Townsend, Sue 3702
Trachtenberg, Inge 2474
Tracy, Honor 2213
Trapido, Barbara 3308
Treadwell, Sophie 1643
Treichler, Paula Antonia 3463
Tremain, Rose 3464
Trench, Melesina 742
Trimmer, Sarah Kirby 637
Trinh, T. Minh-Ha 4147
Tristan, Flora 883
Trollope, Frances Milton 784
Trollope, Joanna 3465
Trotter, Catherine 522
Troubridge, Laura Gurney 1321
Truman, Margaret 2500–2501
Trussoni, Danielle Anne 4881
Truth, Sojourner 860
Tsushima, Yūko 3803
Tsvetaeva, Marina 1757

Tuchman, Barbara 2192
Turkle, Sherry 4738
Turnbull, Agnes Sligh 1689
Turnbull, Margaret 1702
Tusquets, Esther 3010
Tuthill, Louisa Caroline 862
Tweedie, Jill 2828
Tyler, Anne 3309
Tyrwhit, Elizabeth 322
Ueland, Brenda 1758
Ugresic, Dubravka 3941
Uhnak, Dorothy 2871
Ullman, Liv 3108
Ulrich, Laurel Thatcher 3109
Umansky, Ellen M. 4011
Undset, Sigrid 1587
Ung, Loung 4836
Vachss, Alice 4012
Valenzuela, Luisa 3110
Valiente, Doreen 2442
Van Buren, Abigail 2333
Vanderbilt, Amy 2103
Vanzant, Iyanla 4216
Vapnyar, Lara 4851
Vardill, Anna Jane 789
Vendler, Helen Hennessy 2872
Verdelle, A. J. 4558
Vida, Vendela 4852
Vilar, Irene 4805
Villanueva, Alma Luz 3546
Vincent, Norah 4713
Vincenzi, Penny 3164
Viorst, Judith 2780
Viramontes, Helena María 4279
Viva 3467
Volk, Patricia 3468
von Meysenbug, Malwida 940
Vorse, Mary Heaton 1575
vos Savant, Marilyn 3703
Voznesenskaya, Yuliya 3236
Vreeland, Susan 3704
Waddles, Charleszetta 2193
Waite, Mary 534
Walbert, Kate 4598.1
Waldo, Octavia Capuzzi 2686
Walker, Alice 3547
Walker, Barbara G. 2744
Walker, Katharine 1097
Walker, Margaret 2259
Walker, Mary Edwards 1047
Walker, Rebecca 4806
Wallace, Michelle 4149
Wallis, Velma 4559
Walsh, Jill Paton 3065
Walsh, Maria Elena 2745
Walters, Anna Lee 3705
Walters, Barbara 2687
Walters, Dottie 2538
Walters, Lilly 4394
Walters, Minette 3944
Wanatee, Adeline 2144
Wandor, Michelene 3237
Wang Anyi 4280
Wann, Marilyn 4739
Ward, Barbara 2230
Ward, Mary Augusta 1187
Warner, Anna Bartlett 979
Warner, Marina 3706

Warner, Susan 961
Warner, Sylvia Townsend 1789
Washington, Harriet A. 4634
Wasserstein, Wendy 4013
Waters, Sarah 4740
Weaver, Frances 2645
Webb, Beatrice Potter 1239
Webb, Mary 1576
Webster, Margaret 2035
Weinraub, Sally 2503
Weisstein, Naomi 3165
Weldon, Fay 2874
Wells, Carolyn 1368
Wells, Ida B. 1291
Wells, Rebecca 4150
Welty, Eudora 2117
Wertheim, Margaret 4474
West, Jane 694
West, Jessamyn 1959
West, Mae 1790
West, Rebecca 1759
Westheimer, Ruth 2646
Wharton, Anne 462
Wharton, Edith 1292
Wheathill, Ann 388
Wheeler, Kate 4078
Whitbread, Jane 2231
Whitehorn, Katharine 2647
Whiteley, Opal 1858
Whitestone-McCallum, Heather
    4882
Whitman, Marina von Neumann
    2957
Whitman, Sarah Power 884
Whitney, Adeline Dutton 996
Whitson, Beth Slater 1538
Whitton, Charlotte 1839
Widdemer, Margaret 1561
Wieder, Marcia 4396
Wiggin, Kate Douglas 1214
Wilde, Jane Francesca 1010
Wilder, Laura Ingalls 1345
Wildman, Stephanie M. 3945
Wiley, Doreen Gandy 2617
Wilhelm, Gale 2104
Willard, Emma Hart 806
Willard, Nancy 3013
Williams, Anna 561
Williams, Bertye Young 1485
Williams, Carol 3876
Williams, Helen Maria 716
Williams, Joy 3550
Williams, Patricia 4079
Williams, Sherley Anne 3551–3552
Williamson, Marianne 4151
Willis, Gwendolen 1486
Willis, Sarah 4284
Willson, Dixie 1720
Willson, Margaret 4219
Wilson, Barbara 4015
Wilson, Elizabeth 3014
Wilson, Margaret 1589
Wiltz, Christine 3878
Winegarten, Renee 2443
Winn, Marie 3115
Winn, Mary Day 1691
Winslow, Anne Goodwin 1467
Winslow, Thyra Samter 1985

Winterson, Jeanette 4510
Winwar, Frances 1923
Witt, Shirley Hill 2918
Wittig, Monique 2958
Woffington, Peg 586
Wolf, Christa 2689
Wolf, Naomi 4635
Wolff, Charlotte 2008
Wolitzer, Hilma 2748
Wolitzer, Meg 4511
Wollstonecraft, Mary 701
Wolverton, Terry 4286
Wong, Nellie 2919
Wood, Ellen 922
Wood, Sally Sayward 702
Woodhull, Victoria Claflin 1086
Woodman, Marion 2648
Woodruff, Julia 1054
Woolf, Virginia 1590
Worthington, Robin 2829
Wright, Frances 850
Wright, Judith 2260
Wright, Robin 3879
Wucker, Michele 4808
Wurdeman, Audrey 2170
Wurtzel, Elizabeth 4762
Wyatt, Edith Franklin 1423
Wylie, Elinor 1645
Wyse, Lois 2584
Yamada, Eimi 4512
Yamauchi, Wakako 2504
Yang Jiang 2171
Yang Ping 2105
Yaroshinskaya, Alla 4220
Yearsley, Anne 710
Yee, Marian 4989
Yezierska, Anzia 1562
Yglesias, Helen 2261
Yonge, Charlotte 991
Young, Cathy 4661
Young, Iris Marion 3947
Young, Leontine 2148
Young, Louise B. 2359
Younger, Maud 1384
Yourcenar, Marguerite 1986
Zarin, Cynthia Rebecca 4513
Zayas y Sotomayor, María de 398
Zeidner, Lisa 4341
Zeisler, Andi 4221
Zepatos, Thalia 4342
Zhang Jie 3067
Zhang Kangkang 4017
Zong Pu 2649
Zuboff, Shoshana 4081
Zygmuntowicz, Itka Frajman 2585

E. SCIENCE AND MEDICINE
COMPUTER SCIENCE AND TECHNOLOGY

Borg, Anita 3888
Camp, Tracy 4671
Carter, Sandy 4637
Goren-Bar, Dina 4451
Gürer, Denise W. 4409
King, Countess of Lovelace, Ada
    Byron 929
Murray, Janet Horowitz 3679

Perl, Teri 2573
Renne, Tanya 4830
Todosijevic, Jelica 4973

ENGINEERS
Clarke, Edith 1594
Dicciani, Nance K. 3822
Gilbreth, Lillian Moller 1513
Jackson, Lisa P. 4619
Qing, Dai 3250.1
Resnik, Judith 3931
Swallow, Ellen 1112

**HEALTH SCIENCES—
PHYSICIANS, DENTISTS,
PSYCHIATRISTS, MIDWIVES,
HEALERS, ET AL.**
Abdellah, Faye Glenn 2335
Allen, Mary Wood 1099
Anna of Saxony 384
Ataniyazova, Oral 4398
Bachelet, Michelle 4022
Baker, Sara Josephine 1407
Bakke, Kit 3628
Barnhouse, Ruth Tiffany 2446
Barnwell, Ysaye 3633
Barry, James Stuart Miranda 830
Barton, Clara 980
Bashir, Halima 4925
Benes, Francine M. 3557
Blackwell, Elizabeth 981
Blackwell, Emily 1005
Bonner, Ylena Georgievna 2447
Bradwell, Myra R. 1035
Breckinridge, Mary 1565
Brundtland, Gro Harlem 3129
Calderone, Mary Steichen 1989
Caldicott, Helen 3075
Capps, Lois 3076
Carter, Lillian 1862
Cavell, Edith Louisa 1310
Chen, Pauline W. 4356
Chesler, Phyllis 3184
Clancy, Carolyn 4238
Colborn, Theodora "Theo" 2622
Cooper, Diana 1744
Davis-Floyd, Robbie 4037
Delany, Elizabeth "Bessie" 1725
Deutsch, Helene 1608
Elders, Joycelyn "Minnie" 2843
Ferguson, Patricia 4176
Flowers, Margaret 4576.1
Fraiberg, Selma 2314
Galchen, Rivka 4907
Gamble, Vanessa Northington 4177
Gao Yaojie 2597
Genefke, Inge 3503
Gideon, Lillian 2088
Glasgow, Maude 1351
Halifax, Joan 3341
Halprin, Anna 2373
Hamburg, Margaret "Peggy"
    4303.1
Hamilton, Alice 1361
Han Suyin 2291
Healy, Bernadine 3509
Heide, Wilma Scott 2400
Herman, Judith Lewis 3342

Hinkle, Beatrice 1436
Horney, Karen 1631
Hunter, Alberta 1811
Jessop, Violet 1665
Johnson, Adelaide 2023
Jordan, Sara Murray 1613
Joshee, Anandabai 1316
Judith, Anodea 4113
Kelley, Virginia Cassidy 2462
Kenny, Elizabeth 1549
King, Janice 4456
Klein, Melanie 1579
Knopf, Olga 1683
Kruhonja, Katarina 3907
Kübler-Ross, Elisabeth 2560
Levi-Montalcini, Rita 2112
Lyon, Emily 4379
Mahler, Margaret 1853
Mandela, Winnie 2905
Mendenhall, Dorothy Reed 1442
Miller, Jean Baker 2607
Montessori, Maria 1381
Morgan, Elizabeth 3773
Morgan, Marlo 3048
Mori, Nobuko 2811
Morris, Margaret 625
Myss, Caroline M. 4126
Nasrin, Taslima 4627
Nightingale, Florence 974
O'Brien, Mary Mamie 2571
Ojiambo, Josephine 4592
Parker, Pat 3531
Pastan, Linda 2815
Phillips, Debora 4937
Potor, Aurelia 2253
Preston, Ann 921
Prothrow-Stith, Deborah 4267
Ramey, Estelle R. 2300
Riddlestone, Sue 4552
Rolf, Ida P. 1833
Sabin, Florence 1393
Sadik, Nafis 2681
Samar, Sima 4430
Sanger, Margaret 1535
Saunders, Cicely 2329
Schnall, Susan 3454
Shainess, Natalie 2256
Shaywitz, Sally E. 3376
Sherfey, Mary Jane 2865
Smith, Laura Frost 1784
Stewart, Alice 2057
Summerskill, Edith 1943
Swearingen, Terri 4433
Thompson, Clara 1787
Trotula of Salerno 177
Ulrich, Mabel S. 1586
Vassiltchikov, Marie 2304
Wald, Lillian D. 1342
Walker, Mary Edwards 1047
Wattleton, Faye 3469
Whyte, Edna Gardner 1960
Wolff, Charlotte 2008
Zassenhaus, Hiltgunt Margaret
    2279

NATURALISTS
Ackerman, Diane 3808
Adamson, Joy 2336

Galland, China 3410
Laurel, Alicia Bay 3908–3909
Lord, Nancy 4119
Pollard, Josephine 1059
Williams, Terry Tempest 4339
Winn, Marie 3115
Wordsworth, Dorothy 758

**NUTRITIONISTS, CHEFS,
COOKBOOK WRITERS, AND
FOOD SPECIALISTS**
Child, Julia 2174
Davis, Adelle 1992
de Baca, Fabiola Cabeza 1806–1807
Deen, Paula 3734
DeWit, Antoinette 2451
Farmer, Fannie 1221
Fisher, M.F.K. 2085
Hazan, Marcella 2486
Lawson, Nigella Lucy 4541
Leith, Prue 3205
Leslie, Eliza 804
Powter, Susan 4427
Rajalakshmi, R. 2574
Spicer, Susan 4212
van den Beld, Theodora 4148
Waters, Alice 3548

**PSYCHOTHERAPISTS, ANALYSTS,
SOCIAL WORKERS, AND
COUNSELORS**
Addams, Jane 1251
Adelman, Penina V. 4155
American, Sadie 1281
Anastasi, Anne 2076
Anderson, Ruth Ann 3553
Bamber, Helen 2508
Bassoff, Evelyn S. 3477
Bhatt, Ela 2835
Bloom, Amy 4163
Bolen, Jean Shinoda 2965
Bolgar, Hedda 2106
Bonaparte, Marie L. 1564
Borysenko, Joan Z. 3638
Bowen, Louise de Koven 1242
Branch, Anna Hempstead 1454
Breckinridge, Sophonisba Preston
    1324
Breitman, Barbara E. 3955
Bricker-Jenkins, Mary 3326
Briggs, Dorothy Corkille 2477
Canaan, Andrea R. 3729
Carroll, Vinnette 2422
Chess, Stella 2216
Childs, E. Kitch 3024
Conrad, Beatrice 2590
Davis, Laura 4361
Day, Dorothy 1846
Deutsch, Helene 1608
Dunbar-Nelson, Alice 1457
Earhart, Amelia 1847
Estés, Clarissa Pinkola 3567
Fraiberg, Selma 2314
Franz, Marie-Louise von 2240
Freston, Kathy 4676
Freud, Anna 1810
Gawain, Shakti 3827
Goodman, Carolyn 2242

Greenberg, Julie 4721
Grueso, Libia 4578
Hamilton, Eleanor 2109
Herbert, Marie 3270
Hooyman, Nancy R. 3582
Hope, Lugenia Burns 1390.1
Hyman, Judith Partnow 3089
Irigaray, Luce 2717
Joseph, Helen 2024
Kahn, Kathy 3585
Kellor, Frances Alice 1413
Kristeva, Julia 3277
Le Shan, Eda J. 2434
Mahler, Margaret 1853
Mankiller, Wilma Pearl 3591
Marston, Stephanie 3914
Matthews-Simonton, Stephanie 3210
McDougall, Joyce 2567
Meyer, Agnes 1668
Miller, Alice 2466
Miller, Jean Baker 2607
Mitchell, Juliet 3212
Mladjenovic, Lepa 4264–4265
Nemeth, Maria 2812
Orbach, Susie 3685
Perera, Sylvia Brinton 2816
Phillips, Debora 4937
Pincus, Lily 1873
Rankin, Jeannette 1555
Reddy, Helen 3297
Rosenstein, Harriet 2818
Rush, Florence 2328
Sears, Vicki 3303
Semenow, Dorothy 2740
Shain, Merle 2947
Shainess, Natalie 2256
Singer, June K. 2330
Smith, Janna Malamud 4143
Stabenow, Debbie 4008
Steichen, Joanna T. 2868
Stevens, Christine 4688
Stiver, Irene Pierce 2497
Ward, Mary Augusta 1187
West, Cheryl L. 4714
Westheimer, Ruth 2646
Woodman, Marion 2648
Woolsey, Mary 1048
Young, Leontine 2148

SCIENTISTS—BIOLOGICAL
Arditti, Rita 2877
Atakhanova, Kaisha 4439
Borysenko, Joan Z. 3638
Brown, Rachel Fuller 1861
Bunting, Mary Ingraham 2121
Carson, Rachel 2061
Charkowski, Amy O. 4841
Clark, Eugenie 2423
Colborn, Theodora "Theo" 2622
Earle, Sylvia A. 2926
Eastwood, Alice 1247
Elion, Gertrude B. 2312
Fausto-Sterling, Anne 3499
Fleming, Amalia 2175
Galdikas, Biruté M. F. 3657
Gao Yaojie 2597
Gibson, Janet 4178
Giordano, Anna 4697

Goodall, Jane 2892
Grandin, Temple 3748
Hafild, Emmy 4488
Hamilton, Alice 1361
Hazan, Marcella 2486
Hopkins, Nancy 3511
Hrdy, Sarah Blaffer 3665
Hubbard, Ruth 2487
Hunt, Carrie 4372
Hypatia 107
Judson, Olivia 4791
Kaplan, Gisela 3516.1
Kaufman, Paola 4792
Kenyon, Cynthia 4311
Kochladze, Manana 4863
Krim, Mathilde 2559
Lim Wei-ling, Wilina 4980
Maathai, Wangari Muta 3207
McClintock, Barbara 1952
Merian, Maria Sibylla 481
Michiel, Renier Giustina 683
Nüsslein-Volhard, Christiane 3363
Pert, Candace B. 3687
Phelps, Almira Lincoln 840
Potter, Beatrix 1330
Profet, Margie 4465
Quin Guanshu 2679.1
Ramey, Estelle R. 2300
Ray, Dixy Lee 2227
Rogers, Lesley 3452
Sabin, Florence 1393
Sarabi, Habiba 4392
Savage-Rumbaugh, Susan 3937
Simeonova, Albena 4712
Stevens, Nettie Maria 1279
Stopes, Marie Carmichael 1558
Subramaniam, Banu 4145
Swallow, Ellen 1112
Taylor, Jill Bolte 4508
Tilghman, Shirley M. 3701

SCIENTISTS—CHEMICAL

Ataniyazova, Oral 4398
Benston, Margaret Lowe 3020
Blodgett, Katharine "Katie" Burr 1860
Brown, Barbara B. 2621
Brown, Rachel Fuller 1861
Cori, Gerty Theresa 1821
Elion, Gertrude B. 2312
Joliot-Curie, Iréne 1851
Makhubu, Lydia Phindile 3045
Rajalakshmi, R. 2574
Rolf, Ida P. 1833
Saruhashi, Katsuko 2389
Singer, Maxine 2776
Thatcher, Margaret 2537

SCIENTISTS—EARTH AND SKY

Burbidge, E. Margaret 2338
Cannon, Annie Jump 1293
Carson, Rachel 2061
Clark, Eugenie 2423
Earle, Sylvia A. 2926
Halifax, Joan 3341
Harris, Rachel 4893
Hazan, Marcella 2486
Herschel, Caroline 662

Hypatia 107
King, Ynestra 3840
Lappé, Frances Moore 3518
Lubchenco, Jane 3768
Mathews, Jessica Tuchman 3676
Mitchell, Maria 951
Oreskes, Naomi 4463
Payne-Gaposchkin, Cecilia Helena 1919
Primavera, Jurgenne 3605
Rikhvanova, Marina 4594
Rubin, Vera C. 2640
Seager, Joni 4273
Sharman, Helen 4654
Shiva, Vandana 4141
Somerville, Mary 783
Swallow, Ellen 1112
Weed, Becky 4560

SCIENTISTS—MATHEMATICS AND PHYSICS

Agnesi, Maria Gaëtana 581
Burnell, Jocelyn Bell 3395
Chbtelet, Émilie du 557
Chien Shiung Wu 2173
Clarke, Edith 1594
Cohen, Amy 3329
Curie, Marie 1335
Dresselhaus, Mildred Spiewak 2702
Franklin, Rosalind 2370
Henrion, Claudia 4454
Hodgkin, Dorothy Crowfoot 2132
Hopper, Grace Murray 2048
Hypatia 107
Jemison, Mae 4374
Keller, Evelyn Fox 2988
King, Countess of Lovelace, Ada Byron 929
Kovalevskaya, Sofia Vasilyevna 1177
Lonsdale, Kathleen Yardley 1972
Malone-Mayes, Vivienne 2808
Mayer, Maria Goeppert 2054
Megaw, Helen Dick 2071
Meitner, Lise 1514
Merkel, Angela 4261
O'Hara, Maureen 4202
Perl, Teri 2573
Quimby, Edith 1732
Ramey, Estelle R. 2300
Ride, Sally 4069
Sengers, Johanna Levelt 2682
Shiva, Vandana 4141
Somerville, Mary 783
Uhlenbeck, Karen 3382
Williams, Lynda 4475
Yalow, Rosalyn 2416
Young, Louise B. 2359

SCIENTISTS—SOCIAL AND BEHAVIORAL

Adams, Grace 1893
Apter, Terri 3882
Arizpe, Lourdes 3390
Arndt, Bettina "Tina" 3883
Arrien, Angeles 2920
Arslan, Antonia 3069

Assad, Marie B. 2445
Avery-Clark, Constance 4228
Axline, Virginia Mae 2149
Bardwick, Judith M. 2832
Barnard, Jessie 1965
Bateson, Mary Catherine 3124
Bell, Gertrude 1347
Benedict, Ruth 1659
Benet, Sula 1966
Bennett, Georgette 3634
Bernard, Jessie Shirley 1967
Bertell, Rosalie 2651
Bieber, Margarete 1521
Blee, Kathleen M. 4162
Bolgar, Hedda 2106
Bonaparte, Marie L. 1564
Boulding, Elise M. 2362
Brothers, Joyce 2587
Busfield, Joan 3130
Campbell, Anne 4031
Chiang Kai-shek 1863
Chodorow, Nancy 3487
Clendinnen, Inga 2884
Conklin, Beth Ann 4239
Connelly, Joan Breton 4240
Davis-Floyd, Robbie 4037
Dinnerstein, Dorothy 2452
Douvan, Elizabeth "Libby" 2545
Edwards, Marie 2548
Estés, Clarissa Pinkola 3567
Etcoff, Nancy L. 4299
Faraday, Ann 2927
Farro, Maria Elena Foronda 4482
Fernea, Elizabeth Warnock 2595
Field, Joanna 1899
Flekkøy, Målfrid Grude 2703
Follett, Mary Parker 1350
Fossey, Dian 2795
Gilligan, Carol 2979
Gimbutas, Mirija 2399
Grant, Toni 3266–3267
Guidon, Niède 2852
Halifax, Joan 3341
Harding, M. Esther 1680
Harrison, Jane 1176
Hawkes, Jessie 2131
Heide, Wilma Scott 2400
Henley, Nancy M. 2894
Horner, Matina S. 3148–3149
Hrdy, Sarah Blaffer 3665
Hurston, Zora Neale 1727
Ireland, Mardy S. 3833
Jackson, Jacquelyne J. 2802
Janeway, Elizabeth 2201
Kanter, Rosabeth Moss 3429
Kaplan, Louise J. 2666
King, Deborah K. 4254
Kitzinger, Celia 4539
Kiyak, H. Asuman 4054
Klein, Laura Cousino 4768
Kübler-Ross, Elisabeth 2560
Leach, Penelope 3042
Lerner, Harriet Goldhor 3519
Levin, Diane E. 3764
Lightfoot, Sara Lawrence 3520
Loftus, Elizabeth Fishman 3522
Luker, Kristin Carol 3673
Mandela, Makaziwe "Maki" 4191

Martin, Emily 3526
McFate, Montgomery "Mitzi" 4706
McIntosh, Mary 2992
Mead, Margaret 1935
Meadows, Donella "Dana" 3282
Mernissi, Fatima 3211
Millar, Susanna 4544
Moore, Patricia A. 4124
Morgan, Elaine 2383
Murray, Margaret Alice 1298
Myers, Isabel Briggs 1854
Myrdal, Alva Reimer 1953–1954
Norberg-Hodge, Helena 3682
Oakley, Ann 3529
Oaks, Laura Mary 4753
Patkar, Medha 4266
Pipher, Mary 3784
Prell, Riv-Ellen 3786
Rank, Beata 1831
Reinharz, Shulamit 3693
Reinisch, June Machover 3448
Riley, Matilda White 2165
Roe, Anne 2004
Rosaldo, Michelle Zimbalist 3536
Routledge, Katherine 1331
Rowe, Dorothy 2739
Rozman, Deborah 3933–3934
Sassen, Georgia 3936
Savage-Rumbaugh, Susan 3937
Scott-Maxwell, Florida 1601
Shaheed, Farida 4208
Small, Meredith F. 4005
Smith, Dorothy E. 2579
Storkey, Elaine 3460
Streshinsky, Naomi 2536
Tapp, June L. 2743
Taylor, Janelle S. 4873
Tett, Gillian 4761.1
Tiefer, Leonore 3543
Turkle, Sherry 4738
Valian, Virginia 3383
Washburn, Margaret Floy 1395
Webb, Beatrice Potter 1239
Weisstein, Naomi 3165
Wheatley, Margaret "Meg" 3311
Willson, Margaret 4219
Witt, Shirley Hill 2918
Wortham, Anne 3314
Yener, Kutlu Aslihan 3708

F. OTHER

ADVENTURERS, FRONTIER SETTLERS, HEROES, AND PILOTS

Alden, Priscilla 416
Arria the Elder 87
Barr, Nevada 4084
Bonny, Anne 548
Brown, Clara 875
Brown, Tabitha Moffatt 779
Burke, Martha Jane 1190
Burlend, Rebecca Burton 837
Cashman, Nellie 1183
Chuo Wên-chün 69
Clappe, Louise Amelia 954
Cobb, Geraldyn M. 2752
Cochran, Jacqueline 2043
Coleman, Bessie 1742
Collins, Eileen 4359

David-Néel, Alexandra 1348
Davidson, Janine 4745
Earhart, Amelia 1847
Earle, Sylvia A. 2926
Eberhardt, Isabelle 1491
Erauso, Catalina de 392
Erde, Betty Skelton 2550
Fergus, Pamelia Dillin 2482
Fitzgerald, Zelda 1901
Hahn, Emily "Mickey" 2019
Hamilton, Emma 727
Hutton, Lauren 3422
Jemison, Mae 4374
Joan of Arc 252
Johnson, Amy 2091
Johnson, Osa 1797
Judith 48
Kelly, Emily "Pat" 1400
Langston, Laodicea "Dicey" 730
Lindbergh, Anne Morrow 2053
Markham, Beryl 1951
Martin, Martha 1827
Masterson, Martha Gay 1080
Mazuchelli, Elizabeth Sarah 1046
McAuliffe, Christa 3848
Mock, Geraldine "Jerrie" 2532
Morgan, Barbara "Barb" 4063
Murphy, Virginia Backentoe 1058
Nichols, Ruth Rowland 1937
Niemi, Judith 3288
Oakley, Annie 1260
Oliver, Ruth Law 1671
Paddleford, Clementine 1871
Pfeiffer, Ida Laura 857
Pocahontas 404
Resnik, Judith 3931
Ride, Sally 4069
Routledge, Katherine 1331
Rowlandson, Mary 468
Scott, Blanche Stuart 1753
Sharman, Helen 4654
Stinson, Katherine 1736
Telesilla 58
Tiburzi, Bonnie 3873
Whyte, Edna Gardner 1960
Wright, Susanna 546
Yeager, Jeana L. 4153
Zane, Elizabeth "Betty" 703

ATHLETES, SPORTS, AND FITNESS FIGURES
Alfredsson, Helen 4691
Boudrot, Denise M. 4090
Cher 3643
Colledge, Cecilia 2367
Comaneci, Nadia 4606
Connolly, Olga 2789
Devers, Gail 4746
Didriksen Zaharias, "Babe" 2218
Dressel, Brigit 4569
Ederle, Gertrude 2045
El Moutawakel, Nawal 4610
Evert Lloyd, Chris 4243
Fonda, Jane 3029
Gera, Bernice 2759
Gibson, Althea 2598
Goitschel, Marielle 3659
Griffith Joyner, Florence 4487

Hamm, Mia 4859
Harding, Tonya 4820
Johnson, Shirbey 3273
Jones, Marion 4910
Joyner-Kersee, Jacqueline "Jackie" 4621
Kerrigan, Nancy 4793
King, Billie Jean 3434
Krone, Julie 4645
Leslie, Lisa 4864
Matthews, Jill 4682
Mullins, Aimee 4913
Navratilova, Martina 4424
Nelson, Mariah Burton 4384
Newlin, Marjorie 2386
Nyad, Diana 3922
Powter, Susan 4427
Rea, Shiva 4756
Rosenfeld, Bobbie 2005
Rudolph, Wilma "Skeeter" 3226
Sanchez, Cristina 4869
Sharapova, Maria 4957
Shur, Fanchon 2950
Slaney, Mary Decker 4470
Smith, Robyn 3541
Tauziat, Nathalie 4761
Williams, Venus 4944

BUSINESS EXECUTIVES, ENTREPRENEURS, INDUSTRIALISTS, AND CONSULTANTS
Adler, Polly 1894
Alvarado, Linda G. 4083
Arden, Elizabeth 1503
Arizpe, Lourdes 3390
Arnold, Susan E. 4227
Arrien, Angeles 2920
Ash, Mary Kay 2306
Ayer, Harriet Hubbard 1163
Barrows, Sydney Biddle 4086
Berresford, Susan V. 3393
Bettencourt, Liliane Schueller 2418
Browner, Carol M. 4293
Bundchen, Gisele 4931
Caine, Lynn 2588
Calderón, Sila María 3327
Canth, Minna 1125
Castle, Victoria 3889
Chang, Helen Mack 4091
Cheng, Nien 2239
Claiborne, Liz 2655
Cochran, Jacqueline 2043
Cocroft, Susan 1284
Coleman, Deborah A. 4170
Daché, Lilly 1991
Danieli, Cecilia 3401
de Palacio, Loyola 3960
Deen, Paula 3734
Dicciani, Nance K. 3822
Dunn, Lydia 3188
Dyson, Esther 4040
Estaugh, Elizabeth Haddon 524
Ettore, Barbara 4041
Farenthold, Sissy 2551
Fee, Elizabeth 3651
Fiorina, Cara Carleton "Carly" Sneed 4244–4245

Fishback, Margaret 1900
Fisher, Renee 3743
Follett, Mary Parker 1350
Fox, Muriel 2626
Gabor, Zsa Zsa 2287
Garvey, Jane F. 3502
Gilman, Charlotte Perkins 1254
Gilson, Mary Barnett 1494
Gordy Edwards, Esther 2370.1
Graham, Bette Clair 2484
Handler, Ruth 2269
Harper, Martha Matilda 1223
Heldman, Gladys Medalie 2431
Helmsley, Leona 2374
Herman, Susan 3343
Hernandez, Aileen Clarke 2553
Hobson, Laura Z. 1905
Hollander, Xaviera 3421
Holley, Mary Austin 796
Hollman, Peggy 4304
Hutton, Lauren 3422
Jacobs, Rose Gell 1681
Jarrett, Valerie Bowman 4373
Jayapal, Pramila 4702
Johnson, Abigail 4582
Josefowitz, Natasha 2555
Karan, Donna 3836
Kellems, Vivien 1826
Kennedy, Marilyn Moats 3431
Killefer, Nancy 4186
Kim, Sung-Joo 4419
Knight, Sarah Kemble 508
Kramer, Joyce 3357
Kreps, Juanita 2403
Lauder, Estée 2052
Lear, Moya Olson 2246
Leek, Sybil 2296
Leith, Prue 3205
Lesher, Jan 4313–4314
Liu, Peggy 4624
Lopez, Jennifer 4824
Lydia 90
Lyon, Mary 855
Magner, Marjorie 3913
Martin, Lynn 3151
Mathews, Jessica Tuchman 3676
Mayberg, Maude 1750
McCain, Cindy 4260
Mills, Karen Gordon 4262
Moore, Ann S. 3917
Nelson, Paula 3599
Ngilu, Charity Kaluki 4129
Nooyi, Indra 4322
Parisot, Laurence 4501
Partnow, Elaine Bernstein 3291
Partnow, Susan 3782
Perino, Dana 4866
Phillips, Lois 3222
Pinckney, Eliza 591
Poon, Christine A. 4135
Popcorn, Faith 3855
Powers, Donna 3926
Rebolledo, Tey Diana 3052
Roddick, Anita 3370
Rogers, Desiree 4504
Rubinstein, Helena 1383
Ruckelshaus, Jill 3054
Schutz, Susan Polis 3538

Seager, Joni 4273
Shah, Nishita 4941
Shelton, Charlotte 3795
Siebert, Muriel "Mickie" 2823
Siegel, Deborah 4803
Slocumb, Mary 709
Spicer, Susan 4212
Spiotta, Dana 4872
Springer, Carol 3007
Stabenow, Debbie 4008
Stanford, Sally 2007
Stewart, Ella Jane S. 1394
Stewart, Martha 3307
Strand, Polly 2825
Stronach, Belinda 4736
Sutphen, Mona 4760
Swanson, Gloria 1892
Sweeney, Anne 4434
Talmadge, Betty Shingler 2499
Taylor, Elizabeth 2826
Tobias, Sheila 2954
Tolstaya, Tatyana 4074
Tymoshenko, Yulia Volodymyrivna 4557
van den Beld, Theodora 4148
Vernon, Lillian 2616
Versace, Donatella 4337
Walker, C.J. 1343
Walker, Sarah Breedlove 1344
Walters, Anna Lee 3705
Walton, Meredith "Marty" 3011
Wheatley, Margaret "Meg" 3311
Whitestone-McCallum, Heather 4882
Whitman, Meg 4395
Wieder, Marcia 4396
Williams, E. Faye 3312
Willoughby, Denita 4742
Wilson, Heather 4561
Winterson, Jeanette 4510
Woodhull, Victoria Claflin 1086
Wyse, Lois 2584
Zuboff, Shoshana 4081

ECONOMISTS, FINANCIAL SPECIALISTS, AND BANKERS
Al Kuwaiz, Samira 4664
Arroyo, Gloria Macapagal 3717
Bair, Sheila C. 4229
Barrow, Lisa 4669
Bellamy, Carol 3324
Bilmes, Linda J. 4521
Dery, Dominika 4890–4891
Diogo, Luísa Dias 4446
Domini, Amy 4100
Fawcett, Millicent Garrett 1150
Gilson, Mary Barnett 1494
Henderson, Hazel 2853
Hewlett, Sylvia Ann 3664
Jain, Devaki 2856
Keyserling, Mary 2136
MacGuineas, Maya 4771
Malveaux, Julianne 4190
Marlin, Alice Tepper 3525
Narbona Ruiz, Cristina 4065
Nelson, Paula 3599
Orman, Suze 4131
Otero, María 3998

Porter, Sylvia 2207
Prins, Nomi 4867
Quinn, Jane Bryant 3156
Romer, Christina D. 4468
Rouse, Cecilia 4652
Salvatore, Christina 4801
Schapiro, Mary L. 4332
Somers, Helen 2824
Treerat, Nualnoi 4659
Wallace, Cath 4338
Ward, Barbara 2230
Whitman, Marina von Neumann 2957

FARMERS, RANCHERS, HORTICULTURISTS, AND AGRICULTURISTS

Blunt, Anne 1075
Bricker-Jenkins, Mary 3326
Colborn, Theodora "Theo" 2622
Dann, Carrie 2624
Dann, Mary 2450
Greene, Jennifer 3575
Hamer, Fannie Lou 2290
Jekyll, Gertrude 1116
Johnson, Lady Bird 2180
Kincaid, Jamaica 3906
Lopata, Jadwiga 4258
Luxborough, Henrietta Knight 547
Markham, Beryl 1951
McMullan, Margaret 4542
Nearing, Helen 2001
Nghatsane, Linda Olga 4425
Severn, Jill 3794
Strong, Harriet Williams Russell 1131
Swerda, Patricia 2277
Weed, Becky 4560
Williams, Carol 3876

HOUSEHOLDERS, OFFICE WORKERS, LABORERS, SLAVES, AND MISCELLANEOUS

Albert, Octavia V. 1196
Bai, Mukta 230
Benet, Mother 347
Bouza, Erica 3245
Bowes, Elizabeth 348
Boyle, Susan 4566.1
Bradford, Mistress 385
Brockovich, Erin 4522
Brown, Clara 875
Burlend, Rebecca Burton 837
Burr, Theodosia De Visme 620
Calvin, Idelette de Bure 346
Cazalla, Maria 330
Chandler, Mary 531
Clarkstone, Bessie 448
Collier, Mary 532
Copley, Susannah Farnum 706
Davys, Mary 517
De La Cruz, Jessie Lopez 2341
Edwards, Sarah Pierpont 567
Ehrlich, Emma 1769
Elliott, Anna 747
Fergus, Pamelia Dillin 2482
Foster, Doris Ann 3571
Gideon, Lillian 2088
Greene, Catharine 675

Gutmans, Sarel 437
Hagar 5
Hall, Mrs. Daniel 748
Harper, Martha Matilda 1223
Herchenfreda 119
Huerta, Dolores 2716
Jacobs, Harriet 949
Jessop, Violet 1665
Joceline, Elizabeth 371
Lacy, Mary 749
Lamb, Mary Ann 722
Larcom, Lucy 1008
Leapor, Mary 590
Ledbetter, Lilly 3093
Lightner, Candy 3671
Lord, Nancy 4119
Martin, Sarah 824
McCorvey, Norma 3769
Morgan, Elizabeth 3773
Morpurgo, Rahel 820
Nelson, Hannah 4826
Niedecker, Lorine 1978
Niemann, Linda 3681
Nisa 2773
Oakley, Annie 1260
Ormes, Cicely 324
Orr, Mary 4548
Pascalina, Madre 1802
Paston, Agnes 280
Paston, Margaret Mautby 262
Peabody, Elizabeth 666
Peace Pilgrim 2098
Pelham, Mary Singleton Copley 570
Pesotta, Rose 1829
Pfeiffer, Ida Laura 857
Rabi'a al-Adawiya 136
Renard, Cecile 764
Rizk, Sarah
Robinson, Harriet 1003
Rosenthal, Ida 1657
Royall, Anne Newport 745
Ryan, Sarah 594
Salavarrieta, Policarpa 826
Savitsky, Esther 1875
Shubrick, Mrs. Richard 752
Slave girl who was a soothsayer 92
Stanhope, Hester Lucy 773
Stewart, Elinore Pruitt 1483
Strozzi, Alessandra de' Machingi 251
Struven, Mildred Witte 1837
Stubbes, Katherine 377
Susman Ashkenazi, Rachel 364
Terry, Lucy 611
Thornton, Alice 454
Truth, Sojourner 860
Tubman, Harriet 978
Walker, Sarah Breedlove 1344
Wallbridge, Elizabeth 753
Wheatley, Phillis 677
Wilson, Martha 695
Wiseman, Jane 527
Woods, Rose Mary 2305
Xanthippe 59
Zhang, Lijia 4690

INVENTORS

Baker, Sara Josephine 1407

Cochran, Jacqueline 2043
Eglui, Ellen 1543
Gilbreth, Lillian Moller 1513
Graham, Bette Clair 2484
Handler, Ruth 2269
Jones, Amanda Theodosia 1066
Rosenthal, Ida 1657
Strong, Harriet Williams Russell 1131
Walker, C. J. 1343

MILITARY PERSONNEL, SOLDIERS, AND PATRIOTS

Abdellah, Faye Glenn 2335
Antin, Mary 1563
Artemisia 60
Augustín, María 800
Bai, Lakshmi 1016
Barry, James Stuart Miranda 830
Bratton, Martha 746
Cavell, Edith Louisa 1310
Deborah 27
Draper, Mary 582
Erauso, Catalina de 392
Frietschie, Barbara 729
Hopper, Grace Murray 2048
Howard, Michelle J. 4535.1
Joan of Arc 252
Labé, Louise 316
Lute, Jane Holl 4378
Margaret of Anjou 258
Martin, Elizabeth 648
Noor Inayat Khan 2225
Pryor, Sarah Agnes 1031
Richardson, Dorcas 636
Roland, Jeanne-Marie 678
Senesh, Hannah 2413
Sforza, Caterina 269
Slocumb, Mary 709
Taylor, Arie P. 2614
Telesilla 58
Washington, Mary 565
Winnemucca, Sarah 1133
Zenobia of Palmyra 100

OCCULTISTS, WITCHES, AND PROPHETS

Agreda, María de 415
Angela of Foligno 219–220
Audeley, Eleanor 436
Bertken, Sister 257
Boulbie, Judith 556
Bridget of Sweden 234
Catherine of Genoa 263
Catherine of Siena 237
Corey, Martha 538
Deborah 27
Goodman, Linda 2519
Gowdie, Isobel 494
Hildegarde von Bingen 179
Huldah 52
Jones, Amanda Theodosia 1066
Kempe, Margery 245
Krudener, Juliana 721
Leek, Sybil 2296
Mechtild von Magdeburg 215
Miriam 16
Myrta 96

Parry, Blanche 363
Shipton, Ursula 286
Stanhope, Hester Lucy 773
Truth, Sojourner 860
Valiente, Doreen 2442
Weil, Simone 2116
Woodhull, Victoria Claflin 1086

PHILANTHROPISTS AND HUMANITARIANS

Al-Abdullah, Queen of Jordan, Rania 4810
Alvarado, Linda G. 4083
Astor, Brooke 1946
Bedingfield, Natasha 4945
Betsch, MaVynee 2921
Bundchen, Gisele 4931
Ceschina, Yoko Nagae 2788
Colquhoun, Janet 786
Deneuve, Catherine 3402
Diller, Phyllis 2286
Dix, Dorothea 872
Dyson, Esther 4040
Fine, Sylvia 2197
Fletcher, Mary 627
Graham, Isabella 638
Jones, Mother 1028
Karan, Donna 3836
Kieko, Yamamuro 1439
Klagsbrun, Francine 2768
Lauder, Estée 2052
Lear, Moya Olson 2246
Lee, Ettie 1634
Lennox, Annie 4256
Low, Juliette 1257
Maria Theresa 579
Maxwell, Darcy 640
McCain, Cindy 4260
Mercer, Margaret 825
More, Hannah 649
Pickford, Mary 1781
Ricker, Marilla 1096
Roosevelt, Eleanor 1618
Rosenthal, Ida 1657
Russell, Rosalind 2168
Sams, Jamie 4070
Sendzimir, Venda 4140
Sewall, Harriet 959
Shaarawi, Huda 1536
Shakira 4919
Smith, Sophia 851
Sofía of Spain, Queen 3106
Stronach, Belinda 4736
Strong, Harriet Williams Russell 1131
Walker, C.J. 1343
Walker, Sarah Breedlove 1344
Williamson, Marianne 4151
Wright, Frances 850
York, Eva Rose 1240

RELIGIOUS FIGURES, LEADERS, AND THEOLOGIANS

Abigail 34
Abutsu 227
Agnes the Martyr 295
Agreda, María de 415

Alais 202
Alcoforado, Mariana 471
Ambapali 54
Ambrose, Mary 1737
Angela of Foligno 219–220
Anna 43
Armstrong, Karen 3474
Askew, Anne 313
Audeley, Eleanor 436
Ava, Frau 185
Bailey, Urania Locke 964
Baldwin, Monica 1762
Barclay, Aviel 4779
Barnhouse, Ruth Tiffany 2446
Bathurst, Elizabeth 491
Baudonivia 117
Beatrijs of Nazareth 204
Bernadette 1121
Berners, Juliana 266
Bertegund 115
Bertell, Rosalie 2651
Bertken, Sister 257
Besant, Annie Wood 1148
Bingham, Sally 3243
Blackwell, Antoinette Brown 998
Blavatsky, Elena Petrovna 1034
Boulbie, Judith 556
Brenner, Antonia 2543
Bridget of Sweden 234
Brigid of Kildare 110
Brown, Olympia 1062
Cabrini, Frances Xavier 1171
Caesaria 118
Cardin, Nina Beth 4166
Carpio de San Feliz, Marcela de 420
Castillo y Guevara, Francisca Josefa
    del 537
Catherine of Bologna 253
Catherine of Genoa 263
Catherine of Siena 237
Céu, Violante do 417
Chittister, OSB, Joan 2969
Clare of Assisi 201
Clitherow, Margaret 358
Cole-Whittaker, Terry 3134
Combs, Valda Jean 4442
Crosby, Sarah 605
Cruz, Juana Inés de la 487
Daly, Mary 2623
Delilah 24
Devi, Indra 1884
Dyer, Mary 429
Eddy, Mary Baker 982
Edna 44
Edwards, Sarah Pierpont 567
Egburg 137
Egeria 108
Eilberg, Amy 4241
Elisabeth 78
Elizabeth of Thuringia 214
Ellis, Sarah 918
Elwell, Sue Levi 3824
Enheduanna 4
Eve 1
Falk, Marcia 3650
Ferris, Helene 3028
Fiedler, Maureen 3334
Fox, Margaret Askew Fell 432–433

Geller, Laura 3969
Gertrude the Great 221
Gottlieb, Lynn 3899
Gray, Elizabeth Dodson 2660
Greenberg, Julie 4721
Gregoria, Francisca 490
Grossman, Susan C. 4302
Grumbach, Argula von 288
Guevara, Marina de 303
Guyon, Jeanne-Marie de la Motte
    482
Halifax, Joan 3341
Hannah 30
Harris, Barbara Clementine 2712
Hastings, Selina 562
Hebblethwaite, Margaret 4250.1
Héloise 178
Heyward, Carter 3579
Hildegarde von Bingen 179
Hroswitha of Gandersheim 158
Huneberc of Heidenheim 142
Hutchinson, Anne 399
Inanna 6
Isasi-Diaz, Ada Maria 3424
Isaure, Clemence 270
Iselda 208
Isis 3
Jackson, Rebecca Cox 848
Jael 28
Jephthah the Gileadite, Daughter
    of 21
Jerusalem [mother of the dead
    child], Prostitute of 36
Jerusalem [mother of the living
    child], Prostitute of 37
Joan of Arc 252
Job, Wife of 41
Judson, Ann Hasseltine 811
Juliana of Norwich 236
Kassiane 149
Kempe, Margery 245
Kent, Corita 2318
Kieko, Yamamuro 1439
Kleinbaum, Sharon 4490
Krudener, Juliana 721
Kuhlman, Kathryn 2067
Lalleswari 235
Leah 9
Leddy, Mary Jo 3669
Lee, Ann 622
Leek, Sybil 2296
Levy, Naomi 4646
Lewes, Joyce 360
Li Yeh 147
Liadan 129
Lichtenstein, Tehilla 1779
Litman, Jane 3206
Lot's daughter (the elder) 10
Mahadeviyakka 211
Manoah, Wife of 25
Marcelle, Countess de 339
Marchocka, Anna Maria 418
Maribel, Mother 1667
Mary Magdalene 81
Mary, Virgin 79
Mattern, Evelyn 3281
Maximilla 112

Maxwell, Darcy 640
McPherson, Aimee Semple 1713
Mechtild von Magdeburg 215
Mettika 49
Milgrom, Shira 4062
Mirabai 293
Montagu, Lily 1416
Morrissey, Mary Mannin 3918
Mott, Lucretia 839
Murray, Pauli 2139
Mutta 50
Naomi 22
Nicholson, Zoe Ann 3852
Nirmala, Sister 2909
Nirmala Devi, Shri Mataji 2467
Ormes, Cicely 324
Pankhurst, Christabel 1553
Pascalina, Madre 1802
Perpetua, Vivia 99
Phinehas, Wife of 31
Polyxena 84
Pounds, Jessie Brown 1275
Prejean, Helen 3155
Prest, Wife of 361
Priesand, Sally 3787
Pulcheria, Aelia 109
Pulci, Antonia 265
Qurrat al-'Ayn 1195
Rabi'a al-Adawiya 136
Rachel (1) 13
Radegunda 114
Rebekah 11
Renée de France 304
Rogers, Hester Ann 687
Roulet, Elaine 2738
Royden, Maude 1498
Ruether, Rosemary Radford 3004
Ruth 23
Ryan, Sarah 594
Salavarrieta, Policarpa 826
Samaritan Woman 83
Samson, First wife of 26
Sarah 8
Sarah 45
Sasso, Sandy Eisenberg 3790
Schneiders, Sandra Marie 3005
Seton, Elizabeth 765
Seven Brothers, Mother of the 70
Shikishi Naishinno 192
Sibyl, the Jewish 68
Spalding, Catherine 842
Spencer, Anna Garlin 1185
Spider Woman 2
Starbuck, Mary Coffyn 478
Starhawk 4072
Stein, Edith 1735
Sumangalamata 51
Sun Bu-er 184
Susanna 53
Táhirih, Fátimih Baragháni 925
Tarabotti, Arcangela 419
Teish, Luisah 3871
Tekoa, Woman of 39
Teresa [of Calcutta] 2142
Teresa of Ávila 308
Theano 63
Thérèse de Lisieux 1422
Trapnel, Anna 444

Truth, Sojourner 860
Tuite, Marjorie 2441
Vanzant, Iyanla 4216
Waddles, Charleszetta 2193
Wallbridge, Elizabeth 753
Wang Wei 553
Ward, Mary 393
Watkins, Sharon E. 4282
Webb, Mary 1576
Weil, Simone 2116
Weinberg, Sheila Pelz 3707
Wentworth, Anne 455
Wesley, Susanna 512
West, Frances 2781
Wheeler, Kate 4078
Wilkinson, Jemima 674
Williams, E. Faye 3312
Young, Elizabeth 352
Yü Hsüan-chi 152
Zelophehad, Five Daughters of,
    Mahlah, Noah, Hoglah,
    Milcah and Tirzah 18
Zipporah 19

Royalty and Courtiers

Agrippina the Younger 80
Al-Abdullah, Rania, Queen of
    Jordan 4810
Albret, Jeanne d' 327
Aldrude 196
Ankhesenpaton 15
Anna Maria of Braunschweig 337
Anne of Austria 414
Anne of England 504 Artemisia 60
Artois, Mahuat d' 228
Bai, Lakshmi 1016
Basine 111
Bathsheba 33
Beatrix, Queen of the Netherlands
    3072
Boadicea 86
Boleyn, Anne 300
Bonaparte, Marie Letitia 655
Borgia, Lucrezia 281
Bourbon, Catherine de 362
Bryan, Margaret 329
Caroline Matilda 667
Catherine II of Russia 604
Catherine of Aragon 283
Cenci, Beatrice 381
Châtelet, Emilie du 557–558
Christina of Sweden 450
Clinton, Elizabeth 379
Compton, Elizabeth 397
Corday, Charlotte 736
Daisy, Princess of Pless 1411
Diana, Princess of Wales 4568
Eleanor of Aquitaine 183
Elisabeth of Brandenburg 284
Elisabeth of Braunschweig 302
Elizabeth 1898
Elizabeth, Caroline Amelia 737
Elizabeth, Helene Marie Phillipine
    720
Elizabeth I of England 334
Elizabeth II of England 2549

Elizabeth of Thuringia 214
Elizabeth of York 271
Este, Anne d' 333
Este, Beatrice d' 278
Este, Isabella d' 276
Esther 56
Godolphin, Margaret 489
Gormley 169
Grey, Elizabeth Woodville 260
Grey, Jane 336
Grey, Mary 343
Grumbach, Argula von 288
Guercheville, Antoinette de Pons 374
Gulbadan Begam bint Babur
    Badshah 320
Han Ts'ui-p'in 153
Harvey, Alice 386
Hathshepsut 14
Hausset, Madame du 661
Henrietta Maria 424
Iratsume, Kasa no 145
Iratsume, Otomo no Sakano-e no 128
Isabella I 264 Isis 3
Iwa no Hime 106
Izumi Shikibu 165
Jahan, Nur 382
Jefimija 238–239
Jezebel 40
Josephine 717
Juliana 2111

Kamamalu 854
Kazu-no-Michi 1144
Killigrew, Anne 496
Knesebeck, Eleonora von dem 525
Knollys, Lettice 338
Koka, Stewardess of the Empress 210
Lambrun, Margaret 387
Liliuokalani, Lydia Kamekeha
    1083
López de Córdoba, Leonor 243
Lytton, Constance 1365
Makhfi 470
Margaret of Anjou 258
Margaret of Austria 282
Margaret of Nassau 242
Margrethe II 3208
Marguerite of Valois 356
Maria of Hungary and Bohemia
    298
Maria Theresa 579
Maria, Grand Duchess of Russia
    1712
Marie de France 193
Marie-Antoinette 682
Mary I of England 309
Mary II of England 498
Mary of France 290
Mary of Scots 341
Mary, Queen Consort of Great
    Britain 1338

Mathilde 972
Matilda 180
Maxwell, Darcy 640
Medici, Catherine de' 310
Michal 32
Michiel, Renier Giustina 683
Mirabai 293
Monk, Mary 577
Nagako, Kuni 1976
Nijo, The Empress of 151
Noor Al-Hussein 4066
Nukada 123
Oku 124
Orléans, Ann-Marie-Louise d' 452
Orsini, Isabella de' Medici 342
Parr, Catherine 305
Parry, Blanche 363
Penelope 20
Pharaoh's daughter 17
Pocahontas 404
Pompeia Plotina 93
Poppaea Sabina 85
Porcia 77
Pulcheria, Aelia 109
Radegunda 114
Raleigh, Elizabeth 370
Rich, Penelope Devereaux 366
Rieux, Renée de Chateauneuf
    351
Russell, Elizabeth Hoby 326

Salome 82
Satrapi, Marjane 4802
Scindia, Yashodhara Raje 4271
Semiramis 42
Sheba, Queen of 38
Shikibu, Murasaki 166
Shikishi Naishinno 192
Shonagon, Sei 163
Silvia of Sweden, Queen 3456
Sofía of Spain, Queen 3106
Sophia Dorothea of Celle 510
Sugawara no Takasue no musume
    181
Suo 174
Tamar 35
Theodora 113
Toshiko, Kishida 1300
Tse-t'ien Wu 121
Tyrwhit, Elizabeth 322
Ukon, Lady 154
Vernon, Elizabeth 378
Victoria 960
Vidya 133
Visconti, Valentine 247
Wallada al-Mustakfi 172
Walsingham, Frances 373
Wheathill, Ann 388
Willoughby, Catherine 312
Yamatohime 127
Zenobia of Palmyra 100

Ethnicity and Nationality Index

Contributors have been arranged according to the nation of their *birth,* rather than the nation of their residence and/or death: those citations may be found in the Biographical Index. Additionally, to serve multicultural studies programs, women of color have been arranged, whenever possible, according to their race and/or ethnic background within the context of their nation of birth.

Ancient lands and nations no longer extant have been annotated with the present-day nations of their geographic origins. Within appropriate categories, contributors are listed alphabetically.

AFGHAN
Ata, Shahla 4714.1
Barakzai, Shukria 4854.1
Fana, Frozan
Gauhari, Farooka 3745
Gulbadan Begam bint Babur
    Badshah 320
Joya, Malalai 4927
Kaker, Malalai 4822
Majid, Friba 4981
Rawi, Mahboba 4776
Samar, Sima 4430
Sarabi, Habiba 4392

ALBANIAN
Teresa [of Calcutta] 2142

ALGERIAN
Bonal, Denise 2396
Gallaire-Bourega, Fatima 3500
Ghezali, Salima 4450

AMERICAN (U.S.A.)
Abbot, Sidney 3015
Abbott, Berenice 1859
Abbott, Patsy 2690
Abbott, Shirley 2875
Abbott, Wenonah Stevens 1307
Abdellah, Faye Glenn 2335
Abrams, Linsey 4018
Abramson, Jill 4222
Abramson, Lisabeth Hughes 4343
Aburdene, Patricia 3709
Abzug, Bella 2360
Ace, Jane 2009

Acker, Kathy 3710
Ackerman, Diane 3808
Ackerman, Jennifer 4476
Adams, Abigail 646
Adams, Carol J. 4018.1
Adams, Grace 1893
Adams, Léonie 1880
Adams, Maude 1396
Addams, Jane 1251
Addonzio, Kim 4223
Adelman, Penina V. 4155
Adler, Freda 2876
Adler, Margot 3238
Adler, Rachel 3387
Ai 3711
Aiken, Joyce 2750
Akalaitis, JoAnne 3016
Akers, Elizabeth Chase 1043
Akins, Zoö 1646
Akre, Jane 4562
Alam, Glynn Marsh 3389
Albelda, Randy 4288
Albright, Madeleine 2959
Alcosser, Sandra 3472
Alcott, Louisa May 1044
Alden, Ada 1215
Alden, Paulette Bates 3712
Alderman, Ellen 4397
Aldis, Mary Reynolds 1397
Alexander 997
Alexander, Elizabeth 4601
Alexander, Jane 3117
Alexander, Shana 2540
Alger, Abby Langdon 1170
Allen, Candace 4224

Allen, Dede 2506
Allen, Florence Ellinwood 1603
Allen, Mary Wood 1099
Allerton, Ellen Palmer 1060
Allison, Dorothy E. 3880
Allred, Gloria 3240
Allwine, Janine Maria 4225
Allyn, Jeri 4082
Allyson, Karrin 4602
Alsop, Marin 4344
Alston, Theodosia Burr 793
Alta 3319
Alther, Lisa Reed 3473
Alvarado, Linda G. 4083
Ambrose, Mary 1737
American, Sadie 1281
Anastasi, Anne 2076
Anderson, Catherine 3713
Anderson, Edith 4515
Anderson, Laurie 3714
Anderson, Margaret 1647
Anderson, Ruth Ann 3553
Andrews, Lori B. 4156
Andrews, Mary Kay 4226
Andrus, Ethel Percy 1604
Angier, Natalie 4438
Aniston, Jennifer 4778
Annan, Annie Rankin 1157
Anthony, Katharine 1487
Anthony, Susan B. 963
Antler, Joyce 3320
Antrim, Minna 1262
Applebaum, Anne 4665
Applegate, Debby 4763
Arbus, Diane 2444

Arensberg, Ann 3017
Armantrout, Rae 3716
Armstrong, Cora Harvey 3018
Arnold, Margaret Shippen 704
Arnold, Susan E. 4227
Arnow, Harriette 2078
Arrien, Angeles 2920
Arzner, Dorothy 1895
Ascher, Barbara Lazear 3718
Ash, Mary Kay 2306
Ashmun, Margaret Eliza 1452
Askew, Rilla 4020
Astor, Brooke 1946
Astor, Madeline Talmage 1760
Astor, Mary 2037
Astor, Nancy 1519
Atherton, Gertrude 1216
Atkinson, Ti-Grace 3070
Aubry, Erin J. 4812
Auel, Jean M. 2960
Austin, Mary Hunter 1346
Avary, Myrta Lockett 1217
Avery, Byllye Y. 3019
Avery-Clark, Constance 4228
Axline, Virginia Mae 2149
Ayer, Harriet Hubbard 1163
Azara, Nancy 3120
Babbitt, Natalie 2784
Babcock, Barbara Allen 3071
Babitz, Eve 3391
Bacall, Lauren 2476
Bache, Sarah Franklin 647
Bachman, Moira 3171
Bacon, Josephine Dodge 1468
Bacon, Martha 2280

Baez, Joan 3241
Bailey, Pearl 2307
Bailey, Urania Locke 964
Bair, Sheila C. 4229
Baizley, Doris 3555
Baker, Dorothy 2060
Baker, Dorothy Gillam 2038
Baker, Ella J. 1962
Baker, Josephine 2039
Baker, Sara Josephine 1407
Bakke, Kit 3628
Balch, Emily Greene 1333
Baldwin, Christina 3629
Baldwin, Faith 1761
Ball, Lucille 2150
Ballard, Bettina 1963
Bancroft, Anne 2786
Bang, Mary Jo 3630
Bank, Melissa 4518
Bankhead, Tallulah 1964
Bannerman, Helen 1282
Banning, Margaret Culkin 1721
Bara, Theda 1623
Barber, Janette 4158
Bardwick, Judith M. 2832
Barker, Elsa 1356
Barley, Mary 3632
Barnard, Jessie 1965
Barnebey, Faith 2880
Barnes, Djuna 1739
Barnes, Margaret Ayer 1648
Barnes, Melody C. 4668
Barney, Natalie Clifford 1470
Barnhouse, Ruth Tiffany 2446
Barolini, Helen 2509
Barr, Nevada 4084
Barr, Roseanne 4085
Barrett, Andrea 4692
Barrett, Rona 2961
Barrow, Lisa 4669
Barrows, Sydney Biddle 4086
Barry, Kathleen 3123
Barry, Lynda 4346
Barry, Rebecca 4764
Barrymore, Ethel 1520
Barth, Belle 2151
Barton, Clara 980
Barton, Emily 4780
Basinger, Jeanine 2962
Bass, Ellen 3720
Bassoff, Evelyn S. 3477
Bates, Katherine Lee 1241
Bateson, Mary Catherine 3124
Battelle, Phyllis 2417
Bayes, Nora 1540
Beal, Frances M. 3173
Beals, Jessie Tarbox 1370
Beard, Mary Ritter 1471
Beard, Miriam 1926
Bechdel, Alison 4519
Beck, Evelyn Torton 2833
Becker, Robin 4023
Beecher, Catharine Esther 865
Beers, Ethel Lynn 1011
Begley, Sharon 4348
Belcher, Jennifer M. 3556
Belenky, Mary Field 2834
Bell, Christine 4024

Bell, Helen Olcott 1023
Bellamy, Carol 3324
Bellows, Laurel Gordon 3809
Belmont, Eleanor Robson 1505
Bender, Marilyn 2511
Bender, Sheila 3810
Benedict, Agnes E. 1694
Benedict, Ruth 1659
Benes, Francine M. 3557
Benét, Laura 1605
Bengis, Ingrid 3478
Benjamin, Medea 4087
Bennis, Phyllis 4025
Benston, Margaret Lowe 3020
Benton, Suzanne 4159
Berenson, Mary 1302
Berg, Elizabeth 3811
Berg, Gertrude 1882
Bergen, Candice 3635
Berkley, Rochelle "Shelley" 4026
Berman, Ellen 3636
Bern, Sandra Lipsitz 3479
Bernal, Esmeralda 3886
Bernard, Jessie Shirley 1967
Berne, Suzanne 4565
Bernhard, Sandra 4289
Bernikow, Louise 3174
Berresford, Susan V. 3393
Berriault, Gina 2542
Berry, Dawn Bradley 4399
Bethune, Mary McLeod 1453
Betsch, MaVynee 2921
Bialosky, Jill 4603
Bianchi, Martha Dickinson 1323
Biddle, Flora Miller 3722
Biden, Jill 4027
Billings, Victoria 3558
Bilmes, Linda J. 4521
Bingham, Anne Willing 719
Bingham, Sallie 3021
Bingham, Sally 3243
Birch, Alison Wyrley 2419
Bird, Caroline 2237
Bird, Rose 2963
Birkeland, Janis Lynn 3559
Bishop, Elizabeth 2153
Bishop, Wendy Sue 4161
Black, Barbara Aronstein 2836
Black, Shirley Temple 2619
Black, Sophie Cabot 4440
Blackwell, Antoinette Brown 998
Blackwell, Elizabeth 981
Blackwell, Emily 1005
Blais, Madeleine 3723
Blake, Lillie Devereux 1049
Blakely, Mary Kay 3813
Blee, Kathleen M. 4162
Bleecker, Ann Eliza 670
Blodgett, Katharine "Katie" Burr 1860
Bloom, Amy 4163
Bloomer, Amelia Jenks 944
Blume, Judy 3074
Boesing, Martha Gross 2964
Bogan, Louise 1843
Boggs, Lindy 2262
Bolen, Jean Shinoda 2965
Bolton, Sarah Knowles 1101

Bombeck, Erma 2586
Bond, Carrie Jacobs 1283
Bond, Victoria 3887
Bonds, Julia 4088
Bonney, Barbara 4349
Bono, Mary 4566
Boosler, Elayne 4089
Borg, Anita 3888
Borysenko, Joan Z. 3638
Botta, Anne 926
Botume, Elizabeth 1371
Boucher, Sandy 2966
Boudrot, Denise M. 4090
Bourke-White, Margaret 2041
Bovasso, Julie Anne 2693
Bowditch, Katherine 1791
Bowen, 'Asta 4290
Bowen, Catherine Drinker 1844
Bowen, Louise de Koven 1242
Bower, B. M. 1385
Bowles, Gloria 4350
Bowman, Meg 2653
Boxer, Barbara 3176
Boxer, Sarah 4781
Boyle, Kay 1947
Boyle, Sarah 917
Bracken, Peg 2309
Brackett, Anna C. 1070
Bradford, Cornelia 542
Bradley, Marion Zimmer 2694
Bradley, Mary 1061
Bradwell, Myra R. 1035
Brady, Rose 4351
Braid, Bernice 2837
Brainard, Mary Gardiner 1252
Branch, Anna Hempstead 1454
Branch, Mary 1091
Bratton, Martha 746
Braude, Ann Deborah 4291
Braverman, Kate 3954
Breckinridge, Mary 1565
Breckinridge, Sophonisba Preston 1324
Breitman, Barbara E. 3955
Brenner, Antonia 2543
Breslin, Rosemary 4401
Breuer, Bessie 1763
Brewster, Martha 629
Brice, Fanny 1722
Brickell, Edie 4716
Bricker-Jenkins, Mary 3326
Bridges, Madeline 1123
Bridgford, Kim Suzanne 4477
Briggs, Dorothy Corkille 2477
Bright, Susannah "Susie" 4441
Brightman, Carol 3126
Brill, Alida 3888.1
Brine, Mary Dow 933
Brinker, Ruth 2420
Brock-Broido, Lucie 4352
Brockovich, Erin 4522
Brodie, Fawn M. 2238
Brodine, Karen 3726
Bronaugh, Anne 1472
Broner, E.M. 2695
Brooks, Louise 2042
Brooks, Maria 845
Brothers, Joyce 2587

Brotherton, Alice Williams 1159
Brown, Abbie Farwell 1455
Brown, Alice 1218
Brown, Barbara B. 2621
Brown, Charlotte 1577
Brown, Frances 935
Brown, Helen Gurley 2421
Brown, Kathleen 3639
Brown, Lisa 4523
Brown, Mary Elizabeth 1108
Brown, Maxine 3127
Brown, Olympia 1062
Brown, Ophelia Guyon 1541
Brown, Rachel Fuller 1861
Brown, Rita Mae 3481
Brown, Rosellen 3128
Brown, Tabitha Moffatt 779
Brown, Trisha 2967
Browner, Carol M. 4293
Brownmiller, Susan 2922
Brubaker, Pamela K. 3640
Brumberg, Joan Jacobs 3482
Bryan, Mary E. 1081
Bryant, Anita Jane 3177
Buck, Pearl S. 1741
Buell, Mary E. 1386
Bunch, Charlotte 3483
Bunting, Mary Ingraham 2121
Burk, Martha Gertrude 3247
Burke, Billie 1624
Burke, Martha Jane 1190
Burke, Phyllis 4030
Burkett, Elinor 3394
Burks, Maria 4233
Burlingame, Lettie 1243
Burnett, Carol 2838
Burnett, Frances 1164
Burr, Amelia 1507
Burroughs, Nannie Helen 1592
Bush, Barbara 2514
Bush, Laura 3641
Butts, Cassandra Quin 4693
Butts, Mary Frances 1071
Byron, Beverly Butcher 2787
Cabrini, Frances Xavier 1171
Cadden, Vivian 2264
Cahill, Susan 3178
Caine, Lynn 2588
Calderone, Mary Steichen 1989
Caldwell, Sarah 2478
Calisher, Hortense 2154
Camp, Tracy 4671
Canaan, Andrea R. 3729
Cannon, Annie Jump 1293
Cantwell, Mary 2698
Capek, Mary Ellen S. 4032
Capps, Lois 3076
Carabillo, Toni 2544
Caraway, Hattie Wyatt 1508
Cardin, Nina Beth 4166
Carey, Mariah 4813
Carleton, Emma 1172
Carlisle, Andrea 3484
Carnahan, Jean 2839
Carney, Julia A. 986
Carpenter, Liz 2363
Carr, Cynthia 4478
Carson, Norma 3181

Carson, Rachel 2061
Carter, Lillian 1862
Carter, Deana 4717
Carter, Rosalyn Smith 2589
Carter, Sandy 4637
Cary, Alice 966
Cary, Phoebe 992
Caschetta, Mary Beth 4718
Case, Elizabeth York 1092
Case, Sue-Ellen 3328
Casey, Margaret 4353
Cash, Roseanne 4294
Cassatt, Mary 1126
Castillo, Ana 4354
Castillo, Aurora 2215
Castle, Victoria 3889
Cather, Katherine Dunlap 1489
Cather, Willa 1408
Catherwood, Mary 1149
Catt, Carrie Chapman 1244
Caulkins, Frances Manwaring 846
Ceballos, Jacqui Michot 2516
Chamberlin, Judi 3486
Chambers, Jane 3023
Chandler, Loma 2010
Chang, Iris 4765
Chang, Leslie T. 4782
Chang, Tina 4783
Chapman, Maria Weston 893
Charkowski, Amy O. 4841
Chase, Ilka 2011
Chase, Mary 2062
Chase-Riboud, Barbara 3132
Chast, Roz 4235
Chayes, Sarah 4604
Cheever, Susan 3396
Chehak, Susan Taylor 4034
Cheney, Gertrude Louise 2310
Cheney, Lynne Ann 3248
Cher 3643
Chernin, Kim 3183
Chesler, Phyllis 3184
Chesnut, Mary Bokin 987
Chess, Stella 2216
Chicago, Judy 3133
Child, Julia 2174
Child, Lydia Maria 870
Childress, Alice 2364
Childs, E. Kitch 3024
Chittick, Elizabeth L. 2081
Chittister, OSB, Joan 2969
Chodorow, Nancy 3487
Chona, Marie 1134
Chopin, Kate 1184
Christian, Meg 3644
Chua, Amy 4605
Churchill, Jennie Jerome 1201
Chute, Carolyn 3730
Cinciotta, Linda Ann 3398
Claflin, Tennessee 1135
Claiborne, Liz 2655
Clampitt, Amy Kathleen 2365
Clancy, Carolyn 4238
Clappe, Louise Amelia 954
Clarenbach, Kathryn 2366
Clark, C. Hope 4357
Clark, Eleanor 2195
Clark, Eugenie 2423

Clark, Marcia 4169
Clarke, Edith 1594
Clausen, Jan 3959–3960
Clayton, Eva M. 2883
Cleghorn, Sarah Norcliffe 1473
Clemmer, Mary 1087
Cleyre, Voltairine de 1325
Clinchy, Blythe M. 2700
Clingerman, Mildred McElroy 2311
Clinton, Catherine 4093
Clinton, Hillary Rodham 3731
Cloud, Darrah 4296
Clyde, Mary 4962
Coates, Florence Earle 1173
Coates, Grace Stone 1566
Coatsworth, Elizabeth 1766
Cobb, Geraldyn M. 2752
Coblentz, Catherine Cate 1845
Cochran, Jacqueline 2043
Cocroft, Susan 1284
Coffee, Lenore J. 1820
Coffey, Susanna J. 4358
Coffin, Judith G. 4095
Cohan, Alice 4035
Cohen, Amy 3329
Cohen, Charlotte Bonny 3400
Cohen, Deborah S. 3820
Cohen, Leah Hager 4744
Cohen, Mary M. 1202
Cohen, Sherry Suib 2885
Colborn, Theodora "Theo" 2622
Cole, Johnnetta B. 2971
Cole, Mary 816
Coleman, Deborah A. 4170
Cole-Whittaker, Terry 3134
Colins, Janet 2283
Collins, Eileen 4359
Collins, Emily 946
Collins, Judy 3135
Collins, Marva Nettles 2972
Colvin, Claudette 3185
Colwin, Laurie 3488
Combs, Valda Jean 4442
Comden, Betty 2339
Comini, Alessandra 3079
Commire, Anne 3186
Conant, Isabel La Howe 1426
Cone, Helen Gray 1245
Cones, Nancy Ford 1357
Conklin, Beth Ann 4239
Conkling, Grace H. 1509
Conkling, Hilda 2123
Connelly, Joan Breton 4240
Conrad, Beatrice 2590
Cook, Blanche Weisen 3249
Cooke, Rose Terry 1012
Cool, Lisa Collier 4096
Coolbrith, Ina 1102
Coolidge, Grace Goodhue 1523
Coolidge, Susan 1136
Coombs, Mary 3489
Coontz, Stephanie 3490
Cooper, Jane 2481
Copley, Susannah Farnum 706
Corbin, Alice 1567
Corey, Shirley Trusty 2923
Cotton, Elizabeth 1767
Coulter, Ann 4567

Couric, Katie 4402
Covington, Vicki 4097
Cowan, Alison Leigh 4638
Cox, Ana Marie 4856
Craighead, Meinrad 2973
Craigie, Pearl 1334
Craigin, Elisabeth 2701
Cram, Mildred 1695
Crane, Nathalia 2196
Crapsey, Adelaide 1510
Craven, Margaret 1929
Creech, Sharon 3562
Crist, Judith 2424
Crittenden, Ann 3027
Croce, Arlene 2887
Crocker, Hannah Mather 673
Cromwell, Gladys 1626
Cronan, Sheila 3646
Crothers, Rachel 1511
Crouse, Mary Elizabeth 1410
Crowe, Frances 2340
Crowell, Grace Noll 1490
Crowley, Candy 3821.1
Cryer, Gretchen 2924
Cumming, Patricia 2791
Cunningham, Agnes "Sis" 2107
Cunningham, Imogen 1595
Cuomo, Chris J. 4674
Curtis, Jamie Lee 4443
Curtis, Rebecca 4883
Curtiss, Ursula Reilly 2448
Cushman, Charlotte Saunders 936
d'Adesky, Anne-Christine 4479
Dall, Caroline 984
Daly, Mary 2623
Danowitz, Jane 3890
Dargan, Olive 1358
Daughtrey, Martha Craig 3331
Daum, Meghan 4814
Davenport, Doris 3891
Davidson, Janine 4745
Davidson, Laura Lee 1372
Davidson, Lucretia Maria 903
Davidson, Margaret 988
Davidson, Sara 3732
Davis, Adelle 1992
Davis, Bette 2082
Davis, Dorothy Salisbury 2265
Davis, Elizabeth Gould 2124
Davis, Laura 4361
Davis, Lydia 3733
Davis, Olena Kalytiak 4905
Davis, Rebecca Harding 1037
Davis-Floyd, Robbie 4037
Day, Dorothy 1846
Day, Lillian 1768
de Baca, Fabiola Cabeza 1806–1807
De La Cruz, Jessie Lopez 2341
de Lavallade, Carmen 2754
de Matteo, Donna 3252
de Mille, Agnes 2012
Decter, Midge 2592
Deen, Paula 3734
DeGeneres, Ellen 4445
Delmar, Viña 2013
Delmhorst, Kris 4906
Deming, Alison Hawthorne 3647
Deming, Barbara 2285

Denham, Alice 2841
Dennie, Abigail Colman 576
Derricotte, Toi 3254
Deutsch, Babette 1808
DeWit, Antoinette 2451
Dey, Judy Goldberg 4977
Di Prima, Diane 2890
Diamant, Anita 4038
Diaz, Cameron 4857
Dicciani, Nance K. 3822
Dickinson, Emily 1024
Didion, Joan 2925
Didriksen Zaharias, "Babe" 2218
DiFranco, Ani 4816
Dillard, Annie 3563
Diller, Phyllis 2286
Dinnerstein, Dorothy 2452
DiPerna, Diane 4963
DiPerna, Paula 3892
Dix, Dorothea 872
Dix, Dorothy 1265
Dixon, Marlene 2974
Dodge, Mabel 1524
Dodge, Mary Mapes 1039
Dodson, Lisa 4099
Dolan, Jill 4403
Dole, Elizabeth Hanford 2975
Dolliver, Clara G. 1429
Dolson, Hildegarde 2083
Domini, Amy 4100
Donnelly, Liza 4297
Doolittle, Hilda 1650
Doress-Worters, Paula B. 3082
Dorr, Julia 999
Doten, Elizabeth "Lizzie" 1013
Doubiago, Sharon 3648
Douglas, Helen Gahagan 1897
Douvan, Elizabeth "Libby" 2545
Dow, Dorothy 1968
Dowd, Maureen 4102
Dowd, Nancy E. 3893
Dowling, Colette 3083
Draper, Mary 582
Dreifus, Claudia 3495
Drescher, Fran 4404
Dresselhaus, Mildred Spiewak 2702
Drexler, Rosalyn 2546
Drinker, Sophie Hutchinson 1678
Driscoll, Louise 1456
DuBois, Ellen Carol 3737
Dudar, Helen 2084
Duehring, Cindy 4608
Dugaw, Dianne 3823
Dukakis, Olympia 2755
Duke, "Patty" 3649
Dunbar, Roxanne 3140
Dunbar-Ortiz, Roxanne 3084
Duncan, Isadora 1512
Dungy, Camille T. 4858
Dunlop, Becky Norton 4039
Dunn, Jennifer 3256
Dunn, Katherine "Karen" 3565
Dwight, Mary Ann 895
Dworkin, Andrea 3738
Dworkin, Susan 4817
Earhart, Amelia 1847
Earle, Sylvia A. 2926

Earp, Josephine "Josie" Sarah "Sadie" 1266
Eastman, Crystal 1568
Eckenstein, Lina 1220
Eddy, Mary Baker 982
Edelstein, Jean 2593
Ederle, Gertrude 2045
Edson, Margaret 4571
Edwards, Anne 2594
Edwards, Betty 2547
Edwards, Marie 2548
Edwards, Sarah Pierpont 567
Egan, Jennifer 4609
Ehrenreich, Barbara 3257
Ehrlich, Emma 1769
Eilberg, Amy 4241
Eisenhower, Mamie 1824
Elion, Gertrude B. 2312
Elkins, Caroline 4786
Ellerbee, Linda 3496
Elliott, Anna 747
Elliott, Maxine 1388
Ellison, Katherine 4405
Ellman, Lucy 4362
Elmendorf, Mary J. 2369
Elwell, Sue Levi 3824
Emanual, Lynn 3895
Embree, Alice 3566
Emerson, Claudia 4406
Emerson, Jo Ann 3963
Emerson, Mary Moody 763
Emshwiller, Carol 2397
English, Deirdre 3825
Ensler, Eve 4174
Ephron, Delia 3498
Ephron, Nora 3258
Epstein, Cynthia Fuchs 2844
Erbe, Bonnie 4174.1
Erde, Betty Skelton 2550
Espinosa, María 3142
Essbaum, Jill Alexander 4844
Estés, Clarissa Pinkola 3567
Etcoff, Nancy L. 4299
Etheridge, Melissa 4573
Ettore, Barbara 4041
Eugene-Richard, Margie 3332
Evans, Augusta 1063
Evans, Mari 2453
Evert Lloyd, Chris 4243
Fadiman, Anne 4175
Fairley, Darlene 3404
Fairstein, Linda A. 3741
Falk, Marcia 3650
Faller, Heather Roote 4447
Faludi, Susan 4481
Farabough, Laura 4407
Faraday, Ann 2927
Farenthold, Sissy 2551
Farmer, Fannie 1221
Farnham, Eliza 928
Fasig, Lisa Biank 4612
Faugéres, Margaretta Van Wyck 755
Fauset, Crystal Bird 1792
Fausto-Sterling, Anne 3499
Feinberg, Leslie 3896
Feinstein, Dianne 2848
Feld, Merle 3742
Feldt, Gloria 3333

Felton, Rebecca Latimer 1064
Fenwick, Millicent 2127
Ferber, Edna 1663
Fergus, Pamelia Dillin 2482
Ferguson, Anita Perez 4527
Ferguson, Elizabeth Graeme 624
Ferguson, Kathy E. 3966
Ferguson, Marilyn 3085
Fern, Fanny 914
Fernea, Elizabeth Warnock 2595
Ferraro, Geraldine A. 2929
Ferrell, Carolyn 4613
Ferris, Helene 3028
Fey, Tina 4527.1
Fiedler, Maureen 3334
Field, Connie 3826
Field, Kate 1082
Field, Rachel Lyman 1793
Field, Sally 3653
Fields, Annie Adams 1055
Fields, Dorothy 2014
Fields, Suzanne 4574
Fields, Totie 2757
Fine, Sylvia 2197
Fingerhut, Arden 3654
Finley, Karen 4363
Fiorina, Cara Carleton "Carly" Sneed 4244–4245
Fishback, Margaret 1900
Fishel, Elizabeth 3967
Fisher, Carrie 4364
Fisher, Dorothy Canfield 1525
Fisher, M. F. K. 2085
Fisher, Renee 3743
Fiske, Minnie 1312
Fitzgerald, Frances 3189
Fitzgerald, Zelda 1901
Fitzpatrick, Sheila Mary 3259
Flagg, Fannie 3260
Flanagan, Hallie 1705
Flanagan, Mary 3405
Flanner, Hildegarde 1885
Flanner, Janet 1745
Fleeson, Doris 1931
Fletcher, Bridget 597
Fletcher, Lucille 2176
Fleury, Maria de 787
Flexner, Anne Crawford 1430
Flinders, Carol Lee 3406
Flint, Annie Johnson 1326
Flournoy, Michèle A. 4576
Flowers, Margaret 4576.1
Flynn, Elizabeth Gurley 1706
Foderaro, Lisa W. 4675
Fogelin, Adrian 4042
Follett, Mary Parker 1350
Foltz, Clara Shortridge 1165
Fonda, Jane 3029
Fonseca, Isabel 4614
Forbes, Esther 1794
Forbus, Lady Willie 1746
Ford, Betty 2313
Ford, Lena Guilbert 1373
Fossey, Dian 2795
Foster, Doris Ann 3571
Foster, Hannah Webster 697
Foster, Jodie 4615
Fowler, Connie May 4639

Fowler, Karen Joy 3968
Fox, Muriel 2626
Fox, Paula 2454
Fox-Genovese, Elizabeth 3261
Fraiberg, Selma 2314
Frank, Florence Kiper 1628
Frank, Ray 1313
Franken, Rose 1809
Franks, Rebecca 707
Frantz, Marge 2315
Fraser, Arvonne 2517
Fraser, Clara 2455
Fraser, Kathleen 3030
Freeman, Jo 3572
Freeman, Judith 3656
Freeman, Mary Wilkins 1192
Fremont, Helen 3573
French, Marilyn 2658
Freston, Kathy 4676
Freudenberger, Nell 4892
Friday, Nancy 3031
Friedan, Betty 2398
Friedman, Bonnie 4448
Friedman, Lenore 4933
Frietschie, Barbara 729
Frings, Ketti 2241
Frost, Frances 2015
Frucht, Abby 4408
Frye, Marilyn 3262
Fuller, Loie 1286
Fuller, Margaret 910
Fuller, Margaret Witter 1389
Fulton, Alice 4105
Furman, Laura 3574
Furness, Betty 2266.1
Fussell, Betty Harper 2596
Gaard, Greta 4529
Gaeta, Lisa 4615.1
Gage, Frances Dana 904
Gage, Mathilda J. 1007
Gaitskill, Mary 4246
Gale, Zona 1431
Galinsky, Ellen 3408
Gallagher, Mary 3744
Gallagher, Tess 3409
Galland, China 3410
Gamble, Eliza Burt 1103
Gamble, Vanessa Northington 4177
Gandy, Kim 4247
Garber, Marjorie B. 3501
Gardiner, Lisa 1902
Gardinier, Suzanne 4577
Gardner, Ava 2427
Gardot, Melody 4955
Garfield, Lucretia Rudolph 1045
Garland, Judy 2428
Garrison, Deborah 4696
Garrison, Theodosia 1433
Garson, Barbara 3335
Garthwaite, Terry 3143
Garvey, Jane F. 3502
Gates, Ellen 1065
Gaulke, Cheri 4248
Gawain, Shakti 3827
Gaylor, Annie Laurie 4300
Gearhart, Sally Miller 2758
Geddes, Anne 4365
Gelfant, Blanche H. 2429

Geller, Laura 3969
Gellhorn, Martha 2087
Gelpi, Barbara C. 2849
Geniesse, Jane Fletcher 2977
George, Elizabeth 3897
Gera, Bernice 2759
Gerber, Merrill Joan 3087
Gerould, Katherine 1526
Gerson, Kathleen 3746
Gerstenberg, Alice 1629
Geyer, Georgie Anne 2930
Gibbons, Kaye 4530
Gibbs, Lois Marie 4106
Gibbs, Nancy 4531
Gibson, Margaret 3504
Gilbert, Elizabeth 4788
Gilbert, Peggy 2018
Gilbert, Sandra 2978
Gilbreth, Lillian Moller 1513
Gilchrist, Ellen 2931
Gilchrist, Marie 1770
Gildersleeve, Virginia 1493
Gill, Sarah Prince 601
Gillan, Maria Mazziotto 3190
Gillespie, Marcia 3505
Gillibrand, Kirsten 4720
Gilligan, Carol 2979
Gilman, Caroline 843
Gilman, Charlotte Perkins 1254
Gilpin, Laura 1726
Gilson, Mary Barnett 1494
Giltinan, Caroline 1610
Ginsburg, Ruth Bader 2850
Girsh, Faye Joan 2851
Gish, Lillian 1771
Glaser, Lulu 1434
Glasgow, Ellen 1435
Glasgow, Maude 1351
Glaspell, Susan 1474
Glassman, Carol 3336
Glendon, Mary Ann 3088
Glück, Louise Elisabeth 3413
Goddard, Mary Katherine 621
Goddard, Sarah Updike 550
Godwin, Gail 3032
Goedicke, Patricia 2760
Goetz, Cecelia Helen 2316
Golan, Galia 3143.1
Goldberg, Natalie 3828
Goldberg, Whoopi 4301
Goldberger, Nancy Rule 2891
Golden, Marita 3970
Goodale, Dora Read 1327
Goodale, Elaine 1295
Goodenough, J. B. 3337
Goodman, Allegra 4749
Goodman, Amy 4408.1
Goodman, Carolyn 2242
Goodman, Ellen H. 3264
Goodman, Linda 2519
Goodwin, Doris Kearns 3415
Gordon, Bette 4366
Gordon, Mary Catherine 3898
Gordon, Ruth 1825
Gordon-Reed, Annette 4532
Gordy Edwards, Esther 2370.1
Gore, Tipper 3829
Gornick, Vivian 2932

Gottleib, Linda 3265
Gottlieb, Lynn 3899
Gould, Hannah Flagg 810
Gould, Lois 3033
Goulianos, Joan 3144
Graff, E.J. 4452
Grafton, Sue 3191
Graham, Bette Clair 2484
Graham, Jorie 3972
Graham, Katharine 2289
Graham, Laurie 3192
Graham, Margaret Collier 1174
Graham, Martha 1795
Graham, Virginia 2177
Grahn, Judy 3193
Grandin, Temple 3748
Grant, Lee 2599
Grant, Toni 3266–3267
Grasso, Ella 2343
Gratz, Rebecca 788
Grau, Shirley Ann 2659
Gray, Elizabeth Dodson 2660
Gray, Kimi 3660
Gray, Madeline 1949
Green, Anna 1143
Green, Constance McLaughlin 1849
Green, Edith Starrett 2128
Green, Melissa 4533
Greenberg, Blu 2981
Greenberg, Joanne 2801
Greenberg, Julie 4721
Greene, Catharine 675
Greene, Gayle 3416
Greene, Jeanette 2661
Greene, Jennifer 3575
Greenfield, Meg 2710
Gregg, Linda 3339
Griffin, Adele 4819
Griffin, Susan 3417
Griffith, Aline 2457
Griffith, Nanci 4250
Griffith Joyner, Florence 4487
Griffiths, Martha Wright 2178
Griffitts, Hannah 600
Grimes, Martha 2761
Grimké, Angelina 890
Grimké, Sarah Moore 832
Gross, Jane 4453
Gross, Rita M 3506
Gross, Terry 4043
Grossman, Susan C. 4302
Gruber, Ruth 2157
Grumbach, Doris Isaac 2317
Gubar, Susan 3507
Guest, Barbara 2371
Guest, Judith 2982
Guffy, Ossie 2762
Guinan, Texas 1611
Guiney, Louise Imogen 1268
Guitar, Mary Anne 2372
Gullette, Margaret Morganroth 3268
Gürer, Denise W. 4409
Gurung, Jeanette D. 4303
Gutmann, Amy 3900
Gwinn, Mary Ann 4044
Hacker, Marilyn 3340
Hahn, Emily "Mickey" 2019

Haiken, Elizabeth 4964
Hainstock, Elizabeth G. 2630
Hale, Clara Mcbride 2020
Hale, Lucretia Peabody 967
Hale, Nancy 2089
Hale, Sarah Josepha 807
Haley, Gail E. 3146
Halifax, Joan 3341
Hall, Hazel 1651
Hall, Mrs. Daniel 748
Hall, Sharlot Mabridth 1374
Hallman, Linda D. 4179
Halprin, Anna 2373
Halprin, Sally 4965
Halsey, Margaret 2130
Halsted, Anna Roosevelt 2046
Hamburg, Margaret "Peggy" 4303.1
Hamill, Janet 3576
Hamilton, Alice 1361
Hamilton, Edith 1336
Hamilton, Eleanor 2109
Hamilton, Gail 1051
Hamilton, Jane 4411
Hamm, Mia 4859
Hammond, Eleanor Prescott 1328
Hampl, Patricia 3661
Handler, Ruth 2269
Hansberry, Lorraine 2711
Hansen, Grace 2198
Harding, Florence Kling 1255
Harding, M. Esther 1680
Harding, Sandra G. 2934
Harding, Tonya 4820
Hardwick, Elizabeth 2270
Harkness, Madden 3973
Harriman, Florence Hurst 1375
Harris, Barbara 2935
Harris, Corra May 1362
Harris, Janet 2243
Harris, Jean 2458
Harris, Julie 2520
Harris, Marguerite 1886
Harris, Patricia Roberts 2485
Harris, Rachel 4893
Harris, Ruth Mae 3195
Harrison, Barbara Grizzuti 2893
Harrison, Kathryn 4579
Hart, Frances Noyes 1707
Hart, Louise 3034
Hart, Nancy 618
Hartigan, Grace 2430
Hartman, Saidiya 3974
Harvey, Matthea 4876
Haskell, Molly 3147
Hathaway, Helen 1772
Hausman, Bernice L. 4618
Hawes, Elizabeth "Babe" 1969
Hawn, Goldie 3577
Hawthorne, Sophia Amelia Peabody 907
Hayden, Anna Tompson 483
Hayden, Esther 575
Hayes, Elinor Rice 1933
Hayes, Helen 1904
Hayes, Lucy Webb 1041
Head, Edith 1850
Healy, Bernadine 3509

Hebard, Gracy 1269
Hecht, Jennifer Michael 4699
Heckler, Margaret 2764
Hedrick, Joan D. 3510
Heide, Wilma Scott 2400
Heilbrun, Carolyn G. 2552
Heimel, Cynthia 3750
Hejinian, Lyn 3269
Heldman, Caroline 4860
Heldman, Gladys Medalie 2431
Heller, Karen 4412
Hellman, Lillian 2021
Helmsley, Leona 2374
Hempel, Amy 4046
Henley, Beth 4109
Henley, Nancy M. 2894
Henriksen, Louise Levitas 2179
Henrion, Claudia 4454
Hepburn, Katherine 2110
Herman, Judith Lewis 3342
Herman, Susan 3343
Hernandez, Aileen Clarke 2553
Herndon, Rosanna Taylor 2713
Heron, Joan 2854
Herschberger, Ruth 2292–2293
Heschel, Susannah 4368
Hess, Cynthia 4678
Hewitt, Mary Elizabeth 901
Heyward, Carter 3579
Heyward, Jane Screven 2375
Hibbard, Grace 1376
Hickok, Lorena A. 1773
Higginbottom, Heather A. 4861
Higgins, Tracy E. 4700
Higginson, Ella 1287
Hill, Catherine 4979
Hill, Ruth Beebe 2199
Hillman, Brenda 4047
Himmelfarb, Gertrude 2432
Hine, Darlene Clark 3752
Hine, Lorraine 2714
Hinkle, Beatrice 1436
Hinton, S. E. 3831
Hirshfield, Jane 4180
Hite, Shere 3344
Hobson, Laura Z. 1905
Hochman, Sandra 2983
Hochschild, Arlie Russell 3196
Hoffman, Malvina 1630
Hogan, Linda 3753
Hogue, Ilyse 4790
Holiday, Billie 2244
Holland, Barbara 4048
Holland, Norah M. 1476
Holley, Marietta 1073
Holley, Mary Austin 796
Hollibaugh, Amber 3754
Holliday, Judy 2401
Hollman, Peggy 4304
Holman, Sheri 4722
Holmes, Marjorie 2133
Holmes, Mary Jane 1018
Holt, Anne Haw 2895
Holt, Kimberly Willis 4535
Holtzman, Elizabeth 3271
Holtzman, Fanny Ellen 1971
Hooper, Ellen Sturgis 937
Hoover, Eleanor 2521

Hoover, Louise "Lou" Henry 1437
Hooyman, Nancy R. 3582
Hope, Lugenia Burns 1390.1
Hopkins, Nancy 3511
Hopper, Grace Murray 2048
Hopper, Hedda 1709
Horan, Nancy 3832
Horne, Lena 2294
Horne, Marilyn 2896
Horner, Matina S. 3148–3149
Hosmer, Harriet 1026
Houston, Jean 3037
Howar, Barbara 2898
Howard, Jane 2936
Howard, Maureen 2715
Howard, Michelle J. 4535.1
Howarth, Ellen 1014
Howe, Fanny 3197
Howe, Florence 2663
Howe, Julia Ward 956
Howe, Louise Kapp 2899
Howe, Marie 3975
Howe, Tina 3038
Howell, Carol K. 4251
Howell, Margery Eldredge 1774
Howells, Mildred 1399
Howland, Bette 3039
Hoyt, Helen 1664
Hrdy, Sarah Blaffer 3665
Hubbard, Alice 1271
Hubbard, Barbara Marx 2664
Hudson, Helen 2376
Hufstedler, Shirley M. 2523
Hull, Jane Dee 2937
Hulme, Kathryn 1906
Hungry Wolf, Beverly 3977
Hunt, Carrie 4372
Hunt, Swanee 3978
Hunter, Clementine 1652
Hunter, Kristin 2765
Hunter-Gault, Charlayne 3347
Hurst, Fannie 1697
Hurston, Zora Neale 1727
Huston, Anjelica 4049
Hustvedt, Siri 4307
Hutchinson, Ellen M. 1546
Hutten, Bettina von 1438
Hutton, Lauren 3422
Huxtable, Ada Louise 2402
Hyatt, Lesley A. 4700.1
Hyde, Mary 3198
Hyman, Judith Partnow 3089
Ian, Janis 4050
Ifill, Gwen 4308
Ireland, Mardy S. 3833
Irving, Minna 1224
Isaacs, Susan 3423
Iskin, Ruth E. 2377
Ivins, Molly 3512
Jabs, Carolyn R. 3979
Jacker, Corinne 2855
Jackson, Helen Fiske Hunt 1027
Jackson, Jacquelyne J. 2802
Jackson, Janet 4723
Jackson, Lisa P. 4619
Jackson, Maggie 4679
Jackson, Mahalia 2159
Jackson, Rachel Robards 735

Jackson, Rebecca Cox 848
Jackson, Shirley 2346
Jacobi, Kathryn 3756
Jacobs, Deborah 4111
Jacobs, Harriet 949
Jacobs, Jane 2271
Jacobs, Rose Gell 1681
Jacobson, Ethel 2022
Jacobson, Sandra Weinstein 2718
Jacoby, Susan 3584
Jaffe, Rona 2766
Jagan, Janet 2378
James, Alice 1160
James, Bessie Rowland 1814
James, Sarah 3513
James, Selma 2719
James, Sibyl 3666
Jamieson, Kathleen Hall 3667
Jance, J. A. 3514
Janeway, Elizabeth 2201
Janis, Elsie 1698
Janowitz, Tama 4415
Janvier, Margaret 1138
Jardine, Alice A. 4309
Jay, Karla 3758
Jenkins, Carol 3516
Jenkins, Margaret 3759
Jentz, Terri 4416
Jessye, Eva 1815
Jewett, Sarah Orne 1166
Jiles, Paulette 3427
Johnsen, Dawn 4620
Johnson, Lady Bird 2180
Johnson, Abigail 4582
Johnson, Adelaide 2023
Johnson, Diane 2900
Johnson, Eleanor Murdock 1748
Johnson, Georgia Douglas 1653
Johnson, Guion Griffis 1908
Johnson, Josephine Winslow 2135
Johnson, Kory 4926
Johnson, Osa 1797
Johnson, Rheta Grimsley 4184
Johnson, Shirbey 3273
Johnson, Sonia 2985
Johnston, Annie Fellows 1296
Johnston, Mary 1377
Jolie, Angelina 4895
Jones, Amanda Theodosia 1066
Jones, Ann 3040
Jones, Beverly 2602
Jones, Margo 2202
Jones, Rickie Lee 4252
Jong, Erica 3349
Jong-Fast, Molly 4934
Joplin, Janis 3428
Jordan, Sara Murray 1613
Judith, Anodea 4113
Judson, Ann Hasseltine 811
Judson, Olivia 4791
Julavits, Heidi 4767
Justin, Dena 2183
Kael, Pauline 2347
Kagan, Elena 4536
Kahn, Florence Prag 1329
Kahn, Kathy 3585
Kalish, Mildred Armstrong 2460
Kallen, Lucille Chernos 2433

Kamensky, Jane 4641
Kaminer, Wendy 3981
Kanin, Fay 2295
Kanter, Rosabeth Moss 3429
Kaplan, Louise J. 2666
Kaplan, Temma E. 3350–3351
Kaptur, Marcy 3668
Karan, Donna 3836
Karmel, Marjorie 2857
Karon, Jan 3041
Karr, Mary 4310
Kasdorf, Julia Spicher 4623
Kasebier, Gertrude 1194
Kassebaum, Nancy 2804
Katie, Byron 3352
Kauffman, Linda S. 3903
Kaufman, Shirley 2461
Kaufman, Sue 2556
Kaye, Carol 2525
Kaye, Judy 3837
Kearney, Belle 1297
Keenan, Nancy 4114
Kegel, Martha 4455
Kellems, Vivien 1826
Keller, Evelyn Fox 2988
Keller, Helen 1548
Kellerman, Faye 4115
Kellett, Christine H. 3274
Kelley, Florence 1248
Kelley, Kitty 3353
Kelley, Virginia Cassidy 2462
Kellor, Frances Alice 1413
Kelly, Brigit Pegeen 4052
Kelly-Gadol, Joan 2632
Kempton, Sally 3430
Kennedy, Adrienne 2767
Kennedy, Caroline 4417
Kennedy, Marilyn Moats 3431
Kennedy, Rose Fitzgerald 1710
Kennelly, Barbara B. 2989
Kent, Corita 2318
Kenyon, Cynthia 4311
Kenyon, Jane 3763
Kephart, Beth 4538
Kerber, Linda Kaufman 3201
Kerbis, Gertrude Lemp 2557
Kerr, Jean 2463
Kerr, Sarah 4966
Kerr, Sophie 1550
Kerrigan, Nancy 4793
Kesselman, Wendy 3202
Ketcham, Katherine 3904
Keyes, Frances Parkinson 1632
Keyserling, Mary 2136
Kijewski, Karen 3432
Kilbourne, Jean 3433
Kilgallen, Dorothy 2203
Killefer, Nancy 4186
Kilmer, Aline Murray 1682
Kimball, Harriet 1057
King, Billie Jean 3434
King, Carole 3355
King, Coretta Scott 2603
King, Florence 2990
King, Georgiana Goddard 1391
King, Laurie R. 4116
King, Ynestra 3840
King-Hammond, Leslie 3517

Kingsolver, Barbara 4312
Kinsolving, Sally 1477
Kintz, Linda 3587
Kirchheimer, Gloria DeVidas 3356
Kirk, Lisa 2526
Kirkland, Winifred 1401
Kirkpatrick, Jeane 2558
Kissling, Frances 3435
Kitt, Eartha 2604
Kiyak, H. Asuman 4054
Kizer, Carolyn 2527
Klagsbrun, Francine 2768
Klein, Laura Cousino 4768
Kleinbaum, Sharon 4490
Kline, Christina Baker 4680
Klobuchar, Amy 4540
Knight, Sarah Kemble 508
Knopf, Blanche Wolf 1798
Kolata, Gina 3841
Kolb, Barbara 3150
Kolbert, Elizabeth 4584
Koller, Alice 2488
Koontz, Libby 2348
Koppel, Lily 4946
Kort, Michele 3982
Kraemer, Ross Shepard 3842
Kramarae, Cheris 3091
Kramer, Jane 3092
Kramer, Joyce 3357
Kramer, Melinda 4935
Krantz, Judith 2634
Krauss, Nicole 4884
Kreps, Juanita 2403
Krone, Julie 4645
Kuhlman, Kathryn 2067
Kuhn, Maggie 2025
Kumin, Maxine 2529
Kummer, Clare 1684
Kushner, Rachel 4769
La Coste, Marie de 1139
LaFollette, Suzanne 1776
Lakich, Lili 3358
Lamott, Anne 4255
Landers, Ann 2319
Lane, Rose Wilder 1654
Lange, Dorothea 1816
Langer, Susanne K 1817
Langston, Laodicea "Dicey" 730
Lape, Esther 1569
Lappé, Frances Moore 3518
Laramore, Vivian Yeiser 1749
Larcom, Lucy 1008
Larsen, Jensine 4897
Lathbury, Mary 1104
Lauder, Estée 2052
Laurel, Alicia Bay 3908–3909
Lavin, Mary 2184
Lawrenson, Helen 1996
Layton, Elizabeth 2137
Lazarre, Jane D. 3436
Lazarus, Emma 1168
Lazarus, Josephine 1145
le Baron, Marie 1109
Le Guin, Ursula K. 2668
Le Row, Caroline Bigelow 1117
Le Shan, Eda J. 2434
Le Sueur, Marian 1496
Le Sueur, Meridel 1911

Lea, Fanny Heaslip 1615
Leachman, Cloris 2562
Lear, Moya Olson 2246
Lease, Mary 1178
Lebowitz, Fran 3984
Ledbetter, Lilly 3093
Lee, Harper 2563
Lee, Agnes 1352
Lee, Barbara 3670
Lee, Ettie 1634
Lee, Gypsy Rose 2222
Lee, Hannah Farnham 782
Lee, Jennifer 8. 4911
Leech, Margaret 1778
Leffland, Ella 2769
Leibowitz, Annie 3910
Leifer, Carol 4376
Leigh, Carolyn 2564
Leitch, Mary Sinton 1478
L'Engle, Madeleine 2320
Lennart, Isobel 2247
Lennox, Charlotte 584
Leonard, Annie 4585
Lepore, Jill 4725
Lerner, Harriet Goldhor 3519
Lesher, Jan 4313–4314
Leslie, Amy 1256
Leslie, Eliza 804
Leslie, Lisa 4864
Lesser, Elizabeth 4117
LeTendre, Mary Jean 3844
Levin, Diane E. 3764
Levine, Emily 3845
Levine, Judith 4118
Levinson, Nan 3911
Levy, Naomi 4646
Lewinsky, Monica 4877
Lewis, Edith 1551
Lewitzky, Bella 2273
Liebman, Wendy 4586
Lienert, Tania 4885
Lightner, Candy 3671
Lin, Maya 4492
Lincoln, Abbey 2723
Lincoln, Mary Todd 950
Lincoln, Victoria 1997
Lindbergh, Anne Morrow 2053
Lindley, Mary Ann 3766
Lindsay, Sarah 4457
Lingle, Linda 4189
Lippman, Laura 4493
Lipstadt, Deborah 3767
Lipton, Eunice 3278
Litman, Jane 3206
Livermore, Mary 971
Livingstone, Belle 1462
Lockwood, Belva 1029
Loftus, Elizabeth Fishman 3522
Longauex y Vasquez, Enriqueta 3589
Longworth, Alice Roosevelt 1616
Loos, Anita 1686
Lopez, Jennifer 4824
Lord, Nancy 4119
Loud, Pat 2565
Lougee, Carolyn Chappell 3359
Louis, Minnie D. 1105
Love, Barbara J. 3043

Love, Courtney 4681
Lowell, Amy 1440
Lowry, Beverly 3095
Lowry, Lois 3044
Lowry, Mary 3279
Lubchenco, Jane 3768
Luce, Clare Boothe 1973
Luce, Gay Gaer 2724
Luker, Kristin Carol 3673
Lunch, Lydia 4494
Lurie, Alison 2566
Luscomb, Florence 1666
Lute, Jane Holl 4378
Lydon, Susan 3438
Lynn, Loretta 2806
Lyon, Emily 4379
Lyon, Mary 855
Lyon, Phyllis 2489
Maazel, Fiona 4912
Mable, Jackie "Moms" 1800
MacDonald, Betty 2093
Macdonald, Cynthia 2636
MacGuineas, Maya 4771
MacKinnon, Catherine A. 3674
MacLaine, Shirley 2903
MacMurray, Rose 2405
MacPherson, Myra 2939
Macy, Joanna 2669
Maddow, Rachel 4878.1
Madgett, Naomi Long 2465
Madison, D. Soyiini 3912
Madison, Dolley 738
Madonna 4459
Maggio, Rosalie 3439
Magner, Marjorie 3913
Mahoney, Rosemary 4587
Maines, Natalie Louise 4886
Mairs, Nancy 3440
Mallicoat, Helen M. 2070
Malone-Mayes, Vivienne 2808
Malpede, Karen 3590
Malveaux, Julianne 4190
Manley, Joan 2809
Mann, Emily 4120–4121
Mannes, Marya 1998
Maran, Meredith 4056
Marbury, Elisabeth 1211
Marchetto, Marisa Acocella 4625
Marcus, Lisa 4704
Margonelli, Lisa 4705
Marion, Frances 1655
Markham, Lucia Clark 1380
Marlin, Alice Tepper 3525
Marshall, Catherine 2224
Marshall, Lucinda 4381
Marston, Stephanie 3914
Martin, Anne Henrietta 1463
Martin, Del 2407
Martin, Elizabeth 648
Martin, Emily 3526
Martin, Jane Roland 2671
Martin, Judith 3097
Martin, Lynn 3151
Martin, Martha 1827
Marx, Patricia 4259
Mason, Bobbie Ann 3209
Mason, Caroline 989
Mason, Viviane Carter 1913

Massaro, Toni Marie 4316
Massie, Suzanne 3280
Masterson, Martha Gay 1080
Mathews, Jessica Tuchman 3676
Matsui, Doris Okada 3527
Mattern, Evelyn 3281
Matthews, Glenna C. 3098
Matthews, Jill 4682
Matthews-Simonton, Stephanie 3210
Maule, Frances 1533
Maxwell, Elsa 1596
May, Elaine 2810
May, Julia Harris 1052
Mayberg, Maude 1750
Mayer, Bernadette 3592
Mayer, Jane 4317
McAuliffe, Christa 3848
McBride, Mary Margaret 1888
McCain, Cindy 4260
McCall, Dorothy 1699
McCarthy, Abigail 2248
McCarthy, Mary 2185
McCarthy, Sarah J. 3360
McCaslin, Mary 3677
McCaughey, Martha 4726
McClintock, Barbara 1952
McCormick, Anne O'Hare 1582
McCormick, Virginia Taylor 1415
McCorvey, Norma 3769
McCoy, Rose Marie 2435
McCracken, Elizabeth 4727
McCullers, Carson 2297
McDermott, Alice 4193
McFadden, Bernice L. 4728
McFate, Montgomery "Mitzi" 4706
McFerren, Martha 3770
McGill, Alice 2606
McGinley, Phyllis 2027
McGovern, Ann 2725
McGrory, Mary 2323
McHugh, Heather 3849
McIntosh, Maria 879
McIntosh, Peggy 2906
McKellar, Danica 4898.1
McKenna, Elizabeth Perle 4382
McKenney, Ruth 2161
McLaughlin, Patricia 3593
McLeod, Merikay 3771
McMullan, Margaret 4542
McNamara, Jo Ann 2770
McPhee, Jenny 4543
McPhee, Martha S. 4683
McPherson, Sandra 3441
McRae, Carmen 2382
McWhorter, Diane 4060
Mead, Margaret 1935
Meadows, Donella "Dana" 3282
Means, Marianne 2907
Megaw, Helen Dick 2071
Melanie 3772
Mendenhall, Dorothy Reed 1442
Mercer, Margaret 825
Merman, Ethel 2114
Merriam, Eve 2274
Metzger, Deena 2993
Meyer, Agnes 1668
Meyer, Annie Nathan 1339

Meyer, Leisa D. 4647
Meyer, Marlane 4061
Michaelis, Aline Triplett 1635
Michelman, Kate 3361
Midler, Bette 3594
Mikulski, Barbara 2994
Miles, Josephine 2162
Milgrom, Shira 4062
Millay, Edna St. Vincent 1751
Miller, Alice Duer 1443
Miller, Caroline 1974
Miller, Casey Geddes 2350
Miller, Ceci 4461
Miller, Emily 1053
Miller, Helen Hill 1889
Miller, Jean Baker 2607
Miller, Laura 3992
Miller, Lee 2072
Miller, Sue 3442
Miller, Susan 3528
Millett, Kate 2908
Millner, Caille 4928
Mills, Karen Gordon 4262
Mills, Stephanie 3851
Miner, Dorothy Eugenia 1999
Mink, Gwendolyn 4122
Minnelli, Liza 3678
Minow, Martha 4263
Mirrielees, Edith Ronald 1515
Mitchell, Margaret 1914
Mitchell, Maria 951
Mitchell, Martha 2325
Mock, Geraldine "Jerrie" 2532
Moeller, Susan D. 4731
Moffat, Mary Jane 2859
Moirai, Catherine Risingflame 3993
Moïse, Penina 856
Mojtabai, A. G. 3046
Monk, Karen 4982
Monroe, Anne Shannon 1497
Monroe, Harriet 1258
Monroe, Marilyn 2568
Montgomery, Roselle Mercier 1445
Moody, Anne 3213
Moore, Ann S. 3917
Moore, Grace 1936
Moore, Honor 3596
Moore, Julia A 1153
Moore, Liz 4954
Moore, Liz 2436
Moore, Lorrie 4421
Moore, Marianne 1669
Moore, Martha Milcah 632
Moore, Patricia A. 4124
Moore, Susanna 3597
Moore, Virginia 1975
Moorhead, Sarah Parsons 633
Mora, Elizabeth Catlett 2351
Moran, Ellen 4732
Morgan, Angela 1446
Morgan, Barbara 1915
Morgan, Barbara "Barb" 4063
Morgan, Elizabeth 3773
Morgan, Julia 1403
Morgan, Marabel 3047
Morgan, Marlo 3048
Morgan, Robin 3284
Morgan, Ruth 2384

Morphonios, Ellen James 2674
Morris, Esther Hobart 923
Morris, Holly 4733
Morris, Margaret 625
Morris, Mary 2205
Morrissey, Mary Mannin 3918
Morrow, Elizabeth Cutler 1417
Morton, Sarah Wentworth 698
Moseley Braun, Carol 3774
Moses, Claire Goldberg 3285
Moses, Grandma 1259
Moskowitz, Faye S. 2728
Moss, Cyntha 3215
Mossell, N. F. 1212
Mott, Lucretia 839
Moulton, Louise 1067
Mountain Wolf Woman 1571
Mowatt, Anna Cora 957
Mullins, Aimee 4913
Mumford, Ethel Watts 1516
Munk, Erika 3152
Murphy, Sara 1597
Murphy, Virginia Backentoe 1058
Murray, Janet Horowitz 3679
Murray, Judith Sargent 669
Murray, Kathryn 2055
Murray, Patty 3994
Muscio, Inga 4734
Muske-Dukes, Carol 3598
Musser, Tharon 2533
Myerhoff, Barbara 2940
Myers, Dee Dee 4590
Myers, Isabel Briggs 1854
Myerson, Bess 2491
Myss, Caroline M. 4126
Napolitano, Janet 4423
Nathan, Maud 1289–1290
Nation, Carry 1146
Naylor, Gloria 3995
Near, Holly 3921
Nearing, Helen 2001
Neal, Alice 2097
Neiman, Susan 4321
Nelson, Antonya 4591
Nelson, Donna J. 4199
Nelson, Mariah Burton 4384
Nelson, Martha 4128
Nelson, Paula 3599
Nelson, Portia 2385
Nenadic, Natalie 4967
Newlin, Marjorie 2386
Newman, Frances 1598
Newman, Jody 4498
Newman, Naomi 2730
Newton, Frances 2731
Nichols, Anne 1730
Nichols, Martha 4968–4969
Nichols, Mary D. 3600
Nichols, Ruth Rowland 1937
Nicholson, Zoe Ann 3852
Niedecker, Lorine 1978
Niederman, Sharon 3853
Niemann, Linda 3681
Niemi, Judith 3288
Nixon, Pat 2186
Noble, Vicki 3775
Noddings, Nel 2675

Noonan, Peggy 3996
Noor Al-Hussein 4066
Norberg-Hodge, Helena 3682
Norman, Dorothy 2028
Norman, Liane 3049
Norman, Marsha 3776
Norris, Kathleen 3777
Norris, Kathleen Thompson 1552
Norton, Eleanor Holmes 3050
Norton, Grace Fallow 1479
Notley, Alice 3602
Nottage, Lynn 4683.1
Nunez, Sigrid 4067
Nussbaum, Hedda 3362
Nussbaum, Martha C. 3778
Nyad, Diana 3922
Nyro, Laura 3779
Oakley, Annie 1260
Oates, Joyce Carol 3099
O'Brien, Shannon 4499
O'Brien, Virginia 3683
Ochs, Vanessa L. 4201
O'Connell, Roselyn 3997
O'Connor, Flannery 2534
O'Connor, Karen 3100
O'Connor, Sandra Day 2733
Odetta 2734
O'Donnell, Rosie 4628
O'Grady, Ellen 1340
O'Hara, Maureen 4202
O'Keeffe, Georgia 1670
Olds, Sharon 3364
Oliver, Mary 2941
Oliver, Ruth Law 1671
Oliveros, Pauline 2813
Olsen, Frances 3603
Olsen, Tillie 2187
Onassis, Jacqueline Kennedy 2676
O'Neill, Rose 1447
O'Neill, Terry 4202.1
O'Reilly, Jane 2995
Orenstein, Catherine 4754
Oreskes, Naomi 4463
Orlean, Susan 4324
Orman, Suze 4131
Orr, Mary 2140
Orth, Maureen Ann 3444
Osgood, Frances Sargent 915
Ostriker, Alicia Suskin 3051
Owen, Anita 1714
Owen, Mary A. 1179
Owens, Rochelle 2996
Ozick, Cynthia 2638
Packer, Ann 4500
Paddleford, Clementine 1871
Page, Geraldine 2492
Pagels, Elaine 3445
Paglia, Camille 3780
Painter, Charlotte 2572
Painter, Nell 3365
Painter, Pamela 3290
Paley, Barbara "Babe" 2251
Paley, Grace 2437
Paley, Vivian Gussin 2677
Palin, Sarah 4684
Palmer, Alice Freeman 1206
Palmer, Gretta Brooker 2029
Paltrow, Gwyneth 4847

Parent, Gail 3218
Paretsky, Sara 3781
Parker, Dorothy 1780
Parker, Gail Thain 3446
Parker, Kathleen 4797
Parker, Suzy 2814
Partnow, Elaine Bernstein 3291
Partnow, Jessica 4947
Partnow, Susan 3782
Parton, Dolly 3686
Pastan, Linda 2815
Patchett, Ann 4650
Patterson, Eleanor 1572
Patterson, Martha Johnson 1020
Paul, Alice 1637
Payne, Ethel L. 2163
Peabody, Elizabeth 666
Peabody, Elizabeth Palmer 886
Peabody, Josephine Preston 1448
Peace Pilgrim 2098
Pearce, Susan C. 4387
Peelen, Jean 3292–3293
Peery, Janet 3854
Peiss, Kathy 4203
Pelosi, Nancy 3220
Penley, Constance 3924
Perera, Sylvia Brinton 2816
Peri, Janis-Rozena 3221
Perino, Dana 4866
Perkins, Frances 1584
Perl, Teri 2573
Perry, Eleanor 2252
Perry, Nora 1042
Perry, Zenobia Powell 2099
Pert, Candace B. 3687
Pessl, Marisha 4929
Petchesky, Rosalind Pollack 3366
Peterkin, Julia 1554
Peterson, Brenda 4132
Peterson, Virgilia 2002–2003
Phair, Liz 4755
Pharr, Suzanne 3153
Phelps, Almira Lincoln 840
Phelps, Elizabeth 930
Phelps, Elizabeth Stuart 1127
Phillips, Bonnie 3367
Phillips, Debora 4937
Phillips, Jayne Anne 4133
Phillips, Julia 3532
Phillips, Julie 4710
Phillips, Lois 3222
Picon, Molly 1872
Picoult, Jodi 4735
Piercy, Marge 2997
Pierpont, Claudia Roth 4134
Pincus, Joy 4798
Pinkard, Susan 4204
Plain, Belva 2355
Plaskow, Judith 3785
Plath, Sylvia 2817
Pogrebin, Letty Cottin 3154
Polier, Justine Wise 1981
Polk, Sarah Childress 881
Pollard, "Sister" Evelyn 1599
Pollard, Josephine 1059
Pollitt, Katha 3925
Polowy, Carol 4388
Ponsot, Marie Birmingham 2410

Pool, Gail 3689
Poole, Jeannie Gayle 4068
Poon, Christine A. 4135
Popcorn, Faith 3855
Porter, Anne 2164
Porter, Eleanor H 1354
Porter, Katherine Anne 1715
Porter, Sylvia 2207
Post, Emily 1418
Postlethwaite, Diana 4000
Potor, Aurelia 2253
Poulsson, Emilie 1199
Pounds, Jessie Brown 1275
Powell, Dawn 1830
Powell, Maxine 2492.1
Powers, Donna 3926
Prager, Emily 3856
Pratt, Minnie Bruce 3690
Prejean, Helen 3155
Prell, Riv-Ellen 3786
Prentiss, Elizabeth Payson 952
Preston, Ann 921
Preston, Margaret J. 976
Previn, Dory 2679
Priesand, Sally 3787
Priest, Dana 4502
Priest, Ivy Baker 2031
Prins, Nomi 4867
Pritchard, Melissa 3857
Proctor, Edna Dean 1021
Proctor, Mary 4550
Profet, Margie 4465
Propp, Karen 4428
Prose, Francine 3788
Proulx, E. Annie 2942
Pryor, Sarah Agnes 1031
Putnam, Emily James 1318
Quayle, Marilyn 4001
Quimby, Edith 1732
Quindlen, Anna 4136
Quinn, Jane Bryant 3156
Quinn, Sally 3294
Radner, Gilda 3691
Radtke, Joyce 4327
Raine, Nancy Venable 3692
Ramey, Estelle R. 2300
Ramsay, Martha Laurens 699
Randal, Vera 2438
Randall, Margaret 3000
Rank, Beata 1831
Rankin, Jeannette 1555
Raphaöl, Sally Jessy 3447.1
Ras, Barbara 3929
Rascoe, Judith 3295
Raven, Arlene 3533
Ravitch, Diane 3102
Rawalt, Marguerite 1818
Rawlings, Marjorie Kinnan 1832
Ray, Dixy Lee 2227
Raymond, Janice G. 3930
Razovsky, Cecilia 1656
Rea, Shiva 4756
Reagan, Maureen 3296
Reagan, Nancy 2411
Reddy, Maureen 4328
Reed, Donna 2412
Reese, Lizette 1213
Reeves, Nancy 2209

Rehm, Diane 3001
Reid, Willa Mae 3157
Reinisch, June Machover 3448
Reitz, Rosetta 2493
Renfroe, Anita 4629
Renne, Tanya 4830
Reno, Janet 3103
Repplier, Agnes 1236
Resnik, Judith 3931
Resnik, Muriel 2301
Revoyr, Nina 4799
Reynolds, Malvina 1920
Rhode, Deborah L. 4137
Rice, Alice Caldwell 1382
Rice, Ann 3298
Rice, Ruth Mason 1617
Rice, Susan E. 4687
Rich, Adrienne 2680
Rich, B. Ruby 4800
Richards, Ann 2861
Richards, Cecile 4466
Richards, Laura Howe 1180
Richardson, Dorcas 636
Richardson, Margaret "Peggy"
    Milner 3449
Richman, Alyson M. 4868
Richman, Julia 1207
Ricker, Darlene Marie 4269
Ricker, Marilla 1096
Ride, Sally 4069
Riding, Laura 1938
Riley, Janet Mary 2254
Riley, Matilda White 2165
Rind, Clementina Bird 634
Rinehart, Mary Roberts 1480
Ripley, Sarah Alden 841
Rittenhouse, Jessie 1367
Rivers, Caryl 3053
Rivers, Joan 2862
Roach, Pam 3861
Roberts, Cokie 3450
Roberts, Elizabeth Madox 1638
Roberts, Julia 4757
Robinson, Barbara Paul 3299
Robinson, Corinne Roosevelt
    1276
Robinson, Harriet 1003
Robinson, Jill 3002
Robinson, Lillian 3300
Robinson, Mabel Louise 1449
Robinson, Marilynne 3451
Rochlin, Harriet 2494
Rockefeller, Lucy 1084
Roe, Anne 2004
Roe, Rebecca 4138
Rogers, Desiree 4504
Rogers, Estelle H. 4984
Rogers, Ginger 2166
Rogers, Pattiann 3225
Roiphe, Anne 2943
Roiphe, Katie 4777
Rolf, Ida P. 1833
Rollin, Betty 3003
Romer, Christina D. 4468
Ronell, Ann 2102
Ronstadt, Linda 3694
Roosevelt, Eleanor 1618
Roosevelt, Edith Carow 1277

Rosaldo, Michelle Zimbalist 3536
Rose, Phyllis 3371
Rose, Wendy 3862
Rosen, Marjorie 3372
Rosen, Ruth 3608
Rosenberg, Ethel 2255
Rosenberg, Karen 4879
Rosenberg, Tina 4553
Rosenstein, Harriet 2818
Ross, Lillian 2611
Ross, Susan C. 3373
Rossi, Alice S. 2439
Rossner, Judith 2944
Roulet, Elaine 2738
Rourke, Constance 1639
Rouse, Cecilia 4652
Routsong, Alma 2495
Row, Amanda 2774
Rowland, Helen 1481
Rowlandson, Mary 468
Roy, Sara 4330
Royall, Anne Newport 745
Rozman, Deborah 3933–3934
Rubin, Vera C. 2640
Ruckelshaus, Jill 3054
Rudikoff, Sonya 2612
Rudman, Masha Kabakow 2863
Rudner, Rita 4390
Rudolph, Wilma "Skeeter" 3226
Rudy, Kathy 4391
Ruether, Rosemary Radford 3004
Rukeyser, Muriel 2210
Rule, Jane 2775
Runkle, Bertha 1517
Rush, Florence 2328
Russell, Rosalind 2168
Ryan, Kay 3609
Saberi, Roxana 4918
Sabin, Florence 1393
Salisbury, Joyce Ellen 3537
Salter, Mary Jo 4270
Salter, Stephanie 3935
Salvatore, Christina 4801
Samalin, Nancy 3055
Sampson, Edith Spurlock 1874
Sampter, Jessie Ethel 1600
Sanchez, Carol Lee 2911
Sandler, Bernice "Bunny" R. 2641
Sanger, Margaret 1535
Sangster, Margaret E. 1085
Sappington, Margo 3789
Sarandon, Susan 3695
Sassen, Georgia 3936
Sasso, Sandy Eisenberg 3790
Satran, Pamela Redmond 4205
Savage-Rumbaugh, Susan 3937
Sawyer, Diane 3610
Sawyer, Ruth 1556
Scanlan, Susan 3791
Scarf, Maggie 2819
Scattergood, Sally 4832–4833
Schaeffer, Susan Fromberg 3302
Schapiro, Mary L. 4332
Schine, Cathleen 4206
Schlafly, Phyllis 2496
Schlessinger, Laura Catherine 3792
Schmidt, Karen Anne 3611
Schnall, Marianne 4758

Schnall, Susan 3454
Schneiders, Sandra Marie 3005
Schneir, Miriam 2864
Schroeder, Pat 3227
Schulder, Diane B. 3056
Schultz, Tammy S. 4887
Schutz, Susan Polis 3538
Schwarz, Christina 4653
Scofield, Sandra 3455
Scott, Blanche Stuart 1753
Scott, Evelyn 1783
Scott, Joanna 4554
Scott, Melissa 4555
Scott-Maxwell, Florida 1601
Scudder, Janet 1421
Seacrest, Susan 4272
Seaman, Barbara 2946
Sears, Vicki 3303
Sebelius, Kathleen 3864
Sebold, Alice 4630
Sedgwick, Catherine Maria 812
Sedgwick, Eve Kosofsky 4003
See, Carolyn 2913
Seeger, Ruth Crawford 1939
Seidelman, Susan 4139
Seiffert, Marjorie Allen 1640
Sekaquaptewa, Helen 1876
Semenow, Dorothy 2740
Semmel, Joan 2821
Sendzimir, Venda 4140
Senna, Danzy 4834
Seton, Anya 2006
Seton, Cynthia Propper 2577
Seton, Elizabeth 765
Seton, Julia 1701
Seton-Thompson, Grace 1405
Seuling, Barbara 3057
Severn, Jill 3794
Sewall, Harriet 959
Sewall, Sarah 4596
Sexton, Anne 2642
Shainess, Natalie 2256
Shalit, Wendy 4900
Shanker, Wendy 4870
Shaw, Anna Moore 1877
Shaywitz, Sally E. 3376
Shear, Marie 3228
Sheehan, Cindy 4431
Sheehy, Gail 3059
Sheindlin, Judith 3377
Sheldon, Alice Bradley 2257
Sheldon, Karin P. 3613
Shelley, Rebecca 1672
Shelton, Charlotte 3795
Shepard, Alice M. 2741
Shepherd, Karen 3229
Sherfey, Mary Jane 2865
Sherman, Gail Berkeley 4209
Sherman, Susan 3158
Sherrill, Martha 4507
Sherwood, Kate Brownlee 1106
Sherwood, Margaret P. 1306
Shields, Carol 2949
Shivers, Louise 2683
Shlain, Tiffany 4835
Shocked, Michelle 4631
Shore, Dinah 2391
Showalter, Elaine 3305

Shubrick, Mrs. Richard 752
Shulman, Alix Kates 2822
Shur, Fanchon 2950
Sidney, Margaret 1129
Siebert, Muriel "Mickie" 2823
Siegel, Deborah 4803
Sigourney, Lydia Howard 827
Sill, Judee 3539
Sills, Beverly 2684
Silver, Joan Micklin 2951
Silverman, Sarah 4849
Simmons, Laura 1501
Simmons, Ruth 3614
Simon, Carly 3615
Simon, Kate 2190
Simon, Maurya 4004
Simon, Patricia 2914
Simonson, Joy Rosenheim 2356
Simpson, Becky 3006
Simpson, Nancy 3105
Sinclair, Lee 4431.1
Singer, Alyson 4970
Singer, June K. 2330
Singer, Maxine 2776
Sittenfeld, Curtis 4901
Skinner, Cornelia Otis 1940
Sklarek, Norma Merrick 2643
Slaney, Mary Decker 4470
Slater, Lauren 4655
Slaughter, Anne-Marie 4471
Slick, Grace 3159
Sloan-Hunter, Margaret 3796
Slocumb, Mary 709
Small, Meredith F. 4005
Smaller, Barbara 4210
Smeal, Eleanor 3160
Smedley, Agnes 1754
Smiley, Jane 3939
Smith, "Patti" 3696
Smith, Anna Young 688
Smith, Arabella 1130
Smith, Bessie 1878
Smith, Betty 1835
Smith, Elizabeth Oakes 899
Smith, Evelyn Elizabeth 2742
Smith, Hazel Brannon 2228
Smith, Janna Malamud 4143
Smith, Laura Frost 1784
Smith, Lee 3540
Smith, Liz 2469
Smith, Margaret Bayard 777
Smith, Margaret Chase 1857
Smith, May Riley 1110
Smith, Nora Archibald 1250
Smith, Robyn 3541
Smith, Sarah 3797
Smith, Sophia 851
Snitow, Ann 3457
Snortland, Ellen 4211
Snow, Helen Foster 2073
Snow, Phoebe 4144
Snowe, Olympia 3798
Sokoloff, Natalie J. 3542
Sokolow, Anna 2141
Solanas, Valerie 3230
Solis, Hilda 4432
Solomon, Hannah Greenebaum
   1238

Somers, Helen 2824
Sommers, Christina Hoff 4007
Song, Cathy 4333
Sontag, Susan 2866
Soren, Tabitha 4759
Sorrels, Rosalie 2867
Sotomayor, Sonia 4273.1
Southern, Eileen Jackson 2392
Spacks, Patricia Meyer 2685
Spafford, Bertha 1518
Spalding, Catherine 842
Spallone, Patricia 4071
Speare, Dorothy 1879
Spears, Britney 4950
Spellberg, Denise A. 4986
Spencer, Anna Garlin 1185
Spencer, Lilly Martin 985
Spero, Nancy 2580
Speyer, Leonora 1406
Spicer, Susan 4212
Spiotta, Dana 4872
Spofford, Harriet 1068
Spolin, Viola 2056
Spretnak, Charlene 3698
Springer, Carol 3007
Springer, Nancy 3868
Sproat, Nancy Dennis 732
St. Denis, Ruth 1557
St. James, Margo 3060
St. Joan, Jacqueline "Jackie" 3616
St. Johns, Adela Rogers 1804
Stabenow, Debbie 4008
Stafford, Jean 2258
Stanford, Sally 2007
Stannard, Una 2613
Stannow, Lovisa 4987
Stanton, Elizabeth Cady 931
Stanwyck, Barbara 2074
Starbuck, Mary Coffyn 478
Starhawk 4072
Starr, Hattie 1719
Steel, Danielle 3799
Steichen, Joanna T. 2868
Stein, Gertrude 1450
Stein, Linda 3459
Steinem, Gloria 2916
Stern, Edith Mendel 1941
Sternhell, Carol 4009
Stevens, Christine 4688
Stevens, Christine 2332
Stevens, Nettie Maria 1279
Stewart, Elinore Pruitt 1483
Stewart, Eliza "Mother" 938
Stewart, Ella Jane S. 1394
Stewart, Martha 3307
Stifter, Vicky 4073
Stiller, Nikki 4988
Stimpson, Catharine R. 3008
Stinson, Katherine 1736
Stiver, Irene Pierce 2497
Stockton, Annis 623
Stoddard, Elizabeth 990
Stone, Lucy 953
Stone, Merlin 2778
Stone, Sharon 4472
Stowe, Harriet Beecher 916
Strand, Polly 2825
Strasberg, Susan 3107

Streep, Meryl 3869
Streisand, Barbra 3379
Streshinsky, Naomi 2536
Strong, Anna Louise 1642
Strong, Harriet Williams Russell 1131
Strouse, Jean 3617
Strout, Elizabeth 4473
Struven, Mildred Witte 1837
Stuteville, Sarah 4942
Suckow, Ruth 1756
Sullivan, Annie 1332
Sullivan, Leonor 1958
Sumner, Helen L. 1484
Sutley, Nancy 4632
Sutphen, Mona 4760
Svirsky, Gila 3699
Swallow, Ellen 1112
Swanson, Gloria 1892
Swearingen, Terri 4433
Sweeney, Anne 4434
Swenson, May 2212
Swerda, Patricia 2277
Swerdlow, Amy 2470
Swift, Kate 2471
Swindle, Renee 4850
Swit, Loretta 3161
Syfers, Judy 3870
Symes, Lillian 1819
Szasz, Suzy 4213
Szold, Henrietta 1261
Taft, Helen Herron 1280
Tager, Marcia 3231
Taggard, Genevieve 1805
Tall, JoAnn 4274
Tallent, Elizabeth 4275
Talmadge, Betty Shingler 2499
Tannen, Deborah F. 3618
Tapp, June L. 2743
Tappan, Eva March 1203
Tarbell, Ida 1227
Tarule, Jill M. 3462
Tax, Meredith 3700
Taylor, Janelle S. 4873
Taylor, Jean M. 4656
Taylor, Jill Bolte 4508
Taylor, Katherine 4880
Taylor, Renee 2869
Tchen, Christina "Tina" M. 4393
Teasdale, Sara 1619
Tempelsman, Cathy Rindner 4972
Tenneson, Joyce 3619
Terry, Megan 2827
Thaxter, Celia 1069
Thomas, Aline 2143
Thomas, Audrey Grace 2953
Thomas, Edith 1204
Thomas, Helen 2393
Thomas, Lynn M. 3801
Thomas, Marlo 3062
Thomas, Martha "Minnie" 1228
Thomas, Minnie 2870
Thompson, Clara 1787
Thompson, Jean 4010
Thompson, Kay 2169
Thorne, Barrie 3380
Thorpe, Rose Hartwick 1181
Thurman, Judith 3872

Tiburzi, Bonnie 3873
Tiefer, Leonore 3543
Tillman, Lynne 3802
Tillmon, Johnnie 2583
Tinti, Hannah 4874
Tipton, Billy 2229
Tipton, Jennifer 3063
Tobias, Sheila 2954
Todd, Mabel Elsworth 1559
Toklas, Alice B. 1502
Tomassi, Debbie 4598
Tomlin, Lily 3009
Tompkins, Jane P. 3234
Torgovnick, Marianna 3940
Toth, Emily 3545
Towne, Laura 1004
Townsend, Eliza 813
Traister, Rebecca 4527.1
Treadwell, Sophie 1643
Treichler, Paula Antonia 3463
Treiman, Joyce 2440
Trethewey, Natasha 4737
Trevor, Claire 2191
Truman, Margaret 2500–2501
Truman, Bess 1644
Trussoni, Danielle Anne 4881
Tuchman, Barbara 2192
Tucker, Anne 3620
Tuite, Marjorie 2441
Tunnell, Sophie 1621
Turell, Jane Colman 564
Turkle, Sherry 4738
Turnbull, Agnes Sligh 1689
Turner, Kathleen 4276
Turner, Nancy Byrd 1560
Tuthill, Louisa Caroline 862
Tyler, Anne 3309
Tyler, Priscilla Cooper 939
Tyson, Laura D'Andrea 3804
Ueland, Brenda 1758
Uhlenbeck, Karen 3382
Uhnak, Dorothy 2871
Ukeles, Mierle Laderman 3163
Ulrich, Laurel Thatcher 3109
Ulrich, Mabel S. 1586
Umansky, Ellen M. 4011
Unsoeld, Jolene 2779
Vachss, Alice 4012
Valentine, Jean 2917
Valian, Virginia 3383
Van Buren, Abigail 2333
Van Duyn, Mona 2415
Van Horne, Harriet 2394
Van Rensselaer, Mariana Griswold 1186
Van Runkle, Theadora 3235
Van Susteren, Greta 4277
Vance, Linda Susan 3942
Vanderbilt, Amy 2103
Vanderbilt, Gloria 2502
Vega, Suzanne 4509
Vendler, Helen Hennessy 2872
Veneman, Ann M. 3943
Verdon-Roe, Vivienne 4278
Verona, Virginia 1588
Vida, Vendela 4852
Vincent, Norah 4713
Viorst, Judith 2780

Viramontes, Helena María 4279
Viva 3467
Vogel, Paula A. 4076
Volk, Patricia 3468
Vorse, Mary Heaton 1575
vos Savant, Marilyn 3703
Vreeland, Susan 3704
Wagner, Jane 2956
Wagner, Melinda 4436
Wagner, Sally Roesch 3384
Wakoski, Diane 3064
Walbert, Kate 4598.1
Wald, Lillian D. 1342
Walders, Davi 3113
Waldman, Anne 3621
Waldo, Octavia Capuzzi 2686
Walker, Barbara G. 2744
Walker, Katharine 1097
Walker, Mary Edwards 1047
Wallis, Velma 4559
Walters, Anna Lee 3705
Walters, Barbara 2687
Walters, Dottie 2538
Walters, Lilly 4394
Walton, Meredith "Marty" 3011
Wanatee, Adeline 2144
Wann, Marilyn 4739
Ward, Celeste M. 4853
Ware, Katharine Augusta 861
Warner, Anna Bartlett 979
Warner, Susan 961
Warren, Mercy Otis 603
Washburn, Margaret Floy 1395
Washington, Harriet A. 4634
Washington, Kerry 4921
Washington, Martha 613
Washington, Mary 565
Wasserman Schultz, Debbie 4761.2
Wasserstein, Wendy 4013
Waters, Alice 3548
Waters, Ethel 1838
Watkins, Sharon E. 4282
Wattleton, Faye 3469
Wayne, June 2334
Weaver, Frances 2645
Webster, Margaret 2035
Weddington, Sarah 3622
Weed, Becky 4560
Weimer, Joan Myers 3012
Weinberg, Sheila Pelz 3707
Weinstock, Lotus 3470
Weisberg, Ruth 3385
Weisman, Leslie Kanes 3623
Weisstein, Naomi 3165
Welby, Amelia C. 962
Wells, Carolyn 1368
Wells, Rebecca 4150
Wells-Witteman, Alisa 2688
Welty, Eudora 2117
Wertenbaker, Timberlake 4077
West, Cheryl L. 4714
West, Frances 2781
West, Jessamyn 1959
West, Mae 1790
Wharton, Edith 1292
Wheatley, Margaret "Meg" 3311
Wheeler, Mercy 560
Whitbread, Jane 2231

Whiteley, Opal 1858
Whitestone-McCallum, Heather 4882
Whitman, Meg 4395
Whitman, Marina von Neumann 2957
Whitman, Sarah Power 884
Whitney, Adeline Dutton 996
Whitson, Beth Slater 1538
Whyte, Edna Gardner 1960
Widdemer, Margaret 1561
Wieder, Marcia 4396
Wiese, Anne Pierson 4854
Wiggin, Kate Douglas 1214
Wilcox, Ella Wheeler 1209
Wilcox, Margaret R. 2146
Wilder, Laura Ingalls 1345
Wildman, Stephanie M. 3945
Wilhelm, Gale 2104
Wilkinson, Eliza 686
Wilkinson, Jemima 674
Wilkinson, Marguerite 1602
Willard, Emma Hart 806
Willard, Frances 1090
Willard, Nancy 3013
Willebrandt, Mabel Walker 1703
Williams, Ann Claire 3946
Williams, Bertye Young 1485
Williams, Carol 3876
Williams, E. Faye 3312
Williams, Fannie Barrier 1210
Williams, Jody 4014
Williams, Joy 3550
Williams, Lucinda 4218
Williams, Lynda 4475
Williams, Mary Lou 2147
Williams, Patricia 4079
Williams, Pearl 2232
Williams, Terry Tempest 4339
Williams, Vanessa 4660
Williamson, Marianne 4151
Willis, Gwendolen 1486
Willis, Lydia Fish 566
Willis, Sarah 4284
Willner, Ann Ruth 3166
Willoughby, Denita 4742
Willson, Dixie 1720
Willson, Margaret 4219
Wilner, Eleanor 3066
Wilson, Barbara 4015
Wilson, Dorothy Wright 4838–4839
Wilson, Heather 4561
Wilson, Margaret 1589
Wilson, Marie C. 3877
Wilson, Martha 695
Wiltz, Christine 3878
Windsor, Wallis Simpson 1840
Wineapple, Brenda 4152
Winger, Debra 4340
Winn, Mary Day 1691
Winnemucca, Sarah 1133
Winslow, Anne Goodwin 1467
Winslow, Thyra Samter 1985
Winters, Shelley 2395
Witkovsky, Susan 3386
Wohlstetter, Roberta 2194
Wolf, Naomi 4635
Wolitzer, Hilma 2748

Wolitzer, Meg 4511
Wolverton, Terry 4286
Woo, Merle 3313
Wood, Natalie 3116
Wood, Sally Sayward 702
Woodhull, Victoria Claflin 1086
Woodruff, Julia 1054
Woods, Rose Mary 2305
Woodward, Joanne 2749
Woolsey, Mary 1048
Wordsworth, Elizabeth 1098
Wortham, Anne 3314
Worthington, Robin 2829
Wray, Fay 2075
Wright, Robin 3879
Wucker, Michele 4808
Wurdeman, Audrey 2170
Wurtzel, Elizabeth 4762
Wyatt, Edith Franklin 1423
Wylie, Elinor 1645
Wyse, Lois 2584
Yalow, Rosalyn 2416
Yankowitz, Susan 3315
Yeager, Jeana L. 4153
Yglesias, Helen 2261
Young, Iris Marion 3947
Young, Leontine 2148
Young, Louise B. 2359
Young, Rida Johnson 1369
Younger, Maud 1384
Yung, Judy 3167
Zane, Elizabeth "Betty" 703
Zarin, Cynthia Rebecca 4513
Zeidner, Lisa 4341
Zeisler, Andi 4221
Zellweger, Renée 4809
Zepatos, Thalia 4342
Zuboff, Shoshana 4081
Zwilich, Ellen Taaffe 3168

African American
Albert, Octavia V. 1196
Anderson, Marian 1945
Angelou, Maya 2618
Armstrong, Margalynne 4960
Armstrong, Mary F. 1539
Baker-Fletcher, Karen 4517
Bambara, Toni Cade 3121
Barnwell, Ysaye 3633
Bartholet, Elizabeth 3172
Berry, Mary Frances 3073
Blakely, Nora Brooks 4029
Bond, Cynthia 4400
Brooks, Gwendolyn 2281
Brown, Clara 875
Bryant, Castell 3815
Butler, Octavia 3727
Cannon, Katie Geneva 3956
Carroll, Vinnette 2422
Chapman, Tracy 4673
Chisholm, Shirley 2480
Christian, Barbara T. 3397
Cleage, Pearl 3818
Clifton, Lucille 2970
Coleman, Bessie 1742
Collins, Kathleen 2753
Collins, Patricia Hill 3821

Cooper, Anna Julia 1231
Dauenhauer, Nora 2591
Davis, Angela 3493
Davis, Eisa 4951
Davis, Thadious M. 3494
Delany, Elizabeth "Bessie" 1725
Delany, Sarah "Sadie" 1696
Devers, Gail 4746
Dove, Rita Frances 4101
Dunbar-Nelson, Alice 1457
Edelman, Marian Wright 3141
Eglui, Ellen 1543
Elders, Joycelyn "Minnie" 2843
Evers-Williams, Myrlie 2847
Forman, Ruth 4787
Gibson, Althea 2598
Gibson, P.J. 4107
Gideon, Lillian 2088
Gilmore, Glenda Elizabeth 4640
Giovanni, Nikki 3412
Greene, Bella da Costa 1527
Hamer, Fannie Lou 2290
Harper, Frances Ellen Watkins
   1000
Harris, Barbara Clementine 2712
Herron, Carolivia 3751
Hill, Anita 4369
Hill, Lauryn 4894
hooks, bell 4305
Hunter, Alberta 1811
Jackson, Elaine 3425
Jackson-Opoku, Sandra 4183
Jamison, Judith 3426
Jemison, Mae 4374
Johnson, Rebecca L. 4375
Johnson, Shirley Childress 3760
Jones, Gayl 3902
Jones, Marion 4910
Jones, Patricia 4051
Jordan, Barbara 2986
Jordan, June 2987
Joyner-Kersee, Jacqueline "Jackie"
   4621
Kahlil, Aisha 3199
Kennedy, Florynce R. 2272
King, Deborah K. 4254
King, Janice 4456
Lee, Andrea 4188
Lightfoot, Sara Lawrence 3520
Mathis, Deborah 4192
McDowell, Deborah E. 4058
Morrison, Toni 2771
Moscou, Jacqueline 3919
Mullen, Harryette Romell 4197
Murphy, Beatrice M. 2096
Murray, Pauli 2139
Nelson, Hannah 4826
Nelson, Jill 4127
Nelson, Marilyn 3680
Norman, Jessye 3601
Obama, Michelle 4648
Parker, Pat 3531
Parks, Rosa 2206
Parks, Suzan-Lori 4649
Petry, Ann 2100
Pierce-Baker, Charlotte 3447
Piper, Adrian 3688

Plato, Ann 975
Price, Leontyne 2610
Prothrow-Stith, Deborah 4267
Radford-Hill, Sheila 3927
Rahman, Aishah 2999
Reagon, Bernice Johnson 3369
Rice, Condoleezza 4268
Richards, Beah 2387
Roberts, Dorothy E. 4389
Rodgers, Carolyn M. 3607
Sanchez, Sonia 2912
Sapphire 4002
Shalala, Donna 3304
Shange, Ntozake 3865
Smith, Anna Deavere 4006
Smith, Barbara 3697
Stewart, Maria W. 882
Taylor, Arie P. 2614
Teish, Luisah 3871
Terrell, Mary Church 1299
Terry, Lucy 611
Truth, Sojourner 860
Tubman, Harriet 978
Tucker, C. DeLores 2615
Tucker, Cynthia 4336
Vanzant, Iyanla 4216
Verdelle, A. J. 4558
Waddles, Charleszetta 2193
Wade-Gayles, Gloria Jean 3112
Walker, Alice 3547
Walker, C. J. 1343
Walker, Margaret 2259
Walker, Rebecca 4806
Walker, Sarah Breedlove 1344
Wallace, Michelle 4149
Waters, Maxine 3114
Wells, Ida B. 1291
Wheatley, Phillis 677
Williams, Sherley Anne 3551–3552
Williams, Venus 4944
Winfrey, Oprah 4285
Young, Rolanda 4016

Asian American
Allen, Susan Au 3625
Chang, Diana 2882
Chao, Elaine 4167
Chen, Pauline W. 4356
Chin, Marilyn 4295
Houston, Jeanne Wakatsuki 2897
Kim, Elaine Haikyung 3354
Kingston, Maxine Hong 3203
Lim, Genny 3672
Matsumoto, Valerie 4420
Mink, Patsy 2608
Mirikitani, Janice 3283
Ng, Fae Myenne 4385
Tan, Amy 4146
Wong, Nellie 2919
Yamada, May 2475
Yamauchi, Wakako 2504
Yee, Marian 4989

Latina American
Alvarez, Cecilia 3949
Anzaldúa, Gloria Evangelina 3321
Baca, Judy Francisca 3953

Benítez, Sandra Ables 3242
Cervantes, Lorna Dee 4234
Chávez, Denise Elia 3816
Cisneros, Sandra 4237
Cota-Cárdenas, Margarita 3250
Gonzales, Sylvia Alicia 3414
Huerta, Dolores 2716
Moraga, Cherríe 4125
Portillo Trambley, Estela 2609
Pursifull, Carmen M. 2736
Rebolledo, Tey Diana 3052
Richards, Amy 4831
Rodriguez, Graciela "Chely" 4939
Ruiz, Mona Sandoval 4505
Valdés, Gina 3466
Villanueva, Alma Luz 3546
Vallejo, Linda 4075

Multiracial American
Allen, Paula Gunn 3118
Houston, Velina Hasu 4413
Sánchez-Scott, Milcha 4331

Native American
Dann, Carrie 2624
Dann, Mary 2450
Erdrich, Louise 4242
Glancy, Diane 3263
Green, Rayna 3338
Harjo, Joy 4045
Hinck, Jeannie 4110
Littlebear Morena, Naomi 4377
Mankiller, Wilma Pearl 3591
Pocahontas 404
Power, Susan 4593
Quick-to-See Smith, Jaune 3224
Sams, Jamie 4070
Sanchez, Georgiana Valoyce 4940
Silko, Leslie Marmon 3866
Spider Woman 2
Tapahonso, Luci 4214
Wauneka, Annie Dodge 2145
Whiteman, Roberta Hill 3806–3807
Witt, Shirley Hill 2918

ARABIAN
Hind bint Utba 120
Rabi'a bint Isma'il of Syria 139
Safiya bint Musafir 126
Wallada al-Mustakfi 172

ARGENTINEAN
Arditti, Rita 2877
Gambaro, Griselda 2628
Jessop, Violet 1665
Kaufman, Paola 4792
Kirchner, Cristina 4187
Malagrino, Silvia A. 3988
Ocampo, Victoria 1731
Perón, Eva Duarte 2354
Storni, Alfonsina 1755
Teubal, Savina J. 2582
Valenzuela, Luisa 3110
Walsh, Maria Elena 2745

ARMENIAN
Koghtnatsi, Khosrovidoukht 138

Kouchak, Nahabed 401
Siunetsi, Sahakdoukht 148

ASSYRIAN
Semiramis 42

AUSTRALIAN
Adamson, Joy 2336
Anderson, Judith 1841
Arnim, Mary Elizabeth 1322
Bandler, Faith 2361
Bird, Carmel 3175
Brooks, Geraldine 4292
Brown, Eileen Kampakuta 2696
Bruce, Mary Grant 1506
Caldicott, Helen 3075
Chandab, Taghred 4916
Clark, Margaret D. 3399
Clendinnen, Inga 2884
Dunn, Irina 3962
Durham, Judith 3403
Evatt, Elizabeth 2846
Franklin, Miles 1544
Greer, Germaine 3145
Hazzard, Shirley 2763
Hewett, Dorothy Coade 2459
Highbridge, Dianne 3580
Horacek, Judy 4580
Hospital, Janette Turner 3345
Jeffreys, Sheila 3834
Katona, Jacqui 4724
Kenny, Elizabeth 1549
Kidman, Nicole 4750
Langley, Eve 2092
Manos, Helen 3989
Margarula, Yvonne 4460
McLeod, Irene Rutherford 1729
Melba, Nellie 1274
Powter, Susan 4427
Reddy, Helen 3297
Rogers, Lesley 3452
Rowe, Dorothy 2739
Spender, Dale 3458
St. John, Madeleine 3306
Stead, Christina 1957
Sutherland, Joan 2581
Sykes, Roberta 3461
Wertheim, Margaret 4474
Wingfield, Eileen Wani 2747
Wright, Judith 2260

AUSTRIAN
Anne of Austria 414
Bolgar, Hedda 2106
Bregy, Charlotte 435
Cori, Gerty Theresa 1821
Eisler, Riane 2756
Eschenbach, Maria von Ebner 1025
Faschinger, Lilian 3965
Freud, Anna 1810
Hubbard, Ruth 2487
Klein, Melanie 1579
Knopf, Olga 1683
Lenya, Lotta 1868
Lerner, Gerda 2380
Ludwig, Paula 1912
Mahler-Werfel, Alma 1532

Margaret of Austria 282
Maria of Hungary and Bohemia 298
Maria Theresa 579
Marie-Antoinette 682
Meitner, Lise 1514
Pappenheim, Bertha 1249
Pfeiffer, Ida Laura 857
Schumann-Heink, Ernestine 1278
Sheehan, Susan 3058
Suttner, Bertha von 1119

AZERI
Hajiyeva, Lala Shovket 4108
Yunusova, Leyla 4437

AZTECAN (NOW MEXICO)
Macuilxochitl 259

BANGLADESHAN
Ali, Monica 4743
Chowdhury, Seema 4842
Hasina Wajed, Sheikh 3749.1
Nasrin, Taslima 4627
Wazed, Hasina 3805
Zia Rahman, Khaleda 3624

BAVARIAN
Pascalina, Madre 1802

BELGIAN
Beatrijs of Nazareth 204
Calvin, Idelette de Bure 346
De Vinck, Catherine 2425
Fabien, Michèle 3568
Hepburn, Audrey 2662
Irigaray, Luce 2717
Sarton, May 2189
Yourcenar, Marguerite 1986

BELIZEAN
Gibson, Janet 4178

BENGALESE
Chandidas 246
Sinha, Kabita 2777

BOHEMIAN
Gutmans, Sarel 437

BOLIVIAN
Ayllón Soria, Virginia 3952
Otero, María 3998

BOSNIAN (ALSO SEE YUGOSLAVIA)
Filipovic, Zlata 4932

BOTSWANAN
Nisa 2773

BRAZILIAN
Bundchen, Gisele 4931
Cecato, Lica 4355
de Jesus, Carolina Maria 2217
Guidon, Niède 2852
Purim, Flora 3368
Silva, Marina 4469

BRITISH (NOTE: ENGLISH, IRISH, SCOTTISH, WELSH ARE THE PREFERRED CATEGORIES)
Apter, Terri 3882
Atkins, Eileen 2878
Banks-Smith, Nancy 2691
Barrett, Michèle 3885
Bayliss, Claire 4840
Blackburn, Julia 3812
Bonham-Carter, Violet 1660
Bouza, Erica 3245
Budiardjo, Carmel 2512
Burchill, Julie 4524
Burnell, Jocelyn Bell 3395
Burton, Harriet Emma 1424
Busfield, Joan 3130
Byatt, A. S. 2968
Campbell, Beatrix 3728
Carrington, Leonora 2282
Colledge, Cecilia 2367
Cope, Wendy Mary 3560
Corbett, E. T. 1542
Cotton, Nancy 3492
Coward, Rosalind 4171
Cumming, Anne 2284
Davey, Janet 4172
Desai, Kiran 4843
Du Pré, Jacqueline 3564
Ellis, Alice Thomas 2793
Flanders, Laura 4575
Fonteyn, Margot 2342
Ford, Anna 3407
Fremantle, Anne 2108
Graves, Clarissa 1747
Hampson, Daphne 3508
Harris, Joanne 4677
Hazleton, Lesley 3578
Henderson, Hazel 2853
Hocking, Anne 1708
Hodgkin, Dorothy Crowfoot 2132
Jackson, Glenda 2984
Jekyll, Gertrude 1116
Kanner, Barbara "Penny" 2524
Kelly, Emily "Pat" 1400
Lacy, Mary 749
Lahiri, Jhumpa 4752
Lambert, Angela 3204
Lanchester, Elsa 1950
Lejeune, Caroline 1852
Levy, Andrea 4257
Lonsdale, Kathleen Yardley 1972
Mary, Queen Consort of Great Britain 1338
McTaggart, Lynne 4059
Norris, Pippa 4200
Partridge, Frances 1918
Phillips, Angela Marie 3783
Phillips, Anne 4426
Phillips, Marie 4914
Pym, Barbara 2208
Richards, Janet Radcliffe 3535
Russell, Dora 1803
Scott, Robyn 4949
Seymour, Miranda J. 4207
Sharman, Helen 4654
Simon, Rachel 995
Terán, Lisa St. Aubin de 4215

Thomson, Alice 4657
Ward, Barbara 2230
Westwood, Vivienne 3310
Williams, Shirley 2746
Wilson, Elizabeth 3014
Zelter, Angie 4080

BULGARIAN
Simeonova, Albena 4712

BURKINABE
Nacro, Fanta Régina 4626

BURMESE
Aung San Suu Kyi 3554
Win, Aye Aye 4807

BYZANTINE (NOW TURKEY)
Comnena, Anna 176
Kassiane 149
Theodora 113
Pulcheria, Aelia 109

CAMBODIAN
Ung, Loung 4836

CAMEROON
Liking, Werewere 3986

CANADIAN
Allen, Charlotte Vale 3239
Apostolides, Marianne 4875
Arbour, Louise 3715
Arden, Elizabeth 1503
Ashenburg, Katherine 3951
Atwood, Margaret 3119
Barclay, Aviel 4779
Barfoot, Joan 3631
Barlow, Maude 3719
Bertell, Rosalie 2651
Bolt, Carol 3244
Brodribb, Somer 4232
Campbell, Kim 3642
Carr, Emily 1387
Carson, Anne Regina 3957
Ciment, Jill 4168
Diamond, Selma 2368
DiManno, Rosie 4978
Dion, Céline 4766
Doody, Margaret Anne 3138
Dressler, Marie 1412
Eastwood, Alice 1247
Ferron 4103
Firestone, Shulamith 3570
Forbes, Leslie 4484
Fréchette, Louise 3655
Galchen, Rivka 4907
Gallant, Mavis 2426
Galloway, Priscilla 2705
Granholm, Jennifer M. 4486
Gruen, Sara 4909
Haggerty, Joan 3194
Harper, Martha Matilda 1223
Harris, Maureen 3419
Huston, Nancy 4181
Itani, Frances 3348
Jacobsen, Josephine 2090
Johnson, Emily Pauline 1272

Kelley, Edith Summers 1614
Kidder, Margot 3839
Klein, Naomi 4823
Kogawa, Joy 2938
Laing, Dilys 2051
Laurence, Margaret 2561
Laut, Agnes C. 1392
Leddy, Mary Jo 3669
Leveridge, Lillian 1531
Matossian, Mariam 4865
Mavrikakis, Catherine 4588
McCallion, Hazel 2408
McClung, Nellie 1414
McCrory, Colleen 3991
McLachlan, Sarah 4773
McPherson, Aimee Semple 1713
Millar, Margaret Ellis 2249
Mitchell, Joni 3443
Montgomery, Lucy Maud 1444
Moodie, Susanna 880
Munro, Alice 2772
Nattel, Lilian 4383
Orr, Mary 4548
Overall, Christine 3923
Pearson, Patricia 4685
Pickford, Mary 1781
Pollock, Sharon 2998
Rabliauskas, Sophia 4551
Richie, Alexandra 4651
Ritter, Erika 3860
Rosenfeld, Bobbie 2005
Roy, Gabrielle 2115
Schapiro, Miriam 2468
Seager, Joni 4273
Shain, Merle 2947
Smart, Elizabeth 2211
Stronach, Belinda 4736
Tilghman, Shirley M. 3701
Tyler, Robin 3381
Watt-Cloutier, Sheila 4283
Whitton, Charlotte 1839
Winslow, Anna Green 700
Woodman, Marion 2648
York, Eva Rose 1240

Native Canadian
Brant, Beth 3246
Campbell, Maria 3179
Kassi, Norma 4253
Qernertoq 156
Sainte-Marie, Buffy 3301

CARIAN (NOW GREECE & TURKEY)
Artemisia 60

CARTHAGINIAN (NOW TUNESIA)
Perpetua, Vivia 99

CENTRAL AFRICAN REPUBLIC
Tauziat, Nathalie 4761

CHALDEAN (NOW IRAZ)
Sarah 8

CHILEAN
Aguirre, Isidora 2337
Allende, Hortensia Bussi de 2234
Allende, Isabel 3317
Aróstica, Florencia 4345

Bachelet, Michelle 4022
Castedo-Ellerman, Elena 3022
Mistral, Gabriela 1700
Parra, Violeta 2299
Roepke, Gabriela 2388
Roumeau, Jacqueline 4985

CHINESE
Bai Fengxi 2785
Berssenbrugge, Mei-mei 3721
Chang, Jung 4092
Chang Ts'ai-t'ien 1283.1
Chao Li-hua 240
Chao Luan-luan 144
Cheng, Nien 2239
Chiang Kai-shek, Madame 1863
Chien Shiung Wu 2173
Ch'in Chia, Wife of 72
Ch'iu Chin 1425
Chu Shu-chên 197
Chuo Wên-chün 69
Feng Meng-lung 380
Gao Yaojie 2597
Han Suyin 2291
Han Ts'ui-p'in 153
Ho, Lady 67
Ho Shuang-ch'ing 573
Hou Xiaotian 4581
Hsiang Chin-yu 2134
Hsiao Hung 2158
Hsi-chün 73
Hsieh Ping-ying 2049–2050
Hsüeh T'ao 140
Huang O 292
Huang Zongying 2522
Jiang Qing 2221
Kuan Tao-shêng 223
Li Qingzhao 175
Li Yeh 147
Liu, Peggy 4624
Lord, Betty Bao 3094
Manjaa, Nora 4898
Mettika 49
Mutta 50
Pan Chao 8788
Peng Peiyun 2678
Qing Dai 3250.1
Qui Jin 1465
Quin Guanshu 2679.1
Ru Zhijuan 2535
Shen Rong 2948
Shen-ch'iung, Nieh 162
Sumangalamata 51
Sun Tao-hüsan 182
Sun Bu-er 184
Sun Yat-sen, Madame 1786
Sun Yün-fêng 725
T'ang Wan 213
Teng Ying-ch'ao 1983
Ting Ling 2058
Ts'ai Yen 98
Tse-t'ien Wu 121
Tzu Yeh, Tzu 104
Wang Anyi 4280
Wang Ch'ing-hui 233
Wang Wei 553
Wang Yongchen 4281
Xue Tao 141
Yang Jiang 2171

Yang Ping 2105
Yü Hsüan-chi 152
Zhang, Lijia 4690
Zhang Jie 3067
Zhang Kangkang 4017
Zong Pu 2649

ANGLO-CHINESE
Ayscough, Florence 1504
McIntyre, Tami 2409
Yang, Gladys 2358
Yard, Molly 2233

COLOMBIAN
Castillo y Guevara, Francisca Josefa del 537
Gonzalez, Patricia 3971
Grueso, Libia 4578
Paternostro, Silvana 4549
Salavarrieta, Policarpa 826
Shakira 4919

CONGOLESE
Deschryver, Christine Schuler 4694

CORSICAN (ALSO SEE FRENCH)
Bonaparte, Marie Letitia 655

CROATIAN (ALSO SEE YOGOSLAVIA)
Terselic, Vesna 4633
Ugresic, Dubravka 3941

CUBAN
Alonso, Dora 2118
Fornés, Maria Irene 2704
García, Cristina 4449
Isasi-Diaz, Ada Maria 3424
Montero, Mayra 4123
Obejas, Achy 4386

CZECHOSLOVAK
Connolly, Olga 2789
Crespi, Camilla T. 3330
Dery, Dominika 4890–4891
Epstein, Helen 3740
Hauser, Ewa 3662
Kalisch, Shoshana 2631
Krásnohorská, Eliska 1151
Malcolm, Janet 2904
Navratilova, Martina 4424
Pincus, Lily 1873
Vostrá, Alena 3111
Winn, Marie 3115

DANISH
Caroline Matilda 667
Christina, Leonora 442
Dinesen, Isak 1627
Genefke, Inge 3503
Margrethe II 3208
Undset, Sigrid 1587

DOMINICAN REPUBLIC
Vicioso, Sherezada 3875

DUTCH
Beatrix, Queen of the Netherlands 3072
Bertken, Sister 257

Charrière, Madame de 630
de Moor, Margriet 3253
Hadewijch of Brabant 218
Hari, Mata 1475
Hillesum, Etty 2220
Juliana 2111
Keuls, Eva Clara 2633
Molesworth, Mary Louisa 1088
Reinharz, Shulamit 3693
Sengers, Johanna Levelt 2682
Stein, Edith 1735
van den Beld, Theodora 4148

ECUADORAN
Pink, Lady 4686

EDOMITE (NOW ISRAEL AND JORDAN)
Job, Wife of 41

EGYPTIAN
Aboulela, Leila 4663
Ahmed, Leila 3169
Ankhesenpaton 15
Assad, Marie B. 2445
Cleopatra VII 75
Eltahawy, Mona 4747
Hagar 5
Hathshepsut 14
Isis 3
Kamel, Laila Iskandar 3761
Lively, Penelope 2858
Mubarak, Suzanne 3286
Pharaoh's daughter 17
Rizk, Sarah
Shaarawi, Huda 1536
Shebl, Riham 4920
Sibyl, the Jewish 68

EL SALVADORIAN
Méndez, Nora Bermúdez 4795

ENGLISH (ALSO SEE BRITISH)
Adams, Louisa Catherine 766
Adams, Sarah Flower 888
Agnes the Martyr 295
Aguilar, Grace 932 Aiken, Lucy 785
Alden, Priscilla 416
Allingham, Margery 1987
Amanpour, Christiane 4437.1
Amelia 794
Anger, Jane 383
Anne of England 504
Ardagh, Susan Hamilton 1200
Ariadne 535
Armstrong, Karen 3474
Arndt, Bettina "Tina" 3883
Ashford, Daisy 1704
Askew, Anne 313
Asquith, Margot 1301
Astell, Mary 507
Atkinson, Kate 4021
Auber, Harriet 761
Aubin, Penelope 521
Austen, Jane 767
Austin, Sarah Taylor 836
Bacon, Anne Cooke 328
Bagnold, Enid 1693
Bainbridge, Beryl Margaret 2831

Baker, Elizabeth 1469
Baldwin, Monica 1762
Bamber, Helen 2508
Barbauld, Anna Letitia 642
Barber, Lynn 3475
Barber, Margaret Fairless 1355
Barker, Jane 523
Barker, Patricia 3392
Barnard, Charlotte Alington 1022
Barrington, Judith 3476
Bathurst, Elizabeth 491
Bawden, Nina 2510
Baynard, Anne 516
Bedingfield, Natasha 4945
Beeton, Isabella Mayson 1074
Begbie, Janet 2120
Behn, Aphra 472
Bell, Florence 1182
Bell, Gertrude 1347
Benet, Mother 347
Benson, Stella 1740
Berners, Juliana 266
Berry, Dorothy 456
Besant, Annie Wood 1148
Betsko, Kathleen 3125
Bianco, Margery Williams
Bibesco, Elizabeth Asquith 1842
Billington-Greig, Teresa 1488
Billson, Christine 4520
Bingham, Charlotte 3325
Bingham, Madeline 2172
Bisset, Jacqueline 3637
Blackmore, Susan Jane 4028
Blamire, Susanna 653
Blunt, Anne 1075
Boadicea 86
Boleyn, Anne 300
Booth, Cherie 4231
Booth, Evangeline 1308
Boothby, Frances 493
Boothroyd, Betty 2652
Bottome, Phyllis 1606
Boulbie, Judith 556
Bowen, Marjorie 1675–1676
Brackley, Elizabeth 445
Braddon, Mary Elizabeth 1076
Bradford, Elizabeth 500
Bradford, Mistress 385
Bradley, Katharine 1141
Bradstreet, Anne 430
Bray, Ann Eliza 815
Brereton, Jane 529
Brett, Dorothy 1591
Brittain, Vera 1764–1765
Brontö, Anne 965
Brontö, Charlotte 934
Brontö, Emily 945
Brooke, Frances 593
Brookner, Anita 2620
Brown, Tina 4165
Browning, Elizabeth Barrett 892
Bryan, Margaret 329
Burbidge, E. Margaret 2338
Burlend, Rebecca Burton 837
Burney, Fanny 671
Burrell, Sophia 660
Burton, Isabel 1036
Burton, Elaine Frances 1988
Buxton, Bertha 1124

Byron, Mary C. G. 1263
Caldwell, Taylor 1896
Cam, Helen M. 1625
Cameron, Julia Margaret 927
Campbell, Anne 4031
Campbell, Patrick 1309
Carew, Elizabeth 391
Carter, Angela 3182
Carter, Elizabeth 578
Cartland, Barbara 1928
Cartwright, Johanna 473
Castle, Barbara Anne 2122
Cavell, Edith Louisa 1310
Cavendish, Georgiana 690
Cavendish, Jane 441
Cavendish, Margaret 446
Chamber, Anna 774
Chambers, Jessie 1661
Chandler, Mary 531
Chapone, Hester 598
Chard, Sylvia C. 3077
Charke, Charlotte 705
Charles, Elizabeth 1017
Childe-Pemberton, Harriet L. 1723
Christie, Agatha 1724
Churchill, Caryl 3078
Clarkstone, Bessie 448
Clifford, Anne 396
Clinton, Elizabeth 379
Clitherow, Margaret 358
Clive, Catherine 572
Cobbe, Frances P. 983
Coleridge, Mary 1264
Coleridge, Sara 871
Collier, Mary 532
Collins, Anne 485
Collins, Joan 2840
Compton, Elizabeth 397
Compton-Burnett, Ivy 1743
Conran, Shirley 2790
Cook, Eliza 947
Cookson, Catherine 2044
Cooper, Diana 1744
Cooper, Edith 1285
Cooper, Elizabeth 607
Corey, Martha 538
Cornford, Frances Darwin 1649
Cowley, Hannah 643
Craik, Dinah Mulock 1006
Craster, Edmund 1427
Crawford, Louisa Macartney 817
Crosby, Sarah 605
Crowe, Catharine 818
Cunard, Nancy 1822
Custance, Olive 1428
Dane, Clemence 1677
Daniels, Sarah 4360
De Bary, Anna Bunston 1359
De Wolfe, Elsie 1311
Dean, Louise 4815
Delaney, Shelagh 3137
Delany, Mary 549
Dench, Judi 2889
Dhaliwal, Daljit 4607
Diana, Princess of Wales 4568
Doudney, Sarah 1113
Dowriche, Anne 349
Drabble, Margaret 3139
Drew, Elizabeth 1662

Duff, Esther Lillian 2125
Duffy, Maureen 2842
du Maurier, Daphne 2063
Dunant, Sarah 3961
Dunbar, Andrea 4570
Dunn, Nell 2976
Dyer, Mary 429
Eaglen, Jane 4526
Eden, Emily 853
Edwards, Amelia 1040
Egburg 137
Egerton, Sarah F. 514
Eliot, George 955
Elizabeth 1898
Elizabeth I of England 334
Elizabeth II of Great Britain 2549
Elizabeth of York 271
Elliott, Charlotte 809
Ellis, Sarah 918
Elstob, Elizabeth 528
Ephelia 474
Estaugh, Elizabeth Haddon 524
Evans, Edith 1679
Evelyn, Mary 464
Falconar, Harriet 768
Falconar, Maria 759
Fane, Violet 1114
Fanshawe, Ann 449
Fanshawe, Catherine Marie 726
Fawcett, Millicent Garrett 1150
Ferguson, Patricia 4176
Ferguson, Sarah "Fergie" 4483
Field, Joanna 1899
Fielding, Sarah 568
Fields, Gracie 1866
Finch, Anne 497
Fitzgerald, Penelope 2266
Fleming, Joan 2086
Fletcher, Mary 627
Fowler, Ellen Thorneycroft 1253
Fox, Margaret Askew Fell 432
Franklin, Eleanor Anne 847
Franklin, Rosalind 2370
Fraser, Antonia 2796
Fry, Elizabeth 780
Fugard, Sheila 2797
Fyleman, Rose 1492
Gardam, Jane 2629
Gaskell, Elizabeth 911
Gee, Shirley 2798
Gems, Pam 2518
Gibbons, Stella 1948
Gilliatt, Penelope 2799
Gingold, Hermione 1848
Glenconnor, Pamela 1390
Glyn, Elinor 1303
Godolphin, Margaret 489
Godwin, Hannah 819
Goodall, Jane 2892
Gore, Catherine 863
Goudge, Elizabeth 1903
Graham, Sheilah 1995
Green, Mary A. E. 948
Grenfell, Joyce Phipps 2129
Greville, Frances 1267
Greville, Frances Fulke 583
Grey, Elizabeth Woodville 260
Grey, Jane 336
Grey, Mary 343

Griffith, Nicola 4534
Grote, Harriet 833
Grymeston, Elizabeth 367
Gurney, Dorothy 1232
Gwyn, Nell 486
Hadley, Tessa 4410
Hall, Radclyffe 1545
Hallack, Cecily R. 1866.1
Hamilton, Emma 727
Hankey, Katherine 1056
Harington, Lucy 389
Harley, Brilliana 411
Harrison, Jane 1176
Harvey, Alice 386
Haskins, Minnie 1459
Hastings, Flora 896
Hastings, Selina 562
Havergal, Frances Ridley 1072
Hawkes, Jessie 2131
Hay, Lucy 406
Haywood, Eliza 539
Hearne, Mary 569
Heathorn, Henrietta 1001
Heaton, Rose Henniker 1612
Hebblethwaite, Margaret 4250.1
Hemans, Felicia 838
Hepworth, Barbara 1970
Herbert, Mary Sidney 365
Hewlett, Sylvia Ann 3664
Hit-him-home, Joane 475
Hoby, Margaret 375
Holbrook, Ann 781
Holford, Margaret Wrench 711
Holland, Elizabeth 756
Holtby, Winifred 1867
Hope, Laurence 1315
Hoper, Mrs. 631
Hopkins, Jane Ellice 1079
Horsfield, Debbie 4306
Howard, Anne Dacre 359
Howard, Anne Douglas 543
Howard, Isabella 589
Howell, Georgina 3346
Howitt, Mary 864
Hume, Anna 476
Huneberc of Heidenheim 142
Huntington, Helen 1460
Hurnscot, Loran 1907
Hutchinson, Anne 399
Hutchinson, Lucy 438
Inchbald, Elizabeth 676
Ingelow, Jean 968
James, P. D. 2379
Jardine, Lisa 3515
Jeger, Lena May 2245
Jellicoe, Ann 2600
Jennings, Elizabeth 2554
Jewsbury, Geraldine 919
Jewsbury, Maria Jane 867
Joceline, Elizabeth 371
Johnson, Amy 2091
Johnson, Pamela Hansford 2181–2182
Johnston, Jill 2665
Jones, Emily Beatrix 1775
Jones, Mary 663
Joseph, Helen 2024
Joseph, Jenny 2803
Judson, Sarah B. 877

Juliana of Norwich 236
Katz, Lilian G. 2805
Keatley, Charlotte 4537
Keays, Sara 3838
Keith, Penelope 3200
Kemble, Fanny 908
Kempe, Margery 245
Kenney, Annie 1528
Killigrew, Anne 496
Killigrew, Catherine 331
King, Harriet 1094
King, Countess of Lovelace, Ada Byron 929
Kitzinger, Celia 4539
Kitzinger, Jenny 4644
Kitzinger, Sheila 2667
Knollys, Lettice 338
Knowles, Mary 615
Lamb, Caroline 799
Lamb, Mary Ann 722
Landon, Letitia 873
Langtry, Lily 1197
Lansbury, Angela 2530
Lanyer, Aemilia 372
Lathbury, Eva 1910
Lawrence, Gertrude 1934
Lawson, Nigella Lucy 4541
Le Gallienne, Eva 1887
Le Gallienne, Hesper 1777
Leach, Penelope 3042
Leapor, Mary 590
Lee, Ann 622
Lee, Hermione 3843
Lee, Mary Chudleigh 492
Lee, Sophia 664
Leek, Sybil 2296
Leigh, Vivien 2204
Letts, Winifred 1580
Leverson, Ada 1288
Levertov, Denise 2464
Levy, Amy 1273
Lewes, Joyce 360
Lewis, Sarah Anna 994
Liddell, Catherine 1161
Lillie, Beatrice 1869
Lisle, Honor 296
Littlewood, Joan 2223
Llewellyn-Thomas, Beatrice 1711
Lloyd, Marie 1378
Lovell, Marie 878
Low, Juliette 1257
Loy, Mina 1581
Lupino, Ida 2321
Luxborough, Henrietta Knight 547
Lyall, Edna 1225
Lytton, Constance 1365
Macaulay, Rose 1570
MacLeod, Jean S. 2094–2095
Madan, Judith 665
Maitland, Sara Louise 3987
Makin, Bathsua 412
Manley, Delariviere 501
Margaret of Anjou 258
Margolis, Sue 3990
Maribel, Mother 1667
Markham, Beryl 1951
Markova, Alicia 2138
Marsh, Anne 823

Martin, Sarah 824
Martin, Sarah Catherine 739
Martineau, Harriet 874
Mary I of England 309
Mary II of England 498
Mary of France 290
Masters, Mary 610
Matilda 180
Mazuchelli, Elizabeth Sarah 1046
McIntosh, Kinn Hamilton 2726
McIntosh, Mary 2992
McPartland, Marian 2324
Mee, Margaret 2113
Merry, Anne Brunton 743
Mew, Charlotte 1366
Meynell, Alice Christiana 1152
Milbanke, Anne Isabella 834
Mill, Harriet Taylor 902
Millar, Susanna 4544
Mitford, Jessica 2298
Mitford, Mary Russell 805
Mitford, Nancy 2000
Montagu, Elizabeth 585
Montagu, Lily 1416
Montagu, Mary Wortley 533
Montefiore, Judith 797
More, Hannah 649
Morris, Jackie 4589
Mortimer, Penelope 2326
Motley, Annette 4825
Muller, Mary Ann 973
Munda, Constantina 425
Murry, Ann 750
Nesbit, Edith 1234
Nevill, Dorothy 1009
Nightingale, Florence 974
Nonnen, Emily 920
Norton, Caroline Sheridan 905
Oakley, Ann 3529
O'Brien, Mary Mamie 2571
O'Keeffe, Adelaide 771
O'Malley, Mary 3289
O'Neill, Terry
Opie, Amelia 744
Orbach, Susie 3685
Ormes, Cicely 324
Orred, Meta 1140
Orton, Beth 4827
Osborne, Dorothy 453
Ouida 1089
Owen, Jane 426
Page, Louise 4325
Pankhurst, Adela 1636
Pankhurst, Christabel 1553
Pankhurst, Emmeline 1235
Pankhurst, Sylvia 1583
Pardoe, Julia 898
Parr, Catherine 305
Parry, Blanche 363
Paston, Agnes 280
Paston, Margaret Mautby 262
Pateman, Carole 3219
Payne-Gaposchkin, Cecilia Helena 1919
Pennington, Mrs. 617
Pethick-Lawrence, Emmeline 1341
Philips, Joan 515
Philips, Katherine Fowler 459

Pitter, Ruth 1855–1856
Pix, Mary Griffith 509
Porter, Jane 772
Potter, Beatrix 1330
Prest, Wife of 361
Primrose, Diana 457–458
Proctor, Adelaide 1002
Quant, Mary 2910
Radcliffe, Ann 723
Raine, Kathleen Jessie 2101
Raleigh, Elizabeth 370
Rathbone, Eleanor 1404
Ray, Rebecca 4938
Reed, Esther De Berdt 651
Renault, Mary 2033
Rendell, Ruth 2737
Rice-Davies, Mandy 3534
Rich, Penelope Devereaux 366
Richardson, Dorothy Miller 1419
Richardson, Miranda 4467
Richter, Gisela 1585
Riddlestone, Sue 4552
Ridler, Anne Barbara 2188
Roberts, Michele 3932
Robinson, A. Mary F. 1226
Robinson, Mary 693
Roddick, Anita 3370
Rogers, Hester Ann 687
Rolls, Mrs. Henry 912
Rossetti, Christina 1032
Routledge, Katherine 1331
Rowe, Elizabeth Singer 518
Rowling, J. K. 4711
Rowson, Susanna Haswell 715
Royden, Maude 1498
Rubenstein, Gillian 3374
Russell, Anna 2167
Russell, Elizabeth Hoby 326
Russell, Rachel 467
Ryan, Sarah 594
Sackville, Margaret 1574
Sackville-West, Vita 1752
Saunders, Cicely 2329
Saunders, Margaret Baillie 1420
Sayers, Dorothy L. 1782
Scindia, Yashodhara Raje 4271
Scott, Mary 751
Seward, Anna 641
Sewell, Anna 977
Sewell, Sarah Ann 1128
Sharp, Joane 427
Shaw, Anna Howard 1154
Sheepshanks, Mary 3612
Shelley, Mary Wollstonecraft 859
Sheridan, Clare 1641
Sherrington, Grace 353
Sherwood, Mary Martha 769
Shipton, Ursula 286
Siddons, Sarah 684
Sitwell, Edith 1673
Smith, Charlotte 658
Smith, Dodie 1836
Smith, Dorothy E. 2579
Smith, Stevie 1956
Smith, Zadie 4902
Smyth, Ethel Mary 1237
Sophia Dorothea of Celle 510
Southey, Caroline Anne 802

Sowerby, Githa 1482
Sowernam, Ester 428
Speght, Rachel 405
Spence, Jo 2915
St. John, Christopher Marie 1466
Stanhope, Hester Lucy 773
Steele, Anne 580
Stephenson, Isabella S. 1118
Stewart, Alice 2057
Stewart, Mary 2276
Stopes, Marie Carmichael 1558
Storace, Nancy 728
Storey, Violet Alleyn 1922
Storkey, Elaine 3460
Struther, Jan 1942
Stubbes, Katherine 377
Summerskill, Edith 1943
Sutcliffe, Ann 413
Symonds, Caroline 835
Tait, Katherine 2473
Tattlewell, Mary 477
Taylor, Ann 792
Taylor, Elizabeth 2826
Taylor, Jane 795
Taylor, Mrs. 526
Terry, Ellen 1162
Tett, Gillian 4761.1
Thatcher, Margaret 2537
Thomas, Elizabeth 520
Thornton, Alice 454
Thrynne, Frances 679
Tollet, Elizabeth 541
Tonna, Charlotte Elizabeth 821
Townsend, Sue 3702
Tracy, Honor 2213
Trapnel, Anna 444
Trefusis, Elizabeth 718
Tremain, Rose 3464
Trench, Melesina 742
Trimmer, Sarah Kirby 637
Trollope, Frances Milton 784
Trollope, Joanna 3465
Trotter, Catherine 522
Troubridge, Laura Gurney 1321
Tweedie, Jill 2828
Tyrwhit, Elizabeth 322
Valiente, Doreen 2442
Vardill, Anna Jane 789
Vernon, Elizabeth 378
Vestris, Eliza 828
Victoria 960
Vincenzi, Penny 3164
Waite, Mary 534
Wallbridge, Elizabeth 753
Walsh, Jill Paton 3065
Walsingham, Frances 373
Walters, Minette 3944
Wandor, Michelene 3237
Ward, Mary 393
Ward, Mary Augusta 1187
Warner, Marina 3706
Warner, Sylvia Townsend 1789
Webb, Beatrice Potter 1239
Webb, Mary 1576
Weddell, Mrs. 612
Weinraub, Sally 2503
Weldon, Fay 2874
Wentworth, Anne 455

Wesley, Susanna 512
West, Jane 694
Wharton, Anne 462
Wheathill, Ann 388
Whitehorn, Katharine 2647
Whitney, Isabella 340
Wickham, Anna 1622
Williams, Anna 561
Williams, Helen Maria 716
Williams, Sarah "Sadie" 1107
Willoughby, Catherine 312
Wilson, Dagmar 2278
Wilson, Harriette 814
Winegarten, Renee 2443
Winehouse, Amy 4953
Winterson, Jeanette 4510
Winthrop, Margaret 400
Wiseman, Jane 527
Woffington, Peg 586
Wollstonecraft, Mary 701
Wood, Ellen 922
Woolf, Virginia 1590
Woolley, Hannah 443
Wordsworth, Dorothy 758
Wordsworth, Mary 754
Wright, Susanna 546
Wroth, Mary Sidney 395
Yearsley, Anne 710
Yonge, Charlotte 991
Young, Elizabeth 352

FINNISH
Canth, Minna 1125
Gripenberg, Alexandra 1222
Halonen, Tarja Kaarina 3418
Jotuni, Maria 1547
Manner, Eeva-Liisa 2406

FRANKISH (NOW GERMANY)
Baudonivia 117
David-Néel, Alexandra 1348
Radegunda 114

FRENCH (ALSO SEE CORSICA)
Adjani, Isabelle 4287
Aimée, Anouk 2782
Aissé, Charlotte Elizabeth 540
Alais 202
Alamanda 194
Albret, Jeanne d' 327
Ancelot, Virginie 829
Anduza, Clara d' 203
Antoine-Dariaux, Geneviève 4516
Arnould, Sophie 628
Artois, Mahuat d' 228
Atlan, Liliane 2783
Auclert, Hubertine 1158
Aury, Dominique 2059
Bardot, Brigitte 2879
Beauveau, Marie de 571
Beauvoir, Simone de 2080
Bernadette 1121
Bernhardt, Sarah 1122
Bettencourt, Liliane Schueller 2418
Bieiris de Romans 205
Bonaparte, Marie L. 1564
Bourbon, Catherine de 362
Breillat, Catherine 3814

Brunet, Marguerite 606
Caesaria 118
Campan, Jeanne Louise 672
Carroll, Jean 2155
Chanel, Coco 1593
Châtelet, Émilie du 557–558
Choiseul, Louise Honorine de 616
Cixous, Hélène 3025
Clements, Marcelle 3819
Coignard, Gabrielle de 354
Colette 1409
Coligny, Henriette de 431
Corday, Charlotte 736
Cornuel, A. M. Bigot de 421
Cottin, Sophie 762
Cresson, Édith 2886
Curie, Ève 1990
Curie, Marie 1335
Daché, Lilly 1991
Dacier, Anne 488
Danielsson, Marie-Thérèse 2449
Deffand, Marie Anne du 544
Deneuve, Catherine 3402
Deroine, Jeanne-Françoise 889
Desbordes-Valmore, Marceline 801
Deshoulières, Antoinette 469
Desjardins, Marie-Catherine 460
Detourbey, Jean 1078
Dilke, Emilia 1093
Domna H. 207
Drouet, Juliette 894
Du Châtelet, Gabrielle Emilie le
    Tonnelier de Breteuil 558
Eleanor of Aquitaine 183
Elizabeth, Helene Marie Phillipine
    720
Farrar, Eliza Ware 822
Faure, Elie 1458
Fradonnet, Catherine 345
Fradonnet, Madeleine 314
Genlis, Stephanie Félicité 650
Geoffrin, Marie Thérèse Rodet 513
Germain, Sylvie 4249
Girardin, Delphine de 885
Goitschel, Marielle 3659
Gournay, Marie le Jars de 369
Gouges, Olympe de 656
Grignan, Françoise-Marguerite de
    Sévigné 480
Guercheville, Antoinette de Pons
    374
Guilbert, Yvette 1314
Guillema de Rosers 217
Guillet, Pernette du 315
Guyon, Jeanne-Marie de la Motte
    482
Hausset, Madame du 661
Héloise 178
d'Hericourt, Jenny P. 906
Henrey, Robert 2047
Henrietta Maria 424
Houdetot, Sophie de la Briche 609
Hughes, Karen 4370–4371
Isaure, Clemence 270
Iselda 208
Jacquet de la Guerre, Elisabeth-
    Claude 502
Jeanne of Navarre 226

Joan of Arc 252
Joliot-Curie, Iréne 1851
Josefowitz, Natasha 2555
Josephine 717
Kristeva, Julia 3277
La Fayette, Marie Madeleine de 465
Labé, Louise 316
Launey 969
Laurencin, Marie 1633
Leduc, Violette 2068
L'Enclos, Ninon de 439
Lenéru, Marie 1461
Lespinasse, Julie-Jeanne-Eléonore
    de 614
L'Heritier, Marie Jeanne 503
L'Incarnation, Marie de 407
Lombarda 200
Lorraine, Duchess of 232
Maintenon, Françoise de 466
Marcelle, Countess de 339
Marguerite of Navarre 289
Marguerite of Valois 356
Marie de France 193
Messud, Claire 4729
Michel, Louise 1030
Moreau, Jeanne 2637
Necker, Suzanne Chardon 626
Necker de Saussure, Madame 740
Nin, Anaïs 1979
Orléans, Ann-Marie-Louise d' 452
Parisot, Laurence 4501
Parturier, Françoise 2353
Pétigny de Saint-Romain, Marie-
    Louise-Rose 741
Poitiers, Diane de 294
Pompadour, Jeanne-Antoinette
    Poisson de 588
Renard, Cecile 764
Renée de France 304
Reza, Yasmina 4503
Rieux, Virginie des 410
Rieux, Renée de Chateauneuf 351
Rochefort, Christiane 2302
Roland, Jeanne-Marie 678
Roland, Pauline 891
Rosenthal, Rachel 2576
Roth, Stephanie Danielle 4848
Sablé, Madeleine de Souvré de 408
Sagan, Françoise 2945
Sand, George 887
Scudéry, Madeleine de 423
Sévigné, Marie de 451
Signoret, Simone 2414
Staöl, Germaine de 733
Stark, Freya Madeline 1785
Straus, Geneviève 1169
Tencin, Claudine Alexandrine de
    530
Thérèse de Lisieux 1422
Tibergeau, Marchioness de 552
Varda, Agnes 2644
Ventadorn, Marie de 195
Vigée-Lebrun, Elisabeth 685
Vreeland, Diana 1984
Weil, Simone 2116
Wittig, Monique 2958

GAMBIAN
Bensouda, Fatou 4564

GEORGIAN
Kochladze, Manana 4863

GERMAN
Albers, Anni 1881
Albrecht of Johannsdorf, Mistress
    of 229
Anna Maria of Braunschweig 337
Anna of Saxony 384
Arendt, Hannah 2036
Arnim, Bettina von 798
Augusta 689
Ava, Frau 185
Bachmann, Ingeborg 2541
Baum, Vicki 1674
Bedford, Sybille von Schoenbeck
    2152
Blind, Mathilde 1100
Campbell, Jane Montgomery 941
Catherine II of Russia 604
Diehl, Guida 1349
Dietrich, Marlene 1930
Dohm, Hedwig 1050
Dressel, Brigit 4569
Droste-Hülshoff, Anette Elizabeth
    von 852
Elisabeth of Brandenburg 284
Elisabeth of Braunschweig 302
Elizabeth, Caroline Amelia 737
Elizabeth of Thuringia 214
Figes, Eva 2794
Fleisser, Marie-Luise 1932
Follen, Eliza Lee 803
Frank, Anne 2657
Franz, Marie-Louise von 2240
Fuentes, Sonia Pressman 2627
Galdikas, Biruté M. F. 3657
Gertrude the Great 221
Glückel of Hameln 479
Gottschewski, Lydia 2708
Greiffenberg, Catharina Regina
    von 463
Grumbach, Argula von 288
Hagen, Uta 2345
Hegi, Ursula 3663
Herschel, Caroline 662
Hildegarde von Bingen 179
Horney, Karen 1631
Hroswitha of Gandersheim 158
Jhabvala, Ruth Prawer 2601
Kaplan, Gisela 3516.1
Kaufman, Bel 2160
Kelly, Petra 3762
Kemnitz, Mathilda von 1495
Klopstock, Margaret 602
Knesebeck, Eleonora von dem 525
Kollwitz, Käthe 1337
Kolmar, Gertrud 1799
Lasker-Schüler, Else 1364
Lawrence, Frieda 1530
Lehman, Lotte 1685
Lisiewska-Therbusch, Anna
    Dorothea 587
Mann, Erika 2026
Mara, Gertrude Elizabeth 657

Margaret of Nassau 242
Mayer, Maria Goeppert 2054
McDougal, Susan 4318
Mechtild von Magdeburg 215
Merian, Maria Sibylla 481
Merkel, Angela 4261
Mueller, Lisel 2490
Neuber, Frïederika Karoline 545
Nüsslein-Volhard, Christiane 3363
Otto, Louise 958
Räthzel, Nora 3858
Reinshagen, Gerlind 2575
Riedesel, Frederica de 652
Riefenstahl, Leni 1955
Robinson, Therese Albertine Louise
    858
Roth, Friederike 3863
Sachs, Nelly 1734
Schirmacher, Kathe 1319
Schücking, Heffa 4506
Schurman, Anna Maria van 422
Silvia of Sweden, Queen 3456
Süssmuth, Rita 3061
Sylva, Carmen 1120
Tikaram, Tanita 4804
Trachtenberg, Inge 2474
Varnhagen, Rahel Levin 757
Vernon, Lillian 2616
von Meysenbug, Malwida 940
Westheimer, Ruth 2646
Wigman, Mary 1658
Wolf, Christa 2689
Wolff, Charlotte 2008
Zassenhaus, Hiltgunt Margaret
    2279
Zell, Katherine 291
Zetkin, Klara 1229

GHANIAN
Aidoo, Ama Ata 3316
Sutherland, Efua Theodora 2498

GREEK
Anyte of Tegea 66
Aspasia 62
Bakoyannis, Dora 4230
Boumi Pappa, Rita 2040
Corinna 55
Erinna 47
Fleming, Amalia 2175
Huffington, Arianna 3976
Matheopoulos, Helena 3675
Mercouri, Melina 2531
Penelope 20
Phyrne 64
Polyxena 84
Praxilla 61
Rebecca 57
Sappho 46
Slave girl who was a soothsayer
    92
Sofía of Spain, Queen 3106
Telesilla 58
Theano 63 Xanthippe 59

GUADELOUPEAN
Condé, Maryse 3026

GUATAMALEN
Chang, Helen Mack 4091
Corvera, Bernardina Guevara 4855
Menchú, Rigoberta 4495

GUYANESE
Melville, Pauline 3850

HAITIAN-AMERICAN
d'Adesky, Anne-Christine 4479
Danticat, Edwidge 4784

HARAN/HITTITE (NOW TURKEY)
Leah 9

HAWAIIAN
Kamamalu 854
Liliuokalani, Lydia Kamekeha 1083

HEBREW (ALSO SEE ISRAEL)
Anna 43
Deborah 27
Hannah 30
Jephthah the Gileadite, Daughter
    of 21
Jerusalem [mother of the dead
    child], Prostitute of 36
Jerusalem [mother of the living
    child], Prostitute of 37
Manoah, Wife of 25
Michal 32
Miriam 16
Phinehas, Wife of 31
Rachel (1) 13
Seven Brothers, Mother of the 70
Susanna 53
Tamar 35
Tekoa, Woman of 39
Zelophehad, Five Daughters of,
    Mahlah, Noah, Hoglah,
    Milcah and Tirzah 18
Zipporah 19

HONDURAN
Martinez, Judith "Judy" Perez 4315

HONG KONGER
Dunn, Lydia 3188

HUNGARIAN
Bennett, Georgette 3634
Gabor, Zsa Zsa 2287
Kohut, Rebekah Bettelheim 1304
Mahler, Margaret 1853
Nemeth, Maria 2812
Orczy, 1317
Petröczi, Kata Szidónia 499
Schwimmer, Rosika 1499
Senesh, Hannah 2413
Sonneschein, Rosa 1156

ICELANDIC
Sigurdardottir, Johanna 3378

INDIAN
Ambapali 54
Andal 167 Auvaiyar 102
Bai, Lakshmi 1016

Bai, Mukta 230
Basu, Aparna 4930
Bee, Rashida 4347
Bhatt, Ela 2835
Dasi, Binodini 1294
Ded, Lal 248
Devi, Sampat Pal 4525
Gandhi, Indira 2288
Hong, Rani 4862
Honnamma 495
Hosain, Attia 2200
Jahan, Nur 382
Jain, Devaki 2856
Jayapal, Pramila 4702
Joshee, Anandabai 1316
Kamani, Ginu 4622
Kshetrayya 551
Lalleswari 235
Macatti, Okkur 95
Mahadeviyakka 211
Mahodahi 130
Makhfi 470
Marula 191
Mehta, Deepa 3916
Mirabai 293
Mittal, Anuradha 4774
Mukherjee, Bharati 3216
Murray, Margaret Alice 1298
Naidu, Sarojini 1534
Nair, Mira 4422
Namjoshi, Suniti 3287
Nannakaiyar, Kaccipett 103
Nirmala, Sister 2909
Nirmala Devi, Shri Mataji 2467
Nomani, Asra Q. 4708
Nooyi, Indra 4322
Pandit, Vijaya Lakshmi 1917
Patkar, Medha 4266
Qurrat al-'Ayn 1195
Rajalakshmi, R. 2574
Roy, Arundhati 4595
Shah, Nishita 4941
Shiva, Vandana 4141
Shukla, Champa Devi 4142
Sila 131
Silabhlattarika 132
Subramaniam, Banu 4145
Vallana 157
Venmanipputi 97
Vidya 133
Zia, Ather 4922

INDOCHINESE (ALSO SEE MALAYSIAN,
VIETNAMESE)
Duras, Marguerite 2219

INDONESIAN
Alomang, Yosepha 3948
Hafild, Emmy 4488
Hollander, Xaviera 3421
Kennard, Joyce L. 3275
Lim Wei-ling, Wilina 4980
Sukarnoputri, Megawati 3800

IRANIAN
Ebadi, Shirin 3739
Etessami, Parvin 2064
Farrokhzad, Forough 2928

Ghaaem-Maghami, Aalamtaaj 1609
Ghoratolain, Tahereh 942
Guppy, Shusha 2933
Hashemi Rafsanjani, Faezeh 4617
Jarrett, Valerie Bowman 4373
Khakpour, Porochista 4924
Mehri 250
Nafisi, Azar 4320
Nahai, Gina Barkhordar 4546
Rabi'a of Balkh 171
Satrapi, Marjane 4802
Sofer, Dalia 4871
Táhirih, Fátimih Baragháni 924–925
Tohidi, Nayereh 4658

IRAQI
Abdul Rahman, Haifa 4958
Akhyaliyya, Laila 122
Katz, Rita 4642

IRISH (ALSO SEE BRITISH)
Alexander, Mrs. Cecil Frances 943
Azadeh, Carol 4667
Barber, Mary 536
Barry, James Stuart Miranda 830
Blessington, Marguerite 808
Boland, Eavan 3480
Bonny, Anne 548
Bowen, Elizabeth 1883
Brennan, Maeve 2263
Brigid of Kildare 110
Carr, Marina 4672
Carrigan, Ana 3485
Cashman, Nellie 1183
Centlivre, Susanna 511
Colum, Mary "Molly" 1607
Corrigan Maguire, Maireád 3491
Crawford, Julia 866
Daisy, Princess of Pless 1411
D'Arcy, Margaretta 2888
Davys, Mary 517
Demarest, Mary Lee 1219
Devlin, Bernadette 3736
Donoghue, Emma 4785
Dufferin, Helen 900
Dugdale, Bridget Rose 3255
Edgeworth, Maria 734
Enright, Anne 4611
Fee, Elizabeth 3651
Gore-Booth, Eva 1398
Gormley 169
Gray, Agnes Kendrick 1796
Gregory, Augusta 1193
Grierson, Constantia 559
Hamilton, Anna 1115
Hamilton, Elizabeth 691
Hart, Josephine 4367
Herbert, Marie 3270
Hickey, Emily 1137
Hinkson, Katharine Tynan 1270
Hungerford, Margaret Wolfe 1205
Jameson, Anna Brownwell 844
Johnston, Henrietta 506
Jones, Mother 1028
Kavanagh, Julia 993
Keyes, Marian 4643
Liadan 129
Lyon, Mrs. 714

Mary of Warwick 447
McAleese, Mary 4057
Monk, Mary 577
Morgan, Sydney Owenson 770
Murdoch, Iris 2352
Ní Chonaill, Eibhlín Dhubh 645
Oaks, Laura Mary 4753
O'Brien, Edna 2732
O'Casey, Eileen 1980
O'Faolain, Nuala 3217
O'Neill, Henrietta 692
O'Neill, Moira 1305
Pelham, Mary Singleton Copley 570
Pilkington, Laetitia 563
Power, Samantha 4829
Roche, Adi 4329
Shane, Elizabeth 1500
Sheridan, Frances 595
Tighe, Mary 760
West, Rebecca 1759
Wilde, Jane Francesca 1010
Williams, Betty 3471

ISRAELI (ALSO SEE HEBREW)
Aloni, Shulamit 2650
Bar-Yosef, Rivka Weiss 3323
Bat-Miriam, Yocheved 1925
Beruriah 216
Dayan, Yaöl 3136
Esther 56
Goren-Bar, Dina 4451
Gur, Batya 3749
Livni, Tzipora "Tzipi" Malka 4458
Mer-Khamis, Arna 2673
Namir, Ora 2729
Peled-Elhanan, Nurit 4326
Portman, Natalie 4948
Ran, Shulamit 3928
Shalvi, Alice 2578

ITALIAN
Abbagnano, Nicola 1924
Adler, Renata 3068
Agnesi, Maria Gaötana 581
Aldrude 196
Angela of Foligno 219–220
Anguissola, Sofonisba 335
Annunziata, Lucia 4959
Arslan, Antonia 3069
Ascarelli, Devorah 409
Azzopardi, Trezza 4563
Bartoli, Cecilia 4715
Berneri, Marie Louise 2308
Bertana, Lucia dall'Orno 318
Borgia, Lucrezia 281
Caccini, Francesca 394
Carriera, Rosalba 519
Castellani, Maria 2699
Castiglione, Ippolita 319
Catalani, Angelica 778
Catherine of Bologna 253
Catherine of Genoa 263
Catherine of Siena 237
Cenci, Beatrice 381
Christine de Pisan 244
Cibo, Caterina 297
Clare of Assisi 201
Colonna, Vittoria da 287

Compiuta Donzella, La 231
Dalla Costa, Mariarosa 3081
Danieli, Cecilia 3401
d'Aragona, Tullia 301
Datini, Margherita 241
Duse, Eleanora 1246
Este, Anne d' 333
Este, Beatrice d' 278
Este, Isabella d' 276
Fallaci, Oriana 2656
Farnese, Giulia 277
Fedele, Cassandra 272
Fermi, Laura Capon 2065
Ferrante, Elena 4975
Fonte, Moderata 357
Franco, Veronica 344
Gabrielli, Caterina 608
Gambara, Veronica 285
Gandhi, Sonia 3658
Garrick, Eva Maria 596
Gentileschi, Artemisia 403
Ginzburg, Natalia 2267
Giordano, Anna 4697
Giovanelli, Elettra Marconi 2707
Gonzaga, Elisabetta 275
Gonzaga, Giulia 306
Gonzaga, Lucrezia 355
Hazan, Marcella 2486
Krim, Mathilde 2559
Levi-Montalcini, Rita 2112
Loren, Sophia 2902
Magnani, Anna 2322
Malfitano, Catherine 3846
Mancini, Maria Anna 484
Maraini, Dacia 2991
Marinella, Lucrezia 376
Matraini, Chiara Cantarini 307
Medici, Catherine de' 310
Medici, Lucrezia de' 255
Michiel, Renier Giustina 683
Modotti, Tina 1828
Montessori, Maria 1381
Morata, Olimpia 325
Morgantini, Luisa 3214
Morpurgo, Rahel 820
Morra, Isabella da 317
Nogarola, Isotta 254
Orsini, Isabella de' Medici 342
Ortese, Anna Maria 2226
Pierobon, Gigliola 3999
Pulci, Antonia 265
Rame, Franca 2639
Rilliet-Huber, Catherine 724
Schiaparelli, Elsa 1834
Sentinelli, Patrizia 3938
Sforza, Caterina 269
Sforza, Costanza Varano 256
Stampa, Gaspara 323
Strozzi, Alessandra de' Machingi 251
Sullam, Sarah Copia 402
Tarabotti, Arcangela 419
Terracina, Laura 311
Torelli, Barbara 279
Trevisan, Anna F. 2034
Trotula of Salerno 177
Versace, Donatella 4337
Visconti, Valentine 247
Winwar, Frances 1923

IVORIAN
Tadjo, Véronique 4334

JAMAICAN
Brown, Rosemary 2697
Cliff, Michelle 3645
Goodison, Lorna 3747

JAPANESE
Abutsu 227
Agata, Hikari 3388
Albery, Nobuko 3170
Ceschina, Yoko Nagae 2788
Doi, Takako 2625
Eifuku, Empress 225
Emon, Akazome 168
Fukuzoyo Chiyo 554
Fumiko, Hayashi 1993
Harima, Young Woman of 134
Horikawa 186
Iratsume, Kasa no 145
Iratsume, Otomo no Sakano-e no 128
Ise, Lady 155
Ishikawa 143
Itatani, Michiko 4182
Iwa no Hime 106
Izumi Shikibu 165
Kawai Chigetsu-Ni 461
Kazu-no-Michi 1144
Ki no Tsurayuki, Daughter of 159
Kieko, Yamamuro 1439
Kii, Lady 146
Kirino, Natsuo 4053
Koka, Stewardess of the Empress 210
Kometani, Foumiko 2720–2721
Masuda, Mizuko 3847
Michitsuna, Mother of 160
Mori, Nobuko 2811
Motoni, Nomura 897
Nagako, Kuni 1976
Nakatsukasa 164
Nijo, Lady 222
Nijo, Empress 151
Nukada 123
Ohba, Minako 2735
Oku 124
Ono, Yoko 2860
Ono no Komachi 150
Sanu, Chigami 135
Sarashina, Lady 173
Saruhashi, Katsuko 2389
Shikibu, Murasaki 166
Shikishi Naishinno 192
Shonagon, Sei 163
Sugawara no Takasue no musume 181
Sugimoto, Etsu Inagaki 1451
Suo 174
Tanaka, Yukiko 3232
Tomioka, Taeko 2955
Toshiko, Kishida 1300
Tsushima, Yüko 3803
Ukon, Lady 154
Yamada, Eimi 4512
Yamatohime 127

JERUSALEMITE (NOW ISRAEL)
Kamal, Zahira 3586
Lichtenstein, Tehilla 1779
Mary Magdalene 81
Mary, Virgin 79
Shalom, Imma 91
Susman Ashkenazi, Rachel 364

JUDEAN (NOW ISRAEL AND JORDAN)
Abigail 34
Huldah 52
Salome 82

KAZAKHSTAN
Atakhanova, Kaisha 4439

KENITE (NOW ISRAEL AND JORAN)
Jael 28

KENYAN
Abdi, Dekha Ibrahim 4662
Chesoni, Atsango 4961
Kaara, Wahu 4185
Maathai, Wangari Muta 3207
Mawiyoo, Neema "Ngwatilo" 4952
Mpaayei, Florence 4545
Murungi, Kaari Betty 4983
Ngesa, Mildred 4899
Ngilu, Charity Kaluki 4129
Njogu, Ann Wairimu 4775
Ojiambo, Josephine 4592
Okello-Orlale, Rosemary 4709
Patel, Shailja 4828
Ringera, Karambu 4429

KOREAN
Cha, Theresa Hak Kyung 4033
Ho Nansorhon 368
Hwang Chin-I 299
Kim, Myung Mi 4418
Kim, Sung-Joo 4419
Lee, Min Jin 4794
Paik, Younhee 3604

KUWAITI
Al-Abdullah, Queen of Jordan, Rania 4810

LEBANESE
Adnan, Etel 2505
al-Shaykh, Hanan 3611.1
Farhoud, Abla 3569
Khalifeh, Imane 4896

LIBERIAN
Cooper, Helene 4719
Johnson-Sirleaf, Ellen 3090

LITHUANIAN
Gimbutas, Mirija 2399
Goldberg, Lea 2156
Goldman, Emma 1360
Razumovskaya, Lyudmila 3859

MALAYSIAN (ALSO SEE INDOCHINESE)
Anwar, Zainah 4157
Fernandez, Irene 3652
Lim, Shirley Geok-Lin 3521

MEDE (NOW IRAN)
Edna 44
Sarah 45

MEROVINGIAN (NOW AUSTRIA, FRANCE, GERMANY)
Bertegund 115
Herchenfreda 119

MESOPOTAMIAN (NOW ISRAEL)
Eristi-Aya 12
Rebekah 11

MEXICAN
Arizmendi, Yareli 4666
Arizpe, Lourdes 3390
Castellanos, Rosario 2515
Corpi, Lucha 3561
Cruz, Juana Inés de la 487
de Hoyos, Angela 3187
Esquivel, Laura 3964
Gervitz, Gloria 3411
Hernandez, Antonia 3830
Kahlo, Frida 2066
Lagarde, Marcela 3983
Molina de Pick, Gracia 2727

MOABITE (NOW JORDAN)
Ruth 23

MOROCCAN
El Moutawakel, Nawal 4610
Mernissi, Fatima 3211

MOZAMBICAN
Diogo, Luísa Dias 4446

NAMIBIAN
Mensah-Williams, Margaret

NEW ZEALAND
Angus, Rita 2077
Ashton-Warner, Sylvia 2079
Clark, Helen 3958
De Groen, Alma 3251
Frame, Janet 2483
Hulme, Keri 3755
Lawless, Lucy 4770
Mansfield, Katherine 1687
McDougall, Joyce 2567
Mitchell, Juliet 3212
Okin, Susan Moller 3684
Sheppard, Kate 1155
Wallace, Cath 4338
Waring, Marilyn 4217

NICARAGUAN
Astorga, Nora 3884
Chamorro, Violeta Barrios de 2654
Jagger, Bianca 3980

NIGERIAN
Adichie, Chimamanda Ngozi 4915
Anyanwu, Christina 4019
Bello, Mairo 4670
Emecheta, Buchi 3497
Ibrahim, Hauwa 4701

Mohammed, Binta S. 4796
Sofola, Zulu 2952

NORWEGIAN
Boulding, Elise M. 2362
Brundtland, Gro Harlem 3129
Flekkxy, Melfrid Grude 2703
Ostenso, Martha 1916
Skram, Amalie 1147
Spafford, Anna 1111
Torvik, Solveig 3162
Ullman, Liv 3108
Westergaard, Brita 3549

NUMIDIAN (NOW ALGERIA)
Monica 105

PAKISTANI
Aafreen, Ishrat 4514
Abbasi, Talat 4154
Bhutto, Benazir 4160
Jehangir, Asma 4112
Mumtaz, Khawar 4064
Naqvi, Tahira 4198
Sadik, Nafis 2681
Shaheed, Farida 4208

PALESTINIAN (NOW ISRAEL AND JORDAN)
Arafat, Suha 4636
Ashrawi, Hanan 3627
Badawi, Khulood 4903
Baransi-Siniora, Maysa 4904
Naufal, Vera 4547
Nye, Naomi Sihab 4130
Tawil, Raymonda 3233
Zhivago, Um 4990

PANAMANIAN
Hunt, Lynn 3583

PAPUAN
Kajir, Anne 4821

PARAGUAYAN
Lieberman, Alicia F. 3765

PERSIAN
Khatun, Jahan 249
Khatun, Padeshah 224
Lessing, Doris 2349
Mahsati Ganjavi 212
Rabi'a al-Adawiya 136

PERUVIAN
Escot, Pozzi 2845
Farro, Maria Elena Foronda 4482
Macher, Sofia 4380
Moyano, Maria Elena 4462
Tristan, Flora 883
Wheeler, Kate 4078

PHILIPPINE
Aquino, Corazon 2830
Arroyo, Gloria Macapagal 3717
Flores-Oebanda, Cecilia 4528
Geonzon, Winefreda Estanero 2706

Hagedorn, Jessica Tarahata 3901
Marcos, Imelda 2670
Primavera, Jurgenne 3605
Torres, Amaryllis Tiglao 3544
Wiley, Doreen Gandy 2617

PHILISTINE (NOW ISRAEL AND JORDAN)
Delilah 24
Samson, First wife of 26

PHOENICIAN (NOW SYRIA AND LEBANON)
Jezebel 40

POLISH
Adler, Polly 1894
Amir, Anda 1944
Appignanesi, Lisa 3626
Benet, Sula 1966
Burton, Sala 2513
Deutsch, Helene 1608
Gray, Francine Du Plessix 2709
Grossman, Chaika 2344
Hoffman, Eva 3581
Klepfisz, Irena 3276
Landowska, Wanda 1529
Langer, Felicia 2722
Lopata, Jadwiga 4258
Luxemburg, Rosa 1379
Marchocka, Anna Maria 418
Miller, Alice 2466
Modjeska, Helena 1095
Nowakowska, Urszula 4323
Olesnicka, Zofia 350
Rambert, Marie 1733
Rose, Ernestine Louise 913
Ruarowna, Margareta 440
Rubinstein, Helena 1383
Schtok, Fradel 1718
Szymborska, Wislawa 2472
Ulinover, Miriam 1690
Yezierska, Anzia 1562
Zygmuntowicz, Itka Frajman 2585

PORTUGUESE
Alcoforado, Mariana 471
Barreno, Maria Isabel 3122
Carmo, Isabel do 3180
Céu, Violante do 417
Costa, Maria Fatima Velho da 3080
Horta, Maria Teresa 3036
Sigea, Luisa 321

PROVENÇAL (NOW FRANCE)
Almucs de Castelnau 188
Azalais de Porcairages 189
Beatritz de Dia 190
Castelloza 206
Garsenda de Forcalquier 198
Tibors 187

PRUSSIAN (NOW GERMANY)
Bieber, Margarete 1521

PUERTO RICAN
Alvarez, Aida 3881

Burgos, Julia de 2214
Calderón, Sila María 3327
Cofer, Judith Ortiz 4094
Lebron, Lolita 2605
Ramos, Rosa Hilda 3606
Toro, María Suárez 3874
Vilar, Irene 4805

ROMAN (HOLY R- EMPIRE, MUCH OF EUROPE, NORTH AFRICA AND THE NEAR EAST)
Agrippina the Younger 80
Arria the Elder 87
Cornelia 71
Hortensia 74
Hypatia 107
Isabella 199
Lais 65
Maximilla 112
Myrta 96
Pompeia Plotina 93
Poppaea Sabina 85
Porcia 77
Sulpicia 94
Sulpicia 76

ROMANIAN
Cassian, Nina 2479
Comaneci, Nadia 4606
Fiorenza, Elisabeth Schüssler 3086
Schwarcz, Vera 3793
Spewack, Bella 1891

RUSSIAN (ALSO SEE SOVIET)
Akhmatova, Anna 1692
Alliluyeva, Svetlana 2507
Antin, Mary 1563
Bashkirtseff, Marie 1230
Berberova, Nina 1927
Blavatsky, Elena Petrovna 1034
Bonner, Ylena Georgievna 2447
Dashkova, Ekaterina Vorontsova 644
Devi, Indra 1884
Dostoevsky, Anna 1142
Durant, Ariel 1864–1865
Eberhardt, Isabelle 1491
Figner, Vera 1191
Gessen, Masha 4748
Ginzburg, Eugenia 1994
Gorbachev, Raisa Maxima 2800
Gorbanevskaya, Natalya 2980
Gorchakova, Galina 4616
Grushin, Olga 4845–4846
Kollontai, Aleksandra 1402
Kovalevskaya, Sofia Vasilyevna 1177
Krudener, Juliana 721
Krupskaia, Nadezhda Konstanitovna 1363
Kuklina, Ida 2528
Lispector, Clarice 2381
Litman, Ellen 4878
Mamonova, Tatyana Valentina 3096
Maria, Grand Duchess of Russia 1712
Meir, Golda 1870

Mischenko, Vera 4195
Molodowsky, Kadya 1801
Némirovsky, Irène 1977
Nevelson, Louise 1890
Noor Inayat Khan 2225
Orlova, Raisa Davydovna 2327
Panova, Vera Fedorovna 2030
Pavlova, Anna 1573
Perovskaya, Sofia 1198
Pesotta, Rose 1829
Petrushevskaya, Lyudmila 3101
Politkovskaya, Anna 4464
Ptaschkina, Nelly 1982
Rachel (2) 1716
Rand, Ayn 2032
Rikhvanova, Marina 4594
Rosenthal, Ida 1657
Sarraute, Nathalie 1921
Savitsky, Esther 1875
Sharapova, Maria 4957
Stokes, Rose Pastor 1537
Swetchine, Sophie-Jeanne Soymonof 791
Tarasova, Yelena 4971
Tolstaya, Tatyana 4074
Tolstoy, Sophie 1132
Tsvetaeva, Marina 1757
Tucker, Sophie 1620
Turbina, Nika 4889
Vapnyar, Lara 4851
Vassiltchikov, Marie 2304
Voronel, Nina 2873
Voznesenskaya, Yuliya 3236
Young, Cathy 4661
Zaturenska, Marya 1961

SAMARITAN (NOW JORDAN)
Samaritan Woman 83

SAUDI ARABIAN
Hajar, Hanaa 4976
al-Huwaider, Wajeha 4846
Al Kuwaiz, Samira 4664

SCOTTISH (ALSO SEE BRITISH)
Audeley, Eleanor 436
Baillie, Joanna 713
Baker, Mary 1738
Barnard, Anne 659
Barr, Amelia 1033
Barr, Mary A 1188
Bowes, Elizabeth 348
Boyle, Susan 4566.1
Brown, Anna Gordon 654
Brunton, Mary 775
Campbell, Dorothea Primrose 831
Carlyle, Jane Welsh 869
Carswell, Catherine 1522
Cockburn, Alicia 574
Colquhoun, Janet 786
Craig, Agnes 696
Daviot, Gordon 1823
Duffy, Carol Ann 4298
Elliot, Jean 599
Ferrier, Susan Edmonstone 790
Fleming, Marjory 876
Garden, Mary 1432

Glennie, Evelyn 4698
Gowdie, Isobel 494
Graham, Isabella 638
Graham, Janet 592
Grant, Anne 680
Holford, Margaret 776
Home, Anne 639
Home, Grisell 505
Houston, Libby 3272
Jordan, Dorothea 712
Kay, Jackie 4583
Kennedy, A. L. 4703
Keppel, Caroline 619
Lambrun, Margaret 387
Lennox, Annie 4256
Locke, Anne 332
MacDonald, Sharman 4055
MacKay, Shena 3524
Mary of Scots 341
Maxwell, Darcy 640
McWilliam, Candia 4319
Melvill, Elizabeth 390
Mina, Denise 4730
Munro, Rona 4497
Musgrave, Thea 2637.1
Nairne, Carolina 731
Oliphant, Margaret 1019
Oxlie of Morpet, Mary 434
Pyper, Mary 849
Somerville, Mary 783
Spark, Muriel 2331
Turnbull, Margaret 1702
Wright, Frances 850

SEMITE/MESOPOTAMIAN (NOW IRAQ)
Lot's daughter (the elder) 10
Sheba, Queen of 38

SERBIAN
Jefimija 238 Litricin, Vera 3437
Softic-Kaunitz, Elma 4597
Zajovic, Stasa 4689

SINGAPOREAN
Heng, Geraldine 4974
Tan, Hwee Hwee 4888

SOMALIAN
Ahmed, Naima 4600
Dirie, Waris 4695
Hirsi Ali, Ayaan 4789
Jibrell, Fatima 3835

SOUTH AFRICAN
Anglo
Armstrong, Sue 3322
Collen, Lindsey 4036
Freed, Lynn 4104
Fugard, Lisa 4485
Gordimer, Nadine 2456
Handler, Marisa 4917
Head, Bessie 3035
Landsman, Anne 4491
Leith, Prue 3205
Russell, Diana E. H. 3104
Schreiner, Olive 1208

Suzman, Helen 2303
Trapido, Barbara 3308

Asian
Shaikh, Shamima 4556

Black
Duarte, Jessie 4173
Duncan, Sheena 2792
Grae, Jean 4908
Issel, Shahieda 4414
Kgositsile, Baleka 3905
Makeba, Miriam 2807
Mandela, Winnie 2905
Mandela, Makaziwe "Maki" 4191
Mashinini, Emma 2672
Mbete-Kgositsile, Baleka 3915
Mofokeng, Connie 4496
Mosala, Bernadette 4196
Nghatsane, Linda Olga 4425
Ngubane, Thembi 4956
Pillay, Navanethem "Navi" 3223
Sisulu, Nontsikelelo Albertina 2357

Multiracial
Jacobs, Rayda 3757

SPANISH
Agreda, María de 415
'Aisha bint Ahmad al-Qurtubiyya 161
Augustín, María 800
Bazan, Emilia Pardo 1189
Carpio de San Feliz, Marcela de 420
Castro, Rosalia de 1077
Catherine of Aragon 283
Cazalla, Maria 330
Egeria 108
Erauso, Catalina de 392
Gregoria, Francisca 490
Guevara, Marina de 303
Ibarruri, Dolores 1813
Isabella I 264
Kasmuneh 209
Laforet, Carmen 2404
López de Córdoba, Leonor 243
Martínez Sierra, María 1441
Maryam bint Abi Ya'qub al-Ansari 170
Narbona Ruiz, Cristina 4065
O'Neill, Carlotta Monterey 1688
Otero, Caroline 1353
de Palacio, Loyola 3960
Pinar, Florencia del 268
Sanchez, Cristina 4869
Teresa of Ávila 308
Tusquets, Esther 3010
Zayas y Sotomayor, María de 398

SRI LANKAN
de Kretser, Michelle 4444
Kumaratunga, Chandrika Bandaranike 3588

SUDANESE
Bashir, Halima 4925

SUMERIAN (NOW IRAQ)
Enheduanna 4
Inanna 6
Kubatum 7

SWAZI
Makhubu, Lydia Phindile 3045

SWEDISH
Alfredsson, Helen 4691
Bergman, Ingrid 2236
Bok, Sissela Ann 2881
Bremer, Frederika 868
Bridget of Sweden 234
Cedering, Siv 3131
Christina of Sweden 450
Fredriksson, Marianne 2595.1
Garbo, Greta 2017
Grebäck, Kerstin 3267
Hedstrvm, Barbro 3420
Herrstrvm, Christina 4489
Key, Ellen 1167
Kirsebom, Vendela 4751
Lagerlöf, Selma 1233
Lenngren, Anna Maria 681
Liljeström, Rita 2635
Lind, Jenny 970
Lindgren, Astrid 2069
Myrdal, Alva Reimer 1953–1954
Osten, Suzanne 3530
Seaberg, Rönnog 2820
Törnqvist, Mia 4435
Zetterling, Mai 2539

SWISS
Del Ponte, Carla 3735
Dyson, Esther 4040
Gilmore, Jennifer 4818
Giroud, Françoise 2268
Jung, Emma 1578
Kübler-Ross, Elisabeth 2560
Miller, Alyce 4194
Montolieu, Jeanne Isabelle 668
Muller, Karin 4707
Spyri, Johanna 1015

SYRIAN
al-Samman, Ghada 3318
Maysun 125
Zenobia of Palmyra 100

TAIWANESE
Chin, Ann-ping 3817
Lu, Annette 3523

TANZANIAN
Mongella, Gertrude Ibengwe 3595

THAI
Deetes, Tuenjai 4098
Treerat, Nualnoi 4659

THURINGIAN (NOW GERMANY)
Basine 111

TRINIDADIAN
Brand, Dionne 4164

ETHNICITY AND NATIONALITY INDEX

TUNISIAN

Benmussa, Simone 2751

TURKISH

Agduk Agduk, Meltem 4811
Ertük, Yakin 4572
Hanim, Leylâ 1175
Hatun, Mihri 261
Lemke, Birsel 3985
Lydia 90
Sidqi 555
Yener, Kutlu Aslihan 3708
Zana, Leyla 4599

UGANDAN

Manji, Irshad 4772
Museveni, Janet 3920
Were, Beatrice 4741

UKRAINIAN

Dunayevskaya, Raya 2126
Gerasymyuk, Olga 4923
Melen, Olya 4936
Tussman, Malka Heifetz 1788
Tymoshenko, Yulia Volodymyrivna 4557
Yaroshinskaya, Alla 4220

URUGUAYAN

Ibarbourou, Juana de 1812

UZBEKISTAN

Ataniyazova, Oral 4398

VIETNAMESE (ALSO SEE INDOCHINESE)

Binh, Nguyen Thi 2692
Ho Xuan Huong 708

Tam, Ba 4943
Trinh, T. Minh-Ha 4147
Trinh, Trieu Thi 101

WELSH (ALSO SEE BRITISH)

Bovey, Shelley 3724–3725
Mechain, Gwerfyl 267
Morgan, Elaine 2383
Morris, Jan 2569
Owens, Vilda Sauvage 1464
Piozzi, Hester Lynch 635
Sage, Lorna 3453
Sleigh, Sylvia 2275
Waters, Sarah 4740

WEST INDIAN (ALSO SEE INDIVIDUAL NATIONS)

Johnstone, Wilhelmina 1909
Kincaid, Jamaica 3906

Lorde, Audre 2901
Pinckney, Eliza 591
Rhys, Jean 1717
Scott, Hazel 2390

YUGOSLAVIAN (ALSO SEE BOSNIAN, CROATIAN, SLOVENIAN)

Drakulíc, Slavenka 3894
Kruhonja, Katarina 3907
Mladjenovic, Lepa 4264–4265
Slapsak, Svetlana 3867
Todosijevic, Jelica 4973

ZIMBABWEAN

Dangarembga, Tsitsi 4480
Taylor, Debbie 4335

Subject Index

Numbers: numbers preceding colons are contributor numbers (guides to these numbers are found at the top of each page in the Quotations section); numbers following colons reflect specific numbered quotations. If several quotations for that contributor are cited under the same subject, they are separated by commas. Semicolons separate one contributor from another.

Word forms: singular is used except in those instances when the plural helps to distinguish the connotation of the word (as in "speech" and "speeches" or "appearance" and "appearances"); reader should presume plurals when applicable (for example, under "change" is the subheading "nothing"; one *assumes* the phrase "nothing changes")

"The" is used sparingly and must often be assumed (e.g., "dead"); however, when it distinguishes the *meaning* of a subject, it is applied (e.g., "English, the").

The tilde (~) is used in subclassifications to replace the main subject word; its placement varies and is meant to aid definition, thus—"marriage, ~ laws", "population, over- ~", "African American, achievement of ~ women".

Like subjects are often sandwiched together with a slash, as in "mother/hood," "nurse/nursing," and "Europe/an." Entries are filed letter-by-letter.

Capitalization is used to differentiate meaning, as with Nature (the environment) and nature (human behavior) or Earth (the planet) and earth (soil).

Whenever possible, subjects are in the form of nouns or present participles.

Abbreviations: *"vs."* is used throughout, most frequently meaning "as opposed to" or "against", occasionally meaning "versus": its sense should be apparent.

The abbreviation *"re"* is used throughout, in place of "in relation to".

The ampersand (&) is used throughout to replace the word "and".

References: Cross-references are generously sprinkled throughout the index.

Subjects have been classified according to the period in *which they were made:* i.e., even though the USSR no longer exists, quotations related to it are still tagged USSR, whereas pre- or post-Soviet references are tagged *Russia*.

Alphabetization: letter-by-letter method is employed; hyphens and apostrophes are not considered.

For a statement on the purpose and style of the Subject Index, please see the Introduction.

A

abandonment *see also* renunciation, 4563:4; ~ of loved one, 154:2

Abelard, Peter, 178:6

ability *see also* skill; talent, 1480:5; measure of ~, 961:3; 3395:1

abolitionism/abolitionist *see also* slave/ry; 946:2

aboriginal *see also* native; tribalism, 846:1

abortion *see also* pregnancy/pregnant, terminated ~; pro-choice movement, 1943:4; 2084:1; 2272:8; 2281:3; 2850:2; 2970:5; 3257:6; 3361:2; 3839:1; 3925:1; 3982:4; anti-~, 1920:3; 2343:1; 3088:3; 3284:1; 4009:3; battleground of ~, 3769:3; funding for ~, 3160:3; illegal ~, 3366:1; justification for ~, 4713:1; legality of ~, 3622:2; 3925:2; 3999:1; politics of ~, 3100:1; 4987:1; reason for ~, 4814:1; reducing ~, 4370–4371:1; regret over ~, 3769:2; religion and ~, 2084:2; right to ~; 3888.1:2 4566:2; ~ rights (*see also* birth control, right to ~), 3103:1; 3264:2; 3361:1; 3435:1; 4247:1; 4849:1; supporters of ~, 3088:3; ~ wars, 4391:1

Abraham, 2979:2

absence, 172:2; 586:1; 629:1, 4; 1409:13; 2405:1; 4871:2; desire for ~, 3137:1; ~ of husband, 1973:14 absolutes, 2572:1; 4480:1

absolution see also forgiveness, divine ~, 448:1

abstinence, 3413:2; sexual ~ (see celibacy)

absurdity, 1236:9; 1288:1; 1760:1; 2032:11

abuse see also mistreatment, 916:6; 1019:1; 1535:9; child ~, 2158:1; domestic ~, 2496:8; men who ~, 1622:6; 4116:11; victim of ~, 2206:2

Abzug, Bella, 1875:1, 2; 2360:2

academia, confines of ~, 4141:1; fulfillment in ~, 4145:4; women in ~, 4350:1

Academy Award, 3029:1; ~ on television, 2110:2

acceptability, 2416:1

acceptance see also resignation, 396:2; 1689:5; 1701:4; 1741:19; 1759:3; 2224:5; 2554:1; 3653:2; 3772:1; ~ of god's will, 1710:4; ~ of loved one, 4955:2; resigned ~, 2475:2; wisdom of ~, 1667:3

accident see also chance, 907:1; 2066:4; 3099:8; 3704:6; consequences of ~, 3438:2; highway ~, 4140:3

accomplishment see also achievement/achiever, 736:1; 1054:1; 1127:5; 1183:1; 1335:3; 1408:13; 1435:1; 1505:1; 1648:4; 1670:5; 2537:11; 2589:3; 3880:1; 4289:3; lack of ~, 4947:2; owe ~ to God, 2067:1; work for ~, 4629:4

accountability, ~ for crime, 4895:4

accreditation, 2612:1

accusation see also mudslinging; 604:7; 1073:1; 1646:1; 2021:10; 2068:1; 3068:4; false ~, 3741:1

achievement/achiever see also accomplishment; 327:4; 446:9; 695:4; 734:9; 1006:12; 1032:10; 1276:3; 2754:3; individual ~, 2248:3; perspective on ~, 1419:7

acknowledgement, 1545:1

ACLU (American Civil Liberties Union), 1706:2; 3512:6

acquaintance, beginning ~, 408:1; old ~, 1420:2

acquisition/acquisitiveness, 2256:1; 2634:1; 3623:1; 3669:5; 3855:4; 4396:4; addiction to ~, 3829:4; culture as ~, 1227:5; desire for ~, 2028:3

acrimony, 2765:7

acronym, political ~, 2763:4

acting (dramatic) see also actor; performance/performer; theater, 1095:1; 1246:1, 3; 1312:2; 2074:2; 2492:2, 3; 2637:4;

2838:1; 2984:1; 4006:4; comparing ~ performances, 3869:2; desire to ~, 2345:4; ~ in film, 1722:6; love of ~, 2935:2; method ~, 1887:5; ~ school, 1095:5; spirit of ~, 4006:2; stage ~, 2395:1; teaching ~, 2056:5; weary of ~, 2749:1

action, 32:1; 733:1, 13; 976:2; 1183:1; 2668:2; 3133:2; 3317:4; 3918:3; arena of ~, 1171:1; basis for ~, 3968:3; cataclysmic ~, 4680:1; collective ~, 2272:7; 2960:2; consequences of ~, 1747:1; foiled ~, 2488:2; human ~, 4597:3; immutable ~, 1177:3; judged by ~, 4445:1; need for ~, 362:1; 934:2; 1355:2; 1592:5; political ~, 4106:1; 4339:4; 4527:5; responsibility for ~, 2236:3; taking ~, 671:4; 872:3; 2892:2; 3749:3; 4536:3; 4729:3; unconscious ~, 2567:2; women and ~, 2855:3

activism/activist see also agitator; reform/er, 2922:3; 3019:1, 2; 3575:2; 3707:2; 4482:2; 4594:4; 4624:1; 4836:2; ~ and protests, 3245:1; compensation for ~, 3585:3; Jewish women ~, 3082:1; personal ~, 1086:1; political ~, 3505:2; threats to ~, 4927:2; ~ vs. corporations, 4142:0; woman ~, 893:3; 1394:1; 3458:1; 4347:1

activity see also bustle; movement [physical], lack of ~, 3954:1; need for ~, 367:4

actor see also acting [dramatic]; performance/performer; theater; 572:2; 684:5; 1162:1; 1312:2; 1314:1; 1409:2; 1904:1, 5; 2141:2; 2826:3; 3170:1; 4666:2; aspiring ~, 2140:1; behavior of ~, 4364:1; birth of ~, 2428:1; ego of ~, 3107:0; employment for ~, 3837:3; endurance of ~, 1624:1; film ~, 1684:3; 1771:3; 1996:3; great ~, 3252:2; ~ in relation to audience, 1520:3; 3170:4; ~ in relation to family, 781:1; Latina ~, 4331:2; movie ~, 3379:3; out of work ~, 1698:3; 3032:4; timing of ~, 1505:3; tools of ~, 2599:2; 4467:1; type cast ~, 2074:3; 2896:3; versatility of ~, 4301:1; wardrobe for ~, 1850:1; woman ~, 1520:2

Adam, sin of ~, 514:2

Adam & Eve see also Eve; 91:1; 254:2; 357:6; 372:1; 405:2; 944:5, 7; 1057:2; 1669:4; 1910:1; 2126:1; 2778:4; 2979:1

Adams, Abigail, 3248:2

adaptability see also flexibility; 767:; 1409:8; 1977:6; 2645:1; 3309:11; 4023:2; 4117:8

addiction see also drugs; 2480:1; 3396:2; 4750:3

address, form of ~, 2857:3; good ~, 3984:3

ADHD (attention deficit hyperactivity disorder), 2622:3

admiration see also adoration; 585:1; 658:8; 1669:3; 3139:4; need for ~, 713:6; ~ of fans, 3924:1

adolescence/adolescent see also teenager; years of age; young; youth; 1561:2; 1608:3; 1744:1; 2154:2; 2216:2; 2566:2; 2619:4; 2666:1; 3498:1; 4235:2; brain of ~, 3509:2; dichotomies of ~, 1810:2; 2668:19; end of ~, 3560:1; female ~, 2083:1; 2657:2; 3784:2; food and ~, 3137:7; ~ of girl, 3784:1; pre- ~, 2212:1; questions of ~, 2572:4; rigorous ~, 3922:2; task of ~, 2666:4; 3882:2

adoption, 3665:5; 4009:2; 4583:6; ~ and birth mother, 3856:3; anti- ~ activist, 4009:3; fate of ~, 4009:1; ~ in relation to birth, 3603:3; success of ~, 3172:2

adoration see also admiration; 887:24; 1315:3; object of ~, 3287:1

adult/hood, 1858:3; 2185:1; 2931:8; 3391:4; 4144:1; ~ and leadership, 2577:7; early ~, 1844:3; 3455:4; ~ in relation to child, 2133:3; ~ in relation to youth, 2079:3; threshold of ~, 672:3; young ~ , 3882:3; young ~ in relation to parent, 3882:4

adultery see also faithlessness; infidelity; 69:1; 211:1; 446:6; 593:2; 2819:4; 3499:1; 3803:3; 4895:2; ~ among politicians, 3442:5; consensual ~, 4143:1; politics of ~, 4369:3; rewards of ~, 3883:5

advantage, 423:3; 472:15; taking ~, 955:6

adventure/r, 392:2; 1201:6; 1268:4; 1663:4; 1671:1; 2043:1; 2091:1; 2817:11; 2925:1; 3146:3; 3496:2; 3807:0; motivation for ~, 2457:1

adversity see also hardship; life, struggle of ~; obstacle; trouble; 94:1; 313:2; 356:3; 430:8; 502:2; 950:2; 1012:1; 1316:4; attitude toward ~, 4117:2; 4802:5; mastery of ~, 1044:12

advertisement/advertising see also commercialism; marketing; publicity; 1325:2; 1618:2; 1632:4; 1920:2; 2874:6; 3391:3; 3566:3; 4716:1; ~ aimed at children, 3433:2; 3764:1, 3; criticism of ~, 2915:3; deception in ~ (deception ~ in advertising), 2192:17; false ~, 4324:5; function of ~, 3433:3; ~ in U.S.A., 1901:4; influence of

~, 3433:1; 4917:1; men and ~, 3173:1; ~ on Internet, 4040:1; representation of women in ~, 3381:2; sexual ~, 4246:1; simplification of ~, 3778:3; television ~ (see also television, ~ commercials), 2074:1; violence and ~, 3764:2

advice/advisor, 533:8; 3349:14; 4764:1; bad ~, 1332:4; ~ for living, 2845:; 3690:5; good ~, 1250:1; ~ to child, 70:2; 639:2; 1740:1; woman's ~, 1044:11

aesthetics, importance of ~, 2226:3

affectation see also pretense, 598:1; 1435:5

affection, 808:10; 2320:1; lack of ~, 2405:3; physical ~, 1211:5; words of ~, 713:16

affiliation see also community; relationship, woman's capacity for ~, 1608:1

affirmative action, 2128:1; 2658:3; 3625:1; 3881:3; 4079:1

afflicted/affliction, 640:2; 765:1

Afghanistan, 4604:1, 2, 4; 4776:2; ~ Constitution, 4430:4; ~ in relation to United States, 4708:1; 4927:1; Kandahar ~, 4604:1, 4; ~ parliament, 4927:3; strife in ~, 4430:5; support for ~, 4230:3; war in ~, 4430:3; ~ women, 4927:2; 4981:1; women in ~, 4854.1:1

Africa/n see also blacks, 612:2; 642:4; 677:3; 698:4; 768:1; 807:15; 882:2; 2139:5; 2807:3; 2901:9; 2903:3; 3035:2; 3207:3; 3547:13; 3938:1, 3; 4312:2; AIDS in ~, 3740:1; coopting ~ culture, 2680:25; exploitation of ~, 3835:1; game reserves of ~, 3322:2; ~ in relation to United States, 4983:2; ~ in relation to whites, 1822:1; ~ Lovedu tribe, 3040:2; music of ~, 2807:5; ~ nation, 3207:5; ~ Nyasa Tribesman, 2456:3; perception of ~, 3347:4, 5; poverty in ~, 3938:2; ~ queen, 3040:1; rectifying damage in ~, 4335:1; ~ women, 4185:2; women's work in ~, 3040:1

African American see also blacks, 1291:1; 4190:2; history of ~, 4649:1; ~ in politics, 2986:3; ~ spirituality, 3919:1; struggles of ~, 3332:2; style of ~, 2618:16; ~ women, 3384:2; 3505:4

afterlife see also reincarnation; 285:4; 884:2; 950:1; 1039:6; 1059:2; 1127:3; 4038:5

age, ~ 16, 952:1; 4954:1; ~ 25, 4947:2; ~ 30, 4729:3; ~ 50, 3292–3293:1; 4224:2; 4423:3; ~ 60, 3511:4; ~ 70, 1904:4; ~ 80, 3126:3, 3; ~ 90, 2324:2

Age (era), also see specific eras, 1529:2; diseased ~, 2443:5; Gilded ~, 3510:3; Golden ~,

457–458:3; 1583:3; Ice ~, 3224:1; Modern ~, 750:1; Neolithic ~, 2756:3

age/aging (see also longevity) see also adolescence/adolescent; elderly/elders; middle age; old age; people, old ~; years of age; youth; 165:3; 294:2; 368:1; 450:4; 779:2; 786:1; 807:18; 841:2; 1025:11; 1134:2; 1166:6; 1173:1; 1197:1; 1387:4; 1409:7, 11; 1473:3; 1481:8; 1567:2; 1590:27; 1604:2; 1785:5; 1900:3; 2025:5; 2093:3; 2398:14; 2434:6; 2437:9; 2561:1; 2584:2; 2595.1:2, 4; 2645:3; 2704:5; 2940:3, 4; 3089:5; 3099:19; 3113:1; 3300:2; 3443:3; 3468:3; 3582:1; 3743:3; 3862:3; 4180:3; 4224:2; 4311:2; 4376:6; 4623:2; 4761.2:1; 4909:1; anonymity of ~, 2542:1; attitudes on ~, 3268:2, 3; changing face of ~, 3357:3; control of ~, 4311:3; effects of ~, 2456:4; expectations of ~, 4325:2; fear of ~, 1935:17; 1968:1; 1993:1; 2106:2; 2386:1; 3593:2; healthy ~, 2165:1; honoring ~, 947:3; ~ in America, 2882:2; 4124:2; ~ in relation to work, 2048:3; ~ in relation to youth, 870:1; looking your ~, 3743:2; meaning of ~, 3357:1; perversity of ~, 193:1; 1862:2; physical aspects of ~, 2286:3; politics and ~, 931:30; realization of ~, 2236:1; sex and ~, 3690:3; signs of ~, 2479:1; statutory ~, 2185:17; wisdom of ~, 2807:2; women and ~ (see also woman/women, aging ~; woman/women, old ~; woman/women, older ~), 1383:2; 1991:2; 2233:1; 3067:1

ageism see also prejudice; 1761:4; 2025:2; ~ in fashion, 3422:3; ~ in language, 3089:6

agenda, personal ~, 3041:2

aggravation, 1759:2

aggressiveness, 2300:4; ~ in woman, 3611:1

agitator see also activism/activist; reform/er; 1028:4; political ~, 860:8; 1004:1; 1028:1; 1178:1; 1235:8, 10; 1394:1

agnosticism see also God, belief in ~; God, disbelief in ~; 3958:3

agony, 1590:19; lessons of ~, 3447.1:1

agreeableness, 713:9

agriculture, 4841:2; government and ~, 3943:2; ~ industry, 4420:4; natural ~, 3081:5; ~ vs. industrialism, 1896:3; women and ~, 4303:2; 4425:1

aid, ~ for the underclass, 2901:6; foreign ~, 3370:5; proffering ~, 1518:1; public ~, 2354:1

AIDS, 2559:1; 2866:19; 4741:1, 3; ~ cover-up, 2597:1; fear of

~, 2559:3; fighting ~, 3641:5, 6; global implications of ~, 2866:18; ~ in Africa, 3740:1; losses from ~, 4453:1; ~ Names quilt, 2468:5

Ailey, Alvin, 3426:2

aimlessness, 2060:3; 4683:1

air, demanding ~, 4457:2; fresh ~, 3571:1; good ~, 407:1; polluted ~, 670:3; sweet ~, 4411:2

airplane see also flying; 1863:1; 2463:1; ~ crash, 4140:3; emergency landing of ~, 1847:7; flying an ~, 2550:1; mechanical problems with ~, 1736:2; piloting ~, 3873:1; ~ safety, 3502:1; woman piloting ~, 1937:1

Al Qaeda see also Taliban, 3879:2; concerns of ~, 4642:1 Alabama, ~ government, 2661:1; Montgomery ~, 3185:2; Selma ~, 4368:2

alchemy, 306:3

alcohol/ism see also drinking; drunkard; liquor, 2219:7; 2313:1; 2463:6; 3303:2; 4591:1, 2; ~ among Native Americans, 2145:1; dangers of ~, 938:1; 1239:3; 3433:4; denial of ~, 4286:5; living with ~, 944:4; loving an ~, 4193:2

Alcott, Louisa May, 3628:1

Alderson, Federal Reformatory for Women, 1706:8

Aleichem, Sholom, 3276:5

alertness see also vigilance; wakefulness, 649:2

Alexander the Great, 367:4; 2589:3

algorithm, 4028:1

Ali, Muhammed, 1669:16

alienation, feeling of ~, 1855–1856:2; ~ of the elderly, 2907:3; ~ of the young, 2907:3; ~ of Western people, 2607:4

alimony, 1776:7; 3373:1

Allah see also God; Islam; Koran; Muslim; 122:3; 3092:; 3211:2

allegiance, 334:10

Allen, Gracie, 3563:7

Allen, Woody, 2932:8

alliance, ~ of capital and labor, 1636:4

aloneness see also loneliness; seclusion; solitude; 270:1; 1059:3; 1387:2; 1444:3; 1502:4; 1956:1; 1964:5; 2017:2; 2552:12; 2571:2; 2942:4; 3133:1; 3164:4; 3602:2; 3792:3; 4796:1; 4889:2; 4912:3; choosing ~, 3818:3; ~ in public, 2763:5; totality of ~, 3186:1

aloofness, 919:2; 1973:15

Alpes-Maritimes, 2914:1

alphabet, 2196:3; 3576:1

altruism/altruist see also selflessness, 341:7; 784:3; 892:19; 905:2; 982:12; 1240:1; 2068:3; 2534:7; 2662:3; 3788:2

Alzheimer's disease, 2956:1; 3802:4

amaryllis, 2464:3

Amazon River, 3288:1

Amazonia, sustainability in ~, 4469:1

ambiguity, 1982:1; 2149:1

ambition see also aspiration, 260:1; 469:1; 603:3; 669:4; 799:2; 845:6; 887:14; 947:6; 1450:22; 1727:7; 1752:8; 1830:1; 2000:1; 2082:1; 2190:3; 2324:1; 2598:1; 2686:3; 2970:3; 3002:4; 4116:10; 4510:8; 4775:1; danger of ~, 334:8; ~ in women, 4374:1; political ~, 2192:13; ~ to write, 954:4

America see also specific states, regions and cities; United States, 1663:14; 2453:2; 3807:0; 4295:3; 4683:2; adversaries of ~, 4760:2; aging in ~, 1935:17; ~ as role model, 3655:2; beauty of ~, 1241:1; change in ~, 4775:2; culture in ~, 2192:15; destiny of ~, 1496:1; discovery of ~, 4242:5; disintegration of ~, 1776:12; dissolution of society in ~, 1998:5; 3512:5; early ~, 4641:3; equality in ~, 4960:2; fate of ~, 2866:8; fear in ~, 2987:4; founding fathers of ~, 3584:4; freedom in ~, 3248:1; 3903:4; going to ~, 1563:1; history of ~, 4788:3; identity of ~, 4039:6; ~ in 1977, 4416:2; ~ in relation to Arabs, 1518:2; ~ in relation to Chinese, 4765:2; ~ in relation to Middle East, 4066:2; ~ in relation to world, 3220:2; 4129:3; 4174:5; 4611:6; Jews in ~, 4026:2; melting pot in ~, 4702:2; memory in ~, 1911:5; motto of ~, 2185:2; nature of ~, 4192:3; newcomers to ~, 2509:1; ~ on the move, 1888:2; opportunity in ~, 3142:2; pace of life in ~, 2298:1; people of color in ~, 2771:17; poverty in ~, 3276:4; power of ~, 4812:3; racial intolerance in ~, 4812:3; railroad in ~, 1106:2; rebuilding ~, 3774:4; religion in ~, 3584:4; 4201:4; schools in ~, 3584:6; segregation in ~, 2987:5; separation of church and state in ~, 4174:13; settling of ~ (see also settler, ~ of West), 1269:3; 4242:6; sexism in ~ (see sex, ~ in America; sexism); standard of living in ~, 1934:2; subjugation of women in ~, 2987:6; women in ~, 2398:6; 4661:1

American see also United States, 1440:11; 1655:10; 1670:7; 3189:1; 3309:11; 4115:2; 4731:4; ~ and tragedy, 3427:3; ~ business man, 1558:5; ~ character, 807:10; 1201:1; 1292:10; 1741:20; 2192:11, 14; 2439:11;

2925:2; 3142:2; 3714:4; 4146:5; 4424:3; 4815:2; character of ~, 3731:18; 3963:3; 4282:3; ~ child, 2899:3; 3088:2; ~ country women, 1816:1; crassness of ~, 1292:9; ~ culture, 4731:1; ~ democracy (see also democracy, American ~; United States, democracy in ~), 3512:8; ~ energy, 2866:6; ethnic ~, 2994:1; hardiness of ~, 1301:4; ~ identity, 4828:1; ~ inquisition, 1666:6; ~ in relation to government, 3350–3351:2; ~ in relation to Native American, 2911:1; maturity of ~, 1668:7; ~ men, 1686:1; 1934:3; Mexican-~, 2727:1; middle-class ~, 2592:2; ~ mindset, 2402:4; ~ minorities, 4601:5; money and ~, 4412:4; narcissism of ~, 870:5; ~ settlers, 1663:11; ~ smile, 4878:2; ~ soul, 2969:1; typical ~, 2899:1; unity of ~, 3864:2; ~ values (see also values, ~ in Western culture), 1686:12; 1691:1; 2000:3; 2192:17; 3326:3; 3360:2; ~ voters, 3698:2; ~ women, 646:3; 1836:3; 1893:1; 2127:5; 2201:7; 2233:2

American Recovery and Reinvestment Act, 4247:6

American Revolution, heroes of ~, 1794:2

amnesia, 4767:0

amorality, 2036:10

amphetamine, 3059:3

amputee/amputation, 3051:3; 4913:2

Amsterdam, 3941:2

amusement (see also diversion; pleasure) 960:3; 1236:4

analysand, 2740:2

analysis see also psychoanalysis; psychotherapy; therapy, 3158:1; 4907:1; Freudian ~, 3213:2; scientific ~, 1953–1954:1

anarchist/anarchy, 1325:1, 6; 1360:11; 2558:2

anatomy, 4356:2

ancestor/ancestry see also foremother; 731:2; 4257:2; 4952:5; strength from ~, 3254:3 Anderson, Marian, 3601:1

androgyny see also gender, ~ identity; 892:3; 910:4; 1191:1; 1337:7; 2318:3; 2552:3, 4; 2569:2; 2849:1; consciousness of ~, 2330:7; creativity and ~, 2189:8

angel, 964:1; 3470:7; love of ~, 910:15

Angelou, Maya, 4016:1

anger see also rage; 46:1; 194:1; 1015:4; 1407:2; 3031:1; 4046:3; 4133:3; 4818:0; children's ~, 3055:3; dealing with ~, 4305:4; expressing ~, 2657:1; 3147:4; 3818:1; message of ~, 3519:5;

~ of masses, 2900:2; overcome ~, 303:1; repressed ~, 2587:2; 4045:1

Anglican Church, 2712:1

anguish, 1024:10; 1160:9; 1751:24

animal *also see* ape; bear; beast; cat; cow;dog; horse; insect; marine life; pet; primate; wolf; wildlife, 905:6; 955:4; 1269:2; 1270:2; 1330:1; 1450:6, 15; 1669:7; 1797:4; 1948:1; ~ activist, 2879:3; alligator, 863:1; ass, 909:1; barnyard ~, 2201:6; bat, 4406:1; ~ behavior research, 3499:2; buffalo, 1269:2; camel, 1570:6; caribou, 3513:4; 4253:1; chicken, 388:2; children and~, 2529:11; communication with ~, 3427:1; 4084:4; ~ cruelty, 4676:2; doe, 2472:1; dolphin, 4438:2; donkey, 1270:2; eating ~, 4018.1:1; elephant, 1180:5; 1627:4; 2281:7; 3215:1, 2; 4947:3; elk, 1269:1; fox, 2529:10; giraffe, 1627:5; goldfish, 2291:9; hen, 2537:11; 3565:1; ~ in relation to men, 4539:5; ~ instinct, 2135:9; killing ~, 4560:1; laboratory ~, 2332:2; lamb, 807:7; language of ~, 2529:10; leopard, 4589:1; ~ lover, 983:2; mole, 1645:5; monkey, 4485:4; monogamy among ~, 4438:1; mule, 1914:10; otter, 1827:1; play among ~, 4544:1; protecting ~, 2336:2; rabbit, 1330:1; 3590:3; rat, 3009:5; ~ rights, 1669:12; 2332:1; river trout, 1509:3; salamander, 323:1; saving ~, 2529:5; shark, 2783:1; 3550:5; sheep, 469:2; snail, 1605:1; 2775:2; snake ~, 3389:4; ~ sounds, 2117:13; study of ~ life, 3363:2; sunshine and ~, 2164:3; tiger, 1282:1; 1282:2; treatment of ~, 526:1; 870:11; 3748:1; wild ~, 2336:1; 4589:1; worm, 1254:1; young ~, 2460:2; zoo ~, 2281:6

anniversary *see also* marriage; wedding; golden wedding ~ 2011:3

anonymity, 1268:1; 1590:17; 2767:1; 4611:3

Another Mother for Peace, 2553:1

answer, 1450:27; 2409:2; 4703:1; finding ~, 4421:3; 4816:1; preparing ~, 2949:2; simple ~, 1835:5

anthologist/anthology, 2027:1; 2201:3

Anthony, Susan B., 931:28, 30; 1062:4; 1154:1

anthropologist/anthropology, 1336:2; 2481:2; 2691:2; 2858:4; finance and ~, 4761.1:1

anticipation, 955:12; 1129:2; 1160:8; 3855:2

anti-depressants, ~ Prozac, 4965:1

antiquity *see also* history, 935:2

anti-Semitism *see also* Jew/Judaism, 1168:3; 1735:6; 1947:4; 2943:8; dealing with ~, 1905:3; 4187:4; ~ of Jew, 3693:2

anti-violence *see also* pacifism; violence; 2111:3

anti-war movement *see also* pacifism; resistence, ~ to war, 3762:3; alternatives to ~, 4706:1, 2

Antoinette, Marie, 2670:1

anxiety *see also* worry; 1579:3; 1979:16; extreme ~, 4765:4; women's ~, 987:4; 1998:4

apartheid *see also* racism; 2303:3; 2807:1; 3757:1, 4; 4191:1; surviving ~, 2905:5

apartment, small ~, 676:11

apathy *see also* passivity; 1548:10; 1727:10

ape, 3937:1; Bonobo ~, 3937:4; 4590:4; chimpanzee ~, 3937:3; gorilla, 2795:1; protecting gorillas, 4694:3; orangutan, 3657:2, 4

apology, 1317:4; 2305:1

apostle, 308:2

Appalachia, U.S.A., desecration of ~, 4088:1, 2

appearance (physical), 533:14; 1409:6; 1462:2; 1959:1; 3478:4; changing ~, 3643:1; 4497:1; commercialization of men's ~, 4203:4; concern for ~, 2527:1; contemporary ~, 4362:2; deceptive ~, 3856:2; enhanced ~, 1516:2; good ~, 1750:1; 2052:0; ~ in sports, 4761:1; judged by ~, 4445:1; 4566.1:1; ~ of women, 1663:18; 2613:1; 2765:6; 2977:1; 3840:5; 4566.1:2; ~ of youth, 3451:2; youthful ~, 1991:2; 2016:3; 3593:2

appearances (impression), 224:1; 465:3; 547:1; 614:1; 676:6; 790:2; 1025:1; 1085:3; 1615:2; 1914:10; 3059:2; 4813:1; keeping up ~, 1382:4; 2829:2; perfect ~, 2801:1

applause, 2138:1

Apple Computer, Inc., ~ iPods, 4227:3

appreciation *see also* gratitude; respect/ability; 1110:2; 3546:2; ~ of life, 61:2

approval, 767:25; 2056:3

aptitude, 272:1

aquaculture, sustainable ~, 3605:2, 3

Aquarian Age, 3085:1

Aquino, Jr., Benigno, 2830:3

Arab/ia *see also* specific nations, 3346:3; 4130:3; character of ~, 1347:1; image of ~, 2595:2; ~ in relation to Great Britain, 3346:4; ~ in relation to Jews, 2673:4; lack of ~ leadership, 4846:3; marriage in ~, 4846:1; 4986:3; suppression of women in

~, 3547:12; 4846:2, 4; ~ women, 3233:4

Arafat, Yasar, 4636:1

archaeologist/archaeology, 1724:7; 1867:6; 2124:1; 3708:2; end of ~, 1743:8

architect/architecture *see also* building; 1403:1, 2; 3735:1; 4492:2; American ~, 2402:4; Eastern ~, 1391:2; irrelevance of ~, 2402:8; masculine ~, 4273:1; modern ~, 2691:1; styles of ~, 2503:1; women in ~, 2557:1; 2643:2

Arden, Elizabeth, 3370:2

Argentina, 1930:2; 4187:1; militarism in ~, 2877:0; rural ~, 4081:2; schizophrenic ~, 2628:6

argument *see also* bickering; dispute; fight/ing; quarrel, 769:5; 1409:6; 2772:8; 3054:3; ~ between men and women, 2302:1; dislike of ~, 738:1; fallacious ~, 4852:1; friendly ~, 1677:7; sides of ~, 2027:13

aristocrat/aristocracy *see also* nobility, 234:3; 839:5; 2000:2; disdain for ~, 630:1; impoverished ~, 731:2

Aristophanes, 4278:3

Aristotle, 487:9; 585:2

ark, holy ~, 31:1

armed forces/army *see also* specific branches; military; soldier; war; 897:1; 3811:1; discipline in ~, 2192:8; documentary ~, 2949:5; enlisting in ~, 2951:3; lie about ~, 2620:1; limitations of ~, 2386:2; ~ officer, 2951:3; ~ recruitment, 2078:3; standing ~, 701:6; volunteer ~, 1480:1; women and ~, 1047:2

Armenian, 3069:1

Armistice Day, 1784:3

arms *see also* gun; weaponry, 1329:1; call to ~, 582:1; 648:1; 2049–2050:2; ~ race, 2038:1; 3145:5

army, indigenous ~, 4853:1

arrogance, 163:2

art *see also* specific art forms; artist; the Muses; 179:5; 698:3; 798:5; 887:8; 928:3; 936:1, 2; 1093:1; 1167:14; 1246:4; 1258:1; 1314:2; 1443:1; 1633:1; 1658:1; 1670:1; 1775:2; 1817:2; 1881:7; 1901:2; 1938:7; 2116:17; 2141:3; 2144:2; 2154:4; 2331:5; 2342:1; 2347:3; 2352:11; 2546:4; 2593:1; 2599:4; 2658:1; 2668:9, 15; 3051:7; 3117:3; 3533:2; 3620:1; 4797:2; 4934:1; 16th century ~, 335:1; ~ appreciation, 1186:2; 2281:9; ~ as healing process, 2468:5; benefits of ~, 500:1; ~ center, 2266:2; collaborative ~, 4248:1; ~ collector, 2089:6; commercialization of ~, 3585:1; ~ competition,

3869:2; creating ~, 2270:7; 3567:7; 3749:6; demands of ~, 3797:7; economic power of ~, 3117:1; feminism and ~, 2821:1; 3533:1; function of ~, 1705:1, 3; 3420:1; ~ gallery, 2377:1; ~ imitating life, 4816:6; impact of ~, 3168:3; 3722:2; impact of war on ~, 2172:3; ~ in education, 2923:1, 2; ~ in Europe, 2066:1; 3973:1; ~ in relation to government, 1705:3; information on ~, 2347:5; ~ interpretation, 2866:2, 3; lasting ~, 2628:1; making ~, 2273:3; 2973:1; 4075:3; 4629:6; male standard in ~, 2580:1; ~ movements, 1843:4; nature ~, 549:1; necessity of ~, 1512:10; 2518:4; performance ~, 2576:1; 3688:2; place for the ~, 2402:9; political influence in ~, 2771:11; politics and ~, 2680:29; popular ~, 1686:12; 3119:8; portrait ~, 335:1; power of ~, 3117:1; practice of ~, 3688:3; primitive ~, 2572:; public ~, 4638:2; public funding for ~, 3117:2; purpose of ~, 1408:6; 4159:1; relevance of ~, 3182:1; religion and ~, 1408:14; revelations of ~, 1551:1; revolution in ~, 887:7; self-conscious ~, 1186:1; self-discovery in ~, 3971:1; sexuality in ~, 2756:9; source of ~, 1408:14; 3604:1; spirituality and ~, 3120:4; strong ~, 1658:3; ~ student, 1881:6; success in ~, 1573:3; superior ~, 2845:4; teaching ~, 2066:9; violence depicted in ~, 2756:9; visual ~, 3120:2; women in ~, 545:1; works of ~, 1292:11; 1759:7; 2464:11; 3944:3

articulateness, 234:4

artifact, historical ~, 4406:2

artist *see also* specific types; 798:3; 931:10; 1314:2; 1421:1; 1436:5; 1630:2; 1844:9; 2108:1, 2; 2154:4; 3414:2; 3721:2; abilities of ~, 4595:6; American ~, 2827:5; 3648:2; ~ at work, 1230:3; becoming an ~, 3079:1; best work of ~, 2089:5; black women ~, 3517:1; business of ~, 1259:1; celebrity and ~, 2377:2; 4492:1; choosing to be ~, 4182:2; commercialism of ~, 4256:1; creation of ~, 2141:5; creativity of ~, 4210:5; cynicism of ~, 2089:4; dilemma of ~, 4512:1; ego of ~, 3459:1; failure of ~, 1950:2; 3349:4; function of ~, 3756:1; government and ~, 2073:1; growth of ~, 1408:2; ~ in relation to community, 2141:4; inspiration of ~, 2273:1; 2299:1; introspective ~, 3443:6; legacy of ~, 3524:2; legendary ~, 2077:1;

life of ~, 3168:4; male ~, 1436:1; ~ materials, 1881:2; ~ model, 587:1; motivation of ~, 3038:3; need for ~, 2291:5; New York ~, 1881:4; objective of ~, 2089:2; older ~, 2754:1; political power of ~, 2580:2; prerogative of ~, 2347:1; pretensions of ~, 2066:1; rights of ~, 4363:2; role of ~, 2028:2; self-taught ~, 706:1; sensibility of ~, 1970:1; universality of ~, 2860:1; ~ view of Nature, 1817:3; vulnerable ~, 2933:1; wife of ~, 4884:5; woman ~, 844:1; 1126:2; 1185:1; 2468:1, 2; 3133:4; 3517:2; 3620:3; 3816:1; 4407:1; women's movement and ~, 4358:2; work of ~, 3910:1

Ashcroft, John, 4984:2

Asia/n see also specific nations, 1642:1; 3035:2; ~ -American woman, 2475:3; 3283:3; 3313:1; 3521:1; business in ~, 4419:1; children in ~, 1741:24; conquest of ~, 1347:3; coopting ~ culture, 2680:25; economic development in ~, 3354:1; ~ in relation to whites, 1618:7

ASL (American Sign Language), 3760:1; ~ interpreter, 3633:1

aspiration see also ambition, 1152:6; 1254:17; 4641:3; fear of ~, 2999:3; high ~, 2464:12; thwarted ~, 1755:1

assassination, 736:2; 754:2; 2642:2; ~ attempts, 2898:2

assault, see also violence; 511:3

assertiveness, ~ in women, 2552:10

assessment, 1006:15

assistance see also aid; help/fulness; giving ~, 1335:2

assumptions, making ~, 2248:1

astonishment, 1409:26; 4543:1

astrology see also horoscope, 306:3; 1744:2; history of ~, 2519:2

astronaut, 2043:3; woman ~, 3731:19

astronomer/astronomy, 1293:4; 2338:1, 2; new theories of ~, 2640:1; new worlds of ~, 1293:2

atheism, 4084:1; 4789:2; 4888:2

athlete/athletics see also specific types and events; sports, 4384:3; 4621:2; 4910:1; ailments of ~, 4621:1; champion ~, 4243:2; 4650:9; 4864:2; practice for ~, 2367:0; racism in ~, 4944:1; use of drugs in ~, 4487:1; 4569:1; women ~, 2005:2, 3; 4384:1; 4470:2; 4621:3; 4747:1

Atlantic Ocean, 2410:1 atom see also molecule, 492:1; 2210:8; exploring the ~, 2054:1

atomic bomb see also Hiroshima, Japan; nuclear power; 2496:4; effects of ~, 3303:1

atomic energy, 1514:1, 3

atonement see also penitance; purgatory, 3854:3

atrocity, military ~, 4263:4; ~ of past, 1913:2; response to ~, 3342:3

attachment, 805:3; overly emotional ~, 2775:2

attention, attracting ~, 167:1; center of ~, 451:7; 1790:3; 4938:2; demand ~, 3112:3; giving ~, 2116:3; lack of ~, 3419:3; need for ~, 4285:8; paying ~, 4166:2; wanting ~, 2481:1

attitude, 1780:9; 3470:7; cultural ~, 939:1; positive ~, 1613:2; 4624:1; respectful ~, 916:3; youthful ~, 2564:4

Attorney General, U.S., 2496:2

attraction, 4929:3; sexual ~, 3732:4; ~ to extremes, 3723:2; ~ to intellect, 644:1

attractiveness see also beauty; 773:1; effects of poverty on ~, 2765:2; ~ in women, 767:20; 1163:1, 3; 1383:3; 2204:1; ~ of wife, 3388:1

audience see also public, the; 1722:2; 2056:4; ~ in relation to performer (see also performance/performer, ~ in relation to audience), 2903:8; 3691:1; ~ in relation to play, 2518:3; seduction of ~, 4489:1; silence of ~, 2395:1; theater ~, 2755:1; 3170:4; 3186:3

Auschwitz, 2631:2; 4251:1, 4

Austen, Jane, 805:4

austerity, 3453:2

Australia/n, indigenous ~, 2361:1; ~ in relation to United States, 3075:2; Kakadu National Park ~, 4724:2

Austria, women in ~, 3965:2

authenticity, 4668:4

author see writer, power of ~, 3992:7

authoritarianism, 2298:4

authority see also expert/ise; power; 430:10; 818:2; 839:6; 1895:1; 3961:1; 4081:7; basis of ~, 3617:1; challenging ~, 890:3; 2756:19; 4522:2; 4724:3; defiance of ~, 2036:17; ~ for women, 3706:4; ~ of the state, 3118:4; questioning ~, 2582:4; 4174:7; resisting ~, 4802:4; women and ~, 535:2; 3330:1; 4527:4; women in position of ~ (see also woman/women, ~ in authority), 3133:3

autism, 3748:3, 4; 4154:1; 4856:3

autobiography see also memoir; story, personal ~; writing; 2238:3; 2260:5; 2349:22; 2875:1; 3225:2; selling one's ~, 860:14; writing ~, 1867:1

automation, 4081:3; impact of ~ on workforce, 1229:2; ~ in home, 2602:2

automobile, 3578:4; 4076:2; driving ~, 4656:1; energy needs of ~, 4552:2; 4857:1; ~ horn, 3612:3; ~ in America, 3676:1; ~ industry, 4486:2, 3; isolation of ~, 2370:1; mechanics of ~, 2330:1; parking ~, 3770:1; racing ~, 1688:3; sex in ~, 2748:2; ~ workers, 4008:3

autonomy, 2607:1; 3697:2

autumn, 1166:2; 1465:2; 2117:3

avant-garde, 3439:5

avarice see also greed, 1282:1; 3860:1

averageness, ~ in people, 1741:23; ~ in whites, 1725:2

aviation/aviator see also flying; 1736:1; 2532:3; career in ~, 1960:2; goal of ~, 2043:2; ~ school for blacks, 1742:1; spirit of ~, 4066:3; woman ~, 1960:3; 4359:1

avocation see hobby; career; profession

awakening, 122:2; 2464:6; 3563:1; 4573:1; ~ in old age, 2919:2; national ~, 3615:5; ~ of consciousness, 798:2; ~ of womanliness, 2751:1; religious ~, 1959:8

award see also crown; honors; prize; arbitrariness of ~, 3306:4

awareness, 955:26; 1979:6; 2572:3; 3497:1, 4; ~ at cellular level, 4508:2; growing ~, 4758:2; keen ~, 2711:7; lack of ~, 2177:4; ~ of inner self (see also self-awareness), 2724:2; pain of ~, 1751:24; sonic ~, 2813:1

awe, 2689:5

Azerbaijan, 4437:1; elections in ~, 4437:2

B

Baal Shem Tov, 4383:2

baby see also child/ren; childbirth; infant; newborn; 998:5; 1044:19; 1068:2; 1256:1; 1906:5; 2188:4; 2434:4; 2987:1; 3030:1; 3033:5; 3457:2; 3702:2; 3733:4; 4005:4; 4046:4; 4207:3; 4365:1; 4842:1; birth of ~, 2773:2; bringing up ~, 2827:1; ~ clothes, 4210:2; crying ~, 1700:6; face of ~, 907:2; in love with ~, 4133:1; incubator ~, 4533:3; joys of having ~, 1429:1; love of ~, 871:1; newborn ~, 1763:3; 1827:4; observing ~, 3042:1; prenatal care for ~, 1407:1; promise of ~, 2187:19; reason to have ~, 3099:4; selecting traits of ~, 4964:2; sleeping ~, 952:3; 1719:4; smell of ~, 3718:2; smiling ~, 1900:2; tenderness for ~, 4193:4

Bach, Johann Sebastian, 1336:7; 2845:1

bachelor see also single/ness; 2943:5; eligible ~, 767:5

backbone see also character; 1871:3

backlash, basis for ~, 2607:5

backward, looking ~, 1450:29

bad/ness see also evil; good and evil; wickedness, 674:3; 799:7; 1321:1; stave off ~, 367:1

Baghdad, Iraq, 1663:4

Bahá'í, philosophy of ~, 3368:3

Bai, Mira, 293:2

Bailly, Jean Sylvain, 733:17

balance, ~ of life, 1176:1; 4531:3; world out of ~, 3953:1

Ball, Lucille, 4628:1

ballad, 2679:4

ballet see also dancer/dancing; girls and ~, 4067:1

banality, 1852:1; 2577:2

band see also music; marching ~, 731:4

bank/er, 1586:3; 4250:3; ~ deposit/er, 4229:1; ~ failure, 4679:5; ~ industry, 4229:2; ~ loan, 2262:3; ~ microcredit, 3106:1, 2; regulation of ~, 3156:3; ~ regulations, 4468:3; ~ robber, 4600:1; ~ savings, 782:5; shadow ~, 4761.1:5

bankruptcy, 1420:1

baptism, 3066:4; water for ~, 3243:1

barbarian/barbarism see also savage/ry, 880:1; 931:15; 1033:4; 2116:1

Barcelona, Spain, 2404:1

bargain, 585:8

barnyard, 1614:1

bars and pubs see also drinking; 2352:14; 4048:4; 4764:2

bartender, 2311:1

bartering, 3803:2; 4734:4

baseball, 1434:1; 1669:14; 2218:3; 4535:3; ~ fan, 4273.1:3; ~ umpire, 2759:1, 2

baseness see also turpitude, 539:4

bath, 2817:9; ritual ~, 2981:3

Bath, England, 767:1

bathing suit, 1836:4

bathroom, 2561:5

battle, 1549:8; daily ~, 992:5; doing ~, 2843:2; field of ~, 1526:2; ~ for nation, 1224:3; need for ~, 1076:2; postwar ~, 3241:5

bayou, 1457:1

BBC (British Broadcasting Company), 2266:3, 4; women and ~, 3706:3

beach see also sand, 146:1; 1069:1

bear (animal), 4372:1; dancing with ~, 2843:2; ~ in relation to humans, 4372:2; protecting ~, 4372:3

beast see also animals; 4252:4; taming a ~, 450:5

beauty see also attractiveness; prettiness, 59:1; 166:9; 474:1; 507:3; 589:1; 663:2; 864:3; 927:1; 937:1; 1060:2; 1205:1; 1208:9; 1223:3; 1254:4; 1305:1; 1316:1;

1322:5; 1366:2; 1388:1; 1443:1; 1446:5; 1485:1; 1669:9; 1769:1; 2456:7; 2782:1; 3039:5; 3413:4; 3856:1; 4358:1; 4636:2; ~ aids, 4227:2; ~ business, 2613:1; 3370:2; ~ contest, 3399:2; creating ~, 1752:5; desire for ~, 1284:1; 1750:3; destruction of ~, 1715:9; ephemerality of ~, 507:2, 5; 1068:1; fading ~, 85:1; 1134:2; ~ in relation to women, 1940:2; 2369:1; 2799:2; 3637:1; inadequacy of ~, 1619:4; inner ~, 2662:2; 4755:3; invisible ~, 1509:4; lack of ~, 1595:2; 2375:1; 3292–3293:2; loss of ~, 1454:2; ~ magazine, 2083:2; ~ myth, 4635:3; ~ of nature (see also Nature), 2235:1; ~ of women, 3246:3; physical ~, 2763:2; 2814:1; pin-up ~, 3738:4; price of ~, 2890:2; prison of ~, 701:7; privileges of ~, 3402:1; proof of ~, 1336:7; ~ secrets, 4203:1; unnoticed ~, 3854:1

bed/room, 225:1; 1570:2; 2542:2; going to ~ with partner, 1973:14; holiday ~, 2063:6

Bedford Hills Correction Facility, New York, 2458:2

bedouin see also nomad; 125:1

Beecher, Henry Ward, 4763:1

Beecher, Lyman, 3510:3

Beethoven, Ludwig van, 1922:3; 2845:1; 3168:4; 4042:8

beggar/begging, 1562:6; 2420:1

beginner, awe of ~, 3170:3

beginning, 88:2; 544:2; 722:5; 930:3; 1184:2; 1344:2; 1392:5; 1409:19; 1650:2; 1872:3; 1881:6; 2048:2; 2061:2; 2263:3; 2317:1; 2855:1; 3110:4; 4019:3; ~ again, 2135:7; humble ~, 1343:2; 2435:3; new ~, 1006:3; 3217:6; 4945:1; point of ~, 1724:11; practical ~, 974:6

behavior see also specific emotions; comportment; conduct; human nature; socialization; 2069:3; analyzing human ~, 3499:2; authentic ~, 2920:5; childish ~, 922:3; controlling ~, 2148:2; guidelines for ~, 3266–3267:1; refinement of ~, 931:7; reserved ~ 3897:1; ~ towards loved ones, 1085:5; unconscious ~, 2735:3

Behn, Aphra, 462:1; 497:5; 535:1

beingness see also identity, 354:1; 2320:2; state of ~, 1450:5; 2292–2293:2; 2711:4; 3473:2

Beirut, Lebanon, 2505:2

Belafonte, Harry, 2762:1

belief see also convictions; faith; religion; 1783:2; 1848:4; 2327:1; 4587:2; 4890–4891:1; history of ~, 1625:5; ~ in oneself, 2133:5; 2416:4; 3217:5;

3638:2; power of ~, 2694:1; sacred ~, 2613:4

Bellow, Saul, 2638:10

belonging (member) see also connectedness/connection; 1929:5; 3308:2; 3309:10; ~ to another, 1809:1

belongings see also possession, 3562:1; relinquish ~, 404:1

beneficiary/benefit, 2618:12; personal ~, 2483:5

benevolence see also kindness; generosity; 2266:12

bereavement see also grief; 1873:1; 2352:6

Berlin, Germany, personality of ~, 4651:1; political denial in ~, 4651:2

Bernstein, Leonard, 4344:3

best, 46:9; 2564:3; doing one's ~, 992:7; giving your ~, 1123:2

betrayal see also traitor, 1522:1; 1610:2; 1912:1; 2078:5; 2387:5; 2944:2; 3906:6; ~ of nation, 2291:8; pain of ~, 2819:4; 4369:3

betterment, working for ~, 4648:5

Beverly Hills, California, 2634:1

bewilderment see also confusion, 158:5; 713:12

Bhutto, Zulfikar Ali, 4160:7

Bible see also specific Biblical figures and Books; Gospel; Koran; Magnificat; sacrament; scripture; Ten Commandments; 288:1; 516:2; 890:1; 931:25; 979:2; 987:1; 1548:2; 1910:1; 1986:5; 2007:2; 2021:9; 2067:0; 3139:12; history in ~, 3086:1; homosexuality and ~, 3153:1; influence of ~, 931:17; interpretation of ~, 3445:5; knowledge of ~, 2770:2; ~ Old Testament, 2778:4; questioning ~, 3508:1; translation of ~, 832:1; women and ~, 369:1; women in ~, 931:20; 1304:6; 2613:2; 3086:2

bickering see also argument; quarrel, 187:1

Biden, Joseph, 4027:4

bigotry see also racism; prejudice; 2837:3; 3427:4; consequences of ~, 4057:4

bilingual, 2523:1; 3830:3

bill, paying ~, 1892:1

biodiversity see also ecology; environment; loss of ~, 4258:3

biofeedback, 2621:1

biographer/biography see also autobiography, 1487:7; 1551:1; 1628:1; 1659:9; 2189:11; 2270:6; 3843:1; elitism of ~, 3371:3; facts and fiction in ~, 1844:7

biology, 1751:10; ~ as destiny, 3383:2; 4031:1; enthusiasm for ~, 1279:1; ~ in relation to

women, 3665:1; molecular ~, 3701:2

biotechnology, agricultural ~ (see also agriculture), 4774:7; ban on ~, 4774:6; need for ~, 3943:1

bipartisanship, 3798:3; 3864:2

bird, 159:1; 268:1; 490:1; 845:3; 970:1; 1069:1; 1109:3; 1224:1; 1450:6; 1855–1856:3; 1885:1; 4743:4; 4791:5; blue heron, 1868:1; bullfinch, 547:1; caged ~, 1208:10; 1441:1; 1627:3; crow, 4734:3; death of ~, 2135:9; dove, 847:2; eagle, 3686:1; hawk, 654:1; 1885:1, 2; heron, 2117:4; kite, 847:2; ~ lover, 2761:1; magpie, 67:1; nightingale, 46:8; 658:1; owl, 396:1; 751:1; 2212:5; parrot, 511:2; peacock, 2534:8; 2771:6; pigeon, 1450:6; 4270:2; 4902:4; raven, 884:3; rehabilitated ~, 4697:1; rooster, 4385:5; scarcity of ~, 2061:11; ~ song, 723:1; 1272:3; 1355:6; 1605:2; 1710:3; 2100:2; sparrow, 1224:1; 2761:2; stork, 73:1; thrush, 1605:2; warbler, 897:2; ~ watching, 3578:2; whip-poorwill, 1109:3

Birmingham, Alabama, 3260:2; 4060:1; 4097:2; 4268:2

birth see also childbirth; newborn; pregnancy/pregnant; rebirth; 122:2; 459:4; 1537:6; 3019:3; 4053:2; 4643:1; ~ abnormalities, 4347:4; 4398:1; ~ and death, 3413:1; awaiting ~, 3408:1; ~-injured child, 3260:3; miracle of ~, 70:1; ~ of boy, 853:6; ~ of parents, 3089:1; origin of ~, 4740:1; philosophy of ~, 2571:1; ~ right, 3317:4

birth control see also contraception; condom; family ~ planning; vasectomy; 1329:0; 1535:, 7, 11; 1741:25; 1804:2; 2044:1; 2439:6; 2794:1; 3333:1; attitudes toward ~, 2349:2; involuntary ~, 4634:1; ~ pill, 3990:1; ~ programs, 3003:1; prohibition of ~, 4931:1; right to ~ (see also abortion, ~ rights), 2850:2; types of ~, 4781:1

birthday, 76:1; 546:2; 1903:1; ~ celebration, 4763:1; ~ wishes, 624:3

bisexual/ity see also androgyny; homosexual/ity; sex; 1337:7; 1545:3; 2665:2; 2990:1

bitch (pejorative), 1973:1; 4169:1; 4211:1; 4221:0; woman as ~, 3572:1

bitterness see also resentment, 1646:4; 1780:9; 1901:1; 4160:5; eliminating ~, 1310:1 black (color), 3425:1

blackmail see also extortion, diplomatic ~, 1857:

blacks see also Africa/n; African American; 677:2; 1299:5; 1592:3; 1668:4; 2259:1; 3121:3; 3412:2; admiration of ~, 2469:2; ~ Americans, 3195:2; 4301:3; ~ and finance, 4742:2; autonomy of ~, 1291:1; average ~, 1725:2; character of ~, 1070:3; ~ child of slave owner, 1000:2; color of ~, 2456:3; communication between ~ women, 4127:1; ~ community, 3970:1; control of ~, 2711:10; ~ culture of gangstas, 2615:1; dangerous ~, 4164:3; destiny of ~, 807:15; educated ~, 2767:2; education for ~, 1577:1; 4652:3; enslavement of ~ (see also rights, black ~), 3796:1; equal treatment for ~, 2139:4; equality between ~ men and women, 1070:2; ~ experience, 3254:2; 4042:4; exploitation of ~ musicians, 2392:1; ~ family, 3752:5; freedom of ~, 2206:4, 5; ~ hair, 3112:1; ~ heritage, 1453:4; ~ identity, 2485:1; 2762:1; 2767:1; 3461:1; image of ~, 4714:3; ~ in relation to America, 1874:3, 4; ~ in relation to whites, 843:2; 2563:7; 2659:6; 2771:2; 3865:1; 4164:2; marginalization of ~, 4305:2; ~ men, 3995:4; murder of ~, 1291:5; 1299:6; 2244:1; obstacles of ~, 1299:3; oppression of ~, 807:13; 1291:2; 1299:1, 4; 2118:1; 2771:14; 3050:1; 3157:2; ~ passing as white, 4737:2; ~ power movement, 4149:2; prejudice against ~, 2658:3; 3729:2; ~ pride, 1453:4; 1592:4; 2453:1; 2723:1; 2901:1; 4149:1; racism among ~, 1592:2; recreational area for ~, 2921:3; relations between ~ men and women, 4317:2; religions and ~, 4517:1; ~ rights, 3185:1, 3; self-deprecation of ~, 3970:2; self-determination of ~, 4305:10; sexism among ~, 860:8; 2802:1; 4305:6; ~ suffrage, 4763:4; survival skills of ~, 2901:5; ~ teenage girls, 3493:5; the ~ experience, 3821:2; ~ tokenism, 2610:2; ~ women, 882:2; 1299:7; 2380:1; 2618:3; 2771:2, 4; 3157:; 3447:1; 3493:1, 2; 3505:1; 3547:9; 3796:2; 3815:3; 3956:1; 3995:3; 4149:3; 4386:1; 4673:2; ~ women and appearance, 1592:1; ~ women as caretakers, 4191:3; ~ women in America, 4389:1; ~ women in relation to white women, 4442:1, 2; ~ women in South, 4634:1

Blair, Tony, wife of ~, 4231:2

Blake, William, 1358:1

blame see also scapegoat, attached to ~, 4034:2; hierarchy of ~,

4312:3; ~ oneself, 3112:4; placing ~, 2987:7; 3911:5

blasphemy *see also* profaneness; sacrilege; 41:1

bleeding *see also* blood; 2767:4

blessed, 4955:1

blessing, 2997:11

blind/ness, 519:3; ~ in newborn, 1006:2; metaphorical ~, 4074:4; reading by ~, 4544:4

bliss *see also* happiness; joy; 713:10; 966:3; 1240:2

blog/ger *see also* computer, cyberspace, Internet, 4189:4; 4781:4; 4856:1

blonde, ~ bombshell, 2766:1; dumb ~, 2401:2 blood *see also* bleeding, 4565:4

bloom, 3441:1

blush, 873:1; 4105:7

boasting, 1120:1; 2537:11; 2680:7

boat/ing *see also* ship; 4168:4; ~ anchor, 4319:2

body (human) *see also* face; foot; hair; hand; heart; womb, 1932:1; 2950:2; 4237:2; 4598:1; admiration of ~, 4174:3; aging ~, 3357:2; appreciation of ~, 4806:1; ~ arm, 1122:2; awareness of ~, 3827:3; care of ~, 1771:8; comfort of ~, 4603:3; concealed ~, 3619:2; connection to ~, 4113:1; control over ~, 4035:2; enjoyment of ~, 3827:4; expressiveness of ~, 2950:1; fascination with ~ buttocks; 410:1; female ~, 3816:3; 4055:1; 4689:1; girl's ~ image, 3482:1; ~ image, 2155:1; 4174:4; 4541:3; 4812:1; 4831:1; 4875:2; ~ knee, 2910:3; limitations of ~, 2760:3; maintaining ~, 1884:4; male ~, 3119:13; man's leg, 1152:2; ~ mind connection, 1117:3; passions of ~, 2815:3; reclaiming women's ~, 3025:3; relevancy of ~, 3840:2; religion and ~, 928:1; repulsion of ~, 3951:1; rhythms of ~, 2724:3; ~ size (*see also* weight), 767:24; 4010:3; 4739:1; stomach, 790:12; strength of ~, 3922:1; vulnerability of ~, 1715:5; 1986:8; 3840:4; 4416:1; woman's ~, 4038:4

Bohemian, 4478:2

Boleyn, Anne, 300:7; 3102:3

bomb/ing *see also* land mines; dropping ~, 4415:1; suicide ~, 4231:1; 4430:5

Bombay, India, 4752:4

book *see also* fiction; literature; novel/ist; reading; story; textbook; 517:1; 649:4; 769:3; 808:13; 1024:28; 1066:1; 1159:1; 1199:3; 1213:1; 1333:5; 1368:5; 1415:1; 1440:4; 2464:7; 3349:3, 13; 4101:4; 4255:3; ~ as educational tool, 951:5;

~ at home, 4729:2; ~ award, 3306:4; bad ~, 2649:1; banned ~, 3250.1:4; beginning a ~, 3464:; boring ~, 4235:3; ~ by person of importance, 2201:4; children's ~, 2668:28; 2774:1; 3062:2; 4781:3; cook- (*see also* cooking, ~ recipe), 816:1; ~ design, 1999:1; good ~, 1852:2; importance of ~, 3850:5; influence of ~, 3992:6; library ~, 4727:1; lost in a ~, 4639:4; marketing ~, 2809:2; old ~, 4175:4; paperback ~, 2027:10; publication of ~, 1751:31; reading ~, 3044:3; ~ review, 3689:2; science fiction ~, 4710:1; ~ selling, 3440:1; ~ title, 3968:5; travel ~, 3681:1; ~ with substance, 2863:2; writing ~ (*see also* writer; writing), 2270:5

border, building walls at ~, 4948:4; separation by ~, 4952:3; ~ wall, 4423:4

bore/dom *see also* monotony; 683:1; 767:7; 1377:1; 2033:1; 2169:3; 2526:1; 2913:3; 3110:1; 4206:4; 4544:2; avoiding ~, 3957:3

borrowing, 479:3

Bosnia/n, 3867:3; conflict in ~, 3152:4

Boston, Massachusetts, 399:3; 1512:1; 4375:1; 4641:3; ~ Symphony Orchestra, 2478:3; ~ Tea Party, 600:1

botany, 2522:2; studying ~, 1952:6

Botox *see also* cosmetic surgery, 4660:1

Botswana, funerals in ~, 4949:1

bottom, hitting ~, 3567:3; room at ~, 1825:3

boundaries, 4219:1; 4699:2; personal ~, 2832:3

bourgeoisie *see also* class [social]; 2886:2; 3770:2

boxing, 1943:3

boy/hood *see also* child/ren; son; 821:5; 1409:13; 1450:23; 1580:3; ~ at risk, 4007:4; birth of ~, 853:6; conditioning of ~, 2951:3; ~ growing up, 3498:1; ~ in relation to mother, 4052:1; ~ kept indoors, 1650:3; role of ~, 1437:2; 1935:5; teenage ~ (*see also* adolescence/adolescent; teenage/r), 3783:2; trouble with ~, 3783:3; upbringing of ~, 2524:1; violence and ~, 3764:2

boycott, 2716:2, 3

boyfriend *see also* fiancé/e, lover; 4013:6; 4516:3; dissatisfied with ~, 2913:3

Brahms, Johannes, 2845:1; 4344:4

brain *see also* intellect/intelligence; mind; 998:4; 1024:19; 1254:19; 1590:25; 2176:2; 4711:3; ~ capacity, 4348:5; damaged ~, 4508:4; development of ~, 3509:2; 4405:4; diseased ~,

3557:1; ~ donation, 4508:1; female ~, 3027:6; ~ of woman, 1973:9; training of ~, 2547:3; woman's ~, 4590:3

brainwashing, 2602:3

Brandeis, Louis D., 1681:3

brassiere *see also* underwear; 3074:1; 4224:2

bravery *see also* courage; valor; 308:12; 713:7; 730:1; 1497:1; 1560:1; 1914:5; 2642:12; ~ in relation to fear, 4084:5; lack of ~, 2732:7

Brazil/ian, 1930:2; 2153:3; environmentalism in ~, 4469:3; government in ~, 2852:1; hunger in ~, 4774:8; land in ~, 2852:3

bread, 682:1; 2318:1; commercial ~, 1617:3; ~ roll, 3512:1

breakfast, 1322:1; 3097:4; 3443:2; 4870:3

breast, 2368:4; 3498:1; 4085:5; 4586:3; 4678:1; exposing ~, 860:11; ~ fixation, 3147:2; 3372:6; ~ milk, 3376:1; prosthesis ~, 2269:3; ~ size, 3074:1; women's ~, 54:3; 1657:1

breast feeding, 379:1; 998:9; 2210:3; 2946:1; 3467:3; 4133:2; 4696:3; ~ in the workplace, 3404:1

breath/ing, 1559:1; 1620:4

brevity, 408:4; 571:1; 1780:13; 2780:4

Briand, Aristide, 1480:6

bribery, 3317:2; 4780:4

bride *see also* wedding; mother of ~, 3283:5; older ~, 3156:4; shower for ~, 4226:4

bridge (structure), 2987:1

Brisbane, Arthur, 1709:3

British Museum, 1590:13

British Navy, 1187:7

British, the *see also* English, the; Irish, the; Scot/land; Welsh; 652:1

broadcaster *see also* journalism/journalist; obligations of ~, 4562:2

Broadway (New York City) *see also* Manhattan; 2114:1; theater on ~, 2827:3

broken/ness, mending what's ~, 1914:14; ~ spirit, 4352:1

Brontë, Emily, 934:13; 3957:1

Brooklyn, New York, 1835:1; 3512:1; 4004:3

Brooks, Gwendolyn, 4601:4

brothel *see also* prostitute/prostitution; sex industry; 1894:1; ~ keeper, 2007:1

brother *see also* sibling; 1234:1; 3950:5; 4020:1; death of ~, 365:4; 838:7

brotherhood *see also* esprit de corps; fellowship; sisterhood; 3101:2

Brown, John, 1021:1

Brown, Rap, 2762:1

Browning, Elizabeth Barrett, 1440:13

Bruce, Lenny, 4085:4

brutal/ity, ~ of humans, 3374:1

brute/brutishness, 1033:4; ~ force, 2124:4

Brutus, 77:1

Bryn Mawr College, 2771:7

Buber, Martin, 2768:2

Buckingham Palace, bombing of ~, 1898:2

Buddha/Buddhism, 166:13; 1659:5; 2572:5; 2797:1; 3284:6; 4507:1; women and ~, 4933:1

budget *see also* money; ~ cuts, 4486:1; family ~, 1275:2; 2207:1; national ~, 4771:5

building *see also* architect/ure; government ~; wall, 3735:1; importance of ~, 2402:8

bullfighting, 4703:5; 4869:2; women in ~, 4869:1

bum, 2569:6

Bunche, Ralph, 2762:1

buoyancy, 2187:13

burden, bearing one's ~, 2866:16

bureaucracy/bureaucrat *see also* red tape; 1379:6; 1402:4, 5; 1745:2; 2185:7; 2937:2; ~ and paper trail, 4554:5; dependence on ~, 3947:3

burial *see also* cemetery; death; dying; funeral; grave; 2731:1; tears at ~, 916:16

burlesque, 804:3; ~ dancer, 3594:1

Burma, 3558:1; government of ~, 3554:2; 3558:2

Burton, Sir Richard, 1036:3; 2826:2

bus, crowded ~, 3666:2

Bush, George H. W., 3442:5

Bush, George W., 2861:1; 2939:3; 3114:1, 4; 3512:4, 6; 3890:3; 3980:5; 4102:5; 4247:5; 4317:3; 4540:3; 4866:0; abortion and ~, 4035:1; ~ administration, 3774:3; 4060:2, 3; 4118:2; 4502:2; 4823:2; administration of ~, 2977:7; budget of ~, 4771:1; character of ~, 4102:6, 7; economics during ~, 3804:1; 4486:3; election of ~, 4575:1; Iraqi war and ~, 2393:6; 4886:1, 2; science and ~, 3768:5; sex education and ~, 4466:3; women around ~, 4575:2

Bush, Laura, 2907:4; 3641:4

business *see also* commerce; corporation; enterprise; management; 793:1; 808:12; 885:1; 1790:17; 1826:4; ~ acumen, 2052:1; American ~, 2823; 4244–4245:2; ~ associates, 3791:1; big ~, 1666:4; ~ creed, 3370:1; ~ critic, 3966:2; ~ cycles, 4468:4; ~ deals, 3398:1; dislike of ~, 734:6; environmental standards for ~, 4293:1; ~ ethics, 4041:2; feminism and ~, 3966:1; home ~, 2484:2; ~ in relation to employee, 2306:5; 4521:1, 2;; ~ in relation to families, 2517:; interdependence of ~, 2032:9; 2093:1; launching ~, 3599:4; loathsomeness of ~, 1120:5; minding one's ~ (see also nosiness), 1914:11; mix ~ with pleasure, 3860:1; music ~, 2806:1; ~ of others, 452:5; ~ partner (see partner/ship); reading habits of ~ men, 2511:4; small ~, 3527:2; 4262:2; ~ start-ups, 3527:1; success in ~, 4083:1; 4434:1; trust in ~, 3917:3; unconventional ~, 3370:3; woman in ~, 2269:1; 2957:1; 3078:4; 3913:1; 4941:1; women in cosmetic ~, 1383:1

businessperson, 916:1; 1896:10; prescription for ~, 1613:3; ~ woman (see also career, ~ woman), 3183:2

bustle see also activity; 793:1

Byron, Lord George Gordon, 799:7; 869:2; 1153:1; 1922:3

bystander, 2508:4

C

Cabinet, U.S. see also United States, ~ government; 2325:1; woman in ~, 2558:4

Cabrini, Mother, 1804:1

Caesar, Gaius Julius, 403:2

Cairo, 2932:1

cajolery see also flattery; 24:1

Calais, France, 299:1; 593:2

calamity, 658:9; 3500:1

Calamity Jane, 1190:2

calculation, 1975:3

calendar, 3871:1

California see also Beverly Hills, Hollywood, Los Angeles, San Francisco, 1370:4; 2925:5, 10; 3639:1; 3954:5; 4289:2; agriculture in ~, 3317:10; 4420:3, 4; Esalen ~ 1833:1; Leisure World ~ 4004:4; Simi Valley ~, 4960:2; Southern ~, 3266–3267:1

calling, following one's ~, 1815:1; true ~, 3669:3

calm, appearance of ~, 1073:3; continuous ~, 2220:2; intolerance for ~, 1780:7

Calvin, John, 782:7

Calvinism/Calvinist, 339:1; 3446:3

camaraderie, 3197:4; 3772:1

Cambodia, 4942:1

Camelot, 2537:13

camera see also photographer/photography, 1816:2; 2444:4; 4021:1; ~ angle, 1771:4; motion picture ~, 3814:1; ~ on vacation, 2866:12

camp (style), 2866:4

camp/ing, 2647:5

campaign, ~ contributions, 2787:2; political ~, 881:1; 2248:1; political smear ~, 1618:13; ~ promise, 2343:2

campfire, 1701:3

Canada/Canadian, 1387:5; forests of ~, 3991:1; ~ in relation to U.S.A., 3655:3; 4268:5; leadership of ~, 4014:3; mountains of ~, 3991:2; politics in ~, 4736:1; prosperity in ~, 1392:4

cancer, 3599:1; 3691:2; 4815:1; 4962:4; breast ~ (see also breast, prosthesis ~), 2915:1; 3340:5; 3357:4; chemotherapy for ~, 4625:4; cigarettes and ~, 4109:1; colon ~, 4962:1; cure for ~, 3470:5; 4748:2; ~ mastectomy, 3051:2; 3340:4; ~ survivor, 3003:5

candidate see also politics, women in ~; woman ~, 4498:1

candle, 405:5

candor see also frankness; openness; 3009:2; 3413:4; ~ of children, 158:3

capability, 2771:3; individual ~, 1982:3; ~ of women, 522:6; 3511:2

capital punishment see also death sentence; execution; 300:3; 780:1; 887:28; 2242:2; 3155:4; 3921:5; opposition to ~, 3155:2

capitalism see also free enterprise; profit; 1239:1; 1360:8; 1379:3; 1548:5, 9; 1666:5; 2455:2; 2877:1; 2996:3; 2997:1; 3780:1; 4774:4; ~ and family, 2719:1; crisis in ~, 2455:3; evils of ~, 2875:3; 3157:2; impact of ~ on values, 1558:5; 2185:16; ~ in Germany, 1379:2; ~ in relation to women, 3081:6; opposition to ~, 1583:4; problems of ~, 1920:4; ~ vs. communism, 1618:12

capriciousness see also fickleness; whim; 892:5

captive see also prisoner; 84:1; 468:1; 1272:1; 1273:2; ~ on Western Frontier, 468:3

card playing see also gambler/gambling; 742:1; ~ poker, 4298:2

career see also occupation; profession; 1211:5; 2568:2; 4340:2; ~ and glass ceiling, 4309:2; ~ choice, 855:2; 2112:1; 2312:1; 2702:2; 4648:1; commitment to ~, 2626:2; ~ differences between male and female, 3395:2; married to ~, 3900:3; men and ~, 2916:24; new ~, 2647:6; persisting with ~, 2836:1; ~ woman (see also business, ~ woman; woman/women, working ~), 1185:1; 1255:1; 1339:2; 1370:3; 2254:2; 2557:1; 3054:5; 3350:0; 3664:2; 3861:1; 4013:1, 2; 4778:3

carefreeness, 503:1; 2187:8

caregiving, 5:1; 4122:2; crisis in ~, 3608:3; demands of adult ~, 4453:2

carelessness see also thoughtlessness, 1024:9; 1451:1

caring see also nurturing; thoughtfulness, 910:14; 1752:13; 1981:5; 2529:5; 4174:6; ethic of ~, 2979:4; ~ for future, 2756:25; ~ for offspring, 4489:2; ~ for others, 2662:1; genuine ~, 3933–3934:5; gift of ~, 2887:1; lack of ~, 2966:2; price of ~, 2979:2

carnage see also savage/ry; 2831:1; ubiquitousness of ~, 2761:2 carnation, 537:1

Carter, Jimmy, 2589:2; ~ in relation to Middle East, 3767:2

Carter, Rosalyn, 1824:1

cartoon/ist, 4297:3; 4580:2; woman ~, 4297:4; 4976:1

Carver, Raymond, 3409:4

Cassandra, 496:2

Castro, Fidel, 3166:2

cat, 693:3; 795:3; 1051:3; 1230:2; 1409:15; 1650:1; 1922:2; 2349:11; 2953:2; 3488:5; 3716:1; 4982:1; death of ~, 1306:1; ~ fancier, 2426:4; ~ purr, 1444:6; stray ~, 3010:2

catastrophe see also crisis; disaster; fear of ~, 4924:1; surviving a ~, 4988:1

catharsis, 1710:3; 4985:1

Catherine II of Russia, 585:5; 604:9; Jews and ~, 3394:3

Catherine of Aragon, 300:6; 3102:3

Catholic Church, Roman and Catholicism see also confession; Mass; Pope; Vatican, 1095:2; 1980:1; 2331:10; 4240:1; 4459:1; birth control and ~, 2044:1; 4114:1; changes in ~, 1802:2; ~ charities, 1849:4; fears of ~, 1121:1; misogyny of ~, 3284:1; sexism in ~, 3078:3; women and ~, 2746:1, 2; women in ~, 2623:6; 3898:4

Cato, Publius (or Priscus) Valerius, 77:1; 94:1

caucasian, 1450:12

cause see also movement (sociopolitical); devotion to ~, 1874:1; just ~, 1244:4

cause and effect, 1723:3; 3508:3

caution see also prudence; 61:3; 694:4; 1450:11

Cavendish, Margaret, 3492:

celebration see also feast; party (social); 40:1; 2459:2; 2970:2

celebrity see also fame; public life; stardom; 1237:2; 2687:2; 3454:2; 3696:2; 4492:1; ~ and the media, 4607:1; conversing with ~, 2417:1; dangers of ~, 4256:6; exposing ~, 3353:2; hounding of ~, 2017:3; impact of ~, 4165:2; 4717:2; institutionalized ~, 1904:6; spoiled ~, 1850:3;

Third World and ~, 4694:4; using ~ for good, 4948:3; world of ~, 4946:2

celibacy see also abstinence, sexual ~; 3349:9; choice of ~ among women, 971:2

cell, stem ~ research, 3557:2

cemetery see also burial; grave; 945:13; 2731:1; 4784:1

censorship, 3911:5; 3949:1; 3988:1; 4796:4; ~ in library, 4111:4; ~ in media, 1620:5

Central Park (New York City), ~ at night, 3115:5

century, 1010:1; 19th ~, 3098.1; 20th ~, 1677:9; 1859:5; 2527:3; 2621:2; 2881:3; 3124:5; ~ plant, 1974:2

ceremony see also rite/ritual; 2405:6; importance of ~, 2103:1; sweat ~, 4075:1

certainty, 2080:14; 2853:1

Cezanne, Paul, 1126:3

Chaldea (Mesopotamia), 68:1

challenge, 1201:5; 1592:7; 1618:17, 22; 3369:1; facing ~, 1927:2; 2754:3; 3072:1; 4791:6; 4918:3; ~ limits, 3206:2

champion, 3434:1; tennis ~, 2598:2

chance see also destiny; fate; fortune [chance]; luck; 2982:3; 3161:1; 4213:1; 4473:3; 4804:2; ~ meeting, 1042:1

Chanel, Coco, 3029:5

change see also social change; world, changing ~; 635:1; 741:1; 1204:1; 1677:3; 1916:4; 2021:14; 2062:2; 2330:3; 2668:5; 2936:3; 3311:2; 3519:1; 3629:2; 3635:2; 3880:3; 4014:1; 4189:3; 4804:2; ability to ~, 3341:2; 3743:3; agent of ~, 3754:3; attitudes toward ~, 2944:4; 3518:4; choosing ~, 4963:3; constancy of ~, 2739:4; 3972:2; 4117:8; desire for ~, 1654:3; embracing ~, 4186:3; great ~, 1360:15; illusion of ~, 2162:5; 2607:3; ~ in culture, 3871:2; ~ in lifetime, 2861:4; inability to ~, 193:2; 760:2; inevitability of ~, 1187:5; inner ~, 3210:1; instruments of ~, 3755:1; lack of ~, 2277:2; 2680:3; lasting ~, 3393:2; love of ~, 4949:2; making ~, 3434:4; 4151:4; miracle of ~, 1141:3; national ~, 4811:1; ~ of heart, 1341:3; ~ of individual, 887:23; ~ of pace, 2601:4; opportunity for ~, 4763:5; resistance to ~, 1654:3; 4020:5; 4117:3, 5; speed of ~, 4189:2; study of ~, 1787:2; surviving ~, 2901:2; unwillingness to ~, 1876:1; working for ~, 1734:1; 2139:7; 4664:2

changelessness, 172:1

chant/ing, 4625:1

Chanukah, 1168:9

chaos, 3288:3; 3795:1; social ~, 502:2; 1668:5

Chaplin, Charlie, 1781:2

character see also backbone; 1618:13; 1648:5; 1761:7; ~ assassination, 3572:3; forming ~, 1663:5; 2657:5; good ~, 513:3; ~ in books, 3032:6; interesting ~, 2238:4; revealing ~, 3097:7; superior ~, 3346:5; test of ~, 1148:2; 1450:1; woman of ~, 3637:1

charisma see also charm; 3642:1

charity see also philanthropy, 234:2; 734:4; 1251:7; 1618:11; 1778:2; 1906:4; 2027:15; 2116:19; 2354:1; 3518:3; false ~, 945:10; refusing ~, 1193:11; true ~, 3097:5

Charles II of England, 731:5

Charlotte (Sophia), Queen Consort, 822:1

charm see also charisma; 1320:1; exemplary ~, 2620:7; love ~, 4331:3

chasteness/chastity, 115:1; 321:1; 982:2; 4791:3; drawn to ~, 2592:

chauvinism see also nationalism, 3491:1

Chavez, Cesar, 2716:6

cheating, 3421:1

Chechnya, Republic of, 2528:2

cheerfulness see also mirth; 485:2; 593:8; 1006:5; 2684:4; 4743:3

chef see also cook/ing; 4602:2

chemical/chemistry, 662:1; 1832:4; dangers of ~ (see also pollution, ~ by chemicals), 1112:1; 2061:7, 8, 9; 2622:3, 4; 4106:2; 4608:1; ~ industry, 3985:2; ~ testing, 2622:5; ~ waste, 4106:5

Cheney, Dick, 2393:9; 3248:3; 4247:5; 4866:0

Chevron/Texaco Corporation, 3980:6 Chicago, Illinois, 1256:2; 1916:3; 2069:2; 3039:7; 4601:4

Chicago, Judy, 2750:1

Chicano/a see also Hispanic; Mexican American; ~ rights, 2727:1

child abuse see also sexual abuse, 2049–2050:1; 2158:1; 2328:1; 2466:2; 3773:1; dealing with ~, 2466:5

childbirth see also baby; birth; infant, birth of ~; newborn, pregnancy/pregnant; 384:1; 655:1; 1565:1; 1870:10; 1906:5; 1914:9; 1979:5; 2105:1; 2658:7; 2667:4; 3034:3; 3051:4; 4038:4; 4105:4; ~ by Caesarean, 2667:3; 3425:2; dangerous of ~, 3540:3; difficulties of ~, 319:1; early ~, 3399:3; 3673:1; effects of ~, 1933:1; ~ in hospital, 4037:1; men and ~, 2857:1; posture for ~, 2667:6

child care see day care, children's ~; 2844:4; 3386:4; affordable ~, 3608:3; institutional ~, 3746:3; ~ perfectionism, 2844:3; responsibility for ~,

child development, practices of ~, 1381:2

childhood see also child/ren; youth; 671:8; 867:1; 967:3; 1700:8; 1751:26; 1835:4; 1843:6; 2154:1; 2212:2; 2213:2; 2460:3; 2529:2; 2774:1; 4298:5; 4650:8; constancy of ~, 4611:1; ~ delights, 3209:; difficult ~, 1838:3; future of ~, 4298:8; ~ goal, 3553:1; grief in ~, 965:4; importance of ~, 3034:5; ~ in relation to old age, 870:9; ~ is over, 4205:3; ~ learning, 2805:2; length of ~, 3746:1; mysteries of ~, 4448:4; painful ~, 3813:5; politics and ~, 4188:3; privileges of ~, 4751:1; suppression of ~, 2434:3; wounds of ~, 3026:2;

child labor, 1248:1; 1414:1; ~ among poor, 3761:3, 4

childlessness, 970:2; 1648:3; 2817:21; 3712:1; choice of ~, 3833:1; ~ in relation to families with children, 1487:4; reasons for ~, 2036:20

child pornography, eradicating ~, 3456:2, 3

child rearing see also day care, children's ~; instruction, ~ to children; youth; 430:7, 9; 512:1; 672:3; 782:11; 880:7; 965:2; 1073:5; 1251:8; 1332:1; 1390:2; 1468:2; 1776:3; 1853:1; 2023:2; 2098:1; 2148:4; 2322:2; 2434:3; 2439:8; 2477:4; 2492.1:1; 2630:1; 2676:1; 2771:15; 2972:2; 3055:2, 3; 3649:2; 3665:3; 3914:1; 4972:4; ~ by the book, 1831:1; 3033:2; difficulties of ~, 3764:4; 4815:3; egalitarian ~, 3383:3; goals of ~, 2362:2, 8; 3529:1; importance of ~, 3034:1; instruction in ~, 4832–4833:1; length of ~, 2827:1; mistakes in ~, 1332:5; ~ of disabled, 2570:1; permissive ~, 3467:1; 3469:1; purpose of ~, 3631:2; society's obligations to ~, 3393:1

child/ren see also baby; boy; child/ren; childhood; daughter; girl; infant; progeny; son; young; youth; 71:1; 713:8; 722:6; 734:11; 815:1; 870:3; 908:1; 910:17; 993:1; 1100:1; 1104:2; 1167:4; 1176:3; 1315:5; 1381:7; 1382:3; 1409:9; 1480:3; 1552:1; 1563:6; 1615:1; 1668:5; 1974:2; 2160:4; 2216:1; 2217:3; 2317:4; 2323:2; 2756:26; 2827:2; 2883:1; 3386:3; 3765:1; 3944:1; 4390:7; 4477:3; accomplishments of ~, 2863:1; ~

activities, 3115:3; adult ~ in relation to parent, 1409:10; 1697:10, 11; 2080:10; 2715:1; 3002:5; 3031:3; 3309:4; affording ~, 511:11; appearance of ~, 3984:1; ~ as artists, 3386:1; ~ as storytellers, 2677:3; ~ at risk, 3419:1; attitudes toward ~, 2687:4; attractions of ~, 3097:2; caring for ~, 2136:2; 2908:1; conditioning of ~ (see also boy, conditioning of ~; girl, conditioning of ~), 2675:1; 2911:1; controlling ~, 4544:3; creativity of ~, 1758:2; custody of ~, 3498:2; death of ~, 119:1; 183:2; 311:1; 459:5; 827:1; 952:2; 2069:4; 2502:2; 2728:2; 2773:1; 3514:4; 4326:1; demands of ~, 4172:1; desire for ~, 13:1; 2288:5; different ~ (see also difference; disabled/disability, children with ~; handicap), 3896:1; 4538:3; dislike of ~, 3612:4; education of ~, 886:1; 2405:5; 2756:27; ~ emotions, 2148:2; equality for ~, 2703:2; expectation of ~, 2036:8; 2146:1; 2263:1; 4644:2; exploitation of ~, 2201:11; first born ~, 3967:1; formative years of ~, 2630:2; ~ games, 1059:1; games of ~ (see also play/ing; toy), 805:1; 1361:1; gender conditioning of ~, 4030:1; good ~, 4516:4; growing independence of ~, 3042:4; ~ growing up, 2355:4; grown ~, 2437:8; handicapped ~ (see also child/ren; different; disabled/disability, children with ~; handicap), 3636:1; helping ~, 3324:1; honored ~, 444:1; illegitimate ~, 2245:2; importance of ~, 1555:1; 4672:1; ~ in foster care, 3058:1; ~ in poverty, 3141:5; ~ in relation to adults, 3146:2; 4744:1; ~ in relation to child, 2677:1; ~ in relation to mother (see also mother/hood, ~ in relation to child), 1858:1; 2680:15; 2694:4; 2780:6; 3563:7; 3644:1; ~ in relation to other children, 2805:5; ~ in relation to parent (see also parent/hood, ~ in relation to child), 1411:1; 1562:5; 1743:, 4; 1905:8; 2049–2050:1; 2728:2; 3540:1; 4010:1; 4242:4; 4534:1; 4648:10; 4794:5; independent ~, 2069:1; 2244:2; 2630:1; 2801:2; 4972:3; indulgence of ~, 452:2; 1236:1; 2319:2; 2424:2; 2592:4; joy of ~, 329:1; legacy to ~, 3227:2; 4329:2; lessons for ~, 3106:3; liking ~, 1385:1; literature and ~, 3797:8; loss of ~, 43:1; ~ loss of faith, 861:1; love of ~, 722:7; 2020:1; 2762:2; 4143:2; needs of ~, 2031:3; 3077:1; 3141:6; 3783:1;

neglect of ~, 1248:2; 1741:25, 26; 1920:3; 2217:2; 3141:1; news for ~, 1748:1; nurturing ~, 722:4; obligations of ~, 931:24; obligations to ~, 3261:4; ~ of affluence, 166:10; ~ of celebrities, 4934:3; ~ of divorce, 1943:5; ~ of leftists, 2470:1; ~ of loveless marriage, 442:4; ~ of working mother, 4778:3; ~ performing, 1756:4; poverty and ~, 2153:4; 3711:2; 3761:3; prejudice vs. ~, 3728:3; problem ~, 2216:3; respecting ~, 3914:2; restrictions of ~, 807:17; rhymes of ~, 2164:4; rights of ~ (see rights, children's ~); role model for ~, 3682:7; sacrifice for ~, 3290:2; safety of ~, 4433:1; sensitivity of ~, 2148:5; sexually maturing ~, 1337:2; 1579:1; shouting at ~, 4255:6; smart ~, 3984:7; ~ soldiers, 4564:1; spirited ~, 1729:4; spoiled ~, 3042:3; suffering of ~, 1512:9; 2756:23; sweet ~, 4150:2; teaching ~ to care, 2675:6; ~ that kill, 3141:8; thoughts of ~, 1042:3; too many ~, 3730:2; trusting ~, 3077:3; unlovable ~, 4972:2; unwanted ~, 2454:1; 2668:20; 2972:1; 3839:1; 4639:3; war and ~, 2673:3; welcome ~, 3706:4; worthiness of ~, 1659:8

Chile, 4022:3; 4345:1; economy of ~, 4345:3; political rule of ~, 2234:1

China, People's Republic of see also Chinese; Hong Kong; 3067:1; agriculture in ~, 2192:10; authoritarianism in ~, 4690:; censorship in ~, 3250.1:4; children in ~, 4690:1; culture of ~, 3817:1; 4690:2; democracy in ~, 2239:5, 7; energy use in ~, 4624:2; freedom in ~, 1741:; greatness of ~, 4765:3; human rights in ~, 3715:1; ~ in relation to Hong Kong, 3188:1; ~ in relation to Japan, 1863:4; literature in ~, 2358:1; middle class in ~, 4782:1; nuclear power in ~, 2239:6; reproductive health and ~, 2678:1; socialist ~, 1786:3; struggle of ~, 1863:10; unification of ~, 1863:1; women in ~, 1465:3; women in modern ~, 3067:4

Chinese see also China, 1741:12, 27; ~ character, 3094:4; ~ civilization, 1863:9; ~ communism, 3400:1, 2; ~ Cultural Revolution, 2049–2050:2; 2649:2; ~ culture, 4092:1; ~ family, 2058:1; ~ man, 4825:2; ~ proverb, 2642:11; rights of ~, 3250.1:3; ~ society, 2522:2; ~ women, 1425:2; 2398:3; 3167:2; ~ youth, 2049–2050:2

chivalry *see also* gentleman; 217:2; 1291:3; 2876:2

choice *see also* preference; priority; 1326:1; 1412:1; 2210:5; 2667:3; 2756:8; 3066:2; 4122:3; 4500:2; 4711:4; daily ~, 4629:2; ~ for women, 2302:2; life ~, 2965:2; making ~, 2053:5; 2892:2; 3852:2; 3869:1; personal ~, 3916:1; 4798:3; power to make ~, 4126:4; reproductive ~ (*see also* pro-choice), 1535:14; 3930:1; unable to deal with ~, 4830:1

chore *see also* task; domestic ~, 4310:5

choreography *see also* dancer/dancing, 2273:2; 3789:1

Christian Science, 2115:3

Christian/ity *see also specific denominations;* church; cross; life, Christian ~; religion; 352:4; 809:2; 3179:2; 3852:3; ~ and goddess, 2744:3; death and ~, 1089:8; ~ dogma, 4217:1; early ~, 3537:1; evangelical ~, 3294:3; ~ gospel of love, 2756:4; history of ~, 3445:5; homosexuality and ~, 2446:2; hypocrisy of ~, 334:7; 3571:2; identity of ~, 99:1; mythology of ~, 3706:2; nonsense of ~, 439:5; war and ~, 839:4; 1029:4; woman and ~, 1007:1

Christie, Agatha, 2691:3

Christmas *see also* Santa Claus, 871:2; 1006:14; 1044:5; 1129:2, 4; 1199:2; 2793:1; ~ celebration, 3766:1; 4763:1; commercialism of ~, 2647:2; ~ Eve, 2459:2; ~ gift, 1368:2; ~ in South (U.S.A.), 4184:1

chromosome *see also* DNA; genes, Y ~, 4211:4

chronology, 2858:1; 3268:3

church *see also specific denominations,* clergy; religion; 3547:5; 3704:5; attending ~, 1024:13; 1735:2; 3680:1; ~ canon, 2116:22; country ~, 1922:1; death of ~, 2758:1; disillusionment with ~, 3771:2; environmentalism and ~, 3243:1, 3; ~ going, 1713:3; Holy Rule of ~, 1906:4; hypocrisy of ~, 399:3; 633:1; ~ in relation to body, 928:1; ~ in relation to society, 1007:10; integrity of ~, 3771:1; mission of ~, 1929:4; politics and ~, 2985:1; problems with attending ~, 3952:1; purpose of ~, 2193:2; ~ stand on prostitution, 3328:1; temporal interests of ~, 1618:26; women and ~, 291:1; 308:11; 931:20; 2446:1; work for ~, 875:1; youth and ~, 4456:1

Church of England, 1187:3; unacceptability of ~, 309:3

Churchill, Winston, 1869:4; 4048:3

CIA (Central Intelligence Agency), 2544:5

Cicero, 649:9

cigarette, 4168:1; 4908:1; banning ~, 2647:3; health hazards of ~, 4109:1; ~ in public, 2990:1; ~ manufacturer, 3228:2

Cinderella, 2072:1; ~ complex, 3083:2

circle, 3287:1

circumcision *see also* genitalia, mutilation of ~; 19:1, 1; female ~, 3322:1

circumstance, 2620:3; altering ~, 1667:3; making best of ~, 2475:4

citizen/ship, 1168:7; 1656:2; 3981:5; black ~, 1696:1; complacency of ~, 4060:2; distrust of ~, 1251:2; global ~, 4080:1; government and ~, 3049:1; informed ~, 4648:3; loyalty of ~, 309:2; naturalized ~, 3658:1; obligations of ~, 3250.1:1; ~ of the world, 2510:2; 3782:5; renouncing ~, 3344:1; rights of ~, 2916:12; second class ~, 3627:3; solid ~, 4401:2

city *see also specific cities;* megalopolis; town; 76:6; 670:3; 1251:4; 2404:1; American ~, 2848:1; beautification of ~, 4638:2; ~ buildings, 4641:3; ~ development, 2271:5; façade of ~, 4123:6; ~ government, 2408:2; growth of ~, 1849:1; 2271:6; history of ~, 2402:5; influence of ~, 2429:1; inner ~ life, 4787:1; 4894:1; ~ life, 713:3; 1149:5; 1167:8; 1270:1; 1491:2; love of ~, 2771:16; obligations of ~, 4632:1; ~ park, 2271:4; ~ planning, 2271:1, 6; 4273:1, 2; ~ polish, 1689:8; ~ politics, 1849:3; preservation of ~, 2402:6; safety of ~ streets, 2271:3; ~ services, 3163:1; smells of ~, 4519:0; ~ street, 864:6; thriving ~, 935:1; whirl of ~, 804:1

civil disobedience *see also* nonviolence; protest/er; 890:5; 1146:5; 1235:4, 6, 9; 1360:18; 1537:1, 2, 3; 1677:3; 1846:3; 2036:16, 17; 2259:6; reason for ~, 1235:1

civil rights *see also* human rights; liberation; 2850:2; 3314:4; 4268:2; Congress and ~, 2163:1

civil rights movement, 2922:6; childhood memory of ~, 3185:2; 4188:3; engagement in ~, 4368:2; leaders of ~, 4308:3

Civil War, American, 1037:6; 4530:2; black soldiers in ~, 978:3; families and ~, 2895:1; public atmosphere during ~, 1064:2

civility, 1174:2; 4130:3; voice of ~, 4014:1

civilization *see also* culture; society, 963:4; 1351:1; 1625:3; 1687:1; 1935:4; 2032:1; 2352:2; 2668:3; 3451:5; advances of ~, 733:4; 971:1; 1007:10; 2124:1; 2603:1; 2881:3; definition of ~, 2875:3; development of ~, 2443:1; 4113:2; measure of ~, 2875:4; precariousness of ~, 846:1; rebuilding ~, 2860:1; standardization of ~, 1458:1; women and ~, 2552:5

clarity *see also* simplicity, 581:1; 1942:1; 2219:4; 3203:5

class (social), 684:7; 782:1; absence of ~ consciousness, 1506:2; bikers ~, 3845:3; commercial ~, 1009:2; conditions of lower ~, 4549:1; consciousness, 998:3; 1973:6; differences between ~, 880:6; 1544:1; 2716:5; 4925:3; doing away with ~, 1973:6; lower ~ (*see* lower class); middle ~ women, 1151:2; polarization of ~, 839:5; 2994:3; rising middle ~, 1239:1; ruling ~, 2996:3; 2997:1, 2; 3085:3; stodginess of middle ~, 1687:2; taxes on middle ~, 2027:11; upper ~ (*see also* affluence/affluent; wealth), 1787:5; 1866:1; 2130:3; 4464:1; working ~ (*see also* proletariat), 1227:3; 1384:3; 4289:1

class (style), test of ~, 2319:6

classification, 2522:2

classism *also see* class, ~ consciousness, 1829:1; 1977:4; 2736:2; lack of ~, 940:2

classroom *see also* school, ~ atmosphere, 3520:2; challenges of ~, 2677:4; ~ scholar, 3399:2

cleaning *see also* housekeeping, 2586:6; 3776:3; carpet ~, 4485:3; ~ dishes, 3616:2

cleanliness *see also* tidiness, 1304:2; 1601:7; 1979:4; 2093:2; 2272:2; 3951:3; 4237:3; household ~, 2772:1

clergy *see also* church; preacher/ preaching; priest/hood; religious life, 183:1; 361:1; 790:10; ~ attitude toward women, 931:18; impotence of ~, 308:2; ~ in relation to politics, 1802:1; male ~, 2653:2; ~ man, 734:18; pomp of Catholic ~, 286:1; radicalization of ~, 2084:2; women in the ~, 1062:3; 1185:3; 2712:1; 3460:2; 3579:1; 3787:1; work of ~, 4241:1

cleverness, 366:1; 694:4; 1098:1; 1333:4; 2860:5; ~ in women, 894:2

cliché *also see* banality, 4448:2

climate, ~ change (*see also* global warming), 3418:3; 3600:2; 4283:1; 4405:1, 2, 6; 4632:1; 4893:1, 2

civilization *see also* culture; society

Clinton, Hilary Rodham, 2848:4; 2907:5; 3076:2; 3435:2; ~ supporter, 4732:1

Clinton, William Jefferson, 2462:1; 2861:2; 3512:7; 4877:2; impeachment proceedings vs. ~, 2989:1

clique *see also* elitism, government ~, 1863:7

clock *see also* time, ~ piece, 2771:13; nature's ~, 1346:4; ~ watching, 3021:2; 3631:1

closemindedness *see also* narrowmindedness, 980:3; 1230:6; 1549:6; 1660:2

clothing *see also specific articles;* fashion; wardrobe, 944:3; 1015:1; 1023:1; 1025:1; 1047:1; 1780:13; 2129:1; 4404:1; actor's ~, 1850:1; buying ~, 4027:3; ~ design, 2910:1; fit of ~, 4953:1; influence of ~, 4675:1; love of ~, 4648:7; non-military ~, 2472:; practical ~, 1335:6; ready-made ~, 2775:4; sex and ~, 1996:2; taste in ~, 4410:1; women's ~, 944:3; 1958:1; 2511:1; 3029:5

cloud, 1253:1; 3790:3

clown *see also* performance/performers, 1024:29

cloying, 3567:2

CNN, 4437.1:1

coach, personal ~, 4798:1

coalition, meaningful ~, 2901:4

cocaine *see also* drugs, 4934:2; ~ addiction, 1964:2

cockfight, 2537:11

coercion, 1419:5

coffee, ~ house, 4048:4; ~ latte, 3498:3

coffin, 2376:1; 2894:1

coincidence, 4021:3

cold (weather), 1638:1; 4252:3; 4705:4; protection from ~, 3263:2

Colette, 3872:1

collectivism, 2032:6; 2107:2

college *see also* education; school; university, 2012:1; 3102:1; ~ campus malevolence, 3820:1; community ~, 4027:2; compulsory ~, 2237:; ~ drop-out, 4652:3; ~ freshman, 4777:1; goal in ~, 3004:3; going to ~, 4852:1; ~ graduates, 3815:2; high-tech ~, 3091:3; historically black ~, 3614:3; ~ in relation to earnings, 2237:6; investment of ~ fund, 2237:4; ~ life, 699:1; reason to attend ~, 2237:7; women and ~, 2565:1

Colombia, 4549:2; Afro-~, 4578:1; ~ in relation to U.S.A., 4502:2; life in ~, 4549:1; murder in ~, 4553:1; war in ~, 4578:2

colonialism, 1083:2; 1778:3; 4036:1; 4444:3; 4843:1; aftermath of ~, 3682:5; failure of ~,

2230:2; ~ in Africa, 4786:1, 4; injustice of ~, 3947:5

color, 166:9; 192:1; 1311:2

color (skin) also see specific races, women of ~, 3912:1

Columbus, Christopher, 2532:3; 4242:5; 4725:3

combat see also fight/ing; soldier; war, ~ on Western Frontier, 468:2; women in ~, 2614:1

comedian see also comedy; humorist, 1722:3; 1950:1; 3691:5; Jewish ~, 3470:6; woman ~, 2167:1; 2232:1; 2286:4

comedy see also humor, 1412:3; 2286:5; 4085:4; 4158:2; performance of ~, 2838:1; reason for ~, 4013:3; sense of ~, 1639:2; straight man in ~, 3563:7

comfort, 276:3; 869:6; 1130:1; 1292:3; 1751:29; 4280:1; throw off ~, 713:11

command, 14:1; action of ~, 3101:3; possessing ~, 1697:5

commandment, moral ~, 2032:8; power of ~, 2768:2

commerce see business; marketing

commercialism, 1325:2; 2353:2; 2430:1; 2511:2; 3196:2; ~ in United States, 1754:4

commitment, 1553:1

common good see also public welfare, 2986:6; 3085:3; 3513:1; 3608:5

common ground see also universality, 3220:1; 3538:1; seeking ~, 4458:2 common sense see also sense, 1160:6; 1449:1; 1450:30; 2817:4; 3013:3; 3306:3

commoner, 2128:2; life of ~, 2900:1

commonplace see also ordinariness, 1136:1; disinterested in ~, 1955:4

communal society/commune see also community, 2612:5; 3070:1; , ~ living, 2001:5

communication see also specific forms, 308:3; 643:3; 1149:3; 1193:5; 1618:3, 18; 2862:7; 3941:3; 4048:1; ~ among rich, 2502:1; ~ between men and women, 3618:3; desire for ~, 2679:4; difficulties of ~, 1385:2; 2463:3; 4508:4; 4889:4; face-to-face ~, 2656:1; family ~, 2079:8; future ~, 4109:4; global ~, 4665:3; indirect ~, 3356:1; lack of ~, 1759:5; 2021:14; 2063:5; 2149:2; 3753:1; 4197:2; men and ~, 4031:3; mode of ~, 4555:2; political ~, 3378:2; tools of ~, 369:5; 1448:2; women and ~, 4633:3; 4840:2

communism/communist, 1402:3; 1632:3; 1666:5; 1897:1; 1920:5; argument against ~, 1618:12; life under ~, 4890–4891:2

Communist Party, Chinese ~, 2192:9

community see also affiliation; communal society/commune, 1977:7; ~ engagement, 4260:2; ~ experience, 4440:2; exploitation of poor ~, 4088:3; global ~, 4857:3; impoverished ~, 4724:1, 2; ~ in America, 2986:5; ~ in relation to children, 2771:15; lack of ~, 2607:4; 2889:2; 4943:2; loss of ~, 2771:26; post-national ~, 2230:3; power of ~, 4212:2; ~ quality of life, 3068:2; religious ~, 4209:2; sense of ~, 2942:7; 3700:1; women and ~, 3978:5

companion see also friend, brother as ~, 3950:5; identification with ~, 2456:8; lasting ~, 1445:4

companionship see also friendship; sociability, 767:26; 1024:11; 1113:3; 1176:2; 1225:1; 1409:20; need for ~, 2388:1; seeking ~, 153:1

company, choosing one's ~, 1444:3; responsible ~, 3456:3

comparison, making ~, 3967:4

compassion see also humaneness; pity, 693:2; 892:4; 1693:1; 2193:3; 2224:3; 2666:3; 4001:2; 4318:1; 4329:3; creating ~, 2613:4; ~ fatigue, 4731:3; ~ for all, 3978:2; ~ for elderly, 244:10; ~ for past, 887:22; lack of ~, 36:1; 2205:2; power of ~, 3491:5

compatibility, 451:6

competence, 3002:4; 4794:3; attaining ~, 408:2

competition see also contest, 1239:1; 1260:1; 2218:2; 2261:; 2268:2; 2929:2; 4090:1; 4353:1; ~ between men and women, 2324:1; cutthroat ~, 2885:1; 3009:5; emotional cost of ~, 3936:1; gender and ~, 4645:3; healthy ~, 1468:1; individual ~, 2903:6; intellectual ~, 4175:; refrain from ~, 674:1; women and ~, 1960:4; 2423:2; worthy ~, 844:4

competitive/ness, 1960:1; learning to be ~, 4666:

complacency, danger of ~, 4377:2; ~ of citizenry, 4060:2

complaint/complainer, 300:5; 383:4; 596:1; 2363:2; 2948:3

completeness see also unfinished, lack of ~, 3602:2

complex (psychological), 1731:4; Cinderella ~, 3083:2

complexity, 2591:1

complication see also entanglement, ~ everywhere, 2087:1

complicity, 378:1

compliment, 1430:1

comportment see also behavior; conduct, 264:1

composer, 4344:5; 4436:1; intuitive ~, 3928:1; music ~, 4436:3; woman ~, 2637.1:2

composure, 1593:4; 2346:3

compromise, 775:2; 869:7; 1350:7; 1698:2; 1761:2; 1901:1; 3335:5; 3428:5; 3881:2; 4190:3; life's ~, 1654:5; 3881:2; need for ~, 2227:2; ~ oneself, 2862:3; 4126:5; shun ~, 1956:4

compulsion see also obsession, 1578:1

computer see also blog/ger; cyberspace; Internet; Silicon Valley; word processor, 929:1, 2; 2547:3; ~ as companion, 4738:2; children and ~, 3115:4; 4409:2; children and ~ games, 4409:3; gender and ~ games, 4409:4; ~ gone berserk, 3677:2; identity and ~, 4738:3; pornography on ~, 3456:3; power of ~, 4738:4; ~ programming, 4968–4969:1; writer and ~, 3776:3; women and ~ science, 4409:1, 5

computerization, 4081:4

concealment, 671:2

conceit/edness see also egocentricity/ egotism; self-centeredness, 658:7; 799:2; 955:16

concentration, 2771:9; capacity for ~, 3933–3934:1

concentration camp, death in ~, 2036:2; ~ numbers, 1906:1

concept see also idea, carrying out of ~, 736:3; global ~, 2547:3

conception (reproductive) also see birth; fertility, 179:3; 4053:2

concern, 1631:4

conciliation, 717:2

conclusion, drawing ~, 1752:7

condemnation, ~ of others, 1918:2

condescend/er, men ~ women, 4643:4

condom see also birth control, 4741:2

conduct see also behavior; comportment; manners, 275:1; 353:1; 1078:2; 1570:3; 1740:1; 2162:4; 3065:1; cheap ~, 1721:2; control of ~, 614:1; mis- ~, 808:8; poor ~, 671:10; upright ~, 466:1; 732:1

conductor, music ~, 4344:5; woman ~, 4344:1

confession, 1190:2; 1265:3; 4653:1; Catholic ~, 2331:10; forced ~, 381:3

confidence see also self-confidence, 772:4; 1618:16; 2832:1; 4357:1; 4913:1; ~ in oneself, 1461:5; sharing ~, 2711:6; 2893:5

confinement see also imprisonment, 218:1; 2532:1

conflict see also strife; struggle, 1350:2; 1534:2; 2240:3; cause of international ~, 2116:11; inner ~, 716:2; 1034:1; 1631:6; 1647:2; 1887:3; 2556:1; 2842:5; 3099:11; international ~ resolution, 3143.1:3; national ~, 651:1;

~ resolution, 3332:1; 3588:3; 4256:7; 4545:3; 3027:1; 3782:1; simplistic ~, 4308:1

conformist/conformity see also convention; propriety, 863:3; 1844:2; 1863:7; 1996:3; 2560:6; 3496:1; 4020:5; 4503:2; demand for ~, 2927:1

Confucianism, 88:1

confusion see also bewilderment, 867:2; 1669:11; 1942:1; 4411:4; emotional ~, 186:1

Congo, Democratic Republic of, 4312:9; 4694:2; genocide in ~, 4694:3; story of ~, 4312:3; women of ~, 4694:1; 4758:4

Congress, U.S. see also lawmaker; legislation; legislator; politician, 2360:3; 2937:2; 3227:3; 3731:17; ~ in relation to legislation for women, 1086:8; members of ~ (see also lawmakers; legislator), 2127:1; 2787:2; 2861:3; 3469:4; responsibility of ~, 3667:1; seniority system of ~, 2480:5; sexism in ~, 3160:3; under-representation of women in ~, 3160:3; women in ~ (also see government, women in ~); 1555:2; 2178:3; 2360:5

connectedness/connection see also oneness; interconnectedness; unity, 986:1; 1342:5; 2210:13; 3238:1, 2; 3311:1; 3371:1; 3466:1; 4119:4; ~ among people, 2031:2; ~ among women, 3249:1; difficulties of ~, 2607:6; hidden ~, 1731:5; loss of ~, 3698:3; need for ~, 2765:4; ~ of all life, 2320:6; 2425:3; 4005:2; ~ to Nature, 2359:2; ~ with friend, 3955:1; ~ with others, 3792:3; ~ with right person, 1648:2

Connecticut, 4763:2; ~ Yankees, 4763:3

conqueror, myths of ~, 1911:3

conquest, 1025:7; 2617:1; ~ by invading forces, 4597:4; ~ of people, 1347:3

Conrad, Joseph, 2872:3

conscience, 341:7; 506:1; 722:2; 879:2; 916:1; 1174:6; 1198:1; 1605:1; 1979:4; 2563:3; awakened ~, 237:3; clear ~, 353:1; 852:2; 2021:10; guilty ~ (see also guilt/y), 352:1; 1980:1; 2195:1; 2314:1; liberty of ~, 3778:6; overdeveloped ~, 1789:2; political ~, 1297:2; search one's ~, 733:9; trials of ~, 2135:8

conscientious objector see also movement, antiwar ~, 1751:28; 2340:2; 3049:1

conscientiousness, 1697:2; 2871:2

consciousness see also self-consciousness; unconscious/ness,

1387:3; 1692:2; 1817:4; 2240:1; 2756:8; 2849:3; 2911:6; 3497:1; awakening of ~, 798:2; changes in ~, 2756:14; ~ of world, 3827:2; ~ -raising, 2916:3; 3024:1; 3495:1; 3593:1; social ~, 4482:2; stream of ~, 1906:2; 1921:2; 3277:1; 3597:3

conscription *see also* army, soldier, 987:3; 1480:1; 1756:1; 2604:1; mother and ~, 1545:5; ~ of women, 1349:2

consensus, 3335:2; ~ in politics, 2537:10

consequence, ~ of actions, 1747:1

conservation (environment) *see also* ecology, 2061:12; 3657:4; downside of ~, 4567:1; importance of ~, 3513:2; ~ of game, 266:3; politics of ~, 3942:2; river ~, 1726:3

conservatism/conservative (political) *see also* Moral Majority; reactionary, 3939:9; 4629:5; influence of ~, 4523:1; women ~, 2907:1

consistency, 1959:5

consolation, 222:1; 1120:2; 1700:11

conspiracy, Western ~, 4846:4

constancy *see also* loyalty, 334:12; 341:10

Constitution, U.S., 2551:2; defending First Amendment of, ~, 4363:2; exclusivity of ~, 2986:2; Fourteenth Amendment of ~, 1086:2; 4763:4; interpreting ~, 4523:1; preamble of ~, 963:8; preserving ~, 4466:2; proposed flag amendment to ~, 3935:3; representation of women in ~, 2363:1; 2838:2; 3160:2; repudiation of ~, 4022:5; sexism in ~, 953:5

constructiveness, 893:5

consulting, 4186:1

consumer/ism *see also* shopping, 3669:4; 3908–3909:1; 4118:5; 4341:1; 4395:3; 4585:4, 5; ~ awareness, 4857:2; ~ frenzy, 3829:4; healthy ~, 4322:3; ~ in America, 3855:1; power of ~, 4217:3; promoting ~, 4567:1; ~ rights, 4562:1

container, 1368:4

contemplation *see also* meditation, 325:3; 3661:2; life of ~, 1348:2; 2201:5

contempt 2913:2; ~ for men, 678:3

contentiousness, 166:17; 711:4

contentment, 347:1; 578:1; 583:2; 585:7; 808:8; 812:2; 1025:13; 1548:4; 1766:2; 3686:2; ~ of partner, 2079:5

contest *see also* competition, skiing ~, 3659:1

continuity, ~ of life, 3779:1

contraception *also see* birth control, condom, 1535:13; 2946:2; ~ for teenagers, 2843:4; lack of ~, 2646:3; weakness of ~, 4781:1

contract, verbal ~, 1722:7

contradiction *see also* paradox, 2717:2; ~ in terms, 2763:3; ~ of desires, 4056:1

contrariness, 2337:1; rule of ~, 922:5

contrast, life of ~, 1717:3

contribution, ~ of men, 1618:32; ~ to society, 1822:2

control *see also* manipulator; self-control, 1262:6; 1409:; 1576:2; 3951:2; 4148:1; lack of ~, 3213:2; 4667:3; letting go of ~, 1759:3; loss of ~, 522:4; 3099:12; majority ~, 1350:11; measure of ~, 4213:3; ~ of circumstance, 863:1; ~ of mind, 3522:2; ~ of response, 4798:3; ~ of self, 4939:2

controversy, understanding ~, 3258:3

convenience, 684:7; acquisition of ~, 1070:5

convent *see also* nun, 392:1; 1122:1; ~ education, 1715:13; life in ~, 487:15; motivation to enter ~, 487:5

convention/ality *see also* conformist/conformity, 1167:10; 1352:2; 2552:6; 4711:2; breaking through ~, 922:4; sticking with ~, 1355:2

conversation *see also* dialogue, 783:4; 859:6; 1073:4; 1182:2; 1236:8; 1450:13; 1598:2; 1752:4; 1759:5; 2219:1; 2526:1; 3961:2; art of ~, 649:9; 1940:5; 2687:1; cautious ~, 2944:5; cluttered ~, 4410:4; compulsive ~, 1598:3; danger of ~, 1724:4; decline of good ~, 829:2; fascinating ~, 972:2; gender and ~, 3618:1; good ~, 1904:3; ideal ~, 1418:2; idle ~, 916:10; 2991:1; meaningless ~, 643:12; ~ of friends, 467:1; ~ of women, 773:3; ongoing ~, 4326:5; religious ~, 511:2; repetitive ~, 3110:1; spiritual ~, 825:1; stimulating ~, 807:20; strong ~, 635:5; subject of ~, 607:2; 844:2; 2258:1

conversion, 188:1; religious ~, 633:1; 877:1; 1735:5; 4209:1

convictions *see also* belief; principle, 1187:4; 2327:1; courage of ~, 1952:2; one's own ~, 998:2; remaining true to one's ~, 4423:2

cook/ing *see also* chef; recipe, 487:9; 944:1; 1221:1; 1311:3; 1418:4; 1834:2; 2174:3, 6; 2307:3; 2394:1; 2486:1, 2; 2801:6; 3747:4; 4204:1; 4212:1; 4541:1; 4677:3; ~ at school, 4542:1; ~book, 2174:1; ~ bug, 4707:1; dislike of ~, 1324:3; ~ fish, 2172:5; home ~, 4602:2; men and ~, 914:1; 2948:2; Mexican ~,

4204:2; over-~, 2596:4; pleasures of ~, 3734:1; ~ recipe, 2647:1; ~ rules, 4541:2; ~ sauces, 1502:1; spoiling ~, 2172:4; ~ with joy, 1871:4; ~ with liquor, 944:1

Coolidge, Calvin, 1616:1

cooperation *see also* harmony; peace, world ~, 674:1; 1044:15; 1618:18; 2088:2; 2971:1; 3772:3; 4423:2; creative ~, 2971:4; global ~, 2664:3; 3676:3; 3938:1; ~ in business world, 2032:9; learning ~, 4629:3

Copernicus, 4290:1

Copley, John Singleton, 570:1; 706:1

corn, 405:5; 1974:1; 2596:1; ~ field, 3781:2; industrialization of ~, 2596:2; 3781:3

corporation *see also* business; multinationals, 3566:1, 2, 4; actions of ~, 4790:1; 4823:1; American ~, 2885:1; 3587:1; 4100:1; 4225:0; cover up of ~, 2622:2; effects of ~ competition, 2885:1; ~ employees, 4434:1; 4521:1; ethics of ~, 3312:2; ~ executive, 2511:3; 3401:1; globalization and ~, 4771:4; greed of ~, 4106:4; ~ in relation to employees, 1223:1; 3429:1; ~ in relation to environment, 4506:2; ~ leadership, 4977:3; male world of ~, 3139:9; malfeasance of ~, 4347:2; multinational ~, 1666:4; power of ~, 4585:3; ~ profits, 4008:2; racism in ~, 4742:1; ruthless ~, 4506:5; sexism in ~, 3093:3; 4979:2; structure of ~, 2418:3; values of ~, 4227:1

corruption *see also* bribery; debauchery; graft, 477:2; 1689:11; 1846:2; 1894:4; 2491:1; 4464:4; cost of ~, 4540:1; ~ in government, 1133:2; 2291:1; 3317:1; 4525:1; 4604:3; ~ of white race, 807:15; political ~, 1239:2; 2496:1

corset *see also* underwear, 1969:5; 3029:5

cosmetic surgery *see also* Botox, 2568:6; 4964:2, 3, 4; alternatives to ~, 1613:2

cosmetics *see also* specific items; makeup, 1163:4; 1246:3; 3033:7; 4036:4; 4251:8; use of ~, 1539:2

cosmopolitan, 3984:6 cost, ~ of things, 1503:2

costume, athlete's ~, 2367:0

cotton, picking ~, 1652:1; 2604:2

couch, ~ potato, 4598:2

counting, 1450:20; 3782:4

country *see also* nation, cruel ~, 4485:2; free ~, 1552:4; , ~ girl, 4901:2; leaving the ~, 3209:2; love of ~, 4296:1; obscurity of ~, 3485:1; unknown ~, 142:2

country life *see also* countryside; rusticity, 338:1; 670:2; 1032:8; 1357:1; 1362:1; 2201:6; 4081:2; ~ vs. city life, 1506:1; 2771:16

countryside *see also* country life; landscape; outdoors; rusticity, 670:2; 864:6; 1762:1; 4284:1; city visitor in ~, 4105:3; ~ road, 3578:3

couple *see also* lover; marriage; partner/ship [social]; relationship; sex partner, 2490:5; 3349:5; communication between ~, 1950:3; confines of ~, 1507:3; enduring ~, 4354:3; interracial ~, 4806:2; loving ~, 2166:1; obstacles of ~, 3897:6; odd ~, 2014:6; sexual intimacy & ~, 4176:3; 4228:2; 4611:5; 4937:1, 2; ~ splitting up (*see also* divorce), 3921:1; well-suited ~, 2771:24

courage *see also* bravery; valor, 100:1; 196:2; 955:2; 1847:4; 1997:1; 2053:6; 2520:2; 2552:11; 3818:4; 3965:3; 4110:1; 4131:2; 4211:6; influence of ~, 1575:2; lack of ~, 198:1; 4725:3; moral ~, 1764–1765:4; need for ~, 3545:2; pray for ~, 878:1; ~ showing, 3880:1; spiritual ~, 2756:19; ~ tried, 603:6; 682:2

court (judicial) *see also* judiciary, 1693:3; 2963:4, 5; authority of ~, 2963:1; image in ~ room, 4269:1; seeking aid of ~, 2850:3; victory in ~, 3830:1

court (royal), French ~, 465:2; ~ life, 661:2

courter/courtship *see also* lover; romance, 20:1; 559:1; 643:9; 1481:9; lesbian ~, 3218:5

courtesan *see also* mistress [courtesan]; prostitute/prostitution (*see also* sex industry), 1462:4

courtesy *see also* manners; politeness; tact, 533:13; 1842:3; 1940:4; ~ in Japan, 2903:1; lack of ~, 916:18

courtiers *see also* noble [rank]; royal/ty, marriage among ~, 363:1

cow, 1948:1; 2784:3; milking ~, 4258:2; sacred ~, 2288:6

coward/ice, 539:4; 807:14; 965:7; 4822:1; physical ~, 1764–1765:4

cowboy, 3732:4

crack (drug), 2870:1

craft/smanship, 955:37; 1408:10; 2082:3; hand ~, 3855:3; learning a ~, 1881:4; 2890:3

Craven, Earl of, 814:1

craving, ~ more, 3669:4, 5, 6

craziness, 3880:5; ~ in artist, 3901:1

creation, 670:1; 1575:3; 3369:3; controlling ~, 1783:3; Indian ~ story, 4045:4; ~ of woman,

514:1; ~ of world, 2638:1; sustained ~, 2187:15

Creation, the, 2:1; 405:2; 430:1; 593:8; 936:1; 1209:10; Native American ~, 1170:1; purpose of ~, 4321:4; understanding ~, 1752:9

creationism, scientific ~, 4455:1; teaching ~, 4684:5

creativity see also self-expression, 798:4; 931:10; 1254:4; 1337:7; 1495:2; 1574:1, 2; 1658:2; 1782:14; 1903:5; 2089:6; 2623:1; 2801:8; 4070:2; 4155:2; 4519:1; 4757:3; atmosphere of ~, 1733:1; 2430:2; essence of ~, 3971:2; impulse for ~, 2600:2; need for ~, 3397:1; obsession with ~, 1147:1; path of ~, 2993:2; peace of ~, 4176:1; power of ~, 3567:5; purpose of ~, 3732:5; repressed ~, 2642:16; seeds of ~, 4327:1

creator, 3763:1

credence see also truth, 245:3

credibility, 4966:3

credit see also money, 1920:4; 3610:2; ~ card, 1696:3; 3610:2; 4341:1

creed see also belief, faith, religion, 945:1; 1213:2

crime see also specific criminal acts, 1340:1; 1724:3; 1870:17; 2298:4; 4021:2; 4705:3; addictiveness of ~, 3191:1; ~ vs. environment, 4469:3; ~ vs. humanity, 4895:4; ~ vs. women (see also rape), 1870:17; 4685:1; alcohol and ~, 3433:4; commercialization of ~, 3444:1; debating ~ control, 3981:2; definition of ~, 2876:4; ~ of drunk driving, 3671:1; ~ of passion, 3056:1; 3099:12; political ~, 1897:5; 3255:1; punishment of ~ (see also capital punishment), 780:2; urge to commit ~, 1739:3; white collar ~, 2274:1; women and ~, 2458:2

criminal see also juvenile delinquent; outlaw, 4115:2; ~ behavior, 3944:4; bogus ~ plea, 3981:3

criminology, 1987:4

crisis see also catastrophe; disaster, 1409:17; 3976:7; 4731:4; dealing with ~, 651:1; 4282:1; 4687:1; economic ~, 4585:2; 4966:1; families in ~, 4429:4; financial ~, 4230:1; 4867:4; surviving ~, 1905:6

critic/ism see also faultfinding; review [critical]; self-criticism, 507:5; 1153:3; 1218:1; 1278:1; 1421:1; 1423:2; 1450:21; 2154:4; 2424:1; 3158:1; accepting ~, 3731:9; age of ~, 3052:1; art ~, 1186:2; 2377:1; 3585:1; constructive ~, 1354:3; destructive ~, 1354:3; 1399:1;

1758:4; drama ~, 539:1; fear of ~, 1402:5; harmful ~, 1421:2; literary ~, 527:1; 615:1; 2100:1; 3397:2; literary ~ and women, 3234:1; personal ~, 4402:2; sexism in ~, 1511:1; soliciting ~, 1024:1; theater ~, 3776:6; 4306:1

Croat/ia, 3735:3; 3867:3

Cromwell, Oliver, 1181:1; 1378:4

crop see also farm/er, cash ~, 3518:1

cross-culturalism, 3321:3

cross-dressing see also transsexual; transvestite, 535:2; 2229:1

crowd, 966:1; 1979:10; ~ control, 3800:1; psychology of ~, 4917:2

crown see also honors, royalty, 224:1; 772:6; 3910:2

cruelty see also malice; meanness; ruthlessness; viciousness, 4491:1; 4615:1; ~ of humankind, 3343:4; 4765:1; pleasure in ~, 977:2

cruise, women on ~, 2176:1

Crusades, devastation wrought by ~, 176:1

cry/ing see also tears, 126:1; 160:2; 245:2; 317:1, 2; 382:1; 484:1; 693:2; 716:2; 1571:1; 1690:2; 1979:2; 3596:2; 4954:2; ~ adult, 2460:6; ~ in bed, 165:2; men ~, 3464:4; quick to ~, 1444:5

Cuba/n, 4386:2; exiled from ~, 4449:5

cuckold/ry see also adultery, 383:3; 3499:1

cuisine see also food, 4541:1; American ~, 1871:5; French ~, 2174:4; Italian ~, 2174:5

culpability, escape from ~, 3935:1

cult/ism, recruitment by ~, 3565:3

cultural activity, suspicion of ~, 4367:5

culture see also civilization; society; Western culture, 543:3; 1227:5; 1436:3; 1526:3; 4495:4; 4851:4; adaptation to ~, 2260:6; advertising and ~, 3433:3; agrarian ~, 2719:1; American ~, 3009:6; 4699:3; attitudes of ~, 2073:2; cross ~, 3950:3; defining ~, 2671:5; differing ~, 4066:2; dominant ~, 3321:2; erosion of ~, 1929:3; exchange of ~, 3037:4; healthy ~, 3784:5; homosexual ~, 3738:2; influence of ~, 4267:3; male ~, 1683:2; ~ of violence, 3365:5; popular ~, 3780:5; 4252:1; primitive ~, 4168:2; pursuing ~, 1292:6; sanitation and ~, 3163:3; secularism in American ~, 3661:1; shaping ~, 3518:6; transformation of ~, 3747:5; understanding ~, 4670:2; Western ~, 2720–2721:1; woman and ~, 2579:1; 3684:3

cunning, 2997:5

Cupid, 452:4; 660:2; 1581:1

cure see also healing; recovery, 790:6

curfew, 1870:17

Curie, Marie, 1581:2; 1851:1

curiosity, 472:12; 604:4; 1618:23; 2381:6; 4711:6; 4767:1; lack of ~, 2799:2; unanswered ~, 1938:4

custom see also habit; mores; tradition, 453:1; 584:4; 893:4; 1244:1; 1625:3; barbaric ~, 2409:1; break with ~, 2268:5; loss of ~, 1929:3; revolt vs. ~, 946:4

cyberspace see also computer; internet, 3679:1; anarchy of ~, 4968–4969:2

cynic/ism, 1114:3; 1325:4; 2006:2; 2021:5; 2224:4; 3099:5; 3488:1; political ~, 4464:3

D

dam, 4506:4; impact of ~, 3250.1:5; 4266:3, 5

damnation/damned, 674:3; influence of ~, 107:5

dance (ballroom), 3054:1; group ~, 3257:9; learning ~, 2839:3; love of ~, 4533:6; ~ tango, 4919:1

dancer/dancing see also choreography, 259:1; 915:1; 1475:1; 1512:4; 1557:2; 1701:1; 2012:4, 5; 2055:2; 2141:2; 2273:2; 2533:1; 3040:3; 3063:2; 3199:1; American ~, 1795:3; ballerina ~, 1573:3; discipline of ~, 1573:1; growth of ~, 2967:1; 3426:2; healing power of ~, 2373:1, 2; ~ in university, 2012:3; light design for ~, 2533:1; ~ of future, 3915:1; performing ~, 3426:4; primitive ~, 1701:2; 3426:1; social ~, 726:2; spiritual ~, 253:1; teaching others to ~, 3547:1; ~ technique, 2754:2 danger see also risk, 451:4; 1190:1; 1450:16; 2561:7; 4046:1; 4367:3; 4797:1; bond of ~, 805:3; 3422:2; facing ~, 1847:3; 1937:2; 3931:1; living with ~, 2315:3; ~ of life, 2642:5

Dante Alighieri, 1782:13; 2705:3; 2872:3

Danube Delta, 4936:1

Darfur, 4829:2; 4925:1

daring, 1751:27; 2812:4

darkness, 413:1; 999:4; 1234:1; 2196:2; 4115:1; banishing ~, 2791:1; emerging from ~, 2928:1; fear of ~, 2104:1; 3309:2; out of the ~, 1252:2; 2943:10; world of ~, 2195:3; 2694:3

dating see also relationship, 1872:2; 4089:1; ingredients of ~, 3097:6; steady ~, 3939:8

Daud Khan, Mohammad, 4714.1:1

daughter, 1006:13; 1563:6; 3092:1; 3480:3; 4004:2; 4650:4; death of ~, 1111:2; ~ in relation to father (see also father/hood, ~

in relation to child), 2659:3; 4728:4; 4752:2; 4847:3; 4881:1; ~ in relation to mother (see also mother/hood, ~ in relation to daughter), 12:1; 128:1; 1409:11; 1697:9; 2047:1; 2461:1, 3; 2916:20; 3477:1; 3616:2; 4010:4; 4038:2; 4410:1; 4435:1; 4752:1; 4956:1; 4988:2; loss of ~, 2016:2; obedient ~, 4146:3

David, king of Israel, 33:1; 38:1

dawn see also morning; sunrise, 225:1; 725:1; 866:1; 1136:5; 1346:4; 1433:; 1502:8; 1909:2

day see also specific days of the week; specific times of day; end of ~, 1283:3; full ~, 2552:13; holiness of ~, 3563:6; last ~, 1091:1; long ~, 1858:4; many ~, 4889:3; one ~ at a time, 2986:1; sameness of ~, 1192:3; short ~, 1206:4

day care, children's ~ (see also child rearing), 1167:15; 2136:3; 2916:6; 3386:2, 3

daydream see also dream; reverie, 174:1; 671:15; 691:5; 1275:1; 1376:1; activating one's ~, 1002:1; chasing ~, 802:4; dispelling ~, 950:4; woman's ~, 852:4

de Gaulle, Chalres, 2449:1

dead, the see also death; dying, 789:1; 792:4; 955:36; 1100:3; 2188:3; 2732:8; 3374:2; 3451:6; 3598:2, 4; 4146:6; 4884:6; attitude toward ~, 4588:2; communicating with ~, 175:1; disposal of ~, 4718:1; forgiving ~, 3929:4; honoring ~, 2731:3; memento of ~, 945:12; mourning ~, 1429:0; newly ~, 4310:3; power of ~, 1233:9; praise for ~, 389:1; pray for ~, 1028:3; preoccupation with ~, 670:2; respect for ~, 2379:3; speaking ill of ~, 676:8; 1800:4; treatment of ~, 772:5; uncaring ~, 1619:1; walking ~, 1468:5

deaf/ness, 4698:2, 3; interpreting music for ~, 3760:1, 2; tone ~, 1162:2

death see also burial; dead, the; death sentence; dying; grave; mortality, 56:1, 1; 75:4; 280:1; 308:10; 341:9; 355:2; 389:1, 2; 417:1; 479:4; 541:2; 594:1; 629:1; 870:4; 879:4; 934:13; 945:2; 982:9; 1001:1; 1024:17; 1027:8; 1033:7; 1102:3; 1173:5; 1176:7; 1193:4; 1254:16; 1255:2; 1406:3; 1491:3; 1560:2; 1590:20; 1682:5; 1707:2; 1751:14; 1780:18; 1914:9; 2080:12; 2560:7; 2561:4; 2585:3; 2793:3; 2916:13; 3019:3; 3087:1; 3218:4; 3235:1; 3316:4; 3691:6; 3763:2; 3779:1; 3910:3; 3975:1; 4038:5; 4161:2;

4356:1, 3; 4376:4; 4491:2; 4711:1, 9; 4844:1; acceptance of ~, 300:6; 326:1; 439:5; 1024:21; 1507:1; 2001:3; 4376:5; accidental ~, 3850:4; ~ and guilt, 2560:2; ~ and literature, 2872:5; approaching ~, 308:1; 317:2; 476:2; 562:1, 2; 577:2; 682:3; 849:2; 955:35; 1027:4; 4884:1; attitudes toward ~, 3445:6; brush with ~, 1249:6; 4340:1; ~ by stoning, 4701:2; cause of ~, 1090:2; 1751:28; celebration of ~, 1920:5; certainty of ~, 285:1; 2628:2; 4130:1; choosing ~, 2515:2; denial of ~, 2212:3; 3341:3; 4851:2; ~ during wartime (see also war, death and ~), 2560:5; early ~, 459:4; 2015:2; earning one's ~, 2698:1; escaping ~, 1046:1; evilness of ~, 46:2; exaltation in ~, 1456:3; facing ~, 300:4; 442:5; 579:2; 826:1; 1181:2; 1325:6; 2329:2; 2901:9; fear of ~, 1147:3; 2198:2; 2756:3; ~ for a cause, 4462:1; ~ for country, 2288:11; foreknowledge of ~, 1052:1; freedom of ~, 1925:2; 3372:6; 3412:1; 3571:1; helplessness before ~, 3906:1; honorable ~, 113:2; 1291:4; 1813:1; hour of ~, 588:4; 1208:16; iconic ~, 4270:1; illusion of ~, 1689:3; imagining ~, 4611:7; impact of ~, 1751:13; ~ in America, 2560:3; ~ in youth, 2437:13; industry around ~ (see also funeral), 1808:3; inevitability of ~, 39:1; 122:3; 465:4; 483:1; 1808:5; influence after ~, 3865:3; inner ~, 2365:2; Judeo-Christian judgment in relation to ~, 3445:3; knowledge of ~, 3159:3; legacy of ~, 4082:2; lessons of ~, 2560:5; love and ~, 2842:4; mistaken ~, 1549:4; narrow escape from ~, 2977:4; 3309:3; near ~, 3046:2; no ~, 2566:3; ~ of child (see child/ren, death of ~); ~ of comrades, 1813:3, 4; ~ of loved one (see loved one, death of ~; specific relation [e.g. son, death of ~; family, death in ~]); ~ of old person, 3389:5; ~ of soldier, 1139:2; ~ of young, 546:1; 835:2; postponing ~, 3923:2; preoccupation with ~, 896:1; preparation for ~, 779:2; 1687:6; 2380:3; questioning ~, 1032:13; 3635:1; reaction to ~, 2925:15; 3128:2; 3442:3; readiness for ~, 280:2; 3281:4; resort to ~, 1273:1; smile in ~, 2817:7; spiritual ~, 2560:6; staving off ~, 1407:3; sudden ~, 4588:1; terrified of ~, 3396:1; time of ~, 1995:2; unchangeability of ~, 2153:5; undignified

~, 3883:2; violent ~, 3878:1; ~ while on duty, 1379:7; wish for ~, 231:1; 284:1; 451:11; 682:5; 802:3; 813:1; 950:1; 1161:1
death sentence see capital punishment; execution
death toll, 2987:8; ~ from conquest, 1227:2
debasement, 1076:1
debate, endless ~, 3737:1
debauchery see also corruption; seduction, ~ of men, 517:5
Deborah, 882:1; 1304:6
Debs, Eugene V., 1706:1
debt, 283:1; 1516:5; 4412:4; accumulating ~, 922:2; escaping ~, 4725:2; national ~, 4190:6; ~ to the dead, 4116:2
decade see also generation, 1570:1; ~ of 1880s, 1227:7; ~ of 1920s, 1597:1; 4203:2; ~ of 1950s, 2270:3; ~ of 1960s, 2411:2; 2925:14; 3068:4; 3084:2; 3694:2; 3732:2; ~ of 1970s, 4416:2; ~ of 1980s, 3241:6
decadence, 311:2; 2383:2; 2443:4; Western ~, 3086:3
deceit/deception see also duplicity; falseness; hypocrisy/hypocrite; lie/lying; self-deception; subterfuge; trick/ery, 289:9; 383:5; 801:18; 992:3; 1419:2; 1729:3; 3069:3; ~ in advertising (see also advertisement/advertising), 1901:4; man's ~, 383:2
decency, 2474:2; sense of ~, 2026:1
deception, ~ in love, 205:1
decision see also indecision; resoluteness, 2805:3; life ~, 2012:2; ~-making, 733:10; 4273.1:2, 4
Declaration of Independence (U.S.), 1592:6; 3082:3; amending the ~, 1666:3
Declaration of Sentiments, 931:6, 7, 8
decline, feeling of ~, 3268:4
deed (act) see also task, 955:5; 1024:27; good ~, 221:1; 966:2; great ~, 892:19; noble ~, 991:1
defeat see also failure, 899:2; 960:1; 1173:3; 3703:4; 3704:3
defeatism, 2187:10
defector, 4424:2
defense, armed ~ (see also army), 1106:4; ~ of country, 1106:3; ~ spending, 4446:2
Defense Department (U.S.A.), 3271:1; ~ under Rumsfeld, 4502:1
defense mechanism, lack of ~, 4533:4; use of ~, 2112:3
defensiveness, 4816:2
deference, ~ to men, 3377:5
defiance, 947:2; repressed ~, 1936:1
deforestation, ~ in Indonesia, 4488:1
Degas, Edgar, 1126:1

dehumanization see also objectification, 2288:7; 2680:8; capitalism and ~, 3020:3
delicacy, 466:2; ~ of girl, 4762:2
delirium, 1986:2
democracy, 1618:30; 1990:2; 2226:4; 2990:2; 3141:4; 3731:16; 4141:4; American ~ (see also United States, democracy in ~), 1360:13; 1741:11; communication and ~, 4200:3; corruption in ~, 2026:3; creed of ~, 3554:1; 4339:4; destruction of ~, 1666:6; future of ~, 1583:3; ideals of ~, 3907:3; 4200:1; ~ in America, 3344:2; 4129:4; ~ in the home, 1694:2; influence of Christianity on ~, 3445:1; institutions of ~, 2963:5; participation in ~, 3219:1; practicing ~, 1494:3; requirements of ~, 1238:4; root of ~, 1350:1; secrecy in ~, 4620:2; speech in ~, 3911:5; spreading ~, 2393:7; system of ~, 2288:9; the arts in ~, 2345:3; women and ~, 3219:4
Democratic Party (U.S.) see also political party, 2227:1; 2558:3; 3381:1; ~ Convention, 2986:3; sex and ~, 3442:5
democratization, 3059:5; 4605:1
demography, 733:7; immersed in ~, 2710:3
demonstration, 4903:1; political ~ (see also movements, socio-political), 4917:2
demotion (see also employment), 436:1
denial, 2459:1; 2938:3; 3417:5; 3829:2; 4713:1; consequences of ~, 3254:4; ~ in relationships, 1646:3
Denmark/Dane, beer and ~, 1871:8; ~ in relation to Islam, 3208:1
Department of Labor (U.S.), 3151:1
departure see also parting; separation, 2101:2; ~ from homeland, 854:1
dependability, 2201:5
dependence/dependency, 1677:6; 2252:3; 2590:1; 2679:2; 2685:2; 4122:3; breaking with ~, 1743:7; consequences of ~, 3947:3; ~ on another, 869:5
dependent, ~ male, 2518:1
depression (mental), 910:13; 997:2; 2739:3; 2982:5; 4762:1; cure for ~, 1090:1; 1836:2; 2739:5; defining ~, 2739:1; ~ in America, 4219:2; ~ in London, 4219:3
Depression, Great, 1584:2; 1946:1; 4468:1; global impact of ~, 4468:2; ~ in the midwest, 1654:4; migrants of ~, 1654:6; suicide during ~, 2154:3
deprivation, 682:5; 804:6; 1127:4; 1751:29; 2290:2; 2349:9; effects

of ~, 2116:16; relativity of ~, 1200:1
Descartes, René, 2133:2
desert, 470:1; 1462:5; 3550:2; 3812:2; 4339:3; high ~, 3052:4; light on ~, 1670:4
desertion, 2453:3; ~ by husband, 4643:1
design, 2402:3; expression of ~, 3836:3; ~ of living space, 4679:1
desire see also passion, 511:14; 1622:5; 2189:3; 3025:2; 3345:2; 4018:2; 4180:1; fickleness of ~, 1382:1; ~ for opposite sex, 2564:2; fulfilling ~, 1015:2; object of ~, 1446:1; 3883:6; 4168:3; overcome by ~, 2211:1; 2355:1; pitfalls of ~, 193:10; sexual ~, 501:5; 1209:4; suppressed ~, 1474:1; 1755:5; 4194:3; women's ~, 2717:1
desolation, 2454:2; ~ of land (see also wasteland), 2400:1
despair, 247:1; 808:19; 1120:3; 1977:10; 2982:1; 3530:1; 4146:1; courage of ~, 1654:6; ~ of the times, 2818:1; rid of ~, 3763:2; upside of ~, 2220:2
desperation, impact of ~, 4808:5
despot/ism see also tyranny; tyrant, 300:1; 931:5
dessert see sweets
destination, ~ unknown, 2101:2
destiny see also chance; fate; fortune [chance], 93:1; 1110:3; 1230:7; 1435:2; 1651:1; 2012:2; 2771:27; discovering one's ~, 2752:1; 4653:4; women and ~, 2818:2
destruction/destructiveness see also ruin; self-destructiveness, acceptance of ~, 3630:2; ~ by unseen powers, 4515:2; end to forces of ~, 2111:3; inevitability of ~, 4076:1; passion for ~, 2572:2; urge for ~, 2657:4
detachment see also indifference; objectivity, 1903:4; 2224:3; 3321:4
detail, attention to ~, 3548:1
deterioration, ~ of human body, 2456:4; ~ of society, 1187:2
determination, 393:1; 947:2; 2306:2; 2537:6; 2606:2; 2902:1; great ~, 1192:2; 3539:3
determinism, 3583:4
developers (building), 3039:3; community ~, 3550:4; zeal of ~, 4566:1
development, 2362:4; 3197:3; economic ~, 2271:6; 2537:9; 2835:2; 3090:5; 4141:7; hypocrisy of ~, 4821:2; ~ in relation to environment, 2164:1; 3129:7; 4065:1; 4281:1; 4469:2; ~ of society, 2669:3; planned ~, 4551:2; sustainable ~, 2678:3; 4446:1;

women and world ~, 2856:1; 4430:3

developmental disorder, 4154:1, 2

devil see also Satan, 237:2; 436:1; 508:1; 534:2; 870:8; 876:4; 977:2; 1364:1; 2331:12; 3298:1; 3546:3; banishing ~, 113:1; ~ in disguise, 2296:1; ~ within, 3179:2; work of ~, 931:31

devil's advocate, 4001:1

devotion see also God, devotion to ~; piety, 356:5; 436:2; ~ to loved one, 2498:1; 4844:4

dew, 215:1; 322:2; mountain ~, 143:1; ~ on flower, 554:1

dialectic, 2443:2

dialogue see also conversation, ~ between men and women, 3174:4; 3586:1

diamond, ~ bracelet, 1686:1

diaper, disposable ~, 3236:1

diarist/diary see also journal, 1162:3; 1982:1; 2572:; 3109:1; 3139:13; 3399:1; musing over ~, 1440:9; 4946:1; reasons to keep ~, 2657:1, 2; revelations of ~, 1132:4, 5; 4134:3; woman's ~, 2859:1

Diaz, Cameron, 4758:1

dichotomy, feminist ~, 2401:1; ~ of humans (see also people, dichotomy of ~), 1676:2; 2185:1; 2735:5; ~ of life, 568:1; 4814:3

Dickinson, Emily, 1440:13

dictator/ship, 4160:1; art under ~, 2345:3

Diderot, Denis, 587:1

Didrickson, Babe, 4621:4

diet/er see also eating, over- ~; fat/ness; nutrition/ist; obesity; weight, 2085:5; 2757:4; 2765:8; 3990:4; 4794:4; 4870:3; American ~, 1992:2, 4; anti-aging ~, 4311:1; obsession with ~, 2309:1; 4875:2; people and ~, 1112:3; weight loss ~, 1409:5; 2586:4; women and ~, 4541:3

difference see also otherness; outsider, 1502:1; 1693:12; 2671:1; 4009:4; ~ among individuals, 1854:1; blessing ~, 3650:3; fear of ~, 3824:1; getting past ~, 2971:1; intolerance of ~, 4326:5; making ~, 2892:1; 3281:3; 4014:5; 4670:3; possessing ~, 3044:1; recognition of ~, 3650:2

difficulty see also vicissitudes, challenge of ~, 4282:, 4

digestion see also eating, 1882:4; good ~, 616:7

digital systems see also computer, 4147:8

dignity, 3250.1:2; 3743:5; maintaining ~, 3254:1

dilettante, 2066:1

diligence see also effort; industriousness; perseverance, 578:2; 642:1;
695:2; 1435:1; 3170:2; 4487:1; rewards of ~, 706:1; 868:1

dining see also specific meals; eating; feast; food, ~ alone, 843:4; importance of ~ well, 1590:10

dinner, 1614:2; ~ announcement, 3095:2

Diogenes, 544:3

diploma, value of ~, 2237:4

diplomacy/diplomat, 1256:2; 1535:6; 2708:1; 3676:4; advantages of ~, 3797:5; restraints of ~, 2769:1; role of ~, 4887:1

direction, best ~, 2809:1; finding ~, 1901:3; heading in wrong ~, 522:4; lack of ~, 3532:4; 3831:4; right ~, 3406:1; sense of ~, 4735:2; written ~, 3097:8

directness, 3009:2

dirt see also soil, 769:7; 2604:4

disabled/disability see also handicap, 1601:4; 1816:3; children with ~, 2570:1; 3260:3; oppression of ~, 3840:3; overcoming ~, 1922:3; physical ~, 2451:2

disagreement, 808:2; 3250.1:2; philosophical ~, 3469:3

disappearance, 166:11; 1409:13; 2628:3; 3099:22; wish for ~, 1925:3

disappointment, 1015:2; 1114:1; 2187:4; 4962:3; ~ in self, 4727:2; little ~, 694:1

disapproval, 1743:3; 2056:3; 3068:4; expressing ~, 595:1

disarmament, nuclear ~, 4080:2; working for ~, 4080:5

disaster see also catastrophe; crisis; tragedy,1583:1; 1702:2; 1724:13; 2737:1; anticipating ~, 2194:2; cost of ~, 4521:3; facing ~, 2248:2

discipline see also self-discipline, 916:12; 945:8; 2110:3; 3122:2; ~ in relation to liberty, 1381:4

disclosure, 1193:7; 4905:2; need for ~, 3447:2; personal ~, 1759:11; public ~, 3099:17

discomfort, 4727:3

discontent, 391:4; 3776:1; ~ of citizenry, 276:1

discovery, 2742:2; 2776:3; 3593:1; fear of ~, 1124:1; 2657:6; moment of ~, 2112:2

discretion, 1184:11; lack of ~, 166:8

discrimination see also prejudice, eliminating ~, 1618:30; 2608:4; ~ in the workplace, 2643:2; 3093:2, 3, 4; racial ~, 2088:1; response to ~, 1727:1; sex ~, 2641:3; ~ vs. women, 2764:3

disease see also specific disorders; specific illnesses; illness; sickness, 982:7; 2235:1; 4748:1; attitudes toward ~, 3445:6; contagious ~, 3961:6; cures for ~, 4135:3; degenerative ~, 4059:2; dread of
~, 1176:7; study of ~, 1992:3; symptoms of ~, 974:3

disembodiment, 221:2

disembowelment, 2817:14

disfavor, 459:2

disgrace, fall into ~, 2710:1 disillusionment, 1921:4; 4717:1; fear of ~, 1610:3

disloyalty, 522:3

Disney World, 2402:7

disorder, 1554:3; 2415:3; 3759:2

displacement, 158:1

disposition see also human nature; personality; temper/ament, 683:2; good-natured ~, 676:7; importance of ~, 613:1

dispute see also argument, legal ~, 4137:6

dissatisfaction, 292:4; 306:2; 722:8; impetus of ~, 1209:10

dissembling see also falseness, deceit/deception; pretense, 1409:23; 4390:2; difficulty of ~, 639:1; power of ~, 2021:16

dissent, war vs. ~, 4330:3

dissident, political ~, 2447:1

distance, disappearance of ~, 1441:2

distinction see also individuality, 790:7; achieving ~, 1262:8; desire for ~, 451:8; 671:12; woman of ~, 522:1

distraction see also amusement, need for ~, 4298:2

distrust see also paranoia, 356:2; 955:27

dive, perfect ~, 4401:1

diversion see also amusement; pleasure, 578:4; 784:1; incessant ~, 449:3; 734:7; indifference to ~, 435:2

diversity see also multiculturalism; variety, 4199:2; biological ~, 4065:1; celebrating ~, 2971:3; 4702:2; cut off from ~, 1666:2; 4141:2; defining ~, 4135:2; elimination of ~, 1935:4

divestment, 285:3

divine/divinity see also god; goddess, 301:1; 3120:3; experiencing the ~, 4700.1:1; feminine in ~, 1007:3; 3698:1; gender of ~, 2399:1; omnipresence of ~, 1148:6; 3650:4; search for ~, 2380:7

division, class ~, 1155:3

divisiveness, 3466:1

divorce see also alimony; couple, ~ splitting up; marriage, end of ~, 1265:2; 1481:3; 1622:3; 1776:2; 2718:1; 3797:3; 3959–3960:1; 4902:3; ~ among elderly, 1872:5; ~ among rich, 2463:2; children and ~, 1943:5; 3498:2, 5; impermissible ~, 1776:6; ~ lawyer, 2191:1; ~ litigation, 2295:1; New York ~, 1292:1; precipitant ~, 4778:1; reasons for ~, 2943:2; women and ~, 1973:2
DNA see also chromosome; gene, 4005:2; 4084:6; ~ testing, 4748:3

doctor see medical profession; healer; physician; therapist, ; 4059:1; holiday for ~, 2817:15; ~ in foreign culture, 4175:1; ~ in relation to patient; ~ in relation to terminally ill, 2329:1; ~ patient relationship, 3509:3; 4213:2; women ~, 974:11

Dodge, Mabel, 1591:1

dog see also pet, 405:1; 739:1; 1241:2; 1292:12; 1448:1; 1454:5; 1650:1; 1689:14; 1700:7; 1720:2; 1729:1; 2546:3; 3258:5; 3750:2; 3968:4; 3989:1; 4046:2; 4211:1; 4404:3; 4453:3; 4982:1; admiration of ~, 678:3; 1848:2; eyes of ~, 642:3; ~ in relation to master, 1449:4; ~ in relation to people, 983:1; 1693:17; love for ~, 616:1; 983:2; 1230:2; 3217:3; 4168:; loyalty of ~, 1444:7; naughty ~, 141:1; neighborhood ~, 4346:3; pit bull ~, 4684:1; stray ~, 4226:5

dogma, 3470:2

doll, 1138:1; black ~, 4101:2

domestic abuse see also violence, ~ vs. women, 2256:4; 3058:2; surviving ~, 3362:2

domesticity see also tameness, 649:10; 2269:1; 3488:4; early ~, 1935:10; limitations of ~, 931:3; rewards of ~, 1941:2; women and ~, 1419:6; 2855:3

domination, 1986:5; dissolution of male ~, 2794:1; maintenance of ~, 2756:6; ~ of culture, 3988:1; ~ of nature, 3942:1; ~ of women, 3942:1; ~ over others, 2988:3; 4605:3; power of ~, 2032:3; structures of ~, 3858:1; tactics of ~, 3889:2; tools of ~, 2901:10; will to ~, 3738:1

dominion, 3441:3

Don Quixote, 841:1

Donner Party, 1058:2

doom, 4912:3

door, ~ bell, 1793:2

doorman, 2203:2

Dostoevsky, Feodor, 1142:2

double standard see also sexism, 1135:1; 1776:5; ~ in child-rearing, 906:3; ~ in manners, 2177:3; ~ in politics, 4561:2

double talk see also duplicity; pretense, 676:4; 2185:15

doubt see also skepticism; uncertainty, 1072:1; 3609:1; 4285:9; self-~, 3913:1; unfounded ~, 908:5

Douglas, Helen Gahagan, 1618:13

Dover, White Cliffs of (England), 1443:5

Dow Chemicals, fighting ~, 4142:0; malfeasance of ~, 4347:3

dowdiness, 1163:2

downstream, 4312:6

dowry, 300:2

Dracula, 2705:3

drama (play) *see also* stage play; theatre, 2575:2

drawing, learning to ~, 2547:1; symbols in ~, 4735:1

dread *see also* fear, 903:2; 2689:5; 3306:1

dream/ing *see also* daydream; nightmare, 103:1; 838:8; 852:5; 859:1; 1022:1; 1160:5; 1525:3; 1534:1; 1566:3; 1766:1; 1961:1; 2062:1; 2638:14; 3128:3; 3131:1; 3340:2; 3957:2; 4234:3; ~ analysis, 3537:2; animal ~, 2481:2; big ~, 3922:3; color of ~, 3239:3; ~ come true, 1538:1; 3979:1; conscious of ~, 2063:1; controlling one's ~, 1576:2; destroying ~, 1653:1; 3272:2; facts of ~, 1739:2; faded ~, 155:1; following ~, 3179:3; forgotton ~, 3953:1; function of ~, 1739:3; good ~, 162:1; holding a ~, 2812:4; 2942:9; impact of ~, 945:6; importance of ~, 3918:1; in search of a ~, 1866:2; influence of ~, 3276:1; meaning of ~, 3032:3; ~ of evil, 2642:13; ~ of love, 1152:3; realizing one's ~, 2589:3; 4396:1; recurring ~, 4416:3; shared ~, 3694:1; staving off ~, 2970:4; unattainable ~, 2735:1; understanding ~, 2927:2

dreamer *see also* visionary, 1044:17; 1102:2; 3716:4; yearnings of ~, 3747:3

dress *see also* clothing; fashion, fit of ~, 1850:2; stunning ~, 3405:1; unadmired ~, 1144:2

drinking *see also* bars and pubs; drunkard; liquor, 1526:1; 1780:17; 1862:1; 3364:3; 4226:1; 4587:1; 4591:1, 2; ~ beer, 1871:8; ~ champagne, 1462:1; ~ cocktails, 1825:1; 4226:3; ~ habits, 1686:3; ill effects of ~, 1146:3; ~ martini, 1780:17; 4048:3; social ~, 2313:1; succumbing to ~, 2066:8; ~ whiskey, 3547:7; ~ wine, 250:1; 405:3; 790:6; 1146:4; 4677:4

driver/driving, 3147:5; 3612:3; ~ at night, 4963:2; drunk ~, 3671:1; lost ~, 4735:2; victims of drunk ~, 3671:2

drought, 3136:2; 3906:2; casualties of ~, 1654:4; solution for ~, 4266:5

drowning, 424:1

drudgery, 2817:23; freedom from ~, 50:1; ~ of kitchen, 51:1

drug abuse, ~ in America, 4056:2; incarceration for ~, 4987:2, 3;

recovery from ~, 4260:1; teenage ~, 4056:3

drug addict/ion, 2244:7; 2594:1; 2876:3; ~ among Native Americans, 2145:1; fighting ~, 2678:4; treatment for ~, 4987:2; women and ~, 2870:1

drugs *see also specific drugs;* addiction, addictive to ~, 916:6; balm of ~, 692:1; 1188:1; ~ culture, 2088:3; decriminalization of ~, 3634:1; effect of ~, 3302:3; hallucinogenic ~, 1979:17; heroin ~, 4934:2; mescaline ~, 4286:3; psychotropic ~, 3264:1; 3451:4; 3557:3; 4965:1; social ~, 3110:3; speed ~, 3059:3; steroid ~, 4569:1; war on ~, 4987:3; workers on ~, 3585:2

drum/ming, ~ circles, 4688:1

drunkard/drunkenness *see also* alcohol/ism; drinking, 147:1; 289:6; 371:2; 508:2; ~ hangover, 175:5

Du Bois, W. E. B., 2392:2

duality, 1689:3; 2628:2; inner ~, 1629:1; ~ of events, 1211:3; ~ of the sexes, 910:4

duel/ing, 4267:3

dullness, 691:5; 3216:2; longing for ~, 4924:1

Duma (Russian Parliament), 4464:2

Duncan, Isadora, 3921:3

duplicity *see also* deceit/deception; pretense, 334:10; 801:17; 887:25; 2103:3; 2430:1; 2623:2; 3136:1; 3174:1; ~ of life, 2689:4

Duse, Eleonora, 1923:1

dust, 1780:18; 2817:10; 4166:2

duty *see also* obligation; responsibility, 782:9; 855:1; 937:1; 1063:2; doing one's ~, 1469:1; forgetting one's ~, 2288:12; path of ~, 1143:1; performing one's ~, 2332:3; rewards of ~, 913:1

dying *see also* burial; dead, the; death; death sentence; grave, 367:2; 603:9; 1006:11; 2815:2; 3087:2; 3348:4; 3854:2; 4815:1; 4906:2; ~ at home, 2560:4; ~ by violence, 3727:3; choice of ~, 2001:2; 2851:1; deserting the ~, 2329:1; experience of ~, 2948:5; fear of ~ (*see also* death, fear of), 1337:6; prolonged ~, 3883:2; romantic notion of ~, 289:1; ~ slowly, 3416:3; tending the ~, 3416:2; ways of ~, 3302:5; words of the ~, 61:2

dyslexia, 3376:3

E

Earhart, Amelia, 1937:1; 4359:1

earliness, 257:1

earning *see* livelihood; wage, ~ a living, 3873:2; ~ of women, 4979:1

Earp, Wyatt, 1266:2

Earth *see also* planet; world, 1788:1; 2668:22; 2997:7; 3105:1;

3753:2; abundance of ~, 1723:2; ~ as mother, 2183:4; caring for ~, 3075:3; 3081:4; 3227:2; 3243:2; 3384:5; 3418:3; 3762:3; 4174:14; 4338:1; 4573:2; connectedness to ~, 2199:4; 3571:1; 3993:1; 4045:2; damage to ~, 3420:1; 4585:2; 4790:1; desecration of ~ (*see also* environment, destruction of ~), 642:13; 710:1; 2993:5; 3719:3; enduring ~, 412:3; 4854:3; ~ from space, 4063:1; future of ~, 2574:2; interaction with ~, 3518:2; living organism of ~, 3311:6; love of ~, 1355:1; preservation of ~, 2113:1; 3403:1; protecting ~, 179:6; 4274:1; 4936:2; stewardship of ~, 2362:2; 3163:2; 3548:3; 3652:4; 3762:2; 3835:2; story of ~, 2061:6; 4475:4; survival of ~, 2623:8; 3761:1; troubled ~, 2442:5; unfriendly ~, 317:1; use of ~ resources, 2349:26

Earth Day, 2749:0

easiness, 451:6; 585:7

Easter, 1021:3

eating *see also specific meals;* digestion; dining; food, 1834:3; 3468:1; 3518:2; 3964:4; 3990:7; communion of ~ together, 2085:6; ~ disorder, 3685:4; 4875:2; ~ habits, 531:1; 1874:7; 4707:2; ~ habits of youth, 3137:7; man ~, 3995:7; ~ outdoors, 3113:4; over- ~ (*see also* diet/er), 807:11; ~ rats, 2072:2

eBay *see also* Internet, 4395:1, 2, 3

eccentric/ity, 2803:1

ecofeminism *see also* biodiversity; ecology; ecosystem; environment, 3081:5; 3559:2; 4529:1, 2

ecology *see also* conservation [environment]; ecosystem; environment; pollution, 1112:2; 1916:4; community ~, 4552:1; frailty of ~, 4329:4; ignorance of ~, 4398:2; management of ~, 3129:1; principles of ~, 3613:1; unbalanced ~, 1935:14; world ~, 2669:5

economics/economy (system) *see also* finance; inflation, 911:3; 1943:2; 4100:3; ~ and the poor, 2856:3; ~ as cause of exploitation, 2996:4; backbone of American ~, 2341:3; benefits of ~, 4345:3; city ~, 2271:6; cooperative ~, 1666:5; corporate ~, 4585:3; crisis in ~, 3600:2; 4771:6; depressed ~, 801:8; 1584:2; domestic ~, 1275:2; false ~, 585:8; ~ forecasting, 2207:5; global ~, 3324:1; 3652:3; 4761.1:2; 4843:2; growth of ~, 2036:13; 2227:3; 2832:2; 4041:3; improving ~, 4190:6; ~

in relation to art, 1408:14; ~ in the Bible, 3153:1; ~ loophole, 2127:4; market-based approach to ~, 4966:2; materials ~, 4585:2; national ~, 3676:2; ~ of plenty, 2207:3; ~ of scarcity, 2994:3; ~ of world trade, 1471:7; ~ stability, 4322:2; ~ stimulus, 4247:6; sustainable ~, 4468:4; theory of ~, 4288:2; United States ~, 2853:4; 4668:2; unstable ~, 672:4; 1618:6; vital interests of ~, 2116:11; women and ~, 3020:1

ecosystem *see also* ecofeminism; ecology; environment, destruction of ~, 4065:1; mangrove ~, 3605:3, 4; marine ~, 3768:4; ~ of forest, 2926:3; restoring wetlands, 3606:1, 2; understanding ~, 3808:2; 4178:1

ecstasy, physical ~, 3827:4

Ecuador, exploitation in ~, 3980:6

Eden, Garden of *see also* heaven; paradise; utopia, 1313:4; 1977:5

Edinburgh, England, 4725:2

editor, 4161:4; book review ~, 3689:2; crusading ~, 2228:3; woman ~, 1572:1

education *see also* college; instruction; school; study, 543:2; 642:; 981:3; 1286:2; 1381:12; 1519:4; 1694:1; 2160:5; 2331:6; 3520:3; 4042:1; American ~ (*see also* United States, education in ~), 2547:3; ~ and gender, 4007:6; ~ and speech, 1381:6; ~ and technology, 3091:3; arts in ~, 2923:1, 2; 3744:4; ~ at birth, 1381:11; bureaucracy in ~, 2013:1; children and ~, 1606:1; 1715:13; 2405:5; 2424:2; 2916:6; competition in ~, 4652:1; concept of ~, 1381:14; cost of ~, 839:3; curriculum in ~, 4316:1; early ~, 886:1; 2805:2; effect of ~ on morals, 604:11; financial assistance for ~, 951:4; focus of ~, 3782:4; ~ for black children, 2972:3; ~ for women, 558:1; gender and ~, 4179:1; global public ~, 2756:23; goals of ~, 2675:3; 3102:2; 3544:2; good ~, 975:1; government influence of ~, 1493:2; heart of ~, 4652:4; higher ~, 3545:1; holistic ~, 1863:6; impact of early ~, 3229:1; importance of ~, 4430:3; ~ in relation to society, 3390:2; institutes of ~, 2837:2; lack of ~, 823:2; 1431:3; liberal ~, 1419:1; 2771:7; 3755:3; liberal arts ~, 2237:5; lifelong ~, 3061:2; 3168:2; methods of ~, 1070:1; models of ~, 3614:2; money and ~, 2794:4; narrow ~, 1117:2; Nature and ~, 1381:5; ~ of a nation, 3544:1; ~ of environment, 4281:2; ~ of girls, 2725:3; parent ~, 3829:3; partnership ~, 2756:24; physical ~, 2789:1; pleasure of ~, 1336:11; practical ~, 662:1; principles of ~, 3900:1; problems of ~, 2675:6; progressive ~, 1587:1; public ~, 1167:6; 1668:3; purpose of ~, 701:11; 769:1; 1206:2; 3584:1; 4154:3; reforming system of ~, 4208:1; religious ~, 512:1; 516:2; rural ~, 1009:1; self- ~, 1028:2; sex ~ (see sex, ~ education); sexism in ~, 166:1; 244:2; 669:2; 2675:1; 3154:2; 4388:1, 2; timing of ~, 2267:5; tools of ~, 3614:1; university ~, 1105:2; women and ~ (see also woman/women, educated ~), 316:7; 369:2; 412:4; 507:1; 807:4; 827:3; 851:1; 874:3; 1078:1; 1189:3; 2545:1; 2675:2

educator see also professor; teacher, 4902:5

Edward VI of England, 329:1

efficiency, 1789:5; 2408:1; 4743:2; ~ of people, 2724:1

effort see also diligence; endeavor, 2349:5; best ~, 2001:1

egalitarianism see also equality; gylany, 1666:3; 4290:4; men and ~, 2916:2

ego/ism see also identity; self-image, 4703:4; 487:8; 1160:2; building one's ~, 2027:4; competitive ~, 1282:2; feeding ~, 2086:2; lack of ~, 4859:2

egocentricity/egotism see also conceit/edness; self-centeredness; self-interest; selfishness, 408:1; 451:7; 501:3; 858:1; 863:2; 887:25; 911:8; 955:16; 1044:11; 1669:18; 1686:6; 1739:1; 1758:4; 2463:3

Egypt, 974:7; polygamy in ~, 874:14; schooling girls in ~, 3761:2

Eichmann, Adolf, 2036:10; 2884:4

Eiffel Tower (Paris), 1034:4

Eisenhower, Dwight D., 1618:31; ~ and civil rights, 2163:3

elderly/elders see also old age, 1961:2; 2687:3; 3845:2; 4902:8; care for ~, 2844:4; 3341:1; 4453:2; compassion for ~, 2918:1; dangers of ~ care, 2726:2; death of ~, 642:6; 2882:1; 3705:2; image of ~, 3018:2; ~ in America, 2380:8; ~ in public service, 2025:3; ~ in relation to adult children, 2666:2; 3176; ~ in relation to youth, 2368:3; ~ in small towns, 4124:1; intimacy between ~, 4925:2; joy of ~, 2967:2; neighborhoods of ~, 2871:1; pets and ~, 4453:3; respect for ~, 2724:4; responsibility for ~, 3393:1; ro-

mance between ~, 2825:2; secret of ~, 2349:20

Elders, Joycelyn, 3304:1

election see also vote/r, 4189:1; 4498:2; money and ~, 3365:4; political ~, 1618:13; 2742:1; U.S. Supreme Court and ~, 3297:1; women and ~, 4442:4

electricity, 2483:2

elegance, 701:4; 1984:1; 4516:5; 4769:3; ~ in men, 3310:2

Eliot, George, 1019:10; 4000:2

elite, ~ women, 1697:3

elitism see also clique; snob, 1471:5; 1673:11; 1776:1; 2857:3; 3325:3; weapons of ~, 2764:1

Elizabeth I of England, 334:1, 13; 456:2; 457–458:1, 2; 3102:3

Elizabeth, queen of Bohemia, 948:1

Ellis, Sir William and Lady, 822:2

eloquence see also speech, articulate ~, influence of ~, 1149:1

elusiveness, 1317:2; 2185:5

e-mail see also Internet, 3164:3; invitation by ~, 4814:2; ~ love affair, 4341:3

emancipation see also liberation, 50:1; 913:3; 1210:1; ~ for all, 958:2; ~ of women (see also suffrage/suffragist, women's ~), 906:1; 925:2; 1167:2; 2974:2; 3762:1

Emancipation Proclamation (U.S.), 1453:2

embarrassment, 2151:3

embitterment, 2187:11; 2817:2

embrace see also affection, loving ~, 249:1

embryo (human) see also fetus; unborn, legal status of ~, 4156:3

emergency, treating ~, 4731:2

emigrant/emigration see also immigrant/immigration; refugee, 1563:1; 2380:2; haven for ~, 1168:4; Irish ~, 900:2; ~ to America, 3950:1; tribulations of ~, 3203:3

emissions, controlling toxic ~, 4338:2, 3

emotion see also feelings; passion, 1333:2; 2947:1; 3196:3; 3212:3; 3687:2; 3933–3934:4; base ~, 3272:1; control of ~, 3797:5; expression of ~, 1559:2; 1870:12; 2220:5; 4563:3; negative ~, 2819:2; positive ~, 3933–3934:3; range of ~, 1780:15

emotionalism, 1982:5

empathy see also identification, 585:3; 903:1; hyper- ~, 3727:4

Empire State Building (New York), 3133:5

employee see also labor/er; worker, 2294:2; ~ benefits (see workforce, benefits for ~); ~ devoted, 1586:2

employer, ~ attitude toward women, 3078:4; fair ~, 1819:1; ~ hiring

practices, 4536:2; ~ in relation to employee, 1003:3; 1229:5

employment see also job; livelihood; workforce, ~ for all, 1618:6; sustainable ~, 3324:2; 4446:1

empowerment see also power, 3486:1; ~ of others, 2834:1; ~ of women, 2885:2; 3775:1; 4347:5

emptiness see also void, 1579:4; 2187:13; 2588:1; 2791:1; 3290:1; 4180:2; filling ~, 2534:7

encouragement, benefits of ~, 1354:3

encroachment, 3531:2

encyclopedia, 1419:1

endeavor see also effort, 992:7

ending, 1502:5; 1520:1; 2117:10; 4033:3; 4161:2; happy ~, 2185:2

endocrine, ~ disruption, 2622:6

endowment, 1577:2

endurance see also strength, 193:2; 652:3; 1043:5; 1741:19; 3139:3; 3349:7; limit of ~, 3569:1

enemy, 450:2; 791:3; 2617:1; confronting ~, 809:2; consorting with ~, 2413:2; defining ~, 3729:1; engagement with ~, 3143.1:3; making ~, 684:6; ~ of people, 2689:7; ~ to onself, 3430:3; treatment of ~, 652:2; 772:5

energy (activity) see stamina; vigor; vitality

energy (power) see also fuel, 1431:2; 2812:1; alternative ~, 4266:4; clean ~, 3600:1, 2; creative ~, 1436:4; ~ crisis, 2227:2; form of ~, 3687:1; hydropower ~, 3250.1:5; saving ~, 4552:2; solar ~, 2436:2; wasting ~, 4348:3

enfranchisement see also suffrage/suffragist, ~ of women, 1086:2; 1299:8

engineer/ing, challenges of ~, 3822:1; women ~, 1594:1

England see also English, the; Great Britain, 642:7; 767:1; 1245:2; 1669:20; 1823:1; 2276:1; attitude toward money in ~, 2130:3; culture in ~, 3145:13; economics of ~, 1341:1; fame of ~, 864:2; future of ~, 2537:13; homes of ~, 838:2; ~ in relation to Jews, 473:1; ~ in relation to U.S.A., 709:1; 1301:5; 1778:1; leadership in ~, 754:2; 1823:1; mores in ~, 593:2; security of ~, 1443:5; significance of ~, 1928:3; taxes in ~, 2213:1; treatment of servants in ~, 874:11; treatment of women in ~, 874:1; weather in ~, 3137:2; women writers in ~, 883:4

English (language), speaking ~, 2523:1; 2627:2

English Channel, the, 2045:2

English, the see also British, the; England; Great Britain, 1443:4;

2006:1; 2177:4; 2379:2; ~ army, 4257:3; ~ character, 1411:5; 1717:1; faithful ~-man, 509:4; ~ history, 2130:1; ~ language, 472:11; ~-man, 919:2; refinement of ~, 1956:3; rustic ~, 1009:1; ~ values, 2000:3; well-bred ~, 1782:10; ~ women, 2019:6; 2204:1

enigma, 466:5; 726:1; 1532:4

enjoyment see also pleasure, 1175:1; 1314:3; ~ of life, 4313–4314:1; simple ~, 285:2; suffering from ~, 3402:2

enlightenment see also illumination, 315:3; 798:4; 813:1; 1184:2; 1801:2; 2801:3; spreading ~, 1292:13; sudden ~, 3277:1; values of ~, 2694:3

Enlightenment, Age of, 2708:1

enslavement see slave/ry

entanglement see also complication, 2591:1

enterprise see also business, 868:1; 934:2; 966:2; 2794:2; unfinished ~, 2230:2

entertainer see also performance, 1722:2

entertainment see also amusement; diversion; fun; show-business; theater, 1378:1, 2; 2607:3; ~ at home, 1080:2; night of ~, 3428:4; technology and ~, 4434:2

enthusiasm, 1630:1; 2289:2; 3594:2; restrained ~, 1979:3

entitlement, province of ~, 3997:2

entrepreneur/ship see also business, 3599:4; American ~, 4262:3; black female ~, 1343:3; failings of ~, 2616:2; path of ~, 4742:1

environmentalism/environmentalist see also ecofeminism; ecology; ecosystem; pollution; resources, 3129:3; activist for ~, 3129:3; 4439:2; 4676:1; 4758:1, 2; accountability for ~, 3332:1; beauty of ~, 2180:5; caring for ~, 2747:1; children and ~, 4675:2; ; cleaning up ~, 2098:5; contamination of ~, 4088:4; 4106:4, 5; controlling the ~, 2032:14; destruction of ~ (see also Earth, desecration of ~), 2135:5; 3129:1; 3422:4; 3682:3; 3980:6; ~ disaster see also disaster, 2881:2; ~ education, 4281:2; 4482:1; impact of ~, 4067:7; importance of ~, 4392:1; 4712:1; improving ~, 4536:3; ~ in Europe, 4100:1; influence of ~, 4734:3; ~ in relation to development, 3129:7; 4281:1; ~ in relation to women, 4935:1; institutions and ~, 4303:2; international ~, 3418:3; politics and ~, 3677:1; pollution of ~, 1998:5; preserving ~, 2227:2; protecting

~, 3075:3; 3676:2, 3; 3890:3; 4039:2; 4482:3; 4560:2; 4926:2; public concern for ~, 4200:7; raising awareness of ~, 2749:0; reversing ~ destruction, 4469:1; ~ rights vs. human rights, 4039:3, 4; solutions for ~, 4039:1; 4857:1; special interests vs. ~, 4433:2; standards for ~, 4293:1; ~ sustainability, 4469:2; threats vs. ~, 1935:14; 3892:1; work ~ (see also workplace), 2430:2

envy see also jealousy, 67:1; 152:1; 391:4; creating ~, 2511:2; ~ of splendor, 717:1

EPA (Environmental Protection Agency), ~ and automobile industry, 4619:1; 4712:2; failures of ~, 4433:2; women and ~, 3367:1; 4398:3

ephemera, 2760:1

epiphany see also turning point,, 2105:3

Episcopalian, 2943:8

epitaph, 334:13; 827:1; 1006:12; 1027:8; 1892:1; 2082:5

epithet, sexist ~, 3519:4

equality, 931:8; 1148:2; 1637:3; 2116:15; 2656:6; 2883:1; 2985:4; 4185:5; 4444:1; 4897:3; ~ among the poor, 3285:1; ~ at workplace (see also workplace), 2439:4; battle for ~, 4290:2; ~ for all, 1786:2; 2039:1; 2390:2; 2551:1; ~ for women, 372:2; 889:2; 931:15; 1446:3; 1487:6; 1935:4; 1973:10; 2080:7; 3067:4; 3682:2; 4481:2; gender ~, 2641:1; 3684:1; 3715:4; 4288:1; ~ in relationships, 2828:3; ~ in sexist society, 2635:1; legacy of ~, 2553:3; men and ~, 3583:7; 3595:1; ~ of rights, 3852:5; ~ of the sexes, 405:2; 422:4; 673:1; 890:8; 963:4; 998:1; 1029:1; 1041:1; 1081:1; 1178:0; 1228:1; 1498:1; 2733:2; racial ~, 612:1; 2024:1; sexual ~, 195:1, 2; ~ under law, 656:4

equanimity, 3341:2

equity, economic ~, 1178:3; ~ in law, 1243:1

ERA (Equal Rights Amendment) see also feminism/feminist, 1637:2; 1818:1; 1973:10; 2081:12178:1; 3054:4; 3160:5; effects of ~, 2551:2; 2838:2; 2985:1; failure of ~, 2589:1

Eros, 46:4; 3178:2

erosion, 4088:2

erotica/eroticism, 46:4; 1495:1; 1581:1; 2908:2; 2916:7; 3738:5; 3886:1; ~ in art, 2821:2; ~ in film, 3916:3; sacredness of ~, 3579:3; writing ~, 4441:3

error see also mistake, 315:2; 982:10; excusing ~, 539:5;

human ~, 671:10; 2805:3; making ~, 3777:4; past ~, 1136:3; response to ~, 3412:3; results of ~, 497:6; 1002:2

escape/ escapism, 58:1; 250:1; 487:5; 2812:3; ~ from difficulty, 4816:8; ~ from oneself, 2051:3; 4881:1; ~ in entertainment, 2456:11

Eskimo, 3270:2; ~ child, 3270:1; missionary and ~, 3563:5

ESP (extra sensory perception), 2176:2

espionage see also FBI; KGB; spy, usefulness of ~, 3236:1

esprit de corps see also brotherhood; fellowship; sisterhood, 1786:2; ~ of races, 807:19; 2039:1

essay, 1401:2; 1590:6; 2638:11

essence, loss of ~, 3755:2; ~ of matter, 1693:4

Establishment, the, anti- ~, 2036:17; belong to ~, 4336:2; dropping out of ~, 3230:2

Esther, 882:1

estrangement, 3238:1

eternity see also forever; infinity, 986:1; 1254:9; 1470:3; 2668:25; 4543:2; welcome ~, 3806–3807:1

ethics see also morality; principle, 369:4; 2979:4; business ~, 1289–1290:1; 2393:8; changing ~, 2628:4; devoid of ~, 4332:3; grasp of ~, 3778:3; ~ in government, 4100:1; ~ in media, 2393:8; maintaining ~, 4282:1; ~ of legal practice, 4137:1; principles of ~, 2979:2

ethnicity see also race [genetic], 3424:2; 4605:2; interracial ~, 4532:1; sensitivity of one's ~, 1655:10

etiquette see manners, importance of ~, 3097:3

eugenics, 1535:10

eulogy, 3996:3

euphemism, 2763:3; 4444:5

Euripedes, 892:4

Europe/an see also specific nations and major cities, 759:1; 3092:; 4261:2, 4; ~ character, 880:1; cooperation within ~, 4230:2; diversity of ~, 3061:3; ~ economics, 4100:2; ~ in relation to U.S.A., 1778:1; 2002–2003:3; 2011:1; 2656:4; materialism of ~, 2925:2; post-war ~, 1957:6; schools in ~, 3584:6; ~ women, 850:1; women in ~ Eastern, 3662:1

European Union, 4261:1; farm policies of ~, 4258:1

euthanasia see also suicide, assisted ~, 1254:15; 1741:21; 2612:6; legalizing ~, 4984:2

evaluation, ~ of men and women, 4299:1

Evangelical/ism, 4629:5

evasion/evasiveness, 1025:12; polite ~, 676:4

Eve see also Adam & Eve, 379:1; 850:3; 860:7; 1313:4; 2777:1

eve/ning see also night; sunset; twilight, 1663:1; 2153:10

event/fulness, 2464:8; exhaustive ~, 2715:5; personal ~, 2514:3; special ~, 3990:2; ~ unfolding, 1723:3

Everglades (Florida), 3632:1; ~ and tourism, 3632:2

Evers, Medgar, 2847:1

evidence, 3165:5; 3902:3; lack of ~, 334:1

evil see also bad/ness; evildoing; good and evil; wickedness, 231:2; 234:5; 451:3; 845:8; 1233:8; 1347:4; 2036:9; 3298:2; 3547:3; avoiding ~, 289:8; choosing ~, 1790:4; exorcising ~, 2816:3; explore ~, 2101:1; fighting vs. ~, 1677:3; 4711:5; great ~, 858:1; imaginary ~, 1025:14; ~ in relation to religion, 4321:5; lamenting ~, 4517:2; protection from ~, 52:1; responsibility for ~, 4321:3; suppress ~, 677:1; tools of ~, 2776:4 evolution, 2383:3; 2638:3; 2892:2; 4791:4; adherents of ~, 2496:5; conscious ~, 2664:4; 3827:2; culmination of ~, 2664:3; lessons of ~, 998:6; meaningful ~, 2756:25; ~ of humans (see also people, dichotomy of ~), 1940:3; 2756:2; 2892:3; ~ vs. creationism, 4684:5

exaggeration, 451:1; 1570:4; ~ in America, 1095:3

examination see also test, 3158:1; passing ~, 3289:1

excellence see also merit, 122:1; 485:1; 507:5; 2189:2; 2540:2; achieving ~, 2042:2; desire for ~, 775:1; seeking ~, 1513:1

exception, 1515:3

exceptional, desire to be ~, 3419:2; ~ person, 3346:5

excess, 4185:5; fault of ~, 2189:9

excitement, 2117:2; 2196:1

excrement, 4902:4

excuse see also rational/ization, 1753:1; 3349:12; 3377:4; making ~, 2135:2; war as an ~, 1677:1; weak ~, 241:1

execution see also capital punishment; death; lynching, ~ by decapitation, 300:4; 1754:3; facing ~, 300:1; 678:2; 682:2; 801:15; last words at ~, 324:1; mass ~, 333:1

executive see also businessperson, black ~, 4742:3; woman ~, 2823:

exemplar see also role model, 2761:3; poor ~, 1347:7

exercise (physical) see also fitness; gym, 642:9; 821:2; 1733:2; 3257:2; 4259:1; ~ adherents,

3612:5; running as ~, 4153:2; walking as ~, 4445:3

exhaustion see also fatigue; tiredness; weariness, 248:1

exigency, demands of ~, 770:7

exile, 972:3; 1168:6; 2281:11; 3340:2; 3901:2; 4627:3; living in ~, 3941:1; political ~, 2807:4; story of ~, 4057:2; welcoming ~, 1168:5

existence see also life; living, 2817:16; 3340:1; 3555:2; 4906:3; purpose of ~, 2273:3; reason for ~, 1869:1; wonder of ~, 2059:6

existentialism, 2620:9; 2797:1

exodus, 1977:2; ~ from Egypt, 16:1

expansiveness, 1406:

expatriot, 4478:2

expectation see also anticipation, 355:3; 1160:1; 1166:9; 1521:1; 2684:5; 3897:4; disappointed ~, 694:1; false ~, 1442:1; moment of ~, 760:1; no ~, 1902:1; unmet ~, 1914:12

expediency, 2237:2; 4713:1

experience see also practice, 264:3; 1262:10; 1435:13; 1474:4; bowing to ~, 301:2; diverse ~, 3888:2; first-hand ~, 1262:3; gaining ~, 1384:1; importance of ~, 4953:2; inner ~, 2240:2; ~ is best teacher, 1528:1; lack of ~, 1502:6; lessons of ~, 823:2; meaningful ~, 3262:2; new ~, 1025:8; repetition of ~, 2349:10; sexual ~, 4777:2; unbearable ~, 2819:3; understanding ~, 3693:1; youthful ~, 4691:1

experiment, 3291:4; youthful ~, 4691:1

expert/ise see also proficiency, 1093:2; 3418:1

explanation, easy ~, 1631:3; lack of ~, 3353:3; scientific ~, 2487:3

exploitation, 1548:7; 2291:6; 2689:6; ~ by government, 1030:6; ~ by ruling class, 3173:2; capitalism and ~, 3020:3; ~ in the arts, 2424:3; ~ of individual, 1870:6; 3772:2; ~ of masses, 1030:3; ~ of slaves, 916:9; ~ of weak, 540:3; ~ of women (see also woman/women, exploitation of ~), 3565:2; 3870:2

exploration see also search, 670:1; 3497:3; 3620:2; marine ~, 2926:4; ~ of Northwest (U.S.A.), 1392:2

explorer, 2837:1

exposure, 269:1; public ~, 3353:2; ~ to life, 1663:7

expression, ~ of emotions, 4563:3

extinction, ~ of bird life, 2061:11; ~ of human species, 783:1; saving species from ~, 2669:4; threat of ~, 2881:2

extortion see also blackmail, 4877:1

extravagance, 1201:6; 1655:9; 1825:4

extroversion/extrovert, 316:3; 1697:8; 4703:4

eye witness, 511:1

eyeglasses, 1780:3

eyes *see also* sight (human), 382:1; 2642:10; 3099:13; 3630:1; 4804:1; aging ~, 3113:2; loving ~, 1719:2; lying ~, 1714:1; use of ~, 2089:3

F

face (human) *see also* eyes, 533:6; 1623:2; 2476:3; 3064:2; aging ~, 2817:6; angelic expression on ~, 176:2; beautiful ~, 1060:2; examination of ~, 1451:2; expression of ~, 1230:1; 3321:4; features of ~, 773:1; lips, 144:1; 1209:4; mouth, 382:2; nose, 681:1; 1722:1; ~ of loved one, 790:2, 13; ~ of younger self, 1501:1; perfect ~, 4362:2; revealing ~, 3619:2; unlined ~, 2799:1; washing one's ~, 4246:2; ~ wrinkles, 4598.1:1

Facebook *see also* Internet, 4040:4

factionalism, 366:2; 2426:2

factory, 821:6; ~ worker, 3585:2; 3713:1

facts, 1236:2; 1392:3; 2638:7; 2949:5; 3451:1; 4484:2; facing ~, 1782:9; 1825:7; gathering ~, 2938:4; 3335:3; ignoring ~, 1959:6; ~ in relation to truth, 2618:10; not facing ~, 1362:3; perception of ~, 2541:1; telling ~, 734:20

fad/dism, 2607:3; 2956:2; 3443:5

failure *see also* defeat; fault; shortcoming, 887:14; 955:23; 1585:1; 1601:6; 1663:16; 1774:1; 2063:3; 2174:3; 3567:3; 4268:6; disappointment of ~, 3735:4; handling ~, 1687:7; impossibility of ~, 963:12; overcoming ~, 2175:1; 2306:3; women and ~, 3162:1; 4139:1

faint (blackout), 157:1

fairness *see also* justice, 3125:2; 3343:1; lack of ~ (*see also* inequity; injustice), 1832:8; 3570:3

fairy, 1250:2; 1263:2; 1492:2; ~ -land, 1088:3

fairytale *see also* story, 1489:2; 3799:1; ~ ending, 2577:6

faith *see also* belief; religion, 313:3; 375:1; 544:6; 899:1; 1006:16; 1024:4; 1336:10; 1356:1; 1654:8; 2464:10, 13; 2534:11, 13; 2830:4; 3638:5; 4888:2; benefit of ~, 1453:5; 1779:1; blind ~, 3647:2; books and ~, 3992:6; comfort of ~, 856:1; developing ~, 2950:3; devout religious ~, 887:13; forsaking ~, 1619:2; ~ in humankind, 193:9; 653:2;

1741:7; ~ in nature, 2529:6; ~ in oneself, 1025:3; 2464:6; 2902:1; 4746:1; 4910:1; loss of ~, 858:2; 1921:1; 2715:4; maintaining ~, 2142:3; roots of ~, 791:1; ~ tried, 291:2; vulnerability of ~, 4795:1; world of ~, 2199:1

faithfulness *see also* fidelity, sexual ~; loyalty, ~ to god, 90:1

faithlessness *see also* adultery; inconstancy, infidelity, 154:2; 166:16

Fall (biblical), 2383:2; 2534:2

falling, 2978:2

falseness *see also* deceit/deception; duplicity; lie/lying; pretense; tears, crocodile ~, 584:3; 1955:3; 2996:2

fame/famous, the *see also* celebrity; public life; stardom, 496:3, 4; 570:1; 713:1; 985:1; 1089:5; 1122:3; 1213:5; 1274:2; 1593:10; 1595:1; 2021:17; 3444:3; 4914:1; bearing ~, 2656:2; born to ~, 1230:7; desire for ~, 1973:13, 16; ephemerality of ~, 299:2; 2110:4; 4681:1; fraud of ~, 3002:1; immortal ~, 623:1; loneliness of ~, 1674:2; overnight ~, 2754:1; pitfalls of ~, 2931:2; 4813:4; price of ~, 684:3; 4809:1; pursuit of ~, 734:12; rejection of ~, 2935:2; responsibilities of ~, 1945:2; sex and ~, 4696:1; value of ~, 827:9

familiarity, 367:5; 2009:2; 2252:1; deadliness of ~, 4449:3; desire for ~, 3001:2; disadvantages of ~, 916:18; odd ~, 4852:3

family *see also specific family members*, 1404:1; 2514:4; 2613:4; 2908:1; 3054:2; 3885:1; 4251:2; 4312:5, 11; American ~, 2899:3; ~ and independence, 3746:5; ~ authority, 953:8; ~ balanced with work, 3701:1; breakdown of traditional ~, 3490:3; breaking ~ ties, 4193:5; changing ~, 2586:3; 3124:1; 3295:2; 3746:4; commitment to ~, 2626:2; ~ communication, 2079:8; decline of ~, 3140:3; 3261:5; 3365:5; definition of ~, 2916:9; 3752:5; demise of ~, 219–220:1; 3101:1; difficulties of ~ life, 767:17; 801:13; 916:14; discussing ~ members, 1743:1; divine ~, 622:1; 2756:21; divisiveness in ~, 2426:2; dual income ~, 1255:1; 2844:2; ~ duty, 998:7; dysfunctional ~, 4310:1; happy ~, 2349:6; holy ~, 2133:4; ideal of ~, 1570:5; importance of ~, 4766:2; ~ in relation to government policy, 3053:3; ~ in relation to society, 3746:3; insensitivity of ~ members, 1027:2; insulting ~, 1628:1; ~ interaction, 3782:1; interracial ~,

3436:4; ~ jokes, 1740:2; large ~, 887:10; 2762:2; 2827:2; 3226:1; 4788:2; lessons of ~ life, 1254:7; 2494:2; 2903:7; ~ life, 981:5; ~ love, 1700:5; 2184:2; 3145:11; ~ meal (*see* meal, family ~); money and ~, 1288:2; ~ myth, 4744:3; nuclear ~, 2771:15; openness in ~, 3939:1; oversize ~, 2668:20; patriarchal ~, 3342:1; ~ pattern, 3129:6; ~ planning (*see also* birth control), 1535:11; 2678:2; 3333:1; 3731:8; 3982:4; 4242:4; 4466:1; 4477:1; ~ resemblance, 2680:15; responsibility to ~, 1741:24; 4370–4371:2; role of ~ members, 1953–1954:2; 2819:2; separation of ~, 3963:2; size of ~, 1535:1; 2681:2; ~ story, 2713:1; 3442:2; strength of ~, 2936:5; successful ~, 3490:2; supportive ~, 4648:8; traditional ~, 3813:1; traditional ~ myths, 3813:3; unity of ~, 1254:6; ~ values, 3490:1; women in ~, 1229:8

fan (device), 88:4

fanatic/ism, 2354:3

fantasy *see also* dream, 1275:1; 2352:15; 2568:3; 2668:14; 2893:2; ~ come true, 4892:1; ~ creatures, 1916:6; living out ~, 1094:1; 1464:1

farm worker *see also* migrant worker, ~ union, 2716:4

farm/er, 6:1; 593:7; 941:1; 1233:6; 1435:2; 2107:2; 4105:1; 4141:11; 4653:5; American ~, 2341:3; dairy ~, 2156:1; daughter of ~, 3209:2; family ~, 4345:1; French ~, 2914:1; Kansas ~, 1178:1; ~ land, 2942:3; misery of ~, 1654:4; ~ planting beans, 1751:16; ~ regulations, 4258:3; small ~, 4258:1; wisdom of ~, 3472:2; woman ~, 1414:1; 4303:1; women ~, 1131:1; Yankee ~, 807:3

farming *see also* crop; soil, dangers of monoculture ~, 4141:2; effect of ~ on soil, 1916:4; revolution in ~, 1849:2; uncertainty of ~, 1832:3

farsightedness, ~ of nation, 910:11

fascism *see also* Nazi, 1813:3; fight against ~, 2161:1; women and ~, 2699:1

fashion *see also* clothing, 782:8; 957:1; 1018:2; 1019:4; 1593:1, 2, 6; 1834:1; 1900:1; 1963:3; 1969:1, 3; 2265:3; 2368:1, 4; 2655:1; 3642:2; 1990s ~, 4954:3; American ~, 4817:1; ~ and consumerism, 4585:6; caprices of ~, 642:10; dressy ~, 3910:2; Eastern ~, 3836:1; ~ for big women, 4337:1; fur ~, 2825:3; ~ in hats, 2197:1; 3097:9; 4324:3; ~ industry, 2511:2; men and ~,

1969:5, 6; 4390:5; ~ of African Americans, 2618:16; ~ of different peoples, 1316:1; 2409:1; ~ of Muslim women, 4776:1; passing ~, 671:14; power of ~, 1044:10; styles in ~, 1969:4; 4668:4; women and ~, 1346:1; 2910:2; 3422:3; 4226:2

fashionableness, 4928:2

fastidiousness, 1669:1; 2629:5

fat/ness *see also* obesity; plumpness, weight, ~ control, 3685:1, 2; 3750:1; 3841:1; 4739:2; 4870:1; ~ woman, 3724–3725:1

fatalism, 56:1; 888:1; 1470:9; 2560:8

fate *see also* chance; destiny; fortune [chance]; luck, 300:5; 520:1; 523:3; 943:2; 1616:2; 1977:1; 2411:4; 3330:4; 4845–4846:2; 4929:5; conquering ~, 1101:1; foretelling ~, 711:3; ironies of ~, 1445:3; 1615:3; scorning ~, 1349:2; shared ~, 300:6

father/hood *see also* parent/hood, 870:3; 1702:1; 2034:2; 2659:3; 4023:4; 4027:5; 4480:1; 4507:2; 4533:1; 4884:3; absent ~, 4579:1; 4735:5; changing role of ~, 3089:2; controlling ~, 2405:2; death of ~, 869:10; 1261:6; dependence upon ~, 1590:21; dying ~, 2815:2; good ~, 1905:5; homecoming of ~, 1039:2; ~ in relation to child, 1602:2; 3812:3; 3921:2; 4140:1; ~ in relation to daughter(*see also* daughter, ~ in relation to father), 1049:2; 1693:15; 2027:6; ~ in relation to newborn, 3089:3; ~ in relation to son (*see also* son, ~ in relation to father), 2943:7; 3897:5; 4421:2; 4481:5; influence of ~, 2972:2; lack of ~, 3898:1; 4510:3; loving ~, 2184:2; obligation to ~, 45:1; overbearing ~, 2753:1; role of ~, 2916:16; sexual relations with ~, 10:1; symbolic ~, 404:1; touch of ~, 4493:0; unwed ~, 2245:2, 3; visit from ~, 3895:2

fatherlessness *see also* mother/hood, single ~, orphan, 2245:2

fault *see also* shortcoming, 4385:1; accepting one's ~, 802:2; finding ~, 428:3; 501:3; 701:14; 793:2; overcoming ~, 308:5

favor, 387:2; deferred ~, 934:1; political ~, 603:1; receiving ~, 367:3

favoritism, 343:1; 2128:1; 3860:1

FBI (Federal Bureau of Investigation), 2544:5

FDIC (Federal Deposit Insurance Corp.), 4229:1

fear *see also* dread; fright; panic; paranoia, 260:2; 276:2; 426:1; 1173:2; 1247:3; 1621:1; 1682:4; 2118:2; 2669:2; 3099:20; 3590:3; 3878:2; 4045:7; 4133:3;

4711:7; attraction of ~, 4094:2; basis for ~, 1579:2; cast away ~, 1268:3; conquering ~, 3554:5; consequences of ~, 2832:4; constant ~, 3744:1; denial of ~, 4816:2; disguising ~, 857:3; facing ~, 1618:16; 4151:3; 4396:2; freedom from ~, 4777:3; influence of ~, 734:9; lack of ~, 977:3; lessons of ~, 3003:2; 3124:3; living in ~, 1990:1; ~ of difference, 2903:2; ~ of eternal punishment, 1935:12; ~ of future, 2648:6; ~ of life, 1120:6; ~ of minority, 3394:3; ~ of self, 3797:6; rid of ~, 3763:2; unfounded ~, 706:4

feast see also celebration, continual ~, 283:2

feat, see also deed, great ~, 3203:4

fecundity, 123:1; 3039:4

Federal Reserve, U.S., 4468:3

feeding see also nutrition/ist, forced ~, 1235:5

feeling see also emotion; heart; love; passion; sensibility; sentiment, 934:6; 1817:1; 3895:1; 4653:2 ~ affected by others, 3811:3; ambivalent ~, 474:3; deadened ~, 852:6; 3897:1; deep ~, 1669:2; excited ~, 604:1; expressing ~, 576:1; 688:3; 801:14; 3539:1; family ~, 1033:2; inexpressible ~, 845:7; injured ~, 395:1; lack of ~ (see also impassivity), 64:1; 206:3; 2438:2; 2488:1; masking ~, 724:1; maternal ~, 1994:2; mixed ~, 2415:3; ~ of well-being, 3368:1; suppressed ~, 931:22; 1780:6

fellowship see also brotherhood; esprit de corps; sisterhood, place for ~, 320:1

female see woman/women

feminine/femininity see also woman/women; womanhood; womanliness, 1993:1; 2237:3; 2268:4; 2922:5; 3145:17; ~ experience, 2648:3; image of ~, 2894:1; ~ in America, 2595:3; 4958:0; ~ in relation to masculinity, 910:4; loss of ~, 3148–3149:1; power of ~, 2816:1; ~ principle, 2849:1; traits of ~, 1979:11

feminism/feminist see also ERA; suffrage/suffragist; women's liberation; women's movement, 1623:2; 1686:8; 1759:1; 1782:16; 1867:5; 2432:1; 2628:4; 2916:23; 2990:6; 3050:5; 3457:1; 3483:1; 3646:2; 3834:3; 3874:3; 3927:3; 4232:1; 4305:1; 4403:2; 4426:1; 4524:4; 4700:3; 4704:1, 2; 4733:1; 4974:1; abortion and ~, 3261:1; American ~, 3780:11; anti- ~, 3136:5; approaches to ~, 4635:6; backlash vs. ~, 2607:5; 4635:1;

blacks and ~, 2901:8; 3067:4; 3505:1; 3927:1; changing ~, 4290:4; ~ consciousness; 3005:2; ~ critics, 3300:3; decline of ~, 2864:1; dichotomy of ~, 3219:2; discussions of ~, 2658:4; exclusivity of ~, 4674:1; face of ~, 4758:3; failure of ~, 4171:1; 4452:4; goals of ~, 4007:3; ~ icon, 4152:1; ~ in Eastern Europe, 4830:2; ~ in literature, 3446:2; ~ in relation to men, 1401:3; 4309:1; ~ in relation to motherhood, 2943:6; 4831:2; ~ in relation to multiculturalism, 3684:5; ~ in relation to war, 2516:1; ~ in the 21st century, 3927:2; ~ in U.S.S.R., 3096:1; inner conflicts of ~, 3305:3; leaders of ~, 4007:1; literature of ~, 1487:3; ~ movement, 3184:1; 4221:2; perfect ~, 2995:5; pitfalls of ~, 3406:4; polarizing effect of ~, 4007:2; principles of ~, 3326:2; 3495:1; radical ~, 4885:1; relativity of ~, 4796:2; ~ revolution, 2400:5; 2623:3; 3284:7; roles for ~, 4192:2; roots of ~, 1486:1; salvation of ~, 4300:1; strategy of ~, 3380:1; the new ~, 4790:3; transformed by ~, 4009:5; 4511:1; values of ~, 1535:5; 1578:3; 3326:3; 3350–3351:1

Fermi, Enrico, 2065:1

ferocity, 4684:1

fertility see also conception, 1801:3; management of ~, 3145:9; rate of ~, 2622:4; ~ symbol, 3706:1

festivity see also celebration; party (social), attending ~, 423:6

fetus see also pregnancy/pregnant; unborn, 3780:2; bond with ~, 4873:1; disorder of ~, 4798:2; image of ~, 4037:3

fiancé/e see also boyfriend, 265:1

fickleness see also capriciousness, 459:2; 507:3; 892:5

fiction see also book; literature; novel/ist; prose; writing, 584:4; 770:1; 2638:14; 2668:27; 2875:1; 3175:2; 4320:1; creating ~, 1590:16; fantasy ~, 2668:14; historical ~, 1625:4; revelations of ~, 1959:9; tenets of ~, 423:1; ~ writing, 3409:5

fidelity, sexual ~ (see also faithfulness), 292:1, 2

field (land) see also land, disappearing ~, 4150:5

fight/ing see also argument; combat; quarrel; soldier; war, 2659:7; enduring ~, 3622:1; ~ for a cause, 4528:3; good ~, 1468:1; 3639:2; ~ like a man, 548:1; mental ~, 1590:22; military ~, 3136:3; physical ~, 738:1; 1526:1; political ~, 3556:3

film see also actor, film ~; filmmaker/filmmaking; Hollywood; screenplay, 1705:2; 2021:1; 2347:4; 2411:3; 3691:3; ~ about artists, 2472:6; American ~, 2347:3; antiwar ~, 3068:3; ~ as arbiter of morality, 1623:1; 3068:3; ~ as literature, 4800:2; ~ as opiate of the masses, 3372:4; basics of ~, 4366:1; ~ business, 1820:1; ~ director, 2252:4; 3814:1; documentary ~, 1955:1; 3826:2; ~ -goer, 4872:2; good ~, 2347:2; hackneyed ~ script, 1891:1; Hollywood ~, 1763:2; image of women on ~, 3372:2, 3; imitative ~, 1771:5; ~ industry, 2295:2; 4301:2; influence of ~, 1895:2; ~ love scenes, 1771:6; multifaceted ~, 4950:1; ~ music, 4422:2; nudity in ~, 1790:15; orgasms in ~, 3635:3; ~ producer, 3532:1; propaganda ~, 3068:3; ~ romances, 2825:2; science fiction ~, 2866:5; ~ screening, 3147:7; ~ setting, 2962:3; sex in ~, 2168:2; 3528:2; ~ star, 3696:2; Swedish ~, 2426:5; violence in ~, 2168:2; 2424:3; Western ~, 2911:1; 4242:1; women and ~, 2644:2; 3147:3; 3372:6; women in ~, 2599:3; 2644:1; 2962:2; ~ world, 1655:9; ~ writing, 1655:10

filmmaker/filmmaking see also film, 2506:1; 3372:1; 3532:2; 4422:3; ~ in Africa, 4626:1

finance/financing see also economics/economy; investment; stock market; World Bank, anthropology and ~, 4761.1:1; ~ business, 4742:2; crisis in ~, 4468:3; 4867:4; cyber-~, 4761.1:4, 5; micro-~, 3998:2; stability of ~, 4229:3; ~ support of women, 1466:1; women and ~, 4761.1:3; world of ~, 4867:3

fingers (human), 144:2

Finland, citizenry of ~, 3418:4; woman's suffrage in ~, 1222:1

Finley, Karen, 4478:1

fire, ~ control, 4906:5; wild- ~, 2937:1

First Lady, U.S. see also public figure, 1523:1; 2180:4; 2514:1; 2676:3; 3641:3; 3731:11

fisher/fishing, 266:2; 2942:5; life of ~, 2942:7; livelihood of ~, 731:3; ~ tales, 1179:2

fitness see also exercise, ~ fanatic, 4325:1

Fitzgerald, F. Scott, 1901:5

fixation, ~ on trivia, 4279:2

flag, 2196:4; American ~, 1224:3; 3935:3; national ~, 3925:4

flagellation, 420:2

Flanders/Flemish, 226:1

flattery see also cajoling; compliment, 477:5; 539:2; 649:3; 676:2; 887:24; 894:2; 1645:2, 3; 1675–1676:6, 7; 1900:3; love of ~, 2086:2; ~ toward men, 1590:12; ~ toward women, 1749:1

Fleming, Alexander, 2175:2

flesh, repulsed by ~, 2059:5

flight/flying see also airplane; aviation/aviator; journey, ~ by air, 734:8; 1671:1; 1937:2; 2532:2; 2860:4; adventure of ~, 2053:2; love of ~, 2752:1; ~ solo, 1847:2; transcontinental ~, 3002:3; women ~, 2091:1

flirt/ation, 1532:3; 4929:3; men and ~, 1780:3

flood, 588:3; causes of ~, 4088:2

flora see also flower; plant life, ~ around the house, 3337:1; four-leaf clover, 1287:2; identifying ~, 3851:3; greenery of ~, 593:8

Florence, Italy, 277:1

Florida see also Everglades, 735:1; 3039:3, 4; 3297:1; 4324:1; American Beach, Amelia Island ~, 2921:3; South Beach ~, 3444:2

flower see also flora; rose; seed, 721:1; 790:2; 870:6; 1061:1; 1102:2; 3876:3; ~ arranging, 1940:1; 2277:1; 4333:1; ~ at graveside, 856:2; 1670:1; azalea, 1057:2; ~ bloom, 2171:1; bluebell, 1380:1; ~ bud, 840:3; 1085:2; 3906:5; ~ bulb, 760:5; columbine, 1295:2; cut ~, 2817:5; daffodil, 979:1; 2415:2; daisy, 1673:2; 1714:2; dandelion, 1157:1; 1245:4; 3225:1; dried ~, 1077:1; goldenrod, 1087:1; growing ~, 2464:14; heather, 680:1; ~ in bloom, 2078:4; ~ in city, 2180:5; lily, 760:5; 1110:3; 1663:13; 1673:2; morning glory, 3337:1; painting ~, 1670:9; pansy, 1061:1; 1546:1; poppy, 3441:1; strength of ~, 3099:1; violet, 1327:1; wisteria, 3337:1; withered ~, 574:2; 802:5; 835:1, 2

fog see also dew; mist, 3330:2

folklore see also fairytale, 4168:4

folly see also foolishness; silliness, 408:6; 518:2; 533:3; 955:15; cure for ~, 804:3

food see also dining; eating; fruit; meal; nutrition/ist; sweets; vegetable, 564:1; 1743:6; 2085:5; 3205:1; 4427:1; 4677:5; 4870:3; American ~, 2596:1; 3984:4; ~ and relationships, 3001:4; animal as ~, 3748:1; bad ~, 540:1; benefits of ~, 790:6; ~ chain, 1885:1; chicken soup, 2398:12; children and ~, 2771:1; comfort ~, 1871:1; commerce of ~, 1992:4; ~ consumption, 1112:3; 4676:2; Creole ~, 2618:6; different tastes in ~, 3797:4; down to earth ~, 1663:1; ethnic ~, 2398:12; 2709:4; 4843:4; ~ faddist, 1992:1; fresh ~, 2566:1; frozen ~, 2486:3; 3496:3; garlicky ~, 2208:3; good ~, 3548:1; healing powers of ~, 4854:2; hunting for ~, 1832:6; ~ industry, 4345:1, 3; junk ~, 2098:2; lack of ~, 4330:2; learning about ~, 3548:2, 3; localization of ~, 3682:4; memory of ~, 1852:3; milk, 4258:2; oyster, 1871:7; packaged ~, 4258:4; power of ~, 4212:2; preoccupation with ~, 2258:1; prepared ~, 1324:3; ~ production, 3507:1; 4774:3; sea ~, 1871:7; sharing ~, 2085:3; spicy ~, 3391:6; surplus ~, 2341:2; take-out ~, 4843:4; women and ~, 3685:3

fool, 149:3, 4; 450:3; 533:12; 571:2; 578:3; 805:1; 955:16; 1153:2; 1675–1676:10; 2197:2; 3349:11; 3703:3; act the ~, 3714:4; easy to ~, 3857:1; fear of ~, 2561:6; great ~, 487:10; making ~ of oneself, 2011:4; purpose of ~, 790:3; wise ~, 805:2

foolishness see also folly; frivolity; silliness, 955:10; charms of ~, 911:9

foot, ~ binding, 4092:2; 4579:2; mutilation of ~, 4092:2

football see also sports, 2627:1; 4367:5; 4643:2; ~ player, 3648:2

forbidden see also taboo, 1024:30

force see also might; strength, inner ~, 3099:12; life ~, 2874:7; necessity of ~, 2959:1; primitive ~, 3389:4; take by ~, 1441:6

foreboding, 3306:1

foreign aid, 4895:1

foreign land, 142:2; 2011:1

foreign policy, 4268:1; 4829:3

foreigner, 770:4; 3309:10; anxiety towards ~ (see also xenophobia), 3858:1; female ~, 2190:2; resident ~, 3666:1

foreknowledge see also premonition; prophecy, 512:2

foremother see also ancestor/ancestry, 2653:2; 2728:3; courageous ~, 2457:1

foresight, 671:8; 1684:4; 4834:2

forest see also jungle; woods, 642:11; 1509:2; 4533:1; being in ~, 3851:1; degradation of ~, 827:11; 3991:1, 2; dependent upon ~, 4821:3; life of ~, 2926:3; old growth ~, 837:4; preservation of ~, 2937:1; 3657:5; rain ~, 3657:4; virgin ~, 3704:8

forever see also eternity, 1872:1; 3340:1; trapped ~, 784:2

forgetfulness see also forgotten, 808:12; 3593:3; balm of ~, 838:4; 1032:9; 3032:1; oblivion of ~, 3464:2

forgetting, ~ our history, 2680:26; ~ pain, 1006:7; 2629:4

forgiveness see also mercy; reconciliation, 291:3; 391:3; 513:1; 1001:2; 1287:1; 1959:2; 2224:5; 3731:4; 3929:4; 4728:3; conditional ~, 767:8; divine ~ (see also absolution), 448:1; ~ of lover, 1930:4; ~ of self, 697:3; 2716:1; prompt ~, 166:7; results of ~, 3970:1

forgotten see also forgetfulness, 154:1; 682:4, 6; not ~ (see also unforgettable), 127:1

form, ~ and function, 1833:2; defining ~, 4876:3; ~ revolutionized, 1843:8

fortitude, 236:3; 747:2; weakening ~, 566:1

fortune (chance) see also chance; destiny; fate; luck, 193:4; 282:3; 469:3; 2060:2; 4883:1; bad ~, 459:8; 4163:3; 4872:3; changes of ~, 499:1; 574:1; 734:17; 808:18; fickleness of ~, 1825:6; good ~, 643:2; 4750:1; reverses of ~, 694:1; speciousness of ~, 341:3; ~-telling (see also prediction; prophecy), 3755:3; 4889:1

fortune (money) see also wealth, leaving a ~, 3008:4; receiving a ~, 934:8

forward, looking ~, 1450:29 foundation, strong ~, 1743:5

foundling see also orphan, 1462:2

fragility, 4034:1; 4511:2; ~ of life, 3756:3

France see also Francophile; French, 341:5; 349:1; 1889:1; 3278:2; economics of ~, 4501:3; food and ~, 1221:3; government of ~, 733:19; ~ in relation to Germany, 2741:1; lovemaking in ~, 1928:5; mores in ~, 593:2

franchisement see enfranchisement; suffrage/suffragist; vote/r

Francophile, 804:5

Frankenstein, 2705:3

Franklin, Benjamin, 600:2; 3245:2

frankness see also candor, 466:3

fraternity (social club), 4852:1

fraud, pious ~, 472:14

freak/ishness, 2444:2

free enterprise/market see also capitalism, global ~, 3587:1; 4605:1

free press, democracy and ~, 4200:8; in Czechoslovakia, 4424:1; ~ in U.S.A., 4424:1

free spirit, woman of ~, 643:11

free thinker, women ~, 4300:3

free will, 887:1; 1676:3; 2196:4; control of ~, 253:2

freedom see also liberation; liberty; rights, 375:2; 603:5; 821:8; 878:2; 978:1, 5; 998:12; 1022:2; 1168:2; 1231:2; 1379:5; 1405:6; 1525:6; 1608:7; 1741:6, 9; 1917:5; 1928:3; 2004:2; 2154:5;

2612:2; 2673:5; 2688:1; 3067:5; 3145:15; 3400:2; 3505:3; 3948:3; 4320:2; crossing to ~, 978:2; 1609:1; demand for ~, 3284:2; discovering ~, 2398:3; dream of ~, 2139:2; economic ~, 1776:9; equality and ~, 3674:3; escape to ~, 1622:3; fight for ~, 893:1; 963:12; 1553:2; 1706:3; 4110:2; ~ for all, 3412:1; 4451:0; ~ for men, 2027:3; ~ for women, 1890:1; fragility of ~, 3145:1; illusion of ~, 603:7; justice and ~, 3674:3; lack of ~, 1666:6; lack of ~ for workers, 1706:5; legal ~, 1453:2; love of ~, 677:5; 2259:2; momentary ~, 1687:3; need for ~, 1120:6; ~ of expression, 2295:3; ~ of innocence, 469:2; ~ of press, 621:1; 1618:2; 2654:1; 2963:2; ~ of speech, 2652:2; 3050:4; 3312:1; 3592:2; 4225:0; 4789:5; ~ of thought, 1402:5; 2073:1; political ~, 2537:9; poverty and ~, 3110:2; religious ~, 677:5; sacrifice for ~, 600:1; 1030:4; song of ~, 897:2; struggle for ~, 1235:2; studying ~, 4101:6; suppression of ~, 1379:6; ~ to learn, 273–274:6; ~ vs. tyranny, 2036:11; women's ~, 1535:3; women's ~ denied, 946:4

freeway see also highway, 2925:13

French Polynesia, 2449:1

French Revolution, 3583:3; 3983:5

French, Marilyn, 3888.1:1

French, the see also France, 1443:2; ~ character, 1179:1; clarity of ~, 2219:4; ~ conversation, 1940:5; ~ culture, 2192:15; 3548:1; ~ fashion, 1969:2; ~ law, 2085:4; ~ men, 1611:1; 2039:2; sex and ~, 1686:12; ~ soldier, 1531:2; ~ women, 685:2; 719:1

Freud, Sigmund, 1176:8; 1550:1; 1608:6; 1973:7; 2613:3; 2887:2; 3184:6; 4286:1

friction see also conflict, 1044:15; 1090:3

friendliness, American ~, 3119:9

friend/ship see also companion/ship, 149:1; 450:2; 451:9; 459:10; 496:5; 511:4; 705:4; 808:18; 845:1; 945:5; 1006:15; 1123:1; 1254:20; 1276:1; 1283:3; 1500:2; 1516:1; 1593:3; 1597:2; 1918:1; 2429:2; 2931:6; 4125:5; 4404:6; aging ~, 955:34; animal ~ (see also pet), 955:4; best ~, 955:19; 2584:4; ~ between men and women (see also relationship, ~ between men and women), 1754:1; ~ between women (see also woman/women, ~ in relation to women), 331:1; 801:6; 1385:3; 2874:2; 3122:1; 4031:4; 4840:1; breach in ~, 266:1; 1417:1; celibate ~,

3777:1; childhood ~, 3995:1; choosing ~, 1923:1; criticism of ~, 598:1; dear ~, 365:1; 1149:3; death of ~, 1032:3; demanding ~, 1505:4; dependable ~, 782:12; 3355:4; discomfort with ~, 3044:1; equality of ~, 195:1; faithful ~, 266:1; 472:18; finding ~, 4042:11; girlhood ~, 3494:1; good ~, 3678:2; ~ grown apart, 767:2; 1450:7; importance of ~, 4768:1; indispensable ~, 166:4; joys of ~, 696:1; keeping ~, 513:2; limits of ~, 189:2; loss of ~, 212:1; 693:4; 4206:3; love and ~, 1209:8; loyalty of ~, 2559:3; making ~, 4629:3; men and ~, 4031:3; needing a ~, 2917:3; obligation to ~, 918:1; old ~, 46:3; 1166:8; politeness in ~, 1409:14; quarrel with ~, 955:20; single men and ~, 1408:12; spark of ~, 649:5; supportive ~, 2439:3; 3349:5; 4778:2; treasure ~, 2133:1; treatment of ~, 1201:7; true ~, 1409:12; trusting ~, 2680:9; unreliable ~, 540:1; wealthy ~, 1211:4

fright see also fear, 1906:6

frigidity, 1409:16

frivolity see also foolishness, 412:4

frontier, child of ~, 1565:1; ~ life, 954:3; settling of ~, 2192:11

frost, 810:1

fruit, see also food, apple, 46:9; 1843:1; berry, 1397:1; canning ~, 1066:2; eating ~, 2212:4; ~ in relation to flower, 166:3; overripe ~, 533:17; ripe ~, 209:1; 708:1; taste of ~, 1843:1

fuel see also energy, renewable ~, 4432:2

Fujimori, Alberto Ken'ya, 4380:1

fulfillment see also satisfaction, wish ~, 108:1

fun see also entertainment, 2033:4; 3310:1; 3391:5; ~ person, 3065:3

function, ~ and form, 1833:2

fundamentalism see also reactionary; religion, 4747:2; 4904:4; change and ~, 4117:5; Christian ~, 2990:5; interpretation of ~, 4208:3; religious ~, 2756:12; women and ~, 3086:3

fundraising, 2027:15; 2420:1; 3449:1; ~ appeal, 4731:3

funeral see also burial; death, industry around ~; grave, 734:3; 1872:4; 3033:4; 4163:1; attending ~, 4949:1; ~ director, 2561:3; 3598:4; food at ~, 3338:4; ~ parlor, 2894:1; preparation for ~, 3598:3; ~ wake, 2139:1

fur, fox ~, 1669:12; mink ~, 2368:1; wearing ~, 2825:3

furniture, 1663:5

fury, 2438:4

futility, 1328:1; 2286:1

future *see also* tomorrow, 797:1; 1265:1; 1446:3; 1567:2; 2048:2; 2481:3; 3099:21; 3349:6; anxious about ~, 1832:9; ~ attitude toward past, 887:22; better ~, 2349:16; 3039:6; dedicated to ~, 1933:2; facing ~, 1741:; 2971:1; 3799:1; fearing ~, 2070:1; foretelling ~ (*see also* foreknowledge; prophecy), 711:3; 804:8; 4116:8; ignoring ~, 3136:4; inevitability of ~, 4611:1; influencing ~, 3663:4; living for ~, 1654:7; looking to ~, 1355:5; 4949:2; not caring about ~, 2266:1; personal ~, 887:30; planning for ~, 2778:5; prospects of ~, 1104:2; responsibility to ~, 2893:3; survival in ~, 1915:2; vision of ~, 3212:1; women and ~, 2201:13

G

Gaia, 3311:6
galaxy *see also* universe, 2090:4; movement of ~, 2640:2
Galileo, 3704:4
gambler/gambling *see also* card playing, 1462:6; 2258:2; 3317:6; 4510:1; 4563:1; ~ coin toss, 2726:1
game *see also* play/ing; toy, constructive ~, 3782:2; playing ~, 4631:4; rules of ~, 1257:2; violent ~, 4566:3
Gandhi, Mohandas Karamchand ("Mahatma"), 2979:2; 3166:2; 3658:3, 5; assassination of ~, 2185:12; feminism and ~, 3406:3
garbage, 3866:4; 4975:6; disposal of ~, 4585:1; importance of ~, 3163:2
garden/ing, 1116:1; 1232:1; 1580:4; 1751:16; 1752:6; 1785:3; 1916:1; 2566:1; 3095:1; 3120:1; 3876:1, 2, 4; 4420:2; ~ compost, 3550:1; lessons of ~, 910:11; 3120:3; mother's ~, 3547:10; ~ pest, 3550:1; planting a ~, 2997:7; pleasure of ~, 1359:1; 1797:1; tending ~, 3866:6; vegetable ~, 2349:4; 4648:6; ~ weed, 1399:1
Garland, Judy, 2594:1; 3982:2
garrulous/ness, 3849:4; ~ woman, 3091:2
gasoline, ~ station, 4705:3
gay liberation movement *see* homosexual/ity; lesbian/ism, 2407:5; 3481:5; women in ~, 2936:4
geek, 3565:1
gender *see also* sex roles; sexes, 2569:1, 2; 3313:2; 3823:2; 4003:2; 4076:2; 4077:1; 4618:1; 4726:2; concepts of ~, 3383:4; ~ conditioning, 4032:1, 3; continuum of ~, 1590:8; 1752:12; 3410:2; defining ~, 2954:4; ~ differences, 3511:2; 3586:1,

2; 4531:2; ~ equality, 3852:4; ~ exploitation, 3947:2; ~ gap, 4527:1; ~ identity, 1044:4; 1545:3; 2988:5; 3501:2; 4441:1; ~ in America, 2916:21; ~ in the workplace, 3007:1; ~ independence, 4030:2; prison of ~, 2552:3; roles of ~, 3153:3; 3872:1; technology and ~, 4409:2
generation *see also* decade; posterity, 1960s ~, 2036:18; connection between ~, 2680:26; faults of ~, 1449:3; lost ~, 1450:28; new ~, 864:8; 1911:1
generation gap, 1176:1; 1408:7; 1697:1; 2577:7; 2592:3; 2780:2
generosity *see also* largess, 513:1; 992:4; 2799:5; 3730:3; danger of ~, 2266:6; lack of ~, 1444:5; ~ of spirit, 1604:4; sham of ~, 1073:2; ~ toward children, 1487:4; ~ toward poor, 1260:2
Genesis *see also* Bible, 2660:1; 3445:3; misogyny in ~, 4539:2
genes/genetics *see also* DNA; chromosome, 4156:4; aging and ~, 4311:3; commercialism of ~, 3509:1; engineering of ~, 4235:2; male ~, 2124:2; pregnancy and ~, 4964:2; research of ~, 3701:2
genitalia *see also* penis; vagina, female ~, 981:7; mutilation of ~ (*see also* circumcision), 2445:2; 2916:8; 3322:1; 4292:2; 4920:1, 2
genius *see also* great/ness, 487:8; 642:1; 733:18; 870:12; 892:16; 910:10; 955:31; 1044:9; 1079:1; 1095:3; 1396:2; 1450:18; 2080:13; 2116:13; 2342:2; 2405:9; 4140:2; 4845–4846:1; cultivation of ~, 910:14; identifying ~, 3008:2; offspring of ~, 602:2; philosophy and ~, 1063:3; woman ~, 919:3; 955:32; 1081:2; works of ~, 2189:8
Genoa, Italy, 2226:2
genocide *see also* holocaust, 517:4; 1977:2; 3767:1; 4829:2; ~ and the United States, 4829:1; ~ in Kenya, 4786:2; ~ of African women, 4694:1, 2; ~ of Native Americans, 2624:2; 3301:3; responding to ~, 4687:2, 3
gentility, 1318:1
gentleman *see also* chivalry; man/men, 1704:1; 1759:9; characteristics of ~, 934:4; honor of ~, 1418:5; pseudo- ~, 947:4
gentleness *see also* tenderness, 308:9; 1306:1; 2680:17; ~ in men, 1930:6
geologist/geology, lessons of ~, 1090:2
George III of England, 712:1
George IV of England, 737:1
Georgia (Asia), 4863:2

Georgia (U.S.A.), writer in ~, 2534:10
German/y, 2474:1; 2490:7; American women in ~, 1361:2; ~ in 1910s, 1216:3; Nazi ~, 4060:2; ~ occupation of France, 1745:2; ~ philosophy, 1977:3; ~ under Hitler, 2323:3; ~ writer, 1798:1
gesture, 1409:21
Ghana, development of ~, 3974:2; women in ~, 3316:3
ghetto/ization, 2179:1; 2187:3; 2217:1; black ~, 3260:2; ~ life, 2871:1; 4505:1
ghost, 1032:3; 1433:; 4408:1
Gibson, Althea, 2598:2; 4944:1
gift *see also* present (gift); talent, ~ as sales tool, 2052:1; ~ giving, 1368:2; 1390:1; 2536:1; hand-made ~, 88:4; return ~, 2287:1; symbology of ~, 3261:3
Gillespie, Dizzy, 3368:3
Gingrich, Newt, 3512:7
Ginsberg, Allen, 2872:4; women and ~, 2292–2293:1
girl *see also* daughter, 1650:4; 1690:2; 2694:2; 4613:1; action of ~, 2618:9; aspiration of ~, 1408:17; 4558:1; concerns of ~, 3482:2; conditioning of ~ *see also* woman/women, conditioning of ~), 590:1; 669:2; 855:3; 1345:2; 1442:1; 1844:2; 2331:3; 2366:1; 2725:3; 2997:4; 3495:2; disadvantages of ~, 1127:2; dreams of ~, 2100:2; games for ~, 1712:1; ~ growing up, 2979:5; 3498:1; ~ in relation to mother (*see also* mother/hood, ~ in relation to daughter), 1044:13, 13; limitations on ~, 2775:3; lost ~-hood, 3753:6; physical development of ~, 821:2; 4875:2; prayers of ~, 2190:1; respectable ~, 2021:12; savvy ~, 2027:8; school ~, 951:4; sexual discrimination vs. ~, 2822:1; teenaged ~ (*see also* adolescence/adolescent), 1205:2; 1561:2
Girl Scouts of America, 1257:1, 2
girlfriend *see also* lover, 2115:1
Girls Inc., 4939:2
giving *see also* charity, 367:3; 4333:4; fulfillment of ~, 3889:3; luxury of ~, 955:22
Glacier National Park (Montana), 4372:3
gladness *see also* joy, 401:2; 1359:1
glamour, 1940:2; 4337:3
glasnost *see also* government, open ~, 3059:5
global thinking, 2651:2; 2853:3; 3719:2; 3762:3; 4006:3; 4141:12; 4185:1; 4322:1; 4897:1; pacifism and ~, 1244:8
global warming *see also* climate, ~ change, 3264:3; 4463:1; ~ and developed nations, 4893:2; ~

and oil, 3513:3; consumer goods and ~, 4488:2; humans and ~, 4348:4; reducing ~, 3281:3; 4338:2
globalization *see also* internationalism, benefits of ~, 3805:2; corporate ~, 3719:3; 4141:6; downside of ~, 4760:2; impact of ~, 3805:3; 4702:6; 4760:1; opportunities of ~, 4022:3
gloom, 3139:6; 4563:5
glory, 308:10; 617:1; moving towards ~, 1490:1
goal *see also* purpose; pursuit, 2538:2; 3002:; absence of ~, 2021:2; achieving ~, 1666:1; 2106:1; 3022:1; 3663:3; 3736:1; 3922:4; 4714.1:1; common ~, 3307:3; determined ~, 1192:2; differing ~, 3694:1; discovering ~, 3345:4; high ~, 4470:1; idealistic ~, 801:7; life ~, 1367:1; personal ~, 2970:1; pursuit of ~, 1278:2; 1576:3; 4396:2, 3; ~ setting, 2668:4
God *see also* absolution; Allah; goddess; gods; Holy Ghost; Jesus Christ; Providence; religion; theology, 48:2; 91:1; 179:2; 230:2; 298:1; 304:1; 308:12, 13; 312:4; 365:2; 407:4; 414:1; 518:3; 601:1; 679:1; 769:4; 888:1, 2; 892:17; 905:1; 941:1; 943:1; 982:4; 1013:1; 1039:6; 1146:1; 1252:1; 1283:1; 1416:1; 1478:3; 1751:4; 1782:12; 1938:1; 2027:16; 2189:3; 2193:4; 2318:1; 2381:5; 2623:2, 4; 2668:25; 3041:1; 3316:2; 3440:2; 3547:5; 3704:5; 3727:2; 3849:1; 3899:1; 4151:1; 4241:1; 4294:2; 4312:7; 4792:2; alone with ~, 136:2; ~ as love, 1339:3; ~ as woman, 2425:2; awareness of ~, 4302:1; behavior of ~, 1727:5; belief in ~, 284:1; betrayal by ~, 1896:9; capriciousness of ~, 1687:3; 4639:5; closeness to ~, 28:1; 786:3; comfort of ~, 791:2; 4216:2; communing with ~, 801:7; 2116:6; 2711:9; concept of ~, 2240:1; 3508:2; 3787:2; connectedness to ~, 2768:2; creations of ~, 1446:7; death and ~, 280:2; death of ~, 4084:1; defining ~, 3352:3; demands of ~, 824:1; denial of ~ (*see also* agnosticism; atheism), 4789:2; devotion to ~, 263:1; 305:4; 309:2; diversity of ~, 1796:2; enemies of ~, 27:2; 237:5; escape from ~, 502:1; evilness of ~, 4251:4; existence of ~, 412:6; 430:1; 936:3; 1063:3; 1454:5; 2638:1; 2956:1; faith in ~, 27:2; 1092:1; 1459:1; 2438:3; feminine in ~, 1249:5; finding ~, 4650:7;

forgetting ~, 411:2; forgiveness of ~ (*see also* forgiveness, divine ~), 2021:6; gender of ~, 2425:2; 2916:4; 3005:1; 3506:1; 3547:4, 6; 4368:1; gifts of ~, 158:1, 9; 350:1; 790:7; 955:37; 1441:5; 1480:5; 2116:20; glory of ~, 956:1; 2142:2; goodness of ~, 4321:2; grace of ~, 388:2; gratitude to ~, 360:1; 375:2; 753:1; 1698:1; guidance from ~, 848:1; ~ in man's image, 2744:1; ~ in relation to affluence, 2618:2; ~ in relation to Nature, 1359:2; 1454:4; 1490:3; 1751:3; 3136:2; 3790:3, 4; ~ in relation to oppressed, 84:2; ~ in relation to poor, 2794:2; ~ in relation to sinner, 4020:4; ~ in relation to soul, 1091:1; ~ in relation to world, 440:1; ~ in the wilderness, 2464:3; inheritance of ~, 29:1; involved with ~, 3816:2; kingdom of ~, 622:3; knowledge of ~, 297:2; lessons of ~, 118:2; love of ~, 137:1; 236:1; 245:1; 253:1; 289:4; 305:1; 308:2; 420:1; 887:21; 1461:3; 3243:2; 3281:1; mercy of ~, 2265:2; messenger of ~, 252:3; missionary of ~, 3179:1; money and ~, 4126:6; names for ~, 3790:2; obedience to ~, 4251:5; ~ of vengeance, 1339:3; omnipotence of ~, 30:1; 48:4; 442:1; 1062:5; omnipresence of ~, 2021:15; 3969:1; 4383:2; omniscience of ~, 5:1; 211:2; 312:2; 512:2; opposing ~, 3696:3; perpetuity of ~, 1187:5; personal relationship with ~, 4136:12; pity of ~, 1693:4; plan of ~, 1735:3; playing ~, 4084:7; 4298:1; pleasing ~, 214:1; 466:4; power of ~, 1148:5; 1779:2; praise of ~, 16:1, 1; 179:5; 518:1; praying to ~, 892:1; presence of ~, 105:2; 2070:1; providence of ~, 289:6; 322:1; 354:1; 418:1; punishment by ~, 357:6; 420:2; 2728:1; purpose of ~, 25:1; 4321:4; questioning ~, 1167:7; religious preference of ~, 4116:4; revelation from ~, 215:4; searching for ~, 2078:2; 2642:18; separated from ~, 1907:2; servant of ~, 92:1; service to ~, 1735:4; serving ~, 167:2; 479:2; 628:3; 961:5; 1207:1; 1741:17; solace of ~, 867:2; thanks to ~, 2997:9; ~ the father, 1007:4; troubles of ~, 3720:3; trust in ~, 289:7; 341:4; 346:1; 352:2; 1599:2; 1632:2; understanding ~, 48:1; 221:2; 356:4; 2261:2; united with ~, 110:2; 139:1; 303:2; 326:1; 640:2; 3211:4; voice of ~, 761:1; ~ vs. goddess, 2124:3; war and ~, 1317:6;

will of ~, 219–220:1; 281:2; 290:1; 429:1; 943:2; 1108:1; 1110:3; 1710:4; 2618:2; 4684:4; ~ within, 112:1; 263:2; 365:1; 1758:2; 3179:1; 3207:1; 3865:2; women in relation to ~, 412:5; 432–433:3; 882:1; 2985:2; word of ~, 236:3; 288:2, 4; work of ~, 840:3; 2142:5; worship of ~, 136:1; 533:2

goddess, 4:1; 1680:1; 2124:3; 2778:1, 3; 3852:1; 4072:4; destruction of ~, 2744:3; identify with ~, 4237:5; ~ in woman's image, 2744:1; inspiration of ~, 66:1; 2593:2; ~ Isis, 3:1; return of ~, 2816:2; symbology of ~, 2131:4; ~ within, 3775:1; ~ worship, 3182:2

godlessness *see also* atheism, 4611:2

gods, 63:2; belief in ~, 1741:13; creating ~, 3474:4; destroying ~, 1741:4; indifference of ~, 3580:2; inner ~, 2816:4; of love ~, 3178:2; will of ~, 93:1

Godwin, William, 819:1

gold *see also* money; wealth, 340:2; 511:8; 585:4; 3831:3; hidden ~, 474:5; ~ jewelry, 3985:2; ~ obtained via slavery, 916:9; pirate ~, 1184:3; ~ production, 3890:6; strip mining for ~, 3985:1

golf, 2726:3

good and evil *see also* bad/ness; evil; good/ness; wickedness, 893:6; 2116:9; 3298:1; 4729:1; ~ in Christianity, 3211:1

good will, 367:3; 4312:9

good/ness *see also* good and evil, 167:2; 178:2; 193:1; 379:2; 584:7; 674:3; 717:2; 753:1; 1018:2; 1098:1; 1333:4; 1345:1; 1790:12; 1955:3; 2249:2; 2997:10; 3090:1; 3778:1; acquired ~, 1982:3; 3108:1; admiration for ~, 1570:3; doing ~, 757:2; 790:4; 825:3; 4733:2; hidden ~, 1321:1; immortality of ~, 1825:8; power of ~, 1209:7; quest for ~, 273–274:5; 1557:2; seek out ~, 3591:3; sick of ~, 1160:3; ~ works, 825:1; 3200:2; 3518:3

Gorbachov, Mikhail, 4351:1

Gore, Al, 4235:5; 4573:2

Gospel *see also* Bible; Ten Commandments, 234:7; 629:3; 2738:2; living the ~, 2758:1; ~ of one's life, 2738:2; women in ~, 1007:3

gossip *see also* hearsay; rumor, 166:8; 190:2; 405:1; 955:28; 1006:4; 1409:22; 2027:2; 2469:1; 2526:1; 2685:4, 5; 4000:3; 4653:1; 4759:4; fear of ~, 450:; lewd ~, 477:2; malicious ~ (*see also* slander), 472:4;

1089:3; object of ~, 174:1; women's ~, 517:5

governance, 3567:10; 4189:1

governess *see also* teacher, 626:2

government *see also specific forms*; head of state; leader/ship; nation; policy; rule/r; state, 1360:2, 17; 1435:4; 1504:1; 1537:4; 3512:2; 3717:3; abuses of ~, 3652:2; 4380:1; arguments of ~, 4169:3; ~ as model to children, 3838:1; ~ authority, 2916:12; blaming ~, 1896:5; ~ budget, 3766:2; business and ~, 1849:3; ~ censorship, 525:1; common good and ~, 3731:7; control of ~, 4659:1; cooperation of ~, 4014:4; ~ corruption, 1030:2, 6; 3624:1; 4719:2; covert ~, 4594:4; deceipt of ~, 4540:3; ~ department, 2763:4; education and ~, 2916:6; elitism in ~, 1863:7; 1908:1; 2764:2; faults of ~, 3049:2; fighting ~, 2215:1; 2747:2; 4098:1; 4439:1; game of ~, 3111:1; ~ growth, 2227:3; hypocrisy in ~, 1981:3; improving ~, 4186:2; ~ in relation to art/ist, 1705:3; 2073:1; ~ in relation to citizens, 1251:2; 3378:3; 4022:1, 2; 4091:3; 4345:2; ~ in relation to environment, 3129:3; 4398:2; ~ in relation to property, 1235:6; ~ in relation to status quo, 2271:5; ~ institutions, 3682:3; 4118:2; ~ interests, 3049:3; ~ interference, 1756:1; lack of faith in ~, 4247:5; lawless ~, 4620:1, 3; ~ leaders, 2823:3; militant ~, 4160:3; national ~, 2230:3; open ~, 4668:1; oppressive ~, 1666:6; ~ policies, 770:5; ~ promises, 4242:3; representative ~ (*see also* representation), 2409:3; 3774:5; resources of ~, 109:1; responsibility of ~, 2080:4; 2288:1; right-wing ~, 2658:8; secrecy in ~, 2881:1; transitory ~, 2654:3; transparency in ~, 4200:4; U.S. ~, 4174:5; undermining system of ~, 2764:1; unprincipled ~, 1776:8; useless ~, 1636:4; war and ~, 2116:10; welfare ~, 2619:1; women and ~ (*see also* representation), 1360:9; 3877:2; 3978:3; women in ~, 807:9; 963:4; 1251:4; 1618:10; 1844:10; 2027:3; 2360:1, 3; 2537:1; 2811:1; 2848:4; 3162:1; 3227:7; 3869:4; 3877:1; 4066:6; world ~, 1519:1; 1666:5; 2038:2

Grable, Betty, 4013:7

grace, 158:9; 466:2; attaining ~, 4473:3; epitomy of ~, 1044:8; fall from ~, 1441:4; 4411:1; state of ~, 252:5

Graduate, The (film), 2577:6

graffiti, 4686:2

graft *also see* corruption, 1689:11; 3421:3

grammar *also see* language; syntax, 3016:1; adjective, 3044:3; correct ~, 3432:1; noun, 1350:10; verb, 1350:10

Grand Canyon (Arizona), 3890:5

grandchild, 251:3

grandeur, 293:3

grandfather, 1296:1

grandmother, 1601:5; 2584:3; 3977:1; absence of ~, 2990:4; food and ~, 1871:6; influence of ~, 1800:1

grandparent, 870:13; 1776:11; 2577:1

grass, 917:1; 999:5; 1751:3; green ~, 4411:2

Grasse, France, 2914:1

gratification *see also* satisfaction, instant ~, 4364:3

gratitude *see also* appreciation, 373:2; 536:1; 992:4; 1659:7; 1761:8; 2053:1; 2973:2; 4906:6; ~ to parents, 1602:2

gratuity, 2203:2

grave *see also* burial; cemetery; death; dying; funeral, 459:7; 827:8, 9; 999:5; 1734:4; 1751:2; ~ tombstone, 1362:2

Great Britain *see also* British; England; Ireland; Scot/land; Wales, 768:2; 18th century ~, 759:2; colonies of ~, 4786:4; government in ~, 525:1; 2192:4; 3346:1; ~ in Kenya, 4786:3; ~ in relation to Africa, 768:1; 4786:1; ~ in relation to Arabia, 3346:4; ~ in relation to India, 1016:1; ~ in relation to Roman Empire, 86:1; ~ in relation to U.S.A., 600:1; prime minister of ~, 2537:5; victories of ~, 86:1

great/ness *see also* fame, genius, 196:1; 393:1; 955:36; 2406:4; born for ~, 4285:5; characteristics of ~, 887:17; 1301:2; 1975:1; 2032:2; courage of ~, 1764–1765:7; drive for ~, 4295:1; hazards of ~, 701:3; maladies of ~, 4868:3; true ~, 603:8

Greece/Greek, Ancient ~, 4077:3; mind of ~, 1336:1; ~ women, 4240:3; women in ~, 2633:1

greed *see also* avarice, 306:1; 1825:2; 2669:2; 4820:1; excuses for ~, 2794:3

green movement *see also* Kyoto Protocol, 3525:1; big business and ~, 4624:3

Green Party, 3762:2

Greer, Germaine, 3300:1

greeting, 1882:5

greyness, 2464:15

grief *see also* mourning; sorrow, 222:1; 365:4; 645:1; 838:6; 911:4; 1626:1; 1873:2; 1905:4; 1986:4; 2326:5; 2490:3; 2815:1;

2925:16, 17; 3939:2; 4011:1;
4015:2; 4312:13; 4402:1; acceptance of ~, 955:25; duration of ~,
4062:2; love of ~, 4164:1; measure of ~, 1534:5; overcoming ~,
44:1; shock of ~, 2859:2; stages of ~, 3763:5; suppress ~, 2938:1;
unspoken ~, 1072:3; women's ~, 987:4; working through ~,
3963:1

Griffith, D. W., 1709:1

groom/ing, 2875:5; ~ of man, 1663:6; ~ of women, 643:5;
1940:2; 1963:3

group, effectiveness of ~, 1637:2; separating from ~, 3308:2; ~
spirit, 1350:6; success of ~, 1350:4

growing up, 916:5; 1682:1; 1920:1; 2098:1; 2244:3; 2630:3; 2732:9;
2780:8; 2919:1; 3042:4; 3309:2; 3337:2; disappointments of ~,
1044:4; ~ female, 3399:3; ~ poor, 1838:2

growth, 1752:2; 2170:4; 2477:3; 2607:3; 3122:4; 3282:3; 3772:1;
aiding ~ of others, 2607:2; artistic ~ (see also artist), 3426:2;
1408:2; economic ~, 3676:2; inner ~, 1148:7; lack of ~,
3032:5; personal ~ (see also maturity), 887:23, 30; 955:38;
1381:14; 1387:3; 1743:7; 2537:9; 3779:6; possibility of ~,
4775:2

guardian, ~ of child, 1761:9

Guatemala, 4495:1; terrorism in ~, 4091:4

guest see also visit/or, 3069:3; perfect ~, 1612:1; 1669:5; treatment
of ~, 2177:1; welcome ~, 807:20; 4259:2; woman ~, 1596:1

guidance/guide, 4334:1; 4401:2; need for ~, 2797:1; spiritual ~,
2960:1

guilt/y, 455:2; 944:2; 1129:5; 1176:5; 1610:2; 2195:1; 2642:1;
3112:4; 3445:, 4; 3951:3; 4034:2; assumption of ~, 2552:1;
Jewish ~, 2810:1; secret ~, 4385:1; tinge of ~, 341:2

Gulf War, 3525:3

gullibility, 245:3; 306:1; 616:5; 3421:1; ~ of citizenry, 258:1

gun see also arms; marksmanship; shooting; weapon, 2460:5;
3160:2; 4235:6; carrying ~, 2647:3; ~ control, 2846:1;
3864:1; 4174:13; 4432:3; 4759:1; fascination with ~,
2951:3; 4493:3; loaded ~, 4797:1; power of ~, 4160:3; ~
use, 4275:2; ~ violence, 4759:1, 2

guru see also spirit/uality, 3612:1

Guyana, 2378:2

gylany see also egalitarianism; equality, 2399:2 gym see also ex-

ercise; fitness; health club, work out at ~, 2386:2

gymnast, scoring ~, 4606:1

gypsy, character of ~, 1036:3; ~ song, 4614:1

H

habit see also custom, 1590:3; 3918:3; 4516:1; breaking ~,
1433:1; creature of ~, 4354:4; personal ~, 1977:4; simple ~,
769:2

hacienda, life on ~, 2609:1

Hadassah, 1261:10

Hagen, Uta, 3252:2

hair, 4333:2; dyed ~, 4279:1; facial ~, 4158:3; grey ~, 1968:1; loss
of ~, 4962:2; ~ style, 1346:1; 2364:3; 3112:1; 4443:1

Haiti/an, 3114:2; 4808:1

halal see also kosher, 4902:2

Hamas (Islamic Resistance Movement), 3143.1:3

Hamlet, 1891:1; 3797:8

hand (human), 144:2; 722:1; 1741:29; child's ~, 2133:3;
fingers of ~, 1199:1; flaccid ~, 1754:5; holding ~, 2577:3; ~
washing, 3650:1

handbag, 2426:6; 3836:2

handicap see also child/ren, handicapped ~; disabled/disability,
4882:1; physical ~, 1018:3; 4913:3

handshake, 1548:6

Hannah, 379:1; 385:1

haphazardness see also chance, 1515:2

happiness see also bliss; joy, 342:1; 495:2; 544:5; 585:4; 613:1;
697:2; 733:13; 815:1; 887:18, 19; 1032:5; 1292:5; 1408:3;
1433:1; 1435:10, 12; 1440:3; 1483:3; 1690:1; 2002–2003:1;
2029:1; 2032:7; 2117:8; 2184:1; 2352:5; 2680:27; 2684:4;
2757:2; 2920:3; 3258:1; 3379:2; 3763:4; 3766:1; 3944:1; 4503:1;
4756:1; 4876:2; 4907:2; defining ~, 1006:6; domestic ~, 843:5;
ephemerality of ~, 643:7; 658:2; 1573:2; feigned ~, 676:6; finding
~, 593:1; 1354:1; 1411:2; hungry for ~, 1382:5; loss of ~ (see
also unhappiness), 395:2; 575:1; money and ~, 1461:2; road to ~,
691:2; sharing ~, 3164:4

harassment, legal ~, 3896:2; sexual ~ (see also sexism), 4122:4

harbor, 1166:1

hardship see adversity; life, struggle of ~; obstacle; trouble

harm, inflict ~, 451:2

harmony see also cooperation, 457–458:3; ~ with nature, 2117:11

Harris, Katherine, 4575:1

Harvard University, 2392:2; 4928:1; ~ Law School, 4536:1, 3

hate/hatred, 273–274:1; 356:2; 805:3; 955:1; 1245:1; 2181–
2182:1; 2290:1; 2320:7; 2613:5; 2668:17; 3033:8; 3587:2;
3976:1; 4843:3; blindness of ~, 2585:2; eliminating ~, 1310:1;
look of ~, 955:17; object of ~, 1262:8; ~ of parent, 4728:4; ~ of
self (see self-hatred); ~ of wife, 1903:2

hats, women's ~, 4324:3

Havel, Václav, 4553:2

Hawaii/ans, 1083:1, 2

head of state see also specific positions; leader/ship; rule/r;
statesman, 334:5; 341:10; 3850:3; accountability of ~,
341:8; credibility of ~, 258:1; 288:3; demands on ~, 604:5, 10;
friend of ~, 343:1; impotence of ~, 4963:1; pressures of ~, 672:2;
woman ~, 304:2; 3169:4

Headstart, funding for ~, 3229:1

healer, 1007:5; 1179:3

healing see also cure; recovery; remedy, 982:6; 1805:1; 2648:6;
2695:1; 2756:20; 3210:2; 3638:1; 3720:1; 3742:3; 3779:3;
4285:3; 4542:2; 4889:1; alternative ~, 3612:1; 4117:6; ~
arts, 1833:3; ~ oneself, 1779:2; 3827:3; 4174:8; ~ others, 4862:2

health, 276:3; 868:1; 1223:3; 1596:4; 1687:8; 2667:1; 2724:2;
2862:4; 4586:3; ~ and culture, 4177:2; chemicals and ~, 4608:1;
HMO (health maintenance org.), 4586:3; ill ~, 3139:11;
importance of ~, 1430:3; 2286:6; lack of ~, 2621:2; maintaining
~, 1407:3; poor ~, 533:15; principles of ~, 1112:4; promoting
~, 3731:2; protecting ~, 4106:3; reproductive ~, 2678:2; 2779:2;
science of ~, 981:2; seeking ~, 804:1; study of ~, 1992:3; teaching ~, 1565:1; women's ~, 177:1;
4670:5

health care, 4238:1; ~ coverage, 2779:2; ~ industry, 4290:3; single
payer ~, 4576.1:1, 2; universal ~, 4824:1

health club see also gym, 3139:14; 3260:6

hearing (senses), 2668:1

hearsay see also gossip, 1759:11

Hearst, William Randolph, 2470:1

heart see also emotion; feeling; love, 128:3; 271:1; 310:1; 401:1;
522:5; 1664:2; 2415:3; 3409:2; ~ attack, 2567:1; 3003:4; ~ beat,
2817:16; big ~, 1211:2; bountiful ~, 1152:4; care of ~, 3139:7; cold
~, 847:1; fluttering ~, 2196:1; following one's ~, 2965:2;
free ~, 898:2; 1032:5; hard ~, 2205:2; 4858:1; hiding one's ~,
1855–1856:1; light ~, 905:3;

logic of ~, 614:4; lonely ~, 790:9; loving ~, 3355:2; master of ~,
1317:; mind and ~, 3849:3; narrow ~, 3094:2; noble ~, 411:3;
open ~, 2456:8; poetic ~, 2417:2; secrets of ~, 3135:3; stolen one's
~, 242:1; submissive ~, 459:1; weak ~, 1160:9; willing ~, 713:9;
win one's ~, 382:2; 529:2; 660:2; woman's ~, 316:1; 511:8; 894:5

heartbreak, 150:2; 564:3; 1406:4; 1653:2; 2435:1; 3094:1; 3413:3;
4764:3; consolation for ~, 2417:3; pain of ~, 4542:2

heartlessness, ~ in society, 2527:2

heat, 4024:1; coping with ~, 2931:7; intense ~, 4949:3; wasting ~,
4348:3

heathen see also pagan/ism, 560:1

heaven see also paradise; utopia, 240:1; 285:4; 831:1; 974:5;
1219:1; 2462:2; 2561:2; 3391:3; 4629:1; arrival in ~, 1307:1;
3427:4; blocked from ~, 455:2; entrance to ~, 295:1; fly to ~,
4250:2; going to ~, 1085:4; invention of ~, 3159:3; ~ on earth,
892:17; personal ~, 4773:2; reward in ~, 2916:17; road to ~,
808:3; 1730:2; seeking ~, 772:6; unbelief in ~, 1675–1676:3;
women in ~, 3316:2

hedonism see also pleasure, 3278:3

hegemony, science and ~, 2988:4

heir/ess, American ~, 2185:9

hell see also damnation/damned; purgatory, 149:3; 288:4; 415:1;
2705:3; 3094:3; 4580:1; condemned to ~, 1741:12; 3563:5;
world going to ~, 2566:4

Heloise, 178:6

help/fulness, 1120:4; asking for ~, 2543:3; 2961:2; creed of
~, 1696:4; giving ~, 1006:10; 1119:1; ~ oneself, 466:9

helplessness, 4246:3

Hemingway, Ernest, 1780:10; 1930:6; 2546:5; 2668:23; 3597:2

Henry IV of France, 362:1

Henry VIII of England, 3102:3

Hercules, 592:2

here and now see also present [time]; today, 584:6; 3428:2;
appreciating ~, 959:1; dealing with ~, 1914:13; observation of
~, 1186:1

heredity, 472:8; 1535:9; 4337:2; ~ of values, 3154:1

heritage see also roots, 883:1; 1455:1; 1812:2; 2187:12; literary
~, 2192:15; ~ of humanity, 3719:3

hero/ism see also exemplar; idol/atry; rescue; savior; warrior,
42:1; 111:1; 421:2; 423:1; 603:7; 884:2; 1062:4; 1677:5; 1794:2;
2020:1; 2281:8; 3325:1; 3353:1; 3412:4; 3831:1; 3865:1; 3890:1;
4110:1; 4754:1; anonymous ~,

3996:4; anti-~, 3453:3; death of ~, 624:4; ~ in history, 2676:7; military ~, 623:3; misguided ~, 2884:4; need for ~, 1668:8; portraying ~, 1095:1; 2028:1; women ~, 2965:1; 3147:3; women ~ in literature, 1162:4

Herod, 1580:1

Herschel, John Frederick, 662:1

hesitation see also tentativeness, 1790:8

heterosexual/ity see also sex, balance of power in ~, 3237:3; female ~, 3262:3; lovemaking and ~, 3194:2

hiding, 4627:1

high school see also school, training for ~ graduate, 2675:4

highlander, 680:2; 712:1

highway see also freeway, 2659:4; American ~, 4963:2

hijab (head scarf), 2595:4

hill see also mountain, 1509:1; 1566:4; 2123:1

hillbilly, 2570:2

Hilton, Conrad, 3427:2

hindsight, 733:17; 873:5; 1743:8; 2194:2

Hindu, 984:2; deities of ~, 4708:3; poverty and ~, 4142:1

hipness, 2780:2; 3443:5; 4928:2

hippie see also beatnik, 2185:16

Hippocrates see also physician, oath of ~, 3509:3

Hispanic see also Chicano/a; Mexican American, 4083:2; ~ women, 3424:2

historian, 1625:5; 2270:10; 3423:3; 3752:4; confines of ~, 4000:1; limitations of ~, 3752:3

history see also antiquity; women's history, 965:1; 1336:10; 1600:4; 2027:14; 2126:4; 2380:6; 2490:7; 2618:11; 2836:3; 2949:3; 3084:3; 3581:1; 3714:3; 3737:1; 4017:1, 2; 4558:2; 4879:2; American ~, 3301:3; black ~, 3752:1, 4; caught in ~, 2411:4; causality in ~, 3508:3; changing ~, 3298:5; 3361:1; climax of ~, 2038:1; codification of ~, 3277:2; cycles in ~, 2439:10; debate over ~, 3583:5; distorted ~, 2618:18; documenting ~, 4160:4; dullness of ~, 767:23; false ~, 2680:20; importance of ~, 2201:12; inventing ~, 544:1; 4828:1; lessons of ~, 4763:5; living ~, 4737:4; making ~, 4717:2; manipulating ~, 3949:1; oral ~, 3752:2; 3902:1; personal ~, 1670:5; 1715:12; 2938:3; 3897:6; perspective of ~, 1706:3; pre-~, 3004:4; precariousness of ~, 3758:1; progression of ~, 1625:1; reading ~, 2676:7; recorded ~, 1156:1; remembering ~, 4492:3; repetition of ~, 2769:2; 3050:2; revisionist ~, 4930:1;

study of ~, 2836:2; 3359:1; ~ taught in school, 2756:5; telling ~, 3417:6; truth in ~, 357:4; understanding of ~, 3000:2

Hitchcock, Alfred, 2935:1

Hite Report, 3344:3

Hitler, Adolf, 1333:7; 1349:1; 1582:3; 1870:2; 2157:3; 2474:1; 3166:2; 3204:2; and Jews ~, 1870:5; ~ and youth organization, 2026:2; plotting demise of ~, 2304:1

hobby see also avocation; pastime, 1437:1; 4199:2

hockey, 4978:0

holiday see also vacation, 2728:3; American ~, 1868:2

Holiday, Billie, 3982:2

holiness, 976:3; 2352:17; 2569:7; 2997:10; 3579:3; 3932:2

Holland see Netherlands, 1039:1

Holliday, Doc, 1266:1

Hollywood, California see also film; Los Angeles, 1709:2; 1820:1; 2568:5; 3002:1; 3147:1; 3291:2; 3349:15; 3532:3; 4085:6; 4242:1; end of ~, 1686:13; ~ gossip, 3678:1; ~ residences, 2599:1; women in ~, 4472:1

holocaust see also genocide, 1977:2; 2323:3; 3756:2; 3767:1; denial of ~, 3767:2, 3; evil of ~, 3669:1; Jewish ~, 1333:7; 2631:1; 2884:1; perpetrators of ~, 4057:3; remembrance of ~, 2722:5; 2981:2

Holy Ghost see also God; Jesus Christ, 463:2

home see also house; residence, 309:1; 342:1; 649:10; 691:2; 1167:15; 1357:1; 1418:4; 1552:5; 1668:1; 2009:1; 3251:3; 3307:2; 3562:1; 4609:1; 4792:2; 4879:1; 4925:1; annoyances at ~, 916:14; being at ~ anywhere, 1935:20; ~ buyer, 3156:3; childhood ~, 904:1; culture and ~, 3684:4; design of ~, 4679:2; English ~, 1590:7; ~ foreclosure, 4229:3; going ~ (see also homecoming), 22:1; 73:1; 2529:7; 4858:0; ~ industry, 1787:6; leaving ~, 697:1; 1448:3; 4782:2; loving ~, 622:4; men at ~, 911:2; moving to new ~, 2711:1; nursing ~, 2335:2; ~ of the rich, 1301:1; ~ owner, 713:2; 1178:4; 2869:4; 2990:3; privacy of ~, 4700:2; remembrance of ~, 2092:1; safety of ~, 4648:2; sanctity of ~, 2556:5; second ~, 4679:4; settling in new ~, 2464:15; soldier's ~, 1373:1; suburban ~, 1886:1; women and ~, 1311:1; 1165:1; 2219:8; 2416:5; women returning ~, 4192:2

homecoming see also home, going ~, 55:1; 1531:1; 2349:17

homeland, 3929:1; forgetting one's ~, 4449:1

homeless see also vagrant, 2219:2; 3829:1; 4455:2, 3

homeliness, 4050:3; rewards of ~, 1262:1; trials of ~, 2822:2

Homer, 357:5

homesickness, 653:1; 989:1; 3906:8; 4104:1; 4428:2; 4614:4

homesteading, women ~, 1483:1

homework school see also, 968:2; 1875:2; 2780:5

homicide see also killing; murder/er, 3514:3; acceptable ~, 3671:1

homogeneity, 1666:2; ~ of life, 1189:2

homosexual/ity see also bisexual/ity; gay liberation movement; lesbian/ism; sex, 3177:1; 3381:5; 3780:10; acceptance of ~, 4490:2; Christianity and ~, 2446:2; ~ coming out, 4003:1; ~ community, 3381:4; confession of ~, 1905:7; ~ in the Bible, 3153:1; lovemaking and ~, 3194:2; marriage between ~, 3106:4; 3275:2; 4720:2; meeting ~, 3097:1

honesty see also candor; truth, 511:17; 1060:2; 1751:20; 1896:2; 4625:2; ~ with oneself, 4056:1

Hong Kong see also China, 3188:1, 2

honor, 276:3; 521:1; 1418:5; 2192:3; 4835:1; defining ~, 2517:3; money and ~, 308:4; receiving ~, 662:2

honors see also awards, 479:4; shunning ~, 2132:1

hope, 235:1; 276:2; 487:3; 635:3; 801:12; 827:5; 880:5; 1024:5; 1069:2; 1140:1; 1174:1; 1236:3; 1259:2; 1389:1; 1521:1; 1700:11; 2139:3; 2281:4; 2381:3; 2451:1; 2463:5, 7; 2625:2; 2892:4; 3476:4; 3754:3; 4255:2; 4865:2; 4890–4891:1; animated by ~, 734:10; balm of ~, 716:3; disappointed ~, 693:1; 834:1; frail ~, 845:9; 3539:2; fulfilling ~, 4697:2; keeping ~ alive, 1248:3; lack of ~, 3210:3; lost ~, 1024:24; 1692:6; new ~, 1600:1; 2618:11; 4773:4; power of ~, 1534:2; 1713:1; 3799:5; precarious ~, 790:8; remove ~, 1089:7; theology of ~, 2425:1; weary ~, 105:1; 912:1

hopelessness, 381:2; 584:1; 1640:2; 4020:6; ~ in Middle East, 4231:1

horizon, 2371:4; broadening one's ~, 2200:2; 3094:2

hormone, 2300:4; ~ testosterone, 2300:3; 4136:4; ~ therapy, 2946:5

horoscope see also astrology, 2540:1

horror see also fear, 1627:7

horse, 905:6; 1454:1; Arabian ~, 1075:, 1, 2; ~ -back riding, 1440:10; ~ -racing jockey, 3541:1; 4090:1; rider and ~, 3427:1; 4645:2; riding ~, 380:1; 2212:2; 2733:3; 4788:1; ~ stable, 1947:3

horseracing see also jockey, 4645:1

hospital, 892:12; 1764–1765:1; ~ deaths, 2726:2; mental ~, 2642:7; sophistry in ~, 4571:1; ~ use of IV, 4037:2

hospitality, 738:4; 2629:3; 4116:1; 4988:3

host/ess, 1596:6; quandary of ~, 2177:1

hostage, 1935:18; trauma of being taken ~, 3611.1:3

hostility, 2288:3

hotel, ~ flophouse, 3427:2; great ~, 2169:2; 2925:12; ~ room, 3309:5

hour, 641:1

house see also home; residence, 1406:5; 4147:5; 4207:5; ~ bound, 2532:1; building a ~, 2942:10; clean ~, 4237:3; doors of ~, 1088:2; haunted ~, 2978:1; old ~, 1088:1; 1426:1; protection of ~, 3302:2; 3932:1; renovation of ~, 3307:1; room in ~, 4280:5; small ~, 966:1; soul of ~, 4148:2

House of Commons (U.K.), 960:1

House of Representatives (U.S.A.) see also Congress, U.S., 3151:3; women and ~, 3220:4

household see also family, breaking up ~, 155:3; female head of ~, 4093:1; ~ help, 2844:1

housekeeper/housekeeping see also housework; labor/er, household ~; servant, 2439:3; 3465:2; importance of ~, 931:29

housewife see also homemaker/ homemaking; housework; wife, 1249:3; 1254:12; 1490:2; 1499:3; 1566:5; 1941:1; 2015:1; 2054:2; 2353:5; 2568:3; 2709:3; 2793:5; 2817:19; 2885:2; 2932:4; 2995:2; 4085:3; child-centered ~, 3746:2; consciousness of ~, 2468:4; suburban ~, 2398:1; work of ~, 2602:5; 3081:1, 2; working class ~, 2719:2

housework see also cleaning; cleanliness; homemaker/homemaking; housewife; laundry; tidiness, 67:1; 314:1; 358:1, 2; 434:1; 807:19; 930:2; 1044:6; 1112:5; 1127:5; 1206:3; 1212:1; 1254:2; 1663:3; 1697:4; 1866.1:1; 2185:8; 2286:1; 2287:3; 2639:3; 2658:4; 2771:10; 2862:1; 2916:5; 3027:2; 3175:1; 3529:4; 4235:1; 4784:2; demands of ~, 3529:1

housing, fair ~ law, 4960:3; ~ project, 3551–3552:2

HUAC (House Un-American Activities Committee), 1666:6
Hugo, Victor, 894:1
human being *see* human/kind
humaneness *see also* compassion; kindness, 12:1; 860:3; 1672:1; 2097:1
humanism, 3412:7
humanitarianism *see* philanthropy
humankind *see also* individual; people; public, the, 1230:1; 1627:1; 2157:2; 2793:4; 3101:4; 3652:4; 4443:3; 4888:1; attitude toward ~, 1741:17; 1906:1; belief in ~, 2038:2; 2438:3; bonds of ~, 2899:2; 3124:4; characteristics of ~, 177:2; damage to ~, 3420:1; demise of ~, 1751:25; 2505:1; dichotomy of ~, 2656:5; 2892:3; diversity of ~, 783:2; drive of ~, 2664:2; elevating ~, 4951:1; ethos of ~, 3081:3; future of ~, 783:1; healthy race of ~, 2849:2; ~ in relation to animal kingdom, 533:10; ~ in relation to God, 1148:5; ~ in relation to Nature, 1739:4; 2124:5; 3410:1; ~ intellect, 3291:1; loveliness of ~, 4237:4; love of ~, 289:4; 883:3; 1537:5; 1846:4; 3187:1; 3491:1; mystery of ~, 1662:4; nature of ~, 2135:7; needs of ~, 3350–3351:1; ~ of the future, 1764–1765:6; potential of ~, 2669:3; 2574:2; powerlessness of ~, 2590:2; priorities of ~, 1672:1; remains of ~, 3866:4; resources of ~, 2960:2; role of ~, 902:1; selfishness of ~, 1896:11; separateness of ~, 1155:3; strength of ~, 652:3; 733:4; study of ~, 745:2; 769:3; superiority of ~, 694:5; ~ traits, 2908:3; universal ~, 2664:5; what separates ~ from beasts, 2062:1; works of ~, 1785:2
human nature *see also* behavior; disposition, 1435:11; 1724:6; 4285:8; 4845–4846:1; changing ~, 2903:5; complexity of ~, 1239:5; destructiveness of ~, 4510:4
human potential movement, 2936:1; 4897:1, 2
human race *see* human/kind
human rights *see also* civil rights, 2517:4; 3583:6; 3719:5; 3731:6; 4380:2; 4482:3; ~ abuses, 4087:1; 4088:4; advocates for ~, 2512:1; ~ and global warming, 4893:1; ~ and religion, 3739:1; defending ~, 3948:2; democracy and ~, 1463:2; fight for ~, 2491:2; 4528:3; ~ in Africa, 4983:2; ~ in relation to commerce, 2959:5; progress of ~, 3715:5; protection of ~, 3715:3; respect for ~, 3588:2; universal

~, 3213:3; ~ violation, 3696:5; 4022:6
human trafficking, 3456:1; 4528:4; 4670:4; 4862:1
humidity *see also* weather, 2931:7
humility, 234:1; 308:6; 377:1; 388:1; 767:19; 1846:4; 1906:3; 4202:2
humor *see also* comedian; comedy; joke; wit, 1236:11; 1669:7; 2586:7; 2932:8; 2990:7; 3530:1; 4297:4; ~ as weapon, 3165:3; importance of ~, 1236:12; 4648:8; ~ in America, 1639:3, 4; ~ in foreign language, 1590:5; sense of ~, 430:5; 955:30; 1687:2; ~ of oppressed, 1725:3
hunger *see also* starvation, 352:2; 880:2; 1265:6; 1409:1; 1622:4; 1741:2; 2085:2, 6; 2193:1; 2291:2; 2307:4; 2318:1; 2535:3; 3546:3; 3862:1; 4185:5; 4622:3; causes of ~, 4774:8; children and ~, 3417:3; 4266:2; effects of ~, 215:2; grip of ~, 51:1; ~ in relation to economics, 4774:5; satisfying ~, 2659:2; 4755:2; ~ strike, 1235:10; 1365:1; universal ~, 1471:3; worldwide ~, 1030:3; 1618:15
hunter/hunting, 278:1; 1669:12; 1827:1; 1832:6; 2960:2; 4539:4; first ~ trip, 1405:1; modern sports ~, 4192:1
Hurok, Sol, 2431:1
Hurricane Katrina, 4455:3; cleanup of ~, 4542:3; victims of ~, 4190:4; volunteers and ~, 4542:4
hurry, 1842:1; doomed to ~, 684:1
hurt *see also* injury; wound, 395:1
husband *see also* marriage; partner/ship [social]; spouse; wife, 19:1; 265:1; 281:1; 880:3; 919:3; 987:2; 1135:1; 1481:5; 1586:1; 2822:4; 3317:5; 3898:2; 4085:8; 4500:3; bad ~, 3678:2; death of ~, 359:2; 449:4; 613:2; 627:2; 2645:2; 4298:4; disabled ~, 4591:3; disappearance of ~, 4639:3; disapproval of ~, 853:1; dominating ~, 1532:1; hunting for ~, 2185:9; ~ in relation to successful wife, 3078:1; ~ in relation to wife, 26:1; 423:5; 592:1, 2; 1007:7; 1184:6; 2830:3; 2924:2; losing ~, 423:8; loving ~, 498:1; murder of ~, 2676:6; needs of ~, 2287:2; philandering ~, 310:6; power of ~, 646:1; rights of ~, 3417:1; role of ~, 2794:3; several ~, 1804:6; support of ~, 3554:4; ~ with working wife, 1959:10
husband and wife *see also* marriage, 910:6; 3145:3
Hussein bin Talal, 4066:3
Hussein, Saddam, 2615:2
Huxley, Thomas, 1919:1

hymn, singing ~, 4623:1
hyperactivity, 4154:2
hypocrisy/hypocrite *see also* deceit/deception, 212:1; 1552:6; 2036:12; 2044:3; 2185:3; 2323:1; 4050:1; attacking ~, 3732:3; cultural ~, 2911:4; ~ of humankind, 1896:11; ~ of ruling class, 1135:4; ~ of sexism, 963:2
hysteria *see* panic, 3212:2; 3305:2; women & ~, 3626:2

I

ice skating, 4513:1
iceberg, 1760:1
Idaho, 4901:2
idea *see also* concept, 2552:2; 2638:7; age of ~, 1435:8; creative ~, 4210:5; great ~, 1360:12; 3703:5; growth of ~, 2266:9; importance of ~, 3628:3; killing ~, 1990:3; 2116:12; new ~, 4096:2; 4378:3; ready-made ~, 2775:4; trying on ~, 2349:13
ideal/ism, 593:1; 982:12; 1504:1; 4744:5; fidelity to ~, 4557:1; high ~, 2913:4; loss of ~, 3853:3; maintaining ~, 1475:3
idealist, daughter of ~, 2473:1
identification *see also* empathy, ~ in wallet, 4867:2; ~ with another, 3895:3
identity *see also* beingness; ego/ism; self; self-image, 200:1; 804:4; 1024:8; 1160:2; 1562:7; 1647:1; 1700:8; 1716:2; 1739:4; 1791:1; 2072:1; 2199:4; 2320:2; 2381:7; 2577:5; 2689:3; 2765:3; 2870:2; 2884:3; 2983:1; 3033:5; 3068:4; 3135:2; 3193:1; 3338:1; 3491:5; 3546:1; 3869:1; 4583:2; 4711:4; 4799:1; 4872:2; 4924:3; 4964:4; clarity of one's ~, 1510:3; cultural ~, 3414:3; discovering one's ~, 4515:1; 4623:4; evolution of ~, 4964:2; finding ~, 3901:2; group ~, 3008:1; ~ in the technological age, 4738:3; lack of ~, 734:16; 1301:7; 2488:1; 4013:8; 4234:1; maintaining ~, 2283:1; male ~, 2607:4; multiple ~, 4666:1; national ~, 3950:1, 3; personal ~, 3482:1; 4903:3; search for ~, 3371:1; 3547:10; 4367:2; 4906:1; sexual ~, 3153:2; 4123:8; woman's ~, 1680:1; 3133:3
ideograph, drawing ~, 1451:1
ideology, 2221:1; mono- ~, 4830:1; prisoner of ~, 2958:2; respect for ~, 2175:3
idleness *see also* laziness, 367:4; 466:9; 637:2; 1132:2; 1328:1; 2021:11; 2272:6; 2563:1; maintaining ~, 3954:1
idol/atry *see also* hero/ism, 616:4; 649:3; 1677:5; 3362:1; age of ~, 3780:5; desire for ~, 1440:1;

function of ~, 2511:2; ~ of women, 2400:4; ~ worship, 459:1
ignorance *see also* knowledge, lack of ~; stupidity, 315:2; 328:1; 334:9; 413:1; 961:1; 1211:1; 2021:4; 2618:6; 2893:1; 2944:5; 4042:1; advantages of ~, 1549:3; embarrassment of ~, 4306:2; harm of ~, 1663:7; ~ of child, 4644:2; ~ of masses, 951:3; perception of ~, 4558:3
Iliad, The, women in ~, 4577:3
illiteracy, 860:2; 2618:1
illness *see also specific disorders*; disease; sickness, 1867:4; 2046:1; 2866:14; chronic ~, 4533:5; cure for ~ (*see also* cure), 1424:1; 2556:2; life-threatening ~, 3436:5; privacy of ~, 2476:2; psychosomatic ~ (*see also* hypochondria; mental illness; mind, disease of ~), 423:2; 2567:1; treating ~, 4542:2
illumination *see also* light, 2711:5
illusion, 1292:3; 2263:2; 2428:3; 3046:1; creating ~, 3372:1; dupe to ~, 1184:10; giving up ~, 2406:3; lost ~, 808:16; ~ of newness, 4123:5; ~ of self, 887:14; women's ~, 2620:6
image, addicted to ~, 2866:11; bad self-~, 1132:3; creating ~, 1973:15; 2921:2; iconic use of male ~, 3133:5; ~ in wartime, 4731:5; maximizing ~, 2581:2; need new ~, 955:9; power of ~, 4731:6; public ~, 682:7; 2401:1; 3577:1; self-~ (*see* self-image); understanding ~, 3654:1;
imagination, 289:7; 671:3; 762:2; 808:4; 1162:1; 1481:11; 1639:1; 1963:2; 2668:11; 2911:6; 3095:3; 3455:3; 4825:1; 4924:2; importance of ~, 2220:5; lack of ~, 1019:11; power of ~, 3478:3; repressing ~, 3337:2; soaring ~, 658:6; using ~, 4734:4; ~ vs. reality, 1444:4; women and ~, 767:6; 2685:3
imitation, 1450:; 1685:5; 1834:4; 4136:7
immigrant/immigration *see also* emigrant/emigration; refugee, 837:2; 1342:3; 3542:2; 3567:11; 3581:4; 3744:5; 3901:4; 4331:1; 4915:3; barring ~, 4073:1; ~ child/ren, 3542:3; 3786:1; 4275:1; desperation of ~, 4808:5; education of ~, 1413:1; ~ in America, 2656:4; 4295:3; 4449:1; 4702:5, 6; 4808:3; 4943:1; 4948:4; industry and ~, 1849:3; language and ~, 1413:2; ~ parents, 1916:5; ~ policy, 4808:4
immorality *see also* morality, lack of ~, 701:3; 4851:1

immortality, 165:1; 965:6; 1089:5; 1247:2; 1389:1; 1911:4; 2560:7; 3704:3; 4038:6; 4352:2; 4683:3; belief in ~, 1754:2; desire for ~, 4906:4

impassivity see also feeling, lack of ~, 2799:1; 2801:1; learning ~, 960:5

impatience see also patience, 760:1; 1309:1; 2281:2; 2861:4

impeachment, ~ of American president, 2989:1

imperfection, 2472:4

imperialism, 1535:; 2291:6; 4431:1; American ~, 1741:11; British ~, 4786:3

imperturbability, 3216:1

imperviousness, 4825:2

importance see also significance, 961:4; 2969:2; feeling of ~, 1618:24; lack of ~, 1724:2; ~ of others, 2306:4

impossibility see also possibility, 818:2; 1592:7; 2704:2; desire for ~, 4755:2; overcoming ~, 3284:5; 3762:5

impotence, feeling of ~, 2594:2

impression, leaving an ~, 2620:11

Impressionism, 2089:5

imprisonment see also enslavement; prisoner, 243:1; 398:1; 482:1; 3493:3; advantages of ~, 442:3; effects of ~, 2897:1; escaping ~, 2504:3

improvement see also self-improvement, 642:8; 1335:2; 1796:1; continuous ~, 3917:1; ~ for future, 3591:3; ~ of succeeding generations, 1019:8; resisting ~, 770:3

impunity see also guilt, declaration of ~, 4553:2

inaction, 2941:6

inactivity also see lethargy, desire for ~, 4554:4

incentive, lack of ~, 1299:4

incest, 10:1; 35:1; 3342:2; ~ in Bible, 10:1; victims of ~, 3104:3

inclusiveness, 4897:3

income see also salary; wage, ~ in relation to god, 2618:2; inequality of women's ~, 2733:1; living within one's ~, 244:9; ~ of college graduate, 2237:6

incompatibility, 3119:1

incompetence, mark of ~, 1803:1

inconsiderateness see also thoughtlessness, 1209:11

inconstancy see also faithlessness, 472:1

indebtedness, 1367:2; 4500:1

indecency, 1590:2; 1684:1

indecision see also decision, 566:1; 568:1; 671:11; 3356:2

independence, 701:2; 963:10; 967:2; 1126:1; 1204:3; 1681:2; 1851:1; 1935:16; 2244:2; 2269:2; 2867:1; 3240:3; 3547:2;

4027:1; attaining ~, 2765:4; 4813:3; desire for ~, 1381:9; gaining ~, 3115:3; 3882:3; illusion of ~, 2364:2; test of ~, 2159:1; ~ vs. individuality, 1229:5; women of ~, 101:1; 161:1; 357:7; 880:3; 931:19; 1086:1; 1419:6; 1620:2; 1757:2; 4419:3; 4661:1

India/n, 2601:2, 3, 4; 3638:3; 3658:1; Bhopal ~, 4347:1, 2; children in ~, 2288:5; democracy in ~, 2288:4; drought in ~, 4266:3, 5; energy alternatives in ~, 4266:4; fashion in ~, 1316:1; hunger in ~, 2288:6; 4774:8; ~ in relation to Great Britain, 2225:1; ~ in relation to whites, 1618:7; Kashmir ~, 4922:1; Ladakh ~, 3682:1; Narma River of ~, 4506:3; national life in ~, 1534:4; poverty of ~, 2903:4; 4271:1; racism in ~, 1148:1; women in ~, 1316:2; 1534:4; 2835:2; 4525:3; ~ writer, 1917:4; youth in ~, 2288:2

indifference see also detachment, 1675–1676:8; 1687:10; 1780:6; 2413:4; 2477:2; 2491:1; 2966:2; 4021:2; 4889:5

indigenous people, 4495:3; exploitation of ~, 4460:1; Gwich'in ~, 3513:2, 4; 4253:1; oppression of ~, 4495:2; religion and ~, 4495:5; rights of ~, 2361:1; 3948:2

indignation see also specific peoples, 1822:3

indiscretion, 76:5

indispensability, 1208:12

individual/ity see also nonconformist/nonconformity; people; person, singularity, 945:4; 1687:9; 2009:3; 2019:4; 2648:1; 2794:2; 3940:1; dangerous ~, 451:4; 799:7; dignity of ~, 1870:6; effacement of ~, 863:3; finding one's ~, 4136:7; freedom of ~, 2015:1; historicity of ~, 3437:1; ignoring one's ~, 1783:5; impact of ~, 2892:1; importance of ~, 3631:2; 4070:1; ~ in relation to society, 1350:3; 1977:3; 3261:4; intrinsic worth of ~, 3445:1; loss of ~, 1996:3; rugged ~, 4836:3; ~ vs. group, 2903:6; women of ~, 1693:10

individualism, 3583:4

indolence see also laziness, 435:2; 450:4; ~ in children, 166:10

indomitability, 2279:1

Indonesia/n, 2512:2; East Timor ~, 2512:4; resources of ~, 4488:1

indulgence, 1076:6; 3743:4; ~ of society, 2256:1; self- ~, 799:3; 1175:1; slight ~, 1378:3

Industrial Age, 3709:2; ~ in relation to environment, 4469:4

Industrial Revolution, 1239:1

industrialization/industry see also Industrial Age, ~, 1365:2; 3020:3; 4141:8; captains of ~, 2823:3; changing ~, 4227:3; development of ~, 1379:3; dominance of ~, 2061:13; effects of ~, 1037:1; 1787:6; effects of ~ on family function, 1953–1954:2; ~ in relation to Wall Street, 1896:3; inhumanity of ~, 1227:3; local ~, 1009:1; ~ of West, 2288:7; sustainable ~, 4322:3; women and ~, 4409:6

industriousness see also diligence, 637:2; 1019:9

inequality, 2131:3; charges of ~, 3674:5; ~ of the sexes, 3603:2

inequity see also fairness, lack of ~; injustice, ~ of life, 3680:2; ~ of world, 3570:3

inexpressible, 1901:2

infancy/infant see also baby; childbirth; newborn, 713:4; 722:3; 4595:2; birth of ~ (see also childbirth), 401:2; death of ~, 164:1; 311:1; 564:4; 669:1; 756:3; 801:5; 802:1; 4603:2; dependence of ~, 4453:4; environment of ~, 2362:3; ~ in relation to adults, 4438:3; ~ in relation to mother, 2461:2; vulnerability of ~, 2666:5

infatuation see also love, 610:1

inferiority, feeling of ~, 2761:3; sense of ~ (see also self-esteem, low ~), 1618:1

infertility, 1801:3; 4155:2; 4428:1; technology and ~, 4009:2

infidelity see also adultery; philanderer, 166:16; 894:4; excitement of ~, 4286:4; hiding ~, 380:3; rationalization for ~, 2301:3; woman's ~, 443:2

inflation see also economics/economy, 1920:4; 2227:3

influence see also persuasion, 1115:1; ~ on thought, 107:3; sphere of ~, 682:7; 1301:6; wielding ~, 3980:2

information see also technology, information ~,1450:30; 2330:5; 2668:2; addicted to ~, 4127:4; art and systems of ~, 2334:1; giving ~, 2676:2; presenting an issue of ~, 4403:1; lack of ~, 3925:3; ~ leak, 166:15; personal ~, 4031:4; power of ~, 2853:2; 4709:4; public ~, 1857:5; right to ~, 3295:1; seed of ~, 1383:4; seeking ~, 2185:13; sharing ~, 4081:7; useless ~, 1070:4

Information Age, 3709:2

ingenuousness see also naivete, 270:1; 1987:3

inheritance see also legacy, 3070:1; 3599:3; 4095:2; large ~, 3325:4; ~ of American blacks, 2771:21;

pitfalls of ~, 4419:4; ~ rights for women, 9:1; 18:1, 1

inhibition, 2861:5; losing ~, 3290:2

inhospitality, 2475:4

injury see also scar, physical ~, 2508:2

injustice see also fairness, lack of ~; inequity, eliminating ~, 971:1; fighting vs. ~, 1028:1; 1291:4; 1592:6; great ~, 869:7; historical ~, 4025:3; sense of ~, 1297:2; ~ toward the poor, 1086:4; unrectified ~, 2185:10

ink, 3318:2

inner life, 2266:10; 2560:8; 2567:3; 2913:1; 2927:1; 3012:5; 3142:3; 4692:2; 4703:3; 4773:2; examination of ~, 3037:1; 3669:3

innocence see also naivete; purity, 449:1; 693:5; 1089:4; 3051:5; 3961:5; betrayal of ~, 1896:9; desire for ~, 1755:4; loss of ~, 1578:1; 3241:6; 3412:6; maintain ~, 667:1; ~ of child, 4644:2; proclaiming ~, 3805:1; ~ vs. ignorance, 1301:8

innovation/innovator, 1887:2; 3429:2; American ~, 4760:3; great ~, 2032:5; social ~, 2608:2; 2853:3

innuendo, 3356:1

insanity see also madness; mental illness, 2586:5; end to ~, 4427:2; fear of ~, 722:8; understanding ~, 4508:1

insect, 2022:2; 3929:2; ant, 4855:1; bee, 95:1; 215:4; 926:1; 1024:32; butterfly, 741:1; 771:3; 827:1; 1206:1; 3034:4; 3686:2; 3851:5; 4042:5; centipede, 1427:1; cicada, 141:2; cockroach, 4415:1; 4988:1; desert ~, 4420:1; dragonfly, 1226:1; fly, 446:2; 864:1; 1024:17; glowworm, 801:9; grasshopper, 461:1; scorpion, 61:3; spider, 864:1; 4406:4; study of ~, 481:1; swarm of ~, 4249:1; wasp, 737:3

insecticide see also chemical, 2061:10

insecurity, effects of ~, 3236:2

inseparability, 178:7; 193:8

insight see also perception; understanding, 408:7; 860:2; 3470:1; 4252:2; keen ~, 767:10; 955:26; sudden ~, 2030:1

insignificance see also trivia/lity, 165:1

insomnia/c see also sleep/ing, trouble ~; sleeplessness, 152:4; 2817:13; 3679:2; cure for ~, 2896:2

inspiration, 1076:4; 1358:1; 2472:6; 2636:2; 4718:5; 4828:3; ~ for others, 4906:4; ~ of discovery, 1529:4; producing ~, 1550:2

instinct see also intuition, 3030:1; losing one's ~, 981:1; maternal ~,

1254:14; 3712:2; street-fighter's ~, 4595:4
institution *see also* mental institution, changing ~, 3815:1
instruction *see also* education; teaching, 489:2; heavenly ~, 252:2
insult *see also* offense, 4116:6; thoughtless ~, 650:4
insurance, health ~, 4576.1:1, 2
integration, disgust with ~, 4097:2; ~ in America, 2325:2; ~ in music hall, 3127:1; racial ~, 1668:4; 2060:1; 2159:4
integrity *see also* principle, 41:1; 53:1; 283:3; 650:1; 804:2; 1601:7; 2242:1; 2306:1; maintaining ~, 1911:6; 2704:6; 4918:3; religion and ~, 3771:1; trial of ~, 2135:8
intellect/intelligence *see also* mind; thinker/thinking; wit, 469:3; 733:3; 1655:6; 1693:1; 2076:3; 2079:6; 2142:2; 2219:3; 2258:3; 2294:2; 2986:7; 3085:4; appearance of ~, 830:1; freedom of ~, 177:2; ~ gathering, 2194:3; lack of ~, 1236:10; measure of ~, 3473:1; native ~, 2618:1; ~ of men, 669:3; ~ of men and women, 1686:8; ~ of women, 244:2; 405:7; 4115:3; passion of ~, 1843:7; sign of ~, 1461:1; 2687:5; sterile ~, 2439:9; ~ tests, 2076:2; undernourished ~, 3738:3
intellectual/ism, 961:2; 1590:23; 1964:3; 2032:15; anti- ~, 1741:30; gathering of ~, 1503:1; ~ woman, 272:2; 412:2; 528:2; 557:1; 1025:2; 1608:5; 1686:2; 2997:4; 3853:2;
intensity, 4287:1; consequences of ~, 1844:2; constant ~, 1927:1
intention *see also* purpose, ~ gone awry, 2444:3
interact/ion, lack of ~, 4856:3
interconnectedness *see also* connectedness/connection, 2106:3; 2609:5; 2664:5; 2837:2; 2931:4; 3403:1; 3513:1; 3704:7; 3795:2; 3835:2; 3855:5; 4080:1; 4141:12; 4183:2; 4282:, 4; 4665:3; ~ as global citizens, 3782:5; ~ of ecosystems, 4178:1; ~ of world, 4648:9
interdependence, 1174:5; 1342:5; 3591:3; ~ of lovers, 1557:4; ~ of men and women, 4171:1
interior decorating, 3832:3; 4519:1
interior design, 4067:7
internationalism *see also* globalization, 2651:2; 4217:3
Internet *see also* computer; cyberspace; Facebook; World Wide Web; YouTube, 4100:5; 4770:1; 4781:4; ~ advertising, 4040:1; ~ business, 4395:1, 3; children and ~, 3433:2; content on ~, 4040:2;

culture of ~, 4200:5; freedom of ~, 4973:1; music and ~, 4227:3; navigating the ~, 3679:2; power of ~, 4189:4; romance on ~, 3498:4; surfing ~, 4555:1; ~ users, 4040:4; ~ V-pods, 4810:2
interrogation, 2563:5; ~ techniques, 4317:3
interruption, 3965:1
interview, 3475:1; subject of ~, 4043:4
intimacy *see also* togetherness, 767:3; 2109:2; 2552:8; 2577:3; 2772:2; 4603:3; attachments of ~, 3477:2; ~ between elders, 4925:2; ~ between women, 1883:2; intolerance of ~, 2027:12; yearning for ~, 143:1
intolerance, eradicating ~, 4490:3
introductions, 3097:1
introspection *see also* self-analysis; self-examination, 670:2; 827:2; 3680:5; 4136:8; 4603:4; lack of ~, 305:2
introversion, 3598:1
intuition *see also* instinct, 3567:1
invalid, caring for ~, 4310:6
invention/inventor, 511:14; 733:1; 1991:1; 2021:6; 2893:1; labor-saving ~, 2231:1; politics of ~, 1543:1; wife of ~, 1542:1
investigation, thorough ~, 1513:2
investment/investor, *see also* finance, 2230:1; ~ business, 4582:1; risk of ~, 4867:5; socially responsible ~, 4100:4; trust and ~, 4332:2
invincibility, mistaken ~, 4762:2
invisible/ness, 3474:2; power of ~, 1669:15; sense of ~, 3419:4; ~ to another, 4491:3; transforming the ~, 4666:4
invitation, 1790:1; sending ~, 4814:2
Iran/ian, 4320:5; 4546:2; ~ and Islam, 4658:1; ~ government, 4918:2; human rights in ~, 3739:0; ~ in relation to U.S.A., 4576:1; 4658:2; Jews in ~, 4546:1; travel in ~, 2900:5; ~ women, 4617:1
Iraq/i, ~ in relation to Iran, 4802:1; reconstruction in ~, 4596:1; ~ War, 4823:2; 4886:1; war in ~, 2615:2; 3114:4; 3994:2; 4225:0; 4561:1; 4886:2
Ireland/ Irish, the *see also* Great Britain, 900:2; 1398:1; 1669:6; characteristics of ~, 770:2; 1411:5; ~ Famine, 1010:2; identity of ~, 4753:1; ~ in relation to England, 1411:5; 2888:1; 3255:1; independence of ~, 2888:1; Jews and ~, 4057:1; mission of the ~, 870:7; poetry in ~, 3480:1; 4367:4; poverty in ~, 1040:2; ~ Rebellion, 517:4; women of ~, 1305:2

irony *see also* sarcasm, 1236:11; 3597:2; lack of ~, 4319:1; ~ of life, 2444:3
irrationality, 3314:2
irrelevance, 1549:7; 2483:4
irreligiousness, 560:1; 1195:1
irritability, 916:15; 1193:9
IRS (Internal Revenue Service), 2301:1; 3449:2; heading up ~, 3449:1
Iscariot, Judas, 1610:2; 2078:5
Isis, 3:1
Islam *see also* Koran; Moslem, 3208:1; 3739:1; 4708:4; 4789:4; ~ and the divine, 3211:4; apartheid of ~, 3184:7; crises of ~, 4772:2; golden age of ~, 4772:1; ~ in relation to United States, 4708:1; interpretation of ~, 3169:3; ~ nation, 4320:5; trappings of ~, 4157:1; women of ~, 3739:2; 4157:2, 3; 4617:1, 3; 4708:2
island, 1793:1; ~ shore, 1417:2; uninhabited ~, 2472:2
isolation/ism, 1461:3; 1762:2; 1977:11; 2628:4; artistic ~, 1024:16; illusion of ~, 2192:6; removal from ~, 1335:7
Israel/i *see also* Jerusalem; Jew/ Judaism, 27:2; 31:1; 56:2, 2; 1168:8; 1313:3; 1618:21; 1620:7; 2413:3; 3731:15; apartheid in ~, 3184:7; changes in ~, 3143.1:1; conflict of ~, 3699:2; defense of ~, 1870:1; education in ~, 4948:1; eradication of ~, 3394:4; ~ in relation to America, 3143.1:2; 4026:1; ~ in relation to Arab nations, 1261:4; 1618:27; 1870:3, 7; 4903:2; ~ in relation to Palestine, 2650:2; 2722:3; 4458:4, 5; 4810:1; ~ justice, 2722:5; Middle East attitude toward ~, 1870:2; other nations in relation to ~, 48:6; ~ peace movement, 3699:1; ~ policy, 4326:2; prejudice against ~, 1168:10; survival of ~, 4026:2; ~ under attack, 4458:1, 3; visiting ~, 2141:1; ~ women, 2344:2; 2650:1; 3323:1; 4904:2
Italian/Italy, 723:2; 1012:1; 1201:4; 1215:1; alone in ~, 2226:2; ~ American women, 2509:2; ~ architecture, 671:9; government of ~, 733:19; ~ in relation to America, 4959:1; ~ men, 2190:2; ~ Parliament, 1582:2; political system of ~, 4959:2; treasures of ~, 1292:8

J

J. P. Morgan & Co., 4761.1:4
Jackson, Jesse, 4308:1
Jackson, Michael, 4478:3

jail *see also* prison, 2259:6; 2260:4; horrors of ~, 3773:1; shock of ~, 2672:1
Jamaica/n, 3645:1
James, Henry, 1292:11; 3099:25
Jane Eyre, 2978:1
Janus, 895:1
Japan/ese, 1983:1; characteristics of ~, 1659:6; 2019:5; ~ immigrants, 4420:5; Kobe ~ after World War II, 4413:1; ~ language, 3580:2; militarism in ~, 897:1; rural ~, 4507:3; ~ saying, 2475:2; spirituality in ~, 2817:14; travel in ~, 1926:2; ~ values, 2903:1; women in ~, 3232:1
Japanese American, ~internment of, 2504:3; 2897:1; Manzanar Internment Camp (California), 2897:1
jealousy *see also* envy; possessiveness, 1262:9; 1973:3; 2945:6; breeding ~, 2477:1
Jeffers, Robinson, 2669:1
Jefferson, Thomas, 4532:2
Jenkinson, Robert Banks, 754:2
Jerusalem *see also* Israel/i; Palestine/Palestinian, 108:1; 797:3; 2977:6; 4116:5
Jesus Christ *see also* God; Holy Ghost; Messiah; ~, 83:1; 110:1; 178:1; 255:1; 537:1, 2; 597:1; 848:2; 870:8; 877:1; 890:8; 979:1; 982:8; 983:4; 1006:14; 1056:1; 1161:2; 1219:1; 1270:2; 1522:1; 1610:2; 1713:2; 2028:4; 2067:0; 2078:5; 2318:2; 2636:1; 2690:2; 2756:19; 3241:1; 3284:6; 3298:4, 5; 3473:3; 3652:5; 3696:1; 3852:3; 3925:6; 4089:4; 4312:7; 4735:4; 4785:3; 4904:1; ~ and death penalty, 3155:3; ~ and fathers, 4481:6; androgyny of ~, 291:1; 432–433:3; birthday of ~, 4763:1; concept of ~, 3440:3; death of ~, 81:1; faith in ~, 2909:1; ~ imprisoned, 2543:1; ~ in relation to church, 3771:3; ~ in relation to women, 214:3; 372:3; 428:2; 860:6; indifference towards ~, 3412:7; infant ~, 234:6; lack of faith in ~, 2534:2; life of ~, 2133:4; love of ~, 478:1; 567:2; 809:1; miracles of ~, 405:3; mythology of ~, 4300:1; rejection of ~, 3779:2; robe of ~, 312:3; ~ within, 622:2; word of ~, 352:4
Jew/Judaism *see also* anti-Semitism; Israel/i; Jerusalem; Messiah; synagogue; Torah, 932:1, 2; 955:29; 1168:1; 1562:4; 1674:6; 1947:4; 2157:1; 2380:9; 2413:1; 2432:4; 2636:1; 2638:6; 2690:2; 2722:2, 4; 2940:2, 4; 4011:2; 4292:4; 4326:7; 4835:3; ~ and Israel, 1261:3; 1618:27; ~ and money, 4085:2; annihilation of

~, 1870:2; ~ anxiety, 2932:8; ~ banishment from England, 473:1; ~ commandments, 2432:5; ~ community, 4490:1; defense of ~, 1870:5; diaspora of ~, 3394:3; disparagement of ~, 334:7; ~ family, 1202:2; ~ food, 1202:1; goals of ~, 2494:3; growing up ~, 2476:1; history of ~, 4023:2; ~ holiday, 3113:4; ~ home, 1202:0; homosexuality and ~, 4490:2, 2; ~ identity, 1563:4, 5; 3276:2; image of ~, 1905:2; ~ in America, 1207:0; ~ in Eastern Europe, 3581:3; ~ in Middle East, 3233:3; ~ in relation to Arabs, 1261:4; 2673:2, 4; ~ in relation to children, 788:2; ~ in relation to Muslims, 4747:3; ~ in World War II, 1870:5; Kaddish and ~, 4011:1; legacy of ~, 788:2; lesbian ~, 2833:1; memory and ~, 3793:1; 4251:1; observance of ~, 4302:1; Orthodox ~, 3039:2; persecution of ~, 2873:2; purpose of ~, 2437:11; ~ religious service, 931:25; sexism in ~, 2650:1; 4539:1; studying ~, 4201:1; test of ~, 1145:2; transformation of ~, 3969:4; unlit ~ menorah, 2943:10; ~ women activists, 3082:1; women and ~, 797:2; 1249:1; 1261:7, 10; 1281:1; 1304:3, 4; 1313:5, 6; 1681:2; 2398:15; 3028:1; 3206:1; 3320:1, 4; 3785:2; 4779:1; 4817:3

jewel/ry, 485:1; 1686:1; 2801:7; 3836:2

Joan of Arc, 1425:1; 2943:1

job *see also* employment, competition for ~, 4244–4245:2; ~ counselor, 3257:8; creating one's own ~, 1847:5; dressing for ~, 4675:1; ~ for woman, 3071:1; loss of ~ (*see also* unemployment), 4244–4245:3; ~ qualifications, 2400:1; risky ~, 4737:1; routine ~, 3420:4; ~ satisfaction, 4521:2; ~ security, 3151:1

Job, Story of, 4310:4

Jobs, Steve, 4566:4

jockey *see also* horseracing, 3541:1

John the Baptist, 82:1

Johnson, Samuel, 615:1; 635:5

joke *see also* humor; wisecrack, different taste in ~, 1740:2; unappreciated ~, 4109:2

Joplin, Scott, 2680:27

Jordan, go over ~, 1592:5

journal *see also* diarist/diary, 1217:1; 2760:1; travel ~, 4548:1; ~ writing, 3629:3; 3810:1

journalism/journalist *see also* blog/ger; broadcaster; 2393:3; 2904:1; 4019:1; 4463:4; 4759:3; ~ abroad, 4947:1; facts and ~,

4128:2; failure of ~, 4452:3; fears of ~, 2904:3; good ~, 4437.1:4; immersion ~, 4713:5; importance of ~, 4437.1:3; morality of ~, 2219:5; 4277:2; pack ~, 3053:1; truth in ~, 1642:2; 4562:1

journey *see also* travel; trip; voyage, ~ alone, 124:1; ~ by air (*see also* flight/flying), 734:8; charting one's ~, 3689:1; end of ~, 887:26; inner ~, 2680:30; mountain ~, 1689:4; personal ~, 4327:1; preparation for ~, 1687:6; separate ~, 240:1; 3955:1

joy *see also* bliss; happiness; rejoicing, 206:1; 271:1; 356:1; 439:3; 462:2; 1174:4; 1619:3, 7; 1710:3; 1843:11; 1986:4; 3301:4; 3349:12; remembered ~, 801:2; shared ~, 3863:1

joylessness, 1337:4

Judaism *see* Jew/Judaism, 1168:9

judgement *see also* opinion; taste [preference], 455:3; 522:2; 934:6; good ~, 819:1; hasty ~, 313:1; passing ~, 27:1; 585:2; 650:2; 2409:3; 3968:3; 4197:5; poor ~, 671:10; suspending ~, 2834:3; thoughtful ~, 1315:6

Judgement Day, 234:3; 4718:2; facing ~, 2842:1

judiciary *see also* court [judicial]; jurist; jury; law; legal system, independent ~, 3299:1; protecting ~, 2963:3; sexism in ~, 2178:2; women in ~, 3890:2; 4231:3; 4273.1:5

jumping, 4621:2

jungle *see also* forest, life in ~, 4578:1

juniper, 287:6

jurisprudence, 1981:4; 3946:1

jurist *see also* judiciary; lawyer, 1693:4; 2316:1; 4269:2; decision of ~, 2850:4

jury *see also* judiciary, 2563:6; importance of ~, 2871:3

justice *see also* fairness, 75:2; 193:6; 234:2; 326:2; 950:2; 955:13; 1114:3; 1340:1; 1452:1; 1603:2; 1618:4; 1799:1; 1981:5; 2178:1; 2237:2; 2458:3; 2997:10; 3073:2; 3214:3; 4112:1; 4444:2; 4988:0; ~ and accountability, 4263:2; blind ~, 2272:3; cost of ~, 2797:4; 3946:3; environmental ~, 4926:2; ethics of ~, 2979:4; ~ for the poor, 3006:1; ~ in America, 4137:5; 4169:2; ~ in relation to custom, 244:1; international ~, 1167:19; juvenile ~, 3141:2; lack of ~ (*see also* inequity; injustice), 282:2; 4430:3; law and ~, 923:1; moving toward ~, 1625:3; ~ of life, 2874:3; passion for ~, 3669:6; pursuit of ~, 4091:1, 2; 4185:3; quality

of ~, 4838–4839:1; repressive ~, 2116:14; right to ~, 1000:1; satisfaction of ~, 2847:1; seeking ~, 3240:3; sense of ~, 1903:3; social ~, 3418:4; universal ~, 1863:8; war for ~, 4045:9; world ~, 3418:2; 3640:1; 4282:2

justification, moral ~, 2925:3

juvenile delinquent *see also* criminal, 449:2; 1981:4; 2281:6

K

Kansas, 3854:1; ~ Territory, 3939:3; ~ winds, 1346:2

Kant, Immanuel, 4321:2

karma *see also* destiny, 166:5; 1034:3; 4894:4

Kazakhstan, Republic of, 4439:2

Keats, John, 2890:2

Kennedy family, 1710:1; 2676:4; 4417:3; Jackie ~ (*see* Onassis, Jacqueline Kennedy)

Kennedy, John F., 1618:33; 2323:2; 2676:7; 4417:1; assassination of ~, 2180:1

Kenya, human rights in ~, 4983:3; ~ in relation to America, 4775:3; Mau Mau uprising in ~, 4786:2; peace in ~, 4545:1; women in ~, 3916:2

KGB (Komitet Gosudarstvennoy Bezopasnosti), 2447:2

kidnapping, victim of ~, 3611.1:3

kill/er *see also* murder/er, 2783:1; refusing to ~, 3374:3; young ~, 4735:3

killing *see also* massacre; murder/er, 1870:13; 1980:2; 2659:1; 2735:2; 2771:5; 2922:2; 3241:2; 3921:5; ~ children, 3141:8; honor ~, 4292:2; ~ in war time, 226:1; 1870:7; men and ~, 1447:1; 1474:6

kindness *see also* compassion; humaneness, 637:1; 1025:4; 1450:26; 1566:2; 1576:3; 2001:1; 2364:6; 2732:6; 2772:3; 4045:9; lack of ~, 1408:9; response to ~, 1409:18

king *see also* royal/ty, 255:1; 264:2; 374:2; 764:2; attributes of ~, 334:3; death of ~, 113:2; demands upon ~, 320:1; new ~, 898:1; ~ of England (*also see* specific kings), 1898:1; rule of ~, 1675–1676:4

King, Jr., Martin Luther, 2615:1; 2642:2; 3213:1; 3412:1; 4149:1; marching with ~, 4368:2

kiss/ing, 316:4; 533:16; 551:1; 1109:1; 1386:1; 1389:2; 1409:15; 1686:4; 1700:4; 3720:2; 3799:4; 3939:8; 4650:5; 4955:1; routine ~, 1761:1; telling ~, 3751:1; thrill of ~, 845:7

Kissinger, Henry, 2898:4

kitchen, 487:9; 1129:1; 2748:3; 2811:1; 2817:19; 3961:3; clean

~, 2208:2; 3465:2; messy ~, 2596:3; ~ table, 4045:8; working in ~, 3797:4

Klopstock, Frederich Gottlieb, 602:1

knife, 4180:4

knitting *see also* needlecraft, 1869:2

knowledge *see also* information; wisdom, 215:3; 244:5; 273–274:3; 369:4; 372:1; 412:7; 430:5; 533:11; 827:3; 859:5; 977:3; 1209:6; 1264:1; 1548:1; 1593:7; 1663:7; 1944:1; 2135:4; 2162:2; 2472:7; 3317:8; 4251:7; anatomy of ~, 1558:2; burden of ~, 3602:3; changing ~, 2837:2; danger of ~, 859:2; desire for ~, 2956:3; differing ~, 3065:2; ~ for power's sake, 555:1; gaining ~, 1333:5; 4449:2; generational ~, 2747:5; gift of ~, 193:1; 1383:4; humbled by ~, 801:9; intimate ~, 2564:1; lack of ~ (*also see* ignorance), 516:1; 820:3; 2731:2; 4639:1; limits of ~, 2954:1; misused ~, 2776:4; need for ~, 1578:1; ~ of others, 4509:2; ~ of self (*see also* self-knowledge), 734:19; 1780:2; 1844:3; poverty of ~, 3390:1; price of ~, 2066:2; protecting ~, 2606:3; quest for ~, 1803:3; 2711:10; responsibility of ~, 4040:3; seeking ~, 2456:10; thirst for ~, 1206:1; 2771:12; 2981:4; transmitting ~, 1381:14; wonders of ~, 1441:3

Koran *see also* Bible; Islam; Moslem; scripture, 4292:1; 4556:1; 4627:2; studying ~, 2977:3

Korea/n, ~ in relation to blacks, 4006:1; ~ women, 4419:4

kosher *see also* halal, 4902:2

Ku Klux Klan, 2242:3; 4478:4

Kurd/istan, 4599:1

Kyoto Protocol, 4405:6; Russia and ~, 3960:2

L

label, 1408:15; 1999:2

labor/er *see also* employee; industriousness; job; toil; worker, 915:3; 2156:1; ~ agitator, 1706:1; ~ and trade, 1471:2; child ~, 1473:1; 1561:1; constant ~, 801:13; domestic ~, 3081:2; ~ during war, 1471:1; exploitation of ~, 2716:4; exploitation of female ~, 1229:2; farm ~, 1589:4; forced ~, 4782:3; gender of ~, 3020:2; hard ~, 1037:2, 4; 4129:2; household ~ (*see also* housekeeper; servant), 3020:1; indentured ~, 784:2; life of ~, 2806:2; man's ~, 376:1; 2995:3; ~ market (*see also* workforce, control of) ~, 963:9; oppression of ~, 944:6; 2341:1; rewards of ~, 665:1; 1254:3; skilled ~, 1003:2; timeliness of

~, 257:1; unpaid ~ of women, 1007:8; woman ~, 3171:1

labor movement, 2716:2; American ~, 1471:2

labor union, benefits of ~, 1384:5; dictates of ~, 1588:1; ~ member, 1384:4

Labour Party (Great Britain), 1803:2

lady see also woman/women, 224:1; 1201:2; 1209:3; 1482:2; 1704:1; 1768:1; 2002–2003:2; white ~, 2771:2

Lafayette, Marquis de, 733:17

Lagerlöf, Selma, 1233:9

Lagos, Richard, 4022:1

lake, degradation of ~, 4942:2

Lake Victoria, 4942:2

land see also field [land]; landscape; soil, 968:1; 1008:4; 1741:5; 1914:1; 3753:2; 4242:3; beauty of ~, 2235:1; belonging to ~, 2747:3, 5; 2942:3; 3263:1; ~ boundaries, 4952:3; connection to ~, 2156:2; 2604:4; 3052:4; 4623:3; cultivating ~ (see also farming), 593:7; dry ~, 3705:1; knowledge from ~, 4551:3; ~ management, 4551:2; memory of ~, 2609:3; message of ~, 2371:4; need for ~, 3818:1; 4559:2; ownership of ~, 2784:2; 2895:2; 4774:1; protecting ~, 4551:1; 4848:1; stolen ~, 3866:2; uncultivated ~, 1655:5; vast ~, 2535:1; working ~ (see also farming), 2771:8

landlord, 2765:1

landscape, 2914:1; 4067:7; harshness of ~, 2797:3; picture perfect ~, 2858:5; understanding ~, 3851:3

Lange, Jessica, 4013:7

language see also linguist; syntax, 369:5; 1304:1; 1325:3; 2680:5; 2771:20; 3262:2; 3269:3; 3439:3; 3484:1; 3937:3; 4072:2; adopting new ~, 4418:1; ageisms in ~, 3089:6; changing ~, 3439:4; dead ~, 1470:4; English ~, 4639:4; feminine ~, 4197:3; filter of ~, 2350:2; formality of ~, 4079:5; French ~, 1889:2; 2355:2; 3356:5; 3968:2; gender and ~, 4296:2; German ~, 3356:5; Hebrew ~, 3356:5; humor of foreign ~, 1590:5; influence of ~, 3937:2; 4601:3; Italian ~, 3356:5; ~ of jargon, 2931:9; Latin ~, 1408:11; learning ~, 2349:14; liturgical ~, 3028:1; 3506:1; manipulating ~, 2996:5; non-sexist ~, 3228:1; ~ of native tongue, 3941:3; oppressive ~, 2771:18; perspective in ~, 4296:2; philosophy of ~, 3277:2; poetic ~, 4367:7; ~ police, 2931:9; politics of ~, 3283:2;

power of ~, 2958:3; pretentious ~, 804:5; purpose of ~, 643:3; Russian ~, 1692:4; sad ~, 1843:; sexism in ~, 2183:2; 2350:1; 2471:1; 2916:11, 14; 2958:3; 3519:4; 3526:1; 3533:3; 3591:4; 4539:3; 4644:3; 4734:1; ~ skills, 2547:2; Spanish ~, 3830:3; unskilled in ~, 2509:1; unwritten ~, 1929:2; ~ well spoken, 4558:3; Yiddish ~, 2151:2; 2728:4

largess see also generosity, 347:2

Las Vegas (Nevada) 3358:1; 3656:1

lateness, 643:4; 821:4; 2686:2; 4390:4; 4884:4

Latin America/n see also specific nations; Latino/a, 1930:2; 2890:1; 4022:3; anti-Semitism in ~, 4187:4; children in ~, 4919:3; class in ~, 4666:3; ~ in relation to world, 2930:1; ~ men, 1996:1; trade with ~, 4022:4; transformation of ~, 4187:1

Latino/a, ~ and language, 3830:3; education and ~, 3830:2; identity of ~, 4666:1

Lauder, Estee, 4251:8

laugh/ter see also mirth, 8:2, 2; 382:2; 643:8; 1209:1; 1574:4; 1870:12; 2063:4; 2349:15; 2494:1; 2931:5; 4476:2; 4857:4; ~ at oneself, 1520:4; balm of ~, 2184:3; 3442:3; belly ~, 4070:3; bittersweet ~, 1433:2; die ~, 2117:7; good ~, 3596:2; medicine of ~, 3470:5; need of ~, 1711:1; object of ~, 799:4; women and ~, 2490:6; 3165:4

laundry see also housework, 1697:7; 2266.1:1; folding ~, 3409:1

law see also judiciary; lawmaker; lawyer; legal defense; legal system; legislation; rules; trial, 706:3; 734:10; 806:1; 955:11; 1244:1; 1360:12; 1452:1; 2265:4; 2540:5; 2743:3; 3088:1; 3373:2, 4; 3387:1; 4080:4; 4323:2; 4802:4; adjudicating ~, 1874:5; American women and ~, 1484:1; antiquated ~, 4156:1, 2; ~ as indicator of behavior, 2756:10; attitude towards ~, 2085:4; authority of statute ~, 1625:2; bad ~, 1146:2; basis of ~, 2876:5; breaking ~, 1935:15; changing ~, 2551:3; common ~ and parental duty, 3893:1; contempt for ~, 2192:12; correction of ~, 1803:1; due process of ~, 2743:1; 3071:2; enacting ~, 2517:5; enforcing ~, 3556:3; environmental ~, 4482:1; 4936:2; equality under ~, 656:4; 931:7; ~ firm and women, 1738:1; flexibility of ~, 1360:10; gender equity in ~, 931:1; ~ in relation to women, 2876:1; 2900:4; 3674:6; ~ in technological age,

4156:1; ineffectiveness of ~, 2291:1; international ~, 1029:3; justice and ~, 2674:1; litigation, 3068:5; love of ~, 2499:1; marital ~, 874:8; 2540:4; natural ~, 1977:1; obeying ~, 650:1; origins of ~, 1625:3; petty ~, 1089:6; precedent in ~, 1971:2; 4156:3; progress of ~, 1625:1; Puritanical ~, 3896:2; reasons for ~, 934:7; redefine ~, 4079:3; rule of ~, 2876:1; Salic ~, 304:2; 529:3; ~ school, 2349:1; sex discrimination in ~, 3674:4; sexism in ~, 1029:2; 1776:5; 2850:1; 3056:1; 3489:1; 3674:1; sexual harassment and ~, 4122:4; spirit of ~, 4079:4; ~ suit, 1074:1; trust in ~, 326:2; 713:15; unjust ~, 1125:1; vile ~, 2628:3; women ~ students, 1738:1; 2254:1; women in ~ profession, 1971:1; 3331:1; 3809:1; world rule of ~, 1935:11

lawmaker see also Congress, U.S.; politician, 2551:3

Lawrence (T. E.) of Arabia, 1731:1

Lawrence, D. H., 1524:2; 1661:1; sex and ~, 1530:2

lawyer see also law; legal profession, 1782:8; 1844:4; 3156:1; 3306:3; 3674:2; conscience of ~, 3616:1; courtroom ~, 2063:5; 2563:5; craftiness of ~, 2871:3; defense ~, 3099:6; divorce ~, 2463:4; elderly ~, 1746:1; ~ fees, 4137:2; honest ~, 1376:4; ~ in relation to client, 4720:1; ~ in relation to justice, 2433:1; 3946:3; mercenary ~, 340:3; 412:1; wife of ~, 2337:3; woman ~, 1165:2, 3; 3275:1; 4138:2; 4231:3; 4315:1; 4399:1

laziness see also idleness, 1673:2; 2349:5; 2790:1; 3964:1; ~ in men, 4598:2; justification for ~, 1715:3; 1910:2

leader/ship see also specific types; head of state; rule/r, 1021:2; 1584:3; 1959:5; 2608:2; 2733:3; 3193:2; 3213:1; 3311:5; 3393:3; 4112:2; 4244–4245:1; 4702:1; American ~, 3344:2; 3731:22; attitude towards ~, 2830:1; challenge of ~, 4014:2; change in ~, 4559:4; character of ~, 1689:12; 2969:3; 4429:3; charismatic ~, 2977:5; 3166:2; corrupt ~, 3805:1; danger to ~, 276:1; death of ~, 116:1; demands of ~, 3822:2; desire for ~, 3976:4; differences between men and women ~, 4527:3; failed ~, 4088:4; following ~, 2323:4; gender and ~, 2300:5; government ~, 4657:2; impact of ~ on society, 701:3; importance of ~, 4846:3; ~ in relation to war, 1870:8; 4326:6; insufficient ~, 1712:2; intel-

lectual ~, 2032:15; international ~, 3343:6; loss of ~, 1589:2; married to ~, 2905:3; money and ~, 109:1; moral authority of ~, 4282:2; 4545:3; necessity for ~, 334:5; perception of ~, 3166:1; political ~, 3166:3; qualities of ~, 3343:5; repressive ~, 4437:1; resistance to male ~, 2400:3; role of ~, 75:1; spiritual ~, 1618:26; ~ style, 4135:1; tools of ~, 80:1; treacherous ~, 4129:1; women & ~, 176:3; 2357:1; 2823:3; 2930:4; 2943:1; 2965:3; 3078:6; 3090:4; 3384:2; 3558:1; 3978:4, 5; 3997:2; 4066:6; 4714.1:2

leaf, 758:3; 1788:1; autumn ~, 1868:1; summer ~, 3225:3

League of Nations see also United Nations, 1519:3

learning see also education, 273–274:6; 472:2; 616:2; 1193:8, 10; 1876:2; 1896:4; 2025:8; 2056:2; 2079:2; 2189:1; 2409:6; 2563:4; 2618:12; 2954:1; 4081:6; 4667:2; ~ ABCs, 1015:3; age and ~, 2165:3; book ~, 1554:5; ~ by osmosis, 1763:4; child's way of ~, 2434:5; 2630:2, 3; 3042:2; 3077:2; concealed ~, 488:2; desire for ~, 273–274:3; domino effect of ~, 2776:3; experiential ~, 2837:3; ~ from others, 2735:4; 4449:2; 4623:4; importance of ~, 3709:1; joy of ~, 1529:4; 3520:2; lifelong ~, 2165:3; 3418:1; prejudice against ~, 166:1; women and ~, 466:7

Lebanon, Christians of ~, 4918:1

Lebron, Lolita, 4805:1

lechery see also philanderer, 383:3

lecture/r, successful ~, 3820:2

legacy see also inheritance, 287:1; 955:36; 1224:2; 1453:7; 1974:2; 2612:3; 3902:1; 4986:1; leaving a ~, 3008:4; ~ of history, 2585:1; ~ of parents, 2255:2; ~ to self, 1715:1

legal defense, 3103:2

legal profession, impact of ~, 4536:1

legal system see also judiciary; law, bigotry in ~, 2272:3; plea-bargaining in ~, 4838–4839:1; public participation in ~, 2743:2

legend/ary see also myth/ology, 2268:2; living ~, 3379:4; ~ of matriarchy, 2183:3; telling ~ (see also storyteller/storytelling), 2918:2

legibility, 1773:2

legislation see also law, atmosphere of ~, 2824:1; changing ~, 3579:2

Legree, Simon, 987:2

leisure see also pleasure; relaxation, 684:1; 4081:3; 4637:1; cultured ~, 3004:2

Lenin, Vladimir Ilich, 4665:1

Lennon, John, 4270:1

lesbian/ism *see also* gay liberation movement; homosexuality, 1545:2; 1838:4; 2080:5; 2201:9; 2407:1, 2; 2665:3; 2680:21; 2701:1; 3015:2; 3023:1; 3194:1; 3690:4; 3834:3; 4125:2; disclosure of ~, 3644:1; mother of ~, 2667:2; open ~, 3579:4; ~ partnership, 3769:1; politics of ~, 3015:1; 3237:3; roots of ~, 2618:4; sex and ~, 2008:1; 2407:3; sophisticated ~, 3126:1

lesson, ~ at 50, 1412:6; ~ in life, 3978:1; learning ~, 3146:3; 4827:3; ~ of life, 489:2; 745:2; 870:10; 1265:1; 1362:4; 1701:4; 1846:5; 1990:1; 2263:2; 2612:1; 2957:2; 3048:1; 3349:11; 4404:2; painful ~, 1002:4

lethargy *also see* inactivity, ~ of society, 2886:1

letter (communication) *see also* mail, 175:1; 321:1; 453:2; 576:1; 1828:1; ~ home, 3473:2; love ~, 620:2; 754:1; 2170:3; personal ~, 296:1; survival of ~, 1662:8; undelivered ~, 163:1; unopened ~, 2132:1; writing ~, 163:4; 2153:11; 2270:1; 3439:1

letter (symbol) *see also* humanities; literary world, study of ~, 422:3; world of ~, 961:2

liberal/ism, 2743:1; 3139:1; 3379:6; 3780:7; 3939:10; ~ agenda, 4031:1; ~ in United States, 4211:3

liberation *see also specific social movements;* emancipation; freedom; rights, 2126:2; 2623:5; 2796:1; 2901:2; 3686:1; 3729:3; 3754:3; attaining ~, 1897:4; 4927:4; ideology of ~, 3976:1; impact of ~ on individual, 2901:2; ~ of oppressed, 2272:4

Liberia/n, 3090:1; 4719:1, 3; ~ women, 3090:2

liberty *see also* freedom, 49:1; 482:1; 678:1; 782:3; 901:3; 1603:1; 2027:12; 2537:9; 3245:2; civil ~, 677:5; demands of ~, 2654:5; fight for ~, 86:1, 2; 1030:2; peacefully attained ~, 690:1; personal ~, 1301:5; restrictions on ~, 1244:1; sense of ~, 916:7; true ~, 1552:4; women and ~, 632:1; world ~, 4282:2

librarian, 1527:2

library, 451:5; 472:18; 808:13; 3145:14; 4111:1; children and ~, 4111:3; community and ~, 4111:2; fear of ~, 4465:2; private ~, 4175:5; university ~, 3097:8

licentiousness, 465:5

lie/lying *see also* deceit/deception; falseness; trick/ery; 63:2; 304:1; 361:1; 427:1; 511:10; 563:1; 1096:1; 1190:2; 1216:1; 1325:4; 1512:8; 1724:5; 1729:3; 1744:1; 1987:1; 2388:3; 2393:1; 2448:2; 2572:1; 2944:6; 3009:4; 3812:1; 4078:1; 4084:6; accepting ~, 2087:2; believing ~, 4565:2; dull ~, 3781:1; ~ eyes, 1714:1; government ~, 3554:3; paid to ~, 3726:1

life *see also* existence; lifestyle; living, 166:6; 280:1; 297:1; 308:10; 367:2; 733:12; 892:13; 899:2; 1024:22; 1213:4; 1336:9; 1472:1; 1476:1; 1547:1; 1654:8; 1845:2; 1896:8; 2187:14; 2202:1; 2212:3; 2381:4; 2550:3; 3039:9; 3087:1; 3291:4; 3311:4; 3464:1; 3562:2; 3691:7; 4150:1; 4251:6; 4255:5; 4289:5; 4884:6; accepting ~, 2090:1; 2260:2; 2504:1; 3504:2; adventure of ~, 1548:11; 2286:8; affect of politics on daily ~, 2625:1; appetite for ~, 1591:1; approach to ~, 4123:2; battle of ~, 3488:2; beginning of ~, 497:4; brevity of ~, 1024:10; 4603:2; building ~, 2917:4; burning with ~, 1751:12; care of ~, 1471:4; choices in ~, 4160:6; claim on ~, 1601:8; clinging to ~, 1147:3; closed ~, 2021:13; confines of ~, 4740:1; conquering ~, 2618:9; continuance of ~, 1751:5, 18; 2025:5; 3705:2; cost of ~, 1927:2; course of ~, 1689:2; creation of ~, 1965:1; cruelty of ~, 1301:8; cup of ~, 1689:5; cycle of ~, 489:4; 629:2; 1446:2; 1751:32; 1905:1; 3094:4; 3472:2; 3551–3552:1; 3779:1; 4235:4; daily ~, 1713:2; 1734:2; 2680:26; 3109:1; 3442:4; 3555:1; decline of ~, 3268:4; definition of ~, 2793:2; depleted ~, 3038:1; desire for ~, 1782:6; 3862:1; difficulties of ~, 306:2; 411:3; 459:4; 862:2; 1127:4; 1251:6; 2184:3; 2637:5; 2867:2; 2942:1; direction of ~, 674:3; drama of ~, 2387:1; duration of ~, 671:6; 785:4; enemy of ~, 3032:5; enjoyment of ~, 3594:2; exotic ~, 2208:3; experiencing ~, 1872:1; 1927:1; 2248:3; ~ extension, 3535:5; facts of ~, 3139:10; fleeting ~ (*see also* transience, ~ of life), 299:2; 325:4; 412:3; 472:13; 1002:3; 1067:3; 1322:2; 1785:2; ~ force, 179:2; 293:2; 1416:1; 1801:1; full of ~, 2170:1; game of ~, 4929:5; glory of ~, 1347:2; good ~, 234:4; 1114:2; grateful for ~, 2299:3; hard ~, 802:3; hidden ~, 3099:24; holding fast to ~, 2529:1; horror of daily ~, 2817:3; immersion in ~, 3066:4; imprisonment of ~, 945:3; 3033:3; inner ~ (*see* inner life); insignificance of ~, 658:6; irony of ~, 2618:5; ~ is over, 1560:1; larger than ~, 2345:5; lessons of ~ (*see* lesson, of ~); love of ~, 635:2; 1507:1; 1894:2; 2756:3; 3357:4; making best of ~, 1201:10; 3309:7; mastering ~, 863:1; meaning of ~, 2956:3; 3478:1; meaninglessness of ~, 450:2; 603:4; 4062:1; measure of ~, 1094:1; 1701:3; mess of ~, 4297:1; 4341:4; misery of ~, 2953:1; 3847:3; mission in ~, 4411:3; mystery of ~, 1039:5; 1627:2; 3808:4; narrative of ~, 3629:4; narrowness of ~, 1666:2; new ~, 4667:1; observation of ~, 70:2; ~ of ease, 1251:6; 4396:3; open ~, 1120:7; orderly ~, 237:4; 584:4; origins of ~, 3106:3; pace of ~, 2298:1; 2621:2; participation in ~, 4101:1; passage of ~, 1077:1; 1264:4; path of ~ (*see also* path), 248:2; 423:3; 482:2; 1233:5; 1751:17; 1878:3; 2053:5; 2668:4; 2965:2; 3110:4; 3309:8; pattern of ~, 2355:3; 4067:6; physical ~, 4151:2; precariousness of ~, 4501:0; prime of ~, 2331:4; 3059:4; priorities in ~, 2331:5; productive ~, 2645:1; prolonging ~, 3923:2; purpose of ~, 1013:0; 1867:2; 2034:1; 2255:2; 2560:6; 2727:3; 2775:1; 2941:4; 3669:2; 3731:1; 4109:3; 4174:9; 4216:3; quality of ~, 3778:2; randomness of ~, 3330:4; record of ~, 4929:4; respect for ~, 1167:12; 4117:1; reverence for ~, 4278:4; rich ~, 3355:5; 4280:2; sacredness of ~, 1227:2; saintly ~, 1532:2; saving one's ~, 3571:2; secret of ~, 2464:2; 4255:1; simple ~, 3908–3909:1, 2; 4412:1; solitary ~, 2297:7; specialness of ~, 2845:2; spirit in ~ (*see also* religion; religious life; spirit/uality), 325:3; 361:2; 629:3; 1903:6; 4126:1; story of ~, 2490:4; struggles of ~, 175:2; 237:6; 313:3; 316:2; 325:3; 428:1; 711:4; 880:1; 922:6; 1032:4; 1090:3; 1209:9; 1645:1; 1698:2; 1751:29; 2281:4; 2461:1; 2866:16; 3497:2; 4076:1; substance of ~, 1482:3; sustaining ~, 4339:4; tolerating ~, 2154:6; turning point in ~, 1326:1; unblessed ~, 4872:3; understanding ~, 107:1; 2490:2; unfulfilled ~, 2916:13; unhappy ~, 448:2; unpredictability of ~, 336:1; value of ~, 1276:2; 2413:5; 3350–3351:1; 4062:3; 4220:1; wasted ~, 802:4; weariness of ~, 4902:1; web of ~, 2425:3; 3704:7; welcoming ~, 4945:1

Life (magazine), 3697:1

lifeless/ness *see also* dead/ness, 1880:3

lifestyle, 273–274:5; 3154:1; alternative ~, 3612:1; criticizing ~, 4456:1

light *see also* illumination, 1670:6; bright ~, 3216:4; ~ design, 2533:1; shedding ~, 1248:3; swamp ~, 1140:1

Lillie, Beatrice, 1869:1

limb (human), long ~, 4819:2

limitations *see also* restraint, 2056:7; 3811:2; awareness of ~, 289:5; 2150:2; defying ~, 2866:20; knowing one's ~, 4207:4; pushed beyond one's ~, 2206:3; reaching one's ~, 3733:4; setting ~, 2998:2

Lin, Maya, 2680:24

Lincoln, Abraham, 989:3; 1227:6; 1453:2; 3353:3; 3415:5; cabinet of ~, 3415:3, 4; death of ~, 1589:2; intellect of ~, 3415:2

Lincoln, Mary Todd, 1035:1; 4093:1, 2

Lindbergh, Charles, 1635:1

Lindsay, John L., 3421:3

lingerie *see also* underwear, 1780:13; 4205:2

linguist *see also* language, 1780:12

lips (human), 144:1; 1209:4;

lipstick, 4684:1

liquor *see also* alcohol/ism; drinking; drunkard, 508:2; 531:1; 714:1; 1146:4; 1308:1; 2715:3; abstain from ~, 808:1; benefits of ~, 767:22; 790:6; effects of ~, 938:1; taste of ~, 3303:2

list (written), making ~, 1836:6

listening, 1758:3, 6; 2834:3; 3121:4; 4285:8; active ~, 2813:0; 3540:1; compassionate ~, 3782:3; no one ~, 1789:3; ~ without interruption, 3965:1

Liszt, Franz, 887:21

literacy, ~ in relation to economy, 3761:5

literature *see also* book; fiction; narrative; novel/ist; reading; story; writing, 1166:4; 1450:8; 1548:3; 2349:12; 2409:5; 4175:2; 4280:3; American ~, 910:9; ~ and gender, 2472:3; classical ~, 3788:3; educational aspects of ~, 2358:1; escapist ~, 2668:12; essence of ~, 1504:1; great works of ~, 3778:3; illusion of ~, 2945:5; impact of ~, 3778:5; ~ in India, 4595:5; ~ in industrialized nations, 2689:4; masterpieces of ~, 841:1; men in ~, 3144:2; misogyny in ~, 1487:3; need for ~, 1904:2; ~ of an era, 1336:5; patriarchy of ~, 2668:23; roots of women's ~, 3052:2; symbolism in ~, 2978:1; test of ~, 1662:2; trash in ~, 2472:9; women in ~,

1162:4; 1590:9; 2353:2; 3147:3; 3446:2; women's ~, 3052:3; Yiddish ~, 3276:5

litigation, 3068:5; ~ between married couple, 2295:1

Little Rock, Arkansas, 2036:8

livelihood *see also* annuity; employment; job; wage, earning ~, 1044:18; inequities in earning ~, 2127:4; seeking ~, 705:3; value of ~, 4385:3

living *see also* existence; life, 892:11; 1408:13; 1693:5; 1788:3; 2198:2; 2534:4; 2620:3; 3364:1; 3571:1; art of ~, 4125:6; business of ~, 2537:12; ~ each day, 733:21; 801:4; 1265:1; 1994:3; fighting for the ~, 1028:3; ~ for oneself, 1184:12; ~ for others, 1122:4; ~ fully, 1354:2; 1431:5; 2552:13; 2799:5; 3576:3; 3824:2; practice ~, 2686:1; reason for ~, 1899:2; 2281:10; rules for ~, 2866:17; terms of ~, 1675–1676:1; thoughtful ~, 1025:9

loan *see* bank/er

lobbyist, 2356:1; 2856:2

lock, 4975:2

logging, devastation of over-~, 4821:3

logic *see also* rational; reason; sense, 1924:1; 4062:1; belief in ~, 942:1; fallacy in ~, 3567:6; lack of ~, 2087:1; male ~, 2794:5

London, England, 283:1; 771:1; 1341:1; 1934:1; 2069:2; 2079:7; 2932:1; 4730:3; season in ~, 767:15; war-torn ~, 1558:4

London, Jack, 3510:2

loneliness *see also* aloneness, 103:2; 150:1; 160:2; 790:9; 843:4; 955:27; 1141:1; 1152:5; 1325:5; 1406:; 1409:20; 1431:4; 1497:2; 1566:1; 1883:3; 2117:1; 2142:1; 2247:2; 2281:7; 2297:6; 2535:2; 2679:3; 2925:8; 2932:6; 3099:9; 3145:7; 3309:1; 3921:1; strength in ~, 1246:5

loner, 1729:1; 3136:4

longevity, 166:14; 4631:3; consequences of ~, 2647:6; friends and ~, 4768:1; gender and ~, 2300:4; secret to ~, 1620:4; 1859:5

longing *see also* yearning, 172:2; 181:1; 210:1; 1550:2; 1622:5; 3451:3; 3476:4; loss of ~, 2292–2293:3; unsatisfied ~, 1127:5

Los Angeles, 1655:7; 1959:11; 2347:6; 2925:13; 3391:2; 3691:4; 3954:4; 4872:1; ~ and 1960s, 2925:14; East ~, 2215:0

loser/losing, 2153:8; 4631:4

loss, 487:12; 1447:2; 1716:2; 2016:2; 3316:3704:6; fear of ~, 2028:3; irrevocable ~, 3528:1; ~ of loved one (*see* loved one, loss of ~); ~ of precious things, 2780:7; 4510:5; pain of

~, 1662:6; repercussions of ~, 3753:4; replacing ~, 2978:3

lost, the, 801:3; 1921:3; 1929:5; 2010:1; 2297:3; 3755:2; 4052:1; 4400:1; ~ in America, 3209:1; looking for what is ~, 2117:4; ~ seeking help, 4218:3

Louis XVI of France, 672:2, 4

love *see also* heart; infatuation; love affair; loved one; lovemaking; lover; relationship; romance, 46:5; 128:3; 140:1; 191:1; 193:3; 213:1; 215:1; 218:3; 242:1; 261:2; 297:1; 308:8; 316:6; 323:1, 3; 467:2; 472:15, 16; 482:6; 487:7; 517:7; 518:3; 521:1; 541:1; 569:1, 2; 607:2; 610:2; 614:3; 643:8; 676:3; 733:2; 808:7; 870:2; 876:2; 892:8, 9; 945:5; 1072:2; 1208:13; 1209:5; 1246:4; 1276:1, 4; 1302:1; 1305:1; 1360:5; 1369:2; 1381:10; 1406:; 1408:18; 1431:1; 1456:1; 1479:1, 3; 1682:3; 1727:9; 2291:4; 2319:7; 2333:2; 2406:2; 2409:4; 2429:2; 2595.1:1; 2680:10; 2693:1; 2780:3; 2842:4; 2979:6; 3428:2; 3481:3; 3504:1; 4038:5; 4130:2; 4163:2; 4447:1; 4631:1; 4854:4; abiding ~, 1385:4; 1424:2; 4806:2; absence of ~, 1322:4; 1540:1; 1719:1; 1782:4; 3119:4; absolute ~, 1321:2; age and ~, 1752:3; agelessness of ~, 894:3; ~ and marriage (*see* marriage, love and ~); ~ and misery, 1267:1; ~ and old age, 1811:3; anxiety of ~, 20:2; 3797:2; art of ~, 590:2; 1993:2; ~ at first sight, 206:2; 261:1; 294:2; 804:7; 1470:6; attributes of ~, 3035:3; avoiding ~, 3853:4; basis of ~, 1209:8; benefits of ~, 593:6; blinded by ~, 2585:2; brooding over ~, 246:1; complications of ~, 323:2; constant ~, 186:1; 287:2; ~ curtailed, 873:5; cycles of ~, 1027:7; danger of ~, 4078:2; death of ~, 1027:5; definition of ~, 2371:3; 3975:2; demands of ~, 2336:1; 2535:3; 2715:6; 4180:4; denial of ~, 1957:5; desire for ~, 604:8; 2014:4; 4955:2; difficulties of ~, 189:1; 190:1; 585:4; 1076:7; 1751:17; 2945:3; 4894:2; dying for ~, 289:2; ecstasy of ~, 2948:1; effect of ~, 3488:3; end of ~, 165:4; 244:8; 439:6; 472:17; 522:2; 693:1; 858:3; 1914:16; 2000:4; 2079:1; 2732:10; 2772:5; 2879:1; 3217:2; enduring ~, 2611:2; escape from ~, 2058:2; essence of ~, 3808:5; eternal ~, 185:1; 945:9; evanescence of ~, 501:4; 905:5; 1751:11; 2944:3; 3309:6; exploiting ~, 1914:15; expressing ~, 4673:1; falling in

~, 1481:7; 2326:2; 3563:12; 3911:3; 3995:3; false ~, 316:5; 501:2; familial ~ (*see* family, ~ love); fear of ~, 1366:1; fickle ~, 169:1; first ~, 132:1; 3992:8; first bloom of ~, 1646:6; fleeting ~, 106:1; 1751:21; 2322:1; 4050:2; flourishing ~, 2772:4; forlorn ~, 1132:1; free ~, 471:1; 1086:3; ~ fully, 3615:2; 3863:1; futility of ~, 659:3; 808:17; game of ~ (*see also* courtship), 289:3; 802:2; 1440:12; giving ~, 218:2; 2014:1; 2053:8; 4847:2; great ~, 459:6; guarding ~, 203:1; 3592:1; 4912:2; heterosexual ~, 2219:10; honest ~, 3031:2; hopeless ~, 1261:5; how to ~, 1758:3; hungry for ~, 2142:6; idealized ~, 2085:7; 3031:2; ignorance of ~, 4223:3; impossibility of ~, 1230:6; ~ in America, 874:5; ~ in community, 3885:1; incapacity for ~, 215:3; 616:6; 1142:2; 3030:2; inspiring ~, 4905:1; intense ~, 1700:3; joy of ~, 2828:2; learning to ~, 2352:1; 2920:2; lessons of ~, 1334:1; liberation of ~, 2618:15; longevity of ~, 517:2; longing for ~, 1369:1; loss of identity in ~, 3853:4; lost ~, 127:1; 140:2; 155:1; 210:1; 212:2; 401:1; 619:1; 701:15; 744:1; 755:2; 1305:3; 1315:4; 1408:19; 2541:3; magic of ~, 808:14; 2170:2; 3680:4; maintain ~, 2668:7; men and ~, 207:1; 914:1; mercurial ~, 3442:1; misguided ~, 3010:2; money and ~ (*see also* sex, economics of ~), 1741:15; 2115:2; morality of ~, 1167:9; mother ~ (*see* mother/hood, ~ love); mutual ~, 569:3; 642:5; 808:2; 887:18; 4354:1; mystery of ~, 3280:1; 3846:1; nature of ~, 1412:5; 1601:3; 1780:4; need for ~, 1619:4; new ~, 572:1; 3099:16; no cure for ~, 2292–2293:3; object of ~ (*see also* lover), 130:1; 438:2; 472:1; 616:1; 660:3; 864:4; 1262:8; 1692:2; 1719:2; 1741:1; 2543:2; 3000:3; 4223:1; 4256:4; 4287:2; 4386:1; 4813:2; 4815:4; obsessive ~, 75:3; 438:1; 602:1; 1524:3; ~ of humankind (*see* human/kind, love of); ~ of older woman, 3145:16; ~ of partner, 1683:3; ~ of self (*see also* narcissism/narcissist; self-love), 452:1; 624:2; 883:3; 1790:18; ~ of women, 526:2; ~ of work, 4003:3; old ~, 990:2; 1241:3; openness of ~, 2997:9; opposite of ~, 2477:2; pain of ~, 493:2; 526:1; 564:2; 696:1; 2842:3; parental ~ (*see* parent/hood, love of ~); passing ~, 1109:2; passionate ~, 614:5; 2502:3; past

~, 3686:4; patient ~, 4919:2; perfect ~, 237:4; 1901:6; phases of ~, 1986:7; platonic ~, 641:2; 1985:1; poverty and ~, 2765:2; power of ~, 46:7; 823:1; 1209:7; 1360:7; 1722:4; 2053:7; 2296:2; 2658:2; 3481:2; 3491:5; 3779:3; 3816:1; 3933–3934:2; 4113:5; 4305:8; proof of ~, 1422:1; reasons to ~, 400:1; 474:4; 482:4; 507:3; 524:2; 660:1; 1864–1865:1; recognizing ~, 3704:2; redemption of ~, 4510:2; religious ~, 1171:3; relinquishing ~, 4250:1; reminiscences of ~, 133:2; renewal of ~, 3012:3; respect and ~, 540:2; 4123:3; respite from ~, 1364:2; right to ~, 3481:5; risk of ~, 2739:2; romantic ~, 1647:3; 3443:1; rules of ~, 511:12; sacredness of ~, 1692:1; saved by ~, 3355:1; second ~, 1843:10; secret ~, 472:10; 1646:7; servitude toward ~, 2292–2293:2; 3262:1; sex and ~ (*see* sex, love and ~); sexual ~, 4193:3; ~ -sick, 510:1; 573:1; signs of ~, 128:2; 511:6; simplicity of ~, 1729:5; spiritual ~, 1512:10; 2585:3; standardized ~, 1808:3; stolen ~, 847:2; ~ story, 1414:2; substance of ~, 4850:1; superficial ~, 4813:4; surrender of ~, 2059:3; sweetness of ~, 1729:2; ~ through thick and thin, 2711:3; transports of ~, 1751:15; true ~, 178:4; 193:8; 244:6; 315:1; 623:2; 716:1; 992:2; 1018:3; 1025:15; 1647:3; 2620:10; 3067:3; 4792:4; uncertain ~, 3251:2; undependability of ~, 4207:1; understanding ~, 2875:2; 3487:1; undying ~, 1653:3; unexpressed ~, 1646:7; unpredictability of ~, 698:1; unrequited ~, 145:1; 171:1; 539:7; 718:1; 847:1; 990:3; 1043:3; 1100:2; 1406:1; 1467:1; 2732:5; 4858:2; 4883:2; unworldliness of ~, 2036:7; veiled ~, 76:4; vocabulary of ~, 4067:4; voraciousness of ~, 3472:1; wanting ~, 1838:4; welcoming ~, 1214:2; ~ with soul, 892:7; women and ~, 873:3; 887:3; 1089:2; 1674:3; 1693:2; 1832:7; 3074:2; 4975:1; words of ~, 7:1; 431:1; 460:1; 505:1; 551:1; 892:7; 2428:4; young ~, 609:1

love affair *see also* love, 1540:3; 2019:1; 3371:4; 4614:3; adulterous ~, 4421:1; 4953:3; ~ between younger man and older woman, 1322:3; 1752:3; discretion in ~, 1840:1; end of ~, 1780:1; 3615:4; 4730:1; extra marital ~, 4194:3; 4568:3; illicit ~, 4691:2; sporadic ~, 2799:3; starting ~,

4010:5; three-way ~, 4919:1; unhappy ~, 206:3

loved one see also family, 140:2; 166:14; 232:1; 279:1; 289:10; 613:2; 793:3; 835:1; 869:6, 10; 963:11; 1032:1; 1756:3; 2456:14; 2925:16, 17; 3099:19; 3193:3; 3599:3; 3788:5; 4023:1; failing ~, 1601:6; loss of ~ (see also specific relation [e.g. son, death of ~; family, death in ~]), 173:1; 788:1; 1008:6; 1409:20; 1704:2; 2780:7; 3464:5; memory of ~ (see also memory, ~ of loved one); praying for ~, 1118:1; relation between ~, 2261:3; sacrifices for ~, 916:19; searching for lost ~, 2978:2; treatment of ~, 1209:11; withdrawal of ~, 947:7

loveliness see also beauty, 1619:5; 1968:2; 2014:5

lovemaking see also kiss/ing; love; sensual/ity; sexual intercourse, 292:1, 2; 1526:1; 2912:3; 3318:3; 3531:1; 4105:6; conception and ~, 179:3; routine ~, 4198:3; ~ with stranger, 1686:4

lover see also boyfriend; couple; kiss/ing; love; romance, 6:2; 289:3, 6; 315:3; 949:1; 1123:1; 1470:10; 1646:2; 1751:1; 1986:6; 2407:3; 3413:5; 4894:3; absence of ~, 639:2; abuse of ~, 244:8; 1557:4; death of ~, 1052:1; embrace of ~, 420:1; 460:2; eyes of ~, 3563:13; first ~, 1835:4; foreign ~, 1790:6; good ~, 2109:1; importance of ~, 4672:1; invitation to ~, 744:2; past ~, 2637:3; rendezvous with ~, 533:1; reunion of ~, 3733:3; revenge of ~, 4631:2;secret ~, 380:3; separation from ~, 95:1; 134:1; 294:1; 344:2; 1144:2; ~, 2164:2; type of ~, 3995:7; value of ~, 1640:3; ~ via e-mail, 4341:3

Lowell, Robert, 2153:5

lower class also see poor; proletariat, 1167:8; 1535:1; reared among ~, 1838:2

lowliness, 1254:1

loyalty see also constancy; faithfulness, 23:1; 2944:2; ~ to nation, 1413:2

luck see also chance; fortune (chance), 451:10; 1078:3; 1164:2; 1562:1; 1825:7; 2150:1; 3161:1; belief in ~, 3099:5; good ~, 2564:3; hard ~ (see also misfortune), 2364:1; response to ~, 2436:1; ~ sold, 4242:7

lullaby, 1719:4; 2197:3

luminosity, 2812:5

Lupercio, Leonardo, 487:9

lust see also erotica/eroticism; lasciviousness; 118:1; 1640:4;

2680:4; 3964:2; ~ at night, 1581:5; female ~, 2623:7; male ~, 383:2; 4295:1

luxury see also affluence/affluent, 901:1; 1934:2; 4464:1; hazards of ~, 531:1; 649:8

lynching see also execution, 1299:1, 2; defense of ~, 1064:1; ~ in South (U.S.A.), 1227:7; 2244:1

Lyons, France, ~ during war, 801:8

M

Macbeth, 3797:8

machine/ry, 1037:2; 1345:3; 2116:5; 4510:6; ~ as metaphor, 3311:3; era of ~, 3550:4

machoism see also chauvinism, male ~; male supremacy; maleness; masculinity, 2124:4; 3983:1; 4273:1; ~ among black men, 4149:2

Madame Butterfly, 3846:2

Madison Avenue (New York City), 3454:2

madness see also insanity; mental illness, 289:6; 903:2; 1024:15, 29; 1978:3; 2801:3; 3611.1:4; danger of ~, 4123:7; momentary ~, 4015:1

Madonna, 3780:11

magazine, 4165:1; beauty ~, 2083:2; feminism and ~, 1425:2; managing ~, 4128:1; ~ story, 1761:4

magic/ian see also sorcery; supernatural, 3770:3; 4677:2; ~ and language, 4072:2; ~ of women, 3865:4

Magnificat see also Bible; Virgin Mary, 79:1

Mahler, Gustav, 1532:1; ~ in death, 1532:2

mail see also letter, arrival of ~, 4206:2; delivering the ~, 1190:1; pony express ~, 1190:1

Mailer, Norman, 2908:4

makeup see also specific items; cosmetics, 4203:5; film ~, 2037:2; promises of ~, 4203:3

maladjustment, ~ of people, 2027:5

Malcolm X, 2281:8; 3547:12

male supremacy see also patriarchy; sexism, 507:4; 669:3; 910:1; 931:25; 1790:18; 1973:12; 2080:6; 2183:1; 2353:3, 4; 2380:6; 2552:3; 2613:3; 2876:2; 2908:3; 3122:3; 3173:2; 3738:6; 4734:3

malice see also cruelty; spite, object of ~, 3283:1

mammal see animal

Mamonova, Tatyana, 3096:1

management see also business, 4081:5; ~ and change, 3429:3; good ~, 2246:2; public ~, 4186:2; transparency in ~, 1494:2; women in ~, 3998:1; work of ~, 3429:4

Mandela, Nelson, 2905:3

Mandela, Winnie, 2905:1

Manhattan see also Broadway; New York City, 2270:8; 4193:6; apathy in ~, 3158:2; residents of ~, 3217:6; 3498:6

manipulator, 4543:3

Mankiller, Wilma, 3591:2

mankind see human/kind

man/men see also male supremacy; machoism; masculinity; patriarchy; sexes, 625:1; 1044:19; 1189:2; 1230:2; 1450:23; 1468:4; 1780:11; 1832:1; 2949:1; 3284:3; 3430:4; 3468:4; 3560:2; 4211:4; 4259:3; 4978:1; age and ~, 1481:8; 1727:4; 1883:1; 2860:2; ~ and love, 1620:6; 2115:4; 2942:6; ~ and money, 3239:2; ~ and work, 1201:11; 4257:1; ~ at mid-life, 2570:3; ~ attention to women, 254:1; ~ attitude towards women, 2745:1; attractive ~, 1959:1; behavior of ~, 3690:2; business and ~ (see also business), 2093:1; character of ~, 4755:3; characteristics of ~, 1586:4; competitiveness of ~, 3145:5; contemptible ~, 357:3; creativity of ~, 1631:1; danger of ~, 646:2; 3119:13; dependency of ~, 3119:14; desire of ~, 4611:4; difficulties of ~, 3976:2; distrust of ~, 3070:3; domesticity and ~, 911:2; dominant ~, 2042:3; emotions and ~, 2153:3; energy of ~, 3847:2; fond of ~, 2219:11; good ~, 152:2; identity of ~, 1969:6; 3983:1; 3987:1; 4726:4; image of ~, 3173:1; ~ in relation to feminism, 1401:3; ~ in relation to God, 482:5; ~ in relation to home, 1973:11; ~ in relation to men, 1474:6; 3738:2; ~ in relation to women (see also relationship, ~ between the sexes; woman/women, ~ in relation to men), 55:1; 376:1; 412:5; 428:3; 487:6, 11; 507:1; 688:1; 701:9, 12; 776:1; 799:5; 850:3; 1044:11; 1047:1; 1126:1; 1132:6; 1208:6; 1216:2; 1235:3; 1262:2; 1385:3; 1419:4; 1430:2; 1481:4, 9; 1572:1; 1590:14; 1620:2; 1741:18; 1764–1765:7; 1790:10; 1914:7; 1930:1; 1934:3; 1940:6; 1959:3; 2080:3; 2231:1; 2352:16; 2353:6; 2495:1; 2546:2; 2618:7; 2658:6; 2694:4; 2911:4; 2924:3; 3219:3; 3240:1; 3258:2; 3430:1; 3476:1; 4089:2; 4701:1; 4713:2; 4840:2; ~ in relation to working woman, 1151:3; ~ in the house, 1790:9; inner drive of ~, 2033:5; ~ issues, 2883:1; limitations of ~, 1289–1290:2; ~ loving men, 910:15; managing ~, 3198:1; marriage

and ~ (see husband; marriage, men and ~); older ~, 1800:3; oppression of ~, 3407:2; pleasing ~, 734:1; population of ~, 2623:8; 2758:2; power of ~, 310:5; 3078:5; 3144:2; pregnancy and ~, 2745:2; privileges of ~, 3570:1; 4221:1; relationships and ~, 3002:2; role of ~ (see also sex role; sexes), 1128:1; 1935:6, 7; 2144:1; 2709:1; 2942:8; 3140:1; 3519:2; 4713:4; single ~, 3145:8; size of ~, 2966:1; the new ~, 1819:2, 3; ~ treatment of women, 4900:1; weakness of ~, 3236:2

Mann, Thomas, 2026:4

manners see also conduct; courtesy; politeness, 643:1; 2177:3; 4312:15; forgotten ~, 1516:4; good ~ 1418:1; 2103:2; 2195:2; ~ in men, 2117:6; lack of ~ (see also rudeness), 1516:4; 1660:3; 1772:1; 2460:1; learning ~, 2148:4

Mansfield, Katherine, 1843:6

Manson, Charles, ~ murders, 2925:14

manufacture, small scale ~, 1383:5

Mao Tse-tung (or Zedong), 1283.1:1; 3400:2; 4092:3, 4

map, 4725:1

Marat, Jean Paul, 736:2

Marc Anthony, 75:4

Marconi, Guglielmo, 2707:1; 4233:1

Marcos, Ferdinand, 2830:2

Mardi Gras/Carnival, 4808:2

marginalization, 3947:3

Marie Antoinette, 672:1; 685:1

marijuana see also drugs, 3547:7; ~ and Judaism, 1966:3; ~ brownies, 1502:2; history of ~, 1966:1, 2

marine life see also OCEAN; SEA, manatee, 3621:2; shellfish, 1193:3; sea mammal, 3621:2; 4438:2; threats to ~, 4278:2

marketplace, denizens of ~, 2933:2

marksmanship see also guns, 1260:1; 3432:1

Marrakech, 2595:1

marriage see also anniversary; couple; husband; husband and wife; mate; monogamy; polygamy; relationship; spouse; wedding; wife, 62:1; 67:1; 337:1; 351:1; 356:6; 410:2; 934:9; 1254:20; 1303:1; 1309:3; 1435:3; 1468:4; 1481:2, 3, 10; 1540:3; 1583:5; 1611:5; 1646:3; 1663:8; 1674:5; 1693:11; 1787:8; 1803:1; 1967:3; 2319:4; 2423:3; 2426:3; 2540:4; 2587:1; 2799:3; 3050:3; 3067:3; 3317:5; 3349:5; 3611.1:5; 3577:2; 3731:12; 3738:7; 3832:2; 3939:8; 4312:10; 4493:2;

4587:3; abolishing ~, 3646:1; abusive ~, 4505:2; American man and ~, 2231:2; ~ among young, 874:7; analyzing ~, 1321:4; ~ and business, 1914:7; ~ argument, 2286:2; 2319:3; arranged ~, 2952:1; ~ as vocation, 2190:5; attitude towards ~ partner, 1184:13; avoiding ~, 1283.1:1; 2817:11; bad ~, 2565:2; ~ bed, 380:2; benefits of ~, 1182:3; 1693:16; ~ by choice, 290:2; candor in ~, 2331:2; caution towards ~, 1847:6; children and ~, 1776:6; 3099:4; compromises of ~, 3594:6; constraints of ~, 1033:1; contentment in ~, 287:2; 430:6; 843:5; ~ contract, 2626:3; decision to ~, 454:1; demands on ~, 2924:2; difficulties of ~, 69:1; 459:11; 466:10; 592:1; 2187:7; 2464:1; 2982:4; disappointment in ~, 3460:1; duties of ~, 874:6; 1045:1; economics of ~ (see also money, love and ~), 262:1; 283:4; 807:12; egalitarian ~, 1402:1; end of ~, 3099:10; 3349:16; enduring ~, 2828:1; 3468:2; expectations of ~, 3001:3; faithless ~, 2819:4; fear of ~, 251:4; fulfilling ~, 1513:3; good ~, 451:12; 524:1; 533:19; 593:5; 931:9; 2869:3; holding ~ together, 2414:1; horrors of ~, 57:1; illusions of ~, 2434:1; ~ in relation to singles, 3663:2; institution of ~, 3958:1; interracial ~, 4328:1; legal status of women in ~, 3201:1; limitations of ~, 2752:2; loneliness of ~, 2680:16; long-lived ~, 2577:6; love and ~, 405:4; 423:5; 874:9; 1201:3; 1683:3; 4591:3; 4847:1; loveless ~, 604:8; 1167:9; 1208:2; ~ made in heaven, 2609:2; making the right ~, 446:4; men and ~ , 405:3; 2916:24; mixed ~, 2044:2; 4376:1; money and ~, 1995:3; 2931:1; monotony of ~, 472:3; motivation for ~, 569:3; 808:6; 874:10; 2395:2; 2869:1; multiple ~, 1611:2; 2826:2; 3295:2; nature of ~, 4452:1, 2; ~ of daughter, 128:1; ~ officiant, 2191:1; ~ pact, 1688:4; ~ partners, 77:1; 223:1; 839:1; 1036:2; 2589:2; 2810:4; 2819:1; 4473:4; partnership of ~, 2626:1; political ~, 290:1; ~ proposal, 1036:5; 2200:1; rape and ~, 2496:6; reasons for ~, 4818:1; restraints of ~, 441:1; rights of husband in ~, 2494:4; rights of wife in ~, 953:6; same sex ~, 3275:2, 3; 3450:1; 4247:3; 4376:3; 4720:2; sanctity of ~, 1554:2; second ~, 880:3; secret ~, 363:1; separation during ~, 229:1; sex and ~

(see sex, marriage and ~); sexless ~, 3017:1; spiritual life of ~, 1776:2; survival of ~, 1646:3; 3777:1; surviving ~, 2326:1; threat to ~, 1973:3; time for ~, 1036:4; traditional ~, 1965:2; transformation of ~, 3261:2; troubled ~, 4568:3; 4778:1; ups and downs of ~, 4814:3; ~ vows, 626:1; women and ~, 450:6; 482:3; 492:2; 767:6, 13; 874:3; 891:1; 987:1; 998:11, 12; 1277:1; 1280:1; 1512:5; 1519:6; 1622:7; 1718:1; 1894:5; 2421:1; 2602:1; 2822:4; 2932:2; 2974:1; 3898:2;

martyr/dom, 300:1; 1017:1; 1021:1; 1450:25; 2255:1; 2569:7; 2605:1
Marx, Groucho, 3371:4
Marxism/Marxist, 2297:2
Masaryk, Thomas Garrigue, 1480:6
masculinity see also machoism; man/men; virility, 1176:4; 1673:4; 2124:2; 3780:8; image of ~, 2756:1; ~ in relation to femininity, 910:4; principles of ~, 2849:1
masochism, ~ of women, 2059:2, 3
Mass see Catholic Church; Catholicism
mass media see also specific forms; news, 3317:1; 3976:6; age and ~, 3268:3; changes in ~, 2783:3; distortions of ~, 2899:1; honesty in ~, 2710:4; impact of ~, 2915:2; 3516:2; influence of ~, 1920:2; 3565:3; ~ in relation to politicians, 3164:2; ~ in relation to President, 2393:5; ~ in relation to women, 4381:2; 4961:1; ~ in the Digital Age, 3917:2; inflammatory ~, 4157:4; 4803:1; manipulation of ~, 1666:4; message of ~, 3566:3; misogyny in ~, 3312:2; multi- ~, 2330:2; popular ~, 4957:3; power of ~, 4709:3; role of ~, 4709:2; sexism in ~, 3240:2; soundbites in ~, 3996:1; violence in ~, 2424:3; women and ~, 1920:3; 2243:2; 4709:1
massacre see also genocide; murder/er, 517:4
masses, the see also people; public, the, 539:3; 777:1; 1617:2; food for ~, 682:1; passivity of ~, 1402:3
masterpiece, 2066:10; musical ~, 3168:4; ownership of ~, 1842:1
Masters (William) and Johnson (Virginia), 2887:2
masturbation see also sex/uality, 2008:2; 2068:4; 3547:14; children and ~, 1989:1; women and ~, 2646:2; 4494:1
mate see also husband; marriage; spouse; wife, finding ~, 2014:2; 4622:1; 4625:3; listening to ~, 1622:1; matched ~, 3032:8; soul

~ (see also companion, life ~), 1558:1
materialism see also tangibility; worldliness, 1009:3; 1405:6; 1450:20; 1686:1; 2032:13; 2080:1; 2291:7; 2888:2; 3282:3; 3589:1; evils of ~, 4098:2; ~ in America, 1592:3; ~ in name of conservation, 3942:2; pragmatic ~, 1857:3; relinquishing ~, 2484:1; uncontrolled ~, 2080:8
mathematics, 876:1; 968:2; 1177:1, 2; 2054:3; 2808:1; 2954:2, 3; 3329:3; 3441:2; 4454:1; ~ and integers, 4898.1:1; excellence in ~, 3399:2; love for ~, 3329:2; terrified of ~, 4898.1:2; usefulness of ~, 4898.1:3; women and ~, 3382:1
matriarchy, 2183:3; 2399:2; 2880:1; ancient ~, 1351:1; primal force of ~, 2183:1; roots of ~, 1966:2
matter (physical), 492:1
maturity, 734:21; 1142:1; 1440:6; 1520:4; 1618:11; 1787:8; 1901:3; 2780:8; 3048:1; 4766:1; growing to ~, 2148:3; questions of ~, 2572:4; women and ~, 533:5
McAliskey, Róisín, 3736:2
McCain, John, 4665:4; ~ and sexism, 3284:11; ~ and women's rights, 4466:4
McCarthy, Mary, 3126:1
McCarthyism see also inquisition; red-baiting, 1897:1; 2428:2; 3245:2
McClintock, Barbara, 2988:2
McKinley, William, 1616:2; 1778:4, 5
meadow, high ~, 4105:3
meagerness, ~ of life, 2732:9
meal (eating) see also specific meals; dining; food, 2085:1; family ~, 2709:4; 4519:2
meaning see also interpretation; semantics, 1881:1; 3630:5; creating ~, 2739:4; hidden ~, 2772:6; ~ in life, 2727:3; search for ~, 4597:1
meaninglessness, 2925:16
meanness see also cruelty; unkindness, ~ in women, 3162:2
meddlesomeness see nosiness
media see mass media
medical facilities, inadequate ~, 4430:2
medical profession see also specific branches; doctor; medicine; physician, 1024:3; detachment of ~, 3416:1; ethics of ~, 3009:1; lack of acumen in ~, 974:2; purpose of ~, 2560:1; reactionaries of ~, 1549:5; sexism in ~, 2261:1; tools of ~, 1407:4; women in ~, 807:16; 921:1; 1493:1
medical research, involuntary subjects of ~, 4634:2

medical school, 4356:2
Medicare, 2989:2; 3176:0
medicine see also doctor; medical profession; physician, 1613:1; 20th century ~, 1833:3; alternative ~, 4117:6; diagnoses and ~, 1407:4; field of ~, 3363:1; holistic ~, 3045:1; modern ~, 4059:1; prenatal ~, 4824:1; progress of ~, 4156:2; traditional ~ of Africa, 3045:1; workings of ~, 982:6
mediocrity, 391:2; 408:3; 1935:9; intolerance of ~, 1596:5; women and ~, 2403:1
meditation see also contemplation, 2467:3; 3430:5; 3547:14; learning ~, 4788:4
Medusa, 3025:5
meeting, 4902:5; business ~, 4459:; chance ~, 1830:3
megalopolis see also city, 1816:4
melancholy see also sadness, 411:1; 497:2; 2945:1; 4015:2; 4280:6; 4868:3
melodrama, 4988:1
melody see also music; song, 1529:1; 2153:6
membership, constraints of ~, 3325:3
memento see also souvenir, handmade ~, 135:1
memoir see also autobiography, 1217:1; 3722:1; 4655:1
memory see also recollection; remembrance, 711:1; 947:5; 1236:3; 1259:2; 1525:3; 1686:9; 1744:3; 1775:2; 1883:5; 1979:7, 14; 2051:4; 2117:5; 2238:3; 2315:1; 2349:10, 23; 2490:1; 2585:1; 2680:22; 2728:3, 4; 2933:3; 2950:2; 3317:3; 3476:3; 3480:2; 3522:2; 3793:2; 3902:2; 4533:2; 4767:0; 4909:2, 3; 4975:5; aggravated ~, 693:1; burden of ~, 4792:5; eradicating ~, 2659:1; exposing ~, 3847:1; first ~, 1670:6; influence of ~, 3663:4; management of ~, 3000:2; ~ of feelings, 2087:3; ~ of loved one, 1692:2; ~ of past, 2871:4; ~ of the dead, 4067:5; old ~, 1808:4; painful ~, 395:3; recovering ~, 3711:3; rut of ~, 1409:25; sad ~, 873:2; sanitized ~, 2402:5; stirring up ~, 3012:4; suppressing ~, 2938:2; ~ uncovering, 2613:6; use of ~, 3522:3
Mencken, H. L., 4136:13
Menendez, Erik and Lyle, 3981:3
Mennonite, 4623:1
menopause, 3059:6; 3268:5
menstruation, 2300:2; 3237:2; 3349:8; 4239:1
mental health, 2829:1; 3305:2; disturbed ~, 2982:1; sexist concepts of ~, 3626:1; women's requirements for ~, 3184:6
mental illness see also specific kinds; insanity; madness; nervous

breakdown, 822:2; 2801:8; 3649:1; 3799:2; 4094:1; 4713:6; combating ~, 2466:1; eradication of ~, 3130:1; help for ~, 3799:3; hospital for ~, 3574:; illusions of ~, 2801:4; ~ in prisons, 2458:1; ~ in relation to community, 3068:2; recovering from ~, 2908:7; treatment of ~, 872:1; 2483:1; 3264:1

mental institution, 822:2; 2010:1

mental retardation see also disabled/disability, 1480:5; 1741:22; 4535:1; ~ in children, 2684:1

mentor/ing see also teaching, 315:3; 2890:3

mercenary see also soldier, 625:1

merchant see also business, prospects of ~, 4725:4

mercy see also forgiveness, 310:1; 955:14; 2265:2; 2997:10; plea for ~, 892:1; 2311:2; seeking ~, 318:1; show no ~, 3069:1; showing ~, 1181:1

message, 259:1; symbolic ~ 3345:3

messenger, 654:1; 2142:5

Messiah see also Jesus Christ; Jew/Judaism, 1062:6; 1600:3; coming of ~, 3737:1

metal, precious ~, 474:5

metaphor, bad ~, 3124:2

metaphysics, 1105:1; ~ of ontology, 2320:3

Mexican American see also Chicano/a; Hispanic, 3589:3; ~ women, 3589:2

Mexico/Mexican, ~ in relation to U.S.A., 2066:5; marrying a ~, 4237:1

Michigan, 4008:3; 4486:2

microbes, 4841:1

middle age see also age/aging; years of age, 1411:4; 1552:3; 1751:9; 1843:10; 2053:4; 2117:15; 2243:7; 2253:1; 2396:1; 2434:7; 3268:1; blessings of ~, 1473:2; relationships and ~, 3217:1; ~ romance, 1761:4; transitions during ~, 3914:3; women at ~, 2243:2

middle class see also bourgeoisie; class (social), middle ~, ~ dream, 2642:16; gender and ~, 3383:1; loss of ~, 4540:2

Middle East see also specific nations, 1785:4; 3731:15; businesswoman in ~, 4664:1, 2; deserts of ~, 1870:4; ~ in relation to the West, 2595:2; Israel and ~, 1518:2; peace in ~, 2673:2; 3143.1:2; 3214:2, 3; strife in ~, 3879:2; women of ~, 2445:2; 4658:3; women's peace movement in ~, 3699:1

mid-life crisis, men and ~, 2570:3

midnight, 679:1

midwifery see also childbirth, 384:1

might see also force; strength, right of ~, 2118:4

migrant worker see also farm worker, oppression of ~, 2341:1

migration, 3224:1; ~ of people (see also emigrant/emigration), 2219:2

militancy, see also woman/women, militant ~, consequences of ~, 3145:1; meaning of ~, 2901:4

militarism, 287:3; 1548:5; 2512:3; opposition to ~, 1487:2; supporting ~, 1029:4; world ~, 2441:1

military see also armed forces/army; combat; fight/ing; national defense; soldier; war, 1803:1; alternatives for ~, 2098:5; ~ atrocity, 4263:4, 5; counterinsurgency and ~, 4745:2; 4887:3; dealing with ~, 4446:2; ~ dishonorable discharge, 3483:2; ~ in relation to poverty, 3762:4; ~ industrial complex, 1666:4; ~ medal, 3483:2; ~ mind, 2192:2; 3762:1; mission of ~, 4853:1; ~ officer, 1475:2; 2951:1; 3227:6; purpose of ~, 3454:1; ~ recruitment, 4247:2; ~ retinue, 421:1; ~ tactics, 4706:1; women in ~, 3054:4; 4647:1; 4745:1

Millay, Edna St. Vincent, 1843:5

millennium, Christian concept of ~, 3871:1; new ~, 4113:4; shaping new ~, 2965:3

Milton, John, 1922:3

mind see also brain; intellect/intelligence; reason; thinker/thinking, 230:1; 273–274:2; 474:1; 578:1; 798:1; 799:6; 982:4; 1336:3; 1474:3; 1855–1856:2; 2296:4; 2638:15; 2849:2; 3291:1; 3630:1; 3687:1; 4940:2; beauty of ~, 2145:1; capacity of ~, 1024:19; 2437:9; 4348:1, 2; changing one's ~, 2693:2; 3792:1; 4348:6; confines of ~, 982:3; controlling state of ~, 1451:1; 2621:1; cultivation of ~, 308:7; 543:3; 1227:4; damaged ~, 3315:1; depth of ~, 1447:3; development of ~, 2351:1; distressed ~, 867:2; egalitarianism of ~, 422:2; elevated ~, 769:2; empty ~, 3099:2; escape from ~, 2817:24; ~ expansion, 4364:2; expansiveness of ~, 4182:1; facility of ~, 2131:3; feminine ~, 446:7; 673:1; 681:2; flexibility of ~, 1025:10; freedom of ~, 1494:1; 1676:2; gender of ~, 1935:13; growth of ~, 1332:3; influences upon ~, 1200:2; interdisciplinary ~, 1915:2; large ~, 3203:2; life of ~, 693:6; limitations of ~, 710:2; 1488:1; logical ~, 1174:3; maturity of ~, 585:6; nurturance of ~, 3159:1; 4559:3; open ~, 1470:8; power of ~, 770:7; 3922:1; reeduca-

tion of ~, 1341:3; richness of ~, 487:2; shattered ~, 2629:2; sound ~, 1117:3; stagnation of ~, 4480:1; strong ~, 408:3; tranquil ~, 1884:3; trivia of ~, 3563:3; troubled ~, 213:2; woman's ~, 244:11; 1041:1; 2613:2; 2855:3; 3137:4

miner/mining, 954:5; 1037:2; coal ~, 4088:1; exploitative ~, 4088:3; ~ in Romania, 4848:1; life in a ~ town, 954:2; protest ~, 4848:2

minister see also clergy; preacher, reason for being ~, 1354:4

minority, conflict between ~, 4006:1; lack of support for ~, 4068:1; ~ women, 3912:1

minute/moment also see time, 838:5; 3704:1; enjoying ~, 3524:1; ~ of action, 3749:3; ~ of change, 3438:2; significant ~, 1493:3

miracle, 1715:8; 2096:3; 3339:3; 3680:3; human ~, 3203:4

mirror, bad ~, 772:7; image in ~, 3135:2; 3193:1; 3901:3; reflection in ~, 533:14; 691:3

mirth see also cheerfulness; laugh/ter, 446:1

misandry also see sexism, ~ in lesbian community, 2936:4

mischief see also trickster, 1695:3; 1991:1

misery see also unhappiness; woe; wretchedness, 448:2; 470:2; 489:3; 613:1; 1240:2; 3379:2; 4902:4; 4929:1; denial of ~, 1530:3

misfit, 2534:5; 4711:2

misfortune see also luck, hard ~, 281:2; 705:4; 823:2; 870:10; 4213:3; 4673:3; lessons of ~, 616:2

misogyny see also male supremacy; sexism, 193:5; 244:7; 430:4; 477:1; 526:2; 1684:5; 2285:2; 2763:6; 3840:1; 4118:1; 4539:2; ~ among clinicians, 3184:2; ~ in literature, 1487:3; ~ in religion, 3284:1; ~ in the media, 3312:1

missionary, 877:1; 1741:12; 2291:5; 3179:1; guidelines for ~, 3553:1; ~ in Africa, 2456:2; ~ in India, 1016:1; Jesuit ~, 3224:2

Mississippi, 3213:1; trial of ~, 2847:1; ~ River, 2970:6

mist see also dew; fog, morning ~, 106:1

mistake see also error, 1073:1; 3412:3; 4794:2; accepting one's ~, 1312:3; great ~, 1741:10; 2196:5; learning from ~, 697:3; 2913:4; 3137:3; making ~, 3777:4; repeating ~, 2385:1; 4190:5; 4834:2

mistreatment see also abuse, ~ of women, 2541:2

mistress see also courtesan; prostitute/prostitution; sex industry,

374:1; 814:1; 2947:3; 4421:1; ~ in relation to wife, 310:6

Mitchell, Joni, 3982:1

mobility, upward ~, 3332:2

mockery see also ridicule, 56:3; 289:9; 676:1

moderation, 3703:1

modernity, 1574:3

modesty, 489:1; 1673:3; 2406:1; chains of ~, 470:1; end to ~, 2686:4

Mogadishu, Somalia, 4600:1

Mohammed see Muhammed

Moi, Daniel arap, 4129:1

molecule see also atom, 3687:2

moment see minute/moment

monarch/y see also king; queen; rule/r, 258:1; 334:5

monastic life see also priest, 3777:3

money see also credit; gold; economy; finance; profit; thrift; wealth, 88:3; 266:1; 472:7, 19; 479:4; 511:9; 593:9; 722:10; 885:1; 1063:1; 1120:5; 1150:2; 1153:4; 1317:1; 1408:5; 1450:15; 1461:2; 1715:2; 1882:2; 2086:1; 2116:7; 2130:4; 2207:2; 2333:2; 2463:5; 2853:2; 3779:5; 4084:3; 4131:2; 4242:3; 4243:3; 4357:2; 4480:2; 4755:1; 4851:4; acquisition of ~, 1292:2; 1945:1; 2230:1; 2942:2; attitude toward ~, 2000:3; 2454:3; 3134:1; 4761.1:2; attracting ~, 3059:2; borrowing ~, 437:1; 479:3; circulation of ~, 2154:3; counting ~, 511:16; earning ~, 2249:2; French ~, 2368:5; friendship and ~, 767:18; giving ~ to children, 2267:6; happiness and ~, 1724:12; having ~, 2910:1; honor and ~, 308:4; lack of ~, 251:2; 3592:3; 4131:4; 4280:2; love and ~ (see also marriage, money and ~), 2007:4; love of ~, 237:1; lust for ~, 1957:1; making ~, 1946:1; marry for ~, 1973:13; men and ~, 1872:2; 3558:1; misappropriation of ~, 2670:4; perspective on ~, 1911:6; power of ~, 733:15; 3398:1; 3512:5; public ~, 3386:4; relationships and ~, 1481:6; 2115:2; rent ~, 4511:3; saving ~, 782:5; 1618:35; 1994:3; 4743:1; spending ~ (see also spendthrift), 911:3; 1193:1; 1632:5; 3388:2; understanding ~, 3099:3; 4521:4; value of ~, 607:1; 672:4; 3020:1; ~ vs. barter, 3835:3; ~ wallet, 4867:2; women and ~, 1086:5; 1254:3; 2031:1; 3000:1; 3099:3; 3599:2; 3610:1; 4205:1

Mongolia, politics and ~, 4898:1

monogamy see also marriage, 998:6; 2865:1; 3033:2; 4031:2; 4791:2; ~ in Nature, 4438:1; men and ~, 1495:1

monopoly, 1178:2

monotony see also bore/dom, 1574:1; 3110:1

monster, 859:4

Montana, State of, 4560:1

month, ~ of January, 1409:28; 4730:2; ~ of February, 2346:4; ~ of April, 4193:6; ~ of May, 658:2; 1067:2; ~ of June, 1204:2; 4206:1; ~ of August, 2784:1; 4519:0; ~ of September (see September 11); ~ of November, 299:1; ~ of December, 871:2

monument, ~ to women, 1026:1

mood, 2705:1; dark ~, 2955:3; 3974:1

moon, 307:1; 910:2; 1581:3, 5; 2212:6; 2442:3; pull of ~, 4119:2; symbology of ~, 3017:2

Moral Majority see also conservatism; Right Wing, 4217:1

moral standards, 4456:1

moral/ity see also ethics, 783:4; 1068:1; 1201:8; 1636:1; 1731:2; 1957:5; 2268:5; 2352:10; 2432:3; 4741:2; ~ authority, 3098:2; changing ~, 593:2; 2398:10; conflicts of ~, 3814:2; decaying ~, 3261:4; 3981:4; demise of ~, 1857:3; feminine ~, 2668:20; fight over ~ issues, 2828:4; government and ~, 3049:2; 4247:2; impact of art on ~, 2872:3; ~ in nature, 584:5; lack of ~ (see also immorality), 1772:1; lessons in ~, 1623:1; medicine and ~, 3535:5; objecting to ~, 3370:4; ~ of nation, 2192:16; ~ of women, 2916:1; 2979:3; standards of ~, 3911:5; technology and ~, 3535:4; test of ~, 1450:1; upholding ~, 614:1; ~ vs. profit, 2480:3

mores see also custom, changing ~, 681:2

Morgan, J. P., 1527:1; 3617:1, 2

Mormon/ism, 2238:2; 3294:3; 4428:2

morning see also dawn; day; sunrise, 386:1; 1136:4; 1137:1; 1663:1; 2327:2; 3630:4; mood of ~, 1322:1; sunny ~, 3443:2

mortality see also death, awareness of ~, 1905:1; 3059:4; contemplating ~, 3923:3

mortgage, ~ crisis, 3156:3; ~ foreclosure, 1178:4

Moscow, 1917:3; 2507:1; 4845–4846:3

Moses, 17:1; 1462:2; 1592:5; 2339:2; 3284:6; 4904:1

Moslem see also Islam, 2331:7; brotherhood of ~, 3547:12; ~ women in sports, 4617:2

Mother Hubbard, 739:1

mother/hood see also housewife; parent/hood, 80:2; 102:1; 495:1; 792:1; 843:1; 903:1; 933:1; 1044:13; 1129:3; 1167:3; 1208:5; 1254:11; 1409:11; 1598:1; 1602:2; 1686:5; 1759:10; 1965:1; 1994:2; 2034:2; 2051:2; 2187:16; 2219:9; 2254:2; 2397:1; 2602:2, 3; 2667:5; 2773:2; 2874:2; 3027:2, 5; 3221:1; 3376:1; 3436:2; 3455:1; 3477:4; 3514:4; 3813:, 2; 3898:3; 3957:1; 4038:1; 4085:7; 4143:3; 4326:3; 4381:1; 4408:1; 4452:4; 4518:1; 4592:1; 4603:1; 4630:1; 4685:4; advice from ~, 2416:1; 4615:1; aging ~, 2080:10; anguish of ~, 760:4; ~ as servant, 1487:6; ~ as storyteller, 3203:1; aspects of ~, 1487:1; ~ at home, 4210:3; bad ~, 2809:3; benefits of ~, 970:2; challenges of ~, 4405:5; changes of ~, 4405:3; 4590:3; character of ~, 840:1; contemporary ~, 3665:4; death of ~, 579:1; 801:1; 2089:1; 2773:1; 3906:3; 4718:4; decreasing ~, 3664:1; demands of ~, 3529:1; desire for ~, 3712:1; dying ~, 3596:1; education and ~, 2675:2; expectant ~ (see also pregnancy/pregnant), 701:13; function of ~, 1525:2; glorification of ~, 3003:1; 3890:1; good ~, 3477:3; 4162:1; hostility to ~, 3145:19; illness of ~, 2461:3; 3309:3; image of ~, 2452:1; 3436:1; ~ in relation to adult child, 1601:2; 2261:3; 2810:2, 3; 3031:3; ~ in relation to baby, 1628:1; 3665:5; 4133:1; 4390:3; ~ in relation to child, 37:1; 326:3; 364:1; 371:1; 373:1; 379:1; 644:2; 1265:4; 1620:8; 1853:1; 1862:3; 2462:1; 2680:12; 2867:4; 3098:; 3309:2; 3746:2; 3773:1; 3779:6; 3921:2; 4952:1; ~ in relation to daughter (see also daughter, ~ in relation to mother), 726:1; 727:1; 2715:1; 3364:2; 3538:3; 3882:1; 4047:1; 4794:1; ~ in relation to feminism, 2943:6; 4831:2, 3; ~ in relation to husband (see also wife, ~ in relation to husband), 2021:16; ~ in relation to son (see also son, ~ in relation to mother), 168:1; 1481:4; 1661:1; 3648:1, 2; ~ in relation to teen-aged child, 2566:2; indifferent ~, 2405:1; influence of ~, 807:1, 5; 827:13; 1831:2; 3653:1; 4273.1:1; instinct for ~, 3665:2; internalized ~, 2760:2; invincible ~, 1698:4; Jewish ~, 3320:2, 4; joy of ~, 4009:6; lack of maternal instinct in ~, 1831:1; loss of ~, 3574:1; ~ love, 808:11; 2732:11; 2850:5; 3064:3; 4421:6; 4538:2; love for ~, 1369:0; 2785:2; 4865:1; ~ love for child, 4143:2; lower income ~, 1487:1; mirrors of ~, 4805:2; motivations for ~, 1535:8; nursing ~ (see breast feeding); overbearing ~, 734:16; overprotective ~, 2256:3; 3320:3; patience of ~, 1011:3; preparation for ~, 855:3; 931:21; protective ~, 2817:20; requirements of ~, 3665:3; responsibilities of ~, 1254:5; rights of ~, 656:3; 1943:4; role of ~, 4150:1; sexuality of ~, 3894:3; single ~, 2484:1; society's need for ~, 3529:3; special ~, 3403:3; stage ~, 2222:1; starving ~, 4622:2; step-~, 911:7; supportive ~, 1736:1; surrogate ~, 4089:4; taboo of ~, 3568:1; theories of ~, 3519:2; touch of ~, 4493:0; transformed by ~, 4009:5; unable to ~, 4663:3; unknown ~, 4852:2; unwed ~, 2245:1; 2272:5; voice of ~, 4851:5; welfare ~, 2272:5; 3053:2; white ~ of a black child (see also race, mixed ~), 3436:4; working ~, 1167:15; 1870:11; 2416:3; 2844:1, 2, 4; 4664:3; 4696:2; 4761.2:2; young ~, 3038:2

mother-in-law, 4473:2

Mother's Day, 4381:1

motivation, 2206:1; 2479:2; 4880:1

Motown Records, 2370.1:1; ~ artists, 2492.1:3

mountain see also hill, 1358:2; ~ cabin, 4324:5; ~ climbing, 1046:1; 1400:1; 2977:4; Himalaya ~, 1046:3; lure of ~, 1947:1; 4700.1:1; ~ pass, 222:2

mourning see also grief, 138:1; 164:1; 238–239:1; 359:1; 852:1; 1109:4; 1673:7; 4727:4; national ~, 1778:4 movement (physical) see also activity, 1795:1, 2; 2950:1; emotion and ~, 2373:1

movement (socio-political) see also specific movements; protest/er, 2139:7; 3348:3; 3397:3; devotion to ~, 2727:2; environmental ~ (also see environmentalism), 4106:4; 4405:1, 2; 4790:2; ~ for change, 4758:2; ~ for social injustice, 2756:2; global ~, 4897:1; grass roots ~, 2139:6; 3586:2; 4106:1; 4594:2; liberation ~ (also see liberation), 2285:3; 4528:1; men and women in ~, 3595:1; ~ organizations, 3606:3; 4098:1; 4106:3, 6; pro-choice ~, 3435:1; 3888.1:2; 4035:2; pro-life, 3261:1; 3264:2; socialist ~ (also see socialism), 2315:2; struggles of ~, 4266:1; synchronistic ~, 3257:9

movie see film

Mozart, Wolfgang Amadeus, works of ~, 1759:6

MP (Member of Parliament), 3706:5

Ms. (magazine), 2916:18; 3182:3

Mugabe, Robert, 2349:19

Muhammed ibn 'Abdullah, 3284:6; 4904:1; 4986:2; wives of ~, 4846:2

multiculturalism see also diversity, 4426:2; exposure to ~, 4373:2; ~ in relation to feminism, 3684:5

multinationals see also corporation, 4771:4; greed of ~, 4821:1; ~ in Africa, 3835:3; ~ vs. farmer, 3081:5

multi-racial/ism see also race, mixed ~, 2911:3; benefits of ~, 1659:3

multitasking, 3027:5; dangers of ~, 4445:2

mundane, 3704:; ~ activity, 2790:2

murder/er see also killer; killing; massacre, 611:1; 1708:1; 1724:1, 8; 1986:6; 2331:12; 2761:1; 3514:3; 4479:1; avenging ~, 772:2; condoned ~, 288:1; defending victim of ~, 974:8; incarcerated ~, 3155:1; intentional ~, 4298:1; target of ~, 2900:3

Muses see also various art forms, 496:1; 928:3; ill use of ~, 311:2

museum see also specific museums, impact of ~, 3708:1

Museum of Modern Art (New York City), 2546:4

music see also melody; opera; rhythm; singer/singing; song; symphony, 446:2; 798:2; 1406:2; 1751:23; 2012:5; 2267:1; 2845:3; 3037:5; 3403:4; 3441:2; 3776:2; 4811:2; African ~, 3633:2; American ~, 1512:6; ~ appreciation, 2435:4; blues ~, 2159:3; 2382:1; 2435:4; 2493:1; 4583:3; composing ~, 1685:3; 3150:1; 4042:8; ~ conductor, 3675:1; country ~, 2806:3; devotion to ~, 1815:1; ~ education, 2845:1; emotions and ~, 4517:2; experiencing ~, 990:1; 1678:1; 2760:4; 4242:10; folk ~, 1939:2, 3; god of ~, 1204:4; gospel ~, 2159:2; great ~, 1678:2; ~ in one's soul, 1844:8; ~ in relation to dance, 1512:3; ~ in relation to gender, 2637.1:1; inspiration for ~, 2147:4; jazz ~, 1512:7; 2147:3, 4; 2324:4; 2382:1; 2945:2; 4643:3; learning ~, 2734:1; listening to ~, 4436:2; ~ lover, 650:3; ~ lyrics, 1685:1; martial ~ (see also band), 671:16; modern ~, 1939:1; plaintive ~, 3169:1; power of ~, 3252:3; purpose of ~, 3749:2; reading ~, 4698:1; recording ~, 2610:1; response to ~, 4147:6; rock ~, 2544:3; 2924:1; 3159:2; 3257:10; 4681:3; 4735:3; teaching ~, 1368:1; universality of ~, 2788:1; 4256:5; 4688:1; woman ~ conductor, 3887:1; women in ~, 2806:1; writing ~, 1274:3

musical instrument, 179:5; bagpipe, 731:4; case for ~, 4224:1; exploration of ~, 3928:2; flute, 1368:1; guitar/ist, 1649:3; 3187:2; 4218:1;piano playing, 2147:1, 5; playing ~, 561:1; 1844:1; 3168:1; ~ reed, 3169:1; saxophone, 2018:2; violin, 1233:1; wind instruments, 3169:1

musician, 1649:3; 2018:2; 2478:3; 2999:1; 3135:1; band ~, 2924:1; black ~, 2060:1; life of ~, 910:12; motivation of ~, 2299:1; organist ~, 3730:1; woman ~, 2018:1; 2147:2; 2324:3; 2493:1; 3181:1; 3982:1; work of ~, 1529:3

Muslim, 4292:2; 4772:3; ~ as terrorists, 4567:2; ~ countries, 3169:2; ~ culture, 3253:3; extermination of ~, 4597:2; fear of ~, 4326:8; ~ in relation to Jews, 4747:3; ~ internal strife, 4160:9, 10; on being ~, 4772:1; 4789:1; ~ philosophy, 3211:1; ~ politics, 4986:2; poverty and ~, 4142:1; ~ women, 2595:4; 3169:4; 4347:1; 4556:2; 4776:1; 4916:1, 2; ~ women athletes, 4747:1

Mussolini, Benito, 1480:6

mustache, 3498:1

mystery, ~ of women, 3325:2; solving ~, 984:1

mystic/ism see also spirit/uality, 974:5; 1436:6; 2220:1; 3474:3; experience of ~, 3281:2; ~ in relation to God, 3281:1

myth/ology see also legend/ary, 2183:1; 3037:3; comeback of ~, 2456:11; ~ dragon, 1669:13; end of ~, 4474:2; function of ~, 3529:2; ~ in Neolithic Age, 2399:1; ~ mermaid, 1113:3; ~ phoenix, 67:1; 232:1; 323:1; purpose of ~, 3118:, 6; reality and ~, 2756:11; Roman ~, 1896:8; secret of ~, 2744:1; ~ unicorn, 1916:6;

N

Nader, Ralph, 2227:2; 4235:5; 4522:1

nag/ging, 1292:4; 1943:1

Nagasaki, Japan, bombing of ~, 3303:1

Nairobi, Kenya, 2349:21

naiveté see also ingenuousness; innocence, 1242:1; 4410:3

nakedness see nudity

name, 200:1; 827:10; 2257:2; 2660:1; 4242:8; adopting a ~, 860:13; ancient ~, 4780:2; ~ calling, 1964:3; 2725:1; 4169:1; changing ~, 4872:5; defilement of ~, 550:3; first ~, 2857:3; good ~ (see also reputation), 2584:1; importance of ~, 931:23; 3348:1; 4183:2; Indian ~, 1203:1;

4252:2; nick-~, 300:7; town ~, 1455:2; woman's ~, 4367:1

Nanking, China, rape of ~, 4765:1

nap/ping see also sleep; rest, 1613:3

Naples, Italy, 4975:6

Napoleon Bonaparte, 655:1; 689:1

narcissism/narcissist, 695:3; 910:16; 1883:4; 2068:5 narrative see also literature; storyteller/storytelling, electronic ~, 3679:3

narrowmindedness see also closemindedness; provincialism, 1208:7; 2349:7; 2564:4; counteracting ~, 691:4

Nassar, Gamel Abdel, 1870:2

nation/al see also specific countries; country; government, 1168:7; actions of ~, 892:18; 4811:1; appreciation of ~, 1936:2; ~ building, 3717:2; decline of ~, 530:1; 2192:16; die for ~, 4805:1; differences between warring ~, 3241:3; economic welfare of ~, 3617:2; family and ~, 1404:1; hypocrisy of ~, 1167:17; identity of ~, 3682:5; immoral ~, 1863:3; issue ~, 4730:4; just desserts of ~, 3349:15; life of ~, 1208:16; maturing ~, 807:2; multilateralism of ~, 3655:1; poor ~, 2230:1; responsibilities between ~, 1953–1954:3; thriving ~, 733:5; troubled ~, 666:1; 772:3; undeveloped ~, 1953–1954:3; unifying ~, 4803:1; united vs. divided ~, 2986:4; vanity of ~, 440:1

national defense see also armed forces/army; Defense Department (U.S.); military; national security, 2194:3; 2741:1; women and ~, 4745:2; 4887:3

national security see also national defense, 1857:5; 2608:3; 4174:10; defense of ~, 3129:1; health and ~, 4303.1:1

nationalism see also patriot/ism, 1392:1; 2512:3; limitations of ~, 1668:6

native see also aboriginal, 1450:12; 1627:6

Native American see also Eskimo, 468:1; 801:15; 880:1; 1295:1; 1827:3; 2299:2; 2515:1; 2624:1; 3862:4; 4242:9; ambush by ~, 611:1; challenges of ~, 3977:2; ~ character, 1179:1; ~ Chickasaw, 3753:4; Chippewa ~, 1149:1; coopting ~ culture, 2680:25; ~ custom, 3977:1; devastation of ~, 3591:2; ~ greeting, 4070:1; history of ~, 4947:5; ~ in relation to Earth, 3384:5; ~ in relation to United States, 2624:3; 4593:2; ~ in relation to whites, 1133:1, 2, 4; 1571:2; 3940:2; ~ Iroquois women, 3384:1; language of Pima ~, 1877:1; leadership of

~ Cherokee, 3591:1; ~ men in relation to women, 1070:2; missionaries and ~, 3224:2; ~ Mohawk, 1272:1; ~ names, 827:10; ~ Navajo, 1915:1; ~ Navajo youth, 2145:1; oppression of ~, 2911:2; plight of ~, 4110:3; prejudice against ~, 2911:1; ~ Pueblo, 1915:1; Pueblo ~, 3866:5; ~ reservation, 1663:9; 4242:7; revenge of ~, 1203:1; schooling of ~, 1877:1, 2; ~ Shoshone, 2450:1; Shoshone ~, 1269:1; ~ song, 1770:2; survival of ~, 3591:2; ~ trails, 1269:2; ~ tribes, 4242:6; ~ women, 3246:2; 3384:1, 2, 3; women ~, 3597:1; ~ women and war, 1080:3

Natural History Museum (New York), 3708:1

natural resources see also environment, 4039:1; managing ~, 3556:1, 2; ownership of ~, 2297:2

naturalness, 951:1; 2214:2

Nature (world), 273–274:4; 355:2; 879:1; 1008:3; 1189:1; 1359:2; 1405:5; 1446:9; 1450:; 1723:2; 1868:1; 1929:5; 2061:6; 2387:2; 2566:5; 2914:2; 2941:8; absorbed by ~, 1524:5; accidents of ~, 3780:3; altering ~, 1372:1; 2926:1; ~ and science, 2988:1; back to ~, 1377:1; balance of ~, 4329:4; beauty of ~, 1241:1; causality in ~, 3508:3; communion with ~, 2373:4; 3339:1; 3714:1; 4085:1; 4700.1:2; connection to ~, 1405:4; 1726:2; 1785:2; 4045:2; 4132:2; consolation of ~, 3217:4; constancy of ~, 887:6; control of ~, 2061:12; 2124:5; 2756:6, 15; 2988:3, 4; 3072:0; 3140:1; cycles of ~, 4072:3; divinity of ~, 2442:5; force of ~, 4463:2; gender of ~, 4674:2; hatred of ~, 3840:1; identity of ~, 3559:1; in harmony with ~, 3908–3909:1; ~ in relation to humans, 2101:4; 2175:2; joy of ~, 1335:1; laws of ~, 584:5, 6; 951:6; 1977:1; lessons of ~, 769:1; 1554:5; liberation of ~, 4529:1; loss of ~, 2164:1; message of ~, 3714:1; Mother ~, 3:1; mystery of ~, 1957:4; overwhelmed by ~, 4411:2; pleasure in ~, 184:1; ~ preserve (see also park), 4936:1; provisions of ~, 773:4; relating to ~, 4578:1; removed from ~, 3550:3; restoration of ~, 1152:1; 4084:2; revel in ~, 1268:3; reverence for ~, 931:26; rhythms of ~, 2359:2; rights of ~, 4338:1; role of ~ in education, 1381:5; sexes in ~, 656:1; sights of ~, 2195:3; solace of ~, 2657:3; sounds of ~,

3714:1; splendor of ~, 1745:3; 2162:1; study of ~, 2277:1; survival of ~, 3851:2; understanding ~, 887:15; 4474:2; unity of ~, 1293:4; war vs. ~, 4506:1; wisdom of ~, 474:5

Navratilova, Martina, 4424:2

navy, Greek ~, 60:1

Navy, U.S., sonar technology and ~, 4278:2; women in ~, 2550:2

Nazi see also fascism; Hitler, 1632:3; 2026:1; and Jews, 1514:4; ~ death camps, 4321:1; ~ Germany, 3314:2; ~ in Western Europe, 2513:1; ~ Resistance, 2344:2

NEA (National Endowment for the Arts), 4440:1; influencing of ~, 3117:2

Near East, ~ in relation to whites, 1618:7

neatness see also orderliness; tidiness, 2402:2

necessity, 1236:7; 1355:3; 1751:6; 4312:14; benefits of ~, 930:1

need, 511:14; 1788:2; 2381:2; ~ for another, 1576:4; 3033:8; fulfilled ~, 3755:2; increasing ~, 2080:8; individual ~, 3772:1; object of ~, 1208:12; personal ~, 1751:10

needlecraft see also knitting; seamstress; sewing, 325:2; 3110:3

neglect, 1982:2

negotiation, life is a ~, 4013:5

neighbor/hood, 869:4; bonds among ~, 4312:1; caring for ~, 4282:4; ~ cooperative, 2919:3; keeping up with ~, 1418:3; love of ~, 371:3; 1249:1; mixed ~ (see also integration), 3139:1; ruin ~, 479:1

Neolithic era, 2756:3

neon, 3358:1, 2

Neruda, Pablo, 4577:2

nerves/nervousness see also tension, 1432:1; emotions and ~, 4405:3

nervous breakdown see also mental illness, 1647:2; 4034:1; 4346:1

Netherlands, women in, 1211:2

neurosis see also complex (psychological), 2314:1; 2817:12; ~ in society, 1683:1

Nevada, women in ~, 1463:1

New England see also America; United States, ~ attitude, 1761:5; autumn in ~, 1166:2; farming in ~, 1849:2

New Orleans, growing up in ~, 3494:1; ~ homelessness in, 4455:3

New Year, 1053:1

New York/City, 1254:18; 1370:4; 1611:4; 1617:2; 2203:1; 2402:1; 2405:7; 2453:2; 2592:2; 2638:12; 2656:4; 2925:1; 2932:1; 3002:; 3147:6; 3710:1; 3875:1; 4363:1; 4614:4; 4685:3; 4747:4; ~ address, 4947:4; ~ cuisine, 1871:7; good times in

~, 2943:9; people of ~, 1739:6; 2827:4; poverty in ~, 2270:2; robbery in ~, 860:12; social classes in ~, 2066:6; streets of ~, 4614:2; young women in ~, 1888:3

New Zealand, ~ and nuclear power, 4770:3; independence of ~, 3958:2; ~ women, 973:1; 1155:2

newborn see also baby; childbirth; infancy, 2210:4; 4214:1

newness, 782:10; 2036:5; 3906:7

news see also journalism; mass media, 853:3; 2680:20; 4815:6; ~ as entertainment, 3444:4; bad ~, 2732:2; 2748:4; 3119:16; creating ~, 1080:2; criticism of ~, 2915:3; ~ for children, 1748:1; hard ~, 4876:1; ~ industry, 4607:2; ~ of day, 2261:4; 2426:7; 2464:9; 3697:1; television ~, 2618:17; 4437.1:1, 2, 4; unexpected ~, 916:10

newspaper, 767:4; 1087:3; 2394:2; ~ editor, 4127:3; exaggeration in ~, 1937:1; honesty in ~, 2710:4; impartiality of ~, 634:1; ~ oped, 4754:2; power of ~, 2087:2; 2289:3; ~ press conference, 2500–2501:4; ~ printing, 621:2; reading ~, 658:5; ~ reporter (see also war correspondent), 2019:2; 2228:1; role of ~, 2963:2; sensationalism in ~, 1301:3; ~ staff, 2654:1; ~ under dictatorship, 2654:2; working on ~, 1715:4

NHPC Limited (National Hydroelectric Power Corporation), 4506:2; ruthlessness of ~, 4506:5

Nicaragua, art education in ~, 3744:4

Nigeria, 4019:2; women in ~, 4019:1; 4701:1

night see also eve/ning; midnight, 299:1; 723:3; 884:1; 1067:1; 1263:1; 3957:2; 4029:1; beautiful ~, 1745:3; cloak of ~, 2149:1; fear of ~, 508:1; ~ in country, 1444:8; long ~, 2492:1; ~ on town, 3428:4; secrets of ~, 172:1; shelter of ~, 803:1; sleepless~, 165:5; solitude of ~, 4889:2; voices of ~, 1272:2

nightmare see also dream, 2642:16

Nimrod, 1454:1

Nin, Anais, 4134:3

nine-eleven (9/11), see September 11

Nixon, Richard M., 1618:13, 31; 1804:3; 1897:1; 2323:1; 2480:7; 3594:3; 4620:4

Nobel Prize, 3008:3; 3207:2; ~ Committee, 1569:1; ~ for Peace, 4495:2

nobility see also aristocracy; rank, 2670:1; 2736:2

noble (rank) see also courtiers; royal/ty, desire to be ~, 509:3

noise see also sound, 733:14; ~ of the world, 287:5

nomad see also bedouin; wanderer, 786:2; religion and ~, 2854:2

nonconformist/nonconformity see also individuality, 2866:10; 3250:1; 3481:1; hostility toward ~, 1570:2

nonviolence see also pacifism, 2285:3; 2881:3; 3491:4; practicing ~, 3658:6; women and ~, 3699:4

normality, 1450:9; 4538:1; 4615:3; ~ in children, 2684:2

North/erners (U.S.), ~ in relation to South, 879:3

Norway, women in government of ~, 3549:1

nosiness see also business, minding one's ~, 305:2; 1190:2; 1193:2; 1663:15; 1914:11; 2996:1; 3891:1

nostalgia see also sentimentality, 408:8; 653:1; 1719:3; 3139:5; 3269:2; 3686:4; 4422:1; 4614:1

nothing/ness, 482:2; 544:4; 1880:3; 1925:3; 2021:2, 11; 2732:4; 2799:4; 3119:7; 3139:13; 3609:2; 4716:2; achieving ~, 3954:1; doing ~, 3349:7; fear of ~, 1883:6; having ~, 2067:1; opposite of ~, 3716:3; ~ to lose, 4872:4

notoriety, 1950:4

nourishment see also nutrition/ist, self ~, 1901:7

novel/ist see also book; fiction; literature; reading; story; writer, 767:21; 3138:2; 3216:3; 4320:4; art of ~, 166:12; bad ~, 1780:16; ending of ~, 808:15; insights of ~, 1239:5; 4067:9; invention of ~, 3138:1; romantic ~, 598:3; stream of consciousness ~, 2208:1; writing ~, 2483:7; 4362:1; 4653:6

novelty see also originality, 671:14

NOW (National Organization for Women), 2400:5; 4202.1:1, 2

NRA (National Rifle Association), 4235:6

NSF (National Science Foundation), programs of ~, 4007:4

nuclear energy see also atomic bomb, 3762:3; 4594:1; ~ power industry, 3075:1; uses of ~, 2412:1

nuclear weaponry, 2881:2; 4080:2, 3, 5; banishment of ~, 3214:1; 3676:5; protesting ~, 2278:1, 2; testing ~, 2449:1; 2624:1;

nudity, 533:6; 1015:1; 1545:4; 1836:4; 2777:2; 4849:2; public ~, 4723:1

nuisance, 1858:1

numbers see also mathematics, 3707:2; importance of ~, 4493:4; knowledge of ~, 533:10

nun see also convent, 149:5; 450:6; 1737:1; 2770:1; 2909:2; 3142:1; education of ~, 1220:1; favor of ~, 4105:5; hypocrisy of ~, 1441:5

Nuremberg, Germany, ~ Trials, 2036:10

nurse/nursing see also medical profession, 782:13; 974:1; 1764–1765:1; dedication to ~, 1811:1; ~ home, 2335:2; 3341:1; ~ in relation to patient, 1811:1; 2335:1; ~ in war, 1784:4; training of ~, 1549:1

nurturing see also caring, need for ~, 3172:3

nutrition/ist see also diet/er; food; nourishment, 1221:2; 2566:1; 2709:4; effect of ~ on state of mind, 1992:2; good ~, 1992:1; 3003:4; science of ~, 1112:3

Nyro, Laura, 3982:1, 2

O

Oates, Joyce Carol, 2638:10

oath see also promise; swearing; vow, 399:1; 501:1; false ~, 522:3; keeping one's ~, 808:1; legal ~, 1959:7

Obama, Barack, 2839:0; 2907:5; 3076:2; 3195:1; 4129:3; 4417:1; 4423:1; 4432:2; 4471:1; 4561:2; 4648:3; ~ and Hawaii, 3450:2; bipartisanship and ~, 3798:3; black support of ~, 4442:3; character of ~, 4102:6, 7; 4373:3; ~ in relation to Arab world, 4642:1; inauguration of ~, 4601:5; roots of ~, 4775:3; skills of ~, 4693:1; values of ~, 4648:4; women's issues and ~, 4732:1

Obama, Michelle, 4373:1

obedience, 11:2; 302:1; 1171:2; 1741:14; 3723:1; 4650:8; blind ~, 890:5; 3360:2; ~ in child, 1332:1; total ~, 2118:3

obesity see also diet/er; fat/ness; plumpness; weight, 742:1; 1649:2; 2757:1; facts about ~, 4870:2

obituary, 1789:1

objectification see also dehumanization, ~ of others, 2842:2; 3371:2; ~ of women, 283:4; 799:5; 1132:6; 1208:9; 1917:2; 2369:1; 2600:1; 3738:4; 4860:1

objectivity see also detachment; impartiality, 1278:1; 1618:11

obligation see also duty; responsibility, 937:2; feeling of ~, 2297:5

observation, 614:2; 682:4; 1670:1; 3121:4; 4334:2; ~ of sick, 974:2; powers of ~, 477:3; 1348:3

observatory, 2338:2

obsession see also compulsion, 4911:1; ~ with cleanliness, 1979:4

obsolescence, 3197:2

obstacle see also adversity; trouble, 859:3; 2668:16; 3039:9; creat-

ing ~, 1447:4; ~ of glass ceiling, 3731:20; of women ~, 2480:2; overcoming ~, 366:1; 1233:5; 1497:3; 1913:1; 2306:3; 2702:1; 3913:2; 4610:2; 4746:2

obstetrician/obstetrics see also medical profession, 1442:2

occupation (activity) see also profession; trade; vocation, 578:4; 613:4; 2158:2; change of ~, 1557:1; enduring ~, 422:1; sex and ~, 1935:3

occupation (conquest), ~ by invading forces, 2344:1; living under ~, 1977:6

ocean see also marine life; sea; tide; wave, 227:1; exploration of ~, 2926:5; saving ~, 4278:4; swimming in ~, 4127:5; threats to the ~, 3422:4; 3768:2, 3

odds, going vs. the ~, 2422:1

odds and ends, 1097:1

Odysseus, 3037:1

offense, 3258:3; causing ~, 3381:3

Ohio, 4375:1

oil, 820:2; dependence on ~, 3525:3; 3960:1; drilling for ~, 4174:14; 4684:2; foreign ~, 4432:2; ~ industry, 4863:2; ~ on Indian reservation, 1663:9; politics of ~, 4705:1, 2

O'Keeffe, Georgia, 3940:3

Oklahoma, 3705:1; 4020:2, 3

old age see also age/aging; elderly/ elders; longevity; middle age; years of age, 46:6; 54:1; 572:4; 616:6; 635:2; 689:2; 849:2; 887:20, 26, 27; 956:4; 999:3; 1141:2; 1160:1; 1176:6; 1249:4; 1292:7; 1409:8; 1450:14; 1561:4; 1601:1; 1741:28; 1789:6; 1808:4; 1880:1; 2025:6; 2080:12; 2127:2; 2155:2; 2207:4; 2317:2; 2331:1; 2443:3; 2568:6; 2820:1; 2874:3; 4559:1; 4563:2; 4909:3; accepting ~, 4909:4; attaining ~, 989:2; beauty of ~, 2375:2; behavior in ~, 4207:2; dependency in ~, 1265:5; 4453:4; desires of ~, 4055:2; dreams of ~, 2803:1; happy ~, 870:9; 1337:5; 2025:7; horror of ~, 671:6; 3239:1; ~ in relation to youth, 3472:4; infirmities of ~, 1601:4; isolation of ~, 3196:1; limitations of ~, 972:1; sex and ~ (see also sex), 2294:1; women and ~, 170:1; 439:1; 1362:5

Olsen, Tillie, 2663:1

Olympics, women and ~, 4617:2; 4747:1

omen, 2582:3

omnipotence see also power, 1541:1; 4181:2; illusions of ~, 3599:1

Onassis, Jacqueline Kennedy, 4757:2

O'Neill, Eugene, 1688:1, 2, 4

oneness *see also* connectedness; unity, 2032:6; ~ of all life, 1148:6

openness *see also* candor, 721:1; 807:20; 1114:2; 1575:1; 2437:7; 2777:2; 3048:1; 4116:10; 4180:2

opera *see also* music; singer, 671:1; 1274:1; 4349:1; attending ~, 649:11; children and ~, 3097:2; ~ diva, 3675:3; grand ~, 3097:2; heroines in ~, 4616:1; producing ~, 2478:1; ~ singer, 1432:2; 2581:1; ~ voice, 4715:1

opinion *see also* judgement; public opinion; viewpoint, 533:4; 892:15; 1648:1; 2437:6; differing ~, 4752:3; false ~, 2331:9; humble ~, 3241:7; influence of ~, 1662:3; lack of ~, 808:6; 1645:4; 1761:5; right to ~, 435:1

opium *see also* drugs, 1188:1; 4604:3; ~ poppy, 692:1; 1188:1

opportunism/opportunist, 1663:16; 3136:1

opportunity, 1024:9; 1403:3; 1619:9; 2224:1; 2537:8; 4116:10; blind to ~, 1734:3; creating ~, 2823:1; equal ~, 4079:1; ~ for all, 3888:2, 3; ~ for black women, 2422:1; ~ for women, 1508:2; funding for ~, 4983:1; grab ~, 649:2; 1084:1; 1618:19; 4158:1; missed ~, 966:3; recognizing ~, 3001:1; seeking ~, 961:2

opposites, 3197:3; unifying ~, 1350:5

opposition *see also* opponent, 955:3; 1618:29; 2828:4; 4268:3

oppressed/oppressiveness, 392:2; 2116:21; anonymity of ~, 3980:3; attitude to ~, 1299:2; empowering the ~, 3652:1; history of ~, 1911:3; impact of ~, 1294:1; 4074:2; resistance of ~, 3090:3

oppressor/oppression *see also* persecution; tyranny; woman/women, oppression of ~, 666:1; 1945:3; 2272:1; 2291:6; 2863:3; 3645:1; 3945:1; 3947:1; ~ by government, 3558:2; cycle of ~, 945:11; death of ~, 444:1; effects of ~, 2116:4; fighting ~, 2722:2; ranking ~, 4125:2; release from ~, 1341:1; struggle against ~, 1392:1

optimism/optimist, 282:1; 998:2; 1008:4; 1209:2; 1253:1; 1354:1; 1445:1; 1497:1; 1552:2; 1590:27; 1593:9; 1619:9; 1987:3; 2014:3; 2437:2; 3488:1; 4563:5; 4876:2

order (rule), obeying ~, 2192:8; 4263:4; out of ~, 1554:3

orderliness *see also* neatness; tidiness, 1454:3; 1601:7; 1668:2; 1769:1; 2267:2; 2271:2; 2876:5;

4352:3; lack of ~, 821:3; ~ of life, 2281:5

ordinariness *see also* commonplace, 2786:2; 2874:5; 4717:3; appeal of ~, 2522:1

organ (body), donation of ~, 4508:1; selling ~, 3535:3

organization (business), 3311:3; remodeling ~, 3795:4; staff of ~, 3343:2; transformation of ~, 4032:2

organization (order), 1450:17; ~ at home, 1697:4; need for ~, 2272:7; ~ of household, 1074:2; reasons for ~, 3334:1

organizer *see* activism; agitator, political ~, 2922:7

orgasm *see also* sexual intercourse, 1979:9; 2976:1; 3594:4; 4813:5; female ~, 981:7; 1949:1; 2794:1; 2865:1, 3; 3344:3, 4

originality *see also* novelty; singularity; uniqueness, 1530:1; 1758:1; 2032:5; 3317:7; 4711:2; attempts at ~, 1881:4; lack of ~, 425:2; space for ~, 863:3

ornamentation, 3832:3

orphan *see also* fatherlessness; foundling, 842:1; 864:5; 965:4; 988:1; 2094–2095:1; 2562:1; 3172:1

orthodoxy, overturning ~, 2487:2

Orwell, George, 3830:2

ostentation *see also* pomp; pretense, 1673:9

ostracism, 2535:2; ~ by group, 3572:3

otherness *see also* difference, 2380:9; 358 0:1; 4428:2

outcast *see also* stranger, 3547:2; 4197:5

outdoors *see also* countryside; wilderness, 2914:2; children ~, 805:1; renewed by ~, 1566:4; 2872:1

outsider *see also* difference; loner, 1600:2; inhibited ~, 3802:1; uncaring ~, 4479:1

outspokenness, 3304:1; ~ in women, 4174:12

ovary/ovum, 3526:1; 4005:1

overpopulation, 887:10; 1751:25

Ovid, 1120:2

ownership, 1470:5; 3753:4; 4782:4

Oxford University (England), ~ spinster, 3465:1

oxymoron, 2763:3

ozone, ~ layer, 3330:3

P

pacifism/pacifist *see also* antiwar movement; nonviolence; peace; peace movement, 839:4; 1499:1; 1583:2; 2285:1; 2362:6; 2708:1; ~ in film, 3068:3; ~ of women, 310:5; task of ~, 1764–1765:9

pagan/ism, 2442:2; 4312:2; women in ~, 4539:1

pain *see also* suffering, 77:1; 129:1; 451:3; 489:3; 820:3; 1024:14; 1173:6; 1581:4; 1774:1; 2968:1; 3349:12; 4477:2; 4635:4; bearing ~, 4310:4; commonness of ~, 1136:2; eliminating ~, 974:3; 1447:; eternal ~, 317:1; inflict ~, 302:2; 737:3; inner ~, 2999:2; men and ~, 3260:5; ~ of life, 4072:1; past ~, 976:1; physical ~, 1160:9; ~ reduction, 4364:2; repetition of ~, 4307:2; usefulness of ~, 3862:2; 4404:2

Paine, Thomas, 1096:2; 1271:1

painter/painting *see also* art; picture; portrait, 519:2; 1259:3; 1652:1; 1670:2; 2066:7; 2077:1; 2430:3; 2440:1, 2; 3224:3; 3661:3; amateur ~, 1869:4; business of ~, 1259:1; execution of ~, 1147:1; ~ from a woman's perspective, 2275:0; portrait ~, 2275:1; woman ~, 2097:2

Pakistan, educational system in ~, 4208:2; women of ~, 4708:1; 4942:3

Palestine/Palestinian, 2413:3; 3233:2; 4326:7; human rights and ~, 3233:4; ~ in Israel, 2722:6; 4458:4; ~ in relation to Israel, 4025:1; 4810:1; ~ in relation to Jews, 1870:1; 2650:2; occupation of ~, 2722:1, 3; ~ peace movement, 3699:1; terrorism and ~, 3233:1; ~ under occupation, 2673:1; ~ violence, 4025:2; ~ women, 3184:7; 4330:1; 4547:1; 4904:2

Paley, Grace, 2932:7

Palin, Sarah, 2517:1; 2977:8; 4797:5; 4978:0

Pan, 1415:1

panic *see* fear; hysteria, 2184:4

pantheism, 236:1; 293:2; 3179:2; 3303:3; 3547:6

pantyhose, 1958:1

paperwork, 4554:5

Papua/n, 3948:3; corruption in ~, 4821:1; ~ women, 3948:1

Paracelsus, Philippus Aureolus, 1007:5

parade, World War I ~, 1784:5

paradigm, new world ~, 4290:1, 4; ~ shift, 2971:4; 3085:2; 3537:1; 4113:4; 4921:2

paradise *see also* Eden; heaven; utopia, 252:2; 1238:1; 2705:3; 3714:5; 4292:1; banished from ~, 2777:1; earthly ~, 407:1; ~ lost, 472:12; ~ on earth, 1957:3; path to ~, 129:1; reclaiming ~, 1977:5

paranoia *see also* distrust, 1025:14; 2866:21

parasite *see also* sycophancy/sycophant, 1901:7; 1921:5; 2082:2

parent/hood *see also* father/hood; grandparent; mother/hood,

430:9; 511:13; 850:5; 887:11; 931:10; 965:3; 1618:25; 2242:1; 2263:1; 2390:3; 2554:2; 2586:5; 2771:15, 23; 2916:16; 3002:5; 3029:3; 4004:2; 4013:2; 4537:1; 4756:2; 4880:1; adoptive ~, 3603:3; ~ as role model, 812:4; becoming one's own ~, 3574:2; child's perception of ~, 3702:1; death of ~, 2243:4; decision of ~, 3469:5; dependent ~, 659:2; ~ duty toward child, 705:1; 2630:4; evaluating ~, 2148:1; faults of ~, 734:14; fears of ~, 3408:0; first time ~, 1006:1; guidelines for ~, 3954:2; illusions of ~, 2434:1; ~ in conflict with child, 3055:1, 2; ~ in relation to adult child, 3882:4; ~ in relation to child, 302:3; 336:2; 353:2; 479:5; 593:4; 1437:1; 1721:1; 1743:4; 1882:2; 1905:8; 2023:1; 2080:9; 2592:5; 2657:5; 2834:2; 2867:2; 2936:2; 3154:1; 3231:1; 3316:5; 3551–3552:1; 4682:1; 4972:1; ~ in relation to son, 2448:3; insecure ~, 2801:2; joys of ~, 4298:6; love of ~, 2746:1; 4648:10; 4744:4, 5; 4792:1; obligations of ~, 931:24; ~ of soldier, 2078:3; over-protective ~, 4972:3; permissive ~, 2592:4; 3469:1; price of ~, 2027:7; progressive ~, 2577:7; role of ~, 3342:2; silence of ~, 3573:1; supportive ~, 4069:2; unplanned ~, 3712:1; wise ~, 911:6; working ~, 1668:1; 1776:3

Paris, France, 1745:1; 2219:6; 2962:3; ~ during WWI, 2192:5; expatriates in ~, 4188:1; visiting ~, 4847:3

park, 3704:5; national ~, 3890:5

parking lot, 4150:5

Parks, Rosa, 3073:1; 4042:3; 4101:3

Parliament (Great Britain), 1625:2; 4464:2

participation, 1720:1; 2187:6; 2363:2

parting *see also* departure; separation, 72:1; 294:1; 834:1; 1083:3; 1842:4; 1959:4; 1986:3; ~ from homeland, 341:5

partner/ship *see also* couple; husband; lover; mate; wife, benefits of ~, 931:28; ~ between couples, 1244:7; 2869:2; lack of ~, 3076:1; the right ~, 1044:2; unity of ~, 4153:1

party (social) *see also* celebration; festivity, big ~, 880:7; cocktail ~, 2898:1; drinking at ~ (*see also* drinking), 1995:1; ~ for child, 880:7; ~ is over, 2339:3; leaving ~, 2319:4; reason for ~, 3294:2; women guest at ~, 1596:1

passion *see also* desire; emotion; feeling, 321:2; 770:6; 858:1; 1027:6; 1723:4; 1782:13; 1981:2; 2224:6; 2756:7; 2817:1; 3266–3267:2; 3852:2; acting with ~, 3836:3; ~ at mercy of reason, 934:5; buried ~, 1957:4; continuous ~, 1782:2; finding one's ~, 4324:2; great ~, 2322:1; ~ in relation to death, 1867:3; joyless ~, 1782:5; lack of ~, 845:2; power of ~, 1979:15; releasing ~, 1315:2; sexual ~ (*see also* sexuality), 249:1; 316:6; 1524:3; uncontrolled ~, 650:2; 775:2

passivity *see also* apathy; submissiveness, 1442:1; 1727:10; 1948:1; 2118:2; 3094:3; 3360:1

passport, 1501:1

past *see also* time; yesterday, 442:2; 883:1; 955:8; 1022:1; 1409:24; 1455:1; 1502:7; 1563:2; 1576:1; 2082:1; 2154:6; 2226:1; 2239:2; 2715:3; 2874:8; 3099:21; 4307:1; 4444:4; 4677:6; 4845–4846:2; 4903:2; break with ~, 2648:1; 4004:1; concerned about ~, 2228:; creating ~, 3340:3; delving into the ~, 2680:11; 2772:9; examining ~, 1355:5; 1505:5; 2831:2; ignoring ~, 892:10; interpreting ~, 4583:4; inventing ~, 3812:1; leaving the ~, 3711:1; living in ~, 3298:3; looking back on ~, 1944:2; 2135:1; love of ~, 4406:2; pain of ~, 3254:4; 4406:3; passion about ~, 3136:4; prisoner of ~, 3342:4; reality of ~, 3139:5; regret ~, 993:3; 2070:1; remembering ~, 46:3; 1266:2; return to ~, 4161:3; ruined ~, 2931:3; separation from ~, 4667:4; trouble from ~, 4660:2; understanding ~, 2778:5; undoing ~, 3197:1; unsettled ~, 4207:1

Pasteur, Louis, 2175:2

patent, ~ of life form, 4141:9; ~ protection, 4566:4

paternalism *see also* patriarchy; protectiveness, 860:5

path, carving ~, 1269:2; finding one's ~, 1670:2; 3539:1; 4199:1; following one's ~, 1312:3; 2019:4; seeking a ~, 3539:2; straight and narrow ~, 4136:9

patience *see also* impatience, 308:12; 472:9; 585:7; 595:2; 717:2; 1387:6; 1528:3; 3779:4; 4036:2; ~ in women, 2080:15; learning ~, 2498:2

patient, medical ~ (*see also* physician, visit with ~), 2261:1; psychiatric ~, 3486:2; recovery of ~ (*see also* cure; recovery), 3210:2

patriarchy *see also* paternalism; phallocracy; sexism, 1683:2;

2658:5; 2899:2; 2985:4; 3050:1; 3139:9; 3153:3; 3326:1; 3874:4; dangers of ~, 2680:18; end of ~, 4658:5; fight vs. ~, 3983:2, 5; ~ in educational system, 2675:1; ~ in relation to women's speech, 4291:1; perception of ~, 2756:12; perspective of ~ in literature, 4577:2; structures of ~, 3284:8; women and ~, 2979:1; 2985:2

patriot/ism *see also* nationalism, 707:1; 729:1; 730:1; 746:1; 1106:1; 1251:5; 1310:1; 1349:1; 1465:1; 3257:7; authentic ~, 2260:6; blood shed for ~, 3480:4; obligations of ~, 3981:6; ~ protesting injustice, 1343:1; questioning ~, 1570:5; true ~, 1548:8; women and ~, 827:14

pattern, 1440:5; 1701:4; 2144:2; broken ~, 2030:1; ~ of life, 1655:4; 3139:10

Paul, Alice, 2861:5

Paul, St., 291:1; 308:11

pause, art of ~, 1627:6

Pavarotti, Luciano, 3675:2

pawnbroker, 1602:1

pay *see also* salary; wage, ~ discrimination, 3093:4; 4977:2; equal ~, 3093:2; 4977:1; gender disparity in ~, 2300:5; 4979:1; ~ inequity, 4977:3

peace *see also* pacifism, 287:5; 674:4; 1355:6; 1870:16; 2259:2; 2288:1; 2673:5; 2997:10; 3695:1; 4256:7; 4662:2, 3; 4952:2; attaining ~, 234:7; 3707:3; beginnings of ~, 2362:3; co-exist in ~, 2221:1; consequences of ~, 94:2; construction of ~, 1381:13; desire for ~, 1870:2; 3627:2; 4896:1; domestic ~, 965:5; 3782:1; ~ education, 4545:1; fighting for ~, 327:2; 2211:3; god of ~, 625:2; inner ~ (*see also* tranquility), 1268:5; 1903:4; 2320:4; 2920:3; 2961:1; 3984:2; 4508:3; maintaining ~, 980:1; ~ -making, 2288:3; 2362:7; 3214:2; ~ march, 2553:1; meaning of ~, 4545:2; ~ of mind, 3403:2; organize for ~, 1555:8; partners for ~, 1874:8; price of ~, 1990:1; 2098:6; ~ process, 2362:6; 4662:1; radiating ~, 4892:2; requirements of ~, 4066:4; society at ~, 3040:2; songs of ~, 3772:1; trappings of ~, 1550:3; war and ~, 827:7; 1514:1; women and ~ process, 3699:3; 4066:5, 6; world ~ (*see also* cooperation, global ~), 956:3; 1618:22; 1637:4; 1874:1; 1935:11; 3782:5

Peace Corps, 2854:1; 4066:1

peace movement *see also* pacifism, 3068:1

peacekeeping/er, cost of ~, 4378:2; standards of ~, 4378:4

Pearl Harbor (Oahu, Hawaii), 3372:5; study of ~, 2194:1

peasant, stories of ~, 2918:2

pedantry *see also* ostentation, 517:3

pedigree, 731:2; 1024:32

pencil, 3849:2

penis *see also* genitalia, 2151:1; 2613:3; 2639:2; 2860:2; 2955:4; 4010:3; erect ~, 1790:16; 1800:2; erectile dysfunction of ~, 2622:6; symbology of ~, 3780:12; woman's response to ~, 267:2

Pennsylvania, hills of ~, 1037:5

pension, inequities of ~, 2178:4; investing ~, 4041:3

Pentagon, the, ~ budget, 4521:5

people *see also* human/kind; individual; masses; person; public, 892:11; 2310:1; 2817:10; 3316:1; ~ as products, 3196:2; avoiding ~, 2795:1; categorizing ~, 1525:1; 4326:7; damaged ~, 4367:3; differences among ~, 1977:4; disappearance of ~, 2668:18; enjoying ~, 2472:8; ~ in relation to government, 4594:2; interesting ~, 166:17; morality of ~, 2969:3; ordinary ~ (*see also* commoner; ordinariness), 1020:1; 1024:8; ~ power, 3696:4; primitive ~ (*see also* aboriginal), 846:1; 1797:4; private world of ~, 1761:6; types of ~, 1211:1; 1663:2; 3377:3; unimpressive ~, 1184:9; weakness of ~, 745:3

People (magazine), 4128:1

perception *see also* insight; perspective; sensibility; understanding, 197:3; 1262:4; 2756:14; 3135:2; 3341:3; 3497:4; 3808:3; assumptions of ~, 2595:1.3; 3795:3; 4041:1; changing ~, 3743:1; lack of ~, 407:2; ~ of another, 1655:3; 2564:1; 3720:4; personal ~, 2444:1; training in visual ~, 2547:2

perceptiveness, 2437:10

Perceval, Spencer, 754:2

perfection/ism, 694:5; 1171:2; 2648:4; 2732:3; 2829:2; 2982:3; 3488:6; 4255:4; ~ of self, 1731:1; oneness of ~, 4401:1; portrayal of ~, 684:2; standard of ~, 2089:2

performance/performer *see also* actor; entertainer; 2138:1; 2431:1; 3837:2; carnival, ~, 3565:1; coaching ~, 2492.1:2; cooperative ~, 1685:2; goals of ~, 2492.1.3; identity for ~, 4799:1; ~ in relation to audience, 1771:1; 2867:3; protecting ~, 2370.1:1; salary of ~, 608:1; touring ~, 2652:1

perfume, 1516:3; 1593:5; 2100:2; 2405:4

perjury *see also* law, 1233:4

permissiveness, 2592:4; ~ in society, 2442:1

Perovskaya, Sofia, 1191:1

Perry, Zenobia, 3221:1; 4068:1

persecution *see also* oppressor/oppression; pogrom, 538:1; condoned ~, 288:1; ~ of Jews, 2157:3; ~ of women, 874:4; religious ~, 112:1; 1236:6

Persephone, 4327:1

perseverance *see also* diligence; tenacity, 1233:5; 1335:10; 1515:4; 1953–1954:4; 2099:1; 2174:3; 2313:2; 2340:1; 2448:1; 2643:1; 2862:2; 2944:2; ~ despite odds, 1911:2

Persia, 1785:4

persistence *see* perseverance

person *see* individual; people

personality *see also* disposition, complexity of ~, 1444:1; evolution of ~, 2927:1; irritating ~, 4579:4

perspective *see also* perception; 2185:11; point of view, 2266:8; 4197:4; seeing another's ~, 3345:5

persuasion *see also* influence, 2331:8; 3832:1; components of ~, 1669:10; moral ~, 890:2; power of ~, 3314:1

Peru, education in ~, 2845:1

pessimism/pessimist, 2556:4

pet (domestic) *see also specific species*, 3897:2; 4390:7; attitude toward ~, 2648:5; loyal ~, 807:7; ~ owner, 4982:1; therapeutic effects of ~, 4453:3

Petraeus, David H., Iraq War and ~, 4596:2

phallocracy *see also* patriarchy, 2633:2

pharmaceuticals, commercialism of ~, 2622:6; ~ in United States, 2946:4; ~ industry, 4008:2; regulations for ~, 4008:1

pharmacist, 3069:2

philanderer *see also* infidelity, 844:5; 3499:1; woman ~, 646:5

philanthropy *see also* charity, 971:1; 980:2; 1846:4; 3892:2

Philippines, human trafficking in ~, 4528:4

philosopher, 767:; 773:2; 1044:17; 2128:2; austerity of ~, 65:1

philosophy *see also specific branches & theories*, 80:1; 327:2; 539:6; 2331:5; 2352:12, 13; 2571:2; 3688:3; 3778:4; 4699:1; 4716:1; ~ in relation to wisdom, 328:2; living ~, 1348:1; need for ~, 1904:2; simple ~, 1616:3; woman's ~, 487:6

photographer/photography *see also* camera, 869:8; 927:1; 1194:1; 1370:1; 1828:3; 1859:1, 2, 3, 4; 2444:1, 5; 4777:5; animal ~, 3968:4; artistry of ~, 3944:2; defacing ~, 4579:1; impact of ~, 2575:1; 2915:2; perspectives in

~, 2915:4; portrait ~, 3619:1, 3; snap-shot ~, 2866:11; subject of ~, 2868:2; uses of ~, 3988:2

physician *see also specific specialists;* doctor; medical profession, 511:15; 550:2; 635:4; 774:1; 1724:15; 1761:3; 2597:0; 2857:2; 3033:1; 3129:2; 4356:3; advice of ~, 2946:1; education of ~, 1112:4; greedy ~, 533:7; husband of ~, 2948:2; ~ in relation to patient, 2946:4; incompetent ~, 676:5; ~ looking at function, 4465:3; new ~, 4430:2; vicissitudes of ~, 3473:4; visit with ~ (*see also* patient, medical ~), 1160:7; woman ~, 981:6

physicist/physics, 2054:3; ~ in relation to religion, 4474:1; nuclear ~ research, 2173:1; quantum ~, 4475:1, 3, 5; work of ~, 2054:1

physiology, medicine and ~, 4465:3; study of ~, 4465:1

Picasso, Pablo, 3420:3

picture *see also* painter/painting, computers and ~, 4084:6; thinking in ~, 3748:2

piety *see also* devotion; religion, 620:1

pilgrim, American ~, 1159:2

pilgrimage, religious ~, 108:1

pilot *see also* flying, woman ~, 2550:2

pimp *see also* prostitute/prostitution; sex industry, 1894:3

pioneer *see also* settler, American ~, 1374:1; importance of ~, 4846:3; ~ life, 796:2; ~ women, 1663:11; 2653:1

Piozzi, Hester Lynch, 641:2

piracy/pirate, confronting ~, 4535.1:1

Pitcher, Molly, 1106:4

pitfall *see also* trap, 1208:11

pitilessness *see also* compassion, lack of ~, 98:1; 504:1

pity, 1674:4

Pius XII, Pope, 1802:1, 2

place, character of ~, 3126:2; drawn to ~, 869:3; 1731:3; finding one's ~, 2941:1; image of ~, 3485:2; importance of ~, 4854:1; love of ~, 767:27; out of ~, 396:1; proper ~, 1074:2; special ~, 831:2; ~ where one lives, 2483:6

plagiarism, 509:1; 1901:5; 2392:1; 4175:2

plan/ning, 1453:3; 4268:6; concealed ~, 1887:4; defective ~, 523:3; need for ~, 1515:2

planet *see also* Earth; world, abuse of ~, 4298:8; dying ~, 2892:4; habitable ~, 2359:3; 4510:7; leaving ~, 4359:2; survival of ~, 3600:1; 4712:1; sustainability of ~, 3768:1; 4552:3

Planned Parenthood, 3003:1; 4466:1

plant life *see also specific varieties;* flora, century ~, 1974:2; healthy ~, 3550:1; respect for ~, 758:2

plastic surgery, 2155:1; 4174:4; 4390:1; 4635:5; 4971:1

plastics, 2622:2

Plato, 870:2; 3272:1

play *see* stage play

play/ing *see also* game; toy, 3808:6, 7; 4544:1; children and ~, 807:17; 2677:1, 2; 3042:2; importance of ~, 2362:1; lessons of ~, 3782:2; ~ vs. mechanization, 2888:2

playwright/ing *see also* scriptwriter; stage play; theater, 2518:3; 2704:4; 2996:5; feminist ~, 3818:5; woman ~ 493:1; 2518:4; 3237:1, 4; 3776:3

Plaza Hotel (New York), 2169:1, 2

pleasure *see also* amusement; diversion; hedonism; leisure; relaxation, 158:8; 439:2; 517:6; 519:1; 583:2; 649:7; 3802:2; 4050:4; buried ~, 1264:5; business of ~, 734:6; free ~, 1686:10; giving ~, 540:3; ~ in bed, 2691:3; innocent ~, 905:1; momentary ~, 734:2; physical ~, 2059:2; sexual ~ (*see* sexual intercourse); substance of ~, 955:18; temptations of ~, 237:2

plumbing, outdoor ~, 3686:3

plumpness *see also* obesity, 2013:2

Plutarch, 887:17

Poe, Edgar Allan, 884:2

poem/poetry *see also* poet, 801:15; 929:3; 1024:20; 1152:6; 1258:2; 1423:1; 1770:1; 1843:8; 1978:2; 2090:3; 2123:3; 2210:2; 2680:23; 2817:10; 2872:5; 3269:4; 3562:3; 3721:1; 3895:1; 4002:3; 4298:7; 4367:7; 4787:2; ambition to write ~, 3521:2; appreciation of ~, 887:9; bad ~, 756:1; benefit of~, 4305:3; children and ~, 2274:2; creating ~, 4:2; 152:4; 2090:2; English ~, 1336:4; exposure to ~, 3113:3; form of ~, 4105:8; great ~, 2872:4; Greek ~, 1336:4; imagist ~, 1440:14; impact of ~, 2464:2; listening to ~, 4367:6; love of ~, 476:1; 552:1; memorable ~, 991:1; ~ movement, 1673:1; need for ~, 1904:2; ~ of street, 2164:4; publication of ~, 756:2; rhymed verse ~, 670:4; selling ~, 1684:1; Shakespeare's sonnet ~, 2872:2; short ~, 4601:1; solutions in ~, 1938:6; sonnet ~, 1673:9; spiritual ~, 3661:1; subject of ~, 3849:5; writing ~, 2405:4; 2941:7; 3339:2; 3409:5; 4333:3

poet *see also* poem/poetry; writer, 197:1; 523:2; 577:1; 955:24; 1017:1; 1478:1; 1715:12; 1796:2; 1975:2; 2201:2;

2437:16; 2472:5; 2941:6; 3064:1; 3747:1; 3865:3; ~ and war, 2210:1; ~ at work, 2472:6; boy ~, 3995:1; burden of ~, 2872:1; 4828:2; compulsion of ~, 1808:1; death of ~, 869:2; 915:2; 1673:6; dilemma of ~, 1808:2; epitaph for ~, 2064:1; fame for American ~, 2566:6; feminine ~, 2189:10; function of ~, 984:3; heart of ~, 1590:15; ~ in relation to love and death, 1808:3; insights of ~, 1239:5; ~ laureate, 1843:5; love and ~, 2036:6; message of ~, 1700:11; obscure ~, 2208:6; privacy of ~, 2189:6; recognition of ~, 1258:1; role of ~, 3283:4; styles of ~, 1440:13; task of ~, 1808:1; values of ~, 1947:2; woman ~, 430:2; 434:1; 446:10; 462:1; 472:11; 2991:3

pogrom *see also* persecution, 2873:2

point of view *see also* perspective, 1724:9; 2200:2; understanding ~, 4280:4; understanding others ~, 4666:

poison, 75:3; 1675–1676:5; food ~, 1860:2; tiger's whiskers as ~, 2304:1

police, 4673:2; ~ mentality, 2544:5; racism among ~, 3114:3; secret ~, 3907:4; women in ~ work, 4822:2; ~ work, 3944:4

policy *see also* government, making ~, 2853:1; pessimistic ~, 2362:5; public ~, 3085:3

politeness *see also* courtesy; manners; tact, 808:5; 2987:2; lack of ~, 650:4

political appointment, 1402:2

political convention, television and ~, 1618:27

political correctness, 2771:22

political demonstration, 3736:2 political issues, 3220:1; engagement in ~, 4393:1

political party *see also specific parties,* 1164:1; 2227:1; 2697:2; 3317:2; 4174:6; Canadian Conservative ~, 4736:1; Wobblies, 3084:1; women in ~, 2127:3; 3997:3

political prisoner, 4173:1

politician, 1636:3; 2181–2182:2; 2668:6; 2742:1; 2775:5; 2804:1; 3129:2; 3976:6; 4650:6; 4915:1; assassination attempts on ~, 2898:2; attacks on ~, 2537:7; attitude toward women ~, 931:18; black ~, 4308:2, 4; charismatic ~, 3166:2; Christianity and ~, 234:7; connivances of ~, 4449:3; corrupt ~, 4927:3; criticism of ~, 4557:2; decisions of ~, 4948:4; development of ~, 3813:4; education of ~, 4326:4; foolish ~, 745:3; image of ~, 3204:2; ~ in relation to the press, 3164:2;

lax ~, 2198:1; life of ~, 2248:2; qualifications for ~, 4367:5; questioning ~, 4043:2; regard for ~, 2500–2501:3; requirements of ~, 2379:1; sex and ~, 3060:1; straightforward ~, 3248:3; unqualified ~, 2551:1; voting record of ~, 4720:1; widow of ~, 4527:2; woman ~, 3670:1

politics, 833:1; 1360:3; 1435:4; 1526:4; 1764–1765:8; 1897:; 1917:5; 2122:2; 2513:1; 2517:1; 3431:2; 4963:4; accomplishments in ~, 2537:4; analysis of ~, 3700:1; ~ and war, 3415:1; change in ~, 2907:2; citizens and ~, 2959:4; defeat in ~, 1689:12; defining ~, 2954:5; democratic ~, 2856:2; election rules of ~, 3160:3; ethics of ~, 2185:14; 4317:1; gender and ~, 4527:1; identity ~, 3008:1; 4263:1; impact of ~, 2625:2; 4837:2; male ~, 2680:14; men in ~, 2537:2; middle-of-the-road ~, 3335:5; money and ~, 2000:3; 3365:4; obsession with ~, 3996:6; ~ of conflict, 3749.1:2; playing ~, 3523:2; pursuit of ~, 733:16; rules of ~, 1553:4; sexism in ~ (*see* sexism); sexual ~ (*see also* relationship, ~ between men and women), 1254:2; 3020:1; 3284:10; 3326:2; 4125:1; success in ~, 1710:1; 3731:23; vision and ~, 1889:6; weary of ~, 1377:1; women and ~, 865:2; 1360:4; 1519:2; 1681:2; 3731:21; 4700:1; women in ~, 1555:1; 1663:10; 1973:5; 2354:2; 2665:4; 2779:1; 2861:6; 3176:2; 3256:1; 3997:1; 4160:11; 4187:2; 4499:1; 4700:1; work of ~, 3731:10

polling, 3073:1, 2; 3976:6; immersed in ~, 2710:3

pollution *see also* ecology; environment, 1920:4; 1998:5; 3119:3; 3677:1; air ~, 1037:1; 3243:2; chemical ~, 2061:7, 8; ~ from gold mining, 3890:6; ~ in relation to the poor, 4926:1; indoor ~, 4608:2; insidiousness of ~, 2624:1; noise ~, 1055:1; scourge of ~, 2359:3; water ~, 1112:6; 2266.1:1

polygamy *see also* marriage, 874:14; 3033:2; 3286:2; 4796:3

polytheism *see also* gods, 4708:3

pomp *see also* ostentation, 349:2; 518:2; 603:4

pond, 852:2; life in ~, 2529:1

poor *see also* class (social), lower ~; poverty, 355:1; 796:1; 801:10; 900:1; 1835:3; 1878:2; 2270:2; 2463:5; 2485:1; 3660:1; 4722:2; abandonment of ~, 1981:3;

4960:1; aid to ~, 4486:1; appearing ~, 940:; attitude toward ~, 308:4; 3006:2; birth control for ~, 1535:11; caring for ~, 1251:7; children of ~, 3711:2; choices of ~, 3535:3; concerns of ~, 3611.1:1; crime and ~, 3634:2; dreams of ~, 1376:1; early pregnancy among ~, 3493:5; education of ~, 528:1; 2972:3; 3102:1; feeding ~, 2341:2; ignoring ~, 347:2; ~ in relation to rich, 1724:14; 4774:4; lending to ~, 3998:2; location of ~, 2349:18; love among ~, 1205:3; needs of ~, 3006:1; 3009:3; Reaganomics and ~, 3156:2; remembering the ~, 3516:1; rights of ~, 4774:1; sympathy towards ~, 873:4; treatment of ~, 1846:6; vicissitudes of ~ women, 4099:2

Pope see also Catholic Church; Catholicism, 436:1; 1095:2; 2331:11; 3078:3

Pope, Alexander, 529:1

popular/ity, 1490:3; need for ~, 2252:2

population see also overpopulation, ~ control, 2678:2, 3; 2756:; 3282:1; ~ explosion, 863:3; ~ in relation to earth's resources, 3129:4; world ~, 2664:1

populism, 3365:3

pornography, 2352:15; 2546:6; 2866:9; 3091:1; 3204:1; 3738:4; 4061:1; 4366:1; 4403:3; 4539:5; 4912:1; response to ~, 2016:1; 4441:2

portrait see also art; painter/painting, 766:1; 1963:1

possession, 1470:5; 3451:3; ~ of another, 2059:1; 3099:14; 4683:4

possessions (property) see also belongings, 214:2; 1470:5; 1751:8; 2116:18; 2187:8; 2460:4; 2668:26; 3451:3; accumulating ~, 1336:8; loss of ~, 459:8; relinquishing ~, 1822:5; 1846:5; 3231:2; 3303:4; wealth of ~, 1979:1

possessiveness see also jealousy, 1619:8; 2007:3; 2059:1; 2185:5; 2448:3; 2546:2; 2732:4; 3099:14; 4683:4; 4813:2

possible/possibility see also impossibility; potential; probability, 3139:8; 4746:1; anything is ~, 2957:2; envisioning ~, 1436:6

post office see also mail, 3911:3; efficiency of ~, 853:5

post traumatic stress disorder see also mental illness, ~ from war, 2629:2; symptoms of ~, 4416:1, 3

posterity, 2680:6; legacy for ~, 931:27; 1935:14; praise of ~, 827:9

postmodernism, 3014:1; 4232:2

potato, 1858:2

potential see also possible, 218:1; 1008:2; 1698:1; 3417:2; fulfilling one's ~, 1299:3; 1715:11; 2418:1; human ~, 1173:4; 4906:3; maximizing one's ~, 4285:6; 4470:2; realizing one's ~, 62:2; 916:17; 1032:10; 2137:2; 2867:1; 3694:3; women's ~, 3297:4

poverty see also class (social), lower ~; poor, 149:2; 864:4; 869:9; 1040:1; 1068:3; 1342:2; 1562:4, 6; 1563:7; 1673:12; 2063:3; 2086:1; 2244:3; 2697:1; 2765:2; 2794:2; 3110:2; 4807:1; 4895:1; accustomed to ~, 1412:2; ~ among divorced women, 2718:1; complexity of ~, 2364:4; effects of ~, 801:13; 2117:15; 2153:4; 4067:2; eradicating ~, 1178:3; 1618:12; 2603:3; 3640:2; 4187:3; escape from ~, 1961:0; feminization of ~, 2916:19; fighting ~, 2856:3; 3938:2; 4256:2; impact of ~, 3588:1; ~ in America, 3608:4; marriage and ~, 1167:1; mass ~, 801:8; overcoming ~, 1913:1; rising out of ~, 4528:2; spiritual ~, 2142:4; superiority of ~, 4595:4; trial of ~, 824:1; unimportance of ~, 184:1; women and ~, 2544:4

power see also authority; empowerment; omnipotence, 178:2; 1208:3; 1693:7; 2660:1; 3126:4; 3518:5; 4217:2; 4268:3; 4709:4; 4879:2; abuse of ~, 733:6; 782:7; aims of ~, 1335:5; ambition for ~, 1208:11; ~ among men, 2658:5; ~ and truth, 4019:4; blind obedience to ~, 701:12; ~ changing hands, 1488:2; collective ~, 4125:3; concentration of ~, 2025:4; corruptibility of ~, 2916:1; desire for ~, 3031:4; distribution of ~, 4339:1; drunk with ~, 555:1; effects of ~, 1480:6; essence of ~, 3881:1; exercising ~, 2116:18; fear of ~, 733:19; fight for ~, 310:5; 603:4; global ~, 4760:2; history of ~, 2894:3; ~ in relation to health, 4126:2; love of ~, 4113:5; mask of ~, 2189:6; morality of ~, 3559:2; ~ of intellect, 2986:7; ~ of weaponry, 1675–1676:5; political ~, 260:1; 282:2; 1211:6; 4659:2; political super ~ (see also superpowers), 2038:1; position of ~, 4797:3; redefining ~, 3380:1; 4429:2; relinquish ~, 860:9; staying ~, 1660:1; unequal ~, 3821:1; wielding ~, 3595:2; ~ within, 4285:3; women and ~, 446:8; 676:9; 688:1; 860:7; 883:2; 931:12; 1134:1; 2349:24; 2552:9; 2694:4;2885:2; 2977:1;

2991:3; 3143:1; 3174:3; 3652:1; 4120–4121:1; 4299:2; 4527:4; 4754:3; world ~, 1471:7; 4605:3

powerlessness, 1735:1; 2475:1

Powhatan, Chief, 404:1

practice see also experience, 733:1; benefits of ~, 1162:2

prairie, 1589:1

praise, 456:1; 604:7; 1233:7; 1693:8; false ~, 199:1; giving ~, 1043:4; inability to ~, 4:3; inadequate ~, 256:1; ~ of women, 1536:1; posthumous ~, 2291:3; sexist ~, 650:4

prayer/praying see also contemplation; meditation; worship/per, 216:1; 245:2; 479:2; 708:2; 890:4; 932:3; 1018:1; 1032:11; 1422:2; 1667:2; 2098:4; 2133:2; 2220:3; 4045:5; answer to ~, 1444:2; 1541:1; daily ~, 3720:5; defining ~, 3281:5; ~ for health, 3990:6; ~ for others, 3139:2; futility of ~, 3663:1; highest ~, 982:5; incapable of ~, 215:2; 4298:3; ~ in public, 4663:4; intimacy of ~, 1735:2; Jewish ~, 932:2; 1168:6; meaninglessness of ~, 303:2; poetry and ~, 4298:7; silent ~, 982:1

preacher/preaching see also clergy; minister; sermon, 992:1; 1986:6; 2775:5; ineffectiveness of ~, 308:2; woman ~, 1261:1

precedent, disregard for ~, 980:3; legal ~, 1029:5

preconception, 1959:6

predicament, 1848:3

prediction see also fortune-telling; prophecy, 306:3

preference see also choice; priority; taste (preference), different ~, 325:1; 808:3; 1027:6

pregnancy/pregnant see also birth; childbearing; embryo; fetus, 1132:3; 1318:2; 1700:4; 1783:1; 2105:1; 2384:1; 3099:16; 3336:3; 4194:4; 4390:3; 4583:1; 4603:1; 4685:2; ~ among poor, 1535:12; chemical dependency and ~, 3279:1; creativity during ~, 3590:5; healthy ~, 2667:1; limitations of ~, 2980:2; men and ~, 3227:6; 3257:6; ~ out of wedlock, 3730:2; pain of ~, 626:1; quickening of ~, 2188:4; stories of ~, 3818:2; teenage ~, 3493:5; 3673:2; 3794:1; terminated ~ (see also abortion), 2925:7; trying to get ~, 4176:2; 4440:1; unplanned ~, 2646:3; unwanted ~, 3129:5; 3247:1; 3780:2; wish for ~, 362:2; workplace and ~, 2850:6

prejudice see also ageism; discrimination; racism/racist; sexism, 770:6; 1506:2; 1945:4; 2592:1; 3436:3; ~ against foreigners

(see also xenophobia), 1706:6; 4426:3; child's encounter with ~, 1725:5; class ~, 1085:2; eliminating ~, 934:10; 1209:6; 1741:8; facing one's ~, 850:2; law and ~, 3056:2; overcoming ~, 3977:2; ~ toward women, 2794:5; ~ vs. interracial couple, 2378:1; world without ~, 3754:2

premonition, 1925:1; ~ of death, 4571:2

preoccupation, 3099:11

preparation see also readiness, ~ for royalty, 4568:1; importance of ~, 1618:19; 4473:3

Presbyterian, 745:1

presence, appreciating one's ~, 3065:3

present (gift), 420:1

present (time) see also here and now; today, 2226:1; 2456:13; 2931:3; 3716:2; 4413:2; concern with ~, 2552:7; enjoyment of ~, 2275:0; living for ~, 1749:2; 2188:2; 2320:5; 2986:1; 3026:3; 3628:2; 3851:4; 3914:4; scorn for ~, 408:8; significance of ~, 1184:4

preservation, historical ~, 2130:2; 2402:6; ~ of environment, 4392:1; ~ of personal likes, 4280:5

President, U.S., 2596:5; 4761.2:3; 4816:7; characteristics of ~, 2262:2; confidence of ~, 1618:20; ~ during wartime, 3415:6; family of ~, 2500–2501:1; gender of ~, 2300:1; ~ in relation to women, 4114:2; law and ~, 4620:2; news conference with ~, 2393:5; obligations of ~, 4247:2; powers of ~, 4620:3, 4; progressive ~, 4668:1; role of ~, 2540:3; running for ~, 1086:1; 2480:6; trust in ~, 4950:2; values of ~, 3548:3; wife of ~ (see First Lady, U.S.); woman ~, 2975:1; 3435:3; 3731:19, 21; woman candidate for ~, 3731:13; woman in Cabinet of ~ (see Cabinet, U.S.)

pressure, inner ~, 2913:1; performance under ~, 3434:

pretense see also affectation; falseness; ostentation; selfimportance, 572:2; 1497:1; 1715:10; 1722:5; 1914:2, 10; 1938:2; 1940:4; 3191:3; ~ of rich, 1663:17; tendency toward ~, 887:29

prettiness see also beauty, 1741:16; evanescence of ~, 4524:5; trials of ~, 2822:2; 3565:2

prey, ~ upon own kind, 496:6

pride see also proudness; vanity, 234:1; 413:3; 534:2; 880:6; 1027:3; 1453:1; 1716:1; 1907:2; 1909:3; 2193:3; 2352:9; 2353:3;

2500–2501:2; 2642:14; 3132:1; 4116:13; defense of ~, 1027:1; detecting ~, 1451:2; excessive ~, 245:1; 289:9; family ~, 681:1; overcome ~, 303:1; starved ~, 713:13

priest/hood see also clergy, 888:3; 1076:5; 3041:2; 4240:2; confessor ~, 450:5; connivances of ~, 4449:3; disbelief in ~, 439:4; female ~, 1007:2; ~ in relation to grass roots struggles, 2756:17; ~ in relation to women, 3898:4; ordination of women ~, 2446:1

priestess, 1179:3; 3579:1; 4240:1

Priestly, Joseph, 642:2

primate, humans and ~, 3937:4; 4005:2

prime minister, 4657:2; woman ~, 2537:1

Prince Charming, 2620:6

prince/ss see also royal/ty, 109:1; 341:10; 450:5; 4802:3

principle see also convictions; ethics; integrity; standard, 1487:5; 2603:2; basic ~, 4174:6; cardinal ~ of life, 1863:5; female ~, 4354:2; fighting for ~, 686:1; 4450:1; living by ~, 1198:1; organizing ~, 2837:2; reasons for ~, 934:7; sticking to ~, 1209:9; 1724:10

printing, art of ~, 550:1

priority see also choice; preference, 308:10; 1024:18; ~ in family, 4672:1; ~ in relationships, 2079:5; setting ~, 1211:1; 2668:2

prison see also jail, 289:7; 606:1; 3493:4; 3542:1; 3776:; ~ administrator, 2298:3; American ~ system, 4136:1, 2; benefits of ~ life, 1528:2; ~ cell, 3493:3; claustrophobia of ~, 3571:1; federal ~, 1474:7; ideology in ~, 2298:6; ~ life, 2458:1; location of ~, 2437:12; problems of ~, 3319:1; ~ reform, 4278:1; sexual violence in ~, 4987:3; women in ~, 1706:8, 9; 2458:2; 2738:1

prisoner see also enslavement; imprisonment, 2543:1; exploitation of ~, 2298:5; justification of ~, 2298:6; ~ of war, 747:2; 2279:1; ~ on death row, 3571:4; political ~, 1146:5; 1235:9, 10; 1528:2; 1706:7; 1917:1; 2255:1; 4918:4; rehabilitation of ~, 4278:1; treatment of ~, 4665:2; women ~, 2738:1

privacy see also solitude, 1051:2; 1409:9; 2017:1, 2; 2021:13; 2032:1; 2561:1, 5; ~ in colonial society, 3098:1; ~ in digital age, 4397:1, 2; ~ in home, 2503:1; invasion of ~, 4021:1; lack of ~, 3099:17; loss of ~, 863:3; ~ policies, 4700:3; price of ~, 2771:26; respect for ~, 4043:3; right to

~, 2850:2; 3261:5; space for ~, 2715:2; woman's ~, 752:1

privilege, 1693:7; economic ~, 4960:1; ~ in relation to oppression, 3947:1; white ~, 2906:2

prize see also award, 2005:1; meaninglessness of ~, 2110:6

probability see also possible, 4924:2

problem, embracing ~, 4471:1; ~ solving, 2175:1; 2654:4; 2805:4; 4791:6; 4968–4969:1; women and ~ solving, 3061:1

process, 1387:8; pleasure of ~, 3567:4; socio-economic ~, 4429:2

procrastination see also tomorrow, 160:1; 241:1; 691:1; 945:8; 950:3; 1032:6; 1654:7; 1914:13; effects of ~, 734:13

procreation see also progeny; reproduction, 1949:1; 1979:8; men and ~, 1631:1

productivity, public ~, 4186:2

profaneness see also blasphemy; vulgarity, 231:1; 3590:2

profession see also occupation; avocation; career; vocation, dependence upon ~, 1590:21; ~ in United States, 3786:2; irreplaceable ~, 1663:12; sustaining one's ~, 860:14

professor see also teacher, 1844:5

profit see also capitalism; money, 1636:2; 1896:1; 3566:4; 4843:2; laws of ~, 3253:2; ~ motive, 3608:5; ~ of war, 1379:1; ~ vs. morality, 2480:3

profiteering, 1914:4; 1957:6

profligate, 4058:1, 2

profoundness, 1447:3

progeny see also child/ren; procreation, 10:1

progress, 931:11; 1209:10; 1316:4; 1345:3; 2603:1; basis for ~, 998:6; chaos of ~, 2129:2; consequences of ~, 733:6; disadvantages of social ~, 981:1; illusion of ~, 2711:2; lack of ~, 156:1; 3119:5; mistaking motion for ~, 1174:3; ~ of humankind, 906:4; 3067:4; pace of ~, 887:12; resisting ~, 770:3; slowness of ~, 1019:8; social ~, 1608:7; 2612:2

progressive/ness, 1251:5; ~ thinkers, 3284:6

prohibition see also temperance, ~ law, 1393:1

promiscuity see also wantonness, 76:2; 1086:10; 1787:4; 1998:1; 2217:2; 2286:7; 4755:1; 4791:3; ~ in women, 1928:4; ~ on board ships, 2176:1

promise see also oath, 2327:2; 4385:2; broken international ~, 1863:; empty ~, 3241:4; keeping ~, 217:1; 2871:2; ~ to oneself, 1655:8; unfulfilled ~, 4385:4

promotion, job ~, 1343:3; 2360:4

propaganda, 1662:7; 1955:1; 2116:8; 2496:3; American ~, 3147:1

property, 734:15; 1008:3; ~ as political tool, 1235:6; intellectual ~, 4040:2; public ~, 1051:2; respect for ~, 701:10; women as ~, 548:2

prophet, woman ~, 1261:1; 1313:5

propriety, 960:2; 1914:2

prose see also fiction; writing, 3563:10

prosperity see also money; rich; wealth, 94:1; 178:3; 356:3; 367:5; 430:8; 995:1; ~ for all, 958:1; ~ of the few, 3805:2

prostitute/prostitution see also courtesan; mistress; pimp; sex industry, 1636:2; 1894:3, 5; 2007:1, 2; 2259:4; 3738:7; 3834:2; 3923:1; 3930:3; 4053:1; 4086:1; 4089:1; 4728:1; 4844:3; business of ~, 3060:1; client of ~, 487:1; 3060:1; 3421:2; compassion for ~, 1244:3; criminality of ~, 2908:5; earnings of ~, 2862:3; 3123:2; freedom of ~, 1086:7; greed in system of ~, 3059:1; ~ in ancient times, 4018:1; ~ in relation to client, 4725:4; legalization of ~, 3421:3; 3930:2; profiteers of ~, 1894:4; punishing ~, 3060:2; reasons for ~, 3754:1; survival skills of ~, 3834:1

protection/ism see also paternalism, 3486:2; ~ from others, 3802:3; giving ~, 4021:4; ~ of the young, 1251:8

protest/er see also specific movements; civil disobedience, 860:4; 1289–1290:4; 3696:5; ~ against tyranny, 2980:2; 4225:0; male peace ~, 4481:7; organized ~, 4439:1; risks of ~, 4917:2; tactics of ~, 2792:1

Protestant/ism, ~ charities, 1849:4; influence of ~, 2534:12; work ethic of ~, 2771:25

Proust, Marcel, 2556:2; 2945:4; 3371:4

provisions, 439:2; 564:1; ~ of nature, 4855:1

prudence see also caution, 705:2; women of ~, 1843:3

prudishness, 4336:1

psyche see also mind; spirit, 3567:3

psychiatrist/psychiatry see also psychology; therapy, 1176:8; 3356:4; drugs and ~, 3557:3

psychoanalysis see also analysis; psychotherapy; therapy, 1474:1, 3; 1608:6; 1631:5, 6; 3258:4; 3349:10; 4307:3; aim of ~, 2648:2; 2740:2; demystification of ~, 2740:1; method of ~, 2466:5

psychology see also psychotherapy; subconscious, 734:19; 2866:15;

~ of women, 1631:2; 1973:7; 3165:2; sacred ~, 3037:2

psychotherapy see also analysis; psychiatry; psychoanalysis; therapy, 2149:3; 2326:3; 2333:4; 2434:2; 2446:3; 4361:1; 4415:2; ~ patient, 2326:4; 2740:1; successful ~, 2466:4

public see also public, the, destruction of ~ discourse, 3867:3; 4641:2; ~ exposure, 1309:4; image of ~ figure, 4459:2; ~ goods, 2080:4; ~ relations, 4390:2; changing ~ sentiment, 4763:5; ~ welfare (see also common good; social welfare), ignoring ~, 1998:5

public life (see also celebrity; fame), 334:4; 613:3; 790:11; 1031:1; 2209:1; 2411:1; 3490:1; difficulties of ~ life, 1618:34; 3658:2; domesticity and ~, 3536:1; risks of ~, 1935:18; sacrifices of ~, 2905:3; women in ~, 1644:1, 2; 1824:1; 2514:1; 3098:3; 3379:1; 3448:1

public office, running for ~, 2393:2

public opinion see also opinion, 1044:7; 1656:2; fear of ~, 1034:1; 3244:1; ~ in America, 1584:1; manipulating ~, 3317:1; 4731:5; opposing ~, 1590:22; strength of ~, 4863:1; ~ toward women, 1189:4; yielding to ~, 1390.1:2

public policy, 4452:3; women and ~, 2201:13

public servant/service see also service, 1254:8; 2549:1; betrayal by ~, 1239:2; creed of ~, 1857:2; dedicated ~, 2765:5; influences of ~, 2764:2

public speaker, 734:20; 808:4

public, the see also audience; masses, 4574:2; capriciousness of ~, 684:4; 1684:2; impatience of ~, 910:11; influencing ~, 3556:4; intolerance of ~, 1031:1

publication see also publishing, 3744:2

publicity see also advertisement/advertising, 1695:1; 2665:1; 4415:3; benefits of ~, 3003:2; ~ hound, 1826:3

publishing see also printed word; publication, ~ literature (see also literature), 425:1

Puccini, Giacomo, 4616:1

Puck, 1711:1

Puerto Rico, 3327:1; Vieques ~, 3327:2

pun, 643:10

Punch and Judy, 737:2

punctuality see also timeliness, 821:4; 2568:1

punishment see also reprimand; retribution, 398:1; 1129:5; 2426:7; 2534:5; 2771:1; 4312:8; corporal

~, 443:1; 916:6; 1167:5; 2049–2050:1; 2529:8; 2703:1; 3765:2; 4285:1; deserving ~, 1193:6; need for ~, 1903:3

purgatory *see also* hell; remorse, 390:1

purification, ~ from bathing, 2817:9

puritanism *see also* provincialism, ~ in America, 3396:3; tenets of ~, 4291:2

purity *see also* innocence, 409:1; 1645:5; 3961:1; ~ in women, 1755:4

purpose *see also* goal, 872:2; 976:2; 1024:23; 1204:3; 2048:1; clear ~, 4742:1; fulfilling ~, 1315:5; great ~, 1685:3; ~ in life, 1387:1; 1822:2; 1929:6; 2408:4; 2892:5; 2900:3; 3282:3; 4517:1; individual ~, 2032:7; knowing one's ~, 1513:2; 3303:3; search for ~, 2801:5; sense of ~, 1482:2

pursuit *see also* goal, choosing ~, 671:12

Putin, Vladimir, 4464:2

Pygmies, 1797:3

Q

Qin Guanshu, 2522:1

quackery, 774:1

Quaker/ism (Society of Friends), 1959:7; ~ business, 3370:1; egalitarianism among ~, 556:1; feminism and ~, 3011:1; persecution of ~, 432–433:1; philosophy of ~, 432–433:2; responsibility of ~, 1989:4; women and ~, 839:2; 3011:2; 3446:1

qualification, lack of ~, 252:1

quality, ~ vs. quantity, 806:3; woman of ~, 509:3

quarrel *see also* argument; bickering; fight/ing, 827:12; 1734:2; 1832:2; 3514:1; ancient ~, 2187:7; ~ between lovers (*see also* lover, quarrel with ~), 344:1; domestic ~, 694:6; 2286:2; unpredictability of ~, 1689:10

Quayle, J. Danforth, 1725:2; 3227:5

Quebec, Canada, 407:1, 3

queen *see also* royal/ty, 341:1, 8; 931:14; 1040:1; ~ as mother, 2111:2; ~ for a day, 3714:2; independent ~, 334:2; ~ loved by subjects, 4568:2; ~ of England, 424:1

quest, personal ~, 3298:4

question, 2409:2; 3348:2; 3478:1; 4043:1; asking ~, 4135:1; philosophical ~, 2642:6; 4421:3; the right ~, 4294:1

quickness, 767:10; 1590:24; 2912:1

quilt, 4042:2

quotation, 649:6; 734:22; 1268:2; collecting ~, 2866:13; journalistic ~, 2904:2; use of ~, 1237:1; 1406:6

R

race (genetic), 4194:2; bond of ~, 3757:3; creation of ~, 3974:4; 4045:4; differences between ~, 2618:7; mixed ~ (*see also* multiracial/ism), 2911:3; 3321:1, 3; 4806:3; similarities between ~, 2290:2

racism/racist *see also* bigotry; prejudice; segregation, 1000:1; 1148:1; 1291:3; 2206:5; 2228:2; 2563:7; 2658:3; 2711:8; 2807:1; 2906:1, 2; 2911:1; 2919:1; 3035:2; 3140:2; 3354:1; 3945:1; 3995:4; 4196:2; 4368:3; 4478:4; ~ between men and women, 2911:4; challenging ~, 4305:9; covert ~, 4328:2; divisiveness of ~, 3757:1; effects of ~, 1210:4; 1299:4; eliminating ~, 1333:6; 1148:2; eradicating ~, 1792:1; ~ in America, 2866:7; 3050:1; 3114:3; 3974:5; 4308:1; ~ in media, 3312:2; inter-~ bias, 4050:1; ~ in the arts, 2283:1; nationalistic ~, 1659:4; outliving ~, 1725:1; scientific ~, 4634:2; ~ towards offspring, 1196:3; war and ~, 2504:2; white ~, 4812:3

radiation/radiology, 1732:1; 4329:1; effect of ~ on human genes, 2057:1; 2651:1

radical/ism *see also* revolutionary, 2107:1; 3493:6; 3852:4; watered down ~, 1706:2

radio *see also* mass media, 2642:8; censorship in ~, 1620:5; feminist ~, 3874:1; ~ in Third World, 4670:1; ~ story, 1882:6; women and ~, 3874:2

rage *see also* anger, 955:20; 3190:1; 4127:2; acting out ~, 2798:1; out-~, 4377:2; sudden ~, 4136:11

railroad *see also* travel, ~ car, 1505:2; ~ class, 940:2; growth of ~, 1106:2; routes of ~, 1269:2

rain *see also* storm, 2156:2; 2686:2; 3645:2; 4342:1; children and ~, 1650:3; constant ~, 987:5; incessant ~, 3564:1; praying for ~, 3136:2; singing in ~, 2339:1; wisdom of ~ tribes, 3370:6

rainbow, 807:8

rancher, ~ in relation to environment, 4560:2

rank *see also* nobility, 647:2; 1317:1; elimination of ~, 709:2; privileges of ~, 3514:2

rape, 1608:4; 2080:11; 2922:, 1, 2; 3060:2; 3091:1; 3184:5; 3558:4; ~ as war crime, 3223:1; ~ by verbal coercion, 4777:4; crime of ~, 4012:3; defense vs. ~, 4431.1:2; devastation of ~, 3692:2, 3; disclosure of ~, 3692:1; escape from

~, 58:1; ~ in black community, 3447:1; laws on ~, 3417:1; marriage and ~, 2496:6; ~ of wife, 3104:1; perpetrator of ~, 4012:1, 2; ~ prevention, 4431.1:3; purpose of ~, 2633:3; response to ~, 3070:2; ~ survivors, 4431.1:4; vengeance ~, 4138:1; ~ victim, 2876:6; 3112:4; 4572:1; war and ~, 2019:5; 2680:8; 3894:2; 4381:4

rascal *see also* scoundrel, 237:5

rashness, 1704:2; curbing ~, 1874:9

rational/ization *see also* excuse; logic; reason, 396:2; 539:5; 1351:1; 2947:1; 3314:2; overly ~, 3953:1; totally ~, 2997:3

reaction, faulty ~, 772:7

reactionary *see also* conservativism; fundamentalism, 1211:6; ~ to women's progress, 4481:1

reader/reading *see also* book; fiction; literature; novel, 152:3; 405:6; 691:4; 694:2; 867:3; 874:12; 1199:3; 1554:4; ; 2270:11; 3831:2; 3872:2; 3992:8; 4042:10; 4544:4; 4905:2; ~ aloud, 2345:6; 4175:3; attention of ~, 4096:1; ~ books, 4280:4; businessmen and ~, 2511:4; children and ~, 3865:1; ~ comprehension, 890:4; difficulty ~, 3376:3; importance of ~, 1913:3; ~ in relation to business, 2511:3; influence of ~, 3950:2; ~ list, 4235:3; ~ material, 4044:1; reason for ~, 974:4; 3563:11; ~ to children, 1489:2; 3146:2

readiness *see also* preparation, 649:2; 1899:3

Reagan family, 3296:1; Nancy ~, 2341:2; Ronald ~, 2341:2; 3189:4; 3227:4; 3996:5; 4039:5; 4089:3

realism, 1830:4; ~ vs. truth, 3814:3

reality *see also* unreality, 1882:6; 2210:7; 2371:1; 2775:5; 2858:3; 2931:4; 2949:5; 3831:1; 4002:2; 4147:7; 4444:6; 4609:2; accepting ~, 3352:1; ~ and myth, 2756:11; awakening to ~, 2116:2; creating a ~, 3855:2; different ~, 3064:1; facing ~, 1184:10; gradients of ~, 4474:1; ~ in literature, 1852:4; questioning ~, 838:8; subjectiveness of ~, 3795:3; virtual ~, 4147:8

realization *see also* self-realization; understanding, 2240:2

reason *see also* intellect/intelligence; logic; mind; rational/ization; sense; thinker/thinking, 487:8; 489:3; 506:1; 569:2; 658:3; 671:3; 808:16; 911:5; 1209:6; 1924:1; 2311:3; 2320:4; 2817:4; 3039:1; 3165:5; 4527:5; ability to ~, 177:2; civilization of ~, 1998:7; impotence of ~, 865:; ~

in relation to passion, 934:5; lack of ~, 480:1; listen to ~, 466:8; world of ~, 2199:1

rebellion/rebelliousness *see also* revolt; revolution; uprising, 542:1; 747:1; 913:2; 4157:5; benefits of ~, 2466:4; ~ of women, 1244:6; signs of ~, 916:20

rebirth *see also* renaissance; renewal, 1341:1; 1782:6; 1789:; 2297:3; 2313:2; 2642:3

receiving, fully ~, 3889:1

receptionist, 3618:2

recession, moderating ~, 4468:1; psychological ~, 2832:4

recipe *see also* cook/ing, 816:1; 2309:2; 4390:6; easy ~, 4226:6; home-made ~, 4602:1; trading ~, 2893:4; writing ~, 2174:2

recognition, 5:1; 558:2; 2665:1; bestowing ~ on women, 1044:11; lack of ~, 2612:3; need for ~, 4773:1; ~ of truth, 2995:1

recollection *see also* memory; remembrance, sweet ~, 962:1

reconciliation *see also* forgiveness, 187:1; 1076:2; 2654:6; 2706:1; 2772:3; 2938:4

record keeping, errors in ~, 1549:4

recovery *see also* cure; healing; rehabilitation, 2313:2; 3210:2; 4286:2; drug ~, 4260:1; ~ from downfall, 407:2

recreation, 2055:2; 3054:1; benefits of ~, 266:2; weekend ~, 3511:4

recycling, 4552:1; 4857:2

Red Sea, 1326:1

red-baiting *see also* McCarthyism, 1897:1

redemption *see also* salvation, 341:9; 2534:2; 2775:1

Reed, John, 1524:3

reenactment, historical ~, 4737:4

refinement, 853:4; 1160:4; ~ of life, 1110:1; woman of ~, 1956:3

reflection *see also* deliberation; thought, 683:3; 705:2; avoiding ~, 2567:2

reform/er *see also specific movements;* activism; agitator, 564:2; 931:16; 1017:1; 1037:3; 1723:1; 1826:3; 2517:2; agenda of ~, 1235:7; frustrations of ~, 2498:2; supporting ~, 1244:7

refuge, 1168:4; 2556:5; ~ within, 287:6

refugee *see also* immigrant/immigration, 3124:5; 3894:1; 4312:12; 4495:6; ~ in America, 2959:2; needs of ~; 3152:3; 4683.1; welcoming ~, 1888:1

refusal, empty ~, 1368:3

regret *see also* remorse; sorrow, 1561:5; 2267:2; no ~, 4757:1; ~ of past action, 1697:10

regulations *see also* rules, 3512:3

rehabilitation *see also* recovery, 3635:2

reincarnation, 166:5; 801:3; 1033:5; 2296:3; 3989:1

rejection *see also* unwanted, 1977:10; 2142:1; 2224:1; 3419:3; sexual ~, 3883:6

rejuvenation *see also* recovery, 3582:2

relationship *see also* couple; dating; friendship; love; marriage, 870:2; 2590:1; 2767:3; 3772:3; 3806–3807:2; 4364:4; 4500:1; 4721:2; age difference in ~, 722:9; assessing ~, 4718:3; bad ~, 2925:9; balance of ~, 910:2; basis for ~, 2481:1; 2955:2; ~ between men and women (*see also* man/men, ~ in relation to women; politics, sexual ~; sexes; woman/women, ~ in relation to men), 178:6; 179:4; 195:1, 2; 517:8; 949:1; 1184:12; 1212:1; 1578:4; 1764–1765:6; 1780:8; 2080:7; 2426:3; 2541:2; 2924:3; building ~, 2170:3; 3538:2; changing ~, 1353:1; comfort of ~, 2352:3; commitments to ~, 2380:4; communication in ~, 3174:4; dangers in ~, 2893:6; difficulties of ~, 1292:4; 2437:1; 3631:3; 4109:2; disappointment in ~, 1566:2; 4717:1; doomed ~, 4817:2; 4844:5; dynamics of ~, 4752:3; ending ~, 3217:1; fear of ~, 4518:2; fictions of ~, 3340:3; importance of ~ with others, 2812:2; 3638:2; intellectual ~, 4475:1; intertwining of ~, 1419:7; progress of ~, 4101:5; 4750:3; social ~, 3212:; sports and ~, 4643:2; steady ~, 3615:3; suffocating ~, 4844:4; temporary ~, 2932:5; 3301:2; troubled ~, 3519:3; women and ~, 4612:1; 4643:4; ~ working out, 2435:2

relatives *see specific relation,* 1516:1; 3309:9; understanding one's ~, 3657:1; visiting ~, 3356:3; 4193:1

relaxation *see also* leisure; pleasure; rest, 141:3; 2288:10; need for ~, 713:5

relevance, 1731:5

reliability *see also* unreliability, lack of ~ in men, 997:1

religion *see also specific denomination;* belief; church; clergy; faith; fundamentalism; God; irreligiousness; piety; religious life; theology, 533:9; 627:1; 769:4; 860:3; 874:2; 916:2; 1062:2; 1239:4; 1316:5; 1456:2; 1689:6; 1752:9; 1942:2; 2078:1; 2318:2; 2331:5; 2333:3; 2534:12; 3253:1; 3455:3; 3727:1; 4292:3; 4312:7; ancient ~, 2778:1; ~ and history, 3508:2; ~ and patriarchy, 3284:6; art and ~, 1408:14; benefit of ~, 808:19;

celibate women and ~, 971:2; choosing ~, 4201:3; community of ~, 1600:5; consolation of ~, 2572:5; controversies in ~, 633:1; 1261:2; conversion of ~, 3584:3; dangers of ~, 3984:8; decline of ~, 3981:4; devotion to ~, 3961:4; differences between ~, 1730:2; 4904:1; divisiveness of ~, 327:3; 593:3; 808:3; experience of ~, 2187:5; fervor of ~, 790:5; finding ~, 4816:5; function of ~, 3445:; hypocrisy in ~, 4486:1; ~ in America (*see* America, religion in ~); ~ in public schools, 4455:1; ~ in relation to economics, 995:1; 2943:4; ~ in relation to evil, 4321:5; ~ in relation to government, 3360:3; intolerance of ~, 491:1; irrelevance of ~, 3474:2; martyr to ~, 309:3; mission of ~, 4490:3; mystical ~, 3474:3; non-violence and ~, 3658:4; oppression of women in ~, 4627:2; organized ~, 1416:3; 2467:1; patriarchal ~, 2744:2; persecution of ~, 1016:1; personal ~ (*see also* theology, personal ~), 669:5; 1416:3; politics of ~, 4160:1; principle of ~, 310:4; quarrel with ~, 982:11; 4201:2; race and ~, 1210:2; revisioning ~, 2380:7; righteousness of ~, 4952:4; rituals of ~, 1416:2; selling ~, 3460:3; sexism in ~ (*see* sexism, ~ in religion); similarities among ~, 3474:; ~ stand on violent sex, 2756:16; study of ~, 2738:2; symbol of ~, 2756:3; teaching ~, 1207:2; transforming ~, 3474:1; war and ~, 517:4; 2708:1; women and ~, 832:1; 1076:5; 1185:3; 1419:3, 3; 3284:1; 3446:1

religious institution, opportunities for women in ~, 3178:1

religious life *see also* clergy; nun, 1735:5; actions of ~, 1210:3; petty ills of ~, 818:1

relocating, 2711:1; ~ to rural setting, 880:8

remains, human ~, 2542:3

remark, stifle a ~ (*see also* word, unspoken ~), 1309:2

remedy *see also* cure; healing, search for ~, 489:4

remembrance *see also* memory; recollection, 653:3; 744:1; 1014:2; 2585:3; 3629:5; 4251:7; ~ of loved one, 47:1; 1102:1; sad ~, 1032:9; subjectivity of ~, 3784:4

reminiscence, 1395:1

remorse *see also* purgatory; regret, 158:6; 934:3; cure for ~, 1686:11

renaissance *see also* rebirth, dichotomy of ~, 2190:4; women in ~, 2632:1

renewal *see also* rebirth, 1006:3; 1137:1; 1346:3; 1986:9; 2135:7; 2936:3; 2943:10; 2981:3; 4141:5

Reno, Nevada, 1973:2; 2002–2003:1

rent, ~ control, 4584:1

renunciation *see also* abandonment, 482:2; 1470:1

repentance *see also* penitence; purgatory, 188:1; 455:1; 1313:2; 1325:4

repetition, 1409:24; 1751:32; 3902:2; ~ of life, 2349:10; 3110:4; 4123:5

representation *see also* government, representative ~; spokesperson, ~ for all, 1874:6; ~ of people, 3706:5; ~ of women, 1050:1; ~ of women in government, 646:4; 973:1; 1064:3; 3864:3; virtual ~, 4118:4

repression *see also* suppression, 1408:8; 2556:1; 4023:1; effects of ~, 2864:2

reproduction (human) *see also* progeny; procreation; rights, reproductive; ~, control over ~, 3603:4; healthy human ~, 1659:3; ~ technology, 4009:2; 4071:1; urge for ~, 4076:1

republic, aristocracy in ~ (*see also* aristocracy), 2000:2

Republican Party (U.S.), 3512:8; 3798:5; 4395:; 4856:2; deterioration of ~, 4665:4; future of ~, 3798:6; ~ line, 3256:3; moderate ~, 3798:4; sex and ~, 3442:5; 4102:1; women and ~, 2916:22

reputation, 155:2; 453:1; 1172:1; ~ at school, 695:1; damage to ~, 472:17; good ~ (*see also* name, good ~), 235:2; half-earned ~, 3612:2; literary ~, 3371:1; losing one's ~, 1914:3

rescue *see also* savior, 2601:1; dream of ~, 3325:1; wish for ~, 3083:2

research/er *see also* scholar/ship, 1727:8; 2423:1; fruits of ~, 1821:1; 2312:2; funding for ~, 2622:1; goal of ~, 1608:2; neutrality of ~, 4099:1; ~ partner, 2208:5; purpose of ~, 2946:3; scientific ~, 1952:3; social ~, 3693:1; stem cell ~, 3557:2; 3701:3; threats to ~, 3344:1; woman ~, 2389:2

resentment *see* bitterness, 1646:4; 3087:3; 3616:2

residence *see also* home; house, place of ~, 676:11

resignation *see also* acceptance, 791:4; 808:19; 3986:1

resilience *see also* flexibility; toughness, 919:1; 1727:2; 2570:2; 2618:18; 2637:5; 2698:2; 3090:3; 3099:1; cultivating ~, 2011:2; ~ of Chinese, 1741:27

resistance, 762:1; 3547:15; bond of ~ workers, 3406:2; 3985:3; political ~, 1813:5; 3988:2; positive ~, 2210:11; ~ to war, 1251:1

resoluteness/ resolution *see also* decision, 1597:2; lack of ~, 671:13; personal ~, 1804:5

resourcefulness, 926:1

resources (natural) *see also* environmentalism, 2853:2; ~ in relation to population, 3129:4; 3768:1; shrinking ~, 2671:3

respect/ability *see also* appreciation; reverence; self-respect, 1321:3; 1384:2; 1408:4; 1686:7; 2021:12; 2943:3; 3520:4; 3534:1; benefits of ~, 916:3; demonstrating ~, 3314:3; giving ~, 2436:1; middle-class ~, 1675–1676:9; ~ of women, 701:8; shield of ~, 1721:3

responsibility *see also* duty; obligation, 1681:1; 4202:2; 4304:2; 4797:3; ~ at work, 1814:1; consuming ~, 4024:2; effects of ~, 3660:2; 4042:5; ~ for actions, 451:2; ~ for another, 1782:3; no more ~, 2187:8; personal ~, 1051:1; 3440:2; social ~ to child, 3141:2; taking ~, 3663:1; 4285:2; ~ to future, 2893:3

rest *see also* relaxation; sleep/ing, 760:3; 998:10; 1479:2; 4646:1

restaurant, 4082:1; Chinese ~, 4883:1; Indian ~, 4548:2

restitution, 3316:

restlessness, 1751:12; 1780:7

restraint *see also* limitations, 1022:2; 1120:6; 1262:7; 2736:1; 3467:2; imposing ~, 1208:10; ~ of women, 643:6

result, excellence of ~, 2041:1; gaining good ~, 916:3

resurrection, 346:1

reticence, 955:33

retirement *see also* pension, 684:1; 1852:; 2165:1; 2317:3; ~ community, 4004:4; economics of ~, 2207:4; 4210:4; ~ home, 2562:1; investing in ~, 4582:1; mandatory ~, 1699:3; 1811:2; 2025:1; 2082:4

retreat, consequences of ~, 4561:1; political ~, 2185:14

retribution *see also* punishment; vengeance, 1399:1; 1936:1; 2009:4; 2185:6; 2243:6

returning *see also* homecoming, 1166:10; 4563:4

revelation, 798:2; 1355:4; 3364:1; 3420:2; 4573:3; flood of ~, 1701:3; personal ~, 4286:1

Revelation (bible), Book of ~, 2561:2

revenge *see also* vengeance, 120:1; 171:1; 344:1; 533:18; 539:7; 584:1; 1193:4; 4102:2; fantasy of ~, 4263:3; lover's ~, 4631:2; woman's ~, 568:3

reverence see also awe, destroying ~, 2032:4; instinct for ~, 870:5

reverie see also daydream, 755:1; 845:4; 1687:4

review see also critic/ism, 4161:4

revisionism, 2075:1; 4161:3

revolt see also rebellion/rebelliousness; revolution, ~ against oppression, 1135:3; women in ~, 1488:3

revolution/ary see also specific revolutions; radical/ism; rebellion; revolt, 887:7; 889:1; 1030:5; 1360:16; 1425:1; 1776:1, 10; 2036:15; 2108:1, 2; 2210:9; 2680:14; 2719:3; 2901:7; 2930:2; 3137:6; 3145:4; 3249:1; 3583:4; 3585:3; 4234:2; 4990:1; ~ action, 3884:1; claims of ~, 4462:2; empty ~, 3066:5; feminist ~, 3284:7; fighting for ~, 3173:3; goal of ~, 1360:14; impetus for ~, 2268:5; inner ~, 2601:4; language of ~, 3583:1, 2; love of ~, 1828:2; ~ of heart, 1846:4; ~ of self, 3121:2; place for love in ~, 2618:8; role of ~ party, 1379:4; significance of ~, 1989:3; social ~, 1786:1; street ~, 2905:4; ~ thinking, 2105:3; true ~, 2893:3; women and ~ (see also woman/women, revolution and ~), 685:2; 931:19; 1030:1; 2105:2; 2268:3; 3029:4; 3062:1;3180:2; 3230:1; work of ~, 2126:3; 2172:2

reward see also honors, 603:1; 1952:5; earning ~, 4042:5; ~ of actions, 2243:6

rheumatism, 1025:15

rhythm, 1673:10; 3905:1; 3915:1

rich see also prosperity; wealth, 355:1; 767:19; 1596:3; 1607:2; 1843:9; 2289:1; 2426:8; admiration of ~, 1086:4; attitude toward ~, 2634:2; hate ~, 1706:4; ~ in relation to poor, 812:3; 901:1; 1724:14; 1835:3; 1878:2; miseries of ~, 1724:12; problems of ~, 801:11; spoiled ~, 812:1; 3164:5

Richard II, 1823:1

Richards, Ann, 4466:4

riddle, solving ~, 642:9

ridicule see also mockery, object of ~, 2148:5

right (correct), 3717:1; being ~, 1025:6; ~ to differ, 1618:8;

right and wrong see also rightmindedness; wrong, 1723:1; 2450:1; 3306:2; 4500:2

Right Wing (American) see also conservatism; Moral Majority, ~ in relation to family, 2916:9; religious ~, 3903:2

righteousness see also self-righteousness, 1037:6; 1835:2; establish ~, 444:2; pitfalls of ~, 2925:3

rightmindedness see also right and wrong, 68:1; 734:10

rightness, 1452:1

rights see also specific movements; civil rights; freedom; liberation; 963:1; basic human ~, 2670:3; 3824:1; black ~ (see also blacks, freedom of ~), 860:8; children's ~, 656:5; 1535:4; 1634:1; 1776:3; 3342:1; 3434:2; constitutional ~, 3749.1:1; defending ~, 4898:2; denial of ~, 850:4; enforcing ~, 3373:3; equal ~ (see also equality), 1608:7; 1637:1; 1776:1; equal ~ for boys and girls, 3434:2; fight for women's ~, 963:7; 1235:10; fighting for ~, 3185:3; gay ~ (see also gay liberation movement), 4720:2; hindrance to women's ~, 4323:1; human ~, 733:4; 782:4; 890:8; 1618:5; 1776:4; 2846:2; 4739:2; human vs. property ~, 2032:13; inalienable ~, 1592:6; 4374:3; individual ~, 953:1; 978:5; 1007:9; 3088:4; 3891:1; lack of movement for ~, 3342:5; obligations of ~, 3201:2; reproductive ~, 2678:2; 3946:2; 4035:2; standing up for ~, 1588:2; 3185:2; 3881:1; ~ to differ, 1618:8; ~ to information, 3295:1; universal ~, 889:2; 1618:14; 3082:3; women's ~ (see women's rights); workers' ~ (see also labor movement), 3324:2

Rio Grande (U.S.-Mexico), 1726:3

riot/ing see also uprising, causes of ~, 4230:1; race ~, 1291:2; 4006:1; street ~, 3800:1

ripening, 1650:5

risk see also danger, few ~, 2060:4; life without ~, 2043:4; 2227:3; removal of ~, 2619:1; ~ taking, 101:1; 763:2; 1687:9; 1751:27; 3808:4; 3824:2; 4374:4; 4430:1 rite/ritual, 2940:1; 2973:2; 3238:2; 3629:1; 4072:1; 4155:3; creating ~, 2373:3; decline of ~, 2709:2; ~ for newborn, 4721:1; ~ of eating, 2709:4; transformation of ~, 2816:4; woman's ~ of passage, 2778:2

Ritter, Thelma, 3643:1

rivalry, ~ in love, 1044:3

river also see specific rivers, 317:2; 447:2; 642:12; 1726:1; 1929:6; 3389:2; ~ at night, 787:1; flowing ~, 2970:6; life along ~, 4506:3; names of ~, 838:1; protecting ~, 3250.1:6

Rivera, Diego, 2066:3

roaming see also wanderer; wanderlust, 1517:1

Robinson, Jack, 671:4

robot, 4510:6

rock see also stone, 4854:3

rock 'n roll see music, rock ~

Rodeo Drive (Beverly Hills), 2634:1

Roe vs. Wade see also abortion, 3227:5; 3361:1; 3366:1; 3622:1, 2; 35th anniversary of ~, 3333:3; protecting ~, 4379:1; support of ~, 3333:4

Rogers, Samuel, 756:1

role model see also exemplar, 2257:1; 3818:5; choosing a ~, 3062:2; following ~, 1786:3; ~ for teens, 4267:3; impact of ~, 3859:1; importance of ~, 4409:5; women ~, 3133:3

Rolf, Ida, 1833:1

Roman Catholic Church see Catholic Church

Roman Empire, Holy, 94:1; 4077:3; women in ~, 4018:1

romance see also love; lover, 2007:4; 2602:4; 2780:4; 2947:2; beginning of ~, 4878:1; evolution of ~, 4974:2; images of ~, 3808:5; pseudo-~, 4438:1

romanticism, 1830:4; ~ in poverty, 1321:3

Rome, Italy, 2686:2; 3349:15; Christianity in early ~, 96:1; sack of ~, 3152:2

Romney, Mitt, 3294:3

roommates, 919:2

Roosevelt, Eleanor, 1897:, 2; 3980:4

Roosevelt, Franklin Delano, 1584:3, 4; 3166:2

Roosevelt, Theodore, 1021:2

roots see also heritage, 4257:2; clinging to ~, 3389:; cut off from ~, 1562:7

rose, 624:1; 835:1; 1408:20; 1450:4; beauty of ~, 1993:1; ~ bud, 835:2; sending ~, 4631:2; unopened ~, 3287:2

Rose Bowl (Pasadena, California), 2586:6

Rose, Ernestine, 3082:2, 3

Rosh Hashana see also Jew/Judaism, ~ holiday, 4988:3

Roth, Phillip, 2638:10

rouge, 1879:1

Rousseau, Jean Jacques, 616:3

routine see also rut, 821:3; daily ~, 763:1; imprisonment of ~, 2466:3; 2768:1; 4256:3; ~ of life, 4792:3

Rowe, Elizabeth Singer, 564:2

royal/ty see also courtiers; king; noble (rank); prince/ss; queen, 450:5; 720:1; beholden to ~, 320:; compassion of ~, 320:2; English ~, 948:1; ~ family, 2549:2; line of ~, 15:1; marriage among ~, 283:4; mother of ~, 4483:1; notions of ~, 822:1; women of ~, 320:3

rudeness see also surliness, 166:11

ruin see also destruction/destructiveness, 642:7; 799:3; 1378:4;

mocking one's ~, 56:3; road to ~, 671:12

rule/r see also head of state; leader/ship, 14:1; 484:1; 1515:3; 2517:2; ~ by emotion, 4079:5; ~ by people, 3696:4; command of ~, 604:2; demise of ~, 2517:3; difference in ~, 1526:5; ~ of elite, 1675–1676:4; victorious ~, 255:1

rules (regulations) see also law, 3325:3; 4663:2; breaking ~, 3944:4; learning ~; mistaken ~, 497:6; questioning ~, 2201:10

Romania, churches of ~, 4848:1

rumor see also gossip; scandal, 158:7; 671:7

Rumplestiltskein, 2668:10

Rumsfeld, Donald, 4502:1

run away, 4188:1; habitual ~, 3803:1; women who ~, 3033:6

running, 3226:2

Ruskin, John, 1174:3

Russia/n see also Slav; U.S.S.R., 733:11; 1582:1; 4220:2; ~ Army, 2528:1; energy sources in ~, 4594:1; ~ in relation to environmentalism, 4195:1, 2; ~ in relation to United States, 4220:3; 4684:3; ~ in relation to women, 3096:1; Lake Baikal, Siberia ~, 4594:3; life in ~, 1512:2; ~ people, 4957:1; perception of ~, 3280:2; reform in ~, 4351:1; ~ Revolution, 1712:3; time in ~, 4074:1; ~ under communism, 2459:1; ~ wars, 2528:2; ~ women, 3101:5

rut see also routine, daily ~, 2277:2

ruthlessness see also cruelty, 2222:1

S

Sabbath, 1148:4; 3707:1; 4646:2; holiness of ~, 3547:11; Jewish ~, 2768:1; keeping the ~, 1024:13

sabotage, 1537:1

Sacco and Vanzetti, 1706:6

sacredness, ~ of every day, 1148:4; ~ of life, 1568:3; place of ~, 66:1

sacrifice see also self-sacrifice, 48:5; 129:2; 1062:7; 1412:5; 1717:3; 1977:8; 2291:2; 2413:5; 3736:1; necessity of ~, 1577:3; personal ~, 2186:1; reasons for ~, 2979:2; refusal to ~, 2465:1

sacrilege see also blasphemy, 2116:16

Sadat, Anwar, 3343:6

Sade, Marquis de, 2709:5

sadism, 4012:2

sadness see also melancholy, 310:3; 4010:2; 4150:3; lessons of ~, 3309:1

sadomasochism, 2059:1

safe/ty see also security, 1038:1; 2855:2; 2970:1; 3245:2; ~ living, 3186:5; ~ of chemicals, 2622:5; playing it ~, 733:17; 2048:1

sage *see also* wisdom, 1017:1

sailing/sailor, 505:1; 810:2; 2156:1; 2330:4

saint/liness, 1450:25; 1713:4; 1887:3; 2181–2182:1; 3231:3; dealing with ~, 4105:2; lives of ~, 3987:2; study of ~, 3987:2

salad days *see also* youth, 628:3

salary *see also* income; pay; wage, commensurate ~, 608:1

salmon, 1929:6; preserving the wild ~, 4119:3; ~ run, 3972:4

saloon *see* bars and pubs

salt, 3747:2

salvation *see also* redemption, 1381:7; 2842:1; 3446:3

Samaritan, Good, 83:1

sameness *see also* similarity, 1032:2; 2671:1; 3044:2

Samson, 592:2

San Francisco, 1655:7; 2848:1; 19th century ~, 954:1; ~ bay area, 1376:3; diversity of ~, 3283:4

San Juan Capistrano, California, 1655:2

sand *see also* beach, 2705:2

Sand, George, 892:3; 910:5

Sandanistas, art and ~, 3744:4

sandpiper, 1069:1

Sanger, Margaret, 1804:2

sanitation, 3163:3; department of ~, 3163:1

Santa Claus *see also* Christmas, 4211:2; belief in ~, 2619:3

Sao Paulo, Brazil, 2217:1

Sappho, 462:1; 1440:13

Sarah, 379:1; 1304:6

Sarajevo, Bosnia-Herzegovina, sacking of ~, 4597:2

sarcasm *see also* irony, 4743:3

Satan *see also* devil, 304:1; 2028:4; deliverance from ~, 322:1

satire, 688:2; 1830:4

satisfaction *see also* fulfillment, 578:4; 807:11; 808:9; 3755:4; finding ~, 2001:4; lack of ~, 2948:3

Saturday, 2249:1; ~ night, 732:1

Saudi Arabia, businesswoman in ~, 4664:1

sausage, 2499:1

savage/ry *see also* barbarian; brutal/ity, 407:3; 511:13; ~ of man, 496:6; 1913:2; ~ of men, 98:2; ~ within, 1590:18

savior *see also* hero/ine; rescue, 1592:5

SBA (Small Business Administration), 3798:2; 4262:1

scandal *see also* rumor, 166:15; 517:5

scapegoat *see also* blame, 2079:3

scar *see also* injury, 4015:3; 4714:1

scarecrow, 461:1

Scarlet Pimpernel, The, 1317:2

scholar/ship *see also* research, 1735:4; 2188:1; 3095:1; ~ award, 951:4; limitations of ~,

2439:2; mediocrity of ~, 1335:5; old ~, 2671:4

school/ing *see* classroom; college; education; high school; training; university, 843:3; 3520:3; 3844:1; ~ administration, 3141:3; all-male ~, 3596:4; ~ board bureaucracy, 2013:1; ~ book, 1039:4; ~ building, 947:1; Catholic ~, 2529:8; corporal punishment in ~, 1080:1; ~ curriculum, 2348:1; 2671:2, 3; 2675:1; 3584:6; curriculum ~, 4235:3; discrimination in ~, 1618:30; divinity ~, 1097:2; ~ drop-out, 2281:6; 3995:2; finishing ~, 1208:4; 3216:1; 3308:1; free ~, 2794:4; good ~, 3520:1; graduation from ~, 4297:2; ~ house, 1700:2; independence of child at ~, 2267:7; kindergarten ~, 1500:1; learning from ~ life, 1254:7; ~ lunch program, 3417:3; military ~, 1715:13; public ~, 1342:4; 3102:2; 3900:2; punishment at ~, 1167:5; ~ recital, 1756:4; reforming ~ system, 1167:6; religious ~, 1207:0, 2; remedial programs in ~, 4007:4; return to ~, 2749:1; supporting ~, 2348:2; unjustly treated ~ -child, 2267:7; ~ vouchers, 4652:2; ~ years, 1587:1; zero tolerance in ~, 4267:2

science *see also specific branch*; scientist, 356:4; 1062:5; 1236:12; 1333:3; 1335:4; 1496:1; 1654:8; 1668:9; 2004:1; 2331:5; 2776:1, 2; 2988:1; 3441:2; 3515:1; 4374:2; 4438:6; 4465:4; admirers of ~, 1034:5; 4336:1; advances of ~, 733:6; age of ~, 1103:1; appreciation of ~, 3045:2; art and ~, 1821:2; authority of ~, 3651:1; black women of ~, 1543:1; cautions of ~, 1935:1; 4463:1; confusion of ~, 2487:3; contribution towards ~, 3657:3; culture of ~, 4145:1; discoveries of ~, 1514:2; ethics of ~, 3701:3; experimentation in ~, 2298:5; feats of ~, 2742:3; ~ formula, 951:6; health care and ~, 4135:3; history of ~, 2032:10; 4930:2; ~ in America, 3584:5; 3924:3; ~ in relation to government policy, 3768:5; ~ in relation to industry, 1112:1; interest in ~, 3630:3; limitations of ~, 2330:5; male bastion in ~, 3395:1; medical ~, 4059:3; new ideas in ~, 2487:2; patriarchy and ~, 3874:4; physical ~, 4007:5; politics of ~, 2934:1; 4668:3; responsibilities of ~, 2776:4; sexism in ~, 2988:5; 3526:1; social ~, 4902:6; teaching ~, 3701:4; traditions of ~, 1331:1; 2487:1; women and ~, 557:2; 644:3; 951:7; 1293:1;

1732:1; 1860:1; 1861:1; 1972:1; 2071:1; 2112:4; 2702:3; 2988:2; 4145:3; 4474:3

scientist *see also specific types*; science, 2065:1; 3282:2; 4348:6; 4463:4; attitude toward ~, 1952:1; bias of ~, 2487:1; 4463:3; dedication of ~, 2423:1; earth ~, 4463:2; feminist ~, 4145:2; framework of ~ work, 2487:4; 4000:1; funding for ~, 2622:1; ~ in relation to public, 951:3; obligations of ~, 3605:1; research and ~, 2266:7; reward of ~, 1919:1; woman ~, 1889:3, 4; 2389:1; 2522:1; 2682:1; 3511:1, 3

Scot/land *see also* Great Britain, 680:2; 790:10; ~ in relation to France, 712:1; weather in ~, 4730:2

scoundrel *see also* rascal; villain, 699:2; 801:18

scream, 3112:3

screenplay *see also* film; scriptwriter, 1763:2; 3691:4

scripture *see also* Bible; Koran, interpretation of ~, 4126:3

scriptwriter *see also* playwright/ing; screenplay; stage play, 1763:2; 2295:4

scrutiny, self-~, 4565:1

sculptor/sculpture, 920:1; 2636:4; 3120:1; 3420:2

sea *see also* ocean; tide; wave, 1008:7; 1184:1; 1478:2; 1727:11; 2061:2, 3; 2642:9; 2680:13; 2942:5; 4198:1; bell buoy at ~, 1789:4; gazing at ~, 1317:3; history of ~, 2926:2; safe at ~, 810:2; ~ shore, 2061:1, 4; swimming in ~, 2045:1; twilight at ~, 962:2; view of ~, 1909:1

seamstress, labor of ~, 944:6

Seattle, Washington, 4947:6

second best, 486:1

secret/iveness, 193:3; 671:2; 694:3; 1692:5; 1714:2; 1948:2; 2125:1; 2224:4; 2276:2; 2572:3; 3164:1; 3602:1; 3972:1; 4010:5; keeping ~, 1060:1; 1882:1; national ~, 2881:1; ~ of the heart, 4385:2; ~ revealed, 676:10; unable to keep ~, 2514:2; woman's ~, 4868:2

secretary, 2237:1; 2371:3; 3431:1; 3726:1; power of ~, 3284:4

security *see also* safe/ty, 1353:1; 3145:6; 3335:4; 3978:2; complete ~, 1695:2; false ~, 2131:1; financial ~, 2929:3; ~ guard, 4079:2; holding onto ~, 175:1; lack of ~, 1914:8; national ~ (see national security); physical ~, 4126:5; relinquishing ~, 4174:9; search for ~, 1857:1; unreality of ~, 1548:11

sedentariness, 1710:2

seducer/seduction, 48:3; 718:1; 749:1; 2600:1; uninvited ~, 4548:3

seed, 840:3; 1336:2; 1974:2; 4700.1:2; 4774:3; acorn ~, 2659:5; planted ~, 1092:1; 1974:1; spreading ~, 2171:1; symbol of ~, 4141:3; unplanted ~, 801:14

segregation *see also* racism, 2259:5; ~ at beach, 2921:1; ending ~, 2163:3; fighting ~, 1742:2; ~ in schools, 1908:2; ~ in the South, 4042:3

self *see also* ego/ism; identity, 2320:2; 2381:7; 3428:5; defining ~, 2801:5; 4515:1; demolition of ~, 2819:3; divided ~, 887:4; escape from ~, 2014:7; facing one-~, 1682:2; higher ~, 4282:; inner ~, 1401:1; 1761:6; losing one's ~, 3419:4; questioning ~, 811:1; reinvention of ~, 3368:2; unable to escape from ~, 487:5

self-absorption, 2342:3; 2352:5; 4259:3

self-acceptance, 3686:2; 4443:2

self-actualization *see* self-realization

self-analysis *see also* introspection, 450:3; 674:2; 1412:1; 1989:4; 2187:1; 2577:4; 2613:6; 2932:3; 4985:1; ~ through writing, 3810:2

self-awareness *see also* self-realization, 887:23; 1262:4; 1519:5; 2243:5; 2307:2; 2903:10; 2980:1; 3755:3; 4207:4; 4508:2; 4908:1

self-centeredness *see also* egocentricity; self-interest, 775:1; 1673:3; 1739:1; 1977:11; 2079:4; 2180:2

self-confidence *see also* confidence, 1335:10; 1835:2

self-consciousness *see also* consciousness, 2117:14; 4902:7; extreme ~, 3733:1

self-control *see also* control; discipline, 308:9; 403:1; 459:3; 674:1; 733:20; 960:5; 1025:5; 1044:1, 12, 12; 1117:4; 1675–1676:2; 1920:2; 2288:10; 2330:4; 2797:1; 3303:4; 4036:4; 4170:2; lack of ~, 775:2; 3811:3; loss of ~, 1921:3; regained ~, 705:2

self-criticism, 117:1; 3810:2; 4681:2

self-deception *see also* deceit, 887:25; 1184:8; 2349:9; 2413:4; 2925:4; 3631:3; 3732:3; ~ in love affair, 2556:3

self-defense, 3569:1; ~ for women, 4211:5; 4726:3; physical ~, 4431.1:1, 2, 3

self-denial *see* self-sacrifice

self-destruction, 934:11

self-determination, 1741:14; 2286:8; 2941:2; 2987:3; 4102:5;

~ for blacks, 4305:10; ~ for women, 3842:1
self-discipline *see* discipline; self-control
self-esteem *see also* self-respect, 713:6; 744:3; low ~, 1787:7; maintaining ~, 1409:11; 3394:1; ~ of women, 3784:3; roots of ~, 2805:1; shattered ~, 887:14
self-examination *see* self-analysis
self-exposure, 2527:2
self-expression, 2226:4; lack of ~, 416:1
self-hatred, 1242:2; 2137:1
self-help, 2155:3; 2662:3
self-image *see also* ego; identity, 163:3; 2037:1; 2155:2; 2311:1; 2346:3; 2388:2; 2767:2; 3355:2; 3426:3; 3577:3; 4144:2; 4509:1; limited ~, 3246:3
self-importance *see also* pretense, 2351:1
self-improvement *see also* improvement, 695:3; 1796:1
self-incrimination, 381:1
self-interest *see also* self-centeredness; selfishness, 650:2; 1666:1; 3124:4; 4963:3; ~ of society, 1998:5
selfishness *see also* egocentricity/egotism; self-interest, 767:9, 11; 858:1; 998:5; 1160:3; 1265:4; 1552:6; 2620:2; 3968:1; detecting ~, 1451:2; ~ of humankind, 1896:11
self-knowledge *see* self-awareness
selflessness *see also* altruism, 1195:2
self-love, 3743:5
self-made, 4023:4
self-mutilation, 4174:4
self-objectification, 4860:1
self-organizing, 3311:4
self-pity, 501:3; 799:3; 4773:3
self-preservation, 283:3
self-realization *see also* realization; self-awareness, 955:38; 1344:2, 3; 1687:9; 2199:3; 2240:3; 2281:1; 2398:7; 2466:6; 2607:1; 2688:1; 2786:2; 2797:2; 2961:1; 3037:2; 3145:12; 3190:1; 3567:4; 3925:7; 4244–4245:5; 4307:4; 4533:2; lack of ~, 3698:3; ~ of women, 3865:2; pain of ~, 2466:7
self-reliance *see* self-sufficiency
self-respect *see also* respect/ability; self-esteem, 782:2; 1192:1; 1409:6; 1698:1; lack of ~, 241:1; women and ~, 701:9
self-sacrifice *see also* sacrifice, 695:4; 713:11; 804:6; 1043:2
self-satisfaction, 1236:2
self-sufficiency, 713:2; 945:7; 1592:5; 1663:16; 2021:8; 2205:1; 2408:3; 2835:2; 3412:4; 4019:3; 4769:2; ~ in village life, 3682:1; lack of ~, 2208:4
self-supporting, 1335:8

self-trust, 1758:5
selling, 3278:1; 4395:3; creativity in ~, 2809:2; ~ techniques, 2052:1; 3460:3
semen, 3526:1
Senate, U.S., 3890:4; 4720:3; centrism in ~, 3798:1; courage in ~, 2848:3; moralistic ~, 3994:1; women in ~, 1064:3
sense (reason), *see also* common sense; logic; reason, making ~, 2964:1; 3755:3; nonexistence of ~, 2032:11
senses (physical) *see also specific senses*, 230:1; 798:5; 3808:1; 4476:1; aversion of ~, 1409:16
sensibility *see also* feelings; perception, 578:3; 819:1; 1024:15; 1421:1; lack of ~, 757:1
sensual/ity *see also* senses; voluptuousness, 708:1; 1366:2; 2732:10; women and ~, 2539:1
sentimen/tality *see also* nostalgia, 876:3; 1197:1; 2282:1; 2359:1
separation *see also* parting, 680:2; 1144:1; 3750:4; difficulty of ~, 3118:1; ~ from loved one, 989:1; need for ~, 2917:2; ~ of child, 2461:2; ~ of church and state, 3082:3; ~ of lovers, 817:1; 866:2; pain of ~, 4780:3
separatism, 3697:2
September 11 (2001), 1070:3; 1381:3; 1402:1; 1407:1; 1500:1; 1663:19; 1722:7; 2081:1; 2197:1; 2393:1; 2409:1; 2410:2; 2453:3; 2747:1; 2812:5; 2839:3; 3054:1; 3206:2; 3317:10; 3391:6; 3532:4; 3542:2; 3658:5; 3779:2; 3822:2; 3852:1; 3924:2; 3975:2; 4267:2; 4390:4; 4437:1; 4475:4; 4493:1; 4521:4; 4643:2; 4790:2; 4844:2; 4922:1; 2971:2; 3459:2; 3512:6; aftermath of ~, 3981:5; 4118:5; ~ and twin towers, 4614:2; Ground Zero and ~, 2402:9; impact of ~, 3502:1; Muslim response to ~, 4160:8
Serb/ia, 3735:3; 3867:3; ~ in war, 1338:1
serenity *see* tranquility
sermon *see also* preacher/preaching, 1166:3
servant *see also* housekeeper; labor/er, household ~; valet, 34:1; 397:1; 1843:9; 3202:1; 4146:4; 4769:1; advantage of ~, 1739:5; attitude of ~, 4663:1; attitude toward ~, 588:1; 661:1; 862:1; black ~, 2659:6; dependency upon ~, 1381:3; ~ in relation to guests, 2534:1; subservience of ~, 4058:5
service *see also* public servant/service; volunteer/ism, 3141:7; 4304:2; being of ~, 1111:3; community ~, 1656:1; ~ in business, 1223:2; social service, 1304:5; ~

to humanity, 4750:1; ~ to others, 905:2; 1024:23; 1604:1; 2627:3; 3516:1; 3731:3; 4775:1
servility *see also* parasite; sycophancy, 804:2; 2280:1
settle, ~ down, 2532:
settler *see also* pioneer, ~ of New World, 901:2; ~ of West (U.S. Territory), 1149:4 seven wonders, 2153:1
sewing *see also* needlecraft, 88:2; 801:4; 1991:1
sex appeal *see also* sexiness; sexual attraction, 1691:2; 2309:1; 2902:2; changing tastes in ~, 1462:3
sex discrimination *see* sexism
sex education, 1989:2; 2756:18; 2843:3, 4; 3803:4; 3829:3; 4920:1; ~ for college women, 4777:1
sex industry *see also* brothel; prostitute; pimp, 3754:1; 3930:2; red light district of ~, 4005:3
sex partner, 3857:2; disappointment in ~, 2384:2; poor ~, 380:1
sex roles *see also* gender; sexes, 998:7; 1935:8; 2578:3; 2733:2; 2987:1; 3000:1; 3422:1; changing ~, 3372:5; differences of ~, 2209:1; 2995:3; effect of war on ~, 2796:2; evolution of ~, 2398:10
sex symbol, 1790:5; 2168:3; 4276:1
sexes *see also* gender; sex roles, balance between ~, 1752:12; 3953:1; 4948:2; conflict between ~, 1487:3; differences between ~, 669:2; 698:2; 733:2; 998:1; 1135:2; 1167:12; 1209:5; 1254:19; 1289–1290:2; 1555:5; 1693:9; 1702:2; 1727:4; 1800:2; 1935:2, 13; 1967:1; 2076:1; 2300:3; 2400:1; 2472:3; 2537:11; 2569:4; 2679:1; 2818:2; 3031:4; 3125:3; 3165:1; 3349:17; 3379:5; 3383:1, 2; 535:2; 3582:; 4590:1; 4791:3; polarization of ~, 3083:1; relationship between ~ (see relationship), ~ between men and women); schism between ~, 1265:7; 2219:10; similarities between ~, 543:1; stereotyping ~, 3479:2; 3526:1
sexiness *see also* sex appeal, 4913:1; ~ in men, 2977:1
sexism *see also* double standard; male supremacy; prejudice' sexual harassment, 304:2; 650:4; 688:1; 931:2, 27; 1238:2; 1839:1; 2353:1; 2391:1; 2439:4; 2531:1; 3140:2; 3230:1; 3379:5; 3495:2; 3572:2; 3582:; 3611:1; 4480:3; end of ~, 4658:5; ~ in advertising (*also see* advertising), 3381:2; ~ in America, 2916:21; ~ in government (*see also* politics,

sexual ~), 953:5; ~ in language (see language); ~ in press, 1703:2; ~ in religion, 931:25; ~ in song lyrics, 2544:3; ~ in tribal life, 3570:2; ~ in workplace (*see also* workplace, sex and ~), 953:2; 2272:9; 3078:4; 4678:1; institutionalized ~, 2439:4; 3731:6
sexual abuse, 3728:1; 4012:2; 4137:3; ~ in family, 2328:1; ~ of children, 3728:2, 4; preventing ~, 4644:1
sexual attraction *see also* sex appeal, 1977:9; 2439:8; 2683:1; 3194:1; effects of ~, 1790:16
sexual favors, 1830:2; 2286:7; 4696:1; desire for ~, 4813:5
sexual harassment *see also* sexism, 1957:2; 3750:3; 4137:4; ~ online, 3458:3; punishment for ~, 2822:1; victim of ~, 4369:2
sexual intercourse *see also* lovemaking; orgasm; sensual/ity; sex; sexual/ity; 97:1; 2080:11; 2387:3, 4; 2437:5; 2629:1; 2843:5; 3194:2; 4512:2; ~ between intimates, 2772:2; 2977:2; communication and ~, 2407:4; consequences of ~, 2955:1; 3191:2; ecstasy of ~, 1986:2; first encounter with ~, 2748:1, 2; foreplay during ~, 104:1; frequency of ~, 511:7; furtive ~, 3423:1; ~ in literature, 2908:4; ~ in relation to love, 4512:1; invitation to ~, 4050:2; lack of desire for ~, 2925:9; mutually satisfying ~, 1535:2; peer pressure for ~, 2822:3; pleasure in ~, 2955:4; prepared for ~, 3047:1; results of ~, 3319:2; techniques of ~, 2109:1; variety in ~, 2646:1; ~ with many, 1086:10; ~ with stranger, 4192:4; ~ with wife, 4341:2; women and ~, 3883:4
sexual liberation, 1787:4; 3035:1; 3930:1; 4118:3; ~ in the 1960s, 4524:2; women and ~, 4644:3
sex/uality *see also* bisexual/ity; heterosexual/ity; homosexual/ity; sexual intercourse; transsexual/ism, 1524:1, 2; 1596:2; 1751:19; 1755:2; 1949:1; 2025:8; 2284:1; 2502:4; 2569:2; 2841:1; 3780:9; 3797:2; 3814:2; 3959–3960:2; 4003:2; 4089:2; 4791:1; 4877:3; 4937:3; absence of ~, 2566:3; ~ among elderly (*see also* old age), 8:1; ~ among youth, 2843:4; anonymous ~, 3142:4; 3444:2; 3780:10; ~ as connection, 2201:8; ~ as weapon, 2398:9; body and ~, 2893:7; bond of ~, 1754:1; books on ~, 2887:2; children and ~ (*see also* child/ren, sexually maturing ~), 1989:1; commercialization of ~, 3923:1; consequence of

~, 2019:1; 2659:5; dark side of ~, 2709:5; deprivation of ~, 981:8; ~ drive, 2865:2; ~ education (see education, sex ~); enjoyable ~, 3218:3; equality in ~, 3344:4; exploitation of ~, 2911:4; 3099:14; expression of ~, 3823:1; fear of ~, 4777:2; ~ fixation, 2383:2; force of ~, 3702:3; frustrating ~, 3990:2; global context of ~, 4800:1; ~ identity, 3896:3; illicit ~, 3883:5; images of ~, 4118:3; ~ in America, 1686:12; 1691:1; 1930:3; 2383:2; 2398:4; 2656:3; 3147:2; 3911:4; incestuous ~, 10:1; ~ in fiction, 2270:4; ~ in relation to age, 2294:1; ~ in Western world, 3438:1; love and ~ (see also love, sexual ~), 2185:4; 2349:3; male ~ urge, 3780:10; marriage and ~ (see also marriage, sexless ~), 511:7; 1558:3; 4228:2; 2287:4; 4376:2; men and ~, 1495:2; 2353:3; 2539:1; objectification of ~, 1169:1; 2387:3, 4; 3834:2; obsession with ~, 1686:12; 4579:3; one night stand ~, 4192:4; oral ~, 2976:1; 3349:5; 3531:1; 3883:1; overpowering ~, 133:2; ~ partner, 2690:1; peak of ~, 2732:10; power of ~, 3797:; 4713:2; ~ preferences, 4686:3; premarital ~, 4900:2; purpose of ~, 2698:3; 4703:2; refusing ~, 1780:12; sacredness of ~, 2442:1; ~ symbol, 2168:2; teenage ~ (see sexual behavior among ~); understanding ~, 3487:1; ~ values, 1989:2; women and ~, 267:2; 1564:1; 2319:1; 2398:9; 2865:1; 3021:1; 3031:1; 3392:1; 3590:1; 3883:3; 4248:2; 4497:2; 4650:3; 4713:3; the weaker ~, 944:7; youth and ~, 465:1; 2243:3; 2364:5

shade, 1433:3

shadow, 2153:9; 3348:3; language of ~, 1858:3

Shadrach, Meshach, & Abednego, 890:3

Shakespeare, William, 585:2, 3; 631:1; 1095:4; 2130:2; 2872:2; 3145:20; ~ for children, 3797:8; literature and ~, 1590:26; male characters of ~, 1590:9; women heroes of ~, 1162:4

shame, ~ of one's roots, 3472:3; saved from ~, 157:1; women and ~, 63:1

sharing, 1962:1; 2893:3; 3538:2; ~ with strangers, 3097:5

Sharpton, Al, 4308:1

Shaw, George Bernard, 1309:2

Shelton, General Henry Hugh, 4502:1

shepherd, 785:3; 1152:8

Shetland Isles, Scotland, 831:2

ship see also boat/ing; sailing; travel, 55:1; 1477:1; 1478:2; 1727:4; 2048:1; 4160:2; departing ~, 1445:2; on board ~, 1715:7; ~ on fire, 838:3; passenger ~, 1033:6; upkeep of ~, 464:1; ~ -wreck, 307:2; 1665:1; 1760:1

shirt, starched ~, 3423:2

shock see also trauma, 2552:6; effects of ~, 2886:1; tempering ~, 1741:28

shoe, comfortable ~, 4116:3; high heel ~, 4248:2; sturdy ~, 4449:4

shooting see also gun, 3970:3; ~ a person, 3797:1; 3970:3

shopping, 4904:3; compulsive ~, 2634:1; ~ for food, 1992:5; mail order ~, 2616:1; ~ mall, 3623:1; 4289:2; socially conscious ~, 3525:1; window ~, 2115:1

shortcut, 2190:3

shortsightedness, 1073:1

show business see also entertainment, 1686:11; 3039:8

shyness see also timidity, 3200:1

sibling see also brother; sister, 2529:2; comparing ~, 3967:4; competition with ~, 4083:3; ~ fighting, 3058:2; new ~, 2780:6; relations between ~, 3212:4

sight (human), 2346:3; recovered ~, 519:3

significance see also importance, 1999:2; ~ of things, 2034:1

silence see also pause, 477:4; 488:1; 649:9; 721:1; 999:2; 1375:1; 1510:1; 1667:1; 2117:15; 2288:8; 2560:8; 2668:1; 3290:1; 3338:3; 3411:1; 3472:3; 3803:2; 3865:6; 4177:1; beneath ~, 955:26; ~ between loved ones, 1042:2; cruelty of ~, 3692:2; curse of ~, 402:1; dissent of ~, 3122:5; forced into ~, 4305:5; inner ~, 1906:2; ~ of women, 2187:18; power of ~, 2938:1; protective ~, 2938:2

Silicon Valley, 3888:3

silliness see also foolishness, 3000:3

similarity see also sameness, 1535:9

simplicity see also clarity, 533:16; 581:1; 622:4; 1311:3; 3851:4; ~ in lifestyle, 4412:1, 2; need for ~, 1557:3

sincerity, 466:3; 907:2

singer/singing see also music; opera; song, 167:1; 561:1; 657:1; 728:1; 970:1; 1180:3; 1670:8; 1838:1; 1845:1; 2035:1; 2924:1; 3837:1; bad ~, 1959:1; blues ~, 4218:2; criticism of ~, 1256:3; great ~, 3982:2; impact of ~, 4600:2; ~ technique, 2114:2; 2896:1; therapeutic effect of ~, 2684:3; ~ voice, 628:1; women ~, 2425:2; 3143:1

single/ness see also bachelor; loner; mother/hood, single ~, 161:1;

202:1; 940:1; 1044:16; 2297:6; 2391:1; 2421:1; 3067:3; 3819:1; attitude toward ~, 2548:1; blessing of ~, 4846:1; living ~, 2942:4; ~ women, 550:2; 3218:1

singularity see also originality; uniqueness; individuality, 1673:8; 1896:6; 4223:2

sin/ner see also vice, 158:4; 216:1; 332:2; 341:8; 348:1; 472:5; 487:1; 537:2; 575:1; 605:1; 982:9; 1713:4; 1715:9; 2272:6; 3453:3; 3696:1; 3854:3; changing concepts of ~, 2021:7; consequences of ~, 3445:6; disappearance of ~, 2027:5; ~ in relation to wealth, 149:6; love and ~, 261:2; number of ~, 332:1; ~ of betrayal of the young, 2201:11; refusal to ~, 53:1; variety of ~, 2007:2

sister see also brother; sibling, 988:2; 1032:7; 1044:14; 2680:15; 3967:3; 3995:5; 4125:5; closeness to ~, 331:1; 4834:1; comfort of ~, 576:1; competition with ~, 3659:1; hostility between ~, 2725:1; rejected ~, 4484:1; relationship between ~, 2725:2; 3690:1; 3921:3; rivalry between ~, 3967:2; separation from ~, 278:2; trust in ~, 4038:3

sisterhood see also brotherhood; esprit de corps; fellowship, 785:2; 3567:8

Sisyphus, 2866:16

Sitting Bull, 1260:2

skepticism see also doubt, 616:5; 3630:3

skill see also ability; talent; technique, women's ~, 4984:1

skin, ~ color, 4058:3; ~ pigmentation (see also race), 3995:4

skull, 541:2; 789:1

sky, blueness of ~, 1670:3; night ~, 3488:; perception of ~, 1024:19; summer ~, 1024:31

slander/er see also defamation, 275:1; 402:1; 1218:2; victim of ~, 1955:2

slave/ry see also abolitionism; enslavement, 612:2; 759:2; 890:6; 908:2; 916:9; 949:2; 978:1, 4; 987:1; 1135:4; 1890:1; 2210:6; 2958:1; 3974:5; 4634:2; defining ~, 3535:1; disdain for ~, 2771:25; effects of ~, 2864:2; ~-holder, 2210:6; ~ in America, 837:1; 1539:1; ~ in relation to master, 887:1; ~ in the South (U.S.), 1196:1; 1297:1; intolerance for ~, 908:3; legacy of ~, 4652:3; mental ~, 2244:5; modern day ~ (see also human trafficking), 2297:1; personal ~, 316:5; plantation ~, 1554:1; savagery of ~, 1210:5; sex ~,

3561:1; sexual ~, 3123:1, 3; ~ to a cause, 878:1; ~ trade, 642:4; 677:3; 698:4; treatment of ~, 1196:1, 2, 3; 2606:4; women ~, 860:5; 1371:1; 2080:7; 3493:1

sleep/ing see also dream; nap/ping; rest, 55:2; 616:7; 994:1; 999:4; 1048:1; 1065:1; 1067:1; 1352:1; 1534:1; 1734:2; 1964:1; 2101:4; 2642:17; 2668:2; awakening from ~, 4406:1; balm of ~, 1549:2; foregoing ~, 3170:2; going to ~, 1882:3; 2758:3; ~ late, 447:1; little ~, 2135:3; ~ of baby, 952:3; 4513:2; stillness of ~, 803:1; waking from ~, 1380:1

slowness, 2912:1

slums see also tenement, ~ of Nairobi, 2349:21

smallpox, ~ inoculation, 533:7

smell see also nose; senses, 4125:4; bad ~, 2256:2

smile, 511:3; 660:3; 1123:3; 1262:5; 1283:2; 1409:4; 2732:1; 3355:2; 4507:2; 4827:2; brave ~, 912:1; 1209:2; evil ~, 3547:3; imperative ~, 2924:4; phoney ~, 2010:2; transparent ~, 1525:5; wholesome ~, 4878:2; winning ~, 3246:3

smoking see cigarette

Snake River, Northwestern U.S., 3801:1

snob/bery see also elitism, 961:4; 1415:2

snow, 267:1; 1689:3; 4507:4; 4700.1:1; ~-drop, 1359:2; shoveling ~, 2286:1

Snow White, 1790:13

soaring, 2860:4

sobriety, ~ of youth, 2803:1

soccer, woman ~ player, 4859:1

sociability see also companionship, 423:6; 1303:1; 1504:1; 2042:1; decline in ~, 829:2; lack of ~, 945:7

social aid, ~ in 19th century, 1849:4

social change see also change; world, changing ~ 1764–1765:7; 2172:1; 2210:13; 3059:3; 3173:3; 3326:2; 3400:2; 3990:5; 4048:2; middle class and ~, 3469:2; resistance to ~, 2544:5

social engineering, 4584:1

social life see sociability

social movement see movement

social order see also society, 1829:1; lies of ~, 2214:1; ~ of white men, 4389:2; subversion of ~, 899:3

social security, 2517:4; ~ amount, 3093:1; ~ card, 4867:1

social welfare, 1953–1954:1; 2270:2; 2341:2; 2583:3; 2697:1; 3336:2; born on ~, 2088:3; children and ~, 4136:3; concern for human ~, 1953–1954:3; danger of ~, 2536:1; hostility toward

~, 2536:2; single mothers on ~, 4122:1; women and ~, 3336:1
social work, 1390.1:1; 3553:2; public ~, 1324:2
socialism, 1537:5; 1583:6; 2455:1; 3180:2; ~ in America, 3029:2; working for ~, 1786:2
socialist, 1751:7; 2349:16; ~ women, 1229:1
society see also civilization; culture; social order, 369:6; 664:1; 701:14; 738:3; American ~, 2480:8; 3230:3; ~ at its best, 769:2; 3393:2; changing ~, 1009:3; civilized ~, 3314:1; diversity of ~, 1350:9; divisiveness in ~, 2943:8; end of ~, 3145:10; engaging in ~, 869:1; examination of ~, 2439:9; fashionable ~, 735:2; high ~, 2066:6; horrors of ~, 2818:1; hypocrisy in ~, 1474:7; ~ in relation to children, 3728:3; ~ in relation to government, 4345:2; ~ in relation to individual, 1977:3; ~ in relation to women, 3897:4; 4381:3; intellectual ~, 1461:4; judging ~, 3581:2; new ~, 2165:3; obligations of ~, 2929:3; oppressed ~, 3907:4; optimizing ~, 2362:5; opulence of ~, 3778:2; organization of ~, 2172:1; pitfalls of ~, 2439:10; polite ~, 2894:2; proliferation of growth in ~, 2866:20; reform in ~, 4273:2; rules of ~, 3748:5; stability of ~, 2959:4; throw-away ~, 2243:1; traditional ~, 2952:2; youth-oriented ~, 2243:5
sociologist/sociology, 2352:8
Socrates, 1336:8
Sodom & Gomorrah, 348:1
soil see also dirt; farming; land, 4141:10; 4375:1; untilled ~, 308:7
soldier see also armed forces/army; combat; fight/ing; mercenary; military; sailor; war, 287:3; 486:2; 648:2; 1741:3; 2034:4; 3301:1; 3763:3; American ~, 686:1; ~ away from home, 1373:1; black ~, 2078:3; child ~, 4564:1; comradeship between ~, 3972:3; confrontation with ~, 625:1; 636:1; 747:1; 748:1; 752:1; courage of ~, 1784:1; death and ~, 497:3; 599:1, 2; 905:4; 1011:1; 1446:8; 1580:2; doubts of ~, 2609:4; fearless ~, 1245:3; fighting ~, 4458:1; food for ~, 4257:3; function of ~, 1360:9; grief of ~, 838:6; honorable ~, 1106:3; ~ in relation to woman, 1337:3; 3066:3; memorial to ~, 1531:2; mother of ~, 956:2; 1480:2; ordinary ~, 2510:1; ~ resisting orders, 4263:5; responsibility to ~,

2528:1; restrictions of ~, 2614:1; Scottish ~, 680:2; 712:1; superstition of ~, 2276:3; training of ~, 4735:3; woman ~, 703:1; 1106:4; wounded ~, 1139:1
solidarity see also brotherhood; sisterhood; unity, 3755:1; 4091:1; ~ among women, 1967:2; 3096:1; ~ of humanity, 1231:3; ~ of working class, 889:2
solitude see also aloneness; privacy, 136:3; 472:18; 598:2; 1120:8; 1264:2; 1491:1; 1507:3; 2291:4; 2381:1; 2488:3; 2920:4; 3122:4; 3349:2; 4307:4; 4509:3; benefits of ~, 1348:2; desire for ~, 1674:1; joys of ~, 3718:1; need for ~, 4570:1; place of ~, 2208:2; spiritual ~, 4495:6
Solomon, 2979:2
solution, common-sense ~, 2574:1; finding ~, 1952:4; 2220:6; 2706:1; results of ~, 2805:4
Somalia, girls in ~, 4695:1
Somoa, Polynesia, growing up in ~, 1935:
son see also child/ren, 1006:13; 1315:5; 1563:6; 1700:4, 5; ~ at war, 648:2; death of ~, 238–239:1; 385:1; 713:14; 793:3; desire for ~, 1700:3; disappointment in ~, 4714:2; ~ in relation to father (see also father, in relation to son), 4421:2; ~ in relation to mother (see also mother/hood, ~ in relation to son), 3309:4; raising ~, 965:3; value of ~, 3570:2; values bestowed on ~, 906:3
song see also melody; music; singer/singing, 259:1; 4250:4; ~ as memorial, 2631:1; folk ~, 2734:1, 2, 3; ~ interpretation, 2244:4; making a ~, 3187:2; 4865:2; Native American ~, 1770:2; personal ~, 4346:2; political ~, 2107:1; 3905:1; popular ~, 3135:1; 4781:2; stealing ~, 1767:1
sophistication see also worldliness, 2619:4; 2966:2; illusion of ~, 1715:4; ~ in women, 2168:3
sorcery see also magic/ian, 983:3
sorority, 4852:1
sorrow see also grief; regret, 197:2; 356:1; 368:2; 462:2; 966:5; 1136:2; 1209:1; 1292:7; 1465:2; 1619:7; 1640:1; 1727:2; 1741:19; 1832:4; 2102:0; 2174:2; 2267:2; 2454:2; 3451:4; chasing away ~, 1057:1; deep ~, 596:1
soul see also spirit/uality, 114:1; 204:1, 2; 236:2; 308:10; 399:2; 405:7; 439:3; 567:1; 970:1; 1024:7; 1209:6; 1590:1; 1751:4; 2668:8; 2731:3; 2849:2; 2941:3; 3051:1; 3567:11; 4367:2; 4971:1; age of ~, 2220:4; ~ at

rest, 1599:1; awakening of ~, 1322:1; buffeting of ~, 3648:1; caring for ~, 922:7; denying ~, 4117:4; developing ~, 3145:18; dormant ~, 3420:4; entrance of ~, 1033:5; feeding one's ~, 3576:2; 4367:6; freedom of ~, 482:1; 845:5; 2040:1; healing ~, 1762:1; ~ in relation to body, 1524:1; lost ~, 307:2; 3355:1; masculine ~, 515:2; ~ mate (see also soul, united ~), 801:6; 845:1; 3067:2; 4680:2; meager ~, 1208:7; misuse of ~, 4593:1; musical ~, 1844:8; needs of ~, 180:1; neutrality of ~, 770:6; nourishing ~, 3964:3; ~ of men, 4484:3; opening ~, 1446:4; people without ~, 3119:11; restless ~, 4906:1; safeguarding ~, 1857:1; sanctity of ~, 158:2; saving ~, 3571:2; selling your ~, 4244–4245:4; united ~ (see also soul, ~ mate), 450:1; woman's ~, 403:2; 2860:3
sound see also noise, 2419:1; 4698:4; animal ~, 2117:13; ~ of bells, 758:1; ~ of city, 713:3
South Africa, Republic of, 2303:1, 2; 2797:3; 2807:1; 2905:1; 4485:2; blacks of ~, 2905:2; integration in ~, 2024:1; Karoo ~, 2797:3; Nature in ~, 1208:14; racism in ~, 3347:3; 4196:2; women of ~, 2357:1
South America see Latin America
South/erner (U.S.) see also America; United States, 1914:6; 2325:2; 4640:1; ~ after the civil war, 987:6; anti-bellum ~, 1297:1; attitude towards ~, 2096:2; blacks in ~, 843:2; Christianity and ~, 2534:9; ~ in relation to North, 879:3; mentality of ~, 2661:1; stories and ~, 4097:1; waters of ~, 3389:3; woman ~, 1297:1
Southampton, England, 767:1
Southwest (U.S.), 3862:4; 3902:4
souvenir see also memento, 1014:1; American ~, 1926:1
sovereignty, 2654:5
Soweto, South Africa, rebellion in ~, 3158:2
space (outer), 3609:3; 4063:2; 4654:1; astrophysical ~ and art, 2334:1; Cape Canaveral and ~, 3924:2; exploration of ~, 2752:3; ~ program, 4063:1; ~ shuttle, 4069:1; ~ travel, 3848:1; uses of ~, 4069:4; weightlessness in ~, 4069:3
space (area), crowded ~, 966:1; empty ~, 4289:2; living ~, 2098:1
Space Age, demands of ~, 1915:2
Spain, 1353:2; 3349:15; socialism in ~, 1813:6
speaking see also pause; speech; talk/ing, 2288:8; 3409:3; ~ abil-

ity, 1381:6; 2555:1; ~ English, 1304:1; ~ out, 3190:1; ~ well, 2538:1
specialist/specialization, 2061:13; limitations of ~, 2383:1
species, endangered ~, 3621:2
speech see also freedom, ~ of speech; public speaker; speaking; talk/ing; voice, 2101:3; 3996:2; 4147:4; articulate ~, 2878:1; cessation of ~, 4109:4; control of women's ~, 4291:1; gift of ~, 193:1; impromptu ~, 1825:5; lack of ~, 2689:3; parts of ~, 1770:3; politics of ~, 2036:4; prejudicial ~, 3436:3; vernacular ~, 1589:3
speechlessness, 4:3; 46:7
speed see also pace, 3226:2; excitement of ~, 2945:7; ~ of change, 4411:4
spelling, 406:1; ~ English, 1391:1
spending, deficit ~, 4771:5
sperm, 3526:1; 4005:1
Spinoza, 1078:1
spinster see bachelor; single/ness
spirit/uality see also soul, 352:3; 769:1; 1145:1; 1148:3; 1336:3; 1446:5; 1563:5; 1880:2; 2296:3; 2534:6; 2969:2; 3317:8; adopted ~, 2680:25; broken ~, 1981:2; 3703:2; 4352:1; creation of ~, 4290:1; developing ~, 2362:4; divine ~, 798:4; fanatical about ~, 1532:1; free ~, 852:3; 1741:30; hunger for ~, 3012:2; ~ in all things, 3179:2; 3303:3; 4183:1; ~ in relation to body, 887:4; indomitability of ~, 4377:1; insight into ~, 2331:7; 4117:1; manifestation of ~, 148:1; poverty of ~, 3753:3; practicing ~, 3563:4; 4461:1; social activism and ~, 4117:7; stealing ~, 3384:3; unconquerable ~, 646:3; understanding ~, 315:2; uplift ~, 3704:4; woman and ~, 3066:1
spite see also malice, 289:1
spokesperson see also government; representative ~; representation, ~ for one's people, 1700:10
spontaneity, 2056:1; 2478:2; lack of ~, 2466:3
sports see also specific types; athlete/athletics, 2391:2; 2789:1; girls' ~ in schools, 3273:2; 4610:3; lessons of ~, 4610:1; men and ~, 2995:4; Moslem women and ~, 4617:2; mother of modern ~, 3434:5; outdoor ~, 266:2; women and ~, 2218:1; 2366:1, 2; 2759:1, 2; 3273:1; 4384:1, 2; 4761:1; 4864:1
spouse see also companion; life ~; husband; mate; wife, advice to ~, 3641:3; death of ~, 287:4; 2590:3; 2647:4; 4406:5; loss

of ~, 2396:1; role of ~, 1255:1; 4940:1; supportive ~, 1480:4; travel with ~, 3012:3; trust in ~, 1752:11

spring (season), 123:1; 140:1; 151:1; 175:3, 4; 1024:29; 1085:2; 1208:15; 1387:7; 1507:2; 1534:3; 2049–2050:2; 2061:11; 2327:2; 4198:4; 4206:1; alone in ~, 1610:1; approaching ~, 725:2; early ~, 967:1; end of ~, 658:2; food of ~, 1871:2; gifts of ~, 554:2

Springfield, Dusty, 3982:2

spy see also surveillance, characteristics of ~, 3735:2

Sri Lanka, government in ~, 3588:2; human rights in ~, 3715:2

St. Augustine, 3445:2

St. Patrick, 4057:2

St. Paul, 59:2; 96:1

stability, 3464:2; 3844:2; longing for ~, 1654:3

Stael, Germaine de, 724:1; 757:1

stage play see also drama; playwright/ing; scriptwriter; theater, ~ character, 2546:1; comedic ~, 808:15; important ~, 4413:3; ~ in Ancient Greece, 4077:3; new ~, 3252:1; well-made ~, 3200:

stagnation, 156:1

Stalin, Josef, 2459:1; 2507:2

stamina see also vitality; vigor, mental ~, 3709:2

Stamp Act, 647:1

standard see also principle, ~ of living, 4100:; school ~, 4267:2; single ~, 1790:7

Stanford University (California), 3479:1

Stanley Park, British Columbia, 3704:5

Stanton, Elizabeth Cady, 963:11

star (astronomy), 792:2; 962:2; 1440:8; 3131:2; classifying ~, 1293:4; comfort of ~, 1293:3; fascination with ~, 2338:1; guiding ~, 450:1; reach for ~, 2464:4

Starbucks Coffee Co., also see coffee, 3498:3

stardom see also celebrity; fame; public figure, 1686:6; 2222:2; 2377:2; 2431:1; 2826:3; 2867:3; 3577:2; ambition of Hollywood ~, 2110:1; movie ~, 2962:4; 4421:5; ~ quality, 4938:2; self-centeredness of ~, 1685:2

starvation see also hunger, 1010:2; 1040:1; 1076:1; 1120:3

statesman/woman see also head of state; politician, 731:1; women and ~, 1499:4

statistic, 2583:1

statue, 4101:4

status quo, ~ in America, 2544:5; maintaining ~, 4921:2; rejecting ~, 4186:3; upsetting ~, 2866:10

steal/ing see also theft, ~ food, 3546:3; immorality of ~, 771:2; punishment for ~, 2606:1

Steichen, Edward, 1963:1; wife of ~, 2868:2

Stein, Gertrude, 1502:7; 1581:2; 3895:3; 4152:1

stereotype, 4136:5; cultural ~, 4426:3; doing away with ~, 3479:2; effects of ~, 2842:2; female ~, 2401:2; ~ of girls and boys, 4558:1; ~ of women and men, 1533:1

Stevens, Wallace, 2402:9

stillness, 4573:3

stimulant, 3547:7

stinginess see also miser, 2799:5; 3964:1

stock market see also finance; investment, 1848:1; analyzing ~, 2823:2; investing in ~, 4210:1; ~ report, 2668:12

stoicism, 64:1; 1641:1; 1780:6; 2079:7; 2982:5

stone see also rock, 968:1; 2636:4; communion with ~, 2135:6

Stone, Lucy, 998:11

Stonehenge (England), 585:1; 2135:6

storm see also rain, 996:1; 1669:11; 4554:1; ~ at sea, 1180:1; ~ in hills, 1346:2; summer ~, 3413:5

story see also book; novel, 1408:1; 1515:1; 2117:16; 2210:8; 2415:1; 2437:4; 2510:4; 2772:7; 2920:1; 2993:1; 3013:1; 3629:4; 4754:1; 4940:3; angel's ~, 1053:2; bedtime ~, 3203:1; beginnings and endings of ~, 1556:1; creation ~, 2998:1; family ~, 3442:2; 4042:7; fish ~, 1179:2; function of ~, 2668:10; ghost ~, 4819:1; great ~, 4595:3; healing power of ~, 2993:4; importance of ~, 2756:22; 3242:1; influence of ~, 4212:2; jazz ~, 3902:5; listening to ~, 1938:4; love of ~, 1233:3; ~ of national origins, 4753:1; personal ~ (see also autobiography), 2508:1; 3004:1; 3139:15; 3447.1:2; 4074:3; 4867:2; plot of ~, 3345:1; power of ~, 3950:2; retelling ~, 2518:2; sharing ~, 4147:1; untold ~, 1727:6

storyteller/storytelling see also literature; narrative; tradition, oral ~, 166:8; 193:7; 1187:1; 2260:1; 3013:2; 3146:1; 3246:1; 3567:9; 3850:1; 3895:1; 4033:2; 4518:1; 4740:2; art of ~, 166:13; death of ~, 4147:2; Native American Indian ~, 3866:3; importance of ~, 3866:1; 4290:5; timelessness of ~, 1489:1; woman ~, 4147:3

stowaway, 1445:2

Stowe, Harriet Beecher, 987:2

Stradivari, Antonio, 955:37

stranger see also outsider, 1226:1; 1693:12; 3974:3; charm of ~, 3584:1; 4516:2; conversation with ~, 2337:2; male ~, 3284:3; openness with ~, 3145:2; trusting ~, 3026:1

Stratford-on-Avon, England, 2130:2

stream, ~ in wilderness, 1233:5

street, ~ name, 1441:4

strength see also endurance; might, 2991:2; gaining ~, 3292–3293:4; 3523:2; great ~, 1180:2; inner ~, 287:6; loneliness in ~, 1246:5; physical ~, 334:8; 669:3; 807:14; 1300:1; physical ~ of women, 2789:2

stress see also tension, 3828:1; ~ and gender, 4768:2; combating ~, 3933–3934:5; dealing with ~, 3019:4; effects of ~, 2621:2; prolonged ~, 4116:; response to ~, 4590:2

strife see also conflict, 1534:2

struggle see also conflict; endeavor; life, struggles of ~, 4457:2; ~ against might, 1209:9; collective ~, 4305:7; 4578:3; courageous ~, 1552:2; ~ for existence, 2187:18; inner ~, 2903:9

student see also education; scholar/ship; school; study, 2437:3; 3122:2; becoming ~, 4571:3; behavior of ~, 1280:2; curriculum for ~, 2756:24; efficient ~, 1450:2; female ~, 832:3; health of ~, 1117:1; inferior ~, 699:1; needs of ~, 2372:1; outstanding ~, 2960:3; self-esteem and ~, 3394:1

studiousness see also scholar/ship, 334:6; 773:2

study see also student, 107:4; 273–274:2; 356:5; 1283.1:1; desire for ~, 394:1; fields of ~, 4000:1; life of ~, 3621:1; practical ~, 4769:2; process of ~, 961:1; religious ~, 141:3; rewards of ~, 801:9; woman's inclination to ~, 487:14

stupidity see also ignorance, 369:3; 1741:16; 1931:2; 2066:3; 4289:4; illusion of ~, 3577:3; pretense of ~, 1785:1

style, 1182:1; 1969:3; changing ~, 1969:4; developing ~, 1790:5; ~ of one's own, 1019:4; personal ~, 1715:10

subconscious see also psychology; unconscious, 1590:1

sublime, the, 1669:19

submission/submissiveness see also passivity; surrender, 808:6; 1643:1; 1994:3; effects of ~, 2679:2; feigned ~, 310:2

subordinate, 2857:3

subsidy see also annuity, receiving a ~, 969:1

subsistence, ~ from the land, 4559:2; ~ living, 4780:1

subterfuge see also deceit, excitement of ~, 4286:4

suburb/an, 1622:7; 1935:19; 2780:1; 3002:1; 3231:2; African-American ~, 4188:2

success, 711:2; 1332:6; 1450:24; 2022:1; 2063:3; 2236:2; 2306:2; 2426:1; 2530:1; 2612:3; 2637:1, 2; 2687:6; 2707:1; 3470:3; 3776:5; 3936:1; 4285:7; 4510:8; accepting ~, 4285:4; ~ at age 60, 1412:7; cloak of ~, 4813:1; dichotomy of ~, 2809:4; effects of ~, 734:5; 1611:3; enjoying ~, 2610:3; external ~, 1208:16; gender and ~, 1703:1; group ~, 4836:3; ~ in show business, 1620:1; ~ in theater, 1520:2; ingredients of ~, 1998:6; key to ~, 3683:1; 4083:3; lack of ~, 2786:2; ladder of ~, 1790:2; lessons of ~, 2726:4; loneliness of ~, 1494:4; 1674:2; measure of ~, 2724:; overnight ~, 2492:1; pitfalls of ~, 1843:5; 1998:3; recipe for ~, 4313–4314:2; resentment of ~, 1646:4; road to ~, 1344:1; 3913:2; 4864:2; 4957:1; secret ~, 1573:2; secret of ~, 3606:3; 4812:2; sweetness of ~, 1024:2; unexpected ~, 2150:3; women and ~, 808:9; 1847:5; 2416:2; 3083:2; 3148–3149:1; 4973:1

Sudan, racism in ~, 4925:3

suffering see also pain, 919:1; 1774:1; 1843:11; 2968:1; 3087:4; 3445:6; 4410:2; 4929:1; alleviating ~, 4568:4; depth of ~, 1687:5; fellowship of ~, 1764–1765:5; great ~, 1107:1; healing ~, 1822:5; individual ~, 3152:1; Judeo-Christian judgment in relation to ~, 3445:3; lamenting ~, 4517:2; ~ of innocents, 4321:2; ~ of others, 4829:2; private ~, 687:1; reasons for ~, 3352:2; responsibility for ~, 4166:3; unnecessary ~, 2929:1

suffrage/suffragist see also enfranchisement; vote/r, 1154:0; 1488:1; 1553:3; importance of ~, 1158:1; ~ in Nevada, 1463:1; ~ in relation to men, 1341:2; procession for woman's ~, 1637:5; sacrifices for ~, 4598.1:4; struggle for women's ~, 1341:2; 2439:5; universal ~, 887:16; 3757:2; 4444:3; victory of women's ~, 1244:5; women's ~ (see also Declaration of Sentiments), 931:15; 1050:1; 1086:9; 1155:1, 2; 1365:1, 3; 1528:1; 1555:7; 1637:6, 7; 2864:1; 3737:2

Suharto, 2512:1, 4

suicide, 87:1; 1254:15; 1755:3; 2642:15; 4045:3; 4270:3; 4902:2; assisted ~, 3228:3;

3883:2; ~ bomber, 3641:2; contemplating ~, 704:2; 1147:2; 1717:4; 4765:4; crime of ~, 1034:3; encouraging ~, 2063:2; feigned ~, 1409:23; methods of ~, 1780:5; ~ of housewife, 4360:1; potential ~, 3799:2; preparation for ~, 3003:3; regretting ~, 4554:2; sin of ~, 381:2; 1907:1

summer, 2784:1; 3546:2; 4845–4846:3; 4871:1; Indian ~, 996:1; 1087:2; memorable ~, 1109:2

sun, 2:1; 130:1; 133:1; 365:3; 463:1; 772:1; 841:2; 2092:2

Sun Yat-sen, 1786:3

sunbathing, 4198:2

Sunday, 1654:1; 1717:2; 3788:4; 4144:3; ~ morning, 1782:7

sunrise see also dawn; morning, 691:1; 723:1; 1024:12; 1069:2; 3895:4

sunset see also eve/ning; twilight, 1104:1; 1692:5

superficiality see also trivia, 408:5; 2427:1; 2771:24

superiority, 1673:8; 2765:3; 3099:18; 3110:3; attitude of ~, 4953:2; female ~, 357:2; impotence of ~, 2563:4; male ~, 1819:3

supermarket, 4258:4

supernatural, 1033:8

superpower, ~ in relation to underdeveloped nations, 3547:13

superstition, 306:3; 436:2; 759:1; 916:8; 3298:3; defense of ~, 107:2; eschewing ~, 4300:3; teaching ~, 107:8

supportiveness, 916:17; 1354:3

suppression see also repression, 1474:2; 1622:3; 1727:6; 3174:1

Supreme Court, U.S. see also judiciary, 2178:1, 2; 2733:2; 4466:5; ~ and equality, 4273.1:4; ~ and religion, 3935:2; ~ justices, 3274:1; right-wing ~, 2658:8; women in ~, 1029:5

surgeon/surgery see also physician, 1024:3; 1039:3; 2948:4; cosmetic ~, 4964:1; permission for ~, 2261:1

surprise, 451:1; 1450:14; desire for ~, 4733:3; unable to feel ~, 734:21

surrealism, 2066:7

surrender see also submission, ~ arms, 327:1; 618:1; power of ~, 3321:3; refused to ~, 4816:4; ~ to pleasure, 465:6

surveillance see also spy, object of ~, 2447:2; ~ of private citizen, 2544:5

survival see also self-protection, 1058:1; 1111:1; 1870:9; 2970:2; 4295:2; 4413:1; 4749:1; drive for ~, 2664:2; 3276:3; fighting for ~, 4554:1;

~ of humankind, 2032:14; 2800:2; ~ of poor, 3761:1; ~ of the fittest, 1473:4; strength from ~, 3753:5; struggle for ~, 3835:4; tools of ~, 3389:1

survivor, 283:3; 2508:2; 2715:3; 3497:2; 3563:2; 4431.1:4; 4479:2; 4862:2; ~ of Holocaust, 2508:1; stories of ~, 4862:1

suspicion, 334:11; 1975:3; 2068:2; police ~, 4036:3; under ~, 2344:1; unfounded ~, 1689:1

sustenance, 2122:1; local ~, 3682:1

swearing see also oath; vituperation, 1160:4; 1722:9; 4734:1; ~ on television, 2862:5

sweat, 4024:2

Sweden/Swedish, children of ~, 3088:2; sex in ~, 2656:3

Sweet Honey in the Rock, 3760:1

sweetness, 956:4; vulnerability of ~, 845:3

sweets see also food, 1521:2; cake, 1085:3; chocolate ~, 4677:1; cocoa, 2346:2; cookie, 1751:6; ice cream, 3743:4; ice cream truck, 2680:27

Swift, Jonathan, 533:9; 688:2

swimming, 2045:2; 4127:5; long-distance ~, 3922:1; ~ pool, 2925:11; training for ~, 3922:2

sycophancy/sycophant see also flattery; parasite; servility, 1527:1; 2987:9; 3278:1; 4493:1; 4636:2

symbol/ism see also significance, 2196:3; importance of ~, 1154:0; ~ of a people, 1945:2; sacredness of ~, 4123:4; understanding ~, 2960:1; ~ vs. reality, 4118:4

symmetry, ~ in nature, 2162:1

sympathy see also compassion; understanding, 865:3; 1127:1; 1438:2; unwelcome ~, 3251:1

symphony, 4344:4

synagogue see also Jew/Judaism, 4251:3; services in ~, 4104:2

synchronicity, 3759:1

syntax see also grammar; language, localized ~, 4601:3

T

taboo, dichotomy of ~, 1957:5; social ~, 1843:8

tact see also politeness, 1166:7; 1201:9; 2319:5

Taiwan, 3523:1

talent see also ability; skill, 496:1; 1044:9; 1079:1; 1317:1; 1758:1; 2189:7; 2307:1; 2568:2; appreciating ~, 778:1; bogusness of ~, 1844:1; delicacy of ~, 1758:4; developing ~, 4042:9; exceptional ~, 1076:3; ~ in relation to success, 2637:2; ingredients of ~, 2345:1; lack of ~, 578:2; lost ~ of women, 2480:4; pursuing one's ~, 3349:1; supporting ~, 2418:2;

use of ~, 158:1; 1998:6; women and ~, 557:1

Taliban see also Al Qaeda, 4604:1

talk/ing see also speaking; speech; verbosity, 369:5; 1409:22; 2219:1; 2437:5; compulsive ~ (see also garrulousness), 4473:1; ease of ~, 1881:3; empty ~, 3607:2; inability to ~ (see also speechlessness), 452:3; musicality of ~, 892:2; opposite of ~, 3984:5; ~ to oneself, 2311:1; ~ with restraint (see also reticence), 477:3; 571:1; 4514:1; woman ~, 4643:4

tallness, 1673:5

tameness see also domesticity, price of ~, 2529:4

Tanglewood, Massachusetts, 2478:3

Taos, New Mexico, 1524:5

task see also deed, unfinished ~, 1085:1; 1335:3

taste (preference), 642:10; 796:2; 2168:1; decline of good ~, 829:2; discriminating ~, 1382:5

Tatum, Art, 2147:5

tax/ation, 251:1; 647:1; 1914:9; 2027:11; 2374:1; 3421:3; avoiding ~, 2213:1; ~ bias to singles, 1826:2; ~ dodge, 2301:1; elderly and ~, 1725:4; employee ~, 4041:4; fairness in ~, 4771:3; income ~, 1150:1; ~ law, 1826:1; ~ on wealthy, 4118:2; poll ~, 3365:1; U.S.A. ~, 4771:2; use of ~, 2408:2; women and ~, 74:2

taxidermy, 4324:4

tea, 2379:2; preparation of ~, 1192:1

teacher see also governess; professor, 336:2; 353:2; 640:1; 874:13; 951:5; 1381:8; 2160:2, 3; 3193:2; ~ and curriculum, 2348:1; ~ as observer, 1381:1; efficient ~, 1450:2; goal of ~, 1604:3; 1700:1, 2; 3788:1; goal of music ~, 3564:2; good ~, 806:3; 1167:11; guidance of ~, 581:2; high school ~, 3973:2; hiring ~, 4536:2; ~ in relation to student, 2675:5; 3112:2; influence of ~, 807:5; memorable ~, 3439:2; motivation of ~, 4388:1; ~ of adolescents, 4901:3; ~ pay, 2348:2; physical education ~, 3644:2; pride of ~, 2960:3; salary of ~, 4027:3; wages of woman ~, 839:3; woman ~, 827:13

teaching see also education; instruction; training, 528:1; 657:1; 843:3; 1280:2; 2055:1; 2056:7; 3032:2; 3385:1; 3848:2; 4667:2; ~ about food, 3548:2; ~ children, 3077:1, 2; difficulty of ~, 2238:5; ~ ideas, 1332:8; method of ~, 783:3; 806:2; 2372:1; rewards of ~, 2345:2; 4027:2

team/work, 930:3; 3998:1; 4344:2; 4980:2

tears see also crying, 310:3; 341:6; 470:2; 526:1; 2040:2; 2063:4; 2680:; crocodile ~ (see also falseness), 340:1; idleness of ~, 1213:4

technique see also skill, learning ~, 2890:3

technology, 3903:3; 4081:1; 4609:1; 4738:1, 5; alienation of ~, 2080:8; consequences of ~, 3197:2; 3343:4; disasters of ~, 4835:2; domination of ~, 1699:2; future of ~, 3888:1; government and ~, 4332:1; high ~, 4475:2; history of ~, 4930:2; ~ in America, 3566:1; ~ in relation to environment, 4039:2; information ~, 4200:2; learning to use ~, 3925:5; politics of ~, 2934:1; progress of ~, 3535:4; surrounded by ~, 3203:6; uses of ~, 1548:7; 2032:14; 2776:4; wireless ~, 4233:1; women and ~, 2573:1; 4409:6

teenage/r see also adolescence; years of age; youth, 1956:2; 2034:3; 3258:5; 4686:1; American ~, 4056:4; ~ behavior, 4598.1:3; ~ boys, 4797:1; drugs and ~, 4056:3; end of ~, 4613:2; ~ girls, 4050:3; lessons for ~, 2843:3; sexual behavior among ~, 3360:4; 3377:6

teeth, 2772:8; false ~, 2006:1

telegraph, 1448:2

telepathy see also ESP, mental ~, 2296:2

telephone, 1180:5; 2732:5; 2925:6; ~ answering machine, 4580:1; cellular ~, 4650:2; ~ dial-a-prayer service, 2925:8; hands-free ~, 4445:2

television, 2151:1; 2187:9; 2270:9; 2944:7; 3099:15; 3257:5; 3335:3; 3691:3, 5; 4770:1, 2; children's ~, 3764:3; 3791:2; ~ commercials, 2074:1; 2899:1; ~ criticism, 2394:3; ~ documentary, 2949:5; effects of ~ on children, 3115:2; ~ Law and Order, 3147:6; life imitating ~, 4816:6; live ~, 2786:1; madness of ~, 3780:6; ~ news (see news, TV); ~ news personality, 3454:2; nudity on ~, 4723:1; politics and ~, 1618:28; ~ production deadline, 2321:1; racism and sexism in ~, 2898:3; swearing on ~, 2862:5; ~ talk show, 2939:1; watching ~, 3115:1; women on ~, 3407:1

temper/ament see also disposition, bad ~, 591:1; 4146:2; hidden ~, 3856:2

temperance see also self-control; prohibition, 944:1; 946:5; 1308:1; ~ movement, 1090:4

temple, 1313:1

temptation, 1:1, 1; 413:2; 604:1; 605:1; 864:1; 1019:5; 1462:1; 1744:1; resisting ~, 375:1; 934:7; 992:6; 4181:1

Ten Commandments *see also* Bible; Gospel, 322:2; 2768:3

tenacity *see also* perseverance, 1898:1; 2120:1

tenderness *see also* gentleness, 649:1; 1749:1; 2817:8; 3009:6

tenement *see also* slums, 1961:0

Tenet, George, 3735:2

Tennessee, 735:1; 1020:1; 2570:2

tennis, 2177:2

tension *see also* nerves/nervousness; stress, 1884:1; ~ of boredom, 2798:1

tentativeness *see also* hesitation, 955:21

Teresa, Mother, 2909:2

terrorism/terrorist, 3233:1; 3491:3; 3731:14; 4268:4; 4567:2; 4574:2; combating ~, 4303.1:2; fighting ~, 3641:1; 3670:2; 4022:5; 4431:1; mind of ~, 4815:5; response to ~, 4687:2; uses of ~, 4380:1; victims of ~, 1935:18; 3245:3; war vs. ~, 3980:5

test *see also* examination, intelligence ~, 2076:2

Texas, 1663:17; 3455:2; 3770:4; West ~, 4310:2

textbook, 4574:1; lack of reality in ~, 4388:2

Thai/land, 1659:5

Thanksgiving, 1159:2; ~ pie, 1871:6

Thatcher, Margaret, 3078:6; 3300:1; 4524:3

theater *see also* acting actor; playwright/ing; stage play, 572:3; 606:2; 1411:3; 1412:4; 1462:1; 1540:2; 1693:14; 1887:1; 2056:4; 2202:2, 3; 2827:3; 3063:2; 3125:2; 3186:3; ~ actor, 1771:2; ~ affected by church, 3328:1; business of ~, 743:1; caring people in ~, 4120–4121:2; collaboration in ~, 2223:1; control of ~, 3078:5; death of ~, 1246:2; ~ design, 1286:1; 2533:2; ~ director, 572:5; 2704:4; Federal ~ of WPA, 1705:1; flourishing ~, 631:1; goal of ~ group, 3530:2; good ~, 2202:4; 3744:3; great ~, 3291:5; impact of ~, 3063:1; ~ in Germany, 2575:1; ~ in relation to audience, 1364:3; 2628:5; 3170:4; life in ~, 1573:1; 1722:8; ~ lighting, 2533:1; movie ~, 3147:7; need for ~, 1904:2; philosophy of ~, 2202:1; progress of ~, 1705:2; public ~, 1705:3; repertory ~, 1312:1; ~ support, 1964:4; women in ~, 828:1

theft/thief *see also* steal/ing, 1135:4; 1482:1; 1986:6; 4719:2

theology *see also* God; religion, 833:1; 3387:2; bound by ~, 946:1; women's ~, 3424:1

theory, 3052:1; ~ about women, 2685:1; supporting ~, 1848:4

therapist/therapy *see also* analysis; psychotherapy, feminist ~, 3184:3; shock ~, 2483:1; social ~, 2870:2

things, 1700:9; 4871:3; inanimate ~, 1097:2; little ~, 986:1; origination of ~, 4585:1; solicitude toward ~, 1883:3

thinker/thinking *see also* mind; thought, 245:2; 536:1; 663:1; 795:1; 874:12; 1176:2; 1233:6; 1938:8; 2032:8; 2160:1; 2982:2; 3269:1; 3607:2; 4042:6; danger of ~, 2036:19; ~ for oneself, 859:7; futility of ~, 1450:17; learning process of ~, 701:11; ~ like a man, 4524:1; logical ~, 3535:2; negative ~, 4882:1; neutrality of ~, 892:18; ~ person, 1025:9; 1470:2; ~ women, 2680:2; 3465:1

thinness *see also* weight, 1840:2; 2251:1; 3228:4; 3990:7; ~ in women, 4635:2; obsession with ~, 1836:1; 2309:1; 3183:1

Third World, needs of ~, 2651:3; rural areas of ~, 3682:6

thirst, 1751:22; 4051:1; 4485:4; quench ~, 11:1

Thomas, Clarence, 2987:9

Thomas, Dylan, 1673:6

thoroughness, 1689:7; 3369:2

thought *see also* deliberation; reflection; thinker/thinking, 487:13; 653:3; 827:6; 1120:8; 1152:8; 1333:2; 1899:4; 2098:2; 3918:2; 4711:8; applying ~, 4550:1; bodies of ~, 2571:1; buried in ~, 166:2; controlling ~, 669:5; difficulty of ~, 2036:3; expanding ~, 1655:1; expressing ~, 1590:4; immoral ~, 515:1; independent ~, 1019:7; 1590:22; lack of ~, 2931:9; managing ~, 1905:6; power of ~, 1002:2; ~ process, 2199:2; seize ~, 1435:9; source of ~, 1152:7; systems of ~, 1336:9; troubled ~, 121:1; understanding ~, 511:16; Western ~, 4350:1; women and ~, 998:8; 3329:1

thoughtfulness *see also* caring, 1257:1

thoughtlessness *see also* carelessness; inconsiderateness, 1287:3

threat, 588:2; death ~, 4712:2; response to ~, 2819:5

thrift *see also* money, 1201:6; downside of ~, 2482:1; transcending ~, 4310:5

thumb, opposable ~, 2546:4

Tiananmen Square, Beijing, 2239:5; 4581:1

tide *see also* ocean; sea, 1136:4; ~ -book, 1929:1

tidiness *see also* neatness; orderliness, lack of ~, 1441:7

Tiller, George, M.D., 3888.1:2

time *see also* specific times of day; minute/moment, 641:1; 1440:15; 1927:3; 2009:4; 2027:9; 2187:17; 2349:; 2365:1; 2438:1; 2464:5; 2716:6; 3119:6; 3302:4; 3609:3; 4586:2; 4711:7; balm of ~, 683:3; 869:6; 3779:3; confronting ~, 2479:1; division of ~, 1382:3; fluidity of ~, 4447:1; ~ in native culture, 4119:1; intermediate ~, 4216:1; landscape of ~, 2320:5; lost ~, 2053:3; ~ management, 675:1; 945:8; 4696:2; measure of ~, 2456:5; misspent ~, 276:3; passage of ~, 299:2; 546:2; 586:1; 635:4; 713:12; 955:35; 999:3; 1002:3; 1043:1; 1645:1; 2297:8; 2595.1:4; 3010:1; ~ piece (*see also* clock; watch), 767:12; preciousness of ~, 3385:2; ravages of ~, 693:6; relativity of ~, 474:2; 671:5; 838:5; 1663:1; 1730:1; 1825:1; 2519:1; speed of passing ~, 3260:1; spending ~, 2219:13; spending ~ with loved one, 4047:1; telling ~, 2771:13; ~ to oneself, 334:4; unhurried ~, 4448:1; use of ~, 459:12; 580:1; 806:2; 1963:3; 2080:1; 3631:1; 4844:2; wasted ~, 1113:1; 2679.1:1, 1; 3021:2; ~ well-spent, 795:2

timeless/ness, ~ works of art, 4278:3

timeliness/ timing, 2552:2; 3378:1; 4586:2

Times Square, New York, 3358:1

timidity *see also* shyness, 522:5

Titanic, ~ survivor, 1665:1

Title IX, 2608:4; impact of ~, 2641:2

titles, 3182:3; gender and ~, 3591:4

today *see also* here and now; present, 1002:5; 1534:6

togetherness, 892:6; 2349:8; 2917:1; 3558:3

toil *see also* labor/er, 2185:8; ~ in the fields, 1589:4

toilet, 4530:1; ~ paper, 4173:1; 4857:2; ~ training, 2477:4

tokenism, 2610:2; ~ at workplace, 2898:3; resistance to ~, 1874:6

tolerance, 3208:1; 4261:3; 4280:1; ~ of differing opinions, 1126:3; requirements of ~, 3554:6; specious ~, 4136:6

Tolstoy, Leonid, 1132:5

Toluca, Mexico, 2066:1

tomorrow *see also* future, 1087:4; 1460:1; 2826:1; unknown ~, 4827:2

tongue, holding one's ~, 477:3; sharp ~, 2642:11

tool, necessity of ~, 4205:2; women and ~, 4612:1

Torah *also see* Jew/Judaism, 479:1; 2582:2; 3969:3; 4201:1

torch, passing ~, 4628:1

torture, 2040:2; 2508:3; 2905:4; 3503:2; 4795:1; effectiveness of ~, 4317:4; ~ of forced feeding, 1365:1; ~ of prisoner, 2175:4; ~ of women, 330:1; physical ~, 2692:1; purpose of ~, 3503:1; withstanding ~, 4414:1; 4496:1

Tory Party (Great Britain), 618:1

totalitarianism, 2036:1; 4320:3; 4553:2

touch, bond of ~, 3894:4; human ~, 3929:3; 4113:3

toughness *see also* resilience, 1435:6; 1741:20; 2848:2; ~ in men, 3847:2; ~ in woman, 2259:3

tourism/tourist, 2879:2; effect of ~ on historical preservation, 2130:2; ~ in relation to native people, 4098:3; ~ in relation to nature, 1773:1; ~ worker, 2852:2

Toussaint L'Ouverture, François Dominique, 3865:1

town *see also* village, 1376:3; new ~, 1474:8; small ~, 887:2; 2563:1; 2962:1; 3347:1

Town & Country (magazine), 4165:1

toxin, exposure to ~, 4433:1

toy *see also* game; play/ing, war ~, 2951:3; 3270:1; 3782:2

trade *see also* occupation, 2158:2; learning a ~, 1978:2; tools of ~, 4493:3; woman at helm of ~, 2027:3

tradition *see also* custom; habit; rite, 2445:2; 2709:1; 2834:4; 2950:4; at odds with ~, 1846:1; belonging to ~, 2806:3; 3118:5; breaking with ~, 1396:1; 2578:3; challenges to ~, 4531:1; different spiritual ~, 3871:1; family ~, 4417:3; indigenous ~, 4075:2; loss of ~, 887:12; 3121:6; oral ~ (*see also* storyteller), 3866:5; reversing ~, 4808:2; women and ~, 3684:3; worn out ~, 1244:6

tragedy *also see* disaster, 1297:3; 1574:4; 1759:3; common ground of ~, 2502:2; exploiting ~, 3444:1; recovering from ~, 4929:2; response to ~, 3963:3; surviving ~, 2676:8

train *see also* travel, 1233:2; 2982:2; 4737:3; express ~, 1590:24; freight ~, 1767:2; ~ in France, 4657:1

training *see also* school/ing, physical ~, 1348:1; spiritual ~, 1348:1

traitor *see also* betrayal; treason, 2291:8

tranquility, 178:5; 472:18; 1563:3; 3749:1; foe of ~, 671:2; ~ follows pain, 1998:2; satisfied with ~, 934:2

tranquilizer see also drugs, effects of ~, 1884:2

transcience, 2611:1

transformation, 1734:1; 2467:2; 2582:4; 2940:3; 3034:4; 4151:4; demands of ~, 1837:1; individual ~, 2822:5; ~ of self, 2466:6; political ~, 4160:7; time for ~, 3059:6; 3851:5; 4807:2

transgression, 2638:14; requirements of ~, 3906:4

transience, 967:2; 1408:20; 2297:8; 3355:3; 3647:1; 3733:2; 4023:2; ~ of time, 1752:2

transition see also turning point, age of ~, 2162:5; making ~, 4117:2

translation/translator, 836:1; 1336:6; 2162:6; 2668:21

transparency, ~ in the marketplace, 4202:1

transsexual/transgender see also cross-dressing; gender, ~ identity, 2229:1; 3009:1; 3501:2; 3780:4; 3823:2; 4441:1; cultural response to ~, 2569:3; ~ surgery, 2916:15

transvestite, 3501:1; 4123:8

trap see also pitfall, 1149:2; 1406:1; caught in ~, 2241:1; 2297:4; ~ waiting, 4123:1

trauma see also shock, victims of ~, 4263:3

travel/er see also journey; passport; trip; vacation; visit/or, 76:3; 1126:4; 1715:6; 1720:1; 2019:3; 2152:1; 2483:6; 4067:7; 4116:12; 4215:1; 4448:3; ~ abroad, 1019:3; 1822:4; 3012:3; 3394:2; 4190:1; ~ accommodations, 3356:3; ~ alone, 2858:4; American ~, 2900:5; 3681:1; armchair ~, 2117:9; benefits of ~, 642:8; 804:1; 3211:3; ~ by air, 1744:4; ~ by automobile, 2370:1; ~ by land, 857:2; ~ by pack animal, 1347:2; ~ by rail, 940:3; 4737:3; ~ by ship, 4224:3; ~ companion, 4586:1; dangers of ~, 1046:1; desire to ~, 857:1; 1642:1; 3911:1; food and ~, 2689:3; foreign ~, 1292:8; ignorant ~, 553:1; ~ in India, 4548:2; incessant ~, 769:6; ~ journal, 4548:1; lessons of ~, 951:2; lone ~, 4342:2; mind ~, 972:1; need to ~, 1448:3; passing ~, 1264:3; poor ~, 1936:2; reason for ~, 3911:2; ~ safety, 3502:1; solitary ~, 4215:2; spoiled by ~, 671:9; tales of ~, 1752:1; tribulations of ~, 2854:1; women ~, 646:6; 940:3; 1080:4; 4548:3; world ~, 1517:1; 1951:1

treachery, 4116:7

treason see also traitor, 748:1; 1759:8; 2505:2

treasure, hidden ~, 2238:1; 2940:3; personal ~, 722:5

treaty, 116:2

tree see also leaf, 183:1; 635:2; 1775:1; 1832:5; 1978:1; 2659:5; 4132:2; apple ~, 2015:2; arbutus, 1012:2; ~ blossom, 173:1; 222:2; bonsai ~, 3666:2; city ~, 1234:2; 1835:1; cultivating ~, 1073:5; cypress ~, 1376:2; dead ~, 1560:1; felled ~, 827:11; ~ in winter, 758:2; logging ~, 2732:12; oak ~, 3451:7; old-growth ~, 4132:3; palm ~, 4872:1; planting ~, 1008:1; 3207:4; redwood ~, 1773:1; reverence for ~, 931:26; sapling ~, 1008:2; saving ~, 4857:2; willow ~, 725:2; 2102:0

trespass/ing, 3211:2

trial see also law, ~ by fire, 390:2; 1837:1; ~ expert witness, 3522:1; ~ of character (see also mettle, test one's ~), 603:6

tribalism see also aboriginal, 116:2; 1347:6; demise of ~, 4242:2

trick/ster see also deceit/deception; mischief, 292:3; 1419:2

trip see also journey; travel

triumph also see win/ner, 3226:3

trivia/lity see also superficiality, 349:2

trouble see also adversity; obstacle, 282:1; 313:2; 459:9; always in ~, 4692:1; handling ~, 511:18; petty ~, 790:1; 922:1; put away your ~, 2119:1; women and ~, 1435:7

troublemaker, 370:1; 405:1

trousers, 1152:2

Troy, gates of ~, 3152:2

Truman, Bess, 2500–2501:4

Truman, Harry S., 2180:3; 2500–2501:2, 3

trumpet, 3181:1; 4224:1

trust, 798:1; 908:5; 1071:1; 3126:3; 4711:3; gaining child's ~, 1468:2; importance of ~, 3917:3; ~ in one's people, 4038:3; ~ in one's self, 3914:5; ~ in others, 890:7; lack of ~ (see also mistrust), 616:7

truth see also honesty, 166:13; 252:4; 304:1; 367:5; 423:4; 429:2; 455:3; 465:3; 496:2; 839:6; 844:3; 860:10; 910:10; 928:2; 956:1; 982:10; 993:2; 1187:6; 1213:3; 1336:3; 1449:2; 1608:2; 1645:4; 1938:3; 2006:3; 2080:14; 2224:2; 2265:5; 2266:5; 2329:2; 2352:2, 10; 2534:3; 2572:1; 2613:4; 2763:1; 2866:1; 3099:7; 3282:3; 3782:3; 3964:5; 3966:3; 4033:1; 4144:3; 4369:1; all sides of ~, 3547:8; awareness of ~, 1689:9; awful ~, 3476:2; blind to ~, 349:3; communal ~, 3866:5; defense of ~, 107:2; 2161:2; dismiss ~, 514:3; gaining ~, 1619:6; impact of

~, 501:2; ~ in relation to facts, 2618:10; inconvenient ~, 4343:1; 4573:1; locating ~, 1590:13; making up ~, 3009:4; personal ~, 3700:1; refining one's sense of ~, 1408:2; reporting the ~, 1642:2; requirements of ~, 1863:9; sacrifice for ~, 2979:2; seeking ~, 1590:22; 1686:3; selling ~, 2098:3; slanted ~, 1024:25; spark of ~, 2214:1; study of ~, 1034:2; telling ~, 54:2, 3; 1411:1; 1987:1; 2210:10; 2266:3; 2604:3; 2620:8; 4353:1; ~ to children, 1468:2; ~ to self, 2704:6; ~ vs. justice, 4263:2; ~ vs. realism, 3814:3

Truth, Sojourner, 860:13; 3365:2

Tubman, Harriet, 3121:3; 3417:3

Turenne, Henri de, 421:1

Turk/ey, parliament in ~, 4599:2

Turner, Ted, ~ and CNN, 4437.1:1

turning point see also epiphany; transition, 672:3

turpitude see also baseness, end ~, 522:4

Tutankhamun, 15:1

Tuttle, Richard, 3722:2

Tutu, Desmond, 4191:2

Twain, Mark, 1639:3

twilight see also eve/ning; night; sunset, 870:4; 1140:2; 1226:2; 1428:1; 1502:8; 3302:1

twin, Siamese ~, 2628:2

Typhoid Mary, 1407:2

tyranny/tyrant see also despot/ism; oppressor/oppression, 646:1; 677:3; 689:1; 701:12; 713:8; 764:1, 2; 887:1; 1568:1; 1582:3; 1889:5; 1977:7; 2558:2; 2881:3; escape from ~, 901:2; resistance to ~, 963:6; submission to ~, 890:5; suffering under ~, 1010:2; supporting ~, 2890:1; ~ vs. freedom, 2036:11

U

Uganda/n, 3920:1; plight of ~ 4683.1

ugliness, 737:1; 1383:3; 1412:1; 1593:8; 1752:5; 4782:4; 4915:2

Ukraine, women in ~, 4923:1

unattainable, longing for ~, 959:1; 4827:1

unborn see also embryo; fetus, rights of ~, 2656:7; 3139:8; world of ~, 2230:4

uncertainty, 999:1; 1914:8; 4743:4; ~ of life, 1832:3

uncle, 1006:9

unconscious/ness see also subconscious, 2051:1; 2371:2; 2568:4; exploring ~, 2330:1; ~ in woman, 1578:4

uncouthness, 3032:7

Underground Railroad, 978:6

understanding see also insight; perception; realization; sympa-

thy, 1001:2; 1335:9; 1450:13; 2693:1; 2993:3; complete ~, 1697:6; growth of ~, 1899:1; 2135:4; lack of ~, 48:1; 88:3; 114:1; 1715:14; 2281:5; lack of ~ others, 1854:2; 3693:1

undertaker, 2298:2; 2376:2

underworld, 3012:1

unemployment see also job, loss of ~, 1698:3; 2032:12; 3995:6; cause of ~, 3682:3; impact of ~, 3588:1; massive ~, 801:8; white-collar ~, 3257:8

unfinished see also completeness, lack of ~, 916:16; leaving things ~, 922:6; 2230:2

unfortunate see also victim, attending ~, 2116:3

unhappiness see also misery, 628:2; 815:1; 1707:1; 2739:1; writing from ~, 4696:4

unification, 1350:8

uniformity, 3855:3

union see labor union, fleeting ~, 4940:1; protection of ~, 4432:1

uniqueness see also originality; singularity, 1710:1; 2247:1; 2901:3; 3068:4; 3371:2; 3426:3; 3939:2

United Nations see also League of Nations, 1863:8; 1874:2; 3719:1; ~ and environmentalism, 4552:3; membership in ~, 3523:1; ~ peacekeeping, 4378:1; ~ Security Council, 4687:3; U.S. and ~, 1618:9; 4648:9; women in ~, 2856:4

United States see also specific states, regions and cities; America; American, 677:4; 782:10; 1795:2; 2619:2; 2959:2; 3189:1; 20th century ~, 2192:14; age of ~, 1450:19; ~ aide, 4774:2; apathy in ~, 1588:2; art in ~, 706:2; 2827:5; attitudes towards law in ~, 2192:12; ~ budget, 3271:1; criticism of ~, 1962:2; ~ debt, 3668:1; democracy in ~, 647:2; 733:22; 1666:4; 2111:1; 2255:1; 3976:4; ~ economy, 745:4; 4867:4; education in ~ (see also education, American ~), 1493:2; 4760:3; ~ elections, 4684:4; equality in ~, 2290:2; family life in ~, 807:21; ~ fighting communism, 1857:4; flag of ~, 729:1; freedom in ~, 1301:5; ~ government, 1776:8; 2192:13; 2265:1; 2496:1; 3029:2; 3314:4; history of ~, 3301:3; 4601:5; human rights in ~, 2624:4; 4087:1; hypocrisy in ~, 2604:3; image of ~, 2608:1; immigrants in ~, 4797:4; immigration to ~, 4073:1; ~ in relation to Afghanistan, 4927:1; ~ in relation to African nations, 3347:2; ~ in relation to Arab nations, 4576:1; ~ in relation to Asian nations, 984:2; 1874:8; ~

in relation to Canada, 4268:5; ~ in relation to children, 1741:26; 3141:1, 9; ~ in relation to England, 709:1; ~ in relation to Europe, 1778:1; ~ in relation to family, 3053:3; ~ in relation to genocide, 4829:1; ~ in relation to indigenous people, 4253:1; ~ in relation to Iran, 3143.1:3; ~ in relation to Iraq, 4596:1; ~ in relation to Israel, 3696:5; ~ in relation to Native Americans, 2624:1, 2; ~ in relation to other nations, 2720–2721:1; 3980:1; 3994:3; 4225:0; 4596:3; 4705:1; 4760:1; ~ in relation to Philippines, 3544:1; ~ in relation to Russia, 3280:3; 4220:3; ~ in relation to South America, 2890:1; ~ in relation to U.S.S.R., 2038:1; ~ in relation to Vietnam, 2087:4; 2692:1; 3189:2; the poor in ~, 3608:4; internal problems of ~, 2608:1; law in ~, 2085:4; liberty in ~, 3778:6; life in ~, 1512:2; literature in ~, 910:9; men in ~, 1686:1; ~ middle class, 4540:2; ~ military, 3454:1; 3462:1; newspaper in ~, 1301:3; opportunity in ~, 2959:2; oppression in ~, 2272:1; ~ policy, 3719:2; politics in ~, 1663:10; potential of ~, 2480:8; 4596:4; poverty in ~, 1618:12; 2544:4; power of ~, 4481:5; priorities of ~ government, 2899:3; public face of ~, 2959:3; racism in ~, 3050:1; religion in ~, 3424:3; ~ responsibility to world, 1496:1; 2262:1; 3676:5; settlement in ~, 3578:3; space in ~, 1450:10; standard of living in ~, 4100:; starvation in ~, 807:11; status quo in ~, 2866:10; ~ superiority, 3335:1; technology in ~, 3668:1; women in ~, 850:1; 3160:2

unity see also connectedness; oneness; solidarity, 2032:6; 3717:2; 4711:5; global ~, 2467:2; ~ of human race, 1938:5; 3124:4; ~ of living things, 3291:3

universality see also common ground, ~ of the personal, 4304:1

universe see also galaxy; world, 658:6; 2131:2; 3849:1; friendly ~, 3281:2; indifference of ~, 2266:11; laws of ~, 783:1; 3099:8; 4894:4; power of ~, 3604:1; understanding ~, 799:1; vastness of ~, 840:2

university see also college; school, expense of ~, 2237:7; ~ science programs, 4007:5, 6

unkindness see also meanness, 489:3

unknown, the, 1392:2; 4711:9; dealing with ~, 4147:7

unlikable, 163:3

unwanted see also rejection, 3145:15

Updike, John, 2638:10

upper class, see aristocracy; class; rich

uprising see also rebellion; riot, civil ~, 4960:2

usefulness, 405:5; 1113:2; ~ is over, 1254:15

uselessness, feeling of ~, 1785:5

U.S.S.R. (Union of Soviet Socialist Republics) see also Russia/n; Slav, 2507:3; 2873:1; citizen of ~, 3259:1; education in ~, 3584:2; ~ in relation to U.S., 2038:1; interrogation in ~, 2447:1; social relationships in ~, 2041:2; women and ~, 3236:1

utopia see also Eden; heaven; paradise, 1360:15; 1797:3; 2308:1

V

vacation see also holiday, 2346:6; family ~, 2346:5; festivity of ~, 2063:6; lakeside ~, 1149:5; motive for ~, 3218:3

vagina see also genitalia, 267:3, 4; 292:1, 2; 2638:5; 4174:1, 2; 4734:2; ~ clitoris, 2068:4; derogatory terms for ~, 4734:1

vagrant see also homeless, ~ singing, 4218:2

valet see also servant, 421:2

valor see also bravery; courage, 327:4; 446:11

values see also mores; principle; standard, American ~, 3798:1; 4167:1; authoritarian vs. humanitarian ~, 2124:3; basic ~, 957:1; 3594:5; 4648:4; changing ~, 3326:3; 4185:4; confused social ~, 3483:2; core ~, 3933–3934:2; cultural ~, 3445:6; declining American ~, 2192:14; democratic ~, 3749.1:2; development of ~, 3886:2; family ~, 1339:4; 2595:3; 2756:12; feminist ~, 3350–3351:1; global ~, 2669:4; ~ in Western culture, 1339:4; loss of ~, 1976:1; male ~, 2635:1; materialistic ~, 88:3; monetary ~, 2726:4; new ~, 1568:3; ~ of good life, 1990:1; ~ of things, 2775:1; old-fashioned ~, 4459:4; prioritizing ~, 2987:1; 4957:2; questioning ~, 1570:5; redefining ~, 2971:4; shifting ~ of wartime, 1756:2; spiritual ~, 305:3; woman's ~, 3366:2

Vanderbilt family, 1086:4

vanity see also pride, 767:14; 782:6; 1025:16; 1132:5; 1322:5; 1682:2; 2211:2; 2352:9; 2771:6; 3615:1; 3643:1; lack of ~, 2006:1; man's ~, 676:1; pampered ~, 713:13; woman's ~, 544:7; 1438:1; wounded ~, 1027:3

Vanity Fair (magazine), 4165:1

variety see also diversity, 472:6; loss of ~, 3044:2

vasectomy see also birth control, 2946:2

Vatican see also Catholic Church, 4089:4; wealth of ~, 2756:17

VAWA (Violence vs. Women Act), 2496:7

vegetable see also corn; food; seed, bean, 2529:6; lettuce, 2586:4; pea, 3337:1; turnip, 2769:1

vegetarian/ism, 2825:1; 4676:1

veil, burka ~, 3745:1; tradition of ~, 2977:3; wearing ~, 4617:3

Venezuela, 4087:2

vengeance see also retribution; revenge; vindictiveness, 341:6; 887:28; 1021:1; renounce ~, 391:3; woman's ~, 387:1

Venice, Italy, 519:2; walking in ~, 2063:7

Venus, 1368:3

verbosity see also talk/ing, 571:2; vacuous ~, 559:1

Verdi, Giuseppe, 4616:1

Versace, Gianni, 4337:2, 3

veteran see also World War II, veterans of ~; soldier, war ~, 1782:1

Veterans Affairs, budget of ~, 4521:5

Viagra, ~ and women, 3883:3

vicariousness, 1003:1; 1095:1; 2398:7; 3158:1

vice see also sin/ner, 369:3; 496:7; 521:2; 823:3; 1089:4; 1759:4; 2432:2

vice president, 4650:1

viciousness see also cruelty, 1932:1; ~ of youth, 450:2 vicissitudes see also difficulty, 2352:7; ~ of life, 4691:3

victim/ization see also unfortunate, 538:1; 2040:1; 2116:16; 2508:2; 2956:2; 3128:1; 3377:4; 3981:1; blaming the ~, 4808:4; ~ mentality, 955:3; 2352:4; 4285:2; 4661:2; ~ of war, 4828:1; ~ of women, 4480:3; 4615:2; potential ~, 3283:1; questioning ~, 4793:0

Victoria, queen of England, 807:6; 1617:1

Victorian Age, 807:6; 4000:1; morality in ~, 2432:3

Victorian/ism, 1617:1

victory see also winning, 423:9; 562:1; 1549:8; 2244:6; 2680:7; 4424:4; ~ celebration, 4584:2; ~ of war, 800:1

video, 2783:3; ~ games, 4566:3; ~ on internet, 4810:2

Vietnam Memorial (Washington, D.C.), 2680:24

Vietnam War, 2558:1; 2692:1; 2939:2; 3126:4; opposition to ~, 2553:1; ~ protesters, 2604:1

Vietnam/ese, 2087:4; aftermath of ~ War, 3189:3; community in ~, 4943:2; shooting ~, 2987:8

viewpoint see also opinion, 782:1; 1670:1; 4006:3; cultural ~, 1659:1; differing ~, 240:1; 1261:2; fresh ~, 2837:1, 3; new ~ of world, 3085:2

vigilance see also alertness, 2529:5; 3283:1

vigilante/ism, 4525:1, 2

vigor see also vitality, renewal of ~, 1559:1

village see also town, technology and ~, 4200:2

villain see also scoundrel, 1236:5; 2884:2

vindication, 950:5; ~ of heroes, 1706:3

vindictiveness see also vengeance, 2333:1

violence see also subclassifications passim; anti-violence; rape; war, 832:5; 2866:22; 3112:3; 3658:4; 3782:2; 3892:1; 4141:6; 4267:1; 4752:5; 4921:1; abdicating ~, 3640:1; 4726:1; ~ against women, 2496:7; 3219:5; 3483:3, 4; 3983:4; 4355:1; 4572:2; 4685:1; 4750:2; 4961:1; ~ among youth in America, 2771:19; ~ and the media, 4157:4; causes of ~, 3588:1; children and ~, 4633:1; controlling ~, 4590:4; cultural ~, 2441:1; domestic ~, 2256:4; 2496:8; 2843:1; 3812:3; 4202.1:2; eliminate ~, 3983:3; futility of ~, 3027:1; glorification of ~, 2553:1; gun ~, 4759:2; ~ in America, 2866:6; ~ in media, 2911:1; ~ in news, 1301:3; ~ in world, 2881:3; official ~, 3491:2; ~ perpetrated by government, 2881:1; predatory ~, 4539:4; reasons for ~, 4116:11; response of ~, 2818:1; response to ~, 3907:3; 4633:2; sanctity of ~, 2400:3; uprooting ~, 2950:5; widespread ~, 4810:3; youth ~, 3279:1

Virgen de Guadalupe, 4237:5, 6

Virgin Mary also see Magnificat, 78:1; 79:1; 179:1; 234:6; 379:1; 597:1; 1264:3; 2623:5; 2756:21; 3706:1, 2; child of ~, 2695:2

Virgin of Charity, 4386:2

virgin/ity, 21:1; 61:1; 179:1; 265:2; 509:2; 515:1; 523:1; 1680:1; 1986:1; 2268:1; 3318:3; 4404:5; 4900:1; 4931:1; committed ~, 457–458:2; ~ in East and West, 1928:6; losing one's ~, 4459:3

Virginia, 738:4

virility see also masculinity, symbols of ~, 3563:1

virtue, 68:1; 178:1; 196:1; 221:1; 287:1; 300:2; 394:1; 446:11; 700:1; 701:5; 782:2; 1029:1; 1051:3; 1291:3; 1622:2; 1659:7;

2432:2; 3099:7; abandoned ~, 311:2; great ~, 2267:3; ~ in shabbiness, 3453:2; love of ~, 285:3; ~ of women, 88:1; 1262:1; 1940:6; power of ~, 782:9; rewards of ~, 521:2; tried ~, 603:6

virus, 2559:2

Visconti, Bianca Maria, 256:1

vision (conception), 864:7; 2638:4; 2993:3; 4197:4; heavenly ~, 234:6; imaginative ~, 293:1; limited ~, 1197:2; limitless ~, 670:1; 1355:3; new ~, 2971:4; ~ of future, 1874:9; place of ~, 2582:3; sharing ~, 4075:2

visionary see also dreamer, 820:4; 1348:2

visit/or see also guest; travel/er, 1780:8; perfect ~, 767:16; superior ~, 1669:5; surprise ~, 1793:2; ~ to grandfather, 870:13

vista, beautiful ~, 1046:1

visualization, 1779:3; creative ~, 3827:1; ~ of artist, 4358:2

vitality see also vigor, ~ of men, 1790:11

vituperation see also oath; swearing, ~ in media, 2862:5

vocation see also occupation; profession, 2267:4

voice, 4214:2; boring ~, 4109:2; commanding ~, 1697:5; ~ development, 4526:1; 4715:1; finding one's ~, 1845:1; 3013:1; 3718:3; ~ in opera, 1685:4; mimicking ~, 3850:2; ~ quality, 2935:1; seductive ~, 4136:10; singing ~ (see also singer), 970:3; 1432:3; 2610:3; soft ~, 3095:2

void see also emptiness, filling the ~, 4180:3

volcano, 2131:1

volleyball, 3218:2

Voltaire, Francois Marie Arouet, 544:1; 616:4; 668:1

volunteer/ism see also service, 3920:0; obligations of ~, 4542:4; women ~, 1681:3

voluptuousness see also sensual/ity, 3964:2; look of ~, 1532:3; ~ of woman, 3561:2

voodoo, 4312:4

vote/r see also election, 4498:2; American ~, 4761.2:3; power of ~, 1897:4; qualified ~, 953:9; right to ~, 1155:1; 3365:1; 4722:0; 4763:4; woman ~, 3618:3

vow see also oath, 501:4; private ~, 1869:3

voyage see also journey; travel, meeting others on ~, 1033:6

vulgarity see also profaneness, 1695:3; 2151:4; 2232:1; portraying ~, 2074:2

vulnerability, 583:1; 1812:1; 4150:4; 4174:9

W

wage see also income; livelihood; pay; salary, 2583:2; ~ equity, 1029:2; 1151:1; 1229:4; 1819:1; 2733:1; 3093:1; high ~, 1525:4; ~ inequity, 839:3; meager ~, 1367:1; ~ policy, 4095:1; women's ~, 1086:5

waiting, 911:1; 1113:4; 1114:1; 1743:2; 3609:4; 4285:13; ~ in line, 4041:1

Walker, Alice, 3397:1

walking, 1346:3; 4404:4; 4445:3

wall, building ~, 4423:4; 4825:2; putting up ~, 2668:16

Wall Street see also finance; investment; stock market, 1178:2; 4638:1; crisis in ~, 4867:5; ~ regulations, 4867:3

Wallace, Henry A., 1973:4

wanderer see also nomad, 1348:3; 1483:2; 3540:2

wanderlust see also roaming, 1777:1

war see also specific battles and wars; armed forces/army; combat; fight/ing; military; soldier; weapon/ry, 233:1; 259:1; 269:2; 472:15; 486:2; 931:15; 1350:7; 1440:5, 7; 1446:2; 1548:8; 1659:2; 1669:; 1692:3; 1745:5; 2116:10; 2223:2; 2405:8; 2527:3; 2558:5; 2668:3; 2800:2; 2866:22; 3241:3; 3763:3; 4650:2; activity of ~, 1847:1; alternative to ~, 1519:3; 2036:14; 4256:7; anti- ~ film, 3068:3; ~ as solution, 1618:25; ~ at sea, 60:1; ~ battles, 2192:2; bestialities of ~, 3867:1; causes of ~, 2192:1; 3119:10; 4430:3; children and ~, 1810:1; 2689:2; 3125:1; 4326:6; choosing soldiers of ~, 1555:6; civilians and ~, 4887:2; cost of ~, 4378:2; ~ crime, 2036:10; ~ cry, 800:1; cultural ~, 3865:5; death and ~, 1011:1; 1347:5; 3346:2; destructiveness of ~, 1499:2; dichotomy of ~, 2211:3; disillusion of ~, 2800:2; economics of ~, 1227:1; 1379:1, 3; 1741:15; 2098:6; 2291:7; 4412:3; effects of ~ on arts, 2172:3; effects of ~ on men, 1167:18; effects of ~ on people, 3907:2; effects of ~ on victims, 3573:2; elimination of ~, 1029:3; 1333:1; end of ~, 100:1; 327:1; escape from ~, 3392:3; ethical conduct in ~, 4263:5; examination of ~, 1548:9; fallout of ~, 1745:4; 2686:4; futility of ~, 2260:3; 2668:6; 3392:2; germ ~ -fare, 2349:25; god of ~, 625:2; heartlessness of ~, 1778:2; horror of ~, 974:10; 2210:12; 4932:1; images of ~, 4731:6; impact of ~ on youth, 1867:3; ~ in Europe, 1338:1; ~ in God's

name, 4174:13; influence of journalism on ~ (see also war correspondent), 3867:2; justifying ~, 1167:17; 1317:6; 1553:2; 1741:8; 2800:2; 2969:1; 3412:5; lessons of ~, 1677:3; long ~, 2689:1; love and ~, 1751:30; madness of ~, 1530:4; 2656:5; materialism of ~, 1583:2; medical facility in ~, 1784:2; men and ~, 310:5; 4481:7; misery of ~, 98:1; morale during ~, 3415:6; mother and ~, 1545:5; 3653:1; ~ near home, 1583:1; need for workers during ~, 1471:1; nuclear ~, 3780:3; ongoing ~, 4133:4; opportunity in ~, 2510:1; opposition to ~ (see also anti-war movement; pacifism), 1251:1; 1875:1; 2340:2; 2553:1; 3907:1; 4087:3; 4886:2; outrages of ~, 801:5; personal ~, 3611.1:2; preparation for ~, 980:1; 1329:1; 2769:2; preventing ~, 1167:16; profits of ~, 1914:4; 1957:6; public atmosphere during ~, 1064:2; reality of ~, 977:4; religious ~ (see also religion, war and ~), 517:4; 4952:4; responsible for ~, 2657:4; rules of ~, 511:12; sacrifices of ~, 497:3; science and ~, 1514:2; senselessness of ~, 4851:3; sick of ~, 1857:4; spirit of ~, 1471:7; ~ strategy, 1983:1; ~ stories, 1474:5; 3125:1; technological ~ -fare, 3152:2; ~ -time rations, 2072:2; tragedy of ~, 2800:1; understanding ~, 3939:7; victims of ~, 2692:2; violence and ~, 2922:2; ~ vs. terrorism, 3641:1; winning ~, 1555:4; women and ~, 86:2; 310:5; 582:1; 703:1; 746:1; 748:1; 974:9; 1208:18; 1439:1; 1487:2; 1535:7; 1555:3, 9; 1745:5; 2105:2; 2120:1; 2210:1; 2278:3; 2439:7; 2796:2; 2951:2; 3372:5; 3648:1; 3826:1; 4381:4; 4592:3; ~ wound, 1018:3; youth and ~, 1928:1

War and Peace, 2668:10

war correspondent see also writer, 3865:5; distrust of ~, 2930:3

warrior see also soldier, 2985:3; 3203:7; 3241:5

Washington, D.C. see also White House, 1778:5; 1917:3; 2265:1; 2499:2; 3294:1; 4277:1; 4895:3; atmosphere of ~, 2710:2; cheating in ~, 2710:4; color of ~, 4601:2; demands of ~, 4866:1; news mongering in ~, 4102:2; ~ newspaper, 4127:3; notables of ~, 2710:1; Potomac River ~, 1011:1; provincialism in ~, 4665:3; religion in ~, 745:1; social life in ~, 735:2; 2898:1; voting rights for ~, 3050:6;

Washington Monument ~, 3133:5

Washington, George, 565:1; 623:1; 807:1

waste/fulness, 792:3; ~ in New York City, 2569:5; ~ of Earth's resources, 2349:26; recycling ~, 4552:1; sin of ~, 3309:7

wasteland see also desolation, 1058:2

watch see also clock; time, ~ piece, 580:1; 767:12

water see also particular bodies of water; pollution, water ~, 430:3; 1727:11; 2410:2; 3575:3; 4897:4; ~ activists, 4897:5; ~ aquifer, 4272:2; availability of ~, 3906:2; body of ~, 1457:1; buying ~, 4272:1; connection to ~, 3871:3; development and ~, 3556:5; evaporation of ~, 248:1; exploitation of ~, 2527:4; ~ fountain, 2022:3; ~ in relation to women, 3575:1; 4935:2; light on ~, 2153:2; ~ management, 4266:3; 4506:3; ~ of the world, 2123:2; ~ power, 1849:2; right to ~, 3719:1, 4, 5; running ~, 3686:3

Watergate affair, 3284:4

Waters, Ethel, 2520:1

wave (ocean), 1077:1; 1180:4; 1305:4; 2153:7; 3105:1; crashing ~, 4127:5

waywardness, 1790:10, 13; 1964:5; ~ of daughter, 4802:2

weak/ness, 2082:2; ~ in relation to strong, 1930:5; response to ~, 1410:1

wealth see also fortune; money; prosperity; rich, 149:2; 178:2; 349:3; 408:9; 539:3; 628:1; 1009:3; 1150:2; 1193:1; 1840:2; 2000:1; 2251:1; 3806–3807:2; 4289:4; 4901:1; accumulating ~, 1184:5; 4131:1; advantages of ~, 1620:9; concentration of ~, 4659:2; desire for ~, 1450:22; diminished ~, 704:1; distribution of ~, 812:3; 4774:4; effect of ~, 1836:5; futility of ~, 466:6; ~ in relation to beauty, 1301:1; indifference to ~, 487:2; lack of ~, 4908:1; masculinization of ~, 2916:19; memorializing ~, 1362:2; old ~, 2671:4; personal ~, 2670:2; pursuit of ~, 4332:3

weapon/ry see also specific types; arms; war, development of ~, 1379:3; disappearance of ~, 2363:3; elimination of ~, 3491:4; 3676:5; holding a ~, 3389:4; outdated ~, 3547:13

weariness see also exhaustion; fatigue, 1409:2; 4554:3; ~ of life, 1646:

weather *see also specific weather conditions,* 996:1; bad ~, 1033:3; gray ~, 3564:1; hot and cold ~, 2415:2; tropical ~, 3288:2

weaving (craft), 1881:5

wedding *see also* anniversary; marriage, 1184:7; 2198:3; ~ ceremony, 853:2; ~ preparation, 4226:4

weeping *see also* crying, 1870:12; 2102:0

weight *see also* diet/er; fat/ness; obesity; thinness, ~ control, 3018:1; 4493:4; over- ~, 2757:3; 2765:8; 4739:1; 4817:1

welcome, 1211:2

welfare *see* social welfare

West (U.S.), ~ and women, 1746:2; ideal ~, 3613:2; mythology of ~, 2596:5; settling ~, 1374:1; 1654:3

West Indian/Indies, ~ island, 3026:1

West, Benjamin, 807:1

West, Mae, 2295:3

Western culture, 2195:2; ~ in relation to women, 2979:5; self image of ~, 3182:4; spiritual poverty of ~, 2142:4; women in ~, 2709:2

wetness, exposed to ~, 1330:2

Wheatley, Phillis, 2280:1

Whig Party (Great Britain), 618:1

whistleblower, 4195:3; 4562:2

whistling, ~ woman, 2683:2

White House *see also* Washington, D.C., 1824:1; 2514:3; 3227:7; elitism in ~, 2393:4; ~ hospitality, 738:4; 4504:1; ~ in relation to media, 2163:2; ~ press secretary, 4866:2; vegetable garden at ~, 4648:6; woman in ~, 3731:19

white race *see* whites

white supremacy *see also* colonialism; racism, 2390:1; 2456:6; 2723:1; 3140:2; 3572:2; 3945:1; 4485:1; 4734:3; 4786:3; ~ among women, 3589:2; ~ in schools, 1792:2

whiteness (color), 1057:2

whites (race) *see also* Anglo-Saxon; caucasian, 1244:9; 3301:5; 4194:2; conditioning of ~, 2060:1; imperialism of ~, 3384:4; ~ in America, 4328:1; ~ in relation to blacks, 1577:1; 2905:1; ~ in relation to Native Americans (*see also* Native American, ~ in relation to white man), 1571:2; ~ in relation to other races, 3035:2; ~ men in relation to women, 3121:1

Whitman, Walt, 1037:7; 1431:5; 3187:2

Whittier, John Greenleaf, 984:3

whole/ness, 2849:2; 3638:1; 3763:1; 3775:1; 3954:3; 4653:3; ~ of self, 1884:5; ~ of sexes, 2209:1; part of ~, 986:1

wickedness *see also* bad/ness; evil; good and evil, 377:1; 792:4; 916:4; ~ of women, 472:4

widow/er *see also* husband, spouse & wife, death of ~, 627:2; 638:1; 1316:3; 1689:13; 2588:1, 2; 2645:2; 2647:4; 2817:22; 3317:5; 3747:2; difficulties of ~, 228:1; ~ of famous, 2868:1

wife *see also* housewife; marriage; mate; partner/ship; spouse, 374:1; 492:2; 509:2; 832:4; 1254:10; 1317:5; 1764–1765:2; 1843:9; 2439:3; 2874:2; 2947:3; 3388:1; 4013:1; 4421:4; advantages of having ~, 3870:1; American ~, 2231:2; 3870:2; ~ as property, 3104:2; attitude of ~, 446:5; attractiveness of ~, 1163:5; ~ beating, 265:3; 832:5; conniving to be ~, 1208:2; death of ~, 577:2; dependent ~, 2577:5; differences between ~, 2232:2; excellence in ~, 1044:2; idle ~, 1558:5; ~ in relation to family, 3898:3; ~ in relation to husband, 244:9; 288:2; 310:2; 378:1; 738:2; 744:3; 955:7; 1212:2; 1360:1; 1437:1; 1686:7; 1688:2; 2186:1; 2246:1; 3047:1; 3078:2; 3792:2; 3898:2; ~ in relation to in-laws, 23:1; loving ~, 430:6; minister's ~, 1185:3; ~ murder, 3616:1; necessity of having ~, 357:5; 2840:1; obedient ~, 498:1; 702:1; obligations of ~, 391:1; ~ of politician, 2676:5; ~ of public figure, 2905:3; philandering ~, 391:2; praise of ~, 1033:1; relationship to ~, 1646:2; role of ~, 202:1; 239:2; 1953–1954:2; 2370.1:2; 2839:2; sex and ~, 63:1; slavery of ~, 1086:7; society ~, 2033:; unhappy ~, 643:9; 659:1; working ~, 1959:10; wronged ~, 603:2; 847:2

wilderness, 407:3; 3410:1; 3801:1; alone in ~, 779:1; cherish ~, 2529:3; ~ in Canada, 880:4; settling ~, 1008:5

wildlife *see also* animal, connection with ~, 1405:3; glory of ~, 1405:2; ~ in relation to humankind, 1827:2

wildness, 1512:1; 4045:6; ~ in woman, 3250:1; loss of ~, 4788:3

will (intention), 1024:27; 1333:2; 2033:3; strength of ~, 1179:3; 3099:18

willfulness, ~ in woman, 643:11; suppression of ~, 305:1; 512:1

Williams, Jody, 4014:5

Wilson, Woodrow, 1215:2

Wimbledon Tennis Tournament (London), 4424:5

wind *see also* breeze, 173:2; 182:1; 604:3; 723:3; 1032:12; 1204:2;

1346:5; 1638:1; 3790:4; 4045:6; 4193:6; ~ direction, 1916:2

Winfrey, Oprah, 3353:4; 4812:2

winner/winning *see also* triumph; victory, 4243:1; 4631:4; 4705:2; mental attitude in relation to ~, 2431:2

winter, 192:1; 762:3; 908:4; 1024:6; 1552:7; 2483:3; 3137:2; 4705:4; end of ~, 554:2; last flowers of ~, 1012:2; ~ night, 837:3

wireless, 4609:1

wisdom *see also* knowledge; women, wisdom of ~, 244:4; 312:1; 369:3; 449:1; 585:7; 955:15; 1019:6; 1208:8; 1315:1; 1440:8; 1567:1; 1626:1; 1699:1; 2187:2; 2582:1; 2784:3; 3317:8, 9; disregard for ~, 2080:8; gaining ~, 942:1; ~ of rural women, 3390:1; ~ of the universe, 2101:4; search for ~, 827:3

wisecrack/ing *see also* joke, 1780:14 wish, 1492:3; last ~, 2586:1

wit *see also* humor; intelligence, 604:6; 1780:14; 2197:4; 2990:7; ~ in women, 585:9; live by ~, 1596:4

witch/craft, 2183:2; 2442:4; 2742:3; 2944:1; 3174:3; 4072:3; accusations of ~, 1298:1; ~ as healer, 1007:5; church's stand on ~, 1007:6; flying ~, 494:1; ~ hunt, 3121:1; 3257:1; protection from ~, 1250:2; types of ~, 1298:2

withdrawal, 3230:2; 3302:2; mental ~, 4094:1

witness, 2949:4; 4479:2; ~ at first hand, 2639:1; bearing ~, 2631:2

wizard, 2183:2

woe *see also* misery, remembered ~, 801:2

wolf, 588:2; afraid of ~, 2102:1; call of the ~, 4132:1

Wolfowitz, Paul, 2363:3

Wollstonecraft, Mary, 702:1

Wolsey, Cardinal Thomas, 286:1

woman/women *see also* feminine; girl; government, women in ~; lady; sex roles; sexes; womanhood; womanliness; women's history; women's liberation; women's movement; women's rights; women's studies, 289:1; 495:1; 829:1; 910:7; 958:3; 1076:6; 1089:1; 1105:1; 1208:6; 1209:3; 1214:1; 1284:2; 1334:2; 1351:1; 1436:2; 1453:6; 1481:1; 1608:1; 1627:2; 1632:1; 1680:1; 1721:3; 1727:3, 4; 1794:1; 1797:2; 1799:2; 1843:3; 1944:3; 2027:4; 2187:18; 2189:4; 2360:2; 2406:5; 2612:4; 2618:14; 2668:24; 2714:1; 2785:1; 2922:4; 2965:1; 3005:3; 3025:4; 3119:12; 3338:2; 3430:2; 3572:1; 3672:1; 3729:4; 3865:4; 3871:3; 3954:3; 4103:1;

4524:1; 4592:2; 4783:1; 4897:2; 17th century ~, 443:1; 19th century ~, 3305:1; 3626:1; ability of ~, 951:7; 963:5; abuse of ~ (*see also* wife, ~ beating), 383:1; achievements of ~, 244:3; 3330:1; 3434:3; ~ activists (*see* activism); ~ against violence, 3983:4; aging ~ (*see also* old age, women and ~; woman/women, older ~), 294:2; 439:1; 1387:6; 1409:3; ~ alone, 2606:2; ~ among men, 1049:1; anatomy of ~, 4077:2; appearance of ~, 1750:2; 2527:1; ~ as advisers, 1044:11; 3061:1; 4633:3; assertive ~, 1519:5; attitude toward ~, 946:3; awareness of ~, 3784:3; bad ~, 1321:1; beautiful ~ (*see also* beauty, women and ~), 367:6; big ~, 2765:6; black ~ (*see* blacks, women ~); blessing ~, 3969:2; books about ~, 2080:2; capabilities of ~, 334:3; 430:4; 515:2; 910:3; 1836:3; 1839:1; 1982:4; 3256:2; 3297:3; 4520:1; career ~ (*see also* business, ~ woman; career, ~ woman; woman/women, work & ~, working ~); celebrated ~, 2468:3; changing role of ~, 931:11; 2400:2; 2607:1; 2997:6; 3183:2; characteristics of ~, 3027:6; ~ compared to man, 3091:2; conditioning of ~ (*see also* girl, conditioning of ~), 412:4; 590:1; 2054:2; 2398:2; 2642:4; 2997:5; 3567:2; connections between ~, 2680:19; country ~, 599:1; 1816:1; 3390:1; dangerous ~, 3038:4; 4045:1; dependent ~, 938:2; 2252:3; desirability of ~, 2942:6; devaluation of ~, 2233:2; 3603:4; discrimination against ~ (*see also* sexism) 807:12; 3684:2; disposable ~, 2243:1; domination of ~, 2756:13; duplicity of ~, 1928:2; economics and ~, 4288:2; educated ~ (*see also* education, women and ~), 488:2; 1408:11; efforts of ~, 2916:4; empowerment of ~, 3982:3; enticing ~, 1663:18; equality for ~ (*see* equality, ~ for women); evolution of ~, 2916:10; excellence in ~, 3148–3149:1; exceptional ~, 272:2; 522:1; 2021:3; experience of ~, 4615:2; exploitation of ~, 887:5; fashionable ~, 676:7; freedom for ~, 1535:14; 1890:1; function of ~ (*see also* woman/women, role of ~), 1360:9; 1499:3; 3319:2; good ~, 1988:2; hardships of ~, 1933:1; health of ~, 4670:5; history of ~ (*see* women's history); home and ~ (*see* home, women and); humor and ~, 3165:4; ideal ~, 4013:7; ~ idealized, 568:2; 684:2; 1940:6; 2456:6; identity of ~, 2248:3; 2828:5; 2916:9; 3227:1; 3987:1; 4203:2; 4515:1; image of ~, 1062:1; 1131:2; 1893:1; 2126:1; 2192:7; 2353:2; 2644:2; 3607:1; 3618:2; 4939:1; importance of ~, 4419:2; ~ in 20th century America, 1562:2; 3079:2; ~ in authority, 535:2; 1988:1; ~ in business (see business, women in ~), 2957:1; 3078:4; ~ in music, 2493:1; ~ in politics, 4904:2; ~ in prison, 2738:1; ~ in relation to children, 2659:8; ~ in relation to male artists, 1763:4; ~ in relation to men (see also sexes, relationship between ~), 77:1; 152:2; 357:1; 438:1; 446:8; 519:2; 767:13; 806:4; 832:2; 858:2; 883:2; 963:3; 1019:2; 1099:1; 1133:3; 1193:9; 1260:1; 1262:6; 1443:3; 1481:11; 1508:1; 1524:4; 1566:1; 1578:3; 1590:12, 14; 1628:2; 1679:1; 1744:1; 1780:11; 1783:4; 1790:11, 14; 1841:1; 1914:2; 1979:8, 12; 2007:3; 2051:5; 2185:6; 2302:1; 2416:2; 2437:1; 2531:1; 2586:1; 2679:2; 2704:3; 2817:18; 2874:4; 2883:1; 2985:2; 3031:5; 3070:3; 3083:3; 3116:1; 3122:3; 3137:5; 3145:5; 3174:2; 3191:2; 3198:1; 3219:3; 3236:2; 3292–3293:3; 3325:1; 3349:9; 3377:5; 3529:5; 3620:3; 3656:2; 3690:2; 3961:2; 3962:1; 4058:4; 4374:1; 4520:1; 4625:3; ~ in relation to nature, 4674:2; ~ in relation to women (see also friendship, ~ between women; sisterhood), 756:4; 890:7; 981:4; 1764–1765:7; 1883:2; 1967:2; 2817:8; 3961:2; 4045:3; ~ in revolt, 1488:3; ~ in sports (see sports, women and ~); ~ in workplace (see workplace, women in ~); inaccessible ~, 2353:6; independent ~ (see independence, women of ~); inequality of ~, 4288:1; inferiority of ~, 910:1; influence of ~, 823:1; 827:4; 851:1; 893:2; 916:11; 1897:3; 2552:5; 2849:; injustice to ~ (see also woman/women, discrimination against ~), 1776:5; 1870:17; instinct of ~, 3252:4; intellectual ~ (see intellectual/ism, ~ woman); intelligence of ~ (see intellect/intelligence, ~ in women); invisibility of ~, 3284:9; isolation of ~, 2709:3; ~ issues, 2553:2; 3575:1; 4122:3; 4497:3; knowledge of ~, 1664:1; ~ leaders (see leader/ship, women & ~); liberated ~ (see also woman/women, free ~), 1878:1; 1980:1; 2794:1; 2874:1; 3244:1; 3318:1; 3325:2;

3326:2; 3875:2; 3891:2; limitations imposed upon ~, 646:5, 6; 701:12; 963:2; 1230:5; 1683:2; loose ~, 1554:2; 4975:3; love and ~ (see love, women and ~); ~ loving women (see also lesbian/ism), 910:15; marriage and ~ (see marriage, women and ~); married names of ~, 931:23; militant ~ (see also militancy, ~ in women), 1235:4, 5; 2943:1; 2985:3; mind of ~ (see mind, woman's ~); misguidance of ~, 865:4; modern ~, 1586:1; 1804:4; money and ~ (see money, women and ~); morality and ~, 2979:3; multifariousness of ~, 1757:1; need for approval by ~, 3596:3; needs of ~, 910:8; 1620:3; 2364:6; 3184:6; new generation of ~, 1911:7; objectification of ~ (see objectification); obstacles of ~ (see obstacles); ~ of future, 931:27; ~ of genius, 919:3; 1081:2; old ~ (see old age, women and ~); older ~ , 572:4; 691:3; 1782:11; 2967:2; oppression of ~, 422:4; 423:7; 446:3; 472:11; 701:9; 733:8; 850:3; 874:4; 889:1; 906:2; 931:13; 1003:1; 1135:1, 5; 1319:1; 1419:3; 1471:6; 1973:8; 2300:2; 2583:1; 2778:4; 3157:2; 3947:2, 4; 4196:1; 4273:4; 4514:1; 4599:1; ~ organizations, 1238:2; 3267:1; 3334:1; outspoken ~, 4174:12; personal growth of ~, 2423:3; 3133:3; physical strength of ~, 2789:2; 3644:2; place of ~, 3627:3; plain ~, 2110:5; pleasure and ~, 2717:3; politics and ~ (see politics); poor ~, 2716:5; potential of ~, 669:6; 1568:2; power of ~ (see power, women and ~, women in ~); powerlessness of ~, 2544:1; 2709:3; 2894:1; priorities of ~, 3366:2; professional ~ (see also woman/women, career ~), 923:2; progress of ~, 451:1; 1931:1; 2268:3; 3379:5; 3731:20; refuge of ~, 1785:1; relationships and ~ (see relationships, women & ~); ~ represented in literature, 2978:1; repressed ~, 701:8; 852:4; 2755:2; reproductive function of ~, 1564:1; 3349:8; responsibilities of ~, 3336:3; retrospection in ~, 1578:2; revolution and ~ (see revolution, women and ~); rights of ~ (see rights, ~ of women); role of ~, 62:2; 314:1; 487:6; 644:3; 715:1; 820:1; 827:13, 14; 832:3; 865:1; 882:2; 931:4; 971:3; 998:3; 1082:1; 1112:1, 5; 1128:1; 1189:4; 1238:3; 1249:3; 1254:2; 1304:7; 1508:2; 1535:5; 1562:3; 1644:1; 1654:2; 1935:7;

2019:6; 2080:3; 2144:1; 2219:8; 2272:2; 2370.1:2; 2398:5, 11; 2452:1; 2509:2; 2527:5; 2545:1; 2579:1; 2638:5; 2709:1; 2744:2; 2817:17; 2942:8; 2943:1; 2979:1; 2998:2; 3020:1; 3031:4; 3098:2; 3119:14; 3140:1; 3260:4; 3699:4; 3776:3; 3925:5; 3945:2; 4364:5; 4429:1; 4598.1:2; 4700:2; 4790:2, 3; 4923:1; 4935:1; ~ science (see science, women and ~; scientist, woman ~); scope of ~, 1662:1; secrets of ~, 2683:2; self-hatred of ~, 3868:1; sex and ~ (see sex/uality, women and ~); sexual oppression of ~, 3322:1; sisterhood of ~, 4155:1; ~ soldiers (see heroes; soldier, woman ~; warriors); status of ~, 785:1; 3316:3; 3536:1; 4801:1; strength of ~, 860:5; 1663:19; 3709:2; strong ~, 2785:2; 3644:2; 4221:0; struggles of ~ (see also rights, women's ~), 1185:2; subculture of ~, 3125:3; submissive ~, 3845:1; success and ~ (see success, women and ~); super ~, 3488:6; suppressed ~, 1590:17; 2398:8; ~ talk, 825:2; technology and ~, 3888:1; theories on ~, 2685:1; thinking ~ (see thinker, ~ woman); traditional ~, 3136:5; treatment of ~, 4174:11; 4381:3; types of ~, 3313:1; ugly ~, 934:4; underestimating ~, 4984:1; universal cause of ~, 1231:3; unmarried ~ (see single/ness); unsocialized ~, 4478:1; upkeep of ~, 464:1; viewpoint of ~, 1958:2; 3790:1; vilification of ~, 4481:1; violent ~, 4685:1; ~ volunteer, 1681:3; war and ~ (see war, women and ~); weakness of ~, 472:4; wealthy ~, 2289:1; Western ~, 2709:2; wisdom of ~, 487:9; 820:1; 2834:1; 2965:4; ~ without men, 3663:2; work and ~ (see labor/er, woman ~; work, women and ~); working ~ (see also business, ~ woman; career, ~ woman), 923:2; 1239:6; 1384:5; 1535:1; 1537:6; 1586:2; 1920:5; 1957:2; 2321:1; 3118:3; 3171:1; 3926:1; working class ~, 1363:1; wronged ~, 1007:1; young ~, 865:4; 1752:10

womanhood see also femininity; woman/women; womanliness, 3414:1; advances for ~, 2398:13; ancestry of ~, 1208:17; arriving at ~, 4331:3; ideal ~, 1313:6; lessons of ~, 4784:2; repression of ~, 3183:2; saving ~, 963:7; symbols of ~, 325:2; values of ~, 1167:13

womanliness see also femininity; woman/women, 1176:4;

3145:17; 3376:2; abounding in ~, 916:19

womb, 102:1; 1973:9; 3886:1; 4155:1; 4868:2; ~ envy, 3698:1

Women Strike for Peace, 2278:2

Women's Day, 1229:1

women's history, 669:6; 1010:1; 1659:9; 2201:7; 2380:5; 2580:2; 3086:1; 3248:2; 3326:1; 3458:2; 4300:2; 4930:1; progress of ~, 2632:2; 3505:2; 4300:2; restoring women to ~, 3359:2; suppression of ~, 2974:2

women's liberation see also women's movement; women's rights, 372:2; 931:20; 1086:9; 1235:3; 1360:6; 1870:10; 2134:1; 2318:3; 2398:15; 2416:5; 2439:1; 2537:3; 2995:1; 3732:1

women's movement see also ERA; feminism; women's liberation; women's rights, 1151:2; 1319:1; 1553:1, 5; 2380:5; 2553:3; 2618:8; 2658:9; 2680:18; 2716:5; 2810:5; 2922:6; 3249:1; 3521:1; 3608:1; 3646:1; 4013:4; ~ 1920s, 1819:4; accomplishments of ~, 3608:2; commitment to ~, 2985:4; effects of ~, 1666:3; 2398:10; goals of ~, 2544:2; impact of ~, 2330:6; ~ in Iran, 4658:4; ~ in Palestine, 3586:3; ~ in relation to Native Americans, 3246:2; international ~, 3050:5; pioneers in ~, 1244:2

women's rights see also Declaration of Sentiments; women's liberation; women's movement, 9:1; 18:1; 74:1; 701:1; 715:2; 807:12; 821:1; 839:3; 860:1, 15; 931:6, 12, 22; 946:2; 953:1, 2; 1086:6; 1235:1; 1555:7; 2127:5; 2540:5; 2612:2; 2681:1; 2778:2; 2979:3; 3160:1; 3240:1; 3731:5; 3731:6; 4273:3; 4661:2; 4981:1; backlash vs. ~, 4481:3; discovering ~, 656:2; fighting for ~, 1553:6; justness of ~, 4481:4; losing ~, 2658:8; protecting ~, 4466:2

women's studies, 3285:2; 4145:3; 4350:2; discipline of ~, 4145:4

wonder, 1276:5; 1548:4; 2153:1; loss of ~, 2858:2; ~ of life, 2464:9

wood, burning ~, 1560:1

woodcraft, 1149:4

woods see also forest, 4115:1

woodshed, 1948:2

Woolf, Virginia, 3843:2

word, 1024:26; 1440:2; 2101:3; 2381:8; 4884:2; beauty of ~, 1454:4; choosing ~, 2636:3; clumsy with ~, 1385:2; creation and ~, 2456:9; cruel ~, 2437:1; 2642:11; 4595:1; derogatory ~, 3533:3; extracting ~, 1581:2; flattering ~ (see also flattery),

551:1; hackneyed ~, 477:5; interpreting ~, 4194:1; kind ~, 1283:2; last ~, 504:1; 562:2; 588:4; 678:1; 682:3; 820:3; 852:1; 856:2; 1310:1; 4565:3; long ~, 2687:5; meaning of ~, 501:1; new ~, 1408:15; power of ~, 431:1; 1002:2; 1149:2; 1440:4; 1578:2; 1613:1; 2768:2; 2873:3; 3286:1; 3478:2; 4368:1; printed ~ (*see also* publication); 4555:2; sacredness of ~, 4577:1; smooth ~, 1645:3; spoken ~ (*see also* remark), 1554:4; 1929:2; 4641:1; sweet ~, 430:11; 1645:2; trap of ~, 2056:6; unspoken ~, 1323:1; 1677:2; 2149:2; written ~ (*see* writing)

word processor *see also* computer, 4197:1; 4672:2

work *see also* job; labor/er; livelihood, 966:4; 998:10; 1006:8; 1071:1; 1246:6; 1254:8; 1336:11; 1337:1; 1382:2; 1446:6; 1652:2; age and ~, 2165:2; ~ at home, 4679:1; avoiding ~, 916:13; ~ balanced with family, 3701:1; 3393:1; blessing of ~, 1867:2; busy ~, 1659:10; completing ~, 892:14; creative ~, 2941:5; demanding ~, 1505:4; desire not to ~, 1570:5; devotion to ~, 1851:1; enjoying ~, 4313–4314:1; finding ~ (*see also* employment), 2032:12; flexibility at ~, 2832:3; focus on ~, 2342:3; gender and ~, 3007:1; good ~, 1594:1; hard ~, 4342:2; 4980:2; importance of ~, 1903:5; 2026:4; imprint of ~, 3547:17; incessant ~, 734:7; 1414:1; intoxication of ~, 4287:1; joy of ~, 1247:1; 1370:2; 1387:8; 1687:12; 2173:2; laid off from ~, 3921:6; ~ long hours, 1324:1; 2135:3; love of ~, 4003:3; man's ~, 2942:8; men's ~ vs. women's ~, 2041:1; monotony of ~, 1469:1; motivation to ~, 3131:2; palliative of ~, 2839:1; 3963:1; precariousness of ~, 4501:1; purpose of ~, 1646:5; sexism and ~ (*see* sexism, ~ in workplace); spoken ~, 3850:5; time off from ~, 713:5; tired of ~, 1566:4; woman's ~ (*see also* housework), 532:1, 2; 2916:5; 2942:8; 3409:1; women and ~ (*see also* woman/women, working ~), 151:3; 1229:3; 1254:3; 1342:1; 1484:1, 2; 2121:1; 2189:5; 2380:1; 2607:2; 2756:; 2771:10; 3040:1; 3590:4; 3610:1; 3683:2; 3873:2; 4309:2; 4382:1, 2; 4481:3

worker *see also* employee; labor/er, 2997:1; alienation of ~, 2888:2; alliance of ~, 2994:2; bless ~,

3121:5; blue collar ~, 3192:1; domestic ~, 2844:1; excellence in ~, 3343:2; exploitation of ~ (*see also* miner/mining, exploitation of ~), 2297:1; foreign ~, 4808:3; hours of ~, 1494:5; inclusion of ~, 1494:2; male ~, 2852:2; menial ~, 3163:1; old ~, 1961:2; older ~, 3151:2; piece ~, 3713:1; protecting ~, 2835:1; rights of ~ (*see* rights, workers' ~); skilled ~, 4624:2

workforce *see also* employee; employment; labor, ~ market, global ~, 2756:; 4808:3; paper pushers in ~, 3257:4

workplace, evolution of ~, 4679:3; gender in ~, 4409:6; ~ hazards, 2835:1; sex and ~, 1957:2; sexism at ~ (*see* sexism); women in ~, 1484:2; 2360:4; 3709:2;3945:2; writer's ~, 642:2

world *see also* Earth; planet; universe, 428:1; 1669:8; 2034:5; 4457:1; another ~, 4510:7; barren ~, 3547:1; beauty of ~, 4015:2; better ~, 1335:2; changing ~ (*see also* social change), 1705:2; 2437:15; 4720:3; 4729:1; ~ communication, 4810:3; ~ community (*see also* interconnectedness), 3061:2; 3731:1; concept of ~, 2330:3; ~ cooperation, 3655:1; 4446:1; decaying ~, 3806–3807:1; destruction of ~, 1863:2; different kind of ~, 3406:1; divisiveness of ~, 2694:1; harshness of ~, 213:1; hollow ~, 1073:3; ideal ~, 3852:5; improving ~, 953:12; 2437:11; inner ~ (*see also* consciousness), 2162:3; love of ~, 2669:1; madness of ~, 821:7; masterpieces of ~, 1842:2; mortal ~, 301:1; new ~, 2259:2; 2668:18; 4725:3; physical ~, 1779:1; progress of ~, 1715:14; renounce ~, 603:4; 786:2; 811:1; 1675–1676:3; sacredness of ~, 2669:5; saving ~, 1803:3; 2437:14; self-organizing ~, 3311:1; treatment of ~, 2997:8; ~ turns, 2123:2; understanding the ~, 4637:2; ~ unity, 1548:8; ~ without men, 3529:5; ~ without oppression, 3754:2; wounded ~, 3051:6

World Bank, ~ in relation to environment, 4848:2

world order, domination in ~, 2756:2; partnership in ~, 2756:2

World Trade Organization, demonstration vs. ~, 3682:3

World War I, role of British in ~, 1187:7; U.S. and ~, 1756:2

World War II, 1990:3; survivors of ~, 2279:1; veterans of ~, 3668:2; women and ~, 3826:1; 3926:1

World Wide Web *see also* Internet, 4197:3

worldliness *see also* materialism; sophistication; 305:1; 349:2; 350:1; 413:2; 769:1; dangers of ~, 201:1; release from ~, 219–220:1

world's fair, 1256:1

worry *see also* anxiety, 1684:4; 1763:1; 3099:23; 4023:3; 4757:1 worship/per *see also* prayer; 1254:13; 1313:3; 2781:1; 2943:4; ~ services, 1416:2

worth/iness, creating ~, 3743:1; measure of ~, 806:3

wound *see also* hurt; injury, 4015:3; emotional ~, 4252:3; self-inflicted ~, 4533:4

wrestling, sumo ~, 1300:1

Wright, Frances, 913:1

Wright, Frank Lloyd, 3832:1

writer *see also* novel/ist; playwright/ing; poet; war correspondent; writing, 446:3; 517:1; 808:4, 13; 1051:2; 1166:5; 1590:16; 1669:17; 1782:15; 2027:1; 2219:12; 2270:11; 2295:2; 2443:2; 2510:3; 2638:2, 13; 3995:2; 4383:1; ambition of ~, 2912:2; aspiring ~, 584:2; beginnings of ~, 2456:9; ~ block, 3688:1; 3880:4; challenges of ~, 3872:3; comic ~, 3481:4; discipline of ~, 2061:5; drive of ~, 1752:2; freedom for ~, 4074:2; function of ~, 2916:14; ghost ~, 2201:1; goal of ~, 2456:12; government and ~, 2073:1; great ~, 2620:4; homosexual ~, 4583:5; immersed ~, 1717:5; ~ in relation to society, 4133:5; ~ in relation to world, 3895:4; Indian ~, 1917:4; influences on ~, 1662:5; legacy of ~, 1510:2; life of ~, 3578:1; male ~, 2841:2; needs of woman ~, 1590:11; ~ of book (*see* book, ~ writing); 3799:6; ~ of genius, 2116:2; personality of ~, 1662:5; qualifications of ~, 1764–1765:3; quest of ~, 3777:2; reasons for ~, 1230:4; role of ~, 1979:13; self-doubt of ~, 1409:27; Southern ~, 2534:10; Southern black ~, 3547:16; student ~, 4785:1; temperament of ~, 3898:5; understanding ~, 4614:5; woman ~, 142:1; 419:1; 497:1; 535:1; 539:1; 545:1; 1081:1, 2; 1468:3; 1590:17; 1662:1; 1687:13; 2051:6; 2368:2; 3144:1; 3546:1; 3853:1

writing *see also* book, writing ~; fiction; poem/poetry; prose; stage play; writer, 4:2; 308:3; 407:5; 511:5; 663:1; 1011:2; 1408:16; 1450:3; 1515:1; 1669:14; 1693:13; 1758:5; 2059:4; 2117:16; 2518:3;

2546:5; 2668:21; 3025:1; 3095:3; 3318:2; 3563:9; 3576:1; 3621:1; 3744:2; 3850:5; 3880:2; 4016:1; 4033:3; 4067:8; 4109:5; 4787:3; 4975:4; ~ about youth, 4136:13; ~ as propaganda, 1662:7; ~ at night, 4067:3; bad ~, 425:2; beginnings of ~, 2911:5; categorizing ~, 2999:4; ~ character, 2117:12; creative ~, 1408:21; effort of ~, 4653:7; essentials of ~, 3872:4; fear of ~, 801:9; 3186:2; filthy ~, 688:2; ~ for children, 2668:13; 3057:1; futility of ~, 801:14; how to ~, 3563:8; hunger for ~, 4107:1; ~ implements, 1036:1; inspiration for ~, 487:4; joy of ~, 2981:1; lucid ~, 2932:7; method of ~, 2636:2; motive for ~, 4546:3; ~ of everyday, 2529:9; ~ of nature, 2472:1; ~ on oneself, 3903:1; ~ partners, 2869:2; power of ~, 4339:2; 4709:1; preparation for ~, 434:1; 867:3; reality in ~, 1852:4; reasons for ~, 3950:4; sanitized ~, 3099:25; satisfaction of ~, 1687:11; 3810:1; slipshod ~, 1406:7; spiritual ~, 2425:1; studying ~, 3788:3; subject of ~, 2591:1; teaching ~, 4002:1; 4785:2; ~ technique, 2783:2; 3776:4; 4096:1; time for ~, 3175:1; weeping and ~, 3745:2; ~ when unhappy, 4696:4; ~ with whole self, 3409:4; women and ~, 3025:3; 3453:1; word selection in ~, 2195:4

wrong *see also* right and wrong; sin/ner; vice, 3306:2; being ~, 2704:1; committing ~, 2135:2; 4620:1; ~ of women, 821:1; past ~, 3581:3; ~ redressed, 1215:2; righting a ~, 4697:2; stopping ~, 977:1

X

Xenocrates, 64:1

xenophobia *see also* prejudice, ~ against foreigners, 1706:6; 3824:1

Y

yearning *see also* longing, deep ~, 4639:2

years of age, 10 ~, 734:11; 2212:1; 14 ~, 1956:2; 15 ~, 814:1; 1561:2; 20 ~, 887:20; 25 ~, 523:1; 3 ~, 734:11; 30 ~, 450:; 786:1; 2301:2; 2780:2; 3067:1; 38 ~, 658:3; 40 ~, 533:5; 1473:2; 50 ~, 1412:6; 1590:28; 6 ~, 734:11; 70 ~, 807:18; 1601:1; 80 ~, 1601:1; 90 ~, 1160:1; 100 ~, 1746:1, 3

Yeats, William Butler, 1843:2

yesterday *see also* past, 1944:2

yielding *see also* flexibility, 3094:4

yoga, science of ~, 1884:5

Yorkshire, England, women of ~, 1182:2

Young, Loretta, 3643:1

youth/fulness *see also* adolescence/ adolescent; childhood; teenage/r; years of age, 609:1; 658:9; 794:1; 807:17; 852:3; 1025:10, 11; 1173:1; 1305:1; 1440:6; 1470:7; 1789:6; 1878:1; 1982:1; 2143:1; 2561:1; 3089:4; 3443:4; 3732:2; 4050:4; 4672:3; 4897:2; agonies of ~, 1987:2; 3119:2; attitudes of ~, 544:5; 887:20; 2248:1; bias against ~, 4761.2:1; clinging to ~, 2016:3; concerns of ~, 740:1; conditioning of ~ (*see also* boy, conditioning of ~; girl, conditioning of ~), 4160:3; dissatisfaction of ~, 2346:1; end of ~, 786:1; eternal ~, 801:16; expectations of ~, 4531:3; feeling ~, 3869:3; fountain of ~, 2398:14; freedom in ~, 1752:10; guidelines for ~, 2148:3; happiness of ~, 861:1; impatience of ~, 2096:1; improvidence of ~, 1561:3; ~ in relation to elders, 244:10; ~ in wartime, 1928:1; 2033:2; 4815:5; inexperienced ~, 1242:1; longings of ~, 3455:4; lost ~, 628:3; 1236:3; 1619:6; 1719:3; 2732:9; 3118:2; 4954:1; maintaining ~, 1788:3; misspent ~, 2620:5; provisions for ~, 1251:3; rebellion of ~, 2592:3; recollections of ~, 658:4; regained ~, 1781:1; 2735:4; restoring ~, 3582:2; return to one's ~, 947:3; 1043:1; scars of ~, 1208:1; self-involvement of ~, 1905:4; sex and ~ (*see* sex, youth and ~); sheltered ~, 734:16; sign of ~, 2910:3; ~ spreading wings, 1049:2; unpreparedness of ~, 1649:1

YouTube *see also* Internet, communication via ~, 4810:3

Yunus, Muhammad, 3106:1

yuppie, ~ men in relation to women, 3257:3

Z

zealotry, 1896:7

Zen, 3170:3

Zeus, 325:1

Zimbabwe, beauty of ~, 2349:18; independence in ~, 2349:19

Zion/ism *see also* Israel, 1261:3, 8; 2360:6; sinners of ~, 534:1

zoo, 1749:3; 2201:6

Zoroaster, 870:3